France

THE ROUGH GUIDE

KT-389-336

There are more than eighty Rough Guide titles covering
destinations from Amsterdam to Zimbabwe

Forthcoming titles include
China • Jamaica • New Zealand • South Africa
Vienna • Washington DC

Rough Guide Reference Series
Classical Music • The Internet • Jazz • World Music

Rough Guide Phrasebooks
Czech • French • German • Greek • Italian
Mexican Spanish • Polish • Portuguese • Spanish • Thai • Turkish

Rough Guides on the Internet
http://www.roughguides.com/
http://www.hotwired.com/rough

Rough Guide Credits

Text editor:	Graham Parker
Series editor:	Mark Ellingham
Editorial:	Martin Dunford, Jonathan Buckley, Jo Mead, Alison Cowan, Samantha Cook, Amanda Tomlin, Annie Shaw, Lemisse Al-Hafidh, Catherine McHale, Paul Gray, Vivienne Heller, Alan Spicer (Online UK), Andrew Rosenberg (Online US)
Production:	Susanne Hillen, Andy Hilliard, Melissa Flack, Judy Pang, Link Hall, Nicola Williamson, David Callier, Helen Ostick
Marketing and Publicity:	Richard Trillo, Simon Carloss (UK), Jean-Marie Kelly, Jeffrey Kaye (US)
Finance:	John Fisher, Celia Crowley, Catherine Gillespie
Administration:	Tania Hummel, Margo Daly

Acknowledgments

The authors would like to thank Ruth Goodwin, Tammy Rayne, Yves Sabin, Oristelle Bonis, Hélène Rouch, José Lavezzi, Sina, Jacqueline Alencourt, Peter Polish, Jo Wallis, Claudiu and Isabel Lavezzi, Jean and Margaret Llasera, Anne Provensl, Lotfi Ben Othmane, Roland Ivaldi and Cerise Magnani and their daughter Valentine, Thomas Ivaldi, Véronique Ivaldi, Steve, Sana and Sacha Saint Leger, Marlène Puccini, Jean-Pierre Guiochet, Philippe Gamba, Isabelle Carbonel and Yves Bernaud and their friends in Hyères, Florica Kyriacopoulos, Sendrine Camps, Hervée Bethuel, Bettina Daly and Anaïs. Also Sharon Clay for additional Paris research. Thanks also to Graham Parker for his mammoth editing job, Nicola Williamson for her endless patience with revises, Judy Pang for her speedy typesetting, Melissa Flack for emergency cartographic help, as well as Vivien Antwi for checking, Margaret Doyle for proofreading and Sam Kirby for tremendous work on the maps.

Many thanks, too, for the invaluable contributions of readers of the previous edition. The roll of honour appears on p.iv.

The publishers and authors have done their best to ensure the accuracy and currency of all information in *The Rough Guide to France*; however, they can accept no responsibility for any loss, injury, or inconvenience sustained by any traveller as a result of information or advice contained in the guide.

This fourth edition published 1995 by Rough Guides Ltd, 1 Mercer Street, London WC2H 9QJ.
Reprinted in September 1995 and June 1996.

Distributed by the Penguin Group:

Penguin Books Ltd, 27 Wrights Lane, London W8 5TZ
Penguin Books USA Inc., 375 Hudson Street, New York 10014, USA
Penguin Books Australia Ltd, 487 Maroondah Highway, PO Box 257, Ringwood, Victoria 3134, Australia
Penguin Books Canada Ltd, 10 Alcorn Avenue, Toronto, Ontario, Canada M4V 1E4
Penguin Books (NZ) Ltd, 182–190 Wairau Road, Auckland 10, New Zealand

Originally published in the UK by Routledge & Kegan Paul (1986), and Harrap Columbus (1989 & 1992).
Previous edition published in the United States and Canada as *The Real Guide France*.

Typeset in Linotron Univers and Century Old Style to an original design by Andrew Oliver.
Printed in the United Kingdom by Cox and Wyman Ltd (Reading).
Illustrations in Part One and Part Three by Ed Briant.
Illustration on p.1 by Henry Iles; Illustration on p.963 by Jane Strother.
© Kate Baillie and Tim Salmon 1986, 1989, 1992, 1995

No part of this book may be reproduced in any form without permission from the publisher except for the quotation of brief passages in reviews.

1056p. Includes index.

A catalogue record for this book is available from the British Library.
ISBN 1–85828–124–5

France

THE ROUGH GUIDE

Written and researched by
Kate Baillie and Tim Salmon

Additional material by
Theo Taylor and Greg Ward

Additional research by
Chris Scott and Margo Daly

THE ROUGH GUIDES

THANKS TO OUR READERS

A big thank you to the many readers of previous editions of this guide and our other France *Rough Guides* (*Paris, Brittany & Normandy, Provence & the Côte d'Azur*) who took the trouble to write in with their comments and suggestions: Jance Ackroyd, Sophie Aldred, Mary Attard, Hady Amr, J.M. Barisk, Amy Battle, Nada Bernstein, Brigitte Bertl, I. da Boelema, Eilis Boland, Mike Bold, Harry and Jo Bond, Marie-Christine Bourgeois, S. Bradburry, The Brammers, Barbara Bridges, Tim Burford, Lea Carter, Simon Carter and Dawn Judge, Hung-Wah Chang, Toni Clark, Kristi Chavane de Dalmassy, Tony Clarke, Mrs S. Clinton, Sylvie Cobb, Ruth Cooper, Robert Craig, Bob Dellavalle, Juliet Donnelly, Jim Dominy, Peter G. Drake, Marie-Thérèse F. DuBois, Jane Dumayne, Mark Farmer, Pascal Fautrat, Sam Fosket, Mike Foster, Robin Futoran, Charlie Gibbs, Mr and Mrs Gimbel, Judith M. Goodchild, Glyn Green, M. Guérinel, Sarah Hampton, J.G. Harmsen, Jon and Alison Hasluck, Kay Hatfield, Christopher J. Hindmarch, M. Holman, David W. Hope, Father Vincent Hughes, C. Hutt, Kim Johnson, Simon Jones, Jacqueline Jupin, Richard Keen, Richard Kelly, Andy Kettlety, Alan King, Jane Kingsbury, David Lacaillade, Sarah Lamb, Stuart Landels, C. Large, Victoria Lee, Oscar McCarthy, M.D.S. McConnell, Walter T. McGowan, Alison Marks, Fred Mawer, Michel Mendjel, Ida Miller, Laura Moore, Allan Morris, Hannah Murdoch, Chris Nichols, Evan Noble, David Parkin, John Pelling, Mike and Monica Pennington, M. Pocock, David Potts and Margaret Simpson, N.J. Price, Amy Purdom, Anna Raisin, Liz Raymont, Paul Reed, Chris Relton, Geoff Ridden, Alastair Rolfe, Fiona and Gerard Rooney, Vera Rossiter, Oliver Rowe, Greg Sandell, Jennifer Sanderson, Erik Saunes, Natascha Scott-Stokes, Ray and Barbara Seagles, Peter Setrem, Jonathan Sheldrake, James A. Sinclair, Barrie Somerville, Paul Stainforth, Sue Starbury, J. Tapp, A.M. Teasdale, J.P. Towey, Valerie Vastine Orbell, Jack Ward, Roland White, Mrs J. Whitlow, J.L. Whitlow, Derek Wilde, Claire Williams, Jean Williamson, Ken Williamson, June Willis, Stephen Wilson, C.S. Winfield, Angus Wright, J. Wright. Vicky Wright, Helen Wyld.

HELP US UPDATE

We've gone to a lot of effort to ensure that this second edition of *The Rough Guide to France* is accurate and up-to-date. But France never stops changing and, if you feel there are places we've under-rated or over-praised, or know of good hotels we've missed or others that have closed – or deteriorated – then please write. If you can remember the address, the price, the time, the phone number, so much the better.

We'll credit all contributions, and send a copy of the next edition (or any other Rough Guide if you prefer) for the best letters. Please mark all letters " Rough Guide to France Update" and send to :

Rough Guides, 1 Mercer Street, London WC2H 9QJ
or, Rough Guides, 375 Hudson Street, 3rd Floor, New York NY10014.

CONTENTS

Introduction viii

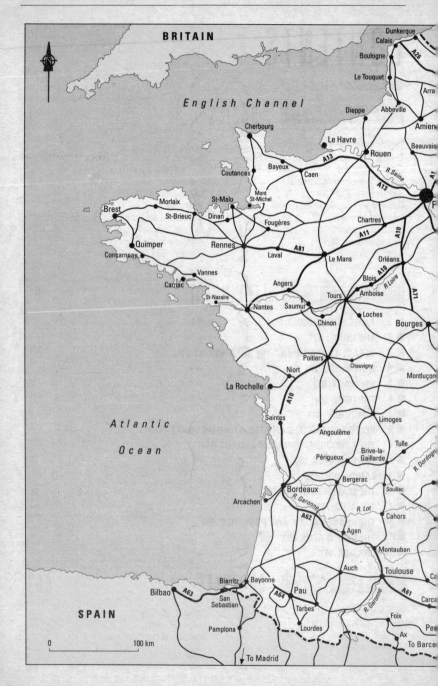

INTRODUCTION

The sheer physical diversity of France would be hard to exhaust in a lifetime of visits. The landscapes range from the fretted rocky coasts of Brittany to the limestone hills of Provence, the canyons of the Pyrenees to the perfect half-moon bays of Corsica and the lushly wooded valleys of the Dordogne to the glaciated peaks of the Alps. Each **region** looks and feels different, has its own style of architecture, its characteristic food, often its own patois or dialect. Though the French word *pays* is the generic term for a whole country, local people frequently refer to their own immediate vicinity as *mon pays*, and to a stranger as coming from another *pays*. And this strong sense of regional identity, sometimes expressed in the form of active separatist movements as in Brittany and Languedoc, has persisted over centuries in the teeth of centralized administrative control from Paris.

Perhaps the most striking feature of the French **countryside** is the sense of space. There are huge tracts of woodland and undeveloped land without a house in sight. Industrialization came relatively late, and the country remains very rural. Away from the main urban centres, hundreds of towns and villages have changed only slowly and organically, their old houses and streets intact, as much a part of the natural landscape as the rivers, hills and fields.

Historical and cultural associations are so widely disseminated across the land that even if you were to confine your travelling to one particular region you would still have a powerful sense of the past without having to seek out major sights. With its wealth of local detail, France is an ideal country for dawdling; there is always something to catch the eye and gratify the senses, whether you are meandering down a lane, picnicking by a slow, green river, or sipping *Pernod* in a village café. There is also endless scope for all kinds of **outdoor activities**, from walking, canoeing and cycling to the more expensive pleasures of skiing and sailing.

If you need more urban stimuli to activate the pleasure buds – clubs, shops, fashion, movies, music, hanging out with the beautiful and famous – then the great **cities** provide them in abundance. Paris, of course, is an outstanding cultural centre, with its elegant boulevards and atmospheric back streets, its art and its ethnic diversity. If your budget can stand it, you can follow the summer migration to the super-chic resorts of the Mediterranean coast – though they are really at their best in late spring.

For a thousand years and more, France has been at the cutting edge of **European development**, and the legacy of this wealth, energy and experience is everywhere evident in the astonishing variety of things to see: from the Gothic cathedrals of the north to the Romanesque churches of the centre and west, the châteaux of the Loire, the Roman monuments of the south, the ruined castles of the English and the Cathars and the Dordogne's prehistoric cave-paintings. If not all the legacy is so tangible – the literature, music and ideas of the 1789 Revolution, for example – much has been recuperated and illustrated in museums and galleries across the nation, from colonial history to fishing techniques, aeroplane design to textiles, migrant shepherds to manicure, battlefields and coalmines.

Many of the **museums** are models of clarity and modern design. Among those that the French do best are museums devoted to local arts, crafts and customs like the Musée Basque in Bayonne and the Musée Dauphinois in Grenoble. But inevitably first place must go to the fabulous collections of paintings, many of which are in **Paris**. This is perhaps because the city nurtured so many of the finest creative artists of the last hundred years, both French, Monet and Matisse for example, and foreign, such as Picasso and Van Gogh.

If you are quite untroubled by a duty to improve your mind in the contemplation of old stones and works of high art, France is well endowed to satisfy the grosser appetites. The French have made a high art of daily life: eating, drinking, dressing, moving and simply being. The **pleasures of the palate** run from the simplest picnic of crusty *baguette*, ham and cheese washed down by an inexpensive red wine through what must be the most elaborate take-away food in the world, available from practically every *charcuterie*; such basic regional dishes as *cassoulet*; the liver-destroying riches of Périgord and Burgundy cuisine; the fruits of the sea; extravagant pastries and ice cream cakes; to the trance-inducing refinements – and prices – of the great chefs. And there are wines to match, at all prices, and not just from the renowned vineyards of Bordeaux, Burgundy and Champagne. If you feel inadequate in the face of all this choice, never be afraid to ask advice, for most French people are true devotees, ever ready to explain the arcane mysteries to the uninitiated.

The people

Visual appearance is important to the French. No effort is too great to make things look good: witness the food shops in even the poorest neighbourhoods of a city, always sparkling clean and beautifully displayed. And it is evident that the people too take pride in looking neat and sharp; they inspect others and expect to be looked at. Life is theatre, lived much more in the public eye – especially in the warm Mediterranean south – than in Anglo-Saxon societies. And for the visitor it's a free and entertaining spectacle.

The French tend to be extremely courteous – it's not unusual for someone entering a restaurant to say "Good evening" to the entire company – and rather formal in their manners. At the same time, if they want something, they may be quite direct. If you are feeling self-conscious about coping with the language, this can seem like rudeness: it isn't. If you observe the formalities and make an effort to communicate, you'll find the French as friendly and interested as anyone else.

As for their reputed arrogance, the French are certainly proud of their culture, something which is reinforced by the education system. Artists and thinkers are held in high esteem in France and their opinions are listened to. Even prime ministers tend to be literate, and are often accomplished authors. But in a world dominated by commercial values and, in addition, the English language, the French (not unnaturally, for their language was once the *lingua franca* of the educated) feel this **culture** is under threat.

Where to go and when

France is easy to travel around. Restaurants and hotels proliferate everywhere and the lower-budget ones are much cheaper than in most other developed western European countries. Train services are highly efficient, as is the road network, especially the (toll-paying) autoroutes, and cyclists are much admired and encouraged. Information is highly organized and available from the tourist offices (*Offices de Tourisme*), a feature of practically every place in the land, as well as from hiking, cycling, camping, hang-gliding and hitchhiking organizations. But although these activities all have their specialist associations, they are not obtrusive; the French will not stand for regimentation, so you're left to your own devices.

There are all kinds of pegs on which to hang a holiday in France: a city, a region, a river or a mountain range, physical activities, cathedrals, châteaux. And in many cases your choice will determine the best time of year to go. Unless you're a skier, for example, you wouldn't choose the mountains between November and May; nor at this time would you head for the seaside – though spring on the Mediterranean coast

THE CLIMATE OF FRANCE

Average Daily Maximum Temperatures

	Jan	Feb	March	April	May	June	July	Aug	Sept	Oct	Nov	Dec
Paris/Ile de France	7.5	7.1	10.2	15.7	16.6	23.4	25.1	25.6	20.9	16.5	11.7	7.8
Alsace	5.5	5.3	9.3	13.7	15.8	23.0	24.1	26.3	21.2	14.9	7.6	4.7
Aquitaine	10.0	9.4	12.2	19.5	18.0	23.7	27.2	25.7	24.2	19.7	15.4	11.0
Auvergne	8.0	6.4	10.1	15.9	17.1	24.2	27.0	24.5	23.3	17.0	11.0	8.3
Brittany	9.3	8.6	11.1	17.1	16.0	22.7	25.1	24.2	21.2	16.5	12.1	9.3
Burgundy	6.1	5.9	10.3	15.3	15.8	23.8	25.8	26.1	21.2	15.5	9.1	6.2
Champagne-Ardenne	6.2	5.6	8.9	13.8	15.1	22.5	23.8	24.9	19.3	15.0	9.6	6.2
Corsica	13	14	16	18	21	25	27	28	26	22	17	14
Franche-Comté	5.4	4.8	9.8	14.6	15.5	23.0	25.0	26.5	21.8	15.2	9.6	5.8
Languedoc-Roussillon	12.4	11.5	12.5	17.6	20.1	26.5	28.4	28.1	26.1	21.1	15.8	13.5
Limousin	6.1	6.1	9.6	16.1	14.9	22.1	24.8	23.6	21.0	16.2	12.8	8.5
Lorraine	5.5	5.3	9.3	13.7	15.8	23.0	24.1	26.3	21.2	14.9	7.6	4.7
Midi-Pyrénées	10.0	9.0	12.3	18.3	19.1	26.4	27.6	27.2	25.0	19.3	15.5	9.8
Nord/Pas de Calais	6.6	5.6	8.3	13.7	14.9	21.5	22.7	24.0	19.3	15.3	8.3	6.9
Normandy	7.6	6.4	8.4	13.0	14.0	20.0	21.6	22.0	18.2	14.5	10.8	7.9
Picardy	6.6	5.6	8.3	13.7	14.9	21.5	22.7	24.0	19.3	15.3	8.3	6.9
Poitou-Charentes	10.0	8.7	11.7	18.2	16.4	22.4	25.3	24.6	22.0	18.4	14.0	9.8
Provence	12.2	11.9	14.2	18.5	20.8	26.6	28.1	28.4	25.2	22.1	16.8	14.1
Rhône Valley	7.4	6.7	10.8	15.8	17.3	25.6	27.6	27.6	23.5	16.5	10.4	7.8
Riviera/Côte d'Azur	12.2	11.9	14.2	18.5	20.8	26.6	28.1	28.4	25.2	22.2	16.8	14.1
Savoy/ Dauphiny Alps	3.1	3.7	7.9	13.8	15.7	22.4	26.8	25.7	22.7	15.9	10.7	6.3
Val de Loire	7.8	6.8	10.3	16.1	16.4	23.6	25.8	24.5	21.1	16.2	11.2	7.0
Western Loire	9.9	8.6	11.3	17.7	16.7	23.3	25.7	24.6	21.8	16.9	12.4	9.5

Average Sea Temperatures

	May	June	July	Aug	Sept	Oct
Channel						
Calais to Le Havre	10	13	16	17	16	14
Cherbourg to Brest	11	13	15	17	16	14
Atlantic						
Brest to Bordeaux	13	15	17	18	17	15
Bordeaux to St-Jean-de-Luz	14	15	18	19	19	17
Mediterranean						
Montpellier to Toulon	15	19	19	20	20	17
Ile du Levant to Menton	17	19	20	22	22	19

All temperatures are in **Centigrade**: to convert to **Fahrenheit** multiply by 9/5 and add 32.
For a recorded **weather forecast** you can phone the Paris forecasting office at ☎45.55.91.09
(☎45.55.95.02 for specific inquiries).

can be very attractive and crowd-free. **Climate**, otherwise, need not be a major consideration in planning when to go. Northern France, like nearby Britain, is wet and unpredictable. Paris perhaps has a marginally better climate than New York, rarely reaching the extremes of heat and cold of that city, but only south of the Loire does the weather become significantly warmer. West coast weather, even in the south, is tempered by the proximity of the Atlantic, subject to violent storms and close thundery days even in summer. The centre and east, as you leave the coasts behind, have a more continental climate, with colder winters and hotter summers. The most reliable weather is along and behind the Mediterranean and on Corsica, where winter is short and summer long and hot.

The single most important factor to take into consideration in deciding when to visit France is tourism itself. As most French people take their holidays in their own country, it's as well to avoid the main French holiday periods – mid-July to the end of August, with August being particularly bad. Almost the entire country closes down, except for the tourist industry itself. You can easily walk half a mile and more in Paris, for example, in search of an open *boulangerie*, and the city seems deserted by all except fellow tourists. Prices in the resorts rise to take full advantage and you can't find a room for love nor money, and not even a space in the campsites on the Côte d'Azur. The seaside is the worst, but the mountains and popular regions like the Dordogne are not far behind. Easter, too, is a bad time for Paris; half Europe's schoolchildren seem to descend on the city. For the same reasons, ski buffs should keep in mind the February school ski break. And no one who values life, limb, and sanity should ever be caught on the roads the last weekend of July or August, and least of all on the weekend of August 15.

PART ONE

THE
BASICS

GETTING THERE FROM BRITAIN

The quickest way of reaching France from Britain is, of course, by air, though it is now rivalled closely by the Channel Tunnel London–Paris rail link that makes the 340-kilometre journey In just three hours. The standard rail- or road-and-sea routes are significantly more affordable, but can be uncomfortable and tiring – and if you're just going for a short break, the journey time can significantly eat into your holiday.

BY AIR

Flying to France – particularly to the south – represents a considerable saving in time compared to the ferry and train/car journey: Nice, for example, is just ninety minutes' flying time from London, Paris only fifty minutes, and Toulouse and Lyon both one-and-a-half hours away. As often as not, if you live outside London, you'll find it pays to go to the capital and fly on to France from there. Direct flights from British regional airports do exist, though prices are unfavourable compared with London fares, usually being £70–120 more expensive.

Air France and *British Airways* fly to Paris nine and seventeen times a day respectively, and at least once a day to Bordeaux, Lyon, Marseille, Nice and Toulouse; *British Airways* also flies to Montpellier once a day. *Brit Air* focuses on destinations in Brittany and Normandy, flying nearly every day to Caen, Le Havre, Rennes, Brest and Nantes; *British Midland* flies to Paris a dozen times a day and Nice twice daily. *Air France* and

British Airways both fly to Corsica, but this involves changing in Paris – *Air France* flies into Ajaccio, Bastia or Calvi; *British Airways* into Calvi. The cheapest fares, though, are generally those from London to Paris for anything between £79 and £120; you should add on between £40 and £80 to fly to a regional airport and £150 to fly into Corsica. To find the best deals you should shop around, ideally a month or so before you plan to leave.

A **scheduled flight** is the most obvious option, with *British Airways* and *Air France* being the main carriers to Paris from London, or you can take the London–Paris leg of a long-haul flight to more distant destinations, like *MAS (Malaysian)* or *PIA (Pakistan International)* – *STA Travel* (see below) are specialists in this. Scheduled flights are rarely the least expensive alternative, but give you the flexibility you may need. An **Apex** (Advance Purchase Excursion) ticket is the cheapest way to travel to Paris on a scheduled flight, and must be reserved two weeks in advance and include one Saturday night. Your return date must be fixed when purchasing and no subsequent changes are allowed. Current costs start at around £108 return to Paris. **Superpex** or **Pex** tickets start at around £155 return to Paris with similar conditions, but may be booked at any time. *Air France* also offers a combined flight and *Eurodomino* train pass (see p.6) costing £209 for three days' or £323 for ten days' inclusive rail travel.

If you shop around, you can often come up with a cheaper flight – often as low as £79. A good place to look for **discount fares** from London to France is the classified travel sections of papers like the Saturday editions of the *Independent* and the *Daily Telegraph*, and Sundays like the *Observer, Sunday Times* and *Sunday Independent*, where agents advertise special deals; if you're in London, check the back pages of listings magazine *Time Out*, the *Evening Standard* or the free travel mag *TNT*, found outside mainline train stations. Independent travel specialists *STA Travel* and *Campus Travel* do deals for students and anyone under 26, or can simply sell a scheduled ticket at a discount price – as can *Nouvelles Frontières*. All these are worth contacting to see what deals they currently have on offer, whether it involves seats on their own or a tour operator's **charter flight** – in theory supposed to be sold in conjunction with accommodation, but it is sometimes possible just to buy the air ticket at a discount through your travel agent. Bear in mind that any travel agent can sell you a **package deal** with a tour operator (see below) and these can also often offer exceptional bargain travel.

PACKAGE TOURS

Any travel agent will be able to provide details of the many operators who operate **package tours** to France (see box below), which can work out to be a competitively priced way of travelling. Some are straightforward travel-plus-beach-hotel affairs, which provide a fixed base,

whereas others offer city breaks, tandem touring, air-and-rail packages or stays in country cottages. If your trip is geared around specific interests – like cycling or self-catering in the countryside – packages can work out much cheaper than the same arrangements made on arrival. A package will also include flights, accommodation and often transfers to and from your hotel or a rental car, which can leave you more time to enjoy your holiday if you're on a tight schedule.

In addition to the addresses in the box, bear in mind that most of the ferry companies (see p.8 for addresses) also offer their own travel and accommodation deals. More complete lists of package operators are available from the **French Government Tourist Office**, 178 Piccadilly, London W1V 0AL (☎0171/491 7622).

AIRLINES AND AGENTS

Air France, 177 Piccadilly, London W1V 0LX (☎0181/742 6600).

Brit Air, 239 Longbridge House, Gatwick Airport, West Sussex, Crawley RH6 0NP (☎01293/502044).

British Airways, 156 Regent St, London W1R 5TA (☎0181/897 4000).

British Midland, Donington Hall, Castle Donington, Derby DE4 2SB (☎0171/589 5599 or ☎01345/554554).

Malaysian Airlines (MAS), 191a Askew Rd, London W12 9AX (☎0181/862 0800).

PIA (Pakistan International), 45–46 Piccadilly W1V 0LD (☎0171/734 5544).

DISCOUNT FLIGHT AGENTS

Campus Travel, 52 Grosvenor Gardens, London SW1W 0AG (☎0171/730 8832); 541 Bristol Rd, Bournbrook, Selly Oak, Birmingham B29 6AU (☎0121/414 1848); 39 Queens Rd, Bristol BS8 1QE (☎0117/929 2494); 5 Emmanuel St, Cambridge CB1 1NE (☎01223/324283); 53 Forrest Rd, Edinburgh EH1 2QP (☎0131/225 6111); 13 High St, Oxford OX1 4DB (☎01865/242067). Also at YHA shops and university campuses.

Council Travel, 28a Poland St, London W1V 3DB (☎0171/287 3337). Eight other offices in Britain.

Masterfare, 269 Old Brompton Rd, London SW5 9JA (☎0171/259 2000). Discount agent with competitive deals.

Nouvelles Frontières, 11 Blenheim St, London W1Y 9LE (☎0171/629 7772). French agency.

South Coast Student Travel, 61 Ditchling Rd, Brighton BN1 4SD (☎01273/570226). Plenty to offer non-students as well.

STA Travel, 86 Old Brompton Rd, London SW7 3LH *and* 117 Euston Rd, London NW1 2SX (tele-sales ☎0171/937 9921); 75 Deansgate, Manchester M3 2BW (tele-sales ☎0161/834 0668); 88 Vicar Lane, Leeds LS1 7JH; 25 Queens Rd, Bristol BS8 1QE; 38 Sidney St, Cambridge CB2 3HX (tele-sales ☎01223/66966); 36 George St, Oxford OX1 2AQ; Strathclyde University, 90 John St, Glasgow G1 1JH. Also on various university campuses.

Thomas Cook, Head office: 45 Berkeley St, London W1A 1EB (☎0171/499 4000).

Wasteels, Platform 2, Victoria Station, London SW1V 1JT (☎0171/834 7066).

Trailfinders, 42–50 Earls Court Rd, London W8 6EJ (☎0171/937 5400).

Note that addresses and telephone numbers may not be in the same location: some airlines and agents use a single telephone-sales number for several offices.

Note also that 0891 numbers are premium rate and charge around 49p per minute before 6pm, 39p after.

FRENCH PACKAGE TOUR OPERATORS AND VILLA AGENCIES

Air France Holidays, Gable House, 18–24 Turnham Green Terrace, London W4 1RF (☎0181/742 3377). Flight and accommodation, fly-drive and air-and-rail packages from many regional destinations. Flight plus a week in a hotel in Nice from £601 per person.

Allez France, 27 West St, Storrington RH20 4DZ (☎01903/742345). Self-drive and fly-drive accommodation packages from Gatwick to various French destinations. London–Paris return flight plus a week's hotel accommodation in Paris at high season starts at around £249 per person.

Bike Events, PO Box 75, Bath, Avon BA1 1BX (☎0225/480130). Biking trips to France.

Brittany Ferries, Brittany Centre, Wharf Rd, Portsmouth PO2 8RU (☎01705/751833). Short breaks in Paris for 3, 6 or 10 days, including ferry crossing with car in peak season: 4 nights £183, 2 nights £113.

British Airways Holidays, Pacific House, Hazelwick Ave, Crawley RH10 1PN (☎01293/615 353). City break flights from regional airports, and package deals from around £149 for a flight and two nights in Paris.

Chambres d'Hôte, Gîtes de France Ltd (Chambres d'Hôte), 178 Piccadilly, London W1V 9DB (☎0171/493 3480). Houses, cottages and chalets all over France from as little as £195 for one week, including ferry crossing for a car with two people.

Corsican Affair, George House, 5–7 Humbolt Rd, London W6 8QH (☎0171/385 8438). Fly-drive, hotel packages and self-catering.

Dominique's Villas, 13 Park House, 140 Battersea Rd, London SW11 4NB (☎0171/738 8772). Small, upmarket agency with a diverse and tempting range of mostly older properties (some quite historic) in the Loire, Dordogne, Provence and on the Côte d'Azur. Most are for large groups, sleeping 6–8 or more.

Gîtes de France, 178 Piccadilly, London W1V 9DB (☎0171/493 3480). Houses, cottages and chalets in the Île-de-France region, mostly about half an hour from Paris by train. One week minimum from Saturday to Saturday or Tuesday to Tuesday from £195 per person, inclusive of car ferry crossing.

Guide Dogs Adventure Group, Hillfields, Burghfield, Reading RG7 3YG (☎01734/835555). Specialists in activity holidays for the visually impaired and unsighted. A week's tandem touring in Normandy for £339 per person with full board, and walking tours in southern France for £430 per person for a week.

Irish Ferries, 2–4 Merrion Row, Dublin 2 (☎01/661 0511). *Paris Rail Breaks* from £146 per person for return from anywhere in Ireland to Rosslare and Cork, ferry crossings and two nights' bed and breakfast.

Keycamp Holidays, 92–96 Lind Rd, Sutton SM1 4PL (☎0181/395 4000). Mobile homes and tents. One week in the south of France from £609 for two adults and two children in high season, including ferry.

Paris Travel Service, Bridge House, Ware SG12 9DF (☎01920/467 467). Wide range of packages from £105 for rail, *Sealink* ferry and basic accommodation. Good for regional flights and rail deals via London.

Plas y Brenin Centre for Mountain Activities, Capel Curig, Betws-y-Coed, Gwynedd, Wales LL24 0ET (☎016904/280). The centre organizes summertime ski-mountaineering courses in the Alps, including parts of the High Level Route. A ten-day course including accommodation but not food costs £440.

Sally Holidays, 92–96 Lind Rd, Sutton SM1 4PL (☎0181/395 3030). Ferry for car and two adults plus two-star hotel in central Paris from £84 per person for the first night, and £27 each subsequent night.

Susie Madron's Cycling for Softies, 2–4 Birch Polygon, Rusholme, Manchester M14 5HX (☎0161/248 8282). An easy-going cycle holiday operator to most regions. Seven-day tours, with flight and accommodation, bike and back-up (not luggage transfer) around £580 per person.

Time Off Ltd, Chester Close, Chester St, London SW1X 7BQ (☎0171/235 8070). Short breaks to Paris by air, bus and train (including Orient Express packages). Two nights in a one-star hotel, travelling by bus, from £121; self-drive packages from £100.

Travelscene Ltd, 11–15 St Ann's Road, Harrow HA1 1AS (☎0181/427 4445). Short breaks in Paris, travelling by air, train or bus. Two nights in a one-star by bus from £99; £78 self-drive.

Vacances en Campagne, Bignor, nr Pulborough RH20 1QD (☎017987 411). Self-catering accommodation all over France and Corsica – from apartments and cottages to large manor houses. High standards, careful information and not cheap, but good value for money.

Venice Simplon-Orient-Express, Sea Containers House, 20 Upper Ground, London SE1 9PF (☎0171/928 6000). From £555 for two nights, flying to Paris, returning in by day-car on the Orient Express.

continued from previous page

VFB Holidays; French Weekenders, Normandy House, High St, Cheltenham GL5 3HW (☎01242/ 580187). Good-value self-catering, ferry and road holidays, plus alpine resorts in the Midi, Alsace and Burgundy. Two nights in a hotel plus flight from £181, or £129 by ferry and car.

Voyages Ilena, 7 Old Garden House, The Lanterns, Bridge Lane, London SW11 3AD

(☎0171/924 4440). Classy hotels and self-catering accommodation all over Corsica; flights and fly-drives too.

Youth Hostels Association, Trevelyan House, St Stephen's Hill, St Albans, Herts (☎01727/855215). Apart from doing cheap accommodation, the association sells combined bike rental and hostel packages.

BY TRAIN

The **Channel Tunnel** has slashed travelling time by train from London to Lille and Paris, with *Eurostar* high-speed trains running from London Waterloo to Lille in two hours and Paris Gare du Nord in three hours. At the time of writing the service is limited to four trains a day to Paris and one to Lille.

Tickets from London to Paris cost £155 return (second class), £195 (first class), or £95 if booked 14 days in advance. Bookings can be made through high street travel agents, by calling *Eurostar* direct, or through *SNCF (French Railways)* in London. At the end of 1995 or the beginning of 1996, night trains using the Chunnel will also operate from Scotland and Wales to Paris.

Now that the *TGV* station at Roissy Charles-de-Gaulle airport is open, you can continue your journey by train to northeastern and southeastern destinations in France without having to go via the capital; by 1996, the *TGV* bypass of Paris from the airport will be extended, allowing direct connections to western and southwestern destinations too.

BY TRAIN AND FERRY/HOVERCRAFT

The opening of the Channel Tunnel has led to competitive cut-rate deals on **train and ferry/ hovercraft** fares via Calais, Boulogne or Dieppe. Crossing the Channel this way works out slightly cheaper than using the Chunnel, but takes considerably longer and is obviously less convenient. You can catch one of the many trains from London Victoria which connect with cross-Channel ferries or hovercrafts, with an onward train service on the other side. Calais-Maritime train station is currently closed for redevelopment, and there's a bus shuttle service until about 8.30pm to Calais-Ville station; taxis cost around 50F.

On the shortest and most economical Channel crossings – Dover–Calais and Folkestone–Boulogne – the choice is between **train and hovercraft**, on which the total journey time from London to Paris is six hours, or **train and ferry**, taking seven or eight hours. Services on these routes are frequent (up to twenty a day in peak season) and tie in well with the trains. By train and ferry, the best deals are on the conveniently scheduled (though slightly slower) night services. Students and anyone under 26 can buy heavily discounted *BIJ* tickets from *Eurotrain* outlets (like *Campus Travel*, see opposite) and most student travel agents; these cost £49 return (departing Tues–Thurs), any other day £70 return, £47 one way; or with *Hoverspeed* (1hr 30min faster), whose prices are £55 return Tues–Thurs, any other day £74 return. *British Rail International*'s cheapest five-day return fare is £57 via Dieppe; the cheapest two-month return is £78 via Dieppe.

TRAIN PASSES

If you plan to use the train network to get around France, there are several **train passes** you might consider buying. **EuroDomino** passes offer unlimited train travel through France for any three (£118), five (£154) or ten (£235) days within a calendar month (passengers under 26 pay £96, £125 and £200 respectively), and are available from accredited *British Rail* travel agents, the *International Rail Centre* at London Victoria (see opposite), or the main *SNCF* stations in France. The pass also entitles you to fifty-percent reductions on train/ferry links to France. *Air France* offers special deals on combined flights and *Eurodomino* train passes (see p.3).

If you're planning to travel beyond France, the **InterRail** pass offers one month's unlimited use of all European train services for £249 to anyone under 26 who has been resident in Europe for at least six months, and is available from *British Rail International* and some travel agents, including branches of *Campus Travel* and *STA Travel* (see p.4). *InterRail* also issues a pass for use solely on the train networks of France, Belgium, the Netherlands and Luxembourg, costing £179 for 15 days' unlimited travel.

BY BUS

At the time of writing, the bus companies have no plans to use the Channel Tunnel, so the choice remains between **bus and hovercraft** and **bus and ferry**. Prices are very much lower than for the same journey by train.

The **Hoverspeed City Sprint** bus/hovercraft service leaves from London's Victoria Coach Station, catches the hovercraft from Dover to Calais or Boulogne, and arrives in Paris between eight and nine hours after setting off. There are two buses per day in winter, four in summer. The regular adult return is £55 (with a student discount of £3), and can be purchased through any travel agent. **Eurolines** runs regular bus/ferry services to over fifty French cities, with adult return fares currently at £55 for Paris, £45 for St-Malo (via Portsmouth), £85 for Lyon, £93 for Strasbourg, £99 for Bordeaux, and £110 for Perpignan/Montpellier. Students and under-26s qualify for a ten-percent discount on certain routes.

USEFUL ADDRESSES

British Rail International, International Rail Centre, Victoria Station, London SW1 (☎0171/834 2345).

Campus Travel, Head office: 52 Grosvenor Gardens, London SW1 (☎0171/730 3402).

Eurolines, 164 Buckingham Palace Rd, London SW1 (☎0171/730 0202).

Eurostar, European Passenger Services, EPS House, Waterloo Station, London SE1 (reservations ☎01233/617 575).

Hoverspeed, Maybrook House, Queens Gardens, Dover CT17 (☎01304/240 202).

Le Shuttle, PO Box 300, Folkestone, Kent CT19 4QW (☎01303/271 100).

SNCF (French Railways), 179 Piccadilly, London W1V 0VA (☎01345/300 003).

Tickets for both *Eurolines* and *Hoverspeed* are available from the companies direct or from most high street travel agents.

BY CAR AND TRAIN

The most convenient way of taking your car across to France is to **drive** down to the Channel Tunnel, load your car on the train shuttle, and be whisked under the Channel in 35 minutes, emerging at Sangatte on the French side, just outside Calais. The Channel Tunnel entrance is off the M20 at Junction 11A, just outside of Folkestone, and the sole operator, *Le Shuttle*, has 21 services daily, including one every hour or so throughout the night. Because of the frequency of the service, you don't have to buy a ticket in advance; just arrive and wait to board; there's a promised loading time of just ten minutes. Inside the carriages, you can get out of your car to stretch your legs during the crossing. **Tickets** are available through *Le Shuttle*'s Customer Service Centre or from your local travel agent. Fares, calculated per car, regardless of the number of passengers, prices are £49 for a day return, £75 for a 5-day return, and £136 for a standard return.

If you don't want to drive far when you've reached France, you can take advantage of *SNCF*'s **Motorail** (☎0171/409 3518), putting your car on the train in Calais or Paris. Calais–Nice, for example, costs from £396 return for car and driver, plus £106 for an additional adult and £53 for children between 4 and 11.

BY CAR OR FOOT AND FERRY/HOVERCRAFT

The cheapest cross-Channel options for most travellers are the **ferry** or **hovercraft** (or high-speed catamaran) links between **Dover–Calais/Boulogne**, **Folkestone–Boulogne** and **Ramsgate–Dunkerque**. However, if your starting point is further west than London, it may well be worth heading direct to one of the south coast ports and catching one of the ferries to Normandy or Brittany – **Newhaven–Dieppe**, **Portsmouth/Southampton/Weymouth/Poole–Le Havre/Caen/Cherbourg/St-Malo** or **Plymouth–Roscoff**. If you're coming from the north of England or Scotland, opting for the **Hull–Zeebrugge** (Belgium) crossing overnight with *North Sea Ferries* makes a lot of sense.

FERRY ROUTES AND PRICES

	Operator	Crossing Time	Frequency	One-way Fares Small car 2 adults	Foot passenger
BRITTANY					
Plymouth–St Malo	Brittany Ferries	8hr 45min	Mar–Nov 1 nightly	£74–179	£24–37
Plymouth–Roscoff	Brittany Ferries	6hr	Feb–Dec 3–17 wkly	£74–161	£23–38
NORMANDY					
Southampton–Cherbourg	Stena Sealink	6–10hr	1–2 daily	£61–166	£12–27
Portsmouth–Cherbourg	P&O European Ferries	4hr 45min	1–3 daily	£75–148	£18–30
Poole–Cherbourg	Brittany Ferries	4hr 15min	Feb–Dec 1–2 daily	£63–132	£18–30
Portsmouth–Caen	Brittany Ferries	5hr 45min	3 daily	£69–145	£20–35
Portsmouth–Le Havre	P&O European Ferries	5hr 45min	2–3 daily	£82–180	£20–35
Newhaven–Dieppe	Stena Sealink	4hr	4 daily	£70–186	£22–26
PAS-DE-CALAIS					
Folkestone–Boulogne	Hoverspeed‡	55 min	5 daily	£103–153	£22–44
Dover–Calais	Stena Sealink	1hr 30min	25 daily	£114–168	£26
Dover–Calais	P&O European Ferries	1hr 15min	20–25 daily	£72–162	£25
Dover–Calais	Hoverspeed‡‡	35–50min	20–24 daily	£72–162	£25
Ramsgate–Dunkerque	Sally Ferries	2hr 30min	5 daily all year	£58–134	£22

Addresses in Britain

Brittany Ferries
Wharf Rd, Portsmouth PO2 8RU
☎01705/827701

Millbay Docks, Plymouth PL1 3EW ☎01752/221321

Poole ☎01202/666466

Hoverspeed
Maybrook House, Queens Gardens, Dover CT17 9UQ ☎01304/240202

‡Seacat high-speed catamaran.

‡‡Hovercraft and Seacat.

North Sea Ferries
King George Dock, Hedon Rd, Hull HU9 5QA
☎0482/795141

P&O European Ferries
Channel House, Channel View Rd, Dover CT17 9TJ
☎01304/203388

Continental Ferry Port, Mile End, Portsmouth PO2 8QW ☎01705/827677

London ☎0181/575 8555

Sally Line
Argyle Centre, York St, Ramsgate, Kent CT11 9DS
☎01843/595522

81 Piccadilly, London W1V 9HF ☎0181/858 1127

Stena Sealink Line
Charter House, Park St, Ashford, Kent TN24 8EX
☎01233/647047

24-hr information, Dover ☎01304/240028

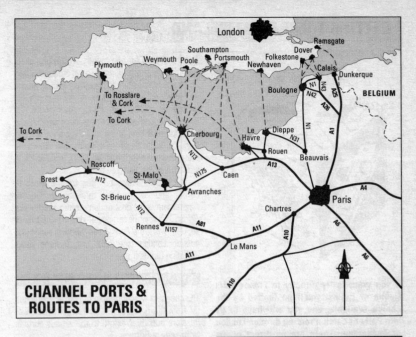

CHANNEL PORTS & ROUTES TO PARIS

Ferry prices are seasonal, and, for motorists, depend on the size of your vehicle, ranging from just £12 one-way for a foot passenger on the Southampton–Cherbourg sailing in low season to £176 for a car with two adults on the Portsmouth–St-Malo route. The popular Dover–Calais routing costs just over £70 for a car and two adults in low season, but cheaper deals are regularly available. Return prices are substantially cheaper than one-way fares, but generally need to be booked in advance – details of routes, companies and current fares are given in the box below. You can either contact the companies direct to reserve space in advance – essential in peak season if you're intending to drive – or any travel agent in the UK or France will do it for you.

The ferry companies will also often offer **special deals** on 3-, 5- and 10-day returns, or discounts for regular users who own a property abroad. The tour operator **Eurodrive** (☎0181/342 8979) can also arrange discounts on ferry crossings and the Chunnel shuttle for people taking their cars across the Channel, and can book accommodation in northern France at competitive rates.

HITCHING

Hitching from Calais or Boulogne to Paris is notoriously difficult, so you'd be well advised to accept through lifts only. The worst black holes – where hitchers become invisible to drivers – are Abbeville and Beauvais, and if you can possibly afford one of the cheaper bus or train tickets, you'll save yourself a lot of trouble. If not, get friendly with drivers on the boat over and try to get a promise of a lift before docking. Dieppe is not that much easier to hitch out of. From Caen's port – Ouistreham – you can get a cheap local bus to the city if your thumb fails you. Hitching in Brittany is much more feasible and single passenger fares on *Brittany Ferries* are reasonable.

It may well be worth contacting the **ride-share organization** *Allostop*, 84 passage Brady, 75010 Paris (☎47.70.02.01; Mon–Fri 9am–7.30pm, Sat 9am–1pm & 2–6pm), which deals with journeys to and from Paris. You pay to register with them (70F for one trip of 500km or more, 60F for 400–500km, 50F for 300–400km, plus 20 centimes per km, including *autoroute* tolls for the driver) and they find a driver who's going to your destination.

GETTING THERE FROM IRELAND

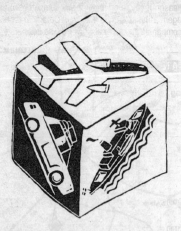

night and valid for one month, with a few seats from IR£149 return. *Budget Travel* organizes charter flights from Dublin to Nice from IR£199 return, and their scheduled flights to Nice at IR£262 include a stopover in Paris. Alternatives via Britain are unlikely to be attractive considering the additional time factor and the cost of a flight from Dublin to Britain. For up-to-date details on the situation, try contacting *USIT*, specialists in student/youth travel (see box).

There are no direct flights from **Belfast** to Paris, and a routing through London or Amsterdam is the best option – often airlines like *British Airways* have special deals from £75 or so; otherwise, the *Paris Travel Service*, based just outside London (see p.5), has package deals including flights from Belfast.

If you want to fly directly to France from Dublin or Belfast you'll be limited by the choice available, and you will have to fly into Paris or catch a routing through London or Amsterdam. There are no direct flights from Ireland to Corsica.

Aer Lingus fly direct from **Dublin** to Charles de Gaulle Paris with Super Apex tickets, booked 7 days in advance, with a stay including a Saturday

BY CAR AND FERRY

The cheapest way of getting to France – although far from the quickest – is by **ferry** from Cork or Rosslare outside Wexford to the various ports in Normandy or Brittany.

Ferry prices vary according to season and, for motorists, the size of their car; note that return prices are substantially cheaper but generally need to be booked in advance. Prices vary from around

---

USEFUL ADDRESSES IN IRELAND

AIRLINES

Aer Lingus, 42 Grafton St, Dublin (☎01/637 0011); 46 Castle St, Belfast (☎0800/626747).

Air Inter, 29–30 Dawson St, Dublin (☎01/677 8899).

British Airways, 60 Dawson St, Dublin (☎0800/626747); 9 Fountain Centre, College St, Belfast (☎0232/245 151).

DISCOUNT FLIGHT AGENTS

Budget Travel, 134 Lower Baggot St, Dublin (☎01/661 3122).

Joe Walsh Tours, 8–11 Baggot St, Dublin (☎01/678 9555); 31 Castle St, Belfast (☎0232/241144).

Thomas Cook, 118 Grafton St, Dublin (☎01/677 1721); 11 Donegal Place, Belfast (☎0232/240 833).

Mainstream package holiday and flight agent, with occasional discount offers.

USIT, 19–21 Aston Quay, Dublin (☎01/778 117); 10–11 Market Parade, Cork (☎021/270 900); 31a Queen St, Belfast (☎0232/242 562). Student and youth specialists.

TOUR OPERATORS

Irish Ferries, 2–4 Merrion Row, Dublin 2 (☎01/6610511). Paris Rail Savers from £169 per person for return from anywhere in Ireland to Rosslare/

Cork, and return between Le Havre/Cherbourg and Paris, plus two nights bed and breakfast. Return to Paris from any Irish Rail station via Le Havre £119.

IR£210 to almost IR£300 for a small car and two adults, regardless of the crossing route; foot passengers will pay between IR£55 and IR£86. Often ferry companies will offer special deals on return fares for a specified period, so check first.

You can either contact the companies direct to reserve space in advance (essential at peak season if you're driving), or any competent travel agent at home can do it for you. Details of routes, companies and fares are given in the box below.

FERRY ROUTES AND PRICES

	Operator	Crossing Time	Frequency	One-way Fares Small car 2 adults (£IR)	Foot passenger (£IR)
Cork–Roscoff	*Brittany Ferries*	13–17hr	April–Oct 1–2 wkly	£210–298	£60–82
Cork–St-Malo	*Brittany Ferries*	18hr	April–Oct 1 wkly	£210–298	£60–82
Cork–Le Havre	*Irish Ferries*	21hr 30min	May–Sept 2 wkly	£210–275	£55–80
Cork–Cherbourg	*Irish Ferries*	17hr 30min	July–Sept 1 wkly	£210–275	£55–80
Rosslare–Cherbourg	*Irish Ferries*	18hr	May–Sept 1–2 wkly	£216–281	£61–86
Rosslare–Le Havre	*Irish Ferries*	21hr	July–Sept 2–3 wkly	£216–281	£61–86
Rosslare–Brest	*Irish Ferries*	15hr	May–Sept 2 wkly	£210–275	£55–80
Cork–Brest	*Irish Ferries*	15hr 30min	May–Sept 2 wkly	£210–275	£55–80

Addresses in Ireland

Brittany Ferries, 42 Grand Parade, Cork
☎021/277801

Irish Ferries, 2–4 Merrion Row, Dublin 2
☎01/661 0511
Cork ☎021/504333
Rosslare ☎053/33158

GETTING THERE FROM NORTH AMERICA

Getting to France from North America is straightforward; there are direct flights from over thirty major cities to Paris (the only transatlantic gateway in France), with connections from all over the continent. Nearly a dozen different scheduled airlines operate flights, making Paris one of the cheapest destinations in Europe. In fact, only London can offer more discounted flights; and while a visit to England may appeal, the price difference is rarely sufficient to make a stopover in London a money-saving idea. Note that Eurail passes (see p.16) are also useful if France is part of a longer European trip, since you can use it to get from any part of Europe to France.

SHOPPING FOR TICKETS

Barring special offers, the cheapest fare is usually an **Apex** ticket, although this will carry certain restrictions: you have to book – and pay – at least 21 days before departure, spend at least seven days abroad (maximum stay three months), and you tend to get penalized if you change your schedule. On transatlantic routes there are also winter **Super Apex** tickets, sometimes known as "Eurosavers" – slightly cheaper than an ordinary Apex, but limiting your stay to between 7 and 21 days. Some airlines also issue **Special Apex** tickets to people younger than 24, often extend-

ing the maximum stay to a year. Many airlines offer youth or student fares to **under 25s**; a passport or driving licence are sufficient proof of age, though these tickets are subject to availability and can have eccentric booking conditions. It's worth remembering that most cheap return fares involve spending at least one Saturday night away and that many will only give a percentage refund if you need to cancel or alter your journey, so make sure you check the restrictions carefully before buying a ticket.

You can normally cut costs further by going through a specialist flight agent – either a **consolidator**, who buys up blocks of tickets from the airlines and sells them at a discount, or a **discount agent**, who deals in blocks of tickets offloaded by the airlines, and often offers special student and youth fares and a range of other travel-related services such as travel insurance, rail passes, car rentals, tours and the like. Bear in mind, though, that penalties for changing your plans can be stiff, and that these companies make their money by dealing in bulk – don't expect them to answer lots of questions. Some agents specialize in **charter flights**, which may

SAMPLE ROUND-TRIP SCHEDULED FARES TO PARIS

Typical lowest discounted fares in low season/ high season, flying midweek.

Atlanta: $600/$670
Boston: $570/$680
Chicago: $590/$720
Cincinnati: $590/$730
Dallas: $660/$780
Houston: $640/$760
Los Angeles: $500/$720
Miami: $600/$700
Montréal: CDN$680/$820
New York: $400/$520
Raleigh-Durham: $600/$700
St Louis: $650/$780
San Francisco: $620/$840
Toronto: CDN$680/$820
Vancouver: CDN$800/$1000
Washington DC: $520/$670

DISCOUNT AGENTS, CONSOLIDATORS AND TRAVEL CLUBS

Air Brokers International, 323 Geary St, Suite 411, San Francisco, CA 94102 (☎1-800/883-3273). Consolidator.

Air Courier Association, 191 University Boulevard, Suite 300, Denver, CO 80206 (☎303/278-8810). Courier flight broker.

Airhitch, 2472 Broadway, Suite 200, New York, NY 10025 (☎212/864-2000). Standby-seat broker: For a set price, they guarantee to get you on a flight as close to your preferred destination as possible, within a week.

Cosmos Tourama, 92-25 Queens Bvd, Rego Park, NY 11374 (☎1-800/338-7092). Travel club.

Council Travel, 205 E 42nd St, New York, NY 10017 (☎800/743-1823). Nationwide US student travel organization with branches (among others) in San Francisco, Washington DC, Boston, Austin, Seattle, Chicago, Minneapolis.

Discount Travel International, Ives Bldg, 114 Forrest Ave, Suite 205, Narberth, PA 19072 (☎800/334-9294). Discount travel club.

Educational Travel Center, 438 N Frances St, Madison, WI 53703 (☎1-800/747-5551). Student/youth discount agent.

Encore Travel Club, 4501 Forbes Blvd, Lanham, MD 20706 (☎1-800/444-9800). Discount travel club.

Globus Gateway, 92-25 Queens Bvd, Rego Park, NY 11374 (☎1-800/221-0090). Travel club.

Holidaze Ski Tours, 810 Belmar Plaza, Belmar, NJ 07719 (☎1-800/526-2827). Ski specialist.

Insight International Tours, 745 Atlantic Ave, Boston, MA 02111 (☎1-800/582-8380). Travel club.

Interworld Travel, 800 Douglass Rd, Miami, FL 33134 (☎305/443-4929). Consolidator.

Last Minute Travel Club, 132 Brookline Ave, Boston, MA 02215 (☎1-800/LAST MIN). Travel club specializing in standby deals.

Moment's Notice, 425 Madison Ave, New York, NY 10017 (☎212/486-0503). Discount travel club.

New Frontiers/Nouvelles Frontières, 12 E 33rd St, New York, NY 10016 (☎1-800/366-6387); 1001 Sherbrook East, Suite 720, Montréal H2L 1L3 (☎514/526-8444). French discount travel firm; also markets charters to Paris and Lyon.

Other branches in LA, San Francisco and Québec City.

Now Voyager, 74 Varick St, Suite 307, New York, NY 10013 (☎212/431-1616). Agent specializing in Courier flights.

Pilgrimage Tours & Travel, 39 Beechwood Ave, Manhasset, NY 11030 (☎1-800/669-0757).

Saga International Holidays, 222 Berkeley St, Boston, MA 02116 (☎1-800/343-0273). Specializes in group travel for seniors.

STA Travel, 48 East 11th St, New York, NY 10003 (☎1-800/777-0112). Worldwide specialist in independent travel with branches in the Los Angeles, San Francisco and Boston areas. STA also has French branches in Paris and Grenoble.

TFI Tours International, 34 W 32nd St, New York, NY 10001 (☎1-800/745-8000). Consolidator; other offices in Las Vegas, San Francisco, Los Angeles.

Travac, 989 6th Ave, New York NY 10018 (☎1-800/872-8800). Consolidator and charter broker; has another branch in Orlando.

Travel Avenue, 10 S Riverside, Suite 1404, Chicago, IL 60606 (☎1-800/333-3335). Discount travel agent.

Travel Cuts, 187 College St, Toronto, ON M5T 1P7 (☎416/979-2406). Canadian specialist student travel organization with branches all over the country.

Travelers Advantage, 3033 S Parker Rd, Suite 900, Aurora, CO 80014 (☎1-800/548-1116). Discount travel club.

Unitravel, 1177 N Warson Rd, St Louis, MO 63132 (☎1-800/325-2222). Consolidator.

Vantage Travel, 111 Cypress St, Brookline, MA 02146 (☎1-800/322-6677). Specializes in group travel for seniors.

Worldtek Travel, 111 Water St, New Haven, CT 06511 (☎1-800/243-1723). Discount travel agency.

Worldwide Adventures, 36 Finch Ave West, North York, ON M2N 2G9 (☎1-800/387-1483). Sightseeing and adventure holidays.

Worldwide Discount Travel Club, 1674 Meridian Ave, Miami Beach, FL 33139 (☎305/534-2082). Discount travel club.

be cheaper than anything available on a scheduled flight, but again departure dates are fixed and withdrawal penalties are high (check the refund policy). If you travel a lot, **discount travel clubs** are another option – the annual membership fee may be worth it for benefits such as cut-price air tickets and car rental.

A further possibility is to see if you can arrange a **courier flight**, although the hit-or-miss nature of these makes them most suitable for a single traveller who travels light and has a very flexible schedule. In return for shepherding a parcel through customs and possibly giving up your baggage allowance, you can expect to get a deeply discounted ticket. For more options, consult *A Simple Guide to Courier Travel* (Pacific Data Sales Publishing). Flights (from about $300 round trip) are issued on a first-come, first-served basis, and there's no guarantee that the Paris route will be available at the specific time you want.

Don't automatically assume that tickets purchased through a travel specialist will be cheapest – once you get a quote, check with the airlines and you may turn up an even better deal. Be advised also that the pool of travel companies is swimming with sharks – exercise caution and *never* deal with a company that demands cash up front or refuses to accept payment by credit card.

Note that fares are heavily dependent on **season**, and are highest from around early June to the end of August; they drop during the "shoulder" seasons, September–October and April–May, and you'll get the best deals during the low season, November through March (excluding Christmas). Note that Friday, Saturday and Sunday travel tends to carry a premium, and that one-way fares are generally slightly more than half the round-trip.

If you have a specific destination in mind in France outside Paris and you're in a hurry – and if you're prepared to pay extra – it's possible to be ticketed straight through to any of more than a dozen **regional airports**. Most of these entail connecting flights on *Air Inter*, *Air France*'s domestic arm, and require a change of planes in Paris (check to make sure there's no inconvenient transfer between Charles de Gaulle and Orly). Some sample round-trip add-on fares from Paris: Bordeaux, $60; Brest, $100; Grenoble, $60; Lyon, $60; Marseille, $100; Nice, $100; Strasbourg, $60; Toulouse, $100.

FLIGHTS FROM THE USA

Transatlantic fares to France from the USA are very reasonable, thanks to intense competition. Any local travel agent should be able to access airlines' up-to-the-minute fares, although they may not have time to research all the possibilities, and you could call the airlines direct. Use the sample fares on p.12 as a guideline.

The most comprehensive range of flights from the US is offered by **Air France**, the French national carrier, which flies nonstop to Paris Charles de Gaulle airport from Anchorage, Boston, Chicago, Houston, Los Angeles, Miami, New York (JFK and Newark) and Washington DC – in most instances daily.

The **major American competitors** tend to be cheaper but offer fewer nonstop routes. *American* and *TWA* have the biggest range of direct routes. *American* flies several times a week to Paris Orly nonstop from Chicago, Dallas, New York (JFK), Miami and Raleigh-Durham, and has good or guaranteed connections from many cities in the south and west. *TWA* flies nonstop to Paris Charles de Gaulle from Boston, New

---

AIRLINES IN NORTH AMERICA

Air Canada (call ☎1-800/555-1212 for local toll-free number).

Air France (☎1-800/237-2747; in Canada, ☎1-800/667-2747).

American Airlines (☎1-800/433-7300).

British Airways (☎1-800/247-9297; in Canada ☎1-800/668-1080).

Canadian Airlines (☎1-800/665-1177).

Continental Airlines (☎1-800/231-0856).

Delta Airlines (☎1-800/241-4141).

Northwest Airlines (☎1-800/225-2525).

PIA Pakistan International Airways (☎1-800/221-2552).

Tower Air (☎1-800/221-2500).

TWA (☎1-800/892-4141).

United Airlines (☎1-800/538-2929).

US Air (☎1-800/428-4322).

Virgin Atlantic Airways (☎1-800/862-8621).

York, St Louis and Washington DC, again with connections from many other cities.

Delta flies direct to Paris Orly from New York, Atlanta and Cincinnati with good or guaranteed connections from over a dozen southern and western cities, and has the only nonstop flight from New York to Nice. *United* flies nonstop to Paris Charles de Gaulle from Chicago, Washington DC, LA and San Francisco. *Tower Air* and *Continental* have direct flights from New York to Paris, with connecting flights from other cities. *US Air* features a direct Philadelphia–Paris routing. *Northwest* flies nonstop from Detroit and Boston to Paris Charles de Gaulle.

Lastly, there are direct flights (often cheap) with *PIA Pakistan International* from New York to Paris Orly.

FLIGHTS FROM CANADA

The strong links between France and Québec's Francophone community ensure regular air services from **Canada to Paris**. The main route is Vancouver–Toronto–Montréal–Paris Charles de Gaulle, although most departures orginate in Toronto, with *Air France* flying almost daily from Toronto to Charles de Gaulle, either nonstop or via Montréal. *Air Canada* and *Canadian Airlines* fly direct to Paris from Toronto and Montréal, again pretty well daily, with guaranteed connections from Vancouver.

Travel Cuts and *Nouvelles Frontières* are the most likely sources of good-value discounted seats; call for details as flights vary from season to season.

FLYING VIA THE UK

Although **flying to London** is usually the cheapest way of reaching Europe, price differences these days are minimal enough for there to be little point travelling to France via London unless you've specifically chosen to visit the UK as well. Having said that, you may well be able to pick up

---

TOUR OPERATORS IN NORTH AMERICA

Abercrombie & Kent, 1520 Kensington Rd, Oak Brook, IL (☎1-800/323-7308). Deluxe hiking, biking, canal, rail and skiing packages.

Actyve Ski Vacations, 252-26 Northern Blvd, Little Neck, NY 11363 (☎1-800/345-5021). Skiing in the Alps.

Adventure Center, 1311 63rd St, Suite 200, Emeryville, CA 94608 (☎800/227-8747). Trekking in France and Corsica.

Adventures on Skis, 815 North Rd, Westfield, MA 01805 (☎1-800/628-9655). Skiing in the Alps.

AESU Travel, 2 Hamill Rd, Suite 248, Baltimore, MD 21210 (☎1-800/638-7640). Riviera packages for under-35s.

Backroads, 1516 5th St, Suite L101, Berkeley, CA 94710 (☎1-800/462-2848). Trendy bike tours.

Butterfield & Robinson, 70 Bond St, Toronto, ON M5B 1X3 (☎1-800/268-8415). Trekking.

CBT Bicycle Tours, 415 W Fullerton, #1003, Chicago, IL 60614 (☎1-800/736-BIKE). European bike tours, some starting or ending in Paris.

Contiki Tours, 300 Plaza Alicante, #900, Garden Grove, CA 92640 (☎800/CONTIKI). Vacations for under-35s.

Cosmos Tourama/Globus, 92-25 Queens Bvd, Rego Park, NY 11374 (☎800/221-0090). Group tours and city breaks; Cosmos has the budget trips.

EC Tours, 10153 1/2 Riverside, Toluca Lake, CA 91602 (☎800/388-0877). City packages, wine tours.

ETT Tours, 198 Boston Post Rd, Mamaroneck, NY 10543 (☎1-800/551-2085). Independent tours and city packages.

Euro-Bike Tours, PO Box 990, DeKalb, IL 60115 (☎1-800/321-6060). Luxury bike tours.

The French Experience, 370 Lexington Ave, Suite 812, New York, NY 10017 (☎1-800/28-FRANCE). Self-drive tours, apartment and cottage rentals, city breaks.

Himalayan Travel, 112 Prospect St, Stamford, CT 06901 (☎1-800/225-2380). Trekking in the French and Corsican interior.

Insight International Tours, 745 Atlantic Ave, Boston, MA 02111 (☎1-800/582-8380). Introductory sightseeing.

Interhome, 124 Little Falls Rd, Fairfield, NJ 07004 (☎201/882-6864). Short-term villa and château rentals.

International Study Tours, 225 W 34th St, New York, NY 10122 (☎1-800/833-2111). Culture/art tours.

Mountain Travel-Sobek, 6420 Fairmount Ave, El Cerrito, CA 94530 (☎1-800/227-2384). Trekking.

Vacance en Campagne, PO Box 299, Elkton, VA 22827 (☎800/327-6097). Short-term rentals of châteaux and country houses in France and Corsica.

Wilderness Travel, 801 Allston Way, Berkeley, CA 94710 (☎1-800/368-2794). Trekking.

a flight to London at an advantageous rate – see pp.3–4 for details of flights from London.

In recent years, **Virgin Atlantic** has offered some of the best fares from New York JFK and Newark, and has now added flights from Miami, Orlando and Boston to its schedules (all into London Gatwick). **British Airways** has entered the fray with a series of rival offers. In summer, the savings are bound to be less, but shop around as there may yet be some European bargains. As well as those from JFK and Newark, *British Airways* has regular nonstop flights from Philadelphia, Boston, San Francisco and Los Angeles – and Detroit via Montréal.

PACKAGE TOURS

Dozens of tour operators specialize in travel to France, and many can put together very **flexible deals**, sometimes amounting to no more than a flight plus car or train pass and accommodation; if you're planning to travel in moderate or luxury style, and especially if your trip is geared around special interests, such packages can work out cheaper than the same arrangements made on arrival. A tour is inevitably more confining than independent travel, but it can help you make the most of time if you're on a tight schedule; a tour can also ensure a worry-free first few days of a trip, and time to find your feet.

There are literally hundreds of **package tour operators** specializing in travel to France. Most can do packages of the standard highlights, but of greater interest are the outfits that help you explore the country's unique points: many organize walking or cycling trips through the countryside, boat trips along canals, and any number of theme tours based around history, art, wine and

so on. The box on p.15 mentions a few of the possibilities, and a travel agent will be able to point out others (remember, bookings made through a travel agent cost no more than going through the tour operator).

TRAIN PASSES

Although there are a number of train passes available for travel within France, all of which are good value (details on pp.6–7), a **Eurail Pass** makes most sense if you're planning to travel through other European countries as well. The pass, which must be purchased before arrival in Europe, allows unlimited free train travel in France and sixteen other countries. The **Eurail Youthpass** (for under-26s) costs US$398 for 15 days, $578 for one month or $768 for two months; if you're 26 or over you'll have to buy a first-class pass, available in 15-day ($498), 21-day ($648), one-month ($798), two-month ($1098) and three-month ($1398) increments. You stand a better chance of getting your money's worth out of a **Eurail Flexipass**, which is good for a certain number of travel days in a two-month period. This, too, comes in under-26/first-class versions: 5 days cost $255/$348; 10 days, $398/$560; and 15 days, $540/$740. A scaled-down version of the *Flexipass*, the **Europass** allows travel in France, Germany, Italy, Switzerland and Spain for 11 days in 2 months for $366/$508; there are also cheaper three- and four-country combinations. A further alternative is to attempt to buy an *InterRail* Pass in Europe (see pp.6–7) – most agents don't check residential qualifications, but once you're in Europe it'll be too late to buy a *Eurail* pass if you have problems. You can purchase *Eurail* passes from one of the agents listed below.

USEFUL RAIL ADDRESSES IN NORTH AMERICA

CIE Tours International, 108 Ridgedale Ave, Morristown, NJ 07690 (☎201/292-3438 or 800/522-5258). A prime source for booking train travel, including *Eurail* passes, in Europe.

CIT Tours, 342 Madison Ave, Suite 207, New York, NY 10173 (☎1-800/223-7987). For *Eurail* passes.

Rail Europe, 226 Westchester Ave, White Plains, NY 10604 (☎1-800/438-7245). Official *Eurail* Pass agent in North America; also sells the widest range of European regional and individual country passes.

ScanTours, 1535 6th St, Suite 205, Santa Monica, CA 90401 (☎1-800/223-7226). *Eurail* and other European country passes.

GETTING THERE FROM AUSTRALASIA

Many people travelling to France from Australia and New Zealand will choose to travel via London, although there are direct flights to Paris. There are also alternative stopover points in Europe, often available at economical fares.

FROM AUSTRALIA

From Australia, you can only fly direct to Paris, but internal add-on flights are "common rated" to the same price. **Discount agents** should be able

to get you at least ten percent off the following low-season published fares: *Garuda International* (via Bali, Jakarta, Singapore or Bangkok, Abu Dhabi, with two stopovers allowed each way), AU$1685 to Paris; *Air France* (on to 87 destinations within France), *British Airways* (via London), *KLM* (Amsterdam), *Lufthansa/Lauda* (Frankfurt), *Alitalia/Qantas* (Rome), *JAL* (overnight in Tokyo), AU$2199; *Aeroflot* (via Moscow to Paris), AU$1700; *Thai International* (Bangkok), AU$2055; *Malaysia* (via Kuala Lumpur), $2099.

TRAVEL AGENTS

Australia

Accent on Travel, 545 Queen Street, Brisbane (☎07/832 1777).

Anywhere Travel, 345 Anzac Parade, Kingsford, Sydney (☎02/663 0411).

Brisbane Discount Travel, 360 Queen St, Brisbane (☎07/229 9211).

Discount Travel Specialists, Shop 53, Forrest Chase, Perth (☎09/221 1400).

Flight Centres, *Australia*: Circular Quay, Sydney (☎02/241 2422); Bourke St, Melbourne (☎03/650 2899); plus other branches nationwide.

France Accommodation, 47, North Blackburn Square, Blackburn, Melbourne (☎03/877 6066).

France and Travel, 55 Hardware Street, Melbourne (☎03/670 7253).

France Unlimited, 232 Flinders Street, Melbourne (☎03/650 9892).

French and International Travel, 383 George Street, Sydney (☎02/299 8696).

French Bike Tours, 16 Goldsmith Street, Elwood, Melbourne (☎03/531 8787).

French Cottages and Travel, 674 High Street, East Kew, Melbourne (☎03/859 4944).

French Tourist Bureau, 12 Castlereagh Street, Sydney (☎02/231 5244).

French Travel Connection, 90 Mount Street, Sydney (☎02/956 5884).

Passport Travel, 320b Glenferrie Rd, Malvern, Melbourne (☎03/824 7183).

Renault Eurodrive, cnr Jamieson and York streets, Sydney (☎02/299 3344); branches in other state capitals.

STA Travel, 732 Harris Street, Ultimo, Sydney (☎02/212 1255 or 281 9866); 256 Flinders St,

Melbourne (☎03/347 4711); other offices in Townsville, Cairns and state capitals.

Topdeck Travel, 45 Grenfell St, Adelaide (☎08/410 1110).

Tourist Travel, 78 Liverpool Street, Sydney (☎02/283 5889).

Tymtro Travel, Suite G12, Wallaceway Shopping Centre, Chatswood, Sydney (☎02/413 1219).

New Zealand

Adventure World, 101 Great South Road, Auckland ☎(09/524 5118).

Budget Travel, PO Box 505, Auckland (☎09/309 4313).

Flight Centres, National Bank Towers, 205–225 Queen St, Auckland (☎09/309 6171); Shop 1M, National Mutual Arcade, 152 Hereford St, Christchurch (☎09/379 7145); 50–52 Willis St, Wellington (☎04/472 8101); branches countrywide.

STA Travel, Traveller's Centre, 10 High St, Auckland (☎09/309 9995); 233 Cuba St, Wellington (☎04/385 0561); 223 High St, Christchurch (☎03/379 9098); other offices in Dunedin, Palmerston North and Hamilton.

OUTDOOR SPECIALISTS

Adventure World, 73 Walker Street, North Sydney (☎02/956 7766); 8 Victoria Avenue, Perth (☎09/221 2300).

Eurolynx, Floor 3, 20 Fort Street, Auckland (☎09/379 9716).

Exodus Expeditions, 81a Glebe Point Road, Sydney (☎008/800 724).

France Ski International, 39/2 Richard Close, North Rocks, NSW (☎02/683 5185).

Snowscene 3360, Pacific Highway, Springwood, NSW (☎008/777 053).

Airpasses, coupons, and discounts on further flights within Europe vary with airlines, but the basic rules are that they must be prebooked with the main ticket, are valid for three months, and are available only with a return fare with the one airline – for example, you have to fly to France with *British Airways* alone to be eligible for their airpass deals. *Air France* offer a **Euroflyer** for use in France and Europe at AU$100 each flight; *British Airways* charge AU$103 for each flight within France. Both airlines also arrange **fly-drive packages**; check with an agent for current deals as prices are very variable. *KLM's* **Passport to Europe** uses coupons for single flights within Europe: 3 coupons for US$405, up to 6 for US$710; *Lufthansa* start at US$375 for three coupons, with extra flights US$105 each, to a maximum of nine.

FROM NEW ZEALAND

From New Zealand, the best discounted deals to Paris from Auckland are: *Japanese Airlines* (NZ$2200, with an overnight stop in Tokyo), *Thai International* (NZ$2265), *Malaysian Airlines* (NZ$2295) and *Garuda* (NZ$2249). For **stopovers** in Europe, *British Airways* charge NZ$2399 via London; *Qantas-Alitalia* are slightly less at NZ$2295 via Rome and London. For **side trips** within Europe, *Qantas-Lufthansa* have a 4-coupon deal on a six-month fare for NZ$2600.

AIRLINE ADDRESSES IN AUSTRALIA AND NEW ZEALAND

Aeroflot, 388 George St, Sydney (☎02/233 7911).

Air France, 12 Castlereagh St, Sydney (☎02/233 3277); 57 Fort St, Auckland (☎09/303 1229). Alitalia, Orient Overseas Building, 32 Bridge St, Sydney (☎02/247 1308); Floor 6, Trust Bank Building, 229 Queen St, Auckland (☎09/379 4457).

Air New Zealand, 5 Elizabeth St, Sydney (02 223 4666); cnr Customs and Queen streets, Auckland (09 366 2424).

Alitalia, Orient Overseas Building, 32 Bridge St, Sydney (☎02/247 7836); Floor 6, Trust Bank Building, 229 Queen St, Auckland (☎09/379 4457).

British Airways, 64 Castlereagh St, Sydney (☎02/258 3300); Dilworth Building, cnr Queen and Customs streets, Auckland (☎09/367 7500).

Garuda, 175 Clarence St, Sydney (☎02/334 9900); 120 Albert St, Auckland (☎09/366 1855).

Japanese Airlines, 17 Bligh St, Sydney (☎02/ 233 4500).

KLM, 5 Elizabeth St, Sydney (☎02/231 6333, 0800/222 747).

Lufthansa/Air Lauda, 143 Macquarie St, Sydney (☎02/367 3800); 109 Queen St, Auckland (☎09/ 303 1520).

Malaysian Air System, 388 George St, Sydney (☎02/231 5066, 0800/269 998); Floor 12, Swanson Centre, 12–26 Swanson St, Auckland (☎09/373 2741).

Qantas, International Square, Jamison St, Sydney (☎02/957 0111, 236 3636); Qantas House, 154 Queen St, Auckland (☎09/303 2506).

Olympic Airways, *S.A.* Floor 3, 37–49 Pitt St, Sydney (☎02/251 2044).

Qantas, International Square, Jamison St, Sydney (☎02/957 0111/236 3636); Qantas House, 154 Queen St, Auckland (☎09/303 2506).

Royal Brunei, Level 52, MLC Centre, 19 Martin Place, Sydney (☎02/223 1566); no New Zealand office.

Singapore Airlines, 17 Bridge St, Sydney (☎02/ 236 0111); Lower Ground Floor, West Plaza Building, cnr Customs and Albert streets, Auckland (☎09/379 3209).

Thai International, 75–77 Pitt St, Sydney (☎02/ 844 0999, 0800/422 020); Kensington Swan Building, 22 Fanshawe St, Auckland (☎09/377 3886).

United 10 Barrack St, Sydney (☎02/237 8888); 7 City Rd, Auckland (☎09/307 9500).

NOTE: *☎008 numbers are toll free, but only apply if dialled outside the city in the address.*

RED TAPE AND VISAS

Citizens of EU countries, Japan, Canada, New Zealand, Finland, Norway, Sweden and the United States do not need any sort of visa to enter France for a tourist stay for up to ninety days. The British Visitor's Passport and the Excursion Pass (for day trips), both obtainable over the counter at post offices in the UK, can be used as well as ordinary passports.

All other passport holders (including British Travel Document holders, Australians and New Zealanders) must obtain a visa before arrival in France.

Obtaining a visa from your nearest French consulate is fairly routine, but check their hours before turning up, and leave plenty of time, since there are often queues.

Three types of **visa** are currently issued: a transit visa, valid for two months; a short-stay (*court séjour*) visa, valid for ninety days after the date of issue and good for multiple entries; and a long-stay (*long séjour*) visa, which allows for multiple stays of ninety days over three years, but which is issued only after an examination of an individual's circumstances. Non-visa citizens who **stay longer than three months** are officially supposed to apply for a **Carte de Séjour**, for which you'll have to show proof of income at least equal to the minimum wage; EU passports are rarely stamped, so there is no evidence of how long you've been in the country. If your passport does get stamped, you can cross the border – to Belgium or Germany, for example – and re-enter for another ninety days legitimately.

CUSTOMS

With the Single European Market you can bring in and take out most things as long as you have paid tax on them in an **EU country** and they are for personal consumption. Customs may be suspicious if they think you are going to resell goods (or break the chassis of your car). Limits

---

FRENCH CONSULATES OVERSEAS

AUSTRALIA 492 St Kilda Rd, Melbourne, Vic 3001 (☎03/820 0921); 31 Market St, Sydney, NSW 2000 (☎02/261 5779).

CANADA *Embassy*: 2 Elysee, pl Bonaventure, Montréal, QUE H5A 1B1 (☎514/878-4381 to 87); *Consulates*: 1 pl Ville Marie, Bureau 22601, Montréal, QUE H3B 4S3 (☎514/878-4381); 1110 av des Laurentides, QUE G1S 3C3 (☎418/688-0430); 130 Bloor Street West, Suite 400, Toronto, ONT M5S 1N5 (☎416/925-80441); 1201-736 Granville St, Vancouver, BC V6Z 1H9 (☎604/681-2301).

IRELAND 36 Ailesbury Rd, Dublin 4 (☎01/694 777).

NETHERLANDS Vijzelgracht 2, Amsterdam (☎20/ 624 8346).

NEW ZEALAND 1 Willeston St, PO Box 1695, Wellington (☎04/720200).

NORWAY Drammensveien 69, 0244 Oslo 2 (☎02/ 41820).

SWEDEN Narvavägen 28, Stockholm 115–23 (☎08/63685).

UK *French Consulate General (Visas Section)*: 1 Cromwell Pl, London SW7 (☎0171/581 5292); 7–11 Randolph Cres, Edinburgh (☎0131/225 7954).

USA *Embassy*: 4101/Reservoir Rd NW, Washington DC 20007 (☎202/944-6000); *Consulates*: 3 Commonwealth Ave, Boston MA 02116 (☎617/266-1680); 737 North Michigan Ave, Olympia Center, Suite 2020, Chicago, ILL 60611 (☎312/787-5359); 10990 Wilshire Bd, Suite 300, Los Angeles, CA 90024 (☎310/479-4426); 934 Fifth Ave, New York, NY 10021 (☎212/606-3621); 540 Bush St, San Francisco, CA 94108 (☎415/397-4330).

still apply to drink and tobacco bought in duty-free shops: 200 cigarettes, 250g tobacco or 50 cigars; one litre of spirits or two litres fortified wine, or two litres sparkling wine and two litres table wine; 60ml perfume and 250ml of toilet water.

Americans can bring home up to $400 worth of goods purchased overseas duty-free, including a litre of alcohol or wine, 200 cigarettes and 100 cigars. If you carry back between $400 and $1000 worth of stuff you'll have to go through the red lane and pay ten percent of the value in duty; above $1000 and the duty depends on the items. **Canadians** are exempt from paying duty on up to $300 worth of goods after spending seven days out of the country (or $100 worth after a trip lasting two to six days). Those goods may include up to 40 ounces of spirits or wine, 24 12-ounce bottles of beer and 200 cigarettes.

Australian citizens can take up to 200 cigarettes and one litre of alcohol home, while **New Zealanders** can take 200 cigarettes, 4.5 litres of beer or wine, and just over one litre of spirits.

COSTS, MONEY AND BANKS

Because of the relatively low cost of accommodation and eating out, at least by northern European standards, France is not an outrageously expensive place to visit. For a reasonably comfortable existence, including hotel room and restaurant or café stops, you need to allow about 500F a day per person. But by counting the pennies, staying at a hostel (between 50F and 70F for bed and breakfast) or camping (around 20F a head if you hunt around) and being strong-willed about extra cups of coffee and doses of culture, you could manage on 200F or even 150F, including a cheap restaurant meal, and possibly less if your eating is limited to street snacks or market food.

For two or more people, **hotel accommodation** can be almost as cheap as the hostels, though a sensible average estimate for a double room would be around 200F. As for **food**, you can spend as much or as little as you like. There are large numbers of reasonable **restaurants** with three- or four-course menus for between 60F and 100F. Having your main meal at midday is always cheaper than in the evening. **Picnic fare**, obviously, is much less costly, especially when you buy in the markets and cheap super-market chains. More sophisticated meals – **takeaway** salads and ready-to-heat dishes – can be put together for reasonable prices if you shop at *charcuteries* (delicatessens) and the equivalent counters of many supermarkets. **Wine** and **beer** are both very cheap in super-markets. The mark-up on wine in restaurants is high, though the house wine in cheaper estab-lishments is still very good value.

Transport will inevitably be a large item of expenditure if you move around a lot, which makes some kind of train pass a good idea, although French trains are in any case good value, with many discounts available (some sample one-way fares: Paris to Nice 423F, Paris to Bordeaux 325F). Buses are cheaper, though prices vary enormously from one operator to another. Bicycles cost about 50F per day to rent. Petrol prices are around 6F a litre for leaded, around 5,5F for unleaded, and around 4F a litre for diesel; there are 3.8 litres to the US gallon. Most motorways have tolls: rates vary, but to give you an idea, Paris to Menton would cost you around 322F just to *use* the *autoroute*.

Museums and monuments have become a lot more expensive in recent years and are likely to prove one of the biggest wallet-eroders. Although **reduced admission** for young people to museums is a function of age – under 26 – not student status, it is worth carrying the *ISIC* (International Student Identity Card), if you are entitled to it, simply because of its universal acceptability as a proof of identity, which is not the case with a British *NUS* card. For reductions as someone over 60 years old, you will need to carry your passport around with you. Several towns operate a global ticket for their museums and monuments. These are detailed in the guide.

CURRENCY AND THE EXCHANGE RATE

French currency is the *franc* (abbreviated as F or sometimes FF), divided into 100 centimes. Francs come in notes of 500, 100, 50, and 20F, and there are coins of 20, 10, 5, 2, and 1F, and 50, 20, 10 and 5 centimes. The exchange rate hovers miserably around 8,10F to the pound. The US dollar rate tends to fluctuate more: at the time of writing it was 5,50F to the dollar; and Australians will pay around 4,25F to the dollar.

CHANGING MONEY

Standard **banking hours** are 9.30am–noon and 2–4pm, and banks are closed Sunday and either Monday or, less usually, Saturday. **Rates of exchange** and **commissions** vary from place to place – a 30F charge for changing 200F is not uncommon; the *Banque Nationale de Paris* usually offers the best rates and takes the least commission. There are **money-exchange counters** at airports and the train stations of all big cities, and usually one or two in the town centre as well; these often keep much longer hours than the high-street banks. You'll also find automatic money **exchange machines** which take dollars and notes of all European currencies but give a very poor rate of exchange. It would be a sensible precaution to buy some French francs before leaving. For cash advances, see p.22.

TRAVELLERS' CHEQUES AND CREDIT CARDS

Travellers' cheques, generally considered one of the safest ways of carrying money, are available from almost any major bank (whether you have an account there or not), usually for a service charge of one or two percent, although your own bank may offer travellers' cheques free of charge provided you meet certain conditions. *Thomas Cook*, *Visa* and *American Express* are the most widely recognized brands. Obtaining **French franc travellers' cheques** can be worthwhile: they can often be used as cash, and French banks are obliged by law to give you the face value of the cheques when you change them, so commission is only paid on purchase.

It pays to get a selection of denominations of travellers' cheques. Make sure you keep the purchase agreement and a record of cheque serial numbers safe and separate from the cheques themselves. In the event that cheques are lost or stolen, the issuing company will expect you to report the loss forthwith to their office in France; most companies claim to replace lost or stolen cheques within 24 hours.

Credit cards are also widely accepted for goods and services: just watch for the window stickers. *Visa* is the most universally recognized: *American Express*, *Mastercard/Access* and *Eurocard* less so. It's always worth checking, however, that restaurants and hotels will accept your card; smaller ones often don't, and even train stations in small towns may refuse them. Be aware that French cards have a smart chip and machines may reject the magnetic strip of British, American or Australasian cards, even if they are valid. If your card is refused because of this, we suggest you say "Les cartes britanniques ne sont pas cartes à puce, mais à piste magnetique. Ma carte est valable et je vous serais très reconnaissant(e) de demander la confirmation auprès de votre banque ou de votre centre de traitement."

CONTACT NUMBERS IN THE CASE OF CREDIT CARD LOSS

American Express ☎47.77.72.00
American Express travellers' cheques ☎05.90.86.00
Visa ☎47.62.75.00
Eurocard ☎47.62.75.00
Barclaycard ☎47.62.75.00
Diners' Club ☎47.62.75.00

All the above numbers are in Paris – dial 16.1 first if phoning from the French provinces.

You can also use credit cards to get **cash advances** from banks and from cash dispensing machines where the appropriate sign is displayed. For *Visa* cards (*Carte Bleue*), you can use the same PIN number as in Britain and the US. For *Mastercard/Access*, you need to apply for a special European PIN number before you go. If your credit card is also a direct debit card, you can use that facility where the cash dispensers show the *Delta* or *Switch* signs. This is the best way of getting money, with no commission charged.

Europeans can use **Eurocheques**, backed up with a card, which can be used for paying shop and restaurant bills in the same way as an ordinary cheque at home. With a PIN number, you can also use them in cash machines which show the same symbol as on your card. Although there is only one-percent commission on each cheque, you have to pay an annual fee for the service of around £10, and you must apply for a card in advance. On the positive side, you can specify the exact amount you want and use the cheques in some places where credit cards are not accepted (though you'll have to write out the sum in French). It takes up to six weeks for the money to be deducted from your account. Also worth considering are post office **International Giro Cheques**, which work in a similar way to ordinary bank cheques except that you can cash them at post offices, which are even more widespread and have longer opening hours than banks.

Before leaving home, check with your bank or credit card company the number to ring if your credit card is **lost or stolen**. For some cards, you have to ring a number in your home country. The numbers in France featured on p.21 (which will tell you British or US contact numbers to ring if necessary) are all in Paris, so remember to dial 16.1 first if phoning from the provinces.

HEALTH AND INSURANCE

Under the French Social Security system, every hospital visit, doctor's consultation and prescribed medicine is charged. Although all employed French people are entitled to a refund of 75–80 percent of their medical expenses, this can still leave a hefty shortfall, especially after a stay in hospital (accident victims even have to pay for the ambulance that takes them there).

To find a **doctor**, stop at any *pharmacie* and ask for an address. Consultation fees for a visit should be around 75–85F and in any case you'll be given a *Feuille de Soins* (Statement of Treatment) for later documentation of insurance claims. Prescriptions should be taken to a *pharmacie* which is also equipped – and obliged – to give first aid (for a fee). The medicines you buy will have little stickers (*vignettes*) attached to them, which you must remove and stick to your *Feuille de Soins* together with the prescription itself. In serious emergencies, you will always be admitted to the **local hospital** (*Centre Hospitalier*); either under your own power or by ambulance.

As getting a refund entails a complicated bureaucratic procedure and in any case does not cover the full cost of treatment, it's always a

Citizens of all EU and Scandinavian countries are entitled to take advantage of French health services under the same terms as residents, if they have the correct documentation. British citizens need form E111, available from post offices. North American and other non-EU citizens have to pay for most medical attention and are strongly advised to take out some form of travel insurance.

better idea to take out ordinary **travel insurance**, which generally allows full reimbursement, less the first few pounds of every claim, and also covers the cost of repatriation.

TRAVEL INSURANCE

Having medical care is the most important reason for taking out medical insurance. The let-out clauses on the cover of money and possessions are getting more and more restrictive; make sure you know exactly what the terms and conditions are. If you're going to ski, rock-climb or engage in any other high-risk activities, the premiums will be higher, but definitely worth it – the cost of a mountain rescue can run into F100,000s.

INSURANCE IN THE UK

In **the UK**, travel insurance schemes to cover medical expenses and theft or loss are sold by all travel agents and banks, from around £45 a month: *ISIS* policies, from *STA Travel* or branches of *Endsleigh Insurance*, are usually good value (see below). Whichever policy you opt for, read the small print to see what is covered before signing up, although most are broadly similar. It is common for money and credit cards to be covered only if stolen from your person. If you have any other insurance policies – house and contents insurance, for example – you'll find some of the optional extra cover in travel insurance only duplicates what you already have at home. Remember that claims can only be dealt with if a report is made to the

local police within 24 hours and a copy of the report (*constat de vol*) sent with the claim; addresses of the Commisariat de police are given in the main towns and cities.

INSURANCE IN NORTH AMERICA

Before buying an insurance policy, check that you're not already covered. **Canadians** are usually covered for medical mishaps overseas by their provincial health plans. Holders of official **student and youth cards** (see overleaf) are entitled to accident coverage and hospital in-patient benefits. **Students** will often find that their student health coverage extends during the vacations and for one term beyond the date of last enrollment. Bank and credit cards (particularly *American Express*) often have certain levels of medical or other insurance included, and travel insurance may also be included if you use a major credit or charge card to pay for your trip. **Homeowners' or renters'** insurance often covers theft or loss of documents, money and valuables while overseas, though conditions and maximum amounts vary from company to company.

After exhausting the possibilities above, you still might want to contact a specialist **travel insurance** company; your travel agent can usually recommend one, or see the box below. Policies are comprehensive (accidents, illnesses, delayed or lost luggage, cancelled flights, etc), but maximum payouts tend to be meagre. Premiums vary, so shop around. The best deals are usually available through student/youth travel agencies –

TRAVEL INSURANCE COMPANIES AND AGENTS

Britain

Endsleigh, 97–107 Southampton Row, London WC1B 4AG (☎0171/436-4451).

STA Travel , 86 Old Brompton Rd, London SW7 3LH (☎0171/937-9921).

North America

Access America, PO Box 90310, Richmond, VA 23230 (☎1-800/284-8300).

Carefree Travel Insurance, PO Box 310, 120 Mineola Blvd, Mineola, NY 11501 (☎1-800/323-3149).

Council Travel, 205 E 42nd St, New York, NY 10017 (☎800/743-1823).

STA Travel, 48 East 11th St, New York, NY 10003 (☎1-800/777-0112; nationwide).

Travel Assistance International, 1133 15th St NW, Suite 400, Washington, DC 20005 (☎1-800/821-2828).

Travel Cuts, 187 College St, Toronto, ON M5T 1P7 (☎416/979-2406).

Travel Guard, 1145 Clark St, Stevens Point, WI 54481 (☎1-800/826-1300).

Travel Insurance Services, 2930 Camino Diablo, Suite 300, Walnut Creek, CA 94596 (☎1-800/937-1387).

ISIS policies, for example, cost $48–69 for fifteen days (depending on coverage), $80–105 for a month, $149–207 for two months, on up to $510–700 for a year. If you're planning to do any "dangerous sports" (skiing, mountaineering, etc), figure on a surcharge of 20–50 percent.

Most North American travel policies apply only to items lost, stolen or damaged while in the custody of an identifiable, responsible third party – hotel porter, airline, luggage consignment, etc. Even in these cases you will have to contact the local police within a certain time limit to have a complete report made out so that your insurer can process the claim. Note also that very few insurers will arrange on-the-spot payments in the event of a major expense or loss; you will usually be reimbursed only after going home.

Full-time students are eligible for the **International Student ID Card (ISIC)**, which entitles the bearer to special fares on local transport and discounts at museums, theatres and other attractions. For Americans there's also a health benefit, providing up to $3000 in emergency medical coverage and $100 a day for 60 days in the hospital, plus a 24-hour hotline to call in the event of a medical, legal or financial emergency. The card, which costs $16 for Americans and $15 for Canadians, is available from *Council Travel*, *STA* and *Travel Cuts* (see p.23 for addresses).

TRAVEL INSURANCE IN AUSTRALIA

In **Australia**, *CIC Insurance*, offered by *Cover-More Insurance Services*, Level 9, 32 Walker St, North Sydney (☎02/202 8000), with some branches also in Victoria and Queensland, has some of the widest cover available and can be arranged through most travel agents. It costs from AUS$140 for 31 days. As with all policies, make sure that you are covered for any activities you might be planning, especially if you are hiking or skiing.

DISABLED TRAVELLERS

France has no special reputation for providing facilities for disabled travellers, but at least information is available. In the major cities and coastal resorts, there are accessible hotels, and ramps or other forms of access are gradually being added to museums and other sites. There are a number of national organizations which provide a national information network: **APF**, the French paraplegic organization, and **CNFLRH**, the French national organization for disabled people (both listed opposite), have regional branches in most **départements**. In listings magazines and brochures, wheelchair access is denoted by "accessible aux handicapés".

Public transport is certainly not wheelchair-friendly, and although many train stations now have ramps to enable wheelchair-users to board and descend from carriages, at others it is still up to the guards to carry the chair. Cars with hand controls are available for rental in France from *ITS* (see opposite).

Up-to-date information about access is difficult to get hold of, but the most comprehensive account of what is available in Paris is contained in **Access in Paris**, obtainable free from the *Access Project* in London, although you are asked to send a £5 donation. Specialist tour operators are listed opposite, and there is a French organization that lists *gîte* accommodation especially equipped for the disabled. The French Tourist Office have a reference guide with useful information on accommodation, transport, accessibility of public places and particular aids such as buzzer signals on pedestrian crossings. The *APF* and *CNFLRH* are the best sources of information, though their details of accommodation with wheelchair access tend to be only for pricey three- and four-star hotels. As far as **airlines** go, *British Airways* has a better-than-average record for treatment of disabled passengers, and from North America, *Virgin Atlantic* and *Air Canada* come out tops in terms of disability awareness (and seating arrangements) and might be worth contacting first for any information they can provide.

For more information, plus first-hand accounts by disabled travellers to France, see *Able to Travel/Nothing Ventured*, a *Rough Guide* special.

CONTACTS FOR TRAVELLERS WITH DISABILITIES

France

APF (*Association des Paralysés de France*), 17–21 bd Auguste-Blanqui, 75013 Paris (☎44.16.83.83). A national organization with regional offices all over France that can provide useful information and lists of new and accessible accommodation. Their guide *Où ferons-nous étape* is available at the office for 70F or by post to a French address for 100F.

Access Project, 39 Bradley Gardens, London W13 8HE. Information service giving details of what facilities for the disabled are available throughout the world.

CNFLRH (*Comité National Française de Liaison pour la Réadaption des Handicapés*), 38 bd Raspail, 75009 Paris (☎45.48.90.13). Information service for disabled travellers, including details of accessible accommodation, holiday centres, etc. They also distribute various useful guides.

ITS, 11 bd Auguste-Blanqui, 75013 Paris (☎45.88.52.37). A Parisian organization that rents out cars with hand controls.

Britain

Holiday Care Service, 2 Old Bank Chambers, Station Rd, Horley, Surrey RH6 9HW (☎01293/774535). Information on all aspects of travel.

Mobility International, 228 Borough High St, London SE1 1JX (☎0171/403-5688). Information, access guides, tours and exchange programmes.

RADAR (*The Royal Association for Disability and Rehabilitation*), 12 City Forum, 250 City Road, London EC1V 8AF (☎0171/250-3222; Minicom ☎0171/637 5315). Information on all aspects of travelling with a disability.

TRIPSCOPE, 63 Esmond Rd, London W4 1JE (☎0181/994 9294). Phone-in travel information and advice service.

North America

Directions Unlimited, 720 N Bedford Rd, Bedford Hills, NY 10507 (☎1-800/533-5343). Tour operator specializing in custom tours for people with disabilities.

Information Center for People with Disabilities, Fort Point Place, 27-43 Wormwood St, Boston, MA 02210 (☎617/727-5540; TDD ☎617/345-9743). Clearing house for information, including travel.

Jewish Rehabilitation Hospital, 3205 Place Alton Goldbloom, Montréal, PQ H7V 1R2 (☎514/688-9550, ext 226). Guidebooks and travel information.

Kéroul, 4545 ave Pierre de Coubertin, CP 1000, Station M, Montréal, PQ H1V 3R2 (☎514/252-3104). Organization promoting and facilitating travel for mobility-impaired people. Annual membership $10.

Mobility International USA, PO Box 10767, Eugene, OR 97440 (Voice and TDD: ☎503/343-1284). Information and referral services, access guides, tours and exchange programmes. Annual membership $20 (includes quarterly newsletter).

Society for the Advancement of Travel for the Handicapped (SATH), 347 5th Ave, New York, NY 10016 (☎212/447-7284). Nonprofit travel-industry referral service that passes queries on to its members as appropriate; allow plenty of time for a response.

Travel Information Service, Moss Rehabilitation Hospital, 1200 West Tabor Rd, Philadelphia, PA 19141 (☎215/456-9600). Telephone information and referral service.

Twin Peaks Press, Box 129, Vancouver, WA 98666 (☎206/694-2462 or 1-800/637-2256). Publisher of the *Directory of Travel Agencies for the Disabled* ($19.95), listing more than 370 agencies worldwide; *Travel for the Disabled* ($14.95); the *Directory of Accessible Van Rentals and Wheelchair Vagabond* ($9.95), loaded with personal tips.

Australia

ACROD (*Australian Council for the Rehabilitation of the Disabled*), PO Box 60, Curtain, ACT 2605 (☎06/682-4333). A body that will provide lists of travel agencies and tour operators for people with disabilities.

Barrier Free Travel, 36 Wheatley St, North Bellingen, NSW 2454 (☎066/551-733). Tour operator for the disabled.

New Zealand

Disabled Persons Assembly, PO Box 10–138, The Terrace, Wellington (☎04/472-2626). Organization that will provide details of tour operators and travel agencies for people with disabilities.

INFORMATION AND MAPS

The French Government Tourist Office gives away large quantities of maps and glossy brochures for every region of France, including lists of hotels and campsites. Some of these, like the maps of the inland waterways, lists of festivals and campsite listings, can be quite useful.

In France itself you'll find a **tourist office** – usually either a *Syndicat d'Initiative (SI)* or *Office du Tourisme* – in practically every town and many villages (tourist office addresses, and in more important cases their opening hours, are detailed in the guide). For the practical purposes of visitors, there is little difference between them: *SI*s have wider responsibilities for encouraging conferences to the town, for example, while *offices du tourisme* deal exclusively with tourism.

From these tourist offices you can get specific local information, including listings of leisure activities, bike rental, laundries and countless other things. And always ask for the free town plan. Many tourist offices also publish hotel and restaurant listings and local car and walking itineraries for their areas. In mountain regions they often share premises with the local hiking and climbing organizers. They are often also willing to give advice about the best places to go in addition to just handing out paper. They may even conduct free town tours. The regional or departmental tourist offices also offer useful practical information.

MAPS

In addition to the various free leaflets – and the maps in this guide – the one extra map you'll probably want is a reasonable **road map** of France. The *Michelin* map no. 989 (1:1,000,000) is the best for the whole country. A useful free map for car drivers, obtainable from filling

---

FRENCH GOVERNMENT TOURIST OFFICES

Australia BNP Building 12th floor, 12 Castlereagh St, Sydney NSW 2000 (☎612/231 5244).

Canada 1981 av McGill College, Suite 490, Montréal, QUE H3A 2W9 (☎514/288-4264); 30 St Patrick St, Suite 700, Toronto ONT M5T 3A3 (☎416/593-6427).

Denmark NY Ostergade 3.3, DK – 1101 Copenhagen (☎33/11 49 12).

Ireland 35 Lower Abbey St, Dublin 1 (☎1/703 4046).

Netherlands Prinsengr. 670, 1017 KX Amsterdam (☎020/627 33 18).

Norway Storgaten 10A, 0155 Oslo 1 (☎22/42 33 87).

Sweden Norrmalmstorg 1 Av, S11146 Stockholm (☎08/679 79 75).

UK 178 Piccadilly, London W1V 0AL (☎0891/244 123).*

USA 610 Fifth Ave, Suite 222, New York, NY 10020-2452 (☎212/757-1125); 645 North Michigan Ave, Chicago, ILL 60611-2836 (☎312/337-6301); 9454 Wilshire Blvd, Beverly Hills, CA 90212-2967 (☎213/271-7838; Cedar Maple Plaza, 2305 Cedar Springs Blvd, Dallas, TX 75201 (☎214/720-4010).

*In Britain, the FGTO has an information service, EuropAssistance, on a premium rate (Mon–Fri 9am–10pm, Sat 9am–5pm; 49p peak rate, 39p cheap rate). This is much easier to get through on; brochures will be sent without postage charge, and specific queries are quickly referred to the relevant organization.

stations and traffic information kiosks in France, is the *Bison Futé* map, showing alternative back routes to the congested main roads, clearly signposted on the ground by special green *Bison Futé* road signs.

For more **regional detail**, the *Michelin* yellow series (scale 1:200,000) is best for the motorist. You can now get the whole series in one large spiral-bound, *Atlas Routier*. If you're planning to **walk or cycle,** check the *IGN* maps – either green (1:100,000 and 1:50,000), or the more detailed blue (1:25,000) series. The *IGN* 1:100,000 series is the smallest scale available that has the contours marked – essential for cyclists, who tend to cycle off 1:25,000 maps in a couple of hours.

MAP OUTLETS

UK

London: *National Map Centre*, 22–24 Caxton St, SW1 (☎0171/222 4945); *Stanfords*, 12–14 Long Acre, WC2 (☎0171/836 1321); *The Travellers Bookshop*, 25 Cecil Court, WC2 (☎0171/836 9132).

Edinburgh: *Thomas Nelson and Sons Ltd*, 51 York Place, EH1 3JD (☎031/557 3011).

Glasgow: *John Smith and Sons*, 57–61 St Vincent St (☎0141/221 7472).

Maps by **mail or phone order** are available from *Stanfords* (☎0171/836 1321).

North America

Chicago: *Rand McNally*, 444 N Michigan Ave, IL 60611 (☎312/321-1751).

Montréal: *Ulysses Travel Bookshop*, 4176 St-Denis (☎514/289-0993).

New York: *British Travel Bookshop*, 551 5th Ave, NY 10176 (☎1-800/448-3039 or ☎212/490-6688); *The Complete Traveler Bookstore*, 199 Madison Ave, NY 10016 (☎212/685-9007); *Rand McNally*, 150 East 52nd St, NY 10022 (☎212/758-7488); *Traveler's Bookstore*, 22 West 52nd St, NY 10019 (☎212/664-0995).

San Francisco: *The Complete Traveler Bookstore*, 3207 Filmore St, CA 92123 (☎415/923-1511); *Rand McNally*, 595 Market St, CA 94105 (☎415/777-3131).

Santa Barbara: *Pacific Traveler Supply*, 529 State St, 93101 (☎805/963-4438; phone orders: ☎805/965-4402).

Seattle: *Elliot Bay Book Company*, 101 South Main St, WA 98104 (☎206/624-6600).

Toronto: *Open Air Books and Maps*, 25 Toronto St, M5R 2C1 (☎416/363-0719).

Vancouver: *World Wide Books and Maps*, 736A Granville St , V6Z 1G3 (☎604/687-3320).

Washington DC: *Rand McNally*, 1201 Connecticut Ave NW, 20036 (☎202/223-6751).

Note that *Rand McNally* now has more than 20 stores across the US; phone ☎1-800/333-0136 (ext 2111) for the address of your nearest store, or for **direct mail** maps.

Australia

Adelaide: *The Map Shop*, 16a Peel St, SA 5000 (☎08/231 2033).

Brisbane: *Hema*, 239 George St, Qld 4000 (☎07/221 4330).

Melbourne: *Bowyangs*, 372 Little Bourke St, Vic 3000 (☎03/670 4383).

Perth: *Perth Map Centre*, 891 Hay St, WA 6000 (☎09/322 5733).

Sydney: *Travel Bookshop*, 20 Bridge St, NSW 2000 (☎02/241 3554).

GETTING AROUND

With the most extensive train network in western Europe, France is a country in which to travel by rail. The nationally owned French train company, the *SNCF* (*Société National des Chemins de Fer*), runs fast, modern trains. In rural areas where bylines have been closed, routes are covered by buses operated by the *SNCF*. It's an integrated service, with buses timetabled to meet trains and the same ticket covering both.

The private bus services are confusing and uncoordinated. Approximate journey times and frequencies can be found in the "Travel Details" at the end of each chapter, and local peculiarities are also pointed out in the text of the guide. For a more private kind of independent transport, by car or bicycle, you'll need to be aware of a number of French road rules and peculiarities. Hitching is less and less popular, but walking, on the extensive network of "GR" footpaths, is recommended, as are the more specialist realms of inland boating and cross-country skiing, both of which have a high profile in France.

TRAINS

SNCF trains are, for the most part, clean, fast and frequent, their staff are courteous and helpful and their coverage is wide. Their high-speed *TGV* (*Trains à Grande Vitesse*) network services the major centres, linking Paris with Lyon, Marseille, Besançon, Le Mans and Toulouse at speeds of up to 200km/h. All but the smallest stations (*gares SNCF*) have an information desk and *consignes automatiques* − coin-operated lockers big enough to take a rucksack − and many rent out bicycles, sometimes of rather doubtful reliability. Train **fares** are reasonable, with only *TGV*s requiring a supplement at peak times and compulsory reservations costing around 20F. It is best to use the counter service for buying tickets, rather than the complicated computerized system, which changes the price of *TGV* tickets depending on the demand.

All **tickets** − but not passes (see below) − must be date-stamped in the orange machines at station platform entrances, and it is an offence not to "*Compostez votre billet*". Train journeys may be broken any time, anywhere, for as long as the ticket is valid (usually 2 weeks), but after a break of 24 hours you must "compost" your ticket again when you resume your journey. On night trains an extra 85F or so will buy you a **couchette** − well worth it if you're making a long haul and don't want to waste a day recovering from a sleepless night.

Regional **rail maps** and complete **timetables** are on sale at tobacconist shops. Leaflet timetables for a particular line are available free at stations. *Autocar* at the top of a column means it's an *SNCF* bus service, on which rail tickets and passes are valid.

DISCOUNTS AND RAIL PASSES

Within France, the *SNCF* itself offers a whole range of **discounted fares** on standard rail prices on *Période Bleue* (blue period) and *Période Blanche* (white period) days, depending on exactly when you want to travel. A leaflet showing the blue, white (smaller discount) and red (peak) periods is given out at *gares SNCF* (train stations).

Apart from these discounts, couples can have a free **Carte Couple**, entitling them to a 25-percent discount on -*TGV*s or on other trains if they start their journey on a blue period day. Over 60s can get the **Carte Vermeille**, which comes in two versions: the **Quatre Temps**, which costs 135F and covers 4 journeys, and the **Plein Temps**, which costs 255F for unlimited travel. Both are valid for one year and offer up to 50 percent off tickets on *TGV*s as well as other journeys starting in blue or white periods. The same percentage reductions are available for under-26s with a **Carissimo** pass, which costs 190F for 4 journeys and 350F for 8, and is valid for one year. This pass also entitles the cardholder to secure the same ticket reductions for up to 3 travelling companions also aged between 12 and 25. Under-16s can obtain the same advantages for themselves and up to 4 travelling companions of any age by purchasing a **Carte Kiwi** (280F for 4 journeys, 430F for unlimited travel), or a **France Railpass**, covering any 3 days in 1 month for \$125 (2nd class) or \$180 (1st), available in the US.

These train passes can be purchased through most travel agents in France or from main *SNCF* stations. For Europe-wide train passes, see pp.6–7 and 16.

BUSES

With the exception of *SNCF* services, **buses** play a generally minor role in France's public transport. They are, however, useful for local and some cross-country journeys. The most frustrating thing about them is that they rarely serve the regions outside the *SNCF* network – which is precisely where you need them. Where they do exist in rural areas, the **timetable** is constructed to suit working, market and school hours – all often dauntingly early. They are, generally speaking, cheaper and slower than trains.

Larger towns usually have a *gare routière* (bus station), often next to the *gare SNCF*.

However, the private bus companies don't always work together and you'll frequently find them leaving from an array of different points (the local tourist office will usually help locate them). The most convenient lines are those run as an extension of rail links by *SNCF*, which always run to/from the *SNCF* station and will also access areas not easily reached by rail.

DRIVING

Driving in France has its disadvantages: costs and breakdown liability are the most pressing, and if you want to feel the country and its culture around you, there's also the strong likelihood of reducing your contact with people. However, you do gain freedom of movement and, especially if you're camping, can be a lot more self-sufficient.

Car rental in France costs upwards of £170/\$120 a week. It is usually cheaper to arrange from Britain or the US before you leave – *Holidays Autos* offer competitive deals on car rental in France. You'll find the big firms – *Hertz, Avis, Europcar* and *Budget* – at airports and in most big cities, with addresses detailed throughout the guide. Local firms can be cheaper but you need to check the small print and be sure of where the car can be returned to. It's normal to pay an indemnity of around 1000F against any damage to the car – they will take your credit card number rather than cash. You should return the car with a full tank (fuel in France costs around 5,90F a litre for unleaded, 6,40F for leaded). Extras are often

CAR RENTAL AGENCIES

UK

Avis, Hayes Gate House, Uxbridge Rd, Hayes, Middlesex (☎0181/848 8733).

Budget, 41 Marlowes Lane, Hemel Hempstead Herts HP1 1XJ (☎0800/181 181).

Eurodollar, Swan National House, Warwick Place, Uxbridge, Middlesex (☎01895/233 300).

Europcar, Wilton Rd, London SW1V 1LA (☎01345/222 525).

Hertz, 1272 London Rd, London SW16 4DQ (☎0181/679 1799).

Holiday Autos, 25 Savile Row, London W1X 1AA (☎0171/491 1111).

North America

Alamo (domestic ☎1-800/354-2322; international ☎1-800/522-9696).

Auto Europe (☎1-800/223-5555).

Avis (domestic: ☎1-800/331-1212; international ☎1-800/331-1084).

Budget (☎1-800/527-0700).

Dollar (☎1-800/421-6868).

Europe by Car (☎1-800/223-1516).

Hertz (domestic: ☎1-800/654-3131; international ☎1-800/654-3001; in Canada ☎1-800/263-0600).

Holiday Autos (☎1-800/422-7737).

National (☎1-800/CAR-RENT).

Rent-A-Wreck (☎1-800/535-1391).

Thrifty (☎1-800/367-2277).

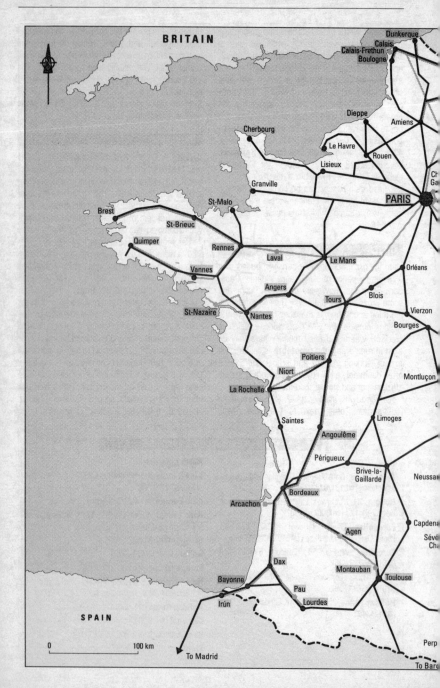

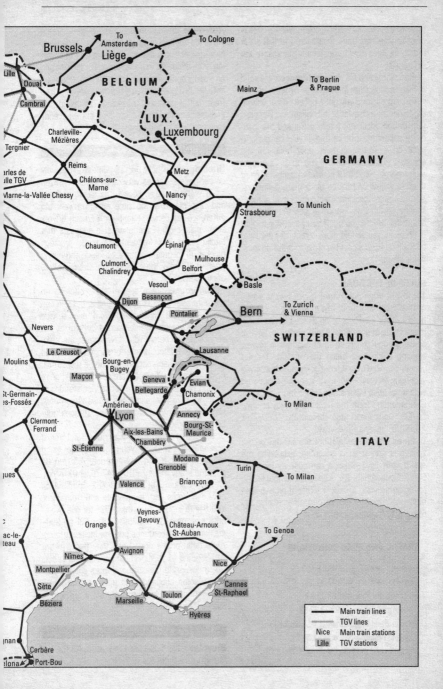

pressed on you, like medical cover, which you may already have from travel insurance. The cost of car rental includes the basic legally necessary car insurance.

British, EU and US **driving licences** are valid in France, though an *International Driver's Licence* makes life easier if you get a police officer unwilling to peruse a document in English. The vehicle's registration document (*carte grise*) and the insurance papers must be carried. If your car is right-hand drive, you must have your headlight dip adjusted to the right before you go – it's a legal requirement – and as a courtesy change or paint them to yellow or stick on black glare deflectors. All the major car manufacturers have garage/service stations in France – get their lists of addresses before you go. If you have an accident or break-in, you should make a report to the local police (and keep a copy) in order to make an insurance claim.

RULES OF THE ROAD

The law of *priorité à droite* – giving way to traffic coming from your right, even when it is coming from a minor road – is being phased out as it is a major cause of accidents. It still applies in built-up areas, so you still have to be vigilant in towns, keeping a look out along the roadside for the yellow diamond on a white background that gives you right of way – until you see the same sign with an oblique black slash, which indicates vehicles emerging from the right have right of way. "*STOP*" signs mean stop completely: "*CEDEZ LE PASSAGE*" means "Give Way".

Fines for driving violations are exacted on the spot, and only cash is accepted. Exceeding the speed limit by 1–30km/h can cost as much as 5000F. Speed limits are: 130km/hr (80mph) on the tolled *autoroutes*; 110km/hr (68mph) on two-lane highways; 90km/hr (56mph) on other roads; and 60km/hr (37mph) in towns.

TRAFFIC AND ROAD CONDITIONS

Paris and Île de France ☎48.99.33.33
Lille and the north ☎20.47.33.33.
Metz and the east ☎87.63.33.33
Rennes and Brittany ☎99.32.33.33
Bordeaux and the southwest ☎56.96.33.33
Lyon and Rhône-Alpes ☎78.54.33.33
Marseille and the Côte d'Azur ☎91.78.78.78

Autoroute driving, though fast, is very boring when it's not hair-raising, and tolls are expensive. Nevertheless, it is the only realistic way of covering large distances in a single day. For information on road conditions call *Inter Service Route* on ☎48.58.33.33 (24hr). Use the *Bison Futé* map, free from petrol stations, especially to avoid the endless jams that build up over the weekends between July 15 and August 15.

HITCHING

Hitching, you'll have to rely almost exclusively on car drivers. Lorries very rarely give lifts. Even so, it won't be easy. Looking as clean, ordinary and respectable as possible makes a very big difference, as conversations with French drivers soon make clear. Experience also suggests that hitching the less frequented D-roads is much quicker. In mountain areas a rucksack and hiking gear will help procure a lift from fellow aficionados.

Autoroutes are a special case; hitching on the *autoroute* itself is strictly illegal, but you can make excellent time going from one service station to another. Remember to get out at the service station before your driver leaves the *autoroute*: the tollbooths are a second best (and legal); ordinary approach roads can be disastrous. If you get stuck at least there's food, drink, shelter and wash facilities at most service stations. It helps to have Michelin's *Guide des Autoroutes*, showing all the rest stops, service stations, tollbooths (*péages*), exits, etc.

For major **long-distance** rides, and for a greater sense of safety, you might consider using the national "hitching" organization, *Allostop*, 84 passage Brady, Paris 75010 (☎47.70.02.01; Mon–Fri 9am–7.30pm, Sat 9am–1pm & 2–6pm), which now only deals with journeys to and from Paris. You pay to register with them (70F for one trip of 500km or more, 60F for 400–500km, 50F for 300–400km, plus 20 centimes per km, including *autoroute* tolls for the driver) and they find a driver who's going to your destination. *Allostop* seems like a desperate measure and lacks spontaneity, but in some circumstances may well be worth considering – sexual harassment is a problem in France (see p.56).

BICYCLES AND MOPEDS

Bicycles have high status in France. All the car ferries carry them for nothing; the *SNCF* makes minimal charges; and the French (Parisians excepted) respect cyclists – both as traffic and, when you stop off at a restaurant or hotel, as customers. These days more and more cyclists are using **mountain bikes**, which the French call *VTTs* (*Vélos Touts Terrains*), even for touring holidays, although if you've ever made a direct comparison you'll soon realize that it's much less effort, and much quicker, to cycle long distances and carry luggage on a traditionally styled touring or racing bike.

Restaurants and hotels along the way are nearly always obliging about looking after your bike, even to the point of allowing it into your room. Most large towns have well-stocked retail and **repair shops**, where parts are normally cheaper than in Britain or the US. However, if you're using a foreign-made bike, it's a good idea to carry spare tyres, as French sizes are different. Inner tubes are not a problem, as they adapt to either size, though make sure you get the right valves.

The **train network** runs various schemes for cyclists, all of them covered by the free leaflet *Train et Vélo*, available from most stations. *Autotrains* (when marked with a bicycle in the timetable) are usually the only ones on which you can travel with a bike as free accompanied luggage. Otherwise, you have to send your bike as registered luggage (135F parcelled up, 180F unparcelled; 15F for packaging). Although it may well arrive in less time, the *SNCF* won't guarantee delivery in under five days; and you do hear stories of bicycles disappearing altogether.

You can normally load your bike straight on to the train at the **ferry** port – as on the boat train at Dieppe – but remember that you must first go to the ticket office of the station to register it (there is time). Don't just try to climb on the train with it, as both you and your bike will end up left behind. In addition to the ferries, *British Airways* and *Air France* both take bikes free. You may have to box them though, and you should contact the airlines first.

At most *SNCF* stations, bikes are also available for rental for 44–55F per day, depending on the type of bike, but you will also be required to leave a deposit of 1000–1500F (credit cards accepted). Bikes – usually mountain bikes – are often available from campsites, youth hostels and *gîtes d'étapes*, as well as specialist cycle shops and some tourist offices. They are more likely to be reliable machines than those from the *SNCFs*, although also more expensive. The bikes are often not insured, however, and you will be presented with the bill for its replacement if it's stolen or damaged. Check whether your travel insurance policy covers you for this if you intend to rent a bike.

For advice on which **maps** to take, see the "Maps" section on pp.26–27. In the UK, the **Cyclists' Touring Club**, Cotterell House, 68 Meadrow, Godalming, Surrey GU7 3HS (☎0483/417217), will suggest routes and supply advice for a small fee, and they run a particularly good insurance scheme.

Companies running specialist bike touring holidays are listed on p.5 & 15.

A CYCLING VOCABULARY

to adjust	*ajuster*	to deflate	*dégonfler*	rack	*le porte-*
axle	*l'axe*	derailleur	*le dérailleur*		*bagages*
ball-bearing	*le roulement à*	frame	*le cadre*	to raise	*relever*
	billes	gears	*les vitesses*	to repair	*réparer*
battery	*la pile*	grease	*la graisse*	saddle	*la selle*
bent	*tordu*	handlebars	*le guidon*	to screw	*visser*
bicycle	*le vélo*	to inflate	*gonfler*	spanner	*la clef*
bottom bracket	*le logement du*	inner tube	*la chambre à air*		*(mécanique)*
	pédalier	loose	*dévissé*	spoke	*le rayon*
brake cable	*le cable*	to lower	*baisser*	to straighten	*rédresser*
brakes	*les freins*	mudguard	*le garde-boue*	stuck	*coincé*
broken	*cassé*	pannier	*le pannier*	tight	*serré*
bulb	*l'ampoule*	pedal	*le pédale*	toe clips	*les cale-pieds*
chain	*la chaîne*	pump	*la pompe*	tyre	*le pneu*
cotter pin	*la clavette*	puncture	*la crevaison*	wheel	*la roue*

MOPEDS AND SCOOTERS

Mopeds and **scooters** are relatively easy to find: everyone in France, from young kids to grandmas, rides one of these, and although they're not built for any kind of long-distance travel, they're ideal for shooting around town and nearby. Places that rent out bicycles will often also rent out mopeds; you can expect to pay 160F a day for a 50cc Suzuki, for example, or 200F for an 80cc motorbike. Crash helmets are compulsory only on machines over 125cc, but you'd be a fool not to wear one even on a moped.

WALKWAYS

Long-distance walkers are well served in France by a network of over 30,000km of long-distance marked **footpaths**, known as *sentiers de grande randonnée* or, more commonly, simply as **GR**s. They're fully signposted and equipped with campsites and rest huts along the way. Some are real marathons, like the GR5 from the coast of Holland to Nice, the trans-Pyrenean GR10 or the *Grande Traversée des Alpes* (the GRX). The *Chemin de St-Jacques* – GR65 – follows the ancient pilgrim route from Le Puy in the Auvergne to the Spanish border above St-Jean-Pied-de-Port and on to the shrine of Santiago de Compostela, while GR3 traces the Loire from source to sea. There are many more.

Each path is described in a **Topoguide** (available in Britain from *Stanfords*, see p.27), which gives a detailed account of the route (in French), including maps, campsites, refuge huts, sources of provisions, etc. In addition many tourist offices can provide guides to their local footpaths, especially in popular hiking areas, where they often share premises with professional mountain guides and hike leaders. The latter organize climbing and walking expeditions for all levels of experience. *Topoguides* are produced by the principal French walkers' organization, the *Comité National des Sentiers de Grande Randonnée*, 8 av Marceau, 75008 Paris (☎47.23.62.32). The main **climbing** organization is the *Club Alpin Français*, 9 rue de la Boétie, 75008 Paris (☎47.42.38.46). In Corsica, you can find out details about rambling and climbing from the *Parc Naturel Régional*, rue Général-Fiorella, 20184 Ajaccio (☎95.21.56.54).

Maps are listed under the "Information and Maps" section on pp.26–27; you might also like to look at the specialized walking sheets produced by *Didier et Richard* of Grenoble for the Alps. Guidebooks worth looking out for are listed on p.1005.

INLAND WATERWAYS

With some 7500km of navigable rivers and canals, **boating** can be one of the best and most relaxed ways of exploring France. Except on parts of the Moselle, there is no charge for use of the waterways, and you can travel without a permit for up to six months in a year. For information on maximum dimensions, documentation, regulations and so forth, ask at a French Government Tourist Office for their booklet *Boating on the Waterways*. They also have brochures on boating in particular regions of France and lists of French and British firms that rent out boats. For a full list write to the *Syndicat National des Loueurs de Bateaux de Plaisance*, Port de la Bourdonnais, 75007 Paris (☎45.55.10.49).

The principal **areas for boating** are Brittany, Burgundy, Picardy-Flanders, Alsace and Champagne. Brittany's canals join up with the Loire, but this is only navigable as far as Angers, with no links eastwards. Other waterways permit numerous permutations, including joining up via the Rhône and Saône with the Canal du Midi in Languedoc and then northwestwards to Bordeaux and the Atlantic. The eighteenth-century Canal de Bourgogne and 300-year-old Canal du Midi are fascinating examples of early canal engineering. The latter completely transformed the fortunes of coastal Languedoc, and in particular Sète, whose attractive harbour dates from that period. Together with its continuation, the Canal du Sète à Rhône, it passes within easy reach of several interesting areas.

The through-journey **from the Channel to the Mediterranean** requires some planning. The Canal de Bourgogne has an inordinate number of locks, while other waterways demand considerable skill and experience – the Rhône and Saône rivers, for example, have tricky currents. The most direct route is from Le Havre to just beyond Paris, then south either on Canal du Loing et de Briare or Canal du Nivernais to the Canal Latéral de la Loire, which you follow as far as Digoin in southern Burgundy, where it crosses the River Loire and meets the Canal du Centre. You follow the latter as far as Châlon, where you continue south on the Saône and Rhône until you reach the Mediterranean at Port St-Louis in the Camargue.

ACCOMMODATION

At most times of the year, you can turn up in any French town and find a room, or a place in a campsite. Booking a couple of nights in advance can be reassuring, however; it saves you the effort of trudging round and ensures that you know what you'll be paying. In most towns, you'll be able to get a double for around 160–220F (£20–27/$29–40), or a single for around 100–150F (£12–18.50/$18–27).

We've detailed a selection of hotels in most of the destinations listed in the guide, and given a price range for each (see box); as a general rule the areas around train stations have the highest density of cheap hotels. Phone numbers as well as addresses are given in the guide, and the "Language" section at the back should help you make a reservation call, though many hoteliers

and campsite managers – and almost all youth hostel managers – speak some English.

Problems arise mainly between July 15 and August 15, when the French take their own vacations *en masse*. The first weekend of August is the busiest time of all. During this period, hotel and hostel accommodation can be hard to come by – particularly in the coastal resorts – and you may find yourself falling back on local tourist offices for help and ideas. Some tourist offices offer a **booking service** – these are detailed in the guide – but they cannot guarantee rooms at a particular price. All tourist offices can provide lists of hotels, the various hostels or the organizations such as *CROUS* (see below) to contact, details of campsites, and bed and breakfast possibilities (*chambres d'hôtes* and *ferme auberges*).

With **campsites**, you can be more relaxed, unless you're touring with a caravan or camper van. Big cities can be difficult throughout the year: we've given a greater range of possibilities for them in the guide and very detailed accommodation listings for Paris, the worst case of all.

HOTELS

Hotel recommendations are given in the text of the guide for almost every town or village mentioned. **Full accommodation lists** for each province are available from any French

ACCOMMODATION PRICE CATEGORIES

All the hotels, youth hostels and guesthouses listed in this book have been price-graded according to the following scale, and although costs will rise slightly overall with the life of this edition, the relative comparisons should remain valid. Paris is far more expensive than the rest of the country. Other big cities have a good variety of cheap establishments; in small towns or villages where the choice is limited, you may not be so lucky. Swanky resorts, particularly those on the Côte d'Azur, have very high July and August prices, but are still less expensive than Paris. If you are staying more than three days it's often possible to negotiate a lower price, particularly out of season. The prices quoted are for the cheapest available double room in high season, although remember that many of the cheap places will have more expensive rooms with en-suite facilities.

What you get for your money varies enormously between establishments. For under 160F the bed is likely to be old and floppy. There won't be soundproofing and showers will be communal, though you may have your own toilet, bidet and washbasin. Over 250F the decor may not be anything to write home about, but rooms will have their own bath or shower and toilet, and perhaps even a TV and telephone. At more than 450F, you should expect a higher standard of fittings and something approaching luxury.

① Under 160F	③ 220–300F	⑤ 400–500F	⑦ 600–700F
② 160–220F	④ 300–400F	⑥ 500–600F	⑧ Over 700F

Government Tourist Office (see p.26) or from local tourist offices, and are especially handy during peak season. All French hotels are **graded** from zero to five stars. The price more or less corresponds to the number of stars, though the system is a little haphazard, having more to do with ratios of bathrooms-per-guest than genuine quality; and ungraded and single-star hotels are often very good. At the cheapest level, what makes a difference in **cost** is whether a room contains a shower: if it does, the bill will be around 30–50F more. **Breakfast**, too, can add 15–30F per person to a bill – though there is no obligation to take it and you will nearly always do better at a café. The cost of eating **dinner** in a hotel's restaurant can be a more important factor to bear in mind when picking a place to stay. Officially it is illegal for hotels to insist on your taking meals, but they often do, and in busy resorts you may not find a room unless you agree to *demi-pension* (half-board). If you are unsure, ask before signing in; cheap rooms aren't so cheap if you have to eat a 150F meal. **Single rooms** are only marginally cheaper than doubles so sharing always slashes costs. Most hotels willingly provide rooms with **extra beds**, for three or more people, at good discounts.

Note that many family-run hotels are closed every year for two or three weeks some time between May and September – where possible we've detailed this in the text. In addition, some hotels in smaller towns and villages close for one or two nights a week, usually Sunday or Monday – if in doubt ring first to check.

In country areas, in addition to standard hotels, you will come across *chambres d'hôte* and *ferme auberge*, bed-and-breakfast accommodation in someone's house or farm. These vary in standard and are rarely an especially cheap option, usually costing the equivalent of a two-star hotel. However, if you're lucky, they may be good sources of traditional home-cooking and French company. The brown leaflets available in tourist offices list most of them.

A very useful option, especially if it's late at night, is the **Formule 1 chain**, well signposted on the outskirts of most big towns. Characterless motels, they provide rooms for up to three people for 130F. With a *Visa, Mastercard, Eurocard* or *American Express* credit card, you can let yourself into a room at any hour of the day or night. Addresses are most easily available on Minitel – 3615 or 3616 Formule 1 – but the hotels are not difficult to find as long as you're travelling by car, and a brochure with full details can be picked up at any one.

YOUTH HOSTELS, *FOYERS* AND STUDENT ACCOMMODATION

At between 50F and 70F per night for a dormitory bed, **youth hostels** – *auberges de jeunesse* – are invaluable for single travellers on a budget. For couples, however, and certainly for groups of three or more people (see above), they don't necessarily work out cheaper than hotels – particularly if you've had to pay a bus fare out to the edge of town to reach them. However, many hostels are beautifully sited, and they allow you to cut costs by preparing your own food in their kitchens, or eating in their cheap canteens. To stay at many of the hostels you're must be a member of the *International Youth Hostel*

YOUTH HOSTEL ASSOCIATIONS

Australia *Australian Youth Hostels Association*, Level 3, 10 Mallett St, Camperdown, NSW (☎02/565-1325).

Canada *Hostelling International/Canadian Hostelling Association*, Room 400, 205 Catherine St, Ottawa, ON K2P 1C3 (☎613/237-7884 or ☎1-800/663-5777).

England and Wales *Youth Hostel Association (YHA)*, Trevelyan House, 8 St Stephen's Hill, St Albans, Herts AL1 (☎017278/45047); 14 Southampton St, London WC2 (☎0171/836 1036).

France *Fédération Unie des Auberges de Jeunesse*, 27 rue Pajol, 75018 Paris (☎44.89.87.27).

Ireland *An Oige*, 39 Mountjoy Square, Dublin 1 (☎01/363111); 56 Bradbury Place, Belfast BT7 (☎01232/324733).

New Zealand *Youth Hostels Association of New Zealand*, PO Box 436, Christchurch 1 (☎03/799-970).

Scotland *Scottish Youth Hostel Association*, 7 Glebe Crescent, Stirling, FK8 2JA (☎01786/51181).

USA *Hostelling International-American Youth Hostels (HI-AYH)*, 733 15th St NW, Suite 840, PO Box 37613, Washington, DC 20005 (☎202/783-6161).

Federation (*IYHF*), which currently costs £9/$25 for over 18s, £3/$10 for under 18s. Head offices are listed in the box opposite.

Slightly confusingly, there are also two rival French youth hostel associations: the *Fédération Unie des Auberges de Jeunesse*, 27 rue Pajol, 75018 Paris (☎44.89.87.27), which has its hostels detailed in the *International Handbook*, and the *Ligue Française pour les Auberges de Jeunesse*, 38 bd Raspail, 75007 Paris (☎45.48.69.84). *IYHF* membership covers both organizations, and you'll find all their hostels detailed in the text. A few large' towns provide a more luxurious standard of hostel accommodation in **Foyers des Jeunes Travailleurs/euses**, residential hostels for young workers and students, where you can usually get a private room for around 60F. They normally have a good cafeteria or canteen.

At the height of summer (usually July & Aug only), there's also the possibility of staying in **student accommodation** in university towns and cities. The main organization for this is *CROUS*, 39 av G-Bernados, 75231 Paris (☎40.51.36.00). Prices are similar to the official hostels, at around 60–75F per person, and you don't need membership.

GÎTES AND REFUGES

In the countryside, a third hostel-style alternative exists. **Gîtes d'étape** are less formal than the youth hostels, often run by the local village or municipality (whose mayor will probably be in charge of the key), and they provide bunk beds and primitive kitchen and washing facilities from around 40F. They are marked on the large-scale *IGN* walkers' maps and listed in the individual GR *Topoguides*. Mountain areas have **mountain refuge huts** on the main GR routes, normally only open in summer. They're extremely basic but invaluable if you get caught by a storm. Costs are around 60F for the night, less if you're a member of a climbing organization affiliated to the *Club Alpin Français*.

If you are planning to stay a week or more in any one place it might be worth considering **renting a house**. You can do this by checking adverts from the innumerable private and foreign owners in British Sunday newspapers (*The Observer* and *The Sunday Times*, mainly), or trying one of the numerous holiday firms that market

accommodation/travel packages (see the boxes on pp.5 or 15 for a brief selection of these).

The easiest and most reliable method, however, is to use the official French Government service, the **Gîtes de France**, based in Britain at 178 Piccadilly, London W1V 9DB (☎0171/493 3480), or in Australia, through *Explore Holidays*, PO Box 256, Carlingford, NSW 2118.

Membership (£3) gets you a copy of their handbook, which contains properties all over France, listed by *département*. The houses vary in size and comfort, but all are basically acceptable holiday homes. There is a photograph and description of each one, and the computerized booking service means that you can instantly reserve one for any number of full weeks. The cost varies with the season from around £115 per week to £300 plus, and may include concessionary ferry rates. *Gîtes Accessible à Tous* (same address; £5 plus 40p postage) lists the *gîte* accommodation especially equipped for the disabled.

CAMPING

Practically every village and town in the country has at least one **campsite** to cater for the thousands of people who spend their holiday under canvas – camping is a very big deal in France. The cheapest – at around 20F per person per night – is usually the **camping municipal**, run by the local municipality. In season or whenever they're officially open, they are always clean and have plenty of hot water; often they are situated in prime local positions. Out of season, those that stay open often don't bother to collect the overnight charge.

If you're planning to do a lot of camping, an **international camping carnet** is a good investment, available from home motoring organizations, or in the US from *Family Campers and RVers* (*FCRV*), 4804 Transit Rd, Building 2, Depew, NY 14043 (☎1-800/245-9755); in Canada, 51 W 22nd St, Hamilton, Ontario LC9 4N5 (☎1-800/245-9755). The carnet is good for discounts at member sites and serves as useful identification. *FCRV* annual membership costs $20, and the carnet an additional $10.

On the coast especially, there are **superior categories** of campsite where you'll pay prices similar to those of a hotel for the facilities – bars, restaurants and sometimes swimming pools. These have rather more permanent status than the *campings municipaux*, with people often spending a whole holiday in the one base. If you plan to do the same, and particularly if you have a caravan, camper or a big tent, it's wise to book ahead – reckon on paying around 35F a head all-in with a tent, 40F with a campervan. Inland, **camping à la ferme** – on somebody's farm – is another possibility (generally without facilities). Lists of sites are detailed in the Tourist Board's *Accueil à la Campagne* booklet.

Lastly, a **word of caution**: never camp rough (*camping sauvage*, as the French call it) on anyone's land without first asking permission. If the dogs don't get you, the guns might – farmers have been known to shoot before asking questions. In many parts of France, *camping sauvage* on public land isn't tolerated – Brittany being a notable exception. On beaches, it's best to camp out only where other people are doing so.

EATING AND DRINKING

French food is as good a reason as any for a visit to France. Cooking has art status, the top chefs are stars, and dining out is a national pastime, whether it's at the bistro on the corner or at a famed house of *haute cuisine*. Eating out doesn't have to cost much, as long as you avoid tourist hotspots and treat the business of choosing a place as an interesting appetizer in itself.

France is also a great place for foreign cuisine, in particular North African, Caribbean (known as Antillais) and Asiatic. Moroccan, Thai or Vietnamese restaurants are not necessarily cheap options but they can be better value for money in city centres.

On the whole, vegetarians can expect a somewhat lean time in France. A few cities have specifically vegetarian restaurants, but elsewhere you'll have to hope you find a sympathetic restaurant (*crêperies* and pizzerias can be good standbys). Sometimes they're willing to replace a meat dish on the *menu fixe* with an omelette; other times you'll have to pick your way through the *carte*. Many vegetarians swallow a few principles and start eating fish and shellfish on holiday. Vegans, however, should probably forget all about eating in French restaurants and stick to self-catering.

BREAKFAST AND SNACKS

A *croissant, pain au chocolat* (a choc-filled croissant) or a sandwich in a bar or café, with hot chocolate or coffee, is generally the best way to eat **breakfast** – at a fraction of the cost charged by most hotels. (The days when hotels gave you mounds of croissants or *brioches* for breakfast seem to be long gone; now it's virtually always bread, jam and a jug of coffee or tea for about 25F.) *Croissants* and sometimes hard-boiled eggs are displayed on bar counters until around 9.30 or 10am. If you stand – cheaper than sitting down – you just help yourself to these with your coffee, the waiter keeps an eye on how many you've eaten and bills you accordingly.

At **lunchtime** and sometimes in the evening, you may find cafés offering a *plat du jour* (chef's daily special) at between 40F and 65F or *formules*, a limited or no-choice menu. The *croque-monsieur* or *croque-madame* (variations on the toasted-cheese sandwich) is on sale at cafés, brasseries and many street stands, along with *frites, crêpes, galettes* (wholewheat pancakes), *gauffres* (waffles), *glaces* (ice creams) and all kinds of fresh sandwiches. For variety, there are Tunisian snacks like *brik à l'œuf* (a fried pastry with an egg inside), *merguez* (spicy North African sausage), Greek *souvlaki* (kebabs) and Middle Eastern *falafel* (deep-fried chickpea balls with salad). Wine bars are good for French regional meat and cheese, usually served with brown bread (*pain de campagne*).

Many people also eat **crêpes** for lunch. These filled pancakes, originally from Brittany, are now available all over France. The savoury buckwheat variety (often called *galettes*) are served as a main course; the sweet white-flour ones are dessert. They taste nice enough, but they are usually poor value in comparison with a restaurant meal; you need at least three, normally at over 20F each, to feel even slightly full. That they always excite children shouldn't fool parents into thinking that *crêperies* are a cheap alternative.

Pizzerias are also common in France. They are somewhat better value than *crêperies*, but quality and quantity vary greatly – look before you leap into the nearest empty seats.

For **picnics**, the local outdoor market or supermarket will provide you with almost everything you need from tomatoes and avocados to cheese and paté. For **takeaway food**, there's nothing to beat the *charcuteries* (delicatessens, mostly pork-based), which you'll find everywhere – even in small villages. These sell cooked meat, prepared snacks such as *bouchées de la reine* (seafood vol-au-vents), ready-made dishes and assorted salads. The cheapest, by far, are the supermarkets' *charcuterie* counters. You purchase by weight, or you can ask for *une tranche* (a slice), *une barquette* (a carton), or *une part* (a portion).

Salons de thé, which open from mid-morning to late evening, serve brunches, salads, quiches, and the like, as well as gateaux, ice cream and a wide selection of teas. They tend to be a good deal pricier than cafés or brasseries – you're paying for the posh surroundings. **Pâtisseries**, of course, have impressive arrays of cakes and pastries.

FULL-SCALE MEALS

There's no difference between **restaurants** (or *auberges* or *relais* as they sometimes call themselves) and **brasseries** in terms of quality or price range. The distinction is that brasseries, which resemble cafés, serve quicker meals at most hours of the day, while restaurants tend to stick to the traditional meal times of noon–2pm and 7–9.30 or 10.30pm. After 9pm or so, restaurants often serve only *à la carte* meals (single dishes chosen from the menu) – invariably more expensive than eating the set *menu fixe*. For the more upmarket places it's wise to make reservations – easily done on the same day. In small towns it may be impossible to get anything other than a bar sandwich after 10pm; in major cities, town centre brasseries will serve until 11pm or midnight and one or two may stay open all night. Don't forget that **hotel restaurants** are open to nonresidents, and often very good value. In many small towns and villages, you'll find the only restaurants are in hotels.

Prices, and what you get for them, are posted outside the restaurant. Normally there's a choice between one or more *menus fixes*, where the number of courses has already been determined and the choice is limited, and choosing individually from the *carte* (menu). **Menus fixes** are normally the cheapest option, and although they often revolve around standard dishes such as steak and chips (*steak frites*) or chicken and chips (*poulet frites*), many restaurants are nowadays offering a much more imaginative variety of fixed menus, and it can be much the best-value way of sampling regional specialities, sometimes running to five or more courses. If you're simply not that hungry, just go for the *plat du jour*. Reckon on paying anything between 60F and 120F for a three- to four-course *menu fixe*: the average cost of a *plat du jour* is between 30F and 70F.

Going *à la carte* does, however, offer greater flexibility and, in the better restaurants, unlimited access to the chef's specialities – though you'll pay for the privilege. A simple and perfectly legitimate tactic is to have just one course instead of the expected three or four. You can share dishes or just have several starters – a useful strategy for vegetarians. There's no minimum charge and prices vary between around 150F and 800F or more.

In the French **sequence of courses**, any salad (sometimes vegetables, too) comes separate from the main dish, and cheese precedes a dessert. You will be offered coffee, which is always extra, to finish off the meal.

Service compris or *s.c.* means the **service charge** is included. *Service non compris, s.n.c.* or *servis en sus* means that it isn't and you need to calculate an additional fifteen percent. **Wine** (*vin*) or a **drink** (*boisson*) is occasionally included in the cost of a *menu fixe*. When ordering wine, ask for *un quart* (0.25 litre), *un demi-litre* (0.5 litre) or *une carafe* (a litre). You'll normally be given the house wine unless you specify otherwise; if you're worried about the cost ask for *vin ordinaire* or the *vin de table*.

The French are much better disposed towards **children** in restaurants than other nationalities, not simply by offering reduced-price children's menus but in creating an atmosphere, even in otherwise fairly snooty establishments, that positively welcomes kids; some even have in-house games and toys for them to occupy themselves with. It is regarded as self-evident that large family groups should be able to eat out together.

A rather murkier area is that of **dogs** in the dining room; it can be quite a shock in a provincial hotel to realize that the majority of your fellow diners are attempting to keep dogs concealed beneath their tables.

CHEESE

Charles de Gaulle once mentioned that "You can unite the French only through fear. You cannot simply bring together a country that has over 265 kinds of cheese." For serious **cheese**-lovers, France is the ultimate paradise. Other countries may produce individual cheeses which are as good as, or even better than, the best of the French, but no country offers a range that comes

---

REGIONAL CUISINE

The **geography of France** explains much of the pride of place the country holds in European cuisines. The French can fish and breed seafood in the Channel waters, the Atlantic Ocean and the Mediterranean as well as catching freshwater fish in a thousand lakes and rivers. Mountains, forests, deltas and plains with climates ranging from the aridly sun-soaked to northern cold and wetness allow an extraordinary variety of produce. Added to this is the historical and social factor of a class of *paysans* – smallholders – who have passed down traditional methods from generation to generation. Though it is true that in recent years industrialization has standardized and sanitized production methods, food imports have greatly increased, and pollution has taken its toll, there remains a strong connection between the countryside and the table, reflected in the different regional cuisines. The gastronomic map of France features certain regions – Alsace, Provence, Brittany and the Pays Basque – in which the preservation of a distinctive cuisine owes much to historical separation. Burgundy, the Auvergne, Normandy and the Dordogne have absorbed classic French cooking from different corners of the country.

Alsace and **Lorraine**'s dishes are based on game, pork, beef and lamb, often stews with dumplings, and flans with pizza-like pastries; the **Atlantic Coast** naturally features much seafood on its menus; in the **Auvergne**, cabbage, pork and bean stew is a favourite, with cheeses, sausages and garlic soups also popular; **Brittany** features plenty of oysters, lobsters and other seafood, with *crêpes* and *galettes* with sweet and savoury fillings, buttery cakes and flans. In **Burgundy**, the famous Charolais beef combined with the local mustard produces some mouth watering variations, with other meat dishes and snails cropping up often; duck and goose in their myriad forms appear often in the **Dordogne**, marinated and served with prunes, preserves and truffles. **Languedoc** has the celebrated Rocquefort cheese as a basis for many dishes, and serves snails in several appetizing ways, along with the rum-flambéed *crêpes languedociennes*. **Lyon** has a special position as the meeting place of north and south, combining sausages and smoked meats with chicken, salads and the tasty *tarte Lyonnais*; **Normandy**, like Brittany, features oysters, mussels and other seafood in its restaurants, and the fresh apples and pears, mushrooms and fish are served imaginatively. The **Pays Basque** specializes in wild pigeon and Bayonne ham, white tuna and the delicious ewe's milk cheese, *brébis*, as well as the rich cherry and chocolate *gâteau Basque*; and **Provence**, with its Mediterranean climate, yields olives, garlic, lavender and delicious fruit and vegetables, all used to perfection in the pastas, fish soups, mixed salads, stock fish and tomato stew and lavender honey. In **Corsica**, it's herbs and plants that give the cuisine its unique flavour, with specialities like smoked pork, game, shellfish, eel and trout, and a range of dishes made with the local chestnuts.

You'll find regional specialities detailed within each chapter.

WINE

French **wines** are unrivalled in the world for their range, sophistication, diversity and status. Individual wines from other countries may be able to compete with the best of French wines, but however hard foreign producers try, the French market is uncrackable. The French simply see no reason to try any wines but their own. Sipping a Nuits St-Georges, Sancerre, Chablis, Châteauneuf-du-Pape or one of the top champagnes – assuming you can afford them – it's hard to disagree.

With the exception of the northwest of the country and the mountains, wine is produced just about everywhere. The **great wine-producing regions** are Champagne, Bordeaux and Burgundy, closely followed by the Loire Valley and Rhône Valley. Alsace also has some great wines, and there are some beautiful wines to be had in the lesser wine regions of Bergerac, Languedoc, Rousillon and Provence.

The quality of the *vins de pays*, though very variable, is still exceptional for the price (from around 45F a litre). Quality wines are denoted by the *appellation d'origine contrôlée*, which strictly controls the amount of wine that a particular area, whether several hundred square kilometres or just two, may produce. Within each *appellation* there is enormous diversity generated by the different types of soil, the lie of the land, the type of grape grown – there are over sixty varietes – the ability of the wine to age, and the individual skills of the wine grower.

It's an extremely complex business and it's not difficult to feel intimidated by the seemingly innate expertise of all French people. Many individual wines and *appellations* are mentioned in the text, but trusting your own taste response is the most important thing. Knowing the grape types that you particularly like (or dislike), whether you like wines very fruity, dry, light or heavy, is all useful when you are discussing your choice with a waiter, wine grower or wine merchant. The more interest you show, the more helpful advice you are likely to receive. The only thing the French cannot tolerate is people ordering Coke to accompany a gourmet meal. We've detailed the main wine-growing regions – and their produce – throughout the guide.

---

anywhere near them in terms of sheer inventiveness. In fact, there are officially over 400 types of French cheese (with new ones being created every year), whose recipes are jealously guarded secrets. Many cheesemakers have successfully protected their products by *AC* (*appellation d'origine controlée*) laws similar to those for wines, which means that the subtle differences between French local cheeses are still not overwhelmed by the industrialized uniformity that has plagued other countries.

Most restaurants keep a well-stocked *plateau de fromages* (cheeseboard), kept at room temperature and served with bread, but not butter. Apart from the ubiquitous Brie, Camembert and numerous varieties of goat's cheese (*chèvre*), there will usually be one or two local cheeses on offer – these are the ones to go for. Your best bet for local produce is a *fromagerie*, which often has 200 varieties or more to choose from. We've indicated the best national and regionally available cheeses in the text.

DRINKING

Wherever you can eat you can invariably **drink**, and vice versa. Drinking is done at a leisurely pace whether it's a prelude to food (*apéritif*), a sequel (*digestif*), or the accompaniment, and **cafés** are the standard places to do it. Every bar or café has to display its full **price list** (usually without the fifteen-percent service charge added), with the cheapest drinks at the bar (*au comptoir*), and progressively increasing prices for sitting at a table inside (*la salle*), or outside (*la terrasse*). You pay when you leave, and it's perfectly acceptable to sit for hours over just one cup of coffee.

Wine – *vin* – is the regular drink. Red is *rouge*, white *blanc*, or there's *rosé*. *Vin de table* or *vin ordinaire* – table wine – is generally drinkable and always cheap, although it may be disguised and priced-up as the house wine, or *cuvée*. Restaurant mark-ups for quality wines can be outrageous, especially in a country where wine is so cheap in the shops. In bars, you normally buy by the glass, and just ask for *un rouge* or *un blanc*; *un pichet* gets you a quarter-litre jug. There are boxes highlighting local wine produce throughout the chapters of this guide.

Familiar Belgian and German brands, plus French brands from Alsace, account for most

FOODS AND DISHES

Basic terms

Pain	Bread	Poivre	Pepper	Verre	Glass
Beurre	Butter	Sel	Salt	Fourchette	Fork
Oeuf	Egg	Sucre	Sugar	Couteau	Knife
Lait	Milk	Vinaigre	Vinegar	Cuillère	Spoon
Huile	Oil	Bouteille	Bottle	Table	Table
				L'addition	Bill

Snacks

Un sandwich/ une baguette...	A sandwich...
au jambon	with ham
au fromage	with cheese
au saucisson	with sausage
à l'ail	with garlic
au poivre	with pepper
au pâté (de campagne)	with pâté (country-style)
croque-monsieur	Grilled cheese and ham sandwich
croque-madame	Grilled cheese and bacon, sausage, chicken or an egg

Oeufs	**Eggs**
au plat	Fried eggs
à la coque	Boiled eggs
durs	Hard-boiled eggs
brouillés	Scrambled eggs

Omelette ...	**Omelette ...**
nature	plain
aux fines herbes	with herbs
au fromage	with cheese

Salade de ...	**Salad of ...**
tomates	tomatoes
betteraves	beets
concombres	cucumber
carottes rapées	grated carrots

Un crêpe...	A pancake...
au sucre	with sugar
au citron	with lemon
au miel	with honey
à la confiture	with jam
aux œufs	with eggs
à la crème de marrons	with chestnut purée

Other fillings/salads

Anchois	Anchovy
Andouillette	Tripe sausage
Boudin	Black pudding
Cœurs de palmiers	Hearts of palm
Epis de maïs	Corn on the cob
Fonds d'artichauts	Artichoke hearts
Hareng	Herring
Langue	Tongue
Poulet	Chicken
Thon	Tuna fish

And some terms

Chauffé	Heated
Cuit	Cooked
Cru	Raw
Emballé	Wrapped
A emporter	Takeaway
Fumé	Smoked
Salé	Salted/spicy
Sucré	Sweet

Soups (*soupes*) and starters (*hors d'œuvres*)

Bisque	Shellfish soup
Bouillabaisse	Marseillais fish soup
Bouillon	Broth or stock
Bourride	Thick fish soup
Consommé	Clear soup
Pistou	Parmesan, basil and garlic paste added to soup
Potage	Thick vegetable soup
Rouille	Red pepper, garlic and saffron mayonnaise served with fish soup

Velouté	Thick soup, usually fish or poultry

Starters

Assiette anglaise	Plate of cold meats
Crudités	Raw vegetables with dressings
Hors d'œuvres variés	Combination of the above plus smoked or marinated fish

Fish (poisson), seafood (fruits de mer) and shellfish (crustaces or coquillages)...

Anchois	Anchovies	*Daurade*	Sea bream	*Louvine,*	Similar to sea
Anguilles	Eels	*Eperlan*	Smelt or	*loubine*	bass
Barbue	Brill		whitebait	*Maquereau*	Mackerel
Bigourneau	Periwinkle	*Escargots*	Snails	*Merlan*	Whiting
Brème	Bream	*Flétan*	Halibut	*Moules*	Mussels (with
Cabillaud	Cod	*Friture*	Assorted fried fish	*(marinière)*	shallots in white
Calmar	Squid	*Gambas*	King prawns		wine sauce)
Carrelet	Plaice	*Hareng*	Herring	*Oursin*	Sea urchin
Claire	Type of oyster	*Homard*	Lobster	*Palourdes*	Clams
Colin	Hake	*Huîtres*	Oysters	*Praires*	Small clams
Congre	Conger eel	*Langouste*	Spiny lobster	*Raie*	Skate
Coques	Cockles	*Langoustines*	Saltwater crayfish	*Rouget*	Red mullet
Coquilles St-	Scallops		(scampi)	*Saumon*	Salmon
Jacques		*Limande*	Lemon sole	*Sole*	Sole
Crabe	Crab	*Lotte*	Burbot	*Thon*	Tuna
Crevettes grises	Shrimp	*Lotte de mer*	Monkfish	*Truite*	Trout
Crevettes roses	Prawns	*Loup de mer*	Sea bass	*Turbot*	Turbot

...and fish terms

Aïoli	Garlic mayonnaise served with salt cod and other fish	*Fumé*	Smoked
		Fumet	Fish stock
Béarnaise	Sauce of egg yolks, white wine, shallots and vinegar	*Gigot de mer*	Large fish baked whole
		Grillé	Grilled
Beignets	Fritters	*Hollandaise*	Butter and vinegar sauce
Darne	Fillet or steak	*A la meunière*	In a butter, lemon and
La douzaine	A dozen		parsley sauce
Frit	Fried	*Mousse/mousseline*	Mousse
Friture	Deep fried small fish	*Quenelles*	Light dumplings

Meat (viande) and poultry (volaille)

Agneau (de pré-salé)	Lamb (grazed on salt marshes)	*Langue*	Tongue
		Lapin, lapereau	Rabbit, young rabbit
Andouille, andouillette	Tripe sausage	*Lard, lardons*	Bacon, diced bacon
		Lièvre	Hare
Bœuf	Beef	*Merguez*	Spicy, red sausage
Bifteck	Steak	*Mouton*	Mutton
Boudin blanc	Sausage of white meats	*Museau de veau*	Calf's muzzle
Boudin noir	Black pudding	*Oie*	Goose
Caille	Quail	*Os*	Bone
Canard	Duck	*Porc*	Pork
Caneton	Duckling	*Poulet*	Chicken
Contrefilet	Sirloin roast	*Poussin*	Baby chicken
Coquelet	Cockerel	*Ris*	Sweetbreads
Dinde, dindon	Turkey	*Rognons*	Kidneys
Entrecôte	Ribsteak	*Rognons blancs*	Testicles
Faux filet	Sirloin steak	*Sanglier*	Wild boar
Foie	Liver	*Steak*	Steak
Foie gras	Fattened (duck/ goose) liver	*Tête de veau*	Calf's head (in jelly)
Gigot (d'agneau)	Leg (of lamb)	*Tournedos*	Thick slices of fillet
Grillade	Grilled meat	*Tripes*	Tripe
Hâchis	Chopped meat or mince hamburger	*Veau*	Veal
		Venaison	Venison

Meat and poultry terms – dishes . . .

Bœuf bourguignon	Beef stew with burgundy, onions and mushrooms	*Coq au vin*	Chicken cooked until it falls off the bone with wine, onions, and mushrooms
Canard à l'orange	Roast duck with an orange-and-wine sauce	*Steak au poivre (vert/ rouge)*	Steak in a black (green/red) peppercorn sauce
Cassoulet	A casserole of beans and meat	*Steak tartare*	Raw chopped beef, topped with a raw egg yolk

. . . and terms

Blanquette, daube, estouffade, hochepôt, navarin and ragoût	All are types of stew	*Rôti*	Roast
		Sauté	Lightly cooked in butter
Aile	Wing	**For steaks:**	
Carré	Best end of neck, chop or cutlet	*Bleu*	Almost raw
Civit	Game stew	*Saignant*	Rare
Confit	Meat preserve	*A point*	Medium
Côte	Chop, cutlet or rib	*Bien cuit*	Well done
Cou	Neck	*Très bien cuit*	Very well cooked
Cuisse	Thigh or leg	*Brochette*	Kebab
Epaule	Shoulder		
Médaillon	Round piece	**Garnishes and sauces:**	
Pavé	Thick slice	*Beurre blanc*	Sauce of white wine and shallots, with butter
En croûte	In pastry		
Farci	Stuffed	*Chasseur*	White wine, mushrooms and shallots
Au feu de bois	Cooked over wood fire		
Au four	Baked	*Diable*	Strong mustard seasoning
Garni	With vegetables	*Forestière*	With bacon and mushroom
Gésier	Gizzard	*Fricassée*	Rich, creamy sauce
Grillé	Grilled	*Mornay*	Cheese sauce
Magret de canard	Duck breast	*Pays d'Auge*	Cream and cider
Marmite	Casserole	*Piquante*	Gherkins or capers, vinegar and shallots
Mijoté	Stewed		
		Provençale	Tomatoes, garlic, olive oil and herbs

Fruit *(fruit)* and nuts *(noix)*

Abricot	Apricot	*Framboises*	Raspberries	*Poire*	Pear
Amandes	Almonds	*Fruit de la passion*	Passion fruit	*Pomme*	Apple
Ananas	Pineapple			*Prune*	Plum
Banane	Banana	*Groseilles*	Redcurrants	*Pruneau*	Prune
Brugnon, nectarine	Nectarine	*Mangue*	Mango	*Raisins*	Grapes
		Marrons	Chestnuts		
Cacahouète	Peanut	*Melon*	Melon	**Terms**:	
Cassis	Blackcurrants	*Myrtilles*	Bilberries	*Beignet*	Fritter
Cérises	Cherries	*Noisette*	Hazelnut	*Compôte de . . .*	Stewed . . .
Citron	Lemon	*Noix*	Nuts	*Coulis*	Sauce
Citron vert	Lime	*Orange*	Orange	*Flambé*	Set aflame in alcohol
Figues	Figs	*Pamplemousse*	Grapefruit		
Fraises (de bois)	Strawberries (wild)	*Pêche (blanche*	(White) peach	*Frappé*	Iced
		Pistache	Pistachio		

Vegetables *(légumes)*, herbs *(herbes)* and spices *(épices)*, etc

Ail	Garlic	*Endive*	Chicory	*Piment*	Pimento
Algue	Seaweed	*Epinards*	Spinach	*Pois chiche*	Chick peas
Anis	Aniseed	*Estragon*	Tarragon	*Pois mange-*	Snow peas
Artichaut	Artichoke	*Fenouil*	Fennel	*tout*	
Asperges	Asparagus	*Flageolet*	White beans	*Pignons*	Pine nuts
Avocat	Avocado	*Gingembre*	Ginger	*Poireau*	Leek
Basilic	Basil	*Haricots*	Beans	*Poivron*	Sweet pepper
Betterave	Beetroot	*Verts*	String (French)	*(vert, rouge)*	(green, red)
Carotte	Carrot	*Rouges*	Kidney	*Pommes de*	Potatoes
Céleri	Celery	*Beurres*	Butter	*terre*	
Champignons,	Mushrooms of	*Laurier*	Bay leaf	*Primeurs*	Spring
cèpes,	various kinds	*Lentilles*	Lentils		vegetables
chanterelles		*Maïs*	Corn	*Radis*	Radishes
Chou (rouge)	(Red) cabbage	*Menthe*	Mint	*Riz*	Rice
Choufleur	Cauliflower	*Moutarde*	Mustard	*Safran*	Saffron
Ciboulettes	Chives	*Oignon*	Onion	*Salade verte*	Green salad
Concombre	Cucumber	*Pâte*	Pasta or pastry	*Sarrasin*	Buckwheat
Cornichon	Gherkin	*Persil*	Parsley	*Tomate*	Tomato
Echalotes	Shallots	*Petits pois*	Peas	*Truffes*	Truffles

Dishes and terms

Beignet	Fritter	*Parmentier*	With potatoes
Farci	Stuffed	*Sauté*	Lightly fried in butter
Gratiné	Browned with cheese or butter	*A la vapeur*	Steamed
Jardinière	With mixed diced vegetables	*Je suis végétarien(ne).*	I'm a vegetarian. Are
A la parisienne	Sautéed in butter (potatoes); with	*Il y a quelques plats*	there any non-meat
	white wine sauce, and shallots	*sans viande?*	dishes?

Desserts *(desserts* or *entremets)* and pastries *(pâtisserie)*

Bombe	A moulded ice cream dessert	*Parfait*	Frozen mousse, some-
Brioche	Sweet, high yeast breakfast roll		times ice cream
Charlotte	Custard and fruit in lining of	*Petit Suisse*	A smooth mixture of
	almond fingers		cream and curds
Crème Chantilly	Vanilla-flavoured and sweet-	*Petits fours*	Bite-sized cakes/pastries
	ened whipped cream	*Poires Belle Hélène*	Pears and ice cream in
Crème fraîche	Sour cream		chocolate sauce
Crème pâtissière	Thick eggy pastry-filling	*Yaourt, yogourt*	Yoghurt
Crêpes suzettes	Thin pancakes with orange		
	juice and liqueur	**Terms:**	
Fromage blanc	Cream cheese	*Barquette*	Small boat-shaped flan
Glace	Ice cream	*Bavarois*	Refers to the mould, could
Île flottante/	Soft meringues floating on		be a mousse or custard
œufs à la neige	custard	*Coupe*	A serving of ice cream
Macarons	Macaroons	*Crêpes*	Pancakes
Madeleine	Small sponge cake	*Galettes*	Buckwheat pancakes
Marrons Mont	Chestnut purée and cream on a	*Gênoise*	Rich sponge cake
Blanc	rum-soaked sponge cake	*Sablé*	Shortbread biscuit
Mousse au	Chocolate mousse	*Savarin*	A filled, ring-shaped cake
chocolat		*Tarte*	Tart
Palmiers	Caramelized puff pastries	*Tartelette*	Small tart

And one final note: always call the waiter or waitress *Monsieur* or *Madame* (*Mademoiselle* if a young woman), never *garçon*, no matter what you've been taught in school.

of the **beer** you'll find. Draft (*à la pression*) is the cheapest drink you can have next to coffee and wine – though the smallest glass, *un demi* (0.25l), is rarely less than ten francs. Bottled beer is exceptionally cheap in supermarkets. British-style ales and stouts are becoming increasingly popular, with a number of special beer-drinking establishments or English-style pubs appearing in the larger cities, and in abundance in the capital. Bear in mind, though, that a small bottle in one of these places will set you back as much as twenty francs.

Strong alcohol is consumed from as early as 5am as a pre-work fortifier, and then at any time through the day according to circumstance, though the national reputation for drunkenness has lost much of its truth. Brandies and the dozens of *eaux de vie* (spirits) and liqueurs are always available. Among less familiar names, try *Poire William* (pear brandy), *Marc* (a spirit distilled from grape pulp), or just point to the bottle with the most attractive colour. Measures are generous, but they don't come cheap: the same applies for imported spirits like whisky (*Scotch*). *Pastis* – the generic name of aniseed drinks such as *Pernod* or *Ricard* – is served diluted with water and ice (*glaçons*). It's very refreshing and not expensive. Two drinks designed to stimulate the appetite are *Pineau* (cognac and grape juice) and *Kir* (white wine with a dash of blackcurrant syrup, or champagne for a *Kir Royal*).

On the **soft drink** front, you can buy cartons of unsweetened fruit juice in supermarkets, although in the cafés the bottled (sweetened) nectars such as apricot (*jus d'abricot*) and blackcurrant (*cassis*) still hold sway. You can also get fresh orange and lemon juice (*orange/citron pressé*), at a price; otherwise it's the standard fizzy cans. Bottles of **mineral water** (*eau minérale*) and spring water (*eau de source*) – either sparkling (*pétillante*) or still (*eau plate*) – abound, from the big brand names to the most obscure spa product. But there's not much wrong with the tap water (*l'eau de robinet*).

Coffee is invariably espresso – small, black and very strong. *Un café* or *un express* is the regular; *un crème* is with milk; *un grand café* or *un grand crème* are large cups. In the morning you could also ask for *un café au lait* – espresso in a large cup or bowl filled up with hot milk. *Un déca* is decaffeinated, now widely available. Ordinary **tea** (*thé*) is *Lipton's* nine times out of ten; to have milk with it, ask for *un peu de lait frais* (some fresh milk).

After overeating, **herb teas** (*infusions* or *tisanes*), served in every café, can be soothing. The more common ones are *verveine* (verbena), *tilleul* (lime blossom), *menthe* (mint) and *camomille* (camomile). *Chocolat chaud* – **hot chocolate** – unlike tea, lives up to the high standards of French food and drink and can be had in any café.

COMMUNICATIONS: POST, PHONES AND MEDIA

POST OFFICES

French **post offices** – *postes* or *PTT*s – are generally open 9am–noon and 2–5pm Monday to Friday, and 9am–noon on Saturday. However, don't depend on these hours: in larger towns you'll find a main office open throughout the day, while in villages, lunch hours and closing times can vary enormously.

You can have letters sent to you **poste restante** at any PTT in the country. If you're travelling around, it's simplest to choose towns of some size, though always specify the main post office (*Poste Centrale*) to avoid possible confusion. **To collect your mail** you need a passport or other convincing ID and should expect to pay a charge of a couple of francs. If you're expecting mail, it's worth asking the clerk to check under your surname *and* all possible first names as well – filing systems tend to be erratic.

Sending letters, the quickest international service is by *aérogramme*, sold at all post offices. You can buy ordinary stamps (*timbres*) at any *tabac* (tobacconist); note that postcards (*cartes postales*) go at a cheaper rate than letters (*lettres*). If you're sending **parcels** abroad, try to check prices in various leaflets available: small *postes* don't often send foreign mail and may need reminding, for example, of the reductions for printed papers and books. **Faxes** can be sent from all main post offices: the official French word is *télécopie*, but everyone understands *fax*.

TELEPHONES

You can make domestic and international phone calls from any telephone box (or **cabine**) and can receive calls where there's a blue logo of a ringing bell. Most call boxes only take **phone cards** (*télécartes*), obtainable from post offices, PTT boutiques, train stations and some *tabacs*; the cheapest card is 46F for 50 units. Coin-only boxes, still common in cafés, bars and rural areas, take 50 centimes, 1F, 5F, 10F pieces; put the money in after lifting up the receiver and before dialling. You can keep adding more coins once you are connected.

For **calls** within France – local or long distance – simply dial all eight digits of the number, except from Paris to the provinces, when you should first dial ☎16; to call a Paris number from anywhere else, first dial ☎16/1. The major **international calling codes**, are given in the box on p.48; remember to omit the initial 0 of the local area code from the subscriber's number.

An alternative to dialling internationally from *cabines* is to use the numbered **booths at main post offices**. You apply at the counter to be assigned a number and then dial. The disadvantage with these – odd considering the French obsession with technology – is that you can't tell how much you're spending. It's worth counting your units and checking – mistakes are sometimes made.

Peak rates are 73c for six-minute local calls, 2.19F a minute for places within 100km, and apply Mon–Fri 8am–12.30pm and 1.30–6pm & Sat 8am–12.30pm. Mon–Sat 12.30–1.30pm and Mon–Fri 6–9.30pm rates are thirty percent less. Mon–Sat 6–8am, Mon–Fri 9.30–10.30pm and Sun 6am–10.30pm rates are fifty percent less. Cheapest rates (65 percent less) are daily 10.30pm–6am.

To avoid payment altogether, you can, of course, make a reverse charge or **collect call** – known in French as "*téléphoner en PCV*". You can also do this through the operator in the UK, by dialling ☎19.00.44 and asking for a "reverse charge call". To get an English-speaking *AT&T* operator for North America, dial ☎19.00.11.

AT&T, MCI, Sprint and other North American long-distance companies all enable their customers to make **credit-card calls** while overseas. Most provide service from France; before you leave, call your company's customer service line

---

IDD CODES

From France dial ☎19 + IDD code + area code minues first 0 + subscriber number

Britain ☎44   Ireland ☎353   USA and Canada ☎1   Australia ☎61   New Zealand ☎64

From Britain to Paris: dial ☎010 331 + 8 digit number
outside Paris: dial ☎010 33 + 8 digit number

From the USA and Canada to Paris: dial ☎011 331 + 8 digit number
outside Paris: dial ☎011 33 + 8 digit number

From Australia to Paris: dial ☎011 331 + 8 digit number
outside Paris: dial ☎011 33 + 8 digit number

From New Zealand to Paris: dial ☎0044 331 + 8 digit number
outside Paris: dial ☎044 33 + 8 digit number

From Paris to the provinces: dial ☎16 + number

From outside Paris to Paris: dial ☎16/1 + number

TIME

France and Corsica are one hour ahead of GMT, except for a short period during October, when it's the same. It is six hours ahead of Eastern Standard Time, and nine hours ahead of Pacific Standard Time. This also applies during daylight savings seasons from the end of March to the end of September.

USEFUL NUMBERS WITHIN FRANCE

Weather ☎36.68.01.01.

Telegrams By phone: internal ☎36.55; external ☎05.26.21.86 (all languages).

Time ☎36.99.

International operator ☎13.

Directory assistance ☎12.

Traffic and road conditions Paris and Île de France ☎48.99.33.33; Lyon and Rhône-Alpes ☎78.54.33.33; Marseille and the Côte d'Azur ☎91.78.78.78; Bordeaux and the southwest ☎56.96.33.33; Metz and the east ☎87.63.33.33; Rennes and Brittany ☎99.32.33.33; Lille and the north ☎20.47.33.33.

---

to find out the toll-free access code in France. Calls made from overseas will automatically be billed to your home number.

MINITEL

Phone subscribers in most French cities have a **minitel**, an on-line computer allowing access through the phone lines to all kinds of directories, databases, chat lines etc. You will also find them in post offices. Most organizations, from sports federations to government institutions to gay groups, have a code consisting of numbers and letters to call up information, leave messages, make reservations etc. You dial the number on the phone, wait for a fax-type tone, then type the letters on the keyboard, and finally, press *Connexion Fin* (the same key ends the connection). If you're at all

computer literate and can understand basic keyboard terms in French (*retour* – return, *envoi* – enter, etc), you shouldn't find them hard to use. Be warned that most services cost more than phone rates.

NEWSPAPERS AND MAGAZINES

A reasonable selection of **English-language newspapers** from the *Sunday Times, European* and *International Herald Tribune* are on sale in most large cities and resorts the day after publication. As for the **French press**, the **national daily** *Le Monde* (Tues–Sun) is the most intellectual and respected, with no concessions to entertainment (such as pictures), but a correctly styled French that is probably the easiest to understand. *Libération* (*Libé* for short; Tues–Sun) is moderately left-wing, independent and colloquial with good, selective coverage; *L'Humanité* is the Communist Party newspaper (*L'Humanité Dimanche* is the bulkier Sunday version), with a diminishing readership. All the other nationals are firmly on the right. The widest circulations are enjoyed by the **regional dailies**. The most important of these is the Rennes-based *Ouest-France* – though for travellers this, like the rest of the regionals, is mainly of interest for its listings.

Weeklies, on the *Newsweek/Time* model, include the wide-ranging left-leaning *Le Nouvel Observateur*, through the right-leaning *Le Figaro*, right up to the *Observateur*'s rightist counterweight, *L'Express*. The best and funniest investigative journalism is in the satirical *Canard Enchaîné*. **Monthlies** include *L'Autre Journal*, which covers culture as well as news, and *Actuel*, which is good for current events. *Le Monde* publishes a beautifully designed monthly, *Le Monde des Débats*, and there are, of course, all the French versions of *Vogue*, *Elle* and *Marie-Claire*, as well as the *Paris-Match* for gossip about stars and royalty. There are also the **comics** (*bandes dessinés* or *BD*), which occupy a far more prestigious status in the bookshops and newsstands than they do in Britain or America. *Charlie-Hebdo* is one with political targets; *A Suivre* is a showpiece for amazing graphic talent.

Some of the huge numbers of homeless people in France (*les sans-logement*) make a bit of money by selling four magazines on the streets that combine culture, humour and self-help with social and political issues – *Macadam Journal* (10F, of which 6F goes to the seller), *Le Réverbère* (10F, collectively owned by the sellers), *Faim de Siècle* (12F, of which sellers keep 6.50F) and *La Rue* (15F, of which 7.80F is kept by the seller).

TV AND RADIO

French TV broadcasts six channels, three of them public, along with a good many more cable and satellite channels, which include *CNN* and the *BBC World Service*. If you've got a **radio**, you can tune into English-language news on the *BBC World Service* on 648kHz or between 6.195 and 12.095MHz shortwave at intervals throughout the day and night. *BBC Radio 4* from 5am to 11.45pm GMT, and the *World Service* from 11.45pm to 5am GMT on 198kHz longwave, are usually quite clear, while the *Voice of America* transmits on 90.5, 98.8 and 102.4FM. *Radio Classique* (FM 101.1) is a classical music station with a minimum of chat and no commercials. For **news** in French, there are the state-run *France Inter* (FM 87.8, 220 longwave), *Europe 1* (FM 104.7, 180 longwave) or round-the-clock news on *France Infos* (FM 105.5).

BUSINESS HOURS AND PUBLIC HOLIDAYS

Basic hours of business are 8am–noon and 2–6pm: almost everything in France – shops, museums, tourist offices, most banks – closes for a couple of hours at midday, although lunch breaks tend to be longer in the south. Food shops often don't reopen till halfway through the afternoon, closing around 7.30 or 8pm just before the evening meal. So if you're looking to buy a picnic lunch, you'll need to buy it before you're ready to think about eating.

The standard **closing days** are Sunday and Monday, and in small towns you'll find everything except the odd *boulangerie* (bakery) shut on both days. This includes **banks**. It's all too easy to find yourself dependent on hotels for money-changing – an alternative

that invariably means poor rates and high commission.

Museums in France are not very generous with their hours, tending to open at around 10am, close for lunch at noon until 2pm or 3pm, and then run through only until 5pm or 6pm. Closing days are usually Tuesday or Monday, sometimes both. Admission charges can be very off-putting, though many state-owned museums have one or two days of the week when they're free, and you can get a big reduction at most places by showing a student card (or passport if you're under 26 or over 60). Churches and cathedrals are almost always open all day every day, with charges only for the crypt, treasuries or cloister and little fuss about how you're dressed. When they are closed you may have to attend Mass on Sunday morning (or at other times which you'll see posted up on the door) to take a look. In small towns and villages, however, getting the key is not difficult – ask anyone nearby or seek out the priest, whose house is known as the *presbytère*.

PUBLIC HOLIDAYS

There are thirteen national holidays (*jours fériés*), when most shops and businesses, though not museums or restaurants, are closed.

January 1 New Year's Day

Easter Sunday

Easter Monday

Ascension Day (forty days after Easter)

Whitsun (seventh Sunday after Easter, plus the Monday)

May 1 May Day/Labour Day

May 8 Victory in Europe Day

July 14 Bastille Day

August 15 Assumption of the Virgin Mary

November 1 All Saints' Day

November 11 1918 Armistice Day

December 25 Christmas Day

FESTIVALS AND ANNUAL EVENTS

It's hard to beat the experience of arriving in some small French village, expecting no more than a bed for the night, to discover the streets decked out with flags and streamers, a band playing in the square and the entire population out celebrating the feast of their patron saint. Apart from Bastille Day (July 14) and the Assumption of the Virgin Mary (August 15), there are traditional folk festivals still thriving in Brittany and the remote rural regions of the south, as well as a full calendar of sophisticated film fests, the Paris Marathon and the Formula I Grand Prix in Monte Carlo, and festivals devoted to music from jazz and folk to rock and classical.

FESTIVALS

Catholicism is deeply ingrained in the culture of French rural areas, and as a result, **religious feast days** still bring people out in all their finery, ready to indulge once Mass has been said. These occasions, along with the celebrations around wine and food production, are usually very genuine affairs. Other festivals, based for example on historical events, folklore or literature, are often obviously money-spinners and shows for municipal prestige – not something to go out of your way for.

One **folk festival** that is definitely worth attending is the **Inter-Celtic** event held at **Lorient** in Brittany every August. Another annual event with deep historical roots is the great gypsy gathering at **Les-Saintes-Maries-de-la-Mer** in the Camargue. Though exploited for every last centime and, in recent years, given a heavy police presence, it is a unique and exhilarating spectacle to be part of.

Bonfires are lit and fireworks set off for **Bastille Day** and for the **Fête de St Jean** on June 24, three days from the summer solstice. *Mardi Gras* – the last blow-out before Lent – is far less of an occasion than in other Catholic countries, although the towns on the Côte d'Azur put on a show at great expense and in questionable taste.

CALENDAR OF EVENTS

January

end-January to beginning February – **Clermont-Ferrand** Festival of short films

February

The week before Lent – **Nice** *Mardi Gras*

The week before Lent – **Nîmes** La Fieria du Carnaval

March

Strasbourg Film Festival

End March/beginning April – **Créteil, outside Paris** International festival of women's films

April

Mid-April – **Paris** Paris Marathon

May

Cannes International Film Festival

From Ascension Day to the following Sunday – **Monte Carlo** Formula 1 Grand Prix

24th – **Les-Stes-Maries-de-la-Mer** Gypsy Festival

24th – **Orcival** Pilgrimage to Notre-Dame d'Orcival

Last week plus first week in June – **Paris** Roland Garros tennis tournament

June

Mid-June – **Le Mans** 24-hour car rally

Mid-June to early July – **Aix** *Aix en Musique*

21st (summer solstice) – **Paris** Gay Pride

Third week – **Calvi, Corsica** Jazz Festival

End June to mid-July – **Douai** Festival of Giants

End June to mid-July – **Montpellier** International Dance Festival

June & July – **La Rochelle** Contemporary Arts Festival

July

First ten days – **Rennes** *Tombées de la Nuit* theatre and music festival

First week for three weeks – **Tour de France**

Second Sunday in July – **Locronan** Breton *Troménie Pardon*

Second week – **Annecy** *Festival de la Vieille Ville*

Mid-July – **Aix** International Dance Festival

Last two weeks – **Avignon** Dance and Drama Festival

Last two weeks – **Juan-les-Pins** International Jazz Festival

Last ten days – **Gannat, near Vichy** World Folk Festival

Last week – **Quimper** *Festival Cornouaille*

Late July to early August – **Prades** Casals Chamber Music Festival in the Abbey of St-Michel-de-Cuxa

End July to mid-August – **Sarlat** Drama Festival

August

Menton Chamber Music Festival

First full week – **Lorient** Inter-Celtic Festival

First full week – **Murat** International Folklore Festival

First full week – **Périgueux** International Mime Festival

15th – **all over France** Assumption of the Virgin Mary – fireworks and *fêtes*

Last week – **Aurillac** International Street Theatre Festival

September

First week – **Dijon** International Folk and Wine Festival

Early September – **Paris** *Fête de l'Humanité* cultural festival sponsored by the Communist Party

Mid-September to December – **Paris** *Festival d'Automne* international theatre and music

Mid-September – **Puy-en-Velay** Festival of the Roi de l'Oiseau

End September to mid-October – **Limoges** International Festival of French-Speaking Communities

Last ten days – **Charleville-Mézières** Triennial World Festival of Puppet Theatre

October

Paris Jazz Festival

Bastia, Corsica Mediterranean Film Festival

Early October – **Paris** Montmartre Vintage Festival

November

Strasbourg International Mime and Clown Festival

Mid-November – **Metz** International Contemporary Music Festival

December

Second week – **Rennes** *Les Transmusicales* international rock festival

MUSIC, FILM AND THEATRE

The best contemporary music you'll hear in France is likely to be distinctly un-French. Paris has no rivals in Europe for the variety of world music to be discovered: West and Central African, Caribbean and Latin American sounds are represented in force both by city-based bands and by club or arena appearances by groups on tour. Throughout the country, though, jazz and classical music lovers will be well served, particularly during the festival season.

In theatre, directors not playwrights dominate. Scripts are there to be shaken up or scrambled. Innovative dance can't compete with the United States, but there are several excellent regional companies and festivals that bring in the best international talent, and film is taken very seriously. The French have treated the cinema as an art form, deserving of state subsidy, ever since its origination with the Lumière brothers in 1895, and TV has only just started to threaten; the international seat of judgement for film is still Cannes, and Paris is the cinema capital of the world.

MUSIC

Standard **French rock** largely deserves its miserable reputation. Leaving aside such figures as the Sixties rocker Johnny Halliday (still France's biggest music star, thirty years on), or the execrable electro-pomp composer Jean-Michel Jarre, names like *U2* and *The Cure* are better known to the French than any home-grown artists. Although most singers — like Patrick Bruel, idol of depressed adolescents — lay claim to the *chansonniers* tradition, few have genuine roots in it, with the notable exception of Patricia Kaas. Vanessa Paradis went so far as to switch to English in order to pursue an international career.

The best "alternative " rock band is **Mano Negra**, whose core members are French-born Spaniard. Their latest album, *Casa Babylon*, has been heavily influenced by their Latin American tours and combines rap, reggae, rock and salsa sounds. Other quality rock musicians include Louis Bertignac and Paul Personne. However, half of all albums bought in France are recorded by British and American bands.

There are numerous **heavy metals bands** with English names like "Megadeath". Then there's **trashpop**, an amalgam of funk, punk and splashes of bebop, heavy metal and psychedelia. An emerging new trend is French "country" music, known as **Astérix rock**, a bawdy, raucous, energetic sound with accordions as the main instruments. *Les French Lovers* and *Les Garços Bhsareto* are two of the current bands making it. French **rap**, much to the disgust of its practitioners, was given subsidies by the last government. Names to look out for are NTM, IAM and MC Solaar, who moves beyond traditional rap to something a good deal more melodic and musical, with superb words that you need to be pretty fluent to appreciate.

One variety of home-grown popular music that survives is the tradition of **chansons**, epitomized by Édith Piaf and developed to its greatest heights by Georges Brassens and the Belgian Jacques Brel. This music is undergoing something of a revival since the return of the 1950s star Juliette Greco to the *Olympia* stage in 1991 brought rapt media attention. Despite the emphasis on poetic lyrics, French **folk songs** can cross frontiers, as Françoise Hardy proved in the 1960s. British or American audiences, however, permeated by rock, are likely to find most of this form unbearably vapid and wimpish. Another retrospective experience is **ballroom dancing** at the old music halls or *guinguettes*.

Jazz is a different matter — in Paris most of all, where you could listen to a different band every night for weeks, from trad, through bebop and free jazz, to highly contemporary experimental. And there are many excellent festivals, particularly in the south (see p.51). If you hear of **Urban Sax** playing at any of these — or elsewhere — go along, if only for the drama of sixty-plus saxophonists performing together.

If your taste is for **classical music** and its descendants, you're also in for a treat. Electronically produced sounds are experimented with at Pierre Boulez's creation of IRCAM beneath Beaubourg. Paris has two opera houses and in the provinces there are no less than twelve companies, of which Strasbourg and Toulouse are said to be the best, and a further dozen orchestras. Monaco's opera house is renowned for drawing the top international stars.

The places to check out for concerts are the *Maisons de la Culture* (in all the larger cities), churches (where chamber music is as much performed as sacred music, often without charge), and festivals – of which there are hundreds, the most famous being at Aix in July.

CINEMA

While it's true that over sixty percent of films shown in **French cinemas** are from the United States, there are *ciné-clubs* in almost every city, censorship is very slight, students get discounts, and foreign films are usually shown in their **original language** with subtitles (look for *version originale* or *v.o.* in the listings). Investment in film production in France is nearly twice the level of that in the UK, and the number of films made annually is three times as great – though, of course, nowhere near the output of the United States. The Paris *Archives du Film* at the *Centre National de la Cinématographie* in the Palais de Tokyo possess the largest collection of silent and early talkie movies in the world, and have embarked on a fifteen-year, 17-million-franc programme to transfer all the pre-1960 stock onto acetate to avoid disintegration.

While the old is treasured and preserved, the new in French cinema revolves around the Nureyev of moviedom, **Gérard Départieu**. Jean-Paul Rappeneau's brilliant 1989 screening of the late nineteenth-century play *Cyrano de Bergerac* was a welcome departure from the style movies of the early 1980s, such as *Diva* and *Subway*, and Départieu has reinvigorated French cinema as an export industry. But there is no current force in French movie-making to touch on the prolific New Wave period of the Sixties, pioneered by **Jean-Luc Godard** and others. Luc Besson, Leos Carax, Agnès Varda, Bernard Tavernier and Patrice Chereau (also well known as a theatre director) are some of the stalwarts, and many foreign directors – notably Kurosawa and Wajda – work or have worked in France, benefiting from public subsidies.

Since *Germinal*, big French films have included the serious two-part period piece *Jeanne la Pucelle* (Joan of Arc) and *Les Visiteurs*, a happy medieval romp. Nostalgia rather than postmodernism seems to be the current mood in French film making. The row over cultural subsidies in the world GATT talks revealed just how threatened France feels by American movie imports, and the top box-office hits throughout the country tend to be transatlantic imports.

The **Cannes Film Festival**, where the prized *Palme d'Or* is handed out, is not, in any public sense, a festival; it's more a screening of what's new for those in the industry. Film fests where anyone can go along include those at **La Rochelle** (*Rencontres Internationales d'Art Contemporain*; June–July); **Créteil** in the Paris suburbs (festival of women's films); **La Ciotat** (silent films; July); **Reims** (thrillers; Oct–Nov); and **Strasbourg** (general films; March).

THEATRE

The earlier **theatre** generation of **Genet**, **Anouilh** and **Camus**, joined by **Beckett** and **Ionesco**, hasn't really had successors. In the 1950s, **Roger Planchon** set up a company in a suburb of Lyon, determined to play to working-class audiences. It became the *Théâtre Nationale Populaire*, the number-two state theatre after the *Comédie Française*, and now does the classics with all due decorum. Bourgeois farces, postwar classics, Shakespeare, Racine and *Cyrano de Bergerac* make up the staple fare in most theatres. There are also plenty of foreign companies, and, for exciting contemporary work, there's the superstar breed of directors like Peter Brook, Ariane Mnouchkine and Jean-Paul Vincent. Spectacular and dazzling sensation tends to take precedence over speech in their productions, with huge casts, extraordinary sets, overwhelming sound and light effects – an experience, even if you haven't understood a word. **Café-théâtre**, though far from avant-garde, is probably less accessible, with satire, *chansons* and dirty jokes the staple ingredients.

For details of **Paris theatres**, see Chapter One. In other cities, the theatres are often part of the *Maisons de la Culture* or *Centres d'Animation Culturelle*; local tourist offices usually have schedules and tickets are not expensive. The two major theatre festivals are the ***Festival Mondial***

BUYING TICKETS

The FNAC shops in all big towns and Virgin Megastores in the main cities have copious listings of what's on and are the best booking agencies for gigs, ballet or theatre. Booking details for festivals are given in the guide.

du Théâtre in Nancy (June) and the *Festival d'Avignon* (July & Aug).

The French regional **dance companies** from La Rochelle, Marseille, Grenoble, Angers and Montpellier easily rival the Paris-based troupes, and the work of choreographers Maguy Marin, Karine Saporta and François Verret are worth looking out for. The current trend is in multidi-mensional performing art, combining movement, mime, ballet, speech, noise, theatrical effects and music from medieval to jazz-rock. Though the famous Lecoq School of Mime and Improvisation in Paris still turns out excellent artists, pure **mime** – as practised by the incomparable Marcel Marceau – hardly exists, except on the streets and at Périgueux's international festival of mime, as well as at the similar bashes in Montpellier, Avignon and Paris.

SPORTS

More than any of the cultural jamborees, it is sporting events that really excite the French – cycling, football, tennis and skiing. At the local level, the gentle sobriety of *boules* is the most obvious manifestation of sporting life.

First and foremost in the French sporting calendar is the *Tour de France* cycle race in July, which takes in most of the country during its three-week run, finishing off with a few laps of the Champs-Élysées. The race leader traditionally wears a yellow jersey (*maillot jaune*), though the French haven't had a victory since Bernard Hinault in 1985.

Here, as everywhere, **football** has quasi-religious standing. The best, though far from the most popular teams in France are currently Paris St-Germain and Nantes. **Nantes** is young and full of unknowns. **Paris St-Germain** is rich and star-studded – with prima donna David Ginola and goalie Bernard Lama – but has no real local following. The most popular clubs remain **St-Étienne**, which first put French football on the international map, and **Olympique Marseille**, now fallen from grace with its flamboyant former owner and European Parliament MP, Bernard Tapie. Punished for its corrupt practices by relegation to Division Two, which it now heads, the club nonetheless retains the loyal support of its home town. It is temporarily rudderless, but the word is that Corsican TV journalist Cangioni is about to take over the club. Meanwhile, France continues to export some of its best players: Jean-Pierre Papin to Bayern Munich, and Eric Cantona and Basil Boli to Britain, to Manchester United and the Glasgow Rangers, respectively.

Although confined mainly to the south and southwest of the country, the sport that arouses most passion in France is **rugby**, currently divided by the debate over whether to give up its amateur status and go professional. The most successful teams at the moment are Toulouse, Agen and Toulon, while Béziers remains the best known for its long reign as champion. The Basque teams of Biarritz and Bayonne are the ones to watch – the Basque country is generally revered as the keeper of the game's soul.

Lastly, in and around the Camargue, the number-one sport is **bullfighting**. Though not to everyone's taste, it is at least a considerably less gruesome variety than that practised by the Spanish – usually bloodless and involving variations on the theme of removing cocades from the base of the bull's horns. It's generally the "fighters", rather than the bulls, that get hurt.

In every town or village square, particularly in the south, you'll see the older generation playing *boules* or *pétanque*. The principle is the same as British bowls but the terrain is always rough (never grass) and the area much smaller. The metal ball is usually thrown upwards from a distance of about 10m, to land and skid towards the wooden marker (*cochonnet*). It's very male dominated, and socially the equivalent of darts or perhaps pool: there are café or village teams and endless championships.

Crowds gather in the Basque country for the national ball game of *pelota*, which is like a lethally (sometimes literally) fast variety of team squash played in a walled court with a ball of solid wood and wicker slings strapped to the players' arms.

SKIING

One sport that millions of visitors come to France to practise rather than watch is **skiing**. And whether downhill, cross-country, or mountaineering, it's also enthusiastically pursued by the French. It can be an expensive sport to practise independently, however, and the best deals are often to be had from package operators (see pp.5, 15, & 17). These can be arranged in France or before you leave (most travel agents sell all-in packages). In France, the umbrella organization to contact is the *Fédération Française de Ski*, 50 rue des Marquisats, 74000 Annecy (☎50.51.40.34).

The best skiing is generally to be had in **the Alps**. The higher the resort the longer the season and the fewer the anxieties you'll have about there being enough snow. These resorts are almost all modern, with the very latest in lift technology. They're terrific for full-time skiing,

but they lack the cachet, charm or the nightlife of the older resorts such as Megève and Courchevel. The **foothills of the Alps** in Provence have the same mix of old and new on a smaller scale. The clientele are Riviera residents and prices are not cheap, though at least you can nip down to the coast for a quick swim when you're bored of snow. The **Pyrenees** are a friendlier range of mountains, less developed (though that can be a drawback if you want to get in as many different runs as possible per day) and warmer, which means more problems with the snow.

Cross-country skiing (*ski de fond*) is being promoted hard, especially in the smaller ranges of the Jura and Massif Central. It's easier on the joints, but don't be fooled into thinking it's any less athletic a sport. For the really experienced and fit, though, it can be a good means of transport, using snowbound GR routes to discover villages still relatively uncommercialized. Several independent operators organize **ski-mountaineering courses** in the French mountains (see pp.5, 15 & 17).

TROUBLE AND THE POLICE

Petty theft is endemic along the Côte d'Azur and pretty bad in the crowded parts of most big cities. Drivers, however, face greater problems, most notoriously break-ins. And any traveller can suffer at the hands of the police if caught without ID.

To safeguard against grab-and-run theft, take normal precautions: keep your wallet in your front pocket and your handbag under your elbow. If you should get attacked, hand over the money and start dialling the cancellation numbers for your travellers' cheques and credit cards, which may offer free "International Rescue" services in which a replacement card or cash can be sent to you within 24 hours. Contact numbers in the case of credit card loss are given on pp.21–22.

Reporting a theft (*faire un constat de vol*) has to be done at the Commissariat de police (addresses are given for all the main cities). It may well involve a lengthy wait and reluctance on the part of the officer who has to fill in the form.

Vehicles are rarely stolen, but car radios and luggage make tempting targets, and foreign numberplates are easy to spot. Good insurance is the only answer, but even so try not to leave any valuables in sight. If you have an accident while driving, you have officially to fill in and sign a *constat à l'aimable* (jointly agreed statement); car

---

EMERGENCIES

Ambulance ☎18
Police ☎17
Fire Service ☎18

It's common for the fire brigade, *les sapeurs pompiers*, to be called for medical problems; they all have paramedical training and equipment.

---

insurers are supposed to give you this with a policy, though in practice few seem to have heard of it.

For noncriminal **driving violations** such as speeding, the police can impose on-the-spot fines. Should you be arrested on any charge, you have the right to contact your consulate (see p.155).

People caught smuggling or possessing **drugs**, even a few grams of marijuana, are liable to find themselves in jail, and consulates will not be sympathetic. This is not to say that hard-drug consumption isn't a visible activity: there are scores of kids dealing in *poudre* (heroin) in the big French cities and the authorities seem unable to do much about it. As a rule, people are no more nor less paranoid about cannabis busts than they are in the UK or North America.

THE POLICE

There are two main types of French police (popularly known as *les flics*): the **Police Nationale** and the **Gendarmerie Nationale**. For all practical purposes, they are indistinguishable; if you need to report a theft, or other incident, you can go to either. A different proposition entirely are the **CRS** (*Compagnies Républicaines de Sécurité*), a mobile force of heavies, sporadically dressed in green combats and armed with riot equipment, whose brutality in the May 1968 battles turned public opinion to the side of the students; they still make demonstrations dangerous. Not quite in the same league, but with an ugly recent history, is the separate **Paris police force**. This bunch are prone to pulling up "nonconformists" – often just ordinary teenagers, predominantly from the country's large North African community – for identity checks. You can be stopped anywhere in France and asked to produce ID. If it happens to you, it's not worth being difficult or facetious.

Lastly, in the Alps or Pyrenees, you may come across specialized **mountaineering sections** of the police force. They are unfailingly helpful,

friendly and approachable, providing rescue services and guidance.

SEXUAL AND RACIAL HARASSMENT

Women are bound to experience **sexual harassment** in France, where many men make a habit of looking you up and down and, more often than not, passing comment. Generally it is no worse than in the UK or North America, but problems arise in judging men without the familiar linguistic and cultural clues.

A "*Bonjour*" or "*Bonsoir*" on the street may be a pick-up line. If you return the greeting, you've left yourself open to a persistent monologue and a difficult brush-off job. On the other hand, it's not unusual to be offered a drink in a bar if you're on your own and not to be pestered even if you accept. This is rarer in big cities than in the countryside, but don't assume that any overture by a Frenchman is a come-on.

Late-night *métros* in the big cities are nowhere near as unnerving as in London or New York, simply because of greater passenger numbers and the fact that people are more inclined to intervene if nasty scenes develop. Hitchhiking is risky – as it is anywhere – and few French women do it except on the Côte d'Azur where public transport is minimal. If you want to hitch it's best to use *Allostop* (see p.32) and take the same precautions as you would at home.

If you need help, go to the police, although don't expect too much from them. The *mairie/ hôtel de ville* (town hall) will have addresses of women's organizations (*Femmes Battues, Femmes en Détresse* or *SOS Femmes*), though this won't be much help outside business hours. You'll find detailed listings for Paris in Chapter One, and we've given contacts for other cities where possible. The national **Rape Crisis** number, *SOS Viol*, is ☎05.05.95.95, but it's not 24hr (Mon–Fri 10am–6pm).

France has its fair share of **racist attitudes** and behaviour. If you are Arab or look as if you might be, your chances of avoiding unpleasantness are very low. Hotels claim to be booked up, police demand your papers, and abuse from ordinary people is horribly frequent. In addition, being black, of whatever ethnic origin, can make entering the country difficult. Changes in passport regulations have put an end to outright refusal to let some British holidaymakers in, but customs and immigration officers can still be obstructive and malicious. In North African-dominated areas of cities, identity checks by the police are common and not pleasant.

The main **antiracist organization** is *SOS Racisme*, with branches throughout the country and the main office at 14 Cité Griset, Paris (☎48.06.40.00), which organizes a rally and concert in Paris every June, and has done a great deal over the last few years to raise consciousness amongst young white French people.

GAY AND LESBIAN FRANCE

France is more liberal on homosexuality than most other European countries. The legal age of consent is 15 and gay communities thrive especially in Paris and many of the southern towns, though lesbian life is rather less upfront. Addresses are listed in the guide, and you'll find details of groups and publications for the whole country in the Paris chapter.

In general, the French consider sexuality to be a private matter. Whether, for example, the former minister of culture, Jack Lang, is gay or not is of no interest to commentators. On the whole, gays tend to be discreet outside specific gay venues, parades and the prime gay areas of Paris and the coastal resorts. Lesbians tend to be extremely discreet.

Hedonistic lifestyles have changed, here as elsewhere, since the advent of AIDS (*SIDA* in French). The resulting homophobia, though not as extreme as in Britain or parts of America, has nevertheless increased the suffering among gay

GAY CONTACTS AND INFORMATION

ARCL (*Archives, Recherches et Cultures Lesbiennes*), Post box (BP) 362, 75526, Paris Cedex 11; answerphone ☎48.05.25.89. Fri 6–8pm – hours may change. *ARCL* publish a yearly directory of lesbian and feminist addresses in France (available at the *Bibliothèque Marguerite Durand* in Paris) and a fairly regular bulletin. They also organize frequent meetings.

David & Jonathan, 92bis rue Picpus, Paris 12e; ☎43.42.09.49 (M° Michel-Bizot). 24hr answerphone for gay Christians.

Maison des Femmes, 8 Cité Prost, off rue Chanzy, Paris 11e; ☎43.48.24.91 (M° Faidherbe-Chaligny). Mon 6–8pm, Wed 3–8pm, Fri 6–8pm; Fri café 8pm–midnight. Run by *Paris Féministe* (see p.155), this is the home of the *Groupe des Lesbiennes Féministes* and the *Mouvement d'Information et d'Expression des Lesbiennes*. A cafeteria operates on Friday nights, and there are occasional events organized.

Minitel. 3615 GPS is the Minitel number to dial for information on groups, contacts, messages etc. The service was set up by *Gai Pied*. There are also any number of chat lines.

Gay media

Exit. Gay newspaper with useful addresses.

Fréquence Gaie, 98.2 FM. 24hr gay and lesbian radio station with music, news, chat, information on groups and events, etc.

Illico. A monthly with lonely hearts and Minitel numbers.

Lesbia. The most widely available lesbian publication, available from most newsagents. Each monthly issue features a wide range of articles, listings, reviews, lonely hearts and contacts.

Spartacus International Gay Guide. Guidebook focusing mainly on gay travel in Europe.

Gay/lesbian travel contacts

Detour Guides, 1016 3rd Ave, Sacramento, CA 95818 (☎916/448-4120). Series covers London, Paris, Amsterdam and several American cities.

Different Drummer Tours, PO Box 528, Glen Ellyn, IL 60137 (☎1-800/645-1275). Scheduled and customized international tours.

Different Strokes Tours, 1841 Broadway, New York, NY 10023 (☎1-800/688-3301). Customized international tours.

International Gay Travel Association, PO Box 4974, Key West, FL 33041 (☎1-800/448-8550 or 305/292-0217). Trade group that can provide a list of gay-owned or gay-friendly travel agents, accommodation and other travel businesses.

Key Tours, 1 Kensington St, London W8 4EB (☎0171/ 229 6961). Gay tour operator.

Uranian Travel, 111 Kew Road, Richmond, Surrey TW9 2PN (☎0171/332 1022). Package holidays and hotel bookings.

men. The Pasteur Institute in Paris is at the forefront of research into the virus, though its gay patients have complained of being treated like cattle. A group of gay doctors and the association AIDES (*Association pour l'Entraide et l'Information SIDA*), however, have consistently provided sympathetic counselling and treatment, and the gay press has done a great deal to disseminate the facts about AIDS and to provide hope and encouragement. Lesbian organizations fight alongside gays on the general issue of anti-homosexuality while campaigning separately on the far more numerous and varied repressions to which women are subject.

WORK AND STUDY

Specialists aside, most Britons, North Americans and Australians who manage to survive for longer periods of time in France do it on luck, brazenness and willingness to live in pretty basic conditions. In the cities, bar work, club work, freelance translating, data processing and typing are some of the ways people scrape by; in the countryside, the options come down to seasonal fruit- or grape-picking, teaching English, busking or DIY oddjobbing.

France has a **minimum wage** (the *SMIC*), currently around 35F an hour. Employers, however, are likely to pay lower wages to temporary foreign workers who don't have easy legal resources. By law, however, all EU nationals are entitled to exactly the same pay, conditions and trade union rights as French nationals. It's worth noting that if you're a full-time non-EU student in France (see opposite), you can get a non-EU **work permit** for the following summer so long as your visa is still valid.

If you're looking for something secure, it's important to plan well in advance. The best

general sources for all jobs in France are the publications *Emplois d'été en France* (Vacation Work, 9 Park End St, Oxford, UK; ☎0865/241978), *Work Your Way Around the World* (Vacation Work, 1507 Dana Ave, Cincinnati, Ohio, USA) and 1000 Pistes de Jobs (*L'Étudiant*, 27 rue du Chemin-Vert, 75011 Paris). *Working Holidays* (Central Bureau, Seymour Mews House, Seymour Mews, London W1H 9PE) is also useful. In France, the evening paper *France Soir* has the best selection of job ads in its Thursday edition.

Teaching English is one of the easiest ways of getting a job in France. It's best to apply from Britain; check the ads in the *Guardian's* "Education" section (every Tuesday), or in the weekly *Times Educational Supplement*. Late summer is usually the best time. You don't need fluent French to get a post, but a *TEFL* (*Teaching English as a Foreign Language*) qualification may well be required. If you apply from home, most schools will fix up the necessary papers for you. It's also quite feasible to find a teaching job when you're in France, but you may have to accept semiofficial status and no job security. For the addresses of schools, look under *Écoles de Langues* in the Professions directory of the local phone book; otherwise contact the *British Council* at 9 rue du Constantine, 75007 Paris, for a list of language schools. Offering **private lessons** (via university noticeboards or classified ads), you'll have lots of competition, and it's hard to reach the people who can afford it, but it's always worth a try.

Au pair work is usually arranged through one of a dozen agencies, all of which are listed in *Working Holidays*. In Britain, *The Lady* is the magazine for classified adverts for such jobs, arranged privately. As initial numbers to ring, try *Euroyouth* (☎01702/341434) or *Avalon au*

Paris (☎01483/63640) in Britain, or *Accueil Familial des Jeunes Étrangers* (☎42.22.50.34) in Paris, or the *American Institute for Foreign Study* (☎203/869-9090) in the US, who can place female au pairs only; any of them will fill you in on the general terms and conditions (never very generous), and the state of the market; you shouldn't get paid less than 1000F a month (on top of board and lodging). It is wise to have an escape route (like a ticket home) in case you find the conditions intolerable – many people have had bad experiences. *Euroyouth* also runs a summer holiday scheme, placing people in French families for 2–3 weeks, where you get free board and lodging in exchange for English lessons.

Temporary jobs in the **travel industry** revolve around courier work – supervising and working on bus tours or summer campsites. You'll need good French (and maybe even another language) and should write to as many tour operators as you can, preferably in early spring. Ads occasionally appear in the *Guardian's* "Media" section (every Monday) in Britain. Getting work as a courier on a campsite is slightly easier. It usually takes in putting up tents at the beginning of the season, taking them down again at the end, and general maintenance and trouble-shooting work in the months between. *Canvas Holidays* (☎01383/644000) are worth approaching, or the *Union Française des Centres de Vacances* (☎45.39.22.23) once you're in France.

An offbeat possibility if you want to discover rural life is being a **working guest** on an organic farm. The period can be anything from a week to a couple of months and the work may involve cheese making, market gardening, bee-keeping, wine producing and building. For details of the scheme and a list of French addresses, write to *Willing Workers on Organic Farms (WWOOF)*, 19 Bradford Road, Lewes, East Sussex BN7 1RB, UK, or the *Service de Remplacement*, c/o Michel Champy, Alancourt Mancy, 51200 Épernay, France, enclosing an SAE.

CLAIMING BENEFIT

If you're an EU citizen – and you do the paperwork in advance – you can sign on for **unemployment benefit**. To do so, you must collect form E303 before leaving home, available in Britain from any DSS office. The procedure is first to get registered at an *ANPE* office (*Agence Nationale pour l'Emploi*), then take the form to your local *ASSEDIC* (benefits office) and give them an address, which can be a hostel or a hotel, for the money to be sent to. You sign once a month at the *ANPE* and receive benefit a month in arrears – theoretically, at least, payments can be delayed in small towns for up to three months. After three months, you must anyway either leave the country or get a *carte de séjour*. EU pensioners can arrange for their pensions to be paid in France, but not, unfortunately, to receive French state pensions.

STUDYING IN FRANCE

It's relatively easy to be a **student** in France. Foreigners pay no more than French nationals (around 1300F a year) to enrol for a course, and the only problem then is to support yourself. Your *carte de séjour* and – if you're an EU citizen – social security will be assured, and you'll be eligible for subsidized accommodation, meals and all the student reductions. In general, French universities are much less formal than British ones and many people perfect their fluency in the language while studying. There are strict entry requirements, including an exam in French, for undergraduate degrees, not for post-graduate courses. For full **details and prospectuses**, contact the Cultural Service of any French embassy or consulate (see p.19).

Language schools are offered at a number of establishments in university towns. They are listed in the hand-out *"Cours de Français pour Étudiants Étrangers"*, also obtainable from embassy or consular cultural sections. Finally, it's worth noting that if you're a full-time student in France, you can get a **work permit** for the following summer as long as your visa is still valid.

DIRECTORY

BEACHES Beaches are public property within five metres of the high-tide mark, so you can kick sand past private villas. Under a different law, however, you can't camp.

CAMERAS AND FILM Film is considerably cheaper in North America than France or Britain, so stock up if you're coming from there. If you're bringing a video camcorder, make sure any tapes you purchase in France will be compatible. Again, American videotape prices are way below French prices.

CHILDREN AND BABIES Kids are generally welcome everywhere, and in most bars and restaurants. **Hotels** charge by the room, with a small supplement for an additional bed or cot, and family-run places will usually babysit or offer a listening service while you eat or go out. Especially in the seaside towns, most **restaurants** have children's menus or will cook simpler food on request. You'll have no difficulty finding disposable nappies (*couches à jeter*), but nearly all baby foods have added sugar and salt, and French milk powders are very rich indeed. *SNCF* charge nothing on **trains and buses** for under-4s, and half-fare for 4–11s (see p.28–29 for other reductions). Most local tourist offices have details of specific activities for children – in particular, many resorts supervise "clubs" for children on the beach. And almost every town down to small ones has a **children's playground** with

a good selection of activities. Something to beware of – not that you can do much about it – is the difficulty of negotiating a child's **buggy** over the large cobbles that cover many of the older streets in town centres.

CONTRACEPTIVES Contraception was only legalized in 1967 but condoms (*préservatifs* or *capotes*) have been available at all pharmacies ever since, as well as, now, from many clubs and street dispensers in larger cities. You can also get spermicidal cream and jelly (*dose contraceptive*), plus the suppositories (*ovules, suppositoires*) and (with a prescription) the Pill (*la pillule*), a diaphragm or IUD (*le sterilet*).

ELECTRICITY This is almost always 220V, using plugs with two round pins.

FISHING You get fishing rights by becoming a member of an authorized fishing club – tourist offices have details.

LAUNDRY Laundries are common in French towns, and some are listed in the guide – elsewhere look in the phone book under *Laveries Automatiques*. The alternative *blanchisserie* or *pressing* services are likely to be expensive, and hotels in particular charge very high rates. If you're doing your own washing in hotels, keep quantities small as most forbid doing any laundry in your room.

LEFT LUGGAGE Luggage lockers of various sizes are available at all *SNCF* stations, in addition to *consigne* (left luggage) for larger items or longer periods.

PETROL The cheapest gas (*essence*) or diesel fuel (*gasoil*) can be bought at out-of-town superstores. Four-star is *super*, unleaded is *sans plomb*.

SAFE SEX Paris has the highest number of people suffering from AIDS of any city in Europe, and studies show that there are almost equal numbers of heterosexual and homosexual people who are HIV positive. Among heterosexuals (excluding drug users) the number of women who are HIV positive has overtaken men. See above for details on contraceptive devices.

SWIMMING POOLS Swimming pools or *piscines* are well signposted in most French towns and reasonably priced. Tourist offices have their addresses.

TIME France is one hour ahead of Britain throughout the year, except for a short period during October, when it's the same. It is six hours ahead of Eastern Standard Time, and nine hours ahead of Pacific Standard Time. This also applies during daylight savings seasons, which are observed in France (as in most of Europe) from the end of March through to the end of September.

TOILETS Usually found downstairs in bars, along with the phone, French public toilets are still often of the hole-in-the-ground squatting variety, and tend to lack toilet paper.

WEATHER ☎36.68.01.01.

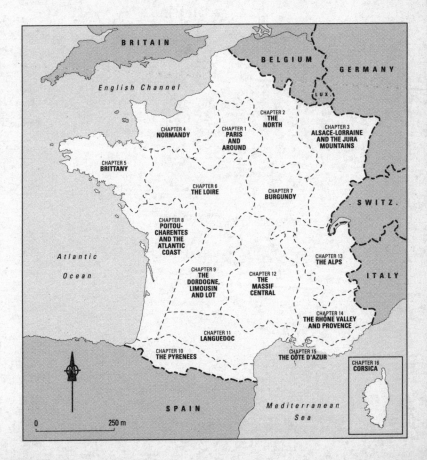

CHAPTER ONE

PARIS AND AROUND

PARIS is the paragon of style – perhaps the most glamorous and the most high-tech city in Europe. And yet it is also deeply traditional, a village-like and in parts dilapidated metropolis whose appeal to outsiders is tempered by the notorious disdain of its inhabitants. While such contradictions and contrasts may be the reality of any city, they are the makings of Paris. Consider the tiny lanes and alleyways of the Latin Quarter, Montmartre or Ménilmontant against the monumental vistas from the Louvre to La Défense or from the Invalides to Trocadéro; the multiplicity of markets, old-fashioned pedestrian arcades and small shops against the giant underground commercial complexes of Montparnasse, the Louvre and Les Halles; or the devotion to *l'informatique* – minitel link-ups for all phone subscribers, touch screen information in shops and métro stations and interactive video in museum displays – while old ladies still iron sheets by hand in the laundries of Auteil.

Paris has long created its own myth. Famous names and events are invested with a peculiar glamour that elevates the city and its people to a legendary realm. It is only in recent decades that Paris has let slip its status as the centre of Western intellectual, artistic and literary movements and as the natural place of European asylum for dissidents and the disillusioned, for those who have been censored, oppressed or forced into exile from every corner of the globe.

Perhaps it is not surprising that, having found themselves for so long at the supposed navel of the world, Parisians feel superior to ordinary mortals.

Some history

The city's history has conspired to create this sense of being apart. From a shaky start the kings of France – whose seat was Paris – gradually extended their control over their feudal rivals, centralizing administrative, legal, financial and political power as they did so, until anyone seeking influence, publicity or credibility – in whatever field – had to be in Paris. **Louis XIV** consolidated this process. Supremely autocratic, considering himself the embodiment of the state – "*L'état, c'est moi*" – he inaugurated the tradition of Paris as symbol: the glorious reflection of the pre-eminence of the state. The Cour Carrée of the Louvre, the Observatoire and Invalides, and the triumphal arches of the Portes St-Martin and St-Denis are his. It is a tradition his successors have been only too happy to follow, whether as king, emperor or president.

Napoléon I added to the Louvre and built the Arc de Triomphe, the Madeleine, and Arc du Carrousel. He instituted the Grandes Écoles, those super-universities for super-competent administrators, engineers and teachers – and totally reorganized the rest of the country, too. **Napoléon III** extended the Louvre even further and had his Baron Haussmann redraw the rest of the city. The **Third Republic** had its World Fairs and bequeathed the Eiffel Tower. Recent presidents have initiated the skyscrapers at La Défense, the Tour Montparnasse, Beaubourg and Les Halles shopping precinct. Many of their projects have been completed by **President Mitterrand**: the high-tech Parc de la Villette complex, the glass pyramid entrance to the Louvre, the Musée d'Orsay, the Grande Arche at La Défense, to which Mitterrand himself has added the Bastille opera house, the Institut du Monde Arabe and the new national library building. The scale of

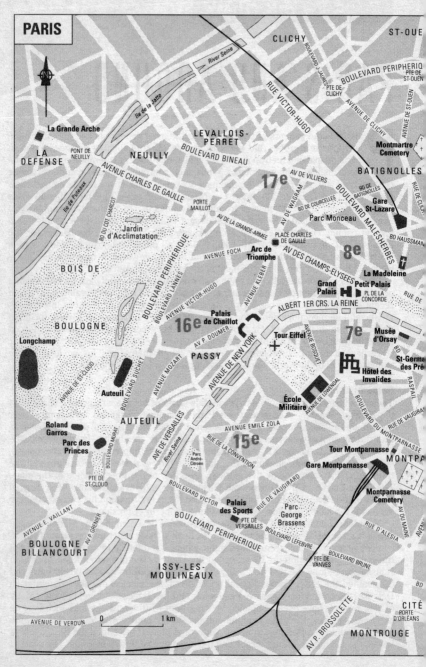

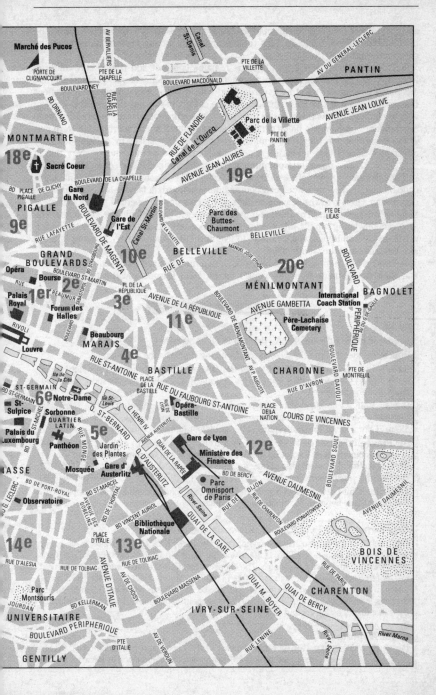

all this publicly financed construction is extraordinary – so, too, the architecture. The new buildings should, and do, feature as prominently on any visitors' itinerary as the classic city sights.

Yet despite these developments Paris remains compact and remarkably uniform, basically the city that Haussmann remodelled in the mid-nineteenth century. He laid out those long geometrical boulevards lined with rows of grey bourgeois residences that are the hallmark of Paris. In doing so, he cut great swathes through the stinking wen of medieval slums that housed the city's rebellious poor, already veterans of three revolutionary uprisings in half a century. If urban renewal and modernization were part of the design, so too was the intention of controlling the masses by opening up more effective fields of fire for artillery and facilitating troop movements. Not that it succeeded in preventing the Commune, the most determined insurrection since 1789.

Though riotous street protests are still a feature of Parisian life, the traditional barricade-builders have long since been booted into the suburban factory-land, or housed in depressing satellite towns, leaving behind ever increasing numbers of people living and begging on the streets. The decaying parts of the city, especially in the east and north, are gradually being rebuilt, introducing a new mix of arty and media types to the under-privileged communities who continue to live in the dank, unsanitary housing of areas like Belleville and the Goutte d'Or.

A large proportion of these downtrodden communities are made up of immigrants and their descendants from the poorer countries of Europe and the former French

POINTS OF ARRIVAL

By Air
Roissy–Charles de Gaulle Airport (☎48.62.22.80; 24hr).

Roissy, northeast of the city, is connected with the centre by the following:

Roissy–Bus. Connects the airport with the Opéra-Garnier (corner of rues Auber and Scribe) every fifteen minutes from 6am to 11pm. At 30F this is the cheapest route and takes around 45 minutes.

Roissy–Rail. A combination of airport bus and *RER ligne B* train to Gare du Nord and Châtelet (every 15 minutes from 5am to 11.15pm), where you can transfer to the ordinary métro. Taking about 35 minutes, this is the quickest route and costs 35F.

Air France bus. This costs 48F and departs from door 6 every 15 minutes from 5.45am to 11pm, stopping at av Carnot by the Arc de Triomphe and terminating at Porte Maillot (métro) on the northwest edge of the city. There are also *Air France* buses from terminal 2 to Gare Montparnasse every hour.

Taxis. Taxis into central Paris cost from 170F to 260F, plus a small luggage supplement, and should take between 45 minutes and one hour.

Orly Airport (☎49.75.15.15; daily 6am–midnight).

Orly, south of Paris, also has a bus–rail link. *Orly-Rail, RER ligne C* trains leave every fifteen minutes from 5.30am to 11.30pm for the Gare d'Austerlitz and other Left Bank stops which connect with the métro. The cheapest option is the **Orlybus** from the airport to Denfert-Rochereau *RER* station in the 14e (27F). Alternatively there are *Air France* buses to the Gare des Invalides and Montparnasse. Both buses leave every ten or fifteen minutes from 6am to 11pm, and journey time is about 35 minutes. A taxi will take about the same time, costing around 130F.

Other Airports
Paris' third airport, **Le Bourget**, is northeast of the centre and handles internal flights only. *USIT/Campus Travel* (see pp.4 & 10) operates a charter service to **Beauvais**. This

colonies of southeast Asia, Africa and the Caribbean. Each ethnic group has brought its own styles and traditions, adding to the superb diversity of the city. However, while most Parisians appreciate the restaurants and the music, racist tensions are undeniable.

... and some highlights

The most tangible and immediate pleasures of Paris are to be found in its streetlife. Few cities can compete with the thousand-and-one cafés, bars and restaurants that line every street and boulevard. And the city's compactness makes it possible to experience the individual feel of the different *quartiers*. You can move easily, even on foot, from the calm, almost small-town atmosphere of **Montmartre** and parts of the **Latin Quarter** to the busy commercial centres of the **Bourse** and **Opéra** or to the aristocratic mansions of the **Marais**. In **Les Halles** you can shop for every brand-name of note, and in the **13ᵉ arrondissement** you can discover strange edibles and fiery spirits in the Chinese supermarkets.

The city's lack of open space is redeemed by unexpected havens like the **Mosque, Arènes de Lutèce** and the courtyard of the **Musée National du Moyen-Age**. The garden of Les Halles has at long last provided greenery in the centre, and there are always the quaysides of the Left and Right Bank and the islands. A grand and imposing backdrop to the streetlife is provided by the monumental architecture of the **Arc de Triomphe, Louvre**, the **Eiffel Tower, Hôtel de Ville**, the bridges and the institutions

---

is a 70km bus journey from Paris, but all air tickets should include the price of the coach into the city at the Bagnolet international terminal.

By Rail

Paris' six **mainline stations** are equipped with cafés, restaurants, *tabacs*, banks, bureaux de change (long waits in season), and are all connected with the métro system. The central number for all *SNCF* **information** is ☎45.82.50.50 and for reservations ☎45.82.50.50.

The **Gare du Nord** (trains from Boulogne, Calais, the UK, Belgium, Holland, northern Germany and Scandinavia; information ☎42.80.03.03, reservations ☎42.06.49.38) and **Gare de l'Est** (serving eastern France, southern Germany, Switzerland and Austria; information ☎42.08.49.90, reservations ☎42.06.49.38) are next door to each other in the northeast of the city. The **Gare St-Lazare** (serving the UK, Dieppe and the Normandy coast; information ☎43.38.52.29, reservations ☎43.87.91.70) is a little to the west of them. Still on the Right Bank but towards the southwest corner is the **Gare de Lyon**, for trains from the Alps, the south, Italy and Greece (information ☎43.45.92.22, reservations ☎43.45.93.33). On the opposite side of the river, the **Gare d'Austerlitz** (☎45.84.14.18) is the terminus of trains from southwest France (except *TGV*'s), the Loire Valley, Spain and Portugal, while **Gare Montparnasse** serves Versailles, Chartres, Brittany and southern Normandy, the Atlantic Coast and *TGV* trains to southwestern France (☎45.38.52.29).

By Bus

Almost all the coaches coming into Paris – international and domestic – use the main **gare routière** at av du Général-de-Gaulle, Bagnolet; the Gallieni métro station links it to the centre. *Citysprint* coaches arrive at and depart from rue St-Quentin, around the corner from the Gare du Nord. Check-in takes place at 135 rue Lafayette (☎42.85.44.55).

Driving

If you're driving in yourself, don't try to go straight across the city to your destination. Use the ring road – the *boulevard périphérique* – to get around to the nearest Porte: it's much quicker, except at rush hour, and easier to find your way.

of the state. Early twentieth-century contributions include the Art Nouveau, Art Deco and Cubist innovations. The habit of breaking architectural moulds has continued through **Beaubourg** to **La Villette**, the **Louvre Pyramid** and the new **Bibliothèque Nationale**, as well as in the stunning smaller-scale examples of postmodernist and deconstructivist tendencies in housing blocks, schools and industrial units scattered throughout the city.

Paris is remarkable too for its museums: the d'Orsay, Beaubourg's modern art, the **Cité des Sciences** at La Villette, the **Palais de Tokyo**, **Marmottan**, **Picasso** and the **Orangerie**.

As for **entertainment**, the city's strong points are in film and music. Paris is a real **cinema** capital, and although French rock is notoriously awful, the best Parisian **music** encompasses jazz, avant-garde, South American, Caribbean, West African and Arab sounds, as well as various combinations in a vibrant world music scene.

Information

The main **Paris tourist office** is at 127 av des Champs-Élysées, 8ᵉ (daily 9am–8pm; closed May 1; ☎49.52.53.54, fax 49.52.53.00).

There are also offices at the **Gare d'Austerlitz** (*Arrivés Grands Lignes*: Mon–Sat 8am–3pm; ☎45.84.91.70); **Gare de l'Est**, bd de Strasbourg, 10ᵉ (*Hall d'Arrivée*; summer Mon–Sat 8am–9pm; winter Mon–Sat 8am–8pm; ☎46.07.17.73); **Gare de Lyon**, 20 bd Diderot, 12ᵉ (*Sortie Grands Lignes*; summer Mon–Sat 8am–9pm; winter Mon–Sat 8am–8pm; ☎43.43.33.24); **Gare du Nord**, 18 rue de Dunkerque, 10ᵉ (*Arrivées des Trains Internationales*; summer Mon–Sat 8am–9pm; winter Mon–Sat 8am–8pm; ☎45.26.94.82); **Gare du Montparnasse**, place Bienvenue, 15ᵉ (*Arrivée Grandes Lignes*; summer Mon–Sat 8am–9pm; winter Mon–Sat 8am–8pm; ☎43.22.19.19); and at the **Eiffel Tower**, Champ-de-Mars, 7ᵉ (Mᵒ Bir-Hakeim; daily May–Sept 11am–6pm).

For recorded tourist information in English phone ☎47.20.88.89 or ☎49.52.53.56.

Consider also using the more youth-orientated **Accueil des Jeunes en France** (*AJF*). They have offices at the Gare du Nord (*Nouvelle Gare Banlieue*; June–Oct 8am–10pm; ☎42.85.86.19); 119 rue St-Martin, 4ᵉ (Mᵒ Châtelet-Les Halles, opposite Centre Beaubourg; Mon–Sat 9.30am–7pm; ☎42.77.87.80), which can also be used as a forwarding address for mail; and at 139 bd St-Michel, 5ᵉ (Mᵒ Port-Royale; March–Oct Mon–Fri 9.30am–6.30pm; ☎43.54.95.86).

City transport

Finding your way around is remarkably easy. Paris proper, without its suburbs, is relatively small, with a **public transport system** that is cheap, fast and meticulously signposted. To help you get your bearings above ground, think of the Louvre as the centre. The Seine flows east to west, cutting the city in two. The area north of the river is known as the Right Bank or *rive droite*; to the south is the Left Bank or *rive gauche*. Roughly speaking, west is smart and east is scruffy. The landmarks you most often catch glimpses of as you move about are the Eiffel Tower, to the west, and the white pimples of the Sacré-Coeur on top of the hill of Montmartre, to the north.

The Métro and *RER*

The **métro**, combined with the overland *RER* (*Réseau Express Régional*) express lines reaching out into the suburbs, is the simplest way of moving around. Trains run from 5.30am to 12.45am; *RER* trains stop at midnight. Stations (abbreviated: Mᵒ Concorde, etc) are frequent, though the interchanges can involve a lot of legwork. **Free maps** are available at most stations, and every station has a big plan of the network outside the entrance and several inside. The lines are colour-coded and designated by numbers for the métro and letters for the *RER* although they are signposted within the system with the names of the terminus stations: for example, travelling from Montparnasse to Châtelet, you follow the sign *Direction Porte-de Clignancourt*; from Gare d'Austerlitz to Grenelle you follow *Direction Boulogne–Pont-de-St-Cloud*. The numerous interchanges (*correspondances*) make it possible to travel all over the city in a more or less straight line.

For the latest in subway technology, use the express stations' **computerized route-finders**, which at a touch of the button give you four alternative routes to your selected destination, on foot or by public transport.

Buses

Don't use the métro to the exclusion of the city's **buses**. They are not difficult to use and you do see much more. There are **free maps** available at métro stations, bus terminals and the tourist office (the *Grand Plan de Paris* shows the complete public transport system). Every bus stop displays the numbers of the buses which stop there, a map showing all the stops on the route and the times of the first and last buses. Each bus also has a map of its own route inside and some have a recorded announcement for each approaching stop. Generally speaking, they start around 6.30am and begin their last run around 9pm.

Night buses (*Noctambus*) run on ten routes from place du Châtelet near the Hôtel de Ville every half hour between 1.30am and 5.30am. There is a reduced service on Sunday. Further information is on the *RATP* (*Régie autonome des Transports Parisiens*) transport board, 53ter quai des Grands-Augustins, 6e (☎43.46.14.14). They also run numerous **excursions**, including some to quite far-flung places, much cheaper than the commercial operators; their brochure is available at all rail and some métro stations.

Tickets and passes

The same **tickets** are valid for bus, métro and, within the city limits and immediate suburbs, the *RER* express rail lines, which also extend far out into the Île de France. Long bus journeys can cost two tickets; ask the driver, if in doubt.

For a short stay in the city, single tickets can be bought in *carnets* of ten from any station or *tabac* – currently 39F, as opposed to 6.50F for an individual ticket. A *Formule 1* **day pass** is also available (27F for the city; 85F to include the outer suburbs and airports). Don't buy from the touts who hang round the main stations; you'll pay well over the odds, quite often for a used ticket. There's a flat rate across the city: you need one ticket per journey. Be sure to keep your ticket until the end of the journey; you'll be fined on the spot if you can't produce one. Only the *RER* has a choice of first or second class, although class distinctions are only in force 9am–5pm.

If you are staying more than a day or two, it's more economical to buy a *Carte Orange*, obtainable at all métro stations and *tabacs* (you need a passport photo). You can get one with either a weekly coupon (*coupon hebdomadaire* or *coupon jaune*; valid Monday morning to Sunday evening; currently 59F for zones 1 and 2, ie within the city and close suburbs) or monthly (*mensuel*) coupon (208F). Alternatively there is a 3- or 5-day **visitor's pass** (*Paris Visites*) at 90F and 140F respectively. The advantage of the latter is that, unlike the *coupon hebdomadaire* whose validity runs unalterably from Monday to Sunday, they can begin on any day. All entitle you to unlimited travel on bus, métro and inner *RER*. On the métro, you put the coupon through the turnstile slot, but make sure to return it to its plastic folder; it is reusable throughout the period of its validity. On a bus you show the whole *Carte* to the driver as you board – don't put it into the punching machine.

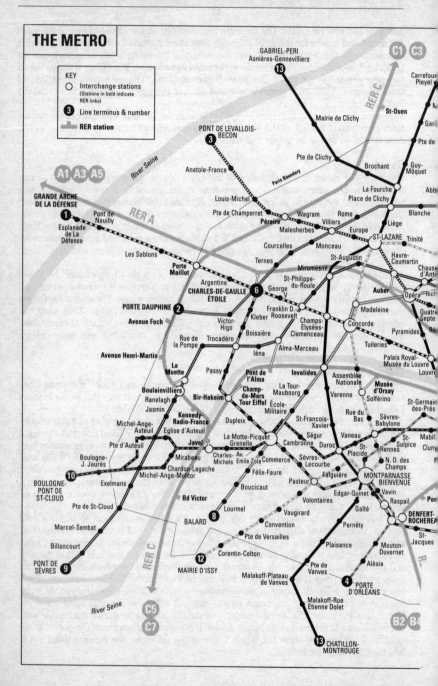

THE METRO

KEY

○ Interchange stations
(Stations in bold indicate RER links)

❸ Line terminus & number

▥ RER station

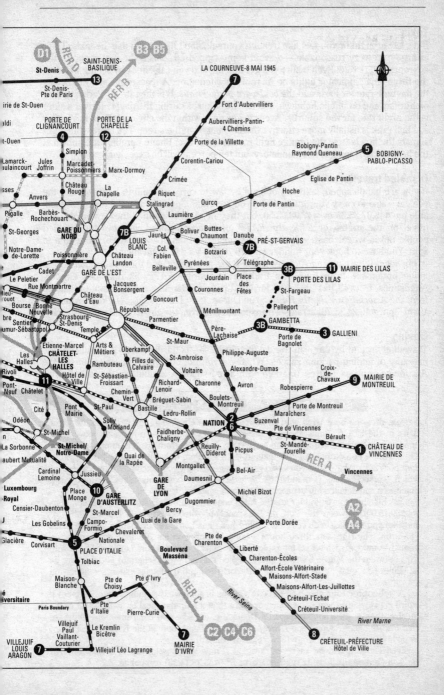

Taxis

If it's late at night or you feel like treating yourself, don't hesitate to use the taxis. Their **charges** are very reasonable. To avoid being ripped off, check the meter shows the appropriate fare rate. Even before you get into the taxi you can check by seeing which of the three small indicator lights on its roof is switched on. A (passenger side) indicates the daytime rate for Paris and the *boulevard périphérique*; B is the rate for Paris at night, on Sunday and on public holidays, and for the suburbs during the day; C (driver's side) is the night rate for the suburbs. Average journeys within the city cost 30–60F. Waiting at a taxi rank is usually more effective than hailing from the street. The large white light signals the taxi is free; the orange light means it's in use. Phone numbers are shown at the taxi ranks. Tipping is not mandatory, but ten percent will be expected.

Disabled travellers

If you are handicapped, taxis are obliged by law to carry you and to help you into the vehicle – also to carry your guide dog if you are blind. Specially adapted **taxis** are available on ☎48.37.85.85 or ☎47.08.93.50, but they need to be notified the day before. For travel on the **métro** or *RER*, the *RATP* offers accompanied journeys for disabled people not in wheelchairs – *Voyage accompagné* – which operates (free) from 8am to 8pm. You have to book your minder on ☎46.70.88.74 a day in advance.

For **wheelchair** users *RER* lines A and B are accessible, and there is an *RER* access guide obtainable from the Paris transport authority, *RATP*, 53 quai des Grands-Augustines, 6ᵉ (☎43.46.14.14), and for blind people a **Braille métro map**, obtainable from the *Association Valentin Haüy*, 5 rue Duroc, 7ᵉ (☎47.34.07.90). *AIHROP* (Mon–Fri 10am–3pm ☎40.24.34.76) arranges transport to and from the airports and within the city.

Driving

Travelling around by **car** – in the daytime at least – is hardly worth it because of the difficulty of finding parking spaces. Whatever you do, don't park in a bus lane or the *Axe Rouge* **express routes** (marked with a red square). Should you be towed away,

---

BOAT TRIPS, BALLOON AND HELI RIDES

Bateaux-Mouches **boat trips** start from the Embarcadère du Pont de l'Alma on the Right Bank in the 8ᵉ (Mᵒ Alma-Marceau; reservations ☎42.25.96.10); rides take between an hour and an hour and a quarter and leave every half hour from 10am to noon and 2pm to 11pm; winter departures at 11am, 2.30pm, 4pm and 9pm only (40F, under-14s 20F, after 8pm 50F/20F). Make sure you avoid the outrageously priced lunch and dinner trips, for which "correct" dress is mandatory. *Bateaux-Mouches* has competitors, all much of a muchness and detailed in *Pariscope* under *Promenades*.

Less blatantly tourist fodder are the canal boat trips run by *Canauxrama* (reservations ☎42.39.15.00) between the Port de l'Arsenal, opposite 50 bd de la Bastille, 12ᵉ (Mᵒ Bastille) and the Bassin de la Villette, 13bis quai de la Loire, 19ᵉ (Mᵒ Jaurès) on the Canal St-Martin. The ride lasts three hours – not a bad bargain for 70F (65F weekend afternoons). A more stylish vessel for exploring the canal is the catamaran of *Paris-Canal* with trips between the Musée d'Orsay, quai Anatole-France, 7ᵉ (Mᵒ Solférino) and the Parc de la Villette, 11 quai de la Loire, 19ᵉ (Mᵒ Porte-de-Pantin); details and reservations on ☎42.40.96.97.

A **helicopter tour** above all the city's sights is somewhat prohibitively priced, but if whirli-gig rides turn you on as much or more than a four-star meal or a stalls seat at the theatre, then a quick loop around La Défense is on. The two companies operating are *Héli-France* (9am–7.30pm) and *Hélicap* (8.45am–7.30pm), both at the Héliport de Paris, 4 av de la Porte-de-Sèvres, 15ᵉ; ☎45.57.75.51 (Mᵒ Balard).

Even classier, and far more extravagant – how about going up in a **balloon**? *Air Balloon Communications*, 12 rue Bonaparte, 6ᵉ (☎43.29.14.13) can oblige.

you'll find your car in the pound (*fourrière*) belonging to that particular *arrondissement*; you'll have to check with the local town hall (*mairie*) for the address.

In the event of a **breakdown** you can call *S.O.S. Dépannage*, 28bis rue Pascal, 5ᵉ (☎47.07.99.99); *Aleveque Daniel*, 116 rue de la Convention, 15ᵉ (☎48.28.12.00), or *Aligre Dépannage*, 92 bd de Charonne, 20ᵉ (☎49.78.87.50), for round-the-clock assistance. Alternatively, contact the police.

See the Listings on p.155 for details of car and bike rental.

Boats

There remains one final mode of transport – by *Batobus* along the Seine. At the moment there are only five stops, though more are planned, and the service operates from April to September. The stops are: port de la Bourdonnais (Eiffel Tower), port de Solférino (Musée d'Orsay), quai Malaquais (Musée du Louvre), quai de Montebello (Notre-Dame) and quai de l'Hôtel de Ville. Boats run every 36 minutes from 10am to 7pm, the total journey time is 21 minutes, and tickets are 15F a stop.

Accommodation

Not surprisingly, Paris **hotels** are the most expensive in France. Compared with other European capitals, however, accommodation isn't exorbitant. It's possible to find somewhere decent and centrally located for under F220 for a double, even as low as F120, for a small room with just a washbasin – as long as you've booked in advance or it's out of season and you're prepared to hunt around a bit. If you're stuck, the **Bureaux d'Accueil** at the main tourist office, the Gare du Nord, Gare de l'Est, Gare de Lyon, Gare Montparnasse and Gare d'Austerlitz will endeavour to find you a room (20F commission for a hotel room, 8F for a hostel). The **Acceuil Jeunes de France** (*AJF*) at the Gare du Nord, at 119 rue St-Martin, 4ᵉ (Mᵒ Châtelet-Les Halles, opposite Beaubourg) and at 139 bd St-Michel, 5ᵉ (Mᵒ Port-Royale), guarantee to find young people a room, but not necessarily a cheap one, for a 10F fee.

Our recommendations below are divided by *arrondissement* (see map, p.76) and listed in ascending price order by the cheapest double rooms available in high season (where there are only very few rooms in the lower categories we show the range).

1ᵉʳ hotels

Hôtel Vauvilliers, 6 rue Vauvilliers; ☎42.36.89.08 (Mᵒ Châtelet/Les Halles/Louvre). Need to book several weeks in advance for this well-established cheapie. ①–②.

Hôtel Henri IV, 25 pl Dauphine; ☎43.54.44.53 (Mᵒ Pont-Neuf/Cité). An ancient and well-known bargain in a beautiful and dead central location. Nothing more luxurious than a *cabinet de toilette* and rather run down. Essential to book. ②.

Hôtel Lion d'Or, 5 rue de la Sourdière; ☎42.60.79.04, fax 42.60.09.14 (Mᵒ Tuileries). Spartan, but clean, friendly and very central. ③–④.

Hôtel Washington Opéra, 50 rue de Richelieu; ☎42.96.68.06 (Mᵒ Palais-Royal). Pleasant and comfortable. ④–⑤.

Agora, 7 rue Cossonerie; ☎42.33.46.02, fax 42.33.80.99 (Mᵒ Les Halles/Châtelet). Charming and peaceful. ⑤–⑦.

Ducs d'Anjou, 1 rue Ste-Opportune; ☎42.36.92.24, fax 42.36.16.63 (Mᵒ Châtelet). A carefully renovated old building overlooking the endlessly crowded place Ste-Opportune in the middle of Les Halles nightlife district. ⑥.

2ᵉ hotels

Hôtel de France, 11 rue Marie-Stuart; ☎42.36.35.33 (Mᵒ Châtelet-Les Halles/Sentier). Bargain prices, perfectly clean, and a great location – don't be put off by exterior. ②.

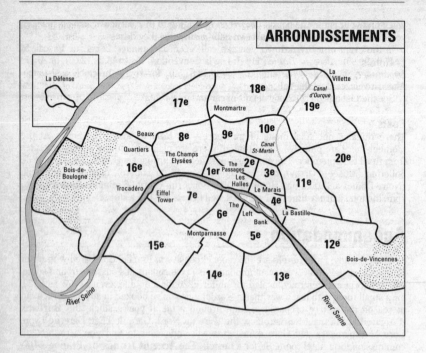

Les Noailles, 9 rue Michodière; ☎47.42.92.90, fax 49.24.92.71 (M° Opéra/4 Septembre). Contemporary styling with traditional pleasures of garden and *terrasse*. ⑤–⑦.

3ᵉ hotels

Hôtel du Marais, 16 rue de Beauce; ☎42.72.30.26 (M° Arts-et-Métiers/Filles-du-Calvaire). The genuine article: a prewar Paris cheapie, untouched, with brown spiral stairs, tiled floors, Turkish loos and an old-fashioned bar on the ground floor. Primitive, certainly, but clean, quiet and with pleasant service. ①.

Hôtel Picard, 26 rue de Picardie; ☎48.87.53.82, fax 48.87.02.56 (M° Arts-et-Métiers/Filles-du-Calvaire). Clean and comfortable, overlooking the Carreau du Temple. Run by a charming and very accommodating Pole. ③.

Hôtel de Saintonge le Marais, 16 rue de Saintonge; ☎48.87.76.41 (M° Filles-du-Calvaire). On the edge of the Marais, near the Picasso Museum. Very relaxing. ⑤–⑥.

4ᵉ hotels

Hôtel Moderne, 3 rue Caron; ☎48.87.97.05 (M° St-Paul/Bastille). Much better than the first impression of the staircase would suggest, and the price is amazing for this area. ①.

Grand Hôtel du Loiret, 8 rue des Mauvais-Garçons; ☎48.87.77.00 (M° Hôtel-de-Ville). Simple, but offering very good value for the price. ②.

Grand Hôtel Jeanne d'Arc, 3 rue de Jarente; ☎48.87.62.11, fax 48.87.37.31 (M° St-Paul). Clean, quiet and attractive. Booking essential. ④.

L'Hôtel du Septième Art, 20 rue St-Paul; ☎42.77.04.03, fax 42.77.69.10 (M° St-Paul/Pont-Marie). Pleasant and comfortable place decorated with posters and photos from old movies. The stairs and bathrooms live up to the black-and-white-movie style. Every room equipped with a safe. ⑤.

Hôtel des Célestins, 1 rue Charles-V; ☎48.87.87.04 (M° Sully-Morland). A very comfortable restored seventeenth-century mansion. ⑥.

Grand Hôtel Mahler, 5 rue Mahler; ☎42.72.60.92, fax 42.72.25.37 (M° St-Paul). Right in the heart of the Marais; breakfast is served in a renovated seventeenth-century vaulted wine cellar. ⑦.

5e hotels

Hôtel du Commerce, 14 rue de la Montagne-Ste-Geneviève; ☎43.54.89.69, fax 43.54.89.69 (M° Maubert-Mutualité). Somewhat gloomy but extremely economical for the heart of the Latin Quarter. Communal washing and toilets. No reservations and lots of competition, so arrive before 10am. ①.

Hôtel des Alliés, 20 rue Berthollet; ☎43.31.47.52, fax 45.35.13.92 (M° Censier-Daubenton). Simple and clean, and bargain prices. ②.

Hôtel le Central, 6 rue Descartes; ☎46.33.57.93 (M° Maubert-Mutualité/Cardinal-Lemoine). Clean and decent accommodation in a typically Parisian old house on top of the Montagne Ste-Geneviève, overlooking the gates of the former École Polytechnique. One of a dying breed. ③.

Hôtel Marignan, 13 rue du Sommerard; ☎43.54.63.81 (M° Maubert-Mutualité). One of the best bargains in town. Totally sympathetic to the needs of rucksack-toting foreigners, with free laundry and ironing facilities, plus a room to eat your own food in – plates provided. Even the maid speaks English. No reservations – turn up early. Rooms for two, three and four people. ③.

Hôtel Esmeralda, 4 rue St-Julien-le-Pauvre; ☎43.54.19.20, fax 40.51.00.68 (M° St-Michel/Maubert-Mutualité). A discreet and ancient house on square Viviani with a superb view of Notre-Dame. ②–⑤.

Grand Hôtel Oriental, 2 rue d'Arras; ☎43.54.38.12, fax 40.51.86.78 (M° Jussieu/Cardinal-Lemoine/Maubert-Mutualité). No longer the old-fashioned cheapie it used to be, but still quite a bargain for this locality – and nice people, too. ④.

Hôtel des Grandes Écoles, 75 rue du Cardinal-Lemoine; ☎43.26.79.23 (M° Cardinal-Lemoine). Refurbished, and comfortable, in a great location with a beautiful garden. ⑤.

Hôtel de la Sorbonne, 6 rue Victor-Cousin; ☎43.54.58.08, fax 40.51.05.18 (M° Luxembourg). An attractive old building, quiet, comfortable and close to the Luxembourg gardens. ⑤.

Le Jardin des Plantes, 5 rue Linné; ☎46.07.06.20, fax 47.07.62.74 (M° Jussieu). Small, friendly hotel with a rooftop terrace for breakfasting. ⑤–⑦.

Hôtel des 3 Collèges, 16 rue Cujas; ☎43.54.67.30, fax 46.34.02.99 (M° Luxembourg). Light and airy rooms with young, helpful staff. ⑤–⑥.

Agora St-Germain, 42 rue des Bernardins; ☎46.34.13.00, fax 46.34.75.05 (M° Maubert-Mutualité). Very pleasant and all the comfort you'd expect for the price. ⑦.

6e hotels

Hôtel de Nesle, 7 rue de Nesle; ☎43.54.62.41 (M° St-Michel). Hippy haven. No reservations – arrive before 10am. ②–③.

Le Petit Trianon, 2 rue de l'Ancienne-Comédie; ☎43.54.94.64 (M° Odéon). Adequate accommodation right in the heart of things. ③–④.

Hôtel St-Michel, 17 rue Gît-le-Cœur; ☎43.26.98.70 (M° St-Michel). Simple, but perfectly acceptable. Great location in a very attractive old street close to the river. ③–④.

Hôtel Récamier, 3bis pl St-Sulpice; ☎43.26.04.89 (M° St-Sulpice/St-Germain–des-Prés). Comfortable, and superbly sited. ⑤.

ACCOMMODATION PRICE CATEGORIES

All the hotels, youth hostels and guesthouses listed in this book have been price-graded according to the following scale, and although costs will rise slightly overall with the life of this edition, the relative comparisons should remain valid. Paris and the large cities will, as anywhere, be more expensive than equivalent accommodation in the countryside or small towns. The prices quoted are for the cheapest available double room in high season, although remember that many of the cheap places will have more expensive rooms with en-suite facilities.

① Under 160F	④ 300–400F	⑦ 600–700F
② 160–220F	⑤ 400–500F	⑧ Over 700F
③ 220–300F	⑥ 500–600F	

Hôtel des Marronniers, 21 rue Jacob; ☎43.25.30.60, fax 40.46.83.56 (M° St-Germain-des-Prés). This three-star costs more than our usual prices, but it is a delightful place with a dining room overlooking a secret garden. Good for a special occasion. ⑥–⑦.

Hôtel de l'Angleterre, 44 rue Jacob; ☎42.60.34.72, fax 42.60.16.93 (M° St-Germain-des-Prés). Classy and elegant, this was once the British Embassy. Later Hemingway lived in room 14. ⑦.

7e hotels

Grand Hôtel Lévèque, 29 rue Cler; ☎47.05.49.15, fax 45.50.49.36 (M° École-Militaire/Latour-Maubourg). Clean and decent; nice people, who speak some English. Good location smack in the middle of the rue Cler market. Book one month ahead. ②–③.

Hôtel du Palais Bourbon, 49 rue de Bourgogne; ☎45.51.63.32, fax 45.55.20.21 (M° Varenne). A handsome old building in a sunny street by the *Musée Rodin*. Rooms are spacious and light. ③–④.

Hôtel Soferino, 91 rue de Lille; ☎47.05.85.54, fax 45.55.51.16 (M° Bac). Attractive place, featuring an old-fashioned cage-lift. ③–⑥.

Hôtel Malar, 29 rue Malar; ☎45.51.38.46, fax 45.51.38.46 (M° Latour-Maubourg/Invalides). Small, with slightly pokey rooms, but in a very attractive street close to the river. Prices include breakfast for two. ④.

Le Pavillon, 54 rue St-Dominique; ☎45.51.42.87, fax 45.51.32.79 (M° Invalides/Latour-Maubourg). A tiny former convent set back from the tempting shops of the rue St-Dominique in a leafy courtyard. A lovely setting, but the rooms are rather small for the price. ⑤–⑥.

Hôtel de la Tulipe, 33 rue Malar; ☎45.51.67.21, fax 47.53.96.37 (M° Latour-Maubourg). Patio for summer breakfast and drinks. Beamy and cottagey. But as with all hotels in this area you are paying for the location rather than great luxury. ⑤.

Hôtel Bersoly's St-Germain, 28 rue de Lille; ☎42.60.73.79, fax 49.27.05.55 (M° Bac). Small but exquisite rooms each named after an artist. Impeccable service. ⑦.

8e hotels

Hôtel d'Artois, 94 rue la Boétie; ☎43.59.84.12 (M° St-Philippe-du-Roule). One of the cheapest in this smartest part of town. ③–⑤.

Hôtel de Penthièvre, 21 rue Penthièvre; ☎43.59.87.63, fax 45.62.00.76 (M° Miromesnil/Champs-Élysées). Good value for the location; pleasant management and a beautiful Siamese cat always stalking the foyer. ④–⑤.

Hôtel de l'Élysée, 12 rue des Saussaies; ☎42.65.29.25, fax 42.65.64.28 (M° St-Philippe-du-Roule). Chandeliers and four-posters – classic luxury. ⑦.

9e hotels

Hôtel des Trois Poussins, 15 rue Clauzel; ☎48.74.38.20 (M° St-Georges). A reliable cheapie at the foot of Montmartre. You can book rooms for the month at under 200F a night. ③.

Hôtel de Beauharnais, 51 rue de la Victoire; ☎48.74.71.13 (M° Le Peletier/Havre-Caumartin). Louis Quinze, First Empire . . . every room decorated in a different period style. ④.

Hôtel Imperial, 45 rue de la Victoire; ☎48.74.10.47 (M° Le Peletier/Chaussée d'Antin). Young, efficient manager speaking excellent English. Fairly nondescript rooms but acceptable. ④.

Hôtel Chopin, 46 passage Jouffroy; ☎47.70.58.10, fax 42.47.00.70 (M° Montmartre). Splendid period building in an old *passage*. Enter on bd Montmartre, near rue du Faubourg-Montmartre. ⑤.

10e hotels

Hôtel du Jura, 6 rue de Jarry; ☎47.70.06.66 (M° Gare-de-l'Est/Château-d'Eau). Primitive, but friendly and decent. ①–②.

Sibour Hôtel, 4 rue Sibour; ☎46.07.20.74, fax 46.07.37.17 (M° Gare-de-l'Est). Good value, if characterless. ②–③.

Adix Hôtel, 30 rue Lucien-Sampaix; ☎42.08.19.74, fax 42.08.27.28 (M° Bonsergent). In a pleasant street close to the St-Martin canal. Reasonable value for money, including three-person rooms at 515F. ④.

Belta Hôtel Résidence, 46 rue Lucien-Sampaix; ☎46.07.23.87, fax 42.09.87.27 (Mᵒ Gare-de-l'Est). Good location on the St-Martin canal bank. Totally renovated, in bland airport style, but comfortable. ⑤–⑥.

Hôtel St-Laurent, 5 rue St-Laurent; ☎42.09.83.50, fax 42.09.83.50 (Mᵒ Gare-de-l'Est). Comfortable base close to the stations. Fine views from the top floor. ⑥.

11ᵉ hotels

Hôtel de l'Europe, 10 rue Louis-Bonnet; ☎43.57.17.49 (Mᵒ Belleville). A very basic flop. ①.

Hôtel des Arts, 2 rue Godefroy-Cavaignac; ☎43.79.72.57 (Mᵒ Voltaire). Not much charm, but hospitable and acceptable at the price. ②–④.

Hôtel de Vienne, 43 rue de Malte; ☎48.05.44.42 (Mᵒ République/Oberkampf). Very pleasant, good-value cheapie, and nice people. ②.

Hôtel de Nevers, 53 rue de Malte; ☎47.00.56.18 (Mᵒ République/Oberkampf). Clean and decent accommodation run by a sympathetic proprietor. Excellent breakfasts. ③–④.

Hôtel Parmentier, 91 rue Oberkampf; ☎43.57.02.09 (Mᵒ Parmentier). Clean and friendly. Better to get a room on the courtyard if you can; the street side is a little noisy. ③.

Hôtel St-Martin, 12 rue Léon-Frot; ☎43.71.09.14 (Mᵒ Boulets-Montreuil). Boring neighbourhood, but a nice hotel – friendly with all the mod cons. ④.

Pax Hotel, 12 rue de Charonne; ☎47.00.40.98, fax 47.00.40.98 (Mᵒ Ledru-Rollin/Bastille). A reasonable establishment if you want to be in the centre of the Bastille's nightlife. ③–④.

Hôtel Beaumarchais, 3 rue Oberkampf; ☎43.38.16.16, fax 43.38.32.86 (Mᵒ Filles du Calvaire/Oberkampf). All rooms with bathrooms and a complimentary copy of *Libération* newspaper every day. Pleasant. ④.

Méridional, 36 bd Richard-Lenoir; ☎48.05.75.00, fax 43.57.42.85 (Mᵒ Bréguet-Sabin). Attractive with light rooms and a garden. ⑥–⑦.

12ᵉ hotels

Paris Hôtel, 93 rue de Charenton; ☎46.28.13.63 (Mᵒ Ledru-Rollin/Gare de Lyon). Basic. ①.

Hôtel des Pyrénées, 204 rue du Faubourg-St-Antoine; ☎43.72.07.46, fax 43.72.98.45 (Mᵒ Faidherbe-Chaligny). Comfortable and quiet behind its posh reception area. ④.

Hôtel du Midi, 31 rue Traversière; ☎43.07.88.68 (Mᵒ Ledru-Rollin). Close to the Gare du Lyon and very pleasant. ③–④.

Hôtel Saphir, 35 rue de Citeaux; ☎43.07.77.28, fax 43.46.67.45 (Mᵒ Faidherbe-Chaligny). On a quiet street of the Faubourg St-Antoine. No special charms but comfortable. ⑤.

13ᵉ hotels

Arian Hôtel, 102 av de Choisy; ☎45.70.76.00 (Mᵒ Tolbiac). Boring but cheap. ②.

Hôtel des Arts, 8 rue Coypel; ☎47.07.76.32, fax 43.31.18.09 (Mᵒ Place d'Italie). Very decent, modest but modern hotel. ③.

Résidence Les Gobelins, 9 rue des Gobelins; ☎47.07.26.90, fax 43.31.44.05 (Mᵒ Les Gobelins). Delightful establishment, but well known so it needs booking well in advance. ⑤.

14ᵉ hotels

Ouest Hotel, 27 rue de Gergovie; ☎45.42.64.99, fax 45.42.46.65 (Mᵒ Pernety). Basic. ②.

Virginia, 66 rue du Père Corentin; ☎45.40.70.90, fax 45.40.95.21 (Mᵒ Pte d'Orléans). In a quiet part of town some way from the centre, but very good value. ②.

Hôtel de la Loire, 39bis rue du Moulin-Vert; ☎45.40.66.88, fax 45.40.89.07 (Mᵒ Alésia/Plaisance). Decent cheapie on a very quiet street, with a little garden for breakfast. ③.

Hôtel Le Royal, 49 rue Raymond-Losserand; ☎43.22.14.04 (Mᵒ Pernety/Gaîté). Reasonable bargain in the middle of the old 14ᵉ. ③.

15e hotels

Mondial Hôtel, 136 bd de Grenelle; ☎45.79.73.57, fax 45.79.58.65 (M° La Motte-Picquet). Friendly and decent, with large rooms and good views in spite of a rather grim appearance. Right under the raised métro. Prices include breakfast. ③.

Pratic Hôtel, 20 rue de l'Ingénieur-Keller; ☎45.77.70.58, fax 40.59.43.75 (M° Charles-Michel). Very nice: clean and friendly. Still some rooms under 220F. Close to the Eiffel Tower. ③.

Tourisme Hôtel, 66 av de la Motte-Picquet; ☎47.34.28.01, fax 40.59.43.75 (M° La Motte-Picquet). The building itself is an unprepossessing barrack-like structure on the corner of bd de Grenelle, but once you're inside the rooms are fine. ④.

Hôtel Wallace, 89 rue Fondary; ☎45.78.83.30, fax 40.58.19.43 (M° Émile-Zola). Unpretentious and charming place with a pretty garden in the courtyard. ⑥.

16e hotels

Hameau de Passy, 48 rue Passy; ☎42.88.47.55, fax 42.30.83.72 (M° Muette). Tucked away in a mews – utterly peaceful and with faultless service. ⑥–⑦.

Hôtel Pergolèse, 3 rue Pergolèse; ☎40.67.96.77, fax 45.00.42.60 (M° Argentine). Modern and very stylish design in a classic Beaux Quartiers building. ⑦.

17e hotels

Hôtel Gauthey, 5 rue Gauthey; ☎46.27.15.48 (M° Brochant). Basic but clean. ①.

Hôtel Avenir-Jonquière, 23 rue de la Jonquière; ☎46.27.83.41 (M° Guy-Môquet). Clean, friendly establishment offering bargain accommodation. ②.

Hôtel des Batignolles, 26–28 rue des Batignolles; ☎43.87.70.40 (M° Rome/Place de Clichy). A quiet and very reasonable establishment in a neighbourhood that prides itself on its village character. Triples for 370F. ④.

Lévis-Hôtel, 16 rue Lebouteux; ☎47.63.86.38, fax 40.53.00.92 (M° Villiers). Only ten rooms, but very nice, clean and quiet, in small side street off the rue de Lévis market. ④.

Hôtel du Roi René, 72 pl Félix-Lobligeois; ☎42.26.72.73, fax 42.63.74.99 (M° Rome/Villiers). Very nice location by a mini-Greek temple and public garden. ⑤.

18e hotels

Idéal Hôtel, 3 rue des Trois-Frères; ☎46.06.63.63 (M° Abbesses). Cheap, clean and a real bargain in a marvellous location on the slopes of Montmartre. ①–③.

Style Hôtel, 8 rue Ganneron; ☎45.22.37.59 (M° Place de Clichy). Wooden floors, marble fireplaces, a secluded internal courtyard, nice people – great value. ②–③.

Hôtel André Gill, 4 rue André-Gill; ☎42.62.48.48, fax 42.62.77.92 (M° Pigalle/Abbesses). Low prices for very adequate rooms in a great location on the slopes of Montmartre. It's very quiet too, in a dead-end alley off rue des Martyrs. ③.

Hôtel Tholozé, 24 rue Tholozé; ☎46.06.74.83 (M° Blanche/Abbesses). Another genuine bargain – clean, friendly and quiet, in a steep, quiet street below the *Moulin de la Galette*. ③.

La Résidence Montmartre, 10 rue Burcq; ☎46.06.51.91, fax 42.52.82.59 (M° Abbesses). Smart and comfortable. ⑥.

19e hotels

Hôtel Rhin et Danube, 3 pl Rhin-et-Danube; ☎42.45.10.13, fax 42.06.88.82 (M° Danube). Way out of the centre but on the airy heights of Belleville and geared to self-catering. The only disadvantage is the building works on the square, which should be finished by mid-1995. ④.

20e hotels

Hôtel Tamaris, 14 rue des Maraîchers; ☎43.72.85.48 (M° Porte de Vincennes). Simple, clean, and attractive, and run by pleasant people. Extremely good value. Close to métro and the terminus of #26 bus route from Gare du Nord. Closed mid-July to mid-August. ②–③.

Hôtel Pyrénées-Gambetta, 12 rue Père-Lachaise; ☎47.97.76.57, fax 47.97.17.61 (M° Gambetta). Perfect for anyone passionate about the Père-Lachaise cemetery. Very pleasant. ④.

Hostels, student accommodation and campsites

There are numerous places offering **hostel** accommodation. In the main you have a choice among three organizations: the official International Youth Hostel Association (IYHF) hostels, hostels run by *MIJE* (*Maison Internationale de la Jeunesse et des Étudiants*), and those run by *UCRIF* (*Union des Centres de Rencontres Internationaux de France*). There is also a handful of privately run hotels.

Rates for bed & breakfast are 106–126F for IYHF hostels (membership card necessary), 115F for *MIJE* hostels and between 100F and 200F for *UCRIF* hostels. There is no age limit for *MIJE* and *UCRIF* and no advance bookings. *MIJE* hostels, mostly centrally situated in historic buildings, have a seven-day stay limit; for the other hostels it varies but is normally less. We've detailed only the most central of the *UCRIF* hostels: for a full list contact their main office at 4 rue Jean-Jacques-Rousseau, 1er; ☎42.60.42.40 (M^o Louvre-Rivoli; Mon–Fri 10am–6pm).

IYHF hostels

Jules Ferry, 8 bd Jules-Ferry, 11e; ☎43.57.55.60, fax 40.21.79.92 (M^o République). In the lively and colourful area at the foot of the Belleville hill. When full, they will help you find a bed elsewhere for the same price.

D'Artagnan, 80 rue Vitruve, 20e; ☎43.61.08.75, fax 43.61.09.12 (M^o Porte-de-Bagnolet). A pleasant modern building on the edge of the city in Charonne. There's also an annexe at *Auberge Ste-Marguerite*, 10 rue Trousseau, 11e; ☎47.00.62.00.

MIJE hostels

Résidence Bastille, 151 av Ledru-Rollin, 11e; ☎43.79.53.86 (M^o Ledru-Rollin/Bastille/Voltaire).
Le Fourcy, 6 rue de Fourcy, 4e; ☎42.74.23.45 (M^o St-Paul).
Le Fauconnier, 11 rue du Fauconnier, 4e; ☎42.74.23.45 (M^o St-Paul/Pont-Marie).
Maubuisson, 12 rue des Barres, 4e; ☎42.72.23.45 (M^o Pont-Marie/Hôtel-de-Ville).
François Miron, 6 rue François-Miron, 4e (M^o Hôtel-de-Ville). Annexe of the *Maubuisson*.

UCRIF hostels

BVJ (*Bureau de Voyages de la Jeunesse*) Centre International de Paris/Louvre, 20 rue Jean-Jacques-Rousseau, 1er; ☎42.36.88.18, fax 42.33.40.53 (M^o Louvre/Châtelet-Les Halles).
BVJ Centre International de Paris/Opéra, 11 rue Thérèse, 1er; ☎42.60.77.23, fax 42.33.40.53 (M^o Pyramides/Palais-Royal).
BVJ Centre International de Paris/Les Halles, 5 rue du Pélican, 1er; ☎40.26.92.45, fax 42.33.40.53 (M^o Louvre/Châtelet-Les Halles/Palais-Royal).
BVJ Centre International de Paris/Quartier Latin, 44 rue des Bernardins, 5e; ☎43.29.34.80, fax 42.33.40.53 (M^o Maubert-Mutualité).

Other hostels

Maison Internationale des Jeunes, 4 rue Titon, 11e; ☎43.71.99.21, fax 43.71.78.58 (M^o Faidherbe-Chaligny). For 18–30-year-olds. Operates like a youth hostel, but does not require *YHA* membership. 95F B&B.

Three Ducks Hostel, 6 pl Étienne-Pernet, 15e; ☎48.42.04.05 (M^o Émile-Zola). A private youth hostel, with no age limit – though as the warden says himself, it's mainly young and noisy. Lock-out 11am–5pm, curfew at 1am. 85F – some rooms for couples. Kitchen facilities. It's necessary to book between May and Oct: send the price of the first night. The same management also runs the *Aloha Hostel*, 1 rue Borronné, 15e; ☎42.73.03.03 (M^o Volontaires).

Young and Happy Hostel, 80 rue Mouffetard, 5e; ☎45.35.09.53, fax 47.07.22.24 (M^o Monge/Censier-Daubenton). Turn up between 8pm and 10pm to book. Noisy, basic and studenty. 95F B&B.

Student accommodation

You can also get **student accommodation** during vacation time. The organization to contact is *CROUS*, Académie de Paris, 39 av Georges-Bernanos, 5e; ☎40.51.36.00.

Campsites

Camping du Bois de Boulogne, Allée du Bord-de-l'Eau, 16ᵉ; ☎45.24.30.00 (Mᵒ Porte-Maillot and then bus #244 to Route des Moulins or a thirty-minute walk). Much the most central campsite, next to the river Seine in the Bois de Boulogne, and usually booked out in summer.

Camping du Parc de la Colline, Route de Lagny, 77200 Torcy, slightly further east than the above; ☎60.05.42.32 (*RER ligne A4* to Torcy, then bus #421 to stop Le Clos). Mid-March to mid-Oct.

Camping du Parc-Étang, Base de Loisirs, 78180 Montigny-le-Bretonneux, southwest of Paris; ☎30.58.56.20 (*RER ligne C* St-Quentin-en-Yvelines. Métro connections for *RER ligne C* at Invalides, St-Michel, Gare d'Austerlitz). April to end Sept.

The City

Paris is an extremely compact city, strictly confined within the 78-square-kilometre limits of its ring road, the *boulevard périphérique,* built over the nineteenth-century city defences. The Seine flows in an arc through the middle from east to west, with its two islands, the Île de la Cité – whose Notre-Dame sits at the historic heart of the capital – and the Île St-Louis. In the centre, north of the river on the **Right Bank**, or *rive droite,* is the Louvre, the banking, media and commercial quarter contained within the *grands boulevards,* the old main market (now the Forum des Halles), and the aristocratic **Marais**. South of the islands is the **Latin Quarter** (quartier Latin), so called for the language of the university that has been here since the thirteenth century, and **St-Germain-des-Prés**, the *quartier* that evolved around the abbey, established on the site of a church of the same name from the sixth century.

These areas make up the first six divisions or *arrondissements* of Paris and contain the highest concentration of major monuments and museums, though by no means all. The outer *arrondissements,* continuing the clockwise spiral centred on the Île de la Cité, were mostly incorporated into the city in the nineteenth century. Those to the east accommodated the poor and the working class, while the west were, and still are, the addresses for the aristocracy and new rich. The project of turning the entire city into a middle-class bastion is still underway.

There are any number of ways of exploring Paris – you certainly don't have to start with the Louvre or Notre-Dame. Our account is structured in chunks of territory that share a common identity even though they do not always correspond exactly with the boundaries of the twenty *arrondissements.* We start with the Île de la Cité, then move to the Right Bank, incorporating the Voie Triomphale, the city's greatest vista leading from the Louvre right out to the northwest perimeter, and move east of the Marais to the now trendy *quartier* of the Bastille. We then continue with the inner *arrondissements* on the Left Bank, followed by the southern *arrondissements,* the rich Beaux Quartiers to the west, and beyond them, outside the city, the modern business district of La Défense, then Montmartre and the northern *arrondissements* and, finally, the east of the city with the old villages of Belleville and Ménilmontant, including the Père-Lachaise cemetery and out to Vincennes.

The Museums

You may find there is sufficient visual stimulation just wandering around Paris streets without exploring what's to be seen in the city's **art galleries and museums**. It's certainly questionable whether the **Louvre**, for example, can compete in pleasure with the Marais, the *quais* or parts of the Latin Quarter. But if established art appeals to you at all, the Paris collections are not to be missed.

The most popular are the various museums of modern art, notably the **Beaubourg** and **Palais de Tokyo**, and the **Musée d'Orsay**, **Orangerie** and **Marmottan**. There are many single-artist collections, of which the **Picasso** and **Rodin** museums are best, and **contemporary art** has a new venue for temporary exhibitions in the revamped **Jeu de Paume** in the Tuileries gardens. No less breathtaking, going back to earlier cultural roots, are some of the **medieval works** in the **Musée National du Moyen-Age**, including the glorious *La Dame à la Licorne* tapestry. Among the city's extraordinary number of technical, historical, social and applied art museums, pride of place goes to the dazzling **Cité des Sciences**, radical in both concept and architecture – and fun. Entertaining, too, if more conventional, is the **Musée National des Arts et Traditions Populaires**, its equivalent for the past.

If you're going to visit a great many museums in a short time, it is worth buying the *Carte Inter-Musées* **museum pass** (60F 1-day; 120F 3-days; 170F 5-days; available from *RER* stations and museums) – valid for 65 museums in and around Paris, and allows you to bypass the ticket queues. A student card is really no help in getting reductions unless you're under 25. Otherwise, for reductions for under-25s, under-18s and over-60s, you will need always need to show your passport alongside your original student card.

Île de la Cité

The **Île de la Cité** is where Paris began. The earliest settlements were sited here, as was the small Gallic town of Lutetia, overrun by Julius Cæsar's troops in 52 BC. A natural defensive site commanding a major east–west river trade route, it was an obvious candidate for a bright future. The Romans garrisoned it and laid out one of their standard military town plans, overlapping onto the Left Bank. While it never achieved any great political importance, they endowed it with an administrative centre that became the palace of the Merovingian kings in 508, then of the counts of Paris, who in 987 became kings of France.

Today the lure of the island lies in its tail-end **square du Vert-Galant** and, at the opposite end, the **cathedral of Notre-Dame**. The central section has been dulled by heavy-handed nineteenth-century demolition that displaced 25,000 people and replaced them by four vast edifices largely given over to housing the law. The litter-blown space in front of the cathedral was a by-product, though that at least has the virtue of allowing a full-frontal view.

Pont-Neuf and the quais, Sainte-Chapelle and the Conciergerie

Arriving on the island by the **Pont Neuf**, the city's oldest bridge, steps behind the **statue of Henri IV** (who commissioned the bridge) lead down to the **quais** and the **square du Vert-Galant**, a small tree-lined green enclosed within the triangular stern of the island. The prime spot to occupy is the extreme point beneath a weeping willow – haunt of lovers, sparrows and sunbathers.

On the other side of the bridge, across the street from the king's statue, seventeenth-century houses flank the entrance to the sanded, chestnut-shaded **place Dauphine**, one of the city's most secluded and exclusive squares. The further end is blocked by the dull mass of the **Palais de Justice**, which swallowed up the palace that was home to the French kings until Étienne Marcel's bloody revolt in 1358 frightened them off to the greater security of the Louvre.

The only part of the older complex that remains in its entirety is Louis IX's **Sainte-Chapelle** (daily April–Sept 9.30am–6pm, Oct–March 10am–5pm; closed public hols; 26F, combined ticket with Conciergerie 40F), built to house a collection of holy relics he had bought at extortionate rates from the bankrupt empire of Byzantium. Though much restored, the chapel remains one of the finest achievements of French High Gothic (consecrated in 1248). Very tall in relation to its length, it looks like a cathedral choir lopped off and transformed into an independent building. Its most radical feature is its fragility: the reduction of structural masonry to a minimum to make way for a huge expanse of stunning stained glass. The impression inside is of being enclosed within the wings of myriad butterflies – the predominant colours blue and red and, in the later rose window, grass-green and blue.

MUSEUMS

1 M. National des Arts et Traditions Populaires
2 Centre Nationale de la Photographie
3 M. Arménien et M. d'Ennery
4 M. des Contrefaçons
5 M. Marmottan
6 Atelier d'Henri Bouchard
7 Maison de Belzac
8 M. de Radio-France
9 Palais Chaillot (M.du Cinéma, M. des Monuments Français et M. de l'Homme)
10 M. Guimet
11 M. des Costumes
12 Palais de Tokyo (M. d'Art Moderne de la Ville de Paris)
13 M. Intercoiffure
14 M. Cernushi
15 M. du Bottier
16 M. de S.E.I.T.A
17 M. de l'Armée
18 M. d'Orsay
19 M. Rodin
20 M. Valentin-Haüy
21 M. Bourdelle
22 M. de la Poste
23 M. Musée Pasteur
24 M. Branly
25 M. Ernest-Hébert
26 M. Zadkine
27 M. Delacroix
28 M. National du Moyen Age
29 M. de la Préfecture de Police
30 Institut du Monde Arabe
31 M. Assistance Publique
32 Orangerie
33 Jeu de Paume
34 M. des Lunettes
35 M. Cognacq-Jay
36 M. de la Perfumerie
37 M. Gustave Moreau
38 M. Renan-Scheffer
39 M. Art juif
40 M. de Montmartre
41 M. d'Art Naïf Max Fourny
42 M. Grévin I
43 M. du Cristal
44 M. des Arts de la Mode (Louvre)
45 M. des Arts Décoratifs (Louvre)
46 M. de la Publicité (Louvre)
47 Centre Culturel des Halles (M. Grévin II/M. Holographie)
48 M. National Techniques
49 Beaubourg
50 M. des Instruments de Musique Mécanique
51 M. de la Serrurerie
52 M. Kwok-On
53 M. Picasso
54 M. Carnavelet
55 M. de l'Histoire de France
56 Maison Victor Hugo
57 M. de la Curiosité
58 M. Adam Mickiewicz
59 Pavillon de l'Arsenal
60 M. Arts Africans et Océaniens
61 M. Edith Piaf
62 Cité de la Musique
63 Cité des Sciences
64 Centre International de l'Automobile

It pays to get to Sainte-Chapelle as early as possible; it attracts hordes of tourists, as does the **Conciergerie** (daily April–Sept 9.30am–6pm; Oct–March 10am–4.30pm; closed bank hols; 26F), Paris' oldest prison, where Marie-Antoinette and, in their turn, the leading figures of the Revolution were incarcerated before execution. The chief interest of the Conciergerie is the enormous late-Gothic *Salle des Gens d'Arme*, canteen and recreation room of the royal household staff. You are missing little in not seeing Marie-Antoinette's cell and various other macabre mementoes of the guillotine's victims.

If you keep along the north side of the island from the Conciergerie you come to **place Lépine**, named for the police boss who gave Paris' *flics* their white truncheons and whistles. There is an exuberant **flower market** here six days a week, with birds and pets – cruelly caged – on Sunday. The police headquarters is right behind.

Notre-Dame

The great west front of the **Cathédrale de Notre-Dame** (daily 8am–7pm; closed Sat 12.30–2pm) is truly impressive, with its strong vertical divisions counterbalanced by the horizontal emphasis of gallery and frieze, all centred by the rose window. It demands to be seen as a whole, though that can scarcely have been possible when the medieval houses clustered close about it. It is a solid, no-nonsense design, confessing its Romanesque ancestry. For more fantastical Gothic, look rather at the north transept façade with its crocketed gables and huge fretted window space.

Notre-Dame was begun in 1160 under the auspices of Bishop de Sully and completed around 1245. In the nineteenth century, Viollet-le-Duc carried out extensive renovation work, including remaking most of the statuary – the entire frieze of Old Testament kings, for instance – and adding the steeple and baleful-looking gargoyles, which you can see closeup if you brave the ascent of the **towers** (daily 10am–6pm; Oct–March closes 5pm; 31F, or 45F combined admission with *crypte archéologique* – see below). Ravaged by weather and pollution, its beauty is partially masked by scaffolding, hiding restoration work that will take several years to complete.

Inside, the immediately striking feature is the dramatic contrast between the darkness of the nave and the light falling on the first great clustered pillars of the choir, emphasizing the special nature of the sanctuary. It is the end walls of the transepts that admit all this light, nearly two-thirds glass, including two magnificent rose windows coloured in imperial purple. These, the vaulting and the soaring shafts reaching to the springs of the vaults are all definite Gothic elements and there remains a strong sense of Romanesque in the stout round pillars of the nave and the general sense of foursquareness, as there does outside. There are free guided tours which take place in French every weekday at noon and Sat at 2pm and in English on Wed at noon. There are also free organ concerts every Sun at 5 or 5.30pm, and four masses on Sun morning and one at 6.30pm. The **trésor** (daily 4.30–6.30pm; 15F), though, is not really worth the entry fee.

Before you leave, walk round to the public garden at the east end for a view of the flying buttresses supporting the choir, and then along the riverside under the south transept, where you can sit in springtime with the cherry blossom drifting down. Out in front of the cathedral, in the plaza separating it from Haussmann's police HQ, is the unappetizing entrance to the **crypte archéologique** (10am–5.30/4.30pm; 26F), in which are revealed the remains of the original cathedral, as well as streets and houses of the Cité as far back as the Roman era.

Le Mémorial de la Déportation

At the east tip of the island is the symbolic tomb of the 200,000 French who died in Nazi concentration camps during World War II – Resistance fighters, Jews and forced labourers among them. The **Mémorial de la Déportation** is scarcely visible above ground; stairs hardly shoulder-wide descend into a space like a prison yard. Within the crypt thousands of points of light represent the dead. Floor and ceiling are black and it ends in a black raw hole, with a single naked bulb hanging in the middle. Either side are empty barred cells. Above the exit are the words "Forgive. Do not forget."

The Voie Triomphale

La Voie Triomphale, or Triumphal Way, stretches in a dead straight line from the site of the original fortress of the Louvre to the modern complex of corporate skyscrapers at La Défense, nine kilometres away. Incorporating some of the city's most famous landmarks – the Champs-Élysées, the Arc de Triomphe and the Tuileries – its monumental constructions have been erected over the centuries by kings and emperors, presidents and corporations, to promulgate French power and prestige.

The tradition dies hard. Further self-aggrandizement has recently been given expression in an enormous, marble-clad cubic arch at the head of La Défense and a glass pyramid entrance in the central courtyard of the much-expanded Louvre.

The Arc de Triomphe and Champs-Elysées

The best view of this grandiose and simple geometry of kings to capital is from the top of the Arc de Triomphe, Napoléon's homage to the armies of France and himself (daily 10am–6/5pm; 31F, under-7s 7F; access from stairs on north corner of av des Champs-Élysées). Your attention, however, is most likely to be caught not by the view but by the mesmerizing traffic movements directly below you, around the massive place de l'Étoile – the world's first organized roundabout. Twelve wide avenues make up the star (étoile), of which the busiest is the Champs-Élysées. Its pavements have recently been widened and new trees planted, but the facelift hasn't managed to bring back glamour to the array of airline offices, car showrooms, hamburger joints and multiscreen cinemas. It only comes to life at Christmas when the fairy lights go on, and on December 31, with everyone happily sitting in a huge traffic jam, hooting in the New Year. Bastille Day's procession of president, tanks and guns is less appealing.

North of the Champs-Élysées is the Musée Jacquemart-André, 158 bd Haussmann, 8e (Mº Miromesnil; Wed–Sun 1–6.30pm; 35F) with a collection of Rembrandts and fifteenth- and sixteenth-century Italian genius represented by Botticelli, Titian, Tintoretto and Donatello. A short way west in the magnificent Hôtel Salomon de Rothschild, 11 rue Berryer, 8e (Mº George V), the Centre Nationale de la Photographie hosts important temporary exhibitions of photography (daily except Tues noon–7pm; 30F).

The best section of the avenue is between place de la Concorde and the Rond-Point roundabout, whose Lalique glass fountains disappeared during the German occupation. It's bordered by chestnut trees and municipal flower beds, pleasant enough to stroll among but not sufficiently dense to muffle the discomfiting squeal of accelerating tyres. The two massive buildings rising above the greenery to the south are the Grand and Petit Palais, with their overloaded Neoclassical exteriors, train-station roofs and exuberantly optimistic flying statuary. On the north side, combat police guard the high walls round the presidential Élysée Palace and the line of ministries and embassies ending with the US in prime position on the corner of place de la Concorde. On Thursdays and at weekends you can see a different manifestation of the self-images of states in the postage-stamp market at the corner of avenues Gabriel and Marigny.

Place de la Concorde and the Tuileries

The Champs-Élysées descends to place de la Concorde, where crossing over to the middle is again a death-defying task. As it happens, some 1300 people did die here between 1793 and 1795, beneath the Revolutionary guillotine: Louis XVI, Marie-Antoinette, Danton and Robespierre among them. The centrepiece of the place, chosen like its name to make no comment on these events, is an obelisk from the temple of Luxor, offered as a favour-currying gesture by the viceroy of Egypt in 1829. It serves merely to pivot more geometry:

the alignment of the French parliament, the **Assemblée Nationale**, on the far side of the Seine with the church of the Madeleine to the north (see p.93). Needless to say, it cuts the Voie Triomphale at a precise and predictable right angle.

The symmetry continues beyond place de la Concorde in the formal layout of the **Tuileries gardens**, disrupted only by the bodies lounging on the grass, kids chasing their boats round the ponds, and gays cruising the terrace overlooking the river. A major project of replanting and tree surgery, recasting statues and some relandscaping of the gardens is now underway. The aim is to have 3000 healthy trees by the year 2000 and a revamped Tuileries which both harks back to Catherine de Médicis' original garden and adds new perspectives to the Louvre. The two buildings flanking the garden at the Concorde end are the Orangerie (see below) by the river and the **Jeu de Paume** by rue de Rivoli (Mº Concorde; Tues noon–9.30pm, Wed–Fri noon–7pm, Sat & Sun 10am–7pm; 32F, under-13s free). This ex-royal tennis court and ex-Impressionists museum has had huge windows cut into its classical temple walls to light the city's newest exhibition space for contemporary art.

A private collection, inherited by the state with the stipulation that it should always stay together, none of the pictures in the **Orangerie** (Mº Concorde; daily except Tues 9.45am–5.15pm; 33F) has been moved to the Musée d'Orsay, with the result that it remains one of the top treats of Paris art museums. Its centrepiece is two oval rooms arranged by Monet as panoramas for his largest waterlily paintings. In addition, there are works by no more than a dozen other Impressionist artists – Matisse, Cézanne, Utrillo, Modigliani, Renoir, Soutine and Sisley amongst them. Cézanne's southern landscapes, the portraits by Van Dongen, Utrillo and Derain of Paul Guillaume and Jean Walter, whose taste this collection represents, the massive nudes of Picasso, Monet's

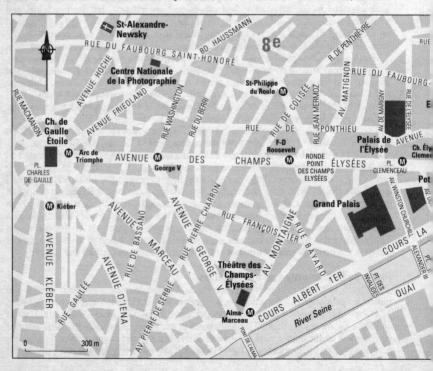

Argenteuil and Sisley's *Chemin de Montbuisson* are the cherries on the cake of this visual fest. What's more, you don't need marathon endurance to cover the lot and get back to your favourites for a second look.

The Louvre

The largest building in Paris, the focal point for centuries as the site of the French court, one of the world's greatest art galleries and the starting point of the Voie Triomphale: the **Louvre** was begun by Philippe Auguste in 1200 as a fortress to store his scrolls, jewels and swords while he himself lived on the Île de la Cité. Charles V was the first French king to make the castle his residence, but not until François 1er in the mid-sixteenth century were the beginnings of the palace laid and the fortress demolished. From then on, almost every sovereign added to it, with Catherine de Médicis, Henri II's widow, contributing the Palais des Tuileries extension across what are now the Tuileries gardens – a construction which was burnt to the ground during the Paris Commune (1871). The whole lot was nearly demolished under both Louis XIV and Louis XV but the Louvre survived to be given further additions by Napoléons I and III, and finally by Mitterrand in the 1980s. It was during the French Revolution that the palace was first opened to the public to display the former kings' art treasures, a collection greatly expanded by Napoléon I's requisitions in his foreign campaigns.

Every alteration and addition up to 1988 created a surprisingly homogeneous building, with a grandeur, symmetry, and Frenchness entirely suited to this most historic of Parisian edifices. Then came the **pyramid**, bang in the centre of the Cour Napoléon. It was an extraordinary leap of daring and imagination, conceived by the American architect Ieoh Ming Pei with no connection to its surroundings, save as a symbol of symme-

LA VOIE TRIOMPHALE

try. Mitterrand also managed to persuade the Finance Ministry to move out of the northern Richelieu wing, which now, with its two courtyards roofed over in glass, houses the French sculpture collection of the museum. A public passageway, the **passage Richelieu**, linking the Cour Napoléon with rue de Rivoli, allows you to look down into these courtyards – a better view of the Cheveux de Marly and Puget's monumental sculptures than you get from within the museum.

Mitterrand's project has also dramatically extended the Louvre under ground, with the **Hall Napoléon** beneath the pyramid (the entrance to the museum) leading into a series of galleries of shops, restaurants and exhibition spaces known as the **Carrousel du Louvre**, plus conference facilities and vast parking areas.

The underground complex is directly accessible from place du Carrousel and from the Palais Royale–Musée du Louvre métro: above ground, from the same station, you can take the Passage Richelieu to reach the Pyramid, or, from Mº Louvre-Rivoli, you can come in through the Three Musketeers' Cour Carrée; and, by the end of 1996, you should be able to cross the Seine into the Tuileries from the Musée d'Orsay on a new Solférino footbridge.

THE MUSEUMS

Lifts and escalators lead from the Hall Napoléon into the three wings of the **Louvre** (Mon 10am–9pm, Wed 9am–10pm, Thurs–Sun 9am–6pm; temporary exhibitions 10am–10pm; everything closed Tues; 40F; after 3pm & Sunday 20F; under-18s free; same-day re-admission allowed), each with four floors: *Sully* around the Cour Carrée; *Denon*, the southern wings, and *Richelieu* to the north. These are then divided into numbered areas and then rooms, with colour codings for the main categories of the collection (explained in the free brochure available in English from the Hall Napoléon information desk). If this sounds complicated, it is: the Louvre requires enormous stamina, will-power and leg muscles – even more so now that it has been so much expanded.

One bonus from the rearrangements, however, has been the opportunity to excavate the remains of the medieval Louvre – Philippe-Auguste's twelfth-century fortress and Charles V's fourteenth-century palace conversion – under the Cour Carrée. These are now on display along with a permanent exhibition on the **Histoire du Louvre** from the Middle Ages right up to the current transformations, in *Sully, entresol* – the floor at the top of the Hall Napoléon's escalators.

The seven basic categories of the museum's collections remain the same: three lots of antiquities, plus sculpture, painting, and applied and graphic arts. **Oriental Antiquities** (*Sully* ground floor 1–5) covers the Sumerian, Babylonian, Assyrian and Phoenician civilizations, plus the art of ancient Persia. **Egyptian Antiquities** (*Sully* ground floor 5–7 & 1st floor 6–8) contains jewellery, domestic objects, sandals, sarcophagi and dozens of examples of the delicate naturalism of Egyptian decorative technique, like the wall tiles depicting a piebald calf galloping through fields of papyrus and a duck taking off from a marsh. Some of the major exhibits are: the pink granite *Mastaba Sphinx*, the *Kneeling Scribe* statue (*Sully* ground floor 6), a wooden statue of *chancellor Nakhti*, the *god Amon*, protector of Tutankhamun, a bust of *Amenophis IV*, *Sethi I* and the *goddess Hathor*. The **Greek and Roman Antiquities** (*Denon* ground floor 2–4, first floor 3; *Sully* ground floor 7–8, first floor 8) include the *Winged Victory of Samothrace* (*Denon* first floor 3) and the late second-century BC *Venus de Milo* (*Sully* ground floor 8) – the biggest crowd-pullers in the museum after the *Mona Lisa*. Venus' antecedents are all on display, too, from the delightful *Dame d'Auxerre* (seventh century BC) and the fifth-century BC bronze *Apollo of Piombino*, still looking straight ahead in the archaic manner, to the classical perfection of the *Athlete of Benevento* and the beautiful *Ephebe of Agde*. In the Roman section are some very attractive mosaics from Asia Minor and luminous frescoes from Pompeii and Herculaneum which already seem to foreshadow the decorative lightness of touch of the Renaissance.

The **Applied Arts** collection (*Sully* first floor 1–6 & 8; *Denon* first floor 8) is heavily weighted on the side of vulgar imperial opulence and ecologically catastrophic abuses such as the entire doors of tortoiseshell in the work of the renowned cabinet-maker Boulle (active round 1700). There are also several acres of tapestry – all of the very first quality and workmanship, but a chore to look at. Better to seek relief in the smaller, less public items – Marie-Antoinette's travelling case, the carved Parisian ivories of the thirteenth century, and the Limoges enamels and Byzantine ivories.

The **Sculpture** section (*Denon* ground floor 5 & 7–10) covers the entire development of the art in France from Romanesque to Rodin and includes Michelangelo's *Slaves*, designed for the tomb of Pope Julius II.

The largest and most indigestible section by far is the **paintings** (*Sully* second floor 1–4; *Denon* first floor 1, 2 & 4–10, second floor 9): French from the year dot to mid-nineteenth century, along with Italians, Dutch, Germans, Flemish and Spanish. Among them are many paintings so familiar from reproduction in advertisements and on chocolate boxes that it is a surprise to see them on a wall in a frame. And unless you're an art historian, it is hard to make much sense of the parade of mythological scenes, classical ruins, piety, acrobatic saints and sheer dry academicism. A portrait, a domestic scene or a still life is a real relief. The early Italians (*Denon* first floor 5 & 7) are perhaps the most interesting part of the collection. All the big names are represented – Giotto, Fra Angelico, Botticelli, Filippo Lippi, Raphael; works to look out for include Uccello's *Battle of San Romano*, a *Crucifixion* by Mantegna, and Paolo Veronese's *Marriage At Cana*, a huge work painted in 1563. If you want to get near the *Mona Lisa* (*Denon* first floor 5), go first or last thing in the day. No one, incidentally, pays the slightest bit of attention to the other Leonardos right alongside, including the *Virgin of the Rocks*. Non-Italian works worth lingering over include Quentin Matsy's moralistic *Moneychanger and his Wife*, Rembrandt's masterful *Supper at Emmaus*, and a number of paintings by Poussin. There are also canvases by the French nineteenth-century artists David, Ingres and Géricault – whose harrowing *Raft of the Medusa* made his name as an artist. Look out, too, for Courbet's later *Funeral at Ornans*, perhaps the best-known Realist painting of all, its events rendered with dour, passive precision.

Upstairs in the *Richelieu* wing (second floor) are the imperial apartments of Napoléon III – you can see why the Ministry of Finance was loathe to vacate the premises.

The other two museums in the Louvre, the **Musée des Arts de la Mode et du Textile** (a museum of fashion) and the **Musée de la Publicité** (dealing with the art of advertising), both in the northern wing along rue de Rivoli west of the Richelieu wing, are being revamped and should open at the end of 1995. Check *Pariscope* for new opening hours and prices.

The *Passages* and Right Bank commerce

In the narrow streets of the 1er and 2e *arrondissements*, between the Louvre and **boulevards Haussmann**, **Montmartre and Poissonnière**, the grandiose financial, cultural and political state institutions are surrounded by well-established commerce – the rag trade, newspapers, sex and well-heeled shopping. In contrast to the hulks of the Bourse, Banque de France and the Bibliothèque Nationale are the once crumbling and secretive **Passages**, shopping arcades long predating the concept of pedestrian precincts, with glass roofs, tiled floors and unobtrusive entrances. Almost all have now been rendered as chic and immaculate as they were originally in the nineteenth century, with mega-premiums on their leases. Many are closed at night and on Sundays.

The *Passages*

Foremost among the *Passages* is the **Galerie Vivienne**, between rue Vivienne and rue des Petits-Champs, with its flamboyant décor of Grecian and marine motifs enticing you to buy Jean-Paul Gaultier or Yuki Torri gear. The neighbouring **Galerie Colbert**, gorgeously lit by bunches of bulbous lamps, has become a showcase extension for the Bibliothèque Nationale. But the best stylistically are the dilapidated three-storey **passage du Grand-Cerf**, at the bottom of rue St-Denis, and **Galerie Véro-Dodat**, off rue Croix-des-Petits-Champs, named after the two pork butchers who set it up in 1824. This last is the most homogeneous and aristocratic of the *Passages*, with painted ceilings and panelled shop-fronts divided by black marble columns. At no. 26, Monsieur Capia keeps a collection of antique dolls in a shop piled high with miscellaneous curios.

North of rue St-Marc the grid of arcades round the **passage des Panoramas** are still a touch rough, with no fancy mosaics for your feet. An old brasserie with carved wood panelling has been restored, and new restaurants have moved in, but there are still bric-a-brac shops, bars, stamp dealers, and an upper-crust printshop with its original 1867 fittings. In **passage Jouffroy** across bd Montmartre, an M. Segas sells walking canes and theatrical antiques opposite a fittings and furnishings shop for dolls' houses, while Paul Vulin spreads his secondhand books further down along the passageway.

The garment business

Mass-produced clothes is the business of **place du Caire**, the centre of the rag-trade district. The frenetic trading and deliveries of cloth, the food market on rue des Petits-Carreaux, and general toing and froing make a lively change from the office-bound quarters further west. Beneath an extraordinary pseudo-Egyptian façade of grotesque Pharaonic heads (a celebration of Napoléon's conquest of Egypt), an archway opens on to a series of arcades, the **passage du Caire**. These, contrary to any visible evidence, are the oldest of all the *Passages* and entirely monopolized by wholesale clothes shops.

The garment business gets progressively more upmarket west of the trade area. The upper end of **rue Étienne-Marcel**, and Louis XIV's **place des Victoires**, adjoined to the north by the appealingly asymmetrical **place des Petits-Pères**, are the centre for new-name designer clothes, displayed to deter all those without the necessary funds. The boutiques on **rue St-Honoré** and its Faubourg extension have the established names, paralleled across the Champs-Élysées by **rue François-1ᵉʳ**, where *Dior* has at least four blocks on the corner with av Montaigne. The aristocractic **place Vendôme**, with Napoléon high on a column clad with recycled Austro-Russian cannons, offers all the fashionable accessories for haute couture – jewellery, perfumes, the original Ritz, a Rothschild office and the Law and Order ministry.

Two shops are worth visiting for their small private collections: **Pierre Marly**, opticians, 380 rue Honoré, 1ᵉʳ (Mᵒ Concorde; Tues–Sat 9am–1pm & 2–7pm; free) has a display of visual aides, from the first medieval corrective lenses to specs worn by contemporary celebrities. Many items are miniature masterpieces. The bespoke shoe- and bootmakers **Di Mauro**, 14 rue du Faubourg St-Honoré, 8ᵉ, *escalier B* in the courtyard on the right (M° Madeleine; Mon–Sat 10am–6pm; free), display their upmarket creations from the 1920s to the present day. Customers willing to pay 5800F upwards often ask for variants of an old style. As long as your visit doesn't coincide with one of them, the grandson of the shop's founder will give a guided tour (in French or Italian only).

Place Madeleine and the Opéra

Another obese Napoleonic structure on the classical temple model is the church of **La Madeleine**, which serves for society weddings and for the perspective across place de la Concorde. There's a **flower market** every day except Monday along the east side of the church and a luxurious **Art Nouveau loo** by the métro at the junction of place and bd Madeleine. But the greatest appeal of the square is for window-gazing gourmets. In the northeast corner – at *Fauchon* – are two blocks of the best **food display** in Paris, with a snack bar for gourmet treats.

Boulevard de la Madeleine, becoming bd des Capucines, leads to the most preposterous building in Paris, the **Opéra de Paris**, whose architect, Charles Garnier, looks suitably foolish in a golden statue on the rue Auber side of his edifice. Excessively ornate and covering three acres in extent, this provided ample space for aristocratic preening, ceremonial pomp and the social intercourse of opera-goers, for whom the performance itself was a very secondary matter. These days, with the new Bastille opera, the Opéra Garnier – as it's now called – is used almost exclusively for ballet. By day you can visit the interior (daily 11am–5pm), including the auditorium, whose ceiling is by Chagall.

Palais Royal

The avenue de l'Opéra was built at the same time as its namesake – and left deliberately bereft of trees which might mask the vista of the Opéra. It leads down to the **Palais Royal**, originally Richelieu's residence, which now houses various government and constitutional bodies, and the **Comédie Française,** where the classics of French theatre are performed. The palace **gardens** to the north were once a gastronomic, gambling and amusement hot spot overlooked by flats lived in by Cocteau and Colette, amongst others. They are now rather austere, although new shops and cafés have opened in the arcades. But folly has returned in the form of black-and-white pillars in different sizes, standing above flowing water in the main courtyard of the palace. The creation of Daniel Buren, kids use these monochrome Brighton-rock lookalikes as an adventure playground, but for most people the palace grounds are just a useful short cut from the Louvre to rue des Petits-Champs. Beyond this street, just to the left, is the forbidding wall of the modern **Bibliothèque Nationale**, where you can see a public display of coins and ancient treasures (1–5pm), so you can at least enter the building should you feel so inclined.

Les Halles to Beaubourg

In 1969 the main **Les Halles** market was moved to the suburbs after more than eight hundred years in the heart of the city. There was widespread opposition to the destruction of Victor Baltard's nineteenth-century pavilions, and considerable disquiet at what renovation of the area would mean. The authorities' excuse was the *RER* and métro interchange they had to have below. Digging began in 1971, and the hole was only finally filled at the end of the 1980s. Hardly any trace remains of the working-class quarter, with its night bars and bistros to serve the market traders, and rents now rival the 16ᵉ.

The Forum des Halles

From Châtelet-Les Halles *RER*, you surface only after ascending levels 4 to 0 of the **Forum des Halles** centre, which stretches underground from the Bourse du Commerce rotunda to rue Pierre-Lescot. The overground section comprises aquarium-like arcades of shops enclosed by glass buttocks with white steel creases sliding down to an imprisoned patio. To cover up for all this, commerce, poetry, arts and crafts pavilions top two sides in a simple construction – save for the mirrors – that just manages to be out of synch with the curves and hollows below.

The gardens above the extensive underground complex do, however, provide much needed greenery and open space, even if the giant head and hand sculptures, on the north side still suggest the dislocation of the place. Beneath the garden, amidst the uninspiring shops, there's scope for various diversions such as swimming, watching games of billiards, discovering Paris through videos (see p.145) and wandering through a tropical garden. Touch-screen computers, with French and English "menus", are on hand to guide you round. After a spate of multilevels, air conditioning and artificial light, you can seek relief in the water cascading down the perfect Renaissance proportions of the **Fontaine des Innocents**, or in the high Gothic and Renaissance **church of St-Eustache**, where a woman preached the abolition of marriage from the pulpit during the Commune.

There are always hundreds of people around the Forum filling in time, hustling or just loafing about. Pickpocketing is pretty routine; the law plus canine arm are often in evidence and at night it can be quite tense, although the area southwards to **place du Châtelet** teems with jazz bars, nightclubs and restaurants and is far more crowded at 2am than 2pm. Back towards the Louvre streets like **de l'Arbre-Sec**, **Sauval** and **du Roule** revive the gentler attractions of pavement window-shopping, while on the riverfront, the three blocks of the **Samaritaine department store** (Mon, Thurs & Sat 9.30am–7pm; Tues & Fri 9.30am–8.30pm; Wed 9.30am–10.30pm) recall the days when art rather than marketing psychology determined the decoration of a store. Built in 1903 in pure Art Nouveau style, its gold, green and glass exteriors and interior ceramic tiles and wrought-iron staircases and balconies have all been restored, though best of all is the view from the roof – the most central high location in the city.

Beaubourg: Musée National d'Art Moderne

In the daytime, the main flow of feet is from Les Halles to Beaubourg, or the **Georges Pompidou national art and culture centre** (Mᵒ Rambuteau/Hôtel-de-Ville; Mon & Wed–Fri noon–10pm, Sat & Sun 10am–10pm; Musée National d'Art Moderne 30F; Galeries Contemporaines 20F; day pass 57F; free Sun 10am–2pm). This famous building by Renzo Piano and Richard Rogers – so revolutionary for the 1970s – is showing severe signs of wear and tear, but it remains one of the most popular Parisian buildings, though as much for the plaza's shifting spectacle by buskers of mime, magic, music and fire as for the more mainstream cultural activities inside. The entire complex is closed until late 1995 for a major structural overhaul.

On the ground floor, the postcard selection and art bookshop betters anything on the streets outside, and there are usually some scattered artworks that you don't have to pay to see. On the second floor, you can consult a wide range of books, tapes, videos and international newspapers for free at the **Bibliothèque Publique d'Information (BPI)**. Whether you want to do this or not, you should ride up the glass intestine of the escalator at least once. As the circles of spectators on the plaza recede, a horizontal skyline appears: the Sacré-Coeur, St-Eustache, the Eiffel Tower, Notre-Dame, the Panthéon, the Tour St-Jacques with its solitary gargoyle and La Défense menacing in the distance. From the platform at the top you can look down on the *château*-style chimneys of the Hôtel de Ville with their flowerpot offspring sprouting all over the lower rooftops.

The **Musée National d'Art Moderne** on the fourth floor of Beaubourg is second to none, with a constantly expanding collection of exclusively twentieth-century art. Contemporary movements and works dated the year before last find their place here along with the late-Impressionists, Fauvists, Cubists, Figuratives, Abstractionists and the rest of this century's First World art trends. The lighting and hanging are superb, although only a sixth of the whole collection is exhibited at any one time.

One of the earliest paintings is Henri Rousseau's *La Charmeuse de Serpent* (1907), an extraordinary, idiosyncratic beginning. In a different world, Picasso's *Femme assise* of 1909 brings in the reduced colours and double dimensions of **Cubism**, presented in its fuller development by Braque's *L'Homme à la Guitare* (1914), and, later, in Léger's solid balancing act, *Les Acrobates en gris* (1942–44). Among **Abstracts**, there's the sensuous rhythm of colour in Sonia Delaunay's *Prismes Electriques* (1914) and a good number of Kandinskys at his most harmonious and playful. Dali disturbs, amuses or infuriates with *Six apparitions de Lénine sur un piano* (1931), and there are more surrealist images from Magritte and de Chirico. Moving to the Expressionists, one of the most compulsive pictures – of 1920s female emancipation as viewed by a male contemporary – is the portrait of the journalist Sylvia von Harden by Otto Dix. The gender of the sleeping woman in *Le Rêve* by Matisse has no importance – it is simply a painting of the human body at its most relaxed. Jumping forward, to Francis Bacon, you find the tension and the torment of the human body and mind in the portraits, and – no matter that the figure is minute – in *Van Gogh in Landscape* (1957). Squashed-up cars, lines and squares, wrapped-up grand pianos and Warhol's *Electric chair* (1966) are there to be seen, while for a reminder that **contemporary** art can still hold its roots, there's the classic subject of *Le Peintre et son modèle* by Balthus, painted in 1980–81.

Elsewhere, the Beaubourg has temporary exhibitions of photographs, drawings, collages and prints (**Salle d'Art Graphique and Salon Photo**); **audiovisual presentations and films** on art history, contemporary art and current exhibitions; and the **Galleries Contemporaines**, where the overflow of the museum's contemporary collection gets rotated and young artists get a viewing. The **Grande Galerie** right at the top of the building is where the big-time exhibitions are held.

Back on the ground, **visual entertainments** around Beaubourg include the clanking gold *Défenseur du Temps* clock in the Quartier de l'Horloge; a *trompe-l'œil* as you look along rue Aubry-le-Boucher from Beaubourg; a nine-digit timepiece counting down the milliseconds to the year 2000 on the south side of the building, overlooking sculptures and fountains by Tinguely and Nicky de St-Phalle in a pool. This waterwork paying homage to Stravinsky shows scant respect for passers-by, and is the ceiling for **IRCAM**, the centre for contemporary music. A new, overground extension to *IRCAM* has appeared beside the old public baths on rue St-Merri – a Renzo Piano creation with a façade of stark terracotta marked like graph paper.

Quartier Beaubourg and the Hôtel de Ville

The **quartier Beaubourg** excels in its selection of small commercial art galleries where you can browse to your heart's content for free. **Rue Quincampoix** and **rue Renard**, the continuation of rue Beaubourg, are particularly promising. Rue Renard runs down to **place de l'Hôtel de Ville**, where the oppressively vertical, gleaming and gargantuan mansion is the seat of the city's government. An illustrated history of the edifice, always a prime target in riots and revolutions, is displayed along the platform of the Châtelet métro on the Neuilly-Vincennes line. After the defeat of the Commune in 1870, the bourgeoisie decided that a Parisian municipal authority worked against the better interests of law and order, property and the suppression of the working class, and for 100 years Paris was ruled directly by the ministry of the interior. The next head of an independent municipality was Jacques Chirac, elected in 1977 and still in control of the city today.

The Marais, the Île St-Louis and the Bastille

Jack Kerouac translates **rue des Francs-Bourgeois** as "street of the outspoken middle classes". The original owners of the mansions lining its length would not have taken kindly to such a slight on their blue-bloodedness. The name's origin is medieval,

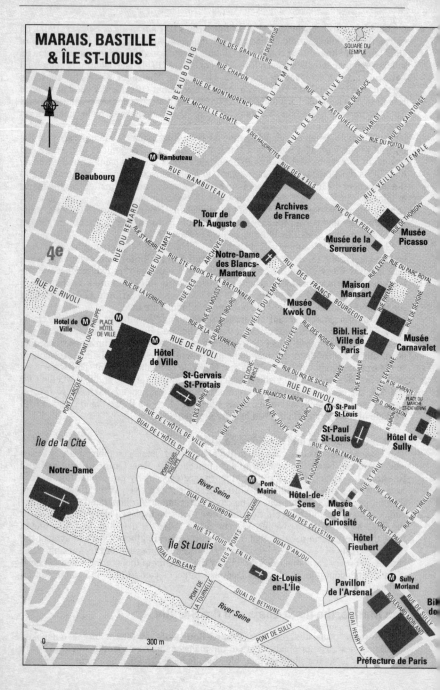

MARAIS, BASTILLE
& ÎLE ST-LOUIS

RUE DES GRAVILLIERS

SQUARE DU
TEMPLE

RUE DES VERTUS

RUE CHAPON

RUE DE MONTMORENCY

RUE MICHEL LE COMTE

RUE BEAUBOURG

RUE DU TEMPLE

RUE DES ARCHIVES

RUE DE BEAUCE

RUE PASTOURELLE

RUE CHARLOT

RUE DU SAINTONGE

RUE DU POITOU

R DES HAUDRETTES

RUE VIELLE DU TEMPLE

M Rambuteau

Beaubourg

RUE RAMBUTEAU

RUE DES 4 FILS

Archives
de France

RUE DE LA PERLE

RUE DE THORIGNY

Tour de
Ph. Auguste

Musée de la
Serrurerie

**Musée
Picasso**

4e

RUE DU RENARD

RUE ST MERRI

RUE DU TEMPLE

RUE STE CROIX DE LA BRETONNERIE

ARCHIVES

Notre-Dame
des Blancs-
Manteaux

RUE DES FRANCS

RUE ELZEVIR

RUE DU PARC ROYAL

Maison
Mansart

RUE PAYENNE

RUE DE SEVIGNE

RUE DE RIVOLI

RUE DE LA VERRERIE

RUE DES

RUE DU MOUSSY

Musée
Kwok On

BOURGEOIS

RUE DES ROSIERS

Hôtel de
Ville

M

PLACE
HÔTEL
DE VILLE

M

RUE PONT LOUIS PHILIPPE

RUE DE LA VERRERIE

RUE DU BOURG TIBOURG

RUE VIELLE DU TEMPLE

RUE DES ECOUFFES

**Bibl. Hist.
Ville de
Paris**

Musée
Carnavalet

RUE DE RIVOLI

Hôtel
de Ville

R DES ECOUFFES

R MALHER

RUE DE SEVIGNE

R DE JARENTE

R D ORMESSON

St-Gervais
St-Protais

R DES BARRES

R CLOCHE-
PERCE

RUE DU ROI DE SICILE

R PAVEE

PLACE DU
MARCHE
STE-CATHERINE

R G L'ASNIER

RUE FRANCOIS MIRON

RUE DE RIVOLI

M St-Paul
St-Louis

R CARON

QUAI DE L'HÔTEL DE VILLE

RUE DE JOUEY

RUE DE FOURCY

**St-Paul
St-Louis**

Hôtel de
Sully

PONT D'ARCOLE

RUE DE L'HÔTEL DE VILLE

RUE CHARLEMAGNE

R FIGUIER

R FAUCONNIER

RUE ST PAUL

RUE CHARLES V

Île de la Cité

Notre-Dame

PONT LOUIS
PHILIPPE

River Seine

M Pont
Marie

Hôtel-de-
Sens

Musée
de la
Curiosité

RUE DES LIONS ST PAUL

RUE BEAUTREILLS

QUAI DE BOURBON

PONT MARIE

QUAI DES CELESTINS

**Hôtel
Fieubert**

RUE ST LOUIS

R DES 2 PONTS

EN ÎLE

Île St Louis

QUAI D'ANJOU

QUAI D'ORLEANS

St-Louis
en-L'Île

**Pavillon
de l'Arsenal**

M Sully
Morland

PONT DE
LA TOURNELLE

QUAI DE BETHUNE

River Seine

PONT DE SULLY

BOULEVARD MORLAND

RUE DE SULLY

Bibl
de

0   300 m

QUAI HENRY IV

Préfecture de Paris

and it was not until the sixteenth and seventeenth centuries that the **Marais**, as the area between Beaubourg and the Bastille is known, became a fashionable aristocratic district. After the Revolution it was abandoned to the masses who, up until some 25 years ago, were living ten to a room on unserviced, squalid streets. Since then, gentrification has proceeded apace and the middle classes are finally ensconced – mostly media, arty or gay, and definitely outspoken.

The renovated mansions, their grandeur concealed by the narrow streets, have become museums, libraries, offices and chic apartments, flanked by shops selling designer clothes, house and garden accoutrements, works of art and one-off trinkets. Though cornered by Haussmann's boulevards, the Marais itself was spared the Baron's heavy touch and very little has been pulled down in the recent gentrification. It is Paris at its most seductive – old, secluded, as unthreatening by night as it is by day, and with as many alluring shops, bars and places to eat as you could wish for.

Rue des Francs-Bourgeois, the Jewish quarter and the place des Vosges

Rue des Francs-Bourgeois begins with the eighteenth-century magnificence of the **Palais Soubise**, which houses the Archives de France. Further down the street are two of the grandest Marais *hôtels*, **Carnavalet** and **Lamoignon**, housing respectively the Musée Carnavalet and the Bibliothèque Historique de la Ville de Paris.

The **Musée Carnavalet**, 23 rue de Sévigné, 3e (M° St-Paul; Tues–Sun 10am–5.40pm, Thurs closes 8.30pm; closed hols; 26F, 35F with exhibitions; disabled access), is a converted Renaissance mansion presenting the history of Paris as viewed and lived by royalty, aristocrats and the bourgeoisie from François I's time to 1900. The rooms for 1789–95 are full of sacred mementoes: models of the Bastille, original *Declarations of the Rights of Man and the Citizen*, tricolours and liberty caps, sculpted allegories of Reason, crockery with revolutionary slogans, glorious models of the guillotine and execution orders to make you shed a tear for the royalists as well. In the rest of the gilded rooms, the display of paintings, maps and models of Paris is a bit too exhaustive to give you an overall picture of the city changing.

The changing exhibitions at the **Musée Kwok-On**, 41 rue des Francs-Bourgeois, 4e (M° St-Paul/Rambuteau; Mon–Fri 10am–5.30pm; 15F), feature the popular arts of southern Asia – the musical instruments, festival decorations, religious objects and, most of all, the costumes, puppets, masks and stage models for theatre, in eleven different countries stretching from Japan to Turkey. The collection includes such things as figures for the Indonesian and Indian Theatres of Shadows, Peking Opera costumes and storytellers' scrolls from Bengal.

The area around **rue des Rosiers** is traditionally the **Jewish quarter** of the city, and remains so, despite incursions by trendy clothes shops. If you sense a certain suspicion of outsiders in this area, the reason is the bomb attacks in recent years on synagogues here and on *Goldenburg's* deli/restaurant. People have died in these assaults, and *Front National* spray cans periodically eject their obscenities on walls and shop-fronts.

At the end of Rue des Francs-Bourgeois you reach the masterpiece of aristocratic urban planning, the **place des Vosges**, vast square of stone and brick symmetry built for the majesty of Henri IV and Louis XIII, whose statue is hidden by trees in the middle of the grass and gravel gardens. Expensive high heels tap through the arcades pausing at art, antique and fashion shops, while toddlers and octogenarians, lunch-break workers and schoolchildren sit or play in the garden, the only green space of any size in the locality. From the southwest corner of the *place*, a door leads through to the formal *château* garden, orangerie and exquisite Renaissance façade of the **Hôtel de Sully**. You can visit the temporary exhibitions mounted by the *Caisse Nationale des Monuments Historiques et des Sites* here or just pass through, nodding at the sphinxes on the stairs, to rue St-Antoine.

Wandering north through the 3ᵉ *arrondissement*, you're likely to end up at the grimly barren **place de la République**, one of the largest roundabouts in Paris. Dominated on the north side by an army barracks, and joining seven major streets all penetrating through the then-surrounding areas of rebellious dissent, this is the most blatant example of Napoléon III's political town planning. In order to build it Haussmann destroyed a number of popular theatres, including the *Funambules* of *Les Enfants du Paradis* fame, and Daguerre's unique diorama.

Musée Picasso

Housed in a grandiloquent seventeenth-century mansion, the Hôtel Salé, the **Picasso museum**, 5 rue de Thorigny, 3ᵉ (Mᵒ St-Paul/Filles-du-Calvaire; daily except Tues 9.15am–5.15pm; Wed closes 10pm; 26F, under-18s free), represents the largest collection of Picassos anywhere. A large proportion of the works from the collection were personally owned by Picasso at the time of his death, and the state had first option on them in lieu of taxes owed. They include all the different media he used, the paintings he bought or was given by his contemporaries, his African masks and sculptures, photographs, letters and other personal memorabilia.

All of which said, it's a bit disappointing. These are not Picasso's most enjoyable works – the museums of the Côte d'Azur, Barcelona and Madrid are more exciting. But the collection here does leave you with a definite sense of the man and his life, partly because these were the works he wanted to keep, and many are accompanied by photographs. The paintings of his wives, lovers and families are some of the gentlest and most endearing here: the portraits of *Marie-Thérèse* and *Claude dessinant Françoise et Paloma*, for example, painted in 1937, as was the portrait of Dora Maar, during the Spanish Civil War when Picasso was going through his worst personal and political crises. This is the period when emotion and passion play hardest on his paintings and they are by far the best. A decade later, Picasso was a member of the Communist Party – his cards are on show along with a drawing entitled *Staline à la Santé* (Here's to Stalin) and his delegate credentials for the 1948 World Congress of Peace. The *Massacre en Corée* (1951) demonstrates the lasting pacifist commitment in his work.

Temporary exhibitions bring to the Hôtel Salé works from the periods least represented: the Pink Period, Cubism (despite some fine examples here, including a large collection of collages), the immediate postwar period and the 1950s and 1960s. There is also a cinema and reference library.

South of rue St-Antoine

In the southern section of the Marais, **below rue St-Antoine**, the crooked steps and lanterns of rue Cloche-Perce, the tottering timbered houses of rue François-Miron, the medieval *Acceuil de France* buildings behind St-Gervais-et-Protais and the smell of flowers and incense on rue des Barres are all good indulgence in Paris picturesque. But shift eastwards to the next tangle of streets and you'll find the modern, chi-chi flats of the "Village St-Paul" and its expensive clusters of antique shops. Rue St-Paul itself has some good addresses, including the **Musée de la Curiosité** at no. 11 (Mᵒ St-Paul/Sully-Morland; Wed, Sat & Sun 2–7pm; 45F), dedicated to the art of illusion with a magician performing impossible sleights of hand every half-hour from 2.30 to 6.30pm.

Further east again at 21 bd Morland, the **Pavillon de l'Arsenal** (Tues–Sat 10.30am–6.30pm, Sun 11am–7pm; free), signalled by a sculpture of Rimbaud, entitled *The man with his souls in front*, is an excellent addition to the city's art of self-promotion, its aim to present the city's current architectural projects to the public and show how past and present developments have evolved as part and parcel of Parisian history. To this end they have a permanent exhibition of photographs, plans and models, including a model of the whole city linked to a touch-screen choice of 30,000 images.

The Île St-Louis

Unlike its larger neighbour, the Île St-Louis has no monuments or museums, just high houses on single-lane streets, a school, church, restaurants and cafés, and the best sorbets in the world *chez M. Berthillon*. It's also where the likes of the Aga Khan and the pretender to the throne of France have their Parisian residences. You can find seclusion on the **southern quais**, tightly clutching a triple-sorbet cornet as you descend the various steps or climb over the low gate on the right of the garden across bd Henri-IV to reach the best sunbathing spot in Paris.

The Bastille

The column with the "Spirit of Liberty" on **place de la Bastille** was erected not to commemorate the surrender in 1789 of the prison – whose only visible remains have been transported to square Henri-Galli at the end of bd Henri-IV – but the July Revolution of 1830 that replaced the autocratic Charles X with the "Citizen King" Louis-Philippe. When Louis-Philippe fled in the more significant 1848 revolution, his throne was burnt beside the column and a new inscription added. Four months later, the workers again took to the streets. All of eastern Paris was barricaded, with the fiercest fighting on rue du Faubourg-St-Antoine. The rebellion was quelled with the usual massacres and deportation of survivors, and it is still the 1789 Bastille Day that France celebrates.

The Bicentennial in 1989 was marked by the inauguration of the **Opéra-Bastille**, Mitterrand's pet project and subject of the most virulent sequence of rows and resignations of any of the *grands projets*. Almost filling the entire block between rues de Lyon, Charenton and Moreau, this bloated building has totally altered place de la Bastille. The column is no longer pivotal; in fact, it's easy to miss it altogether when dazzled by the night-time glare of lights emanating from this hideous "hippopotamus in a bathtub", as one perceptive critic put it.

The opera's construction destroyed no mean amount of low-rent housing, and the **quartier de la Bastille** is now trendier than Les Halles. But as with most speculative developments, the pace of change is uneven: old tool shops and ironmongers still survive alongside cocktail haunts and sushi bars; laundries and cobblers rub shoulders with art galleries and gay bars. **Place and rue d'Aligre** still have their raucous daily market, with food in the covered *halles* and secondhand clothes and junk on the *place*. And on **rue de Lappe**, *Balajo* is one remnant of a very Parisian tradition: the *bals musettes*, or music halls of 1930s "gai Paris", frequented between the wars by Piaf, Jean Gabin and Rita Hayworth. It was founded by one Jo de France, who introduced glitter and spectacle into what were then seedy gangster dives, and brought Parisians from the other side of the city to the rue de Lappe lowlife.

Quartier Latin

On the Left Bank of the river, the pivotal point of the **quartier Latin** is **place St-Michel**, where the tree-lined **boulevard St-Michel** begins. It has lost its radical penniless chic now, preferring harder commercial values. The cafés and shops are jammed with people, mainly young and – in summer – largely foreign.

Rue de la Huchette, the Mecca of beats and bums in the post-World War II years, with its theatre still showing Ionesco's *Cantatrice Chauve* nearly forty years on, is now given over to indifferent Greek restaurants, as is the adjoining rue Xavier-Privas, with the odd *couscous* joint thrown in. Connecting it to the riverside is the city's narrowest street, the **Chat-qui-Pêche**, evocative of what Paris at its medieval worst must have looked like.

Rue St-Jacques

Things improve as you move away from the boulevard. At the end of rue de la Huchette, **rue St-Jacques** is aligned on the main street of Roman Paris, and was in medieval times the road up which millions of pilgrims trudged at the start of their long march to St-Jacques-de-Compostelle in Spain. Just to the right, one block up from rue de la Huchette, the mainly fifteenth-century church of **St-Séverin** (Mon–Thurs 11am–7.30pm, Fri & Sat 9am–10.30pm, Sun 9am–8pm) is one of the city's most elegant, with splendidly virtuoso chiselwork in the pillars of the Flamboyant choir, as well as stained glass by the modern French painter Jean Bazaine.

Back towards the river, **square Viviani** – with a welcome patch of grass and trees – provides the most flattering of all views of Notre-Dame. The mutilated and disfigured church is **St-Julien-le-Pauvre**. The same age as Notre-Dame, it used to be the venue for university assemblies until rumbustious students tore it apart in the 1500s. Round to the left on rue de la Bûcherie, the English bookshop **Shakespeare and Co** is haunted by the shades of James Joyce and other great expatriate literati – though Sylvia Beach, publisher of Joyce's *Ulysses*, had her original shop on rue de l'Odéon.

The river bank and Institut du Monde Arabe

Books, postcards, prints, and assorted goods are on sale from the **bouquinistes**, who display their wares in green padlocked boxes hooked onto the parapet of the **riverside quais**. Continuing upstream, you come to the **Pont de Sully** – with a dramatic view of the apse and steeple of Notre-Dame – and the beginning of a riverside garden dotted with pieces of modern sculpture, known as the **Musée de Sculpture en Plein Air**.

At the end of the Pont de Sully, in the angle between quai St-Bernard and rue des Fossés-St-Bernard, is the **Institut du Monde Arabe** (daily except Mon 10am–6pm; 25F, temporary exhibitions 20F), a cultural centre built to educate in the ways of the Arab world and designed by Jean Nouvel. An elegant glass-and-aluminium mass, cleft in two, with the riverfront half bowed and tapering to a knife-like prow, its broad southern façade comprises thousands of tiny light-sensitive shutters that open and close according to the brightness of the day, mimicking with high-tech ingenuity the *moucharaby*, or traditional Arab lattice-work balcony. Inside, there's a permanent exhibition of glass, rugs, ceramics, illuminated manuscripts, wood carving, metalwork and scientific instruments from the Islamic world. On the first floor, contemporary Arab paintings and sculptures are exhibited, while in the basement *Espace Image et Son* (1–7pm) you can watch TV programmes from around the Arab world and consult a large library of audiovisual material. When you need a rest, take the fastest lifts in Paris up to the café on the ninth floor, which has a brilliant view over the Seine.

Montagne Ste-Geneviève and the Sorbonne

The nearby area around the slopes of the **Montagne Ste-Geneviève**, the hill on which the Panthéon stands, is good for a stroll. The best approach is from **place Maubert** (good **market** Tues, Thurs and Sat mornings) or from the St-Michel/St-Germain crossroads, where the walls of the third-century **Roman baths** are visible in the garden of the Hôtel de Cluny, a sixteenth-century mansion built by the abbots of the powerful Cluny monastery as their Paris *pied-à-terre*. It now houses the **Musée National du Moyen-Age**, 6 pl Paul-Painlevé, off rue des Écoles (Mᵒ Cluny-La Sorbonne/St-Michel; Wed–Mon 9.15am–5.45pm; 27F, under-18s free), a treasure house of medieval art and tapestries. The numerous beauties here include a marvellous depiction of the grape harvest; a Resurrection embroidered in gold and silver thread, with sleeping guards in medieval armour; and a whole room of sixteenth-century Dutch tapestries, full of flowers and birds, a woman spinning while a cat plays with the end of the thread, a lover making advances, a woman in her bath, overflowing into a duck pond. But the greatest wonder of all is *La Dame à la Licorne* ("The Lady with the Unicorn"), six enigmatic scenes featuring a beautiful woman flanked by a lion and a unicorn, late fifteenth century, perhaps made in Brussels. Quite simply, it is the most stunning piece of art you are likely to see in many a long day.

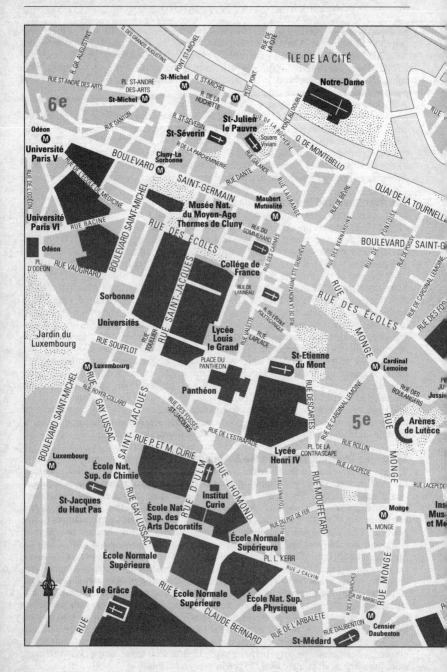

QUARTIER LATIN

Pont Marie Ⓜ

RUE DES DEUX PONTS

LOUIS-EN-L'ILE

LE ST
OUIS

RUE ST-LOUIS-EN-L'ILE

PONT DE LA TOURNELLE

PONT DE SULLY

MAIN

SAINT BERNARD

QUAI SAINT-BERNARD

Musée de la Sculpture
en Plein Air

Institut du
Monde Arab

Universités
Paris VI–Paris VII
Pierre et Marie Curie

Ⓜ

RUE JUSSIEU

RUE CUVIER

TINNE

Jardin des Plantes

Jardin D'Hiver

ut
nan   Galerie
uée   d'Evolution
          Muséum National
          D'Histoire
          Naturelle

RUE GEOFFROY ST-HILAIRE

RUE BUFFON

CENSIER

niversité
Paris III

0   300 m

The grim-looking buildings on the other side of rue des Écoles are the **Sorbonne**, **Collège de France**, and **Lycée Louis-le-Grand**, which numbers Molière, Robespierre, Pompidou and Victor Hugo among its graduates and Sartre among its teachers. All these institutions are major constituents of the brilliant world of French intellectual activity; you can put your nose in the Sorbonne courtyard without anyone objecting. Nearby, the traffic-free **place de la Sorbonne**, with its lime trees, cafés and student habitués, is a lovely place to sit.

The Panthéon and St-Étienne-du-Mont

Further up the hill, the broad rue Soufflot provides an appropriately grand perspective on the domed and porticoed **Panthéon**, Louis XV's thank you to Sainte Geneviève, patron saint of Paris, for curing him of illness. Imposing enough at a distance, it is cold and uninteresting close to – not a friendly detail for the eye to rest on. The Revolution transformed it into a mausoleum for the great, and it is truly deadly inside (April–Sept 10am–5.45pm; Oct–March 10am–noon & 2–4.45pm; closed Tues & public hols; 26F). There are, however, several good cafés down towards the Luxembourg gardens.

More interesting than the Panthéon is the mainly sixteenth-century church of **St-Étienne-du-Mont** on the corner of rue Clovis, with a façade combining Gothic, Renaissance and Baroque elements. The interior, if not exactly beautiful, is highly unexpected. The space is divided into three aisles by free-standing pillars connected by a narrow catwalk, and flooded with light by an exceptionally tall clerestory. Again, unusually – for they mainly fell victim to the destructive anti-clericalism of the Revolution – the church still possesses its rood screen, a broad low arch supporting a gallery reached by twining spiral stairs. There is also some good seventeenth-century glass in the cloister. Further down rue Clovis, a huge piece of Philippe Auguste's twelfth-century **city walls** emerges from among the houses.

There is not much point in going further south on rue St-Jacques: the area is dull and lifeless once you are over the Gay-Lussac intersection, though Baroque enthusiasts might like to take a look at the seventeenth-century church of **Val-de-Grâce**, with its pedimented front and ornate cupola copied from St Peter's in Rome, while around the corner on **bd de Port-Royal** are another big market and several brasseries.

East of the Panthéon

More enticing wandering is to be had in the villagey streets east of the Panthéon. **Rue de la Montagne-Ste-Geneviève** climbs up from place Maubert across rue des Écoles to the gates of the Ministry of Research and Technology. There's a sunny little café outside and several restaurants in rue de l'École-Polytechnique. Rue Descartes runs into the tiny and attractive **place de la Contrescarpe**. Once an arty hang-out where Hemingway wrote – in the café *La Chope* – and Georges Brassens sang, it is now extremely touristy.

The medieval **rue Mouffetard** begins here, a cobbled lane winding downhill to the church of **St-Médard**, once a country parish beside the now-covered river Bièvre. Most of the upper half of the street is given over to eating places, mainly Greek and little better than those of rue de la Huchette. Like any place wholly devoted to the entertainment of tourists, it has lost its soul. The bottom half, however, with its sumptuous fruit and veg stalls, still maintains an authentic neighbourhood air.

The Paris mosque and Jardin des Plantes

A little further east, across rue Monge, are some of the city's most agreeable surprises. Down rue Daubenton, past a delightful Arab shop selling sweets, spices and gaudy teaglasses, you come to the crenellated walls of the Paris **mosque**, topped by greenery and a great square minaret. You can walk in the sunken garden and patios with their polychrome tiles and carved ceilings, but not the prayer room (daily except Fri 9am–noon & 2–6pm; closed Muslim hols). There is a **tearoom** too, open to all, and a **hammam** (see p.156).

Opposite the mosque is an entrance to the **Jardin des Plantes** (daily summer 7.30am–7.45pm; winter 8am–dusk), with a small, cramped, expensive **zoo** (summer Mon–Sat 9am–6pm, Sun 9am–6.30pm; winter Mon–Sat 9am–5pm, Sun 9am–6.30pm; 25F), as well as botanical gardens, hothouses and museums of paleontology, mineralogy, entymology, paleobiology and evolution. The **Galerie d'Evolution**, 36 rue Geoffroy St-Hilaire (Mº Censier-Daubenton; daily except Tues 10am–6pm, Thurs till 10pm; 40F), is housed in a superb turn-of-the-century glass and steel domed building. It presents the diversity of species, the history and science of evolution and the relationships between human beings and the rest of nature.

The gardens are a pleasant space to while away the middle of a day. By the rue Cuvier exit is a fine Cedar of Lebanon planted in 1734, raised from seed sent over from the Oxford Botanical Gardens, and a slice of an American sequoia more than 2000 years old. In the nearby physics labs, Henri Becquerel discovered radioactivity in 1896, and two years later the Curies discovered radium (Pierre ended his days under the wheels of a brewer's dray on rue Dauphine).

A short distance away, with an entrance in rue de Navarre, rue des Arènes and another through a passage on rue Monge, is Paris' other Roman remain, the **Arènes de Lutèce**, an unexpected backwater hidden from the street. It is a partly restored amphitheatre, with a *boules* pitch in the centre, benches, gardens and a kids' playground behind.

Seine Rive Gauche

"Seine Rive Gauche" is the planners' name for the new district being created along the riverfront down from the Gare d'Austerlitz. The star attraction is the new **Bibliothèque Nationale de France**, the world's most advanced library which will be open to all – not just card-carrying academics – in November 1996. It has four 100-metre-high L-shaped transparent towers at each corner of a sunken garden the size of sixteen football pitches, between rue du Chevaleret and the river. Before it opens, you can look at models of the building and the surrounding developments in a teepee right by quai de la Gare métro station.

Hôpital de la Salpêtrière and the Gobelin tapestry workshops

Above bd Vincent-Auriol, to the west of the Gare d'Austerlitz train tracks, is the immense **Hôpital de la Salpêtrière**, built under Louis XIV to dispose of the dispossessed. It later became a psychiatric hospital, fulfilling much the same function. Jean Charcot, who believed that susceptibility to hypnosis was proof of hysteria, staged his theatrical demonstrations here, with Freud a captive member of his audiences. If you ask very nicely in the Bibliothèque Charcot (block 6, red route; entrance from bd de l'Hôpital; Mº St-Marcel), the librarian may show you a book of photographs of the poor female subjects of these experiments. For a more positive statement on women, take a look at the building at 5 rue Jules-Breton, which declares in large letters on its façade, "In humanity, woman has the same duties as man. She must have the same rights in the family and in society."

On the other side of av des Gobelins, rues Berbier-du-Mets and Croulebarbe run over the river Bièvre, covered over in 1910 as a health hazard. The main source of the pollution was the dyes from the **Gobelin tapestry workshops**, 42 av des Gobelins (Mº Gobelins; guided visits Tues, Wed & Thurs 2 & 2.45pm; 26F), in operation here for some 400 years. Tapestries are still being made by the same methods on cartoons by contemporary painters – a painfully slow process which you can watch.

St-Germain

The northern half of the 6e *arrondissement*, asymmetrically centred on **place St-Germain-des-Prés**, is one of the most physically attractive, lively and stimulating square kilometres in the city. The most dramatic approach is to cross the river from the Louvre by the **Pont des Arts**, with the classic upstream view of the Île de la Cité, with barges moored at the quai de Conti, and the Tour St-Jacques and Hôtel de Ville breaking the skyline of the Right Bank. The dome and pediment at the end of the bridge belong to the **Institut de France**, seat of the Académie Française, an august body of writers and scholars whose mission is to safeguard the purity of the French language. This is the grandiose bit of the Left Bank riverfront; to the left is the **Hôtel des Monnaies**, redesigned as the Mint in the late eighteenth century; to the right is the **Beaux-Arts**, the school of Fine Art, whose students throng the *quais* on sunny days, sketchpads on knees.

The riverside

The riverside part of the 6e *arrondissement* is cut lengthwise by **rue St-André-des-Arts** and **rue Jacob**. It is full of bookshops, commercial art galleries, antique shops, cafés and restaurants, but poke your nose into courtyards and sidestreets. The houses are four-to-six storeys high, seventeenth and eighteenth century, some noble, some stiff, some bulging and skew, all painted in infinite gradations of grey, pearl and off-white. Broadly speaking, the further west the posher.

Historical associations are legion: Picasso painted *Guernica* in rue des Grands-Augustins. Molière started his career in rue Mazarine; Robespierre and co. split ideological hairs at the *Café Procope*, now an expensive restaurant, in rue de l'Ancienne-Comédie. In rue Visconti, Racine died, Delacroix painted and Balzac's printing business went bust. In the parallel rue des Beaux-Arts, Oscar Wilde died, Corot and Ampère (father of amps) lived, and the crazy poet Gérard de Nerval went walking with a lobster on a lead.

If you're looking for lunch, **place** and **rue St-André-des-Arts** offer a tempting concentration of places, from Tunisian sandwich joints to seafood extravagance, and a brilliant food market in rue Buci up towards bd St-Germain. Before you get to Buci, there is an intriguing little passage on the left, **Cour du Commerce**, where Marat had a printing press and Dr Guillotin perfected his notorious machine by lopping off sheep's heads in the loft next door. A couple of smaller courtyards open off it, revealing another stretch of Philippe Auguste's wall.

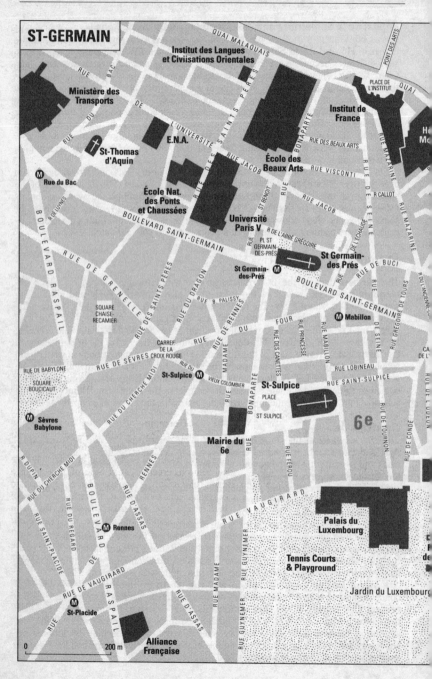

ST-GERMAIN

Institut des Langues
et Civilisations Orientales

QUAI MALAQUAIS

PONT DES ARTS

Ministère des
Transports

PLACE DE
L'INSTITUT

QUAI

Institut de
France

He
Mo

RUE DU BAC

RUE DES SAINTS PÈRES

DE L'UNIVERSITÉ

RUE DE BEAUX ARTS

BONAPARTE

RUE MAZARINE

✝ St-Thomas
d'Aquin

E.N.A.

RUE JACOB

École des
Beaux Arts

RUE VISCONTI

R CALLOT

Ⓜ Rue du Bac

RUE JACOB

École Nat.
des Ponts
et Chaussées

ST BENOÎT

RUE DE SEINE

RUE DE L'ÉCHAUDÉ

RUE DE LEUNES

BOULEVARD SAINT-GERMAIN

Université
Paris V

R DE L'ABBÉ GRÉGOIRE

PL ST
GERMAIN
DES-PRÉS

St Germain-
des Prés

✝

RUE DE BUCI

BOULEVARD

RASPAIL

RUE DE GRENELLE

RUE DES SAINTS PÈRES

St Germain-
des-Prés

Ⓜ

BOULEVARD SAINT-GERMAIN

R DE L'ANCIENNE CO

R GRÉGOIRE DE TOURS

RUE DE SEINE

SQUARE
CHAISE-
RECAMIER

RUE DU DRAGON

RUE B. PALISSY

DU

FOUR

RUE PRINCESSE

RUE MABILLON

Ⓜ Mabillon

RUE DE RENNES

RUE DES CANETTES

CARREF.
DE LA
CROIX ROUGE

RUE DE SÈVRES

RUE DU

RUE LOBINEAU

RUE DE BABYLONE

RUE DU

RUE SAINT-SULPICE

CA
DE L'

St-Sulpice Ⓜ

VIEUX COLOMBIER

St-Sulpice

SQUARE
BOUCICAUT

RUE MADAME

BONAPARTE

PLACE

6ᵉ

Ⓜ Sèvres
Babylone

RUE DU CHERCHE MIDI

ST SULPICE

✝

RUE DE TOURNON

RUE DE CONDÉ

R DUPIN

Mairie du
6e

RUE

RUE FÉROU

RENNES

RUE DU CHERCHE MIDI

BOULEVARD

RUE D'ASSAS

RUE GUYNEMER

RUE DU RÉGARD

Ⓜ Rennes

RUE VAUGIRARD

RUE SAINT-PLACIDE

DE

Palais du
Luxembourg

E
F
de

RASPAIL

RUE DE VAUGIRARD

RUE MADAME

RUE D'ASSAS

RUE GUYNEMER

Tennis Courts
& Playground

Jardin du Luxembourg

Ⓜ St-Placide

RUE

0   200 m

Alliance
Française

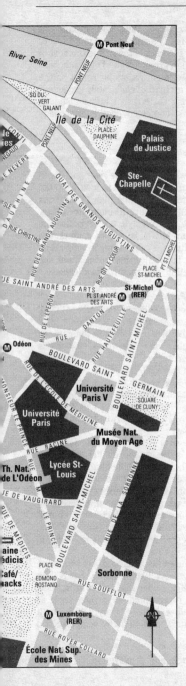

An alternative corner for midday food or quiet is around rue de l'Abbaye and rue du Furstemberg, with a tiny square where **Delacroix's old studio** overlooks a secret garden and is now a museum (at no. 6), with a small collection of the artist's personal belongings as well as temporary exhibitons of his work. This is also the beginning of some very upmarket **shopping territory**, in **rue Jacob**, **rue de Seine** and **rue Bonaparte** in particular.

Place St-Germain-des-Prés

Place St-Germain-des-Prés, the hub of the *quartier*, is only a stone's throw away, with the *Deux Magots* café on the corner and *Flore* just down the street – both renowned for the number of philosophico-politico-poetico-literary backsides that have shined their seats, although nowadays you're more likely to be dragged into some street-clown's act than engaged in high-flown debate.

The tower opposite the *Deux Magots* belongs to the **church of St-Germain**, all that remains of an enormous Benedictine monastery. The interior is its best aspect, with its pure Romanesque lines still clear under the deforming paint of nineteenth-century frescoes.

St-Sulpice and the Palais du Luxembourg

South of bd St-Germain the streets round St-Sulpice are calm and classy. **Rue Mabillon** is pretty, with a row of old houses set back below the level of the modern street. On the left are the **halles St-Germain**, on the site of a fifteenth-century market. **Rue St-Sulpice** – with excellent shops for edibles – leads through to the front of the enormous **church of St-Sulpice**, an austerely classical church, erected either side of 1700, with a Doric colonnade surmounted by an Ionic, and Corinthian pilasters in the towers, only one of which is finished. For many however, the main attraction of **place St-Sulpice** is *Yves Saint Laurent Rive Gauche*, the most elegant fashion boutique on the Left Bank. The least posh bit of the *quartier* is the eastern edge, where the university is firmly implanted, along bd St-Michel, with attendant scientific and medical bookshops, skeletons and instruments of torture as well as a couple of weird and wonderful shops in rue Racine. But there is really no escape from elegance round here.

To the south, rue Férou, where a gentleman called Pottier composed the *Internationale* in 1776, connects with **rue de Vaugirard**, Paris' longest street, and the **Palais du Luxembourg**, constructed for Marie de Médicis, Henri IV's widow, to remind her of the Palazzo Pitti and Giardino di Boboli of her native Florence – today it is the seat of the French Senate. The **gardens** are the chief recreation ground of the Left Bank, with tennis courts, pony rides, children's playground, *boules* pitch, yachts for rental on the pond, and, in the wilder southeast corner, a miniature orchard of elaborately espaliered pear trees. With its strollers and mooners and garish parterres, it has a distinctly Mediterranean air on summer days, when the most contested spot is the shady **Fontaine de Médicis** in the northeast corner.

Trocadéro, Eiffel Tower and Les Invalides

The vistas across the river between the 7e *arrondissement* south of the river and the 8e and 16e on the north are impressive – particularly at night. You have to look from the terrace of the **Palais de Chaillot** on place du Trocadéro, across the river to the **Tour Eiffel** and **École Militaire**, from the ornate 1900 Pont Alexandre III along the grassy Esplanade to the **Hôtel des Invalides**. But the scale and the style are despotic. The Palais de Chaillot, like a latterday Pharaoh's mausoleum (1937), is, however, home to a theatre used for diverse but usually radical productions and several interesting museums, as is its smaller neighbour, the **Palais de Tokyo**. Further upstream on the south bank of the river is the ornate erstwhile train station, now the **Musée d'Orsay**.

The Eiffel Tower and the Palais de Chaillot and Palais de Tokyo

When completed in 1889, the **Tour Eiffel** was the tallest building in the world at 300m, and its 7000 tons of steel, in terms of pressure, still sit as lightly on the ground as a child in a chair. Reactions to it were violent. Outraged critics protested "in the name of menaced French art and history" against this "useless and monstrous" tower. "Is Paris", they asked, "going to be associated with the grotesque, mercantile imaginings of a constructor of machines?" But it stole the show at the 1889 Exposition, for which it had been constructed. In 1986 the tower was given a new system of illumination from within its superstructure, so that it now looks at its magical best after dark, as light and fanciful as a filigree minaret. Going to the top (10am–11pm for stages 1 and 2; 10am–10pm for stage 3) costs 53F (20F and 36F respectively for the first two stages), so it's only really worth the expense on an absolutely clear day.

Facing the Eiffel Tower from the other side of the river is the **Palais de Chaillot**, which contains four museums, the biggest of which is the **Musée de l'Homme** (M^o Trocadéro; daily except Tues 9.45am–5.15pm; closed hols; 25F). Full of high-tech interactive displays, it covers the origins, cultures, languages and genetics of human beings from Polynesia to the Arctic. The **Musée du Cinéma Henri-Langlois** (guided tours only Wed–Sun 10am, 11am, 2pm, 3pm & 4pm; 25F) includes a rare archive screening as well as costumes, sets and cameras. Models of ships and reproductions of church sculpture are the focus of the **Musée de la Marine** (Wed–Sun 10am–6pm; 45F) and the **Musée des Monuments Français** (daily except Tues 10am–5.30pm, Wed till 9pm; 21F).

The Palais de Tokyo on av du Président-Wilson houses the **Musée d'Art Moderne de la Ville de Paris** (M^o Iéna/Alma-Marceau; Tues–Fri 10am–5.30pm, Sat & Sun 10am–7pm; Wed till 8.30pm in summer; closed hols; 27F, under-18s free), with schools and trends of twentieth-century art always richly represented by artists such as Vlaminck, Zadkine, Picasso, Braque, Juan Gris, Valadon, Matisse, Dufy, Utrillo, both Delaunays, Chagall, Modigliani, Léger and many others, as well as by sculpture and painting by contemporary artists.

Among the most spectacular works on permanent show are Robert and Sonia Delaunay's huge whirling wheels and cogs of rainbow colour displayed in the ground-floor corridor; the pale leaping figures of Matisse's *La Danse*; and Dufy's enormous mural, *La Fée Electricité* (done for the electricity board), illustrating the story of electricity from Aristotle to the then modern power station, in 250 lyrical, colourful panels filling three entire walls. The upper floors of the gallery are reserved for all sorts of contemporary and experimental work, including music and photography.

On sale in the bookshop are a number of artists' designs, among them a set of Sonia Delaunay's playing cards, guaranteed to rejuvenate the most jaded cardsharp. Next to it is an excellent and reasonably priced snack bar.

Around the École Militaire

Stretching back from the legs of the Eiffel Tower, the long rectangular gardens of the **Champs de Mars** lead to the eighteenth-century buildings of the **École Militaire**, originally founded in 1751 by Louis XV for the training of aristocratic army officers, and attended by Napoléon, among other fledgling leaders. The surrounding *quartier* is expensive and sought after as an address, but uninteresting to look at, like the **UNESCO building** at the back of the École Militaire. Controversial at the time of its construction in 1958, it looks somewhat pedestrian and badly weathered today. It can be visited, and there are a number of art works inside, the most noticeable being an enormous mobile by Alexander Calder and a quiet Japanese garden. One unexpected corner of this rather austere *quartier* is the wedge of early nineteenth-century streets between av Bosquet and the Invalides. Chief among them is the market street of **rue Cler** with the cross streets rue de Grenelle and rue St-Dominique full of classy little shops, some with their original painted glass panels.

Out on the river bank at quai d'Orsay is the **American Church** which, together with the American College nearby at 31 av Bosquet, is a nodal point in the well-organized life of the large American community. The notice board is usually plastered with job offers and demands. The other quayside attraction is the **sewers**, or *les égouts* (entrance southeast of Pont de l'Alma and quai d'Orsay junction; Sat–Wed 11am–5/6pm, last ticket 1hr before closing; 24F). Guidebooks always bill this as an outing for kids, though this is doubtful. The visit consists of an unilluminating film, a small museum and a very brief look at some tunnels with a lot of smelly water swirling about.

Les Invalides

The **Esplanade des Invalides**, striking due south from **Pont Alexandre III**, is a more attractive and uncluttered vista than Chaillot-École Militaire. The wide façade of the **Hôtel des Invalides** – topped by its distinctive dome and resplendent with new gilding to celebrate the bicentenary of the Revolution – fills the whole of the further end of the Esplanade. It was built as a home for invalided soldiers on the orders of Louis XIV. Under the dome are two churches, one for the soldiers, the other intended as a mausoleum for the king but now containing the mortal remains of Napoléon. Les Invalides today houses the vast **Musée de l'Armée** (daily 10am–5pm; 34F), an enormous national war museum whose largest part is devoted to the uniforms and weaponry of Napoléon's armies with numerous personal items of the emperor, including his campaign tent and bed, and even his dog – stuffed. Later French wars are illustrated, too, through paintings, maps and engravings. Sections on the two world wars are good, with deportation and resistance covered as well as specific battles. Some of the oddest exhibits are Secret Service sabotage devices – for instance, a rat and a lump of coal stuffed with explosives.

Both of the Invalides churches are cold and dreary inside. The **Église du Dôme**, in particular, is a supreme example of architectural pomposity, with Corinthian columns and pilasters, and grandiose frescoes in abundance. Napoléon lies in a hole in the floor in a cold, smooth sarcophagus of red porphyry, enclosed within a gallery decorated with friezes of execrable taste and grovelling piety, captioned with quotations of awesome conceit from the great man: "Cooperate with the plans I have laid for the welfare of peoples"; "By its simplicity my code of law has done more good in France than all the laws which have preceded me"; "Wherever the shadow of my rule has fallen, it has left lasting traces of its value."

Immediately east of the Invalides is the **Musée Rodin**, on the corner of rue de Varenne (M° Varenne; Tues–Sun 10am–5/5.45pm; 27F, garden only 5F), housed in a beautiful eighteenth-century mansion which the sculptor leased from the state in return for the gift of all his work at his death. Major projects like *Les Bourgeois de Calais*, *Le Penseur*, *Balzac*, *La Porte de l'Enfer* and *Ugolini et fils* are exhibited in the garden – the latter forming the centrepiece of the ornamental pond. Indoors (and very crowded) are works in marble like *Le Baiser*, *La Main de Dieu*, *La Cathédrale* – those two perfectly poised, almost sentient, hands. There is something particularly fascinating about the works, like *Romeo and Juliet* and *La Centauresse*, which are only half-created, not totally liberated from the raw block of stone.

The rest of rue de Varenne and the parallel rue de Grenelle are full of aristocratic mansions, including the **Hôtel Matignon**, the prime minister's residence. At the further end, the **rue du Bac** leads right into rue de Sèvres, cutting across **rue de Babylone**, another of the *quartier*'s livelier streets, with the crazy, rich man's folly, **La Pagode** – now a cinema – down on the left beyond the barracks.

Musée d'Orsay

Close to Les Invalides and staring out towards the Jardins des Tuileries over the river, the **Musée d'Orsay**, 1 rue de Bellechasse/quai Anatole-France, houses the painting and sculpture of the immediately pre-modern period, 1848–1914, bridging the gap between the Louvre and the Centre Beaubourg (M° Solférino, *RER* Musée d'Orsay; Tues, Wed, Fri & Sat 9/10am–6pm, Thurs 9/10am–9.45pm, Sun 9am–6pm; 36F, Sun 20F, under-18s free; free guided tours in English by staff lecturer 11am & 2pm). Its focus is the cobweb-clearing, eye-cleansing collection of **Impressionists** rescued from the cramped corridors of the Jeu de Paume, though not – unavoidably – from the coach parties. Scarcely less electrifying are the works of the **Post-Impressionists** brought in from the Palais de Tokyo.

On the **ground floor**, the mid-nineteenth-century sculptors, including Barye, caster of super-naturalistic bronze animals, occupy the centre gallery. To their right, a few canvases by Ingres and Delacroix (the bulk of whose work is in the Louvre) serve to illustrate the transition from the early nineteenth century. Puvis de Chavannes, Gustave Moreau, the Symbolists and early Degas follow, while in the galleries to the left, Daumier, Corot, Millet and the Realist school lead on to the first Impressionist works, including Manet's *Déjeuner sur l'Herbe*, which sent the critics into apoplexies of disgust when it appeared in 1863. *Olympia* is here, too, equally controversial at the time, for the colour contrasts and sensual surfaces – rather than the content – though the black cat was considered peculiar.

To get the chronological continuation you have to go straight up to the top level, where numerous landscapes and outdoor scenes by Renoir, Sisley, Pissarro and Monet owe much of their brilliance to the novel practice of setting up easels in the open to catch a momentary light. Monet's water lilies are here in abundance, too, along with five of his Rouen cathedral series, each painted in different light conditions. *Le Berceau* (1872) by Morisot, the only woman in the early group of Impressionists, is one of the few to have a complex human emotion as its subject – perfectly synthesized within the classic techniques of the movement. A very different touch, all shimmering light and wide brush strokes, is to be seen in Renoir's depiction of a good time being had by all in *Le Moulin de la Galette* – a favourite Sunday afternoon out on the Butte Montmartre. Cézanne, a step removed from the preoccupations of the mainstream Impressionists, is also wonderfully represented. One of the canvases most revealing of his art is *Still Life with Apples and Oranges* (1895–1900), in which the background abandons perspective while the fruit has an extraordinary reality.

The rest of this level is given over to the various offspring of Impressionism. Among a number of pointilliste works by Seurat and others is Signac's horrible *Entrée du Port de Marseille*. There's Gauguin, post- and pre-Tahiti, as well as some very attractive derivatives like Georges Lacombe's carved wood panels; several superb Bonnards and Vuillards and lots of Toulouse-Lautrec at his caricaturial night-clubbing best – one large canvas including a rear view of Oscar Wilde at his grossest; plus all the blinding colours and disturbing rhythms of the Van Goghs. The **middle level** takes in Rodin and other late nineteenth-century sculptors, three rooms of superb Art Nouveau furniture and *objets*, and, lastly, some Matisses and Klimts to mark the transition to the moderns in the Beaubourg collection.

As if these exhibition riches weren't enough, **the building** is itself a handsome structure. It was inaugurated in time for the 1900 World Fair and continued to serve the stations of southwest France until 1939. Orson Welles used it as the setting for his film of Kafka's *Trial*, and de Gaulle used it announce his *coup d'état* of May 19, 1958.

Montparnasse and southern Paris

Montparnasse is very much part of central Paris and has changed very little over the last decades. The rest of southern Paris has been – and still is – subject to large-scale developments, most notably along the riverfronts both east and west. There are lively areas: the **Buttes-aux-Cailles** in the 13e, **Pernety** in the 14e and **rue du Commerce** in the 15e, and three good parks: **Montsouris**, **George-Brassens** and **André Citroën**. It's the least touristy area of town and well worth exploring.

Like other Left Bank *quartiers*, Montparnasse still trades on its association with the wild characters of the interwar artistic and literary boom. Many were habitués of the cafés *Select*, *Coupole*, *Dôme*, *Rotonde* and *Closerie des Lilas*, all still going strong on **bd du Montparnasse**. Another major subcommunity in the *quartier* in the early years of the century consisted of outlawed Russian revolutionaries. They were so many that the Tsarist police ran a special Paris section to keep tabs on them. Trotsky lived in rue de la Gaîté near the cemetery – a fascinating street of old theatres and cafés – and Lenin lodged further south in the 14e *arrondissement*.

Most of the life of the quarter is concentrated between the junction with bd Raspail where Rodin's *Balzac* broods over the traffic, and the station end of bd du Montparnasse, where the colossal **Tour du Montparnasse** has become one of the city's principal landmarks. You can go up on a tour for less than at the Eiffel Tower (summer 9.30am–11pm; winter 10am–10pm; 40F), though for a bit more you could have a drink in the top-floor bar. The tower is much reviled as a building because it is totally out of scale with its surroundings. It has bred a rash of workers' barracks in the area behind it and, in front and beneath it, there's an enormous shopping complex. For food, better to shop at the market in **bd Edgar-Quinet**, where the cafés are full of stall holders.

Montparnasse cemetery, the catacombs and the Observatoire

Just south of bd Edgar-Quinet is the main entrance to the **Montparnasse cemetery**, a gloomy city of the dead with ranks of miniature temples, dreary and bizarre, and plenty of illustrious names for spotters, from Baudelaire to Sartre and André Citroën to Saint-Saëns. In the southwest corner is an old windmill, one of the seventeenth-century taverns frequented by the carousing, versifying students who gave the district its name of Parnassus.

If you are determined to spend your time among the dear departed, you can also get down into the **catacombs** (Tues–Fri 2–6pm, Sat & Sun 9–11am & 2–4pm; 27F) in nearby **place Denfert-Rochereau**, formerly place d'Enfer (Hell Square). These are abandoned quarries stacked with millions of bones cleared from the old charnel houses in 1785, claustrophobic in the extreme, and cold.

Rue Schroeder and bd Raspail on the east side of the cemetery have some interesting examples of twentieth-century architecture, from Art Nouveau to contemporary façades of glass in the Cartier Foundation at 259 bd Raspail. For a more classical style, there's the **Observatoire de Paris**, on bd Arago just east of place Denfert-Rochereau, with a garden open on summer afternoons in which to sit and admire the dome. From the 1660s, when it was constructed, until 1884, all French maps had the zero meridian through the middle of this building. After that date, they reluctantly agreed that 0° longitude should pass through a small village in Normandy that happens to be due south of Greenwich.

Bd St-Jacques, becoming bd Auguste-Blanqui, with its overhead métro line, runs east from place Denfert-Rochereau to place d'Italie, hub of the 13ᵉ. If you head south you'll pass Ste-Anne's psychiatric hospital where the great political philosopher, Louis Althusser, died after being committed for murdering his wife. One block further on is **Parc Montsouris**, a tempting place to collapse but you'll be up against more of the city's obsessionally whistling park police the moment you touch the grass. A beautiful reproduction of the Bardo palace in Tunis, built for the 1876 *Exposition Universelle*, is finally being restored. Lenin took strolls here in 1909 when he was living with his mother, wife and sisters at **4 rue Marie-Rose** (now a small museum). Later walkers in the park no doubt included Dali, Lurcat, Miller, Durrell and other artists who found homes in the tiny cobbled street of **Villa Seurat** off rue de la Tombe. **Square de Montsouris**, running between rue Nansorty and av Reille, is a typical secretive and verdant early twentieth-century street. Close by at 53 av Reille is one of Le Corbusier's earliest Paris commissions.

Rue du Commerce and the western riverfront

It was in the **rue du Commerce**, west of Montparnasse, that George Orwell worked as a dishwasher, described in his *Down and Out in Paris and London*. These days it is a lively, old-fashioned high street full of small shops and peeling, shuttered houses. Towards the end of the street, just past a fading Belle-Époque butchers on the west side, is **place du Commerce**, with a bandstand in the middle, a model of old-fashioned petit-bourgeois respectability. It might be a frozen frame from a 1930s movie. Cafés and *pâtisseries* proliferate as rue du Commerce ends on the pleasant open space of place Etienne-Pernet, where cottagey houses still survive. There's nothing very special to the streets either side of rue des Entrepreneurs.

The western edge of the 15ᵉ *arrondissement* fronts the Seine from the **Porte de Javel** to the Eiffel Tower. From Pont Mirabeau northwards, the river bank is marred by a sort of mini-Défense development of half-cocked futuristic towers with pretentious galactic names, rising out of a litter-blown pedestrian platform some ten metres above street level. Far pleasanter riverside strolling is to be had on the narrow midstream island, the **Allée des Cygnes**, which you can reach from the Pont de Grenelle. A scaled-down version of the **Statue of Liberty** stands at the downstream end.

Between Pont Mirabeau (Mᵒ Javel), Pont de Garigliano and place Balard is a very new and very underused park, the **Parc Citroën**, so named because the site used to be the *Citroën* motor works. The best features are the glasshouses full of exotic smelling shrubs – the gardens are less successful, with far too much concrete.

The Beaux Quartiers and Bois de Boulogne

The **Beaux Quartiers** are the 16ᵉ and 17ᵉ *arrondissements*. The 16ᵉ is aristocratic and rich; the 17ᵉ – or at least the southern part of it – middle-class and rich, embodying the cautious values of the nineteenth-century manufacturing and trading classes. The northern half of the 16ᵉ, towards place Victor-Hugo and place de l'Étoile, is leafy and distinctly metropolitan in feel. The southern part, around the old villages of **Auteuil** and **Passy**, has an almost provincial feel, and is full of pleasant surprises for the walker. There are several interesting pieces of early twentieth-century architecture scattered through the district, especially by Hector Guimard (the designer of the swirly green Art Nouveau métro stations) and by Le Corbusier and Mallet-Stevens, architects of the first "cubist" buildings. Also in the area is the wonderful **Musée Marmottan**.

Auteuil

A good place to start an architectural exploration is the **Église-d'Auteuil** métro station, with several Guimard buildings in the vicinity for aficionados: 34 rue Boileau, 8 av de la Villa-de-la-Réunion, 41 rue Chardon-Lagache, 192 av de Versailles and 39 bd Exelmans. From the métro exit, **rue d'Auteuil**, with a lingering village high-street air, leads to **place Lorrain** with a Saturday market. There are more Guimard houses at the further end of rue La Fontaine, which begins here: no. 60 is perhaps the best in the city. On rue Poussin, just off the *place*, is the entrance to **Villa Montmorency**, a typical 16ᵉ villa, a sort of private village of leafy lanes and English-style gardens. Gide and the Goncourt brothers of *Prix* fame lived in this one.

Behind it is rue Dr-Blanche where, in a cul-de-sac on the right, are Le Corbusier's first private houses (1923), one of them now the **Fondation Le Corbusier** (Mon–Fri 10am–1pm & 2–6pm; closed Aug). Built in strictly Cubist style, very plain, with windows in bands, the only extravagance is the raising of one wing on piers and a curved frontage. They look commonplace enough now, but what a contrast to anything that had gone before. Further along rue Dr-Blanche, the tiny **rue Mallet-Stevens** was built entirely by Mallet-Stevens also in Cubist style.

After taking a left at the northern end of rue Dr-Blanche, and right on bd Beauséjour, a subway under the disused *Petite Ceinture* train line brings you out by av Raphaël and hence to the **Musée Marmottan**, 7 rue Louis-Boilly, 16ᵉ (Mº Muette; Tues–Sun 10am–5.30pm; 35F), the collection of Monet paintings bequeathed by the artist's son. Among them is the canvas entitled *Impression, Soleil Levant* (*Impression, Sunrise*), an 1872 rendering of a misty sunrise over Le Havre, whose title the critics usurped to give the Impressionist movement its name. There's a dazzling collection of canvases from Monet's last years at Giverny, including several *Nymphéas* (water lilies), *Le Pont Japonais*, *L'Allée des Rosiers*, *La Saule Pleureur*, where rich colours are laid on in thick, excited whorls and lines. To all intents and purposes, these are abstractions, much more "advanced" than the work of, say, Renoir, Monet's exact contemporary. *Impression, Soleil Levant* was stolen from the gallery in October 1985, along with four other Monets, two Renoirs, a Berthe Morisot and a Naruse. After a police operation lasting five years and going as far afield as Japan, the paintings were discovered in a villa in southern Corsica and are back on show – with greatly tightened security measures.

Passy

Passy, too, offers scope for a good meandering walk, from place du Trocadéro to Balzac's house and up rue de Passy. To the south of Passy métro station, between av Marcel Proust and the river, is the cobbled **rue d'Ankara** with the gates of an eighteenth-century *château* half hidden by greenery and screened by a high wall. This is the Turkish embassy but was once a clinic where the pioneering Dr Blanche tried to treat the mad Maupassant and Gérard de Nerval, amongst others. From its gates **rue Berton**, a cobbled path with gas lights still in place, follows round the ivy-covered garden wall to an old green-shuttered house with a boundary stone bearing the date 1731. Apart from the embassy security, there is nothing to say that it is not still 1731 in this tiny backwater. The house was Balzac's in the 1840s and now contains **memorabilia** and a **library**.

Just across the road, **rue de l'Annonciation** gives more of the flavour of old Passy. You may not want your Bechstein repaired or your furniture lacquered, but as you approach the end of the street there'll be no holding back the salivary glands. At place de Passy you join the old high street, **rue de Passy**, and a parade of eye-catching brand-name boutiques stretching up to métro La Muette.

Bois de Boulogne

The **Bois de Boulogne**, running all down the west side of the 16e, is supposedly modelled on London's Hyde Park, though it is a very French interpretation. It offers all sorts of facilities: the **Jardin d'Acclimatation** has lots of attractions for kids (see p.148); the **Parc de Bagatelle** features beautiful displays of tulips, hyacinths and daffodils in the first half of April, irises in May, water lilies and roses at the end of June; a riding school; **bike rental** at the entrance to the Jardin d'Acclimatation; **boating** on the Lac Inférieur; **race courses** at Longchamp and Auteuil. The best, and wildest, part for walking is towards the southwest corner. When it was opened to the public in the eighteenth century, people said of it, "*Les mariages du bois de Boulogne ne se font pas devant Monsieur le Curé*" ("Unions cemented in the Bois de Boulogne do not take place in the presence of a priest"). Today's after-dark unions are no less disreputable.

If you have any interest in the beautiful and highly specialized skills, techniques and artefacts developed in the long ages that preceded industrialization, standardization and mass-production, then you should find the fascinating **Musée National des Arts et Traditions Populaires**, 6 av du Mahatma Gandhi, Bois de Boulogne (Mº Les Sablons/Porte-Maillot; daily except Tues 9.45am–5.15pm; 20F, 28F with exhibitions, Sun 14F), beside main entrance to Jardin d'Acclimatation. Boat-building, shepherding, farming, weaving, blacksmithing, pottery, stone-cutting, games, clairvoyance . . . all beautifully illustrated and displayed.

La Défense

Angled a few degrees out from the far western end of the Voie Triomphale, **La Grande Arche** has put the business development of **La Défense** (Mº Grande Arche de la Défense/*RER* La Défense) high on the list of places to which visitors to Paris must pay homage, a beautiful and astounding structure, a 112-metre hollow cube, clad in white marble. Suspended within the hollow – which could shelter Notre-Dame with ease – are the open lift shafts and a "cloud" panoply. It houses a government ministry, international businesses, an information centre on the European Union and, in the roof section, the *Arche de la Fraternité* foundation who stage exhibitions and conferences on issues related to human rights. You can ride up to the roof (July & Aug Mon & Thurs 9am–7pm, Tues & Wed 9am–5pm, Fri 9am–9pm, Sat 10am–9pm, Sun 10am–7pm; otherwise Sun–Fri 9am–6pm, Sat 9am–7pm; 35F). As well as having access to the *Arche de la Fraternité* exhibitions, you can admire the "Map of the Heavens" marble patios and, on a clear day, scan from the marble path on the parvis below you to the Arc de Triomphe and beyond to the Louvre.

Between the Grande Arche and the river is the **business complex** of La Défense, a perfect monument to the horrors of late twentieth-century capitalism. There is no formal pattern to the arrangements of towers. Token apartment blocks, offices of *ELF*, *Esso*, *IBM*, banks and other businesses compete for size, dazzle of surface and ability to make you dizzy. Mercifully, bizarre **artworks** transform the nightmare into comic entertainment. Joan Miró's giant wobbly creatures despair at their misfit status beneath the biting edges and curveless heights of the buildings. Alexander Calder's red iron offering is a *stabile* rather than a mobile and between them a black marble metronome shape without a beat releases a goal-less line across the parvis. A nineteenth-century war memorial perches on a concrete plinth in front of a plastic-look waterfall and, further down, disembodied people clutch each other around endlessly repeated concrete flowerbeds.

You'll find details of all the sculptures in the **Art Défense** exhibition space beside the waterfall, and, if you're desperate to hand over money to the firms surrounding you, there's the enormous *Quatre-Temps* shopping centre to the left of the Grande Arche as you face it, and an FNAC bookshop in the *CNIT* building oppposite. Fun but expensive is **Le Dôme-Imax**, a 180° projection cinema between *Quatre Temps* and the Grande Arche (daily 12.15–8pm; 55F; programme details in *Pariscope*).

The 17ᵉ

The 17ᵉ *arrondissement* is most interesting in its eastern half. The classier western end is cold and soulless, cut by too many wide and uniform boulevards. A route that takes in the best of it would be from **place des Ternes**, with its cafés and flower market, through the stately wrought-iron gates of av Hoche into the small and formal **Parc Monceau**, surrounded by pompous residences. **Rue de Lévis** (a few blocks up rue Legendre from Mᵒ Monceau) has one of the city's most strident, colourful and appetizing markets every day of the week except Monday and is also a good restaurant area, particularly up around rue des Dames, rue Cheroy and the bottom-line rue Dulong.

Further north still, across the St-Lazare train tracks, **rue des Batignolles** is the heart of Batignolles "village", now sufficiently self-conscious to have formed an association for the preservation of its *"caractère villageois"*. At the north end of the street is a semicircular *place* with cafés and restaurants framing a small colonnaded church whose entrance was modelled on the Madeleine. Behind it is the tired and trampled greenery of square Batignolles, with the marshalling yards beyond. The long **rue des Moines** leads northeast towards Guy-Moquet. This is the working-class Paris of the movies, all small, animated, friendly shops, four- to five-story houses in shades of peeling grey, brown-stained bars where men drink standing at the *zinc*.

Montmartre cemetery

From Guy-Moquet it's a short walk back along av de St-Ouen to **rue du Capitaine-Madon**, a cobbled alley with washing strung at the windows, leading to the wall of the Montmartre cemetery, where hopefully you will still find the Hôtel Beau-Lieu. Ramshackle, peeling, on a tiny courtyard full of plants, this epitomizes the kind-hearted, no-nonsense, sepia Paris that every romantic visitor secretly cherishes. Most of the guests have been there fifteen years or more. Tucked down below street level in the hollow of an old quarry, the **cemetery** itself (Mon–Fri 8am–5.30pm, Sat 8am–8.30pm, Sun 8am–9pm) has its entrance on av Rachel under rue Caulaincourt. A tangle of trees and funereal pomposity, it holds the graves of Zola, Stendhal, Berlioz, Degas, Feydeau, Offenbach, Dalida and François Truffaut, among others.

Montmartre and northern Paris

Montmartre lies in the middle of the largely petty-bourgeois and working-class 18ᵉ *arrondissement*, respectable round the slopes of the *Butte*, distinctly less so towards the **Gare du Nord** and **Gare de l'Est**, where depressing slums crowd along the train tracks; on its northern edge lies the extensive St-Ouen flea market. The Butte itself has a relaxed, sunny, countrified air; Pigalle, at the foot of the hill, is full of sex shops and peep shows interspersed with tired-looking women in shop doorways.

Place des Abbesses and up to the Butte

In spite of being one of the city's chief tourist attractions, the **Butte Montmartre** manages to retain the quiet, almost secretive, air of its rural origins. The most popular access route is via the rue de Steinkerque and the steps below the Sacré-Cœur (the funicular railway from place Suzanne-Valadon is covered by the *Carte Orange*). For a quieter approach, go up via place des Abbesses or rue Lepic.

Place des Abbesses is postcard-pretty, with one of the few complete surviving Guimard **métro entrances**. East, at the Chapelle des Auxiliatrices in rue Yvonne-Le-Tac, Ignatius Loyola founded the Jesuit movement in 1534. It is also supposed to be the place where Saint Denis, the first bishop of Paris, had his head chopped off by the Romans around 250 AD, carrying it until he dropped, where the cathedral of St-Denis now stands north of the city.

To continue from place des Abbesses to the top of the Butte, two quiet and attractive routes are up **rue de la Vieuville** and the stairs in rue Drevet to the minuscule **place du Calvaire** with a lovely view back over the city, or up **rue Tholozé**, then right below the **Moulin de la Galette** – the last survivor of Montmartre's forty-odd windmills, immortalized by Renoir – into rue des Norvins.

Artistic associations abound hereabouts. Zola, Berlioz, Turgenev, Seurat, Degas and Van Gogh lived in the area. Picasso, Braque and Juan Gris invented Cubism in an old piano factory in place Emile-Goudeau, known as the **Bateau-Lavoir**, still serving as artists' studios, though the original building burnt down some years ago. And Toulouse-Lautrec's inspiration, the **Moulin Rouge**, survives also, albeit a mere shadow of its former self, on the corner of bd de Clichy and place Blanche.

The **Musée de Montmartre** at 12 rue Cortot (daily except Mon 11am–6pm; 25F), just over the brow of the hill, tries to recapture something of the feel of those pioneering days, but it's a bit of a disappointment, except for the occasionally excellent temporary exhibition. The house itself, rented at various times by Renoir, Dufy, Suzanne Valadon, and her alcoholic son Utrillo, is worth visiting for the view over the neat terraces of the tiny **Montmartre vineyard** and the north side of the Butte. The entrance to the vineyard is on the steep rue de Saules.

Place du Tertre and Sacré-Cœur

The **place du Tertre** is the heart of tourist Montmartre, photogenic but totally bogus, jammed with tourists, overpriced restaurants and "artists" doing quick portraits while you wait. Between place du Tertre and the Sacré-Cœur, the old church of **St-Pierre** is all that remains of the Benedictine abbey that occupied the Butte Montmartre from the twelfth century on. Though much altered, it still retains its Romanesque and early Gothic feel. In it are four ancient columns, two by the door, two in the choir, leftovers from a Roman shrine that stood on the hill – *mons mercurii*, Mercury's Hill, the Romans called it. As for the **Sacré-Cœur** itself, graceless and vulgar pastiche though it is, its white pimply domes are an essential part of the Paris skyline. The best thing about it is the **view** from the **tower** (daily summer 9am–7pm; winter 9am–6pm; 15F), almost as high as the Eiffel Tower and showing the layout of the whole city. Construction was started in the 1870s on the initiative of the Catholic Church to atone for the "crimes" of the Commune. But **square Willette,** the space at the foot of the monumental staircase, is named after the local artist who turned out on inauguration day to shout, "Long live the devil!"

The Flea Market of St-Ouen

Officially open 7.30am to 7pm – unofficially, from 5am – the **puces de St-Ouen** (M°️ Porte-de-Clignancourt) claim to be the largest flea market in the world, the name "flea" deriving from the state of the secondhand mattresses, clothes and other junk sold here when the market first operated outside the city walls. Nowadays it is predominantly a proper – and expensive – antiques market (mainly furniture, but including old café bar counters, telephones, traffic lights, posters, juke boxes and petrol pumps), with what is left of the rag-and-bone element confined to the further reaches of **rue Fabre and rue Lécuyer.**

Pigalle

From place Clichy in the west to Barbès-Rochechouart in the east, the hill of Montmartre is underlined by the sleazy **boulevards of Clichy and Rochechouart**, the centre of the roadway often occupied by bumper-car pistes and other funfair sideshows. At the Barbès end, where the métro clatters by on iron trestles, the crowds teem round the *Tati* department stores, the city's cheapest, while the pavements are lined with West and North African street vendors offering cloth, watches and trinkets. At the place Clichy end, tour buses from all over Europe feed their contents into massive hotels. In the middle, between place Blanche and place Pigalle, sex shows, sex shops, tiny bars where hostesses lurk in complicated tackle, and street prostitutes, both male and female, coexist with one of the city's most elegant private *villas* on av Frochot, and, in the adjacent streets, the best **specialist music shops**.

The Goutte d'Or

Along the north side of bd de la Chapelle, between bd Barbès and the Gare du Nord rail lines, stretches the poetically named quarter of the **Goutte d'Or** ("the Drop of Gold"), a name that derives from the medieval vineyard that occupied this site. It has gradually become an immigrant ghetto since World War I, when large numbers of North Africans were first imported to replenish the ranks of Frenchmen dying in the trenches. It's currently in the throes of redevelopment that inevitably is changing its character, but old men still talk for hours over tea in the numerous tiny cafés; restaurants serve Tunisian delicacies for next to nothing; Raï music resonates from the upper balconies. Understandably, there is a certain suspicion towards outsiders, whether yuppies pondering future property prices or tourists wanting to photograph urban seediness. Wednesday and Saturday, when the **bd de la Chapelle market** attracts large crowds, are perhaps the best days to go.

Canal St-Martin and La Villette

The **Bassin de la Villette** and the **canals** at the northeastern gate of the city were for generations the centre of a densely populated working-class district. The jobs were in the main meat market and abattoirs of Paris or in the many interlinked industries that spread around the waterways. The amusements were skating or swimming, betting on cockfights or eating at the numerous restaurants famed for their fresh meat. Now La Villette is the wonderworld of laser-guided culture, the pride of politicians, and the recipient of over a billion pounds' worth of public spending. It's vast and has become progressively less and less appealing as more and more has been added to it.

The whole Villette complex stands at the junction of the **Ourcq** and **St-Denis canals**. The first was built by Napoléon to bring fresh water into the city. The second is an extension of the Canal St-Martin built as a short cut to the great western loop of the Seine around Paris.

Canal St-Martin and Place de Stalingrad

The **Canal St-Martin** runs underground at the Bastille to surface again in bd Jules-Ferry by the rue du Faubourg-du-Temple, another key point in the annals of revolutionary street fighting. Barricaded by the *Communards* in 1871 and the *quarante-huitards* in 1848, it is now a peaceable, populous, run-down street of small shops, cafés, Arab sweatshops and crummy passages. The southern section of the canal is the most attractive. Plane trees line the cobbled *quais* and elegant high, arched footbridges punctuate the spaces between locks. A few momentoes of the area's old identity remain, such as the façade of the **Hôtel du Nord** of Marcel Carné's film, at 102 quai de Jemappes. But grossly bland and strident apartment blocks have elbowed in among the traditional, solid, mid-nineteenth-century residences, and north of rue des Recollects redevelopment has mutilated both banks.

You have to make a brief detour away from the canalside at **place de Stalingrad**. The centrepiece of the *place*, the beautifully restored Rotonde de la Villette, was one of Ledoux's **toll-houses** in Louis XVI's tax wall, where taxes were levied on all goods coming into the city – a major bone of contention in the lead-up to the 1789 revolution.

Beyond the *place* is the **Bassin de la Villette** dock, now used for Sunday strolls, fishing and canoeing. Recobbled, and with its dockside buildings converted into offices for canal boat trips, the Bassin has lost all vestiges of its former status as France's premier port. At rue de Crimée, where a unique hydraulic bridge crosses the canal, one of the facing pair of warehouses, itself now converted into trendy offices, survives. If you keep to the south bank on quai de la Marne, you can cross directly into the Parc de la Villette.

The Parc de la Villette

The major extravagance of La Villette is the **Cité des Sciences et de l'Industrie** (M° Porte de la Villette; Tues–Sun 10am–6pm; 45F; *Géode* Tues–Sun 10am–8pm 50F, combined ticket with *Cité* 85F, available from *Géode* only; for *Cité des Enfants*, see p.148). This high-tech museum devoted to science and all its applications is built into the concrete hulk of the abandoned abattoirs on the north side of the canal de l'Ourcq. Three times the size of Beaubourg, this is certainly one of the most astounding monuments to be added to the capital in the last decade. Giant walls of glass hang beneath a dark-blue lattice of steel, with white rod walkways accelerating out of the building across a mock fortress moat, crow's-nests and cantilevered platforms, bridges and suspended walkways, the different levels linked by lifts and escalators around a huge central space open to the full forty-metre height of the roof. It may be colossal, but you are more likely to lose yourself mentally rather than physically and come out after several hours reeling with images and ideas, while none the wiser in actual fact about DNA, quasars, bacteria reproduction, rocket launching or whatever.

The **permanent exhibition**, called *Explora*, covers different subjects such as microbes, maths, sounds, robots, flying, energy, space, information, language etc. The emphasis is on exploring and the means used are interactive computers, videos, holograms, animated models and games. In *Expressions et comportements* you can intervene in stories acted out on videos, changing the behaviour of the characters to engineer a different outcome. Hydroponic plants grow for real in a green bridge across the central space. You can steer robots through mazes; make music by your own movements; try out a flight simulation; watch computer-guided puppet shows and holograms of different periods' visions of the universe.

When all this interrogation and stimulation becomes too much, you can relax at the café within *Explora* (*niveau 2* by the planetarium). When you want your head to start reeling again, just join the queue for the **planetarium**. Back on the ground floor there's a **cinema**; an exhibition of current scientific research; and a whole programme of **temporary exhibitions**. Below ground there are **libraries, restaurants** and an **aquarium**.

In front of the complex balances the **Géode**, a bubble of reflecting steel dropped from an intergalactic *boules* game into a pool of water that ripples the mirrored image of the Cité. Inside the bubble, half the sphere is a screen for Omnimax 180° projections, not noted for their plots but a great visual experience. Or there's the Cinaxe projection (between the Cité and the Canal St-Denis), where the seats move in synchronation with the movie (check *Pariscope* for programme details). Close by is a real 1957 French **submarine**, *L'Argonaute*, and towards the bridge over the canal de l'Ourcq, a **dragon slide**. South of the canal are bizarrely landscaped gardens, with peculiar sculptures; over to the east is the **Zenith** inflatable rock-music venue, and to the south the largest of the old **market halls** – an iron-frame structure designed by Baltard, the engineer of the vanished Les Halles pavilions. It is now a vast and brilliant exhibition space, the **Grande Salle**. South of the Grande Salle is the brand new **Cité de la Musique**, in two complexes to either side of the Porte-de-Pantin entrance. The one to the west houses the national music academy and was designed with the worst indulgence to architectural pseudo-intellectualism. It combines waves and funnels, irregular polygons and non-parallel lines, gangways, greenhouses and agressive slit windows. The block opposite, due to be completed in late 1995, will have a concert hall, a museum of music, and commercial outlets for everything to do with music-making.

The Parc de la Villette is accessible from Mº Porte-de-la-Villette to the north or Mº Porte-de-Pantin to the south. There are information centres by the northern entrance and by the canal bridge.

Belleville, Ménilmontant, Père-Lachaise and the Bis de Vincennes

The **eastern districts** of Paris are no longer the revolutionary hotbeds they were in the nineteenth century, and the predominantly working-class identity of the area is changing as a slow process of rebuilding takes place. **Belleville** and **Ménilmontant** have long had large immigrant populations of Slavs, Greeks, Chinese, Vietnamese, Jews, Arabs, Armenians, Senegalese, Malian – still very much in evidence against a backdrop of some much more pleasing architectural additions than previous shelving-unit housin. Exploring the old villagey streets and admiring the best of the new constructions are the main pleasures of this part of town, plus the views down onto the city, and for a focus to wander, the **Père-Lachaise cemetery**.

Parc des Buttes-Chaumont

At the northern end of the Belleville heights, a short walk from La Villette, is the **parc des Buttes-Chaumont** (Mº Buttes-Chaumont or Botzaris), constructed by Haussmann in the 1860s to camouflage what until then had been a desolate warren of disused quarries and miserable shacks. The sculpted beak-shaped park stays open all night and, equally rarely for Paris, you're not cautioned off the grass. At its centre is a huge rock upholding a delicate Corinthian temple and surrounded by a lake which you cross via a suspension bridge or the shorter Pont des Suicides. Louis Aragon, the literary grand old man of the French Communist Party, wrote of this bridge that it claimed victims among passers-by who had no intention of dying, but found themselves suddenly tempted by the abyss. Feeble metal grills erected along its sides have put an end to such impulses.

Belleville and Ménilmontant

The route from Buttes-Chaumont to Père-Lachaise will take you through the one-time villages of **Belleville** and **Ménilmontant**. Many of the old village lanes disappeared in the 1960s and 1970s tower-block mania, but others have now been opened up, and many of the newest buildings make imaginative infill, following the height and curves of their older neighbours. Dozens of cobbled and gardened *villas* remain intact: around place Rhin et Danube just east of Buttes-Chaumont, up steps from place O-Chanute near Porte de Bagnolet, between rue Boyer (with a 1920s Soviet-style building at no. 25) and rue des Pyrénées just north of Père-Lachaise.

The first main street you cross coming down from Buttes-Chaumont, **rue de Belleville**, has become the new Chinatown of Paris. Vietnamese and Chinese shops and restaurants have proliferated over the last few years, adding considerable visual and gastronomic cheer to the area. African and oriental fruits, spices, music and fabrics can be bought at the **bd de Belleville market** on Tuesdays and Fridays. Edith Piaf was dumped, a few hours old, on the steps of no. 72 rue de Belleville, and has a small

museum dedicated to her at 5 rue Créspin-du-Gast (M° Ménilmontant/St-Maur; Mon–Thurs 1–6pm, by appointment on ☎43.55.52.72). Rue Ramponneau, just southeast of the crossroads with bd de Belleville – and now entirely rebuilt – was where the last *Communard* on the last barricade held out alone for a final fifteen minutes.

From almost every street you get fantastic views down onto the city, particularly from **rue de Ménilmontant**, just before it links above rue de l'Ermitage, and just down from one of the best bakeries in Paris, *Ganachaud* at no. 150–154. But the best place to watch the sun setting on the city is the **Parc de Belleville** (M° Couronnes/Pyrenées), which descends in a series of terraces and waterfalls from rue Piat.

Père-Lachaise cemetery

The **cimetière Père-Lachaise** (M° Gambetta, Père-Lachaise and Alexandre-Dumas; daily 7.30am–6pm) is like a miniature city devastated by a neutron bomb: a great number of dead, empty houses and temples of every size and style, and exhausted survivors, some congregating aimlessly, some searching persistently. The cemetery was opened in 1804 after an urgent stop had been put on further burials in the overflowing city cemeteries and churchyards, and to be interred in Père Lachaise quickly became the ultimate symbol of riches and success.

Swarms flock to ex-Doors lead singer Jim Morrison's tomb (division 6), where a motley assembly of European hippies roll joints against a backdrop of Doors' lyrics and declarations of love and drug consumption, graffitied in every western language on every stone in sight. Colette's tomb (division 4), close to the main entrance, is very plain though always covered in flowers. The same is true for Sarah Bernhardt's (division 44) and the great chanteuse Edith Piaf's (division 97). Marcel Proust lies in his family's conventional tomb (division 85), which honours the medical fame of his father.

Corot (division 24) and Balzac (division 48) both have superb busts, Balzac looking particularly satisfied with his life. Chopin (division 11) has a willowy muse weeping for his loss. The most impressive of the individual tombs is Oscar Wilde's, for which Jacob Epstein sculpted a strange Pharaonic winged messenger. The inscription is a grim verse from *The Ballad of Reading Gaol*. Below Wilde's grave you'll find in division 96 the grave of painter Modigliani and his lover Jeanne Herbuterne, who killed herself in crazed grief a few days after he died in agony from meningitis.

But it is the monuments to the collective, violent deaths that have the power to change a sunny outing to Père-Lachaise into a much more sombre experience. In division 97, you'll find the memorials to those who died in the Nazi concentration camps, to executed Resistance fighters and to those who were never accounted for in the genocide of the last world war. The sculptures are relentless in their images of inhumanity, of people forced to collaborate in their own degradation and death. Finally, there is the *Mur des Fedérés* (division 76), the wall where the last troops of the Paris Commune were lined up and shot in the final days of the battle. The man who ordered their execution, Adolphe Thiers, lies in the centre of the cemetery in division 55.

Down to the Faubourg St-Antoine

To the south and west of Père-Lachaise, off **rue de la Roquette** and **rue de Charonne**, there's nothing very special about the passages and ragged streets that make up the 11ᵉ *arrondissement*, except that they are utterly Parisian, with the odd detail of a building, the display of veg in a simple greengrocer's, the sunlight on a café table or the graffiti on a Second Empire street fountain to charm an aimless wanderer.

There are quiet havens from the mania of the Bastille traffic in the courtyards of **rue du Faubourg-St-Antoine**. Since the fifteenth century, this has been the principal artisan and working-class *quartier* of Paris, the cradle of revolutions and mother of street-fighters. From its beginnings the principal trade associated with it has been **furniture-making**; the maze of interconnecting yards and passages are still full of the workshops

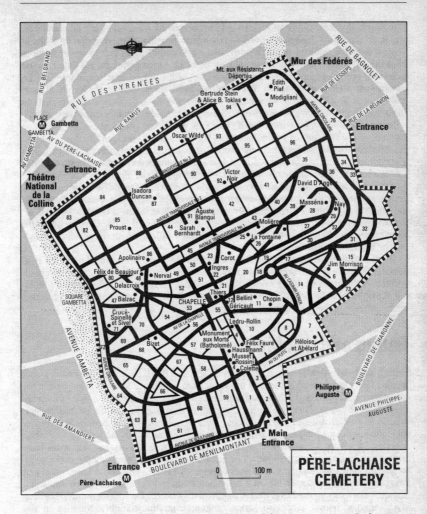

PÈRE-LACHAISE
CEMETERY

of the related trades: marquetry, stainers, polishers, inlayers etc, many of whom are still producing the classic styles of French furniture.

Out to Vincennes

From place de la Nation, a fifteen-minute walk from the Père-Lachaise cemetery, the cours de Vincennes runs out over the *boulevard périphérique* to the Bois de Vincennes, the largest park in the city and taken from the Abbaye de St-Maur in the eleventh century for the king.

Just outside the forest – past the 1930s colonial façade of jungles, hard-working natives and the place names of the French empire – is the **Musée des Arts Africains et Océaniens**, 293 av Daumesnil, one of the least crowded museums in the city (Mº Porte-Dorée; Mon & Wed–Fri 9.45am–noon & 1.30–5.20pm, Sat & Sun 10am–6pm;

27F; Sun half price). It has an African gold brooch of curled-up sleeping crocodiles on one floor and, in the basement, five live crocodiles in a tiny pit surrounded by tanks of tropical fish. Imperialism is much in evidence in a gathering of culture and creatures from the old French colonies: hardly any of the black African artefacts are dated, as the collection predates European acknowledgement of history on that continent, and the captions are a bit suspicious too. These masks and statues, furniture, adornments and tools should be exhibited with paintings by Expressionists, Cubists and Surrealists to see in which direction inspiration went. Picasso and friends certainly came here often.

In the **Bois de Vincennes** itself, you can spend an afternoon boating on Lac Daumesnil (by the zoo) or rent a bike from the same place and feed the ducks on Lac des Minimes on the other side of the wood (or bus #112 from Vincennes métro). The fenced enclave on the southern side of Lac Daumesnil is a **Buddhist centre** with a Tibetan temple, Vietnamese chapel and international pagoda, all of which are visitable. As far as real woods go, the *bois* opens out once you're east of av de St-Maurice, but the area is so overrun with roads that countryside sensations don't stand much chance. To the north is the **Parc Floral**, with lily ponds and a Four Season Garden for all-year-round displays (see p.149 for kids' activities). To the east of it is the **Cartoucherie de Vincennes**, an old ammunitions factory, now home to four theatre companies including the radical *Théâtre du Soleil*.

On the northern edge of the *bois*, the **Château de Vincennes**, royal medieval residence, then state prison, porcelain factory, weapons dump and military training school, is still undergoing restoration work started by Napoléon III. A real behemoth of a building, it's unlikely to be beautified by the removal of the nineteenth-century gun positions or any amount of stone-scrubbing.

Eating and drinking

Eating and drinking is one of the chief delights of Paris, as it is in the country as a whole. There is tremendous variety of foods, from Sengalese to Caribbean, from Thai to eastern European and North African, as well as regional French cuisines, notably from the southwest. There's also the diversity of eating and drinking establishments: luxurious **restaurants** in the traditional style or elbow-to-elbow bench- and trestle-table jobs; spacious **brasseries** and **cafés** where you can watch the world go by while nibbling on a baguette sandwich, or dark, cavernous **beer cellars** and tiny **wine bars** – often run by English expats – with sawdust on the floor and providing the opportunity to sample wines by the glass from every region of France. You could take coffee and cakes in a chintzy *salon de thé*, in a bookshop or gallery, or even in the confines of a mosque. Bars can be medieval vaults, minimalist or postmodern design units, London-style pubs or period pieces in styles ranging from the Naughty Nineties to the Swinging Sixties. The variety is endless and the distinctions between bars, cafés, pubs, ice cream parlours, sandwich bars, brasseries and wine bars can't always be clearly drawn. **Gay** establishments proliferate in the Marais and around the Bastille *quartier*, the only **lesbian** bar in town is *La Champmeslé* in the 2e.

STUDENT RESTAURANTS

Anyone in possession of an International Student Card or *Carte Jeune* (for under-26s) is eligible to eat for 12.30F in the university restaurants known as "*Resto-U's*" managed by *CROUS de Paris*, 39 av Georges-Bernanos, 5e (Mº Port-Royal). They will provide a complete list of addresses and opening hours; tickets come in *carnets* of ten and cost 24.60F if you are over 26 and not a student.

PARIS FOR VEGETARIANS

The chances of finding vegetarian main dishes on the menus of regular restaurants are not good. However, even if you don't eat fish, it is possible to have a vegetarian meal at even the most meat-oriented brasserie by choosing dishes from among the starters (*crudités*, for example, are nearly always available) and soups, or by asking for an omelette.

All the establishments listed below are specifically **vegetarian restaurants** reviewed in the pages which follow.

Aquarius 1, 54 rue Ste-Croix-de-la-Bretonnerie, 4ᵉ. p.126.

Aquarius 2, 40 rue Gergovie, 14ᵉ. p.133.

Bol en Bois, 35 rue Pascal, 13ᵉ. p.133.

Country Life, 6 rue Daunou, 2ᵉ. p.125.

Au Grain de Folie, 24 rue de La Vieuville, 18ᵉ. p.136.

Le Grenier de Notre-Dame, 18 rue de la Búcherie, 5ᵉ. p.127.

Joy in Food, 2 rue Truffaut, 17ᵉ. p.135.

Piccolo Teatro, 6 rue des Écouffes, 4ᵉ. p.127.

La Truffe, 31 rue Vieille-du-Temple, 4ᵉ. p.127.

It's true that the old-time cheap neighbourhood cafés and bistros are a dying breed, while fast-food chains have burgeoned at an alarming speed. Quality is also in decline at the lower end of the restaurant market, particularly in tourist hotspots. But however much Parisians bemoan the changing times, you'll find you're still spoiled for choice even on a modest budget. There are numerous **fixed price menus** for around 80F, particularly at lunchtime, providing staple dishes; for 150F you'll have the choice of more interesting dishes; and for 200F, you should be getting some gourmet satisfaction. There are several **restaurant chains,** the best being *L'Amanguier* and *La Criée* (specializing in seafood). *Batifol* is acceptable if rather uninspired; *Hippopotamus* is very mediocre; and *Le Bistro Romain* is desperately trying to regain its previously good reputation.

The big **boulevard cafés and brasseries** are always more expensive than those a little further removed, and addresses in the smarter or more touristy *arrondissements* set prices soaring. A snack or drink on the Champs-Élysées, place St-Germain-de-Prés or rue de Rivoli, for instance, will be double or triple the price of Belleville, Batignolles or the southern 14ᵉ. Many bars have **happy hours** but prices can double after 10pm, and any clearly trendy, glitzy or stylish place is bound to be expensive.

The different eating and drinking establishments are listed here under *arrondissement*. They are divided into **Restaurants**, including some brasseries, and **Bars and Cafés**, which includes snacks, ice cream parlours and *salons de thé*. You'll also find full lists of **vegetarian** (not Paris' strongest suit) and **late-night** possibilities.

1ᵉʳ
BARS AND CAFÉS

Angélina, 226 rue de Rivoli, 1ᵉʳ (Mᵒ Tuileries). Daily 10am–7pm; closed Aug. A long-established gilded cage, where the well-coiffed sip the best hot chocolate in town. *Pâtisseries* and other desserts of the same high quality. Not cheap.

Aux Bons Crus, 7 rue des Petits-Champs, 1ᵉʳ (Mᵒ Palais-Royal). Mon–Fri 8am–10pm, Sat 8.30am–6pm. A relaxed workaday place which has been serving good wines and cheese, sausage and ham for over eighty years. Wine from 10F a glass; plate of cold meats from 30F.

Café Costes, 4 rue Berger, 1ᵉʳ (Mᵒ Châtelet-Les Halles). Tedious, overpriced, shallow and ugly. The design of the loos is original, but has failed to take account of the effect water smears have on glass.

Le Cochon à l'Oreille, 15 rue Montmartre, 1ᵉʳ (Mᵒ Châtelet-Les Halles/Étienne-Marcel). Mon–Sat 7am-5pm. This classic little café, with raffeta chairs outside and scenes of the old market in ceramic tiles inside, opens early for the local fishmongers and meat traders.

Chez Jo-Jo et Michele, 79 rue St-Honoré, 1ᵉʳ (Mᵒ Louvre-Rivoli). Mon–Sat noon–2pm. A leftover from the market days where local butchers eat. Excellent meat. 69F menu.

Restorama, Le Carrousel du Louvre, 1ᵉʳ (Mᵒ Louvre). Daily 9am–9pm. One vast underground fast-food eating hall served by over a dozen different outlets: rotisseries, hamburgers, pizzas, Tex-Mex, Chinese, Lebanese, Japanese, crêperies, salad bars – easy to eat for under 40F. Access from pl du Carrousel or the Louvre pyramid.

Le Rubis, 10 rue du Marché-St-Honoré, 1ᵉʳ (Mᵒ Pyramides). Mon–Fri 7am–10pm, Sat 8am–4pm. Closed mid-Aug. One of the oldest wine bars, it enjoys a reputation for having among the best wines, plus excellent snacks and *plats du jour*. Very small and very crowded. Glasses of wine from 10F.

Le Sous-Bock, 49 rue St-Honoré, 1ᵉʳ (Mᵒ Châtelet-Les Halles). 11am–5am. Hundreds of bottled beers (around 33F a bottle) and whiskies to sample with simple, inexpensive food. Mussels a speciality (40–50F). Frequented by night owls.

Taverne Henri IV, 13 pl du Pont-Neuf, 1ᵉʳ (Mᵒ Pont-Neuf). Mon–Fri noon–9.30pm, Sat noon–4.30pm; closed Aug. One of the good older wine bars, opposite Henri IV's statue. Yves Montand used to come here when Simone Signoret lived in the adjacent pl Dauphine. Full of lawyers from the Palais de Justice. The food is good but a bit pricy if you have a full meal. Plates of meats and cheeses around 70F, sandwiches 25F, wine 25–50F a glass.

RESTAURANTS

Le Dauphin, 167 rue St-Honoré, 1ᵉʳ; ☎42.60.40.11 (Mᵒ Palais-Royal–Musée-du-Louvre). Daily noon–2.30pm & 7–11.30pm (June–Oct until 12.30am). A genuine bistro with menus under 100F. Seafood platter for 167F. Excellent *lapereau* (young rabbit) *à la grand-mère* and *magret de canard*.

Aux Deux Saules, 91 rue St-Denis, 1ᵉʳ; ☎42.36.46.57 (Mᵒ Châtelet-Les Halles). Daily until 1am. Cheap if unexciting dishes. A leftover from the days of the market. The tile work representing same is the best feature. 69F menu.

Foujita, 41 rue St-Roch, 1ᵉʳ; ☎42.61.42.93 (Mᵒ Tuileries/Pyramides). Mon–Sat noon–2.15pm & 7.30–10pm. Closed mid-Aug. One of the cheaper but best Japanese restaurants, as evidenced by the numbers of Japanese eating here. Quick and crowded; soup, sushis, rice and tea for 85F at lunchtime; plate of sushis or sushamis for under 100F.

L'Incroyable, 26 rue de Richelieu, 1ᵉʳ; ☎42.96.24.64 (Mᵒ Palais-Royal). Tues–Thurs lunchtime & 6.30–9pm, Sat & Mon lunch only; closed Sun & two weeks at Christmas. Hidden in a tiny passage, a very pleasant restaurant serving decent meals for 60F at midday and 70F in the evening.

Osaka, 163 rue St-Honoré, 1ᵉʳ (Mᵒ Palais-Royal). 11.30am–8.15pm. Japanese snack bar with meals for 60F. More expensive sushi, sushimi and tempura bar on the left.

Le Petit Ramoneur, 74 rue St-Denis, 1ᵉʳ; ☎42.36.39.24 (Mᵒ Châtelet-Les Halles). Mon–Fri until 9.30pm. Closed end Aug. Elbow-rubbing cheapie in good bistro tradition, with cheap wine that's better than table wine. Crowded, but a welcome and genuine relief in Les Halles. 63F menu.

Au Pied de Cochon, 6 rue Coquillière, 1ᵉʳ; ☎42.36.11.75 (Mᵒ Châtelet-Les Halles). Open 24 hours. For extravagant middle-of-the-night pork chops and oysters. Seafood platter 192F. *Carte* up to 300F.

Le Relais du Sud-Ouest, 154 rue St-Honoré, 1ᵉʳ; ☎42.60.62.01 (Mᵒ Palais-Royal/Musée-du-Louvre). Mon–Sat till 10.30pm. An ancient map of the southwest of France hangs on the wall; there's an old kitchen range, and traditional southwest specialities are served at candlelit tables. Good value on the 80F menu.

Au Rendez-vous des Camionneurs, 72 quai des Orfèvres, 1ᵉʳ; ☎43.54.88.74 (Mᵒ St-Michel). Daily noon–2pm, 7–11.30pm. Crowded, traditional establishment serving snails, steaks and scallops. 130–180F.

2ᵉ

BARS AND CAFÉS

L'Arbre à Cannelle, 57 passage des Panoramas, 2ᵉ (Mᵒ Rue-Montmartre). Mon–Sat till 6pm. Exquisite wooden panelling, frescoes and painted ceilings; puddings, flans and *assiettes gourmandes* for 54–70F.

La Champmeslé, 4 rue Chabanais, 2ᵉ (Mᵒ Pyramides). Mon–Sat 11am–2am, Sun 5pm–2am. Lesbian bar with two rooms reserved for women and one room for mixed company. Cocktails (from 45F), picture/photo exhibitions, and Thurs night cabaret.

Du Croissant, corner of rue du Croissant and rue Montmartre, 2ᵉ (Mᵒ Montmartre). On July 31, 1914, the Socialist and pacifist leader Jean Jaurès was assassinated in this café for his antiwar activities. The table he was sitting at still remains.

La Micro-Brasserie, 106 rue de Richelieu, 2ᵉ (Mᵒ Richelieu-Drouot). Mon–Sat 8am–2am. A beer cellar that brews its own beer on the spot and offers *moules* and *frites* for 40F.

Tigh Johnny, 55 rue Montmartre, 2ᵉ (Mᵒ Sentier). Daily 4pm–1.30am, last orders 12.30am. A mostly Irish clientele at this bar that serves a reasonably priced Guinness and sometimes has impromptu Celtic bands.

RESTAURANTS

Country Life, 6 rue Daunou, 2ᵉ; ☎42.97.48.51 (Mᵒ Opéra). Mon–Sat 11.30am–2.30pm only. Vegetarian soup, hors d'oeuvres, lasagne and salad for under 60F. Menu details gluten and soya contents. No alcohol, no smoking.

Dilan, 13 rue Mandar, 2ᵉ; ☎42.21.46.38 (Mᵒ Les Halles/Sentier). Daily noon–2pm & 7.30–11pm. Closed Sun midday. An excellent-value Kurdish restaurant. Beautiful starters, stuffed aubergines (*babaqunuc*), fish with yoghurt and courgettes (*kanarya*). Midday menu 60F.

Drouot, 103 rue de Richelieu, 2ᵉ; ☎42.96.68.23 (Mᵒ Richelieu-Drouot). Daily noon–3pm & 6.30–10pm. Admirably cheap and good food, served at a frantic pace, in an Art Deco décor. Menu around 80F.

Le Vaudeville, 29 rue Vivienne, 2ᵉ; ☎40.20.04.62 (Mᵒ Bourse). Until 2am. A lively late-night brasserie, where it's often necessary to queue. Good food, attractive marble-and-mosaic interior. *Carte* from 150F. 119F and 159F menus midday, evening 189F.

3ᵉ
RESTAURANTS

Chez Nénesse, 17 rue Saintonge, 3ᵉ; ☎42.78.46.49 (Mᵒ Arts-et-Métiers). Mon–Fri noon–3pm & 7.30–10.15pm. Closed Aug. Steak in bilberry sauce and figs stuffed with cream of almonds are two of the unique delights of this restaurant, along with home-made chips at Thursday lunchtimes. Under 100F midday, over 200F for dinner.

4ᵉ
BARS AND CAFÉS

Bar Central, 33 rue Vieille-du-Temple (corner rue Ste-Croix-de-la-Bretonnerie), 4ᵉ (Mᵒ St-Paul). Noon–2am. One of the most popular gay bars in the Marais.

Berthillon, 31 rue St-Louis-en-l'Île, 4ᵉ (Mᵒ Pont-Marie). Wed–Sun 10am–8pm. Long queues for these very best of ice creams and sorbets (18F a triple), which are made and sold here on the Île St-Louis. Also available at *Lady Jane* and *Le Flore-en-l'Île*, both on quai d'Orléans, as well as at four other island sites listed on the door.

Bofinger, 3–7 rue de la Bastille, 4ᵉ; ☎42.72.87.82 (Mᵒ Bastille). Daily until 1am. A well-established and popular turn-of-the-century brasserie, with original décor, serving the archetypal fare of sauerkraut and seafood. Menu at 149F, otherwise over 200F.

Café Beaubourg, 43 rue St-Merri, 4ᵉ (Mᵒ Rambuteau). Until 2am. Postmodernist clone of the earlier Philippe Starck *Café Costes*. It's expensive and the service is sour. It shares its rival's loo fetish; they are better here.

Dame Tartine, 2 rue Brise-Miche, 4ᵉ (Mᵒ Rambuteau/Hôtel-de-Ville). Daily noon–11.30pm. Overlooking the Stravinsky pool, serving particularly delicious open toasted sandwiches (27–30F). Inside, decorated with kids' pictures.

L'Ébouillanté, 6 rue des Barres, 4ᵉ (Mᵒ Hôtel-de-Ville). Tues–Sun noon–9pm. Tiny *salon de thé* in picturesque street behind the church of St-Gervais, with reasonable prices and simple fare – chocolate cakes and *pâtisseries* as well as savoury dishes. *Plats du jour* for 60F.

Les Enfants Gatés, 43 rue des Francs-Bourgeois, 4ᵉ (Mᵒ St-Paul). Deep armchairs, painting exhibitions and snacks like goat's cheese and tarragon tart (40F).

Ma Bourgogne, 19 pl des Vosges, 4e (M^o St-Paul). Open daily until 12.30am or 1am in summertime. A quiet and agreeable arty café with tables under the arcades on the northwest corner of the square. Best in the morning when the sun hits this side of the square. Serves somewhat pricy meals too.

Épices et Délices, 53 rue Vieille-du-Temple, 4e (M^o St-Paul). Daily to midnight. Restaurant and *salon de thé* with very pleasant service and food. Aubergine *gratin* 60F.

Au Petit Fer à Cheval, 30 rue Vieille-du-Temple, 4e (M^o St-Paul). Mon–Fri 9am–2am, Sat–Sun 11am–2am; food noon–midnight. Very attractive small *bistrot*/bar with trad décor. Good wine, excellent *gigot d'agneau à romarin* for 58F and oither good-value *plats*.

Le Petit Marcel, 63 rue Rambuteau, 4e (M^o Rambuteau). Mon–Sat, until 2am. Speckled tabletops, mirrors and Art Nouveau tiles, cracked and faded ceiling and about eight square metres of drinking space. Friendly barman and "local" atmosphere.

Le Quetzal, 10 rue de la Verrerie (corner rue Moussy), 4e (M^o St-Paul). Daily until 3am. A fashionable and stylish gay bar, with space for dancing.

Le Rouge Gorge, 8 rue St-Paul, 4e (M^o St-Paul). Mon–Sat noon–2am. The young and enthusiastic clientele sip familiar wines and snack on *chèvre chaud* and smoked salmon salad, or tuck into more substantial fare (*plats du jour* around 60F), while listening to jazz or classical music.

Sacha Finkelsztajn and Florence Finkelsztajn, 27 rue des Rosiers, 4e (Wed–Sun 9.30am–1.30pm & 3–7.30pm) and 24 rue des Écouffes, 4e (Mon & Thurs–Sun 9.30am–1.30pm & 3–7.30pm). Both M^o St-Paul. Marvellous for takeaway snacks and goodies: gorgeous east European breads, cakes, *gefilte* fish, aubergine purée, tarama, *blinis* and *borscht*.

Self-Service Beaubourg, 5th floor, Centre Pompidou, 4e (M^o Rambuteau). Wed–Sun noon–9.30pm. Cheap beer, coffee and snacks; no extra for sitting down on the *terrasse* with superb views.

La Tartine, 24 rue de Rivoli, 4e (M^o St-Paul). Wed–Mon until 10pm. Closed Aug. The genuine 1900s article, which still cuts across class boundaries in its clientele. A good selection of affordable wines, plus excellent cheese and *saucisson* with *pain de campagne*.

Le Temps des Cerises, 31 rue de la Cerisaie, 4e (M^o Bastille). Mon–Fri until 8pm; food at midday only. Closed Aug. It is hard to say what is so appealing about this café, with its dirty yellow décor, old posters and prints of *vieux Paris*, save that the *patronne* knows most of the clientele, who are young, relaxed and not the dreaded *branchés*. There's a cheap *menu fixe*.

Le Trumilou, 84 quai Hôtel-de-Ville 4e; ☎42.77.63.98 (M^o Pont-Marie). Daily to 11pm. The Parisian equivalent of a diner. Pigs trotters, Lyonnais sausage and wonderful sweet chestnut charlotte, all served with wit and panache. 65F and 80F menus. *À la carte* close to 200F.

Yahalom, 22–24 rue des Rosiers, 4^e (M^o St-Paul). Kosher *falafel* 25F; *plats du jour* 45F.

RESTAURANTS

Aquarius 1, 54 rue Ste-Croix-de-la-Bretonnerie, 4^e; ☎48.87.48.71 (M^o St-Paul/Rambuteau). Mon–Sat noon–9.45pm. Austere and penitential vegetarian restaurant: no alcohol, no smoking, and a leavening of Rosicrucianism. Menu at 51F.

Auberge de Jarente, 7 rue Jarente, 4^e; ☎42.77.49.35 (M^o St-Paul). Tues–Sat noon–2.30pm & 6.30–10.30pm. Closed Aug. A hospitable and friendly Basque restaurant, serving first-class food: *cassoulet*, hare stew, king prawns in whisky, *magret de canard*, and *piperade* – the Basque omelette. Menus at 130F and 170F.

La Canaille, 4 rue Crillon, 4e; ☎42.78.09.71 (M^o Sully-Morland/Bastille). Mon–Sat lunchtime & 7.30pm–midnight. Bar in front, restaurant behind. The food is simple, traditional and well cooked. Friendly atmosphere. There are 85F and 125F evening menus, and *à la carte* at 140F.

Chez Caroll Sinclair, 36 bd Henri-IV, 4e; ☎42.72.17.09 (M^o Sully-Morland). Open until 11.30pm. Closed Sat midday and Sun evening. Beautiful fish dishes including seafood soup and excellent desserts. Over 200F *à la carte* but 150F midday weekday menu with wine and 177F evening menu.

Le Farafina, 12 rue Quincampoix, 4e; ☎48.04.50.52 (M^o Châtelet/Hôtel-de-Ville). Tues–Sun 8pm–dawn. *Maffé* (Senegalese meat or fish stew) and *yassa* (chicken and lime) but the main attraction is live African music. Not for the retiring. Around 200F.

Goldenberg's, 7 rue des Rosiers, 4ᵉ; ☎48.87.20.16 (Mᵒ St-Paul). Daily until 11pm. The best-known Jewish restaurant in the capital; its *borscht, blinis,* potato strudels, *zakouski,* and other central European dishes are a treat. Around 200F.

Piccolo Teatro, 6 rue des Écouffes, 4ᵉ; ☎42.72.17.79 (Mᵒ St-Paul). Wed–Sun noon–3pm & 7–11pm. Closed Aug. A vegetarian restaurant with *assiette végétarienne* at 58F; lunch menus at 54F and 74F, evening at 85F and 110F.

Le Ravaillac, 10 rue du Roi-de-Sicile, 4ᵉ; ☎42.72.85.85 (Mᵒ St-Paul). Noon–3pm & 7–10.30pm; closed Sun, Mon lunchtime & Aug. Long-established Polish restaurant. Specialities include meat *perushkis,* beef Stroganoff, and *choucroute.* Excellent quality for the price – around 100F.

La Truffe, 31 rue Vieille-du-Temple, 4ᵉ; ☎42.71.08.39 (Mᵒ St-Paul). Daily noon–4pm & 7.30–11pm. A vegetarian specializing in mushrooms as well as lentil and cheese dishes and delicious fruit tarts.

5ᵉ

BARS AND CAFÉS

Café de la Mosquée, 39 rue Geoffroy-St-Hilaire, 5ᵉ (Mᵒ Monge). Mon–Thurs, Sat & Sun 10am–9.30pm. Closed Aug. In fine weather you can drink mint tea and eat sweet cakes beside a fountain and assorted fig trees in the courtyard of this Paris mosque – a delightful haven of calm. The interior of the salon is beautifully Arabic with cats curled up on the seats. You can have meals in the adjoining restaurant.

La Fourmi Ailée, 8 rue du Fouarre, 5ᵉ (Mᵒ Maubert-Mutualité). Noon–7pm. Closed Tues. Simple, light fare – including brunch on Saturday and Sunday – in this feminist bookshop–cum–*salon-de-thé.* Around 60F for tea and a cake.

La Gueuze, 19 rue Soufflot, 5ᵉ (Mᵒ Luxembourg). Mon–Sat noon–2am. Comfy surroundings – lots of wood and stained glass. Kitchen specials are *pierrades*: dishes cooked on hot stones. Numerous bottles and several draughts, including cherry beer. Close to the university with lots of student habitués.

Le Piano Vache, 8 rue Laplace, 5ᵉ (Mᵒ Cardinal-Lemoine). 9am–1.30am, Sat & Sun evenings only. Venerable student bar with canned music and relaxed atmosphere.

Les Pipos, 50 rue de la Montagne-Ste-Geneviève, 5ᵉ (Mᵒ Maubert-Mutualité/Cardinal-Lemoine). Old carved wooden bar and sculpted chimney piece, its own wines, and a long-established position opposite the gates of the former *grand école.*

Polly Magoo, 11 rue St-Jacques, 5ᵉ (Mᵒ St-Michel/Maubert-Mutualité). A scruffy all-nighter frequented by chess addicts.

Le Violon Dingue, 46 rue de la Montagne-Ste-Geneviève, 5ᵉ (Mᵒ Maubert-Mutualité). Mon & Wed–Sun 6pm–1am. Happy hour 6–9pm. A long, dark, student pub, noisy and friendly.

RESTAURANTS

Auberge des Deux Signes, 46 rue Galande, 5ᵉ; ☎43.25.00.46 (Mᵒ St-Michel). Closed Sat midday, Sun & Aug. A medieval setting and for once, an interesting choice on the *menus fixes* at 140F and 230F.

Bistro de la Sorbonne, 4 rue Toullier, 5ᵉ; ☎43.54.41.49 (Mᵒ Luxembourg). Mon–Sat until 11pm. Help-yourself starters and salads, good ices and *crêpes flambées.* Copious portions. Crowded and attractive student ambience. 70F menu at lunchtime, including wine and service; 95F in the evening.

Brasserie Balzar, 49 rue des Écoles, 5ᵉ; ☎43.54.13.67 (Mᵒ Maubert-Mutualité). Daily until 12.30am; closed Aug. A traditional literary-bourgeois brasserie, frequented by the intelligentsia of the Latin Quarter. About 170F.

Le Grenier de Notre-Dame, 18 rue de la Bûcherie, 5ᵉ (Mᵒ Maubert-Mutalité). Daily noon–11.30pm. Some veggies love this place, others hate it. Substantial fare including couscous, fried tofu, cauliflower cheese. Menus at 75F, 105F and 140F.

Chez Léna et Mimile, 32 rue Tournefort, 5ᵉ; ☎47.07.72.47 (Mᵒ Consier-Daubenton). Until 11pm. Closed Sat & Sun midday. The south-facing high *terrasse* is the main attraction, and the 185F menu with wine and coffee included is excellent. Also 98F menu.

Le Liban à la Mouff, 3 rue de l'Estrapade 5ᵉ; ☎47.07.29.99 (Mᵒ Monge). Closed Tues & Wed midday. A pleasant and unusually cheap Lebanese restaurant. *Kafta* 60F, wonderful milk pudding *mouhallabiah* 28F, large *mezze* for four 440F.

Perraudin, 157 rue St-Jacques, 5ᵉ; ☎46.33.15.75 (*RER* Luxembourg). Mon & Sat 7.00–10.30pm, Tues–Fri noon–2pm & 7.30–10.15pm. A well-known traditional *bistrot* with a midday menu at 60F; *carte* around 150F.

Student restaurants 8bis rue Cuvier, 5ᵉ (Mᵒ Jussieu); 39 av G-Bernanos, 5ᵉ (Mᵒ Port-Royal); 31 rue Geoffroy-St-Hilaire, 5ᵉ (Mᵒ Censier-Daubenton); and 10 rue Jean-Calvin, 5ᵉ (Mᵒ Censier-Daubenton).

Tashi Delek, 4 rue des Fossés-St-Jacques, 5ᵉ; ☎43.26.55.55 (Mᵒ Luxembourg). Lunchtime and evenings until 10.30pm. An enjoyable Tibetan restaurant – run by refugees – where you can eat for as little as 50F, without wine. On the 125F menu you can try the wonderful *beignets* of chicken with ginger sauce.

6ᵉ
BARS AND CAFÉS

Le 10, 10 rue de l'Odéon, 6ᵉ (Mᵒ Odéon). Daily 5.30pm–2am. The beer here is very cheap, which is why it attracts youth, particularly foreigners. Old posters, a juke box, and a lot of chatting-up.

L'Alsace à Paris, 9 pl St-André-des-Arts, 6ᵉ; ☎43.26.21.48 (Mᵒ St-Michel). A very busy and well-worn brasserie, with menus at 110F, 130F and 180F – but also delicious and cheap *tartes flambées* like thin pizzas that you can also take away.

L'Assignat, 7 rue Guénégaud, 6ᵉ (Mᵒ Pont-Neuf). Mon–Sat 7.30am–8.30pm, closed July. Zinc counter, bar stools, bar football and young regulars in an untouristy café close to quai des Augustins. 25F for a sandwich and a glass of wine.

La Closerie des Lilas, 171 bd du Montparnasse, 6ᵉ (Mᵒ Port-Royal). 10am–1am. The smartest, artiest, classiest one of all, with excellent cocktails. No bum's paradise – it's pricy. The tables are name-plated after celebrated habitués (Verlaine, Mallarmé, Lenin, Modigliani, Léger, Strindberg), and there's a pianist in residence.

Les Deux Magots, 170 bd St-Germain, 6ᵉ (Mᵒ St-Germain-des-Prés). Open until 2am; closed Aug. Right on the corner of place St-Germain-des-Prés, it too owes its reputation to the intellos of the Left Bank, past and present. In summertime it picks up a lot of foreigners seeking the exact location of the spirit of French culture, and buskers galore play to the packed terrace.

Le Flore, 172 bd St-Germain, 6ᵉ (Mᵒ St-Germain-des-Prés). Open until 2am; closed July. The great rival and immediate neighbour of *Deux Magots*, with a very similar clientele.

Chez Georges, 11 rue des Canettes, 6ᵉ (Mᵒ Mabillon). Tues–Sat noon–2am; closed July 14–Aug 15. An attractive wine bar in the spit-on-the-floor mode, with its old shop-front still intact in a narrow leading street off place St-Sulpice.

Le Mazet, 60 rue St-André-des-Arts, 6ᵉ (Mᵒ Odéon). Mon–Thurs 10am–2am; Fri and Sat until 3.30am; closed Sun. A well-known hang-out for buskers (with a lock-up for their instruments) and heavy drinkers. What about a *bière brûlée* for an evil concoction – it's flambéed with gin.

La Paillote, 45 rue Monsieur-le-Prince, 6ᵉ (*RER* Luxembourg/Mᵒ Odéon). Mon–Sat 9pm till dawn. Closed Aug. *The* late-night bar for jazz fans, with one of the best collections of recorded jazz in the city. Drinks around 38F.

La Palette, 43 rue de Seine, 6ᵉ (Mᵒ Odéon). Mon–Sat 8am–2am. Once-famous Beaux Arts student hang-out, now more for art dealers and their customers. The service can be uncivil, but the murals and every detail of the décor are superb.

Pub Saint-Germain, 17 rue de l'Ancienne-Comédie, 6ᵉ (Mᵒ Odéon). Open 24 hours. 21 draught beers and hundreds of bottles. Huge, crowded, and expensive. Hot food at mealtimes, otherwise cold snacks. For a taste of "real" French beer try *ch'ti* (patois for 'northerner'), a *bière de garde* from the Pas-de-Calais.

La Taverne de Nesle, 32 rue Dauphine, 6ᵉ (Mᵒ Odéon). 7am–5am. Vast selection of beers. Full of local night birds. Cocktails from 40F.

RESTAURANTS

Aux Charpentiers, 10 rue Mabillon, 6ᵉ; ☎43.26.30.05 (Mᵒ Mabillon). Mon–Sat until 11pm; closed hols. A friendly, old-fashioned place belonging to the *Compagnons des Charpentiers* (Carpenters' Guild), with appropriate décor of roof-trees and tie beams. Traditional *plats du jour* are their forte. Around 220F.

Drugstore Saint-Germain, 149 bd St-Germain, 6ᵉ (Mᵒ St-Germain-des-Prés). Until 2am. The best of the drugstores for salads, sandwiches, snacks and larger meals (see also under 8ᵉ). Basics include *steak tartare*, and *langoustines* done to a T.

Lipp, 151 bd St-Germain, 6ᵉ; ☎45.48.53.91 (Mᵒ St-Germain-des-Prés). Until 12.30am; closed mid-July to mid-Aug. A 1900s brasserie, one of the best-known establishments on the Left Bank, haunt of the successful and famous. Rather more welcoming now that its sour old owner has died and been replaced by a niece. 200–250F. No reservations; be prepared to wait.

Le Muniche, 22 rue Guillaume-Apollinaire, 6ᵉ; ☎46.33.62.09 (Mᵒ St-Germain-des-Prés). Noon–2am. A crowded old-style brasserie with an oyster bar, mirrors and theatre posters on the walls and good old French offal concoctions on the menu. 140F menu.

Orestias, 4 rue Grégoire-de-Tours, 6ᵉ; ☎43.54.62.01 (Mᵒ Odéon). Mon–Sat lunchtime & evening until 11pm. A mixture of Greek and French cuisine. Good helpings and very cheap – with a menu at 44F (weekdays only).

Le Petit Saint-Benoît, 4 rue Saint-Benoît, 6ᵉ; ☎42.60.27.92 (Mᵒ St-Germain-des-Prés). Mon–Fri lunchtime & 7–10pm. A simple, genuine and very appealing local for the neighbourhood's chattering classes. Serves solid traditional fare in a brown-stained, aproned atmosphere – for about 120F.

Le Petit Zinc, 11 rue Saint-Benoît, 6ᵉ; ☎46.33.51.66 (Mᵒ St-Germain-des-Prés). Noon–2am. Excellent traditional dishes, especially seafood, in stunning new Art Nouveau premises, complete with white fringed parasols over the pavement tables. Not cheap – midday menu 158F, seafood platter 440F for two.

Polidor, 41 rue Monsieur-le-Prince, 6ᵉ; ☎43.26.95.34 (Mᵒ Odéon). Mon–Sat until 1am, Sun until 11pm. A traditional *bistrot*, whose visitors' book, they say, boasts more of history's big names than all the glittering palaces put together. Not as cheap as it was in James Joyce's day but good food and great atmosphere. Lunches at 55F during the week and an excellent l00F evening menu.

Le Procope, 13 rue de l'Ancienne-Comédie, 6ᵉ; ☎43.26.99.20 (Mᵒ Odéon). Daily noon–1am. This was the first establishment to serve coffee in Paris. Over 300 years it has retained its reputation as *the* place for powerful intellectuals. Its present décor dates from the Bicentennial of the Revolution, and citizens are still offered 69F and 98F menus – before 7pm. After that it's 289F until 11pm, when a 119F menu is on offer.

Restaurant des Arts, 73 rue de Seine, 6ᵉ (Mᵒ St-Germain-des-Prés). Mon–Thurs till 9pm, Fri lunchtime only; closed Aug. Menu at 78F. A small, crowded, friendly place with simple, homely meals. Young and old, well-heeled and not at all.

Restaurant des Beaux-Arts, 11 rue Bonaparte, 6ᵉ; ☎43.26.92.64 (Mᵒ St-Germain-des-Prés). Daily lunchtime & evening until 10.45pm. The traditional hang-out of the art students from the Beaux-Arts across the way. Menu at 69F including wine. The choice is wide, portions generous, and the queues long in high season; the atmosphere is generally good, though the waitresses can get pretty tetchy.

Student restaurants at 55 rue Mazet, 6ᵉ (Mᵒ Odéon) and 92 rue d'Assas, 6ᵉ (Mᵒ Port-Royal/Notre-Dame-des-Champs). See box on p.122 for details.

Village Bulgare, 8 rue de Nevers, 6ᵉ; ☎43.25.08.75 (Mᵒ Odéon/Pont-Neuf). Noon–2pm & 7.30–10pm; closed Sun evening & Mon midday. The only Bulgarian restaurant in France. Specialities include *kebabtcheta* (veal and lamb stew), *cirène au four* (baked sheep's milk cheese with vegetables), yoghurt and Gamza wine. 80F menu, *à la carte* 150F.

7ᵉ

BARS AND CAFÉS

La Pagode, 57bis rue de Babylone, 7ᵉ (Mᵒ François-Xavier/Sèvres-Babylone). 4–9.45pm, Sun 2–8pm. A real-life pagoda (see p.10) – one of the most beautiful buildings in Paris in which to have tea. Tables in the Chinese garden in summer.

Restaurant du Museé d'Orsay, 1 rue Bellechasse, 7ᵉ (*RER* Musée d'Orsay/Mᵒ Solférino). Tues, Wed & Fri–Sat 11.30am–2.15pm, 4–5.30pm & 7–9.45pm; Thurs 11.30am–2.15pm & 7–9.45pm; Sun 11.30am–2.15pm & 4–5.30pm. Superb views over the Seine in the museum's rooftop restaurant. Hors d'oeuvres, dessert and wine for 72F. Quick and friendly service.

RESTAURANTS

Au Babylone, 13 rue de Babylone, 7ᵉ; ☎45.48.72.13 (Mᵒ Sèvres-Babylone). Mon–Sat lunchtime only; closed Aug. Lots of old-fashioned charm and basics like *rôti de veau*, steak etc, plus wine on the 80F menu.

Le Bourdonnais, 113 av La Bourdonnais, 7ᵉ; ☎47.05.47.06 (Mᵒ École-Militaire). Till 11pm. A gem of a restaurant and a high-class one at that. *À la carte* costs around 400F, but there's a superb midday menu including wine for 220F, evening menu 280F.

Escale de Saigon, 24 rue Bosquet, 7ᵉ; ☎45.51.60.14 (Mᵒ École-Militaire). Mon–Sat noon–2.30pm & 7–10.30pm. A small and inexpensive local Vietnamese, with a 47F menu.

8ᵉ

BARS AND CAFÉS

La Boutique à Sandwiches, 12 rue du Colisée, 8ᵉ (Mᵒ St-Philippe-du-Roule). Mon–Sat 11.45am–11.30pm; closed Aug. Not the best sandwiches in the world, but certainly cheap for this part of town, plus *raclette* and *steak frites* for under 80F at the counter.

Drugstore Élysées, 133 av des Champs-Élysées, 8ᵉ (Mᵒ Étoile). Daily 9am–2am; **Drugstore Matignon**, 1 av Matignon, 8ᵉ (Mᵒ Franklin-Roosevelt). Daily 10am–midnight; closed mid-Aug. All day salads, sandwiches, *plats du jour*, full-blown meals and huge, delicious desserts are available from all three drugstores (see also under 6ᵉ), along with books, newspapers, tobacco, and a multitude of fripperies. Prices are very reasonable.

Ma Bourgogne, 133 bd Haussmann, 8ᵉ (Mᵒ Miromesnil). Mon–Fri 7am–10pm; closed July. A place for pre-siesta glasses of Burgundy; *plats du jour* as well, and meals at 150–200F.

Virgin Megastore Café, 52 av des Champs-Élysées, 8ᵉ (Mᵒ Franklin-Roosevelt). Daily 10am–11.30pm. As popular as the store; coffee and snacks – *tapas* around 35F, sandwiches for 28F – or meals for around 150F.

RESTAURANTS

Aux Amis du Beaujolais, 28 rue d'Artois, 8ᵉ; ☎45.63.92.21 (Mᵒ George-V/St-Philippe-du-Roule). Mon–Sat till 9pm; closed middle two weeks of July. If you can fathom the handwritten menu, you'll find good traditional French dishes of stews and sautéed steaks, and Beaujolais. Around 150F.

L'Élysées Bar Restaurant, 134 rue Faubourg St-Honoré, 8ᵉ (Mᵒ St-Philippe-du-Roule). Tues–Sat noon–2.30pm & 7–9.30pm. Tables outside for *gigot d'agneau* (72F) and *steak tartare frites* (73F). If you don't fancy it, there's the *Lord Sandwich* bar next door.

Fouquet's, 99 av des Champs-Élysées, 8ᵉ; ☎47.23.70.60 (Mᵒ George-V). Daily until midnight. A long-established, expensive watering-hole for ageing stars, politicians, newspaper editors, and advertising barons. The restaurant upstairs (closed weekends and mid-July to Aug) is more expensive than the terrace "grill", but both are outrageous. At around 350F you're paying for the past and present clientele, the prime site on the Champs-Élysées, and the snobbishness of the whole affair.

Yvan, 1bis rue J-Mermoz, 8ᵉ; ☎43.59.18.40 (Mᵒ Franklin-Roosevelt). Mon–Sat noon–2.30pm & 7pm–midnight, closed Sat lunchtime. Fish specialities and pigeon with polenta attract a stylish clientele. Extremely good food and menus at 168F, 188F and 238F.

9ᵉ

BARS AND CAFÉS

Cave Drouot, 8 rue Drouot, 9ᵉ (Mᵒ Richelieu-Drouot). Mon–Fri 8am–10pm; closed July 14–Sept 1. Excellent wines and a reasonably priced restaurant with *plats du jour* and *charcuterie*.

Le Dépanneur, 27 rue Fontaine, 9ᵉ; ☎40.16.40.20 (Mᵒ Pigalle). Relaxed and fashionable all-night bar.

Le Grand Café Capucines, 4 bd des Capucines, 9ᵉ (Mᵒ Opéra). A favourite all-nighter with over-the-top Belle Époque décor and excellent seafood. Boulevard prices mean 20F for an espresso.

RESTAURANTS

Chartier, 7 rue du Faubourg-Montmartre, 9ᵉ; ☎47.70.86.29 (Mᵒ Montmartre). Until 9.30pm. Dark-stained woodwork, brass hat-racks, mirrors, waiters in long aprons – the original décor of a turn-of-the-century soup kitchen. Worth seeing and, though crowded and rushed, the food is not bad at all. Under 100F.

Aux Deux-Théâtres, 18 rue Blanche, 9ᵉ; ☎45.26.41.43 (Mᵒ Blanche). Daily till 12.30am. A place to lash out on champagne, oysters, lobster, gooey desserts affordably. Menu at 165F. Best to go early and book for later.

10ᵉ
BARS AND CAFÉS

L'Opus, 167 quai de Valmy, 10ᵉ (Mᵒ Château-Landon). 8pm–4am; closed Sun. A stylish modern-chintzy atmosphere in a barn-like space. Listen to live classical music (from 10pm) while you sip your cocktails – or dine, in the rather expensive restaurant. Drinks 65–80F average, plus 50F surcharge for the music.

La Patache, 60 rue de Lancry, 10ᵉ (Mᵒ Jacques-Bonsergent). An atmospheric café-bar, survivor from the neighbourhood's pre-gentrification days.

Quasre Shireen, 14 rue Faubourg-St-Denis, 10ᵉ (Mᵒ Strasbourg-St-Denis). Fast-food Indian cheapie with rice and curry for 25F, samosas 5F.

RESTAURANTS

Flo, 7 cours des Petites-Écuries, 10ᵉ; ☎47.70.13.59 (Mᵒ Château-d'Eau). Until 1.30am. Handsome old-time brasserie where you eat elbow to elbow at long tables, served by waiters in ankle-length aprons. Excellent food and atmosphere. From around 200F; really good value menus at 110F and 159F midday, 185F evenings.

Julien, 16 rue du Faubourg St-Denis, 10ᵉ; ☎47.70.12.06 (Mᵒ Strasbourg-St-Denis). Until 1.30am. Part of the same enterprise as *Flo*, with an even more splendid décor. Same good Alsatian cuisine; same prices and similarly crowded. From about 200F, with a 110F menu including wine after 11pm.

Restaurant de Bourgogne, 26 rue des Vinaigriers, 10ᵉ; ☎46.07.07.91 (Mᵒ Jacques-Bonsergent). Lunchtime, and evenings until 10pm; closed Sat evening, Sun and Aug. Homely old-fashioned restaurant with midday menu at 50F and evening menu at 60F.

Terminus Nord, 23 rue de Dunkerque, 10ᵉ; ☎42.85.05.15 (Mᵒ Gare-du-Nord). Daily until 12.30am. A magnificent 1920s brasserie where a full meal costs around 250F, but where you could easily satisfy your hunger with just a main course and still enjoy the décor for considerably less.

11ᵉ
BARS AND CAFÉS

Café de l'Industrie, 16 rue St-Sabin, 11ᵉ (Mᵒ Bastille). 9am–2am; closed Sun. Rugs on the floor around solid old wooden tables, miscellaneous objects on the walls, and a young, unpretentious crowd enjoying the lack of chrome, minimalism or Philippe Starck. One of the best Bastille addresses. *Plats du jour* from 38F.

Café de la Plage, 59 rue de Charonne, 11ᵉ (Mᵒ Bastille). Tues–Sun until 2am. A multiracial clientele and as many women as men in this low-ceilinged, friendly, youthful and often very crowded Irish-run bar. Jazz club downstairs.

Fouquet's, 130 rue de Lyon, 12ᵉ (Mᵒ Bastille). Till midnight. Closed Sat & Sun midday. A smart and expensive café-restaurant underneath the new Opéra, sister establishment to the Champs-Elysées *Fouquet*'s. But with perfect French courtesy they will leave you undisturbed for hours with a 15F coffee. Menu, including wine, at 165F.

Iguana, 15 rue de la Roquette (corner rue Daval), 11ᵉ (Mᵒ Bastille). Mon–Sat 10am–4am. A place to be seen in. Décor of trellises, colonial fans, and brushed bronze bar. The clientele studies récherché art reviews.

Jacques-Mélac, 42 rue Léon-Frot, 11ᵉ; ☎43.70.59.27 (Mᵒ Charonne). 8.30am–8pm (10pm Tues and Thurs); closed Sat & Sun and mid-July to mid-Aug. Some way off the beaten track (between Père-Lachaise and place Léon-Blum) but a highly reputed and very popular *bistrot à vins* whose patron even makes his own wine – the solitary vine winds round the front of the shop (harvest celebrations in the second half of Sept: said to be great fun). The food (*plats* around 38F), wines and atmosphere are great, but you can't book, so it pays to get there early.

Pause Café, 41 rue de Charonne (corner rue Keller), 11ᵉ (Mᵒ Ledru-Rollin). Tues–Sat 8am–2am, Sun till 9pm. A new and fashionable Bastille café, down among the galleries.

La Pirada, 7 rue de Lappe, 11ᵉ; ☎47.00.73.61 (Mᵒ Bastille). Till 2am, Sun till 5pm. Designer *tapas* bar for the designer people of the new Bastille; live music. 60–120F. 68F menu at midday.

RESTAURANTS

L'Abreuvoir, 68 rue de la Roquette (corner rue des Taillandiers), 11^e; ☎43.57.71.74 (M^o Voltaire/ Bastille). Lunchtime, & evenings until 1am; closed Sun midday. Traditional cooking. Local restaurant from pre-trendy days. Midday menu at 59F, otherwise around 120F.

Les Amognes, 243 rue du Faubourg-St-Antoine, 11^e; ☎43.72.73.05 (M^o Faidherbe-Chaligny). Tues– Sat noon–2.30pm & 7.30–11pm; closed 3 weeks in Aug. Excellent and interesting food. The restaurant is popular with the Bastille's new and successful residents. Need to book. A menu at 160F, otherwise well over 200F.

Blue Elephant, 43–45 rue de la Roquette, 11e; ☎47.00.42.00 (M^o Bastille/Richard-Lenoir). Daily to midnight. Closed Sun evening. Superb Thai restaurant in tropical forest decor. Worth every centime. 150F midday menu, otherwise over 250F.

Les Cinq Points Cardinaux, 14 rue Jean-Macé, 11e; ☎43.71.47.22 (M^o Faidherbe-Chaligny/ Charonne). Noon–2pm & 7–10pm. An excellent, simple, old-time *bistrot*, still mainly frequented by locals and decorated with the old tools of their trades. Prices under 55F for lunch; menus 57F and 95F in the evening. The snails in basil and the profiteroles are worth trying.

Chez Justine, 96 rue Oberkampf, 11e; ☎43.57.44.03 (M^o St-Maur/Ménilmontant). Mon lunchtimes only, Tues–Sat lunchtimes and evenings until 10.30pm; closed Aug. Good, substantial traditional cooking, decent wines for around 100F a bottle and a homely, cheerful atmosphere. Menus at 68F midday and 85F and 135F evenings.

La Mansouria, 11 rue Faidherbe-Chaligny, 11e; ☎43.71.00.16 (M^o Faidherbe-Chaligny). Lunchtimes, and evenings until 11.30pm; closed Sun, and Mon lunchtime, plus a fortnight in Aug. An elegant Moroccan restaurant, with the cheapest menu at 99F; otherwise around 170F. Excellent Moroccan crêpes and *tagines*.

Palais de la Femme, 94 rue de Charonne, 11^e; ☎43.71.11.27 (M^o Charonne/Faidherbe-Chaligny). Daily 11.30am–2.30pm & 6.30–8pm. A self-service restaurant in the women's hostel, run separately and open to all. Good solid meals for less than 50F.

Au Trou Normand, 9 rue Jean-Pierre Timbaud, 11e; ☎48.05.80.23 (M^o Filles-du-Calvaire/ Oberkampf/République). Mon–Fri lunchtimes & evenings until 9.30pm, Sat evening only; closed Aug. A small, totally unpretentious and very attractive local *bistrot*, serving good traditional food at knock-down prices. Dinner around 70F.

12^e
BARS AND CAFÉS

Le Baron Rouge, 1 rue Théophile-Roussel (corner of place d'Aligre market), 12e (M^o Ledru-Rollin). 10am–2pm & 5–9.30pm; closed Sun evening and Mon. Another popular and local bar. As well as the wines – around 16F per litre from the barrel – it serves a few snacks of cheese, *foie gras,* and *charcuterie*.

Le Penty Bar, corner of pl d'Aligre and rue Emilio-Castellar, 12e. Small, old-fashioned café making no concessions to 1990s sanitation and still only 5F for a sit-down cup of coffee.

RESTAURANTS

Au Limonaire, 88 rue de Charenton, 12e; ☎43.43.49.14 (M^o Ledru-Rollin/Gare-de-Lyon). Noon– 2.30pm & 8–10pm; closed Aug. Interesting food and wine in a beautiful old-fashioned café, adorned with musical instruments (entertainment in second half of week after 10pm: traditional French singing, etc). Lunchtime *plats* for around 50F; dinner 90–150F.

Le Train Bleu, 1st floor, Gare de Lyon, 20 bd Diderot, 12e; ☎43.43.09.06 (M^o Gare-de-Lyon). Daily until 10pm. You pay not for the food but the ludicrous *fin-de-siècle* stucco and murals of popular train destinations. Lunch menu at 195F, otherwise inflated *à la carte* prices.

13^e
BARS AND CAFÉS

La Folie en Tête, 33 rue de la Butte-aux-Cailles, 13e (M^o Place-d'Italie/Corvisart). Mon–Sat 10am– 2am. Cheap beer, sandwiches and midday *plat du jour*. Jazz Thursday nights; *chansons* Friday and Saturday. A very warm and laid-back address.

Le Merle Moqueur, 11 rue des Buttes-aux-Cailles, 13ᵉ (Mº Place-d'Italie/Corvisart). Daily 9pm–1am. Still going strong and still popular, along with its neighbouring bar-restaurants, **Le Diapason** (no. 15), **Chez Michel** (no. 15), **Resto des Bons Amis** (no. 13) and **Le Palmier** (no. 13).

RESTAURANTS

Bol en Bois, 35 rue Pascal, 13ᵉ; ☎47.07.27.24 (Mº Gobelins). Mon–Sat noon–2.30pm & 7–10pm. Macrobiotic veg and fish restaurant in a street being taken over by veggie/Buddhist concerns. 95F menu, *carte* 110F. Generous portions.

Chez Gladines, 30 rue des Cinq-Diamants, 13ᵉ; ☎45.83.53.34 (Mº Corvisart). Tues–Sun 7.30am–1.30am. Sometimes empty, sometimes bursting, this small corner *bistrot* is always welcoming. Excellent wines and dishes from the southwest. The mashed/fried potato is a must and goes best with *magret de canard* (58F). Around 100F for a full meal.

Lao-Thai, 128 rue de Tolbiac, 13ᵉ; ☎43.31.98.10 (Mº Tolbiac). Thurs–Tues 11.30–2.30 & 7–11pm. Big glass-fronted resto on a busy interchange. Finely spiced Thai and Laotian food, with coconut, ginger and lemon grass flavours. Around 120F.

Phuong Hoang, Terrasse des Olympiades, 52 rue du Javelot, 13ᵉ; ☎45.84.75.07 (Mº Tolbiac: take the escalator up from rue Tolbiac). Mon–Fri noon–2.30pm & 7–11.30pm. Vietnamese, Thai and Singapore specialities on lunch menus at 50F and 68F; *carte* 100–150F. If it's full or doesn't take your fancy, try *Le Grand Mandarin* or *L'Oiseau de Paradis* nearby.

Student restaurant 105 bd de l'Hôpital, 13ᵉ (Mº St-Marcel). See box on p.122 for details.

Le Temps des Cerises, 18–20 rue de la Butte-aux-Cailles, 13ᵉ; ☎45.89.69.48 (Mº Place-d'Italie/Corvisart). Mon–Fri noon–2pm & 7–11pm, Sat 7–11pm: A well-established workers' co-op with elbow-to-elbow seating and a different daily choice of imaginative dishes. 58F and 112F menus.

Thuy Huong and **Tricotin**, Kiosque de Choisy, 15 av de Choisy, 13ᵉ; ☎45.86.87.07 and ☎45.84.74.44 (Mº Porte-de-Choisy). Noon–2.30pm & 7–10.30pm; closed Thurs. *Thuy Huong* is in the inner courtyard of this Chinese shopping centre and is more of a café. *Tricotin* has two restaurants, visible from the avenue, no. 1 specializing in Thai dishes, no. 2 in the other Asiatic cuisines. Not easy to work out what's on the menu (*méduse*, by the way, is jellyfish), but you can depend on the *dim sum*, the duck dishes and the Vietnamese rice pancakes. Around 120F, or 70F at *Thuy Huong*.

14ᵉ
BARS AND CAFÉS

L'Entrepot, 7–9 rue Francis-de-Pressensé, 14ᵉ (Mº Pernety). Mon–Sat 2–11.30pm. Cinema with a spacious café, 58F midday menu, 95F and 125F evening menus.

Mustangs, 84 bd du Montparnasse, 14ᵉ (Mº Montparnasse-Bienvenue). Daily 9am–5am. Young crowd and happy atmosphere. A good place to finish up the evening after night-clubbing in St-Germain. Tex-Mex food, cocktails and beers.

Le Rallye, 6 rue Daguerre, 14ᵉ (Mº Denfert-Rochereau). Tues–Sat until 8pm; closed Aug. A good place to recover from the Catacombs or Montparnasse cemetery. The patron offers a bottle for tasting; gulping the lot would be considered bad form. Good cheese and *saucisson*.

RESTAURANTS

Aquarius 2, 40 rue Gergovie, 14ᵉ; ☎45.41.36.88 (Mº Pernety). Mon–Sat noon–3pm & 7–10.30pm. Imaginative vegetarian meals served with proper Parisian bustle. 60F menu.

Le Berbère, 50 rue de Gergovie, 14ᵉ; ☎45.42.10.29 (Mº Pernety). Daily, lunchtime & evenings until 10pm. A very unprepossessing place décor-wise, but serves wholesome, unfussy and cheap North African food. Couscous from 60F.

Bergamote, 1 rue Niepce, 14ᵉ; ☎43.22.79.47 (Mº Pernety). Tues–Sat lunchtime & evenings until 11pm; closed Aug. A small and sympathetic bistro, in a quiet, ungentrified street off rue de l'Ouest. Only about ten tables; you need to book weekends. There are 61F and 100F *formules* at lunchtime, 125F in the evening; *carte* around 160F.

La Bûcherie, 138 bd du Montparnasse, 14ᵉ; ☎43.20.47.87 (Mº Vavin/Port-Royal). Butcher's shop décor (minus the carcasses), waiters in butchers' aprons, menus on leather . . . and ace steaks. Up to 150F.

La Coupole, 102 bd du Montparnasse, 14ᵉ; ☎43.20.14.20 (Mº Vavin). 7.30–10.30am for breakfast, then noon–2am. The largest and perhaps the most famous and enduring arty-chic Parisian hang-out for dining, dancing and debate. After 11pm menu at 109F including wine. *Carte* 170–310F. Dancing 3–7pm weekends (Sat 60F, Sun 80F) and 9.30pm–4am Fri & Sat (90F).

N'Zadette M'Foua, 152 rue du Château, 14e; ☎43.22.00.16 (Mo Pernety). Mon–Sat evenings, until midnight. A small and tasty Congolese restaurant – *manioc, maboké*, etc. Reservations required weekends. Around 120F.

Au Rendez-vous des Camioneurs, 34 rue des Plantes, 14e; ☎45.40.43.36 (Mo Alésia). Mon–Fri lunchtime & 6–9.30pm; closed Aug. No lorry drivers any more, but good food for under 100F; menu at 60F and a quarter of wine 5F. Wise to book.

La Route du Château, 123 rue du Château, 14e; ☎43.20.09.59 (Mo Pernety). Mon lunchtimes only, Tues–Sat lunchtimes and evenings until 12.30am; closed Aug. Linen tablecloths, a rose on your table, an old-fashioned *bistrot* atmosphere. The food is beautifully prepared and cooked – getting pricy on the *carte* (well over 150F). Menu at 80F.

Student restaurants at 13/17 rue Dareau (Mo St-Jacques) and in the Cité Universitaire (*RER* Cité Universitaire). See p.122 for details.

15e
BARS AND CAFÉS

JeThéMe, 4 rue d'Alleray, 15e (Mo Vaugirard). Tues–Sat 10.30am–7pm; closed Aug. Despite the obnoxious name and the nostalgic décor (plagues of most Parisian *salons de thé*), the sweets, salads and snacks are good, and served at reasonable prices and with rare grace. Also sells coffee, tea and chocolate to take away.

RESTAURANTS

Aux Artistes, 63 rue Falguière, 15e; ☎43.22.05.39 (Mo Pasteur). Mon–Fri lunchtime & 7.15pm–1am, Sat 7.15pm–1am only. An old-time cheapie that has seen many a poor artist in its day. Still crowded and popular, serving a menu at 75F.

ETHNIC RESTAURANTS IN PARIS

AFRICAN AND NORTH AFRICAN
Le Berbère, 50 rue de Gergovie, 14e. North African. p.133.
Le Farafina, 12 rue Quincampoix, 4e. Central African. p.126.
Fouta Toro, 3 rue du Nord, 18e. Senegalese. p.136.
La Mansouria, 11 rue Faidherbe-Chaligny, 11e. Moroccan. p.132.
N'Zadette M'Foua, 152 rue du Château, 14e. Congolese. p.134.
Au Port de Pidjiguiti, 28 rue Étex, 18e. Co-operative, run by a village in Guinea-Bissau. p.137.

EAST EUROPEAN
Le Ravaillac, 10 rue du Roi-de-Sicile, 4e. Polish. p.127.
Village Bulgare, 8 rue de Nevers, 6e. Bulgarian. p.129.

GREEK
Égée, 19 rue de Ménilmontant, 20e. p.137.
Orestias, 4 rue Grégoire-de-Tours, 6e. p.129.

INDO-CHINESE
Blue Elephant, 43–45 rue de la Roquette, 11e. p.132.

Escale de Saigon, 24 rue Bosquet, 7e. Vietnamese. p.130.
Pho-Dong-Huong, 14 rue Louis-Bonnet, 20e. Chinese. p.137.
Phuong Hoang, Terrasse des Olympiades, 52 rue du Javelot, 13e. Vietnamese, Thai and Singaporean. p.133.
Taï Yen, 5 rue de Belleville, 20e. Thai. p.137.
Thuy Huon and Tricotin, Kiosque de Choisy, 15 av de Choisy, 13e. Chinese and Cambodian. p.133.

JAPANESE
Foujita, 45 rue St-Roch, 1er. p.124.

JEWISH
Goldenberg's, 7 rue des Rosiers, 4e. p.127.

KURDISH
Dilan, 13 rue Mandar, 2e. p.125.

LEBANESE
Le Liban à la Mouff, 3 rue de l'Estrapade, 5e. p.127.

TIBETAN
Tashi Delek, 4 rue des Fossés-St-Jacques, 5e. p.128.

Le Commerce, 51 rue du Commerce, 15ᵉ; ☎45.75.03.27 (Mᵒ Émile-Zola). Daily noon–3pm & 6.30–midnight. A double-storey restaurant that has been catering for *le petit peuple* for over a hundred years. Still varied, nourishing and cheap. Midday menu 100F; *plats du jour* 55–65F; 88F and 114F *formules*; *carte* around 145F.

L'Ostréade, 11 bd Vaugirard, 15ᵉ; ☎43.21.87.41 (Mᵒ Montparnasse). Daily to 11pm. A newish seafood brasserie with *tapas* on a 75F *formule* and excellent oysters. Around 175F for a full whack.

Sampieru Corsu, 12 rue de l'Amiral-Roussin, 15ᵉ (Mᵒ Cambronne). Mon–Fri lunchtimes & 7–9.30pm. Decorated with the posters and passionate declarations of international socialism, this restaurant has as its purpose the provision of meals for the homeless, the unemployed, the low-paid. The principle is that you pay what you can and it is left to your conscience how you settle the bill. The minimum requested is 36F for a three-course meal with wine. However poor you might feel, as a tourist in Paris you should be able to pay more. The restaurant only survives on the generosity of its supporters, and it's a wonderful place.

Student restaurant at 156 rue Vaugirard, 15ᵉ (Mᵒ Pasteur). See box on p.122 for details.

16ᵉ
BARS AND CAFÉS

Le Coquelin Aîné, 67 rue de Passy, 16ᵉ (Mᵒ Muette). Tues–Sat 9am–6.30pm. An elegant café on place Passy, meeting place of gilded youth and age. Excellent salads, *tartes,* cakes, at a price – this is not for paupers. 110F menu from noon to 2.30pm.

Kléber, place du Trocadéro, 16ᵉ (Mᵒ Trocadéro). Open until dawn. Good for cinematic views of the Eiffel Tower catching the first light or morning mist filling the valley of the Seine.

RESTAURANTS

Les Chauffeurs, 8 chaussée de la Muette, 16ᵉ; ☎42.88.50.05 (Mᵒ Muette). Daily noon–2.30pm & 7.30–10pm. You can't beat the 59F menu (not available Sun) for this part of the world.

Jean-Claude Ferrero, 38 rue Vital, 16ᵉ; ☎45.04.42.42. (Mᵒ Passy). Closed first 2 weeks in May & last 3 weeks in Aug. A gourmet heaven run by the chef who introduced menus dedicated to mushrooms and truffles. Mushrooms in a delectable sauce are included on the 220F midday menu. *À la carte* 450F upwards.

17ᵉ
BARS AND CAFÉS

Bar Belge, 75 av de St-Ouen, 17ᵉ (Mᵒ Guy-Môquet). Tues–Sun 3.30pm–1am. Belgian beers and *moules frites* for 60F, *coq au vin* 70F and *poulet aux cèpes* 65F.

L'Endroit, 67 pl Félix-Lobligeois, 17ᵉ; ☎42.29.50.00 (Mᵒ Rome/La Fourche). Noon–2am; closed Sun. A smartish late-night bar serving the local youth. Drinks from about 50F.

RESTAURANTS

Joy in Food, 2 rue Truffaut, 17ᵉ; ☎43.87.96.79 (Mᵒ Place-Clichy). Mon–Sat lunchtime, also evenings Tues, Fri & Sat. Minuscule veggie, with its mind on higher things: open meditation sessions at 8pm Wed. Good food and inexpensive.

Sangria, 13bis rue Vernier, 17ᵉ; ☎45.74.78.74 (Mᵒ Porte-de-Champerret). For 75F at midday and 85F in the evening you can help yourself to starters and wine in addition to enjoying three other courses. Very popular and crowded.

18ᵉ
BARS AND CAFÉS

La Petite Charlotte, 24 rue des Abbesses, 18ᵉ (Mᵒ Abbesses). Tues–Sun to 8pm. Crêpes, *pâtisseries* and 58F *formule* on sunny tables.

Le Pigalle, pl Pigalle, 18ᵉ (Mᵒ Pigalle). 24-hr bar, brasserie and *tabac*. A classic, complete with 1950s décor. Prices go up after 10pm.

Le Refuge, corner of rue Lamarck and the steps of rue de la Fontaine-du-But, 18ᵉ (Mᵒ Lamarck-Caulaincourt). A gentle café stop with a long view west down rue Lamarck to the country beyond.

RESTAURANTS

L'Assiette, 78 rue Labat, 18ᵉ; ☎42.59.06.63 (Mᵒ Château-Rouge). Closed Wed and Sat midday. A bit out of the way but very friendly with an 82F menu, delicious *champignons forestières* and chocolate charlotte.

Fouta Toro, 3 rue du Nord, 18ᵉ; ☎42.55.42.73 (Mᵒ Marcadet-Poissonniers). 8pm–midnight; closed Tues. A tiny, crowded, welcoming Senegalese diner in a very scruffy run-down alley northeast of Montmartre. No more than 70F all-in. Unless you come at the 8pm opening time, or after about 10.30pm, you'll almost certainly have to wait.

Au Grain de Folie, 24 rue La Vieuville, 18ᵉ; ☎42.58.15.57 (Mᵒ Abbesses). 12.30–2.30pm & 7–11.30pm. Tiny, simple and cheap, with just the sort of traditional atmosphere that you would hope for from Montmartre. Vegetarian. Soup and tart 60F, menu 100F.

LATE-NIGHT PARIS

For bars and brasseries in Paris to stay open after midnight is not at all unusual; the list below comprises cafés and bars that remain open after 2am, and restaurants that are open beyond midnight.

BARS AND CAFÉS

Le Dépanneur, 27 rue Fontaine, 9ᵉ. All-nighter. p.130.

Drugstore Élysées, 133 av des Champs-Élysées, 8ᵉ (p.130); **Drugstore Matignon**, 1 av Matignon, 8ᵉ (p.130); and **Drugstore Saint-Germain**, 149 bd St-Germain, 6ᵉ (p.129). All until 2am.

Le Grand Café Capucines, 4 bd des Capucines, 9ᵉ. All-nighter. p.130.

Iguana, 15 rue de la Roquette, 11ᵉ. Till 4am. p.131.

Kléber, place du Trocadéro, 16ᵉ. Until dawn. p.135.

Le Mazet, 6 rue St-André-des-Arts, 6ᵉ. Until 2am; Fri & Sat until 3.30am. p.128.

L'Opus, 167 quai de Valmy, 10ᵉ. Till 4am. p.131.

Le Pigalle, place Pigalle, 18ᵉ. Till 5am. p.135.

Polly Magoo, 11 rue St-Jacques, 5ᵉ. All-nighter. p.127.

Pub Saint-Germain, 17 rue de l'Ancienne-Comédie, 6ᵉ. 24-hr. p.128.

Le Quetzal, 10 rue de la Verrerie, 4ᵉ. Till 3am. p.126.

Le Sous-Bock, 49 rue St-Honoré, 1ᵉʳ. Until 5am. p.124.

La Taverne de Nesle, 32 rue Dauphine, 6ᵉ. Until 5am. p.128.

RESTAURANTS

L'Abreuvoir, 68 rue de la Roquette, 11ᵉ. Till 1am. p.132.

Aux Artistes, 63 rue Falguière, 15ᵉ. Until 12.30am. p.134.

Bofinger, 3–7 rue de la Bastille, 3ᵉ. Until 1am. p.125.

Brasserie Balzar, 49 rue des Écoles, 5ᵉ. Until 12.30am. p127.

Chez Gladines, 30 rue des Cinq-Diamants, 13ᵉ. Until 2am. p.133.

La Coupole, 102 bd du Montparnasse, 14ᵉ. Until 2am. p.133.

Aux Deux Saules, 91 rue St-Denis, 1ᵉʳ. Until 1am. p.124.

Le Farafina, 12 rue Quincampoix, 4ᵉ. Till 4am or later. p.126.

Flo, 7 cours des Petites-Écuries, 10ᵉ. Until 1.30am. p.131.

Fouta Toro, 3 rue du Nord, 18ᵉ. Until 1am. p.136.

Julien, 16 rue du Faubourg-St-Denis, 10ᵉ. Until 1.30am. p.131.

Lipp, 151 bd St-Germain, 6ᵉ. Until 12.30am. p.129.

Le Muniche, 22 rue Guillaume-Apollinaire, 6ᵉ. Until 3am. p.129.

Le Petit Zinc, 11 rue Saint-Benoît, 6ᵉ. Until 3am. p.129.

Au Pied de Cochon, 6 rue Coquillière, 1ᵉʳ. 24-hr. p.124.

Polidor, 41 rue Monsieur-le-Prince, 6ᵉ. Until 1am. p.129.

Le Procope, 13 rue de l'Ancienne-Comédie, 6ᵉ. Until 1am. p.129.

La Route du Château, 123 rue du Château, 14ᵉ. Until 12.30am. p.134.

Terminus Nord, 23 rue de Dunkerque, 10ᵉ. Until 12.30am. p.131.

Taï Yen, 5 rue de Belleville, 20ᵉ. Until 1am. p.137.

Le Vaudeville, 29 rue Vivienne, 2ᵉ. Until 2am. p.125.

OVER THE TOP... THE GOURMET RESTAURANTS OF PARIS

If you're feeling slightly crazed – or you happen on a winning lottery ticket – there are, of course, some really spectacular Parisian restaurants. For *nouvelle cuisine* at its very best *Robuchon* (32 rue de Longchamp, 16ᵉ), *Lucas Carton* (9 place de la Madeleine, 8ᵉ), and *Taillevent* (15 rue Lamenais, 8ᵉ) are said to be the pinnacles of gastronomic experience and not just for bills that can reach 10,000F for two. For pride of place if not so much for *plats* there's *Jules Vernes* on the second floor of the Eiffel Tower. Unfortunately, the moment's madness that might inspire you to eat in any of these restaurants would most likely come months too late for you to make reservations.

Marie-Louise, 52 rue Championnet, 18ᵉ; ☎46.06.86.55 (Mᵒ Simplon). Lunchtime, and evenings until 9.30pm; closed Sun, Mon & Aug. A place with a well-deserved reputation. A bit of a trek north, but very much worth the journey for a special meal, for the traditional French cuisine is excellent. Menu at 120F, otherwise around 200F. The dish to try is *bœuf à la ficelle* (poached beef).

À la Pomponnette, 42 rue Lepic, 18ᵉ; ☎46.06.08.36 (Mᵒ Blanche). Lunchtime, and evenings until 9.30pm; closed Sun evening, Mon & Aug. A genuine old Montmartre *bistrot*, with posters, drawings, zinc-top bar, nicotine stains etc. The food is excellent, but will cost you going on 200F *à la carte*; good menu including wine at 150F.

Au Port de Pidjiguiti, 28 rue Étex, 18ᵉ; ☎42.26.71.77 (Mᵒ Guy-Môquet). Lunchtime, and evenings until 11pm; closed Mon & Jan. Very pleasant atmosphere and excellent food for about 80F. It is run by a village in Guinea-Bissau, whose inhabitants take turns in staffing the restaurant; the proceeds go to the village. Good-value wine list.

20ᵉ
BARS AND CAFÉS

Le Baratin, 3 rue Jouye-Rouve, 20ᵉ (Mᵒ Pyrénées). Tues–Fri noon–midnight, Sat & Sun 5pm–midnight. *Bistrot à vins*. Friendly, unpretentious place with a good mix of people, locals and alternative types. Good selection of lesser known wines and whiskies. Midday menu 59F, *à la carte* 150F.

Les Envierges, 11 rue des Envierges, 20ᵉ (Mᵒ Pyrénées). Wed–Fri noon–midnight, Sat & Sun noon–8pm. *Bistrot à vins*. Another purveyor of good-quality lesser known wines to connoisseurs. An attractive bar – though more a place to taste and buy wine than eat – in a great location above the Parc de Belleville.

RESTAURANTS

À la Courtille, 1 rue des Envierges, 20ᵉ; ☎46.36.51.59 (Mᵒ Pyrénées). Lunchtime, and evenings until 11.30pm. Slightly stark modern interior, but good traditional cuisine in an unbeatable situation overlooking the delightful new Parc de Belleville. Get a pavement table on a summer evening and you'll have the best restaurant view in Paris. Midday menus 70F and 100F, *à la carte* 200F.

Égée, 19 rue de Ménilmontant, 20ᵉ; ☎43.58.70.26 (Mᵒ Ménilmontant). Noon–2.30pm & 7.30–11.30pm. Greek and Turkish specialities served with fresh home-made bread. Lunch menu at just 45F, eating *à la carte* is more like 120F.

La Fontaine aux Roses, 27 av Gambetta, 20ᵉ; ☎46.36.74.75 (Mᵒ Père-Lachaise). Till 10pm. Closed Mon, Sun midday & Aug. Small and beautiful restaurant with first-rate midday menu of 103F and evening 156F, both including kir royale, wine and coffee.

Pho-Dong-Huong, 14 rue Louis-Bonnet, 20ᵉ; ☎43.57.42.81 (Mᵒ Belleville). Noon–10.30pm; closed Tues. Spotlessly clean Vietnamese resto, where all dishes are under 50F and come with piles of fresh green leaves. Spicy soups, crispy pancakes, but slow service.

Aux Rendez-Vous des Amis, 10 av Père-Lachaise, 20ᵉ; ☎47.97.72.16 (Mᵒ Gambetta). Lunchtime only, noon–2.30pm; closed Sun and mid-July to mid-Aug. Unprepossessing surroundings for very good, simple and satisfying family cooking – at around 80F, menu at 59F.

Taï Yen, 5 rue de Belleville, 20ᵉ; ☎42.41.44.16 (Mᵒ Belleville). 11.30am–1am. You can admire the koi carps like embroidered satin cushions idling round their aquarium while you wait for the copious soups and steamed specialities. 60F menu, 100F *à la carte*.

Music and nightlife

The strength of the Paris **music scene** is its diversity – a reputation gained mainly from its absorption of immigrant and exile populations. The city has no rivals in Europe for the variety of **world music** to be discovered: Algerian, West and Central African, Caribbean and Latin American sounds are represented in force. **Jazz** fans, too, are in for a treat, with new venues opening all the time, and all styles from New Orleans to current experimental, although in most clubs expense is a real drawback to enjoyment: admission charges are generally high and when they're not levied there's usually a whacking charge for your first drink, and subsequent drinks don't come cheap.

Finally, there is the tradition of **chansons**, epitomized by the sublime Edith Piaf and developed to its greatest heights by Georges Brassens and the Belgian Jacques Brel. This music survives and, indeed, is undergoing something of a revival.

Nightlife recommendations – for **dance clubs and discos** – are to some extent incorporated with those for rock, world music and jazz, with which they merge. Separate sections, however, detail places that are mainly for dancing, or which cater for a primarily gay or lesbian clientele. Bear in mind that some clubs operate very snooty door policies.

Classical music, as you might expect in this Neoclassical city, is alive and well and takes up twice the space of "jazz-pop-folk-rock" in the listings magazines. The Paris **Opéra** has a new palace with Europe's largest opera stage at the Bastille. The need for advance reservations (except for the concerts held in churches) rather than the price is the major inhibiting factor here. If you're interested in the **contemporary** scene of Systems composition and the like, check out IRCAM at Beaubourg. At the end of the section are details of all the **stadium venues** for major events from heavy metal to opera.

Information and tickets

For exhaustive **listings of what's on** in the city, there are the weekly guides, published on a Wednesday: *Pariscope* and *L'Officiel des Spectacles. Pariscope* is probably the easiest to find your way around, but since both are just listings, with a minimum of comment, there is not much difference between them. The best place to get **tickets** for concerts, whether rock, jazz, *chansons* or classical, is *FNAC Musique,* 4 place de la Bastille, 12ᵉ (Mᵒ Bastille); and 2 rue des Italiens, 9ᵉ (Mᵒ Chaussée d'Autin; Mon, Tues, Thurs & Sat 10am–8pm, Wed & Fri 10am–10pm) or the *Virgin Megastore*, 56–60 av des Champs-Élysées, 8ᵉ (Mᵒ Franklin-Roosevelt); and Carrousel du Louvre, Palais du Louvre, 1ᵉʳ (Mᵒ Louvre-Rivoli; both Mon–Thurs 10am–midnight, Fri & Sat 10am–1am, Sun 2pm–midnight).

Music venues

Most of the **music venues** listed below are clubs. A few of them will have live music all week, but the majority host bands on just a couple of nights, usually Friday and Saturday, when admission prices are also hiked up.

Mainly rock

La Cigale, 120 bd de Rochechouart, 18ᵉ; ☎42.23.15.15 (Mᵒ Pigalle). Rita Mitsouko, punk, indie etc. An eclectic programming policy in an old-fashioned converted theatre, long a fixture on the Pigalle scene. Music from 8.30pm.

Le Gibus, 18 rue du Faubourg-du-Temple, 11ᵉ; ☎47.00.78.88 (Mᵒ République). For twenty years English rock bands on their way up have played their first Paris gig at Gibus, the Clash and Police among them. Fourteen nights of dross will turn up one decent band, but it's always hot, loud, energetic and crowded. It's also one of the cheaper clubs. Tues–Sat 11pm–5am, Aug Sat only.

La Locomotive, 90 bd de Clichy, 18ᵉ; ☎42.57.37.37 (Mᵒ Blanche). Enormous high-tech nightclub with three dance floors, one for techno, one for rock and heavy metal, and one for rap and funk. Crowded and popular. Tues–Sun 11pm–5am. Concerts start at 1am. Tues–Fri 50F; Sat & Sun 90F.

New Riverside, 7 rue Grégoire-de-Tours, 6ᵉ; ☎43.54.46.33 (Mᵒ Odéon). Good, friendly club playing rock and pop music in a sixteenth-century cellar. Breakfast included in admission price at the weekend. Free admission for women, except Fri & Sat; otherwise, Mon–Thurs 70F, Fri, Sat & Sun 100F.

Rex Club, 5 bd Poissonnière, 9ᵉ; ☎42.36.10.96 (Mᵒ Montmartre). Live music – rock, funk, soul, raï, rap (mainly on Tues and Sat from 6pm), charging 50–100F. Disco from 11pm, 60–90F. Tues, Wed & Fri–Sun 8pm–6am; sometimes closed Sun.

Le Saint, 7 rue St-Séverin, 5ᵉ; ☎43.25.50.64 (Mᵒ St-Michel). Good value, varied music played in an ancient cellar; popular with students. Tues–Sun 11am–dawn. 50F including one drink Tues–Thurs, 70F Fri–Sun.

Mainly Latin and Caribbean

L'Escale, 15 rue Monsieur-le-Prince, 6ᵉ; ☎43.25.55.22 (Mᵒ Odéon). More Latin American musicians must have passed through here than any other club. The dance sounds, *salsa* mostly, are in the basement (disco on Wed), while on the ground floor every variety of South American music is given an outlet. 11pm–4am. Drinks 80F.

La Plantation, 45 rue de Montpensier, 1ᵉʳ; ☎ 49.27.06.21 (Mᵒ Palais-Royal). In spite of the reputation for welcoming everyone, the doormen are fussy, particularly if you're white. Inside, excellent Cuban, Angolan, Congolese and Antillais music awaits you. Tues–Sun 11pm–dawn. 90F entry, including first drink; further drinks from 50F.

Les Trottoirs de Buenos Aires, 37 rue des Lombards, 1ᵉʳ; ☎42.26.29.32 (Mᵒ Châtelet). Argentinian tango is the only music performed on the stage of "the pavements of Buenos Aires". No one dances except professional artistes, but it's highly recommended. Tues–Sun 9.30pm onwards. 100F entrance, drinks from 50F.

Bals musettes

Balajo, 9 rue de Lappe, 11ᵉ; ☎47.00.07.87 (Mᵒ Bastille). The old-style music hall of *gai* but straight *Paris* – extravagant 1930s décor, working-class Parisians in their weekend best and the music everything to move to from mazurka, tango, waltz, cha-cha, twist to the slurpy *chansons* of between the wars. Thurs, Fri, Sat & Mon 11pm–4.30am. Afternoon sessions cost 30F and run 3–6.30pm Mon, Fri & Sat.

Chapelle des Lombards, 19 rue de Lappe, 11ᵉ; ☎43.57.24.24 (Mᵒ Bastille). This erstwhile *bal musette* still plays the occasional waltz and tango but for the most part the music is salsa, reggae, steel drums, gwo-kâ, zouk, raï and the blues. The doormen are not too friendly and we've heard alarming stories of hassle and harassment inside. 100F entry and first drink; 50F upwards for next drinks. Mon–Sat 10.30pm–dawn; bands Thurs–Sat only.

Le Tango, 13 rue Au-Maire, 3ᵉ; ☎42.72.77.78 (Mᵒ Arts-et-Métiers). The tango has been played here since the turn of the century and the décor looks as if it's retained layers from every decade since. No vetting, cheap admission and drinks, people dancing with abandon to please themselves, not the adjudicators of style. Fri–Sat 11pm–5am.

Mainly jazz

Baiser Salé, 58 rue des Lombards, 1ᵉʳ; ☎42.33.37.71 (Mᵒ Châtelet). A bar downstairs and a small, crowded upstairs room with live music every night from 11pm – usually jazz, rhythm & blues, Latino-rock, reggae or Brazilian. 8.30pm–4am. Drinks from 60F.

Le Bilboquet, 13 rue St-Benoît, 6ᵉ; ☎45.48.81.84 (Mᵒ St-Germain). A very comfortable bar/restaurant with live jazz every night – local and international stars, like baritone player Gary Smulyan. Music starts at 10.45pm. No admission; drinks over 70F a shot. Mon–Sat 9pm–dawn; live music from 10.45pm.

L'Eustache, 37 rue Berger, 1ᵉʳ; ☎40.26.23.20 (Mᵒ Châtelet-Les Halles). Cheap beer and very good jazz by local musicians in this young and friendly Les Halles café – cheapest good jazz in the capital. Mon–Sat 11am–4am; live jazz Thurs, Fri & Sat 10.30pm–2am.

Lionel Hampton Bar, *Hôtel Méridien*, 81 bd Gouvion-St-Cyr, 17ᵉ; ☎40.68.34.34 (Mᵒ Porte-Maillot). First-rate jazz venue, with big-name musicians. Inaugurated by himself, but otherwise the great man is only an irregular visitor. Drinks from 130F. Mon–Sat 10pm–2am.

New Morning, 7–9 rue des Petites-Écuries, 10ᵉ; ☎45.23.51.41 (Mᵒ Château-d'Eau). Host to the big international names but not all it's cracked up to be. The sound is good but the décor, though spacious, is rather cold; no marks either for the ludicrous drink prices. 9pm–1.30am (concerts start around 10pm).

Le Petit Journal, 71 bd St-Michel, 5ᵉ; ☎43.26.28.59 (Mᵒ Luxembourg). Small, smoky bar, long frequented by Left Bank student types, with good, mainly French, traditional and mainstream sounds. Mon–Sat 10pm–2am. Closed Aug. First drink over 100F.

Le Petit Journal Montparnasse, 13 rue du Commandant-Mouchotte, 14ᵉ; ☎43.21.56.70 (Mᵒ Montparnasse). Under the *Hôtel Montparnasse*, and sister establishment to the above, with bigger, visiting names, both French and international. Mon–Sat 9pm–2am. Closed July. Drinks around 80F.

Le Petit Opportun, 15 rue des Lavandières-Ste-Opportune, 1ᵉʳ; ☎42.36.01.36 (Mᵒ Châtelet-Les-Halles). It's worth arriving early to get a seat for the live music in the dungeon-like cellar where the acoustics play strange tricks and you can't always see the musicians. Fairly eclectic policy and a crowd of genuine connoisseurs. Tues–Sat 9pm–3am; music from 11pm. First drink 120F.

Le Sunset, 60 rue des Lombards, 1ᵉʳ; ☎40.26.46.20 (Mᵒ Châtelet-Les-Halles). Restaurant upstairs, jazz club in the basement, featuring the best musicians – the likes of Alain Jeanmarie and Turk Mauro – and frequented by musicians. Mon–Sat 8pm–3am. Admission 100F with drink.

Théâtre Dunois, 108 rue du Chevaleret, 13ᵉ; ☎42.33.22.88 (Mᵒ Chevaleret). Free and experimental jazz – and one of the few places in Paris to hear improvised music, as opposed to free jazz. Cheap and unsnobbish. Daily from 7pm; concerts Mon–Fri & Sun 8.30–11.30pm. 70F entry; 50F for students.

Utopia, 1 rue Niepce, 14ᵉ; ☎43.22.79.66 (Mᵒ Pernety). Good French blues singers interspersed with jazz and blues tapes playing to a young and studentish crowd. No admission charge and cheap drinks. Generally very pleasant atmosphere. Tues–Sat 10.30pm–dawn. Drinks from 50F.

Mainly *chansons*

Le Caveau des Oubliettes, 11 rue St-Julien-le-Pauvre, 5ᵉ; ☎45.54.94.97 (Mᵒ St-Michel). French popular music of bygone times – Piaf and earlier – sung with exquisite nostalgia in the ancient prisons of Châtelet. Mon–Sat 9pm–2am. Entry and first drink 140F.

Le Piston Pélican, 15 rue de Bagnolet, 20ᵉ; ☎43.70.23.93 (Mᵒ Alexandre-Dumas). A scruffy bar seeing a revivial of *café-conc'* – listening to live music for the price of a coffee, but getting a bit too popular for its own good. Wed–Sun 10pm–2am, Tues 7pm–2am.

Nightclubs and discos

La Casbah, 18-20 rue de la Forge-Royale, 11ᵉ; ☎43.71.71.89 (Mᵒ Bastille). Bar upstairs, dancing down. The outstanding feature of this rather fancy and exclusive place is the décor: beautiful and authentic stuff from Morocco – doors, furniture, plasterwork – matched by the *zouave* costumes of the waiters and waitresses. Daily 9pm–5am.

Discophage, 11 passage du Clos-Bruneau (off 31–33 rue des Écoles), 5ᵉ; ☎43.26.31.41 (Mᵒ Maubert-Mutualité). A jam-packed and under-ventilated space, but all such discomforts are irrelevant for the best Brazilian sounds you can hear in Paris. Mon–Sat 9pm–3am, music begins at 10pm; closed Aug.

Flash Back, 37 rue Grégoire-de-Tours, 6ᵉ; ☎43.25.56.70 (Mᵒ Mabillon). Techno and commercial rock in a futuristic decor. 11am–dawn. Closed Monday. 70F entry.

Le Malibu, 44 rue Tiquetonne, 2ᵉ; ☎42.36.62.70 (Mᵒ Étienne-Marcel). Black music from all over West Africa and the West Indies in a crowded basement beneath a restaurant, with no strict admission policy. Wed–Sun 8.30pm–5am. Around 150F.

Le Moloko, 26 rue Fontaine, 9ᵉ; ☎48.74.50.26 (Mᵒ Blanche). A new, fashionable and successful addition to the night scene, frequented by the young and gorgeous, the trendy and posey, all sorts. Jukebox instead of DJs, occasionally live music in the early evening. Daily 9pm–6am. No admission; drinks from 50F.

Le Palace, 8 rue du Faubourg-Montmartre, 9ᵉ; ☎42.46.10.87 (Mᵒ Montmartre). The best night out in Paris, packed nightly with revellers in their best party gear. Some nights it's thematic fancy dress, some nights the music is all African, other times the place is booked for TV dance shows. It's big, the bopping is good, and the clientele are an exuberant spectacle in themselves. Entry 120F weekends, otherwise 100F. 11pm–dawn.

Le Shéhérazade, 3 rue de Liège, 9ᵉ; ☎48.74.41.68 (Mᵒ Liège). Popular with the youthful, mixed, dancing crowd. House music, with occasional variant evenings. Exotic décor in a former Russian cabaret; vodka 80–90F a shot. Mon–Thurs 11pm–dawn, Fri–Sun midnight–dawn. 100F admission plus drink.

Zed Club, 2 rue des Anglais, 5ᵉ; ☎43.54.93.78 (Mᵒ Maubert-Mutualité). *The* rock 'n' roll club. Wed–Sat 10.30pm–3.30am; 50F entry Wed, 50F entry plus drink Thurs, 100F entry and drink Fri & Sat.

Lesbian and gay clubs and discos

Lesbian clubs find it hard to be exclusively female, and you may find that none of them are particularly agreeable. The pleasures of **gay men** are far better catered for, though AIDS has changed the scene and the wicked little bars with obscure back-rooms around Les Halles have all but ceased to exist. High-tech, well-lit, sense-surround disco beat is the current style. For a complete rundown, consult *Paris Scene* (Gay Men's Press, £5.99) or the *Gai-Pied Guide*.

Women

Chez Moune, 54 rue Pigalle, 18ᵉ; ☎45.26.64.64 (Mᵒ Pigalle). In the red-light heart of Paris, this mixed but predominantly women's cabaret and disco may shock or delight feminists. The evening includes a strip-tease (by women) without the standard audience for such shows (any man causing the slightest fuss is kicked out). Sunday tea-dance afternoons at 4.30–8pm are strictly women-only. 10pm–dawn.

Entre Nous, 17 rue Laferrière, 9ᵉ; ☎48.78.11.67 (Mᵒ St-Georges). A small women-only club with an intimate atmosphere and catholic taste in music. Wed & Sat only 11pm–dawn.

Le New Monocle, 60 bd Edgar-Quinet, 14ᵉ; ☎43.20.81.12 (Mᵒ Montparnasse). Revitalized women's cabaret. A scattering of men are allowed in every evening. 11pm–dawn; closed Sun.

Le Privilège-Kat, 3 cité Bergère, 9ᵉ; ☎42.46.50.98 (Mᵒ Rue-Montmartre). A venue run by two stylish women. No men. Fri & Sat 11.30pm–6am. Entry 90F, drinks from 60F.

Men

Le BH, 7 rue du Roule, 1ᵉʳ (Mᵒ Châtelet-Les-Halles). Still one of the cheapest gay discos in the city; exclusively male. 11pm–8am.

La Luna, 28 rue Keller, 11ᵉ; ☎40.21.09.91 (Mᵒ Bastille). Latest high-tech rendezvous for the gay Bastille, complete with mirrors to dance to. Wed–Sun 11pm–6am. Weekend entry 50F, drinks from 45F.

Le Manhattan, 8 rue des Anglais, 5ᵉ; ☎43.54.98.86 (Mᵒ Maubert-Mutualité). Men-only club with a good funky disco. Fri, Sat & Sun 11pm–6am. Admission 48F; drinks from 37F.

Le Palace, 8 rue du Faubourg-Montmartre, 9ᵉ; ☎42.46.10.87 (Mᵒ Rue Montmartre). Gay tea dance every Sunday afternoon, 5pm onwards; entry 40F before 6pm, 69F after; drinks from 50F.

Le Piano Zinc, 49 rue des Blancs-Manteaux, 4ᵉ; ☎42.74.32.42 (Mᵒ Rambuteau). From 10pm when the piano-playing starts, this bar becomes a happy riot of songs, music hall acts and dance, which may be hard to appreciate if you don't follow French very well. Tues–Sun 6pm–2am. Drinks around 40F.

Classical and contemporary music

Paris is a stimulating environment for **classical music,** both established and contemporary. The former is well represented in performances within churches – often for free or very cheap – and in an enormous choice of commercially promoted concerts held every day of the week. Contemporary and experimental computer-based work flourishes.

Concert venues

The **Cité de la Musique** project at La Villette has given Paris two new, major concert venues. The **Conservatoire**, the national music academy, has already opened its doors on av Jean-Jaurès (information and bookings ☎40.40.46.46, 40.40.46.47). Next door, a new **auditorium** – due to be completed by the end of 1995 – will be adaptable to all kinds of novel configurations of instruments.

These apart, the top **auditoriums** are: *Salle Pleyel,* 252 rue du Faubourg-St-Honoré, 8e (M° Ternes; ☎45.61.06.30); *Épicerie-Beaubourg,* 12 rue du Renard, 4e (M° Hôtel-de-Ville; ☎42.72.23.41); *Gaveau,* 45 rue de la Boétie (M° Miromesnil; ☎49.53.05.07); *Théâtre des Champs-Élysées,* 15 av Montaigne, 8e (M° Alma-Marceau; ☎47.23.47.77); and the *Théâtre Musical de Paris,* 1 place du Châtelet, 1er (M° Châtelet; ☎40.28.28.40). **Tickets** are best bought at the box offices, though for big names you may find overnight queues, and a large number of seats are always booked by subscribers. The price range is very reasonable. Classical concerts also take place for **free** at *Radio France,* 166 av du Président-Kennedy, 16e (M° Passy; ☎42.30.23.08).

Opera

The first performance at the **Bastille opera house** – the six-hour-long *Les Troyens* by Berlioz – cast something of a shadow on the project's proclaimed commitment to popularizing its art. Since then it has been plagued by rows and resignations, and opinions differ on the quality of the acoustics and of the productions. To judge the place for yourself, tickets (40–520F) can be booked Monday to Saturday 11am to 6pm on ☎44.73.13.00 or from the ticket offices (Mon–Sat 11am–6.30pm within two weeks of the performance). The cheapest seats are only available to personal callers; unfilled seats are sold at discount to students five minutes before the curtain goes up. For programme details phone ☎43.43.96.96. Note that the old Paris opera house – the Palais Garnier – is now solely used for staging ballet.

More big-scale opera productions are staged at the **Théâtre Musical de Paris** and the **Théâtre des Champs-Élysées** (see above). Rather less grand opera is also performed at the **Épicerie-Beaubourg** (see above), and at the **Opéra-Comique**, Salle Favard, 5 rue Favard, 2e, M° Richelieu-Drouot (☎42.86.88.83). Both opera and recitals are also put on at the multipurpose performance halls (see oposite).

Contemporary music

Beneath the Beaubourg arts centre is the vast laboratory of acoustics and "digital signal processing" – a complex known as **IRCAM** and set up by composer Pierre Boulez. You can play around for free with tapes in the IRCAM lobby (entrance down the stairs by the Stravinsky pool on the south side of Beaubourg). If you're impressed, you might want to attend a performance by the resident *Ensemble Inter-Contemporain* (details from Beaubourg information desk).

Apart from Boulez, other names to look out for are Paul Mefano and his 2E2M ensemble, Jean-Claude Eloy, Pascal Dusapin and Luc Ferrarie. Check *Pariscope* and *L'Official des Spectacles* for details.

Festivals

Festivals are plentiful in all the diverse fields that come under the far too general term of "classical". The **Festival de Musique Ancienne** takes place at the end of May and beginning of June, and focuses on a particular civilization or culture. The **Soirées de Saint-Aignan** at the Hôtel St-Aignan in May feature European music of the eighteenth and nineteenth centuries. There is also a **festival of sacred music** most years, a **Chopin festival**, a **Mozart festival**, and the *Festival de l'Orangerie de Sceaux* of chamber music all summer at the Château de Sceaux to the south of the city.

For details of these and more, pick up the current year's **festival schedule** from one of the tourist offices or the Hôtel de Ville, 29 rue du Rivoli, 4ᵉ (Mᵒ Hôtel de Ville).

The big performance halls

Events at any of the performance spaces listed below will be well advertised on billboards and posters throughout the city. Tickets can be obtained at the halls themselves, though it's easier to get them through agents like *FNAC* or *Virgin Megastore.*

Le Bataclan, 50 bd Voltaire, 11ᵉ; ☎47.05.65.23 (Mᵒ Oberkampf). One of the best places for visiting and native rock bands.

Forum des Halles, Niveau 3, Porte Rambuteau, 15 rue de l'Equerre-d'Argent, 1ᵉʳ; ☎42.03.11.11 (Mᵒ Châtelet). Varied functions – theatre, performance art, rock etc, often with foreign touring groups.

Maison des Cultures du Monde, 101 bd Raspail, 6ᵉ; ☎45.44.72.30 (Mᵒ Rennes). All the arts from all over the world and undominated for once by the Europeans.

Olympia, 28 bd des Capucines, 9ᵉ; ☎ 47.42.25.49 (Mᵒ Madeleine/Opéra). An old music hall hosting occasional well-known rock groups.

Palais des Congrès, place de la Porte-Maillot, 17ᵉ; ☎40.48.25.50 (Mᵒ Porte-Maillot). Opera, ballet, orchestral music, trade fairs and the superstars of US and British rock.

Palais des Glaces, 37 rue du Faubourg-du-Temple, 10ᵉ; ☎42.02.27.17 (Mᵒ République). Smallish theatre used for rock, ballet, jazz and French folk.

Palais Omnisports de Bercy, 8 bd de Bercy, 12ᵉ; ☎43.42.01.23 (Mᵒ Bercy). Opera, Bruce Springsteen, ice hockey, with seats to give vertigo to the most level headed, but an excellent space when used in the round.

Palais des Sports, Porte de Versailles, 15ᶜ; ☎48.28.40.10 (Mᵒ Porte-de-Versailles). Good place for seeing your favourite mega rock star in miniature half a mile away.

Zenith, Parc de la Villette, 211 av Jean-Jaurès, 20ᵉ; ☎42.08.60.00, 42.40.60.00 (Mᵒ Porte-de-Pantin). Seating for six-and-a-half-thousand people in an inflatable stadium designed exclusively for rock and pop concerts. The concrete column with a descending red aeroplane is the landmark you should head for.

Film, theatre and dance

Paris belongs, of course, in the top international touring circuit for **dance and theatre companies**, and hosts the best of the French regional productions, which can be just as good, if not better, than Paris-based work of the companies, particularly in dance. The *Maisons de Culture* in the suburbs also rival the city proper for bold experimental theatre. But that's not to say that performing arts don't flourish in Paris, and as for **film**, the city is, without a doubt, the cinema capital of the world.

Festivals include *Paris Quartier d'Été* from mid-July to mid-August with music, theatre and cinema events around the city; the *Festival d'Automne* between September and December with traditional and experimental theatrical, musical, dance and multimedia productions from all over the world; the *Festival International: Films des Femmes* in March or April (see overleaf); and the *Prix International de Danse* in November.

Information and tickets

The most comphrehensive **film listings** are given in *Pariscope*. You rarely need to book in advance; programmes (*séances*) often start between 1 and 3pm and continue through to the early hours. The average price is 45F and many have lower rates on Monday or Wednesday and for earlier *séances*, and student reductions from Monday to Thursday. The *UGC* and *Gaumont* chains sell five tickets for 150F which can be used by two people at the same time. Almost all of the huge selection of foreign films will be shown at some cinemas in the original – *v.o.* in the listings. Dubbed films will be listed as *v.f.* and English versions of co-productions as *version anglaise* or *v.a.*

Stage productions are detailed in *Pariscope* and *L'Official des Spectacles* with brief resumés or reviews. Prices vary between 50F and 165F for state theatres; 200–300F for others. Many theatres have student discounts from Tuesday to Thursday (most closed Mon). Prices are high for epic productions by top directors which may be seven hours long or even carry over several days. These always need booking in advance. Tickets can be bought directly from the theatres, from *FNAC* shops and *Virgin Megastores* (see p.138) or at two **ticket kiosks**: in the Châtelet-Les Halles *RER* station (Tues–Fri 12.30–7.30pm, Sat 2–7.30pm) and opposite 15 place de la Madeleine, 8ᵉ (Mᵒ Madeleine; Tues–Sat 12.30–8pm, Sun 12.30–4pm). The kiosks sell same-day tickets at half price, but be prepared to queue. Tickets for **café-théatres** average around 80F and it's best to book in advance for weekends directly from the venues.

Many cinemas and theatres have unwaged ushers who will expect a 5F tip.

Film and video

There are over 350 **films** showing in Paris in any one week, covering every place and period, with new works (excepting British movies) arriving long before London and New York. If your French is good enough for subtitles, go and see a Senegalese, Taiwanese, Brazilian or Finnish film that would never be seen in Britain or the US. Or choose your own video clips at the *Vidéothèque de Paris* (see below). The **International Festival of Women's Films** is organized by the *Maison des Arts* in the southeastern suburb of Créteil, and programme details are available from mid-March onwards, from the *Maison des Arts*, place Salvador-Allende, Créteil (Mᵒ Créteil-Préfecture; ☎49.80.38.98), or from the *Maison des Femmes* (see p.155). For the biggest screens of all, check-out the 180° Omnimax projection system at La Villette and La Défense – see p.118 and p.115.

Venues

Cinémathèques, Salle Garance, Centre Beaubourg, 4ᵉ (Mᵒ Rambuteau); Musée du Cinéma, Palais de Chaillot, corner of avs Président-Wilson and Albert-de-Mun, 16ᵉ (Mᵒ Trocadéro); and Palais de Tokyo, 13 av du Président-Wilson, 16ᵉ (Mᵒ Trocadéro). For seriously committed film-freaks the three *cinémathèques* offer a choice of over fifty films a week, many of which would never be shown commercially. Tickets are 25F; 15F for students.

L'Entrepôt, 7–9 rue Francis-de-Pressensé, 14ᵉ (Mᵒ Pernety). One of the best alternative Paris movie houses, which has been keeping ciné-addicts happy for years with its three screens dedicated to the obscure, the subversive and the brilliant. It also shows videos, satellite and cable TV, has a bookshop (Mon–Sat 2–8pm) and a restaurant (daily noon–midnight).

L'Escurial Panorama, 11 bd de Port-Royal, 13ᵉ (Mᵒ Gobelins). A cinema that combines plush seats, a panoramic screen and more art than commerce in its screening policy (and films are never dubbed).

Grand Action & Action Ecoles, 5 and 23 rue des Ecoles, 5ᵉ (Mᵒ Cardinal-Lemoine/Maubert-Mutualité); **Action Christine,** 4 rue Christine, 6ᵉ (Mᵒ Odéon/St-Michel). The *Action* chain specializes in new prints of ancient classics.

Le Grand Rex, 1 bd Poissonnière, 2ᵉ (Mᵒ Bonne-Nouvelle). Just as outrageous as the *Pagode* (see opposite), but in the kitsch line, with a Metropolis-style tower blazing its neon name, 2800 seats and a ceiling of stars and Moorish city skyline as a frame for the largest cinema screen in Europe.

Max Linder Panorama, 24 bd Poissonnière, 9ᵉ (Mᵒ Bonne-Nouvelle). Opposite *Le Grand Rex*, this always shows films in the original, and has almost as big a screen, state-of-the-art sound, and Art Deco decor.

La Pagode, 57bis rue de Babylone, 7ᵉ (Mᵒ François-Xavier). The most beautiful of the city's cinemas, transplanted from Japan at the turn of the century to be a rich Parisienne's party place. The wall panels of the *Grande Salle* auditorium are embroidered in silk; golden dragons and elephants hold up the candelabra; and a battle between Japanese and Chinese warriors rages on the ceiling.

Le Studio 28, 10 rue de Tholozé, 18ᵉ (Mᵒ Blanche/Abbesses). In its early days, after one of the first showings of Bunuel's *L'Age d'Or*, this was done over by extreme right-wing Catholics who destroyed the screen and the paintings by Dali and Ernst in the foyer. The cinema still hosts avant-garde premières, followed occasionally by discussions with the director, as well as regular festivals.

Vidéothèque de Paris, 2 Grande Gallerie, Porte St-Eustache, Forum des Halles, 1ᵉʳ (*RER* Châtelet-Les Halles). This screens four films or videos daily but also has a library of 3500 videos — newsreel footage, film clips, ads, documentaries etc — all with a connection to Paris, that you can access yourself from a computer terminal. You can make your choice via a Paris place-name, an actor, a director, a date and so on, and there are instructions in English at the desk and a friendly "librarian" to help you out. Tues–Sun 12.30–8.30pm; entry 30F/25F.

Drama

Bourgeois farces, postwar classics, Shakespeare, Racine and *Cyrano de Bergerac* – all are staged with the same range of talent or lack of it that you'd find in London or New York. What is rare are home-grown, socially concerned and realist **dramas**. But touring foreign companies make up for that, and for exciting contemporary work, there are the superstar breed of directors such as Peter Brook, Ariane Mnouchkine and Jean-Paul Vincent. Spectacular and dazzling sensation tends to take precedence over speech in their productions, with huge casts, extraordinary sets, overwhelming sound and light effects – an experience, even if you haven't understood a word.

Venues

Bouffes du Nord, 37bis bd de la Chapelle, 10ᵉ; ☎46.07.34.50 (Mᵒ Chapelle). Peter Brook's permanent base in Paris, where he produces such events as the nine-hour show of the Indian epic *Mahabharata*.

Cartoucherie, rte du Champ-de-Manoeuvre, 12ᵉ; ☎43.74.24.08 (Mᵒ Château-de-Vincennes). Home to several interesting theatre companies including Ariane Mnouchkine's workers' co-op, *Théâtre du Soleil*, whose interpretation of several Greek classics, *Les Atrides*, stunned and delighted audiences from France, Britain and the USA in 1994.

Comédie Française, 2 rue Richelieu, 1ᵉʳ; ☎40.15.00.15 (Mᵒ Palais-Royal). The national theatre for the classics.

Odéon Théâtre de l'Europe, 1 place Paul-Claudel, 6ᵉ; ☎44.41.36.36 (Mᵒ Odéon). Contemporary plays and foreign-language productions in the theatre that became an open parliament during May 1968.

Rond-Point Théâtre, Renaud-Barrault, 2bis av Franklin-Roosevelt, 8ᵉ; ☎44.95.98.00 (Mᵒ Franklin-Roosevelt). The permanent home for the Renaud-Barrault troupe (Jean-Louis Barrault was Baptiste in *Les Enfants du Paradis* and died in 1994; Madeleine Renaud, his widow, is one of the great French stage actresses). The performances of Beckett here are unequalled.

Théâtre des Amandiers, 7 av Pablo-Picasso, Nanterre, 92; ☎46.14.70.00 (*RER* Nanterre-Université and theatre bus). The suburban base for Jean-Paul Vincent's exciting productions.

Théâtre de la Bastille, 79 rue de la Roquette, 11ᵉ; ☎43.57.42.14 (Mᵒ Bastille). One of the best places for new work and fringe productions.

Théâtre de la Colline, 15 rue Malte-Brun, 20ᵉ; ☎43.66.43.60 (Mᵒ Gambetta). A national theatre putting on epic directors' works as well as less well-established innovators.

Théâtre National de Chaillot, Palais de Chaillot, pl du Trocadéro, 16ᵉ; ☎47.27.81.15 (Mᵒ Trocadéro). A national theatre where Lyon-based Roger Planchon brings his productions.

Théâtre Silvia-montfort, parc Georges Brassens, 106 rue Briançon, 15ᵉ; ☎45.31.10.96 (Mᵒ Porte-de-Vanves). Plays modern classics and contemporary original works.

Dance and mime

The French **regional dance companies** from La Rochelle, Marseille, Grenoble, Angers and Montpellier easily rival the Paris-based troupes, and the work of choreographers Maguy Marin, Karine Saporta and François Verret are worth looking out for. The current trend is in multidimensional performing art combining movement, mime, ballet, speech, noise, theatrical effects and music from medieval to jazz-rock. Though the famous Lecoq School of Mime and Improvisation still turns out excellent artists, pure mime – as practised by the incomparable Marcel Marceau – hardly exists, except on the streets, and Beaubourg's piazza in particular.

Many of the theatres listed above under drama include these new forms in their programmes. Plenty of space and critical attention is also given to **tap, tango, folk and jazz dancing**, and to visiting traditional dance troupes from all over the world. As for **ballet**, the principal stage is at the old opera house, the *Opéra Garnier*, under the directorship of Patrick Dupont, Nureyev's successor. Other major productions are at the *Théâtre des Champs-Élysées* and the *Théâtre Musical de Paris*.

Venues

Centre Mandapa, 6 rue Wurtz, 13ᵉ; ☎45.89.01.60 (Mᵒ Glacière). The one theatre dedicated to traditional dances from around the world.

Le Déjazet, 41 bd du Temple, 3ᵉ; ☎48.87.52.55 (Mᵒ République). Experimental dance productions, with the emphasis on mime.

Maison de la Culture, 1 bd Lénine, Bobigny; ☎48.31.11.45 (Mᵒ Pablo-Picasso). Home of François Verret's company and venue for prodigious young choreographers' competition in March.

Maison des Arts, place Salvador-Allende, Créteil; ☎49.80.38.98 (Mᵒ Créteil-Préfecture). Maguy Marin's company's home base.

Opéra de Paris-Garnier, place de l'Opéra, 9ᵉ; ☎47.42.53.71 (Mᵒ Opéra). The company has lost their greatest dancer, Sylvie Guillem, but Dupont has coaxed back many other top classical dancers who couldn't take Nureyev's highly emotional directing methods.

Théâtre des Champs-Élysées, 15 av Montaigne, 8ᵉ; ☎47.52.50.50 (Mᵒ Alma-Marceau). Forever aiming to outdo the Opéra with even grander and more expensive ballet productions.

Théâtre Contemporain de la Danse, 9 rue Geoffroy-l'Asnier, 4ᵉ; ☎42.74.44.22 (Mᵒ Pont-Marie). Established producer of innovative work.

Théâtre Musical de Paris, place du Châtelet, 4ᵉ; ☎40.28.28.40 (Mᵒ Châtelet). A major ballet venue, where, in 1910, Diaghilev put on the first season of Russian ballet, assisted by Cocteau, Rodin, Proust and others.

Café-théâtre

Café-théâtre, with its word-play and allusions to current fads, phobias and politicians, can be incomprehensible even to a fluent French-speaker. Puerile, dirty jokes are also its stock in trade. But the atmosphere can be fun and every so often, an original talent will appear.

The Marais has a high concentration of venues: you could try the tiny Blancs-Manteaux, 15 rue des Blancs-Manteaux, 4ᵉ; ☎48.87.15.84 (Mᵒ Hôtel-de-Ville/Rambuteau) or the Café de la Gare, 41 rue du Temple, 4ᵉ; ☎42.78.52.51 (Mᵒ Hôtel-de-Ville/Rambuteau), which has a reputation for novelty.

Daytime entertainment: mainly games and sport

When it's cold and wet and you've peered enough at museums, monuments and the dripping panes of shop-fronts and café vistas, don't despair or retreat back to your hotel. As well as the usual movies and videos, there is a whole host of pleasant ways to pass the time indoors not unique to Paris: **skating, bowling, billiards, swimming**... or outdoors as spectator of or participant in all the **popular sports**.

Information

L'Officiel des Spectacles has the best **listings** of sports facilities (under *Activités Sportives*). Or you can ring *Âllo Sports* on ☎42.76.54.54 (Mon–Fri 10.30am–5pm) or call on the *Direction Jeunesse et Sports*, 25 bd Bourdon, 4ᵉ (Mᵒ Bastille; Mon–Fri 10am–5.30pm) for details of all the municipal facilities. For current sporting events there's the daily sports paper *L'Équipe*. A major venue for all sports including athletics, cycling, show-jumping, ice hockey, ballroom dancing, judo and motorcross, is the *Palais des Omnisports Paris-Bercy* (*POPB*) at 8 bd Bercy, 12ᵉ; ☎40.02.60.60 (Mᵒ Bercy).

Participatory sports

Billiards and bowling You can do both at the *Bowling-Académie de Billiard*, 66 av d'Ivry, 13ᵉ; ☎45.86.55.52 (Mᵒ Tolbiac/Porte d'Ivry; daily 2pm–2am) and at *Bowling Mouffetard* (Centre-Commercial Mouffetard-Monge, 73 rue Mouffetard, 5ᵉ; ☎43.31.09.35 (Mᵒ Monge). Bowling costs around 20F a session, more at weekends; billiards around 50F an hour plus an average 100F deposit.

Boules Pétanque is best performed (or watched) at the Arènes de Lutece in the Latin Quarter and the Bois de Vincennes, but on balmy summer evenings you're likely to see it played in any of the city's parks and gardens.

Ice skating The city's only rink is the *Patinoire des Buttes-Chaumont*, 30 rue Edouard-Pailleron, 19ᵉ; Mᵒ Bolivar (☎46.08.72.20). Mon, Tues, Thurs 3–9pm; Wed 10am–9pm; Fri 3pm–midnight; Sat 10am–midnight; Sun 10am–6pm; entry including skate rental 41F/36F.

Roller-skating There's a special disco rink at *La Main Jaune* on pl de la Porte-de-Champerret, 17ᵉ, Mᵒ Champerret. Open Wed, Sat & Sun 2.30–7pm, Fri & Sat also 10pm–dawn; day sessions 55F; evenings 85F. The main outdoor roller-skating and skateboarding arena is the concourse of the Palais de Chaillot (Mᵒ Trocadéro). Les Halles (around the Fontaine des Innocents) and the Beaubourg piazza are also popular.

Swimming As well as the municipal baths that charge around 20F (check in *L'Officiel des Spectacles* for opening times), try the wealthy *Deligny*, 25 quai Anatole-France, 7ᵉ, on the vast deck above the Seine (Mᵒ Chambre-des-Deputés); the unchlorinated student hang-out *Jean Taris*, 16 rue de Thouin, 5ᵉ (Mᵒ Cardinal-Lemoine); and the 50m long *Piscine Susanne Berlioux/ Les Halles*, 10 pl de la Rotonde, niveau 3, Porte du Jour, Forum des Halles, 1ᵉʳ (*RER* Châtelet-Les Halles).

Spectator sports

Cycling The biggest event of the French sporting year is the grand finale of the *Tour de France* on the Champs-Élysées in the third week of July.

Football and rugby The *Parc des Princes*, 24 rue du Commandant-Guilbaud, 16ᵉ; ☎40.71.91.91, 48.74.84.75 (Mᵒ Porte-de-St-Cloud) is the capital's main stadium for both rugby union and football events, and home ground to the first-division Paris football team *Paris-SG* (*St-Germain*) and the recent rugby champions, *Le Racing*.

Horse-racing The biggest races are the *Prix de la République* and the *Grand Prix de L'Arc de Triomphe* on the first and last Sundays in October at Auteuil and Longchamp, both in the Bois de Boulogne. Trotting races, with the jockeys in chariots, run from August to September on the Route de la Ferme in the Bois de Vincennes. *L'Humanité* and *Paris-Turf* carry details of all races; admission charges are around 25F. If you want to fathom the betting system, any bar or café with the letters *PMU* will take your money on a three-horse bet, known as *le tiercé*.

Running The Paris Marathon is held in May over a route from pl de la Concorde to Vincennes. Up-to-date information from the runners' shop, *Marathon*, 29 rue de Chazelles, 17ᵉ; ☎42.27.48.18 (Mᵒ Monceau).

Tennis The French Tennis Open takes place in the last week of May and first week of June at *Roland-Garros* (2 av Gordon-Bennett, 16ᵉ; ☎47.43.00.47 (Mᵒ Porte d'Auteuil). A few tickets are sold each day, but only for unseeded matches.

Kids' stuff

The biggest attraction for **kids** to have hit the Paris area is, of course, Disneyland Paris (see "Out from the City"), though there are plenty of possibilities for kids to have fun within the city at far less expense. Many of the **museums** and **amusements** already detailed may appeal; the tours around the **sewers** and the **catacombs** certainly could delight some children; for the smaller ones, look out for *Guignol* (the Punch & Judy equivalent) in the city's parks. A number of museums have activities for children, detailed in the booklet *Objectif Musée*, available from the museums or from the *Direction des Musées de France*, 34 quai du Louvre, 1ᵉʳ (closed Tues). The Centre Beaubourg and the Musée d'Art Moderne de la Ville de Paris have children's workshops on Wednesday and Saturday afternoons, for example. Otherwise the most useful **sources of information**, for current shows, exhibitions and events, are the special sections in the listings magazines, "*Pour les jeunes*" in *Pariscope*, in "*Jeunes*" in *L'Officiel des Spectacles* and the town hall's Kiosque Paris-Jeunes, 25 bd Bourdon, 4ᵉ (Mon–Fri only).

Cité des Enfants

The **Cité des Enfants** – for 3- to 6-year-olds and 6- to 12-year-olds – is a totally engaging special section of the Cité des Sciences et de l'Industrie in the Parc de la Villette, 19ᵉ (Mᵒ Corentin-Cariou/Porte-de-la-Villette; Mon–Fri 11.30am, 1.30pm & 3.30pm, Sat & Sun 10.30am, 12.30pm, 2.30pm & 4.30pm; 45F/35F entrance to Cité des Sciences, 20F extra for Cité des Enfants, no charge for accompanying adult). The kids can touch and smell and feel inside things, play about with water, construct buildings on a miniature construction site complete with cranes, hard hats and barrows, experiment with sound and light, and carry out genetic tests with computers. It's beautifully organized and managed, and if you haven't got a child it's worth borrowing one to get in here. The rest of the museum is also pretty good for kids, particularly the planetarium, the Omnimax film shows in the Géode, the Cinaxe films, the Argonaute submarine and the Dragon slide (see p.118).

Jardin d'Acclimatation

This **garden** in the Bois de Boulogne by Porte des Sablons (Mᵒ Sablons/Porte-Maillot; daily 10am–6pm; 10F, under-16s 5F, under-3s free, additional charges for some attractions) is a cross between funfair, zoo and amusement park, with temptations ranging from bumper cars, go-karts, pony and camel rides, to sea lions, birds, bears and monkeys; a magical mini-canal ride (*la rivière enchantée*), distorting mirrors, scaled-down farm buildings, a puppet theatre and a superb collection of antique dolls at the *Grande Maison des Poupées*. There are good animations in the **Musée en Herbe**, and music and movement at the **Théâtre du Jardin pour l'Enfance et la Jeunesse**.

Special attractions on Wednesdays, Saturdays and Sundays, and all week during school hols, include a little train to take you there from M⁰ Porte-Maillot (behind the L'Orée du Bois restaurant; every 10min, 1.30–6pm; 9F).

Outside the *jardin*, in the Bois de Boulogne, **older children** can amuse themselves with **mini-golf and bowling**, or **boating** on the *Lac Inférieur*. By the entrance to the *jardin* there's **bike rental** for roaming the wood's cycle trails.

Parc Floral

The excellent **playground** (M⁰ Château-de-Vincennes then bus #112; summer daily 9.30am–10pm; 10F/5F; winter daily 9.30am until 5 or 6pm; 4F, and 2F for the 6–9s; under-6s always free) in the Bois de Vincennes on rte de la Pyramide has slides, swings, ping-pong and pedal carts; a few paying extras like mini-golf, an electric car circuit, and pony rides (April–Oct daily 2–6pm); and clowns, puppets and magicians on summer weekends. Most of the activities are free and in general you'll be far less out of pocket after an afternoon here than at the Jardin d'Acclimatation. Also in the park a children's theatre, the **Théâtre Astral**, may have mime, clowns and other not-too-verbal shows. A little train tours all the gardens (April–Oct Wed–Sun 10.30am–5pm; 5F).

Parc Zoologique

The top Paris **zoo** in the Bois de Vincennes, 53 av de St-Maurice, 12ᵉ (M⁰ Porte-Dorée; summer 9am–6pm, winter 9am–5.30pm; 30F/15F, under-6s free), and one of the first in the world to get rid of cages and use landscaping to give the animals more room to exercise.

Jardin des Halles

Right in the centre of town at Les Halles at 105 rue Rambuteau, and great if you want to lose your charges for the odd hour (M⁰/*RER* Châtelet-Les Halles; 7- to 11-year-olds only; Tues–Sat 10am–6pm, Sun 1–6pm; closed Mon & during bad weather, winter closes 4pm; 2.50F per hour). There is a whole series of fantasy landscapes that fill this small but cleverly designed space; on Wednesday animators organize adventure games; and at all times the children are supervised by professional child-carers. You may have to reserve a place an hour or so in advance; and on Saturday mornings you can go in and play, too. There's also usually a merry-go-round by the Forum des Halles.

Cirque de Paris

An entire **day at the circus** on the corner of av Hoche and av de la Commune-de-Paris, Nanterre (*RER* Nanterre-Ville; ☎47.24.11.70; Nov–June Wed, Sun & school holidays 10am–5pm; 235F+ adults, 195F+ children). In the morning you are initiated into the arts of juggling, walking the tightrope, clowning and make-up. You have lunch in the ring with your artiste tutors, then join the spectators for the show, after which, if you're lucky, the lion-tamer takes you round to meet his cats. You can, if you prefer, just attend the show at 3pm (70–155F/45–95F).

Shopping

Even if you don't plan – or can't afford – to buy, Parisian **shops and markets** are one of the chief delights of the city. Flair for style and design is as evident here as it is in other aspects of the city's life. Parisians' fierce attachment to their small local traders, especially when it comes to food, has kept alive a wonderful variety of shops, despite the pressures to concentrate consumption in gargantuan underground and multistorey complexes. Among specific areas, the square kilometre around **place St-Germain-des-Prés** is hard to beat, packed with books, antiques, gorgeous garments, artworks and playthings. But in every *quartier* you'll find enticing displays of all manner of consumables.

Bookshops

Books are not cheap in France – foreign books least of all. But don't let that stop you browsing. The best areas are the Seine *quais* with their rows of **stalls** perched against the river parapet and the narrow streets of the quartier Latin, but there are other places where you can sit down with a cup of coffee and a book.

Books in English

Abbey Bookshop/La Librairie Canadienne, 29 rue de la Parcheminerie, 5ᵉ (Mᵒ St-Michel). A Canadian bookshop round the corner from *Shakespeare & Co*, with lots of secondhand British and North American fiction; good social science sections; knowledgeable and helpful staff . . . and free coffee. Mon–Thurs 11am–10pm, Fri & Sat 11am–midnight, Sun 3–8pm.

FNAC Librairie Internationale, 71 bd St-Germain, 5ᵉ (Mᵒ Cluny/*RER* St-Michel). Literally hundreds of foreign newspapers and magazines and tens of thousands of foreign books. Mon–Sat 10am–8pm.

Shakespeare & Co, 37 rue de la Bûcherie, 5ᵉ (Mᵒ Maubert-Mutualité). A cosy, famous literary haunt, with the biggest selection of secondhand English books in town. Also poetry readings and such. Noon–midnight every day.

Tea and Tattered Pages, 24 rue Mayet, 6ᵉ (Mᵒ Duroc/Falguière). Large collection of good-value secondhand books, plus cakes and tea. Daily 11am–7pm.

Books in French

FNAC, Forum des Halles – level-2, Porte Pierre-Lescot (Mᵒ/*RER* Châtelet-Les Halles); 136 rue de Rennes, 6ᵉ (Mᵒ Montparnasse); 26 av des Termes, 17ᵉ (Mᵒ Termes); *CNIT*, 2 place de la Défense (*RER* La Défense). Mon–Sat 10am–7.30pm. Not the most congenial of bookshops, but it's the biggest and covers everything.

Parallèles, 47 rue St-Honoré, 1ᵉʳ (Mᵒ Châtelet-Les Halles). Mon–Sat 10am–7pm. The alternative bookshop with everything from anarchism to New Age. Good for info on current events, including gigs.

Clothes

For **haute couture**, the two traditional areas are av Montaigne, rue François 1ᵉʳ and rue du Faubourg-St-Honoré in the 8ᵉ, and av Victor-Hugo in the 16ᵉ. The fashionable newer designers are to be found around place des Victoires in the 1ᵉʳ and 2ᵉ. There's nothing to stop you from trying on the fabulously expensive creations, apart from the intimidating scorn of the assistants and the awesome chill of the marble portals... and prices which can be well into the stratosphere. The longtime darlings of the glitterati are Jean-Paul Gaultier and Azzedine Alaïa who, in 1991, were prevailed upon to design some gear for the city's **cheapest department store** – *Tati* (main branch at 13 place de la République, 11ᵉ; Mᵒ République). For **clothes** to buy without the fancy labels the best area is the 6ᵉ: round rue de Rennes and rue de Sèvres. The **department stores** *Galeries Lafayette* and *Au Printemps* have good selections of designer prêt-à-porter; the Forum des Halles and the Centre Maine-Montparnasse underground complexes have huge ranges of not particularly cheap shops. The **sales** take place in January and July, with up to forty-percent reductions on designer clothes. **Ends of lines** and **old stock** of the couturiers are sold all year round in discount shops concentrated in rue d'Alésia in the 14ᵉ and rue St-Placide in the 6ᵉ.

Designer fashion

The addresses below are those of the main or most conveniently located shops.

Azzedine Alaïa, 7 rue de Moussy, 4e (M^o Hôtel-de-Ville).

Giorgio Armani, 6 & 25 place Vendôme, 1e (M^o Opéra).

Balmain, 44 rue François-1er, 8e (M^o George-V).

Cacharel, 5 pl des Victoires, 1er (M^o Bourse).

Pierre Cardin, 59 rue du Faubourg-St-Honoré, 8e (M^o Madeleine).

Carven, 6 rond-point des Champs-Élysées, 8e (M^o Franklin-Roosevelt).

Cerrutti, 1 and 15 pl de la Madeleine, 8e (M^o Madeleine).

Chanel, 31 rue Cambon, 1e (M^o Madeleine).

Chloé, 60 rue du Faubourg-St-Honoré, 8e (M^o Madeleine).

Comme des Garçons, 40–42 rue Étienne-Marcel, 2e (M^o Châtelet-Les-Halles).

Courrèges, 40 rue François-1er, 8e (M^o George-V).

Dior, 32 av Montaigne, 8e (M^o Franklin-Roosevelt).

Dorothée Bis, 46 rue Étienne-Marcel, 1er (M^o Châtelet-Les Halles).

Louis Féraud, 88 rue du Faubourg-St-Honoré, 8e (M^o Madeleine).

J-P Gaultier, 6 rue Vivienne, 2e (M^o Bourse).

Givenchy, 8 av George-V, 8e (M^o Alma-Marceau).

Kenzo, 3 pl des Victoires, 1er (M^o Bourse).

Emanuelle Khan, 2 rue de Tournon, 6e (M^o Odéon).

Christian Lacroix, 73 rue du Faubourg-St-Honoré, 8e (M^o Concorde).

Karl Lagerfeld, 19 rue du Faubourg-St-Honoré, 8e; 51 rue François-1^{er,} 8e (M^o Concorde).

Lanvin, 2 rue du Faubourg-St-Honoré, 8e (M^o Concorde).

Ted Lapidus, 35 rue François-1er, 8e (M^o Franklin-Roosevelt).

Guy Laroche, 30 rue du Faubourg-St-Honoré, 8e (M^o Concorde).

Issey Miyake, 3 pl des Vosges, 4e (M^o St-Paul).

Claude Montana, 3 rue des Petits-Champs, 1er (M^o Bourse/Pyramides).

Paco Rabanne, 7 rue du Cherche-Midi, 6e (M^o Sèvres-Babylone).

Nina Ricci, 39 av Montaigne, 8e (M^o Alma-Marceau).

Saint-Laurent, 38 rue du Faubourg-St-Honoré, 8e (M^o Concorde); 6 pl St-Sulpice, 6e (M^o St-Sulpice/Mabillon).

Jil Sander, 52 av Montaigne, 8e (M^o Franklin-Roosevelt).

Valentino, 17–19 av Montaigne, 8e (M^o Alma-Marceau).

Gianni Versace, 62 rue du Faubourg-St-Honoré, 8e (M^o Concorde).

Department stores

Au Bon Marché, 38 rue de Sèvres, 7e. (M^o Sèvres-Babylone). Paris' oldest department store, founded in 1852. The prices are lower on average than at the chicer *Galeries Lafayette* and *Printemps*. Excellent kids' department and an alluring food hall. Mon–Sat 9.30am–6.30pm, Sat closes 7pm.

Au Printemps, 64 bd Haussmann, 9e (M^o Havre-Caumartin). Books, records, a *parfumerie* even bigger than the rival *Galeries Lafayette*, excellent fashion department for women – less so for men. Mon–Sat 9.30am–7pm.

Galeries Lafayette, 40 bd Haussmann, 9^e (M^o Havre-Caumartin). The store's forte is, above all, high fashion. Two complete floors are given over to the latest creations by leading designers for men, women and children. Then there's household stuff, tableware, furniture, a huge *parfumerie*, etc – all under a superb 1900 dome. Mon–Sat 9.30am–6.45pm.

La Samaritaine, 75 rue de Rivoli, 1er (M° Rivoli). The biggest of the department stores, spread over three buildings, whose boast is to provide anything anyone could possibly want. It aims down-market of the previous two. Mon–Sat 9.30am–7pm, Thurs closes 10pm.

Food

You can, of course, find sumptuous foodstores all over Paris; the listings below are for the **specialist places**, palaces of gluttony many of them, with prices to match. Buying food with a view to **economic eating**, you will be invariably best off shopping at the **street markets or supermarkets**, though save your bread buying at least for the local *boulangerie*. The cheapest supermarket chains are *Ed L'Épicier* and *Franprix*. Food markets are detailed at the end of this section.

Bread

Poilâne, 8 rue du Cherche-Midi, 7e (M° Sèvres-Babylone). Bakes to ancient and secret family recipes, but there is always a queue. Mon–Sat 7.15am–8.15pm.

Charcuterie

Divay, 50 rue du Faubourg-St-Denis, 10e (M° Château-d'Eau). *Foie gras, choucroute, saucisson* and suchlike. Tues–Sun 7.30am–1pm & 4–7.30pm, Wed & Sun morning only.
Goldenberg's, 7 rue des Rosiers, 4e (M° St-Paul). Superlative Jewish deli and restaurant. Daily 9.30am–11pm.

Cheese

Barthélémy, 51 rue de Grenelle, 7e (M° Bac). Purveyors of cheeses to the rich and powerful. Tues–Sat 8.30am–1pm & 3.30–7.30pm, Sat closes 6.30pm; closed Aug.
Carmès et Fils, 24 rue de Lévis, 17e (M° Villiers). Tues–Sat 8.30am–1pm & 4–7pm, Sun am only; closed Aug. A family of experts who mature many of the cheeses in their own cellars.

Chocolates and pâtisserie

Debauve and Gallais, 30 rue des Saints-Pères, 6e (M° St-Germain-des-Prés). A beautiful and ancient shop, specializing in chocolate and elaborate sweets. Mon–Sat 10am–7pm; closed Aug.
A la Mère de Famille, 35 rue du Faubourg-Montmartre, 9e (M° Le Peletier). An eighteenth-century *confiserie* serving *marrons glacés*, prunes from Agen, dried fruit, sweets, chocolates and even some wines. Mon–Sat 7.30am–1.30pm & 3–7pm.

Gourmet groceries

Fauchon, 26 pl de la Madeleine, 8e (M° Madeleine). Carries an amazing range of super-plus groceries and wine, all at exorbitant prices. There's a self-service counter for *patisseries* and *plats du jour* if you want a treat. Mon–Sat 9.40am–7pm, summer closes 10pm.
Hédiard, 21 pl de la Madeleine, 8e (M° Madeleine). Since 1850 the aristocrat's grocer. Several other branches throughout the city. Mon–Sat 9.30am–9pm, Sat until 10pm.

Salmon, seafood and caviar

Caviar Kaspia, 17 pl de la Madeleine, 8e (M° Madeleine). Blinis, smoked salmon and Beluga caviar. Mon–Sat 9.30am–12.30pm.

Snails

La Maison de l'Escargot, 19 rue Fondary, 15e (M° Dupleix). They even sauce them and re-shell them while you wait. Tues–Sat 8.30am–8pm, Sun 9am–1pm; closed mid-July to end of Aug.

Vegetarian

Diététique DJ Fayer, 45 rue St-Paul, 4e (M° St-Paul). Dietary, macrobiotic, vegetarian . . . one of the city's oldest specialists. Tues–Sat 9.30am–1.30pm & 2.45–8.45pm.

Wine

Les Caves Taillevent, 199 rue du Faubourg St-Honoré, 8ᵉ (Mᵒ Ternes). The Taillevent restaurant cellars have a very wide range of wines and expert advice. Mon 2–7pm, Tues–Sat 9am–7pm; closed Aug.

Michel Renaud, 12 pl de la Nation, 12ᵉ (Mᵒ Nation). The other end of town and the other end of the scale from the *Taillevent caves* – superb-value French and Spanish wines, champagnes and Armagnac. Tues–Sat 9am–1pm & 2–8.30pm, Sun 9am–1pm.

Music

Cassettes and CDs are not a particularly cheap buy in Paris, but you may come across selections that are novel enough to tempt you, and there are plenty of second-hand bargains. Like the live music, there are Brazilian, Caribbean, Antillais, African and Arab albums that would be specialist rarities in London or the States, as well as every kind of jazz. Bear in mind that the *Cité de la Musique*, soon to open in La Villette, will have a range of shops devoted to all things musical.

Blue Moon, 7 rue Pierre-Sarrazin, 6ᵉ (Mᵒ Odéon). Exclusive imports from Jamaica and Africa: ska and reggae. Mon–Sat 11am–7pm.

BPM Records, 1 rue Keller, 11ᵉ (Mᵒ Bastille). Specialists in house, including acid, hip-hop and rap. Tues–Sat 1–9pm.

Camara, 45 rue Marcadet, 18ᵉ (Mᵒ Marcadet-Poissonnière). The best selection of West African music on cassette and video in town. Daily 10am–7pm.

Crocodisc, 40–42 rue des Écoles, 5ᵉ (Mᵒ Maubert-Mutualité). Folk, oriental, Afro-Antillais, funk, reggae, soul, country, new and secondhand. Some of the best prices in town. Tues–Sat 11am–7pm.

Crocojazz, 64 rue de la Montagne-Ste-Geneviève, 5ᵉ (Mᵒ Maubert-Mutualité). Jazz, blues and gospel: mainly new imports. Tues–Sat 11am–1pm & 2–7pm.

Disc' Inter, 2 rue des Rasselins, 20ᵉ (Mᵒ Porte de Montreuil). Wide-ranging stock of Afro-Caribbean music on CD, cassette, video and vinyl. Mon–Sat 10am–7pm.

Le Disque Arabe, 116bis bd de la Chapelle, 18ᵉ (Mᵒ Porte-de-la-Chapelle). Good range of Arab music. Mon–Sat 10am–8pm.

Dream Store, 4 pl St-Michel, 6ᵉ (Mᵒ St-Michel). Good discounted prices on blues, jazz, rock, folk and classical. Tues–Sat 9.30am–7pm.

FNAC Musique, 4 pl de la Bastille, 12ᵉ, next to opera house (Mᵒ Bastille). Extremely stylish shop in black, grey and chrome with computerized catalogues, every variety of music, books, and a concert booking agency. Branch at 24 bd des Italiens, 9ᵉ, with a greater emphasis on rock and popular music. The other *FNAC* shops (see above under *Books*) also sell music and hi-fi. Mon–Sat 10am–8pm, Wed & Fri 10am–10pm; closed Sun.

Virgin Megastore, 56–60 av des Champs-Élysées, 8ᵉ (Mᵒ Franklin-D-Roosevelt/Carrousel du Louvre); Palais du Louvre, 1ᵉʳ (Mᵒ Louvre–Rivoli). *Virgin* has trumped all Paris music shops; it's the biggest and trendiest. Concert booking agency. Mon–Thurs 10am–midnight, Fri & Sat 10am–1am, Sun noon–midnight.

Sport and outdoor pursuits

Le Ciel est à Tout le Monde, 10 rue Gay-Lussac, 5ᵉ (Mᵒ Luxembourg); 7 av Trudaine, 9ᵉ (Mᵒ Anvers). The best kite shop in Europe. It also sells frisbees, boomerangs, etc, and books and traditional toys. Mon–Sat 10.30am–7pm; closed Mon in Aug.

Au Vieux Campeur, 48 rue des Écoles, 5ᵉ. Maps, guides, climbing, hiking, camping, ski gear, plus a kids' climbing wall. Mon 2–7pm, Tues–Fri 9.30am–8.30pm, Sat 9.30am–8pm.

Markets

Markets, like shops, are grand spectacles. Mouthwatering arrays of **food** from half the countries of the globe, intoxicating in their colour, shape and smell, assail the senses in even the drabbest parts of town. Though the food is perhaps the best offering of the

Paris markets, there are also street markets dedicated to **secondhand goods** (the *marchés aux puces*), **clothes and textiles, flowers, birds, books and stamps**. Note that several of the markets listed below are described in more detail in the guide.

Flea markets (marchés aux puces)

Porte de Montreuil, 20ᵉ (Mᵒ Porte-de-Montreuil). Best of the flea markets for secondhand clothes – cheapest on Mon when leftovers from the weekend are sold off. Sat, Sun & Mon 6.30am–1pm.

Porte de Vanves, av Georges-Lafenestre/av Marc-Sangnier, 14ᵉ (Mᵒ Porte-de-Vanves). The obvious choice for bric-à-brac searching. Sat & Sun 7am–6pm.

St-Ouen/Porte de Clignancourt, 18ᵉ (Mᵒ Porte de Clignancourt). The biggest and most touristy flea market, with stalls selling clothes, shoes, records, books and junk of all sorts, as well as expensive antiques. Sat, Sun & Mon 7.30am–7pm.

Books and stamps

Marché du Livre Ancien et d'Occasion, Pavillon Baltard, Parc Georges-Brassens, rue Brancion, 15ᵉ (Mᵒ Porte de Vanves). Secondhand and antiquarian books. Sat & Sun 9am onwards.

Marché aux Timbres, junction of avs Marigny and Gabriel, 8ᵉ (Mᵒ Champs-Élysées-Clemenceau). The stamp market. Thurs, Sat, Sun & hols 10am-dusk.

Food markets

Markets usually start between 7am and 8am and tail off mid-afternoon. The covered markets have specific opening hours, which are given below along with details of locations and days of operation.

Place d'Aligre, 12ᵉ (Mᵒ Ledru-Rollin). Tues–Sat until noon.

Belleville, bd de Belleville, 20ᵉ (Mᵒ Belleville/Ménilmontant). Tues & Fri.

Buci, rue de Buci and rue de Seine, 6ᵉ (Mᵒ Mabillon). Tues–Sun.

Carmes, place Maubert, 5ᵉ (Mᵒ Maubert-Mutualité). Tues, Thurs & Sat.

Rue Cler, 7ᵉ (Mᵒ École-Militaire). Tues–Sat.

Convention, rue de la Convention, 15ᵉ (Mᵒ Convention). Tues, Thurs & Sun.

Edgar-Quinet, bd Edgar-Quinet, 14ᵉ (Mᵒ Edgar-Quinet). Wed & Sat.

Enfants-Rouges, 39 rue de Bretagne, 3ᵉ (Mᵒ Filles-du-Calvaire). Tues–Sat 8am–1pm & 4–7.30pm, Sun 8am–1pm.

Rue de Lévis, 17ᵉ (Mᵒ Villiers). Tues–Sun.

Monge, place Monge, 5ᵉ (Mᵒ Monge). Wed, Fri & Sun.

Montorgueil, rue Montorgueil and rue Montmartre, 1ᵉʳ (Mᵒ Châtelet-Les Halles/Sentier). Daily.

Mouffetard, rue Mouffetard, 5ᵉ (Mᵒ Censier-Daubenton). Daily.

LATE-NIGHT SHOPPING

Prisunic supermarket, 52 av des Champs-Élysées, 8ᵉ (Mᵒ Franklin-D-Roosevelt). Tues–Sat open till midnight.

Boulangerie de l'Ancienne-Comédie, 10 rue de l'Ancienne-Comédie, 6ᵉ (Mᵒ Odéon). Mon–Sat open 24hrs.

Le Cochon Rose, 44 bd de Clichy, 17ᵉ (Mᵒ Blanche/Pigalle). Grocers open daily except Thurs 6pm–6am.

Le Terminus, 10 rue St-Denis, 1ᵉʳ (Mᵒ Châtelet/Les Halles). *Tabac* open daily to 2am.

La Favourite Bar-Tabac, 3 bd St-Michel, 5ᵉ (Mᵒ St-Michel). *Tabac* open daily to 2am.

Old Navy, 150 bd St-Germain, 6ᵉ (Mᵒ St-Germain-des-Prés). *Tabac* open daily till 5am.

Le Pigalle, 22 bd de Clichy, 18ᵉ (Mᵒ Blanche). Open till 4.30pm.

Select, 62 rue de Grenelle, 7ᵉ (Mᵒ Rue-du-Bac). 24hrs, 7 days a week: food shop.

Shell Garage, 6 bd Raspail, 7ᵉ (Mᵒ Rue-du-Bac). 24-hr food shop and garage.

Port-Royal, bd Port-Royal, near Val-de-Grâce, 5ᵉ (Mᵉ Porte-Royale). Tues, Thurs & Sat. Organic on Sun.

Porte-St-Martin, rue du Château-d'Eau, 10ᵉ (Mᵉ Château-d'Eau). Tues–Sat 8am–1pm & 4–7.30pm, Sun 8am–1pm.

Raspail, bd Raspail, between rue du Cherche-Midi and rue de Rennes, 6ᵉ (Mᵉ Rennes). Tues & Fri; organic on Sun.

Saint-Germain, rue Mabillon, 6ᵉ (Mᵉ Mabillon). Tues–Sat 8am–1pm & 4–7.30pm, Sun 8am–1pm.

Secrétan, av Secrétan/rue Riquet, 19ᵉ (Mᵉ Bolivar). Tues–Sat 8am–1pm & 4–7.30pm, Sun 8am–1pm.

Tang Frères, 48 av d'Ivry, 13ᵉ (Mᵉ Porte d'Ivry). Not really a market, but a vast emporium of all things Oriental, where speaking French will not help you discover the nature and uses of what you see before you. In the same yard there is also a Far Eastern flower shop. Tues–Sun 9am–7.30pm.

Ternes, rue Lemercier, 17ᵉ (Mᵉ Ternes). Tues–Sat 8am–1pm & 4–7.30pm, Sun 8am–1pm.

Listings

Airlines *Air France*, 119 av des Champs-Élysées, 8ᵉ (☎45.35.61.61); *Air Inter*, 49 av des Champs-Élysées, 8ᵉ (☎45.46.90.90); *British Airways*, 12 rue Castiglione, 1ᵉʳ (☎47.78.14.14). Full lists of the rest from any tourist office.

Babysitting There are two main agencies, both with English speakers: *Ababa* (☎45.49.46.46) and *Kid Service* (☎42.96.04.12). Apart from these, you could try the notices at the American Church, 65 quai d'Orsay, 6ᵉ (Mᵉ Invalides), or if you know someone who has a phone, you could dial up Babysitting on "*Elletel*" via their minitel.

Banks and change To change money outside normal banking hours, there are money exchange bureaux open till 11.30pm at the airports, until 11pm at the Gare de Lyon, and automatic exchange machines at the airports, train stations, at the *Crédit du Nord*, 24 bd Sébastapol, 1ᵉʳ (Mᵉ Les Halles), *CCF*, 115 av des Champs- Élysées, 8ᵉ (Mᵉ Georges V), and many exchange bureaux in the streets. Credit cards with international PIN numbers (check with your bank at home) can be used in many cash machines.

Bike rental *Paris-Vélo*, 2 rue du Fer-à-Moulin, 5ᵉ; ☎43.37.59.22 (Mᵉ Censier-Daubenton; Mon–Sat 10am–7pm), or *Cycles Laurent*, 9 bd Voltaire, 11ᵉ (Mᵉ Oberkampf/République; Mon–Sat 10am–12.30pm & 2–7pm).

Car rental Local firms include *Acar*, 77 rue Lagny, 20ᵉ; ☎43.79.76.48 (Mᵉ Porte-de-Vincennes; Mon–Sat 8am–12.30pm & 2–7pm); *Dergi et Cie*, 60 bd St-Marcel, 5ᵉ; ☎45.87.27.04 (Mᵉ Gobelins; Mon–Sat 8am–7pm); *Locabest*, 9 rue Abel, 12ᵉ; ☎43.46.05.05 (Mᵉ Gare-de-Lyon; Mon–Sat 7.30am–7pm); *Rent a Car*, 79 rue de Bercy, 12ᵉ; ☎45.45.15.15 (Mᵉ Bercy; Mon–Sat 8.30am–7pm).

Dental treatment Emergency service: *Urgences Dentaires*, 9 bd St-Marcel, 13ᵉ (Mᵉ St-Marcel; ☎47.07.44.44).

Embassies *Australia*, 4 rue Jean-Rey, 15ᵉ; ☎40.59.33.00 (Mᵉ Bir-Hakeim); *Britain*, 9 av Hoche, 8ᵉ; ☎42.66.38.10 (Mᵉ Courcelles); *Canada*, 35 av Montaigne, 8ᵉ; ☎44.43.29.86 (Mᵉ Franklin-Roosevelt); *Ireland*, 12 av Foch, 16ᵉ, enter from 4 rue Rude; ☎45.00.20.87 (Mᵉ Étoile); *Netherlands*, 7–9 rue Eblé, 7ᵉ; ☎43.06.61.88 (Mᵉ St-François-Xavier); *New Zealand*, 7 rue Léonardo-de-Vinci, 16ᵉ; ☎45.00.24.11 (Mᵉ Victor-Hugo); *Sweden*, 17 rue Barbet-de-Jouy, 7ᵉ; ☎44.18.88.00 (Mᵉ Varenne); *USA*, 2 av Gabriel, 8ᵉ; ☎42.96.12.02 (Mᵉ Concorde).

Emergencies Call ☎18, or *SOS-Médecins* (☎47.07.77.77) for 24-hour medical help; ☎15 or ☎45.67.50.50 for **24-hour ambulance service**.

Feminism Best place to make contact is the *Maison des Femmes*, 8 Cité Prost, off rue Chanzy, 11ᵉ; ☎43.48.24.91 (Mᵉ Faidherbe-Chaligny). It's run by *Paris Féministe* who produce a fortnightly bulletin and organize a wide range of events and actions. It's also home to the lesbian group *MIEL (Mouvement d'Information et d'Expression des Lesbiennes;* recorded information ☎43.79.61.91). A cafeteria run by *MIEL* operates most Friday evenings. Don't be put off by the back-alley entrance, and don't expect English speakers.

Festivals There's not much in the carnival line, though kids armed with bags of flour and aiming to make a total fool of you appear on the streets during **Mardi Gras** (in Feb). There are marching bands and street performers and **Gay Pride** for the Summer Solstice (June 21), and July 14 (**Bastille Day**) is celebrated with official pomp in parades of tanks down the Champs-Élysées, firework displays and concerts. The French Communist Party hosts an annual **Fête de l'Humanité** in September at La Courneuve, just north of Paris, with representatives of just about every CP or ex-CP in the world and information tables, bands and eats that bring in Parisians of most political persuasions, and good times had by all.

Gay and lesbian life A few bars and clubs are listed in the "Nightlife" and "Eating & Drinking" sections. There are numerous gay organizations (far fewer lesbian ones): best place for information is the main gay and lesbian bookshop, *Les Mots à la Bouche*, 6 rue St-Croix-de-la-Bretonnerie, 4e (M^o Hôtel-de-Ville). The Gay Switchboard equivalent is *Écoute Gai* (☎48.06.19.11; Mon–Fri 6–10pm).

Hammams Best of all Paris' Turkish baths is *Hammam de la Mosquée*, 39 rue Geoffroy-St-Hilaire, 5e (M^o Censier-Dauenton). 65F (massage 50F extra). Hours for women are Mon & Wed 11am–8pm, Thurs 11am–9pm, Sat 10am–8pm; for men, Fri 11am–8pm & Sun 10am–8pm; closed August.

Helpline SOS Helpline in English: any problems, call ☎47.05.07.99 (Mon–Fri 9.30am–7pm, Sat 9.30am–1pm). The American Church help and counselling on ☎47.05.07.99 (Mon–Fri 9.30am–7pm, Sat 9.30am–1pm).

Hitching *Allostop*, 84 passage Brady, 10e (Mon–Fri 9am–7.30pm, Sat 9am–1pm and 2–6pm; ☎42.46.00.66).

Hospitals English-speaking hospitals include the *American Hospital*, 63 bd Victor-Hugo, Neuilly-sur-Seine; ☎46.41.25.25 (M^o Anatole-France/Pont-de-Levallois); and the *Hertford British Hospital*, 3 rue Barbès, Levallois-Perret; ☎46.39.22.22 (M^o Anatole-France).

Language schools French lessons from the *Alliance Française*, 101 bd Raspail, 6e, and numerous other establishments. A full list, *Cours de Français pour Étudiants Étrangers*, is obtainable from embassy cultural sections.

Laundries Self-service places have multiplied in Paris over the last few years, and you'll probably find one near where you're staying.

Left luggage There are lockers at all train stations and *consigne* for bigger items or longer periods.

Libraries *The British Council*, 9 rue de Constantine, 7e (M^o Invalides), and the *US Institute*, 10 rue du Général-Camou, 7e (M^o Ecole-Militaire), have paying libraries, with daily newspapers. The library of the Canadian Council, next door to the British, is free. Interesting French collections include the *BPI* at Beaubourg (vast, including all the foreign press), *Forney* (books being a good excuse if you want to visit the medieval bishop's palace at 1 rue Figuiler in the 4e), and the *Historique de la Ville de Paris*, a sixteenth-century mansion housing centuries of texts and picture books on the city at 24 rue Pavée, 4e.

Lost luggage Orly: ☎46.75.40.38; Roissy/Charles de Gaulle: ☎48.62.12.12.

Lost property *Bureau des Objets Trouvés*, 36 rue des Morillons, 15e (M^o Convention; Mon–Fri 8.30am–5pm; ☎45.31.14.80).

Petrol 24-hr filling stations are *Esso*, 338 rue St-Honoré, 1er, and 18 av des Champs-Élysées, 8e; *Shell*, 109 rue de Rennes, 6e; 1 bd de la Chapelle, 10e; 4 av Foch, 16e; *Mobil*, 47 bd de Vaugriard, 15e.

Pharmacies 24-hr service at *Dhery*, 84 av des Champs-Élysées, 8e (M^o George-V; ☎45.62.02.41).

Police Dial ☎17 for emergencies. The main *Préfecture*, if you need to report a theft, is at 7 bd du Palais, 4e (☎42.60.33.22).

Post office Main office at 52 rue du Louvre, Paris 75001 (M^o Châtelet-Les-Halles): open 24hr for telephones and poste restante.

Train information See "Getting Around the City".

Travel firms *USIT Voyages*, 6 rue de Vaugirard, 15e; ☎42.96.15.88 (M^o Odéon), is an excellent and dependable student–youth agency. *Nouvelles Frontières*, 66 bd St-Michel, 6e (☎46.34.55.30), has some of the cheapest charters going and flights just about anywhere in the world. For national and international buses you can get information and tickets at the main terminus in Porte de la Villette – M^o Porte-de-la-Villette (☎42.05.12.10).

VD clinic Free treatment at *A-Fournier*, 25 bd St-Jacques, 5e; ☎40.78.26.00 (M^o Glacière).

Work Not easy: look for ads in *Le Monde*, *Le Figaro* or *The International Herald Tribune*, or try the youth organization *CIDJ*, 101 quai Branly, 15e (M^o Bir-Hakeim), or the French job agency *ANPE* (*Agence Nationale Pour l'Emploi*) – check the phone book for the nearest office. The notice boards at the *British Council Library* (see above) and the American Church are worth a look.

Out from the city

The region around the capital – the Île de France – and the borders of the neighbouring provinces are studded with large-scale **châteaux**. Many were royal or noble retreats for hunting and other leisured pursuits, and some – like **Versailles** – were for more serious state show. They are undoubtedly impressive but don't necessarily provide great fun days out. Indeed, if you have even the slightest curiosity about church buildings, forget the châteaux and make instead for the cathedral of **Chartres**, which is all it is cracked up to be – and more. Closer in, on the edge of the city itself, **St-Denis** boasts a cathedral second only to Notre-Dame among Paris churches – a visit to which can be combined with a walk back along the banks of the **St-Denis canal**. Other waterside wanders include **Chatou** and the Marne-side towns with their memories of carousing, carefree painters and musicians in the 1900s, when these places were open countryside or small villages. Whether the various suburban museums deserve your attention will depend on your degree of interest in the subjects they represent – china at **Sèvres**, French prehistory at **St-Germain-en-Laye**, Napoléon at **Malmaison**, or horses at **Chantilly**. The biggest pull for kids is without question **Disneyland Paris**, out beyond the bizarre satellite town of **Marne-la-Vallée**, but they might also like the air and space museum at **Le Bourget** and the Île-de-France museum at **Sceaux**.

Cathedrals

An excursion to **Chartres** can seem a long way to go from Paris just to see one building; but then you'd have to go a very long way indeed to find any edifice to beat it, although the cathedral of **St-Denis**, right on the edge of Paris, predates Chartres and represents the first breakthroughs in Gothic art. It is also the burial place of almost all the French kings.

Chartres

About 80km southwest of Paris and an hour by train from Paris-Montparnasse, **CHARTRES** is a small and relatively undistinguished town. However, its **Cathédrale Notre-Dame** (daily March–Sept 7.20am–7.20pm; Oct–Feb 7.10am–7pm) is one of the finest examples of Gothic architecture in Europe and, built between 1194 and 1260, perhaps the quickest ever to be constructed. Its façade is dominated by two towers, which rise up above portals heavily laden with sculpture that marks the transition from the Romanesque to Gothic styles – depictions of Christ, the Apostles, and the 24 Elders of the Book of Revelation. Inside, the chairs of the nave cover up the labyrinth on the floor – an original thirteenth-century arrangement and a great rarity, since the authorities at other cathedrals had them pulled up as distracting frivolities. The Chartres labyrinth traces a path over 200m long enclosed within a diameter of 13m, the same size as the rose window above the main doors. The centre used to have a bronze relief of Theseus and the Minotaur, and the pattern of the maze was copied from classical texts – the medieval Catholic idea of the path of life to eternity echoing Greek myth. During pilgrimages the chairs are removed so you may be lucky and see the full pattern.

But there are more than enough wonders to enthral: the geometry of the building, unique in being almost unaltered since its consecration in the thirteenth century; the details of the stonework, the Renaissance choir screen and the hosts of sculpted figures above each transept door; and the shining circular symmetries of the transept windows, virtually all of which are original, dating from the twelfth and thirteenth centuries. Among paying extras, the crypt and treasures can wait for another time but, crowds permitting, it's worth climbing the north tower (times vary, check in the cathedral; 20F). There are gardens at the back from where you can contemplate at ease the

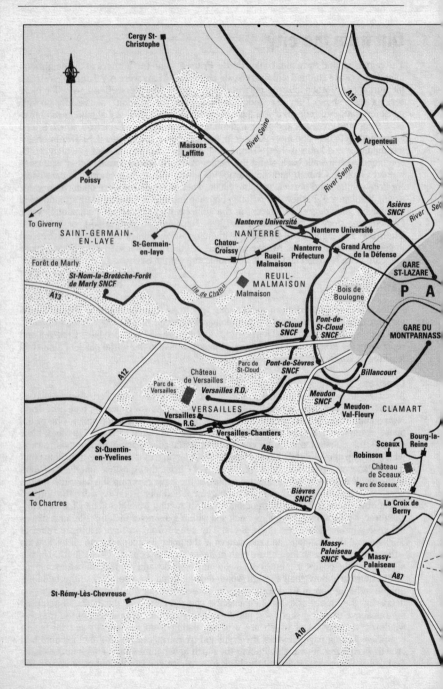

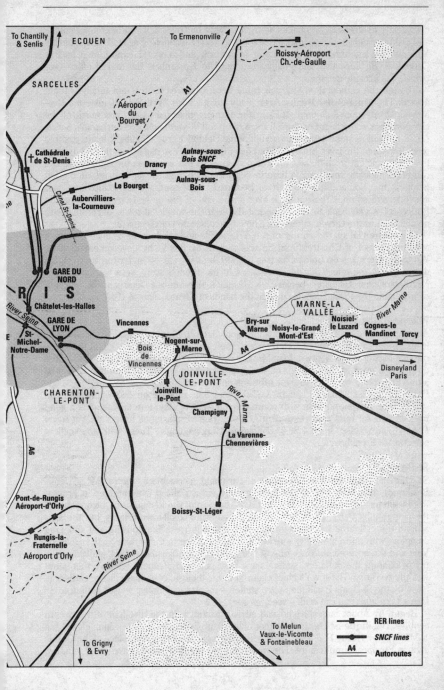

complexity of stress factors balanced by the flying buttresses. If you hear a passionate and erudite Englishman giving guided tours as you're wandering around, it is probably Malcolm Miller, almost an institution in himself and a world expert on Chartres Cathedral. He does two tours daily from April to November; the tourist office (see below) can provide details.

Though the cathedral is why you come here, Chartres itself is not totally without appeal. The **Musée des Beaux Arts** (daily except Tues April–Sept 10am–6pm; Oct–March 10am–noon & 2–6pm; 16F) in the former episcopal palace just north of the cathedral has some beautiful tapestries, a room full of Vlaminck, and Zurbaran's *Sainte Lucie*, as well as good temporary exhibitions. Behind it, rue Chantault leads past old town houses to the river Eure and Pont des Massacres. You can follow this reedy river lined with ancient wash-houses upstream via rue des Massacres on the right bank. The cathedral appears from time to time through the trees and, closer at hand, on the left bank, is the Romanesque church of **St-André**, now used for art exhibitions, jazz concerts and so on. Crossing back over at the end of rue de la Tannerie into rue du Bourg takes you back to the cathedral through the medieval town, decorated with details such as the carved salmon on a house on place de la Poissonerie.

The **memorial** on the corner of rue d'Harleville and bd de la Résistance is to Jean Moulin, Prefect of Chartres until he was sacked by the Vichy government in 1942. When the Germans occupied Chartres in 1940, he had refused under torture to sign a document to the effect that black soldiers in the French army were responsible for Nazi atrocities. He later became de Gaulle's number-one man on the ground, coordinating the Resistance. He died at the hands of Klaus Barbie in 1943.

Practicalities

Arriving at the **gare SNCF** (hourly trains from Gare du Montparnasse), av J-de-Beauce leads straight up to place Châtelet. Past all the coaches on the other side of the *place*, rue Ste-Même crosses place Jean-Moulin with the cathedral down to the left. Rue d'Harleville goes to the right to bd de la Résistance, a section of the main ring road around the old town. The **tourist office** is on the cathedral parvis, at 7 Cloître Notre-Dame (Mon–Sat 9.30am–12.30pm & 2–6.30pm, Sun 10am–noon & 3–6pm), and can supply **free maps** and help with **rooms** if you want to stay. Rue du Cygne is a good place to look for **bars and restaurants**. If you want to splash out, have a meal at *Henri IV* at 31 rue Soleil-d'Or (☎37.36.01.55; closed Mon evening & Tues), with an excellent selection of French wines.

St-Denis

ST-DENIS, 10km north of the centre of Paris and accessible by métro (M° St-Denis-Basilique), has been one of the most heavily industrialized communities in France. Recession has taken its toll, but it is still the bastion of the Red suburbs, stronghold of the Communist Party. Its centre retains traces of its small-town origins, but the area around the cathedral has been transformed into a fortress-like housing and shopping complex, with a thrice-weekly **market** still taking place in the square by the Hôtel de Ville and the covered *halles* nearby; it is a multi-ethnic affair these days, and the quantity of offal on the butchers' stalls – ears, feet, tails and bladders – shows this is not wealthy territory. The town's chief claim to fame, though, is its magnificent cathedral, close by the St-Denis Basilique métro station – much the simplest way of getting to St-Denis (although you can walk – see opposite).

Begun by Abbot Suger, friend and adviser to kings, in the first half of the twelfth century, **Basilique St-Denis** (summer daily 10am–7pm; winter closes 5pm; closed Jan 1, May 1, Nov 1, Nov 11 & Dec 25) is generally regarded as the birthplace of the Gothic style in European architecture. The west front was the first ever to have a rose window, but it is in the choir that you best see the clear emergence of the new style: the slimness and lightness that comes with the use of the pointed arch, the ribbed vault and the long shafts of half-column rising from pillar to roof. It is a remarkably well-lit church, too, thanks to the clerestory being almost one hundred percent glass – another first for St-Denis – and the transept windows being so big that they occupy their entire end walls. Once the place where the kings of France were crowned, the cathedral has been the burial place of all but three since 1000 AD, and their very fine tombs and effigies are distributed about the transepts and **ambulatory** (Mon–Fri 10am–6.30pm, Sat & Sun noon–6.30pm; closed during services; 26F, under-17s free). Among the most interesting are the enormous Renaissance memorial to François 1er on the right just beyond the entrance, and the tombs of Louis XII, Henri II and Catherine de Médicis on the left side of the church. To the right of the ambulatory steps you can see the stocky little general, Bertrand du Guesclin, who gave the English the run-around after the death of the Black Prince, and on the level above him – invariably graced by bouquets of flowers – the undistinguished statues of Louis XVI and Marie-Antoinette. Around the corner on the far side of the ambulatory is Clovis himself, king of the Franks way back in 500, a canny little German who wiped out Roman Gaul and turned it into France, with Paris for a capital.

Not many minutes' walk away on rue Gabriel-Péri, third right off rue de la Légiond'Honneur, the **Musée d'Art et d'Histoire de la Ville de St-Denis** (Mon & Wed–Sat 10am–5.30pm, Sun 2–6.30pm; 15F) is housed in a former Carmelite convent. The exhibits are not of spectacular interest, save for the unique collection of documents relating to the Commune: posters, cartoons, broadsheets, paintings, plus an audiovisual presentation. There is also an exhibition of manuscripts and rare editions of the Communist poet, Paul Éluard, native son of St-Denis.

To get to the **canal** at the St-Denis end, follow rue de la République from the Hôtel de Ville to a church, then go down the left side of the church until you reach the canal bridge. If you turn left, you can walk all the way back to Paris along the towpath – about an hour and a half to Porte de la Villette. There are stretches where it looks as if you're probably not supposed to be there. Just pay no attention and keep going.

Not far from the start of the walk, past some peeling *villas* with unkempt gardens, you come to a now defunct restaurant, *La Péniche*. Rue Raspail leads from there to a dusty square where the town council named a side street for IRA hunger-striker Bobby Sands. Continuing along the canal, you can't get lost. Sacré-Coeur is visible up ahead as you pass cottages with yards open on the water, patches of greenery, sand and gravel docks, waste ground where larks rise above rusting bedsteads and doorless fridges, lock-keepers' cottages with roses and vegetable gardens, decaying tenements and brightly painted shacks, derelict factories and huge sheds where trundling gantries load bundles of steel rods on to Belgian barges.

Châteaux

The mansions and palaces around the capital are all very impressive on first sighting, but they can be hard work to tour around – and none more so than larger-than-life **Versailles**.

That said, **Vaux-le-Vicomte**'s classical magnificence and **Fontainebleau**'s Italianate decoration are easy to appreciate; **Chantilly** has a gorgeous Book of Hours and a bizarre horse connection; **Malmaison** is interesting for its former occupants. The main satisfaction, however, is in breathing country air in the gardens, parks and forests that surround the châteaux, and being able to get back to Paris comfortably in a day. Some, whose principal function these days is to house museums, are described later in this chapter, while the tourist office in Paris can provide full lists of others.

Versailles

The **Palace of Versailles** (Tues–Sun 9am–7pm; Oct–April closes 5.30pm; 40F adults, under-18s free) is one of the three most visited monuments in France. It's hard to know why so many tourists come out here in preference to all except the most obvious sights of Paris. Yet they do, and the château is always a crush of bodies. To **get there**, take the *RER ligne C5* to Versailles-Rive Gauche (40min), turn left out of the station and immediately right to approach the palace. You can get maps of the park from the tourist office on rue des Réservoirs to the right of the palace.

THE CHÂTEAU

It is not a beautiful building by any means, its décor a grotesque homage to one of the greatest of all self-propagandists, Louis XIV, and more than anything else, is impressive for its size – which by any standards is incredible. It was inspired by the young king's envy of his finance minister's château at Vaux-le-Vicomte (see opposite), which he was determined to outdo. He recruited the design team of Vaux-le-Vicomte architect Le Vau, painter Le Brun and gardener Le Nôtre, and ordered something a hundred times the size.

Construction of the château began in 1664 and lasted virtually until the Sun King's death in 1715. It was never meant to be a home; kings were not homely people. Second only to God, and the head of an immensely powerful state, Louis XIV was an institution rather than a private individual. His risings and sittings, comings and goings, were minutely regulated and rigidly encased in ceremony, attendance at which was an honour much sought after by courtiers. Versailles was the headquarters of every arm of the state. More than twenty thousand people – nobles, administrative staff, merchants, soldiers and servants – lived in the palace in a state of unhygienic squalor, according to contemporary accounts.

Following Louis XIV's death, the château was abandoned for a few years before being reoccupied by Louis XV in 1722. It remained the residence of the royal family until the Revolution of 1789, when the furniture was sold and the pictures dispatched to the Louvre. Thereafter it fell into ruin and was nearly demolished by Louis-Philippe. In 1871, during the Paris Commune, it became the seat of the nationalist government and the French parliament continued to meet in Louis XV's opera building until 1879. Restoration only began in earnest between the two world wars.

The most amazing room is perhaps the dazzling **Hall of Mirrors** – or Galerie des Glaces – where the Treaty of Versailles was signed to end World War I. You can also visit the state apartments of the king and queen, and the royal chapel, a grand structure that ranks among France's finest Baroque creations.

Visitors to the château have a choice of **itineraries**. Apart from the state apartments of the king and queen and the Galerie des Glaces, which you can visit on your own, most of the palace can only be viewed in guided groups, and whose times are much more restricted. Long queues are common. Don't set out to see all the palace in one day – it's not possible. Quite apart from the size, tours of both Mme du Barry's apartments and of the Dauphin and Dauphine's apartments take place at 2pm. If you want to be sure of a place on a guided tour, it is wise to phone ahead (*Bureau d'Action Culturelle* for reservations, ☎30.84.76.18; general information, ☎30.84.74.00).

THE PARK

Outside, the **park** (open dawn–dusk) is something of a relief, although it's inevitably a very formal affair. The fountains are turned on every Sunday from 3.30pm to 5pm, May to September (20F park entrance, other times free). The scenery gets better the further you go from the palace. There are even informal groups of trees near the lesser outcrops of royal mania, the **Grand** and **Petit Trianons** (Tues–Fri 10am–12.30pm & 2–5.30pm; Grand Trianon 20F, Petit Trianon 12F). More charming and rustic than either of these is **Le hameau de Marie-Antoinette**, a play-village and farm built in

1783 for Louis XVI's queen to indulge the fashionable Rousseau-inspired fantasy of returning to the natural life. You may find bulldozers and chain saws wreaking havoc, as storm damage in 1990 prompted a massive restoration programme that involves, amongst other things, uprooting 20,000 chestnut trees because they weren't part of Le Nôtre's original creation.

The one competing attraction in Versailles town is a wonderfully snobbish **tearoom** in the *Hôtel Palais Trianon*, where the final negotiations for the Treaty of Versailles took place in 1919. It's near the park entrance at the end of bd de la Reine and much more worthwhile than shelling out for château admission, with trayfuls of *pâtisseries* to the limits of your desire for about 80F. The style of the *Trianon* is very much that of the town in general. The dominant population is aristocratic with the pre-revolutionary titles disdainful of those dating merely from Napoléon. On Bastille Day both lots show their colours with black ribbons and ties.

Vaux-le-Vicomte

Of all the great mansions within reach of a day's outing from Paris, the classical **château of Vaux-le-Vicomte** (daily 10am–6pm; Nov–March 11am–5pm; closed Jan. Château, gardens and Musée des Équipages 48F; garden and museum 27F), 46km southeast of Paris (*RER* Gare de Lyon–Melun, then radio cab on ☎64.52.51.50), is the most architecturally harmonious, the most aesthetically pleasing and the most human in scale. Louis XIV's finance superintendent, Nicholas Fouquet, had it built at colossal expense, using the top designers of the day – Le Vau, the royal architect, Le Brun, the painter, and Le Nôtre, the landscape gardener. The result was magnificence and precision in perfect proportion and a bill that could only be paid by someone who occasionally confused the state's account with his own. The housewarming party, to which the king was invited, was more extravagant than any royal event – a comparison which other finance ministers ensured that Louis took to heart. Within three weeks Fouquet was jailed for life on trumped-up charges, and Louis carted Le Vau, Le Brun and Le Nôtre off to Versailles to work on a gaudy and gross piece of one-upmanship.

Seen from the entrance, the château is a rather austere grey pile surrounded by an artificial moat, and it's only when you go through to the south side, where clipped box and yew, fountains and statuary stand in formal gardens, that you can look back and appreciate the very harmonious and very French qualities of the building – the combination of steep, tall roof and central dome with classical pediment and pilasters.

As to the interior, the main artistic interest lies in the work of Le Brun, who was responsible for the two fine tapestries in the entrance, made in the local workshops set up by Fouquet specifically to adorn his house (and subsequently removed by Louis XIV to become the famous Gobelins works in Paris), as well as numerous painted ceilings, notably in Fouquet's bedroom, the Salon des Muses, his *Sleep* in the Cabinet des Jeux, and the so-called King's bedroom, whose décor is the first example of the style that became known as Louis Quatorze. The two oval marble tables in the Salle d'Hercule are the only pieces of furniture never to have left the château.

Other points of interest are the kitchens, which have not been altered since construction, and – if you read French – a room displaying letters in the hand of Fouquet, Louis XIV and other notables. One, dated November 1794 (ie in mid-Revolution), addresses the incumbent Duc de Choiseul-Praslin as *tu*. "Citizen," it says, "you've got a week to hand over one hundred thousand pounds . . ." and signs off with, "Cheers and brotherhood." You can imagine the shock to the aristocratic system.

Every Saturday evening during May, June and Oct, and July to September Friday and Saturday between 8.30pm and 11pm, the state rooms are illuminated with a thousand candles, as they probably were on the occasion of Fouquet's fateful party (65F entrance). The fountains and other waterworks can be seen in action on the second and last Saturdays of each month between April and October, from 3pm until 6pm.

The **Musée des Équipages** in the stables comprises a collection of horsedrawn vehicles, including the method of transport used by Charles X fleeing Paris and the Duc de Rohan retreating from Moscow.

Fontainebleau

If you were feeling energetic, you could spend the morning at Vaux-le-Vicomte and continue by train from Melun to the **château of Fontainebleau** (daily except Tues 9.30am–12.30pm & 2–5pm; 31F, under-18s free, Sun 20F. Petits Appartements guided tours July–Sept Mon & Wed–Fri 10am, 11am, 2.15pm, & 3pm. Gardens dawn–dusk), 70km southeast of Paris – an instructive and pleasant exercise in rapid châteaux touring.

The vast, rambling château that you see today owes its existence to its situation in the middle of a magnificent forest, which made it the perfect base for royal hunting expeditions. A hunting lodge was built here as early as the twelfth century, but the building only began its transformation into a luxurious palace during the sixteenth on the initiative of François 1er, who imported a colony of Italian artists to carry out the decoration – most notably Rosso il Fiorentino, who completed the celebrated **Galerie François-1er**, a work that was seminal in the evolution of French aristocratic art and design; also notable are the Salle de Bal, the Salon Louis XIII and the Salle du Conseil, with its fine eighteenth-century decoration. The palace continued to enjoy royal favour well into the 1800s, and Napoléon lavished huge amounts of money on it, as did Louis-Philippe.

The **gardens** are equally luscious, but if you want to escape to the wilds, the surrounding **forest of Fontainebleau** is full of walking and cycling trails and its rocks are a favourite training ground for French climbers. Paths and tracks are all marked on Michelin map 196 (*Environs de Paris*). **Trains from Paris** take around 45 minutes from Gare de Lyon (25min from Melun), and there's a local bus to the gates from the train station.

Chantilly

CHANTILLY is the kind of place you go when you think it's time you did something at the weekend – like get out and get some culture and fresh air. It comprises a château, park and two museums, one of which is devoted to live horses. Some 3000 thoroughbreds prance the forest rides of a morning, and two of the season's classiest **flat races** are held here.

The town is 40km north of Paris, accessible **by train** from the Gare du Nord. The footpaths GR11 and 12 pass through the park and forest, for a more peaceful and leisurely way of exploring this bit of country.

The Chantilly estate used to belong to two of the most powerful clans in France: first to the Montmorencys, then, through marriage, to the Condés. The present **château** (daily except Tues March–Oct 10am–6pm; Nov–Feb 10.30am–12.30pm & 2–5pm; 37F, park only 15F) was put up in the late nineteenth century. It's an imposing rather than beautiful structure, too heavy for grace, but it stands well, surrounded by water and looking out in a haughty manner over a formal arrangement of pools and pathways designed by the busy Le Nôtre.

The entrance is across a moat, past two realistic bronzes of hunting hounds. The visitable parts are mainly made up of an enormous collection of paintings and drawings. They are not well displayed, and you quickly get visual indigestion from the massed ranks of good, bad and indifferent, deployed as if of equal value. Some highlights, however, are a collection of portraits of sixteenth- and seventeenth-century French monarchs and princes in the Galerie de Logis; interesting Greek and Roman bits in the tower room called the Rotonde de la Minerve; a big series of sepia stained glass illustrating Apuleius' *Golden Ass* in the Galerie de Psyche, together with some very lively portrait drawings; and, in the so-called Santuario, some Raphaels, a Filippo

Lippi and forty miniatures from a fifteenth-century *Book of Hours* attributed to the French artist Jean Fouquet.

The museum's single greatest treasure is in the library, the Cabinet des Livres, which you can enter only in the presence of the guide. It is *Les Très Riches Heures du Duc de Berry*, the most celebrated of all the Books of Hours. The illuminated pages illustrating the months of the year with representative scenes from contemporary (early 1400s) rural life – like harvesting and ploughing, sheepshearing and pruning, all drawn from life – are richly coloured and drawn with a delicate naturalism, as well as being sociologically interesting. Unfortunately – and understandably – only facsimiles are on display, but they give an excellent idea of the original. Sets of postcards, of middling fidelity, are on sale in the entrance. There are thousands of other fine books on display as well.

Five minutes' walk along the château drive, the colossal stable block has been transformed into a museum of the horse, the **Musée Vivant du Cheval** (May–Aug daily 10.30am–5.30pm; April, Sept & Oct closed Tues; closed Nov–March; 45F). The building was erected at the beginning of the eighteenth century by the incumbent Condé prince, who believed he would be reincarnated as a horse and wished to provide fitting accommodation for 240 of his future relatives. In the main hall, horses of different breeds from around the world are stalled, with a ring for demonstrations (enquire at the ticket desk for details), followed by a series of life-size models illustrating the various activities horses are used for. In the rooms off here are collections of paintings, horseshoes, veterinary equipment, bridles and saddles, a mock-up of a blacksmith's, children's horse toys (including a chain-driven number, with handles in its ears, which belonged to Napoléon III), and a fanciful Sicilian cart painted with scenes of Crusader battles.

Malmaison and Chatou

The château of **MALMAISON** was the home of the Empress Josephine, and – during the 1800–1804 Consulate – of Napoléon, too. According to his secretary, "it was the only place next to the battlefield where he was truly himself". After their divorce, Josephine stayed on here, occasionally receiving visits from the emperor until her death in 1814. The **château** (daily except Tues 10am–noon & 1.30–4.30/5.30pm; guided tours only; combined ticket with Bois-Préau museum 27F) is set in the beautiful grounds of the **Bois-Préau**, about 15km west of central Paris, and is a relatively small and surprisingly enjoyable place to visit. Tours include the private and official apartments, in part with original furnishings, as well as Josephine's clothes, china, glass and personal possessions. There are other Napoleonic bits in the **Bois-Préau museum** (daily except Tues 10.30am–1pm & 2–6pm; same ticket as above).

To get there take the *RER* to La Défense, then bus #158A to Malmaison-Château. Alternatively, if you'd like a walk, take the *RER* to Rueil-Malmaison and follow the GR11 footpath from the Pont de Chatou along the left bank of the Seine and into the château park.

A long narrow island in the Seine, the **Île de Chatou** was once a rustic spot where Parisians came on the newly opened rail line to row and dine and flirt at the riverside *guinguettes* (eating and dancing establishments). One of these, the **Maison Fournaise**, just below the Pont de Chatou road bridge, has finally been restored and is now once again a restaurant (☎30.71.41.91; lunchtimes & evenings until 10pm; winter closed Sun; menu 150F; *carte* 200–250F), with a small **museum** alongside dedicated to the artists of its heyday – Renoir, Monet, Manet, Van Gogh, Seurat, Sisley, Courbet – for whom it was a favourite haunt. One of Renoir's best-known canvases, *Le Déjeuner des Canotiers*, shows his friends lunching on the balcony, which is still shaded by a magnificent riverside plane tree. Vlaminck and his fellow-Fauves, Derain and Matisse, were also habitués. It was in fact from here that Vlaminck set off for the 1905 *Salon des Indépendants* with the truckload of paintings that caused the critics to coin the term Fauvism.

Access to the island is from the Rueil-Malmaison *RER* stop: turn left out of the station, right on the dual carriageway and up to the Pont de Chatou. Bizarrely, there's a twice-yearly **ham and antique fair** on the island, which could be fun to check out (March & Sept).

Museums

Meudon, **Sèvres** and **Sceaux**, once distinct villages, have expanded into each other over the last century, spreading across the steep hills above the Seine. The heights are dominated by luxury apartments these days, but for visitors the main attractions lie in museums: **Rodin** and **Jean Arp** at Meudon, **ceramics** at Sèvres and **Île de France history** at Sceaux. **Le Bourget** to the north, Paris' airport for internal flights, and home to the dreaded French arms trade fairs, has an aerospace museum.

Musée de l'Air et d'Espace

The French were always adventurous, pioneering aviators and the name of **LE BOURGET** is intimately connected with their earliest exploits. Lindbergh landed here after his epic first flight across the Atlantic. From World War I to the development of Orly in the l950s, it was Paris' principal airport. Today its used only for internal flights, but some of the older buildings have been turned into a fascinating **museum of flying machines**. **To get there**, take the *RER* from Gare du Nord to Drancy, where the Germans and the French Vichy regime had a transit camp for Jews en route to Auschwitz. From the station follow av Francis-de-Pressensé as far as the main road, turn left and, by a *tabac* on the left at the first crossroads, catch bus #152. Alternatively, take bus #350 from Gare du Nord, Gare de l'Est or Porte de la Chapelle, or #152 from Porte de la Villette.

The museum (Tues–Sun 10am–5pm; 20F) occupies the old airport buildings, and consists of five adjacent hangars, the first devoted to **space**, with rockets, satellites, space capsules etc. Some are mock-ups, some the real thing. Among the latter are a Lunar Roving Vehicle, the Apollo XIII command module in which James Lovell and his fellow astronauts nearly came to grief, the Soyuz craft in which a French astronaut flew, and France's own first successful space rocket. Everything is accompanied by extremely good explanatory panels – though in French only. The remainder of the exhibition is arranged in chronological order, starting with **Hangar A** (the furthest away from the entrance), which covers the period 1919–39. Several record-breakers are here, including the Bréguet XIX, which made the first ever crossing of the South Atlantic in 1927, and the corrugated iron Junkers F13 that featured so long on US postage stamps; the Germans were forbidden to produce this after World War I and it was taken over instead by the US Mail. Hangar B shows a big collection of World War II planes, including a V-1 flying bomb and the Nazis' last jet fighter, the largely wooden Heinkel 162A. Incredibly, the plans were completed on September 24, 1944, and it flew on December 6. **Hangars C and D** cover the years 1945 to the present day, during which the French aviation industry, having lost eighty percent of its capacity in 1945, has recovered to a pre-eminent position in the world. Its high-tech achievement is represented here by the super-sophisticated best-selling Mirage fighters, the first Concorde prototype and – symbol of national vigour and virility – the Ariane space-launcher (the latter two parked on the tarmac outside). **Hangar E** contains light and sporty aircraft.

Musée des Antiquités Nationales

ST-GERMAIN is not specially interesting as a town, but if you've been to the prehistoric caves of the Dordogne, or plan to go, you'll get a lot from the **Musée des Antiquités Nationales** (Wed–Sun 9am–5.15pm; 20F, under-18s free). It is in the unattractively renovated château (opposite the *RER* station), which was one of the main residences of the French court before Versailles was built.

The presentation and lighting make the visit a real pleasure. The extensive Stone Age section includes a mock-up of the Lascaux caves and a profile of Abbé Breuil, the priest who made prehistoric art respectable, as well as a beautiful collection of decorative objects, tools and so forth. All ages of prehistory are covered, right down into historical times with Celts, Romans and Franks: abundant evidence that the French have been a talented arty lot for a very long time. The end piece is a room of comparative archeology, with objects from cultures across the globe.

From right outside the château, a **terrace** – Le Nôtre arranging the landscape again – stretches for more than 2km above the Seine with a view over the whole of Paris. All behind it is the **forest of St-Germain**, a sizeable expanse of woodland, although crisscrossed by too many roads to be convincing as wilderness.

Musée de l'Île-de-France

The **château of SCEAUX** is a nineteenth-century replacement of the original – demolished post-Revolution – which matched the now-restored Le Nôtre grounds. As a park it's the usual classical geometry of terraces, water and woods, but if you fancy a walk you can get off the *RER* at La-Croix-de-Berny at the southern end. Otherwise it's a five- to ten-minute walk from Parc-de-Sceaux station (15min from Denfert-Rochereau): turn left on av de la Duchesse-du-Maine, right into av Rose-de-Launay and right again on av Le-Nôtre and you'll find the château gates on your left.

The château housing the **Musée de l'Île-de-France** (Wed–Sun 10am–6pm; Oct–March closes 5pm; 20F, disabled access) evokes the Paris countryside of the *ancien régime* with its aristocratic and royal domains; of the nineteenth century, with its riverside scenes and eating and dancing places, the *guinguettes*, that inspired so many artists; and of the new towns and transport of the current age. There are models, pictures and diverse objects: a backpack hot-chocolate dispenser with a choice of two brews; 1940s métro seats; a painting of river laundering at Cergy-Pontoise alongside photos of the new town high-rise; early bicycles and a series of plates and figurines inspired by the arrival of the first giraffe in France in the 1830s. Though some of the rooms hold little excitement, most people, kids included, should find enough to make the visit worth it.

Temporary exhibitions and a summer festival of classical chamber music are held in the **Orangerie**, which, along with the **Pavillon de l'Aurore** (in the northeast corner of the park), survives from the original residence. The concerts take place at weekends, from July to October – details from the museum (☎46.61.06.71), or from the *Direction des Musées de France*, Palais du Louvre, Cours Visconti, 34 quai du Louvre, 1er (☎42.60.39.26).

Musée National de la Céramique

SÈVRES is very easy to reach from central Paris: take the métro to Pont-de-Sèvres/Boulogne-Pont-de-St-Cloud; the **Musée National de la Céramique** (daily except Tues 10am–5pm; 17F, under-18s free) stands just to the right of the main road, close to the riverbank. Ceramics are an acquired taste, maybe, but if you do have it, there is much to be savoured here – not just French pottery and china, but Islamic, Chinese, Italian, German, Dutch and English. There is also, inevitably, a comprehensive collection of Sèvres ware, as the stuff is made right here. Close by, overlooking the river, the **Parc de St-Cloud** is good for fresh air and visual order, with a geometrical sequence of pools and fountains delineating a route down to the river and across to the city.

Meudon-Val-Fleury

MEUDON-VAL-FLEURY, on the *C5/C7 RER* lines, is the most easily accessible patch of Seine countryside. And to give a walk some purpose there is the **Villa des Brillants** at 19 av Auguste-Rodin, off rue de la Belgique (July–Sept Sat & Sun 1.30–

6.30pm; 12F), the house where **Rodin** spent his last years, with an annexe containing some of his maquettes, plaster casts and other bits and bobs.

From the station you make your way up the east flank of the valley through the twisty **rue des Vignes**. You can either go up rue de la Belgique until you reach av Rodin on the left towards the top, or turn down it to the rail line embankment, go through the tunnel and take the footpath on the right, which brings you out by the house. It stands in a big picnickable garden, where Rodin himself is buried, on the very edge of the hill looking down on the decimated Renault works in Boulogne-Billancourt. To the south, on the edge of Meudon's forest, is the **Musée et Jardin de Sculptures de la Fondation Hans Arp** at 21 rue des Châtaigniers, Clamart (Fri–Sun 2–6pm; 20F). This was the home and studio of Dadaists Hans Arp and Sophie Täuber – both the house and garden have examples of their work and the house itself is a curiosity.

Works by Arp, Täuber, Rodin and others are exhibited at the **Musée d'Art et d'Histoire de Meudon**, in what was once Molière's residence at 11 rue des Pierres (Wed–Sun 2–6pm). There are also mementos of various other characters who had some connection with the house, including Wagner.

The New Towns

Since the 1960s a new feature to the Parisian outskirts has been the New Towns or *Villes Nouvelles*. Satellites to the city rather than places in their own right, they have spawned some extraordinary pieces of architecture. **MARNE-LA-VALLÉE,** where Terry Gilliam's totalitarian fantasy *Brasil* was filmed, has long topped the charts for most outrageous designs. It starts ten kilometres east of Paris and hops for twenty kilometres from one new outburst to the next, ending with Europe's first **Disneyland**.

At **NOISY-LE-GRAND** you surface on the Arcades, a stony substitute for a town square, and there you have the poetic panorama of a controlled community environment. The two acclaimed architectural pieces in this monolith are both low-cost housing units, gigantic, quite unlike anything you're likely to have seen before and unmitigatedly horrible. The **Arènes de Picasso** is in the group of buildings to the right of the *RER* line as you look at the lakes from the Arcades, about half a kilometre away. It's soon visible as you approach: two enormous circles like loudspeakers facing each other across a space that would do nicely for a Roman stadium. Prepare to feel as if the lions were waiting. At the other end of Mont d'Est, facing the capital, is the extraordinary semicircle, arch and half square of **Le Théâtre et Palacio d'Abraxas**, creation of Ricardo Boffil. Ghosts of ancient Greek designs haunt the facades but proportion there is none, whether classical or any other.

CERGY-PONTOISE, thirty kilometres northwest of Paris (*RER* line A3, Cergy-St-Christophe), is the start of an "Axe Majeur" pointing towards La Défense. From the *RER*, take the left-hand exit and keep going straight up through pedestrianized squares until you see a high white column. From here, the 3km vista towards La Grande Arche has yet to have its full complement of architectural fantasies, and may not have for a long time given the recession. There are very few cafés and brasseries in Cergy, and those there are seem full of arcade machines and bored men.

Disneyland Paris

Around 32 kilometres east of Paris, **DISNEYLAND PARIS** is a 5000-acre slice of the USA grafted onto a bleak tract of the Bassin Parisien, an area taking up a space one-fifth the size of Paris. The ploy was to make the Disney empire more accessible to Europeans, but it seems that many Europeans are either not interested or would rather opt for the more reliable weather and better rides of Florida's Disneyworld, which is not much more expensive a proposition. The latest marketing ploy to escape the former downbeat connotations of the place was to change the name from Euro Disney to Disneyland Paris in September 1994, hopefully bringing the park in line with its siblings abroad. But for all the jokes about "Euro-dismal", the theatricality and professionalism of the place elevate it head and shoulders above any other theme park.

Before setting out, you should be clear about just what Disneyland Paris is, and what it is not. The physical buzz of shocks, fright and gravitational pulls is not a priority on the Disney agenda. They want you to feel safe and secure at all times; they want it to be a thoroughly *wholesome* experience. And so the park is short on real fear-thrill rides; originally there was only *Big Thunder Mountain*. Now there's the first 360° loop ever in a Disney ride in *Indiana Jones and the Temple of Doom*, and *Discovery Mountain*, due to open in 1995, will have three loops and a corkscrew turn.

The **Magic Kingdom** is divided into four "lands" radiating out from Main Street – Fantasyland, Frontierland, Discoveryland and Adventureland. **Fantasyland** appeals to the youngest kids (*Sleeping Beauty's Castle, Mad Hatter's Tea Cups, Alice in Wonderland's Maze*); **Adventureland** boasts the most outlandish sets (*Aladdin, Indiana Jones, Pirates of the Caribbean, Swiss Family Robinson Treehouse*); **Frontierland** has the *Psycho*-inspired *Phantom Manor* and *Big Thunder Mountain*; and **Discoveryland**, a high-tech 3-D Michael Jackson film, a 360° Parisian exposé in *Le Visionarium*, and the Nautilus submarine of *2000 Leagues under the Sea*. The grand **parade** sallies down Main Street USA at 3pm sharp every day, and Snow White, Dumbo, Pinocchio, Roger Rabbit, Mickey et al strut their stuff with unfoundering joviality. Night-time Electrical Parades and **firework displays** take place several times a week.

Besides the **Disneyland Paris Park**, the complex includes **Festival Disney** – the evening entertainments complex – and the Disney hotels. These, unlike the park, are radically different from their US or Japanese counterparts, having been designed especially for Europeans, who, according to Disney executives, invented fairy tales and castles, but have run out of good ideas since.

The six themed Disney **hotels** may be out of many people's price range, the cheapest room off-season being 300F a night (2 adults, 2 children), rising to over F2000 peak season for a room in the *Disneyland Hotel* inside the Magic Kingdom on Main Street. The complexes are generally a mixed bag of hideous eyesores and over-ambitious kitsch designed by some of the world's leading architectural names – Michael Graves, Antoine Predock, Robert Stern and Frank Gehry – but they do offer an array of eating venues, as well as saunas, jacuzzis, golf, gyms, video games and even a children's theatre.

To enable people to commute to the park from Paris, the French government has built a *TGV* and a *RER* **train station** at Marne-la-Vallée, a 40-minute journey from the Gare de Lyon and costing F66 return; by **car**, take the Serris exit on the A4. If you're coming straight from the airport, there's a half-hourly **shuttle bus** from Charles de Gaulle, and another every 45 minutes from Orly (75F, no reductions for children), plus the trains.

Mid-season **admission** charges are: 1-day pass F225 (under-11s F150), 2-day pass F425 (F285), 3-day pass F565 (F375). A 1-day high-season costs 250F and 175F; 1-day low-season costs 175F and 125F.

travel details

Trains

Gare du Nord to: Amiens (at least hourly; 1hr 45min); Arras (1hr 40min); Lille (2hr 30min).

Gare de l'Est to: Besançon (frequent; 3hr); Metz (frequent; 2hr 30min); Nancy (frequent; 2–3hr); Reims (frequent; 1hr 30min); Strasbourg (frequent; 4hr).

Gare St-Lazare to: Dieppe (2 daily; 2hr 15min); Le Havre (frequent; 2–2hr 30min); Cherbourg (frequent; 3–3hr 30min); Rouen (frequent; 1hr 15min).

Gare Montparnasse to: Brest (frequent; 5hr 30min–6hr); Nantes (frequent; 3hr 30min); Rennes (frequent; 2hr 30min).

Gare d'Austerlitz to: Bayonne (6 daily; 6–8hr); Bordeaux (numerous; 5hr); Poitiers (numerous; 3hr); Toulouse (6 daily; 7–8hr); Tours (numerous; 2hr).

Gare de Lyon to: Dijon (almost hourly *TGV*; 1hr 40min); Dijon (7–8 daily; 2hr 30min); Lyon (almost hourly *TGV*; 2hr 30min); Lyon (7–8 daily; 5–6hr); Grenoble, changing at Lyon (almost hourly *TGV*; 3hr 45min); Marseille (10 daily *TGV*; 5hr); Nice (10 daily; 10hr 30min).

Hitching

Hitching out of Paris isn't easy, especially in high summer when you are likely to face long delays. It's much better to spend a few extra francs taking a train or bus 50km clear of the city. Alternatively, for a small fee, you can register with the hitching organization *Allostop*; they will find you a ride and you just make a small contribution towards petrol (see "Listings" for details).

CHAPTER TWO

THE NORTH

When conjuring up exotic holiday locations, the **north** of France is unlikely to get a mention. Even among the French, the most enthusiastic tourists of their own country, it has few adherents. Artois and Flanders include the most heavily industrialized parts of the country, while across the wheat fields of the more sparsely populated regions of Picardy and Champagne a few drops of rain are all that is required for total gloom to descend. It is likely, however, that you'll arrive and leave France via this region, and there are reasons to stop within easy reach of the channel ports – of which **Boulogne** is by far the most appealing.

The north of France has been on the obvious invaders' path into the country, from northern Europe as well as from Britain, and the events that have taken place in Flanders, Artois and Picardy have shaped French history. The bloodiest battles were those of the First World War, above all the **Battle of the Somme** which took place north of Amiens, and **Vimy Ridge** near Arras, where the trenches have been preserved in perpetuity. Throughout the north, but particularly around the villages of the Somme, there are powerful reminders in monuments and cemeteries of the devastating human wastage of those years.

Picardy boasts two of France's finest cathedrals at **Amiens** and **Laon**. Further south, the *maisons*, vineyards and produce of the **Champagne** region are the main draw, for which the best bases are **Épernay** and **Reims**, the latter with another fine cathedral. Other attractions include the bird sanctuary of **Marquenterre**; the wooded wilderness of the **Ardennes**; industrial archeology in the coal fields around Douai where Zola's *Germinal* was set; the great medieval castle of **Coucy-le-Château**; and the battle sites of the Middle Ages – **Agincourt** and **Crécy** – whose names are so familiar in the history of Anglo-French rivalry.

Though the past is not forgotten, the present life of the region does not feed on it. In city centres from **Lille** to **Troyes**, you'll find your fill of food, culture and entertainment in the company of locals similarly intent on having a good time; and in addition to the more obvious pleasures of the Champagne region, there's the possibility of finding relatively lucrative employment during the harvest season towards the end of September.

ACCOMMODATION PRICE CATEGORIES

All the hotels, youth hostels and guesthouses listed in this book have been price-graded according to the following scale, and although costs will rise slightly overall with the life of this edition, the relative comparisons should remain valid. Paris and the large cities will, as anywhere, be more expensive than equivalent accommodation in the countryside or small towns. The prices quoted are for the cheapest available double room in high season, although remember that many of the cheap places will have more expensive rooms with en-suite facilities.

① Under 160F	④ 300–400F	⑦ 600–700F
② 160–220F	⑤ 400–500F	⑧ Over 700F
③ 220–300F	⑥ 500–600F	

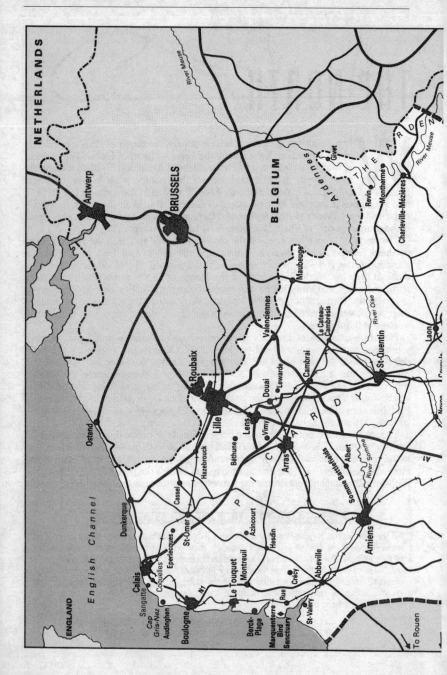

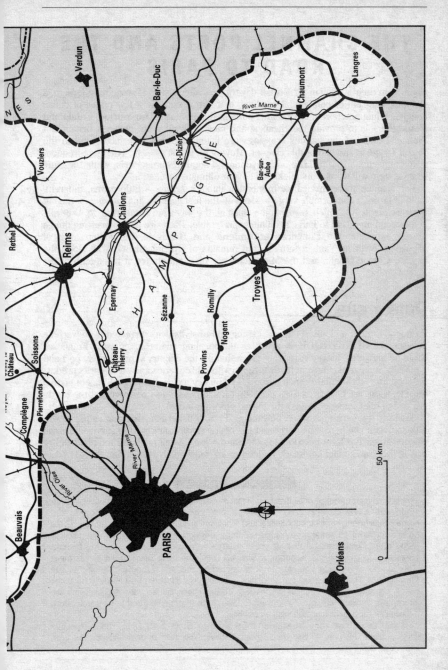

THE CHANNEL PORTS AND THE ROAD TO PARIS

Apart from their attraction for British day-trippers after a sniff of something foreign, a shopping bag full of continental produce, or more commonly a few crates of cheap beer, the chief function of the channel ports in this section – **Dunkerque**, **Calais** and **Boulogne** – is to provide the cheapest and most efficient route between Britain and France. Details of the various crossings are listed in *Basics* (see p.000) and in the *Travel Details* at the end of this chapter. Moving on is just as easy. There are frequent train connections east to **Lille** and beyond, and south towards **Paris**, while the autoroute system will whisk you quickly off to your ultimate destination.

For a much more immediate immersion into *La France* – little towns, different-looking farms, a comfortable verge to sleep off the first *baguette* and *vin rouge* – the old *route nationale* N1, which shadows the coast all the way from Dunkerque to Abbeville before heading inland to Paris, is infinitely preferable. There are also interesting things to see en route: the cathedrals at **Amiens** and **Beauvais**, the hilltop town of **Montreuil** with its Vauban fortress, the remains of Hitler's Atlantic Wall along the bracing **Côte d'Opale**, and the **Marquenterre bird sanctuary** at the mouth of the River Somme.

Dunkerque

Frequently under a cloud of chemical smog and unstylishly resurrected from wartime devastation, **DUNKERQUE** is about as unappealing an introduction to France as could be imagined: hardly surprising given that it's the country's third largest port and a massive industrial centre in its own right, with oil refineries and steel works producing a quarter of the total French output. If you fancy a closer look at all this industrial muscle, there are boat trips from place du Minck, bassin du Commerce, at the northern end of rue Clemenceau (ask the tourist office for times).

Save for the occasions when blockading French fishermen rule *aux quais*, there's little to detain you here. The only buildings of any significance to have survived the last war (or at least to have been rebuilt afterwards) are the tall medieval red-brick **belfry** that is the town's chief landmark (guided tours hourly daily except Sun 9.30–11.30am

---

SHOPPING

The best area for shoppers to head for is the main drag, **bd Alexandre-III**, its continuation, **rue Clemenceau**, and the cross-street, **rue Poincaré**. In addition to the clothes, perfume, fancy tobacconists and kitchenware shops on bd Alexandre-III, *Le Sanglier* stocks all manner of saliva-inducing edibles, including numerous take-out *plats*, while *Pimkie* sees a riotous press of style-conscious shoppers seeking fashion bargains. On place de la République just off the boulevard, the *Uniprix* department store stocks everything you can think of, including masses of food and booze. In rue Poincaré, *Le Manoir* is good for groceries, *Boulangeries Hossaert* and *Poulain* for tarts, cakes, biscuits and the like. As everywhere on this coast, crustaceans and shellfish are a tempting bargain buy, but if you want to take them home, you need to be quick about it and preferably arrive armed with a cool bag.

If you don't have time to wander from shop to shop, *Sally Lines* run a free bus service from the port to the three giant all-under-one-roof **hypermarkets**, *Auchan*, *Carrefour* and *Cora*.

DUNKERQUE 1940

The evacuation of 350,000 Allied troops from the beaches of Dunkerque from May 27 to June 4, 1940, has become one of those heroic wartime legends which conveniently conceals the fact that the Allies, through their own incompetence, almost lost their entire armed forces in the first few weeks of the war.

The German army had taken just ten days to reach the English Channel and could very easily have finished off the job. Unable to believe the ease with which he had overcome a numerically superior enemy, Hitler ordered his generals to halt their lightning advance, giving Allied forces trapped in the Pas-de-Calais enough time to organize Operation Dynamo, the largest wartime evacuation ever undertaken. Initially it was hoped that around 10,000 men would be saved, though thanks to low-lying cloud and the assistance of over 1750 vessels – among them pleasure cruisers, fishing boats and river ferries – 140,000 French and over 200,000 British soldiers were successfully shipped back to England.

In France, the ratio of Brits to French evacuees caused bitter resentment since Churchill had promised that the two sides would go *bras dessus, bras dessous* ("arm in arm"). Meanwhile, the British media played up the "remarkable discipline" of the troops as they waited to embark, the "victory" of the RAF over the Luftwaffe and the "disintegration" of the French army all around. In fact, there was widespread indiscipline in the early stages as men fought for places on board; the battle for the skies was evenly matched; and the French fought long and hard to cover the whole operation, some 150,000 of them remaining behind to become prisoners of war. In addition, the Allies lost 7 destroyers and 177 fighter planes and were forced to abandon over 60,000 vehicles.

& 2.30–5.30pm; 12F); the much restored fifteenth-century **church of St-Éloi**; and, a few blocks south of the church on place Jean-Bart, the turn-of-the-century **Hôtel de Ville**, a Flemish fancy to rival that of Calais.

If you're stuck with time on your hands, however, head for the unexpectedly brilliant **Musée d'Art Contemporain** (daily except Tues 10am–noon & 2–6pm; 6F), with works by Karel Appel, Vasarely, César and many other stars of the postwar era, housed in a suitably serious, pared-down, white ceramic building in a landscaped canalside sculpture park off av des Bains (15min walk north of town centre towards Malo-les-Bains or bus #3 to *Piscine*). Alternatively, there's the **Musée des Beaux-Arts** (daily except Tues 10am–noon & 2–6pm; 12F), on place du Général-de-Gaulle by the post office, with good collections of Flemish, Dutch and French painting, natural history and, inevitably, a display on the evacuation of May 1940 (see box).

Practicalities

The **ferry terminal** is some 15km west of the town and *gare SNCF*, but it's linked by a free shuttle service – laid on by *Sally Lines* (☎28.21.43.44), the only ferry company which operates from Dunkerque – which drops you in the central place Émile-Bollaert. The **tourist office** (Mon–Fri 9am–12.30pm & 1.30–6.30pm, Sat 9am–6.30pm) is on the ground floor of the town belfry. To get there from place Bollaert, walk east one block to place Jean-Bart (named after Louis XIV's licensed pirate), then left up rue Clemenceau. If you're looking to **rent a car**, *Europcar*, 32 place de la Gare (Mon–Fri 8am–7pm, Sat 8am–noon & 2–6pm; ☎20.12.13.33), provides affordable rates.

Two cheap **accommodation** options on place de la Gare are *Terminus Nord* (☎28.66.54.26; ①) and the comfortable two-star *Le Select* (②). More salubrious hotels away from the station include *Hôtel Borel*, overlooking the fishing boats of the Bassin du Commerce on rue Hermitte (☎28.66.51.80; ④), a modern three-star with well set-up rooms; or the equally well-equipped but more old-fashioned *Europ Hôtel*, close by at 13 rue Leughenaer (☎28.66.29.07; ④). There's also a seafront IYHF **youth hostel** on place Paul-Asseman, 2km east of the centre practically at Malo-les-Bains (☎28.63.36.34; curfew 10.30pm; ①; IYHF card required); take bus #3 to *Piscine*.

You could do a lot worse than **eat** at the station buffet, the *Richelieu*. It's not especially cheap but they accept some brands of plastic. Other possibilities include *Aux Halles*, on rue de l'Amiral-Ronarc'h near the tourist office, a pleasant bar/brasserie with a decent *menu complet* for 40F, or a pizzeria/grill with Flemish dishes, the *Auberge du Flamand*, 11 pl Charles-Valentin, near the town hall. For more enjoyable eating options, head for the seaside suburb Malo-les-Bains (see below).

Malo-les-Bains and around

If you can't bear the thought of Dunkerque, you might want to consider staying in **MALO-LES-BAINS**, Dunkerque's surprisingly pleasant nineteenth-century seaside suburb on the east side of town (bus #3 and #9), from whose vast sandy strand the Allied troops were embarked in 1940 (see box). Digue des Alliés is the dirtier, pollution-strewn end of an extensive **beachfront** promenade lined with cafés and restaurants; at the cleaner Digue des Mers end, the beach can almost seem pleasant when the sun comes out, along with determined dog-walkers, joggers and cyclists – that is, if you avert your eyes from the stinking industrial inferno to the west. The suburb actually reveals its turn-of-the-century charm away from the seafront, a few parallel blocks inland along av Faidherbe and its continuation av Kléber, with the pretty green-squared place Turenne sandwiched in between; around here you'll find some excellent *pâtisseries*, *boulangeries* and *charcuteries*.

Moving on from Dunkerque by car, you'll be shepherded quickly (unless you take some pains to avoid it) onto the autoroute system, with links to Belgium, Germany and Paris. Heading west along the coast, on the other hand, brings you to Vauban-walled **GRAVELINES**, 16km from Dunkerque, site of one of France's many nuclear reactors.

Places to **stay** include the *Hirondelle*, 48 av Faidherbe (☎28.63.17.65; closed Aug 15–Sept 7; ④), a modern two-star in a great position, and the unassuming, less expensive *Au Bon Coin*, 49 av Kléber (☎28.69.12.63; ②), with its cosy bar below good for a drink. Both have well-regarded **restaurants** specializing in seafood, the *Hirondelle* more formal and pricier with 82F and 125F menus, *Au Bon Coin* intimate and relaxed. Also on av Kléber are a few ethnic restaurants, including a Vietnamese and a North African one. For a quiet coffee or **snack** in light airy surrounds, try *Le Central* on place Turenne, a corner bar run by a friendly woman and facing the park. Two popular beachfront brasseries, again specializing in seafood, are *L'Iguane*, 15 digue des Alliés, a down-to-earth establishment offering generous servings (couscous too), and the slightly more expensive, colourfully stylish *Le Pavois*, at the nicer end of the beach.

Calais

CALAIS is under 40km from England – the Channel's narrowest crossing – and by far the busiest French passenger port. The port (and its accompanying petro-chemical works) dominates the town; in fact, there's not much else here. In the last war the British destroyed it to impede its use, fearing a German invasion, but ironically, the French still refer to it as "the most English town in France", an influence which began after the battle of Crécy in 1346, when Edward III seized it for use as a beach-head in the Hundred Years' War. It remained in English hands until 1558, when its loss caused Mary Tudor to make her famous schoolroom history quote: "When I am dead and opened, you shall find Calais lying in my heart." The association, however, has been maintained across the centuries by Brits both loved and unloved back home: Lady

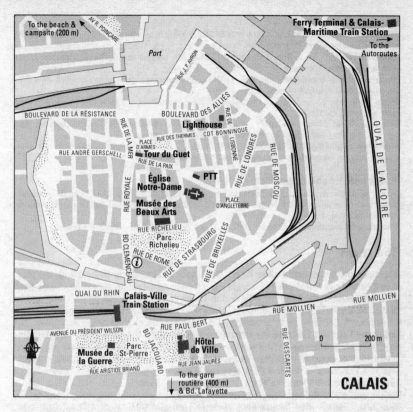

To the beach & campsite (200 m)

AV. R. POINCARE

Port

RUE J. P. AVRON

Ferry Terminal & Calais-Maritime Train Station ■

To the Autoroutes

BOULEVARD DE LA RÉSISTANCE

BOULEVARD DES ALLIÉS

RUE DE

Lighthouse

CDT BONNINQUE

RUE DE LISBONNE

RUE ANDRÉ GERSCHELL

RUE DE LA MER

PLACE D'ARMES

RUE DES THERMES

Tour du Guet

RUE DE LA PAIX

RUE DE LONDRES

RUE DE MOSCOU

QUAI DE LA LOIRE

RUE ROYALE

Église Notre-Dame

■ **PTT**

Musée des Beaux Arts

PLACE D'ANGLETERRE

RUE RICHELIEU

BD CLEMENCEAU

Parc Richelieu

RUE DE ROME

RUE DE STRASBOURG

RUE DE BRUXELLES

ⓘ

QUAI DU RHIN

Calais-Ville Train Station

RUE MOLLIEN

RUE MOLLIEN

AVENUE DU PRÈSIDENT WILSON

RUE PAUL BERT

BD JACQUARD

Hôtel de Ville

RUE DESCARTES

0   200 m

Musée de la Guerre

Parc St-Pierre

RUE JEAN JAURÈS

RUE ARISTIDE BRIAND

To the gare routière (400 m) ▼ & Bd. Lafayette

CALAIS

Emma Hamilton, Lord Nelson's mistress; Oscar Wilde on his uppers; Nottingham lace-makers who set up business in the early nineteenth century; and, most notably today, nine million British travellers per year, plus another million-odd day-trippers.

Arrival and accommodation

Don't bother walking into town from the ferry terminal (Calais-Maritime train station). There's a free daytime **bus** service to place d'Armes and the central Calais-Ville train station in Calais-Sud. The **gare routière** is at the southern end of bd Jacquard, by the municipal theatre. If you're intent on **hitching** to Paris, take a left out of the ferry terminal – the new autoroute bypass begins almost immediately, leading to both the A26 and the old N1. If you're intending to **rent a car**, the main companies are *Avis* (☎21.34.66.50), *Budget* (☎21.96.42.20) and *Hertz* (☎21.96.52.33), located in place d'Armes; cheaper options include *EuroRent*, 1 rue des Thermes (☎21.34.41.99) and *Citer*, 17 rue du Cdt-Bonnique (☎21.96.44.44). For ferry crossings, see p.8.

Should you need to stay, there's plenty of cheap **accommodation** available, though it can be tricky finding a room late in the day in high season. If you're going to miss the boat home, phone before you arrive to book a room. Alternatively, you could use the **tourist office accommodation service** at 12 bd Clemenceau (Mon–Sat 9am–7.30pm Sun 10am–1pm & 4.30–7.30pm; ☎21.96.62.40), for which there is a small charge.

Hotels

Hôtel Albert 1er, 51–53 rue de la Mer (☎21.34.36.08). Only hotel with seafront views, albeit a noisy choice. All rooms are well equipped. ④.

Hôtel Le Littoral, 71 rue Aristide-Briand (☎21.34.47.28). Large rooms and a popular choice, situated in a quiet street opposite Parc St-Pierre. ③.

Meurice, 5 rue Edmond-Roche (☎22.34.57.03). Large, upmarket three-star in a quiet street behind the Musée des Beaux-Arts. ④–⑤.

Hôtel Richelieu, 17 rue Richelieu (☎21.34.61.60). More upmarket, and close to the park. All rooms have shower, TV and toilet. ③.

Hôtel Le Signe, 32 rue Jean-Jaurès (☎21.34.55.18). Behind the Hôtel de Ville, the cheapest place there is after the youth hostel, but very basic and above a rowdy bar. ①.

Hôtel Windsor, 2 rue du Cdt-Bonnique (☎21.34.59.40). Pleasant two-star conveniently placed for the car ferry on the quiet approach road to place d'Armes. ③–④.

Youth hostels and campsites

Youth hostel, av du Maréchal de-Lattre-de-Tassigny (☎21.34.70.20). One block behind the seafront promenade, this ultra-modern hostel was opened in July 1993. Single and double rooms available; disabled facilities. ①.

Camping municipal, 26 av Poincaré (☎21.46.62.00). An exposed site close to the beach.

The Town

The town divides in two: **Calais-Nord**, the old town rebuilt after the war with the place d'Armes and rue Royale as its focus, is separated by canals from sprawling **Calais-Sud**, which focuses on the Hôtel de Ville and the main shopping streets, bd Lafayette and bd Jacquard, named after the inventor of looms who mechanized Calais lacemaking.

Although Calais-Nord is nominally the old town, its charms soon wear thin. The medieval **Tour du Guet** on the drab main square, place d'Armes, is the only building in the quarter to have survived wartime bombardment. From the Tour, rue de la Paix leads to the **church of Notre-Dame**, where Charles de Gaulle married local girl Yvonne Vendroux in 1921. Rather spuriously dubbed the only English Perpendicular church on the continent, it's not a particularly good example of the style, especially in its present state of dereliction. Frill-fanciers can enjoy the unusual lacemaking exhibition in the **Musée des Beaux-Arts et de la Dentelle** (daily except Tues 10am–noon & 2–5.30pm; 10F, Wed free) on rue Richelieu.

Calais-Sud is scarcely more exciting. Just over the canal bridge, the town's landmark, its Flemish extravaganza of an **Hôtel de Ville**, which was finished in 1926 and miraculously survived the war, rears its belfry over 60m into the sky. Somewhat dwarfed by the building, Rodin's famous bronze **Burghers of Calais** records forever the self-sacrifice of these local dignitaries, who offered their lives to assuage the brutal lust of the victor at Crécy, Edward III – only to be spared at the last minute by the intervention of the Queen. For a record of Calais' wartime travails you can consult the **Musée de la Guerre** (March–Nov daily 10.30am–5.30pm; 15F) installed in a former German *Blockhaus* in the Parc St-Pierre across the street.

Eating and drinking

Calais is full of places to **eat**, mostly mediocre to satisfy the day-tripper trade: place d'Armes is full of such examples, with rue Royale offering your best bet. There are plenty of self-service and fast-food outlets at the beach.

Café de Paris, 72 rue Royale. Continues as crowded as ever: popular with locals and tourists alike for its cheap fare; *plats du jour* from 55F.

Channel, 3 bd de la Résistance, overlooking the yacht basin. Generous menus and stylish decor; the popular 90F menu – the lowest – is not available on Sunday, but a big range of yummy desserts always are. Closed Sun evening & Tues.

Le Grand Bleu, 8 rue J-P-Avron. On the waterfront, with the ships of the port in view and vendors selling fresh seafood opposite, a smart modern restaurant specializing in the stuff itself; expensive.

Histoire Ancienne, 20 rue Royale. Brasserie with a charming interior, particularly its old bar; run by a Greek, you'll sometimes find bits of his cuisine on the menu but mainly a good French range. Inexpensive interesting salads should please vegetarians. Closed Sun & Mon.

Palm Beach, 7 rue Royale. Remarkably for the northern French provinces, this is a popular (mostly male) gay bar; cocktails and tacky tropical decor.

Le Toquet, 57 rue Royale. This large old brasserie is a local institution, with lots of fish and seafood; menus from 65F up to 220F. Closed Mon.

Le Troubador, quai du Rhin. Hidden away in a quiet street near the station and tourist office, this bar is a popular hang-out for local music-heads: lots of long hair around the games tables by day and bands by night.

Around Calais

Understandably, most tourists travel non-stop through the **Pas-de-Calais** – France's northernmost *département* – heading for warmer climes and more varied scenery. However, if you're on a short break to one of the channel ports, it's worth making the effort to venture inland; **Cassel** in particular is a minor gem for this part of France.

St-Omer

The first stop inland for many visitors to France is **ST-OMER**, a quiet, unassuming little town, though one which establishes an immediately distinct and foreign character. The landscape seems to expand and the town itself has flights of Flemish magnificence, especially in the **Hôtel de Ville** and some of the recently restored mansions on rue Gambetta. The Gothic **Basilique Notre-Dame** contains some noteworthy statuary, and there are some handsome exhibits in the eighteenth-century **Hôtel Sandelin** museum on rue Carnot (Wed–Sun 10am–noon & 2–6pm, Thurs & Fri till 5pm; 11F) – in particular, a glorious piece of medieval goldsmithing known as the *Pied de Croix de St-Bertin*.

Aside from the pleasant **public gardens** to the west of town, there's also the possibility of exploring the nearby **marais**, a network of very Flemish-seeming waterways cut between plots of land on reclaimed marshes east of the town along the river. You can rent boats from *Taverne Flamande*, 60 route de Clairmarais, or join one of the bâteaux-promenade which leave from the bridge on the D209, 2km west of the *gare SNCF* (daily July & Aug; Sun only May, June & Sept; 40F per person). The round trip takes roughly two hours, the longer one including a ride down the unique vertical boat-lift at Arques. For more information go to the **tourist office** by the **gare routière** on place P-Painlevé.

To get to the centre of town from the exuberant 1903 **gare SNCF**, cross over the canal and walk ten minutes down rue F-Ringot, past the *PTT* and into rue Carnot. **Accommodation** is satisfactory enough: *Le Comte de Luxembourg* in the street of the same name (☎21.38.10.09; ③), and the *St-Louis* at 25 rue d'Arras (☎21.38.35.21; ③–④), are both fine, if not especially cheap. The nearest **campsite** is near the *Forêt de Clairmarais*, 4.5km east of St-Omer (☎21.38.34.80; April–Oct), although there's no transport out there. Place Maréchal-Foch is lined with **cafés** and **restaurants**; try the Anglo-Indian place, *Sitar*, at no. 32, or for Flemish fare, the *Belle Époque*, just off the square at 3 place P-Painlevé.

The Blockhaus at Eperlecques

Another interesting excursion is to the **Forêt d'Eperlecques** (3 or 4 trains daily from Calais to Watten station, on the eastern edge of the forest), 12km north of St-Omer. Here in 1943–44, the Germans – or rather 6000 half-starved slave labourers – built the largest ever **Blockhaus**, or concrete bunker (most of the year guided tours only: March Sun 2.15pm; April, Oct & Nov daily 2.15–6pm; May Mon–Sat 2.15–6pm & Sun 10am–7pm; June Mon–Sat 10am–noon & 2.15–7pm; July & Aug daily 10am–7pm; Sept Mon–Sat 10am–noon & 2.15–7pm, Sun 10am–7pm; 30F), from which to launch V2 rockets against London. Luckily the RAF and the French Resistance prevented its ever being ready for use.

Cassel

Twenty-three kilometres east of St-Omer is the hilltop town of **CASSEL**. Hills are rare in Flanders, and Cassel was much fought over from Roman times onwards. Marshall Foch spent "some of the most distressing hours" of his life here during World War I, and it was up to the top of Cassel's hill that the "Grand Old Duke of York" marched his 10,000 men in 1793, though, as hinted in the nursery rhyme, he failed to take the town.

Cassel consists of little more than its very Flemish Grande-Place, lined with some magnificent mansions. The train station, 3km west of town, is linked only to Dunkerque, so you'll need your own transport to justify the trip. If you have it, it's very worthwhile for exploring the narrow, cobbled streets fanning out from the square: southwards to a fine Gothic **church**; northwards to the **public gardens** from which you have an unrivalled view over Flanders, with Belgium just 10km away. Here among the trees is Cassel's only remaining wooden **windmill** – there used to be 29 pounding their oil mills and driving the locals mad day and night – which revolves on its axis every Sunday. For refreshments, head for the **café** in the nearby nineteenth-century mansion, headquarters of the frequently banned Flemish radio station, *Ulyenspiegel*.

There are one or two small **hotels** should you wish to stay over, including the fabulous eighteenth-century *Schoëbeque* on rue Foch (☎28.42.42.67; ④), where the marshal himself used to stay. Two gourmet **restaurants**, *Le Sauvage* and *Taverne Flamande*, are posed side by side on the Grande-Place, but you can get simpler fare opposite at the Hôtel de Ville.

The Côte d'Opale

The coastal road from Calais to Boulogne – a 42-kilometre route along the D940 – passes along some of the finest stretches of the **Côte d'Opale** (Opal Coast), where sea and sky often merge in an opalescent, oyster-grey continuum and the air is tangy with salt. The long sandy beaches are exposed by huge tidal flows and backed by high chalk cliffs which the French have dubbed the Côte d'Escales, or the "Site des Deux Caps", as Cap Blanc-Nez and Cap Gris-Nez – just under 20km apart – provide spectacular views of the coastline and undulating rural landscape.

The Eurotunnel Information Centre and Cap Blanc-Nez

Right on the outskirts of Calais, **BLÉRIOT-PLAGE** commemorates Louis Blériot's epic first cross-channel flight in 1909. Six kilometres along a foreshore of well-conserved dunes, dreary **SANGATTE** is set to be the French terminal for the Channel tunnel (see box). The site is actually in the village of **COQUELLES**, 4km southeast, where you can visit the rather disappointing **Eurotunnel Information Centre** (daily 10am–7pm; Oct–March closes 6pm; 30F), with an abundance of facts and figures about the new sub-Channel link-up; more interesting are the weekend tours of the site (40min; 15F extra). Thereafter, the road winds up on to the grassy windswept heights of **Cap Blanc-Nez**, topped by an obelisk commemorating the Dover Patrol who kept the Channel free from U-boats during World War I. Better than the Eurotunnel centre for an overall history of "Chunnel" exploits is the **Musée Transmanche** (daily 10am–6pm; Oct–March Sat & Sun only; 20F), housed in the basement of a rather pricey restaurant with panoramic views, *Le Thomé du Gamond*, just off the D940 opposite the turn-off to the Cap Blanc-Nez obelisk. From here, 130m above sea level, you can spot the Channel craft plying the water to the north, and to the south down to **WISSANT** and its enormous beach between the capes from which Julius Cæsar set sail in 55 BC to conquer Britain.

THE CHUNNEL

The notion of building a tunnel (or bridge) across the English Channel has long fired the imaginations of the rulers and engineers of Britain and France. Napoléon was the first to toy seriously with the idea in 1802, but it wasn't until 1878 that the first real attempt was made, this time by the British, who got just 168m in five years before giving up – the tunnel under Shakespeare Cliff remains to this day, unlined and remarkably watertight. Edward Heath and Georges Pompidou had another go in 1973 in a fit of Euro-enthusiasm following the UK entry into the EEC, only for Harold Wilson to call it off after just 300m had been dug on each side. Finally it was left to the gigantic egos of Margaret Thatcher and François Mitterrand to go the whole way and commit both governments to completing the "Chunnel" in the 1990s.

Anglo-French private-sector company *Eurotunnel* had the unenviable task of raising the billions needed to finance the project without government assistance – and of overcoming popular scepticism that this attempt, unlike the rest, would actually succeed. While anti-Chunnel groups sprang up all over Kent and southeast England, protest in the sparsely populated and economically depressed northeast of France focused on places bypassed by the tunnel rail-link. The town of Amiens, notably, set up shop in Victoria, London, selling ten-metre plots of French land in an attempt to foil the planned route.

Today, the two fifty-kilometre-long rail tunnels – along with a central service tunnel and a high-tech system of pumping stations, ventilation shafts and signalling equipment – run about thirty metres beneath the sea bed, linking a terminal at Folkestone to its trans-Channel equivalent outside of Calais. Cars, coaches, motorbikes and trucks are carried through the tunnel on shuttle trains between the two termini within 35 minutes. As well as the shuttle service, around forty high-speed passenger trains a day run in each direction, linking London Waterloo to Paris Gare du Nord and Brussels Midi, cutting journey time from London to Paris to just over three hours. At peak times services operate every fifteen minutes, and even during the quietest times of the night, services still run hourly.

The British, French and Belgian rail lines are currently working on a comprehensive high-speed network to the major cities, promising to make swift, non-stop train travel from Britain to all over the continent a reality.

To Cap Gris-Nez and the Blockhaus at Audinghen

The walk along the cliff tops past Wissant and up to **Cap Gris-Nez**, just 28km from the English coast, is certainly an exhilarating one. Otherwise, the turn-off to the second cape is 1km outside of **AUDINGHEN**, and then a 3km walk, drive or cycle. The entire Côte d'Opale is studded with massive concrete bunkers, or *Blockhäuser*, that were part of the German World War II defences known as the Atlantic Wall. One of them is just after the Cap Gris-Nez turn-off beside the D940. Equipped with a gun that could hit the English coast, it has been converted into a rather rough-and-ready **museum** (daily April–Oct 9am–6pm; Nov–March 9am–noon & 2–6pm; closed Jan; 25F) of the paraphernalia of war. Burrowing two or three floors below ground level, it has curiosity value rather than any great attractions. The best exhibits are British propaganda material and a poster, cautioning troops against the dangers of VD, in which a portly officer, buttons popping with excitement, is propositioned by a German fräulein ("Komm' mit mi'!").

Audinghen itself is a drab, inland town. If you're stuck for somewhere to stay, you'd do better in the charming though faded seaside villages of **AYDRESELLES** and **AMBLETEUSE** further on.

Wimereux

Just 4km north of Boulogne is **WIMEREUX**, a traditional, turn-of-the-century seaside resort. Once favoured by the vacationing miners of the north of France, it still preserves a certain faded charm, with mock-Gothic and Tudor chalets holding out against the encroaching developers' bulldozers. Sale boards proliferate and it all looks set to become heavily gentrified, with a chalet-style apartment development and plenty of signs advertising *moules* and crabs (a plate of *moules frites* will set you back 30F at a roadside café). With all this development, Wimereux at least feels as if it has some life to it, unlike many of the nearby towns. You can see why people are attracted here: the shore is pleasantly sandy and rocky, with plenty of wind-surfing and walks along the cliffs to the north. Signs of upmarket development include the **Galerie du Rayon** at 13 Digue de Mer Vert (Tues–Sat 3–7pm, Sun 4–6pm), a contemporary gallery with some wonderful ceramics and glassware housed in the old post office.

The **tourist office** is on place du Roi-Albert near the river (April–Sept daily 9am–7pm; Oct–March daily 9am–1pm & 3–7pm; closed Sun afternoon). Opposite is a small market on Tuesday and Friday mornings, good for picking up picnicking material. The town itself is easily reached by local **bus** (*ligne 1* goes via the coast, while *ligne 2* goes in land via Wimille, the village just inland from Wimereux) or **train** (to Wimille) about every two hours.

The main street, rue Carnot, has two good **hotels**: *Hôtel des Arts* at no. 143 (☎21.32.43.13; ①; closed Thurs outside high season), with a popular bar and restaurant, and the *Auberge de Maître Hans* at no. 12 (☎21.32.41.04; ②–③). For a sit down **meal**, try *Le Charolais*, 25 rue Napoléon, the narrow road heading for Boulogne; smart but relaxed, it has a set menu from 95F (closed Sat lunch & Sun). Opposite the *Galerie du Rayon* is the young trendy hang-out *Café de la Poste*.

Boulogne-sur-Mer

BOULOGNE is quite different from Dunkerque and Calais – recommendation in itself. It has long been an important harbour and claims to be the largest fishing base in Europe. Rising above the port is an attractive medieval quarter, the **ville haute**, flanked by grassy ramparts and dominated by a grand black-domed cathedral. Below, amid the newer shopping streets of the **ville basse**, are some of the best *charcuteries* and *pâtisseries* in the north, along with an impressive array of fish restaurants. Alone among the northeast channel ports, this is a place that might actually tempt you to stay.

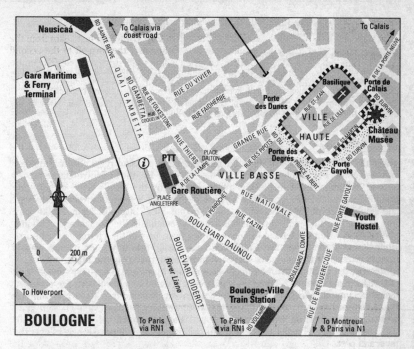

BOULOGNE

Arrival and accommodation

Ferries dock within a few minutes' walk of the town centre. If you arrive by hovercraft, a little further out, you'll be met by a free shuttle **bus** (*Hoverspeed* ☎21.30.27.26; *Sealink SNCF* ☎21.30.25.11). If you intend to stay, stop at the **tourist office** (Mon–Thurs 9am–8pm, Fri & Sat 9am–10pm, Sun 10am–8am), housed in a small Art Deco pavilion across the bridge from the ferry terminal, which can supply a mass of information and advise on availability of rooms, which, in summer, get taken early.

There's plenty of inexpensive **accommodation** in Boulogne if you've missed your boat and need somewhere basic to stay; most of the cheap hotels are close to the port area. For more of an occasion, there are some centrally located upmarket places, but rates remain competitive.

Hotels

Hôtel Arcade, cnr bd Ervin/rue de la Porte-Neuve (☎21.31.21.01). Modern two-star just outside the *haute ville*; all rooms have bathrooms and are soundproof, with telephone and cable TV. Parking available. ④.

Hôtel des Arts, 102–112 quai Gambetta (☎21.31.53.31). Very reasonable hotel right opposite the port; rooms are clean, light and well set up; many with balcony. No lift; be prepared for a long climb. ①.

Hôtel Faidherbe, 12 rue Faidherbe (☎21.31.60.93). Very respectable, well-tended central two-star; all rooms have bathroom and TV. ①–③.

Hôtel Hamiot, cnr rue Faidherbe and bd Gambetta (☎21.31.44.20). Cheap hotel on the main road above a popular bistro. ①.

Le Castel, 51 rue Nationale (☎21.31.52.88). A one star with inexpensive rooms. ①.

Le Metropole, 51 rue Thiers (☎21.31.54.30). In the midst of a fashionable street, a plush three-star. Spacious rooms; central but not noisy. ④–⑤.

La Plage, 124 bd Sainte-Beuve (☎21.31.34.78). Small hotel opposite the Nausicca; reception is inside its rather smart *Mimic d'Anvers* restaurant. Closed Dec 19–Jan 5. ③.

Youth hostels and campsites

IYHF youth hostel, 36 rue de la Porte-Gayole (☎21.31.48.22). Southeast of the old town walls, this friendly and modern youth hostel (IYHF card necessary) is a fair climb, so phone first to check for space. Small dorms; breakfast included. Reception open 5–11pm (curfew 11pm). Open all year. ①.

Camping Moulin Wibert. A three-star place ten minutes by bus along the bd Sainte-Beauve, on the way to the sandy strand of Wimereux. Open April to mid-Oct.

The Town

The quiet cobbled streets of the **ville haute** make a pleasant respite from the noise and congestion of the ville basse. Within the walls, the **Basilique Notre-Dame** proves an odd building, raised in the nineteenth century by the town's vicar, without any architectural knowledge or advice. Against all the odds it seems to work. In the vast and labyrinth **crypt** (Mon–Sat 8am–noon & 2–7pm, Sun 8.30am–12.30pm & 2.30–6pm; July & Aug Sun till 7pm;) you can see frescoed remains of the Romanesque building and relics of a Roman temple to Diana. In the main part of the church sits a bizarre white statue of the Virgin and Child on a boat-chariot, drawn here on its own wheels from Lourdes over the course of six years during a pilgrimage in the 1940s.

Nearby, the **Château Musée** (daily except Tues May–Sept 10am–6pm, Fri till 8pm; Oct–April 10am–1pm & 2–5pm; 20F) has items donated by a local-born Egyptologist, including a good collection of Greek pots. Alternatively – and free – you can climb up the oldest monument in the old town, the twelfth-century **Beffroi** (Mon–Fri 8am–5pm; access via the Hôtel de Ville), or stroll round along the medieval **walls**, decked out with rosebeds, gravel paths and benches for picnicking, with impressive views over the town and port.

Outside the ville haute the place to head for is the town's smart new aquarium at the *Centre National de la Mer* or **Nausicaá**, on bd Sainte-Beuve (mid-May to mid-Sept daily 10am–8pm; mid-Sept to mid-May Mon–Fri 10am–6pm, Sat & Sun 10am–7pm; closed 2 weeks in Jan; 48F). Ultraviolet lighting and New Age music create a suitably weird ambience, while hammerhead sharks circle overhead and giant conger eels conceal themselves in rusty pipes – definitely not for piscophobes. There's plenty of educational stuff, too (in French and English throughout), and a half-hour film show, though only a passing nod towards environmental issues.

Three kilometres north of Boulogne on the N1 stands the **Colonne de la Grande Armée**, where, in 1803, Napoléon is said to have changed his mind about invading Britain and turned his troops east towards Austria. The column was originally topped by a bronze figure of Napoléon symbolically clad in Roman garb – though his head, equally symbolically, was shot off by the British navy in the last war. It is now displayed in the château museum (see above).

Eating and drinking

A large fishing port, Boulogne is a good spot to **eat** fresh fish and seafood. There are dozens of possibilities for eating around place Dalton and the ville haute, but bear in mind the day-tripper trade and be selective. If you're after a **drink**, there is a concentration of bars in the *place* opposite the Hôtel de Ville, and several lively bars in place Dalton, with *Au Bureau*, *Le Saint Germain* and the *Pub J.F. Kennedy* being most popular.

Un Cornet d'Amour, 91 rue Thiers. An excellent *pâtisserie* with a comfortable *salon de thé*, reasonably priced with lots of local ladies taking tea.

L'Cygne, 30 rue des Pipots (☎21.30.01.63).Traditional menus, modest prices, big servings and a modest atmosphere. Menu from 85F, mains (fish and meat) start from 50F. Closed Wed.

SHOPPING

For whatever you're after in the consuming line – clothes, furniture, sheets, hats, plates – you'll find it in Grande-Rue, Thiers, Faidherbe and Nationale. For general **shopping**, head straight for the *Champion* supermarket on the pier, unless you want to hit the serious **hypermarkets**, in which case catch bus #4 for the *Continent*, bus #5 for the *Mammouth*, or the special *Cars Sergent* service, from outside the *SI*, to the monstrous *Auchan* complex, 8km along the N42 to St-Omer. *Centre Commercial Liane*, on the corner of bd Diderot and bd Danoe, is a downmmarket **shopping mall** on two levels; lots of neon, milling teenagers, food stalls, a supermarket and a cheap cafeteria.

More fastidious foodies should cross the Pont de l'Entente-Cordiale into Grande-Rue, slip into *Derrien*'s **charcuterie** and load up with snails, sausages, *foie gras* and pigs' trotters before sidling up to *Luqand*'s *pâtisserie* (open Sun), where the savoury trophies can be followed by chocolates, *tartes aux fraises* and the like. For more indulgence, try *De Marchez*, on the corner of rue Thiers and rue Faidherbe, a large *pâtisserie* and *chocolatier* with a mouth-watering selection. For something altogether healthier, although still indulgent, *Idriss* at 16 Grande-Rue sell only **dried fruits,** many exotic, with a wonderful window display. Check out the fish selection at *Aux Pêcheurs d'Étaples*, a large *wissonnerie* on the Grande-Rue, opposite place Dalton. One other shop that should not be missed is Phillipe Olivier's famous *fromagerie*, just around the corner in rue Thiers, with over 200 cheeses – in various states of maturation – to choose from.

As far as **department stores** go, *Nouvelles Galeries* on rue Thiers has all the lower to middle range of clothes and cosmetics; you'll find plenty of fashion shops on rue Thiers too. Some beautiful Parisian women's clothes can be tried on at *Cloë* on rue Nationale. For a wide selection of **hats**, mainly traditional (including the good old beret), there's *Monteil*, on the corner of rue Faidherbe and rue Thiers, and for **handbags**, wander along to the *Marquinerie Florence*, on rue Faidherbe between rue Thiers and rue Victor-Hugo, with a huge range of over 600 bags. For **shoes**, try *Roger*, at 67 rue Thiers, with an interesting, beautifully made selection for women in particular, some manufactured in Paris, others locally. For fashionable French **lingerie**, try *Aneth*, near the corner of rue Thiers and rue Faidherbe; a staider, more serviceable collection can be found at *Divine* on the other side of the block. That old stand-by, *Prisunic*, a cross between a supermarket and a department store, is on the corner of Grande-Rue and rue Nationale. It's good for cheaper **cosmetics**, but for a more upmarket range, including *Lancôme* and the like, an expensive *parfumeur* is *Douglas Parfumier* on rue Thiers. At *Leclerc*, 15 Grande-Rue, you'll find beautiful **homeware**, including glass, cutlery and plates. You might try *Henry Fournier* on the Grande-Rue near place Dalton for **jewellery and watches** in particular, while for something altogether tackier, check out *St Expedit* next door, selling garnish **religious paraphernalia**. Pens, lighters, pipes and a big range of continental cigarettes can be snapped up at *La Civette*, an upmarket *tabac* in rue Thiers. French **fabrics** are highly regarded and *Antoine Tissus* on place Gustave-Charpentier has rolls of the stuff; for interesting, albeit expensive, **children's clothes,** pop across to *Les Petits Indiens*, opposite, while a range of fantastic French **linen goods** (including some amusing Babar pillowcases and duvet covers) are found at *Texti Linge* on narrow rue Felix-Adam.

The best **bookshop** is *Le Furet du Nord*, 15 Grande-Rue, with a wide selection of **maps** and an excellent *papeterie* downstairs. If you're looking to **cycle** or **bike** from Boulogne, *Motul* is a large motorbike/cycle shop at 106 rue Thiers; it also sells mountain bike supplies. For **camera, video** and **electronic equipment**, try *Audinet* on rue Thiers (close to the corner of rue Faidherbe). From place Lorraine and place Charpentier, rue Faidherbe heads uphill but downmarket with lots of bargain shops, hi-fi and electronics. Electronic/gift places like *Mady*, *Petyt* and *Tentation* are found here, while *Texti* is good for cheap clothes and T-shirts. And don't miss the Wednesday and Saturday **markets** on place Dalton.

Estaminet du Château, rue de Lille (☎21.91.49.66). Opposite Notre-Dame in the *ville haute*, this restaurant has an excellent menu from 60F and inexpensive *à la carte* dishes (quarter roast chicken 30F). Plain food in a nice old stone building, prettily decorated.

L'Étoile de Marrakech, 228 rue Nationale. A friendly Moroccan restaurant where the chef comes out and shakes your hand; olives, bread and spicy sausage come as complimentary starters, and the servings of couscous (from 68F) are incredibly generous. Not far from the train station and youth hostel. Closed Wed.

Hôtel Hamiot, 1 rue Faidherbe. The brasserie remains as popular as ever with locals and tourists alike, a large range from 30F omelettes to 65F and 95F menus. The special on Saturdays is couscous.

L'Huitrière, 2 pl Lorraine. The freshest fish and seafood in a small, unpretentious restaurant hidden behind a blue- and white-awninged *poissonière* front.

Chez Jules, 8 pl Dalton. A large establishment in a lively square specializing in seafood with excellent 120F or 150F menus; simple fish and chips for around 60F.

La Matelote, 80 bd Sainte-Beuve. Opposite the *Nausiccá*, a very smart restaurant featuring a *dégustation* menu at 350F; less well-heeled diners can go for the 120F menu; *à la carte* fish from 110F. Loving care taken over the food and service, but unfortunately it's rather snooty.

Pizzeria Milano, rue Coquelin. Excellent pizzas from 30F to 50F, with takeaway available.

Sucré Salé, 13 rue Monsigny. Smart, modern eatery combining the roles of restaurant, café, bar, *salon de thé* and *pâtisserie*; its speciality is gourmet salads, making it a good choice for vegetarians. Light, airy and sparse, with a wonderful range of teas and coffees. Daily 8am–8pm except Sun afternoon.

From Boulogne to Amiens

Strictly speaking, there's no coast road south of Boulogne. The nearest thing to it, the D940, keeps a fair distance from the shores, as does the main Calais–Paris train line, making transport to the seaside resorts by public transport quite tricky, with the exception of the nobbiest of the lot, **Le Touquet**. If you are passing this way, one recommended diversion is the bird sanctuary at **Marquenterre**, one of only two in the country. A more direct road south is the N1, cutting across some fairly dull countryside to **Amiens** – **Montreuil** being the single significant distraction en route.

Le Touquet and Étaples

Among dunes planted with wind-flattened tamarisks and pines, **LE TOUQUET-PARIS-PLAGE** (to give its full title) is one of those peculiarly French northern resorts, once the height of fashion, now dully suburban. In the 1920s, 1930s and for a spell after World War II, the town ranked alongside places on the Côte d'Azur, with its broad sands and leafy luxury villas. At one time it is supposed to have had flights from Britain every ten minutes. The opening up of long-distance air travel put an end to this era, though not completely, nor forever. The new British rich, sensing a fresh field of elitism, are back in some force. Their private aircraft are now virtually the airport's only traffic.

It is an extraordinary set-up really and not one where many vistors will feel at home. With strict sociological intent, however, take a glimpse at the *Le Manoir Hotel* on av du Golf (☎21.05.20.22; ⑦), the most palatial of the town's bunch, which includes *Le Westminster*, av du Verger (☎21.05.48.48; ⑥–⑦), and *Le Bristol*, 17 rue Jean-Monnet (☎21.05.49.95; ⑥–⑦). And if you've got kids, an expensive treat worth indulging in is Le Touquet's *Aqualud* **swimming complex** right on the front, which boasts no fewer than three giant waterslides (admission 60F); there's also the vast *Bagatelle* amusement park, 10km south of Le Touquet (daily April to mid-Sept 10am–7pm).

To get to Le Touquet, take the train from Boulogne to **ÉTAPLES**, a much more down-to-earth fishing village near the mouth of the River Canche, from where a local bus covers the last 4km; alternatively, you can take one of the four daily buses directly from Boulogne (☎21.31.77.48 for times) from outside the *Café de la Station*; the bus heads down the coast to Berck. The **tourist office** in the Palais de l'Europe on place de l'Hermitage can furnish you with a free map of the town, and if you're looking for somewhere reasonable to **stay** the night, try *L'Union*, 7 rue de Metz (☎21.05.08.88; ①), or *Hôtel Armide*, 56 rue Léon-Garet (☎21.05.21.76; half-board ③). There's also a **campsite**, on the waterfront of the Canche estuary, but this requires three nights minimum stay. Places to **eat** are generally expensive here; worth a treat are *Le Café des Arts*, 80 rue de Paris (closed Mon & Tues), and *Auberge de la Dune aux Loups* on the avenue of the same name (closed Tues & Wed), where you can eat their speciality fish on the terrace. More affordable is *Les Sports*, 22 rue St-Jean, a classic brasserie with menus from 75F.

Montreuil-sur-Mer

Once a port, but now stranded 13km inland, **MONTREUIL-SUR-MER** is a far cry from Le Touquet, even though it's only ten minutes away by train. Strikingly situated on a sharp little hilltop above the River Canche and enclosed by a ring of Vauban walls, it's an immediately appealing place. Lawrence Sterne spent a night here on his *Sentimental Journey*, and it was the scene of much of the action in Victor Hugo's *Les Misérables*, perhaps best evoked by the steep cobbled street of pavée St-Firmin, first left after the Porte de Boulogne, a short climb from the *gare SNCF*.

Two minor Gothic masterpieces grace the main square: the **church of St-Saulvé** and a tiny wood-panelled **chapelle** tucked into the side of the red-brick *Hôtel-Dieu*. To the south there are numerous cobbled lanes to wander down, replete with half-timbered artisan houses. In the northwestern corner of the walls lies Vauban's **citadelle** (daily except Tues 9.30am–noon & 2–6pm; closed Oct; 10F) – ruined, overgrown and, after dark, pretty atmospheric, with subterranean gun emplacements and a fourteenth-century tower that records the coats of arms of the French noblemen killed at Agincourt.

For **accommodation**, there's the gastronomic château-hôtel opposite the citadel (☎21.81.53.04; ⑧). Less ritzy is *Le Darnétal* on place de la Poissonnière (☎21.06.04.87; ②), and there's also an IYHF **youth hostel** (☎21.06.10.83; ①), housed in one of the citadel's outbuildings and giving access to the place long after the gates have been closed to the public.

In the second half of August, Montreuil puts on a surprisingly lively mini-arts **festival** of opera, theatre and dance, *Les Malins Plaisirs*.

Agincourt and Crécy

Two of the bloodiest Anglo-French battles of the Middle Ages took place near the attractive little town of **HESDIN** on the River Canche (a town familiar to Simenon fans from the TV series *Inspector Maigret*). Getting to either site is really only feasible with your own transport, as the nearest train stations are Hesdin or Rue for Crécy (17km), and Blangy-sur-Ternoise for Agincourt (6km).

Twenty kilometres southwest of Hesdin, at the **Battle of Crécy**, Edward III inflicted his first of many defeats on the French in 1346, thus beginning the Hundred Years' War. This was the first appearance on the continent of the new English weapon – the six-foot longbow – and the first use in European history of gunpowder. There's not a lot to see today, just the **Moulin Édouard III** (now a watchtower), 1km northeast of the little town of **CRÉCY-EN-PONTHIEU** on the D111 to **WADICOURT**, site of the windmill from which Edward watched the hurly-burly of battle. Further south, on the D56 to Fontaine, the battered **croix de Bohème** marks the place where King John of Bohemia died, having insisted on leading his men into the fight, in spite of his blindness.

Ten thousand more died in the heaviest defeat ever of France's feudal knighthood at the **Battle of Agincourt** in 1415. Forced by muddy conditions to fight on foot in their heavy armour, the French were sitting ducks to the lighter, mobile English archers. The rout took place near present-day **AZINCOURT**, about 12km northeast of Hesdin on the D928, and a **museum** in the village includes a short film about the battle, with notice boards placed at strategic points on the battlefield to indicate the sequence of fighting. Just east of the village, by the crossroads of the D104 and the road to Maisoncelle, a copse and a **cross** mark the position of the original grave pits whose reputation was once so grim it used to be called "The Carrion".

The Marquenterre bird sanctuary

Ornithologists will need no persuasion, but if you know nothing of birds, the **Parc ornithologique du Marquenterre** (daily mid-March to mid-Nov 9.30am–7pm; guided visits only mid-Nov to Dec Sat 2.30pm & Sun 10am & 2.30pm; 44F) will be a revelation. In terms of landscape, it is beautiful and strange: all dunes, tamarisks and pine forest, full of salty meres and ponds thick with water plants. It is "new" land formed by the erosion of the Normandy coast and the silting of the Somme estuary, where thousands of cattle are grazed today to give their meat the much-prized flavour of the "salt meadows".

One of only two bird sanctuaries in the whole of France, Marquenterre is a tiny reserve in an area that gives new meaning to the word "sanctuary". From the opening of the water-fowl season – on July 14, Bastille Day, ironically – gunshots can be heard, day and night, all around. No species, however rare, is spared.

You'll need to rent binoculars unless you carry your own, and there's no point in trying to manage without. Once inside, there's a choice of two itineraries, the longer being the more interesting. It takes you from resting area to resting area whence you can train your glasses on dozens of species – ducks, geese, oyster-catchers, terns, egrets, redshanks, greenshanks, spoonbills, herons, storks, godwits – some of them fat-cat residents, most taking a breather from their epic migratory flights to and from the ends of the earth. In April and May they head north, and they return from the end of August to October, so these are the best times to visit.

The nearest town of any size is **RUE**, one of a number of attractive fishing villages in the area and now stranded inland by the silting up of the Somme. Rue lies on the main Calais–Paris train line, but the final seven kilometres to the sanctuary is only served by a bus in July and August.

The Somme estuary

After Marquenterre, the bus meanders through yet more dry fishing hamlets, whose crouching cottages are reminders of their former poverty. Some, like **LE CROTOY**, with enough sea still to attract the yachties, are enjoying the inevitable holiday- and second-home boom. Its south-facing beach has attracted numerous writers and painters over the years: Jules Verne wrote *Twenty Thousand Leagues under the Sea* here; Colette, Toulouse-Lautrec and Seurat were also frequent visitors. **Rooms** are available at *Le Baie*, quai Léonard (☎22.27.81.22; ②).

In summer you can take a resuscitated **steam train** (July & Aug Tues–Sun; rest of summer Sun only) around the bay to **ST-VALÉRY-SUR-SOMME**, from whose shores William the Conqueror set sail for England in 1066. With a fully intact **ville haute**, and a quayside of brightly painted fishermen's cottages, it easily outclasses Le Crotoy, its main rival across the estuary. There are **rooms** and fresh seafood available at both ends of the scale: cheap at *Hôtel du Port et des Bains* on quai Blavet (☎22.60.80.09; ①); expensive at the eighteenth-century *Château du Romerel*, quai du Romerel (☎22.26.93.23; ⑤).

Between the two, near **NOYELLES-SUR-MER**, lies one of the most unusual war graves in France – the **Chinese Cemetery**. Nearly a thousand Chinese were drawn from north China to serve as dockers at St-Valéry, one of the major supply ports during World War I, though most of them died in the 1919 yellow fever epidemic. Noyelles is also served by the steam train service, after which it's another two kilometres to the cemetery along the D111 to Nolette.

Abbeville

ABBEVILLE lies about halfway from Calais to Paris and makes a convenient stop-off on the N1; until a German air raid in May 1940, it was also a very beautiful town. Nowadays, all that remain of its former glories are a superbly ornate Flemish-style **gare SNCF**, what's reputed to be the oldest **belfry** in France, and the Gothic **Cathédrale St-Vulfran**, the latter on a par with those at Amiens and Beauvais, but under scaffolding since the war and still closed to the public, although the **tourist office** at 1 place de l'Amiral-Courbet (☎22.24.27.92) organizes guided visits on demand for 10F. If you've time to kill, the best Abbeville has on offer is the eighteenth-century country mansion of **Bagatelle**, 2km south of town – not to be confused with the nearby amusement park of the same name – set in ten hectares of parkland (guided visits early July to early Sept daily except Tues 2–6pm; 30F).

If you are looking for somewhere to **stay**, *Le Condé*, 14–16 place de la Libération (☎22.24.06.33; ②), and *Le Jean Bart*, 5 rue Ste-Cathérine (☎22.24.21.71; ②), have the cheapest rooms in town.

Amiens

Were it not for the cathedral, few travellers would stop at **AMIENS**. Badly scarred during both world wars, and with heavy traffic pounding along the ring road built over its old city walls, it's not an immediately likeable place. Yet there is more to the town than first meets the eye – St-Leu, the canal-laced medieval *quartier*, north of the cathedral, has recently been renovated, the town's university makes its presence felt, and within a few minutes' walk from the train station, the *hortillonages* transport you into a peaceful rural landscape.

Arrival and accommodation

The main **gare SNCF** (Amiens-Nord) and **gare routière** are both situated on the rectangular place A-Fiquet. There's a very modern, helpful **information centre** (Mon–Sat 8am–8pm, Sun 9.30am–8pm; Oct–April 8am–7pm, Sun 9.30am–8pm) within the train station that can book accommodation for Amiens and has masses of info on the city and Picardy generally. In summer, a tourist office is also open in front of the station (daily 10am–7pm), but the main **tourist office** is west of the cathedral, between the Hôtel de Ville and the twelfth-century *beffroi* at 12 rue du Chapeau-de-Violettes (May–Nov Mon–Sat 9am–12.30pm & 2–4pm). Connected to the train station is a new two-storey shopping complex, *Amiens 2*, where you'll find most things you need – including a supermarket and public toilets.

Economical **accommodation** options can be found on rue Alexandre-Fatton, a quiet street opposite the station: at no. 15, the *Hôtel Spatial* (☎22.91.53.23; ①) has free parking and simple doubles, and at no. 17 the *Central Anzac* (☎22.91.34.08; ①) has cheaper rooms still. The upgraded *Victor Hugo*, 2 rue de l'Oratoire (☎22.91.57.91; ②), is right in sight of the cathedral; *Le Prieuré*, 17 rue Porion (☎22.92.27.67; ②), has rooms with

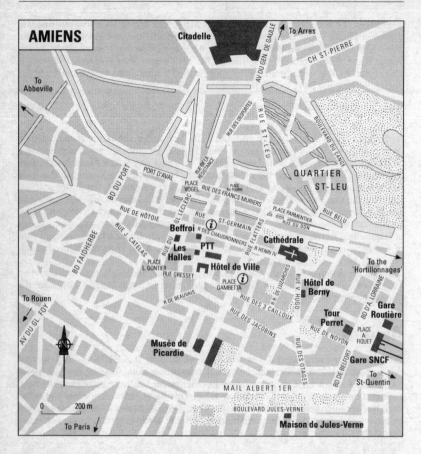

shower, TV, telephone and toilet; and the more upmarket *Le Postillon*, 17 place au Feurre (☎22.91.46.17; ④), is close to the cathedral. Unfortunately for diehard budgeters, both the *Auberge de la Jeunesse* and the campsite have closed down; you could try the UFCV **hostel** on 6 rue St-Fuscien (☎22.89.69.10; ①), but there are only 25 beds and it fills up quickly, more than likely booked by groups.

The City

The **Cathédrale Notre-Dame** (daily April–Sept 8.30am–7pm, Sun to 6pm; Oct–March 8.30am–noon & 2–5pm) provides the city's very obvious focus, whatever your interests. First of all, it dominates all else by its sheer size – it's the biggest Gothic building in France – but its appeal lies mainly in its unusual uniformity of style. Begun in 1220 under the architect Robert de Luzarches, only the tops of the towers were unfinished in 1269, and so the building escaped the influence of succeeding architectural fads that marred the "purity" of some of its slower sisters.

The west front, now in need of a good scrub, is best seen with early afternoon sun falling obliquely across it – not too easy given the climate – to give some good chiaroscuro effects and bring out the detail of the riot of over 4000 pieces of sculpture adorning the three main porches. By way of contrast, the interior is all straight up and no fuss: a light, calm and unaffected space. Ruskin thought the apse "not only the best, but the very first thing done perfectly in its manner by northern Christendom". If there is any pretence, it's in the later embellishments, like the sixteenth-century choir stalls (guided tours only), but they are works of such breathtaking virtuosity you might forgive anyone who could handle a chisel like that for wanting to show off. The same goes for the sculpted panels depicting the life of Saint Firmin, Amiens' first bishop, on the right side of the choir screen. The figures in the crowd scenes are shown in fifteenth-century costume, the men talking serious business among themselves, while their wives listen more credulously to the preacher's words. One of the most atmospheric ways of seeing the cathedral is during a Sunday morning mass (10.15am), when the Gothic structure is uplifted by sublime Gregorian chanting. You can also visit the **treasure** of the cathedral, a collection of gold and silver religious artefacts and some religious art (15F).

Just north of the cathedral is the **quartier St-Leu**, a thoroughly Flemish network of canals and cottages once belonging to Amiens' thriving textile industry. The town still produces much of the country's velvet, but the factories moved out to the suburbs long ago, leaving St-Leu to rot away in peace. That is, until the local property developers moved in: the whole area was certainly in need of renovation, and the rue de Don and rue Belu still retain some of the old character of the *quartier*, but many of the old houses have simply been torn down or turned into chi-chi riverside flats. Despite all that, it remains an interesting area to wander around.

On the edge of town, the canals still provide a useful function as waterways for the **hortillonnages** – a series of incredibly fertile market gardens, reclaimed from the marshes created by the very slow-flowing Somme. Farmers travel about them in black, high-prowed punts and a few still take their produce into the city by boat for the Saturday morning **market**, the *marché sur l'eau*, on the river bank of place Parmentier. If you want to look around the *hortillonages*, turn right as you come out of the station and continue straight ahead for about five minutes until you reach the Chemin de Halage, which you can wander down. A map here shows pedestrian routes and viewpoints – otherwise, watch out for cars on the narrow tow path. If you walk further up boulevard de Beauvais to no. 54, here the *Association des Hortillonages* is the embarkation point for their inexpensive **boat trips** (daily June–Aug, regular departures from 2pm; April–May & Sept–Oct Sat, Sun & hols 3pm; 26F; 45min).

If you're interested in Picardy culture, you might take a look at Amiens' two regional museums. Five minutes' walk south of central place Gambetta, a nineteenth-century mansion houses the **Musée de Picardie** (daily except Mon 10am–12.30pm & 2–6pm; 20F), whose star exhibit is a collection of rare sixteenth-century paintings on wood donated to the cathedral by a local literary society, some of the pictures still in their original frames carved by the same craftsmen who worked the choir stalls. Close by the cathedral, in the seventeenth-century **Hôtel de Berny** (Thurs & Sun mid-April to mid-Sept 1–6pm; Oct to mid-April 2–6pm; 10F), is an annexe to the main museum, with local history collections, including a portrait of Choderlos de Laclos, author of *Les Liaisons Dangereuses*, who was born in Amiens. A third museum or documentation centre is **Jules Verne's house**, 2 rue Dubois, who spent most of his life, and died, in Amiens (Mon–Fri 9am–noon & 2–6pm; *maison* free, *Centre de Documentation* 15F).

Eating, drinking and entertainment

Cheap **brasseries** and **restaurants** spread out around the station, while in the centre, around place Gambetta, there are numerous **snack bars** and **food shops**. In St-Leu, there's *Le Vieil Amiens* on rue Belu (closed Wed), which gives another great view over the canal to the cathedral; *La Poissonade*, place du Don, a seafood snackery even closer to the cathedral; and *Memo*, a Turkish restaurant just off rue des Majots. *Grill Kurdistan*, 13 rue des Majots, is an inexpensive ethnic eatery with plenty for vegetarians; *The Fall In*, on the same street, is a small contemporary café frequented by visitors to the colourfully painted *Maison du Théâtre* next door, serving dirt-cheap couscous and kebabs; and for a more expensive and memorable meal, you couldn't do better than *Les Marissons*, on pont de la Dodane, a converted fifteenth-century boat-shed decked out in Picardy colours.

Away from the old quarter, other recommended eateries are *Au Vieux Beffroi*, next door to the tourist office on rue du-Chapeau-de-Violettes, which specializes in gourmet salads and omelettes – perfect for veggies; *Le Continental*, on the corner of rue des Lombards and rue des Sergents between the cathedral and the Hôtel de Ville, a great local bar for a quiet coffee and a huge baguette; and on the *hortillonnages*, about five minutes' stroll up the chemin de Halage, the *Auberge du Vert-Galant*, a pretty, moderately priced place for outdoor dining and Picardy cuisine. For a do-it-yourself picnic meal, visit the startlingly modern *Les Halles*, an excellent covered food **market** shaped like an ark next to the *beffroi*.

There are plenty of lively **bars** to drink at of an evening in the area too: try the tiny *American 50s Bar* on place du Don (Mon–Sat 4pm–2am), or one of several 'pub'-style bars across the canal on quai Belu.

For one week in May Amiens bursts into life for its annual international **jazz festival**; on the third weekend in June, the local costumes come out for the **Fête d'Amiens**; and in November there's a cinema festival. In August, traditional Picardy **marionettes** give performances (mostly evenings) at the *Maison du Théâtre*, 8 rue des Majots, in the quartier St-Leu: call *Théâtre d'Animation Picard* (☎22.92.42.06) for reservations – tickets are around 70F. If you end up fascinated by the marionettes, you can buy hand-made examples (or at least have a good look close up) from *Jean-Pierre Facquier* at his small workshop at 67 rue du Don.

Beauvais

As you head south from Amiens towards Paris, the countryside becomes broad and flat – agricultural, though not rustic. **BEAUVAIS** seems to fit into this landscape. Rebuilt, like Amiens, after the last world war, it's a drab, neutral place redeemed only by its radiating Gothic cathedral.

The **Cathédrale St-Pierre** rises above the town, its roof, unadorned by tower or spire, seeming squat for all its height. It is a building that perhaps more than any other in northern France demonstrates the religious materialism of the Middle Ages – its main intention to be taller and larger than its rivals. The choir, completed in 1272, was once five metres higher than that of Amiens, though only briefly – it collapsed in 1284. Its replacement, only completed three centuries later, was raised by the sale of indulgences – a right granted to the local bishops by Pope Leo X. This, too, fell within a few years and, the authorities having overreached themselves financially, the church remained unfinished, forlorn and mutilated. The appeal of the building, and its real beauty, is in its glass, its sculpted doorways and the remnants of the so-called Basse-Oeuvre, a ninth-century Carolingian church incorporated into the structure. It also contains a couple of remarkable clocks, including one 12m high that displays the night sky over Beauvais and features the Archangel Michael helping to weigh souls at the Last Judgement.

Stopping at Beauvais to break the journey, you'll probably want to give the rest of the town no more than a passing look. The **church of St-Étienne**, a few blocks to the south of the cathedral on rue de Malherbe, houses yet more spectacular Renaissance stained-glass windows. There's also the **Galerie Nationale de Tapisserie** behind the cathedral (Tues–Sun 9.30–11.30am & 2–4.30/6pm; 15F), a museum of the tapestry for which Beauvais was once renowned, and the **Musée Départemental** (Tues–Sun 10am–noon & 2–6pm; 10F), devoted to painting, local history and archeology, in the sharp, black-towered building opposite. The rousing **statue** in the central square is of local heroine Jeanne Hachette, a fighter and inspiration in the defence of the town against Charles the Bold, Duke of Burgundy, in 1472.

Practicalities

Beauvais is an hour by train from Paris, and the **gare SNCF** is a short walk from the centre of town – take av de la République, then right up rue de Malherbe. Just off the main square, on place Clemenceau, the **tourist office** can provide exhaustive further information. If you want to **stay**, two possible hotels are the *Bristol*, 58–60 rue de la Madeleine (☎44.45.01.31; ③), and *Le Brazza*, 22 rue de la Madeleine (☎44.45.03.86; ③). There's a **campsite** just out of town on the Paris road.

For fine **food** on the square, call in at the restaurant *Le Marignon*, 1 rue de Malherbe (☎44.48.15.15), with menus from 62F to 195F.

THE INDUSTRIAL NORTH AND THE BATTLEFIELDS

Picardy, Artois and Flanders are littered with the monuments, battlefields and cemeteries of the two world wars, but nowhere as intensely as the region northeast of Amiens, between **Albert** and **Arras**. It was here, among the fields and villages of the Somme, that the main battle lines of World War I were drawn. They can be visited most spectacularly at **Vimy Ridge**, just off the A26 north of Arras, where the trenches have been left *in situ*. Lesser sites, often more poignant, are dotted over the countryside around Albert and along the **Circuit de Souvenir**.

A more enduring and more domestic presence in the life of northern France has been that of the **coalfields** and all their related heavy industrial works. At their peak of production they formed a continuous stretch from Béthune in the west to Valenciennes in the east, though the industry is now in terminal decline. At **Lewarde** you can visit one of the pits, while at the big, industrial city of **Lille**, or the pleasant town of **Douai**, you can see what the masters did with takings from the muck.

Lille

LILLE, by far the largest city in the north, is the very symbol of French industry and working-class politics. Its mayor, Pierre Mauroy, was the first Socialist prime minister appointed by Mitterrand in 1981. In every direction the city spreads far into the countryside, a mass of suburbs and heavy industrial plants. Lille exhibits most of the problems and assets of contemporary France – some of the worst poverty and racial conflict in the country, a crime rate rivalled only by Paris and Marseille, and a certain regionalism; *Lillois* sprinkle their speech with a French-Flemish patois and to some extent assert a Flemish identity. But there is also classic French affluence. The city has a lovely central heart, Vieux Lille, some vibrant and obviously prosperous commercial areas, modern residential squares, a large university, a brand new métro system, and a very serious attitude to its culture and restaurants. Although you may not consider Lille a prime destination, if you're travelling through this region, it's worth at least a day and a night.

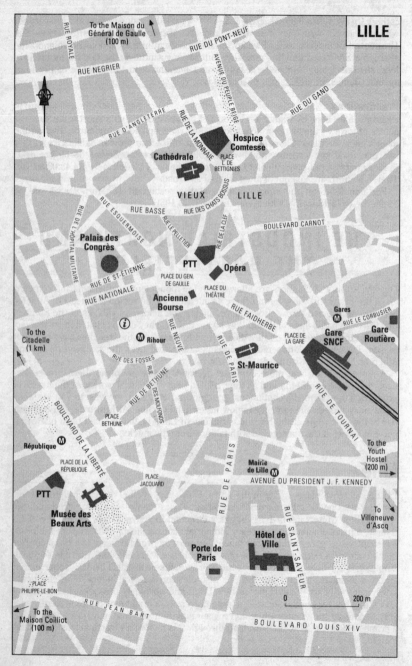

LILLE

To the Maison du Général de Gaulle (100 m)

RUE ROYALE
RUE NEGRIER
RUE DU PONT-NEUF
AVENUE DU PEUPLE BELGE
RUE DU GAND

RUE D'ANGLETERRE
RUE DE LA MONNAIE

Hospice Comtesse
Cathédrale
PLACE L. DE BETTIGNIES

VIEUX LILLE

RUE DE L'HOPITAL MILITAIRE
RUE ESQUERMOISE
RUE BASSE
RUE DES CHATS BOSSUS
RUE LE PELLETIER
RUE DE LA CLEF
BOULEVARD CARNOT

Palais des Congrès
RUE DE ST-ÉTIENNE
PTT
Opéra
PLACE DU GEN. DE GAULLE
PLACE DU THÉÂTRE

RUE NATIONALE
Ancienne Bourse

To the Citadelle (1 km)

(i)
Ⓜ Rihour
RUE NEUVE
RUE FAIDHERBE
Gares Ⓜ
RUE LE CORBUSIER

Gares
PLACE DE LA GARE
Gare SNCF
Gare Routière

RUE DES FOSSES
RUE DE BETHUNE
RUE DES MOLFONDS
RUE DE PARIS
St-Maurice

PLACE BETHUNE

RUE DE TOURNAI

BOULEVARD DE LA LIBERTE
République Ⓜ
PLACE DE LA RÉPUBLIQUE
PLACE JACQUARD

To the Youth Hostel (200 m)

RUE DE PARIS
Mairie de Lille Ⓜ
AVENUE DU PRESIDENT J. F. KENNEDY

PTT
Musée des Beaux Arts

RUE SAINT-SAVEUR

To Villeneuve d'Ascq

PLACE PHILIPPE-LE-BON

Porte de Paris
Hôtel de Ville

To the Maison Coilliot (100 m)

RUE JEAN BART
0   200 m
BOULEVARD LOUIS XIV

Arrival and accommodation

The central Grande-Place is just a few minutes' walk from the **gare routière** and adjacent **gare SNCF** (originally Paris' Gare du Nord, but brought here brick by brick in 1865). Despite being the fifth largest city in France, the centre of Lille is small enough to walk round, and, unless you choose to visit Villeneuve-d'Ascq on the outskirts, you won't even need to use the city's efficient métro system.

The **tourist office** in place Rihour (Mon–Sat 9am–7pm, Sun 10am–noon & 2–5pm) is ten minutes from the station to the end of rue Faidherbe, through place du Théâtre and place du Général-de-Gaulle, housed in what's left of a fifteenth-century ducal palace. They operate a free accommodation booking service for Lille (30F for the rest of France).

There should be few problems finding a cheap place to **stay** if you don't mind the slightly seedy station area. The new youth hostel should be finished by the end of 1995, the Youth Hostel information desk at 156 rue Nationale (☎20.57.08.94) can provide information on cheap accommodation; ask about university lodgings during holiday periods.

Hotels

Carlton, 3 rue de Paris (☎20.13.33.13). Posh four star with all the frills, right down to a red carpet outside. ⑦.

Hôtel Continental, 11 pl de la Gare (☎20.51.85.57). More upmarket version of the *Voyageurs*, complete with satellite TV. ③.

Flandres-Angleterre, 13 pl de la Gare (☎20.06.04.12). Much the classiest of the train station lot: all rooms with bath or shower and toilet. ④.

Hôtel de France, 10 rue Béthune (☎20.57.14.78). Fantastic location right in the centre of the pedestrianized area. Big, clean, comfortable rooms, some with balcony. ①.

Le Grand, 51 rue Faidherbe (☎20.06.31.57). Comfortable two star, all rooms with shower, toilet and TV. ③.

La Paix, 46bis rue de Paris (☎20.54.63.93). Classy two star with leather lounges, gleaming wooden staircase. Great position, all rooms with shower, toilet and TV. ④.

Hôtel des Voyageurs, 10 pl de la Gare (☎20.06.43.14). Slip of a building directly opposite the station, offering basic, cheap rooms – worth it just for the wrought-iron lift. ①.

Youth hostels and campsites

Relais Européen de la Jeunesse, 40 rue Thumesnil (☎20.52.69.75). A *foyer* for the city's young workers. ①.

Camping Le Ramiers, Bondues (☎20.23.13.42). Lille's nearest site is actually in the village of Bondues, about 10km north of the city and linked by bus. Closed Nov–March.

The City

The point to make for is the **Grande-Place** (otherwise known as place du Général-de-Gaulle), which marks the southern boundary of the old quarter, **Vieux Lille**. To the south is the central pedestrianized shopping area which extends along rue de Béthune as far as the adjacent squares of place Béthune and place de la République. On Saturdays especially, the area is so jammed with shoppers that you can hardly move, and crowded outdoor cafés add to the street life. The major festival of the year, the Grande Braderie, takes place over the first weekend of September, when a big street parade and vast fleamarket fill the streets of the *vieille ville* by day, and the evenings see *moules frites* frenzy in all the restaurants, with empty mussel shells piled up in the streets.

Vieux Lille

One side of the Grande-Place is dominated by the old exchange building, the lavishly ornate **Ancienne Bourse**, as perfect a representative of its age as could be imagined. To the merchants of seventeenth-century Lille, all things Flemish were the epitome of wealth and taste; they were not men to stint on detail, neither here nor on the imposing surrounding mansions. Recently cleaned up, the courtyard is now an organized flea market, with stalls selling books, junk and flowers. Lounging around the fountain at the centre of the *place* is a favourite *Lillois* pastime. At its centre is a **column** commemorating the city's resistance to the Austrian seige of 1792, topped by *La Déesse* ("the goddess"), modelled on the wife of the mayor at the time.

North of the Bourse, you can see how the Flemish Renaissance architecture developed, becoming distinctly French and combining brick with stone in grand flights of Baroque extravagance. The superlative example of this style is Lille's **Opéra**, which has a façade so strident it's almost ridiculous. It was built at the turn of this century by Louis Cordonnier, as was the equally inflated **belfry** of the neighbouring Nouvelle Bourse and Chamber of Commerce, now the city's main *PTT*.

Further north, the streets of the old town are pleasant to wander through, though the only specific sight is the **Hospice Comtesse** on rue de la Monnaie. Twelfth-century in origin – though much reconstructed in the eighteenth century – it served as a hospital until as recently as 1945. Its old ward, the **Salle des Malades**, can be visited (daily except Tues 10am–12.30pm & 2–6pm; 10F; Wed & Sat am free). **Rue d'Angleterre** and the streets off it formed until quite recently an entirely Arab quarter of town. Gradually over the last decade, though, the boutiques and designer offices have taken over, and only a few families now remain.

In this unlikely part of town, at 9 rue Princesse, is the house where Charles de Gaulle was born in 1890. Predictably enough, it's now a **museum** (Wed–Sun 10am–noon & 2–5pm; 7F). Another must for military buffs is the nearby **citadelle** that overlooks the old town to the northwest, constructed in familiar star-shaped fashion by Vauban in the seventeenth century. Still in military hands, it too can be visited, though only on Sundays and by guided tour (details from tourist office; 35F).

Amid all the city's secular pomp, Lille's ecclesiastical architecture seems rather subdued. The city's cathedral, the nineteenth-century **Cathédrale Notre-Dame-de-la-Treille**, is undistinguished and still unfinished, making the city's finest church the cathedral-esque **church of St-Maurice**, close to the station off place de la Gare, a classic red-brick Flemish Hallekerke, with the characteristic five aisles of the style.

South of the Grande-Place

Just south of the Grande-Place is **place Rihour**, a modern-looking leafy square with an old palace that now houses the tourist office, hidden behind an ugly war monument of gigantic proportions. Further south, the busiest shopping street, **rue de Béthune**, leads into place Béthune, another fine square, with some excellent cafés, and beyond to the **Musée des Beaux-Arts** on place de la République (daily except Tues 10am–5pm; free). Like so many French art museums, it studiously covers each art genre: paintings, ceramics, tapestries and so on. Here, though, the emphasis is very much on the Flemish painters, from "primitives" like Dieric Bouts, through the Northern Renaissance to Ruisdael, de Hooch and the seventeenth-century schools. It's an instructive display, helped by a small library of art books provided for browsing in the entrance hall. There's an additional scattering of Impressionists, including works by Monet and Corot.

A couple of blocks to the south of the museum, on rue de Fleurus, is **Maison Coilliot**, a ceramics shop and one of the few houses built by Hector Guimard, who made his name designing the Art Nouveau entrances to the Paris métro. Built at the height of the Art Nouveau movement, it's as striking today as it obviously was to the conservative burghers of Lille (there are no other such buildings in Lille), but it also displays the somewhat muddled eclecticism of the style, coming over as half brick-faced mansion, half timber-framed cottage. East of the museum, near the triumphal arch of **Porte de Paris**, the city's **Hôtel de Ville** is also worth a quick look, executed in a bizarre, Flemish Art Deco style, with a tall belfry and viewing platform (April–Sept Sun only).

Villeneuve d'Ascq: Musée d'Art Moderne

One of the best escapes from the urban excess of Lille, amid the spaghetti junction of autoroutes east of the city centre, is the suburb of **VILLENEUVE-D'ASCQ**. Acres of parkland, an old windmill or two, and a whole series of mini-lakes form the backdrop for the **Musée d'Art Moderne** (daily 10am–7/8pm; Oct–May daily 10am–6pm; closed Tues; 25F), housing an unusually good collection in its uninviting red-brick buildings. To get there, take the métro to *Pont-de-Bois*, then bus #41.

The ground floor is generally given over to temporary exhibitions of varying quality by contemporary French artists. The permanent collection starts on the first floor with canvases by Picasso, Braque, Modigliani, Miró and a whole room devoted to Fernand Léger and Georges Rouault. There's also a small room – easy to miss but worth the search – on the top floor, devoted to graphics by many of the above. Meanwhile, outside on the grass, Giacometti and Calder provide some playful picnic backdrops.

Eating

A Flemish flavour and taste for mussels (*moules*) characterize Lille's cuisine. The main area for **cafés**, **brasseries** and **restaurants** is around place Rihour and along rue de Béthune. Rue Royale has a selection of fairly pricey ethnic eateries from Cambodian to Japanese.

Bar de la Cloche, 13 pl du Théâtre. Excellent small brasserie serving twenty different wines by the glass. Inexpensive *plats* from 40 to 60F, *tartines* and cheeses 20–25F. Popular with the older set, relaxed, casual.

Brasserie Jean, pl du Théâtre. Large, bright brasserie specializing in Flemish-style dishes and taking up nearly a whole corner under the *Hôtel Carlton*. There's an excellent 75F menu.

Christian Leclercq, 9 rue Lepelletier. This highly regarded *artisan fromager* also harbours a restaurant out back where you can gorge on anything cheesey – in tarts, salads, fondues and more. Expensive but an experience. Closed Sun & Mon.

La Galetitère, 4 pl Louis-de-Bettignies. Good-value *crêperie* in the old town. Closed Sun & Mon.

Le Grand Café, pl Rihour. As good a place as any for sandwiches and light meals.

La Huîtrière, 3 rue des Chats-Bossus. A wonderful, colourful mosaic-tiled shop showing seaside and rural working scenes and selling everything from fish, seafood, chicken, meats to wine, with huge lobsters alive in their tanks. Behind it is an expensive, chandelier-hung restaurant specializing in fish and seafood at 150–178F a dish; a staggering 480F menu.

Lino, 1 rue des Trois-Couronnes. Top-quality, moderately priced authentic Italian – no pizza here. Cosy rustic decor.

Aux Moules, 34 rue de Béthune. The place to eat mussels; it's been serving them since 1930 in its Art Deco style interior; nothing much over 58F, including other brasserie fare. Daily 11.30am–11pm.

La Petite Cour, rue du Curé-St-Étienne, off rue St-Étienne. Characterful, part stone-wall restaurant serving traditional dishes like *coq au vin blanc* from 50F.

Piccolo Mondo, rue des Molfonds, off rue de Béthune. Lille's best pizza place also serves pasta with several vegetarian alternatives.

Les Saveurs du Liban, 155 rue Nationale. Good choice for vegetarians, an Arab eatery with lots of *hummous*, *tabboleh* and *falafel* on the inexpensive menu. Lunchtime 49F menu. Closed Sun.

Drinking and nightlife

The **Cafés** around the Grande-Place and place Rihour are always buzzing with life. Rue de Paris has lots of tacky, loud, crushed **bars** raging at all hours, if that's your scene, while rue Basse and nearby place Louis-de-Bettignies have some trendier spots. Art and music events are always worth checking up on, with a particularly lively jazz scene. Pick up a copy of the **free weekly listings magazine** *Sortir* from the tourist office, or look in the local paper *La Voix du Nord*.

Bar Jazz, 55 rue Basse. More jazz here in a slick, modern interior. Daily 10am–2am, Sun from 6pm.

Les Ailes du Désir, 57 rue Basse. Groovy bar, an intimate atmosphere and lots of plants adding some greenery. Daily 10am–2am, Sun & Mon from 5pm.

Café au Bureau, rue de Béthune. Done out as all English pubs should be – plenty of brass and dark woodwork. Tables outside crowded with young things watching the parade; 100 kinds of beer.

Le Caveau de la Treille, 9 pl Louis-de-Bettignies (☎20.31.00.51). A basement jazz venue hidden between the church and the hotel of the same name. Tues–Sat 9.30pm–4am.

L'Imaginaire, pl Louis-de-Bettignies, next door to the *Hôtel Treille*. Arty young bar with paintings adorning the walls.

Le Pubstore, 44 rue des Halles. Where students with money hang out; evenings only.

Listings

Autostop ☎20.42.08.88.

Banks All the banks have big branches on rue Nationale and you can guarantee to find one open until 4pm on Saturday. There's a branch of *Barclays* here too.

Books *Le Furet du Nord*, 11 pl Général-de-Gaulle, is a huge bookstore with a wide selection of books in English.

Films There are several cinemas in Lille with a concentration on rue de Béthune. Try your luck at any for original-language versions, although the mainstream *Gaumont* at no. 25 will usually have one of its eight screens in English.

Hospital ☎20.44.59.62.

Laundry There are three outlets of *Lavarama:* at 72 rue Pierre-LeGrand, 148 rue de la Louvière and 148 rue des Stations.

Post office 7 place de la République (Mon–Fri 8am–5pm, Sat 8am–noon).

Taxi *Gare* ☎20.06.64.00; *Rag* ☎20.55.55.20; *Radio Taxi Union* ☎20.06.06.06.

Douai and around

Right at the heart of mining country, 35km south of Lille, and badly damaged in both world wars, **DOUAI** is a surprisingly attractive and lively town, its streets of eighteenth-century houses cut through by both river and canal. Once a haven for English Catholics fleeing Protestant oppression in Tudor England, Douai later became the seat of Flemish local government under Louis XIV, an aristocratic past evoked in the novels of Balzac.

Centre of activity is the **place d'Armes**, overlooked by the massive Gothic belfry on rue de la Mairie of the **Hôtel de Ville**, popularized by Victor Hugo and renowned for its *carillon* of 62 bells – the largest single collection of bells in Europe – which plays a great variety of tunes. It's currently being renovated but still rings every half hour, and there are hour-long concerts every Saturday at 10.45am, on public holidays at 11am, and on summer Monday evenings at 9pm.

One block north of the town hall, on **rue Bellegambe**, is an outrageous Art Nouveau shop-front serving a very ordinary haberdashery store. Rising above the old town, at the end of the street, are the Baroque dome and tower of the **church of St-Pierre**, an immense, mainly eighteenth-century church with – among other treasures – a spectacular carved Baroque organ case. East of the place d'Armes, Douai's oldest church, the twelfth-century **church of Notre-Dame**, suffered badly in the last war but has been refreshingly modernized inside. Beyond the church is the better of the town's two surviving medieval gateways, now a triumphal roundabout, the **Porte Valenciennes**.

With the exception of the 1970s extension to the old Flemish Parliament building, the riverfront west of the town hall is pleasant to wander along. Between the river and the canal to the west, on rue de Chartreux, the **Ancienne Chartreuse** is now a museum (daily except Tues 10am–noon & 2–5pm Sun 3–6pm; 12F) with a top-quality collection of paintings by Flemish, Dutch and French masters, including Van Dyck, Rubens, Rodin and Douai's own Jean Bellgambe.

Practicalities

The **gare SNCF** is a five-minute walk from place d'Armes – left down bd Faidherbe, then right down rue de Valenciennes. The **tourist office** is within the fifteenth-century Hôtel du Dauphin, on the *place* facing the *Hôtel de Paris* (☎27.88.95.63; ③), for **accommodation** that has seen better days. Other budget accommodation includes *L'Homme Sauvage*, 106 rue de Valenciennes (☎27.88.85.03; ③), or the *Grand Cerf*, 46 rue St-Jacques (☎27.88.79.60; ③). A far classier option is *La Terrasse*, a swanky four star in the narrow Terrasse St-Pierre (☎27.88.70.04; ⑤) to one side of the church of the same name; its restaurant is well regarded, with a menu beginning at 135F. Northeast of the place d'Armes is the *PTT*, whence buses leave (*Ligne #1 orange*) for Lewarde.

Lewarde

A visit to the colliery at **LEWARDE**, 7km east of Douai, is a must for admirers of Zola's *Germinal*, perhaps the most electrifying "naturalistic" novel ever written, now transferred to celluloid in Claude Berai's not very satisfactory movie starring Gérard Départieu. The bus from Douai heads east across the flat and featureless beet fields, down a road lined with poor brick dwellings that recall the company-owned housing of *Germinal*, intersected by streets named after Pablo Neruda, Jean-Jacques Rousseau, Georges Brassens and other luminaries of the French and international Left. This is the traditional heart of France's coal mining country, always dispiriting and now depressed by closures and recession. Even the distinctive landmarks of slag heap and winding gear are fast disappearing with demolition and landscaping.

The bus puts you down at the main square in Lewarde, leaving a fifteen-minute walk down the D132 towards Erchin. The **Centre Historique Minier** (daily 10am–5.30pm; office closes 4pm; guided visits 1hr 30min: Nov–March 52F, April–Oct 60F) is on the left in the old Fosse Delloye, sited, like so many pits, amid woods and fields. Visits are guided by retired miners, many of whom are not French, but Polish, Italian or North African – Polish labour was introduced in the 1920s, other nationalities successively after World War II. One Polish guide went down the pit at 14 and was brought up at 38 with silicosis, which had also killed his father at 52. *"Ce n'est pas un métier"*, he said – "it's not what you'd call a career".

The main part of the tour – in addition to film shows and visits to the surface installations of winding gear, machine shops, cages, sorting areas and the rest (you can't yet go underground) – is a surface reconstruction of the pit-bottom roadways and faces, variously modelled and equipped to show the evolution of mining from the earliest times to today. These French pits were extremely deep and hot, with steeply inclined narrow seams that forced the miners to work on slopes of 55° and more, just as Étienne and the Maheu family do in Zola's story.

Accidents were a regular occurrence in the old days: the northern French pits had a particularly bad record in the last years of the nineteenth century. The worst mining disaster occurred at Courrières in 1906, when 1100 men were killed. Incredibly, despite the fact that the owners made little effort to search for survivors, thirteen men suddenly emerged after twenty days of wandering in the gas-filled tunnels without food, water or light. The first person they met thought that they were ghosts and fainted in fright. More incredible still, a fourteenth man surfaced alone after another four days.

Cambrai and Le Cateau

CAMBRAI, like Douai 26km to the north, has kept enough of its character to repay a passing visit, despite the tank battle of November 1917 (see box) and the fact that the heavily defended Hindenburg Line ran through the town centre for most of World War I.

CAMBRAI 1917

At dawn on November 20, 1917, the first full-scale tank battle in history began at **Cambrai**, when over 400 British tanks poured over the Hindenburg Line. In just 24 hours, the Royal Tank Corps and British Third Army made an advance that was further than any undertaken by either side since the trenches had first been dug in 1914. A fortnight later, however, casualities on both sides had reached 50,000, and the armies were back where they'd started.

Although in some respects the tanks were ahead of their time, they still relied on cavalry and plodding infantry as their back-up and runners for their lines of communication. And before they even reached the "green fields beyond", most of them had broken down. First World War tanks were primitive machines, operated by a crew of eight who endured almost intolerable conditions; with no ventilation system, the temperature inside could rise to 120°F. The steering alone required three men, each on separate gearboxes, communicating by hand signals through the din of the tank's internal noise. Maximum speed, 6km/ph, dropped to almost literally a snail's pace – 1km/ph – over rough terrain, and refuelling was necessary every 55km. Consequently, of the 179 tanks lost in the battle at Cambrai, very few had been destroyed by the enemy; the majority broke down and were abandoned by their crews.

The huge, cobbled main square, **place Aristide-Briand**, is dominated by the Neoclassical Hôtel de Ville, and still suggests the town's former wealth, based on the textile and agricultural industries. Cambrai's chief treasure for once is not its cathedral but the **church of St-Géry**, off rue St-Aubert west of the main square, which contains a celebrated *Mise au tombeau* by Rubens. The **Musée Municipal** (March–Dec daily except Tues 10am–noon & 2–5pm) on rue de l'Épée, south of the town square, is also worth a visit. The paintings of Velázquez feature prominently alongside various Flemish masters, works by Utrillo and Matisse, a native of Le Cateau (see below).

Cambrai's **tourist office** is housed in the *Maison Espagnole* on av de la Victoire, south of place Aristide-Briand. Central **accommodation** comprises *Le Mouton Blanc*, 22 rue d'Alsace-Lorraine (☎27.82.30.16; ③), which is a convenient and moderately priced hotel close to the station with a posh restaurant inside and an inexpensive self-service one around the corner. The cheaper hotels are way out on the other side of town on the highway, while the nearest **campsite**, 10km away, is signposted off the D939 to Arras.

Le Cateau

Twenty-two kilometres east of Cambrai along an old Roman road, the small town of **LE CATEAU-CAMBRÉSIS** is the birthplace of twentieth-century Fauvist painter Henri Matisse (1869–1954). As a gift to his home town, Matisse bequeathed it a collection of his works. All of them are now displayed in the **Musée Matisse** (Mon & Wed–Sat 10am–noon & 2–6pm, Sun 10am–12.30pm & 2.30–6pm; .15F) housed in the local château in the centre of town, and although there are no major works here, it still deserves a visit, being the third largest collection of his work in France. Matisse's work occupies the first floor and includes several studies for the chapel in Vence and whole series of his characteristically simple pen-and-ink sketches. Also worth looking at is the work of local Cubist Auguste Herbin on the ground floor, particularly his psychedelic upright piano.

Arras, Albert and the Somme battlefields

Around Arras and Albert, some of the fiercest and most futile battles of World War I took place, and at one time the trenches even cut through the grandiose main square in **Arras**, now restored to its former glory. At nearby **Vimy Ridge**, the Canadians fell in their thousands; at **Notre-Dame de Lorette**, the French suffered the same fate. **Albert** is not a place to linger, but makes a convenient base for exploring the many war cemeteries in the area.

Arras

ARRAS has been rebuilt more times than any other town in France. Its history of conflict dates from the early fifteenth century – a temporary truce was signed here before the Battle of Agincourt (see p.188) – and in addition to the destruction of this century, it has seen capture and bombardment by the Austrians, Spanish, British and Germans.

Oddly enough, the town bears few obvious battle scars. Reconstruction here, particularly after the last war, has been careful and stylish, and two grand arcaded squares in the centre – **Grand' Place** and the smaller **Place des Héros** – preserve their historic, harmonious character. On every side are restored Renaissance mansions, built in relatively restrained Flemish style, and, on place des Héros, there's a grandly ornate **Hôtel de Ville**, its entrance hall housing a permanent photographic display documenting the wartime destruction of the town and sheltering a pair of *géants* (festival giants) awaiting the city's next fête.

Also inside the town hall is the entrance to the belfry viewing platform and **les souterrains** (or *les boves*), cold, dark passageways and spacious vaults tunnelled beneath the centre of the city (Tues–Sat 2.30–6pm; Sun 10.30am–12.30pm & 3–6.30pm; guided tours 30F). Once down, you're escorted around an impressive area and given an interesting survey of local history. During World War I, the rooms – many of which have fine, tiled floors and lovely pillars and stairways – were used as a British barracks and hospital.

Arras' other main sight is its cathedral, the former Benedictine **Abbaye St-Vaast** that was revived from its ruins after eighteenth- and twentieth-century wars. It now houses the **Musée des Beaux-Arts**, its entrance at 22 rue Paul-Donnier (daily except Tues 10am–noon & 2–6pm, Sun 10am–noon & 3–6pm; Oct–March Mon–Fri closes 5pm; 13F), with a mediocre collection of paintings, including a couple of Jordaens and Brueghels, fragments of sculpture, local ceramics and some of the tapestries or "screens" (*arras*; the final "s" is pronounced), which gave the town its name.

On the western edge of town, next to the Vauban barracks, is a **war cemetery** and **memorial** by British Sir Edwin Lutyens, a movingly elegiac, classical colonnade of ivy-covered brick and stone, commemorating 35,928 missing soldiers, the endless columns of their names inscribed on the walls. It's a long time ago now and the number of surviving relatives is dwindling fast; yet there are few sights as poignant as the fading posies left with a card beneath a name, an elderly hand reminding "Dad" she hasn't seen him since she was seven.

It is a mournful corner of town. Around the back of the old brick fortress, in an overgrown moat, is the **Mur des Fusillés**, where some 200 Resistance fighters were shot by firing squad in the last war, most of them of Polish descent, most of them miners, and most of them Communists.

Practicalities

The **tourist office**, 7 pl du Maréchal-Foch, opposite the station (Mon–Sat 10am–noon & 2–5/6pm), is worth consulting on transport and tours of local battlefields (see "Vimy

Ridge and around" below); they also have a small branch bureau in the town hall. To reach the Vimy memorial, you can also **rent a car** from *Hertz*, rue Carnot (☎21.23.11.14), or *Rent-A-Car*, bd Strasbourg (☎21.71.57.57), for a slightly cheaper deal.

If you are **staying** the night there are several hotels: the new *Hôtel Ibis*, pl Ipswich (☎21.23.61.61; ③), a comfortable, reliable two star, fully accessible for the disabled; *Des Trois Luppars*, 47 Grand' Place (☎21.07.41.41; ③), a friendly family-run place with modern facilities in a characterful old building; and *Le Rallye*, 9 rue Gambetta (☎21.51.44.96; ③), near the station. The newly modernized, well-positioned **youth hostel** with an 11pm curfew is at 59 Grand' Place (☎21.21.07.83; IYHF card required; ①), and there's a **campsite** (April–Oct) 1km out of town on the Bapaume road.

Restaurants worth trying include *La Rapière*, 44 Grand' Place, serving good-value regional food with a 78F menu, and the gourmet *La Faisanderie*, a few doors away for a splurge, with *dégustation* menu at 385F. **Pizzerias** abound and two particularly good ones are on rue Petit-Viéziers, *Le Petit Théâtre* and the *Salon de Thé aux Petits*, while *Le Palerme* at 50 Grand' Place also serves pasta. For something different, an excellent *shwarma* place (eat in or take away) is tucked away in rue des Trois-Visages, just around the corner from the cathedral, with a luscious range of Middle Eastern sweets.

Les Grandes Arcades, the hotel on Grand' Place, also serves very good and not wildly expensive **regional food** (including the local speciality *andouillette* or tripe sausage – an acquired taste), and you'll find a good **fromagerie**, *Jean-Claude Leclercq*, at 39 place des Héros. Saturdays are a good day for food and wine, when the squares are taken up with a morning **market**, and *Esto Cave*, an extensive sixteenth-century wine cellar, is open for the sale of fine **wines** (10am–1pm & 3–8pm), run by the delightfully large and quirky proprietor of *Des Trois Luppars*.

Vimy Ridge and around

Eight kilometres north of Arras on the D49, **Vimy Ridge**, or Hill 145, was the scene of some of the direst trench warfare of World War I: almost two full years of battle, culminating in its capture by the crack Canadian Corps in April 1917. It is a vast site, given in perpetuity to the Canadian people out of respect for their sacrifices, and has been preserved, in part, as it was during the conflict. There's an **information centre** (April–Sept daily 10am–6pm; free) supervised by bilingual Canadian students, who run free guided tours and can fill you in on all the horrific details. You really need your own transport to get here, otherwise opt for an organized tour through the tourist office in Arras (see above).

Near the information centre, long worms of neat, sanitized trenches meander over the now grassy ground, still heavily pitted and churned by shell bursts beneath the planted pines. There are examples of dug-outs, hideous places where men used to shelter during heavy bombardments and where makeshift hospitals were set up. Beneath the ground lie some 11,000 bodies still unaccounted for and countless rounds of unexploded ammunition. Signs are still required to warn against straying from the directed paths.

On the brow of the ridge, 1500m north of the information centre, overlooking the slagheap-dotted plain of Artois, a great white **monument** towers, like a giant funerary stele, rent down the middle by elemental force, with allegorical figures half-emerging from the stone towards the top, and inscribed with the names of 60,000 Canadians and Newfoundlanders who lost their lives during the war. An unenviable task to design a fitting memorial to such slaughter, but this one, aided by its setting, succeeds with great drama. At the time, Vimy was seen by many as the birth of the Canadian nation, yet you may feel a certain aversion to the victorious tone of the tourist handouts and the triumphalism of the memorial itself – it took eleven years to build, used up 6000 tonnes of limestone and cost $1.5 million – a huge sum in the Depression years.

Back from the ridge, there's a subdued **memorial** to the Moroccan Division who also fought at Vimy, and in the woods behind, on the headstones of another exquisitely maintained **cemetery**, you can read the names of half the counties of rural England.

La Targette, Neuville-St-Vaast and Notre-Dame de Lorette

At the crossroads (D937/D49) of **LA TARGETTE**, 8km north from the centre of Arras and accessible from there by bus, the **Musée de la Targette** (daily 9am–8pm; Jan Mon–Fri only; 20F) contains an interesting collection of World War I *objets de guerre*. It is the private collection of one David Bardiaux, assembled with passion and meticulous attention to detail, under the inspiration of tales told by his grandfather, a veteran of Verdun. Its interest lies in the absolute precision with which the thirty-odd mannequins of British, French, Canadian and German soldiers are dressed and equipped, down to their sweet and tobacco tins and such rarities as a 1915 British-issue cap with earflaps, very comfortable for the troops but withdrawn because the top brass thought it made their men look like yokels. All the exhibits have been under fire; some belonged to known individuals and are complete with stitched-up tears of old wounds. When you're finished, the *Café Flambeau* serves well-priced food.

More **cemeteries** lie a little to the south of La Targette (10km from Arras and reached by bus), nominally at **NEUVILLE-ST-VAAST**, though the village is actually 1km away to the east. There is a small British cemetery, a huge French one, and an equally large German cemetery, containing the remains of 44,833 Germans. If you haven't been to a German war cemetery before, the macabre, skeletal black crosses – each one represents four soldiers – come as quite a shock. So, too, do the handful of individual Jewish headstones that stand out from the rest. The Polish sculptor Henri Gaudier Brzeska died in action here in 1915 – a Polish **memorial** and Czech **cemetery** face each other across the main street of the village itself.

On a bleak hill a few kilometres to the northwest of Vimy Ridge (and 5km north of Neuville-St-Vaast) is the church of **Notre-Dame de Lorette**, scene of a costly French offensive in May 1915. The original church was blasted to bits during the war and rebuilt in grim neo-Byzantine style in the 1920s, grey and dour on the outside but rich and bejewelled inside. It now stands at the centre of a vast graveyard with over 20,000 crosses laid out in pairs, back to back, each one separated by a cluster of blood-red roses. There are 20,000 more buried in the ossuary, and there's the small **Musée Vivant 1914–1918** (March–Nov daily 9am–8pm; Dec–Feb Sat & Sun 9am–7pm; 20F) behind the church displaying photographs, uniforms and other military paraphernalia. You can reach Notre-Dame de Lorette by bus from Arras, direction *Lens*.

Albert and around

The church at **ALBERT** – now, with the rest of the town, completely rebuilt – was one of the minor landmarks of World War I. Its tall tower was hit by German bombing early on in the campaign, leaving the statue of the Madonna on top leaning at a precarious angle. The British, entrenched over three years in the region, came to know it as the "Leaning Virgin". Army superstition had it that when she fell the war would end, a myth inspiring frequent hopeful potshots by disgruntled troops. Unless you have a really strong battlefield interest, however – in which case you could spend weeks here roaming the region – modern Albert does not invite much of a stay.

As you arrive (trains from Amiens or Arras), the town's new tower, capped now by an equally improbably posed statue, is the first thing that catches the eye. The **tourist office** is close by on rue Gambetta (June to mid-Sept daily 2–5pm) together with a couple of good **hotels**: the moderately priced *Basilique*, 3–5 rue Gambetta (②), whose good restaurant offers pricey Picardy specialities, and the much cheaper *La Paix*, 43 rue Victor-Hugo (☎22.75.01.64; ①), whose restaurant has simpler menus from 60F.

THE BATTLE OF THE SOMME

On July 1, 1916, the British and French launched the **Battle of the Somme** to relieve pressure on the French army defending Verdun. The front ran roughly northwest–southeast, 6km east of Albert across the valley of the Ancre and over the almost treeless high ground north of the Somme – huge hedgeless wheat fields now, their monotony relieved by an undulation as slow as the rhythm of a long sea swell. These windy open hills had no intrinsic value, nor was there any long-term strategic objective – the region around Albert was chosen simply because it was where the two allied armies met.

There were 57,000 British casualties on the first day alone, approximately 20,000 of them dead – making it the costliest defeat the British army has ever suffered. Sir Douglas Haig is the usual scapegoat for the Somme, yet he was only following the military thinking of the day, which is where the real problem lay. As A.J.P. Taylor put it, "Defence was mechanized: attack was not." Machine guns were far more efficient, barbed wire more effective, and, most important of all, the rail lines could move defensive reserves far faster than the attacking army could march. The often ineffective heavy preliminary bombardment favoured by both sides only made matters worse, since the shells forewarned the enemy of an offensive and churned the trenches into a giant muddy quagmire.

Despite the bloody disaster of the first day, the battle wore on until bad weather in November made further attacks impossible. The cost of this futile struggle was 415,000 British, 195,000 French, and around 600,000 German casualties.

The *Circuit de Souvenir*

Was it for this the clay grew tall?
O what made fatuous sunbeams toil
To break earth's sleep at all?

Wilfred Owen, *Futility*

The **Circuit de Souvenir** conducts you from graveyard to mine crater, trench to memorial. There's not a lot to see; nothing, at least, that is going to satisfy any appetite for shocking atrocities or scenes of destruction. Neither do you get much sense of movement or even of battle tactics. But you will find that, even if you started out with the feeling that your interest in war was somehow puerile or mawkish, you have in fact embarked on a sort of pilgrimage, in which each successive step becomes more harrowing and oppressive.

The **cemeteries** are the most moving aspect of the region – beautiful, the grass perfectly mown, an individual bed of flowers at the foot of every gravestone. And there are tens of thousands of them, all identical, with a man's name, if it is known (nearly half the British dead have never been found), and his rank and regiment. Just reading the names of the regiments evokes a world of experience quite different from today's: locally recruited regiments, young men from Welsh border farms, mill towns, and villages, who had never been abroad, wiped out in a morning, men from all corners of the Empire. In the lanes between Albert and Bapaume you'll see the cemeteries everywhere: at the angle of copses, halfway across a wheat field, in the middle of a bluebell wood, moving and terrible in their simple beauty. What follows is necessarily just a selected handful of some of the better-known sites.

A good place to start is the station at **HAMEL** (7km by train north of Albert), where the 51st Highland Division walked abreast to their deaths with their pipes playing. Just across the river, towards the village of **THIEPVAL**, the 5000 Ulstermen who died in the Battle of the Somme are commemorated by the incongruously Celtic **Ulster Memorial**, a replica of the Helen's Tower at Clandeboyne near Belfast. Probably the most famous of

Edwin Lutyens' many memorials is south of Thiepval: the colossal **Memorial to the Missing**, in memory of the 73,357 British troops whose bodies were never recovered at the Somme. A half-hour hike west of Hamel station is the Newfoundlanders' memorial at **BEAUMONT-HAMEL**. Here, on the hilltop where most of them died, a series of **trenches** has been preserved, now grassed over and eroding, where German faced Canadian a few paces apart. It all seems so small scale now and almost more appropriate to the antics of the party of school children witnessed running around here shooting each other with their fingers than to anything as obscene as what took place.

Twelve kilometres east at **LONGUEVAL,** the other side of the Albert–Bapaume road, the **Musée 1914–1918** (daily 9.30am–6pm) consists mainly of a section of trench reconstructed in the back garden of a café and "equipped" with genuine battlefield relics. It's a bit amateurish, but quite interesting if you're passing through. The guide had first collected objects from the battlefield as a boy to sell for pocket money. Farmers apparently still turn up about 75 tons of shells every year – not really surprising when you think the British alone fired one-and-a-half million in the last week of June 1916.

Another fine Lutyens memorial stands at **VILLERS-BRETONNEUX,** some 18km southwest of Albert near the River Somme itself. As at Vimy, the landscaping of the **Australian Memorial** is dramatic – for the full effect, climb up to the viewing platform of the stark white central tower. The monument was one of the last to be inaugurated in July 1938, when the prospects for peace were already looking bleak.

AISNE AND OISE

To the southeast, away from the coast and the main Paris through-routes, the often rainwashed and dull province of Picardy becomes considerably more inviting. Particularly in the *départements* of **Aisne** and **Oise**, where the region merges with neighbouring Champagne, there are some real attractions set amid lush, wooded hills. **Laon, Soissons** and **Noyon** all centre around handsome Gothic cathedrals, while at **Compiègne**, Napoléon Bonaparte and Napoléon III enjoyed the luxury of the magnificent château and embellished it to their hearts' content.

Transport is good for once, too, with a network of bus connections from Amiens and good train and bus links with Paris.

St-Quentin

A pleasant and prosperous industrial centre, **ST-QUENTIN** is a convenient place to pause en route to somewhere else, but unless you have a passion for entomology (see below), the town makes no great demands on your time.

Thanks to St-Quentin's Communist mayor, the central place de l'Hôtel de Ville is now completely closed to traffic. One side of it is dominated by a particularly good-looking, arcaded, late-Gothic **Hôtel de Ville**, whose bells ring protracted, syncopated changes every quarter hour. From the other side, rue St-André leads to the town's skyscrapingly massive but outwardly rather uninspiring Gothic **Basilique**. Inside, its main virtue is its sheer size. In fact, it's a miracle that it is still standing at all, since the retreating Germans mined all 300 pillars in 1918 and were only prevented from setting them off by lack of time – you can still see the marks left by the mines. Another curiosity is the maze in the paving of the nave designed for penitents to figure out on their knees.

Of much greater interest is the **Musée Antoine-Lécuyer** on rue Lécuyer, at the end of rue Raspail (daily except Tues 10am–noon & 2–5pm; Sun 2–6pm only; 8F, Wed free), which contains a big collection of pastel portraits of the leading politicians, nobles,

artists and socialites of eighteenth-century France by locally born Maurice-Quentin de
Latour. The other unique collection, and one of the largest in the world, is that of more
than half a million butterflies and other insects, housed in the **Musée d'Entomologie**,
14 rue de la Sellerie, just off the main *place* (daily except Tues 2–6pm; 7,20F).

Practicalities

To get to the centre from town from the **gare SNCF**, follow rue Général-Leclerc over the
Somme, and up rue d'Isle. The **tourist office** (Mon 1.30–6.30pm, Tues–Sat 9.30am–
12.30pm & 2.30–6.30pm) is housed in the same building as *Musée d'Entomologie*, and will
recommend **accommodation**. Try the basic *Hôtel du Départ*, pl du Monument-aux-
Morts (☎23.62.31.69; ①), just to the right as you come out of the station, or the *Terminus*,
2 rue du Général-Leclerc (☎23.62.31.73; ①), over the bridge from the train station. The
town's **campsite** and **youth hostel** are on bd Jean-Bouin (both ☎23.62.68.66; ①; March–
Nov), 2km from the station by the river – bus #3 to rue H-Dunant.

Laon and around

Looking out over the plains of Champagne and Picardy from the spine of a high narrow
ridge, girt still by its gated medieval walls, **LAON**, 36km southeast of St-Quentin, is one
of the gems of the region. Dominating it all and visible for miles around are the five
great towers of one of the earliest and finest Gothic cathedrals in the country. Of all the
cathedral towns in Aisne, Laon is the one to head for.

Arrival and accommodation

The **tourist office** is right by the cathedral (daily 9am–12.30pm & 2–6.30pm), housed
within the impressive Gothic Hôtel-Dieu, built in 1209. Budget **accommodation** is
mostly in the *ville basse*. Try the av Carnot straight in front of the *gare SNCF*, where you'll
find *Le Welcome* (☎23.23.06.11; ③), or the perfectly decent *Le Carnot* (☎23.23.02.08; ①),
with a good, no-frills restaurant. For rooms in the *ville haute*, the cheapest solution is the
Maison des Jeunes, 20 rue du Cloître, by the cathedral (☎23.20.27.64; ①; no curfew). As
for *ville haute* hotels, *La Paix*, 52 rue St-Jean (☎23.23.21.95; ③; closed Aug) is a good bet,
followed by the simple but comfortable *Les Chevaliers* on rue Serurier (☎23.23.43.78; ②),
an old hotel in the centre. The official IYHF **youth hostel** is 5km out on the Soissons
road and not worth the bother. The **camping municipal** is on the south side of the *ville
basse*, near the *stade municipal*, just off the N44.

The Town

Arriving by train or road, you find yourself in the disappointingly shabby and characterless lower town, or **ville basse**. To get to the upper town or **ville haute**, you can either
walk – a stiff climb up the steps at the end of av Carnot – or take the world's first cable-
hauled, pilotless, rubber-tired aerial métro, the **Poma 2000** (Mon–Sat 7am–8pm; July
& Aug Sun 2.30–6pm; one-way 5,50F, round-trip 8F), pride and joy of Laon. You board
next to the train station and get out by the town hall on place Général-Leclerc; from
there a left turn down rue Serurier brings you nose to nose with Laon's number-one
attraction – its cathedral.

The magnificent **Cathédrale Notre-Dame** (daily 8am–6.30pm; summer till 7pm;
guided tours Sat, Sun & public holidays at 3pm from tourist office), built in the second
half of the twelfth century, was a trend-setter in its day, elements of its design – the
gabled porches, the imposing towers, and the gallery of arcades above the west front –
being repeated at Chartres, Reims and Notre-Dame in Paris. Seen wrapped in thick mist,

the towers seem other-worldly. The creatures craning from the uppermost ledges appear to be reckless mountain goats borrowed from some medieval bestiary and are reputed to have been carved in memory of the valiant horned steers who lugged the cathedral's masonry up from the plains below. Inside, the effects are no less dramatic – the high white nave lit by the dense ruby, sapphire and emerald tones of the stained glass, which at close range reveals the appealing scratchy, smoky quality of medieval glass.

Crowding in the cathedral's lee are a web of quiet, grey, eighteenth-century streets. One – rue Pourier – leads past the *PTT* and onto the thirteenth-century **Porte d'Ardon** which looks out over the southern part of the *ville basse*. A left turn at the post office along rue Hermant leads to the little twelfth-century octagonal **Chapelle des Templiers** – the Knights Templar – set in a secluded garden by the **Musée de Laon**, 32 rue Georges-Ermant (daily except Tues 10am–noon & 2am–5pm; winter 2–6pm; 10F), with a collection of classical antiquities.

The rest of the *ville haute*, which rambles along the ridge to the west of the cathedral into the Le Bourg quarter around the early Gothic **church of St-Martin**, is good to wander in, with grand views from the **ramparts**.

Eating, drinking and entertainment

Rue Châtelaine has a good range of **boulangeries** and **fromageries** for assembling picnics. Simple **snacks** can be had at the *Café de Paris* overlooking the west front of the cathedral; *Crêperie Agora*, an inexpensive Breton place near the cathedral on rue des Cordeliers (open until 1am; closed Sat lunch & Mon); or you could try the *Pizzeria Florentina*, rue Châtelaine. *L'Entr'acte Bar*, next door to the arts complex on place Aubrey, is a fittingly arty place for a drink, its walls covered with intriguing paintings while mellow jazz and blues play in the background. **Restaurants** in Laon tend to be expensive; *La Petite Auberge* at 45 bd Pierre-Brossolette, in the *ville basse* near the station, falls into this category, but serves traditional French cuisine using the freshest ingredients.

There's usually something going on at the *Maison des Arts* on place Aubrey – including the annual ten-day international **film festival** in early April – and a concentration during the *Heures Médiévales* festival in the second and third weeks of September.

Coucy-le-Château and the Forêt St-Gobain

About 30km west of Laon, on the far side of the forest of St-Gobain and set in hilly countryside (a worthwhile cycling trip in itself), lie the straggling ruins of one of the greatest castles of the Middle Ages, **Coucy-le-Château** (daily except Tues April–Sept 9am–noon & 2–6pm; Oct–March 10am–noon & 1.30–4pm). The power of its lords, the Sires de Coucy, rivalled and often even exceeded that of the king – "King I am not, neither Prince, Duke nor Count, I am the Sire of Coucy", was Enguerrand III's proud refrain. The retreating Germans capped the destruction of World War I battles by blowing up the castle's keep as they left in 1917, but enough remains, crowning a wooded spur, to be extremely evocative. The entire modern village of **COUCY-LE-CHÂTEAU-AUFFRIQUE** is contained within the vast ring of walls, entered through the original gates, squeezed between powerful, round flanking towers. There is a footpath all around the outside, and the *Hôtel Bellevue* within (☎23.52.70.12; ①; closed Feb), should you be hungry or stuck here at night.

It's hard to get to Coucy-le-Château without à car, though several Laon–Soissons trains stop at **ANIZY-PINON**, which, if you're otherwise hitching, cuts the distance by about half – and there is an infrequent bus on to Soissons. If you continue into the nearby **Forêt St-Gobain**, include **ST-GOBAIN** itself, 13km north of Coucy, in your itinerary. The original eighteenth-century **glassworks** – the firm is now a vast conglomerate – hides behind a classical façade, pretending it's nothing so vulgar as a factory.

Soissons

Half an hour by train southwest of Laon or 30km down the N2, **SOISSONS** can lay claim to a long and highly strategic history. Before the Romans arrived it was already a town, its kings controlling parts of Britain as well as northern France. And in 486 AD it was here that the Romans suffered one of their most decisive defeats at the hands of Clovis the Frank, making Soissons one of the first real centres of the Frankish kingdom. Napoléon, too, considered it a crucial military base, a judgement borne out this century in extensive war damage.

The town boasts the fine, if little sung, **Cathédrale Notre-Dame** – thirteenth century for the most part with majestic glass and vaulting – at the west end of the main square, place F-Marquigny. More impressive still is the ruined **Abbaye de St-Jean-des-Vignes**, to the south of the cathedral down rue Panleu and rue Racine. The façade of this tremendous Gothic building rises sheer and grand, impervious to the now empty space behind it. The **monastery** (daily except Tues 10am–noon & 2–5pm; guided tours only), save for remnants of a cloister and refectory, was dismantled in 1804. Near the *abbaye* is the impressive eighteenth-century **Hôtel de Ville** with its grand stone gate.

Practicalities

Soissons is relatively compact. From the **gare SNCF** (with good services to Laon and Paris) the main square is a fifteen-minute walk away along av du Général-de-Gaulle and then rue St-Martin. The **gare routière** is closer to the centre by the river on Le Mail: infrequent buses leave for Noyon and Compiègne as well as Laon. The **tourist office** (Mon 2–5pm, Tues–Sat 10am–noon & 2–5pm) is on the place de la République roundabout at the end of av du Général-de-Gaulle.

The town is a useful and attractive place to stay if you're exploring this part of the country, and there are several moderately priced **hotels**: *Hôtel de la Gare* by the station (☎23.53.31.61; closed Mon & Aug; ①), *Hôtel du Nord*, left out from the station on rue de Belleu (☎23.53.12.55; ①), and *Hôtel de la Marine*, 2 rue St-Quentin, in the centre by the river above a rowdy bar (☎23.53.31.94; ①). Rooms are also sometimes available at the two youth *foyers*: women at 8 rue de Bauton; men at 20 rue Malieu. Alternatively there's a **campsite**, 1km from the station on av du Mail. One of the nicest places to eat in Soissons is *La Scala*, an exceptionally good Italian restaurant on rue Petrot-Labarre, which runs off the place Hôtel-de-Ville. Alternatively, the *Lion Rouge*, off place de la République, is a good French fall-back (closed Sun).

Compiègne and around

Thirty-eight kilometres west of Soissons, **COMPIÈGNE**'s reputation as a tourist centre rests on the presence of a vast royal palace, built at the edge of the Forêt de Compiègne – in order that generations of French kings could play at "being peasants", in Louis XIV's words. It's worth a visit certainly for the opulent palace interiors and the car and Second Empire museums, although the town is a bit of a one-horse place with a bland, Sunday-afternoon feel.

Arrival and accommodation

The **gares routière** and **SNCF** (bike rental available) are adjacent to each other, with the centre of town a few minutes' walk away: cross the wide River Oise and go up rue Solférino to place de l'Hôtel-de-Ville. The **tourist office** (Mon–Sat 9.30am–12.15pm & 2–7pm, Sun April–Nov 9.30am–12.30pm & 2.30–5pm) takes up part of the ornate Hôtel de Ville and, for a couple of francs, will provide you with a plan of the town, on which is conveniently marked an exhaustive visitors' route, including the forest paths (see below).

As for **accommmodation**, there are cheapish rooms at the *Hôtel St-Antoine*, 17 rue de Paris (☎44.86.17.18; ①), concealed above a Thai restaurant; *Hôtel de la Tour*, rue des Trois-Barbeaux (☎44.23.37.18; ③; closed Sun); and the *Lion d'Or*, 4 rue du Général-Leclerc (☎44.23.32.17; ①). Much the best place to stay, however, is the *Hôtel de France*, 17 rue E-Floquet (☎44.40.02.74; ①), centrally positioned right next to the Hôtel de Ville, a charming comfortable old place with very reasonable rates. The **youth hostel** is also reasonably central, 1km from the station at 6 rue Pasteur (☎44.40.26.00; ①; bus #3 to rue des Fosses; IYHF card required; curfew 10pm), and there's a **campsite** along av Royale, into the forest beyond the palace.

The Town

The town itself is plain disappointing, though that shouldn't come as a surprise, as a platoon of German soldiers burnt it down in 1942 to provide their commander with evidence of a subjugated community. Several half-timbered buildings remain on the pedestrianized rue Napoléon and rue des Lombards, south of the main place de l'Hôtel-de-Ville. The most striking building, as so often in these parts, is the **Hôtel de Ville** itself – Louis XII-Gothic, with an ebullient nineteenth-century statuary including Joan of Arc, captured in this town by the Burgundians before being handed to the English.

But Compiègne's star attraction is two blocks east of the town hall down rue des Minimes. And for all its pompous excess, there is a certain fascination about the seventeenth- and eighteenth-century **Palais National** (April–Sept 9.15am–6.15pm; closed Tues; guided tours only; last tour leaves 45min before closing; 31F all-inclusive), particularly its interior: the lavishness of Marie-Antoinette's rooms, the sheer, vulgar sumptuousness of the First and Second Empire, and the evidence of the unseemly haste with which Napoléon I moved in, scarcely a dozen years after the Revolution. The palace also houses the **Musée du Second Empire** and the **Musée de la Voiture**, the latter containing a wonderful array of antique bicycles, tricycles and fancy aristocratic carriages, as well as the world's first steam coach. The Grand Théâtre, planned (but never finished) by Napoléon III, has recently been completed at a cost of some thirty million francs. Originally designed with just two seats for Napoléon and his wife, it now seats 900 and is regularly used for concerts.

If you don't want to take the guided tour, a visit to the palace gardens or **petit parc** (daily 7.30am–6.30/8pm) is a pleasant alternative. Serene and formal, they include a long, straight avenue extending far into the **Forêt de Compiègne**, which touches the edge of town. Very ancient, and cut by a succession of hills, streams and valleys, this is grand rambling country for walkers or cyclists – the GR12 goes through it. East of Compiègne, some 6km into the forest and not far from the banks of the Aisne, is a green and sandy clearing guarded by cypress trees, known as the **Clairière de l'Armistice**. Here, in what was then a rail siding for rail-mounted artillery, World War I was brought to an end on November 11, 1918. A plaque commemorates the deed: "Here the criminal pride of the German empire was brought low, vanquished by the free peoples whom it had sought to enslave." To avenge this humiliation, Hitler had the French sign their capitulation on June 22, 1940, on the same spot, in the very same rail carriage. The original car was taken immediately to Berlin, then destroyed by fire in the last days of the war. Its replacement, housed in a small **museum** (daily except Tues 8/9am–noon & 1.30pm/2–5.30/6.30pm; 3F), is similar, and the objects inside are the originals.

If you have an interest in Greek vases, the **Musée Vivenel** on rue d'Austerlitz (daily 9am–noon & 2–6pm; closed Sun am & Mon; 12F) has one of the best collections around, especially a series illustrating the Panathenaic Games from Italy – a welcome dose of classical restraint and good taste compared with the palace. There is also a section on the forest's flora and fauna, which includes a wild boar the size of an armoured car. Another museum of specialist interest is the **Musée des Figurines** by the side of the town hall (same hours and price), with reputedly the world's largest collection of wafer-thin military figurines in mock-up battles from ancient Greece to World War II.

There are a couple of villages worth heading for right in the heart of the forest – **VIEUX-MOULIN** and **ST-JEAN-AUX-BOIS** – and 13km southeast of Compiègne at **PIERREFONDS**, connected by three buses daily from the train station in Compiègne, there's the classic medieval **château de Pierrefonds** (May–Aug Mon–Sat 10am–6pm, Sun 10am–7pm; March, April, Sept & Oct Mon–Sat 10am–12.30pm & 2–5pm, Sun 10am–6pm; Jan, Feb, Nov & Dec daily 10am–noon & 2–5pm, Sun 10am–5.30pm; closed Tues; 26F), built in the twelfth century and heavily restored since to make the model fairytale affair of turrets, towers and moat; the inside displays a varied range of medieval artefacts.

Eating, drinking and entertainment

Compiègne has no shortage of cheap **eateries** like *Cafétéria La Closeraie*, 37 rue Solférino, and *Á la Dernière Minute* on place de la Gare. More rewarding restaurants are *La Pizza Grill*, 10 rue des Boucheries (closed Mon & Aug), and an excellent Vietnamese place, *Le Phnom Penh*, 13 rue des Lombards, which augments its *carte* with Thai dishes and a budget French menu. *Le Bouchon Restaurant Bar à Vin*, 5 rue St-Martin (☎44.40.05.32; Tues–Sat noon–8pm), requires booking for special *dégustation* food and wine nights, with inexpensive *plats du jour* and a wide range of wines served by the glass; and *Le Lombard*, a contemporary-style bar/brasserie on rue Napoléon, whose good range of gourmet salads should please vegetarians.

For just a pastry and coffee, try *Berthelot*, 1 rue Solférino, just by the bridge, with a relaxing atmosphere and magazines to browse through. Lastly, on Saturdays, there's a big all-day **market** in the square by place de l'Hôtel-de-Ville.

Noyon

Further up the Oise, and a possible day trip from Compiègne, is **NOYON**, another of Picardy's cathedral towns. Its quiet provinciality belies a long, illustrious history, first as a Roman prefecture, then as seat of a bishopric from 531. Here, in 768, Charlemagne was crowned king of Neustria – largest of the Frankish kingdoms; in 987, Hugues Capet was crowned king of France; and to cap it all, John Calvin was born here in 1509.

Rowing along the Oise on his *Inland Journey of 1876*, Robert Louis Stevenson stopped briefly at Noyon, which he described as "a stack of brown roofs at the best, where I believe people live very respectably in a quiet way". It is a bit like that, though the **cathedral**, to which Stevenson warmed – "my favourite kind of mountain scenery" – is impressive, at least in passing. Spacious and a little stark, it successfully blends Romanesque and Gothic, and is flanked by the ruins of thirteenth-century cloisters and a strange, exquisitely shaped **Renaissance library** that contains a ninth-century illu-minated bible (guided tours only: book in advance at the tourist office). Close by, signs direct you to the recently reconstructed **Musée Calvin** (daily except Tues 10am–6pm; winter closes 5pm; 10F), ostensibly on the site of the reformer's birthplace. The respectable citizens of Noyon were never among their local boy's adherents and tore down the original long before its tourist potential was appreciated.

If you intend to **stay**, the cheapest hotel is *Le Balto* on place de l'Hôtel-de-Ville (☎44.44.02.97; ①). The local **campsite** is 4km out of town along the N32 to Compiègne. **Buses**, mainly for Compiègne, leave from outside the *gare SNCF*, where you can also rent **bicycles**. Big days in Noyon are Saturday morning, when a colourful **market** spills out across place de l'Hôtel-de-Ville, and the first Tuesday of the month, when a cattle market takes over virtually the entire town centre.

CHAMPAGNE AND THE ARDENNES

Bubbly is the reason most people visit **Champagne**. The Romans continued with wine production here, using vineyards that had already been in existence for centuries, but it wasn't until the blind cellarmaster of a Benedictine Abbey of Hautvillers near Reims, Dom Perignon, experimented with new bottling techniques that champagne as we know it came into existence. The use of strong bottles and cork imported from Spain allowed the French monk to trap the bubbles and taste stars, even though he couldn't see any.

Away from the unusual landscape of the vineyards, the region's rolling plains are an uninspiring sight, growing more wheat and cabbages per hectare than any other region of France, though it seems to bring the villages no great benefit. Some places look so run down you feel the shutters would fall off if you so much as popped a paper

CHAMPAGNE: THE FACTS

Nowhere else in France, let alone the rest of the world, are you allowed to make **champagne**. You can blend wines from chalk-soil vineyards, double-ferment them, turn and tilt the bottles little by little to clear the sediment, add some vintage liqueur, store the result for years at the requisite constant temperature and high humidity in sweating underground *caves* carved from chalk soil, and finally produce a bubbling golden liquid; but you cannot call it champagne. It's perhaps an outrageous monopoly to keep the region's sparkling wines in the luxury class, although the locals will tell you the difference comes from the squid fossils in the chalk, the lie of the land and its critical climate, the evolution of the grapes, the regulated pruning methods, the legally enforced quantity of juice pressed.

Three authorized **grape varieties** are used in champagne: Chardonnay, the only white grape, growing best on the Côte des Blancs and contributing a light and elegant element; Pinot Noir, grown mainly on the Montagne de Reims slopes, giving body and long life; and Pinot Meunier, cultivated primarily in the Marne Valley, adding flowery aromas.

The vineyards are owned either by *maisons* who produce the *grande marque* champagne, or by small cultivators called *vignerons* who sell the grapes to the *maisons*. The *vignerons* also make their own champagne and will happily offer you a glass and sell you a bottle at half the price of a *grande marque* (ask at any *SI* in the Champagne region or at the *CIVC* in Épernay for a list of addresses – see below). The difference between the two comes down to capital. The *maisons* can afford to blend grapes from anything up to sixty different vineyards and to tie up their investment while their champagne matures for several years longer than the legal minimum (one year for non-vintage, three years vintage). So the wine they produce is undoubtedly superior – and not a lot cheaper here than in a good discount off-licence in Britain or the US.

If you could visit the head offices of *Cartier* or *Dior*, the atmosphere would probably be similar to that in the champagne *maisons* whose palaces are divided between Épernay and Reims. Visits to the handful of *maisons* that organize regular guided tours are no longer free, and some require appointments, but don't be put off – they all speak English and, with an individually arranged visit, you're more likely to get a *dégustation*. Their audiovisuals and (cold) cellar tours are on the whole very informative, and do more than merely plug brand names. The professional body regulating the industry is the *Comité Interprofessionel du Vin de Champagne* (*CIVC*), 5 rue Henri-Martin, Épernay; they can provide copious information and a full list of addresses and times for visits, as can any local *SI*.

If you want to work on the **harvest**, contact either the *maisons* direct; the *Agence Nationale pour l'Emploi*, 11 rue Jean-Moët, Épernay (☎26.51.01.33), or 57 rue Talleyrand, Reims (☎26.88.46.76); or try the youth hostel in Verzy where casual workers are often recruited, or work advertised – located at 14 rue du Bassin (☎26.97.90.10).

bag – and few are much more than hamlets, with grocery vans doing the rounds once a week without a *boulangerie* in sight.

At least the official capital of Champagne, the cathedral city of **Reims**, is worth a visit in its own right, and it has a reasonably full cultural calendar. For champagne-worshippers, however, **Épernay** is the place to head for out of preference, where you can sample vintages to your heart's content and go on several underground visits to the *caves* of the different *maisons*. Across the plains, neither **Châlons-sur-Marne**, nor the smaller, further-flung towns like **Chaumont** or **Langres** dotted along the Marne towards its source, are much of an incentive to break your journey. Really the only major attraction in the rest of the region is the town of **Troyes**, some way off to the southwest, which is easily Champagne's most beautiful city.

Reims

Laid flat by the bombs of World War I, **REIMS** (pronounced like a nasal "Rance") doesn't give an attractive first impression if you arrive by car – a seemingly large industrial centre with little to redeem it. However, the town is not as large as it looks and there are other reasons for visiting here – apart from its world champagne status, it possesses one of the most impressive Gothic cathedrals in France, formerly the coronation church of dynasties of French monarchs and avidly painted in all its shimmering glory by Impressionist Monet.

Arrival and accommodation

The cathedral is less than ten minutes' walk from the **gare SNCF** and **gare routière**, and the **tourist office** is conveniently located next door in a picturesque ruin (Mon–Sat 9am–7.30pm, Sun 9.30am–6.30pm); they will book accommodation for 15F.

Accommodation is easy to come by in Reims – much of it affordable – with plenty of centrally located hotels, many on place Drouet-d'Erlon.

Hotels

Au Bon Accueil, 31 rue de Thillois (☎26.88.55.74). A small old hotel in an excellent central location with the cheapest single rates in town – just a little more than the youth hostel. Basic rooms have toilet and shower. ①.

Continental, 93 place Drouet-d'Erlon (☎26.40.39.35). Well situated with quiet rooms, all with bathroom and TV. Parking 25F. ③.

Grand Hôtel des Templiers, 22 rue Templiers (☎26.88.55.08). Very handy for the *maisons* – in the same peaceful street as *Lanson* – this is an upmarket choice in a beautiful shuttered nineteenth-century building. Huge luxurious rooms. ⑧.

New Hôtel Europe, 29 rue Buirette (☎26.47.39.39). Quiet turn-of-the-century four-storey four star. Parking 38F. ④.

Le Paris, 33 place Drouet-d'Erlon (☎26.47.48.89). Cheap and convenient above a lively bar – definitely no frills. ①.

Thillois, 17 rue de Thillois (☎26.40.65.65). A couple of blocks from place Drouet-d'Erlon, this is a convenient cheapie in a quiet street. ①.

Youth hostels

Centre International de Séjour, 1 chaussée Bocquaine (☎26.40.52.60). A large, well-run IYHF youth hostel with single or double rooms, and self-catering, although breakfast is available. It's a fifteen-minute walk from the station on the other side of the canal: best route is to head south down rue de Vesle, the main shopping drag; crossing the canal, the street is left off rue du Colonel-Fabien. Or catch bus #H from Théâtre to stop Pont-de-Gaulle. There's a curfew of 11pm, but no daytime lockout; no IYHF card required. ①.

The City

Reims' historical heart is quite a compact area surrounding the cathedral about a ten-minute walk from the *gare SNCF*, and it's here that you'll find the main collections, Hôtel de Ville, Law Courts and shops. Ten minutes' walk east of here is the popular automobile museum, with the basilica of St-Rémi and the *caves* about fifteen minutes to the south down at the bottom of rue Gambetta.

The cathedral and around

The lure of the thirteenth-century **Cathédrale Notre-Dame** is threefold: first, the kaleidoscopic patterns in the stained glass, with Marc Chagall designs in the east chapel and champagne processes glorified in the south transept; second, a series of unusually lovely tapestries; and third, and best, an inexplicable joke, running around the restored but still badly mutilated statuary on the west front – the giggling angels

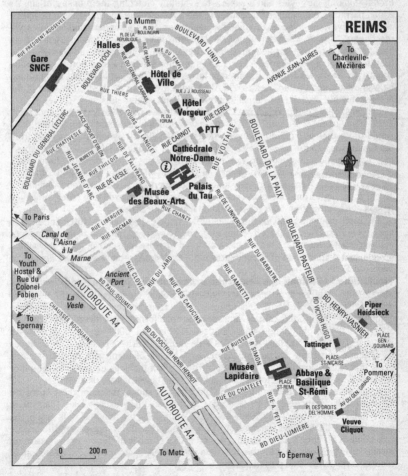

who seem to be responsible for disseminating the prank are a rare delight. Not all the figures on the cathedral's west front are the originals – some have been removed to spare them further erosion by the elements and are now at the former bishop's palace, the Palais du Tau (see overleaf).

Reims Cathedral was where Joan of Arc succeeded in getting the Dauphin crowned as Charles VII in 1429 – an act of immense significance when France was more or less wiped off the map by the English and their allies. In all, 26 kings of France were crowned in the Gothic glory of this edifice. Between July and September the upper parts of the cathedral are open to the public so you can look down and contemplate the vices and virtues of those who made the procession along its nave.

At the **Palais du Tau** (daily 9.30am–noon & 2–5/6pm; July & Aug 9.30am–6.30pm; 26F), next door to the cathedral, you can appreciate the expressiveness of the statuary from close up – a view that would never have been possible in their intended monumental positions on the cathedral. Apart from the grinning angels, there are also some friendly-looking gargoyles and a superb Eve, shiftily clutching the monster of sin. As added narrative, embroidered tapestries of the *Song of Songs* line the walls. The palace also preserves, in a state of unlikely veneration, the paraphernalia of the arch-reactionary Charles X's coronation in 1824, right down to the Dauphin's hat box. In being anointed here in purple pomp – after Revolution, Robespierre and Napoléon had tried to achieve a new France – Louis XVI's brother stated his intention to return the country to the *ancien régime*. His attempt turned out to be short-lived, but the tradition he was calling upon dated back to 496 AD when Clovis, king of the Franks (and of the first identifiably French post-Roman entity), was baptized in Reims.

Just west of the cathedral on rue Chanzy, the **Musée des Beaux-Arts** (daily except Tues 10am–noon & 2–6pm; 10F) is the city's principal museum, which, though ill suited to its ancient building and very diverse, does effectively cover French art from the Renaissance to the present. Few of the works are among the particular artists' best, but the collection does contain one of David's replicas of his famous Marat death scene, a set of 27 Corots, two great Gauguin still-lifes, some beautifully observed sixteenth-century German portraits, and various interesting odds and ends, including an old *tabac* sign from nineteenth-century Reims. As long as you don't feel compelled to look at everything, an hour or so could be happily spent here.

The same cannot be said for the museum five minutes away in the **Hôtel Vergeur**, 36 place du Forum (Tues–Sun 10am–6pm; 20F), you'll have to go through a long guided tour of the whole works, but it's nevertheless a stuffed treasure house of all kinds of beautiful objects, including two sets of Dürer engravings – an *Apocalypse* and *Passion of Christ*.

The Basilique St-Rémi, the Automobile Museum and Salle de Reddition

Most of the early French kings were buried in Reims' oldest building, the eleventh-century **Basilique St-Rémi**, ten minutes' walk from the cathedral on rue Simon (Mon–Fri 2–6.30pm Sat & Sun 2–7pm; 10F), part of a former Benedictine abbey named after the 22-year-old bishop who baptized Clovis and 3000 of his warriors. An immensely spacious building, with aisles wide enough to drive a bus along, it preserves its Romanesque choir and ambulatory chapels, some of them with modern stained glass that works beautifully. The ticket to the basilica includes entrance to the other monastic buildings, where more stone sculpture and tapestries are displayed.

If you have even a passing interest in old cars you should make for the **Centre de l'Automobile Française**, 84 av Georges-Clemenceau (daily except Tues 10am–noon & 2–7pm; Dec–Feb Sat & Sun 10am–noon & 2–5pm; 30F), ten minutes' walk east of the cathedral. All 150 vehicles, dating from 1891 to the present day, are part of the private collection of Philippe Charbonneaux, designer of a number of the postwar classics on display. And, in addition to the full-scale cars, there's an impressive selection of models, antique toys and period posters.

On the opposite side of town, behind the station in rue Franklin-Roosevelt, is the rather more dull **Salle de Reddition**, or Surrender Room (daily except Tues 10am–noon & 2–6pm; Oct–April 10am–noon; 10F), an old schoolroom which served as Eisenhower's HQ from February 1945. In the early hours of May 7, 1945, General Jodl agreed to the unconditional surrender of the German army, thus ending World War II in Europe. The room has been left exactly as it was (minus the ashtrays and carpet), but there's really not enough to warrant a special visit out here unless you're particularly motivated.

Champagne tasting

For the serious business of Reims, head to place des Droits-de-l'Homme and place St-Niçaise, near the Basilique St-Rémi, which are both within striking distance of the majority of the Reims *maisons*, most of which charge a small entrance fee for their tours. Only three can be visited without an appointment: the houses of *Mumm, Taittinger* and *Piper Heidsieck*.

The best of the regular guided tours, and the only one of the three offering a taste, is **Mumm** at 34 rue du Champ-de-Mars (daily 9–11am & 2–5pm; Nov–Feb Mon–Fri only; 20F; 45min). Established in 1827, *Mumm* is familiar for its red-slashed *Cordon Rouge* label – its un-French sounding name being the legacy of its founders, affluent German wine-makers from the Rhine Valley. The tour is fairly informal, with a good amount of wandering freely about its cellar museum and throwing questions at the approachable guides – although you pick up the basics from a pre-tour video. There's not a lot of walking despite 25km of cellars and a reported 35 million bottles of wine, and en route you can gaze at the caged vintage bottles, some from as early as 1911. It all ends with a generously poured glass from a choice of three champagnes: *Cordon Rosé*, the populist choice, the more unusual and expensive *Mumm de Cramant*, made entirely of the *cru* of the Cramant village, and their standard *Cordon Rouge*.

At **Taittinger**, 9 place St-Niçaise (Mon–Fri 9.30am–1pm & 2–5.30pm, Sat & Sun 9am–noon & 2–6pm; Dec–Feb Mon–Fri only; 15F; 1hr; no tasting), there are still more ancient *caves*, with doodles and carvings added by more recent workers, and statues of St-Vincent and St-Jean, patron saints respectively of *vignerons* and cellar hands.

Although founded in 1785, **Piper-Heidsieck** at 51 bd Henry-Vasnier (March–Nov daily 9–11.45am & 2–5.15pm; March–Sept to 6.15pm; Dec–Feb closed Tues & Wed; 20F) is better known in the New World than the Old, having been the champagne of the American movie industry since first appearing – with Laurel and Hardy – in the 1934 classic *Sons of the Desert*. The champagne of the Oscars gives a fair whack of sponsorship for film prizes and festivals too, and really the only folk who'll get anything out of the tour – which ends up at a gallery of celebrity snaps – are confirmed film buffs, and lovers of tackiness could well go for a laugh: the antique *caves* are toured by automatic five-seater car shuttle rather like a ghost train. Out of the darkness and timed to a cliché-ridden narration loom giant fibreglass grapes and vast hands armed with secateurs, or life-size badly proportioned lumpy figures positioned as cellar masters. You emerge to a glittering photo-studded foyer and a snooty atmosphere without a much-needed drink in sight.

Top of the list of appointment-only houses is the **Maison Veuve Clicquot-Ponsardin**, 1 place des Droits-de-l'Homme (☎26.85.40.29). In the early days of capitalism, the widowed Mme Clicquot not only took over her husband's business, but later bequeathed it to her business manager rather than to her children – both radical breaks with tradition. In keeping with this past, the *maison* is one of the least pompous and its video the best. The *caves*, with their horror-movie fungi, are old Gallo-Roman quarries. The **House of Pommery**, 5 place du Général-Gouraud (☎26.61.62.55), has also excavated Roman quarries for their cellars; they claim – in good champagne one-upmanship – to have been the first to do so. Other appointment-only *maisons* are

Ruinart, 4 rue des Crayères (☎26.85.40.29), *Charles Heidsieck*, 4 bd Henry-Vasnier, and *Lanson*, 12 bd Lundy (☎26.78.50.50).

Finally, to get an overview of the various champagnes available (plus wines from all over France), it's worth visiting *La Vino Cave*, 43 place Drouet-d'Erlon (9.30am–1pm & 2.30–7.30pm; closed Mon am & Sun), where you can also buy all the paraphernalia of the bubbly business from champagne flutes to snazzy servers.

Eating, drinking and entertainment

Place Drouet-d'Erlon, a wide pedestrianized boulevard lined with **bars** and **restaurants**, is also where you'll find most of the city's **nightlife**, such as it is. For self-catering, there's a big Wednesday and Saturday **market** in place du Boulingrin (6am–1pm), while vegetarians can top up supplies at *La Vie Claire*, 23 place d'Erlon.

Le Bangkok, 24 rue du Tambour. Excellent, well-priced Thai place. Closed Sat lunch & Sun.

Boyer, 64 bd Henry-Vasnier (☎26.82.80.80). Reputed to be one of France's finest gastronomic restaurants – with prices and style to match – *Boyer* is set in a restored eighteenth-century château.

Chèvres et Menthe, 63 rue de Barbatre. A very good value, plain establishment recommended for vegetarians with its interesting range of gourmet salads from 15F. Daily *carte* dishes might include moussaka (35F) as well as more traditional choices.

Le Colbert, 64 place Drouet-d'Erlon. Traditional cuisine – including an excellent regional Champagne–Ardenne menu (150F) – in a daintily set up, popular restaurant. Menus from 80F and affordable champagne by the glass.

Aux Côteaux, 86 place Drouet-d'Erlon. Bustling friendly place serving unusual pizzas (from 37F) and an equally interesting range of salads. Closed Sun.

Les Cyclades, 13 rue du Colonel-Fabien. Just around the corner from the youth hostel, a very well priced authentic Greek restaurant. Closed Sat lunch, Sun & Aug.

La Grappa, 49 rue du Colonel-Fabien. Handy for the youth hostel, an often crowded Italian – popular with families – serving pasta and pizza, both recommended and priced for budgets.

Le Paris, 33 place Drouet-d'Erlon. A popular spot for locals with very reasonable *plats du jour* (like lasagne for 30F), as well as the usual omelettes, sandwiches, quiches and pizza. Transforms into a lively night spot when the outside tables come into their own.

Au Petit Bacchus, 11 rue de l'Universite. Reasonably priced traditional cooking in an interior of sparse brick floor, bare tables. Closed Sun.

Au Petit Comptoir, 17 rue de Mars (☎26.40.58.58). Close to the *Marché du Boulingrin*, with traditional dishes from 85F (no menus) served in a solid provincial middle-class milieu. Champagne by the glass too. Closed Sat lunch & Sun.

Le St-Niçaise, place St-Niçaise. Cheap but faded brasserie, convenient if you've been visiting the *caves*, otherwise don't bother. Closed Sun evening.

Entertainment

In the summer, over 100 classical **concerts** – many of them free – take place as part of *Les Flâneries Musicales d'Été*; pick up a leaflet at the tourist office. As a university city, Reims' cafés are livelier than most: try the *Café aux Loges* on place Drouet-d'Erlon, where you can play pool or sit at the designer tables and drink till late; or the **jazz bar** *Croque-Notes*, 24 rue Ernest-Renan (Mon–Sat until 2.30am; closed Aug), which has live bands every night.

Épernay

ÉPERNAY, 26km south of Reims, is *the* Champagne town to head for, beautifully situated below rolling, vine-covered hills with wealth-impregnated tree-lined streets, the loveliest being **avenue de Champagne,** worth a stroll to check out the eighteenth- and nineteenth-century mansions and champagne *maisons* – even if you don't fancy visiting any; their tours (should you decide to take them all) could keep you fully occupied for a couple of days. Children over the age of four should be happy enough on the *caves* tours: toddlers may get chilly and scared.

The largest, and probably the most famous *maison* of all, is **Moët et Chandon**, 18 av de Champagne (daily 9.30–11.30am/noon & 2–4/5pm; Nov–March Mon–Fri only; 20F, includes *dégustation*), who own *Mercier*, *Ruinart* and a variety of other concerns, including *Dior* perfumes. By its own reckoning, a *Moët* champagne cork pops somewhere in the world every two seconds – or at least did before the slump of 1990. The cellars are adorned with mementoes of Napoléon, a good friend of the original M. Moët, and the vintage is named after the monastic hero of champagne history, Dom Perignon. True to tradition, the bottles are still turned by hand, a process of *remuage* or riddling explained in detail by the guide; by generous *dégustation* you appreciate why the stuff costs so much.

Of the other *maison* visits, one of the most rewarding is **Mercier**, 70 av de Champagne (Mon–Sat 9.30–11.30am & 2–4.30pm, Sun 9.30–11.30am & 2–5.30pm; Dec–Feb closed Tues & Wed; 20F), whose glamour relic is a giant barrel that held 200,000 bottles-worth when M. Mercier took it to the 1889 Paris Exhibition, with the help of 24 oxen – only to be upstaged by the Eiffel Tower. Visits round the cellars here are by electric train, and are great fun, climaxing in *dégustation*.

Another *maison* worth visiting is **Castellane**, by the station at 57 rue de Verdun (May–Oct daily 10.30am–noon & 2–5.30pm; April pm only), with its tower, a kind of Neoclassical signal box, providing Épernay's chief landmark and giving a clue to the company's turn-of-the-century beginnings. It also houses a champagne-related museum, a visit to which on the tour offers never bettered views of the Marne Valley. If you go on a weekday, you'll see all the processes. The tour is less gimmicky and chic than *Mercier*'s or *Moët*'s, and the *dégustation* a lot more generous.

Newer still, and keen to impress, is **Desmoiselle**, 42 av de Champagne (20F; 45min). Established in the late 1980s, the modern *maison* nevertheless sits upon 200-year-old cellars decorated with beautifully carved figures and fruits; the rather haphazard tour with a pointless *son et lumière* includes *dégustation*.

Épernay has many other *grand maisons* that can be visited by appointment (details from tourist office), but perhaps more worthwhile are the many smaller houses. On rue Chaude-Ruelle, west of av du Champagne with views over the town, there are three: **Janisson-Baradon**, no. 65 (☎26.54.45.85; 20F), **Leclerc-Briant**, no. 67 (☎26.54.45.33; 20F), and **Charles de Cazonore**, no. 39 (☎26.59.57.40; 15F), all offering tours with *dégustation*; they alternate opening at weekends, when it's possible to just turn up, or else make an appointment for weekdays. The tourist office has a comprehensive list of opening hours and details of possible *cave* visits in both the town and the surrounding countryside: Épernay being at the centre of the three champagne-producing zones of the Montagne de Reims, Côte des Blancs and Marne Valley, many are easy to reach.

Finally, die-hard champagne appreciators might wander into the **Musée du Champagne** on av de Champagne (daily except Tues 10am–noon & 2–6pm; 10F). The exhibits themselves are humdrum, but the building is worth a peek, housed as it is in Château Perrier, an impressive example of a nineteenth-century champagne mansion, with a Louis XIII exterior and a flamboyant marble interior featuring a rather grand staircase.

Practicalities

The information-packed **tourist office** is at 7 av de Champagne (Mon–Sat 9.30am–12.30pm & 1.30–7pm; Nov–Feb closes 5.30pm). If you feel like roaming around the *vignerons*, bikes can be rented at the **gare SNCF** or c/o M Buffet, behind the church near the tourist office.

The cheapest **hotels** in Épernay are *St-Pierre*, 1 rue Jeanne-d'Arc (☎26.54.40.80; ①), a quiet street away from the centre; *Hôtel de la Cloche*, 5 place Mendès-France

(☎26.55.24.05; ②) by the train station; and *Le Progrès*, 6 rue des Berceaux (☎26.55.24.75; ②). The *MJC* **youth hostel**, 8 rue de Reims (☎26.55.40.82; ①), has dorm-style accommodation and a cheap cafeteria. The **campsite** is 1.5km to the north on route de Cumières in the Parc des Sports, on the south bank of the Marne.

Places to **eat** include several cheaper, culturally varied places on rue Gambetta, between the *gare* and place de la République. *Le Bel Azur* at no. 33 has Tunisian specialities, while *Le Messina* at no. 17 has pizza and inexpensive pasta. The café of *Le Progrès* is always bursting with folk availing themselves of its hefty sandwiches, while for a more versatile bite, the slickly modern *Brasserie de Rohan* around the corner at 38 rue du General-Leclerc also doubles as a *salon de thé*; *plats du jour* start from 48F, or you could tuck into more expensive seafood specialities. The town's top restaurant is *Les Berceaux*, 13 rue Berceaux (☎26.55.28.84; closed Sun), if you want to unload some cash.

Troyes

TROYES, ancient capital of Champagne, is a gem. Its high narrow streets of restored, half-timbered houses protect an elegant Gothic cathedral, half-a-dozen superb lesser churches, a fistful of Renaissance mansions, and several exceptionally good museums.

Arrival and accommodation

The **gare SNCF** and **gare routière** are side by side off bd Carnot (part of the ring road). Not all buses use the main station, though, and if you're heading for the countryside, it's best to check first with the **tourist office** at 16 bd Carnot (Mon–Sat 9am–8.30pm, Sun 10am–noon & 2.30–5.30pm; mid-Sept to May 9am–12.30pm & 2–6.30pm).

Places to **stay** around the station are plentiful, although for not much more you can find accommodation right in the centre of the old town. Outside term time there may be room in the city's *foyers* – the tourist office has details.

Hotels

Hôtel de la Gare, 8 bd Carnot (☎25.78. 22.84). A basic two star near the station. ①.

Grand Hôtel, 4 av Mal-Joffre (☎25.79.90.90). Right opposite the station, a big three-star hotel with several bars and eateries. ③.

Marigny, 3 rue Charbonnet (☎25.73.10.67). Central hotel in a rickety half-timbered building; basic and inexpensive. ①.

Hôtel de Paris, 54 rue Roger-Salengro (☎25.73.36.32). Pleasant two-star with its own courtyard. Parking 20F. ②.

Le Relais Saint-Jean, rue Paillot-de-Montabert (☎25.73.89.90). Posh hotel in a half-timbered building in a narrow street right in the centre. ⑤.

Select Hotel, 1 rue de Vauluisant (☎25.73.18.52). In the old part of town right next to the museum. Run-down and basic but run by a friendly young family; hall showers free. ①.

Hôtel Splendid, 44 bd Carnot (☎25.73.08.52). Near the station on a very busy road. Shower and TV in rooms. ②.

Hôtel du Théâtre, virtually opposite the *Theatre Madeleine*. A quiet location and friendly management, along with a good-value, old-fashioned brasserie downstairs. ①.

Youth hostels and campsites

IYHF youth hostel, 8 rue Jules-Ferry, Rosières (☎25.82.00.65). 6km out of town opposite the sign saying "Vielaines", a path leads down to this former fourteenth-century priory, where you can stay year round as well as camp in the grounds. Take bus #6B to the last stop, then bus #11, stop *Liberté*. IYHF card required. ①.

Campsite, Pont-Ste-Marie. 2km northeast of Troyes on the D960 via bus #1. April–Oct.

The Town

As tourist pamphlets are at pains to point out, the ring of boulevards round the town is shaped like a champagne cork. In fact it's just as much like a sock – a shape that's just as suitable, since hosiery and woollens have been Troyes' most important industry since the end of the Middle Ages, when Louis XIII decreed that charitable houses had to be self-supporting and the orphanage of the Hôpital de la Trinité set their charges to knitting stockings.

Today the business still accounts for more than half the town's employment. Some of the machines and products can be seen in a **Musée de la Bonneterie**, 7 rue de la Trinité (daily except Tues 10am–noon & 2–6pm; 15F, Wed free), in the sixteenth-century Hôtel de Vauluisant, opposite the church of St-Pantaléon on the rue de Vauluisant. Beautifully restored and visually appealing, it sets an example for all crafts museums with its respect for the traditions and lack of sentimentality. Just one block east is **La Maison de l'Outil**, 7 rue de la Trinité (daily 9am–noon & 2–6pm; 30F) in the beautiful sixteenth-century Hôtel de Mauroy, a surprisingly fascinating museum of tools, with seventeenth- and eighteenth-century exhibits providing a window into the world of the workers who used them, as well as the people who crafted them.

Despite being raked by numerous fires in the Middle Ages, Troyes has retained many of its timber-framed buildings south of the central main shopping street, **rue Émile-Zola**, around the cathedral and particularly in the streets and alleyways of the **old town** off rue Champeaux, the most touristy street. The **church of St-Jean** between the rue Émile-Zola and rue Champeaux (daily 10am–noon & 2.30–5.30pm; July–Sept 10am–5.30pm) is where Henry V married Catherine of France after being recognized as heir to the French throne in the 1420 Treaty of Troyes, his claim to the title being that he had successfully ravaged the already divided country – no doubt without a single one of the qualities attributed to him by Shakespeare. Other Troyes churches worth seeking out are the **church of Ste-Madeleine** on the road of the same name (March–Nov Tues–Sun 2–5pm; July to mid-Sept 10am–5pm), whose delicate stonework roodscreen – used to keep the priest separate from the congregation – is one of the few left in France, and the sumptuous **church of St-Pantaléon**, south-west of church of St-Jean, off place Audiffred (July & Aug daily), which you can only peer into for most of the year; and the gothic **Basilique St-Urbain**, place Vernier (hours as church of St-Jean), its exterior dramatizing the Day of Judgement with the damned and the devils providing a wicked variety of gargoyles. Five minutes' walk from the church of St-Jean up rue Urban IV is **la Cité**, the part of Troyes bounded to the south by the Seine canal and centred on the **Cathédrale St-Pierre-et-St-Paul** (daily mid-Sept to June 9am–noon & 2–6pm; July to mid-Sept 9am–6pm), its pale Gothic nave stroked with reflections from the wonderful stained-glass windows.

Next door to the cathedral, housed in the old bishops' palace, is the **Musée d'Art Moderne** (daily except Tues 11am–6pm; 15F), an outstanding museum displaying part of an extraordinary private collection of art, particularly rich in Fauvist paintings by the likes of Vlaminck and Dérain – along with other works by Degas, Courbet, Gauguin, Matisse (a tapestry and three canvases), Bonnard, Braque, Modigliani, Rodin, Robert Delaunay and Ernst – all of them first class. On the other side of the cathedral, the **Musée St-Loup** (daily except Tues 10am–noon & 2–6pm; 15F, Wed free) is mostly natural history, but is worth a look for the ornate Baroque library on the first floor. In similar vein, the **Hôtel-Dieu**, back down rue de la Cité, has a richly decorated sixteenth-century apothecary (times as above; 10F).

Quite different to the rash of Christian churches in Troyes is the **synagogue** on rue Brunneval, serving a small collection of North African Jewish families but inaugurated in memory of the Jewish scholar Rachi (1040–1105) in 1987. Rabbi Soloman Ben Isaac is better known by his acronym (Rachi in English). He was a member of the small

Jewish community which flourished for a time during the eleventh and twelfth centuries under the protection of the Counts of Champagne. His commentaries on both the Old Testament and the Talmud are still important, both in terms of interpretation and language, to academics today: the Rachi University Institute opposite is devoted to studying his work.

Eating and drinking

Rue Chamoneaux is packed with places to **eat**, many of them trying to lure in the tourists; if you must eat here, crêpes are the thing to have: *Crêperie la Tourelle* – a half-timbered building with its own tiny tower – has inexpensive crêpes and looks out onto church of St-Jean. A popular bar/brasserie, especially in the sunnier months, is *L'Odyssée*, with its tables out on pedestrianized rue Chamoneaux. It has a *plat du jour* for 40F and inexpensive omelettes and sandwiches. The best place for a traditional meal is *Les Quatre Seasons*, 14 rue de Turenne, whose pretty decor runs to fresh flowers, and the prices are attractive too. *Le Provençal* at 18 rue General-Saussier, with quick and cheap standard fare, proves how unnecessary fast food is in France, while at no. 48, *Timgad* provides decent, typically inexpensive Algerian fare. Narrow rue Pithou, near the *Marché des Halles*, hides *L'Etoile*, a small, friendly place with lots of omelettes and menus from 50–70F; there are a couple of tables outside. Vegetarians could find satisfaction here or at *Aux Délices de l'Escargot*, 90 rue Urbain IV, featuring gourmet salads. *Le Cafe du Musée*, 59 rue de la Cité, near the cathedral, has a decent upstairs restaurant and a cool contemporary bar downstairs (daily until 1.30am), with a wide range of beers. *Le Tricasse*, 2 rue Charbonnet, is perennially popular, with tables and the occasional live band, while nearby narrow rue Paillot-de-Montabert has a few good bars, including *Bar des Bougnets des Pouilles*, tiny but consistently packed out. If it's tea rather than alcohol you're after, *Victoria* on rue General-de-Saussier is a rather alternative *salon de thé* with bright yellow walls covered in paintings and tea served in big fat pots.

Self-caterers should head for the *Marché les Halles*, a daily covered market (Mon–Thurs 8am–12.45pm & 3.30–7pm, Fri 7.30am–7pm, Sat 7am–7pm & Sun 9am–12.30pm) on the corner of rue Général-de-Gaulle and rue de la République, close to the Hôtel de Ville. Vegetarians and the health-conscious will think they're in heaven at *Coopérative Hermes*, 39 rue Général-Saussier, a surprisingly good – for France – wholesale/healthfood store.

The Plateau de Langres

The Seine, Marne and Aube and several other lesser rivers rise in the **Plateau de Langres** between Troyes and Dijon. Hunting for sources, though, is a thankless task – there are no bubbling springs promising bigger things to come, and you're more likely to be conscious of undifferentiated water everywhere, rather than emanations from specific fissures. Main routes from Troyes to the Burgundian capital of Dijon skirt this area; the eastern one, which the train follows, takes in **Chaumont** and **Langres**, two towns that could briefly slow your progress if you're in no hurry.

Chaumont

Situated on a steep bank overlooking the Marne valley, **CHAUMONT**, 93km east of Troyes, is one of the few towns worth pausing at on the road to Dijon. The main building to go and look at is the **Basilique St-Jean-Baptiste**. Built with the same dour, grey stone of most Champagne churches, it has, nevertheless, a wonderful Renaissance addition to the Gothic transept of balconies and turreted stairway. The decoration includes a fifteenth-century polychrome *Mise en Tombeau* with muddy tears but expressive faces, and an *Arbre de Jessé* of the early sixteenth-century Troyes school in which all the characters are sitting, properly dressed in the style of the day, in the tree.

As for the rest of the town, there's not much to do except admire the strange, bulging towers of the houses in which the shapes of wide spiral staircases show through. Although not the most animated of places, Chaumont has recently set up an annual international **poster festival** held in the first week of July. Otherwise, try and go on Wednesday or Saturday, when a **market** is held on place des Halles.

If you're looking for a cheap **room**, try *Le St-Jean*, 2 place Aristide-Briand (☎25.03.00.79; ①; closed Sun & end of Aug), on the opposite side of town from the train station; its restaurant serves couscous and paella as well as traditional fare.

Between Troyes and Chaumont, there's one stop-off that might appeal if you have your own transport: the **Cristallerie de Champagne** below the church in Bayel, 7.5km southeast of Bar-sur-Aube on the D396. The glassworks can be visited if you make an appointment (Mon–Sat 9.30am–5.30pm; ☎25.92.05.02), or you can simply call at the shop (Mon–Sat 8.30am–12.30pm & 2.15–5.30pm, Sun 2.30–5.30pm). Most of the exquisite crystal on display is very expensive, but they also sell irregular and end-of-season items at greatly reduced prices.

Langres

LANGRES, 35km south of Chaumont and just as spectacularly situated above the Marne, suffered far less war damage and retains its encirclement of gateways, towers and ramparts. Walking this circuit, with views east to the hills of Alsace and southwest across the Plateau de Langres, is the best thing to do if you're just stopping for an hour or so. Wandering inside the walls isn't unrewarding either – Renaissance houses and narrow streets give the feel of a place time has left behind, hidden by the mists of south Champagne. Langres was the home to the eighteenth-century Enlightenment philosopher Diderot for the first sixteen years of his life, and people like to make the point that if he were to return to Langres today, he'd have no trouble finding his way around.

The **Musée de l'Hôtel du Breuil**, in one of the best of the town's sixteenth-century mansions (daily except Tues 10am–noon & 2–6pm; winter closes 5pm; 10F, Wed free), dedicates a room to Diderot with his encyclopedias, various other first editions of his works, and one of Van Loos' portraits of the savant. In addition, the museum contains a collection of beautiful ivory pieces and sets of dining knives for which this area was famous for several centuries. Local faïence – glazed terracotta – is featured, too, though these nicely crafted pieces are upstaged by the sixteenth-century tiles from Rouen in one of the nave chapels of the **Cathédrale St-Mammès**. This grey stone edifice has not been improved by the eighteenth-century addition of a new façade, but, in addition to the Rouen tiles, there's an amusing sixteenth-century relief of the *Raising of Lazarus*, in which the apostles watch, totally blasé, while the locals look like kids at a good horror movie.

Practicalities

The **tourist office** is just inside the town's main Porte des Moulins (May–Nov Mon–Sat 9am–noon & 2–6.30pm, Sun 10am–noon & 2–6.30pm), on the other side of town from the **gare SNCF** (infrequent connections to Troyes and Dijon); they can give you a useful map with a walking route marked to take in the main sights.

For **accommodation**, there's the basic *Auberge Jeanne d'Arc*, 26 rue Gambetta (☎25.87.03.18; ①), in the centre of town; more comfortable *Les Moulins*, 5 place des États-Unis (☎25.87.08.12; ③), just outside the town's walls near the Porte des Moulins; or the characterful *Hôtel le Cheval Blanc* in a converted church on rue de l'Estrés (☎25.87.23.13; ③). The latter's *Restaurant Diderot* serves good but expensive **food**;

portions are larger and less expensive at the well-regarded dining room of the *Grand Hôtel de l'Europe*, nearby on rue Diderot, with a generous menu for 95F.

The Ardennes

To the north of Reims, the scenery of the **Ardennes** region along the Meuse valley knocks spots off any landscape in Champagne. Most of the hills lie over the border in Belgium, but there's enough of interest on the French side to make it well worth exploring.

In war after war, the people of the Ardennes have suffered protracted last-ditch battles down the valley of the Meuse – which, once lost, gave invading armies a clear path to Paris. The hilly terrain and deep forests (frightening even to Julius Cæsar's legionnaires) gave some advantage to World War II's Resistance fighters when the Ardennes was annexed to Germany, but even peacetime living has never been easy. The main employment over the last century is coming to an end as the slateworks have all closed down, and the ironworks are following suit. The only offering from Paris has been a nuclear power station in the loop of the Meuse at Chooz, to which locals responded by etching "Nuke the Élysée!" high on a half-cut cliff of slate just downstream.

The land is rugged and unsuitable for crops, and tourism is the main growth industry. As yet, the Ardennes is far from developed, which is its greatest attraction. Train and bus connections are good, and there are walking and boating possibilities, too.

Charleville-Mézières

The usual starting point for exploring northwards is the twin towns of **CHARLEVILLE** and **MÉZIÈRES**, which spreads across the meandering Meuse before the valley closes in and the forests take over. Of the two, Charleville is the one to head for, though aside from its main square, its major virtue is as a base for the Ardennes countryside.

Charleville's main sight is the beautifully arcaded central **place Ducale**, the result of the seventeenth-century local duke's envy of the contemporary place des Vosges in Paris. Despite the posh setting, the shops in the arcades remain very down-to-earth – *poissonnières* amongst them – and the cafés charge reasonable prices to sit outside, a very good position on Tuesdays, Thursdays and Saturdays, when the **market** is held here.

The most famous person to emerge from the town was the poet Arthur Rimbaud (1854–91), who actually ran away from Charleville four times before he was seventeen, so desperate was he to escape from such a quiet, provincial town. He is honoured in the **Musée Arthur Rimbaud**, housed in a very grand stone windmill – a contemporary of the place Ducale – on quai Arthur-Rimbaud, two blocks north of the main square (Tues–Sun 10am–noon & 2–6pm; 10F). It contains a lot of pictures of him and those he hung out with, as well as facsimiles of his writings and related documents. A few steps down the quayside is the spot where he composed *Le Bateau Ivre*. After a lifetime of penning poetry in Paris, journeying to the Far East and trading in Ethiopia and Yemen, Rimbaud died in a Marseille hospital, and his body was brought back to his home town – probably the last place he would have wanted to be buried. True Rimbaud fanatics can also visit his **tomb** in the cemetery west of the place Ducale at the end of av Charles Boutet.

Charleville is also a major international **puppetry centre** (its school is justly famous), and every three years at the end of September or early October, it hosts one of the largest puppet festivals in the world, the **Festival Mondial des Théâtres de**

Marionnettes (the next one is in 1997). For ten days, as many as 150 professional troups – some from as far away as Mali and Burma – put on something like fifty shows a day on the streets and in every available space in the town. Tickets are cheap, and there are shows for adults as well as the usual stuff aimed at kids. For booking and information, call ☎24.59.94.94.

Practicalities

The **Bureau Municipal de Tourisme** is at 4 place Ducale (Mon–Sat 9.30am–12.30pm & 1.30–7pm, Sun 9.30am–12.30pm & 2–6pm; mid-Sept to May Tues–Sat 9.30am–noon & 1.30–6pm) and can provide information for the whole region. From the **gare SNCF**, place Ducale is a five-minute bus ride away (take any of the buses going to the right as you come out of the station and ask someone to tell you when you reach place Nevers, just below place Ducale): the **gare routière** is a couple of blocks north of place Nevers, between rues du Daga and Noël.

Three fairly central **hotels** to try are *Hôtel de Paris*, 24 av G-Corneau (☎24.33.34.38; ③), *L'Europe*, 26–28 rue Baron Quinart (☎24.33.23.77; ①) for basic accommodation above a lively bar, and *Le Relais du Square*, 3 place de la Gare (☎24.33.38.76; ③), a smart three-star hotel in a tree-filled square near the station. For the IYHF **youth hostel**, 3 rue des Tambours (☎24.57.44.36; ①; IYHF card necessary; reception to 10am & 5–10pm), take bus #9, direction *La Brouette,* from the station or place Nevers (stop *Auberge de Jeunesse*); they also rent out **bikes**. The town **campsite** is south of place Ducale, over the river past the museum and off to the left.

If you'd prefer to get out into the countryside, the Ardennes office of **Gîtes de France** is at the *Chambre d'Agriculture*, 1 av du Petit Bois (☎24.56.89.65), or ask at the tourist office for the hefty booklet.

There are plenty of places to **eat** and **drink**. For pizzas (from 43F) with a mass of fresh ingredients, and a good range of pasta too, try *Alizée* at 1 av Jean-Jaurès. For something more traditional, *La Côte à l'Os* nearby at 11 cours Aristide-Briand, both a restaurant and a *traiteur*, specializes in *fruits de mer* and local *Ardennais* cuisine; daily chalkboard menus from 68F. Worth checking out for a drink or a coffee is the *Ideal Bar* on rue de la République with its chandelier-style lights and dark wood interior – it's a characterful, down-to-earth local nevertheless; or you could sit under the arcades on place Ducale at *Au Caveau*.

Exploring the Ardennes

Georges Sand wrote of the stretch of the Meuse that winds through the Ardennes that "its high wooded cliffs, strangely solid and compact, are like some inexorable destiny that encloses, pushes and twists the river without permitting it a single whim or any escape". What all the tourist literature writes about, however, are the legends of medieval struggles between Good and Evil whose characters have given names to some of the curious rocks and crests. The grandest of these, where the schist formations have taken the most peculiar turns, is the **Roc de la Tour**, also known as the devil's castle, up a path off the D31, 3.5km out of **MONTHERMÉ**, a slate-roofed little town with nothing of interest except a twelfth-century **church**.

The journey through this frontier country should ideally be done on foot or skis, or by boat. The alternatives for the latter are good old *bateau-mouches* or live-in pleasure boats – not wildly expensive if you can split the cost four or six ways. If you're interested, contact *Loisirs Accueil en Ardennes*, 18 av G-Corneau, Charleville. At the same office you'll also find the *Ardennes Comité de Tourisme*, who can provide walking maps of the region. You can go canoeing with the local club at Revin; contact the tourist office there for details (☎24.40.19.59), but it works out roughly at 130F for a full day,

90F for a half day. For public transport from Charleville, trains follow the Meuse into Belgium, and a few buses run up to Monthermé and **LES HAUTES-RIVIÈRES**, the latter on the River Semoy.

The **GR12** is a good walking route, circling the Lac des Vieux Forges (17km northwest of Charleville – and with canoe hire), then meeting the Meuse at Bogny and crossing over to Hautes Rivières in the even more sinuous **Semoy Valley**. There are plenty of other tracks, too, though beware of *chasse* signs – French hunters tend to hack through the undergrowth with their safety catches off and are notoriously triggerhappy. Wild boar are the main quarry being hunted, and nowhere near as dangerous as their pursuers: the bristly beasts would seem to be more intelligent, too, rooting about near the crosses of the Resistance memorial near Revin, while hunters stalk the forest at a respectful distance. The abundance of wild boar is partly explained when you rootle around on the forest floor yourself and discover, between the trees to either side of the river, an astonishing variety of mushrooms, and, in late summer, wild strawberries and bilberries. For connoisseurs of water, the faintly lemoned spring water of **ST-VLADIMIR** – just out of Haybes on the Hargnies road – makes for a pleasant goal.

travel details

Trains

Amiens to: Paris (very frequently; 1hr 45min–2hr); Compiègne (several daily; 1hr 15min); Laon (several daily; 2hr).

Beauvais to: Paris (6 daily; 1hr 10min).

Boulogne-Ville to: Paris (8 daily; 3 hr); Amiens (8 daily; 1hr 15min); Calais-Ville (9 daily; 30min); Étaple-Le Touquet (9 daily; 20min), Montreuil (9 daily; 30min); Arras (9 daily; 2hr).

Calais-Ville to: Paris (6 daily; 3hr 30min); Amiens (6 daily; 1hr 45min); Boulogne-Ville (9 daily; 30min) and Étaple-Le Touquet (1hr); Lille (frequent; 1hr–1hr 30min).

Dunkerque to: Arras (7 daily; 1hr 20min); Calais-Ville (3 Mon–Sat; 1hr); Paris (7–8 daily; 3hr 10min).

Laon to: Paris (4 daily; 2hr 20min); Soissons (3 daily; 1hr 40min).

Lille to: Arras (*TGV* daily; 40min); Brussels (regularly; 2hr); Longeau (*TGV* daily; 1hr 10min); Lyon (*TGV* daily; 4hr 40min); Paris (very frequently; 2–2hr 30min).

Reims to: Charleville-Mézières (frequently; 55min); Épernay (frequently; 25min); Paris (frequently; 2hr).

St-Quentin to: Compiègne (50min); Paris (frequent; 1hr 45min).

Troyes to: Paris (frequently; 1hr 30min).

Buses

Amiens to: Albert (frequent; 40min); Beauvais (frequent; 1hr 45min); St-Quentin (frequent; 2hr 30min).

Boulogne to: Calais (5 daily; 1hr); Le Touquet (5 daily; 1hr).

Calais to: Boulogne (5 daily; 1hr); Le Touquet (5 daily; 2hr).

Dunkerque to: Calais (several daily).

Épernay to: Troyes (1 daily; 3hr 30min).

Reims to: Troyes (3 daily; 2hr 30min).

Ferries

See Basics, p.8.

CHAPTER THREE

ALSACE-LORRAINE AND THE JURA MOUNTAINS

rance's eastern frontier provinces, **Lorraine** and **Alsace** – usually grouped together under the title Alsace-Lorraine – and the neighbouring *région* of **Franche-Comté**, where the Jura mountains lie, have had a complex and tumultuous history. For a thousand years they have been a battleground, disputed through the Middle Ages by independent dukes and bishops whose allegiance was endlessly contested by the kings of France and the princes of the Holy Roman Empire. These provinces were also the scene this century of some of the worst fighting of both world wars.

The democratically minded burghers of **Alsace**, hugging the German border, had already created a plethora of well-heeled, semi-autonomous towns for themselves centuries before their eighteenth-century incorporation into the French state. Sharing the Germans' taste for Hansel-and-Gretel decoration, they adorned their buildings with all manner of frills and fancies – oriel windows, carved timberwork and Toytown gables – and with Teutonic orderliness they still maintain them, festooned with flowers and in pristine condition. Not that you should ever call an Alsatian German. Alsatian is a Germanic dialect, but their neighbours across the Rhine have behaved in decidedly unneighbourly fashion twice in the last hundred years, annexing them along with much of Lorraine from 1870 to 1918 and again under Hitler. They remain fiercely and proudly Alsatian and French, in that order.

The combination of influences makes for a culture and atmosphere as distinctive as any in France. It is seen at its most vivid in the numerous little wine towns that punctuate the **Route du Vin** along the eastern margin of the wet and woody Vosges mountains, at **Colmar**, and in the great cathedral city of **Strasbourg**, now one of the capitals of the European Union. But the province is not just a quaint setting for coach tours: it's also an industrial powerhouse, making cars, train engines, textiles, machine tools, telephones – you name it – as well as half the beer in France.

ACCOMMODATION PRICE CATEGORIES

All the hotels, youth hostels and guesthouses listed in this book have been price-graded according to the following scale, and although costs will rise slightly overall with the life of this edition, the relative comparisons should remain valid. Paris and the large cities will, as anywhere, be more expensive than equivalent accommodation in the countryside or small towns. The prices quoted are for the cheapest available double room in high season, although remember that many of the cheap places will have more expensive rooms with en-suite facilities.

① Under 160F ④ 300–400F ⑦ 600–700F
② 160–220F ⑤ 400–500F ⑧ Over 700F
③ 220–300F ⑥ 500–600F

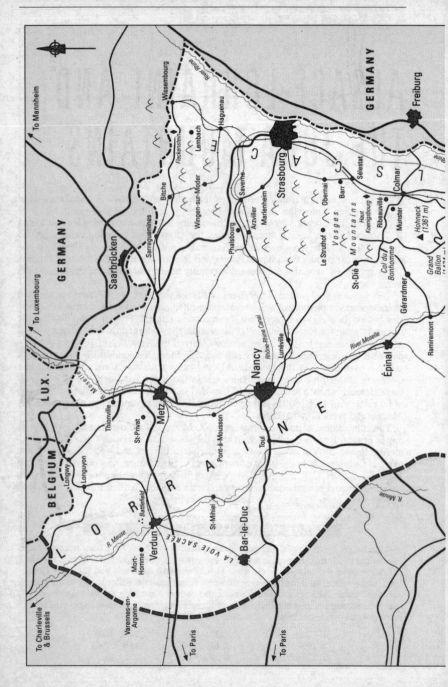

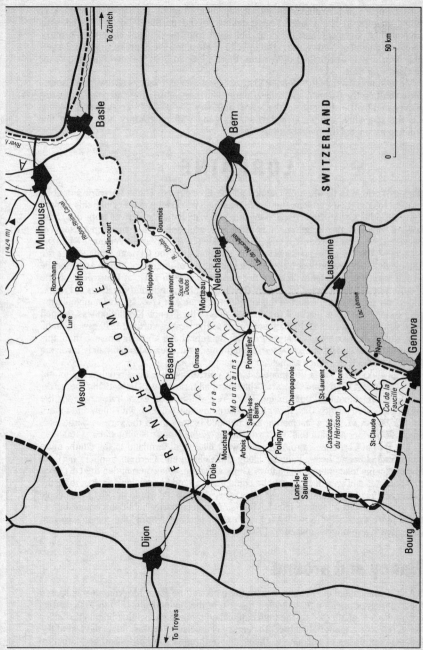

By comparison **Lorraine**, although it has suffered much the same vicissitudes, is rather colourless. It's a large region taking in the northern border shared with Luxembourg, Germany and Belgium, but apart from the elegant eighteenth-century provincial capital of **Nancy**, the cathedral city of **Metz** and the depressing and unforgettable World War I battlefield of **Verdun**, there's little to hold the attention or take up much of your time.

More impressive are the wooded plateaux, pastures and valleys of the **Jura mountains** abutting the German and Swiss frontiers further south, rural and poor, but partly rejuvenated by the attentions of the leisure industry. *Ski de fond* – cross-country skiing – is the speciality, and it's ideal terrain. It's good walking country, too, without the grinding ascents of the neighbouring Alps.

LORRAINE

During World War II, when de Gaulle and the Free French chose **Lorraine**'s double-barred cross as their emblem, they were making a powerful point. For it is this region, above all others, that the French associate with war. Its name derives from the Latin, *Lotharii regnum*: the kingdom of Lothar, who was one of the three grandsons of Charlemagne, among whom his empire was divided by the Treaty of Verdun in 843 AD.

Lorraine has been the principal route of invasion from the German lands across the Rhine ever since, even though the trench-like valleys of the rivers Meuse and Moselle form a main line of defence. Joan of Arc was born here in 1412, at **Domrémy** on the Meuse, when the land was disputed by the dukes of Burgundy and the kings of France, and it only finally became part of the kingdom of France in 1766. In 1792 a mixed army of Prussians and other alarmed royalist enemies of the French Revolution was stopped by Revolutionary forces at the battle of Valmy to the west of Verdun; 1870 saw a humiliating defeat of Napoléon III's armies on the heights above Metz by Prussia; then, this century, the two world wars saw terrible fighting in the area, both ultimately involving American as well as French armies.

Of all the killing fields the bloodiest was **Verdun**, where the French army fought one of the most costly and protracted battles of all time from 1916 to 1918. The battlefield is a site of national pilgrimage. The *SNCF* still lays on extra trains here for the celebration of Armistice Day, though there are now few left alive who knew and mourn the 750,000 dead. For a fascinating and detailed history of all the various battlefields there is no better account than Richard Holmes' *Fatal Avenue* (see *Contexts*, p.1000).

The rest of Lorraine – a rolling, windswept plateau of farmland to the south, moribund coalfields and heavy industry along the Belgian and German frontiers north of **Metz** – seems to stand in the shadows. General Patton, who commanded the US troops that liberated the area in 1944, said he could imagine "no greater burden than to be the owner of this nasty country where it rains every day and the whole wealth of the people consists in assorted manure piles". That is an unnecessarily harsh judgement but, in truth, there's not a lot to hold you here, except perhaps **Nancy**, the region's elegant capital, with a wonderful museum of Art Nouveau.

Nancy and around

NANCY, the capital of Lorraine, lies on the banks of the River Meurthe. It was spared the Prussian occupation that afflicted the rest of the region from 1870 to 1918, and its centre, largely unaffected by the undistinguished modern sprawl that blights the valley sides, remains a model of eighteenth-century classicism. For this, it has the last of the independent dukes of Lorraine to thank, the dethroned King of Poland and father-in-law of Louis XV, Stanislas Leszczynski (see p.250). During the twenty-odd years of his office in the mid-eighteenth century, he ordered some of the most successful urban renewal of the period in all France.

Arrival and accommodation

The part of Nancy that you are likely to want to see extends no more than ten to fifteen minutes' walk either side of **rue Stanislas**, the main axis and shopping street connecting the **gare SNCF** (☎83.56.50.50) and the principal **place Stanislas**, itself a leisurely twenty minutes away on foot. The **tourist office**, on the north side of place Stanislas (Mon–Sat 9am–7pm; Dec & Jan closes 6pm; June–Sept Sun & hols 10am–noon & 2–

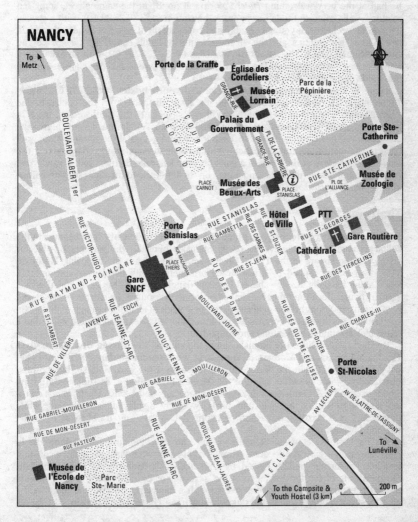

NANCY

To Metz

Porte de la Craffe
Église des Cordeliers
Parc de la Pépinière
Musée Lorrain
Palais du Gouvernement
Porte Ste-Catherine
BOULEVARD ALBERT 1er
COURS LÉOPOLD
GRANDE-RUE
PL DE LA CARRIÈRE
RUE STE-CATHERINE
Musée de Zoologie
PLACE CARNOT
Musée des Beaux-Arts
PLACE STANISLAS
PL DE L'ALLIANCE
RUE VICTOR-HUGO
RUE STANISLAS
Hôtel de Ville
PTT
Porte Stanislas
RUE GAMBETTA
RUE DES CARMES
RUE ST-DIZIER
RUE ST-GEORGES
Gare Routière
RUE MAGINOT
PLACE THIERS
Cathédrale
RUE ST-JEAN
RUE DES TIERCELINS
Gare SNCF
RUE RAYMOND-POINCARÉ
R ST-LAMBERT
AVENUE JEANNE-D'ARC
FOCH
VIADUCT KENNEDY
BOULEVARD JOFFRE
RUE DES PONTS
RUE DES QUATRE-ÉGLISES
RUE ST-DIZIER
RUE CHARLES-III
RUE DE VILLERS
MOUILLERON
RUE GABRIEL-
Porte St-Nicolas
RUE DE MON-DÉSERT
RUE GABRIEL-MOUILLERON
RUE DE MON-DÉSERT
RUE JEANNE D'ARC
AV LECLERC
AV DE LATTRE-DE-TASSIGNY
RUE PASTEUR
To Lunéville
Musée de l'École de Nancy
Parc Ste-Marie
BOULEVARD JEAN-JAURÈS
AV LECLERC
To the Campsite & Youth Hostel (3 km)
0   200 m

5pm; ☎83.35.22.41), is well stocked with all manner of bumph about both city and region. The **gare routière** is just five minutes' walk behind the Hôtel de Ville on the south side of the square, close to the cathedral.

Accommodation

Reasonable **accommodation** is not hard to find in Nancy. On parallel streets a little way south of the train station, there's the *Hôtel Jean-Jaurès*, 14 bd Jean-Jaurès (☎83.27.74.14; ②), slightly weary and worn, and the cheaper *Hôtel Moderne*, 73 rue Jeanne d'Arc (☎83.40.14.26; ①), whose street-side rooms are a little noisy. Right outside the station, the *Central Hôtel*, 6 rue Raymond-Poincaré, the continuation of rue Stanislas (☎83.32.21.24; ③), has comfortable rooms, though better value for money can be had at the very welcoming *Hôtel Poincaré* at no. 81 in the same street, some ten minutes' walk going to the left away from the station (☎83.40.25.99; ②), with a special bargain at weekends: if you stay Friday and Saturday night, you get Sunday thrown in free. Other possibilities are the splendidly quirky family-run *Hôtel Choley*, 28 rue Gustave-Simon, just to the left off rue Stanislas (☎83.32.31.98; ③), with an excellent if rather pricey restaurant, and the more luxurious *Mercure*, 5 rue des Carmes, on the other side of rue Stanislas (☎83.35.32.10; ④–⑤).

There is also a spacious and prettily located **youth hostel** (☎83.27.73.67; curfew 10pm; no IYHF card required; ②), but it's a fair distance from the centre to the Château de Rémicourt in the suburb of Villers-lès-Nancy to the southwest off the N74 Dijon road/av Général-Leclerc, near the Rond-Point du Vélodrome. To get there, take bus #6 on rue des Carmes, direction *Vandoeuvre*, and get off at the *Mangin* stop; walk back to the main road, turn left, then right at the first major intersection, leaving the *École d'Architecture* at the edge of a park on your left; take the next left, a small road running uphill beside the park, and a gate on the left leads to the château. The **camp-site**, *Camping de Brabois* (April–Oct), is nearby.

The Town

Pride of place must go to the wide **place Stanislas**, the middle of which belongs to the solitary statue of its inspirer, the portly Stanislas himself, who was responsible for laying out the square in the 1750s. On the south side stands the imposing **Hôtel de Ville**, its roof-line topped by a balustrade ornamented with florid urns and amorini, while along its walls lozenge-shaped lanterns dangle from the beaks of gilded cocks; similar motifs adorn the other buildings bordering the square. Its entrances are closed by magnificent wrought-iron gates, with the best work of all in the railings of the north-eastern and northwestern corners, which frame gloriously extravagant fountains dominated by lead statues of Neptune and Amphitrite.

In the corner where rue Stanislas joins the square, the **Musée des Beaux-Arts** (10.30am–6pm; closed Mon am & Tues; 20F, Wed free for students; 30F joint ticket with Musée de l'École de Nancy) boasts work by Dufy and Matisse, but nothing outstanding. Time is better spent at the **Musée de Zoologie**, 34 rue Ste-Cathérine (daily except Tues 10am–noon & 2–6pm; school hols daily; 25F). Upstairs is a colossal jumble of stuffed animals and birds, woefully displayed and labelled, while downstairs is a startling aquarium of exotic fish whose colours surpass even the daring of Matisse.

On its north side, place Stanislas opens into the long, tree-lined **place de la Carrière**, a fine eighteenth-century transformation of what was originally a jousting ground. Its further end is closed by the classical colonnades of the **Palais du Gouvernement**, former residence of the governor of Lorraine. Behind it, in the old fifteenth-century Palais Ducal, entered through a handsome doorway surmounted by an equestrian statue of one of the dukes, the **Musée Historique Lorrain**, 64 Grande-

ART NOUVEAU NANCY

A traditional handicraft and metal-working town, at the turn of this century Nancy became a centre of **Art Nouveau** to rival Paris, the most illustrious exponent of the "School of Nancy" being the manufacturer of glass and ceramics, Émile Gallé. The town's moment of glory was short-lived, however, and all that now remains are a handful of buildings and, best of all, the *Musée de l'École de Nancy*, housed in a turn-of-the-century villa. For a post-museum coffee in the same kind of atmosphere, try the Art Nouveau café-restaurant of the former hotel *L'Excelsior*, opposite the train station, built in 1910 and preserved virtually intact to this day.

Rue (daily except Tues May–Sept 10am–6pm; Oct–April 10am–noon & 2–5pm; closed public hols; 20F) is dedicated to the history and traditions of Lorraine. It contains, among other treasures, a room full of superb etchings by the Nancy-born seventeenth-century artist Jacques Callot, whose concern with social issues, evident in series such as *The Miseries of War* and *Les Gueux,* presaged much nineteenth- and twentieth-century art. Next door, in the old Couvent des Cordeliers, the **Musée Régional des Arts et Traditions Populaires** (same hours as above, but closed Mon; 20F) illustrates rural life in the region in days gone by. On the other side of the Palais du Gouvernement, you can play crazy golf, admire the deer or just collapse with exhaustion on the green grass of the **Parc de la Pépinière**, a sort of cross between a formal French garden and an English park. At the end of Grande-Rue the medieval city gate, **Porte de la Craffe**, is now an annexe of the museum (daily except Tues mid-June to mid-Sept 10am–noon & 2–6pm; 5F), containing medieval sculpture.

A half-hour walk southwest of the train station, the **Musée de l'École de Nancy**, 36 rue Sergent-Blandan (daily except Tues 10am–noon & 2–5/6pm; 30F), is housed in a 1909 villa built for the Corbin family, founders of the *Magasins Réunis* chain of department stores. Even if you are not into Art Nouveau, this collection is exciting. Although not all of it belonged to the Corbins, the museum is arranged as if it were a private house. The furniture is outstanding – all swirling curvilinear forms, whether the object is mantlepiece or sofa, buffet or piano – and the standards of workmanship are superlative, with a fair sprinkling of Gallé's work on display, too.

Eating and drinking

There are plenty of places to **eat** and **drink** in Nancy, and good streets for restaurant spotting include Grande-Rue, rue St-Dizier and rue des Ponts. The place Stanislas has several cafés, making good vantage points to watch Nancy go by.

Restaurants

L'Aiglon, 5 rue Stanislas, near the square (☎83.32.21.43). The interesting and well-prepared meals here range 85–140F; For more sophisticated traditional and local cuisine, with dishes like *choucroute, tourte lorraine, baeckeoffe, poule-au-pot,* you can't go wrong. Closed Tues.

Chez Bagot, 45 Grande-Rue (☎83.37.42.43). The *Bagot*'s 118F menu includes such delights as a John Dory *pot-au-feu* and *crème brûlée de crustacées.* Closed Sun, Tues lunchtime & Sept 20–Oct 1.

L'Excelsior, 50 rue Henri-Poincaré, corner of rue Mazagran in front of the train station (☎83.35.24.57). The interior of this restaurant is a delight: a turn-of-the-century Art Nouveau brasserie, frequented by everyone who aspires to being anyone in Nancy. A combination of fun, atmosphere and good food at affordable prices all at one go. It serves excellent fish, shellfish and *choucroute*, with menus at 97F and 140F. It is also the best daytime stop for coffee. Open to 12.30am.

Flunch, 9bis rue Maurice-Barrès, off the south side of pl Stanislas. Palatable no-fuss meals in the national cafeteria chain: a good limited-choice meal for 50F.

Goéland, 27 rue des Ponts (☎83.35.17.25). A renowned and first-rate fish restaurant, whose 165F menu is a bargain; *à la carte* you are quickly up to 400F and more. Part of the same outfit as *Pissenlits*. Closed Sun, Mon lunchtime & Aug 1–15.

Hyppolite, 47 rue des Ponts (☎83.32.97.92). The speciality here is generous servings of *raclette, fondues* and *pierrades*, with prices ranging 50–100F. Closed Sun, Mon, Sat lunchtime & July 15–Aug 15.

Petit Excelsior, 82 rue Jeanne-d'Arc (☎83.27.92.54). A popular bistro serving simple traditional dishes, with a lunchtime menu at 55F and evening ones from 75F (*carte* around 100F). Closed Sat pm & Sun.

Pissenlits, 25bis rue des Ponts (☎83.37.43.97). Serves real old-fashioned bistro fare at 45–75F a *plat*, in an attractive bistro atmosphere. Closed Sun & Mon lunchtime.

Le Vaudemont, 4 pl Vaudemont, at the end of rue Gustave-Simont. Menus ranging 70–130F. Open till midnight.

Café-bars

Bar des Carmes, corner of rue du Lycée and rue des Carmes. For a straight stand-up shot at a tiny and delightful old-fashioned bar.

Le Clavier, pl Stanislas. A popular place to watch the world go by till 4am; closed Sun.

Le Commerce, pl Stanislas. On the corner of rue Stanislas, this is the place to be seen. Till 2am.

Le Stratocaster, 27 Grande-Rue. Slightly downbeat with good taped jazz. Till 2am; closed Sun.

Le Synonyme, 27 rue de la Visitation (☎83.36.51.40). The place for gays, where drinks go for 50–60F a shot. 10.30pm–4am/5am on weekends.

Lunéville

LUNÉVILLE, twenty-minutes' train ride east of Nancy or a half-hour drive along the banks of the River Meurthe, was renowned for the **faïence** (ceramic tile) works set up by Stanislas. There is now a small collection of it – not worth a detour unless you're a specialist – in a museum in the immense eighteenth-century **château** (daily except Tues 10am–noon & 2–6/5pm), dubbed *Le Petit Versailles,* which dominates the town. The rest of the museum is occupied by cavalry uniforms and weaponry, Lunéville being a garrison town; the formal château gardens, host to an extensive rookery, are good for picnicking.

While you're in town, the one thing worth a visit is M. Chapleur's private motorcycle museum, the **Musée de la moto et du vélo** (Tues–Sun 9am–noon & 2–6pm; 20F), directly opposite the gates of the château. Monsieur Chapleur started collecting in the 1930s when he was a mechanic at Citroën. The museum has over 200 models of different origins on display, all overhauled and in working order. And they are beauties, works of art in copper, brass, chrome and steel. Some of the bicycles go back to 1865, and the motorbikes date mostly from 1900 to 1940. Several of the older bikes are probably unique; one certainly is – a 1906 René Gillet 4.5hp belt-driven tandem. Many look like flying bombs and must have been incredibly dangerous to ride: bits of Meccano with a couple of hefty cylinders welded on and capable of 100km/ph in 1900.

Between the *gare SNCF* and the château run the small-scale cottagey streets of the old town, where the newly restored, splendidly Baroque church of **St-Jacques**, Stanislas' gift to the town, raises its enormous twin towers.

From the **gare SNCF**, the rue Carnot north will bring you to the back of the old theatre which adjoins the château, where the **tourist office** is housed (daily 9am–noon & 2–6pm). Should you wish to **stay**, the modest and decent *Hôtel de l'Agriculture* hides away at 14 rue du Rempart (☎83.73.00.61; ②; closed Sun), parallel to the main rue de la République; it also has a restaurant, with meals from 45F. If you want something very special, then the place to go is the *Château d'Adoménil*, a couple of kilometres out of town across the River Meurthe (☎83.74.04.81; ⑥–⑦; closed Sun out of season, Mon & Feb); its seven rooms are beautifully furnished and luxuriously equipped, and overlook water, orchards and a home farm, and its restaurant belongs in the top category (closed Sun evening out of season, Tues lunchtime, Mon & Feb; cheapest menu 210F, *carte* upwards of 400F). At a more humdrum level, **food** at *Le Lunéville*, 43 rue de la République (closed Sun evening, Mon & Aug; menus from 60F), will satisfy most palates. With slightly more interesting food, but a rather stuffy atmosphere, there is *Les Bosquets*, 2 rue des Bosquets, opposite the side entrance to the château gardens (closed Sat & Wed evening; 100–140F).

Metz and around

METZ (pronounced "Mess") lies on the east bank of the River Moselle, close to the *Autoroute de l'Est* linking Paris and Strasbourg and the main train line. Its origins go back at least to Roman times, when, as now, it stood astride major trade routes. On the death of Charlemagne it became the capital of Lothar's portion of his empire, managing to maintain its prosperity in spite of the dynastic wars that followed. By the Middle Ages it had sufficient wealth and strength to proclaim itself an independent republic, which it remained until its absorption into France in 1552.

A frontier town caught between warring influences, it has had more than its share of history's vicissitudes, none more gruesome than those it has endured in the last century and a quarter. In 1870, when Napoléon III's defeated armies were forced to surrender to Kaiser Bill, it was ceded to Germany. It recovered its liberty at the end of World War I in 1918, only to be re-annexed by Hitler in 1940. It was liberated by American troops under the command of General Patton in 1944.

Although its only really important sight is the magnificent cathedral, it is not at all the dour place you might expect from its northern geography and industrial background. The university founded here in the 1970s is at least partly responsible for this liveliness.

Arrival and accommodation

The huge granite **gare SNCF** (☎87.63.50.50) stands opposite the **post office** at the end of rue Gambetta. The **tourist office** (summer Mon–Sat 9am–9pm, Sun 10am–1pm & 3–5pm; rest of year 9am–7pm, Sun 10am–1pm; ☎87.55.53.76) is located by the side of the Hôtel de Ville on place d'Armes in the old town (see below). The **gare routière** stands close to place St-Louis on the eastern edge of the old town.

There is a good range of hotels and budget **accommodation** in Metz, including an official youth hostel, *foyer* and campsite, as well as the odd ritzy establishment. The several reasonable hotels in front of the train station tend to fill up fast in season.

Hotels

Grand-Hôtel de Metz, 3 rue des Clercs (☎87.36.06.93). An ancient and characterful establishment in the course of modernization, right in the heart of the old town near the cathedral. ③.

Hôtel du Centre, 14 rue Dupont-des-Loges (☎87.36.16.33). A well-established cheapie between rue des Clercs and place St-Louis. ②.

Lafayette, 24 rue des Clercs (☎87.75.21.09). A cheap and cheerful establishment on the street which leads from place de la République to the cathedral. ①.

Métropole, 5 pl du Général-de-Gaulle (☎87.66.26.22). Directly in front of the station, this hotel is not particularly welcoming but fine for a stop-over. ②.

Moderne, 1 rue Lafayette (☎87.66.57.33). A functional and friendly hotel just a short distance to the left as you come out of the station. ③.

Hôtel du Théâtre, 3 rue du Pont-St-Marcel, Île Chambière (☎87.31.10.10). Standing on the island in the Moselle below the cathedral, this is a smart and very prettily located hotel. ⑦.

Youth hostels and campsites

IYHF youth hostel, 6 rue Marchant (☎87.75.07.26). Budget accommodation close to the place d'Armes and the cathedral. ①.

Youth hostel, 1 allée de Metz-Plage, Île Chambière (☎87.30.44.02). This clean and friendly youth hostel is on the island by the bridge at the further end of rue Belle-Isle, which crosses the end of rue du Pont-St-Marcel. Bus #3 or #11 from the *gare SNCF*. ①.

Camping municipal, allée de Metz-Plage, Île Chambière. Right next door to the youth hostel. May–Sept.

The City

The tone of the town is set by the **gare SNCF**, a vast and splendid granite structure of 1900 in Rhenish Romanesque, a bizarre cross between a Scottish laird's hunting lodge and a dungeon. Its gigantic dimensions reflect the German intention to use it as the fulcrum of their troop transport system in subsequent wars of conquest against the French. It is matched by the **post office** opposite, and by some imposing bourgeois apartment buildings in the adjacent streets, intended as a model of superior town planning in contrast to the squalid hugger-mugger of the French. Whether you arrive by road or rail, you will find yourself sooner or later in the **Ville Allemande** or German quarter, constructed to the south of the old French quarters on the banks of the Moselle. This was undertaken as part of a once-and-for-all process of Germanification after the Prussian occupation in 1870. Although totally Teutonic in style, it has considerable elegance and grandeur.

Place de la République is bounded to one side by shops and cafés. To the south are army barracks, while to the west, the open end, the formal gardens of the **Esplanade** look out over a pleasantly planted and fountained riverside walk along the Moselle. To the right, as you look down the esplanade, is the handsome classical **Palais de Justice** in yellow stone. To the left, a gravel drive leads past the old arsenal, now converted into a prestigious concert hall by the postmodernist architect Riccardo Bofill. It continues past the **church of St-Pierre-aux-Nonnains**, not much to look at but claiming to be one of the oldest churches in France, with elements from the fourth century – with, nearby, the octagonal thirteenth-century **Chapelle des Templiers.**

From the north side of place de la République, **rue des Clercs** cuts through the attractive, bustling and largely pedestrianized heart of the old city, where most of the best shops are located. Past the **place St-Jacques**, with its numerous café hang-outs, you come to the eighteenth-century **place d'Armes**, where the lofty Gothic cathedral of **St-Étienne** towers above the pedimented and colonnaded classical facade of the **Hôtel de Ville**. It boasts the tallest nave in France after Beauvais and Amiens cathedrals, but its best feature is without doubt the stained glass, both medieval and modern, including windows by Chagall in the north transept and ambulatory.

From here a short walk up rue des Jardins brings you to the city's best museum, the **Musée d'Art et d'Histoire**, 2 rue du Haut-Poirier (daily except Tues 10am–noon & 2–5/6pm; 20F), a treasure house of Gallo-Roman sculpture, but equally strong on mock-ups of vernacular architecture from the medieval and Renaissance periods. The art section is less impressive, although it includes works by Corot and Delacroix.

For the city's most compelling townscape, as well as the most dramatic view of the cathedral, you have only to go down to the river bank and cross to the tiny **Île de la Comédie**, dominated by its classical eighteenth-century square and theatre and a rather striking Protestant church erected under the German occupation. An older and equally beautiful square is the partly arcaded **place Saint-Louis** some ten minutes' walk to the east of the cathedral along the curiously named rue En-Fournirue. On the way, wander up into the Italianate streets climbing the **hill of Ste-Croix** to your left, the legacy of the Lombard bankers who came to run the city's finances in the thirteenth century.

One further thing worth a look if you have come this far is the **Porte des Allemands**, at the end of rue des Allemands: a massive, fortified double gate that once barred the eastern entrances to the medieval city.

Eating and drinking

Metz offers a variety of interesting **eating** possibilities, with plenty of popular **cafés** on place St-Jacques for daytime refreshment. For nightime **drinking**, there is a core of lively places, some with live music.

Restaurants

Café de l'Abreuvoir, 8 rue de l'Abreuvoir, near pl St-Louis. A fashionable place: cosy and noisy with a very French atmosphere and simple, good wine-bar fare (*andouillette* and *quiche lorraine* at around 40F per *plat*). Till midnight/Sat 8pm; closed Sun.

Le Chambertin, 22 pl St-Simplice, off pl St-Louis (☎87.37.32.81). Classic top-notch bourgeois cuisine with such offerings as capons from Bresse, wood pigeon, red mullet, snails and a first-rate menu at 158F. Closed Sun evening, Mon, March 15–30 & Sept 1–21.

Flo, 2bis rue Gambetta, near the station (☎87.55.94.95). A chain of traditional brasseries serving its hallmark excellent seafood, *côte de bœuf* and herring, with a 90F menu that includes wine after 11pm. Till 12.30am.

Le Relais des Tanneurs, 2bis rue des Tanneurs, off the end of rue En-Fournirue (☎87.75.49.09). Traditional French cooking with lots of specialities, including mussels, scallops and *ris de veau*; menus from 65–160F, *carte* around 120F, *plats du jour* 40–60F. Closed Sun & Aug 1–15.

Restaurant du Pont-St-Marcel, 1 rue du Pont-St-Marcel, Île Chambière (☎87.30.12.29). A seventeenth-century establishment on the island, distinctive for its excellent regional cuisine and staff dressed in regional costume. Menus at 98F and 165F, including eel and suckling pig, and wines from the French Moselle. Closed Sun evening & Mon.

À la Ville de Lyon, 7 rue Piques (☎87.36.07.01). Just below the cathedral, this good-value restaurant has a menu at 100F. Closed Sun evening, all day Mon, Feb 17–21 & July 26–Aug 22.

Bars and cafés

Café Jehanne d'Arc, pl Jeanne-d'Arc. Fifteen minutes' walk northeast of pl d'Armes, with medieval beams and frescoes, and occasional music. Till 2 or 3am.

Café Lancieu, 4bis rue du Lancieu, near pl de la République. The place to go for civilized, calm conversation in Second Empire surrounds. Closed Sun.

Café Mathis, 72 rue En-Fournirue. A minute old-time place which spills over into the garden of the former chapel of St-Genest in summertime, opposite a house where Rabelais once lived. Closed Sun.

Irish Pub, 3 pl de Chambre. Crowded and smoky. Till 1am.

L'Oscar, 1 rue Paul-Bezançon (till 2.30am). Live music on Thurs.

Les Trinitaires, 10–12 rue des Trinitaires, north of pl Ste-Croix. For serious jazz, rock, folk and *chanson* fans who like the extra enhancement of Gothic cellars, this is the place to go in town. It's hosted such eminent musicians as Dexter Gordon, Max Roach and Archie Shepp. Live music at 9pm. Closed Sun & Mon.

Le Tunnel, 27 pl du Quarteau at the south end of pl St-Louis. Hang-out of the under-20s, who need their rock music to accompany a drink. Till 2.30am/3.30am weekends.

The battlefields of 1870

Just north of Metz, beyond the Moselle, the land rises to a bleak windswept plateau across which the conquering might of German armies has rolled three times in the last hundred years or so. Stone memorials stand among the fields marking the site of individual, particularly German, regiments' actions.

The D903, christened the Voie de la Liberté on the milestones, and the N3 cross the southern half of the **August 1870 battlefield**, passing the farms of Malmaison and Moscou, whose buildings, disposed in easily fortified squares, became strongpoints of defence in the battles. Moscou was named by one of his veterans, in oddly nostalgic memory of Napoléon I's disastrous Russian campaign.

To the north among the now dying mining communities around **ST-PRIVAT**, you can see a plethora of **memorials** to the Prussian Guards' regiments. If you want to arrive in Verdun in appropriately sombre mood, then there is no better approach than this.

Verdun and the battlefield

At Verdun even the pretence of rationality failed. The slaughter was so hideous that even a trench system could not survive.... In the town, tourists inspect the memorials. One monument shows French soldiers forming a human wall of comradeship against the enemy. In another, France is personified as a medieval knight; resting on a sword, he dominates a steep flight of steps built into the old ramparts. There is another view of reality. Near the railway station, Rodin's statue shows a winged Victory as neither calm nor triumphant, but demented by rage and horror. Her legs are tangled in a dead soldier and she shrieks for survival.

Donald Horne: *The Great Museum*

The small country town of **VERDUN** lies in a bend of the River Meuse, 68km west of Metz. Of no great interest in itself, what makes it remarkable is its association with the ghastly battle that took place on the bleak uplands to the north between 1916 and 1918.

Long a frontier town, in the aftermath of German victory in the 1870–71 war Verdun and its environs became the most heavily fortified military region in France, the lynch-pin of its northeastern defences. For this reason, and in order to break the stalemate of trench warfare, the German General Erich von Falkenhayn chose it as the target for an offensive that, in 1916, was the most devastating ever launched in the annals of war. His intention was "to bleed the French army to death and strike a devastating blow at the morale of the French people". He advanced to within five kilometres of the town, but never succeeded in taking it. Gradually the French clawed back the lost ground, but final victory came only in the last months of the war in 1918 and then only with the aid of US troops under the command of General Pershing.

The best part of a million men died in the battle, both French and German, to say nothing of the numbers scarred for life by their experiences. But it was particularly devastating for the French: the battle was fought on their native soil against the enemy who had humiliated them so badly in 1870, and it decimated the country's young male population. Most of the names inscribed on the thousands of sad memorials that stand in every village, hamlet and town of France belong to men who died at Verdun. It was also the battle that made the reputation of Philippe Pétain, the general who organized the defence of Verdun. Without it, it's arguable that he would have become head of the collaborationist Vichy regime in 1940.

The Town

Given the pounding it received in World War I and the bomb damage of World War II, Verdun is not as grim as you might expect. The liveliest part lies between the river and the steep little hill dominated by the cathedral of **Notre-Dame**, along rue St-Paul/rue Mazel. The **Rodin memorial** stands beside a handsome eighteenth-century gateway at the northern end of rue St-Paul, where it joins av Garibaldi. Another fine gate, the fourteenth-century **Porte Chaussée**, guards the river crossing in the middle of town. Beyond it, further along rue Mazel, a flight of steps climbs up to the **Monument de la Victoire**, where a helmeted warrior leans on his sword in commemoration of the 1916 battle, while in the crypt below a roll is kept of all the soldiers, French and American, who took part. At the end of the street a crooked lane and steps lead to the **cathedral**, whose outward characteristics are Gothic – ironically, its earlier Romanesque origins were only uncovered by shell damage in 1916. The crypt was subsequently dug out, revealing some of the original carved capitals; the new replacements show scenes from the World War I fighting. The rather beautiful **Bishop's Palace** behind it has been converted into a World Peace Centre, hosting exhibitions and conferences.

Rue du Rû, the continuation of rue Mazel, takes you to the underground galleries of the **Citadelle Vauban** (daily April 4–Dec 9.30am–noon & 2–5.30pm; July–Aug 9.30am–8pm; 17F), used as shelter and hospital for thousands of soldiers during the battle. The Unknown Soldier, whose remains now lie under the Arc de Triomphe in Paris, was chosen from among the dead who lie here.

Practicalities

The **tourist office** (Mon–Sat 8.30am–7pm, Sun 9.30am–noon & 1.30–4pm; Oct–April Mon–Sat 9am–noon & 2–5.30/6pm; ☎29.86.14.18) lies just across the River Meuse from the Porte Chaussée opposite the end of the bridge. From May 1 to September 15, staff at the tourist office run daily minibus four-hour **tours of the battlefield** (tours in English, French or German: 2pm only; 145F) – not exactly cheap, but the guides are interesting and the expense is not one that you're likely to repeat. Alternatively, you can **rent bicycles** throughout the year from the *Garage Poncin*, av de Douaumont, and make your own way to the battlefield. The **gare SNCF** and the **bus station** are both on av Garibaldi.

As for **accommodation**, it makes much more sense to stay in Metz or Nancy. However, if you do need to spend the night in Verdun, the most attractive place to stay is the *Hôtel St-Paul*, 12 place St-Paul (☎29.86.02.16; ②; closed Dec 7–Jan 7), close to the Rodin memorial. Decent and inexpensive alternatives are *Hôtel Montaulbain*, 4 rue de la Vieille-Prison (☎29.86.00.47; ①–②), and *Hôtel de France*, 21 av du Général-de-Gaulle (☎29.86.09.85; ①), on the right as you come out of the train station. Although simple and old-fashioned, the latter is a particularly good bargain.

Finding a satisfactory place to **eat** is more problematic. Apart from the *Hôtel St-Paul* (see above), which has a good traditional restaurant with menus from 89F, the best thing is to try one of the brasserie-type places off rue St-Paul/rue Mazel or on the river bank. Two or three of the hotels on av Garibaldi also have restaurants.

The battlefield

The **Battle of Verdun** opened on the morning of February 21, 1916, with a German artillery barrage which lasted ten hours and expended two million shells. It concentrated on the forts of Vaux and Douaumont which the French had built after the 1870 Franco-Prussian War. By the time the main battle ended ten months later, nine villages had been pounded to nothing. Not even their sites are detectable in aerial photos of the time. The heavy artillery shells ploughed the ground to a depth of eight metres and, although much of it is now reforested, there are parts that steadfastly refuse anchorage to any but the coarsest vegetation even today.

The most visited part of the battlefield extends along the hills north of Verdun, but the fighting also spread well to the west of the Meuse, to the hills of Mort-Homme and Hill 304, to Vauquois and the Argonne, and south along the Meuse to St-Mihiel, where the Germans held an important salient until dislodged by US forces in 1918.

The only really effective way to explore the area is by car. The main sights are reached via the D913 or by a minor road, the D112, that leaves the main N3 to Metz opposite the Cimetière du Faubourg-Pavé on the outskirts of Verdun and is soon enclosed by appropriately gloomy conifer plantations. On the right you pass a **monument** to André Maginot, who was himself wounded in the battle and under whose later stewardship at the Ministry of War the famous Maginot Line (see box) was built.

THE MAGINOT LINE

Like the Séré de Rivières forts constructed along the line of the rivers Meuse and Moselle after the 1870–71 war (such as Génicourt, Paroches and Troyon on the Meuse – not open to the public), the **Maginot Line** was designed to keep the Germans out. Constructed between 1930 and 1940, it was the brain-child of the French Minister of War (1929–31), André Maginot. Spanning the entire length of the French–German border, it comprised a complete system of defence in depth. There were advance posts equipped with anti-tank weapons and machine-guns. There were fortified police stations close to the frontier. But the main line consisted of a continuous chain of underground strongpoints linked by anti-tank obstacles and equipped with state-of-the-art machinery. It was of course hugely expensive and, when put to the test in 1940, proved to be worse than useless: the Germans simply violated Belgian neutrality and drove round the other end of the Line.

One of the largest forts, the **Fort de Fermont**, situated about 50km north of Verdun near the small town of Longuyon, is open to the public (daily May–Aug 1.30–5pm; 25F/ 15F). Armed with nine fire points, it was served by six kilometres of underground tunnels and a garrison of 600. The entrance is hidden in woodland. Nothing shows above ground but the scarcely noticeable cupolas of the gun turrets. Below, the tunnels are equipped with power plants, electric trains, monorails, elevators and all the other technological paraphernalia necessary to support such a lunatic enterprise. The place has the feel of a nuclear bunker.

Getting there without your own transport is not easy. There are trains to Longuyon from Metz and Verdun (change at Conflans), but you'll have to hitch or walk the last 5km to the fort.

Shortly afterwards a sign points out a forest ride to the **Fort de Souville**, the furthest point of the German advance in 1916.

The site is not on the main tourist beat and it is a very moving, if rather frightening twenty-minute walk over ground absolutely shattered by artillery fire, with pools of black water standing in the now grassy shell-holes, as if the players in some malevolent game had been abruptly and mysteriously removed. The fort itself lies half-hidden among the scrub, the armoured gun turrets still lowering in their pits, the tunnels to their control rooms dank and dangerous with collapse. A little way beyond the fort, where the D112 meets the D913, a stone lion marks the precise spot at which the German advance was checked. To the left the road continues to Fleury and Douaumont.

Fleury and the Fort de Vaux

The horrifying story of the battle is graphically documented in the **Musée-memorial de Fleury** (mid-March to mid-Sept daily 9am–6pm; mid-Sept to mid-March daily 9am– noon & 2–5/6pm; 18F), which is included in the tourist office's guided tour. Contemporary newsreels and photos present the stark truth; and in the well of the museum, a section of the shell-torn terrain which was once the village of Fleury has been reconstructed as the battle left it.

Also included in the tour is the **Fort de Vaux**, 4km east of Fleury (same hours and admission as Fort de Douaumont below; closed Wed), where after six days' hand-to-hand combat in the confined, gas-filled tunnels, the French garrison, reduced to drinking their own urine, were left with no alternative but surrender. On the exterior wall of the fort a plaque commemorates the last messenger pigeon sent to the command post in Verdun vainly asking for reinforcements. Having safely delivered its message, the pigeon expired as a result of flying through the gas-filled air above the battlefield. It was posthumously awarded the *Légion d'Honneur*.

Douaumont

The principal memorial to the carnage stands in the middle of the battlefield a short distance along the D913 beyond Fleury. It is the **Ossuaire de Douaumont** (April–Sept daily 9am–5.30/6.30pm; March, Oct & Nov daily 9am–noon & 2–5/6pm), a vast and surreal structure with the stark simplicity of a Romanesque crypt or a Carolingian sarcophagus, from which rises a central tower shaped like a projectile aimed at the heavens. Its vaults contain the bones of thousands upon thousands of unidentified soldiers, French and German, some of them visible through windows set in the base of the building. When the battle ended in 1918 the ground was covered in fragments of corpses; 120,000 French bodies were identified, just a third of the total killed.

Across the road, a cemetery contains the graves of 15,000 men who died more or less whole, Christians commemorated by rows of identical crosses, Muslims of the French colonial regiments by gravestones aligned in the direction of Mecca. Nearby, a wall commemorates the Jewish dead, beneath a treeless ridge-top on whose tortured, pitted ground around the remains of the Fort de Thiaumont some of them must have died.

The **Fort de Douaumont** (mid-March to Sept daily 9/9.30am–6/7pm; Sept to mid-March Tues–Sun 10am–noon & 1.30/2–4/5/6pm; closed Jan; 15F) is 900m further on. Completed in 1912 and commanding the highest point of land, it was the strongest of the 38 forts built to defend Verdun. But in one of those inexplicable aberrations of military top brass, the armament of these forts was greatly reduced in 1915. When the Germans attacked in 1916, twenty men were enough to overrun the garrison of 57 French territorials. The fort is on three levels, two of them underground. Its claustrophobic, dungeon-like galleries are hung with stalactites. The Germans, who held it for eight months, had 3000 men housed in its cramped quarters with no toilets, continuously under siege, its ventilation ducts blocked for protection against gas, infested with fleas and lice and plagued by rats which attacked the sleeping and the dead indiscriminately. In one night, when their ammunition exploded, 1300 men died in the blast. When the French retook the fort, it was with Moroccan troops in the vanguard. General Mangin, revered by officialdom as the heroic victor of the battle, was known to his troops as "the butcher" for his practice of shoving colonial troops into the front line as cannon fodder.

Last stop on the guided tour is the so-called **Tranchée des Baïonnettes** (Trench of the Bayonets), where, legend has it, two entire infantry platoons are thought to have been buried alive in an upright position with fixed bayonets during a German bombardment on June 11, 1916. It has become too much of a tourist attraction, however, and its protective concrete roof gives no more aura now than a men's urinal.

Mort-Homme, Vauquois and the Argonne

Because they are so much less visited, the battle sites west of the Meuse are just as evocative. **The hill of Mort-Homme**, above the farming village of Chattancourt, was furiously contested in 1916 as the Germans sought to outflank the main French positions above Verdun. The access road comes to an end at the memorial on top of the hill, where the ground is still a chaos of shell-holes. On the way up you get a chillingly clear picture of how exposed these low hills were before the conifer plantations.

A dozen kilometres further west this exposed country gives way to the friendlier contours of the **Argonne**. Just off the D38, above the prettily rustic hamlet of **VAUQUOIS**, is the steep wooded hill known as the **Butte de Vauquois**. Steps lead to the top, where an astonishing sight awaits you. The whole of the hill-top has been blown away by mine explosions, both French and German. The largest, a German 60-tonner, killed over a hundred French soldiers on May 14, 1916. Of the village of Vauquois, which once stood here, not a trace survives. Extensive networks of trenches and rusting wire entanglements are visible in the woods round about.

ST-MIHIEL AND THE VOIE SACRÉE

In an attempt to cut Verdun off as early as 1914, the Germans captured the town of **St-Mihiel** on the River Meuse to the south of it, which gave them control of the main supply route into Verdun. The only route left open to the French – and that far from safe – was the N35, winding north from Bar-le-Duc over the open hills and wheatfields. In memory of all those who kept the supplies going, the road is called **La Voie Sacrée** (The Sacred Way) and marked with milestones capped with the *poilu*'s (the slang term for the French infantryman) helmet.

Just behind the town of St-Mihiel to the east, on the Butte de Montsec, is a memorial to the Americans who died here in 1918 and a US cemetery at Thiancourt on the main road.

Below the hill lies the village of **VARENNES-EN-ARGONNE**, where Louis XVI and the royal family were recognized and arrested on the night of June 21, 1791, as they tried to escape from Revolutionary France. A plaque marks the spot opposite the Hôtel de Ville and the Post Office. Just uphill is a memorial to American soldiers from Pennsylvania, and the entire area is riddled with tunnels and bunkers from World War I. One that was known as the **Abri du Kronprinz**, off the D38 4km from Varennes, was used by the German Crown Prince during the battle for Verdun.

ALSACE

There's no denying **Alsace**'s attractiveness, with its old stone and half-timbered towns set amid the thickly wooded hills of the Vosges, but it's a quaintness that has become a commodity. **Strasbourg**, the Alsatian* capital, and along with Brussels, one of the main centres of the European Union, escapes the tweeness of some of the smaller towns of the foothills. **Saverne** and **Wissembourg**, to the north, also avoid the worst of the tourist-brochure image, giving access to some spectacular ruined castles in the **northern Vosges**.

South of Strasbourg, along the **Route du Vin**, there are countless picturesque medieval villages and yet more ruined castles that suffer to varying degrees from the attention of the tour buses. A very different, sobering experience is the concentration camp of **Le Struthof**, hidden away in the Vosges forest. **Colmar** is almost excessively cute, yet still worth a visit for Grünewald's amazing Issenheim altarpiece. By contrast, **Mulhouse** is thoroughly industrial but boasts some unusually good museums devoted to cars, trains, electricity and printed fabrics.

Strasbourg

STRASBOURG owes both its name – "the city of the roads" – and its wealth to its position on the west bank of the Rhine, long one of the great natural transport arteries of Europe. Its medieval commercial preeminence was damaged by too-close involvement in the religious struggles of the sixteenth and seventeenth centuries, but recovered with the city's absorption into France in 1681. Along with the rest of Alsace, it suffered annexation by Germany from 1871 to the end of World War I and again from 1940 to 1944.

---

*Note that **four-legged Alsatians** are conspicuous by their absence in what the British assume is their homeland. In fact they originated in Germany, and are known to the rest of the world as German shepherds (*bergers allemands*).

THE FOOD AND WINE OF ALSACE

The cuisine of Alsace is quite distinct from that of other regions of France, because of its German origins, albeit tempered by French refinement. The classic dish is the chopped pickled cabbage of **sauerkraut**, or *choucroute*, which includes the use of juniper berries in the pickling stage and is cooked with goose grease or lard and smoked pork, with ham and a variety of sausages added. The qualification *à l'alsacienne* after the name of a dish usually means with *choucroute*.

Strasbourg **sausages** and boiled **potatoes** are another common ingredient in Alsatian cooking. One of the best culinary incarnations of the spud is the three-meat hot pot, *baeckoffe*, which consists of pork, mutton and beef marinated in wine and cooked between layers of potato for a couple of hours in a baker's oven.

Onions, too, are a favourite dish, either in the form of an onion tart, which is made with a *béchamel* sauce, or *flammeküche* (*tarte flambée* in French), made with a mixture of onion, cream and pieces of chopped smoked pork breast baked on a base of thin pizza-like pastry. **Noodles** are also a common feature, and don't miss the chance of a *matelote* or stew of river fish cooked in Riesling or Vosges trout cooked *au bleu*, briefly boiled in Riesling with a dash of vinegar.

Like the Germans, Alsatians are fond of their **pastries**. The dessert fruit tarts made with cherries or the little yellow *mirabelle* plums – *tarte alsacienne* – are delicious. Cake-lovers should try *kugelhopf*, a moulded dome-shaped cake with a hollow in the middle, made with raisins and almonds, and *birewecks*, made with dried fruit marinated in kirsch.

All of these delights can be washed down with the region's **white wines**, renowned for their dry, clean-tasting fruitiness and compatibility with any kind of food. The best-known of them are Riesling, Gewürztraminer, Sylvaner and Tokay, named after the type of grape from which they are made – unlike other wine-growing regions in the country, the taste of Alsatian wines does not vary from locality to locality. There are, incidentally, a couple of reds – from Otrott and Marlenheim – but it is the whites which make the region's reputation. The term *Edelzwicker* on a label means the wine is a high-quality blend.

Alsace also shares the German predilection for **beer** and has long been the heartland of French hop-growing and brewing. Its fruit brandies are honoured too, especially *kirsch* which is made from cherries, and *quetch* and *mirabelle* from different varieties of plum.

Today those animosities have been submerged in the togetherness of the European Union, of which, as the seat of the Council of Europe, the European Court of Human Rights and the European Parliament, it is one of the capitals. Prosperous, beautiful and modern, with an orderliness that is Germanic rather than Latin, Strasbourg is big enough with a population of over a quarter of a million people to have a metropolitan air, but without being overwhelming. It has one of the loveliest cathedrals in France and one of the oldest and most active universities: this is the one city in eastern France that is definitely worth a special detour.

Arrival and accommodation

The **gare SNCF** (☎88.22.50.50; tourist office annexe, hotel reservations and bureau de change) lies on the west side of the city centre, barely fifteen minutes' walk from the cathedral along rue du Maire-Kuss and rue du 22-novembre. At 17 place de la Cathédrale is the city **tourist office** (June–Sept daily 8am–7pm; Oct–May Mon–Sat 9am–6pm, Sun 9am–12.30pm, 2–5pm; ☎88.52.28.22; guided tours, boat trips etc), with the regional office nearby at 9 rue du Dôme (same hours).

The **airport shuttle** terminates in place Kléber (every 30mins 5.15am–8pm to the airport; from the airport 8am–11pm Mon–Fri, Sat 9.30am–10.30pm, Sun 10.30am–11pm; 36F).

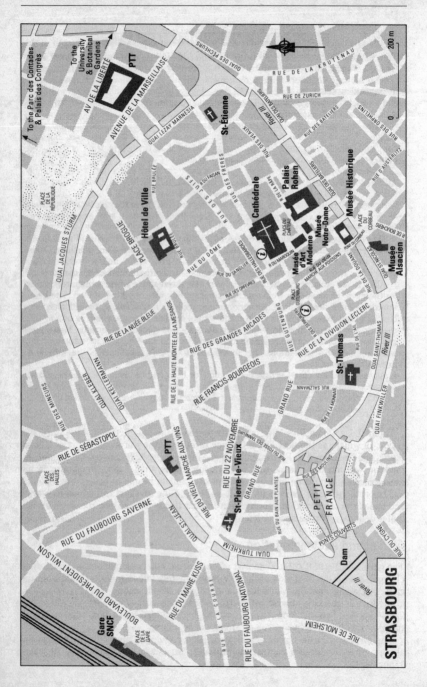

If you're **driving** you'll need to find parking space as most of the city centre is now pedestrians only. The most capacious **car parks** are at Centr'Halles, just north of the centre, and place de l'Étoile, a bit further out to the south. *Parking Heyritz*, near place de l'Étoile, offers a free bus shuttle service into town or free bikes.

Accommodation

When you are looking for a place to **stay**, bear in mind that once a month the European Parliament is in session for three or four days, bringing its hundreds of MPs and their entourages into town, which puts all the city's facilities under pressure, especially hotel accommodation. The youth hostels, at least, are less affected, although it is said that even they play host to one or two Euro-deputies. The station area has the usual clutch of hotels.

HOTELS

Dragon, 2 rue de l'Écarlate (☎88.35.79.80). A very comfortable and fully modernized luxury hotel south of the River Ill. ⑥.

Hôtel Beaucour, 5 rue des Bouchers (☎88.76.72.00). In a handsome old house with its own courtyard, this hotel is very central, just off place du Corbeau. ⑥.

Hôtel Gutenberg, 31 rue des Serruriers (☎88.32.17.15). The central *Gutenberg* is in an old house with period furniture in some rooms. ③–④.

Hôtel de l'Ill, 8 rue des Bateliers (☎88.36.20.01). The best bargain hotel in Strasbourg is the family-run *de l'Ill*, a quiet, comfortable, friendly place only fifty metres from the river, in sight of the cathedral. Closed Dec 25–Jan 1. ②–③.

Hôtel Michelet, 48 rue du Vieux-Marché-aux-Poissons, off pl Gutenberg (☎88.32.47.38). An outwardly unprepossessing but perfectly acceptable old hotel. ①–②.

Hôtel Patricia, 1a rue du Puits (☎88.32.14.60). This hotel is in a great location in the back streets of the old town not far from place Gutenberg. ①–②.

Hôtel-Restaurant Au Cerf d'Or, 6 pl de Hôpital (☎88.36.20.05). Sixteenth-century hotel with its own bar and restaurant (menu from 95F) on the south side of the River Ill. ④.

Hôtel Suisse, 2–4 rue de la Râpe (☎88.34.34.28). A good possibility directly underneath the cathedral's east end. ③–④.

YOUTH HOSTELS AND CAMPSITES

IYHF youth hostel Parc du Rhin, rue des Cavaliers (☎88.60.10.20). Close to the Pont de l'Europe over the Rhine to Germany, you can catch bus #11 or #21 from the station, or #32 from pl Kléber, direction Kehl, stop *Pont du Rhin*. Canteen meals at 50F. ①.

IYHF youth hostel René-Cassin, 9 rue de l'Auberge-de-Jeunesse (☎88.30.26.46). 3km southwest of the city centre; bus #3, #13 or #23 from quai Altorffer by Pont Kuss, stop *Auberge de Jeunesse*; camping and canteen. ①.

CIARUS, 7 rue Finkmatt (☎88.32.12.12). A Protestant hostel near the Palais de Justice, just north of the centre. Curfew 1am; from 75F; bus #10 or #20 from the station to place Pierre. ①.

La Montagne-Verte campsite, 2 rue Robert-Forrer (☎88.30.25.46). Behind the René-Cassin youth hostel, this site is well equipped. Closed Nov–Feb.

The City

It is not difficult to find your way around Strasbourg. The city centre is easily manageable on foot due to the fact that it's concentrated on a small island encircled by the River Ill. Visible throughout the city is the magnificent filigree spire of the pink **cathedral** that dominates not just the city but most of Alsace; it is to the south of this building that you'll find the cream of the museums. To the north of here, **place Kléber** is the heart of the commercial district, and **place Gutenberg** is nominally the main square. About a fifteen-minute walk west on the tip of the island is **Petite France**, where timber-framed houses and gently flowing canals hark back to the city's medieval trades of tanning and dying.

Place Gutenburg and the cathedral

Right at the heart of medieval Strasbourg, with its steep-pitched roofs and brightly painted facades, **place Gutenberg** was named after the printer and pioneer of moveable type, whose statue occupies the middle of the square; he lived in the city in the early fifteenth century. On the west side stands the sixteenth-century **Hôtel de Commerce**, where the writer Arthur Young watched the night-time destruction of the magistrates' records during the Revolution. And on the corner of rue du Vieux-Marché-aux-Poissons the sulptor Jean Arp, was born.

From wherever you are in the city centre, the one landmark you can see is the **Cathédrale de Notre-Dame** (daily 7–11.30am & 12.40–7pm; closed during services; 5F), soaring out of the close huddle of medieval houses at its feet, with a single spire of such delicate, flaky lightness it seems the work of confectioners rather than masons. It's worth slogging up the 328 steps to the spire's **viewing platform** (daily Nov–Feb 9am–4.30pm; March & Oct 9am–5.30pm; April–Sept 9am–6.30pm; July & Aug 9am–7pm; 10F) for the superb view of the old town, and, in the distance, the Vosges to the west and the Black Forest to the east.

The interior, too, is magnificent, the high nave a model of proportion and enhanced by a glorious sequence of stained glass windows. The finest are those in the south aisle next to the door, depicting the life of Christ and the Creation, but all are beautiful, including, in the apse, the modern glass designed in 1956 by Max Ingrand to commemorate the first European institutions in the city. On the left of the nave, the cathedral's organ perches precariously above one of the arches, like a giant gilded eagle, while further down on the same side is the late fifteenth-century pulpit, a masterpiece of intricacy in stone by the appropriately named Hans Hammer.

In the south transept are the cathedral's two most popular sights. One is the slender triple-tiered central column known as the **Pilier des Anges**, decorated with some of the most graceful and expressive statuary of the thirteenth century. The other is the huge and enormously complicated **astrological clock** built by Schwilgué of Strasbourg in 1842: a favourite with the tour-group operators, whose customers roll up in droves to witness the clock's crowning performance of the day, striking the hour of noon, which it does with unerring accuracy, at 12.30pm – that being 12 o'clock Strasbourg time. Death strikes the chimes; the Apostles parade in front of Christ, who occupies the highest storey of the clock; and as each one passes he receives Christ's blessing.

Strasbourg's museums

Most of Strasbourg's **museums** are to be found to the south of the cathedral, between the tree-lined place du Château and the river.

Right next to the cathedral, place du Château is enclosed to the east and south by the Lycée Fustel and the **Palais Rohan** (Mon & Wed–Sat 10am–noon & 1.30–6pm, Sun 10am–5pm; 15F), both eighteenth-century buildings, the latter designed for the immensely powerful Rohan family, who, for several generations in a row, cornered the market in cardinals' hats. There are three museums in the Palais Rohan itself: the **Musée des Arts Décoratifs** (same times and prices as above), **Musée des Beaux-Arts** (same times and prices as above) and **Musée Archéologique** (same times and prices as above). The rooms of the château are not especially interesting: vast, opulent and ostentatious. Of the three collections, only the Arts Décoratifs stands out – and that of slightly specialist interest – with its eighteenth-century faïence tiles crafted in the city by Paul Hannong.

Next door in the mansion lived in by the cathedral architects, the **Musée de l'Oeuvre Notre-Dame** (Mon–Sat 10am–noon & 1.30–6pm, Sun 10am–5pm; 15F) houses the original sculptures from the cathedral exterior, damaged in the Revolution and replaced today by copies; both sets are worth seeing. And there are other treasures here: glass from the city's original Romanesque cathedral; the eleventh-century Wissembourg Christ, said to be the oldest representation of a human figure in stained glass; the architect's original parchment drawings for the statuary (not on display at the time of writing in 1994), done in fascinating detail down to the different expressions on each figure's face.

The **Musée d'Art Moderne** (Mon–Sat 10am–noon & 1.30–6pm, Sun 10am–5pm; 15F), next to the Notre-Dame museum, was originally a fourteenth-century *douane*, but now features an impressive permanent collection featuring such artists as Monet, Picasso, Klimt, Ernst, Klee and the Alsatian Dadaist Hans Arp and his wife, the Swiss Surrealist Sophie Täuber. Only a small selection is on display at any one time, but the museum intends to relocate in 1996 to reveal more of its treasures.

On **place du Marché-aux-Cochons-de-Lait** "sucking-pig market", the **Musée Historique** (closed until 1995), housed in the old Grande Boucherie, is mainly concerned with the city, though it also has an odd-ball collection of mechanical toys upstairs. Last, but by no means least, in a typically Alsatian house on the other side of the river on quai St-Nicolas across the Pont du Corbeau, there's the **Musée Alsacien** (Mon & Wed–Sat 10am–noon & 1.30–6pm, Sun 10am–5pm; 15F), containing pleasing painted furniture and other local artefacts.

The rest of the old town

On the far side of the Pont du Corbeau, the medieval **Cour du Corbeau** still looks much as it must have done in the fourteenth century. Downstream, the **quai des Bateliers** was part of the old business quarter, and it is still worth a wander in the streets leading off it: rue Ste-Madeleine, rue de la Krutenau and rue de Zurich. Two bridges upstream, the Pont St-Thomas, leads to the **chruch of St-Thomas** (April–Nov 10am–noon & 2–6pm; Dec–March 10am–noon & 2–5pm; closed Sun am for services), with a Romanesque façade and Gothic towers. Since 1549 it has been the city's principal

---

THE ALSATIAN LANGUAGE

Travelling through the province, it's easy to mistake the language being spoken in the shops and streets for German. In fact it is **Alsatian** (*Elsässisch*), a High German dialect, known to philologists as Alemannic. To confuse matters further, there are two versions, High and Low Alemannic, as well as an obscure Frankish dialect spoken in the Wissembourg region and a Romance one called *Welche* located in the valleys around Orbey.

Most daily transactions are conducted in French, and *Elsässisch* has still not made it onto the school curriculum. Yet it remains a living language, with a rich medieval literary legacy, and is still spoken by young and old throughout Alsace and even parts of Lorraine. A recent upsurge in nationalist feeling has meant that *Elsässisch* is beginning to appear again on menus and shop signs. In many ways, it's a miracle that it has survived at all, since both French and German rule have tended to discourage the Alsatian language.

During the French Revolution, the language was suppressed in favour of French for nationalistic reasons, only to be ousted by German when the Prussians annexed the region in 1870. On its return to French rule, however, all things Germanic were disdained, and many Alsatians began to speak French once more. The Nazi occupation brought in laws that made the speaking of French and even the wearing of berets imprisonable offences. To top off the linguistic confusion, Strasbourg's Socialist mayor, Catherine Trautman, proposed bilingual French and Alsatian street signs as recently as 1991, but the central government felt uncomfortable with the idea of *strasse* being printed next to *rue* and overturned the decision.

Protestant church. Strasbourg was a bastion of the Reformation, and one of its leaders, Martin Bucer, preached in this church. The amazing piece of sculpture behind the altar is Jean-Baptiste Pigalle's **tomb of the Maréchal de Saxe**, a very capable French military commander active against the Duke of Cumberland in the campaigns of the War of Austrian Succession in the middle of the eighteenth century.

From here, it's a short walk upstream to the **Pont St-Martin**, which marks the beginning of the district known as **La Petite France**, where the city's millers, tanners and fishermen used to live. At the far end of a series of canals are the so-called **Ponts Couverts** (they are in fact no longer covered), built as part of the fourteenth-century city fortifications and still punctuated by watchtowers. Just beyond is a **dam** built by Vauban (daily mid-Oct to mid-March 9am–7pm; mid-March to mid-Oct 9am–8pm; 5F) to protect the city from water-borne assault. The whole area is extremely attractive with winding streets – most notably rue du Bain-aux-Plantes – bordered by sixteenth- and seventeenth-century houses that are adorned with elaborately carved woodwork and decked with flowers. Predictably, it's a top-of-the-bill tourist hot spot.

The area east of the cathedral is good for a stroll, too, where rue des Frères leads to place St-Étienne. **Place du Marché-Gayot**, off rue des Frères behind the cathedral, is also very lively, with a couple of studenty cafés on one side. From the north side of the cathedral, rue du Dôme leads to the eighteenth-century **place Broglie**, with the Hôtel de Ville and *préfet*'s residence and some imposing eighteenth-century mansions around. It was at 4 place Broglie in 1712 that Rouget de l'Isle first sang what later became known as the *Marseillaise* for the mayor of Strasbourg, who had challenged him to compose a rousing song for the troops of the army of the Rhine (see p.451).

The German quarter and the Palais de l'Europe

Across the river here, **place de la République** is surrounded by vast German neo-Gothic edifices erected during the post-1870 Imperial Prussian occupation, a good example being the main **post office** on av de la Liberté. At the centre of the square is a war memorial showing a mother holding two dead sons in her arms, one German and one French, testifying to the split personality of this frontier city whose inhabitants fought on both sides during the war. At the other end of av de la Liberté, across the confluence of the Ill and Aar, is the city's university, where Goethe studied. Adjacent, at the beginning of bd de la Victoire, are the splendidly Teutonic municipal baths, the **Grand Établissement Municipal de Bains**, where you can take a sauna or Turkish bath or just swim.

From in front of the university, the wide straight allée de la Robertsau, flanked by confident turn-of-the-century bourgeois residences, leads to the **Palais de l'Europe**, home of the Council of Europe and the European Parliament. The buildings are surprisingly disappointing, with the one exception of Richard Rogers' contribution for the European Court of Human Rights, with its curving glass entrance and silver towers rising to a boat-like superstructure overlooking a sweep of canal. It is nearing completion at the time of writing. To visit the European Parliament you have to book (☎88.17.20.07); there is no charge.

Opposite the Palais, the **Orangerie** is Strasbourg's best bit of greenery, and plays host to a variety of exhibitions and free concerts.

Eating, drinking and entertainment

For the classic Strasbourg **eating** experience, you have to go to a *winstub*, usually translated as a wine bar, a cosy establishment with bare beams, panels and benches, and a noisy and convivial atmosphere. In the classic version there is a special table set aside for the *patron*'s buddies and regulars. The food tends towards *choucroute*, *tarte à l'oignon*, knuckle of pork and horseradish, ham *en croûte*: the Alsatian classics, washed down with local wines. If you fancy sitting outside with a young and animated crowd, there are several places to eat and drink in the place du Marché-Gayot behind the cathedral.

Restaurants

La Bourse, pl de Lattre-de-Tassigny (☎88.36.40.53). Quite a sedate brasserie meal, in agreeable, spacious surroundings across the river in the direction of place de l'Étoile. 80–120F, 50F menu at lunchtime. Till 11pm.

D'Choucrouterie, 20 rue St-Louis, by the church of St-Louis just across Pont St-Thomas (☎88.36.52.87). *Choucroute* specialist with menus at 150 and 160F, *plats* from about 70F. Closed Jan 1–10; closed Mon.

Mekang, 17 route du Polygone across pl de l'Étoile (☎88.84.26.78). A little out of the way, but does excellent Chinese food. *Plats* 35–45F. Closed Sun.

L'Olivier, 60 rue de Zurich (☎88.36.33.80). Cheap and excellent-value meals – especially at lunchtime – in this Middle Eastern restaurant in the Krutenau quarter. *Plats* 30–40F, with excellent cheap sandwiches. Closed Sun.

Restaurant Le Trasimeno, 41 rue Fossé-des-Treize (☎88.22.66.34). Another foreign possibility is this friendly, good-value Italian pizzeria, with *plats* around 50F. Closed Sat lunchtime & Sun.

La Robe des Champs, 4 rue de l'Écurie (☎88.22.36.82). Potato-fanciers will enjoy the variety of things they can do – inexpensively – with the spud here. Closed Sat lunchtime & Sun.

Le Saint-Sépulcre, 15 rue des Orfèvres, off rue des Hallesbardes (☎88.32.39.97). Traditional *winstub*. Closed Sun & Mon and first fortnight in July.

Salamboo Amilkar, 2 rue de la Croix (☎88.35.40.50). For a couscous, this is the best – if not the cheapest – place to come, with *plats* at around 80F. Closed Sun & Mon.

La Victoire, 24 quai des Pêcheurs (☎88.35.39.35). Another *winstub*, worth experiencing for its lively student ambience rather than the food. Closed Sat evening, Sun and three weeks in Aug.

Winstub Strissel, 5 pl de la Grande-Boucherie (☎88.32.14.73). *Winstub* with Alsatian fare and menus at 35F and 50F (otherwise, 70F or more per *plat*). Closed Sun & Mon.

Zür Zehnerglock, 4 rue du Vieil-Hôpital, near the cathedral (☎88.32.87.09). Quality food and a little live music to sweeten the digestion on Fridays. *Plats* around 75F. Closed Sun & Mon.

Bars and cafés

Académie de la Bière, 17 rue Adolphe-Seyboth, near the church of St-Pierre. For beer-drinkers this is Strasbourg's most famous *bierstub* or beerhall. Daily 9pm–3am.

Les Aviateurs, 12 rue des Soeurs. Expensive place that's big on trendiness and noise. Daily 6pm–3am.

Café des Anges, rue Ste-Cathérine. Easygoing place run by a collective, caters for a slightly older clientele than many bars, with rock or jazz concerts most evenings on the ground floor, with an entrance fee around 20–30F; the basement is free. 11pm–3am; usually closed on Sun.

Le Java, 6 rue Faisan. Good for the younger crowd; the most popular place with concerts and rock music. Till 1am.

Montmartre, 1 pl de la Grande-Boucherie. Near the cathedral, this is a Parisian-style café serving snacks and drinks.

Strasbourg Opéra, pl Broglie. The bar here is smart without being pretentious.

Le Warning Bar, 3 rue Klein. Mostly but not exclusively gay, with a relaxed and agreeable atmosphere, but not cheap. 9pm–4am; closed Mon.

Entertainment

Strasbourg usually has lots going on. In summer pick up the *Saison d'Été* listings leaflet from the tourist office or, for 7F, the weekly listings magazine *L'Hebdoscope*. If you're here during university term-time, you might want to check the notice boards at the university as well. **Free concerts** are held regularly in the Parc des Contades and Parc de l'Orangerie, which also boasts a 24-lane bowling alley. The best of the annual **festivals** starts with music from round the world in mid-June, followed by jazz in July, contemporary world music in mid-September and early October, and mime and clowning in November.

Listings

Bikes Bicycles can be rented from the *gare SNCF* and Parking Heyritz.

Boat trips For information on River Ill boat trips, ask at the tourist office (see above).

Books *Librarie International Kléber*, 1 rue des Francs-Bourgeois, sells new books, French and English; *La Librocase*, 2 quai des Pêcheurs, sells secondhand books. The *Quai des Brumes*, 35 quai des Bateliers, although small, also has a very good range.

Buses Out-of-town buses leave from place des Halles.

Car rental *Avis*, Galérie Marchande, place de la Gare (☎88.32.30.44); *Hertz*, at the airport and 6 bd de Metz by the *gare SNCF* (☎88.32.57.62).

Cinemas *Le Club*, 32 rue du Vieux-Marché-aux-Vins, and *Le Star*, 27 rue du Jeu-des-Enfants (the parallel street) are first-run independent cinemas. The *Odyssée*, 3 rue des Francs-Bourgeois (programme changes every day), is an *Art and Essai* cinema showing classics and contemporary films.

Hiking information *Club Vosgien*, 16 rue Ste-Hélène. ☎88.32.57.96, fax 88.22.04.72.

Hitching *Allostop* ☎88.37.13.13; or look in at the office at 5 rue Général-Zimmer, a couple of blocks south of the university.

Laundry 29 Grand'Rue near the Église St-Pierre.

Markets The city's biggest fruit and vegetable market takes place every Tuesday and Saturday morning on bd de la Marne.

Rape Crisis *SOS Viol* ☎05.05.95.95.

Taxis *Station Centrale* ☎88.36.13.13; *Novotaxi* ☎88.75.19.19.

The northern Vosges

The **northern Vosges** begin at the Saverne gap northwest of Strasbourg and run up to the German border where they continue as the Pfälzerwald. They don't reach the same heights as the southern Vosges, nor do they boast any famous vineyards. As a result, they are spared the mass tourism of the southern range. Much of the region is designated a *Parc Naturel*, and there are numerous hiking possibilities, as well as a couple of attractive towns – **Saverne** and **Wissembourg** – built in the characteristic red sandstone of the Vosges.

HIKING, CYCLING AND DRIVING IN NORTHERN VOSGES

Numerous **cycling** and **motoring** routes designed to bring you into contact with the most interesting sights, villages and landscapes are detailed in the pamphlet *Panorama Nord*, published by the *Office Départemental du Tourisme du Bas-Rhin*, 9 rue du Dôme, 67000 Strasbourg (☎88.22.01.02, fax 88.75.67.64). Independent hikers and cyclists will find further routes marked on the Club Vosgien 1:50,000 and 1:25,000 maps (on sale in bookshops and tourist offices), in addition to the three **GRs** (*Sentiers de Grande Randonnée*), which cross the *Parc Naturel Régional des Vosges du Nord*: GR53–55, GR531 and GR532.

If you are attracted by the idea of having your night-time **accommodation** and **baggage transport** taken care of for you, the *Maison du Parc*, 67290 La Petite Pierre (☎88.70.46.55, fax 88.70.41.04) will organize this for you on a number of routes, whether you're walking or on a bike. The routes vary in length from 2 days to 11 days and the prices from roughly £60 to roughly £300 (for bed and breakfast; demi-pension is available but adds to the cost).

For further information, see the magazine *Les Grandes Traversées des Vosges*, also obtainable from the *Office Régional du Tourisme* (see above for address), or contact the *Club Vosgien*, 16 rue Ste-Hélène, 67000 Strasbourg (☎88.32.57.96, fax 88.22.04.72).

Transport here is patchy, as elsewhere in Alsace, though not hopeless. *SNCF* buses wind their way through the villages and apple orchards around Hagenau, and the Strasbourg–Sarreguemines and Hagenau–Bitche train lines cut across the range. In addition, Saverne and Wissembourg are linked to Strasbourg by train. Even so, the easiest way to explore the region is with your own transport – hilly work, if it's a bike.

Saverne and around

SAVERNE, seat of the exiled Catholic prince-bishops of Strasbourg during the Reformation, commands the only easy route across the Vosges into Alsace, at a point where the hills are pinched to a narrow waist. It is a small and friendly town, not as picturesque as some of its neighbours, but it has the region's characteristic steep-pitched roofs, dormer windows and window-boxes full of geraniums. It's also the best launch pad from which to explore the northern Vosges.

A couple of things are worth seeing in town, not least the vast red sandstone **Château des Rohan** on place de Gaulle, built in a rather austere classical style by one of the Rohans who was prince-bishop at the time, and now housing the none-too-special local museum, the tourist office and youth hostel. The River Zorn and the Marne–Rhine canal both weave their way through the town, the latter framing the château's formal gardens in a graceful right-angle bend. Alongside the château, the **church of Notre-Dame-de-la-Nativité** contains another finely carved pulpit by Hans Hammer. Horticultural distraction can be found in the town's famed rose garden, **La Roseraie**, to the west of the centre by the river, which boasts over a thousand varieties, and the **botanical gardens**, 3km out of town off the N4 Metz/Nancy road.

There are several relatively easy **walks** around Saverne (the tourist office can give details), the most popular being the one to the ruined **Château du Haut-Barr** (2hr return). Follow rue du Haut-Barr southeast along the canal past the leafy suburban villas until you reach the woods, where a signboard indicates the various walks possible. Take the path marked "Haut-Barr" through woods of chestnut, beech and larch, and you'll see the castle standing dramatically on a narrow sandstone ridge with fearsome drops on both sides and views across the wooded hills and eastward over the plain towards Strasbourg. Approaching by road you'll pass an early **telegraph station**, part of the Paris–Strasbourg line dating to around 1800 (daily except Mon June–Aug 11am–5pm).

If you're driving, there are several beautiful small towns and villages within easy reach of Saverne, in particular Bouxwiller, Neuwiller, Pfaffenhoffen and Ingwiller, from where an alternative road to Bitche (see overleaf) leads through the densely wooded heart of the northern Vosges. The **Château of Lichtenburg** (April–Oct 10am–noon & 1.30–6pm, Sun 10am–7pm; closed Mon am), dating back to the thirteenth century and much restored, provides a possible focus to your explorations, just a short way outside Ingwiller.

Practicalities

The Château des Rohan on place de Gaulle contains the **tourist office** in one of its lodges (Mon–Fri 10am–noon & 2–6pm; Sat 10am–noon & 3–5pm; June–Sept Mon–Fri 9am–noon & 2–6pm; Sat, Sun & public hols May–Sept 10am–noon & 3–6pm). Opposite the **gare SNCF**, next to the *Hôtel Fischer*, the **Club Vosgien** has information on hiking.

For **accommodation** in town, there's the splendidly old-fashioned *Hôtel-Restaurant de la Marne*, 5 rue du Griffon (☎88.91.19.18; ①–②; winter closed Fri) overlooking the Marne-Rhine canal in the centre of town. And, if you have a yen for something more comfortable, there are the bright, modern rooms of the *Europe Hôtel* nearby at 7 rue de la Gare (☎88.71.12.07; ③–④). The friendly IYHF **youth hostel** (☎88.91.14.84; ①) is in the château (see above), and there's also a **campsite** about 1km from town below the castle of Haut-Barr (see above; ☎88.91.80.47; closed Oct–March).

Where **food** is concerned, gourmets will appreciate the *Taverne Katz* on the main street, 50 Grand-Rue (☎88.71.16.56; closed Tues & Wed evening; menu at 85F). Not only is it a beautiful old house, with an ornately carved front and warm, plush decor inside, but the food is excellent also: traditional Alsatian cuisine, with a very good *baekoffe* and divine sorbets. There is more good Alsatian food at *Chez Jean*, 3 rue de la Gare (☎88.91.10.19; menus 75–298F; *choucroute* and *preskopf de bœuf au Raifort*). More modest, but very satisfying and with a genuinely local ambience, there's the restaurant of the *Hôtel de la Marne* (see above; menu at 72F).

Wissembourg

WISSEMBOURG, 60km north of Strasbourg and hard against the German border, is a small town of cobbled and higgledy-piggledy prettiness, largely given over to tourism by well-paid German weekenders. The townspeople have one curious linguistic anomaly; they speak a very ancient dialect derived from Frankish, unlike their fellow Alsatians whose language is closer to modern German.

At its centre, at the end of rue Nationale, the main commercial street, stands an imposing Gothic church, the **church of St-Paul-et-St-Pierre**, with a Romanesque belfry and some fine stained glass of the twelfth and thirteenth centuries, once attached to the town's abbey. Beneath the apse, the meandering River Lauter flows under the Pont du Sel beside the town's most striking secular building and first hospital, the **Maison du Sel** (1450). A few minutes' walk away, on the northern edge of the town, another fine old building, with beautifully carved woodwork round its windows, contains the town's folk museum, the **Musée Westercamp**, 3 rue du Musée (June–Sept 10am–noon & 2–6pm; closed Tues, Sun & the morning of public hols). Along the southern edge of town, following the river bank from the Tour des Husgenossen in the western corner, a long section of the **medieval walls** survives intact, built – like the houses – in the local red sandstone.

The **tourist office** is at 9 place de la République (☎88.94.10.11; June–Sept Mon–Fri 9am–noon & 2–6pm, Sat & Sun 10am–noon & 2–5pm; Oct–April daily except Mon 9am–noon & 2–5pm). Should you want to stay, much the most attractive **hotel** is the *Hôtel du Cygne*, 3 rue du Sel, next to the town hall on the central place de la République (☎88.94.00.16; ④; closed Wed, Feb, & first fortnight in July; restaurant about 150F). Otherwise, try the *Hôtel Walck*, 2 rue de la Walck, by the hospital just outside the old town (☎88.94.06.44; ③; closed Sun pm & Mon, Jan 10–30 & June 15–30), with a very good but rather expensive restaurant, with the cheapest menu at 130F. Less expensive

---

THE POLES OF WISSEMBOURG

Stanislas Leszczynski, born in the Polish–Ukrainian city of Lemberg (now Lwóv) in 1677, lasted just five years as the elected king of Poland before being forced into exile by the Russian tzar, Peter the Great. For the next twenty-odd years he lived on a French pension in Wissembourg, along with a motley entourage of Polish ex-pats. After fifteen years of relatively humdrum existence in the town's *Ancien Hôpital* south of the main church, Stanislas' luck changed when he managed, against all odds, to get his daughter, Marie, betrothed to the fifteen-year old king of France, Louis XV. Marie was not quite so fortunate: married by proxy in Strasbourg Cathedral, and having never even set eyes on the groom, she subsequently had a total of ten children, only to be ultimately rejected by Louis, who preferred hunting and the company of his two more powerful mistresses, Madame de Pompadour and Madame du Barry. Bolstered by his daughter's marriage, Stanislas had another brief spell on the Polish throne from 1733 to 1736, but eventually gave it up in favour of the comfortable dukedom of Barr and Lorraine. He lived out his final years in true aristocratic style in the capital, Nancy, which he transformed into one of France's most beautiful towns.

but charmless, the *Hôtel de la Gare*, opposite the *gare SNCF* (☎88.94.13.67; ②), makes an adequate place to lay your head; the hotel restaurant is cheaper, too.

In addition to the hotel restaurants above there are a couple of reasonable places to **eat** on the main rue Nationale: *Aux Dominicains* at no. 36 (☎88.94.90.87; closed Mon evening & Tues; menu at 100F), and an apparently nameless place next door at no. 40 with menus at 55F and 75F – both places serve Alsatian cuisine. A much fancier establishment, with a chef who rings his own inventive changes on the traditional regional cuisine, is *À l'Ange*, 2 rue de la République (☎88.94.12.11; closed Tues evening, Wed, Feb, & first fortnight in Aug) in a beautiful old house by the stream next to place du Marché-aux-Choux. The prices reflect the excellent cooking, influenced by the proximity of Germany: the cheapest menu is the lunchtime 165F. Otherwise, you need to think in terms of twice that.

Nearby **WOERTH**, 25km southwest along the D27, has a **museum** dedicated to an important engagement in the 1870 Franco-Prussian War, reconstructed here with the aid of 4000 lead soldiers (April–Oct 2–5pm; July & Aug closes 6pm). The nearest IYHF **youth hostel** to Wissembourg is also here at 10 rue du Moulin (☎88.54.03.30; mid-March to Oct; bus from Haguenau).

Route des Châteaux

Scattered among the wooded hills to the west of Wissembourg are a host of ruined castles that once stood guard over the frontier with Germany, and the winding D3 and its smaller tributaries that cross the now untenanted frontier take you close to most of them. The ruins of the **Château du Fleckenstein** (daily 9.30am–5/6pm; 10F), 7km north of Lembach, are perhaps the most spectacular, rising above the forest on a narrow sandstone outcrop, just a stone's throw from the German border. Six kilometres further on at Obersteinbach, there's an information centre, the **Maison des Châteaux-Forts**, with displays and maps on the other castles in the area. A rather more modern fortress is the **Four à Chaux**, part of the Maginot Line, just outside Lembach (guided tours: mid-March to April at 10am, 2 & 3pm; May–June 10am, 2, 3 & 4pm; July–Sept 10 & 11am, 2, 3, 4 & 5pm; Oct to mid-Nov 10am, 2 & 3pm).

The road continues westwards through wet, sparsely populated country to the big French army camp at **BITCHE**, 32km from Lembach. It has long been a garrison town, dominated by a squat dark Vauban **fort** built atop its commanding bluff. There is nothing to keep you here, but if you need a **bed**, the *Hôtel de la Gare*, 2 av Trumeler-Faber, is the only reasonable bet (☎87.96.00.14; closed Sat, Sun & Christmas vacation; ①); its restaurant is acceptable, too. Otherwise, in the village of **LEMBACH**, try the homely and unpretentious *Hôtel An Heimbach*, 15 rue de Wissembourg, a very agreeable base for exploring them (☎88.94.43.46; ②–④), a prospect made all the more enticing, if you're feeling prosperous, by the presence directly opposite of the exquisite cuisine of the *Auberge du Cheval Blanc* (☎88.94.41.86; closed Mon, Tues, Feb 7–25 & July 4–22; 165F upwards). There are buses as far as Lembach (twice daily Mon–Sat), 15km from Wissembourg, but after that you'll need your own transport.

The southern Vosges

The **southern Vosges** cover a much greater area than the northern range, stretching as far south as Belfort in Franche-Comté. The major tourist attractions are along the **Route du Vin**, which follows the foot of the mountains along the western edge of the wide flat valley of the Rhine, where every turn in the road reveals yet another exquisitely preserved medieval village – many of them packed out with visitors. **Colmar**, the main centre for the *route*, also suffers from an overdose of visitors. If you want to escape from the crowds, you'll need to head for the hills proper, along the **Route des Crêtes** that traces the central ridge of the Vosges to the west.

The Route du Vin

Alsace is a region both blessed and cursed by tourism and no more so than along the so-called **Route du Vin**, which stretches from Marlenheim, west of Strasbourg, to Thann, near Mulhouse. The problem with Alsace is that, left to its own devices, it stays on the right side of Disneyland but, under the impact of tourism and the desire to make money, it comes close to caricaturing itself.

Set against the "blue line of the Vosges", the *route* winds north–south through the endless terraced vineyards which produce the region's famous fruity white wines. Opportunities for tasting the local produce are plentiful, with free *dégustations* along the roadside, in the *caveaux* of most villages, and at the region's countless wine festivals. You can take a closer look at the vines themselves courtesy of the region's tourist offices, or independently via the various *sentiers vinicoles* (vineyard paths). In the midst of this sea of vines are dozens of flowery and typically picturesque Alsatian villages, dominated from the heights above by an extraordinary number of ancient ruined castles, testimony to the province's turbulent past.

The *Route du Vin* is deceptively hilly work on a bike, but it's definitely easier to get around with your own transport. Otherwise you're dependent either on the train, which narrowly misses some of the best villages, or the region's more or less non-existent bus services.

Obernai and around

If you're heading south, the vineyards may begin at Marlenheim, but picturesque little **OBERNAI**, on the D422, is the first place most people head for on the *route*. Miraculously unscathed during the last two world wars, it has retained almost its entire **rampart system**, including no fewer than fifteen towers, as well as street after street of carefully maintained medieval houses. Not surprisingly, it also gets more than its fair share of visitors, though this shouldn't put you off coming here. The town is just about big enough to absorb the crowds. If you're thinking of **staying** the night, the only reasonably priced **hotels** are the *Maison du Vin*, 1 rue de la Paille (☎88.95.46.82; ②), whose pretty rooms are above a wine shop, and *La Diligence*, 23 pl de la Mairie (☎88.95.55.69; ③).

ROSHEIM, 7km north of Obernai and up in the hills a little to the west of the D422, is relatively off the beaten track for this busy region. Its two main sights are the Romanesque **church of St-Pierre-et-St-Paul**, whose roof is peppered with comical sculptured figures contemporary with the building, and the twelfth-century **Heidenhüs**, thought to be the oldest building in Alsace. The simple, clean, friendly, family-run *Hôtel Alpina*, 39 rue du Lion (☎88.50.49.30; ②), with an attractive terrace and breakfast room, makes a very nice place to stay. **ROSENWILLER**, a couple of kilometres up the hill among the vineyards, has a prettily sited and atmospherically overgrown **Jewish cemetery** at the edge of the woods, testimony to Alsace's once numerous Jewish community.

From Rosheim's *gare SNCF*, 1.5km northeast of the village, a steam train runs up the valley on Sundays and holidays to **OTTROTT**, which produces one of the few red wines of Alsace. An elegantly restored and modernized village house at 11 rue des Châteaux has been transformed into a rather luxurious **hotel**, the *Hostellerie des Châteaux*, with sauna and swimming pool (☎88.95.81.54; ⑤–⑥). Rather than **eat** in its overpriced restaurant, it is better to go, for a really good meal, to *Beau Site* in place de l'Église (☎88.95.80.61; ④; closed Sun evening & Mon; good-value menu at 160F), specializing in the cuisine of the south, but serving local dishes as well.

Ottrott brings you within hiking distance – 6km – of **Mont Ste-Odile** (763m), whose summit is surrounded by a mysterious Celtic wall, originally built in the seventh century BC. It is almost 10km in length and in parts reaches a height of 3.5m. Saint Odilia herself is buried in the small **chapel** on top of the hill, a pilgrimage site to this day. According to tradition, having been cast out by her father at birth on account of her blindness, she miraculously regained her sight during childhood and returned to found the convent on Mont Ste-Odile, where she is said to have cured thousands of blindness and leprosy.

Barr

For some unknown reason **BARR**, west of the main road, is bypassed by many of the coach groups. Every bit as charming as Obernai, it's easy to while away a couple of hours wandering its twisting cobbled streets, at their busiest during the mid-July wine festival and on Sundays when the vintners come to ply their wines. The town has just one specific sight, **La Folie Marco** (daily except Tues July–Sept 10am–noon & 2–6pm; June & Oct Sat & Sun 10am–noon & 2–6pm), an unusually large eighteenth-century house on the outskirts of the town along the road to Obernai, with displays of period French and Alsatian furniture. There are regular *dégustations* in the garden cellar, and a festival of dance and waltz at the end of May.

The nicest place to **stay** in Barr is the *Hôtel Le Manoir*, 11 rue St-Marc (☎88.08.03.40; ④), an attractive residence on the edge of town, whose light and spacious rooms make gracious bedrooms. Alternatively, there's a **campsite** in St-Pierre, 3km south of Barr. The **gare SNCF** is 1km east of town in the neighbouring village of Gertwiller.

Le Struthof concentration camp

Deep in the forests and hills of the Vosges, over 20km west of Barr, **Le Struthof-Natzwiller** (daily April–Aug 8am–noon & 2–6.30pm; Sept–Dec 24 & March 9am–noon & 2–5pm; closed Dec 25–Feb; 10F) was the only Nazi concentration camp to be built on French soil (though at the time, of course, it was part of the Greater German Reich). Like the picture-postcard villages along the *route*, the site is almost perversely beautiful, its stepped terraces cut into the steep hillside, giving fantastic views across the Bruche valley. Set up shortly after Hitler's occupation of Alsace-Lorraine in 1940, it is thought that over 10,000 people died here. When the Allies liberated the camp on November 23, 1944, they found it empty – the remaining prisoners having already been transported to Dachau.

The barbed wire and watchtowers are as they were, though only two of the prisoners' barracks remain, one of which is now a **museum** on the deportations. Captions are in French only, but the pictures alone tell the story. An arson attack by neo-Nazis in 1976 only served to underline the need for such displays. At the foot of the camp is the crematorium with its ovens still intact; a couple of kilometres down the road to the west, towards Schirmeck, the Germans built a gas chamber – proof that Le Struthof was a fully integrated part of the Nazi killing machine. Alongside the gas chamber, in extraordinarily bad taste, is a tourist restaurant. To the east, the two main granite quarries worked by the internees still survive, clearly signposted from the main road.

Sélestat

Back on the *Route du Vin*, **SÉLESTAT**, midway between Strasbourg and Colmar, is a delightful old town, positively cosmopolitan compared with the wine route's villages, and a good base for exploring the central and most popular section of the *route*. The choice of reasonable accommodation is better than average, and the town itself contains a couple of interesting churches and a great museum for bibliophiles.

The oldest and finest of the two churches is the **church of Ste-Foy**. Built by the monks of Conques and much restored since, its clean, austerely Romanesque lines have not been entirely wiped out. Close by to the north, the much larger Gothic **church of St-Georges** sports spectacularly multicoloured roof tiles and some very fine stained glass. For a brief period in the late fifteenth and early sixteenth centuries, Sélestat was the intellectual centre of Alsace, due mainly to its Latin School, which attracted a group of Humanists led by Beatus Rhenanus, whose personal library was one of the most impressive collections of its time. At the **Bibliothèque Humaniste** (9am–noon & 2–6pm; closed Sat pm & Sun; July & Aug also Sat & Sun 2–5pm; 10F), housed in the town's former corn exchange just by St-Georges, Rhenanus' collection is now on display along with some unusual and very rare books and manuscripts from as far back as the seventh century.

Sélestat is comparatively well served transport-wise, with frequent train connections to Strasbourg and Colmar, as well as a branch line which heads north to Strasbourg via Molsheim; the **gare SNCF** is west of the town centre down av de la Liberté. For a place to **stay**, there's none better than the comfortable, friendly *Auberge des Alliés*, 39 rue des Chevaliers, in the middle of town (☎88.92.09.34; ③–④; closed Sun & Mon, Jan 15–30 & June 27–July 10). It includes a good-value restaurant (menus from 98F), which is worth a look in its own right for the splendid tiled stove that stands in the middle. For an unashamedly modern alternative try the *Vaillant* on place de la République (☎88.92.09.46; ③). There's also a **campsite** south of the centre behind Vauban's remaining ramparts. For further information, the **tourist office** is by the ring road on bd du Général-Leclerc (☎88.92.02.66).

Castles around Sélestat

Within easy range of Sélestat are a whole host of **ruined castles**. Seven kilometres north, and accessible by train, the village of **DAMBACH-LA-VILLE**, with its walls and three fortified gates all intact, is one of the highlights of the *route*, and has a cheap **campsite** (June to mid-Sept), 1km east, on the D210 as well as a small but most attractive and inexpensive hotel, *Hôtel à la Couronne*, 13 pl du Marché (☎88.92.40.85; ①–②; closed Thurs, Feb 10–March 1 & mid-Nov to Dec 5). A thirty-minute climb west of the village is the formidable **castle of Bernstein**. In the Middle Ages, Alsace was culturally more German than French and this is a typically German mountain keep, tall and narrow, with few openings and little use for everyday living. Around it are residential buildings, enclosed within an outer wall, the masonry cut into protruding knobs, which gives it a curious pimpled texture.

From **SCHERWILLER**, another attractive village just 3km to the northwest of Sélestat, you can reach the **castle of Ortenbourg** via a steep marked path. Like Bernstein, it has a lofty refuge-tower with courtyards outside, in a very good state of preservation, protected by a rock-cut ditch. A few hundred metres to the southwest of here, **Ramstein castle** was originally built in 1293 to protect the besiegers of Ortenbourg.

The best cluster of castles, however, is southwest of Sélestat. Four kilometres away, **KINTZHEIM** boasts a small but luxurious ruined castle built around a cylindrical refuge-tower. Today it's an aviary, the **Volerie des Aigles**, for birds of prey, with magnificent displays of aerial prowess by eagles and vultures (demonstrations: April, May, Sept daily at 3 & 4pm, Sun & hols 3, 4 and 5pm; June to mid-July daily at 3, 4 & 5pm; mid-July to Aug daily at 2.30, 3.30, 4.30 & 5.30pm; Oct–Nov 11 Wed, Sat & Sun at 3 & 4pm). If you have a yen to watch Barbary apes at play in the Vosgian jungle, you can do just that a couple of kilometres further west at the **Montagne des Singes** (daily April to mid-Oct 10am–noon & 1.30–6pm; mid-Oct to mid-Nov Wed, Sat & Sun only, same hours; 22F).

Another 5km on, the ruins of **Oudenbourg castle**, its sizeable hall preserved among the trees, is dwarfed by the massive **Haut-Koenigsbourg** (daily 9am–noon & 1–4/5/6pm; no lunchtime closure June–Sept; closed Jan 5 to Feb 5; 31F), one of the biggest, most popular castles in Alsace, and – astride its 757-metre bluff – by far the highest. Ruined after an assault in 1633, it was heavily restored in the early years of this century for Kaiser Wilhelm II. It's easy to criticize some of the detail of the restoration, but it's an enjoyable experience and a remarkably convincing re-creation of a castle-palace of the age of Dürer. There are guided tours, but it's best on your own. The views all around are fantastic. There's a winding road down to Bergheim (see below) from here, if you'd rather not retrace your tracks to Sélestat.

Around Ribeauvillé

RIBEAUVILLÉ is the largest town between Sélestat and Colmar – not as pretty as some of its immediate neighbours, but right at the foot of the mountains and well placed for exploring the many castles and villages which surround it. There is **camping** at the *Camping des Trois Châteaux* to the north of town, or the much plusher *Pierre-de-Courbertin* site to the south (closed Feb to mid-March), plus the rather fancy little *Hôtel de la Tour*, 1 rue de la Mairie, in a converted winery (☎89.73.72.73; ④; closed Jan 6–March 19), with Turkish bath and *winstub*. For an alternative to eating at the *winstub*, try the *Brasserie de la Poste* on place de l'Armée (100F or less). For a bed you might also consider Monsieur Bruppacher's *chambre d'hôte* at 28 rue Jean-Macé in the middle of the village of Beblenheim, half a dozen kilometres on towards Colmar (☎89.47.88.33; just over 200F for two). In the vicinity of Ribeauvillé is a threesome of fortresses built by the counts of Ribeaupierre: **St-Ulrich castle**, an hour's haul up a marked path; just north of it the smaller **Girsberg castle**, balanced on a pinnacle which somehow provides room for a bailey, two towers and other buildings; and, further on, the ruins of **Haut-Ribeaupierre**.

BERGHEIM, 3.5km northeast of Ribeauvillé, retains a good part of its old fortifications, with three towers still surviving; and despite being one of the most beautiful Alsatian villages, it rarely attracts the attentions of the tour groups. Also within easy walking range of Ribeauvillé, this time to the south, the village of **HUNAWIHR** is another beguiling hamlet, with a fourteenth-century walled **church** standing out amid the green vines. Hunawihr is at the forefront of the Alsatian ecological movement aimed at reintroducing the stork – the *cigogne* – to the region, and there's a **reserve** to the east of the village.

Lastly, getting closer to the hub of Colmar, there are a couple of tourist targets you may want to avoid, or at least for which you might be advised to time your visits carefully. A couple of kilometres south of Hunawihr, the walled village of **RIQUEWIHR** is exceptionally well preserved with plenty of medieval houses and a château containing a **postal museum**, and consequently suffers more visitors per annum than any other village along the *route*. **KAYSERBERG**, still further to the southwest, also plays host to more than its fair share of tour buses. It boasts a fortified **bridge** and a handsome sixteenth-century wooden altarpiece in the main **church**. But the town's principal renown is as the birthplace of Nobel Peace Prize winner Albert Schweitzer, who spent most of his extremely active, and not always peaceful, life at the leprosy hospital he founded at Lambaréné in French Equatorial Africa, now Gabon. During World War I, he was interned by the French authorities as an "enemy alien", but nowadays he is suitably honoured with a **museum** dedicated to him at 124 rue de-Gaulle.

Two kilometres away in the village of **KIENTZHEIM** there is a very comfortable hotel – not for the budget-conscious – which would make a good base for visiting Colmar, only 10km distant, while avoiding the hassle of being in the town: *Hostellerie de l'Abbaye de l'Alspach*, 2–4 rue Foch (☎89.47.16.00; ④).

Colmar

COLMAR, a fifty-minute train ride south of Strasbourg, has sprawled unattractively on both sides of the train tracks, but the old centre remains typically and whimsically Alsatian, with crooked houses, half-timbered and painted, on crooked lanes – all extremely pretty and very touristy. Colmar's attractions don't stop at its buildings; it is also the proud possessor of one of the last and most extraordinary of all Gothic paintings – the altarpiece for St Anthony's monastery at Issenheim, painted by Mathias Grünewald.

Arrival and accommodation

The **tourist office** on place d'Unterlinden (May–Oct Mon–Fri 9am–6/7pm; Sat 9am–5pm, Sun & hols 10am–1pm & 2–4pm; mid-Nov to April Mon–Fri 9am–noon & 2–6pm, Sat 9am–1pm & 2–5pm, Sun & 10am–noon; ☎89.41.02.29), by the Musée d'Unterlinden, sells *Club Vosgien* hiking maps and a booklet of day walks in the hills behind the town. They'll also give you details of the **buses** to the towns and villages of the *Route du Vin*, which leave from outside the **gare SNCF** on rue de la République, where it's also possible to rent **bikes**.

Accommodation is not as overpriced as you might expect, with a number of reasonable hotels on av de la République, past place Rapp to rue Kléber and the Musée d'Unterlinden. Try *La Chaumière*, at no. 74 (☎89.41.08.99; ②), or the quiet and comfortable *Colbert* at no. 2 (☎89.41.31.05; ③) in the parallel rue des Trois-Épis, continuation of rue de la Gare, which also begins at the station. For more luxurious sleeping, there's the old *Hôtel Bristol*, a relic of the grand old prewar days of tourism, now refurbished as *Terminus-Bristol*, 7 pl de la Gare, directly opposite the station exit (☎89.41.10.10; ⑤–⑥). There are also two **hostels**: the IYHF youth hostel is at 2 rue Pasteur (☎89.80.57.39; ①; curfew midnight), reached by bus #4 from the station or Unterlinden, stop *Lycée Technique* – off the route d'Ingersheim or N415 going west. Alternatively, there's the *Maison des Jeunes*, 17 rue Camille-Schlumberger (☎89.41.26.87; curfew 11pm; ①), two streets over from av de la République, about ten minutes' walk and much nearer to the town centre. The nearest **campsite** is on the east side of town along the N415 Neuf Brisach road (☎89.41.15.94; closed Dec & Jan); take bus #1 from the station, direction *Wihr* to the Port-du-Canal stop.

The Town

From the *gare SNCF*, the **Musée d'Unterlinden** (daily April–Oct 9am–6pm; daily except Tues Nov–March 9am–noon & 2–5pm; 28F) is a ten-minute walk down av de la République, housed in a former Dominican convent. Its *pièce de résistance*, the **Issenheim altarpiece**, although displayed in an exploded format, was designed to make a single piece. On the front was the Crucifixion, almost luridly expressive: a tortured Christ with stretched rib-cage and outsize hands turned upwards, fingers splayed in pain, flanked by his pale, fainting mother, St John and Mary Magdalene. Then it unfolded, relative to its function on feast days, Sundays and weekdays, to reveal an Annunciation, Resurrection, Virgin and Child, and finally a sculpted panel depicting saints Anthony, Augustine and Jerome. Completed in 1515, the painting is affected by Renaissance innovations in light and perspective while still rooted in the medieval spirit, with an intense mysticism and shifts of mood in its subject matter. Other works in the museum are, inevitably, secondary, but there's a surprisingly interesting collection of modern paintings in the basement, including works by Picasso, Léger and Vasarely.

A short walk into the old town, the **Dominican church** on rue des Serruriers has some fine glass and, above all, a radiantly beautiful altarpiece, known as *The Virgin in a Bower of Roses* (mid-March to mid-Nov daily 10am–6pm; 5F), painted in 1473 by Martin Schongauer, who is also represented in the Musée d'Unterlinden. At the other end of rue des Serruriers you come to the **Collégiale St-Martin** on a café-lined square. Known locally as "the cathedral", it's also worth a quick peek for its stonework and stained glass. On the south side of the church is the sixteenth-century **Maison Pfister** with painted panels and, on the opposite side of the street, the birthplace of Frédéric Auguste Bartholdi, the nineteenth-century sculptor responsible for New York's Statue of Liberty. Now the **Musée Bartholdi** (March–Dec daily except Tues 10am–noon & 2–6pm; 10F), it contains Bartholdi's personal effects, plus the original designs for the statue, along with sundry Colmarabilia.

Rue des Marchands continues south to the *Ancienne Douane* or **Koïfhus**, its gaily painted roof tiles loudly proclaiming the city's medieval prosperity. This is the heart of Colmar's old town, a short step away from the archly picturesque quarter down the Grande-Rue, cut through by the River Lauch and known as **La Petite Venise**. The dolly-mixture colours of the old fishing cottages on quai de la Poissonnerie are more touristy even than Strasbourg's Petite France. Twice as tall, but similarly over-restored, are the black-and-white half-timbered tanners' houses on **quai des Tanneurs**, which leads off from the Koïfhus, with open verandahs on the top floor originally designed for drying hides.

Eating and drinking

Restaurants in Colmar are generally overpriced, particularly Alsatian ones. For a quick and easy meal there's a *Flunch* cafeteria at 8 av de la République. A fun establishment for both food and atmosphere is *S'Parisser Stewwele*, 4 pl Jeanne-d'Arc (☎89.41.42.33; closed Tues, Nov 20–Dec 2 & June 20–30; around 60–70F the main course or 160F-plus *à la carte*). Other nice places to try are *Les Tanneurs*, 12 rue des Tanneurs (☎89.23.72.12; closed Wed & Thurs lunchtime, mid-Dec to mid-Jan; local specialities; menu at 89F), and *Le Petit Bouchon*, 11 rue Alspach (☎89.23.45.57; menu at 80F). Otherwise, you could amass a sumptuous picnic from the town's numerous *pâtisseries* and *charcuteries* like *CCA* on the corner of place Unterlinden. There's a fruit and veg **market** every Thursday around the Koïfhus, and every Saturday on place St-Joseph.

Munster and the Route des Crêtes

MUNSTER owes its existence and its name to a band of Irish monks who founded a monastery here in the seventh century, some 19km west of Colmar up the narrowing valley of the River Fecht, overlooked by Le Petit Ballon (1267m) and Le Hohneck (1362m), among the highest peaks of the Vosges. Its name in the world today is particularly associated with a rich, creamy and exceedingly smelly cheese, the crowning glory of many an Alsatian meal. Although of no special interest in itself, the town makes a peaceful and verdant base either for exploring further into the mountain range or for visiting Colmar and other places along the Route du Vin.

It is accessible by **train** from Colmar (*gare SNCF* ☎89.77.34.17). The **tourist office** is in place du Marché (Mon–Fri 9.30am–12.30pm & 2–6pm, Sat 10am–noon & 2–4pm; July–Aug Mon–Sat 9.30am–12.30pm & 2–7pm, Sun 9.30am–12.30pm; June & Sept 9am–noon & 2–6pm, Fri & Sat 9.30am–12.30pm & 2–7pm, Sun 10am–noon).

If you want to **stay**, the large, modern *Hôtel Verte-Vallée*, 10 rue Alfred-Hartmann (☎89.77.15.15; ④), in the depths of the wooded valley, with its squeaky-clean and pastel atmosphere, makes a perfect haven for a day or two. It has a good restaurant specializing in traditional French dishes, with a terrace overlooking the stream (a menu at 78F; *carte* 180F or more). Less well appointed but blessed with stupendous views are two hotels perched high on the north side of the valley in the hamlet of Hohrodberg: *Hôtel Panorama*, 3 rte de Linge (☎89.77.36.53; ③–④) and, with rather awful decor, *Hôtel Roess* (☎89.77.36.00; ③), 100m higher up. Both have restaurants.

Route des Crêtes

Above Munster the main road to Gérardmer crosses the mountains by the principal pass, the **Col de la Schlucht**, where it intersects the so-called **Route des Crêtes**. Built for strategic purposes during World War I, it's a spectacular trail traversing thick forest and open pasture where the herds of cows which produce the Munster cheese graze in

---

HIKING IN THE SOUTHERN VOSGES

There is no shortage of waymarked paths in the **southern Vosges**. Six **GRs** – *Sentiers de Grande Randonnée* or long-distance footpaths – cross the Vosges.

GR7: Ballon d'Alsace to Remiremont.
GR53: Wissembourg to Belfort (part of the route coincides with GR5).
GR59: Ballon d'Alsace to Besançon.
GR531: Wissembourg to the Ballon d'Alsace.
GR532: Soultz-sous-Forêts to Belfort.
GR533: Sarrebourg to Belfort, along the west flank of the Vosges.

There are five treks of between five and eleven days' duration described in *Les Grandes Traversées des Vosges*, published by the *Office Départemental du Tourisme du Bas-Rhin*, 9 rue du Dôme, 67000 Strasbourg (☎88.22.01.02), with details of accommodation, access and so on. They are structured to show different aspects of the Vosges in landscapes, history and traditional culture.

Organized walks, involving guides or luggage transport or both, are arranged by various companies and tourist offices. The Munster *SI*, for instance, place du Marché (☎89.77.31.80), organizes walks from half a day to six days in length (1900F for the latter, including guide, meals and accommodation), as does the *SI* in Ste-Marie-aux-Mines, place du Prensureux (☎89.58.80.50). *Horizons d'Alsace*, 20 rue de Gaulle in Orbey (☎89.71.36.16), and *Tourhotels Alsace*, La Claquette in Rothau (☎88.97.01.95), carry your bags for you.

---

summer and which in winter becomes one long cross-country ski route. Starting in **CERNAY**, 15km west of Mulhouse, it follows the main ridge of the Vosges, including the highest peak of the range, the **Grand Ballon** (1424m), north as far as **STE-MARIE-AUX-MINES**, 20km west of Sélestat, once at the heart of a silver-mining district. From Munster it is also accessible by a twisting minor road through Hohrodberg (see above), which takes you past the beautiful glacial lakes, the **Lac Blanc** and the **Lac Noir**, as well as the eerie World War I **battlefield of Linge**, where the still clearly visible French and German trenches were separated by, literally, a few feet.

Mulhouse and around

Thirty-five kilometres south of Colmar, **MULHOUSE** is a large sprawling industrial city, popularly dubbed by the British the "French Manchester". It was Swiss until 1798 when, at the peak of its prosperity, based on printed cotton fabrics and allied trades, it voted to become part of France. Its only other minor claim to fame is as the hometown of Alfred Dreyfus, the unfortunate Jewish army officer who was wrongly convicted of espionage in 1894 (see *Contexts*, p.973). Not having much of an old town, it is no city for strollers, but it does have four or five unusually good – and rather unusual – museums in the town and its vicinity, delving into the region's manufactuiring past. Wallpaper, firemen, railway, automobiles, fabrics are all given their platform.

Closest to the *gare SNCF*, just along the canal to the right, is the excellent **Musée de l'Impression sur Étoffes**, 3 rue des Bonnes-Gens (June–Sept daily 10am–noon & 2–6pm; winter daily except Tues 10am–noon & 2–6pm; 30F, combined ticket with Musée du Papier-Peint below 45F). It contains a vast collection of the most beautiful fabrics imaginable – eighteenth-century Indian and Persian imports which revolutionized the European ready-to-wear market in their time; silks from Turkestan; batiks from Java, Senegalese materials, some superb kimonos from Japan, and a unique display of scarves from France, Britain and the US.

Again out of the centre of Mulhouse, near the northwestern suburb of **DORNACH**, in the direction of the A36 autoroute, is the rail museum, **Musée Français du Chemin de Fer**, 2 rue Alfred-de-Glehn (daily except Mon April–Sept 9am–6pm; Oct–March 9am–5pm, open Mon during school & public hols; bus #17, stop *Porte-Jeune Place*; 40). Rolling stock on display includes Napoléon III's ADCs' drawing-room, decorated by Viollet-le-Duc in 1856, and a luxuriously appointed 1926 diner from the *Golden Arrow*. There are cranes, stations, signals and related artefacts, but the stars of the show are the big locomotive engines with their brightly painted boilers, gleaming wheels and pistons, and tangles of brass and copper piping. Cold steel they may be, but you could be forgiven for thinking they had life in them – real works of craft. In the same complex is the **Musée du Sapeurs-Pompiers** (times as above), its antique fire engines and other memorabilia the personal collection of a retired local firefighter. These museums have now been joined by a third: **Electropolis – Musée de l'Energie Électrique**, 55 rue du Pâturage (daily except Mon 10am–6pm; closed Dec 25–26 & Jan 1), devoted to the production and uses of electricity.

A couple of kilometres north of the city centre, in the **Musée National de l'Automobile**, 192 av de Colmar (daily 10am–6pm; Oct–April closed Tues; bus #1, #4 or #17, stop *Porte-Jeune Schuman* or *Porte-Jeune Place*; 54F), are over six hundred cars, originally the private collection of local business sharks, the Schlumpf brothers. The vehicles range from the industry's earliest attempts, like the extraordinary wooden-wheeled Jacquot steam "car" of 1878, to 1968 Porsche racing vehicles and contemporary factory prototypes. The largest group is that of locally made Bugatti models: dozens of glorious racing cars, coupés and limousines, the pride of them the two Bugatti Royales, out of only seven that were constructed – one of them Ettore Bugatti's own, with bodywork designed by his son.

Practicalities

Place de la Réunion, nominally the centre of town, is five minutes' walk north of the **gare SNCF** (☎89.46.50.50). The Mon–Fri 9.30am–12.30pm & 2–6pm, Sat 10am–noon & 2–4pm is on the way at 9 av Foch (Mon–Sat 9am–7pm; July–Sept Mon–Sat 9am–8pm, Sun 10am–1pm). Reasonably priced **accommodation** is not easy to find in Mulhouse, but the following are affordable: the rather inconveniently located *Paon d'Or*, 13 av de Colmar (☎89.45.34.41; ①–②); the central *Hôtel de Paris*, 5 passage de l'Hôtel-de-Ville (☎89.45.21.41; ②); and the *Hôtel Schoenberg*, 14 rue Schoenberg, behind the station (☎89.45.19.41; ②). If these are full, the IYHF **youth hostel**, 37 rue de l'Illberg (☎89.42.63.28; ①; bus #1 or #2, stop *Salle des Sports*), is about your best bet, with facilities for camping. There is also a pleasant **campsite** on rue Pierre-de-Coubertin, near the suburb of Dornach, 4km from the city centre on the banks of the Ill (☎89.06.20.66, closed Oct–March).

As at Colmar and Strasbourg, Mulhouse's Alsatian **restaurants** are none too cheap. The *Auberge du Vieux Mulhouse*, right on the main square, place de la Réunion (closed Sun evening; ☎89.45.84.18; menus 53–140F), is one of the few exceptions. The *Winstub Henriette*, 9 rue Henriette (☎89.46.27.83; closed Sat lunchtime & Sun; lunchtime menu at 55F, in the evening around 90–100F for main courses), although not cheap, is a lively and well-frequented establishment specializing in Alsatian cuisine. The *Crêperie Crampous Mad*, 14 rue des Tondeurs (closed Sun), is a good standby (50–100F). Alternatively, you can drown your sorrows at *Gambrinus*, 5 rue des Franciscains, north of place de la Réunion, which boasts over thirty beers on tap and a bit of simple food to wash them down with (45–140F).

In the first week of September, Mulhouse hosts the region's hottest **jazz festival**; to find out what's going on at other times of the year, get hold of a copy of *Mulhouse Poche*, the free listings quarterly.

Rixheim and Pulversheim

In the village of **RIXHEIM**, 6km east of Mulhouse, the **Musée du Papier-Peint**, 28 rue Zuber (June–Sept daily 10am–noon & 2–6pm; winter daily except Tues 10am–noon & 2–6pm; 30F, combined ticket with Musée de l'Impression sur Étoffes above 45F; train to Rixheim or bus #10, stop *Centre Europe*), a subsidiary of the printed fabrics museum, is housed in the former headquarters of the Teutonic Knights. A museum of wallpaper may not be everyone's idea of a fun afternoon out, but this contains a stunning cornucopia of antique painted wallpaper, and there are demonstrations of printing the stuff.

Just past **PULVERSHEIM**, ten kilometres northwest off the D430, Mulhouse attempts to confront environmental issues in the **Écomusée de Haut-Alsace** (daily July–Aug 9am–7pm; June & Sept 9am–6pm; April, May & Oct 10am–6pm; Nov–March 11am–5pm; regional bus, direction *Geubwiller*; April–Nov 65F, Dec–March cheaper). "Eco" may be a somewhat misleading prefix for this open-air museum, but it's certainly plenty of fun for adults and kids, with over fifty traditional Alsatian buildings spanning the centuries, as well as on-site craft workers doing their various things. It's a vast complex already, and there are plans to enlarge it further, to incorporate the nearby potassium mine which recently ceased production.

FRANCHE-COMTÉ
AND THE JURA MOUNTAINS

The **Jura mountains** – gentle in the west, precipitous in the east, with wide, high forested plateaux in between – cover most of the old county of **Franche-Comté**, once part of the realms of the Grand Dukes of Burgundy, but properly French only since the late 1600s. With the exception of the city of **Besançon**, what there is to see is countryside – hundreds of square miles of woodland, lake and pasture that is hard to get around without a car, and is best explored on foot or by bicycle. There are several **GR footpaths** in the area, including the marathon GR5 from the Netherlands to the Med, and the GR9, which snakes its way through the *Parc Régional du Haut-Jura*.

CROSS-COUNTRY SKIING & MOUNTAIN BIKING IN THE JURA

The nature of the Jura's terrain – high plateaux guaranteeing winter snow but without excessively steep gradients – has made it France's most popular **cross-country skiing** destination. Known as *ski du fond*, the goal of any superfit *fondeur* is the 210km *Grande Traversée du Jura (GTJ)*, which roughly follows the long-distance GR5 footpath across the high plateau from Villiers-le-Lac to Hauteville-Lompnes.

The same gentle topography and established infrastructure which enable cross-country skiing has made this region an ideal high-summer venue for **mountain biking**, currently enjoying an upsurge in popularity in the eastern Jura, with hundreds of waymarked cross-country skiing pistes used in season doubling as trails for adventuresome mountain bikers. The 300km **GTJ-VTT**, starting near Montbéliard, has become the greatest long-distance challenge in the area.

The headquarters of the regional tourist board, the **Comité Departmental du Tourisme**, BP 652, 39021, Lons-le-Saunier (☎84.85.89.82), can supply plenty of information, maps and literature – some in English – on outdoor leisure opportunities of all kinds in the Jura.

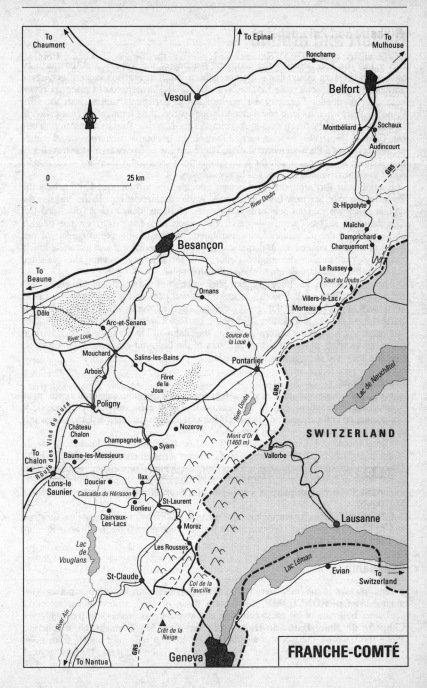

To Chaumont
To Epinal
To Mulhouse
Ronchamp
Belfort
Vesoul
Montbéliard
Sochaux
Audincourt
GR5
0   25 km
River Doubs
St-Hippolyte
Maîche
Damprichard
Charquemont
Besançon
Le Russey
Saut du Doubs
Ornans
Villers-le-Lac
To Beaune
Morteau
Dôle
Arc-et-Senans
Source de la Loue
River Loue
Mouchard
Salins-les-Bains
Pontarlier
Lac de Neuchâtel
Arbois
Fôret de la Joux
Poligny
Route des Vins du Jura
Nozeroy
River Doubs
SWITZERLAND
Château Chalon
Champagnole
Syam
Mont d'Or (1460 m)
Vallorbe
To Chalon
Baume-les-Messieurs
Lons-le-Saunier
Doucier
Ilax
Cascades du Hérisson
St-Laurent
Lausanne
Bonlieu
Clairvaux-Les-Lacs
Morez
Lac de Vouglans
Les Rousses
Lac Léman
St-Claude
Evian
To Switzerland
River Ain
Col de la Faucille
GR5
Crêt de la Neige
To Nantua
Geneva

FRANCHE-COMTÉ

Belfort and around

Nestled in the gap between the southern reaches of the Vosges and the northern outliers of the Jura mountains – the one natural chink in France's eastern geological armour and the obvious route for invaders – **BELFORT** is assured of a place in French hearts for its deeds of military daring. Its name is particularly linked with the 1870 Prussian War, when its long resistance to siege spared it the humiliating annexation to Germany suffered by much of neighbouring Alsace-Lorraine. And its commanding officer, Colonel Denfert-Rochereau, earned himself the honour of numerous street names as well as that of a Parisian métro station. There are few real reasons for the traveller to give it much attention, though the train connections are good. Otherwise, it's a nondescript town, surrounded by zones of heavy industry.

Finding your way around Belfort is easy enough. The town is sliced into two by the River Savoureuse: the **new town** to the west is the commercial hub; to the east lies the quieter **old town**, laid out below the massive red **château** (daily except Tues April–Oct 8/10am–noon & 2–5/7pm; Nov–March 8am–noon & 2–6pm; 10F) on the heights above, built by the ubiquitous fortress-architect Vauban on the site of an earlier fort, and now housing collections of paintings, as well as archeological and historical knick-knackery. Vauban also surrounded Belfort with fortifications, creating the five-sided old town that is still largely unchanged in its street-plan.

The most famous and photographed phenomenon in town is the eleven-metre-high red sandstone **lion** applied to the rockface that you pass on the way up to the castle, fashioned in 1875–80 by the great sculptor of the overblown, Frédéric Auguste Bartholdi, to commemorate the 1870 siege. Bartholdi went on to make his mark by immortalizing his mother's stern visage on the Statue of Liberty in New York Harbor. From the **viewing platform** at the front paw of the lion, you get some stunning views over the town and surrounding countryside.

Practicalities

The **gare routière** and **gare SNCF** are at the end of Faubourg-de-France, the main pedestrianized shopping drag in the new town. The **tourist office** is on place de la Commune, just off Faubourg-de-France (Mon–Sat 9.30am–12.15pm & 1.45–6/7pm July & Aug Mon–Sat 10am–7pm, Sun 9am–noon).

There shouldn't be any problems with finding a **room**: try the *Vauban*, 4 rue du Magasin (☎84.21.59.37; ③), or the *Hôtel du Centre*, across the street (☎84.28.67.80; ②). There's no official **youth hostel**, but the *Foyer des Jeunes Travailleurs*, west of the rail line at 6 rue de Madrid (☎84.21.39.16; ①), does the same job, though it gives priority to under-25s. Belfort's **campsite** is just before the *foyer*, in the Parc des Loisirs (closed Nov–April).

Inexpensive places to **eat** include the pizzeria, *L'Ancêtre*, 4 Faubourg-des-Ancêtres, and *Le Cèdre*, a Lebanese restaurant (not bad for vegetarians) on the Grande-Rue not far from Vauban's stronghold.

Ronchamp

Before you take to the hills, there is one day trip from Belfort worth undertaking – the mining town of **RONCHAMP**, 20km west (train or bus), where the architect Le Corbusier built one of his most enduring and atypical masterpieces in the 1950s, the **Chapelle de Notre-Dame-du-Haut** (daily 9am–7pm; 5F). It stands, all in concrete, above the town on the top of a wooded hill, white and reflective, visible from miles away, with its aerodynamic tower and wave-curved roof cutting into the sky beyond.

Inside, the rough-textured walls are pierced with unequal embrasures, several closed by patterns of primary glass, whose reds, blues and yellows stain the dipping floor. Simplicity itself, with pared-down crucifix and steel altar rail; it's highly atmospheric.

If it's getting late and you're worried about a place to **stay**, there are rooms at *La Pomme d'Or*, 19 rue le Corbusier (☎84.20.62.12; ②), alongside the train line. Youth hostellers can take another twenty-minute train ride west to **VESOUL**, where the IYHF **youth hostel** is at 1 rue Paul-Petitclerc (☎84.76.48.55; ①). Failing either of these, you'll have to beat a retreat to Belfort.

Besançon and the Doubs

The capital of Franche-Comté, **BESANÇON**, is an ancient and attractive grey stone town at the northern edge of the Jura mountains, enclosed in a loop of the River Doubs, whose lugubrious meanders define the layout of the old town. The tongue of land it sits on has been protected since Roman times, when it lay on a major trading route; the indefatigable Vauban added the still-extant fortifications and a citadelle to guard the natural breach in the river. Once a major centre of French clock-making (until the Far East became important in the manufacturing industry), Besançon was also the birth-place of artificial silk – or rayon – in 1890, along with the pioneering Lumière brothers and epic novelist Victor Hugo.

The River Doubs rises on the high plateau 100km to the south of here, making a diversion far to the northwest of the town, gathering tributaries and broadening as it briefly crosses the Swiss border before entering Besançon. A lazy journey upstream to **Pontarlier** can make a rewarding excursion over a couple of days. From Pontalier a direct return north to Besançon can be made by following the River Loue's steep descent through its heavily wooded valley past the pretty mill town of **Ornans**.

The Town

Rue de la République leads from the river to the central **place du 8-septembre** and the sixteenth-century **Hôtel de Ville**. The principal street, **Grande-Rue**, cuts across the square along the line of the old Roman road, overlooked by a craggy hill above the river, where another of Vauban's prodigious citadels rises (see below). At its north-western end – the livelier part of town with shops and cafés – there is the excellent **Musée des Beaux-Arts** (daily except Tues 9.30am–noon & 2–6pm; 20F), with some good nineteenth- and twentieth-century works, two magnificent Bonnards and a wonderful clock collection. Midway down the street, the fine sixteenth-century **Palais Granvelle** houses a not very illuminating local history museum. Continuing up the street, you pass place Victor-Hugo (he was born at no. 140) and arrive at the **Porte Noire**, a second-century Roman triumphal arch spanning the street and partially embedded in the adjoining houses. Beside it, in the shady little square **Archéologique A-Castan**, are the remains of a *nymphaeum*, a small reservoir of water fed by an aqueduct. Beyond the arch is the pompous eighteenth-century **Cathédrale St-Jean** (guided visits at hourly intervals 9.50–11.50am & 2.50–5.50pm; closed Jan & Oct–March Tues, Wed; 20F), which houses the nineteenth-century *Horloge Astronomique*, detailing over a hundred terrestrial and celestial positions and contain-ing some 30,000 parts.

The **citadelle** (daily except Tues April–Sept 9.15am–6.15pm; Oct–March 9.45am–4.45pm; 25F) is a steep, fifteen-minute climb from here, with a crow's-nest view of the town and the noose-like bend in the river that contains it. It houses three worthwhile museums (times as above): the **Musée d'Histoire Naturelle**, which speaks for itself;

the **Musée Populaire Comtois**, with pottery, furniture, a good collection of nine-teenth-century marionettes, as well as some marvellous old farming implements; and – best of all – the **Musée de la Résistance et de la Déportation**, a superb aid to understanding postwar France's political consciousness (English audio commentary available). The first rooms document the rise of Nazism and French fascism through photographs and exhibits, including a bar of soap stamped *RIF* – Pure Jew Fat. Moving on to the Vichy government, there's a telegram of encouragement sent by Marshall Pétain to the French troops of the "legion of volunteers against Bolshevism", fighting alongside the Germans on the eastern front. Finally, as counterbalance, much is made of General Leclerc's vow at Koufra in the Libyan desert, whose capture in January 1941 was the first, entirely French, victory of the war: "We will not stop until the French flag flies once more over Metz and Strasbourg", a vow which he kept, when he entered the latter city at the head of a division in November 1944.

Practicalities

The **tourist office**, by the second bridge on rue de l'Armée-Française (April–Sept Mon–Sat 9am–7pm, Sun 10am–noon; mid-June to mid-Sept Sun 10am–noon & 3–5pm; Oct–March Mon–Sat 9am–6pm; ☎81.80.92.55), provide a free accommodation service. **Buses** south for Pontarlier and Salins-les-Bains leave from the **gare routière** on rue Proudhon off rue de la République. The **gare SNCF** is at the end of av Maréchal-Foch.

Hotels include the *Florel* opposite the station (☎81.80.41.08; ②–③); the *Levant*, 9 rue des Boucheries (☎81.81.07.88; ③); the dead central *Regina*, 91 Grande-Rue (☎81.81.50.22; ④); or the *Hôtel de Paris*, 33 rue des Granges (☎81.81.36.56; ④–⑥), with free parking for guests. There is no official youth hostel, but the *Centre International de Séjour* at 19 rue Martin-du-Gard, 4km northwest of the centre (☎81.50.07.54; ①; bus #8, stop *L'Épitaphe*), fulfils the same function, though at slightly greater expense. Alternatively, there's the *Foyer des Jeunes Filles*, 18 rue de la Cassotte (☎81.80.90.01; ①; women only), and *CROUS*, whose main office is at 38 av de l'Observatoire (☎81.50.26.88); but to get a room you must head for the university itself (open July & Aug; bus #7 direction *Campus*, stop *Université*). **Camping** is at Plage de Chalezeule, 5km out on the Belfort road (March–Oct; bus #1 towards Palente).

For **eating**, the *Levant* hotel has a popular restaurant (closed Sat), or you could try the student restaurant, *Canot*, at the entrance to the old town by Pont Canot (closed evenings July & Aug); the *Pause Café* at no. 9 also makes a nice place for a snack. Two good places for a more substantial meal include the century-old *Restaurant au Petit Polonai*, 81 rue des Granges (closed Sat eve & Sun), a local favourite offering good-value menus from 55F to 110F; and the *Restaurant le Champagney*, 37 rue Battant (☎81.81.05.71; closed Sun), with menus featuring regional specialities up to 135F.

The two biggest **cultural events** of the year in Besançon are *Jazz en Franche-Comté*, which takes place in June and July, and an international young conductors' competition in the first two weeks of September.

Southeast of Besançon

The Doubs runs a course like a hairpin, doubling back on itself repeatedly, with its most dramatic change of course at **AUDINCOURT**, a short way south of Belfort and the place where *Peugeot* bikes are made. The town's chief sight is the modern **church of Sacré-Coeur**, which has windows and a tapestry by Fernand Léger, while **SOCHAUX**, just north of town, is home to the **Musée Peugeot** (daily 10am–6pm; 30F), displaying over a century of automotive manufacture from the Bey of Tunis' one-off quadricycle to contemporary rally winners and concept cars.

From Audincourt, southwards and upstream, the D437 follows the valley of the Doubs, winding and climbing steadily between steep, wooded banks, to the bridging point at **ST-HIPPOLYTE**, where you'll find the riverside *Hôtel Bellevue* (☎81.96.51.53; ③–⑤), and a **campsite** (closed Nov–April). Seven kilometres west along the D39, the *Auberge de Moricemaison* in Valoreille (☎81.64.01.72; ③) offers rustic simplicity and wholesome evening meals (closed Dec–Feb).

A less congested scenic route from Besançon follows the D464 south of the river, but without a car you'd have to hitch all this – manageable but slow. Beyond St-Hippolyte the road climbs onto a wide plateau at around 800–900m altitude, with grassy cattle pastures encompassed by fir-clad ridges and dotted with broad-roofed farms and barns. Once up here, cycling is easy enough. Alternatively, it's a lovely but long hike of well over 50km along the **GR5 footpath** from St-Hippolyte, across the plateau and up the Doubs valley, to the plunging waterfall of the **Saut du Doubs** outside **VILLERS-LE-LAC**, where the **GTJ** marathon cross-country ski piste begins. To reach the fall, it's a four-kilometre walk from the last houses above the north end of the lake in Villiers along a track through the woods. If you want to stay, there's *La Petite Ferme*, rte de Morteau (☎81.68.08.33), and a **campsite** in Goumois on the Swiss border and Villers-le-Lac (closed Nov–March).

By road, Villiers is 47km south of St-Hipployte along the D437, turning east at **MORTEAU**, a village with nothing more than a much altered, thirteenth-century priory church to recommend it. There is accommodation here in the form of a **gîte** on rue des Moulinots (☎81.67.48.72), and up on the plateau, the *Hôtel des Montagnards* also offers a warm welcome (☎81.67.08.86; ③–④).

Pontarlier and around

Thirty kilometres southwest of Morteau by train lies **PONTARLIER**, one of the bigger Jura towns, and not very interesting in itself except as a transit point and recreational base. If you need **accommodation** here, try the *Hôtel de France* at 8 rue de la Gare (②), or the *Hôtel Morteau*, 26 rue Jeanne d'Arc, near the river (☎81.39.14.83; ④); if you're on a strict budget, there's the IYHF **youth hostel** at 2 rue Jouffroy (☎81.39.06.57; ①), as well as two **gîtes** – *Le Gounefay*, rte du Grand-Taureau (☎81.39.05.99), and the *Chalet-Refuge du Larmont* (☎81.39.11.25). Campers are best off asking at the **SI**, near the station between the PTT and the youth hostel. For a couple of places to **eat**, try the *Restaurant Le Petit Vannolles*, 8 rue de Vannolles, for a snack or the *Brasserie de la Poste*, 55 rue de la Republique, for a meal. Good-quality **mountain bikes** can be rented for 80F a day and 60F per day thereafter from *Vélos Pernet*, 23 rue de la République, (☎81.46.48.00), and cross-country **ski gear** from *Sports du Niège* at no. 4 (☎81.39.04.69).

Just south of town, passing a divinely aromatic *Nestlé* factory that will have chocoholics drooling, a steep road to the left ascends 11km up to **Le Grand Taureau**, whose 1328m summit is just a short walk from the road's end and offers a view over the whole Jura Massif and across Switzerland to the Alps. A couple of kilometres further south of Pontarlier, the **Château de Joux** (Easter–June 10am–noon & 2–5pm; July & Aug 9am–6pm; Sept & Oct 10–11.15am & 2–3.30pm) stands over the defile known as La Cluse et Mijoux, the ancient Franco-Swiss frontier. It was originally constructed in the eleventh century, and Vauban had a hand in remodelling and modernizing, but most of what you see today is less than a century old; the fort's history and impressive appearance are of more interest than its present collection of military uniforms housed inside.

Moving on, there are trains and buses to Besançon, trains to Frasne to pick up the *TGV* to Dijon and Paris, and local buses to the six-kilometre-long **Lac de St-Point**, where you can pick up GR5 again to make the ascent of **Mont d'Or** (1463m) overlooking Lake Geneva and the Alps, and to Mouthe, where the River Doubs emerges from an underground cavern.

Ornans and the Valley of the Loue

Some 17km north of Pontarlier, the D67 splits west off the N67 and plunges precipitously into the **Valley of the Loue**. A couple of kilometres above the village of Ouhans lies the source of the river, issuing from an enormous rock beneath a tiered cliff, in winter entirely fringed with icicles. From this point you can continue by foot along the **GR595 footpath** down the valley bounded by densely wooded limestone cliffs, a descent no less dramatic by road as it passes through a string of pretty villages.

Roughly halfway between Pontarlier and Besançon, **ORNANS** is the prettiest of all, an archetypal Franche-Comté town that has become the touristic focal point of the valley. The Loue here is an abrupt trench with the river washing away at the foundations of Ornans' ancient balconied houses: the definitive view of the town is easily appreciated from the numerous footbridges spanning the river. Pierre Vernier, inventor of the eponymous gauge, and the painter Gustave Courbet were both born here: the latter's house is now a **museum** (daily April–Nov 10am–noon & 2–6pm; winter closed Tues), displaying some of his drawings, sculpture and locally painted scenes. There's the riverside *Hôtel Le Progrès*, 11 rue Jacques Gervais (☎81.62.16.79; ④–⑤), or the pricier but finely situated *Hôtel de la Cascade* (☎81.60.95.30; ⑤) in the centre of Mouthier, further down the D67. There are **campsites** and *gîtes d'étapes* in Ornans, Vuillifans and Mouthier Haute-Pierre (both up in the valley).

Dôle and the lowlands

Halfway between Besançon and Dijon on the edge of the flat and fertile valley of the Saône, **DÔLE** is quiet and provincial. The medieval capital of the Comté region until Louis XI ordered its destruction in 1479, it's a place to stay overnight, or rest, and attractive enough in a subdued way. Grey stone houses with barred ground-floor windows stand on narrow streets around its vast, stolid **church of Notre-Dame**, with its lofty belfry. The Rhône–Rhine canal washes the feet of the town, and along its bank below the church runs the narrow rue Pasteur, birthplace of the French biologist and chemist Louis, who discovered the rabies virus (and its cure), and whose name is commemorated in the process of "pasteurization", another of his discoveries. He was the son of a tanner, and his house, like those of his father's workmates, backs on to a pretty waterside walkway leading to an island. The newly renovated house is now a **museum**.

Whatever happens in Dôle happens between the Grande-Rue – leading up from the bridge – and place Grévy, with the **tourist office** at no. 6 (Tues–Sat 8.30am–noon & 2–5/6/7pm). At the top of Grande-Rue is the delightful place aux Fleurs, with its fountain and amusing bronze sculpture of *Les Trois Commères* (The Three Gossips). There are some reasonable **hotels** here, including *Le Grand Cerf*, 6 rue Arney, near place Grévy (☎84.72.11.68; ③); and *La Chaumière* across the river on av Maréchal-Juin (☎87.72.40.32; ③). But the cheapest rooms, as usual, are at the IYHF **youth hostel**, in fact a mixed *foyer*, on place St-Jean XXIII (☎84.82.0036; ①; no curfew; IYHF card required). To get there, take bus #1, direction *Mesnils-Poiset*, stop *Les Paters*; the hostel also does **bike rental**. There's a **campsite**, *Camping du Pasquier*, by the river (☎84.72.02.61; mid-March to Oct). Apart from pizzerias and *crêperies*, like the canalside *La Demi-Lune*, 39 rue Pasteur (closed Wed), you should try *Restaurant Associative*, 8 rue Charles-Sauria, or the station's *Buffet de la Gare*, both of which have good local reputations. The **gare routière** is next to the train station.

The Forêt de Chaux

To the east of Dôle lies the two hundred square kilometres of the ancient **Forêt de Chaux**, France's third largest forest and site of some of the country's earliest industrial endeavours. Set in a clearing in the southern central part of the forest are the ancient settlements of **LA VIEILLE-LOYE** and **TUROT**, since early Christian times centres of charcoal burning – once essential in the production of metals – and until very recently glass manufacture, at one time producing up to one million bottles a year.

Access to the forest – which makes an agreeable alternative to the main roads to Salins-les-Bains or Besançon – is easiest from the N5/N72 Salins road to the south and west. In this part of the forest you'll find many waymarked walking trails wending their way beneath the overhead canopy of oak, chestnut, beech and wattle.

Arc-et-Senans and Salins-les-Bains

At the southeastern edge of the Forest of Chaux, some 7km north of Mouchard, is the unfinished eighteenth-century "salt city" of the **Salins Royale d'Arc-et-Senans** (May–Sept 9am–7pm; Oct–April 9am–noon & 2–5pm). Commissioned by royal decree in 1773 to replace the ageing works at Salins-les-Bains (see below) while utilizing the wood from a nearby forest as fuel, the complex was to have become a model utopian city dreamed up by the revolutionary architect Claude Nicolas Ledoux. His grandiose project reflected the egalitarian social concerns of the pre-revolutionary era: the settlement was to have radiated along the primary axes of a clockface from a nucleus housing the administrative offices, distillation plants, public baths and other municipal utilities.

Sadly, the socio-aesthetic ideals could not overcome the *salin*'s functional deficiencies: the pipeworks linking the new plant with Salins deteriorated rapidly and only half of the central *arc* was ever completed. Salt production continued until the end of the nineteenth century but all that remains today is the impressively restored semicircle of eleven buildings, a monumental epitaph to Ledoux's unconsummated vision.

If you've developed a taste for saltworks, **SALINS-LES-BAINS**, 8km east of Mouchard, is worth a further detour. Confined at the bottom of a narrow valley piercing the flank of the Jura's central plateau, the recuperative spa town of Salins has been producing salt for around a thousand years. The Chalon family moved in on the town in the thirteenth century and the wealth they accrued from the control and sale of the "white gold" essential for the preservation of food enabled them to become among the most influential of the Comté's medieval overlords. This prominence, as well as the town's key position on the route to Switzerland, accounts for the two lofty forts overlooking the town. The **Salines de Salins**, or brine-wells (one hour guided tours daily: Feb–Easter & mid-Sept to Nov 10.30am, 2.30 & 4pm; Easter to mid-Sept hourly 9–11am & 2.30–5.30pm; 21F), are inevitably the town's main attraction: once inside the vaulted underground galleries, you are shown the pumps which drew up the brine solution from the rock salt that was too deep to mine, while other salt-related activities are also innovatively depicted.

For further information, the **tourist office** is next to the eighteenth-century Hôtel de Ville on the central place des Alliés. Having styled itself as a spa town since the 1840s (and still doing so), Salins has some grand **hotels** that once accommodated the fashionably ailing gentry. The *Grand Hôtel des Bains* in place des Alliés (☎84.73.01.34; ⑤) offers grand comforts, or try the *Hôtel des Deux Forts* in place du Vigneron (☎84.37.93.75; ④). *The Hôtel Bon Accueil* on 50 rue de la Liberté, north off the central square (☎84.37.94.31; ②), welcomes the less solvent. There is a **campsite** (mid-June to mid-Sept) on av Général-de-Gaulle.

Lons-Le-Saunier to Arbois

At the base of the central plateau's west-facing rim are a string of towns set picturesquely astride rivers and in the midst of fertile soils that have supported centuries of agriculture, recently accommodating the small, specialist industries so typical of the Jura. The spa town and departmental capital of **Lons-Le-Saunier** offers visitors nothing exceptional, but south of the town a string of vineyards traces the plateau's edge to just beyond **Arbois**, the Jura's wine-making capital. This is the eighty kilometre **Route des Vins du Jura**, where the region's varied and distinctive wines are cultivated and manufactured from a variety of vines.

Between Lons and Arbois, a scenic detour can be made into the hills to visit the ancient, time-locked villages of **Baume-Les-Messieurs** and **château Chalon**. And at **Poligny** more wines and the long-refined flavour of Comté cheese, produced in the Jura since the thirteenth century, are available for sampling at the Maison du Comté.

Lons-Le-Saunier

Once the site of a neolithic settlement, **LONS-LE-SAUNIER** was rebuilt afer a distastrous fire all but destroyed the town in the early seventeeth century, and most buildings date from this era. A wander around some of the older examples makes an agreeable way to fill half a day here.

The central **place de la Liberté**, a ten-minute walk north of the train station, is a good place to start. Should you happen to be in the square on the hour, the **Theatre clock** at the *place's* eastern end will chime a familiar half-dozen notes from *La Marseillaise* to honour Lons' most famous son, Rouget de Lisle, the anthem's composer (see p.451). Originally a stirring composition penned for the Rhine Army, it was renamed in 1792 by troops from Marseille as they entered Paris to proclaim the new Republic. Just north of the place is the attractive, colonnaded thoroughfare of rue du Coerce, where some of Lons' oldest buildings line the street in which de Lisle was born. Continuing north through the place de la Comédie and past the ancient **salt well**, Le Puits Salé, the **Museum of Archeology**, 25 rue Richebourg (Mon–Fri 10am–noon & 2–6pm, Sat & Sun 2–5pm; closed Tues, free entry Wed) presents some absorbing prehistoric displays, including a touching neolithic family scene circa 4000 BC, a dug-out canoe found locally, and a life-size replica of a 210-million-year-old plateosaurus, France's oldest-known dinosaur. The museum, which also mounts various temporary exhibitions, is housed in the old Bel cheese factory, whose enduringly popular *La Vache Qui Rit* cheese spread is now produced in larger premises near the station. Returning south along rue Richebourg to av Jean Moulin, you come to the inevitable **statue** of Rouget de Lisle, designed by Frédéric Bartholdi, the sculptor who went on to refine de Lisle's stirring pose on a much grander scale in the Statue of Liberty. A turn left here leads to the pleasant **Parc Edouard Guenon** and in it the **Thermal Baths** (ring ☎84.24.20.34 for admission details) with their ornate *fin-de-siècle* exterior. Lavishly equipped with a sauna, Turkish bath and jacuzzi, its saline immersions not only soothe the usual aches and pains, but are also renowned for their ability to cure juvenile bedwetting.

Practicalities

Lons' **tourist office** is close to the theatre clock at 1 rue Pasteur (Mon–Sat 8.30–noon & 2–6pm; ☎84.24.65.01) and offers an ample selection of local and regional information. If you want to **stay**, two good hotels are the *Hôtel des Sports*, 21 rue St-Désiré, which leads south of the place de la Liberté (☎84.24.04.42; ②), offering a good-value menu, or the cosy *Nouvel Hôtel*, 50 rue Lecourbe (☎84.47.20.67; ④), just west of the *place*. More inexpensive are the *Foyer Mixte des Jeunes Travailleurs* at 1000 rue des Gentianes, 2km east of the centre (☎84.43.11.96; ①), the women-only *Foyer Bon Accueil*, 1 rue Sebile, near the top of rue du Commerce (☎84.43.11.96; ①), or the rather pricey *Camping de la Marjorie* on the northeast edge of town. For cheap **eating**, try the unsigned *Restaurant-pension de famille Ferrard* in 7 rue Tamisier, left of rue du Commerce, where just 50F will ensure a filling meal. Alternatively, for twice the price and a charming setting, pay a visit to the *Bistrot des Marronniers*, 22 rue de Vallière, west off rue St-Désiré (closed Sun).

Baume-Les-Messieurs and Château Chalon

Twenty kilometres east of Lons is the tiny village of **BAUME-LES-MESSIEURS**, tucked in a cliff-bound valley festooned with foliage on all but the steepest faces. From Lons, the quickest – as well as most interesting – way to get there is to take the N471-Champagnole road and turn down the narrow and steep lanes descending into the valley from the north; the **Belvedere des Roches de Baume**, signposted off the N471, gives stunning views of the village and the verdant Seille valley out as far as the Château Chalon and beyond if the weather is up to it.

In the village, the main attraction is the **abbey**, founded as a monastery by the Irish monk Saint Columba in the sixth century. In spite of hoards of fellow visitors clacking over the ancient stone floors, an atmosphere of monastic tranquility still pervades. Consecrated as the Abbaye de Cluny in 910 by Benedictine monks, it was disbanded by the newly formed Republic in 1792, and today the interior and its twelfth-century **church**, in whose crypt rest many members of the once-dominant Chalon family, remain open to the public.

Two kilometres south of the village, at the very end of the valley, are the **Grottes de Baume** (April–Sept several guided tours daily 9am–6pm; 40min; 25F), one of the many limestone stalactite cave systems throughout the region. Those who are particularly energetic may wish to ascend the stairway cut into the rock on the valley's eastern face; at times exposed and best avoided if conditions are wet, it leads to the clifftop and the Belvedere des Roches de Baume viewpoint described above. Others may opt for a meal at the *Restaurant des Grottes* near the beautiful, fern-draped **waterfall** with a stunning view back down the valley.

Leaving Baume to the north, the limestone cliffs recede as the valley opens out to reveal miles of vineyards that yield the distinctive yellow wine of Château Chalon, produced from the Sauvignon grape. The fortified hilltop village of **CHÂTEAU CHALON** overlooks the vines, and was built around a castle (not open to the public) of the once-influential Comtoise family who give the village its name. A short wander will lead you past promising baskets of *Chalon* (expect to pay around 160F a bottle) to the fortified **church**. Dating from the eleventh century and possessing some impressive stained glass and early examples of vaulting, an archway outside by the porch leads to the **Belvedere de la Rochette**, looking out across the valley back towards Baume.

Poligny and Arbois

Back on the Route des Vins de Jura, the attractive medieval town of **POLIGNY**, at the south of the Culée de Vaux Valley, is noteworthy for its well-preserved, early Romanesque buildings, including the **church of St-Hippolyte**, with its characteristic, bell-like tower, as seen all over Franche-Comté. But the town's principal attraction is the hallowed **Maison de Comté** in av de la Résistance, leading south from the central place des Deportés (daily guided tours July-Aug; 1hr), an old *fromagerie* that now forms the headquarters of the *Comité Interprofessional du Gruyère de Comté*. Displays show the process of cheese-making from extracting milk to producing the finished article, alongside audio-visual presentations exalting the industry. Gruyère officers, an institution of tax collectors founded by Charlemagne, once collected the two-foot-wide *meules* of cheese as payment – each the product of 500 litres of milk; now, with over eight hundred years' experience of production, Comté cheese has earned the distinguished *Appellation d'Origine Contrôlée* (*AOC*) label more commonly reserved for vintage wines.

The attractive medieval houses and other sites of interest in Poligny are indicated on the blue *Walking Through The Old Town* leaflet available from the friendly **tourist office** in rue Victor Hugo, and a **meal** at *La Mottarone*, an eighteenth-century *hôtel particulier* at 17 rue du College (☎84.37.20.30; ③), will end the day nicely.

There's no mistaking that **ARBOIS**, 10km to the north, is the capital of this region's viticulture. Glittering wine emporia line the central place de la Liberté, entreating you to sample the unusual local wines, of which the sweet *vin de paille* is rarest – so called because its grapes are dried on beds of straw, giving the wine a strong aftertaste equal to that of the better-known Château Chalon.

Louis Pasteur lived in the town after his family moved from Dôle, and his boyhood home, the **Maison Pasteur** on av Pasteur, has recently been reopened to the public. Enquire about times at the **tourist office** in rue de l'Hôtel de Ville (☎84.37.47.37), whose basement also houses the **Musée de la Vigne et du Vin** (Mon–Sat l0am–noon & 2–6pm; free), detailing the development and production of wine in the Jura.

If you're **staying** overnight in town, try the *Hôtel Mephisto*, 33 place Faramand, just over the river (☎84.66.06.49; ③), or the *Hôtel Les Messageries* (☎84.66.15.45; ④–⑤), up from the Maison Pasteur. There's a **campsite** called *Camping des Vignes* on av Général-Leclerc (☎84.66.14.12; closed Oct–March), 1km east of the centre. For a **meal**, try the *Restaurant La Cuisance*, with lunchtime menus around 50F and evening menus from 70F to 100F.

The Central Plateau and the Jura mountains

On the broad upland plateau, the Jura landscape unrolls, stretches and rises in increasingly abrupt steps to the mountains bordering the Swiss frontier. It is a region of lakes and pine forests, small farming communities and – at the higher altitudes – huge ski-resorts enveloping tiny villages, semi-deserted in summer. It is the best of the Jura, and as you might expect – despite trains linking **Champagnole**, **Morez** and **St-Claude** with Arbois and Pontarlier – is best appreciated with your own transport or on bikes, available for rental in several locations.

Champagnole and the Forêt de la Joux

Although a main crossroads on the plateau, **CHAMPAGNOLE**, an industrial town largely rebuilt after a major fire in 1798, has little of interest for the passing visitor excepting an **archeological museum** above the tourist office on rue Baronne Delfort, displaying mediumly diverting Gallic and Roman artefacts found in the vicinity. The one reason to come here is to use the town as a base for exploring the countryside and particularly the Forêt de la Joux to the northeast.

Accommodation in town includes the *Hôtel Franc-Comtoijs*, 11 rue Clemenceau (☎84.52.04.95; ④), or the *Hôtel de la Londaine*, 23 rue Baronne Delfort (☎84.52.45.99; ④), both central. There's **hostel** accommodation at the *Accueil Jeunes*, Base de la Roche-sur-Ain (☎84.52.07.76), and a **campsite** on rue Georges-Vallery (closed mid-Sept to May). The **tourist office** is in an annexe of the *mairie* on rue Baronne Delfort (☎84.52.43.67).

Out of Champagnole things take a turn for the better. To the southeast, the D279 passes the château at **SYAM** built in 1818 (summer Sat & Sun only) to the **Gorges de la Langouett**, 17km away. Here, a half-hour walk leads down to the narrow 47-metre high gorge sliced through the cretaceous escarpment by the River Saine. Other river-ine curiosities in the area include the **Pert de l'Ain** near the village of Bourg-de-Sirod, where a half-hour walk from an electricity station leads through the woods, past a waterfall and lesser cascades, to a boulder-strewn chasm where the Ain takes a brief subterranean detour. Another pleasant ten-minute walk a few kilometres northeast – just past the village of Conte – leads to the natural amphitheatre from whose base the **source of the Ain** issues in all but the driest years.

A couple of kilometres north of the source, spread over a small hill surrounded by pastures, is the old walled village of **NOZEROY**, ancestral home of the Chalon family that dominated regional politics in feudal times. The town preserves much of its medie-val charm today with the **Port d'Horloge** – once part of the town's fortifications – fram-ing the beginning of the Grande Rue, with its many ancient houses; Grande Rue ends at the place des Annonciades and the ruins of the thirteenth-century **castle**. The only place to **stay** in Nozeroy is the small *Hôtel des Remparts* in the town centre (☎84.51.13.44; ④), with a couple of medieval-themed restaurants nearby.

North of Nozeroy, on the other side of the D471 Champagnole-Pontarlier road, the **Forêt de la Joux** is considered one of the most beautiful of France's native pine forests. It is criss-crossed by a net of narrow fire roads, but if you don't have a car the Gare de la Joux, in the heart of the forest on the Champagnole-Pontarlier rail line, offers access for exploration on foot or by bicycle. The **Information Centre** near the station will give some suggestions on the many well-marked walking trails through the forest: the most popular area is the **Sapins de la Glacière**, a couple of kilometres east of the Information Centre. The **Route de la Sapins** is the approved tourist drive, sign-posted for 50km from the D471 to the village of Levier and passing lookouts and the 45-metre high **Sapin President** along the way. But the less regimented can just as easily enjoy getting mildly disorientated by following any number of lesser, unmarked roads and discovering the wonder of the forest for themselves.

The Lake District

South of Champagnole the flattened plateau, unable to shed the Haute Jura's winter run-off, collects the meltwaters in a series of natural and not-so-natural lakes: the **Region des Lacs** loosely strung along the valley of the River Ain. Where the ground begins to crumple upward to the eastern summits, gorges and waterfalls highlight each succes-sive step and lookouts survey the tiny, empastured villages, each with their characteris-tic domed belfry beaten from metal or composed from a mosaic of tiles and slates.

Clairvaux-les-Lacs and the Cascades du Hérisson

The *Region*'s main resort town is **CLAIRVAUX-LES-LACS**. It is here that the northern tip of the serpentine **Lac de Ouglans**, dammed 25km downstream, reverts to the River Ain which feeds it. The **Grand Lac**, just south of town, is the focus of summer resort activity, although the lake's attractions are in its beach area and watersports facilities rather than its scenic situation.

Back in town, both the *Hôtel Restaurant Arbez* on place du 8-mai 1945 (☎84.25.81.22; ②), and the *Restaurant La Raillette*, 50 rue Neuve (☎84.25.82.21 ③), offer simple, inex-pensive rooms, while the *Chaumière du Lac* (☎84.25.81.52; ④) and the *Hôtel Bellevue*, on route de Moirans, the D27 south of town (☎84.25.82.37; ③; closed Oct-May), provide more comfortable lodgings, the latter offering a view true to its name.

Surrounded by hills, **Lac Chalain**, 16km north of Clairvaux and near the village of Doucier, has a much more impressive setting, as well as being another venue for water-borne recreation. **Campers** are very well catered for here, with the large, well-appointed *Le Domaine de Chalain* (☎84.24.29.00; closed mid-Oct to April) on the east side of the lake and the terraces of *La Perola* (☎84.25.70.03; May–Sept) on the north side near

Marigny being very popular spots. Both are open to day visitors. In the pretty village of **DOUCIER**, the *Hôtel Roux* (☎85.25.71.21; ③–④) caters adequately for non-campers.

By far the most interesting excursion around here – and one of the Jura's best-known natural spectacles – are the **Cascades du Hérisson**, a series of waterfalls fed by the like-named river. The septet of cascades descend nearly a thousand feet from the plateau in just three kilometres: something worth considering if you plan to under-take a return walk to all the falls. Well-marked from either end of the gorge, the easiest walk, accessible by road via Val-Dessous southeast of Doucier, leads to the best-known and prettiest of the falls, the **Eventail**. A ten-minute stroll from the car park leads to the cascade, which spreads out in ever-widening tiers, giving it the fan-like appearance after which it is named. Continuing upstream – or more precisely uphill – you'll shake off most casual spectators and pass up through the woods of wild oak and springtime daffodils to the dramatic **Grand Saut**, with its clear drop of 60m and pathway passing behind the waterfall: an alarmingly windy – as well as more obviously drenched – spot to shower in. A steep climb leads to smaller *sauts* feeding the odd swimming hole, past a kiosk (with access south to the village of Bonlieu) to the uppermost **Saut Girard**, 4km up from the Eventail and close to the village of **ILAY**. With restaurants and souve-nir shops, the only hotel here is the *Auberge du Hérisson*, much more expensive than it looks (☎84.25.58.18; ⑤; mid-Oct to March).

A short drive up the N78 east of Ilay leads to the near-thousand-metre lookout atop **Pic de l'Aigle**, one of the best spots from where the Jura's topography – its mountains, plateaux and valleys – can be clearly appreciated. On fine days, the views are said to extend as far as Mont Blanc to the east, and west to the plain of the Saone.

The Haute Jura

Rising from the plateau through the pine forests to the scrawny higher pastures, the temperatures dip as the landscape takes a bleaker turn towards the summits of the **Haute Jura**. Main roads struggle up the valleys towards the Swiss border but less demanding routes run along the mountain's narrow folds linking Pontarlier to **Morez** and **St-Claude**. When not passing through woodland or low cloud, they can offer memorable motoring but, skiers and mountain bikers aside, most people come up here for the views from the thousand-metre cols towards the French Alps.

The main towns are valley-bound and claustrophobic and in the resort towns, hotels tend to be expensive or rather soulless places out of season. For all their appeal, the Haute Jura's views always end up pointing one way: across Lac Léman in Switzerland towards the perennial snowscapes of the Alps.

Up to Morez and Les Rousses

The main trans-Jura route into Switzerland is the N5, which begins its ascent to the frontier around St Laurent-en-Grandvaux, great for skiing but unmemorable apart from the picturesque **Lac de l'Abbaye**, 4km south of town on the D437. Also on the Arbois–St-Claude rail line is **MOREZ**, 12km up the road, a town squeezed along the slit-like valley floor and noted for the manufacture of watches and spectacles. The **tourist office** is in the central place Jaurès, along with the **gare routière**, where buses leave for La Cure on the Franco-Swiss border. From the Swiss side there are trains down to Nyon on Lac Léman and on to Geneva itself.

A couple of kilometres before the frontier, **LES ROUSSES** exists purely for skiing – downhill and especially cross-country – but just before it a lane goes down to a very attractive IYHF **youth hostel** in an old, red-shuttered farmhouse by a stream, 2km away at Bief-de-la-Chaille (☎84.60.02.80; closed Oct to mid-Dec & mid-April to mid-May). There's also a **gîte d'étape** at Premanon on the D25 (☎84.60.54.82; closed Sept to mid-Dec, May & June).

From the youth hostel you can see the eerie spheres of the satellite-tracking station on the summit of **La Dôle** (1677m), the Jura's highest peak just over the Swiss border. The **GR9 footpath** passes through here, beginning a magnificent hiking section all along the crest of the ridge to the Col de la Faucille and beyond (see below). Les Rousses has plenty of **hotels**: the *Hôtel de France*, 323 rue Pasteur (☎84.60.01.45; ⑤–⑥), is the town's best, but less extravagant lodgings can be found at the *Hôtel Du Gai Pinson*, 1465 route Blanche (☎84.60.02.15; ④), or the *El Patio*, 344 rue Pasteur (☎84.60.02.01; ④). For a **meal**, try the restaurant at the *Hôtel Restaurant Les Gentianes*, or the *Restaurant Les P'Losses* in the winter sports centre on the Geneva road southwest of town.

St-Claude

From Morez, the train line leaves the N5 and heads along the Gorges de la Bienne to the industrial town of **ST-CLAUDE**, to the southwest, squeezed in even more claustrophobically by even higher mountains than Morez. It's famous for its pipes (the smokers' kind) and diamonds, and there's a **Pipe and Diamond Museum** opposite the fortified cathedral of St Pierre on rue du Marché. The **tourist office** is at 1 av de Belfort (☎84.41.42.62), where the English-language guide *Discovery* is available, floridly describing a two-hour walk around the town.

Should you **stay** here for the night, the *Hôtel Le Media* at 7 rue de la Poyat (☎84.45.49.81; ④), off the main rue du Pré, is marginally better than the *Hôtel de la Poste* on rue Reybert (☎84.45.52.34; ④), opposite the tourist office. Plusher accommodation can be found at the *Jura Hôtel*, 40 av de 1 Gare (☎84.45.24.04; ⑤), or the *Hôtel Le Joly* in Le Martinet, 3km southwest of town on the Col de la Faucille road right next to a campsite. For **eating**, the restaurants at *Le Media* or *Le Bayard* in the central place du Pré are both wholesome and inexpensive.

What gives purpose to the rest of the onward route from either St-Claude or Les Rousses are the superb views from the crest of the great fir-clad ridge that overlooks Lac Léman (Lake Geneva) to the east. The N5 crosses the ridge at the **Col de la Faucille** (1323m). If it's clear, the view is unbelievably dramatic from the Col or the GR footpath, with the whole range of the western Alps stretched out before you, dominated by Mont Blanc with the steely cusp of Lac Léman laid at your feet. There's an even better view from the top of nearby **Mont Rond** (1534m), accessible by chairlift. Of course, if it's not clear, the journey will have been in vain, but if you're carrying on south of Geneva, 30 km away, it's downhill all the way – with the thought of a couple or more revitalizing bars of Swiss chocolate at the day's end.

travel details

Trains

Besançon to: Bourg-en-Bresse (4–5 daily; 2hr 30min); Champagnole (4 daily; 1hr 40min–1hr 30min); Dijon (10 daily; 1hr); Dôle (10 daily; 30min); Lons (several daily; 1–1hr 30min); Morez (4 daily; 2hr 10min–2hr 30min); Morteau (4 daily; 1hr–1hr 45min); Paris-Lyon direct (up to 6 daily; 2hr 30min); St-Claude (4 daily; 2hr 30min–3hr); St-Laurent (4 daily; 1hr 40min–2hr).

Belfort to: Besançon (5 daily; 1hr–1hr 15min); Dôle (5 daily; 1hr 30min); Paris-Est (2 daily; 5hr); Ronchamp (12 daily; 5 min).

Dôle to: Dijon (10 daily; 30min); Paris-Lyon (10 daily; 4hr); Pontarlier 3 daily; 1hr 20min).

Metz to: Longuyon (2 daily; 1hr 30min); Mulhouse (7 daily; 2hr 30min); Nancy (hourly; 1hr); Paris-Est (4 daily; 3hr); Strasbourg (every 2hr; 1hr 30min).

Mulhouse to: Belfort (up to 5 daily; 30–45 min).

Nancy to: Lunéville (hourly; 30min); Paris-Est (hourly; 3hr); Saverne (3 daily; 1hr); Strasbourg (2 daily; 1hr 20 min).

St-Claude to: Bourg (4–5 daily; 1hr 40min–2hr), connecting with *TGV* to Paris.

Strasbourg to: Barr (9 daily; 55min); Basel (hourly; 1hr 30min–2hr); Besançon (8 daily; 2hr 15min); Colmar (hourly; 50min); Dambach (9 daily; 1hr); Dôle (10 daily; 3hr 30min); Ingwillen (6 daily; 30min); Molsheim (9 daily; 20min); Mulhouse (hourly; 1hr 20min); Obernai (9 daily; 40min); Paris-Est (every 2hr; 4hr 30min); Rosheim (9 daily; 25min); Sarreguemines (6 daily; 1hr 20min); St-Dié (3 daily; 1hr 50min); Sélestat (hourly; 20min); Wingen-Moden (6 daily; 40min); Wissembourg (up to 3 daily; 1hr).

Verdun to: Chalons-sur-Marne (up to 5 daily; 1hr 20min); Metz, changing at Conflans (1 daily; 1hr–1hr 15min); Nancy (2 daily; 1hr 40min); Paris-Est (up to 5 daily; 3hr).

Buses

Arbois to: Monchaud (7 daily; 5min).

Belfort to: Ronchamp (1 daily; 45min).

Besançon to: Ornans (4 daily; 30min); Pontarlier (4 daily; 1hr); Salins-les-Bains (3 weekly; 1hr).

Colmar to: Mulhouse (up to hourly; 1hr); Sélestat (hourly; 1hr).

Haguenau to: Pfaffenhoffen (4 daily; 30min); Neuwillen (4 daily; 1hr 10min); Saverne (4 daily; 1hr 40min).

Morez to: Lons (1 most days; 1hr 45min); St-Claude (3 weekly; 1hr).

St-Claude to: Lyon (daily; 3hr 40min).

Saverne to: Molsheim (2 daily; 1hr).

Sélestat to: St-Dié (5–6 daily; 1hr 10min).

CHAPTER FOUR

NORMANDY

T hough now firmly incorporated into the French mainstream, the seaboard province of **Normandy** has a history of prosperous independence as one of the crucial powers of medieval Europe. Colonized by Norsemen from Scandinavia, it began to colonize in turn in the eleventh and twelfth centuries, not only England but as far afield as Sicily and parts of the Near East. Later, as part of France, it was instrumental in the settlement of Canada.

Normandy has always had large ports: **Rouen**, on the Seine, is the nearest navigable point to Paris; **Dieppe**, **Le Havre** and **Cherbourg** have important transatlantic trade. Inland, it is overwhelmingly agricultural – a fertile belt of tranquil pastureland, where the chief goal of most visitors will be the restaurants of towns such as **Vire** and **Conches**. Much of the seaside is a little overdeveloped; the last French emperor created, towards the end of the last century, a "Norman Riviera" around **Trouville** and **Deauville**, and an air of pretension still hangs about their elegant promenades. But the ancient ports – **Honfleur** and **Barfleur** especially – are visual delights, and there are numerous seaside villages with few crowds or affectations. Along the Seine, too, are several idyllic resorts.

Normandy also boasts extraordinary Romanesque and Gothic architectural treasures, although only the much-restored capital, Rouen, has a complete medieval centre. The attractions are more often single buildings than entire towns. Most famous of all is the spectacular *merveille* on the island of **Mont St-Michel**, but there are also the monasteries at **Jumièges** and **Caen**; the cathedrals of **Bayeux** and **Coutances**; and Richard the Lionheart's castle above the Seine at **Les Andelys**. **Bayeux** has, in additions its vivid and astonishing tapestry, and among more recent creations are Monet's garden at **Giverny** and, at **Le Havre**, a fabulous collection of paintings by Dufy, Boudin and other Impressionists. Furthermore, Normandy's vernacular architecture makes it well worth exploring inland – the back roads through the countryside are lined with splendid centuries-old half-timbered manor houses. It is remarkable how much has survived or been restored since the Allied landings in 1944 and the subsequent **Battle of Normandy**, which has its own legacy in a series of war museums, memorials and cemeteries.

ACCOMMODATION PRICE CATEGORIES

All the hotels, youth hostels and guesthouses listed in this book have been price-graded according to the following scale, and although costs will rise slightly overall with the life of this edition, the relative comparisons should remain valid. Paris and the large cities will, as anywhere, be more expensive than equivalent accommodation in the countryside or small towns. The prices quoted are for the cheapest available double room in high season, although remember that many of the cheap places will have more expensive rooms with en-suite facilities.

① Under 160F	④ 300–400F	⑦ 600–700F
② 160–220F	⑤ 400–500F	⑧ Over 700F
③ 220–300F	⑥ 500–600F	

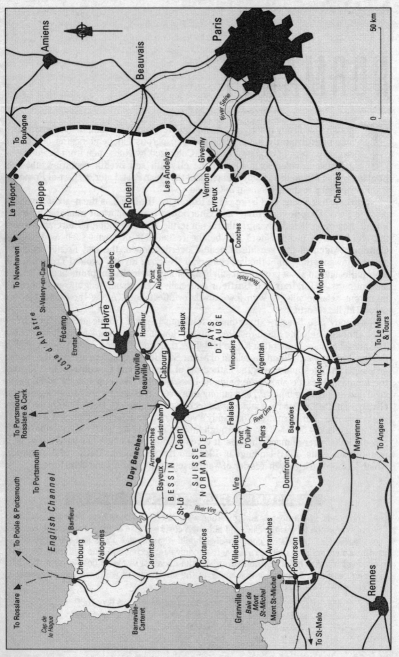

THE FOOD OF NORMANDY

The **food of Normandy** owes its most distinctive characteristic – its gut-bursting, heart-pounding richness – to the lush orchards and dairy herds of its agricultural heartland, and most especially the area southeast of Caen known as the Pays d'Auge. Menus abound in meat such as veal (*veau*) cooked in *vallée d'Auge* style, which consists largely of the profligate addition of cream and butter. Many dishes also feature orchard fruit, either in its natural state or in successively more alcoholic forms – either as apple or pear cider, or perhaps further distilled to produce brandies.

Normans have a great propensity for blood and guts. In addition to gamier meat and fowl such as rabbit and duck (a speciality in Rouen, where the birds are strangled to ensure that all their blood gets into the sauce), they enjoy such intestinal preparations as *andouilles*, the sausages known in English as chitterlings, and *tripes*, stewed for hours *à la mode de Caen*, but rendered no less palatable. A full blow-out at country restaurants in the small towns of inland Normandy – places like Conches, Vire, and the Suisse Normande – will also traditionally entail one or two pauses between courses for the *trou normand*: a glass of *Calvados* while you catch your breath before struggling on with the feast.

Normandy's long coastline ensures that it is also a great place for **seafood**. Many of the larger ports and resorts have long waterfront lines of restaurants competing for attention, each with its *"copieuse" assiette de fruits de mer*. **Honfleur** is probably the most enjoyable of these, but **Dieppe**, **Cherbourg** and **Granville** also spring to mind as offering endless eating opportunities. The menus tend to be much the same as those on offer in Brittany (see p.325), if perhaps slightly more expensive.

The most famous products of Normandy's meadow-munching cows are, of course, their **cheeses**. The tradition of cheese-making in the Pays d'Auge is thought to have started in the monasteries during the Dark Ages. By the eleventh century the local products were already well defined; in 1236, the *Roman de la Rose* referred to *Angelot* cheese, identified with a small coin depicting a young angel killing a dragon. The principal modern varieties began to emerge in the seventeenth century – **Pont l'Evêque**, which is square with a washed crust, is soft but not runny, and **Livarot**, which is round, thick and firm, has a stronger flavour. Although Marie Herel is generally credited with having invented **Camembert** in the 1790s, a smaller and stodgier version of that cheese had already existed for some time. A priest fleeing the Revolution seems to have stayed in Mme Herel's farmhouse at Camembert, and suggested modifications in her cheese-making in line with the techniques he'd seen employed to manufacture Brie de Meaux – a slower process, gentler on the curd and with more thorough drainage. The rich full cheese thus created was an instant success in the market at Vimoutiers, and the development of the railways (and the invention of the chipboard cheesebox in 1880) helped to give it a worldwide popularity.

To the French, at least, the essence of Normandy is its produce. This is the land of Camembert and Calvados, cider and seafood, and a butter- and cream-based cuisine with a proud disdain for most things *nouvelle*. Economically, however, the richness of the dairy pastures has been Normandy's downfall in recent years. EU milk quotas have liquidated many small farms, and stringent sanitary regulations have forced many small-scale traditional cheese factories to close. Parts of inland Normandy are now among the most depressed of the whole country, and in the forested areas to the south, where life has never been easy, things have not improved.

CÔTE D'ALBÂTRE

The Channel ports along Normandy's upper coast, **Dieppe** and **Le Havre**, unquestionably provide a better introduction to France than their counterparts further north in Picardy, though things get livelier and warmer to the west, and it's only a short train or bus ride to Rouen. An impressive display of white cliffs has earned this stretch of seashore the epithet of "Alabaster coast", and occasional surprises can be found beyond the windswept and tide-chased walks, such as a wonderful Lutyens fantasy at **Varengeville** and the Hammer Horror Benedictine distillery at **Fécamp**.

Dieppe and around

Crowded between high cliff headlands, **DIEPPE** is an enjoyably small-scale port. It's industrious, with the commercial docks unloading half the bananas of the Antilles and forty percent of all shellfish destined to slither down French throats. The markets sell fish right off the boats, displayed with the usual Gallic flair, and the sole, scallops and turbot available in profusion at the restaurants may well tempt you to stay. Even if you do immediately head south by train, the line runs along the *quais* of the fishing port, so you can get a whiff of what you're missing.

The town used to be more of a resort; Parisians would take the sea air here in the days before fast cars took them further afield. In the nineteenth century, the French would promenade along the front while the English colony indulged in the peculiar pastime of swimming – hence the extravagant space allotted to the seafront and "salt water therapy centre" (now hemmed in by car parks). The streets at the heart of Dieppe tend to be run down and in continual shadow – little advertisement for the eighteenth-century town planning to which they are supposed to be a monument. Livelier, particularly for its Saturday **market**, is the pedestrianized **Grande-Rue**.

Arrival and accommodation

Dieppe's **tourist office** is on the pont Ango, which separates the ferry harbour from the pleasure port; you can't miss it if you're arriving by ferry (Mon–Sat 9am–noon & 2–7pm; Oct–April closes 6pm; ☎35.84.11.77), alongside the very ordinary Hôtel de Ville. A beach annexe at Rotonde de la Plage is open in summer (July & Aug Tues–Sun 10am–1pm & 3–8pm; May, June & first two weeks of Sept, Sat & Sun 10am–1pm & 3–8pm; ☎34.84.28.70).

There are between three and four daily *Sealink* **ferries** from Dieppe to Newhaven all year round. The **gare maritime** is on quai Henri IV (foot passengers can buy tickets daily 10am–6pm & 10pm–5am, or call ☎35.06.39.19; car terminal open daily 9am–6am, vehicle ticket reservations ☎35.06.39.00) – see p.8 for crossong details. Connecting trains for the ferries draw up alongside on the quay, although the main **gare SNCF** (☎35.98.50.50) is 500m away on bd Clemenceau, 1km from the beach. The **gare routière** (☎35.84.21.97) is right alongside.

Dieppe has plenty of **hotels**; on the whole, prices get progressively cheaper as you head further inland from the seafront, which is actually among the quietest areas of town, especially near the castle end away from the car-ferry traffic.

Hotels

Hôtel Les Arcades, 1–3 Arcades de la Bourse (☎35.84.14.12). Facing the port; particularly suitable for tired passengers arriving at midnight and not wanting to walk more than 200 yards to find a bed. Restaurant with full, good-value menus from 75F. ②.

Hôtel Epsom, 11 bd de Verdun (☎35.84.10.18). Facing the sea, this newly refurbished hotel is bright and cheerful, with TV in all rooms. *English Bar* with tartan carpet and resident pianist. No restaurant. ③.

Hôtel de la Jetée, 5 rue de l'Asile Thomas (☎35.84.89.98). Very welcoming place overlooking the sea, with plain but spacious rooms. ①.

Hôtel Select, 1 rue Toustain (☎35.84.14.66). Very grand red-brick building at the far (western) end of rue de la Baine, opposite the steps up to the château. Serves a "Great British Breakfast" for 59F all day long – to all. No restaurant. ②.

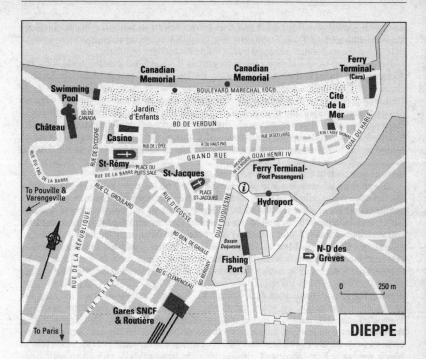

Hôtel Tourist, 16 rue de la Halle au Blé (☎35.06.10.10). Very plain rooms in a converted town house, one block back from the beach behind the Casino (a typical high-class gambling den). No restaurant. ①.

Hôtel Windsor, 18 bd de Verdun (☎35.84.15.23). You pay premium rates for sea-facing rooms in this *logis*, where the panoramic first-floor dining room – *Le Haut Gallion* – has menus from 80F. Lavish buffet breakfasts. ②-④.

Youth hostels and campsites

IYHF youth hostel, 48 rue Louis Fromager, 2km southwest of the *gare SNCF* in the Quartier Janval (☎35.84.85.73). Neither comfortable nor convenient on top a hill and on bus route #2, direction *Val Druel*; get off at the *Château Michel* stop. Open year-round, except for two weeks in December and two weeks in February. ①.

Camping Vitamin, Chemin des Vertus (☎35.82.11.11). Three-star place on the #2 bus route. April–Oct.

Camping du Pre Saint Nicholas, route de Pourville (☎35.84.11.39). Two-star site west along the coast, 3km beyond the château. All year.

The Town

The **place du Puits Salé**, dominated by the huge **Café des Tribunaux**, is at the centre of the old town. The café was built as an inn towards the end of the seventeenth century and briefly became Dieppe's town hall after the previous one was bombarded by the British in 1694. In the late nineteenth century, it was favoured by painters and writers such as Renoir, Monet, Sickert, Whistler and Pissarro. It's now a cavernous café, with sombre wooden panels and dark-brown velveteen walls, the haunt of college students and open until after midnight. For English visitors, its most evocative association is that the exiled and unhappy Oscar Wilde drank here regularly.

For monuments, the obvious place to start is the medieval **castle** overlooking the seafront from the west, home of the **Musée de Dieppe** and two showpiece collections (June–Sept daily 10am–noon & 2–6pm; Oct–May Mon & Wed–Sat 10am–noon & 2–5pm, Sun 10am–noon & 2–6pm; 13F). The first is a group of carved ivories – virtuoso pieces of sawing, filing and chipping of the plundered riches of Africa, shipped back to the town by early Dieppe "explorers". The other permanent exhibition is made up of a hundred or so prints by the co-founder of Cubism, Georges Braque, who went to school in Le Havre, spent summers in Dieppe and is buried just west of the town at Varangeville-sur-Mer (see opposite). Only a small number of prints are displayed at any one time, but in theory you can see the rest if you ask.

An exit from the western side of the castle takes you out onto a path up to the **cliffs**. On the other side, a flight of steps leads down to the **square du Canada**, originally a commemoration of the role played by Dieppe sailors in the colonization of Canada. Now a small plaque is dedicated to the Canadian soldiers who died in the suicidal 1942 raid on Dieppe, justified later as a trial run for the 1944 Normandy landings.

The new **Cité de la Mer**, at 37 rue de l'Asile-Thomas, just back from the harbour, sets out simultaneously to entertain children and to serve as a centre for scientific research, and succeeds in both without being all that interesting for the casual adult visitor (April–Sept Mon 2–7pm, Tues–Sun 10am–12.30pm & 2–7pm; Oct–March Mon 2–6pm, Tues–Sun 10am–noon & 2–6pm; 25F). Kids are certain to enjoy learning the principles of navigation by operating radio-controlled boats (5F for three minutes). Thereafter, the museum traces the history of sea-going vessels, featuring a Viking *drakkar* under construction following methods depicted in the Bayeux Tapestry. Next comes a very detailed geological exhibition covering the formation of the local cliffs, in which we learn how to convert shingle into sandpaper. Visits culminate with large **aquariums** filled with the marine life of the Channel: flat fish with bulbous eyes and twisted faces, retiring octopuses, battling lobsters, and hermaphrodite scallops (the white part is male, and the orange female). Thanks to a typical lack of sentimentality, jars of fish soup, whose exact provenance is not made explicit, are on sale at the exit.

Eating and drinking

The most promising area to look for **restaurants** in Dieppe is along the quai Henri IV, but there are alternatives all over the town – and note that many of the hotels reviewed above also have good dining rooms. All show a marked tendency to change name and owner overnight. Competition for ferry passengers keeps prices extremely low, so this is one of the few Norman towns where you can still find a good menu for around 50F.

The biggest **hypermarket** in the area is *Mammouth*, out of town at the Val Dunel commercial centre on the route de Rouen (RN 27).

Les Ecamias, 129 quai Henri-IV (☎35.84.67.67). Small, friendly traditional French restaurant, at the quieter, seaward end of the main quay not far from the Cité de la Mer. The 58F menu includes *moules marinières* and stuffed shellfish, and they also serve skate with capers.

Marmite Dieppoise, 8 rue Saint Jean (☎35.84.24.26). Between St-Jacques church and arcades de la Bourse. Lunch menu from 80F. Small, rustic and busy, featuring the local *marmite dieppoise* (seafood pot, with shellfish and white fish). Closed Sun pm and Mon, and Thurs pm out of season.

Le Mélie, 2 Grande rue Pollet (☎35.84.21.19). One of Dieppe's best fresh-fish restaurants, right where the fishing boats come in. Menus from 100F.

Les P'tits Bateaux, 23 quai Henri IV (☎35.06.14.74). Sixteenth-century cellar with live music until late; menus at 80F and 110F, last orders midnight. The more upmarket *Pergola* is on the ground floor. Out front, there's a lavish display of seafood on ice, and a macaw.

Les Tourelles, 43 rue du Commandant Fayolle (☎35.84.15.88). Just behind the Casino, and especially good for paellas, though it also serves all the standard seafood dishes. Menus from 65F.

Varengeville

If the museum in Dieppe has awakened your interest in Georges Braque, you may be interested in visiting his **grave** in the clifftop church some way north of **VARENGEVILLE**, 8km west of town (a 25-minute ride on bus #311 or #312, afternoons only). The tombstone is monstrous and the view along the cliffs more appealing than the artist's stained-glass windows.

Back along the road from the church, the **Bois des Moutiers** was one of British architect Edwin Lutyens' first commissions, and is a very un-French ensemble in almost every respect. Enthusiastic guides lead you through the gardens (daily mid-March to mid-Nov 9am–noon & 2–7pm; closed Sat am; 25F), as well as the highly innovative construction and composition of the house (July & Aug Mon & Wed–Sat 9am–noon & 2–7pm, Sun 2–7pm). The colours of the Burne-Jones tapestry hanging in the stairwell were copied from Renaissance cloth in William Morris' studio, with the rhododendrons chosen from similar samples. Paths lead through vistas based on paintings by Poussin, Lorrain and other eighteenth-century artists; no modern roses are allowed to update the colours.

West along the coast

From Dieppe to Le Havre the coast is eroding at a ferocious rate, and it's conceivable that the small resorts here, tucked in among the cliffs at the ends of a succession of valleys, may not last more than another century or so. For the moment, however, they are quietly prospering, with casinos, sports centres and yacht marinas ensuring a modest but steady summer trade.

St-Valery-en-Caux and Fécamp

The first sizeable community west of Dieppe is **ST-VALERY-EN-CAUX**, a rebuilt town which is the clearest reminder of the fighting – and massive destruction – of the Allied retreat of 1940. A monument on the western cliffs pays tribute to the French cavalry division who faced Rommel's tanks on horseback, brandishing their sabres with hopeless heroism, while beside the ruins of a German artillery emplacement on the opposite cliffs another commemorates a Scottish division, rounded up while fighting their way back to Le Havre and the boats home. The *Terrasses*, 22 rue le Parrey (☎35.97.11.22; ④), is the only hotel-restaurant actually facing the sea in St-Valery; the other, much cheaper, *logis* in town, *La Marine*, 113 rue St-Léger (☎35.97.05.09; ③), is tucked away in a back street on the west side of the harbour. The *Restaurant du Port*, 18 quai d'Amont (☎35.97.08.93), has a delicious and very fishy 115F menu.

FÉCAMP, roughly halfway between Dieppe and Le Havre, is a serious fishing port with an attractive seafront promenade. One compelling reason to pay a brief visit is to see the **Benedictine Distillery** on rue Alexandre-le-Grand, in the narrow strip of streets running parallel to the ports towards the town centre. A taste for nineteenth-century operatic horror sets is more important than a liking for the liqueur in question. Tours lasting 45 minutes (daily 9.30–11.30am & 2–5.30pm; 25F) start with a small **museum**, set firmly in the Middle Ages with props of manuscripts, locks, testaments, lamps and religious paintings beneath a nightmarish mock-Gothic roof. The first whiff of Benedictine comes in the grim rust-and-grey-coloured *Salle des Abbés*, and at this point the script abruptly changes – from mysterious monks to PR for an exclusive product. The boxes of ingredients are a rare treat for the nose (take it easy with the myrrh), and there's further theatricality in the old distillery where boxes of herbs are thrown with gusto into copper vats and alembics. (Commercial production has long since moved to an out-of-town site). Finally you are offered a *dégustation* in their bar across the road – neat, in a cocktail, or on crêpes; make sure you hold on to your ticket to qualify.

If your aesthetic sensibilities need soothing after this, the soaring medieval nave and Renaissance carved screens of the **church of the Trinité**, up in the town centre, may do the trick. Alternatively, you could feast your eyes on a Renaissance chancel on a grass floor with the open sky above and an intact Gothic lady chapel: the remains of the **Abbaye de Valmont** (daily except Wed 10am–noon & 2–6pm; Oct–April also closed Sun), 11km east from the coast (bus #261, #311 from Fécamp).

The **tourist office** is opposite the distillery at 113 rue Alexandre-le-Grand (☎35.28.51.01); the **gares SNCF** and **routière** are between the port and the town centre on av Gambetta. The **hotels** in Fécamp tend to be set back away from the sea on odd side streets. It's a popular place; you need to reserve a room at the *Hôtel de l'Univers*, 5 place St-Étienne (☎35.28.05.88; ②), or the *Angleterre*, 93 rue de la Plage (☎35.28.01.60; ②). The **youth hostel** (☎35.29.75.79; reservations ☎35.29.36.35; ①; July to mid-Sept); is near the lighthouse east of the port, along the route du Commandant-Roquigny, on the Côte de la Vierge. A superb **campsite**, the *Camping de Renneville* (☎35.28.20.97), is a short walk away on the western cliffs.

Étretat

ÉTRETAT, another 20km west towards Le Havre, is a very different kettle of fish to Fécamp. Here the alabaster cliffs are at their most spectacular – their arches, tunnels, and the solitary "needle" out to sea will doubtless be familiar from tourist brochures long before you arrive – and the town itself has grown up simply as a pleasure resort. There isn't even a port of any kind; the seafront consists of a sweeping unbroken curve of concrete above the shingle beach.

Étretat is a very pretty little place, centring on the **place Foch** just back from the sea, where the old wooden market *halles* still stand, the ground floor now converted into souvenir shops, but the beams of the balcony and roof bare and ancient. As soon as you step onto the beach you see the cliff formations to either side. To the west, on the **Falaise d'Aval**, a straightforward if precarious walk leads up the crumbing side of the cliff, with lush lawns and pastures to the inland side and German fortifications on the shore side extending to the point where the turf abruptly stops, occasionally ripped by the latest fall of cliff. From the windswept top you can see further rock formations and possibly even glimpse Le Havre, but the views back to the village sheltered in the valley, and the **Falaise d'Amont** on its eastern side – which Maupassant compared to an elephant dipping its trunk into the ocean – are what stick in the memory. The cliff itself presents an idyllic rural scene, with a gentle footpath winding up the green hillside to the little chapel of Notre-Dame.

Étretat's **tourist office** is alongside the main road through the centre of town, on place M-Guillard (daily 10am–7pm; mid-March to mid-June & mid-Sept to mid-Oct daily 10am–noon & 2–6pm; mid-Oct to mid-March Fri 2–6pm, Sat 10am–noon & 2–6pm, Sun 10am–noon; ☎35.27.05.21). Four **hotels** crowd onto all corners of place Foch, all significantly cheaper than the grand sea-view places. Much the most picturesque is the *Hôtel la Résidence* (☎35.27.02.87; ②), a dramatic half-timbered old mansion with beautiful wooden carvings decorating its every nook and cranny; the quality of rooms is variable, and you have to pay well over the odds to get one to match the setting. More dependable, and also without a restaurant, is the *Hôtel des Falaises*, opposite (☎35.27.02.77; ②) – in fact, from its modernized rooms you get a better view of the *Résidence* than if you're actually staying there.

For an absolute blow-out on seafood, you couldn't do better than *La Huitrière* in the place de Gaulle, at the foot of the steps up the Falaise d'Aval (☎35.27.02.82), which has a panoramic first-floor dining room and an enormous range of seafood platters from

82F up to the four-person triple-decker 920F extravaganza. **Campers** will find the *camping municipal* (☎35.27.07.67), 1km out on rue Guy-de-Maupassant.

Le Havre

Most ferry passengers head straight out of the port of **LE HAVRE** as quickly as the traffic will allow to escape a city that most guidebooks dismiss as dismal, disastrous and gargantuan. While it is not the most picturesque or tranquil place in Normandy, it is not the soulless urban sprawl the warnings suggest, even if the port – the second largest in France after Marseille – does take up half the Seine estuary, extending way beyond the town. The city was originally built on the orders of François I in 1517 to replace the ancient ports of Harfleur and Honfleur, then silting up, and its name was soon changed from the mouth-challenging Franciscopolis to Le Havre – "the Harbour". It became the principal trading post of France's northern coast, prospering especially during the American War of Independence and thereafter, importing cotton, sugar and tobacco. In the years before the outbreak of war in 1939, it was the European home of the great luxury liners like the *Normandie*, *Île de France* and *France*.

Le Havre suffered heavier damage than any other port in Europe during World War II. Following its near total destruction, it was rebuilt to the specifications of a single architect, Auguste Perret, between 1946 and 1964 – which makes it a rare entity, and one visibly circumscribed by constraints of time and money. The sheer sense of space can be exhilarating, as the showpiece monuments have a dramatic and winning self-confidence and the few surviving churches and other relics of the old city have been sensitively integrated into the whole. The skyline has been kept deliberately low, but the endless mundane residential blocks, which were thrown up as economically and

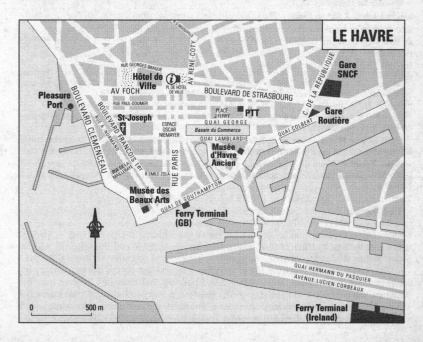

swiftly as possible after the war, get dispiriting after a while. However, with the sea visible at the end of almost every street and open public space and expanses of water at every turn, even those visitors who ultimately fail to agree with Perret's famous dictum that "concrete is beautiful" should enjoy a stroll around his city.

Arrival and accommodation

The **tourist office** is at the back, on the right, of the main Hôtel de Ville (April–Sept Mon–Sat 8.45am–12.15pm & 1.30–7pm, Sun 10am–1pm; Oct–March Mon–Sat 8.45am–12.15pm & 1.30–6.30pm, Sun 10am–1pm; ☎35.21.22.88), and the **post office** is on rue Jules Siegfried (Mon–Fri 8am–7pm, Sat 8am–noon; ☎35.42.45.67).

The **gare SNCF** (☎35.98.50.50) is 1.5km west, on cours de la République, right alongside the **gare routière** (☎35.26.67.23), across bd de Strasbourg. Bus #3 from the *gare SNCF* runs to the *P&O* **European Ferries Terminal** (☎35.21.36.50), served by two daily sailings from Portsmouth, while a separate shuttle goes to the Terminal d'Ireland (☎35.53.28.83) to connect with *Irish Continental* boats from Rosslare and Cork (summer only) – see pp.8 & 11 for crossing details.

Le Havre has two main concentrations of **hotels**: one group faces the *gare SNCF*, and there are more within walking distance of the ferry terminal. The nearest **campsite** is at the *Forêt de Montgeon* site (mid-April to Sept; ☎35.46.52.39), north of the town centre in a 700-acre forest. Take bus #1 from the Hôtel de Ville or *gare SNCF*, direction *Jacques-Monod*, getting off at *Sainte-Cecile* or *Noisetriers*.

Hotels

Hôtel Celtic, 106 rue Voltaire (☎35.42.39.77). Friendly and comfortable option, not too far from the ferry terminal, in the long buildings that flank the espace Oscar Niemeyer, overlooking the Volcano. No restaurant. ②.

Hôtel Foch, 4 rue de Caligny (☎35.42.50.69). Plain cream-coloured cement building, beside the main entrance to the St-Joseph church, offering a good standard of accommodation. ③.

Hôtel Green, 209 bd de Strasbourg (☎35.22.63.10). Double glazing – and easy parking – near the *gare SNCF*. Ten-percent discount on weekends, Sept to March. It doesn't have its own restaurant, but there are plenty nearby. ②.

Hôtel-Restaurant Monaco, 16 rue de Paris (☎35.42.21.01). The closest hotel to the ferry terminal, on quite a busy corner overlooking the quay, with a highly recommended and good-value restaurant (see below). Closed second fortnight in Feb, and Mon from July to Oct. ②.

Grand Hôtel Parisien, 1 cours de la République (☎35.25.23.83). A well-appointed place, with congenial management, facing the *gare SNCF* on the busy corner. Twenty-five percent reductions on Fri & Sat from Dec to March. ②.

Hôtel Séjour Fleuri, 71 rue Emile-Zola (☎35.41.33.81). On a side road off rue de Paris, close to the ferry terminal; not exactly "fleuri", but cheered up by some bright red shutters. No restaurant. ①.

Hôtel Yport, 27 cours de la République (☎35.25.21.08). Another option opposite the *gare SNCF*, this time slightly quieter, being set just back from the street, and unusually hospitable. No restaurant. ①–②.

The Town

One reason visitors tend to dismiss Le Havre out of hand is that it's easy – whether you're travelling by train, bus, or your own vehicle – to get to and from the city without ever seeing its downtown area, and simply see the city as an endless industrial sprawl.

The Perret-designed central **Hôtel de Ville**, a logical first port of call as it houses the tourist office (see above), is a low flat-roofed building that stretches for over hundred metres, topped by a seventeen-storey concrete tower. Surrounded by pergola walkways, flower beds, and flowing water from strata of fountains, it's an attractive, lively place with a high-tech feel, and is often the venue for imaginative civic-minded exhibitions.

Perret's other major creation, clearly visible northwest of the town hall, was the **church of St-Joseph**. Instead of the traditional elongated cross shape, the church is built on a cross of which all four arms are equally short. From the outside it's a plain mass of speckled concrete, the main doors thrown open to hint at dark interior spaces within resembling an underground car park. In fact, when you get inside it all makes sense: the altar is right in the centre, with the 100-metre bell tower rising directly above it. Very simple patterns of stained glass, all around the church and right the way up the tower, create a bright interplay of coloured light, focusing on the altar. A tight spiral concrete staircase winds its way up one corner of the shaft of the tower – not that visitors can climb it, or indeed would want to.

Le Havre's boldest specimen of modern architecture is even newer – the cultural centre known as the **Volcano**, standing at the end of the Bassin du Commerce dominating the **espace Oscar Niemeyer**. The Brazilian architect for which it is named designed this slightly asymmetrical, smooth, gleaming white cone, cut off abruptly just above the level of the surrounding buildings, so that its curving planes were undisturbed by doors or windows; the entrance is concealed beneath a white walkway in the open plaza below.

The **Bassin du Commerce**, which stretches away from the complex, is of minimal commercial significance; kayaks and rowboats can be rented to explore its regular contours, and a couple of larger boats are moored permanently to serve as clubs or restaurants; it's all disconcertingly quiet, serving mainly as an appropriate stretch of water for the graceful white footbridge of the Passarelle du Commerce to cross.

The **Musée des Beaux-Arts**, overlooking the port entrance on bd J-F-Kennedy, is one of the best-designed art galleries in the country (daily except Tues 10am–noon & 2–6pm; free). The lovely collection of French nineteenth- and twentieth-century paintings includes fifty canvases by Eugene Boudin, as well as works by Corot, Courbet, Pissarro, Sisley, Gauguin, Léger, Braque and Lurçat. Raoul Dufy, a native of Le Havre (1877–1953), has a whole room for his drawings and paintings, in which the windows at the base of the walls show water lilies in a shallow moat outside. Water lilies in oil appear along with Westminster and a snowscape sunrise by Monet.

If you have the time to spare, you might like to see what old Le Havre looked like in the prewar days when Jean-Paul Sartre wrote *La Nausée* here. He taught philosophy for five years during the 1930s in a local school, and his almost transcendent disgust with the place cannot obscure the fascination he felt in exploring the seedy dockside quarter of St-François, in those spare moments when he wasn't visiting Simone de Beauvoir in Rouen. Little survives of the city Sartre knew, but pictures and bits gathered from the rubble are on display in one of the very few buildings that escaped, the **Musée de l'Ancien Havre** at 1 rue Jerome-Bellarmato, just south of the Bassin du Commerce (Wed–Sun 10am–noon & 2–6pm; free).

Eating

Few of the **restaurants** in Le Havre are worth making a fuss about, except perhaps for some in the suburb of **Sainte-Adresse**. There are, however, lots of bars, cafés and brasseries around the *gare SNCF*, and all sorts of *crêperies* and ethnic alternatives – couscous, South American, Caribbean – in the back streets of the St-François district.

If you're **shopping** for food to take home, possibilities include the central **market**, just west of place Gambetta and ideal for fresh produce, and two hypermarkets: *Mammouth* at Montivilliers (signposted from the Tancarville road) or the larger *Auchan* at the Mont Gaillard Centre Commercial (follow cours de la République beyond the *gare SNCF*, through the tunnel, then look for signs).

La Huitrière, 12 quai Michel Féré (☎35.21.24.16). Seafood specialists in the St-François quarter, facing the rotating bridge between the English and Irish ferry ports. Even the simplest 82F *assiette* includes clams, shrimps and *langoustines*; the four-person 980F *Abondance* has to be seen to be believed. They also have branches in Étretat and Dieppe.

Lescalle, 39 pl de l'Hôtel de Ville (☎35.43.07.93). Good if not desperately inspiring or original food, served in an opulent dining room overlooking the huge town hall square. Menu from 97F. Closed Aug, plus Mon & Sun pm.

Hôtel-Restaurant Monaco, 16 rue de Paris (☎35.42.21.01). Hotel near the ferry terminal (see above), where the downstairs brasserie has outdoor seating. In the more formal restaurant upstairs, menus begin at 115F, with an unusual Livarot salad starter and salmon steaks served with *langoustines*. Closed second fortnight in Feb, and Mon from July to Oct.

Nice-Havrais, 6 pl Frédéric Sauvage, Ste-Adresse (☎35.46.14.59). Lovely sea views, excellent cooking, especially fish; moderately expensive. Closed Sun, and Mon pm.

La Petite Auberge, 32 rue de Ste-Adresse (☎35.46.27.32). Traditional French food; few surprises but no disappointments. The 125F menu offers particularly good value. Closed Mon and Sun pm.

Tilbury, 39 rue Jean-de-la-Fontaine (☎35.21.23.50). Attractive and unusual place specializing in low-priced lunches, with the emphasis on baked dishes. Closed Mon, Sat am and Sun pm.

THE SEINE VALLEY

The days of the **Seine**'s tidal bore and treacherous sandbanks are over. Heavy ships now serenely make their way up the looping river to the provincial capital of **Rouen**, the largest city of Normandy and the only one to merit a long stay. Further upstream, Monet's wonderful house and garden at **Giverny** and the medieval English frontier stronghold of **Château Gaillard** at Les Andelys also justify taking a slow route into Paris. The immense **Tancarville** suspension bridge spans the opening of the estuary just beyond Le Havre, while at **Caudebec** the yellow stays of the Pont de Brotonne produce magical optical effects on your way across; for unhurried river crossings there are *bacs* (ferries are cheaper for cars than the bridge tolls). Le Havre-to-Rouen buses (#191, #192) follow the north bank, much the best in terms of scenery.

The Parc Naturel Régional de Brotonne

Le Havre and Rouen being such vast industrial conglomerates, you might not expect the countryside between them to hold much appeal. In fact, it's a surprisingly beautiful area, designated the **Parc Naturel Régional de Brotonne** with imaginative projects run by local people to preserve the environment and traditional activities. Details on all aspects of the park can be obtained from the very helpful *Maison du Parc* at 2 rond-point-Marbec in Le Trait, near St-Wandrille (see below). After the oil refineries of Le Havre, the *parc* comes as quite a shock. On the south bank Camargue horses and Scottish highland cattle graze in the Vernier marshes, and upstream the scenery on both sides of the Seine is soft and lush like a sleeping, giant green cat.

The first town of any size on the right bank of the Seine is **CAUDEBEC-EN-CAUX**. Most traces of its long past were destroyed by fire in the last war, after which it was rebuilt. The damage – and previous local history – is recorded in the thirteenth-century **Maison des Templiers**, one of the few buildings to be spared. The town has one inexpensive **hotel**, the *Cheval Blanc* (☎35.96.21.66; ②), and even there the food is pricey. A riverside **campsite**, *Barre Y Va* (☎35.96.11.12), is a little way north of the centre. You can **rent bicycles** from M. Jaubert on rue de la Vicomte. A **market** has been held every Saturday since 1390 in the main square.

Just beyond the Pont de Brotonne as you continue towards Rouen, the medieval **abbey** in **ST-WANDRILLE** was founded – so legend has it – by a seventh-century count who, with his wife, renounced all earthly pleasures on the day of their wedding. The abbey's buildings are an attractive if curious collection: part ruin, part restoration and, in the case of the main buildings, part transplant – a fifteenth-century barn brought here just a few years ago from another Normandy village miles away. Benedictine monks are on hand to show visitors around the abbey every afternoon at 3 and 4pm, and also at 11.30am on Sunday (15F); you can hear their Gregorian chanting in their new church at morning (Mon–Sat 9.30am, Sun 10am) and evening (Mon–Wed, Fri & Sat 5.30pm; Thurs 6.45pm, Sun & hols 5pm) services.

There's a *crêperie* opposite the abbey, and the more upmarket *Deux Coronnes* restaurant in the place de l'Église (π35.96.11.44; closed Sun pm & Mon) is a seventeenth-century inn where delicious menus start at 120F.

In the next loop of the Seine, 12km on from St-Wandrille, comes the highlight of the Seine valley: the majestic **abbey** in **JUMIÈGES** (daily summer 9am–noon & 2–6pm; winter 10am–noon & 2–4pm). Destroyed as a deliberate act of policy during the Revolution, the main outline of today's haunting ruin dates from the eleventh century; William the Conqueror himself attended its consecration in 1067. The towers, nearly 60 metres high, still stand, along with part of the nave, roofless now and even more impressive because of it.

The south bank

Just across the river from Jumièges, near **HAUVILLE** (off the road to Guerande), you can look around a **windmill** (July & Aug daily 2.30–6.30pm; May, June & Sept Sat & Sun 2.30–6.30pm; March, April & Oct to mid-Nov Sun 2.30–6.30pm; 10F), one of six owned by the abbey's Benedictine monks, who farmed and forested the entire area in the Middle Ages. Its outline – based on contemporary castle towers – looks just like a kid's drawing.

If you have time, move on from here to the neighbouring village of **LA HAYE-DE-ROUTOT**. The churchyard has a novelty – a pair of millennia-old **yew trees** that are still alive but have been sufficiently hollowed out to shelter a chapel and grotto – but the feature for which the village is best known (at least in Normandy) is its annual **Fête de Sainte Claire**, held on her feast day, July 16. The centrepiece of this is a towering, conical bonfire, topped by a cross, which must survive to ensure a good year. The smouldering logs are taken home as protection against lightning. Should you miss the big day, a video recording of the goings on is featured in the local **crafts museum**, adjacent to the church, which also displays a traditional functioning bread oven and a clog-specialist shoemaker opposite (March and mid-Sept to Nov Sun & hols 2–6.30pm; April–May Sat, Sun & hols 2–6.30pm; June to mid-July Sat 2–6.30pm, Sun & hols 10am–6.30pm; mid-July to mid-Sept daily 10am–6.30pm; 8F).

For **accommodation** in the *parc* south of the river, there's a *gîte d'étape* at Routot (c/o M. Verhaeghe, π32.57.31.09) and a few rooms available at the *Maison des Métiers* in Bourneville (π32.57.40.41), which is also a beautifully presented **museum** of traditional farming and building techniques (July & Aug daily 2–7pm; mid-Feb to June & Sept to mid-Oct Mon & Wed–Sat 2–6.30pm, Sun 2.30–6.30pm; 10F). The most practical places to stay are on the north bank, either at Caudebec or in **DUCLAIR**, with a couple of cheap hotels: *L'Aigle d'Or*, 75 rue Jules-Ferry (π35.37.50.38; ①), and *Le Tartarin*, 125 pl du Général-de-Gaulle (π35.37.50.38; ①).

Rouen

You could spend a day wandering around **ROUEN** without realizing that the Seine runs through the city. The war destroyed all the bridges, the area between the cathedral and the *quais,* and much of the left bank industrial quarter. The immediate riverside area has never been adequately restored, with the result that what you might expect to be the most beautiful part of this ancient city is in fact an abomination. Instead, enormous sums were devoted to a thorough restoration job on the streets a few hundred yards north of

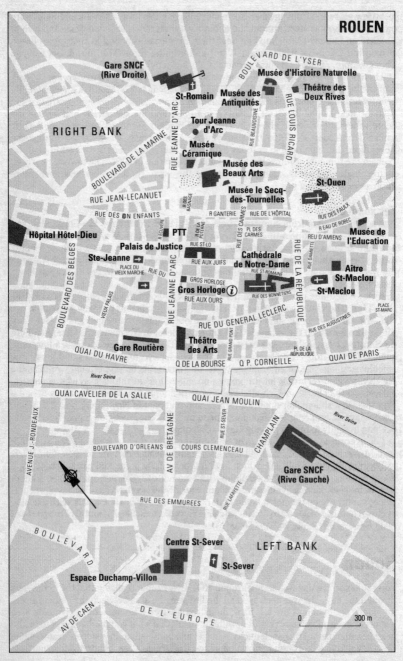

ROUEN

Gare SNCF
(Rive Droite)

BOULEVARD DE L'YSER

Musée d'Histoire Naturelle

St-Romain

Musée des
Antiquités

Théâtre des
Deux Rives

RUE LOUIS RICARD

RUE BEAUVOISINE

RUE JEANNE D'ARC

Tour Jeanne
d'Arc

RIGHT BANK

BOULEVARD DE LA MARNE

Musée
Céramique

Musée des
Beaux Arts

St-Ouen

RUE JEAN-LECANUET

Musée le Secq-
des-Tournelles

R DES
BASNAGE

RUE DES ENFANTS

R GANTERIE

RUE DE L'HÔPITAL

RUE DES FAUX

R EOUVERE

R DE LA
POTENNE

PL DES
CARMES

R EAU DE ROBEC

BOULEVARD DES BELGES

Hôpital Hôtel-Dieu

PTT

R ST-LO

RUE DES CARMES

REU D'AMIENS

Musée de
l'Education

Palais de Justice

RUE AUX JUIFS

RUE DE LA RÉPUBLIQUE

RUE LAMETTE

Ste-Jeanne

PLACE DU
VIEUX MARCHE

RUE DU ARC

Cathédrale
de Notre-Dame

Aître
St-Maclou

VIEUX PALAIS

GROS HORLOGE

RUE ST-ROMAINE

St-Maclou

Gros Horloge

RUE JEANNE D'ARC

RUE AUX OURS

RUE DES BONNETIERS

PLACE
ST-MARC

RUE DU GENERAL LECLERC

RUE DES AUGUSTINES

QUAI DU HAVRE

Gare Routière

RUE GRAND PONT

Théâtre
des Arts

PL DE LA
RÉPUBLIQUE

QUAI DE PARIS

Q DE LA BOURSE

Q P. CORNEILLE

River Seine

QUAI CAVELIER DE LA SALLE

QUAI JEAN MOULIN

River Seine

AVENUE J.-RONDEAUX

AV DE BRETAGNE

BOULEVARD D'ORLEANS

COURS CLEMENCEAU

RUE ST-SEVER

CHAMPLAIN

Gare SNCF
(Rive Gauche)

RUE DES EMMUREES

RUE LAFAYETTE

BOULEVARD

Centre St-Sever

LEFT BANK

St-Sever

Espace Duchamp-Villon

AV DE CAEN

DE L'EUROPE

0   300 m

the river, which turned the centre into an idealized medieval city – it looks authentic and probably isn't in the slightest. Historians consulted on the project suggested that the houses would have been painted in bright, clashing colours – an idea not considered sufficiently evocative or picturesque by the city authorities. Still, the churches are extremely impressive and the whole place faintly seductive.

Outside the renovated quarters, things are rather different. The city spreads deep into the loop of the Seine to the south, and increasingly into the hills to the north, while the riverbank itself is lined with a fume-filled motorway. As the nearest point that large container ships can get to Paris, the port remains the country's fourth largest – albeit in decline. Rouen's docks and industries stretch endlessly away to the south. Many workers live outside the municipal boundaries, which might explain why the left is never elected to the town hall.

Arrival and accommodation

Rouen's **tourist office**, 25 pl de la Cathédrale, opposite the cathedral, stands in the early sixteenth-century House of the Exchequer (Mon–Sat 9am–7pm, Sun 9.30am–12.30pm & 2.30–6pm; Oct–April Mon–Sat 9am–12.30pm & 2–6.30pm; ☎35.71.41.77).

The main **gare SNCF**, at the top end of rue Jeanne-d'Arc (☎35.98.50.50), is referred to as Gare Rive Droite; Gare Rive Gauche on the south bank only handles goods traffic. All town buses except #2A from here run the length of rue Jeanne-d'Arc to the Théâtre des Arts by the river, and the **gare routière** is tucked away in rue des Charettes (☎35.71.81.71) behind the riverfront buildings, one block to the west of the bottom end of rue Jeanne-d'Arc. Out-of-town buses include #191 and #192 to Le Havre along the river via Jumièges and Caudebec, #193 to Dieppe via Totes and Bacqueville, #150 to Dieppe and Le Tréport, and #261 to St-Valéry.

You can rent **bicycles** from *Freeway*, 21 rue des Bonnetiers (☎35.70.04.04), just south of the cathedral. The **post office** is halfway down rue Jeanne-d'Arc, at no. 45, in the centre of town (Mon–Fri 8am–7pm, Sat 8am–noon; ☎35.08.73.73).

There should be no difficulty in finding **accommodation** in Rouen, even at the busiest times. Few of the hotels have restaurants, chiefly because there's so wide a choice of places to eat all over town.

Hotels

Hôtel des Carmes, 33 pl des Carmes (☎35.71.92.31). This beautifully decorated old house in a quiet central square is a short way north (uphill) from the cathedral. Guests are not given keys to stay out late. No restaurant, but there are buffet breakfasts for 35F. ③.

Hôtel de la Cathédrale, 12 rue St-Romain (☎35.71.57.95). One of the very nicest hotels in Rouen, set in a pedestrianized street lined with fourteenth-century timber-framed houses. Quiet, central rooms alongside the cathedral, with a quaint old courtyard with flowers. No restaurant. ③.

Colin's Hotel, 15 rue de la Pie (☎35.71.00.88). A very modern place set around a venerable old courtyard, just the toss of a match from the place du Vieux-Marché. A high standard of comfort has quickly made this the most popular upmarket hotel in town. ⑥.

Hôtel des Familles, 4 rue Pouchet (☎35.71.69.61). Friendly, characterful place near the Gare Rive Droite. It incorporates the old *Hôtel de la Paix*; hence the two entrances. No restaurant. ④.

Hôtel de Québec, 18–24 rue de Québec (☎35.70.09.38). Near place de la République and pont Corneille, this hotel is run by a Parisian couple who are firm Anglophiles. No restaurant. ②.

Hôtel de la Rochefaucauld, 1 rue de la Rochefaucauld (☎35.71.86.58). Basic rooms near the Gare Rive Droite, but not easy to find; bear left from the station exit, and the hotel is opposite the St-Romain church. No restaurant. ④.

Hôtel Sphinx, 130 rue Beauvoisine (☎35.71.35.86). Very basic accommodation at the north end of the street near the Musée des Antiquités. None of the rooms has a shower; there's a charge of 16F per shower, and having an extra bed in the room costs 60F. No restaurant. ④.

Hôtel-Restaurant L'Union, 11–12 pl du Générale-de-Gaulle (☎35.71.46.55). Facing the Hôtel de Ville, overlooking St-Ouen church, and not all that welcoming, but the prices make it worth considering. *Plat du jour* for 39F and a not very inspiring *à la carte*. ①.

Hostellerie du Vieux Logis, 5 rue de Joyeuse (☎35.71.55.30). Cheap and old-fashioned but very comfortable place, officially considered as offering *pension de famille*, with a good-value restaurant. Guests must arrive before 10pm. ③.

Youth hostels and campsites

IYHF youth hostel, 118 bd de l'Europe (☎35.72.06.45). From the *gare SNCF* on the north bank, take bus #12, direction *Parc des Expositions*, as far as the *Diderot* stop. 11pm curfew. ①.

Camping Municipal, rue Jules-Ferry in Déville-lès-Rouen (☎35.74.07.59). Four kilometres northwest of town and reached by taking bus #2 from the Théâtre des Arts.

Camping L'Aubette, 23 Vert Buisson in St-Léger du Bourg-Denis (☎35.08.47.69). Significantly less accessible than the above, and five kilometres east of town.

The Town

Rouen spends a bigger slice of its budget on monuments than any other provincial town – which annoys many a Rouennais – and as a tourist, your one complaint may be the lack of time to visit them all.

The place du Vieux-Marché to the cathedral

The obvious place to start sightseeing is the **place du Vieux-Marché**, where a small plaque and a huge cross, nearly 20-metres high, mark the spot on which Joan of Arc was burned to death on May 30, 1431. A new memorial **church** to the saint has been built in the square – a spikey, wacky-looking thing, said to represent an upturned boat, designed to accommodate some sixteenth-century stained glass rescued from the destroyed church of St-Vincent that once stood here. It is an architectural triumph, and part of an ensemble of buildings that manages to incorporate a covered food **market** – more for show than practical shopping. The square itself is surrounded by fine old brown-and-white half-timbered houses; many on the south side are now restaurants.

From place du Vieux-Marché, **rue du Gros-Horloge** leads east towards the cathedral. Just across rue Jeanne-d'Arc you come to the **Gros Horloge** itself. A colourful, one-handed clock, it used to be on the adjacent Gothic belfry until it was moved down by popular demand in 1529, so that people could see it better. You can climb the fourteenth-century **belfry** that still contains the innards of the clock (Easter–Sept Wed 2–5.45pm, Thurs–Mon 10–11.45am & 2–5.45pm; 11F, combined with Beaux-Arts and Le Secq) for views of the surrounding towers and spires, arraying themselves in startling density.

The **Cathédrale-de-Notre-Dame** somehow remains at heart the Gothic masterpiece that was built in the twelfth and thirteenth centuries, although all kinds of vertical extensions have since been added. The west façade – intricately sculpted like the rest of the exterior – was Monet's subject for a series of studies of changing light, which now hang in the Musée d'Orsay in Paris (see p.110). Inside, the carvings of the misericords in the choir provide a study of fifteenth-century life – in secular scenes of work and habits along with the usual mythical beasts. The **ambulatory** and **crypt** hold the assorted tombs of various recumbent royalty, among them the husband of Diane de Poitiers, and the heart itself of Richard the Lionheart; both are closed on Sundays and during services.

St-Ouen and around

The **church of St-Ouen**, next to the Hôtel de Ville (which itself occupies buildings that were once part of the abbey), is larger than the cathedral and has far less decoration, so that the Gothic proportions have that instant impact rivalled by nothing built since the Middle Ages. The world which produced it – and, nearer the end of the era, the light and grace of the **church of St-Maclou** not far to the south – was one of mass death from the plague; the **Aître St-Maclou** (entrance between 184 and 186 rue Martainville) was a cemetery for the victims. It's now the tranquil garden courtyard of the Fine Arts school, but if you examine the one open lower storey of the surrounding buildings you'll discover the original deathly decorations and a mummified cat. In the square outside are several good antique bookshops, and a few art shops.

Just past the Hôtel de Ville, the **Musée des Antiquités** displays its collection in a seventeenth-century convent on rue Beauvoisine (Mon & Wed–Sat 10am–5.30pm, Sun 10am–noon & 2–6pm; 10F), and is particularly good on tapestries, along with its strong Middle Ages collection.

A five-minute walk south of St-Ouen, on the corner of rue Eau-de-Robec and rue Ruissel, is one of a new breed of intellectually self-conscious French museums – the **Musée de l'Éducation** (Tues–Sat 1–6pm; 10F), which covers the upbringing, education and general influences on children. If you're interested in conservative French ideology it's illuminating. If not, **rue Eau-de-Robec** is a good example of Rouen restoration: a pure, shallow stream makes aesthetic appearances between paved crossings to the front doors of neatly quaint houses, now inhabited by successful antique dealers.

The Musée des Beaux-Arts and around

The **Musée des Beaux-Arts** (Wed 2–6pm, Thurs–Mon 10am–noon & 2–6pm; 11F combined ticket with Gros Horloge and Le Secq des Tourelles), west of St-Ouen, itself is not very enthralling but it does include works by the Rouennais Géricault, Sisley and Monet in the Impressionist section, Dadaist pictures by Marcel Duchamp, and a collection of portraits by Jacques Émile Blanche (1861–1942) of his contemporaries – Cocteau, Stravinsky, Gide, Valéry, Mallarmé and others. But of all Rouen's museums, the most interesting and unusual is the ironmongery museum, **Musée Le Secq des Tourelles**, next to the Beaux-Arts (Wed 2–6pm, Thurs–Mon 10am–noon & 2–6pm; 11F combined ticket with above). Housed in the old and barely altered church of St-Laurent on rue Jacques-Villon, it is a brilliant collection of wrought-iron objects of all dates and descriptions. Close by, in the old Hôtel d'Hocqueville, the **Musée des Ceramiques** features a local speciality.

The Musée Flaubert

To understand more of Flaubert and for an insight into the Rouen that he knew, visit the **Musée Flaubert et de l'Histoire de la Médicine**, at the Hôtel-Dieu Hospital (daily except Mon 10am–noon & 2–6pm; ring several times; free), on the corner of rue de Lecat and rue du Contrat-Social, walkable from the centre (or bus #2a). It's infinitely more relevant to Flaubert's writings than the manuscript copies and personal mementos in the Pavillon museum in Croisset-Canteleu further downstream. Flaubert's father was chief surgeon and director of the medical school, living with his family in this house within the hospital. Even during the cholera epidemic when Gustave was eleven, he and his sister were not stopped from running around the wards or climbing along the garden wall to look into the autopsy lab. Some of the medical exhibits would certainly have been familiar objects to him – a phrenology model, a childbirth demonstrator like a giant ragdoll, and the sets of encyclopedias.

Eating and drinking

Unlike the hotels, which sometimes have cheaper weekend rates, Rouen's upmarket **restaurants** tend to charge more over weekends, when families eat out. The greatest concentration of restaurants is in place du Vieux-Marché, where there's a daily **food market**, while the area just north is full of Tunisian **takeaways**, **crêperies** and so forth.

Restaurants

Auberge St-Maclou, 224–226 rue Martainville (☎35.71.06.67). Half-timbered building in the very shadow of St-Maclou church, with tables on the street outside and an old-style ambience inside. The pedestrian street gets very crowded in summer, but the menus are far from overpriced – the 62F set lunch includes cocktail, wine and coffee. Prices to suit all budgets, and dishes including mussels and duck, as well as excellent desserts. Closed Sun pm and all day Mon.

Des Beaux Arts, 34 rue Damiette (☎35.70.17.15). On a pretty pedestrianized street north of St-Maclou church, there's very good value Algerian cuisine, like couscous or tajine from 50F, with all kinds of sausages and assorted meats. Closed Wed.

Le Boeuf Couronné, 151 rue Beauvoisine (☎35.88.68.28). In a traditional Norman house, and offering extremely traditional Norman cooking – the menu makes a theme of "grandmother's specialities". Assorted stews, skate with mustard, and above all *choucroute* of assorted meats. Menus start at 65F and rise to take in double *choucroute* in champagne. Closed Sun.

Flunch, 60 rue des Carmes (☎35.71.81.81). A large and good self-service place on a street running north from the cathedral, with many fresh dishes. Daily 11am–10pm.

Pascaline, 5 rue de la Poterne (☎35.89.67.44). North of Palais de Justice, near the flower market; a classic bistro with a purple wooden enclosure attached to the front of a half-timbered house. It's somewhat formal, but probably the most reasonable place to sample Rouennais *caneton* (duckling). Menus 55F (with a salad buffet), 75F and 95F.

Le P'tit Bec, 182 rue Eau de Robec (☎35.07.63.33). Friendly lunchtime brasserie that has become Rouen's most popular lunch spot, with a simple 69F menu holding such joys as salmon tagliatelle and chocolate fondants. Lovely outdoor setting on pedestrianized street, beside the running water and next door to a gorgeous blue half-timbered mansion. The only evening it's open is Friday; closed all day Sun.

Le Queen Mary, 1 rue du Cercle (☎35.71.52.09). Named after the boat, and the staff look like they are dressed to sail. Brasserie upstairs with *plats du jour* 38F, *formule express* 50F, and a more expensive restaurant on the ground floor. Off the northwest corner of place du Vieux-Marché. Closed Mon.

Au Temps des Cerises, 4–6 rue des Basnages (☎35.89.98.00). If you've come to Normandy for the cheeses, this is the place to get it all out of your system. Turkey breast in Camembert, goats' cheese crêpes, and above all fondues of every description. Lunch menus from 52F, from 78F in the evening. Trendy and slightly overstyled. Closed Mon lunch and all day Sun.

Walsheim, 260 rue Martainville (☎35.98.27.50). A lively Alsatian place alongside St-Maclou church. *Choucroute* specialists; all sorts of meats nestling on a fine shredded cabbage base. Menu from 59F. Ask to see the two old cider presses. Tues–Sat until midnight, Sun & Mon until 10.30pm.

Bars

Some of Rouen's most agreeable **bars** are in the maze of streets between rue Thiers and place du Vieux-Marché. Incoming sailors used to head straight for this area of the city, and the small bars are still there even if the sailors aren't.

Big Ben Pub, 95 rue du Gros-Horloge (☎35.84.44.50). Right under the big clock, hence the name. This restaurant incorporates an always-packed bar, entered from a side street – 30 rue des Vergetiers. Usually as crowded inside as in the street outside. Mon–Sat noon–2am.

La Boite à Bières, 35 rue Cauchoise (☎35.07.76.47). Half-timbered house, on the corner with rue de Fontenelle, near place du Vieux-Marché. "*Cool et pas cher*"; good choice of beers. Daily 3pm–2am.

Au Grès d'Alsace, 13 pl St-Marc (☎35.71.55.88). More of a restaurant but, despite the title and the renowned *strudel d'Alsace*, there are "frequent evenings of Irish music played by expert Bretons". In a run-down area, on southwest corner of place St-Marc and junction with rue des Augustins.

Scottish Pub, 21 rue Verte (☎35.71.46.22). Bar and restaurant right next to the station, with jazz groups from time to time. Open until 2am, closed Sat lunchtime and Sun.

La Taverne Saint Amand, 11 rue St-Amand (☎35.88.51.34). Popular bar off rue de la République above the cathedral serving draught Guinness.

Nightlife and entertainment

As you would expect in a conurbation of 400,000, there's always plenty going on in Rouen, from classical concerts in churches to alternative events in community and commercial centres. An annual handbook, *Le P'tit Normand*, available in all newsagents, is helpful with addresses and telephone numbers. For current events, pick up the free *Cette Semaine à Rouen* from the tourist office.

Rouen has four **theatres** that mainly work to winter seasons, and a wide assortment of one-night performances (jazz, rock, dance, satire) is presented at *Espace Duchamp-Villon* in place de la Verrerie, Saint-Sever, south of the river (☎35.62.31.31). *Le Bateau Ivre*, 17 rue des Sapins (☎35.70.09.05; closed Sun, Mon & all Aug), puts on musical and café-theatre performances of all kinds, while concerts and other spectacles are held in *Hangar 23* (☎35.70.04.07), a converted warehouse down by the river.

Upstream from Rouen

Upstream from Rouen towards Paris, high cliffs on the north bank of the Seine imitate the coast, looking down on waves of green and scattered river islands. By the time you reach Les Andelys, 25km out of Rouen, you're within 100km of the capital, meaning that accommodation and eating prices tend to be geared towards affluent weekend and day-trippers. Large country estates abound in this agreeable countryside, and public transport is minimal – it's assumed any visitor has, if not a residence, then at least a car. However, infrequent buses run from Rouen to Les Andelys, and trains from Rouen call at Vernon.

The most dramatic sight anywhere along the Seine has to be Richard the Lionheart's **Château Gaillard**, perched high above **LES ANDELYS**. Constructed in a position of impregnable power, it looked down over any movement on the river at the frontier of the English king's domains. It was built in less than a year (1196–97) and might have survived intact had Henry IV not ordered its destruction in 1603. As it is, the dominant outline remains and, for once, there's free access at all times. The best route up is the path off rue Richard-Cœur-de-Lion in Petit Andelys.

The cheapest hotel in Les Andelys, *Au Soleil Levant* at 2 rue du Général-de-Gaulle (☎32.54.23.55; ②), is well back from the riverfront; the *Normandie*, 1 rue Grande (☎32.54.10.52; ②; closed Wed pm & Thurs), has a more attractive Seine-side setting, and a good, if not particularly cheap, restaurant.

Roughly 15km south of the ancient fortifications of Les Andelys on the north bank of the river, you come to **Monet's gardens** – complete with water lily pond – at **GIVERNY** (gardens and house April–Oct daily except Mon 10am–6pm; 35F, 25F gardens only). Monet lived here from 1883 till his death in 1926, and the gardens that he laid out were considered by many of his friends to be his masterpiece. Each month is reflected in a dominant colour, as are all the rooms in the house, which remain as he left them, covered floor to ceiling with his collection of Japanese prints. May and June are the best times to visit, when the rhododendrons flower around the lily pond and the wisteria winds over the Japanese bridge in bloom. But any month, from spring to autumn, is overwhelmingly beautiful in this arrangement of living shades and shapes – the one drawback being the crowds of camera-happy visitors contending to capture their own impressions of the water lilies. Monet enthusiasts may be disappointed by the absence of any of his paintings; to see his renditions of the lilies, you need to go to the Orangerie and Musée d'Orsay in Paris (see p.110)

You can rent bikes at the *gare SNCF* in nearby **VERNON** across the river, or catch the bus to the gardens that leaves from the station at 1.15pm and returns from the car park opposite the gardens at 3.15pm and 5.15pm (15F return). In Vernon itself, there's an IYHF **youth hostel** at 28 av de l'Île-de-France (☎32.21.20.51; ①), while the *Hôtel d'Evreux*, 11 pl d'Evreux (☎32.21.16.12; ②), is a fine, old, seventeenth-century town house offering comfortable accommodation and good food.

BASSE NORMANDIE

As you head west along the coast of Lower Normandy, a succession of somewhat smug and exclusive resorts – of which only **Honfleur** is especially memorable – is followed first by the beaches where the Allied armies landed in 1944, and then by the wilder, and in some places deserted, shore around the **Cotentin Peninsula**. There are two absolutely unmissable sights – the glorious island abbey of **Mont St-Michel**, and the **Bayeux Tapestry**.

The Norman Riviera

The only section of the Norman coast to have any serious delusions of grandeur is the stretch that lies immediately east of the mouth of the Seine. But the scheduled completion of the new bridge across from Le Havre threatens to make such places as **Trouville** and **Deauville** too hectic for comfort, although only **Honfleur** has all that much to lose.

Honfleur

HONFLEUR, the best preserved of the old ports of Normandy and the first you come to on the eastern Calvados coast, is a near-perfect seaside town that lacks only a beach. It used to have one, but with the accumulation of silt from the Seine, the sea has steadily withdrawn, leaving the eighteenth-century waterfront houses of **boulevard Charles V** stranded and a little surreal. The ancient port, however, still functions – the channel to the beautiful *Vieux Bassin* is kept open by regular dredging – and though only pleasure craft now use the moorings in the harbour basin, fishing boats tie up alongside the pier nearby, and you can usually buy fish either directly from the boats or from stands on the pier, still by right run by fishermen's wives. It's all highly picturesque, and very upmarket, but not so very different to the town that was the subject of artists' brushstrokes in the second half of the nineteenth century.

With the construction of a vast new bridge across the mouth of the Seine, now well on its way to completion, Honfleur will become just a few minutes' drive from giant Le Havre across the estuary mouth, and the town's sleepy persona may well change. The population is divided as to whether they should build connecting roads to encourage new trade, or bypasses to keep the traffic as far away as possible.

Arrival and accommodation

Honfleur's **tourist office** can be found on place Arthur-Boudin (Mon–Sat 9am–12.30pm & 2–6.30pm; Easter–Oct also Sun 10am–noon & 3–5pm; ☎31.89.23.30), across from the town hall. For most of the year, the tourist office organizes two-hour guided tours of the town (July–Sept Mon, Wed & Fri 3pm, Tues & Thurs 10pm; March–June & Oct Sat 3pm; 28F). The **gare routière** on the place de la Porte-du-Rouen is served by seven direct **buses** per day from Caen (#20; *Bus Verts* enquiries ☎31.89.28.41); however, the nearest train station is at Pont-l'Evêque (see p.316), connected by the Lisieux bus, #50, a twenty-minute ride away.

If finding budget **accommodation** is one of your main priorities, it probably makes sense for you not to stay in Honfleur at all, and simply to visit for the day. Especially on summer weekends, so many visitors turn up that even the most ordinary hotel can get away with charging rates well above the average for Normandy. No hotels overlook the harbour itself.

Hotels

À l'Amiral, 18 rue Brulée (☎31.89.38.26). Very plain building on a quiet side street just 100m inland from Ste-Catherine church. Garage for bikes and motorbikes. Simple but well-furnished rooms. ③.

Hôtel des Cascades, 17 pl Thiers (☎31.89.05.83). Large hotel/restaurant opening onto both the place Thiers and the cobbled rue de la Ville behind. Slightly noisy rooms upstairs, but a good-value if not all that exciting restaurant with outdoor seating; menus climb from 80F towards the expensive *fruits de mer*. Closed Mon pm, Tues out of season, and mid-Nov to mid-Feb. ③.

Hôtel du Dauphin, 10 pl Berthelot (☎31.89.15.53). Grey slate town house, just around the corner from Ste-Catherine church, with a wide assortment of rooms. Closed Jan. ③–⑤.

Hôtel Le Hamelin, 16 pl Hamelin (☎31.89.16.25). Five basic rooms, some with shower, in plain building very near the Lieutenance in the liveliest part of town. The restaurant downstairs has standard seafood menus from 70F, and manages to squeeze a few tables onto the street. ②–③.

Tilbury, 30 pl Hamelin (☎31.98.83.33). Absolutely central, a stone's throw from the Lieutenance. Well-equipped and comfortable rooms above a *crêperie*. ②–⑤.

Campsite

Camping du Phare, pl Jean-de-Vienne, at the western end of bd Charles V (☎31.89.10.26). April–Sept only.

The Town

Though Honfleur has modern suburbs and developments, it's the old centre, around the **Vieux Bassin** (old docks), you'll gravitate towards. At the *bassin*, sixteenth- and seventeenth-century slate-fronted houses, each of them one or two storeys higher than seems possible, harmonize despite their tottering and ill-matched forms into a backdrop of bobbing small craft and a swing bridge across the mouth of the dock. Here, at the harbour entrance, stands the turreted **Lieutenance**, the dwelling of the King's Lieutenant and the gateway to the inner town from the time that Samuel Champlain sailed from Honfleur to found Quebec in 1608. The church of St-Stephen on the opposite quay is now the **Musée de la Marine**, giving an overview of the town and its naval past, with an accompanying ethnographic collection and rather formal guided tours in high season (April–Sept daily 10.30am–12.30pm & 2.30–6pm; Oct–Dec & mid-Feb to March Mon–Fri 2.30–6pm, Sat & Sun 10.30am–12.30pm & 2.30–6pm; closed Jan to mid-Feb; 25F). Just behind it, two seventeenth-century **salt stores**, used to contain the precious commodity during the days of the much-hated *gabelle*, or salt tax, now stage much more palatable temporary art exhibitions during the summer months.

Honfleur's artistic past – and its present concentration of galleries and painters – owes most to Eugène Boudin, forerunner of Impressionism. He was born and worked in the town, trained the fifteen-year-old Monet, and was joined for various periods by Pissarro, Renoir and Cézanne. At the same time, Baudelaire paid visits to the town, which was also home to the composer Erik Satie. There's a fair selection of Boudin's works in the **Musée Eugène Boudin**, west of the port on place Erik-Satie (daily except Tues 10am–noon & 2–6pm; Sept to mid-March Mon & Wed–Fri 2.30–5pm, Sat & Sun 10am–noon & 2.30–5pm; closed Jan to mid-Feb; 16F), and his crayon seascapes in particular are quite appealing here in context, though the Dufys, Marquets, Frieszes and above all the Monets are the most impressive paintings on show.

Admission also gives you access to one of Monet's subjects featured in the museum, the detached belfry of the **church of Ste-Catherine**. The church and belfry are built almost entirely of wood – supposedly due to economic restraints after the Hundred Years War in the sixteenth century. It's a change from the great stone Norman churches and has the added peculiarity of being divided into twin naves, with one balcony running around both. From **rue de l'Homme-de-Bois** behind you can see yacht masts through the houses overlooking the *bassin* and, in the distance, the huge industrial panorama of Le Havre's docks.

Eating

With its abundance of day-trippers and hotel guests, Honfleur supports an astonishing number of **restaurants**, most specializing in seafood. Surprisingly few face onto the harbour itself; the narrow buildings around the edge seem to be better suited to being snack bars, *crêperies*, cafés and ice cream parlours. If you're buying your own food, look out for the excellent *La Panatérie*, a *boulangerie* selling granary and wholemeal breads on the corner of the rue des Prés and av de la République.

Auberge de la Lieutenance, 12 pl Ste-Catherine (☎31.89.07.52). Not by the Lieutenance, despite the name. Plenty of outdoor seating on the cobbled pedestrian square facing both church and nave. Gourmet dining with a heavy emphasis on oysters; menus start at 96F.

Bistro du Port, 14 quai de la Quarantaine (☎31.89.21.84). The middle of five adjacent and substantially similar restaurants, all with outdoor seating but in a not very picturesque setting beside the main road just east of the harbour. The *Bistro* has a slight competitive edge on prices for its conventional seafood menus, with good 85F and 128F menus.

Le Gars Normand, 8 quai des Passagers (☎31.89.05.28). Right in the thick of things, two small dining rooms crammed into a little house all but next door to the Lieutenance. Menus from 88F, with clams and mussels, but the main courses are very unadventurous.

Au P'tit Mareyeur, 4 rue Haute (☎31.98.84.23). Next door to a fish shop and no distance from the centre, with indoor seating only. Very good fish dishes — red crab soup with garlic — plus plenty of creamy Pays d'Auge sauces and a superb chocolate and Cointreau dessert. Main menu 119F.

Taverne de la Mer, 35 rue Haute (☎31.89.57.77). Magnificent selection of fresh seafood, in a small converted bar not far from Place Hamelin, with no outdoor seating. Starters on the cheapest (118F) menu include deep-fried triangular filo parcels of scallop and salmon served in blackberry vinegar; main courses a seafood *marmitte* in a sweet cider sauce. Also grilled fish on open wood fire.

Le Vieux Honfleur, 13 quai St-Étienne (☎31.89.15.31). The best of the restaurants around the harbour itself, with spacious al fresco dining on the usually shady, pedestrianized eastern side of the harbour. Very simple menus, but the seafood is very good, as befits prices starting at 150F.

Trouville and Deauville

Heading west along the corniche from Honfleur, green fields and fruit trees lull the land's edge, and cliffs rise from sandy beaches all the way to Trouville, 15km away. The resorts aren't exactly cheap but they're relatively undeveloped, and if you want to stop along the coast this is the place to do it. The next stretch, from Trouville to Cabourg, is what you might call the Riviera of Normandy with Trouville as "Nice" and Deauville as "Cannes", within a stone's throw of each other.

TROUVILLE retains some semblance of a real town, with a constant population and industries other than tourism. But it is still a resort – and has been ever since the imperial jackass Napoléon III started bringing his court here every summer in the 1860s. One of his dukes, looking across the river, saw, instead of marshlands, money – and lots of it, in the form of a racetrack. His vision materialized and villas appeared between the racetrack and the sea to become **DEAUVILLE**. Now you can lose money on the horses, cross five streets and lose more in the casino, then lose yourself across 200m of sports and "cure" facilities and private swimming huts before reaching the *planches*, 500m of boardwalk, beyond which rows of primary-coloured parasols obscure the view of the sea. French exclusiveness and self-esteem ooze from every suntanned pore.

Practicalities

Visits to the **tourist office** on place de la Mairie in Deauville (Mon–Sat 9am–12.30pm & 2–6.30pm, Sun 11am–4pm; ☎31.88.21.43) – or the one at 32 quai F-Moureaux in Trouville (Mon–Sat 9am–1pm & 2–7pm, Sun 10am–12.30pm & 2.30–5.30pm; Dec–March Mon–Sat 9am–12.15pm & 2–6pm; ☎31.88.36.19) – are repaid with some spectacularly revolting brochures (in English). The towns share their **gare SNCF** (served by trains from Paris via Lisieux) and **gare routière**, in between the two just south of the marina. Seven of the hourly buses from Caen continue along the coast to Honfleur daily.

As you might imagine, **hotels** are either luxurious or overpriced. The *Café-Hôtel des Sports*, 27 rue Gambetta, behind Deauville's fish market (☎31.88.22.67; ②; closed Sun), is the least expensive, while the *Charmettes*, 22 rue de la Chapelle (☎31.88.17.67; ②), is Trouville's closest equivalent. There are also three **campsites**, two in Trouville and one in Deauville. The *Café Chez Marie* at 44 rue Mirabeau in Deauville (☎31.88.34.29) is a top-quality bistro where prices are high but not outrageous, while the *Bristol* at 1 rue Paul-Besson in Trouville (☎31.88.10.37) is good for fish all day, and especially good value for lunch.

Deauville's **American Film Festival**, held in the first week of September, is the antithesis of Cannes, with public admission to a wide selection of previews.

Cabourg and Dives

The smaller resorts west towards Cabourg are equally crowded and equally short on inexpensive hotels, but they're less snobbish, and there are plenty of campsites. With an eye on the tides you can also walk beneath the **Vaches Noires** cliffs from Villers to Houlgate (4.5km).

At **CABOURG**, the *fin-de-siècle* streets of the town centre fan out in perfect symmetry from what must be the straightest promenade in France, with semicircular avenues linking them together. The resort, contemporary with Deauville, seems to be stuck in the nineteenth century – immobilized by Proust perhaps, who wrote for a while in the **Grand Hôtel**, one of an outrageous ensemble of buildings around the **Jardins du Casino**. The **tourist office** here (Mon–Sat 9.30am–12.30pm & 2–6.30pm, Sun 10am–12.30pm & 2.30–6pm; July & Aug daily 9am–7pm; ☎31.91.01.09) has full details on **hotels**. *L'Oie qui Fume*, 18 av de la Brèche-Buhot (☎31.91.27.79; ②–③; closed Sun pm & Mon, & Jan), is 100m back from the sea on a quiet road half a dozen streets west of the centre; menus at 119F and 169F both feature the eponymous goose.

Just across the river from Cabourg is the somewhat more interesting – and much older – town of **DIVES**, the port from which William the Conqueror sailed for Hastings, and like Honfleur now pushed well back from the sea. Dives has nothing in common with the aristocratic resort, other than its significance for Proust, whose dream vision "land's end church of Balbec" is the town's **Notre-Dame church**. A lively Saturday **market** focuses around the ancient oak *halles*, whose steep tiled roof must be five times the height of its walls; on market days, it's crammed with mouthwatering delicacies and Norman specialities, while more mundane produce and imported jeans are sold in the square alongside and up and down the narrow streets. Dives has a reasonable **hotel**, the *de la Gare* (☎31.91.24.52; ②), and there's a **campsite** on the way to Cabourg (and two more off the Cabourg–Lisieux road).

Caen

CAEN, capital and largest city of Basse Normandie, is not a place where you'll want to spend much time; in the months of fighting in 1944, it was devastated. The central feature is a ring of ramparts that no longer have a castle to protect, and, though there are the scattered spires and buttresses of two abbeys and eight old churches, roads

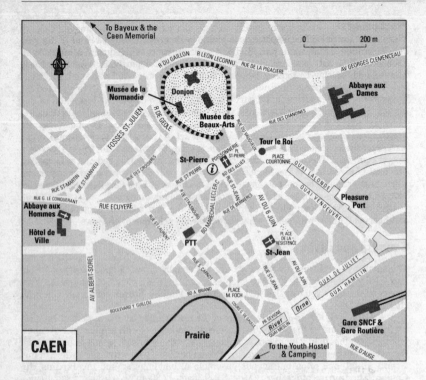

To Bayeux & the
Caen Memorial

Musée de la
Normandie

Donjon

Musée des
Beaux-Arts

Abbaye aux
Dames

Tour le Roi

St-Pierre

PLACE
COURTONNE

Pleasure
Port

Abbaye aux
Hommes

RUE ECUYERE

Hôtel de
Ville

PTT

PLACE
DE LA
RÉSISTENCE

St-Jean

PLACE
M. FOCH

Gare SNCF &
Gare Routière

Prairie

To the Youth Hostel
& Camping

CAEN

and roundabouts fill the wide spaces where prewar houses stood. Approaches are along thunderous dual carriageways through industrial suburbs – once an economic success story, currently hammered by unemployment. Even so, the city that nine hundred years ago was the favoured residence of William the Conqueror remains – in parts – highly impressive.

Arrival and accommodation

Caen's **tourist office** is across the street from the church of St-Pierre in the beautiful sixteenth-century Hôtel d'Escoville at 14 place St-Pierre (Mon–Sat 9am–7pm, Sun 10am–12.30pm & 3–6pm; Oct–May Mon 10am–noon & 2–7pm, Tues–Sat 9am–noon & 2–7pm, Sun 10am–12.30pm; ☎31.86.27.65); for details of forthcoming events in the city, pick up a copy of their free weekly *Caen Scope*. The main **post office** is on place Gambetta (Mon–Fri 8am–7pm, Sat 8am–noon).

The **gare SNCF** (☎31.83.50.50) is 1km south of the town centre, with the **gare routière** so close that you can walk directly to it from platform 1. The *Brittany Ferries* service from Portsmouth, promoted as sailing to Caen, in fact docks at Ouistreham, 15km north (see p.302). Buses from the *gare routière* connect with each sailing.

CTAC, the extensive local bus service (☎31.85.42.76), makes a one-way circuit through town between the *Tour le Roi* stop, just north of the pleasure port, and the *gare SNCF*, travelling north up av du 6-juin and south down rue St-Jean. Digital displays at the main stops show when the next bus is due, and free timetables are available from *CTAC*, 11 bd Maréchal-Leclerc, and the tourist office.

Caen has a great number of **hotels**, though as ever in the bomb-damaged cities of Normandy few could be called attractive. The main concentrations are near the *gare SNCF*, around the pleasure port, and just west of the castle and tourist office. With plenty of dedicated restaurants in town, few hotels other than those specifically mentioned below bother to provide food.

Hotels

Central Hôtel, 23 pl J-Letellier (☎31.86.18.52). By Caen standards, this is a budget hotel; not as quiet as it used to be, but very central. Good views of the château from the higher balconies. ①–②.

Hôtel-Restaurant Petite Auberge, 17 rue des Équipes-d'Urgence (☎31.86.43.30). On the way into town, just off av du 6-juin opposite St-Jean church. Good restaurant, reviewed on p.301. ②.

Hôtel le Quatrans, 17 rue Gémare (☎31.86.25.57). A little way behind the tourist office, but unmissable thanks to its garish neon-lit exterior. The pastel theme continues inside; some might find it a bit cloying, but the service is friendly, and everything works. Cheaper rooms are without showers. ②.

Hôtel Rouen, 8 pl de la Gare (☎31.34.06.03). Reasonable and convenient accommodation, facing the *gare SNCF*. No restaurant. ①–③.

Hôtel St-Etienne, 2 rue de l'Académie (☎31.86.35.82). Old stone house, dating back to before the Revolution, in the characterful St-Martin district not far from the Abbaye aux Hommes. The cheapest rooms do not have showers. ①.

Hôtel St-Pierre, 40 bd des Alliés (☎31.86.28.20). In town, immediately opposite the Tour le Roi, alongside the eponymous bus stop and place Courtonne. Cheaper rooms do not have showers. No restaurant. ①–③.

Hôtel Univers, 12 quai Vendeuvre (☎31.85.46.14). In town, near the port de Plaisance. All rooms have shower or bath. No restaurant. ②.

Youth Hostels And Campsites

IYHF youth hostel Robert-Remé, 68 bis rue E-Restout, Grace-de-Dieu (☎31.52.19.96). About 500m southwest of the *gare SNCF*. Take bus #17 from the town centre (*Tour le Roi*) or *gare SNCF*, direction Grace de Dieu, getting off at stop *Lycée Fresnil*. June–Sept. ①.

Camping OMJ, rte de Louvigny (☎31.72.60.92). The municipal campsite is near the *foyer*, beside the River Orne, (bus #13, direction *Louvigny*, stop *Camping*).

The Town

The **ramparts** of William the Conqueror's château are dramatically exposed, having been cleared of their attached medieval houses by aerial bombardment. World War II took care of the castle as well, and all that remains today is a pleasant garden inside the chunky twelfth-century walls, a partially restored chapel and the foundations of the Norman Exchequer Hall. Within the castle walls have been built two museums – an unmemorable one devoted to **Norman history**, and the far better **Beaux-Arts** (daily except Tues 10am–6pm; 20F, free Sun), which – amid comprehensive displays from fifteenth-century Italian and Flemish primitives to contemporary French artists – includes masterpieces by Poussin, Géricault, Monet and Bonnard, as well as an exceptional collection of engravings by Dürer and Rembrandt.

To the north of the château lie the buildings of the **University**, founded in 1432 by Henry VI of England, but rebuilt in the 1950s. Below the ramparts to the south is the fourteenth-century **church of St-Pierre**, its façade reconstructed since the war – which thankfully spared the magnificent Renaissance stonework of the apse, even though it blew the magnificent thirteenth-century spire to smithereens. Neatly segregated at the west and east of the town stand Caen's two great Romanesque constructions: the Abbaye aux Hommes and the Abbaye aux Dames.

The **Abbaye aux Hommes**, at the end of rue St-Pierre, was founded by William the Conqueror and designed to hold his tomb within the huge, austere Romanesque **church of St-Étienne**, where much of Caen's population sought shelter during the devastating 1944 bombardment; miraculously, considering the extent of the damage to the town, St-Étienne is still essentially Norman, with a few thirteenth-century additions like the spires and east end. Adjoining the church are the abbey buildings, designed during the eighteenth century and now housing the Hôtel de Ville (visitable during office hours); there are some splendid rooms inside, and the carving is especially notable.

At the other end of the town centre, at the end of rue des Chanoines, is the **Abbaye aux Dames**, commissioned by William's wife Matilda in the hope of saving her soul after committing the godless sin of marrying her cousin. Her monument – the church of **La Trinité** – is even more starkly impressive than her husband's, with a gloomy pillared crypt, wonderful stained glass behind the altar, and odd sculptural details like the fish curled up in the holy-water stoup. The convent buildings today house the regional council but are open to the public for free guided tours (daily 2.30pm & 4pm).

Most of the centre of Caen is taken up with busy new shopping developments and pedestrian precincts, where the cafés are distinguished by names such as *Fast Food Glamour Vault*. Outlets of the big Parisian stores – and of the aristocrats' grocers, *Hédiard,* in the cours des Halles – are here, along with good local rivals. The main city **market** takes place on Friday, spreading along both sides of Fosse St-Julien, and there's also a Sunday market in place Courtonne. The **pleasure port,** at the end of the canal which links Caen to the sea, is where most life goes on, at least in summer.

Just north of Caen, at the end of av Marshal-Montgomery in the Folie Couvrechef area, the relatively new **Caen Memorial** – "a museum for peace" – stands on a plateau named after General Eisenhower (daily June–Aug 9am–9pm, last entry 8.15pm; Sept–May 9am–7pm, last entry 5.45pm; closed first fortnight of Jan; 55F, under-10s and World War II veterans free), which ends on a clifftop beneath which the Germans had their HQ in June and July 1944. Funds and material for it came from the US, Britain, Canada, Germany, Poland, the former Czechoslovakia, the USSR and France. One section in this typically French high-tech, novel-architecture conception deals with the rise of fascism in Germany, another with resistance and collaboration in France. A third charts all the major battles of World War II, and finally there's a film documentary on all the conflicts since 1945. Though a touch naive in its historical analysis, it is a great improvement on the older war-glorifying museums of Normandy.

The memorial is on bus routes #12 (Mon–Fri) and #14 (Sat & Sun) from the Tour le Roi stop in the centre of town.

Eating

Caen's town centre offers two major areas for **eating**; cosmopolitan restaurants in the pedestrianized **quartier Vaugueux** and the streets off **rue de Geôle**, near the western ramparts, particularly rue des Croisiers and rue Gémare, with more traditional French restaurants.

L'Alcide, 1 pl Courtonne (☎31.44.18.06). Very conspicuous but rather anonymous-looking bistro-style place, which turns out to be surprisingly good, serving classic French dishes cooked with great attention to detail. Menus from 70F up to 130F.

Le Bœuf Ferré, 10 rue des Croisiers (☎31.85.36.40). Standard gourmet restaurant, all indoors, with stone walls and timbered ceiling. Rich and substantial meals; oysters and scallops to start, followed by *rable de lièvre* with fresh pasta. Midday menu 75F, dinners from 99F. Closed Sat am & Sun, also the first fortnight in March and the second fortnight in July.

Insolite, 16 rue du Vaugueux (☎31.43.83.87). Not the prettiest of this row of half-timbered houses, but some outdoor seating, and a wide assortment of fish dishes. Open until late, with menus at 95F and 160F. Closed Sun pm and Mon.

Le Paquebot, 7 rue des Croisiers (☎31.85.10.10). Sophisticated but relatively inexpensive French cooking in the courtyard of the Abbaye des Croisiers, west of the château. The 60F lunches are a real bargain, but even in the evenings the set menus start at 75F. Closed Sat am & Sun.

Hôtel-Restaurant Petite Auberge, 17 rue des Equipes-d'Urgence (☎31.86.43.30). Plain and simple restaurant, with a nice view of the St-Jean church. Very good value Norman specialities; a 65F menu which doesn't force you to eat tripe. Closed Sun pm and Mon.

Tongasoa, 7 rue du Vaugueux (☎31.43.87.15). Midday menu 55F; evening menus from 85F. Dishes from Madagascar, Réunion and the Seychelles – especially fish, curried, cooked with ginger and tropical fruits, or just plain. Cocktails galore, in lurid colours. Open every day.

The D-Day beaches

Fifty years on, it is all but impossible to picture the scene at dawn on **D-Day**, June 6, 1944, when Allied troops landed along the Norman coast between the mouth of the Orne and Les Dunes de Varneville on the Cotentin Peninsula. For the most part, these are innocuous beaches backed by gentle dunes, and yet this foothold in Europe was won at the cost of 100,000 soldiers' lives. That the invasion happened here, and not nearer to Germany, was partly due to the failure of the Canadian raid on Dieppe in 1942. The ensuing **Battle of Normandy** killed thousands of civilians and reduced nearly 600 towns and villages to rubble but, within a week of its eventual conclusion, Paris was liberated.

The **beaches** are still often referred to by their wartime code names: Sword, Juno, Gold, Omaha and Utah. Substantial traces of the fighting are rare, the most remarkable being the remains of the astounding **Mulberry Harbour** at **Arromanches**, 10km northeast of Bayeux. Further west, at **Pointe du Hoc** on Omaha Beach, the cliff heights are still deeply pitted with German bunkers and shell holes, while the church at **Ste-Mère-Église**, from which the US paratrooper who became entangled in the steeple dangled during heavy fighting throughout *The Longest Day*, still stands, and now has a model parachute permanently fastened to the roof.

Just about every coastal town has its **war museum**. These tend as a rule to shy away from the unbearable reality of war in favour of *Boy's Own*-style heroics, but the wealth of incidental human detail can nonetheless be overpowering.

Veterans and their descendants apart, visitors these days come to this stretch of coast for its **seaside**: sand and seafood (the best oysters are at Courseulles), plenty of

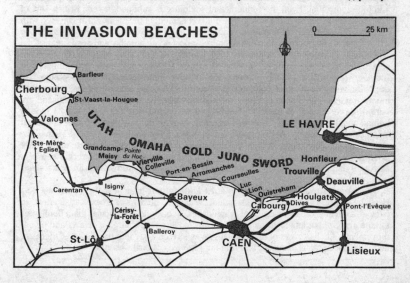

THE INVASION BEACHES

campsites and no Deauville chic. In theory, **buses** run all along this coast. From Bayeux, #74 goes to Arromanches and Corseulles, #70 to Port-en-Bessin and Vierville, #7 to Isigny. From Caen, #30 runs inland to Isigny via Bayeux, #1 to Ouistreham and on to Luc. None of these services, however, except for those linking Caen with the Ouistreham ferries, is reliable – if you don't have a car, you're better off cycling or joining one of the organized **tours** from Bayeux detailed on p.205.

Ouistreham

The small community of **OUISTREHAM**, on the coast 15km north of Caen and connected to it by a fast dual carriageway, gives the impression that it can barely believe its luck at having become a major ferry port. Since *Brittany Ferries* started their service here in 1986, the easternmost of the D-Day resorts has developed an extensive array of

THE WAR CEMETERIES

The **World War II cemeteries** that dot the Norman countryside are filled with foreigners; most of the French dead are buried in the churchyards of their home towns. After the war, some people felt that the soldiers should remain buried in the original makeshift graves dug where they fell. Instead, commissions went about gathering the remains into purpose-built cemeteries devoted to the separate warring nations. It is a moving and salutary experience to visit these cemeteries, and to consider their contrasting styles.

The **British** and **Commonwealth** cemeteries are magnificently maintained, and open in every sense. They tend not to be screened off with hedges or walls, or to be forbidding expanses of manicured lawn, but are instead intimate, punctuated with bright flowers. The family of each soldier was invited to suggest an inscription for his tomb, making each grave very personal and yet part of a common attempt to bring some meaning to the carnage. Some epitaphs are questioning – "One day we will understand"; some are accepting – "Our lad at rest"; some matter of fact, simply giving the home address; some patriotic, quoting the "corner of a foreign field that is forever England". And interspersed among them all, the chilling refrain of the anonymous "A soldier . . . known unto God". Thus the cemetery at **Ryes**, where so many of the graves bear the date of D-Day, and so many of the victims are under twenty, remains immediate and accessible – each grave clearly contains a unique individual. Even the monumental sculpture is subdued, a very British sort of fumbling for the decent thing to say. The understatement of the memorial at **Bayeux**, with its painfully contrived Latin epigram commemorating the return as liberators of "those whom William conquered", conveys an entirely appropriate humility and deep sadness.

An even more eloquent testimony to the futility of war is afforded by the **German** cemeteries, filled with soldiers who served a cause so despicable as to render any talk of "nobility" or "sacrifice" simply obscene. What such cemeteries might have been like had the Nazis won doesn't bear contemplation. As it is, they are sombre places, inconspicuous to minimize the bitterness they must still arouse. At **Orglandes** ten thousand are buried, three to each of the plain headstones set in the long flat lawn, almost hidden behind an anonymous wall. There are no noble slogans and the plain entrance is without a dedicatory monument. At the superb site of **Mont d'Huisnes** near Mont-St-Michel, the circular mausoleum holds another ten thousand, filed away in cold concrete tiers. There is no attempt to defend the indefensible, and yet one feels an overpowering sense of sorrow – that there is nothing to be said in such a place bitterly underlines the sheer waste and stupidity.

The largest **American** cemetery is at **St-Laurent-sur-Mer** near the Pointe du Hoc. Here, by contrast, the atmosphere is one of certainty. The rows of crosses are so neat, so clinical, as to give the appearance of graph paper. At one end, a muscular giant dominates a huge array of battlefield plans and diagrams, covered with surging arrows and pincer movements. Endless rows of impersonal graves stretch away into the distance; there are no individual epitaphs, just gold lettering for a few exceptional warriors.

reasonable hotels and restaurants. Any number of cafeterias and brasseries in the central place Courbonne are eager to liberate passengers from their spare change, while *Le Chanel*, just around the corner at 79 av Michel-Cabieu (☎31.96.51.69; ②), is just about the best value for both eating and sleeping. Ouistreham's road system, at least in summer, is still not quite up to the task of coping with the volume of traffic, and motorists should allow plenty of time to catch their boats. All services are connected by bus with Caen.

Arromanches

At **ARROMANCHES**, 10km northeast of Bayeux, an artificial **Mulberry harbour**, "Port Winston", protected the landings of two and a half million men and half a million vehicles during the invasion. Two of these prefab concrete constructions were built in Britain, while "doodlebugs" blitzed overhead; they were then submerged in rivers away from the prying eyes of German aircraft, and finally towed across the Channel at 4mph as the invasion began. The seafront **Musée du Débarquement**, in Arromanches' main square (daily May–Aug 9am–6.30pm; Sept–April 9–11.30am & 2–5.30pm; closed first three weeks of Jan; 30F), recounts the whole story by means of models, machinery, and movies – and the evidence of your own eyes. A huge picture window runs the length of the museum, enabling you to look straight out to where the bulky remains of the harbour, whose sheer scale is impossible to appreciate at this distance, make a strange intrusion on the beach and shallow sea bed (the other one, slightly further west on Omaha Beach, was destroyed by a ferocious storm within a few weeks). There are war memorials throughout Arromanches, with Jesus and Mary high up on the cliffs above the invasion site and helicopter trips available to overlook the area.

Nonetheless, Arromanches somehow manages to be quite a cheerful place to stay, with a lively pedestrian street of bars and brasseries, and a long expanse of sand where you can rent windsurf boards. Among **hotels**, *La Marine* on quai Canada (☎31.22.34.19; ④; mid-Feb to mid-Nov) is a little expensive but has an excellent restaurant overlooking the sea, serving fishy menus from 85F; further back from the sea is the *Arromanches*, 2 rue du Colonel-Michel (☎31.22.36.26; ②; mid-Feb to Dec).

Other possible bases

A succession of small coastal resorts stretches west from Ouistreham towards the Cotentin Peninsula; in fact, you can set out on foot from the ferry terminal and take your pick of several within a couple of hours' walk. Each tends to have one or two quintessential resort hotels, offering simple rooms upstairs above a large glass-fronted seaview dining room. The largest, Arromanches, is covered separately; of the rest, **LUC** is perhaps the nicest, but the basic experience will be similar wherever you choose to stay. **Accommodation** possibilities include: at Luc-sur-Mer *Beau Rivage* (☎31.96.49.51; ②); at Grandcamp-Maisy, *du Guesclin*, 4 quai Crampon (☎31.22.64.22; ①), and *Grandcopaise*, 84 rue A-Briand (☎31.22.63.44; ②); at Isigny-sur-Mer, *du Commerce*, 5 rue E-Demagny (☎31.22.01.44; ②). There's also a summer-only **youth hostel** in the Stade Municipal at Vierville-sur-Mer (☎31.22.00.33; ①).

Bayeux and around

BAYEUX's perfectly preserved medieval ensemble, magnificent cathedral and world-famous tapestry make it one of the high points of this part of Normandy. Set back from the coast west of Caen, and just fifteen minutes' away by train, it's a much smaller city whose charms can pall somewhat with the influx of summer tourists.

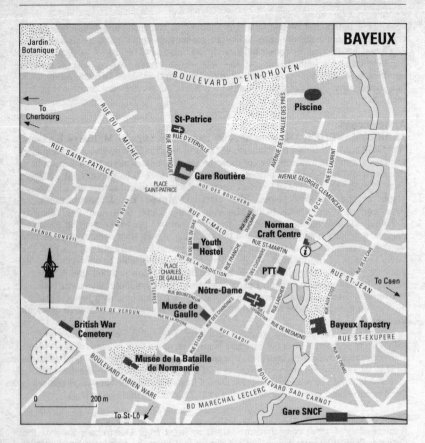

The Town

The seventeenth-century building called the Centre Guillaume-le-Conquérant served as a seminary before the hype surrounding the world-famous **Bayeux Tapestry** began to resound in its stone chambers (daily May to mid-Sept 9am–7pm; mid-March to April & mid-Sept to mid-Oct 9am–12.30pm & 2–6.30pm; otherwise 9.30am–12.30pm & 2–6pm; 20F). But visits to the world-famous Romanesque cartoon are well planned and highly atmospheric, if somewhat exhausting: you start off with a projection of slides on swathes of canvas hung as sails, before moving on to an almost full-length reproduction of the original, complete with photographic extracts and detailed commentary. Upstairs in the plush theatre, there's a film (French and English versions alternate) on the general context and craft of the piece – which you can skip if you feel you know the 1066 story well enough by now. Beyond this – and the souvenirs table – you finally approach the real thing, a seventy-metre strip of linen recounting the story of the Norman Conquest of England with an explanatory surtext in Latin. Although embroidered nine centuries ago – and used as a wagon cover during Napoleonic times – the brilliance of its coloured wools has barely faded, and the tale is enlivened throughout with scenes of medieval life, popular fables and mythical beasts. The quality of the draughtsmanship, and the sheer vigour and detail, are stunning. The work is thought to have been done by nuns in England, working under commission from Bishop Odo, William's half-brother, for the inauguration of Bayeux Cathedral in 1077. Claims advanced by an English historian in the last few years that the tapestry was of more recent origin are not accepted by most authorities. He argued, amongst other things, that the "kebabs" grilled in one beach scene show it to be post-Crusades.

The **Cathédrale Notre-Dame** was the first home of the tapestry and is just a short walk away from its latest resting-place. Despite such eighteenth-century vandalism as the monstrous fungoid baldachin that flanks the pulpit, the original Romanesque plan of the building is still intact, although only the crypt and towers date from the original work of 1077. The crypt is a beauty, its columns graced with frescoes of angels playing trumpets and bagpipes, looking exhausted by their performance for eternity. Next to the cathedral, in the shadow of the 200-year-old Liberty Tree, is a rather dull jumble of porcelain and lace in the **Musée Baron Gerard** on place des Tribunaux (daily June to mid-Sept 9am–7pm; mid-Sept to May 10am–12.30pm & 2–6pm; 15F), for which admission tickets for the tapestry are also valid.

Set behind massive guns, next to the ring road on the southwest side of town, Bayeux's **Musée de la Bataille de Normandie** (daily June–Aug 9am–7pm; mid-March to May & Sept to mid-Oct 9.30am–12.30pm & 2–6.30pm; mid-Oct to mid-March 10am–12.30pm & 2–6pm; 24F) is one of the old school of war museums, with its emphasis firmly on hardware rather than humans. By way of contrast, the understated and touching **British War Cemetery** stands immediately across the road (see box on p.302).

Although Bayeux's newest museum, the **General de Gaulle Memorial** at 10 rue de Bourbesneur, near place de Gaulle (mid-March to mid-Nov daily 9.30am–12.30pm & 2–6.30pm; 15F), is aimed squarely at French devotees of the great man, it does make an interesting detour for foreign visitors. The sheer obsessiveness of the displays, which focus on the three separate day -trips De Gaulle made to Bayeux during the course of his long life, somehow illuminates the extent to which he came to epitomize the very essence of a certain kind of Frenchness – which to foreigners seems scarcely removed from self-parody.

Practicalities

Bayeux's **tourist office** stands in the very centre of town, in what used to be the fish market on the arched pont St-Jean (Mon–Sat 9am–noon & 2–6pm; July to mid-Sept daily 10am–12.30pm & 3–6.30pm; ☎31.92.16.26). The **post office** is just around the corner on rue Larcher (Mon–Fri 8am–7pm, Sat 8am–noon; ☎31.92.01.00).

The **gare SNCF** (☎31.83.50.50) is fifteen minutes' walk away to the west, just outside the ring road, while the **gare routière** is on rue du Manche, alongside place St-Patrice (used as a car park, except during Saturday's market). Travellers without cars who plan to visit the landing beaches and/or the war cemeteries are better advised to join a **minibus trip** with a local operator such as *Bus Fly*, 24 rue Montfiquet (☎31.22.00.08), or *Normandy Tours* on place de la Gare (☎31.92.10.70).

The pick of the **hotels** has to be the *Hôtel-Restaurant Notre-Dame*, 44 rue des Cuisiniers (☎31.92.87.24; ②), with its magnificent view of the cathedral, while *Le Relais des Cèdres*, 1 bd Sadi-Carnot (☎31.21.98.07; ①), is a pretty if not all that friendly guesthouse, not far from the station. Something called the *Family House*, 39 rue Général-Dais (☎31.92.15.20; ①–②), describes itself variously as a youth hostel and a guesthouse; its prices are over the usual odds and it's a bit self-consciously jolly, but it does have its advocates and people return again and again. There's a summer-only **campsite** on bd d'Eindhoven (☎31.92.08.43), on the northern ring road (RN13) near the River Aure.

As for **food**, the *Family House* serves a filling and good-value dinner for around 60F at 8pm each evening; non-guests should phone ahead to reserve a place. Most of the restaurants are in the pedestrianized rue St-Jean – *La Rapière* at no. 53 (☎31.92.94.79) is the most popular. If they are all full, try the Chinese and Vietnamese cooking at *La Paillote d'Or*, 6 rue Génas-Duhomme (☎31.21.79.33).

Cerisy and Balleroy

Heading southwest from Bayeux towards St-Lô, you pass close to the remarkable Romanesque **Abbaye de Cerisy-la-Forêt** (daily 9am–6pm; 6F), halfway along the D572 and 5km to the north of it. With its triple tiers of windows and arches, the delicate workmanship of the nave and choir lap the sunlight into the cream Caen stone and make you sigh in wonder at the skills of medieval Norman masons.

No less notable is the **Château de Balleroy** (daily except Wed 9am–noon & 2–6pm; 40F), 3km southeast of the same junction, where you switch to an era when architects ruled over craftsmen. The main street of the village leads straight to the brick-and-stone château, a masterpiece of the celebrated seventeenth-century architect, François Mansart, and standing like a faultlessly reasoned and dogmatic argument for the power of its owners and their class. Until his recent death, it belonged to the flamboyant American press magnate Malcolm Forbes, pal of Nixon, Ford and Nancy Reagan. His is the enlarged colour photograph sharing the stairwell with Dutch still lifes, and he left his mark on most other aspects of the house, too – only the *salon* remains in its original state of glory, with brilliant portraits of the then royal family by Mignard. The expensive admission also includes a **hot-air balloon museum**, which was one of Mr Forbes' hobbies.

Neither Cerisy-la-Forêt nor the Château de Balleroy is easy to get to without transport, but with a bike or car they shouldn't be missed.

The Cotentin Peninsula

Until *Brittany Ferries* inaugurated its direct services to Brittany, the **Cotentin Peninsula**, in the far west of Normandy hard against the frontier with Brittany, provided many visitors with their first taste of western France. Now that Caen, too, has direct sailings, the port of **Cherbourg** sees only a fraction of the traffic it had twenty years ago, but the peninsula itself remains worth exploring.

Cherbourg

If the murky metropolis of **CHERBOURG** is your port of arrival, best to head straight out and on; the town itself is almost devoid of interest, and there are some really nice places within a very few kilometres to either side. Napoléon inaugurated the transformation of what had been a rather poor, but perfectly situated, natural harbour into a major transatlantic port, by means of massive artificial breakwaters. An equestrian statue commemorates his boast that in Cherbourg he would "recreate the wonders of Egypt". But there are as yet no pyramids nearer than the Louvre, and if you are waiting for a boat, the best way of filling time is to settle into a café or restaurant or do some last-minute shopping. Don't, however, leave your food shopping for the town. Unless you hit the Thursday **market**, held around rue des Halles, the standard fallback is *Le Continent* hypermarket, a real monster opposite the ferry quay.

As for walking off lunch, the only area which really encourages a ramble is over by the mainly fifteenth-century but much altered **Basilique de la Trinité** and the town **beach** – an unexpected pleasure, even if you wouldn't dream of swimming from it. Over

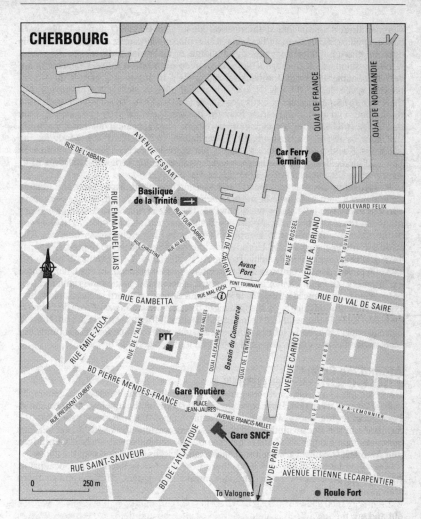

CHERBOURG

RUE DE L'ABBAYE

AVENUE CESSART

Car Ferry
Terminal

QUAI DE FRANCE

QUAI DE NORMANDIE

Basilique
de la Trinité

RUE TOUR CARRÉE

BOULEVARD FELIX

RUE EMMANUEL LIAIS

RUE CHRISTINE

RUE AU BLÉ

QUAI DE CALIGNY

Avant
Port

RUE ALF ROSSEL

AVENUE A. BRIAND

RUE DE TOURVILLE

N

RUE GAMBETTA

RUE MAL FOCH

PONT TOURNANT

RUE DU VAL DE SAIRE

RUE ÉMILE-ZOLA

RUE DE L'ALMA

PTT

RUE DES HALLES

QUAI ALEXANDRE III

Bassin du Commerce

QUAI DE L'ENTREPOT

AVENUE CARNOT

RUE DE L'ERMITAGE

BD PIERRE MENDÈS-FRANCE

RUE PRÉSIDENT LOUBERT

Gare Routière

PLACE
JEAN-JAURES

AV A-LEMONNIER

AVENUE FRANCIS-MILLET

Gare SNCF

RUE SAINT-SAUVEUR

BD DE L'ATLANTIQUE

AV DE PARIS

AVENUE ETIENNE LECARPENTIER

0   250 m

To Valognes

Roule Fort

to the south, you could alternatively climb up to the **Fort du Roule** for a view of the whole port; the fort itself contains a **museum of the war and liberation** (April–Sept Wed–Mon 9am–noon & 2–6pm; Oct–March Wed–Mon 9.30am–noon & 2–5.30pm; 12F).

Practicalities

Several cross-Channel ferry companies sail into Cherbourg. Boats from Portsmouth keep going all year round, operated by *Sealink* and *P&O*, from a terminal on quai de France (☎33.44.20.13). *Brittany Ferries* run their *Trucklines* service from Poole between May and September only (☎33.22.38.98). *Irish Ferries* also operate, in summer only, from Rosslare (☎33.44.28.96) – see pp. 8 & 11 for details of crossings.

Cherbourg's **tourist office** is at 2 quai Alexandre III (Mon 2–6pm, Tues–Fri 9am–noon & 2–6pm, Sat 9am–noon; June–Aug daily 9am–noon & 2–6pm; ☎33.93.52.02). In summer there's also a tourist information kiosk near the *P&O* terminal. The **gare SNCF** (☎33.57.50.50) is on av François-Miller/place Jean-Jaurès; the **gare routière** is opposite, though hidden from view by a building, on av François-Miller.

By the standards of the rest of Normandy, **accommodation** rates in Cherbourg are very reasonable; the main drawback for motorists planning to stay here is the lack of parking space during the day. Reasonably priced options include the clean rooms at the *Croix de Malte*, upstairs at 5 rue des Halles (☎33.43.19.16; ②), one block back from the harbour and around the corner from the theatre; the *Hôtel de la Renaissance*, 4 rue de l'Église (☎33.43.23.90; ②), facing the port in the most appealing quarter of town; and the more basic *Hôtel de la Gare*, 10 pl Jean-Jaurès (☎33.43.06.81; ①), handy for the *gares SNCF* and *routière*. You can't camp, but there is an IYHF **youth hostel** on av Louis-Lumière, 1500m east of the *gare SNCF* (☎33.44.26.31; April–Oct); take bus #1 or #2, direction *Diderot*, and get off at stop *Jean Moulin*.

Restaurants divide readily into the glass-fronted seafood places along the quai de Caligny, each with its *assiette de fruits de mer*, and the more varied, more adventurous and less expensive little places tucked away in the pedestrianized streets and alleyways of the old town. Of the former, *Le Briqueville*, 16 quai de Caligny (☎33.20.11.66), is one of the nicer alternatives, with no outside seating but huge plate-glass windows. The basic 98F menu changes daily, but has very limited choice; once you're prepared to pay 140F you're up to skate in pistachio cream. As for the latter, *La Moulerie*, 73 rue au Blé (☎33.01.11.90), doesn't bother with set menus – there's no need. Instead, it's devoted exclusively to the adoration of mussels, served in colossal ceramic bowls with a choice of ten wine-based sauces varying from sauerkraut through mustard to cumin, plus chips galore, all at around 50F. For a real last-night treat, *Le Grandgousier*, 21 rue de l'Abbaye (☎33.53.19.43), is the definitive French fish restaurant. Menus start at 98F, but this is a place to expect to spend a lot and dine well. Imagine any combination of fish, throw in a bit of caviar and a few crab claws, and you'll find it somewhere on the menu.

Around the Cotentin

Once you get away from Cherbourg, the largely rural Cotentin Peninsula is geographically an area of transition. Little ports such as **Barfleur** on the indented northern headland presage the rocky Breton coast, while inland the meadows resemble the farmlands of the Bocage and the Bessin. The long western flank with its flat beaches serves as a prelude to Mont St-Michel (see p.311), and hill towns such as **Coutances** and **Avranches** contain architectural and historical relics associated with the abbey.

Travelling by bus is not easy in northern Cotentin. Nor is hitching: the local patois has a special pejorative word for "stranger" used for foreigners, Parisians and southern Cotentins alike.

Barfleur

The pleasant little harbour village of **BARFLEUR**, 25km east of Cherbourg, was the biggest port in Normandy seven centuries ago. The population has since dwindled from nine thousand to six hundred, and fortunes have diminished alongside – most recently through the invasion of a strain of plankton that poisoned all the mussels. It's now a surprisingly low-key place, where the sweeping crescent of the grey granite quayside sees little tourist activity.

Barfleur's two best **hotels** are *Le Conquérant*, 16–18 rue St-Thomas-Becket (☎33.54.00.82; ②), a short distance back from the sea, where the rooms face on to an elegant lovely garden courtyard and there's a summer-only *crêperie*, and *Le Moderne*, tucked away south of the main road at 1 place de Gaulle (☎33.23.12.44; ①–④), where some rooms are very inexpensive and the restaurant is superb. Specialities include a grilled salmon trout stuffed with a salmon soufflé, and goats'-cheese *millefeuille*.

Near the town, about a thirty-minute walk, is the **Gatteville lighthouse**, the tallest in France. It guards the rocks on which William, son and heir of Henry I of England (and recently "outed" by historians as being gay), was drowned in 1120, together with 300 of his nobles.

St-Vaast and Valognes

Pretty **ST-VAAST-LA-HOUGUE**, 11 km south of Barfleur, is more of a resort, with lots of tiny Channel-crossing yachts moored in the bay where Edward III landed on his way to Crécy and a string of fortifications from Vauban's time. The *Hôtel de France et des Fuchsias*, 18 rue Foch (☎33.54.42.26; ②–⑤; winter closed Mon & mid-Jan to mid-Feb), with its lovely gardens and good restaurant, is an ideal stopover for ferry passengers – in fact both it and the annexe at the end of the garden are packed throughout the season with British visitors.

VALOGNES, on the main road south from Cherbourg around 18km southwest of St-Vaast, somewhat ludicrously passes itself off as "the Versailles of Normandy". The description might have had some meaning before the war, when the region was full of aristocratic mansions, but now only a scattering of fine old houses remain, along with the very scant ruins of a Gallo-Roman settlement called *Alauna*. The sum total of its attractions are a **cider museum** housed in an old watermill (June–Sept Mon, Tues & Thurs–Sat 10am–noon & 2–6pm, Sun 2–6pm; Easter–May Sat 10am–noon & 2–6pm, Sun 2–6pm; otherwise groups by appointment ☎33.40.22.73; 25F), crammed with bizarre old wooden implements and ancient warped barrels – including a particularly obscene example upstairs – a little public garden and a big empty square, activated only for the Friday **market**. But it's a quiet, convenient alternative to waiting around in Cherbourg: the best place to spend a night is the ivy-covered *Hôtel de l'Agriculture*, 16 rue L-Delisle (☎33.40.00.21; ①).

La Hague and the Nez de Jobourg

If you go west from Cherbourg to **LA HAGUE**, the northern tip of the peninsula, you'll find wild and isolated countryside where you can lean against the wind, watch waves smashing against rocks or sunbathe in a spring profusion of wild flowers. But the discharges of "low-level" radioactive wastes from the **Cap Hague nuclear reprocessing plant** may discourage you from swimming. In 1980, the Greenpeace vessel, *Rainbow Warrior*, chased a ship bringing spent Japanese fuel into Cherbourg harbour. The *Rainbow Warrior's* crew were arrested, but all charges were dropped when 3000 Cherbourg dockers threatened to strike in their support.

The main road, the D901, continues a couple of kilometres beyond the nuclear plant to **GOURY**, where the fields finally roll down to a craggy pebble coastline. Almost the only building here, the *Auberge de Goury* (☎33.52.77.01; summer closed Mon, winter closed Sat), is a really excellent **restaurant**, facing the octagonal lifeboat station and looking out towards a slate-grey lighthouse. It specializes in charcoal-grilled fish and meat, with a wide-ranging cheese board that includes the extraordinary *voluptueuse*, and is very popular at lunchtimes.

From the cape, bracken-covered hills and narrow valleys run south to the cliffs of the **Nez de Jobourg**, claimed in wild local optimism to be the highest in Europe. On the other side, facing north, **PORT RACINE** declares itself rather ludicrously to be the smallest port in France – it consists of one little jetty, some way down a hillside from a tiny and extremely tranquil pension-only hotel, *L'Erguillère* (☎33.52.75.31; ④).

Otherwise, **accommodation** is distinctly lacking in the half-tumbled-down local villages. There are campsites at Omonville-la-Rogue, Vauville and further afield at Urville-Nacqueville, which also has the *Hôtel Beaurivage* (☎33.03.52.40; ②).

South of La Hague a great curve of sand – some of it military training ground – takes the land's edge to **FLAMANVILLE** and another nuclear installation. But the next two sweeps of beach down to **CARTARET**, with sand dunes like mini-mountain ranges, are probably the best beaches in Normandy if you've got transport and a desire for solitude. There are no resorts, no hotels and just two **campsites** – at Le Rozel and Surtainville.

Coutances

The old hill town of **COUTANCES**, 65km south of Cherbourg, confined by its site to just one main street, has on its summit a landmark for all the surrounding countryside: the **Cathédrale de Notre-Dame**. Essentially Gothic, it is still very Norman in its unconventional blending of architectural traditions, and the octagonal lantern crowning the crossing in the nave is nothing short of divinely inspired. The *sons et lumières* on Sunday evenings and throughout the summer are for once a true complement to the light stone building. Also illuminated on summer nights (and left open) are the formal fountained **public gardens**.

Coutances' **gare SNCF** (☎33.07.50.77) is just over 1km southeast of the town centre (at the bottom of the hill), and serves as the stop for **buses** heading north and south. If you want to stay, the **tourist office**, in a new wing behind the Hôtel de Ville in place Georges-Léclerc (Mon–Fri 10am–12.30pm & 2–6pm; ☎33.45.17.79), will be happy to find you **accommodation**. The cream-coloured *Hôtel du Normandie*, behind and below the cathedral at 2 place du Gaulle (☎33.45.01.40; ①), has the usual assortment of rooms, and menus that range from the good-value 52F option to an excellent 95F spread. A better alternative for motorists is the *Relais du Viaduc*, 25 av de Verdun (☎33.45.02.68; ②), at the junction of the D7 and D971, south of town, which serves fine food.

Granville

From Coutances, the D971 runs down to the coast at **GRANVILLE**, the Norman equivalent of Brittany's St-Malo (see p.329), with a history of piracy and the severe citadel of the **haute ville** guarding the approaches to the bay of Mont St-Michel. Though the most lively town and popular resort in the area, it simply doesn't match the appeal of its Breton rival, with its nightmarish traffic and hordes of tourists milling around in summer in the vain hope of finding some way of amusing themselves. The great difference between Granville and St-Malo is that here the fortified citadel contains virtually nothing of interest, just three or four long, narrow, parallel streets of forbidding grey-granite eighteenth-century houses. The views up and down the coast, across to Mont-St-Michel and out to the Îles Chausey, are dramatic, but not unusually so. However, if you want to get to the Channel Islands or the Îles Chausey, whose granite was quarried for the Mont-St-Michel, this is where you embark.

Granville's **tourist office** is below the citadel at 4 cours Joinville (Mon–Sat 9am–12.30pm & 2–7pm; July & Aug Mon–Sat 9am–7.30pm, Sun 10.30am–12.30pm & 4–6pm). Trains between Paris and Cherbourg arrive well to the east at the **gare SNCF** on av Maréchal-Leclerc (☎33.57.50.50), which also serves as the **gare routière**.

With so many visitors in summer, this is a place where it's well worth booking **accommodation** in advance. There are no hotels in old Granville; most of the possibilities are concentrated in the new town. The *Michelet*, 5 rue Jules-Michelet (☎33.50.06.55; ③), which has no restaurant, is reasonably well equipped but characterless, near the casino; options nearer the station include the *Terminus* at 5 place de la Gare (☎33.50.02.05; ①). There's also an IYHF **youth hostel** in the *Centre Regional de Nautisme* (☎33.50.18.95; ①), just off bd des Admiraux Granvillois, 1km south of the station.

Where Granville really does excel is in its waterfront **restaurants**, hard below the citadel walls. The best must be a couple facing the small-boat harbour, towards the end of the peninsula; the *Restaurant du Port*, 19 rue du Port (☎33.50.00.55), has a mouthwatering assortment of very fishy menus, with a garlicky fish soup as its speciality; the

Phare, nearby at no. 11 (☎33.50.12.94; closed Tues pm & Wed), has the standard mussels and *panaché de poissons* on its 82F menu, and a copious *assiette des fruits de mer* on the 128F one. Up in the old town, *L'Echauguette*, 24 rue St-Jean (☎33.50.51.87), serves good simple meals, grilled over an open fire.

South of Granville the crowded towns and small resorts all compete for views and proximity to Mont St-Michel. **ST-JEAN-LE-THOMAS** is the first point from which you can walk at low tide across the bay to the abbey, although it's not a walk to take on a drunken – or any other – impulse. The tide, as they like to tell you, comes up faster than galloping horses. A special phone line on ☎33.50.02.67 gives advice on timing.

Avranches

AVRANCHES is the nearest large town to Mont St-Michel, and it has always had close connections with the abbey. The Mont's original church was founded by a bishop of Avranches, spurred on by the Archangel Michael, who supposedly became so impatient with the lack of progress that he prodded a hole in the bishop's skull – still to be seen in Avranches' **St-Gervais basilica**. Robert of Torigny, a subsequent abbot of St-Michel, played host in the town on several occasions to Henry II of England, the most memorable being when Henry was obliged, bare-footed and bare-headed, to do public penance for the murder of Thomas-à-Becket, on May 22, 1172. The arena for this act of contrition was Avranches Cathedral, designed, most inexpertly, by de Torigny himself: it swiftly "crumbled and fell for want of proper support", and all that marks the site today is a fenced-off platform – the *plate-forme*. A more vivid evocation of the area's medieval splendours comes from the illuminated manuscripts from the Mont, on display in the town **museum** (Easter–Sept daily except Tues 9.30am–noon & 2–6pm; 15F).

Though still some distance from the Mont, Avranches is not a bad place to base yourself. Reasonable **hotels** include *du Jardin des Plantes*, 10 pl Carnot (☎33.58.03.68; ②), which has a good-value basic restaurant; the gloriously old-fashioned *Le Croix d'Or*, 83 rue de la Constitution (☎33.58.04.88; ①; mid-March to mid-Nov), with its gardens and top-notch restaurant; and the *Bellevue*, 2 pl du Général-Patton (☎33.58.01.10; ②). The **youth hostel** is at 15 rue du Jardin-des-Plantes (☎33.58.06.54; ①; year-round).

In high summer, one bus per day runs to Mont-St-Michel from the **tourist office** on place Géneral-de-Gaulle (daily July & Aug 9am–7pm; Sept–June 10am–12.30pm & 2–7pm; ☎33.58.41.30). **Market** day is Thursday, and piped disco music on the streets goes on all summer. The **gare SNCF** is far below the town centre.

Mont St-Michel

The island of **MONT ST-MICHEL** was once known as the Mount in Peril from the Sea, as many pilgrims in medieval times drowned or were sucked under by quicksand while trying to cross the bay to the eighty-metre-high rocky outcrop. The Archangel Michael was its vigorous protector, the most militant spirit of the Church Militant, with a marked tendency to leap from rock to rock in titanic struggles against Paganism and Evil. The abbey dates back to the eighth century, when the Archangel supposedly appeared to a bishop of Avranches, Aubert, who duly founded a monastery on the island poking out of the Baie du Mont-St-Michel. Since the eleventh century – when work on the sturdy church at the peak commenced – new buildings have been grafted onto the island to produce a fortified hotch-potch of Romanesque and Gothic buildings clambering to the pinnacle of the graceful church, forming probably the most recognizable silhouette in France after the Eiffel Tower.

The Mont is barely an island anymore – the causeway (*digue*) that now leads to it is never submerged, and is silting up on both sides; couple this with the ever-constant array of tour buses and cars that use it as a car park, and the distant vision of a once remote and isolated little haven is a million miles away. It was once a large religious community, and there were never more than forty monks resident until it was converted into a prison at the time of the Revolution. On its thousandth anniversary in 1966, the Benedictines were invited to return; today, three nuns and three monks maintain a presence.

The Abbey

The **abbey** (1hr guided tours: summer 9am–6pm; winter 9.30 & 11.45am, 1.45 & 5pm; 36F; also 2hr tours in French 56F), an architectural ensemble which incorporates the high-spired archangel-topped church and the magnificent Gothic buildings known since 1228 as the **Merveille** ("The Marvel") – incorporating the entire north face, with the cloister, Knights' Hall, Refectory, Guest Hall and cellars – is visible from all around the bay, but it becomes if anything more awe inspiring the closer you approach. In Maupassant's words:

> *I reached the huge pile of rocks which bears the little city dominated by the great church. Climbing the steep narrow street, I entered the most wonderful Gothic dwelling ever made for God on this earth, a building as vast as a town, full of low rooms under oppressive ceilings and lofty galleries supported by frail pillars. I entered that gigantic granite jewel, which is as delicate as a piece of lacework, thronged with towers and slender belfries which thrust into the blue sky of day and the black sky of night their strange heads bristling with chimeras, devils, fantastic beasts and monstrous flowers, and which are linked together by carved arches of intricate design.*

The Mont's rock comes to a sharp point just below what is now the transept of the **church**, a building where the transition from Romanesque to Gothic is only too evident in the vaulting of the nave. In order to lay out the church's ground plan in the traditional shape of the cross, supporting crypts had to be built up from the surrounding hillside, and in all construction work the Chausey granite has had to be sculpted to match the exact contours of the hill. Space was always limited, and yet the building has grown through the centuries, with an architectural ingenuity that constantly surprises in its geometry – witness the shock of emerging into the light of the cloisters from the sombre Great Hall.

Not surprisingly, the building of the monastery was no smooth progression; the original church, choir, nave and tower all had to be replaced after collapsing. The style of decoration has varied, too, along with the architecture. That you now walk through halls of plain grey stones is a reflection of modern taste, specifically that of the director of the French Department of Antiquities. In the Middle Ages, the walls of public areas such as the refectory would have been festooned with tapestries and frescoes, while the original coloured tiles of the cloisters have long since been stripped away to reveal bare walls.

Having paid the standard 36F admission fee for a tour in English (or the more detailed French one that takes you higher and deeper), you are also free to wander the generally accessible areas. Intriguing scale models in the reception area show the abbey at four different stages of its historical development. Mass is said at 12.15pm every day, with a nursery provided below for children under eight years old.

The rest of the island

The base of Mont St-Michel rests on a primeval slime of sand and mud. Just above that, you pass through the heavily fortified **Porte du Roi** onto the narrow **Grande Rue**, climbing steadily around the base of the rock and lined with medieval gabled houses and a jumble of overpriced postcard and souvenir shops, maintaining the ancient tradition of prising pilgrims from their money. A plaque near the main staircase records that Jacques Cartier was presented to King François I here on May 8, 1532 and charged with exploring the shores of Canada.

The rather dry **Musée Maritime** (daily Feb to mid-Nov 9am–6pm; 40F, 66F combined ticket) offers an insight into the island's ties with the sea, while the Archangel Michael manages in just fifteen minutes to lead visitors on a voyage through space and time in the **Archéoscope** (as above), with the full majestic panoply of multi-media mumbo-jumbo. Further along the Grande Rue and up the steps towards the abbey church, next door to the eleventh-century **church of St-Pierre**, the absurd **Musée Grévin** contains such edifying specimens as a wax model of a woman drowning in a sea of mud (as above).

Large crowds gather each day at the **North Tower**, to watch the tide sweep in across the bay. During the high tides of the equinoxes (September and March), the waters are alleged to rush in like a foaming galloping horse. Seagulls wheel away in alarm, and those foolish enough to be wandering too late on the sands toward Tombelaine have to sprint to safety.

Practicalities

The island holds a surprising number of **hotels** and **restaurants**, if nothing like enough to cope with the sheer number of visitors. Most are predictably expensive, though virtually all the **hotels** seem to keep a few cheaper rooms (presumably there just isn't the space to refit and expand them in order to put the prices up). The most famous hotel, *La Mère Poulard* (☎33.60.14.04; one room ③, others ⑦–⑧), uses the time-honoured legend of its fluffy omelettes, as enjoyed by Leon Trotsky and Margaret Thatcher (if not simultaneously), to justify extortionate charges. Higher up, however, prices fall to more realistic levels. Both the *Hôtel Croix Blanche* (☎33.60.14.04; ④) and the *Mouton Blanc* (☎33.60.14.04; ②–③) serve good food. The 350-pitch *Camping du Mont-St-Michel* (☎33.60.09.33) is on the mainland a little way short of the causeway, near a grouping of half-a-dozen motel-like hotels.

Most visitors to Mont St-Michel find themselves lodging either at Avranches (see p.311) or **PONTORSON**, 6km inland. The latter has the nearest **gare SNCF** – connected to the Mont by an overpriced bus service (25F day-return), but as ever renting out **cycles**, too. Nothing much about Pontorson itself is worth staying for, although the café attached to the station isn't bad.

The **hotels** are not especially interesting, but both the *Montgomery*, 13 rue du Couesnon (☎33.60.00.09; ③), and the *Le Bretagne*, 59 rue du Couesnon (☎33.60.10.55; ③), along the main road, have very distinguished restaurants. The best budget alternative is the *de France*, 2 rue Rennes (☎33.60.29.17; ①), next to the level crossing beside the station; it has a late, youthful bar, with a pool table and a good jukebox. An IYHF **youth hostel** stands near the cathedral, a kilometre from the station, in the *Centre Duguesclin* on rue Général-Patton (☎33.60.18.65; ①; June–Sept).

FROM THE SEINE TO THE BOCAGE: INLAND NORMANDY

It's hard to pin down specific highlights in **inland Normandy**. The pleasures lie in the feel of particular landscapes – the lush meadows and orchards, the classic half-timbered houses and farm buildings, and the rivers and forests of the Norman countryside. **Gastronomy** is, of course, another major motivation – the cheeses, creams, apple and pear brandies and ciders for which the region is famous. The **Pays d'Auge** country south of Lisieux and the **Vire Valley** to the west are the best for this. The **Suisse Normande** is canoeing and rock-climbing country, and there are endless good walks in the stretch along the southern border of the province designated as the **Parc Naturel Régional de Normandie-Maine**. Of the towns, **Conches** is the most charming, **Falaise** has William the Conqueror as a constant fall-back attraction, and **Lisieux** has religious myths and a spectacularly revolting basilica to back them up.

South of the Seine

Heading south from the Seine you can follow the River Risle from the estuary just east of Honfleur, or the Eure and its tributaries from upstream of Rouen. Between the two stretches the long featureless **Neubourg Plain**. The lowest major crossing point over the Risle is at **PONT-AUDEMER**, where medieval houses lean out at alarming angles over the criss-crossing roads, rivers and canals. From here, perfect cycling roads lined with timbered farmhouses follow the river south.

The size and tranquil ethos of the **Abbaye de Bec-Hellouin**, upstream from Pont-Audemer just before Brionne, give a monastic feel to the whole valley (tours: June–Sept Mon & Wed–Fri 10am, 11am, 3pm, 4pm, & 5pm; Sat 10am, 11am, 3pm, & 4pm; Sun & hols at noon, 3pm, 3.30pm, & 4pm; Oct–May Mon & Wed–Sat 11am, 3.15pm, & 4.30pm; Sun & hols noon, 3pm, & 4pm; closed Tues; 20F). Bells echo across the water and white-robed monks go soberly about their business. From the eleventh century onwards, the abbey was one of the most important centres of intellectual learning in the Christian world; the philosopher Anselm was abbot here before becoming arch-bishop of Canterbury in 1093. Due to the Revolution, most of the monastery buildings are recent – the monks only returned in 1948 – but there are some survivals and appealing clusters of stone ruins, including the fifteenth-century **bell tower of St-Nicholas** and the cloister. Recent archbishops of Canterbury have maintained tradi-tion by coming here on retreat.

The rather twee adjacent town of **BEC-HELLOUIN** holds a **vintage car museum** (mid-June to mid-Sept daily 9am–noon & 2–7pm; mid-Sept to mid-June Fri–Tues 9am–noon & 2–7pm; 25F) and a distinctly un-ascetic **restaurant**, the wonderful *Auberge de l'Abbaye* (☎32.44.86.02; closed Mon pm, all day Tues, and mid-Jan to Feb; ④), which also has half a dozen moderately expensive **rooms**. The *Restaurant de la Tour* on place Guillaume-le-Conquérant nearby (☎32.44.86.15) is a more affordable place to eat, with some outdoor tables.

Brionne and Beaumont-le-Roger

BRIONNE, on the Rouen–Lisieux rail line, is a small town with large regional **markets** on Thursday and Sunday. The fish hall is on the left bank, the rest by the church on the right bank. Above them both, with panoramic views, is an excellent example of a Norman **donjon**. If you decide to **stay**, the *Auberge du Vieux Donjon* (☎32.44.80.62; ③) on the marketplace is good, though pricey.

The River Charentonne joins the Risle near Serquigny. The town is also the meeting point of rail lines and main roads and the banks are clogged with fuming industrial conglomerations. But 7km upstream, at **BEAUMONT-LE-ROGER**, you are back in pastoral tranquillity. The ruins of a thirteenth-century **priory church** slowly crumble to the ground, the slow restoration of one or two arches unable to keep pace. In the village, little happens beyond the hammering of the church bell next door to the abbey by a nodding musketeer. Just across the Risle from here, on the D25 near Le Val-St-Martin, huge stables are spread across an absurdly sylvan setting, and **horses** are available for riding.

The next riverside village, **LA FERRIÈRE-SUR-RISLE**, has an especially beautiful **church**, with some interesting sculpture, and a fourteenth-century covered **market hall**. Paddocks and meadows lead down to the river and two small and inviting **hotels**, the *Croissant* (☎32.30.70.13; ②) and *Vieux-Marché* (☎32.30.70.69; ②).

Conches-en-Ouche and Evreux

Fourteen kilometres east of La Ferrière across the wild and open woodland of the **Forêt de Conches**, **CONCHES-EN-OUCHE** is many a Norman's favourite heartland town, standing above the River Rouloir on an abrupt and narrow spur. At the highest point, in the middle of a row of medieval houses, is the **church of Ste-Foy**, its windows a stunning sequence of Renaissance stained glass. Behind are the gardens of the **Hôtel de Ville**, where a robust, if anatomically odd, stone boar gazes proudly out over a spectacular view. Next to that, you can scramble up the slippery steps of the ruined twelfth-century **castle**. Conches is given a certain edge over other towns with equal lists of historic relics, by the pieces of modern sculpture that seem to lie around every other corner.

Across the main street from the castle is a long **park**, with parallel avenues of trees, a large ornamental lake and fountain, and the **hotel** *Grand Mare* (☎32.30.23.30; ①), which serves up very pricey gastronomic dinners; the *Cygne* (☎32.30.20.60; ②), set around an attractive little courtyard at the north end of town, has a less appealing menu; or there's a **municipal campsite** (☎32.30.22.49). On Thursday the whole town is taken up by a **market**.

If you're heading south to Conches from Rouen, you follow first the River Eure, and then its tributary the Iton, passing through **EVREUX**, capital of the Eure *département*. It's hardly an exciting place, but an afternoon's wander in the vicinity of the **cathedral** – a minor classic with its flamboyant exterior decoration and original fourteenth-century windows – and the **ramparts** alongside the Iton river bank is pleasant. Most of the cheaper **hotels** in the town tend to shut during August. An evening is better spent in Conches or at **PACY-SUR-EURE**, where the *Hôtel de l'Étape* (☎32.36.12.77; ③) nestles at the water's edge.

Lisieux and the Pays d'Auge

The rolling hills and green twisting valleys of the **Pays d'Auge**, which stretches south of the cathedral town of **Lisieux**, are scattered with magnificent half-timbered manor houses. The pastures here are the lushest in the province, their produce the world-famous cheeses of Camembert, Livarot and Pont L'Evêque. And beside them are acres of orchards, yielding the best of Norman ciders, both apple and pear (*poiré*), as well as Calvados apple brandy.

Lisieux

LISIEUX, 35 minutes by train from Caen, is the main town of the Pays d'Auge, and a good place to get to know its cheeses and ciders is at the large **street market** on Wednesday and Saturday. Most people, however, come to Lisieux as a place of pilgrimage based around the cult of Sainte Thérèse, the most popular French spiritual figure of the last hundred years. Passivity, self-effacement and masochism were her trademarks, and she is honoured by the grotesquely gaudy and gigantic **Basilique de Ste-Thérèse**, completed in 1954 on a slope to the southwest of the town centre. Huge mosaics of her face decorate the nave, and every night at 9.30pm as part of a stunningly tasteless (and expensive) laser show, her face is simultaneously projected on every column in the church. The faithful can ride on a white, flag-bedecked fairground train around the holiest sites, which include the infinitely restrained and sober **Cathédrale St-Pierre**.

Lisieux's **tourist office**, 11 rue d'Alençon, is the best place to gather information on the rural areas further inland (Mon–Sat 8.30am–noon & 1.30–6pm; June–Sept daily 8.30am–noon & 1.30–7pm; ☎31.62.08.41). The quantity of pilgrims means that Lisieux is full of reasonably priced places to **stay**: try the *Hôtel de la Terrasse*, 25 av Ste-Thérèse (☎31.62.17.65; ②), or *Hôtel de l'Avenue*, 4 av Ste-Thérèse (☎31.62.08.37; ①), both on the hill near the basilica; or the *Hôtel des Arts*, backing on to the Bishop's gardens at 26 rue Condorcet (☎31.62.00.02; ①). There is also a large **campsite** (☎31.62.00.40), but campers would probably be better off somewhere more rural nearby, such as Livarot or Orbec.

Into the Pays d'Auge

Though the tourist authorities responsible for the Pays d'Auge have laid out a **Route de Fromage** and a **Route du Cidre** – the manor houses of Beuvron-en-Auge on the cider route, and Montpinçon and Lisores on the cheese route, are well worth finding – you won't be missing out if you don't follow these itineraries. For really good solid Norman cooking this is the perfect area to look out for *Fermes Auberges*, working farms which welcome paying visitors to share their meals. Local *Syndicats* can provide copious lists of these and of local producers from whom you can buy your cheese and booze.

There was little left after the war of the old **PONT-L'ÉVÊQUE**, the northernmost of the Pays d'Auge towns. Since then it has become such a turmoil of major roads that it's no place to stay. **CORMEILLES**, on the other hand, is a tiny (Friday) market centre, with several half-timbered restaurants to its credit. **ORBEC** lies just a few miles along a pleasant valley from the source of its river, the Orbiquet. It consists of little more than the main road of classic Norman houses with patterned tiles and bricks between the beams, ending in the huge tower of Notre-Dame church.

The centre of the cheese country is the old town of **LIVAROT**, with the **hotel** and restaurant *du Vivier* (☎31.63.50.29; ①) in its centre. The main attraction is the **Conservatoire du Fromage**, a small-scale working cheese factory (April–Oct Mon–Fri 9am–noon & 2–6pm, Sat 10am–noon; Nov–March Wed–Fri 9am–noon & 2–6pm, Sat 10am–noon; 15F), where visitors can see Camembert, Pont L'Évêque and Livarot cheeses at every stage of their production.

At **ST-PIERRE-SUR-DIVES**, the medieval market hall has been converted into a slightly academic annexe to the Livarot cheese museum. It's an impressive building, though, almost rivalling the Romanesque-Gothic church (whose windows depict the history of the town). A large **market** still takes place every Monday in the adjacent square.

Vimoutiers and Camembert

VIMOUTIERS, due south of Livarot, contains another **cheese museum** (May–Oct Mon 2–6pm, Tues–Sat 9am–noon & 2–6pm, Sun 10am–noon & 2.30–6pm; Nov, Dec, March & April Mon 2–6pm, Tues–Fri 9am–noon & 2–6pm, Sat 9am–noon; 15F). This one specializes in labels – the cheeses underneath are mostly polystyrene. At the tiny village of **CAMEMBERT**, nearby, Marie Harel developed the original soft Camembert cheese early in the nineteenth century, promoting it with a skilful campaign which even involved sending free samples to Napoléon. The **hotels** *Soleil d'Or*, 16 place Mackau (☎33.39.07.15; ①), and *Couronne*, 9 rue du 8-mai (☎33.39.03.04; ②), are good, economical places to stay, and there is also a **campsite**. Just outside the village is the **Escale du Vitou**, a lake, beautifully sited, with everything you need for windsurfing, swimming and horseback riding. In **TICHEVILLE**, roughly 5km southwest on the D12, *La Maison du Vert* (☎33.36.95.84; ②) is a small British-run hotel, highly unusual for Normandy in serving excellent vegetarian (though not vegan) food.

Along the **valley of the Vie** south of Vimoutiers runs the D26 – a route that takes in many of the best features of Normandy, lined along the way with old ramshackle barns and farm buildings. Faded orange clay crumbles out from between the weathered wooden beams of these flower-covered beauties.

Falaise

William the Conqueror, or William the Bastard as he is more commonly known over here, was born in **FALAISE**, 40km southwest of Lisieux. His mother, Arlette, a laundrywoman, was spotted by his father, Duke Robert of Normandy, at the washing-place below the château. She was a shrewd woman, scorning secrecy in her eventual assignation by riding publicly through the main entrance to meet him. During her pregnancy, she is said to have dreamed of bearing a mighty tree that cast its shade over Normandy and England.

Both the keep of the **castle**, and the **Fontaine d'Arlette** on the riverside beneath it, still exist, though so heavily restored as to be scarcely worth the ten-minute tour. The town itself was devastated in the war. The struggle to close the "Falaise Gap" in August 1944 was the climax of the Battle of Normandy, as the Allied armies sought to encircle the Germans and cut off their retreat. By the time the Canadians entered the town on August 17, they could no longer tell where the roads had been and had to bulldoze a new four-metre strip straight through the middle.

The **tourist office** can be found at 32 rue Georges-Clemenceau, the main Caen-Argentan road, which is also the (rather noisy) location of most of Falaise's few **hotels**, such as the *Poste* at no. 38 (☎31.90.13.14; ②). The **campsite**, *Camping du Château* (☎31.90.16.55), next to Arlette's Fountain and the municipal swimming pool, is in a much better location.

The Suisse Normande

The area known as the **"Suisse Normande"** lies roughly 25km south of Caen, along the gorge of the River Orne, between Thury-Harcourt and Putanges. The name is a little far-fetched – there are certainly no mountains – but it is quite distinctive, with cliffs and crags and wooded hills at every turn. The energetic race along the Orne in canoes and kayaks, while the less so are content with pedalos or a bizarre species of inflatable rubber tractor, and high above climbers dangling from thin ropes claw at the sheer rockface. For mere walkers the Orne can be frustrating: footpaths along the river are few and far between and often entirely overgrown.

The Suisse Normande is usually approached from Caen or Falaise and contrasts dramatically with the prairie-like expanse of wheatfields en route. On wheels, the best access is via the D235 from Caen (signed to Falaise then right through Ifs). The *Bus Verts* #34 will take you to **Thury-Harcourt** or **Clécy** on its way to Flers, and there are occasional special summer train excursions from Caen.

Thury-Harcourt and Clécy

At **THURY-HARCOURT**, the **tourist office** on place St-Sauveur can suggest walks, rides and *gîtes d'étape* throughout the Suisse Normande; *SIVOM* at 15 rue de Condé rents out canoes. Unfortunately, there's no very affordable hotel in town, but there are a couple of **campsites** – *Vallée du Traspy* (☎31.79.61.80) and *Camping du Bord de l'Orne* (☎31.79.70.78; June–Sept). In summer, the public park allows access to the riverside.

CLÉCY, 10km to the south, is a slightly better bet for finding a room, although its visitors outnumber its residents in peak season. The village centre is about a kilometre above the river at Pont du Vey. On the way down, in the Parc des Loisirs, is a **Musée du Chemin de Fer Miniature** (Easter–Sept daily 10am–noon & 2.15–6.30pm; 25F), featuring a model railway that may appeal to children. At the bridge is a restored watermill, run as a restaurant and hotel. The river bank continues in a brief splurge of restaurants, takeaways and snack bars as far as the 100-pitch **campsite**. The *logis* in town, *Au Site* (☎31.69.71.05; ②), isn't as good value as the *Alpes Normands* (☎31.69.45.39; ①), a short way along the road facing the church. For advice on accommodation and the wide variety of holiday activities available in Clécy, the **tourist office** is tucked in behind the church.

Pont d'Ouilly

If you're planning on walking, or cycling, one good central spot to base yourself is **PONT D'OUILLY**, at the point where the main road from Vire to Falaise crosses the river. It's a small town, with a few basic shops, an old covered market hall and a promenade (with bar) slightly upstream alongside the weir; you can walk along the riverside down to Le Mesnil Villement. As well as the **campsite** overlooking the river, there's an attractive **hotel**, the *du Commerce* (☎31.69.80.16; ②; closed Mon), with cheap rooms and wonderful food, in a dining room appropriately filled with stuffed animals. About a kilometre north, the much more upmarket *Auberge St-Christophe* (☎31.69.81.23; ③; closed Mon) stands in a beautiful setting on the right bank of the Orne, covered with ivy and geraniums and opposite a roofless and now overgrown Art Deco factory. A *Grand Pardon du Ste-Roche* takes place along the river on the third Sunday in August.

A short distance south of Pont-d'Ouilly is the **Roche d'Oëtre**, a high rock with a tremendous view into the deep and totally wooded gorge of the Rouvre. The river widens soon afterwards into the **Lac du Rabodanges**, formed by the many-arched Rabodanges Dam. It's a popular spot where people practise every watersport, and with a **campsite**, *Les Retours*, perfectly situated between the dam and the bridge on D121.

The Bocage

The region centring on **St-Lô**, just south of the Cotentin, is known as the **Bocage**, from a word that refers to a type of cultivated countryside common in the west of France, where fields are cut by tight hedgerows rooted into walls of earth well over a metre high. An effective form of smallhold farming – at least in pre-industrial days – it also proved to be a perfect system of antitank barricades. When the Allied troops tried to advance through the region in 1944 it was almost impenetrable – certainly bearing no resemblance to the East Anglian plains where they had trained. The war here was hand-to-hand, inch-by-inch slaughter, the destruction of villages often wholesale.

St-Lô

The city of **ST-LÔ**, 60km south of Cherbourg and 36km southwest of Bayeux, is still known as the "Capital of the Ruins". Memorial sites are everywhere and what is new speaks as tellingly of the destruction as the ruins that have been preserved. In the main square, the gate of the old prison commemorates Resistance members executed by the Nazis, people deported east to the concentration camps and soldiers killed in action; when the bombardment of St-Lô was at its fiercest, the Germans refused to take any measures to protect the prisoners and the gate was all that survived. Samuel Beckett was here during the battle and after, working for the Irish Red Cross as interpreter, driver and provision-seeker – for such things as rat poison for the maternity hospitals. He said he took away with him a "time-honoured conception of humanity in ruins".

All the trees in the city are the same height, all planted to replace the battle's mutilated stumps. But the most visible – and brilliant – reconstruction is the **Cathédrale de Notre-Dame**. Its main body, with a strange southward-veering nave, has been conventionally repaired and rebuilt. But the shattered west front and the base of the collapsed north tower have been joined by a startling sheer wall of icy green stone that makes no attempt to mask the destruction.

In contrast to such memories, a lighthouse-like 1950s **folly** spirals to nowhere on the main square; should you feel the urge to climb its stairway, ask at the *mairie* opposite. More compelling, around behind the *mairie*, is a **Musée des Beaux-Arts** (daily except Tues April–Oct 10am–noon & 2–6pm; Nov–March 10am–noon; free). This is full of treasures: a Boudin sunset; a Lurçat tapestry of his dog Nadir and the Pirates; works by Corot, van Loo, Moreau; a Léger watercolour; a fine series of unfaded sixteenth-century Flemish tapestries on the lives of two peasants; and sad bombardment relics of the town.

St-Lô makes an interesting pause but it's virtually abandoned at night. Most of the hotels, restaurants and bars are by the river and **gare SNCF**. Right next to the station, there's the upmarket *Logis Hôtel des Voyageurs*, 5–7 av Briovère (☎33.05.08.63; ④), with a good 100F menu; up in town, try *des Remparts*, 3 rue des Prés (☎33.57.08.06; ②). The **tourist office** is just off the central square at 2 rue Havin, and the **gare routière** is on the rue des 80ᵉ and 136ᵉ, a short way south.

The Vire Valley

Once St-Lô was taken in the Battle of Normandy, the armies speedily moved on for their next confrontation. The **Vire Valley**, trailing south from St-Lô, saw little action – and its towns and villages seem to have been rarely touched by any historic or cultural mainstream. The motivation in coming to this landscape of rolling hills and occasional gorges is essentially to consume the region's cider, Calvados – much of it bootleg – fruit pastries and sausages made from pigs' intestines.

From St-Lô to Tessy

The best section of the valley is south of St-Lô through the Roches de Ham to Tessy-sur-Vire. The **Roches de Ham** are a pair of sheer rocky promontories high above the river. Though promoted as "viewing tables", the pleasure lies as much in the walk up, through lanes lined with blackberries, hazelnuts and rich orchards. Downstream from the Roches, and a good place to stop for the night, is **LA CHAPELLE-SUR-VIRE**. Its **church**, towering majestically above the river, has been an object of pilgrimage since the twelfth century. Next to the bridge on the lower road is the *Auberge de la Chapelle* (☎33.56.32.83; ①), a good but rather expensive restaurant with a few cheap **rooms**.

An alternative base for the Roches, over to the east, is **TORIGNI-SUR-VIRE**, which was the base of the Grimaldi family before they attained princeliness in Monaco. A spacious country town, it boasts a few grand buildings, the scant remains of a sixteenth-century castle and an attractive **campsite**, *Camping du Lac* (☎33.56.91.74). At **TESSY-SUR-VIRE** there's little to see other than the river itself, though the town has a luxurious **campsite**, along with a couple of **hotels** and Wednesday **market**.

Vire

VIRE itself is worth visiting specifically for the food. The town is best known for its dreaded *andouille* sausages, but you can gorge yourself instead on salmon trout fresh from the river, accompanied by local *poiré*. The biggest treats are to be found at the *Hôtel des Voyageurs* (☎31.68.01.16; ①), at the bottom of av de la Gare, by the station. For around 68F you can have a sublime and almost interminable meal in opulent surroundings. Good **restaurants** are to be found, too, at the more central *Hôtel de France*, 4 rue Aignaux (☎31.68.00.35; ②), and *Hôtel du Cheval Blanc*, 2 pl du 6-juin-1944 (☎31.67.19.82; ②). The one problem is what to do when you're not eating; the only action in Vire is at the Friday **market**, again obsessively dedicated to food.

For some exercise (and you'll need it), head 6km south along D76 to **Lac de la Dathée**. Set in open country, the lake is circled by footpaths or can be crossed by rented sailboat or windsurfer – contact the *Maison des Jeunes et de la Culture*, 1 rue des Halles (☎31.68.08.04).

Villedieu-les-Poêles

VILLEDIEU-LES-POÊLES – literally "City of God the Frying Pans" – is a lively though touristy place, 28km west of Vire. Copper souvenirs and kitchen utensils gleam from its rows of shops, and the **tourist office** on place des Costils (☎33.61.05.69) has lists of dozens of local *ateliers* for more direct purchases and details of the copperwork museum. All of which seems a bit overenthusiastic, though there is more authentic interest at the **Fonderie Cornille-Havard** at 13 rue du Pont-Chignon, one of the twelve remaining bell foundries in Europe. Work here is only part-time, but it's always open to visits during the week (daily 8am–noon & 2–5.30pm; early Sept to mid-June Tues–Sat 8am–noon & 2–5.30pm), and you may find the forge lit. If you're charmed into staying, there's a **campsite** by the river (☎33.61.02.44), and excellent basic food and **accommodation** at the *Hôtel de Paris* on route de Paris (☎33.61.00.66; ③).

Southern Normandy

In addition to the two more northerly routes across Normandy described above, motorists heading west from Paris towards Brittany may choose to get just a brief taste of the province by following the line of the N12 through **Alençon** and **Domfront**.

Alençon

ALENÇON, a fair-sized and busy town, is known for its traditional – and now pretty much defunct – lace-making industry. The **Musée des Beaux-Arts et de la Dentelle** (daily except Mon 10am–noon & 2–6pm; 15F) is housed in a former Jesuit school and has all the best trappings of a modern museum. The highly informative history of lace-making upstairs, with examples of numerous different techniques, can, however, be tedious for anyone not already rivetted by the subject. It also contains an unexpected collection of gruesome Cambodian artefacts like spears and lances, tiger skulls and elephants' feet, gathered by a "militant socialist" French governor at the turn of the century. The paintings in the adjoining Beaux-Arts section are nondescript, except for a few works by Courbet and Géricault. Wandering around the town might take you to Ste-Thérèse's birthplace on rue St-Blaise, just in front of the *gare routière* – if, that is, you haven't had a surfeit of the saint at Lisieux. The **Château des Ducs**, the old town castle close by the museum, looks impressive but doesn't encourage visitors. It is a prison, and people in Alençon have nightmarish memories of its use by the Gestapo during the war.

Incidentally, if you feel like taking your food-mixer on a sentimental pilgrimage, or have a few potatoes that need mashing, Alençon is the place for you; it's the centre of operations for *Moulinex*.

Central Alençon can offer visitors a good assortment of shops and cafés, but the main concentration of **hotels** is around the **SNCF** station on the northeast side of town. The two *logis*, *L'Industrie*, 20 pl Général-de-Gaulle (☎33.27.19.30; ①), and the *Grand Hôtel de la Gare*, 50 av Wilson (☎33.29.03.93; ①), are very decent and have fixed-price menus for around 60F. There's an IYHF **youth hostel** out on the D204 towards Colombiers, at 1 rue de la Paix, Damigny (☎33.29.00.48; ①). If you're interested in **horseback riding** – along the Orne – the *Association Départmentale de Tourisme Equestre et d'Equitation de Loisir de l'Orne* has its headquarters in Alençon at 60 Grand-Rue. They can also tell you about the various stud farms open to the public – another speciality of this area.

The **Forêt d'Ecouves**, north of Alençon and inaccessible by public transport, is a dense mixture of spruce, pine, oak and beech, unfortunately a favoured spot of the military – and in autumn of deerhunters, too. You can usually ramble along the cool paths, happening on wild mushrooms and even the odd wild boar. The *gîte d'étape*, on the D26 near Les Ragotières on the edge nearest Alençon, is an ideal spot from which to explore the forest – contact the local *gîte* office at 60 rue St-Blaise in Alençon (☎33.32.09.00).

Carrouges

One alternative base at the western end of the Forêt d'Ecouves is the hill town of **CARROUGES**, with its fine old-style **château** set in spacious grounds at the foot of the hill (mid-June to Aug 9.30–11.30am & 2–6pm; April to mid-June & Sept 10–11.30am & 2–5.30pm; Oct–March 10–11.30am & 2–4pm; 25F). Its two highlights are a superb restored brick staircase and a room in which hang portraits of fourteen successive generations of the Le Veneur family, an extraordinary illustration of the processes of heredity. The town also offers two appealing small **hotels** – the *Hôtel du Nord* (☎33.27.20.14; ①; Sept–June closed Fri) and the tiny *St-Pierre* (☎33.27.20.02; ①).

Bagnoles-de-l'Orne

West of Carrouges, the spa town of **BAGNOLES-DE-L'ORNE** is quite unlike anywhere else in this part of the world. The monied sick and convalescent come from all over France to its thermal baths, and business is so good they maintain a reservations office next to the Pompidou Centre in Paris. The layout is formal and spacious, centring on a lake with gardens where horse-drawn *calèches* take the clients to an enormous casino, and with so many visitors to keep entertained, and spending money, there are innumerable cultural events of a restrained and stressless nature.

Whether you'd actually want to spend time in Bagnoles depends on your disposable income as well as your health. The numerous **hotels** are expensive and sedate places, in which it's possible to be too late for dinner at seven o'clock and locked out altogether at nine, and the **campsite** is rather forlorn. Furthermore, the town as a whole operates to a season that lasts roughly from early April to the end of October; arrive in winter, and you may find everything shut.

Contact the **tourist office** on place République (April–Oct; ☎33.37.85.66) for details on accommodation in Bagnoles and its less exclusive sister town of **TESSE-MADELAINE**. Among the cheaper options in Bagnoles proper are the *Albert 1er* on av Dr-Poulain (☎33.37.80.97; ②), and the *Grand Veneur* on place République (☎33.37.86.79; ②). **Restaurants** in both towns tend to be better value than the hotels; the *de la Terrasse* (☎33.30.80.96) in Bagnoles is well tried and popular.

Domfront

The road west through the Forêt des Andaines from Bagnoles, the D335 and then D908, climbs above the lush woodlands and progressively narrows to a hog's back before entering **DOMFRONT**. Even less happens here than at Bagnoles, but it has the edge on countryside. A public park near the *gare SNCF* leads up to **castle ruins** on an isolated rock. Eleanor of Aquitaine was born in the castle in October 1162, and Thomas-à-Becket came to stay for Christmas in 1166, saying mass in the nearby church of Notre-Dame-sur-l'Eau. The views from the gardens surrounding the mangled keep are spectacular, including a very graphic panorama of the ascent you've made. Domfront is a useful stopover; the *Hôtel de la Poste* on the hill top (☎33.38.51.00; ①) is very reasonable, and there are others down by the station. Be aware though, that the **campsite** has only ten spaces.

The **tourist office** at 52 rue du Dr-Barrabé (☎33.38.53.97) can provide details of the neighbouring forests, the **Forêt de Lande-Pourrie** and **Forêt de Mortain**. The eleventh-century Benedictine vestiges in the church at **LONLAY L'ABBAYE**, 9km out on D22 towards Tinchebray, is one destination. Another is the **Fosse d'Arthur** to the west, a waterfall plunging into deep grottoes, and one of the many claimants to King Arthur's death scene. At the town of **MORTAIN** there are **waterfalls** and a tiny chapel on a high rock from which the neighbouring province of Maine spreads before you.

travel details

Trains

Through services to Paris connect with all ferries at Dieppe, Le Havre and Cherbourg: if you're doing this it's easiest to buy a combined rail-ferry-rail ticket at your point of departure.

Caen to: Coutances (2 daily; 1hr 15min); Cherbourg (10 daily; 1hr–1hr 30min) via Bayeux and Valognes; Le Mans (9 daily; 2hr); Paris-St-Lazare (at least hourly; 2hr 15min); Pontorson, near Mont St-Michel (2 daily; 1hr 30min); Rennes (2 daily; 2hr); St-Lô (2 daily; 1hr); Tours (9 daily; 2hr 30min).

Dieppe to: Paris-St-Lazare (8 daily; 2hr 15min); Rouen (8 daily; 1hr).

Le Havre to: Paris (12 daily; 2hr); Rouen (12 daily; 45min).

Rouen to: Caen (8 daily; 2hr 15min); Fécamp (12 daily; 1hr); Paris-St-Lazare (12 daily; 1hr 15min).

Buses

Caen to: Le Havre (6 daily; 3hr), via Cabourg, Deauville and Honfleur.

Dieppe to: Fécamp (1 daily; 1hr 30min); Paris (5 daily; 2hr 15min).

Lisieux to: Honfleur (5 daily; 45min).

Mont St-Michel to: St-Malo (1–2 daily; 1hr 20min).

Rouen to: Dieppe (2 daily; 1hr 45min); Fécamp (2 daily; 2hr 30min); Le Havre (hourly; 2hr 45min); Lisieux (2 daily; 2hr 30min).

Ferries

Caen (Ouistreham) Brittany Ferries (☎31.36.00.00).1 or 2 daily to Portsmouth (6hr)

Carteret to Jersey. *Vedettes Armoricaines, gare maritime* (☎33.04.60.60); *Vedettes Blanches*, gare maritime (☎33.53.81.17).

Cherbourg *Sealink* (☎33.20.43.38) 1 daytime crossing to Portsmouth (4hr 45min), another to Weymouth (4hr 30min); *Truckline Ferries* (☎33.22.38.98) to Poole (4hr 30min); *P&O* (☎33.44.20.13), 3 daily to Portsmouth (4hr 45min); *Irish Continental* (☎33.44.28.96) to Rosslare (17hr) .

Dieppe *Sealink* (foot passengers ☎35.06.39.19, motorists ☎35.06.39.00) 3–4 daily to Newhaven (4hr).

Granville to Jersey, Guernsey and Chausey Islands. *Vedettes Armoricaines*, 12 rue Clemenceau (☎33.50.77.45); *Vedettes Blanches*, 1 rue Le Campion (☎33.50.16.36); *Jolie France*, gare maritime (☎33.50.31.81).

Le Havre *P&O* (☎35.21.36.50) 2 daily to Portsmouth (5hr 30min); *Irish Ferries* (☎35.53.28.83) daily to Cork (21hr) and to Rosslare (21hr).

CHAPTER FIVE

BRITTANY

No one area – and certainly no one city or town – in **Brittany** encapsulates the province's character; that lies in its people and in its geographical unity. For generations Bretons risked their lives fishing and trading on the violent seas or struggling with the arid soil of the interior. This toughness and resilience is tinged with Celtic culture: mystical, musical, sometimes morbid and defeatist, sometimes vital and inspired.

Though archeologically Brittany is one of the richest sites in the world – the alignments at Carnac rival Stonehenge – its first appearance in history is as the quasi-mythical "Little Britain" of Arthurian legend. In the days when to travel by sea was safer and easier than by land, it was intimately connected with "Great Britain" across the water, and settlements such as St-Malo, St-Pol and Quimper were founded by Welsh and Irish missionary "saints" whose names are not to be found in any official breviary. Brittany remained independent until the sixteenth century, its last ruler, Duchess Anne, only managing to protect the province's autonomy through marriage to two consecutive French monarchs. After her death, in 1532, François I took her daughter and lands, and sealed the union with an act supposedly enshrining certain privileges. These included a veto over taxes by the local *parlement* and the people's right to be tried, or conscripted to fight, only in their province. The successive violations of this treaty by Paris, and subsequent revolts, form the core of Breton history since the Middle Ages.

Bretons have seen their language steadily eradicated and the interior severely depopulated. But people still tend to treat France as a separate country, even if few actively support Breton nationalism (which it's a criminal offence to advocate) much beyond putting *Breizh* (Breton for Brittany) stickers on their cars. But there have been many successes in reviving the language, and the recent economic resurgence, helped partly by summer tourism, has largely been due to local initiatives, like *Brittany Ferries* re-establishing an old trading link, carrying produce and passengers across to Britain and Ireland. At the same time a Celtic artistic identity has consciously been revived, and local festivals – above all August's **Interceltic festival** at Lorient – celebrate traditional Breton music, poetry and dance, with fellow Celts treated as comrades.

For most visitors, it is the Breton **coast** that is the dominant feature. After the Côte d'Azur, this is now the most popular summer resort area in France – for both French

---

ACCOMMODATION PRICE CATEGORIES

All the hotels, youth hostels and guesthouses listed in this book have been price-graded according to the following scale, and although costs will rise slightly overall with the life of this edition, the relative comparisons should remain valid. Paris and the large cities will, as anywhere, be more expensive than equivalent accommodation in the countryside or small towns. The prices quoted are for the cheapest available double room in high season, although remember that many of the cheap places will have more expensive rooms with en-suite facilities.

① Under 160F	④ 300–400F	⑦ 600–700F
② 160–220F	⑤ 400–500F	⑧ Over 700F
③ 220–300F	⑥ 500–600F	

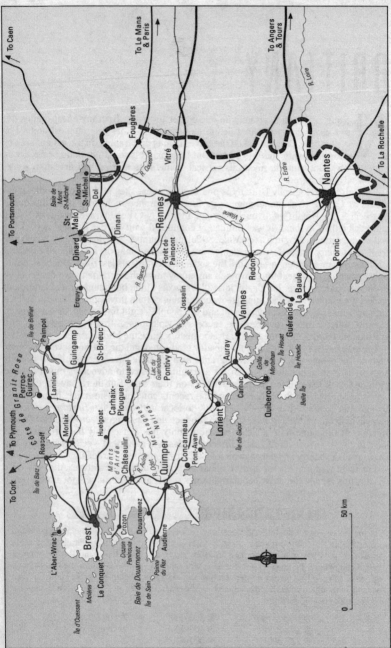

To Caen

To Le Mans & Paris

To Angers & Tours

R. Loire

To La Rochelle

Fougères

Vitré

R. Ouesnon

To Portsmouth

Baie de Mont St-Michel

Mont St-Michel

Dol

Dinan

Rennes

R. Edre

Nantes

St-Malo

Dinard

R. Vilaine

Pornic

Erquy

R. Rance

Forêt de Paimpont

Redon

Vannes

La Baule

Guérande

Ile de Bréhat

Paimpol

Côte de Granit Rose

Perros-Guirec

Guingamp

St-Brieuc

Josselin

Nantes Brest Canal

Auray

Golfe du Morbihan

Ile de Houat

Ile Hoedic

To Plymouth

Lannion

Gouarec

Carhaix-Plouguer

Pontivy

Lac du Guerlédan

Lorient

Carnac

Quiberon

Belle Ile

Roscoff

Morlaix

Huelgoat

Monts d'Arrée

Montagnes Noires

Concarneau

Ile de Groix

Ile de Batz

Châteaulin

R. Aulne

Quimper

Pont-Aven

L'Aber-Wrac'h

Brest

Crozon

Crozon Peninsula

Douarnenez

Baie de Douarnenez

Audierne

R. Odet

To Cork

Molène

Le Conquet

Pointe du Raz

Ile de Sein

Ile d'Ouessant

50 km

0

and foreign tourists. The attractions are obvious: warm white-sand beaches, towering cliffs, rock formations and offshore islands and islets, and everywhere the stone *dolmen* and *menhir* monuments of a prehistoric past. The most frequented areas are the **Côte d'Émeraude**, around **St-Malo**, and the **Morbihan coast** below **Auray** and **Vannes**. Accommodation and campsites here are plentiful, if pushed to their limits from mid-June to the end of August, and for all the crowds there are resorts as enticing as any in the country. Over in **southern Finistère** ("land's end") and along the **Côte de Granit Rose** in the north you may have to do more planning. This is true, too, if you come to Brittany out of season, when many of the coastal resorts close down completely.

Whenever you come, don't leave Brittany without visiting one of its scores of **islands** – the **Île de Bréhat** or **Belle Île** – or taking in cities like **Quimper** or **Morlaix**, testimony to the riches of the medieval duchy. Allow time, too, to leave the coast and explore the interior, particularly the western country around the **Monts d'Arées**. Here you pay for the solitude with very sketchy transport and few hotels, but Brittany is one of the few areas of France where *camping sauvage* (not in campsites) is

FOOD IN BRITTANY

Brittany's proudest addition to the great cuisines of the world has to be the **crêpe** and its savoury equivalent the **galette**; *crêperies* throughout the region attempt to pass them off as satisfying meals, serving them with every imaginable filling. However, there can be few people who plan their holidays specifically around eating pancakes, and gourmets are far more likely to be enticed to Brittany by its magnificent array of **seafood**. Restaurants in resorts such as St-Malo and Quiberon jostle for the attention of fish fanatics, while some smaller towns – like Cancale, which specializes in oysters (*huîtres*), and Erquy, with its scallops (*Coquilles St-Jacques*) – depend wholly on one specific mollusc for their livelihood.

Although they can't quite claim to be uniquely Breton, two appetizers feature on every self-respecting menu. These are **moules marinières**, giant bowls of succulent orange mussels steamed open in a combination of white wine, shallots and parsley (and perhaps enriched by the addition of cream or *crême fraiche* to become *moules à la creme*), and **soupe de poissons**, traditionally served with a little pot of the garlicky mayonnaise known as *rouille* (coloured by the addition of pulverized sweet red pepper) and a bowl of croutons. Jars of freshly made *soupe de poissons* – or even crab or lobster – are always on sale in seaside *poissoneries*, and make an ideal way to take a taste of France home with you. Paying a bit more in a restaurant – typically on menus costing 140F or more – brings you into the realm of the **assiette de fruits de mer**, a mountainous heap of langoustines, crabs, oysters, mussels, clams, whelks and cockles, most of them raw and all (with certain obvious exceptions) delicious. **Main courses** tend to be plainer than in Normandy, for example, with fresh local fish being prepared with relatively simple sauces. Skate served with capers, or salmon baked with a mustard or cheese sauce, are typical dishes, while even the **cotriade**, a stew containing such fish as sole, turbot, or bass, as well as shellfish, is distinctly less rich than its Mediterranean equivalent, the *bouillabaisse*. Brittany is also better than much of France in maintaining its respect for fresh green **vegetables**, thanks to the extensive local production of peas, cauliflowers, artichokes and the like. Only with the **desserts** can things get rather too heavy; **far Breton**, considered a great delicacy, is a stodgy baked concoction of sponge and custard which owes its gravitas to the addition of such ingredients as pig's blood, while *îles flottantes* are meringue icebergs adrift in a sea of *crême brulée* or custard.

Strictly speaking, no **wine** is produced in Brittany itself. However, along the lower Loire Valley, the *département* of Loire-Atlantique, centred on Nantes, is still generally regarded as "belonging" to Brittany – and is treated as such in this chapter. Vineyards here are responsible for the dry white Muscadet – which is what normally goes into *moules marinières* – and the even drier Gros-Plant.

tolerated. There are sporadic *gîtes*, boats to rent on the **Nantes–Brest canal**, and hitching is relatively easy.

Finally, a note on the **pardons**, pilgrimage-festivals commemorating local saints, which guidebooks (and tourist offices) tend to promote as spectacles. These are not, unlike most French festivals, phoney affairs kept alive for tourists, but deeply serious and rather gloomy religious occasions. If you're looking for traditional Breton fun, and you can't make the Lorient festival (or the smaller *Quinzaine Celtique* at Nantes in June/July), look out for gatherings organized by **Celtic folklore groups** – *Circles* or *Bagadou*.

A BRETON GLOSSARY

Estimates of the number of Breton-speakers range from 400,000 to 800,000. You may well encounter it spoken as a first, day-to-day language by the very old, and by the young in parts of Finistère and the Morbihan. Learning Breton is not really a viable prospect for visitors without a grounding in Welsh, Gaelic or some other Celtic language. However, as you travel through the province, it's interesting to note the roots of Breton place names, many of which have a simple meaning in the language. Below are some of the most common:

Aber	estuary	*Hen*	old	*Mor*	sea
Bihan	little	*Hir*	long	*Nevez*	new
Bran	hill	*Inis*	island	*Parc*	field
Braz	big	*Ker*	town or house	*Penn*	end, head
Creach	height	*Koz*	old	*Plou*	parish
Cromlech	stone circle	*Lan*	church	*Pors*	port, farmyard
Dol	table	*Lann*	heath	*Roch*	stone
Dolmen	stone table	*Lech*	flat stone	*Ster*	river
Du	black	*Mario*	dead	*Stivel*	fountain, spring
Gavre	goat	*Men*	stone	*Trez*	sand, beach
Goat	forest	*Menez*	mountain	*Trou*	valley
Goaz	stream	*Menhir*	long stone	*Ty*	house
Guen	white	*Meur*	big	*Wrach*	witch

THE NORTH COAST AND RENNES

Medieval Brittany was obliged vigorously to defend its independence against potential incursors, and today its eastern approaches remain guarded by the heavily fortified citadels of **Fougères** and **Vitré**. Along the coast from Mont St-Michel, only just across the border in Normandy, are some of Brittany's finest old towns. One of the most spectacular introductions to the province is that which greets ferry passengers from Portsmouth; the **River Rance**, guarded by magnificently preserved **St-Malo** on its estuary, and beautiful medieval **Dinan** 20km upstream. To the west stretches a varied coastline culminating in one of the most seductive of the islands, the **Île de Bréhat**, and the colourful chaos of the **Côte de Granit Rose**. Inland all roads curl eventually to **Rennes**, the Breton capital, which lies a short way north of the legendary forest of **Brocéliande** (Paimpont), the location of the Arthurian tales.

The frontier towns

If you're entering Brittany by road from Normandy, Maine or Le Mans, you're likely to pass through **Dol-de-Bretagne**, **Fougères**, or close to **Vitré** – all, at one time or another, heavily fortified strategic sites.

Dol-de-Bretagne

During the Middle Ages, **DOL-DE-BRETAGNE**, 30km west of Mont St-Michel, was an important bishopric. It no longer has a bishop, though its huge granite **cathedral** endures, with its strange, squat, tiled towers. Alongside is the **Musée Historique de Dol** (daily Easter–Sept 9.30am–6pm; Oct 2.30–6.30pm), bloated by the usual array of posed waxworks but with two rooms of astonishing wooden bits and pieces rescued in assorted states of decay from churches, often equally rotting, all over Brittany. These carvings and statues, some still brightly polychromed with their crust of eggy paint, range from the thirteenth to the nineteenth centuries.

Dol still has a few streets packed with venerable buildings, most notably the pretty **Grande-Rue**, where one Romanesque edifice dates back as far as the eleventh century, alongside an assortment of five-hundred-year-old half-timbered houses that look down on the bustle of shoppers below.

All approaches to Dol from the bay are guarded by the former island of **Mont Dol**, now eight rather marshy kilometres in from the sea. This abrupt granite outcrop, looking mountainous beyond its size on such a flat plain, was the legendary site of a battle between the Archangel Michael and the Devil. Various fancifully named indentations in the rock, such as "the Devil's Claw", testify to the savagery of their encounter, which as usual the Devil lost. The site has been occupied since prehistoric times – flint implements have been unearthed alongside the bones of mammoths, sabre-toothed tigers, and even rhinoceroses. Later on, it appears to have been used for worship by the Druids, before becoming, like Mont St-Michel, an island monastery, all traces of which have long vanished. A plaque proclaims that visiting the small chapel on top earns a Papal Indulgence. The climb is pleasant, too, a steep footpath winding up among the chestnuts and beeches to a solitary bar.

There is not a great deal to Dol, for visitors anyway. The **tourist office**, at 3 Grande-Rue (☎99.48.15.37), can direct you to a very reasonable **hotel**, the *Bretagne*, next to the market at 17 place Chateaubriand (☎99.48.02.03; ①–③; closed Oct). The best **campsite** nearby is the *Vieux Chêne* (☎99.48.09.55), 5km west on RN176.

A couple of nice **fish restaurants** can be found in the ancient houses on rue Ceinte, as it winds its way from Grande-Rue to the cathedral; *Le Porche au Pain* at no. 1 and *La Grabotais* at no. 4 (☎99.48.19.89; closed Mon).

Cancale

Along the coast north of Dol, the pinnacle of Mont St-Michel is clearly visible from every vantage point, of which the most spectacular is the **Pointe du Grouin**, a perilous and windy height which also overlooks the bird sanctuary of the **Îles des Landes** to the east. Just south of the *pointe,* and less than 15km from St-Malo across the peninsula, **CANCALE** should not be missed by those who attribute magical properties to **oysters**. In the old church of **St-Méen** at the top of the hill, a small **Musée des Arts et Traditions Populaires** documents the town's obsession with meticulous precision (July & Aug Mon 2.30–6.30pm, Tues–Sun 10am–noon & 2.30–6.30pm; June & Sept Fri–Sun 2.30–6.30pm; closed Oct–May; groups by appointment, ring ☎99.89.79.32; 15F). Cancale oysters were found in the camps of Julius Cæsar, taken daily to Versailles for Louis XIV, and even accompanied Napoléon on the march to Moscow.

From the rue des Parcs next to the jetty of the port, you can see the *parcs* where the oysters are grown at low tide. The rocks of the cliff behind are streaked and shiny like mother-of-pearl; underfoot the beach is littered with countless generations of empty shells. The port area is very pretty and very smart, with a long line of upmarket glass-fronted hotels and restaurants. Cancale's **hotels** mostly insist that you eat if you want to stay; *Le Phare* (☎99.89.60.24; ③) and the *Emeraude* (☎99.89.61.76; ③) on quai Thomas, both of which are set above their own restaurants, and *La Houle*, 18 quai Gambetta (☎99.89.62.38; ③), are among the best value. There's no great reason to recommend any one **restaurant** above the rest, as all serve enticing seafood spreads. As a rule, oysters are no less expensive than on a Paris boulevard, but the daytime-only *Au Pied de Cheval*, 10 quai Gambetta, is an informal place to sample a few, with great baskets of them spread across its wooden quayside tables.

Fougères

FOUGÈRES lies on the main Caen–Rennes road, a town that has a topography impossible to grasp from a map; streets that look a few metres long turn out to be precipitous plunges down the escarpments of its split-levelled site, and lanes collapse into flights of steps. The most dominant feature of Fougères is its robust **castle**, built well below the level of the main part of town, on a low spit of land that separates, and is towered over by, two mighty rock faces (tours on the hour: mid-June to mid-Sept daily 9am–7pm; April to mid-June 9.30am–noon & 2–5.30pm; Oct–March 10am–noon & 2–4.30pm; 15F). Its massive and seemingly impregnable bulk is protected by great curtain walls growing out of the rock, and encircled by a hacked-out moat full of weirs and waterfalls – none of which prevented its repeated capture by such medieval adventurers as du Guesclin. It is, however, eighteenth-century Fougères that is always featured in the summer-night theatrical performances at the château, based on the book that immortalized the town, Balzac's *The Chouans*. It tells, in rampant best-seller vein, the story of the counter-revolutionary *Chouan* rebellion in Brittany during the early 1790s, and makes great play of the strange layout of the town. Within the castle, the focus is more prosaic, and footwear – the main industry of the town – is presented in a **museum** included in the château tours.

The best approach to the castle is from **place des Arbres** beside St-Léonard's church off the main street of the old fortified town. The formal terraces give way to the water meadows of the River Nançon, which you can cross beside a little cluster of medieval houses still standing on the river bank. Alternatively, on the longer route down rue Nationale, you'll pass the **Musée de La Villéon** at no. 51, which commemorates an Impressionist who painted numerous memorable Breton landscapes (mid-June to Aug daily 10.30am–12.30pm & 2.30–5.30pm; Easter to mid-June & first fortnight of Sept Sat & Sun 11am–12.30pm & 2.30–5pm; free).

The **Forêt de Fougères**, a short way out on the D177 towards Vire (see p.319), is one of the most enjoyable in the province. The beech woods are spacious and light, with various megaliths and trails of old stones scattered in among the chestnut and spruce. It's quite a contrast to their normal bleak and windswept haunts to see dolmens sporting themselves in such verdant surroundings.

Practicalities

Fougères's **tourist office** at 1 place Aristide-Briand provides copious information on all aspects of the town and local countryside (July & Aug Mon–Sat 9am–7pm, Sun 10am–noon & 2–4pm; Sept–June Mon–Sat 9.30am–12.30pm & 2–6pm, Sun 10am–noon & 2–4pm; ☎99.94.12.20). The *Grand Hôtel des Voyageurs*, 10 place Gambetta (☎99.99.08.20; ②; closed second fortnight of Aug), is a particularly nice place to **stay**, just round the corner from the tourist office, on the main road. Selecting the cheapest, 85F menu in the excellent downstairs restaurant (closed Sat) gives you the choice of *tournedos de thon* and grants you access to a well-laden *chariot des desserts*. *Hôtel Balzac* at no. 15 in the semi-pedestrian rue Nationale (☎99.99.42.46; ②; all year) is also pleasant, while the *Buffet* at no. 53 (☎99.94.35.76; closed Wed pm & Sun) does more economical meals, with a 54F menu including wine.

St-Aubin-du-Cormier

Halfway between Fougères and Rennes, **ST-AUBIN-DU-CORMIER** has a sad tale to tell concerning English, French and Breton relations. A small monument in a field marks the battlesite where, in 1488, the forces of the Duke of Brittany were defeated by the French army. Many of the Breton soldiers had dressed in the English colours, a black cross on white silk, to scare the French into believing that the duke had extensive English reinforcements. The victorious French were told to spare all prisoners except the English; and so the hapless Bretons were massacred. St-Aubin's castle was then demolished – just one sheer wall survives, with a fireplace visible midway up. Should you wish to **stay** overnight there's the very cheap *Hôtel du Bretagne*, 68 rue de l'Ecu (☎99.39.10.22; ①), a wonderful rambling old building serving very good food.

Vitré

VITRÉ, just north of the Le Mans–Rennes motorway, rivals Dinan as the best-preserved medieval town in Brittany. Its walls are not quite complete, but the thickets of medieval stone cottages that lie outside them have hardly changed. The towers of the **castle** itself have pointed slate-grey roofs in best fairy-tale fashion, looking like freshly sharpened pencils, though, unfortunately, the municipal offices and **museum** of shells, birds, bugs and local history inside are not exactly thrilling (July–Sept daily 10am–12.30pm & 2–6.15pm; April–June daily except Tues 10am–noon & 2–5.30pm; Oct–March Wed–Fri 10am–noon & 2–5.30pm, Sat–Mon 2–5.30pm; 15F).

Vitré is a market town rather than an industrial centre, with its principal **market** held on Mondays in the square in front of **Notre-Dame church**. The old city is full of twisting streets of half-timbered houses, a good proportion of which are bars; **rue Beaudrairie** in particular has a fine selection. An unusual visual treat, if you happen to be using the **post office**, is its modern stained-glass window behind the counter.

Vitré's **gare SNCF** is a little way south of the centre, where the town imperceptibly blends into its newer sectors. Nearby are the **tourist office**, on the promenade St-Yves (Mon–Fri 10am–noon & 1.30–6pm, Sat 10am–noon; ☎99.75.04.46), and most of the **hotels** too. Both the *Petit-Billot* on place du Général-Leclerc (☎99.74.68.88; ②), and *Chêne-Vert* on place de la Gare (☎99.75.00.58; ①; closed late Sept to late Oct; 25F car parking charge), are good value, while rooms on the higher floors of the *Hôtel du Château*, 5 rue Rallon (☎99.74.58.59; ①; closed Sun out of season), on a quiet road just below the castle, have views of the ramparts. Of the **restaurants**, *Le St-Pierre*, 1 place St-Yves, on the corner with the main road (☎99.75.36.52), serves a different menu each day, while *La Soupe aux Choux*, at the top of rue de la Beaudrairie at 32 rue Notre-Dame (☎99.75.10.86; closed Tues), prepares simple but classic French food, with 39F lunches.

St-Malo and the Rance estuary

ST-MALO, walled and built with the same grey granite stone as Mont St-Michel, 45km east, presents its best face to the sea; if you are not planning to arrive by ferry, consider the ten-minute shuttle across the River Rance from Dinard as an alternative to get a perspective on the town. The city was originally a fortified island at the mouth of the Rance, controlling not only the estuary but the open sea beyond. For centuries its pirate-mariners forced English ships passing up the Channel to pay tribute. They brought wealth from further afield, too. Jacques Cartier, who colonized Canada, lived in and sailed from St-Malo, and the Argentinian name for the Falklands, *Las Malvinas*, derives from the islands' first French colonists, *Les Malouins*.

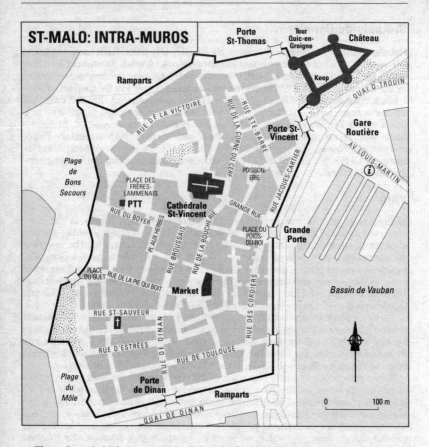

These days, St-Malo is more visited than anywhere in Brittany – and not just for the use of its ferry terminal. The *intra-muros* streets of the **old citadelle** are a unique experience: at times they can be sombre and grim (particularly beneath grey skies), but in high summer or at sunset they become light and almost unreal. Much of what you see today has been lovingly and precisely rebuilt stone by stone, as eighty percent of the city was destroyed in August 1944.

Arrival, information and accommodation

Coming into St-Malo by bus or train, the old city is concealed by modern suburbs and dock-side industry almost until you're in it. Approaches by road are somewhat dismal; the signposts seem designed to confuse and all the roads seem to end on tramlined docksides. Lost and bewildered cars circle the port like seagulls.

The helpful **tourist office** (July–Sept Mon–Sat 8.30am–8pm, Sun 10am–7pm; last fortnight of June and first fortnight of Sept Mon–Sat 9am–7pm, Sun 10am–noon & 2–6pm; Easter to mid-June & last fortnight of Sept Mon–Sat 9am–noon & 2–7pm, Sun 10am–noon & 2–6pm; Oct–Easter Mon–Sat 9am–noon & 2–6pm; ☎99.56.64.48) is housed in a single-storey building beside Bassin Duguay-Trouin in the Port des Yachts.

Officially, the **gare routière** (☎99.40.83.33) is right next to the tourist office, but most buses, whether local or long distance, coincide also with trains at the **gare SNCF** (☎99.65.50.50), 2km out from the citadelle on place Hermine and convenient for neither the old town nor the ferry (take care if you're planning a tight connection). *TIV* (☎99.40.83.33) run buses to Dinard, Dinan, Cancale, Combourg and Rennes, while *Les Courriers Bretons*, 13 rue d'Alsace (☎99.56.79.09), go to Cancale, Mont St-Michel and Fougères, and also run day-trips to Mont St-Michel (summer daily 9.30am, Wed & Sat only in low season; 100F). Dinan buses are also operated by *CAT* (☎96.39.21.05).

As well as the *Brittany Ferries* sailings to Portsmouth from the *Gare Maritime du Naye* (☎99.82.41.41), St-Malo is busy with other **boats**. You'll find details of the various services to the **Channel Islands** in the "Travel Details" at the end of this chapter, and there are also regular ten-minute crossings to Dinard in summer (*Emeraude Lines*; ☎99.40.48.40; single 20F, return 30F), and pleasure cruises around the estuary.

Bicycles can be rented from *Cycles Diazo*, 47 quai Duguay-Trouin (☎99.40.31.63), or *Cycles Nicole*, 11 rue Robert-Schumann (☎99.56.11.06).

Accommodation

St-Malo boasts over a hundred **hotels**, including the seaside boarding houses just off the beach, along with several **campsites** and a couple of **youth hostels**. In high season it needs every one of them, and if you plan to stay the night before catching a summer ferry, make a reservation well in advance.

You pay a premium for the privilege of staying within the city walls, since that's where any nightlife takes place, and it's a fair walk in through the docks from any of the surrounding suburbs. Unfortunately, the *intra-muros* hotels tend to take advantage of high summer demand by insisting that you eat in their own restaurants. Cheaper rates can be found by the *gare SNCF*, or in suburban Paramé, although it's hardly worth being away from the citadelle for the sake of saving a few francs. The youth hostels are notoriously busy. The four municipal **campsites** also tend to be full in July and August, and you may have to travel inland to find space.

HOTELS IN THE CITADELLE

Hôtel Bristol Union, 4 pl de la Poissonerie (☎99.40.83.36). Very correct hotel rooms in a nice little square facing the fish market, just off the Grande Rue. Closed mid-Nov to Jan, no restaurant. ③.

Hôtel-Restaurant Pomme d'Or, 4 pl du Poids-du-Roi (☎99.40.90.24). Modernized rooms in a venerable building, just inside the *citadelle* near the ramparts – take a sharp left after entering through the Grande Porte. Conventional menus start around 80F. ③.

Hôtel-Restaurant Porte St-Pierre, 2 pl du Guet (☎99.40.91.27). Comfortable *logis de France* peeping out to sea over the walls of the *citadelle*, near the small Porte St-Pierre and very handy for the plage de Bon Secours. Menus from 68F to 250F. ③

Hôtel San Pedro, 1 rue Ste-Anne (☎99.56.82.15). Small refurbished hotel in a nice quiet setting, just inside the walls in the north of the *citadelle*. Rooms on the higher floors enjoy sea views. ③.

Hôtel-Restaurant L'Univers, 10 pl Châteaubriand (☎99.40.89.52). One of the grand hotels that face you immediately upon entering the porte St-Vincent. Some good-value rooms, and an excellent 68F menu in the restaurant downstairs, with tables out on the square opposite the château. ③–⑤.

Hôtel-Restaurant aux Vieilles Pierres, 4 rue des Lauriers (☎99.56.46.80). One of the better bargains within the walls, some way from the Grande Porte near place aux Herbes. Open all year. Menus at 75F with fish soup and steak, or 105F for the full spread, in theory totalling six courses but half of those are just intended to keep you ticking over until the next one arrives. ①.

HOTELS OUTSIDE THE WALLS

Hôtel Arrivée, 52 bd de la République (☎99.56.30.78). Budget hotel on a corner very near the *gare SNCF*. Open all year, no restaurant. ①.

Hôtel les Charmettes, 64 bd Hébert, Paramé (☎99.56.07.31). One of Paramé's cheaper options, not on the front itself, though a few rooms have sea views, but very near the beach and the imposing *Grand Hôtel*. Closed Jan, no restaurant. ①.

Hôtel de l'Europe, 44 bd de la République (☎99.56.13.42). Year-round cheap rooms in a genuinely friendly hotel, near the *gare SNCF*. ①.

Hôtel Neptune, 21 rue de l'Industrie (☎99.56.82.15). Cheap rooms – especially good value for groups of three or four – outside the walls, near the *gare SNCF*. Bar but no restaurant. ①.

HOSTELS AND CAMPSITES

Centre des Rencontres International, 37 rue du Père-Umbricht, Paramé (☎99.40.29.80). One of the busiest IYHF hostels in France, although not formally part of the national network, this hostel is 2km northeast of the *gare SNCF* on Paramé's main street, a short way back from the beach on bus routes #1, #2 or #5. It does not operate a curfew. ①.

Maison de l'Hermitage, 13 rue des Écoles (☎99.56.22.00). IYHF hostel half an hour on foot from the station or on bus routes #2 and #4. ①.

La Cité d'Aleth, St-Servan (☎99.81.60.91). Much the nearest campsite to the *citadelle*, on the headland southwest of St-Malo. Reachable in summer on bus #1. Open all year.

Les Ilôts, av de la Guimorais, Rothéneuf (☎99.56.98.72). Inland, to the northeast. June–Sept.

Le Nicet, av de la Varde, Rothéneuf (☎99.40.26.32). On the coast by Pointe de Nicet. Reservations essential. Easter–Sept.

Les Nielles, av John Kennedy, Paramé (☎99.40.26.35). On the beach at the plage du Minhic. Mid-June to mid-Sept.

The *citadelle* and suburbs

The **citadelle** of St-Malo, very much the prime destination for visitors, was for many years joined to the mainland only by a long, single causeway, before the original line of the coast was hidden forever by the construction of the harbour basin. Although its streets of restored seventeenth- and eighteenth-century houses can be crowded to the point of absurdity in summer, away from the more popular thoroughfares random exploration is fun. You can surface to the sunlight on the ramparts to enjoy wonderful views all round, especially to the west as the sun sets over the sea.

Besides the prominent **Grande Porte**, the main gate of the citadelle is the **Porte St-Vincent**. The town **museum** in the castle to the right (June–Sept daily 9.30am–noon & 2–6.30pm; Oct–May daily except Tues 10am–noon & 2–6pm; 19F) is something of a hymn of praise to the "prodigious prosperity" enjoyed by St-Malo during its days of piracy, colonialism and slave trading. Climbing the 169 steps of the castle keep, you pass a fascinating mixture of maps, diagrams and exhibits – chilling handbills from the Nazi occupation, accounts of the "infernal machine" used by the English to blow up the port in 1693, and savage four-pronged *chausse-trappes*, thrown by pirates onto the decks of ships being boarded to immobilize their crews.

You can pass under the ramparts at a couple of points and on to the open shore, where a huge **beach** stretches away beyond the rather featureless resort-suburb of Paramé. When the tide is low, the most popular walk is out to the small island of **Grand-Bé** – sometimes you even need to queue to get on to the short causeway. Solemn warnings are posted of the dangers of attempting to return from the island when the tide has risen too far – if you're caught there, there you have to stay. The island "sight" is the tomb of the nineteenth-century writer-politician **Chateaubriand** (1768–1848), who was described by Marx as "the most classic incarnation of French vanité . . . the false profundity, Byzantine exaggeration, emotional coquetry . . . a never-before-seen mishmash of lies". Suitably enough he features heavily on all the tourist brochures, which – with no apparent irony – extol his "modesty" in choosing so "isolated" a burial spot.

St-Servan, within walking distance along the corniche south of the citadelle, was the city's original settlement, converted to Christianity by St-Malou (or Maclou) in the sixth century; later, in the twelfth century, they moved to the impregnable island we now call St-Malo. The town curves round several small inlets and beaches to face the tidal power dam across the river. Its **Tour Solidor**, three linked towers built in 1382, is open all year for 90-minute guided visits to a museum of clipper ships (summer daily 10am–noon & 2–6pm; Oct–March daily except Tues 2–6pm; 25F).

Finally, the road from St-Malo to Dinard crosses the estuary along the top of the world's first **tidal power dam** which, unfortunately, failed to set a non-nuclear example to the rest of the province. You can see how it works in a half-hour visit (daily 8.30am–9pm) from the entrance on the west bank, just downstream from the lock. If you're catching the bus between St-Malo (St-Vincent gate) and Dinard, get off at Le Richardais for the dam, and at *Gallic* for the centre of Dinard.

Eating

Intra-muros St-Malo boasts even more **restaurants** than hotels, with a long crescent lining the inside of the ramparts between the porte St-Vincent and the Grande Porte. Prices are probably higher than anywhere else in Brittany, however, especially on the open café terraces – the demand is inflated by the numbers of day-trippers and ferry-passengers having last-night blow-outs. Bear in mind that most of the *crêperies* also serve *moules* and similar quasi-snacks.

For last-minute **shopping**, the *citadelle* contains a few specialists, but buying in any quantity is best done in *Le Continent* **hypermarket** on the southwest outskirts of the town. There are **markets** in both St-Malo (*intra-muros*) and St-Servan on Tuesdays and Fridays, and in Paramé on Wednesdays and Saturdays.

All the restaurants listed below are in the *citadelle*.

Astrolabe, 8 rue des Cordiers (☎99.40.36.82). Quality cuisine near the Grande Porte. Lunches for 75F, otherwise the cheapest menu is 105F, featuring *soupe de moules* and duck in honey. Serves until late, open all year, but closed all day Mon, and Tues lunchtime.

Borgnefesse, 10 rue du Puits aux Braies (☎99.40.05.05). This place feels more like the tavern it once was, or a pub, than a restaurant. A heavily pirate-themed dining room has good solid French cooking. 59F lunch with steak, otherwise 95F. Closed Sat lunch & Sun all day.

Le Chalut, 8 rue de la Corne du Cerf (☎99.56.71.58). Quite an exclusive address, a short way in from the porte St-Vincent. A small 90F menu offers the catch of the day, otherwise you pay 175F or 300F for gourmet fish dinners. Reservations preferred, closed Sun pm & Mon.

Le Chasse Marée, 4 rue Groult St-Georges (☎99.40.85.10). Nautical decor and *haute cuisine*, just round the corner from the post office, with a few tables out on the quiet street. The 82F menu, served until 9pm, has oysters followed by red mullet or squid; the 135F features a scallop and duck salad to start, and a mixed fish grill or fish couscous; on the 185F menu you get half a lobster.

Crêperie Chez Chantal, 2 pl aux Herbes (☎99.40.93.97). Sweet and savoury pancakes at very reasonable prices – the seafood fillings are exceptional. Daily noon–11pm.

Le St-Laurent, 7 pl de la Poissonerie (☎99.40.38.38). Brasserie-*crêperie* with seating on a pleasant little square just in from the ramparts. It's of most interest as a self-proclaimed *moulerie*, with mussels cooked in all sorts of sauces – their much-vaunted secret ingredient tastes pretty much like garlic, but there's no harm in that – from around 45F. The ideal place for a lunchtime *moules-frites*.

Dinard

The former fishing village of **DINARD** sprawls around the western approaches to the Rance estuary, just across from St-Malo but a good twenty minutes away by road. While it might not feel out of place on the Côte d'Azur, with its casino, spacious villas and social calendar of regattas and ballet, here in Brittany it's a little incongruous. Its nineteenth-century metamorphosis was largely thanks to the tastes of the affluent English and Americans, though these days age rather than nationality seems to be the common factor uniting most of its summer influx of tourists. Although Dinard is a hilly town, undulating over a succession of pretty little coastal inlets, it attracts great numbers of older visitors; as a result, prices tend to be high, and pleasures sedate.

Central Dinard faces north to the open sea, across the curving bay that holds the attractive **plage de l'Ecluse**. As so often, the buildings that line the waterfront are, with the exception of the casino in the middle, venerable Victorian villas rather than hotels or shops, and so the beach itself has a low-key atmosphere, despite the summer crowds. An unexpected **statue of Alfred Hitchcock** dominates its main access point; standing on a giant egg, with a ferocious-looking bird perched on each shoulder, he was placed here to commemorate the town's annual festival of English-language films.

Enjoyable **coastal footpaths** lead off in either direction from the principal beach, enlivened by notice boards holding reproductions of paintings produced at points along the way. It may well come as a surprise to see that Pablo Picasso's *Deux Femmes Courants sur la Plage* and *Baigneuses sur la Plage*, both of which look quintessentially Mediterranean with their blue skies and golden sands, were in fact painted here in Dinard during his annual summer visits throughout the 1920s. The path that heads east leads up to the Pointe du Moulinet for views over to St-Malo, and then as the **Promenade du Clair du Lune** continues past the tiny and now-exclusive port, and down to the estuary beach, the plage du Prieuré.

Practicalities

Full information on Dinard's hotels, restaurants, local tours and transport facilities can be picked up from the **tourist office**, right in the centre at 2 bd Féart (Mon–Sat 9am–noon & 2–6pm; ☎99.46.94.12). Many visitors simply come over for the day on one of the regular *Émeraude Lines* **boats** from St-Malo; tickets can be bought in Dinard a couple of hundred metres east of the tourist office at 27 av George-V, above the pleasure port.

Dinard tends to be an expensive place to stay, but it does have a wide selection of **hotels** to choose from, including the central and very English *Hôtel-Restaurant Altair*, 18 bd Féart (☎99.46.13.58; ③; closed mid-Nov to mid-Dec), a little way inland from the tourist office, and two nice places near the pleasure port. The *Hôtel-Restaurant Printania*, 5 av George-V (☎99.46.43.07; ②–⑤), on the quiet street as it drops to the port, has a magnificent terrace restaurant, looking over towards St-Malo; the *Hôtel-Restaurant de la Vallée*, 6 av George-V (☎99.46.13.58; ①–⑤; closed mid-Nov to mid-Dec), unfortunately faces the wrong way for views of St-Malo, and its most basic rooms look straight onto a bare cliff. If you're looking for a cheaper bed, Dinard also has some unofficial **youth hostels**, of which the best is the *Centre International du Port Blanc*, over a kilometre west of the centre on rue du Sergent-Boulanger near the plage de Port Blanc (☎99.46.10.32; ①; April–Oct). **Campsites** include the "municipal" *Port Blanc*, also near the plage du Port-Blanc on rue de Sergent-Boulanger (☎99.46.10.74; April–Oct), and *La Ville Mauny* (☎99.46.94.73; April to mid-Oct), in the woods southwest of the centre.

Dinan

The wonderful citadel of **DINAN** has preserved almost intact its three-kilometre encirclement of protective masonry, with street upon colourful street of late medieval houses within. Like St-Malo, it's best seen when arriving by boat up the River Rance, where you can see its castle and fortifications to their best advantage. Behind the houses on the left bank quay where the boats tie up, a steep and cobbled street with fields and bramble thickets on either side climbs up to the thirteenth-century ramparts, partly hidden by trees.

Arrival and accommodation

Dinan's **tourist office** is very central, almost opposite the Tour de l'Horloge in the sixteenth-century Hôtel Kératry at 6 rue de l'Horloge (May–Sept Mon–Sat 9am–7pm,

Sun 10am–1pm & 2–7pm; Oct–April Mon–Sat 8.30am–12.30pm & 2–5.45pm; ☎96.39.75.40). Both the Art Deco **gare SNCF** (☎96.39.22.39) and the **gare routière** (☎96.39.21.05) are in the rather gloomy modern quarter, on place du 11-novembre, ten minutes' walk west of the walled town. In summer, **boats** sail from the port downstream to Dinard and St-Malo, taking anything from three and a quarter to five and a half hours, depending on the state of the tides; for details, contact *Émeraude Lines* in Dinard (☎99.46.10.45) or St-Malo (☎99.40.48.40), or the *Agence Boutin* at 7 Grande Rue in Dinan (☎96.39.12.32).

In addition to the **hotels** listed below, there is a youth hostel and campsite.

HOTELS

Hôtel-Restaurant Duchesse Anne, 10 pl du Guesclin (☎96.39.09.43). Comfort if not luxury, on the quieter side of the square, above a basic restaurant where set menus start at 60F. ②.

Hôtel de l'Océan, 9 pl du 11-novembre (☎96.39.21.51). Extremely convenient and well-run hotel, outside the walls opposite the *gare SNCF*. No restaurant. ①.

Hôtel le Papillon, 27 rue du Quai, port du Dinan (☎96.39.93.76). Simple hotel in romantic location, right on the waterfront down in the port. A long climb up to town for a bit of nightlife, but a lovely place to wake up. No restaurant. March–Nov. ③.

Hôtel Porte St-Malo, 35 rue St-Malo (☎96.39.19.76). Very comfortable rooms in a tasteful small hotel just outside the walls, beyond Porte St-Malo. No restaurant. ①.

Hôtel du Théâtre, 2 rue Ste-Claire (☎96.39.06.91). Very simple rooms above a bar, right by the tourist office and Théâtre des Jacobins. ①.

YOUTH HOSTELS AND CAMPSITES

IYHF youth hostel, Moulin de Méen, Vallée de la Fontaine-des-Eaux (☎96.39.10.83). The hostel is 2km from the *gare SNCF* and unfortunately not on any bus route; to walk there, follow the quay downstream from the port on the town side. ①.

Camping Municipal, 103 rue Chateaubriand (☎96.39.11.96). Just outside the western ramparts. March–Nov.

The Town

For all its slightly unreal perfection, Dinan is not excessively overrun with tourists. There are no very vital museums; the monument is the town itself, and time is best spent wandering from *crêperie* to café, admiring overhanging houses along the way. Unfortunately, you can only walk along one small stretch of the ramparts, from the Jardin Anglais behind St-Sauveur church to a point just short of Tour Sillon overlooking the river. You can get a good general overview from the **Tour de l'Horloge**, dating from the end of the fifteenth century (April–Sept daily 10am–7pm; 13F).

The fourteenth-century keep that once protected the town's southern approach now houses a small local **history museum**. Together with the ancient **Tour Coëtgen**, this is known as the Château de Duchesse Anne (June to mid-Oct daily 10am–6.30pm; mid-Oct to May daily except Tues 1.30–5.30pm; 20F). On the lower floor of the Tour Coëtgen a group of stone fifteenth-century notables looks for all the world like some kind of medieval time capsule, about to de-petrify at any moment.

St-Sauveur church, very much the town's focus, is a real mixture of ages, with a Romanesque porch and an eighteenth-century steeple. Even its nine Gothic chapels feature five different patterns of vaulting in no symmetrical order, and the most complex pair, in the centre, would make any spider proud. A cenotaph contains the heart of Bertrand du Guesclin, the fourteenth-century Breton warrior (and later Constable of France) who fought and won a single combat with the English knight Thomas of Canterbury, in what is now place du Guesclin, to settle the outcome of the siege of Dinan in 1364. Relics of his life and battles are scattered all over Brittany and Normandy; in death, he spread himself between four separate burial places for four different parts of his body (the French kings restricted themselves to three burial sites). North of the church, rue du Jerzual leads down to the gate of the same name and on down (as rue du Petit-Fort) to the port and a majestic old bridge over the Rance, lined with artisans' shops and restaurants.

On the last weekend in September or the first weekend in October – check with the tourist office – the **Fête des Remparts** is celebrated with medieval-style jousting, banquets, fairs and processions, culminating in an immense fireworks display. There's a **market** every Thursday in the places du Champ and du Guesclin (the original medieval fairground).

Eating and drinking

All sorts of specialist **restaurants**, including several ethnic alternatives, are tucked away in the old streets of Dinan. Stroll of an evening through the town and down to the port, and you'll pass at least twenty places. For **bars**, explore the series of tiny parallel alleyways between the place des Merciers and the rue de la Ferronerie. Along rue de la Cordonnerie, the busiest of the lot, the various hang-outs define themselves by their taste in music; *A la Truye qui File* at no. 14 is a sort of contemporary folky Breton dive, while *Morgan's Tavern*, next door at no. 12, is considerably more raucous.

Chez Flochon, 24 rue du Jerzual (☎96.87.91.57). Fine old carved house on the lane up from the port, with a few tables perched on a wooden platform outside so you can watch the world stagger by. Fondues, galettes and crêpes. Closed Sun pm, & Mon in low season.

Crêperie Connetable, 1 rue de l'Apport (☎96.39.02.52). Magnificent old house opposite the *Mère Pourcel* beside the place des Merciers. Sit if you dare at the pavement tables, where all that prevents the upper storeys from crashing down around your ears are a couple of misshapen pillars. Crêpes and snacks in the perfect spot for people-watching.

Mère Pourcel, 3 pl des Merciers (☎96.39.03.80). Beautiful half-timbered fifteenth-century house in the central square. The cheapest menu, at 92F, is a bit minimal, but you reach gourmet class with the crab and fish on the 155F one. Closed Jan, Feb, and Sun pm and Mon out of season.

Le Relais des Corsaires, 7 rue du Quai, port du Dinan (☎96.39.40.17). Just across the road from the waterfront with a restaurant menu from 115F, offering cockles and mussels followed by scallops or monkfish. The *Grill* menu, in theory served in the adjacent *Petit Corsaire* but in low season served in the same building, costs 69F and is "grill" in name only.

Le Saigon, 12 rue Ste-Claire (☎96.85.21.20). Small, friendly Chinese and Vietnamese place near the *Hôtel du Théâtre* (see above). Menus start at 55F. Open every day of the year.

Les Terrasses, 2 rue du Quai, port du Dinan (☎96.39.09.60). A lovely waterfront setting, with good menus from 95F. Closed Tues out of season.

Rennes and around

For a city that has been the capital and power centre of Brittany since the 1532 union with France, Rennes is – outwardly at least – uncharacteristic of the province, with its Neoclassical layout and pompous major buildings. What potential it had to be a picturesque tourist spot was destroyed in 1720, when a drunken carpenter managed to set light to virtually the whole city. Only the area known as **Les Lices**, at the junction of the canalized Ille and the River Vilaine, was undamaged. The remodelling of the rest of the city was handed over to Parisian architects, not in deference to the capital but in an attempt to rival it.

Arrival and accommodation

Rennes' modern **gare SNCF** (☎99.65.50.50), on the express *TGV* line between Paris and Brest, is well south of the Vilaine, fifteen minutes' walk from the central **tourist office** on the Pont de Nemours (Mon 2–6pm, Tues–Sat 9am–6pm; ☎99.79.01.98). The **gare routière** on bd Magenta (☎99.30.87.80) is a couple of blocks north of the *gare*

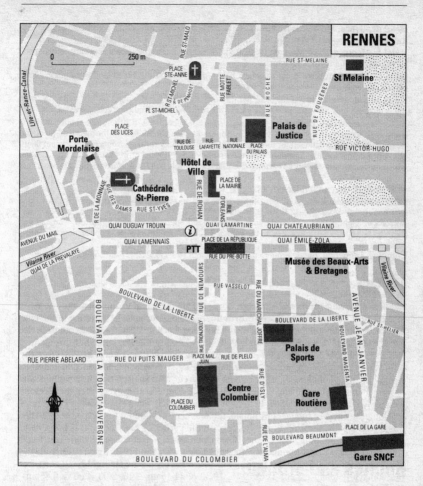

RENNES

0   250 m

RUE ST-MALO

PLACE STE-ANNE

RUE ST-MELAINE

St Melaine

RUE MOTTE FABLET

RUE HOCHE

RUE DE FOUGÈRES

PL ST-MICHEL

R DE PONGET

PLACE DES LICES

Porte Mordelaise

RUE DE TOULOUSE   RUE LAFAYETTE   RUE NATIONALE   PLACE DU PALAIS

Palais de Justice

RUE VICTOR-HUGO

Hôtel de Ville

Cathédrale St-Pierre

RUE DE ROHAN

PLACE DE LA MAIRIE

RUE D'ORLÉANS

RUE DE LA MONNAIE

R DES DAMES   RUE ST-YVES

QUAI DUGUAY TROUIN

QUAI LAMARTINE

QUAI CHATEAUBRIAND

AVENUE DU MAIL

QUAI LAMENNAIS

PLACE DE LA RÉPUBLIQUE

QUAI ÉMILE-ZOLA

Vilaine River

QUAI DE LA PRÉVALAYE

PTT

RUE DU PRÉ-BOTTÉ

Musée des Beaux-Arts & Bretagne

Vilaine River

RUE DE NEMOURS

RUE VASSELOT

RUE DU MARÉCHAL JOFFRE

BOULEVARD DE LA LIBERTÉ

AVENUE JEAN-JANVIER

RUE ST-HÉLIER

BOULEVARD DE LA LIBERTÉ

RUE TRONJOLY

BOULEVARD DE LA TOUR D'AUVERGNE

BOULEVARD MAGENTA

RUE PIERRE ABELARD   RUE DU PUITS MAUGER   PLACE MAL JUIN   RUE DE PLELO

Palais de Sports

Centre Colombier

RUE D'ISLY

Gare Routière

PLACE DU COLOMBIER

RUE DE L'ALMA

PLACE DE LA GARE

BOULEVARD BEAUMONT

Gare SNCF

BOULEVARD DU COLOMBIER

SNCF, but most local buses start and finish on or near place de la République, along-side the tourist office. Rennes is a busy junction, with direct services to St-Malo (*TIV*; ☎99.79.23.44); Dinan and Dinard (*Armor Express*; ☎99.50.64.17), Mont-St-Michel (*Courriers Bretons*; ☎99.56.79.09), and Nantes (*Societé Transports Tourisme de l'Ouest*; ☎40.20.45.20).

Unfortunately, there are very few **hotels** in the old part of Rennes – and those that there are can be very hard to find. If you've arrived by train or bus, it's easier to settle for staying near the *gares SNCF* and *routière*.

HOTELS

Hôtel d'Angleterre, 19 rue du Maréchal-Joffre (☎99.79.38.61). Not brilliant, but relatively cheap, a short way south of the river towards the station. No restaurant. ①.

Central Hôtel, 6 rue Lanjuinais (☎99.30.85.37). Among the nicest of the upmarket hotels, on a quiet little street around the corner from the tourist office, less than 50m south of the river. No restaurant. ③.

Hôtel des Lices, 7 pl des Lices (☎99.79.14.81). Forty rooms, all with TV, in a very comfortable and friendly modern hotel on the edge of the prettiest part of old Rennes. No restaurant. ③.

Hôtel le Magenta, 35 bd Magenta (☎99.30.85.37). Roomy but slightly noisy accommodation opposite the *gare routière*. No restaurant. ①.

Hôtel le Maréchal-Joffre, 6 rue du Maréchal-Joffre (☎99.79.37.74). Small family-run place, south of the river on the way to the station. No restaurant. ①.

Hôtel Riaval, 9 rue de Riaval (99.50.65.58). Friendly hotel with neat budget rooms, well away from the centre, but only a few minutes' walk east of the *gare SNCF*, on a quiet street. No restaurant. ①.

Hôtel-Restaurant Au Rocher de Cancale, 10 rue St-Michel (☎99.79.20.83). Five-room hotel on a lively pedestrian street, between place Ste-Anne and place St-Michel, in the heart of medieval Rennes and ideally positioned for the city's nightlife. Beautifully restored frontage and ground floor, but with modern facilities upstairs. The restaurant, which is closed at weekends, has menus from 58F at lunchtime and 85F in the evening; the 130F exclusively fish menu is excellent. ②.

YOUTH HOSTELS AND CAMPSITES

IYHF youth hostel, 3km out from the centre, next to the Canal d'Ille et Rance – the *Centre International de Séjour*, 10–12 Canal St-Martin (☎99.33.22.33). Charging between 65F and 105F per person per night, it has a cafeteria and a laundry, and operates a midnight curfew. You can get there on bus routes #20 and #22 from the *gare SNCF*, direction St-Gregoire, stop Coëtlogon; neither runs over the weekend, when you have to catch bus #2 instead. Year-round.

Camping municipal, rue de Professeur-Maurice-Audin (☎99.36.91.22). Take bus #3. April–Sept.

The City

Rennes' surviving **medieval quarter**, bordered by the canal to the west and the river to the south, radiates from **Porte Mordelaise**, the old ceremonial entrance to the city, now more prominently exposed following building work in 1990. A few streets from the *porte*, the **place des Lices** is dominated by two empty market halls, but originally it was the venue for tournaments – that is, jousting "lists". It was here, in 1337, that the hitherto unknown Bertrand du Guesclin, then aged seventeen, fought and defeated several older opponents. This set him on his career as a soldier, during which he was to save Rennes when it was under siege by the English. However, after the Bretons were defeated at Auray in 1364, he fought for the French, and twice invaded Brittany.

Along the curving rue de la Monnaie, the one central building to escape the 1720 fire was, symbolically, the **Palais de Justice**, on the corner of rue Hoche. It is possible to see round the building, where the Breton *parlement* – a mixture of high court and council with unelected members – fought battles with the French governor from the reign of Louis XIV up until the Revolution. Tours start from the far right-hand corner of the courtyard (daily except Tues, 9.45, 10.30 & 11.15am, 2.15, 3.00, 4.00 & 4.45pm). Each of the seventeenth-century chambers is more opulently gilded and adorned than the one before, culminating in the debating hall hung with Gobelin tapestries depicting scenes from the history of the duchy and the province. Every centimetre of the walls and ceilings is decorated in Sun King style, although on a relatively small scale.

The **south bank** of the river is every bit as busy, if not busier, than the north – should you feel upon arriving that Rennes feels oddly empty, the chances are that everyone's in the giant **Colombier Centre**, just west of the *gare SNCF*. This vast new mall is Rennes at its most modern, packed with shops of all kinds, plus cafés and snack bars, and featuring an amazing crystal model of itself in its main entrance hall. Slightly nearer the river, **rue Vasselot** has its own array of half-timbered old houses.

Two major museums are housed in former university buildings at 20 quai Émile-Zola, on the south bank of the Vilaine. The **Musée de Bretagne** gives one of the best possible introductions to the history and culture of Brittany (daily except Tues 10am–noon & 2–6pm; 15F). The prehistoric section is good, and includes the bones of a woolly rhinoceros found at Dol, but the greatest strength of the museum is the audiovisual presentation of the transition from the last century to the present. The **Musée des Beaux Arts** owns some Leonardo drawings in addition to more local exhibits (daily except Tues 10am–noon & 2–6pm; 15F). Its specifically Breton room combines paintings of mythical themes – the Île d'Ys legend (see p.360) by Luminais – and of real life – a woman waiting for the fishermen to come back through stormy seas.

Eating and drinking

Most of Rennes' more interesting **bars**, **restaurants** and **nightlife** in general are to be found in the streets just south of place Ste-Anne and St-Aubin church. Rues St-Michel and Penhoët, each with a fine assemblage of ancient wooden buildings, are the epicentre at the moment, while ethnic alternatives can be found along rue St-Malo just to the north – such as the African *Le Maquis* and the Tunisian *Byblos*, adjacent at no. 13. While you're exploring, look around the back of the excellent *crêperie* at 5 place Ste-Anne, through an archway off rue Motte-Fablet, to get an extraordinary glimpse of medieval high-rise housing.

Rue Vasselot is the nearest equivalent south of the river, though if you're just looking for a quick snack, don't forget the various outlets in the Centre Colombier.

La Boutique Antillaise, 5 pl du Bas-des-Lices (☎99.30.54.44). The Caribbean influence goes a little deeper than the colourful cocktails here; you can also get chicken cooked in coconut, court-boullion, and kick off with a *boudin antillais*. A small, friendly restaurant – booking advisable. Midday menu 58F, or upwards of 98F in the evening.

La Chope, 3 rue de la Chalotais (☎99.79.34.54). A little way below place de la République on the south bank. Busy brasserie open until midnight daily except Sun, serving meals from 70F upwards.

Le Chouin, 12 rue d'Isly (☎99.30.87.86). A fine fish restaurant not far from the *gare SNCF*. Menu 99F midday, *à la carte* in the evening. Closed Sun & Mon.

La Khalifa, 20 haut de la pl des Lices (☎99.30.87.30). Assorted Moroccan dishes: couscous 54F and up, brochettes 63F, and tajine 66F, as well as various set menus. Closed Sun in winter.

Le Parc à Moules, 8 rue George-Dattin (☎99.31.44.28). On a small street leading north from the river halfway between the tourist office and the place des Lices. Mussels from Mont St-Michel Bay cooked in twelve different delicious ways for around 45F, and a weekday lunch menu offering *moules-frites* for 49F, plus various more expensive fishy dishes. Closed Sat lunch & Sun.

Ti-koz, 3 rue St-Guillaume (☎99.79.33.89). Classic French cooking in a beautiful sixteenth-century house a little way north of the river tourist office. Lunches from 70F, dinner menus at 98F, 155F and 250F.

Entertainment and nightlife

The varied season of the *Théâtre National de Bretagne*, 1 rue St-Hélier (☎99.30.88.88), runs from mid-October to mid-June. All year round, in a different auditorium on the same premises, *Club Ubu* (☎99.31.55.33) puts on large-scale gigs. There's regular live **jazz** at *Déjazey Jazz Club*, 54 rue St-Malo (daily except Sun; ☎99.38.70.72). The *Barantic* on rue St-Michel is a popular **bar**, putting on occasional live music for a mixed crowd of Breton nationalists and boisterous students.

The presence of so many students – 35,000 all told – gives Rennes a rather more visible level of political and cultural activity than most places in Brittany. The friendly co-operative bookshop *Breizh* at 17 rue Penhöet has cassettes of Breton and Celtic music along with books and posters. *L'Arvor* cinema at 29 rue d'Antrain (☎99.38.72.40) shows *v.o.* (original-language) films, and there's a large selection of English books in the *FNAC* bookshop in the Colombier Centre.

Rennes is seen at its best the first ten days of July, when the **Festival des Tombées de la Nuit** takes over the whole city to celebrate Breton culture with music, theatre, film, mime and poetry in joyful rejection of the influences of both Paris and Hollywood (information: 8 place du Maréchal-Juin, 35000 Rennes; ☎99.30.38.01).

In the second week of December, an annual rock festival, **Les Transmusicales**, attracts big-name acts from all over France and the world at large, though still with a Breton emphasis; over the last decade it has helped to make Rennes an important centre for French rock (information ☎99.31.55.33).

The Forêt de Paimpont

Thirty kilometres to the west of Rennes, the **Forêt de Paimpont**, known also by its ancient name of Brocéliande, is – according to song and legend – the forest of the wizard Merlin. Medieval Breton minstrels, like their Welsh counterparts from whom or with whom the stories originated, set the tales of King Arthur and the Holy Grail both in *Grande Bretagne* and here in *Petite Bretagne*. For all the magic of these shared legends, however, and a succession of likely sites, few people come out here. If you like the idea of roaming around for a day it isn't difficult. The bus from Rennes to Guer runs twice a day past the southern edge of the forest, stopping at Forges-les-Paimpont, and another, around the north corner, to **MAURON**.

Mauron is a good point to start. From the hamlet of **FOLLE-PENSÉE**, just south of the village, it's a circuitous but enjoyable twenty-minute walk to **La Fontaine de Barenton** – Merlin's spring. The path leads off from the end of the road at Folle-Pensée, turning to the right, running through pines and gorse to a junction of forest tracks: here take the track straight ahead for about 100m, where an unobvious path to the left goes into the woods and turns back north to the spring – walled, and filled by the most delicious water imaginable, as you might expect from the elixir of eternal youth. After drinking, stroke the great stone slab beside the spring to call up a storm, roaring lions and a horseman in black armour. Here Merlin first set eyes on Vivianne, who bound him willingly in a prison of air.

The Fountain of Eternal Youth is hidden nearby and accessible only to the pure in heart. The enchantress is supposed to have been born at the now ruinous château at **COMPER**, at the northern edge of the forest near Concoret. Today it serves as the **Centre de l'Imaginaire Arthurien**, which means that each summer it's the venue of different exhibitions and entertainments on Arthurian themes, and also organizes tours of the actual forest (June–Aug daily except Tues 10am–7pm; April, May & Sept daily except Tues & Fri 10am–7pm; 25F).

Another forest walk, more scenic but without a goal, is the **Val sans Retour** (the Valley of No Return), off the GR37 from Tréhorenteuc to La Guette. The path to follow leads out from the D141 just south of Tréhorenteuc to a steep valley from which exits are barred by thickets of gorse and giant furze on the rocks above; at one point it skirts an overgrown table of rock, the **Rocher des Faux Amants**, from which the seduc-tress Morgane le Fay supposedly enticed unwary boys.

Accommodation in the forest

The little market village of **PAIMPONT** is the most obvious and enjoyable base for exploring the forest. It's right at the centre of the woods, backs on to a marshy lake whose shores are thick with wild mushrooms (*cêpes*), and has some excellent **accommodation**. At the *Relais de Brocéliande* in town (☎99.07.81.07; ②), a real flower-bedecked delight, you can stuff yourself for 98F in the restaurant under the gaze of stuffed animal heads, and there's a live parrot whose one note sounds like a submarine. There are also a couple of **campsites**, including the municipal one on the edge of the village (☎97.07.85.25; March to mid-Nov), a *gîte d'étape-chambre d'hôte* in tiny Trudeau on the D40 (☎99.07.81.40; B&B ③), and a lovely **youth hostel**, a couple of kilometres out on the Concoret road (☎97.22.76.75; ①; May–Sept). Information on them all can be picked up from the summer-only Paimpont **tourist office** next to the lakeside abbey (☎99.07.24.83).

There's another *gîte d'étape* at **LES FORGES**, a rural hamlet on the GR37, set by a calm lake south of Paimpont (c/o Mme Farcy; ☎97.06.93.46). Or you could stop at the rather featureless **PLÉLAN-LE-GRAND**, east of the forest on the main Rennes road, which has another affordable **hotel** in the *Bruyères* (☎99.06.81.38; ②). Just outside the village is the *Manoir du Tertre* (☎99.07.81.02; ④; closed Tues & Feb), a very grand old country house, preserved with all its furnishings and operating, with high but not outrageous prices (first menu 135F), as a superb hotel/restaurant.

The north coast from Dinard to Lannion

The coast that stretches from St-Malo to Finistère at the far western end of Brittany is divided into two distinct regions either side of the bay of **St-Brieuc**. First come the exposed green headlands of the **Côte d'Émeraude**; beyond St-Brieuc itself the shore is more extravagantly indented, with a succession of secluded little bays and an increasing proliferation of huge pink granite boulders seen at their best on the **Côte de Granit Rose** near Perros-Guirec.

The Côte d'Émeraude

To the west of the Rance, beyond Dinard, begins the green of the **Côte d'Émeraude**. Though composed mainly of developed family resorts, it also offers wonderful camping, at its best around the heather-backed beaches near **Cap Fréhel**. You can't camp within 5km of the headland itself, a high, warm expanse of heath and cliffs with views extending on good days as far as Jersey and the Île de Bréhat (see p.344). The **Fort la Latte**, to the east, is used regularly as a film set. Its tower, containing a cannonball factory, is accessible only over two drawbridges (guided tours: June–Sept daily 10am–12.30pm & 2.30–6.30pm; Oct–May Sun & hols 2.30–5.30pm; 15F).

The nearest places to stay are the ideal, isolated **campsite** at Pléherel, the *Camping du Pont L'Étang* (☎96.41.40.45; May–Sept), and a basic summer-only **youth hostel** on the D16 just outside Plévenon en route towards the Cap – full address Kérivet-en-Frehel, La Ville Hardrieux (☎96.41.48.98; ①; mid-April to Sept).

Erquy

Further round the headland, the perfect crescent of beach at **ERQUY** curves through more than 180 degrees. At low tide, the sea disappears way beyond the harbour entrance, leaving gentle ripples of paddling sand. Adventurers equipped with suitable boots could walk right across its mouth, from the grassy wooded headland on the left side over to the picturesque little lighthouse at the end of the jetty on the right.

Erquy's **tourist office** on the bd de la Mer (summer daily 9.30am–12.30pm & 2–7pm; otherwise daily except Mon 9.30am–12.30pm; ☎96.72.30.12) coordinates information for the surrounding area. The *Hôtel Beauséjour*, 21 rue de la Corniche (☎96.72.30.39; ③–④; closed Sun pm & Mon in winter), has a good view of the bay and excellent fish dinners from around 70F, while there are several **campsites** on the promontory (dotted with tiny coves) that leads to the Cap d'Erquy north of town, including the *St-Pabu* (☎96.72.24.65; April–Oct) right beside the sea.

Le Val-André

The huge beach in the broader bay of **LE VAL-ANDRÉ** is of finer, sweeter-smelling sand, and the endless pedestrian promenade that stretches along the seafront feels oddly Victorian, consisting solely of huge old houses undisturbed by shops or bars. However, Le Val-André is definitely more of a town than Erquy, and rue A-Charner, running parallel to the sea one street back, is busy with holidaymakers in summer.

Le Val-André's helpful **tourist office** (☎96.72.20.55) is located in the modern casino at the very centre of the waterfront. Of its **hotels**, the tastefully refurbished *Hôtel de la Mer*, 63 rue A-Charner (☎96.72.20.44; ①), uses a fine muscadet to transport *moules marinières* onto a hitherto undreamed-of plane (available on their 89F menu along with rabbit or quail and a delicious raspberry mousse). However, with the success of the business many guests find themselves having to sleep in the characterless *Nuit et Jour* motel, run by the same management. The similar-looking but slightly more imposing *Hôtel Regina*, slightly nearer the centre at 45 rue A-Charner (☎96.72.22.63; ②), is a more dependable if perhaps less exciting choice; a couple of its rooms have attractive balconies. The *Restaurant au Biniou*, 121 rue Clémenceau (☎96.72.24.35; March–Dec), is the best of several adjacent seafood specialists just back from the casino, with an 80F menu featuring stuffed mussels and oysters.

St-Brieuc

The major city on the Côte d'Émeraude, **ST-BRIEUC** is far too busy being the industrial centre of the north to concern itself with entertaining tourists. It's an odd-looking city, with two very deep wooded valleys spanned by viaducts at its core, and it's almost impossible to bypass, however you're travelling. The streets are hectic, with the town centre cut in two by a virtual motorway, unrelieved by any public parks, and not much distinguished either by a mega-shopping complex. Motorists and cyclists, unfortunately, have little choice but to plough straight through rather than attempting to negotiate the backroads and steep hills around. Apart from the sturdy-looking **St-Stephen's cathedral**, the fine views of the valley from **Tertre Aubé** and a handful of half-timbered houses in the streets around place au Lin, there's nothing to keep you here.

If you decide to use the city as a base, one ordinary but economical place to **stay** is the *Hôtel du Parc*, 8 rue Jean-Mermoz (☎96.33.51.02; ①); you can get much more class and comfort at the central *Champ du Mars*, 13 rue de Général-Leclerc (☎96.33.60.99; ③), with a good brasserie downstairs. St-Brieuc also has an IYHF **youth hostel**, two kilometres out, comprising dorms in the magnificent fifteenth-century Manoir de la Ville-Guyomard (☎96.78.70.70; ①); it's on bus route #1 from the station, and has bicycles and canoes for rental.

Among **eating** options in town are the traditional French cooking of *Le Madure*, 14 rue Quinquaine (☎96.51.20.17; closed Sun & Mon), where menus start at 78F, and the "biological" restaurant *Le Grain de Sel*, 19 rue de Maréchal-Foch (☎96.33.19.61; closed Jan, Sat pm, & Sun), which serves **vegetarian** meals and fish made with the fresh organic produce it also sells.

Guingamp

If you skip the Pink Granite Coast and head directly west towards Finistère, you'll pass through **GUINGAMP**, 25km south of the coast, the only town of any size in the centre of this northern peninsula and an old weaving centre – its name possibly the source of the fabric "gingham". It's an attractive place of cobbled streets, but there's not much to see beyond the main square, where a fountain bedecked in griffins and gargoyles is overlooked by a splendid pair of lopsided old timber-frame houses propping each other up, along with the Black Virgin in the basilica.

On the road out towards Morlaix is the miniature "mountain" of the **Ménez Bré**, a spectacular height in these plains. In the mid-nineteenth century, the local rector was observed to climb to the sole mountain's peak on stormy nights, accompanied only by a donkey laden with books. For all his exemplary piety, his parishioners suspected him of sorcery; he was, it turned out, doing early research into natural electrical forces.

North from St-Brieuc

Moving northwest towards Paimpol, the coast becomes wilder and harsher and the seaside towns tend to be crammed into narrow rocky inlets or set well back in river estuaries. **BINIC** is a narrow port surrounded by meadows, with a thin strip of beach and the decent if relatively pricey *Hôtel Benhuyc*, 1 quai Jean-Bart (☎96.73.61.16; ④), while at the sedate family resort of **ST-QUAY-PORTRIEUX**, a little further on, the *Gerbot d'Avoine* (☎96.70.40.09; ②), beside the beach, is the best place to stay, despite the hideous decor of its rooms.

After St-Quay, the coastal road shifts inland, through **PLOUHA**, the traditional boundary between French-speaking and Breton-speaking Brittany. It's a viable proposition to hitch from here to **KERMARIA-AN-ISQUIT**, signposted off the D21 from Plouha, to see the extraordinary medieval frescoes of a *Dance Macabre* in the thirteenth-century **chapel** of the village. They show Ankou, who is death or death's assistant, leading representatives of every social class in a dance of death. An encounter between three living nobles out hunting and three philosophical corpses is also depicted, and there's a statue of the infant Jesus refusing milk from Mary's proffered breast. To get into the chapel you'll need to get a key from Mme Hervé Droniou in the house up the road on the left.

Paimpol

Back on the north coast, **PAIMPOL** is still an attractive town with a tangle of cobbled alleyways and fine grey-granite houses, but has lost something in its transition from working fishing port to pleasure harbour. It was once the centre of a cod and whaling fleet that sailed to Iceland each February, sent off with a ceremony marked by a famous *pardon*. From then until September the town would be empty of its young men. The whole area was commemorated in Pierre Loti's book *Pêcheur d'Islande*; the author, and his heroine, lived in the **place du Martray** in the centre of town.

Thanks to naval shipyards and the like, the open sea is not visible from Paimpol; a maze of waterways leads to its two separate harbours. Both are usually filled with the high masts of yachts, but still also used by the fishing boats that keep a fish market and a plethora of *poissoneries* busy. This is doubtless a very pleasant place to arrive by yacht, threading through the rocks, but from close quarters the tiny port area is a little disappointing, very much rebuilt and quite plain. Even so, it is always lively in summer.

Possible places to **stay** include the luxurious *Repaire de Kerroc'h*, overlooking the small-boat harbour from quai Morand (☎96.20.50.13; ④), which serves gourmet meals from 85F up to 350F; the very hospitable *Hôtel Berthelot* at 1 rue du Port (☎96.20.88.66; ②); and the plainer *Hôtel Origano*, just back from the front at 7 bis rue du Quai (☎96.22.05.49; ②). A year-round IYHF **youth hostel** in the grand old *Château de Kerraoul* (☎96.20.83.60; ①) offers dorm beds and has facilities for **camping**.

As for **restaurants**, *La Cotriade*, on the far side of the harbour on the quai Armand-Dayot (☎96.20.81.08; closed Thurs) is the best bet for authentic fish dishes, with a simple 90F menu, including a *veritable Cassoulet Paimpolais* and a 125F menu that features a delicious crab mousse. Very near the *Origano* hotel, the *Corto Maltese* **bar** serves a fine selection of British and other beers.

Loguivy-sur-Mer

If Paimpol is too crowded for you, it's well worth continuing a few kilometres further across the headland to the little fishing hamlet of **LOGUIVY**. All of the long river inlets along this northern coast tend to conceal tiny coves; at Loguivy, a working harbour manages to squeeze into one such gap in the rocks. There are no hotels, but *chambres d'hôte* (which don't work out any cheaper) are available at **KÉRÉVEUR** (M. Chaboud; ☎96.55.82.76; ②) and **KERLOURY** (I. Le Goaster; ☎96.20.85.23; ②), where Lenin came for his summer holidays in July 1902.

The Île de Bréhat

Two kilometres off the coast at Pointe de l'Arcouest, 6km northwest of Paimpol, the Île De Bréhat – in reality two islands joined by a tiny bridge – gives the appearance of spanning great latitudes. On the north side are windswept meadows of hemlock and yarrow, sloping down to chaotic erosions of rock; on the south, you're in the midst of palm trees, mimosa and eucalyptus. All around is a multitude of little islets – some accessible at low tide, others *propriété privée*, most just pink-orange rocks. All in all, this has to be one of the most beautiful places in Brittany.

As you might expect, this island paradise has attracted Parisians and the like looking for holiday homes. Over half the houses now have temporary residents, and young Bréhatins leave in ever-increasing numbers for lack of a place of their own, let alone a job. In winter the remaining 300 or so natives have the place to themselves, without even a *gendarme*; the summer sees two imported from the mainland, along with upwards of 3000 tourists. As a visitor, though, you should find the Bréhatins friendly enough – it's the holiday-home owners that they really resent.

The beach to swim from at low tide is the **Grève de Guerzido,** on the east side facing the mainland. Near **LE BOURG**, or Bréhat village, which is the centre of all activity on the island, the sea tends to be a bit murky, and the east coast generally is less accessible because of private property. But in the north, even when Le Bourg is blocked up with visitors, you can walk and laze about in near solitude. Bréhat no longer

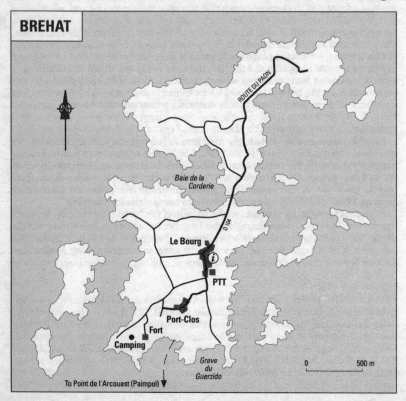

has a castle (blown up twice by the English), but it does have a **lighthouse** and a nineteenth-century **fort**, in the woods near the campsite (see below).

Practicalities

Bréhat is connected regularly by **ferry** from the Pointe de l'Arcouest and is served by regular buses in summer from the *gare SNCF* there. Sailings with *Vedettes de Bréhat* (☎96.55.86.99) are roughly hourly in high summer, and every two hours otherwise, with the last boat back around 7pm; the round-trip costs 35F. Up to three daily guided boat tours circle the island, for a cost of 65F. *Vedettes de Bréhat* also operate occasional trips in summer from Binic, St-Quay-Portrieux, and Erquy.

No cars are permitted on Bréhat itself, and there's barely a road wide enough for its few light farm vehicles. You can rent **bikes** at the ferry port, or take one across with you for 45F (in summer you have to catch a ferry before 10am if you're with bike), but it's easy enough to walk from one end of the island to the other in half an hour.

The **tourist office**, in the old *mairie* in the main square in Le Bourg (daily 10am–1pm & 3–6pm; ☎96.20.04.15), has full details on **accommodation**. The few hotels here are expensive and tend to be permanently booked through the summer, while all close for at least part of the winter. Both the *Vieille Auberge* in Le Bourg (☎96.20.00.24; ⓓ; Easter–Sept) and the *Bellevue* in Port-Clos (☎96.20.00.05; ⓓ; closed Jan) insist on *demi-pension* in high season. However, there's a wonderful **campsite** in the woods high above the sea west of the port (☎96.20.00.36; mid-June to mid-Sept); when that's closed you can pitch your tent almost anywhere.

The Côte de Granit Rose

The whole of the northernmost stretch of the Breton coast, from Bréhat to **Trégastel**, has loosely come to be known as the **Côte de Granit Rose**. There are indeed great granite boulders scattered in the sea around the island of Bréhat, and at the various headlands to the west, but the most memorable stretch of coast lies around **Perros-Guirec**, where the pink granite rocks are eroded into fantastic shapes.

Tréguier

The D786 turns west from Paimpol, passing over a green *ria* on the bridge outside Lézardrieux before arriving at **TRÉGUIER**, one of the very few hill-towns in Brittany. Its central feature is the **Cathédrale de St-Tugdual**, which contains the tomb of Saint Yves, a native of the town who died in 1303 and – for his incorruptibility – became the patron saint of lawyers. Attempts to bribe him continue to this day; his tomb is surrounded by marble plaques and an inferno of candles invoking his aid.

The *Hôtel-Restaurant d'Estuaire* on the waterfront (☎96.92.30.25; ⓓ) is a nice place to **stay** – the sea views are great – with reasonable menus from 65F; *la Poissonerie du Trégor*, up in town at 2 rue Renan (☎96.92.30.27), is an excellent fish **restaurant** which is no more expensive. During the **market** each Wednesday, clothes and so on are spread out in the square by the cathedral, and food and fresh fish down by the port.

Perros-Guirec and Ploumanac'h

PERROS-GUIREC is the most popular resort along this coast, though not perhaps the most exciting, consisting largely of a network of tree-lined avenues of suburban villas. It does stand, however, at one end of the long **Sentier des Douaniers** pathway, which winds round the clifftops to the tiny resort of **PLOUMANAC'H** past an astonishing succession of deformed and water-sculpted rocks. Birds wheel overhead towards the offshore bird sanctuary of Sept-Îles, and battered boats shelter in the narrow inlets or bob uncontrollably out on the waves. There are patches and brief causeways of grass, clumps of purple heather and yellow gorse. Occasionally the rocks have crumbled into a sort of granite grit to make up a tiny beach; one boulder is strapped down by bands of ivy that prevent it rolling into the sea.

Hotels in Perros-Guirec itself include the *Hôtel de la Mairie*, in the place de l'Hôtel-de-Ville (☎96.23.22.41; ②), and two with sea views: the *Gulf Stream*, 26 rue des Sept-Îles (☎96.23.21.86; ②; April to mid-Nov), and the *Bon Accueil*, rue de Landerval (☎96.23.23.45; ④), whose gourmet restaurant is the best in town. Ploumanac'h offers the *Hôtel du Parc* (☎96.91.40.80; ②; April–Sept) and the luxurious *Les Rochers* (☎96.91.44.49; ④; Easter–Sept). The nicest place to **camp** has to be *Le Ranolien* (☎96.91.43.58; Feb–Nov), backing on to the Sentier des Douaniers near a little beach about halfway around, but directly accessible on the other side by road.

Trégastel and Trébeurden

Of the smaller villages further round the coast to the west, **TRÉGASTEL**, with a **campsite**, and **TRÉBEURDEN**, with the IYHF *Le Toëno* **youth hostel** (☎96.23.52.22; ①; open all year), are functional stopovers. Trébeurden has managed to squeeze in an **aquarium** under a massive pile of boulders, and has a couple of huge lumps of pink granite slap in the middle of its fine beach.

The strangest sight along this coast, however, outdoing anything the erosions can manage, is just south of Trégastel on the **route de Calvaire**, where an old stone saint halfway up a high calvary raises his arm to bless or harangue the gleaming white discs and puffball dome of the **Pleumier-Bodou Telecommunications Centre**. A new pink granite "dolmen" commemorates its opening by De Gaulle in 1962, when it was the first receiving station to pick up signals from the American Telstar satellite. The centre is still operating, but is open to visitors on guided tours, along with its Museum of Telecommunications (guided tours daily 10am, 1.30pm, 5.30pm; July & Aug 6pm & 7pm; Feb, March, & Oct–Dec 1.30pm & 5.30pm; Oct–April & Jan closed Sat).

The Bay of Lannion

Despite being significantly back from the sea on the estuary of the River Léguer, **Lannion** gives its name to the next bay west along the Breton coast – and it's the bay rather than the town that is most likely to impress visitors. One enormous beach stretches from **St-Michel-en-Grève**, which is little more than a bend in the road, as far as **Locquirec**; at low tide you can walk hundreds of metres out on the sands.

Lannion

LANNION, set amid plummeting hills and stairways, is an historic city with streets of medieval housing and a couple of interesting old churches – but it's also a centre for a burgeoning and extremely high-tech telecommunications industry, and one of modern Brittany's real success stories, hence its rather self-satisfied nickname, *ville heureuse* or "happy town". In addition to admiring the half-timbered houses around the **place de Général-Leclerc** and along **rue des Chapeliers**, it's well worth climbing from the town up the 142 granite steps which lead to the twelfth-century Templar **Église de Brélévenez**. This church was remodelled three hundred years later to incorporate a granite bell tower, and the views from its terrace are quite stupendous.

The *Hôtel le Bretagne* at 32 av de Général-de-Gaulle (☎96.37.00.33; ③; closed Sat & Sun pm out of season), opposite the station, is a *logis* with a good restaurant; the *Porte de France*, an eighteenth-century coaching inn at 5 rue Jean-Savidan (☎96.46.54.81; ③), is a more luxurious option with no restaurant. There's also a year-round **youth hostel**, conveniently positioned very near the station and the town centre at 6 rue du 73^e Territorial (☎96.37.91.28; ①).

Locquirec

LOCQUIREC, across the bay from Lannion, manages to have beaches on both sides, without ever quite being thin enough to be a real peninsula. Around the main port, smart houses stand in sloping gardens, looking very southern English with their white-washed stone panels, grey slate roofs and jutting turreted windows. On the last Sunday in July, Locquirec holds a combined *pardon de St-Jacques* and Festival of the Sea.

Locquirec veers dangerously close to being over-twee, and none of its **hotels** is all that cheap either – although the *Grand Hôtel des Bains* (☎98.67.41.02; ②) has so gorgeous a setting that perhaps it doesn't matter. Nearby, the *Hôtel du Port* (☎98.67.42.10; ②) also enjoys a sea view, and the municipal **campsite**, a kilometre south along the corniche (☎98.67.40.85), is beautifully positioned, too.

The Cairn du Barnenez

At the mouth of the Morlaix estuary, 6km north of Plouézoch, the prehistoric stone **Cairn du Barnenez** surveys the waters from the summit of a hill (daily July & Aug 10am–1pm & 2–6.30pm; April–June & Sept 10am–12.30pm & 2–6.30pm; Oct–March 10am–noon & 2–5pm; free). As on the island of Gavrinis in the Morbihan (see p.382), its ancient masonry has been laid bare by recent excavations, and provides a stunning sense of the architectural prowess of the megalith builders. Radiocarbon testing has shown the work here to date back to around 4500 BC, which makes this one of the oldest large monuments in the world.

The ensemble consists of two distinct stepped pyramids. Each rises in successive tiers, built of large flat stones chinked with pebbles; the second was added on to the side of the first, and the two are encircled by a series of terraces and ramps. The whole thing measures roughly 70m long by 15–25m wide and 6m high. Both pyramids were long buried under the same eighty-metre-long earthen mound. While the actual cairns are completely exposed to view, most of the passages and chambers that lie within them are sealed off. The two minor corridors that are open simply cut through the edifice from one side to the other, and were exposed by quarrying activities around thirty years ago – which inadvertently provided a good insight into the construction methods. Local tradition has it that one tunnel runs right through this "home of the fairies", and continues out deep under the sea.

FINISTÈRE – LAND'S END

It's hard to resist the appeal of the **Finistère coast**, with its ocean-fronting cliffs and headlands. Summer crowds may detract from the best parts of the **Crozon peninsula** and the **Pointe de Raz**, but there are miles and miles of coast where you can enjoy near solitude. If you've transport, explore the semi-wilderness of the **northern stretches** beyond Brest and the little fishing village of **Le Conquet**, or the misty offshore islands of **Ouessant and Molène**. From the top of **Ménez-Hom** you can admire the anarchic limits of western France, and in the two cities of **Morlaix** and **Quimper**, you'll witness distinctly Breton modern life as well as ancient splendours. Of these, the **parish closes** south of Morlaix reveal much of the mythology of the medieval past.

Roscoff and around

The opening of the deep-water port at **ROSCOFF** in 1973 was part of a general attempt to revitalize the Breton economy. The ferry services to Plymouth and to Cork are intended not just to bring tourists, but also to revive the traditional trading links between the Celtic nations of Brittany, Ireland and southwest England – links which were suppressed for centuries as an act of French state policy after the union of Brittany with France in 1532. In fact, Roscoff has long been a major port. It was here that Mary Queen of Scots landed in 1548 on her way to Paris to be engaged to François, the son and heir of Henri II of France. And it was here that Bonnie Prince Charlie, the Young Pretender, landed in 1746 after his defeat at Culloden.

Roscoff itself has, however, remained a small resort, where almost all activity is confined to **rue Gambetta** and to the **old port** – the rest of the roads are residential back streets full of retirement homes and institutions. One factor in preserving its old character is that both the ferry port and the *SNCF* station are some way from the centre.

The town's main church, **Notre-Dame-de-Croas-Batz** at the far end of rue Gambetta (which becomes rue Amiral-Reveillère), was built in the sixteenth century. Bretons take a particular pride in ornate Renaissance belfries such as the one which embellishes this church, with its sculptured ships and protruding stone cannon. From the side, rows of bells can be seen hanging in galleries, one above the other like a tall, but narrow, wedding cake created by an early Walt Disney. Some way beyond is the grand **Thalassotherapy Institute** of Rock Roum, and a kilometre further on is Roscoff's best **beach**, at Laber, surrounded by expensive hotels and apartments.

The old **harbour** is livelier, mixing an economy based on fishing with relatively low-key pleasure trips to the Île de Batz (see below). The island looks almost walkable; a narrow pier stretches over three or four hundred metres towards it before abruptly plunging into deep rocky waters. The Pointe de Bloscon and the white fisherman's chapel, the **Chapelle Ste-Barbe**, make a good vantage point, particularly when the tide is in; the tide goes out a long way (and dictates the embarkation point for the boat trips). Below the headland are the *viviers,* where you can see trout, salmon, lobsters and crabs being reared for the pot.

In 1828, Henri Ollivier took onions to England from Roscoff, thereby founding a trade which flourished until the 1930s. In the bar of the *Hôtel du Centre* (see below), you can see old photographs of "Johnnies": men in black berets with strings of onions hanging over the handlebars of their bicycles. Older people of the town travelled as children with their fathers as far afield as Glasgow.

Practicalities

Brittany Ferries **boats** from Plymouth (6hr) or Cork (19hr) dock at the new Port de Bloscon (☎98.29.28.28), to the east (and just out of sight) of Roscoff – see pp.8 & 11. The helpful **tourist office** is at 46 rue Gambetta in town (Mon–Fri 9.30am–12.30pm & 2–6pm, Sat 10am–noon; ☎98.61.12.13), and the **post office** at 19 rue Gambetta (☎98.69.72.90). The **gare SNCF** (☎98.69.70.20), a few hundred metres south of the town proper, runs services to Morlaix, with connections beyond. Most buses also go from here, including a direct service to Brest run by *Les Cars du Kreisker* (☎98.69.00.93); another service to Morlaix leaves from the fish hall by the old harbour (*Tourisme Verney*; ☎98.88.56.58). **Bikes** can be rented at *Desbordes François*, 13 rue Brizeux (☎98.69.72.44), and the *gare SNCF*.

For a small town, Roscoff is well equipped with **hotels**, which are well accustomed to late-night arrivals from the ferries. Be warned, however, that most of them close in winter. Very much the obvious places to **eat** are the dining rooms of the hotels themselves, though it's not easy to get a meal much after 9pm. If you'd prefer something lighter, the *à la carte* meals of sweet and savoury pancakes at the central *Crêperie de la Poste*, 12 rue Gambetta (☎98.69.72.81; closed Wed), work out economical, so long as you don't get carried away by the exotic seafood options.

Hotels

Hôtel-Restaurant des Arcades, 15 rue Amiral-Réveillère (☎98.69.70.45). Sixteenth-century building with superb views; menus 48F and upwards. Closed Oct–Easter. ①.

Hôtel-Restaurant Bellevue, bd Jeanne d'Arc (☎98.61.23.38). Seafront *logis*, on the far side of the pleasure harbour to the town centre. There's a lively downstairs bar that can make the hotel noisy. Pleasant rooms, and fine views from the dining room, where the 105F menu offers salmon baked in cheese with mustard. Closed mid-Nov to mid-March. ③.

Hôtel du Centre, 5 rue Gambetta (☎98.61.24.25). *Logis de France* facing the beach, very much run as a family hotel. Menus from 85F. Closed Jan to mid-Feb. ①.

Les Chardons Bleus, 4 rue Amiral-Réveillère (☎98.69.72.03). Friendly and helpful hotel with good restaurant (menus from 75F; closed Thurs out of season) but no sea views. Closed Dec & Jan. ③.

Hôtel de la Gare, 2 rue Ropartz-Morvan (☎98.61.21.42). Cheap rooms, very close to the *gare SNCF*, with a bar and shop but no restaurant. Open all year. ①.

Youth hostels and campsites

IYHF youth hostel, on the Île de Batz (see below).

Camping municipal de Perharidy, 2km west of town (☎98.69.70.86). Just off the route de Santec. Easter–Sept.

Camping du Manoir de Kerestat, 2km south towards St-Pol (☎98.69.71.92). July & Aug.

The Île de Batz

The **ÎLE DE BATZ** (pronounced *Ba*), just off the coast of Roscoff, is a somewhat windswept spot, but well endowed with sandy beaches; for campers looking to have a stretch of coastline to themselves, it could be ideal.

The island's first recorded inhabitant was a "laidly worm", a dragon that infested the place in the sixth century. Such dragons normally symbolize pre-Christian religions, in this case perhaps a Druidic serpent cult. Allegorical or not, when Saint Pol arrived to found a monastery he wrapped a Byzantine stole around the unfortunate creature's neck and cast it into the sea. These days, there are no dragons; there aren't even any trees, just an awful lot of seaweed which is collected and sold for fertilizer.

Several sailings each day from Roscoff, operated by *Armein Excursions* (☎98.61.77.75), arrive at the quayside of the old island town (July to mid-Sept, daily 8am–8pm, every hour on the half hour; mid-Sept to Oct & mid-March to June, eight trips 8.30am–7pm; Nov to mid-March, eight trips 8.30am–6.30pm; 25F return). In July and August, the same company runs boat tours right around the island (Sun 2.15pm).

Walk uphill from the port – site of the basic *Hôtel-Restaurant Roch Ar Mor* (April–Sept; ☎98.61.78.28; ①) – and you will come to the IYHF **youth hostel** at the evocatively-named Creach ar Bolloc'h (☎98.61.77.69; ①; April–Sept). Higher still, on the island's peak (all of 23m above sea level), is a 44m lighthouse which welcomes visitors. And beyond that, it's just the sands and seaweed.

St-Pol-de-Léon

The main road south from Roscoff passes by fields of the famous Breton artichokes before arriving after 6km at **ST-POL-DE-LÉON**. It's not an exciting place but – assuming you've got your own transport – it has two churches that at least merit a pause. The **Cathédrale**, in the main town square, was rebuilt towards the end of the thirteenth century along the lines of Coutances (see p.310) – a quiet classic of unified Norman architecture. The remains of Saint Pol are inside, alongside a large bell, rung over the heads of pilgrims during his *pardon* on March 12 in the unlikely hope of curing headaches and ear diseases. Just downhill is the original **Kreisker Chapel**, with access to the top of its sharp-pointed soaring granite belfry (now coated in yellow moss).

Morlaix

MORLAIX, one of the great old Breton ports, thrived off trade with England in between wars during the "Golden Period" of the late Middle Ages. Built up the slopes of a steep valley with sober stone houses, the town was originally protected by an eleventh-century castle and a circuit of walls. Little is left of either, but the old centre remains in part medieval – cobbled streets and half-timbered houses. Its present grandeur comes from the pink-granite viaduct carrying trains from Paris to Brest way above the town centre. Coming by road from the north, the opening view is of shiny yacht masts paralleling the pillars of the viaduct.

Arrival and accommodation

The **tourist office** in Morlaix is in a central one-storey building, almost under the viaduct in place des Otages (mid-June to mid-Sept Mon–Sat 9am–12.30pm & 1.30–7.30pm, Sun 10am–12.30pm; mid-Sept to mid-June Tues–Sat 9am–noon & 2–6.30pm; ☎98.62.14.94). All **buses** conveniently depart from place Cornic, right under the viaduct, but the **gare SNCF** (☎98.80.50.60) is on rue Armand-Rousseau, high above the town at the western end of the viaduct. To reach it on foot, you have to climb the steep steps of Venelle de la Roche. **Bikes** can be rented from Henri Le Gall, 1 rue de Callac (☎98.88.60.47).

In addition to the many (fairly uninspiring) **hotels** in old Morlaix, there's also a youth hostel and two summer campsites, although the municipal one is now closed.

Hotels

Hôtel les Arcades, 11 pl Cornic (☎98.88.20.03). Not far from the viaduct, opposite the new bus station. No restaurant. ①.
Hôtel Au Roy d'Ys, 8 pl des Jacobins (☎98.88.61.19). Central hotel, across the square from the town museum. The cheapest rooms do not have their own showers; guests have to pay 13F extra to use shared showers. No restaurant, but a downstairs bar. Closed Nov. ①.
Hôtel de l'Europe, 1 rue d'Aiguillon (☎98.62.11.99). Slightly eccentric old place, with an odd line in furnishing but a superb restaurant, where menus start at 95F. ②.
Hôtel-Restaurant les Halles, 23 rue du Mur (☎98.88.03.86). Friendly hotel facing the attractive place des Halles, with a garage for motorbikes and bicycles. Closed Sun. Good cheap restaurant; menus at 48F and 66F. ①.

Youth hostels and campsites

IYHF youth hostel, Île de Batz (see p.349). ①.
Manoir de Kerestat campsite, 2km south towards St-Pol (☎98.69.71.92). July & Aug.
Camping municipal de Perharidy, 2km west (☎98.69.70.86). Just off the route de Santec. Easter–Sept.

The Town

On her way from Roscoff to Paris, Mary Queen of Scots passed through Morlaix in 1548 and stayed at the **Jacobin convent** that fronts place des Jacobins. She was at the time just five years old, and a contemporary account records that the crush to catch a glimpse of the infant was so great that the inner town's "gates were thrown off their hinges and the chains from all the bridges were broken down". The **town museum** in the convent church contains a reasonably entertaining assortment of Roman wine jars, bits that have fallen off medieval churches, cannon and kitchen utensils, and a few modern paintings (entrance on rue des Vigues; daily 9am–noon & 2–6pm; winter closed Tues).

The **church of St-Mathieu**, off rue de Paris, contains a sombre and curious statue of the Madonna and Child; Mary's breast was apparently lopped off by a prudish former priest, to leave the babe suckling at nothing. The whole statue opens down the middle to reveal a separate figure of God the Father, clutching a crucifix. In April 1993, the figure of Christ was stolen, but the thief, who preferred to pray at home, repented in October 1994 and returned it anonymously.

In the eighteenth century, Morlaix's wealth was sustained by boat building, textiles and tobacco, and it still has an active **tobacco factory**, by the port, on quai de Léon (visits Wed pm: ring ☎98.88.15.32), employing 500 people to produce annually 300 million cigars, 50 tons of chewing tobacco and 15 tons of snuff.

After a sizeable fleet was sent by Henry VIII to storm Morlaix, the citizens built the fortified **Château de Taureau** in Morlaix bay, off Pointe de Pen-al-Lann 12 km north of town. In the seventeenth century, it was used as a prison; now it's a sailing school. Meanwhile, the town adopted the motto which it keeps to this day – "If they bite you, bite them back."

Eating

The best hunting ground for **restaurants** in Morlaix is to be found between St-Melaine church and place des Jacobins.

Brocéliande, 5 rue des Bouchers (☎98.88.73.78). In the southeast of town, beyond the place des Halles and St-Mathieu church. Elegant evening-only dining in a *fin-de-siècle* atmosphere; a typical main course from the choice menu costs around 70F.

Dolce Vita, 3 rue Ange-de-Guernisac (☎98.63.37.67). Pizzeria, which also serves pasta dishes. Set menus start at 120F, but you can choose *à la carte*.

La Marée Bleue, 3 rampe Ste-Mélaine (☎98.63.24.21). Well-respected seafood restaurant; the 78F menu isn't at all bad, while for 135F your meal includes a superb *assiette de fruits de mer*.

Le Passé Simple, 21bis pl Charles-de-Gaulle (☎98.88.81.39). Lush and very pleasant restaurant. Excellent seafood on menus starting at just over 50F. Closed Sat lunchtime & Mon.

Nightlife and drinking

Morlaix has recently acquired its own small brewery, set up to produce real ale similar to that its owners had enjoyed on visiting Britain. You should be able to find the resultant brew, *Coreff*, in local **bars**, or you can visit the brewery itself at 1 place de la Madeleine (groups of 10: Tues–Thurs by arrangement; ☎98.63.41.92).

Among bars to look out for while you're in Morlaix are *Ty Coz*, at 10 Venelle Au Beurre (closed Thurs), near the youth hostel, which has boisterous Bretons playing darts, and draught *Coreff* beer, and the lively *Tempo Piano Bar*, facing the port on quai de Tréguier (☎98.63.29.11), where there are regular jazz and blues concerts. The *Club Coätelan* (☎98.72.50.71) in Plougonven, 12km east of Morlaix, also books a wide assortment of jazz, rock and blues performers.

The Parish Closes

Morlaix makes an excellent base for visiting the countryside towards Brest, where *enclos paroissiaux* (walled churchyards incorporating cemetery, calvary and ossuary) celebrate the distinctive character of Breton Catholicism – closer to the Celtic past than to Rome – in elaborately sculpted scenes. Stone calvaries are covered in detailed scenes of the Crucifixion above a crowd of saints, gospel stories and legends; in richer parishes, a high stone arch leads into the churchyard, adjoining an equally majestic ossuary, where bones would be taken when the tiny cemeteries filled up. Most of the parish closes date from the two centuries either side of the union with France in 1532 – Brittany's wealthiest period – and nothing is more telling of the decline in the province's fortunes. The interiors of the churches are often decorated as richly as the architectural ensemble without, while their villages can be battling against poverty.

The most famous *enclos* are in three neighbouring parishes off the N12 between Morlaix and Landivisiau on a clearly signposted route served by *SNCF* bus. At **ST-THÉGONNEC**, the entire east wall of the church is a carved and painted retable, with saints in niches and a hundred scenes depicted, but the pulpit and the painted oak entombment in the crypt beneath the ossuary are acknowledged masterpieces. At **LAMPAUL-GUIMILIAU**, the painted wooden baptistery, the dragons on the beams and the suitably wicked faces of the robbers on the calvary are the key components. Poor Katel Gollet (Katherine the Damned) is depicted tormented in hell at **GUIMILIAU** – for the crime of hedonism rather than manslaughter. In the legend she danced all her suitors to death until the reaper-figure Ankou stepped in to whirl her to eternal damnation. Further on at **LA ROCHE** (15km or so on towards Brest), where the ruined castle above the Elhorn estuary is said to have been her home, it is Ankou who appears on the ossuary with the inscription "I kill you all". If you've got transport, a 5km detour southeast of La Roche brings further variations at **LA MARTYRE** (where Ankou clutches his disembodied head) and its adjoining parish **PLOUDIRY**, the sculpting of its ossuary affirming the equality of social classes – in the eyes of Ankou.

If you have time and interest, other calvaries to take a look at include Pleyben, south of the Monts d'Arrée; Lanrivian, in the centre of Brittany; and Guehenno, southwest of Josselin. Another speciality to be seen in many Breton churches is the intricate carving and paintwork of rood screens: exceptional examples are the St-Fiacre chapel outside Le Faöuet (between Lorient and the Montagne Noire) and the chapel at Kerfons (south of Lannion), though both wonderful works of art are kept locked up except in July and August and for the annual *pardon*.

The *abers* and the western islands

The coast west of Roscoff is some of the most dramatic in Brittany, a jagged series of **abers** – deep, narrow estuaries – in the midst of which are clustered small, isolated resorts. It's a little on the bracing side, especially if you're making use of the numerous **campsites**, but that just has to be counted as part of the appeal. In summer, at least, the temperatures are mild enough, and things get progressively more sheltered as you move around towards **Le Conquet** and Brest.

Around the *abers*

If you're dependent on public transport, the only stop on the Roscoff–Brest bus before it turns inland is **PLOUESCAT**. Here you'll find **campsites** at each of its three adjacent beaches and the *Baie de Kernic* (☎98.69.63.41; ①–③; closed Sun pm & Mon out of season, and all Nov), best bet of the **hotels**. An old wooden market hall can provide picnic provisions and at the edge of the bay, about 1km out from the centre, the *Auberge Le Kersabiec* serves good food.

BRIGNOGAN-PLAGE, on the next *aber*, has a small natural harbour, once the lair of wreckers, with beaches and weather-beaten rocks to either side, as well as its own menhir. The two high-season **campsites** are the central municipal site at Kéravezan (☎98.83.41.65; mid-June to mid-Sept) and the *du Phare*, east of town (☎98.83.45.06; May–Sept), while the hotel *Castel Regis* (☎98.83.40.22; ③; April–Sept) is expensive but beautifully sited among the rocks, right at the headland. There are also schools of sailing and riding. Further west, at **PLOUGUERNEAU**, the **hotel/restaurant** *Les Abériades* (☎98.04.71.01; ②; closed Sun pm & Mon out of season) makes a good base.

The *aber* between Plouguerneau and **L'ABER-WRAC'H** has a stepping-stone crossing just upstream from the bridge at Llanellis, built in Gallo-Roman times, and its long cut stones still cross the three channels of water (access off the D28 signposted Rascoll), and continue past farm buildings to the right to "Pont du Diable".

L'Aber-Wrac'h itself is a promising place to spend a little time. It's an attractive, modest-sized resort, within easy reach of a whole range of sandy beaches and a couple of worthwhile excursions. Beyond the tiny fishing port, the Baie des Anges stretches away towards the Atlantic, with the only sound the cry of seagulls feasting on the oyster beds. The *Hôtel la Baie des Anges* (☎98.04.90.04; ②; Easter–Oct), festooned with ivy and purple clematis, commands lovely views out to sea from the start of its endless curve.

For drivers and cyclists there's a beautiful corniche road west of **TRÉMAZAN**, whose ruined castle was the point of arrival in Brittany for Tristan and Iseult. Odd little chapels dot the route, and the views of sea and rocks are unhindered before turning inland just before Le Conquet.

Le Conquet

LE CONQUET, at the far western tip of Brittany, 24km beyond Brest, is a wonderful place, scarcely developed, with a long beach of clean white sand, protected from the winds by the narrow spit of the Kermorvan peninsula. It is very much a working fishing village, with grey stone houses leading down to the stone jetties of a cramped harbour. It occasionally floods, by the way, causing great amusement to locals who watch the waves wash over cars left there by tourists taking the ferry out to Ouessant and Molène. A good walk 5km south brings you to the lighthouse at **Pointe St-Mathieu**, looking out to the islands from its site among the ruins of a Benedictine abbey.

The *Hôtel de Bretagne*, in town at 16 rue Lt-Jourden (☎98.89.00.02; ②; Easter–Dec; closed Fri pm & Sat out of season), offers cheap **rooms** looking out across the peninsula, and reasonable meals from 65F. There are also two well-equipped **campsites**, *Le Théven* (☎98.89.06.90; mid-April to mid-Sept) and *Quère* (☎98.89.11.71; June–Sept). **Market** day is Tuesday.

The Île d'Ouessant and Île de Molène

The **Île d'Ouessant**, Ushant in English, lies 30km northwest of Le Conquet, and its lighthouse at **Creac'h** (said to be the strongest in the world) is regarded as the entrance to the English Channel. It's at the end of a chain of smaller islands and half-submerged granite rocks. Most are uninhabited, or like **Beniguet** the preserve only of rabbits, but the **Île de Molène**, midway, has a village and can be visited. Both Molène and Ouessant are served by at least one ferry each day from Le Conquet and Brest; however, it is not practicable to visit more than one in a single day.

Île d'Ouessant

You arrive on the **Île d'Ouessant** at the new **harbour** in the ominous-sounding Baie du Stiff. There is a scattering of houses here and dotted around the island, but the single town – with the only hotels and restaurants – is 4km away at **LAMPAUL**. Everybody from the boat heads there, either by the bus that meets each ferry or on bicycles rented from one of the many waiting entrepreneurs – a good idea, as the island is a bit too big to explore on foot.

Lampaul has not a lot to it and quickly becomes very familiar. The best beaches are sprawled around its bay, and, in case you should forget the perils of the sea, the town cemetery's **war memorial** lists all the ships in which townsfolk were lost, alongside graves of unknown sailors washed ashore and a chapel of wax "*proëlla crosses*" symbolizing the many islanders who never returned. You can also visit the **Éco-Musée** – a reconstruction of a traditional island house – at nearby **Niou** (April & May daily except Mon 2–6.30pm, Sun 10.30am–6.30pm; June–Sept daily 10.30am–6.30pm; Oct–March daily except Mon 2–4pm; 15F). The **Creac'h lighthouse**, closed to the public, is a good point from which to set out along the barren and exposed rocks of the north

TIMETABLE OF ISLAND FERRIES

From:	Le Conquet	Brest	Ouessant		Molène	
	All year	All year	April–Sept	Oct–March	April–Sept	Oct–March
Mon	9.30am	8.30am	5pm	4.30pm	5.30pm	5pm
Tues	9.30am	8.30am	5pm	4.30pm	5.30pm	5pm
Wed	9.30am	8.30am	5pm	4.30pm	5.30pm	5pm
Thurs	9.30am	8.30am	5pm	4.30pm	5.30pm	5pm
Fri	9.30am	8.30am	10.30am*	4.30pm	11am*	5pm
	6.30pm[1]		5pm		5.30pm	
Sat	9.30am	8.30am	11am*	11am*	11.30am*	11.30am*
	1.30pm		5pm	2.45pm	5.30pm	3.15pm
Sun	9.30am	8.30am	4pm*	4.30pm	4.30pm	5pm
	5pm[1]		6.30pm		7pm	

Sailings indicated [1] operate between April and September only.

Ferries from **Le Conquet** go to Molène (122F return) and Ouessant (140F return).
Ferries from **Brest** go to Molène (150F return) and Ouessant (170F return).
All ferries from **Ouessant** and **Molène** go to Brest and Le Conquet, except those marked with an asterisk, which run to Le Conquet only.
Discounted fares: 25 percent for students; 50 percent for children 4–10; children under 4 free.

For all details, including the weather (liable to affect sailings), call *Penn Ar Bed* ☎98.80.24.68.
Penn Ar Bed also run some summer services from **Camaret** (p.358) and **Douarnenez** (p.359).

coast. The star-shaped formations of crumbling walls are not extraterrestrial relics, but built so that the sheep – peculiarly tame here – can shelter from the winds.

Staying overnight, you could camp almost anywhere on the island, making arrangements with the nearest farmhouse (which may well let you a room). In Lampaul, the adjacent **hotels** *Océan* (☎98.48.80.03; ①) and *Fromveur* (☎98.48.81.30; ②) both offer a fairly basic standard of accommodation; the *Fromveur* specializes in traditional island cooking, which consists of attempting to render seaweed and mutton as palatable as possible, while the *Océan* also organizes musical evenings. There is also a small official **campsite**, the *Pen ar Bed* (☎98.48.84.65). All the hotel **restaurants** serve menus for under 100F, but if you just come for a day, it's a good idea to buy a picnic before you set out – the Lampaul shops have limited and rather pricey supplies.

Île de Molène

The **Île de Molène** is quite well populated for a sparse strip of sand. Its inhabitants make their money from seaweed collecting and drying – and to an extent from crabbing and from crayfish, which they gather on foot, canoe and even tractor at low tide. The tides here are more than usually dramatic, halving or doubling the island's territory at a stroke. It's not called "the bald isle" for nothing. Few people do more than look at Molène as an afternoon's excursion from Le Conquet, but it's quite possible to stay here and to enjoy it, too. There are **rooms** – very chilly in winter – at *Kastell An Doal* (☎98.07.39.11; ②), one of the old buildings by the port, and it's also possible to arrange to stay in a private house (☎98.07.39.05 for details).

Brest

BREST is set in a magnificent natural harbour, known as the Rade de Brest, and sheltered from the ocean storms by the Crozon peninsula to its south. It has always played an important role in war, and in trade whenever peace allowed. Today it is the base of the French Atlantic Fleet with a dry dock that can accommodate ships of up to 500,000 tons; the town, as a ship repair centre, ranks sixth in the world.

During World War II, Brest was continually bombed to prevent the Germans from using it as a submarine base. When the Americans liberated it on 18 September, 1944, after a six-week siege, they found the town devastated beyond recognition. The architecture of the postwar town is raw and bleak. There have been attempts, as in Caen, to green the city, but despite the heaviest rainfall in France, the site has proved too wind-swept to respond fully to these efforts.

Arrival and accommodation

Brest's **tourist office** on av Clemenceau faces place de la Liberté (June–Sept Mon–Sat 9am–7pm, Sun 10am–noon & 2–4pm; Oct–May Mon–Sat 9.30–12.30pm & 2–6.30pm; ☎98.44.24.96). The **gare SNCF** (☎98.80.50.50) and **gare routière** (☎98.44.46.73) are together in place du 19ᵉ RI at the bottom of av Clemenceau. Brest is very much at the end of the train system, though now connected to Paris in just four hours thanks to the *TGV*. Bus services include those to Plouescat and Roscoff (*Les Cars du Kreisker*; ☎98.69.00.93); to the Crozon peninsula via Landevennec (☎98.27.02.02); and to Le Conquet (*Sarl Saint Mathieu Transport*s; ☎98.98.12.02).

As well as the sailings to Ouessant detailed opposite, in summer (May–Sept; *Vedettes Armoricaines*; ☎98.44.44.04) three **boats** per day make the 45-minute crossing from Brest's Port de Commence to **Le Fret** on the Crozon peninsula, where they are met by buses for Crozon, Morgat and Camaret.

The vast majority of Brest's **hotels** remain open throughout the year; only a few, however, bother to maintain their own restaurants. Several lie within easy walking distance of the stations, in the vicinity of the central place de la Liberté.

Hotels

Hôtel Bellevue, 53 bd Victor-Hugo (☎98.80.51.78). Six-storey soundproofed building, equipped with a lift. Not easy to find, but not far from the *gare SNCF* and well on the way to the lively St-Martin area; look for St-Michel church. No restaurant. ②.

Hôtel de la Gare, 4 bd Gambetta (☎98.44.47.01). Right opposite the stations. You pay a little more for an uninterrupted view of the Rade de Brest. No restaurant. ②.

Hôtel du Musée, 1 rue Ducouëdic (☎98.45.70.20). Plain unadorned rooms, just off the rue de Siam down near the Pont de Recouvrance. Closed Sun. No restaurant. ①.

Hôtel le Regent, 22 rue d'Algésiras (☎98.44.29.77). A clean, newish hotel, very near the tourist office, but without its own restaurant. ③.

Hôtel St-Louis, 6 rue d'Algesiras (☎98.44.23.91). Friendly and reasonably comfortable option, just off the main square near the tourist office. No restaurant. ②.

Youth hostels

IYHF youth hostel, rue de Kerbriant, Port de Plaisance du Moulin-Blanc (☎98.41.90.41). It's 3km east of the *gares SNCF* and *routière* in a wooded setting near the Océanopolis, on bus route #7, or the *Bus Albatros*. Price includes breakfast. All year. ①.

The Town

As a tourist centre, Brest has little to offer. Few relics of the past remain. The fifteenth-century **castle** looks impressive on its headland and offers a superb panorama of the city, but once inside it is not especially interesting. Three of its towers house the **National Maritime Museum** (daily except Tues 9.15am–noon & 2–6pm; 25F). The fourteenth-century **Tour Tanguy** on the opposite bank of the River Penfeld, with its conical slate roof, serves as the **Museum of Old Brest** (July & Aug daily 10am–noon

& 2–7pm; June & Sept daily 2–7pm; Oct–May Wed & Thurs 2–5pm, Sat & Sun 2–6pm; free). Dioramas convey a vivid impression of just how attractive the city used to be.

Océanopolis, next to the Port de Plaisance du Moulin-Blanc, incorporates the largest aquarium in Europe (May–Sept daily 9.30am–6pm; Oct–April Mon 2–5pm, Tues–Fri 9.30am–5pm, Sat & Sun 9.30am–6pm; 50F). Under its white dome, half a million gallons of water contain all kinds of fish, seals, molluscs, seaweed and sea anemones, and there are films and lectures all day. If all this fails to impress or excite you, you can always walk along the **Cours Dajot**, which displays the docklands in all their glory. It holds schools of various naval disciplines, arsenals, the marine records office, and the **Pont de Recouvrance**, the largest drawbridge in Europe.

Eating and drinking

Most of Brest's restaurants are to be found in the immediate area of the stations. There are a lot of lively **bars** in town.

Bar Écossais, rue Jean-Jaurès. Positively festooned with Scottish memorabilia, this bar attracts a lively Celtic crowd.

Maison de l'Océan, 2 quai de la Douane (☎98.80.44.84). Blue-hued fish restaurant down by the port, open every day and serving wonderful assortments of seafood from 70F.

Café de la Plage, pl Guerin. A favourite haunt of students at the top end of rue Jean-Jaurès, near the St-Martin church.

Le Ruffé, 1 rue Yves-Collet (☎98.46.07.70). A new and attractive place between the *gare SNCF* and the tourist office. Prides itself on good, traditional French seafood dishes, served on menus costing 60F and upwards. Daily except Sun until 11.30pm.

La Taverne St-Martin, 92 rue Jean-Jaurès (☎98.80.48.17). A few hundred metres east (and up) from the tourist office. Warm, friendly brasserie/restaurant behind a half-timbered façade, open from 8am until 1am daily. Lunch from 60F, dinner from 85F, plus lots of snacks. Steak tartare is the speciality.

Le Tire Bouchon, 20 rue le l'Observatoire (☎98.44.15.18). Wide-ranging menus from 100F, but a *plat du jour* for lunch at around 40F. Closed all Aug, plus Sat lunch and all day Sun.

The Crozon peninsula

The **Crozon peninsula**, a craggy outcrop of land shaped like a long-robed giant, arms outstretched to defend bay and roadstead, is the central feature of Finistère's torn chaos of estuaries and promontories. Much the easiest way for cyclists, and travellers relying on public transport, to reach the peninsula from Brest is via the ferries to Le Fret (see previous page).

Motorists heading for Crozon have to follow a circuitous route skirting this complex coast through **Plougastel-Daoulas**. At the church here, the calvary shows more torment for Katel Gollet (Katherine the Damned), in this case being raped by devils, but with a more sympathetic sculpting of Katel herself than at Guimiliau.

The Musée de l'École Rurale

Still inland from the peninsula, 3km north of the Menez-Hom hill at the intersection of the Argol-Dineault and Trégarven–Menez-Hom roads and not on any bus routes, is the village of **TRÉGARVAN**. Its **Musée de l'École Rurale** (Jan–March Mon–Fri 2–5pm; April & May daily 2–6pm; June daily 1.30–7pm; July & Aug daily 10.30am–7pm; Sept daily 1.30–7pm; Oct–Dec daily except Sat 2–5pm; 15F), housed in what used to be the local secondary school, is one of those small, quirky French museums that sound slightly ludicrous on paper but are fascinating on the spot.

The school was closed down due to lack of numbers in 1974, then reopened a decade later as a re-creation of a Breton classroom circa 1920. At that time, all the kids

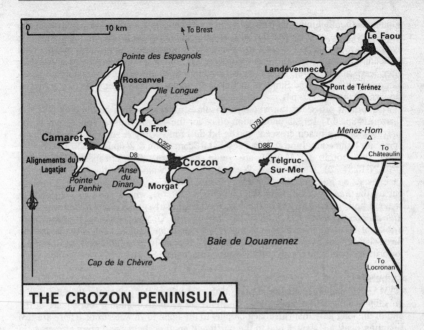

THE CROZON PENINSULA

would have spoken Breton at home, but were forbidden to speak it here. The teacher gave a little wooden cow to the first child to utter a word in the mother tongue, and they could get rid of the *vache* only by squealing on the next offender. The lesson, to parents and pupils alike, was obvious: that Breton was backward and a handicap. Breton was suppressed, with considerable efficiency, throughout the province, and only recently have things begun to change. While a few years back *SNCF* had to be taken to account before it would accept a cheque made out in Breton, there is now a Breton bank. A battle for a Breton TV channel is also underway.

Onto the peninsula

As you approach the Crozon peninsula, it's well worth making a slight detour to climb the hill of **Menez-Hom**, "at the giant's feet", for a fabulous view of the land and water alternating out to the ocean. Getting down to the coastal headlands themselves can be a bit of a disappointment after this vision: those extremities that don't house military installations tend to be too crowded. But it is the cliffs that tourists head for here, and some of the **beaches**, like **La Palue** on the southern arm, are almost deserted.

Crozon and Morgat

The first town on the peninsula proper, **CROZON**, is not much more than a one-way traffic system to distribute tourists among the various resorts – though it does keep a market running most of the week. **MORGAT**, just down the hill, is a more realistic and enticing base. It has a long crescent beach that ends in a pine slope, and a well-sheltered harbour full of pleasure boats raced down from England and Ireland. The main attractions are **boat trips** around the various headlands, such as the **Cap de la Chèvre** (which is a good clifftop walk if you'd rather make your own way). The most popular is the 45-minute tour of the **Grottes** (May–Sept), multicoloured caves in the cliffs, accessible only by sea but with steep "chimneys" up to the clifftops, where in bygone days saints would lurk to rescue the shipwrecked. Organized by two rival companies on the quay, the trips run every quarter of an hour in high season; they often leave full, however, so it's worth booking a few hours in advance. It's also possible, on Wednesdays and Sundays in July and August, to take a ferry service across to Douarnenez (☎98.27.09.54).

The **tourist office** for the whole peninsula is in what used to be the *gare SNCF* at Crozon (☎98.26.17.18); an information office for the Crozon-Morgat area stands at the start of Morgat's beach crescent on the bd du France (July & Aug Mon–Sat 9.30am–7pm, Sun 10am–1pm; June & Sept Tues–Sat 9.30am–noon & 2–6pm; ☎98.27.07.92).

All the **hotels** in Morgat are quite expensive. The cheapest, *des Grottes* (☎98.27.15.84; ②), is a long but pleasant walk from what centre there is, and in any case insists on guests paying for *demi-pension*. Better, if you can afford it, is to splash out on the *Kador*, 42 bd de la Plage (☎98.27.05.68; ③), where you can eat excellent seafood and enjoy the view of the bay, or the similarly grand *Hôtel-Restaurant de la Ville d'Ys* on the port (☎98.27.06.49; ③; Easter–Sept). Or you could always **camp**. With a total of 865 pitches available, campers are spoilt for choice; best perhaps are the three-star sites at *Plage de Goulien* (☎98.27.17.10; mid-June to mid-Sept) and *Les Pins*, towards the pointe de Dinan (☎98.27.21.95; June to mid-Sept).

Camaret

CAMARET is another sheltered port, at the very tip of the peninsula. Its most distinguishing feature is the pink-orange **Château de Vauban**, standing four-square at the end of the long jetty that runs back parallel to the main town waterfront. There are two **beaches** nearby – a small one to the north and another, larger and more attractive, in the low-lying (and rather marshy) *Anse de Dinan*. In high season, *Penn Ar Bed* (☎98.70.02.37) operate an irregular **ferry** service from Camaret to the Île de Sein (162F return), and also to Ouessant (162F return); many boats returning from Ouessant continue to Douarnenez, so it's feasible to catch a ride on to there as well.

A little walk away from the centre, around the port towards the jetty, the quai du Styvel contains a row of excellent **hotels**. Both the *Vauban* (☎98.27.91.36; ①) and *du Styvel* (☎98.27.92.74; ①) are exceptionally hospitable, though the food in *du Styvel* is marginally better with a 68F menu offering *moules à la crème*, and crabs, oysters and scallops rearing their assorted heads on the 92F menu; both have rooms that look right out across the bay. There are also various **campsites** to fall back on, such as the four-star *Lambézen* (☎98.27.91.41; April to mid-Oct). Back along the quayside in the centre of town, *La Voilerie*, 7 quai Toudouze (☎98.27.83.87), is an excellent **fish restaurant**.

South towards Quimper

The Atlantic inlet to the south of the Crozon peninsula is officially the **Baie de Douarnenez**, although it has also earned itself the grim title of the **Baie du Trépassés** (Bay of the Dead), thanks to the shipwrecked bodies washed up here over the centuries.

Locronan

The fantasy village of **LOCRONAN**, a short way inland en route towards Quimper, is a sort of time capsule, perfectly preserved from its medieval days as a sail-making centre; subsequent economic decline has meant that its old buildings have never been destroyed or superseded. It's long been popular with film directors, such as Roman

Polanski, who used it as the setting for *Tess*, but the town's main source of income is high-budget tourists who buy carved wooden statues by local artisans, pottery from the Midi or leather jackets, provenance unknown. Every sort of craft artefact is sold in this village, some of it produced in open **ateliers**, others through the hands of third parties whose sleek cars are parked beside the shops. One of the artisans suggested converting the loft above his studio to a *gîte d'étape* for young people, but the idea was rejected by the powers that be. As it is, there are a couple of **hotels**, *du Prieuré* (☎98.91.70.89; ③), and the *Fer à Cheval* (☎98.91.70.67; ③), both normally reserved well in advance.

Douarnenez

Sufficient quantities of tuna, sardines and assorted crustaceans are still landed at the port of **DOUARNENEZ**, in the superbly sheltered Baie du Douarnenez, south of the Crozon peninsula, to keep the largest fish canneries in Europe busy. However, the catch has been declining ever since 1923, when eight hundred fishing boats brought in 100 million sardines during the six-month season. Over the last fifteen years or so, Douarnenez has therefore set out – at phenomenal expense, the subject of considerable local controversy – to redefine itself as a living museum of all matters maritime.

The whole area of **Port-Rhu**, on the west side of town, now constitutes the remarkable **Port-Musée** (daily June–Sept 10am–7pm; Oct–May 10am–noon & 2–6pm; tickets sold in Boat Museum, June–Sept 60F, Oct–May 48F). The entire waterfront is taken up with fishing and other vessels gathered from all over Europe, which visitors are invited to roam in and out of, up and down ladders and all over the decks, through oily metallic-smelling engine rooms and sleeping quarters divided into wooden compartments. Sail-makers and net-menders work on the jetties, and children can operate a scaled-down eighteenth-century crane by walking inside a wooden treadmill. Across the street, the associated **Boat Museum** (same times) doubles as a working boatyard, where visitors can join in the construction of seagoing vessels, using techniques from all over the world. Once again, the emphasis is on fishing, and the craft on show include a *moliceiro* from Portugal and coracles from Wales and Ireland. With cafés and snack bars on site, there is easily enough here to spend a whole day without seeing it all, though even the most boat-hungry appetite may well be fully slaked after a couple of hours.

Of the three separate harbour areas still in operation, much the prettiest is the **port de Rosmeur**, on the east side, which is nominally the fishing port used by the smaller local craft. Its quayside, lined with cafés and restaurants, curves between a pristine wooded promontory to the right and the fish canneries to the left, which continue around the north of the headland. You can buy fresh fish at the waterfront, or go on a sea-fishing excursion yourself. The various **beaches** around the town look pretty enough, but they are dangerous for swimming.

The **tourist office** is at 2 rue du Dr-Mével (daily mid-June to mid-Sept 9am–7pm; mid-Sept to mid-June 9am–noon & 1.30–6pm; ☎98.92.13.35), just up from the Port-Musée. The holiday trade is as yet just a sideline here, and not much accommodation is available. Choose between either of the **hotels**: *de la Rade*, 31 quai du Grand-Port (☎98.92.01.81; ①), which has a bar downstairs and a restaurant on the first floor looking out on the port du Rosmeur, or the *des Halles*, a little higher up alongside the market *halles* (☎98.92.02.75; ①; closed Sun & all Jan), which has no restaurant. Close by on the bay there's a **campsite**, *Croas Men* (☎98.74.00.18), at Tréboul/Les Sables Blancs.

During the summer, *Penn Ar Bed* (☎98.70.02.37) run occasional **ferries** from the port de Rosmeur out to the Île de Sein (140F return), and also to Ouessant (170F return) via Camaret.

Quimper and the Land's End Pointes

QUIMPER, capital of the ancient diocese, kingdom and later duchy of Cornouailles, is the oldest Breton city. According to legend, the first bishop of Quimper, Saint Corentin, came with the first Bretons across the Channel some time between the fourth and seventh centuries to the place they named Little Britain. He lived by eating a regenerating and immortal fish all his life, and was made bishop by one King Gradlon, whose life he later saved when the seabed city of Ys was destroyed. According to one version, Gradlon built Ys in the Baie de Douarnenez, protected from the water by gates and locks to which only he and his daughter had keys. But Saint Corentin suspected her of evil doings, and was proven right: the princess's keys unlocked the gates, the city flooded and Gradlon escaped only by obeying Corentin and throwing his daughter into the sea. Back on dry land and in need of a new capital, Gradlon founded Quimper.

Modern Quimper is very relaxed, active enough to have the bars – and the atmosphere – to make it worth going out café-crawling. Still "the charming little place" known to Flaubert, it takes at most half an hour to cross it on foot. The word "kemper" denotes the junction of the two rivers, the Steir and the Odet, around which are the cobbled streets (now mainly pedestrianized) of the medieval quarter, dominated by the cathedral towering nearby. As the Odet curves from east to southwest, it is crossed by numerous low flat bridges, bedecked with geraniums, and chrysanthemums in the autumn. You can stroll along the boulevards on both banks of the river, where several ultramodern edifices blend in a surprisingly harmonious way with their ancient – and attractive – surroundings. Overlooking all is **Mont Frugy**, denuded following the devastation of the hurricane of 1987. There is no great pressure in Quimper to rush around monuments or museums, and the most enjoyable option may be to take a boat and drift down "the prettiest river in France" to the open sea at Bénodet.

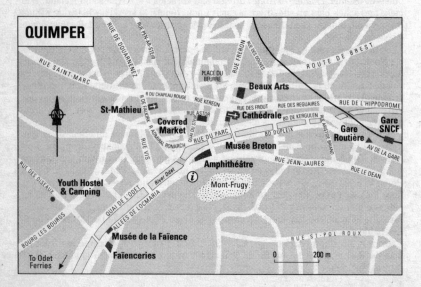

Arrival and accommodation

Quimper's **tourist office**, which seems to move every couple of years, can now be found in a small building on the south bank of the Odet at 7 rue de la Déesse, place de la Résistance (July & Aug Mon–Sat 8.30am–8pm, Sun 9.30am–12.30pm & 3–6pm; last fortnight of June and first fortnight of Sept Mon–Sat 9am–noon & 2–6pm, Sun 9.30am–12.30pm & 3–6pm; mid-Sept to mid-June Mon–Sat 9am–noon & 2–6pm; ☎98.53.04.05).

The **gare SNCF** (☎98.90.50.50) and **gare routière** (☎98.90.88.89) are next to each other on av de la Gare, 1km east of the centre. **Bus services** include those to Bénodet, which leave from place de la Resistance (*Compagnie Amoricaine de Transport*, 5 bd de Kérguelen, ☎98.95.02.36); to Audierne and Pointe du Raz, from the *gare routière* or bd Kérguelen (also *CAT*); to Pont l'Abbé and St-Guénolé, from place St-Corentin (*Cariou Castric Lecoeur*, ☎98.47.04.08); and to Concarneau and Pont-Aven, also from place St-Corentin (*Sarl Transports Caoudal Réné*; ☎98.56.96.72).

Between May and September you can **sail** from Quimper down the Odet to Bénodet, which takes about 1hr 15min, on *Vedettes de l'Odet* (Bénodet ☎98.57.00.58, Quimper ☎98.52.98.41). Between two and four boats each day leave from the end of quai de l'Odet; times vary with the tides so check with the tourist office (who also sell tickets).

There are remarkably few **hotels** in the old streets in the centre of Quimper, though there are some near the station, and a youth hostel only open during the summer.

Hotels

Hôtel-Restaurant Celtic, 13 rue de Douarnenez (☎98.55.59.35). Economical rooms a little way out from the centre. Restaurant closed Sat pm and Sun, except in July & Aug. ③.

Hôtel Gradlon, 30 rue du Brest (☎98.95.04.39). Central but quiet, and exceptionally friendly. The rooms are not cheap, but they're very nicely decorated. No restaurant. ④.

Hôtel-Restaurant La Tour d'Auvergne, 13 rue des Réguaires (☎98.95.08.70). Comfortable rooms in a refurbished hotel tucked away in a quiet street just east of the cathedral. Closed Sun Oct–April. Good menus from 110F. ③.

Hôtel-Restaurant le Transvaal, 57 rue Jean-Jaurès (☎98.90.09.91). Comfortable old-fashioned *logis* just south of the Odet, with a good restaurant whose menus start at 68F. Garage available. ③.

Youth hostels and campsites

IYHF youth hostel, 6 av des Oiseaux in Bois de Seminaire (☎98.55.41.67). Hostel 2km downstream from town, on bus route #1 (direction *Penhars*; stop *Chaptal*). You can camp next door to the hostel (enquiries to the Hôtel de Ville, place St-Corentin; ☎98.55.61.09). April–Sept. ①.

Orangerie de Lannion campsite, route de Bénodet (☎98.90.62.02). Four-star site. May–Sept.

The Town

The enormous **Cathédrale St-Corentin** is said to be the most complete Gothic cathedral in Brittany, though its neo-Gothic spires date from 1856. When the nave was being added to the old chancel in the fifteenth century, the extension would either have hit existing buildings or the swampy edge of the then unchanneled river. The masons eventually found a solution and placed the nave at a slight angle – a peculiarity which, once noticed, makes it hard to concentrate on the other Gothic splendours within. The exterior, however, gives no hint of the deviation, with King Gradlon now mounted in perfect symmetry between the spires.

The heart of old Quimper lies west of place St-Corentin, in front of the cathedral. This is where you'll find the liveliest shops and cafés, housed in the old half-timbered buildings, such as the Breton *Keltia-Musique* record shop in place au Beurre and the

Celtic shop, *Ar Bed Keltiek*, nearby at 2 rue Grallon. The old market hall burned down in 1976, but the light and spacious new **Halles St-Francis** in rue Astor, built to replace it, are quite a delight, not just for the food but for the view past the upturned boat rafters through the roof to the cathedral's twin spires.

In the **Musée des Beaux-Arts**, alongside the Hôtel de Ville at 4 place St-Corentin (July & Aug daily 10am–7pm, 30F; Sept & April–May daily except Tues 10am–noon & 2–6pm; Oct–March Mon & Wed–Sat 10am–noon & 2–6pm, Sun 2–6pm, 25F), are amazing collections of drawings by Cocteau, Gustav Doré and Max Jacob (who was born in Quimper), paintings of the Pont-Aven school, and Breton scenes by the likes of Eugène Boudin. Only the old Dutch oils upstairs let the collection down.

Pottery has been made in and around Quimper since 1690 and, as you walk through the town, it is impossible to ignore its presence – you are invited to look and to buy on every corner. On weekdays, it's also possible to visit the two major *ateliers*, both to the southwest in the suburb of Locmaria just off the route de Bénodet; *H-B Henriot*, allées de Locmarion (☎98.90.09.36), and the more modern *Keraluc*, 71 rue du President-Sadat (☎98.53.04.50). There's also a pottery museum, the **Musée de la Faïence Jules Verlinque**, not far west of the tourist office on the south bank at 14 rue Jean-Baptiste-Bosquet (May–Oct Mon–Sat 10am–6pm).

Eating and drinking

Though the pedestrian streets west of the cathedral are unexpectedly short on places to eat, there are quite a few **restaurants** further east on the north side of the river, en route to the *gare SNCF*. Rue Aristide-Briand here is a particularly promising area, with some lively bars. For *crêperies*, place au Beurre, north of the cathedral, is a good bet.

L'Ambroisie, 49 rue Élie-Fréron (☎98.95.00.02). Upmarket French restaurant on the main road north from the cathedral, with menus from 105F; closed Mon pm, except in summer.

L'Astragale, 3 rue Aristide-Briand (☎98.90.53.85). Very popular Spanish place, with excellent seafood paellas ranging from *La Primera*, 65F, up to the super-abundant *Zarzuela*, 140F.

Le Capucin Gourmand, 29 rue des Réguaires (☎98.95.43.12). Gourmet French cooking, not far east of the cathedral. Menus start at 160F – for which you can opt for snail ravioli in garlic – and zoom on up to 350F. Closed Sat lunch & Sun.

Ceili, 4 rue Aristide-Briand. Lively Celtic bar.

La Krampouzerie, 9 rue du Sallé, pl au Beurre (☎98.95.13.08). One of the best of Quimper's many *crêperies*. Closed Sun, & Mon in winter.

Trattoria Mario, 35 rue des Réguaires (☎98.95.42.15). Italian meals of pizza and fresh pasta, behind the post office. Closed Sun lunch.

Entertainment and culture

Quimper's **Festival de Cornouaille** started in 1923 and has gone from strength to strength since. This great jamboree of Breton music, costumes, theatre and dance is held in the week before the fourth Sunday in July, attracting guest performers from the other Celtic countries and a scattering of other, sometimes highly unusual, ethnic-cultural ensembles. The whole thing culminates in an incredible Sunday parade through the town. The official programme does not appear until July, but you can get provisional details in advance from the tourist office. Accommodation is at a premium in Quimper while the festival is on.

Not so widely known are the **Semaines Musicales** that follow in the first two weeks of August. The music is predominantly classical and tends to favour French composers such as Berlioz, Debussy, Bizet and Poulenc. Founded in 1978, it serves to bring the rather stuffy nineteenth-century theatre on bd Dupleix alive each year.

Down the Odet – and out to the headlands

Once out of its city channel, the Odet takes on the shape of most Breton inlets, spreading out to lake proportions then turning narrow corners between gorges. The family resort of **BÉNODET** at the mouth of the river (reachable by boat from Quimper – see p.361) has a long sheltered beach on the ocean side, with amusements for children and beachside nurseries. Among the nicest **hotels** are the *Hôtel-Restaurant Le Minaret*, an odd-looking building in a superb position overlooking the sea (☎98.57.03.13; ③; April–Sept), and the *Hôtel-Restaurant la Poste*, in the centre of the village on av de la Plage (☎98.57.01.09; ②). Bénodet also has several large **campsites** – if anything, rather too many of them – such as the enormous four-star *du Letty*, southeast of the village by plage du Letty on rue du Canvez (☎98.57.04.69; mid-June to early Sept).

The Pays de Bigouden

The southwest corner of Brittany, the **Pays de Bigouden**, is the least touristed area of the province. Traditions have endured: it's the place you're most likely to see women wearing coiffes for nonpromotional reasons, and the local variety is fairly startling – thirty-centimetre-high tubes of lace that always stay on, defying the strong gusts of wind. World **windsurfing championships** are held at **Pointe de la Torche**, at the southern end of the Baie d'Audierne, and there are usually some aficionados twirling about with effortless ease. But warning signs about swimming should not be ignored. For safer seas framed by white sand beaches, there's the coast from Penmarch to Loctudy and beyond. It's about an hour on the bus from Quimper to this southern tip, and it's one of the more frequent services.

Land's End

An hour and a half's bus ride east of Quimper takes you to the land's end of France, the **Pointe du Raz**. As you approach, the vision of the ocean is blocked by a gaggle of souvenir shops, and then military installations, but once past these you reach plummeting fissures, filling and draining with deafening force, and you can walk on precarious paths above them (shoes that grip are a good idea). A short way back towards Audierne, the fading graffiti on walls and hoardings is the only reminder that this is **PLOGOFF** where ecologists, autonomists and, principally, the local people fought riot police and paratroopers for six weeks in 1980 to stop the opening move in a nuclear power station project. Mitterrand pledged to abandon the plans if elected, and did so.

Audierne

Though on the whole the exposed southwestern extremities of Brittany are not areas you'd immediately associate with a classic summer sun-and-sand holiday, **AUDIERNE**, 25km west of Douarnenez on the Bay of Audierne, is an exception. An active fishing port, specializing in prawns and crayfish, it spreads along the northern shore of the Goyen estuary a short way back from the sea. From the town centre, the road continues just over 1km to the long, curving, and surprisingly sheltered **beach** of Ste-Evette.

The **hotel** *Au Roi Gradlon*, in a superb position at the very mouth of the estuary (closed Sun pm & Oct–May Mon; ☎98.70.04.51; ③), consists of several floors, concealed from the road, that drop down to the beach.

The Île de Sein

Boats to the little **Île de Sein**, 8 km out to sea, off the end of the Pointe du Raz, leave from Ste-Evette beach, just outside Audierne. Services are operated by *Vedette-Biniou* (June to early July & first half of Sept daily at 10am; early July to Aug daily at 10am, 1.30pm & 5pm; 105F return, or 85F day-return on Sun only; ☎98.70.20.15), and *Penn Ar*

Bed (April–Aug 1–3 departures daily, first at 9.30am; Sept–March daily except Wed 9.30am; 112F return; ☎98.70.02.37).

The island was made famous during World War II, when the entire male population answered General de Gaulle's call to join him in exile in England. It was reputed also to have been the very last refuge of the Druids in Brittany, a misty and inaccessible spot where they held out long after the rest of the country was Christianized. Roman sources tell of a shrine served by nine virgin priestesses. Sein is hardly bursting with facilities for tourists, but can offer one summer-only **hotel**, the *Armen* (☎98.70.90.77; ①; June–Sept), and a handful of restaurants.

Concarneau, Pont-Aven and Quimperlé

The first major town east of Bénodet is **CONCARNEAU**, a fishing port doing a reasonable job of passing itself off as a holiday resort. Its greatest asset is its **Ville Clos**, the old walled city situated across a slender causeway on an irregular rocky island in the bay. It has been inhabited for at least a thousand years and was originally a priory founded by King Gradlon of Quimper. It has also been fortified for centuries – its current **ramparts** are as Vauban remodelled them in the seventeenth century, and you can walk along the top of them (Easter to Sept daily 9am–7pm), admiring the climbing roses and clematis on the restaurants, snack bars, and gift shops below.

The **Musée de la Pêche**, immediately inside the Ville Clos in an old sardine cannery (daily mid-June to mid-Sept 9.30am–7pm; mid-Sept to mid-June 9.30am–12.30pm & 2–6pm; 30F), provides an insight into the traditional life Concarneau shared with many other Breton ports. It details the history and practice of whaling, tuna fishing – with drag nets the size of central Paris – herring fishing and sardine processing.

The Ville Clos is almost completely devoid of **hotels**, though there are a few expensive rooms in the upmarket **restaurant** *Le Galion*, 15 rue St-Guénolé (☎98.97.30.16; ④; closed Sun pm, Mon, & Feb), otherwise noteworthy only for the meagre portions from its expensive *nouvelle* menus. Most of the other hotels on offer skulk in the backstreets of the mainland, and tend to be full most of the time. However, right opposite the entrance to the Ville Clos, the *Hôtel les Voyageurs*, 9 pl Jean-Jaurès (☎98.97.08.06; ①), offers basic accommodation, while the *Bonne Auberge*, Le Cabellou (☎98.97.04.30; ②; May–Sept), is a reasonable *logis*. Probably the best bet of all is the IYHF **youth hostel** (☎98.97.03.47; ①; open all year), for once very near the city centre and enjoying magnificent ocean views. It's just around the tip of the headland on the place de la Croix, with a good *crêperie* opposite and a **windsurfing shop** a little further along.

Gauguin and Pont-Aven

PONT-AVEN, 14km east of Concarneau and just inland from the tip of the Aven estuary, is a small port packed with tourists and art galleries. This was where Gauguin came to paint in the 1880s, before he left for Tahiti in search of a South Seas idyll. He produced some of his finest work in Pont-Aven, and his influence was such that the **Pont-Aven School** of fellow artists – the best known of whom was Émile Bernard – developed here; but for all the local hype, the town has no permanent collection of Gauguin's work. The **Musée Municipal** (March–Dec daily 10am–12.30pm & 2–7pm; 20F) in the *mairie* holds changing exhibitions of the school and other artists active during the same period, but you can't count on paintings by the man himself.

Gauguin aside, Pont-Aven is pleasant in its own right. Just upstream of the little granite bridge at the heart of town, the **promenade Xavier Grall** criss-crosses the tiny river itself on landscaped walkways, offering glimpses of the backs of venerable mansions, dripping with red ivy, and a little "chaos" of rocks in the stream itself. A longer walk – allow an hour – leads into the **Bois d'Amour**, wooded gardens which have long provided inspiration to painters, poets and musicians.

The **tourist office**, 5 pl de l'Hôtel de Ville (July & Aug daily 9am–1pm & 2–7pm; Sept–Nov & March–May daily 9am–12.30pm & 2–6.30pm; Dec–Feb Mon–Sat 9am–12.30pm & 2–6.30pm; ☎98.06.04.70) sells an excellent English-language guide-booklet to the town, plus route maps of local walks, for a mere 1F. Much the best of the town's three **hotels** is the central *Hôtel des Ajoncs d'Or*, 1 pl de l'Hôtel de Ville (☎98.06.02.06; ③), where the gourmet menus start at 100F. The nicest of the local **campsites** is *Le Spinnaker* (☎98.06.01.77; May–Oct), set in a large wooded park.

Quimperlé

The final town of any size in Finistère, **QUIMPERLÉ** straddles a hill and two rivers, the Isole and the Elle, cut by a sequence of bridges. It's an atmospheric place, particularly in the medieval muddle of streets around **Ste-Croix church**. This was copied in plan from schema brought back by crusaders of the Church of the Holy Sepulchre in Jerusalem and is notable for its original Romanesque apse. There are some good **bars** nearby and, on Fridays, a **market** on the square higher up on the hill. Both the **hotels** – *L'Europe* (☎98.96.00.02; ①) and *Auberge de Toulföen* (☎98.96.00.29; ①; closed Oct) – have reasonable rooms.

Le Pouldu

At the mouth of the River Laïta, which constitutes the eastern limit of Finistère, the community of **LE POULDU** was another of Paul Gauguin's favourite haunts. It is divided into two distinct sections. The tiny **port**, on one bank of the narrow wooded estuary, is shielded from the open sea by a curving spit of sand. The **beach**, more developed than in Gauguin's day but still very picturesque, is a couple of kilometres away, and the headland separating the two is indented with delightful little sandy coves.

The *Hôtel des Bains* (☎98.39.90.11; ②; May–Aug) drops down to the beach from the main road, with large glass-fronted rooms commanding superb views, and menus starting at 85F, while the appealingly weatherbeaten white *Hôtel de Pouldu* (☎98.39.90.66; ②; April–Sept) stands next to the port. Le Pouldu also makes an ideal spot to **camp** for a few days; among sites near the beach is the *Vieux Four* (☎98.39.94.34).

INLAND BRITTANY:
THE NANTES–BREST CANAL

The **Nantes–Brest canal** is a meandering chain of waterways from Finistère to the Loire, linking rivers with stretches of canal built at Napoléon's instigation to bypass the belligerent English fleets off the coast. Finally completed in 1836, it came into its own at the end of the century as a coal, slate and fertilizer route. The building of the dam at Lac Guerlédan in the 1920s chopped the canal in two, leaving a whole section unnavigable by barge. Road transport had already superseded water haulage; now tourism is breathing life back into the canal.

En route it passes through riverside towns, such as **Josselin** and **Malestroit**, that long predate its construction; commercial ports and junctions – **Pontivy**, most notably – that developed in the nineteenth century because of it; the old port of **Redon**, a patchwork of water, where the canal crosses the River Vilaine; and a sequence of scenic splendours, including the string of lakes around the **Barrage de Guerlédan**, near Mur-de-Bretagne. As a focus for exploring **inland Brittany**, whether by barge, bike, foot or all three, the canal is ideal. Not every stretch is accessible but there are detours to be made away from it, such as the wild and desolate **Monts d'Arrée** to the north of the canal in Finistère.

The Finistère stretch

The **Monts d'Arrée** stretch from the base of the Crozon peninsula almost to Morlaix. These hills, rising at their peaks to only 380m at the wild-looking ridge encircling the Lac de Brennilis, give the impression of being higher than they are, due partly to sparse habitation and partly to the lack of anything higher in the whole province.

They form part of the **Parc Naturel Régional d'Armorique**, an area, in theory at least, of conservation and rural regeneration along traditional lines. The administrative centre is at **MENEZ-MEUR**, off the D342 near the Forêt de Cranou – just inland from the Brest–Quimper motorway. Menez is an official **animal reserve**, with wild boar and deer roaming free and a **museum of Breton horses** (June–Sept daily 10.30am–7pm; May daily except Sat 1.30–5.30pm; Feb–April & Oct–Dec Wed, Sun & hols 10am–noon & 1–6pm). At the reserve gate you can pick up a wealth of detail on the park and all its various activities (☎98.68.81.71).

East of Sizun, 3km along D764 to Commana, is the abandoned hamlet of **MOULINS-DE-KÉROUAT** (*Milin-Kerroc'h* in Breton – and on the Michelin map), which has been restored as an **Eco-Musée** (July & Aug daily 11am–7pm; mid-May to June daily 2–6pm; mid-March to mid-May & mid-Sept to Oct daily except Sat 2–6pm; otherwise by appointment ☎98.68.87.76; 15F). Kérouat's last inhabitant died in 1967 and like many a place in the Breton interior it might have crumbled into indiscernible ruins. The largest of its houses belonged in the last century to the mayor of Commana, who also controlled the mills, and its furnishings are therefore those of a rich family.

The **ridge** around Brennilis is visible as a stark silhouette from the underused **campsite** at NESTAVEL-BRAZ on the eastern shore of the lake. From this deceptively tranquil vantage point, the army's antennae near Roc Trévezel to the north are obscured, as are those of the navy at Menez-Meur to the west. Right behind you, however, is the **Brennilis nuclear power station**, which Breton nationalists attacked in 1975 with a rocket launcher; it survived. Perhaps appropriately, across the lake where the tree-lined fields around the villages end, is **Yeun Elez**, one of the legendary "holes to hell". You can walk around the lake – gorse and brambles permitting; be very careful not to stray from the paths into the surrounding peat bogs. The ridge itself is followed most of the way by a road, but in places it still feels like miles from any habitation.

Huelgoat and its forest

HUELGOAT is the halfway point between Morlaix and Carhaix on the minor road D769, making a pleasant overnight stop, next to its own small **lake**. Spreading north and east from the village is the **Forêt de Huelgoat**, a landscape of trees, giant boulders and waterfalls tangled together in primeval chaos – or at least up until 1987; just how fragile it really was, just how miraculous had been its long survival, was demonstrated by the hurricane of that October, which smashed it to smithereens in the space of fifteen minutes. After several years of cleaning up, the forest has now returned to a fairly close approximation of its former glories, and it is once again possible to walk for several kilometres along the various paths that lead into the depths of the woods.

One or two of Huelgoat's **hotels** were also hard hit by the post-hurricane decline in tourism to survive, but the *Hôtel du Lac*, beside the lake at 12 rue du Général-de-Gaulle (☎98.99.71.14; ①; Feb–Oct), still offers basic **rooms** and good food. Also beside the lake, the *Camping du Lac* (☎98.99.78.80; June–Sept) is complete with swimming pool.

Along the canal

As late as the 1920s, steamers would make their way across the Rade de Brest and down the Aulne River to **Châteaulin**, the first real town on the canal route. If you're walking the canal seriously, **Pont-Coblant** and **Pleyben** are just 10km further away on the map, but be warned that the meanders make it a several-hour hike. Pick your side of the water, too; there are no bridges between Châteaulin and Pont-Coblant.

Châteaulin

CHÂTEAULIN is a quiet place, where the main reason to stay is the canal itself – or river as it is here. Most bars sell permits for its salmon and trout fishing (as do fishing shops, some of which rent out tackle). You should have little difficulty finding a room at the **hotel** *Le Christmas* on rue des Écoles (☎98.86.01.24; ①), which climbs from the town centre towards Pleyben. Within a couple of minutes' walk upstream from the statue to Jean Moulin (the Resistance leader who was *sous-préfet* here from 1930 to 1933) and the town centre, you're on towpaths full of rabbits and squirrels and over-hung by trees full of birds.

Pont-Coblant and around

PONT-COBLANT is the first point on the canal at which you can **rent boats** – either canoes or houseboats (see the travel details at the end of this chapter). A small village, it also has a very basic (and cheap) forty-bed unofficial **youth hostel** (contact the *Moulin de Pont-Coblant*, 29190 Pleyben, ☎98.73.34.40 to reserve a bed) and a **campsite**.

Just 4km north of Pont-Cobland is **PLEYBEN**, renowned for its **parish close** (see p.351). On its four sides the calvary traces the life of Jesus like a comic strip, with a naivety that is echoed by the hand-drawn and coloured exhibition in the repository of local customs, traditions, folktales and fountains.

Châteauneuf-du-Faou and onwards

CHÂTEAUNEUF-DU-FAOU is similar to Châteaulin, sloping down to the tree-lined river. It's a little more developed, though, with a tourist complex, the *Penn ar Pont* (☎98.81.81.25), with swimming pool, *gîtes* and camping, as well as **cycle** and **boat rental**. The canal proper separates off from the Aulne a few kilometres to the east at Pont-Triffen, staking its own path on past Carhaix, and out of Finistère. **CARHAIX**, an ancient road junction, has cafés and shops to replenish supplies, but not much to recommend it. Beyond it the canal – as far as Pontivy – is navigable only by canoe.

The central stretch: Gouarec to Redon

Although the canal is limited to canoeists between Carhaix and Pontivy, it's worth some effort to follow on land, particularly for the scenery from Gouarec to Mur-de-Bretagne. At the centre is the trailing **Lac de Guerlédan**, created by the construction of a barrage near Mur, and backed, to the south, by the enticing **Forêt de Quénécan**. Approaching by road, the canal path is easiest joined at Gouarec, covered by the five daily buses between Carhaix and Loudéac.

Gouarec

At **GOUAREC**, the River Blavet and the canal meet in a confusing swirl of water that shoots off, edged by footpaths, in the most unlikely directions. The old schist houses of the town are barely disturbed by traffic or development, nor are there great numbers of tourists. For a comfortable overnight stop, the *Hôtel du Blavet* (☎96.24.90.03; ②) is in an ideal waterside position; don't be put off by its extravagant menus – they have afford-able meals as well. The municipal **campsite**, *Le Bout du Pont* (☎96.24.90.22; mid-June to mid-Sept), is next to the canal.

Quénécan Forest

For the 15km between Gouarec and Mur-de-Bretagne, the N164 skirts the edge of **Quénécan Forest**, within which is the series of artificial lakes created when the Barrage of Guerlédan was completed in 1928. Though sadly once again damaged by the hurricane, it's a beautiful stretch of river, a little overrun by campers and caravans but peaceful enough nonetheless. The best places to stay are just off the road, past the villages of **ST-GELVEN** and **CAUREL**. At the former, you can walk down to Lac Guerlédan and the **campsite** at **KERMANEC**. From just before Caurel, the brief loop of the D111 leads to tiny, sandy beaches – a bit too tiny in season – with **campsites** *Les Pins* (☎96.28.52.22) and *Les Pommiers* (☎96.28.52.35). At the spot known as **BEAU RIVAGE** is a complex containing a campsite, hotel, restaurant, snack bar and mooring for a 140-seat glass-topped cruise boat.

Mur-de-Bretagne

MUR-DE-BRETAGNE is set back from the eastern end of the lake, a lively place with a wide and colourful pedestrianized zone around its church. It's the nearest town to the barrage – just 2km distant – and has a **campsite**, the *Rond-Point du Lac* (☎96.26.01.90; mid-June to mid-Sept), with facilities for windsurfing and horseback riding. There's also a **youth hostel** a short way along the N164 at **ST-GUEN** (☎96.28.54.34; April–Oct) – take the Loudéac bus and get off at *Bourg de St-Guen*.

Pontivy

You can again take **barges** all the way to the Loire from **PONTIVY**, the central junction of the Nantes–Brest canal, where the course of the canal breaks off once more from the Blavet. When the waterway opened, the small medieval centre of the town was expanded, redesigned and given broad avenues to fit its new role. It was even briefly renamed Napoléonville, in honour of the man responsible for its new prosperity.

These days, Pontivy is a bright market town, its twisting old streets contrasting with the stately riverside promenades. At its northern end, occupying a commanding hill-side site, is the **Château de Rohan**, built by the lord of Josselin in the fifteenth century (mid-June to Sept daily 10am–noon & 2–6pm; Oct to mid-June Wed–Sun 10am–noon & 2–5pm; 15F). Used in summer for low-key cultural events and temporary exhi-bitions, the castle still belongs to the Josselin family, who are slowly restoring it. At the moment, one impressive façade, complete with deep moat and two forbidding towers, looks out over the river – behind that, the structure rather peters out.

Pontivy has several **hotels**, among them the low-priced *Robic*, 2 rue Jean-Jaurès (☎97.25.11.80; ①), whose good restaurant has menus from 55F, and there's a spartan IYHF **youth hostel** (☎97.25.58.27; ①), 2km from the *gare SNCF* on the Île des Recollets.

Bréhan and the Abbaye de Timadeuc

Following the canal beyond Pontivy to Rohan is difficult unless you're on it. Between Rohan and Josselin is the Cistercian **Abbaye de Timadeuc**, which you can enter only to attend mass. But it's beautiful from the outside, with its front walls and main gate covered in flowers at the end of an avenue of old pinès. The abbey also provides an excuse to stay at nearby **BRÉHAN**, a quiet little village whose **hotel**, the *Cremaillère* (☎97.51.52.09; ①), must be one of the best deals anywhere in the province, both for good rooms and excellent food at low prices.

Josselin

A short way south from Timadeuc, you come to the three Rapunzel towers embedded in a vast sheet of stone of the **château** in **JOSSELIN** (July & Aug daily 10am–noon & 2–6pm; June & Sept daily 2–6pm; Feb–May & Oct to mid-Nov Wed, Sun & hols 2–6pm; closed mid-Nov to Jan; 15F). The Rohan family used to own a third of Brittany, the present duke contents himself with the position of local mayor. The pompous apartments of his residence are not very interesting, even if they do contain the table on which the Edict of Nantes was signed in 1598. But the Duchess's collection of dolls, housed in the **Musée des Poupées**, behind the castle, is something special (same hours as museum; June & Sept also open 10am–noon; 20F).

The town is full of medieval splendours, from the gargoyles of the **basilica** to the castle **ramparts**, and the half-timbered houses in between. **Notre-Dame-du-Roncier** is built on the spot where, in the ninth century, a peasant supposedly found a statue of the Virgin under a bramble bush. The statue was burned during the Revolution, but an important *pardon* is held each year on September 8.

Josselin's **tourist office** is in a superb old house on the place de la Congrégation, up in town next to the castle entrance (Mon–Sat 9am–noon & 2–6pm; ☎97.22.36.43). Just across from the basilica, the *Hôtel de France* (☎97.22.23.06; ③; closed Sun pm & Mon between Oct & March) is an ivy-covered *logis* which is amazingly quiet considering its central location, where you can choose on the 77F menu between duck in cider or trout with almonds, while the *Hôtel du Chateau* (☎97.22.20.11; ①) is a lovely medieval building by the river, facing the castle. There's also a *gîte d'étape* nearby, right below the castle walls, where you can rent **canoes** (☎97.22.21.69). Much the best **restaurant** in town, a short walk east of the basilica as the road starts to drop towards the river, is the *Frères Blot* at 9 rue Glatinier (☎97.22.22.08); lunch menus start at 75F.

Guéhenno and the Domaine de Kerguéhennec

One of the largest and best Breton calvaries is at **GUÉHENNO**, south of Josselin on the D123. Sculpted in 1550, the figures include the cock that crowed after Peter's denials, Mary Magdalene with the shroud and a recumbent Christ in the crypt. Its appeal is enhanced by the naivety of its amateur restoration. After damage caused by Revolutionary soldiers in 1794 – who amused themselves by playing *boules* with the heads of the statues – all the sculptors approached for the work demanded exorbitant fees, so the parish priest and his assistant decided to undertake the task themselves.

Another unusual sculptural endeavour, this time contemporary, is taking place at the **Domaine de Kerguéhennec**, which is marked a short way off the D11 near St-Jean-Brevelay. This innovative **sculpture park** is gradually building up a fascinating permanent international collection, set around the lawns, woods and lake of an early eighteenth-century château (April–Nov daily except Mon 10am–6pm; 25F).

Over to the east, off the D151, **LIZIO** has also set itself up as a centre for arts and crafts, with ceramic and weaving workshops its speciality. A **Festival Artisanal** is held on the second Sunday in August, along with street theatre (and pancakes). There are several **gîtes** in the town and a **campsite**.

Malestroit and around

Not a lot happens in **MALESTROIT**, which celebrated its thousand years in 1987. But the town is full of unexpected and enjoyable corners. As you come in to the main square, the **place du Bouffay** in front of the church, the houses are covered with unlikely carvings – an anxious bagpipe-playing hare looking over its shoulder at a dragon's head on one beam, while an oblivious sow in a blue buckled belt threads her distaff on another. The **church** itself is decorated with drunkards and acrobats outside, torturing demons and erupting towers within. Beside the grey canal, the matching grey slate tiles on the turreted rooftops bulge and dip, while on its central island overgrown houses stand next to the stern walls of an old mill.

If you arrive in Malestroit by barge (this is a good stretch to travel), you'll moor very near the town centre. The helpful **tourist office** stands on the bd du Pont-Neuf, next to the main bridge over the river (daily 10am–noon & 2–6pm; ☎97.75.14.57); they can provide details of **boat rental**. Nearby on the same road is the **gare routière**, served by buses from Vannes and Rennes, while across the river there's a **campsite** down below the bridge, in the impasse d'Abattoir next to the swimming pool (☎97.75.13.33; May–Oct). However, the only **hotel** is a few hundred metres away on the far side of the old centre. The unexciting *Hôtel St-Michel*, at 1 Faubourg St-Michel (☎97.75.13.01; ①), is at the start of the D10 towards Serent; it has a bar but no restaurant.

The Musée de la Résistance Bretonne

Two kilometres west of Malestroit (and with no bus connection), the village of **ST-MARCEL** hosts a **Musée de la Résistance Bretonne** (June–Sept daily 10am–7pm; Oct–May daily except Tues 10am–noon & 2–6pm; 25F). The museum stands on the site of a June 1944 battle in which the Breton *maquis*, joined by Free French forces parachuted in from England, successfully diverted the local German troops from the main Normandy invasion movements.

The museum's strongest feature is its presentation of the pressures that made many French collaborate: the reconstructed street corner from which all life has been jerked out by the occupiers; the big colourful propaganda posters offering work in Germany, announcing executions of *maquis*, equating resistance with aiding US and British big business; and against these the low-budget, flimsily printed Resistance pamphlets. All the labelling is in French, which non-speakers may find rather frustrating.

The Parc de Préhistoire de Bretagne

Twenty kilometres southeast of Malestroit, near Rochefort-en-Terre, the new and very heavily publicized **Parc de Préhistoire de Bretagne** is a theme park aimed overwhelmingly at children (April to mid-Oct daily 10am–6pm; mid-Oct to Nov Sun 2–6pm; 45F). Landscaped areas contain dioramas of gigantic (if stationary) dinosaurs and human beings at various stages in their evolution; the story ends shortly after a bunch of deformed but enthusiastic Neanderthals hit on the idea of erecting a few megaliths.

Redon

Thirty-four kilometres east of Malestroit, at the junction not only of the rivers Oust and Vilaine and the canal, but also of the train lines to Rennes, Vannes and Nantes and of six major roads, **REDON** is not easy to avoid. And you shouldn't try to, either. A wonderful grouping of water and locks, it's a town with history, charm and life.

Until World War I, Redon was the seaport for Rennes. Its industrial docks – or what remains of them – are therefore on the Vilaine, while the canal, even in the very centre of town, is almost totally rural, its towpaths shaded avenues. Shipowners' houses from the seventeenth and eighteenth centuries can be seen along quai Jean-Bart by the *bassin* and quai Duguay-Truin next to the river. A rusted wrought-iron workbridge, equipped with a gantry, still crosses the river, but the main users of the port now are cruise ships heading down the Vilaine to La Roche-Bernard.

Redon was once also a religious centre, its first abbey founded in 832 by Saint Conwoion. The most prominent church today is **St-Sauveur**. Its unique four-storeyed Romanesque belfry is squat, almost obscured by later roofs and the high choir, and best seen from the adjacent cloisters; the Gothic tower is entirely separated from the main building by a fire. Inside the church, you'll find the tomb of the judge who tried the legendary Bluebeard – Joan of Arc's friend, Gilles de Rais.

Practicalities

Redon's **tourist office** (May–Sept daily 10am–noon & 3–6pm; Oct–April Mon–Sat 10am–noon & 3–6pm; ☎99.71.06.04) is in the place du Parlement, next to the modern *halles* (scene of a Monday **market**), while the **gare SNCF** (☎99.71.74.10) is five minutes' walk west of the town centre. What long-distance buses serve the town – it takes less than an hour to get to Rennes, Nantes or Vannes – also operate from here. **Bicycles** can be rented from *Cycles Gicquel* in place St-Sauveur (☎99.71.02.82), and **canoes** and **barges** from the *Comptoir Nautique* at 2 quai Surcouf (☎99.71.46.03).

Most of the **hotels** are concentrated in town and near the *gare SNCF* rather than in the port area. The large white *Hôtel le France* looks down on the canal from 30 rue Duguesclin, on the corner of quai de Brest (☎99.71.06.11; ③); its recently renovated rooms offer a considerable degree of comfort for the price, but it has no restaurant. Nearer the station, the *Hôtel Chandouineau*, 10 av de la Gare (☎99.71.02.04; ④), is luxurious, with just seven bedrooms, and its restaurant serves gourmet menus from 120F.

THE SOUTHERN COAST

Brittany's **southern coast** takes in the province's – and indeed Europe's – most famous prehistoric site, the alignments of **Carnac**, with the associated megaliths of the beautiful, island-studded **Golfe de Morbihan**. The beaches are not as spectacular as in Finistère, but there are more safe places to swim and the water is warmer. Of the cities, **Lorient** has Brittany's most compelling **festival** and **Vannes** has one of the liveliest medieval town centres. Further east, **La Baule** does a good impression of a Breton St-Tropez, and you can escape to the islands of **Belle-Île, Hoëdic** and **Houat**. Inevitably it's popular, and in summer you can be hard pressed to find a room, but if you're prepared to make reservations, or you're camping, there shouldn't be much problem.

Lorient and around

LORIENT, Brittany's fourth-largest city, lies on an immense natural harbour protected from the ocean by the Île de Groix and strategically located at the junction of the rivers Scorff, Ter and Blavet. A functional, rather depressing port today, it was once a key base for French and English colonialism, and was founded in the mid-seventeenth century for trading operations by the *Compagnie des Indes*, an equivalent of the Dutch and English East India Companies. Apart from the name, little else remains to suggest the plundered wealth that once arrived here. During the last war, Lorient was a major target for the Allies; the Germans held out until May 1945, by which time the city was almost completely destroyed. The only substantial remains were the U-boat pens – subsequently greatly expanded by the French for their nuclear submarines.

Across the estuary in Port-Louis there's a **museum of the Compagnie des Indes**, a pretty dismal temple to imperialism. Time would be more enjoyably spent on a boat trip, either up the estuary towards Hennebont (see below) or out to the Île de Groix. This 8km-long steep-sided rock is a short way out to sea and has no permanent population, though there is an IYHF **youth hostel** (☎97.86.81.38; ③; April–Oct), with a **campsite** alongside (☎97.86.53.08). The coast around Lorient itself is unenticing and plagued with thick drifts of seaweed.

The Inter-Celtic Festival

The overriding reason people come to Lorient is for the **Inter-Celtic Festival**, held for ten days from the first Friday to the second Sunday in August. The biggest Celtic event in Brittany, or anywhere else for that matter, sees representatives from all seven Celtic countries. In a popular celebration of cultural solidarity, with up to 250,000 people in attendance at over 150 different shows, five languages mingle and Scotch and Guinness flow with French and Spanish wines and ciders. There is a certain competitive element, with championships in various categories, but the feeling of mutual enthusiasm and conviviality is paramount. Most of the activities – embracing music, dance and literature – take place around the central place Jules-Ferry, and this is where most people end up sleeping, too, as accommodation is pushed to the limit.

For schedules of the festival, and further details of temporary accommodation, contact the *Office du Tourisme de Pays de Lorient* on place Jules-Ferry, 56100 Lorient (☎97.21.24.29), bearing in mind that the festival programme is not finalized before May. For certain specific events, you need to reserve tickets well in advance.

Practicalities

Lorient's **tourist office**, beside the pleasure port on the quai de Rohan (July & Aug Mon–Fri 9am–7pm, Sat 9am–noon & 2–7pm, Sun 10am–noon & 2–5pm; Sept–June Mon–Fri 9am–12.30pm & 1.30–6pm, Sat 9am–noon & 2–6pm; ☎97.21.07.84), can provide full details on local boat trips, and organizes some excursions itself.

Unless you arrive during the festival, there's a huge choice of **hotels**. Among reasonable, fairly central options are two on rue Lazare-Carnot as it curves away south of the tourist office: all the rooms in the *Victor Hugo Hôtel* at no. 36 (☎97.21.16.24; ①–③) have TV, and there's an action-packed 95F menu offering langoustines, wild pheasant pâté and duck *à l'orange*, while the *Hôtel d'Arvor*, at no. 104 (☎97.21.07.55; ①), also has a good-value restaurant. There's also an IYHF **youth hostel**, next to the River Ter at 41 rue Victor-Schoelcher, 3km out on bus line C from the *gare SNCF* (☎97.37.11.65; ①; closed mid-Dec to Jan). The *Poisson d'Or* on rue Maître-Esvelin (☎97.21.57.06) is a great **fish restaurant**, with menus from 95F.

Lochrist

Twelve kilometres or so northeast of Lorient is **LOCHRIST**, where the great chimneys of the Hennebont ironworks still stand, smokeless and silent, looking down on the Blavet. Strikes and demonstrations failed to prevent the closure of the foundry in 1966, and the only work since has been to set up the **Musée Forges d'Hennebont**, which documents its 100-year history from the workers' point of view (daily Mon 2–4pm, Tues–Fri 9am–noon & 2–4pm; summer closes 6pm; 25F). Some of the men put out of work have contributed their memories and tools; for others the museum was a final bitter irony. It is excellent though, both in content and presentation, despite the sense of defeat after seeing the joyful pictures of successful strikes in the 1930s. If it's on your route it's worth a stop: the bus station is just opposite, on the other side of the river.

Auray

Some people find **AURAY**, with its over-restored ancient quarter, slightly dull – but it is a lot less crowded than Vannes, a lot cheaper than Quiberon town, and usefully placed for exploring Carnac, the Quiberon peninsula and the Gulf of Morbihan.

The centre of the town today is **place de la République**, with its eighteenth-century Hôtel de Ville. In a neighbouring square, linked to the place de la République by rue du Lait, is the seventeenth-century **church of St-Gildas**, with its fine Renaissance porch. A **covered market** adjoins the Hôtel de Ville, but on Mondays an open-air market fills the surrounding streets with colour – and stops all traffic for a considerable radius.

However, Auray's showpiece is undoubtedly the ancient quarter of **St-Goustan**, with its delightful fifteenth- and sixteenth-century houses. The bend in the River Loch, an early defended site, was a natural setting for a town – and, with its easy access to the gulf, it soon became one of the busiest ports of Brittany. Today, as you look at it from the Promenade du Loch on the opposite bank, with the small seventeenth-century stone bridge still spanning the river, it is not difficult to imagine it in its heyday. In 1776, Benjamin Franklin landed here on his way to seek the help of Louis XVI in the American War of Independence.

Practicalities

Auray's **tourist office** is on the ground floor of the Hôtel de Ville, place de la République (Mon–Sat 9.30am–noon & 2–6pm; ☎97.24.09.75). A small annexe is maintained in July and August at the *gare SNCF*, twenty minutes' walk from the centre, from where buses run through the centre of Auray and on to La Trinité, Carnac and Quiberon.

The most appealing place to **stay** in Auray is down by the port in the St-Goustan quarter, where the *Hôtel du Marin*, 47 rue de Petit-Port (☎97.24.14.58; ①), offers simple accommodation over a bar. Up in town, *Hôtel le Celtic*, on the way into town at 30 rue Clemenceau (☎97.24.05.37; ①), is also pleasant, and the nearby *Olympic Bar*, 19 rue Clemenceau (☎97.24.06.69), is a friendly restaurant-bar with menus at 58F and 90F. There are also a couple of hotels out near the station, including the *Hôtel Terminus* on place de la Gare (☎97.24.00.09; ①), which has a snack bar and *crêperie*.

North of Auray

A short way north of Auray, on the B768 to Baud, beyond the station on the left, is the grandiose **Abbaye de Chartreuse**, housing a black-and-white marble mausoleum with sculpted reliefs by David d'Angers of the 1790s Royalist rebellion (daily 10am–noon & 2–5.30pm; free). Another counter-revolutionary failure is recalled by the **Champs des Martyres**, nearby to the right of the D120, where 350 *chouans*, counter-revolutionary Bretons during the early 1790s, were executed. Two kilometres farther along the D120 towards Brech, you come to the **Écomusée St-Degan** (July to mid-Sept daily 2–6pm; 20F), consisting of a group of reconstructed farm buildings, representing the local peasant life at the beginning of this century. It's all a bit too rustically charming, but at least it escapes the glass cases and wax models of most folk museums.

Ste-Anne-d'Auray

Perhaps the largest of the Breton **pardons** takes place at **STE-ANNE-D'AURAY** on July 26. Some 25,000 pilgrims gather for the occasion to hear Mass in the church, mount the *scala sancta* on their knees, and buy trinkets from the street stalls. The origin of this *pardon* lies in the discovery in 1623 of a statue of Saint Anne by a local peasant, one Nicolazic. He claimed to have been directed to the spot by visionary appearances of the saint (the Virgin's mother) and to have been instructed by her to build a church. Illiterate, speaking only Breton, and with no more than a subsistence livelihood, he managed to raise the necessary funds and construct his church (since destroyed, along with the statue during the Revolution). On his deathbed, twenty years later, the church authorities were still accusing him of making up his story, and the debate continues today with the ongoing campaign to have Nicolazic canonized.

Ste-Anne's status as a pilgrimage centre led to its being chosen as the site for the vast **Monument aux Morts** erected to the memory of the 250,000 Breton dead of the Great War. Even the 200 metres of closely inscribed wall that surrounds the monument is insufficient to list all the victims by name. All in all, Ste-Anne is a sad and solemn place, not really somewhere to stop, despite its abundant hotels.

Carnac

The **alignments** at **CARNAC** – rows of 2000 or so menhirs, or standing stones, stretching for over 4km to the north of the village – constitute the most important prehistoric site in Europe, long predating Knossos, the Pyramids, Stonehenge or the great Egyptian temples of the same name at Karnak. Mercifully, they now stand a few kilometres in from the sea, meaning you can combine a reasonably tranquil visit to the stones with a stay in the popular, modern seaside resort, pretty hectic by Brittany's mild standards.

The alignments

According to local legend, the standing stones at Carnac are Roman soldiers turned to stone by Pope St-Cornély. Another theory, with a certain amount of mathematical backing, says the giant menhir of Locmariaquer and the Carnac stones were an observatory for the motions of the moon – a sort of three-dimensional neolithic graph paper for plotting the movements of heavenly bodies. But history has seen them used as ready-quarried stone, and dug up and removed by peasants to protect their precious crops from academic visitors when prehistoric archeology became fashionable. It's impossible to say how many have disappeared, nor really to prove anything from what's left; and in any case their actual arrangement may never have been particularly important, with their significance lying in some great annual ceremony as each one was erected.

Aside from strolling in wonder among them, you can get a good deal of information, and entertainment, too, from the **Musée de Préhistoire** on rue du Tumulus in Carnac-Ville (July & Aug Mon–Fri 10am–6.30pm, Sat & Sun 10am–noon & 2–6.30pm; Sept–June daily except Tues 10am–noon & 2–5pm; 30F). It combines serious scholarship with large blow-ups of the French Astérix cartoons, and traces the history of the area from about 450,000 years ago up to and after the Romans.

Seeing the stones

Thanks to increasing numbers of visitors (and despite local opposition), the principal alignments have recently been fenced off, and you can no longer wander among them. Inevitably, that means some of the magic has been lost. Now you have to settle for seeing the stones from a distance, either from the road or from the roof of the grandly named **Archéoscope** alongside the site – a vantage point perhaps a dozen feet above ground level. Inside the Archéoscope, a small theatre puts on half-hour audiovisual presentations about the megaliths (mid-Feb to mid-Nov daily 10am–noon & 2–6.30pm; 40F; call for the times of English-language performances ☎97.52.07.49).

If you want to set off on your own, you can rent **bicycles** from several of the town's campsites, or from *Le Randonneur*, 20 av des Druides, Carnac-Plage (☎97.52.02.55). The *Grande Metairie* site also arranges tours on **horseback**.

Probably the best way of all to see the alignments is from the **air**. The year-round *Quiberon Air Club* (☎97.50.11.05) and the summer-only *Thalass Air* (☎97.30.40.00) both operate short flights over the Morbihan from the Aérodrome de Quiberon, near the tip of the Quiberon peninsula at Roc'h Priol (☎97.50.11.05).

The Town

Carnac itself, divided between the original **Carnac-Ville** and the seaside resort of **Carnac-Plage**, is extremely popular and swarming with holiday-makers in July and August. For most of these, the alignments are, if anything, only a side show. But, as a holiday centre, it has its special charm, especially in late spring and early autumn when

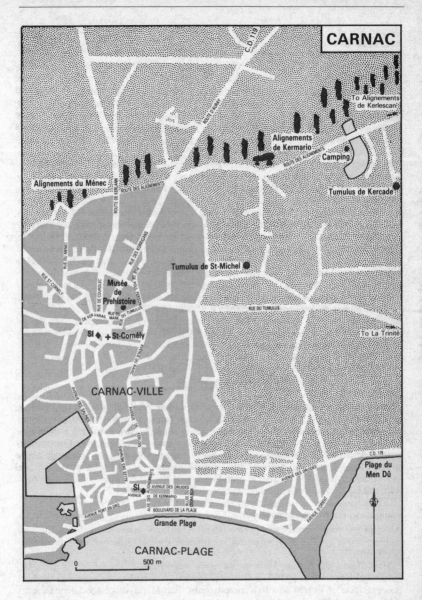

it is less crowded – and cheaper. The town and seafront remain well wooded, and the tree-lined avenues and gardens are a delight, the climate being mild enough for ever-green oak and Mediterranean mimosa to grow alongside native stone pine and cypress.

The town's five **beaches** extend for nearly two miles in total. The small plage Légenèse, nearest the yacht club, is reputed to be the beach on which the ill-fated

Chouan Royalists landed in 1795. The two most attractive beaches, usually counted as one of the five, are **plages Men Dû** and **Beaumer**, which lie to the east towards La Trinité beyond Pointe Churchill.

Practicalities

The main **tourist office** for Carnac is slightly back from the main beach at 74 av des Druides (July & Aug Mon–Sat 9am–7pm, Sun 10am–1pm & 2–6pm; Sept–June Mon–Sat 9am–noon & 2–6pm; ☎97.52.13.52); an annexe in the place de l'Église in town is open between Easter and September. Both provide comprehensive maps and details. **Buses** to Auray, Quiberon and Vannes stop near the tourist office on av des Druides, and on rue Saint-Cornély in Carnac-Ville. The *Tire Bouchon* **rail** link with Auray and Quiberon runs between July and September; the nearest station is at Plouharnel, 4km northwest.

Hotels in Carnac are at a premium in July and August. Carnac-Ville is marginally cheaper than Carnac-Plage, although the distinction is blurred where the two merge. In **Carnac-Ville**, *Hôtel Chez Nous*, 5 pl de la Chapelle (☎97.52.07.28; ③; April–Oct), is central and convenient, with a nice garden, but no restaurant; the similar *Hôtel d'Arvor*, 5 rue St-Cornély (☎97.52.96.90; ③; April–Oct), is run by a couple who speak good English. In **Carnac-Plage**, the *Hôtel-Restaurant Hoty*, 15 av de Kermario (☎97.52.11.12; ②; closed Dec & Jan), is the best value. As befits a family-oriented place, there are as many as eighteen **campsites** in and around Carnac. Among the best are the *Men Dû* (☎97.52.04.23; April–Sept) near the sea, inland from plage du Men Dû, and the more expensive *Grande Metairie* (☎97.52.24.01; June to mid-Sept) near the Kercado tumulus.

Most of the **restaurants** worth recommending are in hotels, such as the bright and cheerful *Bistrot du Pêcheur* in the *Hôtel La Marine*, 4 pl de la Chapelle (☎97.52.07.33; ④; April–Sept), or the old stone *Hôtel Ratelier* on Chemin de Douet (☎97.52.05.04; ③; closed Sun, Mon & Jan), with menus from 90F. There's a **market** in Carnac on Wednesday and Sunday mornings.

The Presqu'île de Quiberon

The **Quiberon Peninsula**, south of Carnac, is well worth visiting on its own merits; **QUIBERON** is quite a lively port, and you can get boats out to the islands or walk the shores of this narrow peninsula. The ocean-facing shore, known as the **Côte Sauvage**, is a wild and highly unswimmable stretch, where the stormy seas look like flashing scenes of snowy mountain tops. The sheltered eastern side has safe and calm sandy beaches, and plenty of campsites.

Quiberon

The town of **QUIBERON** itself centres on a miniature golf course surrounded by bars, pizzerias and some surprisingly good clothes and antique shops. The cafés by the long bathing beach are the most enjoyable, along with the old-fashioned *Café du Marché* next to the PTT.

Port-Maria, the fishing harbour and **gare maritime** for the islands of Belle-Île, Houat and Hoedic (see pp.377 & 378), is the most active part of town and has the best concentration of **hotels** and **fish restaurants**. Port-Maria was once famous for its sardines, canned locally, but those days are long gone.

Practicalities

Between July and September, the special *Tire Bouchon* train links Quiberon's **gare SNCF**, which is a short way above the town proper, with Auray. There are also **buses** right to the **gare maritime** from Vannes (#23 and #24) and Auray (#24) via Carnac.

The **tourist office** at 7 rue de Verdun (July & Aug Mon–Sat 9am–8pm, Sun 10am–noon & 5–7pm; Sept–June Mon–Sat 9am–12.30pm & 2–6.30pm; ☎97.50.07.84), downhill and left from the *gare SNCF*, has an illuminated map outside that purports to monitor exactly which hotels are full, hour by hour.

For most of the year, it's hard to get **accommodation** in Quiberon. In July and August, the whole peninsula is packed, while in winter it gets very quiet indeed. The nicest area in which to stay is along the seafront in Port-Maria.

HOSTELS

Pension Au Bon Accueil, 6 quai de Houat (☎97.50.07.92). One of the best value of Port-Maria's seafront hotels. The rooms are basic but inexpensive, and the friendly dining room downstairs serves good fish soup and seafood specialities on menus that start at 71F. April–Oct. ①.

Hôtel-Restaurant de Kermorvan, 45 rue de Kermorvan (☎97.50.11.33). A good fallback in summer, near the *gare SNCF*. Reasonable meals, and a nice garden. April–Oct. ②.

Le Neptune, 4 quai de Houat (☎97.50.09.62). Alongside *Au Bon Accueil* in Port-Maria, and offering a little bit more luxury. Some rooms enjoy seafront balconies, and the usual seafood menus, of which the cheapest costs 78F. Closed Jan, & Mon in low season. Seaview rooms ④; inland-facing rooms ③.

L'Océan, 7 quai de l'Océan (☎97.50.07.58). Seems to have given up the unequal struggle to keep a restaurant going, but still has reasonably priced rooms. Easter–Sept. ①.

Hôtel au Vieux Logis, St-Julien (☎97.50.07.92). Attractive flower-draped building in St-Julien village, a couple of kilometres north of Quiberon just east of the main road. There are cosy little rooms, and good homely menus from 70F. Hotel closed mid-Oct to mid-March, restaurant closed Oct–April. ②.

YOUTH HOSTELS AND CAMPSITES

Les Filets Bleus IYHF youth hostel, 45 rue du Roc'h-Priol (☎97.50.15.54). 1.5km southeast of the *gare SNCF*. May–Sept. ①.

Do-Mi-Si-La-Mi campsite, St-Julien (☎97.50.22.52). On the sheltered east coast north of Quiberon town. April–Oct.

Camping municipal, in Kerne (☎97.50.05.07). One of the few sites on the Côte Sauvage, above the cliffs, 1km northwest of Port-Maria. July & Aug.

EATING

Once again, the most appealing area in which to browse the menus is along the waterfront in Port-Maria, with its seafood **restaurants** competing to attract ferry passengers. Hotel-owners are very insistent on persuading guests to pay for half-board – at the *Bon Accueil*, for example, that's no great hardship – but there are plenty of alternatives to choose from if you do manage to escape their clutches.

Ancienne Forge, 20 rue Verdun (☎97.50.18.64). Set back from the road down from the *gare SNCF*, with unadventurous but good-value seafood menus from 78F. Closed Jan, and Wed in low season.

De la Criée, 11 quai de l'Océan (☎97.30.53.09). Fresh fish from the quayside. 89F menu with stuffed mussels, and fish smoked on the premises. Closed Jan, Sun pm, & Mon in low season.

Les Pecheurs, rue de Port-Maria (☎97.50.12.75). Small and not especially attractive place down by the port, where the dependably traditional approach to cooking extends to keeping the portions good and large. Full fishy menus from 70F. Closed Jan, & Mon in low season.

Belle-Île

BELLE-ÎLE, 45 minutes by ferry from Quiberon, has its own Côte Sauvage on its Atlantic coast, while the landward side is fertile, cultivated ground, interrupted by deep estuaries with tiny ports. To appreciate the island's contrasts, some form of transport is advisable – you can **rent bikes** at the port and main town of **LE PALAIS**, and if you're in a small car the ferry fare is relatively low.

The island once belonged to the monks of Redon; then to the ambitious Nicholas Fouquet, Louis XIV's minister; later to the English, who in 1761 swapped it for

Menorca in an unrepeatable bargain deal. Docking at Le Palais, the abrupt star-shaped fortifications of the **citadelle** are the first thing you see (daily April–Sept 9.30am–7pm; Oct–March 9.30am–noon & 2–5pm; 15F). Built along stylish and ordered lines by the great fortress builder, Vauban, it is startling in size – filled with doorways leading to mysterious cellars and underground passages, endless sequences of rooms, dungeons, and deserted cells. It only ceased being a prison in 1961, having numbered a succession of state enemies and revolutionaries among its inmates, including Ben Bella of Algeria. Less involuntarily, painters such as Monet and Matisse, the writers Flaubert and Proust, and the actress Sarah Bernhardt all spent time on the island. And presumably Alexandre Dumas, too, as Porthos' death, in *The Three Musketeers*, takes place here. A **museum** documents the island's history, in fiction as much as in fact.

For exploring the island, a coastal footpath runs on bare soil the length of the **Côte Sauvage**. At the Sauzon end you'll find the **Grotte de l'Apothicairerie**, so called because it was once full of cormorants' nests, arranged like the jars on a pharmacist's shelves. It's reached by descending a slippery flight of steps cut into the rock. Be careful: most years someone falls and drowns. Inland, on the D25 back towards Le Palais, you pass the two **menhirs**, Jean and Jeanne, said to be lovers petrified as punishment for wanting to meet before their marriage. Another larger menhir used to lie near these two; it was broken up to help construct the road that separates them.

Belle-Île's second town, **SAUZON**, is set at the mouth of a long estuary, 6km to the west of Le Palais. If you're staying any length of time, and you've got transport, it's probably a better place to base yourself.

Getting to Belle-Île

Throughout the year, at least five **ferries** each day (ten in high summer) sail from Port-Maria, at the southernmost tip of the Quiberon peninsula, to Belle-Île. They are operated by the *Compagnie Morbihannaise et Nantaise de Navigation* (82F return; Le Palais ☎97.31.80.01; Port-Maria ☎97.50.06.90); the crossing takes 45 minutes. The usual port of call in Belle-Île is **Le Palais**, but in July and August the same company sends a few boats direct to **Sauzon**, which takes about half an hour, and also runs a limited service between Sauzon and **Lorient** (1hr 30min; Lorient ☎97.21.03.97).

Between July and September, and occasionally out of season as well, day trips organized by *Navix* (165F; ☎97.46.60.00) set out regularly from Vannes, Port-Navalo and La Trinité, and slightly less frequently from Locmariaquer, Auray and Le Bono.

Practicalities

The island's **tourist office** is next to the **gare maritime** as you arrive in Le Palais (daily July–Sept 8.30am–12.30pm & 2–7.30pm, Oct–June 9.30am–noon & 2–6pm; ☎97.31.81.93).

Accommodation in Le Palais includes the reasonably priced *Hôtel du Commerce*, pl Hôtel-de-Ville (☎97.31.81.71; ②), and the newly refitted *Hôtel-Restaurant de Bretagne* on quai Macé (☎97.31.80.14; ②), with an excellent sea-view restaurant. There's a municipal **campsite**, *Les Glacis* (☎97.31.41.76; April–Sept), and an IYHF **youth hostel** at Haute-Boulogne (☎97.31.81.33; ①; all year), close to town along the cliffs from the *citadelle*. Sauzon has one good hotel in a magnificent setting, the *du Phare* (☎97.31.60.36; ②) – where guests must eat its delicious 90F fish dinners – and two **campsites**, *Pen Prad* (☎97.31.64.82; April–Sept) and *À la Source* (☎97.31.60.95; May–Sept).

Houat and Hoëdic

The islands of **Houat** and **Hoëdic** can also be reached by ferry from Quiberon-Port Maria (*Compagnie Morbihannaise et Nantaise de Navigation*; ☎97.50.06.90; 82F return). There is at least one sailing every day of the year, except for the first Thursday of each month in winter; the crossing to Houat takes forty minutes, and to Hoëdic another twenty-five. On Tuesdays, Thursdays and Saturdays in July and August, *Navix* run day trips to Houat only from Port-Navalo and La Trinité (105F; ☎97.46.60.00).

You can't take your car to these two very much smaller versions of Belle-Île. Both have a feeling of being left behind by the passing centuries, although the younger fishermen of Houat have revived the island's fortunes by establishing a successful fishing cooperative. Houat in particular has excellent **beaches** – as ever on its sheltered (eastern) side – that fill up with campers in the summer. Camping is not strictly legal here; Hoëdic on the other hand has a large municipal **campsite** (☎97.30.63.32). There is a small and not particularly cheap **hotel** on each island; on Houat it's the *Hôtel-Restaurant des Îles* (☎97.30.68.02; ③; Easter–Sept) and on Hoëdic *Les Cardinaux* (☎97.52.37.27; ③; closed mid-Jan to mid-Feb).

Vannes and the Golfe de Morbihan

It was from **VANNES** that the great Breton hero, Nominöe, set out to unify Brittany – giving the Franks a terrible pasting and pushing the borders past Nantes and Rennes, where they remained up until the French Revolution nearly a millennium later. Here, too, the Breton *États* assembled to ratify the Act of Union in the building known as *La Cohue*. **Vieux Vannes**, the old centre of chaotic streets crammed around the cathedral and enclosed by ramparts, gardens and a tiny stream, has every reason to vaunt its historic charms.

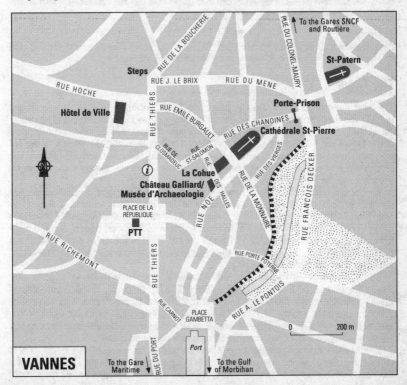

Arrival and accommodation

Vannes' **tourist office** is at 1 rue Thiers (Mon–Sat 9am–noon & 2–6pm; July & Aug Mon–Sat 9am–7pm, Sun 10am–noon; ☎97.47.24.34), on the corner of rue du Drézen, near place Gambetta. The **gare SNCF** (☎97.42.50.50) is 25 minutes' walk north of the town centre. Buses to Auray, Carnac, Quiberon and other destinations leave from the **gare routière** alongside. **Boats** around the gulf are operated from the **gare maritime**, a little way south of the centre on the parc du Golfe, by *Navix* (☎97.46.60.00) and *Compagnies des Îles* (☎97.46.60.00).

In peak season, Vannes can get claustrophobic, but it offers a better choice of **hotels** than anywhere else around the gulf. Much the nicest place to stay, if you can get a room, is **place Gambetta** overlooking the port.

HOTELS
Hôtel la Bretagne, 36 rue du Méné (☎97.47.20.21). Just outside the walls, around the corner from the Porte-Prison. Simple rooms above the *Taverne de Maître* brasserie, which specializes in *choucroute* and has a wide assortment of draught lagers. ①.
Hôtel le Marina, 4 pl Gambetta (☎97.47.22.81). Pleasantly refurbished rooms, right in the thick of things by the port, with sea views and bright sun in the morning. Downstairs there's a bar rather than a restaurant. ②.
Hôtel-Restaurant la Voile d'Or, 1 pl Gambetta (☎97.42.71.81). Extremely central, taking up half of the grand crescent at the head of the port, but the actual rooms are neither especially grand nor expensive. Standard menus in the restaurant that spreads out into the square below start at 89F, with the usual *soupe de poissons* and *steak frites*. ②.

CAMPSITE
Camping Couleau, av du Maréchal-Juin (☎97.63.13.88). The nearest campsite, at the far end of av du Maréchal-Juin, beyond the Aquarium, alongside the gulf. April–Sept.

The Town

The new town centre of Vannes is **place de la République**; the focus was shifted outside the medieval city in the nineteenth-century craze for urbanization. The grandest of the public buildings here, guarded by a pair of sleek and dignified bronze lions, is the **Hôtel de Ville** at the top of rue Thiers. By day, however, the streets of the old city, with their overhanging, witch-hatted houses and busy commercial life, are the chief source of pleasure. **Place Henri IV** in particular is stunning, as are the views from it down the narrow side streets.

La Cohue, which fills a block between rue des Halles and place du Cathédrale, has recently become the **Musée de Vannes** (June–Sept daily 10am–noon & 2–6pm; Oct–May Mon & Wed–Sat 10am–noon & 2–6pm, Sun 2–6pm; 15F), having served at various times over the past 750 years as high court and assembly room, prison, revolutionary tribunal, theatre and market-place. Upstairs it still houses the collection of what was the local Beaux Arts museum, while the main gallery downstairs is the venue for different temporary exhibitions.

The **Cathédrale St-Pierre** is a rather forbidding place, with its stern main altar almost imprisoned by four solemn grey pillars. The light – purple through new stained glass – illuminates the dessicated finger of the Blessed Pierre Rogue, who was guillotined on the main square in 1796. For a small fee, you can in summer examine the assorted treasures, in the chapter house, which includes a twelfth-century wedding chest, brightly decorated with enigmatic scenes of romantic chivalry.

The **Musée Archéologique** on rue Noé is said to have one of the world's finest collections of prehistoric artefacts (Mon–Sat 9.30am–noon & 2–6pm; 15F). But unlike the excellent display at Carnac, it's all pretty lifeless – some elegant stone axes, more recent Oceanic exhibits by way of context, but nothing very illuminating. Further collections of fossils, shells and stuffed birds, equally traditional in their display, are on show around the corner in the **Hôtel de Roscannec** at 19 rue des Halles (same hours).

The huge **Aquarium**, in the parc du Golfe on the right bank of the port from place Gambetta, claims the best collection of tropical fish in Europe, 400-odd electric eels, and a crocodile "discovered in the Paris sewers" (daily June–Aug 9am–7pm; Sept–May 9am–noon & 1.30–6.30pm; 50F).

Eating and drinking

Dining out in old Vannes can be an expensive experience, whether you eat in the intimate little restaurants along the rue des Halles, or down by the port. The leading venues for **live music** are *Le Studio*, on place Bir-Hakeim, which puts on jazz, blues, and African bands when they come to town, and *Le Contretemps*, 22 rue Hoche (☎97.42.40.11), which is more a jazz-buffs' hang-out. During the first week of August, the open-air **Vannes Jazz Festival** takes place in the Théâtre de Verdure.

Le Cordon Bleu, 13 rue des Halles (☎97.42.74.12). One of the less pricey options on this narrow, cobbled street, but every bit as good as its rivals, with a strong emphasis on Breton dishes and ingredients. Evening menus from 75F. Closed Sun & Mon lunchtime in low season.

La Jonquière, 9 rue des Halles (☎97.54.08.34). Very central option, with a modern-minded approach and efficient multilingual staff. For 60F you can take your pick from buffets of hors d'œuvres and desserts; set menus start at 73F, and the *Menu Mer* at 149F gets you a full *assiette*.

Le Lys, 51 rue Maréchal-Leclerc (☎97.42.29.30). Gourmet restaurant, a short way east of the walled city. The *nouvelle*-tinged seafood concoctions get progressively more inventive as the menus rise from 115F, but the portions are never less than reasonable. Closed Sun pm, & Mon in low season.

Villa Romana, 16 rue des Vierges (☎97.47.88.63). Pizzas from a wood-fired oven, most for under 50F, plus pasta and fresh fish. Best for lunch, on the terrace on the old ramparts, over the gardens.

Morbihan – and its islands

It comes as rather a surprise to discover that Vannes is on the sea. Its harbour is a channelled inlet of the ragged-edged **Golfe de Morbihan**, which lets in the tides through a narrow gap between the peninsulas of **Rhys** and **Locmariaquer.** By popular tradition the **islands** scattered around this enclosure used to number the days of the year, though for centuries the waters have been rising and there are now fewer than one for

---

GULF TOURS

In season, dozens of different **gulf tours** leave each day from Vannes, Port Navalo, La Trinité-sur-Mer, Auray, and Larmor-Baden. Full details are available from the Vannes tourist office, but briefly the options are these:

Navix (☎97.46.60.00), who are based in **Vannes**, run deluxe *vedettes* around the gulf itself, including half-day (70F) and full-day (95F) tours, excursions to the gulf islands of Île-aux-Moines and the Île d'Arz, and also gastronomic cruises for lunch (July & Aug daily except Mon; departs noon) and dinner (July & Aug Wed, Fri & Sat; departs 8pm). They also go out to the islands of Belle-Île and Houat. Other *Navix* sailings depart from **Port Navalo** (65–95F, plus some more expensive dinner cruises), and, to no very fixed schedule, from Auray, Le Bono, Locmariaquer and La Trinité.

Compagnie des Îles (☎97.46.18.19), also based in **Vannes**, run gulf tours (70F & 95F) and excursions to the Île-aux-Moines (65F) from there. They also operate similar cruises of varying lengths from **Port Navalo** (65–130F) and **La Trinité** (95–115F) in July & Aug.

Vedettes Blanches Armor (☎97.57.15.27) operate the usual gulf tours and trips to the Île-aux-Moines (mid-June to mid-Sept), as well as a regular shuttle service to Gavrinis from **Larmor-Baden**, which is connected by a daily bus from Vannes.

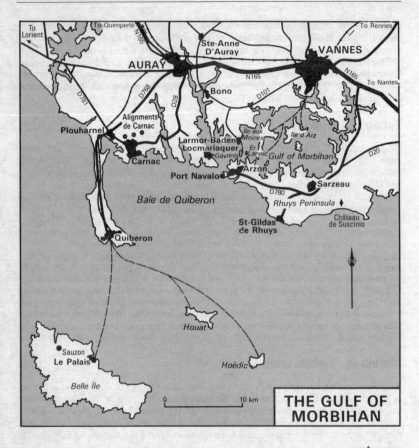

To Lorient
To Quimperlé
To Rennes
Ste-Anne D'Auray
VANNES
AURAY
N165
To Nantes
Bono
D101
Alignments de Carnac
Île aux Moines
Île d'Arz
Plouharnel
Larmor-Baden
Locmariaquer
Er
Gavrinis
Lannic
Gulf of Morbihan
Carnac
Port Navalo
Arzon
Sarzeau
Baie de Quiberon
D780
Rhuys Peninsula
St-Gildas de Rhuys
Château de Suscinio
Quiberon
Houat
Sauzon
Le Palais
Hoëdic
Belle Île
0   10 km

THE GULF OF MORBIHAN

each week. Of these, thirty are owned by film stars and the like, while two – the Île-aux-Moines and Île d'Arz – have regular populations and ferry services and end up in summer being like *Safeway* on a Saturday morning. The rest are the best, and a **boat tour** around them, or at least a trip out to Gavrinis near the mouth of the gulf, is a fairly compelling attraction. As the boats thread their way through the baffling muddle of channels you lose track of what is island and what is mainland; and everywhere there are megalithic ruins, stone circles disappearing beneath the water, and solitary menhirs on small hillocks.

Er Lannic and Gavrinis islands

A dramatic group of menhirs, arranged in a figure of eight, is to be seen on the tiny barren island of **Er Lannic** – though only at low tide when the water gives these smaller islets the appearance of stranded hovercraft skirted with mud. The best island for megalithic monuments is, however, **Gavrinis**. It contains, almost consists of, a tumulus that has been partially uncovered to reveal a chamber in which all the slabs of stone are carved with curving lines like fingerprints, axeheads and spirals – purely decorative according to archeologists. The island is a fifteen-minute **ferry** ride from

Larmor-Baden; in summer, the boat trips include guided tours of the cairn (June–Sept daily, every half-hour 9.30–11.30am & 1.30–5pm; 52F).

Locmariaquer

Thanks to the complex patterning, the stone of the roof on Gavrinis has been identified as part of the same piece as the dolmen known as the **Table des Marchands** at **LOCMARIAQUER**, twelve kilometres south of Auray. Locmariaquer also has the **Grand Menhir Brisé**, supposedly the crucial central point of the megalithic observatory of Carnac. Before being floored by an earthquake in 1722, it was by far the largest known menhir – 22m high and weighing more than a full jumbo jet at 347 tonnes. It now lies on the ground in four pieces, with a possible fifth missing, close to the *Table des Marchands*. Both are fenced off and closed between 12.30 and 2.30pm. There are more prehistoric constructions around the town, which has a couple of small **hotels**, like the *Lautram* on place de l'Église (π97.57.31.32; ②; April–Sept), and *l'Escale* (π97.57.32.51; ②; June to mid-Sept), and several **campsites**, including the excellent *La Ferme Fleurie* (π97.57.34.06).

The Presqu'île de Rhuys

The tip of the Presqu'île de Locmariaquer is only a few hundred metres away from Port Navalo and the **Presqu'île de Rhuys**. This peninsula has a micro-climate of its own, warm enough for pomegranates, figs, bougainvillea and the only Breton vineyards. Oysters are cultivated on the muddy gulf shores, but the currents of the gulf make this no place for swimming. The ocean beaches are the ones to head for: east from St-Gildas-de-Rhuys is the most enticing and least crowded stretch, with glittering gold-and silver-coloured rocks. For details on the whole peninsula, call in at the new information centre just off the main road as you come into Sarzeau.

Near **SARZEAU**, which also has accommodation if you're stuck, is the impressive fourteenth-century **Château de Suscinio**. This completely moated castle, once a hunting lodge of the Dukes of Brittany, is set in marshland at the edge of a tiny village and contains a sagging but still vivid mosaic floor. You can take a precarious stroll around its high ramparts (April–Sept daily except Wed 9.30am–noon & 2–7pm, Wed 2–7pm; Oct–March Tues, Sat, Sun & hols 9.30am–noon & 2–5pm; 20F).

Further on is **ARZON**, probably the best of its towns if you're spending any length of time on the peninsula; **stay** at the *Hôtel Étoile de la Mer* (π97.53.84.46; ②), or either of the two big **campsites**, *Le Tindio* (π97.53.75.59; April–Oct) or *Port Sable* (π97.53.71.98; April to mid-Oct). Near the tip of the peninsula, clearly visible to the north of the main road, is the **Tumulus de Thumiac**, from the top of which Julius Cæsar is said to have watched the sea battle in which the Romans defeated the Veneti.

South to the Loire

South of the **Vilaine**, in leaving the Morbihan *département* you are technically also leaving Brittany itself. The roads veer firmly east and west – to Nantes or La Baule, avoiding the marshes of the **Grande-Brière**. For centuries these 20,000 acres of peat bog have been deemed to be the common property of all who lived in them. The scattered population, the *Brièrois*, made and make their living by fishing for eels in the streams, gathering reeds and – on the nine days permitted each year – cutting the peat. Tourism has arrived only recently, and is resented. The touted attraction is renting a punt to get yourself lost for a few hours with your pole tangled in the rushes.

Guérande

On the edge of the marshes of the Grande-Brière, just before you come to the sea, is the gorgeous walled town of **GUÉRANDE**, which derived its fortune from controlling the salt pans that form a checkerboard across the surrounding inlets. This "white country" is composed of bizarre-looking *œillets*, each 70 to 80 square metres in extent, in which sea water, since Roman times, has been collected and evaporated. Guérande today, a tiny little place, is still entirely enclosed by its stout fifteenth-century **ramparts**. A spacious promenade leads right the way around the outside, passing four fortified gateways; for half its length the broad old moat remains filled with water.

Within the walls, pedestrians share the narrow cobbled streets with the odd car, the houses are bright with window boxes, and there's a **market** next to St-Aubin church. Nearby, the pretty *Roc-Maria*, 1 rue des Halles (☎40.24.90.51; ③; closed Wed & Thurs in low season), offers cosy rooms above a *crêperie* in a fifteenth-century house.

La Baule

There is something very surreal about emerging from the Brière to the coast at **LA BAULE** – an imposing, moneyed landscape where the dunes are no longer bonded together with scrub and pines, but with massive apartment buildings and luxury hotels. Sited on the long stretch of dunes that link the former island of Le Croisic to the mainland, it owes its existence to a storm in 1779 that engulfed the old town of Escoublac in silt from the Loire, and thereby created a wonderful crescent of sandy beach.

Neither La Baule's permanence nor its affluence seems in any doubt these days. This is a resort that very firmly imagines itself in the south of France: around the crab-shaped bay, bronzed nymphettes and would-be Clint Eastwoods ride across the sands into the sunset against a backdrop of cruising lifeguards, horse-dung removers and fantastically priced cocktails. It can be fun if you feel like a break from the more subdued Breton attractions – and the beach is undeniably impressive. It's not a place to imagine you're going to enjoy strolling around in search of hidden charms; the back streets have an oddly rural feel, but hold nothing of any interest.

Full details on staying in La Baule can be had from the **tourist office**, away from the seafront in a new office at 8 place de la Victoire (mid-May to mid-Sept daily 9am–7pm; mid-Sept to mid-May Mon–Sat 9.30am–noon & 2–6pm; ☎40.24.34.44). La Baule has two **gares SNCF**, the barely used La-Baule-les-Pins and the main La-Baule-Escoublac near the tourist office on place Rhin-et-Danube (☎40.66.50.50), where the *TGV*s from Paris arrive. The **gare routière** is at 4 place de la Victoire (☎40.60.25.58).

Few of the **hotels** are cheap, particularly in the high season, and in low season more than half of them are closed. The cheapest year-round options are near the main *gare SNCF*, less than 1km from the beach; these include *Hôtel Violetta*, 44 av Clemenceau (☎40.60.32.16; ②), and *Hôtel-Restaurant la Coquille*, 10 av Clemenceau (☎40.60.38.47; ①). Right in the centre, less than fifty metres from the sea not far from the tourist office, is the *Lutetia* at 13 av des Evens (☎40.60.25.81; ④), whose restaurant (closed Sun pm & Mon) offers magnificent fish cookery for 110F and upwards. The best of the **campsites**, 2km back from the beach, is *La Roserie*, 20 av Sohier (☎40.60.46.66; April–Sept).

Le Croisic

The small port of **LE CROISIC**, sheltering from the ocean around the corner of the headland, is a more realistic and more attractive place to stay than La Baule. These days it's basically a pleasure port, but fishing boats do still sail from its harbour, near the very slender mouth of the bay, and there's a modern **fish market** near the long Tréhic jetty, where you can go to see the day's catch auctioned. The hills on either side of the harbour, Mont Lenigo and Mont Esprit, are not natural; they are formed from the ballast left by the ships of the salt trade. If you are staying, choose between the

hotels *Les Nids*, 83 bd Général-Leclerc (☎40.23.00.63; ③), or the purple-and-white *Estacade*, near the end of the port at 4 quai de Lénigo (☎40.23.03.77; ③), where the 78F menu includes *soupe de poissons* and fish of the day.

Close by, all around the rocky sea coast known as the **Grande Côte**, are a whole range of **campsites**, including the *Océan* (☎40.23.07.69; April–Sept). For equally good beaches and a chance of cheaper **hotel** accommodation, you could go east from La Baule to **PORNICHET** (though preferably keeping away from the plush marina) or to the tiny **ST-MARC**, where in 1953 Jacques Tati filmed *Monsieur Hulot's Holiday*.

St-Nazaire

The best sandy coves in the region are to be found on the western outskirts of **ST-NAZAIRE**, linked by wooded paths and almost deserted. But it's a gloomy city. It was bombed to extinction in World War II, and its shipyards, in more or less continuous operation since constructing Julius Cæsar's fleet, are now closing. The one reason you might want to stay is the relative ease of finding inexpensive **hotel** space – so elusive in this area in summer. Options include the *Lapeyre*, 2 rue de la Paix (☎40.22.55.09; ③), and the new *Korali* opposite the station (☎40.01.89.89; ②). There's also a **hostel**, the *Foyer du Jeune Travailleur*, at 30 rue Soleil-Levant (☎40.22.51.04; ①). Even if St-Nazaire is a familiarly depressing town in total industrial decline, it has one inspiring piece of engineering – the **Pont St-Nazaire**, a great elongated S-curved suspension bridge over the mouth of the Loire. Driving across it incurs a heavy toll, but bikes go over for free.

Nantes

NANTES, the former capital of Brittany, is no longer officially part of the province: it was transferred to the Pays de la Loire in 1962 when the modern administrative regions were established. Nonetheless, such bureaucracy is not taken too seriously in the city, and its history is closely bound up with Breton fortunes. A considerable medieval centre, it later achieved great wealth from colonial expeditions, the slave trade and shipbuilding – activities in turn surpassed by more recent industrial growth. Despite the tower blocks masking the Loire and motorways tearing past the city, it remains to its inhabitants an integral part of Brittany.

Arrival and accommodation

Nantes' **tourist office**, housed in the colonnaded Palais de la Bourse in place du Commerce (Mon–Sat 10am–6pm; ☎40.47.04.51), provides a free book-size guide, including an excellent town map, and runs various guided tours of the city. There's a subsidiary office alongside the château at 1 rue de la Château (Wed–Sun 10am–1pm & 1.30–6pm). The main **post office** is on place Bretagne (☎40.12.60.60).

The **gare SNCF** (☎40.08.50.50), a little way east of the château, is served by three or more *TGV*s daily from Paris (just 2 hours away). It has two exits; for most facilities (tramway, buses, hotels) use *Accès Nord*. There are two central **bus** stations. Local buses use the Gare des Bus on cours Franklin, alongside place du Commerce, while the long-distance **gare routière** (☎40.47.62.70) is 400m away on allée Baco, near place Ricordeau. Modern rubber-wheeled **trams** run along the old riverfront, past the *gare SNCF* and the two bus stations. Flat-fare tickets are valid for one hour, rather than just a single journey, though one-day tickets are also available. **Bicycles** can be rented from *Seguir Bernard*, 38 rue des Alouettes (☎40.46.56.32), as well as the *gare SNCF*.

Although it holds plenty of **hotels** to suit all budgets, Nantes is one of those cities where you won't necessarily stumble upon a suitable place just by walking or driving around at whim. Instead, there are two main concentrations; one, as ever, in the immediate vicinity of the *gare SNCF*, and one in the narrow streets around the place Greslin.

Hotels

Hôtel Amiral, 26bis rue Scribe (☎40.69.20.21). Well-maintained little hotel, suitable for young night-owls, on lively pedestrianized street just north of place Graslin. Room rates for Saturday and Sunday nights are 50F lower, though still within the price category shown here. ③.

Hôtel Grand, 2 rue Santeuil (☎40.73.46.88). Comfortable rooms, between place Royale and place Graslin. No restaurant of its own, but the expensive *Restaurant Margotte* is on the ground floor. ④.

Hôtel Maeva, 3 rue du Marais (☎40.89.60.60). Basic rooms, between the post office and the Hôtel de Ville. The owner is half-English. Room rates for Saturday and Sunday nights drop by 30F, but are still within the price category shown here. No restaurant. ②.

Hôtel l'Océan, 11 rue Maréchal-de-Lattre-de-Tassigny (☎40.69.73.51). A pleasant hotel, with helpful management, just below place Graslin near the Mediathèque. Parking space is available around the back. No restaurant. Closed last two weeks of Dec. ①.

Hôtel St-Daniel, 4 rue du Bouffay (☎40.74.41.25). Simple but pleasant and well-lit rooms, on a cobbled street just off place du Bouffay in the heart of the old city. Much in demand in summer. ①.

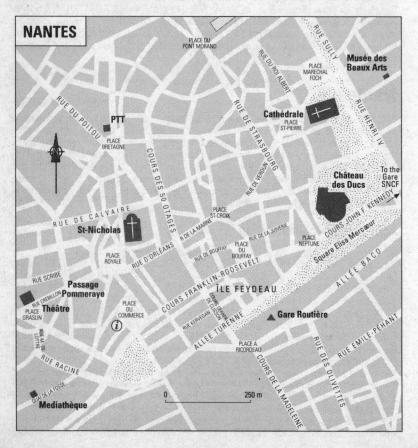

Hôtel Terminus, 3 allée du Commandant-Charcot (☎40.74.24.51). Very near the *gare SNCF*, on the way towards the château. All rooms have double beds and TV. A reasonable restaurant, so long as you skip the very limited 50F menu and head for those at 80F and upwards. ②.

Youth hostels

IYHF youth hostel, Cité Universitaire Internationale, 2 pl de la Manu (☎40.20.57.25). Summer-only hostel, using student accommodation in a postmodern former tobacco factory. Dorms and individual rooms. This is the easier hostel to reach, within 100m of the *gare SNCF* and accessible by taking tramway #1 towards Malachère and getting off at *Manufacture*. July & Aug. ①.

IYHF youth hostel, 1 rue Porte-Neuve (☎40.20.00.80). 2km from the *gare SNCF* on bus routes #36, #40 or #41, direction *place Viarne*, stop *Le Marchix*. Doesn't require youth hostel membership. Open all year. ①.

The City

The Loire, the source of Nantes' riches, has dwindled from the centre. As recently as the 1930s the river crossed the city in seven separate channels, but German labour as part of reparations for World War I filled in five. What are still called "islands" in the centre are now surrounded and isolated, not by water, but by hectic dual carriageways. These are not easy to cross, but they do at least mean that Nantes is separated into a series of discernible districts: the older medieval city is concentrated around the cathedral, with the château prominent in its southeast corner, and the elegant nineteenth-century town lies to the west, across the cours de 50 Otages.

The Château des Ducs

Though no longer on the waterfront, and damaged over the centuries, the **Château des Ducs** still preserves the form in which it was built by two of the last rulers of independent Brittany, François II and his daughter Duchess Anne, born here in 1477. The list of famous people who have been guests or prisoners, defenders or belligerents of the castle is impressive. It includes Bluebeard, publicly burnt to death in 1440; John Knox as a galley-slave in 1547–49; Bonnie Prince Charlie preparing for Culloden in 1745. The most significant act in the castle, from the point of view of European history, was the signing of the **Edict of Nantes** by Henri IV in 1598. It ended the Wars of Religion and granted a certain degree of toleration to the Protestants, but had far more crucial consequences when it was revoked by Louis XIV in 1685.

You can walk into the courtyard and up onto the low but solid ramparts for free; there are also a couple of **museums** (daily 10am–noon & 2–6pm, closed Tues out of season; 30F). The first – housed in the old, well-graffitied prison of the Tour de la Boulangerie – is the **Musée des Arts Populaires**, illuminating Breton history and folklore with murals and dioramas. The city's trading history is the subject of the **Musée des Salorges**, which has a good selection of figureheads and model ships. You can also contrast the pitiful trinkets, beads and bracelets traded for West African slaves – for which Nantes was a major centre – and the accounts and diagrams of the voyages, with the pomp of the barge used for Napoléon's ball in Nantes in August 1808.

The cathedral

In 1800 the Spaniards Tower, the castle's arsenal, exploded, shattering the stained glass of the **Cathédrale de St-Pierre-et-St-Paul** over 200m away. This was just one of many disasters that have befallen the church. It was used as a barn during the Revolution; bombed during World War II; and damaged by a fire in 1971, just when things seemed in order again. Restored and finally reopened, its soaring height and lightness are emphasized by the clean white stone. It contains the tomb of François II and his wife

Margaret, the parents of Duchess Anne – with somewhat grating symbols of Power, Strength and Justice for him and Fidelity, Prudence and Temperance for her.

The nineteenth-century town

The financier Graslin took charge of the development of the western part of the city in the 1780s, when Nantes' prosperity was at a high due to the sugar and slave trades. **Place Royale**, with its distinctive fountain, was first laid out in the closing years of the eighteenth century, and has been rebuilt since it was bombed in 1943; the 1780s also produced the nearby **place Graslin**, named after its creator, with the elaborately styled **Grand Théâtre**, whose Corinthian portico contrasts with the 1895 Art Nouveau of *La Cigale* brasserie on the corner.

West of the place Royale on rue Crebillon, a spectacular nineteenth-century multi-level shopping centre, the **Passage Pommeraye**, drops down three flights of stairs towards the river. The attention to detail lavished upon it is on a scale undreamed of in modern malls, giving a glimpse of early consumerism; each of the gas lamps that light the central area is held by an individually crafted marble cherub.

Just south of here is the elongated former **Île Feydeau**, a typical victim of the modern "development" of Nantes. Its eighteenth-century houses, seen at their best in rue Kervegan, retain some of their baroque charm – but the road is bisected by cours Olivier-de-Clisson and its horrendous traffic jams. The one thing of interest here today is the **Musée Jules-Vernes**, 3 rue de l'Hermitage (Mon & Wed–Sat 10am–noon & 2–5pm, Sun 2–5pm; 8F), commemorating the birthplace of the first serious writer of science fiction.

Rue Voltaire runs west of the place Graslin, leading to the **Musée d'Histoire Naturelle** at no. 12 (Tues–Sat 10am–noon & 2–6pm, Sun 2–6pm; 30F), centring on a vivarium, whose miserable animals are not for the squeamish (the soft-shelled turtle in particular tugs at the heartstrings). But don't let this put you off the eccentric assortment of oddities of its museum collection: rhinoceros toenails, a coelecanth and an aepyornis egg, and slightly tatty stuffed specimens of virtually every bird and animal imaginable. There is an Egyptian mummy, too, as well as a shrunken Maori head and a complete tanned human skin – taken in 1793 from the body of a soldier whose dying wish was to be made into a drum.

Further along is Viollet-le-Duc's **Palais Dobrée** (daily except Mon 10am–noon & 1.30–5.30pm; 20F), a nineteenth-century mansion given over to two museums, one of which claims to feature Duchess Anne's heart in a box.

Eating

Unlike hotels, **restaurants** fill the winding lanes of the old city; it shouldn't take long to come up with something if you wander the pedestrian streets in the centre. Nantes is big enough to have all sorts of ethnic alternatives as well, with Algerian, Italian, Chinese, Vietnamese and Indian places in addition to those listed here.

La Cigale, 4 pl Graslin (☎40.69.76.41). Famous late nineteenth-century brasserie, offering fine meals in opulent surroundings. Fish is a speciality. Menus 75F and 135F, served until midnight to provide post-performance refreshments for patrons of the adjacent theatre.

Le Gavroche, 139 rue des Hauts-Pavés (☎40.76.22.49). Top gastrononomic haunt, decked out in garish pink. Menus from 135F, but you get your money's worth. Closes Sun pm, Mon & Aug.

La Mangeoire, 16 rue des Petites-Écuries (☎40.48.70.83). Very good country food. The 60F lunch menu is a real bargain, while the 128F dinner is a delight; if you can't stomach the dozen snails, there's a mixed fish grill. Closed Sun & Mon June–Sept, otherwise closed Sun pm & Mon.

Le Petit Bacchus, 5 rue Beaurigard (☎40.47.50.46). Red-painted half-timbered house, with the atmosphere and décor of a World War I *estaminet*, just off cours des 50-Otages in a little alley leading down to the cours F-Roosevelt. Lovely 75F menu featuring duck *à l'orange* or fish of the day.

Le Sumo, 4 rue Thurot (☎40.48.57.20). Quite a rarity – a Japanese restaurant, just off the place du Commerce within a few metres of the tourist office. *Sushi* and *sashimi* menus at 80F, or entire set meals with skewered chicken, beef or salmon plus soup and salad for around 50F. Closed Sun.

The coast south of the Loire

In summer Nantes empties, as everyone heads west to the beaches, either to the more upmarket resorts beyond St-Nazaire, or south of the Loire and the almost unbroken line of holiday apartments and *Pepsi* and *frites* stands of the **Pays de Retz** coast. **PORNIC** is the one exception among these resorts, with a still-functional fishing port and one of Bluebeard Gilles de Reis's many castles. It is a small place: you can walk past the harbour and along the cliffs to a tiny beach where the rock walls glitter from the phosphorescent sea-water. The **hotels** in town are not cheap; the *Relais St-Gilles* (☎40.82.02.25; ③), just down the road from the post office, is the most reasonable.

Between the coast and Nantes, the countryside is a series of marshes and mostly inaccessible lakes. The largest, the **Grand-Lieu**, contains two drowned villages, **MURIN** and **LANGON**. Along the estuary itself, the towns are depressed and depressing, their traditional industries struck hard by unemployment.

travel details

Trains

Brest to: Landerneau (7 daily *TGV*s; 12min); Landivisiau (7 daily *TGV*s; 20min); Morlaix (7 daily *TGV*s; 35min); Paris-Montparnasse (7 daily *TGV*s, 4hr; 4 ordinary services daily, 6hr); Quimper (6 daily; 1hr 30min); Rennes (7 daily *TGV*s, 1hr 10min).

Nantes to: La Baule (10 *TGV*s daily; 1hr); Croisic (10 *TGV*s daily; 1hr 15min); Paris (10 *TGV*s daily; 2hr 15min); Quimper (10 *TGV*s daily; 3hr 30min); Vannes (10 *TGV*s daily; 1hr 45min).

Quimper to: Lorient (4 daily *TGV*s; 30min); Redon (2 daily *TGV*s; 1hr 40min); Vannes (4 daily *TGV*s; 1hr).

Rennes to: Brest (8 daily *TGV*s, 2hr 10min; 10 daily slower services also stop at via Lamballe, Guingamp, and Plouaret); Caen (4 daily; 3hr); St Brieuc (8 daily *TGV*s; 45min); Morlaix (8 daily *TGV*s; 1hr 40min); Nantes (4 daily; 1hr 30min); Paris-Montparnasse (8 daily *TGV*s, 2hr 10min; 5 ordinary services daily, 3hr 15min); Quimper (4 daily; 2hr 30min); Vannes (4 daily; 1hr).

St-Malo to: Caen (8 daily; 3hr 30min); Dinan (8 daily; 1hr); Rennes (12 daily; 1hr; *TGV* connections for Paris). All trains pass through Dol (25min).

Buses

Brest to: Le Conquet (4 daily; 30min); Quimper (6 daily; 1hr 30min); Roscoff (5 daily; 1hr 30min).

Fougères to: Vire, Normandy (2 daily; 1hr 30min); Vitré (4 daily; 35min).

Morlaix to: Carantec (4 daily; 20min); Carhaix (3 daily; 1hr 30min); Huelgoat (3 daily; 45min); Lannion (2 daily, not Sun; 1hr); Plougasnou and St Jean-le-Doigt (5 daily; 30min); Quimper (1 daily; 2hr); Roscoff (2–4 daily; 50min).

Quimper to: Audierne (3 daily; 1hr); Bénodet (8 daily; 45min); Camaret (5 daily; 1hr 30min); Concarneau (6 daily; 30min); Crozon (5 daily; 1hr 20min); Locronan (5 daily; 25min); Pointe du Raz (3 daily; 1hr 15min); Quimperlé (6 daily; 1hr 30min).

Rennes to: Dinan (hourly; 1hr); Dinard (8 daily; 1hr 40min); Fougères (7 daily; 1hr); Josselin (8 daily; 1hr); Vannes (8 daily; 2hr).

St-Brieuc to: Cap Fréhel via Val André and Erquy (4 daily; 1hr 40min); Dinan (4 daily; 1hr); Lannion via Guingamp (4 daily; 1hr 40min); Paimpol (8 daily; 1hr 30min).

St-Malo to: Cancale (4 daily; 35min); Combourg (2 daily; 1hr); Dinan (4 daily; 45min); Dinard (8 daily; 30min); Fougères via Pontorson (3 daily; 2hr); Mont St-Michel (4 daily; 1hr 30min); Rennes (3 daily; 2hr).

Vannes to: Carnac (3 daily; 1hr 15min); Quiberon (3 daily; 1hr 45min).

Ferries

St-Malo *Brittany Ferries* (St-Malo ☎99.82.41.41, Portsmouth ☎0705/827701) to: Portsmouth (1 daily mid-March to mid-Nov, otherwise less frequently; 9hr daytime crossing). Regular ferries to Dinard (10min) in season, operated by *Emeraude Lines* (☎99.40.48.40), who also sail to Dinan up the River Rance, and along the Brittany coast to Cap Fréhel, Cézembre and Dinard (May–Sept). They also go to Jersey (mid-March to mid-Nov), and to Guernsey and Sark (April–Sept), and to Îles Chausey and Granville in Normandy. *Condor Hydroglisseurs* (☎99.56.42.29) run services to Jersey (April–Sept 4 daily; Oct 2 daily; second half of March and first half of Nov 1 daily), Guernsey (April–Oct 2 daily; second half of March and first half of Nov 1 daily), and Sark (April–Oct daily), and on from the Channel Islands to Weymouth. *Channiland* (☎99.40.40.90) go to Jersey (mid-March to mid-Nov 1–4 daily), slightly less frequently to Guernsey and Sark.

Roscoff to: **Plymouth** (6hr) and **Cork** (13–17hr). Both services *Brittany Ferries* (Roscoff ☎98.29.28.28, Plymouth ☎0752/21321, Cork ☎215/07666). See p.11 for more details. Also to the Île de Batz (several times daily in season, irregularly out; 15min).

For details of ferries to **Ouessant** and **Molène** see p.353–354; to **Bréhat**, see p.345; to **Groix**, see p.371; to **Sein**, see p.363; to **Belle-Île**, see p.377; and for tours of the **Gulf of Morbihan** see p.381.

For general information on renting **barges** for use on the inland waterways, contact the *Comité de Promotion Touristique des Canaux Bretons*, Office du Tourisme, place du Parlement, 35600 Rennes (☎99.71.06.04).

CHAPTER SIX

THE LOIRE

Intimidated by the density of châteaux and all their great Renaissance intrigues and associations, many people tend to make bad use of time spent in the Loire. This is a pity, for if you pick your castles selectively, rid yourself of a sense of duty to the guided tours, and spend days on river banks supplied with cheese, fruit and white Loire wines, it can be one of the most enjoyable of all French regions.

The Loire's central region of **Touraine** is known as "the heart of France" and has the best wines, the most scented flowers and delicious fruit, two of the best châteaux in **Chenonceau** and **Azay-le-Rideau**, and, it's argued, the purest French accent in the land. It also takes in three of the Loire's most pleasurable tributaries: the Cher, Indre and Vienne, each with its own individual attractions. If you have just a week to spare for the region, then these are the parts to spend it in. The most imposing palaces and hunting lodges are upstream around **Blois** – including the Renaissance turreted fantasy of **Chambord** – with the wild and watery region of the **Sologne** to the east, good for long walks and rides, as well as the fascinating troglodyte dwellings carved out of the rockfaces around **Saumur**.

As well as the select handful of châteaux, the region has a few unexpected sights: most unmissably the gardens at **Villandry**, outside Tours, the Romanesque abbey at **St-Benoît-sur-Loire** and the stunning tapestries in **Angers**, capital of the ancient wineproducing county of **Anjou**. Of the cities, **Tours** and Angers provide the best urban bases, **Orléans** has charm, and **Le Mans**, though some way north of the Loire Valley in the topographically uninspiring *département* of **Sarthe**, is the least touristy and most authentically lively, even outside race times. Further upstream, and quite some distance south of the Loire itself, the marshy farming land of **Berry** contains few sights, apart from the magnificent cathedral and medieval town of **Bourges**, lying between the Loire and the Cher.

The lowest – and best – stretch of the **Loire** flows through Touraine, languidly floating by long islands of reed and willows before it reaches its estuary. But the Loire is still the wild river of whirlpools, quicksands, shifting banks and channels, with vicious currents and a propensity to flood. Plans to control the water levels of the central stretch with dams have been dropped, thanks to hard campaigning by conservationists,

---

ACCOMMODATION PRICE CATEGORIES

All the hotels, youth hostels and guesthouses listed in this book have been price-graded according to the following scale, and although costs will rise slightly overall with the life of this edition, the relative comparisons should remain valid. Paris and the large cities will, as anywhere, be more expensive than equivalent accommodation in the countryside or small towns. The prices quoted are for the cheapest available double room in high season, although remember that many of the cheap places will have more expensive rooms with en-suite facilities.

① Under 160F	④ 300–400F	⑦ 600–700F
② 160–220F	⑤ 400–500F	⑧ Over 700F
③ 220–300F	⑥ 500–600F	

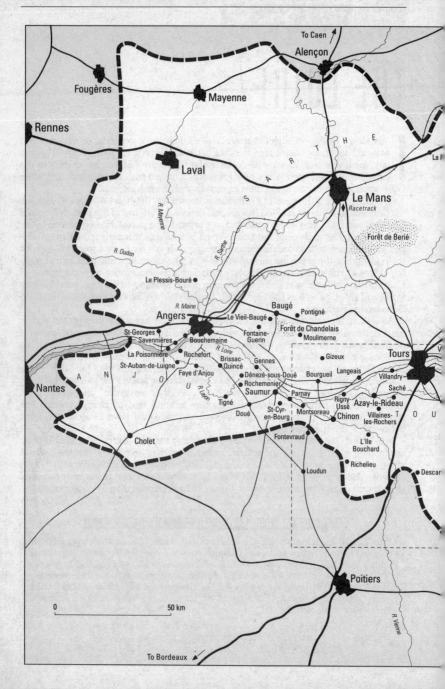

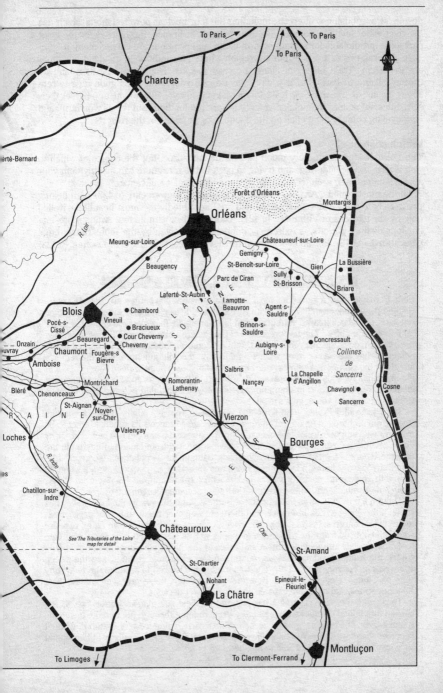

despite strong business interests, including the four nuclear power stations which use the river water for their cooling. The longest river in France, the Loire is for the most part too unpredictable for swimming or boating, and no goods are carried along it.

In general, this is a prime tourism region where air-conditioned cars and bus tours are the norm. Train lines run along the river towards Nantes and Brittany and up through Tours to Paris, but if you're exploring on your own, it's a good idea to rent some means of transport, at least for occasional forays. Buses can be sparse, their schedules not geared to outsiders, and trains are too limiting. But this is wonderful and easy cycling country, best of all on the floodbanks, or *levées*, of the river itself.

Which châteaux?

The Loire **châteaux** are very much part of the landscape, but the choice of which to visit is vast and bewildering, and trying to pack in the maximum can quickly dent your appreciation of their architecture, settings and historical significance.

Of the most famous, **Azay-le-Rideau** (p.427) and **Chenonceau** (p.423) both belong exclusively to the Renaissance period and are undoubtedly the most beautiful, rivalled only by the gardens of **Villandry** (p.421). **Blois** (p.410), with its four wings representing four distinct periods, is extremely impressive, followed by the monstrously huge **Chambord** (p.413). For an evocation of medieval times, the citadel of **Loches** (p.428)

THE FOOD AND DRINK OF THE LOIRE

Fish from the river features on most restaurant menus. Favourites are *filet de sandre* (pickerel), salmon, often flavoured with sorrel, stuffed bream and eels softened in mature red wine, and plates heaped with deep-fried little smelt-like fishes served under the name "*la friture de la Loire*". The favoured meat of the eastern Loire is **game**. Pheasant, guinea fowl, pigeon, duck, quails, young rabbit, venison and even wild boar are all hunted in the Sologne. They are served in rich sauces made from the wild mushrooms of the region's forests or the common *champignon de Paris*, cultivated on a huge scale in caves cut out of the limestone rock along the Loire and its tributaries. Both Tours and Le Mans specialize in *rillettes* or potted pork; in Touraine *charcuteries* you'll also find *pâté au biquion*, made from pork, veal and young goat's meat.

The Loire valley is also great **fruit**- and **vegetable**-growing country. There are green-gages from orchards in Anjou, called *Reine Claudes* after François I's queen. Market stalls overflow with summer fruits, and old varieties of apples and pears can still be found. *Tarte Tatin*, an upside-down apple tart, is said to have originated from Lamotte-Beuvron in the Sologne. Tours is famous for its French beans, Saumur for its potatoes. Asparagus (the best from Vineuil) appears in soufflés, omelettes and other egg dishes, as well as on its own with vinaigrette made (if you're lucky) with local walnut oil. Finally, from Berry, comes the humble lentil, whose green variety often accompanies salmon or trout.

Though not as famous as the produce of Bordeaux and Burgundy, the Loire valley has some of the finest **wines** in France, and there are well over twenty different *appellations* to discover. Sancerre, halfway along the river, produces some well-known flinty, very dry white wines made from the Sauvignon grape, as well as some good reds and a rosé (see p.442). There are the mellow whites and rosés of the Anjou vineyards in the west (see p.403), the fruity sparkling *méthode champenoise* wines around Saumur, and the sweet, still wines of Vouvray (see p.419). The Cabernet grape is used to produce the rich, ruby reds of Chinon (see p.430) and Bourgueil (see p.422); these are some of the best Touraine wines, and many are capable of maturing over decades.

To go with the wine, Touraine has some of the best soft goat's **cheese**: Ste-Maure, shaped into a long cylinder with a piece of straw running through the middle; the small, round *crottin de Chavignol* goat's cheese from Sancerre, eaten fresh or matured, when it becomes hard with a very sharp flavour; the pyramid-shaped Pouligny-St-Pierre and Valençay; and the flat, round Selles-sur-Cher.

is hard to beat; other feudal fortresses include the lesser-known **Fougères-sur-Bièvre** (p.413), the ruined **Chinon** (p.430), **Langeais** (p.422), still furnished in fifteenth-century style, **Meung-sur-Loire** (p.399), with its vile dungeons, and **Amboise** (p.420).

Many châteaux that started life as serious military defences were turned into luxurious residences by their regal or ducal owners: good examples are **Brissac** (p.442), **Chaumont** (p.412), with its nineteenth-century stables, **Ussé** (see p.427) and **Sully** (p.401); at Ussé and Sully it is the setting and exterior appearance that are most striking, so you can admire them without forking out for admission. **Le Plessis-Bourré** (p.442) is a fine example of late fifteenth-century elegant residence and strong defences combined. At **Valençay** (p.426), the interior of the Renaissance château is Napoléonic; **Cheverny** (p.412) is the prime example of seventeenth-century magnificence; its neighbour **Beauregard** (p.413) encloses a sixteenth-century core with seventeenth-century additions but is most famous for its portrait gallery. Other châteaux are more compelling for their contents than for their architecture: **Argent-sur-Sauldre** (p.404), with a brilliant ceramics collection; **St-Brisson** (p.403), with art exhibitions and medieval weaponry demonstrations; cadillacs at the château in **St-Michel-sur-Loire** (p.422); a museum of living donkeys at **Gizeux** (p.422); and **La Bussière** (p.402), celebrating fish and fishing in a fine lake setting with Le Nôtre gardens. At **Saumur** (p.432), a museum of the horse rivals the attraction of the castle itself, while at **Angers** (p.436) the extremely impressive medieval castle pales into insignificance when set against the tapestry of the Apocalypse it houses, the greatest work of art in the Loire valley.

Entry prices can be pretty steep, particularly for the privately owned châteaux. There is no consistency in the concessions offered: if you're over 65, under 25, a student, or still at school, check for any reductions and make sure you've got proof of age or a student card with you.

Orléans and around

ORLÉANS is the most northern city on the Loire, sitting at the apex of a huge arc in the river as it switches direction and starts to flow southwest. The proximity to Paris, just over a hundred kilometres away, is a problem for this ancient city. Not only do many Orléanais go to Paris for their evenings out, they commute to work there as well. To counter its subordinate position as a country suburb to the capital, Orléans feels compelled to recoup its faded glory from the turning point in the Hundred Years' War (1339–1453), when Paris was infested by disease and the English, and Orléans itself as the key city to central France, were under siege.

Despite a rich early history of being a centre of revolt against Julius Cæsar in 52 BC (for which it was burnt to the ground), besieged by Attila the Hun in the mid-fifth century, and elevated to the position of temporary capital of the Frankish kingdom in 498, it is Joan of Arc's deliverance of the city in 1429 that the town feels bound to commemorate. Crazed or divinely inspired, the seventeen-year-old peasant girl had presented herself to the Dauphin, the uncrowned Charles VII, at Chinon (see p.430), rallied French troops at Blois and then led them up the Loire to confront the English at Orléans. She informed the encircling army that God had sent her to throw them out of France, and proceeded to break all military rules and raise the siege. The Maid of Orléans is honoured everywhere in town, though nothing contradicts the overriding feeling that she was, and is, a myth.

There's been a lot of new building and tarting up of the city over the last five years. It may not have provided much aesthetic improvement, which is difficult given the beauty of Orléans' ancient buildings, but it's been a valiant and not entirely vain attempt to bring back some pride to the place.

Arrival and accommodation

The **Centre d'Arc**, a hideous shopping centre on place d'Arc, is the first thing you'll see stepping out of the **gare SNCF** (info ☎38.53.50.50; reservations ☎38.62.56.65). The **tourist office** is in the Centre d'Arc on the south side overlooking place Albert-1er (Mon–Sat 9am–6.30pm, Sun 10am–noon; July & Aug Mon–Sat 9am–6.30pm, Sun 9.30am–12.30pm & 3–6.30pm; ☎38.53.05.95), where you can pick up *Orléans Poche*, a free **listings magazine** telling what's going on around the town. The **gare routière**, on rue Marcel Proust (☎38.53.94.75), is a short way northeast off rue Prince Albert 1er.

Accommodation in Orléans is good, with a few cheap hotels near the unusually appealing station area, and a youth hostel and campsites not too far out.

Hotels

Hôtel de Blois, 1 av de Paris (☎38.62.61.61). The *Blois* is above a brasserie opposite the station and can be noisy unless you get a back room. Rather dingy but certainly a bargain. ①.
Hôtel Charles Sanglier, 8 rue Charles-Sanglier (☎38.53.38.50). A comfortable enough and very central hotel. ②.
Jackotel, 18 Cloître St-Aignan (☎38.54.48.48). Charming hotel with a small garden and views onto the cloisters of St-Aignan. ③–④.
Marguerite, 14 pl du Vieux-Marché (☎38.53.74.32). Not a particularly special place, except for its location on the market square. ③.
Hôtel de Paris, 29 Faubourg Bannier (☎38.53.39.58). Small, very cheap but pleasant rooms, just across place Gambetta from the *gare SNCF*. ①–②.
Saint-Aignan, 3 pl Gambetta (☎38.53.15.35). Pleasant service in a good-value hotel. ③–④.

Youth hostels and campsites

Youth hostel, 14 rue du Faubourg-Madeleine (☎38.62.45.75). The hostel is on the continuation of rue Porte-Madeleine to the west of town by bus #B, direction *Paul-Bert* from the *gares SNCF* and *routière*. Reception is open 7.15–9.30am and 5.30–10/10.30pm; curfew 10/10.30pm. Mid-Feb to Nov; mid-Feb to March closed Sat. ①.
Olivet campsite, rue du Pont-Bouchet in Olivet (☎38.63.53.94). Seven kilometres south of Orléans between the River Loiret and the Loire; bus #O or #S to *Aumône*. April–Sept.
St-Jean-de-la-Ruelle campsite, rue de la Roche, St-Jean-de-la-Ruelle (☎38.88.39.39). The closest campsite to Orléans is 2.5km away out on the Blois road, reached by bus #D, stop *Roche aux Fées*. April–Sept.

The City

Saint Joan turns up all over town. In pride of place in the large, central **place du Martroi**, at the end of rue de la République, rises a bulky mid-nineteenth-century likeness of her on horseback, with a series of copper-green friezes around the base, depicting scenes from her action-filled life. To the east, the **Cathédrale Ste-Croix** (daily 9am–noon & 2–6pm), battered for the best part of 600 years by various wars, is full of Joan of Arc, who celebrated her victory over the English here. In the north transept, her pedestal is supported by two jagged and golden leopards, representing the English, on an altar carved with the battle scene. In the nave, the late nineteenth-century stained glass windows tell the story of her life, starting from the north transept, with caricatures of the loutish Anglo-Saxons and snooty French nobles. Across place d'Étape from the cathedral, outside the red-brick Renaissance **Hôtel de Ville**, Joan appears again, in pensive mood, her skirt now shredded by twentieth-century bullets.

You are spared the Maid in the **Musée des Beaux-Arts**, opposite the Hôtel de Ville (daily except Tues 10am–noon & 2–6pm; 16F), where the main collections are of fourteenth- to sixteenth-century Italian, Dutch and Flemish work on the second floor and eighteenth-century French portraits on the first floor. If you'd rather escape to more recent times, however, head down to the modern art collection in the basement, with canvases by Picasso, Miró, Braque, Dufy, Renoir and Monet, as well as Auguste Rodin's studies of Gauguin, and photographs of Picasso by Man Ray.

If you follow rue Jeanne d'Arc east from the cathedral and turn left down rue Charles-Sanglier you'll find the ornate sixteenth-century **Hôtel Cabu**, which houses a collection of rather beautiful bronze animals from the Gallo-Roman period, along with medieval ivories and more Joan of Arc mementos. The entrance is on square Abbé Desnoyers (daily 10am–noon & 2–6pm; 11F).

At the end of rue Jeanne-d'Arc, on place Général-de-Gaulle, is the semitimbered **Maison de Jeanne d'Arc** (Tues–Sun 10am–noon & 2–6pm; Nov–April 2–6pm; 35F). The building is a 1960s reconstruction of the house where Joan stayed and its contents are fun, most of all for children, with good models and displays of the breaking of the Orléans siege. Despite the consistency in artists' renderings of the saint, it seems the

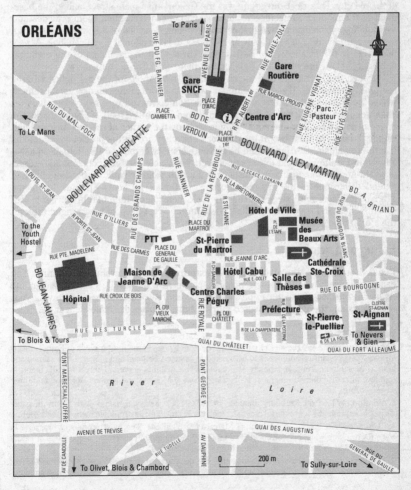

pageboy haircut and demure little face are part of the myth – there is no contemporary portrait of her, save for a clerk's doodle in the margin of the trial proceedings, kept in the Paris archives.

If you read French, the **Centre Charles Péguy**, 11 rue Tabour (Mon–Fri 2–6pm; free), down the road from Joan's house in a Renaissance mansion, is worth a visit. It takes its themes from the life and work of Charles Péguy (1873–1914), a Christian Socialist writer from Orléans. Though there are cartoons and drawings, the main exhibits are texts. Among various books and pamphlets, there's Zola's front-page *J'accuse* letter to the president and the explanations by both sides in the Dreyfus affair, when a Jewish army officer was convicted of treason in 1894 on forged evidence; and documentation of the 1907 general strike call for the 40-hour week (which only became effective in 1936).

If you head back east, and down towards the river, you'll find the scattered vestiges of the old city. **Rue de Bourgogne** was the Gallo-Roman main street, and in the basement of the modern Préfecture at no. 9, a spartan civic reception room provides odd surroundings for an excavated first-century dwelling – or bits of it – and the walls of a ninth-century church. It's not a site as such: ask the receptionist if you can look. Across the street is the façade of the **Salles des Thèses**, all that remains of the medieval university of Orléans where the Reformation theologian Calvin studied law.

Between the Préfecture and the river, the narrow streets of the old industrial area surround the former **Dessaux vinegar works**, a turn-of-the-century establishment whose buildings encircle the house Isabelle Romée moved to a few years after her daughter Joan was burned at the stake in Rouen. Down the road, a plaque marks the house of Joan's brother and companion-in-arms on the corner of rue des Africains and rue de la Folie. At least two of the quarter's churches are on the precious-monuments list: the remains of **St-Aignan** and its eleventh-century crypt, and the Romanesque **St-Pierre-le-Puellier**, an old university church that's now used for concerts and exhibitions. St-Aignan was destroyed during the English siege, rebuilt by the Dauphin and extended into one of the greatest churches in France by Louis XII. But during the Wars of Religion more sieges of the city took their toll on the church, leaving it with just the choir and transepts standing. Visits to the crypt need to be arranged through the tourist office.

Eating and drinking

Rue de Bourgogne is the main street for **restaurant** menu browsing and nightlife. You can choose from among French, Spanish, North African, Middle Eastern, Indian and Asian cuisines, all of which can be sampled at very reasonable prices. For buying your own provisions there are the covered **market halls** on place du Châtelet, near the river.

Restaurants

Les Antiquaires, 2 & 4 rue au Lin (☎38.53.52.35). Run by one of the master chefs of France, this is Orléans' best restaurant and needs to be booked in advance. Seafood and ginger, Loire salmon and a soup of summer fruits and honey are some of the delights served. There's a 110F menu at midday; otherwise there's a menu at 190F. Closed Sun & Mon, second week in April and first three weeks of Aug.

L'Aviation, 473 bd du Faubourg Bannier (☎38.73.91.88). Seasonal menus with plenty of game dishes in autumn and a wonderful crayfish omelette. From 100F; gastronomic menu around 200F.

La Chancellerie, 95 rue Royale, cnr pl Matroi (☎38.53.57.54). The most prominent brasserie in town for drinking wine, beer or cocktails till midnight, indulging in ice cream concoctions or eating good solid *plats du jour* from 50F; menus from 65F. Closed Sun.

Le Dakar, 224 rue du Faubourg Bourgogne, the continuation of rue Bourgogne (☎38.62.88.04). Caribbean and African specialities from 80F in pleasant surroundings. Closed Sun and Mon midday.

Le Restaurant des Plantes, 44 rue Tudelle (☎38.56.65.55). On the south side of the river, this restaurant serves traditional dishes such as *magret de canard* and snails. 95F weekday menu, otherwise from 120F. Closed Mon and first 3 weeks in Aug.

La Ripaille, 14 pl du Châtelet (☎38.54.56.85). Simple grilled meat and fish with salads served up in a convivial atmosphere. Menus from 70F.

Bars and nightlife

Club Paxton's Head, 264–266 rue de Bourgogne. Funky jazz cellar with local jam sessions Wed night and concerts at 11pm Fri and Sat. Tues–Sat 10pm–3am.

Le Miami Club, 17 bd Jean-Jaurès. A bar with billiards, videos, loud music, and a Happy Hour from 5pm opening to 8.30pm. Closed Sun and Mon.

Le Saint Patrick, 1 rue de Bourgogne. Irish brasserie and bar with a fine selection of beers and whiskeys, plus pool, darts and music some nights. Mon–Fri 11am–1am, Sat 7pm–1am.

Listings

Banks There are banks around place Martroi.

Bike rental Available from the tourist office and the youth hostel.

Car rental *Avis*, 13 rue Sansonnières (☎38.62.27.04); *Budget*, 5 rue Sansonnières (☎38.54.54.30); *Europcar*, 81 rue A-Dessaux (☎38.73.00.40); *Hertz*, 47 av de Paris (☎38.62.60.60).

Festivals *Fête de Jeanne d'Arc*, a period piece parade on May 7–8; *Festival de Jazz d'Orléans* in early July; *Semaines Musicales Internationales d'Orléans*, Nov–Dec; programme details and bookings from the tourist office.

Medical assistance *SAMU* (☎38.63.33.33); *Centre Hospitalier*, 1 rue Porte Madeleine (☎38.51.44.44).

Police 63 rue du Faubourg St-Jean (☎38.81.63.00).

Poste Restante Place de Gaulle, 45031 Orléans Cedex 1.

Public transport Bus information available from *SEMTAO* office (☎38.71.98.38), in the Centre d'Arc shopping mall in place Albert 1er.

Taxis ☎38.53.11.11.

Youth Information Centre *Régional d'Information Jeunesse*, 5 bd de Verdon (☎38.54.37.70).

Meung-sur-Loire

Little streams, known as *Les Mauves*, flow between the houses in the village of **MEUNG-SUR-LOIRE**, 14km southwest of Orléans on the Blois rail line, leaving slimy green high-water marks during the summer months. But the sound of water is always pleasant and Meung is no bad place to spend an afternoon.

Meung has had a number of literary associations throughout the years. Over seven hundred years ago one Jean de Meung added 18,000 lines to the already 4000-line-long *Roman de la Rose* (Romance of the Rose), written half a century earlier in 1225 by Guillaume de Lorris. This extended tale of courtly love, all very formal and allegorical, enthused Chaucer, who wrote his own version before moving on to more material topics. More recently, the town featured in the works of Georges Simenon – his fictional hero, Maigret, takes his holidays here.

The town's most notable and imposing building is its grisly **château**, built for the Bishops of Orléans in the early Middle Ages (Sat & Sun 10–11.30am & 2–5pm; July–Sept daily 9am–5.30pm; April–June daily 10–11.30am & 2–5.30pm; Oct to mid-Nov daily 10–11.30am & 2–5pm; 25F). The exterior of the château on the side facing the old drawbridge looks suitably spooky, retaining its thirteenth-century pepperpot towers, even though much of the interior is due to nineteenth-century remodelling. The highlight of the guided tour is, of course, the dreaded dungeon, where you're better off with minimal imagination; it was here that the poet François Villon (1431–1485) – originator of the much-quoted line *"Où sont les nieges d'autan?"* ("Where are the snows of yester-year?") – was imprisoned and where he is supposed to have written his famous *Grand Testament*. He is the only known survivor of this monstrous prison, where people were abandoned to die.

If you feel remotely inspired to pen a few poetic lines yourself as you loiter over lunch, the *Café du Commerce*, on place de l'Église, is the ideal scenario (closed Mon; several menus under 120F).

Beaugency

BEAUGENCY is a pretty little town, 6km southwest of Meung along the Loire; in spite of its size and picturesque qualities, it has played its part in the conniving games of early medieval politics. In 1152, the marriage of Louis VII of France and Eleanor of Aquitaine was annulled by the Council of Beaugency in the church of Notre-Dame, allowing Eleanor to marry Henry Plantagenet, the future Henry II. Her huge lands in southwest France passed to the English crown, which already controlled Normandy, Maine, Anjou and Touraine, and the struggles between the French and English kings over their claims to these territories – and to the French throne itself – lasted for centuries.

Liberated by the indefatigable Joan of Arc on her way to Orléans in 1429, Beaugency was a constant battleground in the Hundred Years' War due to its strategic significance as the only Loire bridge-crossing at that time between Orléans and Blois. Remarkably, the 26-arch **bridge** still stands and gives an excellent view of the once heavily fortified medieval heart of the town. The two central squares – **place St-Firmin**, with its statue of Joan and a tower of a church destroyed during the Revolution, and **place Dunois** – are atmospherically lit by flickering gaslights. Place Dunois is bordered by the massive eleventh-century **Tour de César** that was formerly part of the rather plain fifteenth-century **Château Dunois**, now housing a small museum of traditional Orléanais life, whose guided tours can definitely be given a miss. The square is completed by the rather severe Romanesque **abbey church of Notre-Dame**, the venue for the Council's fatal matrimonial decision in 1152.

Today the town casts a much more romantic image of the medieval period, and wandering the streets of the attractive old town and idling along the shaded river bank are probably the best ways of passing the time peacefully here. But if the urge to sight-see is strong, go and look at the **embroidered wall hangings** in the council chamber of the **Hôtel de Ville** on place du Docteur-Hyvernaud, two blocks north of place Dunois (open office hours, ask at reception; free). One set illustrates the four continents as perceived in the seventeenth century, with the rest dramatizing pagan rites such as gathering mistletoe and sacrificing animals.

If you want to stay in town, the cheapest **hotel** is the *Hôtel des Vieux Fossés*, 4 rue des Vieux Fossés (☎38.44.51.65; ①–②). If you want somewhere special, the *Hôtel de l'Abbaye*, 2 quai de l'Abbaye (☎38.44.67.35; ⑤–⑦), is a beautiful eighteenth-century abbey with painted ceilings and beds on raised platforms. Much cheaper, equally pleasant, but less grand is the *Hôtel de la Sologne*, 6 pl St-Firmin (☎38.44.50.27; ③–⑤). There's also an IYHF **youth hostel** in the suburb of Vernon at 152 rte de Châteaudun, 2km north off the main Orléans-Blois road from the east side of town (☎38.44.61.31; ①).

There are no very special restaurants in Beaugency, but a good place to **drink** is *Le Moulin Rouge* at 2 rue de la Bonde, east of rue du Pont (Tues–Sun 5pm–1am). It has good beers and live blues, jazz and rock some weekends.

East to the Burgundy border

Upstream from Orléans, single-lane roads run along the top of the flood banks of the Loire, ideal for cycling. To the north is the rambling **Forest of Orléans**, densely planted and criss-crossed with roads. Beyond it, a bland, treeless wheat plain stretches to Paris, and the immediate countryside to the south is likewise drab: sticking to the Loire itself is the best advice.

Along the river are plenty of lesser-known attractions, most notably **St Benoît's abbey**, the **château of Sully**, the small town of **Gien**, the **aqueduct at Briare** and the vines of **Sancerre** right on the Burgundy border, which certainly make the most popular dry whites of the region.

If you're out on, or in, the river, or even camping on the bank, beware that the Loire's placid flow along these reaches is deceptive; it can swell within 24 hours and has been known to break its banks.

Germigny-des-Prés and St-Benoît

An afternoon's bike ride, or a short drive, east out of Orléans, crossing to the north bank at **CHÂTEAUNEUF-SUR-LOIRE** – where there is a château with very pleasant gardens of magnolias and rhododendrons – brings you to **GERMIGNY-DES-PRÉS**, whose church was built in 806 in the form of a Greek cross (daily 9am–7pm). The eastern apse is original, with a rare early gold and silver mosaic on the dome, showing angels and the Ark of the Covenant. It survived because it was covered by distemper and only discovered by accident in the middle of last century, when children were found playing with coloured glass cubes in the church.

A few kilometres further south along the D60, **ST-BENOÎT-SUR-LOIRE** offers an even more impressive ancient edifice: the **Abbaye de Fleury**, where a marble mosaic of Roman origin covers the chancel floor of one of the most awe-inspiring Romanesque churches in France, built in pale yellow and cream-coloured stone between 1020 and 1218 (daily 7am–10pm; guided visits daily at 3pm, Mon–Sat 10.30am; English possible; 25F). The oldest part of the church, the porch, illustrates the Vision of the Apocalypse by the fantastically sculpted capitals and by the layout that follows the description of the New Jerusalem in Revelations – foursquare, with twelve foundations and three open gates on each side. The rest of the abbey was destroyed during the Revolution.

Sully-sur-Loire

SULLY-SUR-LOIRE lies on the south bank of the Loire, 7km east of St-Benoît and accessible by bus from Orléans. The grand **château** here is pure fantasy (daily mid-June to mid-Sept 10am–6pm; March to mid-June & mid-Sept to Nov 10am–noon & 2–5/6pm; closed Dec–Feb; guided visits only; 12F), despite savage wartime bombing that twice destroyed the nearby Loire bridge and caused incidental damage to the château itself. The interior is not particularly interesting, apart from the immaculate fourteenth-century chestnut timberwork of the keep, but from the outside, rising massively out of its gigantic moat, the château has all the picturebook requirements of pointed towers, machicolations and drawbridge. Whether sunlit or floodlit, it is a treat.

The castle originally belonged to one of Charles VII's favourites, La Trémoille, who infuriated Joan of Arc by encouraging the Dauphin to forget about the throne and loaf about in Sully eating nice dinners of deer and wild boar. After Joan's failure to liberate Paris in 1430, he attempted to ground her by virtually imprisoning her in the castle – to no avail. The castle changed hands in 1602, this time being snapped up by Henri IV's minister, the Duke of Sully, who added the moat and park, and pushed out the river bank to protect his glorious creation from the vagaries of the Loire. After Henri's death, the arrogant minister was forced into retirement, which he spent writing in his castle. In the eighteenth century young Voltaire, exiled from Paris for libellous political verse, also spent time at the château, sharpening his wit on the company of enlightened thinkers with whom the Duke of Sully of the time liked to surround himself.

From June 15 to July 15 the **International Music Festival** features concerts of contemporary, jazz and classical music in the château's Salle des Gardes and in a medieval-style pavillion in the park – you can find out more details from the **tourist office** on place du Général-de-Gaulle at the southern end of the old town (☎38.36.23.70).

The best place to **stay** in Sully is in the spacious rooms of the *Hostellerie du Grand Sully*, 10 bd du Champ de Foire (☎38.36.27.56; ③–④). Alternatively, there's a serene municipal **campsite** (☎38.36.23.93) with a great location by the river, practically in the grounds of the château.

Gien and around

The fifteenth-century red- and black-brick **château** at **GIEN** – where the young Louis XIV and his bride Anne d'Autriche hid during the revolts against taxation known as the *Frondes* – has been turned over to a **Musée de la Chasse**, with weapons, victims stuffed or skeletal, horns and antlers, plus paintings, pottery and tapestries venerating the sport (Tues–Sun 10am–noon & 2–5pm; May Mon–Fri 10am–noon & 2–5pm, Sat & Sun 9.30am–6.30pm; June–Sept daily 9.30am–6.30pm; closed Dec & Feb; 25F). The squat building itself is hardly worth the climb to reach it, though the interior is quite striking, with its combination of timbered ceilings and brick; it's worth remembering that one of the material gains of the French Revolution of great importance for rural people was the right to hunt, although the exhibits here are dominated by depictions of royal and aristocratic hunting as a sport.

The town of Gien is pretty enough, having been restored to its late fifteenth-century quaintness after extensive wartime bombing, and the sixteenth-century stone **bridge** spanning the river gives excellent views of its medieval mass as you approach from the south. Gien also has a history of fine china making, and there's a **museum** of the art in the cellars of the old workshops within the present-day factory on place de la Victoire, 1km west of the château and bridge (Mon–Sat 9am–noon & 2–6.30pm, Sun 10am–noon & 2–6pm; Feb–May Mon–Sat 9am–noon & 1.45–6.15pm, Sun 10am–noon & 2–6pm; Nov–Jan Mon–Sat 10am–noon & 1.45–6.15pm, Sun 10am–noon & 2–6pm; 16F). There are some beautiful nineteenth-century pieces and a video showing current fabrication techniques which you can see for real in the factory during the week (appointment only; ☎38.67.00.05).

The **tourist office** on place Jean-Jaurès, between the château and the river (☎38.67.25.28), is extremely helpful, with a lot of information on the region, and will make hotel reservations for you. Possible **hotels** in town are the *Relais Normand*, 64 pl de la Victoire (☎38.67.28.56; ①–②), or *Le Rivage*, 1 quai de Nice (☎38.37.79.00; ④–⑥), very hospitable and well situated by the bridge. The *Camping Touristique de Gien*, 500m west of the bridge across the river on rue des Iris (☎38.67.12.50), is quiet and well equipped, with a good view of the town. As for **food**, *Le Rivage* does good menus from 155F, or you could try *Coté Jardin* south of the river, 14 rte de Bourges (☎38.38.24.67; closed Sat midday), with menus from 100F.

La Bussière and the Château de St-Brisson

Twelve kilometres northeast of Gien is another château dedicated to the evolving techniques of catching supper, this time fishing. The **Château de La Bussière** is parked like a yacht on its lake, connected to a formal arrangement on its mainland of gardens and huge outbuildings (daily except Tues April–Nov 11 10am–noon & 2–6pm; July & Aug daily; 25F). Initially a fortress, the château was turned into a luxurious residence at the end of the sixteenth century, but only the gateway and one pepperpot tower are recognizably medieval. Inside, tanks of freshwater fish and a coelacanth, one of the oldest fishes known, with paddle-like fins and a world-weary expression, are the key exhibits, but the seventeenth-century kitchens and old laundry are quite fun as well.

On the south side of the Loire, halfway between Sully and Gien, medieval weaponry is the theme at the **Château de St-Brisson** (ring ☎38.36.71.29 for details; 25F). Demonstrations are given at 3.30pm and 4.30pm every other Sunday during summer in the moat, using bows and arrows, battering rams and devices to lob stones around. The château also has an art gallery with changing exhibitions of painting, sculpture and photography, which makes up for the rather unattractive mix of styles (from the twelfth century to the seventeenth century) of the building itself.

Briare

The small village of **BRIARE**, 10km from Gien on the Orléans–Nevers road and the Paris–Nevers rail line, centres on its Belle-Époque iron aqueduct, the **Pont Canal**, linking the Canal de Briare to the north with the Canal Lateral à la Loire, which runs south to the Sâone. The design of the Pont Canal came from the workshops of Gustav Eiffel of Eiffel Tower fame, but parts of the canal scheme date back to the early seventeenth century, when internal waterways linking the Mediterranean, Atlantic and Channel coasts were devised. You can walk along the aqueduct's extraordinary 625-metre span, with its wrought-iron crested lamps and railings, hopefully without a *bateau-mouche* spoiling the effect.

At the **Musée de l'Automobile**, 500m out of town on the Nevers road (daily noon–6pm; 30F), the junk-shop approach to curating lends a relaxed atmosphere. Crammed into an assortment of warehouses, the absorbing exhibits range from electric bubble cars and penny-farthings to modern racing cars, steam engines and model car collections, all in a state of theme-less disorder. You can wander at your leisure and, having seen the tank in the garden, finish the visit in a suitably anomalous railway bar done out with antique furniture and racing trophies. The museum also rents out **bikes** if you want to peddle along the towpaths or south into the Forest of St-Brisson.

The **tourist office**, 9 pl de la République (daily 10am–noon & 2–5pm; ☎38.31.24.51), can provide details of canal boats and canoe rental, as well as providing maps of footpaths, towpaths and the locks (the one at Chatillon-sur-Loire, 4km upstream, is particularly appealing). For **accommodation**, there's a modern hotel right next to the bridge, the *Hostellerie du Pont Canal*, 19 rue du Pont-Canal (☎38.31.22.54; ④).

Sancerre

Unless you're heading upstream towards Nevers, there's not much justification for stopping at **SANCERRE**, given that you can buy its wines anywhere. But there's something appealing about seeing the vineyards whose fruit you are drinking, plus, of course, the advantages of visits to *vignerons*, who tend to be small-scale traditional winemakers. Sancerre is an extremely dry wine made from the Sauvignon grape. The white is the most renowned but there are good reds as well, and the rarer rosé is exquisite. To go with the wines, the local cheese speciality is the *crottin de Chavignol* from a neighbouring village to the west.

The village huddles at the top of a steep, round hill with the vineyards below. There's a lovely hotel with superb views to the north, the *Panoramic*, Rempart des Augustines (☎48.54.22.44; ③–④), along with two excellent **restaurants**: *La Pomme* *d'Or*, 1 rue de la Panneterie (☎48.54.13.30; closed Sun midday & Mon), with menus from 80F, and *La Tour*, 31 Nouvelle Place (☎48.54.01.36), with menus from 100F.

You can visit some of the **vignerons** in the area, like M. Raimbault at the *Caves de la Mignonne* (☎48.54.07.06), on the D955 towards St-Satar on the left; M. Archambault at *Caves du Clos de la Perrière* on the D134 in Verdigny-en-Sancerre (☎48.54.16.93), to the west of St-Satur; and M. Laporte at the *Cave de la Cresle* on the D57 (☎48.54.04.07), to the northwest. In Chavignol, you'll see signs for visits to *fromageries*, where you can try the hard goat's-cheese *crottins*.

La Sologne

Between the Loire and the Cher, from Gien in the east almost as far as Blois in the west, lies the area known as the **Sologne**, marked to the southeast by the low, abrupt **Collines du Sancerrois**, northwest of Sancerre. The autoroute, main road and rail line from Orléans to Bourges run almost together through the middle of the area.

Depending on the weather and the season it can be one of the most dismal areas in central France: damp, flat, featureless and foggy. But at other times its forests, lakes, ponds and marshes have a quiet magic – in summer when the heather is in bloom and the ponds are full of water lilies, or in early autumn when you can go hunting for wild mushrooms, egg-yolk orange *chanterelles* smelling of apricots, or *cèpes*, with caps like suede and bulging pure white stalks. Wild boar and deer roam here, not to mention ducks, geese, quails and pheasants; the human population is small.

Two *Grands Randonées* run through the Sologne, the **GR41** and **GR3C**, and there are numerous other paths, well signposted and detailing the accessibility for bicycles. From Easter to the end of October, tourist offices in most of Sologne's towns and villages can provide maps, details of bike rental or horse riding, as well as accommodation details. If you're exploring the Sologne after October 1, when the hunting season begins, don't stray from the marked paths.

Domaine du Ciran

Halfway between Ménestreau-en-Villette and Marcilly-en-Villette and 6km east of La Ferté-St-Aubin, just off the D108, is the little hamlet of **CIRAN**. Its tiny château has a **Musée de la Vie Traditionelle**, with photos showing such delights as dogs being used to pull carts, among other local revelations (daily 10am–noon & 2–5.30/6pm; winter closed Tues; 20F). But the main reason to come here is to explore the 300 hectares of the **Domaine de Ciran** and see its working farm, a typical Sologne set-up where the principal activities are deer breeding, keeping goats and making *chèvre*, as well as growing acres of asparagus. You may well catch a glimpse of wild deer in the forested parts of the *domaine* as well as herons and geese around the ponds, and even coypus rustling about. It's also possible to come across wild boar, so be careful, though they are not very threatening unless they're with their babies. The six-kilometre signed walk – for which waterproof footwear is advisable – gives you an excellent taste of the different landscapes of the Sologne.

Argent-sur-Sauldre and around

The thirteenth-century château just outside the village of **ARGENT-SUR-SAULDRE**, on the D940 between Gien and Bourges, houses the unmissable **Musée Vassil Ivanoff** in its grounds (May–Sept Mon–Fri 2–7pm, Sat & Sun 10am–noon & 2–6pm; 16F), containing a small, fascinating collection of modern ceramics. The Bulgarian Ivanoff came to France in the 1920s and settled in La Borne, a small village in the

There is much dispute as to where the magical party in **Alain-Fournier's novel** *Le Grand Meaulnes* was set, despite the fact that it was clearly an imaginary mixture of many places. Fournier was born in La Chapelle d'Angillon, 24km south of Argent-sur-Sauldre on the D940. He spent much of his childhood in the château there, but went to school in Epineuil-le-Fleurial (the Ste-Agathe of the novel) well beyond the Sologne and Bourges, some 25km south of St-Armand-Montrond (turn right off the Montluçon road from Bourges to cross the Cher at Meaulne). Albicoco's film of the book was shot around Epineuil, and the elementary school described in the book can be visited outside class hours. But the "domain with no name" where the *"fête étrange"* takes place is certainly in the Sologne: "In the whole of the Sologne", he wrote, "it would have been hard to find a more desolate spot." Nançay, between Salbris and La Chapelle d'Angillon on the D944, has a **Musée Imaginaire du Grand Meaulnes** dedicated to the novelist within the **Galaria Capazza**, an excellent gallery of contemporary art housed in one of the outbuildings of the château (Sat, Sun & hols 9.30am–12.30pm & 2.30–7.30pm; 16F).

Sancerre hills that has mutated into a highly commercialized pottery centre; there Ivanoff produced a collection which has been described as a revolution in clay. The works on display in the museum – sensual forms expressing all the complexities of the human condition – demonstrate a range of his experimentation with different surface textures and glazes, the most successful of which is a unique, ox-blood red.

The other museum in the château is the **Musée des Métiers et Traditions de France** (mid-April to mid-Oct Mon–Thurs 2–6.30pm, Fri 10am–noon & 2–7pm, Sat & Sun 10am–12.30pm & 2.30–7pm; 25F), a nostalgic meander through eighteenth- and nineteenth-century country crafts and trades, including bizarre machines for making brooms and clogs, looms, a windmill gear, and a display about the production of weathercocks. The exhibits continue into the roofspace, giving a good opportunity to view the rafters of the château.

For **accommodation** and good **food** in Argent, the comfortable *Relais de la Poste* (☎48.73.60.25; ③) is directly opposite the château. Otherwise, there's a very pleasant hotel, *La Solognote*, Grande Rue, in the village of **BRINON-SUR-SAULDRE**, 16km west of Argent (☎48.58.50.29; ④–⑤; closed Wed out of season, mid-Feb to mid-March, last week in May & three weeks in Sept; restaurant closed Wed, and out of season Tues eve).

Close to Argent, 11km southeast on the D8 near Concressault, is a new witchcraft museum at La Jonchère, the **Musée de la Sorcellerie** (Easter–Oct daily 10am–6/7pm; 25F). It's a bit over the top, with its animated reconstructions of witchcraft trials, and it certainly doesn't address the issue from a feminist point of view, but kids will probably enjoy it, and some of the prints and paintings of legendary witches are fun.

Romorantin-Lanthenay

ROMORANTIN-LANTHENAY, 67km due south of Orléans, is the biggest town in the Sologne and best visited on the last weekend in October for the **Journées Gastronomiques**, a major food festival when every restaurant and hundreds of street stalls tempt you with traditional and novel dishes centred on game, wild mushrooms, apples and pumpkins. Throughout the year, if you're feeling very rich and indulgent, you can **eat**, and **stay**, at the *Grand Hôtel du Lion d'Or*, 69 rue G-Clemenceau (☎54.76.00.28; ⑥–⑦; meals well over 500F).

The **Musée de Sologne** in the old mills in the centre of Romorantin (Mon & Wed–Sat 10–11.30am & 2–5.30pm, Sun 2–5.30pm; free) presents the history, ecology and traditions of the area; it's being done up and should be very interesting if the Sologne has struck a chord with you. If you want more information about the Sologne, the **tourist office** on place de la Paix (☎54.88.79.80) has plenty of information.

Bourges

BOURGES, chief town of the rather dispiriting region of Berry, south of the Sologne, is some way from the Loire Valley proper but historically linked to it. The miserable Dauphin Charles VII, mockingly dubbed "King of Bourges" by the English, retreated to the city after Henry V's victory at Agincourt had put all of northern France under English control. Today's city has a substantial calendar of festivals and some good restaurants, but the main attraction is the glorious great Gothic cathedral, closely followed by the mansion belonging to the Dauphin's financial advisor Jacques Cœur.

Arrival and accommodation

The cathedral, with the **tourist office** facing its south façade at 21 rue Victor-Hugo (Mon–Fri 9am–noon & 2–6pm, Sun 10am–1pm; July–Sept 9am–7pm, Sun 9am–1pm & 2.30–7pm ☎48.24.75.33), lies to the south of the city centre. **Rue Moyenne** is the main street leading north from rue Victor-Hugo, with rue Porte-Jaune parallel to it from the cathedral parvis. The **gare routière** is west of the city beyond bd Juranville on rue du Prado, while the **gare SNCF** is 1km to the north of the centre, on av P-Sémard. If you feel like pedalling through the surrounding flat countryside, you can **rent bikes** from *Loca Bourges*, 118 rue Barbès, or from the youth hostel.

Hotels

Hôtel de l'Agriculture, 15 rue du Prinal (☎48.70.40.84). On the corner with bd Juranville, nondescript but a reasonable choice. ③.

Hôtel d'Angleterre, pl des Quatre-Piliers (☎48.24.68.51). Right by the Palais de Jacques-Cœur in the centre. Pleasant service and a decent level of comfort, as you'd expect from the price. ④–⑤.

Le Christina, 5 rue de la Halle (☎48.70.56.50). A large but good hotel on the west of town. ③–④.

Hôtel l'Étape, 4 rue Raphael-Casanova (☎48.70.59.57). Good value and handy for the *gare SNCF* and the *gare routière*. ①.

Hôtel de France, 4 pl Henri-Mirpied (☎48.70.31.12). Very centrally located and reasonably priced hotel whose spacious rooms need a lick of paint. Despite that, a friendly place with genuine old-world charm. ③.

Hôtel Olympia, 66 av d'Orléans (☎48.70.49.84). Small but pleasant rooms. ③–④.

Youth hostels and campsites

IYHF youth hostel, 22 rue Henri-Sellier (☎48.24.58.09). A short way southwest of the centre, overlooking the River Auron. Bus #1 to Maison de la Culture, stop *Auberge de Jeunesse*; only a ten-minute walk from the *gare routière*. Key provided for returning at night. Summer 7am–10pm, mid-March to mid-June & mid-Oct–mid to Nov 8.30am–noon & 3–8pm; 60F, IYHF membership needed. ①.

Centre International de Séjour, 17 rue Félix-Chédin (☎48.70.25.59). A skateboard haven with every kind of ramp, plus plenty of cultural activities and meals for around 50F. For students under 25 only. A short walk north of the *gare SNCF*. ①.

Camping municipal, 29 bd de l'Industrie (☎48.20.16.85). South of the youth hostel by bus #6 to *Justices* from place Cujas, stop *Joffre*, or a ten-minute walk from the *gare routière*.

The City

The centre of Bourges sits on a hill, rising from the River Yèvre in the shadow of its magnificent early Gothic **Cathédrale St-Étienne** (daily 7am–noon & 2–6/7pm). The exterior of the twelfth-century building is characterized by the delicate, almost skeletal appearance of flying buttresses supporting an entire nave that has no transepts to break up its bulk. A much-vaunted example of Gothic architecture, it is modelled on Notre-Dame in Paris but incorporates improvements on the design of the better-known building; for example in the increased height of the inner aisles, which appear to ascend almost to vanishing point.

The tympanum above the main door of the west portal could engross you for hours with its carved figures, their faces alive with expression and bodies full of movement, representing the Last Judgement. The naked figures are very detailed, with thirteenth-century imagination given full rein in depicting the devils, complete with snakes' tails and winged bottoms and faces appearing from below the waist, symbolic of the soul in the service of sinful appetites. A cauldron filling with merry souls – one of whom appears to be wearing a bishop's mitre – contrasts sorely with the depiction of the gloomy-looking saved, while God, sitting in judgement, appears exceptionally sanctimonious.

Apart from the soaring effect of the aisles, the interior's best feature is its mostly twelfth- to thirteenth-century stained glass. There are geometric designs in lovely muted colours in the main body of the cathedral, but the most glorious and astonishingly bright windows are around the choir, all created between 1215 and 1225. You can follow the stories of the Prodigal Son, the Rich Man and Lazurus, the life of Mary, Joseph in Egypt, the Good Samaritan, Christ's crucifixion, the Last Judgement and the Apocalypse; binoculars come in handy for picking up the exquisite detail. But the most memorable way of seeing the cathedral is to come on a Sunday morning, when the powerful eighteenth-century organ is played and the sun is shining brightly through the windows, or attend one of the concerts on Tuesday evenings.

In the **crypt**, you can see the design of the fourteenth-century rose window of the west front cut into the floor, suggesting that this was where it was assembled. Tickets for guided visits to the crypt (20F) also allow you to climb to the top of the north **tower**, rebuilt in Flamboyant style after the original collapsed in 1506.

The rest of Bourges

Having seen the cathedral, many people move straight on, but the rest of the town is worth at least a couple of hours of wandering. Bourges has its fair quota of ancient *hôtels* and burghers' houses, displaying the wealth of the city that was built to rival the ruling provincial city of Dijon.

The finest survivors from Bourges's heyday are contained within the loop of roads northwest of the cathedral to either side of rue Moyenne and rue Porte-Jaune, and although the town's museums are not particularly interesting, they are housed in some beautiful medieval buildings. **Rue Bourbonneux**, parallel to rue Moyenne to the east of the cathedral, is worth a wander for the richly decorated **Hôtel Lallemant** (daily 10am–noon & 2–6pm; free); now a diverting enough museum of medieval artefacts, with displays of sculpture, tapestries and furniture; halfway along the road, you can take a narrow passage up to the remains of the Gallo-Roman town **ramparts**, lined with old houses and trees. **Rue Gambon** is noteworthy for the Maison de la Reine Blanche and the Hôtel-Dieu, and close by is the pleasant square of **place Notre-Dame**, with its eponymous church, clearly showing the shift from Gothic to Renaissance; the fifteenth-century **Hôtel des Echevins** on rue E-Branly (daily 10am–noon & 2–6pm; 20F) has a mellow courtyard that makes a contrasting entrance to the twentieth-century art collection within.

The continuation of rue E-Branly, **rue Jacques-Cœur**, was the site of the head office, stock exchange, dealing rooms, bank safes and home of Charles VII's finance minister, Jacques Cœur (1400–56), a medieval shipping magnate, moneylender and arms dealer who dominates Bourges as Joan of Arc does Orléans, while Charles VII just doesn't get a look in. The **Palais de Jacques-Cœur** (guided tours: daily 9–11.15am & 2–5.10pm; Nov–April 10–11.10am & 2–4pm; 26F) is one of the most remarkable examples of fifteenth-century domestic architecture – the visit is memorable and especially fun for children, starting with the fake windows on the entrance front from which two realistically sculpted half-figures look down – possibly the man himself and his wife. There are hardly any furnishings inside, but the decorations on the stone-work, including numerous hearts and scallop shells, clearly show the mark of the man who had it built. In the Salle du Trésor, there are carved scenes from the romance of Tristan and Iseult. The tour includes the kitchen, with its original water-heating system, and dining hall, with minstrels' gallery; it's also the only mansion where you are shown the original loos.

Eating and nightlife

Bourges's main centre for **eating** is place Gordaine, at the end of rue Coursarlon, off rue Moyenne. The square is attractively medieval, a lovely place to sit and eat in the daytime, despite the continuous piped music: try *La Brownie* (☎48.24.04.70; closed Sun), a lively place serving honest-to-goodness American hamburgers and salads from 40F; or *Le Comptoir de Paris* (☎48.24.17.16), a very popular and friendly restaurant with a terrace overlooking the square and *plats du jour* from 50F with wine, or menus from 80F. The *Arome du Vieux Bourges*, also on the square, is a coffee shop offering all kinds of delicacies. A short walk from here towards the cathedral, *D'Antan Sancerrois*, 50 rue Bourbonnoux (☎48.65.96.26; closed Mon, & Tues midday), features local goodies cooked in wine and served in a medieval dining hall from 90F (no menus); out of the old town is *L'Île d'Or*, 39–41 bd Juranville (☎48.24.29.15; closed Sun eve, Mon midday first half of Sept), with a very generous menu for around 130F.

For sweet tooths, the *pâtisserie* on the corner of rue d'Auron and rue des Armuriers (100m southwest of the PTT; go down the cour des Jacobins) isn't Jacques Cœur's birthplace as claimed, but that doesn't detract from eating their good pastries in a partly medieval room. For chocolates and the local sweet speciality of *fourrées au pral-iné* try the imposing *Maison Forestines* on place Cujas.

Nightlife and festivals

For a small city, Bourges doesn't do too badly for late-night **venues**, which include *Le Beau Bar*, 10bis rue des Beaux-Arts, a student hang-out open till 3am; *Le Perfecto*, 63bis rue Littré, with live music midweek and bopping every night; *Le Guillotin*, place Gordaine, a bar and restaurant with café-théâtre; and *Le Pub des Jacobins*, rue des Armuriers, with live music.

Bourges' **festival** programme is also impressive, with several major events in town. The *Printemps de Bourges* features every sort of music and all the performing arts for one week between mid-April and the beginning of May (ring ☎48.24.30.50). More upbeat is the *Festival Synthèse*, an electronic and acoustic music bash during the first week of June (ring ☎48.20.41.87); and *Les Ballades* in mid-July to mid-August, with a month-long celebration of theatre, music and open-air and street performances.

St-Chartier, Nohant and La Châtre

If you're heading through the damp and dismal **Berry** countryside for Limoges from Bourges, rather than taking the main road through Châteauroux, you could go via **La Châtre**, where George Sand and Chopin spent some time. If the date is close to July 14, then a stop at the small village of **St-Chartier**, 9km north of La Châtre, should defi-nitely be considered to take part in the huge folk festival.

St-Chartier

ST-CHARTIER is known to most as being the venue of one of the best folk festivals in Europe, the *Rencontres Internationales de Saint-Chartier*, an annual festival of folk and traditional music and dance that started as a hurdy-gurdy and pipe festival but has spread its horizons over the years. It takes place around the old château, the village church and in the surrounding parkland. Traditional instrument makers set up their stalls, and there are dance workshops, competitions, concerts and a festive ball in the main square every night.

To give some idea of the festival's range, the 1994 line-up of performances included Mongolian dancers and singers from Siberia, an Asturian folk band, music from Finland, an Italian medieval ensemble, Celtic folk and hiphop from Scotland, Cajun and Romanian dance bands, and a group specializing in the ancient music of France and England.

The festival takes place over four or five days around July 14, and inclusive tickets cost around 300F, or you can just go for the day for about 150F. There are free **camping sites** all around the village for the duration. Details are available from the *Comité George Sand*, 141 rue Nationale, 36400 La Châtre (☎54.06.09.96).

On the rte de Verneuil from St-Chartier there's a country park **hotel**, the *Château de la Vallée Bleu* (☎54.31.01.91; ④–⑤), which is agreeably peaceful and serves excellent food (menus from 130F).

Nohant and La Châtre

NOHANT, on the main Châteauroux–La Châtre road 5km from St-Chartier, is where nineteenth-century novelist George Sand, or Amandine Aurore Lucie Dupin as she was born, spent half her life. The **Château de Nohant** – not really a château but a very pleasant eighteenth-century country house – is open for quick guided tours (daily 9–11.15am & 2–5.30pm; July & Aug 9am–6.30pm; mid-Oct to March 10–11.15am & 2–3.30pm; 26F). You're shown the dining room table where Flaubert, Turgenev, Dumas, Delacroix, Balzac and Liszt all dined on many occasions. The piano that George Sand gave Chopin, her guest for ten years, sits in the living room surrounded by the family portraits. There's also the puppet theatre made by Chopin and Sand's son Maurice, the pair no doubt trying to outdo each other in their well-documented rivalry for Sand's attentions.

Chopin's music is honoured in a week-long **piano festival**, "*Chopin chez George Sand*", at Nohant and La Châtre towards the end of July. Tickets range from 80F to 160F; bookings and programme details from La Châtre's tourist office (see below).

There's more of Sand in nearby **LA CHÂTRE**, where every other place name is connected with the novelist. The **Musée George Sand et de la Vallée Noire**, 71 rue Venose (daily 9am–noon & 2–5pm; summer closes 7pm; 8F), dedicates a floor to the writer, with plenty of pictures: George Sand's caricatures of her friends, a photo of Chopin, her son Maurice's illustrations for his mother's work and the doodles on her manuscripts. Apart from this, the town's most distinctive feature is the background noise of gentle tapping as competitors in the annual **stone sculpture competition** set to work each June. You can watch them at it and admire the results, which stay in the town.

The very helpful **tourist office** is on square George-Sand (daily 10am–noon & 2–6pm; ☎54.48.02.87), and can find you a **room** in the area. A good place to try is *Le Paradis Breton*, 4 rue Alphonse-Fleury (☎54.48.02.87; ①), pleasant with just five very cheap rooms. *Le Lion d'Argent*, 2 av Lion d'Argent (☎54.48.11.69; ③–④), is well equipped with a swimming pool and bikes for rental. Its restaurant (closed Sun out of season; menus from 80F) serves generous helpings of traditional dishes and has a good wine selection. There's also a new **youth hostel** by the Indre on the east side of the town on rue du Moulin Borgnon (☎54.06.00.55; ①; AJ membership required) and a riverside **campsite**, the *Camping Solange Sand* (☎54.48.37.83; mid-March to mid-Nov), at Montgivray, 2.5km from La Châtre. The restaurant *Jardin de la Poste*, 10 rue Basse-Mouhet (☎54.48.05.62; closed Sun eve, Mon & mid-Sept to Oct 5), should leave you feeling well satisfied without paying much more than 100F.

Blois and around

The biggest drawback of a visit to the former seat of the dukes of Orléans at **BLOIS** is the modern town around it, and particularly the broad, fast-moving boulevard that rings the château as if it were a mere traffic island rather than a sensational piece of architecture. There are, however, plenty of places around place Victor-Hugo that offer excellent views of the exterior of the building, Italian loggias and all, and it's worth braving the traffic for the pleasure of a non-guided visit around rooms steeped in power and intrigue.

If you want to get out into the countryside, there are several stretches of woodlands around Blois, including the **Forêt de Blois** to the west of the town on the north bank of the Loire, the **Parc de Chambord** and the **Forêt de Boulogne** around the château further upstream.

On the south bank of the river, within a twenty kilometre radius south and east of Blois, are a handful of impressive and easily visited **châteaux**. By car you could call at all of them in a couple of days. But they make ideal cycling targets or, if you strike out along minor roads and woodland rides with a map, walking destinations. Of the two most imposing examples, **Chaumont** has frequent daily trains from Blois (Onzain *gare SNCF* on the other side of the river), and **Chambord** is a flat, beautiful ride – although to get there on public transport you have to use the expensive châteaux tour buses that leave from Blois, Tours or Amboise.

The Château

All six kings of the sixteenth century spent time at the **Château be Blois** (daily 9am–6pm; Nov to mid-March 9am–noon & 2–5pm; 30F), and in the early nineteenth century it was given to Louis XVIII's brother to keep him away from Paris. Hence the courtiers' mansions that fill the town and, given its earlier non-royal ownerships, the château's building montage of distinct, unmatching wings – medieval, Gothic, Renaissance and classical. Much of the château can be visited, from its oldest part – the thirteenth-century manorial assembly hall of the Salle des États – to the flamboyant Gothic east wing of Louis XII and the Italianate north wing of François I, with its double loggias and gallery, and the great staircase with the spiral of the balconies and its windows not quite in alignment.

The Blois horror story is the murder by Henri III of the Duc de Guise and his brother the cardinal of Lorraine, the perpetrators of the execution of Huguenots at Amboise (see p.420). The king had summoned the States General to a meeting in the Grand Salle, only to find an overwhelming majority supporting de Guise, along with the stringing up of Protestants, and aristocratic rather than royal power. He panicked and had de Guise ambushed and hacked to death in a corridor of the palace. The cardinal was murdered in prison the next day. Their deaths were avenged a year later when a monk assassinated the king himself.

The château was also home to Henri III's mother and manipulator, Catherine de Médicis, who died here a few days after the murders in 1589. The most famous of her suite of rooms is her study, where, according to Alexander Dumas, she kept poison hidden in secret caches in the skirting boards and behind some of the 237 narrow carved wooden panels. In a later century, revolutionaries were tried in tthe Grande Salle for conspiring to assassinate Napoléon III, a year before the Paris Commune.

Otherwise, the interior of the château is wonderfully colourful, or dreadfully garish if you're a purist, thanks to the mid-nineteenth-century restoration. The floors have intricate designs in tiling or parquet, walls are painted with repeating patterns, and the arches, pillars and fireplaces of the superb Salle des États are a riot of colour. Two ornamental regal emblems recur ostentatiously: the porcupine in Louis XII's wing and the salamander in François I's.

In addition, the château houses three small museums: the **Beaux Arts**, with plenty of regal portraits and a rather good collection of forged ironwork including locks and keys; seventeenth-century **sculptures** in white Loire tufa, rescued from many of the neighbouring châteaux before their detail weathered away; and an **archeological collection**, with several fine examples of Merovingian and Carolingian glass and ceramics.

Practicalities

Blois is easy to get around: av Jean-Laigret is the main street leading south from the **gare SNCF** to place Victor-Hugo and the château, and past it to the town centre. The **gare routière** is on place Victor-Hugo (☎54.78.15.66), with buses leaving for Cheverny and Chambord (mid-June to mid-Sept; 65F). The **tourist office**, 3 av Jean-Laigret (Mon–Sat 9am–12.30pm & 2–7pm, Sun 10.30am–12.30pm & 4.30–7pm; Oct–March Mon–Sat 9.15am–noon & 2–6pm; ☎54.74.06.49), organizes hotel rooms for a small fee and changes money. During summer the tourist office has information desks open in the pedestrian precinct and place du Château (July & Aug daily 10am–7pm). **Bikes** can be rented from *Cycles Leblond*, 44 Levée des Tuileries or 17 rue du Sanitas.

Hotels worth trying are the inexpensive *St-Nicolas*, 2 rue du Sermon (☎54.78.05.85; ①), and *Saint-Jacques*, 7 rue Ducoux (☎54.78.04.15; ②), both near the *gare SNCF*, or the slightly more expensive *Hôtel du Bellay*, 12 rue des Minimes (☎54.78.23.62; ②–③). *Le Savoie*, next to the *Saint-Jacques* at 6 rue Ducoux (☎54.74.32.21; ②–③), is more appealing, but if you want somewhere classy, the best choice is the *Mercure*, 28 quai St-Jean (☎54.56.66.66; ⑤), overlooking the river to the east of the town centre.

The IYHF **youth hostel**, 18 rue de l'Hôtel-Pasquier, Les Grouets (☎54.78.27.21; ①; March to mid-Nov), is further out, 5km downstream, between the Forêt de Blois and the river. Take bus #4, direction *Les Grouets*, stop *Auberge*. The Blois **campsite** is across the river 2km from the town centre on the Lac de Loire at Vineuil (☎54.74.22.78; bus #3c, stop *Mairie Vineuil*; bicycle and boat rental).

There are plenty of cheap **eating** places around the town centre: rue St-Lubin, rue des Violettes and rue Foulérie are good streets to try. *La Garbure*, 36 rue St-Lubin (☎54.74.32.89; closed Sat & Wed midday), serves specialities from the southwest for under 100F, and the *garbure*, a filling duck soup, is excellent. *La Tocade*, 9–11 rue Chant-des-Oiseaux, is a popular brasserie with good-value set menus. For straightforward meat grills, *La Forge*, 18 rue du Bourg-Neuf (☎54.74.43.45), is good and a friendly place (from 100F). More upmarket restaurants include *Le Bocca d'Or*, 15 rue Haute (☎54.78.04.74), with one menu at around 100F, and *Au Rendez-Vous des Pêcheurs*, 27 rue Foix (☎54.74.67.48; closed Sun midday & Mon), with delicious fish dishes, especially the salmon, and a menu for around 150F.

Château de Chaumont

Catherine de Médicis forced Diane de Poitiers to hand over Chenonceau on the Cher (see p.423) in return for the **Château de Chaumont** (daily 9.30am–6pm; Oct–March 10am–4.30pm; 31F), 16km downstream from Blois. Diane got a bad deal, but this is still one of the more fascinating châteaux.

Chaumont started life as a Gothic fortress – complete with towers, moat and drawbridge – defending the river and valley below; during the Renaissance, the carcass of the building was dressed up with Renaissance frippery. The wings you see today form three sides of a square, the fourth side having been demolished in 1739 to improve views over the river, which are spectacular. Chaumont's interior, unlike those of many Loire châteaux, is furnished in an early nineteenth-century style which, combined with its unkempt air, gives it a surprising, homely feel. Look out for the tiled floor with its depictions of hunting scenes, and a copy of a sixteenth-century portrait of the young Catherine de Médicis in the Salles des Fêtes, on the first floor.

More interesting than anything inside the château, however, are the remarkable Belle-Époque **stables**, with their porcelain troughs and elegant electric lamps for the benefit of the horses at a time before the château itself was wired – let alone the rest of the country. If you want to get a further feel of the château's equestrian character, the best way is to rent either a horse or a pony and trap, available daily in the château grounds from May to October (☎54.20.90.60; winter daily except Tues).

A nineteenth-century mansion turned **hotel**, the *Château des Tertres* (☎54.20.83.88; ⑤) is in easy reach of Chaumont on the north side of the river on the road to Monteaux from Onzain. There is a **campsite** in Chaumont itself (☎54.20.95.22).

Château de Cheverny

Seventeenth-century addicts are in for treat 15km southeast of Blois with the **Château de Cheverny** (daily 9.30am–noon & 2.15–5/5.30/6pm; June to mid-Sept 9.15am–6.45pm; April–May 9.15am–noon & 2.15–6.30pm; 30F). Built between 1604 and 1634 and never altered, it presents an immaculate picture of symmetry and harmony. The stone from Bourré on the River Cher, from which it is built, lightens with age, so the château looks as if it were whitewashed yesterday. Its interior decoration has only been added to, never destroyed: the display of paintings, furniture, tapestries and armour against the gilded, sculpted and carved walls and ceilings is extremely impressive. The richness can be almost too much to take in; some highlights are the painted wall panels telling stories from Don Quixote in the dining hall, the lily, daffodil and iris motifs in the Salles des Gardes, the bindings of the books in the library and the embroidered Persian silk canopy on the king's bed.

The château is still lived in by a descendant of the original owner, and he takes his hounds and horses out deer hunting every Tuesday and Saturday from October to March. Tourists are bused in to watch the local aristos tie their silk cravats while huntsmen make revolting noises on their horns. There's a room full of deer-head trophies and even the feeding of the hounds is turned into a spectacle. The **son et lumière** every Saturday evening at 10pm from mid-July to August is also dedicated to the hunting theme.

Near Cheverny you can stay in the luxurious *Château du Breuil* (☎54.20.31.31; ⑥–⑦; menus from 200F; half-board obligatory in season) on the road to Fougères-sur-Bièvre (see below), or, more reasonably, at the *Hôtel des Trois Marchands* (☎54.79.96.44; ②–④) in **COUR CHEVERNY**, Cheverny's larger neighbour. The hotel's **restaurant** is not bad at all, with menus from 100F. Another good place to eat is *Le Pousse Rapière* in Cheverny (☎54.79.94.23). There's a **campsite** on the D102 in Cheverny (☎54.79.90.01), and another on rue de Poussard in Cour Cheverny (☎54.79.95.63).

Château de Fougères

If you're on a château binge, the grim, medieval **Château de Fougères** provides a good contrast to Cheverny (daily 9am–noon & 2–6pm; Oct–March Wed–Mon 10am–noon & 2–4.30pm; 20F). It lies in the village of **FOUGÈRES-SUR-BIÈVRE**, 10km southwest of Cheverny, and was built in 1470 by Louis XI's chancellor, who was clearly sceptical about long-term peace. It is a veritable fortress, with spiky towers, and the theme of war running through the building, with sculptured soldiers and battle scenes above arches and on door lintels and chimneys. Come the sixteenth century – here as elsewhere – Italianate windows were fashioned onto former blank walls and steep roofs, but it still looks as if it expects an attack and is concealing its defences as a tactic. It could hardly be a more peaceful place now, and is rarely overrun with visitors.

Château de Beauregard

A cyclable ride from Blois, the relatively little visited **Château de Beauregard**, 7km south of Blois on the D956 to Contres (July & Aug daily 9.30am–6pm; April–June, Sept & Oct daily 9.30–11.45am & 2–6pm; Oct–March daily except Wed 9.30–11.45am & 2–4.45pm; 25F) lies amid the Forêt de Russy. It was – like Chambord – one of François I's hunting lodges, but its transformation in the sixteenth century involved beautification rather than aggrandizement. It was added to in the seventeenth century; the result is a restrained – by Loire standards – and serene white building, very much at ease in its manicured geometric park.

The highlight of the château is a portrait gallery of 363 paintings of kings, queens and their cohorts in a richly decorated gallery, with a floor of Delft tiling depicting an army on the march. The paintings are arranged by reign, beginning with Phillipe VI at the start of the Hundred Years' War and ending with Louis XIII, who inherited the throne in 1610. The gallery includes some characters, like Rabelais, not directly involved with the shifty-eyed monarchs and their power brokers. The paintings are gradually being restored, often revealing other portraits beneath in the process.

Château de Chambord

The **Château de Chambord**, François I's little "hunting lodge", is the largest of the Loire châteaux (daily 9.30am–5.45pm; July & Aug closes 6.45pm; Sept 21–June 12 9.30–11.45am & 2–5.45pm; Oct–March closes 4.45pm; 32F) and one of the most extravagant commissions of its age. Its patron's principal object – to outshine the Holy Roman Emperor Charles V – would, he claimed, leave him renowned as "one of the greatest builders in the universe", and the result is undoubtedly impressive. The palace has over 440 rooms, is surrounded by 34 kilometres of wall, and even involved having the Loire diverted to accommodate its grand plan.

The Italian architect Domenico de Cortona was chosen to design the château in 1519 in an effort to introduce prestigious Italian Renaissance art forms to France; but the labour was supplied by French masons, with an overall result that is essentially French medieval: the massive round towers, with their conical tops, and the explosion of chimneys, pinnacles and turrets on the roof bring to mind Flamboyant Gothic. The details, however, are pure Italian: the Great Staircase (attributed by some to da Vinci), panels of coloured marble, niches decorated with shell-like domes, and free-standing columns. Wandering through, you can get a good feel for the contrasting architectural styles.

The building has its fans, though for many, its mix of styles makes it the single ugliest building in the Loire – except perhaps for the nuclear power station at St-Laurent-des-Eaux, just to the north. Visits, at least, are unguided, and there's plenty of entertainment to be had from roaming around inside – up and down the double spiral staircase (devised so courtiers could ascend and descend without meeting up on the steps) around the spectacular chimneys and through endless rooms and corridors.

The **Parc de Chambord** around the château is an enormous walled game reserve, red deer being the main beast you're likely to spot. You can explore on foot, bike or on horseback, with mounts rented from the *Centre Equestre* near the château.

In **BRACIEUX**, a small village just beyond the southern wall of the Parc de Chambord, 8km from the château, there's the pleasant little *Hôtel de la Bonnheure*, 9bis rue R-Masson (☎54.46.41.57; ③–④), or if that's booked up, the *Hôtel du Cygne*, 20 rue R-Brun (☎54.46.41.07; ③–④). There's also a **campsite** in the village (☎54.46.41.84). In the village of **CHAMBORD** itself, the *Hôtel Saint-Michel* (☎54.20.31.31; ④–⑤) has the château in direct line of view.

Tours and around

Chief town of the Loire Valley and capital of the Touraine region, **TOURS** has long had a reputation as a staid, bourgeois city. An English travel writer wrote in 1913:

> *Tours has an immense air of good breeding . . . you have visions of portentously dull entertainments in lofty gilded saloons where everything is rather icily magnificent.*

The city is now only an hour's journey from Paris on the *TGV* line, and this, together with the building of a new conference centre, has meant an influx of business people and young commuters. With an increasing student population as well, a gradual, enlivening change is being effected. It's busy (as you'll soon discover if you're looking for a place to park) but somehow it's not a very endearing city. However, it has a prettified and fairly animated old quarter, some good museums – of wine, crafts, stained glass and an above-average Beaux-Arts museum – and a great many fine buildings, not least of which is St-Gatien's cathedral. And if you don't have your own transport, it's the obvious Touraine base, within striking distance of a snatch of notable châteaux – **Villandry**, **Langeais** and **Amboise** – as well as the celebrated wine-producing towns of **Vouvray** and **Bourgeuil**.

Arrival and accommodation

The cathedral district is to the northeast, and, a short way southeast facing the mammoth "hypercentre" that shelters the Centre International de Congrès, there's the **gare routière** (☎47.05.30.49) and **gare SNCF** (☎47.20.50.50); some trains, including most *TGV*s, stop at **St-Pierre-des-Corps**, an industrial estate outside the city. Frequent shuttles link the two stations (about 8min) or you can take bus #2 or #3 from St-Pierre-des-Corps to place Jean-Jaurès (15min). The **tourist office** is close by on the corner of

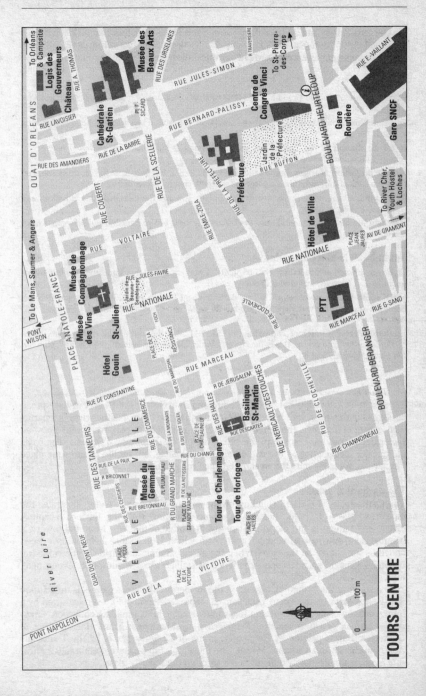

TOURS CENTRE

rue Bernard-Palissy and bd Heuteloup (Mon–Sat 8.30am–7pm, Sun 10am–12.30pm & 3–6pm; Oct–April Mon–Sat 9am–12.30pm & 1.30–6pm, Sun 10am–1pm ☎47.70.37.37). Unless there's a conference in town, **accommodation** shouldn't be a problem.

Hotels

Hôtel Akilene, 22 rue du Grand Marché (☎47.61.46.04). Reasonably priced, comfortable and situated in the old town. ③.

Le Francillon, 9 rue des Bons-Enfants (☎47.66.44.66). A beautiful half-timbered house with rooms to match. ⑤.

Hôtel du Manoir, 2 rue Traversière, cnr rue J-Simon (☎47.05.37.37). A converted nineteenth-century townhouse offering exceptional service. ③–④.

Manoir du Grand Marigny, near Fondettes (☎47.42.29.87). Just 5km from the centre of Tours on the north bank of the river, this is a gorgeous sixteenth-century manor house. ⑥–⑦.

Mon Hôtel, 40 rue de la Préfecture (☎47.05.67.53). Towards the cathedral, this is a clean and comfortable cheapie. ①–②.

Hôtel du Musée, 2 pl François-Sicard (☎47.66.63.81). Right by the cathedral and museum, a quiet and unassuming hotel. ②–③.

Youth hostels and campsites

Le Foyer, 16 rue Bernard-Palissy (☎47.05.38.81). A workers' hostel that sometimes has free rooms for under-25s. Closed Sat afternoon & Sun.

IYHF youth hostel, av d'Arsonval in Parc de Grandmont (☎47.25.14.45). Reception 5pm–9/10pm; late-night key available with deposit. Take bus #6 or #2 from place Jean-Jaurès to Chambray, stop *Auberge de Jeunesse*. Closed Dec & Jan. ①.

Edouard Peron municipal campsite (☎47.54.11.11). On the north bank of the Loire, about 1500m from the town centre, this is the closest municipal campsite to town. Take bus #7, stop *Ste-Radegonde*. May 11–Sept 8.

The City

The centre of Tours lies between the Loire and its tributary the Cher, but has spread far across both banks, with industrial Tours north of the Loire. Neither river is a particular feature of the town, though there are parks on islands in both rivers and a newish footbridge across the Loire from the site of the old castle on quai d'Orléans. The city's old quarter focuses not on the cathedral or the château, but on the picturesque place Plumereau, some 600m to the west of the main rue Nationale.

The cathedral *quartier*

The **Cathédrale St-Gatien**, standing on the square of the same name, illustrates the entire evolution of Gothic designs in France, starting with the thirteenth-century chevet and ending in the glorious Flamboyant Gothic of the west front and towers, a mesmerizing overdose of sculpted pattern to which Renaissance belfries have been added as the cherry on the cake. When the sun is shining, the inside of the cathedral becomes a magic kaleidoscope experience of stained glass windows projecting neat, multihued shards of colour.

Just south of the cathedral, housed in the former archbishop's palace, is the **Musée des Beaux-Arts** (daily except Tues 9am–12.45pm & 2–6pm; 30F), overshadowed by a huge Lebanon cedar. The museum has some beauties in its rambling collection: *Christ in the Garden of Olives* and the *Resurrection* by Mantegna; Frans Hals' portrait of Descartes; Balzac painted by Boulanger; prints of *The Five Senses* by the Tourainais Abraham Bosse; and a sombre Monet. The museum's top treasure, Rembrandt's *Flight into Egypt*, is unfortunately difficult to see through the security glass.

On the other side of the cathedral, between rue Albert-Thomas and the river, is the site of the ancient royal **château** of Tours, of which just two medieval towers remain. The **Tour de Guise**, now embedded in the seventeenth-century Pavillon de Mars, houses a waxworks museum, **Historial de Touraine** (daily 9am–noon & 2–6pm; July & Aug 9am–6.30pm; Nov to mid-March 2–5.30pm; 33F), which makes the various courtly murders, marriages and machinations seem like a bad Disney cartoon. But you can push mock medieval French history out of your mind, replacing it with gently waving multicoloured fish in the **Aquarium Tropical** in the same buildings (daily July & Aug 9am–6.30pm; mid-March to June & Oct to mid-Nov 9.30am–noon & 2–6pm; mid-Nov to mid-March 2–5.30pm; 28F). In the fifteenth-century **Logis des Gouverneurs** alongside (mid-March to mid-Dec Wed & Sat 3–6.30pm; free), across the remnants of the city's Gallo-Roman wall, there's an exhibition of historical artefacts that does give quite a plausible sense of how the city has developed over the centuries, called *Vivre à Tours* (Life in Tours).

Along rue Nationale

At the head of **rue Nationale**, Tours' main street, statues of Descartes and Rabelais overlook the Loire. A short walk back from the river and you come to the **church of St-Julien**, whose old monastic buildings house two of the town's most compelling museums.

The **Musée de Compagnonnage** is in the eleventh-century guesthouse and sixteenth-century monks' dormitory at 8 rue Nationale (daily 9am–6pm; mid-Sept to mid-June Wed–Mon 9–11am & 2–4.30/5.30pm; 20F). Here, for once, the people who built – rather than ordered – the châteaux and cathedrals are celebrated. As well as documents of the origins and militant activity of the *compagnonnage* (the guilds), there are masterpieces (in the original sense of the term) of various crafts from cake making and carpentry to locksmithery and brick laying, with their relevant tools exhibited alongside.

The **Musée des Vins** in the twelfth-century cellars of the abbey at 16 rue Nationale (Wed–Mon 9–11.30am & 2–4.30/5.30pm; 10F) takes you through a comprehensive treatment of the history, mythology and production of wine, though there's nothing on recent technical innovations and no quaffing to look forward to. Behind the museum, a Gallo-Roman wine press from Cheillé sits in the former cloisters of the church.

If you take a left into rue Colbert and right into rue Jules-Favre, you can wander into the **Jardin de Beaune-Semblançay**, with its sixteenth-century fountain standing in front of the sad façade of the mansion that belonged to François I's finance minister. Back on rue Colbert, at no 39, is the house where Joan of Arc is said to have had her suit of armour made.

Vieux Tours

The old part of Tours crowds around **place Plumereau**, over to the west of rue Nationale. Between the two, the **Hôtel Gouin**, 25 rue du Commerce, has a Renaissance façade to stop you in your tracks. Inside, it exhibits a surprising collection for an archeological museum, including a medicine chest belonging to Jean-Jacques Rousseau, and examples of early technical advances in physics, such as the Archimedes screw and a vacuum pump (daily 10am–12.30pm & 2–6.30pm; mid-May to Sept daily 10am–5.30pm; Oct to mid-March daily except Fri closes at 5.30pm; 18F).

But it's the old town's half-timbered houses and bulging stairway towers dating from the twelfth to fifteenth centuries that are the city's showpiece. Some of the earlier buildings look like cut-out models, but the Renaissance stone-and-brick constructions are sturdier – particularly the **Écoles des Langues Vivantes** on rue Briconnet, with its wonderful sculpted dogs, drunks, frogs and monsters. West of rue Bretonneau, around place Robert-Picou, modern artisans' workshops cluster between medieval dwellings.

Off rue Briconnet, at 7 rue du Mûrier, you'll find the **Musée du Gemmail** (July & Aug daily 10am–6.30pm; Palm Sunday to mid-Oct Tues–Sun 10am–noon & 2–4/6pm; 28F), a museum of nonleaded stained glass. Some of the works are displayed in an underground twelfth-century chapel, and artists include such leading lights as Picasso and Jean Cocteau. They shine with an extraordinary intensity and, through the use of layering, have a far greater colour range than traditional stained glass.

To the south an enormous church once stood, with its nave stretching along rue des Halles from rue des Trois Pavées Ronds almost to place de Châteauneuf. Only the north tower, the Tour de Charlemagne, and the western clock tower remain of the ancient **Basilique de St-Martin**. The new church, a late nineteenth-century neo-Byzantine affair, guards the shrine of St-Martin, bishop of Tours in the fourth century and famous for giving half his cloak to a freezing beggar.

Eating and drinking

Place Plumereau is set out with the tables of expensive **cafés** and **restaurants**; the bars in most of the surrounding streets are equally overpriced and exclusive, with silly names like *The Sherlock Holmes*. The most promising restaurant streets are rue du Grand-Marché and rue de la Rôtisserie, on the periphery of old Tours, and rue du Commerce and rue Colbert.

Sugar and chocolate freaks should detour to **pâtisseries** like *La Marotte*, 3 rue du Change, *La Chocolatière*, 6 rue de la Scellerie, and *Sabat*, 76 rue Nationale. The main **market** halls are to the west of St-Martin at the end of rue des Halles.

Académie de la Bière, 43 rue Lavoisier. A serious establishment near the cathedral for those with a measure of dedication to good ale; you can choose from among 150 types of beer while playing darts.
Atomic Café, off place Plumereau. Teeming with people in a good atmosphere, this refreshingly rough-looking bar is situated in a medieval courtyard just off the square.
Jean Bardet, 57 rue Groison (☎47.41.41.11). Tours' top restaurant and one of the best in France. Extremely sophisticated and health-conscious food with a minimum of butter and cream and a maximum of rare herbs and old varieties of vegetables. Unfortunately, you can reckon on paying over 600F *à la carte* and not much less on the fixed menus, starting at 400F.
Brasserie de l'Univers, 8 pl Jean-Jaurès (☎47.05.50.92). Big and beautiful Belle Époque brasserie with its original painted glass. Grilled meat and fish, pizzas and menus from 60F. Service till midnight.
L'Ecuelle, 5 rue du Grand-Marché (☎47.66.49.10). Old-fashioned French cooking with menus from 60F. Closed Mon.
London Pub, rue du Commerce. Lively bar in the old town, popular with students of all nationalities.
La Rôtisserie Tourangelle, 23 rue du Commerce (☎47.05.71.21). Salmon pancakes, beef from Chinon, guinea fowl and other goodies, and an excellent-value 140F menu. Closed Sun evening & Mon.
Le Singe Vert, 5 rue Marceau (☎47.61.50.50). Another Belle Époque brasserie with lunchtime menus from 70F. Open till midnight.
Les Trois Canards, 16 rue de la Rôtisserie (☎47.61.58.16). Traditional Tours dishes of veal and duck on very cheap menus from 50F. Closed 2 weeks in April & Oct.
Les Tuffeaux, 19 rue Lavoisier (☎47.47.19.89). An attractive setting for delicious classic cuisine, menus from 110F. Closed Sun, and Mon midday.
Van Gogh, rue du Commerce. Fun student bar close to the place Plumereau.

Nightlife

Nightlife in the city is a lot more promising than in other Loire towns, with a fairly impressive selection of nightclubs, bars and cabaret-cafés. *Le Feeling*, 16bis rue de la Longue-Echelle, close to place du Grand-Marché (closed Sun; free admission), is a disco with mainly Latin American sounds and reasonably priced drinks. Other clubs with a young clientele include *Le Boléro*, 57 rue de la Scellerie (daily 10.30pm–dawn; Tues & Thurs student nights 55F, Sat & Sun 75F), with various "theme" nights, and *L'Excalibur* in a vaulted cellar at 35 rue Briçonnet (daily 10.30pm–4am; Mon–Fri 60F, Sat & Sun 70F; free admission for women). **Cafés with shows** include the popular *Petit Faucheaux*, 23 rue des Cerisiers, best known for jazz but also featuring comedians, and darts, cards and chess at any time; and *Le Bateau Ivre*, 146 rue Edouard-Vaillant, with a varied programme including jazz, rock, theatre and comedy. *Le Vieux Mûrier* on place Plumereau has live music and an amazing decor of diverse objects.

Listings

Bike rental From the *gare SNCF*; *Loisirs Plus*, corner of bd Heuteloup and rue de Buffon; *Au Col de Cygne*, 46bis rue Dr-Fournier; *Grammont Motocycles* 93 av de Grammont.

Books English books from 2 rue du Commerce and 20 rue Marceau.

Car rental *ELS Sobal*, 6 rue George-Sand (☎47.61.12.28); *Europcar*, 76 rue Bernard-Palissy (☎47.64.47.76); Hertz, 57 rue M-Tribut (☎47.20.40.24).

Change In the *gare SNCF* or 24hr automatic change machine on the wall of the Vinci centre on rue Bernard-Palissy. Most banks are on or close to place Jean-Jaurès.

Châteaux tours *Service Touristiques de Touraine*, gare SNCF (☎47.05.46.09); *Touraine Evasion*, 19 rue Edouard-Vaillant (☎47.60.30.00).

Cinema *Olympia*, rue de Lucé (programme details ☎47.39.04.97). Showings of classic movies in their original language every Wed from May to Sept; *Studios*, 2 rue des Urselines (☎47.05.22.80), shows the arty, obscure and old favourites, also in the original language.

City transport Bus tickets flat fare of 6.50F for an hour's journey. Route map from *SEMITRAT* on place Jean-Jaurès.

Laundries 21–23 pl Michelet; 56 rue du Grand-Marché.

Medical assistance SOS Médecins ☎47.38.33.33; SAMU ☎47.66.85.11; Hôpital Bretonneau, 2 bd Tonnelé (☎47.47.47.47); late-night pharmacy, phone police for address (see below).

Police 70–72 rue Marceau (☎47.60.70.69).

Post restante 1 bd Béranger, 37000 Tours.

Taxis ☎47.20.30.40.

Vouvray

The main reason to visit **VOUVRAY**, 10km east of Tours on the north bank, is for its wines, though it has its own charm in the villagey centre clustered around its thirteenth-century **church**. The tourist office at the Hôtel de Ville can provide addresses of *vignerons*, but all the roads leading up the steep valleys are lined with *caves*. The view of the vines from the top of the hill is almost intoxicating in itself. A living **Musée du Vin et de la Vigne** (daily 10am–7pm; 28F, tasting included) demonstrates the traditional methods of wine making, all still in use, and solves such mysteries as how you get a champagne-size cork into the neck of an ordinary-size wine bottle. Vouvray's wonderful *Foire aux Vins* takes place from August 11 to 15. From Tours, bus #61 runs from place Jean-Jaurès to place St-Vincent just south of the tourist office in Vouvray.

If you choose to **stay** in Vouvray, there's the very cheap *Le Vouvrillon*, av Brûlé (☎47.52.78.80; ①), *Le Val Joli* on the N152 (☎47.52.70.18; ②–③), and a **campsite** between the Loire and the Cisse (☎47.52.68.81). Between Amboise and Tours, there are rather better hotel options, notably the *Hostellerie de la Lanterne*, 48 quai de la Loire in Rochecorbon (☎47.52.50.02; ③–④), an attractive old coach house with comfortable rooms and a decent restaurant (menus from 100F).

Amboise

Twenty kilometres upstream of Tours, **AMBOISE** is a prim little town trading on long-gone splendours, its one saving grace being Leonardo da Vinci's residence of Clos-Lucé and its mind-expanding exhibition on the great man's works. It is also one of Mick Jagger's favourite foreign residences – perhaps because few people recognize him here.

The one concession to twentieth-century art in Amboise is a **fountain** by Max Ernst of a turtle topped by a teddy bear (or ET figure), standing in front of the Friday and Sunday **market** on the riverside. Behind, rising above the river, what's left of the **château** where Charles VIII was born and died is interesting enough (daily 9–11.55am & 2–6.25pm; July & Aug 9am–6.25pm; Oct 24–March 25 closes at dusk; 32F). It was in the late fifteenth century that Charles VIII decided to turn the old castle of his childhood days into a vast, extravagant and luxurious palace. Not long after the work was completed, he managed to hit his head, fatally, on a door lintel. The château continued to be enlarged under Louis XII and François I but later wars and lack of finance have left less than half the total standing.

The **Tour des Minimes**, the original fifteenth-century entrance, is architecturally the most exciting part of the castle, designed for the maximum number of fully armoured men on horseback to get in and out as quickly as possible. From the top you step out onto the roof, with the Loire presenting one of its best panoramas. Before you've had time to orientate yourself, the guide launches into the story of how the hooks along the battlements were once smeared with the blood and guts of rebellious Huguenots. Caught plotting to get rid of the Catholic de Guise family, the power behind young François II, they were summarily tried in the Salle des Conseils and the whole town was hung about with their corpses.

The last French king, Louis-Philippe, stayed in this château, hence the abrupt switch from solid Gothic furnishings to 1830s post-First Empire style. People imprisoned in the castle include Louis XIV's finance minister Fouquet of Vaux-le-Vicomte fame (see p.163), and, in the mid-nineteenth century, Abd el-Kader, an Algerian resistance leader who spent fifteen years fighting against the French. A striking portrait of him hangs in the château.

A man of far greater renown today than any of the French kings was invited here by François I to bolster and encourage the French Renaissance. Leonardo da Vinci made his home at the **Clos-Lucé**, at the end of rue Victor-Hugo (daily summer 9am–7pm, winter 9am–6pm; 34F), now a museum to him and his work, with some forty models of Leonardo's inventions, constructed according to his detailed plans. It's wonderful to see the mechanical manifestations of da Vinci's technological achievements, but even the best model – the wooden tank – does not have the same effect as Leonardo's sketch. Leonardo died here in 1519.

A contrast to Leonardo's output is the **Musée de la Poste** in the Hôtel Joyeuse, 6 rue Joyeuse (Tues–Sun 9.30am–noon & 2–6.30pm; winter 10am–noon & 2–5pm; 16F), whose exhibits trace the history of the postal delivery service, from the pony express to air and sea mail.

If you take the main road south out of Amboise and turn right just before the junction with the D31, you'll come to a very unlikely building in this land of châteaux. It's a **pagoda** which was once part of a château, built in the eighteenth century. You can climb to the top for fabulous views and explore the park (daily July & Aug 9am–7.30pm; April–June & Sept 9.30am–5.30/6pm; Oct to mid-Nov & Feb 18–March 9.30am–12.30pm & 2–5.30/6pm; 25F). In September, an international **fireworks festival** takes place here (details and bookings on ☎47.57.20.97).

Close to the château on rue Victor-Hugo, you'll find the **Caveau de Dégustation-Vente des Vins de Touraine Amboise** (daily March–Sept 10am–7.30pm), a good place to try some wines if you haven't got time to visit individual vineyards. Amboise celebrates its wines in a *Foire aux Vins* on August 15. And if you're heading towards Chenonceaux, you'll pass a farmhouse by a crossroads and a petrol station some 4.5km out from Amboise on the D81. Here, M. Delecheneau sells his *sec* and *demi-sec* white wine and sublime *demi-sec* rosé across the kitchen table. He'll show you his barrels named after cows (Dauphine, Jolie, Violette, etc) and the wine press his grandfather used.

Practicalities

Amboise's overpriced **hotels** don't exactly encourage long stays. Ones worth trying are the central *Français*, 1 pl Chaptal (☎47.57.11.38; ③), *Le Lion d'Or*, 17 quai Charles-Guinot (☎47.57.00.23; ③; half-board compulsory in season), just below the château, and the very pretty *Hôtel du Parc*, 8 av Leonardo-de-Vinci (☎47.57.06.93; ③–⑤). On the budget end of the scale, there's a good **campsite** on the island across from the castle, the *Île d'Or* (☎47.57.23.37), with a **hostel**, the *Centre Charles Péguy* (☎47.57.06.36; ①; reception 3–8pm; closed Mon all year & Sun in winter) next door.

The **restaurants** in town don't stay open beyond 10pm, but try the dependable *Lion d'Or* (menus from 130F), or there are two *crêperies*, on the approach to the château (closed Thurs), and at 7 rue Corneille (closed Sun & Mon during term time).

The **tourist office** is on quai du Général-de-Gaulle, on the riverfront (☎47.57.09.28). If you want to rent bikes, try the **campsite**, *L'Arbelle*, rte des Ormeaux (☎47.57.57.17), or *Cycles Richard*, 2 rue Nazelles.

Villandry

Even if gardens aren't your thing, it's highly recommended you devote some time to getting out to the garden at **VILLANDRY** (daily 8.30am–8pm; April–May 9am–7pm; mid-Sept to March 9am–dusk; gardens 26F, château & gardens 40F). Thirteen kilometres west of Tours along the Cher – a superb cycle trip – this recreated Renaissance garden is no ordinary formal pattern of opposing primary colours, but more like a tapestry of that period, one that changes with the months and only fades in winter. Carrots, cabbages and aubergines are exalted to coloured threads woven beneath rose bowers; herbs and ornamental box hedges are part of the same artwork, divided by vine-shaded paths. From a terrace above, you can see the confluence of the Cher and the Loire and châteaux on the northern bank.

Just past the château, 1km down the D121 towards Druye, there's an upmarket farmhouse restaurant, the *Domaine de la Giraudière* (☎47.50.08.60; daily mid-March to Nov 12), that serves elaborate meals for 150–200F, with some excellent specialities based on goat's cheese. In **SAVONNIÈRES**, between Villandry and Tours, there's *Le Faisan*, rte de Villandry (☎47.50.00.17; ②–③), and the *Ferme Auberge de la Tuilerie* (☎47.50.00.51; Easter–Oct; closed Tues), a farm serving straightforward and very pleasant family meals, with a set menu from 110F; cross the Cher, follow the D288, take the first left along the bank of the Cher and the farm is on your left.

St-Michel-sur-Loire, Langeais, Bourgueil and Gizeux

The **Château de Langeais** sits on a high terrace on the river's north bank in the middle of the town with the same name, looking sturdily severe (daily 9am–noon & 2–5pm; mid-July to Aug 9am–10pm; mid-March to mid-July & Oct 9am–6.30pm; 35F). It is purely fifteenth century, with furnishings to match, and significant to the French because it was built to stop any incursions up the Loire by the Bretons. This threat ended with Charles VIII and Duchess Anne of Brittany's marriage in 1491, which was celebrated in this castle. A diptych of the couple doesn't show them looking very joyous at their union – Anne had little choice in giving up her independence. There are fine tapestries on show, but this is a visit only for real château addicts. Langeais has a pleasant hotel, the *Hosten*, 2 rue Gambetta (☎47.96.70.63; ④–⑤; closed June 20 to July 12), with a good but expensive restaurant.

Five kilometres further west along the river bank, the little town **ST-MICHEL-SUR-LOIRE** has its **Musée Cadillac** located in the Château de Planchoury (daily 10am–6pm; Sept–April daily except Tues; closed Jan; 30F). This is the largest collection of Cadillacs outside the USA, comprising fifty different models of the American dream machine collected from all over the world, and all in remarkable condition.

If you want to do some wine buying, **BOURGUEIL** is just 13km west of St-Michel-sur-Loire. The Abbaye de Bourgueil has been making wine for nearly a thousand years and this is the best place to taste it. The *Close de l'Abbaye* (Mon–Sat 2.30–7pm; ☎47.97.76.30) in the abbey close, just east of the town centre, is open for visits. Bourgueil's *Foire aux Vins* is held the first weekend in March; on the third Tuesday in July they celebrate garlic; and on the third Tuesday in October, it's chestnuts that are honoured.

If you're heading north towards the Sarthe, an interesting stop is **GIZEUX**, 12km north of Bourgueil or 15km on a back-road route from St-Michel, whose fourteenth- to sixteenth-century **château** extends like a game of dominoes around its gardens (May–Sept Mon–Sat 10am–6.30pm, Sun 2–6pm; 35F). It contains some fine Renaissance paintings and beautiful seventeenth-century frescoes, but its speciality is the humble donkey: the **Musée Vivant de l'Ane** (April–Oct Mon–Sat 10am–6.30pm, Sun 2–6pm; 30F, combined ticket with château 50F) has gathered together pack saddles and all the means of controlling and cajoling these stubborn beasts of burden, and has sixty different breeds for you to sympathize with in the park.

The Cher

The **Château de Chenonceau** spans the slow-moving **River Cher**, 20km southeast of Tours, perhaps the best of all the Loire châteaux for architecture, site, contents, organization and atmosphere. **Montrichard** and **St-Aignan** are two places to go to escape the endless stream of castle tours, but for still-unsatiated château buffs, there's **Valençay** on the way south towards the upper stretches of the Indre.

The Château de Chenonceau

Unlike the Loire, the gentle River Cher flows so slowly and passively between the exquisite arches of the **Château de Chenonceau** that you are almost always assured of a perfect reflection (daily 9am–7pm; mid-Sept to Oct 9am–6pm; Nov to mid-Feb 9am–4.30pm; mid-Feb to mid-March 9am–5.30pm; 40F).

The building of the château was always controlled by women. Cathérine Briconnet, whose husband bought the site, hired the first architects in 1515 and had them begin building on the foundations of an old mill that stood on the granite bed of the Cher. The château's most characteristic feature, the set of arches spanning the River Cher, was begun later in the century by Diane de Poitiers (mistress of Henri II) and completed by the indomitable Catherine de Médicis (wife of Henri II), after she evicted Diane and forced her to hand over the château in return for the much more sober Chaumont (see p.412). Mary, Queen of Scots, child-bride of François II, also spent time here until her husband's early death. Then, after a long period of disuse, one Mme Dupin brought eighteenth-century life to this gorgeous residence, along with her guests Voltaire, Montesquieu and Rousseau, whom she hired as tutor to her son. Restoration back to the sixteenth-century designs was completed by another woman in the late nineteenth century. It is now a profitable business, owned and run by the Menier chocolate family firm.

The best approach to the château is not straight up the path to the front door, but through the gardens laid out under Diane de Poitiers. After the pay-booths, cross the stream and follow signs to the maze. Walk along the stream through the woods, turn right to the Cher and, upriver, there's a magnificent view of the château.

During summer the place is teeming with people but visits are unguided – a luxurious relief, for there's an endless number of arresting tapestries, paintings, ceilings, floors and furniture on show. On the ground floor the Chambre de François I features a portrait of Diane de Poitiers by Primaticcio and a case containing copies of her signatures. Another exceptional picture is Zurbaran's half-dressed *Archimedes* with his clothes inside out and a face full of fear and justified suspicion that his theories will be misunderstood. The Salle des Gardes on the same floor, its painted rafters emblazoned with the device of Catherine de Médicis, is used to exhibit Flemish tapestries. The elegant gallery across the Cher, despite the plastic potted plants, is worth spending time in if only to evoke the parties – all naked nymphs and Italian fireworks – held there by Catherine.

There's a *son et lumière* show, "Les Dames de Chenonceau", tracing the history of the château from fortified mill to elegant residence, on June 3 and 4, then every evening from June 24 to Sep 3 (10.15pm; 40F). In July and August you can take boats out onto the Cher, and there's a crèche if you've got small children.

Practicalities

The **tourist office** for Chenonceaux, Chisseaux and Franceuil is at 13bis rue du Château in Chenonceaux (☎47.23.94.45). All the **hotels** in the village of Chenonceaux are on rue du Docteur-Bretonneau within easy reach of the station and the château. The *Hôtel du Roy* at no. 9 (☎47.23.90.17; ①–③) is excellent value for a comfortable hotel. At no. 6, the *Hôtel du Bon Laboureur et du Château* (☎47.23.90.02; ④–⑤) is the most luxurious option. *Le Renaudière*, no. 24 (☎47.23.90.04; ④–⑤), is very welcoming, with decent food on menus from 95F. If these are all booked up you could try *Le Cheval Blanc* at 5 place Charles-Bidault in **BLÉRÉ**, 5km downstream (☎47.30.30.14; ③–④), a

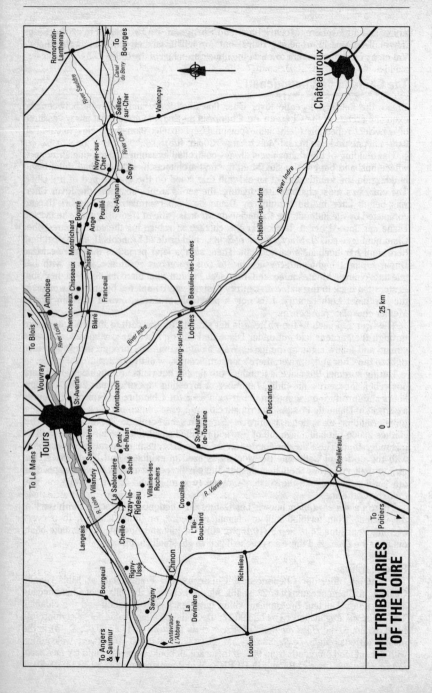

THE TRIBUTARIES
OF THE LOIRE

very pleasant place serving finely cooked meals, with menus from 98F, or the *Clair Cottage*, 27 rue de l'Europe at **CHISSEAUX** (☎47.23.90.69; closed Jan & Feb; ②–③), 2km east of Chenonceaux. For **camping**, there's *Le Moulin Fort* (☎47.23.86.22; Easter to mid-Sept) in **FRANCEUIL**, south of the river.

Montrichard and Bourré

If you're beginning to feel peeved that only dead royals had all the fun, take yourself to the *Fraise-Or*, 3km east of Chenonceaux, just beyond Chisseaux on the road to **MONTRICHARD**. It's an old-fashioned **distillery** (Easter–Sept daily 9–11.30am & 2–6pm; 15F) specializing in fruit liqueurs and complete with shiny copper stills. The visit includes a *dégustation* of three of their eighteen liqueurs and *eaux-de-vie*, based on various fruits, herbs, spices, nuts and, best of all, rose petals.

Montrichard itself is one of those laid-back market towns with its full complement of medieval and Renaissance buildings plus ruined fortress, of which just the **keep** remains. Its Romanesque church was where the disabled twelve-year-old princess, Jeanne de Valois, who would never be able to have children, married her cousin the Duc d'Orléans, who subsequently became King Louis XII after the unlikely death of Charles VIII at Amboise. Politics dictated that he marry Charles VIII's widow Anne of Brittany, so poor Jeanne was divorced and sent off to a nunnery in Bourges.

Montrichard's **tourist office** is in the Maison Ave Maria (daily 10am–noon & 2–5.30pm), an ancient house with saints and beasties sculpted down its beams, on rue du Pont. If the gentle pace of Montrichard takes your fancy, some **hotels** to try are *La Tête Noir*, 24 rue de Tours (☎54.32.05.55; ②–④), by the river, or the cheaper *Hôtel de la Gare*, 20 av de la Gare (☎54.32.04.36; ①–③). The **campsite** *L'Etourneau* (☎54.32.10.16; June to mid-Sept) is on the banks of the Cher, and you can rent **canoes** from the *Club Nautique* (☎54.71.49.49). On the D17, the smaller of the two roads from Montrichard to St-Aignan (see below), between Angé and Pouillé, a good-value **restaurant**, *Le Bousquet*, serves simple meat dishes cooked over a charcoal grill and cheap jugs of local *AOC* wine in an old wine cellar (☎54.71.44.44; July & Aug Tues evening to Sun; rest of the year weekends & holidays only; menus from 71F).

Three kilometres to the east of Montrichard, in **BOURRÉ**, are the quarries for the famous château-building stone that gets whiter as it weathers. Some of the caves are now used to cultivate mushrooms, a peculiar process that you can witness at the **Caves Champignonnières**, 40 rte des Roches (guided visits: daily April–Oct at 10am, 11am, 2pm, 3pm, 4pm & 5pm; 18F). There's also a pleasant *gîte d'étape* in the lock keeper's house at Bourré, the *Vallagon* (☎54.32.50.59; 50F). In Pouillé, on the N76, the *Auberge Le Bien-Allé* (☎54.71.47.45; closed Sun evening), in an attractive eighteenth-century country house overlooking the Cher, has similar fare, with menus starting from 88F.

St-Aignan

ST-AIGNAN, 15km upstream from Montrichard, presents a striking silhouette to the river, composed of its huge Romanesque collegiale church and sixteenth-century château, with the houses of this small and very charming town clustered below.

La Collégiale de St-Aignan (Mon–Sat 9am–7pm, Sun 1–7pm) has some of the best ecclesiastical decoration in the region. Its capitals are adorned with mermaids, a multi-bodied snake biting its own necks, a man's head tunnelled by an eagle, doleful dragons and other wonders of the twelfth-century imagination, while in the crypt are some very well preserved, brightly coloured medieval frescoes.

St-Aignan lends itself to aimless wandering, with the **château grounds** accessible to the public and some pleasant walks down by the river – or a swim if you feel inclined. On the road bridge above the long island facing the town is the *Maison du Vin*, open for tastings and sales of *Côteaux du Cher* wines (July & Aug). On the mainland east of the bridge at 21 quai JJ-Delorme, the *Agence des Trois Provinces* runs boat trips (☎54.75.15.24; departures April–Oct 10.30am, 3pm & 5pm; 50F), or you can rent a **house boat** (2100F–2500F for four people for a weekend) and explore the Berry Canal, which joins the river at St-Aignan. At the *Base Nautique Les Couflons*, a couple of kilometres upstream in Seigy, you can windsurf, canoe and sail. **Bikes** can be rented in town from *Le Tandem*, 54 rue Constant-Ragot.

For a good break from ancient aristocratic artefacts, St-Aignan has the **Zoo Parc de Beauval** (daily 9am–dusk; 50F), 2km to the south of town on the D675. The space given to the animals is ample, and it's part of the European programme for breeding threatened species in captivity to reintroduce them to the wild. From a human viewpoint the park is very attractive, with sumptuous flowerbeds giving way to suitably wild areas of woods, little streams and lakes where the islands provide natural enclosures for some of the monkeys. Two hothouses with tropical flowers and greenery are home to an extraordinary collection of tropical birds and to a large group of chimpanzees and two families of orang-utans. But the creature most children will want to take home with them is the rare white tiger, in particular the ultimate fantasy cuddly pet, Katharina, the first cub to be bred in France.

The **tourist office** is on the island by the road bridge, opposite the *Maison du Vin*. If you're staying the night, **hotels** worth choosing from include *Le Moulin*, 7 rue Novilliers (☎54.75.15.54; ①; closed Sun), to the west of the bridge, with meals for only 52F, or *Le Grand Hôtel*, 7-9 quai J-J-Delorme (☎54.75.18.04; ①–④; closed Sun evening & Mon; menus from 80F). Otherwise, you'll have to look for rooms in **NOYER-SUR-CHER** on the other side of the river. St-Aignan has an excellent **campsite**, near Seigy, the *Camping des Cochards* (☎54.75.15.59; mid-March to mid-Oct).

St-Aignan has few restaurants and none of them is special. Besides the two hotels, you could try *Le Crepiot*, 36 rue Constant-Ragot (☎54.75.21.39; closed Mon & Tues midday), with a terrace where you can eat grills, crêpes and so forth.

Valençay

There is nothing medieval about the fittings and furnishings of the **Château de Valençay**, 20km southeast of St-Aignan on the main Blois–Châteauroux road (daily June–Sept 9am–5.15pm; March–May, Oct & Nov 9am–11.15 & 2–5.15pm; 32F). This proud and overbearing castle was built to show off the wealth of a sixteenth-century financier. Two hundred and fifty years later it was used to illustrate the power of Napoléon's France, as residence of the empire's foreign minister, the Prince de Talleyrand. The contrast of eras is one of the chief interests of Valençay.

Inside the château there hangs an arrogant portrait of the minister, a great political operator and survivor, by François Bonneau. A bishop before the Revolution, with a reputation for having the most desirable mistresses, he proposed the nationalization of church property, renounced his bishopric, escaped to America during the Terror, backed Napoléon and continued to serve the state under the restored Bourbons. One of his tasks for the emperor was keeping Ferdinand VII of Spain entertained for six years here after the king had been forced to abdicate in favour of Napoléon's brother Joseph. The Treaty of Valençay, signed in the château in 1813, put an end to Ferdinand's forced guest status, giving him back his throne.

The interior consequently is largely First Empire, with elaborately embroidered chairs on spindly legs, Chinese vases, ornate inlays and studdings to all the tables, finicky clocks and chandeliers: in short, the sort of furnishings dominated by strict rules of etiquette. Some of the Renaissance period rooms, in which it's easier to imagine more passionate and rougher lifestyles, are being opened.

The château **park** (summer 9am–noon & 2–6pm; winter 2–6pm) keeps a collection of unhappy looking camels, zebras, llamas and kangaroos. There's also yet another **car museum** (same hours and ticket as the château) with pre-World War I Michelin maps and guides.

Azay-le-Rideau and around

Even without its **château** (daily April–Oct 9.30am–5.30pm; July & Aug closes 6.30pm; winter 10am–noon & 2–4.30pm; 31F), **AZAY-LE-RIDEAU** would bask in its serene setting: an island in the Indre, an old mill by the bridge, the Carolingian statues embedded in the façade of the church of St-Symphorien, and a quiet village. The château exterior, however, on its little island in the Indre, is one of the loveliest in the Loire: pure turreted Renaissance and required viewing. While the guided tours of the interior, furnished in period style, don't add much to the experience, the portrait gallery is worth seeing, since it has the whole sixteenth-century royal Loire crew – François I, Catherine de Médicis, the de Guises, and the rest – the highlight being a seminude painting of Gabrielle d'Estrée, Henri IV's lover.

The downside is that **hotels** in Azay-le-Rideau don't come cheap, though *Le Balzac*, 4 & 6 rue A-Richer (☎47.45.42.08; ③), and *Le Grand Monarque*, 3 place de la République (☎47.45.40.08; ③–⑥; half-board compulsory in season), are both comfortable possibilities. Upstream from the château is a large **campsite**, the *Camping du Sabot*, near to the swimming pool and sports centre (☎47.45.42.72), signed off the D84 to Saché. The **restaurant** of *Le Grand Monarque* is very acceptable, with a midday menu for around 100F, or try *L'Automate Gourmand*, 1 rue Parc (☎47.45.39.07; closed Tues & Mon evening out of season), with weekday menus from 120F.

A rotating gourmet **night-time market** operates between Azay-le-Rideau, Bourgeuil and Langeais, from 5pm to midnight, June to September, and involves lots of drinking and delicious snacks. Azay's **tourist office** on place de l'Europe (☎47.45.44.40) can give you the dates. You can rent **bikes** at the station or from *Le Provost*, 13 rue Carnot.

Ussé

Fourteen kilometres west of Azay-le-Rideau, as the Indre approaches its confluence with the Loire, is the **Château d'Ussé** in **RIGNY-USSÉ** (daily 9–11.45am & 2–5.30/6.30pm; mid-July to Aug 9am–6.15pm; Sept 27 to Nov 11 10–11.45am & 2–5.30pm; closed Nov 12 to mid-March; 54F). With its shimmering white towers and spires and idyllic wooded setting (best seen after dark when floodlit), this is the ultimate fairytale château, so much so that it's supposed to have inspired Charles Perrault's transcription of the Sleeping Beauty fairy story. Going inside for the visit – despite a display of models illustrating the Sleeping Beauty myth which might be of interest to children – isn't half as compelling, and perhaps not worth the rather excessive entrance fee.

Villaines-les-Rochers

Six kilometres south of Azay-le-Rideau is the troglodyte village of **VILLAINES-LES-ROCHERS**, famous for its wickerwork cooperative set up in 1849 by the local curate to keep the village economically sustainable; you can still visit the **Coopérative de**

Vannerie (Mon–Sat 9am–noon & 2–7pm, Sun 2–7pm; April–Sept Mon–Sat 9am–noon & 2–7pm, Sun 10am–noon & 2–7pm). Villaines now produces a third of all wickerwork articles in France. You can visit the **workshops** that are dug into the rock, providing perfect humid conditions for keeping the willow supple, and buy baskets, chairs and so forth from the *Maison d'Exposition*.

Upstream along the Indre

Following the D84 from Azay-le-Rideau eastwards along the north bank of the Indre you get glimpses of various privately owned châteaux. North of the hamlet of La Sablonnière, on the top of a hill surrounded by vines with beautiful views of the Indre valley and the village of **SACHÉ**, is where Alexander Calder, sculptor of mobiles and stabiles, had his last atelier. He also worked at La Chevrière just down the slope to the east.

An Alexander Calder mobile decorates the main square of Saché, but it is the novelist Balzac who gets the honours here. The house where he often stayed and wrote several of his novels, notably the locally set *Le Lys dans la Vallée*, is inevitably a **Musée Balzac** (daily 9am–noon & 2–6pm; July & Aug 9.30am–6.30pm; Feb to mid-March; Oct & Nov 9.30am–noon & 2–4pm; closed Dec & Jan; 21F).

Loches and around

Apart from Azay-le-Rideau near the confluence with the Loire (see above), **LOCHES** is the obvious place to head for on the River Indre. Its walled citadel is by far the most impressive of the Loire valley fortresses, with its unbreached ramparts and the Renaissance houses below still partly enclosed by the outer wall of the medieval town.

The **old town** is announced by the Tour St-Antoine belfry, close to place du Marché (Wednesday market), linking rue St-Antoine with Grande Rue. Two fifteenth-century gates to the old town still stand: the **Porte des Cordeliers** by the river at the end of Grande Rue, and the **Porte Picois** to the west, at the end of rue St-Antoine; rue du Château, lined with Renaissance buildings, leads to the twelfth-century towers of **Porte Royale**, the main entrance to the citadel.

The Citadel

The Porte Royale contains the **Musée de Terroir**, a traditional museum of rural life and crafts (daily except Fri 9–11.45am & 2–4/5/6pm; 15F). Beyond the gateway, down to the left is the **Musée Lansyer** with works by the local nineteenth-century painter Lansyer, overshadowed by a Japanese collection that includes a complete samurai suit of armour (daily except Fri 9–11.45am & 2–4/5/6pm; 15F). Straight ahead is the Romanesque church, the **Collégiale de St-Ours**, with its odd roofline of four turrets, two of which are supported by octagonal pyramids. The porch has some entertaining twelfth-century monster carvings and the stoup, or basin for holy water, is a Gallo-Roman altar.

The northern end of the citadel is taken up by the **Logis Royal**, or Royal Lodgings of Charles VII and his three successors (Thurs–Sun 9am–noon & 2–5pm; July & Aug 9am–6pm; mid-March to June & Sept 9am–noon & 2–6pm; 26F). The medieval half of the palace saw two women of some importance to Charles: Joan of Arc, victorious from Orléans, came here to give the defeatist Dauphin another pep talk about coronations, and later the less significant but much sexier Agnès Sorel, Charles's lover, resided here. Even the pope took a fancy to her, which allowed Charles to be the first French king to have an officially recognized mistress on tap. She was buried at

Loches and her tomb now lies in the fifteenth-century wing, her alabaster recumbent figure restored after anticlerical revolutionary soldiers ironically mistook her for a saint. Also in the same room there's a portrait of her in full regalia and a painting of the Virgin in her likeness; the seminudity in both was no artist's fantasy, but a courtly fashion trend set by Sorel.

While little remains today in the Logis Royal to give much impression of the highlife of kings' favourites, the nastiness of being out of favour is clear at the other end of the citadel. Here are the dungeons and two keeps, the larger one, the **donjon**, initiated by Foulques Nerra, the eleventh-century Count of Anjou, with cells and a torture chamber added in the fifteenth century (daily 9.30am–12.30pm & 2.30–6.30pm; July & Aug 9.30am–6.30pm; Oct to mid-March Thurs–Sun 9.30am–12.30pm & 2.30–5.30pm; same ticket as Logis). There is not much left of the fifteenth-century extension, thanks to the people of Loches, who destroyed most of the torture equipment during the Revolution, and although the very professional guides make up for the lack of exhibits with their spiel, they can't quite express the goriness. You can climb unescorted to the top of the keep, even if the surrounding countryside is unexciting.

At the end of the tour you can stay underground for a lesson in mushroom cultivation in the **Galerie du Champignon** (Easter–Sept Wed–Sun 10.30am–12.30pm & 2.30–6.30pm; 18F), or follow the signed path along the ancient **moat** and **ramparts** around the back of the citadel.

Practicalities

From the *gare SNCF* on the east side of the Indre, av de la Gare leads to place de la Marne, with the **tourist office** on your left (☎47.59.07.98) and the **gare routière** a short way down rue de Tours from the *place*. Loches is only an hour's train or coach journey away from Tours, but you may well want to **stay**, particularly if you're camping. The *Hôtel George Sand*, 37 rue Quintefol (☎47.59.39.74; ③–⑤), just below the eastern ramparts, has its best rooms at the back looking onto the river; its restaurant is not at all bad, with menus from 85F. The *Hôtel Tour Ste-Antoine*, 2 rue des Moulins (☎47.59.01.06; ③), is the only hotel in the old town itself, but the *France*, 6 rue Picois, near the Porte Picois (☎47.59.00.32; ③), is pleasanter, with an excellent restaurant, whose menus start at 82F. The *Camping Municipal de la Citadelle* (☎47.59.05.91; April–Nov) is between two branches of the Indre by the swimming pool and stadium, looking up at the east side of the citadel.

Beaulieu-les-Loches

Just across the Indre from Loches is the village of **BEAULIEU-LES-LOCHES** – an extraordinary, unvisited place, thoroughly medieval in appearance and with its parish church built into the spectacular ruins of an abbey contemporary with the Loches keep. Its other church, **St-Pierre**, holds the bones of Foulques Nerra, the eleventh-century count of Anjou responsible for Loches' grisly *donjon*.

In Beaulieu-les-Loches, there's a decent low-budget **hotel**, the *Hôtel de Beaulieu*, 3 rue Foulques Nerra (☎47.91.60.80; ②).

Chatillon and Châteauroux

If you follow the Indre upstream into the region of Berry, the river itself tends to be the only source of interest – other than the Romanesque church in the pretty town of **CHATILLON-SUR-INDRE**, on the Touraine–Berry border. **CHÂTEAUROUX**, the largest town on the banks of the Indre and a local route hub, is a grey and officious sort of place, but further south the river flows past George Sand's old haunt of Nohant and La Châtre.

Chinon

CHINON lies on the north bank of the Vienne, 12km from its confluence with the Loire and surrounded by some of the best vineyards in the Loire valley. The spectacular line of towers and ramparts on the high ridge to the east of the town look as if they must enclose one of the best of this region's châteaux, but all is ruins within. In an attempt to make up for the loss, a medieval quarter below has been restored in over sanitized fashion, and the town's total dedication to tourism has removed whatever charm Chinon might have possessed.

The Town

A fortress of one kind or another existed at Chinon from the Stone Age until the time of Louis XIV, the age of the most recent of its ruins. It was a favourite residence of Henry Plantagenet, who held title to it long before he inherited the throne of England. He added a new castle to the first medieval fortress on the site, built by his ancestor Foulques Nerra, and died here. His son Richard the Lionheart is also said to have breathed his last in Chinon after being wounded in a battle against the French, though he was probably dead on arrival. Richard's son John, with no English inheritance, stayed in Chinon off and on but after a year's siege in 1204–5, Philippe Auguste finally took the castle and put an end to the Plantagenet rule over Touraine and Anjou.

Over two hundred years later, Chinon was one of the few places where Charles VII could safely stay while Henry V of England held Paris and the title to the French throne. Charles' situation changed with the arrival here in 1429 of a peasant girl from Domrémy in Lorraine, with a manic light in her eyes and a conviction so strong in her God-given mission that she was able to talk her way into the castle. Joan of Arc proposed, as proof of her divine guidance, that she would be able to recognize the Dauphin. The court officials, no doubt thinking that humiliating this overprecocious seventeen-year-old would be an entertaining pastime for Charles, agreed. To their amazement, despite the Dauphin disguising himself in a crowd of courtiers, Joan instantly went down on her knees before him, begging him to allow her to lead his army against the English. And to their horror, Charles said yes.

Today, all that remains in the **château** (daily July & Aug 9am–7pm; mid-March to June & Sept 9am–6pm; Oct 9am–5pm; Nov–March 9am–noon & 2–5pm; 23F) is the scene of this encounter, the Grande Salle, with a wall and first-floor fireplace. Visits to this and to the restored Royal Lodgings – both guided – are not wildly exciting. More interesting is the Tour Coudray, over to the west, covered with intricate thirteenth-century graffiti carved by imprisoned and doomed Templar knights. Joan is said to have stayed here, too, and to have watered her horse at the pump and prayed in the church on rue Voltaire after her journey from eastern France.

Below, the town continues its celebration of the long dead, and in sterile fashion: medieval streets vaunting their olde-worlde-ness, overpriced cafés and brasseries, and a wine- and barrel-making museum with tacky, animated models and free tasting of the worst wine. On the first weekend in August tourists are regaled with a bogus reconstruction of a medieval market. The **Marché à l'Ancienne** on the third Saturday of August is similar tourist fodder, the costumes this time of nineteenth-century peasants and the parades led by live pigs, geese and goats.

If you like boats, the models of barges and other vessels that used to carry goods along the Vienne and the Loire in the last century are likely to be the most appealing exhibits of the **Musée du Vieux Chinon** at 44 rue Haute St-Maurice (July–Sept daily 10am–12.30pm & 2.30–7pm; 15F).

Practicalities

The **gare SNCF** lies to the east of the town with rue du Docteur P-Labussière and rue du 11-novembre, leading to the **gare routière** on place Jeanne d'Arc, where Joan is sculptured in mid-battle charge. Keep heading west, either along the river bank or across place Mirabeau into rue Rabelais, and you'll soon reach the medieval quarter. The **tourist office** is at 12 rue Voltaire (daily 10am–noon & 2–5.30pm; ☎47.93.17.85), below the eastern end of the castle.

If you need a **room**, the two cheapest alternatives are the *Point du Jour*, 102 quai Jeanne-d'Arc (☎47.93.07.20; ①–②), and the *Jeanne d'Arc*, 11 rue Voltaire (☎47.93.02.85; ①–②). In a grand eighteenth-century house east of St-Mexme church, the *Hôtel Diderot*, 4 rue Buffon (☎47.93.18.87; ③–④), is a more comfortable option. Dorm rooms and **bikes** for rental are available at the *Centre Animation Accueil*, close to the *gare SNCF* on rue Descartes (☎47.93.10.48; curfew 10.30pm; ①); turn left out of the station onto av Gambetta, and first right into rue Descartes. The **campsite**, *Camping de l'Île Auger* (☎47.93.08.35; mid-March to Oct), overlooks the old town and château from the south bank of the Vienne; turn right from the bridge along quai Danton.

The most reasonably priced decent **restaurant** is *Les Années 30*, 78 rue Voltaire (☎47.93.37.18; closed Wed, Thurs & Nov–Easter; menus from 75F), although Chinon's best one is *Au Plaisir Gourmand*, 2 rue Parmentier (☎47.93.20.48; closed Sun evening & Mon), where you can try *filet de sandre* or wonderful *langoustines* on menus from 175F. These apart, you'll have to make do with indifferent pizzas and crêpes, or pay over the odds for "gargantuan" menus (see below for the Rabelais connection) in the restaurants of the medieval quarter.

You can leave Chinon by **boat**. *Le Club Chinonais de Canoë-Kayak*, on the south bank by the campsite (☎47.93.39.59), offers groups trips up to L'Île Bouchard or down to Candes (July & Aug 10am–6pm), or you can rent **canoes** and **kayaks** on Saturday afternoon and Sunday (around 80F for half a day).

Around Chinon

Although the town of Chinon has been ruined by commercialism, it's a short walk out into the open countryside, with the added interest of some of the region's troglodyte dwellings on the way. The **Coteaux Sainte-Ragonde** (GR3) leads from St-Mexme's church at the eastern end of rue Jean-Jacques Rousseau. The route is lined with cave dwellings, some of which are still inhabited, and ends at the **Chapelle Ste-Radegonde**, a rock-cut church which is part of a complex of cave dwellings in which Saint Radegonde lived with her followers. The sixth-century German princess renounced the world and her husband – probably not a great sacrifice since he eventually murdered her brother – in order to devote her life to God.

The other good excuse for getting out of Chinon is to discover the delights of the Chinon *appellation* ruby-red **wines**. The vineyards extend from **CROUZILLES**, just beyond L'Île Bouchard, 18km upstream, to **SAVIGNY-EN-VÉRON**, near the confluence of the Vienne and the Loire. *Vin de Pâques* (Easter wine) is the name given to the wine that should be drunk young, but most Chinon will age for thirty years, sometimes even longer. Though reds dominate there are also a dry white and dry rosé. The Chinon tourist office can provide a list of wine growers to visit (see above).

The man who vies with Joan of Arc for shops and streets named in his honour in Chinon is the French satirical writer François Rabelais (1494–1553), who wrote approvingly of wine, food and laughter in serious and rather difficult humanist texts, and whose most famous creations are the giant father and son Gargantua and Pantagruel. He was born at **LA DEVINIÈRE**, 6km southwest of Chinon, in a steep-roofed farmhouse that is now a **museum** to the great man (May–Sept daily 10am–7pm; Oct, Nov, Feb–April Thurs–Sun 9am–noon & 2–5/6pm; 20F), completely furnished in the style of the time, right down to the stone kitchen sink.

Saumur and around

Unlike many small Loire towns, **Saumur** is not completely dominated by its château. Nor is it dominated by the military – which it might well be as the home of the French Cavalry Academy, and its successor the Armoured Corps Academy, since 1763; even the local sparkling wines are based elsewhere. Saumur itself is simply peaceful and pretty. The Hôtel de Ville strives busily to attract festivals and conferences, and, when they're successful, finding a room can be a problem. Even at the best of times, reservations are essential.

From Saumur down to Angers is the loveliest stretch of the Loire, with the bizarre draw of **troglodyte dwellings** carved out of cliffs as early as the twelfth century. The land to the south, under grapes and sunflowers, gradually rises away from the river, with long-inactive windmills still standing. Across the water cows graze in wooded pastures. For transport you can either take the train or one of three buses – #5 along the south bank, #11 crossing halfway, or #10 staying north of the river.

Arrival and accommodation

Arriving at the **gare SNCF**, you'll find yourself on the north bank of the Loire: turn right onto av-David-d'Angers and either take bus #A to the centre or cross the bridge to the island on foot. From the island the old **Pont Cessart** takes you to the main part of the town on the south bank. The **gare routière** is in the centre, a couple of blocks from the Pont Cessart on place St-Nicolas. Saumur's main street, rue d'Orléans, cuts back through the south bank sector: the **tourist office** is just across the river on the left, on place de la Bilange (daily 10am–noon & 2–5.30pm; ☎41.51.03.06). The old quarter, around St-Pierre and the castle, is reached along rue Dacier, also to the left of rue d'Orléans.

Hotels

Anne d'Anjou, 32 quai Mayaud (☎41.67.30.30). An eighteenth-century listed building with service and comfort to match. ④–⑥.

Hôtel de Bretagne, 55 rue St-Nicholas (☎41.51.26.38). A few rooms above a bar. Not the quietest place but central and clean. Closed Sun pm. ①–②.

Hôtel Central, 23 rue Daillé (☎41.51.05.78). A small, quiet and comfortable hotel. ③.

Hôtel Le Cristal, 10–12 pl de la République (☎41.51.09.54). One of the nicest hotels, with river views from most rooms and very friendly proprietors. ③.

Hôtel La Croix de Guerre, 9 rue de la Petite-Bilange (☎41.51.05.88). Not wildly appealing but with some very cheap rooms; above a café. Closed Sun. ①–②.

Hôtel du Roi René, 94 av du Général-de-Gaulle (☎41.67.45.30). On the Île d'Offard with lovely river and château views. ④.

St-Pierre, 3 rue Haute St-Pierre (☎41.50.33.00). Large, well-equipped and very comfortable rooms in the old quarter. ④–⑦.

Youth hostels and campsites

Youth hostel, rue de Verden, Île d'Offard (☎41.67.45.00). From the station, take the second left off av du Général-de-Gaulle; it's at the east end of the island. Reception 8–10am & 5–10pm; late-night key available. Boat and bike rental available. ①.

Camping municipal, rue de Verden, Île d'Offard (☎41.67.45.00). Next door to the youth hostel. You can even swim in the Loire from the north side of the island.

La Chantepie, on the D751, St-Hilaire-St-Florent (☎41.67.95.34). An alternative to the municipal campsite, a couple of kilometres west of Saumur.

The Town

The **château** is the town's main crowd-puller (daily Wed–Mon 10am–noon & 2–5pm; mid-June to mid-Sept 9am–7pm; July & Aug Wed & Sat till 10pm; April to mid-June & last two weeks in Sept 9am–noon & 2–6pm; 33F), a great, square building high above the town, recognizable as the gleaming white, turreted subject of one of the scenes of the *Très Riches Heures du Duc de Berry*. Its symmetry and witch-hat towers give it an air of fantasy, particularly on a misty morning or under night-time illumination. It was built in the fourteenth century and turned into a much more decorative and comfortable residence by Duke Réné of Anjou in the fifteenth. The star-shaped fortifications around it were added in 1590 during the Wars of Religion, when Saumur was a Protestant stronghold.

The dungeons and the watchtower can be visited on your own; for the two larger museums within the château, relaxed guides take over. The **Musée des Arts Décoratifs** in the former royal apartments has a huge and impressive collection of European china, plus several fifteenth-century tapestries, one of which portrays wonderfully snooty-looking medieval ladies out hunting. But it's the **Musée du Cheval**, in the attic of the château, that's the real treat. Progressing from a horse skeleton, through the evolution of bridles and stirrups over the centuries, you finally reach an amazing and diverse international saddlery collection. One of the best pieces is a Russian sleigh on which a fishy female figure looks up at a cherub wearing what seems to be a Roman helmet. The **Musée de la Figurine-Jouet**, located in an ancient powder magazine on the ramparts (Sun 2–6pm; April–Sept daily 10am–12.30pm & 2–6pm; separate ticket from château entrance, 12F), offers a display of ancient toys: farm and zoo animals, circus and theatre figures, cowboys and Indians, and model soldiers.

Back down in the town, a real soldier will escort you around the **Musée de la Cavalerie** (Tues–Thurs 9am–noon & 2–5pm, Sat 2–5pm; free), if you knock at the guarded gate on av Maréchal-Foch, west of rue d'Orléans. Among the uniforms, weapons and battle scenes (including some very recent engagements), there's a particularly moving room, dedicated to the cavalry cadets who held the Loire bridges between Gennes and Montsoreau against the Germans for three days in 1940, after the French government had surrendered. The history of tank warfare is covered in the separate **Musée des Blindés**, northeast of place du Chardonnet (daily 9am–noon & 2–6pm; 15F).

The early medieval pointy-spired **church of St-Pierre** is most notable for its interesting selection of dragons, there are at least seven monsters carved in stone and wood or woven into the sixteenth-century tapestries that tell the legend of Saint Florent, an early scourge of the beautiful beasts that symbolize sin. Saumur's oldest church, **Notre-Dame de Nantilly**, by the public gardens south of the château, contains more sixteenth-century tapestries, with immensely crowded and detailed scenes.

SAUMUR WINES

The **Maison du Vin** at 25 rue Beaurepaire in Saumur has information on locally produced wines and addresses of wine growers. The speciality here is sparkling – *méthode champenoise* – wine, which can rival lesser-quality champagnes. Names to look out for are *Veuve Amiot* and *Gratien-Meyer*. A good red is the *Saumur Champigny* from around the village of the same name. The *Caves Coopératives* at St-Cyr-en-Bourg, a short train hop south of Saumur and near the station, have kilometres of cellars, and you can taste different wines with no obligation to buy.

Beyond the town centre

For a slightly less bellicose diversion, you can visit the **École Nationale d'Équitation**, or demilitarized National Riding School, in St-Hilaire-St-Florent, a suburb to the east of the centre; take bus #B from the town centre. The school provides guided tours in which you can watch training sessions (mornings only; closed Aug) and view the stables (Mon 2.30–4pm, Tues–Fri 9.30–10.30am & 2.30–4pm, Sat 9.30–10.30am; 30F morning visits, 20F afternoons; wheelchair access). Displays of dressage and anachronistic battle manoeuvres by the crackshot Cadre Noir, the former cavalry trainers, are regular events (programme details from the tourist office or the school on ☎41.50.21.35; 60F).

Performances of a far greater diversity are celebrated in the **Musée du Masque**, a short walk back down towards Saumur from the Riding School, on rue de l'Abbaye (daily 10am–1pm & 2.30–7pm; mid-Oct to March Sat & Sun only; 25F). This is very much geared for children, with waxwork models of clowns and storybook characters wearing masks dating from the 1870s to the present day.

Another museum in St-Hilaire-St-Florent, of a very different nature, is the **Musée de Champignon** (mid-Feb to mid-Nov daily 10am–7pm; 32F; wheelchair access), which runs informative (if a bit dank and cold) tours through some of the region's five hundred kilometres of underground *caves de champignons*, used to grow seventy percent of France's commonest cooking mushrooms, the *champignon de Paris*. The entrance is one kilometre downriver, along the D751 from the last bus stop in St-Hilaire-St-Florent.

Finally, in Saumur's suburb north of the Loire, St-Lambert-des-Levées, you can visit an **oil mill** at 29 rue Bouju (Thurs & Fri only by appointment; ☎41.67.43.00; 10F), which makes one of those specialist ingredients loved by professional cooks: walnut oil. Take the second right after the bridge, signed to La Croix Verte.

Eating and drinking

There are several cheap **eating** places around place St-Pierre: *Auberge St-Pierre*, 6 pl St-Pierre (☎41.51.26.25; closed Mon out of season), sometimes has *langoustines* on a fairly cheap menu; opposite is *Les Forges de St-Pierre*, 1 place St-Pierre (☎41.38.21.79), with an acceptable 50F menu; and *La Quichenotte*, 2 rue Haute St-Pierre (☎41.51.31.98; closed Mon), serves good crêpes. *Les Chandelles*, 71 rue St-Nicolas (☎41.67.20.40; closed Wed), offers more sophisticated food, with an excellent weekend lunch menu for 89F. You can also eat in the château grounds at *L'Orangerie* (☎41.67.12.88; closed Sun evening and Mon out of season), a restaurant and *salon de thé*, with an 86F menu.

There are a couple of **bars** on place St-Pierre, like *Le Swing*, with its ancient Wurlitzer jukebox and fruit cocktails, and *Le Richelieu*, with good music, Guinness and pool. The *Café de la Poste*, opposite the post office on place du Petit-Thouars, is a student meeting place that serves cheap snacks, and the bar of *Le Cristal* hotel (see p.432) is also popular.

Troglodyte dwellings

The "falun" or soft shellstone found in the Loire Valley lends itself to **troglodyte dwellings**, homes carved out of rocky outcrops, of which there are more in this area – between Saumur and Angers – than anywhere else in France. It's reckoned that in the twelfth century half the local population here lived in semisubsumed homes carved out of the rock. Today, some of the rock dwellings have surprising uses, along with the more predictable "Troglo" bars and restaurants.

Away from the Loire cliffs on the plains to the south, troglodyte villages were built by digging holes like large craters and then carving out the walls. The best example is at **ROCHEMENIER**, north of Doué-la-Fontaine, about 20km southwest of Saumur, where an **underground village** housed a small farming community with its own underground chapel (April–Oct daily 9.30am–noon & 2–7pm; Nov, Feb & March Sat & Sun 2–6pm; 20F), and was only abandoned in the 1930s. The visit includes a typical troglodyte dwelling, along with a museum of domestic items, including wine and oil presses.

Just 3km north, at **DÉNEZÉ-SOUS-DOUÉ**, there are underground carvings thought to have been sculpted by a secret sixteenth-century sect of libertarians. The cartoon-style figures mock religion, morality, the state and the ruling class, with scenes of sex, strange deformities, and perverted Christian imagery (daily July & Aug 10am–7pm; April–June, Sept & Oct 2–7pm; 20F). There are also concerts in the cave on Wednesday evenings (April–Oct).

Equally bizarre is the **Zoo de Doué** on the D960 to Cholet, 2km southwest of Doué-la-Fontaine (daily 9am–7pm; Oct–March 10am–noon & 2–6pm; 48F), established in one of the region's complexes of quarried falun caverns. The natural setting has been used to full advantage for a cave of fruit bats, a vivarium (formerly a cave dwelling but now home to pythons, anacondas and the like), and a lynx enclosure so spacious and overgrown it's actually hard to spot a cat.

At **PARNAY**, about 7km upstream from Saumur on the south bank of the Loire, you can taste and buy wines from a troglodyte mansion, the **Château du Marconnay**, 75 rte de Saumur (April–Sept Tues–Sun 10am–12.30pm & 2.30–6.30pm; 15F). Further on, just before Turquant, in **LE VAL-HULIN**, are the last producers of the once common Saumurois dried whole apples, known as *pommes tapées* – each apple, after drying, is given a little expert tap to make it a more amenable shape for bottle storage. You can tour one of the workshops at **Le Troglo des Pommes Tapées** (July & Aug Tues–Sun 10am–noon & 2.30–6.30pm; June & Sept Tues–Fri 2.30–6.30pm; Easter–May & Nov 1–11 Sat, Sun & hols 10am–noon & 2.30–6.30pm), where you are taken through the apple drying and tapping process and top off the visit with a tasting.

The Abbaye de Fontevraud

The **Abbaye de Fontevraud**, 13km southeast of Saumur on bus #16, is a key site in French and English history, due to its role as the burial place of both countries' monarchs (guided or independent visits: daily 9am–7pm; mid-Sept to May 9.30am–12.30pm & 2–5.30pm; 23F). The community was established in 1099 as both a nunnery and a monastery with an abbess in charge – an unconventional move, even if the post was filled solely by queens and princesses. The remaining buildings date from the twelfth century and are immense, built as they were to house and separate not only the nuns and monks but also the sick, the lepers and repentant prostitutes. There were originally five separate complexes, of which three still gracefully stand in Romanesque solidity. Used as a prison from the Revolution until 1963, its most famous inmate was the writer Jean Genet.

The **abbey church** is an awe-inspiring space, not least for its emptiness. This was the burial ground of the Plantagenet kings, and four tombstone effigies remain: Henry II, his wife Eleanor of Aquitaine who died here, their son Richard the Lionheart and daughter-in-law Isabelle of Angoulême, King John's queen. There's something a bit spooky about them, carved as they were at the time of their deaths – instead of being almost imaginary characters in the stories told at so many of the Loire châteaux, their deathly figures here come to life. Its strange domed roof, the great cream-coloured columns of the choir and the graceful capitals of the nave add to the atmosphere.

Through the spacious **cloisters** adjoining the church, you pass through an exquisitely carved doorway to enter the **chapterhouse**, decorated with sixteenth-century murals, to which many of the abbesses had their portraits added. The **refectory**, on the opposite side of the cloisters to the church, is another vast impressive space with Gothic vaulting surmounting the Romanesque walls. All the cooking for the religious community, which would have numbered several hundred, was done in the perfectly restored Romanesque kitchen, an octagonal building as extrordinary from the outside, with its 21 spiky chimneys, as it is from within.

The abbey is now the *Centre Culturel de l'Ouest (CCO)*, the cultural centre for western France, and is used for a great many activities, from concerts to lectures, art exhibitions and theatre. Programme details are available at the abbey (☎41.51.73.52) or from the Saumur tourist office (see p.432).

Angers

ANGERS, the capital of the ancient county of Anjou, stands on the banks of the Maine, which feeds the Loire just south of the city with the waters of the Mayenne, Sarthe and Loir rivers. Long known as "Black Angers" from the gloomy-coloured slate and stone quarried here since the ninth century, the town can initially present a forbidding aspect, but it's a friendly place with a lively atmosphere. The overriding reason for coming here is to see its two prize tapestry series, more stirring and stunning than all the châteaux and their contents put together, the fourteenth-century *Apocalypse* and the twentieth-century *Chant du Monde*.

Arrival and accommodation

The **gare SNCF** is south of the centre (☎40.08.50.50), about a ten-minute walk from the château. Bus #2 makes the journey to the tourist office and château, bus #22 to place du Raillement, which is handy for cheap hotels. The **gare routière** is up past the Pont de Verdun on place de la Poissonnerie (☎41.88.59.25). **Local buses** operate on a flat ticket rate of 6F; you can pick up a route **map** from *Cotra*, espace Lorraine. The main **tourist office**, which runs an accommodation service, is on place Kennedy, facing the château (Mon–Sat 9am–7pm, Sun & public hols 10.30am–1pm & 2–6.30pm; mid-Sept to mid-June Mon 10am–12.30pm & 2–6.30pm, Tues–Sat 9am–12.30pm & 2–6.30pm; ☎41.23.51.11).

As you'd expect from a large city, there's a wide range of **accommodation** on offer, and finding a room shouldn't present too many problems, though it's still wise to book ahead in summer.

ANGERS' MUSEUMS

A single 45F ticket allows access to the tapestries, together with the town museums and galleries.

Hotels

Hôtel Centre, 12 rue St-Laud (☎41.87.45.07). Quiet and comfortable hotel. Closed Sun. ①–③.

Hôtel Continental, 12–14 rue Louis-de-Romain (☎41.86.94.94). Central, well-equipped place with good service. ③–④.

Hôtel de la Coupe d'Or, 5 rue de la Gare (☎41.88.45.02). One of several hotels close by the station, if you don't want to lug your bags far. ①.

Hôtel les Lices, 25 rue des Lices (☎41.87.44.10). A real bargain hotel in the centre of town. ①–②.

Hôtel du Mail, 8 rue des Ursules (☎41.88.56.22). Old-fashioned and attractive hotel. ②–④.

Hôtel St-Julien, 9 pl du Ralliement (☎41.88.41.62). Generous and pleasant rooms, all well sound-proofed. ②–④.

Youth hostels and campsites

Centre d'Accueil du Lac du Maine, 49 av du Lac de Maine (☎41.22.32.10). Rather expensive hostel-style accommodation southwest of the town on bus #6 (#26 on Sun), either from the *gare SNCF* or bd Générale-de-Gaulle to stop *Bouchemaine*. You can rent canoes at the *Base Nautique* in the complex. There's also a campsite here. ①.

Foyer Darwin, 3 rue Darwin (☎41.72.00.20). Cheaper hostel than the above; take bus #8 to *CFA*. ①.

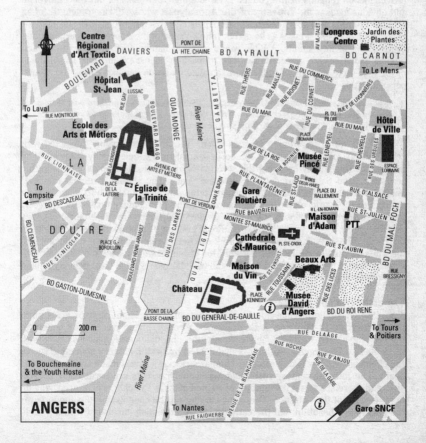

The City

The **château** forms the most lasting impression of Angers, a squat, sturdy fortress by the river, its moat now filled with formal flower arrangements and softened by trees. It's just a quarter-hour stroll east to the **cathedral** and several smaller churches and museums that cluster around it.

Across the pont Verdun from the château is the suburb of **La Doutre**, where the **Hôpital St-Jean** houses the modern response to the castle's Apocalypse tapestry, *Le Chant du Monde*. Further out of Angers in its suburbs are a rash of interesting museums, easily reached by bus, exalting everything from early aeroplanes to Cointreau and communication methods.

The château and Apocalypse tapestry

The **Château d'Angers** (daily 9am–12.30pm & 2–6pm; June to mid-Sept 9am–7pm; April & May 9am–12.30pm & 2–6.30pm; 31F) is a formidable early medieval fortress whose sense of impregnability is created by seventeen circular towers like elephants' legs gripping the rock below the kilometre-long curtain wall. Inside there are a few miscellaneous remains of the counts' royal lodgings and chapels, but the immediate and obvious focus is the **Tapestry of the Apocalypse**, whose 100-metre length (of an original 140m) is well displayed in a modern gallery. Woven between 1375 and 1378 for Duke Réné of Anjou, it takes as its text St John's Vision of the Apocalypse, as described in the Book of Revelations. A bible would come in handy since, though the French biblical quotations are given, the English "translation" is just explanation. The vision is of the lead-up to the Day of Judgement signalled by seven angels blowing their trumpets. After this . . .

> hail and fire mingled with blood . . . were cast upon the earth and the third part of trees was burned up and all green grass . . . and as it were a great mountain burning with fire was cast into the sea and the third part of the sea became blood . . . (Rev. 8:7-8).

The battle of Armageddon rages, as Satan, "the great red dragon" (depicted with seven heads), and his minions of composite animals mark their earthly followers. The holy forces retaliate by breaking the seven vials of plagues. It all ends with heavenly Jerusalem, and Satan buried for a thousand years. The slightly flattened medieval perspective has a hallucinatory quality, extraordinarily beautiful and terrifying, evoking the end of the world either in accordance with the first-century text or as a secular holocaust. If you can take in anything else after that, there are more tapestries, of a gentler nature, in the sporadically open Royal Lodgings and Governor's Lodge within the castle. Those feeling in need of a drink can head straight out of the castle and into the **Maison du Vin de l'Anjou** (closed Mon & Sun in winter; Mon only in summer), where the very professional and helpful staff will offer you wine to taste before you buy, and provide lists of wine growers to visit.

The cathedral and around

Ten minutes' along the quayside from the château, a long flight of steps leads up to the **Cathédrale St-Maurice**. It's a dramatic approach, giving you the full benefit of the building's early medieval façade. Inside, the unusually wide, aisle-less nave with its dome-like Plantagenet vaulting is illuminated by twelfth-century stained glass. In the choir one window is dedicated to Thomas à Becket – it was made shortly after his death. The fifteenth-century rose windows in the transepts are particularly impressive, and there are modern examples of stained glass in the chapel of Notre-Dame de la Pitié, right of the entrance. The stone carving on the capitals and the supports for the gallery are beautiful, but the cathedral is overzealously furnished with a grandiose high altar and pulpit and a set of tapestries that can't compete with Angers's other woven treasures.

In front of the cathedral, on **place Ste-Croix**, is the town's favourite carpentry detail, the unlikely genitals of one of the carved characters on the medieval **Maison d'Adam**. The building is now used by crafts people for presenting their wares (Mon 1–7pm, Tues–Sat 10am–7pm). There's a small **daily market** on the square.

Heading north from place Ste-Croix, you pass **place du Ralliement**, hub of modern Angers and currently undergoing a face-lift, into rue Lenepvue, where a Renaissance mansion houses the **Musée Pincé** (daily 9.30am–12.30pm & 2–7pm; mid-Sept to mid-June Tues–Sun 10am–noon & 2–6pm; 10F). It's a mixed bag of antiquities plus collections from China and Japan, the latter by far the more interesting, with a reconstruction of a tea-room and a gallery full of delicate prints, including the famous wave engulfing a boat with Mount Fuji in the background by Hokusaï.

Apart from its cathedral, the other great Gothic edifice in Angers is the chancel of the **church of St-Serge**, on av Mairie-Talet across bd Carnot, north of the centre near the congress centre. Though nothing much to look at from outside, the interior of the church has some of the most perfect vaulting rising from the slenderest of columns. Close by is the pleasant **Jardin des Plantes** (summer 8am–8pm; winter closes 5pm; free).

Arguably the greatest stone works in Angers, however, are the creations of the famous local sculptor David d'Angers (1788–1856), whose statue of Saint Cecilia adorns the cathedral chancel; his best works, some original, some copies and casts, are exhibited in a brilliant gallery built by glassing over the ruins of a thirteenth-century church, the **Église Toussaint**, 37bis rue Toussaint (daily 9.30am–12.30pm & 2–7pm; mid-Sept to mid-June Tues–Sun 10am–noon & 2–6pm; 10F). David d'Angers was a prime activist in the mid-nineteenth-century Republican struggles in Paris and was close friends with many of the great Romantic artists and thinkers of the time, many of them featuring here in busts or bronze medallions.

The **Musée des Beaux-Arts** collection next door, entered from 10 rue du Musée (same hours; 10F), has delightfully purposeful babies as cupids in Boucher's *Génie des Arts*, Lorenzo Lippi's beautiful *La Femme au Masque*, the highly operatic *Paolo et Francesca* by Ingres, and other representative works from the thirteenth to the twentieth centuries.

La Doutre and *Le Chant du Monde* tapestry

The district facing the château from across the Maine is known as **La Doutre** (literally, "the other side"), and has a few mansions and houses dating from the medieval period, despite redevelopment over the years.

At the north of the area, a short way from the Pont de la Haute Chaine (about fifteen minutes' walk from the château), the **Hôpital St-Jean** was built by Henry Plantagenet in 1174 as a hospital for the poor, a function it continued until 1854, and now houses the city's great twentieth-century tapestry in the **Musée Jean Lurçat et de la Tapisserie Contemporaine** at 4 bd Arago (daily Tues–Sun 10am–noon & 2–6pm; June to mid-Sept 9.30am–1pm & 2–7pm; 15F). The tapestry sequence, **Le Chant du Monde**, was designed by Jean Lurçat in 1957 in response to the Apocalypse tapestry, but he died nine years later before its completion (the artist's own commentary is available in English). It hangs in a vast vaulted space, the original ward for the sick, or Salle des Malades. The first four tapestries deal with *La Grande Menace*, the threat of nuclear war: first the bomb itself; then Hiroshima Man, flayed and burned with the broken symbols of belief dropping from him; then the collective massacre of the *Great Charnel House*; and the last dying rose falling with the post-holocaust ash through black space – the *End of Everything*. From then on, the tapestries celebrate the joy of life and the interdependence of its myriad manifestations: fire, water, champagne, the conquest of space, poetry and symbolic language.

Modern tapestry is an unfamiliar art, and the colours and Lurçat's style are so unlike anything else that initially you may be overwhelmed, but the old hospital building is impressive. You can admire the seventeenth-century pharmacy, the chapel's fine thirteenth-century stained glass windows and soaring Gothic vaulting, or wander around the Romanesque cloisters that still preserve their original woodwork. There are more modern tapestries, too, in the building adjoining the Salle des Malades. Built up around the donation by Lurçat's widow of several of his paintings, ceramics, other tapestries and cartoons for *Le Chant du Monde*, this has become one of the best showcases for contemporary tapestry in a changing programme of exhibitions. If you want to see the different stages involved in carrying out a modern tapestry commission or restoring old tapestries, call in at the neighbouring **Centre Regional d'Art Textile**, 3 bd Daviers (Mon, Tues, Thurs & Fri 10am–noon & 2–5pm; free), where you can watch artists at work.

South of the Hôpital St-Jean, on La Doutre's central square, place de la Laiterie, the ancient buildings of the **Abbaye de Ronceray** are used as an art and technology college, and when the school mounts exhibitions (or if you take one of the tourist office's guided tours of the town) you can visit the Romanesque galleries of the old abbey and admire their beautiful murals. Inside the adjacent twelfth-century **church of the Trinité** on the square, an exquisite Renaissance wooden spiral staircase fails to mask a great peice of medieval bodging used to fit the wall of the church around a part of the abbey that juts into it.

Suburban museums

The **Château de Pignerolles** in the satellite village of **ST-BARTHELEMY D'ANJOU**, to the east of Angers (signposted off the N147), is home to the **Musée Européen de la Communication**, a typically histrionic French science and technology museum, which promises a complete history of communication "from the tom-tom to the satellite" (daily 10am–12.30pm & 2.30–6.30pm; 50F). It's quite good fun, with everything from Leonardo's helicopter drawings to German submarines brought into play, and whizzo scenes of the future, but don't expect to come out much the wiser. For something completely different, you could go on a guided tour around the **Distillerie Cointreau**, just off the ringroad between Angers and St-Barthelemy d'Anjou (mid-June to mid-Sept Mon–Fri 10 & 11am, 2, 3, 4 & 5pm; Sat & Sun 3 & 4.30pm; 20F), reached on bus #7, where the famous orange liqueur has been distilled since the mid-nineteenth century. You'll learn a lot about the Cointreau brothers and how marvellous the drink is, a little bit about distilling techniques, and nothing, of course, about the recipe. You get a little sip at the end, but the highlight is definitely the rows of gleaming copper stills.

Northwest of the city at the Angers-Avrillé aerodrome, one of the most romanticized twentieth-century means of transportation – early aeroplanes – are on show in the **Musée des Ailes Anciennes** (daily 2–5pm; free). There are around forty well-restored examples on display, starting with a classic 1935 Potez 60; take bus #6 from the centre.

Eating and drinking

The streets around place du Ralliement and place Romain have a wide variety of **bars** and **restaurants**, many of them very cheap.

Le Connétable, 13 rue des Deux Haies (☎41.88.57.04). A good Breton *crêperie*, from 50F.

La Dolce Vita, 9 rue Baudrière (☎41.87.23.71). Pizzas and other Italian dishes popular with students. Menus from 65F.

L'Entr'acte, 7 pl Kennedy (☎41.87.46.20). High-class classic French cuisine with the best Anjou wines. Menus from 100F. Closed Sun evening & Mon.

Le Petit Mâchon, 43 rue Bressigny (☎41.81.04.76). Low-priced local wines to go with *andouilletes*, pig's trotters and the like. Closed Sun evening & Mon.

La Rose d'Or, 21 rue Delâge (☎41.88.38.38). Delicious salmon and trout; menus from 110F. Closed Sun evening & Mon.

Le Soufflé, 8 pl Pilori. A café specializing in soufflés from 50F. Closed first 2 weeks Aug.

Nightlife

Bars that stay open late congregate around rue St-Laud and the other pedestrian streets around, and tend to have a young clientele. Over to the east of the city, the *Spirit Factory*, 14–16 rue Bressigny (open till 1am), is a cavernous bar with beer brewed on the premises, serving late night *moules frites*. Up on the northern boulevard ring, *Bogie's Pub*, 38 bd Ayrault, has live rock Sunday nights, good Guinness, and a young, exuberant crowd until 2am.

Listings

Bike rental *Cycl'et Mob*, 67 bd Eugène-Chaumin (☎41.47.46.28).

Boat rental *Anjou Plaisance*, rue de l'Ecluse, Grez-Neuville (☎41.95.68.95), and *Maine-Anjou-Rivières*, Le Moulin, Chenillé-Changé (☎41.95.10.83), rent out boats of all kinds for exploring the Oudon, Mayenne and Sarthe rivers.

Car rental *Anjou Location Auto*, 32 rue Denis-Papin (☎41.88.07.53); *Europcar*, 26 bd Charles-de-Gaulle (☎41.88.80.80); *Hertz*, 14 rue Denis-Papin (☎41.88.15.16).

Emergencies ☎15; *Centre Hospitalier*, 1 av de l'Hôtel-Dieu ☎41.35.36.37; for late-night pharmacies, phone the police on ☎41.47.75.22.

Festivals The *Festival du Théâtre Masqué* takes up the last two weeks in March, with theatre troupes from all over the world (details from *Centre George Brassens*, Avrillé; ☎41.34.63.47); the *Festival d'Anjou* is a prestigious theatre festival using châteaux throughout the Maine-et-Loire *département* as venues in July (details on ☎41.81.49.49).

Laundries 17 rue Marceau; 25 pl Grégoire-Bordillon; 15 rue Plantagênet; 5 pl de la Visitation.

Market A Saturday market is held on place Grégoire-Bordillon.

Police 15 rue Dupetit-Thouars.

Post restante 1 rue Franklin-Roosevelt, 49052 Angers.

Taxis ☎41.87.65.00.

Travel agencies *Havas Voyages*, 3 rue d'Alsace (☎41.88.41.45); *Nouvelle Frontières*, rue Plantagênet (☎41.88.41.41).

Anjou vineyards, châteaux and churches

By lazing around the Loire and its tributaries between visits to vineyards, you could fill a good summer week around Angers, as long as you're mobile. Otherwise it is a two-bus-a-day problem, or no buses at all. Worthy exceptions are the **Savennières vineyards**, which you can reach by train (see box overleaf), and you can rent rowing boats during the summer at **St-Aubin-de-Luigne**, 20km southwest of Angers and just south of Rochefort, at the tourist office, next to the campsite.

If you have your own car, there are a couple more châteaux in these parts: **Brissac-Quincé**, 20km south of the town (on the #9 bus), and **Le Plessis-Bourré** near Ecuillé (impossible to get to by public transport), 17km to the north. For a more accessible glimpse of a real monster of a mansion, try the **Château Serrant**, just outside St-Georges-sur-Loire on bus route #18 from Angers. **Baugé**, north of the Loire and over to the east, is famous for a religious relic and is a pleasant little town for a short stopover, with four or five buses daily from Angers.

Château de Brissac

The **Château de Brissac** at **BRISSAC-QUINCÉ** (Wed–Sun 9.30–11.20am & 2.15–5.15pm; July to mid-Sept daily 9.30am–5.45pm; closed Nov–March; 40F) has been owned since 1502 by the same line of dukes. Of the original fortress, only the fifteenth-century fortified towers remain, and they were long due to be pulled down in deference to the symmetry of the seventeenth-century additions.

The interior is a riot of aristocratic bad taste, but it has some beautiful ceilings, as well as an interesting portrait in the Gallery of Ancestors of Madame Clicquot, the first woman to run a champagne business, and her granddaughter, the present duke's grandmother, apparently one of the first women to get a driving licence. The château has had a vineyard since 1515 and has its own label, and the current *vignerons* are the brothers Daviau at the Domaine de Bablut (visits by appointment only; ☎41.91.22.59).

Château du Plessis-Bourré

Five years' work at the end of the fifteenth century produced the fortress of **Le Plessis-Bourré** (Mon, Tues, Fri–Sun 10am–noon & 2–6pm, Thurs 2–6pm; Dec 26 to mid-Feb daily except Wed 2–6pm; July & Aug daily 10am–6pm; closed mid-Nov to mid-Feb; 37F), 2km southeast of Ecuillé between the Sarthe and Mayenne rivers. It still looks as if it expects an attack any day from across its vast, full moat, spanned by an arched bridge with a still-functioning drawbridge. But inside, all is Renaissance elegance and comfort at its best. The treasurer of France at the time, Jean Bourré, built the château to receive important visitors, among them Louis XI and Charles VIII, and it is appropriately flamboyant. Everywhere is painted with secular and allegorical scenes interwoven with mottos, some enigmatic, some moralistic: a unicorn poses as Lust, a grisly operation is performed by a barber, people carouse and cook. In one of the turreted staircases, the ceiling supports are carved with symbols from alchemy. Less exotic but still impressive are the furnishings of the state rooms and the collection of fans displayed in the library. A visit to the château is capped by a tour of the attics with their ship's keel rafting, and a stroll out onto the roof to follow the sentry's walk.

Château de Serrant

At the **Château de Serrant**, 15km east of Angers beside the N23, the combination of dark-brown schist and creamy tufa give a rather pleasant biscuit-cake effect to the outside (guided tours: daily 9–11.30am & 2–6pm; April–June, Sept & Oct daily except Tues; closed Nov–March; 35F). But it has those heavy slate bell-shaped cupolas pressing down on massive towers, which ruin any impression of lightness and grace. The building was begun in the sixteenth century and has been added to, discreetly for the most part, up until the eighteenth century. In 1755 it belonged to an Irishman, Francis Walsh, to whom Louis XV had given the title Count of Serrant as a reward for Walsh's help against the old enemy, the English. Walsh had provided the ship for Bonnie Prince Charlie to return to Scotland for the 1745 uprising.

Inside are endless tapestries, paintings and furniture; a Renaissance staircase and some richly carved ceilings; a bedroom prepared for Napoléon (who never came); and a library of well over ten thousand books. If you've already had your fill of château tours, then give this one a miss.

Baugé

In **BAUGÉ** – as easily reached by car from Saumur as Angers, 25km north of the river – the nuns at the **Chapelle des Incurables** claim to have a cross made from the True Cross. The wood is certainly Palestinian, though its history prior to its donation to an Angevin crusader is dubious. It is, anyhow, the double-armed cross that became the emblem of the dukes of Anjou and Lorraine and, in this century, of the Free French Forces. To see it, ring at 8 rue de la Girouardière (Wed–Mon 2.30–4.15pm; free).

The **tourist office** in Baugé (daily 10am–noon & 2–5.30pm) is worth visiting merely for its location in a fifteenth-century **castle**, one of Duke Réné of Anjou's favourite residences and once home to his magnificent Apocalypse tapestry, now in Angers (see p.338). Take a look, too, at the Hôpital de Baugé, east of the château up rue Anne-de-Melun, for its seventeenth-century **pharmacy**, to which the hospital receptionist will direct you (Wed–Sat 10am–noon & 3–5pm; Sun 3–5pm; July & Aug Tues–Sat; free), with its beautiful woodwork shelves, parquetry floor and sculpted ceiling, and the vials, flacons and contents just as they were in 1874.

Staying in Baugé, there's a reasonably priced hotel-restaurant, the *Boule d'Or*, 4 rue Cygne (☎41.89.82.12; ③; closed Mon & Sun out of season), as well as a pleasant **campsite** by a river just southeast of the town, *Le Pont des Fées* on chemin du Pont des Fées (☎41.89.14.79; mid-May to mid-Sept). Decent brasserie fare is available at *Le Commerce* **café** on place du Marché (☎41.89.14.15; closed Wed pm & Sun; menus around 65F).

Le Mans and around

LE MANS is 81km northwest of Tours in the *département* of Sarthe, some way from the Loire Valley but included here as a good, relatively untouristy base between Normandy and the Loire Valley, with swift transport connections down to Angers and Tours. The city is taken over by car fanatics in the middle of June for the famous 24-hour race, but for the rest of the year it's still lively enough, with some interesting museums and one of the most beautiful old quarters of any city in France. It was here, in 1129, that Geoffrey Plantagenet, Count of Maine and Anjou, married Matilda, daughter of Henry I of England, and where their son, the future Henry II, was born.

Arrival and accommodation

Place de la République forms the hub of Le Mans today, with its assortment of Belle Époque façades and more modern office blocks. Beneath the square in the underground shopping centre is the city **bus terminal**; buses #3, #5 and #16 run between here and the **gare SNCF** via av Général-Leclerc, where the **gare routière** is located. From place de la République, rue Bolton leads east into rue de l'Étoile, where you'll find the **tourist office** (daily 9.30am–noon & 2–5.30pm; ☎43.28.17.22) in a turreted seventeenth-century building on the corner with av de la Préfecture. **Bikes** can be rented from *Top Team* on place St-Pierre in the old town, or *Métayer Loisirs*, 73 av Jean-Jaurès (the continuation of rue Nationale).

Unless your visit coincides with one of the big racing events during April, June or September, you should be able to find **accommodation** easily without having to book.

Hotels

Arcade, 40 rue du Vert-Galant (☎43.24.47.24). Overlooking the Sarthe a short way south of the old town; top-floor rooms are the best. ③–④.

Hôtel Chantecler, 50 rue de la Pelouse (☎43.24.58.53). Quiet and well-equipped rooms, even though the hotel is a bit on the impersonal side. ③–⑤.

Hôtel du Saumon, 44 pl de la République (☎43.24.03.19). A very central place that's more comfortable than you'd expect for the price. ①–②.

Hôtel Select, 13 rue du Père-Mersenne, off av du Général-Leclerc (☎43.24.17.74). Small and pretty basic hotel, but ok. ①.

Hôtel de la Terrasse, 15 bd de la Gare (☎43.24.91.00). A cheapie right near the station, for when you don't want to bother looking further. ①.

Youth hostel

IYHF Le Flore youth hostel, 23 rue Maupertuis (☎43.81.27.55). Quite close to the centre: take av du Général-de-Gaulle from place de la République, continue along av Bollée; rue Maupertuis is the third on the left. ①.

The City

The **old town**'s complicated web of streets lies on a hill above the River Sarthe to the north of the central place de la République. The medieval streets are a hotchpotch of intricate Renaissance stonework, medieval half-timbering, sculpted pillars and beams and grand classical façades, still encircled by the original third- and fourth-century Gallo-Roman **walls**, supposedly the best preserved in Europe and running for several hundred metres. Steep, walled steps lead up from the river and longer flights descend on the southern side of the enclosure, using old Gallo-Roman entrances. If you're intrigued, you can see pictures, maps and plans of Vieux Mans, plus examples of the city's ancient arts and crafts, in the **Maison de la Reine Bérengère** (daily 9am–noon & 2–6pm; 5F), one of the Renaissance houses on rue de la Reine-Bérengère.

Rearing up the hill from the east is the immense Gothic apse of the **Cathédrale St-Julien**, with a Romanesque nave and radiating chapels, on **place du Grente** (also called du Château), at the crowning point of the old town. According to Rodin, the now badly worn sculpted figures of the south porch were rivalled only in Chartres and Athens. Some of the stained glass windows here were in place when the first Plantagenet was buried in the church, but the brightest colours in the otherwise austere interior come from the tapestries.

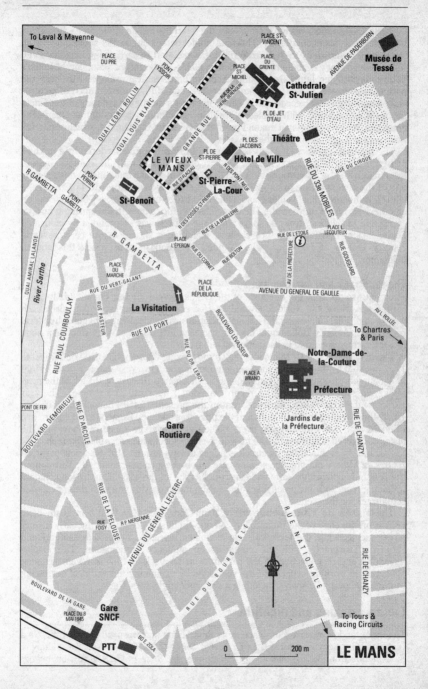

To Laval & Mayenne

PLACE DU PRE

QUAI LEDRU ROLLIN

QUAI LOUIS BLANC

PONT YSSOIR

PLACE ST-VINCENT

AVENUE DE PADERBORN

Musée de Tessé

PLACE DU GRENTE

PLACE ST-MICHEL

RUE DE LA REINE-BERENGERE

Cathédrale St-Julien

GRANDE RUE

PL DE JET D'EAU

Théâtre

RUE DU 33e MOBILES

RUE DU CIRQUE

PL DE ST-PIERRE

PL DES JACOBINS

Hôtel de Ville

LE VIEUX MANS

RUE ST-JUSSAL

R GAMBETTA

PONT PERRIN

PONT GAMBETTA

RUE ST-PIERRE

St-Pierre-La-Cour

R DES FOSSÉS-ST-PIERRE

RUE DE LA BARRIERIE

RUE DES PONT NEUF

St-Benoît

PLACE L'EPERON

RUE DE L'ETOILE

PLACE L LECOUTEUX

QUAI AMIRAL LALANDE

River Sarthe

R GAMBETTA

PLACE DU MARCHE

RUE DU VERT-GALANT

RUE DU CORNET

RUE BOLTON

AV DE LA PREFECTURE

RUE GOUGEARD

RUE PAUL COURBOULAY

PLACE DE LA RÉPUBLIQUE

La Visitation

AVENUE DU GENERAL DE GAULLE

AV L ROLLEE

To Chartres & Paris

RUE PASTEUR

RUE DU PORT

BOULEVARD LEVASSEUR

RUE DU DR LEROY

PLACE A. BRIAND

Notre-Dame-de-la-Couture

Préfecture

PONT DE FER

BOULEVARD DEMORIEUX

RUE D'ARCOLE

Gare Routière

Jardins de la Préfecture

RUE DE CHANZY

RUE DE LA PELOUSE

RUE FOISY

R P MERSENNE

AVENUE DU GENERAL LECLERC

RUE DU BOURG BELE

RUE NATIONALE

RUE DE CHANZY

BOULEVARD DE LA GARE

PLACE DU 8 MAI 1945

Gare SNCF

BD E. ZOLA

PTT

0   200 m

LE MANS

To Tours & Racing Circuits

In the 1850s a road was tunnelled under the quarter – a slum at the time – helping to preserve its self-contained unity. The road tunnel comes out on the south side, by an impressive **monument to Wilbur Wright** – who tested an early flying machine in Le Mans (see below) – and into place des Jacobins, the vantage point for St-Julien's double-tiered flying buttresses and apse. From here, you can walk east through the park to the **Musée Tessé** (daily 9am–noon & 2–6pm; 5F), a mixed bunch of pictures and statues including Georges de la Tour's light at its most extraordinary in the *Extase de St-François*, along with copies of brilliant medieval populist murals in Sarthe churches. It also contains an enamel portrait of Geoffrey Plantagenet, which was originally part of his tomb in the cathedral.

The modern centre of Le Mans is **place de la République**, bordered by a mixture of Belle-Époque buildings.and more modern office blocks, with the Baroque bulk of the **church of the Visitation**, built in 1730 and with a balustrade inside designed by one of the sisters of the order. Just south of here is **Notre-Dame de la Couture**, a church with Plantagenet vaulting and a fine Last Judgement scene over the doorway on an otherwise rather ugly façade. The name has nothing to do with dressmaking but is a corruption of "*culture*" from the days when the church was surrounded by cultivated fields. Inside there are various treasures, including a shroud of the early seventh-century Bishop of Le Mans, who founded the monastery to which this church belonged.

The racetrack and car museum

Stretching south from the outskirts of the city is the **car racing circuit** (daily 9am–5pm; free), where the world-renowned *24 Heures du Mans* car race takes place each year in mid-June, continuing the city's associations with automobiles, begun when local bell-founder Amadée Bollée built his first car back in 1873 – Le Mans still has a huge *Renault* factory operating in its southwest suburbs.

The first big race at Le Mans was the Grand Prix de l'Automobile Club de l'Ouest in 1906, initiated by the newly formed automobile club, and two years later, Wilbur Wright took off in his prototype aeroplane, alongside what is now the fastest stretch of the racetrack, and stayed in the air for a record-breaking 1 hour and 31.5 minutes. The year 1923 saw the first 24-hour car race, run on the present 13.459 kilometre-long circuit. Thirty-three contestants took part, and the prize was taken by Lagache and Léonard in a Chenard and Walcker, covering over 2000km at an average speed of 92km/ph. The distance covered is now over 5000km, with average speeds in excess of 220km/ph.

Entrance to events at the racetrack is pricey today – around 310F for a seat at the *24 Heures du Mans* – but practice sessions are much cheaper, at around 90F. Throughout the year motorcycles, go-karts and even trucks race on the 4.25-kilometre-long Bugatti training circuit, so some practising vehicle is bound to provide you with the appropriate soundtrack for the scene.

The **Musée de l'Automobile** (daily 10am–7pm; Oct–May Wed–Sun 10am–6pm; 35F) is on the edge of the Bugatti and 24-hour circuits. It documents the early history of car racing, while the technical side examines research, automobile anatomy and automated assembly, with the emphasis on audience participation. The display includes a superb collection of 150 cars from as far back as 1885 to recent winners, almost all in working order, and the visit ends by examining the world of car racing through audiovisual displays, including a simulated high-speed track.

Eating, drinking and nightlife

The **cafés** and **brasseries** on place de la République stay open till late and there's a very good, if pricey **restaurant**, *Le Grenier à Sel* (☎43.23.26.30; closed Sat midday & Sun; menus from 120F), and a very cheap one, *La Brise* (☎43.28.20.52), on nearby place l'Éperon. Sophisticated fish dishes are served at *La Feuillantine*, 19bis rue Foisy (☎43.28.00.38), with menus under 100F during the week. The best restaurants, however, are located in the labyrinthine streets of the old town, particularly on and around Grande-Rue. Good value for a blow-out is *Le Flambadou*, 14bis rue St-Flaceau (☎43.24.88.38), which offers a very meaty menu, including a fantastic *cassoulet landaise*, from around 200F. *Le Pantagruel* on place St-Pierre (☎43.24.87.63) is a good bet for fish and *fruits de mer*, with menus from 90F.

The *À la Truie qui File* **charcuterie**, 36 rue du Docteur-Leroy, near place de la République, provides excellent picnic fodder, including the Mans version of *rillettes* or potted pork. There's a daily **market** in the covered halls on place du Marché, and a bric-à-brac market on Wednesday, Friday and Sunday mornings on place du Jet d'Eau, below the cathedral on the new town side, with food as well on Sunday.

Le Mans has a lively night-time scene. There are a couple of good **late-night bars** on bd Émile-Zola, and a jazz bar, *Le Stan*, on place de l'Éperon (until 4am). **Nightclubs** are ubiquitous, but a couple worthy of mention are *Le City Bird* on place d'Alger and *Le Yani's Club* on rue des Ponts Neufs.

The Abbaye de L'Epau

If car racing holds no romance, there's another outing from Le Mans of a much quieter nature. The Cistercian **Abbaye de l'Epau** (daily 9.30am–noon & 2–6pm; mid-Sept to mid-April closed Thurs; 15F), 4km out of town off the Chartres–Paris road (bus #14 from place de la République in Le Mans, stop *Pologne*), was founded in 1229 by Queen Bérengère, consort of Richard the Lionheart. It stands, in a rural setting, on the outskirts of the Bois de Changé and is more or less unaltered since its fifteenth-century restoration after a fire. The visit includes the dormitory, with the remains of a four-teenth-century fresco, the abbey church and the scriptorium, or writing room. The church contains the recumbent figure of Queen Bérengère over her tomb.

travel details

Trains

Angers to: Le Mans (frequent, 1hr 30min; 11 *TGV*s daily, 35min); Nantes (frequent, 45min; 11 daily *TGV*s, 20min); Paris (frequent, 3hr 15min; 11 *TGV*s daily, 1hr 30min); Saumur (frequent; 45min); Savennières-Béhuard (4–5 daily; 15min); Tours (at least 10 daily; 1hr 30min).

Gien to: Briare (4 daily; 20min); La Charité (4 daily; 1hr); Cosne (5 daily; 20min); Nevers (5 daily; 1hr 5min); Paris (5 daily; 1hr 30min).

Le Mans to: Angers (frequent; 1hr 15min, or *TGV*s 30min); Nantes (frequent, 1hr 45min; 11 *TGV*s daily, 55min); Paris (frequent, 1hr 45min; 11 *TGV*s daily, 55min); Rennes (frequent; 2hr); Saumur (3 daily; 2hr).

Orléans (many trains require a change at Les Aubrais-Orléans 5mins away) to: Beaugency (frequent; 25min); Blois (frequent; 1hr); Châteauroux (frequent; 1hr 10min); Meung-sur-Loire (frequent; 15min); Paris (2 hourly; 1hr 10min); Tours (several daily; 1hr 15min).

Tours to: Angers (at least 10 daily; 1hr 30min); Azay-le-Rideau/Chinon (6 daily; 30min–1hr); Blois (at least hourly; 30min); Bourges (5 daily; 2hr); Chenonceaux-Chisseux/St-Aignan (5 daily; 30min–1hr); Langeais (several daily; 20min); Loches (6 daily; 1hr); Montrichard (7 daily; 35min); Orléans (at least hourly; 1hr 15min); Paris (at least hourly; 2hr 30min or *TGV*s 1hr); Saumur (at least 10 daily; 45min); Le Mans (at least 10 daily; 1hr 15min).

Buses

Angers to: Doué (6 daily; 55min); Saumur (3–4 daily; 1hr 30min).

Blois to: Cheverny (1 or 2 daily; 20min); Orléans (4 daily; 1hr 30min); St-Aignan (3 daily; 40min).

Bourges to: Cosne (4 daily; 1hr 50min); Sancerre (3 daily; 1hr).

Gien to: Argent-sur-Sauldre (3 daily; 35min); Bourges (2 daily; 1hr 50min).

Orléans to: Blois (4 daily; 1hr 30min); Châteauneuf-sur-Loire (4 daily; 35min); Gemigny (4 daily; 45min); Gien (3 daily; 1hr 40min); St-Benoit (3 daily; 50min); Sully (3 daily; 1hr 5min).

Saumur to: Chinon (daily; 45min); Doué (6 daily; 30min); Fontévraud (3 daily; 30min).

Tours to: Amboise (7 daily; 30min); Azay-le-Rideau (3 daily; 40min); Chenonceaux (3 daily; 1hr); Chinon (3 daily; 1hr); Loches (4 daily; 45min); Montrichard (3 daily; 1hr 15min); Ste-Maure (2 daily; 45min); Richelieu (2 daily; 1hr 30min).

CHAPTER SEVEN

BURGUNDY

Peaceful, rural **Burgundy** is one of the most prosperous regions in modern France, but for centuries its powerful dukes remained independent of the French crown. During the Hundred Years' War, they even sided against the French with the English, selling them the captured Joan of Arc. By the fifteenth century their power extended over all of Franche-Comté, Alsace and Lorraine, Belgium, Holland, Picardy and Flanders. Their state was the best organized and richest in Europe, its revenues equalled only by Venice. It only finally fell to the French kings when Duke Charles le Téméraire was killed besieging Nancy in 1477.

There is evidence everywhere of this former wealth and power, both secular and religious: in the dukes' capital of **Dijon**, in the great abbeys of **Vézelay** and **Fontenay**, in the ruins of the monastery of **Cluny** (whose abbots' influence was second only to the pope's), and in the châteaux of **Tanlay** and **Ancy**.

Because of its monastic foundations, Burgundy became – along with Poitou and Provence – one of the great church-building areas in the Middle Ages. Practically every village has its Romanesque church, especially in the country around Cluny and Paray-le-Monial, clearly influenced by the architecture of the substantial Roman remains that survive around **Autun**. But Burgundy's historical range stretches even further. **Bibracte** on the atmospheric hill of Mont-Beubray was an important Gallic capital, and **Alésia** was the scene of Julius Cæsar's epic victory over the Gauls in 52 BC, while in more modern times the rustic backwater of **Le Creusot** became a powerhouse of the Industrial Revolution, with manufacturers of train engines, artillery pieces and nuclear boilers using the ample forests and iron ore deposits to fuel the forges.

For voluptuaries, **wine** is, of course, the region's most obvious attraction, and devotees head straight for the great **vineyards**, whose produce has played the key role in the local economy since Louis XIV's doctor prescribed wine as a palliative – perhaps an analgesic – for the royal dyspepsia. If you lack the funds to indulge your taste for expensive drink, go in September or October when the *vignerons* are recruiting harvesters.

ACCOMMODATION PRICE CATEGORIES

All the hotels, youth hostels and guesthouses listed in this book have been price-graded according to the following scale, and although costs will rise slightly overall with the life of this edition, the relative comparisons should remain valid. Paris and the large cities will, as anywhere, be more expensive than equivalent accommodation in the countryside or small towns. The prices quoted are for the cheapest available double room in high season, although remember that many of the cheap places will have more expensive rooms with en-suite facilities.

① Under 160F	④ 300–400F	⑦ 600–700F
② 160–220F	⑤ 400–500F	⑧ Over 700F
③ 220–300F	⑥ 500–600F	

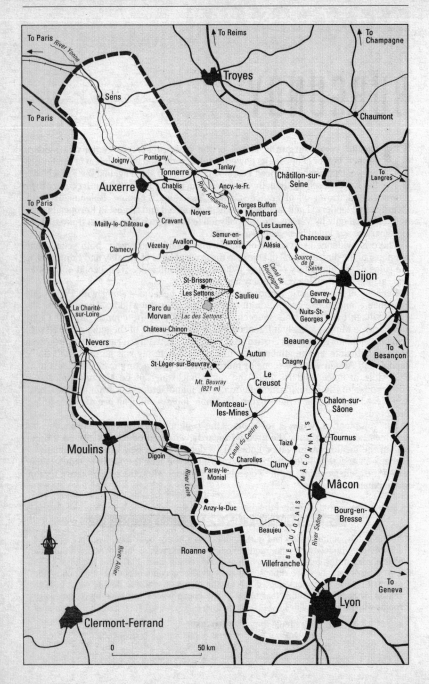

To Paris *River Yonne*
To Reims
To Champagne
Troyes
Sens
To Paris
Chaumont
Joigny Pontigny
Tonnerre Tanlay
Châtillon-sur-Seine
Auxerre Chablis
Ancy.-le-Fr.
River Armançon
To Langres
Noyers Forges Buffon
Montbard
Mailly-le-Château Cravant
Les Laumes
Semur-en-Auxois
Chanceaux
Clamecy Vézelay Avallon Alésia
Source de la Seine
St-Brisson *Canal de Bourgogne*
Dijon
Les Settons Saulieu
Gevrey-Chamb.
La Charité-sur-Loire Parc du Morvan *Lac des Settons*
Nuits-St-Georges
Château-Chinon
Beaune
Nevers Autun
To Besançon
St-Léger-sur-Beuvray Chagny
Mt. Beuvray (821 m) Le Creusot
Chalon-sur-Sâone
Montceau-les-Mines
Canal du Centre Taizé Tournus
Moulins Digoin Charolles Cluny
M Â C O N N A I S
River Loire Paray-le-Monial Mâcon
Anzy-le-Duc Bourg-en-Bresse
River Allier Beaujeu *B E A U J O L A I S* *River Sâone*
Roanne Villefranche
To Geneva
Clermont-Ferrand Lyon

0   50 km

THE FOOD OF BURGUNDY

The **cuisine** of Burgundy is known for its richness, due in large part to two factors: the region's heavy red wines and its possession of one of the world's finest races of beef cattle, the Charollais. The **wines** are used in the preparation of the sauces which earn a dish the designation of *à la bourguignonne*. Essentially, this means cooked in a red wine sauce to which baby onions, mushrooms and *lardons* (pieces of bacon) are added. The classic Burgundy dishes cooked in this manner are *bœuf bourguignon* and *coq au vin*. It is important that the wine should be a good one. Another term which frequently appears on menus is *meurette*, another red wine sauce but made without mushrooms and flambéed with a touch of *marc* brandy. It is used with eggs, fish and poultry as well as red meat.

Snails (*escargots*) are hard to avoid in Burgundy, and the local style of cooking them involves stewing for several hours in the white wine of Chablis with shallots, carrots and onions, then stuffing them with a butter of garlic and parsley and finishing them off in the oven. **Other specialities** include the parsley-flavoured ham (*jambon persillé*), hams from the Morvan hills cooked in a cream *saupiquet* sauce, calf's head (*tête de veau* or *sansiot*), a *pauchouse* of river fish – poached in white wine with onions, butter, garlic and *lardons* – a *poussin* from Bresse, a saddle of hare (*rable de lièvre à la Piron*), a *potée bourguignonne*, or soup of vegetables cooked in the juices of long-simmered bacon and pork bits.

Like other regions of France, Burgundy produces a variety of **cheeses**. The best known are the creamy white *Chaource*, the soft *St-Florentin* from the Yonne Valley, the orange-skinned *Époisses* and the delicious goat cheeses from the Morvan. And then there is *gougère*, a kind of cheesecake, best eaten warm with a glass of Chablis.

Between bouts of gastronomic indulgence, you can engage in some moderate activity: for **walkers** there's a wide range of hikes, from the gentle to the relatively demanding, in the **Morvan Regional Park** and the **Côte d'Or**. There are also several long-distance canal paths, which make great **bike** trips. As for the waterways themselves, aficionados rate most highly the **Canal de Bourgogne** and the **Canal du Nivernais**, both of which can be cruised by rented barge (ring the *Comité Régional du Tourisme de Bourgogne*, BP 1602, 21035 Dijon (☎80.50.10.20, fax 80.30.59.45).

THE ROAD TO DIJON

The old **road to Dijon**, the Nationale 6, runs from Paris down to the Côte d'Azur, the route taken by the National Guardsmen of Marseille when they marched on Paris singing the *Marseillaise* in 1792.* The route enters the province of Burgundy just south of Fontainebleau, near where the River Yonne joins the Seine, and it follows the Yonne Valley through the historic towns of **Sens** and **Auxerre**. Scattered in a broad corridor to the west and east of the road, in the valleys of the Yonne's tributaries, the Armançon, Serein, Cure and Cousin rivers, is a fascinating collection of many abbeys, châteaux, towns, villages and other sites as ancient as the history of France. It makes for a route far more interesting, albeit slower, than speeding around the bland curves of its modern replacement, the **Autoroute du Soleil**.

---

*The *Marseillaise*, the French national anthem, started life as the song of the Revolutionary Army of the Rhine in 1792. It was written by an officer of the army by the name of Rouget de l'Isle in response to a challenge from the mayor of Strasbourg to compose a suitable tune and song. Taken up by the *fédérés* from Marseille who marched to Paris in July 1792 to support the Revolutionary government, it was christened *La Marseillaise*.

Sens

The name of **SENS** commemorates the *Senones*, the Gallic tribe whose shaggy troops all but captured Rome in 390 BC; they were only thwarted by the Capitoline geese cackling the garrison awake. Its heyday as a major ecclesiastical centre was in the twelfth and thirteenth centuries, but it lost its preeminence in the ensuing centuries largely through damage caused by the Hundred Years' War and the wars of religion. Nowadays, it is a quiet and unexciting place on the banks of the River Yonne, although the cathedral, its treasury and the adjacent museum make a stop worthwhile.

Contained within a ring of tree-lined boulevards where the city walls once stood, the town's ancient centre is still dominated by the **Cathédrale St-Étienne**, close to the intersection of Grande Rue and rue de la République, which, together with their prolongations, neatly quarter the *centre ville*. Begun around 1130, this was the first of the great French Gothic cathedrals. Though an early example, the Gothic elements of airiness, space and weightlessness are fully realized, in the height of the nave, the arcading of the aisles and the great rose window. The architect who completed it, William of Sens, was later to rebuild the choir of Canterbury Cathedral in England, the missing link being Thomas-à-Becket, who had previously spent several years in exile around Sens. The story of his murder is told in the twelfth-century windows in the north aisle of the choir, just part of the cathedral's outstanding collection of stained glass. The **treasury**, which can be entered either from the cathedral or the museum (see below for times), is also uncommonly rich, containing Islamic, Byzantine and French vestments, jewels and embroideries.

Just to the south is the thirteenth-century **Palais Synodal**, with its roof of Burgundian glazed tiles restored by the nineteenth-century "purist" Viollet-le-Duc, like so many other buildings in this region. Its vaulted halls, originally designed to accommodate the ecclesiastical courts, now house an excellent **museum** (daily 10am–noon & 2–6pm; Oct–May Wed, Sat, Sun 10am–noon & 2–6pm, Mon, Thurs, Fri 2–6pm; 13F, free Wed), making all possible use of available space to display a prize collection of exhibits found in the region, including statuary from the cathedral and Gallo-Roman mosaics. Prize exhibits include the **Villethierry treasure**, which consists of 867 items of bronze jewellery in a jar, and thought to be a jeweller's horde; a collection of bone combs; and the façade of Sens' second-century public baths. The vaults of the building – partly constituting the remains of a Gallo-Roman building, including baths heated through the pavement – have now been incorporated into the museum, along with displays of Gallo-Roman metalwork, jewellery and textile crafts, many of which were discovered when the basement was excavated.

Facing the cathedral across place de la République are fine wood and iron *halles*, where a **market** is held on Monday, Friday and Saturday mornings. The *place* stands right in the centre of town where the main streets, **rue de la République** and **Grande-Rue**, intersect. Lined with old houses now converted into shops, they are mainly reserved for pedestrians. There are two particularly finely carved and timbered houses on the corner of rue Jean-Cousin: the **Maison d'Abraham** and the **Maison du Pilier**, with **Maison Jean Cousin** on rue du Général-Alix.

Practicalities

At the far end of Grande-Rue, the road crosses two broad arms of the River Yonne and leads straight ahead to the **gare SNCF** (☎86.64.20.54), about fifteen minutes' walk from the cathedral. The **tourist office** is on place Jean-Jaurès (daily except Sun 9am–noon & 1.30–6.15pm; July & Aug closes 7.30pm; ☎86.65.19.45), just north of the Hôtel de Ville, where rue de la République becomes rue Leclerc.

For places to **stay**, try the *Hôtel du Centre*, 4 pl de la République, opposite the cathedral (☎86.64.31.78; closed March, Oct, Wed evening & Thurs; ②), or the *Hôtel Esplanade*, 2 bd du Mail, the broad boulevard leading away from place Jean-Jaurès (☎86.65.20.95; closed Aug; ②). Also by the cathedral and a cut above the others is the old-time provincial *Hôtel de Paris et de la Poste*, 97 rue de la République (☎86.65.17.43; ④–⑤), with an excellent restaurant specializing in traditional country cuisine (menu at 145F, *carte* considerably more). The **campsite**, *Entre-deux-Vannes*, is on av de Sénigallia (☎86.65.64.71; closed mid-Nov to mid-March), just out of town.

For cheap **eating**, the self-service place, *Brasserie le Senonais*, 99 rue de la République, and good *crêperie*, *Aux 4 Vents*, 3 rue de Brennus, do the trick. There's also inexpensive Chinese food at the *Saigon* on Grande-Rue near the bridge, with a number of reasonable restaurants around place de la République, including the *Restaurant de le Cathédrale*, 11 pl de la République (☎86.65.17.79), with good traditional fare and menus at 75F and 115F.

Joigny

Travelling south of Sens towards Auxerre, the next place of any size on the Yonne is the prosperous little town of **JOIGNY**, its elegant old houses ranged up the slope above the river. It's not worth a prolonged visit, but makes a pleasant rest stop. Buildings worthy of attention are the **Château des Gondi**, built by Cardinal Gondi in the sixteenth century and borrowing Italian influences from the château at Ancy-le-Franc (see p.458); remains of the twelfth-century **ramparts** on Chemin de la Guimbard; and a number of half-timbered houses on **rue Montant-au-Palais**, the street leading up to the church of St-Jean, including the best-known **Maison du Pilori**, combining Gothic and Renaissance styles, with some carvings strangely reminiscent of crocodile heads.

The **tourist office** is on quai Ragobert (daily 9am–12.15pm & 2–6.15pm; winter Tues–Sat; ☎86.62.11.05), by the **gare routière**. Cheap **hotels** include the simple but adequate *Relais de L'Escargot*, 1 av Roger-Varrey (☎86.62.10.38; ①), and the *Lion d'Or*, 5 rue Roger-Varrey (☎86.62.17.00; ②). A much classier establishment is *Rive Gauche* on chemin du Port-au-Bois (☎86.91.46.66; ④–⑥), with a very reasonable restaurant overlooking the river (menus 92–250F).

For reasonable **eating**, the *Marmite de Joigny* on rue Gabriel-Cortel (☎86.62.31.81; closed Wed) has a good 95F menu. There's a snazzy bar and pizzeria, the *Montmartre*, on place de Jean-de-Joigny. But the nicest place both to stay and eat is a little way out of town to the west, 6km along the D182 towards St-Julien-du-Sault: *Le P'tit Claridge* in Thèmes (☎86.63.10.92; ②; closed Sun evening & Mon, Sept 1–15 & Feb 1–15), with a restaurant offering a very good value menu at 90F.

Auxerre

A pretty old town of narrow lanes and handsome squares, **AUXERRE** stands on a hill a further 50km up the Yonne. It looks its best seen from Pont Paul-Bert and the riverside **quays**, where houseboats and barges moor. Its churches soar dramatically and harmoniously above the surrounding rooftops, and the most interesting of them is the disused abbey church of **St-Germain** (daily except Tues 9am–12.30pm & 2–6.30pm; Fri 9am–8pm; mid-Sept to mid-June 9am–noon & 2–6pm; 18F), at the opposite end of rue Cauchois from the cathedral. Partial demolition has left its belfry detached from the body of the building, but what gives it special interest is the **crypt**, one of the few surviving examples of Carolingian (ninth century and earlier) architecture, with its plain barrel vaults still resting on their thousand-year-old oak beams. Deep inside, the faded ochre frescoes of St Stephen (St-Étienne) are among the most ancient in France, dating back to around 850 AD.

The **cathedral** itself (Easter–Nov Mon–Sat 9am–noon & 2–4pm; Sun 2–4pm; crypt 5F, treasury 5F) still remains unfinished, despite the fact that its construction was drawn out over more than three centuries from 1215 to 1560; the southernmost of the two west front towers has never been completed. Compensation for this lies in the richly detailed sculpture of the porches and the glorious colours of the original thirteenth-century glass that still fills the windows of the choir, despite the savagery of the Wars of Religion and the Revolution. There has been a church on the site since about 400 AD, though nothing visible survives earlier than the eleventh-century **crypt**. Among its frescoes is a unique depiction of a warrior Christ mounted on a white charger, accompanied by four mounted angels.

From in front of the cathedral, rue Fourier leads to place du Marché and off left to the Hôtel de Ville and the old city gateway known as the **Tour de l'Horloge** with its fifteenth-century coloured clock face. The whole quarter, from place Surugue through rue Joubert and down to the river, is full of attractive old houses. Of somewhat recondite interest, the **Musée Leblanc-Duvernoy**, in an eighteenth-century *hôtel* at 9 rue Egleny, contains a collection of faïence and china of local provenance, furniture and tapestries (daily 2–6.30pm; mid-Sept to mid-June closes 6pm; 10F).

Practicalities

If you arrive by train at the **gare SNCF** in rue Paul-Doumer (☎86.46.93.94), you'll find yourself across the river from the town: follow signs for the *centre ville* and cross Pont Paul-Bert. The **tourist office** is here by the river at 2 quai de la République (Mon–Sat 9am–1pm & 2–7pm; Sun 10am–1pm & 3–6.30pm; Oct–May Mon–Sat 10am–12.30pm & 2–6pm; ☎86.52.26.27), with an annexe in place des Cordeliers in summer. There is a **Bureau d'Informations Jeunesse** at 70 rue du Pont (☎86.51.68.75), with information on travel and leisure activities. The **gare routière** lies in place des Migraines off the *boulevard périphérique* (☎86.46.90.66); the **market** happens in place de l'Arquebuse, also on the *périphérique* at the end of rue du Temple.

For a simple and inexpensive **stay**, try the central *Hôtel de la Renommée*, 27 rue d'Egleny (☎86.52.03.53; ①; closed Sun & 3 weeks in Aug), whose restaurant has menus at 56F and 89F. Two more comfortable but less central hotels are the *Normandie*, 41 bd Vauban, one of the outer boulevards (☎86.52.57.80; ③–④), and *Les Clairions* on av Worms in the Clairions district off the N6 to Paris (☎86.46.85.64; ③–④). But if you are looking for something a bit special, *Le Maxime* is the place, overlooking the river at 2 quai de la Marine (☎86.52.14.19; ④; closed mid-Dec to Jan). Cheapest of all are the *foyers*: at 16 av de la Résistance near the train station (☎86.46.95.11; ①; canteen 39F), across the tracks by the footbridge; and at 16 bd Vaulabelle (☎86.52.45.38; ①), at the back of the courtyard of the *Peugeot* and *Citroën* garage. For campers, there's a pleasant **camping municipal**, 8 rte de Vaux, going south (☎86.52.11.15; April–Sept), next to the riverside football ground.

Finding somewhere to **eat** is easy, as there are numerous reasonably priced restaurants. *La Renaissance* at 93 rue du Pont, near the river, is a convenient brasserie (menu at 61F). In the same street at no. 37, *La Primavera* does Greek, Italian and Mediterranean food well (☎86.51.43.36; closed Wed evening and Sun, & three weeks in Aug; menus 75–125F). *Le Quai*, in the very pretty place St-Nicholas, opening on to the river not far from the tourist office, does *plats du jour* at lunchtime for 58F – though it is really a place for a drink. *Hôtel-Restaurant de la Poste*, 9 rue d'Orbandelle near place des Cordeliers in the centre (☎86.52.12.02; closed mid-Nov to mid-Dec; menus from 89F upwards), is good value and has interesting dishes of oysters, curry, *ris de veau* and *médaillon de lotte*. For good traditional cuisine, there's *Le Saint Pélerin*, 56 rue St-

Pélerin (near the Pont Paul-Bert; ☎86.52.77.05; closed Sun & Mon) with a menu at 100F. Finally, top of the range in culinary terms, *Le Jardin Gourmand*, 56 bd Vauban, for all its inventiveness and sophistication still offers a menu at 98F, and an even better value one at 140F (☎86.51.53.52; closed Mon, Tues lunchtime, Dec 6–23, Feb 21–28 & May 9–17).

Around Auxerre

On or close to the D965 and the Paris–Dijon rail line in the open, rolling country east of Auxerre lie several minor attractions, ranging from Greek treasures to Cistercian abbeys and Renaissance châteaux. The valley of the aptly named Serein River is the location of the villages of **Chablis**, famed for its excellent vineyards, and time-locked **Noyers-sur-Serein**, while to the south, a string of villages along the **upper valley of the Yonne** provide a glimpse of a gentler, more intimate countryside, with the possibility of a quiet night's rest for the long-distance traveller keen to get away from the main roads and towns.

Pontigny

The ravages of time – in particular, the 1789 Revolution – have destroyed most of the great monastic buildings of the Cistercian order of monks, whose rigorous insistence on simplicity and manual labour under their most influential twelfth-century leader, Saint Bernard, was a revolutionary response to the worldliness and luxury of the Benedictine abbeys of Cluny (see p.486). Cîteaux and Clairvaux, the first Cistercian foundations, are unrecognizable today: the only places you can get an idea of how Cistercian ideas translated into bricks and mortar are at Pontigny and Fontenay (p.459).

PONTIGNY lies 18km northeast of Auxerre, and its beautifully preserved twelfth-century **abbey church** stands on the edge of the village, where its functional mass rises from the meadows. There is no tower, no stained glass and no statuary to distract from its austere, harmonious lines. The effects of cream-coloured stone flooded with light and permeated with the smell of freshly cut flowers are only slightly marred by the nineteenth-century choir screen that cuts the nave in two. Begun in the early 1100s and finished in the late, it spans the transition between the old Romanesque and the new Gothic, evident especially in the choir, and was much copied in the country round about – in Chablis, for example.

Surprisingly, three Englishmen played a major role in the abbey's early history, all of them archbishops of Canterbury: Thomas-à-Becket took refuge in the abbey from Henry II in 1164, Stephen Langton similarly lay low here during an argument over his eligibility for the primacy, and Edmund Rich died here: his tomb in the church is a goal of pilgrimages to this day. The abbey was also the origin of a tourist attraction with which a nearby village is more often associated: the famous **Chablis wine**. It was the monks of Pontigny who originally developed and refined the variety, and the village and its unassuming neighbouring hamlets are better places to sample the wine than in the expensive wine bars of Chablis itself.

There is a simple **hotel** in Pontigny: the *Relais de Pontigny* on the N77 (☎86.47.42.83; ①), whose rooms have neither bath nor shower. With more cash, it's better to go for the *Relais St-Vincent*, 14 Grande-Rue in nearby Ligny-le-Chatel, 4km along the D91 (☎86.47.53.38; ③–④; restaurant from 70F). Another hotel possibility is the *Soleil d'Or* at Montigny-la-Resle on the N77 (☎86.41.81.21 or 86.41.86.88; ③; closed Jan; restaurant from 88F). Ligny also has a **campsite** by the Serein off the D8 Auxerre road (mid-May to Sept).

Chablis

Sixteen kilometres to the south, the pretty red-roofed town of **CHABLIS** is the home of the region's famous light dry white wines. It lies in the valley of the River Serein – brim-full of fish waiting to be poached – between the wide and mainly treeless upland wheatfields typical of this corner of Burgundy. While wandering around you could take a look at the side door of the **church of St-Martin**, decorated with ancient horseshoes and other bits of rustic ironwork left as ex-votos by visiting pilgrims. Legend has it that Joan of Arc was one of them.

Nearby, if you need to **stay** the night, *Hôtel de l'Étoile*, 4 rue des Moulins (☎86.42.10.50; closed Sun evening, Mon in winter & Dec 20–Jan 13; ②; restaurant from 90F) is reasonable; and there's an attractive **campsite**, the *Camping du Serein*, beside the river just outside the village (June 4–Sept 18). If you're seeking sustenance, *Le Vieux Moulin*, 18 rue des Moulins (☎86.42.47.30; closed Mon evening & Tues) is good enough, with menus from 58F.

CHABLIS: THE WINE

The neatly staked **vineyards**, originally planted by the monks of Pontigny (see above), cover the sunny, well-drained, stony slopes on both sides of the valley. The grape is the *chardonnay*, which is to white wine what the *pinot noir* is to red: raw material of all the greatest Burgundies. But the town milks its product for all it's worth. Overpriced wine bars and stuffy restaurants abound. You don't get the opportunity to taste the cheaper varieties and there's haughty disapproval if you hope to spend less than 100F a bottle. Better to head for the cooperative, *La Chablisienne*, on bd Pasteur (Mon–Sat 8am–noon & 2–6pm, Sun 9.30–noon & 2–6pm), or better still, drink in one of the other villages like Pontigny or Maligny. If you want to buy a good wine, go for the ones with an *appellation*; the *grands crus*, from the northern slopes of the valley, are the best, with the *premiers crus* next in line. For information on the Chablis *appellation*, ask at the *Maison de la Vigne et du Vin*, 26–28 rue Auxerrois (☎86.42.42.22).

Noyers-sur-Serein

Twenty-three kilometres to the southeast – there's no alternative to hitching if you don't have your own transport – you come to the beautiful little town of **NOYERS-SUR-SEREIN**, sealed from the modern world in a medieval time warp. Its half-timbered and arcaded houses, ornamented with rustic carvings – particularly those on place de la Petite-Étape-aux-Vins and round place de l'Hôtel-de-Ville – are corralled inside a loop of the river and the town walls, and pleasant hours can be passed wandering the path between the river and the irregular walls with their robust towers. The Serein here is as pretty as in Chablis, but Noyers, being remarkably free of commercialism, has more authentic charm.

The town's main sight is the **Musée de l'Art Naïf** (Sat & Sun 2.30–6.30pm; June–Sept daily 11am–6.30pm; 15F), comprising the remarkable collection of art historian Jacques Yankel. The naïve painters (also known as "Sunday artists") had no formal training and were often workers lacking academic education (one, Augustine Lesage, worked as a miner for sixty years before he started painting). The perspectives are sometimes awkward, tending to lack depth, and meticulous detail is employed to compensate for this flatness. Some star exhibits include Gérard Lattier's morbid comic-strip-style work and the excellent collages of Louis Quilici.

There's a **hotel** – also the best place to **eat** – in place du Grenier-à-Sel in the town centre: the creeper-covered seventeenth-century *Hôtel de la Vieille Tour* (☎86.82.87.69; ②–③), with just five rooms beautifully furnished in old wood, and views across the gardens to the river. The restaurant is at the entrance to the village by the Porte Peinte (☎86.82.81.07; Easter–Oct closed Wed evening & Thurs) and has simple and good menus at 60F, 75F and 90F.

The valley of the Yonne

If you're travelling south from Auxerre and want a break from the main roads, there's a twisting minor road that leaves Auxerre as the D163 and follows the course of the **River Yonne** through a score of peaceful rural villages. Several have places both to stay and eat, making for a much more restful overnight stop than the towns.

VAUX and **ESCOLIVES-SAINTE-CAMILLE**, the first villages you come to, both have attractive Romanesque churches. **VINCELOTTES** and **IRANCY**, on the opposite bank of the river, are flower-decked and picturesque. Irancy produces the only red wine in this area, much loved of Louis XIV, while Vincelottes was the port for shipping it. It also has a small but pleasant **hotel**, *L'Auberge des Tilleuls*, 12 quai de l'Yonne (☎86.42.22.13; ③–④; closed Jan, Feb, Oct–Easter Wed evening & Thurs), whose restaurant has menus from 110F.

Six kilometres upstream in **CRAVANT**, the *Hôtel Hortensias* beside the church makes another pleasant stopover (☎86.42.24.63; ③; closed Nov 12–Dec 1, 3 weeks in Feb, plus Sun evening and Mon in winter; restaurant from 72F). Better still, with a most attractive and attentive restaurant, is *Le Castel* in **MAILLY-LE-CHÂTEAU**, a further 10km along the river on place de l'Église (☎86.81.43.06 or 86.81.49.26; ②–④; closed Wed and mid-Nov to mid-March), serving tasty snails, *coq au vin* and *magret de canard* at around 150F *à la carte* (menus 72–170F). The village is on high ground above the river, but don't miss the riverside quarter with its ancient houses huddling under the cliffs.

Half a dozen kilometres further upstream, more cliffs flank the east bank of the river: the **Rochers du Saussois**. About 50m high, they are a series of broken rock walls, ideal for rock-climbing, which is indeed what they are used for, with routes of all sorts of different grades. From here south to Clamecy, the river is at its most attractive, becoming more and more of a mountain stream.

The Canal de Bourgogne

From Migennes near Joigny on the N6, the River Armançon, in tandem with the **Canal de Bourgogne**, branches off to the north of the River Yonne. Along or close to its valley are several places of real interest: the Renaissance châteaux of **Tanlay** and **Ancy-le-Franc**, the eighteenth-century ironworks and **Fontenay monastery** near Montbard, and the site of Julius Cæsar's victory over the Gauls at **Alésia**. It is a route which is particularly worthwhile if you don't have your own transport, for all these places are served by trains on the Dijon–Migennes line (with connections to Sens and Auxerre).

Tonnerre and around

On the Paris–Sens–Dijon train route, **TONNERRE** is a useful starting point for exploring this corner of the region. A pleasant little town, its principal sight is a vast and well-conserved **medieval hospital** (guided tours: June–Sept daily 10am–noon & 1–7pm; April, May & Oct Sat, Sun & hols only 1–6pm; 20F), right on the main road in the middle of town. In the chapel is a super-expressive and realistic piece of Burgundian *tableau* statuary, an Entombment of Christ, in the style pioneered by Claus Sluter.

A couple of blocks from the hospital, the **Hôtel d'Uzès** saw the birth of Tonnerre's quirkiest claim to fame, an eighteenth-century gentleman with the impossible handle of Charles-Geneviève-Louise-Auguste-Andrée-Timothée Éon de Beaumont. He tickled his contemporaries' prurience by going about his important diplomatic missions for King Louis XV dressed in women's clothes. His act was so convincing that while he was in London bookmakers took bets on his real sex. Oddly enough, he was also a fearsome swordsman, though history does not relate what he wore to fight in. When he died, the results of the autopsy were eagerly awaited by the gossip columnists of the day.

The **tourist office** is directly opposite the hospital at 10 rue du Collège (daily except Sun 9.30am–12.30pm & 2.30–6.30pm; Nov–March Tues–Sat 9am–noon & 2–6pm; ☎86.55.16.48). The cheapest **accommodation** is at the *Hôtel du Centre*, 65 rue de l'Hôpital (☎86.55.10.56; ①–②), an old-fashioned provincial hotel with a reasonable little **restaurant** with menus from 62F. Slightly posher, there's *Hôtel de la Fosse Dionne*, 37 rue de l'Hôtel-de-Ville (☎86.55.11.92; ②–③), near the beautiful old *lavoir* or public washing-place, also with restaurant and a menu from 80F. The **campsite** (May–Sept) is between the River Armançon and the now more-or-less defunct Canal de Bourgogne.

The châteaux of Ancy-le-Franc and Tanlay

Close to Tonnerre are two of the finest – though least-known and least-visited – châteaux in France: Tanlay and Ancy-le-Franc. The former has the edge for romantic appeal, the latter for architectural purity.

The **Château of Ancy-le-Franc**, 8km from Tonnerre, was built in the mid-sixteenth century for the brother-in-law of the notorious Diane de Poitiers, mistress of Henri II (guided tours: April–Nov 11 10am–noon & 2–6pm; 40F). More Italian than French, with its rather gloomy, austere classical countenance, it is the only accepted work of the Italian Sebastiano Serlio, one of the most important architectural theorists, who was brought to France in 1540 by François I to work on his palace at Fontainebleau. The inner courtyard is more elaborate, and some of the apartments are sumptuous, decorated by the Italian artists Primaticcio and Niccolo dell'Abbate, who also worked at Fontainebleau. The most impressive rooms are La Chambre des Arts with medallions by Primaticcio and La Galerie des Sacrifices with monumental battle scenes in monochrome by Abbate.

If you want to stay, Ancy has two small **hotels**, the *Hôtel du Centre*, 34 Grande-Rue (☎86.75.15.11 or 86.75.14.13; ②–③; closed Fri evening in winter & Dec 12–Jan 5; good restaurant from 78F), and *Hôtel de la Poste*, 79 Grande-Rue (☎86.75.11.08; ②; restaurant from 75F; winter closed).

The **Château of Tanlay** (guided tours: daily except Tues April–Oct 9.30am, 10.30am & 11.30am; afternoons every 45min from 2.15 to 5.15pm; 36F), 15km along the canal from Tonnerre, is by contrast much more French and full of *fantaisie*. It is only slightly later in date, about 1559, but those extra few years were enough for the purer Italian influences visible in Ancy to have become Frenchified. It also feels much more feudal, the village crouching humbly at its gate and its approach road – a long straight tree-lined avenue – like a private drive, tying down the land on either side, proclaiming ownership.

Encircling the château are water-filled moats, and a wooded hill provides an effective backdrop. Standing guard over the entrance to the first grassy courtyard is the grand lodge, and it's here that you enter the château proper across a stone drawbridge. Domed and lanterned turrets terminate the wings of the *cour d'honneur*, urns line the ridge of the roof, from whose slates project carved and pedimented dormers. The white stone and round medieval towers, leftovers from the original fortress, add to the irregularity and charm. Inside, the most remarkable, if overpowering, room is the Grande Galerie, entirely covered by monochrome *trompe-l'œil* frescoes.

Montbard and around

The area around **MONTBARD** offers some insights into Burgundy's early industrial heritage. Blessed with iron ore deposits, extensive forest for charcoal burning, and water for hydraulic power, this part of the country became the cradle of the French industrial revolution during the eighteenth century (see "Le Creusot", p.470). The earliest foundries were small-scale rural affairs, dependent on one man's knowledge, with minimal and costly production, despite the invention of the blast furnace (*haut fourneau*) and the use of water power to drive hammers and bellows.

The town itself is of no great interest, and its current predicament is typical of 1990s industrial Europe: a one-industry town – it makes steel tubes – it is seeing the bottom drop out of its livelihood. It was the family home of the celebrated botanist, the Comte de Buffon (see below), and the only things worth a look are the pretty terraced gardens of the **Parc Buffon**, laid out by the great man, and the **museum** opposite devoted to his works (May–Oct daily except Tues 10am–noon & 3–6pm), with a rather specialist display of books, manuscripts and drawings.

The **tourist office** is in rue Carnot (daily 10am–noon & 2.30–6.30pm; Nov–March 2–6pm; ☎80.92.03.75). There's **accommodation** opposite the train station at *Hôtel de la Gare*, 10 rue Maréchal-Foch (☎80.92.02.12 or 80.92.41.72; closed Dec 22–Jan; ③), and a **campsite** near the swimming pool on rue Michel-Servet (Feb–Oct). There's a cheap little **restaurant**, the *Auberge du Donjon*, on rue Févret.

Forges de Buffon

Just outside Montbard, 6km north on D905, beside the River Armançon and the Canal de Bourgogne, are the remains of one of the most influential eighteenth-century foundries, the **Forges de Buffon** (daily except Tues 2.30–6pm; July & Aug Wed, Thurs & Fri 10am–noon), built in 1768 by Georges-Louis Buffon, distinguished scientist, landowner and lord of Montbard. Production was never more than 400 tons of iron a year, but Buffon's main interest was the experimental. The site, now owned by an Englishman and being restored as part of the growing French interest in industrial archeology, comprises model dwellings for workers (woodmen, ox-drivers and miners along with foundry workers) as well as the **foundry workshops**. These are situated on the banks of the river, designed in a most unindustrial classical style, with special viewing galleries for royal visitors and a grand staircase. There's not a great deal to see (some reproductions of machinery made by kids from the local school), but you get a unique insight into a precapitalist approach to industry. The foundry's most notable product was the railings, still in place, of the Jardin des Plantes in Paris.

The best approach to the Forges de Buffon is a pleasant hour's walk along the canal path. If that doesn't appeal, there are buses to St-Rémy, from where it's a mere two-kilometre hike to **BUFFON**. Here, on the main road, the *Marronier* hotel (☎80.92.33.65; ①) offers simple and pretty rooms right on the Canal de Bourgogne, with a very acceptable restaurant from 50F.

Fontenay Abbey

Six kilometres east of Montbard and accessible from the GR213 footpath, the privately owned **Abbey of Fontenay** (45min guided tours daily on the hour 9am–noon, on the half hour 2.30–6pm; 30F), founded in 1118, is the only Burgundian monastery to survive intact, despite conversion to a paper mill in the early nineteenth century. It was restored earlier this century to its original form and is one of the most complete monastic complexes anywhere, comprising caretaker's lodge, guesthouse and chapel, dormitory, hospital, prison, bakery, kennels, dovecote, abbot's house, as well as church, cloister, chapter house and even a forge. There's not much to be seen in the forge, but it is interesting that there should have been such a large one here, in the same countryside where France's industrial ironmasters set up shop 500 years later.

On top of all this, the abbey's physical setting, at the head of a quiet stream-filled valley enclosed by woods of pine, fir, sycamore and beech trees, is superb. There is a bucolic calm about the place, but you still feel a *frisson* of unease at the spartan simplicity of Cistercian life. Not a scrap of decoration softens the church; not one carved capital – the motherly statue of the Virgin arrived after St Bernard's death; there's no direct lighting in the nave, just an other-worldly glow from the square-ended apse, beautiful but daunting, the perfect structural embodiment of St Bernard's ascetic principles. The final scenes of the Gérard Depardieu movie *Cyrano de Bergerac* were filmed here.

Venarey-les-Laumes and around

One train stop south of Montbard (or three hours on the footpath) brings you to **VENAREY-LES-LAUMES**, home to another ailing metal tube factory. It was here, or rather behind and above the town, on the flat-topped hill of Mont Auxois, that the Gauls, united for once under the leadership of Vercingétorix, made their last stand against the military might of Rome at the **Battle of Alésia** in 52 BC. Julius Cæsar himself commanded the Roman army, surrounding the hill with a huge double ditch and earthworks and starving the Gauls out, bloodily defeating all attempts at escape. Vercingétorix surrendered to save his people, was imprisoned in Rome for six years until Cæsar's formal triumph, and then strangled. The battle was a great turning point in the fortunes of the region, marking the end of Gallic independence and an end to life in Europe before Greece and Rome. Thereafter, Gaul remained under Roman rule for 400 years. The site of **Alésia**, treeless and exposed, is back along the ridge 3km from the modern village of Alise-Ste-Reine (see below). While you can see little more than the layout today, it is extensive, and the interest of the whole area lies in imagined atmosphere rather than in anything concrete.

Towards the top of Mont Auxois, the village of **ALISE-STE-REINE** has a small **museum** (daily July to mid-Sept 9am–7pm; April–June & mid-Sept to Nov 10am–6pm) displaying finds from the Gallic town of Alésia and Cæsar's earthworks (the line of them still clearly visible in aerial photographs). On the first weekend of September the martyrdom of Sainte Reine is celebrated in a costume procession through the village, a custom that goes back to the year 866. Sainte Reine was a young Christian girl who was put to death in 262 for refusing to marry the proconsul of the Gauls, Olibrius. This martyrdom was the occasion for the conversion of Alésia.

Directly above the village, steps climb up to a great bronze **statue of Vercingétorix**. Erected by Napoléon III, whose influence popularized the rediscovery of France's pre-Roman roots, the statue represents Vercingétorix as a romantic Celt, half virginal Christ, half long-haired 1970s matinée idol. On the plinth is inscribed a quotation from Vercingétorix's address to the Gauls as imagined by Julius Cæsar: "United and forming a single nation inspired by a single ideal, Gaul can defy the world." Napoléon signs his dedication, "Emperor of the French", inspired by a vain desire to gain legitimacy by linking his own name to that of a "legendary" Celt.

Accommodation in Venarey-les-Laumes can be found at *Hôtel-Restaurant de la Gare*, 6 av de la Gare (☎80.96.00.46; ③; closed Fri & Sun evening; with restaurant, from 100F). The **campsite** is off the D954.

The Château de Bussy-Rabutin

Six kilometres northeast of Alise on the D954 you can see the handsome **Château de Bussy-Rabutin** (guided tours: daily 10 & 11am, on the hour 2–6pm; Oct–March Mon & Thurs–Sun 10 & 11am, 2 & 3pm; 26F), built for Roger de Rabutin, member of the Academy in the reign of Louis XIV and a notorious womanizer. The scurrilous tales of life at the royal court told in his book, *Histoires amoureuses des Gaules*, earned him a spell in the Bastille, followed by years of exile in this château, which contains some interesting portraits of great characters of the time, including the famous female beauties of the age, each underlined by a sharp little comment of the kind: "The most beautiful woman of her day, less renowned for her beauty than the uses she put it to."

Châtillon and the source of the Seine

If you're interested in pre-Roman France, there is one compelling reason for going to **CHÂTILLON-SUR-SEINE**: the so-called **Treasure of Vix**. Housed in the town's **museum** in the Maison Philandrier, 7 rue du Bourg, close to the centre (mid-June to mid-Sept daily 9am–noon & 1.30–6pm; mid-Sept to mid-Nov & mid-April to mid-June daily except Tues 9am–noon & 2–6pm; mid-Nov to mid-April daily except Tues 10am–noon & 2–5pm; 20F), it consists of the finds from the sixth-century BC tomb of a Celtic princess buried in a four-wheeled chariot. In addition to pieces of the chariot, these include staggeringly beautiful jewellery, Greek vases and Etruscan bowls. But the best on show is a gloriously simple gold tiara, actually found on the princess's head, and the largest bronze vase (*krater*) of Greek origin known from antiquity. It stands an incredible 1.64m high on triple tripod legs, and around its rim is a superbly modelled high-relief frieze depicting naked hoplites and horse-drawn chariots, with Gorgons' heads for handles. How these magnificent objects found their way to such a remote place is a mystery. One explanation lies in the fact that the village of **VIX**, 6km northwest of Châtillon, is the highest navigable point on the Seine, and it is thought that the Celtic chieftains who controlled it received such gifts, possibly from traders in Cornish tin shipped south from Britain via here on its way to the Adriatic, and perhaps to the bronze workers of Bibracte, the capital of the Aedui (see p.470).

The town of Châtillon has a few points of interest. On the rocky bluff overlooking the steep-pitched roofs of Châtillon's old quarter are the ruins of a **castle** and the early Romanesque **church of St-Vorles**. At its foot in a luxuriantly verdant spot, a **spring** swells out of the rock to join the infant Seine.

The **tourist office** is off place Marmont as you come into town from Chaumont (daily 9am–noon & 2–6pm; April–Oct Sun only; ☎80.91.13.19). There is a very welcoming **hotel**, the *Jura* on rue Docteur-Robert (☎80.91.26.96; ①–②; closed Sun evening). More expensive are the *Hôtel Sylvia*, standing in attractive grounds at 9 av de la Gare (☎80.91.02.44; ①–③), and the *Hôtel de la Côte d'Or*, 2 rue Charles-Ronot (☎80.91.13.29; ②–⑤), with its excellent restaurant from 95F.

The source of the Seine

To get to the **source of the Seine** you have to hitch 43km down N71 to the hamlet of **COURCEAU**, or take the GR2 footpath. From there, by road, take D103 through the upland hamlet of St-Germain, all crumbling stone farms and barns; or, better still, because rides are unlikely, pick up the GR2 at the bridge in Courceau for a two-hour walk.

The Seine, no more than a trickle here, rises in a tight little vale of beech woods. The spring is now covered by an artificial grotto complete with a languid nymph, Sequana, spirit of the Seine. In Celtic times it was a place of worship, as is clear from the numerous votive offerings discovered there, including a neat bronze of Sequana standing in a bird-shaped boat, now in the Dijon museum (see p.476). If you're here alone, it's a good place for rustic reverie, but if your arrival coincides with a coachload of Parisian day-trippers (the site belongs to the city of Paris) you'd be wise to retreat downstream. There's a **campsite** at **CHANCEAUX**, 5km away on the N71 (mid-April to Sept).

Semur-en-Auxois

Thirteen kilometres west of Alésia, the small fortress town of **SEMUR-EN-AUXOIS** sits on a rocky bluff, an extraordinarily beautiful little place of cobbled lanes, medieval gateways and ancient gardens cascading down to the River Armançon: only the patina of centuries could achieve such harmony of shape and colour. All roads here lead to place Notre-Dame, a handsome square dominated by the large thirteenth-century

church of Notre-Dame, another Viollet-le-Duc restoration, characterized by its huge entrance porch and the narrowness of its nave. The twin-towered west front has had many of its statues removed and the niches left bare. The best view is from the east in place de l'Ancienne-Comédie, past the finely sculpted north transept door (the life of Doubting Thomas), with a couple of Burgundy snails, symbol of Burgundy's culinary traditions, carved on the flanking columns. Inside, the windows of the first chapel on the left commemorate American soldiers of the First World War – a reminder that the battlefields were not far away. Also on the left are further, fine fifteenth-century windows dedicated by the butchers' and drapers' guilds and illustrating their trades, and a masterly Sluteresque painted Entombment.

Down the street in front of the church and off to the left you come to the four sturdy towers of Semur's once powerful **castle**, dismantled in 1602 because of its utility to enemies of the French crown. There is a dramatic view of it from the **Pont Joly** on the river below. Less specifically, the whole town is full of interesting buildings: there is scarcely a street without something of note, and there's a pleasant shady walk around the **fortifications**. On rue J-J-Collenot, the **library** (Wed 2–6pm), which is part of the otherwise not very interesting **museum** (mid-June to Sept Wed & Fri 2.30–6.30pm), has a fantastic collection of illuminated manuscripts and early printed books.

Practicalities

The **tourist office** is on the small place Gaveau (Mon–Sat 8.30am–noon & 2–6.30pm; July & Aug daily; ☎80.97.05.96), at the junction of rues de l'Ancienne-Comédie, de la Liberté and Buffon, where the medieval Porte Sauvigny and Porte Guillier combine to form a single long, covered gateway.

Hôtel des Gourmets, 4 rue de Varenne (☎80.97.09.41; ①–②; closed Mon evening, Tues & Dec), has the cheapest **hotel rooms** in town and an excellent, reasonably priced **restaurant**, with good home cooking from 90F, as has the *Hôtel de la Côte d'Or*, 3 place Gaveau (☎80.97.03.13 or 60.97.29.83; ②–③; closed Wed & Nov 24–Dec), with a restaurant serving traditional Burgundy cuisine like *coq au vin, truite farcie* and *ris de veau aux morilles* from 95F. Alternatively, there's the modern and comfortable *Hôtel du Lac* down by the lake at Pont-et-Massène (☎80.97.11.11; ②–③; closed Sun evening, Mon & mid-Dec to Jan), also with a good restaurant featuring *coq au vin, jambon persillé* and *tête de veau* (menus 88F–185F). There is a **youth hostel**, 1 rue du Champ-de-Foire, to the left off rue de la Liberté (☎80.97.10.22; ①), and a similar but more expensive establishment founded by a group of unemployed, the *Centre CRAC*, 10 rue du Couvent (☎80.97.03.81; ①). Both provide canteen meals for around 40F. The **campsite** is at Lac-de-Pont, 3km south of town.

Cheese connoisseurs might like to take a short twelve kilometre hop further west on the Avallon road to **ÉPOISSES**, not just for its village and **château** (July & Aug daily except Tues 10am–noon & 2–6pm), but for its distinctive soft orange-skinned cheeses washed in *marc de Bourgogne*.

THE MORVAN

The **Morvan** lies smack in the middle of Burgundy between the valleys of the Loire and the Saône, stretching roughly from Clamecy–Vézelay–Avallon in the north to Autun and the Charollais in the south. It is a land of wooded hills, close and rounded rather than mountainous, although they rise to 900m above Autun. The villages and farms are few and far between, for the soil is poor and the pastures only good for a few cattle. In the old days timber was the main business: supplying firewood and charcoal to Paris; but in modern times, far from main roads and rail lines, the region's chief export has been its escaping young. It earned a reputation as one of the poorest and most backward regions in the country. In fine weather it is beautiful; in foul it is rather depressing.

The creation of a *Parc naturel régional* in 1970 did something to promote the area as a place for outdoor activities and refuge from commuterdom. But more than anything it was the election of François Mitterrand, local politician and mayor of Château-Chinon for years, as president of the Republic that rescued the Morvan from oblivion. In addition to lending it some of the glamour of his office, he has taken concrete steps to beef up the local economy.

Avallon

Approaching **AVALLON** along the N6 from the north, you wouldn't give the place a second look. But the southern aspect is altogether more promising, as the town stands high on a ridge above the wooded valley of the River Cousin, looking out over the hilly, sparsely populated country of the Morvan regional park. Once a staging-post on the Romans' *Via Agrippa* from Lyon to Boulogne on the Channel coast, it is a small and ancient town of stone façades and comatose cobbled streets, bisected north to south by the narrow **Grande-Rue-Aristide-Briand**. Under the straddling arch of the fifteenth-century **Tour de l'Horloge**, whose spire dominates the town, this street brings you to the pilgrim **church of St-Lazare**, on whose battered Romanesque façade you can still decipher the graceful carvings of signs of the zodiac, labours of the months, and the old musicians of the Apocalypse. Almost opposite, in a fifteenth-century house, is the tourist office, with the municipal **museum** (Easter–Oct daily 10am–12.30pm & 2–6.30pm; 15F) behind it. Exhibits include a room of modern silverware designed by local boy Jean Despres, and a second-century mosaic from a Gallo-Roman villa. Continuing down the street, now called rue Bocquillot, brings you to the lime-shaded **Promenade de la Petite Porte**, with precipitous views across the plunging valley of the Cousin. You can walk from here around the outside of the **walls**. From the **Parc des Chaumes**, on the east side of town, there is a great view back to the old quarter, snug within its walls, with garden terraces descending on the slope beneath.

Practicalities

The **tourist office**, 6 rue Bocquillot (daily Easter–Oct 9am–12.30pm & 2–6.30pm; July & Aug 9.30am–7.30pm; Nov–March closed Sun & Mon; ☎86.34.14.19). **Bike rental** is from the **gare SNCF** at the end of av Président-Douma. The main shopping centre is concentrated in the new town north of the city walls, but there's a Saturday **market** in place Vauban.

For cheap **accommodation**, the bargain-priced *Hôtel du Parc*, opposite the train station at 3 place de la Gare (☎86.34.17.00; ①–②), is a clean and friendly place with an inexpensive restaurant and bar frequented by locals. The *Hôtel de Paris*, not far from the station at 45 rue de Paris (☎86.34.10.05; ①), is also cheap but less interesting. Modern, but more comfortable and very welcoming, there's the *Dak' Hôtel* on the Dijon road (☎86.31.63.20; ③–④). The road alongside the River Cousin is an attractive, though more roundabout route to nearby Vézelay (see below), and five kilometres from town you'll reach the perfect little *Moulin de Ruats*, an expensive hotel (☎86.34.07.14; ④–⑤; closed mid-Nov to Feb 2), but with a very good restaurant and *al fresco* rural dining beside the river (closed Tues lunchtime & Mon and same period as hotel; from 150F). The *Foyer Mixte de Jeunes Travailleurs*, 10 av Victor-Hugo (☎86.34.01.88; ①), has canteen meals at 40F, and you'll find the attractive **camping municipal** de Sous-Roche (☎86.34.10.39; March–Oct), and camping *à la ferme* at *Les Chatelaines* (☎86.34.16.37; April to mid-Oct), a couple of kilometres out of town in the Cousin valley.

Reasonable **eating** is to be found on place Vauban at the *Hôtel du Centre* (☎85.34.03.53), or at *Cheval Blanc*, 55 rue de Lyon, and there's a snack bar on place Vauban – the *Pub Vauban* – with hamburgers and the like.

Vézelay

If you can get a reliable bike, cycling is a pleasant way of covering the distance to **VEZELAY** (around 20km from Avallon). Alternatively, there are buses from Avallon (*Cars de la Madeleine*; one a weekday) and trains to Sermizelles on the Auxerre–Avallon line with an *SNCF* bus link on to Vézelay.

A hundred years ago the village of Vézelay was abandoned, although its abbey church, **La Madeleine** (sunrise–sunset; closed during Sun mass 10.30am–12.15pm; 10F), one of the seminal buildings of the Romanesque period, had already been saved from collapse by Viollet-le-Duc in 1840. Quintessentially picturesque and popular with the coach tours, it is undeniably an attractive place.

As you emerge puffing from the climb into the rather desolate square in front of the church, Viollet's reproduced west front looks disappointingly unauthentic. But veer to the right into the garden on the south side and you get an angle on the long buttressed nave and Romanesque tower that corrects the balance and sheds light on the nautical imagery of "nave" – *navis*, ship or hull.

The colossal narthex was added to the nave around 1150 to accommodate the swelling numbers of pilgrims attracted by the supposed presence of the bones of Mary Magdalen. Inside, your eye is first drawn to the superlative sculptures of the central doorway, on whose tympanum an ethereal Christ swathed in swirling drapery presides over a group of apostles and peoples going about their business with cows, fish, crossbows and so forth – among those featured are giants, pygmies (one mounting his horse with a ladder), a man with breasts and huge ears, and dog-headed heathens. Better preserved are the charmingly small-scale medallions of the zodiac signs and labours of the months in the outer arch. In the flanking portals are depicted nativity scenes on the right, and Christ on the road to Emmaus after the resurrection on the left.

From this great doorway you look down the long body of the church, vaulted by arches of alternating black and white stone, to a choir of pure early Gothic (completed in 1215), luminous with the delicacy of the inside of a shell by contrast with the heavier, more sombre Romanesque nave. Its arches and arcades are edged with fretted mouldings, and the supporting pillars are crowned with 99 finely cut capitals, depicting scenes from the Bible, classical mythology, allegories and morality stories. The finest of all is "The Mystic Mill" at the end of the fourth bay on the right, showing Moses pouring grain (Old Testament Law) through a mill (Christ), the flour (New Testament) being gathered by St Paul.

Saint Bernard preached the Second Crusade at Vézelay in 1146. Because the church was too small, he preached in the open, down the hill; a **commemorative cross** marks the spot. Richard the Lionheart and Philippe Auguste, king of France, also made their rendezvous here before setting off on the Third Crusade in 1190. But the abbey's heyday came to an end in 1280 when it was discovered that the Magdalen's bones belonged to someone else. Its decline was hastened by Protestant vandalism in the sixteenth century, and the whole establishment was disbanded during the Revolution.

Before moving on, be sure to take a look at the beautiful Gothic church in the village of **ST-PÈRE**, a half-hour walk from the abbey at the foot of the hill. The village is also home to one of the greatest restaurants in the land, *Marc Meneau* (upwards of 350F).

Practicalities

Vézelay's small **tourist office** (daily except Wed & Sun Easter–Oct 10am–1pm & 2–6pm; July & Aug daily) is on the right in rue St-Pierre as you go up towards the abbey, and *SNCF* **buses** for Sermizelles and buses for Avallon leave from Garage de la Madeleine on the main square.

For **accommodation**, reasonable-value hotels include the *Hôtel de la Terrasse*, right outside the church (☎86.33.25.50; ②–③), with only four rooms; and *Le Cheval Blanc* on place Champ-du-Foire (☎86.33.22.12 or 86.33.34.29; ①; restaurant from 70F), although at weekends and in high season you'll find it best to avoid either eating or sleeping here. There are also two **youth hostels**: the *Centre de Rencontres Internationales* on rue des Écoles, run by the *Amis de Pax Christi* (☎86.33.26.73; ①; July & Aug), and an IYHF-affiliated hostel about 1km along the route de l'Étang (☎86.33.24.18; ①; Easter–Sept; IYHF card required), which also has **camping** space.

For a rather special and romantic stay, you could try the lovely creeper-covered *Moulin des Templiers* by the river near **PONTAUBERT** back towards Avallon (☎86.34.10.80; ③–④; closed Nov to mid-March). Another possibility is Clamecy (see below), or, for **campers**, a beautiful site in the little farming village of **BRÈVES** right beside the Yonne midway between Vézelay and Clamecy (closed mid-Sept to mid-June).

Clamecy

A more workaday place to stay is **CLAMECY**, 23km to the west of Vézelay on the banks of the River Yonne. In sharp contrast to its rustic neighbours, it has a distinctly industrial feel as the centre of the Morvan's logging trade from the sixteenth century to the completion of the Canal du Nivernais in 1834. Individual woodcutting gangs working in the hills floated their logs down the Yonne and its tributaries as far as Clamecy, where they were made up into great rafts for shipment on to Paris. This contact with the capital – and cradle of new egalitarian political ideas – led to the early spread of revolutionary thoughts among the workers and peasantry of the Morvan, who staged a number of violent insurrections even before 1789. The history of the logging trade is documented in the **museum** on rue de la Mirandole (Easter–Oct daily except Tues 10am–noon & 2–6pm; 15F).

There's nothing special to see in town, apart from the many fifteenth- to eighteenth-century buildings in the centre, but it does have an interesting history and a bizarre connection with Bethlehem. In 1168 William IV, crusading Count of Nevers, died in Palestine, bequeathing one of his properties in Clamecy to the bishopric of Bethlehem, to serve as a sanctuary in the case of Palestine falling into the hands of the infidel. When the Latin Kingdom of Jerusalem fell, the first bishop arrived to claim his legacy, and from 1225 until the Revolution fifty bishops of Bethlehem suceeded each other in Clamecy, honouring the little town with the title of bishopric. A curious little **chapel** by the bridge, built in 1927 in reinforced concrete, commemorates the connection.

The **tourist office** is on rue du Grand-Marché, opposite the church of St-Martin. For places to **stay**, try the lovely old-fashioned *Hôtel de la Poste* on place Émile-Zola not far from the bridge (☎86.27.01.559; ③–④; closed Sun evening & Mon; restaurant from 95F) or the good-value *La Boule d'Or*, 2 pl Bethléem (☎86.27.11.51; ①–②), with an attractive restaurant, located in a renovated thirteenth-century chapel just across the river, near the modern Chapel of Bethlehem on the road to Auxerre. For **campers**, there's a good riverside site on the edge of town on the route de Chevroches (May–Sept). For places to **eat** outside the hotels, try *La Vieille Rome*, also by the church on place du 19-août (closed Sun eve & Mon; 70–120F).

Saulieu and the Parc du Morvan

SAULIEU, having suffered something of a decline with the depopulation of the Morvan, then the construction of the A6 autoroute that took away the traffic from the old N6, is once more a relatively thriving market town, chiefly known for its gastronomic reputation dating back to its days as a post house in the seventeenth century. Saulieu is far from easy to get to without your own transport, as bus connections are unhelpful, while the train from Dijon takes three-and-a-half hours and involves two changes. By car, the drive takes just 40 minutes.

The old town – on the west side of the N6 – is pretty enough, but it's not somewhere you'd want to stay long. Its main sight is the twelfth-century **Basilique St-Andoche**, noted for its lovely capitals, probably carved by a disciple of Gislebertus, the master sculptor of Autun (see p.468). Next door, the **Musée François-Pompon** (Mon & Wed–Sat 10am–12.30pm & 2–6pm, Sun 10.30am–noon & 2–5pm; 20F) is also surprisingly interesting, with good local folklore displays and a large collection of the works of the local nineteenth-century animal sculptor, François Pompon.

The **tourist office** (Mon–Sat 9.30am–noon & 2–6pm, Sun 10am–noon; July & Aug Mon–Sat 9.30am–6pm; ☎80.64.00.21) is on the N6 near the hospital, in the direction of Paris. There is a Pompon statue of a bull in the little garden almost opposite. The **gare SNCF** (☎80.64.05.32) is straight up av de la Gare opposite the market place/car park.

Should you need to stay, two reasonable **hotels** to try are *La Vieille Auberge*, 15 rue Grillot (☎80.64.13.74; ③; closed Tues evening, Wed & mid-Dec to mid-Jan; restaurant from 70F) and *Le Lion d'Or*, 5 rue Courtépée – by the hospital (☎80.64.16.33; ②–③; closed Sun evening, Mon, & Jan 1–15), whose restaurant food starts at 68F *à la carte*. There are also a couple of *gîtes d'étape* (Easter–Nov) and a **camping municipal** (☎80.64.00.21; April–Oct), 1km out along the Paris road.

Saulieu's culinary fame is expensive to put to the test. An exception is the excellent **restaurant** of the *Hôtel de la Poste*, 1 rue Grillot (☎80.64.05.67; ②–③), which has menus starting at 98F; the other eating establishment of note is *La Côte d'Or* at 2 rue d'Argentine in the middle of town (☎80.64.07.66), run by one of the country's top-rated chefs, where the cheapest meal is a weekday lunchtime menu at 290F.

The Parc du Morvan

The **Parc Régional du Morvan** was only officially designated as such in 1970, when 170,000 hectares of hilly countryside were set aside in an attempt to protect the local cultural and natural heritage with a series of nature trails, animal reserves, museums and local craft shops. The official information centre for the park, the **Maison du Parc** (Mon–Fri 8.45am–12.15pm & 1.30–5.30pm; ☎86.78.70.16), is at **ST-BRISSON**, 13km from Saulieu. There's no public transport there, but if you're walking or cycling it's a good place to head for as they have all available information on routes and facilities in the park, as well as a small **museum** (July to mid-Sept daily 2–6pm; 15F) devoted to the World War II Resistance movement in the region, and a **herbarium** of regional plants. The *maison*, about a kilometre outside St-Brisson on the D6, is located in beautiful grounds, which include a deer park. At weekends the same service is provided by the exhibition centre next to the museum.

A map, *Saulieu Vélo Tout-Terrain en Morvan*, marks cycling and walking routes. For **walkers** the most challenging trip is the **GR13** footpath, which crosses the park from Vézelay to Mont-Beuvray, taking in the major lakes, which are among the park's most developed attractions. There are also less strenuous possibilities: for example, the four-kilometre walk to Lac Chamboux, leaving Saulieu by the D26 and taking a track to the left (blue and yellow markers) after about ten minutes. For a starting point deeper into the park, there is a bus to Moux.

Accommodation in the park includes a number of hotels and campsites. There are several campsites round the Lac des Settons, and municipal sites in St-Brisson (☎86.78.70.80; May–Aug) and in **MOUX** (☎86.76.18.81; June–Sept), 10km to the east of Settons, which also has a reasonable hotel, *Le Beau Site* (☎86.76.11.75 or 86.76.15.84; ①–②; closed Dec 22–Feb 10, plus Sun & Mon evening out of season), whose good restaurant has meals from 60F. Montsauche, northwest of Settons, is a good bet for provisions, including camping gas, and also has a *camping municipal* (☎86.84.51.05). **Bikes** are available from a number of outlets, including the train station in Saulieu (☎80.64.05.32), *Camping du Midi* on Lac des Settons (☎86.84.51.97) and *La Margelle* pizzeria in Montsauche (☎86.84.54.55).

Château-Chinon

The most substantial community in the park itself is the rather ugly village of **CHÂTEAU-CHINON**, set in beautiful country (bus connection to Autun). President Mitterrand was a local council member here until 1983, and the town has been the home base of his political life for half a century. Thanks largely to him, it boasts a major hosiery factory and military printing works.

In the **Musée du Septennat** (daily 10am–6pm; Oct–May Sat, Sun & public holidays only; July & Aug closes 7pm; 12F) you can see the extraordinary variety of gifts Mitterrand has received as head of state. The museum is light and airy, purpose-built to hold a collection of some of the finest handicrafts from their many countries of origin: carpets from the Middle East, ivory from Togo, Japanese puppets, beaded spears from Burundi and bizarre gifts, like a table decorated with butterfly wings.

Mitterrand's preferred **hotel** is the *Vieux Morvan*, 8 place Gudin (☎86.85.05.01 or 86.85.02.78; ③–④; closed Jan), with a nice, bright restaurant with view, from 80F. If you're not budgeting for such expense, you might be better off in the *Hostellerie l'Oustalet* on the route de Lormes (☎86.85.15.57; ①–②; closed Sept 20–Oct; restaurant from 55F), or in the comfortable *Lion d'Or* (☎86.85.13.56; ②; restaurant from 65F).

Autun and around

With its Gothic spire rising against a backdrop of Morvan hills, **AUTUN**, even today, is scarcely bigger than the circumference of its medieval **walls**, and they in turn followed the line of the Roman fortifications which predated them. The emperor Augustus founded the town in about 10 BC as part of a massive and, in the long term, highly successful campaign to pacify and Romanize the broody Celts of defeated Vercingétorix. Augustodunum, as it was called, was designed to eclipse by its splendour the memory of Bibracte (see below), the neighbouring capital of the powerful tribe of the Aedui. And it did indeed become one of the leading cities of Roman Gaul.

The Town

Traces of the Roman period are still much in evidence. Two of the city's four Roman gates survive: **Porte St-André**, spanning rue de la Croix-Blanche in the northeast, and **Porte d'Arroux** in Faubourg d'Arroux in the northwest. In a field just across the River Arroux stands a lofty section of brick wall known as the **Temple of Janus**, which was probably part of the sanctuary of some Gallic deity, while on the east side of the town you can see the rather meagre remains of what was the largest **Roman theatre** in

Gaul, with a capacity of 15,000 – in itself a measure of Autun's importance at that time. It's in av du 2ème-Dragon just off the Dijon road. It's not an evocative site – the remaining seats now overlook a football pitch – but in July and August its authenticity is enhanced by the performances of a play in which 600 locals, dressed in period costume, reconstruct the Gallo-Roman past of the town.

The influence of the monuments of this ever-present Roman past proves very much in evidence in Autun's great **Cathédrale St-Lazare**, built in the twelfth century, getting on for a thousand years after the Romans had gone. It stands in the most southerly and best fortified corner of the town, and although its external appearance has been much altered by the addition of Gothic tower, spire and side chapels in the fifteenth century, and the twin towers flanking the front in the nineteenth, the Romanesque – and Roman – elements are very clear inside, and the church's greatest claim to artistic fame lies in its sculptures, the work of Gislebertus, generally accepted as one of the greatest Romanesque sculptors. The tympanum of the Last Judgement above the west door

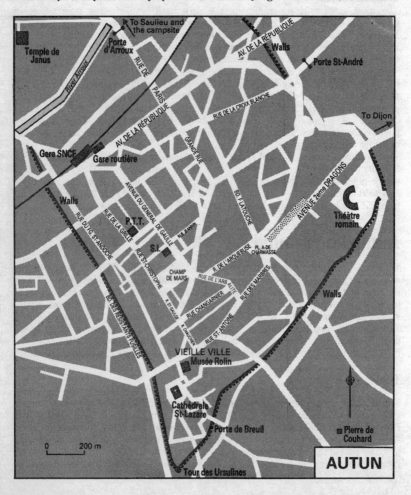

AUTUN

bears his signature – *Gislebertus hoc fecit*: "Gislebertus made this" – beneath the feet of Christ. To the left and right of Christ are depicted the elect entering heaven; the apostles; the Archangel Michael disputing souls with Satan, who tries to cheat by leaning on the scales; and the flames of hell licking at the damned. Luckily, during the eighteenth century the local clergy decided it was an inferior work and plastered it over, saving it from almost certain destruction during the Revolution. The interior, whose pilasters and arcading were modelled on the Roman architecture of the city's gates, was also decorated by Gislebertus, who himself carved most of the capitals. Conveniently for anyone wanting a close look, some of the finest are now exhibited in the old chapter library, up the stairs on the right of the choir, among them a beautiful *Flight into Egypt* and *Adoration of the Magi*.

Just outside the cathedral on rue des Bancs, the **Musée Rolin** (daily except Tues April–Sept 9.30am–noon & 1.30–6pm; Oct 10am–noon & 2–5pm; Nov–March 10am–noon & 2–4pm; 12F) occupies a Renaissance *hôtel* built by Nicolas Rolin, chancellor of Philippe le Bon, and is definitely worth a look. In addition to interesting Gallo-Roman pieces, the star attractions are Gislebertus' representation of Eve as an unashamedly sensual nude and the Maître de Moulins' brilliantly coloured *Nativity*.

The most enigmatic of the Gallo-Roman remains in the region, however, is the **Pierre de Couhard**, off Faubourg St-Pancrace to the southeast of the town. It's a 27-metre-tall stone pyramid situated on the site of one of the city's necropolises, thought to date from the first century, and most probably either a tomb or a cenotaph.

Practicalities

Whether you arrive at the **gare SNCF** (☎85.52.28.01) or **gare routière** next door, you'll find yourself on av de la République, bisected at right angles by av Charles-de-Gaulle which leads to the wide square of the Champs-de-Mars and into the old town. The **tourist office** is at 3 av de Gaulle (Mon–Sat 9am–noon & 2–6pm; Oct–Easter Mon–Fri 9am–noon & 2–7pm; Sat 9am–noon; ☎85.52.20.34).

There is a good choice of **accommodation**. Opposite the station, the *Hôtel de France*, 18 av de la République (☎85.52.14.00; ①–②), and *Hôtel Commerce et Touring* at no. 20 (☎85.52.17.90; ①–②; closed Oct; reasonable restaurant from 65F) are both decent and inexpensive. For something a bit better, there are a couple of old coaching inns just off the Champs-de-Mars, both comfortable and with some character: *Hôtel St-Louis*, 6 rue de l'Arbalète (☎85.52.21.03; ③; closed Dec 20–Jan 28; restaurant from 82F), where the great Napoléon slept; and *Hôtel La Tête Noire* opposite at 1–3 rue de l'Arquebuse (☎85.52.25.39; ②–③; restaurant from 85F). The municipal **campsite** is just across the river beyond Porte d'Arroux (☎85.52.10.82; April–Oct).

In addition to the hotel restaurants, the Champs-de-Mars has a couple of **brasseries**, but, best of all, in the bottom corner by the Hôtel de Ville, try the innovative cooking of the *Chalet Bleu*, 3 rue Jeannin (☎85.86.27.30; closed Mon evening, Tues & Feb 6–22) which, though expensive *à la carte*, has a weekday menu at 85F and a very good value one at 120F.

Mont-Beuvray and Bibracte

The base for the climb up Mont-Beuvray to the 2000-year-old site of the Gallic capital of Bibracte is **ST-LÉGER-SOUS-BEUVRAY**, about 26km southwest of Autun and reached along the N81 and D61 through typical Morvan countryside of wooded hills and scattered farms, coarse marshy pastures and brown streams. There's a morning and afternoon bus to St-Léger, or you can tackle the seven-hour walk on **GR131** from the Croix de la Libération outside Autun. If you need to spend the night, there's a **youth hostel** (☎85.82.55.46; ①) and **camping municipal** in St-Léger.

From here, it's the best part of two hours further by the path, or 8km by the road, to **BIBRACTE** at the top of the hill, at an altitude of 800m – if you want to recapture a Celtic mood, it's worth doing this last stretch on foot along a path winding up through woods of conifers and beech. The settlement of Bibracte, the lines of which you can still follow through the trees, was inhabited from 5000 BC; in 52 BC it was the scene of an assembly of all the Gallic tribes, which resulted in the election of Vercingétorix as their commander-in-chief, in one last desperate attempt to fight off Roman imperialism. Although it is two millennia since Bibracte was abandoned – probably on Roman orders – vague memories of its significance were preserved in the folk tales of the Morvan and a fair was held on the summit every May until the beginning of World War I. Close to the fortified earthwork that surrounds the site, great ceremonial stones like the **Pierre de la Wivre** are still standing.

Le Creusot

LE CREUSOT means one thing to French ears: the **Schneider iron and steel works**, maker of the first French railway engine in 1838, the first steamship in 1839, the 75mm field gun – mainstay of First World War artillery – the iron-work of the Pont Alexandre-III and the Gare d'Austerlitz in Paris. Its successor, *Creusot-Loire*, now manufactures specialized steels and boilers for the nuclear industry and, like many steel works in Britain, employs far fewer people.

Arriving in Le Creusot through the wooded hills from Autun, 25km away, the sight of this erstwhile industrial powerhouse, whose origins go back to the exploitation of the region's coal in the sixteenth century, comes as a bit of a shock. You arrive suddenly, over the brow of a hill, to see abandoned factories and workers' housing spilling down the bottom of a valley.

A small street of rustic-looking workers' dwellings survives in the **Combes des Mineurs**, while in place du 8-mai on the Montchanin road out of town a colossal 100-ton Schneider **drop-hammer** has been set up as a monument to past glories. Climb to the rue des Pyrénées above the Combe des Mineurs, from where you can see Le Creusot spread before you, including the modern *Creusot-Loire* steel works, the gleaming white Château de la Verrerie and the terraces of pastel-coloured houses, against a backdrop of hills which are the northeast border of the Massif Central.

The town's main attraction is the **Écomusée de la Communauté Urbaine du Creusot-Montceau-les-Mines** in the Château de la Verrerie on place Schneider (Mon–Fri 9am–noon & 2–6pm, Sat & Sun 2–6pm; 15F). Built as a glassworks in 1786–87 – Louis XVI was a shareholder before losing his head – the château was sold to the Schneider family in 1838 and was transformed into their private home and the administrative centre of their business empire. The Schneiders were paternalistic but despotic employers, providing housing, schools and health care for their workers, but expecting "gratitude and obedience" in return. When a certain Dumay, one of their workers whose political interests and involvement in strikes they had been watching with disapproval, became mayor in 1870 and proclaimed adherence to the Paris Commune, he was sentenced to hard labour for life; the army organized a private police force to keep an eye on workers' reading matter and church attendance, handed out building plots for "good behaviour", and rigged municipal elections in favour of "their" candidates. In the end they became so unpopular they had to turn the château into a kind of Fort Knox. But, by one of history's delightful ironies, the last Schneider married the granddaughter of Jules Guesde, father of the French Communist Party. The château remained in the family's possession until the widow of the last incumbent bequeathed it to the town in 1969. The peculiar cone-shaped constructions in the court-yard were the glass furnaces, recently transformed into a theatre and a chapel.

Today, the exhibits in the *écomusée* tell the story of he
the area, with superb period photos, coin-slot push-butt
cranes, reconstructed workshops, models of locomotive
great *Mistral* train's run from Paris to Marseille. Many ex
are on display, with a video explaining methods of producti

Practicalities

The **tourist office** in the Château de la Verrerie (Mon & We...
Sat 2–7pm; winter 10am–noon & 2–6pm; ☎85.55.02.46) ca...mation on
tours of the town, the *TGV* industry workshops and some of the coal mines in the vicinity. Frequent buses connect Le Creusot with the *TGV* station 6km away in Montchanin, connecting with Paris.

If you need to **stay** overnight, *Hôtel des Voyageurs*, 5 pl Schneider (☎85.55.22.36; ②–③; closed Fri & Sun evening), is acceptable and has a good restaurant, as is the *Hôtel Moderne* near the station at 41 rue Maréchal-Leclerc (☎85.80.80.80; ③; closed Aug), also with a restaurant. But the town does not have the sort of charm that makes a stay even remotely inviting.

DIJON AND THE CÔTE D'OR

If the much touted image of "rural Burgundy" has conjured up an image of slightly backward and ramshackle rustic charm in your mind, you'll have to do some adjusting when you encounter the slick prosperity of **Dijon** and the wine-producing country to the south, known as the **Côte d'Or**. It may look peacefully pastoral, but there is nothing medieval about the methods or the profits made in today's wine business. For any trace of the older traditions you have to head into the southwestern corner of the region.

Dijon

DIJON owes its origins to its strategic position in Celtic times on the tin merchants' route from Britain up the Seine and across the Alps to the Adriatic. It became the capital of the dukes of Burgundy in around 1000 AD, but its golden age occurred in the fourteenth and fifteenth centuries under the auspices of dukes Philippe le Hardi (the Bold), who as a boy had fought the English at Poitiers and been taken prisoner, Jean sans Peur (the Fearless), Philippe le Bon (the Good), who sold Joan of Arc to the English, and Charles le Téméraire (the Rash). They used their tremendous wealth and power – especially their control of Flanders, the dominant manufacturing region of the age – to make Dijon one of the greatest centres of art, learning and science in Europe. It lost its capital status on incorporation into the kingdom of France in 1477, but has remained one of the country's pre-eminent provincial cities, especially since the rail and industrial booms of the mid-nineteenth century. Today, it is smart, modern and young.

Arrival, information and accommodation

Dijon is not an enormous city. The part you'll want to see is neatly confined in the centre and eminently walkable. Whether you arrive by road or rail from either Paris and the north or Lyon and the south, you will find yourself almost inevitably at the **gare SNCF** (☎80.41.50.50). The **gare routière** is next to the *gare SNCF* at the end of av Maréchal-Foch, five minutes from place Darcy.

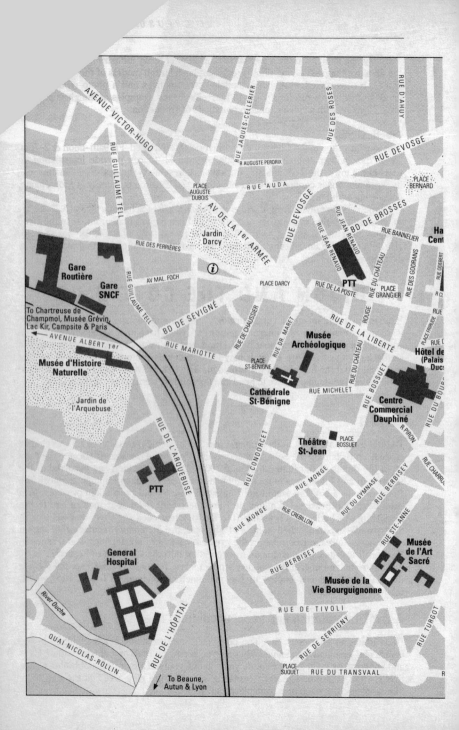

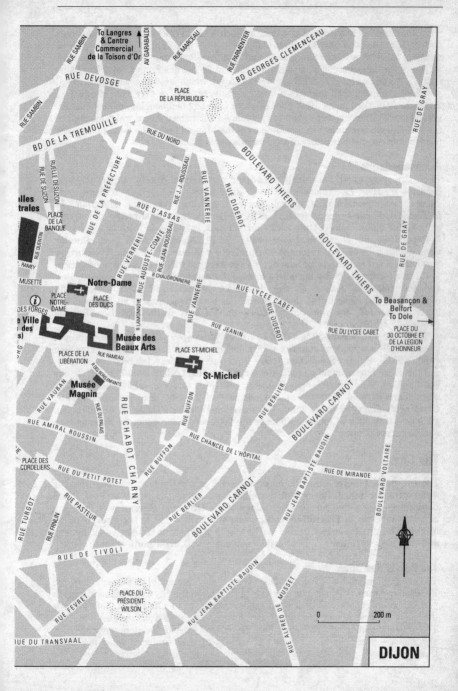

DIJON

From immediately outside the station, av Foch leads to place Darcy in five minutes on foot. You pass the **tourist office** (daily 9am–noon & 2–7pm; mid-April to May & mid-Sept to mid-Nov 9am–8pm; June to mid-Sept 9am–9pm; ☎80.43.42.12) on your left as you reach the square. There's another office at 34 rue des Forges (Mon–Fri 9am–noon & 2–6pm; winter closed Fri am; ☎80.30.35.39), which also houses the *Club Alpin*, a walking company that produces a booklet, *Promenez-vous en Côte d'Or*, showing all the region's marked paths. Both offer services such as hotel booking, money change, guided tours of the city, and – most worthwhile – a 15F museum card which allows free access to all the museums listed below except the Musée Grevin; the tourist office also produces an excellent directory of local facilities, called *Divio*.

Accommodation

There are some good, reasonably priced and very central **hotels**. Among the best bargains are *Hôtel Le Chambellan*, 92 rue Vannerie (☎80.67.12.67; ②–③), with some cheaper attic rooms and a special deal with the traffic wardens, and *Hôtel Le Jacquemart*, 32 rue Verrerie (☎80.73.39.74; ②–③). Both are in attractive old streets close to the dukes' palace. Only a little further away, at 3 rue du Nord near place de la République, the *Hôtel République* (☎80.73.36.76; ②) offers more good value for money with a 50-percent discount on Sunday if you stay two nights. Two further possibilities are *Hostellerie Le Sauvage*, 64 rue Monge (☎80.41.31.21; ③; closed Sept 1–15) in a former coaching inn with a lovely little courtyard for its restaurant tables, and the *Hôtel du Palais*, 23 rue du Palais (☎80.67.16.26; ②–③), clean and modernized and close to the ducal palace. For something quite a lot cheaper, but likely to be full, try the central *Hôtel du Théâtre*, 3 rue des Bons-Enfants (☎80.67.15.41; ①).

There are two **hostels**: the IYHF *Centre de Rencontres Internationales*, a proper youth hostel in a modern complex with a self-service canteen, at 1 bd Champollion (☎80.72.95.20; ①; bus #5, direction *Épirey*, from place Grangier – last bus around 8pm), and the *Foyer International d'Étudiants* on rue Maréchal-Leclerc (☎80.71.51.01; ①; bus #4, direction *St-Apollinaire*, stop *Billardon*; also with canteen), which takes visitors when there is room. Both are on the east side of the city. The nearest **campsite**, *Camping du Lac* (☎80.43.54.72; bus #12, direction *Fontaine d'Ouche*, or #18, direction *Plombières*), is off bd Chanoine-Kir near the lake: follow the signs for Paris and it's about 1km out of town.

The City

The **rue de la Liberté** forms the major east–west axis in the town, running from the wide, attractive **place Darcy** and the eighteenth-century triumphal arch of **Porte Guillaume**, once a city gate, past the **palace of the Dukes of Burgundy** on the semi-circular **place de la Libération**, and moving still further east to the **church of St-Michel**. The street is pedestrianized and lined with smart shops and elegant old houses, and most places of interest are within fifteen minutes' walk to the north or south of it.

The Palais des Ducs

The geographical focus of a visit to Dijon is inevitably the seat of its former rulers, the **Palais des Ducs**, which stands precisely at the hub of the city overlooking Mansart's perfectly proportioned and deliciously mellow **place de la Libération**, built towards the end of the seventeenth century as place Royale to show off a statue of the Sun King. Though still functioning as the town hall, the palace's exterior has undergone so many alterations – especially in the sixteenth and seventeenth centuries when it became Burgundy's parliament – that the dukes themselves would scarcely recognize it. The only outward reminders of the older building that stood here are the fourteenth-century **Tour de Bar** above the east wing, which now houses the Musée des Beaux-Arts (see below), and the fifteenth-century **Tour Philippe-le-Bon** (daily 9am–noon & 2.30–5.30pm, tours every 45mins; Nov–Easter Wed pm, Sat & Sun, tours at 9am, 10am, 11am, 1.30pm, 2.30pm & 3.30pm; 15F), from whose terrace they say you can see Mont Blanc on a very clear day.

The palace is now home to the excellent **Musée des Beaux-Arts** (daily except Tues & public hols 10am–6pm; 12F, Sun free), with a collection of paintings representing many different schools and periods, from Titian, Rubens and Schongauer to Monet, Manet and other Impressionists, with substantial numbers of Italian and Flemish works and quantities of religious artefacts, ivories and tapestries. One of the most interesting exhibits is a small room devoted to the intricate woodcarving of the sixteenth-century designer and architect Hugues Sambin, whose work appears throughout the old quarter of the city in the massive doors and façades of the aristocratic *hôtels*. Visiting the museum also provides the opportunity to see the surviving portions of the original ducal palace, including the vast **kitchens** needed to service the dukes' gargantuan appetites and the magnificent **Salle des Gardes**, richly appointed with panelling, tapestries and a minstrels' gallery. Here are displayed the **tombs** from the Chartreuse de Champmol (see below) of Philippe le Hardi and Jean sans Peur and his wife, Marguerite de Bavière. Both follow the same pattern: painted effigies of the dead, attended by angels holding their helmets and heraldic shields and accompanied by a cortège of brilliantly sculpted mourners.

The Quartier Notre-Dame

Architecturally more interesting than the palace, and much more suggestive of the city's former glories, are the lavish town houses of its rich burghers. These abound in the streets behind the palace: rue Verrerie, rue Vannerie, rue des Forges, rue Chaudronnière (look out for no. 28, *Maison des Cariatides*). Some are half-timbered, with storeys projecting over the street; others are in more formal and imposing Renaissance stone. Particularly fine are the **Hôtel de Vogüé**, 12 rue de la Chouette, and at no. 34, the **Hôtel Chambellan** (1490), housing the tourist office and *Club Alpin*. There's a good view of the latter from the courtyard, with its open galleries reached by a spiral staircase, with a marvellous piece of stonemason's virtuosity at the top, where the vaulting of the roof springs from a basket held by the statue of a gardener. For a glimpse of what must be nearly genuine medieval character, take a look in the cobbled alleys by the **Tour St-Nicholas**, off rue Jean-Jacques-Rousseau.

Also in this quarter behind the dukes' palace, in the angle between rue de la Chouette and rue de la Préfecture, is the **church of Notre-Dame**, built in the early thirteenth century in the Burgundian Gothic style, with an unusual west front adorned with tiers of spectacularly leaning gargoyles. Inside, the north transept windows contain some beautiful fragments of the original stained glass, while in the south transept, there is a twelfth-century black wooden Virgin that has long been an object of veneration to the citizens of Dijon. Outside on rue de la Chouette, in the north wall of the church, is a small sculpted owl – *une chouette* – polished by the hands of passersby who for centuries have touched it for luck and which gives the street its name. High on the south tower of the west front is a Jaquemard clock, liberated from Courtrai in Belgium in 1382, when Philippe le Hardi defeated the people of Ghent and took the clock as a present for Dijon.

From here rue de la Musette leads to the **market square**, the whole area full of sumptuous displays of food and always thronged with people. There are several good and attractive cafés and restaurants, too. The market operates from 6am on Tuesday, Friday and Saturday, spilling over into the surrounding streets, with bric-à-brac in rue de Soissons on the north side and clothes in the beautiful little **place François Rude**, named after the sculptor and a favourite hang-out with its cafés and fountain graced by the bronze figure of a grape harvester.

South of the place de la Libération

On the south side of the axis place Darcy–church of St-Michel, and especially in the *quartier* behind place de la Libération, there is a concentration of magnificent *hôtels* from the seventeenth and eighteenth centuries, built for the most part by men who had bought themselves offices and privileges with the Parliament of Burgundy, established by Louis XIV in 1477 after the death of Duke Charles le Téméraire (the Bold) as a concession designed to win the compliance of this newly acquired frontier province. One of them, 4 rue des Bons-Enfants, houses the **Musée Magnin** (daily except Mon 10am–6pm; Oct–May 10am–noon & 2–6pm; 12F, Sun 8F). The building, a seventeenth-century *hôtel particulier*, complete with its original furnishings, is more interesting than the exhibition of paintings by good but lesser-known artists, the personal collection of Maurice Magnin, donated to the state in 1938. Other noteworthy houses are to be found nearby in rue Vauban, some showing the marks of Hugues Sambin's influence in their decorative details (lions' heads, garlands of fruit, tendrils of ivy and his famous *chou bourguignon*, or Burgundy cabbage): notably, nos 3, 12, 21 and 23. Also worth a look for its elaborate west front is the **church of St-Michel**, a ten-minute walk to the east behind place du Théâtre.

In the same area, in rue Ste-Anne near place des Cordeliers, are two museums. The **Musée de la Vie Bourguignonne**, 17 rue Ste-Anne (daily except Tues 9am–noon & 2–6pm; 10F, Sun free), housed in a stark, well-designed modern setting within a former convent, is all about nineteenth-century Burgundian life, with costumes, furniture, domestic industries like butter, cheese and bread making, along with a reconstructed kitchen. Practically next door at no. 15, the **Musée d'Art Sacré** (daily 10am–6pm; Oct–May 9am–noon & 2–6pm; 8F, Sun free) contains an important collection of church treasures, including a seventeenth-century statue of Saint Paul, the first in the world to be treated with gamma-rays – carried out in Grenoble as part of the Nucle-art project. Formerly crumbling to dust, it is now solid. There's a free guided visit that really perks up these special-interest exhibits.

Around the cathedral

A little further to the west, at the end of rue du Dr-Maret in the direction of place Darcy, the **cathedral** – the once great abbey church of St-Bénigne – is no longer of very great interest, although its garish tiled roof and nineteenth-century spire dominate the skyline impressively enough. Its circular crypt is the original tenth-century Romanesque church. A little historical curiosity, however, is the fact that Raoul Glaber was a monk here: Glaber is famed as the historian who described the great burgeoning of Romanesque churches across France once the Apocalyptic dangers of the first millennium were safely passed and the earth began "clothing herself in a white garment of churches".

In the chestnut-shaded garden next to it, the **Musée Archéologique,** 5 rue du Docteur-Maret (daily except Tues 9.30am–6pm; Oct–June 9am–noon & 2–6pm; 10F, Sun free) has some extremely interesting finds from the Gallo-Roman period, especially funerary bas-reliefs depicting the perennial Gallic preoccupation with food and wine and a collection of ex-votos from the source of the Seine, among them the little bronze of the goddess Sequana (Seine) upright in her bird-prowed boat. Also on show is Sluter's bust of Christ from the Chartreuse.

On a more profane level, the neighbouring streets – especially **rue Monge** and **rue Berbisey** – are very active at night with lots of bars and restaurants. The latter ends in a curious post-Modernist perspective joke: a sort of parody of a medieval housing estate. In place Bossuet at the start of rue Monge there is a theatre whose programmes are worth keeping an eye on, the Théâtre du Parvis St-Jean.

The Musée d'Histoire Naturelle and around

One of the greatest of Dijon's artistic monuments, however, lies some 1.5km west of the city centre along av Albert-1er, close to the *gare SNCF*; the **Chartreuse de Champmol** (daily 8am–6pm; free), founded by Duke Philippe le Hardi in 1383 to be the burial place of his dynasty – Dijon's equivalent of the cathedral of St-Denis in Paris. To adorn it, Philippe recruited a talented team of artists, foremost among them the Dutchman Claus Sluter, pioneer of realism in sculpture and founder of the Burgundian school. Although it was practically destroyed in the Revolution and most of the surviving works of art are in the city's museums, two of Sluter's finest – the so-called *Well of Moses* featuring six highly realistic portrayals of Old Testament prophets, and the portal of the chapel – remain *in situ*. The site is now part of a psychiatric hospital, and you enter at 1 bd Chanoine-Kir; bus #12, direction *Fontaine d'Ouche*, from the station to stop *Hôpital des Chartreux*. On the way from the station to the Chartreuse de Champol, you pass Dijon's waxworks, the **Musée Grevin** at 13b av Albert-1er (daily 9.30am–noon & 2–7pm; 36F), a not wildly interesting experience, consisting principally of scenes from Burgundy's history. You're better off strolling in the botanical garden, the **Jardin de l'Arquebuse**, site of the **Natural History Museum** (Mon & Wed–Sat 9am–noon & 2–6pm, Sun 2–6pm), with just about every stuffed bird and mammal you can think of, plus an exquisite collection of butterflies.

Eating, drinking and entertainment

Dijon has an inordinate number of **pâtisseries** in the town, full of high-quality, tempting confectionery in which marzipan and fruit feature prominently. The more exotic places also promote the Dijon specialities: *pain d'épices*, a gingerbread made with honey and spices and eaten with butter or jam (from *Mulot et Petitjean*, 13 pl Bossuet), and *cassissines* – blackcurrant candies. **Chocolate**, best made on the premises, is another speciality – try *Au Parrain Généreux*, 21 rue du Bourg, or *L'Instant Gourmand*, 41 rue des Godrans.

And you can hardly forget that Dijon is also the high temple of **mustard**; there is the shop of leading producer **Maille** at 28 rue de la Liberté, selling a range from the mild to the cauterizing. Finally, a couple of ideas for buying good but affordable **wine**: first and foremost, there's *Nicot*, 48 rue Jean-Jacques-Rousseau, where you can taste, seek advice or take courses; alternatively, try *La Cave du Clos*, 3 rue Jeannin, or *Nicolas*, 6 rue François-Rude.

Restaurants

If you want to shell out to sample some of Dijon's cuisine – local and otherwise – in style, the listings that follow are just a small selection from a large number of excellent **restaurants** in town.

L'Armstrong, 42 rue Berbisley (☎80.30.74.06). Cheap traditional food with live jazz on Friday and Saturday evenings.

Bistrot des Halles, 10 rue Bannelier (☎80.30.11.00). Serious gourmet eating at a poor man's version of the top-rank Jean-Billoux establishment on place Darcy; around 160F, lunchtime menu at 92F.

Chabrot, 36 rue Monge (☎80.30.69.61). Particularly good on salmon, with 69F menu at lunchtime, 98F in the evening, *carte* over 200F. Closed Sun & Mon lunchtime.

Le Clos des Capucines, 3 rue Jeannin, at the end of rue Jean-Jacques-Rousseau (☎80.65.83.03). In a beautiful medieval setting, this restaurant has very good traditional, rich Burgundy cuisine (*jambon persillé, escargots, bœuf bourguignon*) at very reasonable prices. Menus at 83F and up to 197F, *carte* around 200F. Closed Sat lunchtime & Sun.

Côte St-Jean, 13 rue Monge (☎80.50.11.77). Rather chic restaurant offering such delights as a fricassé of lobster, duck tournedos, a *gratin* of pears and almonds. Menus 85–200F, *carte* over 200F. Closed Sat lunch & Tues.

Coum' Chez Eux, 68 rue Jean-Jacques Rousseau (☎80.73.56.87). A restaurant that continues to provide genuine down-home regional cooking: *jambonneau* with lentils, leek pie, homemade *terrines,* rabbit sautéed Morvan-style. It also has an informal and agreeable atmosphere. A little to the south of République, closed Sat lunchtime & Sun; *carte* around 110F.

Le Dôme, 16bis rue Quentin (☎80.30.58.92). Good for simple *plats,* this place has a good selection of interesting but lesser known wines; menus 45–63F, *formule* at 83F in the evening.

Flunch cafeteria, 24 bd de Brosses. For a quick self-service meal, you can eat your fill here for as little as 60F. At lunchtime it pays to come early; otherwise there'll be a terrible queue. Daily 11am–3pm & 6–10pm.

Le Germinal, 44 rue Monge (☎80.44.97.16). The best place in town for frogs' legs and inexpensive Burgundy specialities. 56F for an express lunchtime menu.

Grille Laure, 8 pl St-Bénigne (☎80.41.86.76). Right by the cathedral, this restaurant is in a great location for eating pizzas, pasta, grills for around 100F. Closed Sun lunch.

Hostellerie de l'Étoile, 1 rue Marceau (☎80.73.20.72). Serves an excellent traditional meal in an attractive dining-room just off pl de la République. Closed Sun evening and Mon; menus from 110F, *carte* around 200F.

Hostellerie Le Sauvage, 64 rue Monge (see under accommodation). First-class grills in a great little courtyard. Lunchtime menu at 75F, *carte* around 130–150F. Closed Sat lunch & Sun from May to Oct.

Le Marrakech, 20 rue Monge (☎80.30.82.69). Serves excellent *tajines* and couscous, with a *carte* at 110–130F.

Le Potimarron, 4 av de l'Ouche (☎80.43.38.07); closed Sun & Mon; menus at 75F and 85F, *carte* 70–90F). Vegetarian and macrobiotic dishes as well as organic meat and fish.

Le P'tit Resto, 13 rue d'Ahuy, north of rue Devosge (☎80.80.56.22.81). Wild décor and a lively atmosphere, the best place for a simple filling meal. Good-value lunchtime menu at 49F. Closed Sun and Mon & Sat lunchtimes.

University restaurants, 3 rue du Dr-Maret in the town centre; 6 bd Mansart; 6 rue du Recteur-Bouchard, near the university to the southeast of the city. Students can eat for 11.50F (11.30am–1.15pm & 6.40–7.45pm).

Villa Tan, 16 rue Perrières, near the station (☎80.43.23.40). A good Chinese near the station, with 69F menu at lunchtime, evening at 85F, *carte* 100–130F.

Bars and nightclubs

Dijon is an important university city as well as one of France's main conference centres, so **nightspots** and cultural centres at both ends of the range are worth exploring. There's a good choice in rue Berbisey.

L'Acropole, 4 bd du Dr-Petitjean. Near the university on #9 bus route. Popular with students for cheap lunchtime snacks, games and occasional gigs. Till 1am; closed Sun.

L'An-Fer, 8 rue Marceau. One of the livelier discos. Tues–Thurs 10.30pm–3am/Fri & Sat till 4am; admission 50F weekdays/60F weekends.

Le Brighton, 33 rue Auguste-Comte. English pub with 200 different kinds of beer and dancing. 5pm–3am/summer 3pm–3am; *demi* 20F in the evening.

Café de la Cathédrale, 4 pl St-Bénigne, next to the *Café au Carillon.* Two bars popular with students, in front of the cathedral. Daily 6.30pm–1am.

Le Café des Grands Ducs, 96 rue de la Liberté. Popular rendezvous for young people, with original decor and table jukeboxes. Daily till 2am winter/3am summer.

L'Escapade, Varois et Chaignot. Outdoor pool, and a huge dance floor. Young and popular. Thurs 10pm–3am, Fri & Sat 10pm–4am; admission 60F, women free on Fri.

Le Grand Café, rue du Château. A very pleasant bar/brasserie with an Art Deco interior.

Hunky Dory, 5 av Maréchal-Foch. Dynamic bar with excellent decor, billiards, karaoke, dancing and live music. Sat & Sun till 3am/4am.

Le Privé, 20 av Garibaldi. Older clientele, dancing to rock and Lambada. Tues–Thurs 10pm–3am/ Fri & Sat till 4am; admission 60F Fri & Sat.

Pub Kilkenny, 1 rue Auguste-Perdrix. Noisy, popular Irish bar: draught Guinness and week-night Irish bands. Daily till 3am.

Rhumerie la Jamaïque, 14 pl de la République. Cocktails (35–65F) and ice-creams laced with alcohol in an exotic venue. Jazz bar in the basement. 3pm–3am; closed Sun.

L'Univers, rue Berbisey. The city's punk bar, with rock concerts in the cellar.

Listings

Buses Distances are small enough to make walking easy, but if you plan to use buses a lot it's worth getting a pass and bus map from *STRD*, in the middle of place Grangier.

CROUS Student information service, 3 rue du Dr- Maret near place Darcy (☎80.40.40.40).

Cinemas *L'Eldorado*, 21 rue Alfred-de-Musset (☎80.66.12.34), is a three-screen arts cinema showing all films in original language with a concentration of foreign films. *Le Devosge*, 6 rue Devosge (☎80.30.74.79), shows some films in the original, and tries to deviate from the obvious classics.

Festivals The city has a good summer music season, with classical concerts through June in its *Été Musical* programme. *L'Estivade*, June 20–Aug 15, puts on endless music, dance and street theatre performances. *Fête de la Vigne* at the beginning of Sept is a traditional costume/folklore jamboree, while the *Foire gastronomique* at the beginning of Nov celebrates all things edible.

Hitching For Paris, follow av Albert-1ᵉʳ to Lac Kir; for Beaune and Lyon, cross the canal from place du 1ᵉʳ-mai and continue down av Jean-Jaurès.

Laundries 41 rue Auguste-Comte, 28 rue Berbisey, 36 & 42 rue Guillaume-Tell (near the station).

Markets Tues, Fri & Sat mornings along the four streets surrounding the covered market – rue Bannelier, rue Quentin, rue C-Ramey, rue Odebert.

Swimming pool *Oxygène-Parc Aquatique*, Centre Commercial de la Toison d'Or, bus #16; 10am– 8pm/10pm Fri & Sat; closed Tues & Thurs outside school hols; adults 39F, kids 29F. Toboggans, jacuzzi, & water slides.

Travel agents *Agence Wasteels*, 20 av Maréchal-Foch near the station, is a youth-orientated travel agent. *Nouvelles Frontières* is at 7 place des Cordeliers.

The Côte d'Or

The attractive countryside of the **Côte d'Or** is characterized by the steep scarp of the *côte*, wooded along the top and cut by steep little valleys called *combes*, where local rock climbers hone their skills (**footpaths GR7 and GR76** run the whole length of the wine country as far south as Lyon). Spring is a good time to visit this region, when you avoid the crowds and the landscape is a dramatic symphony of browns – trees, earth, vines, with millions of bone-coloured vine stakes wheeling past as you travel through, like crosses in a vast war cemetery.

The villages, strung along the N74 through Beaune and beyond, have names – Gevrey-Chambertin, Vougeot, Vosne-Romanée, Nuits-St-Georges, Pommard, Volnay, Meursault – that all sound like Pavlov's bell to the ears of wine buffs and are familiar to the most casually interested; but they turn out to be sleepy, dull and exceedingly prosperous places, full of houses inhabited by well-heeled *vignerons* in expensive suits and fat-cat cars. You make a very good living on a patch of four or five hectares (ten to twelve acres), the average-sized plot, the proof being that none is ever up for sale.

There are numerous *caves* where you can taste (usually for a charge of 30–40F) and buy the local elixir, but, remember, the former is meant to be a prelude to the latter. And there's no such thing as a cheap wine here, red or white, 100–120F being the minimum. The *Hautes Côtes* (Nuits and Beaune), wines from the top of the slope, are cheaper, but they lack the connoisseur cachet of the big names.

THE WINES OF BURGUNDY

Burgundy farmers have been growing grapes since Roman times, and their rulers, the dukes, frequently put their **wines** to effective use as a tool of diplomacy. Today they have never had it so good, which is why they're reticent about the quirks of soil and climate and the tricks of pruning and spraying that make their wines so special. Vines are temperamental: frost on the wrong day, sun at the wrong time, too much water or poor drainage, and they won't come up with the goods. And they like a slope, which is why so many wines are called *Côte de* something.

Burgundy's best wines come from a narrow strip of hillside called the **Côte d'Or** that runs southwest from Dijon to Santenay. It is divided into two regions, **Côte de Nuits** and **Côte de Beaune**. With few exceptions the reds of the Côte de Nuits are considered the best: they are richer, age better and cost more. Côte de Beaune is known particularly for its whites: Meursault, Montrachet and Puligny.

The single most important factor determining the "character" of wines is the **soil**. In the Côte d'Or, the relative mixture of chalk, flint and clay varies over very short distances, making for an enormous variety of taste. Chalky soil makes a wine *virile* or *corsé*, in other words "heady" – *il y a de la mâche*, they say, "something to bite on" – while clay makes it *féminin*, more *agréable*.

These and other more extravagant judgements are made after the hallowed procedure of **tasting**; in order to do it properly, by one account, you have to "introduce a draft of wine into your mouth, swill it across the tongue, roll it around the palate, churn it around, emitting the gargling sound so beloved of tasters, which is produced by slowly inhaling air through the centre of your mouth, and finally eject it". The ejection is what has to be learned.

For an **apéritif** in Burgundy, you should try *kir*, named after the man who was both mayor and MP for Dijon for many years after World War II – two parts dry white wine, traditionally *aligoté*, and one part *cassis* or blackcurrant liqueur. To round the evening off there are many liqueurs to choose from, but Burgundy is particularly famous for its **marcs**, of which the best are matured for years in oak casks.

Beaune

BEAUNE, the principal town of the Côte d'Or, has many charms but is totally devoted to tourism. If you want a base for getting around in the area, it's cheaper and pleasanter to use Dijon or Chalon, as both are easily accessible by train and *Transco* buses, which service all the villages down the N74. Beaune is situated at a major autoroute junction (A6 from Paris/Lyon–A31 from Metz) and its hotels are pricey and likely to be full.

Beaune's town centre is a tightly clustered, rampart-enclosed *vieille ville*, and its chief attraction is the fifteenth-century hospital, the **Hôtel-Dieu** (daily March 3–Nov 21 9am–6.30pm; Jan–March 26 & Nov 22–Dec 12 9am–11.30am & 2–5.30pm; 27F), on the corner of place de la Halle. Once past the turnstile of the Hôtel-Dieu you find yourself in a cobbled courtyard surrounded by a wooden gallery overhung by a massive roof patterned with diamonds of gaudy tiles, green, burnt sienna, black and yellow – and similarly multicoloured steep-pitched dormers and turrets. Inside is a vast paved hall with a painted timber roof, the Grande Salle des Malades, which until quite recently continued to serve its original purpose of accommodating the sick. The last item on the tour is a splendid fifteenth-century altarpiece of the Last Judgement by Rogier van der Weyden, commissioned by Nicolas Rolin, who also founded the hospital in 1443 (King Louis XI commented: "It was only fair that a man who had made so many people poor during his life should create an asylum for them before his death."). It is here that a major wine auction takes place during the annual *Trois Glorieuses*, the prices paid setting the pattern for the season.

The private residence of the dukes of Burgundy on rue d'Enfer now contains the **Musée du Vin** (daily 9.30am–6pm; mid-Nov to March closed Tues; 20F), with more giant wine presses and an interesting collection of tools of the trade. At the other end of rue d'Enfer the church of **Notre-Dame** is about the only thing free in town. Inside are five very special tapestries from the fifteenth century, depicting the Life of the Virgin and commissioned, once again, by the Rolin family.

There are two other museums, both in the Hôtel de Ville: the not-very-interesting **Musée des Beaux-Arts** and the **Musée Marey** (both daily April–Nov 21 2–6pm; 20F), devoted to early movie photography. On the outskirts of the town, by the auto-route A6 Beaune-Tailly-Merceuil rest area, there's an open-air park called the **Archéodrome**, illustrating the history of Burgundy with film and reconstructions of a neolithic house, Cæsar's siege of Alésia (see p.460), a farm with ancient breeds of farm animals and so on. It costs from 20 to 50F for adults, 15 to 40F for kids, depending on how many of the displays you wish to use.

Practicalities

Beaune's **gare SNCF** is outside the old walls to the east of town in av du 8-septembre (☎80.22.13.13). If you arrive by bus, you're likely to be dropped at the main **gare routière** on the southwest side of town, just outside the walls at the end of rue Maufoux, a five-minute walk from the town's highlights. The **tourist office** is in place de la Halle opposite the Hôtel-Dieu (May–Sept daily 9am–midnight; April till 10pm; Oct–Nov till 8pm; Dec–March Mon–Sat 9am–7.15pm, Sun 9am–noon & 2–6pm; ☎80.22.24.51), and they are the best people to consult about all things to do with the region's wines. You can rent **bikes** from the English-speaking *Butterfield and Robinson*, 5 rue Cîteaux, behind the train station.

If you're going to **stay** in Beaune, a couple of cheap possibilities are the *Hôtel Foch*, 24 bd Foch (☎80.24.75.59; ②), to the west of the town outside the walls (from the tourist office take av de la République and turn right when you reach the circular boulevards), and the *Hôtel Rousseau*, 11 pl Madeleine (☎80.22.13.59; ①–②), a friendly, no-frills establishment off rue du Faubourg-Madeleine, the continuation of rue d'Alsace when coming from the town centre. For a more comfortable stay, try *Le Home*, 138 rte de Dijon, on the way into Beaune (☎80.22.16.43 or 80.24.90.74; ④–⑤). The pretty *Les Cent Vignes* **camp-site**, 10 rue Dubois (☎80.22.03.91), is about 1km out of town, off rue du Faubourg-St-Nicolas (the N74 to Dijon), before the bridge over the autoroute; booking is advisable as it fills up through the day.

Eating can be an expensive business here. The best places to look for something cheap are rue Monge, place Carnot and rue Madeleine. *Le Carnot*, 18 rue Carnot, is a good cafeteria; and decent, reasonably priced restaurants include the *Brelinette*, 6 rue Madeleine, where menus start at 58F. If you are looking for something more sophisti-cated, *Le Bénaton*, 25 rue du Faubourg-Bretonnière (☎80.22.00.26; closed Wed evening & Thurs), has a good-value 90F menu, with a choice of calf's head, *jambon persillé*, chocolate gâteau and *coq au vin*, although *à la carte* will set you back quite a bit more; there's also *Bernard Morillon*, 31 rue Maufoux (☎80.24.12.06; closed Mon, Tues lunch-time, Feb 1–20 & Aug 15–22); and *Le Gourmandin*, 8 pl Carnot (☎80.24.07.88; closed Sun evening & Tues), with a good menu at 85F. All these places get very crowded in season, so it is wise to book.

Château du Clos-de-Vougeot

Though the whole French wine culture is fascinating, it is debatable whether making a special detour to see these vineyards is really worthwhile. The only "sight" you should perhaps go out of your way for is the **Château du Clos-de-Vougeot** (guided tours: daily 9–11.30am & 2–5.30pm; April–Sept 9am–6.30pm, Sat closes 5pm; 15F), 15km

north of Beaune between Gévry-Chambertin and Nuits-St-Georges, where you get to
see the mammoth thirteenth-century wine presses installed by the Cistercian monks to
whom these vineyards belonged for nearly 700 years until the Revolution. The château
today is the home of a phony chivalrous order founded in 1934, the Confrèrie des
Chevaliers du Tastevin (about which you get a video promo after the tour), whose principal reason for existence seems to be commerce and snobbery, though no doubt the
food and wine are treated seriously at the trade's annual beanfeast – the so-called *Les
Trois Glorieuses* on the third Saturday in November.

FROM THE SAÔNE TO THE LOIRE

The **Saône Valley** is prosperous and modern, nourished by the autoroute, tourism,
industry and the wine trade. But turn your back on the river and head west and at once
you enter a different Burgundy: close, hilly pasture and woodland, utterly rural and
more populated by cattle than people. This is the hinterland – the Deep South – of
Burgundy, where every village clusters under the tower of a Romanesque church,
spawned by the influence of Cluny in the 1000s and 1100s. It is only when you reach the
Loire and encounter the main traffic routes again that you re-enter the modern world.

It is beautiful country for cycling, but all is not lost if you don't have your own transport. Buses run a back route through the Mâconnais, and there are train connections
between Dijon and Paray-le-Monial and between Dijon and Nevers.

Chalon-sur-Saône

CHALON, sizeable port and industrial centre on a broad meander of the Saône, is not
a place you'd want to stay very long, but its old riverside quarter does have an easy
charm. Today it's a thriving business centre, and trade fairs frequently possess the
town, but more festive occasions are also an important part of its appeal and good
reasons to stop if you're around at the right time. Three major events are a carnival in
March, which features a parade of giant masks, confetti battle and "laughter evening";
a national festival of street artists in July; and a film festival in October.

The **old town** is just back from the river around Grande-Rue and rue du Châtelet.
At the junction of these two streets you'll find a fifteenth-century timber-framed
house, and there are a number of half-timbered jettied façades around the quarter.
Nearby, 200m to the west on place de l'Hôtel-de-Ville, is the **Musée Denon** (daily
except Tues 9.30am–noon & 2–5.30pm; 10F, Wed free), whose most vaunted exhibit
is the 18,000-year-old Volgu flint, rated one of the finest stone tools yet discovered.
Apart from the usual collection of bits and pieces excavated nearby, look out for the
local furniture.

The one attraction you definitely won't want to miss is the **Musée Niepce** (daily
except Tues 9.30–11.30am & 2.30–5.30pm; July & Aug 10am–6pm; 10F) on the river
quay just downstream from Pont St-Laurent. Niepce, who was born in Chalon, is
credited with inventing photography in 1816, and the museum possesses a fascinating
range of cameras from the first machine ever to the *Apollo* moon mission's equipment,
plus a number of 007-type spy-camera devices, all attractively displayed under a set of
glass domes. Upstairs is a library of works on the subject of photography, to be
thumbed through at leisure, and a space for temporary exhibitions, with some big
names in the history of the art.

The other interesting target in town is the **Maison des Vins** on Promenade Ste-
Marie (daily 8am–12.30pm & 1.30–8pm), where you can taste and buy Côte

Chalonnaise wines, chosen from the wines of 44 local villages by a choice committee of professional wine tasters.

Practicalities

The **tourist office** is on bd de la République (Mon–Sat 9am–12.30pm & 1.30–6.30pm, Sun 11am–1pm & 3.30–6.30pm; July & Aug Mon–Sat till 7.30pm, Sun 11am–1pm & 3.30–6.30pm; ☎85.48.37.97), giving out excellent listings and a useful map, and just five minutes' walk from the **gare SNCF** at the end of av Jean-Jaurès (☎85.93.50.50).

The most attractive **hotel** in town is undoubtedly the *Hôtel St-Jean*, right on the river bank at 24 quai Gambetta (☎85.48.45.65; ③). For something a little cheaper, there's *Hôtel Central*, 19 pl de Beaune on bd de la République (☎85.48.35.00; ②), and *Nouvel Hôtel*, 7 av Boucicaut (☎85.48.07.31; ②) – from the station turn left at the end of av Jean-Jaurès and left again. Also in the centre on place Beaune, there's the *Hôtel St-Hubert* (☎85.48.70.43; ③–④), in a restored old house. The town is convenient for hostellers, with a riverside **youth hostel** on rue d'Amsterdam (☎85.46.62.77; ①; closed mid-Dec to mid-Jan), about a ten-minute walk along the bank north of the Pont St-Laurent; alternatively, take bus #11 from the tourist office. *Camping de la Butte* (☎85.48.26.86), 3km east of town in St-Marcel, is accessible on bus #9, or, if you're walking, cross either Pont St-Laurent or Pont J-Richard and head east.

The nicest places to **eat** are in rue de Strasbourg on the island across Pont St-Laurent. Try the *Île Bleue*, whose speciality is seafood from a modest 79F, at no. 3 (☎85.48.39.83), or *Le Bistrot* at no. 31 (☎85.93.22.01; from 75F). There are also some Indian places in the street, plus a piano bar, *L'Oiseau de Nuit* (daily except Sun 10pm–3am), and the *Boogie Blues Bar* in the cross-street, rue d'Uxelles. In the centre, there's the *Brasserie Neptune* in place Beaune.

Tournus

TOURNUS is a beautiful small town on the banks of the Saône, just off the autoroute and N6, 27km south of Chalon and 30km north of Mâcon. Squeezed between the N6 and the river, the narrow huddled streets have the inward-looking, self-protecting feel of a Mediterranean town, belying a prosperous past when commercial traffic thronged the busy riverside quays. The quays are quiet today, and Tournus's modern prosperity is based on agriculture, light industry – domestic appliances, in particular – and, increasingly, tourism. But the quays still make a delightful picnic spot, looking out over the broad sweep of the river and its wide flat valley beneath huge piling cloudscapes.

You enter the town from the N6 through a **gateway** flanked by medieval towers – once the entrance to a monastery compound – and are confronted by the old **abbey church of St-Philibert**, one of the earliest and most influential Romanesque buildings in Burgundy. The first construction dates back to around 900 AD and the foundation of the monastic community by monks fleeing Norman raids on their home community of Noirmoutier off the Atlantic coast. The façade of the church, with its powerful towers and simple decoration of Lombard arcading, has the massive qualities and clean, pared-down lines more associated with a fortress. It is equally sturdy inside, with its colossal round pillars and rough-looking masonry in the narthex, and is the oldest surviving part of the building along with the crypt. The nave provides something of an architectural rarity as the vaults of its ceiling run side to side instead of down the axis of the church; an ingenious idea, forced on the builders by the need to make good the damage caused by a disastrous fire around 1000 AD, and one which made possible the creation of windows in the ends of the vaults opening directly into the nave – very unusual given the state of the art.

Beside the church, the **Musée Perrin de Puycousin** (April–Oct daily except Tues 9am–noon & 2–6pm; 10F) is a moderately interesting exposition of local life and costumes, while **Musée Greuze** nearby at 4 rue du Collège (April–Oct Mon & Wed–Sat 9.30am–noon & 2–6.30pm; Sun 2–6.30pm) has an interesting display of portraits and domestic scenes of eighteenth-century painter Jean-Baptiste Greuze, a local of the town.

Practicalities

The **gare SNCF** (☎85.51.07.30) is on av Gambetta, across the road from the old town and a ten-minute walk from the **tourist office**, place Carnot (Mon–Sat 9am–noon & 2–6pm, Sun 10am–noon; July & Aug 9am–noon & 3–7pm, Sun 10am–noon; ☎85.51.13.10).

If you're planning to **stay**, the nicest reasonably priced hotel is *Hôtel aux Terrasses*, 18 av du 23-janvier (☎85.51.01.74; ③–④; closed Jan, Sun evening & Mon; excellent restaurant from 85F), at the southern end of the old town where the continuation of rue de la République rejoins the N6. Alternatively, there's the cheaper *Hôtel de l'Abbaye*, 12 rue Léon-Godin (☎85.51.11.63; ①–②; closed Nov to mid-March; restaurant from 72F), and, standing in splendid isolation on the east bank of the river, the *Hôtel Saône* (☎85.51.20.65; ③; closed Nov–Dec; restaurant from 95F). **Campers** should head for *Le Pas-Fleury* (☎85.51.16.58), a site just south of the town; take av du 23-janvier out of town to the N6, direction *Lyon*.

For further **eating** possibilities outside of the hotels, there are a number of cafés and brasseries in and around place de l'Hôtel-de-Ville.

Mâcon and the Mâconnais

MÂCON is a lively, prosperous place on the banks of the River Saône, 58km south of Châlon and 68km north of Lyon, with excellent transport connections between the two. It's a centre for the wine trade and numerous light industries, with a surprisingly sunny southern seaside feel thanks to its long café-lined **river bank**. There are no great sights here, but it's worth finding the time for a riverside drink and a wander in the streets immediately behind quai Lamartine.

Lamartine, the nineteenth-century French Romantic poet (see box below), was born here in 1790 and his name is much in evidence. He is remembered in the handsome eighteenth-century mansion, the Hôtel Senecé in rue Sigorgne, that houses the **Musée Lamartine** (April–Oct Mon & Wed–Sat 10am–noon & 2–6pm, Sun 2–6pm; Nov, Dec & March 2–6pm; 10F), part of which is dedicated to documents and other memorabilia to do with his personal, political and poetic lives. Nearby, on the corner of place des Herbes where a summertime fruit and veg market is held, stands the town's main tourist curiosity, an extraordinary wooden house built around 1500 and known as the

---

ALPHONSE LAMARTINE (1790–1869)

Often referred to as the French Byron, **Alphonse Lamartine** is one of the best known of the French Romantic poets. He was born and grew up in Milly, about 15km west of Mâcon, and published his first poetic work, *Méditations poétiques*, in 1820. In 1825 he published *Le Dernier Chant du Pélerinage d'Harold* as a tribute to Byron.

After the 1830 revolution in Paris, he became involved in politics, being elected to the Chambre des Députés in 1833 and quickly acquiring a reputation as a powerful orator on the weighty questions of the day, like the abolition of slavery and of capital punishment. His finest hour was as the leading figure in the provisional government of the Second Republic, which was proclaimed from the Hôtel de Ville in Paris on February 23, 1848. He withdrew from politics when reactionary forces, under the leadership of General Cavaignac, let the army loose on the protesting workers of Paris and Marseille in June 1848, after which he retired to St-Point (see p.486).

Maison du Bois. The town's not-very-exciting art and history museum, **Musée des Ursulines**, is at 5 rue des Ursulines (Mon & Wed–Sat 10am–noon & 2–6pm, Sun 2–6pm; 20F), housed in a seventeenth-century convent.

One tastebud-enlivening experience – and the quickest way to bone up on the Mâcon, Beaujolais and Châlonnais wines – is to visit the **Maison Mâconnaise des Vins** on the N6 at 484 av Lattre-de-Tassigny (daily 8am–9pm), where the N6 comes into town along the riverside from Châlon; you can taste and buy wines and eat regional dishes like *andouillette, petit salé* and goat's cheese for a very palatable 100F.

Practicalities

The **tourist office**, 187 rue Carnot (Mon–Sat 10am–7pm, Sun & hols 2–6pm; out of season Mon–Sat 10am–noon & 2–6pm; ☎85.39.71.37), can provide information about the wine-growing villages of the region and how to get to them. The **gare SNCF (gare routière** adjacent) lies on rue Bigonnet at the southern end of rue V-Hugo, but note that *TGV* trains leave from Mâcon-Loché station 6km out of town.

For places to **stay**, there should be no difficulty. The *Hôtel d'Europe et d'Angleterre* on the river at 92 quai Jean-Jaurès has a splendid air of former times (☎85.38.27.94; ①–③). The *Grand Hôtel de Bourgogne* on the top side of place de la Barre at 8 rue Victor-Hugo (☎85.38.36.57; ④; restaurant from 78F) also has character and an attractive atmosphere. Two other possibilities close to the *gare SNCF*, at the southern end of rue Victor-Hugo, are: the *Terminus* (☎85.39.17.11 or 85.38.02.75; ④; restaurant from 88F), and *Hôtel de Genève*, 1 rue Bigonnet (☎85.38.18.10; ③–④; restaurant from 67F). If you want to **camp**, there's a site (☎86.38.16.22; closed Nov to mid-March) 3km north out of town on the N6.

For **food**, apart from what's on offer in the hotels, and for some activity in the evening, the best thing is to head for the river. The *Lamartine*, 259 quai Lamartine, pulls in both diners and drinkers. An alternative is the *Grande Brasserie* at 129 quai Lamartine.

Brou

BROU is an uninteresting suburban village outside Bourg-en-Bresse, 32km east of Mâcon, which happens to have an early sixteenth-century **church** (daily; 26F). If you're heading east to Geneva or the Alps, take a look, but don't lose a lift or miss a train for it. Aldous Huxley found it "a horrible little architectural nightmare", its monuments "positively and piercingly vulgar". Certainly, it was a very rich woman's expensive folly, crammed with virtuoso craftsmanship from the dying moments of the Gothic style; it was undertaken by Margaret of Austria after the death of her husband, Philibert, Duke of Savoy, as a mausoleum for the two of them and Philibert's mother. Interesting to see, but soulless, without a trace of vision or inspiration. It is no longer a place of worship.

BOURG-EN-BRESSE is the place to base yourself if you want to visit Brou's church, just a short bus #1 ride away. The **tourist office** is in Centre Albert-Camus, 6 av Alsace-Lorraine (☎74.22.49.40), with an annexe by Brou church in summer. Wednesday is market day in place Carriat, and on the first and third Wednesdays of each month there's a livestock market as well. An attractive place to **stay** is the *Hôtel du Mail* near the station at 46 av du Mail (☎72.21.00.26; ②–③; closed Sun eve, Mon, Dec 22–Jan 12 & July 12–26). The **camping municipal** (☎74.45.37.21; closed mid-Oct to March) is on av des Sports, the N83 northeast of town heading for Lons-le-Saunier.

The Mâconnais

The **Mâconnais** wine-producing country lies to the west of the valley of the Saône, a strip hardly twenty kilometres wide, stretching from Mâcon to Tournus. The land rises sharply into steep little hills and valleys, at its prettiest in the south, where the region's best white wines come from: the villages of **POUILLY, VINZELLES, PRISSÉ** and **FUISSÉ**, where, should you yearn for rustic rest, the *Hôtel La Vigne Blanche* will provide just the setting you're looking for (☎85.35.60.50; ②–③; closed mid-Dec to mid-Jan), along with good regional cooking in its restaurant for only 80–120F.

Directly above these villages rises the distinctive and precipitous 500m rock of **Solutré**, which in prehistoric times – around 20,000 BC – seems to have served as some kind of ambush site for hunters after migrating animals, with the bones of 100,000 horses found in the soil beneath the rock, along with mammoth, bison and reindeer carcasses. The history and results of the excavations are displayed in a new museum at the foot of the rock: **Musée Départmental de Préhistoire** (daily except Tues June–Sept 10am–1pm & 2–7pm; March–April & Oct–Dec 10am–noon & 2–5pm; 17F). A steep path climbs to the top of the rock where you get a superb view, as far as Mont Blanc and the Matterhorn on a clear day, as well as your immediate surroundings. You look down on the huddled roofs of **SOLUTRÉ-POUILLY** and the slopes beneath you covered with the vines of the Chardonnay grape that makes the exquisite greenish Pouilly-Fuissé wine. It's at its most enchanting in early spring when the earth still shows its *terre-cuite* colours, punctuated by bursts of white cherry blossom and the blue drift of bonfire smoke from prunings amid the neatly staked rows of vines.

Aside from the sheer pleasure of wandering about in such reposeful landscapes – not so, however, if you are trying to tackle this very hilly country on a bike – there are some places to make for. One such is the sleepy hamlet of **ST-POINT**, where the poet Lamartine (see p.484) spent much of his life and all of his retirement in the little **château** (Mon, Tues & Thu–Sat 10am–noon & 2–6pm, Sun 2–6pm; 20F; ring bell to visit), next to the Romanesque church where he is buried. There is **camping à la ferme** behind the château at the *Auberge Fontaine Verdine* (☎85.50.52.99).

The Beaujolais

Imperceptibly, as you continue south, the Mâconnais becomes the **Beaujolais**, a larger area of terraced hills producing lighter, fruity red wines, now fashionable very early. The Beaujolais grape is the Gamay which, in contrast to other parts of Burgundy, thrives here on this granite soil. Of the four *appellations* of Beaujolais, the best are the *crus*, including Morgon and Fleurie, which come from the northern part of the region between St-Amour (the northernmost *cru*), and Brouilly in the south. If you have transport, you can follow the *cru*-trail south from Mâcon by turning right at Crêches-sur-Saône up the D31 to St-Amour, and then south along the D68. *Beaujolais Villages*, which produces the best *nouveau*, comes from the middle of the Beaujolais region, south of the *cru* belt, while plain *Beaujolais* and *Beaujolais supérieur* are produced in the vineyards southwest of Villefranche, not far from Lyon (see below).

The well-marked **route de Beaujolais** winds down through the wine villages to **VILLEFRANCHE**, not far from Lyon and a good base for the route. Here, the **tourist office** at 290 rue de Thizy (☎74.68.05.18) has all the information about *caves*, visits and wine tours. There are numerous cheap **hotels**, almost all near the **gare SNCF**. A good one to try is the friendly and clean *Hôtel la Colonne*, 6 pl Carnot (☎74.65.06.42; ②), with a popular cheap **restaurant**, open every night – including Sunday, when everything else in the village is dead. Most of the cafés on rue Nationale are good for snacks or cheap menus, too.

Cluny

The abbey of **CLUNY** is the major tourist destination of the region. The voice of its abbot once made monarchs tremble, as his power in the Christian world was second only to that of the pope. The monastery was founded in 910 in response to the corruption of the existing church, and it took only a couple of vigorous early abbots to build the power of Cluny into a veritable empire. Gradually, its spiritual influence declined, and Cluny became a royal gift. Both Richelieu and Mazarin did stints in the monastery as abbot.

Now, although the reputation of the place still pulls in the tourist coaches, little remains apart from the very attractive village. The Revolution suppressed the monastery, and Hugues de Semur's vast and influential eleventh-century **church**, the largest building in Christendom until the construction of St Peter's in Rome, was dismantled in 1810. Now all you can see of the former **abbey** (daily 10.30–11.30am & 2–4pm; July–Sept 9am–7pm; April–June 9.30am–noon & 2–6pm; ; Oct 9.30am–noon & 2–5pm; 26F) is an octagonal belfry, the south transept and, in the impressive granary, the *bâtiment du Farinier*, the surviving capitals from its immense columns – disappointing but evocative. From the top of the **Tour des Fromages** (Mon–Sat 10am–noon & 2.30–6.30pm; April–June & Oct daily 10am–12.30pm & 2.30–7pm, Sun 2.30–7pm; July–Sept daily 10am–7pm) you can reconstruct it in your imagination: you enter the tower through the tourist office at 6 rue Mercière. The **Musée Ochier** (same hours as abbey; 13F), in the fifteenth-century palace of the last freely elected abbot, helps to flesh out the picture with reconstructions and fragments of sculpture, while the octagonal Romanesque belfry of the parish **church of St-Marcel** also recalls the belfries that once adorned the abbey.

Also worth a look are the beautiful old houses in rue Mercière/rue Lamartine and, in particular, rue de la République/rue d'Avril, where nos. 25 and 6 are nearly as old as the abbey itself. At the back of the abbey is one of France's national stud farms, **Haras National** (daily 9am–7pm; free), which can also be visited.

Practicalities

The **tourist office** at 6 rue Mercière (daily 10am–12.30pm & 2.30–7pm, Sun 2.30–7pm; July–Sept 10am–7pm; Nov–March daily except Sun 10am–noon & 2.30–6.30pm; ☎85.59.05.34) will help you find a **room**; otherwise, try the *Hôtel de l'Abbaye* on av de la Gare (☎85.59.11.14; ③; closed Jan to mid-Feb), which has reasonable rooms, as does the *Hôtel du Commerce*, 8 place du Commerce (☎85.59.03.09; ①–②). *Hôtel Saint-Odilon*, across the river on the left before the campsite (☎85.59.25.00; ③; closed Dec 20–Jan 5), is quite new, but not to be shunned for that. There's a municipal **hostel**, *Cluny Séjour* on rue Porte-de-Paris (☎85.59.08.83; ①; closed Dec–Jan), and a **camping municipal**, *St-Vital* (☎85.59.08.34; June–Sept), across Pont de la Levée in the direction of Tournus and on the right.

For a **meal**, other than a *crêperie* or snack, try *Les Marronniers*, 20 av de Gaulle (closed Sun evening & Mon) or, for some good country cooking, *Le Potin Gourmand*, 4 pl Champ-de-Foire (☎85.59.02.06; closed Sun evening, Mon & Jan 4–Feb 5; best value menus at 78F & 110F).

Taizé

Another powerful attraction for the converted might be the modern ecumenical community at **TAIZÉ**, 10km north of Cluny. It was founded in 1940, and its monks are drawn from both Protestant denominations and the Roman Catholic Church, with an unashamedly populist outlook, attracting hordes of youngsters who come to take part in discussion groups and camp out under canvas. If you are seriously interested – and it is not likely to be to the taste of the merely curious – write to *Communauté de Taizé*, 71250 Cluny.

Paray-le-Monial and the Charollais

Fifty kilometres west of Cluny, across countryside that becomes ever gentler and flatter as you approach the broad valley of the Loire, is **PARAY-LE-MONIAL**, whose major attraction is its **Basilique du Sacré-Cœur**. Not only is it a superb building in its own right, with a marvellously satisfying arrangement of apses and chapels stacking up in sturdy symmetry to its fine octagonal belfry, it's also the only place, albeit on a smaller scale, where you can get an idea of what the abbey of Cluny looked like (see above). Both churches are contemporary and the result of the same Hugues de Semur's influence.

The town itself is the archetypal country town, quiet and unpretentious, straddling the slow waters of the River Bourbince and the Canal du Centre. The only thing that disturbs its calm is the arrival of pilgrims of the Sacré-Coeur, or Sacred Heart, a cult which originated here with Marguerite-Marie Alacoque, a local nun who received revelations advocating the worship of the sacred heart. The cult was later adopted by the entire Roman Catholic Church. The first pilgrimage took place in 1873, encouraged as a means of combating the socialist ideas espoused by the Paris Commune, and it raised the money to construct the church of the Sacré-Cœur on the hill of Montmartre in Paris (see p.116). Paray is now second only to Lourdes as a pilgrim centre, its best-known visitor of recent times being Pope John Paul II, who visited in 1986.

The one secular building definitely worth a look, aside from just browsing down the main street – rue de la République/rue des Deux-Ponts/rue Victor-Hugo – is the highly ornamented **Maison Jayet**, now the Hôtel de Ville on place Guignaud, built in the 1520s.

Practicalities

The **tourist office** is in av Jean-Paul-II (daily 9am–noon & 2–7pm; July & Aug 9am–7pm; ☎85.81.10.92), and you can rent bikes from the **gare SNCF** on the south side of the canal (☎85.81.07.97).

For **accommodation**, try the *Hostellerie des Trois Pigeons*, 2 rue Daugard, just beyond the Hôtel de Ville (☎85.81.03.77 or 85.81.58.59; ②–③; closed Dec; restaurant from 100F), or, near the station, *Hôtel du Nord*, 1 av de la Gare (☎85.81.05.12 or 85.81.10.92; ①–②; closed Jan; restaurant from 68F). A further possibility is the *Hôtel aux Vendanges de Bourgogne*, 5 rue Denis-Papin (☎85.81.13.43 or 85.88.87.59; ②–③; closed Nov 25–Dec 15 & Sun evening in winter; good-value restaurant from 68F), south of the Canal du Centre off the N79; or, the *Grand Hôtel de la Basilique*, 18 rue de la Visitation (☎85.81.11.13; ②–③; closed Nov to mid-March; restaurant from 69F), bang opposite the chapel that stands on the spot where Sainte Marguerite had her revelations and consequently rather sought after by the pilgrims. The **camping municipal**, *Le Pré-Barré* (☎85.81.05.05; all year), is by the river on bd Dauphin-Louis. If you want to explore the little villages throughout the Maconnais (see below), there's no better base than the Merle family's organic farm at Vitry-en-Charollais (☎85.81.10.79; around 210F with breakfast for two and 70F a head for dinner), with delicious home cooking, about 6km southwest of Paray-le-Monial.

The Charollais

The **Charollais** is cattle country, taking its name from the little market town of Charolles on the main N79 road, and in turn giving its name to one of the world's most illustrious breeds of cattle: the white, curly-haired and stocky Charollais, bred for its lean meat. The fields south of Paray, appropriately enough, are full of the beasts. Throughout this landscape, scattered across the rich farmland along the Arconce River, are dozens of small villages, all with more or less remarkable Romanesque churches, offspring of Cluny in its vigorous youth.

ANZY-LE-DUC, about 15km south off the main D982 to Roanne, boasts an exquisite complex of buildings: a perfect Romanesque church with jackdaw chatter echoing off the octagonal belfry, side by side with the remains of the old priory incorporated into a sort of fortified farm looking out over the Arconce Valley, the whole built in a rich, warm stone. **MONTCEAUX-L'ÉTOILE**, a little nearer, has its special charm too: a quiet, worn church with beautiful sculptures adorning the porch, standing likewise above the Arconce Valley, and, a little way down the village street, a curious tower-like house where a Marquis of Vichy is said to have practised alchemy with the notorious Italian wizard, Cagliostro. There is **camping à la ferme** on the Paray side of the village.

Ten kilometres to the west, the Arconce flows into the Loire just upstream from **DIGOIN**. Although it's not a place you are likely to do more than pass through, the nineteenth-century **bridge** carrying the Canal du Centre over the Loire is worth a look and the riverside quays make a quiet, sunny picnic spot. The town is now France's chief centre of pottery-manufacture, and has two very good **restaurants**, neither of them cheap: *Hôtel de la Gare*, 79 av de Gaulle (☎85.53.03.04 or 85.53.14.70; ③; closed mid-Jan to mid-Feb & Wed outside July & Aug; restaurant from 125F), and *Hôtel Les Diligences*, 14 rue Nationale (☎85.53.06.31 or 85.88.92.43; ③–④; closed Nov 20–Dec 10 & Mon evening and Tues outside July & Aug; restaurant from 95F with a particularly good-value menu at 130F). There's **camping** by the Loire on the Moulins road (☎85.53.11.49; closed Nov–Feb).

Nevers

At the western confines of Burgundy, **NEVERS** is a small provincial city on the confluence of the rivers Loire and Nièvre. In France it is known for its *nougatine* candies and fine porcelain, a hallmark since the seventeenth century, still produced in just three workshops and sold in a few elegant, expensive shops (*faïenceries*) around town. Parts of the **old town**, best viewed from the bridge over the Loire, date back to the twelfth century and make for a relaxed stroll away from the busier town centre. This, combined with an open-air concert programme in summer and a few lively bars and restaurants, makes Nevers an excellent stopover if you're travelling in the region. Movie buffs might also know that Alain Resnais' *Hiroshima Mon Amour* was filmed here.

The Town

The town centres around **place Carnot**, close to the fifteenth-century **ducal palace**, former home of the dukes of Nevers, with octagonal turrets and an elegant central tower decorated with sculptures illustrating the family history of the first duke, François de Clèves, in the mid-seventeenth century. The building now houses an annexe of the law courts. Nearby, opposite the Hôtel de Ville, the **Cathédrale de St-Cyr** reveals a sort of wall display of French architectural styles from the tenth to the sixteenth centuries; it even manages to have two opposite apses, one Gothic, the other Romanesque. But more interesting and aesthetically satisfying is the late eleventh-century church of **St-Étienne** on the east side of the town centre. Behind its plain exterior lies one of the prototype pilgrim churches, with galleries above the aisles, ambulatory and three radiating chapels around the apse.

From the station, av de-Gaulle leads to place Carnot via the city **Parc Roger-Salengro**, whose north side edges onto the **convent of St-Gildard**, where Bernadette of Lourdes ended her days. Her embalmed body is displayed in a glass-fronted **shrine** (daily 6.30am–7.30pm; winter 7am–noon & 1.30–7pm) in the convent chapel.

Crossing to the other side of av de-Gaulle, five minutes' walk from the station by place Mossé and the bridge over the Loire, you pass a section of the old town walls and the **Tour Goguin**, partly dating back to the eleventh century. If you turn in here to the right you come to the **Porte de Croux,** a cream stone tower with intact machicolations and a steep tiled roof like those of its surrounding buildings; inside, the small local **archeology**

museum (daily except Tues 10am–noon & 2–6pm; free) displays mainly Greek and Roman statuary. Nearby in rue du 14-juillet, a seventeenth-century **faïencerie** sells antique pieces such as huge Nivernais plates. To your right again you get back to the oldest quarter of town around the cathedral – rue Morlon and rue de la Cathédrale – with its dilapidated half-timbered houses, alleys and stairs descending to the river.

To the north of the ducal palace on the way out of town towards Orléans, **Porte de Paris**, a triumphal arch, straddles rue des Ardilliers. It commemorates one of Europe's major conflicts, the battle of Fontenoy, fought out between Charlemagne's sons in 841 AD. The stakes were Charlemagne's empire, and the outcome the division of his lands east and west of the Rhine, which formed the basis of modern France and Germany.

Practicalities

The **tourist office**, 31 rue Pierre-Bérégovoy (formerly rue du Rempart), near place Carnot (☎86.59.07.03), provides a map and information on events in the summer music festival. The **gare SNCF** and **gare routière** are on rue du Chemin-de-Fer. **Bike rental** is available from *Laroche*, 28 rue St-Genest.

There are several **hotels** in the area of the *gare SNCF*, not all of which are affected by traffic noise: *Hôtel Thermidor*, 14 rue Claude-Tillier (☎86.57.15.47; ①–②), reached by turning left out of the station and right after *Bar des Messages*, is good value and quiet; a little further away but also worth trying are *Hôtel Beauséjour* at 5 rue St-Gildard (☎86.61.20.84; ①–②), and the neighbouring *Hôtel Villa du Parc*, 16 rue de Lourdes (☎86.61.09.48; ①–②). An alternative, on the north side of the park, is *Hôtel de Verdun*, 4 rue de Lourdes (☎86.61.30.07; ①–②). The **camping municipal** is on the other side of the Loire, just over the bridge.

Avenue de-Gaulle has a few inexpensive **restaurants** and **cafés**, like *Gambrinus* at no. 37 (closed midday Sat & Sun). *Le Goemon*, 9 rue du 14-juillet (closed Sun & Mon evening), is a *crêperie* with good salads, and live jazz on Saturday nights. *Le Florentin Pizzeria*, rue St-Genest (leading to Porte de Croux), has cheap pizzas and pasta. For fresh, tasty food in a friendly place, there's no better than *La Grignote* at 7bis rue Ferdinand-Gambon near the market (☎86.36.24.99; closed Mon, Tues & Wed evenings), with certain *plats* for as little as 30F, *carte* around 100F. More upmarket, the well-situated and classy *Les Jardins de la Porte de Croux*, 17 rue de la Porte-de-Croux (☎86.59.12.71; closed Sun evening & Mon; menus from 120F, *carte* around 200F), has good fish dishes at a price, and a big rear garden.

travel details

Trains

Autun to: Auxerre (4–5 daily; 3hr); Avallon (4–5 daily; 2hr); Sens (4–5 daily; 4hr).

Auxerre to: Autun (4–5 daily; about 3hr); Avallon (4–5 daily; 1hr 5min); Paris (7–8 daily; 1hr 45min).

Avallon to: Autun (4–5 daily; about 2hr); Auxerre (4–5 daily; 1hr 5min); Dijon (4 daily; 2 hr); Paris (2–3 weekly; 2hr); Semur-en-Auxois (3 daily; 40min).

Beaune to: Dijon (about 7 daily; 20min); Lyon (about 7 daily; 2hr); Paris (2 *TGV*s daily; 2hr).

Bourg-en-Bresse to: Dijon (2 daily direct trains; 1hr 45min–2hr 30min); Geneva (4 *TGV*s daily; 1hr 30min); Lyon (14 daily; about 1hr); Mâcon (4 *TGV*s daily; 20min); Mâcon (8 daily; 30min); Paris (4 *TGV*s daily; 2hr).

Dijon to: Beaune (frequent; 25min); Chalon (frequent; 40min); Laroche-Migennes (6 daily; 1hr 40min); Les Laumes (6 daily; 30min); Lyon (20 daily; 1hr 45min–2hr 30min); Tournus (frequent; 1hr); Mâcon (frequent; 1hr–1hr 20min); Montbard (6 daily; 45min); Nuits-St-Georges (frequent; 20min); Paris (9 direct *TGV*s daily; 1hr 40min); Paris (6 daily stopping; 3hr); Sens (6 daily; 2hr 10min); Tonnerre (6 daily; 1hr 15min); Villefranche (frequent; around 1hr 40min).

Mâcon to: Bourg-en-Bresse (4 *TGV*s daily; 20min); Dijon (around 14 daily; 1hr 10min); Geneva (4 *TGV*s daily; 1hr 50min); Lyon (around 14 daily;

40min); Paris (5 direct *TGV*s daily; 1hr 40min).

Nevers to: Autun (3 daily; 1hr 30min); Clermont-Ferrand (5 daily; 1hr 50min); Le Creusot (5 daily; 1hr 30min); Dijon (5 daily; 2hr 30min); Étang (3 daily; 1hr–1hr 50min); Montchanin (6 daily; 1hr 30min); Paris (around 5 daily non-stop; 2hr) ; Paris (several daily stopping; 3hr).

Paray-le-Monial to: Chagny (5 daily; 1–1hr 30min); Chalon (5 daily; 1hr 10min–1hr 40min); Dijon (2 daily; 1hr 45min); Montchanin (2 daily; 50min).

Sens to: Auxerre (3–5 daily; 45min); Autun (3–5 daily; 4hr); Avallon (3–5 daily; 2hr); Dijon (11 daily; 2hr 10min); Joigny (11 daily; 27min); Laroche-Migennes junction (11 daily; 30min); Montbard (11 daily; 1 hr 27min); Paris (frequent; 1hr–1hr 30min); Tonnerre (11 daily; 55min).

Tonnerre to: Dijon (6 daily; 1hr 15min); Paris (6 daily; 1hr 45min).

Buses

Autun to: Beaune (1 daily; 1hr 10min); Chalon (2–3 daily; 1hr 20min); Château-Chinon (1 daily; 1hr); Le Creusot (several daily; 30min); Dijon (1

daily; 2hr 20min); Montchanin *TGV* station (several daily; 1hr); St-Léger-sous-Beuvray (2–3 daily; 1hr 15min).

Avallon to: Dijon (1 daily; 2hr 30min–3hr); Vézelay (1 daily; 30min).

Bourg-en-Bresse to: Lyon (1 daily; 1hr 40min).

Cluny to: Chalon (7 daily; 1hr 20min); Charolles (2–5 daily; 45min); Mâcon (7 daily; 45min); Paray (2–5 daily; 1hr).

Dijon to: Autun (daily; 2hr 30min); Avallon (daily; 2hr); Beaune (daily; 1hr); Châtillon-sur-Seine (4 daily; 1hr 30min); Chaumont (1 daily; 2hr 20min); Langres (1 daily; 1hr 40min); Nuits (daily; 35min); Saulieu (1 daily; 1hr 30min).

Mâcon to: Chalon (7 daily; 2hr 15min); Charolles (2–5 daily; 2hr); Cluny (7 daily; 45min); Paray-le-Monial (2–5 daily; 2hr 20min).

Semur to: Auxerre (1 daily; 2hr 50min); Les Laumes (1 daily; 40min); Montbard (1 daily; 1hr 10min); Saulieu (1 daily; 45min).

Sens to: Auxerre (4 daily; 2hr 5min); Joigny (4 daily; 1 hr 10min); Troyes (4–5 daily; 1hr 45min).

CHAPTER EIGHT

POITOU-CHARENTES AND THE ATLANTIC COAST

N ewsstands selling *Sud-Ouest* remind you where you are: the western coast of France is not the Mediterranean, even though in summer the quality of the light, the warm air, the fields of sunflowers and the shuttered siesta-silence of the farmhouses give you the first exciting promises of the south.

The coast, on the other hand, remains unmistakably Atlantic – dunes, pine forest, reclaimed marshland and misty mud flats. While it has great charm in places, particularly out of season on the islands of **Noirmoutier**, **Ré** and **Oléron**, it's a family, camper-caravanner seaside, lacking the glamour and excitement of the Côte d'Azur, except, perhaps, in Biarritz (covered in *The Pyrenees*, p.609). The principal port in the north of Poitou-Charentes, **La Rochelle**, is one of the prettiest and most distinctive towns in France. The sandy beaches are beautiful everywhere, though can occasionally be disappointing where the water is murky and shallow for a long way out: this applies more to the northern stretches. On the dune-backed **Côte d'Argent**, south of Bordeaux, however, the sea can be lively, not to say dangerous, and often surfable.

Inland, the valley of the **Charente River**, slow and green, epitomizes blue-overalled, Gauloise-smoking, peasant France. The towpath is accessible for long stretches, on foot or mountain bike, and there are boat trips from **Saintes** and **Cognac**. The **Marais Poitevin**, too, with its groves of poplars and island fields reticulated by countless canals and ditches, is both unusual landscape and good walking or cycling country.

But perhaps the most memorable aspect of the countryside – and especially of towns like **Poitiers** – is the presence of exquisite Romanesque churches. This region formed a significant stretch of the medieval pilgrim routes across France and from Britain and northern Europe to the shrine of Saint Jacques (Saint James, or Santiago as the Spanish know him) at Compostela in northwest Spain, and was well endowed by its followers. The finest of the churches, among the best in all of France, are to be found

---

ACCOMMODATION PRICE CATEGORIES

All the hotels, youth hostels and guesthouses listed in this book have been price-graded according to the following scale, and although costs will rise slightly overall with the life of this edition, the relative comparisons should remain valid. Paris and the large cities will, as anywhere, be more expensive than equivalent accommodation in the countryside or small towns. The prices quoted are for the cheapest available double room in high season, although remember that many of the cheap places will have more expensive rooms with en-suite facilities.

① Under 160F	④ 300–400F	⑦ 600–700F
② 160–220F	⑤ 400–500F	⑧ Over 700F
③ 220–300F	⑥ 500–600F	

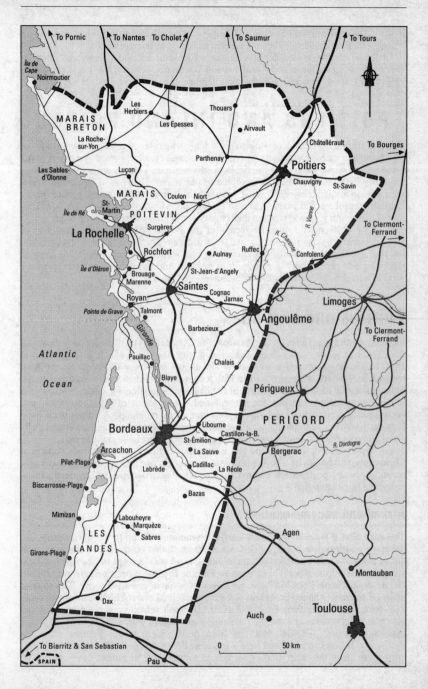

in the countryside around Saintes and Poitiers: informal, highly individual and so integrated with their landscape they often seem as rooted as the trees.

Lastly, of course, remember that this is a region of seafood – fresh and cheap in every market for miles inland – and, around **Bordeaux**, some of the world's top vineyards that you can visit and taste the merchandise.

POITIERS AND INLAND POITOU

Most of the old province of **Poitou** is a huge expanse of rolling wheat land and sunflower and maize plantations where the combines crawl and giant sprinklers shoot great arcs of white water over the fields in summertime. Villages are strung out along the valley bottoms. Heartland of the domains of Eleanor, Duchess of Aquitaine, whose marriage to King Henry II in 1152 brought the whole of southwest France under English control for 300 years, it is also the northern limit of the *langue d'oc*-speaking part of the country, whose Occitan dialect survives among old people even today.

West of **Poitiers** the open landscape of the Poitou plain gradually gives way to *bocages* – small fields enclosed by hedges and trees. The local farmers' cooperatives say that grubbing up woodland and creating vast windswept acreages in the name of efficiency and productivity is going out of fashion. And not just for aesthetic reasons: wind erosion has left scarcely fifteen centimetres of top soil.

Poitiers and around

Heading south from Tours on the *Autoroute de l'Aquitaine*, you'd hardly be tempted by the cluster of towers and office blocks rising from the plain, which is all you see of **POITIERS**. But approach more closely and things look very different. No seething metropolis, Poitiers is a country town with a charm that comes from a long and sometimes influential history – as the seat of the dukes of Aquitaine, for instance – discernible in the winding lines of the streets and the breadth of civic, domestic and ecclesiastical architectural fashions represented in its buildings. A hilltop town overlooking two rivers, with plenty of pedestrian precincts, restaurants and pavement cafés – and some wonderful central gardens – it makes for comfortable sightseeing.

For the dedicated, there are the two Romanesque churches not far from Poitiers at **Chauvigny** and **St-Savin** – both with some great sculpture and frescoes – as well as a recently opened postmodern cinema theme-park, **Futuroscope**, to the north, that's become a huge attraction.

Arrival and accommodation

The **gare SNCF** is on bd du Grand-Cerf, a ten-minute walk up to the town centre, but the **gare routière** is a bus #11 ride from the train station off the D4 on the way north out of town towards Châtellerault; most buses, however – except to Loudun and local villages – leave from place Thézard below Parc de Blossac. Contact *Rapides de Poitou*, 20 rue de la Plaine (☎49.46.27.45), for buses to St-Savin and Chauvigny. The **tourist office**, 8 rue des Grandes-Écoles off place du Maréchal-Leclerc (Mon–Sat 9am–noon & 1.30–6pm; July & Aug 9am–7pm; ☎49.41.21.24), won't actually reserve rooms but can give you hotel options in town, and also supplies walkers with a guide to the regional opportunities: the **GR364** sets out from here, reaching the Vendée coast via Parthenay. **Bikes** can be rented from *Cyclamen*, 49 rue Arsène-Orillard (☎49.88.13.25), **cars** from near the train station on bd du Grand-Cerf, including *Citer*, at no. 48

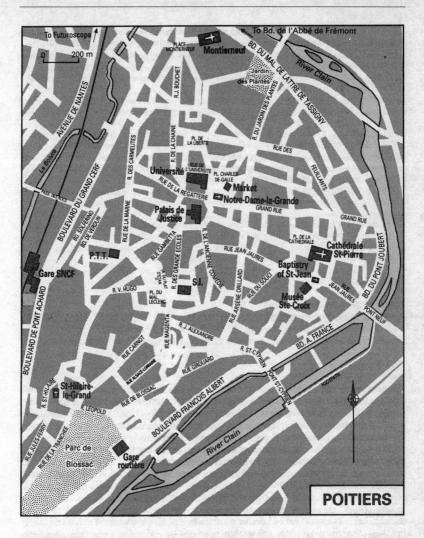

POITIERS

(π49.58.51.58), *Eurorent* at nos. 95–97 (π49.58.24.20), and *Locadoc* at no. 63 (π49.59.77.72).

There are plenty of **hotels** along the bd du Grand-Cerf by the train station, although the area is not particularly salubrious; for more entertaining surroundings it's only a short uphill walk – bd Solférino, then to the right up the steep steps – to the town centre on place du Maréchal-Leclerc.

Hotels

Le Carnot, 40 rue Carnot (π49.41.23.69). Tiny basic hotel over a noisy local bar with as central a location as the swish *Grand Hotel de l'Europe*, opposite. ①.

Hôtel du Chapon Fin, pl du Maréchal-Leclerc (☎49.88.02.97). A substantial old two-star hotel in a great position right near the grand Hôtel de Ville; the spacious rooms all have showers. ②–③.

Hôtel Continental, 2 bd Solférino (☎49.37.93.93). Comfortable two-star in the centre with soundproofed rooms all with bath or shower and TV. ③.

Le Grand Cerf, 137 bd du Grand-Cerf (☎49.58.20.85). Much of a muchness with the *Paris* and the other hotels in the street. Closed Aug 6–27 & Mon. ①.

Grand Hôtel de l'Europe, 39 rue Carnot (☎49.88.12.00). Upmarket in the manner of its name and dead central, but its front courtyard set back from the street means it's very quiet. Covered parking 20F. ③–⑤.

Hôtel Jules Ferry, 27 rue Jules-Ferry (☎49.37.80.14). Friendly family-run establishment situated in a peaceful residential street near the church of St-Hilaire; clean and nicely decorated. ②.

Hôtel de Paris, 123 bd du Grand-Cerf (☎49.58.39.37). A once superior hotel by the station, now run-down and inexpensive; unfortunately traffic makes it noisy front and back. If a little unfriendly, the simple, good-value restaurant compensates. Closed Mon. ①–②.

La Petite Villette, 14 bd de l'Abbé-de-Frémont (☎49.41.41.33). One-star hotel easily accessible from the station; just continue along bd du Grand-Cerf till you reach the roundabout and turn right. Closed Sun. ①–②.

Hôtel du Plat d'Étain, 7 rue du Plat-d'Étain (☎49.41.04.80). Situated in a central quiet street just off the main shopping precinct, this hotel is well run and attractive. ①–④.

Le Terminus, 3 bd Pont-Achard (☎49.58.20.21). A better class of station-located lodging with an excellent brasserie. Rooms are very clean, modern and sound-proofed. ②–③.

Le Victor Hugo, 5 rue Victor-Hugo (☎49.41.12.16). A central bargain above an agreeable bar – only five rooms, most of them simple. ①.

Youth hostels and campsites

IYHF youth hostel, 17 rue de la Jeunesse (☎49.58.03.05). Large, modern hostel often overrun with school groups. Take bus #3 from the *gare SNCF* to Bellejouanne, 3km away. ①.

Camping municipal, rue du Porteau (☎49.41.44.88). Two kilometres north of the town on bus #7.

The Town

The two poles of communal life in Poitiers are the tree-lined **place du Maréchal-Leclerc**, with its popular cafés and lively outdoor culture, and **place Charles-de-Gaulle** to the north, where a big and bustling **market** takes place (Mon–Sat 7am–6pm, Sun 7.30am–1pm). Between the two is a warren of prosperous streets – as far along as the half-timbered medieval houses of **rue de la Chaine** – with the rue Gambetta cutting north past the **Palais de Justice** (guided visits: July & Aug daily 10am & 3pm; 35F), whose nineteenth-century façade hides a much older core. A guided tour of the interior will bring you to the twelfth-century great hall of the dukes of Aquitaine, a magnificent room nearly 50m long, where Jean, Duc de Berry, held his sumptuous court in the late fourteenth century seated on the intricately carved dais at the far end. In one corner, stairs give access to the old **castle keep**. Joan of Arc was once put through her ideological paces here by a committee of bishops worried about endangering their own immortal souls and worldly positions by endorsing a charlatan or a heretic – they also had her virginity checked by a posse of respectable matrons. The stairs lead out on to the roof with a fantastic view over the town.

Right behind you, you can look down upon one of the greatest and most idiosyncratic churches in France, **Notre-Dame-la-Grande** (daily 8am–7pm), begun in the twelfth-century reign of Eleanor and now freshly renovated; strangely enough, pigeon droppings and pollution weren't the major concern, but the salt from the market stalls of fishmongers and salt merchants seeping into the ground and eventually into the church's façade.

The weirdest and most spectacular thing about it is the west front. You can't call it beautiful, at least not in a conventional sense. It is squat and loaded with detail to a degree that the modern eye finds fussy. And yet it is this detail which is enthralling, ranging from the domestic to the disturbingly anarchic: in the blind arch to the right of the door, a woman sits in the keystone with her hair blowing out from her head; in the frieze above, Mary places her hand familiarly on Elizabeth's pregnant belly. You see the newborn Jesus admired by a couple of daft-looking sheep and gurgling in his bath-tub. Higher still are images of the apostles, and at the apex, where the eye is carried deliberately and inevitably, Christ in Majesty in an almond-shaped inset. Such elaborate sculpted façades – and domes like pine cones on turret and belfry – are the hallmarks of the Poitou brand of Romanesque. The interior, crudely overlaid with nineteenth-century frescoes, is not nearly as interesting.

Another unusual church lies towards the southern tip of the old town, where the hump of the hill narrows to a point now occupied by the **Parc de Blossac**, a great spot to sit among the clipped limes and gravelled walks, to watch the *boules* and munch a baguette. The eleventh-century **church of St-Hilaire-le-Grand** on rue du Doyenné unbelievably was pruned of part of its nave in the last century, but the chevet from the outside is still a fine sight; the apse has a particularly beautiful group of chapels surrounding it. Inside, there is the usual ambulatory to accommodate the many pilgrims who flocked here, one of whom perhaps caused the fire around 1100 that destroyed the original wooden roof and necessitated the improvised arrangement that makes St-Hilaire architecturally unique: eight heavy domes introduced for the re-roofing had to be supported somehow, hence the forest of auxiliary columns that make three aisles either side of the nave.

The cathedral and around

Poitiers' **Cathédrale St-Pierre**, at the east of the old town, is an enormous building on whose broad, pale façade pigeons roost and plants take root. Some of the stained glass dates from the twelfth century, notably the crucifixion in the centre window of the apse, in which the features of Henry II and Eleanor are supposedly discernible. The choir stalls, too, are full of characteristic medieval detail: a coquettish Mary and child, a peasant killing a boar, the architect at work with his dividers, a baker with a basket of loaves. But it's the grand eighteenth-century Orgue Clicquot that is the cathedral's most striking feature, often playing its deafening tunes, with organized concerts in the summer.

Opposite – literally in the middle of rue Jean-Jaurès – you come upon a chunky, square edifice with the air of a second-rate Roman temple. It is the mid-fourth-century **Baptistère St-Jean** (daily except Tues 10.30am–12.30pm & 3–6pm; Nov–March 2.30–4.30pm; July & Aug daily; 4F), reputedly the oldest Christian building in France and, until the seventeenth century, the only place in town you could have a proper baptism. The "font" was the octagonal pool sunk into the floor. The guide argues that the water pipes uncovered in the bottom show that the water could not have been more than 30 to 40cm deep, which casts doubt upon the popular belief that early Christian baptism was by total immersion. There are also some very ancient and faded frescoes on the walls, including the Emperor Constantine on horseback, and a collection of Merovingian sarcophagi. Striking a postmodern note between the cathedral and baptistry is the small domed shape of **Espace Mendès-France** (Tues–Fri 10am–7pm, Sat & Sun 2–7pm), containing a state-of-the-art planetarium (32F) and laserium (42F).

Next to the baptistery is Poitiers' museum, the **Musée Ste-Croix** (Tues–Fri 10am–noon & 1–5pm, Sat & Sun 10am–noon & 2–6pm; 15F, Tues free), featuring an interesting collection of farming implements like its *alambic ambulant* or itinerant still, of a kind in use until surprisingly recently. There is also a good Gallo-Roman section with some handsome glass, pottery and sculpture, notably a white marble Minerva of the first century.

If you still have an appetite for buildings, there's a seventh-century subterranean chapel, the **Hypogée Martyrium**, on rue de la Pierre-Levée across the Pont Neuf, and the **Pierre Levée dolmen** itself, where Rabelais came with fellow students to talk, carouse and scratch his name. Descartes, Poitiers University's other most illustrious student, was rather more serious.

Alternatively, you could take a more relaxed walk along the **riverside path** – on the right across Pont Neuf – upstream to Pont St-Cyprien. On the far bank, you can see a characteristic feature of every French provincial town: neat, well-manured *potagers* – vegetable gardens – coming down to the water's edge with a little mud quay at the end and a moored punt, where *monsieur* spends many a weekend hour patiently waiting for a fat carp.

Eating and nightlife

As for **eating**, there are good opportunities for fine food whatever your culinary persuasions. If you know where to head, the town offers everything from cheap fast food to high-priced restaurants with so many recommendations you can't see in the windows for stickers. There's a good range of ethnic options if you're bored with French cuisine. If you're not too long in the tooth, you could also try wangling a university restaurant ticket; ask *CIJ* at 64 rue Gambetta or phone ☎49.01.83.69.

Alain Boutin, 65 rue Carnot (☎49.88.25.53). A better bet for regional dishes like *cailles au pineau* (quails cooked in a brandy liqueur) with a smaller, more carefully chosen selection than the *Poitevin*; menus from 73F to 160F. Closed Sat lunch and Sun.

Le Cappucino, 5 rue de l'Université. One of a number of Italian restaurants in this area. Closed Sun eve & Mon.

Makossa, 20 rue des Vieilles-Boucheries (☎49.01.74.72). Plain and simple African restaurant, with lots of cheap options and vegetarian dishes.

Le Poitevin, 76 rue Carnot (☎49.88.35.04). Regional food at reasonable prices, although the huge menu and predictably "rustic" interior are worrying.

Patatorium, 185 Faubourg du Pont-Neuf, just over the Pont Neuf. French and Moroccan food in café connected to an exhibition centre and record store. Tues–Sat 2–7pm.

Pizza Rosa and Snooker Bar, espace Régratterie, off rue de la Régratterie. Very cheap pizza slices to eat at the bar, and English beers in the Snooker Bar on the same courtyard.

Chez Pierrot, Montierneuf. Inexpensive restaurant with several studenty bars nearby.

Jack Rolland, 16 rue Carnot (☎49.88.14.41). Specializes in exquisite fish dishes, with menus starting at 140F. If that's too pricy, there are several less expensive options in this street. Closed mid-July to mid-Aug, Sun eve & Mon.

Le Saint-Hilaire, 65 rue Théophraste-Renaudot (☎49.41.15.45). In a magnificent medieval cellar with stained glass and ancient columns, this is an extraordinary place to dine, and not as expensive as it looks, with menus from 69F to 110F.

Le Saint Nicholas, 7 rue Carnot (☎49.41.44.48). Actually in small traffic-free lane off rue Carnot, meaning you can eat outside peacefully; traditional food served with a contemporary feel. Menus 79F and 109F. Closed Wed.

La Trattoria, 7 rue de la Régratterie (☎49.88.19.88). Flash pizzeria and a good find for vegetarians, with plenty of flesh-free pasta sauces and a stack of gourmet salads. Closed Sun.

Futuroscope

Poitiers' newest attraction is the giant high-tech film theme park called **Futuroscope: Le Parc Européen de l'Image**, 8km north of the city, a collection of virtual-reality rides which draw lookers-on into the action on screen, with the result that you feel you're flying, being flung around, rocketing down a ski slope or catapulting through the solar system in a vertigo-inducing 3-D nightmare. Not for those with fragile constitutions.

The futuristic **cinema pavilions** are set in several acres of greenery around a series of undulating man-made lakes. The fifteen screens take some getting around, with plenty of walking between them, so arrive early to beat the queues. To see everything in the park in one day, with time off for lunch, takes about ten exhausting hours, and as well as seeing the screen entertainment, you've got to give yourself time to ride the oversized floating bicycles on the park's lakes. To orientate yourself, head first for **La Gyrotour** where a lift takes you to the top of the high rotating tower and you can get the full effect of the futuristic scenario.

All the films are in French, with English commentaries on headphones often available, but as these are not very effective, and as it's the visual impact that's most important anyway, it's better to do without; recommended screenings are listed below. Apart from the films, there's a **laser show** *La Symphonie des Eaux*, a display of music, colour and effects focused on the park's dancing fountains (April–Oct Sat 10.30pm; July to early Sept daily).

The park's opening hours vary with the seasons (daily Feb, March & Oct 9am–6pm; April–June 9am–7pm; July 9am–8pm; Aug 9am–9pm; Sept 9am–6.30pm; Dec 22–Jan 4 10am–6pm; ☎49.49.30.80), and the only public transport to the park is the #17 bus from Poitiers' Hôtel de Ville, which runs twice a day during school term time. A system of taxi shuttles from Poitiers' *gare SNCF*, with specific leaving and return times, is the best option (40F per person plus 10F supplement between 10.45pm & 11pm; you must book your return in advance). **Tickets** are valid for one or two days (one-day pass adult 135F; child 100F; two-day pass both 230F); to avoid queues at the park, you can purchase tickets in advance from a booth at Poitiers' *gare SNCF*. **Food** is predictably expensive inside the park, with even a humble sandwich costing over the odds; a picnic lunch can cut costs substantially.

The presentations – a selection

Le Pavillon de Vienne. Moving seats parade before a huge wall of multiple images patchworking into a film on the region, which also tells the story of *Futuroscope*.

Le Cinéma Dynamique. You literally have to hang on to your seat for this one: a fast and thrilling ride as the seats move in sync with the images on the screen, among them a train and a speeding bobsleigh.

Imax Solido. The screen within a dome in conjunction with 3-D vision glasses gives a breathtaking view of the effects of the sun's energy on life, the universe and everything. Better than LSD, or so we've been told.

Le Cinéma 360°. Spain's contribution to Seville Expo '92 is now housed here permanently. Several screens surround, and you have to turn your head to take in a film about Andalucia.

Paysages d'Europe. Very slow – for a change – and good for the faint at heart and those in need of a rest, as a boat floats serenely past images of the continent.

Le Pavillon de Communication. A high-tech system of projection fires multiple images in rapid succession and attempts to tell the story of human communication. Dizzy-making.

Le Tapis Magique. Probably the most stunning presentation, with a vast screen in front of you, and another under your feet, creating the incredible feeling that you're flying to Mexico on a giant Monarch butterfly.

Le Pavillon du Futuroscope. Using holographic images, a robot tells the story of the universe and its atoms.

Chauvigny

Twenty-three kilometres east of Poitiers, **CHAUVIGNY** is a busy market town on the banks of the Vienne with half a dozen porcelain factories and lumber mills providing work for the area. Overlooking the bustling *ville basse*, the old town has several ruined medieval castles, but its pride is a set of sculpted capitals in the **church of St-Pierre**; take rue du Château opposite Notre-Dame on the central **place de la Poste**, winding up the spur on which the old town stands, continue past the ruins of the **Château**

Baronnial, which belonged to the bishops of Poitiers, and the better-preserved **Château d'Harcourt**, then you'll come to the attractive and unusual east end of St-Pierre.

Inside, the church is damp and in poor repair, but the choir capitals are a visual treat. Each one is different, evoking a terrifying, nightmarish world. Graphically illustrated monsters – bearded, moustached, winged, scaly, human-headed with manes of flame – grab hapless mortals, naked, upside down and puny, and rip their bowels and crunch their heads. The only escape offered is in the naively serene events of the nativity. On the second capital on the south side of the choir, for instance, the angel Gabriel announces Christ's birth to the shepherds, their flock represented by four sheep that look like Pooh's companion Eeyore, while just around the corner the archangel Michael weighs souls in hand-held scales and a devil tries to grab one for his dinner. The oddest scene is on the north side: a Siamese-twin dancer grips the hindlegs of two horse-like monsters that are gnawing his upper arms. You get a strong feeling that here was an artist who came from the same peasant background as his audience, prey to the same fears of things that went bump in the night or lurked in the wet woods.

If you can manage it, making your visit coincide with the Saturday **market** gives an extra dimension to a day trip here. Held between the church of Notre-Dame and the river, it offers a mouthwatering selection of food – oysters, prawns, crayfish, cheeses galore and pâtés in pristine aspic. The cafés are fun, too, bursting with noisy wine-flushed farmers mixing business with pleasure.

If you do want to **stay** here overnight, *Le Lion d'Or*, 8 rue du Marché (☎49.46.30.28; ③; closed mid-Dec to mid-Jan), is comfortable enough. Chauvigny also has a **munici-pal campsite**, just east of the centre on rue de la Fontaine (☎49.46.31.94).

St-Savin

You need to get an early start if you want make a single day trip by public transport to see both Chauvigny and **ST-SAVIN**, 42km east of Poitiers and scarcely more than a hamlet in comparison with bustling Chauvigny.

The bus puts you down beside the abbey near the modern bridge over the poplar-lined River Gartempe; walk downstream a little way to the medieval bridge for a perfect view of the **abbey church** (Mon–Sat 9am–12.30pm & 2.30–5pm, Sun 9–11am & 2.30–5pm; July–Sept closes 7pm) – built in the eleventh century, possibly on the site of a church founded by Charlemagne – rising strong and severe above the gazebos, vegetable gardens and lichened tile roofs of the houses at its feet. Inside, steps descend to the narthex and from there to the floor of the nave, stretching out to the raised choir: high, narrow, barrel-vaulted and flanked by bare round columns, their capitals deeply carved with interlacing foliage. The whole of the vault is covered with paintings. The colours are few – red and yellow ochres, green mixed with white and black. Yet the paintings are full of light and grace, depicting scenes from the stories of Genesis and Exodus. Some are instantly recognizable: Noah's three-decked ark, Pharaoh's horses rearing at the engulfing waves of the Red Sea, graceful workers constructing the Tower of Babel.

If you do get caught in St-Savin, try the *Hôtel du Midi* (☎49.48.00.40, closed Jan, Sun evening & Mon; ③) on route Nationale.

Parthenay and around

Directly west of Poitiers, and served by regular *SNCF* buses, stands the attractive small town of **PARTHENAY**, once an important staging point on the pilgrim routes to Compostela and now the site of a major weekly cattle market each Wednesday. It's not a place to make a special detour for, but it's worth a stopover if you're heading north to Brittany or west to the sea.

Parthenay has nothing very remarkable to see, although its medieval heart is interesting enough. The main part of town – essentially the medieval core, and fairly restricted in area at that – lies ahead to the west, towards the River Thouet. Rue Jean-Jaurès and rue de la Saunerie cut in through the largely pedestrian shopping precinct to the Gothic **Porte de l'Horloge**, the fortified gateway to the old citadel on a steep-sided neck of land above a loop of the Thouet.

The *mairie* faces the attractively simple Romanesque **church of Ste-Croix** across a small garden with a view over the ramparts and the **gully of St-Jacques**, with its medieval houses and vegetable plots climbing the opposite slope. Further along rue de la Citadelle is a house where Cardinal Richelieu used to visit his grandfather, and then a handsome but badly damaged Romanesque door, all that remains of the castle chapel of **Notre-Dame-de-la-Couldre**. Of the **castle** itself practically nothing is left: from the tip of the spur where it once stood you look down on the twin-towered **gateway** and the **Pont St-Jacques**, a thirteenth-century bridge through which the nightly flocks of pilgrims poured into the town for shelter and security. To reach it, turn left under the Tour de l'Horloge and down the **Vaux St-Jacques**, as this medieval lane is called. It is highly evocative of that period, with its crooked half-timbered dwellings crowding up to the bridge. They are only now beginning to be restored. Some look as if they have received little attention since the last pilgrim shuffled up the street.

Practicalities

Finding your way around is easy. From the **gare SNCF**, av de Gaulle leads directly west to the central square, with the **tourist office** on the right-hand corner (☎49.64.24.24). If you're after shelter, a reasonable **hotel** by the main square is *Grand Hôtel*, 85 bd Meilleraie (☎49.64.00.16; ③; closed Sat evening & Sun out of season). Another possibility is the fancier two-star *Hôtel du Nord*, 86 av de Gaulle, opposite the station (☎49.94.29.11; closed Sat; ③). **Campers** have to head to the three-star site at **LE TALLUD** (☎49.94.39.52; open all year), part of the 14-hectare *Base de Loisirs* riverbank recreation area, about 3km west of Parthenay on the D949.

As for **eating**, Parthenay has the usual provincial range of restaurants: Italian, Tunisian and Chinese, as well as traditional French. Best of the latter is *Le Fin Gourmet*, 28 rue Ganne (☎49.64.04.53; closed Sun night & Mon), where high-quality cuisine combines well with a jovial atmosphere on Wednesdays; affordable for all, with menus from 59F to the full gastronomic whack at 150F.

Around Parthenay

There are three more beautiful Romanesque churches you might like to see within easy reach of Parthenay. One – with a sculpted façade depicting a mounted knight hawking – is only a twenty-minute walk on the Niort road, at **PARTHENAY-LE-VIEUX**. The others are at **AIRVAULT**, 20km northeast of Parthenay and easily accessible on the Parthenay–Thouars *SNCF* bus route, and **ST-JOUIN-DE-MARNES**, 9km northeast of Airvault (you'll have to hitch or walk that). Or, you could go on north to **THOUARS** to see the abbey church of St-Laon, 21km from Airvault or 16km from St-Jouin (cheap hotels and *camping municipal*), and combine St-Jouin with a visit to the sixteenth-century **Château d'Oiron**, 8.5km northwest of St-Jouin.

Niort

NIORT is a stopover rather than a destination, most immediately and conveniently if your goal is the Marais Poitevin, the so-called "Green Venice" (see below). In itself Niort is a pleasant morning's stroll and, if you're in a car, probably the best place to stay. If you're on foot, it's the last place before the marshes to get a really wide choice of provisions.

The most interesting part of the town is the mainly pedestrian area around **rue Victor-Hugo** and **rue St-Jean**, full of stone-fronted or half-timbered medieval houses. Coming from the *gare SNCF*, take rue de la Gare as far as av de Verdun with the tourist office and main post office on the corner. Turn right into place de la Brèche. Rue Ricard leaves the square on the left; rue Victor-Hugo is its continuation, following the line of the medieval market in a gully separating the two small hills on which Niort is built. Up to the right, opposite the end of rue St-Jean, is the old **town hall**, a triangular building of the early sixteenth century with lantern, belfry and ornamental machicolations, perhaps capable of repelling drunken revellers but no match for catapult or sledgehammer.

At the end of the street is the river, the **Sèvre Niortaise**, not to be confused with the Sèvre Nantaise which flows northwards to join the Loire at Nantes. There are gardens and trees along the bank and, over the bridge, the ruins of a glove factory, the last vestige of Niort's once thriving leather industry. At the time of the Revolution, it kept more than thirty cavalry regiments in breeches. Today Niort's biggest industry is insurance: the most bourgeois town in France, so it is said, because of the prosperity brought by the large number of major insurance firms making their headquarters here. Accordingly, restaurants are usually packed at lunch-time, and well-heeled shoppers throng the pedestrianized streets, giving a fairly lively – if affluent – feel.

Just downstream, opposite a riverside car park, is the **market hall** (with a café doing a good cheap lunch) and, beyond, vast and unmistakable on a slight rise, the keep of a **castle** begun by Henry II of England. Now housing a **museum** (daily except Tues summer 9am–noon & 2–6pm; winter closes 5pm; 15F, free Wed), it displays mainly local furniture and costumes, an extraordinary variety of which were still commonly worn in the villages until the beginning of the twentieth century.

If you want to see the surrounding Marais area (see below), you can make a bike tour in three days – the pleasantest way to see it. It's completely flat and small enough to pretty well cover.

Practicalities

The excellent **tourist office** (Mon–Fri 9.30–5pm, Sat 9.30am–noon; July & Aug Mon–Fri 9.30am–7pm, Sat 10am–5pm, Sun 10am–1pm; ☎49.24.18.79), with plenty of information to hand about walking itineraries around the Marais, is on place de la Poste. It also offers a free room reservation service (☎49.24.98.92) if you're looking to stay; for more rustic accommodation in the Marais itself, contact *Relais des Gîtes Ruraux* at 15 rue Thiers (☎49.24.00.42). The **gare SNCF** is on rue Mazagran and has **bicycles** for rental. Beware that the *gare* has no *consigne automatique*, charging a hefty 30F for each piece of left luggage. If you're using the buses, the **gare routière** is just off place de la Brèche on rue Viala. If you need money, there's an **exchange facility** at *Société Générale*, rue Ricard (Mon–Fri 8.30am–5pm).

There's the usual crop of **hotels** close to the station, including the two-starred *L'Univers*, 22 rue Mazagran, place de la Gare (☎49.24.41.70; ①–②), and *Terminus*, 82 rue de la Gare (☎49.24.00.38; ②–③; closed Sat). More centrally, the *Saint-Jean*, 21 av St-Jean-d'Angély (☎49.79.20.76; ①–②), is another good bet for cheap, comfortable rooms, while several more upmarket hotels cluster on av de Paris, including *Le Paris*, at no. 12 (☎49.24.93.78; ③), and the more exclusive three-star *Grand Hôtel* at no. 32 (☎49.24.22.21; ③–④). The three-star **camping** de Noron (☎49.79.05.06) is on bd S-Allende next door to the stadium, bus #6 from place de la Brèche.

Two **restaurants** to head for are *Les Quatre Saisons*, 21 rue du Faison (☎49.24.96.97; closed Sun), for Marais Poitevin specialities served super fresh (*menu* *du marché* 69F, *menu régional* 110F), and *Le Lutin*, at 92 rue de la Gare (☎49.24.05.34), a surprising find so close to the station. Colourful and comfy with a generous 55F *menu du jour*, it has lots of fish and regional dishes on the *carte*.

The Marais Poitevin

The **Marais Poitevin** is a strange, lazy landscape of fens and meadows, shielded by poplar trees and crisscrossed by an elaborate system of canals, dykes and slow-flowing rivers. Recently declared a National Park, the French know it as *La Venise Verte* – the Green Venice – and a tourist industry of sorts has been developing around the villages. But the marshes are not yet dead, or completely phoney, and the flat-bottomed punts remain the principal means of transport for many farmers – indeed there's no dry-land access to many of the fields. Be sure to avoid weekends, when the evidence of the coming transformation is all too clear.

Access to the eastern edge of the marsh is easiest at the whitewashed village of **COULON**, on the River Sèvre, just 11km from Niort by bike or occasional bus. As you would expect in a marshland village, Coulon's houses are small, low and obviously poor. Punts, with or without a guide, can be rented here by the half-day at 6 rue de l'Église (☎49.35.02.29) – fun on a sunny day with a picnic.

There are two **hotels** in the village, both likely to be full in season: the family-run *Central*, 4 rue d'Autremont (☎49.35.90.20; ③; closed mid-Jan to early Feb; late-Sept to mid-Oct, Sun & Mon), and the pricey *Au Marais*, 46–48 quai Louis Tardi (☎49.25.90.43; ③–⑤; closed late-Dec to late-Jan). A better bet if you're **camping** is the attractively sited *Camping Venise Verte* in a meadow about 2km downstream (a 25-minute walk), or the *Camping Municipal la Niquière* (☎49.35.81.19; mid-June to mid-Sept), north of Coulon on the road to Benet. The best **eating** option here is the regional cuisine of *Le Central*'s characterful restaurant; with generous servings, a well-deserved reputation and a menu from 88F, you'd be wise to book.

For getting around the Marais, **bicycles** are ideal. There's an excellent place to rent them in **ARÇAIS**, a village 10km west of Coulon, called *La Bicyclette Verte* in rue du Coursault (☎49.35.42.56; 1hr 20F, half-day 50F, day 70F, week 380F; guided 5hr circuit including breakfast 175F), which also has children's bikes and tandems. If you're walking the marshes, it's best to stick to the lanes since cross-country routes tend to end in fields surrounded by water and you have to backtrack continually. Once you're away from the riverside road from Coulon to Arçais, there's practically no traffic, just meadows and cows. At the seaward end of the marsh – the area south of **LUÇON** – the landscape changes, becoming all straight lines and open fields of wheat and sunflowers. The villages cap low mounds that were once islands.

WESTERN POITOU: LA ROCHELLE AND THE ISLANDS

The coast of Poitou – especially the islands – is great for young families, with miles of safe sandy beaches and shallow water. Beware, however, that in August, unless you're camping or have booked something in advance, accommodation is a near-insuperable problem. Out of season you can't rely on sunny weather, but that shouldn't deter you if you like the slightly melancholy romance of quiet misty seascapes and working fishing ports. **La Rochelle** and **Royan** in the south are the best bases, and are both served by train. Away from these centres – if you're not driving – you'll have to take pot luck with the rather quirky bus routes.

Les Sables-d'Olonne and around

The area around **LES SABLES-D'OLONNE** and northwards has been heavily developed with Costa-style apartment blocks. If you're passing through, though, there's a surprisingly good modern art section in the **Musée de l'Abbaye Ste-Croix** on rue Verdun (daily except Mon 10.30am–noon & 2.30–6.30pm; 30F, free Wed) and an **automobile museum**, 8km southeast of town on the road to Talmont (daily 9.30am–noon & 2–6pm; July & Aug daily 9.30am–7pm; Oct to mid-March Sat & Sun 9.30am–noon & 2–6pm; 36F). The main reason to stay, though, is the town's vast curve of clean, beautiful **beach**, which lures hordes in the summer.

Hotels get booked up well in advance for July and August, but a couple worth trying are *Le Merle Blanc* near the beach at 59 av Aristide-Briand (☎51.32.00.35; ①–③; closed Oct to mid-March) and *Hôtel les Olonnes*, 25 rue de la Patrie (☎51.32.04.12; ②–③; closed Sun night & Mon). Budget options include a beachside IYHF **youth hostel**, 3km from the centre at 92 rue du Sémaphore (☎51.95.76.21; ①; April–Sept), a bus line #2 ride away in the direction of *Côte Sauvage* (stop Armandèche); a municipal **campsite** (☎51.95.10.42; March–Oct) on rue des Roses, 400m from the beach; and several more campsites in the Pironnière district, 3km south of town on the D949. For more accommodation options, ask at the **tourist office** on rue du Maréchal Leclerc (daily 9am–12.15pm & 2–6.30pm; July & Aug 9am–7pm; ☎51.32.03.28), or at the local office of *Gîtes de France*, 124 av Aristide-Briand (☎51.62.33.10).

Les Épesses

Some 80km inland from Les Sables (on the N160 if you're driving), at the ruined **Château du Puy du Fou** in the village of **LES ÉPESSES**, a remarkable lakeside extravaganza happens during the summer months (Fri & Sat only June & July 10.30pm; Aug 10pm; 1hr 45min; 110F). This is a weird affair: the enactment of the life of a local peasant from the Middle Ages to World War II, complete with fireworks, lasers, dances on the lake and *Comédie Française* voice-overs. The story, summarized in a brief English text, is interesting but incidental – the spectacle is the thing.

To get to Les Épesses by public transport, you'll need to get to **CHOLET** (reasonably connected by train) and take a bus south from there; Puy du Fou itself is 2.5km from Les Épesses, on the D27 to **CHAMBRETAUD**. There is one reasonably priced hotel in Les Épesses called *Le Lion d'Or*, 2 rue de la Libération, and a wider choice (*Relais*, *Le Centre* or *Chez Camille*) 10km west at **LES HERBIERS**.

The Île de Noirmoutier

The twenty-kilometre-long **Île de Noirmoutier** was an early monastic settlement of the seventh century: now it has bowed to pilgrims of a different ilk, serving as a tourist resort, and a relatively plush one at that. It's been spared the high-rise development of its adjoining coast, and it's villas that are in great demand; but although tourism is the island's main economy, it doesn't dominate everything. Salt marshes here are still worked, spring potatoes sown and fishes fished. The island can be reached in three hours by bus from Les Sables, and is connected to the shore by a toll bridge.

The island town, **NOIRMOUTIER-EN-L'ÎLE**, is a low-key type of place but still has a twelfth-century **castle**, a **church** with a Romanesque crypt, an excellent **market** (Tues & Fri) and most of the **nightlife** on the island in the form of piano bars with longer-than-usual café hours. There are **campsites** dotted around the island – maps from the **tourist office** on the main road from the bridge at **MARMATRE**. **Bike rental** is from *Vel-hop*, 55 av Joseph-Pineau in Noirmoutier, or *Fabre*, rue du Centre,

Marmatre. Among hotels to try in the town are *Le Bois de la Chaize*, 23 av de la Victoire, *La Marée*, 2bis Grande-Rue, or at **BARBATRE**, in the south of the island, *La Fosse*, 57 rue de la Pointe, or *Le Marina*, 1 route du Gois.

As for exploring the island, the western coast, with its great curves of sand, resembles the mainland, while the northern side dips in and out of little bays with rocky promontories between. Inland, were it not for the saltwater dykes, the horizon would suggest that you were miles from the sea. It is a strange place with only one hostile element apart from the storms in spring – a vicious mosquito population. The more southerly resorts, though built up, have not been the main targets for the developers. In the village centres there are still the one-storey houses that you see throughout La Vendée and southern Brittany – whitewashed and ochre-tiled with decorative brickwork around the windows and S- or Z-shaped coloured bars on the shutters.

La Rochelle

LA ROCHELLE is the most attractive and unspoiled seaside town in France. Thanks to the foresight of 1970s mayor Michel Crépeau, its historic seventeenth- to eighteenth-century centre and waterfront were plucked from the clutches of the developers and its streets freed of traffic for the delectation of pedestrians. A real shock-horror outrage at the time, the policy has become standard practice for preserving old town centres across the country – more successful than Crépeau's picturesque yellow bicycle plan, designed to relieve the traffic problem (see below).

La Rochelle has a long history, as you would expect of such a sheltered Atlantic port, and the inevitable English connection. Eleanor of Aquitaine gave it a charter in 1199, which released it from its feudal obligations, and it rapidly became a port of major importance, trading in salt and wine and skilfully exploiting the Anglo-French quarrels. The Wars of Religion, however, were particularly destructive for La Rochelle. It turned Protestant and, because of its strategic importance, drew the remorseless enmity of Cardinal Richelieu, who laid siege to it in 1627. To the dismay of the townspeople, who reasoned that no one could effectively blockade seasoned mariners like themselves, he succeeded in sealing the harbour approaches with a dyke. The English dispatched the duke of Buckingham to their aid, but he was caught napping on the Île de Ré and badly defeated. By the end of 1628 Richelieu had starved the city into submission. Out of the pre-siege population of 28,000 only 5000 survived. The walls were demolished and the city's privileges revoked.

After this disastrous interlude, La Rochelle later became the principal port for trade with the French colonies in the Caribbean Antilles and Canada. Indeed, many of the settlers, especially in Canada, came from this part of France.

Arrival and accommodation

Finding your way around La Rochelle is straightforward. Arriving at the elaborate **gare SNCF** on bd Joffre, take av de Gaulle opposite to reach the town centre; on the left as you reach the waterfront, the efficient **tourist office** on quai de Gabut (Mon–Sat 9am–noon & 2–6pm; June Mon–Sat 9am–7pm & Sun 11am–5pm; July & Aug Mon–Sat 9am–8pm & Sun 11am–5pm; ☎46.41.14.68) dispenses excellent free **maps**. Most things you'll want to see are in the area behind the waterfront: in effect, between the harbour and the place de Verdun, where the **gare routière** and the bus terminal for *Autoplus*, the town's efficient **public transport** system, are located. There is another local bus terminal at 44 cours des Dames. The town's other attractions, including an aquarium and an alternative beach, are just under 2km southwest at Les Minimes, reached by bus #10 from place Verdun or by the more entertaining *bus de mer*, a small boat which

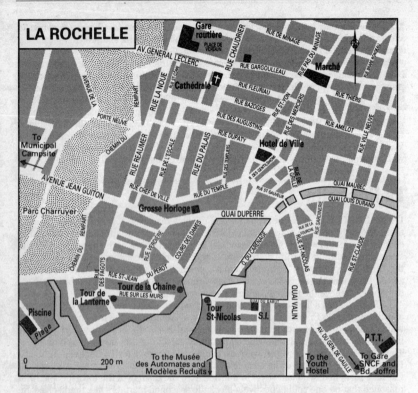

runs from the old port to Port des Minimes, stopping off at av Marillac en route (Sat & Sun hourly 10am–6pm; July & Aug half-hourly 10am–11pm, except 1pm; April–Sept hourly 10am–7pm except 1pm; scheduled timetable is often disrupted, so don't depend on it; 10F one-way). *Interîles* has guided day trips from La Rochelle to the Île d'Oléron (July–Sept 9.30am–8.15pm; 175F doesn't include lunch; ☎46.50.51.88). The **CDIJ Youth Centre**, 14 rue des Gentilshommes, has an information service, including *Allostop*, for young people.

Accommodation in La Rochelle can be a bit of a problem in the summer season, so book ahead, even if you're camping. Expect to pay seaside-type prices in the hotels, especially in season. A useful alternative to hotels are self-catering apartments which abound, particularly around Les Minimes and its *Village Informatique*. The tourist office has a handy board of rented accommodation, and is able to reserve rooms for a 10F fee (see above). There's a handful of cheapies in the town centre, but be sure to book in advance from May until well into autumn.

Hotels

L'Atlantic, 23 rue Verdière, off cours des Dames (☎46.41.16.68). Eighteenth-century ivy-clad affair with some studio apartments behind the waterfront. ④.

De Bordeaux, 43 rue St-Nicholas (☎46.41.31.22). Comfortable, friendly hotel, nicely situated between the train station and the port in a characterful pedestrianized street. ①–②.

Les Estuvales, Village Informatique, Les Minimes (☎46.45.12.34). A short walk along the seafront parkland to the beach of Les Minimes, these small modern self-catering apartments – normally occupied by university students during term-time – are good value. Minimum one week rent (week-end to weekend); deposit (100F) and own bed linen required. From 1200F per week.

Fasthotel, Village Informatique, Les Minimes (☎46.45.46.00). Small, quiet hotel made up of modern bungalows, near the port des Minimes and the beach. ②.

Hôtel de France-Angleterre et Champlain, 20 rue Rambaud (☎46.41.23.99). The old, venerable half is *Le Champlain*; and the new Great Western addition is the *Hôtel de France-Angleterre*; both what you'd expect from a modern and an old-fashioned three-star; close to the extensive park-lands. ④.

Hôtel François-I, 15 rue Bazoges (☎46.41.28.46). Historic building with a walled courtyard. ②–⑤.

Hôtel Henri-IV, 31 rue des Gentilshommes (☎46.41.25.79). Excellent and very popular hotel right in the town centre. If you haven't booked don't bother trying to get in. ①–②.

De l'Océan, 36 cours des Dames (☎46.41.31.97). Comfortable two-star air-conditioned rooms in an enviable position, many with views of the port. ④.

Le Printania, 9 rue Brave-Rondeau (☎46.41.22.86). Pleasant, unpretentious and central place in a peaceful street. ①–③.

Hôtel St-Nicolas, 13 rue Sardinerie (☎46.41.71.55). Nice, old, colonnade-fronted two-star stone hotel in a great central location right opposite pleasant rue de la Fourche. ④.

Youth hostels and campsites

IYHF youth hostel, av des Minimes (☎46.44.43.11). A good budget choice. If you feel like walking follow the signs left as you come out of the *gare SNCF*; otherwise take bus #10 from place de Verdun. ①.

Camping Municipal de Port-Neuf, on the northwest side of town. Take bus #6 from Grosse Horloge, direction *Port-Neuf*.

Camping Le Soleil, Port des Minimes (☎46.44.42.53). Near to the hostel. Take bus #10 from place Verdun to Les Minimes. May–Sept.

Getting around

Once you've stowed your luggage, you can use **bikes** to get around: on quai du Carénage, facing restaurant-lined cour des Dames across the Vieux Port, is the free municipal **bike park**, part of the *Autoplus* system and heir to Michel Crépeau's original no-identity-check, no restrictions, pick-up-and-leave scheme: you get two hours of free bike time after handing over a piece of ID; after this it's a generous 6F per hour (office open daily 9am–12.30pm & 1.30–7pm). You can also rent bikes from the *gare SNCF*, from M. Salaün-Benard, 3 place de la Solette on the left bank of the canal, from *Dock Moto*, bd Émile-Delmas near the bridge to the Île de Ré, and from *Vel'Oxygène*, 29 bd de la République (☎46.56.07.58). **Car rental** is available from *Ada/Budget*, 1 av de Gaulle; *Citer Sorda*, 99 bd Cognehors; *Locarwest*, 14 quai Georgette; or *Tonic Car*, 16 quai Georges-Simenon. *Autoplus* also have a nifty **taxi system** with flat rates between any two of 46 "bornes" – terminal posts with a card-activated calling system, operating 24 hours. You can buy the cards and find out the inexpensive going rate at *Boutique Autoplus*, 5 rue de l'Aimable-Nanette, near the tourist office (Mon–Fri 9am–noon & 2–6pm, Sat 9am–noon). **Boat trips** around La Rochelle and to neighbouring islands are organized by *Océcars*, 14 cours des Dames (☎46.41.78.95).

The Town

The **Vieux Port** is very much the focus of the town, with pleasure boats bobbing in front of the two sturdy towers guarding the entrance to the port. Leading north from the Porte de la Grosse Horloge, the **rue du Palais** runs towards the cathedral and several of the museums on rue Thiers. Between the harbour and the **Port des Minimes**, a new marina development 2km south of the town centre, there are several excellent museums for children and a large frigate permanently moored providing some insight into the town's seagoing past.

The Vieux Port

Dominating the inner harbour, the heavy Gothic gateway of the **Porte de la Grosse Horloge** straddles the entrance to the old town. The quays in front are too full of traffic to encourage loitering; for that, it's best to head out along the tree-lined cours des Dames towards the fourteenth-century **Tour de la Chaine** (daily 10am–noon & 2–6.30pm; mid-Feb to mid-March 2–6pm; 20F), so called because of the heavy chain that was slung from here across to the opposite tower, **Tour St-Nicholas**, to close the harbour at night. Today the only night-time intruders are likely to be yachties from across the Channel, whose craft far outnumber the working boats – mainly garishly painted trawlers. Beyond the tower, steps climb up to **rue Sur-les-Murs**, which follows the top of the old sea wall to a third tower, the **Tour de la Lanterne** or Tour des Quatre Sergents, named after four sergeants imprisoned and executed for defying the Restoration monarchy in 1822 (daily except Tues 9.30am–12.30pm & 2–5pm; June–Aug daily 9.30am–7pm; April, May & Sept daily except Tues 9.30am–12.30pm & 2–6.30pm; 20F). There's a way up onto what's left of the **city walls**, planted with unkempt greenery. Beyond is the beach, backed by casino, hot dog stands and amusement booths, along with an extensive, truly beautiful belt of park that continues up the western edge of the town centre.

The rue du Palais and around

The real charm of La Rochelle lies on the city's main shopping street, **rue du Palais**, leading up from the Vieux Port. Lining the street are eighteenth-century houses, some grey stone, some half-timbered with distinctive Rochelais-style slates overlapped like fish scales, while the shop fronts are set back beneath the ground-floor arcades. Among the finest are the **Hôtel de la Bourse** – actually the Chamber of Commerce – and the **Palais de Justice** with its colonnaded façade, both on the left-hand side. A few metres further on, in **rue des Augustins**, there is another grandiose affair built for a wealthy Rochelais in 1555, the so-called **Maison Henri II**, complete with loggia, gallery and slated turrets, where the regional tourist board has its offices. Place de Verdun itself is dull and characterless, with an uninspiring, humpbacked eighteenth-century classical **cathedral** on the corner. Its only redeeming feature is the marvellously opulent Belle-Époque **Café de la Paix**, all mirrors, gilt and plush, where La Rochelle's ladies of means come to sip lemon tea and nibble daintily at sticky cakes. And there is a tempting *charcuterie* and seafood shop next door.

To the west or left of rue du Palais, especially in **rue de l'Escale**, paved with granite setts brought back from Canada as ballast in the Rochelais cargo vessels, you get the discreet residences of the eighteenth-century shipowners and chandlers, veiling their wealth with high walls and classical restraint. A rather less modest gentleman had installed himself on the corner of **rue Fromentin**: a seventeenth-century doctor who adorned his house-front with the statues of famous medical men – Hippocrates, Galen and others. In rue St-Côme closer to the town walls is the **Musée d'Orbigny-Bernon** (Mon & Wed–Sat 10am–noon & 2–6pm; Sun 2–6pm; 16F), consisting mainly of exhibits of local ceramics.

LA ROCHELLE'S MUSEUMS

If you intend to get around a number of La Rochelle's excellent **museums**, a 37F ticket covers the Nouveau Monde, the Orbigny-Bernon and the Beaux-Arts, as well as two more not listed here – the Histoire Naturelle and the Musée Océanographique.

East of rue du Palais, and also starting out from place des Petits-Bancs, rue du Temple takes you up alongside the **Hôtel de Ville**, protected by a decorative but seriously fortified wall. It was begun around 1600 in the reign of Henri IV, whose initials, intertwined with those of Marie de Médicis, are carved on the ground-floor gallery. It's a beautiful specimen of Frenchified Italian taste, adorned with niches and statues and coffered ceilings, all done in a stone the colour of ripe barley. And if you feel like quiet contemplation of these seemingly more gracious times, there's no better place for it than the terrace of the *Café de la Poste*, right next to the post office, in the small, traffic-free square outside. For more relaxed vernacular architecture nearly as ancient, carry on up rue des Merciers, the other main shopping area, to the cramped and noisy **market square**, close to which you'll find the **Musée du Nouveau Monde** (Mon & Wed–Sat 10.30am–12.30pm & 1.30–6pm; Sun 3–6pm; 16F), whose entrance is in rue Fleuriau. Out of the ordinary, this museum occupies the former residence of the Fleuriau family, rich shipowners and traders who, like many of their fellow-Rochelais, made fortunes out of the slave trade and Caribbean sugar, spices and coffee. There is a fine collection of prints, paintings and photos of the old West Indian plantations; seventeenth- and eighteenth-century maps of America; photogravures of Native Americans from around 1900, with incredible names like Piopio Maksmaks Wallawalla and Lawyer Nez Percé; and an interesting display of aquatint illustrations for Marmontel's novel *Les Incas* – an amazing mixture of sentimentality and coy salaciousness. Nearby in rue Gargoulleau is the **Musée des Beaux-Arts** (daily except Tues 2–5pm; winter till 5pm; 16F), whose works are centred around a few Rochelais artists and illustrate the history of art from the Primitives to the present day.

Back towards the port, from the maze of pedestrianized streets around the Hôtel de Ville, head down rue St-Sauveur, with its large gloomy church, across quai Maubec and quai Louis-Duard to **rue St-Nicholas** and adjoining **rue de la Fourche** – more like a square with its huge shady tree and outdoor café – both pedestrianized and boasting several antiques dealers, secondhand bookshops and a vintage clothes shop. The two streets share a Saturday flea/antiques market.

Towards Port des Minimes

Heading south across the entrance to the port from the Tour St-Nicholas are a couple of excellent museums. You first come to the **Musée Maritime**, housed in the *France I* (daily 10am–6.30pm; 38F), a frigate moored permanently in the Bassin des Chalutiers and kitted out to give you some idea of the realities of ocean life, with cabins, galleys and decks to explore as well as a few informative exhibitions. A ten-minute walk southwest brings you to the **Musée des Automates** on rue de la Désirée (daily 10am–noon & 2–6pm; June–Aug 9.30am–7pm; 35F, under-10s 20F), a fascinating collection of three hundred automated puppets, drawing you into an irresistible fantasy world. Some of the puppets are interesting from an historical angle; others, like one that writes the name "Pierrot", are interesting from a mechanical viewpoint. Further down the same street is the **Musée des Modèles Réduits** (same hours & prices as the Automates, joint ticket for both museums 60F, under-10s 25F). The prices may be a bit prohibitive for families – especially considering the whole tour takes barely half an hour – but this does combine well with a visit to the neighbouring Musée des Automates. Scale models of every variety and era are on show, starting in typical French fashion with cars and including models of a submerged shipwreck and La Rochelle train station.

The **Port des Minimes** is about 2km southwest of the *vieux port*, forming a modern development around a large sheltered yachting harbour, where little white boats cluster on the still waters. Close to the water's edge, the high-tech **Aquarium** (daily 10am–noon & 2–7pm; May & June 9am–7pm; July & Aug 9am–11pm; 39F) is one of France's biggest, with species from around the world.

Eating, drinking and nightlife

For **eating**, try the rue du Port/rue St-Sauveur area just off the waterfront, or else rue St-Nicolas-du-Pérot or rue St-Jean (which has everything from *crêperies* and pizzerias to expensive gourmet restaurants and several ethnic eateries including Indian and Chinese places); particularly worth seeking out are the town's many excellent **fish restaurants** or the fish dishes that dominate most restaurant menus.

Restaurant le Bistrot de l'Entr'acte, 22 rue St-Jean-du Pérot (☎46.50.62.60). Expensive posh place with turn-of-the-century decor, little table lamps and a mainly fish and seafood *carte* of some originality; people rave about the 145F menu. Closed Sun.

A Côté de Chez Fred, rue St-Nicholas (☎46.41.07.03). A characterful corner restaurant with all sorts of charming fishing and seafaring paraphernalia, not crossing the fine line to tackiness. A blackboard *carte* changes depending on what's in next door at the *Poissonerie Chez Fred*. Guaranteed to be super fresh and mouthwatering. Small and very popular so best to book. From 39F entrée to 112F main. Closed Sun.

Pub Lutèce, rue St-Sauveur. Reasonably priced brasserie with outdoor tables.

La Marie-Galante, 35 av des Minimes (☎46.44.05.54). Pretty yellow-and-white striped awnings over the outdoor seating facing the yachts in this peaceful stretch. Fish of the day 50F; fresh fish its speciality, generous menus from 75F.

Molly's Lone Star Restaurant, 20 rue Verdière, opposite the *Atlantic Hotel*. American Tex-Mex style food – well-priced – in generic ranch surrounds. Daily noon–1am.

Les Pyramides, 59 rue St-Jean-du-Pérot. Serves a mixture of expensive Egyptian and Greek food in bright, pleasant surroundings.

Le St-Sauveur, 24 rue St-Sauveur (☎46.41.18.16). Opposite the cathedral, an unpretentious restaurant with good fish dishes (68–98F *à la carte*), particularly the fish soup entrée; good for families, with a fish tank filled with tropical types providing some entertainment for bored children. Menus 68F, 98F and 128F. Closed Sun & Mon night.

Teatro Bettini, 3 rue Thiers (☎46.41.07.03). Crowded noisy pizzeria (46–50F pizzas, many with delicious seafood toppings) with upbeat pink decor. Air-conditioning and gelati to beat the heat. Also pasta (35–48F) and fish. Closed Sun & Mon lunchtimes.

Café-Resto à la Villette, 4 rue de la Forme, behind the market. Tiny, authentic place popular with locals; good *plats du jour*. Closed Mon.

Bars and nightlife

Popular daytime **bars** to hang out at here include the dark and down-to-earth wine bar *Cave de la Guignette*; or for groovy, beautiful types, the outdoor tables of *Cave St Nicholas* and *Café de Solette*, around the corner on shady rue de la Fourche.

To find out what's going on where **nightlife** is concerned, pick up the three-weekly *Sortir* from the tourist office, with theatre, cinema, and mainstream and classical music listings. Otherwise, head for the *Fun House* at 33 rue St-Nicholas for rock/alternative **live music**; the street itself is also promising for nightlife and bars. Bands play in *Bar Sawasdee Rhumerie* at no. 27, while a good **late-night bar** opposite, at no. 26, is *L'Eden* (daily from 3pm). An older crowd heads for rue des Templiers, with its two **music bars**: the *Piano Pub* and the *Mayflower*. **Nightclubs** worth checking out include *L'Oxford*, plage de la Concurrence, and *Le Triolet*, 8 rue des Carmes.

The Île de Ré

A half-hour drive from La Rochelle, the **Île de Ré** is a low, narrow island some 30km long, fringed by sandy beaches to the southwest and salt marshes and oyster beds to the northeast, with the interior a motley mix of small-scale vine, asparagus and wheat cultivation. All the buildings on Ré are restricted to two storeys and are required to incorporate the typical local features of whitewashed walls, curly orange tiles and green-painted shutters, which give the island villages a southerly holiday atmosphere.

Out of season the island has a slow, misty charm, and life in its little ports revolves exclusively around the cultivation of oysters and mussels. In season, though, it's extraordinarily crowded, with upwards of 400,000 visitors passing through. The crowds mainly head for the southern beaches; those to the northeast are covered in rocks and seaweed, and the sea is too shallow for bathing.

The island is connected to the mainland at **LA PALLICE**, a suburb of La Rochelle, by a three-kilometre-long toll bridge constructed in 1988 (110F round trip per car). La Pallice was once a big commercial port with important shipyards, and although it still serves as a naval base, times have changed. As you drive past, you'll notice some colossal weather-stained concrete sheds, submarine pens built by the Germans to service their Atlantic U-boat fleet during World War II. Too difficult to demolish, they are still in use. As an alternative to the toll bridge connection, *Interîles*, 14 cours des Dames, La Rochelle, also run a bus and boat service to **SABLONCEAUX** on Ré (49–59F return), and combine trips to the Îles de Ré and Oléron (see p.515).

ST-MARTIN, the island's capital, is an atmospheric north-coast fishing port with whitewashed houses clustered around the stone quays of a well-protected harbour, from where trawlers and flat-bottomed oyster boats, piled high with cage-like devices used for "growing" oysters, slip out every morning on the muddy tide.

The quayside *Café Boucquingam* recalls the military adventures of the Duke of Buckingham, who attacked the island unsuccessfully in the mid-seventeenth century. To the east of the harbour, you can walk along the almost perfectly preserved **fortifications** – redesigned by Vauban in the late seventeenth century after Buckingham's attentions – to the citadel, long used as a prison. It was from here that the *bagnards* – prisoners sentenced to hard labour on Devil's Island in Guyana or New Caledonia in the Pacific – set out. Most did not return. One who eventually did was the notorious Papillon.

Practicalities

Rébus runs **bus** services all over the island from La Rochelle, leaving from place Verdun via the train station every hour; crossing to Sablonceaux just across the bridge costs 10F. For frequent travelling, ten trip cards are better value: La Rochelle–Sablonceaux costs 72F, La Rochelle–St-Martin 195F, anywhere on the island–La Rochelle 230F, but the timetable can be awkward if you want to tour the island.

The alternative is to rent a **bike** from the Sablonceaux bus depot or from *Cyclo-Surf Location*, 14 rue Henri-Lainé in seaside La Flotte between Sablonceaux and St-Martin; *Clos Vauban*, av V-Bouthillier in St-Martin; and 2 rte Joachim in La Couarde on the southern side of the island.

Hotels are plentiful in all the island's villages, though obviously packed to the gills through July and August. Most reasonably priced are the one-star *Le Sénéchal*, 6 rue Gambetta in Ars-en-Ré, on the other side of the island on a protected bay (☎46.29.40.42; ②–④); *L'Océan*, 4 rue St-Martin in Le-Bois-Plage (☎46.09.23.07; ③–④); and in La Flotte, the *L'Hippocampe*, 16 rue du Château-des-Mauléons (☎46.09.60.68; ①–③), and *Le Français*, 1 quai de Sénac (☎46.09.60.06; ③–⑤; closed mid-Nov to mid-March).

There are even more **campsites** on the island than there are hotels, and it shouldn't be difficult finding a place, except perhaps in desirable locations near the southern beaches at the height of the rush. A few names, if you want to book ahead, are the *Camping du Soleil* in Ars-en-Ré (☎46.29.40.62); *L'Île Blanche* in La Flotte (☎46.09.52.43); and *L'Océan*, La Passe in La Couarde (☎46.29.87.70; Easter–Sept).

Good-value **food** is available on the quayside in St-Martin at *Les Remparts*, 4 quai Daniel-Rivaille, which has a piano bar upstairs. *La Salicorne*, 16 rue de l'Olivette in La Couarde (☎46.29.82.37), has a high standard of cuisine starting at 90F for lunchtime menus, as does *Le Bistrot de Bernard*, 23 rue de l'Église in Le Bois-Plage.

Rochefort and around

ROCHEFORT dates from the seventeenth century. It was created by Colbert, Louis XIII's navy minister, as a naval base to protect the coast from English raids. Built on a grid plan with regular ranks of identical houses, the town may be a joy to the military mind or to a new town planner, but if you're looking for hidden back alleyways or irregular architecture you'll be disappointed. The seventeenth-century warehouse buildings and old arsenal are unrestored and cannot be visited, although there are still a couple of sights worth making a special effort for.

Many of the towns along the pretty surrounding coastline are served by the Aunis and Saintonge buses, although you will find the simplest solution to travelling along this whole section of coast is renting a car or even cycling. Unless you have your own transport, Rochefort is a useless base for nearby Royan or the Île d'Oléron. Bus times are inconvenient and buses to Oléron generally involve a wait at Boucrefranc.

Arrival and accommodation

Should you want to stay, hotels need to be booked in advance to ensure reasonably priced accommodation. The efficient **tourist office** will reserve rooms for a charge of 15F (Mon–Sat 9am–8pm; mid-Sept to mid-June 9am–12.30pm & 2–6.30pm; ☎46.99.08.60) and is on av Sadi-Carnot off rue du Dr-Pelletier, two blocks north of the **gare routière**.

The cheapest **hotel** rooms in town are at *Les Messageries* on place de la Gare (☎46.99.00.90; ①). The *Hôtel de France*, 55 rue du Dr-Pelletier (☎46.99.34.00; ①–②) – left out of the *gare routière* – also has some cheap but dingy rooms, while a better bet is the extremely comfortable and friendly two-star *Caravelle*, 34 rue Jaurès, off av C-de-Gaulle (☎46.99.02.53; ①–④), which leads to the naval museum from directly opposite the *gare routière*, or the central but old-fashioned *Colbert*, 23 rue A-de-Puyravault (☎46.99.08.28; ①–③), left out of the *gare routière* and third right, opposite the post office. More upmarket choices include the two-star *Hôtel Roca Fortis*, 14 rue de la République (☎46.99.26.32; ②), an old hotel with typical shuttered windows, with some rooms overlooking a garden. *Hôtel des Vermandois*, 33 rue Émile-Combes, next door to the Loti Museum (☎46.87.09.87; ③), is another oldie but with modern fittings: one room is accessible for the handicapped, and several are family studios. *La Corderie Royale* on rue Audebert (☎46.99.35.35; ⑥) is the town's poshest place to stay: a three-star within the seventeenth-century ropeworks.

For budget accommodation there's a small, modern IYHF **youth hostel**, centrally located for once at 20 rue de la République (☎46.99.74.62; ①). The **camping municipal** (☎46.99.14.33) is a long haul if you've arrived at the *gare SNCF*: take av du Président-Wilson and keep going straight, until you reach the bottom of rue Toufaire, where you turn right, then left – about half an hour all the way.

The Town

If you have a taste for the bizarre, then there's one good reason for visiting Rochefort – the house of the novelist Julien Viaud, alias Pierre Loti. Forty years a naval officer, he wrote numerous best-selling romances with exotic oriental settings and characters, and revealed his immense vanity by refusing to marry any woman taller than himself. The **Maison de Loti** at 141 rue Pierre-Loti (guided tours: July–Sept Mon–Sat 10 & 11am, 2, 3, 4 & 5pm; Sun 2, 3, 4 & 5pm; Oct–Jun Mon–Sat; closed Dec 20–Jan 20; 40F) is part of a row of modestly proportioned grey stone houses, outwardly a model of petit-bourgeois conformity and respectability, inside an outrageous and fantastical series of rooms decorated to exotic themes. There's a medieval banqueting hall complete with Gothic fireplace and Gobelin tapestries, a monastery refectory with windows pinched from a ruined abbey, a Damascus mosque; a Turkish room, with kilim wall-hangings and a ceiling made from an Alhambra mould. To suit the mood of the place, Loti used to throw extravagant parties: a medieval banquet with swan's meat and hedgehog and a *fête chinoise* with the guests in costumes he had brought back from China, where he took part in the suppression of the Boxer rebellion.

A possible rainy hour's worth of museum is the **Centre International de la Mer** (daily 9am–6/7pm; July & Aug 9am–8pm; 25F, guided tours 30F) situated in the Corderie Royale, or the royal ropeworks, off rue Toufaire. At 372 metres, the Corderie is the longest building in France and a rare example of seventeenth-century industrial architecture, substantially restored after damage in World War II. From 1660 until the Revolution, it furnished the entire French navy with rope, and the building now houses an appropriate exhibition on ropes and rope-making, including machinery from the nineteenth century. If you don't fancy visiting the museum, it's definitely worth a wander around the extensive building and its lawns along the River Charente. If you're desperate to find out more about the town's history and naval importance, head for the diverting enough **Musée d'Art et d'Histoire**, 63 av Charles-de-Gaulle (Tues–Sat 1.30–5.30pm; July & Aug daily 1.30–7pm; 10F).

Lastly, in the seventeenth-century Hôtel de Cheusses, the **Musée de la Marine** on place de la Gallossinnière (daily except Tues mid-Nov to mid-Oct 10am–noon & 2–6pm; 25F) houses an excellent collection of model ships, figureheads, navigational instruments and other naval paraphernalia.

Eating and drinking

For inexpensive **meals**, try *Le Gallion*, a self-service restaurant by the arsenal on rue Toufaire, and there's a more than adequate Vietnamese/Chinese, *L'Asie*, at 45 rue Toufaire. Probably the best restaurant in Rochefort is *Le Tourne-Broche*, 56 av Charles-de-Gaulle (☎46.99.20.19; closed Sun night), with the freshest of ingredients and stylish service; *dégustation* menu 150F, lunchtime express 90F. For an excellent morning *café crème*, try the down-to-earth local bar *La Civette*, just off place Colbert on rue de la République; there's a very pleasant **salon de thé**, *La Tartelière*, at 55 av Charles-de-Gaulle, which serves affordable Antillaise snacks. *Le Comptoir des Îles* on place Colbert serves good **beer**, and you can finish the evening playing billiards, snooker or pool around the corner at *Le Roller*, 48 rue de la République.

Fouras and the Île d'Aix

FOURAS, some 30km south of La Rochelle, is the embarkation point for the tiny Île d'Aix (see below), where Napoléon spent his last days in Europe. It's a dull town, redeemed only by a clutch of popular beaches and the *presqu'île*, the peninsula that extends three kilometres out to sea from the town centre, terminating at the ferry dock, **Pointe de la Fumée**. The peninsula is bordered by oyster beds, and off its westernmost tip at low tide can be seen the *bouchots à moules*, lines of mussel-encrusted stumps. At high tide this is a popular place to fish for *crevettes* – shrimp. The finger of land is hemmed by sea-dashed fortresses – originally intended to protect the Charente, and particularly La Rochelle, against Norman attack – which were later employed against Dutch invasions in the seventeenth century and English ones in the eighteenth. The seventeenth-century **Fort Vauban** (mid-June to mid-Sept Tues & Fri 9.30am–noon) now houses a small, uninspiring, local maritime museum, but its esplanade offers a magnificent panorama of neighbouring forts and islands.

Fouras' **tourist office** is situated in the Fort Vauban (mid-June to mid-Sept Tues & Fri 9.30am–noon). As for places to **stay**, Fouras has a posse of overpriced hotels, the exception being an excellent establishment behind the *gare routière*, the *Hôtel Continental*, 9 av Lucien-Lamoureux (☎46.84.58.38; ②). There are also three **camp-sites** around the town: the *Fumée* (☎46.84.26.77) near the ferry port; the *L'Espérance* off av Philippe-Jannet (☎46.84.24.18); and the *Cadoret* near to plage Nord, on av du Cadoret (☎46.84.02.84). The best-value **food** in town is probably from *Restaurant La Jetée* at Pointe de la Fumée (☎46.84.60.43; closed Mon night, Wed out of season & Jan), serving excellent seafood at affordable prices (menus 90–140F).

Île d'Aix

Less frequented than the bigger islands, the Île d'Aix is small enough – just 2km long – to be walked around in about three hours, giving a greater sense of its island status than is felt on the Île de Ré. Access is by frequent ferry (half-hourly in season) from Pointe de la Fumée (☎46.41.76.24), or with *Interîles* from La Rochelle (May–Sept 2–4 daily).

The crescent-shaped island is well defended, with a pair of forts and ramparts around its southern tip. The island, and particularly **Fort Liédot**, served as a prison for members of the Paris Commune and later held Russian prisoners in the Crimean and First World wars. There's a **museum** (Thurs–Tues 10am–noon & 2–6pm; free) in the house constructed to Napoléon's orders and inhabited by him for a week in 1815 while he was planning his escape to America, only to find himself en route to St Helena and exile. Extensive displays fill ten rooms with the emperor's works of art, clothing, portraits and arms. The white dromedary from which he conducted his Egyptian campaign is lodged nearby in the **Musée Africain**, with its entire collection devoted to African wildlife (ring ☎46.84.66.09).

The only **hotel** on the island is the surprisingly named *Napoléon* on rue Gourgard (☎46.84.66.02; ③), and there's also a **campsite**, the *Fort de la Rade* (☎46.84.50.64).

Brouage and Marennes

Eighteen kilometres southwest of Rochefort, **BROUAGE** is another seventeenth-century military base, this time created by Richelieu after the siege of La Rochelle. It's surrounded by salt marshes, now reclaimed and transformed into meadows grazed by white Charolais cattle and intersected by dozens of reed-filled drainage ditches, where herons watch and yellow flag blooms. It's a strangely beautiful landscape with huge skies specked with wheeling buzzards and kestrels, and being flat as a pancake, it's good cycling and walking country. To reach the town from Rochefort, you cross the

---

OYSTERS

Marennes' speciality is fattening the **oysters** known as *creuses*. It's a lucrative but precarious business, extremely vulnerable to storm damage, changes of temperature or salinity in the water, the ravages of starfish and umpteen other improbable natural disasters.

Oysters begin life as minuscule larvae, which are "born" about three times a year. When a "birth" happens, the oystermen are alerted by a special radio service, and they all rush out to place their "collectors" – usually arrangements of roofing tiles – for the larvae to cling to. There the immature oysters remain for eight or nine months, after which they are scraped off and moved to *parcs* in the tidal waters of the sea: sometimes covered, sometimes uncovered. Their last move is to the *claires* – shallow rectangular pools where they are kept permanently covered by water less salty than normal sea water. Here they fatten up and acquire the greenish colour the market expects. With "improved" modern oysters, the whole cycle takes about two years, as opposed to four or five with the old varieties.

Charente on the D733 near the disused **Pont Transbordeur**, a great iron gantry with a raft-like platform suspended on hawsers, on which a dozen cars were loaded and floated across the river – a technological wonder in its time. From there, either turn right for Soubise and Moëze or go on to St-Agnant.

The way into Brouage is through the **Porte Royale** in the north wall of the totally intact fortifications dating from the mid-seventeenth century. Locked within its 400m square, the town now seems abandoned and somnolent; even the sea has retreated, and all that's left of the harbour are the partly freshwater pools, or *claires*, where oysters are fattened in the last stage of their rearing.

Within the walls, the streets are laid out on a grid pattern, lined with low two-storey houses. On the second cross street to the right is a **memorial** to Samuel de Champlain, the local boy who founded the French colony of Québec in 1608. In the same century, Brouage witnessed the last painful pangs of a royal romance: here, Cardinal Mazarin, successor to Richelieu, locked up his daughter, Marie Mancini, to keep her from her youthful sweetheart, Louis XIV. Geopolitics of the time made the Infanta of Spain a more suitable consort for the King of France than his daughter – in his own judgement. Louis gave in, while Marie pined and sighed on the walls of Brouage. Returning from his marriage in St-Jean-de-Luz, Louis dodged his escort and stole away to see her. Finding her gone, he slept in her room and paced the walls in her footsteps.

Half a dozen kilometres south, on a narrow, drier spit of land, past the graceful eighteenth-century **Château de la Gataudière** (not open to the public) – built by the man who introduced rubber to France – you come to the village of **MARENNES**. This is the centre of oyster production for an area that supplies over sixty percent of France's requirements. If you want to visit the oyster beds and see how the business works, you can do so here; just ask at the **tourist office** on place Chasseloup-Laubat (☎46.85.04.36) or out of season at the *mairie*, 6 rue Foch (☎46.85.25.55).

For **accommodation** in Marennes, there's the inexpensive *Hôtel de France* at 8 rue de la République (☎46.85.00.37; ①), with a restaurant where you can eat generously and well; and a **youth hostel** (☎46.85.22.78; ①; July & Aug only) catering for diehard budgeters.

The Île d'Oléron

The **Île d'Oléron** is France's largest island after Corsica and a favourite of day-trippers and families in the summer months for its beautiful sandy beaches. It's up the road from Marennes, joined to the mainland by a toll bridge (44F round trip). Buses from Rochefort are awkward, with irritating changes at Saintes or Boucrefranc, and it's easier to go direct from Saintes on one of the several daily *Citram* buses that stop at all the main towns on the island; alternatively, take one of *Interîles*' guided daytrips from La Rochelle (see p.506).

Flat and more wooded than the Île de Ré, Oléron has plenty of greenery, with the extensive pine-studded **Forêt des Saumonards** in the northeast of the island; here you can eyeball a dazzling panorama of the surrounding *parcs à huitres* and the mighty **Fort Boyard** stranded in the midst of sea between Oléron and the Île d'Aix to the northeast. At the island's southern tip, the larger **Forêt de St-Trojan** creeps up the western coast along **La Grande Plage**, a popular spot but far enough from the main towns. The island interior is pretty and distinctive. Waterways wind right into the land, their gleaming muddy banks overhung by round fishing nets suspended from ranks of piers. There are so many oyster *claires* that, from above, the island must look like an Afghan mirrored cushion, and the stretch from Boyardville to St-Pierre – with its pines, tamarisks and woods of evergreen oak – is the most attractive.

The island's most interesting attraction is off the D126 between St-Pierre and Dolus, right in the middle of the island. The bird park of **Le Marais aux Oiseaux** (Sun

10am–8pm; June–Aug daily 10am–8pm; Sept, April & May daily 10am–noon & 2pm–dusk; 35F) was originally established as a hospital for injured birds found in the wild, but is now a breeding centre with many examples of rare or endangered species. From 300 to 400 species of birds are given the freedom of twenty hectares of beautiful countryside, while sixty species are caged for observation alongside public walkways.

Most of the little towns on the island, inevitably, have been ruined by the development of hundreds of holiday homes – and it can be a real battle in the summer season to find a place to stay. There are a few places that still retain some amount of charm, not least of which is the main town in the south of the island, **LE CHÂTEAU**, named after the **citadel** that still stands, along with some seventeenth-century **fortifications**; the town thrives on its traditional oyster farming and boat building, and there's a lively **market** in place de la République every morning. The chief town in the north – and most picturesque of the island's settlements – is **ST-PIERRE**, whose market square has an unusual thirteenth-century **monument**, or *lanterne aux morts*. A few kilometres to the northeast, **BOYARDVILLE** has no interest except for the ranks of *bouchots* – stakes for growing mussels – along the shore. It's tempting to help yourself, but these are private property and you'll be in trouble if someone sees you; instead, head to the major attraction around here: the superb stretch of sandy beach at **LA BRÉE-LES-BAINS**. Halfway down the west coast is the pretty fishing port of **LA COTINIÈRE**, with a daily morning fish market (except Sunday), *Criée aux poissons*, where the fishermen traditionally cry out their wares.

Practicalities

The **tourist office** is on place de la République in Le Château (Tues–Sat 10am–noon & 2.30–6pm; June–Aug Mon–Sat 9am–12.30pm & 2.30–7pm, Sun 10am–noon; ☎46.47.60.51), also the location of a couple of affordable restaurants. St-Pierre's **tourist office** is on place Gambetta (Tues–Sat 9.15am–12.30pm & 2–6pm; June–Aug daily 9.15am–12.30pm & 2–7.30pm; ☎46.47.11.39); **bikes** are available in St-Pierre from *Lespagnol*, rue de la République, and from *Lacellerie Michel*, rue Maréchal-Foch.

Inexpensive **accommodation** on the Île d'Oléron can be had at *Les Tamaris* in the port of St-Denis (☎46.47.86.04; ①; closed Oct to mid-March), and at the *Hôtel de la Petite Plage à Domino*, rue de l'Océan, St-Georges (☎46.76.52.28; ②). In the medium price range, *L'Albatross*, 11 bd du Dr-Pineau, St-Trojan-les-Bains (☎46.76.00.08; ③; closed mid-Nov to mid-Feb), is a quiet, comfortable two-star. There are **campsites** all over the island: at La Brée, where the best beaches are, there's *Pertuis d'Antioche* (☎46.47.92.00), 150m from the beach off the D273. Further down the east coast, *Signol* at Boyardville (☎46.47.01.22) is pleasantly sited near pine forests. If you want to stay a week or so, you could rent a **holiday apartment**, easy enough outside of July and August; ask for a list at any of the tourist offices, or contact the *Agence Centrale Oléronaise* (☎46.75.32.53).

Places to **eat** abound on the island, and St-Pierre has the greatest choice of restaurants and brasseries. One place worth mentioning is in La Cotinière: *L'Écailler*, 65 rue Port (☎46.47.10.31; closed Sun & Mon, mid-March to mid-April & Oct), for a slap-up, super-fresh seafood meal facing the port.

Royan and around

Before World War II, **ROYAN**, at the mouth of the Gironde, was a fashionable resort for the bourgeoisie. It is still popular – though no longer exclusive – and the modern town has lost its elegance to the dreary rationalism of 1950s town planning: broad boulevards, car parks, shopping centres, planned greenery. Ironically, the occasion for this planners' romp was provided by Allied bombing, an attempt to dislodge a large contingent of

German troops who had withdrawn into the area after the D-Day landings. But the **beaches** – the most elegant and fashionable of which is in the suburb of **Pontaillac** to the northwest – are beautiful: fine pale sand, meticulously harrowed and raked near town and wild, pine-backed and pounded by the Atlantic to the north.

There is one sight worth seeing in Royan – the 1950s **church of Notre-Dame**, designed by Gillet and Hébrard, in a tatty square behind the main waterfront. Though the concrete has weathered badly, the overall effect is dramatic and surprising. Tall V-sectioned columns give the outside the appearance of massive fluting, and a stepped roofline rises dramatically to culminate in a 65-metre belltower, like the prow of a giant vessel. The interior is even more striking. Using uncompromisingly modern materials and designs, the architects have succeeded in out-Gothicking Gothic. The stained glass panels, in each of which a different tone predominates, borrow their colours from the local seascapes – oyster, sea, mist and murk – before a sudden explosion of colour in the Christ-figure above the altar.

The most attractive area in Royan is around **boulevard Garnier**, which leads southeast from Rond-Point-de-la Poste along the beach and once housed Parisian high society in purpose-built, Belle Époque holiday villas. Some of these have survived, including **Le Rêve**, 58 bd Garnier, where Émile Zola lived and wrote; **Kosiki**, 100 av du Parc (running parallel to bd Garnier), a nineteenth-century folly of Japanese inspiration; and **Tanagra**, 34 av du Parc, whose façade is covered in sculptures and balconies.

Various **cruises** are organized from Royan in season, including one to the **Cordouan lighthouse**, first erected by the Black Prince and commanding the mouth of the Gironde River. There's a twenty-minute **ferry** crossing (one-way pedestrians 14F, cycles 14F, motorbikes 50F, cars 112F) to the headland on the other side of the Gironde, the **Pointe de Grave**, from where a **bicycle trail** and the **GR8** head down the coast through the pines and dunes to the bay of Arcachon (see p.541).

Practicalities

The **tourist office** (Mon–Sat 9am–12.30pm & 2–6pm; July & Aug Mon–Sat 9am–7pm, Sun 10am–1pm & 3–7pm; ☎46.05.04.74; free accommodation booking service) and **PTT** are close to the Rond-Point-de-la-Poste at the east end of the seafront; the **gare routière** and **gare SNCF** are in the nearby cours de l'Europe. You can rent **bikes** from the *gare SNCF*, M. Hay, 20 bd de Lattre-de-Tassigny near the train station, or *Cycl'Océan* at 23 & 37 cours de l'Europe; **car rental** is available from either *Europcar*, 13 pl du Dr-Gantier (☎46.05.20.88), or *Avis*, 78 av de Pontaillac (☎46.38.48.88).

Accommodation in Royan is expensive and in short supply in season, when your best bet is to camp up the coast to the north or visit for the day from Saintes or Rochefort. If you're booking ahead, try the *Nouvel Hôtel de la Plage*, 18 av de Cognac (☎46.39.00.18; ②), a cheapie at Pontaillac beach to the west of town; frequent Aunis and Saintonge buses run from the train station via place Charles-de-Gaulle. There's also the more comfortable and central two-star *Les Bluets*, 21 façade de Foncillon (☎46.38.51.79; ③), with sea or garden views; the *Hôtel de l'Hôtel de Ville*, 1 bd Aristide Briand (☎46.05.00.64; ①–②), also close to the beach; and *Hôtel de la Plage*, right amidst the action at 26–28 Front de Mer (☎46.05.10.27; ②–③). Finally, for those who want air-conditioning and beachfront balconies, the three-star *Family Golf Hotel*, 28 bd Frédéric Garnier (☎46.05.14.66; ⑤), fits the bill unless you're put off by its rather ugly 1950s exterior. Alternatively, 3km southeast of Royan, in **ST-GEORGES-DE-DIDONNE**, there's an excellent little hotel, the *Colinette*, 16 av de la Grande-Plage (☎46.05.15.75; ②), in pleasant surroundings 100m from the sea.

There are a number of **campsites** in the region and around Royan itself, including the *Clairefontaine* (☎46.39.08.11; June–Sept), a fairly pricey site at av Louise, allée des Peupliers in **PONTAILLAC**, and the municipal *La Triloterie* (☎46.05.26.91) off av d'Aquitaine – the road to Bordeaux.

Eating, drinking and nightlife

As for **food**, good-value menus are to be found at the huge, old-fashioned *Relais de la Mairie*, 1 rue du Chay, quite far from the centre off av de Pontaillac (☎46.39.03.15), and from *Les Filets Bleus*, near the cathedral at 14 rue Notre-Dame (☎46.05.74.00), specializing in seafood dishes and gourmet salads, with *plats du jour* from 55F and menus from 85F. The smart *Le Chalet*, 6 bd de la Grandière (☎46.05.04.90; closed Wed), serves imaginative seafood dishes reasonably cheaply and is crammed with French families on Sundays, when you'd be wise to book. Several **crêperies, pizzerias** and **snack bars** are situated on Front de Mer, the brassy strip leading from the tourist office to the beach and Port-de-Plaisance, with the *Crêperie de la Plage* at no. 40 recommended. The town's best-value bistro, though, is packed-out *Le Tiki*, on the beachfront right by the tourist office; it dishes out an above-average variety of *plats du jour* from 37F as well as fish, pizza and grills. Self-caterers can head for the large covered **market**, the Marché Central, at the end of bd A-Briand, open every day (except Mon out of season) but particularly crowded and lively on Wednesday and Sunday mornings.

Nightlife is fairly restricted considering the size of Royan: there's a disco, *Tropicana*, and a jazz bar at Plage de Pontaillac, and a piano bar, *Le Mylord*, and jazz bar, *Le Yachtman*, at Voûtes-de-Port.

Palmyre and Talmont

It's worth knowing about the **zoo park** in **PALMYRE** (daily 9am–noon & 2–6pm; April–Sept 9am–7pm; 55F), 10km northwest of Royan up the D25 coast road, especially if you're travelling with children, although its tacky advertising, with chimps dressed in human clothes, may put you off. Once you're inside, there are plenty of exotic species – from elephants and wild cats to gorrillas and monkeys – housed in spacious enclosures covering fourteen hectares. To reach it, there are buses all day from Royan's *gare routière* and the place de-Gaulle.

An ideal bicycle or picnic excursion just over an hour's ride from Royan is to **TALMONT**, 16km up the Gironde on the GR360, and apart from a few ups and downs through the woods outside Royan, it's all level terrain. The low-crouching village clusters about Talmont's twelfth-century **church of Ste-Radegonde**, standing at the edge of a cliff above the Gironde. With gabled transepts, a squat tower, an apse simply but elegantly decorated with blind arcading – all in weathered tawny stone and pocked like a sponge – it stands magnificently, in sun or cloud, against the forlorn browny-grey seascapes typical of the Gironde. The entrance is through the north transept, where the rings of carving in the arched doorway depict acrobats standing on each other's shoulders and, in the outer braid, two tug-of-war teams hauling roped lions up the arch. The inside is as unpretentiously beautiful as the exterior.

THE CHARENTE

It is hard to believe that the peaceful fertile valley of the **River Charente**, which has given its name to the two modern *départements* that cover much of this chapter, was once a busy industrial waterway, bringing armaments from **Angoulême** to the naval shipyards at **Rochefort**. Today peaceful, low ochre-coloured farms crown the valley slopes, with green swathes of vineyard sweeping up to the walls, and the graceful

PINEAU DES CHARENTES

Roadside signs throughout the Charente advertise **Pineau des Charentes**, a sweet liqueur that's a blending of grape juice stopped in its fermentation by adding cognac from the same vineyard. It's best drunk chilled as an apéritif; the locals also like it with oysters and love cooking with it. Favourite dishes include *moules au Pineau* (mussels cooked with tomatoes, Pineau, garlic and parsley) and *lapin à la saintongeaise* (rabbit casseroled with Pineau rosé, shallots, garlic, tomatoes, thyme and laurel).

turrets of minor châteaux – properties of wealthy cognac-producers – poke up from out of the woods. The towns and villages may look old-fashioned, but the prosperous shops and classy new villas are proof that where the grape grows, money and modernity are not far behind.

The **valley** itself is easy to travel as the main road and train lines to Limoges run this way. North and south, Poitiers, Périgueux (for the Dordogne) and Bordeaux are also easily reached by train. Otherwise, for cross-country journeys, you are heavily reliant on your own transport.

Saintes and around

SAINTES was formerly much more important than its present size suggests. Today a busy market for the surrounding region, it was capital of the old province of Saintonge and a major administrative and cultural centre in Roman times. It still retains some impressive remains from that period, as well as two beautiful Romanesque pilgrim churches and an attractive centre of narrow lanes and medieval houses. It also has the doubtful distinction of being the birthplace of Dr Guillotin, whose instrument of decapitation came into its own during the Revolution.

The Town

The abbey church, the **Abbaye-aux-Dames** (daily 10am–12.30pm & 2–7pm; Oct–May Mon, Tues, Thurs, Fri & Sun 2–7pm, Wed & Sat 2–7pm; 15F), is as quirky as Notre-Dame in Poitiers. It stands back from the street – rue St-Pallais – in a sanded courtyard behind the smaller Romanesque church of St-Pallais. An elaborately sculpted doorway masks a plain, broad interior space roofed with two big domes. Its rarest feature is a tower, flanked with pinnacles and by turns square, octagonal and lantern-shaped, capped with the Poitou pine cone. It was built in the eleventh century.

From here rue Arc-de-Triomphe brings you out on the river bank beside an imposing Roman arch – the **Arc de Germanicus** – which originally stood on the bridge until it was demolished in the mid-nineteenth century to make way for the modern crossing. The arch was dedicated to the emperor Tiberius, his son Drusus and nephew Germanicus in 19 AD. In a stone building next door is an **archeological museum** (daily except Tues 10am–noon & 2–6pm; winter Sun 10am–noon only; free) with a great many more Roman bits and pieces strewn about, mostly rescued from the fifth-century city walls into which they had been incorporated. This whole area comes alive on the first Monday of every month when a sprawling **market** extends from the abbey right through here and up most of av Gambetta.

A footbridge crosses from this point to the covered market on the west bank of the river and place du Marché at the foot of the rather uninspiring **Cathedral of St-Pierre**, which began life as a Romanesque church but was significantly altered in the aftermath of damage inflicted during the Wars of Religion, when Saintes was a Huguenot stronghold. Its enormous, heavily buttressed tower, capped by a hat-like

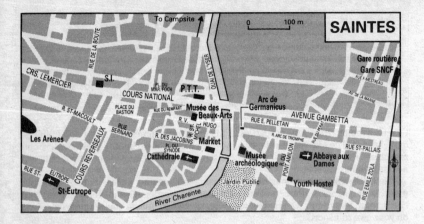

dome instead of the intended spire, is the town's chief landmark. In front, the lime trees of place du Synode stretch away to the municipal buildings, with the old quarter up to the right and the Hôtel Martineau library in the rue des Jacobins with an exquisite central courtyard full of trees and shrubs. Back towards the bridge, a seventeenth-century mansion on rue Victor-Hugo houses the **Musée des Beaux-Arts** (daily except Tues 10am–noon & 2–5/6pm; 10F), containing a collection of local pottery and some unexciting paintings.

Saintes' Roman heritage is best seen at **Les Arènes**, an amphitheatre whose ruins lie at the head of the valley, just a fifteen-minute walk from town (open reasonable hours; approach the concierge). The amphitheatre was dug into the end of the valley in the early first century, making it one of the oldest surviving. Although most of the seats are now grassed over, it is still an evocative spot, and you can easily picture the Roman population of Saintes – twice what it is today – turning out in its finery for a spectacle.

On the way back from the amphitheatre, it's no extra trouble to take in the eleventh-century **church of St-Eutrope**. The upper church, which lost its nave in 1803, has some brilliant capital-carving in the old choir, best seen from the gallery. But it's the crypt – entered from the street – which is more atmospheric and primitive: here massive pillars carved with stylized vegetation support the vaulting in semi-darkness, and there is a huge old font and the third-century tomb of Saintes' first bishop, Eutropius himself.

Practicalities

Saintes' **tourist office** is housed in grand old Villa Musso, 62 cours National (Mon–Sat 10am–noon & 2–6pm; June–Sept Mon–Sat 9am–7pm, Sun 10am–5pm; ☎46.74.23.82), and organizes **boat trips** to Cognac during the summer.

The **gare SNCF** is on av de la Marne at the east end of av Gambetta, with several **hotels** in the vicinity. The stylish *Hôtel de France* (☎46.93.01.16; ③) and the small, old-fashioned *Parisien* (☎46.74.28.92; ②) on this street are worth spending a bit extra on. One cheapie that you should look into is the *Té-Gé-Vé* (☎46.93.07.06; ①), actually a good snack bar at 45 av de la Marne with a few rooms above it. Another good choice off av Gambetta is the very friendly, family-run *Hôtel St-Pallais*, 1 pl St-Pallais (☎46.92.51.03; ①), in the courtyard of an abbey with a congenial bar downstairs: coming from the *gare SNCF* take rue du Perat to the left. More central is *Les*

Messageries in tiny rue des Messageries, off rue Victor-Hugo (☎46.93.64.99; ③). There's a bang up-to-date **youth hostel**, 6 rue Pont-Amilion (☎46.92.14.82; ①), just beyond St-Palais church. Over the river, a right turn (north) on the far bank leads to the **camping municipal** (☎46.93.08.00) on riverside rue de Courbiac.

For **eating**, there's a good restaurant, the *Petit Bidou*, by the river on place Blair, and a popular *crêperie* at 20 rue Victor-Hugo, off rue Alsace-Lorraine, the pedestrianized shopping street. *Le Jardin du Rempart*, 36 rue du Rempart, serves top-value menus from 65F, including salads, seafood and grills, while *Le Ciboulette*, 36 rue Pérat (☎46.74.07.36; closed Sun), serves lots of Charentais specialities at moderate prices. Out of town, the *Restaurant de la Charente* (☎46.11.00.73; closed Sun), 10km upstream at Chaniers, is the Sunday haunt of prosperous locals and makes a more expensive but fulfilling gastronomic experience.

Around Saintes

If you have a car, you could explore several of the marvellous Romanesque churches within easy reach of Saintes, notably the twelfth-century structure with a striking spire in **FENIOUX**, 29km to the north towards St-Jean-d'Angély, and the detailed façade of the church in **RIOUX**, 12km to the south. There is also the fine **Château of Roche-Courbon**, 18km northwest off the Rochefort road – once described as the Sleeping Beauty's castle – with some stylish interiors and gardens.

One place worth any amount of trouble to get to is the twelfth-century pilgrim **church of St-Pierre** at **AULNAY**, 37km northeast of Saintes, and sadly not served by public transport. Aulnay church's finest sculpture is on the west front, the south transept and apse, with some more fine work inside. On the building's main façade, two blind arches flank the central portal. The tympanum of the right depicts Christ in Majesty; the left, Saint Peter, crucified upside down with two extraordinarily lithe and graceful soldiers balancing on the arms of his cross to get a better swing at the nails in his feet. On the south side, the doorway is decorated with four bands of even more intricate carving. The apse, too, is a beauty, framed by five slender columns and lit by three perfectly arched windows, the centre one enclosed by figures wrapped in the finest twining foliage. Inside, there is more extraordinary carving: capitals depicting Delilah cutting Samson's hair, devils pulling a man's beard, human-eared elephants, bearing the Latin inscription *"Hi sunt elephantes"*, "These are elephants" – presumably for the edification of ignorant locals.

You might also like to visit **NUAILLÉ-SUR-BOUTONNE**, 9km west of Aulnay, which boasts another remarkable church; and even nearer, just down the D129 east of Aulnay, you can walk to **SALLES-LES-AULNAY** (20mins), or **ST-MANDÉ** (1hr), with humbler churches of the same period, each in its way as charming as that of Aulnay.

Cognac

Anyone who does not already know what **COGNAC** is about will quickly nose its quintessential air as they stroll about the medieval lanes of the town's riverside quarter. For here is the greatest concentration of *chais* or warehouses, where a high-quality brandy is matured, its fumes blackening the walls with tiny fungi. Cognac is cognac, from the tractor driver and pruning-knife wielder to the manufacturer of corks, bottles and cartons. Untouched by recession (80 percent of production is exported), it is likely to thrive as long as the world has sorrows to drown – a sunny, prosperous, respectable, self-satisfied little place.

The Town

Cognac has a number of medieval stone and half-timbered buildings in the narrow streets of the old town – rue Saulnier and rue de l'Îsle d'Or make atmospheric back-drops for a stroll, and picturesque **Grande-Rue** winds through the heart of the old quarter to the *chais*. On the right is all that remains of the **castle** where King François I was born in 1494.

To the left are the *chais* and offices of the **Hennessy Cognac Company** (Mon–Fri 9–11am & 2–5pm; free), a seventh-generation family firm and widely thought the best of the houses to visit. The first Hennessy, an officer in the Irish brigade serving with the French army, hailed from Ballymacnoy in County Cork and gave up soldiering in 1765 to set up a little business here. The Hennessy visit begins with a film explaining what's what in the world of cognac. Only an *eau de vie* distilled from grapes grown in a strictly defined area can be called cognac, and this stretches from the coast at La Rochelle and Royan to Angoulême. It is all carefully graded according to soil properties: chalk essentially. The inner circle, from which the finest cognac comes – Grand Champagne and Petit Champagne (not to be confused with bubbly) – lies mainly south of the River Charente.

Hennessy alone keep 180,000 barrels in stock. All are regularly checked and various *coupages* or blendings made from barrel to barrel, of which only the best are kept – depending on the well-honed tastebuds of the *maître du chais*. For six generations the job of *maître* has been in the same family; the present heir apparent has already been under his father's tutelage for sixteen years and is still not fully qualified.

Another important cog in the cognac mechanism is Europe's second biggest bottle-maker, the modern **St-Gobain glassworks**, which lies 2km south of town; guided tours of the trade can be arranged through the tourist office (see below).

Practicalities

From the **gare SNCF**, go down rue Mousnier, right on rue Bayard, past the **PTT**, up rue du 14-juillet to the central place François-I, dominated by an equestrian statue of the king rising from a bed of begonias. Close by is the **tourist office** at 16 rue 14-juillet (daily 9am–12.30pm & 2–6.15pm; July & Aug 9am–6.30pm; ☎45.82.10.71), where you can ask about visiting the various *chais*, the St-Gobain glassworks and river trips – upstream through the locks to Jarnac is a particularly beautiful excursion.

As for **rooms**, the tourist office can book hotels on its list; the cheapest are *Tourist Hôtel*, 166 av Victor-Hugo (☎45.82.09.61; ①), for no-frills lodgings above a boisterous bar on the noisy Angoulême road, and *Le Cheval Blanc*, 6–8 pl Bayard (☎45.82.09.55; ①), with a simple inexpensive restaurant downstairs. For something a bit more expensive and more comfortable, try *La Résidence*, 25 av Victor-Hugo (☎45.32.16.90; ②–④), a two-star with a clean modern interior, or *L'Étape*, a little further out on the N141 at 2 av d'Angoulême (☎45.32.16.15; ①–③). For a more characterful resting place, the *Hôtel d'Orleans*, 25 rue d'Angoulême (☎45.82.20.33; ①–③), is in a calm pedestrianized street in the old part of town. Upstream from the bridge, the oak woods of the Parc François-I, where there's swimming in the river or a pool, stretch along the river bank to the Pont Chatenay and the town **campsite** (☎45.32.13.32).

Eating out shouldn't pose a problem. If you'd like a change from French food, head for *El Gringo Loco*, 30 rue Bellefonds off rue Victor-Hugo (☎45.35.05.89; closed Sat lunch & Mon), for fairly authentic Mexican and Tex-Mex-style meals moderately priced. The casual *Restaurant La Fresse*, 42 allée de la Corderie (☎45.82.06.37; closed Sun night), serves up excellent Charentais specialities with inexpensive prices, and there's a good list of local wines. Those after a dining experience find it at *La Boîte-à-Sel*, 68 av Victor-Hugo (☎43.32.07.68; closed Mon), a seasoned restaurant with an emphasis on fresh natural produce; the good-value 75F menu gets you a *plat* from the 102F *menu de marché* and a dessert or entrée; the excellent *menu des gourmets* will set you back 190F. There are a couple of reasonable **cafés** on the place François-I.

Around Cognac

The area around Cognac is gentle enough for some restful walks taking in some pretty little Charentais villages. The best is the towpath or *chemin de hâlage* that follows the south bank of the Charente upstream to Pont de la Trâche, then on along a track to the pretty town of **BOURG-CHARENTE**, with an excellent **restaurant** called *La Ribaudière* at the bridge, an interesting castle and a Romanesque church; the walk takes about three hours in all. A byroad leads back to **ST-BRICE** on the other bank, past sleepy farms and acres of shoulder-high vines. From there, another lane winds 3km up the hill and over to the ruined **abbey** of **CHÂTRE**, abandoned amid brambles and fields. Alternatively, at the hamlet of **RICHEMONT**, 5km northwest of Cognac, you can swim in the pools of the tiny River Antenne below an ancient church on a steep bluff lost in the woods.

Further afield, 18km northwest of Cognac between the villages of Migron and Authon, there's the fascinating **Écomusée du Cognac** (ring ☎46.94.91.16; free), which illustrates the history of the distillation process and the various tools involved, finishing off with a tasting of cognacs, liqueurs and cocktails. Follow the D731 to St-Jean-d'Angely out of cognac for 13km as far as Burie, then turn right on the D131, 4km from Migron.

Angoulême

Today, the cathedral city of **ANGOULÊME** has a failing economy. The papermills that dominated the town used to employ thousands of workers and bolstered the city's prosperity; now they are almost completely defunct. But in the past, the former capital of the Angoumois province was a much-coveted city, being heavily fought over in the fourteenth-century Anglo-French squabbles and again in the sixteenth century during the Wars of Religion, when it was a Protestant stronghold. After the revocation of the Edict of Nantes, a good proportion of its citizens – among them many of its skilled papermakers – emigrated to Holland, never to return.

The Town

The **old town** occupies a steep-sided plateau overlooking a bend in the Charente, its scruffy labyrinthine streets only just beginning to undergo gentrification; it's still a lively place, with lots of interesting restaurants and shops. On the southern edge of the plateau stands the **cathedral**, whose west front – like Notre-Dame at Poitiers – is a fascinating display board for some expressive and lively twelfth-century sculpture, culminating in a Risen Christ with angels and clouds about his head, framed in the habitual blaze of a halo. The lively frieze beneath the tympanum to the right of the west door commemorates the recapture of Spanish Zaragoza from the Moors, showing a bishop transfixing a Moorish giant with his lance and Roland killing the Moorish king.

Next to the cathedral in the old bishop's palace, there's more art on show at the **Musée des Beaux Arts** (daily except Tues 10am–noon & 2–6pm; 15F), with its emphasis on seventeenth- to nineteenth-century paintings, many by Charentais artists. From the front of the cathedral, you can walk all around the **ramparts** encircling the plateau, with long views over the surrounding country, now largely filled with urban sprawl. There are **public gardens** below the parapet at the far end of the fortifications, and a gravelly esplanade by the *lycée* where locals gather to play *boules*.

Angoulême's most fascinating museum lies outside the city walls on the River Charente: the **Centre National de la Bande Dessinée**, 121 rue de Bordeaux (Wed–Fri noon–7pm, Sat & Sun 2–7pm; 30F; bus #3 or #5), devoted entirely to comic strips. Housed in a turn-of-the-century brewery, with contemporary high-rise and glass additions, the museum gets across the message that comics ("BD") – from politics to pornography – are high art in France, with a changing array of three hundred original cartoons, mostly French and dating from the 150-year-old beginning of strip comics to their darker, underground contemporaries. The all-time Gallic favourite, Astérix, is featured, as well as Tin Tin, Belgian Hergé, old favourites like the Peanuts and Mickey Mouse, and a slew of less well known treats. To make comic fiends further salivate, there's a vast cartoon library, much of it in English, and you're welcome to relax on cushions and devour.

Another riverfront museum close by is the **Atelier-Musée du Papier**, 134 rue de Bordeaux (daily except Mon 2–6pm; free), located in a disused cigarette-paper factory a fitting tribute to the declining Charentais paper industry. While exhibits get into the history and technicalities of papermaking, art isn't forgotten, with contemporary creations on show utilizing paper, cardboard and pulp.

Practicalities

Angoulême is easily accessible by train from Cognac, Limoges and Poitiers. The main **tourist office**, 2 pl St-Pierre (π45.95.16.84), is by the cathedral and can provide route details for walks in the area – *circuits pédestres*; there's another branch office outside the **gare SNCF**, from which av Gambetta, with the **gare routière** and several cheap hotels, leads uphill to the town centre through place Pérot.

Both tourist offices can help with **accommodation**, although if you want to go it alone, the cheapest rooms in town are at *Les Messageries* on place de la Gare (π45.92.07.62; ①), above a family-run bar across from the station; another family-run joint, the more peaceful *Le Crab*, 27 rue Kléber (π45.95.51.80; ①–②), left out of the station then first right off av Maréchal-de-Lattre-de-Tassigny; and *Hôtel Gaste*, 381 rte de Bordeaux (π45.91.89.98; ①), a long haul from the station on the opposite side of town but known for its cordiality and its good food. A little pricier are the *Hôtel des Pyrénées*, 80 rue St-Roch (π45.95.20.45; ②), the *Hôtel d'Orléans*, 133 av Gambetta (π45.92.07.53; ②), and the excellent old *Hôtel du Palais*, 4 pl Francis-Louvel (π45.92.54.11; ③), well situated on a shady, café-filled square. Alternatively, there's a wonderfully positioned IYHF **youth hostel** (π45.92.45.80; ①; with canteen) on an island in the Charente; take bus #7 from place du Champ-de-Mars. The **camping municipal** (π45.92.83.22) is nearby, beyond the Pont de Bourgines.

Likely **restaurant** areas are rue de Genève, with a number of options including traditional French and international, and the narrow, pedestrianized rue Massilon; *Le Mektoub*, 28 rue des Trois-Notre-Dames, is good for inexpensive North African cuisine, and just near the excellent daily covered market of Les Halles, *Le Chat Noir*, on rue du Chat, is crowded with lunchers after its cheap salads and snacks. One of the best restaurants in the region, with menus starting at 85F, is *La Ruelle*, 6 rue Trois-Notre-Dames (π45.92.94.64; closed Sat lunch & Sun). A slightly cheaper traditional option is *Le Gastro Cave*, located in a cellar in the same street at no. 3 (π45.92.45.47; closed Wed & Thurs lunchtime), which serves regional specialities with menus from

68F, while *La Marine* on nearby rue Ludovic–Trarieux is its opposite, a modern and airy oyster/wine bar.

Around Angoulême

LA ROCHEFOUCAULD, 15km from Angoulême, is the site of a huge Renaissance **château** on the banks of the River Tardoire, still belonging to the family that gave its name to the town. The stately pile only opens its elaborate portals in August, when there is a brigade-sized cast for the *son et lumière*; outside that time, you can't see the courtyard, the château's best architectural feature. Two **hotels**, if you need them, are the *Hôtel de France*, 13 Grande-Rue (☎45.63.02.29; ②), and *La Vieille Auberge*, Faubourg de la Souche (☎45.62.02.72; ②). The **camping municipal** is on rue des Flots.

East of Angoulême the country becomes hillier and more wooded, with buttercup pastures grazed by liver-coloured Limousin cattle. The small, quiet town of **CONFOLENS**, with its ancient houses stacked on a hill above the river, is about 40km northeast of Rochefoucauld (buses do the 55km trip from Angoulême) and off the main N141 to Limoges. The town's chief claim to fame since 1957 has been the huge **International Folklore Festival**, held every year in the second and third weeks of August (for info contact ☎45.84.00.77).

If you're planning an **overnight** stay, try the *Hôtel de Vienne*, 4 rue de la Ferrandie (☎45.84.09.24) – or there's a **camping municipal**.

AQUITAINE

In Roman times, **Bordeaux** was capital of the province of *Aquitania Secunda*. With the marriage of Eleanor of Aquitaine and King Henry II of England in 1152, it quickly became the principal English foothold for their three-hundred-year Aquitanian adventure, and it was to their presence, and particularly their taste for its red wines – imported back to England and termed "claret" – that the region owed its first great economic boom. The second boom, which financed the building of the gracious eighteenth-century centre of Bordeaux, came with the expansion of colonial trade in the eighteenth century.

The surrounding countryside is not the most enticing. The vineyards throughout the **Médoc** region are mainly flat and monotonous: you go for the wines, not the scenery. More interesting is the vast pine-covered expanse of *Les Landes* and the huge wild Atlantic beaches of the **Côte d'Argent**. But it is not a landscape that charms. Its appeal, like desert, is more in its size and uniqueness – and you definitely need your own transport to explore it.

Bordeaux and around

The city of **BORDEAUX** is something of a disappointment for the casual visitor. It's big, with a population of over half a million, and obviously rich – as it has been since the Romans set up a lively trading centre here. Yet the only part you could call attractive is the relatively small eighteenth-century centre, paid for by the expansion of colonial trade. The rest is scruffy and, even with its long history, contains far fewer sights than many a lesser place. But if you're just passing through – it's the main regional transport centre – there are a couple of sights worth checking out, and plenty of cheap places to sleep and eat.

THE WINES OF BORDEAUX

With Burgundy and Champagne, the **wines** of Bordeaux form the "Holy Trinity" of French viticulture. Despite producing as many whites as reds, it is the latter – known as claret to the British – that have graced the tables of the discerning for centuries. The countryside that produces them stretches north, east and south of the city, enjoying near perfect climactic conditions and a soil which ranges from limestone hills to sand and pebbles. It is the largest quality wine district in the world, turning out around 500 million bottles a year – over half the country's quality wine output.

The Gironde estuary, fed by the Garonne and the Dordogne, determines the lay of the land. The **Médoc** lies northwest of Bordeaux between the Atlantic coast and the River Gironde, with its vines deeply rooted in poor gravelly soil, producing good, full-bodied red wines; the region's eight *appellations* are Médoc, Haut Médoc, St-Estèphe, Pauillac, St-Julien, Moulis en Médoc, Listrac-Médoc and Margaux. Southwest of Bordeaux are the vast vineyards of **Graves**, producing the best of the region's dry white wines, along with some punchy reds, from some of the most prestigious communes in France – Pessac, Talence, Martillac and Villenave d'Ornon amongst them. They spread down to Langon and envelop the areas of **Sauternes** and **Barsac**, which both produce extremely sweet white dessert wines, considered among the best in the world.

On the east side of the Gironde estuary and the Dordogne, the **Côtes de Blaye** feature some good quality white table wines, mostly dry, and a smaller quantity of reds. The **Côtes de Bourg** specialize in solid whites and reds, spreading down to the renowned **St-Émilion** area. Here, there are a dozen producers who have earned the accolade of *Premiers Grands Crus Classés*, and their output is a full, rich red wine that doesn't have to be kept as long as the Médoc wines. Less-known neighbouring areas include the vineyards of **Pomerol**, **Lalande** and **Côtes de Francs**, all producing reds similar to St-Émilion but at more affordable prices.

Between Garonne and Dordogne is the area known as **Entre-Deux-Mers**, which yields large quantities of inexpensive, drinkable table whites and relies mainly on the Sauvignon grape. The less important sweet whites of **Ste-Croix du Mont** come out of the area south of **Loupiac**, which itself produces sweet whites. Stretching in a thin band along the north bank of the Garonne, the vineyards of the **Côtes de Bordeaux** feature fruity reds and a smaller number of dry and sweet whites.

Arrival and accommodation

Arriving by train, you'll find yourself at the **gare St-Jean**, with its own small tourist office (daily 9am–noon & 12.45–7pm; ☎56.91.64.70), right at the heart of a somewhat insalubrious area, half an hour's walk south of the city centre (and off our map to the bottom right); buses #7 or #8 will save you the **hike**. They also rent out bikes. Tickets are available on the **buses** (7F), but it's cheaper if you buy a *carnet* of ten from a *tabac*. You must punch your ticket on the bus; then it is valid for half an hour, even if you change bus and direction. The **gare routière** is just a short walk north of the centre on rue Fondaudège near place Tourny. The **tourist office**, 12 cours du 30-juillet (daily 9am–7pm; June–Sept Mon–Sat 9am–8pm, Sun 9am–7pm; ☎56.44.28.41), can book accommodation free of charge; it also has useful information on the city and surrounding vineyards, to which it also books tours (see above for details).

The area right by the station – particularly rue Charles-Domercq and cours de la Marne – is full of one- and two-star **hotels**, reasonably priced but no great treat to stay at. The hotels listed below are either in the city centre itself or in the quieter neighbourhood around the *gare routière*.

The **classification** of Bordeaux wines is an extremely complex affair. Apart from the usual *appellation d'origine contrôlée* (*AOC*) labelling – guaranteeing the origin but not the quality of the wine – the wines of the Médoc châteaux are graded into five *crus*, or growths. These were established as long ago as 1855, based on the prices the wines had fetched over the previous hundred years. Four were voted the top of the tree or *Premier Grand Crus Classés*: Margaux, Lafitte, Latour and Haut-Brion. Yet with the exception of Château Mouton-Rothschild, which moved up a class in 1973 to become the fifth *Premier Grand Cru Classé*, there have been no official changes, so that the divisions between the *crus* should not be taken too seriously. Since then – to confuse matters further – additional categories have been devised, for instance *Crus Bourgeois*, which has three categories of its own. The wines of Sauternes were also classified in 1855.

If you are interested in **buying wines**, it is possible to find bargains at some of the châteaux, and the advantages of buying at source include the opportunity of tasting the wines before purchasing and the possibility of receiving expert advice about the different vintages. In Bordeaux, the best place to go is *La Vinotèque* next to the tourist office (Mon–Sat 9.15am–7.15pm). In recent years tales of machine oil and chemical additives have shaken many people's confidence in wine-drinking; as a result, there's a growing fashion for organic methods and "green" wines, already available on many good labels.

To **visit the châteaux**, the Bordeaux tourist office has a leaflet detailing all the places that allow visits and wine-tasting. For general **information** on the region's wines, the place to go is the slick *Maison du Vin* in Bordeaux (Mon–Fri 8.30am–6pm, Sat 9am–12.30pm & 1.30–5pm), with many leaflets in English detailing the types of Bordeaux wine. In addition, each wine-producing village has its own tourist office and *Maison du Vin* who can provide the same service. Since getting to any of these places except St-Émilion without your own transport is hard work, the simplest thing is to take one of the Bordeaux tourist office's own **guided tours** (mid-may to mid-Oct), with a different wine area for each day of the week so you can go on a few; full-day tours leave Wednesdays and Saturdays and include lunch (9.30am–6.30pm; 240F); half-day tours leave at 1.30pm the rest of the week (5hr; 130F). The tours, which don't insult anyone's intelligence, are worth the price; generally interesting and informative, the guide translates into English the wine-maker's commentary and any answers to questions you might have. Tastings are generous and expert tuition on how to go about it is part of the deal.

Hotels

Hôtel de Bayonne, 4 rue Martignac (☎56.48.00.88). Impressive eighteenth-century building with classic 1930s decor, just around the corner from the *Grand Théâtre*, and suitably expensive. ④–⑦.

Hôtel Blayais, 17 rue Mautrec (☎56.48.17.87). A good, clean, central bet, and one of the city's most economical. ①.

Hôtel de la Boétie, 4 rue de la Boétie (☎56.81.76.68). Surprisingly cheap for such a central location, this hotel is on a quiet street near the *Musée des Beaux-Arts*. ①.

Hôtel du Centre, 8 rue du Temple (☎56.48.13.29). As the name implies, it's very central; a comfortable two-star with breakfast thrown in for free. ②.

Dauphin, 82 rue du Palais-Gallien (☎56.52.24.62). Very pleasant place near the *gare routière* and the *palais*, so not too far from the action. ①.

Hôtel Etche-Ona, 11 rue Mautrec (☎56.44.36.49). In a very central location in a quiet street, this is at the cheaper end of the upmarket bracket. ②–④.

Grand Hôtel Française, 12 rue Temple (☎56.48.10.35). In a quiet street off the busy pedestrianized rue de la Porte-Dijeaux, this elegant old building has comfortable three-star rooms with all conveniences, including air-conditioning. ④–⑤.

Hôtel Notre Dame, 36 rue Notre Dame (☎56.52.88.24). Quiet, attractive establishment in a small street at the centre of Bordeaux's antiques trade. ③.

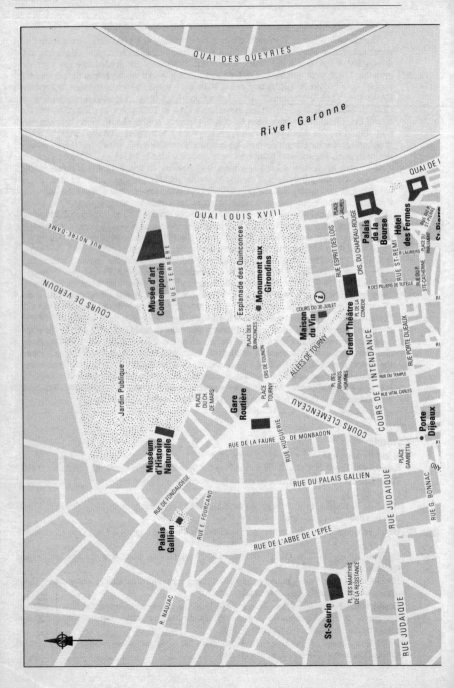

QUAI DES QUEYRIES

River Garonne

QUAI LOUIS XVIII

RUE NOTRE-DAME

COURS DE VERDUN

RUE FERRÈRE

Musée d'art Contemporain

Esplanade des Quinconces

Monument aux Girondins

RUE ESPRIT DES LOIS

PLACE J.-JAURÈS

CRS. DU CHAPEAU-ROUGE

Palais de la Bourse

Hôtel des Fermes

QUAI DE I

FINE RUE ST-PIERRE

PLACE DU PARLIAMENT

St-Pierre

RUE ST-REMI

R LAURIERS

R DES PILLIERS DE TUTELLE

STE-CATHERINE

RUE D.P.

PLACE DES QUINCONCES

Jardin Publique

COURS DU 30 JUILLET

Maison du Vin

PL. DE LA COMÉDIE

Grand Théâtre

ALLÉES DE TOURNY

CRS DE TOURNON

PLACE DU CH DE MARS

Gare Routière

PLACE TOURNY

PL. DES GRANDS HOMMES

COURS DE l'INTENDANCE

RUE DU TEMPLE

RUE VITAL CARLES

RUE PORTE DIJEAUX

Muséum d'Histoire Naturelle

RUE DE LA FAURE

DE MONBADON

RUE HUGUERIE

COURS CLEMENCEAU

Porte Dijeaux

PLACE GAMBETTA

RUE DE FONDAUDÈGE

RUE DU PALAIS GALLIEN

Palais Gallien

RUE E FOURCAND

RUE JUDAIQUE

RUE G. BONNAC

ARD

RI

RUE DE L'ABBÉ DE L'EPÉE

R. NAUJAC

St-Seurin

PL. DES MARTYRS DE LA RÉSISTANCE

RUE JUDAIQUE

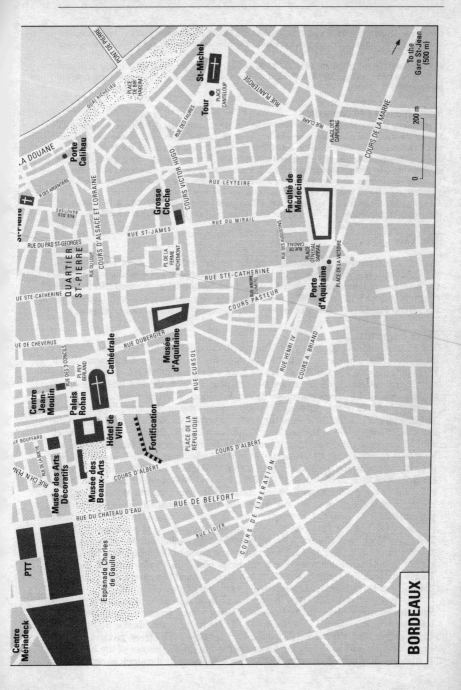

BORDEAUX

To the
Gare St-Jean
(500 m)

COURS DE LA MARNE

200 m

0

PLACE DES
CAPUCINS

RUE CLARE

RUE PLANTEROSE

RUE LEYTEIRE

Faculté de
Médecine

RUE DU MIRAIL

RUE DES AUGUSTINS

PLACE
GENERAL
SARRAIL

RUE DE
CANDALE
RUE ANDRE
DUMERO

PLACE DE LA VICTOIRE

Porte
d'Aquitaine

COURS PASTEUR

RUE STE-CATHERINE

COURS DE LIBERATION

RUE HENRI IV

COURS A. BRIAND

RUE LIGIER

COURS D'ALBERT

PLACE DE LA
RÉPUBLIQUE

RUE DE BELFORT

RUE DE CURSOL

Musée
d'Aquitaine

RUE DUBERGIER

PL DE LA
FERME
RICHEMONT

RUE ST-JAMES

Grosse
Cloche

COURS VICTOR HUGO

RUE DES FAURES

PLACE
CANTELOUP

Tour

St-Michel

PLACE
DE BIR
HAKEIM

QUAI RICHELIEU

PONT DE PIERRE

LA DOUANE

Porte
Cailhau

R DES ARGENTIERS

RUE DES
BAHUTIERS

St-Pierre

RUE DU PAS ST-GEORGES

UE STE-CATHERINE

QUARTIER
ST-PIERRE

RUE BUDOR

COURS D'ALSACE ET LORRAINE

UE DE CHEVERUS

RUE DES 3 CONCILS

PL PEY
BERLAND

Cathédrale

Centre
Jean-
Moulin

Palais
Rohan

Hôtel de
Ville

Fortification

UE BOUFFARD

RUE CH N PENL

RUE DE LA BRETTE

Musée des Arts
Décoratifs

Musée des
Beaux-Arts

COURS D'ALBERT

RUE DU CHATEAU D'EAU

Esplanade Charles
de Gaulle

PTT

Centre
Mériadeck

Hôtel des Quatre Sœurs, 6 cours du 30-juillet (☎57.81.19.20). Pleasant hotel in an ideal central spot next to the tourist office above an excellent, affordable brasserie. All rooms with telephone and TV. ④.

Hôtel Studio, 26 rue Huguerie (☎56.48.00.14). Not only one of the cheapest hotels in Bordeaux, but of a good standard too; all rooms have a shower and WC; disabled access also. Right near the *gare routière*. ①.

Youth hostels and campsites

IYHF youth hostel, 22 cours Barbey (☎56.91.59.51). Situated off cours de la Marne, the hostel is a ten-minute walk from *gare St-Jean*, or take bus #7 or #8. Curfew 11pm. Kitchen and laundry facilities. Drawbacks include the seedy area, a 9.30am–6pm lockout and very poor security. ①.

Maison des Étudiantes, 50 rue Ligier (☎56.96.48.30). Friendly hostel, with a good chance of getting your own room, although students pay less and get preference. The hostel is women-only from October to June, and also accepts men in July and August. There's a kitchen but you'll need your own pots. No curfew. Bus #7 or #8 to stop *cours de la Libération*. ①.

Camping les Gravières, Pont-de-la-Maye, Villeneuve-d'Ornon (☎56.87.00.36). A three-star site, 8km south of *gare St-Jean*, in a forest by the River Garonne. Take bus #B from place de la Victoire.

The City

Bordeaux is reasonably spread out along the western side of the River Garonne, with the eighteenth-century **old town** lying between the **Place de la Comédie** to the north, the pompous buildings of the river bank, and the **cathedral** to the west. North of the centre is Europe's largest square, the **Esplanade des Quinconces**, and further still, the **Jardin Public**, containing some very scant remains of Bordeaux's Roman past.

Vieux Bordeaux

The elegant, eighteenth-century city centres on the **quartier St-Pierre** and stretches up to the Grand Théâtre to the north, the cathedral to the west and the cours Victor-Hugo to the south. The narrow streets are lined with grand mansions from Bordeaux's glory days, and much of the area has been done up over the last ten years or so, though some of the streets remain seedy in anticipation of the restorer's touch.

The social hub of the eighteenth-century city was the impeccably classical **Grand Théâtre** on place de la Comédie at the northern end of rue Ste-Catherine. Built on the site of a Roman temple by the architect Victor Louis in 1780, this lofty building is faced with an immense colonnaded portico topped by twelve Muses and Graces. Inside, the interior is likewise opulently decorated in *trompe l'œil* paintings; the best way to see it is to attend one of the operas or ballets staged throughout the year, with seats in the Gods from as little as 35F (☎56.48.58.54 for info and bookings), or ask at the tourist office about the guided tours they sometimes offer. Smart streets radiate from here: the city's main shopping street, **rue Ste-Catherine**, runs south and has been partially pedestrianized to ease the consumer flow; there's the ritzy cours de l'Intendance running west, and the sandy, tree-lined allées de Tourny leads to a **statue of Claude Boucher**, Marquis of Tourny – the eighteenth-century administrator who was prime mover of the city's "Golden Age" and supervised much of the rebuilding. Back in the narrow streets of the old town, the harmonious **place du Parlement** and **place St-Pierre** are both lined with typical Bordelais mansions and peppered with wrought-iron balconies and arcading, making impressive examples of town planning.

The riverfront was also given the once-over by early eighteenth-century planners, with the imposing **place de la Bourse** creating a focal point on the quayside. The impressive bulk of the old customs house of 1733 contains the **Musée des Douanes** (daily except Mon 10am–noon & 1–5pm; summer closes 6pm; free), giving a rundown on Bordeaux's port and seafaring history and retracing the history of the administration and work of French customs. The square is balanced by the **stock exchange** looking out over the quayside and the broad River Garonne; further south down the river-bank, the fifteenth-century **Porte Cailhau** takes its name from the stones (*caillou – cailhau* in dialect) unloaded on the neighbouring quay to be used as ballast for boats. Crossing the river just south of here, the only testimony to a nobler past is the impressive **Pont de Pierre** – "Stone Bridge", though in fact it's brick – built at Napoléon's command during the Spanish campaigns, with seventeen arches in honour of his victories. The views of the river and quays from here are memorable, although – apart from a few sleazy bars – the once-impressive quayside is little more than a noisy six-lane freeway now.

Place Gambetta, the cathedral and around

Cours de l'Intendance, a street lined with chic shops, links place de la Comédie with café-lined **place Gambetta**, a pivotal square for the city's museums, shops and the cathedral. Once a majestic space conceived as an architectural whole in the time of Louis XV, place Gambetta's house-fronts are arcaded at street level and decorated with rows of carved masks; in the middle of the square, a so-called English garden soaks up some of the traffic fumes, belying the fact that the guillotine lopped 300 heads here at the time of the Revolution. In one corner stands the eighteenth-century arch of the **Porte Dijeaux**, an old city gate.

By the esplanade Charles-de-Gaulle, to the west of the place Gambetta, is Bordeaux's acknowledgement of twentieth-century architectural fashions, the modern shopping centre called the **Centre Mériadeck**. Herald of a brighter future to some Bordelais – and a carbuncle to others – it delivers its streets to the automobile and elevates its humans to midair plazas and walkways. Despite some interesting shapes and textures, it's not user friendly, and your most likely welcome will be an embrace around the legs by yesterday's windblown newspaper.

South of place Gambetta is the **Cathédrale St-André** (daily 8am–noon & 2–7pm; July & Aug Mon–Sat 8am–noon & 2–7pm, Sun 8am–noon & 3–6pm), whose most eye-catching feature is the great upward sweep of the twin steeples over the north transept, an effect heightened by the adjacent but separate *campanile*, the fifteenth-century **Tour Pey-Berland**. The interior of the cathedral, begun in the twelfth century, is not particularly interesting, apart from the choir that provides one of the few complete examples of the florid late-Gothic style known as *Rayonnant*, and there's also some fine carving in the north transept door and the Porte Royale to the right that's worth closer examination.

The attractive **place Pey-Berland** surrounds the cathedral, harbouring an enticing array of pavement cafés, like the old-fashioned *Musée* on the south side, and another on the west by the classical Hôtel de Ville, formerly Archbishop Rohan's palace; it's here – or at least close to it – that the cream of Bordeaux's museums lie. A handsome eighteenth-century house in rue Bouffard, the Hôtel de Lalande, houses the **Musée des Arts Décoratifs** (daily except Tues 2–6pm; 18F, free Wed), whose extensive collection includes some beautiful, mainly French, porcelain and faïence, period furniture, glass, miniatures, Barye animal sculptures and prints of the city in its maritime heyday. Just around the corner on cours d'Albret next to the Hôtel de Ville, the **Musée des Beaux-Arts** (daily except Tues 10am–6pm; 20F, free Wed) has a small but worthy selection of fine art, featuring works by Perugino, Veronese, Delacroix, Rubens, Matisse and Marquet (a native of the city), as well as Kokoshka's superb painting of the city's cathedral. And smaller still is the Resistance museum and archive, the **Centre Jean-Moulin** just off the square to the north (Mon–Fri 2–6pm; free), one of the most comprehensive of its type in the country.

A short walk past the Tour Pey Berland down cours Pasteur, the imaginatively laid-out **Musée d'Aquitaine** (daily except Tues 10am–6pm; 15F, free Wed) is one of the best of the city's museums. A stimulating variety of objects and types of display emphasizes regional ethnography and covers the three main facets of the region's development: maritime, commercial and agricultural. Drawings and writings on the period enable you to see why eighteenth-century Bordeaux was so extolled by contemporary writers, who compared it to Paris. Take a look at the section on the wine trade before venturing off on a vineyard tour in the region (see box, p.526). Parallel rue Ste-Catherine is straddled by a heavy Gothic tower, the sixteenth-century **Grosse Cloche**, originally part of the medieval town hall.

North of the centre

North of the Grand Théâtre, cours du 30-juillet leads into the bare, gravelly – and frankly unattractive – expanse of the **Esplanade des Quinconces**, said to be Europe's largest municipal square. At the quayside end are two tall columns, erected in 1829 and topped by allegorical statues of Commerce and Navigation; at the opposite end of the esplanade is the **Monument aux Girondins**, a glorious *fin-de-siècle* ensemble of statues and fountains built in honour of the influential local deputies to the 1789 Revolutionary Assembly, later purged by Robespierre as moderates and counter-revolutionaries. During the last war, in a fit of anti-French spite, the occupying Germans made plans to melt the monument down, only to be foiled by the local Resistance, who got there first and, under cover of darkness, dismantled it piece by piece and hid it in a barn in the Médoc for the duration of the war.

To the northwest, and a welcome relief, is the **Jardin Public** (daily summer 7am–9pm; winter 7am–6pm), containing the city's botanical gardens and, further west still, the dilapidated third-century amphitheatre, **Palais Gallien** – all that remains of *Burdigala*, Aquitaine's Roman capital. To the east of the gardens, closer to the river, is the city's new **Musée d'Art Contemporain** on rue Ferrère (Tues–Sun 11am–7pm; 20F, free noon–2pm). There are no permanent collections, so it's hit-and-miss as to whether you'll like the stuff on display, although the building alone – a converted nineteenth-century warehouse for exotic goods – is worth the trek. It provides one of the best settings in Europe for the sculpture and installation-based work shown in four exhibitions annually, the vast space giving the work – like that of the gallery's British favourite, Richard Long – real power. There's also a superb collection of glossy art books in the first-floor library and an elegant designer café-restaurant on the roof.

Eating and drinking

Bordeaux is packed with **restaurants**, many of them top-notch, and because of its position close to the Atlantic coast, fresh seafood features prominently on many a Bordelais menu. Being a student town, there are also plenty of lively **cafés** and **bars**, with a reasonable choice of dance clubs and jazz spots.

For **picnic fodder**, there is a marvellous, round, covered **market** near the church of Notre-Dame behind cours de l'Intendance. And on rue de Montesquieu, off place des Grands-Hommes, Jean d'Alos runs the city's best *fromagerie*, with over 150 farm-produced cheeses.

Cafés and restaurants

Salubrious place du Parlement has its fair share of fine **dining establishments**, while the quartier St-Pierre – particularly rue des Bahutiers – is full of enticing cafés and restaurants, not all of them pricey. There are numerous cheap eating places around the station, and ethnic restaurants in the area around church of St-Michel and more centrally in rue des Augustin near the place Victoire, with everything from Greek, Indian, Vietnamese and African to Chinese.

Aero Bar, cours du Chapeau-Rouge. Popular lunch-time café with outdoor tables.

Café des Arts, cnr rue Ste-Catherine and cours Victor Hugo. Large, somewhat tired brasserie – but still popular. Wholesome, inexpensive meals and terrace drinks.

Le Bistro de Quinconces, 4 pl des Quinconces (☎56.52.84.56). Fashionable, fun bistro which doubles as a *salon de thé* in the daytime and a tapas bar in the evening; outdoor tables in a great spot facing the fountains. Modern, eclectic *carte* includes pasta (42–55F).

Restaurant Chez Joël D, 13 rue des Pilliers-de-Tutelle. Airy, modern *bar à huîtres*, where the smart set quaffs oysters and Bordeaux by the glass. Daily noon to midnight.

Au Clair de la Lune, rue des Bahutiers (☎56.81.09.18). Plain, clean, spacious Berber restaurant, with couscous. From 45F. Closed Tues.

Restaurant le Dégustoir, 8 rue Andre-Dumerq (☎56.91.25.06). In a narrow street off rue Ste-Catherine, this simple little place, its whitewashed walls lined with wines, serves inexpensive *plats*, mostly 65–80F, to go with the wonderful wine selection, not vice versa. Open only at night, closed Sun & Mon.

Restaurant le Bistrot de Édouard, 16 pl du Parlement (☎56.81.48.87). A premier spot to try Bordelaise specialities (*carte* 64–97F) under canopies in this lovely square with its fountain. The express lunch menu (57F) is particularly good value, combining a *plat du jour*, a dessert, glass of Bordeaux and a coffee.

La Flambée, 26 rue du Mirail. Fairly cheap seafood.

Chez Gilles, 6 rue Lauriers (☎56.81.17.38). Well-recommended, simple restaurant off place du Parlement, with a good-value 85F *menu du jour* that sensibly gives you the choice of two glasses of Bordeaux or dessert. Closed Sat lunch & Sun.

Chez Phillipe, 1 pl du Parlement (☎56.81.83.15). Bordeaux's top fish restaurant; fish of the day 100–160F, *menu du jour* 180F. Closed Sun, Mon & Aug.

Jean Ramet, 7–8 pl Jean-Jaurès (☎56.44.12.51). Simple, summery decor in an unstuffy – although predictably expensive – highly rated gourmet restaurant. Closed Sat lunch & Sun.

Saloon de Tea, 9 pl du Parlement. An ambient young café, walls covered in paintings, serving inexpensive Mexican snacks. Tables outside on the pretty square, and usually a game of chess in progress.

Le Tire Bouchon, 15 rue des Bahutiers (☎56.44.24.63). Congenial, friendly atmosphere for good French cooking; lunch is very popular. Menus 80–135F. Closed Sun & Sat lunchtime.

Aux Trois Arcades, pl du Parlement. Good for vegetarians – big fresh salads feature.

Bars

Bordeaux's student population ensures a collection of young, lively **bars**, a host of which are found on place de Victoire and down cours de la Somme running off it. There are also several happening bars on rue de Candale, between place de Victoire and restaurant-crowded rue des Augustins. For drinking in the early hours, head for place des Capucins.

Le 18, 18 rue Louis-de-Foix. Gay bar and disco.

Chez Auguste, pl de la Victoire. A regular student hang-out.

Aviatic Bar, pl Général-Sarrail. One of several bars whose tables fill this shady square off rue Ste-Catherine, this one particulary young and hip.

Le Blueberry, rue des Augustins. Bordeaux's grunge haunt, with suitably heavy sounds and peeling poster-covered walls.

Le Bœuf Sur Le Toit Pub, rue de Candale. Looking a bit like an American bar, with a rhythm-and-blues soundtrack for a happily rough-and-ready crowd. *McEwans* served.

Bar Le Bruit du Frigo, rue des Bahutiers. Small, arty and interesting. Open from 2pm.

Connemara, 18 cours d'Albret, next door to the Musée des Beaux-Arts. For the homesick pining for a pint of *Guinness*, this is Bordeaux's lively Irish pub, with a cheap fish-and-chip restaurant attached.

La Plana, 22 pl de la Victoire. Slick contemporary decor, with cool young folk eying up the world from tables outside.

Tardi Café, cours de la Somme. With blaring soul music, this place is lively and packed.

Nightlife and entertainment

To find out the latest **events and happenings** in and around Bordeaux, it's best to get hold of a copy of the regional newspaper *Sud-Ouest*; or there's the bimonthly listings booklet *Confetti* for 2F. *Bordeaux 95*, a free monthly mag available from the tourist office, has a listings section with the highbrow culture events around town. To buy **tickets** for city and regional events, head for the box office (☎56.48.26.26) in the nineteenth-century Galerie Bordelaise arcade, wedged between rue Ste-Catherine and rue Piliers-de-Tutelle.

For **jazz**, hit either *L'Alligator*, 3 place du Général-Sarrail (closed Sun), or *Le Borie*, 43 rue Borie, both of which host jazz ensembles towards the end of the week. *The Cricketers*, 72 quai de Paludate, the southward continuation of quai Richelieu, has a more regular live spot but of more variable quality. *Do Re Mi*, 18 rue des Augustins (☎56.92.72.33), hosts indie line-ups, including many grunge groups touring from the US. Since dance clubs come and go, *Black Records*, 41 rue du Loup (☎56.52.79.41; Mon–Sat 2–8pm), is a source of flyers and the latest club info; they also sometimes organize raves themselves.

Listings

Airlines *Air France*, 29 rue Esprit-des-Lois (☎56.44.64.35); *British Airways*, Galerie Frantel, Centre Mériadeck (☎56.81.24.59).

Airport Bordeaux-Mérignac, 10km west of the city (☎56.34.84.84), with its own tourist office (daily 8am–7pm; ☎56.34.39.39). It's connected on weekdays by half-hourly shuttle to and from the tourist office on cours du 30-juillet (40min).

Bike rental *Gare St-Jean* (open 24hr).

Books *Mollat*, 83–91 rue Porte Dijeaux, the city's largest bookstore, has French and English titles, and a separate record store next door. *Bradley's*, 32 pl Gambetta, has a fair selection of English- and French-language textbooks, as well as a bulletin board for job adverts.

Car rental Numerous rental firms are located at the airport and near *gare St-Jean*. A selection of the latter include *Citer*, at 68 rue Tauzia (☎56.92.19.62); *Leader Rent A Car* at no. 50 (☎56.92.60.40); *Avenir* at no. 87 (☎56.92.21.63); *Budget* at 12 rue Charles Domercq (☎56.91.41.70); and *Europcar* in the same street at no. 35 (☎56.31.20.30).

Cinema Head for the art-house cinema, *Centre Jean Vigo*, 6 rue Franklin, near the Marché des Grands-Hommes (☎56.44.35.17; 34F entry, Mon 27F), where you're more likely to find original-language screenings.

Consulates *Britain*, 15 cours de Verdun (☎56.52.28.35; Mon–Fri 9am–noon & 2.30–5pm); *Canada*, Immeuble Croix-du-Mail, 8 rue Claude-Bonnier (☎56.96.15.61; Mon–Fri 9am–12.30pm & 1.30–4.45pm); *USA*, 22 cours du Maréchal-Foch (☎56.52.65.92; Mon–Fri 9am–noon & 2–5pm).

Hitching *Allostop*, 77 cours d'Argonne (☎57.95.91.11).

Laundries On cours de Marne and rue de la Boétie.

Money exchange *American Express*, 14 cours de l'Intendance (Mon–Fri 8.45am–noon & 1.30–6pm); on Sundays you can change money at the tourist office or *Thomas Cook* at the train station.

Travel agents *Council Travel*, 9 pl Charles-Gruet (☎56.44.68.73); *USIT*, 284 rue Ste-Catherine (☎56.33.89.90).

Women visitors Counselling and information at *CIDF*, 5 rue Duffour-Dubergier (☎56.44.30.30; Mon–Fri 9am–12.30pm & 1.30–4pm).

Young people *CIJA*, 125 cours Alsace-Lorraine. As well as the usual useful information on events, job offers and language courses, there's a desk selling train and *Euroline* tickets.

The Médoc

The landscape of **the Médoc**, a slice of land northwest of Bordeaux wedged between the forests bordering the Atlantic coast and the River Gironde, is itself rather monotonous. Its gravel plains occupying the west bank of the brown, island-spotted Gironde estuary rarely swell into anything resembling a hill, but, paradoxically, this poor soil is ideal for viticulture – vines root more deeply if they don't find the sustenance they need in the topsoil, and firmly rooted, they are less subject to drought and flooding. The region's eight *appellations* – Médoc, Haut Médoc, St-Estèphe, Pauillac, St-Julien, Moulis en Médoc, Listrac-Médoc and Margaux – produce only red wines, from the grape varieties of Cabernet Sauvignon, Cabernet Franc, Merlot and to a lesser degree, Petit Verdot. Cabernet Sauvignon gives body, bouquet, colour and maturing potential to the wine, while Merlot gives it its "animal" quality, making it rounder and softer. The D2 wine road, heading off the N15 from Bordeaux, passes through Margaux, St-Julien, Pauillac and St-Estèphe, and while the scenery might not be stunning, the many famous – albeit mostly inaccessible – châteaux are.

The problem of accommodation is much worse in the Médoc than in the rest of the wine region, so it's a good idea to visit on a day trip from Bordeaux. Considering it's one of the most prestigious wine-growing areas in Bordeaux, it's surprisingly unwelcoming for visitors, with places to eat, and particularly affordable ones, also in short supply. There are regular *Citram* buses to Pauillac, but it's worth considering car rental (see Bordeaux, above).

Château Margaux and Fort Médoc

Easily the prettiest of the Bordeaux châteaux, **Château Margaux** is an eighteenth-century villa in extensive, sculpture-dotted gardens close to the west bank of the Garonne, 27km north of Bordeaux. Its wine, a classified *Premier Grand Cru* and world famous in the 1940s and 1950s, went through a rough patch in the two succeeding decades but improved in the 1980s after the estate was bought by a Greek family. The château (by appointment only; ☎56.88.70.28) is not included in any tours, and advance booking is essential.

In the small village of **MARGAUX** itself, there's an unusually friendly *Maison du Vin* (daily 9am–7pm; Nov to mid-May 9am–noon & 2–6pm; ☎57.88.70.82; English spoken) that can book accommodation and reserve visits to the *appellation*'s châteaux. Nearby, the enterprising cellar *L'Âme du Vin* provides free tastings from lesser-known Margaux châteaux, giving you a chance to try and buy some very good wines. Besides the local bars, you can **eat** at the *Restaurant Le Savoie* (☎56.88.30.08; closed Sun), next to the *Maison du Vin*, with good traditional food and menus from 80F. The only place to stay is the wildly expensive four-star *Le Relais de Margaux* (☎57.88.38.30; ⑦), with restaurant. Otherwise, head 10km back southeast along the D2 and then the D209 to **MACAU**, where there's a good *ferme-auberge*, *Château Guittot-Fellonneau* (Guy and Maryse Constantin, ☎57.88.47.81; ③). Another wine-making family, the Meyres, offer both *chambre* and *table d'hôte* 10km west of Margaux in **LISTRAC-MÉDOC** at *Château Cap-Leon Veyrin* (☎56.58.07.28; ③), on a twenty-acre vineyard.

The seventeenth-century **Fort Médoc**, off the D2 road between Margaux and St-Julien by the banks of the estuary, is a good place to tuck into a few purchases between châteaux. It was designed by the prolific military architect Vauban to defend the Gironde estuary against the British. The remains of the fort are scant but scrambleable, and in summer its toytown aspect has a leafy charm, marred only by a splendid view of the nuclear power station across the river just north of Blaye. Since 1990, the annual Fort-Medoc **jazz festival**, with big-name international acts, has been held here in mid-July (☎56.58.91.02 for details).

A couple of kilometres south, **LAMARQUE** is a very pretty village, full of flowers and with a sweet church. It's a pleasant place to stop for lunch at a very agreeable restaurant/bistro, *Relais du Medoc*. From here, seven or eight ferries (pedestrians & cycles 14F, motorbikes 38F, cars 64F; prices one-way) cross the Gironde daily to Blaye, another place fortified by Vauban and an important, although little known, Bordeaux wine-growing centre (see p.540). If you've missed the boat-crossing, there are plenty of small *caves* in Lamarque to check out while you wait.

Pauillac and around

PAUILLAC is the largest town in the Médoc region and central to the most important vineyards of Bordeaux: no fewer than three of the top five *Grands Crus* come from around here. The town's rapid growth in recent years, however, is due not to its vineyards but to the giant oil refinery which now dominates the town and accounts for the bleak, industrial appearance of the place.

Pauillac tries to make amends for this with a huge *Maison du Tourisme et du Vin* along the waterfront (Mon–Sat 9.30am–12.30pm & 2–6.30pm; ☎56.59.03.08). They don't reserve rooms but can provide you with a list of *gîtes*, rent out bikes and make appointments for you to visit the surrounding châteaux. It's not a great place to **stay**, but should you wish or need to, try the *Hôtel Yachting*, Port de Plaisance (☎56.59.06.43; ③), or the well-recommended riverfront **campsite** on rte de la Rivière (☎56.59.10.03; May to mid-Sept). Campsites are rare in the Médoc; the only other alternative is the two-star *Camping Le Bled* at Bernos (☎56.58.03.45; mid-June to mid-Sept), over 8km southwest near **ST-LAURENT-DE-MÉDOC**, a peaceful, shady and clean option. Alternatively, there's an excellent *chambre d'hôte* about 8km northwest near the village of **CISSAC**: *Château Vieux Braneyre* (the Gugès family, ☎56.59.54.03; ②; dinner 130F), in a large eighteenth-century house attached to a vineyard.

The most famous of the **Médoc châteaux** can be visited by appointment only, either direct or through the *Maison du Vin*: Châteaux Lafite-Rothschild (☎56.73.18.18; English spoken), Château Latour (☎56.59.00.51; English spoken), and Château Mouton-Rothschild (☎56.59.22.22). Their vineyards occupy larger single tracts of land than elsewhere in the Médoc, and consequently the quality of the wines differs to a greater extent than other châteaux on neighbouring land: a good vintage Lafite is perfumed and refined, whereas a Mouton-Rothschild is strong and dark and should be kept for at least ten years. **Château Mouton-Rothschild** and its wine **museum** (Mon–Fri only, closed Aug; ☎56.59.22.22) are not included in tours from Bordeaux and must be booked in advance. As well as the viticultural stuff, you also get to see the Rothschilds' amazing collection of postwar art, which includes work by Picasso, Dali and Warhol.

St-Estèphe

North of Pauillac, the wine commune of **ST-ESTÈPHE** is Médoc's largest *appellation*, consisting predominantly of *Crus Bourgeois* properties and growers belonging to the local *cave coopérative*, **Marquis de St-Estèphe**, on the D2 towards Pauillac (open for tastings; July to mid-Sept daily 9am–noon & 2–7pm; Oct–June Mon–Fri to 6pm, Sat closes 5pm). One of the *appellation*'s five *crus classés* is the distinctive **Château Cos d'Estournel**, with its over-the-top eighteenth-century French version of a pagoda; the château can be visited by appointment (☎56.73.15.55; English spoken). The village of St-Estèphe itself is a sleepy affair dominated by its landmark, the sweet eighteenth-century **church of St-Étienne**, with its highly decorative interior. The small, homespun *Maison du Vin*, presided over by a friendly old lady, is hidden in the church square.

For an elegant place to **stay**, back in the village, *Hôtel Château Pomys* (☎56.59.73.44; ④) is a mansion set in its own park. There are also several good *chambres d'hôtes*, including Jean-Pierre Fatin (☎56.59.35.28; ②) and Françoise Leeman (☎56.59.72.94; ③), both with *table d'hôte*. The other half of St-Éstephe is its port, where you'll find a typical roadside **restaurant**, *Le Peyrat*. In front of a grassy river stretch, it's casual and friendly, with simple, generous dishes; menus from 49F.

Sauternes

The **Sauternes** region, on the left bank of the River Garonne, 40km southeast of Bordeaux, is an ancient wine-making area, originally planted during the Roman occupation. The distinctive golden wine of the area is certainly sweet, but also round, full-bodied and spicy, with a long aftertaste. It's not necessarily a dessert wine, either: try it with some Roquefort cheese or with *foie gras*. Gravelly terraces with a limestone sub-soil help create the delicious taste, but mostly it's due to a peculiar microclimate of morning autumn mists and afternoons of sun and heat which causes *Botrytis Cinerea* fungus, or "noble rot", to flourish on the grapes, letting the sugar concentrate and intro-ducing some intense flavours. When they're picked, they're not a pretty sight: carefully selected by hand, only the most shrivelled, rotting bunches are selected. The wines of Sauternes make up some of the most highly sought after in the world, with bottles of Château d'Yquem, in particular, fetching thousands of francs.

SAUTERNES itself is a fairly quiet little village dominated by the rather intimidating **Maison du Sauternes** (daily summer 9.30am–7.30pm; winter 9.30am–12.30pm & 2–6pm) at one end of the village, and with a pretty church and a vineyard at the other. The *maison* is a room full of treasures, the golden bottles with white and gold labels being quite beautiful objects in themselves. Although they do tastings, they're unfortu-nately rather snooty about it, even if you buy. There are lots of other, smaller *caves* in the village, many offering tastings.

The best place to **stay** in town is the charming *Château du Commerce*, 2km out of town (☎56.76.65.94; ②–③), a medieval fortified farm surrounded by vineyards with its swimming pool, run by a friendly English couple; she cooks, and is commended by even the French press (menus 75–178F), and he runs the small-scale winery and comfortably rustic split-level accommodation. Otherwise try the excellent *chambre d'hôte* in the village (M. Beringuey, ☎56.76.60.17; ③).

There are some good **eating** opportunities, too. Opposite the church is *Auberge Les Vignes*, a typical country restaurant with a red-and-white-checked-curtains kind of decor and regional specialities, like *lapin au Sauternes* (70F), with a lunch menu at 60F. You could also try nearby *Le Saprien*, combining regional-style elements with modern eclec-tic additions and featuring menus from 107F to 250F. For something refreshingly downmarket, there's a typical scruffy local **bar** across the road. Besides the wines sold at the *maison*, there are lots of **caves** in the town, many offering tastings.

Entre-Deux-Mers

The landscape of **Entre-Deux-Mers** (literally "between two seas") – so called because it is sandwiched between the tidal waters of the Dordogne and Garonne – is much more attractive than the other wine regions, with its gentle hills and scattered medieval villages. Its wines, including the Premières Côtes de Bordeaux, are mainly dry whites produced by over forty *caves coopératives*, and are regarded as good but inferior to the Médocs or super-dry Graves to the south. It's also a region which can be explored, at least in part, by public transport, should you feel like avoiding the tourist office tour.

La Sauve

The one place you should really try to see is the ruined **abbey** 3km east of Créon at **LA SAUVE**, an important stop for pilgrims en route to Santiago de Compostela in Spain (daily 10am–noon & 2–6pm; 20F). The bus from Bordeaux's tourist office drops you off in the middle of a tranquil valley of small vineyards and corn fields, but you can see the ruin as you approach. Once it was all forest here, the abbey's full name, La Sauve-Majeure, being a corruption of the Latin *silva major* (big wood). It was founded in 1079, and the treasures of what remains are the twelfth-century Romanesque apse and apsi-dal chapels and the outstanding sculpted capitals in the chancel. The finest are the ones illustrating stories from the Old and New Testaments (Daniel in the lions' den, Delilah shearing Samson's hair and so on), while others show fabulous beasts and decorative motifs. There is a small **museum** at the entrance, with some excellent photos of the ruins, along with keystones from the fallen roofs. But what makes the visit so worthwhile is not just the capitals themselves, but the remote, undisturbed nature of the site. If you have the time, stroll over to the abbey's parish **church** along rue de l'Église, visible on the hill.

St-Macaire and around

If you're heading south through Entre-Deux-Mers, **LANGON** is the first town of any size you come to. But **ST-MACAIRE**, across the Garonne from Langon, is far better for a rest or food stop. St-Macaire still has its original **gates** and **battlements** and a beautiful medieval church, the **Église-Prieuré**. There's also the *Maison du Pays* that serves as an **écomusée** (☎56.63.32.14) and information centre for the region and its produce, with plenty of information for walkers, and free maps. In July and August, the museum runs a programme of visiting winemakers hosting tastings of their products. Next door to the *maison* is an excellent **restaurant**, *Le Compostelle*, with 55F and 100F menus, often crowded with French families, particularly for Saturday lunch. Just below the ramparts is the small, well-run *Camping Les Remparts*.

LA RÉOLE, on the north bank 18km further east, has a wealth of medieval architecture along a well-signposted walk through its narrow, hilly streets, and likewise makes an excellent stop for food or accommodation. France's oldest **town hall**, constructed for Richard the Lionheart in the twelfth century, and the well-preserved simple **Abbaye des Bénédictins** – with a fantastic view over the River Garonne and the surrounding countryside – reward a stroll through the town, although little remains of the fortified **castle**.

La Réole's **tourist office** on place de la Libération (Mon 3–6pm, Tues–Sat 9am–noon & 3–6pm; ☎56.61.13.55) conducts tours of the city in July and August. For **accommodation**, the two-star *Hôtel de l'Abbaye*, 42 rue Armand-Caduc (☎56.61.02.64; ②), is in the same street as the abbey. A good **restaurant** is *Les Fontaines* on rue André-Benac (closed Sun night & Mon), with classic French cuisine in unstuffy surroundings and menus at 75F, 95F and 135F. A lively Saturday **market** on av Jean-Jaurès along the Garonne provides good picnic provisions if you're passing.

Thirteen kilometres south of Langon, the town of **BAZAS** has a laid-back, southern air. Its most attractive feature is the wide, arcaded place de la Cathédrale, overlooked by the lichenous grey **Cathédrale St-Jean-Baptiste** that displays a harmonious blend of Romanesque, Gothic and classical in its west front. A good place to **stay**, despite its kitschy decor, is the medium-priced *Hostellerie St-Sauveur*, 14 rue du Général-de-Gaulle (☎56.25.12.18; ②). To **eat**, head for the *Restaurant des Remparts*, espace Mauvezin, near the *mairie* (☎56.25.95.24; closed Mon), for delicious local specialities and menus from 68F.

Circling back east and north towards Sauternes, you could pass through **UZESTE**, a quiet little place where Pope Clement V – who caused a schism by moving the papacy

---

THE TRUTH ABOUT CADILLAC

According to the tourist office in the medieval town of **Cadillac**, 11km northwest of Langon on the Garonne, the founder of Detroit, Michigan – the home of *General Motors* – Antoine Laumet, originally came from Cadillac. Sadly, this is just too good to be true, and he was born in 1658 in St-Nicolas-de-la-Grave, halfway between Agen and Toulouse, and never set foot in Cadillac itself. On emigrating to Canada, he took the name of Lamothe-Cadillac, a family who had nothing whatsoever to do with the town of Cadillac. In 1701, he founded the city of Detroit, and in 1958, in honour of the 300th anniversary of his birth, *General Motors* named their new limousines "Cadillacs".

to Avignon in the fourteenth century – erected the old **church** on the square. Beyond lies **VILLANDRAUT**, where Clement was born and built a colossal moated **castle**, whose ruinous curtain walls and corner towers still stand beside the road.

St-Émilion and around

ST-ÉMILION, 35km east of Bordeaux and a short trip by train or *Citram* bus from Bordeaux, is well worth a visit in its own right. The old grey houses of this fortified medieval village straggle down the south-hanging slope of a low hill with the green froth of the summer's vines crawling over its walls. Many of the growers still keep up the old tradition of planting roses at the ends of the rows, which in pre-pesticide days served as an early-warning system against infection, the idea being that the commonest bug, *oidium*, went for the roses first, giving three days' notice of its intentions.

St-Émilion is part of the Libourne region of Bordeaux, the area's two other well-known *appellations* being Fronsac and Pomerol. The region yields clay-limestone soil in St-Émilion and Fronsac and sandy or gravelly in Pomerol, both ideal for the Merlot grape, with seventy to eighty percent of the vineyards stretching across the area's hills and plateaux planted with this variety, giving the wine its soft, fruity quality.

There are two distinct wine districts of St-Émilion: the **plateau** and the **Côtes de St-Émilion**. The product of the former are called Graves wines because of the gravelly soil in which they are grown. *Côtes* wines grow in alkaline soil, which gives them added strength: St-Émilion *Côtes* contain an average of one percent more alcohol than Médoc wines.

The town's **belfry** belongs to the rock-hewn subterranean **Église Monolithe** beneath it (guided tours only: daily every 45min 10–11.30am & 2–5pm; April–Oct until 5.45pm; 33F from the tourist office), built on the site of St-Émilion's hermitage, now in a dark hole in someone's back yard, supposedly the cave where Saint Émilion lived a hermit's life in the eighth century. The rough-hewn ledge served as his bed and a carved seat as his chair, where infertile women reputedly still come to sit in the hope of getting pregnant.

Above the cave, the half-ruined thirteenth-century **Trinity Chapel** was built in honour of Saint Émilion and converted into a barn during the Revolution, although fragments of frescoes are still visible, including one of Saint Valérie, patron saint of wine-growers. On the other side of the yard, a passage tunnels beneath the belfry to the **catacombs**, where three chambers have been dug out of the soft limestone, used as ossuary and cemetery from the eighth to the eleventh centuries. In the innermost chamber – discovered by a neighbour enlarging his cellar some fifty years ago – a large tombstone bears the inscription: "Aulius is buried between saints Valérie, Émilion and Avic".

The ninth- and twelfth-century monolithic **church** itself is an incredible place. Simple and huge, the entire structure – barrel-vaulting, great square piers and all – has been hacked out of the rock by faithful eighth-century pilgrims, and provided a secure hiding place for the windows of Chartres Cathedral during the 1939–45 war. The whole interior was painted once, but only faint traces survived the Revolution, when a gunpowder factory was installed in the church. These days, every June, the wine council – La Jurade – assembles here in distinctive red robes to evaluate the previous season's wine and decide whether each *viticulteur*'s produce deserves the *appellation contrôlée* rating.

Behind the tourist office, the town comes to an abrupt end with a grand view of the **moat** and old **walls**. To the right is the twelfth-century **collegiate church of the Cordeliers**, with a handsome but badly mutilated doorway and a lovely fourteenth-century **cloister** (daily 10am–noon & 2–6.30pm).

You should take advantage of the produce of this well-respected wine region, whose most famous wine originates at **Château Ausone**, south of St-Émilion. The cellars (which can be visited) have been dug out of limestone directly beneath the vineyards. If you are interested in seeing the vineyards, ask at the **Maison du Vin** (Mon–Sat 9.30am–12.30pm & 2–6pm, Sun 10am–12.30pm & 2.30–6.30pm; ☎57.74.42.42) at the top of the hill by the prominent belfry.

Practicalities

The super-efficient and helpful **tourist office** on place des Créneaux by the belfry (daily 9.30am–12.30pm & 1.45–7pm; ☎57.24.72.03) is a good source of information and organizes French or English tasting tours in various châteaux in the region (June–Sept only 2pm & 4.15pm, 2hr; 51F); they have a very detailed hand-out of châteaux open to the public for those who want to visit independently. If you haven't got a car, **bikes** can be rented from *Location VTT*, opposite the Collegiate Church (☎57.74.42.55). For those who want to off-load small children to get down to some serious wine-tasting, *Les P'tits Lutins*, place P-Meyrat (☎57.24.63.30; 17F an hour), offers daycare for those aged three months to six years.

If you're short of funds or without your own transport, St-Émilion is best left as a day trip from Bordeaux as there's a chronic shortage of budget **accommodation** within the town. However, the tourist office can furnish you with an extensive list of *chambres d'hôte* in the immediate area, and many of them are very reasonably priced. Within the town itself, the two-star *Auberge de la Commanderie* on rue des Cordeliers (☎57.24.70.19; ③–⑤) is the only remotely affordable place to say; the rest are all expensive three-stars like the *Hostellerie de Plaisance* on place du Clocher (☎57.24.72.32; closed Dec–Feb; ⑥–⑧; disabled facilities), with its brilliant views. Three kilometres northwest in the village of **MONTAGNE**, there's a fantastic three-star campsite, *La Barbanne* (☎57.24.75.80), with its own swimming pool.

There's nowhere to buy groceries in town, but you should try the town's speciality once you're here: macaroons were devised here by the Ursuline sisters in 1620, and the one authentic place to buy them is at 1 rue Gaudet, where the tiny mouth-melting biscuits are baked to the original recipe. A good place to **eat**, though, is the relaxed contemporary-style bistro *L'Envers du Décor* on rue du Clocher, with *plats du jour* for 50F and wine by the glass, which you can accompany with gazpacho, cheese, salads and other light snacks.

Blaye

The green slopes behind the river, the **Côtes de Bourg** and **Côtes de Blaye**, were home to wine production long before the Médoc was planted. The wine is a rather heavier, plummier red, and cheaper than anything found on the opposite side of the river, and the **Maison du Vin des Côtes de Blaye** on cours Vauban, the main street of the pretty little town of **BLAYE**, serves up a representative selection of the local produce, with some ridiculously inexpensive wines, the priciest being around 40F.

The town was fortified yet again by Vauban, and the **citadelle** deserves a wander. People still live within it, and it's a strange combination of peaceful village and tourist attraction, typically with an old man sunning himself outside his tiny home, a revolving postcard rack only feet away. A beautiful spot, it has grass, trees, birds and a spectacular view over the Gironde estuary.

The riverfront **tourist office**, opposite the fort (daily 9am–1pm & 2–6pm; June–Sept 9.30am–12.30pm & 2–7pm; ☎57.42.12.09), is really helpful and can reserve rooms free of charge and give out details on wine-tasting in the region. If you fancy **staying** here, there's the expensive *Hôtel La Citadelle* on place d'Armes (☎57.42.17.10; ④); alternatively, there's a **camping municipal** within the *citadelle* (☎57.42.00.00). *Hôtel Bellevue* is a pleasant ivy-covered two-star on the main riverfront drag (☎57.42.00.36; ①), or there's the *Auberge du Porche* around the corner at 5 rue Ernes-Régnier, the street opposite the tourist office (☎57.42.22.69; ④), whose rooms are pricey for what you get but whose food is very good value, with local specialities as well as crêpes and grills, couscous and paella.

The Côte d'Argent

The **Côte d'Argent** is the long stretch of coast from the mouth of the Gironde estuary to Biarritz, which – at over 200km – is the longest, straightest and sandiest in Europe. The endless beaches are backed by high sand dunes, while behind lies the largest forest in western Europe: **Les Landes**. Despite these attractions, the lack of conventional tourist sights means that the coast still gets comparatively few visitors, and away from the main resorts, it is still possible to find deserted stretches of coastline.

Arcachon and around

On summer weekends, the Bordelais escape en masse to **ARCACHON**, the oldest resort on the Côte d'Argent and a forty-minute train ride across flat, sandy forest from Bordeaux. The beaches of white sand are magnificent but crowded, and its central jetties, Thiers and Eyrac, are busy with boats going off on an array of interesting cruises to places like the Île aux Oiseaux and the Dune de Pyla.

The town itself is a sprawl of villas great and small, the most exclusive area being the **ville d'hiver** (winter town), whose wide shady streets are full of fanciful Second Empire mansions overlooking the seaside **ville d'été** (summer town). Well worth a wander, the area can be reached by following the lively pedestrianized and restaurant-filled rue de Maréchal-de-Lattre-de-Tassigny, running perpendicular to the seafront bd de la Plage; at the end of this mouthful of a street, a lift carries you up to the flower-filled, wooded **Parc Maresque** (daily 9am–1pm & 2.15–7pm, 1F up & down), with the *ville d'hiver* beyond it. From the park, there are fine views over the seafront.

A well-stocked, modern **tourist office**, place Roosevelt, can be reached by following av Gambetta back from seafront place Thiers (Mon–Sat 9am–12.30pm & 2–7pm, Sun 9am–12.30pm; July & Aug Mon–Sat 9am–7pm, Sun 9am–12.30pm; ☎56.83.01.69); it organizes excellent guided visits of the Médoc vineyards (Tues & Thurs 2–7pm; 120F). Boats leave the jetties of Thiers and Eyrac on **cruises** (ring *UBA* ☎56.54.60.32 to book fishing trips) to the Île aux Oiseaux (2hr; 65F), an exploration of the Arcachon basin with a look at the Dune de Pyla (2hr 30min; 70F), and a visit to an oyster farm with tasting (1hr 15min; 50F). There's also a regular June to September boat service from here to Cap Ferret on the opposite peninsula (30min; 45F return).

The tourist office doesn't reserve rooms, and you'll be hard pushed to find an inexpensive **hotel**; a couple of reasonable ones include *Le Provence*, 106 bd de la Plage (☎56.83.10.78; ③), and the small, friendly *St-Christaud*, 8 allée de la Chapelle (☎56.83.38.53; ①, July & Aug *demi-pension* only ④). Pricier options include the modern two-star *Les Mimosas*, bis 77 av de la République (☎56.83.45.86; ③; access for the disabled), and in the *ville d'hiver*, the luxurious *Hôtel Sémiramis* in the wonderfully grand *Villa Térésa*, 4 allée Rebsomen (☎56.83.25.87; ⑤–⑦). Alternatively, there are many **holiday apartments** to rent; ask for the booklet *Locations de Vacances Cléconfort* from the tourist office. **Camping** is another option with plenty of sites around the Arcachon Basin, but only the three-star *Le Camping Club*, allée de la Galaxie (☎56.83.24.15; open all year), is actually within the town. Set in an expanse of bird-filled woodland, it's worth the high summer prices. Hostellers can take the boat to Cap Ferret, where there's an IYHF **youth hostel** (☎56.60.64.62; ①; July & Aug).

A great **restaurant** to sample some of the local seafood is the colourful, jam-packed *La Marée*, 86 rue de Lattre-de-Tassigny; not only is it inexpensive, but if you're lucky you can sit out on one of two tiny wrought-iron balconies.

The Dune du Pyla and Le Teich

The Côte d'Argent's chief curiosity is the **Dune du Pyla**, at 114m, the highest sand dune in Europe – a veritable mountain of wind-carved sand, about 8km south of Arcachon. Buses leave from the *gare SNCF* (where you can also rent bikes) every half hour in July and August – about five a day at other times. From the end of the line the road continues straight on uphill for about fifteen minutes, and if you're driving, it costs 15F to use the obligatory car park. There is the inevitable group of stands selling ice cream, galettes and junk, but from the top you get a superb view over the bay of Arcachon and the forest of the Landes stretching away to the south. It's a great sandy slide down to the sea and a long haul back up. You can take a boat trip into the Arcachon basin and past the Dune du Pyla (see above).

At **LE TEICH**, about 14km east of Arcachon in the southeast corner of the Bassin d'Arcachon, one of the most important expanses of wetlands remaining in France has been converted into a bird sanctuary, the **Parc Ornithologique du Teich** (daily 10am–6pm; 31F), one of only two in the country. The only **accommodation** in Le Teich is the **campsite** beside the sanctuary, but you can easily come here on a day trip by train from Arcachon.

Les Landes

Travelling south from Bordeaux by road or rail, you pass for half a day through an unremitting, flat, sandy pine forest known as **Les Landes**. Until the nineteenth century it was a vast, infertile swamp, badly drained because of the impermeable layer of grit deposited by the glaciers of the quaternary age and steadily encroached upon by the shifting sand dunes of the coast. Today it supports nearly 10,000 square kilometres of trees and since 1970 has been designated a *parc naturel régional*.

At **LABOUHEYRE**, on the N10 and the train line from Bordeaux to Bayonne, you can take a restored steam train as far as **SABRES** (June–Sept at least daily; check at other times), via the **Écomusée de Marquèze** (daily 10.15am–5.40pm; Nov–Palm Sunday Sat & Sun only; 30F), set up by the park authorities to illustrate the traditional *landais* way of life, when shepherds used to clomp around the scrub on long stilts.

travel details

Trains

Angoulême to: Bourdeaux (frequent; 1hr); Limoges (4 daily; 1hr 30min–2hr); Poitiers (several daily; 1hr); Royan (frequent; 2hr).

Bordeaux to: Angoulême (frequent; 1hr); Arcachon (frequent; 45min); Bayonne-Biarritz (frequent; 1hr 40min–2hr 30min); Bergerac (6 daily; 1hr 30min); Brive (5 daily; 2hr 30min); Lourdes (4–5 daily; 2hr 30min–3hr); Marseille (5 or 6 daily; 6–7hr); Nice (4 daily; 9–10hr); Paris-Austerlitz (frequent; 5hr 30min); Paris-Montparnasse (frequent; 3hr); Périgueux (5 daily; 1hr 20 min); Poitiers (frequent; 2hr); Saintes (7–11 daily; 1hr 20min); Sarlat (up to 4 daily; 2hr 20min); St-Jean-de-Luz (6 daily; 2hr 15min); Toulouse (frequent; 2hr 20min).

Poitiers to: Angoulême (several daily; 1hr); Bayonne (several daily; 4hr); Biarritz (several daily; 4hr 30min); Bordeaux (several daily; 2hr 10min); Châtellérault (frequent; 20min); Dax (2–3 daily; 2hr–3hr 30min); Hendaye (2 daily; 4hr 55min); Irun (1 daily; 5hr 5min); Limoges (several daily; 2hr 30min); Niort (4–5 daily; 1hr); Paris-Austerlitz (frequent; 2hr 50min); Paris-Montparnasse (frequent; 2hr 10min); La Rochelle (frequent; 1hr 45min); St-Jean-de-Luz (6 daily; 4hr 40min); Surgères (frequent; 1hr 25min).

La Rochelle to: Bordeaux (several daily; 4hr); Nantes (several daily; 1hr 50min); Rochefort (several daily; 20min); Saintes (several daily; 1hr).

Royan to: Angoulême (frequent; 2hr); Cognac (frequent; 1hr); Saintes (frequent; 40min).

Les Sables-d'Olonne to: Nantes (several daily; 1hr 30min); Paris-Montparnasse (several daily; 4hr 45min).

Buses

Bordeaux to: Blaye (frequent; 1hr 45min); Pauillac (daily but infrequent; 1hr); St-Émilion (5 daily; 1hr 15min).

Parthenay to: Airvault (several daily; 25min); Niort (several daily; 50min); Thouars (several daily; 1hr).

Poitiers to: Le Blanc (3 daily; 1hr 25min); Châteauroux (3 daily; 3hr 30min); Chauvigny (3 daily; 35min); Limoges (daily; 3hr); Parthenay (several daily; 1hr–1hr 30min); Ruffec (daily; 2hr 30min); St-Savin (3 daily; 1hr).

Les Sables d'Olonne to: Luçon (4 daily; 2hr); Nantes (4 daily; 5hr 30min).

Saintes to: St-Denis-d'Oléron (2 daily; 2hr).

CHAPTER NINE

THE DORDOGNE, LIMOUSIN AND LOT

T he land covered in this chapter forms a large westward-pointing triangle. Its base is the western edge of the uplands of the Massif Central and its apex almost exactly **Castillon-la-Bataille** on the River Dordogne, a little way downstream from **Bergerac**. It is the area which was most in dispute between the English and the French during the Hundred Years' War and most in demand among English visitors and second-home buyers in recent times. And there is a satisfying historical irony in this, for it was at Castillon on July 17, 1453, that John Talbot – veteran English general of the Hundred Years' War – was killed and his army defeated in what was to prove the last battle of that war.

Although it does not coincide exactly with either the modern French administrative boundaries or the old provinces of Périgord and Quercy, which constitute the core of the region, it has a physical and geographical homogeneity because of its great rivers: the **Dordogne** with its tributaries, the **Lot** and the **Aveyron**, all of which drain the waters of the western Massif Central into the mighty **Garonne**, which forms the southern limit of the chapter.

There are no great cities in the area; its charm lies in the landscapes and the dozens of harmonious small towns and villages, so that it is impossible to establish a hierarchy of attractiveness. Some, like **Sarlat** and **Rocamadour**, are so well known that they are overrun with tourists. Others, like **Figeac**, **Villefranche-de-Rouergue**, **Gourdon**, **Montauban**, **Monflanquin** and the many *bastides* (fortified towns) that fill the area between the Lot and Dordogne, boast no single notable sight but are perfect organic ensembles.

The landscapes are surprisingly homogeneous, too. From **Limoges** in the province of Limousin in the north to **Montauban** in the south towards Toulouse, the country is gently hilly, full of lush little valleys and miles of woodland, mainly oak. **Limousin**, at the north of this area, is slightly greener and wetter, the south more arid. But you can travel a long way without seeing a radical shift, except in the uplands of the **Plateau de Millevaches**, where the rivers plunge into gorges and the woods are beech, chestnut

---

ACCOMMODATION PRICE CATEGORIES

All the hotels, youth hostels and guesthouses listed in this book have been price-graded according to the following scale, and although costs will rise slightly overall with the life of this edition, the relative comparisons should remain valid. Paris and the large cities will, as anywhere, be more expensive than equivalent accommodation in the countryside or small towns. The prices quoted are for the cheapest available double room in high season, although remember that many of the cheap places will have more expensive rooms with en-suite facilities.

① Under 160F	④ 300–400F	⑦ 600–700F
② 160–220F	⑤ 400–500F	⑧ Over 700F
③ 220–300F	⑥ 500–600F	

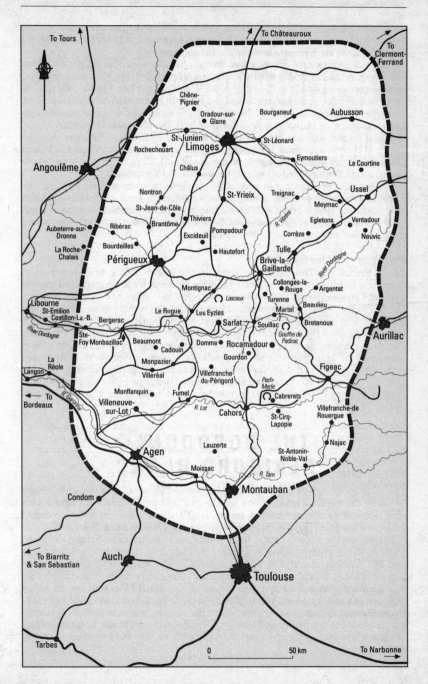

and conifer plantations. The other characteristic landscape is the *causses*, dry scrubby limestone plateaux like the **Causse de Gramat** between the Dordogne and the Lot and the **Causse de Limogne** between the Lot and Aveyron.

Where the rivers have cut their way through the limestone, the valleys are walled with overhanging cliffs riddled with fissures, underground streambeds and caves. And in these caves – especially in the valley of the Vézère around **Les Eyzies** – are some of the most developed prehistoric paintings and reliefs to be found anywhere in the world. The other great artistic legacy of the area is the Romanesque sculpture, visible in its finest examples on the churches at **Souillac** and **Beaulieu-sur-Dordogne**, but all modelled on the supreme example of the cloister of St-Pierre in **Moissac**. And the dearth of luxurious châteaux is compensated for by the numerous splendid fortresses of purely military design: **Bonaguil**, **Najac**, **Excideuil**, **Beynac** and, for lovers of the romantic ruin, the untended remains of **Chalusset** and **Ventadour**.

The wartime Resistance was very active in these out-of-the-way regions, and the roadsides are dotted with tiny memorials to individuals or small groups of men, killed in ambushes or shot in reprisals. There is one monstrous monument to wartime atrocity: the ruined village of **Oradour-sur-Glane**, still as the Nazis left it after massacring the population and setting fire to the houses.

Dordogne – an identity crisis

To the French, the **Dordogne** is a river. To the British, it is a much looser term, covering a vast area roughly equivalent to what the French call Périgord, and starting south of Limoges, taking in the Vézère and Dordogne valleys and much in between. The Dordogne is also a *département*, with fixed boundaries that pay no heed to either definition. The central part of the *département*, around Périgueux and the River Isle, is known as *Périgord Blanc*, after the light, white colour of its rock outcrops; the southeastern half around Sarlat as *Périgord Noir*, said to be darker in aspect than the *Blanc* because of the preponderance of oak woods. To confuse matters further the tourist authorities recently added another two colours to the Périgord patchwork: *Périgord Vert*, the far north of the *département*, so called because of its pastureland; and *Périgord Pourpre* in the southwest, purple because it includes the wine-growing area around Bergerac.

THE DORDOGNE:
PÉRIGORD BLANC

The close green valleys of **Périgord Blanc** – so-called because of the white chalky limestone the terrain is made up of – are like an Englishman's dream of England: very rural, with plenty of space and few people, large tracts of woodland and uncultivated land – and sunshine. Perhaps that's why so many of them have set up home here.

Périgueux, the region's capital, is interesting for its domed cathedral and its Roman remains, whose existence alone is a reminder of how long these parts have been civilized. But it is in the countryside that the region's finest monuments lie. One of the loveliest stretches is the **valley of the Dronne**, from **Aubeterre** on the Charentes border through **Brantôme** to the marvellous Renaissance château of **Puyguilhem**, the abbey of **Boschaux** and the perfect village of **St-Jean-de-Côle**, and on to the great fortress of **Excideuil** and the Limousin border, where the country begins to change, becoming not mountainous but higher and less cosy. Truffle-lovers might like to take a look at **Sorges**, where there is a marked path through truffle country and a museum to explain it all.

THE FOOD AND WINE OF PERIGORD

The two great stars of Périgord cuisine are **foie gras** and **truffles** (*truffes*). *Foie gras* is eaten on its own, in succulent slabs, often combined with truffles to accompany a huge variety of dishes from scrambled eggs to stuffed carp. In fact, you can be sure that this is what you are getting with any dish that has *sauce Périgueux* or *à la périgourdine* as part of its name. Truffles also come *à la cendre*, wrapped in bacon and cooked in hot ashes.

The other mainstay of Périgord cuisine is the grey Toulouse **goose**, whose fat is used in the cooking of everything, most commonly perhaps in the standard potato dish, *pommes sarladaises*. The goose fattens well: *gavé* or crammed with corn, it goes from six to ten kilos in weight in three weeks, with its liver alone weighing nearly a kilo. When the liver has been used for *foie gras*, the meat is cooked and preserved in its own thick yellow grease as *confits d'oie*, which you can either eat on its own or use in the preparation of other dishes, like *cassoulet*. **Duck** is used in the same way, both for *foie gras* and *confits*. *Magrets de canard*, or slices of duck breast, are one of the favourite ways of eating duck and appear on practically every restaurant menu.

Another common goose delicacy is *cou d'oie farci* – goose neck stuffed with sausage meat, duck liver and truffles, which you can also buy in pots; a favourite salad throughout the region is made with warm *gésiers* or goose gizzards. Try not to be put off by this, or your palate will miss out on some delicious experiences – like the stuffed **sheep's feet** or *tripoux* that is really an Auvergnat dish but is quite often served in neighbouring areas like the Rouergue. Other less problematic specialities include stuffed *cèpes* or wild mushrooms, *ballottines* or fillets of poultry stuffed, rolled and poached, the little flat discs of goat's cheese called *cabécou* and the sweet light bread called *fouasse*, rather like the Greek *tsoureki*.

The **wines** should not be scorned either. There are the fine dark, almost peppery reds from Cahors, and both reds and whites from the vineyards of Bergerac, of which the sweet, white Monbazillac is the most famous. Pecharmant is the fanciest of the reds, but there are some very drinkable Côtes de Bergerac, much like the neighbouring Bordeaux and far cheaper. If you are thinking of taking a stock of wine home, you could do much worse than make some enquiries in Bergerac itself, Ste-Foy, or any of the villages in the vineyard area.

Périgueux

PÉRIGUEUX, capital of the *département* of the Dordogne, is a small but busy and prosperous market town for a province made rich by tourism and specialized farming. Its name derives from the *Petrocorii*, the local Gaullish tribe, but it was the Romans who transformed it into an important settlement. A few Roman remains, as well as a medieval *vieille ville*, survive to this day.

Arrival and accommodation

At the southern end of bd Montaigne is the unattractive place Francheville, with the **gare routière**, an underground car park and the **tourist office** at no. 26 (Mon–Sat 9am–noon & 2–6pm; mid-June to mid-Sept Mon–Sat 9am–7pm, Sun & hols 10am–5pm; ☎53.53.10.63), next to the Tour Mataguerre, the last surviving bit of the town's medieval defences. Perigueux's **gare SNCF** (☎53.09.50.50) lies at the end of rue Président-Wilson. If you have no transport of your own, it might be worth contacting Monsieur Delmotte, who runs **minibus and taxi tours** to sites in the surrounding country (150–200F in the minibus, more in the taxi; reservations ☎53.53.70.47). And, if you are a mime fan, keep an eye out for the annual **International Mime Festival** at the beginning of August.

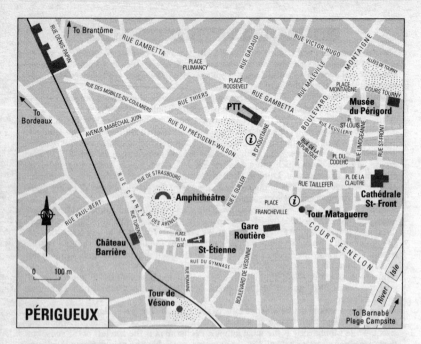

PÉRIGUEUX

Opposite the train station, along rue Denis-Papin, you'll find a number of reasonable **hotels**. The cheapest is the acceptable but rather worn *Hôtel des Voyageurs*, 26 rue Denis-Papin (☎53.53.17.44; ①), followed by the much larger *Hôtel du Midi et Terminus* at no. 18 (☎53.53.41.06; ②–③), with a good regional restaurant serving menus from 65F. More attractive options are the *Hôtel des Arènes*, 2 rue du Gymnase, in a quiet street behind the church of St-Étienne (☎53.53.49.85; ③), and – close to the centre – the *Univers*, 18 cours de Montaigne (☎53.53.34.79; ②–③), with a pretty terrace and restaurant. Best of all is the *Hôtel du Périgord*, 74 rue Victor-Hugo, the westward continuation of cours Tourny (☎53.53.33.63; ③; closed Oct 18–Nov 4), in an attractive house with an exuberantly flowery garden behind; it has a good restaurant as well, with menus from 87F. There is also an IYHF **youth hostel** at the *Résidence Lakanal*, 32 bd Lakanal (☎53.53.52.05; ①; reception 5–7/8pm) – follow the rail line south of the station to the far edge of town, or take rue Littré from place Francheville to rue Bertrand-de-Born.

The City

The main hub of the city's contemporary life is the tree-shaded **boulevard Montaigne** with its cafés and brasseries, which marks the western edge of the *vieille ville*. It runs down to the large place Bugeaud, from where it is only a short walk along rue Taillefer to the domed and coned **Cathédrale St-Front** (daily 8am–12.30pm & 2.30–7.30pm), its square, pineapple-capped belfry surging far above the roofs of the surrounding medieval houses. Unfortunately it's no beauty, having suffered from the zealous attentions of the purist nineteenth-century restorer Abadie, best known for the white elephant of the Sacré-Cœur in Paris. The result is too white, too new, too regular, and the roof is spiked all over with ill-proportioned nipple-like projections serving no obvious purpose; "a supreme example of how not to restore", Freda White tartly observed in her classic travelogue, *Three Rivers of France*. It's a pity, for it was one of the most distinctive Romanesque churches undertaken in France, modelled on St Mark's in Venice and the Holy Apostles in Constantinople. Nevertheless, the Byzantine influence is still evident in the interior in the Greek-cross plan – unusual in France – and in the massive clean curves of the domes and their supporting arches. The big Baroque altarpiece, carved in walnut wood, in the gloomy east bay, is worth a look, too, depicting the Assumption of the Virgin, with a humorous little detail in the illustrative scenes from her life of a puppy tugging the infant Jesus' sheets from his bed with its teeth.

At the west end of the cathedral in **place de la Clautre** beneath the blank façade of the original eleventh-century building, there is a twice-weekly **market** on Wednesday and Saturday. From the terrace below you look across to the wooded hills beyond the River Isle, while north and south of the square crowd the renovated buildings of the medieval **old town**. The longest and finest street is the narrow **rue Limogeanne**, lined with Renaissance mansions, now turned into shops and *pâtisseries*. The surrounding streets are also scattered with fine Renaissance houses; particularly handsome are the **Hôtel de Gamançon**, 3 rue de la Constitution, now the seat of the *Conservation des Monuments Historiques*, and the more sedate **Hôtel de Crenoux** next door. Another curious one is at 17 rue de l'Éguillerie, on the corner of the attractive **place St-Louis**, where a turretted watchtower leans out over the street. There are other old houses down along the river by the Pont des Barris, notably the fifteenth-century **Maison des Consuls**.

At the northern end of rue Limogeanne, out on the broad tree-lined cours Tourny, is the city's museum, the **Musée du Périgord** (daily except Tues 10am–noon & 2–6pm; Oct–March closes 5pm; 10F), with some very beautiful Gallo-Roman mosaics, an extensive and important prehistoric collection, and some exquisite Limoges enamels near the exit, especially the portraits of the twelve Cæsars.

La Cité

Roman Périgueux, known as **La Cité,** lies to the west of the town centre towards the *gare SNCF*. The main vestige is concealed in the Jardin des Arènes – the ruins of an enormous **amphitheatre**, dismantled in the third century and now an atmospheric ruin, while over by the train line in an attractive public garden at the end of rue Romaine is the high brick **Tour de Vésone**, the last remains of a temple to the city's guardian goddess. More bits and pieces – chiefly jumbled masonry – are visible nearby in the so-called **Maison Romane** and also the **Porte Normande** off rue Turenne, essentially defensive works hastily cobbled together to keep the invading Visigoths at bay in the fourth century.

The rather mutilated church in this neighbourhood – the result of Huguenot anger in 1577 – is the former cathedral, the **church of St-Étienne**, condemned to life as a traffic island in place de la Cité.

Eating and drinking

Surprisingly, there is no great abundance of good **restaurants** in Périgueux. Apart from the brasseries around bd Montaigne and the hotel restaurants listed opposite, the best general area to look is around rue Limogeanne and the delightful place St-Louis. A couple of places to try are *Lou Chabrol*, 22 rue Eguillerie (closed Sun; regional cuisine 80–130F), *La Tartine*, 10 rue St-Silain (closed Sun), with snacks and *plats* from about 50F, and *Au Petit Chef*, 5 pl du Coderc (lunchtime only, from 55F; closed Sun) – all close to rue Limogeanne. If you fancy a change from strictly French fare, *Le Canard Laqué*, 2 rue Lammary, is a good and popular Chinese place with menus from 65F, with the *Texas* in rue de la Sagesse representing the US (closed Sun) – it even serves Californian wine.

Brantôme and the valley of the Dronne

Although **Brantôme** itself is very much on the tourist trail, the country both to the west and east of the town along the **River Dronne** remains largely undisturbed. It is tranquil, very beautiful and restoring, best savoured at a gentle pace, perhaps by bike or even by canoeing along the river.

Brantôme

BRANTÔME, 27km north of Périgueux on the Angoulême road and beloved of British tourists, sits in a bend of the River Dronne, whose still, water-lilied surface mirrors the limes and weeping willows of the riverside gardens. On the north bank of the river are the church and convent buildings of the **ancienne abbaye** that for centuries has been Brantôme's focus. Its stone façades, now masking the secular offices of the **Hôtel de Ville**, have that pallor and blank stare so characteristic of the self-denying institutional life. Not that there was much of the flagellant about this monastery's most notorious abbot, Pierre de Bourdeilles, the sixteenth-century author of scurrilous tales of life at the royal court.

Take a look inside the **église abbatiale**, for the palm-frond vaulting of the chapter-house and the font made from a carved and grounded pillar capital; there is also a fine stone staircase at this end of the Hôtel de Ville. But Brantôme's best architectural feature is the Limousin-style Romanesque **belfry** standing behind the church against the wooded and cave-riddled scarp that forms the backdrop to the village.

There are no other specific sights in Brantôme, but a walk through the nearby **gardens** and along the pleasant balustraded **river banks** is a must.

Practicalities

The **tourist office** (Easter–Oct 10am–noon & 2–5.30pm) is in a lime-shaded Renaissance pavilion down on the river bank, and there are three daily buses from Périgueux (Mon–Sat), connecting with the *TGV* in Angoulême.

The best cheap **accommodation** and food in town is to be had at the *Hôtel Vensaveau*, 8 pl de Gaulle (☎53.05.71.42; ②–③; closed mid- to end Oct; brasserie 80–100F), opposite the *Hôtel Chabro* (☎53.05.70.15; ③–⑤; closed Feb, mid-Nov to mid-Dec & Sun evening & Mon out of season), whose restaurant *Les Frères Charbonnel* has a good menu at 160F. There's also a **campsite** to the north of the village on the D78 (☎53.05.75.24; June–Sept).

Outside the hotel **restaurants**, the café/brasserie *Au Fil de l'Eau* on quai Bertin, with tables down by the river, is as cheap as Brantôme's restaurants come, as long as you don't go for the *omelette aux truffes*. If you're feeling rich, you could treat yourself to a meal for upwards of 160F in the beautiful *Moulin de l'Abbaye* **hotel** by the tourist office (☎53.05.80.22; ⑧; closed Mon lunchtime & Oct 24–April 28), which also does rooms at luxury prices.

Bourdeilles

BOURDEILLES, 16km down the Dronne from Brantôme by a beautiful back road, is relatively hard to reach. Perhaps the most appealing way is by canoe – you can rent kayaks or canoes from Porte des Réformés in Brantôme (see above). It's a sleepy backwater, an ancient rural village clustering around its **château** on a rocky spur above the river (daily except Tues 10am–noon & 2–6pm; July & Aug 10am–7pm; mid-Oct to Dec & Feb 9–March 2–5pm; closed Jan–Feb 8; 25F). The château consists of two buildings: one a thirteenth-century fortress, the other an elegant Renaissance residence begun by the lady of the house as a piece of unsuccessful favour-currying with Catherine de Médicis – unsuccessful because Catherine never came to stay and the château remained unfinished. Climb the octagonal keep to look down on the town's clustered roofs, the weir and the boat-shaped mill parting the current, and along the Dronne to the cornfields and the manors hidden among the trees.

The château is now home to an exceptional collection of furniture bequeathed to the state by its former owners. Among the more notable pieces are some splendid Spanish dowry chests; a sixteenth-century Rhenish entombment with life-sized statues, embodying the very image of the serious, self-satisfied medieval burgher; and a fifteenth-century primitive Catalan triptych of an exorcism, with a bull-headed devil shooting skywards out of a kneeling princess.

There are no facilities in town to speak of, apart from a **camping municipal** by the river below the castle (mid-June to mid-Sept).

Ribérac and around

Surrounded by an intimate, hilly countryside of woods and hay meadows and drowsy hilltop villages, **RIBÉRAC**, 30km downstream from Bourdeilles, is a pleasant if unremarkable town, whose greatest claim to fame is its major Friday **market**, bringing in producers and wholesalers from all around. However, with its two or three good **hotels**, it makes an agreeable base from which to explore the quiet, lush Dronne landscape. The cheapest of them is the *Hôtel L'Univers* at 2 av de Verdun on the corner of the wide central place de Gaulle (☎53.90.04.38; ①), with a good restaurant charging around 70–80F for an average meal. Much more attractive and very good value is the *Hôtel de France* on the opposite side of the square at 3 rue Marc-Dufraisse (☎53.90.00.61; ②–③), with a terrace garden and a restaurant of some originality and local renown (menus 68–270F, *carte* around 200F). For an even more rustic sojourn there's an old-fashioned country **hotel** in **VERTEILLAC**, 12km to the north: *Le Périgord* (☎53.91.62.79; closed Feb & Mon; ①; family cuisine 75–120F), which would put you almost within walking distance of some delightful little villages. There's also a **camping municipal** on the Angoulême road outside Ribérac.

For further ideas about *chambres d'hôtes* in the surrounding country Ribérac's **tourist office** on place de Gaulle, close to the *Univers*, is the place to ask (Mon & Wed 1.30–6.30pm, Tues, Thurs & Fri 9am–noon & 1.30–6.30pm; July to mid-Sept Mon–Sat 9am–noon & 1.30–6.30pm, Sun 10am–noon; ☎53.90.03.10); they can also provide information about Romanesque churches in outlying villages of Ribérac that could provide a focus for leisurely wandering. **Bikes** can be rented from the *Peugeot* bike shop at 19 rue Jean-Moulin.

Aubeterre-sur-Dronne and around

A little touristy, but very beautiful with its ancient galleried and turretted houses, **AUBETERRE-SUR-DRONNE** hangs on a steep hillside above the river, clustered around a beautiful central square shaded by plane trees. The village's principal curiosity is the cavernous **Église Monolithe** (daily 9.30am–12.30pm & 2–6pm; Oct–June closed Tues; 16F), carved out of the soft rock of the cliff face in the twelfth century, with its rock-hewn tombs going back to the sixth. A tunnel connects with the **château** on the bluff overhead. There is also the extremely beautiful **church of St-Jacques**, with an eleventh-century façade sculpted and decorated in the richly carved Poitiers style on the street leading uphill from the square.

The **tourist office** is on the main square (July–Oct daily 10am–noon & 2–6pm; closed Mon am), almost next door to the elderly *Hôtel de France*, now under English ownership (☎45.98.50.43; ②). There is a **campsite** just below the village, and the delightful *Hostellerie du Château* (☎45.98.50.11; ②), where you can also eat for around 120F. There is a daily bus to Angoulême in term time, and Chalais, which is on the Angoulême train line, is only 12km away.

South of Aubeterre, towards **LA ROCHE-CHALAIS**, the country gradually changes. Farmland gives way to extensive forest of oak and sweet chestnut, bracken and broom, interspersed with sour, marshy pasture, very sparsely populated. It's ideal cycling and picnicking country.

La Roche-Chalais has a couple of more sophisticated places to **eat** and **sleep**, along with a **campsite**. The *Hôtel Soleil d'Or*, 14 rue de l'Apre-Côte (☎53.90.86.71; ④; restaurant from 110F), has a magnificent view over the surrounding country and very comfortable rooms. There is also a small **restaurant** on the square by the church, *Au Petit Gourmet* (closed Sat evening & Sun; menu at 55F), opposite the **tourist office**, which provides local walking routes and information about visits to farms in the vicinity. There are also **campsites** in Bonnes and St-Aulaye, and St-Aulaye also has a simple, old-fashioned **hotel** just off the village square in place Champ-du-Foire called *Chez Jean-Pierre* (☎53.90.82.29; ①), with a restaurant offering a menu at 55F.

Villars and around

A dozen kilometres northeast of Brantôme lies the hamlet of **VILLARS**, a village with no particular sight but surrounded by beautiful countryside and making an excellent and not overexpensive base for visiting the **Château de Puyguilhem** and **St-Jean-de-Côle**. A short distance north of the hamlet are the **Grottes de Villars** (daily mid-June to mid-Sept 10–11.30am & 2–6.30pm; otherwise Sun only 2–6.30pm; 50F), where local cavers discovered prehistoric paintings – notably of horses and bison – in 1958.

Villars' one **hotel**, *Le Relais de l'Archerie*, is housed in a nineteenth-century mini-château with terrace and gardens (☎53.54.88.64; ②–③; restaurant from 80F), or there is alternative accommodation and food only 6km away at Champagnac-de-Belair at the *Hôtel des Voyageurs* (☎53.54.21.29; ②; restaurant from 70F).

Château de Puyguilhem

About a kilometre outside Villars, the appealing **Château de Puyguilhem** (daily except Tues 9.30am–noon & 2–6pm; Feb & March daily except Tues 10am–noon & 2–7pm; July–Sept 7 daily 9am–noon & 2–7pm; mid-Oct to mid-Dec daily except Tues 10am–noon & 2–5pm; closed mid-Dec to Jan; 25F) sits on the edge of a valley and is backed by oak woods. The building you see today was erected at the beginning of the sixteenth century on the site of an earlier and more military fortress. Today's octagonal tower and broad spiral staircase, steep roofs and elaborate sculpted false dormer windows and magnificent fireplaces combine to form a perfect example of French Renaissance architecture. From the gallery at the top of the stairs you get a close-up of the roof and window decoration, as well as a view down the valley, which once was filled by a lake.

In the next valley, and very much worth the travelling time, lies the ruined Cistercian **Abbey of Boschaux** on the edge of a tobacco field in the middle of the woods, reached by a lane not much bigger than a farm track. Its charm lies as much in the fact that it is – for once – unfenced, unpampered and uncharged for, as in the pure, stark lines of its twelfth-century architecture.

On the way, perched on the intervening hilltop overlooking Puyguilhem, is a farm called *Lafarge* that does **bed and breakfast** for around 180F and delicious home-cooking from 75F.

St-Jean-de-Côle

Midway between Villars and Thiviers on the main Périgueux–Angoulême road, **ST-JEAN-DE-CÔLE** must rank as one of the loveliest villages in the Dordogne. Its ancient houses huddle together in typical medieval fashion around a wide sandy square dominated on one side by the huge single-nave **church of St-Jean-Baptiste**, built in the eleventh century, and the rugged-looking **Château de la Marthonie** (July & Aug 10.45am–noon & 2–7pm; 21F) on the other. The château, first erected in the fourteenth century, has acquired various additions in a pleasingly organic kind of growth.

The **tourist office** (daily April–Sept 10am–noon & 2–6pm) is also on the square, as well as the most attractive *Coq Rouge* **restaurant** (☎53.62.32.71; closed Wed), whose excellent menus will set you back between 85F and 140F – it's wise to book, though. Equally, you can eat at the wisteria-covered *Hôtel St-Jean* on the main road through the village (☎53.52.23.20; ②–③; restaurant 60–150F). There's a **campsite** at **LES VERGNES** on the Villars road.

Thiviers and Sorges

If you're heading along the main road from Périgueux to Angoulême, stop off at **THIVIERS**, on the Périgueux-Limoges train line, a village with some pretty old houses round the church; its **tourist office** is on the central square (Tues–Fri 10am–noon & 3–6pm, Sat 9am–12.15pm & 3–6pm; July & Aug daily 10am–noon & 3–6pm) and has a small **truffle museum** (same hours; 10F), giving a blow-by-blow rundown of the origins of the luxury fungus.

Further along, **SORGES** is strung out along the road, and has less to offer aesthetically than Thiviers, but with two reasonable **hotels**, now part of the same establishment: *Hôtel de la Mairie* by the church and *Hôtel de la Truffe* on the main road (☎53.05.02.11; ③; good local restaurant from 70F). The **tourist office** (daily except Mon 10am–noon & 2–6/7pm) contains another **truffle museum**, and can also direct you to a marked path that gives an idea of how and where truffles live.

The Château de Hautefort

Forty kilometres northeast of Périgueux, the **Château de Hautefort** (Sun 2–5pm; March–June, Sept & Oct 9.45am–noon & 2–6pm; July & Aug 9.45am–noon & 2–7pm; 35F) enjoys a majestic position at the end of a wooded spur above its feudal village. A magnificent example of good living on a grand scale, the castle has an elegance that is out of step with the usual rough stone fortresses of Périgord. You approach across a wide esplanade flanked by formal gardens, cross the moat by a drawbridge through the oldest part of the building and enter a stylish Renaissance courtyard backed by an arcaded gallery and enclosed by slated towers. Once the property of well-known troubadour Bertrans de Born, it passed into the hands of the Hautefort family in the seventeenth century and was extensively remodelled. It was the childhood home of Marie de Hautefort, the young beauty who so captivated Louis XIII.

It is impossible to get from Périgueux to Hautefort and back in one day using public transport: although there is a morning **bus** from Périgueux via Cubjac (Wed & Sat), on other days there's only an evening service. You could get a Brive train as far as La Bachellerie from Périgueux, and hitch the final 15km. By car the most attractive route is along the River Auvézère via Cubjac and **TOURTOIRAC**, where Antoine-Orélie I, "King of Araucania", died in 1878. This bizarre character was a Périgueux lawyer who, deciding he was destined for higher things, borrowed money and set sail for Patagonia, where he proclaimed himself king of the Araucanian Indians.

Excideuil

EXCIDEUIL, connected by a bus service from Périgueux (Mon–Sat), is about 15km from Hautefort on the other side of the D704 Limoges road. In addition to its busy Thursday **market** and the tight streets of the old town, its real interest is the **castle,** splendidly impressive on its ridge overlooking the valley of the Loue and dominated by its skyscraping medievàl keeps. You can enter the precinct but not the privately owned castle itself. It is, however, a classic and well worth seeing. An additional bonus is the typically French *Hostellerie du Fin Chapon* just below the castle at 3 place du Château (☎53.62.42.38; ②; restaurant 65F at lunchtime, evening from 90F), with simple but agreeable rooms. The **tourist office** is next door. There is also a simple but prettily sited **campsite** by the river on the Limoges side of town.

THE DORDOGNE: PÉRIGORD NOIR

Périgord Noir covers the central part of the valley of the Dordogne, around its junction with the River Vézère, and its name refers to the high density of trees growing here. This is distinctive Dordogne country: deep-cut valleys whose water-smooth cliffs have been gradually eroded, with fields of maize in the alluvial bottoms and dense oak woods on the heights, interspersed with patches of not-very-fertile farmland. Plantations of walnut trees (cultivated for their oil), flocks of low-slung grey geese (their livers enlarged for *foie gras*) and prehistoric-looking round stone huts called *bories* are other hallmarks of the region, which for the purposes of this chapter we have extended to include Bergerac in the west and Argentat in the east.

The absolute highlight of the area must be the **prehistoric cave paintings** in the Vézère Valley. But there are also the **bastides** – medieval military settlements – and some lovely villages in the Dordogne Valley itself, as well as the breathtaking church of St-**Amand-de-Coly**, sculptures in the porch of the church at **Beaulieu-sur-Dordogne**, and, lastly, the wines of **Bergerac**.

Many of these places, especially round **Sarlat** and the caves, get very crowded in summer and yet the crowds stick very much to the beaten track. If you want to escape the masses, take the back roads and you will have them to yourself.

Bergerac and around

BERGERAC, capital of what is now known as *Périgord Pourpre* – because of the region's wines – lies on the river bank in the wide plain of the Dordogne. Once a flourishing port for the wine trade, it is still the main market centre for the surrounding maize, vine and tobacco farms. Devastated in the Wars of Religion, when most of its Protestant population fled overseas, Bergerac is now essentially a modern town with some interesting and attractive reminders of the past.

From the *gare SNCF*, it's a ten-minute walk down cours Alsace-Lorraine and its continuation to the **vieille ville**, a calm and pleasant area to wander through, with drinking fountains on the street corners and numerous late medieval houses. In rue de l'Ancien-Pont, the splendid seventeenth-century Maison Peyrarède houses an informative **Musée du Tabac** (Tues–Sat 10am–noon & 2–5/6pm; Sun 2.30–6.30pm; 12F), detailing the history of the weed, with collections of pipes and tools of the trade.

Bergerac has a couple of other museums, the best of which is the small **Musée Éthnographique Régional** on the central place de la Myrpe (Tues–Fri 10am–noon & 2–5.30pm, Sat 10am–noon, Sun 2–6.30pm; 15F), with displays on viticulture, barrel making and the town's once-bustling river-trading past. Outside on the square is a statue in honour of **Cyrano de Bergerac**, the town's most famous association, recently turned into the most expensive French film ever made, starring Gérard Dépardieu. The big-nosed lead character in Edmond Rostand's play, though fictional, was inspired by the seventeenth-century philosopher of the same name, who, sadly, had nothing to do with the town.

Practicalities

The **gare SNCF** is on cours Alsace-Lorraine, ten minutes' walk from the old town. The **tourist office** is at 97 rue Neuve-d'Argenson (summer daily 9am–7pm; winter Tues–Sat 9am–noon & 1.30–5.30pm; ☎53.57.03.11). You can rent **bicycles** from 11 place Gambetta or 114 bd de l'Entrepôt. There is a vast **market** in the covered *halles* off the Grande-Rue in the old town on Wednesday and Saturday.

For **accommodation** in town, there are several small hotels in the back streets. A cheap choice is the *Hôtel Pozzi*, 11 rue Pozzi (☎53.57.24.90; ①–②). For something more comfortable, try the slightly stuffy *Le Cyrano*, 2 bd Montaigne (☎53.57.02.76; ②–③), which has an excellent restaurant with menus in the range of 90–200F. There's also a **camping municipal**, *La Pelouse* (☎53.57.06.67; open all year), a short way west of the centre by the river. Good but inexpensive **eating** can be had at *L'Imparfait* in rue des Fontaines.

Château de Monbazillac

Half a dozen kilometres south of Bergerac and best reached by **bicycle** (see above), the small but handsome sixteenth-century **Château de Monbazillac** (daily 10am–noon & 2–5/6pm; June–Sept 10am–12.30pm & 2–7pm; 20F) sits on gently rising slopes among its long-famous vineyards. The wine – out of fashion for many years – is white, velvety and sweet, best consumed with desserts or chilled as an apéritif. Red Bergeracs, on the other hand, often produced by small growers on the slopes north of the river and for many years known only to local connoisseurs, are beginning to enjoy much greater popularity, particularly among the British, at prices far more reasonable than the better known clarets of Bordeaux. The tour of the château includes a glass of *Monbazillac* at the end.

Sainte-Foy-la-Grande and around

Driving west from Bergerac along the River Dordogne, the first place you come to of any size is the *bastide* town of **SAINTE-FOY-LA-GRANDE,** whose narrow central streets still retain a number of ancient houses, in particular that occupied by the **tourist office** at 102 rue de la Republique (Tues, Thurs & Sat 10am–12.30pm & 2.30–6pm, Mon, Wed & Fri 2.30–6pm; July & Aug daily 10am–12.30pm & 3–7pm; ☎57.46.03.00). It is worth a stop for its mouthwatering Saturday **market** and the exceptional helpfulness of the tourist office, with its good list of *chambres d'hote* and local wine-tasting sessions. **Bikes** can be rented from *Ets David*, 29 rue Jean-Jacques-Rousseau, or *Ets Roturier*, 41 rue Victor-Hugo; in the absence of a car, this would be the best means of going on to the sights that lie in the surrounding countryside. The only other realistic option is the 12.30pm bus to Lamothe-Montravel, which still leaves you with a three- or four-kilometre walk to either destination.

It is 13km from Sainte-Foy to **MONTCARET,** whose attraction is a third-century **Roman villa** with superb mosaics and baths (daily 10am–noon & 2–6pm; April–Sept 9am–noon & 2–6pm; 15F), with an adjoining museum displaying the many objects exhumed on the site. It is another 3.5km to the **Château de Montaigne** (daily 9am–noon & 2–7pm; Sept–June closed Mon & Tues; 25F), built by the sixteenth-century Michel Eyquem de Montaigne, whose chatty, digressive essays on the nature of life and humankind have influenced many writers since. All that remains of the original building is Montaigne's tower-study, its beams inscribed with his maxims; the rest of it was rebuilt in pseudo-Renaissance style after a fire in 1885.

The *bastide* country

During the long struggles of the thirteenth and fourteenth centuries for control of the southwest of France, both the English and the French combatants constructed dozens of new towns – principally in the disputed "frontier" areas between the Dordogne and Garonne rivers – in an attempt to consolidate their hold on their respective territories. These towns, known as *bastides*, were essentially fortified settlements, walled and gated and built on a rational grid-plan round a central arcaded market square, in marked contrast to the haphazard organic growth of the usual medieval town. As an incentive to local people, anyone who was prepared to build, inhabit and defend them was granted various perks and concessions, including a measure of self-government remarkable in feudal times.

There is a heavy concentration of these settlements in the country to the south of Bergerac between the rivers Dordogne and Lot. Many retain no more than vestiges of their original aspect, but two of the finest that are almost entirely intact are to be found within a fifty-kilometre radius of Bergerac: **Monpazier** and **Monflanquin**.

Monpazier and around

MONPAZIER is one of the most complete of the surviving *bastides*, and still relatively free of the commercialism that suffocates a place like Domme (see p566). Built in 1284 by King Edward I of England – who was also Duke of Aquitaine – it hasn't spread that far beyond its original limits; but picturesque and placid though it is today, the village has a hard and bitter history, being twice – in 1594 and 1637 – the centre of peasant rebellions, provoked by the misery that followed the Wars of Religion* and brutally suppressed: the 1637 peasants' leader was broken on the wheel in the square.

It is now severely depopulated. As the street ends the fields begin, and you look out over the surrounding country. There is an ancient *lavoir*, where women used to wash clothes, a much-altered church and a gem of a central square – sunny, still and slightly menacing, like a Sicilian piazza at siesta time. Deep, shady arcades pass under all the houses, which are separated from each other by a small gap to reduce fire risk; at the corners the buttresses are cut away to allow the passage of laden pack animals.

The best place for an overnight **stay** in Monpazier is the *Hôtel de France*, 21 rue St-Jacques (☎53.22.60.06; ③; closed Dec), with an agreeable regional restaurant from 70F. There are **campsites** in the direction of Bergerac (*Lac de Véronne*) and Villeréal (*Moulin de David*). Alternatively there is *camping à la ferme*, 5km along a country lane in a great spot at Le Bouyssou (☎53.22.66.58), signposted as you enter Monpazier.

Another possibility is to base yourself in one of the attractive villages within a twenty-kilometre radius: **BELVÈS** watches over the surrounding country from a ridge-top just 5km from Siorac on the Dordogne, and its *Hôtel Le Home* on the through road

---

* Sully, the Protestant general, describes a rare moment of light relief in the terrible wars, when the men of the Catholic *bastide*, Villefranche-de-Périgord, planned to capture Monpazier on the same night as the men of Monpazier planned to capture Villefranche. By chance, both sides took different routes, met no resistance, looted to their hearts' content and returned home congratulating themselves on their luck and skill, only to find in the morning that things were rather different. The peace terms were that everyone should return everything to its proper place.

at the top of the hill provides good cheap accommodation and food (☎53.29.01.65; ①; restaurant 53–85F). Make sure you take a look at the heart of the old village and place des Armes, with its old pillared **market** and the **tourist office** (☎53.29.01.40; list of B&Bs). The nearest **campsite** is at Les Nauves, 4.5km off the Monpazier road, or there's *camping à la ferme* at *Gratecap* in St-Amand-de-Belves.

VILLEFRANCHE-DU-PÉRIGORD lies 20km further south in the midst of wooded country above the River Lemance. Built in 1261 in lovely warm-coloured stone, it retains much of its *bastide* layout. At the end of the main street, whose medieval **halle** is splendid, is the *Petite Auberge* (☎53.29.91.01; ③; closed Fri evening; restaurant from 77F), on the way out of the village.

Biron, Villeréal and Monflanquin

Eight kilometres south of Monpazier, dominating the countryside for miles around, is the vast **Château de Biron** (daily except Tues 9/9.30am–noon & 2–6pm; July & Aug 9am–noon & 2–7pm; 25F), begun in the eleventh century and added to piecemeal afterwards. You can only see the place on a guided tour – and that means everything, including the grassy courtyard within its walls, where there is a restored Renaissance chapel and guardhouse with tremendous views over the roofs of the feudal village below.

A single street runs through the village of **BIRON**, past a covered **market** on timber supports iron-hard with age, and out under an arched gateway. Well-manured vegetable plots interspersed with iris, lily and Iceland poppies lie under the tumbledown walls. At the bottom of the hill, another group of houses stands on a small *place* with a broken well in front of a half-ruined **church**, its Romanesque origins covered by motley alterations. The *Auberge du Château* serves a very good value lunchtime menu at 50F (☎53.63.13.33).

West of Biron, the *bastide* of **VILLERÉAL** was founded a decade or so earlier than Monpazier – around 15km to the northeast – by Alphonse de Poitiers in an attempt to check English expansion in the Dordogne. It failed to do so and was taken by the English during the Hundred Years' War. Its most outstanding feature is the oak-beamed *halles* in the central square, which dates from the fourteenth century. You can **stay** at the *Hôtel de l'Europe*, 1 rue Mirabeau (☎53.36.00.35; ②; closed Oct), or at one of the many nearby **campsites**, the closest of which is the *camping municipal* (☎53.36.05.63; mid-June to mid-Sept), off the D207 to Bergerac.

Some 25km further south in the direction of Villeneuve-sur-Lot, pretty **MONFLANQUIN**, founded by Alphonse de Poitiers in 1256, is just as perfectly preserved as Monpazier, less touristy and even more impressively positioned on the top of a hill that rises sharply from the surrounding country and is visible for miles. It conforms to the regular pattern of right-angled streets leading from a central square to the four town gates. The square – place des Arcades – with its distinctly Gothic houses, derives a special charm from being on a slope and tree-shaded. Take a look at the fortified church too. The **tourist office** is on the place des Arcades (☎53.36.40.19), and can furnish you with lists of *chambres d'hôte*. There's a **campsite** at **COULON** on the Cancon road.

Beaumont and the Abbaye de Cadouin

BEAUMONT, 17km north of Villeréal on the D676, is another thirteenth-century English *bastide*, founded by Edward I. Like many *bastides*, its church, **Église St-Front**, was built for military as well as religious reasons – a kind of final outpost of defence in times of attack, hence the bulky tower at each of the four corners and the well inside. There's the *Hôtel des Voyageurs* in rue Romier, with very nice, inexpensive rooms and traditional Périgord cuisine (☎53.22.30.11; ②; restaurant from 80F), as well as a **camp-site**, *Les Remparts* (☎53.22.40.86; April–Oct), to the southwest of town off the D676.

Around 15km northeast, and only 6km south of **LE BUISSON** on the Dordogne, is the twelfth-century Cistercian **Abbaye de Cadouin**. Until 1935 it drew flocks of pilgrims to wonder at a piece of cloth thought to be part of Christ's shroud: since that date, when the shroud was shown not to be authentic, the main attraction has been the finely sculpted capitals of the flamboyant Gothic **cloister** (daily except Tues 10am–noon & 2–5pm; July & Aug daily 9am–noon & 2–6/7pm; 12F). Beside it is a Romanesque **church** with a stark, bold front and wooden belfry roofed with chestnut shingles – chestnut trees abound around here, and the timber was used in furniture making and the nuts ground for flour in the once-frequent famines. Inside the church, the nave is slightly out of alignment; this is thought to be deliberate and perhaps a vestige of pagan attachments, for the three windows are aligned so that at the winter and summer solstices the sun shines through all three in a single shaft. There's a **camping municipal** on the Montferrand road (Easter–Oct).

Sarlat and the valley of the Vézère

The **Vézère Valley** contains some extraordinarily beautiful country – hilly, wooded and close, fretted by other luxuriant valleys, some with streams, some without. Typically, the valley sides are smooth, with slightly overhanging cliffs worn away by the millennial action of water courses and riddled with caves that have been used as dwellings and sanctuaries for thousands of years.

It was here in the valley that the first skeletons of **Cro-Magnon people** – the first *homo sapiens*, tall and muscular with a large skull – were unearthed in 1868 by labourers digging out the Périgueux-Agen train line, and here, too, that an incredible wealth of archeological and artistic evidence of the lifestyle of late Stone Age people has since been found. The many cave paintings are remarkable not only for their great age, but also for their exquisite colouring and the skill with which they are drawn.

The international renown of these caves – combined with the well-preserved medieval architecture of **Sarlat** – has made this one of the most heavily touristed inland areas of France, with all the concomitant problems of crowds, high prices and tack. It is really worth coming out of season, but if you can't, seek accommodation away from the main centres, and always drive along the back roads – the smaller the better – whenever there is a more direct route available.

Sarlat

SARLAT-LA-CANÉDA, capital of *Périgord Noir*, is held in a hollow between hills 10km or so back from the Dordogne valley. You hardly notice the modern town, as it is the mainly fifteenth- and sixteenth-century houses of the *vieille ville* in mellow, honey-coloured stone that draw the attention.

The **vieille ville** is an excellent example of medieval organic urban growth, violated only by the straight swathe of the **rue de la République** – now thankfully pedestrianized – which cuts through its middle. The west side alone remains relatively un-chic; the east side is where most people wander. As you approach the old town from the station, turn right down rue Lakanal which leads to the large and unexciting **Cathédrale St-Sacerdos**, mostly dating from its seventeenth-century renovation. Opposite stands the town's finest house, **Maison de La Boétie** – one-time home of Montaigne's friend Étienne de La Boétie – with its gabled tiers of windows and characteristic steep roof stacked with heavy limestone tiles (*lauzes*).

GÎTES D'ÉTAPE AROUND SARLAT

There are a number of **gîtes** in the vicinity of Sarlat, some on or near the GR6. For walkers, cyclists and campers they could provide much more enjoyable and hassle-free accommodation than anything in the towns.

Beynac: *La Grange* (☎53.49.40.93).

Cenac: M. et Mme Sardan (☎53.28.32.77).

St-Vincent-le-Paluel: M. et Mme Saulière, at *Le Communal* on the GR6 7km east of Sarlat (☎53.31.00.21). Camping possible.

Castelnaud-la-Chapelle: *gîte municipal*, below the château (☎53.29.51.21).

Le Breuil: *Lo Cobana* or *Les Cabanes du Breuil*, on the GR6, just north of the D6 midway between Les Eyzies and Sarlat (turn north at Benives; ☎53.29.66.23). Camping and meals.

Ste-Nathalène: *Le Grand Touron*, about 8km east of Sarlat (☎53.31.07.67).

For a better sense of the medieval town, wander through the cool, shady lanes and courtyards around the back of the cathedral – **cour des Fontaines** and **cours des Chanoines**. To one side of the cours des Chanoines is the curious twelfth-century coned tower, the **Lanterne des Morts**, whose exact function has escaped historians, though the most popular theory is that it was built to commemorate Saint Bernard, who performed various miracles when he visited the town in 1147.

There are more wonderful old houses in the streets to the north, especially **rue des Consuls**, and up the slopes to the east. Eventually, though, Sarlat's labyrinthine lanes will lead you back to the central **place de la Liberté**, where the big Saturday **market** spreads its stands of geese, flowers, *foie gras*, truffles and mushrooms in season, as well as various people trying to make a living from the hordes who hit Sarlat in the summer. Another recent development is the increasing number of museums that are cropping up in Sarlat as the town turns more and more to tourism. The only one worth anything more than a passing nod is the **Musée des Miniatures**, 17 rue de la République (Mon–Sat 10am–12.30pm & 2–7pm; July & Aug daily; 20F), with its array of precisely crafted scaled-down objects. Staying just on the right side of kitsch, it's a firm favourite with the many kids who are dragged around Sarlat with their parents.

Practicalities

The **gare SNCF** (☎53.59.00.21) is just over a kilometre south of the old town, and there's a free bus shuttle into town. If you have no transport of your own, you can rent **bicycles** from *Sarlat Sport* on rue Jean-Leclaire, from the youth hostel, the train station, or *Cycles Cumenal*, 52 av Gambetta. The **tourist office** lodges in the sixteenth-century Hôtel de Maleville on place de la Liberté (Mon–Sat 9am–noon & 2–6pm; mid-June to mid-Sept Mon–Sat 9am–7pm; Sun 10am–noon & 4–6pm; ☎53.59.27.67). For a small fee, they'll find you a room in town or B&B accommodation in the surrounding area, though it's almost impossible to find cheap digs in season.

Hotels worth trying include the *Marcel*, 8 av de Selves (☎53.59.21.98; ②–③; March to mid-Nov); the very central *Hôtel de la Mairie* on place de la Liberté (☎53.59.05.71; ②–③); and *Les Récollets*, 4 rue J-J-Rousseau (☎53.59.00.49; ②–④). There is a very pleasant IYHF **youth hostel** at 15 av de Selves (☎53.59.47.59; ①; May–Sept; no curfew), a ten-minute walk from the *vieille ville* along the Périgueux road. The nearest **campsite**, *Les Périères* costs almost as much as a hotel; much better to try *Les Acacias*, about 2km beyond the rail viaduct in La Canéda (☎53.59.29.30; Easter–Sept).

Restaurants are generally overpriced in Sarlat. However, *Le Commerce* in rue Albert-Cahuet, just off rue de la République, with its menus at 50F and 70F and regional specialities like *confits*, offers reasonable value for money, as does the fancier *Auberge de la Salamandre* in rue des Consuls, in spite of its touristy aspect (from 85F). For something a bit special, try *Criquettamu's*, 5 rue des Armes (menus from 55–130F), which serves up *foie gras*, *magret* and *morilles* mushrooms. Otherwise, you could try the brasserie fare of the *Café Bar de la Salamandre* on place de la Grande-Rigaudie.

A very nice alternative to both staying and eating in Sarlat would be to put up in the little hilltop hamlet of **MARQUAY** about halfway to Les Eyzies, at the *Hôtel des Bories* (☎53.29.67.02; ②–③; April–Oct), with a marvellous view, swimming pool and excellent restaurant (from 85F): it is vital to book several months in advance for July and August.

Les Eyzies

The main base for visiting the prehistoric painted caves of the Vézère Valley is **LES EYZIES-DE-TAYAC**, an unattractive one-street village completely dedicated to tourism. But while you're here, visit the **Musée National de Préhistoire** (daily except Mon April to mid-Sept 10.30am–12.30pm & 2.30–6pm; July & Aug closes 7pm; 15F), exhibiting numerous prehistoric artefacts and copies of one of the most beautiful pieces of Stone Age art, two clay bisons from the Tuc d'Audoubert cave in the Pyrenees, as well as the small bas-relief of an exaggerated female figure holding what looks like a slice of watermelon, found near Laussel (see below), known as the *Vénus à la Corne* (Venus with the horn of plenty): the original is in the Musée d'Aquitaine in Bordeaux (see p.531).

In April 1990, local farmer M. Pataud opened his own extensive private collection of prehistoric finds, next door in the **Musée de l'Abri Pataud** (daily except Mon July & Aug 9.30am–7pm; Sept–Dec & Feb–June 10am–noon & 2–5.30pm; 25F). Much of the stuff was discovered during archeological digs in the 1950s and 1960s on Pataud's own farmland, which, it transpired, lay over an *abri* (shelter) used by reindeer hunters for over 20,000 years.

Practicalities

The **tourist office** is on Les Eyzies' one street (Mon–Sat 9am–noon & 2–6pm; July & Aug daily 9am–7pm; ☎53.06.97.05). In addition to **bicycle rental**, they also give out information on private rooms in the area (roughly 150F per person). **Hotels** are pricey and likely to ask for *demi-pension*: the cheapest is the *Hôtel du Périgord*, near the Grotte de Font-de-Gaume on the D47 (☎53.06.97.26; ①–②; closed Dec–Feb; good restaurant from 65F), followed by the *Hôtel de France* on rue du Moulin (☎53.06.97.23; ②–④; closed Nov–March; restaurant 65F). Alternatively, stay in Le Bugue, 10km downstream, where the *Hôtel de Paris*, 14 rue Paris (☎53.07.28.16; ①–②), has much cheaper rooms.

There's a riverside **campsite**, *La Rivière* (☎53.06.97.14; mid-March to mid-Oct), on the rte de Périgueux, and a cheaper one in the direction of Le Bugue, *Le Pech Denissou*. There are hostel-priced beds at a very attractive self-catering **gîte d'étape**, *La Ferme Eymaries* (☎53.06.94.73; April–Oct), thirty minutes by foot from the village; to find it, cross the bridge on the Périgueux road, turn sharp left and continue to the rail track, where there's a signpost to the right.

Eating out in Les Eyzies can be expensive unless you go for the no-nonsense brasserie-style food at *La Grignotière*, near the tourist office, or the hotels mentioned above.

The Caves

There are more **prehistoric caves** around Les Eyzies than you could possibly hope to visit in one day. Besides, the compulsory guided tours are tiring, so it's best to select just a couple of the ones listed below.

No one ever lived in these caves, and there are various theories as to why these inaccessible spots were chosen. Most agree that the caves were sanctuaries, and if not actually places of worship, they at least had religious significance. One theory is that making images of animals that were commonly hunted – like reindeer and bison – or feared – like bears and mammoths – was a kind of sympathetic magic intended to help men either catch or evade these animals. Another is that they were part of a fertility cult: sexual images of women with pendulous breasts and protuberant rumps are common, and it seems, too, that certain animals were associated with the feminine principle. Others argue, from parallels with Australian aborigines who used similar images to teach their young vital survival information as well as the history and mythological origins of their people, that these cave paintings served educational purposes. But much remains unexplained – for instance, the abstract signs that appear in many caves and the arrows which clearly cannot be arrows, because Stone Age arrowheads looked different from these representations.

The size of the caves varies – **Font-de-Gaume** is only 130m long, but many caves, like **La Roque St-Christophe**, are far longer, with terrifyingly difficult access through twisting slippery passages, passable only on your belly. The artists had just the most primitive lamps to light their way and paint by.

Grotte de Font-de-Gaume

Since its discovery in 1901, dozens of polychrome paintings have been found in the tunnel-like **Grotte de Font-de-Gaume** (daily except Tues 9am–noon & 2–6pm; Oct & March 9.30am–noon & 2–5.30pm; Nov–Feb 10am–noon & 2–5pm; 31F; maximum 20 on each tour), 1.5km along the D47 to Sarlat. Beware that tickets sell out fast and only two hundred people are allowed to tour the cave per day, so get to the ticket office as early as possible.

The cave mouth is no more than a fissure from which a resurgent stream once flowed. Concealed by rocks and trees, it now stands above a small lush valley, but when Stone Age people first settled here during the last Ice Age – about 25,000 BC – the Dordogne was the domain of roaming bison, reindeer and mammoths.

Inside, the cave is a narrow twisting passage of irregular height. There's no lighting, and you quickly lose your bearings in the dark. The first painting you see is a frieze of bison, at about eye level: reddish-brown in colour, massive, full of movement, and very far from the primitive representations you might expect. Further on, in a side passage, two horses stand one behind the other, forelegs outstretched as if to attempt – as the guide suggests with some relish – *un début d'accouplement* (the beginnings of copulation). But the most miraculous of all is a frieze of five bisons discovered in 1966 during cleaning operations. The colour, remarkably sharp and vivid, is preserved by a protective layer of calcite. Shading under the belly and down the thighs is used to give three-dimensionality with a sophistication that seems utterly modern. Another panel consists of superimposed drawings, a fairly common phenomenon in cave painting, sometimes the result of work by successive generations, but here an obviously deliberate technique. A reindeer in the foreground shares legs with a large bison behind to indicate perspective.

Stocks of artists' materials have also been found: kilos of prepared pigments; palettes – stones stained with ground-up earth pigments; and wooden painting sticks. Painting was clearly a specialized, perhaps professional, business, reproduced in dozens and dozens of caves located in the central Pyrenees and areas of northern Spain.

Grotte des Combarelles

Discovered in 1910, the innermost part of the **Grotte des Combarelles** (daily except Tues 9am–noon & 2–6pm; Oct & March 9.30am–noon & 2–5.30pm; Nov–Feb 10am–noon & 2–5pm; 31F), 2km along the D47 towards Sarlat, is covered with engravings from the Magdalenian period about 12,000 years ago, many superimposed as they were drawn over a period of 2000 years. They include horses, reindeer, mammoths and crude human figures. Among the finest are the heads of a horse and a lioness.

Unlike Font-de-Gaume, afternoon tickets are not for sale in the morning – arrive early for both sessions to be sure of a place.

Abri du Cap Blanc and the Château de Commarque

Not a cave but a rock shelter, the **Abri du Cap Blanc** (July & Aug 9.30am–7pm; Sept–Oct & March–June 10am–noon & 2–6pm; 25F), 7km east of Les Eyzies, contains a sculpted frieze of horses and bison dating from the Middle Magdalenian period, 14,000 years ago; and of only ten surviving prehistoric sculptures in France, this is undoubtedly the best. The design is deliberate, with the sculptures polished and set off against a pock-marked background. But what makes this place extraordinary is not just the large scale, but the high relief of some of the sculptures. This was only possible in places where light reached in, which in turn brought the danger of destruction by exposure to the air. Cro-Magnon people actually lived in this shelter, and a female skeleton has been found that is some 2000 years younger than the frieze.

If you're looking for a non-cave detour, continue a little further up the primitive-looking and heavily wooded Beune valley from Cap Blanc, to the elegant sixteenth-century **Château de Laussel** (closed to the public). On the opposite side of the valley stand the romantically overgrown ruins of the **Château de Commarque**. Built in the thirteenth century, it was occupied by the English during the Hundred Years' War, and substantial sections of the fortifications still stand. You can reach it on foot via the GR6 footpath, which leaves the D47, past the Font-de-Gaume and just after *Pizzeria Girouteaux*.

Grotte du Grand Roc

As well as prehistoric cave paintings, you can see some truly spectacular stalactites and stalagmites in the area around Les Eyzies. Some of the best examples are off the D47 to Périgueux, 2km north of Les Eyzies, in the **Grotte du Grand Roc** (daily 9am–7pm; April, May & mid-Sept to Nov 11 9.30am–6pm; Nov 12–Jan 2 & Jan 23–March 26 10am–5pm; 30F), whose entrance is high up in the cliffs that line much of the Vézère Valley. There's a great view from the mouth of the cave and, inside, along some fifty metres of tunnel, a fantastic array of rock formations.

La Roque St-Christophe

The enormous prehistoric dwelling site, **La Roque St-Christophe** (daily 10am–6pm; July to mid-Sept 10am–7pm; late Dec–Feb 11am–5pm; closed late Nov–late Dec; 27F), 9km northeast of Les Eyzies along the D706 to Montignac, is made up of about one hundred caves on five levels, hollowed out of the limestone cliffs. The caves are 700-800m long and lie 80m above the ground, where the River Vézère once flowed. The earliest traces of occupation go back over 50,000 years. The view is pretty good, and the guided tour instructive, but most of the finds are actually on display at the Musée National de Préhistoire in Les Eyzies (see p.560).

Montignac and the Lascaux caves

Some 26km up the Vézère valley, **MONTIGNAC** is the main base for visiting the **Lascaux caves**. It's a more attractive place than Les Eyzies, with several wooden-balconied houses leaning appealingly over the river, and a lively annual **arts festival** in mid-July, including international folklore. On place Bertran-de-Born in the old hospital, the **Musée Eugène-Le-Roy** (Mon–Sat July & Aug 9am–7pm; Sept–Dec & Feb–June

9.30am–noon & 2–5.30pm; free) displays local crafts and trades, and includes a reconstruction of the household of Jacquou le Croquant, the peasant protagonist of the novel
of the same name by Eugène le Roy, the Dordogne's native novelist, who lived and
died here in Montignac. The novel describes the harshness of peasant life in the early
nineteenth century and the depredations of the local squirearchy in spite of the
reforms of the Revolution.

The **tourist office** shares the old hospital building with the museum on place
Bertran-de-Born (Mon–Sat July & Aug 9am–7pm; Sept–Dec & Feb–June 9.30am–noon
& 2–5.30pm). **Bikes** can be rented from *Cycles Recross* on rue du 4-septembre.

Accommodation, as everywhere around here, is a problem. *Le Bon Accueil*
(☎53.51.82.99; ②) and *Hôtel de la Grotte* (☎53.51.80.48; ①; restaurant from 60F), both
on rue du 4-septembre, and the *Périgord* on place Tourny (☎53.51.80.38; ①) are reasonably priced. For rooms and food, there's the *Soleil d'Or*, also on the main rue du 4-
septembre (☎53.51.80.22; ③–⑦), whose restaurant has a menu at 90F; otherwise it will
be upwards of 150F. And there is a cheap **camping municipal** on the river bank 500m
away (April–Oct).

There are other worthwhile hotel options in the area. One of the most attractive,
though not the cheapest, is *La Table du Terroir* at **LA CHAPELLE-AUBAREIL,** about
15km beyond the Lascaux caves (☎53.50.72.14; ②–④), which has a swimming pool and
an excellent restaurant (menus from 70F). Another, offering equally good food, is the
Hôtel Laborderie further to the south at Tamnies on the Les Eyzies–St-Genies road
(☎53.29.68.59; ②–⑤; April–Oct; restaurant from 95F). For other possibilities, ask the
tourist office in Montignac for their extensive list of B&B and farm **campsites**. A
particularly good spot for campers with a taste for luxury is the site at the exquisite
riverside village of St-Léon-sur-Vézère.

Grotte de Lascaux

The **Grotte de Lascaux** was discovered in 1940 by four boys who were, according to
popular myth, looking for their dog and fell into a deep cavern decorated with marvellously preserved animal paintings. Executed by Cro-Magnon people 17,000 years ago,
the paintings are among the finest examples of prehistoric art in existence. There are
five or six identifiable styles, and subjects include the bison, mammoth and horse, plus
the biggest known prehistoric drawing, of a five-and-a-half-metre bull with astonishingly expressive head and face. In 1948, the cave was opened to the public, and over
the course of the next fifteen years, more than a million tourists came to Lascaux.
Sadly, because of deterioration from the body heat and breath of visitors, the cave had
to be closed in 1963 and can now only be visited by prior appointment. If you want to
see the original you can put your name on the waiting list, but there's a two-year back-
log. Since 1983, though, it has been possible to see an exact replica – known simply as
Lascaux II.

Lascaux II

Two kilometres south of Montignac on the D104e, **Lascaux II** (Tues–Sun 10am–noon
& 2–5.30pm; July & Aug daily 9.30am–7pm; 45F) was opened in 1983, the result of
eleven years' painstaking work by twenty artists and sculptors, under the supervision
of Monique Peytral, using the same methods and materials as the original cave painters. While the visit can't offer the excitement of a real cave, the reconstruction – which
cost over 500 million francs – rarely disappoints the thousands who trek here every
year. The guided tour lasts 40 minutes (commentary in French, with English translations available), and the tickets include entrance into the **prehistoric theme park**,
5km down the Vézère at **LE THOT**, with Disneyesque mock-ups of prehistoric scenes
and live examples of some of the animals that feature in the paintings: European bison,

long-horned cattle and Przewalski's horses, rare and beautiful animals from Mongolia believed to resemble the prehistoric wild horse: notice the erect mane.

During July and August, tickets must be bought from Montignac tourist office from 9am – there are 2000 on sale a day, but they go fast.

St-Amand-de-Coly

Nine kilometres east of Montignac, the village of **ST-AMAND-DE-COLY** boasts a superbly beautiful fortified Romanesque **church**, a magical venue for concerts in the summer Périgord festival (see p.547). Despite its bristling military architecture, the twelfth-century church manages to combine great delicacy and spirituality. With its purity of line and simple decoration, it is at its most evocative in the low sun of late afternoon or early evening. Its defences left nothing to chance: the walls are four metres thick, a ditch runs all the way around, and a passage once skirted the eaves, with numerous positions for archers to rain down arrows, and blind stairways to mislead attackers.

There is a guard on hand to give guided tours, including an informative and evocative 30-minute film. Although not officially sanctioned, he will usually agree to show you the roof and galleries if you make a special request. If you don't mind heights, you'll be rewarded with a magnificent view down into the church, and you can climb secret stairs for a bird's-eye view of the roof. Next to the church, the small *Hôtel la Gardette* (☎53.51.68.50; ②; restaurant from 60F) makes it possible to stay overnight in this tiny, idyllic place.

Villages and castles of the upper Dordogne

East of St-Cyprien, the River Dordogne is at its most appealing, forming great loops between rich fields, wooded hills and craggy outcrops. The ten kilometres between **Les Milandes** and **Domme** are particularly spectacular, with cliff-top châteaux facing each other across the valley, mostly dating from the Hundred Years' War, when the river marked the frontier between French-held land to the north and English territory to the south.

Further upstream there are marvellous examples of Romanesque sculpture in the churches at **Souillac** and **Beaulieu**, and superbly preserved medieval villages at **Martel** and **Carennac**, both much less touristy than Sarlat or the *bastide* village of Domme. Without a car, though, you can only reach Souillac, Vayrac and Beaulieu. One way to join them up might be to paddle downstream by canoe (see box on p.567 for details).

Châteaux: Les Milandes, Fayrac and Castelnaud

The first château you come to east of St-Cyprien is **Les Milandes** (May–June & Sept to mid-Oct daily 9.30–11.30am & 2–6pm; July & Aug 9.30am–6.30pm; 30F), perched high on the south bank. Built in 1489, it was the property of the de Caumont family until the Revolution, but its most famous owner is the *Folies-Bergères* star, **Josephine Baker** (see box), who owned it in 1936–69. The stories surrounding the place are more intriguing than the château itself, which contains de Caumont treasures as well as Ms Baker's effects.

Further along on the same side of the river, the **Château de Fayrac** was an English forward position in the Hundred Years' War, built to watch over Beynac, on the opposite bank, where the French were holed up, and is all slated pepperpot towers, unfortunately closed to the public. But you can visit the ruins of the **Château de Castelnaud** (daily 10am–6pm; July & Aug daily 9am–8pm; mid-Nov to Feb daily except Sat 2–5pm;

JOSEPHINE BAKER AND THE RAINBOW TRIBE

Born on June 3, 1906, in the black ghetto of East St Louis, Illinois, **Josephine Baker** was one of the most remarkable women of this century. Her mother washed clothes for a living and her father was a drummer who soon deserted his family, yet by the late 1920s Josephine was the most celebrated cabaret star in France, primarily due to her role in the legendary *Folies Bergères* show in Paris. On her first night, de Gaulle, Hemingway, Piaf and Stravinsky were among the audience; her notoriety was further enhanced by her long line of illustrious husbands and lovers, which included the crown Prince of Sweden and the crime novelist Georges Simenon; she mixed with the likes of Le Corbusier and Adolf Loos, and kept a pet cheetah called Mildred, with whom she used to walk around Paris. During the war, she was active in the Resistance, for which she won the *Croix de Guerre*. Later on, she became involved in the civil rights movement in North America, where she insisted on playing to non-segregated audiences, a stance which got her arrested in Canada and tailed by the FBI in the US.

By far her most bizarre project was the château of **Les Milandes**, which she bought in 1936, after her marriage to the French orchestra leader Jo Bouillon. Having equipped the place with two hotels, three restaurants, a mini-golf course, tennis court and an autobiographical wax museum, she opened the château to the general public as a model multicultural community, popularly dubbed the *"village du monde"*. In the course of the 1950s, she adopted babies (mostly orphans) of different ethnic and religious backgrounds from around the world. By the end of the decade, she had brought twelve children to Les Milandes, including a black Catholic Colombian and a Buddhist Korean, along with her mother, brother and sister from East St Louis.

Over 300,000 people a year visited the château in the 1950s, but the conservative local population were never very happy about Les Milandes and the "Rainbow Tribe". In the 1960s, Baker's financial problems, divorce and two heart attacks spelled the end for the project, and despite a sit-in protest by Baker herself (by then in her sixties), the château was sold off in 1969. Josephine died of a stroke while on stage, in 1975, and was given a grand state funeral at La Madeleine in Paris, mourned by thousands of her adopted countryfolk.

24F), a little to the south of Fayrac and the true rival to Beynac in terms of impregnability – although it was successfully captured by the bellicose Simon de Monfort as early as 1214. The English held it for much of the Hundred Years' War, and it wasn't until the Revolution that it was finally abandoned. Fairly heavily restored in the last two decades as it is, none of the architecture can match the views up and down the valley.

Beynac

Clearly visible on an impregnable cliff edge on the north bank of the river, the eye-catching village and castle of **BEYNAC-ET-CAZENAC** was built in the days when the river was the only route open to traders and invaders. By road, it is 3km to the **château** (daily May–Sept 10am–6pm; March, April, Oct & Nov 10am–noon & 2.30–5.30pm; 29F), but a steep lane leads up through the village and takes only fifteen minutes by foot. It is protected on the landward side by a double wall; elsewhere the sheer drop of almost 200m does the job. The flat terrace at the base of the keep, which was added by the English, conceals the remains of the houses where the beleaguered villagers lived; one of the houses has been partly excavated. Richard the Lionheart held the place for a time, until a gangrenous wound received while besieging the castle of Châlus, north of Périgueux, ended his term of bloodletting.

Originally, to facilitate defence, the rooms inside the keep were only connected by a narrow spiral staircase – in stone, not wood as in the reconstruction, because of the danger of fire. The division of domestic space into dining rooms and so forth only came about when the advent of artillery made these old *châteaux-forts* militarily obsolete.

From the roof, there is a stupendous – and vertiginous – view upriver to the **Château de Marqueyssac**, whose beautiful seventeenth-century gardens are open to the public in the summer.

In the main street below the castle is the *Hôtel Bonnet* (☎53.29.50.01; ②–③; closed mid-Oct to March; good restaurant from 120F), as well as a riverside **campsite**, *Le Capeyrou* (June–Sept).

La Roque-Gageac

The village of **LA ROQUE-GAGEAC** is almost too perfect, its ochre-coloured houses sheltering under dramatically overhanging cliffs. Regular winner of France's prettiest-village contest, it inevitably pulls in the tourist buses, and since the main road separates the village from the river, the noise and fumes of the traffic can become oppressive. The best way to escape is to slip away through the lanes and alleyways that wind up through the terraced houses. The other option is to take the rowing-boat ferry service to the small island, where you can picnic and enjoy a much better view of La Roque than from among the crowds milling around beneath the village, at its best in the burnt-orange glow of the evening sun.

Most people just come here for the afternoon, so there's usually space if you want to **stay** the night, most cheaply at *La Belle Étoile* (☎53.29.51.44; ③–⑤; closed mid-Oct to Palm Sunday). In low season this can be a good deal, but in high season, prices rocket and availability plummets. There are also four **campsites** in the vicinity, and a good **restaurant** serving Périgord cuisine at Les Veyssières, *La Sanglière* (☎53.28.33.51; from 95F), half-a-dozen kilometres is in the direction of Sarlat.

Domme

High on the scarp on the opposite bank of the river, **DOMME** is one of the best preserved of the *bastides*. Somewhat petrified by too careful grooming, Domme's attractions include three original thirteenth-century **gateways** and a section of the old **walls**. From the northern edge of the village, known as the *barre*, marked by a drop so precipitous that fortifications were deemed unnecessary, you look out over a wide sweep of river country. Underneath the village are hundreds of metres of **caves** (daily 9am–noon & 2–6pm; July & Aug 9.30am–7pm; Nov 2–6pm; Dec–March 2–5pm; 25F) in which the townspeople took refuge in times of danger. You enter the complex opposite the **tourist office** on the main square (same times as caves).

There is a nice and surprisingly reasonable **hotel** at the beginning of Grand'rue, *Lou Cardil* (☎53.28.38.92; ②; April–Oct). There are **canoes** to rent down by the river at **CÉNAC** (see box), along with a **camping municipal**. If you come down here, don't miss the round tile roof of the chapel or the beautifully proportioned twelfth-century **church** on rue St-Cybranet.

Souillac

The first place of any size east of Sarlat is **SOUILLAC**, at the confluence of the Borrèze and Dordogne rivers. Virginia Woolf stayed here in 1937, and was pleased to meet "no tourists.... England seems like a chocolate box bursting with trippers afterward." There are still few tourists, since Souillac's only real point of interest is the twelfth-century **church of Ste-Marie**, just off the main road. Roofed with massive domes like the cathedrals of Périgueux and Cahors, its spacious interior creates just the atmosphere for cool reflection on a summer's day. On the back of the west door are some of the most wonderful Romanesque sculptures, including a seething mass of beasts devouring each other. The greatest piece of craftsmanship, though, is a bas-relief of

Isaiah, fluid and supple, thought to be by one of the artists who worked at Moissac (see p.599). Behind the church, a new museum has opened to try and draw a few more visitors to Souillac – the **Musée de l'Automate** (daily 10am–noon & 3–6pm; July & Aug 10am–7pm; Nov–March closed Mon & Tues; 25F). Those under twelve are the ones most likely to enjoy the mostly nineteenth-century mechanical dolls, who dance, sing and perform magical tricks.

The **tourist office** is on the main road next to the delightful *Grand Hôtel* (☎62.32.78.30; ③–④; April–Oct), where you can sleep in the owner's former apartment with its massive fireplace for 500F; the hotel also has an excellent restaurant from 68F–220F. But there is cheaper accommodation in the pretty place du Puits in the old quarter, at the *Auberge du Puits* (☎65.37.80.32; ①–②; closed Sun evening & Nov, Dec), with good food from 70F. Alternatively, there's the large riverside **campsite**, *Les Ondines* (☎65.37.86.44; May–Sept), and a *gîte d'étape* at Le Gachou on the Martel road (☎65.32.27.17). You can rent **bicycles** from the *gare SNCF*, 1.5km northwest of the centre, or from *Évasion Sport*, 36 bd L-J-Malvy.

Martel

About 15km east of Souillac and set back even further from the river, **MARTEL** is a minor medieval masterpiece, built in a pale, almost white, stone, offset by the warm reddish-brown roofs, yet it suffers none of the crowds endured by the likes of Sarlat.

THE TALE OF HENRY SHORT-COAT

At the end of the twelfth century, Martel was the stage for one of the tragic events in the internecine conflicts of the Plantagenet family. When Henry Plantagenet (King Henry II of England) imprisoned his estranged wife Eleanor of Aquitaine, his sons took up arms against their father. The eldest son, **Henry Short-Coat** (Henri Court-Mantel to the French) even went so far as to plunder the viscounty of Turenne and Quercy. Furious, Henry II immediately stopped his allowance and handed over his lands to the third son, Richard the Lionheart. Financially insecure, and with a considerable army of soldiers to feed and clothe, Henry Short-Coat began looting the treasures of every abbey and shrine in the region. Finally, he decided to sack the shrine at Rocamadour, making off with various artefacts, including Roland's famous sword, *Durandal*. This last act was to be his downfall, for shortly afterwards he fled to Martel and fell ill with a fever. Guilt-ridden and afraid for his life, he confessed his crimes and asked his father for forgiveness. Henry II was busy besieging Limoges, but sent a messenger to pardon him. On the messenger's arrival in Martel, Henry Short-Coat died, and Richard the Lionheart became heir to the English throne.

Another Turenne-administered town (see p.579), its heyday came during the thirteenth and fourteenth centuries, when the viscounts established a court of appeal here.

The main square, **place des Consuls**, is mostly taken up by the large eighteenth-century covered *halles*, but on every side there are reminders of the town's illustrious past, most notably in the superb Gothic **Hôtel de la Raymondie**. Begun in 1280, it served as the Turenne law courts, though it doubled as the town's refuge, hence the distinctive corner turrets. Facing the *hôtel* is the **Tour des Pénitents**, one of the many medieval towers which gave the town its epithet, *"la ville des sept tours"*. Henry Short-Coat (see box above) died in the striking building in the southeast corner of the square, the **Maison Fabri**; one block south, rue Droite leads east to the town's main church, the **church of St-Maur**, built in a fiercely defensive, mostly Gothic style, with a finely carved Romanesque tympanum depicting the Last Judgement above the west door.

If you'd rather **stay** here than in Souillac, head for the *Quercy Turnne* on av J-Lavayssière (☎65.37.30.30; ①–②; closed Dec–March), with traditional cuisine from 75F. There's also a **camping municipal**, *La Callopie* (May–Oct), on the road to Quatre-Routes, and a little riverside campsite, 5km away in the village of **GLUGES**, where there are a couple of nice restaurants with menus from 60F, and canoe and kayak rental down by the water. **Bikes** can be rented from *Copeyre* in Martel (☎65.37.33.51).

Carennac and Castelnau-Bretenoux

CARENNAC is without doubt one of the most beautiful villages in this part of the Dordogne. Elevated just above the south bank of the river, 13km or so east of Martel, it's best known for its typical Quercy architecture, its Romanesque priory, where the French writer Fénelon spent the best years of his life, and for its greengages.

Carennac's feature, as so often in these parts, is the Romanesque tympanum above the west door, in the Moissac style. Christ sits in majesty with the Book of Judgement in his left hand, with the apostles and adoring angels below him. Inside the church, you can gain access to the old **cloisters** (daily 10am–noon & 2–7pm; 7F), which contain an exceptionally expressive life-size entombment of Christ, quite simply one of the best in the Dordogne.

There are two comfortable and reasonably priced **hotels** in the village, both with good restaurants specializing in traditional regional cuisine: the *Hôtel Fénelon* on the main street (☎65.10.96.46; closed Jan 10–March 10; restaurant from 87F; ③), and the

Auberge du Vieux Quercy (☎65.10.96.59; ②–③; closed mid-Nov to mid-March), whose restaurant has a particularly good value menu at 90F. There's also a **camping municipal** in town (May to mid-Sept).

Another 10km further upstream, the sturdy towers and machicolated red-brown walls of the eleventh-century **Château de Castelnau-Bretenoux** (daily except Tues 9am–noon & 2–5/6pm; July & Aug 9.30am–6.30pm; 25F) dominate a sharp knoll above the Dordogne, making a harmonious whole with the village piled at its feet. Most of it has now been restored and refurnished. Below, on the banks of the River Cère, you come to the graceful little *bastide* of **BRETENOUX**, with two sides of its cobbled and arcaded square still intact.

For **accommodation** in Castelnau, there's the *Hôtel de la Cère* (☎65.39.71.44; ③), and a grassy and shady **campsite** beside the river. **Bikes** can be rented from *Ets Bladien* (☎65.38.41.56).

Beaulieu-sur-Dordogne

Beautifully situated on the banks of the Dordogne, 8km upriver from Castelnau-Bretenoux, **BEAULIEU-SUR-DORDOGNE** boasts another of the great masterpieces of Romanesque sculpture on the porch of the **church of St-Pierre** in the centre of town. This doorway is unusually deep-set, with a tympanum presided over by an Oriental-looking Christ with one arm extended to welcome the chosen. All around him is a complicated pattern of angels and apostles, executed in characteristic "dancing" style, similar to that at Carennac. The dead raise the lids of their coffins hopefully, while underneath a frieze of monsters crunches heads. Take the opportunity also to wander through to the peaceful medieval **quartier de la Chapelle** to the north of the town centre, which boasts some handsome fourteenth-century houses with sculpted façades.

The *Hôtel Fournié* (☎55.91.01.34; ③) has comfortable rooms and a cheap restaurant from 85F; equally appealing is the magnificent half-timbered and turreted IYHF **youth hostel**, in the Quartier de la Chapelle (☎55.91.13.82; ①; April–Sept). There are river-bathing and canoeing possibilities, and a riverside **campsite** close by.

Argentat

An *SNCF* bus can take you still further upstream to **ARGENTAT**, the last major town on the Dordogne and the last part of the river accessible by anything other than foot. Beyond Argentat, the Dordogne changes character entirely, due to the series of hydroelectric dams (*barrages*) that turn the river into a succession of grand reservoirs.

Argentat's whitewashed houses and rather sombre grey slate rooftops make a distinct change from the warm yellow stone of the rest of the Dordogne. It's easy enough to while away an hour or so sitting at one of the river bank cafés or exploring the cobbled *petites ruelles* which slope down to the river. But there's nothing else to make you stay, except for the comfortable, reasonably priced **rooms** at the *Hôtel Fouillade*, 11 pl Gambetta (☎65.28.10.17; ①–②; closed Nov 4–Dec 10), with a **restaurant** from 70F.

THE LIMOUSIN

The **Limousin** – the country around Limoges – is hilly, wooded, wet and not particularly fertile: ideal pasture for the famous Limousin breed of cattle. This is herdsman's country, from where – presumably – the widespread use of the shepherd's cape known as a *limousine* gave its name to the big, wrap-around, covered twentieth-century car.

The modern Limousin region stretches south to the Dordogne valley to include Brive and Tulle. But while these places, together with **Limoges** itself, are not without interest, the star of the show is the countryside, especially in the east on the **Plateau de Millevaches** round **Eymoutiers**, **Meymac** and **La Courtine**. Happily, there is a mountain rail line connecting Limoges and Ussel. Although it is remote and underpopulated, there are plenty of small hotels, *gîtes* and campsites to accommodate the wanderer.

Limoges

LIMOGES is not a city that calls for a long stay, but it is worth a look for a magnificent train station and the craft industries that made the city's name a household word: enamel in the Middle Ages and, since the eighteenth century, some of the finest china ever produced. If these appeal, then the city's unique museum collections – and its Gothic cathedral – will reward a visit. But it has to be said that the industry today seems a spent tradition, hard hit by recession and changing tastes among the rich. The local *kaolin* (china clay) mines that gave Limoges china its special quality are exhausted, and the workshops survive mainly on the tourist trade.

Arrival and accommodation

The magnificent **Gare des Benedictins** (☎55.77.58.11) lies at the end of av de Gaulle, 500m northeast of the old quarter. The main **gare routière** is a five-minute walk away, although some buses leave from a second station on place des Charentes. The **tourist office** is on bd de Fleurus, also five minutes' walk from place Jourdan (daily 9am–8pm; mid-Sept to mid-June 9am–noon & 2–4.30pm; ☎55.34.46.87), and has a money-changing facility when the banks are closed.

A conveniently central **hotel** is the comfortable and agreeable *Hôtel de la Paix*, right in the quietest corner of the place Jourdan (☎55.34.36.00; ②–④). Slightly cheaper and very nice, on the other side of the town centre at 28 bd Victor-Hugo is the *Beaux-Arts*, between place d'Aine and place Dussoubs (☎55.79.42.20; ①–②); and cheaper still is the **youth hostel** in the *Foyer des Jeunes Travailleuses* at 20 rue Encombe-Vineuse, off rue François-Chenieux close to place Carnot (☎55.77.41.43; ①). The nearest **campsite** is *La Vallée de l'Aurence* (☎55.38.49.43), 5km north of town on the N20 Paris road.

The City

Limoges is built on high ground overlooking the River Vienne. The small city centre lies encircled by modern boulevards, with the tower of the **Cathédrale St-Étienne** a landmark for miles around. Begun in 1273, the building was planned on the model of the cathedral of Amiens, though only the choir, completed in the early thirteenth century, is pure Gothic. The rest of the building was added piecemeal over the centuries, the western part of the nave not until 1876. The most striking external feature is the sixteenth-century façade of the north transept, built in full Flamboyant style with elongated arches, clusters of pinnacles and delicate tracery in window and gallery. At the west end of the nave, the tower, erected on a Romanesque base that had to be massively reinforced to bear the weight, has octagonal upper storeys, in common with most churches in the region. It once stood as a separate *campanile* and probably looked the better for it. Inside, the effects are much more pleasing, and the rose stone looks warmer than on the weathered exterior. The sense of soaring height is accentuated by all the upward-reaching lines of the pillars, the net of vaulting ribs, the curling, flame-like lines repeated in the arcading of the side chapels and the rose window, and, above all, as you look down the nave, by the narrower and more pointed arches of the choir.

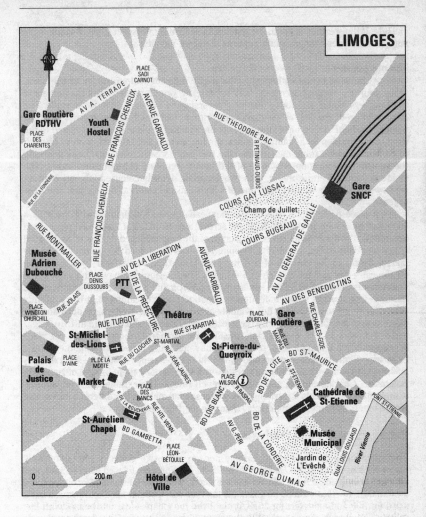

The best of the city's museums – with its showpiece collections of enamelware dating back as far as the twelfth century – is the **Musée Municipal de l'Évêché** (daily except Tues 10am–noon & 2–5pm; July–Sept 10–11.45am & 2–6pm; free) in the old Bishop's Palace overlooking a classic eighteenth-century formal garden next to the cathedral. There's an interesting progression to be observed here, from the simple, sober, Byzantine-influence *champlevé* (copper filled with enamel), to the later, especially seventeenth- and eighteenth-century work that used a far greater range of colours and indulged in elaborate virtuoso portraiture. By the nineteenth century, however, the spirit and vigour had dissipated, and although there are contemporary artisans in the city using the medium, their work, too – judging from this display – is not much more successful. There is also a permanent exhibition of **wartime Resistance** housed in an outbuilding (same hours; free).

Outside, if the weather is good, the **garden** is an inviting prospect (daily 7.45am–5.30/ 9pm; free), descending gracefully towards the River Vienne.

The old quarter

Over to the west of the cathedral is the partly renovated **old quarter** of the town. Make your way through to rue de la Boucherie, for one thousand years the domain of the Butchers' Guild, and today featuring several good but expensive restaurants. The dark, cluttered **chapel of St-Aurélien**, with a fourteenth-century cross outside, belongs to them. At the top of the street is the **market** in place de la Motte, and to the right, partly hidden by adjoining houses, the fourteenth- and fifteenth-century **church of St-Michel-des-Lions**, named after the two badly weathered Celtic lions guarding the south door and topped by one of the best towers and spires in the region. The inside is dark and atmospheric, with two beautiful, densely coloured fifteenth-century windows either side of the choir, one of which – in the south aisle – depicts the Tree of Jesse.

From place de la Motte, rue du Clocher leads to rue Jean-Jaurès, with the **PTT** a couple of blocks up to the left. Straight across, **rue St-Martial** leads past place de la République – where the fourth-century crypt of the long-vanished **Abbey of St-Martial** (July–Sept daily 9.30am–noon & 2.30–5pm; 15F) was discovered during building operations in 1960 – to the **church of St-Pierre-du-Queyroix**, whose belfry was the model for the cathedral and the church of St-Michel. The interior, partly twelfth century (the exterior was remodelled in the sixteenth century), gains a sombre strength from the massive round pillars which still support the roof. Like the cathedral, it has a slightly pink granite glow. There is a fine window at the end of the south aisle depicting the Dormition of the Virgin, signed by the great enamel artist Jean Pénicault in 1510.

To the west of the old quarter, the **Musée Adrien-Dubouchée** lies off place Winston-Churchill and close to place Dussoubs, featuring collections of porcelain and extensive china displays from around the world (daily except Tues 10am–noon & 1.30–5.30pm; 15F). Various celebrity services are included, among them images of Napoléon Bonaparte, Charles and Di, and sundry French royals. The exhibits are well laid out, with explanatory panels describing the processes for making the different wares, and form a much more interesting display than you might expect.

Eating, drinking and festivals

There is an abundance of agreeable and not too expensive places to **eat**. Two lovely places for a light lunch are *La Parenthèse*, 22 rue du Consulat (closed Mon & Sun), and *La Louisiane*, place d'Aine (closed Mon & Sun), with delicious salads and pastries – around 50F. *Le Khédive* at 39 bd Carnot is another very popular spot, and you can get a salad for 30F and a dessert for 15F. At night the rue Charles-Michels buzzes with life; there's a whole selection of ethnic restaurants. For more classic French eating, there's the rather posh *Brasserie Le Versailles*, also on place d'Aine, with menus at 69F and 130F; the business people's haunt of *Rive Gauche*, 3 av Garibaldi, close to place Jourdan, with a wide selection of seafood (closed Sun; menus at 59F and 79F); and for serious, first-class meat eating, the *Bœuf à la Mode*, 60 rue François-Chenieux (closed Sun; menus 80–170F).

For **drinks** at any time of the day, people sit out in the not-very-attractive place de la République. The *Lord John Pub* on av de-Gaulle near the train station – complete with darts – is a popular hang-out. The *Top Bar* at 17 rue Charles-Michels is frequented by the youthful members of Limoges' smart set, and the *Rolls* at 13 rue du Temple (till 4am; closed Sun–Tues) is where they go to dance – a rather gentle, intimate place, with occasional live music.

Festivals

There is an annual international **exhibition of china and enamel** in July and August, organized at various venues around the town. For French speakers, there is an interesting gathering of writers, dramatists and musicians from other French-speaking countries at the **Festival International des Francophonies** in September and October. Gourmets should make sure their visit coincides with the third Friday in October, for the **Fête des Petits Ventres**, when the entire population turns out to gorge on everything from pig's trotters to sheep's testicles in the rue de la Boucherie.

Around Limoges

There is a clutch of villages within a day's reach of Limoges. The Limoges tourist office has worked out a route linking places of interest on the south bank of the Vienne – like the **châteaux** of **Rochebrune**, **Rochechouart** and **Châlus** – detailed in a leaflet called the *Route Richard-Cœur-de-Lion*, due to its associations with the English king. Visiting all of them really requires a car, but some at least are accessible by a combination of public transport and patient hitching.

Oradour-sur-Glane

Twenty-five kilometres northwest of Limoges and a few kilometres north of the N141 road to Angoulême, the village of **ORADOUR-SUR-GLANE** stands just as the soldiers of the SS *das Reich* Division left it on June 10, 1944, after killing all the inhabitants in reprisal for attacks by French *maquisards*. It seems irreverent to approach it as a "sight"; perhaps it should be treated more as a shrine.

A gate into the **old village** admonishes: "*Souviens-toi*" ("Remember"), and the main street leads past roofless houses gutted by fire. Telephone poles, tram cables and gutters are fixed in tormented attitudes where the fire's heat left them; prewar cars rust in the garages; a yucca, grown into an enormous clump, still blooms in the notary's garden; last year's grapes hang wizened on a vine whose trellis has long rotted away.

Behind the square is a **memorial garden**, a plain rectangle of lawn hedged with beech. A dolmen-like slab on a shallow plinth covers a crypt containing relics of the dead, and the awful list of names. Beyond, by the stream, stands the **church** where the women and children – five hundred of them – were burnt to death.

The **modern village** of Oradour has been constructed beside the old, with a 1950s concrete church trying to be impressive but struggling with the task of commemorating what happened here.

There are buses from place des Charentes in Limoges, although it might be more convenient to take the train to **ST-JUNIEN** and then bus back to Oradour. The *Hôtel au Rendez-vous des Chasseurs*, Pont-à-la-Planche (☎55.02.19.73; ②; closed Feb, Nov 1–15; good restaurant specializing in game from 68F) makes a good place to put up in St-Junien.

Rochechouart and Les Salles-Lavauguyon

Twenty kilometres southwest of Oradour, across the Vienne, is the pretty walled town of **ROCHECHOUART** and its **château**, an hour by bus from the *gare SNCF* in Limoges. With its oldest parts dating from the thirteenth and fifteenth centuries and with a fine interior courtyard and frescoed hunting gallery added in Renaissance times, the château now serves as town hall, magistrates' court and **Musée d'Art Contemporain** (July & Aug daily except Tues 10am–noon & 2–6pm; March–June &

Sept to mid-Dec Wed–Sun 2–6pm), with some interesting experimental modern art exhibitions. While you're in town, take a look at the wind-carved spiral spire on the **church of St-Sauveur**. The **tourist office** is at 6 rue Victor-Hugo.

A further 20km to the southwest – though it is really only practicable by car – is the Romanesque **church of St-Eutrope** in **LES SALLES-LAVAUGUYON**, boasting some very early frescoes from around 1100, only uncovered by restorers in 1986. Les Salles-Lavauguyon lies well to the west of the D675 Rochechouart–Nontron road, 11km from Vayres-la-Chaise or 7.5km from St-Mathieu. If you're really keen on walking, the Rochechouart tourist office's *Walking Route*, which joins Rochechouart with Les Salles-Lavauguyon, is a handy publication.

Châlus and Nexon

CHÂLUS is best reached direct from Limoges, 35km along the N21 or one hour by bus. Its principal point of interest is the ruined **château** (July to mid-Sept daily 10am–noon & 2–6pm; April–June Sun & holidays only; free), where Richard the Lionheart was mortally wounded by an archer shooting from the still extant keep in 1199. Richard, son of Eleanor of Aquitaine and himself as much French as English, was campaigning to suppress a local rebellion against English rule. The archer was flayed to death for his marksmanship. For real enthusiasts, there are two further castles, **Brie** and **Montbrun**, a short distance west of Châlus and both visitable on request from the respective concierge. For an overnight **stay** in Châlus, there's the friendly *Hôtel du Centre*, 8 pl de la Fontaine (☎55.78.41.61; ①–②), with good-value menus at 60F and 80F in its restaurant.

Eighteen kilometres east, past another early medieval fortress at **RILHAC-LASTOURS**, the village of **NEXON**, also directly accessible by bus and train from Limoges, is of more general interest, with a fine, heavily restored late medieval **château** (only open to the public in summer), set in magnificent parklands with a **stud farm** (daily 9am–noon & 2–7pm), renowned for its Anglo-Arab breeds. You can **camp** in Nexon at the *Étang de la Lande* and, for a **meal**, try the *Dexet* in av de la Gare.

Chalusset and Solignac

A dozen kilometres south of Limoges in the lovely wooded valley of the Briance, the Château de Chalusset and the abbey of Solignac make the most attractive day's outing from the city. There are daily buses to Le Vigen (on the St-Yrieix line), although the times do not allow for a return the same day.

It is a fifteen-minute walk from Le Vigen to Solignac. You can see the Romanesque **abbey of Solignac** ahead of you, with the tiled roofs of its octagonal apse and neat little brood of radiating chapels. The twelfth-century façade is plain with just a little sculpture, as the granite of which it is built does not permit the intricate carving of limestone. Inside it is beautiful, a flight of steps leading down into the nave with a dramatic view the length of the church. There are no aisles, just a single space roofed with two big domes, and no ambulatory either – an absolutely plain Latin cross in design. It is a simple, sturdy church, with the same feel of plain robust Christianity as the crypt of St-Eutrope in Saintes (see p.519).

There is a very pleasant, simple **hotel** in the village, *Les Sarrazins* (☎55.00.51.48; ①), which serves a copious meal for 53F, and another in **LE VIGEN**, *Les Touristes* (☎55.00.52.11; ①–②; restaurant from 50F).

The **Château de Chalusset** is a one to one-and-a-half hour walk up the valley of the Briance in the other direction – uphill quite a lot of the way. After about three-quarters of an hour, at the highest point of the climb, there is a little ornamental belvedere in the trees on the right of the road, giving a dramatic view across the valley to the ruined keep of the castle rising above the woods. It is a further kilometre down to the bridge on the Briance, where a path follows the river bank for five minutes before winding up into the steep woods. You come first to a secondary keep, the **Tour Jeannette**, and then to the main bulk of the castle. Half-submerged in a jungle of oak and chestnut, hazel and broom, with wildflowers growing from its creviced walls, it is a splendidly dramatic and romantic ruin.

Built in the twelfth century, it was in English hands during the Hundred Years' War and, in the lawless aftermath, became the lair of a notorious local brigand, Perrot le Bearnais. Dismantled in 1593 for harbouring Protestants, it is now a private site and at the time of writing, a little discreet trespassing is required to reach it. Entry has been prohibited because of the danger of falling masonry, and you do need to be careful.

St-Léonard-de-Noblat

ST-LÉONARD-DE-NOBLAT, 25 minutes by train from Limoges or 45 minutes by bus, is a beautiful little market town of narrow streets and medieval houses with jutting eaves and corbelled turrets. There's a very lovely eleventh- and twelfth-century **church**, whose six-storey tower looks out over the rising hills and woods where the River Vienne threads its course down from the heights of the Massif Central. The interior is strong and simple, with barrel vaults on big, square piles, a high dome on an octagonal drum and domed transepts – the whole in grey granite.

If you're in a car, St-Léonard can make a pleasant base for visiting Limoges. A good place to **stay** is the *Modern Hôtel* in the old town, 6 bd Pressemanne (☎55.56.00.25; ②; restaurant from 105F). Alternatively, try the *Beau Site* at Royèrcs near the Vienne (☎55.56.00.56; ③; closed Jan–March). There is also a **camping municipal** beside the river below the town. The **tourist office** on rue Roger-Salengro (☎55.56.25.06) publishes route maps for local walks and will point you to *chambres d'hôte* possibilities round about.

Aubusson

AUBUSSON is 90km east of Limoges and served by regular buses and trains. A neat grey-stone town in the bottom of a ravine formed by the River Creuse, it is of no great interest in itself. What makes it unique is its enormous reputation as a centre for weaving tapestries, second only to the Gobelins in Paris. If you're interested, the place to aim for is the **Musée Départemental de la Tapisserie** in av des Lissiers (daily 9am–12.30pm & 2–6.30pm; closed Tues am in summer, Tues all day in winter). For information about further exhibits, ask at the **tourist office** in rue Vieille. If you want to stay, there are two inexpensive **hotels** in the main Grande-Rue: *Hôtel du Lissier*, nos. 84–86 (☎55.66.14.18; ②; with restaurant), and *Hôtel du Chapitre*, at nos. 53–55 (☎55.66.18.54; ②). The town's **campsite** is by the river on the Felletin road.

Ussel and the Plateau de Millevaches

Millevaches, the plateau of a thousand springs, is undulating upland country 800-900m in altitude, a sort of step on the northern edge of the Massif Central. It is a wild and sparsely populated landscape, and the villages here are few and far between; the ones there are appear small, grey and sturdy, inured like their mainly elderly inhabitants to the buffeting of upland weather. It is a country of conifer plantations and natural woodland – of beech, birch and chestnut – interspersed with reed-fringed tarns, dam-created lakes and pasture grazed by sheep and cows, where you still find people haymaking with rake and pitchfork.

STEAM TRAINS ON MILLEVACHES

In July and August every year **steam train trips** are run on the beautiful Limoges-Ussel mountain line. Prices are in the range of 50–160F (adults) and 30–80F (children), according to the length of the journey. You can do Limoges–Meymac, Limoges–Eymoutiers, Eymoutiers–Bujaleuf and Meymac–Ussel. For dates and times, consult the brochure *Trains Touristiques à Vapeur en Limousin* or the tourist offices in Limoges, St-Leonard-de-Noblat, Bujaleuf, Pyrat-le-Château, Île de Vassivière, Eymoutiers, Bugeat, Meymac or Treignac.

The small towns, like **Eymoutiers and Meymac**, have a primitive architectural beauty and an old-world charm largely untouched by modern development. It is an area to walk or cycle in, or at least savour at a gentle pace, and there are a surprisingly large number of attractive old-fashioned hotels.

Obviously, getting around by car is easiest, but there is access by public transport. **Ussel,** the main town, is on the main road and rail link between Brive and Clermont-Ferrand and is also connected by a cross-country line through Meymac and Eymoutiers to Limoges.

Ussel

On the eastern edge of the plateau is **USSEL**, 90km west of Clermont-Ferrand and 60km northeast of Tulle, where the land begins its gradual descent to the uppermost reaches of the Dordogne valley, thickly wooded and cut by numerous deep tributary valleys. The town is pleasant enough, with some attractive sixteenth- and seventeenth-century houses scattered about the central part, and a giant battered granite eagle on the place Voltaire is all that remains of a Roman settlement hereabouts. It's not a place with much to see.

One building worth a look is the house of the local lords, the **Maison des Ducs de Ventadour**, who moved here from their draughty fortress in the hills to the south (see opposite). Just off place de la République behind the church, it has a very provincial and rather amateurish Renaissance grandeur, perhaps aping their rich metropolitan cousins. Also worth a quick look is the local **Musée des pays d'Ussel**, one half of which is dedicated to traditional crafts and trades of the region and located in the eighteenth-century Hôtel du Juge Choriol on rue Michelet, parallel to av Thiers (daily 9am–noon & 2–6pm; mid-Sept to June by arrangement; 15F).

The N89, the main Clermont road, passes through the town centre. The **tourist office** is on the wide place Voltaire (Mon–Sat 9.30am–noon & 2–5pm; July & Aug Mon–Sat 9am–1pm & 3–7pm, Sun 10am–1pm & 3–6pm; Sept daily 9am–noon & 2–6pm; ☎55.72.11.50). At the top of the hill, the N89 becomes av Carnot and begins to descend towards the **gare SNCF** (☎55.23.50.50) – on the left at the bottom of the slope.

Perhaps the quietest place to **stay** is the *Hôtel L'Auberge* at 6 av Gambetta, opposite the Post Office (☎55.96.17.30; ②; restaurant from 70F). Alternatively, try its *Logis de France* twin, *Hôtel Le Midi*, 24 av Thiers (☎55.72.17.99; ②–③; restaurant from 50F). There is a **camping municipal** just off the road to Tulle, and several brasserie-type **eating** places on av Carnot, and a cluster of hotel-restaurants in front of the station.

Meymac and around

Pepper-pot turrets and steep slate roofs adorn the ancient grey houses of beautiful **MEYMAC**, 17km west of Ussel, packed tightly around the twelfth-century Romanesque **church**, with striking pink capitals flanking its porch; next to it are the remains of the original Benedictine **abbey**, whose foundation a thousand years ago brought the town into being.

Grand-Rue, the main street, ends in steps that climb past the round **bell-tower**, the town's landmark, to the lime-shaded square in front of the town hall. The **tourist office** is opposite, the other side of a prettily jetting fountain (Mon–Fri 3–4.30pm; May–Sept Mon–Sat 10am–12.30pm & 3–4.30pm, Sun 10am–12.30pm), and can arrange **bike rental** and give out **hiking information**.

There are two simple but pleasant **hotels** on the main road, of which the more gracious is the *Hôtel Limousin*, 76 av Limousine (☎55.95.12.11; ①–②; menus 55F & 95F). The other, close by, is *Les Voyageurs* (☎55.95.11.92; ①; restaurant from 53F). A muncipal **campsite** is close at hand on the Sornac road.

One of the most touted sights in the area is the remains of a **Roman villa** and second-century **temple** at **CARS**. Although there is nothing very spectacular to see, the very presence of Roman influence here is interesting. And, if you want to stay, there is one of the loveliest, simple, old-fashioned country **hotels** just a few kilometres away at Perols-sur-Vézère, Madame Gioux's *Hôtel des Touristes* (☎55.95.51.71; ①–②), with genuine home cooking from 60F; another is the perfectly adequate *Hôtel des Touristes* in nearby Bugeat (☎55.95.50.20; ①; closed two weeks in Sept & Sun evening), where there is also a **campsite**.

Five kilometres further, the six houses of **VIAM** perch prettily on the shores of an artificial lake. Its innocence has been slightly marred by water-sporting, but it has an exquisite and proportionately minute, lopsided **church**, whose door is blocked by a small iron gate, like Bugeat's church – presumably a local device to keep wandering farm animals out. There is no accommodation in Viam, but 6km on towards Eymoutiers there is a **gîte d'étape** by the Étang de Goussolles (Mme Sarrazin; ☎55.95.54.99; June & Sept).

Eymoutiers

EYMOUTIERS, on the banks of the River Vienne, 45km from Limoges, is another attractive upland town of tall, narrow, stone houses crowding round a much-altered Romanesque **church**. Not interesting enough for a prolonged stay, it nonetheless makes another agreeable stopover – especially for campers, as it has a simple but magnificently sited **campsite** on top of a hill overlooking the town (access off the Meymac–Tulle road). If you prefer a **bed**, you can find a perfectly comfortable one – and food – in the very unprepossessing looking *Hôtel St-Psalmet*, on the wide square opposite the *gare SNCF* (☎55.69.10.06; ①–②). A further, very rural alternative is the *Hôtel des Touristes* back on the St-Léonard road in the tiny village of **BUJALEUF** (☎55.69.50.01; ①; restaurant from 60F).

Château de Ventadour

The **Château de Ventadour**, like Chalusset, is a magnificent ruin, and all the more romantic for having no fence, no caretaker and no admission charge. It stands on the very tip of a high narrow spur way above the river valleys converging at its feet, with a lone tower rising above the trees and undergrowth, which someone has begun to clear. Built in the twelfth century, the château was abandoned in around 1600 by its owners, the dukes of Ventadour, in favour of a more comfortable house in Ussel. The celebrated troubadour Bernard de Ventadour was born here, child of a castle servant.

The castle is about 6km from Egletons on the Tulle–Ussel road. You take the dead-end turning to the farming hamlet of Moustier. But far the most dramatic approach is from below, up the winding road from **NEUVIC** – itself an ancient village, rather spoilt by the presence of an artificial lake which has elevated it to resort status. It does however, have an interesting **Musée de la Résistance**, based on the life of Henri-Queville, a former government minister and *résistant* (Sun & hols 10am–noon & 3–6pm; mid-June to mid-Sept daily 10am–noon & 3–6pm; closed Nov–April; 25F).

There are **hotels** in Egletons, but it is much nicer to stay in Clergoux or Gimel-les-Cascades (see under Tulle).

Brive-la-Gaillarde and around

BRIVE-LA-GAILLARDE is a major rail junction and the nearest thing to an industrial centre for miles around, but it makes an agreeable base for exploring the Corrèze *département* and its beautiful villages, as well as the upper reaches of the Vézère and Dordogne rivers.

Though it has no commanding sights, Brive-la-Gaillarde does have a few distractions. Right in the middle of town is the much-restored **church of St-Martin**, originally Romanesque in style, though now only the transept, apse and a few comically carved capitals survive from that era. Saint Martin himself, a Spanish aristocrat, arrived in pagan Brive in 407 on the feast of Saturnus, smashed various idols, and was promptly stoned to death by the outraged onlookers.

Numerous streets fan out from the surrounding square, **place du Général-de-Gaulle**, with a number of turreted and towered houses, some dating back to the thirteenth century. The most impressive is the sixteenth-century **Hôtel de Labenche** on bd Jules-Ferry, now housing the town's archeological finds (daily except Tues 10am–6/6.30pm; 22F).

From the **gare SNCF**, it's a ten-minute walk south along av Jean-Jaurès to the old town, south of which is the attractive square Auboiroux, with the **PTT** and **gare routière** nearby. The **tourist office** is north of the ring road on place 14-juillet (Mon–Sat 9am–noon & 2–6pm; July & Aug 9am–12.30pm & 2–7pm, Sun 10am–1pm), alongside a modern timber-framed **market** (Tues, Thurs & Sat).

There are numerous cheap **hotels** on av Jean-Jaurès towards the station, like the *Majestic et Voyageurs*, 67 av Jean-Jaurès (☎55.24.10.20; ②), but best of all the inexpensive hotels is *Hôtel Champanatier*, shuttered and creeper-covered and slightly out of the way at 15 rue Dumyrat, just west of the station (☎55.74.24.14; ①–②; restaurant from 53F). A real bargain is the *Hôtel-Bar de Corrèze* at 3 rue de Corrèze, off the main rue Toulzac, with a shopfront that belongs to a bygone age (☎55.24.14.07; ①; menu at 60F). In addition, there's a clean modern IYHF **youth hostel** on the other side of town from the train station at 56 av Maréchal-Bugeaud (☎55.24.34.00; ①; curfew 11pm), 25 minutes by foot from the *gare SNCF*, with a **campsite**, *Les Îles*, just across the river.

For alternative places to **eat**, try the *Brasserie Théâtre* opposite the tourist office, *Le Boulevard* at 8 bd Jules-Ferry or, close to St-Martin in the centre, *Les Viviers St-Martin*, 4 rue Traversiens, with a 65F menu at lunchtime.

Uzerche and Arnac-Pompadour

A half-hour train ride north of Brive along the course of the bubbling River Vézère, the town of **UZERCHE** is impressively located above a loop in the river's course. It's worth a passing visit as the town has several fine old buildings. From the **gare SNCF**, the old town is a five-minute walk south along the main road which tears through the town. The **tourist office** – behind the main church – provides information on landmarks, but the place is so small you can easily find your own way around. For a grand view of Uzerche, and well worth the extra detour, turn left onto rue du Champ-de-Foire as you come down from the station; pass the church and keep on to rue Ste-Eulalie, turning right at the end to cross the river on rue du Pont. If you need a place to **stay**, the *Hôtel Ambroise* by the river (☎55.73.28.60; ③) is about all there is.

Roughly 20km west of Uzerche (40min by train, on a different line, from Brive), is **ARNAC-POMPADOUR**, a town dominated by its grey, turreted **château**, presented in 1745 by Louis XV to his mistress, Madame de Pompadour, though she never actually visited it. Set in the green countryside of southern Limousin – reminiscent of parts of Ireland – the château is home to one of France's best known **stud farms** (*haras*), first created by Louis XV in 1761, although today only the terraces can be visited. For horse-lovers it's a must, and it's interesting even for the non-fanatic. Its forte is the Anglo-Arab breed, descendants of horses brought back from the Crusades, and the stallions are kept at the Puy-Marmont stables west of the château (mid-July to late Feb; free guided tours every 40 min; closed Sat), the mares 4km away at La Jumenterie de la Rivière (afternoons only). From May to October there are frequent race meetings and open days. In spring the fields are full of mares and foals, the best being kept for breeding, the rest sold worldwide as two-year-olds.

The **gare SNCF** is southeast of the town, close to the racecourse and opposite the château. There's even a reasonable place to **stay**, and **eat**, by the station: the *Hôtel-Restaurant de l'Hippodrome* (☎55.73.35.03; ③).

Turenne

TURENNE, just 16km south of Brive (one bus on Tues, Thurs, Fri during term time), is the first of two very picturesque villages close to the town. Capital of the viscounty of Turenne, whose most illustrious *seigneur* was Henri de la Tour d'Auvergne – the "Grand Turenne", whom Napoléon rated the finest tactician of modern times – the village today would still seem familiar to him. The same mellow stone houses still crowd in the lee of the sharp bluff whose summit sprouts the towers of their castle, one forming part of someone's house. The other, known as **La Tour de César**, can be visited (daily 9am–noon & 2–7pm; Oct to mid-March Sun only 10am–noon & 2–5pm; 25F), and is worth climbing for the views away over the ridges and valleys to the mountains of Cantal.

Collonges-la-Rouge

COLLONGES-LA-ROUGE, 7km east of Turenne, is the epitome of rustic charm with its red-sandstone houses, pepper-pot towers and pink-candled chestnut trees, although you need to time your visit carefully, as the village is now very much on the tourist bus circuit. Though small scale, there is a grandeur about the place, as if the resident Turenne administrators were aping, within their means, the grandiloquence of their superiors. On the main square a twelfth-century **church** testifies to the imbecility of shedding blood over religious differences: here, side by side, Protestant and Catholic conducted their services simultaneously. Outside, the covered **market hall** still retains its old-fashioned baker's oven.

If you want to **stay** somewhere nearby, it's best to head downhill a few minutes to **MEYSSAC**, a town built in the same red sandstone, though less grandly, for the cheaper **accommodation** at the very pleasant *Relais du Quercy* (☎55.25.40.31; ①–③), or the **campsite**, *Moulin de Valane* (☎55.25.41.59; April–Oct).

Getting to Collonges without your own wheels is difficult (bus Tues only July & Aug), though worth the effort. The prettiest route on foot from Turenne is along the back lanes through meadow and walnut orchards via **SAILLAC** (3hr), whose Romanesque **church** sports an elaborately carved tympanum upheld by a column of spiralling animal motifs.

Tulle and around

Seen from the distance, **TULLE**, 29km east of Brive, is a strange and unattractive-looking place. Strung out along the bottom of the narrow and deep valley of the Corrèze, it looks grey, run-down and industrial. But once you get down to the riverside and the area around the cathedral, it reveals itself to be full of fascinating winding lanes and stairways bordered by very handsome houses – many as old as the fourteenth century – with an imposing **hôtel de ville** at the end of rue du Trech, the main commercial street. If not worth a prolonged stay, Tulle certainly makes an interesting stopover.

The **Cathédrale Notre-Dame**, whose construction was drawn out from Romanesque to Gothic periods, stands on the riverside quays in place Émile-Zola. The cloister beside it has a small **museum** (Sun–Tues, Thurs & Fri 10am–noon & 2–6pm, Wed & Sat 2–6pm; Oct–March closes 5pm; free), containing a mishmash of exhibits ranging from archeology to accordions, along with a large contingent of firearms, which once formed one of the town's major industries, along with lace. Next door is a collection of documents to do with the Resistance at the **Musée Départemental de la Résistance et de la Déportation**, 2 quai Edmond-Perrier (Mon–Fri 9am–noon & 2–

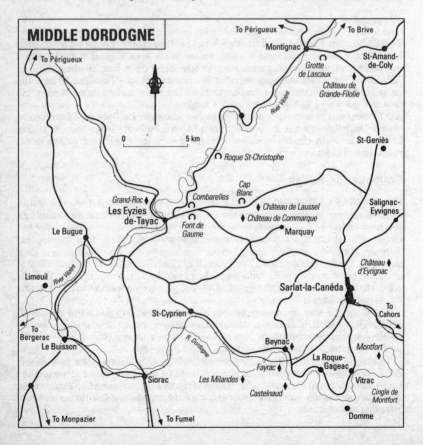

6pm; 25F), particularly the terrible reprisals wreaked by the Germans when they recaptured the town from the Resistance on June 8, 1944 and hanged ninety-nine people.

The **tourist office** is opposite the cathedral at 2 place Émile-Zola (Mon–Sat 9.30am–12.30pm & 2.30–6.30pm; July to mid-Sept Mon–Sat 9.30am–6.30pm, Sun 10am–noon; ☎55.26.59.61), and you'll find the **bus and train stations** side by side on the southwest edge of the town on av Winston-Churchill. The **market** takes place every Wed and Sat by the cathedral.

By far the most attractive place to **stay** is also the simplest: the *Hôtel au Bon Accueil*, 10 rue du Canton (☎55.26.70.57; ①; closed Feb, Easter and a week at Christmas; restaurant from 65F), in an old beamed house with stone mullion windows right across the river from the cathedral. Other places to stay include *Le Pont-Dunant* by the Pont Dunant bridge some way downstream from the centre (☎55.20.15.42; ①–③; restaurant from 50F), and the *Toque Blanche* at 29 rue Jean-Jaurès (☎55.26.75.41; ②), overlooking the car park by the very unattractive municipal offices, but only five minutes from the cathedral; the rooms here are acceptable but nothing special, whereas the **restaurant** is renowned, with an affordable menu at 100F. There is a **campsite** by the river on the Ussel side of town (May–Sept).

Gimel and Clergoux

If you're travelling by car, you might consider staying in one of the villages in the hilly wooded country northeast of Tulle. **GIMEL-LES-CASCADES**, in particular, is very beautiful and, out of season at least, very quiet. It is a minute hamlet, about 10km away and clinging to the edge of a steep valley beside a spectacular waterfall, the **Montane**, which has sadly been turned into a paying "sight" (25F). There is also a superb twelfth-century reliquary, known as the *Chasse de St-Étienne*, in the treasury of the local **church**.

There is a certain amount of local animosity to "the American" who has bought the attractive **hotel**, *Hostellerie de la Vallée* (☎55.21.40.60; ②–③; good restaurant from 95F), and, they would have you believe, most of the village. Two further possibilities for accommodation are the delightfully friendly and unpretentious *Hôtel Maurianges*, near the defunct Monteil train station, fifteen minutes up the road from Gimel, and serving delicious and copious home-cooked meals for 70F (☎55.21.28.88; ①–②; restaurant closed Sat & Sun evening – they prefer you to phone in advance for the restaurant); and in **CLERGOUX**, another 15km east, the lovely creeper-covered *Hôtel Chammard* (☎55.27.76.04; ①; closed Nov-March; no restaurant). There is also a slightly expensive **campsite** by the beautiful lakelet, the Étang de Ruffaud, near Gimel, where you can swim and get a reasonable meal in the lakeside bar.

THE LOT

The core of this section is formed by the old provinces of Haut Quercy and Quercy: the land between the Dordogne and the Lot and between the Lot and the Garonne, Aveyron and Tarn. We have extended it slightly eastwards to include the gorges of the River Aveyron and Villefranche-de-Rouergue on the edge of the province of Rouergue.

It is hotter, drier, less well known and, with few exceptions, less crowded here than the Dordogne, which does not mean that the area is less interesting. The cave paintings at **Pech-Merle** are quite the equal of those at Les Eyzies. **Najac**, **Penne** and **Peyrerusse** have ruined castles to rival those of the Dordogne. Towns like **Figeac** and **Villefranche-de-Rouergue** are without equal, as are villages like **Cardaillac** and **St-Antonin-Noble-Val**, and stretches of country like that below Gourdon, around **Les Arques** where Ossip Zadkine had his studio, and the **Célé Valley**.

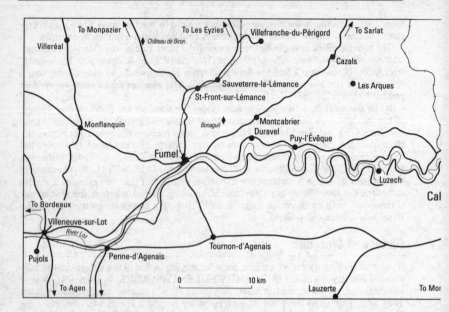

Again, without transport, many places are out of reach. Some consolation, however, is the existence of the Brive–Toulouse train line that makes Figeac, Villefranche-de-Rouergue and Najac accessible, while Agen, Moissac and Montauban are on the Bordeaux–Toulouse line.

Rocamadour and around

Tucked under a cliff in the deep and abrupt canyon of the Alzou stream, the spectacular setting of **ROCAMADOUR** is hard to beat; the village itself must have been beautiful once, too, but for centuries now it has been inundated by religious pilgrims (and latterly more secular-minded coach tours), whose constant stream has turned the place into something of a nightmare, with every house displaying mountains of unbelievable junk. The reason for its popularity since medieval times is the supposed miraculous ability of the cathedral's Black Madonna. Nowadays, pilgrims are outnumbered by tourists, who come here to wonder at the sheer audacity of its location, built almost vertically into its rocky backdrop.

Legend has it that the history of Rocamadour began with the arrival of Zacchaeus, husband of Saint Veronica, who fled to France to escape religious persecution and lived out his last years here as a hermit. When in 1166 a perfectly preserved body was found in a grave high up on the rock, it was declared to be Zacchaeus, who thereafter became known as Saint Amadour. Rocamadour soon became a major pilgrimage site and a staging post on the road to St-Jacques de Compostelle in Spain. Saint Bernard, numerous kings of England and France and thousands of others crawled up the chapel steps on their knees to pay their respects and seek cures for their illnesses. Henry Short-Coat (see p.568) was the first to plunder the shrine, but he was easily outclassed by the Huguenots, who tried in vain to burn the saint's corpse but finally resigned themselves simply to hacking it to bits. What you see today, therefore, is not the real thing but a

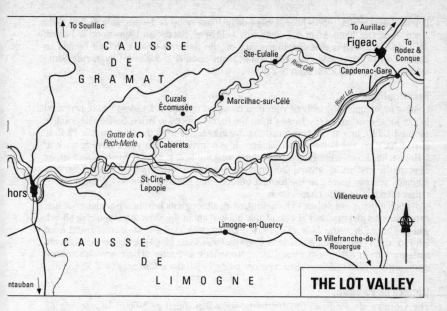

To Souillac

To Aurillac

C A U S S E
D E
G R A M A T

Ste-Eulalie

River Célé

Figeac

To
Rodez &
Conque

Capdenac-Gare

Cuzals
Écomusée

Marcilhac-sur-Célé

River Lot

Grotte de
Pech-Merle

Caberets

St-Cirq-
Lapopie

hors

Villeneuve

Limogne-en-Quercy

To Villefranche-de-
Rouergue

C A U S S E
D E
L I M O G N E

ntauban

THE LOT VALLEY

nineteenth-century reconstruction, carried out in the hope of reviving the flagging pilgrimage.

The Town

Rocamadour is easy enough to find your way around – there's just one street, rue de la Couronnerie, strung out between two medieval gateways, while above sits the **Parvis**, the main complex halfway up the cliff, with no fewer than seven churches. The indolent take the lift dug into the rockface (30F up and back), while the devout drag themselves on their knees up the 223 steps of the *Via Sancta* to the smoke-blackened and votive-packed **Chapelle Notre-Dame** where the miracle-working twelfth-century Black Madonna resides. The tiny, macabre statue of walnut wood is appropriately lit in the mysterious half light of her protective black cage, but the rest of the chapel is unremarkable. High up in the rock above the entrance to the chapel is a sword, supposedly Roland's legendary blade *Durandal*.

There's no relief for the nonreligious in the **Musée Francis Poulenc** (daily 9am–noon & 2–6pm; July & Aug 9am–6pm; 10F), which contains sacred art treasures, reliquaries and various historical documents. It's dedicated to the French composer Francis Poulenc (1899–1963) because he was one of the modern pilgrims who received miraculous inspiration from the shrine, though in his case the results were musical rather than medical.

You can climb still further to the ancient **ramparts** above the chapel, or take the winding shady path, *La Calvarie*, past the stations of the cross: either way the views across the valley are stunning.

There are three different wildlife centres in Rocamadour: the **Rocher des Aigles** (April–Oct daily 10am–noon & 2–6pm; 30F), a breeding centre for birds of prey (demonstrations of falconry at 11am and hourly 3–6pm); the **Forêt des Singes**, off the D673, where 150 barbary apes roam the relative freedom of a reserve in the plateau behind L'Hospitalet (April–June & Sept daily 10am–noon & 1–6pm; July & Aug daily 10am–7pm; Oct 10am–noon & 1–5pm; Nov 1–11 Wed, Sat & Sun 10am–noon & 1–5pm; 30F); and the **Jardin des Papillons**, just off the route de Gramat, which breeds an international cast of wild butterflies (daily 10am–noon & 2–5.30pm; July & Aug 9am–6.30pm; closed mid-Oct to March; 22F).

Practicalities

Getting to Rocamadour without your own transport is awkward, unless you're prepared to pay for the summer-only **buses** from the tourist offices in Brive, Sarlat and Souillac (around 120F), or walk or take a taxi the five kilometres from the Rocamadour-Padirac **gare SNCF** on the Brive–Capdenac line. If you arrive **by car**, you'll have to park in L'Hospitalet, 1.5km from Rocamadour (and with the best view of the town there is), or else in the car park, several hundred metres below the town. If you're carrying luggage, you can leave it at the **tourist office** in the Hôtel de Ville on the main street, rather than lug it up the chapel steps.

Rocamadour is not a place to hang around in, although its **hotels** are actually not that expensive; it's just that they're completely booked out in the summer. If you ring ahead, you might get in at the *Lion d'Or*, Porte Figuier (☎65.33.62.04; ②–③; restaurant from 59F), or the *Terminus* on place de la Carretta (☎65.33.62.14; ②–③; closed Dec–March; restaurant from 68F), both closed from November to Easter. There are also several **campsites** in L'Hospitalet, the nearest one being *Le Relais du Campeur* (☎65.33.63.28).

Gouffre de Padirac

The **Gouffre de Padirac** (guided tours: daily 9am–noon & 2–6pm; July & Aug 8/8.30am–6.30/7pm; closed mid-Oct to March; 39F) is about 20km east of Rocamadour on the other side of the main Brive–Figeac road. It is an enormous limestone sink-hole, about 100m deep and over 100m wide. There are some spectacular formations of stalactites and waterfalls created by the accumulation of lime, and beautiful underground lakes, but it is very, very touristy – so much so that it's best avoided at weekends and other peak periods, or you'll wait an age for tickets. Visits are partly on foot, partly by boat, and the guided tours last an hour and a half. In wet weather you'll need a waterproof jacket. If you have no car, the nearest **gare SNCF** is Rocamadour-Padirac, over 10km to the west; the only alternative to walking or hitching is the summer-only bus, which costs over 50F for the round trip.

St-Céré

East of Padirac and about 9km from Bretenoux on the River Bave, a minor tributary of the Dordogne, is the medieval town of **ST-CÉRÉ**, dominated by the brooding ruins of the **château de St-Laurent-les-Tours** and full of ancient houses crowding around place du Mercadial. The two powerful keeps of St-Laurent, partially rebuilt, date from the twelfth and fifteenth centuries and were part of a fortress belonging to the Turennes. In wartime, the artist Jean Lurçat operated a secret Resistance radio post here; after the war he turned it into a studio, and it's now a museum of his work, mainly his huge tapestries but also sketches, paintings and pottery (daily mid-July to Sept 9.30am–noon & 2.30–6.30pm; also 2 weeks at Easter; 15F). The town itself has just one distraction, the **Musée Automobile du Haut-Quercy**, out on the rte de Monteil (Easter–May daily except Tues 10am–noon & 2–6pm; June–Sept daily 10am–noon & 2–7pm; 15F), with over thirty automobiles dating from 1900 to 1950.

St-Céré has two reasonable places to **stay**: *Hôtel Victor Hugo*, 7 av du Maquis, by the river (☎65.38.16.15; ③; restaurant from 55F; closed Oct 1–21 & March 1–15 as well as Mon), and *La Truite Dorée*, 4 av de la Monzie (☎65.38.17.54; ①–③; closed July 1–15 & Sun in winter), with a good restaurant from 58F.

Bikes can be rented from M. St-Charmant in rue Faidherbe – and one of the best trips you could pedal is to the hugely pretty little village of **AUTOURE**, in a tight side valley, about 10km to the west of St-Céré.

Gourdon and around

GOURDON lies between Sarlat and Cahors, conveniently served by the Brive–Toulouse train line, and makes a quiet, pleasant base for visiting some of the major places in this part of the Dordogne. It's 17km south of the River Dordogne and pretty much at the eastern limit of the luxuriant woods and valleys of Périgord, which give way quite suddenly, at the line of the N20, to the arid limestone landscape of the Causse de Gramat. It is a beautiful town, its medieval centre of yellow stone houses attached like a swarm of bees to a prominent hilltop, neatly ringed by modern boulevards containing all the shops.

In the Middle Ages, Gourdon was an important place, deriving wealth and influence from the presence of four monasteries. It was besieged and captured in 1189 by Richard the Lionheart, who promptly murdered its feudal lords. Legend has it that the archer who fired the fatal shot at him during the siege of Chalus was the last surviving member of this family. But more than anything, it was the devastation of the Wars of Religion that dispatched Gourdon into centuries of oblivion.

From whichever direction you approach, all roads lead to place de la Libération in front of the fortified **gateway** over rue du Majou, the narrow main street of the old town. It is lined all the way up with splendid stone houses, some, like the **Maison d'Anglars** at no. 17, as old as the thirteenth century. At its uphill end, rue du Majou debouches into a lovely square in front of the massive but not particularly interesting fourteenth-century **church of St-Pierre**. **Market days** are Tuesday and Saturday in the *place*. There is a handsome **Hôtel de Ville** on one side and, in place des Marronniers behind the church, the family home of the Cavaignacs, who supplied the nation with numerous prominent public figures in the eighteenth and nineteenth centuries, including the notoriously brutal general who put down the Paris workers' attempts to defend the Second Republic in June 1848. From the square, steps climb to the top of the hill, where the castle once stood and where there is a superb view over the Dordogne Valley and surroundings.

A couple of kilometres along the Sarlat road in the direction of Cougnac from Gourdon, there is a very interesting **cave**, the **Grottes de Cougnac**, discovered in 1949 (daily 9.30–11am & 2–5pm; July & Aug daily 9.30am–6pm; closed Nov–March; 28F). It has beautiful rock formations as well as some fine prehistoric paintings rather similar to those at Pech-Merle (see p .593).

Practicalities

The **tourist office** is on the left at the beginning of rue du Majou (Mon–Sat 10am–noon & 2–4pm; July & Aug Mon–Sat 9.30am–1pm & 2–7pm, Sun 9.30am–1pm; June & Sept Mon–Sat 9.30am–noon & 2–6pm, Sun 10am–noon), and has extensive lists of B&B options in the area. They also organize **day trips** by bus to Rocamadour, Sarlat and other local sights (80–120F). **Bikes** can be rented from the **gare SNCF** or *Gourdon Forme* on route de Salviac.

If you want to **stay** in the town itself, the *Hôtel Bissonnier*, 51 bd des Martyrs, on the eastern side of the ring road near the *PTT* (☎65.41.02.48; ①–④; closed Dec–Jan 10), is very agreeable and has a restaurant with such local specialities as *confits* and stuffed duck's neck available *à la carte* (menu from 70F). Not so pleasant but a little cheaper is the *Terminus* in av de la Gare (☎65.41.03.29; ②–③; restaurant from 70F), by the train station. The **camping municipal**, *Écoute s'il pleut*, is on the north side of town.

For a pleasant independent **restaurant**, with a tiny outside terrace, try the *Croque-Note* on the corner of rue Jean-Jaurès and bd Gabanès on the south side of the old town (80–130F).

Les Arques

Twenty-five kilometres southwest of Gourdon on the Fumel road, you come to a pretty but not remarkable *bastide* called **CAZALS**; a left turn here takes you along the bottom of the valley of the Masse and up its left flank to the exquisite hamlet of **LES ARQUES**. This is quiet, remote, small-scale farming country, emptied of people by the slaughter of rustic sons in World War I and by migration to the towns in search of jobs and money.

Les Arques' main claim to fame is the Russian cubist/expressionist sculptor Ossip Zadkine, who bought the old house by the church here in 1934. Some of his sculptures adorn the space outside the church as well as its lovely interior, and his studio, which now belongs to the City of Paris, houses a **museum** with a number of his other works (daily 11am–7pm; mid-Sept to mid-June Sat, Sun & school hols 2–5pm; 15F). It is particularly interesting if you know the delightful secret garden of his house and studio in Paris.

The other reason to come here is the now superannuated village school, transformed into a most unusual **restaurant**, *La Récréation* (☎65.22.88.08), where you get a copious and delicious meal to eat beneath the wisterias and chestnut trees of the school yard for about 90–130F. On a summer night with the swifts screaming overhead, it is idyllic.

On the other side of the valley and well signposted, the tiny Romanesque **chapel of St-André-des-Arques** reputedly has some very lovely fifteenth-century frescoes discovered by Zadkine, but it is not easy to get the key from the house next door.

Cahors

CAHORS, on the River Lot, was the capital of the old province of Quercy. In its time, it has been a Gallic settlement; a Roman town; a briefly held Moorish possession; governed by the English; a bastion of Catholicism in the Wars of Religion, sacked in consequence by Henri IV; a university town for four hundred years; and birthplace of Gambetta, after whom so many French streets and squares are named. Despite all this, modern Cahors is a sunny southern backwater. Its two most interesting sights are its **cathedral** and the remarkable fourteenth-century **Pont Valentré**.

While you're in the Cahors area, don't miss out on the local **wine**, heady and black in colour but dry to the taste and not at all plummy like the Gironde wines from Blaye and Bourg, which use the same Malbec grape.

The Town

Small and easily walkable, the town squats on a peninsula formed by a tight loop in the River Lot, and is protected on the northern side by a rank of fourteenth-century **fortifications**, with the **Barbacane de St-Jean** making a breach in the walls.

Right in the middle of the town is the **cathedral**, consecrated in 1119, the oldest and simplest in plan of the Périgord-style churches. The exterior of the church is not exciting: a heavy square tower dominates the plain west front, whose best feature is the elaborately decorated portal in the street on the north side, where a Christ in Majesty dominates the tympanum, surrounded by angels and apostles, while cherubim fly out of the clouds to relieve him of his halo. Side panels show scenes from the life of Saint Stephen. The outer ring of figures over the portal shows a line of naked figures being stabbed in the behind and hacked with axes.

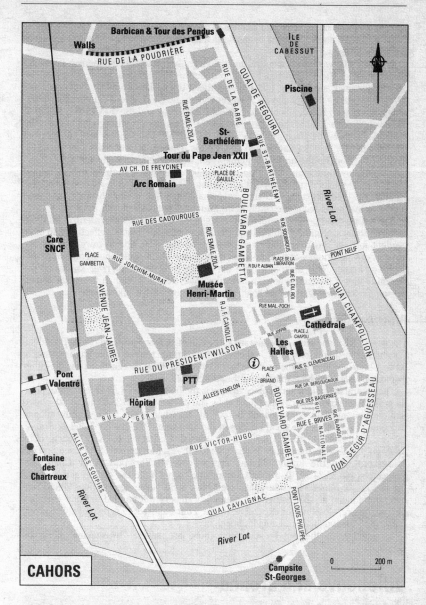

CAHORS

Inside, the cathedral is much like St-Étienne at Périgueux, with a nave lacking aisles and transepts, roofed with two big domes; in the first are fourteenth-century frescoes of the stoning of Saint Stephen. The Gothic choir and apse are extensively but crudely painted. To their right a door opens into a delicate cloister in the Flamboyant style, still retaining some intricate carving, though damaged. On the northwest corner pillar a graceful girl with broad brow and ringlets to her waist serves as a model for the Virgin. In the northeast corner, an arch opens on to a courtyard by the fine Renaissance **archdeacon's house**.

In the area between the cathedral and the river, there's a warren of narrow lanes and alleys, most of them handsomely restored during the last ten years. Many of the houses, turreted and built of flat, thin, southern brick, date from the fourteenth and fifteenth centuries. Rues Nationale, Bergougnoux and rue Lastié are particularly interesting, along with rue des Soubirons, rue St-Barthélémy and rue du Château-du-Roi to the north. Take a look at the impressive **Hôtel d'Issale** in rue Bergougnoux and the **Maison Roaldès** in place Henri-IV; also go out of your way to see the **Hôpital Grossia** in rue des Soubirous and the **Palais Duèze**, opposite the church of St-Barthélémy, built for the brothers of Pope John XXII in the fourteenth century.

Immediately south of the cathedral, the lime-bordered **place Jean-Jacques-Chapou** commemorates a local trade-unionist and Resistance leader, killed in a German ambush on July 17, 1944. Next to it is the covered **market** and a shop bearing the name *Gambetta* that belonged to the family of the famous deputy of Belleville in Paris.

The reason most people venture to Cahors is the dramatic **Pont Valentré**. Its three powerful towers, originally closed by portcullises and gates, made it effectively an independent fortress, guarding the river crossing on the west side of town. One of the finest surviving bridges of its time, it is, rightly, one of the most photographed monuments in France. Just upstream from the bridge is a resurgent river known as the **Fontaine des Chartreux**, flowing from the valleyside. The Roman town was named *Divona Carducorum* after it, and it still supplies Cahors with drinking water.

Practicalities

The **gare SNCF** and **gare routière** are at the end of av Jean-Jaurès off rue du Président-Wilson. For further information on the area, make for the **tourist office** on the corner of bd Gambetta and allées Fénelon close to the cathedral. **Bicycle rental** is possible either from *Ets Combes*, 117 bd Gambetta, or the *gare SNCF*.

The central and characterful place to **stay** is the budget-priced *Hôtel de la Paix*, place de la Halle, opposite the covered market by the cathedral (☎65.35.03.40; ①–②; closed Sun; restaurant from 60F) – don't be put off by what might be a slightly offhand welcome. There are three good options in the area round the station: *Hôtel de France*, 252 av Jean-Jaurès (☎65.35.16.76; ②–④; closed Christmas to New Year), *Hôtel Melchior*, opposite the station (☎65.35.03.38; ①–②; restaurant from 68F; closed Sun out of season), and the lovely old-time creeper-covered *Terminus*, 5 av Charles-de-Freycinet (☎65.35.24.50; ③–⑤), just around the corner from the station and boasting the famous *Le Balandre* restaurant (closed Mon & Sun evenings and July to mid-Sept lunchtime; menu at 120F, otherwise double). Campers will be glad to know there's a new **campsite**, albeit rather expensive, by the Pont Cabessut to supplement the grotty *municipal camping* by Pont Louis-Philippe.

In addition to the hotel-restaurants, there are several **brasseries** along bd Gambetta.

Villeneuve and around

VILLENEUVE-SUR-LOT, 75km west and downstream from Cahors and capital of the Lot-et-Garonne *département*, does not have a great deal to commend it: there are no very interesting sights, though the handful of attractive timbered houses in the old town go some way to compensate. If you're reliant on public transport, it's worth remembering there's no train station, and bus links are poor.

The town's most striking landmark is the red-brick tower of the church of **Ste-Catherine**, completed as late as 1937 in typically garish neo-Byzantine style, but rather unusually built on a north–south axis; inside, the church retains some attractive stained glass from the previous fourteenth-century building. In the streets around the main square, **place La Fayette**, a couple of towers alone survive from the fortifications of this originally *bastide* town; here is also thirteenth-century **Pont Vieux**, resembling the Pont Valentré in Cahors but devoid of towers. There is, however, and rather unexpectedly, a good museum, the **Musée Gaston Rapin** on bd Voltaire (daily except Tues 2–7pm; free), on the south bank of the river beyond the Porte de Pujols, with sections on traditional crafts and local history, as well as typically very good, temporary exhibitions.

The **tourist office** is in the theatre on bd de la République (Mon–Sat 9.30am–noon & 2–6pm; closed Sun; ☎53.70.31.37). Market days are Tuesdays and Saturdays in place la Fayette. If you're looking for **accommodation** and don't fancy the **camping municipal** on the N21, try the central, clean and welcoming *Hôtel de l'Espoir,* 5 pl de la Marine (☎53.70.71.63; ③), the *Remparts,* 1 rue Marcel (☎53.70.71.63; ①), or the *Hôtel Les Platanes,* 40 bd de la Marine (☎53.40.11.40; ①–②). For a bit more luxury and a beautiful setting, there's the *Hôtel Les Chênes,* 3km to the south at Bel-Air, Pujols (☎53.49.04.55; ③–④), with the very fancy and expensive **restaurant** *La Toque Blanche* nearby (☎53.49.00.30; closed June 20–27 & Nov 28–Dec 5; 190F upwards). For something simpler, *Chez Câline* in rue Notre-Dame offers menus from 75F.

Pujols and Penne d'Agenais

For a pleasant short walk – about half an hour from the Porte de Pujols – you can climb south to the tiny walled village of **PUJOLS** to see the faded Romanesque frescoes in the **church of Ste-Foy** and take in some great views over the surrounding country. Another side trip could be to the beautiful but touristy old fortress town of **PENNE D'AGENAIS**, 8km upstream on a steep hill also on the south bank of the Lot, with remains of a thirteenth-century castle teetering on a cliff-edge; take the **bus** to St-Sylvestre on the north bank and walk. There are great views from the top. The **tourist office** in rue du 14-juillet can supply comprehensive lists of B&Bs and *gîtes* in the area round about (daily 10am–noon & 2–5pm). There's a **campsite** by the river and a **gîte d'étape** near the gare SNCF on the Agen–Paris line.

The château de Bonguil, Puy L'Evêque and Luzech

From Villeneuve as far as Fumel, the Lot Valley is ugly and industrial, but upstream from here, the vine-cloaked banks are dotted with small and ancient villages. An *SNCF* bus threads through them, and because there are six daily it's possible to get off, look around and pick up the next bus – not that any of the villages is worth more than a brief stay.

The first place worth heading for east of Fumel – the **Château de Bonaguil** (daily Feb 6–Nov 10 10.30am–noon & 2.30–5.30pm; 25F) – is more difficult to get to. It's spectacularly perched at the end of a wooden spur commanding two valleys, about 8km northeast of Fumel. Built during the fifteenth and sixteenth centuries with a double ring of walls, five huge towers and a narrow boat-shaped keep designed to resist artillery, it was the last of the medieval castles to be constructed.

Back on the Lot, **PUY-L'ÉVÊQUE**, 15km east of Fumel, is probably the prettiest village in the entire valley, with many grand houses built in honey-coloured stone and overlooked by both a **church** and the **castle** of the bishops of Cahors. For the best view, stand on the suspension bridge which crosses the Lot. If you want to **stay** over, the *Hôtel Henri* has cheap and decent rooms (☎65.21.32.24; ①–②), and there's a **camping municipal** by the river.

Several bends in the river later – 15km by road – you come to **LUZECH**, with scant Gaulish and Roman remains of the town of *L'Impernal,* and the **Chapelle de Notre-**

Dame-de-l'Île, dedicated to the medieval boatmen who transported Cahors wines to Bordeaux. It stands in a huge river loop, overlooked by a thirteenth-century **keep**, with some picturesque alleys and dwellings in the quarter opposite place du Canal.

St-Cirq-Lapopie

If you have your own transport you could easily make a side trip to the cliff-edge village of **ST-CIRQ-LAPOPIE**, perched high above the south bank of the Lot. The village was saved from ruin when poet André Breton came to live here earlier this century, and is now an irresistible draw for the tour buses with its cobbled lanes, half-timbered houses and gardens; but it's still worth the trouble, especially if you visit early or late in the day. Public transport in the form of an *SNCF* bus will get you from Cahors to Gare-St-Cirq in the valley bottom; thereafter, there's no alternative but to leg it up the steep hill. For **accommodation**, there is the very pretty *Auberge du Sombral* (☎65.30.26.37; ④; closed Tues, Wed & Nov 11–March), with an excellent restaurant and a menu at 95F, and a **campsite**, *Camping de la Plage*, down by the river – a slightly regimented site, but with access to the river and its swimming and canoeing possibilities. There's another camp-site at **LA TRUFFIÈRE**, 3km to the southeast and over the rim of the valley; about 20km upstream, there is a **gîte** at **CAJARC** (Mme Mignot; ☎65.40.65.20).

Figeac and around

FIGEAC lies on the River Célé, 71km east of Cahors and some 8km north of the Lot. It's a beautiful little town with an unspoilt medieval centre, in whose narrow streets you begin to get a sense of the south. It has the added advantage of being away from the main tourist beat.

Like many another provincial town hereabouts, it owes its beginnings to the founda-tion of an abbey in the early days of Christianity in France, one which quickly became wealthy because of its position on the pilgrim routes to both Rocamadour and Compostella. In the Middle Ages it became a centre of tanning, which partly accounts for the many houses whose top floors have *soleilhos*, or open-sided wooden galleries used for drying skins. Again, as so often, it was the Wars of Religion that pushed it into eclipse, for Figeac threw in its lot with the nearby Protestant stronghold of Montauban and suffered the same punishing reprisals by the victorious royalists in 1662.

Both roads and train line funnel you automatically into the town centre, where the **Hôtel de la Monnaie** surveys place Vival (Mon–Sat April–Sept 10am–12.30pm & 2.30–7pm; Oct–March 11am–noon & 2.30–5.30pm; 25F). It is a splendid building whose origins go back to the thirteenth century, when it served as a kind of depot for coins stamped out in the city's mint. The building now houses the tourist office, as well as a none-too-exciting museum of old coins and archeological bits and pieces found in the surrounding area. In the streets radiating off to the north of the square – Caviale, République, Gambetta and their cross-streets – there is a delightful range of houses of the medieval and classical periods, both stone and half-timbered with brick noggings, adorned with carvings and colonnettes, ogees, and interesting bits of iron work. At the end of these streets are the two small squares of **place Carnot** and **place Champollion**, both of great charm. The former is the site of the old *halles*, under whose awning a restaurant now spreads its tables.

Champollion, the Egyptologist who cracked Egyptian hieroglyphics by deciphering the triple text of the Rosetta Stone, was born in the house at 4 impasse Champollion, off the square, and the building now houses a very interesting **museum** dedicated to his life and work (daily except Mon 10am–noon & 2.30–6.30pm; July & Aug daily 10am–noon & 2.30–6.30pm; Nov–Feb daily except Mon 2–6pm only; 20F). At the end of this alley, a larger-than-life reproduction of the Rosetta Stone forms the floor of the tiny **place des Écritures**, beside a little garden planted with tufts of papyrus.

On the other side of place Champollion, rue Boutaric leads up to the cedar-shaded **church of Notre-Dame-du-Puy**, most interesting for its views over the roofs of the town. More interesting is the **church of St-Sauveur** off place des Herbes near the tourist office, with its lovely Gothic chapterhouse decorated with heavily gilded but dramatically realistic seventeenth-century carved wood panels illustrating the life of Christ.

Practicalities

At the heart of the town on place Vival, you'll find the **tourist office** in the Hôtel de la Monnaie (Mon–Sat 10am–12.30pm & 2.30–7pm; Oct–March 11am–noon & 2.30–5.30pm; ☎65.34.06.25). The **gare SNCF** (☎65.34.10.37) and **gare routière** are a few minutes' walk to the south across the river at the end of rue de la Gare and avenue des Poilus.

The nicest place to **stay** in the heart of Figeac is the *Hôtel Champollion* on place Champollion (☎65.34.04.37; ②–③), the only drawback being the absence of a restaurant. For a cheap alternative, there is the newly renovated *Hôtel du Faubourg*, just to the east of the centre on the Rodez road (☎65.34.21.82; ①–③; restaurant 65F). And there are two possibilities across the river: the great old *Chez Marinette* at 51 allées Victor-Hugo (☎65.34.10.16; ②–③; closed mid-Jan to Feb 10, plus Sun evening & Mon out of season), with a 1930s lounge and excellent regional cuisine (particularly good menus at 75F and 125F) and, opposite the station, the *Terminus*, 27 av Clemenceau (☎65.34.00.43; ②–③; closed Oct 24–Nov 8), also with a good restaurant from 80F. A further possibility, and an attractive one, is to go on to Capdenac-Gare, 7km away, and stay at the riverside *Auberge la Diège* (☎65.64.70.54; ①–③; closed Dec 24–Jan 3 & Fri out of season), where you can also eat from 58F. The tourist office can recommend *chambres d'hôte*, and there's a **campsite** by the Célé on av de Cahors, by the sports ground, where you can also rent **canoes**.

For **eating** somewhere other than a hotel restaurant, the *Puce à l'Oreille*, 5 rue St-Thomas, behind place Carnot, has a good reputation, but is quite expensive, with just one menu at 75F (*carte* 200F or so; Sept–June closed Mon). For a light meal, there's the *crêperie La Chandeleur* (about 50F) in rue Boutaric, off place Champollion.

Cardaillac

Home of one of the great families of Quercy in the Middle Ages, the old part of the village of **CARDAILLAC**, about 10km to the north of Figeac off the N140, is gathered on the tip of a steep ridge above wild wooded valleys: an organic pile of houses, primitive machinery and crumbling fortifications of such antiquity that you wonder how they have survived so long. The village has created what they call a **musée éclaté**, consisting of a tour of several old houses and giving an insight into the lifestyle and practices of yore, like bread-making, drying chestnuts and preparing prunes (mid-June to mid-Sept daily 10am–noon & 2.30–7pm; other times by arrangement on ☎65.34.17.23; 10F). An additional plus point is the minute but delightful **hotel** *Chez Marcel*, on the through road (☎65.40.11.16; ①), with a first-rate **restaurant** (closed Mon) offering such delights as a *gigot* of lamb from the *causse* and the regional offal speciality, *tripoux*.

Foissac, Peyrerusse-le-Roc and Decazeville

Coming out of Figeac on the road to Villeneuve, you pass one of the so-called **aiguilles**, or stone needles, that used to ring Figeac. They are an incredible 8m high and date from the 1100s; no one knows whether they were milestones, boundary markers for the abbey, or something completely different.

Some 20km further south, and west of the road to Villeneuve, is the village of **FOISSAC**, which has given its name to a local **cave** (Sun 2–6pm; July & Aug daily 10am–6.30pm; June & Sept daily 10–11.30am & 2–6pm; 25F); in addition to the weird and wonderful geological formations here, there is an unusual prehistoric **potter's workshop** dating from about 4000 BC.

Coming out of Figeac on the Decazeville road, you very quickly reach **CAPDENAC**. Take the time to leave the main road and look at the old village, its **castle** remains and **ramparts**, perched on the height commanding this almost strangulated bend in the Lot. Another 20km south of here, along the winding valley-bottom road beside the River Diège, is another magical hilltop village: the ruined **PEYRERUSSE-LE-ROC**, once an important fortress guarding the local silver mines but abandoned to the elements since the seventeenth century.

Somewhat surprising in such a quintessentially rural part of France, **DECAZEVILLE**, some 28km southeast of Figeac, owes its place in the annals of the nation's history to coal mining and the role its well-organized Communist miners played in the local *maquis* and Resistance. It was the centre of the Rouergue – as this province of France is known – coalfield, and only came into being in the nineteenth century. The last mines ceased working in 1965 after prolonged industrial action by the miners, with the all-too-familiar economic and social consequences. The enormous crater of the last working mine, an opencast one known as **La Découverte,** is unmissable as you leave town on the Aubin road. The one curiosity in Decazeville is the presence in the **church of Notre-Dame** of a dozen early paintings by the Symbolist, Gustave Moreau, although you would need to be a committed devotee to come all this way for that reason alone.

Four kilometres south, neighbouring **AUBIN** has a mining museum, the **Musée de la Mine** on the main square opposite the tourist office (daily 10am–noon & 2–6pm; mid-Sept to May Sat & Sun 3–6pm; free), and a rather romantic bronze statue of a miner. Exhibits include an interesting collection of tools, clothing and equipment and documentary evidence about strikes, accidents and local history.

The valley of the Célé

The **River Célé** joins the Lot at **CABRERETS**, 41km west of Figeac, and for this last stretch of its course, it flows through a luxuriant canyon-like valley cut into the limestone uplands of the Causse de Gramat. A twisting minor road follows the river here: a silent, backwater of a place, hot in summer, frequented mainly by canoeists (frequent opportunities to rent craft). The **GR651** follows the same route, sometimes close to the river, sometimes on the edge of the *causse* on the north bank.

Two villages, in particular, are worth a stop. The first is **ESPAGNAC-STE-EULALIE**, about 18km west of Figeac. It's a tiny and beautiful hamlet across an old stone bridge on the south bank of the river, under the limestone outcrops of the *causse*. A gorgeous hatted lantern crowns the belfry of the **church** (daily 10.30am–noon & 1.30–3.30pm), and under a weathered tower next door, an ancient gateway leads to the *gîte d'étape* (☎65.40.05.24). There are two **campsites** in Brengues, the next hamlet, as well as the *Hôtel de la Vallée* (☎65.40.02.50; ②–③).

But the next place of real interest is **MARCILHAC**, 4km downstream, whose semi-ruinous **abbey** with its gaping walls and broken columns has the most romantic atmosphere. Very early and rather primitive ninth-century Carolingian sculpture decorates the doorway, and there are some handsome Romanesque capitals in the chapterhouse. In the damp interior are frescoes from around 1500 and old coats-of-arms of the local nobility, for Marcilhac was once mightily powerful, having even Rocamadour under its sway. During World War II, Marcilhac was the scene of the one of the *maquis'* first theatrical gestures of turning the tables on the occupier: on November 11, 1943 –

Armistice Day – Jean-Jacques Chapou's group (see Cahors, p.588) briefly occupied the village and laid a wreath at the war memorial.

There's a **gîte d'étape** in the abbey, as well as a **camping municipal** nearby and the small and attractive *Hôtel des Touristes* on the main street (☎65.40.65.61; ①; restaurant from 70F). You can also swim from the small village beach.

Écomusée du Quercy

Set back from the north side of the River Célé, about 13km from Marcilhac in Cuzals, the **Écomusée du Quercy** (June–Sept daily except Sat 9.30/10am–6.30/7pm; May Sun & holidays only 10am–7pm; Oct Sun only 1–5.30pm; 44F) is one of the better open-air museums, and was set up in the 1980s to preserve the distinctive rural architecture of France. Reconstructions that range from a half-timbered eighteenth-century farmhouse to a garage from the 1920s are scattered around the site, which is centred around a twentieth-century château burnt down by the Nazis in the last war. The information is dished out with an appealing blend of humour and didactics, and the whole place is less blatantly commercial than many other *écomusées*.

Grotte de Pech-Merle

Discovered in 1922, the **Grotte de Pech-Merle** (Easter–Sept daily 9.30am–noon & 2–6pm; rest of year phone ☎65.31.23.33; 35F) is bigger and less accessible than those at Les Eyzies, and doesn't suffer from the same problems of overcrowding and the consequent dangers of deterioration. It is well hidden on the scrubby hillsides above Cabrerets, which lies 15km from Marcilhac and 4km from Conduché, where the Célé flows into the Lot.

The cave itself is far more beautiful than those at Padirac or Les Eyzies, with galleries full of the most spectacular stalactites and stalagmites – structures tiered like wedding cakes, hanging like curtains, or shaped like whale baffles, discs or cave pearls. On the down side, the cave is wired for electric light and the guide, who talks like a recorded message, makes sure you're processed through in the scheduled time.

The first drawings you come to are in the so-called Chapelle des Mammouths, executed on a white calcite panel that looks as if it's been specially prepared for the purpose. There are horses, bison charging head down with tiny rumps and arched tails, and tusked, whiskery mammoths. You then pass into a vast chamber where the glorious horse panel is visible on a lower level; it's a remarkable example of the way in which the artist used the contour and relief of the rock to do the work, producing an utterly convincing mammoth by just two strokes of black. The cave ceiling is covered with finger marks, preserved in the soft clay. You pass the skeleton of a cave hyena that has been lying there for 20,000 years – wild animals used these caves for shelter and sometimes, unable to find their way out, starved to death in them. And finally, the most moving and spine-tingling experience at Pech-Merle – the footprints of a Stone-Age adult and child preserved in a muddy pool.

The admission charge includes a film and excellent **museum**, where prehistory is illustrated by colourful and intelligible charts, a selection of objects (rather than the usual 10,000 flints), skulls and beautiful slides displayed in wall panels.

There's a **gîte d'étape** and a **campsite** close by at Cabrerets.

Montauban and the valley of the Aveyron

MONTAUBAN today is a prosperous middle-sized provincial city, capital of the largely agricultural *département* of Tarn-et-Garonne. It lies on the banks of the River Tarn, 53km from Toulouse, close to its junction with the Aveyron and their joint confluence with the Garonne, where the wide alluvial plain of the three rivers stretches flatly for miles around it. But this is where the lines of communication run, and Montauban lies, conveniently, on the southwest Bordeaux–Toulouse autoroute and train line.

Its origins go back to 1144 when the count of Toulouse decided to create a *bastide* here as a bulwark against English and French royal power. In fact, it is generally regarded as the first *bastide*, the model for those rationally laid out medieval new towns, and that plan is still clearly evident in the beautiful town centre.

Montauban has enjoyed various periods of great prosperity, as one can guess from the proliferation of fine town houses. The first followed the suppression of the Cathar heresy and the final submission of the counts of Toulouse in 1229 and was greatly enhanced by the building of the Pont-Vieux in 1335, making it the best crossing-point on the Tarn for miles around. The Hundred Years' War did its share of damage – as did Montauban's opting for the Protestant cause in the Wars of Religion – but by the time of the Revolution it had become once more one of the richest cities in the southwest, particularly successful in the manufacture of cloth.

Arrival and accommodation

Montauban couldn't be easier to find your way around. The visitable part is the small kernel of central streets based on the original *bastide*, and is enclosed within an inner ring of boulevards between bd Midi-Pyrénées on the east and the river on the west. The **tourist office** is on the northern corner of bd Midi-Pyrénées by the hideous market square, place Prax-Paris (Mon–Sat 9am–noon & 2–6pm; July & Aug daily; ☎63.63.60.60). From here the unattractive place Roosevelt rue de l'Hôtel-de-Ville leads directly to the Pont Vieux and across the river to av de Mayenne, at the end of which are both the **train** (☎63.63.50.50) and **bus stations** (☎63.63.88.88). There's a daily **market** on place Nationale and a bigger one on Saturday outside the tourist office in place Prax-Paris. The main summer **festival** is jazz in the first half of July, with well-known foreign artists taking part.

If you are planning to **stay** the night, there are two perfectly adequate hotels right on the cathedral square. The cheaper of the two is the attractive, old-time *Hôtel du Commerce*, 9 pl Roosevelt (☎63.66.31.32; ①–②). The other, on the corner of **rue de la Résistance,** is the *Hôtel du Midi*, 12 rue Notre-Dame (☎63.63.17.23; ①–④; restaurant from 79F). Alternatively, there is a comfortable hotel with an equally good restaurant just outside the train station: the *Hôtel d'Orsay*, 31 rue Roger-Salengro (☎63.66.06.66; ③–④; closed Sun & Dec 23–Jan 4; restaurant from 100F).

The Town

The greatest delight in Montauban is simply to wander the streets of the city centre, with their lovely pink brick houses; the town is only a ten- or fifteen-minute stroll from end to end. The finest point of all is the **place Nationale**, rebuilt after a fire in the seventeenth century and surrounded on all sides by exquisite double-vaulted arcades. It's surely one of the most successfully executed town squares anywhere, still the hub of the city's social life and definitely the first place to head for coffee, drinks or food.

The adjacent **place du Coq** on rue de la République is also pretty, and if you follow the street down it brings you out by the **church of St-Jacques**, first built in the thirteenth century on the pilgrim route to Compostella and featuring a distinctive octagonal Toulousain belfry, visible from all over town; nearby is the wonderful **Pont-Vieux** of 1335, whose seven arches spanning the Tarn raised Montauban's profile as an important river crossing point. From here, the wide view of the river is impressive.

At the near end of the bridge, the former Bishop's residence is a massive half-palace, half-fortress, begun by the Black Prince in 1363 but never finished because the English lost control of the town. It is now the **Musée Ingres** (daily except Mon 9.30am–noon & 1.30–6pm; 15F), so called because it houses drawings and paintings that early nine-teenth-century classical artist Jean-Auguste-Dominique Ingres, a native son of Montauban, left to the city on his death. It is a collection the city is very proud of, but unlikely to be of great interest to anyone but a definite Ingres fan. The same is true of the substantial collection of the works of Bourdelle, the ubiquitous monumental sculptor, also a native son. There is a gruesome item in the middle of the basement room, known as a *banc de question*, used for extracting confessions by torture in the Montauban courts.

Across the road there is an interesting museum of local crafts, tools, costumes, furniture and the like, with a natural history collection upstairs, under the name of the **Musée du Terroir et d'Histoire Naturelle** (Tues–Sat 10am–noon & 2–6pm).

The **Cathédrale Notre-Dame**, ten minutes up rue de l'Hôtel-de-Ville, is a cold fish: an austere and unsympathetic building erected just before 1700 as part of the triumphalist campaign to reassert the glories of the Catholic faith after the cruel defeat and repression of the Protestants. But it is a bit of an architectural rarity in France, where there are few cathedrals built in the classical style.

Eating and drinking

In addition to the hotel restaurants mentioned above, the simplest way of finding a place to **eat** is to go to the place Nationale, where you'll find *plats* under the arcades from around 35–45F at the *Agora* at no. 9, or *Brasserie des Arts* at no. 4, while on place de la Cathédrale the *Attrape-Cœur* does *crêpes*, and the *Bodega*, 40 rue de la République, *tapas*. For finer French fare, one of the top places is *Ambroisie*, 41 rue de la Comédie (closed Sun & July 12–31), with an interesting menu at 110F (*carte* upwards of 200F), or the *Ventadour*, 23 quai Villebourbon, magnificently sited in an old house on the river bank and specializing in regional cuisine (closed Mon evening, Sun & Aug 7–31; with a menu at 80F, *carte* 200F or more).

The place Nationale is also the obvious place to go for a **drink**, and you could add *Le Bouchon* wine bar to the list of places to try out. Other attractive options are the *Palais* on the neighbouring place du Coq, and for beers, *Le Flamand* at the corner of République and Soubirous-Bas, or *L'Irlandais* in rue Gillaque, just off place Nationale.

The valley of the Aveyron

About 25km east of Montauban, the flat alluvial plains break quite suddenly into abrupt hilliness, the tops rising between 300m and 400m in altitude. Through these hills the **River Aveyron** – and its main tributary, the Viaur – have cut deep, thickly wooded valleys peopled with numerous ancient villages.

One of the finest and most substantial is **ST-ANTONIN-NOBLE-VAL**, 50km east of Montauban. It sits on the bank of the Aveyron beneath the beetling cliffs of the **Roc d'Anglars**. It has endured all the vicissitudes of the old towns of the southwest: it went Cathar, then Protestant and each time was walloped by the alien power of the kings from the north. Yet in spite of all, it recovered its prosperity, manufacturing cloth and leather goods, endowed by its wealthy merchants with a marvellous heritage of medieval houses in all the streets leading out from the lovely **place de la Halle** and its prolongation.

There's a cafe most conveniently and picturesquely placed at the end of the ancient *halle*, with a view of the town's finest building, the Maison des Consuls, whose origins go back to 1120. It now houses the town museum, **Musée du Vieux Saint-Antonin** (July–Sept 10am–noon & 3–6pm; 20F), with collections of objects to do with the former life of the place, as well as a section on local prehistoric sites.

The **tourist office** is in the current town hall (☎63.30.63.47; July & Aug daily 9.30am–12.30pm & 2–6.30pm), and will supply information about B&Bs, canoeing on the Aveyron and walks in the region round about. By the bridge as you cross from the Montauban road, there's a simple and attractive **hotel** immediately on the left, the *Hôtel des Thermes* – so called because St-Antonin once tried to be a spa – with a terrace overlooking the water (☎63.30.61.08; ②; restaurant offers 55F menu at lunchtime, 85F for dinner). The local **campsite**, *Camping Anglars*, is by the riverside (July & Aug).

Twenty kilometres downstream you come to the beautiful ridge-top village of **PENNE**, once a Cathar stronghold, with its ruined **castle** impossibly perched on an airy crag. Everything is old and leaning and bulging, but holding together, nonetheless, with a harmony that would be impossible to create purposely.

Another hilltop **castle** commands its village at **BRUNIQUEL** (May–Oct 10am–12.30pm & 2–7/6pm; 15F), a few kilometres further on. You can also visit a handsome house in the village, the aristocratic **Maison des Comtes de Payrol** (mid-June to mid-Sept daily 10am–noon & 2–6pm; April to mid-June & mid- to end-Sept Sat, Sun and hols only 10am–noon & 2–6pm; 10F). There's also a small **hotel** called the *Étape du Château* (☎63.67.25.00; ①–②; restaurant from 82F), whose proprietor is a mountain bike freak and will take you out on trips. The *Le Payssel* **campsite** is about 600m along the bottom road, and there's a **gîte** 3km along the GR46 towards Gaillac (☎63.67.27.21), which also serves meals to non-residents.

Najac

NAJAC occupies an extraordinary site on a conical hill isolated in a wide bend in the already deep valley of the Aveyron, 25km south of Villefranche-de-Rouergue and on the main Brive–Toulouse train line, with one direct train to Paris every day. Its photogenic castle, which graces many a travel poster, sits right on the peak of the hill, while the half-timbered and stone-tiled village houses tail out in a single street along the narrow back of the spur that joins the hill to the valleyside. It's all very attractive and consequently touristy, with the inevitable resident knick-knack shops and craftspeople.

The **castle** (daily April–Sept 10am–noon & 2.30–5/6/7pm; 15F) is a model of medieval defensive architecture and was endlessly fought over because of its commanding and impregnable position in a region once rich in silver and copper mines. You can see clearly all the devices for restricting an attacker once he was inside the castle: the covered passages and stairs within the thickness of the walls, the multistorey archers' positions, and, of course, the most magnificent all-round view from the top of the keep. In one of the chambers of the keep you can see the stone portraits of Saint Louis, king of France, Alphonse de Poitiers, his brother, and Jeanne, the daughter of the count of Toulouse, the couple whose marriage was arranged in 1229 to end the Cathar wars by bringing the domains of Count Raymond and his allies under royal control. It was Alphonse de Poitiers who "modernized" the castle and made the place we see today. Signatures of the masons who worked on it are clearly visible on many stones.

Below the rather dull central *place* stretches the **faubourg**, a sort of elongated square bordered by houses raised on pillars as in the central square of a *bastide*, which reduces to a narrow waist of a street overlooked by more ancient houses and leading past a fountain to the castle gate. At the foot of the castle, in the centre of what was the medieval village, stands the very solid-looking **church of St-Jean**, which the villagers of Najac were forced by the Inquisition to build at their own expense in 1258 as a punishment for their conversion to Catharism. In addition to a lovely silver reliquary and an extraordinary iron cage for holding candles – both dating from the thirteenth century – the church has one architectural oddity: its windows are solid panels of stone from which the lights have been cut out in trefoil form. Below the church, by a derelict farm, a stretch of **Roman road** survives and, at the bottom of the hill, a thirteenth-century **bridge** spans the Aveyron.

The modern village balances on the shoulder of the spur round an open square with the *Oustal del Barry* hotel on the downhill side (☎65.29.74.32; ②–④; April–Oct), whose rather expensive restaurant is renowned for its subtle and inventive cuisine (menus at 100F and 130F, otherwise a great deal more). The **tourist office** is on the *faubourg*.

Villefranche-de-Rouergue

No medieval junketting, not a craft shop in sight, **VILLEFRANCHE-DE-ROUERGUE** must be as close as you can get to what a French provincial town used to be like, and it's also where you are as likely to hear Occitan spoken as French. It's a small place, lying on a bend in the Aveyron, 35km due south of Figeac and 61km east of Cahors across the Causse de Limogne. Built as a *bastide* by Alphonse de Poitiers in 1252 as part of the royal policy of extending control over the recalcitrant lands of the south, the town became rich on copper from the surrounding mines and its privilege of minting coins; from the fifteenth to the eighteenth centuries, its wealthy men built the magnificent houses that grace the cobbled streets to this day.

Rue du Sergent-Bories and rue de la République, the main commercial street, are both very attractive, but they are no preparation for **place Notre-Dame**, the loveliest *bastide* central square in the region. It's built on a slope, so the uphill houses are much higher than the downhill, and you enter at the corners underneath the houses – all the houses are arcaded at ground-floor level, providing for a market where local merchants and farmers spread out their weekly produce. The houses are unusually tall and some are very elaborately decorated, notably the so-called **Maison du Président Raynal** on the lower side at the top of rue de la République, with its extraordinary spiral staircase leading out of a narrow medieval courtyard; you can push open the door and look in.

The east side of the square is dominated by the **church of Notre-Dame** with its colossal – nearly sixty-metre high – porch and bell-tower. The interior has some fine late-fifteenth-century stained glass, carved choir stalls and misericords. Behind it is the covered market, with a weekly Thursday **market**, which – as the locals will tell you – is the quintessential Villefranche experience, and you won't hear any French spoken.

On the boulevard that forms the northern limit of the old town, the seventeenth-century **Chapelle des Pénitents-Noir** (daily except Tues July & Aug 10am–noon & 2–6pm; Sept 1–15 closes 5pm) boasts a splendidly baroque painted ceiling and an enormous gilded retable; another ecclesiastical building worth a slight detour is the **Chartreuse St-Sauveur**, about one kilometre out of town on the Gaillac road. It was completed in the space of ten years from 1450, giving it a singular architectural harmony, and has a very beautiful cloister and choir stalls by the same master as Notre-Dame in Villefranche, which, by contrast, took nearly 300 years to complete.

Aside from the pleasing details of many of the houses you notice as you explore the side streets, the town reserves one other most unexpected surprise. The **municipal library** in the seventeenth-century chapel of the order of the Pénitents-Bleus at 27 rue Sénéchal (☎65.45.59.45) includes an amazing collection of jazz records, books, papers, recordings and documents belonging to the late Hugues Panassié, famous French jazz critic and one of the founders of the *Hot Club de France*. Much of the material is unrecorded or unobtainable elsewhere and is open to perusal by researchers and enthusiasts. CD selections are on sale both here and at the tourist office.

Practicalities

The **tourist office** sits on place du Giraudet (daily 10am–noon & 2–5pm; ☎65.45.13.18) at the corner of the bridge. For those who want to stay overnight, there are two agreeable **hotels**: *Hôtel Lagarrigue* just behind the Post Office on place Bernard-Lehz in the old town (☎65.45.01.12; ①–③; closed Oct 1–15 and two weeks in Feb); and *L'Univers*, 2 pl de la République at the end of the bridge opposite the tourist office (☎65.45.15.63;

②–④; good traditional restaurant from 80F, closed Fri evening and Sat except July–
Sept & Nov 12–27). For an even more sumptuous meal, as well as a comfortable sleep,
there's *Le Relais de Farrou*, 3km out on the Figeac road (☎65.45.18.11; ③–④; restaurant
from 105F, closed Sun evening & Mon out of season). For cheaper accommodation,
there's the *Foyer des Jeunes Travailleurs* **hostel**, which has seen better days but has a
lovely situation on the river bank behind the Hôtel de Ville and tourist office at 13 rue
Émile-de-Rodat (☎65.45.09.68; ①; meals at 35F). There is also a **gîte d'étape** by the
river at La Gasse, 1km out of town on the D269 back road to La Bastide-L'Évêque, at
the start of **GR62b** (☎65.45.10.80; May–Oct), plus a **campsite**, 1.5km to the south on
the D47 to Monteils (April–Sept). Finally, in the covered market is the workers' diner,
Café de la Halle, where you can eat a copious meal for 50F at shared tables, if you don't
feel too self-conscious in such a French and local ambience.

Agen and around

AGEN, capital of the Lot-et-Garonne *département*, is a pleasanter town than it first
appears. It was quartered by modern boulevards in the nineteenth century in its own
version of a Haussmann clean-up, and it is down these roads that you're funnelled into
the town, with the result that you see nothing of interest.

The town lies on the broad, powerful River Garonne halfway between Bordeaux and
Toulouse, and lived through the Middle Ages wracked by war with England and internecine strife between Catholics and Protestants. But it was able to extract some advantage from disputes in possession, as it seesawed between the English and French,
gaining more and more privileges of independence as the price of its loyalty – a tradition that it maintained at the time of the Revolution and after by being staunchly republican (the churches still bear the legend: *Liberté, Fraternité, Égalité*).

Its pre-Revolutionary wealth derived from the manufacture of various kinds of cloth
and its thriving port on the Garonne, which in those days was alive with river traffic.
But the industrial revolution put paid to all of that. Agen's prosperity now is based on
agriculture – in particular, its famous prunes and plums, said to have been brought
back from Damascus during the Crusades.

The Town

The interesting part of Agen centres on **place Goya**, where boulevard de la
République, leading to the river, crosses boulevard du Président-Carnot. On the south
side of bd de la République, the main shopping area is around place Wilson, rue
Garonne and the partly arcaded place des Laitiers. A left turn at the end of rue Garonne
brings you to the wide place du Dr-Esquirol and an exuberant turn-of-the-century
municipal **theatre**; opposite this is the **Musée Municipal des Beaux-Arts** (daily
except Tues 10am–noon & 2–6pm; free), magnificently housed in four adjacent
sixteenth- and seventeeth-century mansions adorned with stair turrets, Renaissance
window details, different roof angles. The collections include a rich variety of archeological finds, Roman and medieval, furniture and paintings – among the latter some
Goyas. Not far from the museum, in place du Bourg at the end of rue des Droits-de-
l'Homme, the cute little thirteenth-century **church of Notre-Dame** is worth a look.

Behind the theatre rue Beauville, with heavily restored but beautiful medieval
houses, leads through to rue Voltaire, which is full of ethnic restaurants, and rue
Richard-Cœur-de-Lion, leading to the **Église des Jacobins**, a big brick Dominican
church of the thirteenth century, its barn-like interior divided by a single centre row
of pillars, very like its counterpart in Toulouse. Beyond lie the river and the public
gardens of **Le Gravier**, where a market is held every Wednesday and Saturday;

there's a footbridge across the Garonne, with a **canal bridge** dating from 1839 just downstream.

Opposite place Wilson on the north side of bd de la République, the arcaded rue Cornières leads through to the **Cathédrale St-Caprais**, somewhat misshapen but with a finely proportioned Romanesque apse and radiating chapels still surviving. There is a piece of the original fortifications still showing in rue des Augustins close by – the **Tour du Chapelet** – dating from around 1100. Again nearby, in rue du-Puits-du-Saumon, is one of the finest houses in town, the fourteenth-century **Maison du Sénéchal**, with an elaborate open loggia on the first floor.

Practicalities

From the central place Goya, bd du Président-Carnot leads to the **gare SNCF** and **routière**. The **tourist office** is at 107 bd Carnot (Mon–Sat 9am–12.30/1pm & 2–6.30/7pm; July & Aug Mon–Sat 9am–7pm, Sun 10am–noon; ☎53.47.36.09).

There are several reasonable **hotel** options in Agen. Right next to the tourist office, the *Stim'Otel*, 105 bd Carnot (☎53.47.39.11; ③; restaurant from 65F), looks a bit dire but is actually comfortable and welcoming. Also very central and in a more attractive street is the *Hôtel des Ambans*, 59 rue des Ambans, near place Goya (☎53.66.28.60; ②), while the nice-looking *Périgord* overlooks a large traffic roundabout at the eastern end of bd de la République at 42 cours du 14-juillet (☎53.66.10.01; ②–③; restaurant from 100F). At the other end of the boulevard, close to the river, *Hôtel des Îles*, 25 rue Baudin (☎53.47.11.33; ②), has slightly cheaper rooms. There is also an IYHF **youth hostel**, a bit of a trek at 17 rue Leo-Lagrange, not far from the canal bridge on the main D656 to Cahors (☎53.66.18.98; ①; bus direction *Lalande*); it's possible to **camp** here as well.

The best places to **eat** really well at reasonable prices are the *Bistrot Apicius*, 8 rue Sentini (☎53.66.07.81; lunchtime menu 48F, dinner from 70F), and *Le Petit Vatel*, 52 rue Richard-Cœur-de-Lion (☎53.47.66.00; closed Sat lunchtime & Mon; from 99F), which has a delicious variety of seafood. Alternatively, try *L'Étable* by the footbridge on the river at 41bis Peristyle du Gravier along Le Gravier (closed Sat & Sun lunchtime, & Mon; from 60F), or the various places in Agen's rue Voltaire. If you like crêpes, there's no more agreeable place to eat them than the *Crêperie des Jacobins*, right opposite the Église des Jacobins (see above).

Moissac

There is nothing very memorable about the modern town of **MOISSAC**, 40km east of Agen, largely because of the terrible damage done by the flood of March 1930, when the Tarn burst its banks, destroying 617 houses and killing 120 people.

Luckily, the one thing that makes Moissac a household name in the history of art survived, the cloister and porch of the **abbey church of St-Pierre**, a masterpiece of Romanesque sculpture and model for hundreds of churches and buildings elsewhere. The fact that it has survived countless wars, including siege and sack by Simon de Montfort in 1212 during the crusade against the Cathars, is something of a miracle in itself: during the Revolution it was used as a gunpowder factory and billet for soldiers, who damaged many of the sculptures, and in the 1830s it only escaped demolition to make way for the Bordeaux–Toulouse train line by a whisker.

Legend has it that Clovis the Frank first founded a monastery here, though it seems more probable that its origins belong to the seventh century, which saw the foundation of so many monasteries throughout Aquitaine. The first Romanesque church on the site was consecrated in 1063 and enlarged in the following century. The famous **south porch**, with its magnificent tympanum and curious wavy door jambs and trumeau, dates from this second phase of building. It depicts Christ in Majesty, right hand raised in benediction, the Book in his hand, surrounded by the evangelists and the elders of the Apocalypse, a grouping whose influence, assimilated with varying degrees of success, can be seen in the work of artists who decorated the porches of countless churches across the south of France. There is more fine carving in the capitals inside the porch, and the interior of the church, which was remodelled in the fifteenth century, is interesting too, especially for some of the wood and stone statuary it contains.

The adjoining **cloister** is now entered through the tourist office (daily 9am–noon & 2–5pm; July & Aug 9am–7pm; mid-March to June & Sept to mid-Oct 9am–noon & 2–6pm), and if you want to experience the silent contemplation for which it was originally built, you must get there first thing in the morning. The cloister surrounds a garden shaded by a majestic cedar, and its pantile roof is supported by 76 alternating single and double marble columns. Each column supports a single inverted wedge-shaped block of stone, on which are carved with extraordinary delicacy all manner of animals and plant motifs, as well as scenes from Bible stories and the lives of the saints: Daniel in the lions' den, the evangelists, Saint Peter being crucified upside down, John the Baptist being decapitated, and many, many others. An inscription on the middle pillar on the west side explains that the cloister was made in the time of the Abbot Ansquitil in the year of Our Lord 1100. It is difficult to know how best to look at them. The least that can be said is that you need peace and time.

Practicalities

The **tourist office** is outside the church cloister (daily 9am–noon & 2–5pm; July & Aug 9am–7pm; mid-March to June & Sept to mid-Oct 9am–noon & 2–6pm), with the **gare SNCF** and **gare routière** both on av Pierre-Chabrie. There's a weekly Saturday **market** in place des Recollets at the end of rue de la République, which leads away from the abbey, a marvel of colour and temptation.

Overlooking the south side of the square, the *Hôtel au Chapon Fin* makes a pleasant and reasonable place to **stay** (☎63.04.04.22; ①–③; closed Mon & Nov; restaurant from 80F). Alternatively, old red-brick *Le Pont Napoléon*, at the end of the bridge of the same name, makes a rather finer stopping place at 2 allées Montebello (☎63.04.01.55; ②–③; closed Nov 11 to mid-March), with a good restaurant with menus from 85F and a terrace overlooking the river. For **campers**, there's a shady site across the river and to the left by an old mill on a little island, the Île du Bidounet (April–Sept), where there is also a **gîte d'étape**. For simple, quick **eating**, there's the *Salons du Cloître* right outside the church (from 42F).

Around Moissac

As you head north towards Cahors, leaving the wide flat valleys of the Tarn and Garonne behind you, the land rises gradually to gently undulating country, green and woody, cut obliquely by parallel valleys running down to meet the Garonne and planted with vines and sunflowers, maize, and apple and plum orchards. It's a very soft landscape, and villages are small and widely scattered. The pace of life seems about equal with that of a turning sunflower.

Should you find yourself taking this route, then the place to make a halt is **LAUZERTE**, one of Raymond of Toulouse's *bastides* and of great military importance as it commands the road to Cahors, the route down which the pilgrims of St-Jacques came pouring every spring, as they still do today, or at least the hardy who follow the GR65 on foot. The town is short on sights, but there are some old houses, a pretty arcaded central square and a good baroque altarpiece in the church, as well as views of the countryside round about.

There's a very pleasant **hotel** at the entrance to the village for those who want to stay: *Hôtel du Quercy* (☎63.94.66.36; ①–②; closed Oct & Sun & Mon pm out of season), which also serves excellent food for 95–50F at lunchtime. There's a **campsite** and **gîte d'étape** for walkers on the GR65, plus the possibility of B&B at *Le Luzerta* at Vignals just below the village (closed Jan–March & Wed; ③; restaurant).

travel details

Trains

Agen to: Belvès (3–4 daily; 1hr 10min); Bordeaux (frequent; 1hr 10min–1hr 50min); Le Buisson (3–4 daily; 1hr 10min); Les Eyzies (3–4 daily; 1hr 40min); Moissac (5 daily; 30min); Mont-de-Marsan (2 daily; 2hr 30min); Montauban (frequent; 40–50min); Monsemprou-Libos (6 daily; 45min); Périgueux (3–4 daily; 2hr 15min–2hr 50min); Toulouse (frequent; 1hr 20min); Villefranche-du-Périgord (3–4 daily; 1hr).

Bergerac to: Bordeaux (10–11 daily; 1hr–1hr 50min); Montcaret (3 daily; 25–30min); St-Émilion (3 daily; 50min); Ste-Foy-la-Grande (8 daily; 15min).

Brive to: Aurillac (5–6 daily; 1hr 45min); Bordeaux (6–7 daily; 2hr 30min–3hr); Cahors (11 daily; 1hr–1hr 15min); Clermont-Ferrand (3 daily; 3hr 40min); Figeac (6 daily; 1hr 20min); Gourdon (8 daily; 45min); Limoges (frequent; 1hr–1hr 10min); Montauban (6 daily; 2hr); Paris-Austerlitz (frequent; 4–5hr); Périgueux (3–4 daily; 1hr–1hr 30min); Rocamadour-Padirac (5–6 daily; 30–40min); Souillac (8 daily; 30min); Toulouse (6 daily; 2hr 30min); Uzerche (several daily; 30min); Villefranche-de-Rouergue (3 daily; 2hr–2hr 20min).

Cahors to: Brive (11 daily; 1hr–1hr 15min); Montauban (6 daily; 40min); Toulouse (6 daily; 1hr 10min).

Figeac to: Aubin (4–5 daily; 30min); Brive (6 daily; 1hr 20min); Decazeville (4–5 daily; 20min); Najac (4–5 daily; 40min); Rodez (4–5 daily; 1hr 45min); Toulouse (4–5 daily; 2hr 30min); Villefranche-de-Rouergue (4–5 daily; 40min).

Limoges to: Angoulême (4 daily; 2hr); Brive (3 daily; 2hr 10min); Eymoutiers (4 daily; 50min); Meymac (3 daily; 1hr 40min); Nexon (3 daily; 25min); Paris-Austerlitz (frequent; 3hr 30min); Périgueux (10 daily; 1hr–1hr 30min); Poitiers (3 daily; 2hr); Pompadour (3 daily; 1hr 15min); St-Léonard (4 daily; 20min); St-Yrieix (3 daily; 45min); Thiviers (7 daily; 40min–1hr); Ussel (3 daily; 2hr).

Montauban to: Agen (frequent; 35–45min); Bordeaux (frequent; 2hr 30min); Moissac (7 daily; 20min); Toulouse ((frequent; 35min).

Périgueux to: Agen (3–4 daily; 2hr 20min); Belvès (3–4 daily; 1hr 10min); Bordeaux (10–12 daily; 1hr 20min–2hr); Brive (5–6 daily; 1hr–1hr 30min); Le Buisson (3–4 daily; 50min); Les Eyzies (3–4 daily; 35min); Limoges (11 daily; 1hr); Monsemprou-Libos (3–4 daily; 1hr 45min); Villefranche-du-Périgord (3–4; 1hr 25min).

Sarlat to: Bergerac (6 daily; 1hr 20min); Beynac (2 daily; 20min); Bordeaux (5–6 daily; 2hr 30min–3hr 30min); Le Buisson (7 daily; 35–45min); Ste-Foy-la-Grande (5 daily; 1hr 30min–1hr 45min).

Buses

Agen to: Villeneuve-sur-Lot (several daily; 1hr 45min).

Argentat to: Beaulieu-sur-Dordogne (July & Aug 3 daily; 40min).

Bergerac to: Bordeaux (1 daily; 1hr 15min); Castillon (1 daily; 1hr 15min); Montcaret (1 daily; 1hr 10min); Ste-Foy-la-Grande (1 daily; 45min).

Brive to: Argentat (1 daily; 1hr 20min); Arnac-Pompadour (1 daily; 1hr 45min); Collonges-le-Rouge (2 daily; 20–35min); Meyssac (2 daily; 40min); Sarlat (1 daily; 2hr 15min); Turenne (1–2 daily; 35min); Uzerche (2 daily; 1hr 30min); Vayrac (1–2 daily; 55min).

Cahors to: Cajaro (3–5 daily; 1hr); Conducté (3–5 daily; 30min); Figeac (3–5 daily; 1hr 45min); Fumel (6–8 daily; 1hr 10min); Luzech (6–8 daily; 30min); Monsemprou-Lisbos (6–8 daily; 1hr 20min); Puy l'Évêque (6–8 daily; 45min).

Limoges: Aubusson (2 daily; 2hr); Châlus (1 daily; 1hr); St-Léonard (3 daily; 35min).

Périgueux to: Angoulême (3 daily; 1hr 40min); Bergerac (3 daily; 1hr 30min); Brantôme (3 daily; 40min); Excideuil (3 daily; 1hr 15min); Montignac (1–2 daily; 1hr); Ribérac (3–4 daily; 1hr); Sarlat (1–2 daily; 1hr 40min).

Ribérac to: Angoulême (2 daily; 1hr 30min).

Tulle to: Argentat (4 daily; 50min–1hr 15min).

CHAPTER TEN

THE PYRENEES

Basque-speaking and wet in the west; craggy, snowy, patois-speaking in the middle; dry and Catalan in the east: the **Pyrenees** are physically beautiful, culturally varied and a great deal less developed than the Alps. The whole range is marvellous walkers' country, especially the central region around the **Parc National des Pyrénées**, with its 3000-metre peaks, streams, forests, flowers and wildlife. If you're a committed hiker, it's possible to go all the way across the mountains, from the Atlantic to the Mediterranean, along the **GR10** or the more difficult **Haute Randonnée Pyrénéenne** (HRP); and there are numerous local walking centres as well – **Cauterets, Luz-St-Sauveur, Barèges, Ax-les-Thermes** – with hikes to suit all temperaments and abilities. The hiking season is from mid-June through to September; earlier in the year, few refuges are open and you will run into snow even on parts of the GR10. Whatever you intend, bear in mind that these are big mountains and should be treated with respect: to cover any of the main walks you'll need hiking boots and, despite the southerly latitude, warm and windproof clothing.

As for the more conventional of the tourist attractions, the **Basque coast** is lovely but very popular, suffering from seaside sprawl and a massive surfeit of campsites. **St-Jean-de-Luz** is by far the prettiest of the resorts, and once-smart **Biarritz** surely the most overrated; **Bayonne** is the most attractive town, with an excellent Basque museum, although, sadly, this is in abeyance right now due to local political wrangles. The foothill towns are on the whole rather dull, although **Pau** is worth at least a day or two, while **Lourdes** is such a monster of kitsch that it just has to be seen. The east – the Catalan-speaking **Roussillon** – has beaches every bit as popular as those in the Basque country, but on the whole is less inviting. Its interior, however, is another matter: craggy landscapes are split by spectacular canyons, with a crop of fine Romanesque abbeys, of which **St-Martin-de-Canigou** and **Serrabonne** are the most dramatic, along with a climate bathed in Mediterranean heat and light.

ACCOMMODATION PRICE CATEGORIES

All the hotels, youth hostels and guesthouses listed in this book have been price-graded according to the following scale, and although costs will rise slightly overall with the life of this edition, the relative comparisons should remain valid. Paris and the large cities will, as anywhere, be more expensive than equivalent accommodation in the countryside or small towns. The prices quoted are for the cheapest available double room in high season, although remember that many of the cheap places will have more expensive rooms with en-suite facilities.

① Under 160F	④ 300–400F	⑦ 600–700F
② 160–220F	⑤ 400–500F	⑧ Over 700F
③ 220–300F	⑥ 500–600F	

Hiking in the Pyrenees

If you're planning on doing even very basic walking or other outdoor activities – canoeing, riding, cycling, paragliding – in the Pyrenees, a good contact point for **ideas, information** and **publications** (in French) is *Randonnées Pyrénéennes*, 29 rue Marcel-Lamarque, 65007 Tarbes (☎62.93.66.03; information centre, ☎62.93.57.57).

There are plenty of walkers' **guidebooks** to the area, both in French and English (see p.1005). There are also three small area guides produced by Arthur Battagel for *West Col*, which include the Spanish side of the range. The best **maps** are the *IGN* 1:25,000 series; #273, #274 and #275 cover the Parc National des Pyrénées.

Wherever you plan to hike, **preparation** is crucial. Before taking to the hills, check the weather forecasts, and be sure you are properly equipped with water, food, maps, bivvy bag, whistle, knife, as well as warm, wetproof and windproof clothing and suitable boots – not to mention ice axe and crampons if you are going anywhere near snow, which you shouldn't be doing unless you are already experienced. Above all, don't take any chances: sunny and warm weather in the valley doesn't necessarily mean it will be the same higher up. Mountain conditions can change very quickly, and if you don't have any mountain-walking experience yourself, it's probably best not to undertake anything more than a well-frequented path unless accompanied by someone with experience.

Don't overdo things. One kilometre in twelve minutes (5km/h) is a fairly average walking pace; if you're going uphill, you need to add at least an extra ten minutes per 100m of altitude gained in calculating how long a trek is going to take you. If you are out of practice it'll take longer, no matter how youthful and vigorous you are. By the same token, if you overdo it on your first day, you'll be plagued by blisters and aching muscles on the second day. Work yourself in gently; otherwise you could easily ruin your holiday. The best rule of thumb is: if in doubt, don't do it.

THE PAYS BASQUE

The three **Basque provinces** – Labourd, Basse-Navarre and Soule – share with their Spanish neighbours a common language, Euskara, and a strong sense of separate identity. The language is universally spoken, and Basques refer to their country as a land in itself, Euskal-herri, or, across the border in Spain, Euskadi. Unlike the Spanish, however, few French Basques favour an independent state or secession from France. There is no equivalent of the Basque nationalist organization ETA here, and the old sympathy, which allowed refuge to Spanish Basques wanted on terrorist charges, has waned. It was hatred of the Franco regime that provided the political momentum.

Administratively, the three French Basque provinces were organized together with Béarn in the single *département* of Basses-Pyrénées, now Pyrénées-Atlantiques, at the time of the 1789 Revolution, when the Basques' thousand-year-old *fors* (rights) were abolished. It was a move designed to curtail their nationalism, but ironically has probably been responsible for preserving their unity.

Apart from the language and the *beret basque*, the most obvious manifestation of Basque national identity are the ubiquitous *frontons* or *jaï alaï*, the huge concrete courts in which the national game of *pelota* is played. This game is a bit like fives: pairs of players wallop a hard leather-covered ball, either with their bare hands or a long basket-work extension of the hand called a *chistera*, against a high wall blocking one end of the court. It's quite extraordinarily dangerous – as you'd expect at speeds of up to 200km/h – and knock-outs and worse are not uncommon. Trials of strength, rather like Scottish Highland games, are also popular: tugs-of-war, lifting heavy weights, turning massive carts, sawing through giant tree trunks and the like.

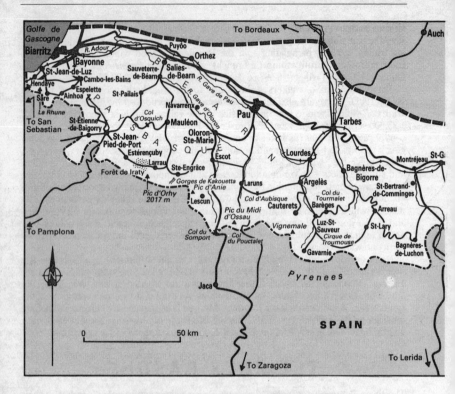

Although **Basque cooking** shares many of the dishes of the southwest, it does have some distinctive recipes of its own. One of the best known is the Basque omelette, **pipérade**, made with tomatoes, chillis and sautéed Bayonne ham (salt cured and resembling Parma ham), mixed into the eggs, so that it actually looks more like scrambled eggs. **Poulet basquaise** is common too, especially as takeaway food at the *traiteur*: pieces of chicken browned in pork fat and casseroled in a sauce of tomato, chilli, onions and a little white wine. And in season there is a chance of **palombe**, the wild doves netted or shot as they migrate north over the Pyrenees. A dish that is popular a bit further inland is the thick potato and cabbage soup, **garbure**, which is enlivened with a piece of pork or *confited* goose or duck.

With the Atlantic close at hand, seafood is a speciality. The Basques inevitably have their version of fish soup, called *ttoro*. Another great delicacy are the **elvers** or *piballes*, which are netted as they come up the Atlantic rivers from the Sargasso Sea. **Squid** are common, served here as *chiperons*, either in their own ink or stewed with onion, tomato, peppers and garlic. All the locally caught fish – cod (*morue*), tuna (*thon*), sardines (*sardine*) and anchovies (*anchois*) – are regular favourites, too.

Cheeses mainly comprise the delicious ewe's-milk *tommes* from the high pastures of the Pyrenees. Among sweets, one that is on show everywhere is the **gâteau basque**, which is made of sweet flan pastry garnished with black cherries or filled with *crème pâtissière*.

As for liquid, the only Basque **wine** is the very drinkable red *Irouléguy*, with the potent green or yellow *Izzara* for liqueur.

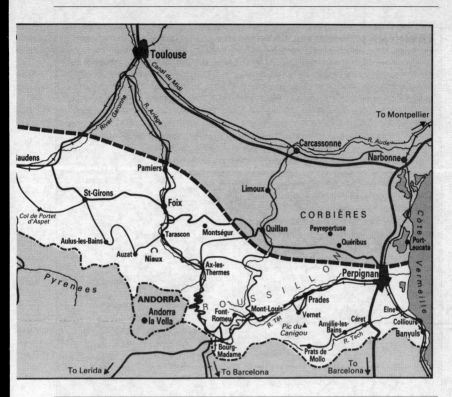

The Côte Basque

Hardly more than 30km long and well served by bus and train, the Basque coast is easily accessible, and reasonably priced hotel accommodation is not that difficult to find – although space can be limited in summer. **Anglet** has a couple of marvellous beaches and suits budgeters, with a choice of youth hostels, while still being close enough to the ritzy nightspots of **Biarritz**, itself a rather exhausting place to stay in full season. Families will certainly prefer **St-Jean-de-Luz** – in any case much the most attractive town.

Bayonne

BAYONNE stands back some 6km from the Atlantic – a position that has protected it from any real exploitation by tourism – bestriding the confluence of the River Adour with the much smaller Nive. Although purists dispute whether it is truly a Basque rather than a Gascon city, it is the effective economic and political capital of the Pays Basque. To the layperson, at least, there seems no doubt about its Basque flavour, with its tall half-timbered houses and woodwork painted in the peculiarly Basque tones of green and red. Here, too, Basques in flight from Franco's Spain came without hesitation to seek refuge among their own. For many years the Petit Bayonne quarter was a hotbed of Basque nationalist ferment, until the French government clamped down on such dangerous tendencies.

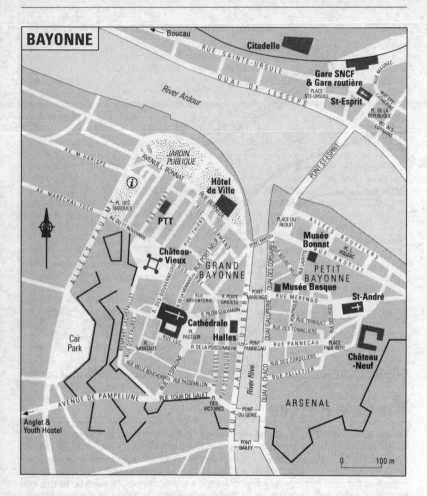

BAYONNE

Boucau

RUE SAINTE-URSULE

Citadelle

Gare SNCF
& Gare routière

QUAI DE LESSEPS

PLACE
STE-URSULE

St-Esprit

River Ardour

RUE MAUBEC

RUE STE-
CATHERINE

PL. DE LA
RÉPUBLIQUE

BD AEL
LORRAINE

AV. M-HARISPE

AVENUE L. BONNAT

JARDIN
PUBLIQUE

AV. MARECHAL-FOCH

Hôtel
de Ville

PONT ST-ESPRIT

PL. DES
BASQUES

RUE BERNEDE

ALLÉES PAULMY

AV. DU 11 NOVEMBRE

RUE THIERS

RUE MARHALET

PTT

RUE PORT-NEUF

PLACE DU
REDUIT

ALLÉES

BOUFLERS

Musée
Bonnat

PL.
POUZAC

Château-
Vieux

RUE DE LA LORMAND

PONT MAYOU

GRAND
BAYONNE

QUAI DES CORSAIRES

RUE LAFITTE

RUE BASTIAT

PETIT
BAYONNE

RUE DES GOUVERNEURS

RUE LAGINAL

PONT
MARENGO

RUE MERENGO

Musée Basque

St-André

RUE DES FAURES

RUE ARGENTERIE

R. PORTE
CASTETS

RUE TRINQUET

RUE DES LISSES

RUE DES TONNELIERS

RUE PILORI GUILHAMIN

Cathédrale

PL
PASTEUR

Halles

RUE PANNECAU

PLACE
PAUL-BERT

Car
Park

REMPART LA CHEVALLIER

R. DES BAQUES

PONT
PANNECAU

RUE DES CORDELIERS

Château
-Neuf

PL
MONTAUT

RUE LUC

R. DE LA POISSONNERIE

RUE PEILETIER

RUE VIEILLE BOUCHERIE

RUE PASSEMILLON

RUE ESPAGNE

RUE BOSSE

QUAI GALUPERIE

River Nive

QUAI A-D'ACO

ARSENAL

AVENUE DE PAMPELUNE

RUE TOUR DE SAUT

PL
DES
VICTOIRES

QUAI JAUREGUIBERRY

PONT
DU GENIE

Anglet &
Youth Hostel

PONT
BAILEY

0   100 m

The city's origins go back to Roman times, its Latin name of *Lapurdum* being corrupted to Labourd, then extended to cover the whole of this westernmost of the three Basque provinces. For 300 years until 1451, it enjoyed prosperity and security under English domination. Around 1500, Sephardic Jews fleeing the Spanish Inquisition arrived, bringing their chocolate manufacturing trade with them, and later the city reached the peak of its commercial success as centre of the armaments industry, giving its name to the bayonet. Later, its prestige suffered a blow in the 1789 Revolution when the three Basque provinces were merged and Pau became capital of the single *département*. More recently, there has been a renewal of economic activity based on the processing of by-products from the natural gas field at Lacq near Pau, but this, too, has been affected by the current hard times, leaving Bayonne with a higher-than-average level of unemployment.

These problems don't immediately impinge on the visitor, however, and first impressions are likely to be favourable. It's a small-scale, easily manageable city. Whether your intention is to head inland or down the coast, it may – as the nodal point of all major road and rail routes from the north and east – be your first encounter with the Pays Basque. Cheaper and quieter than neighbouring Biarritz, it could be worth considering as a base even for a seaside sojourn.

Arrival and accommodation

The **gare SNCF** (☎59.55.50.50) and **gare routière** are next door to each other, just off place de la République on the north bank of the river, across the wide Pont St-Esprit from the city centre. The **tourist office** is nearby in place des Basques (Mon–Fri 9am– 6.30pm, Sat 9am–5pm; July & Aug Mon–Sat 9am–7pm, Sun 10am–1pm; ☎59.59.31.31).

The best and most agreeable budget **hotel** is the old-fashioned *Hôtel des Arceaux*, 26 rue Port-Neuf (☎59.59.15.53; ①–②), below the cathedral; the cheapest is the basic but spotless *Hôtel des Basques* on place Paul-Bert (☎59.59.08.02; ①). A clean and reasonable alternative is the *Hôtel Monbar*, 24 rue Pannecau (☎59.59.26.80; ③). Other possibilities are the *Hôtel de Bordeaux*, 4 rue Maubec (☎59.55.04.07; ⑤), and *Hôtel Vauban*, 13 pl Ste-Ursule (☎59.55.11.31; ③), both close to the station. For something a bit smarter, try the *Loustan* on place de la République (☎59.55.16.74; ④–⑤), overlooking the river, opposite the station.

Another possibility is the IYHF **youth hostel** at 19 rte des Vignes in Anglet, between Bayonne and Biarritz (see p.610); take the *ligne bleue* bus, direction *Biarritz-La Négresse*, from the Hôtel de Ville to Cinq Cantons; make a left down promenade de la Barre, then fifth left into promenade des Sables, and right into rte des Vignes – about 25 minutes on foot. **Campers** can choose between *La Chêneraie* (☎59.55.01.31; mid-March to mid-Oct), off the N117 Pau road close to the Bayonne-Nord exit from the autoroute, and the pleasanter *Camping Barre de l'Adour* at 130 av de l'Adour (☎59.63.16.16; mid-June to mid-Sept), by the mouth of the Adour. Or try one of the Anglet sites (see p.610).

The City

Although there are no great sights in Bayonne, it's a pleasure to wander the deep narrow streets of the town. Vauban's defences still encircle Bayonne, with the Nive neatly paring it into two; the cathedral is on the west bank in **Grand Bayonne**, and the museums east of the river in **Petit Bayonne**.

The **Cathédrale Ste-Marie**, on the magnolia-shaded place Pasteur, has twin towers and a steeple rising with airy grace above the houses. It's best seen from a distance, as up close the yellowish stone reveals bad weathering, with most of the decorative detail lost. Inside, its most impressive features are the height of the nave and some sixteenth-century glass, set off by the prevailing gloom. Like other southern Gothic cathedrals of the period (about 1260), it was based on more famous northern models, in this case Soissons and Reims. On the south side is a quiet, secretive cloister with a lawn, cypress trees and beds of begonias.

The smartest streets in town radiate out from the cathedral: rue d'Espagne, the old commercial centre, and rue de la Monnaie, leading into rue du Port-Neuf, with its aromatic *pâtisseries* and *confiseries*. Behind the cathedral, along rue des Faures and the streets above the old walls, there is a distinctly Spanish feel, with washing strung at the windows and strains of music drifting from dark interiors.

Below the cathedral, the riverside **quays** of the Nive are the city's most picturesque focus, with sixteenth-century arcaded houses on the Petit Bayonne side, one of which used to contain the excellent Basque ethnographic museum, the **Musée Basque**. Unfortunately, the museum is closed at the time of writing because the floors are unsound, but when it reopens, the exhibits will illustrate Basque life through the centuries, and include reconstructed farm buildings, house interiors, implements and tools, *makhilas* – a kind of walking stick, often elaborately carved from medlar wood. There's also a section on Basque seagoing activities (Columbus' skipper was a Basque and another Basque, Sebastian de Caro, made the first circumnavigation of the globe in 1519–22), and rooms on *pelota* – its history and stars – and famous Basques.

The city's second museum, the **Musée Bonnat**, close by at 5 rue Jacques-Lafitte (daily except Tues 10am–noon & 3–7pm; mid-Sept to mid-June Mon, Wed, Thurs 3–7pm, Fri 3–9pm, Sat & Sun 10am–noon & 3–7pm; 15F), is an unexpected treasury of art, with an array of works that includes thirteenth- and fourteenth-century Italian primitives, especially a *Virgin and Child* by Matteo di Giovanni and Isenbrandt, Brussels tapestries, paintings by Goya, Constable, Rubens, Géricault and Delacroix, and some fine society portraits by Léon Bonnat, whose personal collection formed the basis of the museum.

Apart from savouring the wide river skies, there is little to draw you to the northern bank of the Adour. There is a **synagogue** in rue Maubec, a reminder that it was here that Bayonne's Jewish community settled first on arrival from Spain. The **church of St-Esprit** opposite the station is all that remains of a hostel that once ministered to the sore feet and other ailments of the St-Jacques pilgrims – worth a look for an interesting wood sculpture of the *Flight into Egypt*. Just behind the station, Vauban's massive **citadelle** was built in 1680 to defend the town against Spanish attack, though it did not see much action until the Napoleonic wars, when its garrison resisted a siege by Wellington for four months in 1813.

If you have a car, it's worth making an evening trip northwest through the industrial suburb of **BOUCAU** and out to the breakwater that protects the mouth of the Adour. Sit at the bar and watch the leaden-backed Atlantic rollers come in; if you are tempted to bathe from the beautiful white beach that stretches from here to Bordeaux, just remember that there are lethal currents close inshore and you must be extremely careful.

Eating, drinking and entertainment

Apart from the much-frequented *Café du Théâtre* on place de la Liberté, there are no obvious major gathering points in the city. The best place to look for **eating and drinking** places is in the back streets of the Petit Bayonne quarter on the right bank of the Nive, especially round rue Pannecau, rue des Cordeliers and rue des Tonneliers. The *Xan Xan Gorri*, a friendly and popular wine bar at 9 rue des Cordeliers (open until 2am) serves *tapas*-style food in the evenings; the nearby *Bar des Amis* at 13 rue des Tonneliers (open until 9.30pm; from 45F) is a cheap and cheery local restaurant. More sophisticated, with greater choice, is the *Restaurant de la Tour* at 5 rue des Faures (closed Sun), behind the cathedral, which has menus for 60–120F. Good for a midday meal or a dawn snifter (it opens at 5am) is the *Bar du Marché* in rue des Basques, directly opposite the market, with *plats du jour* for less than 40F. *Le Pécharmant*, near the station in the rue Maubec, is also good for an agreeable evening's food and wine (from 85F). But for the city's real gastronomic treat, you have to go to *Le Cheval Blanc* at 69 rue Bourgneuf, whose cheapest menu at 95F is still very good.

VAUBAN

Sébastien Le Prestre, Seigneur de Vauban (1633–1707), was one of the most celebrated engineers in the history of France. He's best known for his military works, both fortified towns and strong points, erected during the reign of Louis XIV as part of his strategic plan to secure the frontiers of France, particularly in the north and east. Examples of his work exist all over France, built according to his designs, if not actually supervised by him. The walls of Bayonne, Gravelines, Sisteron and Concarneau, and the fortesses in Belfort, Lille, Besançon, Belle-Île and Mont-Louis are good examples of his work.

He was also known as a progressive social thinker, the author of a scheme to tax farmers in proportion to the richness of their lands, an idea which did not find favour with the king, as well as a number of improvements in the irrigation and fertilizing of agricultural land.

As far as **festivals** go, Bayonne's biggest thrash of the year is the *Fêtes Traditionelles*, opening on the first Wednesday in August, and consisting of five days and nights of continuous boozing and entertainment, finishing up with a *corrida* on the following Sunday. This is followed by three or four days of bullfighting, starting on August 15. The last two years have also seen a jazz festival in mid-July, which is set to become a regular feature, and every October there is a Franco-Spanish theatre festival.

Biarritz

A few minutes by rail or road from Bayonne, **BIARRITZ** was once the Monte Carlo of the Atlantic coast, transformed by Napoléon III in the mid-nineteenth century into a playground for monarchs, aristos and *glitterati* up until World War II. Today, however, it has something of a faded air, and the overriding impression is the town's slightly sad combination of chic and shabby.

The focus of Biarritz is the **Casino Municipal**, with the rest of the town an amorphous sprawl, and the only bit really worth a stroll are the streets between here and the Plage du Port-Vieux. One centre of Biarritz life is the oblong **place Clemenceau**, where you can nibble a cake or sip a lemon tea at Dodin's *pâtisserie* or Miremont's *salon de thé* – prissy and frightfully superior places. To the west, the faded old-time hotels of **place Ste-Eugénie**, and **place Attalaye**, down by the port, are also worth a look as you go by, as is the workaday **rue du Port-Vieux**, nearby.

The **shore**, however, is beautiful. White breakers crash on sandy strands, where the beautiful people bronze their limbs cheek-by-jowl with suburban families and ageing Californian and Australian surf bums, against a backdrop of casinos and ocean-liner hotels, Gothic castles and unfinished apartment blocks. The **beaches** – served by a special bus or *navette* in summer – extend from Plage de la Milady in the south through Plage Marbella, Côte des Basques, Plage du Port-Vieux, Grande Plage, Plage Miramar to the Pointe St-Martin to the north, though most of the action takes place between the Plage du Port-Vieux and the huge **Hôtel du Palais** overlooking the Plage Miramar, formerly the Villa Eugénie, built by Napoléon III in the mid-nineteenth century for his wife, whom he had met and courted in Biarritz.

Just beside the **Plage du Port-Vieux**, the most sheltered and intimate of the beaches, a rocky promontory sticks out into the sea, ending in an iron catwalk anchoring the **Rocher de la Vierge**, an offshore rock adorned with a white statue of the Virgin that has become Biarritz's trademark. Around it are scattered other rocky islets where the swell heaves and combs. It seems irresistible to lovers, for the seaward view is always obscured by pairs of backs and interlocking arms apparently in thrall to the ocean. On the bluff above the Virgin stands the **Musée de la Mer** (daily 9am–noon & 2–7pm; July & Aug 9am–7pm; 40F), hardly a must, but with interesting exhibits to do with the fishing industry, the region's birds, and an aquarium of North Atlantic fish.

Just below is the postcard-pretty harbour of the **Port des Pêcheurs,** backed by tamarisks and pink and blue hydrangeas. The fishermen have gone, but you could afford a snack at one of the waterfront *tapas* bars or indulge in some good if overpriced seafood at the doughty *Chez Albert* (menus for 160–200F). Beyond lies the **Grande Plage**, taking you in one immaculate sweep of sand past the tatty casino all the way to the lighthouse on the Pointe St-Martin.

Practicalities

Everything happens in the area around the casino on Grande-Plage. The **tourist office** is on square d'Ixelles (daily 9am–6.45pm; July & Aug daily 8am–8pm; ☎59.24.20.24). The **gare SNCF** (☎59.55.50.50) is 3km away at the end of av Foch/av Kennedy in the *quartier* known as La Négresse (bus #2 from the Hôtel de Ville).

Accommodation is heavily booked in July and August, but is less expensive than you might expect. Try the family-run, friendly and clean *Hôtel de la Marine* on the corner of rue des Goélands and rue du Port-Vieux (☎59.24.34.09; ②), or *Hôtel Palym*, 7 rue du Port-Vieux (☎59.24.16.56; ①–③). Slightly more expensive but superbly placed overlooking the Plage du Port-Vieux, *Le Welcome* (☎59.24.10.42; ②–④) has a very charming English-speaking *patronne* and a restaurant, pizzeria and bar. There's an IYHF **youth hostel**, halfway between Biarritz and Bayonne at 19 rte des Vignes in Anglet (see below), reached by taking the bus to the beaches (get off by the *Fontaine-Laborde* campsite, turn up the road by the camp, then left into promenade des Sables and left again into rte des Vignes). **Campers** should try *Biarritz-Camping* at 28 rue d'Harcet, the continuation of av de la Plage (☎59.23.00.12; May–Sept; heavily booked in July & Aug), behind Plage de la Milady, to the south of town.

Finding a reasonable place to **eat** is not easy, but there's always the friendly *Bistrot des Halles* on rue du Centre, by the market (around 110F), and the *Crêperie Bretonne* at 30 rue Mazagran (50–60F).

Anglet

Immediately north of Biarritz, **ANGLET** sprawls up the coast from the Pointe St-Martin to the mouth of the Adour. There is nothing to see except for two superb beaches – the **Chambre d'Amour**, so named for two lovers trapped in their trysting place by the tide, and the **Sables d'Or**, much favoured by the surfers and with boards for rental. Here, too, the swimming is very dangerous and you should heed the warning signs.

There are buses from the Hôtel de Ville in Biarritz, and the *navette des plages* shuttle runs during the summer. Alternatively you can walk it in about thirty minutes, along av de l'Impératrice, av MacCroskey, then second left down to the seaside bd des Plages. Anglet is also a good place to stay if you're hostelling, with an IYHF **youth hostel** at 19 rte des Vignes (☎59.63.86.49; ①). There are also two **campsites**: *Fontaine Laborde* (June–Sept), near the hostel, and *Chambre d'Amour* (April–Sept) in rte de Bouney. For **eating**, there is no alternative to picnicking or making do with overpriced snacks and pizzas from the seaside establishments.

St-Jean-de-Luz

With its fine sandy bay and magnificent harbourfront houses, **ST-JEAN-DE-LUZ** is far and away the most attractive resort on the Basque coast, but happily has not been submerged by tourism. As the only natural harbour on the coast between Arcachon and Spain, it has been a major port for centuries, with whaling and cod fishing the traditional preoccupations of its fleets. It remains one of the busiest fishing ports in France, and the principal one for landing anchovy and tuna.

The Town

The wealth and vigour of St-Jean's seafaring past is evident in the town, most notably in the surviving seventeenth- and eighteenth-century houses of the merchants and ship-owners. One of the finest, adjacent to the Hôtel de Ville on the plane tree-lined **place Louis XIV**, is the turreted **Maison Louis XIV** (June–Sept daily 10.30am–noon & 3–6pm; 20F), built for the ship-owning Lohobiague family in 1635, but taking its name from the fact that the young King Louis stayed here in 1660 during the preparations for his marriage to Maria Teresa, Infanta of Castile; she lodged in the equally impressive pink Italianate villa with loggias overlooking the harbour on **quai de l'Infante.**

In the school-book history of St-Jean-de-Luz, this wedding was a major event. The couple were married in the **church of St-Jean-Baptiste** on **rue Gambetta**, the main shopping street today, although the door through which they left the church has been walled up ever since. The extravagance of the event defies belief. Cardinal Mazarin alone presented the queen with 12,000 pounds of pearls and diamonds, a gold dinner service and a pair of sumptuous carriages drawn by teams of six horses – all paid for by money made in the service of France. Plain and fortress-like on the outside, the church is the biggest of all Basque churches inside, with a barn-like nave roofed in wood and lined on three sides with tiers of dark oak galleries. These are a distinctive feature of Basque churches, and were reserved for the men, while the women sat at ground level in the nave. Equally Basque is the elaborate gilded retable of tiered angels, saints and prophets behind the altar. The walled-up door through which Louis and his bride passed is on the right of the main entrance. Hanging from the ceiling is an *ex-voto* model of the Empress Eugénie's paddle-steamer, *Eagle*, which narrowly escaped wrecking on the rocks outside St-Jean in 1867.

On the other side of the harbour, **CIBOURE** looks like a continuation of St-Jean but is in fact a separate *commune*. Its streets are even prettier, especially opposite the end of the bridge from St-Jean, the waterfront **quai Maurice-Ravel** (the composer was born at no. 12) and the parallel **rue Pocolette** behind. Wide-fronted, half-timbered, gaily painted and sometimes balconied, the houses epitomize the local Labourdian Basque style. The octagonal tower protruding above the houses belongs to the sixteenth-century **church of St-Vincent**, where you'll find more characteristic Basque galleries and a Baroque altarpiece; the entrance is in rue Pocolette through a paved courtyard with gravestones embedded in it.

From the bridge, the **fish dock** sticks out into the harbour, stacked with nets and blackened lobster traps, with grubby blue-painted tuna boats, redolent of diesel oil, tied up alongside. Upstream, smaller boats lie heeled over on the tidal mud flats of the little River Nivelle against a backdrop of green fields and the emerald flanks of the 900-metre peak of La Rhune (3–4 buses daily Mon–Fri from *gare SNCF* to Col de St-Ignace and Sare for ascent of La Rhune; see p.613).

Practicalities

The **gare SNCF** (☎59.55.50.50) is on the southern edge of the centre, 500m from the beach. The **tourist office** is close by on place Maréchal-Foch, behind the Hôtel de Ville (daily 9am–noon & 2–7pm; July & Aug same hours, but Sun 10am–noon). On Friday and Tuesday there is a **market** in the adjacent bd Victor-Hugo. **Bikes** can be rented at the station or *ADO* on av Labrouche. **Pelota** matches take place every Saturday at the *fronton* at the far end of rue Gambetta.

Opposite the train station, on and around av Verdun, are several reasonable **hotels**: try the *Hôtel Toki-Ona*, 10 rue Marion-Garay (☎59.26.11.54; ②; closed Nov–March), the *Hôtel de Verdun*, 13 av de Verdun (☎59.26.02.55; ①–③), or the *Hôtel de Paris*, 1 bd du Comandant-Passicot, on the corner of av Labrouche (☎59.26.00.62; ②–③). A more expensive alternative is the *Hôtel Agur* at 96 rue Gambetta, run by an Englishman (☎59.26.21.55; ③–④). There are numerous **campsites**, all grouped in the so-called *zone des campings* to the left of the N10 between St-Jean and Guéthary.

Leading off place Louis XIV – with its cafés and free summertime concerts in the bandstand – **rue de la République** has numerous touristy restaurants. *Le Kaiku*, in a handsome old house at no. 17, has an excellent reputation for its fish and seafood, but will cost upward of 200F. A cheaper, more family-oriented place is *La Sardinerie* (open 11.30am–2.30pm & 6–10pm; mid-June to mid-Sept) in the car park behind the Hôtel de Ville, where dishes of tuna, sardines or omelettes cost in the region of 40–50F. Popular *Chez Pablo* at 5 rue Mademoiselle-Etcheto, behind the market, does excellent Basque food in a friendly atmosphere for around 130F. Another classic for seafood and dessert is *Le Tourasse* on rue Tourasse (menu at 110F).

Hendaye and the Spanish frontier

HENDAYE, 16km south of St-Jean-de-Luz, is the last town in France before the Spanish frontier. Neither the town itself, **Hendaye-Ville**, nor the seaside quarter,

Hendaye-Plage, is of any intrinsic interest, although the latter has a fine beach and modern tourist amenities.

The town, served by the Paris–Bordeaux–Irun main rail line, lies on the estuary of the River Bidassoa, which forms the border with Spain here. Just upstream, a tiny wooded island known as the Île des Faisans was once used as a meeting place for the monarchs of the two countries. In 1659 it was the scene of the signature of the Treaty of the Pyrenees and in the following year of the marriage contract between Louis XIV and Maria Teresa, when the painter Velázquez, responsible for the nuptial decor, caught the cold which resulted in his death. Another interesting encounter was the meeting between Hitler and Franco at Hendaye station on October 23, 1940, when Hitler refused to commit himself to supporting Franco's colonial claims on Morocco. You might also like to see the house in rue des Pêcheurs, on the waterfront below bd de Gaulle, where the author Pierre Loti died in 1923.

If you are planning to **stay**, hotel prices are cheapest in Hendaye-Ville. The **camp-sites** are mainly grouped around Hendaye-Plage. *Le Moulin,* off the D658 (between the N10 and coastal D912), is one of the cheaper ones. For further information, consult the **tourist office** at 12 rue des Aubépines in Hendaye-Plage (☎59.20.00.34).

Around Hendaye: up the coast and inland

The best thing about Hendaye is in fact getting there, for the stretch of **coast** from St-Jean south has remained miraculously unspoilt, especially in the region of the **Pointe Ste-Anne** promontory, accessible from the **Chemin Piéton Littoral** footpath, which runs parallel to the coastal D912 Corniche Basque road. It is equally accessible from the beach at Hendaye-Plage.

Inland, both trans-Pyrenean walking routes – the **GR10 and HRP** – begin their course in Hendaye-Plage at the former casino on the front. The first stage is dull and gives no sense of the glories that lie ahead: along bd Général-Leclerc, through the town on rue des Citronniers, under the rail line, then 50m east on the N10 before following the waymarks to the right towards the A63 autoroute. A cattle track passes underneath and continues to the tiny hilltop village of **BIRIATOU**, where the walking starts to get interesting. If you are not concerned about the romance of starting at the very beginning, splash out on a taxi and start at Biriatou. A short steep section leads to a Basque **church** with a collection of weather-worn Celtic-type tombstones, next door to the pretty *Auberge Hirribarren,* a temporary haven for many escaping Allied soldiers during World War II. From here the main footpaths and a number of local variations rise rapidly above the coast to semi-isolation, where only the buzzing power lines (soon left behind) and the occasional walker or jogger disturb the peace.

Inland: Labourd and Basse Navarre

If you don't have your own transport, the simplest forays into the soft, seductive landscapes of the Basque hinterland into the **Labourd** area, behind Biarritz and Bayonne, and further into the **Basse Navarre**, are along the St-Jean-de-Luz–Sare bus route and the Bayonne–St-Jean-Pied-de-Port train lines. Either gives a representative sample of places.

La Rhune, Ascain and Sare

The 900-metre cone of **La Rhune** on the Spanish border is the last skyward thrust of the Pyrenees before they decline into the Atlantic. It is *the* landmark of Labourd, in spite of its unsightly TV mast, and since it is also equipped with a rack-and-pinion rail service it is predictably popular with the seekers of views – and very fine they are, way up the Basque coast and east to the rising Pyrenees. Three or four **buses** a day ply the

30-minute route from the *gare SNCF* in St-Jean-de-Luz, stopping at Ascain, Col de St-Ignace (for the rail service to La Rhune) and Sare.

ASCAIN, where Pierre Loti wrote *Ramuntcho,* is like so many Labourd villages – pretty as a picture and in danger of caricaturing itself, with its galleried church, *fronton* and half-timbered houses. To shake off this sweetness you could walk up La Rhune from here in about two and a half hours, or take the little train from **Col de St-Ignace** (July–Sept daily every 35min from 9am; May–June & Oct to mid-Nov Sat & Sun 10am & 3pm; Easter & spring holiday daily 10am & 3pm; 35F). The ascent takes 30 minutes, but you need to allow up to two hours for the round trip.

It is worth going on to **SARE**, even if you've missed the bus. You can either walk on the **GR10** from the station just below the summit of La Rhune in about an hour and a quarter or follow the road from St-Ignace in about the same time. If you plan to continue further east, you can make an overnight stop at the *Hôtel Lastiry* on place du Fronton (☎59.54.20.07; ②; restaurant from 70F), or the *Hôtel Baratchartea* (☎59.54.20.48; ②–③; restaurant from 90F), or at one of two **campsites** just south of the village, *La Petite Rhune* (☎59.54.23.97; June–Sept), and *Goyenetche* (☎59.54.21.71; April–Oct).

Instead of going back to St-Jean-de-Luz, an easy three-to-four-hour stint on the GR10 would take you on to **AINHOA** to link up with the valley of the Nive (see below). Another gem of a village, once patronized by the Duke of Windsor and now touristy in season, it consists of scarcely more than a single street lined with substantial, mainly seventeenth-century houses, whose stone lintels are carved with the dates of their construction and details of their families' history. The heavy-towered church is worth a look with its rich altarpiece of prophets and apostles in niches, framed by Corinthian columns and capped with pediments. There is a **gîte d'étape** at the Maison Elissaldia (☎59.29.25.29), and cheap **rooms** in the *Hôtel-Bar Irubera* (☎59.29.91.49; ①). For a **meal**, there's a good but not inexpensive restaurant at the *Hôtel Oppoca* (from 125F), also on the main street. There is a **campsite**, the *Xokoan*, 3km away at **DANCHERIA** on the Spanish frontier.

The Valley of the Nive

The **River Nive** is the only public transport artery east into the Basque interior, with four or five trains a day making the riverside journey from Bayonne to St-Jean-Pied-de-Port in about an hour. The luminous green landscape, scattered with villages untouched by speculative development, remains as peaceful and harmonious as you approach the mountains as it was in the lowlands.

Cambo-les-Bains

The first major stop is **CAMBO-LES-BAINS**, an old spa town whose favourable microclimate made it an ideal centre for the treatment of tuberculosis in the last century; the locals also claim that camelias flower a month earlier here than elsewhere in the region. It is an attractive town, green and open, but suffers from the usual genteel stuffiness of spas. The "new" town, with its ornate houses and hotels, radiates out from the baths over the heights above the River Nive, while the old quarter, typically Basque with its whitewashed houses and galleried church, lies beside the river.

The main thing to see here is the **Villa Arnaga**, just out of town on the Bayonne road (May–Sept daily 10am–noon & 2.30–6.30pm; March 20–April & Oct 2.30–6pm; 25F), built for Edmond Rostand, author of *Cyrano de Bergerac,* who came here to cure his pleurisy in 1903. It's a larger-than-life Basque house overlooking an almost surreal formal garden with discs and rectangles of water and segments of grass punctuated by blobs, cubes and cones of box, lined by limes and blue cedars, with a distant view of green hills. It's very kitsch inside, with a minstrels' gallery, fake pilasters and allegorical frescoes, chandeliers and numerous portraits and other memorabilia.

The **tourist office** is in the Parc St-Joseph in the upper town centre (Mon–Sat 8.45am–12.15pm & 2–6.30pm; ☎59.29.70.25). For an **overnight stay**, try the *Auberge de Tante Ursule* in Bas Cambo (☎59.29.78.23; ②–③; good restaurant from 80F), by the *fronton;* the nearest year-round **campsite** is *Ur-Hégia* on rte des Sept-Chênes (☎59.29.72.03).

Espelette and Itxassou

It's 5km southwest from Cambo by bus to **ESPELETTE,** a village of wide-eaved houses, with a church notable for its heavy square tower, carved doors, painted ceiling and disc-shaped gravestones. The village's principal source of renown is its large red pimentoes, much used in Basque cuisine, and its *pottok* sales. *Pottoks* are a small stocky Basque breed of pony, once favoured for work in British coal mines but now reared mainly for meat and riding – herds of them are a common sight on the upland pastures. The annual sales take place on the last Wednesday in January; the pimento jamboree takes place on the last Sunday in October. There is a very good **hotel-restaurant** in the village, too, the *Euzkadi* on the Cambo road (☎59.93.91.88; ③), with menus specializing in Basque country cooking from 80F (closed Mon). The *Hôtel Chilar*, on the same road, has slightly cheaper rooms (☎59.93.90.01; ③).

About the same distance from Cambo-les-Bains, next stop up the rail line (though there's only one train a day), **ITXASSOU** is another lovely village, quieter than most of the others in the area, surrounded by green wooded hills. Nearby, the River Nive cuts through a narrow looping defile by the so-called **Pas de Roland** – hardly more than a roadside boulder with a hole in it, supposedly struck by the hooves of the great knight's horse (see opposite). Even without a car, it would be a great place for a gentle recharge of the batteries, especially if you were to stay at the *Hôtel Arzamendi* on place du Fronton (☎59.29.75.29; ②–③), which has attractive, old-fashioned rooms and a restaurant with prices from 60F; the proprietor speaks excellent English. Nearly as enticing is the *Etchepare,* on the same square (☎59.29.75.14; ③; closed Nov–March), also with a restaurant from 60F.

St-Étienne-de-Baïgorry

The next major stop is the station of Ossès-St-Martin-d'Arrossa, where *SNCF* **buses** meet the trains for the eight-kilometre journey south to **ST-ÉTIENNE-DE-BAÏGORRY**. Like other Basque villages, St-Étienne is divided into quite distinct quarters, more like separate hamlets than a unified village. A prosperous, sleek place, its business is still very much agriculture rather than tourism, with the Pays Basque's only vineyards centred here, producing a good, strong red wine named *Irouléguy* after a neighbouring village; a local shop offers **dégustation**.

There are no great sights here. There's a seventeenth-century **church** with a sumptuous Baroque retable, a picturesque bridge posing against a backdrop of romantic castle and distant hills, and the hills themselves. St-Étienne lies in the mouth of the **Vallée des Aldudes**, with the **GR10** running along the **Cresta de Iparla** ridge to the west, the classic ridge walk of the Basque country. The GR10 goes directly up from the village, or you could hitch a ride on the D949 to the Col d'Ispéguy. There are plenty of other gentler walks, too.

The **tourist office** is opposite the church (Mon–Sat 9am–noon & 2–5pm; ☎59.37.47.28). The *Hôtel Hargain* has **rooms** (☎59.37.41.46; ③–④; closed mid-Nov to March), as well as a restaurant with menus from 70F. There's another good restaurant in the *Hôtel Manechenea* beyond Lespars (☎59.37.41.68; ②; restaurant from 75F; closed Dec & Jan). There's a **camping municipal**, *Camping Irouléguy,* on the banks of the river (mid-June to mid-Sept), and another, *Camping à la Ferme Mendy,* in the Lespars quarter to the north, with a **gîte d'étape** (☎59.37.42.39).

St-Jean-Pied-de-Port

The old capital of Basse Navarre, **ST-JEAN-PIED-DE-PORT** lies in a circle of hills at the foot of the Roncevaux pass into Spain. It owes its name to its position "at the foot of the *port*" – a Pyrenean word for "pass". Only part of France since the Treaty of the Pyrenees in 1659, it was an important pilgrim stopping-off point in the Middle Ages. The routes from Paris, Vézelay and Le Puy converged here, and it was the pilgrims' last port of call before struggling over the pass to the Spanish monastery of Roncesvalles (Roncevaux in French), where Roland, Charlemagne's general celebrated in medieval romance, sounded his horn in vain (see below).

The town lies on the River Nive, enclosed by walls of pinky-red sandstone. Above it rises a wooded hill crowned by the inevitable Vauban **fortress**, while to the east a further defensive system guards the road to Spain. The more recent overspill, pleasant but unremarkable, spreads down across the main road on to lower ground.

The **old town** consists of a single cobbled street, **rue de la Citadelle**, running downhill from the fifteenth-century **Porte St-Jacques** – so named because it was the gate by which the pilgrims entered the town – to the **Porte d'Espagne**, commanding the bridge over the Nive, with a view of balconied houses overlooking the stream. Many of the painted houses bear inscriptions on their lintels from the sixteenth, seventeenth and eighteenth centuries. A fourteenth-century plain red church, **Notre-Dame-du-Bout-du-Pont**, stands beside the Porte d'Espagne, and, opposite, a short street leads through the **Porte de Navarre** to the modern road. Off to the left is the town *fronton*, where a bare-handed **pelota match** – the most macho kind – is held every Monday at 4.30pm.

On the other side of the river, the **tourist office** is in place de Gaulle opposite the *mairie* (Mon–Sat 9am–noon & 2–7pm; July & Aug Mon–Sat 9am–12.30pm & 2–7pm, Sun 10.30am–12.30pm; ☎59.37.03.57). The **gare SNCF** is at the end of av Renaud, on the northern edge of the centre. Among **hotels** in town, the *Remparts*, 16 pl Floquet (☎59.37.13.79; ②; restaurant from 60F), just before you cross the Nive coming into town on the Bayonne road, is the cheapest; more expensive are the *Ramuntcho*, just inside the city walls at 1 rue de France (☎59.37.03.91; ③–④), with a good and reasonably priced restaurant from 80F; *Hôtel Itzalpea*, 5 pl du Trinquet (☎59.37.03.66; ③; restaurant from 68F); and *Hôtel Central* on place de-Gaulle (☎59.37.00.22; ③–④; restaurant from 98F; closed mid-Dec to mid-Feb). There is also a **gîte d'étape**, 49 rte d' Uhart, the Bayonne road (M. Etchegoin; ☎59.37.12.08), and a **camping municipal** (May–Sept) on the banks of the Nive, just beyond the *fronton;* another campsite, the *Narbaïtz*, is 2.5km from here along the Bayonne road.

Walks around St-Jean

Numerous tracks lead south from St-Jean up into the mountains towards the Spanish border. It is sheep country, and if you are interested in getting an idea of what the old pastoral life was like, this is a good place to do it. If you are a walker, the last leg of the **GR65** pilgrim route starts from St-Jean and follows the line of the old Roman road across to Spanish Asturia.

THE CHANSON DE ROLAND

Roland, with his sword Durandal, is the hero of the medieval **Chanson de Roland**. But he was also an historical character, as warden of the Breton marches who in 778 accompanied the Emperor Charlemagne on a campaign against the Moors in Spain, in the course of which the Navarrese capital of Pamplona was sacked. In revenge, the Basques ambushed and decimated Charlemagne's rearguard, commanded by Roland, as it withdrew through the gorges above Roncevaux. The *chanson* has it that infidel Saracens were the dastardly foe, but this was propaganda designed to make poor Roland's end more heroic.

TRANSHUMANCE

Like other shepherds in southern or Mediterranean climes, the Basques are forced to take their flocks to the high **mountain pastures** in summer in search of better grazing. They live out on the mountainside in stone huts with a couple of dogs, milking the ewes twice a day and making cheese, the *fromage de brebis*, whose soft and hard versions are a speciality throughout the pastoral Pyrenees. Most of the pastures today are accessible by car, at least at the gentler Basque end of the Pyrenees, so the shepherds' life is not as isolated as it used to be – though there are still areas in the higher mountains that are only accessible with mules or ponies. A measure of the pre-eminence of sheep in the Basque economy is the Basque word for rich, *aberats* – whose literal meaning is "he who owns large flocks".

Much of the grazing is owned in common by various communes, who have over the centuries made elaborate agreements to ensure a fair share of the best pasture and avoid disputes. One of the oldest of these *faceries*, as they are called, concluded by the inhabitants of Roncal and Baretous in 1375, is still in force, renewed each year on payment of three white heifers.

Follow rue d'Espagne in St-Jean out through the city walls. The waymarks begin on the first telephone pole on the left. A little further on you turn up a lane to the right; GR10 and GR65 run together here. Follow the lane, between grassy banks, past fields and isolated farms. The farmhouses have immensely broad roofs, one side short, the other long enough to cover space for stalls and tools; it's all very quiet and rural, with long views out across the valleys. The climb becomes steeper above a little group of houses known as **HOUNTO**. It is no good asking the way, even if you can find someone to ask, as the Basque names are impossible to pronounce if you don't know the language, although everyone speaks French. Above Hounto you come out on top of a grassy spur. The GR65 turns left up what looks like an old drove road to rejoin the tarmac higher up by two small sheds at the edge of beech woods. It is about two hours to these sheds. You get your first glimpse of the higher Pyrenean peaks to the east. Above the trees you come out on grassy uplands dotted with sheepfolds or *cayolars*.

The route continues along the track to a fork (3hr 30min) with a small white statue of the Virgin. Here, the GR65 turns right towards Spain (another 90min) and the GR10 turns left. For a while it follows the road before veering away to the right to Béhérobie (see below), while the road continues its twisting descent to the tiny hamlet of Esterençuby (see opposite), then down along the Nive and back to St-Jean-Pied-de-Port.

East of St-Jean

The **GR65** passes to the north of the espadrille-manufacturing town of **MAULÉON**, about 30km east of St-Jean, but if you are vaguely following the pilgrim route by car, then the road from St-Jean through Col d'Osquich and on towards Navarrenx is the most attractive to take.

There's a couple of reasonable and agreeable **hotels** just after Ordiarp at Musculdy: *Hôtel du Col d'Osquich* (☎59.37.81.23; ②–③; restaurant from 70F; closed Nov–March) and *Hôtel le Chistera* (☎59.28.06.74; ①; restaurant from 60F), as well as a riverside **campsite**, *Le Saison* (June–Sept), just outside Mauléon on the Tardets road, and another, *Le Landran* (Easter–Oct) at Ordiarp, back towards the Col d'Osquich.

Into the mountains

Le bout du monde – the end of the earth – is what they used to call the tiny settlement of **Ste-Engrâce**, locked in its cul-de-sac valley beneath the Spanish frontier at the easternmost extremity of the Basque country. And although a new road has been built, the place still feels very remote, especially if you've approached it over the hills from St-Jean-Pied-de-Port, either on foot by the GR10 or along the tortuous lane that accompanies it.

There are no shops, no hotels, and no villages except **Larrau**. It's a land of open skies, where griffon vultures turn on the thermals without so much as a flick of their huge wings, of countless flocks of sheep and thousands of acres of whispering beech woods. Although the overall distance is not very great, the slowness of the road and the grandeur of the scenery seem to magnify it. There is no public transport. Carrying a tent would give you the greatest flexibility: no one objects if you pitch it discreetly, and to be on the safe side you can always ask the nearest shepherd. For the latest on **weather information** in the western Pyrenees, call ☎59.92.13.49.

Esterençuby, Béhérobie and the Col d'Errozaté

From St-Jean-Pied-de-Port, the D301 follows the deepening valley of the Nive for 8km, past small red- and green-shuttered farms to the village of **ESTERENÇUBY**, and on a further four or five kilometres to **BÉHÉROBIE**. The river, now no more than a mountain stream, runs sparkling down between steep green slopes, whose only crops are hay and bracken. In late June and early July, entire families are out on the mountainside, scything the meadows or turning the sweet-smelling hay with wooden rakes. In the farmyards, stacks of bracken impaled on wooden stakes are dried for winter bedding.

At Béhérobie, the road climbs up to the right to the border and the **Col d'Arnostéguy**. In the valley bottom beside the infant Nive, the only building is the *Hôtel de la Nive* (☎59.37.10.57; ②; closed Jan; restaurant from 50F), invariably booked out in October for the wood pigeon shooting season, but with a terrace overhanging the river, making a marvellous place for a quiet stay. There is an equally attractive hotel a little way back towards Estérençuby, the *Artzain-Etchea* (☎59.37.11.55; ②–③; restaurant from 90F; closed mid-Nov to late Dec).

Just before the bridge at Béhérobie, a lane keeps up to the left, then drops down to cross a tributary stream of the Nive by an ancient barn and cottage with beautiful shady pools to bathe in: this is the **GR10**. To the right, a secondary path heads into the beech woods, bringing you to the bank of the Nive in about half an hour – a fantastic picnic spot – while the GR10 itself bears left over a bridge by the cottage, before climbing back to the right, contouring high along the sides of the valley until, after about an hour, you emerge above the tree line in a huge ravine of shining knee-deep grass. If you feel like continuing, it's another hour to the 1076-metre-high **Col d'Errozate**, or two hours to the 1345-metre-high summit of **Errozaté**.

The Iraty Forest

A kilometre or so on the Estérençuby side of Béhérobie, a lane turns up left towards the **Forêt d'Iraty**. It is very steep and full of tight hairpins, but, as you climb higher up the steep spurs and round the heads of labyrinthine gullies, ever more spectacular views open beneath you. You can see way back over the valley of the Nive, St-Jean and the hills beyond. Stands of beech fill the gullies, shadowing the lighter grass whose green is so intense it seems almost theatrical – an effect produced, apparently, by the juxtaposition of outcrops of rock whose purplish hue brings out the cadmium yellow in the grass.

Along the cols and ridges stand ranks of shooting butts, from which the well-heeled urban bourgeoisie open fire every October on the millions of migrating *palombes*, as they call wood pigeons in the southwest, heading north over the western Pyrenees from Spain. Many other species – not destined to be eaten – can be seen, too, among them honey buzzards, black kites, red kites, cranes and storks. Herds of healthy-looking horses and ponies and big sleek caramel cows with bells at their throats on wooden collars marked with their owners' names wander across the road. Flocks of white sheep graze on the hillsides. There are superb places to camp, with views west to the orange and crimson striations of the sunset and the revolving beacon of the Biarritz lighthouse visible in the dark.

Over the col below **Occabé** (1456m) the road loops down past scattered sheepfolds to the **plateau d'Iraty**, where there is a small lake and a snack bar, and flat ground to camp on. A road leads south to Ochagavia in Spain via the **Chalet Pedro** (1km), where the GR10 swings right and up on to the flat-topped Occabé (90min), with its Iron Age **stone circle** and views across the forest and south to the Sierra de Abodi. Continuing east from the plateau, the road enters the densest part of the forest, climbing past a **campsite** half-hidden in the magnificent beeches, to an unsightly collection of chalets at the **Col de Bargaguiac** (*gîte d'étape*: ☎59.28.51.29) and the **Col d'Orgambideska**, which is one of the prime viewing – and killing – fields for the autumn bird migrations. As you come over the top, the ground drops sharply away into the **Valley of Larrau**, 600m lower. To the right, the brilliant grassy swards of the **Pic d'Orhy** (2017m) culminate in swirling strata of rock below the summit, barring the way to Spain. And ahead, for the first breath-stopping time, you see the serrated horizon of peaks that dominate the **Cirque of Lescun**, a harbinger of the central Pyrenees.

Larrau, the gorges and Ste-Engrâce

The first thing you notice coming into **LARRAU** from the west is how different the architecture is. In contrast to the gaily painted façades and tiled roofs of Labourd and Basse Navarre, the houses here are grey and stuccoed, with slate roofs, the mood secretive and inward-looking. And although it's the biggest place since St-Jean-Pied-de-Port, it is nonetheless very small and quiet – almost dead out of season.

There are two friendly and simple **hotels** with restaurants, the *Hôtel Etchémaïté* (☎59.28.61.45; ①–②; good restaurant from 75F; closed late Jan), and *Hôtel Despouey* (☎59.28.60.82; ①–②; restaurant from 65F; closed Nov–Feb). There is a **campsite** and a **gîte d'étape** 3km away at **LOGIBAR** (☎59.28.61.14), close to the mouth of the **Gorges d'Holzarte** – one of several in the region, cutting deep into northern slopes of the ridge that forms the frontier with Spain. A short track leads from Logibar across the turbulent and freezing stream to a car park, from where a steep path, part of the GR10, climbs through the beech woods to the junction of the Holzarte gorge with the Olhadybia in about one hour. Slung across the mouth of the latter is a spectacular Himalayan-style **suspension bridge**, which bounces and swings dizzily as you walk out over the 180-metre drop. The **GR10** continues to Ste-Engrâce in seven hours, or down to the beginning of the Gorges de Kakouetta in about six. But it is definitely worth coming this far; in June and July, the open spaces are full of flowers – columbines, cranesbills, orchids and vetches and, if you're lucky, you might see the beautiful, long-stemmed *bimbette des Pyrénées*.

The Gorges de Kakouetta and Gorges d'Ehujarré

Ten kilometres east of Larrau, you reach the **Gorges de Kakouetta** (Easter to Nov daily 8am–nightfall; 25F) by turning right off the D26 and down the D113. Just over halfway down, the minuscule hamlet of **LA CASERNE** is the site of the only **food shop** for miles around – opposite the *mairie* – and the *Ibarra* **campsite** (June–Sept). Kakouetta is on the tourist trail, but do not be put off: the gorge is truly dramatic and, outside peak season, is not crowded at all. It pays to be well shod for the path is precarious and very slippery in places; you are glad of the handrail. The walls of the gorge are very high – up to 300m and scarcely more than 5m apart – and are jungle-thick with luxuriant vegetation. The hothouse atmosphere is produced by the myriad seepages and waterfalls that fill the air with a fine spray, refracting and filtering what sunlight gets in, and there's a range of ferns that you wouldn't expect to see outside a houseplant nursery. The path continues for about an hour with a small cave at the end and just before it a full-blown waterfall spewing out of a hole in the rock.

The **Gorges d'Ehujarré** are in Senta, the easternmost of the three hamlets that comprise Ste-Engrâce (see below). It's a straightforward walk – the route has been used for centuries for moving sheep up to the pastures of Pic Lakhoura – but requires about seven hours.

Ste-Engrâce and around

STE-ENGRÂCE remains a beautifully remote and peaceful little collection of houses spread in three little clusters along the main road, enclosed by hay meadows and green mountainsides. It seems largely untroubled by the rhythms of the twentieth century, although the main road now continues east over the head of the valley, reducing its isolation. Life is not so simple for the locals: there is no work and the young won't stay. But for the outsider not caught in the rural poverty trap, it has great charm. Its hallmark is the eleventh-century Romanesque **church** in the hamlet of Senta, which features in all the coffee-table books on the Pyrenees. It stands just as it should, with its heavily buttressed walls, belfry and penthouse roof, a sharply defined and angular assertion of humanity against the often mist-shrouded bulwarks of the mountains behind. Very simple inside, it has some good carved capitals, and the graveyard is full of traditional disc-shaped headstones.

There's a **gîte d'étape** (☎59.28.61.63) opposite the church, with an adjacent field to pitch a tent, and a **café-bar** that will serve meals. There's also the *Hôtel de la Pierre-St-Martin* (☎59.28.63.12; ③) at Calla.

On from Ste-Engrâce

The new road up to the typically ugly modern ski resort of **ARETTE-LA-PIERRE-ST-MARTIN** gives fabulous views of the valley of Ste-Engrâce, through magnificent forests of pine and beech, though if the cloud is down, which it often is, you'll be lucky to see much at all. Just south of the resort is the **Col de la Pierre-St-Martin**, where every July 13 the mayors of Barétous and Roncal exchange heifers in renewal of an ancient grazing treaty (see p.616). Also nearby is the **Gouffre de la Pierre-St-Martin**, at 728m one of the deepest potholes in the world, but grilled over to prevent accidents. To the east begins the descent into the valley of the Aspe, which belongs to the ancient county of Béarn.

THE CENTRAL PYRENEES

The area immediately east of the Pays Basque – the **Central Pyrenees** – is home to the area's highest mountain peaks and is the most spectacular part of the region. The southernmost part is protected, contained within the **Parc National des Pyrénées Occidentales**. Getting to the area is simple enough, at least as far as the foothill towns, by train on the Bayonne–Toulouse line. But travelling around can be very slow: the few buses that run – and most of the other traffic – keep to the north–south valleys, which is frustrating when you want to switch from one valley system to the next without having to come all the way out of the mountains each time.

The **GR10** provides a good link if you are ready to walk all the way, and it's possible to hitch, at least up the valleys and across the main passes at **Col d'Aubisque** and **Col du Tourmalet**, though you will find you invariably get left on the top by drivers, who come up for the view and go back the same way.

Highlights – apart from the lakes, torrents, forests and 3000-metre peaks around **Cauterets** – are the *cirques* of **Lescun**, **Gavarnie** and **Troumouse**, each with its distinctive character. And for less hearty interests, there is many a flower-starred mountain meadow accessible by car, in which to quaff and gorge on a well-chosen picnic. The only real urban centres are **Pau**, which you may use as your entry-point to the area, dull **Tarbes**, and the strikingly tacky pilgrimage target of **Lourdes**. Great monuments of the bricks and mortar kind – with the exception of the fortified church at **Luz-St-Sauveur** – are equally scarce.

The Parc National des Pyrénées Occidentales

The **Parc National des Pyrénées Occidentales** was created in 1968 to protect at least part of the high Pyrenees from the development brought about by modern tourism – ski resorts, roads, mountain-top restaurants, car parks and other amenities – and it runs for more than 100km along the Spanish border, from the Pic de Labigouer, south of Lescun, in the west, to beyond the Pic de la Munia, east of Gavarnie. Wavering between 1070m and 3298m at its highest point, Vignemale, south of Cauteret, the park takes in spectacular cirques of Gavarnie and Troumouse, as well as over two hundred lakes, six valleys and over 350km of marked walking routes.

Through the banning of hunting – apart from the traditional mountain peasants' pursuit of poaching or *braconnage* – it has also provided sanctuary for many rare and endangered species of birds and mammals. Among them are chamois, marmots, genets, griffon vultures, golden eagles, eagle owls and capercaillies, to say nothing of the rich and varied flora. The most celebrated animal – and the most depleted by hunting – is the Pyrenean brown bear, whose prewar numbers ran to as many two hundred, but now amount to barely a dozen individuals. Although largely herbivorous, bears will take the occasional sheep or cow, and the mountain shepherd communities are their remorseless enemies. To appease them, the park pays prompt and generous compensation for any losses, but this is not always enough to overcome the innate fear of the bear. The park has become the object of an aggressive media campaign, slating it for not doing enough to protect the bears – an accusation which angers the hard-pressed rangers, who complain that distant planners have no conception what it is really like trying to reconcile legitimate local economic needs with the protection of wild species and paths, illicit camping and other problems caused by modern tourism.

The **GR10** runs through the entire park on its 700-kilometre journey from coast to coast, starting at Argelès-sur-Mer on the Mediterranean and ending up at Hendaye-Plage on the Atlantic shore; the tougher trail of the **Haute Randonnée Pyrénéenne** (HRP) also finishes its course in Hendaye-Plage and closely shadows the GR10, but takes in much more rugged terrain. Hikers are strongly advised to wear appropriate clothing, carry detailed maps and guides, and heed the words of warning on p.603. This terrain is not the place for an easy stroll.

There are **Maisons du Parc** in Cauteret, Gavarnie, Gabas and Etsaut, giving information about the park's wildlife and vegetation, lists of accommodation options and the best walks to do. There are over twenty refuges and plenty of hotels, campsites and hostels throughout the park, listed in the text of this chapter and highlighted on the map opposite. The four towns listed above also make good bases for venturing into the mountains.

Pau and around

From humble beginnings as a crossing on the Gave de Pau for flocks en route to and from the mountains, **PAU** became the capital of the ancient viscounty of Béarn in 1464, and of the French part of the kingdom of Navarre in 1512. In 1567 its sovereign, Henri d'Albret, married the sister of the king of France, Marguerite d'Angoulême, friend and protector of artists and intellectuals, who transformed the town into a centre of the arts and nonconformist thinking. Their daughter was Jeanne d'Albret, an ardent Protestant,

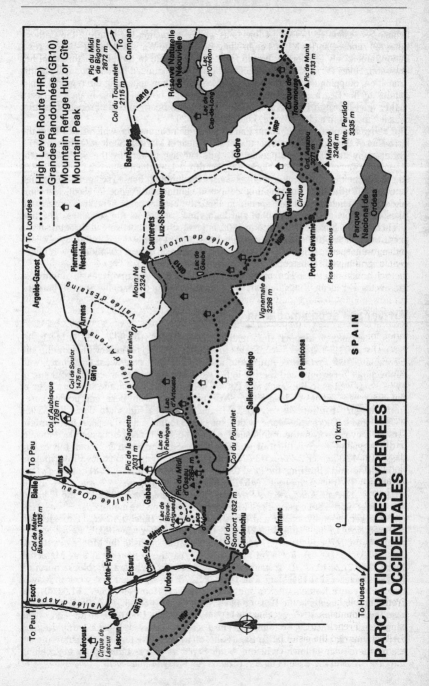

PARC NATIONAL DES PYRENEES
OCCIDENTALES

whose zeal offended her own subjects as well as attracting the wrath of the Catholic king of France, Charles X, thus embroiling Béarn in the Wars of Religion – whose resolution, albeit only temporary, had to await the accession to the French throne of her own son, Henri IV, in 1589. An adroit politician, he renounced his faith to facilitate this transition, quipping that "Paris is worth a Mass" and then appeasing the regional sensibilities of his Béarnais subjects by announcing that he was giving France to Béarn rather than Béarn to France. He did not incorporate Béarn into the French state; that was left to his son and successor, Louis XIII, in 1620.

The least expected thing about Pau is its English connection, which dates from the arrival of Wellington and his troops after the defeat of Marshal Soult at Orthez in 1814. Seduced by its climate and persuaded of its curative powers by the Scottish doctor Alexander Taylor, the English flocked to Pau throughout the nineteenth century, bringing along their peculiar cultural obsessions – fox hunting, horse racing, polo, croquet, cricket, golf (the first eighteen-hole course in continental Europe in 1860), tearooms and parks. When the rail line opened in 1866, the French came here, too: writers and artists like Victor Hugo, Stendhal and Lamartine, as well as the socialites. The first French rugby club opened in Pau in 1902, after which the sport spread throughout the southwest. In the 1950s, natural gas was discovered at nearby Lacq, bringing new jobs and subsidiary industries, as well as massive production of acid pollution, now reduced by filtration but still substantial.

Pau is within easy reach of numerous small, picturesque villages in **northwest Béarn**, as well as the FR65 footpath that runs some 60km down to the Spanish border.

Arrival and accommodation

Pau's international **airport** (information ☎59.33.21.29; *Air Inter* ☎59.33.14.03; *Air Littoral* ☎59.33.26.64) has direct flights to London and Paris. The town lies on the still incomplete **A64** *Pyrénéenne* **autoroute** and on the **main east–west rail route**, with connections to Bayonne and Biarritz in the west, and Lourdes, Tarbes and Toulouse in the east, as well as to Bordeaux and Paris. The **gare SNCF** is on the southern edge of the city centre, across av Jean-Biray: *SNCF* buses leave from here, and private buses from the **gare routière** in rue Michel-Houneau. **Buses** run south down the Vallée d'Ossau and to Oloron-Ste-Marie, with connections to the Vallée d'Aspe. A **free funicular** carries you up from the train station to the bd des Pyrénées, opposite place Royale, at the far end of which is the **tourist office** (Mon–Sat 9am–noon & 2–6pm; July & Aug daily 9am–12.30pm & 2–7pm; ☎59.27.27.08). Several organizations have **information on walking and climbing**: the local *CAF*, 5 rue Fournets (☎59.27.71.81), *Amis du Parc National,* 32 rue Samonzet (☎59.27.15.30), *Pyrénéa-Sports*, 12 rue des Bains (☎59.27.23.11), and *Randonneurs Pyrénéens*, 9 rue Latapie (☎59.30.22.48); the *Librairie des Pyrénées* in rue St-Louis stocks a wide range of books on the mountains.

For a very friendly, cheap and quiet **hotel**, try the *Hôtel d'Albret*, 11 rue Jeanne-d'Albret, close to the castle (☎59.27.81.58; ①). A good alternative that's almost equally central is the *Hôtel du Musée,* 17 rue Mathieu-Lalanne, opposite the Musée des Beaux-Arts (☎59.82.38.00; ①). For a bit more comfort, try the *Commerce* at 9 av Maréchal-Joffre (☎59.27.24.40; ③–④; restaurant 50–130F), or the *Colbert*, a few blocks north off rue Montpensier at 1 rue Manescan (☎59.32.52.78; ③–④; closed first week in May & Sept). For **youth hostels**, there's one at 30 rue Michel-Houneau (☎59.72.61.00; ①), the IYHF *Logis des Jeunes* in the Base de Plein Air at Gelos (☎59.06.57.37; ①), just over the river, and the *Maison Européenne de la Jeunesse*, 18 rue Bourbaki, at the end of rue Montpensier (☎59.62.50.50; canteen). The *Logis des Jeunes* also has a **campsite**, and there is a municipal one on bd du Cami-Salie, off av Sallenave towards the autoroute, on the northern edge of town (Whitsun to mid-Sept), as well as *Camping du Coy*, behind the *gare SNCF* at the Base Plein Air, Bizanos (mid-May to mid-Oct).

The Town

Pau has no great sights or museums, which leaves you free to enjoy its relaxed and friendly elegance at leisure. The parts to wander are the streets behind the **boulevard des Pyrénées**, especially the western end, which stretches along the rim of the scarp above the Gave de Pau, from the castle to the casino in the English-style **Parc Beaumont**. On a clear day, the view from the boulevard is out of this world, encompassing a sixty-mile sweep of the highest Pyrenean peaks, with the distinctive Pic du Midi d'Ossau slap in front of you.

In the narrow streets around the castle and down in the gully of the Chemin du Hédas are numerous cafés, restaurants, bars and boutiques, with the main **market** in the *halles* on place de la République each Wednesday and Saturday morning. The **château** itself (daily 9.30–11.45am & 2–5.45pm, mid-Oct to mid-April closes 4.45pm; guided tours only for royal apartments; 27F) is very much a landmark building. Not much remains of its original appearance beyond the brick keep built by Gaston Fébus in 1370, with handsome Renaissance windows and other details on the inner courtyard added by Henri d'Albret. Louis-Philippe renovated it in the nineteenth century after it had stood empty for two hundred years, and Napoléon III and Eugénie titivated it further to make it suitable for weekend house parties. The visitable apartments are essentially theirs, with some fine tapestries and bits of Henri-IV memorabilia, like the turtle shell that allegedly served him for a cradle, while the ethnographic **Musée Béarnais** (8F) on the top floor has a good collection of costumes, Pyrenean animals, birds, butterflies and objects illustrating pastoral life.

A short distance northeast of the château, the mildly interesting **Musée Bernadotte**, 5 rue Tran (daily except Mon 10am–noon & 2–6pm; 10F), is the birthplace of the man who, having served as one of Napoléon's commanders, went on to become Charles XIV of Sweden. As well as fine pieces of traditional Béarnais furniture, the house contains some valuable works of art collected over his lifetime. Pau's other museum, the **Musée des Beaux-Arts** in rue Mathieu-Lalanne (daily except Tues 10am–noon & 2–6pm; 10F), has a splendidly eclectic collection of works, including Spanish, Italian, Dutch and French schools, and works by El Greco, Rubens and Degas.

Eating and drinking

Of the several **restaurants** in the area of the château, *La Brochetterie*, 16 rue Henri-IV, serves good grills and fish in a pleasant, family atmosphere for around 100F *à la carte*, or from 75F for a *menu fixe*. *La Taverne du Roy*, 7 rue de la Fontaine, on the north side of the Hédas gully (closed Sat noon & Sun), offers more interesting Spanish-influenced menus from 80F, or if Chinese food takes your fancy, there's the excellent *Lotus d'Or*, 1 pl Grammont, with menus from 89F. Other inexpensive possibilities include the lunchtime-only *Royalty*, 4 rue Serviez (menus from 50F), crêpes and salads at *Chez Maman*, 6 rue du Château (menus 40–120F), and decent pizzas at the *Taste-Croûte*, 16 rue Latapic (menus from 40F). For a bit of a splash without breaking the bank, try *La Gousse d'Ail*, 12 rue du Hédas (closed Sun), with traditional French dishes from 98F, or near the station, *Au Fin Gourmet*, 24 av Gaston-Lacoste (menus from 85F).

Brasseries include the popular *Le Berry* on place Clemenceau and the *Forum* in av de l'Université. The small *O'Gascon* on the corner of rue Bordenave-d'Abère and rue du Château is a fun **bar**, as are the typical student hang-outs of *Le Sully*, at 13 rue Henri-IV, which sometimes has live music, *Bar de la Poste* in cours Bosquet, and *Le Béarnais*, at the eastern end of rue Guichenné.

Around Pau

Thirty kilometres northwest of Pau and renowned for the exploits of its basketball team, **ORTHEZ** was the original capital of Béarn, its wealth due in large part to its beautiful and still surviving thirteenth-century **fortified bridge**, which controlled the most important commercial route across the Gave de Pau for English and Flemish textiles, Aragonese wool, olive oil and wine. It was also a major centre on the pilgrim routes to Compostella; the modern route, the **GR65**, crosses the river just 8km east of Orthez at Aragnon; you can follow it 60km south to the Spanish frontier. The town also serves as a gateway to the hinterland of the Pays Basque: *SNCF* buses run from Puyôo, 12km west, to Salies-de-Béarn, Sauveterre and Mauléon.

The **tourist office** occupies the sixteenth-century **Maison Jeanne d'Albret**, and there are other fine old houses in the centre of town, especially in **rue Moncade**. The **church of St-Pierre**, close to the tourist office, still has some interesting Gothic sculptures, though it was badly damaged when the town was sacked by Jeanne d'Albret's Protestant general Montgomery in 1569. Should you need to **stay** overnight, there is the *Hôtel Terminus,* 14 rue St-Gilles (☎59.69.02.07; ②), and a **campsite**, *La Source* (June to mid-Sept), on the east side of the town.

Fifteen kilometres from Orthez (*TPR* bus from Pau), **SALIES-DE-BÉARN** is a typical Béarnais village of winding lanes and flower-decked houses with brightly painted woodwork. The River Saleys, hardly more than a stream, runs through the middle of it, separating the old village from the nineteenth-century development that sprang up to exploit the saline waters for which it has long been famous. It is a charming, if unremarkable place, good for an overnight stop, with a **camping municipal** (mid-March to mid-Oct), and a tiny IYHF **youth hostel** (☎59.38.29.66; ①), both on the rugby pitch.

Heading south again, the D933 winds over hilly farming country to **SAUVETERRE-DE-BÉARN**, another pretty country town beautifully sited on a scarp high above the Gave d'Oloron. From the terrace by the thirteenth-century **church** you look down over the river and the remains of another fortified bridge. At the end of the terrace a ruined **castle** dominates the steep slope, its empty joist sockets making perfect pigeon holes. For **accommodation**, there is the *Hostellerie du Château* in rue Léon-Bérard (☎59.38.52.10; ③; closed Jan), and a **campsite** by the bridge.

Just across the river, the D936 bears left along the flat valley bottom to **NAVARRENX**, 18km away on the Pau–Mauléon bus route, an old-fashioned market town built as a *bastide* in 1316 and still surrounded by its ancient **walls**; you enter by the fortified **Porte-St-Antoine**. The pleasure of the place is its sleepy rural atmosphere. The *Hôtel du Commerce* by the Porte St-Antoine (☎59.66.50.16; ①–③; closed mid-Oct to Nov 2; excellent restaurant from 100F), makes an agreeable place to **stay**, and there's also a **camping municipal** in Chemin des Lauriers (mid-June to mid-Sept).

The **GR65** passes through the town. You pick up the markers on the telephone poles in Susmiou at the western end of the bridge. Turn left over the bridge on the Mauléon road, then right on a back road shortly after. The path meanders west, following by-roads, farm tracks and footpaths to the vicinity of St-Palais, where it turns southwest to follow the main St-Palais–to–St-Jean-Pied-de-Port road. To hitch to Mauléon, keep going to the intersection with the Sauveterre–Oloron road and go straight on. It is wooded, hilly country all the way.

Lourdes

LOURDES, about 30km southeast of Pau, has just one function. Over six million Catholic pilgrims arrive here each year, and the town is totally given over to looking after and exploiting them. Lourdes was hardly more than a village before 1858, when Bernadette Soubirous, the fourteen-year-old daughter of an ex-miller, had the first of eighteen visions of the Virgin Mary in a cave here. Since then, Lourdes has grown a great deal, and it is now one of the biggest attractions in this part of France, many of its visitors hoping for a miraculous cure for scientifically intractable ailments.

The first large-scale **pilgrimage** took place in 1873, organized by a reactionary Catholic movement called the *Assomptionnistes*, who took over the management of Lourdes, shoving aside the local priest who had wanted to organize the pilgrimages himself. Over a hundred years later, it's hard to be charitable about the place. Practically every shop is given over to the sale of indescribable religious kitsch: Bernadette in every shape and size, adorning barometers, thermometers, plastic tree trunks, key rings, perfume bottles, bellows, candles, sweets, and illuminated plastic grottoes. Clustered around the miraculous grotto are the churches of the **Cité Réligeuse**, an annex to the town proper that sprang up last century. The first to be built was the flamboyant **Basilique du Rosaire et de l'Immaculée Conception** (1871), swiftly followed by the massive subterranean **Basilique St-Pie-X**, which claims to be able to house 20,000 people at a time. But the less said about their architecture the better: Woody Allen, who joked that he would come here when he'd completed psychoanalysis, would be impressed. The **Grotte de Massabielle** itself, where Bernadette had her visions, is the focus of the pilgrimages, but it's no more than a moisture-blackened overhang by the riverside with a statue of the Virgin in waxwork white and baby blue. Suspended in front are a row of rusting crutches, offered as ex-votos by the putative cured.

Lourdes' only secular attraction is its **château**, poised on a rocky bluff guarding the approaches to the valleys and passes of the central Pyrenees. Briefly an English stronghold in the late fourteenth century, it later became a state prison. Inside, it houses the surprisingly excellent **Musée Pyrénéen** (daily except Tues 9–11am & 2–5pm; July & Aug daily 9–11am & 2–6pm; 26F). Its collections include Pyrenean fauna, all sorts of fascinating pastoral and farming gear, and an interesting section on the history of Pyrenean mountaineering. In the rock garden outside are some beautiful models of various Pyrenean styles of house, as well as of the churches of St-Bertrand-de-Comminges and Luz-St-Sauveur.

Practicalities

Lourdes' **gare SNCF** is on the northeast edge of the town centre, at the end of av de la Gare; the **gare routière** is in the central place Capdevieille, and the **tourist office** is in place Peyramale (daily 9am–noon & 2–7pm, Sun 10am–noon; mid-Oct to Easter Mon–Sat 9am–noon & 2–6pm; ☎62.42.77.40).

Although it is very thin on good restaurants, Lourdes has more **hotels** than any city in France outside Paris. There's masses of cheap accommodation in the small central streets around the castle, while **hostel** accommodation can be had at the *Centre Pax Christi*, 4 rte de la Forêt (☎62.94.00.66; ①), and *Camp des Jeunes*, Ferme Milhas, av de Monseigneur-Rodhain (①), both on the western edge of town, although the lattter is reserved for genuine pilgrims. The nearest **campsites** (both May to mid-Oct) are the *Poste*, 16 rue de Langelle, just south of the *gare SNCF*, and the *Fronton*, 60 rue de Bagnères, the next parallel street to the south.

Tarbes

Twenty minutes away by train to the north, **TARBES** is useful as a base for visiting Lourdes or launching into the mountains to the south, although apart from that, there is little to draw your attention. If you have an interest in military history, the **Musée Massey** (daily 10am–noon & 2–6pm; 25F), in the very attractive **Jardin Massey** near the train station, houses an extensive collection of cavalry uniforms – principally nineteenth- and twentieth-century hussars, but including samples of other European and US cavalry regiments. They are splendidly extravagant, the epitome of that old-fashioned quality of "dash", which was supposed to make ladies' hearts flutter at glittering balls. The Napoléonic stud farm, **Les Haras**, 70 av du Régiment-de-Bigorre, set in acres of beautiful grounds, is also worth seeing (July to mid-Sept, Oct 21–29 & Dec 21–

31 daily 2–3.15pm & 4.30pm; 20F). The farm is best known for the *cheval Tarbais*, bred from English and Moorish stock as a cavalry horse, and you can watch them drilling at certain times of the year (July–Feb Mon–Fri 2.30–5.30pm). A final sight is the house where **Maréchal Foch**, supreme Allied commander in World War I, was born at 2 rue de la Victoire (Thurs–Mon 8am–noon & 2–5.15pm; 15F), a missable repository of various family and personal mementos.

The **gare SNCF** is on av Joffre, north of the centre (☎62.37.50.50), and the **gare routière** on the other side of town on place au Bois, off rue Larrey. The **tourist office** is on place de Verdun, where rue Massey meets rue Lassalle (Mon–Sat 8.30am–noon & 2.30–6pm; ☎62.51.30.31). Tarbes has some reasonable **hotels** in the vicinity of the station, like the *Hôtel Izard*, 70 av Joffre (☎62.93.06.69; ③; good restaurant from 56F), or *Hôtel Normandie*, 33 rue Massey (☎62.93.08.47; ①–②), as well as an IYHF **youth hostel** at 88 av Alsace-Lorraine (☎62.36.63.63; ①).

The valleys of the Aspe and Ossau

The parallel north–south valleys of the **Aspe** and **Ossau** are the French Pyrenees at their most *sauvage*, and the region in which the Pyrenean brown bear most tenaciously resists extinction. About a dozen survive on the slopes of the valleys, in the **Cirque de Lescun** and in the adjoining parts of Spain.

Tourism is less developed here, especially in the Aspe Valley, because of the unreliable snow conditions for skiing, but what tourism has failed to do, a major road-building scheme threatens to achieve two-fold. To see the best of the region you should get out your map and walk, camping – with permission, of course – in the isolated farms along the way.

Along the Aspe

The valley of the Aspe begins at the grey town of **OLORON-STE-MARIE**, around 45km west of Lourdes, where the mountain streams of the Aspe and Ossau meet. It is served by train from Pau as well as by *Citram* buses, with five daily *SNCF* buses continuing down the valley to Urdos and three to Canfranc in Spain. The town's claim to fame is as the centre of the manufacture of the famous woollen pancake-shaped *beret Basque*, once the standard apparel for all French men but now seldom seen on any but greybeards. However, the only real points of interest for the visitor are the town's two churches: **Ste-Croix**, one of the oldest Romanesque buildings in Béarn, with unusual interior vaulting copied from the Great Mosque at Cordoba, and the **Cathédrale Ste-Marie**, which boasts an unusually beautiful Romanesque portal in Pyrenean marble, supported by two chained slaves. In the upper arch, the elders of the Apocalypse play violins and rebecs, while in the second arch scenes from medieval life are represented – a cooper, the slaying of a wild boar, fishing for salmon. The gallant knight on horseback over the outer column on the right is Gaston IV, Count of Béarn, who commissioned the portal on his return from the first Crusade at the beginning of the twelfth century, hence the reference to Saracens in chains among the sculptures. The magnificent studded doors were a present from Henri IV. Inside, well away from the main area of worship, is a stoup reserved for the use of the Cagots, a stark reminder of the centuries-long persecution and segregation of this mysterious group of people, thought by some to have been lepers and by others to have been perhaps of Visigoth origin.

Oloron's **tourist office** is in place de la Résistance (Tues–Sat 9am–noon & 2–6pm; summer Mon–Sat 9am–12.30pm & 2–7.30pm, Sun 9am–12.30pm). Should you find yourself stuck here, there are a couple of reasonable **hotels** – the *Hôtel de la Paix*, 24 av Sadi-

Carnot near the train station (☎59.39.35.78; ②–③), and *Le Nautilus* in place Clemenceau (☎59.39.04.72; ②), as well as a **camping municipal** on the D919 Arrette road (☎59.39.11.36; June–Oct).

The Goutte d'Eau and Chemin de la Mâture

The narrow enclosed world of the valley proper begins south of Oloron at the village of **ESCOT**, where a beautiful side route, the D294, climbs through beech woods to the **Col de Marie Blanque** and down to Bielle in the Vallée d'Ossau. It's a steep green world where the eye is perpetually carried upwards. South of Escot, the road follows the river through narrow defiles, past the attractive riverside villages of **SARRANCE**, where there is **gîte accommodation** at *Accueil au Monastère* (☎59.34.72.07); there's also a **youth hostel** close by up the mountain at Lourdios (☎59.34.46.39; ①); buses run as far as Asasp. Beyond Sarrance, **BEDOUS** has more **accommodation** – and food – at the cheap and very friendly *Le Choucas Blanc*, 4 rue Gambetta (☎59.34.53.71; ①), and a **gîte d'étape** (☎59.34.73.23) in nearby **OSSE-EN-ASPE**. There's another **gîte** a little further south at **L'ESTANGUET**, near the turning for Lescun (☎59.34.72.30). Beyond here, **CETTE EYGUN** has, in its old train station between the road and the river, an extremely friendly **restaurant-bar-gîte**, *La Goutte d'Eau* (☎59.34.78.83; food around 65F) – cooperatively run, and also a centre for information about the surrounding mountains. There is additional accommodation in an old train carriage parked on the tracks, and camping space on the banks of the river.

Beyond Eygun, the road continues up the valley to **ETSAUT**, where there's a food shop, a *gîte d'étape* (☎59.34.88.98), a **Maison du Parc** (☎59.34.88.30) for information on walks and accommodation in the Parc National des Pyrénées Occidentales (see p.620), and the *Hôtel des Pyrénées* (☎59.34.88.62; ③). **BORCE**, an attractive medieval village on the west flank of the valley, is home to another *gîte d'étape* (☎59.34.70.87) and the squat, menacing **Fort du Portalet**, in which Léon Blum was imprisoned by Pétain's Vichy government, and then Pétain himself after the liberation of France. Just before the fort, at the Pont de Cebers, the GR10 to the left leads to the **Chemin de la Mâture**, an eighteenth-century mule path hacked out of the precipitous rock slabs that form the sides of a dizzy ravine, facilitating the transport of tree trunks felled for use as ships' masts. The path is broad enough, but if you don't like heights, keep away from the edge. The GR10 reaches the **Lacs d'Ayous refuge** opposite the Pic du Midi d'Ossau (see p.629) in about five hours. Further on, at **URDOS**, you pass through French customs; you can **stay** at the *Hôtel des Voyageurs* (☎59.34.88.05; ①–③). From here, three buses a day continue over the **Col de Somport** and the Spanish frontier post (daily 8am–10pm; mid-June to mid-Sept open 24hr) and on to Canfranc in Spain, the terminus for trains from Jaca.

Lescun

Six steep kilometres above the N134 at L'Estanguet, the ancient grey stone houses of **LESCUN** huddle tightly together on the north slopes of a huge and magnificent green cirque. The bowl of the cirque and the lower slopes, dimpled with vales and hollows, have been gently and harmoniously shaped by generations of farming, while to the west it is overlooked by the great grey molars of **Le Billare** and **Le Petit Billare**, beyond whose shoulders bristle further leaning teeth of rock and the snow-slashed bulk of the **Pic d'Anie** (2504m). Below the village in the hollow of the cirque, the *Camping Le Lauzart* must be one of the best sites anywhere, with an uninterrupted view of the peaks and no sound to disturb beyond the chiming of cow bells. If you're on foot, be sure to take provisions with you – it is some way from the village and the only food shop. Lescun also has a **hotel**, the *Pic d'Anie* (☎59.34.71.54; ③; restaurant evenings only), and a **gîte d'étape**, 1500m west of the village (☎59.34.71.61).

The obvious **walk** in the area is along the GR10 in the direction of La-Pierre-St-Martin. From Lescun, the path keeps close to the road as far as the refuge of *Labérouat*

(☎59.34.50.43) – around a two-hour walk – then crosses meadows before entering beech forest beneath the organ-pipe crags of **Les Orgues de Camplong**, with fantastic views of the pine-stippled ridges of the Billares. It emerges above the tree line in a long, flower-strewn, hanging valley by the primitive **Cabane d'Ardinet**, reaching the shepherds' hut at **Cap de la Baitch** (1700m) in a further ninety minutes. From there you can either continue on the GR towards La-Pierre-St-Martin via the Pas d'Azuns, or swing south for the Col des Anies and the Pic d'Anie (see below) – a good two to three hours.

Along the Ossau

The **Ossau Valley** is notable mainly for the distinctive Pic du Midi and some beautiful lakeland settings. The valley is served by both *Citram* and *SNCF* **buses** as far as Laruns. At weekends in July and August, one *SNCF* bus goes on to Gabas and Artouste-Fabrèges, while *Citram* continues to Gourette every day from July to mid-September and again in the skiing season.

Between Pau and Laruns, the only place worth stopping at is **ARUDY**, principally to see the **Maison d'Ossau** (Sat & Sun 2.30–6.30pm; July & Aug daily 10am–noon & 2.30–6.30pm; free), which offers a comprehensive account of the prehistoric Pyrenees and an exhibition of the flora and fauna of the Parc National.

LARUNS, enclosed in the valley bottom by steep wooded heights, is of little interest in itself, although there are some fine old farms towards the river in the quarter known as Le Pon. If you **stay** here for the night, try *Hôtel de France* in rue de la Gare (☎59.05.33.71; ②–③; closed Dec), *Hôtel Le Lorry* on rte des Cols (☎59.05.31.22; ②), or *L'Embaradère* refuge, 13 av de la Gare (☎59.05.41.88; ①; meal from 60F). The nearest **campsites** are *Le Gourzy* and *Le Lauguère* in Le Pon. The **tourist office** is in the main place de la Mairie (daily 9am–12.30pm & 2–6.30pm; ☎59.05.13.41). If you are heading for the Pic du Midi d'Ossau, it is best to stock up with provisions in Laruns.

Gabas

The road to **GABAS**, 13km away, winds steeply into the upper reaches of the Gave d'Ossau Valley, south of Laruns. On days when there is no bus, you should get a lift without much difficulty from other walkers or employees of the Parc National des Pyrénées Occidentales (see p.620), especially early in the morning. Primarily a base for climbers and walkers, there is nothing to it beyond a minuscule chapel, the **Maison du Parc** and its useful walking information (daily 10am–noon & 2–5.30pm), a *CAF* **refuge** (☎59.05.33.14; meals from 65F), and a couple of **hotels** – *Le Biscau* (☎59.05.31.37; ①–③; restaurant from 45F), and *Le Vignau* (☎59.05.34.06; ②–③), both with restaurants.

Pic du Midi d'Ossau

The **Pic du Midi**, with its rocky twin-peaked 2884-metre summit, is a classic Pyrenean landmark, visible for miles around. From Gabas, it is a steep 4.5-kilometre climb up a wooded ravine to the artificial **Lac de Bious-Artigues**, so named because it flooded the *artigue* – a Pyrenean word for mountain pasture – that formerly existed beside the infant *gave*. Just below the dam are the stony terraces of *Camping Bious-Oumettes* (July & Aug), that also has a small provisions shop open around mid-June to September. Beside the lake, right under the Pic, is the *Refuge Pyrénéa Sports* (☎59.05.32.12; June 6–Oct). The area within immediate reach of the road gets very crowded in summer and the refuges are likely to be full at weekends; it's worth phoning ahead.

A round trip of the peak, excluding the summit, takes about seven hours. It can be broken by a **stay** at the *CAF Refuge de Pombie* (☎59.05.31.78; mid-June to Sept), below the vast southern walls of the dam. From the lake, follow the GR10 up the left bank of the *gave* and past the turning to the Lacs d'Ayous (see below). Cross the Pont de Bious and continue upstream across an expanse of flat meadow until you come to a signpost indicating **Lac de Peyreget** to the left. There follows a steepish zigzagging climb to the timber line and a long traverse right to the junction with the HRP path (1hr from *Pyrénéa Sports*). Keep left, with the ground falling away on your right. At the **Lac de Peyreget**, you can either follow the HRP steeply left towards the **Col de Peyreget**, or alternatively keep right – due south – to the **Col d'Iou**. From the latter, traverse left, following the contour to the **Col de Soum**, where you turn north towards the **Refuge de Pombie** (about 4hr). The path continues north back to *Pyrénéa Sports* (about 3hr) via the **Col de Suzon**, where the standard ascent of the Pic begins, the **Col de Moundelhs** and the **Col Long de Magnabaigt**.

There is a path off the mountain from the Col du Soum, and another from the Pombie refuge. The latter leads due east down the valley of the Pombie stream, through meadows full of daffodils, orchids, violets and fritillaries in June, where you might catch a glimpse of izards. At the **Cabane de Puchéou**, a shepherd's hut, cross to the left bank of the stream and carry on down to the next bridge. The HRP continues on the left bank past the Cabane d'Arrégatiou and comes out at the southern end of the **Lac de Fabrèges**. The right-hand path crosses the bridge and descends through woods to the **Gave de Brousset** at Soques (about 2hr from Pombie), where you join the Col du Pourtalet road (which leads to the Spanish frontier) and can hitch back to Gabas.

Lac d'Artouste

A short distance out of Gabas the Pourtalet road passes the **Lac de Fabrèges**, from where a *téléférique* swings up to the 2032-metre Pic de la Sagette to connect with a **miniature rail line** that runs for 10km through the mountains to the **Lac d'Artouste**. Built in the 1920s to service a hydroelectric project, it was later converted for tourist purposes. Weather permitting, the train normally starts operating in early June and keeps going until mid- or late September. It is a beautiful trip, lasting about four hours, including time to walk down to the lake (74F, with a special 96F deal for walkers, allowing them to go out on the first train and return on the last). The first train leaves at 10am, but you need to allow half an hour on the *téléférique*. Don't forget to take warm clothes, as you'll be at an altitude of 2000m.

The Lacs d'Ayous

In the opposite direction from Gabas, this is another classic walk, in some ways more impressive than doing the Pic itself, especially if you spend the night by the lakes to get the quintessential dawn view of the peak silhouetted against the rising sun and reflected in the slaty waters of Lac Gentau.

It's a steady ninety-minute climb from *Pyrénéa-Sports*. Instead of crossing the Pont de Bious, turn up the GR10 to the right through woods of pine and beech, with ever-widening views of the valley scattered with herds of horses and cows and flocks of sheep. The meadows are full of orchids and the stream banks thick with azalea-like alpenrose. You pass the three small **Lacs d'Ayous**. The third and largest is **Lac Gentau**, whose reddish shallows are full of minnows that presumably turn into the trout so sought after by numerous fishermen. On its banks there's an expanse of flat, soft meadow for camping, while above it stands the *Refuge d'Ayous* at 1960m (☎59.05.37.00; June 6 to mid-Sept). Over the Col d'Ayous behind it, the GR10 continues west to the Chemin de la Mâture and the Aspe Valley (see p.626).

The Col d'Aubisque and the road to Cauterets

The only way of reaching Cauterets by road without going back towards Pau is via the **Col d'Aubisque**, a grassy, rounded ridge 17km long and nearly 1000m above Laruns. There's a café on the top, served in July and August by a single afternoon bus from Laruns. It is also hitchable; if you're hitching on, remember that the next possible stopping place is 18km away, so it's best to stay close to the café.

The col is an important grazing ground, with tremendous views over the valleys below and the rocky precipices of the 2613-metre **Pic de Ger** to the south. It is also a favourite place for slaughtering the migrating wood pigeons in autumn, as witness the numerous shooting butts along the ridge. The *Tour de France* passes this way, making the col an irresistible challenge to any French cyclist worth his or her salt. You see swarms of them toiling up, making it a matter of pride to find the breath for a cheery *bonjour*.

Cauterets and the cirques of Gavarnie and Troumouse

Cauterets, 25km due south of Lourdes, and **Gavarnie**, a further 20km southeast, are established resorts on the edge of the Parc National des Pyrénées Occidentales, and the country they give access to is so spectacular that you should not miss it. Both towns are served by *SNCF* buses from Lourdes via the valley of the Gave de Pau. As ever, if you pick your season right or even the time of day, you can still enjoy the most popular sites in relative solitude. At Gavarnie, for instance, few people stay the night, so it is quiet in the early morning and evening, and **Troumouse**, which is just as impressive in its way (though much harder to get to without a car), has very few visitors. As for more conventional sights, there are interesting churches at **Luz-St-Sauveur** and **St-Savin**.

Aucun and St-Savin

Between Lourdes and Cauterets, 8km southwest of the dull town of Argelès-Gazost, **AUCUN** is worth a short detour for its small but fascinating private folk museum, the **Musée du Lavedan** (May–Oct Mon–Sat 10am–noon & 2–5.30pm; 15F), while, heading south from Argelès, it's worth taking a look at the twelfth century **abbey church** at **ST-SAVIN**, to the right of the main road, with its fortifications and fine Romanesque doorway. Inside it boasts a magnificient Spanish wooden Christ, an interesting stoup, and amusing organ cabinet carved with grotesque faces that were designed to pull grimaces as the music played.

Cauterets and around

Thirty kilometres south of Lourdes, **CAUTERETS** is a pleasant if unexciting little town that owes its fame and its rather elegant Neoclassical architecture to its waters, much in demand now for the treatment of rheumatism and ear, nose and throat complaints. In modern times, it has also become one of the main Pyrenean ski and mountaineering centres, and a good base for the Parc National des Pyrénées Occidentales.

The town's origins as a spa began with Count Raymond de Bigorre's grant of land to the monks of St-Savin in 945. In the seventeenth century, Marguerite d'Angoulême came to take the waters and wrote her *Heptameron* here, but the town reached its heyday in the eighteenth and nineteenth centuries: Hugo visited, as did Chateaubriand, Baudelaire, Debussy, Edward VII and many other celebrities.

The modern town is so small that there is no difficulty in finding your way around. Most of it is still squeezed between the steep wooded heights that close the mouth of the Gave de Cauterets Valley. Next door to the **gare routière** on the north edge of the centre, the **Maison du Parc** (daily 9am–noon & 2–6pm) has a small museum of the flora and fauna, and film shows on Wednesday and Saturday in season. In the small centre of the town, two minutes' walk from here, you'll find the **tourist office** in place Clemenceau (Mon–Sat 9am–12.30pm & 2–6pm, Sun 9am–noon; July & Aug Mon–Sat 9am–7pm, Sun 9am–noon & 4–7pm; ☎62.92.50.27). Not far away, the **Maison de la**

Montagne, 5 av Leclerc (☎62.92.58.16), has information on the state of the mountain paths and climbs, book and map shops, and places to **eat**.

If you're staying, affordable **hotels** include *Le Béarn*, 4 av Leclerc (☎62.92.53.54; ①), *Le Centre-Poste*, 10 rue de Belfort (☎62.92.52.69; ①–②), and *Le Bigorre*, 15 rue de Belfort (☎62.92.52.81; ①–②; rooms for 4 280F; restaurant from 75F; closed Nov–April). For something a little more upmarket, try the *César*, 3 rue César (☎62.92.52.57; ①–③; closed March 20–May & Oct 1–26). The cheapest accommodation is in the **gîtes** – *Le Cluquet*, on av du Dr-Domer past the *télésiège du Lys* and the tennis courts (☎62.92.52.95; summer only; space for camping), *Le Pas de l'Ours*, 1 rue Galliéni (☎62.92.58.07), and *Captur* at Concé, just outside town on the Lourdes road (☎62.92.54.02). There are several **campsites** along the Lourdes road, one of the quietest being *Les Bergeronnettes* (June–Sept), across the river on the right before you reach the roadside *Les Glères*.

For **food**, the *Brasserie Le Paris* in place Clemenceau is a friendly and very reasonable establishment. Other places to try include the cafés *Le Béarn* and *Le Commerce* in av Leclerc and the pizzeria *Giovanni* in rue de la Raillère.

Around Cauterets: some hikes

The classic excursion from Cauterets is up the Val de Jéret to the **Pont d'Espagne**, where the Gave de Gaube and Gave du Marcadau hurtle together in a boiling spume of spray, before rushing down to Cauterets over a series of spectacular waterfalls. For a beautiful and tourist-free route, take the **Parc National path** from **LA RAILLÈRE**, 3km from Cauterets (regular buses). It runs all the way beside the stream through woods of beech and pine to come out by the café-bar at Pont d'Espagne (about 2hr up, 90min down).

From Pont d'Espagne, you can fork right up the **Marcadau Valley** to the *Refuge Wallon* (about 5hr round trip), or left up into the alpine valley of the Gave de Gaube, with the lovely little **Lac de Gaube** backed by the snowy wall and glaciers of **Vignemale** (3298m). There is even a *télésiège* (27F return) to save you the first part of the ascent. Beyond the lake, the path continues to the *CAF Refuge des Oulettes* below the north face of Vignemale (about 3hr from Pont d'Espagne), from where you can return to La Raillère via the *Refuge de Baysellance* and the beautiful and quieter **Lutour Valley** (7hr round trip).

A less-frequented walk from Cauterets is to the **Lac d'Ilhéou** along the **GR10** (about 3hr). To avoid the initial steep climb you can take the *télécabine du Lys* (36F return) to the **gare intermédiaire de Cambasque**, crossing the stream there and continuing up the right bank to the **Cabane de Courbet**, where you follow a track, first on the left bank, then on the right. After a short distance, the GR10 leaves the track and climbs up the slope to the left, steadily gaining height to cross a chute of boulders beside the long white thread of the **Cascade d'Ilhéou** waterfall. Over the rim of the chute, you come to a small lake, with the **Refuge d'Ilhéou** in sight ahead on the shore of the lake – it's very pretty in June, with snow still on the surrounding peaks and ice floes drifting on its still surface.

For other ideas for hiking, ask at the Cauterets tourist office (see p.630).

Luz-St-Sauveur and the road to Bagnères de Bigorre

The only approach to Gavarnie and Troumouse, best known of the Pyrenean cirques, is through **LUZ-ST-SAUVEUR**, on the GR10 and the daily bus route from Lourdes. It, too, was a nineteenth-century spa, patronized by Napoléon III and Eugénie, and it owes its elegant Neoclassical façades in the centre to this period.

Its principal sight is the **church of St-André**. Built in the late twelfth century and fortified in the fourteenth by the Knights of St John, it's a classic of its kind, with a crenellated outer wall and two stout towers. The entrance, beneath one of the towers, sports a handsome porch surmounted by a Christ in Majesty carved in fine-grained local stone. The lanes around about are crammed with **market stalls** every Monday.

The **tourist office**, with a *Bureau des Guides* (daily 9am–noon & 2.30–6pm; ☎62.92.81.60), is in the central place du 8-mai, by the crossroads for Gavarnie. Two **hotels** to try are the *Remparts* (☎62.92.81.70; ①–②; restaurant from 75F; closed May to mid-June & Oct to mid-Dec), beside the church, and the *Londres* (☎62.92.80.09; ④; closed Nov & Dec) on the riverbank in the town centre. There's another **campsite** and **gîte d'étape** at *Les Cascades* (☎62.92.82.15), uphill from the church. The *Camping Le Toy* is near the tourist office (☎62.92.86.85; Jan–April & June–Sept). Another very agreeable and only slightly more expensive place to stay is the *Hôtel La Brèche de Roland* (☎62.92.48.54; ③–④; closed Oct–mid-Dec; restaurant from 75F), 12km south in **GÈDRE**, where the road divides for the Cirque de Troumouse. There are a couple of campsites nearby as well.

The road to Bagnères de Bigorre

From Luz-St-Sauveur begins the 18-kilometre pull up to the **Col du Tourmalet**, one of the major torments of the *Tour de France*. The only village in between is **BARÈGES**, 7km away, linked with Lourdes by buses via Luz. It has been popular as a spa – its waters renowned for the treatment of gunshot wounds – since 1677, when it was visited by Madame de Maintenon with her infant charge, the seven-year-old Duc de Maine, son of Louis XIV; today it is a skiing and mountaineering centre. The **GR10** passes through and numerous other trails lead off into the **Néouvielle Massif**, full of lakes and highly recommended as a walking area.

Above Barèges, the road continues up a huge denuded valley, with clusters of stone *bergeries* dug into the slope. At its head, the **Pic du Midi de Bigorre** (2872m) comes into view, crossed by the Col du Tourmalet, which at 2115m is the highest road pass in the Pyrenees. It's a desolate, windy spot with a track – you have to pay – leading off left to the Pic and its observatory, still going strong and continuously staffed since its opening in 1882. There's a small **museum** inside (summer daily 1–6pm; 15F), featuring an unprepossessing array of observatory bits and pieces.

Over the col, the road descends steeply past the monstrously ugly ski resort of **LA MONGIE** into lovely woods of spruce, pine and beech, continuing down to the gentle green **Campan Valley**, whose meadows are dotted with farms all turned south in ranks to face the sun. The architecture is quite distinct from the valleys to the west. The roofs are still slate, but house and barn are built in line as one building, with the balconied living quarters always to the right as you face the sun. In the village of **CAMPAN** there is an interesting sixteenth-century **covered market**, old houses and another curious-looking fortified **church**. School buses cover the 6km from here to **BAGNÈRES DE BIGORRE**, another Pyrenean spa town trying to refurbish its somewhat faded image, but not a place to make a special stop. *SNCF* **buses** leave for Tarbes from the **gare SNCF** on av de Belgique just north of the town centre. Two buses daily continue south to Ste-Marie-de-Campan and, in summer, on to the Lac de Payolle, from where it is possible to hitch on over the pine-covered Col d'Aspin to Arreau in the Aure Valley. The **tourist office** is in allées Tournefort (Tues–Sat 9am–noon & 2.30–6pm; ☎62.95.50.71), close to the leafy allées des Coustous, the main drag, lined with cafés. If you need to stay, there are reasonable **rooms** at the *Hôtel de Nice* (☎62.95.04.65; ①–②) and the *Hôtel de l'Horloge* in rue de l'Horloge (☎62.95.00.20; ①), near the market. There are several **campsites** around the town, too.

The Cirque de Gavarnie

South of Luz-St-Sauveur, **GAVARNIE**, a further 8km up the ravine from Gèdre, is connected with Luz by two daily bus services, or, if you're really into hiking, you could walk it on the GR10 that runs through the Parc National des Pyrénées Occidentales (see p.620). The village is a tacky and unpleasant mess of souvenir shops, car parks and snack bars. Poor and depopulated, it has found the attractions of mass tourism, much of it the excursion trade from Lourdes, too seductive to resist; the town stinks, too, from the droppings of the dozens of mules, donkeys and horses used to ferry visitors up to the cirque. However, the **Cirque de Gavarnie** itself is magnificent – Victor Hugo called it "Nature's Colisseum" – a natural amphitheatre scoured out by a glacier, of which barely the roots of the tongue remain. Nearly 1700m high, it consists of three sheer bands of rock discoloured by the striations of seepage and waterfalls, and separated by sloping ledges covered with snow. To the east, it is dominated by the jagged peaks of **Astazou** and **Marboré**, both over 3000m. In the middle, a corniced ridge sweeps round to Le Taillon, hidden behind the Pic des Sarradets, which stands slightly forward of the rim of the cirque, obscuring the **Brèche de Roland**, a curious vertical slash, 100m deep and about 60m wide, said to have been hewn from the ridge by Roland's sword, Durandal (see p.615).

Practicalities

For **weather information and snow conditions**, ask the *CRS* mountain rescue unit opposite *La Bergerie* or ring ☎62.32.97.77; for **park information**, there's the *Maison du Parc* (daily 10am–noon & 2.30–5.30pm; ☎62.92.49.10) as you come into the village.

As for **hotels**, the historic and unspoilt *Les Voyageurs* at the entrance of the village is much the nicest (☎62.92.48.01; ③–⑤); its "Golden Book" contains the signatures of Count Henry Russell, the eccentric pioneer of Pyrenean mountaineering, George Sand, Flaubert and Hugo among others; its beds witnessed the conception, so the whisper goes, of Napoléon III in an illicit encounter between Hortense de Beauharnais and a local *berger*. Otherwise, the best bets are the *CAF* **refuge**, *Les Granges de Holle* on the Port de Gavarnie road (☎62.92.48.77; closed Nov), which also does meals, or the **gîte d'étape** *Le Gypaète*, near the *Voyageurs* (☎62.92.48.01). If you are carrying a **tent**, there's nothing to beat Gavarnie's *Camping La Bergerie* (☎62.92.48.41; mid-May to Oct; bar and breakfast) on the true right bank of the *gave*, on the cirque side of the village. The facilities leave something to be desired, but the site is away from the crowds and its view gives right into the cirque. The other campsite, *Le Pain de Sucre* (☎62.92.47.55; July–Sept), is on the Luz side of the village. For a place to **eat**, *La Ruade* (June–Sept), also by the *Voyageurs*, is the best.

The cirque and around

It's an easy fifty minutes' walk from Gavarnie to the cirque. Luckily, the scale of it is sufficient to dwarf the tourists, but it is still best to go up before 10am or after 5pm, when the grandeur and silence are almost alarming and the dung less overpowering. The track ends at the *Hôtellerie du Cirque*, once a famous meeting place for mountaineers and now a snack bar. To get to the foot of the cirque walls, you have to clamber over slopes of frozen snow. Take care not to stand too close, especially in the afternoon, because of falling stones. To the left, the **Grande Cascade**, at 423m the highest waterfall in Europe, wavers and plumes down the rock faces – a fine sight in the morning, when it appears to pour right out of the eye of the sun. Scaling the cliffs is obviously a matter for climbers, but the relatively intrepid can get a powerful impression of the majesty of the place – and a superb vantage point for photography – by climbing the first stage of the **HRP path** to the *CAF* **Refuge des Sarradets**, which begins in the right-hand corner of the cirque at the edge of the first band of rock. The first hundred metres or so could be a little nerve-wracking if you are not used to heights, but in dry weather they are perfectly safe.

If you do not want to retrace your steps, an enjoyable and not too demanding walk back to Gavarnie is via the path from the *Hôtellerie* and up the east flank of the Gavarnie Valley to the **Refuge des Espuguettes** (about 3hr). It is a beautiful path, cut into rocky pine-shaded slopes. At the top, you emerge into open meadows, with the *Cabane de Pailla* in a hollow and the *Refuge des Espuguettes* (July–Sept) on a grassy bluff about a 45-minute climb above you; it's well worth the effort for the views of the cirque and the Brèche de Roland. The committed may want to go from here on to **Piméné**, the bare peak above you. It's a couple of easy – but slightly tedious – hours' climbing, and the view is fantastic: the Cirque d'Estaubé, Monte Perdido and away into Spain. To return to Gavarnie, turn right at the signpost below the refuge (allow 90min).

La Brêche de Roland

La Brêche de Roland is *the* walk to do in Gavarnie. It is high, and involves crossing a glacier, which means being properly equipped, preferably with ice axe and crampons. It is, however, extremely popular in summer, so there is a good chance of being able to team up with someone more experienced.

There are three approaches to the *Brêche*, all converging on the *Refuge des Sarradets* (☎62.92.40.41; May–Sept); contact the *CRS* in Gavarnie (☎62.92.48.24) for reservations at the refuge, which are always necessary in high season. The easiest route is up the road to the Port de Gavarnie/Col de Boucharo, where a clear path climbs under the north face of Le Taillon to join (1hr) the footpath coming directly from Gavarnie. This path starts beside the church, climbs steadily up the valley of Pouey Aspé, then zigzags steeply up to join the Port de Gavarnie path (4hr). From the junction of these two paths, it's less than an hour to the refuge. The third route (about 6hr in all from Gavarnie) is via the **Échelle des Sarradets** section of the HRP path (see above). The *Brêche* is about 40 minutes above the refuge.

The Cirque de Troumouse

A vast, wild, desolate place, much bigger than Gavarnie and, in bad weather, rather fright-ening, the **Cirque de Troumouse** lies up an equally desolate valley, whose only habita-tions are the handful of farmsteads that make up the hamlet of **HÉAS** – until the making of the road one of the loneliest outposts in France. There is **camping à la ferme** on the road to Héas, and **chambres d'hôte** in the hamlet. As you reach the head of the valley there is a toll gate, after which the road climbs in tight hairpins up treeless slopes to the *Auberge Le Maillet* (☎62.92.48.97; ①; June–Sept) by the side of a small tarn. After this it climbs again, even more steeply, beneath bare shining crags, to a car park with a white statue of the Virgin Mary crowning a grassy knoll, enclosed by the wide sweeping walls of the cirque and enough pasture to feed thousands of sheep. The close moorland turf is channelled with streams and cut into dingles and hummocks, where gentians and saxi-frage, sedums and houseleeks grow among the rock crevices. Beneath the walls of the cirque is a scatter of clear blue glacial lakelets, the **Lacs des Aires**. A *Parc National* path does the circuit from Héas.

The Comminges

Stretching from **Bagnères-de-Luchon** (Luchon for short) almost as far as Toulouse, the **Comminges** is an ancient feudal county that encompasses the upper valley of the River Garonne. It also boasts one of the finest buildings in the Pyrenees, the magnificent cathedral of St-Bertrand-de-Comminges, the product of three distinct periods of architecture. The mountainous southern part is what you will want to see, and access is via the unprepossess-ing little town of St-Gaudens, from where there are daily bus and train services to Luchon.

Valcabrère and St-Bertrand-de-Comminges

The village of **VALCABRÈRE** lies a short way south of Montréjeau (on the main Bayonne–Toulouse rail line), reached by *SNCF* bus (direction *Luchon*) to the hamlet of

Labroquère, by the Garonne, and strolling across the river. It's a little place of rough stone barns and open lofts for hay drying, with an exquisite Romanesque church in **St-Just-St-Pasteur** (daily 9am–noon & 2–7pm; Nov–April Sat & Sun 2–7pm), whose square tower rises above a cemetery full of cypress trees. The porch is elegantly sculpted and the apse, decorated with a kind of inverted arcading, is quite remarkable. Both interior and exterior are full of recycled masonry from the old Roman settlement of **Lugdunum Convenarum**, whose remains are visible at the crossroads just beyond the village. Founded by Pompey in 72 BC, this was a town of some 60,000 inhabitants at its apogee, making it one of the most important in Roman Aquitaine. Josephus, the Jewish historian, says it was the place of exile of Herod Antipas and his wife Herodias, who had John the Baptist decapitated. It was destroyed by Vandals in the fifth century and again by the Burgundians in the sixth century, after which it remained deserted until Bishop Bertrand began to build his cathedral around 1120.

Further on is **ST-BERTRAND-DE-COMMINGES**, whose grey fortress-like **cathedral** (Mon–Sat 9am–noon & 2–6pm, Sun 9–10.30am & 2–6/7pm; July & Aug daily 9am–7pm; April–June & Sept daily 9am–noon & 2–7pm) commands the plain from the knoll ahead, the austere white-veined façade and heavily buttressed nave totally subduing the clutch of fifteenth- and sixteenth-century houses that gather at its feet. To the right of the west door a mainly Romanesque cloister looks out across a green valley to hills, where a local *maquis* unit had its lair during the war. In the aisleless interior, the small area at the west end reserved for the laity has a superbly carved sixteenth-century oak organ loft, pulpit and spiral stair, although the church's great attraction are its choir stalls, built by Toulousain craftsmen and installed in 1535 in the great Gothic choir – an addition ordered by the future Pope Clement V. The elaborately carved stalls – 66 in all – are a feast of virtuosity, mingling piety, irony and malicious satire, each one the work of a different craftsman. It is in the misericords and partitions separating them that the ingenuity and humour of their creators is best seen: each of the gangways dividing the misericords has a representation of a cardinal sin on top of the end partition. In the middle gangway on the south side, for example, Envy is represented by two monks, faces contorted with hate, fighting over the abbot's baton of office, pushing against each other foot to foot in a furious tug-of-war. The armrest on the left of the roodscreen entrance depicts the abbot birching a monk, while the bishop's throne has a particularly lovely back panel in marquetry, depicting Saint Bertrand himself and Saint John. In the ambulatory a fifteenth-century shrine depicts scenes from Saint Bertrand's life, with the church and village visible in the background of the top right panel.

In July and August the cathedral and St-Just in Valcabrère play host to a **music festival**. Across the small square in front of the cathedral, the *Hôtel du Comminges* (☎61.88.31.43; ②–③; closed Jan) makes a nice place to **stay** and has a restaurant. The nearest **campsite** is *Es Pibous* on the St-Just road (mid-May to Sept), with *La Vieille Auberge* nearby serving good basic food. Cars are no longer allowed in the village itself, but a minibus operates a shuttle service from the nearby car park. Fifteen kilometres northwest, the unprepossessing little town of **ST-GAUDENS** has an IYHF **youth hostel**, at 3 rue de la Résidence (☎61.95.65.37; ①), and a reasonable **hotel** – the *Esplanade*, 7 pl Mas-St-Pierre, by the church in the town centre (☎61.89.15.90; ③–④).

The Grottes de Gargas

About 6km from St-Bertrand in the direction of Mazères-de-Neste, the **Grottes de Gargas** (guided tours: Mon, Wed, Sat & Sun; July & Aug daily 2.30–6pm; 20F) are renowned for their 231 prehistoric painted hand prints. Outlined in black, red, yellow or white, they mostly seem mutilated or deformed – perhaps the result of disease or ritual sacrifice, although no one really knows. There are representations of animals as well.

Bagnères-de-Luchon

There's none of the usual spa town fustiness about **BAGNÈRES-DE-LUCHON**. It is small, but the main street, the **allées d'Étigny**, has a distinctly metropolitan elegance and bustle, lined with cafés and numerous places to eat. There is not, however, anything to see, apart from the slightly moth-eaten **Musée du pays de Luchon** by the tourist office (daily 9am–noon & 2–6pm; 10F), which has an extraordinarily eclectic collection of archeological finds, old skis, art and displays on the Pyrenees, and the nineteenth-century **baths** at the end of allées d'Étigny in the **Parc des Quinconces** (guided tours: Tues & Thurs 2pm).

Luchon is best as a comfortable base for exploring the surrounding mountains. The **gare SNCF**, which is also the **gare routière**, is in av de Toulouse across the River One in the northern part of the town. The **tourist office** is at 18 allées d'Étigny (daily 9am–7pm; Nov–March Mon Sat 9am–noon & 2–6pm, Sun 2–6pm) and includes a *Bureau des Guides* for walking information.

For an all-in **accommodation** package including food and mountain sports, the *Accueil des Jeunes*, 12 allées des Bains (☎61.79.00.14; ①), is the cheapest deal going for under-25s, but it is mainly for groups, and there is no guarantee that passing individuals will find room. An excellent-value **hotel** is the *Deux Nations* at 5 rue Victor-Hugo (☎61.79.01.71; ①–②), with an equally good restaurant and menus from 54F. Alternatively, try the *Bon Accueil*, 1 pl Maréchal-Joffre (☎61.79.02.20; ③), also with a good restaurant. There are numerous **campsites** in and around the town. Less cramped than the in-town ones, *Camping La Lanette* is only 1500m away across the River Pique in Montauban-de-Luchon (down rue Lamartine from allées d'Étigny). However, the best deal of all for sleeping and eating is the romantically sited *Le Jardin des Cascades* (☎61.79.83.09; ②), in a wild steep garden uphill from the church in tiny **MONTAUBAN**, a kilometre to the east. In summer you can eat on a shaded terrace overlooking Luchon and the mountains to the west, where the hang-gliders and *parapentes* float hazily in the sunset. The food and service are excellent, the price around 180F per person, including wine.

Around Luchon: some hikes

There are two classic hikes south of Luchon. To get to **Lac d'Oô**, you can either follow the **GR10** to Superbagnères (3hr), then on west to the *Refuge d'Espingo* (☎61.79.20.01; June–Sept) and the lake (another 5hr), or take the road to **Granges d'Astau**, where there is a **gîte d'étape** (☎61.79.35.63) and **refuge** (☎61.79.14.92; July–Oct). From there it's an hour's walk to the lake or two hours to the Espingo refuge. It's possible to continue into Spain via the Port d'Oô or the Lac du Portillon.

For the second hike to **Port de Vénasque** on the Spanish frontier, walk – or hitch – down the D125 to its end about 30 minutes' walk from the **Hospice de France**, an ancient inn founded by the Knights of St John. From here a signposted path climbs the narrow valley to the frontier ridge past four small lakes where there is a small unstaffed *CAF* refuge. After that it's a steep climb up a scree (subject to avalanches in spring) to the narrow passage of the **Port de Venasque** (3hr), with superb views of the **Maladetta Massif** and the **Pico d'Aneto**, the highest summit of the Pyrenees (3404m).

THE EASTERN PYRENEES

The dominant climatic influence of the **Eastern Pyrenees** is the Mediterranean. The climate is hotter and drier here, and the landscape more arid, with Mediterranean plants like the cistus, broom and thyme making their appearance and the lower slopes planted with vines. The way of life is laid-back and outdoor oriented, and the proximity of Spain is evident; in fact, much of the region is Catalan, incorporated into France a mere three hundred years ago. As with the rest of the Pyrenees, the countryside is spectacular and densely networked, with well-organized hiking trails. The historical sights, with the exception of the prehistoric caves at **Niaux** and the Cathar castle of **Montségur**, are most richly concentrated in the east towards the coast, in what is essentially French Catalonia – **Perpignan** and the coastal resorts of the Côte Vermeille, the **Pic du Canigou** and the beautiful church at **Arles-sur-Tech**.

Along the River Ariège

The first clear herald of the approaching Mediterranean, whether you're coming from the western Pyrenees or heading south from the major transport nodule of Toulouse, is the **Valley of the Ariège**, thorny scrub and white eroded limestone cliffs beginning to make their appearance from Tarascon onwards. Transport is no problem as long as you stick to the valley, but for side trips – into the Couserans and the hike to Montségur – you really need a car.

Foix and around

Administrative centre of the *département* of Ariège, **FOIX** lies 82km south of Toulouse on the main Paris–Barcelona train line and the N20 road to Ax-les-Thermes and the Spanish border. It is an agreeable country town of narrow alleys and half-timbered houses, with an attractive old quarter squeezed between the rivers Ariège and Arget, filled with houses from the sixteenth and seventeenth centuries.

Dominating all are the three distinctive hilltop towers of the **Château des Comtes de Foix**, which contains the somewhat tedious **Musée d'Ariège** (daily 10.30am–noon & 2–5.30pm; July & Aug 9.45am–6pm; June & Sept 9.45am–noon & 2–6pm; free). The counts were determined opponents of the territorial ambitions of the Capetian kings of France, and their resistance was finally broken in 1229 when the feudal overlordship of the French king was imposed on them. Foix's age of glory came in 1290 when its counts married into the house of Béarn. Although they transferred their court to Orthez in the fourteenth century, this was the beginning of a powerful Pyrenean mini-state, whose influence lasted three centuries and came to include the kingdom of Navarre, leading finally to the throne of France with the accession of Henri III of Navarre as Henri IV of France in 1589.

The **gares SNCF and routière** are together in av de la Gare, off the N20 on the right bank of the Ariège. The **tourist office** is at 45 cours Gabriel-Fauré (Mon–Sat 8am–noon & 2–6pm, Sun 9am–noon; ☎61.65.12.12). For a place to **stay**, there's the rather superior *Hôtel Audoye-Lons* on place G-Duthil, by the Pont-Vieux (☎61.65.52.44; ①–④; restaurant from 70F), or the cheaper *Hôtel Eychenne* at 11 rue Noël-Peyrevidal (☎61.65.00.04; ①–③). There's also a **camping municipal**, *Lac de Labarre*, on the N20 (May–Oct). Except on Sundays, there's a daily **bus** service east via Lavelanet to Quillan and four buses a day west to St-Girons.

Mas d'Azil

West of Foix, the **Mas d'Azil** is one of the most impressive, albeit overcommercialized, prehistoric caves in the region, although it's not easy to reach without your own transport. It lies 12km north of the Foix–St-Girons bus route: get off at Vic after La-Bastide-de-Sérou and take the D15. It's a pretty road, but without a lift it'll take a good two hours on foot. Failing that, four *Semvat* buses a day run from Toulouse.

Inhabited in prehistoric times for more than 20,000 years and used as a refuge by Cathars and Protestants in more recent years, the caves include displays of tools, animal bones and other objects found during excavation (guided tours: June–Sept daily

10am–noon & 2–6pm; April & May 2–6pm; Oct–March by appointment, ☎61.69.97.22; 20F, joint ticket with museum).

In the village of **LE MAS-D'AZIL**, 1km beyond the cave, the **Musée de la Préhistoire** (daily 2–6pm; June–Sept 10am–noon & 2–6pm; 20F, joint ticket with cave) contains, among other engravings and tools from the cave, a beautiful carved antler known as *le faon aux oiseaux*, perhaps used as a spear-thrower. If you wish to **stay**, there's a **camping municipal** (July to mid-Sept), 1500m distant on the Pamiers road, or the *Hôtel Gardel* on the main square (☎61.69.90.05; ②).

Tarascon and the Vicdessos Valley

TARASCON-SUR-ARIÈGE lies 16km south of Foix, where the N20 crosses the Ariège. Once a centre for the local iron-mining industry — there is still an aluminium plant in operation — it is an unexciting little town enclosed by high wooded ridges. However, it is useful as a base for the Vicdessos Valley and the prehistoric cave of Niaux.

The **cafés** on the east bank of the river, dominated by the clock tower, are pleasant, sunny places to sit. Apart from that, it is worth taking a stroll up the narrow **rue de Barri** to the wide square by the church, a pleasant expanse with just one arcaded side and a single wooden house still standing, to the **Porte d'Espagne**, the only surviving piece of the town walls. Above the gate is the minuscule **Exposition Gadal**, a museum of prehistoric artefacts and Cathar memorabilia (daily except Mon 9.30am–noon & 2.30–7pm; 15F), dating back to the time when hunted *bonshommes*, the Cathar "priests", took refuge in the caves hereabouts after the fall of Montségur (see p.641).

Quietest and most attractive of the **hotels** is the *Francal* on the riverside quai Sylvestre (☎61.05.60.24; ②–③; restaurant from 65F). Otherwise try the *Bellevue*, also on the river at the head of the bridge on place Jean-Jaurès (☎61.05.60.45; ①; restaurant from 50F), or the *Hostellerie de la Poste* on the N20 (☎61.05.60.41; ②–③; good restaurant from 65F). For **camping**, the *Pré Lombard* site is on the left bank of the river, ten minutes' walk upstream from the bridge, while the **gare SNCF** is a few minutes' walk to the right. The **tourist office** is on place du 19-mars-1962 (☎61.05.63.46).

Niaux and the prehistoric caves

Just south of Tarascon, by the aluminium plant, the D8 cuts up right into the green valley of the Vicdessos past the riverside remains of a Catalan ironworks. The hamlet of **NIAUX** lies in the valley bottom, 5km further on. The tiny settlement has a diverting **Musée Paysan** (daily 10am–noon & 2–6pm; July & Aug 9am–8pm; 25F), with an unrivalled collection of tools, furnishings, old photos and odds and ends illustrating the vanished traditions of peasant Ariège, and is also home to a **campsite** (June to mid-Sept).

But the real reason people descend on the little hamlet is for the **Grotte de Niaux**, a huge cave complex under an enormous rock overhang high on the south flank of the valley (guided visits: daily 11am, 3pm & 4.30pm; July–Sept every 45min 8.30–11.30am & 1.30–5.15pm; reservations essential daily 9.30–11am & 2.30–4.30pm; ☎61.05.88.37; 40F). There are about four kilometres of galleries in all, with paintings of the Magdalenian period (circa 11,000 BC) widely scattered throughout, although the twenty people allowed in the cave at any one time are led through just a fraction of the complex. The paintings you can see are in a vast chamber, a slippery 800-metre walk from the entrance of the cave along a subterranean riverbed. The subjects are horses, ibex, stags and bison. No colour is used, just a dark outline and shading to give body to the drawings, which have been executed with a "crayon" made of bison fat and manganese oxide. They are an extraordinary mix of bold impressionistic strokes and delicate attention to detail: the nostrils, pupils and the tendons on the inner thighs of the bison are all drawn in.

Two other caves in the vicinity are **La Grotte de la Vache** in **ALLIAT** (daily except Tues July & Aug 10am–5.30pm; April–June, Easter & Sept 2.30–4pm; 35F), right across the valley from Niaux, a relatively rare example of an inhabited cave where you can observe hearths, bones, tools, etc, *in situ*. Another cave, **Bedeilhac** (July & Aug daily except Tues 10am–5.30pm; April–June, Easter & Sept 2.30–4pm; 40F), is in the side of the jagged Roc de Sédour ridge overlooking Tarascon on the D618 Massat road.

Vicdessos and Auzat

From Niaux, the road continues deep in the valley bottom, beneath the romantically pinnacled ruins of the **Château of Miglos**, to **VICDESSOS** and **AUZAT**, the latter with an unsightly aluminium works. The villages themselves are not of much interest except as bases for exploring the magnificently wooded country round about. The **GR10** passes nearby on its way from Mérens, above Ax-les-Thermes, to Aulus-les-Bains (see overleaf), and from the **gîte d'étape** at **MOUNICOU** (☎61.64.87.66), beyond Auzat, you can undertake the gruelling ascent of the **Pic de Montcalm**.

For **accommodation**, Auzat and Vicdessos have one hotel each, the *Hôtel Denjean* in Auzat (☎61.64.88.36; ①) and the *Hôtel Hivert* in Vicdessos (☎61.64.88.17; ①–②; restaurant from 60F). Both have year-round **campsites**. **GOULIER**, across the valley, has a **gîte** (☎61.64.85.19), and in **CAPOULET**, back towards Niaux, a Dutch couple offer very comfortable, inexpensive **chambres d'hôtes** (☎61.05.89.88). The **tourist office** in Auzat is also extremely helpful (Mon–Sat 8am–noon & 2–6pm, Sun 2–6pm; July & Aug daily 8am–noon & 2–7pm).

Into the Couserans

From Vicdessos, a really stunning route – the D18 – climbs the **valley of the Suc**, tunnelling through trees, past abandoned barns and occasional cottages in lush meadows, by waterfalls and streams, to the pass at the **Port de Lers** (1517m). On the far side, herds of grey cows graze the alpine meadows down to the Étang de Lers, where there is a snack bar. Then the road climbs again to another col overlooking the head of the valley of the little **River Garbet**. Below, the steep slopes are luxuriant with beech, while straight ahead you look into a high-walled crenellated cirque formed by the **Pic Rouge de Bassiès** and the **Pic des Trois Comtes** above the **Étang de Garbet**, where the heights are underlined by wedges of snow lying beneath the sheerest faces.

Aulus-les-Bains

Down in the Garbet Valley, the road heads west to **AULUS-LES-BAINS**, a remote village lying among moist and fragrant meadows ringed by dramatic peaks. This is the beginning of the **Pays de Couserans**, one of the poorest, least developed and most depopulated regions of the Pyrenees. Aulus, like other spa towns, enjoyed its moment of glory and fell again into rustic somnolence, from which it is trying to resurrect itself once more. This is country for walking and enjoying the landscapes: there's nothing else, and, remote though it is, it is not inaccessible – there are two daily weekday buses and one on Saturdays to St-Girons. The classic walk here involves heading south along the GR10 to the **Cascade d'Ars** (round trip about 5hr).

For all information, consult the **tourist office** in the allée des Thermes (☎61.96.01.79). Among places to **stay**, try the *Hôtel La Terrasse* (☎61.96.00.98; ②–③; closed Oct–May; restaurant from 110F), or the *Hôtel de France* (☎61.96.00.90; ①–②; closed Oct–Dec; restaurant from 90F). There's also a **gîte d'étape** in the village and **camping** at *Le Couledous*, 500m to the north.

For routes on to St-Girons, both the Garbet and Ustou valleys are beautiful. For a brief stopover, there is a great little inn by the river, a little way beyond Ustou at **PONT DE LA TAULE**, called the *Auberge des Deux Rivières* (☎61.66.83.57; ②–③), with a restaurant.

St-Girons

With several *SNCF* buses a day from Boussens, on the main Tarbes–Toulouse rail line, and connections on to Aulus, Ustou, Massat and St-Lary, **ST-GIRONS** may be your first taste of this out-of-the-way region. Apart from its long association with making cigarette papers, the most striking thing about St-Girons is its pavements, made of a local dark-grey marble veined with white, and with finely chiselled gulleys to take rainwater from down-pipes. And although there are no other memorable sights, it's a far from unpleasant town.

The simplest centre for orientation is the **Pont-Vieux**. Straight ahead on the right bank of the River Salat, the bridge points you into the old commercial centre of the town, with some marvellously old-fashioned shops, their fronts and fittings unchanged for generations. To the right is the typically provincial **place des Poilus**, its cachet largely due to the faded elegance of the *Grand Hôtel de France* and the equally old-fashioned *Hôtel de l'Union*, opposite, where you can still stay (see below). The *Grand Café de l'Union* on the square is a splendid balconied period café that faces the *mairie*. Beside it, along the river bank, a wide gravelled *allée* of plane trees, the **Champ de Mars**, provides the site for a big general market on the second and fourth Mondays of every month, and to a regular produce market every Saturday morning.

The **tourist office** is down on the river bank (☎61.66.14.11). If you're **staying** over, the *Grand Hôtel de France* (☎61.66.00.23; ①–③) has a good restaurant with menus from 85F. The *Hôtel de l'Union* is a little cheaper (☎61.66.09.12; ②–③), or there's the *Centre de Séjour du Parc de Paletès* (☎61.66.06.79; ①) – take av des Évadés from the church behind the *mairie* and keep going for about 2km – with space for camping, some rooms, and a nice terrace restaurant overlooking the valley. On the left bank of the river, place des Capots is the terminus for **buses**, where there are also a couple of cheap **places to eat**. Another workaday eating place is the restaurant of the old *Hôtel Madrid* (menus from 55F), opposite the end of the Pont-Vieux.

St-Lizier

ST-LIZIER, a five-minute ride by bus from the old *gare SNCF* on the St-Gaudens road, totally outclasses St-Girons in the tourism stakes. It sits on a hilltop, and is full of history; it's walled, arcaded, cobbled, cathedralled, half-timbered, pretty and lifeless.

Architecturally the most interesting building in town is the **Cathédrale de St-Lizier**, with some lovely Romanesque basketwork carving on the supporting columns and its distinctive octagonal Toulouse-style tower posing photogenically against the mountains to the south. Inside are some fine medieval frescoes, especially its representation of Christ in the apse. There is a second cathedral, **Notre-Dame-de-Sède**, which boasts fine seventeenth-century choir stalls and can be visited along with the **bishop's palace** (daily 7.30am–noon & 2–7pm; 15F), with its collections of religious relics. But that, really, is about it. If you want to know more, the **tourist office** is next door to the cathedral (mid-June to mid-Sept daily 10am–noon & 2–6pm; ☎61.96.77.77).

Ax-les-Thermes and around

Twenty kilometres south of Tarascon, still on the river, the spa town of **AX-LES-THERMES** is completely walled in by mountains. It is small and pleasant enough, but once you've wandered a couple of streets in the quarter to the right of the N20, which forms the main street, there is nothing to see, and Ax's principal value is as a base for exploring the surrounding mountains and as a staging-post on the way to Andorra or on down the N20 to Font-Romeu and, ultimately, Perpignan and the Mediterranean.

Rue de l'École and rue de la Boucarie are really the only old bits in town, with a few medieval buildings adding a certain amount of atmosphere. But the **church of St-Vincent**, with its Romanesque tower hovering above place du Breilh, is the only surviving structure of architectural interest. Just across the road you can dangle your feet for free in the **Bassin des Ladres**, a pool of hot sulphurous water which is all that remains of the hospital founded in 1260 by Saint Louis for soldiers wounded in the Crusades.

The **tourist office** on place du Breilh (Mon–Sat 8am–noon & 2–6pm, Sun 9am–noon; ☎61.64.20.64) has hiking information and lists of walks. There are two particularly nice **places to stay** in Ax: the *Hôtel La Terrasse* at 7 rue Marcaillou (☎61.64.20.33; ①–②), run by a jazz-loving couple and with a restaurant from 65F; and *Le Couloubret*, more like a private house than a hotel (☎61.64.21.88; ②; closed Nov–April), behind the sad-looking casino by the church of St-Vincent. A third possibility is *Hôtel Les Pyrénées* (☎61.64.21.01; ①–③; closed Nov to mid-Dec), with a restaurant from 55F, on the main av Delcassé opposite the casino. There is a **campsite**, *Le Malazéou*, on the river bank just before the **gare SNCF** as you come into town from Tarascon. The most atmospheric places to **eat** are the old *Grand Café*, next to *Hôtel Les Pyrénées*, and *Brasserie Le Club* on place Roussel, which has jazz and food. Alternative places are the pizzeria opposite the *Hôtel de France* on the main road, and the *Terminus Bar* near the station.

Eight kilometres south along the N20, **MÉRENS-LES-VALS** lies on the GR10, which heads east to the Carlit Massif and Font-Romeu/Mont-Louis (see p.566). It has a **gîte d'étape** *(*☎61.64.32.50), and you could use it to link up with the GR7, making a tour of the **Réserve Nationale du Burrus** via the lakeside *Refuge d'En Beys* (☎61.64.24.24; July–Sept).

Montségur

The ruined walls of the **castle** at **MONTSÉGUR** ring the summit of a rocky pyramid, with the houses of the village strung out in terraced lines – not the usual fetal huddle – at the foot of the castle rock. Silent and depopulated now, the town comes to life only with the influx of tourists, but it was once the temporary capital of the banned Cathar church, with a population of some five hundred bishops, clergy and ordinary believers on the run from the persecution of the Inquisition.

The easiest approach to Montségur is probably from Lavelanet, about 12km to the north (see below), or Villeneuve-d'Olmes, 6km closer; but by far and away the most dramatic route is on foot from Comus (around 4hr), where there is a *gîte d'étape* (see opposite). Head west along the GR7B, following a lane beside the stream for about 3km until the lane doubles back hard to the left, leaving the stream to continue into the deep sunless ravine of the **Gorges de la Frau**. The path descends steeply on the old mule road until you hit the dead end of the D5 from Bélesta. Continue along the tarmac to the first farm on the left, where the route turns up the lane between the buildings, becomes a track, then a narrow footpath beside a stream in a deep gully thickly wooded with beech, ash, wild cherry and fir. It crosses to the left flank of the gully and the angle of ascent increases sharply, bringing you finally to an ancient quarry mule road that turns sharply and horizontally right back across the head of the valley to a signposted locality called Liam; from a patch of rough meadow here you get your first glimpse of the ruined walls of Montségur castle. Turn left at the signpost, down a good path with open pastures in a shallow valley on your right with a tarmacked lane. When you hit the tarmacked lane, turn left for a short distance and then right on a clear path down through trees to a riverside campsite. Cross the river to a road and make your way across allotment-like vegetable plots to the village of Montségur.

Before undertaking the hike up to Montségur's **château** (June 21–Sept daily 10am–1pm & 2–7pm, same ticket covers both visits 25F), it's worth a glance at the one-room **museum** (daily 10am–1pm & 2–7pm; Oct–April ask at the *mairie*), with its collection of bits and pieces from the castle. A footpath from the top of the village shortens the way up to the saddle of the hill, where the last steep half-hour climb to the castle begins in the *Prats dels Cramats*, the field where the Cathar martyrs were burned (see below). All that remains of the castle are its stout and now truncated curtain walls and

THE FALL OF THE MONTSÉGUR

In the early years of the thirteenth century, Montségur's castle was reconstructed by a local feudal lord as a strong point for the **Cathars** under attack by the Crusade, and in 1232 the town became the capital of the outlawed Cathar Church, harbouring fugitives from the Inquisition under the protection of a garrison commanded by Pierre-Roger de Mirepoix.

Provoked by a raid on Avignonet in May 1242, which successfully assassinated the Inquisitors, the forces of the Catholic Church and the king of France laid siege to the castle in the spring of 1243. By March 1244, Pierre-Roger, despairing of relief, agreed terms with them. At the end of a fortnight's truce, the 225 Cathars who still refused to recant were burnt on a communal pyre on March 16.

Four men who had made good their escape recovered the Cathar "treasure", which had been hidden in a cave for safekeeping since the preceding Christmas and vanished. Two of them later reappeared in Lombardy, where it seems probable these funds were used to support the refugee Cathar community established there. But numerous legends have grown up, especially in German writings, identifying this "treasure" with the Holy Grail and the Cathars themselves with the Knights of the Round Table.

the terribly cramped keep. A somewhat precarious stairway leads to the top of the walls, whence you look out over miles of forested hills and snowy peaks, giving a sense of solitude and airy isolation that is in itself highly evocative.

There are a couple of **hotels**, the nicest of them the old-fashioned *Hôtel Couquet* (☎61.01.10.28; ②), run by one Mme Couquet and fronted by pollarded lime trees. There is a café and restaurant on the first floor (menus from 60F). The alternative is the more expensive *Hôtel Costes* (☎61.01.10.24; ②; closed mid-Dec to Feb; restaurant at 65F and 90F), or the **gîte d'étape** in the village (☎61.01.20.97). Another *gîte* lies in Comus, attached to the *Centre École Pleine Nature* (☎68.20.33.69), 45 minutes' walk below Montaillou.

Montaillou

About 11km southeast of Montségur as the crow flies, the almost deserted hamlet of **MONTAILLOU** lies above the road to the right just after Prades, over the steep Col de Chioula (1400m). There's little to see today, apart from the stump of a castle tower, once 45m high to facilitate visual communication with Montségur, but the pretty little settlement's interest lies in a fascinating study undertaken in the 1980s by French historian Le Roy Ladurie. Based on Inquisition records, his book covers the years around 1300, when the Inquisition was trying to extirpate the Cathar heresy from its last strongholds. What the poor victims revealed to their interrogators amounts to an extraordinarily detailed and intimate portrait of contemporary life. Much of the book reads like good gossip: who is sleeping with whom, where the sheep are being pastured this year and which paths are best for crossing into Spain.

The remaining inhabitants still bear the names of their Cathar ancestors, and the graveyard is full of them.

Lavelanet and Mirepoix

LAVELANET has nothing to offer beyond its bus connections and a very clean and modern **camping municipal** (March 20–Oct), from which you can just see Montségur nudging over the brow of the intervening ridges. There is a *crêperie*, and a couple of restaurants are off the main square.

If you are heading north in the Carcassonne direction, take a look at **MIREPOIX**. It's a late thirteenth-century *bastide* built around one of the loveliest surviving arcaded market squares in the country, bordered by houses dating from between the thirteenth and the fifteenth centuries, with a relatively harmonious modern *halle* on one side and a not very exciting cathedral behind it. *Hôtel Le Commerce*, on the boulevard encircling the old town near the church (☎61.68.10.29; ②–③), is a safe place to **stay**, with a very agreeable restaurant in its lime-shaded courtyard (menus 65–130F). There's a **camping municipal** on the Limoux road (☎61.68.84.90).

Along the Aude

South of Carcassonne, the road and the rail line both climb steadily up the twisting valley of the **River Aude**, between scrubby hills and vineyards and ever deeper and more forested ravines to Quillan. From there, the road squeezes through the **Gorges de l'Aude** in a sunless bottom before emerging once again towards the river's headwaters above Les Angles on the east side of the Carlit Massif in the high Pyrenees. It is a magnificent drive, and quite hitchable, being one of the main routes to Andorra; public transport runs out at **Axat**, some 10km beyond Quillan.

Limoux and Quillan

The first stop on the D118 road, 24km south of Carcassonne, **LIMOUX** is served several times daily by both the *SNCF* and the private *Cars Teissier* buses. It stands astride the Aude, which for much of the year is a powerful grey flood of snow melt. Life revolves around the pretty **place de la République** in the heart of the old town, with its Friday market, and the nineteenth-century **promenade du Tivoli**, in effect a bypass road. Known in the past for its woollens and the tanning of hides brought down from the mountains, the town's claim to fame today is the production of its excellent sparkling wine, *Blanquette de Limoux,* much cheaper than champagne and not at all inferior. If you've got your own transport, the Romanesque abbeys of **St-Hilaire** and **St-Polycarpe**, under 10km away in the lovely green hills to the east, are worth the effort.

For a place to **stay**, there's the *Hôtel Flassian*, 2 av du Languedoc (☎68.31.78.18; ①), *Hôtel des Arcades*, 96 rue St-Martin (☎68.31.02.57; ③), and, best and most expensive, the *Hôtel Moderne et Pigeon* on place Général-Leclerc (☎68.31.00.25; ⑤; closed early Dec to mid-Jan), with its excellent restaurant (from 135F). Just upstream from the main part of town, on the right bank of the river, is an agreeable poplar-shaded **camping municipal** (June–Sept). For an unusual and characterful place to **eat**, try the *Maison de la Blanquette* on promenade du Tivoli, which promotes the local wines and serves excellent food (closed Wed pm, Jan 1–21 & Oct 18–31; menus from 70F). If you are interested in sampling or buying any wine, the best place to go is the cooperative, *Aimery-Sieur d'Arques* in av du Mauzac (June–Aug daily 8am–7pm). The **tourist office** is on promenade du Tivoli (Mon–Fri 9am–noon & 2–6pm, Sat 9am–noon, Sun 2–7pm; July & Aug daily 9am–7pm; June & Sept daily 10am–1pm & 2–7pm; ☎68.31.1.82).

QUILLAN, 27km further upstream, is a pleasant little town, useful as a staging post on the way south into the mountains or east to the Cathar castles – it has daily bus connections with Perpignan via St-Paul-de-Fenouillet. The only monument of interest is the ruined **castle** that was burned by the Huguenots in 1575 and partly dismantled in the eighteenth century; the remnants are still worth a scramble if you happen to be in town.

For an overnight **stay**, try the *Hôtel Terminus*, 45 bd de-Gaulle (☎68.20.05.72; ①–③; closed mid-Dec to Jan), or the slightly more expensive *Cartier* on the same street at no. 31 (☎68.20.05.14; ②–④; closed Dec 21–Feb); both have restaurants. The **campsite** *La Sapinette* is at 21 rue René-Delpech (☎68.20.13.52), or there's another campsite by the river at Pont d'Aliès (☎68.20.53.27; April to mid-Nov; canteen), another 11km along the D117, or a couple of cheap hotels in **AXAT**, 8km southeast: the *Hôtel de la Poste* (☎68.20.50.35; ②), which has a dining room overlooking the river, and the *L'Ensoleillé* (☎68.20.51.43; ②).

The Gorges du Rebenty and Gorges de l'Aude

From Pont d'Aliès, just north of Axat, there is a beautiful route west up the **valley of the Rebenty** on the tiny D107 through woods of beech, fir and oak, with a magnificent early summer display of orchids and other Pyrenean flowers. It's a marvellous cycling route, too, except for the agony of the climb out of the valley. The road continues to Ax-les-Thermes over the Col du Pradel, or you can escape on to the Plateau de Sault at **ESPEZEL**, some 20km west of Axat.

The narrowest and deepest stretch of the scenic **Gorges de l'Aude** is the eighteen or so kilometres between Axat and Usson. If you want to admire the scenery, don't drive: the road is much too dangerous to allow your eyes to wander. Towards the end there is a magnificent cave to investigate, the **Grotte de l'Aguzou**. It's expensive, but as near the real thing as you can get without being a pukka caver; you spend the entire day underground, accoutred like a professional (visits by arrangement only: ☎68.20.45.38; 200F), although the visits must be arranged a week in advance and there must be a minimum of four people. *Camping sauvage* is allowed by the river, or there is a **gîte d'étape** at **FONTANES-DE-SAULT**, 3km away (☎68.20.37.07).

Continuing upstream, the road divides just after Usson-les-Bains. On a shaggy bluff between the arms of the fork, dwarfed in turn by the heights either side, stand the forlorn ruins of the **Château d'Usson**, allegedly the hiding place for the "Cathar treasure" during the 1244 siege of Montségur (see p.642). Passing its foot, a road winds up through the attractive grey tiers of houses at **MIJANÈS** – where there's a **hotel**, the *Relais de Pailhères* (☎68.20.45.76; ②) – to the pass at the **Col de Pailhères**, which is at its loveliest in June when a cornice of snow still lines the crests above the small round lake.

From Mijanès another road branches up the valley to **QUÉRIGUT**, passing through the village of **LE PLA**, where there is a primitive **campsite**. There's also a thrice-weekly bus from Quillan to Quérigut, run by *Petit Charles* of Carcanières, on Monday, Wednesday and Friday afternoons, that passes through the village. Quérigut, where there is another **campsite** and the *Hôtel du Donezan* (☎68.20.42.40; ②), stands at the head of a slope of neglected terraces, guarded by the ruin of its **castle**, last refuge of the Cathars who held out for eleven years after the fall of Montségur. Above, the forest begins: miles of beech and pine, interspersed with lush meadows, stretching to the windy plateau above Font-Romeu. This is the **Donezan** region, beautiful but the poorest, most neglected and depopulated corner of Ariège.

French Catalonia

The area that makes up the eastern fringe of the Pyrenees and the flatter stretch of land down to the Mediterranean coast is known as **Roussillon**, or **French Catalonia**. Catalan power first came into its own in the tenth century under the independent counts of Barcelona, who then became kings of Aragon as well in 1137. They attempted to create a joint power base with Occitan France under the counts of Toulouse, but that came to an unhappy end with the death of Pedro I at the battle of Muret in 1213, when he came to the aid of Raymond VI of Toulouse against Simon de Montfort in the anti-Cathar crusade. The height of Catalan power was reached in the thirteenth and fourteenth centuries, when the Franco-Catalan frontier was fixed along the base of the Corbières hills north of Perpignan. But Jaime I made the mistake of dividing his kingdom between his two sons at his death. What is now the French part became the kingdom of Majorca with its capital at Perpignan, but, coveted by the rival brother, the king of Aragon, it sought alliance with the kings of France, who saw this as a splendid opportunity to straighten out their southern border, thus ensuring continuous squabbling that was only finally ended by the Treaty of the Pyrenees, negotiated by Louis XIII in 1659.

After the Treaty, the French began a ruthless process of Frenchification, successful in Perpignan where the bourgeoisie tended to identify their commercial interest with a central power; but the mountain hinterland remained largely unchanged until modern times, when the collapse of traditional agriculture, compulsory education and the devastation of the vineyards by phylloxera combined to drive the peasantry off the land – a process which still continues today, albeit at a slower rate.

Although there is no real separatist impetus among French Catalans today, their sense of identity is still strong: the language is very much alive, and the national colours of yellow and red are much in evidence wherever you go. The **Pic du Canigou**, which completely dominates the French Catalan province of Roussillon, is much larger in presence than its actual 2784m, and it remains a powerful symbol of Catalan nationalism, attracting hordes of Catalans from Barcelona to celebrate the summer solstice. The little town of **Prades** has grown into a centre of Catalan education and a local symbol of resistance with the opening of the first Catalan-language primary school in France, as well as being the seat of a Catalan summer university.

Most of the region's attractions are easily reached from the region's one major town, **Perpignan**, itself a friendly, vibrant place. The coast and immediate hinterland above the Spanish frontier is beautiful, though predictably crowded, and the finest spots are in the **Tech** and **Têt valleys** which cut back west into the Pyrenees, where you can view the Romanesque monasteries of **Serrabonne**, **St-Michel-de-Cuxa** and **St-Martin-du-Canigou**, Vauban's fortress town of **Villefranche-de-Conflent**, the museum at **Céret** with its unique series of Picasso ceramics, and **Mont Canigou** itself and its foothill orchards of peaches and cherries.

Perpignan

This far south, climate and geography alone would ensure a palpable Spanish influence. But in addition, a large part of **PERPIGNAN**'s population is of Spanish origin, refugees from the Civil War and their descendants. The southern influence is further augmented by a substantial admixture of north Africans, both Arabs and white French settlers repatriated after Algerian independence in 1962.

While there are no memorable monuments to visit, Perpignan is a lively, pleasant city that lives its life very much on the public street. Its heyday was in the thirteenth and fourteenth centuries, when the kings of Majorca held their court here, and it is from this period that most of its historical interest derives. Well placed on the main Mediterranean coast's international lines of communication, it is much the best base for exploring the eastern end of the Pyrenees, and the Cathar castles of the Corbières, described in Chapter 11, *Languedoc*.

Arrival and accommodation

The **gare SNCF** (☎68.51.10.44) is also the terminus for long-distance **buses** on av Général-de-Gaulle, about a fifteen-minute walk from the **regional tourist office** on quai de Tassigny (daily 10am–noon & 2–5.30pm; ☎68.34.29.94). Further along the River Basse is the **municipal tourist office** in the Palais des Congrès at the end of bd Wilson (summer daily 9am–8pm; winter Mon–Sat 8.30am–noon & 2–6.30pm). The **gare routière** for local buses is at the junction of Pont Arago and av Général-Leclerc.

There are some cheap **hotels** near the station, of which the best is *Le Berry*, 6 av de la Gare (☎68.34.59.02; ①). Another, very cheap possibility is the *Expéditeurs* on the rather desolate av Leclerc, at no. 19 (☎68.35.15.80; ①), with a good cheap restaurant. The *Bristol* is more agreeably situated close to the city gate, 5 rue des Grandes-Fabriques (☎68.34.32.68; ①–③), as is the comfortable and more expensive *Athéna*, 1 rue Quéya, near place de la République (☎68.34.37.63; ①–③). Another attractive and classier alternative is the *Hôtel de la Poste et de la Perdrix*, 6 rue Fabriques-Nabot (☎68.34.42.53; ③),

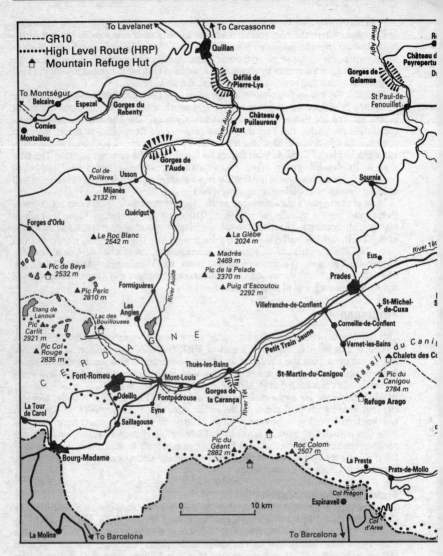

also nearby. In addition, there is a welcoming IYHF **youth hostel** (☎68.34.63.32; ①), behind the public gardens of La Pépinière by Pont Arago (entrance around the back of the police HQ on av de Grande-Bretagne), and two **campsites**, *La Garrigole* on rue Maurice-Lévy, and *Le Catalan* on rte de Bompas, both signposted from the centre.

The City

The best place to begin your exploration of the city is at **Le Castillet**, built as a gateway in the fourteenth century and now home to the **Casa Pairal**, an interesting museum of

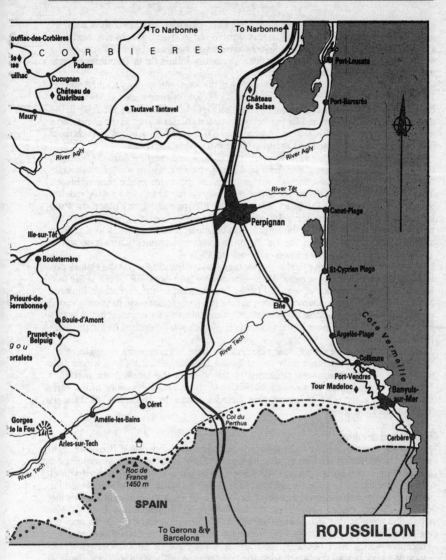

Roussillon's Catalan folk culture (summer daily except Tues 9.30–11.30am & 2.30–6.30pm; winter daily 9–11.30am & 2–5.30pm; free), featuring religious art, agricultural and pastoral exposés and all sorts of local crafts. From the roof there is a great view of the dominant pile of Canigou, and, if you know where to look, you can see the **Château de Quéribus**, standing clear of its ridge to the northwest. A short distance down rue Louis-Blanc you come to the **place de la Loge**, focus of the renovated and pedestrianized heart of the old town. Dominating the cafés and brasseries of the narrow square is Perpignan's most interesting building, the Gothic **Loge de Mer**. Designed to hold the city's stock exchange and maritime court, and decorated with gargoyles and lacy balustrades, its ground floor has been taken over by an incongruous fast-food joint. Side by side next door are the **Hôtel de Ville**, with its magnificent wrought-iron gates and Maillol's statue of *La Méditerranée* in the courtyard, and the fifteenth-century **Palais de la Députation**, once the parliament of Roussillon.

From place de la Loge, rue St-Jean runs down to the fourteenth-century **Cathédrale St-Jean** on place Gambetta, its external walls built of bands of river stones sandwiched by brick. The interior is most interesting for its elaborate Catalan altarpieces, shadowy in the gloom of the dimly lit nave, and for the tortured wooden crucifix known as the *Dévôt Christ* in a side chapel to the south. Dating from around 1400, it's of Rhenish origin and was probably brought back from the Low Countries by some travelling merchant.

From the cathedral, rue de la Révolution-Française and rue de l'Anguille lead into the close, dilapidated maze of the **Arab and gypsy quarter**, where women congregate on the private inner lanes but are seldom seen on the more public thoroughfares. There are North African shops and cafés, especially on rue Llucia, and a daily **market** on **place Cassanyes**. At the heart of the quarter, the wide and grimy **place du Puig** is overlooked by a Vauban **barracks** converted into public housing. Just past it, at the top of a shady uphill street, is the elegant Catalan **church of St-Jacques**, dating from around 1200, on the edge of the **La Miranda** gardens (summer 10am–7pm; winter 10am–5.30pm), laid out by a section of the old city walls.

Crowning the hill that dominates the southern part of the old town is the **Palais des Rois de Majorque** (daily summer 10am–6pm; winter 9am–5pm; 20F), built in the thirteenth century to provide a seat for Jaime I's son, king of the recently conquered Majorca. Vauban's walls surround it now, but the two-storey palace and its great arcaded courtyard have Spanish–Moorish sophistication and finesse – for instance, in the beautiful marble porch to the lower of the two chapels – which you don't often find in the heavier styles of the north.

Finally, at 16 rue de l'Ange near place Arago, there is Perpignan's museum of art, the **Musée Rigaud** (summer daily except Tues 9.30am–noon & 2.30–7pm; winter daily 9am–noon & 2.30–6pm; free), dedicated to the work of the locally born portraitist Hyacinthe Rigaud, who became official painter to the court of Versailles in the early eighteenth century. The collection also includes works by Dufy, Maillol, Picasso, Tapiès, Appel and others.

Eating and drinking

For **eating**, there is nothing to beat the popular and reasonably priced *Perroquet*, right outside the station on the corner of av de-Gaulle, with a good selection of very reasonably priced Catalan dishes (around 75F; closed Thurs pm & Fri). The *Expéditeurs* hotel-restaurant is almost as good (menu from 65F; closed Sat pm & Sun), or, for something smarter, there is the elegant brasserie *Le Vauban* on quai Vauban near Le Castillet (menus 70–90F; closed Sun). Even the fast-food establishment in the Loge de Mer won't disappoint. Other good places are the *Relais St-Jean* in place Gambetta near the cathedral, with hearty Catalan home cooking (from 58F); the *Casa Sansa* at 2 rue Fabriques-Wadel, with excellent food and a lively Spanish atmosphere (95F and upwards); and, best of the bunch from the point of view of the food, *L'Opéra Bouffe* in impasse de la Division, between place Argo and place de la Loge (around 150F).

There are plenty of places for a leisurely **drink** in Perpignan. The *Café de la Grande Poste*, on place de Verdun under the plane trees in front of Le Castille, is a great place to watch the world go by. It is here, too, that in summertime, on Tuesday and Thursday evenings, you will see the Catalan dance, the *sardana*, being performed by kids, grandparents – anyone whom the spirit moves. The *Bodega Castillet* in the nearby alley, rue Fabrique-Couverte, is a favourite bar with the locals, and there are several cafés on place Arago.

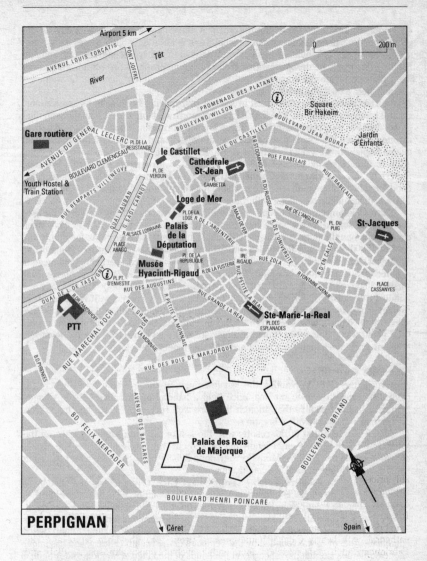

PERPIGNAN

Around Perpignan

CANET-PLAGE is the best place near Perpignan to test the waters of the Mediterranean, although there is nothing to recommend the place, except that its beach is wide and sandy and the sea is wet; take a 25-minute bus ride east from Promenade des Platanes in Perpignan (2–3 an hour). The same goes for the other resorts around here: Port-Leucate, Port Bacarès (complete with weathered Greek ferry beached to make a casino and nightclub) and St-Cyprien.

Perhaps more interesting, 15km north and served by several trains a day, is the **Château de Salses** (summer daily except Tues 9–11am & 3–6pm; winter daily 9am–noon & 3–5pm; 25F), built for the king of Aragon in the early fifteenth century, and one of the first forts to be designed with a ground-hugging profile to protect it from artillery fire. Its superior design apparently put Vauban's nose so out of joint that he wanted it demolished, a task that proved impossible.

Another place, with not so much to see but very moving because of its associations, is the vine-girt village of **TAUTAVEL**, 25km northwest off the St-Paul-de-Fenouillet road. In 1971 the remains of the oldest known European human being – dated to around 450,000 BC – were discovered near the village, and a reconstruction of the skull is on display in the village's **Musée de la Préhistoire** (daily 10am–noon & 2–6pm; July & Aug closes 8pm; free; ☎68.29.07.76), along with various finds from the cave where he was unearthed, the **Caune d'Arago**, a few kilometres north, which can itself be visited by arrangement with the museum between June and August. The local wines are worth sampling, too, along with those of Estagel and Rivesaltes.

Thirteen kilometres to the south, on the way to the resorts of the Côte Vermeille (see below) and served by the same buses and trains, lies the town of **ELNE**. This small place once had the honour of seeing Hannibal camp at its walls en route for Rome, and used to be the capital of Roussillon, until it was displaced by Perpignan as seat of the kings of Majorca. Today, it's worth a stop for its fortified, partially Romanesque **cathedral** and extremely beautiful **cloister** (daily 10–11.45am & 2–4.45pm; April & May daily 9.30am–12.15pm & 2–5.45pm; June–Sept daily 9.30am–6.45pm). Though only one side of the cloister is strictly Romanesque, immaculately carved with motifs such as foliage, lions, goats and Biblical figures, the three fourteenth-century Gothic ones have been made to harmonize perfectly – it's the best introduction to Roussillon Romanesque you could want. Below the cathedral there are still a few streets of the old town left, twisting back down to the drab and unremarkable modern development.

The Côte Vermeille

Known as the **Côte Vermeille**, the last few miles of shore before Spain, where the Pyrenees sweep down to the sea, once held a handful of attractive seaside villages. Tourism has put paid to that, though they are well served by buses and trains from Perpignan and can provide a breather.

ARGELÈS, the first of the resorts with the last of the wide sandy beaches on this stretch of coast, is lively and friendly but packed out with foreign tourists. The **Musée Catalan** in rue de l'Égalité (Mon–Fri 9am–noon & 3.30–6pm, Sat 9am–noon) has some interesting exhibits of local arts and traditions.

A few kilometres south is overly quaint **COLLIOURE**, set on its bay and once by far the prettiest of these places, inspiring Matisse and Derain in 1905 to embark on their explosive Fauvist colour experiments. Palm trees line the curving beach, while behind the town, slopes of vines and olives rise to ridges crowned with ruined forts and watch towers. The **Château des Templiers** (daily 2.30–7.30pm; July & Aug 10.30am–7.30pm), which dominates the town, was founded by the Templars in the twelfth century, and has undergone numerous alterations, especially at the hands of the kings of Majorca and Aragon in the fourteenth century and again after the Treaty of the Pyrenees gave Collioure to France. Today, it is largely given over to summertime exhibitions. Collioure's other landmark is the distinctive round belfry of the seventeenth-century **church of Notre-Dame-des-Anges**, formerly the harbour lighthouse; inside the nave are some exuberant Baroque altarpieces. Behind it two small **beaches** are divided by a causeway leading to the **chapel of St-Vincent**, built on what used to be a rocky islet, while to the left a concrete path follows the rocky shore to the bay of **Le Racou** back towards Argelès.

Behind the château lies the **old harbour**, where half a dozen brightly painted lateen-rigged fishing boats are often beached, all that remains of Collioure's traditional fleet. The attractive surrounding streets of pink- and beige-washed houses are the centre of tourist activity. The **tourist office** is here on place du 18-juin (Mon, Tues & Thurs–Sat 9.30am–noon & 2–6pm; July & Aug Mon–Sat 9.30am–noon & 3.30–7pm, Sun 10am–noon; ☎68.82.15.47). Two pleasant places to **stay** are the *Triton* (☎68.82.06.52; ②) and *Boramar* (☎68.82.07.06; ①–③; closed Nov–March), both on the main beach close to the through road. Cheaper, though a little grim, is the *Majorque*, 16 av de-Gaulle (☎68.82.29.22; ①). The best **campsite** is the seaside *La Girelle* (April–Sept), but there are numerous others in the area should it be full.

PORT-VENDRES, 3km further down the coast, is a functional sort of place. Although the harbour has never been as busy as it was in the nineteenth century, with colonial trade and ferries from North Africa, it still lands more fish than any other place on this stretch of coast. If you're interested, the boats come in between about 4.30 and 6pm every day, except Sunday. You can watch them unload and then auction the catch on the dock at the far end of the harbour. Otherwise, there is little to see here.

South towards **BANYULS**, 7km further on, where the **GR10** finally comes down to the sea, the road winds through attractive scenery with the Albères hills rising steeply on the right. The town, built round a broad sweep of pebble beach, is pleasant but lacks the charm of Collioure and the energy of more popular resorts. There are, however, two things to do before moving on. One is to visit the seafront **aquarium** of the Laboratoire Arago, run by the Sorbonne's marine biology department (daily 9am–noon & 2–6.30pm; summer closes 10pm; 18F), whose tanks contain a comprehensive collection of the region's fish and submarine life. The other is to sample the dark, full-bodied *Banyuls* **wine**, an *appellation* which, apart from Banyuls itself, applies only to the vineyards of Collioure, Port-Vendres and Cerbère. The best place to do this is the *Cellier des Templiers* on rte du Mas-Reig, just under the rail line at the foot of the steep brown stone terraces of Banyuls' own vineyards (daily 9am–7pm; closed Oct–April). For further information consult the **tourist office** opposite the Hôtel de Ville on the seafront (July & Aug daily 9am–12.30pm & 2.30–7pm; April–June & Sept Tues–Sat 2–6pm). There's a **hotel**, *Le Manoir* at 20 rue du Maréchal-Joffre (☎68.88.32.98; ①–③), and if you're **camping**, there's a municipal site on the rte du Mas-Reig (April to mid-Oct).

A magnificent winding drive snakes up from Banyuls through the vineyards to the **Tour Madeloc**, a watchtower built by Jaime I of Majorca at the end of the thirteenth century on the crest of a ridge at about 650m. On a clear day, you can see down into Spain, along the coast, across to Montpellier and over the Corbières, with the castles of Quéribus and Peyrepertuse easily visible.

Vallespir and the valley of the Tech

The first stop on the D115, the main road which follows the **Tech Valley** inland all the way up to the Spanish border at Prats-de-Mollo, is **CÉRET**, capital of the Vallespir region, and served like the rest of the valley by regular buses from Perpignan's *gare routière*. It is a delightful place, friendly and bustling, with a wonderfully shady old town overhung by huge plane trees. The streets are typically narrow and winding, opening onto small squares like the **place des Neuf-Jets**, so called because of its trickling fountain. There's a large and varied Saturday **market** spilling out of place Pablo-Picasso into the main street, av d'Espagne, where two remnants of the medieval walls, the **Porte de France** and **Porte d'Espagne**, are visible. In summer, Céret is also a big centre for *corridas*; the arena is on the other side of town from the market, out towards the Amélie-les-Bains road. Other high points include the Easter Sunday procession of the Resurrected Christ, at a time of year when Céret's famous cherry harvest is also getting under way. And there is an international *sardana* jamboree on the second to last Sunday in August.

Céret's main sight, however, is the remarkable **Musée d'Art Moderne** (daily except Tues 10am–6pm; July & Aug daily 10am–7pm; 25F), just off bd Maréchal-Joffre.

In the early years of this century, Céret's charms, coupled with the presence here of the Catalan artist and sculptor Manolo, drew a number of avant-garde artists to the town, including Matisse and Picasso, who personally dedicated a number of pictures to the museum; it also contains work by Chagall, Dali, Dufy and Manolo, among others. Among the Picassos is a marvellous series of ceramic bowls illustrating bullfighting scenes, and a sketch of a *sardana*.

You can get more information on the *corridas* and other aspects of the town from the **tourist office** on av Clemenceau (daily 10am–noon & 2–5.30pm; ☎68.87.00.53). If you're **staying**, the *Hôtel Vidal* in the place du 4-septembre (☎68.87.00.85; ②–③; restaurant from 68F) is a very attractive and reasonably priced place to stay. The **camping municipal** is just out of town on the Maureillas road.

For **eating**, there is a good, cheap restaurant-*crêperie*, *Le Pied dans le Plat*, on place des Neuf-Jets, while gourmets with money to spare can try the best food for miles around at *Les Feuillants* (☎68.87.37.88; closed Sun noon, Mon & Feb; 220F upwards), whose sophisticated ambience features utterly delicious Catalan cuisine.

To the Spanish frontier

West of Céret, past the leaping single span of its fourteenth-century **Pont du Diable**, the view opens north towards the towering imminence of the Canigou Massif. **AMÉLIE-LES-BAINS**, the next place you come to, is hardly worth a stop, being a rather stodgy health spa for the elderly and rheumatic. If an **overnight stay** is necessary, *Hôtel La Chaumière* at 2 av du Vallespir (☎68.39.05.35; ②), right on the river in the middle of town, is an attractive place, and there are various **campsites**, including the *Hollywood* back towards Céret at La Forge (mid-April to mid-Nov).

ARLES-SUR-TECH, 4km up the valley, is a more interesting spot. It has a beautiful Romanesque **church**, whose Carolingian origins in the ninth century are thought to account for its back-to-front alignment of altar at the west end and the entrance at the east. The massive interior is impressive, but the church's most renowned feature is the **cloister** (daily 10am–noon & 2–5.30pm; free), whose pointed white marble arches and twin columns prefigure the Gothic, showing its relative lateness compared to other examples of Romanesque in the region, like Serrabonne (see opposite). Twin towers flank the church, while against the wall outside the east front – whose plainness is beautifully relieved, as the sun turns, by the shadow of blind arcading – stands a very ancient sarcophagus, known as the **Sainte Tombe**, which has the mysterious and scientifically inexplicable habit of slowly filling with very pure water. The **GR10** passes through Arles, climbing north towards the Cortalets refuge on Canigou and south towards the Roc de France.

The **tourist office** is in rue Barjau, and you can **stay** at the attractive *Hôtel des Glycines* on rue du Jeu-de-Paume (☎68.39.10.09; ②–③), with a good restaurant (from 85F) and wisteria-shaded terrace. The **campsite** is on the west side of town.

A couple of kilometres from Arles in the direction of Prats-de-Mollo, on the right, is the entrance to the **Gorges de la Fou**, some 2km in length, very narrow and up to 250m deep (daily April–Sept 10am–6pm; Oct 10am–5pm; closed in bad weather; ☎68.39.16.21; 25F). It's spectacular, but unfortunately something of a tourist trap, with a car park, admission charge, snacks, and a metal catwalk all along the bottom of the gorge.

After the gorge, the road climbs on towards the border, between valley sides thick with walnut, oak and sweet chestnut, to **PRATS-DE-MOLLO**. Prats is the last French town before the border with Spain, and has a very Spanish atmosphere. Most of the population seems to sit around or play *pétanque* in El Firal, the main square. It's surprisingly unspoilt for a border town, and its **ville haute** makes a wonderful wander, with steep cobbled streets and a weather-worn grey church with marvellous ironwork on the door under the porch. The encircling walls were rebuilt in the seventeenth century after the suppression of a local revolt against the taxation newly imposed by Louis XIV after the Treaty of the

Pyrenees brought these lands under his sway. The **Fort Lagarde** (April–Nov pm only; free), on the heights above the town, also dates from this period, built to keep the local population in check as much as keeping the Spanish out. For a **bed**, try *Hôtel des Touristes* in av du Haut-Vallespir (☎68.39.72.12; ②–③), or if you're **camping**, there's a municipal site 1km along the road towards La Preste.

From here it is only 13km to the border on the **Col d'Ares**. The next place of any size on the other side is **CAMPRODÓN**, a village about 18km away. Alternatively, if you're feeling energetic, you can bus or hitch the 8km north to the spa town of La Preste, and then walk over the **Col Prégon**. It's about an hour's steep climb to the top, followed by another hour's more gentle descent down to the small village of **ESPINAVELL** – leave the road at the first turning on the right before you get into La Preste, and then take the path from La Forge.

From Tech to Têt

The only practical route between the **valleys of the Tech and the Têt**, especially if you're hitching, is the D618 across the eastern spurs of Canigou from Amélie-les-Bains to Bouleternère. It's 43 slow kilometres of mountain road, twisting and climbing through magnificent woods of holm oak, cork oak, regular oak, chestnut, ash and cherry, with explosions of yellow broom and tangles of wild honeysuckle, past isolated half-derelict farms or *mas*, some still tenanted by survivors of the post-1968 migration from the towns. About halfway along, the three-house hamlet of **BELPUIG** stands on the road. One of its buildings is the **Chapelle de la Trinité**, a tiny, dark Romanesque church in grey and yellow stone with elaborate doors and a particularly fine crucifix from the twelfth century. Past the cemetery and up the hill beside a pine plantation, a path climbs to the ruined **Château de Belpuig**, some fifteen minutes' walk from the road with long-range views over the surrounding country.

From here the road descends into the valley bottom, through the pretty hamlet of **BOULE D'AMONT**, before climbing again to the remarkable **Prieuré de Serrabonne** (daily 10am–6pm; 25F), some 4km up an asphalt lane above the road. Even without its carvings, Serrabonne (consecrated in 1151) would still be impressive purely by virtue of its location: high on the scrub-covered mountainside, with massive views over the rocky Boulès Valley and into the valley of the Têt. Yet it is also one of the finest examples – perhaps *the* finest – of Roussillon Romanesque. The interior of the church is breathtakingly simple, making the beautiful carvings on the capitals of the pillars in the tribune even more striking: vividly carved lions, centaurs, griffins and human figures with oriental faces and haircuts – motifs brought back from the Crusades – all in the local pink marble. The altar is made of the same stone, as are the pillars and equally elaborate capitals of the cloister, which is set to one side of the church on a high terrace. Despite the rigours of monastic life here – all abandoned now – the settlement was well developed, and the remains of terraced cultivation and irrigation systems are still visible.

When you reach the Têt at Bouleternère, a 4km detour would take you to **Ille-sur-Têt**, where there is a very interesting museum of sacred art, the **Centre d'Art Sacré** (daily except Tues 10am–noon & 2–7pm; Oct–April 10am–noon & 3–6pm; 20F), whose exhibits include both temporary and permanent shows.

Canigou and the valley of the Têt

The upper part of the Têt Valley, known as the **Pays de Conflent**, is utterly dominated by **Canigou**. The valley bottoms are lush with peach and apple orchards – with the possibility of work as a picker from June onwards – but the mountain presides over all, vast and uncompromising.

The valley capital is **PRADES**, easily accessible by train and bus on the Perpignan–Villefranche–La Tour-de-Carol route and, whether or not you stay, the obvious starting point for all excursions in the Canigou region. It is an attractive place, although there are no great sights beyond the **church of St-Pierre** in the town centre, but it enjoys a standing way out of proportion to its size or economic power. This is largely thanks to the Catalan cellist, Pablo Casals, who set up home here as an exile and fierce opponent of the Franco regime in Spain. In 1950 he instituted the internationally renowned **music festival** now held every year in the abbey of St-Michel-de-Cuxa (see overleaf) from the end of July to the middle of August. Prades is also a centre of ardent Catalan feeling. It hosts a summertime Catalan university (mid- to end Aug) and boasts the first Catalan-language primary school in France.

The **tourist office** at 4 rue Victor-Hugo (Mon–Fri 9am–noon & 2–6pm; July & Aug Mon–Sat 9am–12.30pm & 2.30–7pm, Sun 2.30–7pm; ☎68.96.27.58) is a mine of information about the area and can sort out advance bookings for the music festival. For **accommodation**, try the *Hostalrich* on the rte Nationale (☎68.96.05.38; ④), or *Les Glycines* (☎68.96.51.65; ②). If you have a car, you could try across the river in Molitg-les-Bains or, better still, up in Vernet-les-Bains (see opposite). The **camping municipal** (May–Oct) is by the river on the road to Molitg.

For an undemanding walk, head over to **EUS** on the far side of the valley from Prades. The upper, medieval, part of the village grouped round its **fortress church** has been largely taken over by Parisians and foreigners, to the displeasure of the farming inhabitants of the lower, more modern part – a common occurrence in these picturesque but depopulated villages. To the left of the church, an old mule road climbs up through the scrubland to the derelict village of **COMES**, with a single shepherd and his family in residence, in about one hour.

Climbing the Pic

You can get at least part of the way up the **Pic du Canigou** by car or on foot. **Cars** – and you would be well advised not to try it in a much-loved saloon – can get as far as the *Chalet des Cortalets* refuge either by the track from Villerach or the even steeper and rougher mining road that begins by the *Al Pouncy* **campsite** near Fillols and passes the *Refuge de Balatg* and the now vandalized *Cabane des Cortalets*, where herds of cows and horses graze untended. (They are the best barometer of mountain weather, the locals say, descending to lower altitudes when bad weather is imminent.) Both routes take about an hour. You can also **rent a jeep** and driver from *LeBohec* (☎68.05.20.48), *Amalric* (☎68.96.26.47), or *Calas* (☎68.05.03.08) in Prades, or from the *Garage Louis Villaceque* (☎68.05.51.14), *Bruzan* (☎68.05.62.28) in Vernet-les-Bains, or *Taurigna* (☎68.05.63.06) in Fillols. For **walkers**, the standard ascent is from Vernet on a path that begins about 1km along the road to Fillols, joining up with the **GR10** at the *Refuge de Bonaigua* (about 3hr) which you leave (about 90min) below the **Pic Joffre** to follow the HRP up the ridge to the summit (about 1hr). It is not for faint hearts, because the final ascent up a chimney is rather exposed. There is a five-hour alternative, starting from Casteil, passing the *Refuge Mariailles* (☎68.67.67.07; food served; open all year) on the GR10, then following the HRP for the last stretch via the *Refuge Arago*.

From the *Chalet des Cortalets* (☎68.96.36.19; May–Oct), which has a restaurant, or the smaller *CAF* refuge next door, it's an easy ninety-minute walk to the top. Strike west from the refuge through the last trees, past the little lake with a magnificent view into the *cirque* below the summit, round the back of the Pic Joffre, and up the long stony ridge to the cross and Catalan flag that crown the summit.

Although the **ascent** by this route is straightforward in good weather, you should be properly shod and clothed and have good large-scale maps. If you are not experienced and encounter frozen snow, turn back: a German couple slid to their deaths on the slopes between Pic Joffre and the summit in 1991. Midsummer is a great time to do the climb. Catalans for miles around, including half the population of Barcelona, gather on the top on the night of June 21, which often coincides with the full moon, to light the bonfire from which a flame is carried to kindle all the *feux de St-Jean* of the Catalan villages, although the scene around the refuge can be pretty horrendous, with tents, stereos and litter galore.

Vernet-les-Bains

A quiet and not unpleasant little spa, **VERNET-LES-BAINS** can make a useful base for picking up provisions and information. It has a **tourist office** in place de la Mairie (Mon–Fri 10am–noon & 2–5pm, Sat 10am–noon; June–Sept daily 9.30am–12.30pm & 3–7pm, Sun 9.30am–12.30pm) and plenty of **eating and drinking** possibilities in the main square. It's also a good place to **stay** the night, either at *Hôtel Moderne*, 7 av des Thermes ☎68.05.52.17; ③), or *Hôtel des Thermes*, 22 av des Thermes (☎68.05.50.06; ②; closed Dec–Feb). There's a **campsite**, *Camping Le Cady*, just up the road towards Casteil. In Casteil itself, there is a **gîte d'étape** in av St-Saturnin (☎68.05.51.30). Returning to the valley bottom at Villefranche-de-Conflent, you might want to stop off and look at the magnificent Romanesque church in **CORNEILLA** (key from the care-taker next door).

The abbeys near Vernet

Close to Prades and Vernet are two of the loveliest abbeys in the country. **St-Michel-de-Cuxa** (Mon–Sat 9.30–11.50am & 2–5pm, Sun 2–5pm, until 6pm in summer), 3km from Prades, dates from around 1000AD, and although it was mutilated after the Revolution, it is still beautiful, with its crenellated tower silhouetted against the wooded slopes of Canigou. The bare stone crypt and church – the altar slab was rediscovered doing duty as a balcony on a house in the village of Vinça – are impressive enough, but the glory of the place is the **cloister**. Although some of the capitals were shipped off to the Cloisters Museum in New York earlier this century, those that remain are a feast for the eyes. Carved in the twelfth century in rose-pink marble from Villefranche, they are decorated with exact and highly stylized human, animal and vegetable motifs. The monastery is still inhabited by a small community of Benedictines from Monserrat in Spain.

St-Martin-du-Canigou is just 2km from Vernet-les-Bains, or a half-hour walk above the hamlet of Casteil – with restaurants under the apple orchards, and a **campsite**, *Camping St-Martin*, with swimming pool. Resurrected from its ruins at the turn of the century, the monastery occupies a narrow promontory of rock at over 1000m altitude. Quiet and serene, it is surrounded by the deep shade of chestnut and oak woods, and above it rise the precipitous slopes and eroded pinnacles of Canigou. Below, the ground drops sheer into the ravine of the Cady stream that rushes down from the Col de Jou. The buildings are visitable, in silent groups (summer daily except Tues 10am & 11.45am, 2pm, 3pm, 4pm & 5pm; winter daily 10am, 11.45am, 2.30 & 4.30pm; 15F). What you see is a beautiful little garden and cloister overlooking the ravine, a low dark atmospheric chapel beneath the church and the church itself. Founded in the tenth century, St-Martin was the inspiration for the Romanesque architecture of the region. The graves of the founder, Count Guifred of Cerdagne, and his wife lie in the rock by the church door. It is possible, on request, to do a week's retreat as part of the community.

From the reception building a **path** leads up to a rocky viewpoint from which you can look down on the monastery and away across the valley to the surrounding mountains. As you go up, you pass a signpost to Moura on a path which leads first to the Col de Segalès on the GR10, then, on the HRP, to the *Refuge Arago* and finally to the summit of Canigou – the last stretch involving a rather steep hands-and-feet scramble which might alarm the inexperienced. For a different route back to Casteil, a path drops down into the Cady ravine just at the start of the monastery buildings.

Villefranche-de-Conflent and the Petit Train Jaune

A medieval garrison town suffering from arrested development, **VILLEFRANCHE** is a tourist classic and lives off it. But it is interesting: founded around 1100 by the counts of

Cerdagne to bar the road to Moorish invaders, remodelled by Vauban in the seventeenth century after rebelling against annexation by France, its streets and fortifications have remained untouched by subsequent development. The **church of St-Jacques** is worth a look, and you can walk the **walls** for a fee (daily summer 10am–7.30pm; winter 9am–noon & 2–6pm; 20F). If you do so, you will see why Vauban constructed the **Libéria fortress** on the heights overlooking the town to protect it from "aerial" bombardment. The way up to the Libéria (daily except Mon 9am–6pm) is a stairway of a thousand steps beginning just across the old bridge and rail line at the end of rue St-Pierre. If you don't fancy the climb, ask at the **tourist office** (summer daily 9am–7pm; winter Mon–Fri 9am–5pm; ☎68.96.22.96) by the church for the minibus. For **hiking and other miscellaneous information**, ask at the *Association culturelle de Villefranche* at 38 rue St-Jean. For **accommodation**, it's better to try Vernet or Prades.

Villefranche is the terminus for trains from Perpignan (**gare SNCF** ☎68.96.09.18). From here up to **La Tour-de-Carol** on the Spanish frontier, transport is by *SNCF* bus, or, far nicer, the narrow-gauge **Petit Train Jaune**, which climbs to the valley head at a pace that allows you a walker's or cyclist's proximity to the scenery, especially in summer when some of the carriages are open air.

On up the Têt

Just beyond Thuès-Entre-Valls, southwest of Villefranche on the left of the main N116, the wild wooded canyon of the **Gorges de la Carança** cuts south into the mountains towards Spain. A path follows the gorge to a junction with the GR10 at the refuge of the *Ras de la Carança* (3–4hr), while a further path continues on to meet the HRP on the frontier in another four hours.

At **FONTPÉDROUSE**, 5km beyond Thuès, a road branches south across the river and up a grassy spur above the River Aigues towards the village of Prat-Balaguer. From the top of the rise directly opposite Fontpédrouse, a path leads down to the Aigues where water from **hot springs** forms three separate pools at different temperatures, where you can skinny-dip for free.

Another 10km up the main road brings you onto the wide **plateau of the Cerdagne**, whose once powerful counts controlled lands from Barcelona to Roussillon and endowed the monasteries of St-Michel-de-Cuxa, St-Martin-du-Canigou and Ripoll, now well inside Spain. It's an area that has never been sure whether it is Spanish or French. After the French annexation of Roussillon, it was partitioned, with Spain retaining – as it does today – the enclave of Lliva.

The first place you come to is the little garrison town of **MONT-LOUIS**, built by Vauban in 1679 and still used as a base for paratroops and marines. There isn't much to see, but it is a far pleasanter place to stay than the monstrous ski resort of **FONT-ROMEU** just down the road, and it has a **tourist office** (mid-June to mid-Sept daily 10am–noon & 2–6pm) and a delightful **hotel**, the *Lou Raballou* (☎68.04.23.20; ③–④), towards the back of the town near the barracks, with an excellent restaurant (menus from 120F). There is a **campsite** at **PLA DE BARRES**, 3km away on the road to the Lac des Bouillousses (June–Sept), a **gîte d'étape** at La Cassagne farm (☎68.04.21.40), half an hour back down the main road, and a **youth hostel** 12km west along the N116 at Saillagousse (☎68.04.71.69; ①).

Of things to do round about, there is a good four-hour walk from the pretty mountain village of **EYNE** up a valley renowned for its flowers and medicinal plants to the Col d'Eyne, and numerous walks in the **Carlit Massif** around the **Lac des Bouillousses** – where there's a *CAF* refuge (☎68.04.20.76), though the lake itself and parts accessible by car get very crowded in season. The region's curiosity is the **Four solaire**, or solar power station (daily 10am–12.30pm & 1.30–5.30pm), at **ODEILLO** just below Font-Romeu, although the most impressive part of this, a screen composed of thousands of mirrors, can in fact be seen from the road.

travel details

Trains

Bayonne to: Biarritz (frequent; 10min); Bordeaux (frequent; 1hr 50min); Boussens (4 daily; 3hr); Cambo-les-Bains (4 daily; 20min); Hendaye (frequent; 35min); Lannemazan (4 daily; 2hr 40min); Lourdes (4 daily; 1hr 40min); Montréjeau (4 daily; 2hr 50min); Orthez (4 daily; 50min); Pau (4 daily; 1hr 15min); St-Gaudens (4 daily; 3hr); St-Jean-de-Luz (frequent; 30min); St-Jean-Pied-de-Port (4 daily; 1hr 10min); Tarbes (4 daily; 2hr); Toulouse (4 daily; 4hr).

Foix to: Ax-les-Thermes (5 daily; 45min); Barcelona (2 daily; 5hr 15min–6hr 15min); Latour-de-Carol (5 daily; 1hr 40min–2hr 10min); Tarascon (5 daily; 20min); Toulouse (6–8 daily; 50–70min).

Luchon to: Montréjeau (3 daily; 35min).

Montréjeau to: Boussens (25min); Luchon (3 daily; 35min); Pau (several daily; 1hr 35min); Saint-Gaudens (several daily; 10min); Tarbes (several daily; 35min); Toulouse (several daily; 1hr 15min); Lourdes (several daily; 50min).

Pau to: Oloron-Ste-Marie (4 daily; 30min).

Perpignan to: Argelès (frequent; 18min); Banyuls (33min); Barcelona (6 daily; 2hr 15min–5hr); Cerbère (frequent; 55min); Collioure (23min); Elne (frequent; 10min); Leucate (frequent; 25min); Narbonne (frequent; 40min); Port-Bou (frequent; 50min); Port-la-Nouvelle (frequent; 33min); Port-Vendres (frequent; 27min); Prades (7 daily; 40min); Rivesaltes (frequent; 7min); Salses (frequent; 15min); Villefranche-de-Conflent (7 daily; 52min).

Quillan to: Carcassonne (3 daily; 1hr); Limoux (3 daily; 30min).

Tarbes to: Lourdes (frequent; 20min).

Buses

Bayonne to: Biarritz (frequent; 15min); Cambo-les-Bains (7 daily; 30min); San Sebastian (4 daily); St-Jean-de-Luz (frequent; 40min).

Biarritz to: Bayonne (4 daily; 15min); Orthez (4 daily; 1hr 45min); Pau (4 daily; 2hr 30min); St-Jean-de-Luz (frequent; 35min); Salies-de-Béarn (4 daily; 1hr 20min).

Foix to: Ax-les-Thermes (3 daily; 55min); Carcassonne (1 daily except Sun; 2hr 35min); Lavelanet (1 daily except Sun; 35min); Mirepoix (1

daily except Sun; 1hr 30min); Pamiers (4–6 daily; 25min); Quillan (1 daily; 3hr); Tarascon (3 daily; 20min); Toulouse (4–6 daily; 1hr 50min).

Lannemazan to: Arreau (4–5 daily; 30min); St-Lary (4–5 daily; 1hr).

Lourdes to: Árgelès-Gazost (several daily; 20min); Bagnères-de-Bigorre (3 daily; 45min–1hr); Barèges (2–3 daily; 1hr); Cauterets (5 daily; 50min); Gavarnie (June to mid-Sept 3 daily; 1hr 15min); Lannemazan (3 daily; 1hr); Luz-St-Sauveur (2–3 daily; 45min); Pau (4 daily; 1hr 15min); Pierrefitte-Nestalas (10 daily; 30min); Tarbes (frequent; 30min).

Pau to: Artouste and Gabas (summer Sat & Sun 1 daily; 1hr 45min); Eaux-Bonnes (4 daily; 1hr 15min); La Gourette (4 daily; 1hr 45min); Laruns (4 daily; 1hr 5min); Lourdes (4 daily; 1hr 30min); Mauléon (1 daily; 1hr 50min); Navarrenx (1 daily; 1hr 35min); Tarbes (6 daily; 1hr); Orthez (1 daily; 1hr 10min).

Perpignan to: Amélie-les-Bains (10 daily; 1hr 10min); Argelès (12 daily; 30min); Arles-sur-Tech (1hr 20min); Collioure (5 daily; 45min); Banyuls (5 daily; 1hr 10min); Céret (frequent; 55min); Font-Romeu (1 daily; 2hr 25min); Latour-de-Carol (3 daily; 2hr); Mont-Louis (3 daily; 1hr 30min); Port-Vendres (5 daily; 55min); Prats-de-Mollo (5 daily; 1hr 50min); Prades (7 daily; 1hr); La Preste (5 daily; 2hr 5min); Villefranche-de-Conflent (7 daily; 1hr 15min).

Quillan to: Carcassonne (4 daily; 1hr 15min); Comus (2 daily; 1hr 5min); Perpignan (2 daily; 1hr 30min).

St-Girons to: Aulus-les-Bains (1–2 daily; 1hr 15min); Boussens (several daily; 45min); Foix (4 daily; 1hr); Sentein (1 daily; 1hr); Toulouse (2–4 daily; 2hr 30min).

St-Jean-de-Luz to: Cambo-les-Bains (3 daily; 45 min); Espelette (3 daily; 35 min); Hasparren (3 daily; 1hr 5min); Hendaye (frequent; 35min); Sare-la-Rhune (3 daily; 30min).

Tarascon to: Auzat (Mon, Fri & Sat 1 daily; 1hr 20min).

Tarbes to: Bagnères-de-Bigorre (several daily; 40min); Lourdes (frequent; 30min); St-Lary (1 daily; 2hr 10min); Tarbes-Ossun-Lourdes airport (1 daily; 30min–1hr).

CHAPTER ELEVEN

LANGUEDOC

Languedoc is more an idea than a geographical entity. The modern region covers only a fraction of the lands where once **Occitan** or the *langue d'oc* – the language of *oc*, the southern Gallo-Latin word for *oui* – was spoken. These stretched south from Bordeaux and Lyon into Spain and northwest Italy.

The heartland today is the **Bas Languedoc**, the coastal plain and dry, stony, vine-growing hills between Carcassonne and Nîmes. It is here that the Occitan movement has its power base, demanding greater independence and recognition of its linguistic and cultural distinctiveness. Its appeal derives from widespread resentment against

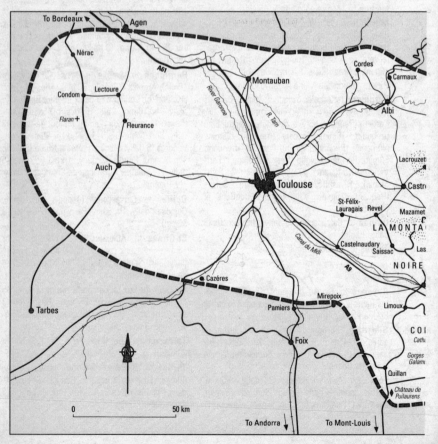

subservience to the bureaucrats of remote and alien Paris. In recent times this has been focused on Parisian determination to drag the province into the twentieth century, with massive tourist development on the coast and the drastic transformation of the cheap wine industry. But it is also mixed up in the collective folk-memory with the brutal repression of the Protestant Camisards around 1700, the thirteenth-century massacres of the Cathars, and the subsequent obliteration of the brilliant *langue d'oc* troubadour civilization. It is a hostility that has made an essentially rural and conservative population vote – paradoxically – massively for the Left.

It's a quirky, eccentric part of the world, and, although things are changing under the impact of a modernized economy, the Occitanian identity remains strong. Thousands of students take the language at school and follow courses at the universities of Montpellier and Toulouse, and a number of writers use Occitan as their normal medium of expression.

Toulouse, the cultural capital, though included in this chapter, lies outside the official region but is a deserved high spot among numerous and various other attractions. There are great stretches of dramatic landscape and river gorges, from the **Cévennes** foothills in the east to the **Montagne Noire** and the **Corbières** hills in the west. There's

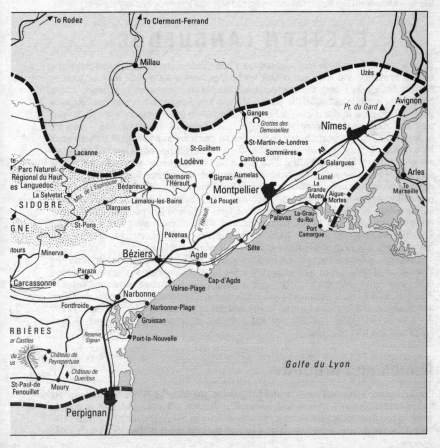

superb ecclesiastical architecture in **Albi** and **St-Guilhem-le-Désert**, medieval towns in **Cordes** and **Carcassonne**, with the unforgettably romantic **Cathar castles** to the south. **Nîmes** has extensive Roman remains, and there are great swathes of beach where – away from the major resorts – you can still find a mile or two to yourself.

EASTERN LANGUEDOC

Heading south from Paris via Lyon and the Rhône Valley, you can go one of two ways: east to Provence and the Côte d'Azur – which is what most people do – or west to Nîmes, Montpellier and the comparatively untouched northern Languedoc coast. **Nîmes** itself, while not officially part of the modern Languedoc region, makes for a good introduction to the region, a hectic modern town impressive both for its Roman past and for some scattered attractions – the **Pont du Gard** for one – nearby. **Montpellier**, also, is worth a day or two, not so much for any historical attractions as for a heady vibrancy and ease of access to the ancient villages, churches and fine scenery of the upper **Hérault Valley**. This is the part of Languedoc most affected by the spread of Protestantism in the sixteenth century, an experience that has marked the region's character more than any other. The Protestants, with their attachment to rationality and self-improvement, espoused the cause of French over Occitan, supported the Revolution and the Republic, fought Napoléon III's coup against the 1848 revolution and adhered to the anticlerical and socialist movement under the Third Republic. They dominated the local textile industry in the nineteenth century and, interestingly, were extremely active in the Resistance to the Nazis.

They also suffered a great deal for their cause, as did the whole region. After the Revocation of the Edict of Nantes in 1685 – the treaty that restored religious toleration at the end of the sixteenth century – persecution drove their most committed supporters, especially in the Cévennes to the north, to form clandestine *assemblées du Désert* and finally, in 1702, to take up arms in the first guerrilla war of modern times, *la guerre des Camisards*. These conflicts are still very much present in the minds of both Huguenot and Catholic families.

Nîmes and around

On the border between Provence and Languedoc, the name of **NÎMES** is inescapably linked to two things – denim and Rome. The latter's influence is highly visible in some of the most extensive Roman remains in Europe, while the former, equally visible on the backsides of the populace, was first manufactured in the city's textile mills (denim = *de Nîmes*), and exported to the southern USA in the nineteenth century to clothe slaves. It's worth a visit, in part for the ruins and, nowadays, for the city's new-found energy and direction, inspired by its mayor of the last thirteen years, Jean Bousquet. The former boss of the fashion house *Cacharel* has enlisted the services of a galaxy of architects and designers – including Norman Foster, Jean Nouvel and Philippe Starck – in his bid to wrest southern supremacy from neighbouring Montpellier.

Arrival and accommodation

The **gare SNCF** is ten minutes' walk southeast of the city centre at the end of av Feuchères, which leads down from Esplanade de-Gaulle, with the **gare routière** just behind in rue Ste-Félicité. There's a **tourist office annexe** in the station which handles hotel bookings (daily 9.30am–12.30pm & 2–6.30pm), and a **main tourist office** at 6 rue Auguste, by the Maison Carrée (Mon–Fri 8am–7pm, Sat 9am–noon & 2–5pm, Sun 10am–noon; July & Aug Mon–Fri 8am–8pm, Sat 9am–7pm, Sun 10am–5pm; ☎66.67.29.11).

There are several recommended **hotels** within easy walking distance of the station. *Hôtel La Couronne* is just to the right at 4 square de la Couronne (☎66.67.51.73; ①), but be warned that the street-side rooms can be very noisy. The *Concorde* is on the other side of the boulevard at 3 rue des Chapeliers beside the Palais de Justice (☎66.67.91.03; ①). Closer in to the centre, *Le France* is at 4 bd des Arènes (☎66.67.23.05; ②), *La Mairie* is at 11 rue des Greffes near the Hôtel de Ville (☎66.67.65.91; ④), and *Les Voyageurs* at 4 rue Roussy off bd Amiral-Courbet (☎66.67.46.52; ②). Slightly more expensive but still central, there's *La Bourse* at 2 rue Tedenat, off bd Victor-Hugo (☎66.67.33.64; ③–④), the *Hôtel des Tuileries*, 22 rue Roussy (☎66.21.31.15; ③), or the *Hôtel Carrière*, 6 rue Grizot (☎66.67.24.89; ②).

There's an IYHF **youth hostel** with tent space on chemin de la Cigale, 2km north-west of the centre (☎66.23.25.04; ①); take bus #8 from the *gare SNCF* to stop *Stade*. The last bus goes at 8pm. The **camping municipal** is on route de Générac, 5km south of the city centre, beyond the new Stade Costières and the autoroute.

The City

Most of what you'll want to see is contained within the boulevards Libération, Amiral-Courbet, Gambetta and Victor-Hugo. The focal point of the city, the first-century AD Roman **arena** (daily 9am–7pm; 20F), known as Les Arènes, lies at the junction of rues Libération and V-Hugo. One of the best-preserved Roman arenas anywhere, its arcaded two-storey façade conceals massive interior vaulting, riddled with corridors and support-ing raked tiers of seats with a capacity of more than 20,000 spectators, whose staple fare was the blood and guts of gladiatorial combat. When Rome's sway was broken by the barbarian invasions, the arena became a fortress and eventually a slum, home to an incred-ible 2000 people when it was cleared in the early 1800s. Today it has recovered something of its former role, with the passionate summer crowds still turning out for some real-life bloodletting – Nîmes is the premier European bullfighting scene outside Spain.

Behind the arena, through the beautiful little **place du Marché**, rue Fresque leads towards the city's other famous landmark, the **Maison Carrée** (daily 9am–noon & 2–5.30pm; July & Aug closes 7pm; free), a neat, jewel-like temple, celebrated for its integ-rity and almost Greek harmony of proportion. Built in 5 AD, it is dedicated to the adopted sons of the Emperor Augustus: all part of the business of blowing up the impe-rial personality cult. No surprise then that Napoléon, with his love of flummery and ennobling his cronies to boost his own legitimacy, should have taken it as the model for the church of the Madeleine in Paris. The temple stands in its own small square opposite rue Auguste, where the Roman forum used to be. Around it are scattered

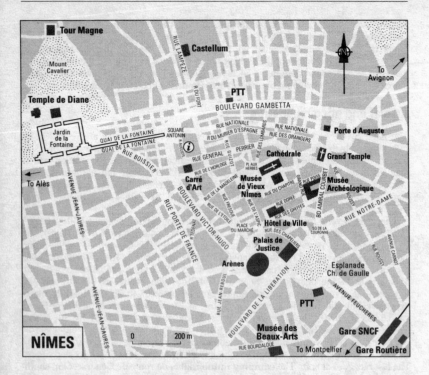

pieces of Roman masonry. The unlit interior is home to three enormous canvases by the American painter Julian Schnabel. On the north side of place de la Maison Carrée, there's a new example of French architectural boldness, the **Carré d'Art** by Norman Foster, housing nearly 300 works representing the principal movements in French art (daily 9am–noon & 2–5.30pm; free).

Though already a prosperous city on the *Via Domitia*, the main Roman road from Italy to Spain constructed in 118 BC, Nîmes did especially well by Augustus. He gave it its walls, remnants of which surface here and there around the town, and its gates, as the inscription on the surviving **Porte d'Auguste** at the end of rue Nationale – the Roman main street – records. He also, indirectly, gave it the chained crocodile of its coat of arms. The device was copied from an Augustan coin struck to commemorate his defeat of Antony and Cleopatra. And he settled his veterans on the surrounding land.

Cutting back east into the old quarter from the Maison Carrée, **rue de l'Horloge** leads to the delightful **place aux Herbes**, with two or three cafés and bars and a fine twelfth-century house on the corner of rue de la Madeleine. In the former bishop's palace, the **Musée du Vieux Nîmes** (daily except Mon 11am–6pm; 20F) has displays of Renaissance furnishings and décor and documents to do with local history. Opposite, the **Cathédrale Notre-Dame-et-St-Castor** sports a handsome sculpted frieze on the west front illustrating the story of Adam and Eve, and a pediment inspired by the Maison Carrée. It is practically the only existing medieval building in town, as most were destroyed in the turmoil that followed the *Michelade*, the St Michael's Day massacre of Catholic clergy and notables by Protestants in 1567. Despite brutal repression in the wake of the *Camisard* insurrection of 1702, Nîmes was, and remains, a doggedly Protestant stronghold. Apart from that, the cathedral is of little interest, having been seriously mutilated in the Wars of Religion and significantly altered in the last century. Alphonse Daudet was born in its shadow, as was Jean Nicot – a doctor, no less – who introduced tobacco into France from Portugal in 1560 and gave his name to the world's most popular drug.

Banned from public office, the Protestants put their energy into making money. The results of their efforts can be seen in the seventeenth- and eighteenth-century *hôtels* they built themselves in the streets around the cathedral – rues de l'Aspic, Chapitre, Doré, Grand-Rue, among others. Their church is the serious-looking **Grand Temple** on bd Amiral-Courbet. On the same street, the **Musée Archéologique** (daily except Mon 11am–6pm; 20F), housed in a seventeenth-century Jesuit chapel at no. 13, is full of Roman bits and bobs. There's another museum, the **Musée des Beaux-Arts**, south of the Arènes in rue de la Cité-Foulc (daily except Mon 11am–6pm; 20F), that prides itself on a huge Gallo-Roman mosaic showing the *Marriage of Admetus*, but it is pretty ordinary apart from that.

The interior of the **Hôtel de Ville**, between rue Dorée and rue des Greffes, has been redesigned by the architect Jean-Michel Wilmotte, combining high-tech with classical stone. Most of the other major examples of revolutionary building are out on the southern edge of town: Jean Nouvel's pseudo-Mississippi-steamboat housing project, **Nemausus**, off the Arles road behind the *gare SNCF*, named after the deity of the local spring which gave Nîmes its name, and the magnificent sports stadium, the **Stades des Costières**, by Vittorio Gregotti, close to the autoroute along the continuation of av Jean-Jaurès. There's also a **bus depot** by Philippe Starck on av Carnot, just east of the centre.

Perhaps the most refreshing thing you can do while in Nîmes is head out to the **Jardin de la Fontaine**, northwest of the centre at the top end of av Jean-Jaurès, France's first public garden, created in 1750. At its foot flows the gloriously green and shady **Canal de la Fontaine** built to supplement the rather unsteady supply of water from the *fontaine*, the Nemausus spring, whose presence in a dry, limestone landscape gave Nîmes its existence. Behind the formal entrance, where fountains, nymphs and formal trees enclose the so-called **Temple of Diana**, steps climb the steep wooded slope, adorned with grots and nooks and artful streams, to the **Tour Magne** (daily 9am–noon & 2–5.30pm mid-June to mid-Sept 9am–7pm; 10F), a 32-metre tower from Augustus' city walls, with a terrific view out over the surrounding country – as far, it is claimed, as the Pic du Canigou on the edge of the Pyrenees.

Eating, drinking and entertainment

For **eating**, bd de la Libération and bd Amiral-Courbet harbour a stock of reasonably priced brasseries and pizzerias, and the café scene is lively along here, too, as it is in bd Victor-Hugo, where the *Napoléon* and *Café de la Bourse* are city classics. *La Truye qui Filhe*, 9 rue Fresque (closed Sun), is an agreeable self-service in the old town. *Les Persiennes*, 5 pl de l'Oratoire, 300m west of the arena (closed Mon), is good for traditional family cooking, and the popular and congenial *Nicolas*, 1 rue Poise (closed Mon), off bd Amiral-Courbet, is highly recommended, if a little pricier. *Les Vendanges* wine bar at 1 rue de la Violette makes a nice alternative, though the various *plats* work out quite expensive. Other places for a good feed include the *Hôtel de France*'s restaurant, with a *carte* from 100F, and a *gratinée de brandade de morue-Gardiane* to die for. *Le Magister*, 5 rue Nationale, has a menu from 140F.

For **music**, there's the jazz bar *Le Mondial* on bd Gambetta, and the *Café de Lyon* on bd Victor-Hugo also serves live sounds. For up-to-the-minute information, you can't do better than ask at Laurent Maréchal's music shop, *Broc 'n Roll*, 3 rue des Flottes, near the Maison Carrée.

Between May and September, dozens of other events take place, most notably **bullfights**, which are Nîmes' particular passion and raise the city's temperature to fever pitch. The principal *fierias* to watch out for are the **La Fieria du Carnaval** in February, when the inflatable "roof" of the *Arènes* is pulled over for protection from the weather; the ten-day madness of the Whitsun **Fieria de Pentecôte**, including bull-running in the streets; and the **Fieria des Vendanges** in the third week of September. You can pick up information on these and other happenings at the tourist office on rue Auguste.

The Pont du Gard and Uzès

Several buses a day head east from Nîmes' *gare routière* along the Avignon road to Uzès, at the source of the Eure – the start of the fifty-kilometre-long aqueduct built by the Romans in 19 AD to bring fresh water into Nîmes. With just 17m difference in altitude between start and finish, it was quite an achievement, running as it does up hill and down dale, through a tunnel, along the top of a wall, cut into trenches, and over rivers. The greatest surviving stretch is the bridge that carries it over the River Gard, the **Pont du Gard**, 21km from Nimes, at which Uzès buses stop. Today it is something of a tourist trap, but is nonetheless a supreme piece of engineering, a brilliant combination of function and aesthetics. It made the impressionable Rousseau wish he'd been born Roman.

Three tiers of arches span the river, with the covered water conduit on the top, rendered with a special plaster waterproofed with a paint apparently based on fig juice. Whatever the recipe, it's in need of a powerful descaler to remove the lime deposits of centuries. You can walk across the bridge, if the height does not bother you, although the whole structure narrows as it rises and is slightly bowed on the upstream side for extra resistance to flooding. A visit was a must for French journeymen masons on their traditional tour of the country, and many of them have left their names and home towns carved on the stone work. You can also see markings left on individual stones in the arches by the original builders, like *FR S III – frons sinistra*, front side left no. 3.

UZÈS is 17km further on, an attractive old town perched on a hill above the River Alzon, though a bit of a backwater until renovation put it on the tourist circuit. Half a dozen medieval towers – the most fetching is the windowed Pisa-like **Tour Fenestrelle**, tacked on to the much later cathedral – rise above its tiled roofs and narrow lanes of Renaissance and Neoclassical houses, the residences of the seventeenth- and eighteenth-century local bourgeoisie, grown rich like their Protestant co-religionists in Nîmes on textiles. From the mansion of **Le Portalet**, with its view out over the valley, walk past the classical **church of St-Étienne** and into the medieval **place aux Herbes**, where there's a Sunday morning market, and up the arcaded **rue de la République**. The Gide family used to live off the square, the young André spending summer vacations with his granny there. To the right of rue de la République the castle of **Le Duché** (daily 9.30am–noon & 2.30–6.30pm; 25F), still inhabited by the same family a thousand years on, is dominated by its original keep, the **Tour Bermonde**. Today, there are guided tours around the castle building and exhibits of local history and vintage cars. Opposite, the courtyard of the eighteenth-century **Hôtel de Ville** holds summer concerts.

For details of these and other summer events, including more bull-running *corridas*, consult the **tourist office** in av de la Libération (☎66.22.68.88), next to the **bus station**. Should you need a **bed**, the *Hôtel La Taverne*, 7 rue Xavier-Sigalon (☎66.22.47.08; ③), and the *Hostellerie Provençale*, 1 rue Grande-Bourgade (☎66.22.11.06; ②), are the best bets, with the *Hôtel Marie d'Agoult* on the Arpaillargues road west of town (☎66.22.14.48; ⑤), offering excellent food and luxurious surroundings. Alternatively, there is a **camping municipal** off av Pascal (mid-June to mid-Sept), the Bagnols-sur-Cèze road running east of town.

More Roman ruins... and Sommières

About 25km west of Nîmes, off the Sommières road out of Lunel and close to the A9 autoroute, the Roman **Via Domitia** crosses the vineyards from the village of Gallargues to the bank of the River Vidourle, where one isolated arch of the original **Roman bridge** remains. On the west bank a fine stretch of the old **cobbled way** is visible climbing the slopes of the former Roman settlement of **Ambrussum**, a fortified staging-post on the road. From the top of the hill you look down on the modern international traffic still passing the same way, on the autoroute and parallel rail line. About 10km to the north, 28km from Nîmes, still on the Vidourle, the little medieval town of **SOMMIÈRES**, with a much modified Roman bridge, is where Lawrence Durrell spent the last years of his life. There is nothing special to see: just wander the hilly old streets.

There are three daily buses from Nîmes (Sat & Sun 1 daily), which pass through the village of **NAGES**, between Sommières and Nîmes, where there are the ruins of another Roman town. There is a **camping municipal** in rue Eugène-Rouch, and a pleasant, inexpensive **hotel**, *Le Commerce*, 15 quai Gaussorgues (☎66.80.97.22; ②), with a restaurant, or the fancier *Auberge du Port Romain*, 2 av Émile-Jamais (☎66.80.00.58; ④), set in an old château.

Montpellier

A thousand years of trade and intellect have made **MONTPELLIER** a teeming, energetic city. Benjamin of Tudela, the tireless twelfth-century Jewish traveller, reported its streets crowded with traders, Christian and Saracen, Arabs from the Maghreb, merchants from Lombardy, from the kingdom of Rome, from every corner of Egypt, Greece, Gaul, Spain, Genoa and Pisa. A few hiccups – like being sold to France in 1349, almost total destruction for its Protestantism in 1622, and depression in the wine trade in the early years of this century – have done little to dent this progress. Today it vies with Toulouse and Nîmes for the title of most dynamic city in the south, with a recent national survey nominating Montpellier. The reputation of its university especially, founded in the thirteenth century and most famous for its medical school, is a long-standing one, its 50,000 students still setting the intellectual and cultural tone of the city – the average age of which is said to be just twenty-five.

Arrival and accommodation

The **gare SNCF** and **gare routière** are next door to each other at the opposite end of rue Maguelone from the central place de la Comédie. The **airport**, Montpellier-Fréjorgues (also known as *Méditerranée*), is 8km to the southeast beside the Étang de Mauguio (buses 25F; 20min). The **tourist office** is off place de Comédie, in allée du Tourisme down some steps towards the *Sofitel* hotel (daily 9am–6pm; summer 9am–7pm; ☎67.58.67.58), and there's an annexe in the *gare SNCF*.

Most **hotel** accommodation is conveniently concentrated in the streets between the train station and place de la Comédie. The cheapest and simplest – entirely acceptable despite the price – is *Hôtel des Touristes*, 10 rue Baudin (☎67.58.42.37; ①); *Parady's*, 14 rue Broussairolles (☎67.58.42.54; ①), is also passable if you are looking for something cheap. The other recommended hotels in the area are comfortable and clean, if somewhat lacking in character: best of the bunch are *Le Mistral*, 25 rue Broussairolles (☎67.58.45.25; ②), and the *Hôtel de la Comédie*, 1bis rue Baudin (☎67.58.43.64; ③), although far the nicest and the most central of the hotels are the *Hôtel du Palais*, 3 rue du Palais (☎67.60.47.38; ④), off to the right at the top end of av Foch, and *Hôtel Le Guilhem*, 18 rue JJ-Rousseau (☎67.52.90.90; ④). Two other good hotels, a little further out, are *La Plantade*, 10 rue Plantade, off rue du Faubourg-du-Courreau (☎67.98.61.45; ①), and the *Hôtel du Polygone*, 16 av du Pont-Juvénal, near L'Antigone (☎67.65.81.41; ②). A little out of the centre in a quieter *quartier* is the comfortable *Ulysse*, 338 av St-Maur (☎67.02.02.30; ③), with free parking. There is a **youth hostel** at 2 impasse de la Petite-Corraterie in the old town (☎67.79.61.66; ①). **Campers** should head towards the coast, to the semi-engulfed suburbs of Lattes and Pérols, in the direction of **PALAVAS**, where you'll find *Eden Camping* (June–Sept) and *L'Oasis Palavasienne* on the D986, and *Camping l'Estelle* on the edge of **PÉROLS**.

The City

Montpellier's hub, **place de la Comédie** – *L'Oeuf* to the initiated – is a colossal oblong square, paved with cream-coloured marble, with a fountain in the middle and cafés either side. One end is closed by the **Opéra**, an ornate nineteenth-century theatre; the other opens on to the **Esplanade**, a beautiful tree-lined promenade which ends in the **Corum** concert hall, a sort of robotic bunker-palace in pink granite, with splendid views from the roof. The city's most trumpeted museum, the **Musée Fabre** (Tues–Fri 9am–5.30pm, Sat & Sun 9am–5pm; 20F), is close by on bd Sarrail and contains a large

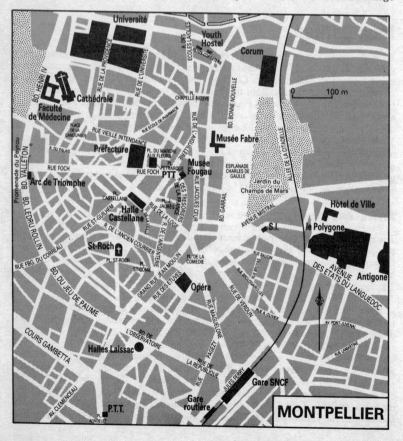

and historically important collection of seventeenth- to nineteenth-century French, Spanish, Italian, Dutch, Flemish and English painting, including works by Delacroix, Raphael, Jan van Steen and Veronese.

From the top side of the *Oeuf*, rue de la Loge and rue Foch, opened in the 1880s in Montpellier's own Haussmann-izing spree, slice through the heart of the old city. Either side of them, a tangled maze of narrow lanes slopes away to the encircling modern boulevards. Few buildings survive from before the 1622 siege, but the city's busy bourgeoisie quickly made up for the loss, proclaiming their financial power in lots of austere seventeenth- and eighteenth-century mansions. Known as *Lou Clapas* ("the rubble"), the quarter is a curious mix of chic restoration and squalid disorder, a pleasure to wander through – the chic tending to the south side, the lively to the north up rue de l'Aiguillerie.

First left off rue de la Loge is **Grand-Rue Jean-Moulin**, where Moulin, hero of the Resistance, lived at no. 21. To the left, at no. 32, the present-day Chamber of Commerce is located in one of the finest eighteenth-century *hôtels*, the **Hôtel St-Côme** (Mon–Fri 9am–5pm; free), originally built as a demonstration operating theatre for medical students. On the opposite corner, rue de l'Argenterie forks up to **place Jean-Jaurès**, on which, through the Gothic doorway of no. 10, is the so-called palace of the kings of Aragon, who ruled Montpellier for a stretch in the thirteenth century. With its morning **market** and cafés, the square is a nodal point in the city's commercial life. Close by is the **Halles Castellane**, Montpellier's answer to Paris' famous iron-framed *Halles*.

A short walk from place Jean-Jaurès, the *Hôtel de Varenne* on place Pétrarque houses two local history museums of somewhat specialized interest, the **Musée du Vieux Montpellier** (Tues–Sat 9.30am–noon & 1.30–5pm; free), concentrating on the city's history, and the more interesting, private **Musée Fougau** on the top floor (Wed & Thurs 3–6.30pm; free), dealing with the folk history of Languedoc and things Occitan. Off to the right, the lively little rue des Trésoriers-de-France has one of the best seventeenth-century houses, the *Hôtel Lunaret*, at no. 5 – also the **Musée de la Société Archéologique** (guided tours only Mon, Wed & Fri at 2.30pm; 20F).

On the hill at the end of rue Foch, from which the royal artillery bombarded the Protestants in 1622, the formal gardens of the **Promenade du Peyrou** look out across the city and away to the Pic St-Loup, which dominates the hinterland behind Montpellier, with the distant smudge of the Cévennes beyond. At the farther end a swagged and pillared water tower marks the end of an eighteenth-century aqueduct modelled on the Pont du Gard. Beneath the grand sweep of its double tier of arches there is a huge Saturday **flea market**, which on Sundays moves to Nîmes. At the city end of the promenade, a vainglorious **triumphal arch** shows Louis XIV-Hercules stomping on the Austrian eagle and the English lion, tactlessly reminding the locals of his victory over their Protestant "heresy".

Lower down the hill on bd Henri-IV, the **Jardin des Plantes** (daily 9am–noon & 2–6pm; Nov–April 8.30am–noon & 2–5pm; closed Sun; free), lovely but slightly rundown with its alleys of exotic trees, is France's oldest botanical garden, where, in the poet Paul Valéry's words, "the pensive, the careworn and talkers-to-themselves come towards evening". Across the road is the long-suffering **cathedral** with its massive porch, sporting a patchwork of styles from the fourteenth to the nineteenth centuries. Inside is a memorial to the bishop of Montpellier who sided with the half-million destitute vinegrowers who came to demonstrate against their plight in 1907 and were fired on by government troops for their pains. Above it, on rue de l'École-de-Médecine in the university's prestigious medical school, the **Musée Atger** (Mon–Fri 1.30–4.30pm; free) has a distinguished academic collection of French and Italian drawings, and the macabre **Musée d'Anatomie** (Mon–Fri 2.15–5pm; free) displays all sorts of revolting things in bottles. Close by is the pretty little **place de la Canourgue**, and, beyond, down rue d'Aigrefeuille, the old university quarter, with some good **bookshops** on rue de l'Université.

L'Antigone

South of place de la Comédie stretches the controversial quarter of **L'Antigone**, a chain of postmodern squares and open spaces designed to provide a mix of fair-rent housing and offices, aligned along a monumental axis from the place du Nombre-d'Or, through place du Millénaire, to the glassed-in arch of the Hôtel de la Région. It's more interesting in scale and design than most attempts at urban renewal, but it has failed to attract the crowds away from the place de la Comédie and is often deserted. The enclosed spaces in particular work well, with their theatrical references to classical architecture, like oversized cornices and columns supporting only sky. The more open spaces are, however, disturbing, with something totalitarian and inhuman about their scale and blandness.

Eating and drinking

Montpellier's year-round vitality supports some varied **restaurants** and **bars** to suit all budgets and tastes. **Cafés** line every square, large and small, while some of the more expensive restaurants use the city's ancient interiors to stunning effect. And Montpellier's youthful population ensures an energetic bar and nightclub scene right through to the early hours.

Le Bouzon, pl St-Lazère. African, Indian and Antillais dishes. Large portions with some delicious sauces but slow service. Meals end with a free dip in the Rum Chest, with some wicked, chilli-flavoured potions. Closed Mon evenings in winter.

Le Cercle des Anges, 3 rue Collow (☎67.66.35.13). Another memorable extravagance, similar if not superior to *La Diligence* in price, quality and service, but set in superbly ornate halls or on the less grand back terrace during fine weather. Closed Sun & Mon lunch.

Crêperie de Deux Provinces, 7 rue Jacques-Cœur. Fast and friendly crêpes between 12F and 46F. Closed Sun.

La Diligence, 2 pl Pétrarque (☎67.66.12.21). Atmospheric vaulted medieval setting for exquisite and innovative French dishes. Menus from 135F to 280F with the former offering a good-value dip into the finest French cuisine. Closed Sat lunch & Sun.

Le Kashmire, 6 rue de la Vieille (☎67.52.98.67). Excellent Indian food served in fittingly palatial surroundings. From 130F.

Le Memestrel, 2 impasse Perrier (☎67.60.62.51). Classy restaurant offering good-value French cuisine served in a former granary. Lunchtime menu from 90F, and 130F in the evenings. Closed Sun & Mon.

Le Petit Jardin, 20 rue JJ-Rousseau (☎67.60.78.78). Quiet, off-street restaurant with garden (summer only) offering quality menus and service for 80–100F.

Pizza du Palais, rue du Palais-de-Guilhem. Among the best of Montpellier's good-value pizzerias, with a lunchtime menu from 50F.

Le Regency, 4 Cité-Benoît (☎67.64.42.69). A specialist in couscous and other traditional dishes from the Maghreb.

Salmon Shop, 5 rue de la Petite-Loge. A novel "mountain cabin" interior offering oak-smoked salmon main courses in half-a-dozen guises at around 70F.

Thanh Long, 3 rue Durand. Inexpensive Vietnamese dishes from as little as 40F. Closed Sun.

Tripti Kulai, 20 rue Jacques-Cœur. Vegetarian dishes with flair from 50F. Closed Sun.

Le Verdi, 10 rue Aristide-Olivier (☎67.58.68.55). Long established as the city's finest Italian restaurant. Closed Sun.

Drinking and entertainment

There's always plenty of **drinking** activity in the place de la Comédie, place du Marché-aux-Fleurs, place Castellane and place St-Côme. *Melody sur Place* by the cathedral, and the *Brasserie des Facultés* on bd Henri-IV, near the medical school, are well-populated student haunts. By night, the obligatory *Irish Tavern*, 13 rue de la Lunaret, is a crowded and smoky young hang-out, *La Pleine Lune*, 28 rue du Faubourg-de-

Figuerolles, is the place for a beer, as is the *Vert Anglais* on place Castellane or the *Baghdad Café*, 18 rue Alger, behind the train station. The *Summertime Café*, 98 av du Pont-Juvenal (closed Sun), is fashionable for its cocktails and live jazz, with the tiny *Le bec de Jazz* on rue du Gagne-Petit being a more intimate alternative. If you fancy swapping peanuts and beers with fashion-bikers, roll up to the *Malibu Bar* on rue Valedeau, while just around the corner things really get cracking after midnight at *Le Mex* in rue Collot, when the tequilla lady offers you a free shot. Still the old perennial for late-night dancing and live gigs is the *Rockstore* near the station on 20 rue de Verdun, with *Mimi La Sardine*, southeast of the centre at 1317 av de Toulouse, a more spacious, up-and-coming dance complex. For what's on at either of these venues look out for posters around town or check out the weekly *Le Sortir* listings magazine.

Listings

Bikes Free single-speed bikes are available from *Vélos pour Tous* in the Esplanade de Gaulle, but you have to leave a deposit of 800F. Daily summer 9am–9pm; winter 10am–5pm.

Books The *Librairie Sauromps*, at the entrance to the *Polygone* shopping centre, is the biggest bookshop in town with a full range of *IGN* maps, regional guides and all of *Rough Guides* French titles.

CROUS Service for foreign students, 11 rue Baudin (Mon–Fri 9–11.30am & 1–4.30pm).

Doctors *SAMU* (☎67.33.78.95); *SOS Médecins*, 148 rue Marius-Carrieu (☎67.45.62.45).

Festivals Montpellier is renowned for its cultural life, and hosts a number of annual festivals. *Le Printemps des Comédiens* (mid-June to mid-July) is a theatre festival; *Montpellier Danse*, from end June to mid-July, is a festival of dance. There's also the music festival, *Le Festival de Radio-France et de Montpellier*, held in the second half of July, and the *Festival du Cinéma méditerranéen*, in the second half of October. The tourist office will provide information about programmes and booking.

Markets The best central food markets are *Halles Castellane* on rue de la Loge and the open-air one on pl Jean-Jaurès. There's also a Sunday morning car boot fair at La Pailloto.

Post office The main office is on pl Rondelet.

Shopping The most convenient place is the *Polygone* mall, with a *FNAC* and *Galeries Lafayette*.

Swimming The nearest beaches for a dip are at Palavas, the best slightly to the west of the town.

Wine Try the *Caves Notre-Dame* wine cellar at 134b av de la Mer (☎67.65.31.76), on the main road heading southeast from Pont Juvenal to the airport, with an especially large range of French wines with excellent Bordeaux, Burgundy, Champagne sections and local produce. Ones to look out for include *Mas de Daumes Gassac*, best in its full and tannic red; the well-structured and award-winning *Château de Valcombe*, 1992, from the Nîmes area, and among the muscats for which Languedoc is famous, the *Muscat vin doux*.

The Coast: Aigues-Mortes to Agde

On the face of it the **Languedoc coast** isn't particularly enticing, the beaches bleak and treeless strands, often irritatingly windswept and cut off from their hinterland by marshy *étangs*. But the area does have long hours of sunshine, 200km of sand still only sporadically populated, and relatively unpolluted water. This could change, as the French government has poured money into this area for the last couple of decades at an amazing rate, building seven new resorts in twice as many years. But for the moment, as long as you steer well clear of the new towns – ugly, soulless places for the most part, anyway – deserted beaches are still there for the walking.

First built of the new resorts, on the fringes of the Camargue, **LA GRANDE-MOTTE** is an extravagant futuristic vision of concrete and glass pyramids and cones ranged around a broad sandy beach. In summer, its seaside and streets are crowded with seminaked bodies; in winter, it's a depressing, wind-battered place with few permanent residents. Both *Camping Lous Dibols* and *Camping le Garden* offer excellent facilities and are just a couple of minutes' walk from the beach.

A little way east are **PORT-CAMARGUE**, with a sparkling new marina, and **GRAU-DU-ROI**, which manages to retain something of its character as a working fishing port. Tourist traffic still has to give way every afternoon at 4.30pm when the swing bridge opens to let in the trawlers to unload the day's catch on to the quayside, whence it is whisked off to auction – *la criée*, conducted today largely by electronic means rather the harsh-voiced shouting of former times. For a reasonable place to **stay**, try the *Hôtel du Quai d'Azur* on rue du Vidourle near the harbour entrance (☎66.53.41.94; ②), or the well-shaded *Camping Abri de Camargue* south of town.

Eight kilometres inland lies the appealingly named town of **AIGUES-MORTES**, built as a fortress port by Louis IX in the thirteenth century for his departure on the Seventh Crusade. Its massive walls and towers remain virtually intact. Outside the walls, amid drab modern development, flat salt pans lend a certain otherworldly appeal, but inside all is geared to the tourist. If you visit, consider a climb up the **Tour de Constance** on the northwest corner (daily 9.30am–noon & 2–4.30pm; July to mid-Sept 9.30am–7.30pm; April–May & mid-Sept to Oct 9am–noon & 2–5.30pm; June daily 9am–6pm; 26F), where Camisard women were imprisoned (Marie Durand was incarcerated for 38 years), and walk the wall, gazing out over the weird mist-shrouded flats of the Camargue.

Palavas and Maguelone

A dozen kilometres by road, **PALAVAS** is the bathing station for the citizens of Montpellier – a concrete sprawl with little to recommend it apart from the presence of the sea, though there is plenty of summertime activity in the discos and the rip-off quayside bars and restaurants. The best place to swim and sunbathe is a little way to the west off the long flat strand that borders the marsh, where some of Europe's only flamingos feed and herons, egrets and other seabirds squabble and dive. Here is the **Cathédrale de Maguelone** (daily 9am–6pm), dating mainly from the twelfth century, pale and grey and fortress-like on an island of vines and pines in the middle of the marsh, the only remains of a settlement decimated by Louis XIII because of its Protestant leanings. Cavernous and cool, the strong and simple church interior is the venue for a music festival in the second half of June. In the Dark Ages the island served as a base for Arab corsairs until Charles Martel drove them out in 737. Construction of the church began in the mid-tenth century.

Sète

Some 28km southeast of Montpellier, twenty minutes away by train, **SÈTE** has been an important port for three hundred years. The upper part of the town straddles the slopes of the Mont St-Clair, which overlooks the vast Bassin de Thau, breeding ground of mussels and oysters, while the lower part is intersected by waterways lined with tall terraces and seafood restaurants. It has a lively workaday bustle in addition to its tourist activity, at its height during the summer *joutes nautiques*.

The pedestrian streets, crowded and vibrant, are scattered with café tables. Climb up from the harbour to the **cimetière marin**, the sailors' cemetery, where the poet Paul Valéry is buried. A native of the town, he called Sète his "singular island", and the **Musée Valéry** in rue Denoyer (summer daily 10am–noon & 2–6pm; winter closed Tues; free), opposite the cemetery, has a room devoted to him, as well as a small but strong collection of modern French paintings. Georges Brassens has a room to himself, too.

Singer-songwriter, an associate of Sartre, and the radical voice of a whole generation in France, **Brassens** was also born and raised in Sète and is buried in the Cimetière le

Py on the other side of the hill, in spite of his song "Plea to be buried on the beach at Sète". If you're feeling energetic, you should keep going up the hill, through the pines to the top, for a view that's fabulous, if it isn't engulfed in sea mist. Below the sailors' cemetery, couched neatly above the water, is Vauban's **Fort St-Pierre**, which hosts a Brassens festival in mid-June.

Practicalities

The **gare routière** is awkwardly placed on quai de la République, and the **gare SNCF** further out still on quai Midi-Nord – though it is on the main bus route which circles Mont St-Clair (last bus about 7pm). The **tourist office** has a central office at 60 Grand'Rue Mario-Roustan (Mon–Sat 9am–5pm; summer daily 9am–8pm; ☎67.74.96.96), a summer desk at the **gare SNCF** and a main office on quai d'Alger, opposite the **ferry port** for boats to Morocco (tickets and information from the tourist office, 4 quai d'Alger; ☎67.74.96.96).

For **accommodation,** try *Hôtel Le Family* right on the quayside at 28 quai de Lattre-de-Tassigny (☎67.74.05.03; ②), or *Hôtel P'tit Mousse* on rue de Provence (☎67.53.10.66; ②), off the Corniche. For somewhere more comfortable there's *Les Mouettes*, 12 quai de la Résistance (☎67.74.76.68; ③), or the *Grand Hôtel*, 17 quai de Lattre-de-Tassigny, living up to its grandiose name (☎67.74.71.77; ③). The IYHF **youth hostel** (☎67.53.46.68; ①) is high up in the town on rue Général-Revest. **Campers** should ask the tourist office for details of the numerous campsites in the area. When leaving, keep in mind that **hitching out** is horribly difficult: you're better off taking a train or bus to the nearest town and trying from there.

There's inexpensive **food** at *L'Hostel* on Promenade JB-Marty from 52F for a menu and, a few doors down, local seafood for twice the price at *Le Chante-Mer* at no. 16.

Agde

Midway between Béziers and Sète at the western end of the Bassin de Thau, **AGDE** is historically the most interesting of the coastal towns. Originally Greek, and maintained by the Romans, it thrived for centuries on trade with the Levant. Outrun as a seaport by Sète, it later degenerated into a sleazy fishing harbour.

Today, it is a major tourist centre with a good deal of charm, notably in the narrow back lanes between rue de l'Amour and the riverside, where fishing boats tie up. The town's most distinctive and surprising feature is its colour – black – from the volcanic stone of the Mont St-Loup quarries which built it. But it has few sights apart from its heavily battlemented **cathedral**. The **waterfront** is attractive, and by the bridge the Canal du Midi slips quietly and modestly into the River Hérault on the very last leg of its journey from Toulouse to the Bassin de Thau and Sète.

Hotel rooms are expensive, but if the budget is reasonably healthy, the *Donjon* on place Jean-Jaurès (☎67.94.12.32; ③) and *Les Arcades*, 16 rue Louis-Bages (☎67.94.11.66; ③), are comfortable and close to the river. If you're **camping**, it's best to seek guidance from the **tourist office** in place Molière near the bridge. Places to **eat** are numerous. The most convenient area to look is in La Promenade. Three specific restaurants to try are the *Orient Express* pizzeria at 8 rue Jean-Roger (menu 50–65F), the *Clara Belle* at 11 rue André-Chassefière, and the tiny *Hanh-Phuc*, 5 bd Georges-Pompidou, offering Vietnamese dishes from 130F.

To get down to the sea at Cap d'Agde, there is a half-hourly bus service, which you can pick up at the **gare SNCF** at the end of av Victor-Hugo, at the bridge and in La Promenade. To explore the **Canal du Midi**, there are boat trips from *Bateaux du Soleil*, 7 quai du Chapitre. Alternatively, you could walk or cycle the tow path (bike rental is available from the *gare SNCF*).

Cap d'Agde

CAP D'AGDE, 7km from Agde, lies to the south of Mont St-Loup. The largest and by far the most successful of the new resorts, it sprawls laterally from the volcanic mound of St-Loup in an excess of pseudo-traditional modern buildings that offer every type of facility and entertainment – all expensive. It is perhaps best known for its colossal **quartier naturiste**, one of the largest in France, with the best of the beaches, space for 20,000 visitors, and its own restaurants, banks, post offices and shops. Access is possible, though expensive, if you're not actually staying there. But if you want to get inside for free, you can simply walk along the beach from neighbouring Marseillan-Plage and remove telltale fabrics en route.

If you have time to fill, the unattractively named **Musée de la Clape** (April–Sept daily 9am–noon & 2–7pm; winter daily except Mon 9am–noon & 3–6pm; free) displays antiquities discovered locally, many of them from beneath the sea. It's worth a visit for the beautiful little Hellenistic bronze known as the **Ephèbe d'Agde**, until recently one of the treasures of the Louvre in Paris.

Inland from Montpellier

For getting out into the country of the Bas Languedoc, there are two good routes from Montpellier, both served by regular buses: the D986 to Ganges and the N109 to Lodève.

The Ganges route

The Ganges road weaves north across the plateau of the *garrigue*, a landscape of scrubby trees, thorns and hot-smelling herbs cut by torrent beds. The distance is dominated by the high limestone ridge of the **Pic St-Loup** until you reach the first worthwhile stopping place, **ST-MARTIN-DE-LONDRES**, 25km on, whose name derives from the Occitan word *loundres* – otters. It's a lovely little place of arcaded houses and cobbled passageways, set around the roadside place de la Fontaine, where the **tourist office** is housed in a round tower. Its pride is an exceptionally handsome early Romanesque **church**, reached through a vaulted passage just uphill from the square. The honey-coloured stone is simply decorated with Lombard arcading, the plain rounded porch with a worn relief of St-Martin on horseback, while the interior has an unusual clover-shaped ground plan. There's a **campsite** just out on the Pic St-Loup road, and the *Hôtel des Touristes* on the main road through the village (☎67.55.70.95; ②). In town you can also rent **mountain bikes**, and a couple of outfits offer rafting and canoeing down the gorge from April to October; call *Canoë St-Guilhem Le Desert* (☎67.57.44.99) or *Rapido* (☎67.55.75.75).

About 6km south, off the Gignac road near Viols-le-Fort (on the bus route) and the Château de Cambous, there is a marvellous **prehistoric village** (Sun & hols 2–6pm; July & Aug daily 2–7pm; 25F), dating from 2000 BC and only discovered in 1967. The site consists of a group of cabins, each about twenty metres long, their outlines clearly delineated, with the holes for the roof supports and the door slabs still in place. A reconstruction shows them to have been much like the sheep stalls in the old *bergeries* that dot the plateau.

Further north, almost as far as Ganges, through dramatic river gorges, you reach the **Grotte des Demoiselles** (daily 9.30am–noon & 2–5pm; April–Sept 8.30am–noon & 2–7pm; 25F), the most spectacular of the region's many caves: a set of vast cathedral-like caverns hung with stalactites descending with millennial slowness to meet the limpid waters of eerily still pools. Deep inside the mountain, it is reached by funicular (regular departures).

GANGES itself, 46km from Montpellier and also connected by regular buses (which continue to Le Vigan on the southern edge of the Cévennes), is an attractive and busy market town (Friday's the day) of small squares, tree-lined walks and vaulted alleys designed for defence in the Wars of Religion – it, too, was a Protestant town, peopled by refugees from the plains, who made it famous for its silk stockings. It was here that the last-ditch revolt of the Camisards earned its name. The rebels sacked and pillaged a shirt factory and went off wearing the shirts – *chemises/camises*.

For a place to **stay**, try *Hôtel de la Poste*, place de l'Ormeau (☎67.73.85.88; ③), or *Hôtel Aux Caves de l'Hérault*, on av Jeu-de-Ballon (③), both in the town centre near the market. The **tourist office is** on place de l'Ormeau.

The Gignac route

The second inland route runs west to the small town of **GIGNAC**, 30km from Montpellier, amid vineyards where a fine eighteenth-century bridge spans the Hérault. There's no hotel here, but the *Camping Le Pont* will serve campers. Otherwise make for the town of **ANIANE**, 5km to the north – with the imposing classical **church of St-Sauveur** and the *Hostellerie St-Benoît* (☎67.57.71.63; ③), with a pool – and then across the eleventh-century **Pont du Diable**, 3km further on. It is supposedly the earliest medieval bridge in the country, and children used to dive into the pool beneath until it was banned. The narrowest part of the Hérault gorge begins here.

The glorious abbey and village of **ST-GUILHEM-LE-DÉSERT** lies in a side ravine, 6km further on. A ruined **castle** spikes the ridge above, and the ancient tiled houses of the village ramble down the banks of the rushing Verdus, everywhere channelled into carefully tended gardens. The grand focus is the tenth- to eleventh-century **abbey**, founded at the beginning of the ninth century by Saint Guilhem, comrade-in-arms of Charlemagne and scourge of the Saracens. It is a beautiful and atmospheric place, though architecturally impoverished by the dismantling and sale of its cloister – now in New York – in the nineteenth century. It stands on place de la Liberté, surrounded by honey-coloured houses and arcades with traces of Romanesque and Renaissance domestic styles in some of the windows. The interior of the church is plain and somewhat severe compared to the warm colours of the exterior, best seen from rue Cor-de-Nostra-Dama/Font-du-Portal, where you get the classic view of the perfect apse.

There are a couple of easy and worthwhile **walks** you can make from here – up the valley of the Verdus into the red-stained walls of the **Cirque du Bout-du-Monde** (from place de la Liberté, take rue du Bout-du-Monde out of the village and continue for about half an hour), or up the zigzagging path of the **GR74**, through the sweet-scented shrubs and flowers towards the castle ridge (also about half an hour). From the crest of the ridge the view down on to the village is magnificent. The path divides here: one branch leads back right to the ruins of the castle, while the other continues along the GR74 to the Ermitage Notre-Dame-de-Belle-Grâce (90min), and on to join the GR7 at St-Maurice-Navacelles on the Causse de Larzac.

In season the village is on every tour operator's route, making early mornings and late afternoons the best times for visiting. An overnight **stay** is possible at the *Hôtel Fonzes* on the main road (☎67.57.72.01; ③; closed Dec–Feb), or at *Camping Moulin de Siau* (mid-June to mid-Sept). Three kilometres back down the road, cave enthusiasts will enjoy the **Grotte de Clamouse** (Sun & school hols 2–6pm; July 10–Aug daily 9am–7pm; April–July 9 9am–noon & 2–6pm; 35F).

Clermont-l'Hérault and around

Eight kilometres west of Gignac, **CLERMONT-L'HÉRAULT** – accessible by bus from Montpellier – is the principal market town of the area and a major producer of grapes for the table. The most interesting quarter to explore is between the huge Gothic

cathedral, fortified in 1351 for protection against English raiders, and the ruined **château** on the hill above. From the plane-shaded **place de la République** outside the cathedral, follow the back streets, passage des Jacobins, rue de la Fontaine-de-la-Ville, rue Barbès, then right past the church of Notre-Dame-de-Gorjan, uphill to the steps that lead to the château. Tumbledown and overgrown, it affords a fantastic view of the surrounding country and makes a good place to picnic.

The **tourist office** is at 9 rue René-Gosse, close to the cathedral. For a place to **stay**, try *Hôtel La Ramasse* on place des Martyrs (☎67.96.02.68; ②) or the *Grand Hôtel* at 2 rue Coutellerie (☎67.96.00.04; ②), the northern continuation of place des Martyrs; if you're **camping**, there's a local site, *Le Salagou*. You'll find reasonable **meals** at the *Restaurant des Remparts* at 3 rue Louis-Blanc, two streets behind rue René-Gusse, as well as an attractive *ferme-auberge* on the D9E right off the Bédarieux road, west of Mourèze (☎67.96.15.62; ②).

Nearby, though not really worth the trouble without a car, is the cramped medieval village of **MOURÈZE**, set in the weirdly eroded landscape of the **Cirque de Mourèze**. Nearer – only 3km away – on the main road to Bédarieux, and far more interesting, is **VILLENEUVETTE**, a model factory and workers' settlement created in the seventeenth century for the production of woollen cloth and subsidized by the royal government under Colbert's policy of trying to break the industrial supremacy of the Dutch and English. Although production ceased in 1954, the handsome buildings are still intact and partly inhabited. There is also a very nice, if somewhat pricey, **hotel** adjoining – *La Source* (☎67.96.05.07; ③–⑤), with a good restaurant and garden.

Three other interesting and little-visited places east of Clermont are only feasible if you have a car. The first is a very fine **dolmen**, like a miniature version of Agamemnon's tomb at Mycenae on the end of a low ridge overlooking the D32 – best reached from the village of **LE POUGET**, where it is signposted. Continuing along the D139, you come within sight of the pale grey ruins of the keep and chapel of the **Château d'Aumelas**, romantically silhouetted on the edge of the plateau of the *causse*. To reach it by road – considerably further – you need to bear right on to the D114 and then take a dirt track opposite a farm. It's a beautiful and silent place, and the chapel is in near-perfect condition.

Two kilometres further along the D114, down an unsigned and bumpy track leading right on to the *causse*, there is a marvellous and remote silvery chapel, **St-Martin-de-Cardonnet**, built in the twelfth century – all that remains of an ancient priory.

On to Lodève

Heading north from Clermont to **LODÈVE**, 19km away, the new A75 *autoroute* brings heavy traffic down from Clermont-Ferrand. It passes through countryside further scarred by uranium mining – the area around the village of St-Martin-du-Bosc has some of the highest soil concentration of radioactivity in the world.

Lodève, entirely enclosed by vine-terraced hills at the confluence of the Lergues and Soulondres rivers, is almost in the shadow of the Causse de Larzac. There are really no sights here, but Lodève is a pleasant old-fashioned place to pause on your way up to Le Caylar or La Couvertoirade on the Causse. The hub of life is **Grand-Rue** and **rue de la République**, where the cafés and restaurants are. The **cathedral** is worth a look, as is the unusual World War I **Monument aux morts** in the adjacent park, provided by the local artist Paul Dardé – more of whose work is on display in the unmemorable **town museum** in the Hôtel Fleury.

A good place to **stay** is the *Hôtel du Nord* at 18 bd de la Liberté (☎67.44.10.08; ②), with a good restaurant from 60F, or the *Hôtel de la Paix*, 11 bd Montalangue, by the bridge (☎67.44.07.46; ②). There is a big Saturday market for food shopping. The **tourist office** is at 7 place de la République, next door to the **gare routière**, where you can catch buses to Montpellier, Béziers, Millau, Rodez and St-Affrique.

FROM BÉZIERS TO THE HILLS

The southern portion of Languedoc cuts a slender triangle west, its watery coastal flats rising to low undulating hills as you move inland. Though the coast is not generally noteworthy, **Narbonne** and **Béziers** are enjoyable diversions on the way to the more refreshing and spectacular upland delights of the **Monts de l'Espinouse** and the **Parc Naturel Régional du Haut Languedoc** (see p.679).

Béziers and around

Though no longer the rich city of its nineteenth-century heyday, **BÉZIERS** is still the capital of the Languedoc wine country and a focus for the Occitan movement, as well as being the birthplace of Resistance hero Jean Moulin. The fortunes of the movement and the vine have long been closely linked; Occitan activists have helped to organize the militant local vine-growers, and there were ugly events during the mid-Seventies, when blood was shed in violent confrontations with the authorities over the importation of cheap foreign wines and the low prices paid for the essentially poor-grade local product. Things are calmer now, as the conservatism of Languedoc farmers has given way to more modern attitudes in the face of public demand for something better than the traditional table wine. As a result, some of the steam has also gone out of the movement; interest today is more in the culture than in anti-Paris separatist feelings.

The City

The finest view of the old town is from the west, as you come in from Carcassonne or the *Béziers-ouest* exit from the A9. Crossing the willow-lined River Orb by the Pont-Neuf, you look upstream at the sturdy arches of the **Pont-Vieux**, with the cathedral crowning the steep-banked hill above, looking more like a castle than a church, with its crenellated towers silhouetted against the blue line of mountains behind. The best approach is up the medieval lanes at the end of Pont-Vieux, rue Canterelle and passage Canterellettes. The **Cathédrale St-Nazaire** is mainly Gothic, the original building having been burnt in 1209 during the sacking of Béziers, when Simon de Montfort's crusaders massacred some five thousand people at the church of the Madeleine for refusing to hand over about twenty Cathars.

From the top of the cathedral **tower**, there's a superb view out across the vine-dominated surrounding landscape. Next door, you can wander through the ancient **cloister** (daily 9.30am–noon & 2–6pm; free) and out into the shady **bishop's garden** overlooking the river. In the adjacent **place de la Révolution**, a monument commemorates the people who died resisting Napoléon III's *coup d'état* in 1851 and their leader, Mayor Casimir Péret, who was shipped off to Cayenne where he drowned in a Papillon-style escape attempt. Also on the square, the Hôtel Fabrégat houses a **Musée des Beaux-Arts** (Tues–Sat 9am–noon & 2–6pm, Sun 2–6pm; free), which, apart from an interesting collection of Greek Cycladic vases, won't keep you long.

The city's other museum, the **Musée du Biterrois** in the old St-Jacques barracks on av de la Marne near the train station (Tues–Sat 10am–noon & 2–6pm, Sun 2–7pm; free) displays a variety of entertaining exhibits, ranging from Greek amphorae and nineteenth-century door-knockers to distilling manuals, clogs and wine-presses. Away from the medieval streets round the cathedral, the centre of life in Béziers is the **allées Paul-Riquet**, a broad, leafy esplanade lined with cafés, *crêpes* stalls, restaurants, banks and shops, named after the seventeenth-century tax-collector who lost health and fortune in his obsession with building the **Canal du Midi** to join the Atlantic and the

Mediterranean. Laid out in the last century, the *allées* run from an elaborate nine-teenth-century theatre on place de la Victoire to the gorgeous little park of the **Plateau des Poètes**, with its ponds and palms and lime trees designed in the so-called English manner by the man who created the Bois de Boulogne in Paris.

Practicalities

If you arrive at the **gare SNCF** on bd Verdun, the best way into town is through the landscaped gardens of the Plateau des Poètes opposite the station entrance and up the allées Paul-Riquet. Halfway along on the left is place Jean-Jaurès, where you'll find the **gare routière**. The **tourist office** is at the end of the next street on the left, at 27 rue du 4-septembre (summer daily 9am–7pm; rest of year Mon–Sat 9am–noon & 2–6.30pm, Sun 10am–noon).

For a place to **stay**, try the *Angleterre* at 22 pl Jean-Jaurès (☎67.28.48.42; ①), or – rather better – the *Hôtel des Poètes*, 80 allées P-Riquet (☎67.76.38.66; ②), or the *Hôtel du Théâtre*, 13 rue de la Coquille (☎67.49.31.58; ②). There's no **campsite** in town, but the nearest is 9km south towards Valras-Plage. For **food**, check out the *La Terrasse*, 29 place Jean-Jaurès, with a menu from 70F, the slightly less expensive *L'Hacienda*, 14 rue des Balances (closed weekend lunchtimes and Mon), north of the square, or the fine interior of *Le Cep d'Or*, 7 rue Viennet (closed Mon evening & Tues), with menus at 70–110F.

Béziers has one of the star **rugby** clubs in France. Its HQ, for *aficionados*, is at 6 place des Trois-Six. **Bullfighting** is also big in Béziers, with the main *feria* on August 15. The principal cultural activity is a **music festival** in the second half of July. For more information on the Occitan movement, call in at the **Centre International de Documentation Occitane** at 7 rue Rouget-de-l'Isle (Mon–Fri 9am–noon & 2–6pm; ☎67.28.71.62).

Pézenas and the Oppidum d'Ensérane

PÉZENAS lies 18km east of Béziers on the old N9. Market centre of the coastal plain, it looks across to rice fields and shallow lagoons, hazy with heat and dotted with pink flamingos. Despite its size, local tourist pamphlets have dubbed it the Versailles of Languedoc – a reference to its long-standing political importance as the seat of the provincial *États-Généraux* for Bas Languedoc. It has, however, retained the air of a gentrified resort, with its seventeenth-century centre, the **vieille ville**, carefully protected from development.

The town also plays up its association with Molière, who visited several times with his troupe in the mid-seventeenth century, when he enjoyed the protection of the local Conti lords. He put on his own plays at the **Hôtel Alphonse** on rue Conti, which now has an ice-cream parlour in its coach-house. When in town, he lodged at the Maison du Barbier-Gély in the unspoiled **place Gambetta**, today occupied by the **tourist office** (daily 10am–noon & 2–5.30pm). Although he figures prominently in the **Musée Vulliod St-Germain** (Mon & Fri–Sun 10am–noon & 3–5pm; July & Aug daily except Tues 10am–noon & 3–6pm; free), housed in an eighteenth-century palace just off the square, it does not fully convince with its re-created interiors and seventeenth- and eighteenth-century paintings.

The tourist office sells a guide to all the town's eminent houses, but you can just as easily follow the explanatory plaques posted all over the centre. Included in the route is the former **Jewish ghetto** on rue des Litanies and rue Juiverie. **Place de la République** is the location of an enormous Saturday **market**, and it's also the place to take a bus to Montpellier, Béziers or Agde. For somewhere to **eat**, try looking on place du 14-juillet, a five-minute walk away.

Seven kilometres southwest of Béziers on the N9 Narbonne road, a sign to the north leads up a hill to **L'Oppidum d'Ensérane**, the site of a 2600-year-old neolithic settlement with a small **museum** displaying recovered relics (daily 10am–noon & 2–5.30pm; free). But more unusually the hill overlooks the extraordinary, radial pattern of fields emanating from the now dry **Étang de Montady**, an egalitarian method of water management dating from pre-Roman times. If you want to spend the night in town, look up the *Hôtel Genieys*, southeast of the centre on 9 rue Aristide-Briand (☎67.98.13.99; ②–③).

Narbonne and around

On the Toulouse–Nice main train line, 25km west of Béziers, **NARBONNE** was the capital of Rome's first colony in Gaul, *Gallia Narbonensis*, and a thriving port and communications centre in classical times and again in the Middle Ages. Plague, war with the English and the silting-up of its harbour finished it off in the fourteenth century. Today, despite the ominous presence of the Malvesi nuclear power plant just 5km out of town, it's a pleasant provincial city of tree-lined walks and esplanades converging on graceful squares.

In the summer of 1991 it acquired notoriety as a new flashpoint in France's continuing problems with its ethnic minorities, but with a difference. This time a long-suffering and long-forgotten minority forced itself on public attention. Among its mixed population of relative newcomers – fugitive Spanish Republicans, returning French settlers from Algeria and Algerian migrant workers – Narbonne has for thirty-odd years been home to a group of **Harkis**, Algerians who had enlisted in the French forces and fought with them against their own people in the Algerian war of independence in the late Fifties. After the war they were settled in France for their own protection, and since then have received little or no help. This summer's unrest was the protest of their children, angry at finding themselves still last in the pecking order in spite of their parents' sacrifice.

The only surviving legacy of Rome in Narbonne is the **horreum** at the north end of rue Rouget-de-l'Isle (daily except Mon 10–11.50am & 2–6pm; Nov–May closes at 5pm; 15F), an unusual and interesting site consisting of two "streets" lined with small cubby-hole shops. Well preserved though now entirely underground, it was used to store grain and other produce. At the opposite end of the same street, close to the attractive tree-lined banks of the **Canal de la Robine**, which bisects the town, is Narbonne's other principal attraction, the enormous Gothic **Cathédrale St-Just-et-St-Sauveur**. With the Palais des Archévêques and its forty-metre keep, it forms a massive pile of masonry that completely dominates the restored lanes of the old town, and – like the cathedral of Béziers – can be seen for miles around. In spite of its size, it is actually only the choir of a much more ambitious church, whose construction was halted to avoid weakening the city walls. The immensely tall interior has some beautiful fourteenth-century stained glass in the chapels on the northeast side of the apse and imposing Aubusson tapestries. The high north tower is open for a panoramic view of the surrounding vineyards.

The adjacent **place de l'Hôtel-de-Ville** is dominated by the great towers of St-Martial, the Madeleine and Bishop Aycelin's keep. From there the passage de l'Ancre leads through to the **archbishop's palace**, housing a tedious **museum of art** (daily 10–11.50am & 2–6pm in summer; winter till 5pm, closed Mon; 20F) but a good **archeology museum** (same hours; free) with interesting Roman remains, including a milestone from the *via Domitia* bearing the name of Domitius Ahenobarbus – vital to the dating of the construction of the road.

If you're going across into the southern part of the town, beyond the bisecting **Canal de la Robine** and the built-over Pont des Marchands, the small paleo-Christian crypt of the church of **St-Paul**, off rue de l'Hôtel-Dieu (daily 10am–noon & 2–6pm; free), is worth a quick look, as is perhaps the eerily empty deconsecrated church of **Notre-Dame-de-la-Mourgié** (summer 10am–noon & 2–6pm; winter closes 5pm; free), though the jumbled Roman stones of the **Musée Lapidaire** it houses aren't very exciting.

Practicalities

The **gare routière** is on the canalside quai Victor-Hugo, and the **gare SNCF**, on the north side of town at the end of av Pierre-Sémard. If you want to head straight to the **tourist office** (daily 10am–noon & 2–5.30pm; ☎68.65.15.60), it's in place Salengro next to the cathedral.

The best budget **accommodation** is the modern and friendly *MJC Centre International de Séjour* in place Salengro (☎68.32.01.00; ①) or, from May to September only, the *Foyer des Jeunes Travailleurs Le Capitole*, at 45 av de Provence (☎68.32.07.15; ①). For a couple of reasonable **hotels**, try the distinctive green *Hôtel du Lion-d'Or*, 39 av Pierre-Sémard (☎68.32.06.92; ②), which has a good restaurant, or the less expensive *Hôtel de la Gare*, 7 av Sémard (☎68.32.10.54; ①), opposite the station. Fancier hotels include *La Dorade*, 44 rue Jean-Jaurès facing the canal (☎68.32.65.95; ③), and the plush *La Résidence*, 6 rue du 1er-Mai (☎68.32.19.41; ④). The nearest **campsite** is the *Languedoc* on chemin de Cresseil, off av de la Mer on the southeast side of town on the Narbonne-Plage road.

You'll find a string of al fresco snackeries along the terraces bordering the Canal de la Robine in the town centre. Otherwise, the **restaurant** at the *Hôtel du Lion-d'Or* (see above) has a good local reputation, with menus beginning at 85F. For something a little fancier, there's *Le Petit Comptoir* at 4 bd du Maréchal-Joffre (closed Sun & Mon), where the 98F menu changes weekly.

Fontfroide and the Étang de Bages

For a side trip from Narbonne – only 15km, but nigh impossible without transport of your own – the lovely **abbey** of **FONTFROIDE** (daily 10am–noon & 2–5pm; mid-June to mid-Sept 10am–noon & 2–5.30pm; July & Aug 10am–6pm; 32F) enjoys a beautiful location, tucked into a fold in the dry cypress-clad hillsides. The extant buildings go back to the twelfth century, with some elegant seventeenth-century additions in the entrance and courtyards, and were in use from their foundation in the eleventh century until 1900, first by Benedictines, then Cistercians. It was one of their monks, Pierre de Castelnau, whose murder as papal legate set off the Albigensian Crusade against the Cathars in 1208.

Visits to the recently restored abbey are only possible with a guide, and star features include the cloister with its marble pillars and giant wisteria, the church itself, some fine ironwork, and the rose garden. The stained glass in the windows of the lay brothers' dormitory are fragments from churches in eastern France damaged in World War I. Incidentally, if you do have transport, the **D611** is a beautiful route south into the Corbières.

Just south of Narbonne, the **Étang de Bages et de Sigean** forms a large lagoon frequently visited by flamingos. A scenic drive leads out over the *étang*. It is a notably arty community with some houses featuring unusually decorous ceramic drainpipes. **Les Palais des Naïfs** at 9 av de la Méditerranée (summer daily except Tues 10am–10pm; other times 2–8pm; 15F) houses a unique collection of naive art through the ages and is well worth a visit.

South of Bages, the road continues along the edge of the *étang* to **PEGRIAC-DE-MER**, which leads on to the **Réserve Africaine Sigean** (daily 9am–6pm), a better-than-average wildlife park with over 150 species from Africa and the rest of the world.

The coast: Valras to Gruissan

The coast close to Béziers and Narbonne enjoys the same attributes – and problems – as the rest of the Languedoc shoreline: fantastic sand but not a stitch of shade, and endless tacky development buffetted by a wind that would flay the shell off a tortoise.

For a quick escape from Béziers, you can take a twenty-minute bus ride across the flat vine-covered coastal plain to **VALRAS** at the mouth of the River Orb, whose old-fashioned family resort status is still just discernible. Further south, St-Pierre and Narbonne-Plage (reachable by bus from Narbonne) are horrible, and the only redeeming feature of this stretch of coast is the mini-landscape of the **Montagne de la Clape**, a former island, pine-covered and craggy, and not more than 200m above sea level in spite of its name. At its further end the fishing village of **GRUISSAN**, 13km from Narbonne (there are buses), built in concentric rings around the hub of the **Tour Barberousse**, is the only real place of character left, and it, too, is under assault by the developers. Out along the beach is a section of houses originally built on stilts to keep them clear of the sea, but since the danger of flooding has receded many have now added ground floors. Some may find the place faintly familiar – the early scenes of Jean-Jacques Beineix's film *Betty Blue* were shot here.

The one really worthwhile thing to do is go up to the **Chapelle Notre-Dame-des-Auzils** about 4km up a winding lane on to the Montagne – a quiet and beautiful spot in the pine woods that is highly atmospheric. From the road a path climbs up to the ridge where the chapel stands. All along it are ranged moving **memorials** to the people of Gruissan lost at sea in merchant ships, trawlers and warships, from Haiti to the Greek island of Skiros. The inside of the chapel is full of ex-votos offered by grateful seamen and their families, many of them now painted on to the walls, the originals having been stolen in the Sixties.

The Parc Naturel Régional du Haut Languedoc

Embracing Mont Caroux in the east and the Montagne Noire in the west, the **Parc Naturel Régional du Haut Languedoc** is the southernmost extension of the Massif Central. The west, above Castres and Mazamet, is Atlantic in feel and climate, with deciduous forests and lush valleys, while the east is dry, craggy and calcareous. Except in high summer you can have it almost to yourself. Buses serve the **Orb Valley** and cross the centre of the park to **La Salvetat** and **Lacaune**, but you really need transport of your own to make the most of it.

Bédarieux to St-Pons: the valleys of the Orb and Jaur

Some 34km north of Béziers, the pleasant if unremarkable town of **BÉDARIEUX** lies right on the edge of the park. Served by buses from both Béziers and Montpellier, and by train from Béziers, it makes a good base for entering the park, especially as the service continues on along the Orb and Jaur valleys to St-Pons beneath the southern slopes of the Monts de l'Espinouse.

The best part of town is across the river around **place des Herbes**, where the tall and crumbly old houses are redolent of a rural France long since vanished in more prosperous areas. On the square itself are a couple of extremely old-fashioned shops, one selling excellent fresh sheep's milk cheese, *fromage de brebis* – worth keeping an eye open for anywhere in the park, where sheep are the only creatures that thrive. Also on the square, the *Hôtel Le Central* makes a cheap and atmospheric place to stay (☎67.95.06.76; ②), with a good and inexpensive restaurant. There's a municipal **campsite** on bd Jean-Moulin (mid-June to mid-Sept), and a **tourist office** at 77 rue Alexandre.

The Orb Valley and Mons

Continuing **west**, the road is an easy hitch (if you don't want to wait for the bus) through spectacular scenery, with the peaks of the Monts de l'Espinouse rising up to 1000m on your right. The spa town of **LAMALOU-LES-BAINS**, 8km on, is notably livelier than neighbouring settlements lacking the attraction of recuperative springs where the likes of André Gide, Dumas *fils* and crowned heads of Spain and Morocco soothed their aches and pains. At the west end of the town by the main road, the **cemetery** is an untypically grand necropolis crowned with ornate mausoleums.

At the village of Colombières, 5km to the west, a path leaves the road to take you up into the **Gorges de Madale** where it joins the GR7, which crosses the southern part of the park to Labastide–Rouairoux beyond St-Pons.

A further seven or eight kilometres brings you to **MONS**, where there is a **gîte** (☎67.97.72.80; M. Cabrol), **camping** at *Le Clap* on the D14, and the small *Auberge des Gorges d'Héric* (☎67.97.72.98; ①; closed Sept) – with good-value restaurant by the suspension bridge at Tarassac, 2km away. From the village a road climbs 5km up the dramatic **Gorges d'Héric** to the hamlet of Héric, with the **Gorges de l'Orb** winding their way southwards back to Béziers along the D14.

Olargues and St-Pons-de-Thomières

Shortly after, you reach the medieval village of **OLARGUES** scrambling up the south bank of the Jaur above its thirteenth-century single-span bridge. The steep twisting streets, presumably almost unchanged since the bridge was built, lead up to a thousand-year-old belfry crowning the top of the hill. With the river and gardens below, the ancient and earth-brown farms on the infant slopes of Mont Caroux beyond, and swifts screaming round the tower, you get a powerful sense of age and history. There's a tiny **tourist office** on rue de la Place. The old station is served only by *SNCF* buses now, and the hotel no longer offers rooms, but there's *Camping Le Baous* by the river.

ST-PONS-DE-THOMIÈRES, 18km further west, is a little larger and noisier: it's on the Béziers–Castres and Béziers–La Salvetat bus routes, as well as the *SNCF*'s Bédarieux–Mazamet bus route. It is the "capital" of the park, with the **Maison du Parc** at 13 rue du Cloître by the cathedral – a strange mix of Romanesque and classical. It also boasts a small and reasonably interesting **Museum of Prehistory** (Wed, Sat & Sun 2–5pm; May–Sept daily 10am–noon & 3–6pm; 15F). If you need to **stay**, there are several cheap **hotels** – try *Hôtel Le Somail*, 2 av de Castres (☎67.97.00.12; ③), or ask at the **tourist office** near the cathedral (☎67.97.06.65); there's also a **gîte d'étape** at *La Ferme Tailhos* (☎67.97.27.62). There's no nearby campsite, however.

North, the D907 leads to La Salvetat in the heart of the park.

The uplands of the park

There's no transport, but the prettiest route into the park to Mont Caroux and L'Espinouse is the D180 from Le Poujol-sur-Orb 2km west of Lamalou-les-Bains. The road winds up through cherry orchards to the village of **COMBES**, where there is a **Bureau des Guides** and a **gîte d'étape** on the GR7 (☎67.95.66.55), and thence through the **Forêt des Écrivains-Combattants**, named after the French writers who died in World War I. Just above the hamlet of Rosis, the road levels out in a small mountain valley, whose slopes are brilliant yellow with broom in June.

Douch and Héric

A left fork leads to the hamlet of **DOUCH**, beneath the 1040-metre summit of **Le Caroux** – a perfect place where time has really stood still. Half a dozen rough stone houses, inhabited by a handful of elderly residents, cluster tightly together for protection against the elements. There's a **gîte d'étape** and a small **hotel**. In the meadows below nestles a jewel of a church with an ancient cemetery full of graves like iron cots.

The University of Toulouse maintains a research unit here to survey the largest mouflon population in France. If you go out early in the morning or just before dark in the evening, there is a good chance of seeing the short-fleeced sheep, and wild boar, too, as they come out to feed. The road provides some good vantage points a little further north round the **Col de l'Ourtigas** and the Pas de la Lauze.

The best short **walk** to do is down the GR7 to the hamlet of **HÉRIC** in the gorge of the same name. The path starts on the left at the end of the road in Douch and follows the telephone line. Once over the col and into the head of the gorge it becomes a beautiful paved mule track looping down through beech and chestnut woods. In the past people lived off the chestnuts, selling them, eating them and making flour from them. It takes about forty minutes to reach the two or three brown stone houses of Héric, inhabited for several generations by the Clavel family (and 90min to climb back up). They run a **gîte** and can provide **food**, too (☎67.97.77.29). Alternatively, make the popular 3km ascent of Le Caroux, south of the village with fine views from the summit along L'Espinouse (see below), south to Béziers, the sea and even the Pyrenees, possibly.

Into the Agout Valley

Continuing north from Douch, the road climbs another 12km above deep ravines and spectacular views to the summit of L'Espinouse. The Col de l'Ourtigas is a good place to stretch your legs and take in the grandeur surrounding you. Here the landscape changes from Mediterranean cragginess to marshy moor-like meadow and big conifer plantations, and the road begins to descend west into the valley of the River Agout. It runs through tiny **SALVERGUES**, with plain workers' cottages and a striking fortress-church, **Cambon**, where the natural woods begin, and postcard-pretty **FRAISSE-SUR-AGOUT** – home to *Camping Le Pioch* and a refuge at the *Maison du Parc* (☎67.97.61.14; ①) and the pricier *Auberge de l'Espinouse* (☎67.97.56.14; ③) – to **LA SALVETAT-SUR-AGOUT**. Situated between the artificial lakes of La Raviège and Laouzas, this is another attractive mountain town built on a hill above the river, with car-wide streets and houses clad in huge slate tiles. It's usually half asleep except at holiday time, when it becomes a busy outdoor activities centre. With several **campsites** and the *Hôtel-Restaurant Cros* (☎67.97.60.21; ②; closed Nov–March), it's a convenient stopover for the centre of the park. There's a municipal **campsite** by the sports ground off the D907, and a **tourist office** in rue de la Poterne at the top of the hill.

Lacaune

Twenty kilometres further north, **LACAUNE** makes another agreeable stop if you're heading for Castres. Surrounded by rounded wooded heights around the 1000m mark, it is very much a mountain town, one of the centres of Protestant Camisard resistance at the end of the seventeenth century, when its inaccessibility made the region ideal for clandestine worship. There are bus connections most days – not at very convenient times, usually afternoon or very early morning – to Castres, Albi and Bédarieux.

The air is fresh. The town, though somewhat grey in appearance because of the slates and greyish stucco common throughout the region, is cheerful enough. For a place to **stay**, the *Fusiès*, an erstwhile coaching inn opposite the church on rue de la République (☎63.37.02.03; ④; closed first half of Jan), offers an old-fashioned classiness and has a restaurant (closed Nov–Jan), while the *Hôtel Calas*, a little way up the hill (☎63.37.03.28; ③; closed first half of Jan), is simpler and also has a reasonable restaurant (closed Oct–Feb).

From here to Castres the most agreeable route is along the wooded **Gijou Valley**, following the now defunct train track, past minuscule Gijounet and **LACAZE**, where a nearly derelict **château** stands picturesquely in a bend of the river and the small *Auberge du Gijou* has a restaurant and three bargain-priced rooms.

CARCASSONNE AND THE CATHAR CASTLES

Right on the main Toulouse–Montpellier train link, **Carcassonne** couldn't be easier to reach; and for anyone travelling through this region it is a must – one of the most dramatic, if also most visited, towns in the whole of Languedoc.

Carcassonne is a good historical introduction to the wild and ruinous **Cathar strongholds** to the north and south. These castles and fortified villages were the ultimate refuges of the Cathars, a sect strong in this part of France, who were literally hounded to death, first in the Albigensian Crusade, promulgated by the Vatican and launched in 1208 under the leadership of the abbot of Cîteaux, then by the notoriously cruel Simon de Montfort, and finally by the king of France. The name of the sect derives from the Greek word for clean or pure, *katharos*, and they abhorred the materialism and worldly power of the established Church, supporting the simple and humble Christianity of the Sermon on the Mount – and although their adherents probably never accounted for more than ten percent of the population, there were many members of the nobility and the influential classes involved. Their clergy or *parfaits* renounced the physical world as inherently evil, the creation of the Devil.

Cathars who were caught were burned in communal conflagrations, a hundred or two hundred at a time. Their lands were laid waste or seized by northern barons, de Montfort himself grabbing the properties of the count of Toulouse. The effect of this brutality was to unite Catholic and Cathar in southern solidarity against the barbarian north. Though military defeat became irreversible with the capitulation of Toulouse in 1229 and the fall of the castle of Montségur in 1244, it took the informers and torturers of the Holy Inquisition another seventy years to root them out completely.

If you're interested, the *Centre National d'Études Cathares* (☎68.77.10.21) in the Château Villegly, at Conques-sur-Orbiel, 8km northeast of Carcassonne, is the place to contact for more **information**, with all local bookshops offering plenty of Cathar literature and souvenir picture books, some in English.

Carcassonne and around

CARCASSONNE owes its division into two separate "towns" – the **Cité** and the **Ville Basse** – to the wars against the Cathars. Following Simon de Montfort's capture of the town in 1209, its people tried in 1240 to restore their traditional ruling family, the Trencavels. In reprisal King Louis IX expelled them, only permitting their return on condition they built on the low ground by the River Aude.

Arrival and accommodation

Arriving by **train**, you'll find yourself in the *ville basse* on the north bank of the Canal du Midi at the northern limits of the town. You can rent **bicycles** from the *gare SNCF*. To reach the **town centre** from the train station, you cross the canal bridge by an oval lock, pass the Jardin Chénier and follow rue Clemenceau, which will take you through the central **place Carnot** and out to the exterior boulevard on the southern side of town (a fifteen-minute walk). If you arrive by bus, the **gare routière** is just off bd de Varsovie on the northwest side of town, south of the canal (for the bus up to the Cité, take no. 4 from square Magenta).

The **tourist office** is at 15 bd Camille-Pelletan (daily July–Aug 9am–7pm; Oct–Easter 9am–noon & 2–6.30pm/7pm; Sept & Easter–June 9am–noon & 2–7pm; Sun during school hols 10am–noon; ☎66.25.07.04) at the end of square Gambetta, where the main road from Montpellier enters the town across the Pont-Neuf over the River Aude. If you're aiming to walk in the Montagne Noire (see p.685), you should consult the *Comité Départemental des Randonnées*, 13 rue de la République.

Accommodation

With the exception of the modern, clean, but frequently booked up IYHF **youth hostel** on rue Trencavel (☎68.25.23.16; ①), the price of staying in the Cité can be high; if you don't mind paying, try the *Hôtel des Remparts*, 3–5 pl des Grand Puits (☎68.71.27.72; ③–④), or *Le Donjon*, 2 rue Comte-Roger (☎68.71.08.80; ④–⑤). There are, however, some very reasonably priced **hotels** in the *ville basse*. Pride of place goes to the *Hôtel Bonnafoux*, 40 rue de la Liberté (☎68.25.01.45; ②), old fashioned but spotlessly clean. *Hôtel de la Poste*, 21 rue de Verdun (☎67.25.12.18; ②), *Le Cathare*, 59 rue Jean-Bringer (☎68.25.65.92; ②), and the *Hôtel Central*, 27 bd Jean-Jaurès (☎68.25.03.84; ③), are acceptable if fairly basic alternatives. More upmarket, the *Bristol*, 7 av Foch (☎68.25.07.24; ③), is situated on the canal bank opposite the *gare SNCF*, and the *Terminus* is at 2 av Maréchal-Joffre (☎68.25.25.00; ⑤).

There are also two *foyers* worth checking out: *Foyer de la CAF*, 2 rue Zola (☎68.47.42.90; ①), and the *MJC Centre International de Séjour*, 91 rue A.-Raymond (☎68.25.86.68; ①). The **campsite**, *Les Campéoles*, is just west of the Cité off route de St-Hilaire and the D104, and there's a rural campsite, *Le Martinet Rouge*, in the village of Brousses-et-Villaret, 14km north of town off the D118 Castres road.

The Cité

The attractions of the *ville basse* notwithstanding, what everybody comes for is the **Cité**, a double-walled and turretted fortress crowning the hill above the River Aude. From a distance it's the epitome of the fairy-tale medieval town. Viollet-le-Duc rescued it from ruin in 1844, and his "too-perfect" restoration has been furiously debated ever since. It is, as you would expect, a real tourist trap. Yet, in spite of the chintzy cafés, arty-crafty shops and the crowds, you'd have to be a very stiff-necked purist not to be moved at all.

Walking from the *ville basse*, across the Pont-Vieux, up rue Barbacane, past the church of St-Gimer, you enter the Cité through the sturdy bastion of the **Porte d'Aude**, all now peacefully integrated with the ancient lichened houses standing in their garden plots below. For a map, room, or details, the **tourist office** run a summer annexe in the **Porte Narbonnaise**, the other main gateway, on the east side.

There is no charge for admission to the streets or the grassy *lices* – lists – between the walls, although cars are banned from 10am to 6pm. However, to see the inner fortress of the **Château Comtal** and to walk the walls, you have to join a guided tour (daily Jan–March 10am–12.30pm & 2–5pm; April & May 9.30am–12.30pm & 2–6pm; June–Sept 9am–7pm; Oct–Dec 10am–12.30pm & 2–5pm; 26F). The tours – in English from June to September – assume some knowledge of French history, pointing out the various phases in the construction of the fortifications, from Roman to Visigothic to Romanesque and to the post-Cathar adaptations of the French kings.

In addition to wandering the narrow streets, don't miss the beautiful church of **St-Nazaire** towards the southern corner of the Cité at the end of rue St-Louis. It's a serene combination of Romanesque nave with carved capitals and Gothic transepts and choir adorned with some of the loveliest stained glass. In the south transept is a tombstone believed to belong to Simon de Montfort.

Eating, drinking and entertainment

For a place to **eat**, try the *Brasserie La Rotonde* on the corner of rue Clemenceau by the Jardin Chénier; alternatives include the Indo-Chinese *Le Long An*, 84 rue 4-septembre, and *Le Vietnam*, 3 rue de Verdun, the *Crêperie Kreiz–Avel*, 15 rue de Verdun (closed Sun noon), or the *Bon Pasteur*, 29 rue Armagnac (closed Sun & Mon). The *Hôtel Cathare* (see above) also has a reasonable restaurant. For picnic provisions, the **market** (Tues, Thurs & Sat) is on rue de Verdun. In the evening, the Cité makes a compellingly atmospheric if expensive place to eat, with a number of open-air restaurants. Try *Le Balaclein*, 6 pl du Château (closed Thurs), with its large terrace and good-value pizzas, and in the same square, *L'Auberge de Dame Carcas*, with a menu from 85F.

There is **dance, theatre and music** in the annual *Festival de Carcassonne* throughout July and, in the first fortnight of August, *Les Médiévales*, a medieval junket of lasers and special effects on themes like the Cathars and the Holy Grail.

The Canal du Midi and Minerve

For 240km from the River Garonne at Toulouse via Castelnaudary, Carcassonne and Béziers to the Étang de Thau between Agde and Sète, the **Canal du Midi** traces a peaceful green alley, lined with plane trees and yellow irises, across the whole of western Languedoc. Both landscape and canal – navigable by houseboat, but no longer by modern barge – have remained much as they were when the canal was constructed between 1666 and 1681.

The canal was the brainchild of **Pierre-Paul Riquet**, a minor tax-collector from Béziers, who succeeded in firing the imagination of Louis XIV against the soberer counsel of his minister, Colbert, with the idea of joining the Mediterranean and the Atlantic via the Garonne. Riquet ruined himself financially in the process, but the canal was a great success for a couple of centuries as a means of moving freight and passengers. It's also a great architectural monument, marrying function and aesthetics in perfect classical style, as in the 1676 **Pont de Répudre** close to Paraza about 45km east of Carcassonne, where the canal crosses a marshy stream among the sun-beaten vineyards.

Today, the way to use the canal is to hike it, bike it or rent a boat, with numerous villages to stop at along the way. To **rent a boat**, contact *Crown Blue Line*, Le Grand Bassin, B.P. 21–11400 Castelnaudary (☎68.23.17.51); *Connoisseurs Cruisers*, 7 quai d'Alsace, Narbonne (☎68.65.14.55); *Bateliers du Midi*, 5 quai Elie-Amouroux, 34310 Capestang (☎67.93.38.66); and *DNP Luc Lines*, 20 quai du Canal, 30800 St-Gilles (☎66.87.27.74). For more **information**, canal boat hotels and day cruises, ask for the English version of the *Tourisme Fluvial* brochure from the Carcassonne tourist office (see above).

Minerve

The village of **MINERVE** lies a dozen kilometres north of the canal in the middle of the Minervois wine country, on a shelf-like terrain of rocky outcrops and magnificent views. Its location is extraordinary, isolated on an island of rock between the gorges of the Briant and Cesse rivers, the latter of which has cut its course through two enormous tunnels in the rock known as the *Ponts naturels*.

The village turned Cathar at the beginning of the thirteenth century, which made it a target for Simon de Montfort's crusade. On July 22, 1210, after a seven-week siege, he took the castle and promptly burned 180 *parfaits* (or clergy). There is a memorial to them by the **church** and, inside, one of the most ancient altars in Gaul, dated 456 – but you won't be allowed in for love nor money. Nothing remains of the castle but the ruins of a tower.

If you want to stay, **camping** is free: ask at the *mairie* by the church. There's a *gîte d'étape* (✆68.91.22.92) in the village as well as the *Hôtel Chantovent* (✆68.91.14.18; ②; closed Jan & Feb; closed Sun pm and Mon out of season). The **tourist office** (daily 10am–noon & 3–5pm) has information about other accommodation possibilities in the area.

The Montagne Noire

There are two good routes from Carcassonne into the **Montagne Noire**, which forms the western extremity of the *Parc du Haut Languedoc* (see p.679): Carcassonne–Revel and Carcassonne–Mazamet by the valley of the Orbiel. Neither is served by public transport, but both offer superlative scenery.

The Revel route: Saissac, Revel and around

The **Revel route** follows the N113 out of Carcassonne, then the D629 through Montolieu (17km) and Saissac. **MONTOLIEU**, semifortified and built on the edge of a ravine, has set itself the target of becoming France's book capital, with shops overflowing with secondhand and antiquarian tomes. Book lovers should drop in at the *Librairie Booth* by the bridge over the ravine.

SAISSAC, another 8km on, is much more an upland village. Conifers and beech woods, interspersed with patches of rough pasture, surround it. Gardens are terraced down the steep slopes. Remains of towers and fortifications poke out among the ancient houses, and on a spur below the village stand the romantic ruins of its castle and the church of St-Michel. The *Hôtel de la Montagne Noire* (✆68.24.46.36: ②) stands on the road, and there's farmhouse accommodation at *Domaine de l'Albelot* (✆68.24.44.03; ③), 3km east of town on the D903 St-Denis road; look for the *Chambres d'hôtes* sign on the left. There are also two **campsites**, and if you have your own transport, the best place for miles around and an experience in itself is the *Camping du Bout du Monde* (✆68.94.20.92; all year round), signposted to the left about 8km up the road after the hamlet of La Régine. It's at a beautiful tumbledown farm called Rodes, near Verdun-en-Lauragais. You camp among the broom at the edge of the woods (though it's also a *gîte d'étape*), but, best of all, the owner is a genius of a cook, and she uses only their own farm-grown produce.

Some 14km west of Saissac on the D103 (or just a few kilometres southwest of the *Bout du Monde* campsite), the ancient village of **ST-PAPOUL** with its walls and cathedral makes a gentle side trip. The fourteenth-century **cloister** is always open, as is the cathedral, although it's currently undergoing restoration. A guide in several languages is lent to visitors, detailing the history of the site. The **Château de Ferrals**, 3km east, though not visitable, is worth a sneaking glance from the road.

Back on the "main" D629, continuing on from La Régine, the road winds down through the forest, past the Bassin de St-Férréol constructed by Riquet to supply water to the Canal du Midi, and on to REVEL, 15km away. Revel is a *bastide* dating from 1342, with an attractive arcaded central square with a superb wooden-pillared *halle* in the middle. Now a prosperous market town (market day is Saturday), it makes an agreeably provincial stopover. The *Hôtel du Midi*, 34 bd Gambetta (✆61.83.50.50; ②), has a restaurant, much appreciated by local gourmets, with menus from 90F. A simpler place to stay and eat is the *Adelscott*, 19 bd de la République (☎61.83.51.39; ①).

Lastours and the valley of the Orbiel

This is the region known as the **Cabardès**. Cut by the deep ravines of the Orbiel and its tributary streams, it's covered with Mediterranean scrub lower down and forests of chestnut and pine higher up. The area is extremely poor and depopulated, with rough stone villages and hamlets crouching in the valleys, and its people lived off beans and chestnut flour and the meat from their pigs, and worked from very ancient times in the region's copper, iron, lead, silver and gold mines. Nothing now remains of that tradition save for the gold mine at Salsigne (of which more below).

The most memorable site in the Orbiel Valley is the **Châteaux de Lastours**, the most northerly of the Cathar castles, 16km north of Carcassonne. As the name suggests, there is more than one castle – four, in fact, their ruined keeps jutting superbly from a sharp ridge of scrub and cypress that plunges to rivers on both sides. The two oldest castles, Cabaret (mid-eleventh century) and Surdespine (1153), fell into de Montfort's hands in 1211, when their lords gave shelter to the Cathars. The other two, Tour Régine and Quertinheux, were added after 1240, when the site became royal property, and a garrison was maintained here as late as the Revolution. Today, despite their ruined state, they look as impregnable and beautiful as ever. A path winds up from the roadside, bright in early summer with iris, cistus, broom and numerous other flowers.

The **Salsigne gold mine**, over the hill to the west of the village of **LASTOURS**, atop a bleak windswept plateau, is a huge and unsightly opencast pit. A forlorn row of miners' cottages stands nearby, with *PCF* slogans and a *Mine Occupée* sign, the only evidence of political passions anywhere in the district. Apparently the only material now going through the treatment plant comes from Greece – thousands of tons of rubble shipped through Port-La Nouvelle and Marseille to be sifted for a few ounces of the stuff that glisters.

About 7km upriver from Lastours, the road and river divide. The left fork leads to the village of **MAS-CABARDÈS**, hunkered down defensively in the river bottom. The right goes to **ROQUEFÈRE**, whose ancient *château* hosts summertime theatre. In a riverside apple orchard near the Orbiel–Rieutort confluence is a very welcoming and beautifully sited **campsite** and **gîte d'étape**, *Les Eaux Vives* (☎68.26.31.05).

From Roquefère a steep, serpentine road winds up through magnificent scenery to the tiny hamlet of **CUPSERVIES**, balanced on the edge of a sudden and deep ravine where the Rieutort stream drops some 90m into the bottom. A couple of kilometres further, by the crossroads at **CANINAC**, there's a very early – tenth century – **chapel of St-Sernin** in the middle of the woods. To get here without transport, there's a marked footpath from Roquefère, which then returns via Labastide-Esparbairenque (a four-and-a-half-hour round trip). For other walking ideas, ask at *Les Eaux Vives*.

The Cathar castles

The Cathars' rejection of the organized debauchery and materialism of the Church of the time brought about the wrath of their Catholic peers, who regarded their anarchistic beliefs as heresy. The castles dotted throughout this region of Languedoc were not built by the Cathars, but they used the fortresses as military bases against the Catholic terrorists, who crushed the sect over a period of a hundred years.

The best of the so-called Cathar castles – they sought refuge in them, but did not build them – are in the arid, herb-scented hills of the **Corbières** to the south of Carcassonne. **Walking** is undoubtedly the most direct way to experience them, and there are numerous paths, of which the **GR36**, crossing from Carcassonne to St-Paul-de-Fenouillet, and the *Sentier Cathare*, crossing east to west from Port la-Nouvelle to Foix, are the most exciting. The *Sentier Cathare* is divided into twelve stages with *gîtes d'étape*, described in the *Sentier Cathare* pamphlet produced by *Comité Départemental de Randonnée*, 13 rue de la République, BP 143, 11003 Carcassonne.

Without transport or walking boots, the best way to tackle them is from the south, for the most spectacular ones are close to the **Perpignan–Quillan road**, which has a bus service. With transport it becomes possible to explore the wilder back roads and utterly ruinous castles like Durfort and Termes and cross the cols where orchids and cowslips shudder in the spring winds and the views southward all end in the snowy Pyrenean bulk of Canigou.

Although there are numerous *gîtes*, *chambres d'hôtes* and basic campsites, hotel accommodation is rare in this region; there are **youth hostels** at **ST-MARTIN LYS**, 11km southeast of Quillan (☎68.20.53.27; ①), at the remote village of **BUGARACH**, 15km east as the crow flies of Quillan (☎68.69.84.37; ①), and at the similarly inaccessible **LE BOUSQUET**, the same distance south of Quillan (☎68.20.54.79; ①).

Puilaurens

From Quillan the road runs south through the incredibly narrow **defilé de Pierre-Lys** to the Pont d'Aliès before swinging 17km east to the village of Lapradelle and the first of the castles, the **Château de Puilaurens** (July–Sept daily 10am–6pm; 10F).

You can either drive up, or there's a shorter and fairly gentle path from the hamlet of **PUILAURENS**. It's a steep climb up to the castle, perched on top of a high, wooded hill at 700m. There are fine crenellated walls built around the very top of the rock outcrops and a keep. Although the existence of a castle here dates from the tenth century, it seems more likely that it was fortified to something like its present extent in the early thirteenth century, when it passed from the king of France to the count of Roussillon, and then to the king of Aragon. It sheltered many Cathars up to 1256, when Chabert de Barbera, effective controller of power in the region, was captured and forced to hand over his strongholds here and at Quéribus further east, to secure his release. The castle remained strategically important, being close to the Spanish border, until 1659, when France annexed Roussillon and the border was pushed away to the south. The view from the battlements, which you can climb up to at one point, is quite breathtaking.

Five kilometres south of the village is the *Hostellerie du Grand Duc* in **GINCLA** (☎68.20.55.02; ③).

Quéribus, Cucugnan and Duilhac

The **Château de Quéribus**, 30km further east towards Perpignan, stands on the ridge above the vine-ringed village of Maury – with a good chance of a lift up the six-kilometre side road. Again, it is spectacularly situated, balanced on a pillar of rock above a sheer cliff, whose crevices nourish a beautiful variety of wild flowers (Easter–Oct 10am–6pm/8pm, though nobody ever seems to shut the gate). Until 1659 this was the border with Spain.

Because of the extreme, cramped topography of the rock, the space within the walls is stepped in terraces, dominated by the polygonal keep and accessible by a single stairway. Inside, at the heart of the keep, is the remarkable **chapel** of St-Louis-de-Quéribus, surprisingly high and wide when you consider the keep's tortured position, and supported by a single pillar. The stairs to the roof are broken, but from the window halfway up there are fantastic views to Canigou and Perpignan, with other castles and watchtowers of the Spanish Marches dotting the peaks and ridges. To the northwest you're within easy eye contact of Peyrepertuse.

The history of Quéribus is similar to that of Puilaurens, though the fortifications visible today are thirteenth century. It was the last stronghold of Cathar resistance, holding out until 1255, eleven years beyond the fall of Montségur. Never reduced by siege, its role as a sanctuary for the Cathars ended with the capture of the luckless Chabert.

If you're provided with water and food, you could camp discreetly on the slopes to the north of the castle behind the ticket office. There is no accommodation in Cucugnan, the village to the north below, though its two **restaurants** – *Auberge de Cucugnan* (closed Wed & first half of Sept) with a 90F menu, and *Auberge du Vigneron* with an 80F menu – draw in the gourmets from miles around. The nearest **rooms** are in **DUILHAC** about 4km away below Peyrepertuse at the *Auberge du Vieux Moulin* (☎68.45.47.12; ②), or in the *gîte d'étape* (☎68.45.01.74). There is also an *alimentation* in the village, with bread, open even on Sunday morning.

Peyrepertuse

The access road for the **Château de Peyrepertuse** (Easter–Oct daily 9am–7/8pm; 15F) starts in Duilhac (see above). Alternatively, you can walk up from Rouffiac on the north side by the GR36, marked "Fontaine de la Jacquette" just outside the village; in summer it's a tough, hot climb that takes the best part of an hour. But either way the effort is rewarded, for Peyrepertuse is one of the most awe-inspiring castles anywhere, clinging to the crest of a long, wickedly jagged spine of rock on the top of a mountain ridge, surrounded by sheer drops of hundreds of metres.

You enter on the north side through thickets of box wood. The heaviest fortifications enclose the lower eastern end of the ridge, with a keep and barbican controlling the main gate. The castle is much larger than the others despite its precarious hold on the earth, with extensive buildings inside the outer wall, culminating in a keep and tower shutting off the highest point of the ridge, where such a pit of air opens at your feet that no artificial defence is necessary.

Surprisingly, the castle was taken by the French without much difficulty in 1240, and most of the existing fortifications were built after that. Whatever you do, don't go up in a thunderstorm; there can be some fierce ones in summer, and the ridge brings down the lightning as sure as a high-tension cable.

If you need to stay the night and are camping, you might prefer **ROUFFIAC**, with its **campsite and hotel**, the *Auberge de Peyrepertuse* (☎68.45.40.40; ① – with restaurant), but no shop. There is, however, a bus on Wednesday and Saturday to St-Paul-de-Fenouillet on the main Perpignan D117 road, returning at noon; there's also one on Monday to and from Perpignan.

Moving on from Peyrepertuse, by car or by the GR36, you can return to St-Paul-de-Fenouillet through the narrow **Gorges de Galamus**, and in many places you can get down to the river for a swim. There is even a *gîte d'étape* in the eagle's-nest **Hermitage St-Antoine** (☎68.59.20.49), built into the side of the ravine.

Alternatively, the drive eastwards offers more castles, including **Padern** and the especially fine **Aguilar**, near Tuchan, which overlooks the hills and vales of the *Côtes de Roussillon-Villages* wine area, with magnificent views from the twisty climbing roads. From here you have the possibility of heading either north towards Narbonne or south through Tautavel to Perpignan.

TOULOUSE AND THE WEST

With its own sunny, cosmopolitan charms, **Toulouse** is a very accessible kick-off point for any destination in the southwest of France. Of the immediately surrounding places, **Albi** is the number-one priority, with its highly original cathedral and unique collection of Toulouse-Lautrec paintings. Once you've made it that far, it's worth the extra hop to the time-warped medieval town of **Cordes**.

Toulouse

TOULOUSE, with its beautiful historic centre, is one of the most vibrant and metropolitan provincial cities in France. This is a transformation that has come about since the war, under the guidance of the French state, which has poured in money to make Toulouse the think-tank of high-tech industry and a sort of premier transnational Euroville. Always an aviation centre – St-Exupéry and Mermoz flew out from here on their pioneering airmail flights over Africa and the Atlantic in the 1920s – Toulouse is now home to *Aérospatiale*, the driving force behind Concorde, Airbus and the Ariane space rocket. The national Space Centre, the European shuttle programme, the leading aeronautical schools, the frontier-pushing electronics industry . . . it's all happening in Toulouse, whose 60,000 students make it second only to Paris as a university centre. But it's not to the burgeoning suburbs of factories, labs, shopping and housing complexes that all these people go for their entertainment, but to the old *ville rose* – pink only in its brickwork, no longer in its politics.

This is not the first flush of pre-eminence for Toulouse. From the tenth to the thirteenth centuries the counts of Toulouse controlled most of southern France. They maintained the most resplendent court in the land, renowned especially for its troubadours, the poets of Courtly Love, whose work influenced Petrarch, Dante and Chaucer and thus the whole course of European poetry. Until, that is, the arrival of the papal thugs in the Albigensian Crusade; in 1271 Toulouse became crown property.

Arrival, information and accommodation

The part of the city you'll want to see is a rough hexagon clamped around a bend in the wide, brown River Garonne. Arriving by train or bus, you'll find yourself at the **gare Matabiau** (☎61.62.50.50 for information), about a twenty-minute walk from the heart of the city. There's a **tourist office** annexe here, shower facilities, a **city bus terminal**, with the **gare routière** to the right at 70 bd Pierre-Sémard, and the *SEMVAT* regional bus depot a short distance away on the corner of rue Bertrand-de-Born and rue Stalingrad, in a *quartier* whose former red-light seediness has all but disappeared. The main **tourist office** in square Charles-de-Gaulle is housed in the sixteenth-century *donjon* that used to house the city archives (Mon–Sat 9am–1pm & 2–5.30pm; ☎61.11.02.22).

The best guide to what's going on in and around the city – and usually there is a lot, from opera to cinema – is the weekly **listings magazine** *Le Flash* (6F), which comes out on a Wednesday. The monthly *Toulouse Culture* from the tourist office has more exclusively highbrow interests.

Hotels

Hôtel Albert-1er, 8 rue Rivals (☎61.21.17.91). Set in a quiet street just off the Capitole, a small, comfortable and good-value establishment. ②.

Hôtel Anatole-France, 46 pl Anatole-France (☎61.23.19.96). Quiet and less obviously charming place by the university. ①–②.

Hôtel des Arts, 1bis rue Cantegril, off rue des Arts (☎61.23.36.21). Simple, friendly and recently renovated. ①–②.

Hôtel des Beaux-Arts, 1 pl du Pont Neuf (☎61.23.40.50). A classy upmarket hotel by the river. ④–⑤.

Hôtel Grand Balcon, 8 rue Romiguières, on the corner of pl du Capitole (☎61.21.48.08). A real classic frequented by St-Exupéry and co in their pioneering days, it has retained its decor and period charm. Closed Aug 4– 25. ②.

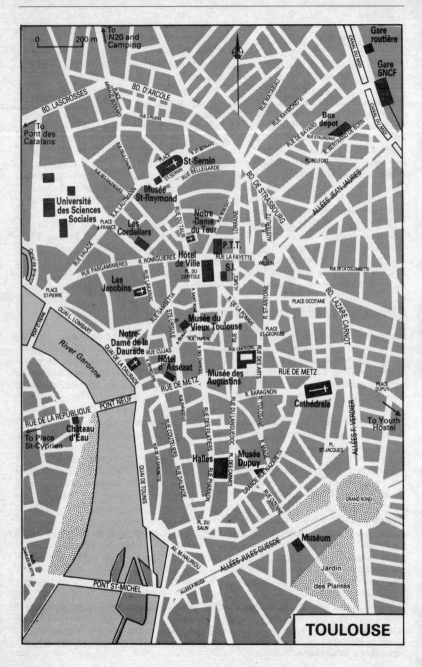

TOULOUSE

Hôtel Mermoz, 50 rue Matabiau (☎61.63.04.04). Immaculate if ordinary rooms compared to the splendid *Mermozabilia*-laden communal ones. Close to the station. ⑤.

Hôtel du Tour, 2 rue du Tour (☎61.21.17.54). Centrally located and comfortable place just off the Capitole. ③.

Youth hostels and campsites

IYHF youth hostel, 125 av Jean-Rieux, 3km south of the train station (☎61.80.49.93). Pokey but friendly hostel in a *quartier* with several cheap eating places and a late-night grocery. Walk south along the canal and turn left into av Jean-Rieux at the fifth bridge. ①.

Camping municipal, chemin du Pont-de-Rupé, off the main N20 Bordeaux road. Scruffy but usable site north of the city, not worth the trouble unless you have some form of transport. Take av des Minimes from the Canal du Midi and fork left at the Barrière de Paris into av des États-Unis. The campsite is signposted, but keep a sharp look-out to your left. It's across the train tracks, near the *Sesquières* leisure centre. Buses #2 and #5 from pl Jeanne-d'Arc.

The City

In addition to the pleasures of soaking up the atmosphere of the streets, old Toulouse offers some real architectural goodies in the two **churches of St-Sernin** and **Les Jacobins** and the ornate **Renaissance mansions** – *hôtels particuliers* – of the merchants who grew rich on the woad-dye trade, which formed the basis of the city's economy from the mid-fifteenth to mid-sixteenth centuries, when the importing of indigo from the Indian colonies wiped it out.

Toulouse's centre of gravity is the **place du Capitole**. Southeast lies the small and attractive **place St-Georges**, a major focus for the fashion-conscious young, with its bars, cafés and street performers. To the south, across the central dividing boulevard of rue de Metz, the central streets around the *halles* in place des Carmes – rue du Languedoc, prolongation of rue d'Alsace-Lorraine and rue des Filatiers – are busy with shoppers, while towards the river and the allées Jules-Guesde they are quietly residential, with some beautiful houses overlooking secret gardens. Across the *allées*, the **Jardin des Plantes**, with the adjacent gardens of the Grand-Rond, provide the city centre's only green space.

Place du Capitole and the *hôtels*

The heart of the city, seat of its government since the twelfth century, is the huge **Capitole**, or town hall, where once sat the *capitouls*, the relatively democratic and independent city council – an institution found in other Languedoc towns under the name of *consulat*, that may have inspired the son of Simon de Montfort who created the first English parliament. Today the Capitole's medieval origins are disguised by an elaborate pink and white classical façade (1750) of columns and pilasters. Appropriately, the square it dominates – **place du Capitole** – is a great meeting-place and talking-shop with numerous cafés and a mammoth Wednesday **market** of clothes, trinkets and food.

From this square radiate the labyrinthine and now largely pedestrianized streets of the old city, elegantly constructed almost exclusively of the flat Toulousain brick, whose rosy colour gives the city its nickname of *ville rose*. It's an attractive material, lending a small-scale, detailed finish to otherwise plain façades and setting off admirably any wood- or stonework. Along these streets many of the Renaissance *hôtels* survive, not usually open to the public, so you have to do a lot of nonchalant sauntering into courtyards to get a look at them. Best known is the **Hôtel Assézat**, towards the river end of rue de Metz, a vast brick extravaganza adorned with Doric, Ionic and Corinthian columns. Several others can be found just to the south: on rue de la Dalbade, where no. 25, the **Hôtel Clary**, is unusual for being built in stone; on rue Pharaon; place des Carmes; rue du Languedoc; and then northwards on rue St-Rome, rue des Changes, rue de la Bourse, and rue du May, where at no. 7 the **Musée du Vieux-Toulouse** (Mon–Sat 3–6pm; May & Oct Thurs 2.30–5.30pm only; closed Nov–April; 8F) in the Hôtel du May illustrates rather unexcitingly the city's history.

A short distance west of place du Capitole, on rue Lakanal, the church of **Les Jacobins** is an ecclesiastical building you can't miss. Started in 1230 by Dominicans who had set up here in the wake of their founding father, Saint Dominic (who himself had come to preach against the Cathars), the church is a huge fortress-like rectangle of unadorned brick, buttressed – like Albi – by plain brick piles, quite unlike the architecture you normally associate with Gothic. The interior is a single space divided by a central row of ultra-slim pillars from whose minimal capitals spring an elegant splay of vaulting ribs – twenty-two from the last in line, like palm fronds. Beneath the altar lie the bones of the philosopher Saint Thomas Aquinas. On the north side you step out into the calming hush of a cloister with a formal array of box trees and cypress in the middle and a superb view of the belfry.

The Cathedral and the rue de Metz

Cutting the old town in half, the late nineteenth-century **rue de Metz** runs towards the river from the **Cathédrale St-Étienne**, an eminently missable hotch-potch of a building, constructed in so many phases that its ends literally do not know its beginnings. Close by, the **Musée des Augustins**, 21 rue de Metz (daily except Tues 10am–2pm & 2–6pm, Wed closes 10pm; 8F), incorporates the two surviving cloisters of an Augustinian priory, with outstanding collections of Romanesque and medieval sculpture, much of it saved from the now-vanished churches of Toulouse's golden age. Many of the pieces form a fascinating, highly naturalistic display of contemporary manners and fashions: merchants with forked beards touching one another's arms in a gesture of familiarity, the Virgin represented as a pretty, bored young mother looking away from the child who strains to escape her hold, and a headless Saint Barbara looking more like a fashionable young woman than a saint.

The rue de Metz leads west to the **Pont-Neuf** (begun in 1544, despite its name), to link up with the St-Cyprien quarter on the left bank, where the **château d'eau**, erected in 1822 to supply clean water to the city's drinking fountains, now houses the **Galerie municipale du Château d'Eau**, place Laganne (daily 1–7pm; Nov–March Mon & Wed–Fri noon–6pm, Sat & Sun 1–7pm), an influential photography exhibition space and information centre, with frequent changes of exhibition. On the right bank, the **riverside** is at its best, with a grassy waterside walk backed by the plane-tree-lined *quais* in front of the art school and eighteenth-century church of La Daurade. Downstream you come to Pont St-Pierre, then the wildest and quietest stretch of *quai*, between the mouth of the lovely tree-lined Canal de Brienne and the Chaussée du Bazacle, formerly a ford across the Garonne.

A short walk along Grande-Rue-Nazareth from the cathedral brings you to the **Musée Paul-Dupuy**, 13 rue de la Pléau (daily except Tues 10am–noon & 2–6pm; Wed closes 10pm, closed Sun am; 10F), a surprisingly good collection of arts and crafts from the Middle Ages to today, including watches and clocks, pottery, enamels from Limoges and furniture.

St-Sernin, Les Jacobins and St-Étienne

From the north side of place du Capitole, **rue du Taur**, full of new and secondhand bookshops, takes you past the belfry wall of **Notre-Dame-du-Taur**, whose diamond-pointed arches and decorative motifs represent the acme of Toulousain bricklaying skills, to place St-Sernin. Here you're confronted with the largest Romanesque church in France, the **basilica of St-Sernin**, begun in 1080 to accommodate the passing hordes of St-Jacques pilgrims, and one of the loveliest examples of its genre. Its most striking external features are the octagonal brick belfry with rounded and pointed arches, diamond lozenges, colonnettes and mouldings picked out in stone, and the apse with nine radiating chapels. Entering from the south, you pass under the Porte Miégeville, whose twelfth-century carvings launched the influential Toulouse school of sculpture. Inside, the great high nave rests on brick piers, flanked by double aisles of diminishing height, surmounted by a gallery running right around the building. To get into the **ambulatory** (Mon–Sat 10–11.30am & 2.30–5pm; 10F) you have to pay a small fee, but it's well worth it for the exceptional eleventh-century marble reliefs on the end wall of the choir.

Right outside St-Sernin is the city's archeological museum, **Musée St-Raymond** (Mon & Thurs–Sat 10am–noon & 2–6pm, Wed 10am–noon & 2–10pm, Sun 2–10pm; 8F), housed in what remains of the poor students' block of the medieval university and containing a large collection of Roman objects, lamps, keys, bronze figurines, the labours of Hercules in relief and similar items. On Sunday mornings the square holds a lively **flea market**.

Eating, drinking and entertainment

There are several good areas to look for a place to eat. One of the most popular is the North African quarter around **place Arnaud-Bernard** just north of the church of St-Sernin: or try the square itself, where there is an organic fruit and veg market; or in the adjoining streets – rue Arnaud-Bernard, rue de la Chaine and rue des Trois-Piliers.

Rue du Taur has several **Vietnamese** places and **sandwich bars**. There's an **all-night crêperie**, *St-André*, at 39 rue St-Rome and another *crêperie*, *Le Bolbu*, at no. 8 in the adjoining rue du May (closed Sun). Or fill up on the cheap and plentiful fare of *La Place du May* (closed Sun lunch) at 4 rue du May.

Auberge Louis XIII, 1bis rue Tripière. With its pleasant courtyard during warm weather, this place serves generous portions of wholesome local dishes in relaxed rustic surroundings for around 100F. Closed Sat, Sun & Aug.

La Bascule, 14 av Maurice-Haurion. Traditional if rather conventional restaurant offering regional dishes. Closed Sun & Mon pm.

Brasserie les Beaux-Arts, Pont Neuf. With its Belle-Époque decor, this is among Toulouse's most popular and fancier *brasseries*.

Le Colombier, 14 rue Bagard (☎61.62.40.05). Menus from 100F, with a long-renowned *cassoulet* in the 170F menu. Closed Sat lunch & Sun.

Chez Émile, 13 pl St-Georges (☎61.21.05.56). For a treat, head for one of the city's best restaurants, with menus starting at around 130F to over twice that. Closed Sun & Mon.

La Grillothèque, 16 bd de Strasbourg. Among the more popular of the many *brasserie*-type establishments along this busy boulevard.

Mami's, *Hôtel des Pyrénées*, rue de la Colombette. Similar to the *Auberge Louis XIII*, with menus from 50F.

Restaurant Mille et une Pôtes, 1bis rue Mirepoix (☎61.21.97.03). Sample all the pâtés under the sun and some unusual pasta-based desserts. Menus 57F and 90F. Closed Sun.

Restaurant à la Truffle de Quercy, 17 rue Croix-Baragnon (☎61.53.34.24). An old established family-run restaurant with inexpensive Franco-Spanish dishes and *cassoulet*.

St-André, 39 rue St-Rome. Popular all-night *crêperie*.

Tantina de Burgos, 27 rue de la Garonette (☎61.55.59.29). Rather lost in a nondescript street, this Toulousain institution has great-value Spanish dishes as well as a popular *tapas* bar. Closed Sat lunch, Sun & Mon.

Cafés

Regular daytime **café-lounging** can be pursued around the popular student/arty hang-out of place Arnaud-Bernard. *Café St-Sernin*, nearby in rue St-Bernard by the eponymous church, is an easy-going, sunny place to sit. Place du Capitole, with its huge Wednesday market, is another very popular meeting-place. The most distinguished establishment is the *Bibent* at no. 5 on the south side, with its exuberant plasterwork, marble tables and cascading chandeliers. Place St-Georges is still very popular, though its clientele is no longer convincingly bohemian. Place Wilson has its enthusiasts. A trendy, designerish number is the *Café Classico* at 37 rue des Filatiers. Nearby, *Le Diagonal*, at 37 pl des Carmes, is *the* modish, hip night-time bar (open till 2am; closed Sun).

Bars and nightlife

L'Apocalypse, Montaudran (☎61.54.67.60). Disco particularly popular in summer.

Barrio Latino, 144 av de Muret (☎61.59.00.58). A salsa bar/restaurant as well as a prime venue for the city's Latin American sounds.

Le Bijou, 123 av de Muret (turn left at the end of Pont St-Michel; ☎61.42.95.07). Bar with concerts and dancing. Popular and musically interesting joint. Closed Sun.

Le Bikini, route de Lacroix-Falgarde (☎61.55.00.29). Casual disco renowned for its rock.

Le Blue's Note, 14 rue Peyrolières (☎61.22.16.12). Popular night-time bar hang-out with established groups. 6pm–2am; closed Sun.

Le Broadway, 11 rue des Puits-Clos (☎61.21.10.11). Popular gay disco.

La Cav' Ragtime, 14 pl Arnaud-Bernard (☎61.22.73.01). Good bar offering jazz, salsa and blues until 2am, or 5am on Saturday nights.

Didjeridoo Bar, 6 rue Jouxt-Aigues (☎61.14.10.61). Bar that serves mostly jazz with a nightly Happy Hour 7–8pm.

Erich Coffie, 9 rue Joseph-Vié, just west of the river in the *quartier* St-Cyprien. (☎61.42.04.27). One of the city's liveliest and most enjoyable music bars (food available) with a fairly eclectic music policy. 9–2am; closed first half of Aug.

Le Mandala, 23 rue des Amidonniers (☎61.21.10.05) on the corner of av Séjourné near the Pont des Catalans. At the time of writing, this is the bar where serious jazz fans and musicians head.

Mélodie en sous-sol, 23bis bd Riquet (☎61.62.35.91). A disco in a subterranean cavern determined to lead the way in sound and fashion.

Le New Shanghai, 12 rue de la Pomme (☎61.23.37.80). Mixed gay and straight disco.

Le Piano Bar, 8 pl Arnaud-Bernard (☎61.21.78.36). Bar offering the opportunity to talk to the accompaniment of the playing.

Le Wist, Angle 6, rue St-Rome (open Thurs–Sun). Disco known for its rock sounds.

Entertainment

The July–August *Musique d'Été* **festival** features Toulouse's own *Orchestre National du Capitole,* whose home base is the *Halle aux Grains* in place Dupuy (☎61.22.29.22), as well as visiting ensembles. September is the regular slot for the *Festival International Piano*, which takes place mainly in the beautiful cloister of the Église des Jacobins.

Major venues in town for theatre and cinema are: the splendid *Théâtre du Capitole* in place du Capitole (☎61.23.21.35) for music, dance and opera; *Le Sorano*, 35 allées Jules-Guesde (☎61.25.66.87), for theatre; and *Odyssud*, 4 av du Parc, Blagnac (☎61.30.45.31). There's a *cinémathèque* at 3 rue Roquelaine (☎61.48.90.75), with programmes that change daily.

Listings

Airlines *Air France*, 2 bd de Strasbourg (☎61.62.70.76); *Air-Inter*, 76 allées Jean-Jaurès (☎61.30.68.68); *British Airways* (☎61.30.45.50).

Airport 7km west at Blagnac; ☎61.42.44.00 for info.

Airport bus From the *gare routière* Mon–Fri 5.20am–10.20pm, Sat & Sun 6am–8.20pm.

Ambulance ☎61.31.56.56.

Books *Gibert*, corner of rue du Taur/place du Capitole, good general bookshop; *Librairie Occitania*, 46 rue du Taur, for regional books; *IGN*, 43 rue Peyrolières, for maps and guides.

Canal boats 2 port St-Étienne (☎61.36.24.24).

Car, scooter and bike rental *A2L*, 54 rue du cimetière, St-Cyprien (☎61.59.33.99).

CRIJ 17 rue de Metz (☎61.21.20.20).

CROUS 7 rue des Salenques: for student services.

Laundry By far the best is *Laundromatique*, 20 rue Arnaud-Bernard.

Pharmacist 24hr; 17 rue Rémusat (☎61.21.81.20).

Police rue du Rempart-St-Étienne (☎61.29.70.00 or 17).

Post office 9 rue Lafayette.

Taxis 24hr: square Wilson (☎61.21.55.46); gare Matabiau (☎61.62.37.34); pl Esquirol (☎61.21.56.42).

Weather forecast ☎36.65.02.31; for the Pyrenees ☎36.65.04.04.

Albi and around

ALBI, 77km and an hour's train ride northeast of Toulouse, is a small industrial town with two unique sights: a museum containing the most comprehensive collection of Toulouse-Lautrec's work (Albi was his birthplace) and the most remarkable Gothic cathedral you'll ever see. Its other claim to fame comes from its association with Catharism; though not itself an important centre, it gave its name – Albigensian – to both the heresy and the crusade to suppress it.

If you've any choice in the matter, you might decide to visit Albi at **festival time**. The town hosts three good festivals over the course of the year: jazz in May, theatre at the end of June/beginning of July, and music at the end of July/beginning of August. During July and August there are also free organ recitals given in the cathedral (Wed 5pm).

The City

The **Cathédrale Ste-Cécile** (daily 8.30–11.45am & 2–5.45pm, except during services; 3F), begun about 1280, is visible the moment you arrive at the train station, dwarfing the town like some vast bulk carrier run aground, the belfry its massive superstructure. If the comparison sounds unflattering, perhaps it is not amiss, for this is not a conventionally beautiful building; it's all about size and boldness of conception. The sheer plainness of the exterior is impressive on this scale, and it is not without interest: arcading, buttressing, the contrast of stone against brick – every differentiation of detail becomes significant. Entrance is through the south portal, by contrast the most extravagant piece of flamboyant sixteenth-century frippery. The interior, a hall-like nave of colossal proportions, is covered in richly colourful paintings of Italian workmanship (also sixteenth century). A rood screen, delicate as lace, shuts off the choir: Adam makes a show of covering himself, Eve strikes a flaunting model's pose beside the central doorway, and the rest of the screen is adorned with countless statuary.

Next to the cathedral, a powerful red-brick castle, the thirteenth-century Palais de la Berbie, houses the **Musée Toulouse-Lautrec** (daily 9am–noon & 2–6pm; Oct–May 10am–noon & 2–5pm; Oct–April closed Mon; 20F), containing paintings, drawings, lithographs and posters from the earliest work to the very last – an absolute must for anyone interested in *Belle Époque* seediness and, given the predominant Impressionism of the time, the rather offbeat painting style of its subject. The artist's house at 14 rue Toulouse-Lautrec is visitable in theory, but the hours are very uncertain, dependent on the whim of the owners.

Opposite the east end of the cathedral, rue Mariès leads into the shopping streets of the **old town**, mostly impeccably renovated and restored. The little square and covered passages by the **church of St-Salvy** on the right are worth a look as you go by.

Eventually you come to the broad **Lices Pompidou**, the main thoroughfare of modern Albi, leading down to the river and the road to Cordes. Less touristy, it is the best place to look for somewhere to eat and drink.

Practicalities

From the **gare SNCF** on place Stalingrad it's a ten-minute walk into town along av de-Gaulle. The **gare routière** is on the right in place Jean-Jaurès just as you reach the limits of the old town. The **tourist office** in one corner of the Palais de la Berbie (Mon–Sat 9am–noon & 2–6pm, Sun 10.30am–12.30pm & 3.30–5.30pm; July & Aug Mon–Sat 9am–7.30pm, Sun 10am–1pm & 3.30–6.30pm; ☎63.54.22.30).

Of Albi's **hotels**, the *Terminus* (☎63.54.00.99; ①), right opposite the station on the corner of place Stalingrad, or, in the heart of the old town near the cathedral, *Hôtel St-Clair*, 8 rue St-Clair (☎63.54.25.66; ③), are reasonable enough. Two cheaper possibilities are *La Fouillade* (☎63.54.21.86; ①–②) and *Le Parking* (☎63.54.09.07; ①), both on place Pelloutier across from place Jean-Jaurès. Otherwise, there's a **youth hostel**, 13 rue de la République (☎63.54.53.65; ①), and **camping municipal** in the *Parc de Caussels*, about 2km east on the D999 Millau road.

The simplest and cheapest place for a **meal** is *Le Petit Bouchon*, 77 rue de la Croix-Verte off place du Vigan. On the square itself, there's the *Grand Café de la Poste*, with useful supermarkets and inexpensive cafeterias nearby. An alternative is the vegetarian *Le Tournesol* in rue de l'Ort-en-Salvy on the west side of the *place* or *Auberge Saint-Loup*, 26 rue Castelviel at the west end of the cathedral, a reasonable, traditional restaurant. More expensive restaurants include *Le Jardin des Quatre Saisons*, 19 bd de Strasbourg (closed Mon), just across the river, with good value for its prices, and *La Tete de l'Art*, 7 rue de la Piale, off place St-Claude, a gallery/restaurant with menus from 85F to 125F.

Around Albi

Somewhat unexpectedly, the country between Albi and Carmaux, 16km to the north, has long been a coal-mining and industrial area, associated in particular with the political activity of Jean Jaurès, father figure of French socialism. Elected deputy for Albi in 1893, after defending the striking miners of Carmaux in his newspaper, *La Dépêche*, he then championed the glassworkers in 1896 in a strike which led to the setting up of a pioneering workers' cooperative, *La Verrerie Ouvrière*, which still functions today, albeit automated and monitored by computer. The **tourist offices** in Carmaux (place Gambetta) and Albi publish a list of interesting industrial sites in the area, including the pit at **CAGNAC-LES-MINES**, which you can visit as a museum, including a trip down the shaft (visits: Mon–Sat 2.30pm, 3.30pm & 4.30pm, Sun 3pm & 4pm; 25F; ☎63.36.94.36).

Of more conventional tourist interest, the town of **CORDES** is 24km northwest of Albi, a brief train ride (as far as Vindrac 3km away, with **bike rental** from the station) or bus ride on Tuesday and Saturday, or an easy hitch. It was founded in 1222 by Raymond VII, Count of Toulouse, and remains pretty much untouched, perched on its conical hill. It was a Cathar stronghold, and the ground beneath the town is riddled with tunnels for storage and refuge in time of trouble. It is worth seeing as it is such a perfect example of a medieval walled town, complete with thirteenth- and fourteenth-century houses climbing its steep cobbled lanes. It is also, however, a major tourist attraction: medieval banners flutter in the streets and artisans practise their crafts – unfortunately, the kiss of death. The **Musée Historique Charles Portal** (July & Aug daily 2–6pm; April–June, Sept & Oct Sun 2–5pm; 10F) depicts the history of one of the southwest's oldest and best-preserved *bastides*. It's not a good place to stay, with no very affordable or recommendable **hotels**, but *Le Château* in the village of **NOAILLES** (☎63.56.81.26; ②; May–Nov; breakfast only), 5km south of Cordes, is authentically dilapidated and makes a memorable visit. There's also a **campsite** 1km away down the Gaillac road.

Castres and around

In spite of its industrial activities, **CASTRES**, 40km south of Albi, has kept a lot of its charm, in the streets on the right bank of the Agout and, in particular, the riverside quarter where the old tanners' and weavers' houses overhang the water. The centre is a bustling, business-like sort of place, with a **market** from Wednesday to Saturday on place Jean-Jaurès.

The Hôtel de Ville is home to the **Musée Goya** (daily except Mon 9am–noon & 2–5pm/6pm; July & Aug daily; 15F). That is something of a misnomer, for it's really a collection of sixteenth- and seventeenth-century mainly Spanish painting, with just three Goyas, including a good self-portrait, the huge canvas of the *Philippines Junta*, and a fair number of predictably macabre drawings.

Castres' other specialist museum is the **Musée Jean-Jaurès**, dedicated to its native son. It's located in place Pélisson (same hours as the Musée Goya; 10F), and getting to it takes you through the streets of the old town, past the splendid seventeenth-century **Hôtel Nayrac**. The museum, which is beautifully laid out according to the latest notions of museum design, was opened in 1988 by President Mitterrand – appropriately enough, because Mitterrand's Socialist Party is the direct descendant of Jaurès' SFIO, founded in 1905, which split at the Congress of Tours in 1920, with the "Bolshevik" element leaving to form the French Communist Party. The museum, although slightly hagiographic as you might expect, nonetheless pays well-deserved tribute to one of France's boldest and best political writers, thinkers and activists of modern times. Jaurès supported Dreyfus, founded the newspaper *L'Humanité*, campaigned against the death penalty and colonialism, and was murdered for his courageous pacifist stance at the outbreak of World War I – oddly enough, by a man called Villain! There could be no better epitaph than his own last article in *L'Humanité*, in which he wrote: "The most important thing is that we should continue to act and to keep our minds perpetually fresh and alive.... That is the real safeguard, the guarantee of our future."

Practicalities

Arriving from Toulouse by train, you'll find the **gare SNCF** a kilometre southwest of the town centre on av Albert-Ier. The **gare routière** is on place Soult, with bus services to Mazamet and Lacaune. Whether you come by train or bus or drive into Castres, however, you will inevitably find yourself by the municipal theatre, with the **tourist office** (Mon–Sat 9.15am–12.30pm & 2–6.30pm/7pm) and the classical Mansart-designed Hôtel de Ville opposite, with a beautiful formal garden in front, of yew and clipped box and pristine avenues of limes, designed by the celebrated seventeeth-century landscapist Le Nôtre.

For a place to stay, there are several reasonable **hotels**. Among the cheaper are *Le Périgord*, 22 rue Émile-Zola (☎63.59.04.74; ①), *Hôtel de France*, 8 rue des Trois-Rois (☎63.59.04.89; ②), and *Hôtel Rivière*, 10 quai Tourcaudière (☎63.59.04.53; ②). Best of the lot, and only a little more expensive, is the grandiose and old-fashioned *Grand-Hôtel* right on the river bank at 11 rue de la Libération (☎63.59.00.30; ③). If you're **camping**, there's a site in a riverside park on av Roquecourbe, 2km north-west of the centre.

In addition to the hotel restaurants, you can **eat** at the *brasseries*, *Grand Café de l'Europe* and *Le Glacier* on place Jean-Jaurès, where there's also a **market** every Tuesday, Thursday, Friday and Saturday. Alternatives are *La Feuillantine* opposite the Jaurès museum (closed Wed), *La Périchole*, 6 rue d'Empare, and, going more upmarket, *Aux Crus d'Alsace*, 21 rue Thomas, or *L'Eau à la Bouche*, 6 rue Malpas (closed Sun eve & Mon).

Le Sidobre

Just east of Castres rises the westernmost extremity of the *Parc du Haut Languedoc* (see p.679), cut by deep river valleys and covered with marvellous woods. It's an area renowned for its granite: huge boulders litter the woods, often carved by the millennia into zoomorphic or other shapes – *les Trois Fromages* and *l'Oie*, for example – that give them commercial value in the eyes of the tourist industry. This is the **Sidobre** – certainly best explored on foot: the **GR36** footpath passes this way.

LACROUZETTE, 15km from Castres, is the main town and is capital of the granite industry. The demand for tombstones being impervious to recession, the town continues to prosper, judging by the number of Jaguars and Mercs in what is otherwise a thoroughly dreary place. However, if you're on your way up the Agout and Gijou valleys (see pp.681 & 682) to Lacaze and Lacaune and feel homesick for the English tongue, the English-run *Hôtel Relais du Sidobre* (☎63.50.60.06; ②) makes a convenient and pleasant stopover.

The Gers

West of Toulouse, the *département* of **Gers** lies at the heart of the historic region of Gascony. In the long struggle for supremacy between the English and the French in the Middle Ages it had the misfortune to form the frontier zone between the English base at Bordeaux and the French at Toulouse – hence the large number of fortified villages or *castelnaux* (the Gascon for *bastide*) dominating the hilltops. It is attractive if unspectacular rolling agricultural land dotted with ancient semifortified farms. Settlement is sparse and – with the exception of Auch, the capital – major monuments are largely lacking, which keeps it well off the beaten tourist trails.

The region's traditional sources of renown are its stout-hearted mercenary warriors – of whom Alexandre Dumas' d'Artagnan and Edmond Rostand's Cyrano de Bergerac are the supreme literary exemplars – and its rich cuisine and Armagnac. The food and brandy still flourish: Gers is the biggest producer of *foie gras* in the country. Other traditional dishes are *magret* of duck, Henri IV's *poule au pot* (the chicken that he promised to provide for every peasant's Sunday dinner), *confit* of chicken and goose

---

ARMAGNAC

Armagnac is a dry brown brandy distilled in the district extending into the Landes and Lot and Garonne *départements*, divided into three distinct areas: Haute Armagnac (around Auch), Ténarèze (Condom) and Bas Armagnac (Eauze), in ascending order of output and quality. Growers of the grape like to compare brandy with whisky: equating malts with the individualistic, earthy Armagnac distilled by small producers, while the blended whiskies resemble the more consistent, standardized output of the large-scale cognac houses. Armagnac grapes are grown on sandy soils and, importantly, the wine is distilled only once, giving the spirit a lower alcohol content but more flavour. Aged in local black oak, Armagnac matures quickly, so young Armagnacs are relatively smoother than corresponding cognacs.

Armagnac was distilled originally for medicinal reasons, and many claims are made for its efficacy. Perhaps the most optimistic are those of the priest of Eauze de St-Mont, who held that the eau-de-vie cured gout and hepatitis. More reasonably, he also wrote that it "stimulates the spirit if taken in moderation, recalls the past, gives many joy above all else, conserves youth. If one retains it in the mouth, it unties the tongue and gives courage to the timid."

Many of the producers welcome visitors and offer tastings, whether you go to one of the bigger *chais* of Condom or Eauze, or follow a faded sign at the bottom of a farm track.

and *daube de porc* – *cassoulet*, too, flavoured with the sausage of neighbouring Toulouse. Then there's *croustade*, a tart of apple and Armagnac, the speciality of Gascon *pâtissiers*. And to wash it all down there are the red wines of Madiran, Buzet and Saint-Mont and the whites of the Côtes de Gascogne.

Auch

The sleepy, provincial capital of Gers, **AUCH** is most easily accessible by rail from Toulouse, 78km to the east. The old town, which is the only part worth exploring, stands on a bluff overlooking the tree-lined River Gers with the cathedral prominent at its edge.

It is this building – the **Cathédrale Ste-Marie** – which makes a trip to Auch worthwhile. Although not finished until the latter part of the seventeenth century, it is built in basically late Gothic style, almost expiring Gothic in fact, with a classical façade. But what is of particular interest are the choir stalls and the stained glass. Both were begun in the early 1500s, but the windows are of clearly Renaissance inspiration, while the choir remains Gothic. The stalls are thought to have been carved by the same craftsmen who executed the stalls at St-Bertrand-de-Comminges, and show all the same extraordinary virtuosity and detail. The eighteen windows, unusual in being a complete set, parallel the scenes and personages depicted in the stalls. They are the work of a Gascon painter, Arnauld de Moles, and are equally rich in detail.

Immediately south of the cathedral, the tree-filled place Salinis by the fourteenth-century ecclesiastical court and prison, the forty-metre-tall **Tour d'Armagnac**, leads to a monumental stairway descending to the river with a statue of d'Artagnan on one of the terraces. From the west front of the cathedral, rue d'Espagne, with its old houses, connects with rue de la Convention and what is left of the narrow medieval stairways known as the **Pousterles**, which gave access to the lower town. Opposite the cathedral front, on the corner of place de la République and **rue Dessolles**, the tourist office inhabits a splendid half-timbered house dating from the fifteenth century, with other fine houses further along the street and the only reasonably priced eating places in town.

Just below rue Dessolles on place Louis-Blanc, the former Couvent des Jacobins houses one of the best collections of pre-Colombian and later South American art in France, left to the town by an adventurous son, M. Pujos, who had lived in Chile in the last years of the nineteenth century. Now known as the **Musée des Jacobins** (May–Oct daily except Mon 10am–noon & 2–6pm; Nov–April daily except Sun & Mon 10am–noon & 2–4pm; 10F), it also boasts a comprehensive collection of traditional Gascon tools, pottery, furniture and so forth, as well as paintings and Roman remains.

Practicalities

The **tourist office** (Sun & Mon 2–5.30/6pm; Tues–Sat 9am–noon & 2–5.30/6pm; winter Tues–Sat) is in an old timber-framed house on the corner of place de la République and rue Dessolles. Beyond the tourist office, place de la Libération leads to the allées d'Étigny, with the **gare routière** off to the right.

For a very central place to **stay**, try the modest *Hôtel des Trois Mousquetaires* at 5 rue d'Espagne near the cathedral (☎62.05.13.25; ②). Slightly superior alternatives are the *Hôtel de Paris*, 38 av de la Marne (☎62.63.26.22; ②), and *Le Relais de Gascogne*, 5 av de la Marne (☎62.05.26.81; ②). To reach av de la Marne from the *gare SNCF*, turn right on av de la Gare, follow it to the end and turn left.

There's also a rather drab IYHF **youth hostel**, *Foyer des Jeunes Travailleurs* (☎62.05.34.80; ①), in a housing development at **LE GARROS**, about 25 minutes' walk from the station: take rue Voltaire opposite the station, turn left at the end and keep straight on until you reach the *Nervol* gas station, where you turn left, then right at the end into rue du Bourget. The **camping municipal** is also off to the right of rue Augusta, and there's a GR653 *gîte d'étape*, 4km east at the Château St-Cricq (☎62.63.10.17).

Fleurance, Lectoure and Condom

Outside Auch is a handful of quiet **country towns** with no great sights, but with the surrounding countryside they make for a lazy taste of French provincial life. They are all connected by bus from Auch, but away from the main roads – the N21 for Fleurance and Lectoure, and the D930 for Condom – you'll be stymied without your own transport.

FLEURANCE, 24km north of Auch, has a typical *bastide* central square, **place de la République**, bordered by arcaded shops and houses, with the difference that its medieval *halle*, now the town hall, was most successfully converted into mellow classical stone in the nineteenth century. The **church** is worth a look, too, for its octagonal Toulouse-style belfry and, more particularly, the three stained-glass windows executed by Arnaud de Moles, the artist of Auch cathedral. The **tourist office** is at 100 rue Pasteur (daily 10am–noon & 2–5.30pm), and if you want to stay, the *Hôtel Capelli* at 72 rue Gambetta (☎62.06.11.88; ②) makes a good place to do so.

Eleven kilometres further north sits **LECTOURE**, the smallest and prettiest of these three towns, built astride a high ridge looking out over the surrounding farmland. Capital of the colony of *Novempopulania* in Roman times and of the counts of Armagnac until their demise at the hands of Louis XI in 1473, it is now renowned for its melons. In the middle of the main street its **Cathédrale de St-Gervais-et-de-St-Protais** raises its enormous tower above the town, while down the rue Fontelié among the scarcely altered medieval houses you come to the **Fontaine de Diane** which, except for the handsome *mairie* with its **Musée Lapidaire** (daily 10am–7pm; 10F), containing some interesting Roman bits and pieces, pretty much exhausts the sights.

There is a **GR65** *gîte d'étape* in rue St-Gervais by the cathedral (☎62.68.76.98; open April–Oct), and just around the corner the superb but unfortunately named *Hôtel de Bastard* in rue Lagrange (☎62.68.82.44; ③–④).

Condom and around

Some 43km north of Auch and 21km west of Lectoure, **CONDOM**'s road signs have been interfered with predictably by passing Brits: there's sadly no connection between the place and the device. Unremarkable in every other sphere, Condom is nonetheless good for a quick visit or an overnight stop, with its cathedral and attractive old streets in the centre. Armagnac drinkers will be interested in the **Musée de l'Armagnac**, 2 rue Jules-Ferry (Mon–Sat 10am–noon & 2–6pm; 10F), and the **Chais Ryst-Duperon** where the liquor is aged (June–Sept Mon–Fri 9am–noon & 2–5pm, Sat 10am–noon & 2.30–7pm, Sun 2.30–6.30pm). For places to taste and buy Armagnac, ask the **tourist office** in place Bossuet. If you want **to stay**, try the *Hôtel Continental* at 22 rue Maréchal-Foch (☎62.28.00.58; ②), the *Hôtel Le Logis des Cordeliers* in rue de la Paix (☎62.28.03.68; ③) or, for a splurge, the *Hôtel des Trois Lys* (☎62.28.33.33; ⑤); both *Le Logis* and *Trois Lys* have pools. There's another GR65 **gîte** at the *Centre Salvandy* (☎62.28.23.80), and a **camping municipal** near the river on the road to Eauze. For a straightforward place to **eat**, try the pizzeria *L'Origan* at 4 rue Cadéot in the town centre (closed Sun & Mon).

Just 5km west of Condom, the tiny twelfth-century village of **LARRESSINGLE** is certainly very pretty, but is totally given over to the heritage industry as the "Carcassonne du Gers", with twee tearooms inside – and it only takes one coachload of visitors to swamp it.

More interesting is the very fine **abbey** of **FLARAN**, 8km along the road to Auch (daily except Tues July & Aug 9.30am–7pm; Sept–June 9.30am–noon & 2–6pm; 20F). Built by the Cistercians in 1151 in pale white stone, it has the same scrubbed, ascetic appeal as Fontenay in Burgundy, with scarcely a hint of ornament – an effect totally destroyed by the decadent, incongruous plasterwork introduced into the monks' dormitory in the seventeenth century. Used as an Armagnac store until 1970, after undergoing many other vicissitudes in its long history, the monastery has only recovered its true identity in the last twenty years.

travel details

Trains

Béziers to: Agde (several daily; 12min); Arles (3–4 daily; 2hr); Avignon (5–6 daily; 2hr); Bédarieux (4 daily; 40min); Carcassonne (frequent; 1hr); Marseille (3–4 daily; 2hr 30min); Millau (4 daily; 2hr); Montpellier (3–4 daily; 1hr); Nîmes (3–4 daily; 1hr 30min); Paris (frequent; 8hr 40min); Narbonne (frequent; 20min); Perpignan (frequent; 1hr); Sète (3–4 daily; 30min).

Carcassonne to: Arles (daily; 3hr 20min); Avignon (daily; 3hr); Béziers (several daily; 1hr); Bordeaux (daily; 3hr 20min); Marseille (3–4 daily; 4hr); Montpellier (several daily; 2hr); Narbonne (frequently; 40min); Nîmes (several daily; 2hr 30min); Quillan (several daily; 1hr); Sète (several daily; 1hr 30min); Toulouse (8 daily; 45min).

Montpellier to: Paris (5–6 *TGV*s daily; 5hr); Arles (3–4 daily; 1hr); Avignon (frequent; 1hr); Béziers (frequent; 1hr); Carcassonne (frequent; 2hr); Lyon (frequent; 30min); Marseille (3–4 daily; 1hr 40min); Mende (1 daily; 3hr 10min); Narbonne (frequent; 1hr 20min); Perpignan (frequent; 2hr); Sète (frequent; 30min); Toulouse (frequent; 3hr 15min).

Narbonne to: Arles (3–4 daily; 2hr); Avignon (frequent; 2hr 20min); Béziers (frequent; 20min); Bordeaux (8 daily; 2hr 45min); Carcassonne (frequent; 40min); Cerbère (several daily; 1hr–1hr 30min); Marseille (daily; 2hr 40min); Montpellier (frequent; 1hr 20min); Nîmes (frequent; 1hr 50min); Perpignan (several daily; 30–40min); Port-Bou (several daily; 1hr 20min–1hr 40min); Sète (frequent; 50min); Toulouse (8 daily; 2hr).

Nîmes to: Arles (3–4 daily; 20min); Avignon (frequent; 30min); La Bastide-St-Laurent (4 daily; 2hr 10min); Béziers (frequent; 1hr 30min); Carcassonne (frequent; 2hr 30min); Clermont-Ferrand (4 daily; 5hr); Génolhac (4 daily; 1hr 25min); Marseille (3–4 daily; 1hr); Montpellier (frequent; 30min); Narbonne (frequent; 1hr 50min); Paris via Alès (4 daily; 40min); Paris (5–6 *TGV*s daily; 4hr 30min); Perpignan (frequent; 2hr 30min); Sète (frequent; 1hr); Villefort (4 daily; 1hr 40min); Vichy (4 daily; 6hr).

Sète to: Arles (3–4 daily; 1hr 30min); Avignon (frequent; 1hr 30min); Béziers (frequent; 30min); Carcassonne (frequent; 1hr 30min); Marseille (3–4 daily; 2hr 10min); Montpellier (frequent; 30min); Narbonne (frequent; 50min); Nîmes (frequent; 1hr); Perpignan (frequent; 1hr 30min).

Toulouse to: Albi (several daily; 1hr); Auch (several daily; 1hr); Ax-les-Thermes (daily; 1hr 45min); Barcelona (several daily; 7hr 15min); Bayonne (4 daily; 4hr); Bordeaux (8–10 daily; 2hr 45min); Brive (4 daily; 4hr 10min); Castres (several daily; 1hr 20min); Foix (several daily; 1hr 5min); Paris (8–10 daily; 8hr); Tarbes (4 daily; 2hr); Lourdes (4 daily; 2hr 20min); Mazamet (5–6 daily; 1hr 40min); Pau (4 daily; 2hr 30min); Pamiers (daily; 50min); Tarascon (several daily; 1hr 20min); La-Tour-de-Carol (daily; 1hr 55min); Luchon (4–5 daily; 2hr – some involve bus from Montréjeau); Lyon (6 daily; 6hr); Marseille (10 daily; 4hr 30min).

Buses

Auch to: Agen (4–6 daily; 1hr 30min); Bordeaux (daily; 3hr 40min); Condom (1 daily; 40min); Fleurance (4–6 daily; 20min); Lectoure (4–6 daily; 40min); Montauban (Mon–Sat 2 daily; 2hr); Tarbes (3–4 daily; 2hr 10min).

Bédarieux to: Lacaune (1 daily; except Tues & Sun); Olargues (4–5 daily; 40min); Pont-de-Tarassac (4–5 daily; 30min); St-Pons-de-Thomières (4–5 daily; 1hr).

Béziers to: Castres (2 daily; 3hr 30min); Mazamet (2 daily; 3hr); Montpellier (frequent; 1hr 35min); Narbonne (5 daily; 40min); Pézenas (several daily; 40min); La Salvetat (1–2 daily; 2hr 10min); St-Chinian (1–2 daily; 50min); St-Pons-de-Thomières (1–2 daily; 1hr 20min).

Carcassonne to: Castelnaudary (3 daily; 1hr); Quillan (2 daily); Toulouse (3 daily; 2hr 30min).

Montpellier to: Aigues-Mortes (frequent; 1hr 30min); Bédarieux (4–5 daily; 1hr 35min); La Cavalerie (daily; 1hr 50min); Clermont-l'Hérault (4–5 daily; 1hr); Ganges (daily; 1hr 15min); Gignac (6 daily; 45min); La Grande-Motte (frequent;

45min); Grau-du-Roi (frequent; 1hr); Lodève (daily; 1hr 5min); Millau (daily; 2hr 15min); Nîmes (frequent; 1hr 45min); Palavas (frequent; 20min); Rodez (daily; 3hr 55min); St-Martin-de-Londres (daily; 50min); Sète (frequent; 1hr); Le Vigan (daily; 1hr 40min); Viols-le-Fort (several daily; 40min).

Narbonne to: Béziers (4–5 daily; 40min); Carcassonne (1 daily; 1hr 20min); Gruissan (4–5 daily; 35min); Narbonne-Plage (several daily); Perpignan (3 daily; 1hr 40min).

Nîmes to Aigues-Mortes (6 daily; 50min); Avignon (several daily; 1hr 30min); Ganges (3–4 daily; 1hr 20min); La Grande-Motte (5 daily; 1hr 15min); Grau-du-Roi (6 daily; 1hr); Montpellier (hourly; 1hr 30min); Pont-du-Gard (several daily; 40min); Sommières (1–3 daily; 50min); Uzès (several daily; 55min); Le Vigan (3–4 daily; 1hr 40min).

Sète to: Montpellier (several daily; 1hr).

Toulouse to: Albi (several daily; 1hr 30min); Auch (1 daily; 3hr 35min); Ax-les-Thermes (several daily; 3hr 10min); Castres (2–3 daily; 1hr 30min); Foix (several daily; 2hr); Pamiers (several daily; 1hr 25min), Tarascon (several daily; 2hr 25min).

CHAPTER TWELVE

THE MASSIF CENTRAL

One of the loveliest spots on earth . . . a country without roads, without guides, without any facilities for locomotion, where every discovery must be conquered at the price of danger or fatigue . . . a soil cut up with deep ravines, crossed in every way by lofty walls of lava, and furrowed by numerous torrents.

So one of George Sand's characters described the Haute-Loire, the central *département* of the **Massif Central**, and it's a description that could still be applied to some of the region. Thickly forested and sliced by numerous rivers and lakes, these once volcanic uplands are geologically the oldest part of France and culturally one of the most firmly rooted in the past. Industry and tourism have made few inroads here, and the people remain rural and taciturn, with an enduring sense of regional identity. They also have a largely unfounded reputation for unfriendliness.

The Massif Central takes up a huge portion of the centre of France, but only a handful of towns have gained a foothold in its rugged terrain: **Le Puy**, spiked with jagged pinnacles of lava, is the most compelling, with its steep streets and majestic cathedral; the spa of **Vichy** has an elegance and charm, newly invigorated by the fashion for fitness; even heavily industrial **Clermont-Ferrand**, the capital, has a certain cachet in the black volcanic stone of its historic centre and its stunning physical setting beneath the **Puy de Dôme**, a 1464-metre-high volcanic plug. There is pleasure, too, in the unpretentious provinciality of **Aurillac** and in the untouched medieval architecture of smaller places like **Murat**, **Besse**, **Salers**, **Orcival**, **Sauveterre-de-Rouergue**, **La Couvert-oirade** and in the hugely influential abbey of **Conques**. But, above all, this is a country where the sights are landscapes rather than towns, churches and museums.

The heart of the region is the **Auvergne**, a wild and unexpected landscape of extinct volcanoes, stretching from the grassy domes and craters of the **Monts-Dôme** to the eroded skylines of the **Monts-Dore**, and deeply ravined **Cantal mountains** to the rash of darkly wooded pimples surrounding Le Puy. It is one of the poorest regions in France and has long remained outside the main national lines of communication. Much of it is above 1000 metres in height and snowbound in winter; it is only now that an autoroute is

---

ACCOMMODATION PRICE CATEGORIES

All the hotels, youth hostels and guesthouses listed in this book have been price-graded according to the following scale, and although costs will rise slightly overall with the life of this edition, the relative comparisons should remain valid. Paris and the large cities will, as anywhere, be more expensive than equivalent accommodation in the countryside or small towns. The prices quoted are for the cheapest available double room in high season, although remember that many of the cheap places will have more expensive rooms with en-suite facilities.

① Under 160F	④ 300–400F	⑦ 600–700F
② 160–220F	⑤ 400–500F	⑧ Over 700F
③ 220–300F	⑥ 500–600F	

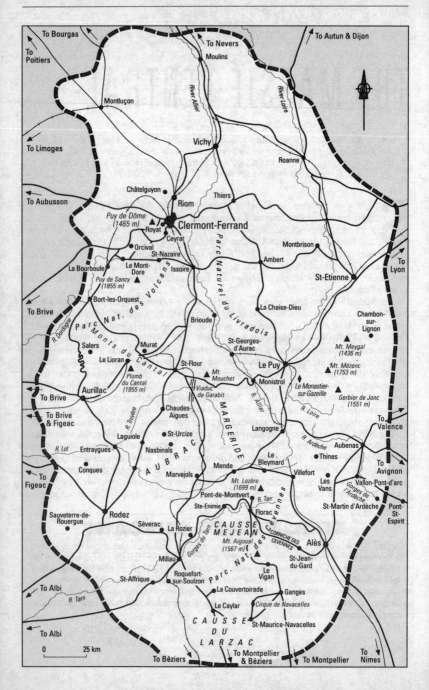

THE FOOD OF THE MASSIF CENTRAL

Don't expect anything very refined from the **cuisine of the Auvergne and Massif Central**: it is solid peasant fare as befits a poor and rugged region. The best-known dish is *potée auvergnate*, basically a **cabbage soup** to which other ingredients are added, often a piece of salt pork. It's easy to make and very nourishing. The ingredients – potatoes, pork or bacon, cabbage, beans, turnips – although added at different intervals, are all boiled up together.

Two potato dishes are very common – **la truffade** and **l'alicot**. For *truffade*, the potatoes are sliced and fried in lard, and then you add fresh Cantal cheese; for an *alicot*, the potatoes are puréed and mixed with cheese. Less palatable for the squeamish, but not at all off-putting in taste, there's *tripoux*, usually a stuffing of either sheep's feet or calf's innards cooked in a casing of stomach lining. **Fricandeau**, a kind of pork pâté, is also wrapped in sheep's stomach.

By way of dessert, **clafoutis** is a popular fruit tart in which the fruit is baked with a batter of flour and egg simply poured over it. Classically, the fruit used is black cherries, but it can also be pears, blackcurrants or apples.

The Ardèche in the east produces some wines, but this is not a region noted for its vineyard. **Cheese** is a different story. There are the four great cow's milk cheeses: St-Nectaire (see p.717), Cantal, Fourme d'Ambert and Bleu d'Auvergne. But the region also produces – on the edge of the Causse du Larzac – the prince of all cheeses, made from sheep's milk: **Roquefort**, whose making is described on p.731.

under construction through the middle. There is little arable land, just thousands of acres of upland pasture, traditionally grazed by sheep brought up from the southern lowlands for the summer. Nowadays, cows far outnumber the sheep, some raised for beef and some still for the production of Auvergne's four great cheeses (see box above). The population has emigrated for generations, especially to Paris, where the café and restaurant trade has long been in the hands of Auvergnats. The same flight of population has affected the equally infertile but beautiful and more Mediterranean southern part of the region: the hills and valleys of the **Cévennes**, where Robert Louis Stevenson and his donkey made one of the more famous literary hikes in 1878.

Many of France's greatest rivers rise in the Massif Central: the **Dordogne** in the Monts-Dore, the **Loire** on the slopes of the Gerbier de Jonc in the east, and in the Cévennes the **Lot** and the **Tarn**. It is these last two rivers which create the distinctive character of the southern parts of this chapter, dividing and defining the special landscapes of the *causses*, or limestone plateaux, with their stupendous gorges.

This is territory, above all, for walkers and lovers of the **outdoors**, and everywhere you go, tourist offices will supply ideas and routes for walks and bike rides, both long and short.

THE PARC DES VOLCANS

The **Parc Naturel Régional des Volcans d'Auvergne** encompasses the whole of the western edge of the Massif Central, from **Vichy** in the north to **Aurillac** in the south. It consists of three groups of extinct volcanoes – the **Monts-Dômes**, the **Monts-Dores** and the **Monts du Cantal** – with the high plateaux of Artense and the Cézallier that link them. It is big, wide-open country, sparsely populated and with largely treeless pasture for the cows whose milk produces Cantal and St-Nectaire cheese.

The park organization, whose headquarters are at the **Maison du Parc**, Château de Montlosier, 20km southwest of Clermont-Ferrand on the Mont-Dore road (Mon–Fri 8.30am–12.30pm & 1.30–5.30pm; ☎73.65.67.19), oversees the various subsidiary *maisons du parc*, each a kind of museum devoted to different themes or activities: fauna and flora, shepherd life, peat bogs and so on. While you can obviously just turn up at these places by car, it is true that you get a much closer understanding of what the park and its landscapes and activities are all about if you walk or bike around.

Four **GR footpaths** cross or make circuits within the park. The **GR40** runs from north to south. The **GR441** makes a circuit round the Monts-Dômes, the **Tour de la Chaîne des Puys**. The **GR400** encircles the Cantal mountains, and the **GR30** the lakes of the Artense plateau and Cézallier, under the title of the *Tour des Lacs d'Auvergne*. There are also lots of shorter walks – ask at the local tourist office for more information, and where to rent mountain bikes.

The towns in the area are few and of secondary interest, although **Orcival, Murat** and **Salers** are out-of-the-ordinary in the beauty stakes. **St-Nectaire** contains an exceptionally beautiful small church in the distinct Auvergne version of Romanesque; and **St-Flour** and **Aurillac** have an agreeable provincial insularity.

Clermont-Ferrand and around

CLERMONT-FERRAND lies at the northern tip of the Massif Central. Although its situation is magnificent, almost encircled by the wooded and grassy volcanoes of the Monts-Dômes, it has for a century been a typical smokestack industrial centre, the home base of *Michelin* tyres, which makes it a rather incongruous capital for such a rustic, even backward province as the Auvergne.

Its roots, both as a spa and a communications and trading centre, go back to Roman times. It was just outside the town, on the plateau of Gergovia to the south, that the Gauls under the leadership of Vercingetorix won their only, albeit indecisive victory against Julius Cæsar's invading Romans. In the Middle Ages, the two towns of Clermont and Montferrand were divided by commercial and political rivalry and ruled respectively by a bishop and the Count of Auvergne. Louis XIII united them administratively in 1630, but it was not until the rapid industrial expansion of the late nineteenth century that the two really became indistinguishable. Indeed, it was Clermont that took the ascendancy, relegating Montferrand to a suburban backwater.

Michelin came into being thanks to the inventions of Charles Mackintosh, the Scotsman of raincoat fame. His niece married Édouard Daubrée, a Clermont sugar manufacturer, and brought with her some ideas about making rubber goods that she had learnt from her uncle. In 1889, the company became *Michelin and Co*, just in time to catch the development of the automobile and the World War I aircraft industry. The family ruled the town and employed thirty thousand of its citizens until the early 1980s, when the industry went into decline. In the fifteen years since, the workforce has been halved, causing rippling unemployment throughout Clermont's economy. Many of those who have lost their jobs are Portuguese immigrants, imported over the last thirty years to fill the labour vacuum and well integrated with the local population.

As in many other traditional industrial towns hit by recession and changing global patterns of trade, Clermont has had to struggle to reorient itself, turning to service industries and the creation of a university of 30,000 students. Nonetheless, many people have moved elsewhere in search of work, reducing the population by nearly a tenth. The town has changed physically too, as many of the old factories have been demolished.

Arrival and accommodation

The **gare SNCF** is on av de l'URSS (☎73.92.50.50), connected by frequent buses with place de Jaude, at the western edge of the cathedral hill (10mins). The **gare routière** (☎73.93.13.61) is next to the main tourist office on bd Gergovia, and there's a city transport information kiosk called *Boutique T2C* on place de Jaude (☎73.26.44.90). If you're flying into town, the **airport** is at Aulnat, 7km east, with daily flights to Paris and other internal destinations, as well as to London during the summer (☎73.62.71.00).

The main **tourist office** is on the southern ring road at 69 bd Gergovia (June–Sept Mon–Sat 8.30am–7pm, Sun 9am–noon & 2–6pm; Oct–May Mon–Fri 8.45am–6.30pm, Sat 9am–noon & 2–6pm, Sun 9am–1pm; ☎73.93.30.20), but there are more conveniently placed annexes immediately to the left outside the train station exit (Mon–Sat 9.15–11.30am & 12.15–5pm; Oct–May Mon–Fri only; ☎73.91.87.89) and in place de Jaude (June & Sept Mon–Sat 9am–noon & 2–6pm; July & Aug Mon–Sat 8.30am–7pm, Sun 9am–noon & 2–6pm; ☎73.93.24.44). The **departmental office** is at 26 rue St-Esprit (☎73.42.21.23), and the **regional office** at 43 av Julien (☎73.93.04.03). Specific hiking or mountain bike information is available from *Chamina*, 5 rue Pierre-le-Venerable (☎73.92.81.44).

Accommodation

The cheapest and friendliest **hotel** is the old-fashioned-looking *Hôtel de Zurich*, 65 av de l'URSS (☎73.91.97.98; ①). Unprepossessing from the outside but perfectly comfortable within, there's also the *St-André* opposite the station at 25 av de l'URSS (☎73.91.40.40; ②–③), as well as the *Albert Elisabeth*, a few moments' walk up av Albert-Elisabeth, at no. 37 (☎73.92.47.41; ②–③), and the cheap *Ravel* nearby in rue Maringues opposite the old Marché St-Joseph (☎73.91.51.33; ①). There are several more moderately priced hotels close to the station, although the area is hardly attractive.

Cheap and cheerful but much more attractively situated, there's the *Blaise Pascal*, near the cathedral at 6 rue Massillon (☎73.91.31.82; ①), or, close to place de Jauder, the *Regina*, 14 rue Bonnabaud (☎73.93.44.76; ①–②; menus at 50F & 75F), and the more upmarket *Hôtel de Lyon*, 16 pl Jaude (☎73.93.32.55; ④), and *Hôtel Gallieni*, 51 rue Bonnabaud (☎73.93.59.69; ③–④).

The IYHF **hostel** is just across the street to the right from the train station at 55 av de l'URSS (☎73.92.26.39; ①; closed Nov–Feb), and there's also the **Foyer St-Jean** just north of the cathedral at 17 rue Gaultier-de-Biauzat (☎73.37.14.31; ①). For **campers**, there are *campings municipaux* at **ROYAT** to the west (☎73.35.97.05; April–Oct; bus #14B), Ceyrat to the south (☎73.61.30.73; all year; bus #4, stop *Preguille*), and **COURNON** to the east (☎73.84.81.30; all year; bus #3, stop *Rives d'Allier*).

The City

The most dramatic and flattering approach to Clermont is from the Aubusson road or along the scenic train line from Le Mont-Dore (see p.714), both of which cross the chain of the Monts-Dômes just north of the Puy de Dôme. This way you descend through the leafy western suburbs with marvellous views over the town, dominated by the black towers of the cathedral atop the volcanic stump that forms the hub of the old town.

Clermont's reputation as a *ville noire* becomes immediately understandable when you enter the city's medieval quarter, clustered in characteristic medieval muddle around the cathedral, and the only part of the city worth wandering through. It is due not to industrial pollution but to the black volcanic rock used in the construction of many of its buildings. The **Cathédrale Notre-Dame** stands at the centre and highest point of the old town; Freda White evocatively described its sombre grey-black-stone lava from the quarries at nearby Volvic (see p.712) as "like the darkest shade of a pigeon's wing". Begun in the mid-thirteenth century, it was not finished until the nineteenth, under the direction of Viollet-le-Duc, who was the architect of the west front and those typically Gothic crocketed spires, whose overmethodically cut stonework at close range betrays the work of the machine rather than the mason's hand. The inter-

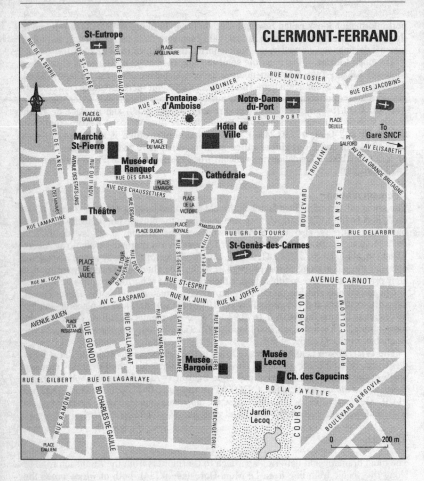

CLERMONT-FERRAND

ior is swaddled in mysterious gloom, illumined all the more startlingly by the brilliant colours of the medieval windows in the choir: look closely at the window in the second chapel on the left, where in the third panel on the right you can see woodmen and boatmen at work, and stone-cutters in the centre panel. If the day is fine, climb the **Tour de la Bayette** (Mon–Sat 9.30–11.30am & 2.30–6pm, Sun 9.30–11.30am; 10F) by the north transept door: you look back over the rue des Gras to the 1464-metre Puy de Dôme (see p.710) looming dramatically over the city, white morning mist retreating down its sides like seaweed from a rock.

A short step northeast of the cathedral, down the elegant old rue du Port, stands Clermont's other great church, the Romanesque **Basilique Notre-Dame-du-Port** – a century older than the cathedral and in almost total contrast both in style and substance, built from softer stone in pre-lava-working days and consequently corroding badly from exposure to Clermont's polluted air. For all that, it's a beautiful building in pure Auvergnat Romanesque style, featuring a Madonna and Child over the south door in the strangely stylized local form, both figures stiff and upright, the child more like a dwarf than an infant. Inside, it exudes the broody mysteriousness so often generated by the Romanesque style. Put a coin in the slot and you can light up the intricately carved ensemble of leaves, knights and biblical figures on the church's pillars and capitals. It was here in all probability that Pope Urban II preached the First Crusade in 1095 to a vast crowd who received his speech with the Occitan cry of "Dios lo Volt" (God wills it) – a phrase adopted by the crusaders in justification of all subsequent massacres.

For general animation, shopping, drinking and eating, the streets between the cathedral and place de Jaude are best, with the main morning market taking place in the hideously modernized **place St-Pierre** just off rue des Gras. **Place de Jaude** remains another monument to planners' aberrations, in spite of the shops, a couple of cafés well placed to take the morning sun and an attempt to disguise its awfulness with trees and fountain. Smack in the middle of the traffic, a romantic equestrian statue of Vercingetorix lines up with the Puy de Dôme.

Away from these central streets, there is nothing to tempt the pedestrian, save perhaps **rue Ballainvilliers**, whose eighteenth-century façades recall the sober, sombre elegance of Edinburgh and lead to the city's most interesting museum, the **Musée Bargoin** (Tues–Sat 10am–noon & 2–5pm, Sun 10am–noon; May–Sept closes 6pm; 21F), with some remarkable archeological finds from round about. These include lots of fascinating domestic bits: Roman shoes, baskets, bits of dried fruit, glass and pottery, as well as a remarkable burial find from nearby Martres-de-Veyre dating back to the second century AD: a young girl's plaited blonde hair, her thigh-length boots, dress, belt and goatskin shoes. There is also an extraordinary collection of wooden limbs found during building operations, buried in a covered-over spring in the suburb of Chamalières: the gifts of people whose ailments had been cured thanks to these waters. Upstairs is a very handsome exhibition of oriental carpets and kilims.

The two other museums are not of great interest. **Musée Lecoq**, directly behind the the Musée Bargoin (same hours & charges), is devoted mainly to natural history – and named after the gentleman who also founded the public garden full of beautiful trees and formal beds just across the street. **Musée du Ranquet**, 34 rue des Gras (Tues–Sat 10am–noon & 2–5pm, Sun 10am–noon; May–Sept closes 6pm; 12F), is housed in a noble sixteenth-century house, containing, most interestingly, a collection of traditional tools and domestic objects and two versions of seventeenth-century philosopher and scientist Blaise Pascal's calculating machine.

Montferrand is today little more than a suburb of larger Clermonts, standing out on a limb to the north, but it's good for a stroll if you're really keen. Built on the *bastide* plan, its principal streets, rue de la Rodade and rue Jules-Guesde (the latter named for the founder of the French Communist Party, for Montferrand was home to many of the *Michelin* factory workers), are still lined with the fine town houses of its medieval merchants and magistrates.

Eating and drinking

If you are staying in the station area, there are a couple of reasonable places to eat without going further afield. The best is the *Auvergnat*, the restaurant of the *Hôtel St-André*, 27 av de l'URSS (around 130F), whose repertoire includes some standard Auvergne dishes like the *potée auvergnate*. Less expensive is the *Hôtel des Commerçants*, opposite the station (from 65F), and as a standby, there's the station buffet itself.

In the centre of town, among the cheaper places, the one must is the everlastingly popular *Crêperie 1513*, 3 rue des Chaussetiers, opposite the cathedral, which occupies a superb Renaissance mansion built in 1513 (till 1am, 2am at weekends; around 50F). In the same street at no. 29, *Le Bougnat* offers local regional cuisine at affordable prices (closed Sun & Mon; from 80F). Close by at 36 rue des Gras, there's good pizza and pasta at *Le Bistrot Vénitien* for about 55F (closed Sun & Mon lunch). On the other side of the cathedral, there's good Vietnamese cooking at around 50F at the *Mai Lan*, 41 bd Trudaine (closed Sun & Mon lunch), and crêpes for 30–40F at the *Pescajoux* in the old rue du Port at no. 13.

For a more specialized gastronomic experience, there's nothing to beat the refined and inventive cooking of *Gérard Anglard* at 17 rue Lamartine, off place de Jaude, especially the lunchtime menu at 100F (closed Sun & Aug 1–15; 160F upwards). Also good value, especially at lunchtime, is the *Clos St-Pierre*, next to the St-Pierre market below the cathedral (closed Sun; 53F at lunchtime, otherwise 160F plus). And, if you don't mind the drive – barely 5km southeast off the old N9 Issoire road – the *Petit Bonneval* at **PÉRIGNAT-LÈS-SARLIÈVE** makes an agreeable and delicious stop for dinner on a summer evening (☎73.79.11.11; menus at 98F & 135F, and upwards).

For a daytime drink or coffee, *Le Suffren*, on the corner of place de Jaude, is one of the most popular and agreeable places to hang out. Also fashionable, especially for a nighttime drink, there's *Le Dérailleur*, 9 av Georges-Clemenceau, while young rockers head for the suburban village of **ORCINES**, beneath the Puy de Dôme, to *Phidias* or *Boudu's*, still going strong on rte de la Baraque (☎73.62.18.34; until 4am; closed Sun & Mon).

The Puy de Dôme

Visiting Clermont without going to the top of the 1464-metre **Puy de Dôme** would be like visiting Athens without seeing the Acropolis – touristy, perhaps, but absolutely spectacular. And if you choose your moment – early in the morning or late in the evening – you can easily avoid the worst of the crowds.

Clearly signposted from place de Jaude, it is about 15km from the city centre by the D941. The last 6.5km is a private road and costs 20F. Alternatively, you can leave the car at the **Col de Ceyssat** and climb the Puy itself on foot in about an hour. In July and August, there's a bus on Monday and Thursday (54F).

The result of a volcanic explosion about 10,000 years ago, the Puy is an abrupt 400m from base to summit. Although the weather station buildings and enormous television mast are pretty ugly close up, the staggering views and sense of airy elevation more than compensate. Even if Mont Blanc itself is not always visible way to the east – it can be if conditions are favourable – you can see huge distances, all down the Massif Central to the Cantal mountains. Above all, you get a bird's-eye view of the other volcanic summits to the north and south, both the rounded domes, largely forested since the nineteenth century, and the perfect 100-metre-deep grassy crater of the **Puy de Pariou**, just to the north.

Immediately below the summit are the scant remains of a substantial **Roman temple** dedicated to Mercury (free entry), some of the finds from which are displayed in the Musée Bargoin in Clermont-Ferrand (see p.709). Beside it is a memorial commemorating the exploits of Eugène Renaux, who landed a plane here in 1911 in response to the offer of a 100,000 franc prize by the Michelin brothers. Today the aviators are hang-gliders and paragliding enthusiasts drifting like gaudy birds around the stern of a ship.

Riom

Just 15km north of Clermont-Ferrand, **RIOM** is sedate and provincial. One-time capital of the entire Auvergne, its Renaissance architecture now secures the town's status as a highlight of the northern Massif. In 1942, just before the first trains of Jewish deportees were shipped to Nazi Germany, Léon Blum, Jewish Prime Minister and architect of the Socialist Popular Front government, was put on trial in Riom by

Pétain, France's collaborationist ruler, in an attempt to blame the country's ills on the Left. Defending himself, Blum turned the trial into an indictment of collaboration and Nazism. Under pressure from Hitler, Pétain called it off, but nonetheless deported Blum to Germany, an experience which he survived, to give evidence against Pétain himself after the war.

You may not want to stay for more than a morning's wandering, but it provides a worthwhile stopover for lunch if you're on the way up to Vichy. It's an aloof, old-world kind of place, still Auvergne's judicial capital, with a nineteenth-century **Palais de Justice** that stands on the site of a grand palace built when the dukes of Berry controlled this region in the fourteenth century. Only the **Sainte-Chapelle** survives of the original palace, with some fine stained glass and tapestries (guided visits only: July & Aug Mon–Fri 3–5.30pm; Sept Wed & Fri 3–5.30pm; May & June Wed 3–5.30pm; 15F).

There is an interesting museum on the region's folk traditions nearby at 10bis rue Delille, the **Musée Régional d'Auvergne** (daily except Tues 10am–noon & 2.30–5.30pm; 15F), with the **Musée Mandet's** displays of Roman finds and unexciting paintings not far away at 4 rue de l'Hôtel-de-Ville (same hours and price). At 44 rue du Commerce, the **church of Notre-Dame-du-Marthuret** holds Riom's most valued treasures, two statues of the Virgin and Child – one a Black Madonna, the other, the so-called *Vierge à l'Oiseau*, a touchingly realistic piece of carving that portrays the young Christ with a bird fluttering in his hands. A copy stands in the entrance hall of the church (its original site), where you can see it with the advantage of daylight.

Riom's **tourist office** is at 16 rue du Commerce in the town centre (Mon–Sat 9am–noon & 2–6pm). If you decide to **stay**, the *Grand Hôtel Desaix*, 1 pl Martyrs-de-la-Résistance (☎73.38.20.36; ②), and *Hôtel du Square*, 26 bd Desaix (☎73.38.46.52; ②–③), are both good value and have their own restaurants with inexpensive menus.

Around Riom

SNCF buses run to **MOZAC**, on the edge of town, with a twelfth-century **abbey church**, its Romanesque sculpture beautiful as ever, and continue to the bourgeois spa-resort of **CHÂTEL-GUYON** in around ten to twenty minutes. With thirty different **hot springs**, great views over the surrounding countryside and *puys*, and a couple of well-equipped **campsites**, this is as good a place as any if you want to rest up for a night. For an easy stroll from here, you can wander out along the leafy **valleys of the Sardon and Prades**.

VOLVIC TO LASCHAMP WALK

For a good day's walk and a really hands-on exploration of the *puys*, take the train from Clermont to Volvic-Gare. Follow the D90 road beside the train line for about 1km until you join up with the **GR441** path, where the road turns right under the train line. Keep along your side of the train track for a few minutes longer and follow the GR441 round to the left, almost doubling back southwest along the line of the wooded Puys Nugères, Jumes and Coquille to the northern foot of the Puy de Chopine (2–3hrs). Here you join up with the **GR4** and follow the combined GR4–441 across the Orcines–Pontgibaud road to the summit of the Puy de Dôme (about 2hr 30min from the road). From the Puy, descend to the Col de Ceyssat in half an hour (good chance of a lift back to Clermont), or continue to **LASCHAMP** (50min), where there is a **gîte d'étape** (7–8hr, although a fit and experienced walker could do it in six).

You should not set off without either the relevant section of the GR4 *Topoguide* or, preferably, the IGN 1:25,000 map, the *Chaîne des Puys*, which also marks the GR441 from Volvic-Gare. If you don't feel up to a walk, there is a really beautiful train ride from Clermont to the town of Le Mont-Dore (see p.714), all round the chain of the *puys*.

The little town of **VOLVIC** is also close by, renowned for its spring water and the quarries that furnished the black rock that built Clermont's cathedral, as well as so many other Auvergnat buildings. Its **Maison de la Pierre** (guided tours only: May–Sept daily 10am–noon & 2–5.30pm; daily except Tues mid-March to April & Oct to mid-Nov; 21F) features a surprisingly engaging display about the use of lava rock, including a historical and geological explanation, as well as a tour of the disused quarries – a warm jacket is advised.

Vichy

VICHY is famous for two things: its World War II puppet government under Marshal Pétain and its curative sulphurous springs, which attract thousands of ageing and ailing visitors, or *curistes*, every year. There's no mention of Pétain's government in town, but the fact that Vichy is one of France's foremost spa resorts colours everything you see here. The population is largely elderly, genteel and rich, and swells several-fold in summer; they come here to drink the water, wallow in it, inhale its steam or be sprayed with it, and the town is almost entirely devoted to catering for them, while trying to rejuvenate its image by appealing to a younger, more fitness-conscious generation.

The Town

All of this should make Vichy a place to avoid, yet it's hard to dislike. There's a real *fin-de-siècle* charm about the town and a curious fascination in its continuing function. The town revolves around the **Parc des Sources**, a stately tree-shaded park that takes up most of the centre. At its north end stands the **Hall des Sources**, an enormous iron-framed greenhouse in which people sit and chat, or read newspapers, while from a large tiled stand in the middle the various waters emerge from their spouts, beside the just-visible remains of the Roman establishment. The *curistes* line up to get their prescribed cupful, and for a small fee you can join them. The *Célestins* is the only one of the springs that is bottled and widely drunk: if you're into a taste experience, try the remaining five. They are progressively more sulphurous and foul, with the *Source de l'Hôpital*, which has its own circular building at the far end of the park, an almost unbelievably nasty creation. Each of the springs is prescribed for a different ailment and the tradition is that – apart from the *Célestins* – they must all be drunk on the spot to be efficacious; a dubious but effective way of drawing in the crowds.

Although all the springs technically belong to the nation and treatment is partially funded by the state, they are in fact run privately for profit by the *Compagnie Fermière*, first created in the nineteenth century to prepare for a visit by the Emperor Napoléon III. The *Compagnie* not only has a monopoly on selling the waters but also runs the casino and numerous hotels, including Vichy's grandest, the *Pavillon Sévigné*. Even the chairs conveniently dotted around the Parc des Sources belong to the *Compagnie*.

Directly behind the Hall des Sources, along the leafy **Esplanade Napoléon III** (the emperor's interest in the waters brought Vichy to public notice in the mid-nineteenth century), is the enormous **Grand Établissement Thermal**, the thermal baths, decorated with Moorish arches and domes and blue ceramic panels of voluptuous mermaids. In the entrance hall, a massive third-century Roman milestone from the Vichy-Clermont road is displayed, with an expensive shopping arcade leading off. And behind this is the latest addition to the town's amenities: the spanking-new, modern **Bains Callou**.

To provide distraction for the *curistes*, a grand **casino** was built at the southern end of the Parc des Sources, which from May to September is the venue for regular concerts and opera productions, with lighter music oom-pah-ing out from the open-air bandstand in the park behind it.

After the waters, Vichy's curiosities are limited. There is pleasant, wooded riverside in **Parc de l'Allier**, created again for Napoléon III. And, not far from here, the old town boasts the strange **church of St-Blaise**, actually two churches in one, with a 1930s Baroque structure built onto the original Romanesque one – an effect that sounds hideous but is rather imaginative. Inside, another Auvergne Black Virgin, Notre-Dame-des-Malades, stands surrounded by plaques offered by the grateful healed who stacked their odds with both her and the sulphur.

Practicalities

Vichy's **gare SNCF** (☎70.46.50.50) is on the eastern edge of the city centre at the end of rue de Paris. The **gare routière** is on the corner of rue Doumier and rue Jardet, by the central place Charles-de-Gaulle. The building that used to house the wartime Vichy government at 19 rue du Parc is now home to the **tourist office** (daily 9am–noon & 2–6pm, Sat 9am–noon; May–Sept 9am–7pm; ☎70.98.71.94), though they are, not surprisingly, very careful to make no reference at all to what once went on upstairs.

There are so many **hotels** that finding a place to stay is not difficult, and there are several around the *gare SNCF* if you don't want to venture further. It's more agreeable to try the freshly decorated and tranquilly bourgeois *Midland*, 2 rue de l'Intendance, off rue de Paris (☎70.97.48.48; closed Oct 11–April 27; ③; good restaurant from 85F); the *Provence* nearby at 6 av Victoria (☎70.98.22.73; ③–④; closed Dec–Feb; restaurant from 85F); or the historic *Hôtel Londres*, 7 bd de Russie, behind the casino (☎70.98.28.27; ①–③; closed mid-Oct to March).

If you prefer something a little cheaper, there are two good choices in the old part of town: the *Hôtel Allier Clairvaux*, 2 pl Vieille-Eglise, opposite the church of St-Blaise (☎70.32.15.13; ①–③; closed mid-Oct to mid-April; restaurant from 55F); and nearby *Hôtel du Bourbonnais*, 20 pl d'Allier (☎70.32.16.10; ①; closed Oct–April), a simple, old-fashioned French hotel with home-cooking for 55F. But for real charm and a lovely view over the park, the best bargain must be the *Belle-Île*, 72 bd des États-Unis (☎70.98.20.61; ①; closed Dec & Jan). The **youth hostel** has moved to the *Foyer Sonacotra*, 76 av des Celestins (☎70.98.43.39; ①), towards the station. There's a **camping municipal**, across the river by the Pont de Bellerive (☎70.32.67.74, May–Sept).

For **eating**, apart from the hotel-restaurants listed above, the simplest solution is to head for the area around the junction of rue Clemenceau and rue de Paris, where there are several brasseries and cafés. For something rather more elegant. and not cheap, the beautiful *Brasserie du Casino*, 4 rue du Casino (closed Thurs lunch, Wed, March 1–15 & Nov, around 150F), is quite an experience. Even more chic and expensive, with excellent food, there's the restaurant of the *Pavillon Sévigne*, 50 bd JF-Kennedy (200F plus).

The Monts-Dore

The **Monts-Dore** lie about 50km southwest of Clermont. Also volcanic in origin – the main period of activity was around five million years ago – they are much more rugged and more obviously mountainous than their gentler, younger neighbours, the Monts-Dôme. Their centre is the precipitous, plunging valley of the River Dordogne, which rises on the slopes of the **Puy de Sancy**, at 1885 metres the highest point in the Massif Central, just above the little town of **Le Mont-Dore**.

In spite of their relative ruggedness, there are few crags and rock faces. Their upper slopes, albeit steep, are grassy and treeless for miles and miles. They are known as *montagnes à vaches* – mountains for cows, as they traditionally provided summer pasture land for herds of cows, raised above all for their milk and the production of **St-Nectaire** cheese. The herdsmen who milked them morning and evening and made the cheese set up their primitive summer homes in the dozens of now mainly ruined stone huts, or *burons*, that scatter the landscape.

Although these traditional activities still continue, many of the upland herds are now beef cattle being fattened for the autumn sales, often for export to Italy, Germany and Spain. And tourism has become an important part of the local economy, although mostly unobtrusive and low key, with mainly walkers in summer and cross-country skiers in winter.

Le Mont-Dore and the Puy de Sancy

Squeezed out along the narrow wooded valley of the infant Dordogne, grey-slated **LE MONT-DORE** is a long-established spa resort, with Roman remnants testifying to just how old. Its popularity goes back to the eighteenth century when metalled roads replaced the old mule paths and made access possible, but reached its apogee with the opening of the railway around 1900. It is an altogether wholesome and civilized sort of place.

The **Établissement Thermal** – the baths, which give the place its *raison d'être* – are right in the middle of town (daily guided tours 10am–noon & 2–5.30pm; 15F). Early every morning, the *curistes* stream into its neo-Byzantine halls – an extravaganza of tiles, striped columns and ornate ironwork – for a hopeful remedy in this self-proclaimed "world centre for treatment of asthma".

Walkers also frequent the town, the principal attraction being the 1885-metre **Puy de Sancy**, whose jagged skyline blocks the head of the Dordogne Valley, 3km away (5 buses every afternoon mid-May to Sept; 10F). Accessible by *téléférique* (31F return) since the 1930s, it's one of the busiest tourist sites in the country. As a result, the path from the *téléférique* station to the summit has had to be railed and paved with baulks of timber to prevent total erosion. Combined with the scars of access tracks for the ski installations, this has done little for its beauty.

However, with a little sweat and effort, it is not hard to escape to wilder areas of the mountain. The **GR30** passes this way and on down to La Bourboule. It will give you a good sense of the typical landscape: long views over meadows full of gentians and violets, grazed by sheep and cows. Start out along the summit path and at the first intermediate peak, take a right and go downhill. The GR30 is signposted. It follows the western ridge of the Dordogne Valley for about an hour and 30 minutes, before turning 90 degrees left, away from the valley. Keep straight ahead at this point, go down a gravelly track, with the rocky dome of **Le Capucin**, above Le Mont-Dore, directly in front of you. The track enters the woods to the left of this bump by a ruined house. Five minutes later, on the right, just past a concrete water-pipe junction, a path drops steeply down through beech trees to Le Capucin *téléférique* station and down again to Le Mont-Dore (3hrs). Coming up, you would need to allow 4–5 hours. The path starts behind the *Panorama Hotel*, near the tourist office.

A shorter, though steep, climb up from the town would take you directly to the summit of Le Capucin (2hr), with great views of the Puy de Sancy and across the Dordogne Valley.

Practicalities

Without a car, Le Mont-Dore is most easily accessible by train from Clermont (see p.706). The stations, both **train** (☎73.65.00.02) and **bus** (☎73.37.31.06), are at the entrance to the town. Ten minutes' walk takes you to the centre, where the **tourist office** sits in the park on av de la Libération (Mon–Sat 9am–12.30pm & 2–6.30pm; ☎73.65.20.21); they will advise about other walking and cycling possibilities (VTT rental), as well as day bus excursions to some otherwise rather inaccessible places round about.

Accommodation is not hard to come by, as the town is brimming with hotels. Try *Les Cascades* at the back of town beyond the baths at 26 av Clemenceau (☎73.65.01.36;

①–③); the *Nouvel Hôtel* near the baths at 4 rue Jean-Moulin (☎73.65.11.34; ①–③); or the *Russie*, also nearby at 3 rue Favart (☎73.65.05.97; ①–②). Cheaper still, but fine for a no-frills stay, is the *Centre* at 8 rue St-Julien (☎73.65.01.77; ①). There's a nice modern **youth hostel** on the Puy de Sancy road (☎73.65.03.77; ①; meals), and a *gîte d'étape* (☎73.65.25.65; meal), and two municipal **campsites**, *Les Crouzets*, opposite the station, and *L'Esquiladou*, on the right off the road to La Bourboule.

As far as **eating** is concerned, there are large numbers of brasseries and cafés in the centre offering *plats* for 40–50F. A particularly agreeable place to try is *Le Bougnat*, 23 av Clemenceau, which offers various Auvergnat traditional dishes on its menus from 75F (closed Tues).

La Bourboule

LA BOURBOULE is just 7km down the road. Known as the sister to Le Mont-Dore, it is another traditional spa – the "capital of allergies" – but with a more open feel and, due to its lower altitude, temperatures a degree or two warmer. The big **casino**, the domed **Grands Thermes baths** and several other turn-of-the-century buildings which used to house privately run baths are ornate, gilded and wonderfully vulgar, with a faded, permanently off-season look to them – much like the whole town. All in all, it's a cool, tranquil place to unwind: as the tourist office's leaflet says, "You will be able to put your vital node to rest in La Bourboule."

Behind the Hôtel de Ville, the large wooded **Parc Fenestre** has a *téléférique* taking you right up to **Plateau de Charlannes** at 1300m, where it's possible to stroll in the woods or ski in winter; the **tourist office** in the Hôtel de Ville on place de la République (☎73.81.07.90) sells a booklet of local walks.

Hotels here are plentiful, three good bargains being the *Aviation Hôtel* in rue de Metz (☎73.65.50.50; ②–③; closed Oct–Dec; restaurant from 85F), *Le Pavillon*, av d'Angleterre (☎73.65.50.18; ③–④; closed Oct–April; restaurant from 75F), and the *Lutétia* on rue des Frères-Roziers (☎73.81.05.75; ①). There is also a good selection of **campsites**, with the *camping municipal* on av Lattre-de-Tassigny, and another at **MURAT-LE-QUAIRE**, 4km away, along the Mont-Dore road.

WALKS AROUND LA BOURBOULE

Fit and serious walkers may want to conquer the **Puy de Sancy**, a six-hour hike south of La Bourboule on the GR30-41, passing after about two hours the two fine waterfalls of the **Cascade de la Vernière** and **Plat à Barbe** – themselves a satisfying destination for a walk. For the summit of Puy de Sancy, see under Le Mont-Dore, opposite. An easier walk out of La Bourboule is to the 1500-metre summit of the **Banne d'Ordanche**: pick up the GR path to the east of the town where it crosses the D130 road and the train line, then take the signposted GR41 where it diverges from GR30.

During winter months, both Le Mont-Dore and La Bourboule double as ski resorts – centres of a **ski-de-fond** (cross-country) network of circular pistes, some over 20km long. Skiable paths also connect La Bourboule to other ski centres in the locality – Sancy, Besse, Chastreix and Picherande. Downhill skiing is possible, too, on the Puy de Sancy.

Orcival

Twenty-seven kilometres southwest of Clermont and about twenty kilometres north of Le Mont-Dore, lush pastures and green hills punctuated by the abrupt eruptions of the *puys* enclose the village of **ORCIVAL** (buses from Clermont), the home town of ex-President Valéry Giscard d'Estaing. A pretty if over-touristed little place, founded by the monks of La Chaise-Dieu in the twelfth century, it makes a suitable base for hiking in the region.

WALKS AROUND ORCIVAL

If you're keen on walking in the area, possibilities out of Orcival include trips to **Lac de Servières** and **Lac de Guéry**. The first takes two and a half hours, the second some five hours. For Lac de Servières, follow the **GR141–30** south through the woods above the valley of the Sioule. The lake is a beauty; it's 1200m up, with gently sloping shores surrounded by pasture and conifers. You can either head southeast to the **gîte d'étape** at **PESSADE** (☎73.79.31.07), or continue to the larger Lac de Guéry, lent a slightly eerie air by the black basaltic boulders strewn across the surrounding meadows, where there is a romantically situated lakeside **hotel**, the *Lac de Guéry* (☎73.65.02.76; ③; closed mid-Oct to mid-Dec; restaurant from 75F) .

If you are driving to Mont-Dore, only 9km further on from here, just before the Lac de Guéry, the road takes you round the head of the **Fontsalade Valley**, where two prominent rocks composed of banks of basalt organ-pipes rise spectacularly from the woods: the **Roche Tuilière** and the **Roche Sanadoire**. A Chamina footpath takes you on a two-hour walk round the valley, starting from the roadside belvedere overlooking Sanadoire. A little higher up, on the bare slopes of the **Puy de l'Aiguiller**, a roadside memorial commemorates some English airmen killed in an accident while making a parachute drop to the *maquis* in March 1944.

Orcival is dominated by the stunning Romanesque **church of Notre-Dame**, built of the same grey volcanic stone as the cathedral in Clermont and topped with a spired octagonal tower and fanned with tiny chapels. Inside, attention focuses on the choir, neatly and harmoniously contained by the semicircle of pillars defining the ambulatory. Mounted on a stone column in the centre is the celebrated **Virgin of Orcival**, a gilded and enamelled statue of Mary enthroned, holding an adult-looking Child in her lap. The statue has been the object of a popular cult since the Middle Ages and is still carried through the streets on Ascension Day.

There's modest **accommodation** at the *Hôtel du Mont-Dore* beside the church (☎73.65.82.06; ①–②; closed mid-Nov to Dec; restaurant from 54F), as well as at the *Hôtel Les Tourists* (☎73.65.82.55; ②–③; closed Nov–Jan; restaurant from 60F), the *Hôtel Vieux Logis* (☎73.65.82.03; ①–②; closed Oct to mid-Dec; restaurant fom 65F), and a **gîte d'étape**, *La Fontchartoux*, 1km away on GR30/GR441, with meals available in the adjoining restaurant run by the *gîte* proprietor (☎73.65.83.04; ①–②). **Campers** are better off at **ST-BONNET**, 5km away in the next valley.

St-Nectaire and around

ST-NECTAIRE lies some way to the south of Orcival, midway between Mont-Dore and Issoire. It comprises the tiny spa of **St-Nectaire-le-Bas**, with its main street lined with grand but fading Belle Époque hotels, and the old village of **St-Nectaire-le-Haut**, overlooked by its magnificent Romanesque **church**, which gives the place its renown. It is, like the church in Orcival and Notre-Dame-du-Port in Clermont, one of the jewels of the Auvergne's Romanesque architecture, with the same delightful features: patterned stonework, intricate arrangement of apse and radiating chapel, richly carved capitals within.

In the narrow valley bottom, where the main street runs, two of the old **hotels** are being refurbished and provide a quiet and comfortable place to stay. One, in particular, the *Hôtel Régina* (☎73.88.54.55; ②–③), has an excellent restaurant with menus at 68–115F. The *Thermalia* (☎73.88.50.28; ②–③), next door, has more character and also provides a good meal from 85F. The best-value **campsite** is the *Clé des Champs*, and there is also a **gîte d'étape** called *Le Clos du Vallon* (☎73.88.50.92; April–Oct) for walkers on the GR30, which heads north from here to Lac Aydat in five hours, or west to the forest-girt **Lac Chambon** in three hours via Murol. There's another *gîte* on the way at **PHIALEIX** (☎73.79.32.43; April–Oct).

For shorter walks out of St-Nectaire, take the D150 past the church through the old village towards the 919-metre **Puy de Mazeyres**, and turn up a path to the right for the final climb to the summit (1hr), where you get a superb aerial view of the country round about. Alternatively, follow the D966 along the Couze de Chambon Valley to **SAILLANT**, where the stream cascades down a high lava rock face in the middle of the village.

Murol

MUROL, 6km west of St-Nectaire by road (July & Aug twice daily bus to Clermont), is an attractive, sleepy little place best known for its powerful medieval **château**, dramatically situated on top of a basalt cone commanding the approaches for miles around (Sun & hols 10am–noon & 2–6pm; June–Aug daily 10am–6pm; April, May & Sept daily 10am–noon & 2–6pm; 20F). In summer, a local organization re-enacts the medieval life of the castle in costume (40F).

There are several small family-run **hotels** here. Try the *Hôtel des Pins* on rue de Levat (☎73.88.60.50; ③; closed Oct–April), or the *Hôtel de Paris* on place de l'Hôtel-de-Ville (☎73.88.60.09; ①–②; closed Oct–March), both with reasonable restaurants from 55F. Of the **campsites**, the best value is the *Ribeyre*, a short distance away at **JASSAT** (☎73.88.64.29; May to mid-Sept).

Besse

Eleven kilometres due south of Murol, **BESSE** is one of the prettiest and oldest villages hereabouts. Its winding streets of noble lava-built houses – some as old as the fifteenth century – sit atop the valley of the Couze de Pavin, with one of the original fortified town **gates** still in place at the upper end of the village.

Its wealth was due to its role as the principal market for the farms on the eastern slopes of the Monts-Dore. Its cooperative is still one of the main producers of St-Nectaire cheese (see below), and the annual ceremonies of the *Montée* and *Dévalade*, marking the ascent of the herds to the high pastures in July and their departure in autumn, are still celebrated by the procession of the Black Virgin of Vassivière from the **church of St-André** in Besse to the chapel of **LA VASSIVIÈRE**, west of **Lac Pavin** (July 2 and the first Sunday after Sept 21) and back again in autumn.

The lake lies 5km west of the village, on the way to the purpose-built ski resort of **SUPER-BESSE** (not very reliable because of the snow conditions). It's a perfect volcanic lake, filling the now wooded crater. The GR30 goes through, passing by the **Puy de Montchal**, whose 1407-metre summit gives you a fine view over several other lakes and the rolling plateau south towards **ÉGLISENEUVE-D'ENTRAIGUES**, 13km

---

ST-NECTAIRE CHEESE

St-Nectaire is an *appellation contrôlée*, to which only cheeses made from herds grazing in a limited area to the south of the Monts-Dore are entitled. It is made in two stages. First, a white creamy cheese or *tomme* is produced. This is matured for two to three months in a cellar at a constant temperature, resulting in the growth of a mould on the skin of the cheese which produces the characteristic smell, taste and whitish or yellowy grey colour.

There are two kinds: St-Nectaire **fermier** and St-Nectaire **laitier**. The *fermier* is the strongest and tastiest and some of it is still made entirely on the farm. Increasingly, however, individual farmers make the *tomme* stage, but then sell it on to wholesalers for the refining. The *laitier* is much more an "industrial" product, made from the milk of lots of different herds, sold on to a co operative or cheese manufacturer for all its stages.

by road, where the Parc des Volcans' **Maison du Fromage** gives a blow-by-blow account of the making of the different cheeses of Auvergne (daily May–Sept 2–6pm; July & Aug 10am–7pm; 16F).

The **tourist office** is next to the church in the town (Mon–Sat 9am–noon & 2–6pm, Sun 10am–noon & 3–6pm; Oct to mid-Dec Mon–Fri 9am–noon & 2–6pm, Sat 9am–noon), and will provide information and advice about walking, mountain biking and skiing. For a place to **stay**, there is none better than the attractive old *Hostellerie du Beffroi*, 24 rue Abbé-Blot (☎73.79.57.87; ③–④; closed mid-Oct to early Nov), whose good restaurant serves up a range of local specialities from 90F.

The Monts du Cantal

The **Cantal Massif** forms the most southerly extension of the Parc des Volcans. Still nearly 80km in diameter and once 3000m in height, it is one of the world's largest, albeit extinct volcanoes, shaped like a wheel without a rim. The hub is formed by the three great conical peaks that survived the erosion of the original single cone: **Plomb du Cantal** (1885m), **Puy Mary** (1787m) and **Puy de Peyre-Arse** (1686m).

From this centre a series of deep-cut wooded valleys radiates out like spokes. The most notable are the **valley of Mandailles** and the **valleys of the Cère and Alagnon** in the southwest, where the road and train line run, and in the north the **valleys of Falgoux and the Rhue**. Between the valleys, especially on the north side, are huge expanses of gently sloping grassland, most notably the **Plateau du Limon**. And it is these which for centuries have been the mainstay of life in the Cantal: summer pasture for the cows whose milk makes the firm yellow Cantal cheese, pressed in the form of great crusty drums. But this traditional activity has long been in serious decline; as elsewhere, many of the herds are now beef cattle. Tourism is on the increase, in particular walking, riding and skiing.

The main walking routes are the fairly arduous **GR400**, which does a circuit of the whole massif, and the **GR4**, which crosses it from the north to the southeast. There are also more than fifty shorter routes, details of which are obtainable through *Chamina* publications. The two main summits, Plomb du Cantal and Puy Mary, are – for better or worse – accessible to all: the former by *téléférique* from Super-Lioran, the latter by a veritable highway of a footpath from the road at Pas de Peyrol. The best section of the GR4–400 for an experienced hiker with limited time is the three-hour stretch between Super-Lioran and the Puy Mary, with the possibility of taking in a couple of extra summits on the way. For motorists, there's the long, sinuous **Route des Crêtes**, which does a rather wider circuit than the GR400. But, be warned, if you hit a period of bad weather, you'll drive a long way in low gear, seeing no more than white banks of mist illumined by your headlights.

The main centres within the massif lie on the N122 between Murat and Aurillac: **LE LIORAN**, where the road and rail tunnels begin, and **SUPER-LIORAN**, the downhill and cross-country ski centre, with the *Auberge du Tunnel* (☎71.49.50.02; ①–②) and two *gîtes d'étape*, as well as a **tourist office** (daily 9.30am–noon & 2–6pm; ☎71.49.50.08). **THIEZAC**, 10km south, has a tourist office (Mon–Sat 9.30am–noon & 2.30–6pm; ☎71.47.03.50), as well as the *Hôtel La Belle Vallée* (☎71.47.00.22; ②–③; closed mid-Nov to mid-Dec, restaurant from 80F), three *gîtes d'étape* and a **camping municipal**, *La Bedisse* (mid-June to mid-Sept). Further south at **VIC-SUR-CÈRE** there's a **tourist office** (Mon–Sat 9.30am–noon & 2.30–6pm; ☎71.47.50.68), and accommodation at the *Hôtel des Bains*, 9 av de la Promenade (☎71.47.50.16; ②–③; closed mid-Sept to April; restaurant from 70F), and the riverside **camping municipal** (April–Sept).

Aurillac

AURILLAC, the provincial capital of the Cantal, lies on the west side of the mountains, 98km east of Brive and 160km from Clermont-Ferrand. In spite of its good mainline train connections and the fact that its population has almost doubled in the last forty years, it remains one of the most out-the-way French provincial capitals. It was until recently a major manufacturer of umbrellas, although that seems doomed to eventual extinction, like its older traditional lacemaking and tanning industries. It is now mainly an administrative and commercial centre, with important cattle markets in the suburb of Sistrières on Mondays. Although there are no important sights, it makes a very agreeable and unpretentious place to stop over on your way into the Massif Central from the west.

The most interesting part of town is the kernel of old streets, now largely pedestrianized and full of good shops, just to the north of the central **place du Square**. **Rue Duclaux** leads through to the attractive **place de l'Hôtel-de-Ville**, where the big Wednesday and Saturday markets are held in the shadow of the handsome grey-stone **Hôtel de Ville**, built in restrained Republican-classical style in 1801 in the aftermath of the Revolution. Beyond it, the continuation of **rue des Forgerons** leads to the beautiful little **place St-Géraud**, with a round twelfth-century fountain overlooked by a Romanesque house that was probably part of the original abbey guesthouse, and the externally rather unprepossessing **church of St-Géraud**, which nonetheless has a beautifully ribbed late Gothic ceiling.

At the back of the church, past a delightful small garden, **rue de la Fontaine** comes out on the river bank by the Pont du Buis, with a shady walk back along cours d'Angoulême on the other side to the Pont-Rouge and **place Gerbert**, where there is an ancient *lavoir*, or washing place, by the *Birdland* restaurant and disco. On a steep bluff overlooking this end of town is the eleventh-century keep of the Château St-Étienne, containing the town's only worthwhile museum, the **Musée des Sciences** (Tues–Fri 10am–noon & 2–6pm, Sat 10am–noon; 15F), with a good section on volcanoes and a splendid view over the mountains to the east.

Southeast of the town towards Aubrac, the road leads through **CARLAT**, once an important feudal fiefdom, as well as the particularly attractive villages of **MUR-DE-BARREZ**, **BROMMAT** and **ALBINHAC**, with some lovely old houses and curious churches in the latter two villages.

Practicalities

The **tourist office** is in a small kiosk on the downhill side of place du Square in the town centre (Mon–Sat 9am–noon & 2–6.30pm; July & Aug daily 9am–7pm, Sun 9am–1pm; ☎71.48.46.58), with a number of guidebooks and maps on sale, as well as a money change facility when the banks are closed. The **gare SNCF** and **gare routière** are together on place Sémard, twenty minutes' walk from the place du Square along av de la République and rue de la Gare.

Right outside the station in Aurillac, if you are looking for a bargain place to **stay**, is the splendidly old-fashioned, unmodernized *Hôtel Terminus*, 8 rue de la Gare (☎71.48.01.17; ①–③), with perfectly adequate rooms for as little as 92F. For something more central and comfortable, try either *Le Square*, 15 pl du Square (☎71.48.24.72; ②–③; reasonable restaurant from 58F), or the *Hôtel Delcher*, just off the square at 20 rue des Carmes (☎71.48.01.69; ①–③; good food from 69F).

There is nowhere particularly exciting to **eat**, but the *Bistro-Cabaret Licence IV* on the corner of av Gambetta and rue Paul-Doumer is friendly and very good value, despite looking like a fast-food joint, serving some properly cooked regional specialities and good desserts (50–100F). Alternatively, there is the riverside *Birdland* by the Pont-

Rouge, done out in the French version of pub style, with pizzas for around 40F and menus for 75–115F (closed Sun); if you're looking for some **nightlife**, the *Bateau-Lavoir* **disco** is part of the same establishment (daily 11pm–4/5am; 40F weekdays, 50F weekends). Finally, Aurillac's most unexpected event is an annual **international street theatre festival** during the last full week in August, which attracts performers from all over Europe and fills the town with rather more exotic characters than are normally to be seen about its provincial streets.

Salers

SALERS lies 42km north of Aurillac, at the foot of the northwest slopes of the Cantal and within sight of the Puy Violent. Scarcely altered in size or aspect since its sixteenth-century heyday, it remains an extraordinarily homogeneous example of the architecture of that time. If it appears rather grand for a place so small, it's because the town became the administrative centre for the highlands of the Auvergne in 1564 and home of its magistrates. Exploiting this past is really all that is left to it, and as a result it is pretty touristy.

If you arrive by the Puy Mary road, you'll enter town by the **church**, which is worth a look for the super-naturalistic statuary of the Entombment of Christ (1496) hidden in a side chapel. In front of you, the cobbled **rue du Beffroi** leads uphill, under the massive clock tower, and into the central **place Tyssandier-d'Escous**. It is a glorious little square, surrounded by the fifteenth-century mansions of the provincial aristocracy with pepper-pot turrets, mullioned windows and carved lintels, among them the sturdy **Maison du Bailliage**, and, nearby, the Maison des Templiers with the small **Musée des Templiers** (Sat & Sun 2.30–5.30pm; May–Sept Mon–Sat 10am–noon & 2.30–6pm, Sun 10am–noon; 17F), with a missable collection of local interest. And, before you are done, be sure to make your way to the **Promenade de Barrouze** for the view out across the surrounding countryside and the Puy Violent.

Any further information you might need can be obtained from the **tourist office** in place Tyssandier-d'Escous (daily 10am–noon & 2.30–6pm; July & Aug 10am–noon & 2.30–7pm; Sept–Nov 11 10am–noon & 2.30–6.30pm; closed Nov 12–March; ☎71.40.70.68). If you are planning to **stay**, try the *Hôtel des Remparts* near the Promenade de Barrouze (☎71.40.70.33; ②–④; closed Oct 20–Dec 19), whose good restaurant specializes in Auvergnat peasant cuisine (from 68F), or the small *Hôtel du Beffroi* in rue du Beffroi (☎71.40.70.11; ②–③; closed mid-Nov to Jan), likewise with good solid regional food (from 60F). There's a **camping municipal** on the Puy Mary road (mid-May to mid-Oct).

Murat

MURAT, on the eastern edge of the Cantal, is the closest town to the high peaks. It is also the easiest of access, lying on the N122 road and main train line, about 12km northeast of Le Lioran. There is no one particular sight to see here, and it's the ensemble of grey stone houses that attracts, many dating from the fifteenth and sixteenth centuries and crowded together on their medieval lanes. They make a magnificent sight, especially as you approach from the St-Flour road, with a backdrop of the steep basalt cliffs of the **Rocher Bonnevie**, once the site of the local castle and now surmounted by a huge white statue of the Virgin Mary. Facing the town, perched on the distinctive mound of the **Rocher Bredons**, on your left as you approach, there's a very lovely little Romanesque **chapel of St-Pierre**. And once you reach the town, one of the finest of the old houses is now open to the public as the **Maison de la Faune** (July & Aug Mon–Sat 10am–noon & 2–6pm, Sun 2–6pm; May–June & Sept–Oct closes 5pm; 22F), a modest museum illustrating the wildlife of the Parc des Volcans area.

The **monument** to deportees on the place de l'Hôtel-de-Ville and the name of the **avenue des 12-et-24-juin-1944**, opposite the tourist office, both commemorate one of the blackest days in Murat's recent history. On June 12, a local Resistance group interrupted a German raid on the town and killed a senior SS officer. In reprisal, the Germans burnt several houses down on June 24 and arrested 120 people, 80 of whom died in deportation.

The **tourist office** is on the main place de l'Hôtel-de-Ville by the monument (Mon–Sat 10am–noon & 2–6pm; July & Aug Mon–Sat 10am–noon & 2–7pm, Sun 10am–noon; ☎71.20.09.47), and you can rent **mountain bikes** opposite from *La Godille*, or *Bernard Escure* in place Gandilhon-Gens-d'Armes. The **gare SNCF** (☎71.20.07.20) is on the main road, av du Docteur-Mallet, where there are also some good places to **stay**; the most comfortable is the *Hôtel Les Breuils*, a handsome bourgeois house at 34 av du Dr-Mallet (☎71.20.01.25; ②–④; closed Nov 3–Dec 21), and there's the equally friendly and simple *Les Globe-Trotters* at no. 22 (☎71.20.07.22; ②–③; closed Oct 1–14: nice restaurant from 60F), and *Les Messageries* at no. 18 (☎71.20.04.04; ②; restaurant from 75F). The **campsite**, *Les Stalapos*, is open winter as well as summer (☎71.20.03.80; Dec 20–April & June–Sept).

St-Flour and the Margeride

ST-FLOUR, seat of a fourteenth-century bishopric, stands dramatically on a cliff-girt basalt promontory above the River Ander, 92km west of Le Puy and 92km south of Clermont-Ferrand, along the new, toll-free A75 autoroute. Its position on the main road from northern France to Languedoc, and the proximity of raw materials for its tanning and leather industries from the nearby grasslands of the Cantal, ensured prosperity in the Middle Ages; the town fell into somnolent decline in modern times, only partially reversed in the last thirty years.

While the lower town that has grown up around the station is of little interest, the wedge of old streets that occupies the point of the promontory surrounding the cathedral has considerable charm. If you are in a car, the best thing is to leave it in the park on the chestnut-shaded **Promenades**, which begin by the **memorial** to Dr Mallet, his two sons and other hostages and assorted citizens executed in reprisals by the Germans during World War II.

The narrow streets of the old town converge from here towards the **place d'Armes**, where the fourteenth-century **Cathédrale St-Pierre** stands, backing onto the edge of the cliff, with a terrace giving good views out over the countryside. From the outside, the plain grey volcanic rock of the cathedral makes for a rather severe and uninspiring appearance; it's an impression that is partly mitigated inside by the fine vaulting of the ceiling and the presence of a number of works of art, most notably by a carved, black-painted walnut figure of Christ of unknown origin, but dating from the thirteenth century.

Facing the cathedral on the place d'Armes are some attractive old buildings, housing a couple of cafés under their arcades, while at the north and south extremities of the square are the town's two museums. At the north end, the fine fourteenth-century building that was once the headquarters of the town's consuls contains the **Musée Douet**'s somewhat rag-bag collections of furniture, tapestries and paintings (May–Sept daily 9am–noon & 2–7pm; winter closes 6pm; 20F); the view from the cliffs behind the museum gives a sense of the impregnable position of the town. At the south end of the square, the current Hôtel de Ville, formerly the bishop's palace built in 1610, houses the much more interesting **Musée de la Haute-Auvergne** (daily 10am–noon & 2–6pm; Oct–May closed Sun; 20F, joint ticket for the two museums 35F), whose collections illustrate the trades, tools, costumes, traditions and activities of the region.

The **gare SNCF** is on av des Martyrs in the lower town (☎71.60.03.37), but the **tourist office** is on the Promenades, opposite the memorial (Mon–Sat 9am–noon & 2–6pm; June to mid-Sept 9am–noon & 2–7pm, Sun 10am–noon & 3–6pm; ☎71.60.22.50). For a place to **stay**, try the attractive, modernized *Hôtel des Voyageurs* at 25 rue du Collège on the north side of the old town (☎71.60.34.44; ①–④; good restaurant from 88F), or the *Hôtel du Nord* at 18 rue des Lacs on the south side (☎71.60.28.00; ①), whose good and popular restaurant serves local specialities (from 55F). Another agreeable place to eat is *Chez Geneviève*, 25 rue des Lacs, where menus start at 50F and you can eat a *pôtée auvergnate* for 49F.

The Margeride

South and west of St-Flour stretch the wild, rolling, sparsely populated wooded hills of the **Margeride**, one of the strongholds of the wartime Resistance groups. If you have your own transport, the D4 makes a slow but spectacular route east (92km) to Le Puy, crossing the forested heights of **Mont Mouchet**, at 1465m the highest point of the Margeride. A side turning, the signposted D48, takes you to the national Resistance **monument** by the woodman's hut, which served as HQ to the local Resistance commander during the June 1944 battle to delay German reinforcements moving north to strengthen resistance to the D-day landings in Normandy. It is now a **museum** (May–Oct 7 daily 9am–noon & 2–7pm; 20F), sketching the progression of the Resistance movement in the area. The views back west from these heights to the Cantal are superb.

Further south, the new autoroute crosses the gorge of the River Truyère beside the delicate steel tracery of the **Viaduc de Garabit**, built by Gustave Eiffel of tower fame in 1884 to carry the newly constructed rail line. Not far away, about 20km south of St-Flour and perched above the waters of the lake created by the damming of the Truyère for hydroelectric power, are the romantic ruins of the keep of the **Château d'Alleuze**, stronghold in the 1380s of one Bernard de Garlan, a notorious leader of lawless mercenaries employed by the English in the Hundred Years' War to sow panic and destruction in French-held parts of the country.

THE SOUTHWEST: AUBRAC AND ROUERGUE

In the southwest corner of the Massif Central, the landscapes start to change and the mean altitude begins to drop. The wild, desolate moorland of the **Aubrac** is cut and contained by the savage gorges of the **Lot and Truyère rivers**. To the south of them, the arid but more southern-feeling plateaux of the *causses* form a sort of intermediate step to the lower hills and coastal plains of Languedoc. And they in turn are cut by the dramatic trenches formed by the **gorges of the Tarn**, **Jonte** and **Dourbie**, along with the spectacular caves of the **Aven Armand** and **Dargilan**. These are places best avoided at the height of the holiday season, when they turn into overcrowded outdoor playgrounds for amateur canoeists, parties of schoolchildren, motorists and campers.

The bigger towns, like **Millau** and **Rodez** in the old province of **the Rouergue**, also have much more of a southern feel. Both are worth a visit, although their attractions need not keep you for more than half a day. Rodez has a fine cathedral and Millau is worth considering as a base for exploring the *causses* and river gorges of the Tarn and Jonte.

The two great architectural draws of the area are **Conques**, with its medieval village and magnificent abbey, which owes its influence to the St-Jacques pilgrim route (now the GR651), and the perfect little *bastide* town of **Sauveterre-de-Rouergue**.

The mountains of Aubrac

The **Aubrac** lies to the south of St-Flour, east of the valley of the River Truyère and north of the valley of the Lot. It is a region of bleak, windswept uplands with long views and huge skies, dotted with glacial lakes and granite villages hunkered down out of the weather. The highest points are between 1200 and 1400 metres, and there are more cows up here than people; you see them grazing the boggy, peaty pastures, divided by dry stone walls and turf-brown streams. There are few trees: a scatter of willow and ash along the streams and the occasional stand of hardy beeches on the tops, and only abandoned shepherds' huts testify to more populous times. It is an area which in bad weather is invisible, but which, in good, has a bleak beauty, little disturbed by tourism or modernization.

Once this was sheep country, where shepherds from the dry summer lowlands of Quercy and Languedoc brought their flocks for the season. They were displaced in the nineteenth century by cows, raised for their more commercially exploitable production of milk and cheese, destined for the growing towns. And these in turn, as available labour shrank with the depopulation of the villages, ceded the pastures to beef cattle, as in the Cantal further north.

Aumont-Aubrac and Aubrac

The waymarked **Tour d'Aubrac footpath** does a complete circuit of the area in around ten days, starting from the town of **AUMONT-AUBRAC**, where you'll find the *Hôtel Prunières* (☎66.42.80.14; ②; restaurant from 70F), a **camping municipal** (☎66.42.80.02), and a **gîte d'étape** at the *Relais de Peyre* (☎66.42.85.88); there's also a daily train connection on the Millau-St-Flour line. The marathon **GR65** from Le Puy to Santiago de Compostela in Spain also crosses the area from northeast to southwest en route to Conques. In fact, the tiny village of **AUBRAC** (not to be confused with Aumont-Aubrac), which gave its name to the region, owes its existence to this St-Jacques pilgrim route, as around 1120, a way station was opened here for the express purpose of providing shelter for the pilgrims on these inhospitable heights. Little remains of it today, beyond the windy **Tour des Anglais**, which harbours a **gîte d'étape** (☎66.44.25.51), and the *Hôtel Moderne* (☎65.44.28.42; ②–③; May–Oct; restaurant from 100F).

St-Urcize and Nasbinals

Lying in the wildest and most starkly beautiful part of the Aubrac, the close-huddled village of **ST-URCIZE**, 13km north of the town of Aubrac, hangs off the side of the valley of the River Lhere, with a lovely Romanesque church at its centre and a devastating World War I **memorial,** with so many names on it you wouldn't have thought it possible such a small place could furnish so much cannon fodder. It is ghostly out of season, for most of the unspoiled granite houses are owned by people who live elsewhere. Should you wish to stay, there is a **campsite**, a **gîte d'étape** (☎71.23.20.57), and the welcoming *Hôtel Remise* (☎71.23.20.02; ①–②; excellent food from 75F); the *Relais de l'Aubrac* (☎66.32.52.06; ②–③; restaurant from 55F; closed Nov 11–Dec 25) lies at the point where the road to Nasbinals crosses the River Bes at the Pont-du-Gournier, around 5km from St-Urcize.

NASBINALS, 8km to the southeast, is rather bigger and livelier, and something of a cross-country ski resort in winter. It, too, has a beautiful small-scale **church** of the twelfth century, joined on to the adjacent house with a round fortified tower incorporated in the transept wall by the entrance. Just below the building, the *Auberge Gourmande* (☎66.32.56.76; ①) has dormitory beds, while above it the *Hôtel La Route d'Argent* (☎66.32.50.03; ②) provides comfortable accommodation and good food from 75F. The village **tourist office** is on the other side of the road (Tues–Sat 9.30am–noon & 2–5pm) and can rent out mountain bikes. There is also a **campsite** and **gîte d'étape** (☎66.32.50.65; meals available), both on the St-Urcize road.

Laguiole

Seventeen kilometres west of St-Urcize and 24km north of Espalion, **LAGUIOLE** passes for a substantial town in these parts. It is a name which means but one thing in France: knives, and specifically ones with a long, pointed, stiletto-like blade and bone handle that fits the palm; the genuine article should bear the effigy of a bee stamped on the clasp that holds the blade open. It is an industry that started in the last century, moved to industrial Thiers outside Clermont-Ferrand and moved back to Laguiole in 1987, when the Société Laguiole opened a factory designed by Philippe Starck on the St-Urcize road, with a giant knife like a yacht's automatic pilot projecting from the roof of the windowless all-aluminium building. Of all the numerous outlets selling knives in the village, only the Société's are made entirely in Laguiole. They have a shop on the main through road, on the corner of the central marketplace opposite the **tourist office kiosk** (daily 10am–12.30pm & 2–6pm; July & Aug 9am–12.30pm & 3–7pm; ☎65.44.35.94); their wares include knives designed by Starck himself at high prices.

There is nothing of great importance to see in the village, though the **Musée du Haut-Rouergue** (July & Aug daily 3.30–6.30pm; 15F), with its collection of objects illustrative of the pastoral life, might be of interest. Nonetheless, it is a relatively metropolitan base for exploring round about, with several **hotels** on the main street. Try the *Aubrac* (☎65.44.32.13; ②–③; restaurant from 60F) opposite the marketplace; both the *Régis* (☎65.44.30.05; ②; restaurant from 75F), and the *Grand Hôtel Auguy* (☎65.44.31.11; ②–③), with a good restaurant from 105F; are side by side on the main street.

Alternatively, there's a sort of *chambre d'hôte* at LE COMBAÏRE, in a quiet rural setting, 3km west on the D42 (☎65.44.33.26; *demi-pension* 152F), *gîtes d'étape* at LE VAYSSAIRE (☎65.48.44.69) and SOULANGES-BONNEVAL (☎65.44.42.18; meals available), 5km on the D541, and a **camping municipal** (☎65.44.39.72; mid–June to mid–Sept) on the St-Urcize road. Communications, however, are not good, and if you don't have a car, your only chance of getting in or out is the daily bus to Rodez.

Marvejols

MARVEJOLS lies at the southeast extremity of the Aubrac on the main N9 road (the autoroute has not yet arrived) and the Paris–Béziers train line. The country changes drastically as you approach. The bare, granite-strewn plateau opens into a wide deep basin, wooded with pines and punctuated by the erosion-formed table-topped pinnacles they call *trucs* hereabouts. It is a small, undeveloped and unpretentious country town, its ancient streets beautifully contained within its surviving medieval gates. There is little to do beyond savouring the atmosphere.

The **tourist office** is in the main gateway on the main road (Mon–Sat 10am–noon & 2–5.30pm; ☎66.32.02.14), and **accommodation** comes in the form of the *Hôtel Henri IV*, next to the tourist office (☎66.32.09.81; ②; restaurant from 65F), or the agreeable *Hôtel Les Rochers* (☎66.32.10.58; ①–③; good restaurant from 65F), opposite the **gare SNCF**, which is 800m uphill to the right off the N9 in the direction of Chirac (☎66.32.00.10). There's also a **camping municipal** beside a tributary stream on the other side of the River Colagne from the town.

WOLVES AND THE BÊTE DU GÉVAUDAN

In Marvejols, at the junction of the bridge across the Colagne and the N9, there stands a hideous, flattened-out bronze statue of a semi-wolf that represents the terrible legendary **Bête du Gévaudan**, supposedly the culprit of a series of horrific attacks in the eighteenth century. Between 1764 and 1767, the whole area between here and Le Puy was terrorized, and twenty-five women, sixty-eight children and six men were slain. The king sent his dragoons, then his best huntsman, who eventually found and killed an enormous wolf, but the mysterious deaths continued until one Jean Chastel shot another wolf near Saugues.

It has never been established if a wolf was really guilty of these deaths – a wolf that attacked women and children almost exclusively, that moved about so rapidly, that never touched a sheep. Was it perhaps a human psychopath?

If you would like reassurance about the temperament of real wolves, visit the **Parc Zoologique du Gévaudan** in the hamlet of Ste-Lucie just off the N9, 9km north of Marvejols, where about 80 wolves live in semiliberty (daily 10am–4.30pm; closed Jan; 32F), the first to do so in France since the beginning of the century.

Rodez and the upper valley of the Lot

A particularly beautiful and out-of-the-way stretch of country lies on the southwestern periphery of the Massif Central, bordered roughly by the valley of the **River Lot** in the north and the **Viaur** in the south. The upland areas are open and wide, with views east to the mountains of the Cévennes and south to the Monts de Lacaune and the Monts de l'Espinouse. **Rodez**, capital of the Rouergue, with a fine cathedral, is the only place of any size, accessible on the main train and bus routes. But the most dramatic places are in the river valleys, in particular the great abbey of **Conques** and the towns of **Entraygues** and **Espalion**.

Rodez

Until the 1960s, Rodez and the Rouergue were synonymous with back-country poverty and underdevelopment. Today it is an active and prosperous provincial town with a charming, renovated centre, even though the approach, through spreading commercial districts, is uninspiring.

Built on high ground above the River Aveyron, the **old town** is predictably dominated by the massive red-sandstone **Cathédrale Notre-Dame**, and the surrounding flattish uplands of the Causse du Comtal ensure that the building is visible for miles around. No matter from what direction you approach the town centre, you will find yourself in the **place d'Armes**, where the cathedral's plain, fortress-like west front and the early classical seventeenth-century bishop's palace sit side by side – both buildings were incorporated into the town's defences. The cathedral was begun in 1277 and was one of the first Gothic buildings in southern France, its plain façade only relieved by the elaborately flowery later addition of a rose window. Towering over the square is the cathedral's 88-metre **belfry**, decorated with pinnacles, balustrades and statuary almost as fantastical as Strasbourg cathedral's. The impressively spacious interior, architecturally as plain as the façade, is adorned with a magnificently extravagant seventeenth-century walnut organ loft and choir stalls by André Sulpice, who crafted it in 1468.

If you leave by the splendid south porch, you find yourself in the tiny place Rozier in front of the elegant fifteenth-century **Maison Cannoniale**, whose courtyard is guarded by jutting turrets. From the back of the cathedral to the north and the south, a network of well-restored medieval streets connects place de Gaulle, place de la

Préfecture and the attractive place du Bourg, with its fine sixteenth-century houses. In place Foch, just south of the cathedral, the Baroque chapel of the old **lycée** is worth a look for its amazing painted ceiling, while in place Raynaldy, the new **Hôtel de Ville** and the **mediathèque** are interesting examples of attempts to graft modern styles onto old buildings.

Practicalities

The **tourist office** is on place Foch, just off bd Gambetta and the place d'Armes, near the cathedral (Mon–Fri 9am–noon & 2–6pm, Sat 10am–12.30pm & 3–5pm; July & Aug 9am–1pm & 2–7pm, Sun 10am–noon; ☎65.68.02.27). To leave the town by bus or train, you'll need to head either for the **gare routière** on av V-Hugo (☎65.68.11.13), or the **gare SNCF** on bd Joffre (☎65.42.50.50), on the northern edge of town.

For reasonable if somewhat charmless hotel **accommodation**, try the *Hôtel Victor-Hugo* at 19 av V-Hugo (☎65.68.14.59; ①), or the better *Hôtel du Clocher* to the left off the east end of the cathedral at 4 rue Séguy (☎65.68.10.16; ①–③). Equally central but more upmarket is *La Tour Maje* in bd Gally behind the tourist office, a modern building tacked on to a medieval tower (☎65.68.34.68; ③–④). Budget accommodation is also on hand at the *Foyer Ste-Thérèse*, 21 rue Bonald (☎65.42.63.30; ①) – parallel to rue Séguy – and at the new IYHF **youth hostel** in Onet-le-Château, 3km to the north, at 26 bd des Capucines, Quatre-Saisons (☎65.42.35.45; ①; good canteen at 46F), which you can reach by taking bus #1 or #3 – direction *Quatre Saisons*, stop *Marche d'Oc/Les Rosiers/Capucine*. **Campers** can make their way to the *camping municipal* on the river bank in the quartier Layoule, about one kilometre from the centre.

As for **eating**, there are no great gastronomic treats in Rodez. *Le Bistroquet*, 17 rue du Bal, off place d'Olmet (closed Sun & Mon), does good salads and grills for around 70F, and the prettily situated brasserie *Le Kiosque* in the garden on av V-Hugo (closed Sun) does seafood and some good regional dishes for around 120F. Otherwise, try the espace Embergue at the end of rue Bonald, and the area behind the cathedral. For a **drink**, a good place to go is the *Café de la Paix* on place Jean-Jaurès, or the *Majesté* bar in the Tour Maje, if you want some gentle music to accompany it.

Sauveterre-de-Rouergue and the gorges of the Viaur

Forty kilometres southwest of Rodez and 6.5km northwest of Naucelle, **SAUVETERRE-DE-ROUERGUE** makes the most rewarding side trip in this part of the Rouergue. It is a perfect, otherworldly *bastide*, founded in 1281, with a wide central square, part cobbled, part gravelled, and surrounded by stone and half-timbered houses built over arcaded ground floors. Narrow streets lead off to the outer road, lined with stone-built houses the colour of rusty iron. On summer evenings, *pétanque*-players come out to roll their bowls beneath chestnut and plane trees, while swallows and swifts swoop and dive overhead.

There are several nice **hotels**, including the cheap and charming *Hôtel La Grappe d'Or* on the outer road (☎65.72.00.62; ①–②; Oct–April closed Thurs pm), whose restaurant offers an excellent menu at 70F, with dishes like *gésiers chauds*, *tripoux*, cheese, ice cream and *fouace* (a kind of sweet cake) as well as a half-carafe of wine. More expensive is the *Sénéchal* at the entrance to the village (☎65.71.29.00; ②–③; closed Feb, Sept–June closed Sun pm & Mon), also with an excellent restaurant (from 95F). There's also a **campsite** (☎65.47.05.32; June–Oct).

The country round about, known as the **Ségala**, is high (around 500m) and wide, cut by sudden and deep river valleys full of lush greenery. The most spectacular of them is the valley of the **River Viaur** to the south and west of Sauveterre, for which a car is essential. If you are heading west towards Najac (see p.596), there is a marvellous back-country route through **LA SALVETAT**, crossing the Viaur at **BELLECOMBE** and again at **MOULIN-DE-BAR**, where there is a riverside **campsite**, *Le Gomvassou*. The wartime Resistance was very active hereabouts and there are numerous memorials to the Resistance fighters who lost their lives in the aftermath of the D-day landings. There is a particularly interesting one beside the tiny church in **JOUQUEVIEL**, further downstream, dedicated to a unit of Polish volunteers and 161 escaped Soviet POWs.

Conques

CONQUES, 37km north of Rodez, is one of the great villages of southwest France. It occupies a spectacular position on the flanks of the steep wooded gorge of the little **River Dourdou**, a tributary of the Lot. The only public transport to the village is a daily service to Rodez, leaving there in the afternoon and returning the following morning; in July and August, there are also bus connections two or three times a week with Villefranche-de-Rouergue and Entraygues/Espalion, as well as Rodez, allowing you to visit Conques and return the same day.

It was the famous abbey which brought the village into existence. Its origins go back to a hermit called Dadon who settled here around 800 AD and founded a community of Benedictine monks, one of whom pilfered the relics of the martyred girl, Sainte Foy, from the monastery at Agen. Known for her ability to cure blindness and liberate captives, Sainte Foy's presence brought the pilgrims flocking to Conques in ever-increasing numbers, which earned the abbey a prime place on the pilgrim route to Compostella.

The abbey church

At the village's centre, dominating the landscape, stands the renowned Romanesque **church of Sainte-Foy**, whose giant pointed towers are echoed in those of the medieval houses that cluster tightly about it. Begun in the mid-eleventh century, its plain fortress-like façade rises on a small cobbled square beside the tourist office (see below) and pilgrims' fountain, the slightly shiny silvery-grey schist prettily offset by the greenery and flowers of the terraced gardens.

In startling contrast to this plainness, the elaborately sculpted Last Judgement in the tympanum above the door admonishes all who see it to espouse virtue and eschew vice. Christ sits in judgement in the centre. On his right hand are the chosen, among them Dadon the hermit and the emperor Charlemagne, while his left hand directs the damned to Hell, as usual so much more graphically and interestingly portrayed with all its gory tortures than the boring bliss of Paradise, depicted in the bottom left panel.

The inside of the church is designed to accommodate the pilgrims and channel them down the aisles and round the ambulatory, where they could gawp at Sainte Foy's relics displayed in the choir, segregated by a lovely wrought-iron screen. There is some fine carving on the capitals, especially in the triforium arches: too high up to see from the nave, so you need to climb to the organ loft, which gives you a superb perspective on the whole interior.

The other unrivalled asset of this church is the survival of its original medieval treasure of extraordinarily rich, bejewelled **reliquaries**, including that of Sainte Foy – bits of which are as old as the fifth century – and one known as the *A of Charlemagne*, thought to have been the first in a series given as presents by the emperor to monasteries he founded. This part of the treasure is kept by the now ruined **cloister**; the rest of it is in the same house as the tourist office (both same hours as tourist office; 25F). Even as far back as 1010, cleric Bernard d'Angers was moved to write: "The crowd of people prostrating themselves on the ground was so dense it was impossible to kneel down.... When they saw it for the first time (i.e. Sainte Foy), all in gold and sparkling with precious stones and looking like a human face, the majority of the peasants thought that the statue was really looking at them and answering their prayers with her eyes."

The village

The **village** of Conques is very small, largely depopulated and mainly contained within the medieval **walls**, parts of which still survive, along with three of its eleventh- and twelfth-century **gates**. The houses date mainly from the late Middle Ages, and the whole ensemble of cobbled lanes and stairways is a pleasure to stroll through. There are two main streets, the old **rue Haute**, or upper street, which was the route for the pilgrims coming from Estaing and Le Puy and passing on to Figeac and Cahors through the **Porte de la Vinzelle**; and the lane, now **rue Charlemagne**, which leads steeply downhill through the **Porte de Barry** to the river and the ancient **Pont Romain**, with the little **chapel of St-Roch** off to the left, from where you get a fine view of the village and church, if you don't opt for the even better views from the road on the far side of the valley. The new and rather grandiose **European centre for medieval art and civilization**, hidden in a bunker right at the top of the hill (June–Sept 10am–12.30pm & 2–6.30pm), has a constant programme of exhibitions and displays.

Walkers can use sections of the **GR65** and **GR62**, both of which pass through the village, and the tourist office will provide information about shorter local walks.

Practicalities

The **tourist office** is on the square beside the church (Mon–Sat 9am–noon & 2–6pm, Sun 9–11am & 2–6pm; July & Aug daily 9am–7pm; ☎65.72.85.00). There is hostel-type **accommodation** at the *Résidence Dadon* (☎65.72.82.98; ①) directly above the abbey, and a *gîte d'étape* next door (Mme Guibert; ☎65.72.82.98), as well as various hotel possibilities, both here and in the surrounding country. In the village, try the *Auberge St-Jacques* (☎65.72.86.36; ①–③), with restaurant menus from 81F and *plats du jour* at 50–60F, or, 7km up the Dourdou at **ST-CYPRIEN**, the *Auberge du Dourdou* (☎65.69.83.20; closed Oct–Feb; ②–③), whose restaurant menus feature good, simple country cooking from 75F. There are **campsites** in Conques (☎65.69.82.23; April–Sept), St-Cyprien (☎65.72.80.52) and Grand-Vabre (☎65.72.87.28; April–Oct), 5km downstream.

The upper valley of the Lot: Grand-Vabre to Entraygues and Espalion

The most beautiful stretch of the **Lot Valley** are the 21.5 kilometres between the bridge of Coursavy, below **Grand-Vabre**, and **Entraygues**: deep, narrow and wild, with the river running full and strong, as yet unaffected by the dams higher up, with scattered farms and houses high on the hillsides among long-abandoned terracing.

There is a *Logis de France* hotel, the *Hôtel du Pont* (☎71.49.94.21; ①–②; restaurant from 80F), in the old stone hamlet of **ST-PROJET** (2.5km), and two more 4km further east in **VIEILLEVIE**, where canoe rental is also available. Try the *Hôtel de la Terrasse* (☎71.49.92.23, ①–③; restaurant from 70F), or the simpler *Relais des Pêcheurs* (☎71.49.98.82; ①–②; restaurant from 65F). A further possibility is the very agreeable *Auberge du Fel*, some 10km further on, high on the north slopes of the valley in the hamlet of **LE FEL**, which by an unexpected accident of climate produces a little local wine (☎65.44.52.30; ①–③; closed Dec–March; excellent restaurant with menus from 65F). There is also a beautifully sited **camping municipal** high on the hillside (☎65.44.51.86; June–Sept).

Entraygues and around

ENTRAYGUES, with narrow riverside streets and attractive grey houses, has the feel of a sleepy mountain town. It lies right in the angle of the junction of the Lot with the equally beautiful River Truyère. The brown towers of a thirteenth-century **château** overlook the meeting of the waters. A magnificent four-arched **bridge** of the same date crosses the Truyère a little way upstream.

The **tourist office** is on the main street (Mon 2–6pm, Tues–Fri 9.30am–12.30pm & 1.30–5.30pm, Sat 9.30am–12.30pm; July & Aug Mon–Sat 9.30am–7pm, Sun 9.30am–12.30pm; June & Sept Mon 9.30am–12.30pm, Tues–Sat 9.30am–12.30pm & 2–6pm; ☎65.44.56.10) and will provide information about walking, mountain-biking and canoeing in the area. The *Hôtel de la Truyère*, on the river bank at the end of the bridge, makes a splendid place to stay (☎65.44.51.10; ②–③; closed Mon & mid-Nov to mid-March; restaurant from 70F). Alternatively, try the *Hôtel du Centre* (☎65.44.51.19; ①–③; closed one week at Christmas; restaurant from 75F). There are also two **campsites**: *Le Val-de-Saures* (☎65.44.56.92; May–Oct) and *Le Roquepailhol* (☎65.44.57.79), and two **gîtes d'étape** – Mme Galan (☎65.44.50.73) and *Le Battedou* (☎65.48.61.62) – on the GR65 at **GOLINHAC**, about 7km south of Entraygues on the other side of the Lot. There is one bus per weekday to Aurillac in the north and Rodez to the south.

There are further accommodation options at **ESTAING**, another beautiful village grouped round a rocky bluff and castle in a bend of the Lot about 10km beyond Golinhac. The *Hôtel aux Armes d'Estaing*, named for the family who occupied the castle for five hundred years, offers attractive rooms and very good food in the centre of the village (☎65.44.70.02; ①–③; closed Jan; restaurant from 60F). There is also a **camping municipal** (☎65.44.72.77) and **gîte d'étape** on the GR65 (☎65.44.71.74). A date to watch out for, however, is the first Sunday in July when the place fills up with people, many in medieval dress, who come to honour the relics of Saint Fleuret, bishop of Clermont, who died here in 621 and was buried in the fifteenth-century church by the castle.

Espalion

The substantial little town of **ESPALION** lies in a mild, fertile opening in the valley of the Lot, 10km from Estaing and 32km northeast of Rodez, and was the first taste of the south to the muleteers, pilgrims and other travellers coming down from the rude heights of the Massif Central and places north. Home town of the composer Francis Poulenc, as well as Benoit Rouqayrol and Louis Denayrouze, inventors of diving suits, Espalion is best known in France for its exiles, in particular its countless sons and daughters who set up in the café business in Paris from the 1850s onwards.

The only interesting part of town is the **riverside quarter**, with its galleried and balconied old houses, once used as tanneries, hanging over the water. The finest view of the area is from the Pont Neuf, for just upstream there is a lovely red sandstone packhorse **bridge** with a domed and turreted **château** dating from 1572 right behind it (not open to the public).

Surprisingly, there are two interesting little museums dedicated principally to the life of the region: **Musée Joseph Vaylet** on bd Poulenc, the main road (July–Sept 10am–noon & 3–7pm; 15F), which contains mainly furniture and domestic objects plus an exhibition of diving gear (thanks to the two Espalionnais mentioned above); and the **Musée du Rouergue** on place Frontin (July & Aug daily except Sat 10am–12.30pm & 2–7pm, Sat 2–7pm; May, June & Sept 2–6pm; 15F), formerly the town jail, with displays of local customs, the story of the exiled café-owners, regional music, cooking and the traditions of the pilgrim routes.

Don't miss the glorious little **church of St-Hilarion**, built in the eleventh and twelfth centuries on the spot, so the story goes, where the Saracens lopped off the head of Saint Hilarion during the reign of Charlemagne. It sits on the edge of the cemetery, about fifteen minutes' walk to the left of the bridge on the château side of the river, past the campsite. Very small and built in the red sandstone, with a wall belfry and wide porch with sculpted tympanum and dozens of figures adorning the corbel ends of the apse and a beautiful Virgin and Child above the south transept door, it's a delight.

Also well worth a visit is the **Château de Calmont d'Olt** (May–Oct 9am–7pm; July & Aug daily, otherwise closed Thurs & Fri; 20F) for its unbeatable views of the town and the country beyond. It's a rough and atmospheric old fortress dating from the eleventh century, on the very peak of an abrupt bluff, 535m high and directly above the town on the south bank. There are reconstructions of medieval siege works and a catapult in the grounds.

For **accommodation**, there's no better place to stay than the *Hôtel Moderne* on the crossroads in the middle of town at 27 bd Guizard (☎65.44.05.11; ③–④; closed Nov). Its rooms are comfortable, but more importantly, its restaurant is first-rate, especially for its river fish (from 100F). A cheaper but friendly and welcoming alternative, the *Hôtel Central,* is on av de la Gare (☎65.44.05.25; ①–②; closed Dec–March), to the left on the other side of the river, near rue Droite, the pedestrian shopping street, which crosses the old bridge.

For uncomplicated **eating**, there are several brasseries on the main through street. But for something special, Espalion has a second first-rate restaurant in the *Méjane* by the old bridge (closed Sun evening & Wed, and Feb 25–March 17), specializing in regional cuisine with a post-nouvelle influence: from l00F with a lunchtime menu at 80F. There is a riverside **campsite** behind the château, but it's unnecessarily fancy and expensive and gets very crowded in season: better, if you have the time and the means, to go to the prettier, simpler and cheaper riverside *Belle Rive* in the attractive village of **ST-CÔME**, another 4km upstream, where there is also a **gîte d'étape** in a beautiful old house (☎65.44.07.24; closed Nov–March) lying on the GR65, GR6 and GR620.

Millau and the Gorges du Tarn

MILLAU, subprefecture of the Aveyron *département* and second town after Rodez in the old province of Rouergue, occupies a beautiful site in a bend of the River Tarn at its junction with the Dourbie. It is enclosed on all sides by impressive white cliffs formed where the rivers have worn away the edges of the *causses*, especially on the north side, where the spectacular table-top hill of the **Puech d'Andan** stands sentinel over the town. From medieval until modern times, thanks to its proximity to the sheep pastures of the *causses*, it was a major manufacturer of leather goods, especially gloves. Although outclassed by cheaper producers in the mass market and suffering serious unemployment as a result, Millau still leads in top-of-the-range goods.

Arrival and accommodation

The **tourist office** (Mon–Fri 9am–noon & 2–6pm, Sat 9am–noon; July & Aug daily 9am–12.30pm & 2–7pm; April–June & Sept Mon–Sat 9am–noon & 2–6pm; ☎65.60.02.42) is a short distance away on the corner of av Alfred-Merles, at the end of which you'll find both bus and train stations. **Bikes and outdoor equipment** can be rented from *Roc et Canyon*, 55 av Jean-Jaurès.

For an overnight **stay**, there's the *Hôtel Le Commerce*, 8 pl du Mandarous (☎65.60.00.56; ①–②; closed one week at Christmas); it's best to take a room at the back to avoid any noise from the square, but all are clean and proper. A bit more expensive is *Les Causses* in an attractive building at 56 av Jean-Jaurès, the N9 (☎65.60.03.19; ②–④), with a reasonable restaurant (from 55F). For a totally different ball game, try the *Millau Hôtel Club*; it's the two glass bubbles by a swimming pool just across the river by the Pont du Larzac (☎65.59.71.33; ③; restaurant around 120F). The official **youth hostel** is about 1km down av Jean-Jaurès at 26 rue Lucien-Costes (☎65.60.15.95; ①; canteen meals for around 35F). There are also several **campsites**: the municipal *Millau-Plage* is on the left bank of the Tarn, north of the confluence with the Dourbie – take the bridge at the end of av Gambetta (☎65.60.10.97; April–Sept).

The Town

There are no remarkable sights in Millau; it is simply a very pleasant, smallish provincial town whose clean and well-preserved old streets have a summery, southern charm. It owes its original prosperity to its position on the ford where the Roman road from Languedoc to the north crossed the Tarn, marked today by the truncated remains of a medieval **bridge** surmounted by a watermill jutting out into the river beside the modern bridge.

Whether you arrive from north or south, you will find yourself sooner or later in **place du Mandarous**, the main square, where av de la Republique, the road to Rodez, begins. South of here, the **old town** is built a little way back from the river to avoid the floods and contained within an almost circular ring of shady boulevards. The rue Droite cuts through the centre, linking the three squares: place Emma-Calve, place des Halles and place Foch. The prettiest by far is **place Foch**, with its cafés, shaded by two big plane trees and bordered by houses supported on stone pillars; some are as old as the twelfth century. In one corner, the **church of Notre-Dame** is worth a look, for its octagonal Toulouse-style belfry, originally Romanesque. In the other, there's the very interesting **Musée archéologique et la Maison de la Peau and du Gant** (Mon–Sat 10am–noon & 2–6pm; April–Sept daily; 22F), whose collections revolve around the bizarre combination of archeology and gloves but include France's one and only complete 180-million-year-old plesiosaurus and the magnificent red pottery of the Graufesenque works (see below). The other two squares have been the subject of some rather questionable attempts at reconciling old stones and Richard Rogers-inspired contemporary urban design, but the **clock tower** off place Emma-Calve (July & Aug 10–11.30am & 3.30–6.30pm; June & Sept 10–11.30am & 3–5.30pm; 15F) is worth a climb for the great all-round view. Take a look also in the streets off the square – rue du Voultre, rue de la Peyrollerie and their tributaries – for a sense of the old working class and bourgeois districts.

Clear evidence of the town's importance in Roman times is to be seen in the **Graufesenque pottery works**, just upstream on the south bank (daily 9am–noon & 2–6.30pm; 20F), whose renowned sigillated ware was distributed throughout the Roman world. It was a huge production line in its day, involving four hundred potters and a hundred kilns; today, there is an archeology museum with a permanent exhibition of the bowls, vases and cups that were produced.

Eating and drinking

If you are just looking for a quick **meal**, the best place to go is place du Mandarous, where there are numerous brasseries and cafés. For light meals and music – in summer – you could try the *Locomotive* at 33 av Gambetta (till 1am; around 40F). For more substantial traditional restaurant fare, it's best to head for bd de la Capelle on the east side of the old town next to place Foch, where three agreeable establishments spread their tables under the trees: *La Mangeoire* at no. 8 (☎65.60.13.16; from 85F), with some good grilled fish, meat and game dishes; *La Marmite*, next door (☎65.61.20.44), which features menus from 90F, including the local potato and cheese dish, *aligot*; and *Le Cyrano* at no. 2 (☎65.60.28.25; from 58F).

Roquefort-sur-Soulzon

Twenty-one kilometres south of Millau, the little village of **ROQUEFORT-SUR-SOULZON** has nothing to say for itself except cheese, and almost every building is devoted to the cheese-making process.

What gives the cheese its special flavour is the fungus, *penicillium roqueforti*, that grows exclusively in the fissures in the rocks created by the collapse of the sides of the valley on which Roquefort now stands. Legend has it that once upon a time a local shepherd one day forgot his lunch of bread and cheese, and found it some months later, covered with mould. He bit tentatively and discovered to his surprise than instead of ruining the cheese, the mould had much improved its taste.

While the sheep's milk used in the making of the cheese comes from different flocks and dairies as far afield as the Pyrenees, the crucial fungus is grown here, on bread. Just two grammes of powdered fungus are enough for 4000 litres of milk, which in turn makes 330 Roquefort cheeses; they are matured in Roquefort's many-layered cellars, first unwrapped for three weeks and then wrapped up again. It takes three to six months for the full flavour to develop.

Two of the cheese manufacturers have organized **visits**: *Société* (daily 9.30am–4pm/ 6pm in summer; 17F) and *Papillon* (daily 9–11.30am & 2–5pm; June–Sept 9.30am– 12.30pm & 1.30–6.30pm; 17F) and each visit consists of a short film, followed by a tour of the cellars – not, in fact, very interesting.

The Gorges du Tarn

Jam-packed with tourists in July and August but absolutely spectacular nonetheless, the **Gorges du Tarn** cut through the limestone plateaux of the Causse de Sauveterre and the Causse Méjean in a precipitous trench 400–500m deep and 1000–1500m wide. Its sides, cloaked with woods of feathery pine and spiked with pinnacles of eroded rock, are often sheer and always very steep, creating within them a microclimate in sharp distinction to the inhospitable plateaux above. The permanent population is tiny, although there is plenty of evidence of more populous times in abandoned houses and once cultivated terraces. Because of the press of people and the subsequent overpricing of **accommodation**, the best bet, if you want to stay along the gorge, is to head up on to the Causse Méjean, where there are several small family-run hotels and *chambres d'hôte*.

The most attractive section of the gorge runs for 53km from pretty **LE ROZIER**, 21km northeast of Millau, to **ISPAGNAC**. If you want to **stay** in Le Rozier, try the *Hôtel Arnal* (☎65.62.62.91; ①; closed Sept–April) or *Hôtel Doussière* (☎65.62.60.25; ②–③; closed Nov 12–March), or for budgeters, there's a **camping municipal** (☎65.62.64.98; closed Oct–March). **ST-CHÉLY-DU-TARN** has the very prettily sited *Auberge de la Cascade* (☎66.48.52.82; ②; restaurant from 60F; closed mid-Oct to mid-March).

A narrow and very twisty road follows the right bank of the river from Le Rozier, but it's not a very good way to see the scenery. For the car-borne, the best views are from the road to St-Rome-de-Dolan above Les Vignes, and from the roads out of La Malène and the attractive **STE-ÉNIMIE**, where you'll find a well-informed **tourist office** (Mon–Sat 9am–noon & 2–7pm; July & Aug daily; ☎66.45.53.44). La Malène has a *camping municipal* (☎66.48.51.16; Easter to mid-Oct) and the nearby *La Blanquière* site (☎66.48.54.93; May to mid-Sept), which is beautifully sited on the road to La Vigne.

But it's best to walk if possible, or follow the river's course by boat or canoe, and there are literally dozens of places to rent canoes. For walkers, the **GR6a**, a variant of the GR6 which crosses the *causses*, climbs steeply out of Le Rozier between the junction of the Tarn with the equally spectacular gorges of the River Jonte on to the Causse Méjéan, then follows the rim of the Tarn gorge for a while before descending to rejoin the GR6 at Les Vignes (4–5hr).

Also eminently worth seeing are two beautiful **caves** about 25km up the Jonte from Le Rozier: the **Aven Armand** (March–Oct daily 9am–12.15pm & 1.15–5.30pm; 40F; ☎66.45.61.31) on the edge of the Causse Méjean, and the **Grotte de Dargilan** (April– Oct daily 9am–noon & 1.30–6pm; 35F; ☎66.45.60.20) on the south side of the river on the edge of the Causse Noir. **HYELZAS**, near the Armand-Aven cave, has a *gîte d'étape* (M. Pratlong ☎66.45.65.25), and **LE VIALE** a *chambre d'hôte* (Mme Vernet; ☎66.48.82.39: 220F or 240F for two, including breakfast; closed Nov–April).

THE CÉVENNES AND ARDÈCHE

The **Cévennes** are mountains and the **Ardèche** a river that has given its name to a *département*. Mountains and *département* overlap, but together they form the southeastern defences of the Massif Central, overlooking the Rhône Valley to the east and the Mediterranean littoral to the south. The bare upland landscapes of the inner or western edges are those of the central Massif. The outer edges, Mont Aigoual and its radiating valleys and the tributary valleys of the Ardèche, are distinctly Mediterranean: deep, dry, close and clothed in forests of sweet chestnut, oak and pine.

Remote and inaccessible country until well into the twentieth century, it has bred rugged and independent inhabitants. For centuries it was the most resolute stronghold of Protestantism in France, and it was in these valleys that the persecuted Protestants put up their fiercest resistance to the tyranny of Louis XIV and Louis XV. In World War II, it was heavily committed to Resistance. In the aftermath of 1968, it became the promised land of the hippies – *zippies*, as the locals called them, not quite getting the point; they moved into the countless abandoned farms and hamlets, whose native inhabitants had been driven away by hardship and poverty. The odd hippie has stuck it out, true to the last to the alternative life. In more recent times, it has been colonized by Dutch and Germans.

The author Robert Louis Stevenson crossed it in 1878 with Modestine, a donkey he bought in miserable Le Monastier-sur-Gazeille near the astounding town of **Le Puy** and sold at journey's end in the former Protestant stronghold of **St-Jean-du-Gard**, a now-famous route described in *Travels with a Donkey* (see p.1000).

The Parc National des Cévennes

The **Parc National des Cévennes** was created in 1970 to protect and preserve the life, landscape, flora, fauna and architectural heritage of the most typical parts of the Cévennes. North to south, it stretches from **Mende** on the Lot to **Le Vigan** and includes both **Mont Lozère** and **Mont Aigoual**, which exemplify both types of upland landscape. Access, to the periphery at least, is surprisingly easy thanks to the Paris–Clermont–Alès–Nîmes train line and the Montpellier–Mende link.

The quickest way of getting around the park is by car, with the usual disadvantages, and a bike would be very tough going because of the relentlessly hilly terrain. **Walking**, as so often, is best for real contact with the land and its flavours. There are numerous GRs: the **7**, **6**, and **60** cross all or part of the range, and other paths complete various circuits. The **GR66** does the tour of Mont Aigoual in 78.5km, the **GR68** of Mont Lozère in 110km. Another good route is the 130-kilometre **Tour des Cévennes** on the GR67.

If you do go off hiking, remember that these are proper mountains for all their southerly latitude. You need good hiking boots, warm and weatherproof clothing, emergency shelter, adequate food, maps and guidebooks. The current weather situation is obtainable on: ☎36.68.02.07 – Ardèche; ☎36.68.02.30 – Gard; ☎36.68.02.48 – Lozère.

The **main information office** for the park is at Florac (see p.735). It publishes numerous leaflets on the flora, fauna and traditions of the park, plus activities and routes for walkers, cyclists, caneoists and horse riders, plus a list of the **gîtes d'étape**.

In July and August, it is wise to book ahead for accommodation; otherwise you could find yourself sleeping out.

Mende and the Mont Lozère

Capital of the Lozère *département*, **MENDE** lies well down in the deep valley of the Lot at the northern tip of the Parc des Cévennes, 28km east of Marvejols and 40km north of Florac, with train and bus links to the Paris-Nîmes and Clermont–Millau lines. It's a very attractive, unspoilt southern town, well worth a visit and a nice place to make an overnight stay.

In front of the **cathedral** stands a statue of Pope Urban IV, who was born locally and used his office to the benefit of his natal soil. It was he who launched the construction of the cathedral in 1369, although it took several centuries to complete; its two unequal towers standing against the haze of the mountain background are the town's landmarks. There's a fine view back along the pine-clad Lot Valley from the porch, and inside is a handsome choir and eight great Aubusson tapestries suspended from the clerestory.

But most pleasure resides in a quiet wander in the narrow medieval streets and minuscule squares behind the cathedral. In **rue Notre-Dame**, which separated the Christian from Jewish quarters in medieval times, the thirteenth-century house at no. 17 was once a synagogue. Nearby, in rue de l'Épine, is the municipal **Musée Ignon-Fabre** (Mon–Sat 10am–noon & 2–5pm; 15F), worth half an hour for the Bronze Age finds from the Causse Méjean. And while you're at it, carry on down to the river to see the medieval packhorse bridge, the **Pont Notre-Dame**, with its worn cobbles arching over the water.

The **tourist office** is at 14 bd Henri-Bourillon, to the right as you reach the centre of town from the N88 (Mon–Fri 8.30am–12.30pm & 2–6pm, Sat 9am–noon; July & Aug Mon–Fri 8.30am–12.30pm & 2–8pm, Sat 9am–noon; ☎66.65.02.69). The departmental tourist office is in the same building, with all the information you could want on the Lozère. The **gare SNCF** (☎60.48.00.39) is across the river north of the centre; the **gare routière** is in place du Foirail off the end of bd H-Bourillon.

For a place to **stay,** there's the *Hôtel du Palais*, right in front of the cathedral on place Urbain V (☎66.49.01.59; ①–③). Just the other side of the square, in rue d'Aigues-Passes, the plastic-looking *Hôtel du Gevaudan* (☎66.65.14.74; ①; restaurant from 58F) is nicer than it looks. For more comfort, try the much prettier *Hôtel de France* on bd Lucien-Arnault, the northern part of the inner ring road (☎66.65.00.04; ②–④; closed mid-Dec to Jan; restaurant from 85F).

Mont Lozère

Mont Lozère is a long, high, windswept desolate barrier of granite and yellow grass-land, rising to 1699m at the summit at **Finiels**, still grazed by herds of cows. Snowbound in winter and wild and dangerous in bad weather, it has claimed many a victim among lost travellers. In some of the squat granite hamlets on the northern slopes, like Servies, Auriac and Les Sagnes, you can still hear the bells known as *clochers de tourmente* that tolled in the wind to give travellers some sense of direction when the cloud was low.

If you're travelling by car from Mende, the way to the summit is via the village of **LE BLEYMARD**, about 30km to the east on the bank of the infant River Lot, with its *Hôtel La Remise* (☎66.48.65.80; ②; restaurant from 70F; closed Dec–Jan). From here, the D20 winds 7km up through the conifers to **LE CHALET**, with its **gîte d'étape** (☎68.48.62.84; food available), where it is joined by the GR7, which has taken a more direct route from Le Bleymard. This is the route that Stevenson took, waymarked as the *Tracé Historique de Stevenson*. Road and footpaths run together as far as the **Col de Finiels,** where the GR7 strikes off on its own to the southeast. The source of the River Tarn is about 3km east of the col, the summit of Lozère, 2km to the west. From the col, the road and Stevenson's route drop down in tandem, through the lonely hamlet of **FINIELS** to the pretty but touristy village of **LE PONT-DE-MONTVERT**.

At Le Pont, a seventeenth-century **bridge** crosses the Tarn by a stone **tower** that once served as a tollhouse. In this building in 1702, the Abbé du Chayla, a priest appointed by the crown to reconvert the rebellious Protestants enraged by the revocation of the Edict of Nantes, set up a torture chamber to coerce the recalcitrant. Incensed by his brutality, a group of them under the leadership of one Esprit Séguier attacked and killed him on July 23. Reprisals were extreme; nearly 12,000 were executed, so precipitating the Camisards' – most of them shepherds and peasant farmers – guerrilla war against the state.

At the edge of the village, there is also an *écomusée* on the life and character of the region, the **Maison du Mont Lozère** (June–Sept daily 10.30am–12.30pm & 2.30–6.30pm; rest of year Thurs, Sat, Sun & school hols only; 25F). If you are tempted to **stay**, there's the small *Hôtel des Cévennes* (☎66.45.80.01; ①–③; closed Nov–March; restaurant from 73F), overlooking the bridge. There's also a **gîte d'étape** in the Maison du Mont Lozère (☎66.45.80.10; not available June & Aug).

Florac and Mont Aigoual

FLORAC, 39km south of Mende, lies in the bottom of the trench-like valley of the Tarnon just short of its junction with the Tarn. Behind it rises the steep wall that marks the edge of the Causse Méjean. When you get here, you have already passed the frontier between the northern and Mediterranean landscapes; the dividing line seems to be the **Col de Montmirat** at the western end of Mont Lozère. Once you begin the descent, the scrub and steep gullies and the tiny abandoned hamlets, with their eyeless houses oriented towards the sun, speak clearly of the south.

The village, with some 2000 inhabitants, is strung out along the left bank of the Tarnon, the main road forming the main street, **avenue Jean-Monestier,** with the **tourist office** about halfway along (Mon–Fri 9am–12.30pm & 2–5pm; July & Aug daily 9am–12.30pm & 2–7.30pm; Sept Mon–Sat 9am–12.30pm & 2–7.30pm; ☎66.45.01.14). There is little specific to see, although the close lanes of the village up towards the valley side have their charms, especially the plane-shaded **place du Souvenir**. A redschist castle is up near here, housing the **Centre d'Information du Parc National des Cévennes** (daily 9am–noon & 1–4.30pm; June to mid-Sept 9am–7pm; ☎66.49.53.00). **Mountain bike rental** is available from *VTT Evasion* (☎66.45.09.56) on the Esplanade, or *Cévennes Evasion* in place Boyer (☎66.45.18.31).

The **accommodation** on offer is not fantastic. The nicest and cheapest place is *Chez Bruno* on the tree-lined **Esplanade/place du Souvenir** (☎66.45.11.19; ①; restaurant from 65F). More expensive, there's the *Hôtel du Parc* on av Jean-Monastier (☎66.45.03.05; ①–③; restaurant from 85F; closed Dec to mid-March). The *Hôtel Central et de la Poste* has a lovely terrace over the stream, but the rooms are a bit grim (☎66.45.00.01; ①–③; restaurant from 70F; closed mid-Jan to Feb). Better perhaps to try the *Lozérette* in **COCURES**, 5km back towards Mont Lozère, on the Pont-de-Montvert road (☎66.45.06.04; ③; restaurant from 78F; closed Nov–March).

Three **gîtes d'etape** include M. Martinez, 18 rue du Pêcher (☎66.45.24.54; closed Nov–March); Mme Rives, rue de l'Église (☎66.45.14.93; closed Jan–March), and M. Serrano in Pont-du-tarn, 1km north (☎66.45.20.89). The best-value **campsites** are the municipal one at Pont-du-tarn out on the road towards Ispagnac (☎66.45.18.26; April–Oct), and two more on the other side of town on the Corniche de Cévennes road, beside the River Tarno.

Mont Aigoual

By road it's 24km up the beautiful valley of the Tarnon to the **Col de Perjuret,** where a right turn will take you on to the **Causse Méjean** to the weird rock formations of **Nîmes-le-Vieux**, and a left turn takes you along a rising ridge a further 15km to the 1565-metre summit of **Mont Aigoual** (GR6, GR7, GR66), from where, they say, you can see a third of France, from the Alps to the Pyrenees, with the Mediterranean coast from Marseille to Sète at your feet. It is not a craggy summit, although the ground drops away pretty steeply into the valley of the River Hérault on the south side, but the view and the sense of exposure to the elements is dramatic enough. There is a **CAF refuge** and **gîte d'etape** in the observatory (☎67.82.62.78; May–Sept), with another *gîte* on the approach road at Cabrillac (☎66.45.62.21; April–Oct).

The descent to Le Vigan (see opposite) by the valley of the Hérault is superb; a magnificent twisty road follows the deepening ravine through dense beech woods, to come out at the bottom in rather Italianate scenery, with tall, close-built villages and vineyards beside the stream. If you're benighted, there's the *Hôtel du Touring et de l'Observatoire* (☎67.82.60.04; ②; restaurant from 68F) at **L'ESPÉROU**, a rather soulless mountain resort just below the summit. Better to go down to **VALLERAUGUE** and stay at *Le Petit Luxembourg* (☎67.82.20.44; ③; good restaurant from 75F).

The Causse du Larzac

In the 1970s, the **Causse du Larzac** was continually in the headlines over sustained political resistance to the high-profile presence of the French military. Originally there was a small military camp outside the village of **LA CAVALERIE** on the N9, long tolerated for the cash its soldiers brought in. But in the early 1970s, the army decided to expand the place and use it as a permanent strategic base, expropriating a hundred or so farms. The result was explosive. A federation was formed – *Paysans du Larzac* – which attracted the support of numerous ecological, left-wing and regionalist groups in a protracted campaign of resistance under the slogan "Gardarem lo Larzac". Successful acts of sabotage were committed, and three huge peace festivals were held here, in 1973, 1974 and again in 1977. The army's plans were scotched by Mitterrand when he came to power in 1981, but you still find Larzac graffiti from here to Lyon, shorthand for opposition to the army, the state and the Parisian central government, and in favour of self-determination and independence for the south.

The best way to immerse yourself in the empty, sometimes eerie atmosphere of Larzac is to walk: **GRs 7**, **71** and **74** cross the plateau, though you shouldn't attempt them without a *Topoguide*. Further information is available from the *Fédération interdépartementale des sentiers de pays*, BP600, Millau (☎65.61.06.57). If you have no time for anything else, the area between La Couvertoirade, Le Caylar and Ganges in the foothills of the Cévennes will give you a real sense of life on the *causse*.

LA COUVERTOIRADE lies 5km off the main road, a perfect Templar village, still completely enclosed by its towers and walls and almost untouched by renovation. Its forty remaining inhabitants live by tourism, and you have to pay to enter the place (daily 10am–noon & 2–5pm; July & Aug daily 9.30am–6pm; 25F). Just outside the walls on the south side is a *lavogne*, a paved water hole of a kind seen all over the *causse* for watering the flocks, whose milk is used for the making of Roquefort cheese (see p.731). If you want to stay, there's the GR71 **gîte d'étape** in the far corner from the entrance. Half a dozen kilometres south, the village of **LE CAYLAR** clusters in similar fashion at the foot of a rocky outcrop, the top of which has been fashioned into a fortress – worth clambering up for the aerial view of the surrounding *causse*: mean little patches of cultivated ground stolen from among the merciless upthrusts of rock.

If you've got your own transport and a good map, the backroad from here, via St-Michel to St-Maurice-Navacelles, is strongly recommended. Wild box grows along the lanes, often meticulously clipped into hedges. Here and there among the scrubby oak and thorn or driving home along the road at milking time, you pass flocks of sheep. Occasional farmhouses materialize, like *Les Besses* – one of the few still in use – huge, self-contained and fortress-like, with the living quarters upstairs and the sheep stalls down below. **ST-MAURICE** itself, on the GR7 and GR74, is small and sleepy, with a shop and the *Hôtel des Tilleuls* (③) opposite a moving World War I memorial by Paul Dardé. There is no official campsite, but if you ask you are directed to a grassy place by the cemetery, where a traditional *glacière* – a stone-lined pit for storing snow for use as ice before the days of refrigerators – has been restored. Its chief advantage is as a base for visiting the **Cirque de Navacelles**, 10km north on the D130 past the beautiful ruined seventeenth-century sheep farm of *La Prunarède*. The *cirque* is a widening in the 150-metre deep trench of the Vis gorges, formed by a now dry loop in the river that has left a neat pyramid of rock sticking up in the middle like a wheel hub. An ancient and scarcely inhabited hamlet survives in the bottom – a bizarre phenomenon in an extraordinary location, and you get literally a bird's-eye view of it from the edge of the cliff above. Both road and GR7 go through. Continuing to Le Vigan or Ganges via Montdardier, you pass a prehistoric **stone circle** on the left of the road, a silent and evocative place, especially in a close, wet, *causse* mist. There are other stones and dolmens in the vicinity.

Le Vigan and the Huguenot strongholds

Only 64km from Montpellier and 18km from Ganges, **LE VIGAN** makes a good starting point for exploring the southern part of the Cévennes. It's a leafy, cool and thoroughly agreeable place, at its liveliest during the **Fête d'Isis** at the beginning of August and the colossal fair that takes over the Parc des Châtaigniers from September 9 to 22.

The prettiest part of the town is around the central place du Quai by the **Protestant church**, or Temple, where there is a concentration of cafés and brasseries. The **tourist office** is nearby in place du Marché (Mon–Fri 8.30am–12.30pm & 1.30–6.30pm, Sat 9am–12.30pm & 1.30–7pm; July & Aug 8.30am–12.30pm & 1.30–7pm, Sun 10am–noon; ☎67.80.01.72), which also has a money exchange facility. For somewhere to **stay**, try the simple but very nice *Hôtel du Commerce*, 26 rue des Barris (☎67.81.03.28; ①–②). The best alternative is a couple of kilometres out of town, south towards Montdardier on the D48: the handsome old *Auberge Cocagne* in **AVÈZE** (☎67.81.02.70; ①–③; restaurant from 55F; closed Dec 21–Feb). There are **campsites** in Avèze (☎67.81.04.02; July & Aug), or a little way upriver from Le Vigan on the opposite bank is the well-shaded riverside *Val de l'Arre* (☎67.81.02.77; April–Sept). There's a **gîte d'étape** at 1 rue de la Carrierrasse (☎67.81.01.71). On place du Marché by the tourist office, the *Brasserie d'Assas* is as good a place to **eat** as any.

From Le Vigan, or more particularly from the Pont de l'Hérault bridge, a beautiful lane (D153) winds northeast through typical south Cévennes landscape – deep valleys thick with sweet chestnut and thinly peopled with isolated farms half-buried in greenery – from Sumène to St-Jean-du-Gard, a distance of around 45km but very slow. **SUMÈNE** is a run-down but lovely old place, the entrance to its close, narrow streets still blocked by its medieval **gates**. It was once a centre for silk spinning, which for a couple of centuries until the 1900s was the mainstay of economic life in the Cévennes – that and the cultivation of the sweet chestnut, which provided the staple diet for the entire population.

At **COLOGNAC**, where there are a few fields, there is a **gîte d'étape** (M. Chartreux; ☎66.85.28.84) and another in the valley bottom outside the big village of **LASALLE** (Mme Cros, Parc des Glycines: ☎66.85.21.31), where there is also the *Hôtel des Camisards* in the main street (☎66.85.20.50; ②–③: restaurant from 65F; closed mid-Nov–April).

St-Jean-du-Gard and around

Thirty-two kilometres west of Alès, **ST-JEAN-DU-GARD** was the centre of Protestant resistance during the Camisard war during 1702–4 (see below). It straggles along the bank of the River Gardon, crossed by a magnificent eighteenth-century bridge, with a number of picturesque old houses still surviving in the main street, **Grand-Rue**. One of them contains a splendid **Musée des Vallées Cévénoles**, a museum of local life, with displays of tools, trades, furniture, clothes, domestic articles and a fascinating collection of pieces to do with the silk industry (Sun 2–6pm; July & Aug daily 10.30am–7pm; May, June & Sept Tues–Sat 10.30am–12.30pm & 2–7pm, Sun 2–7pm; Oct–April Sun 2–6pm only; school hols Tues–Fri & Sun 2–6pm; 16F). Ancient cars and horsedrawn vehicles are on display at the museum, **Le Voyage dans le Temps** (Sun & hols 9am–7pm; July & Aug daily 9am–7pm; 27F). And the last of the Cévennes spinning mills, the **Maison Rouge** in rue de l'Industrie, is visitable (same times & price); it ceased work in 1964.

The **tourist office** is just off the main street by the post office (daily 9–11.30am & 1.30–5pm; July & Aug 9am–6pm; ☎66.85.32.11). They can advise you about the times of the steam train that operates between St-Jean and Anduze in summertime (52F return). There is a big **market** all along Grand-Rue on Tuesday mornings.

The finest place to **stay** is the *Hôtel Orange* in Grand-Rue (☎66.85.30.34; ③; good restaurant from 65F; closed Jan–March). Good and cheap, there's also the *Central*, 11 rue Pelet-de-la-Lozère (☎66.85.30.20; ①; restaurant from 80F). **LE MOULINET** has a **gîte d'étape** (M. Launay; ☎66.85.10.98) and a **camping municipal** by the river at Mas de la Cam, 3km north along the D907 (☎66.85.12.02; April–Sept).

The Musée du Désert

The minuscule hamlet of **MAS SOUBEYRAN** is a picture of beautiful rough stone houses in a gully above the village of Mialet, about 12km east of St-Jean. But it is here that one of the region's most poignant museums lies: the **Musée du Désert** (March–Nov daily 9.30am–noon & 2.30–6pm; 20F), in the house of Roland, one of the Camisards' self-taught but most successful military leaders. It is pretty much as it would have been in 1704, the year of his death.

It catalogues the appalling sufferings and sheer dogged heroism of the Protestant Huguenots in defence of their freedom of conscience: the "desert" they had to traverse between the Revocation of the Edict of Nantes in 1685, which had guaranteed a measure of freedom, and the promulgation of the Edict of Tolerance in 1787, which restored their rights – a process which was not completed until the Declaration of the Rights of Man in the first heady months of the Revolution in 1789.

During this period they had no civil rights, unless they abjured their faith. They could not bury their dead, baptize their children, or marry. Their priests were forced into exile on pain of death. Troops were dispatched to put pressure on the recalcitrant, the infamous *dragonnades*, which involved the forcible billeting of troops in private homes, at the expense of the occupants. As if this was not enough, the soldiers would beat their drums continuously for days and nights in people's bedrooms in order to deprive them of sleep. People were put to death and sent to the galleys for life; their houses were destroyed.

Not surprisingly, such brutality led to armed rebellion, inspired by the prophesying of the lay preachers who had replaced the banished priests, calling for a holy war.

There are documents and private letters and lists of those who died for their beliefs, including the names of 5000 who died as galley slaves and the women who were immured in the Tour de Constance prison in Aigues-Mortes. There are also the chains and rough uniform of a *galérien* (galley slave).

Prafrance and the Mine Témoin

Twelve kilometres from St-Jean in the direction of Anduze, **PRAFRANCE** has an extraordinary and very appealing garden consisting exclusively of bamboos of all shapes and sizes: **La Bambouseraie** (March–Oct daily 9.30am–7pm; Nov–Dec Wed–Sun 10am–5pm; closed Jan–Feb; 28F), the result of its creator's pet passion.

If you want to leave the area by train, the place to head for is **ALÈS** on the Nîmes–Paris line. This was a major coal-mining centre, although 25,000 jobs have been lost and all but two open-cast pits closed in the last thirty years. Today, it has a superb museum on the history and techniques of coal mining, known as the **Mine Témoin**, in the underground workings of a real former mine on chemin de la Cité Ste-Marie in the Rochebelle district (daily June–Aug 9.30am–7pm; April–May & Sept–Nov 9am–12.30pm & 2–5.30pm; 33F; visit 1.5hr).

Aubenas and the northern Cévennes

A small but prosperous and surprisingly industrial town of around 14,000 people, **AUBENAS** sits in the middle of the southern part of the Ardèche *département* overlooking the middle valley of the River Ardèche. It is 91km southeast of Le Puy and 42km west of Montelimar on the Rhône. With a character and nontourist-dependent economy of its own, it makes a much better base than places further downstream around Vallon-Pont-d'Arc, with their nightmarish crowds.

The central knot of streets with their cobbles and bridges, occupying the highest point of town around **place de l'Hôtel-de-Ville**, have great charm, particularly towards place Grenette and place 14-juillet. The *hôtel* itself is the old feudal **château**, from which the local seigneurs ruled the area right up until the Revolution (guided tours: July & Aug daily at 10am & 11am, 3pm, 4pm & 5pm, Sun 10am & 11am only; rest of year fewer tours; free). There's a magnificent view of the Ardèche snaking up the valley below from under an arch beside the castle, as there is from the end of **av Gambetta** two hundred yards downhill, where the **tourist office** is located on the corner (Tues–Sat 9am–noon & 2–6pm; July & Aug daily 9am–noon & 2–6pm, Sun 10am–noon & 3–6pm; ☎75.35.24.87).

There are two inexpensive and old-fashioned provincial **hotels** within spitting distance of the castle: *Hôtel des Négociants* on place de l'Hôtel-de-Ville (☎75.35.18.74; ①–②), with good, nourishing meals from 59F, and *Chez Jacques*, 9 rue Béranger-de-la-Tour, in the opposite corner of the tree-lined place (☎75.93.88.74; ①–③; good food from 65F). There are several **campsites**, the cheapest being *Le Trou d'Oo* down by the river at **VILLE** off the Nl02 (☎75.35.04.39; April–Sept). A fancier and more expensive place to eat is *Le Fournil*, 34 rue du 4-septembre, at the end of Béranger-de-la-Tour (from 100F).

The Gorges de l'Ardèche

The **Gorges de l'Ardèche** begin at the **Pont d'Arc**, an extraordinary and very beautiful arch that the river has cut for itself through the limestone, just downstream from Vallon, itself 39km south of Aubenas. And they continue for about 35km to **ST-MARTIN-D'ARDÈCHE** in the valley of the Rhône.

The gorges are fantastic. They wind back and forth with reptilian sinuosity, much of the time dropping 300m straight down like a knife cut in the almost dead-flat scrubby

Plateau des Gras. But they are also an appalling tourist trap; the road which follows the rim, with spectacular viewpoints marked out at regular intervals, is jammed with traffic and anyway you don't really see very much. The river, down in the bottom, which is where you really want to be to appreciate the grandeur of the canyon, is likewise packed with canoes in high season. But it is walkable, depending on the water level, but you would need to bivouac midway at either Gaud or Gournier. Generally speaking, if you can't go out of season, give it a miss.

The plateau itself is riddled with caves. **Aven Marzal**, a stalactite cavern north of the gorge (daily 10am–noon & 2–6pm; July & Aug daily 10am–7.30pm; 35F) has a prehistoric **zoo**, which consists of reconstructions of dinosaurs and friends (same hours; 32F), but the frequency of visits to the cave depends on the number of visitors waiting.

Best of the area's caves is the **Aven Orgnac** to the south of the gorge (July & Aug 9.30am–6pm; April–June & Sept 9.30am–noon & 2–6pm; March, Oct & Nov 9.30am–noon & 2–5pm; closed Dec–Feb; 35F), one of France's most spectacular and colourful stalactite formations. There's also a very good prehistory **museum** (same hours but opens 10am; 27F, joint ticket at 46F). Further upstream near **VALLON-PONT-D'ARC**, a complex series of cave paintings was discovered in December 1994, after being left untouched for 20,000 years. Adorned with an elaborate sequence of Stone Age paintings depicting woolly rhinos, bison, lions and bears, the cave system is currently being investigated by archeologists, and there is no intention of opening it to the public at the moment.

Accommodation in the area is a problem in season. Vallon has several hotels worth a try, including the *Hôtel du Château* on place de la Mairie (☎75.88.02.20; ①–②), and *Le Manoir de Raveyron* on the river (☎75.88.03.59; ②–③; restaurant from 95F: closed mid-Oct to mid-March), and plenty of **campsites**, the cheapest being the municipal one (☎75.88.04.73; April–Sept). There's a **gîte d'étape** on place de la Mairie (☎75.88.07.87), and the **tourist office** (☎75.88.04.01).

Eight kilometres upstream, there is a well-priced **camping municipal** at **RUOMS** (☎75.93.99.16; May–Sept). And in **GROSPIERRE**, about 14km to the west, there's the *Hôtel Les Peupliers* (☎75.93.95.41 ①; meal from 65F).

The valley of the Chassezac and the Corniche du Vivarais

Between Aubenas and Les Vans, 27km to the southwest, several wild mountain streams flow out of the northern part of the Cévennes to join the Ardèche. One of the most beautiful is the **Chassezac**, which rises north of Villefort and carves a dry, twisting ravine covered with pine, bracken and sweet chestnut down to **LES VANS**.

The centre of the town is occupied by the wide and cheerful **place Léopold-Ollier**, on one side of which is the eccentrically decorated *Hôtel des Cévennes* (☎75.37.23.09; ①; closed Oct 3–17), whose décor, friendly welcome and good cooking (from 85F) make a stop here worthwhile. Other attractions are the remains of the old town and, just outside, the weird rock formations of the **Bois de Paiolive**. There is a **gîte d'étape** across the river at **CHAMBONAS** (☎75.37.24.99).

Thines to the Col de Meyrand

THINES is a dozen twisting kilometres up the Chassezac from Les Vans, past isolated farms, abandoned terracing and numerous tumbling streams, then a further 5km or so up a side valley. The lane that leads to it is no wider than a car, and nature encroaches on either side. Traces remain of the old mule road, and in the torrent bed are the stumps of packhorse bridges long since carried away. Among the scrubby oaks are beehives made from old tree trunks.

The village itself is at the end of the road high on a spur, looking back down the valley: just a handful of squat, grey stone houses tightly grouped around a very lovely twelfth-century **church**, decorated with bands of red and white stone, the faces of its sculptures smashed during the Wars of Religion. At the top of the village, where the **GR4** and the local **GRP** enter from the scrubby heights behind, there is a strange **rock-cut relief** commemorating Resistance people killed here in August 1943. There's also a **gîte d'étape** (Mme Bacconnier; ☎75.36.94.33) and *ferme auberge* (Mme Archambault; ☎75.36.94.47).

If your car is reasonably robust, you can get up on to the D4 on the 1000-metre ridge above Thines by a track that starts just above the bridge over the stream below the village. This is the so-called **Corniche du Vivarais Cévenol**, which you would otherwise have to make a long detour to reach. **SABLIÈRES**, another desolate Cévennes village, lies in the valley of the Drobie down to your right.

The landscape changes completely up here. The Mediterranean influence is left behind; it's windswept moorland, with natural beechwoods and mountain ash around the few bleak farms and plantations of conifers on the tops. The land rises steadily to over 1400m above the **Col de Meyrand**, itself at 1370m, whence it is possible to escape back down to the main road and train line at **LUC**, which is 18km to the west.

Le Puy-en-Velay and the northeast

Smack in the middle of the Massif Central, 78km from St-Étienne and 132km from Clermont, **LE PUY** is one of the most remarkable towns in the whole of France. Both landscape and architecture are totally theatrical. Slung between the higher mountains to east and west, the landscape erupts in a chaos of volcanic acne: everywhere a confusion of abrupt conical hills, scarred with dark outcrops of rock and topknotted with woods. Even in the centre of the town, these volcanic thrusts burst through.

In olden times, Le Puy enjoyed influence and prosperity because of its ecclesiastical institutions. It was – and in a limited way, still is – a major centre for pilgrims embarking on the 1600-kilometre trot to Santiago de Compostella. The starting point is place du Plot (also the scene of a lively Saturday market) and rue St-Jacques. History has it that Le Puy's Bishop Godescalk, in the tenth century, was the first pilgrim to make the iourney. And in the Wars of Religion it managed to resist the Protestant fervour of much of the Massif Central. Today, however, it has fallen somewhat on hard times, and its traditional industries – tanning and lace – have essentially gone bust.

Even today Le Puy is somewhat inaccessible for the capital of a *département*; the three main roads out all cross passes more than 1000m high, which causes problems in winter. But it is far from rundown, and it still produces its famous green lentils.

Arrival and accommodation

If you arrive at the **gare SNCF** (☎73.92.50.50) or **gare routière** (☎71.09.25.60), facing each other in place Maréchal-Leclerc, you'll find yourself barely ten minutes' walk from the central place du Breuil and the **tourist office** (Mon–Sat 8.30am–noon & 1.45–6.30pm; June–Aug daily 8.30am–9.30pm; ☎71.09.38.41), with the **Comité Départemental du Tourisme** at 12 bd Philippe-Jourde (same hours).

The choice of **hotels** is rather limited. Three to try on bd Maréchal-Fayolle, the main boulevard connecting the station and place Breuil, are the odd-looking *Dyke Hôtel* at no. 37 (☎71.09.05.30; ②–③), the *Régional* at no. 36 (☎71.09.37.74; ①), and the rather handsome old *Régina* at no. 34, with a tempting terrace (☎71.09.14.71; ②–③;

restaurant from 87F). For those watching the pennies, there's a good official **youth hostel** at the *Centre Pierre-Cardinal*, 9 rue Jules-Vallès (☎71.05.52.40; ①), just off rue Lafayette. The municipal *Camping de Bouthézard* is off av d'Aiguilhe in the northwest corner of town.

The old town

It would be hard to lose your sense of direction in Le Puy, for the town centre is marked by the highly visible **Rocher Corneille**, 755m above sea level and 130 abrupt metres above the lower town at its feet, with a colossal 16-metre statue at its summit of the Virgin and Child in brick-red, cast from 213 guns captured at Sebastopol and coloured to match the tiled roofs below. You can climb to the top of the Rocher Corneille (9.50F) for stunning views of the city, the church of St-Michel atop the needle-pointed pinnacle of the Rocher d'Aiguilhe, a few hundred metres northwest, and the surrounding volcanic countryside.

Reached by the steep cobbled streets and steps that terrace the Rocher, the main focus of the **old town** is the Byzantine-looking **Cathédrale Notre-Dame-de-France**, begun in the eleventh century and decorated with parti-coloured layers of stone and mosaic patterns and roofed with a line of six domes. It is best approached up the rue des Tables, where you get the full theatrical force of its five-storied west front towering above you. The steps continue under the porch, leading round the south side past the so-called **Fever Stone**, whose origins may have been as a prehistoric dolmen and which was reputed to have the power of curing fevers. In the rather exotic eastern gloom of the interior, a black-faced Virgin in spreading golden robes stands upon the main altar, the copy of a revered original destroyed during the Revolution; the copy is still paraded through the town every August 15. Other lesser treasures are displayed at the back of the church in the sacristy, beyond which is the entrance to the exceptionally beautiful twelfth-century **cloister** (Mon–Sat 8.30am–noon & 1.45–6.30pm, Sun 9.30am–4.30pm; July–Sept daily 9.30am–7.30pm; 20F), with its carved capitals, cornices and magnificent views of the cathedral and the towering Virgin and Child overhead. The surrounding ecclesiastical buildings and the **place du For**, on the south side of the cathedral, all date from the same period and form a remarkable ensemble.

It's a long haul up the 265 steps to the **church of St-Michel** atop the 82-metre needle-pointed lava pinnacle of the **Rocher d'Aiguilhe**, a ten-minute walk northwest of the cathedral. The little Romanesque church, built on Bishop Godescalk's return from his pilgrimage (see above) and consecrated in 962, is a beauty in its own right, and its improbable situation atop this ridiculous needle of rock is quite extraordinary (daily 10am–noon & 2–5/7pm; mid-June to mid-Sept daily 9am–7pm; winter pm only; 10F).

Back in the lower town, lacemakers – a traditional, though now commercialized industry – do a fine trade, with doilies and lace shawls hanging enticingly outside souvenir shops. But it's surface only; deeper into Le Puy's maze of narrow streets the old lanes are uncluttered and wonderful. In the new part of town, beyond the squat **Tour Pannessac**, which is all that remains of the city walls, **place de Breuil** joins **place Michelet** and forms a social hub backed by the spacious Henri Inay public gardens, where the **Musée Crozatier** (Mon & Wed–Sat 10am–noon & 2–6pm, Sun 2–6pm; Oct–April closes 4pm; closed Feb; 15F) is best known for its collections relating to the region's traditional lacemaking activities. Busy bd Maréchal-Fayolle converges with place Cadelade, where there's another of Le Puy's crazier aspects: the extraordinary bulbous tower of the **Pages Verveine distillery**. The verveine (verbena) plant is normally used to make *tisane* (herb tea), but in this region provides a powerful digestive liqueur instead.

Eating and drinking

Apart from the brasseries on the main drag opposite the tourist office, there are several good and not too expensive places to eat. The best, and most expensive, is the *Tournayre* at 12 rue Chenebouterie (closed Sun eve, Mon except July & Aug and first fortnight in Oct; ☎71.09.58.94; from 95F), specializing in the region's cuisine. Two cheaper establishments, both in rue Raphael, which begins at the bottom of rue des Tables, are the *Nom de la Rose* at no. 48 (closed Nov–March), specializing in Mexican food for 60–70F, and the Middle Eastern *La Felouque* at no. 49 (from 68F). Two others, both offering regional cuisine, are *Le Chat Botté*, 8 av de la Cathédrale (from 60F; closed Sun & mid-Jan to mid-Feb), and *Le Rancheterre*, 26 rue Francheterre, off place Carnot (closed Sat lunchtime & Sun eve; from 85F).

For **coffee** or a **snack**, the favourite hang-out is the *Brasserie Le Majestic* on bd Maréchal-Fayolle. For an evening drink, you can always try *Harry's Bar* on rue Raphael (Mon–Sat till 1am), near the corner with rue des Tables, where all the traditional lace shops catering for the tourists are – nonetheless pretty for that.

North of Le Puy

North of Le Puy, the D906 crosses a vast and terminally depopulated area of pine-clad uplands – now a national regional park – and continues all the way to Vichy. After 42km you come to the little town of **LA CHAISE-DIEU**, renowned for the **abbey church of St-Robert** (daily 10am–noon & 2–5pm; July & Aug 9am–noon & 2–7pm; free), whose square towers dominate the town. Founded in 1044 and restored in the fourteenth century at the expense of Pope Clement VI, who had served as a monk here, the church was destroyed by the Huguenots in 1562, burnt down in 1692, and remained unfinished when the Revolution brought a wave of anticlericalism. It was only really finished in this century. Its interior contains the tomb of Clement VI, some magnificent Flemish tapestries of Old and New Testament scenes hanging in the choir, which also boasts some fine Gothic stalls, and a celebrated fresco of the **Danse Macabre**, depicting Death plucking at the coarse plump bodies of 23 living figures, representing the different classes of society. "It is yourself", says the fifteenth-century text below, as indeed it might easily have been in an age when plague and war were rife.

Nearby on the place de l'Echo, the **Salle de l'Echo** (same times; free) is another product of the risk of contagion, if not from plague then from leprosy. For in this room, once used for hearing confession from the sick and dying, two people can turn their backs on each other and stand in opposite corners and have a perfectly audible conversation just by whispering.

La Chaise-Dieu's **tourist office** is on place de la Mairie (daily except Mon 10am–noon & 2–6pm; mid-Sept to March Tues–Sat; ☎71.00.01.16). The *Hôtel Monastère et Terminus* on av de la Gare (☎71.00.00.73; ①–③; restaurant from 75F) and *Hôtel au Tremblant* on the D906 (☎71.00.01.85; ①–③; restaurant from 90F) offer reasonable comfort for a night's stay. There's also a **camping municipal** on the Vichy side of the D906 (☎71.00.07.88; June–Sept), and a **gîte d'étape** (M. Brivadis; ☎71.00.01.05). There's also a **classical music festival** that takes place here in the first week of September.

Ambert and Thiers

Twenty-five kilometres north of La Chaise-Dieu, the little town of **AMBERT** was an important centre of cottage industry in the Middle Ages. From the fourteenth to eighteenth centuries it was the centre of papermaking in France, supplying in particular the printers of Lyon, a connection which brought the region into contact with new ideas, in particular the revolutionary teachings of the Reformed church. Although those small-scale operations have long since been sidelined, there is a still a **paper mill** in operation at Richard-de-Bas just east of the town, with its **Musée historique du papier** (daily 9am–noon & 2–6pm; July & Aug 9am–8pm; 20F), featuring exhibits and explanations from papyrus to handmade samples from medieval days. In the town itself, there's a small **museum** (daily except Mon 9–11.30am & 2–6.30pm; July & Aug 9am–6.30pm; closed Jan 15–30; 21F) devoted to the manufacture of the soft blue Fourme d'Ambert cheese, the region's speciality.

THIERS, another 49km to the north, has an illustrious industrial history: it is the country's great manufacturer of knives. In spite of serious decline, especially since decolonization and the loss of such huge captive markets, it still accounts for some 65 percent of French production. It is an interesting little town, built over the steep slopes of the valley of the Durolle, whose water power drove the forges and blade-makers' wheels for centuries. There's the **Maison des Couteliers**, devoted to the knife, at 58 rue de la Coutellerie in the centre (daily except Mon 10am–noon & 2–6pm; June–Sept daily; 21F), while all along the deep valley bottom you can see where the old workshops were. It's probably best to visit by train from Clermont (30mins; frequent trains), but should you want to **stay**, try the *Fimotel* by the *gare SNCF* (☎73.80.64.40; ③), although the nicest place is at **PONT-DORE**, around 4km out of town, on the old Clermont road: *Chez La Mère Depalle* (☎73.80.06.49; ③), with its good restaurant (from 95F).

East of Le Puy

East of Le Puy lies the barrier of the mountains of the Vivariais, rounded and wooded with beech, pine and fir, interspersed with open cow pastures. The highest points are the **Gerbier de Jonc** (1551m) and **Mont Mezenc** (1753m), with long views west across the whole of the Massif Central.

The Gerbier is a curious tump rising out of the otherwise flattish surrounding uplands, about 50km southeast of Le Puy, with the River Loire rising on its upper slopes. To get out there you take the D535 through **MONASTIER-SUR-GAZEILLE**, where Stevenson bought his donkey and started his journey. Although the village is pretty, with a particularly lovely church, there is something forlorn and unfriendly about it. The rather bleak *Hôtel de Provence* above the village would do for a night's stay (☎71.03.82.37; ①; restaurant from 60F). The riverside **camping municipal** (☎71.03.82.24; June–Sept) and **gîte d'étape** (☎71.03.82.24) are more welcoming.

There are a couple of places within a few kilometres of the Gerbier that make better places to **stay**. In **LE BÉAGE**, there's the *Hôtel Beauséjour* (☎75.38.85.02; ①–③; restaurant from 57F), and **STE-EULALIE** has *Hôtel de la Poste* (☎75.38.81.09; ②–③; restaurant from 78F). Fifty kilometres further north, and about 40km east of Le Puy, behind the gentle bulk of **Mont Meygal** (1436m), lies the area known as the *Montagne Protestante*, because its people converted very early and have remained staunch Protestants ever since, albeit with some fairly far-out tendencies among them. Black stone farmhouses stand in isolation among the pastures strewn with autumn crocus and the dark woods of fir. At the centre of the region lies **CHAMBON-SUR-LIGNON**, a rambling, not very attractive village with a rather faded air, made famous, however, for its extraordinary wartime record as a haven for several thousand Jewish children. Everyone knew of their presence, everyone was involved in protecting them and no one ever betrayed them, bound together in their obdurate resolve by religious conviction. Their story is told in a documentary, made by one of the surviving children who emigrated to the USA, in **Les Armes de l'Esprit** (daily 10am–noon & 2–6pm; 20F). Albert Camus also stayed nearby in 1942 and wrote part of *La Peste* here. The **tourist office** is on the central square (daily 9am–12.15pm & 3–6.30pm, Sun 11am–noon). More local information can be had from the tourist office in **TENCE**, a rather more aesthetic village, 8km down the road (Tues–Sat 9am–noon & 2–6pm; ☎71.59.81.99).

St-Étienne

ST-ÉTIENNE, 78km northeast of Le Puy, is not an appealing town. Almost unrelievedly industrial, it was a major armaments manufacturer, enclosed for miles around by mineworkings, warehouses and factory chimneys. But like so many other industrial centres, it has fallen on hard times and the demolition gangs have moved in to raze its archaic industrial past, which does not add to its charms.

The centre is bland and characterless, the mood one of decline since the closure of the coalfields, but its **Musée d'Art Moderne** at La Terrasse (daily except Tues 10am–7pm; free) justifies a detour for anyone interested in twentieth-century art – a quite unexpected treasure house of contemporary work, both pre- and post-World War II, with a good modern American section, in which Andy Warhol and Frank Stella figure prominently, along with work by Meunier, Rodin, Matisse, Léger and Ernst, and rooms filled entirely with French art, imaginatively laid out to exciting effect. The **Musée d'Art et d'Industrie**, 2 pl Louis-Comte (daily except Tues 9am–noon & 2–6pm; free), is also good on St-Étienne's industrial background, including the development of the revolutionary Jacquard loom.

Bus #10 runs from the **train station** into the centre of town, and the **tourist office** is on place Roannelle (daily except Sun 9am–12.30pm & 1.30–6pm). If you are forced to stay, try *Hôtel de la Tour*, 1 rue Mercière (☎77.32.28.48; ①–②), *Le Cheval Noir*, 11 rue François-Gillet (☎77.33.41.72; ①–③), or *Hôtel Terminus du Forcz*, 29 av D-Rochereau, leading to the station (☎77.32.48.47; ②–④).

travel details

Trains

Alès to: Genolhac (3–4 daily; 40min); Langogne (3–4 daily; 1hr 30min); Nîmeş (6–7 daily; 35min); Villefort ((3–4 daily; 1hr).

Aurillac to: Brive: (4 daily; 1hr 40min).

Clermont-Ferrand to: Aurillac (6 daily; 2hr 30min); Béziers (1 daily; 6hr); Brive (3 daily; 3hr 40min); Limoges (2 daily; 3hr 30min); Le Lioran (6 daily; 2hr); Lyon (6 daily; 2hr 45min–3hr); Le Mont Dore (6 daily; 1hr 30min); Millau (3 daily; 4hr 20min); Murat (6 daily; 1hr 20min); Neussargues (6 daily; 1hr 30min); Paris (5 daily; 5hr); Le Puy (3 daily; 2hr 10min); Riom (10 daily; 10min); St-Flour-Chaudes-Aigues (5 daily; 2hr); Thiers (6 daily; 35min); Vic-sur-Cère (6 daily; 2hr 15min); Vichy (10 daily; 35min); Volvic (5 daily; 24min).

Mende to: La Bastide-Puylaurens (2 daily; 1hr); Langogne (2 daily; 1hr 30min); Marvejols (3 daily; 40min); Montpellier (1 daily; 3hr); Nîmes (3 daily; 2hr 30min–4hr).

Millau to: Aumont-Aubrac (5 daily; 1hr 30min); Béziers (6 daily; 2hr); Marvejols (5 daily; 1hr 10min); Paris (2 daily direct; 8hr 30min).

Le Puy to: St-Étienne (8 daily; 1hr 20min).

Rodez to: Millau (*SNCF* bus & train, 2 daily; 1hr 20min).

St-Étienne to: Clermont-Ferrand (3–6 daily; 2hr 40min); Paris (3 daily *TGV*s; 2hr 50min); St-Germain-des-Fosses (2 daily; 3hr); Lyon (3 daily TGV; 45min).

St-Flour to: Neussargues (2–3 daily; 25 min).

Vichy to: Clermont-Ferrand (frequent; 38min); Nîmes (1–2 daily; 7hr); Paris (4 daily; 3hr 30min).

Buses

Ambert to: St-Étienne (1 daily; 2hr).

Aubenas to: Alès (2–3 daily; 2hr 10min); Joyeuse (8 daily; 25–40min); Privas (7 daily; 1hr); Valence (7 daily; 2hr); Vallon-Pont-d'Arc (4 daily; 45min); Les Vans (5 daily; 1hr 10min).

Aurillac to: Brommat (change at Mut-de-Barrez, 3 weekly; 2hr); Décazeville (1 daily; 2hr); Carlat (3–4 daily; 30min); Entraygues (1 daily; 1hr 30min); Mandailles (1 daily; 1hr 20min); Murat (1 daily; 1hr 40min); St-Flour (1 daily; 2hr 10min); Ste-Geneviève-sur-Argence (change at Mur-de-Barrez, 3 weekly; 2hr 30min); Super-Lioran (1 daily; 1hr 20min); Thiézac (2 daily; 55min); Vic-sur-Cère (2–3 daily; 40min).

Chambon-sur-Lignon to: St-Agrève (2 daily; 30min); Valence (2 daily; 2hr 40min).

Clermont-Ferrand to: Ambert (1–2 daily: 1hr 45min); Aydat (1–2 daily; 40min); Besse (July & Aug 2 daily; 1hr 35min); Bort-les-Orgues (1–2 daily: 2hr 15min); Chaubon (July & Aug 2 daily; 1hr 35min); La Chaise-Dieu (1 Mon; 2hr); Mauriac (1–2 daily: 2hr 45min); Moulins (4 daily: 2hr 30min); Murol (July & Aug 2 daily; 1hr 10min); Le Puy (1 daily: 2hr 15min); St-Flour (2 weekly; 2hr); St-Nectaire (July & Aug 2 daily; 1hr); Superbesse (July & Aug 2 daily; 1hr 45min); Thiers (several daily: 1hr); Vichy (5 daily: 2hr).

Conques to: Entraygues (July & Aug Tues, Thurs, Sat 1 daily; 35min); Espalion (July & Aug Tues, Thurs, Sat 1 daily; 1hr 20min); Najac (July & Aug Tues & Fri 1 daily; 2hr 30min); Rodez (July & Aug Tues, Thurs, Sat 1 daily; 1hr); St-Geniez-d'Olt (July & Aug Tues, Thurs, Sat 1 daily; 2hr 15min); Villefranche-de-Rouergue (July & Aug Tues & Fri 1 daily; 2hr).

Florac to: Alès (1–2 daily; 1hr 30min).

Mende to: Langogne (2 daily; 1hr); Marvejols (*SNCF* 3 daily; 50min); Le Puy (2 daily; 2hr); St-Chély-d'Apcher (1 daily; 1hr 10min); St-Étienne (*SNCF* 2 daily; 2hr 40min).

Millau to: Aven Armand (July & Aug 1–2 daily; 1hr 45min); Meyrueis (1–3 daily; 1hr 15min); Rodez (4 daily; 1hr 30min); Rozier (3–5 daily; 35min); Toulouse (2 daily; 4hr); Ste-Émie (July & Aug 2 daily; 1hr 50min).

Neussargues to: Allanche (*SNCF* 2–3 daily; 20min); Bort-les-Orgues (*SNCF* 2–3 daily; 1hr 45min); Condat (*SNCF* 2–3 daily; 30min); Riom-ès-Montagnes (*SNCF* 2–3 daily; 1hr 15min); St-Flour (*SNCF* 2–3 daily; 30min).

Le Puy to: Aubenas (1 daily; 3hr 15min); La Chaise-Dieu (*SNCF* 2 daily; 1hr); Clermont-Ferrand (1 daily; 3hr); Monistrol d'Allier (3 weekly; 50min); St-Étienne (4 daily; 2hr 10min); Saugnes (3 weekly; 1hr 10min).

Rodez to: Albi (3 daily; 2hr); Conques (July & Aug Tues, Thurs & Sat 1 daily; 1hr); Entraygues (1 daily; 2hr); Espalion (3–4 daily; 45min); Laguiole (1 daily; 1hr 45min); Mende (1 daily; 3hr 30min); Millau (4–5 daily; 1hr 30min); Montpellier (3 daily; 3hr 20min); Montauban (1 daily; 3hr 15min); Mur-de-Barrez (1 daily; 2hr 45min); Séverac-le-Château (several daily; 45min); Toulouse (2–4 daily; 3hr 30min); Villefranche-de-Rouergue (1–2 daily; 1hr 30min).

St-Affrique to: Le Caylar (1 daily; 1hr 40min); Lodève (1 daily; 2hr 10min); Millau (2 daily; 50min); Montpellier (1 daily; 3hr 25min); Rodez (1 daily; 2hr 15min).

St-Agrève to: Chambon-sur-Lignon (4 daily; 20min); St-Étienne (4 daily; 2hr); Tence (4 daily; 35min).

St-Chély-d'Aubrac to: Espalion (1 daily; 30min).

St-Flour to: Chaudes-Aigues (2 daily; 1hr); Laguiole (Tues, Thurs & Sat 1 daily; 3hr); Massiac (3 daily; 35min).

St-Martin-d'Ardèche to: Avignon (1 daily; 1hr 40min); Pont St-Esprit (2 daily; 15min); Vallon-Pont d'Arc (2 daily; 1hr 10min).

Vichy to: Ambert (*SNCF* 5 daily; 2hr 10min); Thiers (*SNCF* several daily; 40min).

Le Vigan to: Ganges (4 daily; 25min); Montpellier (3 daily; 2hr); Nîmes (4 daily; 2hr).

Villefranche-de-Rouergue to: Conques (July & Aug Tues & Fri 1 daily; 2hr); Décazeville (July & Aug Tues & Fri 1 daily; 30min); Najac (July & Aug Tues & Fri 1 daily; 30min).

CHAPTER THIRTEEN

THE ALPS

R ousseau wrote in his *Confessions*, "I need torrents, rocks, pine trees, dark forests, mountains, rugged paths to go up and down, precipices at my elbow to give me a good fright." He might have added wild flowers – best seen in the first half of July – as these are certainly the great summer joys of **the Alps**.

Formed by the collision of two continental plates 200 million years ago, the Alps form a natural boundary between France and Italy. The region contains some of France's most invigorating landscapes, with roads and train lines winding their way around (and often through) limestone cliffs, valleys with tiny settlements shoe-horned into sequestered corners, and rivers fuelled by shifting snow. But the area is hardly an isolated region: over the past thirty years the Alps have been turned into one great resort, with the spectacular **Chamonix-Mont Blanc** area the worst black-spot for overcrowding.

The best, though not the only, way to appreciate the area is on foot. There are a handful of **officially designated parks** covered in this chapter: the national parks of **Écrins**, between Grenoble and Briançon, and **Vanoise**, to the north of Briançon; and the regional parks of **Vercors**, southwest of Grenoble, and – perhaps the least touristy – **Queyras** to the south, both straddling the border with Italy. All of them have circular trails, requiring between one and two weeks' walking. The **Tour of Mont Blanc** path also takes just over a week to complete, and there are two trans-alpine routes: the **Grande Traversée des Alpes**, which crosses all the major massifs from St-Gingolph on Lake Geneva to Nice, 300km south on the Mediterranean, and **Le Balcon des Alpes**, a gentler, village-to-village itinerary through the western foothills.

The handful of towns in the Alps offer good facilities for campers and hikers, and often provide attractions of their own. **Grenoble**, an old town in a stunning setting, is the economic and intellectual capital of the region, with a lively student population and plenty of nightlife; **Chambéry** and **Annecy** make the most of their spectacular positions; and **Briançon**, to the east, is the highest town in Europe on a major communication route into Italy, and is close to three of the parks.

ACCOMMODATION PRICE CATEGORIES

All the hotels, youth hostels and guesthouses listed in this book have been price-graded according to the following scale, and although costs will rise slightly overall with the life of this edition, the relative comparisons should remain valid. Paris and the large cities will, as anywhere, be more expensive than equivalent accommodation in the countryside or small towns. The prices quoted are for the cheapest available double room in high season, although remember that many of the cheap places will have more expensive rooms with en-suite facilities.

① Under 160F	④ 300–400F	⑦ 600–700F
② 160–220F	⑤ 400–500F	⑧ Over 700F
③ 220–300F	⑥ 500–600F	

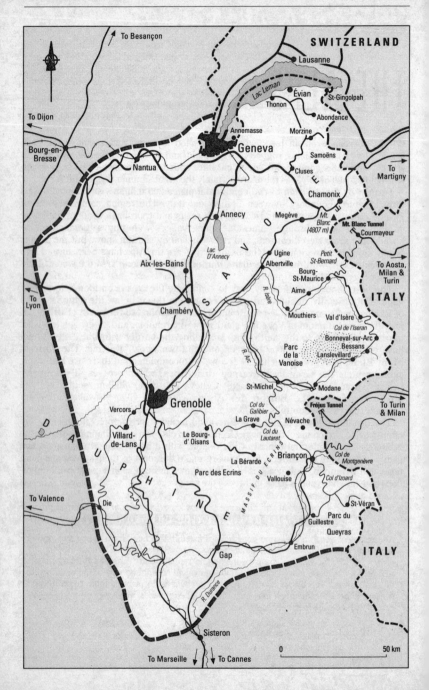

Hiking in the Alps

The Alps are as crowded in mid-summer as they are in winter, with **hiking** much in vogue during the warmer months. You are more or less obliged to go in high season if you want to walk; unreliable weather aside, anywhere above 2000m will be snowbound until the beginning of July. It's worth remembering too that some high passes such as the Col du Galibier and the Col de l'Iseran in the east of the region can remain closed well into June, requiring long detours or excursions into Italy via alpine tunnels.

The **official parks** attract hordes of people, but luckily the scale of the Alps is big enough to absorb considerable numbers while the mountains retain their beauty. All **routes** are clearly marked, equipped with refuge huts and *gîtes d'étape*, and are described in *Topoguides* (see p.1005). The *CIMES* office in Grenoble (see p.750) will provide information on all GR paths. In addition, local tourist offices often produce detailed maps of walks in their own areas.

You should not undertake any high-level **long-distance hikes** unless you are an experienced hillwalker; if you aren't, but nonetheless like the sound of some of these trails, read a specialized hiking book before making any plans, or simply limit your sights to more local targets. You can find plenty of day walks from bases in or close to the parks; and there are some satisfying road routes, too. The Vercors, Chartreuse, Aravis, Faucigny and Chablais areas are the gentlest and quietest introductions.

As for **accommodation**, you can **camp** freely on the fringes of the parks, but once inside you are supposed to pitch a tent only in an emergency and move on after one night. A tent will give you greatest flexibility, since **hotels** are often seasonal (closed in late spring and late autumn), overbooked and their prices inflated. Using **gîtes** and **refuges** is a better solution as they save you having to carry camping equipment, even if they do limit your movements.

The obvious, winter alternative is to **ski**: although this book is not designed as a skier's guide, a short round-up of the resorts is included on p.768.

Grenoble

The economic and intellectual capital of the French Alps, **GRENOBLE** is a lively, thriving, modern city, beautifully situated on the Drac and Isère rivers, surrounded by mountains and home to a university of more than 35,000 students. The city's prosperity was originally founded on glove-making, but in the nineteenth century its economy diversified to include mining, cement, papermills, hydroelectric power (white coal, as they called it) and metallurgy. Today, it is a centre of chemical and electronics industries and nuclear research, with the big, new laboratories of the Atomic Energy Commission on the banks of the Drac.

Grenoble has also been at the forefront of social, environmental and cultural innovation, particularly during the twenty-year mayoralty of Hubert Dubedout, who was killed in a climbing accident in 1986. His Villeneuve housing project (between av Jean-Jaurès and cours de la Libération), though tatty and of ill repute today, started out as an idealistic attempt to provide integrated living space for a complete mix of social classes, including Arab and other immigrant workers, together with open schooling and other community-based programmes. The current mayor, previously Chirac's environment minister, has revived one of Dubedout's ideas in the construction of the city's pride and joy, its pollution-free tram network.

Arrival and accommodation

The most interesting sections of the city are mainly on the south bank of the Isère and easily accessible on foot, just ten minutes east of the **gare SNCF** down av Félix-Viallet,

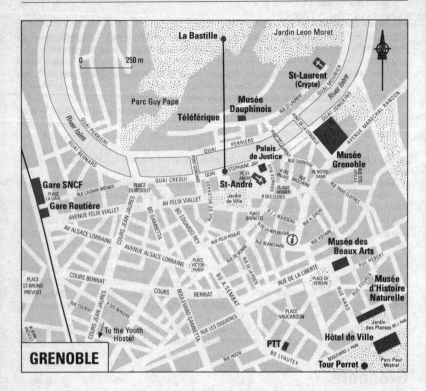

GRENOBLE

with the **gare routière** next door. Not far from place Grenette, you'll find the **tourist office** at 14 rue de la République (Mon–Sat 9am–6pm, Sun 10am–12.30pm; summer Mon–Sat closes 7pm; ☎76.42.41.41), who can give you free copies of the glossy *Grenoble* magazine (available in English), and you'll also find the local *SNCF* and **public transport** information offices here. **Walkers and climbers** should check out the *CIMES* office at 7 rue Voltaire (Mon–Fri 9am–6pm, Sat 10am–noon & 2–6pm; ☎76.54.76.00), and maybe also the *Club Alpin Français* at 32 av Félix-Viallet (☎76.87.03.73). If you fancy a **mountain-bike** tour and haven't brought your machine with you, head for the *Mistral Shop*, 13 pl Ste-Claire, where you can rent a **bike** for 80F a day and buy a *forfait évasion* bus ticket to get you and the bike clear of the town.

For **hotels**, the train station is the most convenient area, with the *Hôtel Terminus* right opposite (☎76.87.24.33; ③) and the nearby *Hôtel des Alpes*, 45 av Félix-Viallet (☎76.87.00.71; ③), both offering comfortable, spacious rooms. The *Bellevue* (☎76.46.69.34; ④) has a better location, as its name suggests, on the corner of quai Stéphane-Jay and rue Belgrade near the *téléférique*. Still in the town centre, the *Grand Hôtel*, 5 rue de la République (☎76.44.49.36; ⑤), offers comfort in the three-star category. Less expensive establishments include the *Lakanal* on 26 rue des Bergers, off cours Jean-Jaurès (☎76.46.03.42; ①–②), while the least expensive central rooms are in the *Hôtel du Moucherotte*, 1 rue Auguste-Gaché, near place Ste-Claire (☎76.54.61.40; ②), and *Hôtel de la Poste* at 25 rue de la Poste (☎76.46.67.25; ②), off place Vaucanson – the entrance may be grubby, but the hotel itself is spotless and friendly.

There's also an IYHF **youth hostel** at 18 av du Grésivaudan, Échirolles (☎76.09.33.52; ①; open all day, year-round), a four-kilometre bus ride south (#1 or #8 from cours Jean-Jaurès) to the *La Quinzaine* stop, by a large *Casino* supermarket with a cafeteria serving good, reasonably priced meals. Other hostel-type possibilities include *Le Foyer de l'Étudiante* – for both sexes, despite the name – at 4 rue Ste-Ursule (☎76.42.00.84; ①), during the summer vacation only, and *Le Foyer La Houille Blanche*, 57 av du Grand-Châtelet, 500m southeast of Parc Paul Mistral (☎76.54.56.01; ②; July–Sept). **Campers** should make for the left bank of the Drac, west of town, where there are campgrounds in Sassenage (*Camping de Sassenage*) and Seyssins (*Les Trois Pucelles*), both around a fifteen-minute bus ride away.

The City

The **old town** centres on the **church of St-André**, originally built in the thirteenth century as the ruling counts of Albon's palace chapel, but heavily restored since and now of little architectural interest. Opposite the church on the place St-André is the sixteenth-century **Palais de Justice** (working hours only; free), with its interior of fine panelling. The narrow streets clustering around the church are far more interesting, leading back towards places Grenette, Vaucanson and Verdun through the liveliest and most colourful quarter of the city, a focus of life for shoppers and strollers alike.

Close to place Grenette, at 1 rue Hector-Berlioz, is the **Musée Stendhal** (Tues–Sun 10am–noon & 2–6pm; free), birthplace of the author of *Le Rouge et Le Noir* and decorated in a style with which Stendhal would have been familiar. Much of his childhood was spent nearby at his grandfather's house, **La Maison Stendhal**, at 20 Grand-Rue just behind the St-André church (same hours; free), which features still more Stendhaliana for the obsessed. Cap it all off with a walk through the **Jardin de Ville** and along the riverside. Further along the river bank is Grenoble's newest cultural showcase, the **Musée Grenoble** on place Lavalette (daily except Tues 11am–7pm, Wed till 10pm; 25F), actually an art gallery which chronologically displays over 10,000 paintings, drawings and sculptures from ancient Egyptian to contemporary times.

South of the old town, the handsome nineteenth-century place de Verdun forms a pleasingly symmetrical focal point, bordered on the east side by the **Musée de Peinture et de Sculpture** (daily except Tues 10am–noon & 2–6pm; 20F, free on Wed), which has an impressive collection of contemporary and representative works by the big names in twentieth-century art. Walking past the *préfecture* will bring you to the **Natural History Museum**, standing amid the fine trees of a public garden (Mon–Sat 9.30am–noon & 1.30–5.30pm, Sun 2–6pm; closed Tues; 15F, free on Wed) and boasting a huge collection of fossils and rocks, animals and birds, including specimens of all the alpine birds of prey, unfortunately very badly displayed.

Opposite, at the edge of the **Parc Paul Mistral**, stands the steel, glass and concrete **Hôtel de Ville**: all straight lines and square corners, but refreshingly contemporary – one of the earliest of France's now numerous and bold architectural experiments with its public buildings. In the park behind is an earlier and more frivolous structure, an 87-metre concrete tower designed in 1925 by Auguste Perret, one of the pioneers of modern French architecture. The concrete looks shabby now and you could hardly call it attractive, but it is bold and unapologetically modern.

The St-Laurent quarter and the Fort de la Bastille

At the base of the Fort de la Bastille, the old **St-Laurent quarter** runs in a narrow strip along the north side of the river. This is the original site of *Curalo*, a third-century Gaulish town built around the base of the foothills of Mont Rachais, and was re-colonized by Italian immigrants in the nineteenth century. The eleventh-century **church of St-Laurent** has a crypt which dates from the Merovingian period (sixth century) and features some interesting capital carvings.

Along rue St-Laurent and up a cobbled path opposite the footbridge by the Palais de Justice, the **Musée Dauphinois**, 30 rue Maurice Gignoux (daily except Tues 9am–noon & 2–6pm; 15F, Wed free), occupies the former convent of Ste-Marie-d'en-Haut. Imaginatively laid out, it is largely devoted to the history, arts and crafts of the province of Dauphiné (unlike neighbouring Savoie, which was only relinquished by the Italians in 1860, Dauphiné has been French since the fourteenth century). There are exhibits on the life of the mountain people, *"les gens de là-haut"* ("the people from up there"), who like most poor mountaineers were obliged to travel the world as pedlars and knife-grinders. Many, too, were involved in smuggling, and there is a fascinating collection of body-hugging flasks used for contraband liquor. The most unusual section is the so-called *Roman des Grenoblois*, the story of the people of Grenoble told in an excellent audiovisual presentation through the lives of various members of a representative selection of families, ranging from immigrant workers to wealthy industrialists.

The best way to get an overview of Grenoble and its stunning environs is to take the **téléférique** (frequent departures Tues–Sat 9am–midnight, Sun till 7.30pm, Mon 11am–7.30pm; one-way 20F, return 31F) from the riverside quai Stéphane-Jay to the **Fort de la Bastille** on the steep slopes above the north bank of the Isère, built to guard the approaches to the medieval city. You are whisked steeply and swiftly into the air in a quartet of ageing transparent eggs, and though the fort is of little interest, the view is undeniably impressive. At your feet the Isère, milky-grey and swollen with melted snow, tears at the piles of old bridges that join the St-Laurent quarter on the Isère's north bank to the nucleus of the medieval town, whose red roofs cluster tightly around the church of St-André. To the east, snowfields gleam in the gullies of the Belledonne Massif (2978m). Southeast is Taillefer and south-southeast the dip where the *Route Napoléon* passes over the mountains to Sisteron and the Mediterranean – this is the road Napoléon took after his escape from Elba in March 1815 on his way to rally his forces for the campaign that led to his final defeat at Waterloo. To the west are the steep white cliffs of the Vercors Massif; the highest peak, dominating the city, is Moucherotte (1901m). The jagged peaks at your back are the outworks of the Chartreuse Massif. Northeast on a clear day you can see the white peaks of Mont Blanc up the deep glacial valley of the Isère, known as La Grésivaudan. It was in this valley that the first French hydroelectric project went into action in 1869.

Eating and drinking

The focus of Grenoble's **eating and drinking** are the places Grenette, St-André and Notre-Dame. Place St-André, with its daily **market**, is frequented day and night by the young and cool. The streets to the east, round place des Herbes, rue Renauldon and rue Chenoise, form the run-down Arab quarter, much the best area for cheap and copious food; try *Le Djerba*, 9 rue Chenoise. Back on place Notre-Dame, there's the reasonably priced *Le Progrès* and *Le Tonneau de Diogène* for standard French fare, and for fancier traditional cuisine under 100F, try *La Panse*, 2 rue de la Paix (closed Sun & mid-July to mid-Aug). The *Brasserie St-Christophe* on rue d'Alembert, behind the train station, is a less budget-orientated place for a meal, and a walk along the quai Perrière on the north bank of the Isère will reveal an almost continuous bank of Italian restaurants: *La Chantelle* is said to make the best pizzas. As for a **drink**, *La Bagatelle* in place St-André is Grenoble's liveliest bar at the moment, and Grenoble's students hang out in the bars of place St-Bruno.

The Vercors and Chartreuse massifs

Both the **Vercors Massif** and **Chartreuse Massif** are very close to Grenoble, particularly the Vercors, which stretches out to the southwest, parallel to the River Drac on the west side of the N75. Chartreuse is northwest of the city, running up the west bank of the River Isère towards Chambéry.

Both ranges are relatively gentle and not too high, so if you're starting your Alpine ventures here, you can use them to break your feet in. The Grenoble *CIMES* office publishes route descriptions with extracts from the IGN 1:25,000 map. Neither massif is heavily populated, and the lack of industry – apart from age-old pastoralism – makes them authentic and unspoilt alpine destinations, popular with all types of energetic outdoor enthusiasts from cavers to mountain bikers.

The Vercors Massif

Simplest and most accessible of the *CIMES* walks is no. 4: a four-hour circular walk to **ST-NIZIER**, just over the rim of the **Vercors Massif**. Start by taking bus #5 from place Victor-Hugo and get off in Seyssinet village by the school. For most of the way you follow **GR9** with its red and white waymarks. The path starts about 200m uphill from the school on the right. It is not difficult, but the path crosses the D106 a few times, and the continuation is not always obvious, so it is worth getting the leaflet. It is about two-and-a-half hours to St-Nizier (return the same way) by a beautiful path through thick woods with long views back over Grenoble to the mountains beyond. The lovely purplish Martagon lily blooms in the woods in early July. St-Nizier has **hotels**: *des Alpes* (☎76.53.41.82; ②) and *Concorde* (☎76.53.42.61; ②) and a small **campsite**. It is a further three-and-a-half hours (there and back) to the top of **Moucherotte** on GR91.

One good way to explore the Vercors further is to base yourself in the mountains in **VILLARD-DE-LANS**, 18km southwest of Grenoble, and backpack around. Comfortable **accommodation** in town includes the inexpensive *Hôtel du Centre* (☎76.95.14.12; ②), the *Hôtel le Gerbier* (☎76.95.10.50; ③), and the smart *Hôtel Le Pré Fleuri* (☎76.95.10.96; ④); the *Villa Primrose* (☎76.95.13.17; ③) offers a particularly warm welcome and self-catering facilities. There are two other good, though more strenuous, walks described in *CIMES* leaflets 6 (Villard-de-Lans to Claix, near Grenoble; 1700m descent; 7hr) and 11 (circuit of Mont Aiguille, starting from Clelles, 1hr by train south of Grenoble; 6hr 30min or 9hr).

By road through the Vercors

The Vercors Massif is very pretty and undeveloped, but the only way to get around, apart from walking, is to drive or hitch. To get started, take the #11/14 trolley just off place Victor-Hugo to *Sassenage Air Liquide* and get off at *La Rollandière,* one stop before the terminus. Start hitching on the road to **LANS-EN-VERCORS**, more or less opposite the stop. The road winds up through a steep wooded gorge before coming out into a wide valley full of hay meadows towards Lans and **VILLARD**. Turn right at Villard on the Pont-en-Royans road into the **Gorges de la Bourne**. The gorge becomes rapidly deeper and narrower with the road cut right in under the rocks, the river running far below, and tree-hung cliffs almost shutting out the sky above. Take a left fork here and climb up to a lovely green valley before descending to St-Martin and **LA CHAPELLE**, where there's the reasonably priced *Hôtel du Nord* (☎75.48.22.14; ②), and the *Maison de l'Aventure* hostel (①); thence the road climbs again to the wide dry **plateau of Vassieux**, bordered to the east by a rocky ridge rising from thick pine forest and to the west by low hills covered with scrubby vegetation.

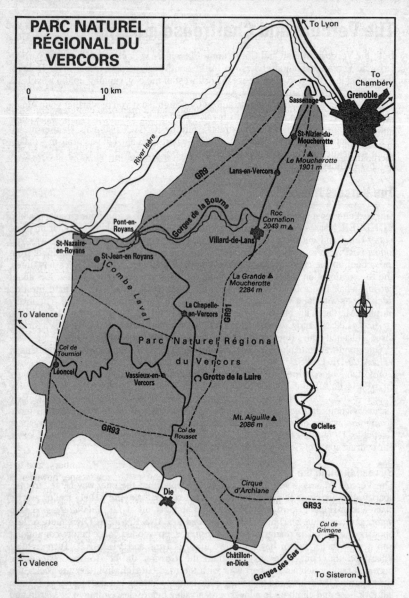

PARC NATUREL RÉGIONAL DU VERCORS

0 — 10 km

To Lyon

To Chambéry

Grenoble

Sassenage

River Isère

St-Nizier-du-Moucherotte

GR9

Le Moucherotte 1901 m

Lans-en-Vercors

Gorges de la Bourne

Roc Cornafion 2049 m ▲

Pont-en-Royans

Villard-de-Lans

St-Nazaire-en-Royans

St-Jean-en-Royans

Combe Laval

La Grande Moucherotte 2284 m ▲

La Chapelle-en-Vercors

To Valence

Col de Tourniol

Parc Naturel Régional du Vercors

Léoncel

Vassieux-en-Vercors

Grotte de la Luire

Mt. Aiguille ▲ 2086 m

Clelles

GR93

Col de Rousset

Die

Cirque d'Archiane

GR93

Col de Grimone

To Valence

Châtillon-en-Diois

Gorges des Gas

To Sisteron

Vassieux

It was around the village of **VASSIEUX**, 10km south of La Chapelle, that the fighters of the Vercors *maquis* suffered a bloody and bitter defeat at the hands of the SS in July 1944. During 1942–43 they had been gradually turning the Vercors into a Resistance stronghold, to the annoyance of the Germans who finally, in June 1944, decided to wipe them out. They encircled and attacked the *maquisards* with vastly superior forces and parachuted an SS division on to Vassieux. The French appealed in vain for Allied support and were very bitter about the lack of response. The Germans took vicious reprisals, and despite their attempts to disperse into the woods, 700 *maquisards* and civilians were killed and several villages razed. The Germans' most ferocious act was to murder the wounded, along with their nurses and doctors, in the **Grotte de la Liure**, a cave off the La Chapelle–Col de Rousset road.

Vassieux itself, a dull little village now rebuilt, has a memorial cemetery and small **Musée de la Résistance du Vercors** (April–Oct 9am–6pm; free), with documents, photos and other memorabilia to do with the *maquis* and the battle. In the field outside are the remains of two gliders used by the German paratroops. If you wanted to **stay** here, there's a *gîte d'étape* (Mme Chapays) or the basic but comfortable *Hôtel La Cornefine* by the roundabout (☎75.48.28.57; ①).

Die to Grimone

From Vassieux, the **Col de Rousset** road winds south through 8km of woods of pine and fir before taking the final steep twisting descent of 10km to **DIE**, with terrific views of the white crags and pinnacles of the southeast end of the massif. Although an attractive little place, Die is worth no more than a brief stop. Its most alluring feature is the bubbly white wine it produces, Clairette de Die. If you do plan to **stay** the night here, there is a **camping municipal**, or the *Hôtel St-Dominique* (☎75.22.03.08; ②).

Six kilometres south along the River Drôme at the **Pont de Quart** the road forks left for **CHÂTILLON**, 6km away – not a bad place to wait on a hot day, for you can swim in the river below the bridge. Châtillon village is lovely, lying in a narrowing valley bottom surrounded by apple and peach orchards, vineyards, walnut trees and fields of lavender; it also has a couple of good **hotels** and a **camping municipal**.

From here on, the road enters the sunless trench of the **Gorges des Gats**, winding up between sheer rock walls to **GRIMONE**, a mountain hamlet on the flanks of a grassy valley with fir trees darkening the higher slopes. The **Col de Grimone** is visible above the village. A path cuts across the valley directly to the col. From the col, it's about 7km down to the main Grenoble road, a tarmac trudge alleviated by the view eastwards to the mountains.

The Chartreuse Massif and Grande Chartreuse monastery

The **Chartreuse Massif** stretches north from Grenoble towards Chambéry, and like Vercors, it is not easy to visit without your own vehicle. The landscape, however, is spectacular: precipitous limestone peaks, mountain pastures and thick forest. The **Grande Chartreuse monastery**, the main local landmark, lies up the narrow Gorges des Guiers Mort, southeast of St-Laurent-du-Port. It is not open to visitors, though there is a **museum** nearby at **LA CORRERIE**, illustrating the life of the Carthusian order to which the monastery belongs (April–Sept Mon–Sat 9am–noon & 2–5.30pm; bus to Voiron, where the *Caves de la Grande Chartreuse* offer a free visit and tasting of the sticky yellow or green liqueur).

Just south of St-Pierre, at the gorge's eastern end, a narrow road leads a couple of kilometres south to the village of **ST-HUGUES**. Its otherwise ordinary-looking **church of St-Hugues** (daily except Tues 9am–noon & 2–7pm; free) has been transformed inside by local artist Jean-Marie Pirot (aka Arcabas), who was originally commissioned to redecorate the interior in 1953 and ended up making it his life's work. His paintings, tapestries, statues and, most notably, the stained glass make an unusual and striking impression and have earned Arcabas and the church a world-wide reputation.

Chambéry

CHAMBÉRY, 55km north of Grenoble, lies just south of the Lac du Bourget in a valley separating the Chartreuse Massif from the Bauges mountains: historically, an important strategic position commanding the entrance to the big Alpine valleys leading to the passes into Italy. The earliest settlement was on the rock of Lemenc, behind the train station, and the church of St-Pierre-de-Lemenc, off bd de Lemenc, hides a sixth-century baptistery in its crypt.

The present town grew up around the château built by Count Thomas of Savoie in 1232, when Chambéry became capital of the ancient province, and flourished particularly in the fourteenth century. Although superseded as capital by Turin in 1563, it remained an important commercial and cultural centre and the emotional focus of all French Savoyards: "the winter residence of almost all the nobility of Savoy", Arthur Young reported in 1789, before its mid-nineteenth-century incorporation into France.

The Town

Halfway down the broad, leafy bd de la Colonne is the splendidly extravagant **Fontaine des Éléphants**, with the heads and shoulders of four large bronze elephants projecting from a stone pediment supporting a tall column, on top of which stands a statue of Comte de Boigne, a native son who made a fortune in the French East India Company in the eighteenth century and spent some of it on his home town. Past this, on the right, and you're at the **Musée Savoisien**, square de Lannoy-de-Bissy (daily 10am–noon & 2–6pm; closed Tues; 10F), which records the lost rural life of the Savoyard mountain communities. On the first floor are some very lovely paintings by Savoyard primitives and painted wood statues from various churches in the region; up above are tools, carts, hay-sledges, old photos, and some very fine furniture from a house in Bessans, including a fascinating kitchen range made of wood and lined with *lauzes* – slabs of schist.

Next to the museum, in the enclosed little place Métropole, the **cathedral** has a handsome, though much restored, Flamboyant façade. The inside is painted in elaborate nineteenth-century *trompe l'œil*, imitating the twisting shapes and whorls of the Flamboyant style. During the Revolution it became the seat of the National Assembly of the Allobroges in a Revolutionary attempt to revive pre-Roman tribal identity.

A passage leads from the square to **rue de la Croix-d'Or**, with numerous restaurants and, to the right, the long, rectangular **place St-Léger**, with a fountain and more cafés, forming the hub of the city's social life, where street musicians and players perform on summer evenings. Rousseau and Mme de Warens lived here in 1735, and also had a country cottage, *Les Charmettes*, just 2km south of the town on the rustic chemin des Charmettes. It's now a small **museum** (daily 10am–noon & 2–6pm; Oct–March 10am–noon & 2–4.30pm; closed Tues; 10F), containing personal possessions of the famous couple.

Towards the further end of the square, the town's smartest street, **rue de Boigne**, leads back to the Elephant Fountain. Past this intersection, on the left, a narrow medieval lane, rue Basse-du-Château, brings you out beneath the elegant apse of the **Ste-Chapelle**, the castle chapel, whose lancet windows and star vaulting are the building's best feature. It was built to house the Holy Shroud, that much-venerated and today highly controversial piece of linen brought back from the Crusades and reputed to bear the image of the dead Christ. The dukes took it with them to Turin, where it still lies in the cathedral. The entrance to the **château** (guided tours: 5 daily in July & Aug; 2 daily June & Sept; March–May, Oct & Nov Sat 2.15pm, Sun 3.30pm; 20F) is on the left. A massive and imposing structure, it was the home of the dukes of Savoie until they transferred to Turin, and is now occupied by the *préfecture*, although you can still visit the fine chapel.

Practicalities

The **gare SNCF** is on rue Sommeiller, 500m north of the old town, with the **gare routière** just outside in place de la Gare. Five minutes' walk away on tree-lined bd de la Colonne, where all the **city buses** stop, is the **tourist office** at no. 24 (Mon–Sat 9am–noon & 2–6pm; ☎79.33.42.47).

If you're **staying**, inexpensive accommodation is not hard to find. Try the *Hôtel du Château*, 37 rue Jean-Pierre Veyrat (☎79.69.48.78; ①); the *Home Savoyard*, 15 pl St-Léger (☎79.33.47.80; ②); or *Les Voyageurs*, 3 rue Doppet (☎79.33.57.00; ①). More expensive are the *Revard*, 41 av de la Boisse (☎79.62.04.64; ③), and the *Hôtel les Princes*, 4 rue de Boigne (☎79.33.45.36; ③–④). But for rural peace and a lovely view there's no better than the *Hôtel aux Pervenches* (☎79.33.34.26; ②), next to Rousseau's house in the village of **LES CHARMETTES**, 2km south of the centre. For **hostel** beds, try the *Maison des Jeunes et de la Culture*, 311 Faubourg-Montmélian (☎75.75.13.23; ①). The nearest **campsite** is *Camping Nivolet* (☎79.33.19.48) at **BASSENS**, reached on bus *ligne C*, direction *Albertville*, from the tourist office.

You'll find good **food** at restaurants and cheap pizzerias around the rue de la Croix-d'Or, with both the *Restaurant La Tête de Lard*, 99 rue Juiverie (closed Sun & Mon), and the *Café chez Chabert*, 7 rue Basse-du-Château, offering menus from 65F, and the *Restaurant Vanoise*, 44 rue Pierre-Lanfrey, offering as fine a meal as you'll find in town, with menus between 90F and 170F, and a terrace during summertime.

Annecy

At the edge of the turquoise Lac d'Annecy and bounded to the east by the turreted peaks of La Tournette and to the west by the long wooded ridge of Le Semnoz, **ANNECY** is one of the most popular resort towns of the French Alps. Historically, Annecy enjoyed a brief flurry of importance in the early sixteenth century, when Geneva opted for the Reformation and the fugitive Catholic bishop decamped here with a train of ecclesiastics and a prosperous, cultivated elite.

The Town

The most interesting part of Annecy lies at the foot of the castle mound, a warren of lanes, passages and arcaded houses, below and between which flow branches of the **Canal du Thiou**, draining the lake into the River Fier. The houses, canal-side railings and numerous restaurants and cafés are stacked with displays of geraniums and petunias – picture-book pretty and inevitably full of tourists.

From rue de l'Îsle on the canal's south bank, the narrow Rampe du Château leads up to the **château**, former home of the counts of Genevois and the dukes of Nemours, a junior branch of the house of Savoy. There has been a castle on this site from the eleventh century. The Nemours, finding the old fortress too rough and unpolished for their taste, added living quarters in the sixteenth century, which now house the miscellaneous collections of the **Musée du Château** (daily except Tues 10am–noon & 2–6pm; 10F), with archeological finds from Roman Boutae, Bronze and Iron Age metallurgy with comparative photos of similar still-surviving skills like scythe- and axe-making, Savoyard popular art, furniture and wood carving, and an excellent display illustrating the geology of the Alps.

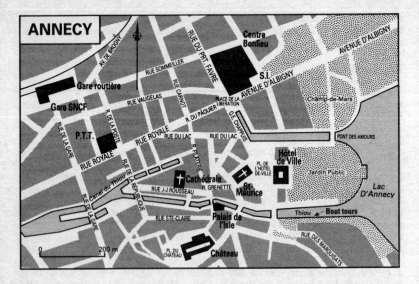

At the base of the château is **rue Ste-Claire**, the main street of the old town, with arcaded shops and houses. No. 18 is the **Hôtel Favre**, where in 1606 Antoine Favre, an eminent lawyer, and François de Sales founded the literary-intellectual *Académie Florimontane* "because the Muses thrive in the mountains of Savoie". At the west end of the street is its original medieval gateway. Down at the canalside, there is a good view back to the grand old **Palais de l'Îsle** (prison, mint and courtroom in its time) from the bridge.

On rue J-J Rousseau, running parallel to the canal, is the uninteresting Gothic **cathedral**, where Rousseau sang as a chorister; just past it is an eighteenth-century **bishop's palace**, now the police commissariat, built on the site of the house where Mme de Warens, Rousseau's lover, lived. The 16-year-old Rousseau, on the run from his miserable engraver's apprenticeship in Geneva, came to lodge with her on Palm Sunday 1728; she was 28. His admirers have placed his bust in the courtyard of the commissariat.

Five minutes' walk east is the **Hôtel de Ville**, backed by shady public gardens, leading to the lakeside lawns of the extensive **Champ de Mars**. Opposite the Hôtel de Ville is the fifteenth-century **church of St-Maurice**, originally built for a Dominican convent and dedicated to the commander of a Theban legion sent to put down a rebellion in the late third century; converted to Christianity, he and his soldiers refused to sacrifice to the pagan gods of Rome and were put to death for their scruples. Inside the church, the apse, with attractive Flamboyant windows, is badly distorted, the walls leaning outwards to an alarming degree; on the left of the choir is a fine fresco dated 1438, all in tones of grey.

Practicalities

The **gare SNCF** is northwest of the centre, five minutes' walk north of the rue Royale. The road's continuation is the arcaded **rue Paquier**, which contains the modern shopping precinct of **Centre Bonlieu**, housing the **tourist office** (Mon–Sat 9am–noon & 1.45–6.30pm, Sun 9am–noon & 3–6pm; July & Aug Mon–Sat 9am–6.30pm, Sun 9am–noon & 1.45–6.30pm; ☎50.45.00.33), which can help you find accommodation and will supply an excellent 1:50,000 map of the Annecy area, showing walking trails. There's **bike rental** from the *gare SNCF* and *Loca Sport*, 37 av de Loverchy, and **round-the-lake boat trips** stopping off at various points along the lake – expect to pay around 10F per hour – from *Compagnie des Bateaux* or *Bateaux Dupraz* by the mouth of the Thiou canal.

The best inexpensive **hotels** are the *Rives du Lac*, 6 rue des Marquisats (☎50.51.32.85; ①–②), and the *Central Hôtel*, 6 bis rue Royale (☎50.45.05.37; ①–②). For more upmarket options try the *Hôtel Alery*, 5 av d'Alery (☎50.45.24.75; ③), *Hôtel des Alpes*, 12 rue de la Poste (☎50.45.04.56; ③–④), or the *Hôtel du Château*, 16 rampe du Château (☎50.45.27.66; ③). The **youth hostel** is called *Grande Jeanne*, rte du Semnoz (☎50.45.33.19; ①), and is a good five-kilometre walk from the old town in a clearing by a small zoo, although a new location is expected to open in the town centre for 1995. There is a **camping municipal** off bd de la Corniche – turn right up the lane opposite Chemin du Tillier; it's on the left past the *Hôtel du Belvédère*. There are other sites all around the shore of the lake.

Among Annecy's many **restaurants**, the *Restaurant La Cave*, 10 faubourg des Annonciades, and the *Restaurant des Arts*, 4 passage de l'Isle, are both pleasantly situated in the heart of the old town and feature menus from 58F. Also nearby is the *Taverne du Fréti*, 12 rue Ste-Claire (closed Mon except July & Aug), which specializes in the region's cheeses and includes *raclettes*, a rather convoluted method of grilling and melting half-rounds of cheese to mouthwatering effect.

Around Annecy

While Annecy's high-season crowds may be bearable for only a day or two, the town's hinterland offers a number of agreeable ways to stretch your eyes and legs. As well as the **boat tours** mentioned (see above), cycling is an enjoyable means of appreciating Lac Annecy. The forty-kilometre road circuit of the lake is a very popular Sunday morning activity among sporty Annéciens and a traffic-free **cycle route** follows the west bank of the lake. The surrounding hills offer walking and mountain biking excursions (as well as more specialized pursuits) to suit all, with the ascent of **La Tournette** (2351m) filling a day and less demanding walks to be found in the forested **Semnoz Mountains** on the lake's west side.

Ten kilometres west of Annecy, the **Gorges du Fier** and nearby Château Montrottier combine both natural and historical spectacle within a short distance of each other, and if you're leaving Annecy to the north, the **Ponts de la Caille** are also worthy of a passing inspection.

Around the lake

Although a road rings Lake Annecy, a far more tranquil way of appreciating the lakeside is aboard one of the frequent boats that depart from Annecy's canalside port, with the possibility of stopovers or returning later in the day. The lakeside village of **MENTHON-ST-BERNARD** sits on the east shore. Signposted just out of Menthon-St-Bernard is the striking edifice of **Château de Menthon** (July & Aug daily noon–6pm; May, June & Sept, Thurs, Sat & Sun 2–6pm; 22F). Inhabited since the twelfth century and birthplace of Saint Bernard (the patron saint of mountaineers for having established hospices on the Franco–Swiss mountain passes which now bear his name), the fortress was extensively renovated in the last century in the romantic Gothic-revival style and possesses a fine collection of period furniture and views across the lake back to Annecy. By the lakeside, the *Buvette du Port* offers *plats du jour* for around 45F.

Likewise **TALLOIRES**, a couple of kilometres down the road, is a lovely little lake-side village and an ideal place to stop for a meal (or possibly the night) while undertaking a lakeside tour. Its ninth-century Benedictine abbey is now the *Hotel de l'Abbaye* (☎50.60.77.33; ⑥–⑧), one of the many comfortable and pricey seasonal hotels the village supports. Other slightly less extravagant establishments include the *Hôtel Charpenterie* (☎50.60.70.43; ③) or the *Villa Tranquille* (☎50.60.70.43; ④; June–Sept).

Returning to Annecy along the west side of the lake, the village of **DUINGT** inhabits a peninsula where there are two more thousand-year-old **châteaux**, one in ruins and the other partly rebuilt. Like Menthon-St-Bernard and Talloires, it boasts a lakeside beach and gives the opportunity to rent pleasure craft. The town has a few good-value hotels such as the *Hôtel Le Chalet* (☎50.68.66.51; ①); or for a slightly pricier and far more tranquil overnight stay, head 7km south to the village of **DOUSSARD**, where the *Hôtel Marceau*, 115 rue de la Chappelière (☎50.44.30.11; ⑤), offers very comfortable accommodation in attractive surroundings.

La Tournette and the Semnoz Mountains

For experienced hill walkers wanting to get their feet into a stiff but straightforward mountain ascent, **La Tournette** (2351m) dominates the east side of the lake with its patchy snowfields and crenellated summits, and can offer a full day's exercise as well as giddying views of Lac Annecy far below and eastwards to Mont Blanc. Better still, a road just north of Talliores crosses the **Col de la Forclaz**, after which a narrow road turns left before the hamlet of **MONTMIN**, ending in a steep but drivable track up to the **Col de l'Aulp**. Having gained 1400m of altitude, less than a thousand metres remain to the summit. From the col, the climb is immediate, steep and clear, leading to the **refuge**, where late snow and increasing exposure demand extra care. Some scrambling (with fixed chains and handrails) leads up to a broad, exposed shoulder where scree slopes are traversed leading, with a little more scrambling, to the summit. To the east, the **Chaîne des Aravis** stretches before the snowbound massif of Mont Blanc on the horizon, just 50km away, while in the other direction the turquoise lake and Annecy itself lie at your feet.

Facing La Tournette on the lake's opposite shore the wooded ridges of the **Semnoz Mountains** offer less radical hiking possibilities. From the village of Duingt, a four-hour walk leads southwards up the Taillefer ridge, involving just over 300m of ascent to the 765-metre summit of **Taillefer** itself. From the town church follow the signs for **Grotte de Notre Dame du Lac**, a steep walk up the ridge, and follow the red and yellow markers thereafter. Towards the summit of Taillefer, there is some scrambling, but nothing too difficult, and 1500m after the peak the path turns round and returns north via the hamlet of **LES MAISONS**.

The highest peak in the Semnoz is the **Crêt de Châtillon**, 16km directly south of Annecy along the D41. At 1699m it offers panoramic views, most impressively east past La Tournette towards Mont Blanc. A twenty-minute walk across meadows from the road's highest point leads to the cross on the summit and an orientation table pointing out the surrounding features. If you fancy spending the night here, the *Hôtel Semnoz Alpes 1704* (☎50.01.23.17; ②) is close to the summit.

The Gorges du Fier and Pont de la Caille

The River Fier, which trickles out of the lake through Annecy's picturesque canals, has cut a narrow crevice through the limestone rock at the **Gorges du Fier** (mid-March to mid-Oct daily 9am–noon & 2–6pm; mid-June to mid-Sept 9am–7pm; 22F). Signposted off the D14 at Lovagny, a footpath leads down into the 300-metre-long gorge which is traversed along a high-level walkway pinned to the gorgeside. As you pass by the gorge, you'll catch glimpses of the **Château de Montrollier** (guided visits: late March to mid-Oct 9–11.30am & 2–5.30pm; 25F), which can be reached by continuing along the path for another 3km or by road from the car park. The castle, which dates from the thirteenth century, possesses an eclectic collection of furniture, earthenware and lace as well as exotic objects from former French colonies in West Africa and the Far East, amassed during the last century by one Léon Mares.

Sixteen kilometres north of Annecy, just after the N201 Geneva road parts from the autoroute, the highway spectacularly bridges the gorge of the River Usses, 140m below. Known as the **Pont de la Caille**, the present bridge was built in 1925, at which time it possessed one of the longest single spans in Europe. Next to it is the stunning spectacle of the original bridge, built under the orders of the King of Sardinia, Charles Albert, in 1839, and now disused. Its castellated towers, supported by two dozen cables, are an impressive example of bold, mid-nineteenth-century engineering.

Parc Régional du Queyras

The train line from Grenoble to Gap seems an obvious approach to the **Parc Régional du Queyras**, spreading southeast of Briançon, a landscape that becomes increasingly Mediterranean in appearance, with low scrub covering the mountainsides, poor shallow soil and white friable rock. The train line first follows the **route Napoléon**, the road taken by the Emperor on his escape from Elba in 1815 (see also p.845), running through the town of **VIZILLE**, where there's a vast Renaissance **château**, now containing a museum of the French Revolution, with original uniforms, documents, flags and arms (Wed–Sun 9.30am–noon & 2–5/6pm; 20F). This was the meeting place in 1788 of the Estates of Grenoble, whose demand for liberty for all Frenchmen and suspension of parliament is often thought of as the catalyst for the French Revolution. Beyond Vizille the train line and road diverge, the road climbing steeply to the village of **LAFFREY**, where Napoléon, finding his way barred by troops from Grenoble, melodramatically threw open his coat, challenging: "Soldiers, I am your emperor! If anyone among you wishes to kill me, here I am!" The commanding officer ordered the soldiers to fire, but, instead, there were cries of *"Vive l'Empéreur!"*, and with his own party augmented by these soldiers, Napoléon went on to enter Grenoble in triumph. He wrote in his memoirs: "As far as Grenoble, I was merely an adventurer. At Grenoble, I became a prince."

The park has some good walking opportunities, with the **GR58** path making a circuit of the park, running through St-Véran and L'Échalp, and the **GR5** crossing through Avrieux and Ceillac on its way towards Briançon.

Embrun and Mont-Dauphin

EMBRUN, 26km south of Briançon, stands on a rock overlooking the huge artificial **Lake Serre-Ponçon**, now developed as a summer resort with campsites and windsurfing schools. It has been a fortress town for centuries. Hadrian made it the capital of the Maritime Alps, and from the third century to the Revolution it was the seat of an important archbishopric. The town's chief sight is its twelfth-century **cathedral**, with a porch in alternating courses of black and white marble in the Italian Lombard style, its roof supported on columns of pink marble resting on lions' backs – an arrangement that inspired numerous imitators throughout the region. The **tourist office**, in a former chapel of the Cordeliers (April–Sept daily 10am–noon & 2–5pm), doubles as a bureau for **mountain guides**, organizing a daily programme of walks in the surrounding mountains. There is an IYHF **hostel** at **SAVINES-LE-LAC**, where the road crosses the lake (☎92.44.20.16; ①).

Eighteen kilometres up the road you come to **MONT-DAUPHIN**, where **buses** leave for Ville-Vieille and St-Véran within the Queyras park. They meet the Paris–Briançon trains: the 7.40am bus going all the way to St-Véran (arriving 9.10am, every day except Sun throughout the year), others only as far as Ville-Vieille (the 4.55pm operates only in the summer season). It is, however, easy to get a lift in these parts; there are always climbers and hikers with transport. Mont-Dauphin itself is just a station, with – opposite – an abandoned but formidably bastioned village, one of many alpine fortifications designed by Vauban in the seventeenth century commanding the entrance to the valley of the Guil.

Guillestre and around

The road into the Queyras park follows the River Guil from Mont-Dauphin, through to the village of **GUILLESTRE**, its houses in typical Queyras style with open granaries on the upper floors, its church with a lion-porch emulating the cathedral at Embrun. You may want to **stay** here for the night: there are *Le Martinet* (☎92.45.00.28; ③) and the *Barnières* (☎92.45.04.87; ③), several **campsites** and an IYHF **youth hostel** in rte de la Gare (☎92.45.04.32; ①), with another one (☎92.46.50.39; ①; July 7–Sept 9) high up at the Col de Vars, 20km along the Barcelonnette road.

Northeast beyond the village, in the **Combe du Queyras**, the river gorge narrows to a claustrophobic crack with walls up to 400m high. Far below the road, the clear stream boils down over red and green rocks. It was only in this century that road-building techniques became sufficiently sophisticated to cope with these narrows. Previously they had to be circumvented by a detour over the adjacent heights.

Ville-Vieille and around

At the upper end of the Combe, the valley broadens briefly, and ahead you see the ruinous fort of **Château-Queyras** barring the way so completely that there is scarcely room for the road to squeeze around its base – Vauban at work again, though the original fortress was medieval. Just beyond is **VILLE-VIEILLE**, where the road for St-Véran branches right over the Guil and up the ravine of the Aigue Blanche torrent. A smaller place than Guillestre, it has only a few old houses still intact and a **church** with its square tower and octagonal steeple flanked by four short triangular pinnacles characteristic of this corner of the Alps. A Latin inscription in the porch says the church was destroyed in 1574 by the "impiety of the Calvinists" and restored by the "piety" of the Catholics. There is a painted sundial on the tower, which is also characteristic of the region.

Straight on, the road follows the Guil through the villages of Aiguilles, Abriés, La Monta (all with *gîtes d'étape*), to the **Belvédère du Viso**, close to the Italian border and **Monte Viso**, at 3841m the highest peak in the area. Above the Belvédère is the **Col de la Traversette**, where in 1480 the Marquis of Saluces drove a seventy-metre tunnel through the mountain. It has been reopened at various times through history, but is finally closed now.

East of L'Échalp, a variant of the **GR58**, which does the circuit of the park, climbs up to the **Col de la Croix**, used in former times by Italian peasants bringing their produce to market in Abriès. South of the village, the path climbs to the pastures of **Alpe de Médille**, where you can see across to Monte Viso, then on past the lakes of **Egourgéou**, **Bariche** and **Foréant** to **Col Vieux** and west to the **Refuge Agnel**; from here you can continue on to St-Véran.

St-Véran

At 2040m, **ST-VÉRAN** claims to be the highest permanently inhabited village in Europe. It lies on the east side of the valley of the Aigue Blanche torrent, backed by acres of steep lush mountain pasture, 7km south of Ville-Vieille. Opposite, rock walls and slopes of scree rise to snowy ridges. In the valley bottom and on any treeless patch

**PARC NATUREL
RÉGIONAL DU
QUEYRAS**

To Grenoble

To Névache

Sestrière

Col de
Montgenèvre

To Turin
& Milan

Briançon

0   10 km

ITALY

To Gap

GR5

Le Laus

Bric Froid
3302 m

Pic de
Rochebrune
3320 m

C. d'Izoard
2360 m

GR58

Casse
Déserte

Brunissard

La Chalp

Château-
Queyras

Abriès

River Guil

Arvieux

Ville Vieille

L'Echalp

To Briançon

Molines-en-Queyras

GR58

Grand Queyras
3114 m

GR5

Mt. Granero
3002 m

GR58

Mont-
Dauphin

St-Véran

Refuge
Agnel

Col Agnel

Combe du Queyras

Ceillac

Notre-Dame-
de-Clousis

Mt. Viso
3841 m

Guillestre

To Gap

Font Sancte
3385 m

ITALY

Col de Vars
2111 m

GR5

------- Grandes Randonnées (GR)
⌂ Mountain Refuge Hut or Gîte
▲ Mountain Peak

of ground, no matter how steep, you can see the remains of abandoned terraces. They were in use up until World War II, though, as with most high alpine villages, traditional farming activity has now practically died out. Today the principal economic activity is entertaining tourists.

The village's houses are part stone and part timber, and there are several refurbished old drinking fountains, made entirely of wood. The stone **church** stands prettily on the higher of the two "streets", its white tower silhouetted against the bare crags across the valley. The columns of its porch rest on crudely carved lions, one holding a man in its paws. The interior is surprisingly rich, with Baroque altars and retables.

Just south of the village, past a triple cross adorned with the instruments of Christ's passion and an inscription urging the passer-by to choose between the saintly and conventional or rebellious life (*"l'homme révolté qui n'est jamais content"*), the **GR58**, waymarked and easy to follow, turns right down to the river, beside which there are some good spots to **camp**. The path continues up the left bank through woods of pine and larch as far as the chapel of Notre-Dame-de-Clausis. There, above the timberline, it crosses to the right bank of the stream and winds up damp grassy slopes to the **Col de Chamoussière**, about three-and-a-half hours from St-Véran. The ridge to the right of the col marks the frontier with Italy. In the valley below, you can see the Refuge Agnel, about an hour away, with the **Pain de Sucre** (3208m) behind it. From there you can continue to L'Échalp (see above). In early July, there are glorious flowers in the meadows leading up to the col: violets, Black Vanilla Orchids, pinks and gentians.

There are several reasonable **hotels** in St-Véran, including the *Hôtel Étoile des Neiges* (☎92.45.82.19; ①), *Le Perce-Neige* (☎92.45.82.23; ①) and the *Hôtel Le Grand Tétras* (☎92.45.82.82; ③). There's also a **gîte d'étape** (☎92.45.83.96) and the *Refuge des Gabelous* (☎92.45.81.39; closed May & Sept 10–Dec 20). If you are feeding yourself, there are only two small shops and they have a tendency to run out of bread, fruit and vegetables.

Walking back down to Ville-Vieille takes about two-and-a-half hours. It's all road work save for an initial short-cut to **MOLINES**, but it's downhill and pretty. Molines and its neighbours **LA RUA** and **FONTGILLARDE** seem to have preserved their traditional rural character better than St-Véran, with well-kept houses and hay meadows still mown – there is nothing prettier than these little patches of alpine meadow, always steep and irregular in shape, full of wild flowers and neatly scythed by hand.

Queyras to Briançon

The direct route from Queyras to Briançon, crossing the 2360m **Col d'Izoard**, is a beautiful trip and saves backtracking to Mont-Dauphin – there are no buses along the route.

The road turns up right just west of Château-Queyras along a wooded ravine to the village of **ARVIEUX**, lying in a high valley surrounded by fields and meadows, just 16km from Briançon. A **church** with the characteristic tower and steeple stands guard at the entrance to the village. The **GR5** passes through, but if you want to **stay**, *Hôtel Casse Déserte* has dormitory accommodation (①). Further up the valley at **LA CHALP** and **BRUNISSARD** are **gîtes d'étape**.

Going up to the col, above the timberline, you cross the **Casse Déserte**, a wild, desolate region with huge screes running down off the peaks and weirdly eroded orangey rocks. From there the view extends over miles and miles of mountain landscape. On the other side, the road loops down through thick forest to **LE LAUS**, a cluster of old stone houses with long, sloping, wooden roofs set in meadows beside the stream, before swinging west into the deep valley of the Durance at Briançon, dominated by the vast **Massif des Écrins**.

Briançon and the Parc National des Écrins

Imposing and fortified, built on a rocky height overlooking the valleys of the Durance and Guisane, around 10km west of the Italian border, **BRIANÇON** guards the road to the desolate and windswept **Col de Montgenèvre**, one of the oldest and most important passes into Italy, marked by a column commemorating Napoléon's construction of the road. Originally a Gallic settlement, the town was fortified by the Romans to guard their *Mons Matrona* road from Milan to Vienne. During the Middle Ages, it was the capital of the *"république des escartons"*, a federation of mountain communities grouped together for mutual defence and the preservation of their liberties and privileges. But in marked contrast to the relatively untouristy Queyras, Briançon and the other towns and villages on this side of the Écrins park are crawling with people in summer.

The **old town**, mainly eighteenth century, is enclosed within another set of Vauban's walls. If you come in a car the best thing is to stop at the **Champ de Mars** at the top of the hill and look around from there otherwise you'll have to struggle up from the unprepossessing modern town that has grown up on the more accessible ground at the foot of the hill. You enter the walls by the **Porte Pignerol**. In front of you the narrow main street, bordered by ancient houses, tips steeply downhill. It is known as the *grande gargouille* because of the stream running down the middle. To your right is the sturdy, plain **church of Notre-Dame**, designed by Vauban, again with an eye to defence. Beyond it there is a fantastic **view** from the walls, especially on a clear starry night, when the snows on the surrounding barrier of mountains give off an icy, silvery glow. Vauban's **citadel** above the Porte Pignerol, the highest point of the fortifications, can be visited, but only as part of an organized tour (ask the tourist office).

Briançon's **tourist office** is by the Porte Pignerol (Mon–Sat 9am–noon & 1.30–6.30pm, Sun 9am–noon & 2–6pm; ☎92.21.08.50), and has a mountain guides' desk. For places to **stay**, try the *Hôtel aux Trois Chamois* in the Champs de Mars (☎92.21.02.29; ②–③), with obligatory *demi-pension* (full board July & Aug) – and the food is good. Alternatives in the old town include *Le Rustique* on rue Pont-d'Asfeld to the left of Grande-Rue (☎92.21.00.10; ②) and *L'Escale*, 59 Grande-Rue (☎92.21.00.69; ②). More expensive is the *Edelweiss* at 32 av de la République (☎92.21.02.94; ③), the main road down to the new town. There's a **youth hostel** at Serre-Chevalier (☎92.24.74.54; ①), behind the village of **LE BEZ**, 8km north on the main Grenoble road – hitchable and also served by local buses. The nearest **campsite** is *Camping la Schappe* (mid-June to mid-Sept) in the lower town at the end of rue Centrale, which starts opposite the tourist office. Turn left after the bridge on the Durance. There is also a *gîte d'étape* at **LE FONTENIL**, 2km along the Montgenèvre road.

As for **eating** options outside the hotels, there are plenty of reasonably priced restaurants in the town, such as *Le Pied de la Gargouille*, 64 Grande-Rue (closed Wed), opposite the library, or the *Restaurant Le Possé Simple*, 3 rue Porte-Meane (closed Sun evening & Mon), both with menus for around 65F. For a quick bite, there are also some *crêperies* at the top of Grande-Gargouille, the *Café du Centre* on place du Temple by the church, or the nearby *Entrecôte* in Porte Gargouille.

Névache

For a really beautiful day excursion from Briançon, head for the valley of the **River Clarée**. Without your own transport, you'll have to hitch or walk, but that should be no hardship because the scenery is truly magnificent.

Leave Briançon by the Montgenèvre road and take the left fork after two kilometres. A lane follows the wooded river bank in the bottom of a narrow ravine parallel to the Italian frontier. On foot you could follow the **GR5**, which passes through the main villages. If you want to spend a night up here, the depopulated and half-ruined hamlet of **PLAMPINET** has both hotel and hostel-type **accommodation** in a vast renovated farm, *La Cleida* (☎92.21.32.48; ①), as well as at the *Auberge de la Clarée* by the bridge (①). And there is more at **NÉVACHE**, where the valley widens. There's already been a good deal of holiday development here, though the old village nucleus of wide-roofed houses still huddles protectively around the **church** – this is worth a look for its carving, Baroque altarpiece, and a few items in the treasury, including some venerable, spiked eleventh-century doors. In addition to hotels, there are three **gîtes**: *Le Creux des Souches*, *Le Pontée* and *Paschalet*.

The finest country is beyond Névache towards the head of the valley, where in May the meadows are running with snow melt and carpeted with crocuses, and fat marmots whistle from the rocks. Six kilometres past the village, there are two **refuges** by the first bridge – *Fontcouverte* and *La Fruitière* – another at the end of the road, as well as a *CAF* refuge on the slopes of Mont Thabor, none of which are open for much more than the summer season.

The Parc National des Écrins

The **Parc National des Écrins** covers 93,000 hectares (230,000 acres) of alpine terrain, some 50km southeast of Grenoble, its highest peaks rising to around 4,100m in the **Massif de Pelvoux** in the north of the park. The usual approach to the park is from the train station at **Argentières-la-Bessée**, a scruffy, depressed little place, south of Briançon towards Mont-Dauphin. From here a small road cuts west into the valley towards **Vallouise**, with the ice-capped monster of **Mont Pelvoux** itself (3946m) rearing in front of you all the way. It's terrain for serious climbers and walkers.

To reach Écrins, it's best to set out from Grenoble by bus via Bourg-d'Oisans to Briançon.

The Vaudois and Les Vigneaux

From the train station of the unnoteworthy **ARGENTIÈRES-LA-BESSÉE**, the first village you reach is **LA BATIE**, where there are remains of the so-called **Mur des Vaudois**. Despite the name, the origins of the wall are uncertain. It was probably built either to keep out companies of marauding soldiers-turned-bandits, or to control the spread of plague in the fourteenth century. These Vaudois (Waldensians in English) are not to be confused with the inhabitants of the Swiss canton of Vaud. They were members of a religious sect, precursors of Protestantism, founded in the late twelfth century by Pierre Valdo, a merchant from Lyon, who preached against worldly wealth and the corruption of the clergy. Practising as he preached, he gave his wealth to the poor. Excommunicated in 1186, the Vaudois came more and more to deny the authority of the Church, and they sought refuge from persecution in the remote mountain valleys of Pelvoux, especially in the area around Vallouise and Argentières. Their numbers were also probably augmented by refugees from the Inquisition's persecutions of the Cathars in Languedoc.

There was a crop of executions for sorcery in the early fifteenth century, and many of the victims were probably Vaudois, burnt to death in wooden cabins built for this purpose. In 1488, Charles VIII launched a full-scale crusade against them. There is a spot west of Ailefroide, known as **Baume Chapelue**, where they were smoked out by the military and butchered. They were finally exterminated in the eighteenth century after the revocation of the Edict of Nantes, when 8000 troops went on the rampage, creating total desolation and "leaving neither people nor animals".

On the right, a couple of kilometres beyond La Batie, the village of **LES VIGNEAUX** shrugs off such a past: a lovely place, surrounded by apple orchards and backed by the fierce crags of Montbrison. The **church** has a fine old door and lock under a vaulted porch. Beside it on the exterior wall of the church are two bands of paintings depicting the Seven Deadly Sins. In the upper band, the sins are naive representations of men and women riding various beasts (a lion, hound and a monkey) and chained by the neck. A man carrying a leg of mutton and drinking wine from a flask represents gluttony; a woman with rouged cheeks, green stockings and displaying an enticing expanse of thigh represents lust. In the lower band they are all getting their comeuppance, writhing in the agonies of hell fire.

Vallouise

VALLOUISE lies under a steep wooded spur at the junction of two valleys, the Gyrond (or Gyr, as it is called upstream of Vallouise) and the Gérendoine, 13km southwest of Briançon. The great glaciered peaks visible up the latter valley are Les Bans; up in front still is Mont Pelvoux. The nucleus of the old village – narrow lanes between sombre stone chalets – is again its **church**, fifteenth century with a characteristic tower and steeple and a sixteenth-century porch on pink marble pillars. A fresco of the Adoration of the Magi adorns the tympanum above the door, itself magnificent with carved Gothic panels along the top and an ancient lock-and-bolt with a chimera's head at one end. Remains of an enormously long-legged figure, partially painted over, cover the end wall of the apse. Inside, as at Les Vigneaux, are more frescoes, including at the back of the church six naive statues on painted wood.

The **GR54,** which does the circuit of the Écrins park, passes through Vallouise; and the stage on from here to Le Monetier via **Lac de l'Eychauda** is one of the best. Another good walk is to the hamlet of **PUY AILLAUD**, high on the west flank of the Gyr Valley. The path starts just to the right of the church and zigzags up the steep slope behind it with almost aerial views of the valley beneath.

Vallouise has a **campsite** and **gîte d'étape**, and several **hotels**: the *Edelweiss* is the least expensive (③; Dec–April & July–Sept), but all rooms in the village are likely to be full in July and August. The Vallouise *Maison du Parc des Écrins* provides **hiking information**. There is a minibus service as far as Ailefroide in summer, starting from the bar next to the *Edelweiss* hotel; to walk takes two hours or so.

Ailefroide

AILEFROIDE, another 6km from Vallouise under the last slopes of Pelvoux, is also a major centre for climbers and walkers. There is a **Bureau des Guides**, and three **campsites**. A path follows the road on up the valley as far as the so-called **Pré de Madame Carle** by the old *Refuge Cézanne* (1hr 30min). In fact, it is not a meadow at all but a jumble of rocks brought down by the torrent from which you can see the **Barre des Écrins** towering above the Glacier Noir. At 4102m, this is the highest peak in the massif – and one of the major Alpine climbs. From the bridge another path runs north up to the **Refuge du Glacier Blanc** on the edge of the glacier at 2550m (about 2hr 30min). Anywhere beyond this on the **Pelvoux Massif** is snow and ice – strictly experienced climbers' territory.

Up the Romanche Valley

Coming into the mountains from Grenoble along the **N91**, you have various alternative approaches to the Parc des Écrins – and the possibility of a substantial two-day circuit between **La Grave** and **Le Casset**, a tiny hamlet just northwest of Le Monetier-les-Bains. The road itself is grand enough, twisting through the precipitous valley of the Romanche and up and over the 2058-metre **Col du Lautaret**, which is kept open all year round and served regularly by the Grenoble–Briançon bus.

La Bérarde and Le Bourg-d'Oisans

To reach **LA BÉRARDE**, right in the midst of the park's mightiest peaks at the end of the Vénéon Valley, you leave the road just after Le Bourg-d'Oisans (49km from Grenoble). A tiny hamlet and mountaineering centre 38km up a very narrow lane, La Bérarde has a *CAF* refuge, mountain rescue base and the small *Hôtel Tairraz* (☎76.79.53.46; ②; late May to late Sept). There are plenty of accessible valley walks without the need to risk your neck, including the approach to the back side of the magnificent, near-4000-metre bulk of **Le Meije**, with its dazzling square glacier, the **Glacier Carré**.

Although **LE BOURG-D'OISANS**, 20km southeast of Grenoble, is of no great interest in itself, it's a good place to catch your breath and pick up information from the **tourist office** on quai Girard, by the river in the middle of town (Mon–Sat 9am–noon & 2–6pm; ☎76.80.03.25) and the **park information centre** on av Gambetta (June–Aug Mon–Fri 10am–noon & 2–5pm). There are also numerous places to **stay**, with a **camp-**

SKIING THE ALPS: THE RESORTS

Skiing in the French Alps is based around resorts that are either purpose-built or have been ruthlessly modernized. It's a highly organized industry, and you can ski away from your front door in the morning and ski straight back at night, rarely having to queue much along the way. The downside is that these resorts offer little else. Many are astonishingly ugly functionalist brutes isolated in the middle of open snow fields – even worse if you see them in summer – which offer nothing in the way of après-ski and often little entertainment at all. There's certainly none of the alpine atmosphere here that you might associate with Austria, for example.

What you get instead at the best of the resorts is a series of vast linked territories with some of the best high-altitude skiing in Europe. At **Val d'Isère** or **Chamonix**, you can at least get some of the atmosphere of older-established resorts as well, though both are too large to be at all picturesque. Val d'Isère is very British-oriented in the ski season and one of the liveliest resorts in France, with a magnificent ski terrain linked to **Tignes** (among the ugliest of the resorts), and endless challenges and off-piste possibilities, plus impressive new facilities built for the Olympics – the downhill and other blue riband events were held here. Chamonix is bigger still, with even more going on, but as a place to ski is definitely less attractive – the local pass covers a wide area, but it's positively un-French in the lack of links between ski areas and relatively awkward transport. The other obvious choice is **Les Trois Vallées** – Courchevel, Méribel and Val Thorens/Les Menuires – which claims to be *"le plus grand domaine skiable du monde"*. This may be true, but it often seems less exciting than the Val d'Isère area: of the resorts, **Courchevel** (actually four separate villages at different heights) is the most glamorous; **Méribel**, in the central valley, is the best placed but full of British yuppies in season; **Val Thorens** and **Les Menuires** are the ugly ducklings in terms of both architecture and cachet. Of the smaller resorts, the pick are probably **Les Arcs**, cleverly designed with varied terrain but no walking at all; **Flaine**, especially good for beginners; **La Plagne**, one of the less ugly modern places with a vast area, though no great challenges; and **L'Alpes d'Huez** and **Valmorel**, among the newest and prettiest developments.

At any of these places you can simply turn up, buy a pass (90–200F a day, 450–800F a week) and rent equipment for a day. If you want to stay longer you'll almost certainly get a better deal by arranging a package before you leave – and accommodation can often be very hard to arrange on the spot.

ing municipal on rue Humbert near the town centre and a concentration of sites across the river on the L'Alpe d'Huez road. Among the better-value **hotels** to try are *Beau Rivage* (☎76.80.03.19; ③), with a good hotel-restaurant, the *Hôtel des Alpes* on the main road (☎76.80.00.16; ②), and the *Hôtel Le Florentin* on rue Thiers (☎76.80.01.61; ②–③). If you like the idea of cycling in sharp mountain air, **bikes** can be rented from *Cycles d'Oisans* on rue Viennois – not such a crazy undertaking as you might think, for if you keep to the valley bottoms, the gradients aren't too fearsome.

L'Alpe d'Huez

One place you're unlikely to be cycling to is the ski resort of **L'ALPE D'HUEZ**, signposted just outside Le Bourg. It is situated more than a vertical kilometre above the valley floor, and the eleven-kilometre road which crawls up the valley side has been a stage in the Tour de France for many years and features 21 hairpins, each individually numbered. As you ascend you get a fine view of the acutely crumpled strata of rock exposed by passing glaciers on the south side of the Romanche Valley. Undoubtedly a skier's paradise in winter, the purpose-built resort itself has little character in July and August, when it's only partially open. The extensive network of *télécabines*, extending as far as the 3327-metre **Pic du Lac Blanc**, at the bottom of the Chaîne des Rousses ridge north of the resort, does support some summertime skiing, but they can also be used to undertake some superb **high mountain walks**. Two recommended ones, detailed in the *Pathmaster* Dauphiné guide, are the eight-kilometre *Lac Blanc and Refuge de la Fare* walk, which winds through the bleak wilderness past the lakes encircling the Dôme des Petites Rousses to the east of the glacier-clad *chaîne*, or the less exposed ten-kilometre hike to the gorges of the Sarennes Valley to the east of the resort along the GR54. Both walks will require the *IGN* 3335 Est 1:50,000 map. A narrow and impressively scenic road through the Sarennes Valley also offers an alternative descent back to the Romanche Valley floor when the Col de Sarennes is free of snow.

Up the valley to La Grave and Valloire

A few kilometres out of Le Bourg, the ascent into the **Gorges de l'Infernet** commences as the slate-black valley walls close around you, broadening out again as you cross the Barrage du Lac du Chambon where roads diverge to the resort of Les Deux-Alpes and the Col de Sarennes to the north. Continuing towards La Grave you'll pass two waterfalls issuing from the north side of the valley: early summer run-off will enhance the slender, 300-metre plume of the **Cascade de la Pisse** and, 6km further on, a near-vertical cauldron of churning white water, the **Saut de la Pucelle**, gives practitioners of the new waterfall-abseiling craze something to think about.

LA GRAVE, 26km from Le Bourg at the foot of the Col du Lautaret, faces the majestic glaciers of the north side of 3983-metre **La Meije**. It's a good base for walking: the **GR54** climbs up to Le Chazelet on the slopes northwest of the village and continues to the **Plateau de Paris** and the **Lac Noir**, which numerous walkers recommend for its breathtaking views of La Meije. A similar and less energetic appreciation of these stunning vistas can be made by taking the **cable car** close to the 3200-metre summit of Le Rateau, just west of La Meije (late June to early Sept; 98F return), a 35-minute ride that's very good value for money when you consider the view of the barely accessible interior of the Écrins is normally seen by only the most intrepid mountain walkers. And from La Grave it's only 11km to the top of the col, with the still higher **Col du Galibier** just beyond. There is no public transport up Galibier, which is closed by snow from mid-October to mid-June.

The **Col du Lautaret** has been in use for centuries. The Roman road from Milan to Vienne crossed it, and its name comes from the small temple (*altaretum*) the Romans built to placate the deity of the mountains. They called it *"collis de altareto"*. Around the col is a huge expanse of meadow long known to botanists for its glorious variety of alpine flowers, seen at their best in mid-July. There is a **Jardin Alpin** right on the col, maintained by the University of Grenoble (July to mid-Sept daily 8am–noon & 2–6pm), which includes plants from mountain ranges throughout the world. This is a great spot for picnicking or lounging while waiting for a ride, for the view into the glaciers hanging off La Meije is intoxicating. Indeed, on a clear sunny day the dazzling luminosity of the ice and the burning intensity of the sky above are such that you can hardly bear to look.

The **Col du Galibier** is less frequented – a tremendous haul up to 2556m, utterly bare and wild, with the huge red-veined peak of the Grand Galibier rearing up on the right and a fearsome spiny ridge blocking the horizon beyond. The pass used to mark the frontier between France and Savoie, and you can see fine views of Mont Blanc to the north. A monument on the south side of the col commemorates Henri Desgranges, founder of the Tour de France. Crossing the col is one of the most gruelling stages in the race, with a long, brutal ascent and terrifying descent at breakneck speed. The road loops down in hairpin after hairpin, through **VALLOIRE**, a sizeable ski resort, whose church is one of the most richly decorated in Savoie, over the Col du Télégraphe at 1570m and down into the deep wooded valley of the Arc, known as **La Maurienne**, with the Massif de la Vanoise rising abruptly behind. Valloire has a **gîte d'étape** (☎79.59.01.54) and pleasant, reasonably priced **hotels** in *Les Gentianes* (☎79.59.03.66; ②), and the *Hôtel Christiania* (☎79.59.00.57; ③).

Le Casset

LE CASSET, back on the D28 just before Monetier-les-Bains, is a hamlet of dilapidated old houses clustered around a church with a bulbous dome. The site is superb: streams and meadows everywhere, reaching to the foot of the larch-covered mountain-sides, the Glacier du Casset imminent, white and dazzling above the green of the larches. The **GR54** goes through the village. A good day's walk is to follow it as far as the **Col d'Arsine**, about three hours, from which point you can either turn back or go on down to La Grave on the north side of the park, making an overnight stop at the *Refuge de l'Alpe* (①), below the col.

The path crosses the Guisane and follows a track through the woods, first on the left and later on the right bank of the Petit Tabuc stream. From the end of the track you cross some grassy clearings before entering the trees again and climbing up to a milky-looking lakelet, the **Lac de la Douche**, at the foot of the Glacier du Casset. From here a clear path zigzags up a very steep slope, coming out in a long valley and eventually leading to the Col d'Arsine. Masses of ground-hugging red rhododendrons grow along the banks of the stream. About halfway up are some tumbledown huts, the **Chalets d'Arsine**, by a series of blue-grey tarns. Up on the left are a whole series of glaciers. The biggest is the **Glacier d'Arsine**, hanging from the walls of the long jagged ridge suspended between the Montagne des Agneaux and the Pic de Neige Cordier to the west. Early in the morning there are colonies of marmots playing above the banks of the stream.

There are a **campsite** and **gîte d'étape** (☎92.24.45.74) near the church, with another (☎92.24.76.42) at neighbouring **LES BOUSSARDES**. But provided you choose a spot where the hay has already been mown it seems you can camp anywhere. There are a café and grocery store in the village, which in season is overcrowded. Other budget accommodation nearby includes a **gîte d'étape** (☎92.24.41.13) in **MONETIER** and the IHYF **youth hostel** at the ski resort of **SERRE-CHEVALIER** (☎92.24.74.54; ①), near the village of Le Bez (see p.765).

Parc National de la Vanoise

The **Parc National de la Vanoise** occupies the eastern end of the **Vanoise Massif**, the area contained between the upper valleys of the Isère and Arc rivers. It is extremely popular, with over 500km of marked paths, including the **GR5**, **GR55** and GTA (*Grande Traversée des Alpes*), with numerous refuges along the trails. For information on the spot, the tourist offices in **Modane**, **Val d'Isère** and **Bourg-St-Maurice** are helpful. The *Maison du Parc* at 135 rue St-Julien in Chambéry also gives advice and sells maps.

Access to the **Vanoise** park is easiest from Chambéry, with frequent trains to Modane.

Modane and the Arc Valley

MODANE, 32km due north of Briançon, is a dreary little place, destroyed by Allied bombing in 1943 and now little more than a rail junction. Nonetheless, it's a good kick-ing-off point for walkers on the south side of the park – easily accessible by train and with a well-sited grassy **camping municipal** just up the road to the Fréjus tunnel (which leads to Bardonecchia in Italy). If you're road weary, try the *Hôtel Bellevue*, 15 rue Replat (☎79.05.20.64; ②–③).

The **GR5** sets out from the northern edge of the transpontine section of Modane and leads up to the **Refuge de l'Orgère**, where a path joins up with the **GR55** leading north to Pralognan, over the **Col de la Vanoise** and right across the park to Val Claret on the Lac de Tignes – a tremendous walk. The GR5 itself keeps east of La Dent

Parrachée mountain, describing a great loop through the **Refuge d'Entre-Deux-Eaux**
before continuing up the north flank of the Arc Valley and over the Col de l'Iseran to
Val d'Isère. Southwest of Modane, you can continue along the GR5 to include the **Tour
de Mont Thabor**, a 6–8- day walk encircling the 3181-metre heights of Mont Thabor –
ask for details at the tourist office in Modane.

The Arc Valley

The **Arc Valley**, dark and enclosed below Modane, widens and lightens above it, with
meadows and patches of cultivation in the valley bottom and the lighter foliage of
larches gracing the mountainsides. It is hardly a joyous landscape, especially under a
stormy sky. Bare crags hang above the steep meadows on the north flanks, glaciers
threaten to the south and east. The villages, though attractive, are poor and humble
places, the houses squat and built of rough grey stone, the homes of people who have
had to struggle to wring a living from harsh weather and unyielding soil. It is surprising at first to find such a wealth of exuberant **Baroque art** in the outwardly simple
churches in small villages like Avrieux, Bramans, Termignon, Lanslevillard and

Bessans. But probably it is precisely because of the harshness and poverty of their lives that the mountain people sought to express their piety with such colourful vitality. Schools of local artists flourished, particularly in the seventeenth and eighteenth centuries, inspired and influenced by itinerant Italian artists who came and went across the adjacent frontier.

In **LANSLEBOURG**, 20km upstream of Modance, **Haute Maurienne Information** (☎79.05.90.02) organize tours of the churches in Avrieux, Bramans, Termignon, Lanslevillard and Bessans, all within a twenty-kilometre radius of each other along the Arc Valley. Lanslebourg is also the start of the climb to the **Mont Cenis pass** over to Susa in Italy, another ancient trans alpine route. Last stop before the perils of the trek, it was once a prosperous and thriving town. Relief at finishing the climb from the French side was tempered by an alarming descent *en ramasse*, a sort of crude sledge, which shot downhill at breakneck speed much to the alarm of travellers. "So fast you lose all sense and understanding", a terrified merchant from Douai recounted in 1518. Lanslebourg has a **campsite** and an IYHF **youth hostel** (☎79.05.90.96), or alternatively try the *Hôtel de la Vieille Poste* (☎79.05.93.07; ③).

BESSANS, further up the valley, retains its village character better than most. Its squat dwellings are built of rough stone with tiny window openings, and roofed with heavy slabs to withstand the long hard winters. Most have south-facing balconies to make the most of the sun and galleries under deep eaves for drying *grebons*, the bricks of cow dung and straw used locally for fuel. The **church** has a collection of seventeenth-century painted wooden statues and a retable, signed by Clappier. The Clappiers were a local family who produced several generations of artists. On the other side of the small cemetery, the **chapel of St-Antoine** has exterior murals of the Virtues and Deadly Sins and fine sixteenth-century frescoes; ask the priest to unlock the chapel – his house is on the right of the road leading east from the village square. Two kilometres up the road you pass the **chapel of Notre-Dame-des-Grâces** on the right, with another ex-voto by Jean Clappier. For **accommodation** try the *Hôtel Le Mont Iseran* (☎79.05.95.97; ③), or on the opposite side of the river, the hamlet of **LE VILLARON** has a *gîte d'étape*.

BONNEVAL-SUR-ARC, 10km upstream and 1835m above sea level, lies at the foot of the **Col de l'Iseran** in a rather bleaker setting close to the timberline. At the head of the Arc Valley to the east, you can see the huge glaciers of the **Sources de l'Arc**. Better preserved and more obviously picturesque than Bessans, Bonneval stops a lot of tourists on their way to and from the col. It is in danger of becoming twee, with its houses clustered tightly around the church, with only the narrowest of lanes between them. You sense how very isolated these places were until only a few years ago, cut off for months by heavy snow, forced in upon their own resources. Several graves in the churchyard record deaths by avalanche. For a place to **stay** in town, try *La Marmotte* (☎79.05.94.82; ④; late June to Sept).

Col de l'Iseran and Haute Tarentaise

As with all the other high alpine passes, the **Col de l'Iseran** has been used for centuries by local people. Despite the dangers of weather and the arduous climb, it was by far the quickest route between the remote upper valleys of the Arc and Isère. The volume of traffic was too small to disturb the nature of the tiny communities that eked out an existence on the approaches, but twentieth-century roads and the development of winter sports have changed all that. Small mountain communities have metamorphosed into monster modern developments, catering to an upmarket ski crowd.

From October to June, the pass is usually blocked by snow. But in summer, being the highest pass in the Alps (2770m), it is one of the sights that tourists with cars feel they must see; consequently it's relatively easy to hitch. A word of warning, though: if you do try, don't do it in light summer clothing, especially on a cool cloudy day, as temperatures can still hover around freezing point and blizzards are not unknown.

The climb begins above Bonneval (see opposite), with splendid views of the glaciers at the head of the Arc, and then follows the rocky gully of the Lenta stream through a narrow defile and out into a desolate cirque, where the Lenta rises and masses of anemones bloom in the stony ground. Behind the chalet on the col, a path climbs west to the **Pointe des Lessières** (round trip 2hr 30min), where on a clear day you have views of the Italian side of Mont Blanc and the whole of the frontier chain of peaks.

Val d'Isère and Tignes

VAL D'ISÈRE, at the foot of the col on the north side, can be reached by buses from Bourg-St-Maurice, 23km northwest, and makes a convenient centre for walking (details from the tourist office), but is no place to stay unless you're feeling extremely rich. Once a tiny mountain village, Val d'Isère has become a hideous agglomeration of cafés, supermarkets and apartments for skiers – with some of the finest skiing in Europe. There's a **campsite** on the edge of the resort at **LE LAISINANT** and an IYHF **youth hostel** (☎79.06.35.07; ①) about 12km away at **TIGNES**, an unattractive, purpose-built resort on the artificial Lac de Chevril. But thereafter the valley is lovely, deep and wooded, with villages perched on grassy shoulders high on either flank.

The Isère Valley

If you're interested in exploring the valley, make for the village of **LES BREVIÈRES**. Seven kilometres beyond, a lane turns left into the valley bottom to **LA SAVINAZ** and **LA GURRAZ**, whose creamy church tower is a landmark for miles around. High above, though looking dangerously close, the green ice cliffs that terminate the Glacier de la Gurraz hang off the edge of **Mont Pourri** (3779m). From the turn, the lane veers steeply down through trees and hay meadows full of flowers, past ruined houses, to the river. The climb up the opposite bank is hard going, past impossibly steep fields. You take a right fork for La Gurraz across a rickety plank bridge in the jaws of a defile. It's about an hour's walk, once you're on the lane.

LA GURRAZ shouldn't disappoint you. Tiny and untouched by tourism, its dozen old houses have wide eaves and weathered balconies spread with sweet drying hay, and firewood stacked outside. The houses are all sited in the lee of a knoll for protection against the avalanches that come thundering off the glacier above, thousands of tons of snow and rock, almost sheer down into a cirque behind. If you are unlucky enough to be out of doors when an avalanche occurs, the blast knocks you off your feet and can even suffocate you. There are no provisions available, so bring your own. Other hamlets on the opposite flank of the valley are just interesting, the prettiest being **LE MONAL**, in the mouth of a small hanging valley, also accessible by car from **LA THUILE**, further along the Bourg-St-Maurice road.

From La Gurraz, a signposted path climbs to **Refuge de la Martin** in an hour and a half. It zigzags up the slope behind the village of La Savinaz, on to a spur by a ruined chalet, where a right-hand path goes up the rocks overhead to the edge of the glacier. The refuge path continues left along the side of a deep gully, whose flanks are thick with the white St Bruno's lily. It crosses a ferocious torrent by a plank bridge and follows a mule track up to the mountain pastures by the refuge, where cows and sheep graze. The **Mont Pourri glaciers** are directly above. Opposite is the big **Glacier de la Sassière** and up to your right Val d'Isère, with the Col de l'Iseran behind.

Bourg-St-Maurice

If you continue down the valley, **BOURG-ST-MAURICE** is the midpoint of the Tarentaise, and although of little interest itself, it can be a useful place to stop. The big purpose-built ski resorts of **LES ARCS** and **LA PLAGNE** are nearby and the classic pass into the Italian Val d'Aosta, the **Col du Petit St-Bernard**, right behind. With its Swiss twin, the Grand St-Bernard, it was the only route around the Mont Blanc massif until the tunnel was opened in 1965. It's a rather spooky crossing, reaching a height of 2188m, with a couple of barrack-like buildings and a row of stat-ues of St Bernard. It's at its most dramatic when you're coming over from the Italian side in the early evening, right into the eye of the setting sun. (There is one daily bus crossing in July and August.)

There are no very appealing **places to stay** in the town. It's best to look on Grande-Rue, the old main street, where you could try the *Hôtel du Centre* (☎79.07.05.13; ②–③) or the slightly more expensive *Vallée de l'Arc* (☎79.07.04.12; ②). There are other places on the dreary main road, av Leclerc, where you'll also find the **gares SNCF** and **routière**, with the **tourist office** almost opposite (Mon–Sat 10am–noon & 2–5.30pm). The town's **campsite**, *Camping le Versoyen*, is in rte des Arcs (☎79.07.03.45), on the right past the sports ground on the Val d'Isère road.

Towards Chambéry

Heading west towards Chambéry, there are a couple of places worth a brief stop. The first is the alpine village of **AIME**, 6km from Bourg-St-Maurice, whose main Grande-Rue presents a pretty and little-spoilt succession of buildings. Its principal sight is the rough stone **church of St-Martin**, whose origins go back to a first-century Roman temple, swept away by the Isère in the third century – an indication of how dangerous these mountain rivers could be in the days before flood control. What survives today is basically early Romanesque.

The other place that rewards a brief detour is **CONFLANS**, a small medieval town on a spur overlooking grim, modern **ALBERTVILLE** (centre of the 1992 winter Olympics), and rather too cutely revived for its own good. From the public garden by the Tour Sarrazine, you can contemplate the contrast in town planning styles: spreading below are gaunt, rectangular blocks of apartments separated by rushing highways, against a steep backdrop of verdant slopes, vineyard terraces and hay meadows.

Mont Blanc

Mont Blanc, right on the Italian border, is the biggest tourist draw in the Alps, but so spectacular it's worth seeing despite the crowds. If you're going to walk in the area, you soon get away from most of the visitors. Annecy is the easiest place to approach the mountain from, and, of the two road routes, the one via the old ski resort of Megève is the more interesting.

The mountain was first climbed in 1786 by Dr Paccard and Jacques Balmat, both natives of Chamonix inspired by the offer of a reward by de Saussure, a Genevan natu-ralist. Alpine exploration and climbing developed quickly in the nineteenth century, although early techniques were primitive and very dangerous: even when guides began to use rope at all, they did not rope themselves to their parties. When Edward Whymper, one of the most renowned alpinists of the age, made the first successful ascent of the Matterhorn in 1865, his party lost four members because the old, worn piece of rope they casually attached themselves to simply snapped.

The two main approach roads to the "Blonk" – as English climbers insist on call-ing the mountain – come together at Le Fayet, where the **tramway du Mont Blanc** begins its 75-minute haul to the **Nid d'Aigle**, a vantage point on the northwest slope. Chamonix-Mont Blanc, the base camp for all Mont Blanc activities, is just 30km further on.

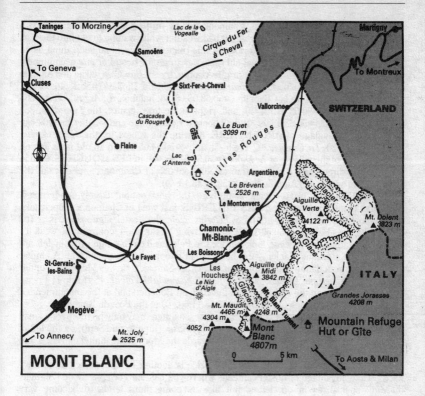

MONT BLANC

Chamonix-Mont Blanc

While **CHAMONIX** may have long since had its village identity submerged in a sprawl of tourist development, the glaring snowfields, eerie green glaciers and ridges of shark-toothed *aiguilles* surrounding Mont Blanc are nothing less than outstanding. The town itself is of little or no interest while being extremely expensive, and it crawls with tourists in the high summer season. The **Musée Alpin** off av Michel-Croz in the town centre (June–Sept daily 2–7pm; Christmas–Easter 3–7pm; free) will interest mountaineers, but is not as exciting as you would expect; among various bits of equipment, documents and letters is Jacques Balmat's account of his first ascent of Mont Blanc, written in almost phonetically spelled French.

Practicalities

The **tourist office** in Chamonix is at 45 place du Triangle de l'Amitié (daily summer 8.30am–7.30pm; winter 8.30am–12.30pm & 2–7pm; ☎50.53.23.33) and can help with booking accommodation. For up-to-the minute **walking and climbing information**, consult the tourist office or the nearby *Maison de la Montagne* (☎50.53.03.40), which also houses the *Bureau des Guides, Office de Haute Montagne* and a meteorological service. The tourist office also publishes a large-scale **map of summer walks** in the area, while the guides run rock- and ice-climbing schools and will, if you wish, accompany you on any expedition they reckon is within your capabilities.

One of the biggest headaches in Chamonix can be **finding a bed**, especially if, as a walker or climber, you're having to sit out bad weather while waiting to get into the hills – the weather in Chamonix is notorious in this respect. There is no such thing as an inexpensive hotel, and the only real alternative is to go for hostel or *gîte* accommodation, of which there is a fair supply. For **gîte rooms**, try *Au Bon Coin*, 80 av de l'Aiguille du Midi (☎50.53.15.67; ②), *Les Planards*, 161 chemin du Biollay (☎50.53.46.86; ③), *Simond et Golf*, 14 rue de la Chapelle (☎50.53.06.08; ②; half-board), *Aiguille Verte*, 683 rue Joseph-Vallot (☎50.53.01.73; ②), and, right in the town centre, the *Lion d'Or*, 255 rue du Dr-Paccard (☎50.53.15.09; ②; half-board). Better value and smaller crowds can be found in the village of **ARGENTIÈRE**, 8km up the valley: try the *Hôtel Carrier* (☎50.54.02.16; ②), *La Boerne*, 292 Tré-le-Champ (☎50.54.05.14), in an old farm just on the Swiss side of the village, or *Le Dahu* (☎50.54.01.55; ②); in **LES HOUCHES**, 5km in the opposite direction – a rather drab satellite suburb of Chamonix – check out the *Hôtel Bel'Alp* on rue de l'Aiguille Vert (☎50.54.43.13; ③).

The IYHF **youth hostel** itself is perhaps the best option; largely modernized, comfortable and friendly, it's at **LES PÈLERINS**, just west of Chamonix proper; take the bus to Les Houches and get off at *Pèlerins École*: the hostel, signposted, is at 103 Montée Jacques-Balmat (☎50.53.14.52; ①). Arriving by car or on foot from the west, it's very easy to miss the turning: look out for the Pèlerins-d'en-Bas sign on your left not long after the Bossons glacier – the hostel road is opposite, on your right. A similar grade of accommodation can be found at *Chalet Ski-Station*, 6 rte des Moussoux, under the Brévent *téléférique* (☎50.53.20.25; ①); *Le Chamoniard Volant*, 45 rte de la Frasse (☎50.53.14.09; ①) on the right towards the Bois du Bouchet; and at the recommended *La Montagne*, 789 pde des Crémeries (☎50.53.11.60; ①) in the Bois du Bouchet.

Campsites are numerous, though in high season there may only be room for a small mountain tent. Two convenient sites are *Les Molliases* (June to mid-Sept), on the left of the main road going west from Chamonix towards the Mont Blanc tunnel entrance, and *Les Rosières* (year round) off the rte des Praz.

Getting a square **meal** at an affordable price is another of Chamonix's little drawbacks. Take advantage of hostel canteens where you can. *La Poêle*, 79 av de l'Aiguille-du-Midi, specializes in omelettes, but like its competitors tends to become very crowded. *Le Fer à Cheval* on place du Mont-Blanc is a treat and its prices for *fondues* are very reasonable in spite of its desperate popularity. There are sandwiches and baps at *La Belouga*, 56 rue Paccard, standard *brasserie* fare at the *Brasserie des Sports* in rue Joseph-Vallot just past the *Marché U* supermarket, and a self-service cafeteria, *Le Grillandain*, in av Mont-Blanc (11am–10pm). Once, at least, you should take a look at *Le Choucas* right in the centre of town, opposite the *Casino* supermarket in rue Paccard, the hang-out of the climbers when they're not celebrating their successes at the *Wild Wallabies* bar in rue de la Tour.

Around Chamonix

There are two touristy things to do around Chamonix that in other circumstances you might baulk at. Here, though, if you don't do them there is not much else, unless you're an experienced walker or climber. The first is to take the **rack railway** from the Gare du Montenvers through the pine woods up to the vast glacier known as the **Mer de Glace** (trains every 20 min 8am–6pm in July & Aug, other times hourly 9am–5pm; closed mid-Nov to mid-Dec; 45F), a favourite with Victorian travellers. Once you get there you have the option of taking a short cable-car ride down into the **ice cave** carved out of the Mer de Glace every year, or – best of all – taking the very expensive *téléférique* (20min; summer daily from 7am; return 160F) to the **Aiguille du Midi** (3842m): even if mountains don't excite you, you won't regret the outlay. The ascent is still one of the longest cable-car ascents in the world, rising no less than 3,000 metres above the valley floor in two impossibly steep stages – and penny-pinching by buying a ticket only as far as the Plan du Midi, which is used principally by climbers heading up to the routes on the Aiguilles du Chamonix, is a waste of money: go all the way or not at all. If you do go up, make the effort to go before 9am, as all over the Alps the summits tend to cloud over towards midday and huge crowds may force you to wait for hours if you go up later. Take warm clothes, as even on a summer day it will be well below zero on the top. You need a steady head, too; the drop beneath the little bubble of steel and glass is truly appalling.

The Aiguille is a terrifyingly exposed granite pinnacle on which the *téléférique* docks and a restaurant is precariously balanced. The view is incredible. At your feet is the snowy plateau of the **Col du Midi**, with the glaciers of the Vallée Blanche and Géant crawling off left at their millennial pace. To the right a steep snowfield leads to the easy ridge route to the summit with its cap of ice (4807m).

Away to the front, rank upon rank of snow-and-ice-capped monsters recede into the distance. Most impressive of all, closing the horizon to your left, from the east to south, is a mind-blowing cirque of needle-sharp peaks and precipitous cliffs: the Aiguille Verte, Triollet, the Jorasses, with the Matterhorn and Monte Rosa visible in the far distance across a glorious landscape of rock, snow and cloud-filled valleys – the lethal testing-ground of all truly crazed climbers.

Chamonix Valley: some hikes

Opposite Mont Blanc, the north side of Chamonix Valley is enclosed by the lower but nonetheless impressive **Aiguilles Rouges**, with another *téléférique* to Le Brévent (15min), the 2525-metre peak directly above the town. Classic walks this side of the valley include the **Lac Blanc**, starting from Les Praz and the Flégère *téléférique* (20min), and the **Grand** and **Petit Balcon Sud** trails, giving spectacular views of Mont Blanc. A highly recommended **two-day hike** is the **GR5** stage north from Le Brévent to the village of **Sixt** (see below) via **Lac d'Anterne**, with a night at the **Refuge d'Anterne**. The classic long-distance route is the two-week **Tour du Mont Blanc** (TMB), described in a *Topoguide*, Andrew Harvey's *Tour of Mont Blanc* and *Chamonix-Mont Blanc: A Walker's Guide* – see p.1005.

Northern pre-Alps: the Cirque du Fer-à-Cheval

The **Northern pre-Alps**, climbing back from the shore of Lake Geneva, are cooler, softer and greener country than the rest of the Alps. They are less well known than the mightier ranges further south and consequently are a lot less crowded. For walkers, there's considerable potential – the only real problem is access off the main routes. To get into the **Giffre Valley**, with its **Fer-à-Cheval** hikers' circuit, you need to hitch or bus over to Taninges and thence to **Samoëns** and **Sixt**.

Samoëns

The gentle and attractive village of **SAMOËNS**, 21km from Cluses, lies at the foot of the Aiguille de Criou, with the tall peak of Le Buet in the distance. Its principal architectural claim to fame is its very late Gothic **church** on a Romanesque base, with a doorway of crouching lions like those in the Queyras. Built in the sixteenth century, it was already well behind its times, given that the Renaissance was in full swing elsewhere – although this architectural conservatism is very much a pattern in remote alpine valleys.

The village is chiefly known for its stonemasons and for Marie-Louise Cognacq-Jay, who left to seek her fortune in Paris at the age of fifteen in 1853, and found it – as the founder of the famous French department store, *La Samaritaine*. Hers was an exceptional success but was part of the pattern of local life: up to World War I the men of the village would set out every spring with their tools on their backs to seek work in the cities of France and Switzerland. Their guild, *les frahans*, evolved its own peculiar dialect, *le mourne*, so they could communicate secretly among themselves. There are a **campsite** and two **gîtes d'étape** in Samoëns – *Les Couadzous* (☎50.34.41.62), in the centre, and *Les Moulins*, 1km away on the road up to **LES ALLAMANDS**. For a **hotel**, try *Les Drugeres* (☎50.34.43.84; ③) or the *Gai Soleil* (☎50.34.40.74; ③) at the north end of town.

Sixt and the Cirque du Fer-à-Cheval

East of Samoëns, the valley narrows into the **Gorge des Tines** before opening out again at **SIXT**, 7km away, another pretty village on the confluence of two branches of the Giffre, the Giffre-Haut which comes down from Salvagny, and the Giffre-Bas which rises in the **Cirque du Fer-à-Cheval**.

The cirque begins about six kilometres from Sixt – there is a footpath along the left bank of the Giffre-Bas. It is a vast semicircle of rock walls, up to 700m in height and 4–5km long, blue with haze on a summer's day and striated with long, tumbling chains of white water from the waterfalls. The left-hand end of the cirque is dominated by a huge spike of rock known as the Goat's Horn, *La Corne du Chamois*. At its foot the valley of the Giffre bends sharply north to its source in the glaciers above the Fond de la Combe. The bowl of the cirque is thickly wooded except for a circular meadow in the middle where the road ends.

There are a **tourist office** and a **park office** in Sixt (both Mon–Sat 10am–noon & 2–5.30pm), though nowhere to buy provisions. The park office produces a folder of walks in the region – useful and well illustrated. They recommend, in particular, the walk to the **Refuge du Lac de la Vogeale** (3hr 30min); the **Chalets de Sales** via the spectacular **Cascade du Rouget** waterfalls on GR5 and GR96; and the GR5 stage to the **Lac d'Anterne**, and on to Le Brévent and Chamonix. Sixt also has a **gîte d'étape**, the *Auberge de Rouget* (②), and the *Hôtel Beau Site* (☎50.34.44.05; ②).

Évian and Lake Geneva

Some 60km north of Mont Blanc is the dolphin-shaped volume of **Lake Geneva** – Lac Léman to the French – forming a natural border with Switzerland. Around 70km long, 13km wide and an amazing 310m deep, the lake is fed and drained by the Rhône. It is a real inland sea, subject to violent storms, as Byron and Shelley discovered to their discomfort in 1816. On a calm day, though, sailing slowly across its silk-smooth surface is a serene experience. The most agreeable way to reach any of the lakeside towns is by boat across the lake from Geneva (3hr from Évian).

There probably isn't any point in visiting **ÉVIAN** unless you are a well-heeled invalid or gambler, except as the end of a pleasant, leisurely trip on the lake. The famous water is now bottled at Amphion, 3km along the lakeside, but the **Source Cachat** still bubbles away behind the Évian company's beautiful nineteenth-century offices, all wood, coloured glass, cupolas and patterned tiles. Anyone can go along and help themselves to spring water. The **waterfront** is elegantly laid out with squares of billiard-table grass, brilliant flowerbeds and trees. It is pretty, restful and not very exciting, like most spa towns. For a little distraction, there are daily ferries across the lake to Lausanne in Switzerland. For further information about things to do, ask the **tourist office** in place d'Allinges (Mon–Fri 8.30am–noon & 2–6.30pm; June–Sept also Sat & Sun 10am–noon & 3–6pm; ☎50.75.04.26).

If you stay, there is an IYHF **youth hostel** on av de Neuvecelle (☎50.75.35.87; ①) – the D21 towards Abondance – as well as several **hotels** that would make a somewhat larger hole in your budget, and one or two that may wipe it out completely. Two affordable options are the *Régina*, 25 rue Nationale, near the port, at the east end of the street (☎50.75.21.09; ②–③; restaurant from 80F), and the *Hostellerie du Lac* on the lakeside av Grande-Rive (☎50.75.02.92; ①; closed Oct to mid-March). The nearest **campsite** is the *Grande Rive* off av Grande-Rive (April–Sept).

If you choose to take one of the boat trips to Geneva from Évian, the boat calls first at **THONON-LES-BAINS**, flanked, just outside the town, by the fifteenth-century **Château de Ripaille**, built by Duke Amadeus VIII and used by him as a retreat before and after his stint as anti-pope. *"Faire la ripaille"* has come to mean "have a really riotous time" in French, which is rather unfair to the duke, who led a much quieter life than popular imagination wanted to believe. The château today contains the **Musée du Chablais**, illuminating local history, archeology and crafts (Mon–Sat 10am–noon & 3–5pm; free).

The next port of call is the walled village of **YVOIRE**, its houses packed on a low rise behind the shore, guarded by a massive fourteenth-century **castle** and wholly devoted to tourism. Mont Blanc and a host of other peaks appear shining in the distance.

travel details

Trains

Annecy to: St-Gervais (10 daily; 1hr 15min–2hr); Grenoble (several daily; 2hr); Chambéry (several daily; 45min); Lyon (several daily; 2hr); Paris (frequent, including 8 *TGV*s; 4hr 30min).

Annemasse to: Annecy, changing at La-Roche-sur-Foron (4 or 5 daily, 1 through train; 1hr 30min); Évian (very frequent; 35min); Paris (1 daily through train; 8hr).

Briançon to: Marseille (3 daily; 4hr 30min).

Chambéry to: Aix-les-Bains (several daily; 10min); Annecy (frequent; 45min); Bourg-St-Maurice (5 daily; 2hr); Geneva (several daily; 1hr 30min); Grenoble (several daily; 1hr); Lyon (very frequent; 1hr 30min–2hr 30min); Modane (frequent; 40min–1hr 20min); Paris (frequent; 5hr 30min).

Geneva to: Paris (4 daily; 3hr 45min).

Grenoble to: Annecy (several daily; 2hr); Chambéry (several daily; 1hr); Briançon, changing at Veynes-Dévoluy (2 daily; 4hr); Gap (2 daily; 2hr 30min); Lyon (very frequent; 1hr 30min–1hr 45min); Paris-Lyon (several daily; 7hr 15min – 3hr 12min by *TGV*).

St-Gervais to: Chamonix (7 daily; 35min).

Buses

Bourg-St-Maurice to: Aosta (1 daily July–Aug: 2hr 30min); Val d'Isère (1–2 daily; 50min–1hr 20min).

Chambéry to: Aix-les-Bains (several daily; 20min); Annecy (several daily; 1hr); Grenoble (several daily; 1hr).

Chamonix to: Annecy via La-Roche-sur-Foron (3 daily; 3hr); Annecy via Megève (1 daily; 3hr); Geneva (1 daily; 2hr 30min); Grenoble (1 daily; 3hr 30min).

Grenoble to: Alpe-d'Huez (2 daily; 45min); Briançon (several daily; 2hr); Bourg-d'Oisans (5 daily; 1hr 20min); Chambéry (several daily; 1hr); Col du Lautaret (1 daily; 2hr); Gap (1 daily; 2hr 45min); La Grave (1 daily; 1hr 40min); Monetier-les-Bains (1 daily; 2hr 25min); Villard-de-Lans (at least 1 daily; 45min).

CHAPTER FOURTEEN

THE RHÔNE VALLEY AND PROVENCE

O f all the areas of France, Provence is the most irresistible. Geographically it ranges from the high mountains of the **southern Alps** to the plains of the **Camargue** and has the greatest European canyon, the **Gorges du Verdon**. Fortresses like **Sisteron** and **Tarascon** guard its old borders and countless citadels perch defensively at strategic heights. The sensual inducements of Provence include warmth – even in winter – food and wine, and the perfumes of Mediterranean vegetation. Along with its coast – which we've covered in the following chapter, *The Côte d'Azur* – it has attracted the rich and famous, the artistic and reclusive, and countless arrivals who have found themselves unable to conceive of a life spent elsewhere.

In appearance, despite the throngs of foreigners and French from other regions, **inland Provence** remains remarkably unscathed. The history of its earliest known natives, of the Greeks, the Romans that squeezed them out, raiding Saracens, schismatic popes, and shifting allegiances to different counts and princes, is still in evidence. Provence's complete integration into France dates only from the nineteenth century, and though the Provençal language is rarely heard today, the common accent is distinctive even to a foreign ear, and in the east the intonation is Italian.

Unless you're intending to stay for months, the main problem with Provence is choosing where to go. In the west along the **Rhône valley** are the Roman cities of **Orange**, **Vaison-la-Romaine**, **Carpentras** and **Arles**, and the papal city of **Avignon**, with its brilliant summer festival. **Aix-en-Provence** is the mini-Paris of the region and home to Cézanne, for whom the **Mont Ste-Victoire** was an enduring subject. Vasarely's works are on show in Aix and **Gordes**; Van Gogh's links are with **St-Rémy** and Arles. The Gorges du Verdon, the **Parc National du Mercantour** along the

---

ACCOMMODATION PRICE CATEGORIES

All the hotels, youth hostels and guesthouses listed in this book have been price-graded according to the following scale, and although costs will rise slightly overall with the life of this edition, the relative comparisons should remain valid. Paris and the large cities will, as anywhere, be more expensive than equivalent accommodation in the countryside or small towns. The prices quoted are for the cheapest available double room in high season, although remember that many of the cheap places will have more expensive rooms with en-suite facilities.

① Under 160F	④ 300–400F	⑦ 600–700F
② 160–220F	⑤ 400–500F	⑧ Over 700F
③ 220–300F	⑥ 500–600F	

Italian border, **Mont Ventoux** northeast of Carpentras, and the flamingo-filled lagoons of the **Camargue** are only a selection of landscapes that really should not be missed.

Before you reach Provence there are the **vineyards of the Rhône valley** and, before them, the French centre of gastronomy and second largest city of the country, **Lyon**. With its choice of restaurants, clubs, culture and all the accoutrements of an affluent and vital western city, it stands in opulent contrast to the medieval hilltop villages of Provence.

FOOD OF PROVENCE AND THE RHONE VALLEY

Lyon is renowned as a gastronomic centre, combining southern and northern ingredients. Its rich and hearty food is very meat and offal oriented, with sausages of every variety and a fine selection of cheeses. A Lyonnais salad includes bacon and a soft-cooked egg; potatoes also tend to be cooked with egg, cheeses and cream; and meat, fish or cheese are turned into fat, filling *quenelles*, or dumplings. *Pâtisseries* specialize in extremely rich chocolate gâteaux.

Olives were introduced to Provence by the ancient Greeks two and a half thousand years ago and today accompany the traditional Provençal apéritif of *pastis*; they appear in sauces and salads, on tarts and pizzas, and mixed with capers in a paste called *tapenade* to spread on bread or biscuits. They are also used in traditional meat stews, like *daube Provençale*. Olive oil is the starting point for most Provençal dishes; spiced with chillis or Provençal herbs (wild thyme, basil, rosemary and tarragon), it is also poured over pizzas, sandwiches, and of course as vinaigrette and mayonnaise with all the varieties of salad.

The ingredient most often mixed with olive oil is the other classic of Provençal cuisine: **garlic**. Whole markets are dedicated to strings of pale purple garlic. Two of the most famous concoctions of Provence are **pistou**, a paste of olive oil, garlic and basil, and **aïoli**, the name for both a garlic mayonnaise and the dish in which it's served with salt, cod and vegetables.

Vegetables have double or triple seasons in Provence, often beginning while northern France is still in the depths of winter. Ratatouille ingredients – tomatoes, capsicum, aubergines, courgettes and onions – are the favourites, along with asparagus. Courgette flowers, or *fleurs de courgettes farcies*, stuffed with *pistou* or tomato sauce, is one of the most exquisite Provençal delicacies.

Sheep, taken up to the mountains in the summer months, provide the staple meat, of which the best is *agneau de Sisteron*, often roasted with Provençal herbs as a *gigot d'agneau aux herbes*. But it is **fish** that features most on traditional menus, with freshwater trout, salt cod, anchovies, sea bream, monkfish, sea bass and whiting all common, along with seafood.

Cheeses are invariably made from goat's or ewe's milk. Two famous ones are *Banon*, wrapped in chestnut leaves and marinated in brandy, and the aromatic *Picadon* from the foothills of the Alps.

Sweets of the region include chocolates, notably from Valrhona in Tain L'Hermitage and from Puyricard near Aix, almond sweets called *calissons* from Aix, candied fruit from Apt and nougat from Montélimar. As for **fruits**, the melons, white peaches, apricots, figs, cherries and Muscat grapes are unbeatable. Almond trees grow on the plateaux of central Provence along with lavender, which gives Provençal **honey** its distinctive flavour.

But more significant are the Côtes du Rhône **vineyards**, of which the most celebrated is the Crozes-Hermitage *appellation*. Once past the nougat town of Montélimar and into Provence, the best wines are to be found in the villages around the Dentelles, notably Gigondas, and at Châteauneuf-du-Pape. To the west are the light, drinkable, but not particularly special wines of the Côtes du Ventoux and the Côtes du Lubéron *appellations*. Huge quantities of wine are produced in Provence, many of the vineyards planted during World War I in order to supply every French soldier with his ration of a litre a day. With the exception of the Côteaux des Baux around Les Baux, and the Côtes de Provence in the Var *département*, the best wines of southern Provence come from along the coast.

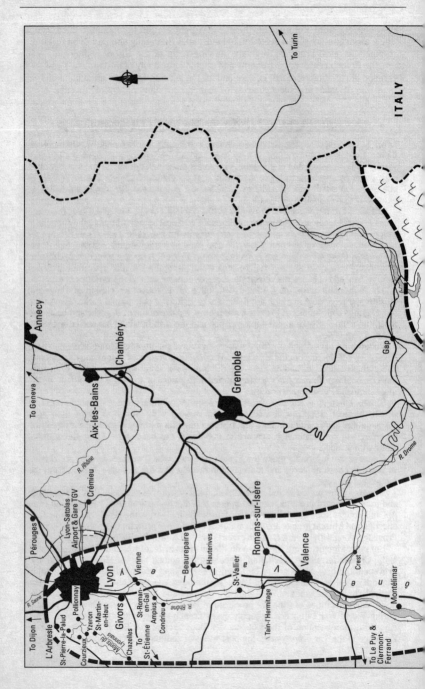

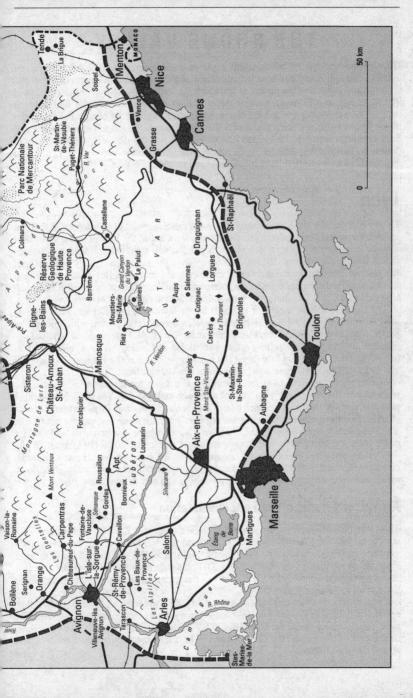

THE RHÔNE VALLEY

The **Rhône valley**, the north–south route of ancient armies, medieval traders and modern rail and road, is now as industrialized as the least attractive parts of the north. Though the river is still a means of transport, its waters now also cool the reactors of the Marcoule and Tricastin nuclear power station between Montélimar and Avignon and act as a dumping ground for the heavy industries along its banks. Following the River Rhône holds few attractions, with the exceptions of the stretch of **vineyards** and fruit orchards between the Roman city of **Vienne** and the distinctly southern city of **Valence**. But the big magnet is, of course, the gastronomic paradise of **Lyon**, with hundreds of sophisticated bars, restaurants and movies.

Lyon

LYON is physically the second biggest city in France, a result of its uncontrolled urban sprawl. Viewed at high speed from the *Autoroute du Soleil*, the impression it gives is of a major confluence of rivers and roads, around which only petrochemical industries thrive. In fact, silk was the city's main industry from the sixteenth century right up until the postwar dominance of metalworks, chemicals and transport. But what has stamped its character most on Lyon is the commerce and banking that grew up with its industrial expansion. It is this that gives it its staid, stolid and somewhat austere air.

The city is now busy forging a new role for itself within a new Europe. International schools and colleges, the new HQ for Interpol, a second *TGV* station with links to the north that bypass Paris, high-tech industrial parks for international companies, research institutes at the cutting edge of medicine and biology – Lyon, more so than any other French city, has embraced the monetarist vision of the European Union and is acting, with some success, as a postmodern city-state within it.

Most French people would find themselves in Lyon for business rather than for recreation: it's a get-up-and-go place, not a lie-back-and-rest one. You probably wouldn't plan a two week stay – as you might in Provence's cities – but Lyon certainly has its charms. Foremost among these is **gastronomy**; there are more restaurants per Gothic and Renaissance square foot of the old town than anywhere else on earth, and the city could form a football team with its superstars of the international chef circuit. While the **textile museum** is the second famous reason for stopping here, Lyon's nightlife, cinema and theatre (including the famous Lyonnais puppets), its antique markets, music and other cultural festivities might tempt you to stay at least a few days.

Arrival, city transport and accommodation

The **Lyon-Satolas international airport** (information ☎72.22.75.05) and its new *TGV* station are off the Grenoble autoroute, 20km to the southeast of the city, with a 45-minute *Satobus* bus link to the town centre (42F). If you're thinking of flying in from Paris, be aware that it's quicker to go by *TGV*. It's only from the air, however, that you can appreciate architect Santiago Calatrava's design of a huge bird alighting, or taking flight from the station roof.

Central Lyon has two train stations: the **Gare de Perrache** on the Presqu'île (information ☎78.92.50.50) is used mainly for ordinary trains rather than *TGV*s, with the **gare routière** alongside. **La Part-Dieu TGV station** stands in the 3e *arrondissement* to the east of the Presqu'île. Central Lyon is linked to the suburbs by a modern and straightforward **métro**.

There's a **Bureau d'Information** in the Centre Perrache at the station where you can pick up a métro, bus, tram and funicular map or just hop two stops on the métro to place Bellecour, where the **central tourist office** is on the southeast corner (summer Mon–Fri 9am–7pm, Sat 9am–6pm, Sun 10am–6pm; winter Mon–Fri 9am–6pm, Sat 9am–5pm; ☎78.42.25.75). There are also **tourist offices** on av Adolphe-Max in St-Jean in the old town, and at 3 av Aristide-Briand in Villeurbanne.

At métro stations or the city transport *TCL* offices the cheapest way to buy **tickets** is in a *carnet* of six (around 40F, discounts for students), or there's the *Ticket Liberté*, valid for 24 hours (20F). The ordinary tickets are flat rate within an hour's duration and limited to three changes using any combination of transport. The métro runs from 5am to around midnight.

Accommodation

As a result of Lyon's commercial pre-eminence, hotel **rooms** can be a problem to find, particularly on weekdays. If you don't book ahead, you could end up paying well over the odds for inferior accommodation. Hotels in Perrache (2ᵉ) and Bellecour (2ᵉ) fill up quickly, but you may be luckier around Terreaux (1ᵉʳ).

If you're on a real budget, stop by the **CROUS** offices, 59 rue de la Madeleine, 7ᵉ (métro *Jean-Macé*; ☎78.80.13.13), where they may be able to fix you up in student lodgings or residences closer to the centre during vacation time.

HOTELS

Hôtel d'Ainay, 14 rue des Remparts d'Ainay, 2ᵉ (☎78.42.43.42). Preferable to its many equally cheap neighbours because of its decent-sized rooms, but it does fill fast. Closed first two weeks in Aug. ①–②.

Hôtel Alexandra, 49 rue Victor-Hugo, 2ᵉ (☎78.37.75.79). Large, well-run old hotel. ③–④.

Celtic, 10 rue François-Vernay, 1ᵉʳ (☎78.28.01.12). Large, fairly comfortable and cheap place. ②–③.

Hôtel Croix-Paquet, 11 place Croix-Paquet, 1ᵉʳ (☎78.28.51.49). Good-value hotel, whose friendly reception makes up for the lack of mod cons in this hotel close to place de Terreaux. ①–②.

Hôtel Foch, 59 av Mal-Foch, 6ᵉ (☎78.89.14.01). Pleasant hotel close to the park, with sound-proofed rooms and a video library. Closed mid-July to mid-Aug. ④–⑤.

Hôtel Globe et Cécil, 21 rue Gasparin, 2ᵉ (☎78.42.58.95). Attractive place with good service and a touch of originality in the decor. ⑤–⑦.

Hôtel de la Marne, 78 rue de la Charité, 2ᵉ (☎78.37.07.46). Convenient, clean and excellent value. ②–④.

Hôtel St-Pierre-des-Terreaux, 8 rue Paul-Chenevard, 1ᵉʳ (☎78.28.24.61). A very relaxed place with discreet charm. ③–④.

Hôtel le Terme, 7 rue Ste-Catherine, 1ᵉʳ (☎78.28.30.45). A cheap and shabby but well-situated hotel. ①–②.

Hôtel du Théâtre, 10 rue de Savoie, 2ᵉ (☎78.42.33.32). This hotel has rather expensive rooms, but is comfortable and well run by a pleasant young couple. ③–④.

Hôtel Vaubecour, 28 rue Vaubecour, 2ᵉ (☎78.37.44.91). One block back from the Saône quays, this place is comfortable, friendly and well furnished for the price. ①.

YOUTH HOSTELS AND CAMPSITES

IYHF youth hostel, 51 rue Roger-Salengro, Vénissieux (☎78.76.39.23). The official hostel is 4km southeast of the centre; take buses #53 or #80 from Perrache, or #36 from Part-Dieu, stop *États-Unis-Viviani* or *Viviani Joliot-Curic*. ①.

Centre International de Séjour de Lyon, 48 rue Commandant-Pégoud, 8ᵉ (☎78.01.23.45). Not far from the youth hostel, although a lot more expensive; the advantage of this hostel is that it's out of earshot of the main ring road. Take bus #53 from Perrache or #36 from Part-Dieu, stop *États-Unis-Beauvisage*. Open 24hr. ①.

Porte de Lyon campsite, Dardilly (☎78.35.64.55). East along the N6 from Lyon or by bus #19 (direction *Ecully-Dardilly*) from the Hôtel de Ville. Pleasant, though expensive.

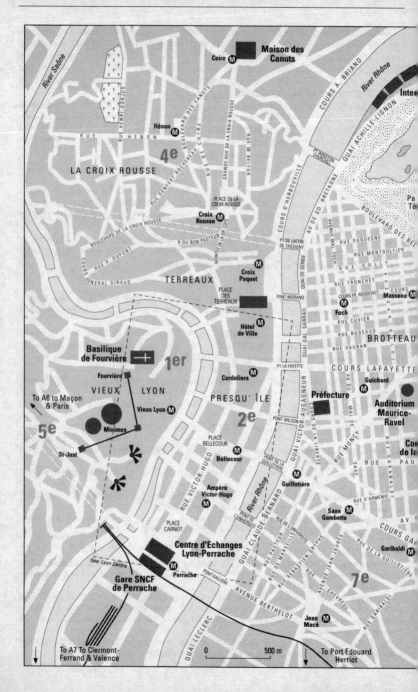

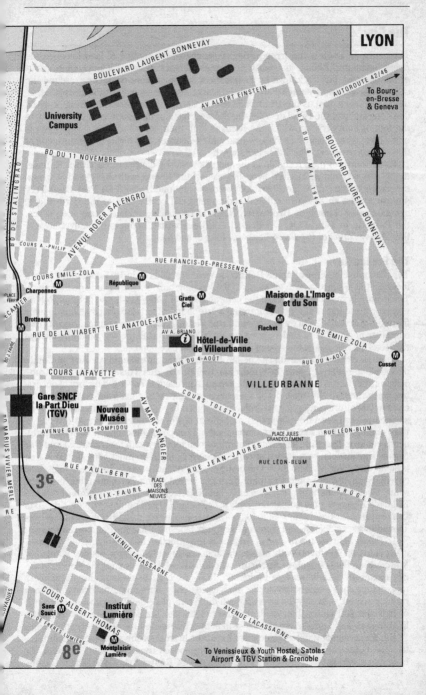

The City

The centre of Lyon is the **Presqu'île**, or peninsula, the tongue of land between the rivers Saône and Rhône, just north of their confluence. Most of it lies within the 2e *arrondissement*, but it's known by its *quartiers*, which include **Bellecour**, around the central square, and **Perrache** around the station. At the top end of the Presqu'île, as the Saône veers west, is the 1er *arrondissement*, known as **Terreaux**, centring on place des Terreaux and the Hôtel de Ville. On the west bank of the Saône is the **old town**, at the foot of Fourvière, on which the Romans built their capital of Gaul. Vieux Lyon is made up of three villages: St-Paul, St-Jean and St-Georges, and forms the eastern end of the 5e *arrondissement*. The 9e lies to its north.

To the north of the Presqu'île is the old silk-weavers' district of **La Croix Rousse**, the 4e *arrondissement*. Modern Lyon lies east of the Rhône, with the 7e and 8e *arrondissements* to the south; the 3e *arrondissement* in the middle, with **La Part-Dieu TGV station** amidst an assertive cultural and commercial centre; and to the north the 6e *arrondissement*, known as **Brotteaux**. North of Brotteaux is Lyon's main open space, the **Parc de la Tête d'Or**. The district of **Villeurbanne**, home to the university and the *Théâtre National Populaire*, lies east of the 6e and the park.

The Presqu'île

The pink gravelly acres of **place Bellecour** were first laid out in 1617, and today form a focus on the peninsula, with views up to the looming bulk of Notre-Dame-de-Fourvière. The square is vast, dwarfing even the central statue of Louis XIV in the guise of Roman emperor. Running south, **rue Auguste-Comte** is full of antique shops selling heavily framed eighteenth-century artworks, and **rue Victor-Hugo** is a pedestrian precinct that continues north of place Bellecour on rue de la République all the way up to the back of the Hôtel de Ville below the area of La Croix Rousse (see opposite).

South of place Bellecour on rue de la Charité, running parallel to rue August-Comte on the Rhône side, is Lyon's best museum, the **Musée des Tissus** (Tues–Sun 10am–5.30pm; 20F, free Wed). It doesn't quite live up to its claim to cover the history of decorative cloth through the ages, but it does have brilliant collections from certain periods, most notably third-century Greek-influenced and sixth-century Coptic tapestries, woven silk and painted linen from Egypt. The fragment of woven wool *aux poissons* (second to third century AD) has an artistry unmatched in European work until at least the eighteenth century. There are silks from Baghdad contemporary with the *Thousand and One Nights*, and carpets from Iran, Turkey, India and China. The most boring stuff is that produced in Lyon itself, with seventeenth- to eighteenth-century hangings and chair covers. Sadly, there's almost nothing from the period of the Revolution, but there are some lovely twentieth-century pieces – Sonia Delaunay's *Tissus simultanés*, Michel Dubost's *L'Oiseau Bleu* and Raoul Dufy's *Les Coquillages*. The dull **Musée des Arts Décoratifs** next door (Tues–Sun 10am–noon & 2–5.30pm; same ticket as Musée des Tissus) has seventeenth- and eighteenth-century tapestries, furniture and ceramics.

To the right at the top of quai St-Antoine is the **quartier Mercière**, the old commercial centre of the town, with sixteenth- and seventeenth-century houses lining rue Mercière, and the **church of St-Nizier**, whose bells used to announce the closing of the city's gates. In the silk weavers' uprising of 1831 (see box), workers fleeing the soldiers took refuge in St-Nizier only to be massacred. The bourgeoisie had certainly been running scared, with only the area between the rivers, place des Terreaux and just north of St-Nizier still under their control. Unfortunately for the *canuts* (the silk workers), their bosses could call on outside aid – which they did, to the tune of 30,000 extra troops.

The monumental nineteenth-century **fountain** in front of the even more monumental **Hôtel de Ville** on place des Terreaux symbolizes rivers straining to reach the ocean; opposite is the large bulk of the **Musée des Beaux-Arts** (Wed–Sun 10.30am–

6pm; 20F), second only to the Louvre in its collections. The paintings progress chronologically around the building from medieval to modern, but be warned that seeing more than ten rooms at a time is exhausting. There are some wonderful works among the modern stuff: Gino Severini's *La Famille du Peintre* of 1939; spring and summer light in Bonnard's canvases beside wintry port scenes by Marquet; Van Dongens and de la Fresnayes throwing amused looks at their women friends; one of Monet's Thames series; *La Petite Niçoise* by Berthe Morisot. Of the early nineteenth-century collection, *La Maraichère*, attributed to David, is outstanding, and you can work your way back through Rubens, Zurbaran, El Greco, Tintoretto, and a hundred others. Downstairs are numerous objects lifted at the turn of the century from Egypt, Iran and elsewhere, some ancient, some fourteenth- and fifteenth-century. The **Musée St-Pierre d'Art Contemporain** is in the same building complex (entrance at 16 rue Eduoard-Herriot; daily except Tues noon–6pm; 20F) and has temporary exhibitions of art from the 1960s onwards.

La Croix-Rousse

La Croix-Rousse is the old silk-weavers' district, north of the Presqu'île. It's still a working-class area, but barely a couple of dozen people operate the modern high-speed computerized looms that are kept in business by the restoration and maintenance of France's palaces and châteaux. You can watch traditional looms in mesmerizing action at **La Maison des Canuts** at 10–12 rue d'Ivry, one block north of place de la Croix-Rousse (métro Croix-Rousse; Mon–Fri 8.30am–noon & 2–6.30pm, Sat 9am–noon & 2–6pm; Aug closed Mon; 10F), and see some rare and beautiful cloths, including silk, damask and brocade, produced by this ancient home weavers' cooperative.

The streets running down from **boulevard de la Croix-Rousse** – as well as many across the river in Vieux Lyon – are intercut with alleyways and tunnelled passages known as *traboules*. Their exits and entrances are sometimes visible; others have doors like any street door that often lead to an upstairs apartment and the traboule. Try going up past the right of St-Polycarpe on **rue Réné-Leynaud** above place Terreaux, then take the *traboule* opposite 36 rue Burdeau, go right around **place Chardonnet**, through 55 rue des Tables-Claudiennes, opposite 29 rue Imbert-Colomés and up the stairs into 14bis, across three more courtyards, and you should come out at **place Colbert**.

THE SILK STRIKE OF 1831

The modern silk-weaving machines are no different in principle from the Jacquard loom of 1804, although they made it possible for one person to produce 25 centimetres in a day instead of taking four people four days. But silk workers, or *canuts* – whether masters and apprentices, or especially women and child workers – were badly paid whatever their output. Over the three decades following the introduction of the Jacquard, the price paid for a length of silk was reduced by over fifty percent. Attempts to regulate the price were ignored by the dealers, even though hundreds of skilled workers were languishing in debtors' jails. On November 21, 1831, the *canuts* called an all-out strike. As they processed down the Montée de la Grande Côte with their black flags and the slogan "Live working or die fighting", they were shot at and three people died. After a rapid retreat uphill they built barricades, assisted by half the National Guard who refused to fire canon at their "comrades of Croix-Rousse". For three days, until the reinforcements were brought in, the battle raged on all four banks, the silk workers using sticks, stones and knives to defend themselves. Some 600 people were killed or wounded, and in the end the silk industrialists were free to pay whatever pitiful fee they chose. But the uprising was one of the first instances of organized labour taking to the streets during the most revolutionary fifty years of French history.

Vieux Lyon

Reached by one of the three *passerelles* or footbridges crossing the Saône from Terreaux and the Presqu'île, **Vieux Lyon** is made up of the three villages of St-Jean, St-Georges and St-Paul at the base of the hill overlooking the Presqu'île.

South of place St-Paul, the streets of Vieux Lyon, pressed close together beneath the hill of **Fourvière**, form a backdrop of Renaissance façades, bright night-time illumination and a swelling chorus of well-dressed Lyonnais in search of supper or a midday splurge. One of the most impressive buildings at the northern end is the sixteenth-century **Hôtel Paterin** at 4–6 rue Juiverie, a galleried mansion best viewed from the bottom of Montée St-Barthélémy, just up from place St-Paul.

A short way south, the **Musée Historique de Lyon** on place du Petit-Collège (daily except Tues 10.45am–6pm, Fri till 8.30pm; 20F) has a good collection of Nevers ceramics, but the **Musée de la Marionette**, on the first floor of this fifteenth-century mansion (same hours; 20F) is a lot more entertaining. As well as the eighteenth-century Lyonnais creations, *Guignol* and *Madelon* (the French equivalents of Punch and Judy), there are glove puppets, shadow puppets and rod-and-string toy actors from all over Europe and the Far East. If you want to see them in action, check out the times of performances at the **Théâtre de Guignol** in the conservatory on rue Louis-Carrand by quai de Bondy (Oct–May Sun 3pm; for weekday shows, ring ☎78.28.92.57).

The central pedestrianized **rue St-Jean** ends at the twelfth- to fifteenth-century **Cathédrale St-Jean**. The damage of religious wars and revolutions to the most recent part, the west façade, is slowly being reversed, but the thirteenth-century stained glass above the altar and in the rose windows of the transepts is in perfect condition. In the northern transept is a fourteenth-century clock, rivalling modern digital watches for superlative functions: you can compute religious feast days till the year 2019, and most days on the strike of noon, 2pm and 3pm, the figures of the Annunciation go through an automated set-piece.

Just beyond the cathedral, opposite av Adolphe-Max and Pont Bonaparte, is the **funicular station** and the Vieux Lyon métro, from which you can ascend to the town's Roman remains (direction *St-Just*; stop *Minimes*). The antiquities consist of two ruinous **theatres** (entrance at 6 rue de l'Antiquaille; daily 9am–sunset; free) – the larger of which was built by Augustus and extended in the second century by Hadrian to seat 10,000 spectators – and an underground museum of Lyonnais life from prehistoric times to 7 AD, the **Musée de la Civilisation Gallo-Romain**, 17 rue Cléberg (Wed–Sun 10am–noon & 2–6pm; 20F). Here, a mosaic illustrates various Roman games; bronze inscriptions detail ecomomic, legal and bureaucratic matters; there's a Gaulois lunar calendar and models aid the imagination in reconstructing the theatres outside. It's a very short walk from the Gallo-Roman museum to the late nineteenth-century creation of **Basilique de Fourvière**, an unenchanting miasma of multicoloured marble and mosaic – you can reach it from the funicular station by Vieux Lyon métro (*Fourvière* terminus). As a visual antidote, make your way to the belvedere behind, with its view of the graceful curving rivers.

Modern Lyon

On the skyline from Fourvière, you'll see a gleaming cylinder with a pointed top and other Manhattanish protuberances around it. This is **La Part-Dieu**, a business-culture-commerce conglomerate including one of the biggest public libraries outside Paris, a mammoth concert hall and a shopping centre said to be the largest in Europe (métro *Part-Dieu*). On the corner of rue Garibaldi and cours Lafayette in front of these less than homely structures are the **main market halls** of Lyon.

For a break from city buildings head north to the **Parc de la Tête d'Or** (tram #4 from *Part-Dieu* or métro to *Masséna*, then walk up rue Masséna), where there are

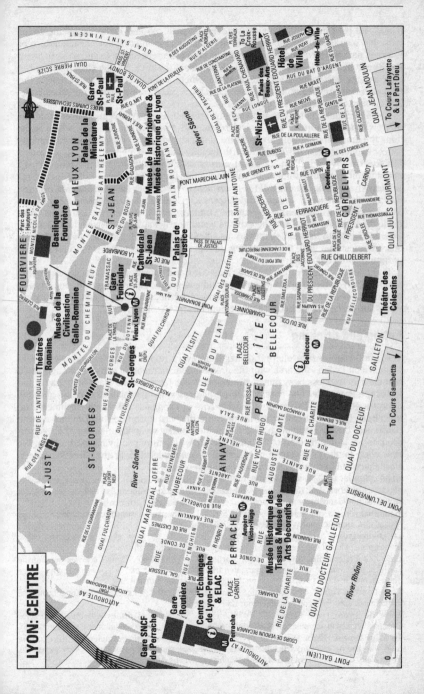

ponds and rose gardens, botanical gardens, a small zoo and lots of amusements for kids. It's overlooked by the bristling antennae of the international headquarters of Interpol, part of a new **Cité Internationale**, with conference centres and so forth along the Rhône bank, across quai Archille Lignon from the park. To the east, dividing the park and the university, is bd de Stalingrad, where antique fanciers can browse in the **Cité des Antiquaires** arcades at no. 117 (Thurs, Sat & Sun 9.30am–12.30pm & 2.30–7pm; closed Sun afternoon in summer).

In Villeurbanne, not far to the east of Part-Dieu, is **Le Nouveau Musée/Institut d'Art Contemporain**, 11 rue Dr-Dolard (bus #1 stop *Nouveau Musée*), which questions the function of art and architecture and their relation to society, with exhibitions by contemporary artists. It's also worth looking out for exhibitions at Villeurbanne's **Maison du Livre de l'Image et du Son** on av Émile-Zola, by métro Flachet, which might feature anything from medieval illuminations to CD-ROMS.

Further south, on the edge of the 8ᵉ *arrondissement*, is the **Institut Lumière**, 25 rue du Premier-Film (daily except Mon 2–6pm; 25F; métro line D, *Monplaisir/Lumière*). The building was the home of Antoine Lumière, father of Auguste and Louis, who made the first ever films, and the exhibits feature early magic lanterns and the cameras used by the brothers, along with various art photographs. The Institut also hosts various film festivals and is celebrating the centenary of cinema with an excellent programme of films, lectures and special exhibitions until January 1996.

Right down in the south of the city, in the **Gerland quartier** (7ᵉ), new developments are underway in the creation of a marina and a new park on the eastern Rhône bank to provide an illusion of nature around the mirrored Institut Pasteur and the thrusting wings and arches of the École Normale Supérieure.

Eating and drinking

You'll find **restaurants** offering dishes from every region of France and overseas in Lyon. Vieux Lyon is the area with the greatest concentration of eateries, though you'll find cheaper and less busy ones between place des Jacobins and place Sathonay at the top of the Presqu'île. The possibilities are endless, but on weekends booking ahead is always a good idea. The most affordable type of Lyonnaise eating establishment, the **bouchon** ("cork"), derived its name from the vast quantities of Lyonnaise wine consumed there. Tradition has it that wine bottles were lined up as the evening progressed, and at the end of the night the bill was determined by measuring from the first cork to the last. There are several *bouchons* located in the streets between Cordeliers and Terreaux, particularly in rue Mercière.

Alain Chapel, Mionnay (☎78.91.82.02). Nineteen kilometres north of Lyon, this restaurant is almost as good as *Paul Bocuse* and in the same price bracket. Superb fish dishes, spicy pigeon stuffed with wild mushrooms, lime soufflé... every dish is a work of art.

L'Amphitryon, 33 rue St-Jean, 5ᵉ (☎78.37.23.68). Usually packed restaurant featuring Lyonnais specialities; menu for under 100F. Service till midnight.

Le Boulevardier, 5 rue de la Fromagerie, 1ᵉʳ (☎78.28.48.22). Very cheap mussels and chips; menus from 65F and jazz piano some Friday nights. Daily till midnight.

Café des Fédérations, 8 rue du Major-Martin, 1ᵉʳ (☎78.28.26.00). Typical *bouchon* serving the earthiest of Lyonnaise specialities (marinated tripe, black pudding and fish *quenelles*) in an atmosphere to match: there's even sawdust on the floor. Closed Sat, Sun and Aug.

Chez Léa "La Voûte", 11 place Antoine-Gourju, 2ᵉ (☎78.42.01.33). Excellent traditional Lyonnaise cooking and especially good salads. From 120F. Closed Sun.

Léon de Lyon, 1 rue Pléney, 1ᵉʳ (☎78.28.11.33). Sophisticated dishes and many traditional Lyonnais recipes in an upmarket brasserie setting. From 450F but with a lunchtime menu for 250F.

La Mère Brazier, 12 rue Royale, 1ᵉʳ (☎78.28.15.49). A beautiful setting complements the excellent food, like Bresse chicken, artichoke hearts on *foie gras*, truffle crêpes – but it's very expensive. From 350F. Closed Sun, Sat midday and evening in July, and Aug.

Merle, Halles de la Part-Dieu, 102 cours Lafayette, 3ᵉ (☎78.62.30.29). Bar and resto in the market halls for seafood and snails. Around 150F for full whack.

La Meunière, rue Neuve, 1ᵉʳ (☎78 28 62 91). Booking is essential in this excellent *bouchon*, but it's worth it for the 140F menu of course after course of Lyonnaise specialities. Other menus start at 85F. Closed Sun & Mon.

Paul Bocuse, 40 rue de la Plage, Collonges-au-Mont-d'Or (☎72.27.85.85). Lyon's most famous restaurant, named after its celebrity chef-owner, is 9km north of the city, on the west bank of the Saône. Traditional French gluttony is the bill of fare, with stunning *crême brûlée* and *baba au rhum*. 500F upwards.

La Tour Rose, 22 rue Bœuf, 5ᵉ (☎78.37.25.90). Gastronomic palace with concoctions like asparagus with an oyster mousse or salad of lobster and spinach with a creamed truffle sauce. From 320F.

Le Vieux Fourneau, 1 rue Tramassac, 5ᵉ (☎78.37.06.42). A good menu at a decent price in a lively ambiance. Closed Mon & Aug; service till midnight.

Nightlife and entertainment

If you haven't overindulged yourself at the meal table, Lyon is almost as good a place for **nightlife** as it is for eating, with a good range of clubs, cinema, opera, jazz, classical music concerts and theatre. The tourist office brings out a bimonthly brochure, *Spectacles Evénements,* with broad mainstream listings. Or there's the weekly *Lyon Poche* available from newsagents (every Tuesday; 7F).

Look out for **stage productions** by the *Théâtre Nationale Populaire* (*TNP*), 8 place Lazare-Goujon (☎78.03.30.40), based across the street from Villeurbanne's town hall. Less radical stuff will be shown at the city's gilded *Théâtre des Célestins* in place des Célestins, 2ᵉ (☎78.42.17.67). The **opera house** is on place de la Comédie, 1ᵉʳ (☎72.00.45.45), with cheap tickets sold just before performances begin. For avant-garde, classic and obscure **films**, usually in their original language, check the listings for the cinemas *CNP Terreaux, Ambiance, Opéra* and *Le Cinéma*.

BARS AND CLUBS

Albion Public House, 12 rue Ste-Catherine, 1ᵉʳ. English pub with draught beer where you can play darts and listen to jazz, rhythm and blues and soul on Sat and Sun nights. Mon–Sat 5pm–2am, Sun 1am.

Antidote, 108 rue St-Georges, 5ᵉ. Irish pub with free concerts of rock, folk, blues and jazz in the basement. Daily 5pm–2am.

Cirque, 14 rue Thomassin, 2ᵉ. Reasonably priced disco with rock, new wave, techno and acid-jazz. Tues–Sun from 10.30pm.

Country Rock, 1 quai des Célestins, 1ᵉʳ. Fifties country music, cocktails and American food. Daily noon–3am.

Écossais, 7 rue Charles-Dullin, 2ᵉ. Scots-style piano bar serving 100 different whiskies. Mon–Sat 6pm–4am.

Espace Gerson, 1 place Gerson, 5ᵉ. Has café-théâtre some nights, otherwise jazz or performance art, plus darts and billiards. Mon–Sat 5pm–2am.

Mylord, 112 quai Pierre-Scize, 5ᵉ. Gay disco with drag shows and an interesting decor of statues and a sculpted stone bar. Mon–Sat 10.30pm–4am.

Paradiso Club, 24 rue Pizay, 1ᵉʳ. Funky music and transvestite or burlesque cabaret. Daily 10pm–dawn.

Pont-Neuf, 9 quai de Bondy, 5ᵉ. Jazz concerts every Sat night in a vaulted cellar. Daily 7pm–1am.

La Ruche, 22 rue Gentil, 2ᵉ. Café-bar haunt of Lyon trendies. Daily 5pm–1am.

Le Village, 8 rue St-Georges, 5ᵉ. Lesbian club with a friendly atmosphere. Shows, songs and cabaret acts, plus mixed night Thurs – men must be accompanied. Tues–Fri from 6pm, Sat from 8pm.

Zoo, 9 rue Mercière, 2ᵉ. Disco with theme nights Tues, rock nights Wed and every kind of dance beat the rest of the week. Tues–Sat from 11pm.

Listings

Bike rental *Locasport*, 62 rue du Colombier, 7ᵉ; *Motobécane François*, 139 av Maréchal-de-Saxe, 4ᵉ.

Boat trips *Bateaux-Mouches Lui*, *Société Naviginter*, 13bis quai Rambaud, 2ᵉ (☎78.42.96.81) from quai des Célestins; up the Saône or down to the confluence to the Île Barbe (daily April–Nov). The *Société Naviginter* also run a boat, *Elle*, down the Rhône to Vienne.

Books English bookshop, *Eton*, 1 rue du Plat, near place des Terreaux.

Car rental *Europcar*, 86 av Félix-Faure, 3ᵉ (☎78.95.94.94); *Rent-a-Car*, 74 rue de Bonnel, 3ᵉ (☎78.95.81.81); *Hertz* at Centre Perrache (☎78.42.24.85), and Gare de la Part-Dieu (☎72.33.89.99).

Changing money *AOC*, 20 rue Gasparin; *Thomas Cook*, Gare de la Part-Dieu (Mon–Fri 6am–8pm, weekends & holidays 6am–6pm); tourist office, place Bellecour (Mon–Fri 9am–7pm, Sat 9am–6pm, Sun 10am–6pm).

Consulates *Canada*, 74 rue de Bonnel, 3ᵉ (☎72.61.15.25); *Ireland*, 4 rue Jean-Desparmet (☎78.76.44.85); *UK*, 24 rue Childebert (☎78.37.59.67); *US*, 7 quai du Général-Sarrail, 6ᵉ (☎78.24.68.49).

Emergencies *SOS Médecins* (☎78.83.51.51); hospitals: Hôtel-Dieu, 1 place de l'Hôtel-Dieu, 2ᵉ (☎78.42.70.80), Hôpital Édouard-Herriot on place d'Arsonval, 3ᵉ (☎78.53.81.11). Pharmacy open till midnight: *Blanchet*, 5 place des Cordeliers, 2ᵉ.

Police The main *commissariat* on place Antonin-Poncet, 2ᵉ (☎78.28.92.93).

Post office PTT, place Antonin-Poncet, Lyon 69002.

Taxis ☎78.28.23.23 or 78.26.81.80.

Around Lyon

Within easy reach of the city, the **Monts du Lyonnais** to the south and west of Lyon may not reach spectacular heights, but they offer quiet and solitude among steep, forested hills and unassuming villages surrounded by cherry orchards, the region's main source of income. Tourism is low key, but food and accommodation in the hostels of the mountain villages are rarely a problem for visitors to the area's parks and museums. **Bus** services from Lyon to the larger villages are reasonably frequent, and to the east of Lyon, the small medieval cities of **Pérouges** and **Crémieu** can easily be reached by train. The mountains can be visited every Sunday from June until the middle of September by steam train, leaving from **L'Arbresle**, just west of Lyon (frequent trains from Lyon-Perrache); it's a scenic service but not very useful for getting anywhere.

Worth a visit if you're not returning straight to Lyon, the **Musée de la Mine** at **ST-PIERRE-LA-PALUD**, 15km west of the city (March–Nov Sat, Sun & hols 2–4pm; 25F), is guaranteed to instill admiration for the endurance of the miners who put up with working conditions like those simulated in the reconstructed mine shaft which forms the main exhibit. Going down into the copper sulphate mine shaft while an ex-miner explains its workings in meticulous detail (two hours, in French) is not recommended if you're claustrophobic. Back on the surface, you move on to an exhibition on the former mining village and pit.

Most of the villages in the Lyonnaise mountains have some form of *auberge* serving food and providing a bed for the night. A typical, attractive example is the tiny village of **YZERON**, 12km south of the wildlife park, on whose main square are a tourist office (Mon–Fri 10am–12.30pm & 2–5.30pm), a *crêperie* and the excellent *Auberge de Tonton* (☎78.81.01.52; ③), which serves duck and salmon as part of a 130F menu. There are a couple of hotels and restaurants in the village of **ST-MARTIN-EN-HAUT**, eight winding kilometres south of Yzeron, and a **camping municipal** just outside the village on the D122 (☎78.48.62.16; all year).

Pérouges and Crémieu

Twenty-nine kilometres northeast of Lyon on the N84, **PÉROUGES** is a pretty little city of cobbled alleyways, whose charm has not gone unnoticed by the French film industry – historical dramas like *The Three Musketeers* and *Monsieur Vincent* were filmed within the town walls – nor by some of the residents of the city, who have fought long and hard for preservation orders on its most interesting buildings.

Local traditional life is also thriving in the hands of a hundred or so workers who still weave locally grown hemp. No particular monument stands out, but the central square of the city, the **place du Halle**, and its main street, the **rue du Prince**, have some of the best-preserved French medieval remains. The **lime tree** on place du Halle is a symbol of liberty, planted in 1792. The place both to **stay** and eat in Pérouges is the *Ostellerie du Vieux Pérouges* (☎74.61.00.88; ⑤–⑦), in a medieval town house on place Tilleul; its **restaurant** (out of season closed Wed & Thurs lunchtime) serves traditional mountain dishes of rabbit and carp, with menus from 180F.

CRÉMIEU, to the south on the D517, is less compelling, despite its local sausages (*sabodet*), monumental architecture and early origins – the city can be traced back to 835 AD. It was once an important commercial centre, signified by the fourteenth-century **market buildings** on rue du Lt-Col-Bel, and a border post of the kingdom of Dauphiné, with a number of imposing doorways all that remain of the medieval fortifications of the city.

Vienne and around

On leaving Lyon, it's tempting to head straight for the Med, and the first stretch of motorway between Lyon and Vienne is unlikely to distract you from that goal. There is nothing here but oil refineries, steel, chemical and paper works, cement, fertilizer and textile factories, all spewing plumes of grey and orange pollution into the air and water. **VIENNE** is still a bit too close to all this for comfort. Taking a reluctant exit off the *Autoroute du Soleil* en route to Provence is well worth the trouble, however, as the town contains extensive remnants of its ancient history as a major seat of Roman power in Gaul. Every street corner seems to sprout some monument: a Roman temple, a medieval church or cloister. The old quarter is criss-crossed with pedestrian precincts which make for enjoyable menu-browsing around **rue des Clercs** and **place Charles-de-Gaulle.** And there's a feeling that despite the distant rumble of the autoroute calling you to sunnier climes, the town has maintained a character and sense of purpose.

The Town

Roman monuments are scattered liberally around the streets of Vienne, and it requires little effort to take in the magnificently restored **Temple d'Auguste** on place du Palais, a scaled-down version of Nîmes's Maison Carrée, or the scanty remains of the **Théâtre de Cybèle**, off place de Miremont. The **Théâtre Antique** (Mon & Tues 2–5pm, Wed–Sat 10am–noon & 2–5pm; May–Sept daily) is more of a haul, off rue du Cirque at the base of Mont Pipet to the north, but it's worth making the trip for the view of the town and river from the very top seats. The theatre is the venue of an **international jazz**

MUSEUMS

The Théâtre Antique, Cloître de St-André-le-Bas, Musée des Beaux-Arts et Archéologie and the Musée Lapidaire can be visited on a single ticket (20F).

festival for the first two weeks of July, when it plays host to some of the biggest names on the jazz circuit.

The **Musée Lapidaire** (Mon & Tues 2–5pm, Wed–Sat 10am–noon & 2–5pm) is in the **church of St-Pierre**, possibly the first cathedral ever built in France. Since its origins in the fifth century, the building has suffered much destruction and rebuilding, but despite a short period when it was used as a factory in the nineteenth century, it is still one of Vienne's most graceful and attractive buildings. The museum itself is predictably dominated by finds from Vienne's Roman past, including mosaics, the most spectacular being the *mosaïque d'Orphée*, depicting birds and animals whose subtle colouring is beautifully preserved. It may, however, no longer be in the museum as most of the mosaics are in the process of being restored, ready to be exhibited in the new museum at St-Roman-en-Gal (see opposite). Close by is the most prominent – and vaunted – of Vienne's monuments, the **Cathédrale St-Maurice**, whose unwieldy façade, a combination of Romanesque and Gothic, appears as if its upper half has been dumped on top of a completely alien building. The interior, with its ninety-metre-long vaulted nave, is impressive though, and there are some superb stained glass windows.

The buildings of the twelfth-century **Cloître de St-André-le-Bas** on rue des Clercs (Mon & Tues 2–5pm, Wed–Sat 10am–noon & 2–5pm) lend themselves well to a shady, quiet pottery museum containing a collection which includes eleventh-century turned wooden vessels. The cloister itself is a tiny grassed courtyard surrounded by a colonnade, and sets of pillars whose capitals are diversely decorated with mythological and biblical figures. The other major museum in Vienne is the **Musée des Beaux-Arts et Archéologie** on place de Miremont (Mon & Tues 2–5pm, Wed–Sat 10am–noon & 2–5pm), with an unfortunate preponderance of eighteenth-century French pottery, but also some pretty pieces of third-century Roman silverware.

Off the D41, leading from the modern road bridge in the direction of Grenoble, there's a fifteenth-century humpback bridge crossing the Gere (a tributary of the Rhône), on the far side of which – and the main reason for crossing it – is the **church of St-Martin**, containing twentieth-century frescoes by Maurice Denis celebrating the Eucharist, and an ancient wooden sculpture of Christ.

Practicalities

The cours Brillier runs at right angles to the river, with the **tourist office** at no. 3, near quai Jean-Jaurès (Mon–Sat 9am–noon & 2–6/7pm; ☎74.85.12.62), and the **gare SNCF** at the other end (☎78.92.50.50). Halfway up the *cours*, rue Boson leads up to the west front of the cathedral.

If you plan to **stay** over, the *Hôtel de la Poste*, 47 cours Romestang (☎74.85.02.04; ③–④), between the station and place de Miremont, has an excellent restaurant and good rooms overlooking the *cours*. For small budgets try the *Hôtel du Musée*, 17 rue du Musée (☎74.85.17.51; ①–②), with spacious rooms close to place de Miremont. *Le St-Maurice* (☎74.85.08.48; ②–③) is well situated at 18 place St-Maurice in front of the cathedral. If you have your own transport, you could stay at the *Château des Sept Fontaines*, 5km northwest on the N7 at **SEYSSUEL** (☎74.85.25.70; ④–⑤), with a large garden, sauna and gym, and comfortable rooms. There's also an *IYHF* **youth hostel** on the other side of the park from the tourist office at 11 quai Riondet (☎74.53.21.97; ①). The *Camping de Leveau* is on the rte de Leveau (☎74.85.23.15; April–Sept).

The old town has a number of promising places to **eat**, including a good selection of cheapies in rue de la Table Ronde (near St-André-le-Bas), including *L'Estancot* at no. 4 (☎74.85.12.09; closed Sat midday & Sun), and *Au Petit Chez Soi* at no. 6 (☎74.85.19.77; closed Sun) with *moules frites* and menus under 100F. *Le Bec Fin*, 7 place St-Maurice (☎74.85.76.72; closed Sun evening & Mon during school holidays), offers a filling menu of pâté and *quenelles* for 108F, but is very expensive *à la carte*. For café loafing and seafood eats, head for *Le Grand Café Glacier* at 61 cours Romestang. Vienne's superlative restaurant is *La Pyramide*, 14 bd Fernand-Point (☎74.53.01.96; closed Wed & Thurs midday), where the cheapest menu is 280F for weekday lunches and *à la carte* is over 500F.

St-Roman-en-Gal

Across the Rhône from Vienne, several hectares of Roman ruins constitute the site of **ST-ROMAN-EN-GAL**, also the name of the town which faces Vienne from the other bank of the Rhône. The excavations, to the right of the N86 as you head away from Vienne towards Lyon, are low lying but immaculately restored and well preserved, particularly the frescoes. They attest to a significant community dating from the first century BC to the third AD, and give a vivid picture of the daily life and domestic architecture of Roman France. Particularly evocative is the **House of the Sea Gods** (April–Sept 9am–noon & 2–5pm; open till 7pm; 10F combined ticket with Vienne's museums), with a beautiful mosaic floor featuring bearded Neptune and other marine images. A new museum is being built at the site which should open in September 1995.

Between Vienne and Valence

Between Vienne and Valence are some of the oldest, most celebrated **vineyards** in France: the renowned Côte Rotie, Hermitage and Crozes-Hermitage *appellations*. If you've got any spare luggage space, it's well worth stopping to pick up a bottle from the local coop; even their *vin ordinaire* is superlative and unbelievably cheap, considering its quality. Just south of Ampuis on the west bank, 8km south of Vienne, is the tiny area producing one of the most exquisite French white wines – Condrieu, and close by one of the most exclusive – Château-Grillet – an *appellation* covering just this single château (Mon–Sat by appointment; ☎74.59.51.56).

Between **St-Vallier** and **Tain l'Hermitage**, the Rhône becomes quite scenic, and after Tain you can see the Alps. You may even conclude that it's worth slowing down. In spring you're more likely to be conscious of orchards everywhere rather than vines. Cherries, pears, apples, peaches and apricots, as well as bilberries and strawberries, are cultivated in abundance.

Tain-l'Hermitage and around

TAIN L'HERMITAGE, accessible from both the N7 and the A7, is unpretentious and uneventful. The only reason to stay here is to drink wine and eat chocolate. You can sample a good selection of the renowned *Hermitage* and *Crozes-Hermitage* wines at the *Cave Coopérative des Vins Fins*, 22 rte de Larnage (daily 8am–noon & 2–6pm; ☎75.08.20.87), and the celebrated chocolates in question are made by *Valrhona* and available at their shop on av du Président-Roosevelt on the N7, past the junction with the RN95 as you're heading south. The **tourist office** at 70 av Jean-Jaurès (Mon–Fri 9.30am–noon & 2–6pm, Sat 9.30am–noon; ☎75.08.06.81), on the RN7 further north, will provide you with a coupon for a free tasting at *Valrhona* and lists of vineyard addresses.

If you need to **stay**, there are several reasonably priced hotels on place Taurobole, off av Jean-Jaurès in the centre of town: *L'Éscale*, 9 place Taurobole (☎75.08.31.67; ①; closed Nov), and *Le Taurobole*, 2 place Taurobole (☎75.08.25.88; ②–③; closed Sun eve & Mon). More upmarket, *Les 2 Côteaux*, 1 rue Joseph-Péala, running off Jean-Jaurès south of place Taurobole (☎75.08.33.01; ①–④; closed Feb), is beside the Rhône.

If you're looking for a cheap **meal** in Tain, the *crêperie La Récré*, 8 place Taurobole (☎75.08.19.00), is an alternative to the stuffier establishments on av Jean-Jaurès. Tain's best restaurant, *Reynaud*, 82 av du Président-Roosevelt (☎75.07.22.10; closed Sun midday & Mon), has an excellent-value 160F menu, with *à la carte* upwards of 300F.

On the third weekend of September, the different wine-producing villages celebrate their cellars in the *Fête des Vendanges*. But at any time of the year you can go bottle hunting along the N86 for some 30km north of Tain along the right bank, following the *dégustation* signs and then crossing back over between **SERRIÈRES** and **CHANAS**.

Hauterives

HAUTERIVES, 25km northeast of Tain, is a small village with a remarkable creation – a manic, surreal **Palais Idéal** built by a local postman by the name of Ferdinand Cheval (1836–1912). The eccentric building took him thirty years to carve, and he designed a likewise bizarre tombstone. Various Surrealists have paid homage to the building; psychoanalysts have given it their all, but it defies all classification (daily 9.30am–noon & 2–5.30pm; Easter–Sept 9am–6.30pm; July & Aug till 7.30pm; 16F). If you want to stay here, there's the *Camping du Château* (☎75.31.82.97; May–Sept) and one **hotel**, *Le Relais* (☎75.68.81.12; ①–②).

Romans-sur-Isère

South of Hauterives and 15km east of the Rhône at Tain is **ROMANS-SUR-ISÈRE**. It's not the most exciting of towns, and its museum of shoemaking – the industry that has kept it going for the last five centuries – isn't one you would automatically alter your itinerary for. But the extensive **Musée de la Chaussure et d'Ethnographie Régionale**, in the former Convent of the Visitation at 2 rue Ste-Marthe (Tues–Sat 9–11.45am & 2–5.45pm, Sun 2.30–6pm; mid-June to mid-Sept Tues–Sat 10am–6pm, Sun 2.30–6pm; 25F), turns out to be well worth the stop. Your toes will curl in horror at the extent to which women have been immobilized by their footwear from ancient times to the present on every continent, while at the same time you can't help but admire the craziness of some of the shoes.

If you need information there's a **tourist office** on place Jean-Jaurès (Mon–Fri 9am–7pm, Sat 9am–6pm, Sun 9.30am–12.30pm; Nov–March Mon–Fri 9am–12.15pm & 1.45–6.30pm, Sat 9am–6pm, Sun 9.30am–1.30pm; ☎75.02.28.72). Romans has plenty of beautiful old streets and buildings to admire, and its region has two gastronomic specialities: a ringed spongy bread flavoured with orange water, known as a *pogne*, and *ravioles*, cornflour-based raviolis with an eggy, cheesy, buttery filling. You can sample these at the restaurant *La Cassolette*, 16 rue Rebatte (☎75.02.55.71; closed Sun & Mon & three weeks from last week in July).

Romans' **hotels** include *Les Balmes*, northwest of the town centre in the quartier Les Balmes (☎75.02.29.52; closed Sun evening; ③), with a reputed and not expensive restaurant (closed Mon midday). A cheaper option for rooms is the *Magdeleine*, 31 av Pierre-Sémard (☎75.02.33.53; ①–②; closed Sun out of season), or the *Terminus*, 48 rue Pierre-Sémard (☎75.02.46.88; ①–②). The municipal **campsite**, *Les Chasses* (☎75.72.35.27; May–Sept), is a kilometre off the N92 northeast of the city, near to the aerodrome.

Valence and Montélimar

At an indefinable point along the Rhône, there's an invisible sensual border. By the time you reach **VALENCE**, you know you've crossed it. The quality of light is different here and the temperature higher, bringing with it the scent of eucalyptus and pine. The colours and contours have suddenly become worlds apart from the cold lands of Lyon and the north. Valence is the obvious place to celebrate your arrival in the Midi (as the French call the south), with plenty of good bars and restaurants in the old town.

Arrival and accommodation

If you come in on the autoroute, running along the Rhône's left bank, you exit onto av Gambetta, with the old town, its ramparts replaced by boulevards, to your left. The N7 follows the eastern edge of the old town and runs straight through place du Général-Leclerc, where you'll find the **tourist office** (Mon–Sat 10am–12.30pm & 2–5.30pm; ☎75.43.04.88). The **gare SNCF** is alongside the N7, 500m south of the square; the **gare routière** and **PTT** are on place Aristide-Briand, which runs south off av Gambetta.

For mid-range hotel **rooms**, try *California*, 174 av Maurice-Faure (☎75.44.36.05; ③), *Hôtel de France*, 16 bd Général-de-Gaulle (☎75.43.00.87; ④), or *St-Jacques*, 9 faubourg St-Jacques; (☎75.42.44.60; ③). Cheaper options include the *Hôtel d'Angleterre*, 11 av Félix-Faure (☎75.43.00.35; ①–②), and the *Splendid*, 20 av P-Sémard (☎75.44.09.18; ①–②), by the station. The *IYHF* **youth hostel** *L'Epervière*, on chemin de l'Epervière (☎75.42.32.007; ①), is by the Rhône, 2km south of the city. It's quite expensive but has good sports facilities – swimming pool, sailing – and bike rental. The **camping municipal** is in the youth hostel grounds (☎75.42.32.00; all year).

The Town

The focus of Vieux Valence, the **Cathédrale St-Apollinaire**, was founded in 1095 and largely reconstructed in the seventeenth century after a local baron went on the rampage, avenging the execution of three Protestants during the Wars of Religion. More work was carried out later, including the horribly mismatched nineteenth-century tower, but the interior still preserves its original Romanesque grace.

The **church of St-Jean**, to the north, has preserved its Romanesque tower and porch capitals, and between the church and cathedral are some of the oldest and narrowest streets of Vieux Valence. They are known as **côtes**: côte St-Estève just northwest of the cathedral; côte St-Martin off rue du Petit-Paradis; and côte Sylvante off rue du Petit-Paradis' continuation, rue A-Paré. Diverse characters who would have walked these steep and crooked streets include Rabelais, a student at the university founded here in 1452 and suppressed during the Revolution, and the teenage Napoléon Bonaparte, who began his military training as a cadet at the artillery school.

Though Valence lacks the cohesion of the medieval towns and villages further south, it does have several vestiges of the sixteenth-century city, most notably the Renaissance **Maison des Têtes** at 57 Grande-Rue, with its eroded but still discernibly bizarre statuary, and the **Maison Dupré-Latour** on rue Pérollerie, with a superbly sculptured porch and spiral staircase. Valence's **municipal museum** on place des Ormeaux (Mon, Tues, Thurs & Fri 2–5pm; Wed, Sat & Sun 9am–noon & 2–6pm; 12F, free Sun & July) is hard work. The tedium is only relieved by the Roman mosaic of the labours of Hercules, some modern sculpture and abstract art, and an eighteenth-century collection of red pencil drawings by Hubert Robert, a reminder of the days when the Rhône valley was an essential part of the Grand Tour of Classical Europe.

A good place if you need to fill in time is the **Parc Jouvet** overlooking the river (and the motorway) south of av Gambetta. At evening-time around sunset, or even better at dawn, this is definitely the best place to be in the city – with a bottle of *Cornas* or sparkling *St-Peray* from the vineyards across the water.

Eating, drinking and entertainment

For **restaurants**, *L'Épicerie-Restaurant*, 18 place Belat (☎75.42.74.46; closed Sat lunchtime & Sun), is one of the most congenial places to eat, with art exhibitions on the fifteenth-century walls, jazz some nights, and imaginative food at reasonable prices. *Le Coelacanthe*, 3 place de la Pierre (☎75.42.30.68; closed Mon & Sat midday and Sun), serves wonderful fish with menus starting at 85F. For Greek and Armenian food, try *Le Bosphore* at 14 rue Balthazar-Baro (☎75.55.24.33), and, for a cheap midday *plat du jour*, go to the *Le Coq au Vin* in rue de l'Hôtel-de-Ville. If you want to eat very well and are prepared to pay over 350F for the pleasure, *Restaurant Pic*, 285 av Victor-Hugo (☎75.44.15.32; closed Sun evening & Wed), is the city's top-notch eating house. Roast lobster with truffles, asparagus with *hollandaise* and caviar, and frozen nougat are some of the delights.

Montélimar

In **MONTÉLIMAR**, 40km south of Valence, every street proclaims the glory of the nougat that has been made here for centuries and is the town's sole *raison d'être*. But it's quite a lively place and its *vieille ville* has some charm.

The main street of the old town, **rue Pierre-Julien**, runs from the one remaining medieval **gateway** on the nineteenth-century ring of boulevards at place St-Martin, south past the **church of Ste-Croix** with its well-populated square, and on to place Marx-Dormoy. Leading off it are plenty of medieval lanes with sixteenth- and seventeenth-century townhouses, and around the pastel façades and old arcades of **place du Marché**, you'll find *Le Métro* bar, done up as an old Paris métro station with a young clientele playing chess and backgammon. Above the old town to the east is the impressive fourteenth-century fortress, the **Château des Adhémar** on rue du Château (guided visits: 10am–noon & 2–7pm; Nov–March closed Tues), with an interesting medieval chapel and relics from the castle's history. If you just want to sample and buy some of the town's moreish nougat, try *Chabert et Guillot*, 9 rue Charles-Chabert, just south of the *gare SNCF*.

The **gare SNCF** is a short way west of the old town, with the **tourist office** in the adjacent park on the allée Champs-de-Mars (Mon–Sat 10am–noon & 2–5.30pm; ☎75.01.00.20); they can fix up visits to a nougat factory. There are plenty of **hotels** around the boulevards, including the luxury *Le Parc Chabaud*, near place Marx-Dormoy at 16 av d'Aygu (☎75.01.65.66; ④–⑦), and the very pleasant *Le Sphinx*, 19 bd Marre-Desmarais (☎75.01.86.64; ③–④). Within the old town you could try *Hôtel Pierre*, 7 place des Clercs (☎75.01.33.16; ①–②; closed Feb) – peaceful, apart from the nearby bell of Ste-Croix tolling the hours. There's a **campsite** not too far away, the *International Deux Saisons* (☎75.01.88.99; mid-Feb to Nov), 500m east on the D540, then right towards Alexis.

Enticing smells emanate from *La Papillote* **restaurant** on place du Temple (☎75.01.99.28; closed Sun & Mon; menus under 100F). For a greater outlay, you can feast on good traditional food at the *Relais de l'Empereur*, 1 place Max-Dormoy (☎75.01.29.00; menus from 150F). Good salads for around 60F are to be had at *Le Garden Bar*, 8 place des Clercs (☎75.53.00.70; closed Sun), and *crêperies* and other snack food places are almost as ubiquitous as *confiseries* (sweet shops).

WESTERN PROVENCE

The richest area of Provence, the Côte d'Azur apart, is the **west**. Most of the large-scale production of fruits, vegetables and wine is based here in the low-lying plains beside the Rhône and the Durance rivers. The only heights are the rocky outbreaks of the **Dentelles** and the **Alpilles**, and the narrow east–west ridges of **Mont Ventoux**, the **Lubéron** and the **Mont Ste-Victoire**. The two dominant cities of inland Provence, **Avignon** and **Aix**, both have rich histories and contemporary fame in their festivals of art. Around the Rhône delta, the **Camargue** is a unique self-contained region, as different from the rest of Provence as it is from anywhere else in France.

Orange and around

ORANGE was the former seat of the counts of Orange, a title created by Charlemagne in the eighth century, and passed to the Dutch crown in the sixteenth century. Its most memorable member was Prince William, who ascended the English throne with his consort Mary, but the town is today best known for its spectacular Roman theatre, now host to two important summer **music festivals**. While the rest of the town is attractive enough, with its medieval street plan, there's not a lot to detain you once you've visited the theatre and adjacent museum and taken a quick look at the Roman triumphal arch at the northern approach to the town centre. If your visit coincides with the strip-cartoon festival in May, then there'll be plenty of entertainment both in the works on display and in the number of weird and wonderful artists around.

Arrival and accommodation

The **gare SNCF** is about 1500m east of the centre, at the end of av Frédéric-Mistral. The nearest bus stop is at the bottom of rue Jean-Reboul, the first left as you walk away from the station. Bus #2, direction *Nogent*, takes you to the Théâtre Antique and the next stop, *Gasparin*, to the **tourist office** on cours Aristide-Briand (Mon–Sat 9am–7pm, Sun 10am–6pm; Oct–March Mon–Sat 9am–6pm; ☎90.34.70.88). The **gare routière** is close to the centre on place Pourtoules.

Of the **hotels**, the *Fréau*, 3 rue Ancien-Collège (☎90.34.06.26; ①–②; closed Aug), is central, simple and cheap; advance bookings are advisable. Others to try are *L'Arène* on place de Langes (☎90.34.10.95; ④–⑤), with spacious rooms and all mod cons, the very comfortable *Le Glacier*, 46 cours Aristide-Briand (☎90.34.02.01; ③–④), or the cheap but not very inviting *Le Milan*, 22 rue Caristie (☎90.34.13.31; ①). Orange's **campsite**, *Le Jonquier*, rue Alexis-Carrel (☎90.34.19.83; mid-March to Oct), to the northwest, is equipped with tennis courts.

The Town

Days off in Orange circa 5 BC were most entertainingly spent from dawn to dusk at the huge Roman **theatre** (daily 9am–6.30pm; Oct 5–March 9am–noon & 1.30–5pm; 15F joint ticket with museum), watching farce, clownish improvisations, song and dance, and occasionally, for the sake of a visiting dignitary, a bit of Greek tragedy in Latin. The acoustics allowed a full audience of 10,000 to hear every word. The hill of St-Eutrope into which the seats were built – along with a vast awning from the top of the stage wall – protected the spectators from the weather. It is the best-preserved example in existence, and the only one with the stage wall still standing – 103m across and 36m high, and completely plain like some monstrous prison wall when you see it from outside. The interior, although missing much of its original decoration, has its central, larger-than-life-size statue of Augustus, and the columned niches for other lesser statues.

The best view of the theatre in its entirety is from St-Eutrope hill. If you go past the Forum or gymnasium remains, across place Silvian and take montée de Chalon to the left off rue de Tourre, you can follow a path up the hill until you are looking directly down onto the stage. The ruins around your feet are those of the short-lived seventeenth-century **castle of the princes of Orange**. Louis XIV had it destroyed and the principality of Orange annexed to France – a small price to pay for the ruler of the Netherlands who was also to become king of England.

The **municipal museum**, across the road from the theatre entrance (Mon–Sat 9am–7pm, Sun 10am–6pm; Oct 5–March Mon–Sat 9am–noon & 1.30–5pm, Sun 9am–noon & 2–5.30pm; 15F joint ticket with theatre), has documents concerning the

Orange dynasty, including a suitably austere portrait of the very first Orangeman, Guillaume "the Taciturn". It also has Roman bits and pieces and an unlikely collection of works by one Frank Brangwyn, a Welsh painter who had no connections with Orange. The pictures here are stark portrayals of British workers early this century.

If you've arrived by road from the north you will have passed the town's second major Roman monument, the **Arc de Triomphe**, whose intricate frieze and relief celebrates imperial victories against the Gauls. It was built around 20 BC outside the town walls to proclaim the importance of the Roman settlement.

The rest of Orange's old town is very small, hemmed in between the **Parc de la Colline St-Eutrope** and the River Meyne, featuring some pretty fountained squares and houses with ancient porticos and courtyards.

Eating, drinking and entertainment

For **food**, cheap *frites* with *plats du jour* to eat in or take away can be had at *La Fringale* on rue de Tourre (till 11pm; closed Sun midday and Wed out of season). *Le Yaca*, 24 place Silvain (☎90.34.70.03; closed Wed and Tues evening out of season), gives a generous choice of efficiently served dishes for 80F in an old vaulted chamber. If it's full, try the neighbouring *Galois* (☎90.34.32.51). The *Café des Thermes* on rue des Vieux-Fossés is a billiards bar with youngish clientele. For a standard **drinking** place, place de la République, opposite the *mairie*, has *Les Négociants* and the less chic *Commerce*, which has a much better jukebox.

Orange also hosts some major **festivals** throughout the year – the Festival BD (*Bandes-Dessinés* or strip cartoons; details from *Sabords 84*, ☎90.51.19.95) in May, the *Chorégies d'Orange*, a programme of opera, oratorios and orchestral concerts in July (details and tickets from *Les Chorégies d'Orange*, place Silvain; ☎90.34.24.24), and the *Nuits d'Eté du Théâtre Antique* in June, featuring ballet, opera and rock concerts (details from the *Centre Culturel Mosaïque*, place Silvain; ☎90.51.89.58). Both music festivals use the Roman theatre as their main venue.

Sérignan and Châteauneuf

The village of **SÉRIGNAN-DU-COMTAT** is just a short drive northeast of Orange. This was the final home of **Jean-Henri Fabre**, a remarkable self-taught scientist, famous for his insect studies, who composed poetry, wrote songs and painted his specimens with artistic brilliance as well as scientific accuracy. In the 1860s he had to resign from his teaching post at Avignon because parents and priests thought his lectures on the fertilization of flowering plants to be licentious, if not downright pornographic. In his **house**, which he named the *Harmas* (Mon & Wed–Sun 9–11.30am & 2–4pm; summer till 6pm; winter 2–6pm only; 10F), you can see his jungly garden, the study with his complete classification of the herbs of France and Corsica and, on the ground floor, a selection from his extraordinary watercolour series of the fungi of the Vaucluse. At the crossroads in the centre of the town (the *Harmas* is on N976 towards Orange) there's a flattering statue of Fabre in front of the red-shuttered buildings of the church and *mairie*.

Châteauneuf-du-Pape

If you're heading down to Avignon, the slower route through **CHÂTEAUNEUF-DU-PAPE** (also taken by four buses daily) exerts a strong pull. The village takes its name from the summer palace of the Avignon popes. But neither the miserable ruins of the fourteenth-century **château** (freely acccessible) nor the medieval streets around **place**

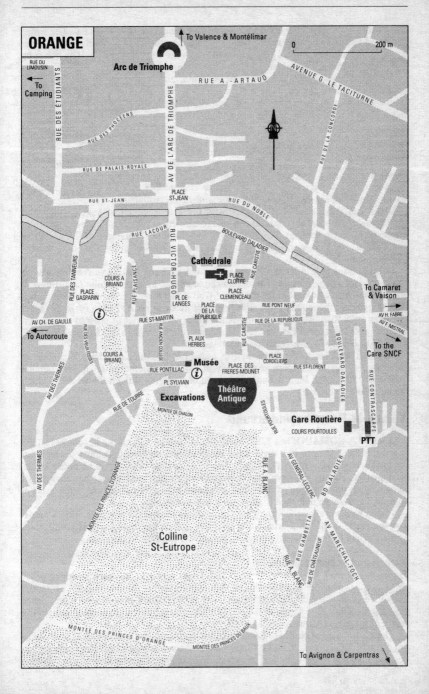

du Portail – the hub of the village – give Châteauneuf its special appeal. The wines produced by the local vineyards – warmed at night by the large pebbles that cover the ground, soaking up the sun's heat during the day – are its real attraction. The rich ruby red is one of France's most renowned, but the white, too, is exquisite.

The *appellation Châteauneuf-du-Pape* does not, alas, come cheap, and there's no single place where you can taste a good selection from the scores of *domaines*. For a casual introduction, the *Cave Père-Anselme* on av Bienheureux-Pierre-de-Luxembourg has a **Musée des Outils de Vigneron** (daily 9am–noon & 2–6pm; free) and free tastings of its own and other Rhône wines to attract visitors. To reach the *cave*, take av Baron-Leroy from place du Portail, then right towards Avignon. Otherwise, the **tourist office** on place du Portail (Mon–Sat 9am–12.30pm & 2–6pm; July & Aug Mon–Sat 9am–7pm, Sun 10am–5pm; ☎90.83.71.08), or the *Fédération des Syndicats de Producteurs* on rte d'Avignon, can provide a complete list of producers, or you can visit an *Association de Vignerons* such as *Prestige et Tradition* at 3 rue de la République (daily 8am–noon & 2–6pm), who bottle the wine of ten producers.

If you can make your visit coincide with the first weekend of August you'll find free *dégustation* stalls throughout the village as well as parades, dances, equestrian contests, folkloric floats and so forth, all to celebrate the reddening of the grapes in the **Fête de la Véraison**. As well as wine, a good deal of grape liqueur – *marc* – gets consumed.

Getting too drunk to leave Châteauneuf is not advisable unless you're prepared to pay dearly for your excesses. The options are confined to three **hotels**: *La Garbure*, 3 rue Joseph Ducos (☎90.83.75.08; ③; closed Wed & last three weeks in Aug), which has only five rooms; the four-star *Hostellerie du Château des Fines Roches* on rte de Sorgues-Avignon (☎90.83.70.23; ⑤–⑦; closed Sun evening & Mon out of season) with seven rooms, and *Le Clement V* on rte de Nimes in the village of **ROQUEMAURE** (☎66.87.67.58; ③–⑤), upstream from Châteauneuf.

You can **eat** for under 100F at the brasserie *La Mule du Pape*, 2 rue de la République, and much more expensively at *La Mère Germaine* on place Fontaine (☎90.83.70.72; closed Mon & Sun evening out of season) – though the weekday lunch menu at 160F is brilliant.

Vaison-la-Romaine and around

VAISON-LA-ROMAINE lies 27km northeast of Orange and hit the headlines in 1992 when the River Ouvèze that divides the medieval and eighteenth-century towns burst its banks, destroying riverside houses, the modern road bridge, and an entire industrial quarter. Though the town has recovered remarkably, its character has changed. It seems much more commercialized and less friendly – perhaps because of the mass of ghoulish tourists who flocked to the town to see the damage.

It still, however, has the strong attractions of its medieval *haute ville*, with a ruined cliff-top castle, a medieval bridge that held out against the floods, a cloistered former cathedral and the exceptional excavated remains of two Roman districts.

Arrival and accommodation

Buses to and from Carpentras, Orange and Avignon stop at the **gare routière** on av des Choralies near the junction with av Victor-Hugo, east of the town centre. The **tourist office** is on place du Chanoine Sautel (Mon–Fri 9.30am–noon & 2–5.45pm, Sat & Sun 10am–noon & 2–5.45pm; ☎90.36.02.11), between the two archeological sites in the north of the modern town.

There's not a great choice of **hotels** and few bargains. The best deal is at *Le Burrhus* on place Montfort (☎90.36.00.11; ②–③) above all the terraced cafés. For really stylish lodgings, Vaison's best hotel and restaurant is *Le Beffroi*, a sixteenth-century residence on rue de l'Évêché in the *haute ville* (☎90.36.04.71; ⑤–⑥). On rte de St-Marcellin, 1km east of town down av Geoffroy from the Pont Romain, you'll find the *Centre Culturel à Cœur Joie*, with simple rooms (☎90.36.00.78; ①). For **campers**, there's the central *Camping du Théâtre Romain* on chemin du Brusquet, off av des Choralies, Quartier des Arts (☎90.28.78.66; April–Oct).

The Town

The *haute ville* lies on the south side of the river, with **rue du Pont** climbing up towards place des Poids and the fourteenth-century **gateway** to the town. More steep zigzags take you past the Gothic gate and overhanging portcullis of the **belfry** and into the heart of this sedately quiet, uncommercialized and rich *quartier*.

On the north bank from the **Pont Romain**, a Roman bridge that has been patched up over the years, Grande-Rue leads up to the central streets of rue de la République and cours Henri-Fabre, after which it becomes av Général-de-Gaulle. The two excavated **Roman residential districts** lie to either side of this avenue: Puymin to the east and La Villasse to the west (daily 9am–12.30pm & 2–5.45/6.45pm; ticket for both plus Puymin museum and cathedral cloisters 32F).

The Puymin excavations contain the theatre, several mansions and houses, a colonnade known as the *portique de Pompée* and the museum for all the items discovered. The excavations of La Villasse reveal a street with pavements and gutters with the layout of a row of arcaded shops running parallel, more patrician houses (some with mosaics still intact), a basilica and the baths. The houses require a certain amount of imagination, but the street plan of La Villasse, the colonnade with its statues in every niche, and the theatre, which still seats 7000 people during the July festival, make it easy to visualize a comfortable, well-serviced town of the Roman ruling class.

Most of the detail and decoration of the buildings are displayed in the **museum** (Sept–March closed 1–2.30pm; joint ticket 32F) in the Puymin district. Tiny fragments of painted plaster have been jigsawed together with convincing reconstructions of how whole painted walls would have looked. There are mirrors of silvered bronze, lead water pipes, taps shaped as griffins' feet, dolphin door knobs, weights and measures, plus impressive busts and statues.

Tickets can be bought at the Puymin entrance just by the tourist office or in the cloisters of the former **Cathédrale Notre-Dame**, west down chemin Couradou, which runs along the south side of La Villasse. The apse of the cathedral is a confusing overlay of sixth-, tenth- and thirteenth-century construction, using pieces quarried from the Roman ruins. The **cloisters** (daily 9am–12.30pm & 2–5.45/6.45pm; ticket for both plus Puymin museum and excavations 32F) are fairly typical of early medieval workmanship – pretty enough but not wildly exciting. The only surprising feature is the large inscription visible on the north wall of the cathedral, a convoluted precept for the monks.

Eating and drinking

The **restaurant** to head for is *Le Bateleur*, 1 place Théodore-Aubanel, downstream from the Pont Romain on the north bank (☎90.36.28.04; closed Sun evening, Mon & Oct). The lamb stuffed with almonds and the *rascasse soufflé* are highly recommended, and there's a 120F menu, with *à la carte* at around 180F. *L'Auberge de la Bartavelle*, 12 place Sus-Auze (☎90.36.02.16; closed Mon), has specialities from southwest France from 100F to 200F. Homemade bread and savoury tarts are to be had at *La Gloriette et Pomponette* at 22 Grande-Rue (☎90.28.77.74; closed Sun, and Thurs out of season), as well as traditional menus for around 110F. You can get crêpes and pizzas in the old town and brasserie fare on place de Montfort, the obvious drinking place to gravitate towards. For a more local atmosphere, try *Vasio Bar* on cours Taulignan.

Mont Ventoux

Some 20km east of Vaison rises **Mont Ventoux**, whose outline repeatedly appears upon the horizon from the Rhône and Durance valleys. White with snow, black with storm-cloud shadow or reflecting myriad shades of blue, the barren pebbles of the uppermost 300m are like a weather-vane for all of western Provence. Winds can accelerate to 250km per hour around the meteorological, TV and military masts and dishes on the summit, but if you can stand still for a moment the view in all directions is unbelievable. A road, the D974, climbs all the way to the top, though no buses take it.

If you want to make the ascent on foot, the best path is from **LES COLOMBETS** or **LES FÉBRIERS**, two hamlets off the D974, east of **BÉDOIN** – whose **tourist office** on the Espace M L -Gravier (Mon–Sat 9.30am–noon & 2–6pm, Sun 9.30am–noon; ☎90.65.63.95) can give details, plus addresses of campsites and *gîtes ruraux*.

Mont Ventoux is a sporadic highlight of the Tour de France, hence its appeal in summer for committed cyclists. Around the treeline is a **memorial** to the great British cyclist Tommy Simpson, who died here from heart failure, on one of the hottest days ever recorded in the race; his last words were "Put me back on the bloody bike."

The Dentelles and around

The **Dentelles**, a row of jagged limestone pinnacles, run across an arid, windswept, and near-deserted upland area, the **Massif Montmirail-St-Amand**, just south of Vaison-la-Romaine. Their name refers to lace – the limestone protrusions were thought to resemble the contorted pins on a lace-making board – though the word's alternative connection with "teeth" is equally appropriate.

The area is best known for its wines. On the western and southern slopes lie the wine-producing villages of **GIGONDAS, BEAUMES-DE-VENISE, SABLET, SÉGURET, VACQUEYRAS** and, across the River Ouzère, **RASTEAU**. Each one carries the distinction of having its own individual *appellation contrôlé* within the *Côtes du Rhône* or *Côtes du Rhône Villages* areas: in other words, their wines are exceptional. In addition, some of the villages are alluringly picturesque, with Séguret super-conscious of its Provençal beauty.

The most reputed **wine** in the Dentelles is made at Gigondas – it's almost always red, and quite strong with an aftertaste of spice and nuts. You can taste the produce from forty different *domaines* and buy *en vrac* (in bulk) – a real bargain for this wine – at the *Cave des Vignerons* (closed Wed) on place de la Mairie in the village. The most distinctive wine, and elixir for those who like it sweet, is the pale amber-coloured Beaumes-de-Venise muscat which you can buy from the **Cave des Vignerons** (8.30am–noon & 2–6pm; closed Sun) on the D7 just outside Beaumes.

Besides *dégustation* and bottle buying, you can go for long walks in the Dentelles, stumbling upon mysterious ruins or photogenic panoramas of **Mont Ventoux** and the Rhône valley. The pinnacles are favourite scaling faces for apprentice rock-climbers – though their wind-eroded patterns can be appreciated just as well without risking your neck on an ascent.

The **tourist office** in Gigondas is on place du Portail (Mon–Sat 9.30am–noon & 2–6pm, Sat 9.30am–noon; ☎90.65.85.46), and either the *Cave des Vignerons* or *mairie* in Beaumes can provide lists for the villages of particular *domaines* or *caves* grouping several *vignerons*. It's possible to get to Beaumes, Vacqueyras, Gigondas, Séguret and Sablet by public transport, with two **buses** daily from Vaison and Carpentras. There are **campsites** in Sablet (☎90.46.96.27), Beaumes (☎90.62.95.07) and Vacqueyras (☎90.65.84.24) and a **gîte d'étape** on the rte de Sablet in Séguret (☎90.65.93.31). In Beaumes, the *Auberge St-Roch* on av Jules–Ferry (☎90.62.94.29; ②; closed mid-Aug to mid-Sept) and *Le Relais des Dentelles* (☎90.62.95.27; ②), past the old village and over the river, are quiet, old-fashioned hotels; note that both are closed on Monday. Gigondas has *Les Florets*, 2km from the village towards the Dentelles (☎90.65.85.01; ④–⑤; half-board obligatory in season), and the very upmarket *Hôtellerie de Montmirail*, which you reach via Vacqueyras (☎90.65.84.01; ⑥–⑦). The *gîte d'étape* at the entrance to Gigondas (☎90.65.80.85) is the place to go for walking and climbing information and for bike rental, as well as to stay.

In Sablet, the *Café des Sports* on the last spiral of the dome-shaped village feeds you for under 100F, with no fooling around with menus. The restaurant at *Les Florets* (see above) has a good 155F menu, or there's *L'Oustalet* on place du Portail in Gigondas (☎90.65.85.30). Places to stop for a drink or food are few and far between once you leave the main villages.

Carpentras

With a population of around 30,000, **CARPENTRAS** is a substantial city for this part of the world, lying 22km southeast of Orange. It is also a very old city, its known history starting in 5 BC as the capital of a Celtic tribe. The Greeks who founded Marseille came to Carpentras to buy honey, wheat, goats and skins, and the Romans had a base here. For a brief period in the fourteenth century, it became the papal headquarters and gave protection to Jews expelled from France.

For all its ancient remains, Carpentras seems incapable of working up an atmosphere to imbue the present with its past. The local history museum – the **Musée Comtadin** on bd Albin-Durand (Wed–Sun 10am–noon & 2–4/6pm; free) – is dark and dour and filled with dry regional bits and pieces. The erotic fantasies of a seventeenth-century cardinal frescoed by Nicolas Mignard on the **Palais de Justice**, formerly the episcopal palace, were effaced by a later incumbent. The *palais* is attached to the **Cathédrale St-Siffrein** and behind, almost hidden in the corner, stands a **Roman arch** inscribed with happy imperial scenes of prisoners in chains. Fifteen hundred years after its erection, Jews – coerced, bribed or otherwise persuaded – entered the cathedral in chains to be unshackled as converted Christians. The door they passed through – the **Porte Juif** – is on the southern side and bears strange symbolism of rats encircling and devouring a globe. Apart from the Porte Juif, though, the cathedral is exceedingly dull, as is the space around it. The **synagogue** (Mon–Fri 10am–noon & 3–5pm, 4pm on Fri, closed Jewish feast days; free), near the Hôtel de Ville, although the oldest in France, was rebuilt in the seventeenth century.

Buses (the trains are freight only) arrive either on av Victor-Hugo or a short distance away on place Terradou. From the latter, rue de la République runs north to the cathedral, past which rue d'Inguimbert leads off right towards the synagogue and Hôtel de Ville. The **tourist office** is at 170 allée Jean-Jaurès (summer daily 9am–7pm; winter Mon–Sat 9am–12.30pm & 2–6.30pm; ☎90.63.00.78) and hands out free maps. If you want to **stay**, *La Lavande* at 282 bd A-Rogier (☎90.63.13.49; ①–②) has eight basic doubles but is often full. If so, *Le Théâtre*, 7 bd Albin-Durand (☎90.63.02.90; ①–②), is another low-cost option, with *Le Cours*, 65 bd Albin-Durand (☎90.63.10.07; ①–③), running a close second. The most pleasant hotel is *Le Fiacre*, 153 rue Vigne (☎90.63.03.15; ②–⑤), an old town house with a garden close to the tourist office.

As far as **eating** goes, *Le Marijo* at 73 rue Raspail (☎90.60.42.65; closed Fri evening & Sun) is excellent, with menus under 130F. *Le Vert Galant*, 12 rue Clapies (☎90.67.15.50; closed Sat midday & Sun), serves more sophisticated fare, with a lunchtime menu for around 100F, otherwise from 160F. Takeaway Thai, Chinese and Vietnamese food is available from *La Perle d'Asie* on place du Théâtre. Café-crawling is best done on place Aristide-Briand or around the cathedral.

Avignon

AVIGNON, great city of the popes and for centuries one of the major artistic centres of France, can be very daunting. The monuments and museums are huge; it's always crowded in summer and it can be stiflingly hot. But it is an immaculately preserved medieval town with endless impressively decorated buildings, ancient churches, chapels and convents, and more places to eat and drink than you could cover in a month. During the **Festival d'Avignon** in July and the beginning of August, it is *the* place to be.

Central Avignon is enclosed by medieval walls, built by one of the nine popes that based themselves here throughout most of the fourteenth century, away from the anarchic feuding or, in the case of the last two, away from the rival popes in Rome. Avignon was a lively place while the papacy had its headquarters here. According to Petrarch, the overcrowded, plague-ridden papal entourage was "a sewer where all the filth of the universe has gathered". In 1403 the anti-Pope Benoit, who had built the walls in a fit of justified paranoia during the shifting alliances of the Great Schism, was ousted and the city had to content itself with mere cardinals.

Arrival and accommodation

Both the **gare SNCF** (☎90.82.50.50) and the **gare routière** are close to Porte de la République on bd St-Roch. Cours Jean-Jaurès runs inside the gate, with the **tourist office** a little way up on the right at no. 41 (Mon–Fri 9am–1pm & 2–6pm, Sat 9am–1pm & 2–5pm; April–Sept also Sun 9am–1pm & 2–5pm; ☎90.82.65.11), which has an annexe at the other end of town by the Pont d'Avignon. If you're driving, it's best to park to either side of Pont Daladier outside the walls on the west side of the city. The city's two main local **bus termini**, with *TCRA (Transports en Commun de la Région d'Avignon)*

THE FESTIVAL

Unlike most provincial festivals of international renown, the **Festival d'Avignon** is dominated by theatre rather than classical music, though there is also plenty of that, as well as lectures, exhibitions and dance. It uses the city's great buildings as backdrops to performances, and takes place every year for three weeks from the second week in July. The year 1995 will be its 49th. During festival time everything stays open late and everything gets booked up; there can be up to 200,000 visitors, and getting around or doing anything normal becomes virtually impossible.

Recent festivals have seen plays by Euripides, Shakespeare, Heinrich von Kleist, Edward Bond and Samuel Beckett, a gay fable about AIDS from New York, the equestrian theatre of the Zingaro people from India, and dance events ranging from the Ballet de l'Opéra National de Paris to the Bill T Jones/Arnie Zane company. As well as the mainstream festival, there's a fringe contingent known as the **Festival Off**, using eighty different venues and the streets for a programme of innovative, obscure or bizarre performances.

The **main festival programme**, with details of how to book, is available from the second week in May from the *Bureau du Festival d'Avignon*, 8bis rue de Mons, 84000 Avignon (☎90.82.67.08). Ticket prices are reasonable (between 100F and 150F) and go on sale from the second week in June. As well as phone sales, they can be bought from *FNAC* shops in all major French cities. During the festival, tickets are available until 1pm for the same day's performances. The **Festival Off programme** is available from mid-May from *Avignon Public Off* BP5, 75521 Paris Cedex 11 (☎48.05.20.97). During the festival, the office is in the Conservatoire de Musique on place du Palais. Tickets prices range from 50F to 70F and a *Carte Public Adhérent* for 65F gives you 30F off all shows.

offices for route maps and tickets (6F each or 36F for ten), are by Porte de la République (stops *Poste, Cité Administrative, Gare routière* and *Gare)*, and place Pie, right in the centre of town.

Accommodation

Even outside festival time, finding a **room** in Avignon can be a problem: cheap hotels fill fast and it's never a bad idea to book in advance. It's worth remembering, too, that Villeneuve-lès-Avignon is only just across the river and may have rooms when its big neighbour is full. Between the two, the Île de la Barthelasse is an idyllic spot for camping, and you may find the odd farmhouse advertising rooms.

Vaucluse Tourisme Hébergements (Mon–Fri 9am–6pm, Sat 10am–5pm; ☎90.82.05.81), located in the main tourist office in summer and in place Campana in winter, can provide comprehensive information on accommodation in Avignon and the region and book rooms for a small fee.

HOTELS

Hôtel de l'Angleterre, 29 bd Raspail (☎90.86.34.31). An old, traditional hotel with some reasonably priced rooms, well away from night-time noise in the southeast corner of the old city. ②–④.

La Ferme Jamet, Île de la Barthelasse (☎90.86.16.74). A sixteenth-century farm on the island in the Rhône (signposted right off Pont Daladier as you cross over from Avignon) with a choice of farmhouse bedrooms and period furniture, your own outhouse building, an ultramodern flat or a gypsy caravan. Tennis courts and swimming pool. ④.

Hôtel Innova, 100 rue Joseph-Vernet (☎90.82.54.10). A small, friendly hotel that's well worth booking. ②.

Hôtel Le Magnan, 63 rue Portail-Magnanen (☎90.86.36.51). Quiet hotel just inside the walls by Porte Magnan a short way east from the station, and with a very pleasant shaded garden. ③–④.

Hôtel Mignon, 12 rue Joseph-Vernet (☎90.82.17.30). Good-value and stylish hotel. ②–③.

Hôtel de Mons, 5 rue de Mons (☎90.82.57.16). A central, imaginatively converted thirteenth-century chapel. All the rooms are odd shapes and you breakfast beneath a vaulted ceiling. ③.

HOSTELS AND CAMPSITES

Pavillon Bleu Bagatelle, Île de la Barthelasse (☎90.86.30.39). Dormitory beds; take bus #20 from the PTT or from Porte de l'Oulle opposite pont Daladier. ①.

Residence La Madeleine, 4 impasse des Abeilles, 25 av Monclar-Nord (☎90.85.20.63). Studios with kitchenettes for two, three or four people. Turn right out of the station and first right, away from the old town. ①.

Camping Bagatelle, Île de la Barthelasse (☎90.86.30.39). A campsite with dormitory rooms; the closest to the city centre. Bus #20 to stop *Bagatelle*. Open all year. ①.

Camping municipal St-Bénézet, Île de la Barthelasse (☎90.82.63.50). A site about 3km from the centre overlooking Pont St-Bénézet. Bus #20 to stop *Bénézet*. March–Oct.

The City

Avignon's walls still form a complete loop around the city. They appear far too low to be a serious defence, but half the full height is buried since it was impossible to excavate the moat during the nineteenth-century restoration work.

From the station, the cours Jean-Jaurès becomes **rue de la République**, the main axis of the old town, leading straight up to **place de l'Horloge**, the city's main square. Beyond that is **place du Palais**, with the city's major sight, the **Palais des Papes**, home of the medieval popes, and the **Rocher des Doms** park and the porte du Rocher overlooking the Rhône by the **Pont d'Avignon**, or pont St-Bénézet as it's officially known.

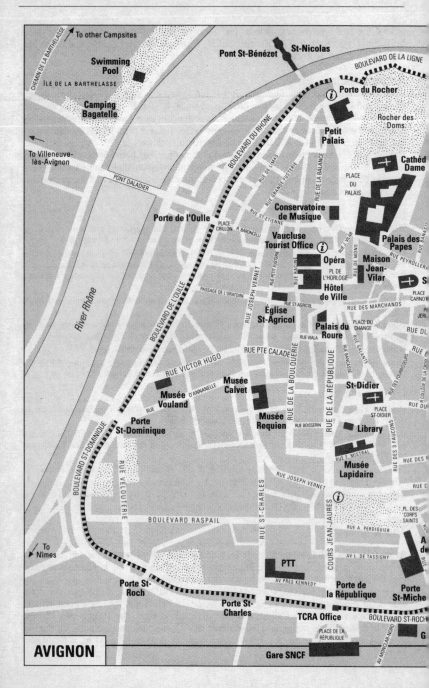

AVIGNON

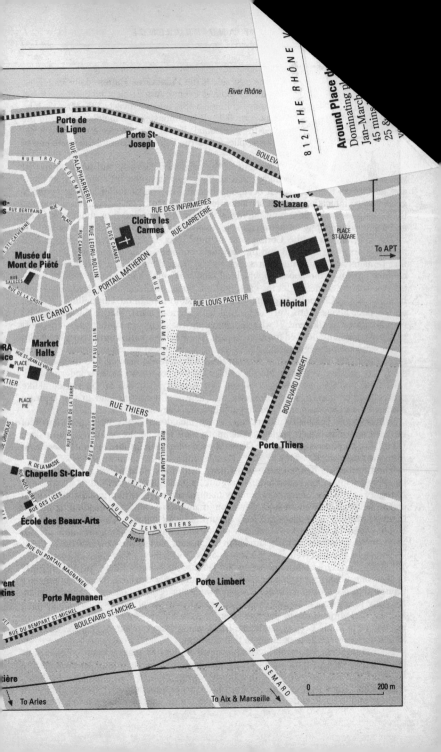

Around Place d

Dominating p
Jan–March
45 mins
25 &

River Rhône

Porte de
la Ligne

Porte St-
Joseph

BOULEVARD

RUE TROIS
COLOMBES

RUE PALAPHARNERIE

RUE S PILAIS

RUE BERTRAND

RUE STE-CATHERINE

RUE DES INFIRMIERES

Cloître les
Carmes

RUE CARRETERIE

Porte
St-Lazare

PLACE
ST-LAZARE

To APT

Musée du
Mont de Piété

RUE SALUCES

RUE DE LA CROIX

PL DES CARMES

RUE CAMPANA

RUE LEDRU ROLLIN

R. PORTAIL MATHERON

RUE GUILLAUME PUY

RUE LOUIS PASTEUR

Hôpital

RUE CARNOT

Market
Halls

RA
ce

RUE ST-JEAN LE VIEUX

PLACE
PIE

XTIER

RUE PAUL SAIN

PLACE
PIE

RUE DU FOUR DE LA TERRE

RUE THIERS

RUE GUILLAUME PUY

RUE PHILONARDE

BOULEVARD LIMBERT

Porte Thiers

GRIVOLAS

R. DE LA MASSE

Chapelle St-Clare

RUE NOEL BIRET

RUE DES LICES

RUE ST-CHRISTOPHE

École des Beaux-Arts

RUE DES TEINTURIERS

Sorgue

RUE DU PORTAIL MAGNANEN

ent
tins

Porte Magnanen

Porte Limbert

RUE DU REMPART ST-MICHEL

BOULEVARD ST-MICHEL

AV

P

SEMARD

ière

0   200 m

To Arles

To Aix & Marseille

Palais

ace du Palais on the east side is the **Palais des Papes** (daily 9am–7pm; , Nov & Dec daily 9am–12.45pm & 2–6pm; Aug 21–Sept till 8pm; last ticket before closure; guided tours in English 46F, unguided visits 38F; May 13–June Aug 13–Sept evening visits 9pm; 60F). It is a monster of a building, doing to the rtical what Versailles does to the horizontal. If you want to get a dramatic neck-cricking view of the whole towering pile, follow rue Peyrolerie around the south end of the Palais.

Inside the palace, so little remains of the original decoration and furnishings that you can be deceived into thinking that all the popes and their retinues were as pious and austere as the last official occupant, Benoît XII. The denuded interior certainly gives sparse indication of the corruption and decadence of fat, feuding cardinals and their mistresses, the thronging purveyors of jewels, velvet and furs, musicians, chefs and painters competing for patronage, the riotous banquets and corridor schemings.

The visit begins in the **Consistoire** of the **Vieux Palais**, where sovereigns and ambassadors were received and the cardinals' council was held. The only decoration that remains are fragments of frescoes moved from the cathedral and a nineteenth-century line-up of the popes, in which all nine look remarkably similar thanks to the artist using the same model for each portrait. Some medieval artistry is in evidence, however, in the **Chapelle St-Jean**, off the Consistoire, and in the **Chapelle St-Martial** on the floor above. Both were decorated by a Sienese artist, Matteo Giovanetti, and commissioned by Clement VI who demanded the maximum amount of blue – the most expensive pigment, derived from lapis lazuli. The **kitchen** on this floor also gives a hint of the scale of papal gluttony with its square walls becoming an octagonal chimney-piece for a vast central cooking fire. In the **Palais Neuf**, Clement VI's bedroom and study are further evidence of this pope's secular concerns, with wonderful food-orientated murals and painted ceilings. But austerity resumes in the cathedral-like proportions of the **Grande Chapelle** or Chapelle Clementine and in the **Grande Audience**, its twin in terms of volume on the floor below.

When you've completed the circuit, which includes a heady walk along the roof terraces, you can watch a glossy but informative film on the history of the palace (English headphones available). There are also concerts: programmes are available from the ticket office.

The **Cathédrale Notre-Dame-des-Doms**, next to the Palais des Papes, might once have been a luminous Romanesque structure, but the interior has had a bad attack of Baroque. In addition, nineteenth-century maniacs mounted an enormous gilded Virgin on the belfry, which would look silly enough anywhere, but when dwarfed by the 50-metre towers of the popes' palace is absurd. There's greater reward behind, in the **Rocher des Doms** park. As well as ducks and swans and views over the river to Villeneuve and beyond, it has a sundial in which your own shadow tells the time.

The **Petit Palais** (Wed–Sun 9.30am–noon & 1.30–5.30pm; May–Sept 10.30am–6pm; 18F, Oct–March free Sun), just below the Dom rock, also has treats, though the scale of the collections in this episcopal palace is dauntingly extreme. There are almost a thousand paintings and sculptures, most of them thirteenth- to fifteenth-century Italian. It's easy to get stuck on the mastery of colour and facial expressions of a Simone Martini or Fabriano, or to pass out from a surfeit of Madonnas and Childs before you've got to Louis Bréa or Botticelli. But a visual feast is assured, however short or long a time you decide to dedicate to this museum.

Behind the Petit Palais, and well signposted, is the half span of Pont St-Bénézet, or the **Pont d'Avignon** of the famous song (daily except Mon 9am–5pm; April–Sept 9am–6.30pm; 10F). One theory has it that the lyrics say "*Sous le pont* (under the bridge)", rather than "*Sur le pont* (on the bridge)", and refer to the thief and trickster clientele of a tavern on the Île de la Barthelasse (which the bridge once crossed) dancing with glee at the arrival of more potential victims. Repairing the bridge from the ravages of the Rhône was finally abandoned in 1660, three and a half centuries after it was built, and only four of the original 22 arches remain. It can be walked, danced or sat upon, but beware the precipitous, barely protected drops on either side.

Around place de l'Horloge

The café-lined **place de l'Horloge**, frenetically busy most of the time, is the site of the city's imposing **Hôtel de Ville** and **clock tower**, and the **Opera**. Around the square, on rues de Mons, Molière and Corneille, famous faces appear in windows painted on the buildings. Many of these figures from the past were visitors to Avignon, and of those who recorded their impressions of the city, it was the sound of over a hundred bells ringing that stirred them most. Of a Sunday morning, traffic lulls permitting, you can still hear a myriad different peals from churches, convents and chapels in close proximity. The fourteenth-century **church of St-Agricole**, just behind the Hôtel de Ville, has recently been restored and proves one of Avignon's best Gothic edifices.

To the south, just behind rue St-Agricole on rue Collège du Roure, is the beautiful fifteenth-century **Palais du Roure**, a centre of Provençal culture (Tues 3pm only; free). The gateway and the courtyard are definitely worth a look; there may well be temporary art exhibitions, and if you want a rambling tour through the attics to see Provençal costumes, publications and presses, photographs of the Carmargue in the 1900s and an old stage coach, you need to turn up on Tuesday.

To either side of place de l'Horloge and northwards are the most desirable Avignon addresses – both now and three hundred years ago. High, heavy façades dripping with cupids, eagles, dragons, fruit and foliage range along **rue Joseph-Vernet**, **rue Petite-Fusterie** and **rue St-Étienne**.

The Banasterie and Carmes quartiers

The **quartier de la Banasterie** behind the Palais des Papes is almost solid seventeenth- and eighteenth-century, and the heavy wooden doors, with their highly sculptured lintels, today bear the nameplates of lawyers, psychiatrists and doctors. The most spectacular doorway in this area, which like the others is firmly closed, is the Renaissance creation of the **church of St-Pierre** on place St-Pierre. In the scene of the Annunciation on the right-hand door, Mary looks as if she's saying "Who the hell are you?" to Gabriel, who points to the dove as his credentials.

Between Banasterie and **place des Carmes** are a tangle of tiny streets guaranteed to get you lost. Pedestrians have priority over cars on many of them, and there are plenty of tempting café or restaurant stops. At 24 rue Saluces, you'll find the peculiar **Musée du Mont de Piété**, an ex-pawnbroker's shop and now the town's archives (Mon–Fri 8.30–11.30am & 1.30–5.30pm; free). It has a small display of papal bulls and painted silk dessicators for determining the dry weight of what was the city's chief commodity.

Rue de la République to place Pie

Between rue de la République and the hideous **market hall** on **place Pie** (every morning except Mon) is the main pedestrian precinct centring around **place du Change**. **Rue des Marchands** and **rue du Vieux-Sextier** have their complement of chapels and late-medieval mansions, in particular the **Hôtel des Rascas** on the corner of rue des Marchands and rue Fourbisseurs, and the **Hôtel de Belli** on the corner of rue Fourbisseurs and rue Vieux-Sextier.

More Renaissance art is on show in the fourteenth-century **church of St-Didier**, chiefly the altarpiece in which the realism of Mary's pain has prompted the somewhat uncomfortable name Notre-Dame-du-Spasme. There are also some original frescoes in the left-hand chapel.

Musée Calvet and around

The excellent **Musée Calvet**, 65 rue Joseph-Vernet (daily except Tues 10am–noon & 2–6pm; check with tourist office or museum on ☎90.86.33.84), has a bit of everything – from an Egyptian mummy of a five-year-old boy to a Vaserely tapestry, with Renaissance armchairs, Géricault adventure tableaux, Utrillos, Laurençons and Dufys, Dutch still lifes, Gallo-Roman pots, sixteenth-century clocks and masses of wrought iron. The eighteenth-century palace housing this eclectic collection is in itself a delight to walk around, and its layout, unlike the Petit Palais, makes it easy to return to treasures glimpsed while passing earlier.

The remaining crop of museums is considerably less compelling. Next door to the Musée Calvet is the **Musée Requien** (Tues–Sat 9am–noon & 2–6pm; free). Its subject is natural history and its sole advantage is in being free and having clean loos. With little more to recommend it is the **Musée Lapidaire**, a museum of Roman and Gallo-Roman stones housed in the Baroque chapel at 27 rue de la République (daily except Tues 10am–noon & 2–6pm; 12F, Nov–April free). Finally, at the **Musée Vouland** at the end of rue Victor-Hugo near Porte St-Dominique (Tues–Sat 9am–noon & 2–6pm; Oct–May 2–6pm only; 25F) you feast your eyes on the fittings, fixtures and furnishings that French aristocrats indulged in both before and after the Revolution. There's some brilliant Moustiers faïence, exquisite marquetry and Louis XV ink-pots with silver rats holding the lids – but little that you can't see better *in situ* elsewhere.

Southeast: to rue des Teinturiers

Through the park by the tourist office (where there's an old British red phone box) you come to **place des Corps-Saints**, a lively area of cafés and restaurants whose tables fill the square. Just to the north, rue des Lices runs eastwards, past the École des Beaux-Arts, to **rue des Teinturiers**, the most atmospheric street in Avignon. Its name refers to the eighteenth- and nineteenth-century business of calico printing. The cloth was washed in the Sorgue which still runs alongside the street turning the wheels of long-gone mills, and although the water is fairly murky and sometimes smelly, this is still a great street for evening strolls, with a large number of cheap restaurants.

Eating, drinking and nightlife

Good-value midday **meals** are two-a-penny in Avignon and eating well in the evening needn't break the bank. The large terraced café-brasseries on place de l'Horloge, rue de la République, place du Change and place des Corps-Saints all serve quick basic meals. Rue des Teinturiers is good for menu-browsing if you're budgeting, and the streets between place de Crillon and place du Palais are full of temptation if you're not.

Restaurants

L'Ailtoli, place des Corps-Saints. Fast food but not junk food from a *charcuterie*. From 40F.

Brunel, rue Balance (☎90.85.24.83). Opposite *Le Mesclun* and run by the same management, this upmarket restaurant serves superb regional dishes, with menus from 200F. Closed Sun & Mon, and mid-July to mid-Aug.

Hiély-Lucullus, 5 rue de la République (☎90.86.17.07). This is one of Avignon's top gastronomic palaces, serving beautiful Provençal cuisine. The Rhône wines are the very best, and will add a good whack to an already groaning bill if you order *à la carte*. But at lunchtime, except Sun, there's a 130F menu, wine included. Closed Mon & Tues midday, and the last two weeks of June.

Le Mesclun, 46 rue Balance (☎90.85.24.83). Different *plats du jour* for around 50F each day, with cod topped with garlic mayonnaise on Friday.

Le Petit Bédon, 70 rue Joseph-Vernet (☎90.82.33.98). The "Pot-belly" does the best meal for under 150F to be had anywhere in the city. Closed Mon evening & Sun, and the last two weeks in Aug.

Le Port des Barques, 25 place Pie (☎90.82.63.82). Renowned for seafood and white wine. Menu from 130F. Closed Sat midday and Sun, and second half of Aug.

La Tache d'Encre, 22 rue des Teinturiers (☎90.85.46.03). The food isn't brilliant but the musicians – jazz, rock, chansons, African or salsa – usually are; there's live music on Friday and Saturday nights, occasionally weekdays, too; booking advisable. Congenial atmosphere; menus under 100F. Closed midday Sat & Sun.

Le Venaissin, 16 place de l'Horloge (☎90.86.20.99). In the height of summer, you'd be lucky to get a table here – it's the only cheap brasserie on place de l'Horloge that serves more than *steak frites*; two menus under 100F.

Cafés and bars

Barhoo, place des Corps-Saints. Young and lively café-bar.

Le Bistrot d'Avignon, 1 rue Jean-Vilar. Café-wine bar for upmarket imbibing of Rhône specialities.

Le Carnot, cnr rue Carnot and rue de la Croix. Young and noisy place with bar football.

Les Célestins, place des Corps-Saints. A young, fairly trendy clientele.

Grand Café du Commerce, 21 rue St-Jean-de-Vieux. Pleasant café for all tastes.

Pub Z, cnr rue Bonneterie and rue Artaud. Café catering for the designer chic; all black and white in honour of the zebra.

Nightlife

There's a fair amount of **nightlife** and cultural events in Avignon, with the **Opéra** on place de l'Horloge (☎90.82.23.44) mounting a good range of productions; *Le Chêne Noir*, 8bis rue Ste-Catherine (☎90.86.58.11), a theatre company worth seeing, with mime, musicals or Molière on offer; and plenty of **classical concerts** performed in churches, usually for free.

For **live music**, *AJMI Jazz Club*, 8bis rue Ste-Catherine (☎90.86.08.61), hosts live jazz every Thursday night and features major acts and some adventurous new groups. *Le Bistroquet*, Quartier du Mouton on Île de la Berthelasse, is a cool rock bar, and the restaurant *La Tache d'Encre* (see above) has some good live sounds on Friday and Saturday nights. The tourist office hands out a free bimonthly calendar called *Rendez-Vous*, and also stocks the monthly rock fanzine *Rock in Town*, which gives details of local gigs.

Listings

Bike rental *Dopieralski*, 84 rue Guillaume-Puy; *Masson Richard*, place Pie; *Vélomania*, 1 rue de l'Amelier.

Boat trips *Le Mireio*, allée de l'Oulle (☎90.85.62.25; all year round, 2-week advance booking recommended), upstream towards Châteauneuf-du-Pape and downstream to Arles.

Car rental *Ardam Location*, 110 av du Grand Gigognan (☎90.82.10.31), is the cheapest option. Located on bd St-Ruf are *ACA* at no. 15 (☎90.85.69.11), *Europcar* at no. 27 (☎90.82.49.85), and *Eurorent* at no. 3 (☎90.86.06.61).

Emergencies Doctor: *SOS Médecins* (☎90.82.65.00); Hospital: Centre Hospitalier de la Durance, 305 rue Raoul-Follereau (☎90.89.91.31); all-night chemist: call police at bd St-Roch on ☎90.80.51.00 for addresses.

Exchange *Chaix Conseil*, 43 cours Jean-Jaurès, or *AOC*, 20 & 26 rue Grande Fusterie.

Police bd St-Roch, near the *gare SNCF* (☎90.80.51.00).

Post office PTT, av du Président-Kennedy, Avignon 84000.

Taxis pl Pie (☎90.82.20.20).

Women *Vaucluse Information Femmes*, 9 rue Carnot (☎90.88.41.00; daily except Fri 9am–noon & 2–6pm).

Villeneuve-lès-Avignon

VILLENEUVE-LÈS-AVIGNON rises up a rocky escarpment above the west bank of
the Rhône, looking down upon its older neighbour from behind far more convincing
fortifications. Historically, Villeneuve operated largely as a suburb to Avignon, with
palatial residences constructed by the cardinals and a great monastery founded by
Pope Innocent VI.

To this day, Villeneuve is technically a part of Languedoc and not Provence, and
would score better in the hierarchy of towns to visit were it further from Avignon,
whose monuments it can almost match for colossal scale and impressiveness. In
summer, at least, it benefits, providing venues for the Avignon Festival as well as alternatives for accommodation overspill; and it's certainly worth a day, whatever time of
year you visit.

Arrival and accommodation

From Avignon's **gare SNCF** (see p.808), the Villeneuve–Les Angles #10 bus runs
direct to Villeneuve every half-hour to place Charles-David (stop *Bellevue*), taking less
than ten minutes, or five if you catch it from Porte d'Oulle. After 8pm you'll have to take
a taxi or walk – it's only 3km. On place Charles-David you'll find the **tourist office**
(Mon–Fri 9.30am–noon & 2–5/7pm, Sat 9.30am–noon; ☎90.25.61.55; annexe in
summer at entrance to La Chartreuse) and, on Thursday mornings, a **market** of food,
clothes and bric-à-brac. Rue Gabriel-Péri leads west off the place past the *mairie* to
place St-Marc. From here, the main street, rue de la République, runs due north.

For reasonably priced **accommodation**, try the *Hôtel Beauséjour*, 61 av Gabriel-Péri
(☎90.25.20.56; ①–③), overlooking the river near the Pont du Royaume, or, much
cheaper and in the heart of town, the *Central*, 15 rue de la République (☎90.25.44.12;
①). If money is less of an object, *Le Prieuré*, 7 place du Chapitre (☎90.25.18.20; ⑥–⑦),
is indisputably the first choice, both for the rooms and for its restaurant. For half the
price, you could stay in equally ancient surroundings at *L'Atelier*, 5 rue de la Foire
(☎90.25.01.84; ③–⑤), a sixteenth-century house with huge open fireplaces and a walled
garden. Alternatively there's a Louis XIV mansion, *Les Cèdres*, 39 bd Pasteur
(☎90.25.43.92; ③–④), with pool and restaurant.

The **YMCA hostel**, 7bis chemin de la Justice (☎90.25.46.20; ①), is an attractive alternative, beautifully situated overlooking the river by Pont du Royaume, with balconied
rooms for two to six people and an open-air swimming pool; if you're staying more than
one night you have to pay full or half board (bus stop *Pont d'Avignon* on the Les
Angles–Villeneuve bus, or *Général-Leclerc* on the Villeneuve–Les Angles bus). The
Résidence P L Loisil on av Pierre-Sémard (☎90.25.07.92; ①), to the left at the top of rue
de la République, offers accommodation in rooms for three to four people and cheap
meals. For **campers**, the *Camping Municipal de la Laune* is in chemin St-Honoré
(bookings through tourist office; April–Sept) off the D980, near the sports stadium and
swimming pools.

VILLENEUVE'S MUSEUMS AND MONUMENTS

A **Passeport pour l'Art** (45F) gives you entry to the Fort St-André, Tour Philippe-le-Bel,
La Chartreuse du Val de Bénédiction, the Collégiale Notre-Dame and its cloister and the
Musée Pierre-de-Luxembourg. The ticket is available from each of the monuments and
from the tourist office.

The Town

For a good overview of Villeneuve – and Avignon – make your way to the **Tour Philippe-le-Bel** at the bottom of montée de la Tour (bus stop *Philippe-le-Bel*). This tower was built to guard the French end of Avignon's Pont St-Bénézet (or Pont d'Avignon see p.812–13), and a climb to the top (daily except Tues 10am–12.30pm & 3–7pm; Oct–March 10am–noon & 2–5.30pm; closed Feb) will be rewarded with stunning views.

Even more indicative of French distrust of its neighbours is the enormous **Fort St-André** (daily 10am–noon & 2–5pm; April, June & Sept 9.30am–12.30pm & 2–6.30pm; July & Aug 9.30am–7.30pm; July & Aug 9.30am–7.30pm), whose bulbous double-towered gateway and vast white walls loom over the town. Inside, refreshingly, there's not a hint of a postcard stall or souvenir shop – just tumbledown houses and the former abbey, with its gardens of olive trees, ruined chapels, lily ponds and dovecotes. Its cliff-face terrace is the classic spot for artists to aim their brushes, or photographers their cameras, over Avignon. You can reach the approach to the fortress, montée du Fort, from place Jean-Jaurès on rue de la République, or by the "rapid slope" of **rue Pente-Rapide**, a cobbled street of tiny houses leading off rue des Recollets on the north side of place Charles-David.

Almost at the top of rue de la République, on the right, allée des Muriers leads from place des Chartreux to the entrance of **La Chartreuse du Val de Bénédiction** (daily 9am–6.30pm; Oct–March closes 5.30pm). This Charterhouse, one of the largest in France, was founded by the sixth of the Avignon popes, Innocent VI, whose sharp profile is outlined on his tomb in the church. The buildings, which were sold off after the Revolution and gradually restored this century, are totally unembellished. With the exception of the Giovanetti frescoes in the chapel beside the refectory, all the paintings and treasures of the monastery have been dispersed, leaving you with a strong impression of the austerity of the Carthusian order. You're free to wander around unguided, through the three cloisters, the church, chapels, cells and communal spaces, which have little to see but plenty of atmosphere to absorb. Contemporary inspiration and creativity are given rein here in summer by *CIRCA*, a cultural organization that invites contemporary artists to take up residence.

Another festival venue is the fourteenth-century **Collègiale Notre-Dame** and its cloister on place St-Marc (daily except Tues 10am–12.30pm & 3–7pm; Oct–March 10am–noon & 2–5.30pm; closed Feb). Notre-Dame's most important treasure is a rare fourteenth-century smiling Madonna and Child made from a single tusk of ivory, now housed, along with many of the paintings from the Chartreuse, in the **Musée Pierre-de-Luxembourg**, just to the north opposite the *mairie* (daily except Tues 10am–12.30pm & 3–7pm; Oct–March 10am–noon & 2–5.30pm; closed Feb). The spacious layout includes a single room, with comfortable settees and ample documentation, given over to the most stunning painting in the collection – *Le Couronnement de la Vierge*, painted in 1453 by Enguerrand Quarton as the altarpiece for the church in the Chartreuse, and notable for its detail.

Eating and drinking

Villeneuve's centre has perfectly reasonable places to **eat** for under 120F. Try *La Calèche*, 35 rue de la République (☎90.25.02.54; closed Sun, and Thurs out of season), or Italian *La Mamma Lucia* on place V-Basch; (☎90.25.00.71; closed midday Wed & Sat). For a blow-out meal *La Magnaneraie*, 37 rue Camp de Bataille (☎90.25.11.11), off rue de la Magnanerie, is the posh and perfect answer, with a menu for 170F (*à la carte* over 400F). Alternatively, *Aubertin*, 1 rue de l'Hôpital (☎90.25.94.84; closed Sun evening out of season), serves a midday 150F menu in the shade of the old arcades by the Collègiale Notre-Dame (*à la carte* 300F upwards).

St-Rémy-de-Provence and the Alpilles

The watery and intensely cultivated scenery of the Petite Crau plain south of Avignon changes abruptly with the eruption of the **Chaîne des Alpilles**, whose peaks look like the surf of a wave about to engulf the plain. At the base of the Alpilles nestles **ST-RÉMY**, a dreamy place whose old town is contained within a circle of boulevards no more than half a kilometre in diameter. Outside this ring, the modern town is sparingly laid out, so for once you don't have to plug your way through dense developments to reach the centre. It is a beautiful place, as unspoilt as the villages around it.

Arrival and accommodation

There's no train station in St-Rémy, and **buses** from Avignon, Aix and Arles drop you in place de la République, the main square abutting the old town on the east. The **tourist office** on place Jean-Jaurès (Mon–Sat 9am–noon & 2–6pm; June–Sept Mon–Sat 9am–noon & 3–7pm, Sun 9am–noon; ☎90.92.05.22) is just south of the centre, reached by following bd Marceau/av Durand-Maillane. They have excellent free guides to **cycling and walking routes** in and around the Alpilles and can provide addresses for renting **horses**. If you want to rent a **bike** or **car**, go to *Florelia*, 35 av de la Libération, the road to Cavaillon (☎90.92.10.88). It's difficult to get to Glanum or Les Baux (see p.820) except by foot or taxi; some taxi numbers are ☎90.92.48.20, ☎90.92.10.82 and ☎90.92.09.95.

The town has a fairly wide choice of **accommodation**, though real bargains are hard to come by. In the old town, pleasant hotels with some cheap rooms are *Le Provence*, 36 bd Victor-Hugo, on the eastern edge of the old town (☎90.92.06.27; ③–④; closed Oct to mid-March); and *Les Arts-La Palette*, above the *Café des Arts* at 30 bd Victor-Hugo (☎90.92.08.50; ③–④; closed Wed & Fri). The *Ville Verte* on av Fauconnet, on the corner of place de la République (☎90.92.06.14, ②–③), is central and has some rooms with disabled facilities, a garden and pool, and also organizes walking, climbing and cycling trips. In the middle of the old town, there's a new hotel and restaurant, the *Mexican Café*, 4 rue du 8-mai-1945 (☎90.92.17.66; ③), with just five rooms. *Le Castellet des Alpilles*, 6 place Mireille (☎90.92.07.21; ③–⑤; closed Mon, and Tues midday), south of the old town past the tourist office, is small and friendly, with some rooms with great views. Close by the tourist office, the *Hôtel des Antiques*, 15 av Pasteur (☎90.92.03.02; ④–⑤; closed Nov–March), is a nineteenth-century mansion with huge grounds, pools and wonderfully aristocratic furnishings in the dining room and salons.

There are three **campsites** near St-Rémy: the municipal *Le Mas de Nicolas*, 2km along the rte de Mollèges (☎90.92.27.05; all year); *Monplaisir*, 1km along the rte de Maillane (☎90.92.22.70/☎90.92.12.91; closed mid-Nov to March); and *Pegomas*, 1km along the rte de Cavaillon (☎90.92.01.21; closed Nov–March).

The Town

To reach the old town from place de la Résistance, take av de la Résistance, which runs alongside the town's main church, the **Collégiale St-Martin** (organ recitals July–Sept Sat morning), and start wandering up the alleyways into immaculate, leafy squares. For an introduction to the region, a good first visit is to the **Musée des Alpilles** on place Favier, housed in the Hôtel Mistral de Mondragon (daily 10am–noon & 2–6pm; July & Aug closes 8pm; Nov & Dec closes 5pm; closed Jan–March; 14F). The museum features interesting displays on folklore, festivities and traditional crafts, plus some intriguing local landscapes, some creepy portraits by Marshall Pétain's first wife, and souvenirs of local boy Nostradamus.

You can buy a combined 30F ticket for the Musée des Alpilles and the neighbouring **Musée Archéologique** in the Hôtel de Sade (guided visits several times daily 10am–4/5/6.30pm; closed Jan–March; 14F), displaying finds from the archeological digs at the Greco-Roman town of Glanum (see overleaf), for which the combined ticket is also valid. The hour's tour may be a bit much for the noncommitted, but there are some stunning pieces, in particular the temple decorations.

In addition to the two fifteenth- to sixteenth-century hôtels that house the museums, you'll find more ancient stately residences as you wander through the **old town**, particularly along rue Parage. On rue Hoche is the birthplace of **Nostradamus** – though only the façade is contemporary with the futuristic savant, and it's not open for visits. The Hôtel d'Estrine, 8 rue Estrine, houses the **Centre d'Art Présence Van Gogh** (Tues–Sun 10.30am–12.30pm & 2.30–6.30pm; free, 20F for exhibitions), which hosts contemporary art exhibitions and has a permanent exhibition of Van Gogh reproductions and extracts from letters, as well as audiovisual presentations on the painter, who was in an asylum nearby (see below).

Eating, drinking and festivals

You'll find plenty of **brasseries** and **restaurants** in and around old St-Rémy. *Le Jardin de Frédéric*, 8 bd Gambetta (☎90.92.27.67; closed Wed), has a 120F midday menu, and usually some interesting dishes on offer. There are a few good options on rue Carnot, leading from bd Victor-Hugo east through the old town to bd Marceau, including the *Haricot Vert Palace* at no. 48, *La Gousée d'Ail* at no. 25 (☎90.92.16.87; closed Wed), where veggies can feast on pasta with pesto and almonds, and *Le Gaulois* at no. 57 (☎90.92.11.53), which, though not brilliant, has a generous menu under 100F.

Lou Planet, 7 place Favier near the Musée des Alpilles, is a scenic spot to dine on crêpes, and *Le Bistrot des Alpilles*, 15 bd Mirabeau (☎90.92.09.17; closed Sun), is a popular brasserie for *gigot d'agneau* and *tarte citrone* (70F midday menu, evening one 160F). For **café** lounging, head for the *Café des Arts*, 30 bd Victor-Hugo (open till 12.30am; closed Feb), where the works of local painters are exhibited.

The best time to visit St-Rémy is during the **Fête de Transhumance** on Whit Monday, when a 2000-strong flock of sheep, accompanied by goats and donkeys, does a tour of the town before being packed off to the Alps for the summer. Or come for the **Carreto Ramado**, on August 15, a harvest thanksgiving procession in which the religious or secular symbolism of the floats reveals the political colour of the various village councils. A pagan rather than workers' **May Day** is celebrated with donkey-drawn floral floats on which people play fifes and tambourines.

South of St-Rémy

About 1.5km south of the old town, following av Vincent-Van-Gogh past the tourist office, you'll come to **Les Antiques** (free access), a triumphal arch celebrating the Roman conquest of Marseille, and a mausoleum thought to commemorate two grandsons of Augustus. Save for a certain amount of weather erosion, the mausoleum is perfectly intact; the arch less so, but both display intricate patterning and the unaesthetic proportional sense of the Romans.

The old **monastery of St-Paul-de-Mausole**, a hundred yards or so east of the *Antiques*, is the place where, in 1889, Vincent Van Gogh, then living in Arles, had himself placed for psychiatric observation. The hospital is still a psychiatric clinic today. Although the regime was more prison than hospital, Van Gogh was allowed to wander out around the Alpilles and painted prolifically during his twelve-month stay. The *Champs d'oliviers*, *Le Faucher*, *Le Champ clôturé* and *La Promenade du soir* are among the 150 canvases of this period. The driveway with a statue of the artist, the church and cloisters can be visited (daily 9am–noon & 2–6pm; free). Take av Edgar-Leroy or allée St-Paul from av Vincent-Van-Gogh, go past the main entrance of the clinic and into the gateway on the left at the end of the wall.

Not very far beyond the hospital is a signposted farm called **Mas de la Pyramide** (daily 9am–noon & 2–5/6pm; wait by the gate if there's no immediate answer to the bell; 9F). It's an old troglodyte farm in the Roman quarries for Glanum with a lavender and cherry orchard surrounded by cavernous openings into the rock filled with ancient farm equipment and rusting bicycles. The farmhouse is part medieval and part Gallo-Roman, with pictures of the owner's family who have lived there for generations.

Glanum

One of the most impressive ancient settlements in France, **GLANUM** (daily 9am–noon & 2–5pm; April–Sept 9am–7pm; 26F, combined ticket 30F) was dug out from alluvial deposits at the very foot of the Alpilles, just 500m south of Les Antiques. The site was originally a neolithic homestead; then, between the second and first centuries BC, the Gallo-Greeks, probably from Massalia (Marseille), built a city here, on which the Gallo-Romans, from the end of the first century BC to the third century AD, constructed yet another town. Successive Barbarian invasions obliterated the town, which was subsequently used as a quarry for the new settlement at St-Rémy (see above).

Though Glanum is one of the most important archeological sites in France, it can be very difficult to get to grips with. Not only were the later buildings moulded on to the earlier, but the fashion at the time of Christ was for a Hellenistic style. You can distinguish the Greek levels from the Roman most easily by the stones: the earlier civilization used massive hewn rocks while the Romans preferred smaller and more accurately shaped stones. The leaflet at the admission desk is helpful, as are the attendants if your French is good enough.

The site is bisected by a road running from north to south, with several **Hellenic houses** to the northwest. East of here are the **Thermes**, a complex of furnaces, bathing chambers and pools, and beyond this the **Maison du Capricorne** with some fine mosaics. A **forum** dating from Roman times is south of here, near a restored **theatre** and the superb sculptures on the Roman **Temples Geminées** (twin temples). The temples also have fragments of mosaics, fountains of both Greek and Roman periods, and first-storey walls and columns. As the site narrows in the ravine at the southern end, you find a Grecian edifice around a **sacred spring** – the feature that made this location so desirable. Steps lead down to a pool, with a slab above for the libations of those too disabled to descend. An inscription records that Agrippa was responsible for restoring it in 27 BC and dedicating it to Valetudo, the Roman goddess of health.

Les Baux and the Val d'Enfer

At the top of the Alpilles ridge, 7km southwest of St-Rémy, lies the distinctly unreal, fortified village of **LES BAUX**, where the ruined eleventh-century citadel is hard to distinguish from the edge of the plateau, whose rock is both foundation and part of the structure.

Once Les Baux lived off the power and widespread possessions in Provence of its medieval lords, who owed allegiance to no one. When the dynasty died out at the end of the fourteenth century, however, the town, which had once numbered 6000 inhabitants, passed to the counts of Provence and then to the kings of France, who eventually, in 1632, razed the feudal citadel to the ground and fined the population into penury. From that date until the nineteenth century, both citadel and village were inhabited almost exclusively by bats and crows. The discovery in the neighbouring hills of the mineral bauxite (from Les Baux) brought back some life to the village, and tourism has more recently transformed the place. Today the population stays steady at around 400, while the number of visitors exceeds 1.5 million each year.

The **lower town** has a great many very beautiful buildings, and the view beside the statue of Provençal poet Charloun Riev beyond the upper town at the southern edge of the plateau is superb. There are half a dozen museums in town, the best being the **Musée d'Art Contemporain** in the Hôtel des Porcelets (daily 10am–12.30pm & 2–6.30pm; winter closed Wed; 20F), whose highlight is its collection of paintings of the twentieth-century figurative artist Yves Brayer. The **Musée Iconographicque** in the sixteenth-century Hôtel de Manville on impasse du Château (daily 9.30am–noon & 2–6.30pm; 20F) gives a lengthy explanation of the printing process and its history, and the **Musée des Santons** in the old Hôtel de Ville (daily 8am–8pm; 10F) has a strange display of traditional Provençal crib figures and Christmas cribs. Pick of the bunch is the **Musée de l'Olivier**, featuring paintings of olive trees and their artistic treatment by Van Gogh, Gauguin and Cézanne (March–Nov daily 8am–7.30pm; summer till 9pm; combined ticket with the *ville morte*).

But the reason everyone comes to Les Baux is to see the **Ville Morte**, or upper town, whose ruined houses are half carved out of the rocky escarpment on which they sit. You enter the site via a turnstile after paying at the **Musée Lapidaire** (daily 9.30am–noon & 2–6.30pm; 25F), with its collection of archeological remains, grave goods from a nearby Celtic cemetery and exhibitions on bauxite. The expanse of the ruins is impressive, with some restored towers and staggering views over the edge of the escarpment. You can wander freely among the ruins, picking your way past the partially restored **chapel of Ste-Catherine** and the **Paravelle Tower**, which gives good views over the town and the castle ruins.

The **tourist office** is at the end of Grand-Rue (April–Nov daily 9.30am–12.30pm & 2.30–6.30pm; ☎90.54.34.39). It's difficult to get to Les Baux from St-Rémy unless you have a car – see above for taxi numbers. Nothing in Les Baux comes cheap, least of all **accommodation**, but if you're feeling rich and want to treat yourself, just below Les Baux on the southern side is the beautiful hotel-restaurant *Le Mas d'Aigret* (☎90.54.33.54; ④–⑦), with a generous 90F lunchtime menu, including wine and coffee; dinner menus are from 190F.

The Val d'Enfer

Within walking distance of Les Baux, along the D27 leading northwards, is the valley of quarried and eroded rocks named the **Val d'Enfer** – the Valley of Hell. Here, quarries have been turned into an audiovisual experience under the title of the **Cathédrale des Images** (daily except Tues March 20–Nov 11 10am–6/7pm; 35F), signposted to the right downhill from Les Baux's car park. The projection is continuous, so you don't have to wait to go in. You're surrounded by images projected all over the floor, the ceilings and the walls of these vast rectangular caverns, and by music that resonates strangely in the captured space. The content of the show, which changes yearly, does not really matter. It just is an extraordinary sensation, wandering on and through these changing shapes and colours. As an erstwhile worksite put to good use, it couldn't be bettered.

Arles

ARLES is a major town on the tourist circuit, its fame sealed by the extraordinarily well-preserved Roman arena, **Les Arènes**, at the city's heart, and backed by an impressive variety of other stones and monuments, both Roman and medieval. It was the key city of the region in Roman times, then, with Aix, main base of the counts of Provence before unification with France. For centuries it was Marseille's only rival, profiting from the inland trade route up the Rhône whenever the enemies of France were blocking Marseille's port. It was a centre for counter-revolutionary activity in 1792 and is to this day an arch-reactionary town, whose one claim to contemporary fame is the trendily folkloric rock group, the *Gypsy Kings*.

Arrival and accommodation

Arriving by train eases you gently into the city, with the **gare SNCF** conveniently located a few blocks to the north of the Arènes. Most buses also arrive here at the adjacent **gare routière**, though for Aix, Marseille and the Crau, the stop is in the centre at 22 bd G-Clemenceau. Rue Jean-Jaurès, with its continuation rue Hôtel-de-Ville, is the main axis of old Arles. At the southern end it meets bd Georges-Clemenceau and bd des Lices, with the **tourist office** directly opposite (Mon–Sat 9am–6pm; Easter–Sept Mon–Sat 9am–7.30pm, Sun 9am–1pm; July & Aug Mon–Sat closes 8pm; ☎90.18.41.20); there's also an annexe in the *gare SNCF*. You can rent **bikes** from *Peugeot* on 15 rue du Pont or *Dall'Oppio* in rue Portagnel (March–Oct), and **cars** from *Europcar* (☎90.93.23.24), *Avis* (☎90.96.82.42) or *Hertz* (☎90.96.75.23), all on bd Victor-Hugo.

Arles is well used to visitors and there's little shortage of **hotel** rooms at either end of the scale. The best place to look for cheap rooms is in the area around Porte de la Cavalerie near the station. If you get stuck, the tourist office will find you accommodation for a small fee.

Hotels

Hôtel Calendal, 22 place Pomme (☎90.96.11.89). Generous rooms overlooking a garden. ②–④.

Hôtel Constantin, 59 bd de Craponne, off bd Clemenceau (☎90.96.04.05). Pleasant, well kept and comfortable, with prices kept down by the proximity of the Nîmes highway (some traffic noise) and its location some distance from the centre. ②.

Hôtel Diderot, 5 rue Diderot (☎90.96.10.30). Comfortable and clean; a lot nicer than any of the others in this price category. ②–③.

Hôtel le Forum, 10 place du Forum (☎90.93.48.95). Spacious rooms in an old house at the ancient heart of the city, with a swimming pool in the garden. Closed mid-Nov to mid-Feb. ③–⑦.

Hôtel Gauguin, 5 place Voltaire (☎90.96.14.35). Comfortable, cheap and well run. Advisable to book. ①–②.

Hôtel Musée, 11 rue du Gd-Prieuré (☎90.96.04.49). Quiet location opposite Musée Réattu. ②–④.

Hôtel Lamartine, rue Marius-Jouveau (☎90.96.13.83). A gloomy but adequate hotel. ①–②.

Hôtel le Rhône, 11 place Voltaire (☎90.96.43.70). Slightly more character than its neighbours. ②.

Youth hostels and campsites

IYHF youth hostel, 20 av Maréchal-Foch (☎90.96.18.25). The hostel is open all year; reception 7.30–10am and 5–11.30pm; 2am curfew; bus #3 from bd des Lices to Fournier. ①.

La Bienheureuse, 7km out on the N453 at Raphèles-les-Arles (☎90.98.35.64). Best of Arles's half-dozen campsites; the restaurant here is furnished with pieces similar to those displayed in the Musée Arlaten, and full of pictures of popular Arlesian traditions. Open all year; regular buses from Arles.

Camping City, 67 rte de Crau (☎90.93.08.86). The closest campsite to town on the Crau bus route. Mid-March to mid-Sept.

The City

The centre of Arles fits into a neat triangle between bd E-Combes to the east, bds Clemenceau and des Lices to the south, and the Rhône to the west. With the exception of Les Alyscamps, down across the train lines to the south, all the Roman and medieval monuments are within easy walking distance in this very compact city centre.

Les Arènes and Roman Arles

Roman Arles provided grain for most of the western empire and was one of the major ports for trade and shipbuilding. Under Constantine, it became the capital of Gaul, Britain and Spain. While being on the key road and river routes, however, it found itself isolated once the empire crumbled between the Rhône, the Alpilles and the marshlands of the Camargue – an isolation that allowed it to preserve considerable vestiges of an arrogant past. Today, all of the city's Roman remains have been classified by UNESCO as world heritage sites. Most are covered on a general ticket, though parts that you can see for free include the remnants of the aqueduct within the medieval ramparts east of the Arènes, and of the Roman bridge on the other side of the river opposite rue Marius-Jouveau.

The amphitheatre, known as the **Arènes** (daily 9am–12.10pm & 2–6.40pm; April closes 6.10pm; March & Oct closes 5.40pm; Feb & Nov 9–11.40am & 2–4.40pm; Dec & Jan 9–11.40am & 2–4.10pm; 15F), is the most impressive of the Roman monuments. To give an idea of its size, it used to shelter over two hundred dwellings and three churches built into the two tiers of arches that form its oval surround. This medieval quarter was cleared in 1830 and the Arènes was once more used for entertainment. Today, though not the largest Roman amphitheatre in existence and missing its third storey and most of the internal stairways and galleries, it is a very impressive structure and a stunning venue for performances. It can still seat 20,000 spectators.

The **Théâtre Antique** (daily 9am–12.15pm & 2–6.45pm; April closes 6.15pm; March & Oct closes 5.45pm; Feb & Nov 9–11.45am & 2–4.45pm; Jan & Dec 9–11.45am & 2–4.15pm; 15F), just south of the Arènes, comes to life in July during the dance and theatre festival and for the *Fête du Costume*, in which local folk groups parade in traditional dress. The theatre is not as well preserved as the arena, with only one pair of columns standing, all the statuary removed and the sides of the stage littered with broken bits of stone. At the river end of rue Hôtel-de-Ville, the **Thermes de Constantine** (same hours and admission as theatre) are all that remain of the imperial palace that extended along the waterfront. The Forum was on the site of **place du Forum**, still the centre of life in Arles. You can see the pillars of an ancient temple embedded in the corner of the *Nord-Pinus* hotel.

The Romans had their burial ground southwest of the centre, and it was used by well-to-do Arlesians well into the Middle Ages. Now only one alleyway, foreshortened

---

BULLFIGHTING

Bullfighting in Arles and the Camargue is not usually the Spanish-style *mise-à-mort*. Though the bulls probably don't enjoy their appearances very much, it is the bullfighters, or *razeteurs*, who get hurt, not the beast. Bulls are fêted and adored, and before retirement are given a final tour around the arena while people weep and throw flowers.

It's a passion with the populace, who treat the champion *razeteurs* like football stars. The shows involve various feats of daring, but the most common form is where the bull has a cockade at the base of its horns and ribbons tied between them. Using blunt razor-combs the *razeteurs* have to cut the ribbons and get the cockades. There's no betting but people add to the prize money as the game progresses. The drama and grace of the spectacle is the stylish way the men leap over the barrier away from the bull. You are much closer to the scene than with other dangerous sports and there are occasional casualties. For some shows involving horsemen, arrows are shot at the bull, though these don't go in deep enough to make the animal bleed.

All this may leave you feeling cold, or sick, but it's your best way of taking part in local life and of experiencing the Roman arena in Arles. The tourist office, local papers and publicity around the arena will give you the details – be sure to check shows are not *mise-à-mort*.

by a train line, is preserved. To reach **Les Alyscamps** (same hours and admission as theatre), follow av des Alyscamps from bd des Lices. Sarcophagi still line the shaded walk, whose tree trunks are azure blue in Van Gogh's rendering. There are numerous tragedy masks, too, though any with special decoration have long since been moved to serve as municipal gifts, as happened often in the seventeenth century, or to reside in the museums. But there is still magic to this walk, which ends at the ruins of a Romanesque church.

The cathedral, museums and medieval Arles

Arles's central **place de la République** fronts the main door of the **Cathédrale St-Trophime**, one of the most famous examples of twelfth-century Provençal stone carving in existence. It depicts the Last Judgement, trumpeted by angels playing with the enthusiasm of jazz musicians while the damned are led naked in chains down to hell and the blessed, all female and draped in long robes, process upwards.

The cathedral itself was started in the ninth century (during the Carolingian period) on the spot where, in 597 AD, Saint Augustine was consecrated as the first bishop of the English. It was largely completed by the twelfth century. A font in the north aisle and an altar illustrating the crossing of the Red Sea in the north transept were both originally Gallo-Roman sarcophagi. The high nave is decorated with d'Aubusson tapestries, in which the one depicting Mary Magdalene bathing Christ's feet has a cat jumping from one oil container to another chased by a dog being ridden by a child. The creamy white vaulted galleries above the **cloisters** (daily 9am–12.15pm & 2–6.45pm; March from 9.30am; Oct–Feb 10am–12.15pm & 2–5.15/5.45pm; 15F) are given over to the **Musée Nécropole** which displays, very beautifully, objects of everyday Roman life as well as coffins and urns. It includes wonderful mosaics of Jupiter carrying off Europa and of Orpheus charming the animals, along with a bust of Augustus dated after the Christianization of the Roman Empire, suggesting that the cult of emperor worship continued secretely.

To see yet more fallen, chipped and time-eroded stones, take the short cut through the ground floor of the classical **Hôtel de Ville** and turn left into rue Balze. The **Musée d'Art Chrétien** and **Cryptoportiques du Forum** (to reopen in 1995: check with tourist office for details) both contain sarcophagi – once the Romans had been converted they gave up their old and much more practical habit of cremating the dead. From a flight of stairs in the museum you can descend to the cryptoporticus, a huge, dark, dank and wonderfully spooky underground Roman gallery, built as a granary.

It sometimes seems that life stopped in Arles after the Middle Ages – if not after the Romans. For a corrective, head for the **Musée Arlaten** on rue de la République (daily 9am–noon & 2–5/6/6.30pm; Oct–June closed Mon; 18F). The museum was set up in 1896 by Frédéric Mistral, the Nobel Prize-winning novelist who was responsible for the turn-of-the-century revival of interest in all things Provençal and whose statue stands in place du Forum. The collections of costumes, documents, tools, pictures and paraphernalia of Provençal life is alternately tedious and intriguing. The evolution of Arlesian dress is charted in great detail for all social classes from the eighteenth century to World War I and includes a scene of a dressmaking shop.

In the **Musée Réattu** (same hours and admission as Cloître St-Trophime), opposite the Roman baths, you can finally return to twentieth-century artworks, assuming that you ignore the rigid eighteenth-century classicism of works by the museum's founder and his contemporaries. Of the moderns, Picasso is the best represented, with the sculpture *Woman with Violin* and 57 ink-and-crayon sketches from between December 1970 and February 1971 which he donated to the museum. Amongst the split faces and clowns is a beautifully simple portrait of his mother. There are works by contemporary artists – an ever-shifting pattern in ball bearings by Pol Bury, Mario Prassinos' black-and-white studies of the Alpilles, César's *Compression 1973* – and, from time to time, exhibitions of photography on the top floor.

If you walk to the back of the Réattu museum, you'll see its gargoyles jutting over the river. There are lanterns along the river wall (and wonderful sunsets), though much of the river front and its bars and bistros, where workers drank and danced away their woes, were destroyed during the war.

Another casualty of the bombing was the "Yellow House" where Van Gogh lived before entering the hospital at St-Rémy, and where his friend Gauguin stayed until Vincent attacked him with a razor blade. Van Gogh arrived in February 1888 and began painting straight away, producing such celebrated canvases as *The Sunflowers*, *Van Gogh's Chair*, *The Red Vines* and *The Sower*. He used to wander along the river bank wearing candles on his hat, watching the light of night-time. *The Starry Night* is the Rhône at Arles; the *Café Evening* is now a shop on place du Forum; the *Café de Nuit* has been replaced by a *Monoprix* supermarket across the square from where the "Yellow House" once stood.

Eating and drinking

Arles has a good number of excellent-quality and cheap restaurants. If you're looking for quick meals, or just want to watch the world go by, there's a wide choice of brasseries on the main boulevards. The best ice creams are to be had at *Fonfon* at the bottom of bd des Lices, towards the motorway.

L'Affenage, 4 rue Molière (☎90.96.07.67). Provençal specialities in generous portions on a 135F menu.

Hostellerie des Arènes, 62 rue du Réfuge (☎90.96.13.05). The service may be a bit abrupt but the food is real French family cooking. Good pizzas and menus from 75F. Closed Tues.

Lou Marquès, *Hôtel Jules-César*, bd des Lices (☎90.93.43.20). The top gourmet palace in the top grand hotel. The specialities, which include *baudroie* (monkfish), *langoustine* salad and Camargue rice cake, are all served with the utmost pomposity. Menus from 200F. The other restaurant in the hotel, *Le Cloître*, has a a midday menu at around 100F. Closed Nov & Dec.

Le Médiéval, 9 rue Truchet (☎90.96.65.77). A top-value four-course menu at 125F.

La Paillote, 28 rue Dr-Fanton (☎90.96.33.15). Very friendly place with a good 90F menu. Closed Thurs out of season.

Poisson Banane, 6 rue Forum (☎90.96.02.58). Menu under 80F and, naturally, the Caribbean speciality of fish and banana. Very cool. Evenings only till 12.30am; closed Wed.

Le Tambourin, 65 rue Amédée-Pichot (☎90.93.13.32). Fish and seafood in a pleasant atmosphere. Menus under 100F. Closed Mon.

Le Vaccarès, 9 rue Favorin (☎90.96.06.17). Overlooks place du Forum and serves both new and traditional dishes in a light, inventive fashion. The lamb with *tapenade* and the fish *à la poutargue* are exceptional. Menus from 135F; *à la carte* over 300F. Closed Sun and Mon.

The Camargue

The Camargue is one of those geographically enclosed areas that are separate and unique. Its boundaries – the Petit Rhône, the Grand Rhône and the sea – are invisible until you come upon them. Its horizons are infinite because land, lagoon and sea share the same horizontal plain. Both wild and human life have traits peculiar to this drained, ditched and now protected delta land. Today, the whole of the Camargue is a *Parc Naturel Régional*, with great efforts made to keep an equilibrium between tourism, agriculture, industry and hunting on the one hand, and the indigenous ecosystems on the other.

The region is home to the **bulls** and the **white horses** that the Camargue *gardiens* or herdsmen ride, although neither beast is truly wild – both run in semiliberty. The Camargue horse, whose origin is unknown, remains a distinct breed, born dark brown or black and turning white around its fourth year. It is never stabled, surviving the humid heat of summer and the wind-racked winter cold outdoors. The *gardiens* likewise are a hardy community. Their traditional homes, or *cabanes*, are thatched and windowless one-storey structures, with bulls' horns over the door to ward off evil spirits. They still conform, to some extent, to the popular cowboy myth, and play a major role in guarding Carmarguais traditions. Throughout the summer, with spectacles involving bulls and horses in every village arena, they're kept busy and the work carries local glamour. Winter is a good deal harder, and fewer and fewer Carmarguais property owners can afford the extravagant use of land that bull-rearing requires.

The Camargue bulls and horses are just one element in the area's exceptionally rich **wildlife**, which includes flamingos, marsh- and seabirds, waterfowl and birds of prey; wild boars, beavers and badgers; tree frogs, water snakes and pond turtles; and a rich flora of reeds, wild irises, tamaris, wild rosemary and juniper trees. These last, which grow to a height of six metres, form the **Bois des Rièges** on the islands between the **Étang du Vaccarès** and the sea, part of the central national reserve to which access is restricted to those with professional credentials.

After World War II, the northern marshes were drained and re-irrigated with fresh water. The main crop planted was rice, and so successful was it that by the 1960s the Camargue was providing three-quarters of all French consumption of the grain. Vines were also reintroduced – in the nineteenth century they had survived the disease that devastated every other wine-producing region because their stems were under water. There are other crops – wheat, rapeseed and fruit orchards – as well as trees in isolated clumps. To the east, along the last stretch of the Grand Rhône, the chief business is the production of salt, which was first organized in the Camargue by the Romans in the first century AD. It's one of the biggest saltworks in the world, with salt pans and pyramids adding a somehow extraterrestrial aspect to the Camargue landscape.

Though the Étang du Vaccarès and the central islands are out of bounds to humans, there are paths and sea dykes from which their inhabitants can be watched. One of the best observation points for flamingos is the path running alongside the **Étang du Fangassier**, which provides views of the nearby flamingo nesting ground. The ideal months for bird-watching are April to June – the mating period – with the greatest number of flamingos present between April and September.

Practicalities

Infrequent **buses** run between Arles and Stes-Maries, where you can rent **bikes** at *Camargue Vélos*, 27 av Frédéric-Mistral (☎90.97.94.55), *Bruns Sports* on place Mireille (☎90.97.81.83), *Le Vélociste* on place des Remparts (☎90.97.83.26), and *Le Vélo Sanitois* on rte de Cacharel (☎90.97.86.44). The other means of transport to consider is riding, as there are around thirty farms that rent out **horses** by the hour, half-day or day. The tourist office in Stes-Maries (see opposite) has a complete list.

For transport as an end in itself, there's the **paddle steamer** *Le Tiki III*, which leaves for river trips from the mouth of the Petit Rhône, off the rte d'Aigues-Mortes, 2.5km west of Stes-Maries (☎90.97.81.68), and the *Soleil*, which leaves from the port in Stes-Maries (☎90.97.85.89).

Be wary of taking your car or bike along the **dykes**, as although maps and road signs show which routes are closed to vehicles and which are accessible only at low tide, they don't warn you about the road surface. The other problem is **theft** from cars. There are well-organized gangs of thieves with a particular penchant, as locals will testify, for foreign licence plates.

If you stay in the area, be warned that **mosquitoes** are rife from March through to November; staying right beside the sea will be okay, but otherwise you'll need serious chemical weaponry. Biting flies are also prevalent and can take away much of the pleasure of this hill-less land for bicycling. The other problem is the **winds**, which in autumn and winter can be strong enough to knock you off your bike (though fortunately you won't have to cope simultaneously with biting insects and high winds). Conversely, in summer the weather can be so hot and humid that the slightest movement is an effort. There's really no ideal time for visiting the area.

Into the Camargue: the road to Les-Saintes-Maries

For a good general introduction to the area, the **Musée Carmarguais** (daily 9.15am–5.45/6.45pm; Oct–March daily except Tues 10.15am–4.45pm; 25F), on the way to Stes-Maries from Arles, halfway between Gimeaux and Albaron, documents the traditions and livelihoods of the Camarguais people through the centuries, using self-consciously modern museum techniques. At **PONT DE GAU**, just 4km short of Stes-Maries, the **Centre d'Information du Parc** provides information on the whole of the Camargue (daily 9am–noon & 2–6pm; Oct–March closed Fri; free). Just down the road is the **Parc Ornithologique** (daily 8am–sunset; closed Dec–Jan; 25F), with some of the less easily spotted birds kept in aviaries, plus trails across a thirty-acre marsh and a longer walk, all with ample signs and information.

Les Saintes-Maries-de-la-Mer

LES-SAINTES-MARIES-DE-LA-MER is best known for its annual festival on May 24–25, when the town is swamped with Gypsies asking favours from their patron saint Sarah. It's also a good base from which to explore the Camargue, with plenty of reasonably priced accommodation and restaurants.

Arrival and accommodation

The **tourist office** is located on av Van-Gogh, and will happily weigh you down with information detailing all the town's festivals and events (daily summer 9am–1pm & 3–7pm; winter 9.30am–noon & 2.30–6pm).

From April to October **rooms** in Stes-Maries should be booked in advance, and for the Gypsy festival, several months before. Prices go up considerably during the summer and at any time of the year are more expensive than at Arles. Hotels in outlying *mas* (farmhouses) tend to be very expensive. **Camping** on the beach is not officially tolerated, but even at Stes-Maries people sleeping beneath the stars rarely get told to move on. The fifteen-kilometre seaside Plage de Piemanson, south of Salin-de-Giraud, 10km east of Stes-Maries, is a favoured venue for *camping sauvage* in summer.

HOTELS

La Brise de Mer, 31 av G-Leroy (☎90.97.80.21). Overlooking the sea, with a moderately priced restaurant. Obligatory half-board in July and August. ④–⑤.

Mas de Calabruhn, rte de Cacharel (☎90.97.83.23). Tastefully furnished spacious rooms. Obligatory half-board in season. ⑤–⑦.

Le Méditerranée, 4 rue Frédéric-Mistral (☎90.97.82.09). Centrally located, with some of the cheapest rooms in town. March–Nov. ②–③.

Hostellerie du Pont de Gau, rte d'Arles, Pont de Gau (☎90.47.81.53). Middle-priced hotel with old-fashioned Camarguais decor, 4km from Stes-Maries. Closed Jan to mid-Feb. ③.

Le Sauvageon, Petite route du Bac, the road linking the D38 and D570 (☎90.97.89.43). Pretty little *auberge* in its own garden. ②–③.

Les Vagues, 12 av Théodore-Aubanal (☎90.97.84.40). Another low-priced option on the road leading out of town towards Aigues-Mortes. ②–③.

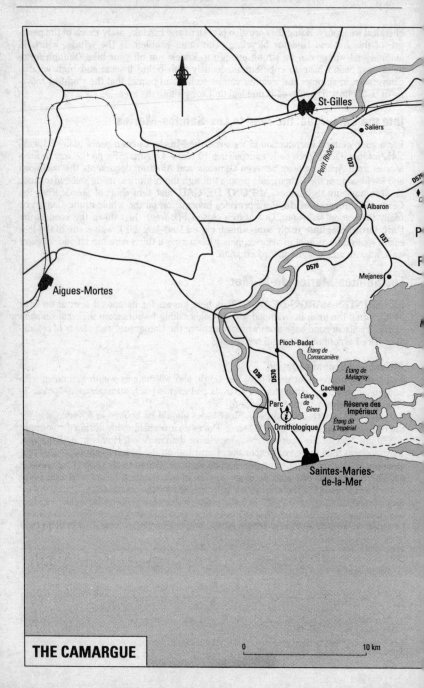

THE CAMARGUE

0   10 km

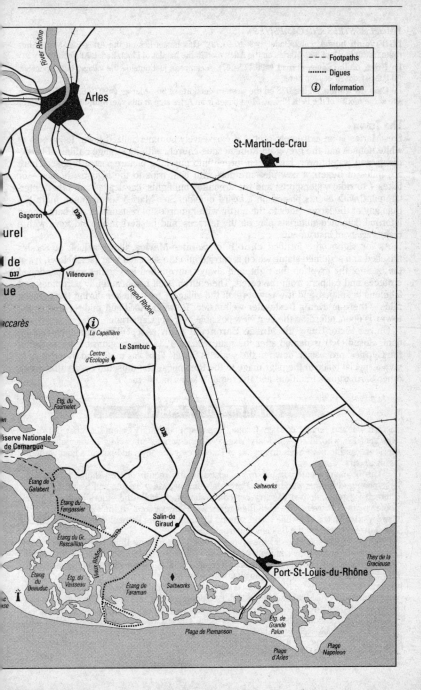

YOUTH HOSTELS AND CAMPSITES

IYHF youth hostel, Pioch-Badet (☎90.97.91.72). This hostel lies on the Arles–Stes-Maries bus route, 10km north of Stes-Maries on the Arles road in the hamlet of Pioch-Badet. All year. ①.

La Brise, on the Cacharel road (☎90.47.84.67). A campsite just outside the village, but expensive. All buses from Arles stop here.

Le Clos du Rhône, on the D38 on the western outskirts of Stes-Maries (☎90.97.85.99). Expensive site at the mouth of the Petit Rhône. Most buses from Arles stop at this site. Mid-June to mid-Sept.

The Town

Stes-Maries is an extremely pretty, if excessively commercialized town. Its streets of white houses and the grey-gold Romanesque church, with its strange outline of battlements and watchtower, have been turned into one long picture-postcard pose. There are miles of **beach**; a new pleasure port with boat trips to the lagoons; horses – or bikes – to ride; watersports; and the arena for bullfights, cavalcades and other entertainment, with events posted on a board outside. Stes-Maries seems much more fun than any of the larger cities to the north, with hundreds of restaurants and bars whose informal flamenco-guitarists play on the terraces, and buskers in the old town with a crazy variety of instruments.

As for sights, the fortified **church of Saintes-Maries** allows a look at Sarah's tinselled and sequined statue which is carried into the sea each year (see below). It's at the back of the crypt on the right, and always surrounded by candles and abandoned crutches and calipers from the cured. The church itself has beautifully pure lines and fabulous acoustics, and it was where all the villagers took shelter during the Saracen raids – there is even a freshwater well inside. Between April and mid-November the **tower** is open, affording the best view possible over the Camargue.

On rue Victor-Hugo, the **Musée Baroncelli** (daily except Wed 9am–noon & 2–5/6pm; closed Oct) is named after the man who, in 1935, was responsible for initiating the Gypsies' procession down to the sea with Sarah. This was motivated by a desire to give a special place in the pilgrimage to the Romanies. The museum covers this event, other Carmarguais traditions and the region's fauna and flora.

THE LEGEND OF SARAH

Sarah was the servant of Mary Jacobé, Jesus' aunt, and Mary Salomé, mother of two of the apostles, who, along with Mary Magdalene and various other New Testament characters, are said to have been driven out of Palestine by the Jews and put on a boat without sails or oars.

The boat apparently drifted to an island in the mouth of the Rhône, where the Egyptian god Ra was worshipped. Here Mary Jacobé, Mary Salomé and Sarah, who was herself Egyptian, settled to carry out conversion work while the others headed off for other parts of Provence. In 1448 their relics were "discovered" in the fortress church of Stes-Maries on the erstwhile island, around the time that the Romanies were migrating to western Europe from the Balkans and from Spain.

Whatever the explanation, the Gypsies have been making their pilgrimage to Stes-Maries since at least the sixteenth century. It's a time for weddings and baptisms, as well as music, dancing and fervent religion. After mass on May 24, the shrines of the saints are lowered from the high chapel to an altar where the faithful stretch out their arms to touch them. Then the statue of Black Sarah is carried by the Gypsies to the sea. On the following day the statues of Mary Jacobé and Mary Salomé, sitting in a wooden boat, follow the same route, accompanied by the mounted *gardiens* in full Camargue cowboy dress, Arlesians in traditional costume, and all present. The sea, the Camargue, the pilgrims and the Gypsies are blessed by the bishop from a fishing boat, before the procession returns to the church with much bell ringing, guitar playing, tambourines and singing. Another ceremony in the afternoon sees the shrines lifted back up to their chapel.

Eating and drinking

Few of the restaurants in Stes-Maries are bargains, though there are any number to choose from, and out of season the quality improves and prices come down. Right in the centre of town on place des Impériaux, *L'Impérial* (☎90.97.81.84; closed Nov–March & Tues except July & Aug) serves pleasant fish dishes on a 115F menu, with a fast *formule* on offer for under 100F. The best places to try local fish specialities are at **BEAUDUC**, over the dykes on the spit of sand on the opposite side of the bay from Stes-Maries. There are restaurants here amidst the shacks and caravans on the beach, like *Chez Juju* and *Chez Marc et Mireille*.

From Avignon to Gordes

If you're heading east from Avignon towards Apt and the Lubéron, two worthwhile stops are the exquisitely romantic **Fontaine-de-Vaucluse** and the picturesque **Gordes**, with its Vasarely connections and the nearby **Abbaye de Senanque**. Between Gordes and Apt are the old ochre quarrying villages of **Roussillon**, **Gargas** and **Rustrel**. Visiting all these places without your own transport is not that easy; Fontaine is accessible by bus from **L'Isle-sur-la-Sorge**; Gordes from **Cavaillon**, 24km southwest of Avignon, and Roussillon only infrequently from Apt.

L'Isle-sur-la-Sorgue and Fontaine-de-Vaucluse

The source of the Sorgue, the same stream that runs alongside rue des Teinturiers in Avignon, is at **L'ISLE-SUR-LA-SORGUE**, 23km southwest of Avignon and one of the most powerful natural springs in the world. At the top of the gorge above the village is a mysterious tapering fissure deeper than the sheer 230-metre cliffs that barricade its opening. This is where the waters of the Sorgue appear, sometimes in spectacular fashion, bursting down the gorge (in March and April normally), other times seeping stealthily through subterranean channels to meet the riverbed further down. The best time to admire it is in the early morning before the crowds arrive.

A few kilometres east, **FONTAINE-DE-VAUCLUSE** was once a rustic backwater lauded by fourteenth-century poet Petrarch, but now is given over to the day-trip trade. If you're intrigued by the source of the river and speak French, visit the **Norbert-Casteret Musée de Spéléologie** (Wed–Sun 10am–noon & 2–6.30pm; June–Aug daily; closed Nov–Jan; 27F) in the underground commercial centre alongside the chemin de la Fontaine, the path to the source. At the upper end of the centre, you'll find a re-creation of the medieval method of pulping rags to paper – using river power – with a vast array of printed matter on the product for sale.

On chemin de la Fontaine, there's also an impressive new **Musée de la Résistance** (daily except Tues 10am–noon & 2–6pm; July & Aug daily except Tues 10am–7pm; mid-Oct to Dec Sat & Sun 10am–noon & 1–5pm; March to mid-April Sat & Sun 10am–noon & 2–6pm; 10F). A few doors down, the **Musée de la Justice et l'Injustice** (same times and price), with a horrible collection of torture and execution equipment, is frankly one to avoid. Across the river, through an alleyway just past the bridge, is the much more comforting **Musée de Petrache** (mid-April to mid-Oct Wed–Sun 9.30am–noon & 2–6.30pm; winter Sat & Sun only; 15F), with beautiful old books dating back to the fifteenth century and pictures of Petrarch, his beloved Laura and of Fontaine, where he passed sixteen years of his unrequited passion.

The cheapest and most beautifully situated of Fontaine's **hotels** is the *Hostellerie Le-Château* (☎90.20.31.54; ④), but like everything else it's likely to be booked solid in summer. The hotel's **restaurant** (closed Tues evening and Wed) serves fresh trout on a menu for around 100F. There's also an *IYHF* **youth hostel** on chemin de la Vignasse, 1km south on the road to Lagnes (☎90.20.31.65; ①; reception 8–10am & 5–11pm; closed Dec–Jan), and a **campsite**, *Les Pres* (☎90.20.32.38; all year), 500m downstream from the village, with tennis courts and swimming pool.

Gordes and around

Just 5km east of Fontaine as the crow flies, but 18km by road, is **GORDES**, a picturesque Provençal village that is a favourite spot for the country residences of Parisian media personalities, film directors, artists and the like: reasons enough to skip the place entirely, were it not for its **château**. This houses a **Didactic Museum** (daily except Tues 10am–noon & 2–6pm; July–Aug daily; 25F), founded in 1970 by the Hungarian artist Victor Vasarely, who establishment critics deride as the inventor of "op art", a movement using optical illusions to bend the viewer's mind. The upper floor charts the complex evolution of Vasarely's creative development. It's fascinating to see the training he gave himself in every aspect of visual experience. On the first floor are gorgeous tapestries of cubes turning into spheres and colours chasing their way through squares, circles and diamonds.

The **tourist office** is in the château (daily 9am–noon & 2–6pm; ☎90.72.02.75). If you're looking for somewhere to **stay**, the most reasonably priced hotel is *Le Provençal* (☎90.72.10.01; ③), with just seven rooms. *Les Romarins* (☎90.72.12.13; ⑤–⑦), overlooking the village on the rte de Sénaque, is an old country house with comfortable, traditionally styled rooms. The best eating place in town is the *Comptoir du Victuailler* on place du Château (☎90.72.01.31; closed Tues evening & Wed out of season), always full of Parisians in summer and with 100F and 135F lunchtime menus in July & Aug, otherwise 300F upwards.

Four kilometres north of Gordes, amidst fields of lavender in a hollow of the hills, stands the twelfth-century Cistercian **Abbaye de Sénanque** (Mon–Sat 10am–noon & 2–6pm, Sun 2–6pm; Nov–Feb Mon–Fri 2–5pm, Sat, Sun & school holidays 2–6pm; 18F). It is still in use as a Cistercian monastery and you can visit the church, cloisters and all the main rooms of this huge and austere but venerable building; a shop sells the monks' produce, including liqueur, as well as honey and lavender essence.

The other stone construction of note in the vicinity of Gordes is the **Village des Bories**, 3.5km east off the D2 to Cavaillon, a strange collection of dry-stone dwellings inhabited, despite their prehistoric appearance, from the Middle Ages right up to the nineteenth century (daily 9am–sunset; 25F). You can wander around the site and into the cottages.

The best and most surreal detour in the vicinity is to the old ochre mines – which you can look into but not enter – between Gordes and Apt (best approached by bus from Apt). The houses in the village of **ROUSSILLON**, 8km to the east, radiate all the different shades of the seventeen ochre tints once quarried here. You can **stay** at the *Résidence des Ocres* (☎90.05.60.50; ③) or at the *Arc-en-Ciel* **campsite** (☎90.05.73.96; mid-March to Oct) among pine trees on an ochre floor, 2km along the D104 to Goult.

There are other quarries in the neighbouring village of **GARGAS** and, more dramatically, near **RUSTREL**, known as the Rustrel Colorado. They're more difficult to get to – and hence not so inundated with coach parties – but yield the distinctive cream-, coffee- and vanilla-coloured sands that rival Vasarely's works for colour sensation.

The Lubéron

After its descent from the Alps, the River Durance makes a wide southern curve before joining the Rhône, skirting the massive rock-fold known as the **Lubéron** that runs for 50km between Cavaillon and Manosque. The Lubéron has long been escape country for well-heeled Parisians, Dutch and British, but has also attracted a good number of artists; the artists' organization *Artifices* currently organizes summer exhibitions and visits to studios in Apt and the surrounding villages (details on ☎90.74.01.26). But the main attraction is the countryside itself and the tiny, immaculately preserved villages.

The Lubéron's northern face is damper, more alpine in character, extremely cold in winter, and dotted with tiny villages clinging stubbornly to the foothills. The southern slopes, by contrast, are Mediterranean in scent and feel. It's almost all wooded, except for the summer sheep pastures at the top, and there's just one main route across it, through the Combe de Lourmarin.

Apt and the Parc Naturel Régional du Lubéron

The sole town base for exploring the Lubéron is **APT**, though in itself it's not much of a town for sightseeing, nor is it renowned for the charm and friendliness of its people. Its large confectionery factory spews mucky froth into a concrete-channelled River Coulon and as late as early spring, when mimosa is blossoming down on the coast, the temperature around Apt can drop to well below freezing. It cheers up, however, every Saturday for the weekly **market** when cars are barred from the town centre to allow artisans and cultivators from all the surrounding countryside to set up stalls. As well as featuring every imaginable Provençal edible, the market is accompanied by barrel organ, jazz musicians, stand-up comics, aged hippies and assorted freaks.

Arriving by **bus** – Apt's *gare SNCF* is freight only – you're most likely to be dropped at **place de la Bouquerie**, the main square lined with cafés and restaurants. The **tourist office** is at 2 av Philippe-de-Girard (Mon–Sat 8.30am–noon & 2–6/7pm; ☎90.74.03.18), just up to your left as you face the river. There's a good choice of **accommodation** in Apt, unlike the more scenic hilltop villages, where all rooms are reserved months before the summer season. At the opposite end of the town from place de la Bouquerie is the *Hôtel L'Aptois*, 6–8 cours Lauze de Perret (☎90.74.02.02; ②–③), with some cheap rooms. *Le Ventoux*, 67 av Victor-Hugo (☎90.74.07.58; ②–④), is flanked by petrol stations, but proves pleasant once you're inside, with probably the best-value restaurant in town. The cheapest rooms in Apt are bang in the centre at *Le Palais*, 12 place Gabriel-Péri (☎90.74.23.54; ①–②; closed Mon), above a rather uninspired pizzeria. **Campers**, for once, are treated to a municipal ground within easy walking distance of the town – *Les Cèdres* on av de Viton (☎90.74.14.61; all year), northeast of the town centre.

Outside Apt, you could try the *Auberge du Presbytère* on place de la Fontaine in **SAIGNON**, a perched village 4km southeast of Apt (☎90.74.11.50; ②–④), or the *St-Paul* (☎90.75.21.47; ③–⑤), with beautiful rooms and wonderful views from its wooded hillside site outside the village of **VIENS**, 16km east. The *gîte*, the *Relais de Roquefure* (☎90.04.88.88), off N100 in the Avignon direction, has horses and bikes for rental.

If you haven't stuffed yourself with chocolates and candied fruit (Apt's speciality), you can **eat** a cheap and extremely edible four-course meal at *Le Brémondy* on place St-Pierre (☎90.04.70.39; closed Sun). *La Calèche*, 4 rue Cély, is similarly priced, or there's the restaurant of *Le Ventoux* hotel (see above). Pricey Argentinian specialities and much cheaper pizzas are available at *Argentin 12*, 12 quai Général-Leclerc, with live music weekend nights. Outside Apt, on the Avignon road opposite the big supermarket, is *Le Perroquet*, a restaurant with jazz and blues at the weekend. In **CHÊNE**, 2.5km west of Apt, there's extremely good food and a chance to try the local goat's cheeses plus lavender *crème brûlée*, at *Bernard Mathys* (☎90.04.84.64; closed Tues & Wed; menus from 160F).

The Parc Naturel Régional du Lubéron

A large area of the Lubéron has been designated the **Parc Naturel Regional du Lubéron**, with the aim of conserving the natural fauna and flora and limiting development. The park is administered by the **Maison du Parc**, 1 place Jean-Jaurès in Apt

(☎90.74.08.55; Mon–Sat 8.30am–noon & 2–7pm), which is the place to go for information about every aspect of the Lubéron: the fauna and flora, footpaths, cycle routes, pony-trekking, and *gîtes* and campsites. The *maison* houses a small **fossil museum** designed for kids (Mon–Sat 8.30am–noon & 2–6/7pm; 10F) and has a shop where you can taste local wines and produce, along with exhibitions and videos on the ecology and environment of the Lubéron.

Given the region's general dearth of public transport, the only practical and pleasurable way to explore is by hiking or cycling. Two **bike** rental places are *D Devoncoux*, 17 quai Général-Leclerc, and *Garage Maretto*, a few doors down. There are special cycle paths, courtesy of the park, from Apt to Cavaillon (40km), from Apt to La Bégude (12km) and on to Volx, all signposted in brown.

The Abbaye de Silvacane

If you're heading for Aix-en-Provence from Apt, you'll pass close to another ancient Cistercian abbey contemporary with Sénanque (see p.832), 29km south of Apt, just across the Durance – the **Abbaye de Silvacane**, (daily except Tues 10am–noon & 2–5/6pm; free), which, after a long history of abandonment and evictions, monks are again inhabiting. It is isolated from the surrounding villages on the bank of the Durance and its architecture has hardly changed at all over the last 700 years; you can visit the stark, pale-stoned splendour of the church, its cloisters and surrounding buildings.

Aix-en-Provence

AIX-EN-PROVENCE would be the dominant city of central Provence were it not for the great metropolis of Marseille, just 25km away on the coast. Historically, culturally and socially, however, they are moons apart and the tendency is to love one and hate the other. Aix is complacently conservative and a stunningly beautiful place, its riches based on land owning and the liberal professions. The youth of Aix are immaculately dressed, and immediately striking is the number of American undergraduates speaking fluent French and acting as if this were home.

From the twelfth century until the Revolution, Aix was the capital of Provence. In its days as an independent fiefdom, its most mythically beloved ruler, King Réné of Anjou, held a brilliant court renowned for its popular festivities and patronage of the arts. Réné also introduced the muscat grape to the region, and today he stands in stone in picture-book medieval fashion, a bunch of grapes in his left hand, looking down the majestic seventeenth-century replacement to the southern fortifications, the cours Mirabeau.

Arrival and accommodation

Cours Mirabeau is the main thoroughfare of the town, with the multifountained place Général-de-Gaulle, or La Rotonde, at its west end, the main point of arrival. The **gare SNCF** is on rue Gustavo Desplace at the end of av Victor-Hugo (☎91.08.50.50), the avenue leading south from the square; the **gare routière** is between the two western avenues, av des Belges and av Bonaparte, on rue Lapierre (☎42.27.17.91). The **tourist office** is at 2 place Général-de-Gaulle (daily 9am–10pm; ☎42.16.11.16), between av des Belges and av Victor-Hugo.

From mid-July to mid-August (festival time) your chances of getting an unbooked **hotel** room are pretty slim, and you must reserve a couple of months in advance at least. Outside this time, there is a decent range of accommodation to choose from.

Hotels

Hôtel des Arts-Sully, 69 bd Carnot (☎42.33.11.77). The cheapest rooms to be found in the centre of Aix are a bit noisy, but the hotel is very welcoming. You can't book, so turn up early. ②.

La Caravelle, 29 bd Roi-Réné (☎42.21.53.05). By the boulevards to the southeast of the city. The more expensive rooms overlook courtyard gardens. ③–⑤.

Hôtel Casino, 38 rue Victor-Leydet (☎42.26.06.88). Nothing very special, but with some cheap rooms. ②–④.

Hôtel de France, 63 rue Espariat (☎42.27.90.15). Right in the centre and with very comfortable rooms. ③–④.

Le Manoir, 8 rue d'Entrecasteaux (☎42.26.27.20). Tucked away in a quiet street in the centre, with agreeable air-conditioned rooms. ④–⑥.

Hôtel Pasteur, 14 av Pasteur (☎42.21.11.76). Next door to *Hôtel Paul* and not quite so attractive, but with an excellent-value restaurant. ①–③.

Hôtel Paul, 10 av Pasteur (☎42.23.23.89). Just outside the boulevard ring, but comfortable and excellent value. Rooms for three and four people. ②.

Hôtel des Quatre-Dauphins, 54 rue Roux-Alphéran (☎42.38.16.39). Old-world charm and compulsory breakfast in the *quartier* Mazarin. ④.

Youth hostels and campsites

IYHF youth hostel, 3 av Marcel-Pagnol (☎42.20.15.99). Though the building and its position can't be faulted, the forms and regulations are over the top – you can't use your own sleeping bag and you must be an official member. If you're in a group of two or more you'd be better off in a hotel. Take bus #8 or #12, direction *Jas de Bouffan*, stop *Vasarely*. Reception is open 7.30–10am & 5.30–10pm; no cooking facilities; restaurant April–Oct. Closed Dec 20–Feb 1. ①.

CROUS, Cité Universitaire des Gazelles, 38 av Jules-Ferry (☎42.26.47.00). This student organization can sometimes find cheap rooms on campus during July and August. Take bus #5, direction *Gambetta*, stop *Pierre-Puget*.

Arc-en-Ciel, rte de Nice, Pont des Trois Sautets (☎42.26.14.28). 3km southeast of town on bus #3, and not particularly cheap. Very good facilities. Open all year.

Airotel Camping Chanteclerc, rte de Nice, Val St-André (☎42.26.12.98). Also 3km from the centre on bus #3, and equally expensive. Facilities are excellent. Open all year.

The City

As a preliminary introduction to Aixois life, a café-stopping stroll beneath the gigantic plane trees that shade the **cours Mirabeau** – Aix's main promenade, running from place Général-de-Gaulle to rue Thiers – is mandatory. The north side is one long line of cafés; the south side banks and offices, all lodging in seventeenth- to eighteenth-century mansions of a uniform hue of weathered stone, with ornate wrought-iron balconies and Baroque decorations.

Vieil Aix

To explore the network of jumbled little lanes and narrow roads that make up **Vieil Aix**, the heart of Aix, wander north from leafy **cours Mirabeau** to anywhere within the ring of cours and boulevards. The layout of the old town is not designed to assist your sense of direction, but each street is alive with people, bars and shops and makes a fascinating place to wander. The architectural backdrop is of treats from the sixteenth and seventeenth centuries, with every fifty metres or so puncuated by a fountained square in which to rest from the constant buzz of upmarket commerce.

The **church of the Madeleine** on the central place des Prêcheurs is decorated with paintings by Rubens and Van Loo, born in Aix in 1684, and a three-panel medieval Annunciation. The **Hôtel de Ville**, just north of place Richelme, displays perfect classical proportions and embroidery in wrought iron above the door. On the south side of the square, a delicate though fairly massive foot hangs over the architrave of the old

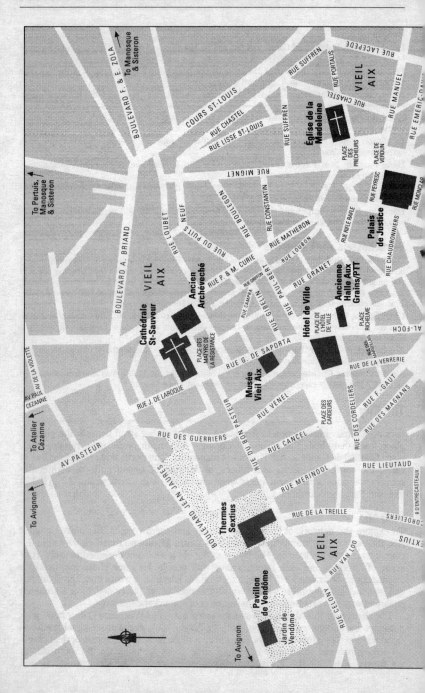

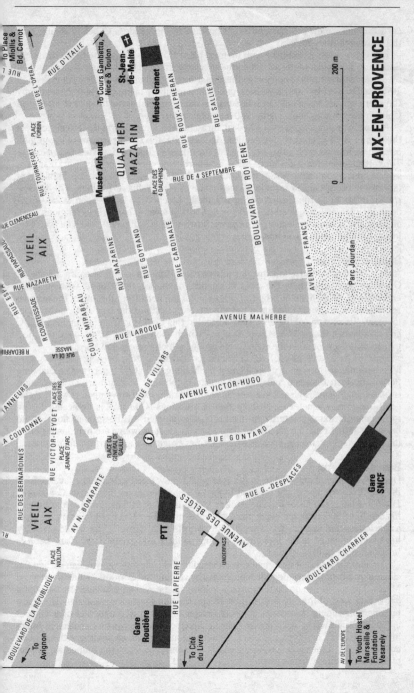

AIX-EN-PROVENCE

200 m

0

corn exchange, now the **post office**. It belongs to the goddess Cybele, dallying with the masculine River Rhône.

Rue Gaston-de-Saporta takes you up from place Hôtel-de-Ville to the **Cathédrale St-Sauveur**, a conglomerate of fifteenth- to sixteenth-century building works, full of medieval art treasures. The best of these is a triptych commissioned by King Réné in 1475, *Le Buisson Ardent*, whose side panels are regularly opened up and discussed by the sacristan (daily except Tues & Sun), revealing an elaborately depicted Mary and Child in the burning bush, loaded with symbolic references.

A short way down from the cathedral, through place des Martyrs-de-la-Résistance, is the former Bishop's palace, the **Ancien Archevêché**, the setting for part of the grandiose music festival each July and housing the **Musée des Tapisseries** (daily except Tues 10am–noon & 2–5.45pm; 13F), a superb collection of quality workmanship. There's also a contemporary section with annual exhibitions, for which the definition of tapestry is broadened to include textiles made of rope, raffia or feathers. The **Musée du Vieil Aix** at 17 rue Gaston-de-Saporta (daily except Mon 10am–noon & 2.30–6/2–5pm; 15F) is worth a look while you're in this part of town. It has a set of religious marionettes and a huge collection of *santons* (Provençal crib figures), but you won't be losing out that much if you miss it.

Quartier Mazarin

Aix's other central museums are in the **quartier Mazarin**, south of cours Mirabeau. On place St-Jean-de-Malte the most substantial of the lot, the **Musée Granet** (daily except Tues 10am–noon & 2–6pm; 15F), exhibits the finds from the site of the original settlement of Aix, the Oppidum d'Entremont, 3km north of the city. Also in the basement are the remains of the Romans who routed this Celtic-Ligurian township in 90 BC and established their city of *Aquae Sextiae* – which evolved into Aix – around the thermal springs they found in the vicinity and around which there is still a spa.

Upstairs is a very mixed bag of paintings: Italian, Dutch, French, mostly seventeenth- to nineteenth-century, appallingly badly hung and lit. The portraits of Diane de Poitiers by Jean Capassin and Marie Mancini by Nicolas Mignard are an interesting contrast, and there is also a self-portrait by Rembrandt, and rows upon rows of eighteenth- and early nineteenth-century French paintings. One wall is dedicated to the most famous Aixois painter, Paul Cézanne, who studied on the ground floor of the building, at that time the art school. Two of his student drawings are here, as well as a handful of minor canvases such as *Bethsabée*, *Les Baigneuses* and *Portrait de Madame*.

Beyond Vieil Aix

One of Cézanne's many studios in Aix is at what is now 9 av Paul-Cézanne, overlooking the city from the north and reached by bus #1, stop terminus *Beisson*, or *Coutheron/Puyricard* bus, stop *Cézanne*. The **Atélier Cézanne** is exactly as it was at the time of his death in 1906; coat, hat, wine glass and easel, the objects he liked to paint, his pipe, a few letters and drawings. . . everything save the man himself, who would probably have been horrified at the thought of it being public (daily except Tues 10am–noon & 2/2.30–5/6pm; 14F).

For a totally different experience, both visually and conceptually, you can escape the cloying grandeur of seventeenth-century Aix by visiting the **Fondation Vasarely** on av Marcel-Pagnol in Jas-de-Bouffan (daily except Tues 9.30am–12.30pm & 2–5.30pm; 35F), 4km west of the city centre (bus #8 or #12, stop *Fondation Vasarely*). There are innumerable sliding showcases, showing images related to all the themes of architect/artist Vasarely's work, including his "plastic alphabet" and designs for apartment buildings. Downstairs, however, the seven high hexagonal spaces, each hung with six huge colour-wonder dimension-doubling designs, is where you'll get the immediate impact of this extraordinary man's work.

Collective cultural life is the basis of the **Cité du Livre** in the old matchmaking factory at 8–10 rue des Allumettes, a short way southwest from the tourist office (Tues, Thurs & Fri noon–6pm, Wed & Sat 10am–6pm; free). It includes libraries, a cinema, theatre space, a *videothèque d'art lyrique* (where you can watch just about any French opera performance) and any number of exhibitions. But best of all are the two entrances at the ends of the conglomerate of buildings: giant books leaning together as if on a shelf, an imaginative design statement.

Eating, drinking and entertainment

Aix is stuffed full of **restaurants** of every price and ethnic origin. Place des Cardeurs, just northwest of the Hôtel de Ville, is nothing but restaurant, brasserie and café tables, while rue de la Verrerie running south from the place has an immense variety of Indian, Chinese and North African restaurants. Rue Van Loo is a good place for low-budget restaurants. The café-brasseries on cours Mirabeau are also tempting, and in between them you'll find cheaper snackeries and peddlars of delicious fresh fruit juice.

Cafés and restaurants

L'Aligote, 6 place des Cardeurs (☎42.63.00.26). Specialities from southwest France from 150F.

De l'Archevêché, place des Martyrs-de-la-Résistance (☎42.21.01.12). Good midday pasta, tapas and salads for under 80F.

Les Bacchanales, 10 rue Couronne (☎42.27.21.06). Salmon with *cêpes*, rabbit with marjoram; inventive cooking with menus from 75F. Open till 1am in summer.

Le Basilic Gourmand, 6 rue du Griffon (☎42.96.08.58). Classic Provençal food on an 80F midday menu, accompanied by exhibitions of paintings.

Le Bistrot Latin, 18 rue Couronne (☎42.38.22.88). *Escargot* and black olive sauce profiteroles and honey and garlic rabbit are two of the top dishes here. Midday menu 89F, evening from 118F. Closed Sun evening and Mon midday.

La Bodéga, cnr rues de la Treille/Muletiers (☎42.96.54.00). Spanish resto serving paella Valenciennes for around 150F on Fri & Sat. Closed Sun.

Le Clos de la Violette, 10 av Violette (☎42.23.30.71). Aix's most renowned restaurant with dishes that might not sound very seductive, like stuffed lamb's feet and *pieds et pâquets* (tripe and salt pork), but are in fact gastronomic delights. More obviously alluring are the puddings: a *clafoutis* of greengages and pistachios with peach sauce and a tart of melting dark chocolate. 185F menu midday, otherwise menus start at 300F and *à la carte* from 450F. Closed Mon midday and Sun.

Les Deux Garçons, cours Mirabeau. Reasonably priced café-brasserie for cours Mirabeau. The erstwhile haunt of Camus is done up in the faded style of the old Orient Express and still attracts a motley assortment of intellectuals.

L'Hacienda, cnr rue Mérindol/place des Cardeurs (☎42.27.00.35). Outdoor tables and a 60F midday menu including wine, with delicious hacienda beef *à la carte*.

Le Jasmin, 6 rue de la Fonderie (☎42.38.05.89). Iranian food for around 100F. Closed Sat & Sun evenings.

Kéops, 28 rue de la Verrerie (☎42.96.59.05). Egyptian cuisine featuring falafel, stuffed pigeon and gorgeous milk-based desserts. From 120F.

Pizza Chez Jo/Bar des Augustins, place des Augustins. Cheap pizzas and traditional *plats du jour*, usually packed.

Le Platanos, 13 rue Rifle-Rafle (☎42.21.33.19). Very cheap and popular Greek resto with menus under 100F.

Nightlife and festivals

The best **jazz club** in town is *Hot Brass*, rte d'Eguilles-Célony (☎42.21.05.57; 10.30pm onwards); rather cheaper is *Le Scat Club de Jazz*, 11 rue de la Verrerie (☎42.23.00.23), with all kinds of jazz from 10pm onwards. *La Chimère*, montée d'Avignon, on the north-ern bypass towards Sisteron (☎42.23.36.28; Wed–Sun from 11pm), is a gay bar and disco, and *La Mazarin*, 6 rue Laroque, an independent **cinema** showing original-version films.

During the annual **music festivals**, *Aix en Musique* (mid-June to first week in July) and the *Festival International d'Art Lyrique* (last two weeks of July), the alternative scene – of street theatre, rock concerts and impromptu gatherings – livens up the town out of all recognition. The international festival's mainstream events are extremely expensive: if you want to try to get tickets apply to the *Comité Officiel des Fêtes* at Complexe Forbin, cours Gambetta (☎42.63.06.75). The office for the International Dance Festival (ten days in mid-July) operates from the same address.

Listings

Bike rental *Troc Vélo*, 62 rue Boulégon (Mon–Sat 9am–noon & 3–7pm). You can leave your passport rather than a deposit.

Books *Paradoxe*, 6 av de France, for English books; *Vents du Sud* on place du Petit-Marché, is the best French bookshop in town.

Car rental *ADA Discount*, 114 cours Sextius (☎42.96.20.14); *Avis*, 11 rue Gambetta (☎42.21.64.16); *Budget*, 16 av des Belges (☎42.38.37.36); *Europcar*, 55 bd de la République (☎42.27.83.00).

Changing money *American Express*, 15 cours Mirabeau; *Change d'Or*, 22 rue Thiers; automatic machine outside *Crédit Lyonnais*, place Jeanne-d'Arc.

Emergencies *Hospital Centre Hospitalier*, chemin de Tamaris (☎42.33.50.00); *SOS Médecins* ☎42.26.24.00; for a late-night chemist, ring the *gendarmerie* on ☎42.26.31.96.

Police Av de l'Europe (☎42.93.97.00).

Post office 2 rue Lapierre 13100 AIX.

Taxis ☎42.26.29.30, ☎42.27.62.12 or ☎42.21.61.61.

Travel agents *Nouvelles Frontières*, 52 Cours Sextius (☎42.26.47.22).

Women Contacts and information from *CIDF Information Femmes*, 24 rue Mignet (☎42.20.69.82).

Mont Ste-Victoire

Mont Ste-Victoire, a rough pyramid whose apex has been pulled off-centre, lies 10km east of Aix. Ringed at its base by the dark green and orange-brown of pine woods and cultivated soil, the limestone rock reflects light, turning blue, grey, pink or orange. In the last years of his life **Cézanne** painted and drew Ste-Victoire more than fifty times, and, as part of his childhood landscape, it came to embody the incarnation of life within nature. Two of his greatest canvases, *Mont Ste-Victoire* and *Paysage d'Aix*, are intricately colour-sculpted representations of solid physical nature – not the play of light or tricks of perception of the Impressionists.

You may, however, be more interested in climbing Mont Ste-Victoire and in the view from it. The southern face has a sheer 500-metre drop, but from the north, the two-hour walk requires nothing more than determination. The **GR9**, also called the *Chemin des Venturiers*, leaves from a small car park on the D10 just before **VAUVENARGUES**, 14km east of Aix (three buses daily). Having reached the 945-metre summit, marked by a monumental cross that doesn't figure in any of Cézanne's pictures, you can follow the path east along the ridge and descend south to **PUYLOUBIER** (about 15km from the summit).

At Vauvenargues, a perfect weather-beaten, red-shuttered fourteenth-century **château** (not open to the public) stands just outside the village, with nothing between it and the slopes of Ste-Victoire. Picasso bought the château in 1958, lived there until his death and now lies buried in the gardens, his grave adorned with his sculpture *Woman with a Vase*.

EASTERN PROVENCE

In **eastern Provence**, it is the landscapes not the cities that dominate. The gentle hills and villages of the **Haut-Var**, the northern half of the Var *département*, make for happy motorized – or cycling – exploration, before the foothills of the Alps gradually close in, eventually reaching heights of over 3000m in the far northeastern corner around **Barcelonnette**. Winter visitors are almost exclusively skiers, while the summer brings a variety of dedicated hikers, bird watchers, botanists and climbers. The **Parc National du Mercantour** is the best area to experience this mountainous terrain, but the most stunning geographical feature is the **Gorges du Verdon** – Europe's answer to the Grand Canyon – in the heart of Provence.

Between Valence and Montélimar, the River Drôme joins the Rhône at **Livron-sur-Drôme**. Following the river upstream by train to **Sisteron**, or by road to Sisteron or Barcelonette, is one of the most dramatic ways of entering eastern Provence.

Haut-Var villages

Between **ST-MAXIMIN-DE-LA-STE-BAUME**, 35km east of Aix and famous for the supposed relics of Mary Magdalene, and **DRAGUIGNAN**, an eminently avoidable military town, a network of small roads links a dozen villages, all of which are ideal for Provençal-style loafing. The roads wind through farmland, vineyards and woods, alongside streams and lakes.

East of the **Lac de Carcès**, between Cabasse and Carcès, off the D19, is the last of the three great Cistercian monasteries of Provence. Even more so than Silvacane and Sénanque, the **Abbaye du Thoronet** (Mon–Sat 9am–7pm, Sun 9am–noon & 2–7pm; Oct–March 9am–noon & 2–5pm; 18F) has been unscathed by the vicissitudes of time, and during the Revolution was kept intact as a remarkable monument of history and art; today it is unused. It was first restored in the 1850s, and a recent campaign has brought it to clear-cut perfection. As with the other two abbeys, it's the spaces, here delineated by walls of pale rose-coloured stone, that are the essence of the experience.

LORGUES, further east, has a serious gourmet stop in the **restaurant** *Chez Bruno* on rte de Vidauban (☎94.73.92.19; closed Sun evening & Mon; menu at 270F, *à la carte* around 400F), where there were wonderfully wild local ingredients in their chestnut and *chanterelle* soup, truffle dishes, pheasant, guinea-fowl and *crème brûlée* with figs in wine.

Heading 13km northwest, **ENTRECASTEAUX** has an ancient stone **laundry** by the river that's still used, and a very beautiful **château** (daily 10am–noon & 2–6pm; Oct–Dec & April–June closes 5pm; Jan–March 2–5pm; 30F), which is lived in and decorated in a sparse but luxurious contemporary style.

COTIGNAC, 9km west of Entrecasteaux, is the Haut-Var village *par excellence*, with a shaded main square for *pétanque* and passageways and stairs bursting with begonias, jasmine and geranium and leading through a cluster of medieval houses. More gardens sprawl at the foot of the bubbly rock cliff that forms the back wall of the village. Places to **stay** in the village include the rather oversmart *Lou Calen* at the bottom of cours Gambetta (☎94.79.60.10; ④–⑤) and the recently renovated *Du Cours*, 18 cours Gambetta (☎94.04.78.50; ③).

North of Cotignac, **SILLANS-LA-CASCADE** has a beautiful walk, signposted off the main road, to an immense waterfall and aquamarine pool, and a good place to **eat** in the *Auberge de la Dame d'Argent*. Its larger neighbour, **SALERNES**, makes tiles and pottery and has the good, old-fashioned *Grand Hôtel Allègre*, on rte de Sillans

(☎94.70.60.30; ②–③). **VILLECROZE** to the northeast and **TOURTOUR** beyond are both suitably picturesque, each with exceptional hotel-restaurants: *La Bastide de Tourtour* on rte de Flayosc (☎94.70.57.30; restaurant closed Mon & Tues midday in season plus Mon evening out of season; ⑤–⑦), which has a 150F weekday lunchtime menu (otherwise from 310F), and 3km from Villecroze on the same road, *Au Bien-Être* (☎94.70.67.57; ④–⑥; restaurant closed Mon & Sun evening out of season), with menus from 115F.

Aups

Between Salernes and the Lac du Ste-Croix, **AUPS** is an off-the-beaten-track market town which would make a good base for both the Gorges du Verdon (see below) and the Haut Var villages – if you have your own transport. The village is a favourite with the British, and its **church of St-Pancrace**, designed by an English architect 400 years ago, has recently had its doors restored by two local British carpenters. Aups remains, however, very much an agricultural Provençal town: it specializes in truffles, and, if you're here on a Thursday between November and mid-March, you can witness the **truffle market**.

On the marketplace, **place Martin-Bidoué**, a monument commemorates the town's citizens who died in 1851 defending the republic and its laws, the year being that of Louis Napoléon's *coup d'état*. Peasant and artisan resistance was strongest in Provence, and the defeat of the insurgents was followed by a bloody massacre of men and women. This might explain the enormous *"République Française, Liberté, Egalité, Fraternité"* sign on the church, proclaiming it as state property.

One other surprising feature of Aups is a museum of modern art, the **Musée Simon Segal** in the former chapel of a convent on av Albert-1er (mid-June to mid-Sept 10.30am–noon & 3–6pm; 10F). The best works are those by the Russian-born painter Simon Segal, but there are interesting local scenes in the other paintings, such as the Roman bridge at Aiguines, now drowned beneath the artificial lake of Ste-Croix.

The **tourist office** is on av Georges-Clemenceau (Mon–Sat 10am–noon & 3–6pm; ☎94.70.00.80). All the **hotels** are good value: *Le Provençal* on place Martin-Bidoué (☎94.70.00.24; ①) is the cheapest; the *Grand Hôtel* on place Duchâtel (☎94.70.10.82; May–Sept; ②–③) is the most expensive. More luxury is to be had at *L'Escale du Verdon*, 1km out on the rte de Sillans-la-Cascade (☎94.84.00.04; ④; May–Sept). There are three **campsites** close to town: at *Camping Les Prés*, to the right off allée Charles-Boyer towards Tourtour (☎94.70.00.93; all year), you can rent **bikes**.

For **meals**, your first choice should be the hotel-restaurant *St-Marc* (☎94.70.06.08; ②–③; closed second & third week of June), a nineteenth-century mill on rue Aloisi. Serving local dishes, truffles and boar in season, it offers a very cheap midday menu and evening menus from 95F (closed Tues evening & Wed). There's also the good-value *Framboise* on place Maréchal-Foch (closed evenings out of season) and for snacks *La Pizza boulangerie-pâtisserie* on place Général-Giraud.

The Gorges du Verdon and around

The vast military terrain of the Camp de Canjuers blocks any approach from the south to the **Gorges du Verdon**. The road north from Draguignan to Comps-sur-Artuby is one of the few public roads through the military terrain. From Comps, the road runs west through 16km of deserted heath and hills with each successive horizon higher than the last. When you reach the canyon, it is as if a silent earthquake had taken place during your journey.

EXPLORING THE CANYON

By far the best way to explore the canyon – if your legs are up to it – is in its depths. To follow the river from Rougon to Mayreste on the **Sentier Martel** takes two days; or just the section between Rougon and Les Malines, about eight hours. Access to the gorge depends on the French electricity board, which controls the volume of the Verdon. Anyway, it must be done in a guided group (crossing the torrent by rope is no simple matter on your own). Unaccompanied shorter excursions into the canyon include the fairly easy descent from the *Falaise des Cavaliers* (west of the *Balcons*), crossing via the *Passerelle de l'Estellié* and ascending to the *Chalet de la Maline* – it's about two hours one way. Another walk of similar length can be done from the *Point Sublime*, passing through the *Couloir Samson*, a 670-metre tunnel with occasional "windows" and a stairway down to the chaotic sculpture of the river banks.

You should get details of the route and advice on weather conditions before you set out. You'll need drinking water, a torch (for the tunnels), and a jumper for the cold shadows of the narrow corridors of rock. Always stick to the path and don't cross the river except at the *passerelles* – the electricity board may be opening dams upstream....

From this vantage point, known as the **Balcons de la Mescla**, you are looking down 250m to the base of the V-shaped, 21-kilometre-long gorge incised by the River Verdon through piled strata of limestone. Ever changing in its volume and energy, the river falls from Rougon at the top of the gorge, disappearing into tunnels, decelerating for shallow, languid moments and finally exiting in full, steady flow at the **Pont de Galetas**. The huge artificial **Lac de Ste-Croix**, filled by the Verdon as it leaves the gorge, is great for swimming when the water levels are high; otherwise the beach becomes a bit sludgy. West from the *Balcons* runs the *Corniche sublime*, the D71, built expressly to give the most breathtaking and hair-raising views. On the north side, the **Route des Crêtes**, the D952, does the same, at some points looking down a sheer 800-metre drop to the sliver of water below.

The entire circuit around the gorge is 130km long and it's cycling country solely for the preternaturally fit. Even for drivers it's hard work, as the hidden bends and hairpins in the road are perilous and, in July and August, so is the traffic.

Public transport around the canyon is less than comprehensive. There's just one bus between Aix, Moustiers, La Palud, Rougon and Castellane on Monday, Wednesday and Saturday from July to mid-September; the rest of the year just on Saturday.

La Palud-sur-Verdon

The loop of the Route des Crêtes joins at **LA PALUD-SUR-VERDON**, the tiny village on the northern face of the gorge and the best base to explore it. Life in the village revolves around the *Lou Cafetier* bar-restaurant. There are one or two other places to eat and a market on Wednesday morning around the church.

The **tourist office** is on the main road in La Palud (mid-June to mid-Sept Tues–Fri 10am–noon & 4.40–6.30pm, Sat 10am–noon; ☎92.77.32.02), with a nearby **Bureau des Guides** (Mon–Sat 10am–12.30pm & 2–5.30pm; ☎92.77.30.50). The *Cabanon du Verdon* has maps and books for sale, and organizes guided walks all year round (M. Bettus, ☎92.77.38.58), as does *Le Perroquet Vert*, a climbing shop (☎92.77.33.39). If you want to **stay**, there's *Le Provence* on the rte de la Maline (☎92.77.36.50; ④–⑥), and the slightly cheaper *Auberge des Crêtes*, 1km east towards Castellane (☎92.77.38.47; ③–④). The same management runs the *Auberge du Point Sublime* in **ROUGON** (☎92.83.60.35; ③), which lives up to its name and is not wildly expensive. The **youth hostel**, *Le Trait d'Union*, with camping in its grounds, is half a kilometre below the village

(☎92.77.38.72; ①; March–Nov), and there's also a municipal **campsite** 800m to the west of the village (☎92.77.38.13) and a **gîte**, *L'Étable*, on the rte des Crêtes (☎92.77.30.63), with a restaurant. The *Chalet de la Maline*, on the rte des Crêtes to the south of the town (☎92.77.38.05), is a mountain **refuge** run by the *Club Alpin Français*.

Moustiers-Ste-Marie

Given the choice, **MOUSTIERS-STE-MARIE** is one place to avoid, particularly during the high season, when the road west out of the gorge through the town is one long traffic jam and the village a tourist trap. There's a glut of hotels, restaurants, souvenir stands and a veritable surfeit of *ateliers* making glazed pottery – Moustiers's traditional speciality. The pottery, like the village itself, is pastel coloured and pretty and on sale in *Liberty* or *Bloomingdales*, but if you want to lug plates home with you, here's your chance.

Aiguines

AIGUINES is perched high above the lake, with a turreted château (not open to the public) and a history of wood-turning – the *boules* for *pétanque* made from ancient box wood roots used to be its speciality. There's the tiny **Musée des Tourneurs sur Bois** (daily except Tues 10am–noon & 2–6pm; 10F), a museum devoted to the intricate art of wood-turning, and some very expensive and beautiful woodwork to be viewed at the *Infiniment Rond* gallery on rue Haute (March–Sept daily).

For **rooms**, there's the hotel-restaurant *Du Vieux Château* (☎94.70.22.95; ②; break-fast included), or the rather characterless *Altitude 823* (☎94.70.21.09; ③–④; half-board compulsory). Of the seven **campsites**, *Les Galetas* (☎94.70.20.48; April–Nov 10) is almost within diving distance of the lake, a long way down from the village. The best place to stay – as long as you don't suffer from vertigo – is the *Hôtel du Grand Canyon du Verdon* by the Falaise des Cavaliers (☎94.76.91.31; ⑤–⑥) on the *Corniche sublime*, a good 20km from Aiguines and with stunning views. The restaurant serves reasonable food from 125F.

Castellane

Twelve kilometres upstream from La Palud on the *Route Napoléon* (see opposite), **CASTELLANE**'s only distinguishing feature is the abrupt, massive rock to the east of the town. Since there's little else to do you might as well climb up to it – thirty minutes' worth from behind the modern church. The gorge itself is out of sight, but the view is still worth the trouble.

The **tourist office**, at the top of rue Nationale (Mon–Sat 9.30am–noon & 3–6pm; ☎92.83.61.14), can provide a full list of the many hotels and campsites in the village and its environs. The *Auberge Bon Accueil* on place Marcel-Sauvaire (☎92.83.62.01; ②–③) is one of the cheapest; the *Nouvelle Hôtel du Commerce* on place de l'Église (☎92.83.61.00; ④) is the swanky option, but also has an amazing 110F menu on which you can eat arti-choke hearts and raviolis stuffed with wild mushrooms and goat's cheese, a burbot and fennel *bouillabaisse* and cheese or dessert. The closest **campsite** to town, off the D952 or rte de Moustiers, is the *Frédéric-Mistral* (☎93.82.62.27; all year). **Mountain bikes** can be rented on the rte de Draguignan opposite the *gendarmerie*.

Riez

A much more pleasant option, though not in the immediate vicinity of the gorge, is low-key **RIEZ**, 15km west of Moustiers. There are pottery workshops here, too, but the main business is derived from the lavender fields that cover this corner of Provence.

Just over the river on the road south is a lavender distillery making essence for the perfume industry. At the other end of the town, 1km along the road to Digne, is the **Maison de l'Abeille** (House of the Bee), a research and visitors' centre (daily 9am–7pm; free). Visitors can buy various honeys (including the local speciality, lavender honey) and hydromel – the honey alcohol of antiquity made from nectar – and if you show interest, you'll get an enthusiastic tour.

In size, Riez is more village than town, but it soon becomes clear that it was once more influential than it is now. Some of the houses on **Grande-Rue** and **rue du Marché** – the two streets above the main allées Louis-Gardiol – have rich Renaissance façades, and the **Hôtel de Ville** on place Quinquonces is a former episcopal palace. The sixth-century **cathedral**, which was abandoned 400 years ago, has been excavated just across the river from allées Louis-Gardiol. Beside it is a **baptistery**, restored in the nineteenth century but originally constructed, like the cathedral, around 600 AD (the key is available from the Hôtel de Ville). If you recross the river and follow it downstream, you'll find the even older and much more startling relics of four **Roman columns** standing in a field.

A rather more strenuous walk, heading first for the clock tower above Grande-Rue and then taking the path past the cemetery and on uphill (leaving the cemetery to your left), brings you to a cedar-shaded platform on the hilltop where the pre-Roman Riezians lived. The only building now occupying the site is the eighteenth-century **Chapelle Ste-Maxime**, with a gaudily patterned interior.

Riez is in danger of losing its out-of-the-way charm, as pedestrian precincts are introduced and buildings are being given facelifts. The musty old *Hôtel des Alpes* on the allées (☎92.77.80.03; ②–③), once the town's only **hotel**, hasn't changed, however. But there's a new, executive-style hotel on the other side of the river, the *Hôtel Carina* (☎92.77.85.43; ③), which has views and comfort to make up for its lack of character. Alternatively, there's a **campsite** over the river on the D11 before the distillery. The **tourist office** (Mon–Fri 10am–12.30pm & 2–5.30pm; ☎92.77.82.80) is at the end of the allées on place Quinquonces, and the **restaurant** *Les Abeilles* on allées Louis-Gardiol (☎92.77.89.29; closed Mon) has a 50F menu, including wine.

Along the Route Napoléon to Sisteron

North of Castellane, the **Route Napoléon** passes through the barren scrubby rocklands of some of the most obscure and emptiest parts of Provence. The road was built in the 1930s to commemorate the great leader's journey north through Haute Provence on return from exile on Elba in 1815, in the most audacious recapture of power in French history. Using mule paths still deep with winter snow, Napoléon and his 700 soldiers forged ahead towards Digne-les-Bains and Sisteron on their way to Grenoble – a total of 350km – in just six days. One hundred days later, he lost the battle of Waterloo and was permanently incarcerated on the island of St-Helena.

There are bus connections between Castellane and Annot, four stops down from Barrême (and about 30km to the east as the crow flies), and in summer the stretch between Annot and Puget-Théniers can be done by steam train. Timetables are available from the tourist office in Castellane, the *gare SNCF* in Barrême, and the Digne tourist office or *gare SNCF*. The narrow-gauge *Chemin de Fer de Provence (CFP)* also runs from Digne to Nice, one of France's great regular scenic train rides.

Sisteron

Sticking to the *Route Napoléon*, you will reach **SISTERON**, the most important mountain gateway to Provence. The site had been fortified since time immemorial and even now, half destroyed by the Anglo-American bombardment of 1944, its citadel stands as a fearsome sentinel over the city and the solitary bridge across the River Durance.

The **Citadelle** (mid-March to mid-Nov daily 9am–7pm; 15F) can easily take up half a day. There are no guides, just recordings in French attempting to recreate historic moments, such as Napoléon's march, of course, and the imprisonment in 1639 of Jan Kazimierz, the future king of Poland. Most of the extant defences are Vauban's work, when it was a front-line fort against neighbouring Savoy. The eleventh-century castle was destroyed in the mid-thirteenth century during a pogrom against the local Jewish population.

The best view is from the *Guérite du Diable* look-out post. The outcrop on which the citadel sits abruptly stops here, 500m above the narrow passage of the Durance. From mid-July to mid-August, the festival known as *Nuits de la Citadelle* has open-air performances of music, drama and dance in the citadel grounds. There are also art exhibitions in the vertiginous late medieval chapel, **Notre-Dame-du-Château**, restored to its Gothic glory and given very beautiful, subdued stained-glass windows in the 1970s.

Back in Sisteron's old town, you'll see three huge **towers** built into the ramparts around the expanding town in 1370. To their left is the Romanesque **Cathédrale Notre-Dame-des-Pommiers**. From the cathedral, rue Deleuze leads to **place de l'Horloge**, where the Wednesday and Saturday **market** is held and which, on the second Saturday of every month, hosts a fair.

Arriving by train at Sisteron, turn right out of the **gare SNCF** along av de la Libération until you reach place de la République, where you'll find the **tourist office** (Mon–Sat 9am–noon/12.15pm & 2–6/7pm, Sun 10am–noon & 2–5pm; ☎92.61.12.03) and the **gare routière**. Rooms come very cheap in the run-down *Hostellerie Provençal* on av J-Moulin (☎92.61.02.42; ①) and nearby *Andrônes* (☎92.61.01.68; ①), both very central. The genteel and old-fashioned *Grand Hôtel du Cours* on allée du Verdon (92.61.04.51; ③–⑤) is the best hotel in town. Sisteron's **campsite** is across the river and 3km along the D951 (☎92.61.19.69; all year).

The food in Sisteron's **restaurants** is nothing special, though the view down the valley from the terrace of the *Hôtel-Restaurant de la Citadelle*, 126 rue Saunerie, certainly is. The *Grand Hôtel du Cours* (see above) offers the local lamb on a 105F menu, and there are plenty more eating places along rue Droite and rue Saunerie. *Le Mondial* bar at the top of rue Droite stays open late, as does *Le Primerose* on place de l'Horloge.

Digne-les-Bains

DIGNE-LES-BAINS, 25km east of Sisteron, is the chief town of the Alpes-de-Haute-Provence *département*, and lies in a superb position between the Durance valley and the start of the real mountains. For years its main activity was administering thermal spring cures for rheumatism and respiratory disorders, never a good sign for tourism. The old town and the two cathedrals were in a pretty miserable state, with repair works now underway, and well-designed new blocks are replacing some of the slums in the old town. It can still be a bit of a dispiriting place, but its varying attractions make it a must for geologists, admirers of Tibet and intrepid woman travellers.

Covering over 150,000 hectares to the east of Dignes, the **Réserve Naturelle Géologique de la Haute Provence** is the largest geological reserve in Europe, with fossils dating back 300 million years. Guided day trips are organized by the tourist office from the second week in July to the third week in August, on Sunday, Monday and Thursday. The **Centre de Géologie**, with a range of fairly interesting videos and exhibitions, is in the Quartier St-Benoît, north of the town along av St-Benoît to Barles, across the bridge and down to the left (daily 9am–noon & 2–5.30pm, Fri closes at 4.30pm; Nov–March Mon–Fri; 13F).

The town's connection with Tibet is through the explorer Alexandra David Neel, who managed to spend two months in the forbidden city of Lhasa disguised as a beggar in 1924. She spent the last years of her long life in Digne, dying there at the age of 101, and her house, *Samten Dzong* at 28 av du Maréchal-Juin, is now the **Fondation Alexandra David Neel** (guided visits: daily 10.30am, 2pm & 4pm; July–Sept 10.30am, 2pm, 3.30pm & 5pm; free), devoted to her memory. The Dalai Lama himself has visited the place twice. Also a cut above the normal is the town's **municipal museum** at 64 bd Gassendi (Tues–Sun 1.30–5.30pm; July & Aug 10.30am–noon & 1.30–6.30pm; 15F), with some great sixteenth- to nineteenth-century paintings and homages to local seventeenth-century mathematician and savant Pierre Gassendi.

The **tourist office** is on the Rond-Point du 11-novembre-1918 (Mon–Sat 9am–noon/12.30pm & 2–6/7pm; ☎92.31.42.73), and the **gare routière** is to the north, on av Demontze. The **gare SNCF** and the **Chemin de Fer de Provence** are both to the west over the river on av Pierre-Sémard. A very cheap **hotel** option is the *Origan*, 6 rue Pied-de-Ville (☎92.31.62.13; ①), with an excellent restaurant (closed Sun) and menus starting from 100F. *Le Grand Paris*, 19 bd Thiers (☎92.31.11.15; ④–⑤), is considerably more luxurious and also has a good and expensive restaurant (300F upwards).

Northeast Provence

Depending on the season, the northeastern corner of Provence is two different worlds. In winter, the sheep and shepherds find warmer pastures, leaving the snowy heights – ranging from 1000m to 3000m – to horned mouflons, chamois and the perfectly camouflaged ermine. The villages, where shepherds came to summer markets, are battened down for the long, cold haul. Other villages – or rather gatherings of Swiss-style chalets, sports shops and discos – come to life, with a ski lift instead of a church or marketplace as the focal point.

In spring, the fruit trees in the narrow valley orchards blossom, and melting waters swell the Vésubie, the Tinée and the Roya, sometimes flooding villages and carrying whole streets away. In summer and autumn the ski resorts are ghostly, and from the valleys to the peaks, sunlight is filtered through chestnut and olive trees and then pine forests edged with wild raspberries, up to rocks with eagles' nests, moors and sheep pastures where wild rhododendrons and gentians grow.

An area of 68,500 hectares along the Italian border has been designated the **Parc National du Mercantour**, with the small towns of **St-Étienne-de-Tinée**, **St-Martin-Vésubie**, **St-Sauveur-sur-Tinée** and **Barcelonnette** making the best bases for exploring it. East of the park, the **upper Roya valley**, with good transport links, is worth exploring, and **Sospel** is a real delight.

The Parc National du Mercantour

The **Parc National du Mercantour** is a long, narrow band of mountainland running 80km along the Italian border, from south of the town of Barcelonnette almost as far as Sospel, 16km north of the Mediterranean. The park is little populated and a haven for wildlife, with colonies of golden eagles, chamois, marmots and ibex, and many species of alpine plants only found in this area. The Vallée des Merveilles, with its thousands of open-air rock drawings dating back thousands of years (see overleaf), forms the chief touristic site within the park.

Organized walks, mountain shelters and information centres make discovering this patch of wilderness relatively simple. The **GR52** runs through the southern section of the park, from Sospel through Madone de Fenêstre, with the **GR5** cutting across the middle section from St-Sauveur to St-Étienne-de-Tinée. For more detailed information,

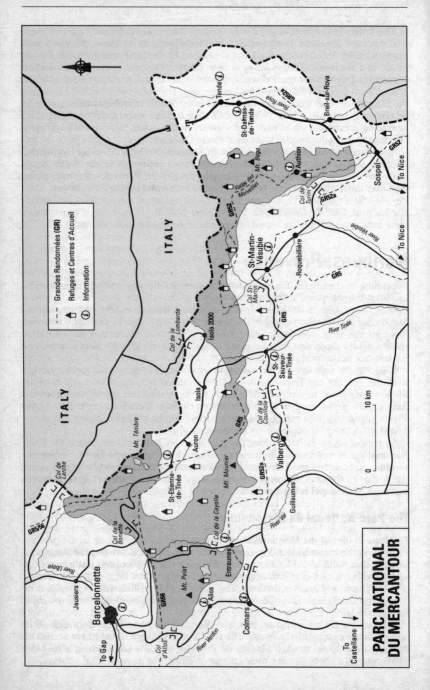

PARC NATIONAL
DU MERCANTOUR

contact one of the **Maisons du Parc** in Barcelonnette, St-Étienne-de-Tinée, St-Martin-Vésubie and St-Sauveur-sur-Tinée (see below), which provide maps and accommodation details as well as advice on footpaths and weather conditions. They can also give addresses for horse and bike rental. For hiking, the best guide is no. 13 in the *Footpaths of Europe* series, *Walking the GR5: Larche to Nice*, which covers much of the national park (see p.1005).

Transport other than by foot is a problem. Apart from the Turin–Nice train line down the Roya valley close to the Italian border, there are regular bus connections going out from Barcelonnette or from Sospel but they don't meet, and there are only infrequent buses between villages on market days. Camping is not allowed in the park but there are plenty of sites outside its limits, never too far away. There are *gîtes d'étape* in many of the villages, and, in the back country, more basic refuges or mountain huts, accessible only by foot and more expensive than a youth hostel. These tend to be on GR5 and GR52 (signed red on white) which run through sections of the park.

The Vallée des Merveilles

The first person to stumble upon the lakes and tumbled rocks of the **Vallée des Merveilles**, in the east of the park, was a fifteenth-century traveller who had lost his way. He described it as "an infernal place with figures of the devil and thousands of demons scratched on the rocks": a pretty accurate description, except that some of the carvings are of animals, tools, people working, and symbols that could mean anything. There are around 100,000 of them, dated to some time in the second millennium BC, and that is about all that's known about them.

The most direct route into the valley is the ten-kilometre hike that starts at *Les Mesches Refuge*, 10km west of St-Dalmas-de-Tende, on the D91 and the Turin–Nice train line. When you're nearly there, you'll find the *Refuge des Merveilles* (☎93.04.64.64), where you can get sustenance and shelter. Never underestimate these mountains' ability to turn blue skies and sun into violent hailstorms and lightning: the route takes between five and six hours there and back, excluding time spent looking at (and for) the carvings.

The closest base to the valley is **ST-DALMAS-DE-TENDE**, where you can **stay** at the *Hôtel Terminus* on the rte de la Vallée des Merveilles, near the station (☎93.04.60.10; ①–②). There's a **Maison du Parc** nearby (☎93.04.67.00).

Barcelonnette

From Gap in the Hautes Alpes, the most direct road into Provence brings you to **BARCELONNETTE**, a place of immaculate charm in which snow-capped mountains are visible at the end of each short boulevard. It is not very big, and a more ideal spot for doing nothing would be hard to find. The central square, **place Manuel**, has café tables from which to gaze at the blue sky and a white clock tower commemorating the centenary of the 1848 revolution. It also makes a good base to explore the Parc National du Mercatour, ten kilometres to the east.

Barcelonnette's **tourist office** is on place Frédéric-Mistral (Mon–Sat 9.30am–noon & 3–5/6pm; ☎92.81.04.71), and its **Maison du Parc** is at 10 av de la Libération in the nearby village of **LA SAPINIÈRE** (☎92.81.21.31). Probably the best place to **stay** in the centre of town is the *Azteca* on rue François-Arnaud (☎92.81.46.36; ④–⑥), decorated in Mexican style. The *Choucas Hôtel* (☎92.81.15.20; ①–②) and the *Grand Hôtel* (☎92.81.03.14; ①–③), both overlooking place Manuel, are two cheaper options. Otherwise, try the *Cheval Blanc*, just down the road at 12 rue Grenette (☎92.81.00.19; ③), or the *Provençal*, 30 rue Manuel (☎92.81.03.39; ②). There are two **campsites** on the D902 leading to the Col de la Cayolle, and *Le Peyra*, 10 av de Peyra (☎92.81.24.06; June–Sept), the cheapest and closest to town.

Excellent **food** can be had at *La Mangeoire*, in an old sheep barn on place des Quatre-Vents (☎92.81.01.61; closed Mon, Tues and middle of May; 100F menu, à la carte 230F upwards). There are more basic but dependable dishes at *Le Troubadour* on place Frédéric-Mistral (☎92.81.24.24; closed Thurs; menus from 75F), and *Ubayoglace*, 6 rue Bellon, serves incredible homemade ices and fruit sorbets.

The road from Barcelonnette to Sospel

The road across the Cime de la Bonette pass – the D2205 from Barcelonnette – claimed to be the highest in Europe, reaches over 2800m and gives a feast of high-altitude views. You may have to brake for a two-foot-long furry marmot or for an army truck, as the military are rather fond of this deserted spot, but the green and silent spaces of the approach, circled by barren peaks, are magical.

At **ST-ÉTIENNE-DE-TINÉE**, nestling close to the border of the park, you can recover from vertigo and maybe see the sheep fairs, held every three weeks or so between March and October. For **accommodation**, the *Hôtel-Restaurant Pinatelle* on rte d'Auron (☎93.02.40.36; ①; half-board compulsory; Jan–Sept) is the cheapest place to stay, and there's a **campsite** on bd Rouery, *L'Archiardy* (☎93.02.41.43; all year). The *Maison du Parc* is in the quartier de l'Ardon (☎93.02.42.27).

From St-Étienne, the **GR5** footpath heads off into the mountains, past the ski resort of **AURON**, after which there's nothing but white quartz and white heather, with only the silvery sound of crickets competing with the water's roar. The GR5 eventually rejoins the road at **ST-SAUVEUR-SUR-TINÉE**, another sheep-fair town, with a *Maison du Parc* on the main road (☎93.02.01.63). From there, roads and paths both go east towards lovely **ST-MARTIN-VÉSUBIE**, whose main street is cobbled and no more than an arm's-length wide, with a stream of channelled water running down the middle and overhung by roofs and balconies. *La Bonne Auberge* (☎93.03.20.49; ③) and *La Châtaigneraie* (☎93.03.21.22; ⑤), both on the allées de Verdun, are **hotel-restaurants**, and there are no cheaper places to stay in the village. The **campsite**, *La Mério*, is on the rte de la Colmaine (☎93.03.30.38; June to mid-Sept), and there's a **gîte**, *Le Touron*, just under 1km away on the Nice road (☎93.03.21.32). You can treat yourself to a terrific pizza at *La Treille*, 70 rue Cagnoli, the main street of the old village. The **tourist office** on place Félix-Faure (Mon–Sat 10am–12.30pm & 2–5.30pm; ☎93.03.21.28) provides details on paths and *gîtes*/refuges in the vicinity, and the **Maison du Parc** on rue Kellerman-Serrurier can provide practical information for exploring the Mercantour park (☎93.03.23.15).

Sospel and the Roya valley

The road from the Vésubie valley joins the **Roya valley** at **SOSPEL**, a dreamy Italianate town spanning the gentle River Bévéra. You may find it overtranquil after the excitements of the high mountains or the flashy speed of the Côte d'Azur, but it can make a pleasant break.

The main street, **avenue Jean-Médecin**, follows the river on its southern bank. The central bridge, the **Vieux Pont**, was built in the eleventh century to link the town centre on the south bank with its suburb across the river. The liveliest part of town is **place de La Cabraïa**, by the western modern bridge.

The best approach to the old town is from place St-Pierre to the east, along the gloomy, deeply shadowed **rue St-Pierre**. Suddenly it opens up into **place St-Michel**, one of the most beautiful series of peaches-and-cream baroque façades in all Provence, made up of the **Cathédrale St-Michel**, two chapels and several arcaded houses. The road behind the cathedral, rue de l'Abbaye, or the steps between the chapels, lead up to an ivy-covered **castle** ruin, from which you get a good view of the town. An even better view can be had from the **Fort St-Roch**, part of the ignominious inter-war Maginot Line, along chemin de St-Roch, which houses the **Musée de la Résistance**, illustrating the courageous local resistance movement during the last war (June–Sept Tues–Sun 2–6pm; April & May Sat & Sun 2–6pm; 10F).

The **gare SNCF** is southeast of the town on av A-Borriglione, which becomes av des Martyrs-de-la-Résistance, before leading down to the park on place des Plantanes opposite place St-Pierre. The **tourist office** is now housed in the Vieux Pont (Mon–Sat 10am–noon & 2.30–6pm; ☎93.04.18.44). If you want to **stay**, the *Auberge du Pont-Vieux*, 3 av J-Médecin (☎93.04.00.73; ①–②), is Sospel's cheapest hotel. The *Auberge Provençale*, on rte du Col de Castillon 1.5km uphill from the town (☎93.04.00.31; ③–④), is much nicer, with a pleasant garden and terrace from which to admire Sospel. There are five **campsites** around the town, the closest of which is *Le Mas Fleuri* in Quartier La Vasta (☎93.04.03.48; all year), with its own pool, 2km along the D2566 to Moulinet following the river upstream.

There are various **eating** places along av J-Médecin. At *L'Escargot d'Or*, 3 rue de Verdun (☎93.04.00.43; closed Fri), just across the eastern bridge, you can eat for between 100F and 150F on a terrace above the river.

The upper Roya valley

LA BRIGUE, one stop up the line from St-Dalmas-de-Tende, is the best place to stay in the upper Roya valley, with some good-value hotels. While you're here, make the trip 4km east of town to the sanctuary of **Notre-Dame-des-Fontaines**, whose frescoes were executed by one Jean Canavéso at around the same time the waylaid fifteenth-century traveller was freaking out about the devils and demons of the Vallée des Merveilles (see p.849). The frescoes, which cover the entire building, are the sort of thing that wouldn't be shown on television. The goriest detail is a devil extracting Judas's soul from his disembowelled innards. The chapel is open all year; a key is available from the restaurants and *tabacs* in La Brigue. There are three **hotels** in La Brigue: *Le Mirval* (☎93.04.63.71; ②–③; April–Oct), *Auberge St-Martin* (☎93.04.62.17; ①–②; late-Feb to Nov), and the *Fleurs des Alpes* (☎93.04.61.05; ①–②).

One more stop north on the train line brings you to **TENDE**, where the French spoken has a distinctly Italian accent. A **Musée des Merveilles** about the Bronze Age, with reproductions of the Vallée des Merveilles engravings, is planned to open soon (details from *Office de Tourisme de la Haute Roya*, av du 16-septembre-1947; ☎93.04.73.71). That apart, there's the old town to explore in which many of the door lintels are engraved with the symbols of bygone trades. Tende is a busy place with plenty of shops and restaurants, though nothing very special on the gourmet front. To **stay**, there's the *Hôtel du Centre* on place de la République (☎93.04.62.19; ①), or the slightly more upmarket *Le Cheval Blanc* (☎93.04.62.22; ②–③).

travel details

Trains

Aix-en-Provence to: Briançon (3 daily; 4hr 30min); Gap (3 daily; 2hr 15min); Manosque (6 daily; 45min); Marseille (very frequent; 30min); Sisteron (3 daily; 1hr 20min).

Arles to: Avignon (frequent; 20min); Marseille (frequent; 50min).

Avignon to: Arles (frequent; 20min); Châteauneuf-du-Pape (2–3 daily; 6min); Montpellier (frequent; 50min); Marseille (frequent; 55min); Orange (8 daily; 25min); Perpignan (frequent; 3hr).

Breuil-sur-Roya to: La Brigue (9 daily; 30min); Tende (9 daily; 45min).

Lyon (La Part-Dieu or Perrache) to: Arles (frequent; 2hr 45min); Avignon (very frequent; 2hr 10min); Bordeaux (3 daily; 7–9hr); Bourg-en-Bresse (5–6 daily; 1hr 50min); Dijon (5 daily; 2hr); Grenoble (2–3 daily; 1hr 15min); Marseille (very frequent; 3hr 40min); Montélimar (frequent; 1hr

35min); Orange (frequent; 2hr 10min); Paris (frequent *TGV*s; 2hr 10min; 3–4 ordinary trains daily; 5hr); Roane (frequent; 1hr 30min); St-Étienne (3 daily; 47min); Strasbourg (5 daily; 5hr); Tain l'Hermitage (5 daily; 1hr 5min); Valence (very frequent; 55min); Vienne (7 daily; 20 min).

Lyon Perrache to: Nîmes (*Le Cevenol* scenic train; 8hr 30min).

Lyon (Satolas or La Part-Dieu) to: Lille Europe (7 *TGV*s daily; 2hr 55min); Valence (5 *TGV*s daily; 40min).

Buses

Aix-en-Provence to: Barcelonnette (4 daily; 4hr); Draguignan (2 daily; 2hr 25min); Marseille (4 daily; 25min); Sisteron (4 daily; 2hr).

Arles to: Aix (3 daily; 1hr 55min); Les Baux (1–3 daily; 30min); Stes-Maries-de-la-Mer (3–8 daily; 1hr).

Aups to: Cotignac (1–2 daily; 20min); Entrecasteaux (1–2 daily; 10min); Salernes (1–2 daily; 10min); Villecroze (1–2 daily; 20min).

Avignon to: Apt (4 daily; 1hr 10min); Arles (3 Mon–Sat; 45min); Carpentras (frequent; 45min); Cavaillon (frequent; 45min); Châteauneuf-du-Pape (2 daily; 30min); Digne (2 daily; 3hr 10min); L'Isle-sur-la-Sorgue (1 daily; 40min); Orange (frequent; 45min–1hr 10min); St-Rémy (6–9 daily; 40min).

Carpentras to: Aix (3 daily; 1hr 50min); Apt (3 weekly during school time; 1hr 5min); Beaumes (2 daily; 15min); Cavaillon (3 daily; 45min); Gigondas (2 daily; 40min); L'Isle-sur-la-Sorgue (2 daily; 20min); Orange (5 daily; 40min); Sablet (2 daily; 45min); Vacqueyras (2 daily; 25min); Vaison (2 daily; 45min).

Digne to: Apt (2 daily; 2hr 5min); Barcelonnette (1 daily; 1hr 45min); Château-Arnoux–St-Auban (7 *SNCF* buses daily; 35min); Riez (1 daily; 1hr 30min); Sisteron (2 daily; 1hr 10min); Veynes-Devoluy (7 *SNCF* buses daily; 1hr 35min–1hr 50min).

Draguignan to: Aups (1–2 daily; 1hr 10min); Moustiers-Ste-Marie (1–2 daily; 2hr); Nice airport (2 daily; 1hr).

Gordes to: Cavaillon (2 daily; 45min).

Orange to: Carpentras (5 daily; 40min); Châteauneuf-du-Pape (4 daily; 25min); Sablet (3 daily; 50min); Seguret (3 daily; 55min); Sérignan (5 daily; 20min); Vaison-la-Romaine (4 daily; 1hr 10min).

St-Rémy to: Les Baux (2 daily; 15min).

Sospel to: Menton (3 daily; 55min).

CHAPTER FIFTEEN

THE CÔTE D'AZUR

The **Côte d'Azur** has to be the most built-up, overeulogized and expensive stretch of coastline anywhere in the world. There are only two industries to speak of – tourism and building, plus the related services of estate agents, yacht traffic wardens and Rolls Royce valets. Posters for extreme right-wing politician Le Pen go undefaced, and construction companies pick their labourers from lines of North African immigrants just as galley owners before them chose their slaves. Meanwhile, a hotel serves tender meat morsels to its clients' pets in a restaurant for dogs.

On the other hand, in every gap between the monstrous habitations – in the **Estérel**, the **St-Tropez** peninsula, the **islands** off **Cannes** and **Hyères**, the **Massif des Maures** – the remarkable beauty of the hills and land's edge, the scent of the plant life, the mimosa blossom in February and the strange synthesis of the Mediterranean pollutants that make the water so translucent, devastate the senses. The chance to see the works of innumerable artists seduced by the land and light also justifies the trip. See, for example, Cocteau in **Menton** and **Villefranche**, Matisse, Dufy and Chagall in **Nice**, Picasso in **Antibes** and **Vallauris**, and collections of Fauvists and Impressionists at St-Tropez, Nice and Hauts-de-Cagnes. And it must be said that places like **Monaco** and **Cannes**, the star excrescences of the coast, have a twisted entertainment value, just as the down-to-earthness of **Marseille** has its own strong attraction.

The months to avoid are July and August, when all hotels are booked up, the overflowing campsites become health hazards, local people are overworked, and the vegetation is at its most barren.

FROM MARSEILLE TO TOULON

From the vast and wonderful scruffiness of **Marseille** to the rather squalid naval base of **Toulon**, this stretch of the Mediterranean is definitely not what most people think of as the Côte d'Azur: there is no continuous corniche, few villas in the Grand Style, and

---

ACCOMMODATION PRICE CATEGORIES

All the hotels, youth hostels and guesthouses listed in this book have been price-graded according to the following scale, and although costs will rise slightly overall with the life of this edition, the relative comparisons should remain valid. Paris and the large cities will, as anywhere, be more expensive than equivalent accommodation in the countryside or small towns. The prices quoted are for the cheapest available double room in high season, although remember that many of the cheap places will have more expensive rooms with en-suite facilities.

① Under 160F	④ 300–400F	⑦ 600–700F
② 160–220F	⑤ 400–500F	⑧ Over 700F
③ 220–300F	⑥ 500–600F	

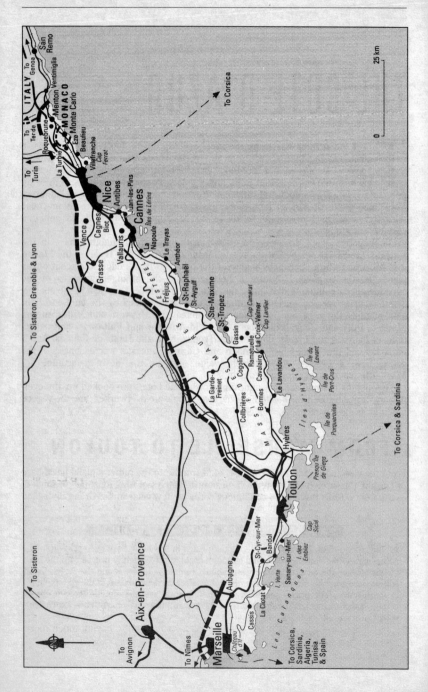

FOOD AND WINE OF THE CÔTE D'AZUR

The **Côte d'Azur**, as part of Provence, shares its culinary fundamentals of olive oil, garlic and the herbs that flourish in dry soil, its gorgeous vegetables and fruits, plus Menton's lemons, the goat's cheeses and, of course, the predominance of fish.

The fish soups of **bouillabaisse**, famous in Marseille, and **bourride**, served with a chilli-flavoured mayonnaise known as **rouille**, are served all along the coast, as are **fish** covered with Provençal herbs and grilled over an open flame. **Seafood** – from spider crabs to clams, sea urchins to crayfish, crabs, lobster, mussels and oysters – are piled onto huge *plateaux de mer* – not necessarily representing Mediterranean harvest, more the luxury associated with this coast.

The **Italian influence** is even stronger on the coast than it is inland, particularly in Nice, with delicate raviolis stuffed with asparagus, prawns, wild mushrooms or *pestou*, pizzas with wafer-thin bases and every sort of pasta as a vehicle for anchovies, olives, garlic and tomatoes. **Nice** has its own specialities, such as *socca*, a chickpea flour pancake, *pissaladière*, a tart of fried onions with anchovies and black olives, *salade Niçoise* and *pan bagnat*, which combines egg, olives, salad, tuna and olive oil, and *mesclum*, a salad of bitter leaves including dandelion. *Petits farcies* – stuffed aubergines, peppers or tomatoes – are a standard feature on Côte d'Azur menus, and in inland Provence as well.

The Italian **dessert** tiramisu, made of marscapone cheese, chocolate and cream, appears in Nice, while St-Tropez has its own sweet speciality in the *tarte Tropezienne*. The sweet chestnuts that grow in the Massif des Maures are candied or turned into puree. Outlets for ice cream and sorbets are ubiquitous.

As for **wine**, the rosés of Provence might not have the great status in the hierarchy of wines, but for baking summer days they are hard to beat. The best of the Côte wines come from Bandol: Cassis too has its own *appellation*, and around Nice the Bellet wines are worth discovering. Fancy cocktails are a Côte speciality, and *pastis* is the preferred thirst quencher at any time of the day.

work is geared to an annual rather than summer cycle. **Cassis** is the exception, but Marseille is the overriding attraction here – a city that couldn't be confused with any other, no matter where you were dropped in it.

Marseille

The most renowned and populated city in France after Paris, **MARSEILLE** has – like the capital – prospered and been ransacked over the centuries. It has lost its privileges to sundry French kings and foreign armies, refound its fortunes, suffered plagues, religious bigotry, republican and royalist Terror and had its own Commune and Bastille-storming. It was the presence of so many Marseillaise Revolutionaries marching their way from the Rhine to Paris in 1792 which gave the name to the *Hymn of the Army of the Rhine* that became the national anthem, "La Marseillaise" (see p.451).

Today, it can't be denied that Marseille is a deprived city, that it is neither particularly beautiful nor clean, that it has acres of grim 1960s housing estates. You might not choose to live here, but it's a wonderful place to visit – a real, down-to-earth port city with a trading history going back over 2500 years. It's just as cosmopolitan as Paris with the advantages of being nearly 800km farther south, having much more down-to-earth, informal inhabitants, and lacking the usual trappings of the rest of the Côte.

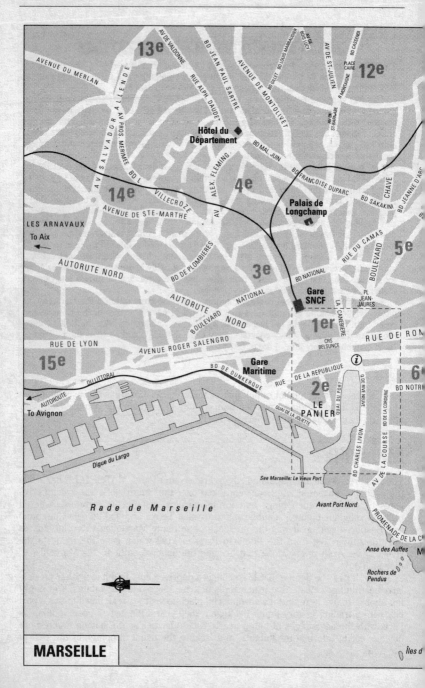

MARSEILLE

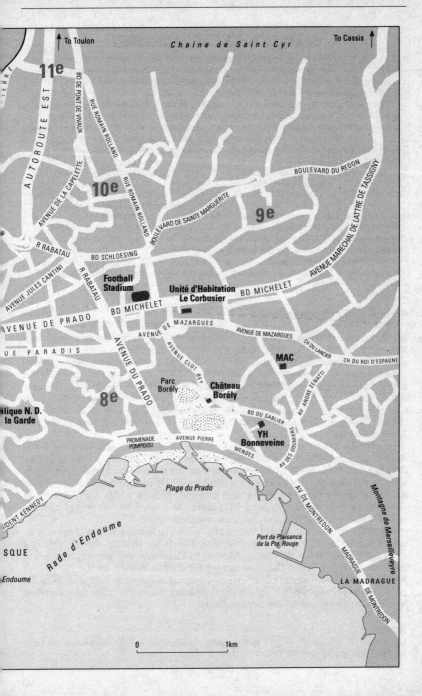

POWER AND POLITICS

Marseille has all the social, economic and political ills of France writ large. In addition, it has to contend with its notoriety for protection rackets and shoot-outs, corruption, drug-money laundering and prostitution. This reputation is a bit unfair – not because it's ill-founded, but because the rest of the Côte d'Azur is just as bad.

Since 1989 the city has been in the hands of **Robert Vigouroux**, an independent socialist lacking the charisma of his predecessor Gaston Deferre. Vigouroux has concentrated on prestige cultural improvements (or not, in the case of the dreadful Musée de la Mode, said to have been a "little gift" for his wife) and attracted very little new investment to the city. For a long while the fear was that the National Front leader Jean-Marie Le Pen would end up in the town hall.

But then **Bernard Tapie** appeared on the scene: a millionaire businessman who entered politics with the express intention of seeing off Le Pen. Tapie won the hearts of the Marseillais by making their football team, *Olympic de Marseille* or *OM*, great again. Despite allegations of the team cheating to win the league in 1993, followed by investigations into not just the team's finances but the whole of Tapie's business empire, around 70 percent of the city's electorate voted for him in the European elections of 1994. He remains an MGP and fantastically popular in the city, even though he has been declared bankrupt and cannot stand for any French office until 1999.

However, there is still significant grassroots support for Le Pen, and the dominating fear and violence in the city comes from racism rather than any Mafia activities.

Arrival and accommodation

The main **tourist office** is at 4 La Canebière (June–Aug daily 8am–8pm; Sept–May Mon–Sat 9am–7.30pm, Sun 10am–5pm; ☎91.54.91.11), down by the Vieux Port. It's just a fifteen-minute walk from the **gare SNCF St-Charles** on the northern edge of the 1er *arrondissement* on esplanade St-Charles (☎91.08.50.50), which itself is just round the corner from the **gare routière** on place Victor-Hugo (☎91.08.16.40). From the *gare SNCF*, a monumental Art Deco staircase leads down to bd d'Athènes and thence to La Canebière, Marseille's main street. The city's **airport**, the *Aéroport de Marignane* (☎42.78.21.00), is 20km northwest of the Vieux Port; a shuttle bus runs to the *gare SNCF* St-Charles.

Once you're in the city centre, the best way to get around is to walk. However, if you need to get across the city fast, the **bus**, **tram** and **métro** network is pretty efficient, though not particularly cheap. It's worth knowing that the métro only runs from 5am to 9pm, except when the city's mercurial football team, *OM*, are playing. After 9pm, buses run along roughly the same routes until midnight. **Tickets**, which can be bought in *carnets* of six from métro stations or *RTM* kiosks, or singly from bus drivers, must be validated on the bus, on tramway platforms or at métro gates.

Since Marseille is not a great tourist city, finding a room in July or August is no more difficult than during the rest of the year. **Hotels** are plentiful, though if you get stuck for a room, the main tourist office on La Canebière (see above) offers a free **accommodation service**. The most inexpensive options, as ever, are the city's **youth hostels**, both quite a way from the centre. **Camping** is currently only possible at the Bois-Luzy hostel (tents only), but it's worth phoning the tourist office (see above) to ask if the town's campsites have been reopened.

Hotels

Hôtel Alizé, 35 quai des Belges, 1er (☎91.33.66.97). Comfortable, soundproofed rooms, the more expensive looking out on to the Vieux Port. ③–④.

Hôtel Caravelle, 5 rue Guy-Mocquet, 1er (☎91.48.44.99). Friendly, quiet and close to La Canebière and cours Julien, just off bd Garibaldi. ②.

Hôtel Le Corbusier, Cité Radieuse, 280 bd Michelet, 8e (☎91.77.18.15). Stylish hotel on the third floor of the architect's prototype tower block; book in advance. ②–④.

Hôtel Edmond-Rostand, 31 rue Dragon, 6e (☎91.37.74.95). Helpful management, great charm and atmosphere, and well known, so you should book in advance. ①–②.

Hôtel Esterel, 124 rue Paradis, 6e (☎91.37.13.90). A hotel in a good, animated location with all the mod cons. ③–④.

Hôtel Manon, 36 bd Louis Salvator, 6e (☎91.48.67.01). Pleasant, though a little noisy, between the Préfecture and cours Julien. ①.

Hôtel Pavillon, 27 rue Pavillon, 1er (☎91.33.76.90). In a central location and very friendly, apart from a yapping black poodle. ①.

Hôtel Relais St-Charles, 5 bd Gustave Desplaces, 1er (☎91.64.11.17). Just north of the station, a comfortable and quiet hotel. ②–③.

Hôtel Le Richelieu, 52 Corniche Kennedy, 7e (☎91.31.01.92). One of the more affordable of the Corniche hotels overlooking the plage des Catalans. ③.

Le Saint Ferréol's Hôtel, 19 rue Pisançon, cnr rue St-Ferréol, 1er (☎91.33.12.21). Pretty décor, marble baths with jacuzzis, in a central pedestrianized area. ④–⑤.

Youth hostels

IYHF youth hostel, 76 av de Bois-Luzy, 12e (☎91.49.06.18). Cheap, clean youth hostel in a former château a long way out from the centre. Curfew 11pm. No card needed. Camping also available. Reception 7–10am & 5–10.30pm; bus #8 direction *St-Julien* from Centre Bourse, stop *Bois Luzy*. ①.

IYHF youth hostel, 47 av J-Vidal, impasse du Dr-Bonfils, 8e (☎91.73.21.81). Not so cheap or secure as the *Bois Luzy* hostel, but the lack of curfew and proximity to the beach make up for it. Reception 7.30–9.30am & 5–11pm; bus #41 or métro *Rond-Point du Prado*, then bus #44 direction *Roy d'Espagne*, stop *Vidal-Collet*. ①.

The City

Like Paris, Marseille is divided into *arrondissements* – in this case sixteen – which spiral out from the focal point of the city, the **Vieux Port**. Due north lies the "old town", **Le Panier**, still home to much of Marseille's Algerian population. The wide boulevard leading from the head of the Vieux Port, **La Canebière** divides bourgeois Marseille, on the south side, from the North Africans' commercial district, **quartier Belsunce**, to the north. Drifting east past the city's red-light area is a vaguely bohemian, studenty area of bars, restaurants and music shops around **place Jean-Jaurès** and the trendy **cours Julien**. Heading **south** from La Canebière, the city's more glitzy commercial quarter gradually gives way to the favoured residential districts between rue de Rome's continuation, **av du Prado**, and the **Corniche**. The city's sandy **beaches** are down south, at the end of the Corniche.

The Vieux Port

The cafés around the east end of the **Vieux Port** indulge the sedentary pleasures of observing street life, despite the fumes of exhausts and half-dead fish straight off the boats on quai des Belges and the lack of any quayfront claim to beauty. The clientele of Cannes and St-Tropez – and, no doubt, the ancient Greeks who built the port of *Massalia* in the first place – would find it all unbearably tacky. But it remains as it has always been, the life centre of the city.

Two **fortresses** guard the harbour entrance. **St-Jean**, on the north, dates from the Middle Ages when Marseille was an independent republic, and is now only open when hosting exhibitions. Its enlargement of 1660, and the construction of **St-Nicolas**, on the south side of the port, represent the city's final defeat as a separate entity. Louis

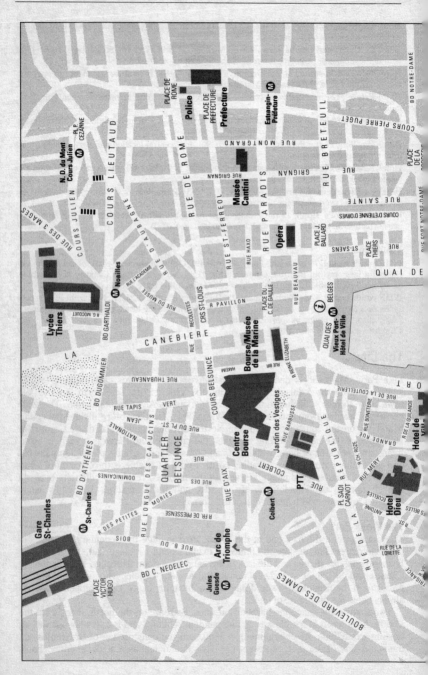

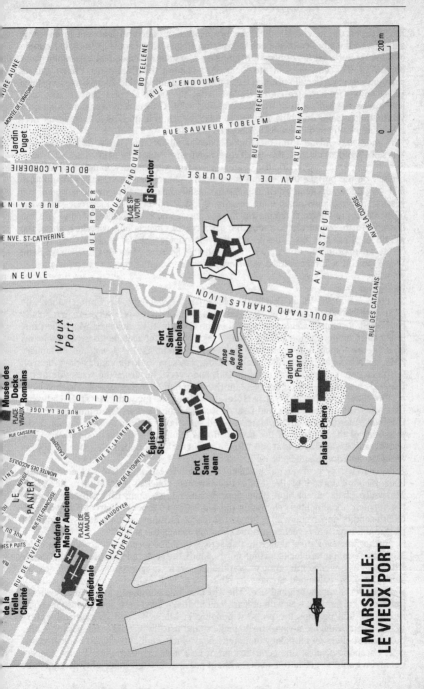

MARSEILLE:
LE VIEUX PORT

XIV ordered the new fort to keep an eye on the city after he had sent in an army, suppressed the city's council, fined it, arrested all opposition and – in an early example of rate-capping – set ludicrously low limits on Marseille's subsequent expenditure and borrowing. The best view of the Vieux Port is from the **Palais du Pharo** and its surrounding park (small entrance fee) on the headland beyond Fort Nicolas or, for a wider angle, from **Notre-Dame-de-la-Garde**, the city's Second Empire landmark which tops the hill south of the harbour (bus #60). Crowned by a monumental gold Virgin that gleams to ships far out to sea, the church itself is a monstrous neo-Byzantine riot (daily 7.30am–5.30/7.30pm).

A short way inland from the Fort St-Nicolas, above the Bassin de Carénage, is Marseille's oldest church, the **Basilique St-Victor** (Mon–Sat 10am–noon & 3–5pm, Sun 3–5pm; small fee charged). Originally part of a monastery founded in the fifth century on the burial site of various martyrs, the church was built, enlarged and fortified – a vital requirement given its position outside the city walls – over a period of 200 years from the middle of the tenth century. It looks and feels like a fortress – the walls of the choir are almost three metres thick – and it's no ecclesiastical beauty. You can descend to the **crypt** and **catacombs**, a warren of chapels and passages where the weight of stone and age – not to mention the photographs of skeletons exhumed – create an appropriate atmosphere to recall the horrors of early Christianity; Saint Victor himself, a Roman soldier, was slowly ground to death between two millstones.

Le Panier

To the north of the Vieux Port is the oldest part of Marseille, **Le Panier**, where, up until the last war, tiny streets, steep steps and houses of every era irregularly connected, forming a *vieille ville* typical of the Côte. In 1942, however, Marseille came under German occupation and the quarter became an unofficial ghetto for *Untermensch* of every sort, including Resistance fighters, Communists and Jews; and in January 1943, the Nazis gave the 40,000 inhabitants one day's notice to quit and packed them off to the camps. Dynamite was carefuly laid, and everything from the waterside to rue Caisserie was blown sky-high, except for three old buildings that appealed to the fascist aesthetic: the seventeenth-century **Hôtel de Ville** on the quay, the **Hôtel de Cabre** on the corner of rue Bonneterie and Grande-Rue, and the **Maison Diamantée** on rue de la Prison. After the war, archeologists reaped some benefits from this destruction in the discovery of the remains of the Roman docks equipped with vast food-storage jars, which can be seen *in situ* at the **Musée des Docks Romains** on place de Vivaux (daily except Mon 10am–5pm; 10F).

Surrounded by postwar quick-and-cheap concrete buildings, the sixteenth-century diamond-point façade of the Maison Diamantée conceals the **Musée de Vieux Marseille** (daily except Mon 10am–5pm; summer 11am–6pm; 15F), with a wonderful hotch-potch of mementos celebrating old Marseille – a modelled street scene of nineteenth-century insurrectional fighting, Provençal furniture and costume, recipes for plague antidotes and revealing pre-1943 photographs of the area.

Further into Le Panier along rue Caisserie, you'll find steps leading up to place des Moulins. A couple of blocks further north stands the restored **Hospice de la Vieille Charité**, a seventeenth-century workhouse with a gorgeous Baroque chapel surrounded by columned arcades in pink stone, with only the tiny grilled exterior windows recalling its original use. The Hospice was admittedly much nicer when a hundred local families – all with at least ten children – lived here, just prior to its restoration. It's still perhaps the prettiest building in Marseille, and its **cultural centre** (daily except Mon 10am–5pm) hosts major – and usually brilliant – temporary exhibitions and shelters an ethnology and archeological museum plus a good bookshop and café. Locals do scoff at this gentrification of Le Panier and jokingly ask how concert-goers are going to get to the centre without passing through this eighty-percent Arab quarter, and it's true that when there are no major exhibitions the centre can often be almost deserted, with more life outside where old tenement buildings have been demolished and superb murals painted on the surrounding exposed walls.

Inside the Hospice are two museums: **Musée d'Archéologie Méditerranéene** (daily except Mon 10am–5pm; 15F, 25F for both museums) contains some very beautiful pottery and glass, an Egyptian collection with a mummified crocodile and the Celto-Légurian finds from Roquepertuse. The **Musée des Arts Africain, Océaniens et Amérindiens** (daily except Mon 10am–5pm; 15F, 25F for both museums) is less appealing: dark and spooky with a horrible collection of dried heads.

At the western end of Le Panier overlooking the modern docks are Marseille's twin **cathedrals**: the mid-nineteenth-century neo-Byzantine **Major**, overshadowing its predecessor, the twelfth-century Romanesque **Major Ancienne** that stands, much diminished, alongside (guided tours only: Tues–Sun May–Sept 9am–noon & 2.30–6pm; Oct–April 9am–noon & 2–5pm). Opposite the cathedrals, on esplanade de la Touret, is a very professional mural illustrating the ancient Greeks arriving at Marseille, and at the end of the esplanade, opposite Fort St-Jean, the small Romanesque **church of St-Laurent** was built on the site of a Greek Temple of Apollo.

The expansion of Marseille's present docks started in the first half of the nineteenth century. Like the new cathedral, wide boulevards and Marseille's own Arc de Triomphe – the **Porte d'Aix** at the top of Cours Belsunce/rue d'Aix – the docks were paid for with the profits of military enterprise, most significantly the conquest of Algeria in 1830. The Third Empire was the next boom time for Marseillais traders, with the opening of the Suez Canal in 1869, giving the city a crucial advantage over other French ports.

La Canebière

La Canebière – the broad, leafy boulevard that runs for about a kilometre down to the port – is the undisputed hub of the town, its name taken from the hemp (*canabé*) that once grew here and provided the raw materials for the town's thriving rope-making trade. Fashioned originally with the Champs-Élysées in mind, La Canebière is a more patchwork affair of hotels, cafés and shops, neatly providing a division between the monied southern *quartiers* and the ramshackle **quartier Belsunce** to the north: an extraordinary, dynamic, mainly Arab area and a great trading ground. Hi-fis, suits and jeans from France and Germany are traded alongside spices, cloth and metalware from across the Mediterranean on flattened cardboard boxes in the streets – and not a French middleman in sight.

One block west, the **Centre Bourse** provides a stark contrast in a fiendish giant hypermall of noise, air-conditioning and overlighting – useful, nevertheless, for mainstream shopping. Behind it is the **Jardin des Vestiges**, where the ancient port extended, curving northwards from the present quai des Belges. Excavations have revealed a stretch of the Greek port and bits of the **city wall** with the base of three square towers and a gateway, dated to the second or third century BC. A museum in the Centre Bourse complex, the **Musée d'Histoire de Marseille** (daily except Mon 10am–5pm; summer 11am–6pm; 15F), presents the rest of the finds, including a third-century wreck of a Roman trading vessel. Further along La Canebière, where it crosses the place de la Bourse, is the **Musée de la Marine** (daily except Tues 10am–noon & 2–6pm; 15F), housed on the ground floor of the Neoclassical stock exchange, filled with intricate models and paintings of ships on the high seas.

The Palais Longchamp and the Hôtel du Département

The **Palais Longchamp** was built 2km east of the port in 1869 (bus #80 & #41 or métro *Longchamp-Cinq-Avenues*), at the end of bd Longchamp, and forms the grandiose conclusion of an aqueduct that brought water from the Durance to the city. Although the aqueduct is no longer in use, water is still pumped into the centre of the colonnade connecting the two palatial wings. Below, an enormous statue looks as if it honours some great feminist victory – three muscular women above four bulls wallowing passively in a pool from which a cascade drops four or five stories to ground level.

The palace's north wing is the city's **Musée des Beaux-Arts** (daily except Mon 10am–5pm; summer 11am–6pm; 15F), a hot and slightly stuffy place, but with a fair share of delights. Most unusual, and a very pleasant visual treat, are three paintings by Françoise Duparc (1726–76), whose first name has consistently found itself masculinized to François in catalogues both French and English. The nineteenth-century satirist from Marseille, Honoré Daumier, has a whole room for his cartoons. Plans for the city, sculptures, and the famous profile of Louis XIV by the Marseille-born Pierre Puget are on display along with graphic contemporary canvases of the plague that decimated the city in 1720. Almost opposite the Palais Longchamp, the **Musée Grobet-Labadi** (daily except Mon 10am–5pm; 15F) is a typical late nineteenth-century bourgeois townhouse filled with exquisite objects, but not wildly interesting.

Northwest of the Palais Longchamp at the end of bd Mal-Juin stands the brand new **Hôtel du Département** (M° St-Just). Deliberately set away from the centre of town in the run-down St-Just–Chartreux *quartier*, the new seat of local government for the Bouches-du-Rhône *département* is the biggest public building to be erected in the French provinces this century. It was designed by the English architect William Alsop, who used his hallmark ovoid glass tube shapes above and alongside vast rectangular blocks of blue steel and glass. The building is accessible during working hours, and the enormous glass foyer – with a capacity for 4000 people – is used for shows and exhibitions.

South of La Canebière

The prime shopping district of Marseille is encompassed by three streets running **south from La Canebière**: rue Paradis, rue St-Ferréol and rue de Rome, a continuation of cours Belsunce/rue d'Aix. A few blocks to the east you'll run into the city's red-light district, where sex is a visible commodity day and night. Marseille's main collection of twentieth-century and contemporary art, the **Musée Cantini**, is here at 19 rue Grignan (daily except Mon 10am–5pm; summer 11am–6pm; 15F). You'll find works by artists as diverse as Miró, Artaud, Dufy, Léger, Balthus, Bacon, as well as Vasarely, Max Ernst's huge *Monument aux Oiseaux*, but the overdose of recent acquisitions means that the contents have to rotate.

Four kilometres south of La Canebière on bus #21 or #22 is an entirely different kind of architecture from that in the city centre – Le Corbusier's seventeen-storey block of flats called the **Cité Radieuse**, designed in 1946 and completed in 1952. The *Cité* only fails to amaze now because so many architects the world over have tried to imitate Le Corbusier's revolutionary model. Each apartment has two levels and balconies on both sides of the building with unhindered views of mountains and sea. One floor has shops, restaurants and a post office; the third floor is now a hotel (see p.859); and on the top floor you can admire the sculptural and ceramic roof-decoration, along with a pool, gym and running track.

The corniche, beaches and the Château d'If

The most popular stretch of sand close to the city centre is the **plage des Catalans**, a few blocks south of the Palais du Pharo at the mouth of the Vieux Port. This marks the beginning of Marseille's **corniche**, av J-F-Kennedy, which follows the cliffs past the dramatic statue and arch that frames the setting sun of the **Monument aux Morts des Orients**. South of the monument, steps lead down to an inlet, **Anse des Auffes**, which is the nearest Marseille gets to being picturesque. Small fishing boats are beached on the rocks, the dominant sound is the sea, and narrow stairways and lanes lead nowhere. Further down the corniche, at the **Malmousque peninsula**, there's a **coastal path** you can follow, with steps down to tiny bays and beaches – perfect for swimming when the Mistral wind is not inciting the waves. You can see along the coast as far as Cap Croisette and, out to sea, the abandoned monastery on the Îles d'Endoume and the Château d'If (see below). The end of the corniche is marked by a copy of Michelangelo's *David*, a stone's throw from the artificially constructed **plage du Prado**, best of the local beaches, with remarkably clean water. For buses along the corniche, #83 runs from the Vieux Port to av du Prado and #80 from the *Estrangin-Préfecture* métro to the Anse du Vallon de l'Oriel. From av du Prado, #19 runs to Madrague, and #20 on out to Cap Croisette.

A short way inland from the plage du Prado, 3.5km south of the Vieux Port, at the end of av du Park Borély off av du Prado, is the city's best green space, the **Parc Borély**, with a boating lake, rose gardens and palm trees, and a botanical garden (Mon–Fri 10am–3.30pm, Sat 1–5.30pm; free). A museum of decorative arts has long been planned within the stern eighteenth-century château, but has not yet materialized. Further south from the park, at 69 bd d'Haïfa, 8ᵉ (stop *Haïta-Marie Louise*), is the new contemporary art museum, **MAC** (daily except Mon 10am–5pm; summer 11am–6pm; 15F). The permanent collection – in perfect, pure-white surrounds – includes works from the 1960s to the present by the Marseillais artists César and Ben, along with Buren, Christo, Klein, Niki de Saint-Phalle, Tinguely and Warhol. There's also a cinema, the **Cinémac** (☎91.25.01.07), showing feature films, shorts and videos on different themes each month.

Boats leave the quai des Belges in the Vieux Port regularly for the fifteen-minute journey out to the **Château d'If** (summer every hour 9am–5pm; winter 9am, 11am, 2pm, 3.30pm & 5pm; 45F), best known as the penal setting for Alexandre Dumas's *The Count of Monte Cristo*. After having made his watery escape after five years of incarceration as the innocent victim of treachery, the hero of the piece, Edmond Dantès, describes the island as: "Blacker than the sea, blacker than the sky, rose like a phantom the giant of granite, whose projecting crags seemed like arms extended to seize their prey." The reality, for most prisoners, was worse: they went insane or died (and sometimes both) before reaching the end of their sentences. Only the nobles living in the less fetid upper-storey cells had much chance of survival – like one de Niozelles who was given six years for failing to take his hat off in the presence of Louis XIV, and Mirabeau who was doing time for debt.

There's nothing else to the island apart from the château (times coincide with boats; 26F), originally built in 1524 for François I and only later used as a prison. It's horribly well preserved, but you can stalk around the cells and take in the magnificent view from the terraces.

Eating and drinking

The Marseillais **eat** just as well, if not better, than the ancient aristos and skin-stretched stars of the Riviera. Fish and seafood are the main ingredients, and the super-star of dishes is the city's own expensive invention, *bouillabaisse*, a saffron- and garlic-flavoured fish soup with bits of fish, croutons and *rouille* to throw in and conflicting theories about which fish should be included and where and how they must be caught.

For a wide range of good **restaurants**, cours Julien (Mᵒ Notre-Dame du Mont–Cours Julien) is the best place to head for. More upmarket and fishy is the pedestrian precinct around place Thiars, behind the south quay of the Vieux Port; rue Pavillon, parallel to La Canebière to the south, is good for **lunches** and **snacks**; Le Panier and the quartier Belsunce are also good for menu-browsing.

As Marseille is a Mediterranean city, people tend to stay up late in summer. Around the Vieux Port and place Jean-Jaurès to cours Julien are the two areas where there are always lots of people around and cafés and restos open well after midnight.

Restaurants

Chez Angèle, 50 rue Caisserie, 2ᵉ (☎91.90.63.35). Packed Le Panier local, with a bargain *menu fixe* for basic French food.

L'Assiette Marine, 142 av Mendez-France, 8ᵉ (☎91.71.04.04). Serves fresh pasta in lobster sauce, aubergine and lamb with truffles, and other exquisite dishes, just north of the plage du Prado. Menus at 135F and 300F.

Auberge "In", 25 rue du Chevalier-Roze, 2ᵉ (☎91.90.51.59). In a health-food shop on the edge of Le Panier. Vegetarian *menu fixe* served lunchtimes and early evenings. Closed Sun.

Les Arcenaulx, 25 cours d'Estienne-d'Orves, 1ᵉʳ (☎91.54.77.06). Superb food for 250–300F a head in this intellectual haunt, which is also a bookshop. Cheap midday menus on weekdays. Closed Sun & Mon.

La Coupole, 5 rue Haxo, 1ᵉʳ (☎91.54.88.57). Elegant brasserie serving a midday *plat du jour* with a glass of wine for 100F. Seafood salads a temptation. Daily 7am–midnight.

Dar Djerba, 15 cours Julien, 6ᵉ (☎91.48.55.36). Excellent Tunisian restaurant with beautiful tiling – ignore the stuffed camel's head. Around 150F.

Chez Étienne, 43 rue Lorette, 2ᵉ. Another old-fashioned Le Panier bistro; hectic, cramped and crowded. Full meal 150–250F but you can just have a pizza. No bookings. Closed Sun & Mon.

La Kalena, 2 rue de la République, 1ᵉʳ. Popular Moroccan place, with grills and couscous from 60F. Closed Sun & Mon midday.

Maurice Brun, 18 quai Rive-Neuve, 7ᵉ (☎91.33.35.38). A Marseille institution which has recently changed hands and doubled its space. Still authentic Provençal cooking, but attracting a less stuffy clientele.

Chez Michel, 6 rue des Catalans, 7ᵉ (☎91.52.30.63). There's no debate about the *bouillabaisse* ingredients here. A basket of five fishes, including the elusive and most expensive one, the *racasse*, is presented to the customer before the soup is made. Quite simply *the* place to eat this dish. Expect to pay 250F for the *bouillabaisse* alone.

Tom Pouce, 2 rue des Convalescents, 1ᵉʳ. Very cheap, studenty Tunisian resto in the *quartier* Belsunce.

Cafés and bars

Bar Le Petit Nice, 26 pl Jean-Jaurès, 1ᵉʳ. The place to head for on Saturday morning after market.

Bar de la Samaritaine, 2 quai du Port, 2ᵉ. Sunny bar, with the best panorama of the Vieux Port.

Le Cadratin, 17 rue St-Saëns, 1ᵉʳ. Friendly and cheap bar with Sixties music playing on the juke-box and a great mix of people, both foreign and local.

Café Parisien, 1 pl Sadi-Carnot, 2ᵉ. Very beautiful old-fashioned café, where people play cards and chess. Occasional painting exhibitions.

Nightlife

Marseille's **nightlife** has something for everyone, with plenty of live rock and jazz, as well as the more choice pastimes of theatre-, opera- and concert-going. The *Virgin Megastore* at 75 rue St-Ferréol is the best place to go for **tickets and information** on gigs, concerts, theatre, free films and whatever cultural events are going on. They also stock a wide selection of English books and run a café on the top floor, open, like the rest of the store, seven days a week until midnight. Other places to head for info are the book and record shop *FNAC* on the top floor of the Centre Bourse (Mon–Sat 10am–7pm), the café, travel agency and comic shop, *La Passerelle*, 26 rue des Trois-Mages (noon–midnight), and the New Age music shop *Tripsichord* next door. At any of these places, you can pick up a copy of *Taktik*, Marseille's independent free weekly listings paper, which comes out on a Wednesday.

Live music

La Cave à Jazz, 24 quai de Rive-Neuve, 7ᵉ. Jazz club and a place for rock, fashion, theatre and dance.

Cité de la Musique, 4 rue Bernard du Bois, 1ᵉʳ (☎91.39.28.28). Jazz cellar and auditorium.

Maison de l'Étranger, 9 av Général Leclerc, 3ᵉ (☎91.28.24.01). A club not far from the *gare SNCF* St-Charles, which puts on regular world music gigs, especially Raï.

La Maison Hantée, 10 rue Vian, 6ᵉ (☎91.92.09.40). *Café-théâtre* and cinema alternates with country music, r'n'b and rock. Closed Mon.

May Be Blues, rue Poggioli, 6ᵉ (☎91.42.41.00). Relaxed blues/jazz club. No entry charge, though drinks go up once the music starts. Closed Mon & Tues. 8pm–2am.

Au Moulin, 47 bd Perrin (☎91.06.33.94; métro *St-Just*). An obscure venue in the northwest of the city specializing in weird and wonderful European bands.

Le Stendhal, 92 rue Jean-de-Bernady, 1ᵉʳ (☎91.84.74.80). Wide selection of malt whiskies and beers, including *Courage*, and live music Tuesdays and Thursdays. Red and black interior, naturally enough.

Film, theatre and concerts

Ballet National de Marseille, 20 bd Gabès, 8ᵉ (☎91.71.03.03). Roland Petit's famous dance company's home base.

Bastide de la Magalone, 245 bd Michelet, 9ᵉ (☎91.39.28.28). Classical music concerts.

Chocolat Théâtre, 59 cours Julien, 6ᵉ (☎91.42.19.29). Theatre-restaurant-exhibition space with shows ranging from male striptease to avant-garde improvisations.

Cinéma Paris, 31 rue Pavillon, 1ᵉʳ (☎91.33.15.59). The only cinema in Marseille which regularly shows *v.o.* (*version originale* – undubbed) films.

Espace Julien, 33 cours Julien, 6ᵉ (☎91.47.09.64). A mixed bag arts centre, with theatre, jazz, dance and exhibitions.

Nightclubs

The **clubs** around cours d'Estienne-d'Orves – mainly jazz, some Caribbean – are for trendy kids from the upper-crust *arrondissements*, with prices to match. One of the more pleasant jazz clubs is *La Pelle Mêle*, 45 cours d'Estienne-d'Orves, 1ᵉʳ (☎91.54.85.26), with *Le Pourquoi Pas*, 1 rue Fortia, 1ᵉʳ (☎91.33.50.54), offering Caribbean music and punch to get drunk on. *Rose Bonbon*, 7 rue Venture, 1ᵉʳ, just off rue Paradis, is as good a place as any if you're determined to bop.

Listings

Airlines *Air France*, 14 La Canebière, 1ᵉʳ (☎91.54.92.92); *Air Inter*, 8 rue des Fabres, 1ᵉʳ (☎91.91.90.90); *British Airways* (☎91.90.77.10) and *TWA* (☎91.91.66.44), both 41 La Canebière, 1ᵉʳ.

Bike rental *Green Bike*, 135 av Clot Bey, 8ᵉ (☎91.25.36.26). Touring bikes and mountain bikes at around 90F a day.

Consulates *Canada*, 24 av du Prado, 6ᵉ (☎91.37.19.37); *Eire*, 148 rue Sainte, 1ᵉʳ (☎91.54.92.29); *UK*, 24 av du Prado, 6ᵉ (☎91.53.43.32); *USA*, 12 bd Peytral, 6ᵉ (☎91.54.92.00).

Disabled *Office Municipal pour Handicappés*, 128 av du Prado, 8ᵉ (☎91.81.58.80). Information on disabled access and facilities. Also operates a transport service; call ☎91.78.21.67 a day ahead.

Emergencies Ambulance: *SAMU* (☎91.49.91.91); Hospital: *Hôtel-Dieu*, 6 pl Daviel, Le Panier, 2ᵉ (☎91.96.47.89); Doctor: ☎15, or *SOS Médecins* (☎91.52.91.52); Crisis line: *SOS Amitié* (☎91.76.10.10).

Money exchange *Thomas Cook* at *gare SNCF* St-Charles (Mon–Fri 6am–8pm, weekends & holidays 6am–6pm); *Comptoir Marseillais de Bourse*, 20 La Canebière (Mon–Fri 9am–7.30pm).

Post office 1 pl de l'Hôtel-des-Postes, 13001, Marseille.

Police *Commissariat Centrale*, 2 rue Antoine Becke, 2ᵉ (☎91.39.80.00; daily 8am–noon & 2–6pm).

Women's centre *CODIF* runs a library and information centre at 81 rue Senac, 1ᵉʳ (☎91.47.14.05).

Cassis, La Ciotat and Bandol

It's difficult to imagine two towns more dissimilar so close to one another on the Côte; **Cassis** would be more at home round the corner from St-Tropez, while **La Ciotat**, still visibly dominated by its now defunct shipbuilding industry, is more akin to the industrial giants of Marseille and Toulon.

Cassis

A lot of people rate **CASSIS** the best resort this side of St-Tropez – its inhabitants most of all. An old Provençal fishing port hemmed in by high white cliffs, its modern development has been limited to a model toytown on steep inclines in which foreign traffic is not encouraged. Portside posing and drinking aside, there's not much to do except sunbathe and look up at the ruins of the town's medieval **castle**, built in 1381 by François le Baux and refurbished by Monsieur Michelin, the authoritarian boss of the family tyres and guides firm.

The favoured lazy pastime, though, is to take a boat trip to the **calanques** – long, narrow, deep fjord-like inlets that have cut into the limestone cliffs. Several companies operate from the port, but check if they let you off or just tour in and out, and be prepared for rough seas. Or, if you're feeling energetic, you can take the well-marked footpath from the route des Calanques behind the western beach; it's about 90 minutes' walk to the furthest and best, **En Vau**, where you can climb down rocks to the shore. Intrepid pine trees find root-holds, and sunbathers find ledges on the chaotic white cliffs. The water is deep blue and swimming between the vertical cliffs is an experience not to be missed.

Practicalities

The **gare SNCF** is 3km out of town, with precious few buses to the centre, apart from the one that drops you at the **gare routière** on place Montmorin in the centre of town.

Cheap **rooms** just don't exist in Cassis, but the least expensive are the modern *Laurence*, 8 rue de l'Arène (☎42.01.88.78; ③–④), close to the port, or the *Grand Jardin*, 2 rue P-Eydin (☎42.01.70.10; ④–⑤). For a little more – and a view over the port – try *Le Golfe* on place du Grand-Carnot (☎42.01.00.21; ⑤). Further out, there's also the *Hôtel Joli Bois*, rte de la Ginesete (☎42.01.02.65; ②; closed Mon in winter, *demi-pension* obligatory in season), just off the main road to Marseille, 3km from Cassis. Far more isolated is the gorgeously scenic but rather inaccessible IYHF **youth hostel** *La Fontasse* in the hills above the *calanques* west of Cassis (☎42.01.02.72; reception 8–10am & 5–11pm; open all year); from the D559 (stop *Les Calanques*), a road leads down towards the Col de la Gardiole, and when it becomes a track, take the left fork, and after another 2km you'll find the hostel. Rain water, beds and electricity are the only mod cons, but if you want to explore this wild uninhabited stretch of limestone heights,

---

THE COSQUER CAVE

In 1991, diver **Henri Cosquer** filmed and photographed a series of wall paintings in a cave near Cassis, whose sole entrance has been underwater since the end of the last ice age. The depictions of hundreds of animals and human hands are similar in style to those found as Lascaux in the Dordogne. They took a long time to be authenticated, as few archeologists specializing in the paleolithic (old Stone Age) period had the necessary diving experience to take a look. It is not certain whether a dry entrance can be drilled from above, and public access isn't ever likely.

the people running it will advise you enthusiastically. To get to Cassis you can descend to the *calanques* and walk along the coast (about 1hr). If you're **camping**, don't bother going into town – the campsite, *Les Cigales* (☎42.01.07.34; mid-March to mid-Nov), is just off the D559 from Marseille before av de la Marne turns down into Cassis, a gruelling one-kilometre walk from the port.

Restaurant tables are in abundance along the portside quai des Baux; prices vary greatly, but if you can afford it, your best bet has to be to follow your nose, and seek out the most enticing fish smells. The authentic Provençal *ratatouille* and freshly caught fish at *Chez Gilbert*, 19 quai Baux (☎42.01.71.36), are hard to beat, with a 110F menu. *El Sol* at no. 23 (☎42.01.76.10; closed Wed) costs a bit less.

La Ciotat

The old shipbuilding town of **LA CIOTAT**, halfway towards Toulon from Marseille, rests on its bygone reputation for its active naval dockyards. They were closed five years ago, and while the golden-stoned Vieux Port remains charming, the massive cranes and derricks of the shipyards are a depressing reminder of the town's demise.

La Ciotat is not a town for keyed-up museum or monument motivation; neither is it made for quayside lounging. Nevertheless, the **old town** has the charm of most other Provençal ports, and the **beaches** are excellent. There are **boat trips** out to the tiny offshore Île Verte from the quai du Vieux Port (30min; ☎42.83.11.44, 42.71.53.32), and to a number of nearby *calanques* from quai Ganteaume (☎91.43.73.60). For fans of celluloid, there's also the original **Eden cinema** on the corner of bd Jean-Jaurès and G-Clemenceau overlooking the pleasure port, where the locally born Lumière brothers showed their first moving images in 1895. The modern **Cinéma Lumière**, with a mural of the brothers, is in the covered market halls on place E-Gras, a few blocks away; a commemorative plaque at the *gare SNCF* confirms its star performance in one of the Lumière films.

After the contrast of the shipbuilding leftovers with the fishing boats and golden stone quayside buildings, the strangest sight in La Ciotat itself is the cluster of rock formations on the promontory beyond the shipyards in the **Parc du Mugel** (daily 9am–12.40pm & 2–7pm; Oct–March 10am–noon & 2–6pm; closed Dec; free), which you can reach on bus #3 (direction *La Garde*, stop *Mugel*). A path leads up from the park's entrance through overgrown vegetation to a narrow terrace overlooking the sea. Here, the cliff face looks like the habitat of some gravity-defying, burrowing beast rather than the erosions of wind and sea.

Practicalities

The **gare SNCF** is 4km from the Vieux Port, but a bus meets every train to shuttle you down there. The old town and port look out across the Baie de la Ciotat, whose inner curve provides the beaches and resort lifestyle of La Ciotat Plage. The town's **tourist office** is at the corner of bd Anatole-France and quai Ganteaume in the Vieux Port (daily 10am–noon & 2–6pm): if you're here in the middle of June, they can provide details of the annual **Festival du Cinéma**.

Hotels are cheap by Côte d'Azur standards. Probably the best bet in the old town is *La Marine*, 1 av F-Gassion (☎42.08.35.11; ②–③), and *Beaurivage*, 1 bd Beaurivage (☎42.83.09.68; ②–④), best for La Ciotat Plage. La Ciotat has nine **campsites**, three of them by the sea, of which *St-Jean*, 30 av St-Jean (☎42.83.13.01; end March–Sept; bus #4, direction *gare SNCF*, stop *St-Jean Village*) is the closest to the centre.

La Ciotat's **restaurants** are not gastronomically renowned, though *Coquillatges Franquin*, 13 bd Anatole-France (☎42.83.59.50), serves perfectly respectable fish dishes. On quai Stalingrad, *Le Louveteau* and *L'Escalet* both have very cheap *menus* *fixes*, and *La Fresque*, 18 rue des Combattants (☎42.08.00.60), is very good. Apart from the Vieux Port, bd Beaurivage in La Ciotat Plage is probably the most productive street for menu-browsing.

Bandol

Between Les Lecques, behind St-Cyr, and **BANDOL**, a large and classy resort halfway between La Ciotat and Toulon, you can follow a coastal footpath about 8km (signed in yellow), giving you access to a rare stretch of unbuilt-up coast, with secluded beaches and *calanques*. Inland lie the vineyards producing some of the best wines on the Côte, the *appellation Bandol*.

Bandol itself is an expensive resort, with plenty of flash yachts in its harbour and an unwelcome tendency to keep sprouting more apartment blocks in the hills behind. But the town's glory is the wine produced under its name: the **Maison des Vins de Bandol** on allées Vivien (☎94.29.45.03), just behind the tourist office, will provide addresses of vineyards in the area for tasting. The *Domaine de Terrebrune*, 724 chemin de la Touelle (☎94.74.01.30), produces a wonderful deep and dusky red wine and has an expensive but very good Provençal restaurant, with menus from 200F (closed Mon evening & Sun out of season).

The town's other great attraction lies in its offshore island, the Île de Bendor, owned by Paul Ricard, the rags-to-riches *pastis* man. Boats to Bendor leave every half-hour from quai Charles-de-Gaulle in Bandol, just east of the **tourist office** on allées Vivien (daily 7am–8.30pm; June–Sept 7–2am; journey time 7min). The island is a diving, yachting and windsurfing centre, and promotes the teaching of painting and drawing though the *Fondation Paul Ricard*. The monthly exhibitions in the *Fondation's* Galerie d'Art can be very good, but the real treat on the island is a **museum of wines and spirits** from all over the world, the *Exposition Universelle des Vins et Spiritueux* (daily except Wed Easter–Sept 10am–noon & 2.15–6pm; free). The curator claims that no society anywhere or at any time has not discovered alcohol. There's also cheap youth accommodation on the island in a hostel run by the *Club Nautique* (☎94.29.52.91; ①; no membership necessary, but book ahead).

Bandol's **tourist office** is on allées Vivien (daily 10am–noon & 2–6pm). You can rent **bikes** at *Holiday Bikes* on rte de Marseille (☎94.32.21.89), down av Loste, west of the *gare SNCF*. They come in handy for doing some energetic rounds of the vineyards. **Accommodation** possibilities include the *Relais Fleuri*, 177 av de la Gare (☎94.29.41.40; ①–②), Bandol's cheapest hotel; there's also the very pleasant *Golf Hôtel*, right on the beach of Renecros, the bay on the west side of town (☎94.29.45.83; ③–⑤), and *La Reserve* on av Libération (☎94.29.30.00; ③–⑤), with soundproofed rooms on the sea front at the east end of town. In the centre of Bandol, you'll find good **restaurants** in rue de la République and allée Jean-Moulin, running parallel to the promenade. Try the *Auberge du Port*, 9 allée Jean-Moulin (☎94.29.42.63), famous for its fish dishes, with menus from 110F and *à la carte* over 300F.

Toulon and around

TOULON is not an attractive town. It was half destroyed in the last war and rebuilt in anonymous concrete blocks, defacing the previously picturesque harbour and seeing a slew of military, shipbuilding and armaments buildings spring up close to the centre; today the arsenal created by Louis XIV is one of the major employers in southeast France.

Despite being home to the French navy's Mediterranean fleet and lying on a naturally sheltered port – best viewed from the summit of Mont Faron behind the city or

Notre-Dame du Mai on the high cliffs of Cap Scié – the town has lost its shipbuilding industry. The traditional yards of La Seyne-sur-Mer are being axed, closing the book on a centuries-old and often notorious industry. Until the eighteenth century, slaves and convicts were still powering the king's galleys, and, following the Revolution, convicts were sent to Toulon with iron collars round their necks for sentences of hard labour – their crimes often petty. After 1854, convicts were deported to the colonies, in whose conquest ships from Toulon played a major part.

The **old town**, crammed in between bd de Strasbourg and quai de Stalingrad on the old port and now subject to major demolition and rebuilding – is pleasant enough during the day. Full of fountains, more often than not of dolphins, it boasts an excellent **market** (Thurs–Sun) around rue Landrin and cours Lafayette, as well as a covered **fish market** on place de la Poissonnerie. Big chunks of the old town, once presided over by the city's considerable North African population, have disappeared with the construction of a gleaming new *lycée* and shopping centre, but towards the quays you'll still find every other door leads to a cheap restaurant, bar, jazz dive, nightclub or sex shop. As night falls, men outnumber women ten to one on the streets – and most of the women are working. This is less true in the **Mourillon quartier** to the east (bus #3), where trendy nightlife glitters down the Littoral Frédéric-Mistral and the beaches face the open sea.

Toulon's sea-level museums are not particularly intriguing unless you're obsessed with military history and model ships. The **Musée d'Art**, 113 bd Maréchal-Leclerc (daily 1–7pm; free), is very disappointing, with all the best paintings held in reserves and never on show. The exhibitions are arranged around themes and the artists whose works you may or may not see include Brueghel, Carracci, Puget and the Van Loos; amongst the moderns Vlaminck, Friez, Ziem and Rodin; and of contemporaries, Francis Bacon, Christo, Gilbert and George, and Sol Le Witt. The most impressive public artwork in the city is Pierre Puget's sculpture **Atlantes**, which holds up all that is left of the old town hall on quai de Stalingrad. It's thought that Puget, working in 1657, modelled these immensely strong, tragic figures on galley slaves.

The best way to pass an afternoon in Toulon is to leave the town 542m below you by ascending the summit of **Mont Faron**. Take bus #40, stop *Téléphérique* on bd Amiral-Vence in Super Toulon and you'll find a **funicular** (Tues–Sun 9.15am–noon & 2.15–6pm, Mon 2.15–6pm; winter Mon–Sat only; 30F). It's a bit pricey, but a real treat.

At the top there's the **Musée-mémorial du Débarquement en Provence**, a memorial museum to the Allied landings in Provence of August 1944 (summer 9am–7pm; winter 9–11.30am & 2–5.30pm; 20F), with screenings of original newsreel footage. In the surrounding park are two restaurants, and a little further up to the right, a **zoo** specializing in big cats (daily 2–6pm; May–Sept 10am–noon & 2–7pm; 25F). Beyond the zoo, you can walk up the hillside to an abandoned fort and revel in the clean air, the smell of the flowers and the distance from the urban sprawl below.

Practicalities

The **gare SNCF** and **gare routière** are on place Albert-1er. Turning left and down bd de Tessé three blocks brings you to place Mazarin, with av Colbert running to the right, where you'll find the extremely helpful **tourist office** at 8 av Colbert (daily 10am–noon & 2–5.30pm; ☎94.22.08.22), with information on the surrounding area and further afield.

One of the cheapest **hotels** in Toulon is the *Hôtel des Allées*, 18 allées Amiral Courbet (☎94.91.10.02; ①–②), where English is spoken and you can find rooms for up to four people; another inexpensive central option is the *Little Palace*, 6–8 rue Berthelot (☎94.92.26.62; ①–②), in the old town by the Opéra. In Toulon's most desirable suburb, La Mourillon, east of the centre, *La Corniche*, 17 Littoral Frédéric-Mistral (☎94.41.35.12; ③), has some very pleasant rooms, half of them with views over the sea.

There's also a friendly and pleasant **hostel**, *Foyer de la Jeunesse*, 12 pl d'Armes (☎94.22.62.00; ①), just west of the old town, ten minutes' walk from the *gare SNCF*, with meals for 25F.

One of the pleasures of Toulon is **eating**. There are plenty of brasseries, cafés and restaurants along the quayside, some selling just sandwiches, while others offer wonderful seafood-based *menus fixes* for under 100F; the Littorial Frédéric-Mistral in chic Le Mourillon is choc-a-bloc with good restaurants, and well worth the #3 or #13 bus ride from the city centre. Toulon's oldest restaurant, *Au Sourd*, 10 rue Molière, in the old town (☎94.92.28.52; closed Sun, Mon & Aug), specializes in fish dishes including *bouillabaisse*, with a good menu at 140F and *à la carte* at around 300F. *Le Bistrot de la Corniche*, 1 Littoral Frédéric-Mistral (☎94.32.09.09; closed Sun evening and Tues out of season), is a delightful place overlooking the sea, and features extremely good-value *plateaux de fruit de mer* and Bandol wines, with menus from 100F.

THE CENTRAL RESORTS AND ISLANDS

Out of season, the stretch of coastline between **Hyères** and **Cannes** – the Côte d'Azur proper – and its backdrop of wooded hills hold their own against the cynicism engendered by tourist brochure overkill. The magic lies in the scented Mediterranean vegetation, silver beaches glimpsed between purple cliffs, secluded islands and medieval hilltop villages. Granted, you're unlikely to tread new ground or make any discoveries of your own, and the seasonal traffic jams and spot-the-square-foot-of-sand beaches are to be avoided, but – out of season – it's still possible to feel very happy to be here.

There are no cities along this stretch: **Hyères**, which preserves a certain air of gentility, and the **St-Raphael-Fréjus** conurbation are the biggest towns. Of the resorts, **Cavalaire** is probably the least status-conscious; **St-Tropez** is a must, for a day's visit at least; and out to sea, the **Îles d'Hyères**, also known as the Îles d'Or, shelter some of the best fauna and flora in Provence. Inland, the dark wooded hills of the **Massif des Maures** form a backdrop to most of this coast, with the ancient villages of **Collobrières** and **La Grande Freinet** providing contrasting targets – the former as unchanged as you could hope for, the latter still enchanting, but increasingly hemmed in by luxury villas.

Hyères

Lacking a central seafront, **HYÈRES,** the oldest resort on the Côte – listing Queen Victoria and Tolstoy among its early admirers – lost out on snob-appeal when the Côte clientele switched from winter convalescents to quayside strutters. It has the unique distinction on the Côte of not being totally dependent on the summer influx and is consequently very appealing. The old town is neither a tourist trap nor a slum, and the surrounding orchards, nursery gardens, vineyards and fields of early vegetables – taking up land which elsewhere would have been developed into a rash of holiday shelving units – are crucial to Hyères's economy. The town exports exotic plants, of which the most important is the date palm that graces every street in Hyères (and numerous desert palaces in Arabia). The only blight on all this is the presence of an air force base, just north of the main port, from which test pilots play up and down the coast with the latest fiendish multimillion-franc exports.

Arrival and accommodation

The first port of call for many is the Toulon-Hyères **airport** (☎94.22.81.60), between Hyères and the Mediterranean, 3km away. Arriving by **train**, you'll find yourself at the end of av Edith-Cavell, 1500m south of central place Clemenceau, linked by frequent buses to the **gare routière** on the square. The **tourist office** is in the *Rotunde Jean-Salusse* on av de Belgique, two blocks south from place Clemenceau (daily 10am–noon & 2–5.30pm; ☎94.65.33.40). **Bikes** and **mopeds**, which you may well need, can be rented from *Holiday Bikes* on rte du Palyrestre, between the airport and the *gare SNCF* (☎94.38.46.08), or the *Mistral Centre* on the rte de Gens (☎94.58.26.87).

The **hotels** in the old town include the *Hôtel du Soleil* on rue du Rempart (☎94.65.16.26; ②–④), in a renovated house at the foot of the parc St-Bernard, and the smaller *Hôtel du Portalet*, 4 rue de Limans (☎94.65.39.40; ①–③). Right in the centre of the modern town, the *Hôtel de la Poste*, 7 av Lyautey (☎94.65.02.00; ④), is a good cheap option. By the sea, *Le Calypso* on Hyères-Plage (☎94.58.02.09; ③) has reasonable rates, and the *Hôtel Port Hélène* at the eastern end of Almanarre beach (☎94.57.72.01; ①) does a very good deal on studio apartments for four.

There's no youth hostel near Hyères, but there are plenty of **campsites** on the coast: *Capricorne* (☎94.65.18.55; mid-April to Oct) at **LES SALINS**; *Le Parc* (☎94.66.31.77; July & Aug) at **L'AYGUADE-CEINTURON** (signed off the D42 just after the airport); and the *Camping Caravaning de la Presqu'île de Giens* (☎94.58.22.86; April–Oct) are amongst many.

The Town

Walled and medieval, old Hyères lies on the slopes of 204-metre-high Castéou hill, 5km from the sea and with the ruins of a thirteenth-century **castle** on its summit. From the top of the keep and the ivy-clad towers that outreach the oak and lotus trees, you can see the modern palm-lined expansion of the town and, beyond, the peculiar **Presqu'île de Giens**, leashed to the mainland by an isthmus and a parallel sand bar enclosing salt marshes. The isthmus, known as **La Capte**, is covered by houses and hotels; the much narrower sand bar just carries the rte de Sel. Out to sea, east of Giens, the three **Îles d'Hyères** are visible.

From place Clemenceau a medieval gatehouse, the **Porte Massillon**, opens onto rue Massillon and the **old town**. At **place Massillon**, you encounter a perfect Provençal square, animated by a daily market and with terraced cafés overlooking the twelfth-century **Tour St-Blaise**, the remnant of a Knights Templar lodge. To the right of the tower, a street leads uphill to **place St-Paul**, from which you have a panoramic view over a section of medieval town **wall** to the Mont des Oiseaux and the Golfe de Giens.

Wide steps fan out from the Renaissance door of the former collegiate **church of St-Paul** (daily 2.30–5pm; summer 3–6pm), whose distinctive belfry is pure Romanesque, as is the choir, though the simplicity of the design is masked by the collection of votive offerings hung inside. The decoration also includes some splendid wrought-iron horror movie candelabras, and a Christmas crib with over-life-size *santons*. Today, the church is only used for special services – the main place of worship is the mid-thirteenth-century former monastery **church of St-Louis** on place de la République.

To the right of St-Paul, a Renaissance house bridges rue St-Paul, its turret supported by a pillar rising beside the steps. Through this arch you can head up via rue St-Bernard to the **parc St-Bernard**, full of almost every Mediterranean flower known, and on up to the ruined citadel.

The switch from medieval to eighteenth- and nineteenth-century Hyères – bordered by **av des Îles-d'Or** and its continuation, **av Général-de-Gaulle**, the boundary of the old and new town – is as abrupt as it is radical, with wide boulevards and open spaces, opulent villas and waving palm fronds. If you're keen on the history of this coast, the **Musée d'Art et d'Archéologie** on place Lefèvre (Mon, Wed, Thurs & Fri 10am–noon & 3–6pm; free) may be interesting. It displays the finds of the archeological digs at **L'Almanarre**, the original Greek settlement of Olbia, 5km south of the existing town, as well as traditional tools of the fishing industry and salt works, plus a diverse selection of paintings, including some beauties by the eighteenth-century Rotari of the Venetian school.

Eating and drinking

For **eating and drinking**, there are the terraced café-brasseries in place Massillon; and, all around this corner of the old town, a good choice of *crêperies*, pizzerias and little bistros that serve *plats du jour* for around 80F. The best restaurant in the old town has to be *Chez Ma-Mie*, 3 rue de l'Oratoire (☎94.35.39.20; evenings only, closed Wed), with a cosy atmosphere and a wonderful chocolate fondue with fresh fruit dips; menus are 150–250F. *La Bergerie*, 16 rue de Limans (☎94.65.57.97), is a friendly and down-to-earth pizzeria, with excellent salads and pizzas that are cooked under your nose in a coal-fired oven. On the edge of the new town, *Les Jardins de Bacchus*, 32 av Gambetta (☎94.65.77.63; closed Sun evening plus Mon out of season), is a good place to try novel concoctions like pigeon with *foie gras* and caramelized pears on salmon with prawns and bacon; menus start at 130F, and *à la carte* at around 350F. Overlooking the Port d'Hyères is *La Parillada de Puerto* (☎94.57.44.82; closed Nov–March), with Spanish specialities based on fresh fish and menus from 150F.

Around Hyères

The **Presqu'île de Giens**, besides the peculiarity of its attachment to the mainland (last broken by storms in 1811), is a fairly nondescript and upmarket resort. It has some fine cliffs facing the sea, and in rough weather you can understand why so many wrecks have been discovered here. **La Tour Fondue**, a Richelieu construction on the eastern side, overlooks the small port that serves the Îles d'Hyères.

Boats for the islands also leave from **PORT D'HYÈRES**, beside Hyères-Plage back on the mainland. Traffic fumes and the proximity to the airport make the **beaches** here rather undesirable despite the pines and ubiquitous palms. Better to head down **La Capte** – the wider arm of the peninsula – or west of L'Almanarre, or up the coast past **Le Centurion Plage** and **Ayguade Plage** to the little fishing port of **LES SALINS D'HYÈRES**. East of Les Salins, where the coastal road finally turns inland, you can follow a **path** between abandoned saltflats and the sea to a naturist beach.

The Îles d'Hyères

A haven from tempests in ancient times, then the peaceful home of monks and farmers, the **Îles d'Hyères** became, from the Middle Ages onwards, the target of piracy and coastal attacks by an endless succession of assorted aggressors.

The three islands – Porquerolles, Port-Cros and Levant – are covered in half-destroyed, rebuilt or abandoned forts, dating from the sixteenth century, when François I started a trend of underfunded fort building, up to the twentieth century, when the German gun positions on Port-Cros and Levant were put out of action by the Americans. Porquerolles and Levant are not yet free of garrisons, thanks to the knack of the French armed forces for getting prime beauty sites for bases. But this has prevented the otherwise inevitable Côte build-up, and, in the nonmilitary areas, the government ensured

---

FERRIES TO THE ÎLES D'HYÈRES

Departures are from:

La Tour Fondue on the Presqu'île de Giens (☎94.58.21.81; bus #66 from the Port d'Hyères). All-year services to Porquerolles (20min).

Toulon, quai Stalingrad (☎94.92.96.82). June–Sept services to Porquerolles (1hr 30min).

Le Lavandou, 15 quai Gabriel-Péri (☎94.71.01.02). Year-round daily services to Levant (30min) and Port-Cros (35min), thrice-weekly service to Porquerolles (50min; daily mid-July to Aug).

Cavalaire (☎94.64.08.04). Summer-only services to all three islands (Levant 45min; Port-Cros 60min, Porquerolles 2hr 30min).

Port d'Hyeres (☎94.57.44.07). Services to Port-Cros (1hr 15min; all year) and on to Levant (1hr 30min; all year).

---

protection of the islands' very fragile environment by setting up the *Parc National de Port-Cros* and the *Conservatoire Botanique de Porquerolles*.

The islands' wild, scented greenery, combined with sea and sun, constitute the essence of what makes this part of France so desirable, and the endless signs forbidding smoking (away from the ports), flower-picking and littering are understandable. You can **stay** on the island: expensively on Porquerolles and Port-Cros, less so in Levant's nudist colony, the tiny morsel of the island not ruled by the military.

Île de Porquerolles

Porquerolles is the most easily accessible of the Îles d'Hyères and has a permanent village, also called **PORQUEROLLES**, around the port, with a few hotels and restaurants, plenty of cafés, a market and interminable games of *boules*. It dates from a settlement of Napoléon's veterans, whom the emperor felt deserved an island paradise for their retirement, and the village still focuses around the central **place d'Armes**, named after its original function as a military exercise ground. In summer its population explodes to over 10,000, but there is some activity all year round.

This is the only cultivated island of the three and has its own wine, called *appellation Côtes des Îles*; in fact, Porquerolles is big enough to get lost on – around 7km long by 2km wide – amid its stunning landscapes. The **lighthouse** due south of the village and the **calanques** to its east make good destinations for an hour or two's walk, though don't even think of swimming on this side of the island. The southern shoreline is all cliffs, with scary paths meandering close to the edge through heather and exuberant *maquis* scrub. The longest beach is the **plage de Notre-Dame**, 3km northeast of the village just before the *terrain militaire* that takes up the northern tip. The nearest beach to the village, 1km away (continue away from the port past the *Arche de Noë* and take the first, well-signed right) is the **plage d'Argent**, a 500-metre strip of white sand around a curving bay, backed by pine forests and a single restaurant.

You can rent **bicycles** from outlets all over the island, but the cheapest option is to pay for the bike with your ferry ticket in the Tour Fondue on the Presqu'île de Giens and pick it up as you land in Porquerolles. **Hotels** in Porquerolles are generally expensive, and need to be booked months in advance. All the hotels have obligatory pension except for the *Relais de la Poste*, place d'Armes (☎94.58.30.26; ⑤–⑥; May–Oct). Madame Rossi offers a few *chambres d'hôtes* at *La Bicoque*, rue du Phare (☎94.58.30.14; ②; Easter–Sept; book well in advance). There's no campsite on Porquerolles and *camping sauvage* is strictly forbidden, so it's inadvisable to miss the last ferry to the mainland. **Restaurants** in the village are pure tourist fodder and very expensive, but if you arrive in the morning you will be able to buy picnic provisions.

Île de Port-Cros

The dense vegetation and mini-mountains of **Port-Cros** make its exploration much tougher than Porquerolles, even though it is less than half the size. Aside from ruined forts and the handful of buildings around the port, the only intervention on the island's wildlife are the classification labels to some of the plants and the extensive network of paths. You're not supposed to stray from these signposted routes and it would be very difficult to do so given the thickness of the undergrowth. Sadly, staying on Port Cros is not much of an option, as the sole island hotel is prohibitively expensive, as are the few restaurants around the port, though you can get a sandwich or a slice of pizza. Again, camping is forbidden.

The entire island is a protected zone, and has the richest fauna and flora. Kestrels, eagles and sparrow hawks nest here; there are shrubs that flower and bear fruit at the same time, and more common species like broom, lavender, rosemary and heather flourish in abundance. It takes a couple of hours to walk from the port to the nearest beach, **plage de la Palu**; a similar time to cross the island via **Vallon de la Solitude** or **Vallon de la Fausse Monnaie**. You can also follow a 10-kilometre **circuit of the island**.

Île du Levant

The **Île du Levant** – ninety percent military reserve – is almost always humid and sunny. Cultivated plant life goes wild, with the result that giant geraniums and nasturtiums climb three-metre hedges, overhung by gigantic eucalyptus trees and yucca plants. The tiny bit of the island spared by the military is a **nudist colony**, set up in the village of **HELIOPOLIS** in the early 1930s. About sixty people live here all the year round, joined by thousands who come just for the summer, and tens of thousands of day-trippers.

Visitors who come to the colony for just a couple of hours tend to be treated as voyeurs. If you **stay**, even for one night, you'll generally receive a much friendlier reception, although this option tends to be open only to campers or big spenders: the **hotels** on Levant, apart from two exceptions, *Le Gaetan* (☎94.05.91.78; ③–④) and *La Source* on chemin de l'Aygade, close to the port (☎94.05.91.36; Easter to mid-Oct; ③–④), are even more expensive than those on Porquerolles; all require advance booking and most full- or half-board. The best-deal **campsite** is *Le Colombero* (☎94.05.90.29; Easter–Oct).

Levant has a better choice of **restaurants** than the other islands, though prices and quality still don't match, even taking into account the cost of transporting supplies. The restaurant of *La Source* (see above) is reasonable, with a good 130F menu.

The Corniche des Maures

The Côte really gets going with the resorts of the **Corniche des Maures**, as multi-million-dollar residences lurk increasingly in the hills, even more luxurious yachts in the bays, and seafront prices become alarming. You can sip the divinest cocktail under the warmest moon, purchase swimwear made of leopard skin, or have your car stereo nicked while you're waiting at the lights. This is the place where the rich and famous go to seed: Douglas Fairbanks Jr, the late Grand Duke of Luxembourg, and a host of sundry titled names have pushed this coastline into legend.

The Corniche des Maures includes beaches that shine silver, with tall dark pines, oaks and eucalyptus to shade them; rocks glitter purple, green and a reddish hue, and there are no trains and no motorways.

Sheer expense aside, **transport** is the one big problem: this is very much auto-land. Buses are extremely slow, especially in high season, and cycling doesn't get you very far unless you're *Tour de France* material.

Bormes-les-Mimosas and around

Seventeen kilometres east of Hyères, **BORMES-LES-MIMOSAS**, like all good Provençal villages, is indisputably medieval, with a ruined but restored **castle** at the summit of its hill, protected by spiralling lines of pantiled houses backing onto short-cut flights of steps. Attractions include **Musée d'Art et d'Histoire** at 65 rue Carnot (Thurs, Sat & Sun 9am–noon & 3–5pm; Oct–May Thurs & Sun 10am–noon & 3–5pm; free), with its turn-of-the-century regional painting; a mindlessly ugly pleasure port down by **La Favière**, flanked by torso-covered beaches; and addresses in the **old town** such as "alleyway of lovers", "street of brigands", and "arse-breaker street" (*rue Roumpi-Cuou*). The mimosas here, and all along the Côte d'Azur, are no more indigenous than the people passing in their Porsches: the tree was introduced from Mexico in the 1860s, but the town still has some of the most luscious climbing flowers of any Côte town.

To the southwest of Bormes is one of those rare unbuilt-up stretches of coast around **BREGANÇON** and **CABASSON**, good wine-growing terrain and harbouring a presidential residence in the castle at Cap de Bregançon. Unfortunately, access to the sea is heavily controlled, with three beaches charging hefty parking fees (and a small charge for pedestrians and cyclists). The beach by the castle past Cabasson is the best.

Three reasonable **hotels** in old Bormes are *La Terrasse*, 19 pl Gambetta (☎94.71.15.22; ①–②), with ordinary, clean rooms; *Le Provençal* on rue de la Plaine-des-Anes (☎94.71.15.25; ②–③), with a pool and seaside restaurant, if rather shabby rooms; and the *Bellevue* on place Gambetta (☎94.71.15.15; ②–③), rather plain and old-fashioned. The numerous **campsites** are by the sea off the road to Cap Bénat, closer to Le Lavandou than to Bormes. In high season you should book. Some names and addresses in descending order of price are: *Camp du Domaine*, 2581 rte de Bénat, La Favière (☎94.71.03.12; mid-March to Oct), *La Célinette*, 30 impasse du Moux, La Favière (☎94.71.07.98; April to mid-Oct), and *Les Cyprès* on av de la Mer, La Favière (☎94.64.86.50; Easter–Oct). For more information, the **tourist office** in Bormes is on place Gambetta (daily 10am–noon & 2–6pm; ☎94.71.15.17).

Good **restaurants** include *La Tonnelle des Délices* on place Gambetta (☎94.71.34.84; last orders 10pm), for traditional Provençal fare, menus from 125F, *à la carte* 300F. *L'Escoundudo* is in a similar price bracket at 2 ruelle du Moulin (☎94.71.15.53; closed Mon out of season), with a delicious tomato and hot goat's cheese tart; and *Pâtes... et Pâtes* on place du Bazar (☎94.64.85.75; closed Tues) serves the best pasta for 100–150F. More ordinary dinners can be had at the cheaper hotels listed above and at *La Pastourelle*, 41 rue Carnot (☎94.71.57.78).

Le Lavandou to La Croix Valmer

Fishing fleets still bring in their catches to the quaysides of the seaside towns and villages of the Corniche des Maures with the fancy restaurants providing the demand, but there are very few coves and headlands that would be recognizable to someone who tended nets in the early decades of this century.

LE LAVANDOU, a few kilometres east of Bormes, is a characterless pleasure port with little to offer the yachtless traveller. Ageing photos of old Lavandou festooning the

tourist office on quai Gabriel-Péri (☎94.71.00.61) only serve to remind of the contrast with today's glittering resort, where the sea is hardly visible for yachts and the remaining beach is continually invaded by the construction of further mooring space. And while tourism has caused the village's population to swell from a few hundred at the turn of the century to around 5000, the number of boats in the original fishing fleet has dropped from fifty to just twelve, and these are difficult to spot for yachts and schooners.

To the east, Le Lavandou merges into **ST-CLAIR, CAVALIÈRE, PRAMOUSQUIER** and **LE RAYOL**, after which there's a brief breathing space of impenetrable scrub behind high cliffs before the particularly gross resort of **CAVALAIRE-SUR-MER**.

The coastal road turns inland just before **LA CROIX-VALMER**, probably the best base around here, with its coastal suburb of Gigaro marking the start of a wonderful coastal conservation area, the **Domaine de Cap Lardier**, around the southern tip of the St-Tropez peninsula. La Croix-Valmer's **tourist office** is in Jardin de la Gare (daily 10am–noon & 2–6pm; ☎94.79.66.44). A budget-priced **hotel** for this part of the world is *La Cigale*, RN 559 (☎94.79.60.41; ①; half-board obligatory in season), right on the main road and consequently not very quiet; better value is *La Bienvenue* on rue L-Martin (☎94.79.60.23; ②–④), right in the centre of the village. At the other end of the scale is *Le Château de Valmer* on rte de Gigaro (☎94.79.60.10; ⑦), a seriously luxurious old Provençal manor house in walking distance of the sea. You can **camp** at the four-star *Selection campsite* on bd de la Mer (☎94.79.61.97; Easter–Sept, need to book mid-summer), 400m from the sea with excellent facilities. Good, inexpensive pizzas are guaranteed at *L'Italien* on plage de Gigaro, at almost the last commercial outlet before the conservation area.

The Massif des Maures

The secret of the Côte d'Azur is that however grossly vulgar the conglomeration of the coast, Provence is still just behind – old, sparsely populated, village orientated and dependent on the land for produce, not real estate. Between Marseille and Menton, the most bewitching hinterland is the **Massif des Maures**, stretching from Hyères to Fréjus. The highest point of these hills stops short of 800m, but the quick succession of ridges, the sudden drops and views and then closure again, and the curling, looping roads are pervasively mountainous. Where the lie of the land gives a wide bowl of sunlit slopes, vines are grown. Elsewhere the hills are thickly forested, with aleppo and umbrella pines, holly, cork oaks and sweet chestnut trees.

Much of the Massif is inaccessible even to walkers. However, the **GR9 footpath** follows the highest and most northerly ridge from Pignans on the N97 past Notre-Dame-des-Anges, La Sauvette, La Garde-Freinet and down to the head of the Golfe de St-Tropez. The best place for information about **walking** is the *Comité Départemental de Tourism* at St-Raphaël or the Toulon tourist office. If you're **cycling**, the **D14** that runs 42km through the middle, parallel to the coast, from Pierrefeu-du-Var, north of Hyères, to Cogolin near St-Tropez, is manageable and stunning, climbing from 150m to 411m above sea level.

Collobrières and La Chartreuse de la Verne

At the heart of the Massif is the ancient village of **COLLOBRIÈRES**, reputed to have been the first place in France to learn from the Spanish that a certain tree plugged into bottles allows wine to keep longer. From the Middle Ages until very recent times cork production has been the major business of the village. The church, the *mairie* and the houses don't seem to have been modernized this century, yet the **Confiserie Azurienne** exudes efficiency and modern business skill in the manufacture of all things chestnut: ice cream, jam, nougat, purée, and *marrons glacées* (shop 9am–noon & 2–6pm).

If you're too overdosed on sticky chestnut to move, there are two **hotels**: *Notre-Dame*, 15 av de la Libération (☎94.48.07.13; ②–④), and *Auberge des Maures*, 19 bd Lazare Carnot (☎94.48.07.10; ②–④), both small so they need to be booked in advance. There's also a **camping municipal** (May–Oct; ☎94.48.07.01). For **food**, other than chestnuts, the *Restaurant de la Petite Fontaine*, 1 pl de la République (☎94.48.00.12; last orders 9pm; closed Sun pm & Mon), is congenial and affordable, but books up fast. If you want to buy some local **wines**, there's *Les Vignerons de Collobrières* close to the *Hôtel Notre-Dame*.

Hidden in the forest, 12km from Collobrières off the D14 towards Grimaud, is the ruin of a huge monastery, **La Chartreuse de la Verne** (daily 10am–7pm; Nov–June daily except Tues; closed Oct), abandoned at the time of the Revolution. It is very picturesque and beautifully situated, and the recent restoration has incuded the overhauling of the monk's baking oven, which now serves up freshly made bread.

La Garde-Freinet

LA GARDE-FREINET, 8km northwest of La Croix-Valmer, was the Saracens' headquarters in the Maures under the name of Le Fraxinet, and their fortress above the village was the base from which attacks on the interior were made. The foundations, beside the ruins of a fifteenth-century **castle**, are still visible. Follow the signs to the GR9 at the northern end of the village; a path leads from a car park down to a cross and then up to the fort – about 1km in all, and steep. Today the main occupiers of the village are Oxbridge professors and other Anglos with time on their hands. The location is desirable, with top-notch medieval charm in the **old town** around the church; tasteful villas hide behind walls and trees, and there are easy walks to stunning panoramas and **markets** twice a week (Wed & Sun). You'll find all the modern necessities here, and it's just the right distance – about 25km – from St-Tropez.

For **rooms**, *La Sarrasine* on rue Longue or the D588 after it turns west at the top of the village (☎94.43.67.16; ①–③) is good value for this part of the world and has an excellent restaurant; *Hôtel Fraxinois* on rue François-Pelletier (reception at the *Tabac-Presse*, ③) is also reasonable. The two **campsites** are the municipal *Saint-Eloi* (☎94.43.62.40; June–Sept) on the D558 towards Grimaud, and *La Ferme de Bérard* (☎94.43.21.23) at a neighbouring farm.

La Garde's renowned **restaurant** is *La Faucado* at 31 bd de l'Esplanade (☎94.43.60.41; last orders 10pm; closed Tues out of season; booking essential); it's a bit overpriced but serves some beautiful dishes from local produce. Around place Vieille you'll find other cheaper eateries, and on place du Marché there's a young, arty café-cocktail bar and art gallery, *Le Lézard,* with jazz sessions on Saturday nights.

Grimaud

GRIMAUD, 10km due west of St-Tropez, is a film set of a *village perché*, where the cone of houses enclosing the eleventh-century church and culminating in the ruins of a medieval castle appears as a single, perfectly unified entity, decorated by its trees and flowers. The most vaunted street in this ensemble is rue des Templiers, which leads up to the pure Romanesque **church St-Michel** and a house of the Knights Templars. The view from the **castle** ruins is superb. If you're stopping **to eat**, the *Café de France* on place Neuve (last orders 10pm; closed Tues) serves good local dishes for a reasonable price on a vine-covered terrace.

Cogolin

What makes **COGOLIN** special is the combination of tourism with traditional craft manufacturing – of wind instrument reeds, pipes, cane furniture, silk yarn and knotted wool carpets. They're all serious businesses for the one-off, made-to-order, high-quality and high-cost Côte d'Azur market. One immediate consequence though is that Cogolin is alive all the year round, so even out of season you might well want to stay here.

Visits to Cogolin's **craft factories** are easily arranged; the tourist office provides a complete list of addresses and times, or you can wander down av Georges-Clemenceau and take your pick. For **carpets**, one of the best is the *Manufacture des Tapis de Cogolin*, 6 bd Louis-Blanc (Mon–Fri 8am–noon & 2–6pm; closed third week in Aug). And world-famous musicians visit *Rigotti* on rue Barbusse (Mon–Fri 8am–noon & 2.30–5.30pm; closed Aug) to replace the reeds of their oboes, bassoons and clarinets.

The best place to taste at least twelve of the local **wines** is at *Les Maîtres Vignerons de la Presqu'île de St-Tropez* (Mon–Fri 8am–noon & 2–6pm), on the rte de Cogolin just off the major roundabout at La Foux, the last town before St-Tropez.

The **tourist office** is on place de la République (daily 10am–noon & 2–5.30pm; ☎94.54.63.17). For reasonable **hotel** rates, try the *Hôtel du Golfe*, 13 av Clemenceau (☎94.54.40.34; ③–④), and the *Coq* on rue Général-du-Gaulle (☎94.54.63.14; ③–④). The **restaurant** at the *Coq* is okay (closed Wed): otherwise take a look around place Jean-Jaurès and rue Nationale. Alternatively, try the Lebanese specialities at *Le Bedouin*, 4 rue Nationale (☎94.54.67.16; closed Sun), or *aïoli*, opposite, at *La Taverne du Siffleur* (☎94.54.67.02).

St-Tropez and its peninsula

The origins of **ST-TROPEZ** are unremarkable: a little fishing village that grew up around a port founded by the Greeks of Marseille that was destroyed by the Saracens in 739 and finally fortified in the late Middle Ages. Its sole distinction from the myriad other fishing villages along this coast was its inaccessibility. Stuck out on the southern shores of the Golfe de St-Tropez, away from the main coastal routes on a wide peninsula that never warranted real roads, St-Tropez could only easily be reached by boat. This held true as late as the 1880s, when the novelist Guy de Maupassant sailed his yacht into the port during his final high-living binge before the onset of syphilitic insanity.

Soon after de Maupassant's fleeting visit, the painter and leader of the Neo-Impressionists, Paul Signac, was sailing down the coast when bad weather forced him to moor in St-Tropez. He instantly decided to build a house there, followed by a stream of others – Bonnard, Marquet, Dufy, Dérain, Vlaminck, Seurat and Van Dongen – and by the eve of World War I, St-Tropez was pretty well established as a hang-out for bohemians. The 1930s saw a new influx of artists, this time of writers as much as painters: Anaïs Nin's journal records "girls riding bare-breasted in the back of open cars… an intensity of pleasure…", and in 1956 Roger Vadim arrived to film Brigitte Bardot in *Et Dieu Créa la Femme*. The international cult of Tropezian sun, sex and celebrities took off – even the 1960s hippies who flocked to the revamped Mediterranean mecca of liberation managed to look glamorous – and the resort has been big-money mainstream ever since.

Arrival and accommodation

The **tourist office** on quai Jean-Jaurès (summer daily 9am–8pm; winter Mon–Sat 9am–12.30pm & 2–6.30pm; ☎94.97.45.21) can help with hotel reservations, although with more and more people wanting to pay homage to St-Trop, accommodation is a problem. Between April and September you won't find a room unless you've booked months in advance and are prepared to pay exorbitant prices. If you have your own transport, you may be better off staying in La Croix-Valmer or La Garde-Freinet (see pp.877–879). Otherwise, you'll arrive at the **gare routière** on av Général-Leclerc. You can **rent bikes** and **mopeds** from 5 rue Quaranta.

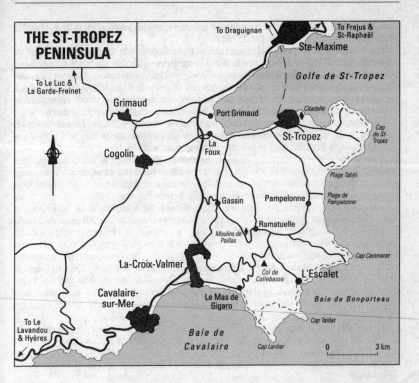

THE ST-TROPEZ PENINSULA

To Le Luc &
La Garde-Freinet

To Draguignan

To Frejus &
St-Raphaël

Ste-Maxime

Golfe de St-Tropez

Grimaud

Port Grimaud

Citadelle

St-Tropez

Cap de St-Tropez

La Foux

Cogolin

Plage Tahiti

Gassin

Pampelonne

Plage de Pampelonne

Ramatuelle

Moulins de Paillas

Cap Cammarat

La-Croix-Valmer

Col de Collebasse

L'Escalet

Cavalaire-sur-Mer

Le Mas de Gigaro

Baie de Bonporteau

To Le Lavandou & Hyères

Cap Taillat

Baie de Cavalaire

Cap Lardier

0   3 km

Out of season you may be luckier, though in winter few **hotels** stay open. One of the cheaper options is *Les Chimères*, Quartier du Pilon (☎94.97.02.90; March to mid-Dec; ②–④), a short way back from the *gare routière* towards La Foux; if they're booked up try the more central *Laetitia*, 52 rue Allard (☎94.97.04.02; ③–⑤; April to mid-Oct); or the rather scruffy *La Méditerranée*, 21 bd Louis-Blanc (☎94.97.00.44; ③–④; March–Oct). If you're prepared to blow more cash, *Le Baron*, 23 rue de l'Aïoli (☎94.97.06.57; ⑥–⑦), overlooking the citadel, is a bit quieter than those in the centre, or there's the luxury *La Ponche* on place du Révelin (☎94.97.02.53; ⑦), an old block of fishers' houses with a host of famous arty names in its guest book.

Camping near St-Tropez is also a problem. The nearest are the two sites on the plage du Pampelonne which charge extortionate rates and are massively crowded in high summer. Otherwise, 6km away off the road to Bourrian near Gassin is the three-star *Camping Parc Montana* (☎94.56.13.03; April–Sept), which also has caravans for rental. Within a three-kilometre radius of Ramatuelle (see over) are *Les Tournels* on rte de Camarat (☎94.79.80.54) and *La Croix du Sud*, rte de St-Tropez (☎94.79.80.84; May–Sept).

The Town

Beware of coming to St-Tropez in high summer, unless by yacht and with limitless credit. The 5.5km of road east from Le Foux has summer traffic jams as bad as Nice or Marseille; the pedestrian jams to the port are not much better; the hotels and restaurants are full and too expensive; overnighting in vehicles is prohibited; the beaches, as Bardot put it, are covered in turds and condoms and every other sort of rubbish.... So save your visit, if you can, for a spring or autumn day and you'll understand why this place has had such history and such hype.

The road into St-Tropez divides as it enters the village into av Général-Leclerc and av du 8-mai-1945, which will lead you to the **Vieux Port**, with the old town rising above the eastern quay. And here you have the classic St-Trop experience: the quayside café clientele *face-à-face* with the yacht-deck martini sippers, and the latest fashions parading in between, defining the French word *frimer*, which means to stroll ostentatiously in places like St-Tropez. It's surprising just how entertaining this spectacle can be.

Up from the port, at the end of quai Jean-Jaurès, rue de la Mairie passes the town hall, with a street to the left leading down to the rocky **Baie de la Glaye**. Further up, along rue de la Ponche, you reach the **fishing port** with its tiny beach, where roads lead up to the sixteenth-century **citadel**. Its **Musée de la Marine** (daily except Tues 10am–5/6pm; free) is not much fun, but the walk around the **ramparts** on an overgrown path has the best views of the gulf and the back of the town – views that haven't changed since their translations to oil on canvas before the war.

The paintings, suitably, you can see at the **Musée de l'Annonciade** (daily except Tues 10am–noon & 2–6pm or 3–7pm; closed Nov; free), reason in itself for a visit to St-Tropez. It was originally Signac's idea to have a permanent exhibition space for the Neo-Impressionists and Fauvists who painted here, though it was not until 1955 that the collections of various individuals were put together in the deconsecrated sixteenth-century chapel on place Georges-Grammont, just west of the port. The *Annonciade* features works by Signac, Matisse and most of the other artists who worked here: grey, grim, northern views of Paris, Boulogne and Westminster, and then local, brilliantly sunlit scenes by the same brush: a real delight and unrivalled outside Paris for the 1890–1940 period of French art.

The beach within easy walking distance of St-Tropez town is **Les Graniers**, below the citadel just beyond the port des Pêcheurs. From there, a path follows the coast around the **Baie des Canoubiers**, with its small beach, to Cap St-Pierre, Cap St-Tropez, the very crowded **Les Salins** beach and right round to **Tahiti-Plage**, about 11km away.

Tahiti-Plage is the start of the almost straight, five-kilometre north–south **Pampelonne** beach, famous bronzing belt of St-Tropez and world initiator of the topless bathing cult. The water is shallow for 50m or so, and the beach is exposed to the wind, and sometimes scourged by dried sea vegetation, not to mention slicks of industrial pollutants. Though you'll stumble across people in the nude on all stretches of the beach, only some of the bars welcome people carrying wallets and nothing else.

To get to the beaches from St-Tropez, there's a frequent minibus service from place des Lices to Salins, Tahiti and Pampelonne, or a bus from the *gare routière* to Tahiti, Pampelonne and L'Escalet; otherwise, you could rent a bike or moped (see "Arrival and accommodation"). If you're driving, you'll be forced to pay high parking charges at all the beaches, or to leave your car or motorbike some distance from the sea and easy prey to thieves.

Eating and drinking

There are **restaurants** to cover every budget in St-Tropez, as well as plenty of snack bars and takeaway outfits, particularly on rue Georges-Clemenceau and place des Lices.

Chez Angèle, 1 rue des Charrons, an alleyway off rue Aillard (☎94.97.47.74). Tiny, homely and serving acceptable if very ordinary dishes. *Plats du jour* 80F, menu from 90F. Closed midday Sun & Wed.

Auberge des Maures, rue du Dr Boutin, off rue Aillard (☎94.97.01.50). Roast lamb, stuffed peppers and gooey chocolate cake at reasonable prices; menu from 130F.

Bistrot des Lices, 3 place des Lices (☎94.97.29.00). Turn-of-the-century decor for traditional preening and overpriced eats (menus start at 240F). July & Aug evenings only, closed Tues out of season.

Café des Arts, place des Lices (☎94.97.02.25). The number-one brasserie on the square. Old-timers still gather in the bar at the back. Menus from 200F.

Café Sénéquier, on the port. The top quayside café, horribly expensive, but selling sensational nougat (which you can also buy from the shop at the back).

Glaces Alfred, rue Sibille. Ice creams made on the premises.

Joseph, 5 rue Cepoun San Martin and 6 rue Sibille (☎94.97.03.90). Good *bouillabaisse* and *bourride*, and great desserts. Menus from 160F, *à la carte* 300F upwards.

Restaurant de la Citadelle, cnr rue Citadelle and rue Aire du Chemin. *Moules marinières*, fish soup, *pissaladières*, and other standard regional fare. Not brilliant, but reasonably priced with *plats du jour* for 58F.

Snack Thierry et Roland, cnr bd Vasserot and rue F-Sibilli. Generous takeaway sandwiches for around 25F. In the same block of outlets you'll find pizzas, roast chicken and a *charcuterie*.

La Tarte Tropezienne, 1 rue G-Clemenceau. *Patisserie* claiming to have invented this sponge and cream custard cake.

Nightlife

In season St-Tropez stays up late, as you'd expect. If you get tired of the portside spectacle or window shopping in the amazing range of foodshops, go and see the animation of place des Lices, where games of *boules* continue until dusk. If you're mad enough to want to pay to see – and be seen with – the **nightlife** creatures of St-Trop, clubs include the young and boppy *Aphrodisiaque*, 35 rue Allard (every night in summer; Sat in winter); *L'Esquinade* on rue du Four, which stays open latest (but summer only); and the gay disco *Le Pigeonnier*, 13 rue de la Ponche (every night in summer; Sat in winter).

Gassin and Ramatuelle

Though the coast of the **St-Tropez peninsula** sprouts second residences like a cabbage patch gone to seed, the interior is almost uninhabited, thanks to government intervention, complex ownerships and the value of some local wines.

The hilltop village of **GASSIN**, 6km southwest of St-Trop, the shape and size of a small ship perched on a summit, was once a Moorish stronghold and is now, of course, highly chic. It's an excellent place for a blow-out dinner, sitting outside by the village wall with a spectacular panorama east over the peninsula and its richly green and flowering countryside. You can **stay** at *Bello Visto*, 9 pl des Barrys (☎94.56.17.30;.④), whose **restaurant** is the least outrageously priced out of the handful here, and you'll find cheapish *crêpes* and pizzas at *Au Vieux Gassin* nearby.

Gassin's lower neighbour **RAMATUELLE**, 2km towards the sea, is bigger, though just as old, and is surrounded by some of the best *Côte de Provence* vineyards. The twisting, arcaded streets are full of arts and crafts of dubious talent, but it's all very pleasant nonetheless. **Hotels** worth trying are *Chez Tony*, 31 rue Clemenceau (☎94.79.20.46; ③), and *Lou Castellas* on rte des Moulins (☎94.79.20.67; ③). The most beautiful French actor ever to have appeared on screen, Gérard Philippe (1922–59), is buried in Ramatuelle's **cemetery**. His ivy-covered tomb, shaded by a rose bush, is set against the wall on the right as you look down.

Port Grimaud

Just north of La Foux and 6km west of St-Tropez on the main coast road, the ultimate Côte d'Azur property development half stands and half floats at the head of the Golfe de St-Tropez. **PORT GRIMAUD** was created in the 1960s as a private lagoon pleasure city, with waterways for roads and yachts parked at the bottom of every garden. All the houses are in exquisitely tasteful old Provençal style and their owners – Joan Collins for example – more than just a little well heeled. In a way it's surprising that the whole enclave isn't wired off and patrolled by Alsatian dogs.

The main visitors' entrance is 800m up the well-signed road off the N98. You don't have to pay to get in but you can't explore all the islands without renting a boat. Even access to the church is controlled by an automatic paying barrier, though the fee is admittedly nominal. The brasseries, English-style pubs, restaurants and cafés, however, are less easily affordable and their ambience, during the day at least, is of patronizing benevolence that mere tourists are allowed in at all. Affordable accommodation doesn't feature on the Port Grimaud landscape: stay further down the coast in St-Tropez or at Ste-Maxime.

Ste-Maxime and around

STE-MAXIME faces St-Tropez across its gulf, making a classic Côte stereotype: a palmed corniche and pleasure boat harbour, beaches crowded with well-heeled windsurfers and waterskiers, and an outnumbering of estate agents to any other businesses by something like ten to one. It sprawls a little too much – like many of its neighbours – but the magnetic appeal of the water's edge is hard to deny.

To enjoy the resort, however, requires money. If your budget denies you the pleasures of promenade cocktail sipping and seafood-platter picking (not to mention waterskiing, wet-biking and windsurfing), you might as well choose somewhere rather prettier to swim, lie on the beach and walk along the shore.

For the spenders, **Cherry Beach** – on the east-facing plage de la Nartelle, 2km from the centre towards Les Issambres – is the strip of sand to head for. As well as paying for shaded cushioned comfort, you can enter the water on a variety of different vehicles, eat grilled fish, have drinks brought to your mattress, and listen to a piano player as dusk falls.

High up in the Massif des Maures on the road to Le Muy, some 10km north of Ste-Maxime, the **Musée du Phonographe et de la Musique Mécanique** lies in the **Parc St-Donat** (Easter to mid-Oct Wed–Sun 10am–noon & 2.30–6.30pm; 25F). The museum is the result of one woman's forty-year obsession with collecting audio equipment, and she has amassed a wide selection of automata, musical boxes and pianolas, as well as various outstanding pieces: one of Thomas Edison's "talking machines" of 1878, the first recording machines of the 1890s and an amplified lyre (1903). Almost half the exhibits still work. If you get a tour from Madame herself, you'll find it hard to resist her enthusiasm for the history of this branch of twentieth-century technology.

Practicalities

The **tourist office** on the promenade Simon-Lorrièrre (☎94.96.19.24) can give you all the relevant information on trips and pleasures and will advise on hotel vacancies – once again, very rare in summer. If you're heading for St-Tropez from Ste-Maxime, an alternative to the bus, at not much greater cost, is to go by **boat**; the service from Ste-Maxime's *gare maritime* runs from July to September with frequent daily crossings of twenty minutes. **Bikes** can be rented at 8 av St-Exupéry (☎94.43.90.19).

Among the cheaper **hotels** is the small *Castellamar*, 21 av G-Pompidou (☎94.96.19.97; ③), on the west side of the river but still close to the centre and the sea. For pleasanter and more expensive surroundings, there's the *Hôtel de la Poste*, 7 bd Frédéric-Mistral (☎94.96.18.33; ⑤–⑥), an ugly modern place but with very nice rooms and right in the centre; or the *Marie-Louise*, 2km southwest in the Hameau de Guerre-Vieille (☎94.96.06.05; ④), tucked away in greenery but in sight of the sea.

For non-beach **eating**, the *Hostellerie de la Belle Aurore*, 4 bd Jean-Moulin (☎94.96.02.45; closed mid-Oct to mid-March), offers gourmet food on a sea-view terrace; or, for half the price, there's the *Le Calypso*, (☎94.96.42.55; closed Tues), serving traditional fish dishes. Otherwise there are snack bars and brasseries along the seafron.

Fréjus and St-Raphaël

The major conurbation of **Fréjus** and **St-Raphaël**, 3km away on the ... ...as a history dating back to the Romans. Fréjus was established as a naval base u. er Julius Cæsar and Augustus, St-Raphaël as a resort for its veterans. The ancient port at Fréjus, or *Forum Julii*, had two kilometres of quays and was connected by a walled canal to the sea, which was considerably closer then. After the battle of Actium in 31 AD, the ships of Antony and Cleopatra's defeated fleet were brought here.

The area between Fréjus and the sea is now the suburb of **Fréjus-Plage** with a hideous 1980s development of a marina – **Port-Fréjus**. Both Fréjus and Fréjus-Plage merge with St-Raphaël, which in turn merges with Boulouris to the east.

Despite the obsession with facilities for the seaborne rich – there were already two pleasure ports at St-Raphaël before Port-Fréjus was built – this is no bad place for a stopover. There's a wide price range of hotels and restaurants (in St-Raphaël more than Fréjus), good transport links, and some interesting sightseeing to be done in Fréjus.

Arrival and accommodation

About four trains a day also stop at Fréjus' **gare SNCF** (☎94.51.30.53); **buses** between Fréjus and St-Raphaël are much more frequent and take ten minutes on the St-Raphaël–Draguignan line. The **gare routière** is on place Paul-Vernet (☎93.99.50.50), which is opposite the small **tourist office**, 325 rue Jean-Jaurès (daily 10am–noon & 2–5.30pm; ☎94.17.19.19).

St-Raphaël's **gare SNCF** (☎94.91.50.50) in the centre of town is the main station on the Marseille–Ventigmilia line. The **gare routière** is on av Victor Hugo (information ☎94.95.16.71), and the **tourist office**, which has an accommodation service and information on all the surrounding region, is just to the left out of the *gare SNCF* on rue W-Rousseau (daily 10am–noon & 2–5.30pm; ☎94.19.52.52). You can rent **bikes** from *Patrick Moto*, av Général-Leclerc (☎94.53.65.99), and **cars** from *ADA St-Raphaël Automobiles* (☎94.83.11.41), *Avis* (94.95.60.42) and *Europcar* (☎94.95.56.87), all on place P-Coulet.

There's a goodly range of **hotels, youth hostels** and **campsites** in Fréjus, St-Raphaël and in the surrounding area. Of the many campsites around here, the two east of town are preferable.

Fréjus

Aréna, 139 av Général-de-Gaulle, Fréjus (☎94.17.09.40). Pretty rooms, if a bit small, in a converted bank in Fréjus centre. Very friendly reception. ④–⑤.

Excelsior, promenade Réné-Coty (☎94.95.02.42). All mod cons overlooking the plage du Veillat seafront of the town centre. ⑤–⑥.

Hôtel Sable et Soleil, 158 rue Paul-Alène, Fréjus-Plage (☎94.51.08.70). A pleasant, small, modern hotel 300m from the sea. ②–③.

Résidences du Columbier, 1239 rte de Bagnols, Fréjus (☎94.51.45.92). A series of modern bungalows in a pine wood north of the town; all rooms have their own garden and terrace. ④–⑤.

La Riviera, 90 rue Grisolle, Fréjus (☎94.51.31.46). Very small hotel in the centre of Fréjus. Not very modern, but clean and perfectly acceptable. ②–③.

IYHF youth hostel, chemin du Counillier, 2km from the centre (☎94.52.18.75). A shuttle bus leaves for the hostel from St-Raphaël *gare routière* at 6pm, or you can take a regular #4, #8 or #9

...phaël or Fréjus, *direction L'Hôpital* to the *Les Chênes* stop and walk up av du Gal-d'Armée
...alies; the chemin du Counillier is the first left. You can also camp here. Closed 10am–6pm;
11pm curfew. ①.

St-Raphaël

La Bellevue, 22 bd Félix-Martin (☎94.95.00.35). Good value for its central location. ③–④.

La Bonne Auberge, 54 rue de la Garonne (☎94.95.69.72). More salubrious than *Les Templiers* and close to the old port. ②–③.

Les Templiers, place de la République (☎94.95.38.93). About the cheapest hotel you can get, above a bar in the old part of town north of the station. ①.

Centre International Le Manoir, chemin de l'Escale, Boulouris (☎94.95.20.58). 5km east of St-Raphaël, close to the beach by the Boulouris *gare SNCF*, with trains or buses every half hour from St-Raphaël. More luxurious than the other hostel. Closed 4–5pm; 105F b&b. ①.

Les Campeoles campsite, Le Dramont (☎94.95.52.13). East along the Esterel coast. March to mid-Oct.

Le Val Fleury campsite, Boulouris (☎94.95.21.52). Four-star site east of the town. Open all year.

Fréjus

The population of **FRÉJUS**, remarkably, was greater in the first century BC than it is today if you just count the residents of the town centre, which lies well within the Roman perimeter. But very little remains of the original Roman walls that once buffeted the city, and the harbour that made Fréjus an important Mediterranean port began to silt up and was finally filled in after the Revolution. Still, there is enough remaining to evoke a feel for the ancient town.

The Roman town

Doing a tour of the Roman remains gives you a good idea of the extent of *Forum Julii*, but they are scattered throughout and beyond the town centre and take a full day to get around. Turning right out of the *gare SNCF* and then right down bd Severin-Decuers brings you to the **Butte St-Antoine**, against whose east wall the waters of the port would have lapped, and which once was capped by a fort. It was one of the port's defences, and one of the ruined **towers** may have been a lighthouse. A path around the southern wall follows the quayside (odd stretches are visible) to the medieval **Lanterne d'Auguste**, built on the Roman foundations of a structure marking the entrance of the canal into the ancient harbour.

In the other direction from the station, past the Roman **Porte des Gaules** and along rue Henri-Vadon, you come to the **amphitheatre**, smaller than those at Arles and Nîmes, but still able to seat around 10,000 – today it's used for bullfights and rock concerts. Its upper tiers have been reconstructed in the same greenish local stone used by the Romans, but the vaulted galleries on the ground floor are largely original. The Roman **theatre** is north of the town, along av du Théâtre-Romain, its original seats long gone, though again it is still used for shows in summer. Northeast of it, at the end of av du XVème-Corps-d'Armée, a few arches are visible of the forty-kilometre **aqueduct**, once as high as the ramparts. Closer to the centre, where bd Aristide-Briand meets bd Salvarelli, are the arcades of the **Porte d'Orée**, positioned on the former harbour's edge alongside what was probably a **bath complex** (daily except Tues 9am–noon & 2–4.30/6.30pm; 10F).

The cathedral

The cathedral lies on the place Formigé – the marketplace and heart of both contemporary and medieval Fréjus – flanked by the fourteenth-century **bishop's palace**, now the Hôtel de Ville, and **chapterhouse**; the rue Sièyes leading off from here contains some picturesque seventeenth- and eighteenth-century mansions.

The oldest part of the **cathedral** close is the **baptistry** (both daily 9am–noon & 4–6pm; free), built in the fourth or fifth century and so contemporary with the decline and fall of the city's Roman founders. Its two doorways are of different heights, signifying the enlarged spiritual stature of the baptized.

Parts of the cathedral itself are tenth century, and it has some finely carved Renaissance doors, but one of the most beautiful and engaging components of the close is the **cloisters** (daily except Tues April–Sept 9am–7pm; Oct–March 9am–noon & 2–4.30/6.30pm; 20F). In a small garden of scented bushes, around a well, slender marble columns, carved in the twelfth century, support a fourteenth-century ceiling of wooden panels painted with apocalyptic creatures. Out of the original 1200 pictures, 400 remain, each about the size of this page. The subjects include multiheaded monsters, mermaids, satyrs and scenes of bacchanalian debauchery. On the upper storey of the cloisters is an **archeological museum**, whose star pieces are a complete Roman mosaic of a leopard and a statue of double-headed Hermes.

Modern Fréjus

Unlikely remnants of the more recent past come in the shape of a **Vietnamese pagoda** and an abandoned **"Soudanese" mosque**, both built by French Colonial troops. The pagoda (daily 9am–noon & 2–6.30pm; free), still maintained as a Buddhist temple, is on the crossroads of the RN7 to Cannes and the D100, about 2km out of Fréjus. The mosque is on the left off the D4 to Bagnols, in the middle of an army camp 2km from the RN7 junction. A strange, guava-coloured, fort-like building of typical West African style, it is decorated inside with fading murals of desert journeys gracefully sketched in white on the dark pink walls.

Fréjus has a **modern art gallery** (Sat & Sun 10am–6pm, Mon–Fri by appointment on ☎94.40.76.30; 25F), bizarrely located in the *Zone Industrielle du Capitou* just by turnoff 38 from the motorway; from place Paul-Vernet, take bus #2 to *Z.I. Capitou*. It has no permanent collection but some quite interesting temporary exhibitions.

Fréjus is a sound bet if you have kids to entertain, with a number of activity centres in the vicinity designed specifically for them. One of these is a **water amusement park**, *Aquatica* (daily June–Sept 10am–6pm; July & Aug 10am–7pm; 85F, children 65F), off the RN98 to St-Aygulf. Water scooters, toboggans and pedal boats are the principal forms of transport down chutes into an enchanted river; and there are lakes, a huge swimming pool with artificial waves and also a beach for the less energetic. To get there, take the St-Raphaël–Fréjus bus and get off at the *Géant Casino* stop.

The **Safari Park**, which lies just north of the motorway (turnoff 38), can be visited either by car or on foot (daily May–Sept 9.30am–6pm; Oct–April 10am–5pm; 65F); take the Fayence bus from St-Raphaël to the *Camps Lecocq* stop and it's only a ten-minute walk from there. Between Fréjus and St-Aygulf on the RN 98 is a 600-metre **go-cart track**, *Azur Karting* (daily except Tues 11am–9pm; summer 11am–midnight).

Eating and drinking

One of the best **restaurants** here is *Les Potiers*, 135 rue des Potiers (☎94.51.33.74), with menus of fresh seasonal ingredients for very reasonable prices. The restaurant at *L'Arena* hotel (see p.885) is excellent for fish, with menus starting at 110F. Cheaper eats can be found on place Agricola, and at Fréjus-Plage there's a string of eating houses including *Chez Jo*, 47 bd de la Libération (☎94.51.32.47; closed Tues evening & Wed), serving *plateau des fruits de mer* and a terrific *bourride*; and *La Scala*, 491 bd Alger (☎94.52.31.41; closed Wed out of season), for Italian specialities.

At Fréjus, **market days** are Wednesday and Saturday. On the second Saturday of June, the Foire de St-François takes over the town, and on October 6 there's a garlic fair.

St-Raphaël

A large and characterless resort, **ST-RAPHAËL** became fashionable at the turn of the century, though you wouldn't know it today, the town having lost its Belle Époque mansions and hotels through bombardment in the last war.

However there is a tiny **old quarter** around a crumbling Romanesque **church** by place Carnot on the other side of the rail line, and fragments of the Roman **aqueduct** that brought water from Fréjus stand outside the church in a little courtyard off rue des Templiers. Opposite is the **Musée d'Archéologie** (Mon–Sat 11am–noon & 2–4pm; mid-June to mid-Sept daily except Tues 10am–noon & 3–6pm; 10F). It features underwater archeology and local finds, as well as local history. If the church is locked you can get a key here.

The **beach** stretches between the old port in the centre and the newer **Port Santa Lucia**, with opportunities for every kind of water sport. You can also take boat trips to St-Tropez, the Iles d'Hyères and the much closer *calanques* of the Esterel coast from the *gare maritime* on the south side of the Vieux Port. When you're tired of sea and sand there's **bowling** at the *Bowling Raphaëlois* on promenade Réné-Coty and **billiards** close by at *Le Candy*. And if you want to lose whatever money you have left on slot machines or blackjack, the **Grand Casino** on Square de Gand overlooking the Vieux Port will be only too happy to oblige (daily 11am–4am).

Eating and drinking

You'll find reasonably priced **cafés** and **brasseries** around place Victor-Hugo and place de la République, and any number of pizzerias, *crêperies* and restaurants of varying quality around the Port Santa Lucia and along the promenades. Look out especially for *Le Sirocco*, 35 quai Albert-1er (☎94.95.31.31), a smart restaurant specializing in fish with a good menu for around 110F plus a view of the sea; or *Pastorel*, 54 rue de la Liberté (☎94.95.02.36; closed Sun evening & Mon), with menus from around 160F; there are decently priced Provençal wines, *aïoli* on Fridays and wonderful hors d'œuvres. Food markets are held every day on place Victor-Hugo and place de la République, with fish on place Ortolan.

For **drinking**, try the selection of beers at the *Blue Bar* on bd de la Libération on plage du Veillat (open till 4am in summer), or for expensive cocktails the *Madison Club* at the casino, or *Coco-Club* at Port Santa Lucia.

THE RIVIERA

The **Riviera**, the seventy-odd kilometres of coast between **Cannes** and the Italian border, was once an inhospitable shore with few natural harbours, its tiny local communities preferring to cluster round feudal castles high above the sea. It wasn't until the nineteenth century that the first foreign aristocrats began to choose to winter in the region's mild climate. But the real transformation came with the onslaught of 1950s mass tourism. Nowadays, it's an almost uninterrupted promenade, lined by palms and megabuck hotels, with speeding sports cars on the corniche roads and yachts like ocean liners moored at each resort.

Attractions, however, still remain, most notably in the legacies of the artists who stayed here: Picasso, Léger, Matisse, Renoir and Chagall. **Nice**, too, has real substance as a major city.

Cannes and around

The film industry and all other manner of business junketing represent **CANNES'** main source of income in an ever-multiplying calendar of festivals, conferences, tournaments and trade shows. And the spin-offs, of servicing the day and night needs of the jetloads of agents, reps, dealers, buyers and celebrities, are even more profitable than providing the strictly business facilities. Cannes might be more than its film festival, but it's a grotesquely overhyped urban blight on this once exquisite coast – a contrast reinforced by the sublime **Îles de Lérins**, a short boat ride offshore and the best reason for coming here.

The old town, known as **Le Suquet** after the hill on which it stands, used to be the home for the city's poorer residents. The streets that lead you to the summit are now well gentrified, though still good for cheaper eats and drinks, and provide a great panorama of the twelve kilometres of beach.

At the very top of Le Suquet, the remains of the fortified priory lived in by Cannes's eleventh-century monks and the beautiful twelfth-century chapelle Ste-Anne house the **Musée de la Castre** (daily except Tues 10am–noon & 2–5/6pm, July–Sept 10am–noon & 3–7pm; 10F). Along with pictures and prints of old Cannes and an ethnology and archeology section, the museum has an extraordinary collection of musical instruments from all over the world.

You'll find nonpaying **beaches** to the west of Le Suquet, along the plages du Midi and just east of the Palais des Festivals. But the sight to see is **La Croisette**, the long boulevard along the seafront, with its palace hotels on one side and private beaches on the other. It is possible to find your way down to the beach without paying, but not easy (you can of course walk along it below the rows of sunbeds). The beaches, owned by the deluxe *palais-hôtels* – the *Majestic*, the *Carlton* and the *Noga Hilton* – is where you're most likely to spot a face familiar in celluloid or a topless hopeful, especially during the film festival, though you'll be lucky to see further than the sweating backs of the paparazzi who buzz around them. At the quays at the end of La Croisette and the Vieux Port, you'll find millionaires eating their meals served by white-frocked crew on their yacht decks, feigning oblivion of landbourne spectators a crumb's flick away. As an alternative to the dubious entertainment of watching *langoustines* disappear down overfed mouths, you can buy your own food in the **Forville covered market** two blocks behind the *mairie*, or wander through the day's flower shipments on the allées de la Liberté back from the Vieux Port.

Strolling on and off the main streets of Cannes – **rue d'Antibes**, **rue Meynardier** and the **promenade de la Croisette** – is like wading through a hundred current issues of *Vogue*. If you thought the people on the beach were wearing next to nothing, now you can see where they bought the sunglasses and swimming suits, the moisturizers and creams for every hour of the day, the watch, the perfume, and the collar and leash for little Fou-Fou.

Practicalities

The **gare SNCF** is on rue Jean-Jaurès, five blocks north of the **Palais des Festivals**, an orange, concrete megabunker on the seafront and the main venue for Cannes's big events, of which the premier celeb-puller is the **International Film Fesival** in May. There are **tourist offices** at the train station and in the Palais des Festivals (both daily 10am–noon & 2–5.30pm). The **gare routière** is on place B-Cornut Gentille between the *mairie* and Le Suquet.

If something or someone compels you to spend a night in Cannes, you'll find the best concentration of **hotels** in the centre, between the *gare SNCF* on rue Jean-Jaurès

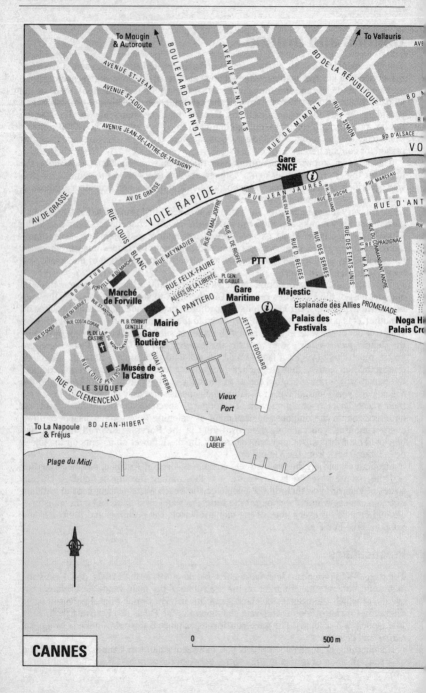

CANNES

0   500 m

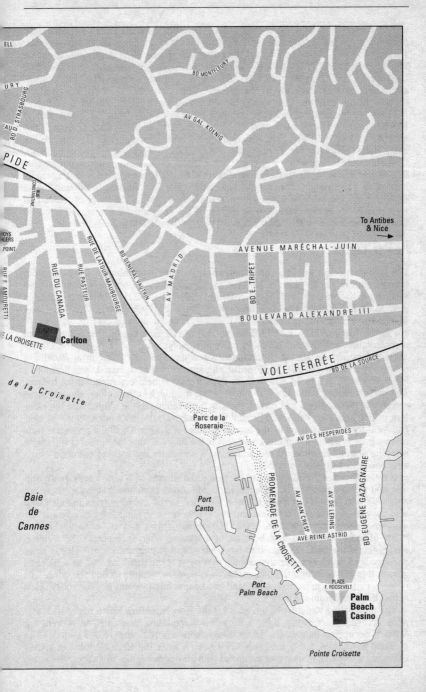

and La Croisette, around the central axis of rues Antibes and Félix-Faure. The *Hôtel National*, 8 rue Maréchal-Joffre (☎93.39.91.92; ③), is clean, adequate and close to the station; two more central options are the rather uninspiring *Hôtel Bourgogne*, 13 rue de 24-août (☎93.38.36.73; ②–④; closed Dec), one of the cheapest in town, and the *Hôtel Chanteclair*, 12 rue Forville (☎93.39.68.88; ②–③), better than average. The town's **camp-site**, the *Camping Bellevue*, 67 av Maurice-Chevalier (☎93.47.28.97; Feb–Oct), is slightly cheaper than most and nearer the sea in Cannes-La Bocca, a western suburb.

There are hundreds of **eateries**, covering the whole range from 75F *menus fixes* to 1000F blow-outs. The best areas for the cheaper end are rue Meynadier, Le Suquet and quai St-Pierre on the Vieux Port, with nothing but brasseries and cafés. Try *Au Bec Fin* in the *Hôtel Cybelle-Bec Fin*, 12 rue du 24-août (☎93.38.35.86; closed Sat evening & Sun), for traditional cooking with a very good choice of *plats du jour* and generous portions, or *Le Bouchon d'Objectif*, 10 rue de Constantine (☎93.99.21.76; closed Sun), with huge help-ings on its 118F menu. There are fish specialists, like *Lou Souléou*, 16 bd Jean-Hibert (☎93.39.85.55; closed Wed & Tues evening), which serves a good range of seafood on very reasonably priced menus, with a view of the sea, and *La Croisette*, 15 rue du Commandant-André (☎93.39.86.06; closed Tues), with excellent grilled offerings.

Îles de Lérins

The **Îles de Lérins** would be lovely anywhere, but at fifteen minutes' ferry ride from Cannes, they're not far short of paradise facing purgatory. **Boats** leave from the *gare maritime* in the old port (summer 14 crossings daily 7.30am–5.15pm; winter 5 crossings daily 7.30am–2.45pm). The last boats back leave St-Honorat at 4.45pm and Ste-Marguerite at 6 or 7pm (summer times). Tickets cost 60F for a round-trip; one-way it's 40F for Ste-Marguerite, 45F for St-Honorat. Taking a picnic is a good idea as the handful of restaurants on the islands have a lucrative monopoly.

Owned by monks almost continuously since its namesake and patron founded a monastery here in 410 AD, **St-Honorat**, the smaller southern island, was home to a famous bishops' seminary, where Saint Patrick trained before setting out for Ireland. The present **abbey** buildings date mostly from the nineteenth century, though some vestiges of the medieval and earlier constructions remain in the church and the clois-ters (which only men can visit). Behind the cloisters on the sea's edge stands an elev-enth-century **fortress**, used by the monks in times of danger. Of all the protective forts against invaders built along this coast, this is the only one that looks as if it still might serve its original function. At the same time it shows its age without cosmetic recon-struction or picture postcard ruins.

But the forces of this island today are peace and silence, with pine leaves gently stir-ring and the sea mapping out its minuscule tide. Apart from one restaurant, there are no shops, bars, hotels or cars: just vines, lavender, herbs and olive trees mingled with wild poppies and daisies; and pine and eucalyptus trees shading the paths beside the white rock shore mixing with the scents of rosemary, thyme and wild honeysuckle.

Ste-Marguerite can at first be a bit of a letdown after St-Honorat. The water is sludgy round the port, the lagoon at the western end is stagnant and the aleppo pines and woods of evergreen oak are so thick that most of the paths are cast in sepulchral gloom. It is still beautiful, though, and large enough for visitors to find seclusion. The western end is the most accessible, and the best points to swim are the rocky inlets across the island from the port.

The dominating structure of the island is the **Fort Ste-Marguerite** (daily 10.30am–noon & 2–4.30pm/6.30pm; 10F), a Richelieu commission that failed to prevent the Spanish occupying both of the Lérin islands between 1635 and 1637. Later, Vauban rounded it off, presumably for Louis XIV's *gloire* – since the strategic value of greatly enlarging a fort facing your own mainland without upgrading the one facing the sea is pretty minimal. There are cells to see, including the one in which Dumas' *Man in the Iron Mask* is supposed to have been held, and a **Musée de la Mer** (same times as fort), of mostly Roman local finds but also remnants of a tenth-century Arab ship. Access is free to the grassy ramparts of this vast construction.

Vallauris

Picasso stayed ten years just northeast of Cannes in **VALLAURIS**, the place where he first began to use clay, thereby reviving one of the traditional crafts of this little town in the hills above the Golfe Juan. Today the main street, **av Georges-Clemenceau**, sells nothing but pottery – much of it the garishly glazed bowls and figurines that could feature in souvenir shops anywhere. The **Madoura workshop**, where Picasso worked, is off rue 19-mars-1962, to the right as you come down av Georges-Clemenceau, and still has the sole rights on reproducing Picasso's designs – for sale, at a price, in the shop (Mon–Fri only).

The bronze statue of **Man with a Sheep**, Picasso's gift to the town, stands in the main square and marketplace, place de la Libération, beside the church and castle. The local authorities also suggested he should decorate the early medieval deconsecrated **chapel** in the castle courtyard (daily except Tues 10am–noon & 2–6pm; 8F), which he finally did in 1952: his subject was *La Guerre et la Paix* (war and peace). The space is tiny and has the architectural simplicity of an air-raid shelter, and at first glance it's easy to be unimpressed by the painted panels covering the vault – as many critics still are – since the work looks mucky and slapdash, with paint runs on the plywood panel surface. But stay a while and the passion of this violently drawn pacifism slowly emerges. On the War panel, a music score is trampled by hooves and about to be engulfed in flames; a fighter's lance tenuously holds the scales of justice and a shield that bears the outline of a dove. Peace is represented by Pegasus, the winged horse of poetry; people dancing and suckling babies; and the freedom of the spirit to mix up images and concepts with unmalicious mischief.

Vallauris is no place to stay, though it does boast a good cheap **restaurant**, the *Vieux Bourg*, on rue Lascaris in the old town. **Buses** from Cannes and Golfe-Juan run every hour to Vallauris and finish up at the place de la Libération, close to the castle.

Grasse

GRASSE, 16km inland from Cannes and with some stunning views over the Côte, is the world capital of *parfumiers* and has been for almost 300 years. These days it likes to flaunt itself, promoting its perfumed image as a chic eighteenth-century village with a medieval heart surrounded by acres of scented flowers. Making perfumes is presented as a mysterious process, an alchemy, turning the soul of the flower into a liquid of luxury and desire, and the industry is at pains to keep quiet about modern innovations and techniques.

Grasse is the official starting point of the *Route Napoléon* (see p.845) but is equally easy to visit as a day trip from the coast.

The Town

Vieux Grasse, despite its touristy shops and full range of restaurants, is surprisingly humble, a working-class enclave where lines of washing festoon the high, narrow streets – rates of pay for the pickers of raw ingredients for perfume essences are notoriously low. The inhabitants say it's like a village where everyone knows each other, and out of season that's certainly the atmosphere that prevails.

Place des Aires, at the top of the old town, is the main meeting point for all and sundry and the venue for the daily flower and vegetable **market**. It is ringed by arcades of different heights and the elegant wrought-iron balcony of the *Hôtel Isnard* at no. 33, and at one time was the exclusive preserve of the tanning industry. At the opposite end of Vieux Grasse lie the **cathedral** – containing various paintings, including three by Rubens and a wondrous triptych by the sixteenth-century Niçois painter Louis Bréa – and the **bishop's palace**, now the Hôtel de Ville, both built in the twelfth century.

A museum you might like to take a quick flit through is the **Musée d'Art et d'Histoire de Provence**, 2 rue Mirabeau, housed in a luxurious town house commissioned by Mirabeau's sister for her social entertainment duties (Wed–Sun 10am–noon & 2–5pm; June–Sept daily 10am–1pm & 2–7pm; closed Nov; 10F). As well as all the gorgeous fittings and the original eighteenth-century kitchen, the historical collection adds a nice eclectic touch. It includes wonderful eighteenth- to nineteenth-century faïence from Apt and Le Castellet, Mirabeau's death mask, a tin bidet and six prehistoric bronze leg bracelets.

The perfume factories

There are thirty *parfumeries* in and around Grasse, most of them making not perfume but the essence that is sold on to *Dior, Lancôme, Estée Lauder* and the rest. Perfume contains 20 percent essence (*eau de toilette* and *eau de Cologne* considerably less) and the bottles are extremely small – one litre of jasmine essence reputedly costs 90,000F – but the major cost in this multibillion-dollar business is marketing. The grand Parisian couturiers whose clothes, on strictly cost-accounting grounds, serve simply to promote the perfume, go to inordinate lengths to sell their latest fragrance, spending hundreds of millions of francs a year on advertising alone.

A good place to get an overview of the business is the **Parfumerie Fragonard** – actually two venues, one in the centre of town at 20 bd Fragonard, and the other 3km towards Cannes at Les Quatre Chemins, first set up by the painter's enterprising cousin. The first shows traditional methods of extracting essence and has a collection of bejewelled flagons. The one outside town is far more informative and admits to modernization of the processes. A map of the world shows the origins of all the various strange ingredients, which include civet (extract of cat's genitals), ambergris (intestinal goo from whales) and musk from Himalayan goats. Other *parfumeries* to tour include *Galimard*, 73 rte de Cannes, and *Molinard* at 60 bd Victor-Hugo (closed Sun). These – and all the others – are free, and they also have shops and give frequent tours in both French and English.

Practicalities

Grasse's **gare routière** lies to the east of the old town at the *Parking Notre-Dames-des-Fleurs*; a short way uphill is place de la Foux and the **tourist office** (daily 10am–noon & 2–6pm; ☎93.36.03.56).

Three possible **hotels** at the cheaper end of the market are: *Napoléon*, 6 av Thiers (☎93.36.06.37; ①–②), close to the tourist office; *Ste-Thérèse*, 39 bd YE-Baudoin (☎93.36.10.29; ③), west of the old town and uphill; and *Pension Michèle*, 6 rue du Palais-de-Justice (☎93.36.80.80; ②–③).

Bars and **restaurants** in the old town are good value. *Le Vieux Bistrot*, 5 rue des Moulinets (lunch only; closed Sun) serves great, simple food. The *Crêperie Bretonne* (till 11pm; closed Sun) and *La Galerie Gourmand* on rue Fabrières are good stand-bys, and you'll find plenty of other menus to choose from on rue de la Fontette and rue Droite. The bars on place des Aires give the most opportunity for encounters with the locals – the spit and sawdust *Bar-Tabac L'Ariel* is a good place to start.

Antibes and around

ANTIBES and its environs is the only place left on the Côte d'Azur – Monaco excepted – where the really, *really* rich and the very, *very* successful still live, or at least have residences. Yet it's not immediately obvious why this area should be so desirable: it's just as built up as the rest of the Riviera, with no open countryside separating Golfe-Juan a few miles west from Antibes, and none on the Cap d'Antibes that isn't surrounded by high electric fences. The centre of Antibes remains predictably pretty with a seventeenth-century **church**, though very little of the town's medieval stucture is left.

The sixteenth-century **castle** is a beautifully cool, light space, with hexagonal terracotta floor tiles, windows over the sea and a terrace garden with four sculptures by Germaine Richier, Miró, César and others. In 1946, Picasso was offered the dusty building – by then already a museum – as a studio. Several extremely prolific months followed before he moved to Vallauris, leaving all his Antibes output to what is now the **Musée Picasso** (daily except Tues 10am–noon & 3–7pm; winter 10am–noon & 2–6pm; closed Nov; 20F). Although Picasso donated other works later on, the bulk of the collection belongs to this one period. There's an uncomplicated exuberance in the numerous still lifes of sea urchins, the goats and fauns in Cubist nondisguise, and the wonderful *Ulysses et ses Sirènes* – a great round head against a mast around which the ship, sea and sirens swirl; and a whole room full of drawings. Picasso is also the subject here of other painters and photographers, including Man Ray and Bill Brandt, and there are works by contemporaries, among them a tapestry of construction workers by Léger.

Practicalities

Antibes' **gare SNCF**, a block back from the head of the port, lies at the north end of av Robert-Soleau; the **tourist office** is at the other end on place Général-de-Gaulle (daily 10am–noon & 2–6pm; ☎93.90.53.00), and the **gare routière** off the adjoining place Guynemer. The triangular-shaped **old town** lies to the south and east of these points – pick up a free map of Antibes and its environs from the tourist office and walk down rue de la République to place Nationale, the heart of old Antibes. **Bicycles** can be rented from *Deux Roues Location*, 33 bd Guillaumont, and *Fun Location*, 113 bd Wilson.

The most economical **hotels** are both close to the *gare routière*; the *Brasserie Nouvelle*, 1 av Niguet (☎93.34.10.07; ②), and *Le Nouvel Hôtel*, 1 av du 24-août (☎93.34.44.07; ③–④). For greater comfort, try the *Mas Djoliba*, 29 av Provence (☎93.34.02.48; ⑤–⑥), between the old town and the beach, which has a large garden and is very pleasant.

There's a **youth hostel** on Cap d'Antibes, the *Relais International de la Jeunesse* on bd de la Garoupe (☎93.61.34.40; ①; June–Sept; closed 10am–5.30pm) which needs booking well in advance; you'll have to get bus #2a from Antibes to L'Antiquité, and there's a midnight curfew. Of the many **campsites** along the coast north of Antibes, *Idéal-Camping* (☎93.74.27.07), opposite the *gare SNCF* at La Braque (one stop north of Antibes), has the advantage of being open all year, but *Le Logis de La Braque* (☎93.33.54.72; May–Sept) offers the same prices with many more facilities.

Rue James-Close, off rue de la République, is packed with good-value **restaurants**: try the excellent *La Marmite* at no. 20 (☎93.34.56.79; closed Mon; around 120F). For pizza, there's *Il Giardino*, 21 rue Thuret, though you may have a long wait to be served, and *La Famiglia*, a cheap family-run outfit at 34 av Thiers (closed Wed). *Chez Olive* on square Albert-1er (closed Sun eve & Mon) does a good midday menu for under 80F during the week, and for traditional Provençal food in a charming setting, try *Le Marquis*, 4 rue Sade (☎93.34.23.00; closed Tues midday & Mon; around 150F). For something really special, *Les Vieux Murs*, near the castle at av Amiral de Grasse (☎93.34.06.73), does a superb meal for 250–300F, including wine. There's also a wonderful **market** every day except Monday 6am–1pm on cours Masséna. If you've run out of things to read, *Heidi's English Bookshop* at 24 rue Aubernon (daily 10am–7pm) is the cheapest English bookshop on the coast.

Juan-les Pins

JUAN-LES-PINS, just 1.5km west of Antibes, is another of those overloaded Côte d'Azur names: the summer St-Moritz, the night-time playground for the most expensively outfitted and consistently photographed myths, who retreat at dawn to well-screened cages on Cap d'Antibes. Beyond the image, the place has very little in the way of history. Unlike St-Tropez, it was never a fishing village, just a pine grove by the sea, where Napoléon happened to land on his return from exile in 1815. It wasn't until the 1930s that the place began to take off as a full-blown Côte resort. Now its greatest attraction is the annual jazz festival in the second week of July.

The **tourist office** is at 51 bd Guillaumont (daily 10am–noon & 2–6pm; ☎93.61.04.98) and can provide tickets and information about the festival. **Hotels** are extortionately priced here; you're certainly better off in Antibes, a very short train journey away. You can get brasserie **food**, crêpes, pizzas and similar snacks from street stalls till the early hours, and many shops and bars also keep going in summer till 3 or 4am – worth remembering if you arrive mid-morning and wonder why the place is dead. *Le Crystal* on av Georges-Gallice is the brasserie at the hub of the milling crowds; its neighbouring **bars**, *Le Pam-Pam* and *Le Festival,* 137 and 146 bd Wilson respectively, compete, both with South American music and glittering cocktails, and are packed in high season.

Biot

Seven buses a day cover the 8km from Antibes to the village of **BIOT**, where early- to mid-twentieth-century painter Fernand Léger lived for a few years at the end of his life. A stunning collection of his works can be seen at the **Musée Fernand Léger** (summer daily except Tues 10am–noon & 2–5/6pm; 30F), just southeast of Biot.

Léger's art has the capacity for instant pleasure – the pattern of the shapes, the colour – though he can also draw it back to harsh horror as in the charcoal black to brown on off-white paper in *Stalingrad*. It's interesting to compare his life and work with Picasso, his fellow pioneer of Cubism and long-time comrade in the Communist Party. While Léger's commitment to collective working-class life never wavered, Picasso only waved at it when he needed it. Picasso wanted to embrace the whole world and be embraced in return. He chose a complex, dominating, sometimes perverted persona in which to do it, while Léger stuck within the reality of himself and the world, an outlook captured by Alexander Calder's wire sculpture portrait of Léger in the museum.

Above the Baie des Anges

Between Antibes and Nice, the **Baie des Anges** laps at twentieth-century resorts with two fine examples of concrete corpulence, the giant petrified sails with viciously pointed corners of the Villeneuve-Loubet-Plage marina, and an apartment complex, one kilometre long and sixteen storeys high, barricading the stony beach.

The old towns and softer visual stimulation lie inland. **Cagnes** is another artists' town – Renoir's in particular – as is **St-Paul-de-Vence**, which houses the wonderful modern art collection of the Fondation Maeght. **Vence** has a small chapel decorated by Matisse, and is a reasonable place to stay.

Cagnes

CAGNES is made up of Cros-de-Cagnes by the sea, Haut-de-Cagnes on the hilltop and Cagnes-sur-Mer in between.

At the top of place de-Gaulle, the main square in **Cagnes-sur-Mer**, av Auguste-Renoir runs right and crosses the road to La Gaude. A short way further on, chemin des Collettes leads off to the left up to **Les Collettes**, the house that Renoir had built in 1907 and where he spent the last twelve years of his life. It is now a memorial **museum** (daily except Tues 10am–noon & 2–5/6pm; 20F), and you're free to wander around the olive and rare orange groves that surround it. One of the three studios in the house — north facing to catch the late afternoon light – is arranged as if Renoir had just popped out. As well as ten of Renoir's own works, there are portraits of him by his closest friends – Albert André, Aristide Maillol and others – and several works by occasional visitors such as Dufy and Bonnard.

Haut-de-Cagnes is a favourite haunt of successes in the contemporary art world, as well as those of decades past, and it lives up to everything dreamed of in a Riviera *village perché*. The ancient village backs up to a crenellated feudal **château** (daily except Tues 10am–noon & 2–5/6pm; 5F), which houses museums of local history, fishing and olive cultivation, along with the **Musée d'Art Moderne Méditerranéen** – with changing exhibitions of the painters who have worked on the coast in the last hundred years. It also contains the **Donation Suzy Solidor**, which consists of wonderfully diverse portraits by all the great twentieth-century painters of the lesbian cabaret star who inspired the music hall song "If you knew Suzy, like I knew Suzy". In addition, if you're here between July and September, you can see the entries from forty-odd countries for Haut-de-Cagnes' big event of the year, the *Festival International de la Peinture*.

Practicalities

The **gare SNCF** is southwest of the town centre alongside the autoroute. You need to turn right on the northern side of the autoroute along av de la Gare to reach the town centre. If you want to rent a **bike**, take the second right, rue Pasqualini, where you'll find *Cycleset Cyclomoteurs Marcel* at no. 5 (☎93.20.64.07). The sixth turning on your right, rue des Palmiers, leads to the **tourist office** at 6 bd Maréchal-Juin (daily 10am–noon & 2–5.30pm; ☎93.20.61.64) and a **bicycle rental** place, *Location 2 Roux*, at 3 rue du Logis. Bus #7 runs from the *gare SNCF* to square Bourdet; from here you can take bus #9 to Haut-de-Cagnes or bus #5A to chemin des Collettes. If you are coming directly from Cannes or Antibes on the Nice bus, you can get off at the *Bésat–Les Collettes* stop by the chemin des Collettes.

Economical **hotels** in Cagnes include *La Caravelle*, 42 bd de la Plage (☎93.20.10.09; ①), and *Le Saratoga*, 111 av de Nice (☎93.31.05.70; ①–②), both in Cros de Cagnes, and *Le Christia-Flore*, centrally located at 10 bd Maréchal-Juin (☎93.20.61.1; ①–②). *Les Collettes*, close to Renoir's house at 38 chemin des Collettes (☎93.20.80.66; ④–⑤), has very pleasant rooms with views of the sea.

All the best places to **eat** are in Haut-de-Cagnes. The *Restaurant des Peintres*, 71 montée Bourgade (☎93.20.83.08; closed Wed), serves light Provençal delicacies with a 110F menu, wine included, for lunch on weekdays. *Le Clap*, despite the unfortunate name, at 4 rue Hippolyte Guis, off montée Bourgade (☎92.02.06.28; closed Wed), has reasonable menus starting from 85F. *Place du Château* is the centre of not just the town's but the whole district's nightlife. *Le Jimmy's* is a famous **piano bar** and the best place for afternoon terrace drinking.

St-Paul-de-Vence: the Fondation Maeght

Further into the hills, the fortified village of **ST-PAUL-DE-VENCE** is home to yet another artistic treat, and one of the best in the whole region: the remarkable **Fondation Maeght** (daily 10am–7pm; Oct–June 10am–12.30pm & 2.30–6pm; 45F). The Nice–Vence **bus** that stops at place de-Gaulle in Cagnes-sur-Mer has two stops in St-Paul: the *fondation* is signposted from the second. Admission includes the permanent collections, temporary exhibitions, bookshop, library and cinema, and it's worth every last centime.

Once through the gates, any idea of dutifully seeing the catalogue of priceless museum pieces crumbles. Giacometti's *Cat* is sometimes stalking along the edge of the grass; Miró's *Egg* smiles above a pond and his totemed *Fork* is outlined against the sky. It's hard not be bewitched by the Calder mobile swinging over watery tiles, by Léger's *Flowers, birds and a bench* on a sun-lit rough stone wall, by Zadkine's and Arp's metallic forms hovering between the pine trunks, or by the clanking tubular fountain by Pol Bury. The building itself is a superb piece of architecture: multilevelled and flooded with daylight, making inside and outside hard to distinguish, and the collection it houses of sculpture by Braque, Miro, Chagall, Léger and Matisse is undeniably impressive.

Vence

A few kilometres north, with abundant water and the sheltering Pré-Alpes behind, **VENCE** has always been a significant town. In the 1920s, however, it became yet another haven for painters and writers – André Gide, Dufy, D.H. Lawrence and Marc Chagall all spent time here, and Lawrence and Chagall died here, in 1930 and 1985 respectively. The old town is blessed with numerous ancient houses, gateways, fountains, chapels and a cathedral that boasts a Chagall mosaic, but the work which people come to Vence to see is that of Henri Matisse.

Towards the end of World War II, Matisse moved to Vence to escape the Allied bombing of the coast, and his legacy is the town's most famous and exciting building, the **Chapelle du Rosaire**, at 466 av Henri-Matisse, on the road to St-Jeannet from the Carrefour Jean-Moulin at the top of av des Poilus (Tues & Thurs 10–11.30am & 2.30–5.30pm; closed Nov to mid-Dec; free). The chapel was his last work – consciously so – and not, as some have tried to explain, a religious conversion. "My only religion is the love of the work to be created, the love of creation, and great sincerity" – a statement from 1952 when the five-year project was completed.

The drawings on the chapel walls – black outline figures on white tiles – were executed by Matisse with a paintbrush fixed to a six-foot long bamboo stick specifically to remove his own stylistic signature from the lines. He succeeded in this to the extent that many people are bitterly disappointed, not finding the "Matisse" they expect. The only source of colour in the chapel comes from the light diffused through green, blue and yellow stained-glass windows, changing with the day's light. Yet it is a total work – every part of the chapel is Matisse's design – and one that the artist was content with. It was his "ultimate goal, the culmination of an intense, sincere and difficult endeavour".

Practicalities

Vence is a real town with affordable places to **stay** and **eat**. Arriving by bus, you'll be dropped at the **gare routière** on place du Grand-Jardin, with **bicycle rental** at *Vence Motocycles*, the **tourist office** nearby (daily 10am–noon & 2–5.30pm) and, just beyond, the main gate into the old town. For **hotels**, *La Closerie des Genets*, 4 impasse Maurel (☎93.58.33.25; ③), off av M-Maurel to the south of the old town, and *La Lubiane*, 10 av Joffre (☎93.58.01.10; ③–④), to the west up av Henri-Isnard and av des Poilus, both have low-priced rooms. For a bit more luxury, including a pool, there's *La Roseraie*, 14 av

Henri Giraud (☎93.58.02.20; ④–⑤). There's a **campsite** 3km west off the road to Tourette-sur-Loup, *La Bergerie* (☎93.58.09.36; March–Oct).

For a special **meal**, try *La Farigoule* at 15 av Henri-Isnard (☎93.58.01.27; closed Fri), or, on the same street but half the price, *La Vieille Douve* (☎93.58.10.02; closed Thurs). Prices tend to be higher in the old town, but there's a wider selection; try the pizzas at *Le Pêcheur*, 1 pl Godeau (closed Fri lunchtime). **Drinking** is a young and noisy affair at *Henry's Bar* on place du Peyra, and ostentatiously cool at *La Régence* on place du Grand-Jardin.

Nice

The capital of the Riviera and fifth largest town of France, **NICE** scarcely deserves its glittering reputation. Living off inflated property values and fat business accounts, its ruling class has hardly evolved from the eighteenth-century Russian and English aristocrats who first built their mansions here; today it's the *rentiers* and retired people of various nationalities whose dividends and pensions give the city its startlingly high ratio of per-capita income to economic activity. And their votes ensured the monopoly of municipal power held for decades by the right-wing dynasty, whose corruption was finally exposed in 1990 when the mayor fled to Uruguay.

The traffic is a nightmare, miniature poodles would appear to be mandatory, the phones are always vandalized and the beach isn't even sand: this should be by rights one of the most loathsome cities on the Riviera. And yet Nice manages to be delightful. The sun and the sea and the laid-back, affable Niçois cover a multitude of sins. The medieval rabbit-warren of the old town, the Italianate façades of modern Nice and the rich, exuberant, turn-of-the-century residences that made the city one of Europe's most fashionable winter retreats have all survived intact. It has also retained momentos from its ancient past, when the Romans ruled the region from here, and earlier still, when the Greeks founded the city. The bus and train connections make Nice by far the best base for visiting the rest of the Riviera.

Arrival and accommodation

Arriving by **air**, you can get a bus (every 20min) from outside the end door of *Aérogare I* to the junction of av Gustav V and the promenade des Anglais, or on to the **gare routière** (☎93.85.61.81) if you're continuing your journey straight out of town. The *gare routière* is for once very central, close to the old town beneath the promenade du Paillon on bd Jean-Jaurès; the **gare SNCF** (☎93.87.50.50) is a little further out, a couple of blocks west of the top end of av Jean-Médecin (bus #12 will take you to place Masséna).

The main **tourist office** is beside the *gare SNCF* on av Thiers (Mon–Sat 8.45am– 12.30pm & 2–6pm; July–Sept Mon–Sat 8.45am–7pm, Sun 8.45am–12.30pm & 2–6pm; ☎93.87.07.07). It's one of the most useful and generous of Côte tourist offices and a lot better than its annexes at 5 av Gustav V and at Nice-Ferber on the road from the airport. Any of these offices can supply you with a free listings magazine, *7 Jours 7 Nuits*, which comes out every Wednesday and covers the whole Riviera.

For **getting around** the city, buses are frequent and run until 12.15am. Fares are flat rate and you can buy a single ticket on the bus or a *carnet* of five tickets. There are also one-day, five-day or weekly passes, all of which can be bought at *tabacs*, kiosks, newsagents and from *TN*, the transport office at 10 av Félix-Faure, where you can also pick up a free route map. **Bicycles**, **mopeds** and **motorbikes** can be rented from *Nicea Location Rent* at 9 av Thiers, just by the *gare SNCF*.

Before you start doing the rounds, it's well worth taking advantage of the **reservation service** offered, for a small fee, by the tourist office at the train station. The area

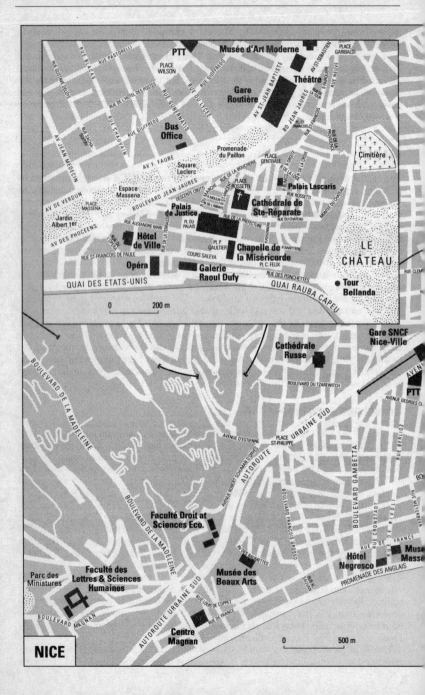

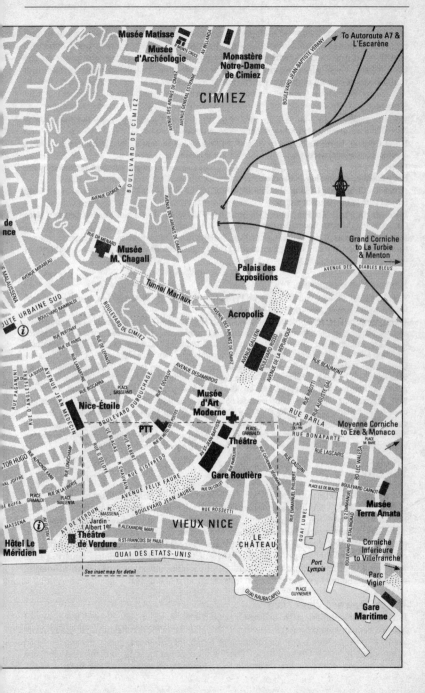

around the station teems with cheap, seedy **hotels**, but it's perfectly possible to find reasonably priced rooms in Vieux Nice. In summer, there's a fairly good choice of **youth accommodation**, or if you want to pay nothing, this is the one place on the Côte d'Azur where **sleeping on the beach** is tolerated. In fact, so many people do it that it becomes an all-night party throughout the summer.

Hotels

Hôtel le Capitole, 4 rue de la Tour (☎93.80.08.15). A good if potentially noisy location in Vieux Nice with a warm atmosphere though not overgenerous rooms. ④–⑤.

Hôtel Central, 10 rue de Suisse (☎93.88.85.08). Very small and not too bad if you can get a room overlooking the courtyard. ③.

Hôtel de Lépante, 6 rue de Lépante (☎93.62.20.55). Quiet and central, but don't be fooled by the Belle Époque exterior; inside the rooms are plain. ⑤.

Hôtel les Orangers, 10bis av Durante (☎93.87.51.41). A cheapie that all American students head for and unfailingly recommend. ③.

Hôtel de la Place du Pin, 10 rue Bonaparte (☎93.56.42.19). Not a bad location between place Garibaldi and the port. Rooms are reasonable, if a little dingy. ③.

Hôtel St-François, 3 rue St-François (☎93.85.88.69). On a busy pedestrian thoroughfare in the old town, above a restaurant hosting live jazz on Friday nights. An ideal base if you're not bothered by noise. ③–④.

Hostels and campsites

Abadie Guest House, 2nd floor, 22 rue Pertinax (☎93.85.81.21). Privately run hostel with rooms for one to five people, no curfew and no lock out. ①.

IYHF youth hostel, rte Forestière du Mont-Alban (☎93.89.23.64). Nice's hostel is 4km out of town and, for two people, not a lot cheaper than sharing a hotel room. The last bus from the centre leaves at 7.30pm and there's a curfew at 11.30pm. No card required. Take bus #14 from place Masséna, direction *place du Mont-Boron*, stop *L'Auberge*. Reception 7–10am & 5–11pm. ①.

Clairvallon Relais International de la Jeunesse, 26 av Scuderi (☎93.81.27.63). Slightly cheaper than the youth hostel but 10km north of the centre and with a 10.30pm curfew. Location apart, it's pleasantly informal and has a pool; take bus #15 or #15A, stop *Scudéri*. Reception till 6pm. ①.

MJC Magnan, 31 rue Louis-de-Coppet (☎93.86.28.75). This hostel is not too far from the centre and close to the beach. Take buses #3, #9, #10, #12, #22 or #24, stop *Magnan*. June to mid-Sept. ①.

Camping Terry, 768 rte de Grenoble, St-Isodore (☎93.08.11.58). The only campsite anywhere near Nice, 6.5km north of the airport on the N202 and not on any bus route. Unless you have a camper-van or caravan to park, it's probably better to sleep in the open air on the town beach.

The City

It doesn't take long to get a feel for the layout of Nice. Shadowed by mountains that curve down to the Mediterranean east of its port, it still breaks up more or less into old and new. **Vieux Nice**, the old town, groups about the hill of **Le Château**, its limits signalled by **boulevard Jean-Jaurès**, built along the course of the River Paillon. Along the seafront, the celebrated **promenade des Anglais** runs a cool 5km until forced to curve inland by the sea-projecting runways of the airport. The central square, **place Masséna**, is at the bottom of the modern city's main street, **avenue Jean-Médecin**, while off to the north is the exclusive hillside suburb of **Cimiez**.

The château and Vieux Nice

For initial orientation, with brilliant sea and city views, fresh air and the scent of Mediterranean vegetation, the best place to make for is the **Château park** (daily 7am–7pm). It's where Nice began as the ancient Greek city of *Nikea*, hence the mosaics and stone vases in mock Grecian style. There's no château as such, but the real pleasure lies in looking down on the scrambled rooftops and gleaming mosaic tiles of Vieux

Nice and along the sweep of the promenade des Anglais. To reach the park, you can either take the lift by the Tour Bellanda, at the eastern end of quai des États-Unis, or climb the steps from rue de la Providence or rue du Château in the old town.

Only a handful of years ago, any ex-pat or police officer would tell you that **Vieux Nice** was a dangerous place, brimming with drug-pushers, dark-skinned muggers and car thieves. That was always a gross exaggeration, but it still reveals how much the *quartier* has changed of late. In the early 1980s, a process of gentrification started with the renovation of low-rent flats, although a fair number of the old residents remain. There are still little hardware stores selling brooms and bottled gas; clothes lines are hung high across the streets; and tiny cafés are full of blue-overalled men. This life co-exists with the expensive boutiques and new restaurants mushrooming here.

The streets of the old town are too narrow for buses – it's an area made for walking. The central square is **place Rosetti**, where the soft-coloured Baroque **Cathédrale de St-Réparate** just manages to be visible in the concatenation of eight narrow streets. There are two cafés to relax in, one sun-lit, one shaded, and a magical ice cream parlour. The real magnet, though, is **cours Saleya** and the adjacent place Pierre-Gautier and place Charles-Félix: these are wide-open, sun-lit spaces alongside grandiloquent municipal buildings and Italianate chapels and the site of the city's main vegetable and fabulously colourful **flower market** (daily 6am–1pm). Over on place St-François, in the north of Vieux Nice, is the **fish market**, its odours persisting till late at night, when all the old streets are hosed down with enough water to go paddling.

On rue Droite, the **Palais Lascaris** (daily except Monday 9.30am–noon & 2.30–6pm; closed Nov) is a seventeenth-century palace built by a family whose arms, engraved on the ceiling of the entrance hall, bear the motto "Not even lightning strikes us". It's all very noble, with frescoes, tapestries and chandeliers, along with a collection of porcelain vases from an eighteenth-century pharmacy. Between cours Saleya and the sea at 77 quai des États-Unis is the **Raoul Dufy Musée-Gallerie** (Tues–Sat 10am–noon & 2–6pm, Sun 2–6pm; free), with the town's lovely collection from the Beaux Arts, including many works painted in Nice, plus temporary exhibitions.

Place Masséna and around

The stately, red ochre **Place Masséna** is the hub of the new town, built in 1835 across the path of the River Paillon, with good views north past fountains and palm trees to the mountains. A balustraded terrace and steps on the south of the square lead to Vieux Nice; the new town lies to the north. It's a pretty and spacious expanse, without being very significant – in fact the only things of interest here are the sundry ice cream vendors who shelter their goods under the arcades during summer. It's a short walk west to the **Jardins Albert-1er** on the promenade des Anglais, where the Théâtre de Verdune occasionally hosts concerts.

From place Masséna, the covered course of the Paillon to the north marks the site of one of the city's most prestigious projects. At its worst, up beyond traverse Barla, is the multimedia, megabuck conference centre grotesquely called the **Acropolis**. Though theoretically a public building – with exhibition space, a cinema and bowling alley (daily 11–2am) – international business often limits casual entry. Downstream from the Acropolis, a new and vast marble monument to the ambition of the city's leaders has recently opened, the **Musée d'Art Moderne et d'Art Contemporain**, or MAMAC

(Mon & Thurs–Sun 11am–6pm, Wed 11am–10pm; free). Neo-Realism and Pop Art make up most of the gallery's permanent collection, including works by, among others, Andy Warhol, Yves Klein, Roy Lichtenstein and Christo, and plenty of stuff by the pile-of-bricks/crushed-egg-cartons school of art.

Heading north from place Masséna, **avenue Jean-Médecin** is the city's main shopping street, named after the former mayor, father of corrupt mayor Jacques Médecin. The late nineteenth-century architecture and trees set the scene for some serious designer boutiques, *pâtisseries* and the **Nice-Étoile shopping complex** between rue Biscarra and bd Dubouchage, with all the mainstream clothes and household accessory chains, plus *FNAC* for books and records.

The promenade des Anglais and the beaches

The debouchment of the Paillon into the sea marks the beginning of the world-famous palm-fringed **promenade des Anglais**, created by nineteenth-century English residents for their afternoon's sea-breeze stroll along the Mediterranean sea coast. Today it's the city's unofficial high-speed racetrack, bordered by some of the most fanciful turn-of-the-century architecture on the Côte d'Azur, and stretching all the way past the old town to the airport.

Most celebrated of all is the opulent **Negresco Hotel** at no. 37, built in 1906, and filling up the block between rues de Rivoli and Cronstadt. There's nothing to stop you wandering in to take a look at the Salon Louis XIV and the Salon Royale. The first, on the right of the foyer, has a seventeenth-century painted oak ceiling and mammoth fireplace, plus royal portraits that have all come from various French châteaux. The Salon Royale, in the centre of the hotel, is a vast domed oval room, decorated with 24-carat gold leaf and the biggest carpet ever to have come out of the Savonnerie workshops. The chandelier is one of a pair commissioned from *Baccarat* by Tsar Nicholas II – the other hangs in the Kremlin.

Just before the *Negresco*, with its entrance at 65 rue de France, the **Musée Masséna** (daily except Mon 10am–noon & 2–5pm; April–Sept closes 6pm; free) is one of those dire historical museums committed to making its subjects – in this case the history of Nice, Garibaldi and Napoleonic times – as inaccessible and uninteresting as possible.

Behind the promenade, the pedestrianized **rue Masséna** and the end of **rue de France** are where tourists are supposed to congregate – and they do. It's all hotels, bars, restaurants, ice cream and fast-food outlets, with no regard for quality or style. Skirting this, the chief interest in western Nice is in the older architecture: eighteenth and nineteenth-century Italian Baroque and Neoclassical, florid Belle-Époque, and unclassifiable exotic aristo-fantasy. The trophy for the most gilded, exotic and elaborate edifice goes to the **Russian Orthodox Cathedral**, off bd Tsarewitch at the end of av Nicolas II (summer 9am–noon & 2.30–6pm; winter 9.30am–noon & 2.30–5pm; 10F).

A kilometre or so down the promenade and a couple of blocks inland at 33 av des Baumettes is the **Musée des Beaux-Arts** (Tues–Sun May–Sept 10am–noon & 3–6pm; Oct–April 10am–noon & 2–5pm; free; bus #38, stop *Chéret*). It has too many whimsical canvases by Jules Chéret, who died in Nice in 1932, a great many Belle Époque paintings to go with the building, a room dedicated to the Van Loos, and there are modern works that come as unexpected delights: a Rodin bust of Victor Hugo and some very amusing Van Dongens, such as the *Archangel's Tango*. Monet, Sisley – one of the famous poplar alleys – and Degas also grace the walls.

The **beach** below the promenade des Anglais is all pebbles and mostly public with showers provided. It's not particularly clean and you need to watch out for broken glass. There are, of course, the mattress, food and drinks concessionaries, but nothing like to the extent of Cannes.

There's a small, more secluded beach on the west side of Le Château below the sea wall of the port. But the best, and cleanest, place to swim, if you don't mind rocks, is the string of coves beyond the port that starts with the **plage de la Reserve** opposite parc Vigier (bus #32 or #3). From the water you can look up at the nineteenth-century fantasy palaces built onto the steep slopes of the **Cap du Nice**. Further up, past **Coco Beach** (bus #3 only, stop *Villa La Côte*), rather smelly steps lead down to a coastal path which continues around the headland. Towards dusk this becomes a gay pick-up place.

Cimiez

The northern suburb of **Cimiez** has always been a posh place. Its principal streets – av des Arènes-de-Cimiez and bd de Cimiez – rise between plush, high-walled villas to what was the social centre of the town's elite some 1700 years ago, when the city was capital of the Roman province of *Alpes-Maritimae*. Part of a small amphitheatre still stands, and excavations of the **Roman baths** have revealed enough detail to distinguish the sumptuous and elaborate facilities for the top tax official and his cronies, the plainer public baths and a separate complex for women. The new **Musée d'Archéologie**, 160 av des Arènes – entrance from rue Monte-Croce (May–Sept 10am–noon & 2–6pm; Oct–April 10am–noon & 2–5pm; closed Sun am & Mon) – displays all the finds.

The Roman remains and the Musée Matisse back onto an old olive grove, one of the best open spaces in Nice and venue for the July jazz festival. At its eastern end are the sixteenth-century buildings of the **Monastère Notre-Dame de Cimiez** (Mon–Sat 10am–noon & 2–6pm). The oratory has brilliant murals illustrating alchemy, with three masterpieces of medieval painting by Louis Bréa and Antoine Bréa in the church.

The seventeenth-century villa between the excavations and the arena is the **Musée Matisse** (daily except Tues 11am–7pm; Oct–March 10am–5pm; 25F, under-18s free), which has been recently expanded and reopened after a long closure. Matisse spent his winters in Nice from 1916 onwards, staying in hotels on the promenade – from where *A Tempest at Nice* was painted – and then from 1921 to 1938 renting an apartment overlooking place Charles-Félix; he died in Cimiez in November 1954, aged 85. The collection is a bit disappointing, though not if you love the gouaches cut-outs – *Les Abeilles* and *La Danseuse Créole* are delightful – and there are studies for *La Danse*, the huge blue and pink mural in the Palais de Chaillot in Paris, models for the chapel he designed in Vence (see p.898), and a nearly complete set of the bronze sculptures.

At the foot of Cimiez hill, just off bd Cimiez on av du Docteur-Menard, **Chagall's Biblical Message** is housed in a perfect museum (daily except Tues 10am–noon & 2–5.30pm; July–Sept 10am–7pm; 23F, Wed free), built specially for the work and opened by the artist in 1972. The rooms are light and white and cool, with windows allowing you to see the greenery of the garden beyond the indescribable shades between pink and red of the *Song of Songs* canvases. The seventeen paintings are all based on the Old Testament and complemented with etchings and engravings. To the building itself, Chagall contributed a mosaic and stained-glass window.

Buses #15 from place Masséna run past the Chagall museum and up to bd Arènes. Alternatives for Cimiez, but not for the Chagall, are buses #17, #25 and #22.

Theme and leisure parks

Right out by the airport is a vast new tourist attraction, the **Phoenix Parc Floral de Nice**, 405 promenade des Anglais (April–Sept 9am–7pm, otherwise 9am–5pm; closed Jan & Mon except bank hols & school hols; 45F; exit St-Augustin from the motorway or bus #9, #10, #23, #24 & #26 from Nice). It's a cross between botanical gardens, bird and insect zoo, and a tacky theme park: automated dinosaurs and mock Mayan temples along with alpine streams, ginkgo trees, butterflies and cockatoos. The greenhouse full of butterflies fluttering around is the star attraction, but the assumption that the world's fauna and flora is yours to admire may make you feel a bit uneasy.

Halfway between the city and the airport on bd Impératrice-Eugénie, and more manageable in size, is the **Parc des Miniatures** (daily 9.30am–sunset; 47F; bus #22), with scaled models of Côte d'Azur buildings, past and present.

Eating and drinking

Nice is a great place for **food** indulgence, whether you're picnicking on market fare, snacking on Niçois specialities or dining in the palace hotels. The Italian influence is strong in all restaurants, with pasta on every menu; seafood is also a staple. For **snacks**, many of the cafés sell sandwiches with typically Provençal fillings such as fresh basil, olive oil, goat's cheese and *mesclum*, the unique green salad mix of the region. If you want to buy the best bread or croissants in town, seek out *Espuno*, 22 rue Vernier, in the old town.

Most areas of Nice reveal excellent restaurants. **Vieux Nice** has a dozen on every street catering for a wide variety of budgets. Another good hunting ground is the **port quaysides** and the area behind.

Restaurants

La Barale, 39 rue Beaumont (☎93.89.17.94). This cavernous, cluttered comedy-set of a provincial restaurant is more of a social than a gastronomic experience. But feed you it will, with one set six-course menu that includes *pissaladière* (onion tart with anchovies), *socca* (a chick-pea flour pancake), ravioli and a sticky delicious tart. Evenings only until 9pm; closed Sun, Mon & Aug.

Le Bateleur, 12–14 cours Saleya. Generous and delicious pizzas for under 50F, plus live bands of dubious talent. Open till 2.30am.

Café de Turin, 5 pl Garibaldi. This is the place for oysters, mussels, clams and sea urchins, with a glass or two of wine, either in the tiny sawdust-swept *salle* inside or outside on the pavement. Watch out for costly extras though, and the long queue for tables which forms every night in summer from 7pm. Daily 8.30am–11pm; no bookings.

Chantecler and **La Rotonde**, *Hôtel Negresco*, 37 promenade des Anglais (☎93.88.39.51). *Chantecler* is the best restaurant in Nice and well over 500F *à la carte*, but chef Dominique Le Stanc provides a lunchtime menu, wine and coffee included, for 250F, which will give you a good idea of how sublime Niçoise food at its best can be. At *La Rotonde* you can taste less fancy but still mouth-watering dishes on a 150F lunchtime menu or *plats du jour* for 75F. *À la carte* around 250F. Closed mid-Nov to mid-Dec.

L'Estrilla, 13 rue de l'Abbaye (☎93.62.62.00). You need to book in summer for this popular restaurant that serves such Niçois specialities as courgette flower fritters. Closed Sat midday and Sun. Around 150F.

Chez Flo, 4 rue Sacha-Guitry (☎93.80.70.10). A big brasserie behind *Galeries Lafayette*, serving *choucroute*, *confit de canard*, seafood and great *crème brûlée*. Around 200F. Open till 1am.

Nissa Socca, 5 rue Ste Réparate (☎93.80.18.35). *Socca*, pizzas and other Niçois snacks. Hot, sweaty and cheap. Closed Monday.

La Noisetine, cours Saleya, near rue Gassin. One of the cheapest places to eat on the cours Saleya with generous and tasty crêpes, huge salads, nice desserts and fresh fruit juices. Open till midnight.

Chez René Socca, 2 rue Miralhéti, off rue Pairolière. The cheapest meal in town: you can buy helpings of *socca*, *pissaladière*, stuffed peppers, pasta or *calamares* at the counter and eat with your fingers on stools ranged haphazardly across the street; the bar opposite serves the drinks. Closed Mon.

Cafés and wine bars

Caves Ricord, 2 rue Neuve. An old-fashioned wine bar with faded peeling posters and drinkers to match. A wide selection of wine by the glass, plus pizzas and other snacks. Daily 8am–7pm.

L'Hermitage, 9 rue St-Vincent. Also known as the *Bar des Oiseaux* for the birds that fly down from their nests in the loft and the pet parrot and screeching myna bird that perch by the door. Serves delicious and copious baguette sandwiches. Erratic opening hours, sometimes closed all afternoon.

Les Ponchettes, cours Saleya. At the far end of the marketplace, with cane seats fanning out a good fifty metres from the café doors. Open late in summer.

Scarlet O'Hara, 22 rue Droite. Tiny Irish folk bar on the corner of rue Rosetti serving the creamiest, priciest *Guinness* this side of the Irish Sea. Daily 7pm–12.30am; closed Mon & first half of July.

Les Trois Diables, cours Saleya. Wall-to-wall leather jackets and classic grooves from the Fifties and Sixties.

Nightlife and festivals

Given the city's staid, affluent population, the luxury hotel bars tend to dominate the late-night scene. The old town offers more hope, though even here out of season not much goes on beyond midnight. As for Niçois nightclubs, bouncers judging your wallet or exclusive membership lists are the rule.

B52, 8 Descente Crotti. Small dance floor, young clientele and good value. Daily 10.30pm–4am, free entry until 1am.

Le Baby Doll, 227 bd de la Madeleine. Lesbian disco, not exclusively female. Daily.

Le Blue Boy, 9 rue Jean-Baptiste Spinétta. Lesbians and heteros are welcome at this, Nice's best gay venue off bd François-Grosso. There are two bars, two dance floors, DJs who know what's what, and a floorshow every Wednesday night. Daily 11pm–dawn; entrance charge on Wed & weekends.

La Douche, 34 cours Saleya. One of the cheapest and friendliest of the cours Saleya bars with billiards. Open till 2am. Daily.

Findlater's, 6 rue Lépante. Probably the best of the bouncer clubs – basically a video-bar with a small dance floor, young, trendy clientele, and predictable music. Closed Mon.

Le Las Vegas, 8 rue Marechal-Joffre. Mainstream venue with two discos and late-night restaurant.

Chez Wayne, 15 rue de la Préfecture. Popular bar on the edge of the old town run by an ex-pat who shares the French penchant for good old rock'n'roll. Live bands – of greatly varying quality – some nights. Daily 10am–midnight.

Festivals

Details of Nice's lively **festival** calendar are available from the city listings magazines or the *Comité des Fêtes*, 5 promenade des Anglais (☎93.87.16.28). The **Mardi Gras Carnival** opens the year's events in February, with the second and third week of July taken up by the **Parade du Jazz** in the Parc de Cimiez. At the end of July, the **Festival de Folklore International** and **Batailles des Fleurs**, involving unspontaneous flower-throwing, seize the town, and in December, there's the more sedate **Festival du Cinéma Italien**.

Listings

Airport information ☎93.21.30.30.

Emergencies Doctor, *S.O.S Médecins*, ☎93.83.01.01; casualty, *Hôpital St-Roch*, 5 rue Pierre-Dévoluy; ☎93.03.33.33; ambulance ☎93.92.55.55.

Money exchange *Thomas Cook* at the *gare SNCF* and 2 pl Magenta (Mon–Sat 8am–7pm, Sun & hols 9am–7pm; June–Sept Mon–Sat 8am–11pm).

Police 1 av Maréchal-Foch (☎93.92.62.22).

Post office pl Wilson, 06000 Nice.

Pharmacist The *pharmacie* at 7 rue Masséna is open 7.30am–8.30pm.

Taxis ☎93.52.32.32.

The Corniches

Three **corniche roads** run east from Nice to the independent principality of **Monaco** and to **Menton**, the last town of the French Riviera. These bends are the classic location for commercials for three-litre cars – and films where people driving them are killed; it was here that Princess Grace met her fate. Napoléon built the **Grande Corniche** on the route of the Romans' *Via Julia Augusta*; and the **Moyenne Corniche** dates from the first quarter of the twentieth century, when aristocratic tourism on the Riviera was already causing congestion on the lower, coastal road, the **Corniche Inférieure**.

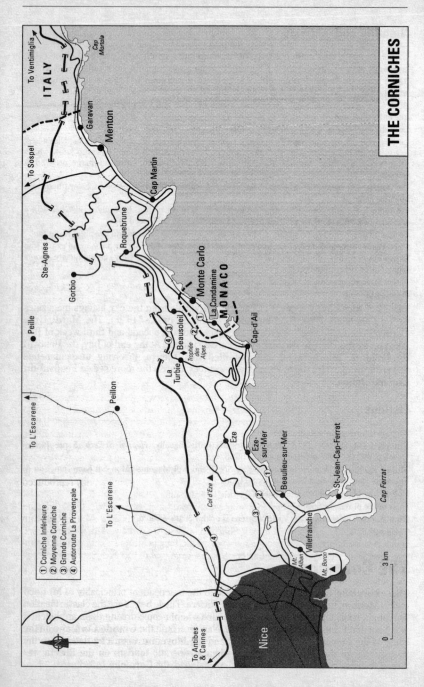

THE CORNICHES

Buses take all three routes; the **train** follows the lower corniche; and all three are superb means of seeing the most mountainous stretch of the Côte d'Azur. Staying in a **hotel** anywhere between Nice and Menton is going to be exorbitant, and it makes more sense to base yourself in Nice and treat these routes as pleasure rides.

The Corniche Inférieure

The characteristic Côte d'Azur mansions that represent the stylistically incompatible fantasies of their original owners parade along the **Corniche Inférieure**. Or they lurk screened from view on the promontories of Cap Ferrat, their gardens infested with killer cacti and piranha ponds if the plethora of *"Défense d'entrer – Danger de Mort"* signs is anything to go by.

VILLEFRANCHE-SUR-MER is just over the other side of Mont Alban from Nice, and has been spared architectural eyesores only to be marred by lurking US and French warships attracted by the deep waters of the bay. But as long as your visit doesn't coincide with sailors' shore leave, the old town on the waterfront, with its active fleet of fishing boats, sixteenth-century citadel and its rue Obscure running beneath the houses, feels almost like the genuine article – an illusion which the quayside restaurants' prices quickly dispel.

The tiny fishing harbour is overlooked by the medieval **Chapelle de St-Pierre**, (daily except Mon 9.30am–noon & 2–4/6pm; 12F), decorated by Jean Cocteau in 1957 in shades he described as "ghosts of colours". The colours fill drawings in strong and simple lines, portraying scenes from the life of Saint Peter and homages to the women of Villefranche and to the Gypsies. Above the altar, Peter walks on water supported by an angel to the outrage of the fishes and the amusement of Christ. The fishermen's eyes are drawn as fishes; the ceramic eyes on either side of the door are the flames of the apocalypse, and the altar candelabras of night-time fishing forks rise above single eyes. On June 29 each year, local fishers celebrate the feast day of Saint Peter and Saint Paul with a mass, the only time the chapel is used.

Only a few kilometres further along the coast on the pretty Baie des Fourmis, **BEAULIEU** is sheltered by a ring of hills that ensure its temperatures are amongst the highest on the Côte. The most interesting thing in town is undoubtedly the **Villa Kerylos** (mid-March to June & Oct daily 10.30am–12.30pm & 2–6pm; July–Sept 10am–6/7pm; Dec–March Tues–Fri 2–5.30pm; 30F), just east of the casino on av Gustav-Eiffel, a near-perfect reproduction of an ancient Greek villa. Théodore Reinach, the archeologist who had it built, lived here for twenty years, eating, dressing and acting like an Athenian citizen, taking baths with his male friends and assigning separate suites to women. However perverse the concept, it's a visual knockout, with faithfully reproduced mosaics and vases and lavish use of marble and alabaster.

On the main road along the neck of the Cap Ferrat peninsula, between Villefranche and Beaulieu, stands the **Villa Ephrussi** (daily 10am–6/7pm; Nov–March Sat, Sun 10am–6pm; 30F). Built in 1912 for a Rothschild heiress, it overflows with decorative art, paintings, sculpture and artefacts ranging from the fourteenth to the nineteenth centuries, and from European to Far Eastern origins. In addition, the villa is surrounded by huge, elaborate gardens.

The Moyenne Corniche

Of the three roads, the **Moyenne Corniche** is the most photogenic, a real cliff-hanging, car-chase highway. Eleven kilometres from Nice, the medieval village of **EZE** clings to its rock just below the corniche, a picture of old streets, a fourteenth-century chapel and spectacular views out to the azure Med waters as far as Corsica. On the down side, there is no other *village perché* in all of Provence so infested with antique, dealers, pseudo artisans and other caterers to the tourist, and it requires a major mental feat to recall that the labyrinth of tiny vaulted passages and stairways was designed not for charm but from fear of attack.

From place du Centenaire, just outside the old village, you can reach the shore through open countryside, via the **sentier Frédéric-Nietzsche**. The philosopher is said to have conceived part of *Thus Spake Zarathustra*, his shaggy dog story against believing answers to ultimate questions, on this path – which isn't quite as hard-going as the book. You arrive at the Corniche Inférieure at the eastern limit of Eze-sur-Mer (coming upwards, in the other direction, it's signposted to *La Village*).

The Grand Corniche

At every other turn on the **Grande Corniche**, you're invited to park your car and enjoy a *belvédère*. And at certain points, such as Col d'Eze, you can turn off upwards for even higher views. Eighteen stunning kilometres from Nice, you reach the village of **LA TURBIE** and its **Trophée des Alpes**, a sixth-century BC monument to the power of Rome and the total subjugation of the local peoples. Originally a statue of Augustus Cæsar stood on the 45-metre plinth which fell into rack and ruin over the centuries. Painstakingly restored in the 1930s, it now stands statueless. Viewed from a distance, it still looks impressive, but if you want a closer inspection, you'll have to buy a ticket (daily April–Sept 9am–7pm; Oct–March 9am–noon & 2–5pm; 20F).

As the corniche descends towards Cap-Martin, it passes the eleventh-century castle of **ROQUEBRUNE** and its village nestling round the base of the rock. The **castle** (summer daily 10am–noon & 2–7pm; winter daily except Fri 10am–noon & 2–5pm) has been kitted out enthusiastically in medieval fashion, while the village itself is almost too good to be true, with lovely gardens next to the seventeenth-century **church of Ste-Marguerite**. To get to the *vieux village* from the **gare SNCF**, turn east and then right up av de la Côte d'Azur, then first left up escalier Corinthille, across the Grand Corniche and up escalier Chanoine JB Grana.

Between the Roquebrune station and the sea, a **coastal path** runs west to Monaco and southeast around the wealthy enclave of **Cap Martin**, giving you access to a wonderful shoreline of white rocks and wind-bent pines. The path is named after Le Corbusier, who spent several summers in Roquebrune and died, tragically, by drowning off Cap Martin in 1965. His grave – designed by himself – is in the **cemetery** (square J near the flagpole), high above the old village on Promenade 1er DFL.

Monaco

Monstrosities are common on the Côte d'Azur, but nowhere – not even Cannes – can outdo **MONACO**. This tiny independent principality, no bigger than London's Hyde Park, has lived off gambling and catering for the desires of the idle international rich for the last hundred years. Meanwhile, it has become one of the greatest property speculation sites in the world – a sort of Manhattan-by-Sea without the saving aesthetic grace of the skyscrapers rising from a single level.

The principality has been in the hands of the ruling Grimaldi family since the fourteenth century, and legally Monaco will once again become part of France when the royal line dies out. The current ruler, Prince Rainier, is the one constitutionally autocratic ruler left in Europe, under whose nose every French law is passed for approval prior to being applied to Monaco, and while there is a parliament, it has limited functions and is elected by Monégasque nationals – only sixteen percent of the population. But there is no opposition to the ruling family. The citizens and residents pay no income tax and their riches are protected by rigorous security forces – Monaco has more police per square metre than any other country in the world.

One time to avoid Monaco – unless you're a motor-racing enthusiast – is the second week in May, when racing cars burn around the port and casino for the Formula 1 **Monaco Grand Prix**. Every space in sight of the circuit is inaccessible without a ticket, making casual sightseeing out of the question.

The Principality

The three-kilometre-long state consists of the old town of **Monaco-Ville** – the principality's capital – around the palace on a high rocky promontory, with the new suburb and marina of **Fontvieille** in its western shadow. **La Condamine** is the old port quarter on the other side of the rock; **Larvotto**, the bathing resort with artificial beaches of imported sand, reaches to the eastern border; and **Monte-Carlo** is in the middle.

Monaco-Ville

Hub of Monaco-Ville is the **place du Palais**, decorated with cannon given to the principality by Louis XIV. On its western side rises the pastel pink wedding-cake façade of the toy **Prince's Palace** (daily 9.30am–6.30pm; Oct 10am–5pm; closed Nov–May; 30F), where you can admire suitably over-the-top princely spaces including the Salle du Trône, where the civil part of Prince Rainier and Grace Kelly's marriage was enacted. The west wing is devoted to the **Napoléon museum and palace archives** (daily except Mon 10.30am–12.30pm & 2–5pm; Oct daily 10am–5pm; closed Nov; 20F), showing a range of medals, uniforms, personal items and flags in a rather dry fashion.

From the square lead the narrow streets of the glacé-iced **old town**, where every other shop sells royal mugs and similar assorted junk, and the buildings are so well preserved they look like a medieval Ideal Home exhibition. The Romanesque-style **cathedral**, overlooking the Jardins St-Martin, went up in only 1875 and provided a suitably starchy backdrop for the society wedding of Prince Rainier to American glamour queen Grace Kelly in 1956.

The one point of real interest in the old town, however, is the aquarium in the basement of the **Musée Océanographique** (daily 9am–7/8pm; Oct–March 9.30am–7pm; bus #1 or #2, *Monaco-Ville*; 60F), where the fishy beings outdo the weirdest Zandra Rhodes creations. Less exceptional but still peculiar cactus equivalents can be viewed in the **Jardin Exotique** high above Fontvieille (daily 9am–6pm; May–Sept 9am–7pm; 35F).

Monte-Carlo

Monte-Carlo is the area of Monaco where the real money is flung about – a core of opulent private villas, casinos, the ritzy *Hôtel de Paris* and designer shops vying to outdo each other in the luxury stakes.

The famous Monte-Carlo **casino** has to be seen. Entrance is restricted to over-21s and you may have to show your passport; dress code is rigid, with shorts and T-shirts frowned upon, and skirts, jackets, ties and so forth more or less obligatory for the more interesting sections. Any coats or large bags involve hefty cloakroom fees.

In the first gambling hall, the **Salons Européens** (open from noon; 50F), slot machines surround the American roulette, craps and blackjack tables, the managers are Vegas-trained, the lights low and the air oppressively smoky. Above this slice of Nevada, however, the decor is turn-of-the-century Rococo extravagance, while in the adjoining *Pink Salon Bar*, female nudes smoking cigarettes adorn the ceilings.

The heart of the place are the **Salons Privés** (from 4.15pm), through the Salles Touzet. You must look like a gambler, not a tourist (no cameras), to get in, and dispense with 100F at the door. More richly decorated than the European Rooms and much bigger, the atmosphere is that of a cathedral in the early afternoon or out of

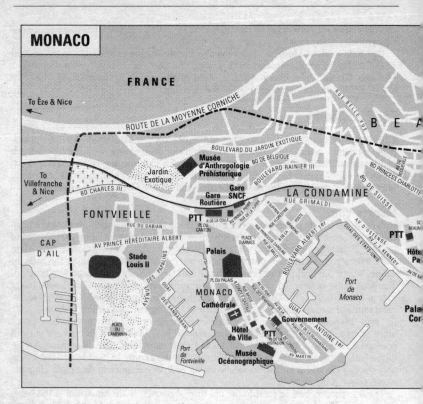

season. No clinking coins, just quiet-voiced croupiers and sliding chips. Elderly gamblers pace silently, fingering 500F notes (the maximum unnegotiated stake here is 500,000F), closed-circuit TV cameras above the chandeliers watch the gamblers watching the tables, and no one drinks. On midsummer evenings the place is packed out and the vice loses its sacred and exclusive touch.

Adjoining the casino is the gaudy opera house, and around the palm-tree-lined place du Casino are more casinos and the city's palace-hotels and *grands cafés*. The *American Bar* of the **Hôtel de Paris** is, according to its publicity, the place where "the world's most elite society" meets. As long as you dress up and are prepared to be challenged if you haven't ordered a 200F drink, you can entertain yourself free of charge against the background of Belle Époque decadence, watching people whose bank accounts are possibly the most interesting thing about them.

Practicalities

The **gare SNCF** is on av Prince-Pierre in La Condamine, a short walk from the main **gare routière** on place d'Armes. Buses following the middle and lower corniches stop here; other routes have a variety of stations, of which the **tourist office** at 2a bd des Moulins, near the casino, can give details (Mon–Sat 9am–7pm; Sun 10am–noon; ☎92.16.61.66). Local bus #4 runs from the *gare SNCF* to the *Casino-Tourisme* stop, close to the tourist office and place du Casino. One free and very useful public service is the incredibly clean

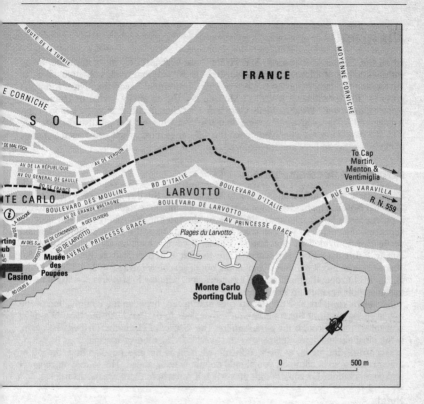

and efficient **lifts** linking the lower and higher streets (marked on the tourist office map). **Bicycles** can be rented from *Auto-Motos*, 7 rue de la Colle, off av Prince-Pierre.

Monaco has no campsite, and caravans are illegal in the state – as are bathing costumes, bare feet and bare chests once you step off the beach. Campervans have to be parked at the *Parking des Écoles* in Fontvieille, and then only between 8am and 8pm. If you stay more than a day, La Condamine is the best area for **hotels**, though don't expect bargains. You could try *Cosmopolite*, 4 rue de la Turbie (☎93.30.16.95; ③–④) near the station, or its neighbour the *Hôtel de France*, 6 rue de la Turbie (☎93.30.24.64; ③–④). Another reasonable option is *Helvetia*, 1 rue Grimaldi (☎93.30.21.71; ④–⑤). You may be able to get a dorm-style bed at the *Centre de Jeunesse Princess Stéphanie*, near the station at 24 av Prince-Pierre (☎93.50.83.20; ①), but you can't make reservations in summer, and the hostel is only open to those under 26 or students under 31.

La Condamine and the old town are replete with **restaurants**, but good food and reasonable prices don't exactly match. Around the station you'll find generous pizzas at *Bacchus*, 13 rue de La Turbie (closed Sat & 2nd week in July), and a good 70F menu at *La Cigale*, 18 rue de Millo (Mon–Fri only; closed Aug; ☎93.30.16.14). *Castelroc* in the old town on place du Palais (☎93.30.36.68; midday only, closed Sat) has a generous 100F menu. *Le Pinocchio* nearby at 30 rue Comte F-Gastaldi (☎93.30.96.20, evening only in season, closed Wed out of season) is a dependable Italian, with menus starting at 85F. It simply isn't worth going upmarket in Monaco unless you're prepared to hit 700F-a-head bills – in which case, dine at *Louis XV* in the *Hôtel de Paris* by the casino.

Menton

Of all the Côte d'Azur resorts, **MENTON** – the warmest and most Italianate, being within a couple of kilometres of the border – is the one that retains an atmosphere of aristocratic tourism, being even more of a rich retirement haven than Nice. It doesn't go in for the ostentatious wealth of Monaco nor the creativity cachet of Cannes and some hilltop towns. What it chiefly glories in is its climate and year-round lemon crops. It is ringed by protective mountains, and hardly a whisper of wind disturbs this sun-trap of a city. Winter is when you notice the difference most, when you'd need a change of clothes between here and the exposed central resorts.

Arrival and accommodation

Roquebrune and Cap Martin merge into Menton along the three-kilometre shore of the **Baie du Soleil**. The modern town is arranged around three main streets parallel to the promenade du Soleil. The **gare SNCF** is on the top one, bd Albert-1er, from which a short walk to the left as you come out brings you to the north–south av de Verdun and av de Boyer divided by the Jardins Biovès – central location for citrus sculptures during February's **Fête du Citron**. The **tourist office** is at 8 av Boyer (Mon–Sat 10am–noon & 2–5.30pm, Sun 10am–noon; out of season Mon–Sat; ☎93.57.57.00), in the Palais de l'Europe; the building was once a casino, but now hosts various cultural activities and contemporary art exhibitions.

The **gare routière** and the **urban bus station** are between the continuation of the two avenues north of the train line on the esplanade de Carei. All the local bus lines (flat rates) pass through the *gare routière*. The district of **Garavan**, further east again, is the most exclusive residential area and overlooks the modern marina.

Accommodation is, as ever, difficult. Menton is no less popular than the other major resorts, so in summer, you should definitely book ahead. The tourist office won't make reservations for you, though they will tell you where there are rooms free.

Hotels

Hôtel Beauregard, 10 rue Albert-1er (☎93.35.74.08). Classically furnished rooms and no attempt to foist breakfast on you. Closed Oct–Dec. ③.

Hôtel Belgique, 1 av de la Gare (☎93.35.72.66). More mundane option than the above, but no less clean and conveniently close to the station. Closed Dec. ③–④.

Napoléon, 29 porte France, Garavan (☎93.35.89.50). Wonderful views from the rooms. ④–⑤.

Hôtel Terminus, pl de la Gare (93.57.69.87). The cheapest rooms in Menton. ②.

M. Paul Gazzano, 151 rte de Castellar (☎93.57.39.73). *Chambres d'hôtes* two kilometres from Menton, a delightful house with a terrace looking down over the wooded slopes to the sea. ③.

Hostels and campsites

IYHF youth hostel, plateau St-Michel (☎93.35.93.14). The hostel is up a gruelling flight of steps from behind the *gare SNCF*, or take bus #6 from the *gare routière*, direction *Ciappes de Castellar*, stop *Camping St-Michel*. No advance booking, no card needed, 11pm curfew. Reception closed 10am–5pm. ①.

Camping St-Michel, plateau St-Michel (☎93.35.81.23). Reasonably priced campsite in the hills above the town, with plenty of shade and good views out to sea. March–Nov.

The Town

The **promenade du Soleil** runs along the pebbly beachfront of Menton's aptly named Baie du Soleil, stretching from the quai Napoléon III past the casino towards Roquebrune. The most diverting building on the front is a seventeenth-century fort by the quai Napoléon III south of the old port, now the **Musée Jean Cocteau** (daily 10am–noon & 3–7pm; mid-Sept to mid-June 10am–noon & 2–6pm; free), set up by the artist himself. It contains pictures of his Mentonaise lovers in the *Inamorati* series, a collection of delightful *Animaux fantastiques* and the powerful tapestry of *Judith and Holophernes* simultaneously telling the sequence of seduction, assassination and escape. There are also photographs, poems, a portrait by friend Picasso, and ceramics.

As the *quai* bends around the western end of the Baie de Garavan from the Cocteau museum, a long flight of black and white pebbled steps leads up into the **vieille ville** to the **Parvis St-Michel**, an attractive Italianate square hosting concerts during the summer and giving a good view out over the bay. The frontage of the **Église St-Michel** proclaims its Baroque supremacy in perfect pink and yellow proportions, and a few more steps up to another square will reward you with the beautiful façade of the **chapel of the Pénitents-Noirs** in apricot-and-white marble, with pastel campaniles and disappearing stairways between long-lived houses.

In the middle of the modern town, the **Salles des Mariages** (Mon–Fri 8.30am–12.30pm & 1.30–5pm; 5F), or registry office, forms part of the **Hôtel de Ville** on place Ardoino and was decorated in inimitable style by Jean Cocteau in 1957. It can be visited without matrimonial intentions by asking the receptionist by the main door. On the wall above the official's desk, a couple face each other with strange topological connections between the sun, her headdress and his fisherman's cap. A *Saracen wedding party* on the right-hand wall reveals a disapproving bride's mum, the spurned girlfriend of the groom and her armed, revengeful brother among the cheerful guests. On the left-hand wall is the story of *Orpheus and Eurydice* at the moment when Orpheus has just looked back. Meanwhile, on the ceiling are *Poetry rides Pegasus*, tattered *Science juggles with the Planets* and *Love*, open-eyed, waiting with bow and arrow at the ready. Adding a little extra confusion, the carpet is mock panther-skin.

On av de la Madone, at the other end of the modern town, an impressive collection of paintings from the Middle Ages to the twentieth century can be seen in the **Palais Carnolès** (Wed–Sun 10am–noon & 2–7pm; mid-Sept to mid-June 2–5.30pm; bus #3; free), the old summer residence of the princes of Monaco. Of the early works, the *Madonna and Child with St Francis* by Louis Bréa is exceptional. The most recent include canvases by Graham Sutherland, who spent some of his last years in Menton.

If it's cool enough to be walking outside, the public parks up in the hills and the gardens of **GARAVAN**'s once elegant villas make a change from shingle beaches. The best of all the Garavan gardens used to be **Les Colombières**, just north of bd de Garavan (daily 10am–noon & 2–6pm; closed Oct–Dec; bus #8, direction *bd de Garavan*, stop *Colombières*; 20F). They have been allowed to fall into ruin but plans are always afoot to resuscitate them, so you might be lucky. Designed by the artist Ferdinand Bac, they lead you through every Mediterranean style of garden. There are staircases screened by cypresses; balustrades to lean against for the soaring views through pines and olive trees out to sea; fountains, statues and a frescoed swimming pool. Otherwise, nearer to the *vieille ville* on the same bus route, there's the public **Parc du Pian**, shaded by olive trees, and the **Jardin Exotique** (20F), both below bd de Garavan.

Eating and drinking

Surprisingly, Menton is not blessed with streets of gorgeous Provençal **restaurants**. If you're not bothered about what you eat as long as it's cheap, the pedestrianized rue St-Michel is promising ground. For a proper **restaurant** meal in very elegant surroundings, there's *La Veranda* in *Hôtel Les Ambassadeurs*, 2 rue du Louvre (☎93.28.75.75), with an evening bistro menu for 160F. Menton also has two excellent Moroccan restaurants, both around the 200F mark: *La Mamounia*, 51 porte de France, Garavan (☎93.57.95.39), and *Le Darkoum*, 23 rue St-Michel (☎93.35.55.44).

travel details

Trains

The **Ventimiglia line** follows the coast more or less all the way from Marseille to Menton, running inland only over the stretch between Toulon and St-Raphaël. About five trains daily do the full journey; trains from Marseille to Nice are also frequent, as are trains from Nice to Menton.

Major stops on the Ventimiglia line from Marseille are: Toulon (40 min); St-Raphaël (1hr 50 min); Cannes (2hr 15mins); Antibes (2hr 30min); Nice (2hr 50min); Monaco (3hr 15 min); Menton (3hr 30min).

Cannes to: Menton (18 daily; 1hr 25min).

Marseille to: Antibes (frequent; 2hr 30min); Cannes (frequent; 2hr 15min); Cassis (frequent; 20min); La Ciotat (frequent; 25min); Hyères (1 daily; 1hr); Lille (3 TGVs daily; 5hr 30min); Menton (5 daily; 3hr 30min); Monaco (5 daily; 3hr 15min); Nice (frequent; 2hr 50min); Paris Gare de Lyon (4 TGVs daily; 4hr 10min); St-Raphaël (frequent; 1hr 50min); Toulon (frequent; 40min).

Nice to: Beaulieu-sur-Mer (frequent; 11min); Cagnes-sur-Mer (frequent; 15min); Cap d'Ail (frequent; 18min); Cap Martin-Roquebrune (frequent; 28min); Eze (frequent; 14min); Marseille (frequent; 2hr 15min–2hr 30min); Menton (frequent; 35–40min); Paris-Gare de Lyon (7 daily; 10hr 40min–12hr); Villefranche-sur-Mer (frequent; 7min).

St-Raphaël to: Dijon (15 daily; 7hr 50min); Lyon (15 daily; 4hr); Marseille (15 daily; 1hr 30min); Paris-Gare de Lyon (15 daily; 9hr 30min–10hr).

Toulon to: Hyères (4 daily; 20min).

Buses

Cannes to: Grasse (frequent; 45min); Nice airport (frequent; 45min); Vallauris (frequent; 15min).

Hyères to: Bormes (4 daily; 25min); Giens (14 daily; 25min); Le Lavandou (4 daily; 35min); Toulon SNCF (10 daily; 30min); St-Tropez (7 daily; 1hr 35min); La Tour-Fondue (9 daily; 20min).

Hyères/Toulon airport to: Cavalaire (2 daily; 1hr); La Croix-Valmer (2 daily; 1hr 20min); Le Lavandou (2 daily; 30min); Port Grimaud (2 daily; 1hr 20min); Ste-Maxime (2 daily; 1hr 30min); St-Tropez (2 daily; 1hr 30min).

Le Lavandou to: Bormes-les-Mimosas (1 daily; 10min); Cogolin (1 daily; 40min); La Garde-Freinet (1 daily; 1hr 20min).

Nice to: Beausoleil (5 daily; 50min); Biot (frequent; 50min); Cagnes-sur-Mer (frequent; 20min); Cannes (frequent; 1hr 30min); Menton (frequent; 45min); St-Paul (frequent; 40min); La Turbie (4 daily; 25min); Vence (frequent; 55min).

St-Raphaël to: Bagnols-en-Fôret (4 daily; 20min); Boulouris (7 daily; 15min); Cannes (7 daily; 1hr 10min); Cannes via N7 (6 daily; 50min); Fayence (4 daily; 45min); Fréjus (frequent; 10min); Nice airport (5 daily; 1hr 5min); St-Tropez (7 daily; 1hr 25min).

St-Tropez to: Bormes-les-Mimosas (1 daily; 45min); Cogolin (9 daily; 15min); Fréjus (9 daily; 1hr 10min); Gassin (3 daily; 20min); Grimaud (9 daily; 20min); Ramatuelle (3 daily; 25min); Ste-Maxime (9 daily; 40min); St-Raphaël (9 daily; 1hr 20min).

Toulon to: Cavalière (7 daily; 1hr 20min); La Croix-Valmer (7 daily; 1hr 50min); Hyères (7 daily; 35min); Le Lavandou (7 daily; 1hr 10min); St-Tropez (7 daily; 2hr 10min).

Ferries

For Îles d'Hyères and Îles de Lérins services see p.875 and p.892.

Marseille to: Ajaccio, Corsica (4–7 weekly; 9hr, 12hr overnight); Bastia, Corsica (3–4 weekly; 7hr, 12hr overnight); Porto-Vecchio, Corsica (July–Sept 1–3 weekly; 12hr overnight); Propriano, Corsica (April–Sept 1 weekly; 12hr overnight); L'Île Rousse, Corsica (April–Sept 2 weekly; 8hr).

Nice to: Ajaccio, Corsica (1–6 weekly; 12hr overnight); Bastia, Corsica (3–6 weekly; 12hr overnight); Calvi, Corsica (April–Sept 1–3 weekly; 5hr); L'Île Rousse, Corsica (April–Sept 1–3 weekly; 5hr).

St-Raphaël to: St-Tropez, Port Grimaud and the Îles de Lérins (summer excursions operated by MMG, quai Nomy).

Toulon to: Ajaccio, Corsica (April–Sept 1–4 weekly; 10hr overnight); Bastia, Corsica (April–Sept 1–3 weekly; 12hr overnight); Propriano, Corsica (June–Sept 1 weekly; 12hr overnight).

CHAPTER SIXTEEN

CORSICA

A round one and a half million people visit **Corsica** each year, drawn by a
climate that's mild even in winter and by some of the most astonishingly
diverse landscapes in all Europe. Nowhere in the Mediterranean has beaches
finer than Corsica's perfect half-moon bays of white sand and transparent
water, or seascapes more inspiring than the granite cliffs of the west coast. Even
though the annual influx of tourists now exceeds the island's population sixfold, tourism hasn't spoilt the place: there are a few resorts, but overdevelopment is rare and
high-rise blocks are nonexistent.

The island has always been of strategic and commercial appeal, set on the western
Mediterranean trade routes. Greeks, Carthaginians and Romans came in successive
waves, driving native Corsicans into the interior. The Romans were ousted by Vandals,
and for the following thirteen centuries the island was attacked, abandoned, settled and
sold as nation states, with generations of islanders fighting against foreign government.
Two hundred years of French rule have had a limited effect on Corsica, and the island's
Baroque churches, Genoese fortresses, fervent Catholic rituals and a Tuscan-
influenced indigenous language show a more profound affinity with neighbouring Italy.
Corsica has had a rather uneasy relationship with its motherland, relegated to the position of an outpost of France and largely neglected economically.

Capital of the north, **Bastia** was the principal Genoese stronghold, and its fifteenth-
century old town has survived almost intact. Of the island's two large towns, this is the
more purely Corsican, and commerce rather than tourism is its main concern. Also
relatively undisturbed, the northern **Cap Corse** harbours inviting sandy coves and
friendly fishing villages such as **Erbalunga** and **Centuri Port**. Within a short distance
of Bastia, the fertile region of the **Nebbio** contains a plethora of churches built by
Pisan stoneworkers, the prime example being the cathedral of Santa Maria Assunta at
the appealingly chic little port of **St-Florent**.

To the west of here, **L'Île-Rousse** and **Calvi**, the latter graced with an impressive
citadel and fabulous sandy beach, are major targets for holidaymakers. The spectacular
Scandola nature reserve can be visited by boat from the tiny resort of **Porto**, from
where walkers can also strike into the wild **Gorges de la Spelunca** and **Fôret
d'Aitone**. **Corte**, at the heart of Corsica, is the best base for exploring the stupendous

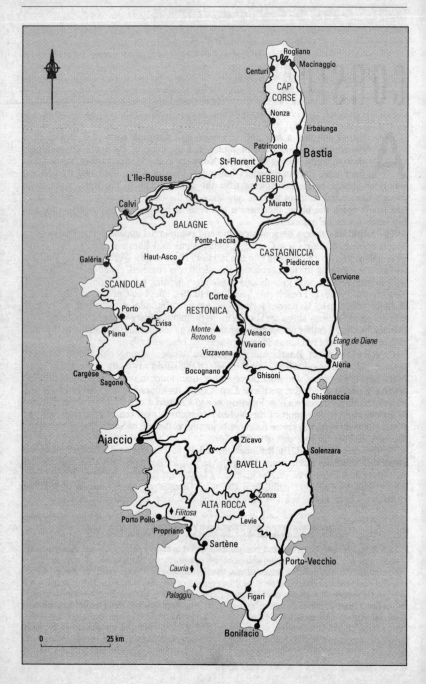

mountains and gorges of the interior which form part of the **Parc Naturel Régional** that runs almost the entire length of the island.

Sandy beaches and rocky coves punctuate the west coast all the way down to **Ajaccio**, Napoléon's birthplace and the island's capital. Its pavement cafés and palm-lined boulevards are thronged with tourists in summer, most sampling the watersport facilities of the expansive and beautiful **Golfe d'Ajaccio**. Slightly fewer make it to nearby **Filitosa**, greatest of the many prehistoric sites scattered across the south. Brash **Propriano**, the spot that has perhaps suffered most from the tourist boom, lies close to stern **Sartène**, seat of the wild feudal lords who once ruled this region and still the quintessential Corsican town.

More megalithic sites are to be found south of Sartène on the way to **Bonifacio**, a comb of ancient buildings perched atop furrowed white cliffs at the southern tip of the island. Equally popular **Porto-Vecchio** provides a springboard for excursions to the amazing beaches of the south. The eastern plain has less to boast of, but the Roman site at **Aléria** is worth a visit for its excellent museum.

Getting to Corsica

Ferries to Corsica from Marseille, Nice and Toulon are run by *SNCM Corsica Marittima*, and the crossing takes between seven and twelve hours on a regular ferry, and from two-and-a-half to three-and-a-half hours on the fast service from Nice. Crossings cost between 135F and 300F per person for a one-way crossing, plus between 220F and 600F per vehicle, with promotional discounts throughout the year; there is no extra supplement on the fast ferry. You can **book** through *SNCM Corsica Marittima* in France at 61 bd des Dames, Marseille 13002 (☎91.56.30.10); at the *Gare Maritime*, quai du Commerce, Nice 06303 (☎93.13.66.66); or 21 & 49 av de l'Infanterie

---

THE FOOD OF CORSICA

It's the maquis herbs – thyme, marjoram, basil, fennel and rosemary – which give Corsican cooking a unique flavour that's enhanced by olive oil and spices, especially in the south of the island, where flavours are less subtle than in the north.

You'll find the best **charcuterie** in the north, where pork is smoked and cured in the cold cellars of village houses – it's particularly tasty in the Castagniccia, where wild pigs feed on the chestnuts which were once the staple diet of the locals. Here you can also taste chestnut fritters (*fritelli a gaju frescu*) and chestnut cake (*pulenta*) sprinkled with sugar or *eau de vie*. **Brocciu**, a soft fromage frais made with ewe's milk, is found everywhere on the island, forming the basis for many dishes, including omelettes stuffed with *brocciu* and mint, and *canneloni al brocciu*. *Fromage Corse* is also very good – a unique hard cheese made in the sheep-rearing central regions, where *cabrettu a l'istrettu* (kid stew) is a speciality.

Game – mainly stews of hare and wild boar but also roast woodcock, partridge and wood pigeon – features throughout the island's mountain and forested regions. Here blackbirds (*merles*) are made into a fragrant pâté, and eel and trout are fished from the unpolluted rivers. **Fish** like red mullet (*rouget*), sea bream (*loup de mer*) and a great variety of shellfish is eaten along the coast – the best crayfish (*langouste*) comes from around the Golfe de St-Florent, whereas oysters (*huîtres*) are a speciality of the eastern plain.

Of the local **wine**, you should be sure to try the Santa Barba or Fiumicicoli wines of the Sartène area, which come in both rosé and red, and the Patrimonio, a robust white wine from Cap Corse. The favoured *apéritifs* are the sweet muscat produced on Cap Corse and the drink known as *Cap Corse*, a fortified wine flavoured with herbs. Note that **tap water** is particularly good quality in Corsica, coming from the fresh mountain streams.

> ### THE CORSICAN LANGUAGE
>
> **Corsican**, originally a Latin-based language with similarities to Romanian, developed an Italianate vocabulary and syntax during Pisan and Genoese occupation. Arabic and French influences have added to the complexity of Corsican, which was predominantly an oral tongue until around two hundred years ago – hence the confusing variety of spellings for place names, despite attempts at standardization. The commonest variants come about through the transposition of ll and dd – as in "casteddu" and "castellu". Buildings and monuments are often labelled in different languages (San Pietro/San Pietru), and on maps you'll find mountain passes, rivers and regions marked in a mixture of Italian, French and Corsican. Deep in the country, many old people are still easier with Corsican than French. Pronunciation is generally as for Italian, but look out for two tricky clusters of consonants – chj/chi and ghj/chi, pronounced ty or dy.

de Marine, Toulon 83000 (☎94.16.66.66); or through *Southern Ferries*, 179 Piccadilly, London W1V 9DB (☎0171/491 4968).

From **Marseille**, there are ferry connections to Ajaccio (Jan–Oct 2–4 weekly; 10hr overnight), Bastia (Jan–Oct 2–3 weekly; 12hr), L'Île Rousse (Aug 1 weekly; 8hr) and Propriano (April–Aug 1 weekly; 12hr overnight). You can also catch ferries from **Nice** to Ajaccio (1–6 weekly 11hr 30min overnight), Bastia (1–6 weekly, 6hr; fast 1 daily except Wed, 3hr 30min), Calvi (April–Sept 1–3 weekly, 5hr; fast 1 daily except Sat, 2hr 30min), L'Île Rousse (March–Sept 1–3 weekly; 5hr). From **Toulon**, you can take the ferry to Ajaccio (April–Sept 1–4 weekly; 10hr overnight), Bastia (April–Sept 1–3 weekly; 12hr overnight), or Propriano (June–Sept 1–4 weekly; 8hr).

Bastia and around

The dominant tone of Corsica's most successful commercial town, **BASTIA**, is one of charismatic dereliction, as the city's industrial zone is spread onto the lowlands to the south, leaving the centre of town with plenty of aged charm. The old quarter known as the **Terra Vecchia** makes a tightly packed network of haphazard streets, flamboyant Baroque churches and lofty tenements, their crumbling golden-grey walls set against a backdrop of fire-darkened hills. **Terra Nova**, the historic district on the opposite side of the old port, is a tidier area that's now Bastia's yuppie quarter.

The city dates from Roman times, when a base was set up at Biguglia to the south, although Bastia began to thrive under the Genoese, when wine was exported to the Italian mainland from Porto Cardo, forerunner of Bastia's Vieux Port, or Terra Vecchia.

Despite the fact that in 1811 Napoleon appointed Ajaccio capital of the island, initiating a rivalry between the two towns which exists to this day, Bastia soon established a stronger trading position with mainland France. The Nouveau Port, created in 1862 to cope with the increasing traffic with France and Italy, became the mainstay of the local economy, exporting chiefly agricultural products from Cap Corse, Balagne and the eastern plain.

Arrival, information and accommodation

Bastia's **Poretta airport** is 16km south of town off the Route Nationale (☎95.54.54.54); buses into the centre coincide with flights, dropping passengers at the train station for a fare of 35F. **Ferries** arrive at the Nouveau Port, just a five-minute walk to the centre of town; the *SNCM* office is at 15 bd de Gaulle (☎95.32.69.04). **Buses** from Ajaccio stop in bd Paoli, Bastia's main thoroughfare, whereas those coming from Porto Vecchio and Calvi stop in av du Maréchal-Sebastiani, which leads from the station to place St-

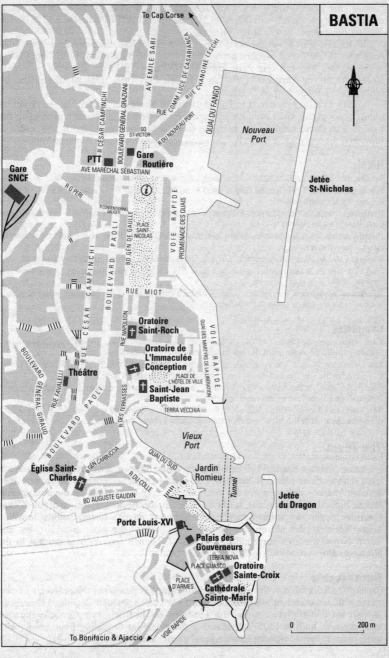

BASTIA

To Cap Corse

AV EMILE SARI

R CÉSAR CAMPINCHI

BOULEVARD GÉNÉRAL GRAZIANI

RUE COMM LUCE DE CASABIANCA

RUE CHANOINE LESCHI

QUAI DU FANGO

SQ ST-VICTOR

R DU NOUVEAU PORT

Nouveau Port

Jetée St-Nicholas

PTT

Gare Routière

AVE MARÉCHAL SÉBASTIANI

Gare SNCF

R G PERI

R CONVENTIONNEL SALICETI

PLACE SAINT-NICOLAS

BD GÉN DE GAULLE

VOIE RAPIDE

PROMENADE DES QUAIS

BOULEVARD PAOLI

RUE CÉSAR CAMPINCHI

RUE MIOT

RUE NAPOLEON

Oratoire Saint-Roch

Oratoire de L'Immaculée Conception

QUAI DES MARTYRS DE LA LIBÉRATION

VOIE RAPIDE

Théâtre

RUE FAVALELLI

BOULEVARD GÉNÉRAL GIRAUD

BOULEVARD PAOLI

R DES TERRASSES

PLACE DE L'HÔTEL DE VILLE

Saint-Jean Baptiste

TERRA VECCHIA

Vieux Port

Église Saint-Charles

R GÉN CARBUCCIA

QUAI DU SUD

R DU COLLE

BD AUGUSTE GAUDIN

Jardin Romieu

Tunnel

Jetée du Dragon

Porte Louis-XVI

Palais des Gouverneurs

TERRA NOVA

PLACE GUASCO

Oratoire Sainte-Croix

PLACE D'ARMES

Cathédrale Sainte-Marie

VOIE RAPIDE

To Bonifacio & Ajaccio

0   200 m

Nicolas, the main square. For local bus information, call ☎95.31.06.65. For long-distance buses to Ajaccio call *Ollandini*, 9 av du Maréchal Sebastiani (☎95.32.22.05), or *Rapides Bleus* at no. 1 (☎95.31.03.79).

The **tourist office** is at the north end of place St-Nicolas (Mon–Sat 9am–noon & 2–6pm; ☎95.31.00.89) and supplies a map of the town and a list of hotels and apartments in the region. You can rent **cars** from *Avis/Ollandini*, 9 av du Maréchal Sebastiani (☎95.32.57.30), or *Europcar*, 1 rue du Nouveau Port (☎95.31.59.26). **Bikes** can be rented from *Locacycles*, 8 bd Graziani.

You are usually guaranteed to find somewhere to **stay** in Bastia, but the choice of hotels is not great. Apart from the upmarket *Posta-Vecchia*, the classier places line the road to Cap Corse north of the port; the more basic ones are found in the centre of town, and there are a few even cheaper small *pensions* around the Nouveau Port.

Hotels

Forum, 20 bd Paoli (☎95.31.02.53). Attractively chic, with spacious rooms and bar. ③.

Hôtel de la Paix, 1 bd Général Giraud (☎95.31.06.71). Elegantly decorated. Worth the climb up the hill and the extra cost. ④.

Pietracap, route de San Martino, Pietranera (☎95.31.64.63). Luxury hotel with swimming pool. Closed mid-Dec to Feb. ⑤.

Posta-Vecchia, quai des Martyrs de la Libération (☎95.32.32.38). Large chic hotel with wonderful views across the sea. ①.

Riviera, 1 rue du Nouveau Port (☎95.31.07.16). Comfortable hotel that's handy for the port. ③.

Sud Hôtel, av de la Libération, Lupino (☎95.30.20.61). Charming place with a car park and friendly owners. About 1km south of town. ③.

Hôtel des Voyageurs, 9 av du Maréchal Sebastiani (☎95.31.08.97). In the touristy part of town – but useful for the buses going to Porto Vecchio. ③.

Campsites

Esperenza, route de Pineto (☎95.36.15.09). About 11km south of Bastia, beyond San Damiano (see below) and with fewer facilities. Hourly buses in summer from the *gare routière*.

Les Orangers, Miomo, 4km north along the route to Cap Corse (☎95.33.24.09). Shady and attractive site near the sea; the half-hourly bus to Erbalunga will drop you here.

Sables Rouges, on the beach (☎95.31.71.26). The closest campsite, situated 1km south of town at L'Arinella beach, but rather dirty and crowded.

San Damiano, Pineto, 10km south of Bastia (☎95.33 68.02). Huge and spacious with excellent facilities; take the road to the left across the bridge at Furiani roundabout. Buses as for the Esperenza.

The Town

Bastia isn't a large town and all its sights can easily be seen in a day without the use of a car. The spacious **place St-Nicolas** is the focus of town life: open to the sea and lined with shady trees and cafés, it's the most pleasant spot for soaking up the atmosphere. Running parallel to it on the landward side are **boulevard Paoli** and **rue César Campinchi**, the two main shopping streets, but all Bastia's historic sights lie within **Terra Vecchia**, the old quarter immediately south of the place Saint-Nicolas, and **Terra Nova**, the area surrounding the citadel. There's not much of interest in the **Nouveau Port** area, north of the *place*, other than restaurants and bars.

Terra Vecchia

From place Saint-Nicolas the main route into Terra Vecchia is **rue Napoléon**, a narrow street with some ancient offbeat shops and a pair of sumptuously decorated chapels on its east side. The first of these, the **Oratoire de St-Roch**, is a Genoese Baroque extravagance, built in 1604 and reflecting the wealth of the rising bourgeoisie, with walls of finely carved wooden panelling and a magnificent gilt organ.

A little further along stands the **Oratoire de L'Immaculée Conception**, built in 1611 as the showplace of the Genoese in Corsica, who used it for state occasions. Overlooking a pebble mosaic of a sun, the austere façade belies the flamboyant interior, where crimson velvet draperies, a gilt and marble ceiling, frescoes and crystal chandeliers create the ambience of an opera house. The sacristy houses a tiny **museum** (daily 9am–6pm) of minor religious works, of which the wooden statue of Saint Erasmus, patron saint of fishers, dating from 1788, is most arresting.

If you cut back through the narrow steps beside the Oratoire de St-Roch, a two-minute walk will bring you to place de l'Hôtel de Ville, commonly known as **place du Marché** after the market that takes place here each morning. Shouldering the south end of the square is the **church of St-Jean-Baptiste**, an immense ochre edifice that dominates the **Vieux Port**. Its twin campaniles are Bastia's distinguishing feature, but the interior is less than impressive – built in 1636, the church was restored in the eighteenth century in a hideous Rococo overkill of multicoloured marble. Decorating the walls are a few unremarkable Italian paintings from Napoléon's uncle, Cardinal Fesch, an avid collector of Renaissance art (see p.944).

Around the church extends the oldest part of Bastia, a secretive zone of dark alleys, vaulted passageways and seven-storey houses. By turning right outside the church and following rue St-Jean you'll come to rue General-Carbuccia, the heart of Terra Vecchia. Corsican independence campaigner Pascal Paoli (see p.957) once lived here, at no. 7, and Balzac stayed briefly at no. 23 when his ship got stuck in Corsica on the way to Sardinia. Set in a small square at the end of the road is the **church of St-Charles**, a Jesuit chapel whose wide steps provide an evening meeting place for the locals; opposite stands the **Maison de Caraffa**, an elegant house with a strikingly graceful balcony.

The **Vieux Port** is the most appealing part of town: soaring houses seem to bend inwards towards the water, peeling plaster and boat hulls glint in the sun, while the south side remains in the shadow of the great rock that supports the citadel. Site of the original *Porto Cardo* (see above), the Vieux Port later bustled with Genoese traders, but since the building of the ferry terminal and commercial docks it has become a backwater. It's livelier at night, with the glow and noise from the harbourside bars and restaurants, which continue round the north end of the port along the wide quai des Martyrs, where live bands clank out pop classics for the tourists in summer.

The best view of Bastia is from the jetée du Dragon, the quay that juts out under the citadel. To reach the citadel you can walk through the **Jardin Romieu**, the eighteenth-century terraced garden that ascends the cliff on this side of the harbour, now a notorious hang-out for dubious characters.

Terra Nova

The military and administrative core of old Bastia, **Terra Nova** (or the citadel) has a distinct air of affluence, its lofty apartments now colonized by Bastia's yuppies. The area is focused on **place du Donjon**, which gets its name from the squat round tower that formed the nucleus of Bastia's fortifications and was used by the Genoese to incarcerate Corsican patriots – Sampiero Corso was held in the dungeon for four years in the early sixteenth century. Next to the tower a strategically placed terrace bar commands a magnificent view that extends to Elba on a clear day.

Facing the bar is the impressive fourteenth-century **Palais des Gouverneurs**. With its great round tower, arcaded courtyard and battered orange paintwork, this building has a distinctly Moorish feel and was built for the governor and local bishop during the town's Genoese heyday. When the French transferred the capital to Ajaccio it became a prison, then was destroyed during Nelson's attack of 1794. The subsequent rebuilding was not the last, as parts of it were blown up by the Americans in 1943, and today the restorers are trying to regain something of the building's former grandeur. Part of the palace is given over to the **Musée d'Éthnographie** (Mon–Sat 9am–noon & 2–6pm;

25F), which presents the history of Corsica from prehistoric times to the present day. Its dusty vaulted chambers contain some fascinating historical titbits like a diminutive Roman sarcophagus decorated with hunting scenes, busts of famous Corsicans and an original 1755 Flag of Independence, with its distinctive Moorish emblem.

On the terrace of the museum stands the conning tower of the **submarine Casabianca**, which played a major part in the liberation of Corsica in World War II by ferrying weapons and ammunitions from Algeria. The sub was named after twelve-year-old Giocante de Casabianca, who died at Aboukir in 1798 when he refused to leave his father's ship after it had been attacked by Nelson's fleet – giving Felicia Hemans her inspiration for the poem beginning "The boy stood on the burning deck".

Back in place du Donjon, if you cross the square and follow rue Notre Dame you come out at the **church of Ste-Marie**. Built in 1458 and overhauled in the seventeenth century, it was the cathedral of Bastia until 1801, when the bishopric was transferred to Ajaccio. The over-restored façade is an ugly shade of peach, and there's nothing of interest inside except a small silver statue of the Virgin. Virtually next door, in rue de l'Evêché, stands the **Oratoire Ste-Croix**, a sixteenth-century church decorated in Louis XV style, all rich blue paint and gilt scrollwork. It houses another holy item, the Christ des Miracles, a blackened oak crucifix which in 1428 was discovered floating in the sea surrounded by a luminous haze. Beyond the church, the narrow streets open out to the tiny **place Guasco**, a delightful square at the heart of the citadel that typifies the exclusivity of Terra Nova. A few benches offer the chance of a rest before descending into the fray.

The beaches

Crowded with schoolchildren in the summer, the pebbly town **beach** in Bastia is only worth visiting if you're desperate for a swim. To reach it, go left at the flower shop on the main road south out of town, just beyond the citadel. A better alternative is the long beach of **L'Arinella** at Montesoro, a further 1km along the same road, the beginning of a sandy shore that extends along the whole east coast. A bus to L'Arinella leaves from outside *Café Riche* on boulevard Paoli every twenty minutes; just get off at the last stop and cross the train line to the sea. There are a couple of sailing and windsurfing clubs here, and a bar.

Eating and drinking

Numerous pizza vans are scattered about town, evidence of a strong Italian influence that's also apparent in the predominance of **pizzerias** and pasta places in the Nouveau Port area. The town also boasts some excellent inexpensive **restaurants** serving Corsican specialities: the posh places on the quai des Martyrs do the best *aziminu*, a Corsican version of *bouillabaisse*. Most of the good restaurants are to be found around the Vieux Port and on the quai des Martyrs, with a sprinkling in the citadel.

Drinking is serious business in Bastia, with the Casanis *pastis* factory on the outskirts of town in Lupino making the town's favourite drink. There are many bars and cafés all over town, varying from the stark and brightly lit bars of Terra Vecchia that are the haunt of old men, to the elegant, dimly lit cafés on place St-Nicolas. For a more sedate atmosphere, bd Paoli and rue Campinchi are lined with chi-chi *salons de thé* offering elaborate creamy confections, local chestnut cake and doughnuts.

Restaurants

U Cantarettu, Vieux Port. Corsican lasagne and sublime pizzas, along with a nightly concert of popular Corsican ballads courtesy of the owner; he doesn't do requests.

Casa Corsa, 1 quai des Martyrs. The freshest fish, and regional specialities such as *fiadone*, a kind of eggy cake.

Le Caveau du Marin, 4 quai des Martyrs. Welcoming little place decked out like a fishing hut, sharks' teeth and all. Seafood pasta a speciality.

Le Depôt, 22 rue César Campinchi. Rich, delicious pizzas with crême fraiche and Roquefort toppings, baked in a wood oven. Trendy modern decor, loud music.

Le Dernier Métro, 3 rue des Zéphirs. Elegant restaurant with a good reputation for classic French cuisine. Expensive.

Chez Jack, 19 rue César Campinchi. Tiny but comfortable family bistro with inexpensive French cuisine and sardonic service.

Le Paradou, pl Galetta. Inexpensive pasta, pizzas and steaks, just behind the Vieux Port. Popular with young Bastiais.

A Scaletta, Vieux Port. Entrance on the steps leading from the port to the church of St-Jean-Baptiste. Fresh fish, served on a precarious balcony overlooking the boats. Generous Corsican speciality menu at F65. Eau-de-vie on the house if you're lucky.

U Tianu, 4 rue Monsigneur Rigo. Sparse, trendy nationalist hang-out in a small insalubrious street off quai des Martyrs. Excellent *charcuterie* and a different menu everyday, featuring local dishes such as blackbird paté and hare and olive stew. Not to be missed.

Bars and cafés

Bar Corsica, 2 rue Spinola. Tucked away behind the Vieux Port, this is the place to hear traditional Corsican singing.

L'Escale, 12 rue Luce-de-Casabianca. Spacious bar with pool tables opposite the Nouveau Port.

L'Impériale, 6 bd Général-de-Gaulle. Busy café at the centre of place Saint-Nicolas. The only place which sells cigarettes late at night, so people are always coming and going.

Café Napoléon, 16 bd Général-de-Gaulle. Recently refurbished, elegant café, famous for its surly waiter, a character straight out of Asterix.

Les Palmiers, 8 bd Général-de-Gaulle. Popular café with young Bastiais. Good draught beer.

Café Riche, 29 bd Paoli. Large and busy café that's a centre for gambling, next door to the first betting shop in Corsica.

Le Richelieu, 1 bd Général-de-Gaulle. Stark and unpretentious bar with a pinball machine and a huge picture of Bastia's football team. Open very late.

La Marana, Mariana and the Étang de Biguglia

Traditionally the summer haunt of prosperous Bastia families, the sixteen-kilometre littoral known as **LA MARANA** lies a few kilometres south of Bastia. The beach here offers shady pine woods, restaurants and bars, though the sea is quite polluted. All this part of the coast is divided into holiday residences or sections of beach attached to bars, the latter freely open to the public. Try **A Pagoda**, about 5km along the road – popular with the young crowd, it has a disco and a large open-air bar. Another good spot is **Pineto**, the furthest beach along the road and therefore the least crowded in the summer, where the bus terminates.

Fed by the rivers Bevinco and Golo, the **Étang de Biguglia** is the largest lagoon in Corsica, with reed, moustached and cetti warblers during summer. In winter, Biguglia is a stop-off point for migrating grey herons, kingfishers, great crested grebes, little grebes, water rails and various species of duck, such as the spectacular red-crested pochard, immediately identifiable by its red bill, red feet and a bright red head.

The Roman town of **MARIANA**, just south of Étang de Biguglia, can be approached by taking the turning for Bastia's Poretta airport, 16km along the N193, or the more scenic coastal route through La Marana. It was founded in 93 BC as a military colony, but today's houses, baths and basilica are too ruined to be of great interest. It's only the square baptistery, with its remarkable mosaic floor decorated with dancing dolphins and fish looped around a bearded Neptune, that is worth seeking out.

Adjacent to Mariana stands the **church of Santa Maria Assunta**, known as La Canonica. Built in 1119 close to the old capital of Biguglia, it is the finest of around three hundred churches built by the Pisans in their effort to evangelize the island. Modelled on a Roman basilica, the perfectly proportioned edifice is decorated outside with Corinthian capitals plundered from the main Mariana site and with plates of Cap Corse marble, their delicate pink and yellow ochre hues fusing to stunning effect.

About 300m metres to the south of La Canonica stands **San Parteo**, built in the eleventh and twelfth centuries over the site of a pagan burial ground. A smaller edifice than La Canonica, the church also displays some elegant arcading and fine sculpture – on the south side, the door lintel is supported by two writhing beasts reaching to a central tree, a motif of oriental origins.

Cap Corse

Until Napoléon III had a coach road built around **Cap Corse** in the nineteenth century, the promontory was effectively cut off from the rest of the island, relying on Italian maritime traffic for its income – hence its distinctive Tuscan dialect. For all the changes brought by the modern world, Cap Corse still feels like a separate country, with wild flowers in profusion, vineyards and quiet, traditional fishing villages.

Forty kilometres long and only fifteen across, the cape is divided by a spine of mountains called the Serra, which peaks at Monte Stello, 1037m above sea level. The coast on the east side of this divide is characterized by tiny ports or marines, tucked into gently sloping river-mouths, alongside coves which become sandier as you go farther north. The villages of the western coast are sited on rugged cliffs, high above the rough sea and tiny rocky inlets that can be glimpsed from the corniche road.

For those without transport a circular tour bus operates daily from Bastia all year round. There's also a regular bus to **Erbalunga**, a placid fishing village 10km north of Bastia, where the buildings, ending in one of the ruined look-out towers for which the cape is famous, rise directly from the sea.

Erbalunga

Built along a rocky promontory 10km north of Bastia, the small port of **ERBALUNGA** is the highlight of the east coast, with aged, pale buildings stacked like crooked boxes behind a small harbour and ruined Genoese watchtower. A little colony of French artists lived here in the 1920s, and the village has drawn a steady stream of admirers ever since. It gets a fair number of tourists throughout the year, and come summer it's transformed into a veritable cultural enclave, with concerts and arty events adding a spark to local nightlife. The town is most famous for its Good Friday procession, known as the *Cerca* (The Search), which evolved from an ancient fertility rite.

A port since the time of the Phoenicians, Erbalunga was once a more important trading centre than Bastia or Ajaccio. With the increasing exportation of wine and olive oil, in the eleventh century it became the capital of an independent village state, ruled by the da Gentile family, who lived in the **palazzo** that dominates place de Gaulle.

In the harbour, a few **bars** shaded by an enormous chestnut tree look out across the water to the one **hotel**, the *Castel'Brando*, is sited at the entrance to the square (☎95.30.10.30; ④; closed Nov–March); it's an elegant old stone-floored building, but it's closed in winter and doesn't have a restaurant. For a restaurant meal you have the choice of *Le Pirate*, right on the sea some thirty metres from place de Gaulle, which has been here for years and serves mainly fish, and *Chez Antoine*, directly overlooking the jetty, which serves basic but excellent fish dishes and regional food, such as pasta with wild boar.

Macinaggio and around

A port since Roman times, well-sheltered **MACINAGGIO**, 20km north of Erbalunga, was developed by the Genoese in 1620 for the export of olive oil and wine to the Italian peninsula. Pascal Paoli landed here in 1790 after his exile in England, whereupon he kissed the ground and uttered the words "O ma patrie, je t'ai quitté esclave, je te retrouve libre" ("Oh my country, I left you as a slave, I rediscover you a free man") – a plaque commemorating the event adorns the wall above the ship chandlers. There's not much of an historic patina to the place nowadays, but with its boat-jammed **marina** and its line of colourful seafront awnings, Macinaggio has a certain appeal in itself. In addition, its proximity to some of the best beaches on Corsica make it irresistible.

The best place to **stay** is *Hôtel Les Îles*, opposite the marina (☎95.35.43.02; ③; closed winter), which has cosy rooms overlooking the port and a good restaurant. Otherwise your best bet is *U Libecciu*, behind the marina on the road that leads north off the D80 road to Rogliano (☎95.35.43.22; ③; closed mid-Oct to Feb), with spacious rooms and an excellent restaurant. *U Ricordu*, on the south side of the road to Rogliano (☎95.35.40.20; ⑤; includes breakfast), is along the same lines, and has a swimming pool. As for **restaurants**, the *Pizzeria San Columbu*, at the end of the port facing out to sea, does a passable seafood pizza, or you can have a Corsican feast at *Les Îles*, with good fresh fish dishes.

If you head away from town to the north, there are some stunning stretches of white sand and clear sea. The **Baie de Tamarone**, 2km along this stretch, has deep clear waters, making it a good place for diving and snorkelling. Just behind the beach the road forks, and if you follow the left-hand track for twenty minutes you'll come to the isolated Romanesque **Chapelle Santa-Maria**. Raised on the foundations of a sixth-century church, the building comprises a tenth-century chapel and a twelfth-century chapel merged into one, hence the two discrepant apses.

Three kilometres north of the chapel you come to **Plage Santa Maria**, a perfect arc of white sand overlooked by the huge Tour Chiapelle. Dramatically cleft in half and entirely surrounded by water, the ruined three-storied building was one of three built on the northern tip of the cape by the Genoese in the sixteenth century (the others are at Tollare and Barcaggio) as lookout posts against the increasingly troublesome Moorish pirates. As Macinaggio grew in importance, the towers began to be used also by health and customs officers, who controlled the maritime traffic with Genoa. Pascal Paoli established his garrison here in 1761, having been unsuccessful in his attempt to take Macinaggio, and contemplated building a rival port.

Centuri

From Macinaggio you can drive west across the promontory along an eight-kilometre hairpin road over the **Col St-Nicolas** (303m) and the **Col de Serra** (365m). Once you've passed over the second col you soon come to **CAMERA**, the first hamlet of the commune of **CENTURI**, where the bizarre cylindrical turrets of the **Château de Général Cipriani** (not open to the public) peer from the woods beneath the road. The smaller hamlet of **CANELLE**, overlooking Centuri-Port and accessible from Camera along the road heading north or on foot from the port, is known for its enormous fig trees, whose drooping branches overhang the houses and shadow the road.

When Boswell arrived here from England in 1765, the former Roman settlement of **CENTURI-PORT** was a tiny fishing village, recommended to him for its peaceful detachment from the dangerous turmoil of the rest of Corsica. Not much has changed since Boswell's time: Centuri-Port exudes tranquillity despite an influx of summer residents, several of them artists who come to paint the fishing boats in the slightly prettified harbour, where the grey stone wall is highlighted by the green serpentine roofs of the encircling cottages, restaurants and bars. The only drawback is that you'll find the small beach disappointingly muddy and not ideal for sunbathing.

Centuri-Port has more **hotels** than anywhere else on Cap Corse. The least expensive place, *Hôtel-Restaurant du Pêcheur* (☎95.35.64.47; ②; closed winter), the yellow building in the harbour, is also the most pleasant and fills up quickly in the high season; its rooms are agreeably cool, with thick stone walls, and it has a popular restaurant. The *Vieux Moulin* (☎95.35.60.15; ③; closed Oct–March) occupies a prime location behind the harbour on the right as you enter the village, but the rooms are stuffy and the obligatory 150F menu is not up to much. Otherwise you have *Hôtel U Marinara* (☎95.35.62.95; ②; closed Oct–March), behind *du Pêcheur*, also with a restaurant. For **campers** there's *Camping l'Isolettu*, 400m south (☎95.35.62.81), an uninviting option but the only choice in the vicinity.

Nonza

Eighteen kilometres south of Centuri and set high on a black rocky pinnacle dropping vertically into the sea, the village of **NONZA** is one of the highlights of the Cap Corse shoreline. It was formerly the main stronghold of the da Gentile family, and the remains of the **fortress** are still standing on the furthest rocks on the overhanging cliff.

Nonza is also famous for **Saint Julia**, patron saint of Corsica, who was martyred here in the fifth century. The story goes that she had been sold into slavery at Carthage and was being taken by ship to Gaul when the slavers docked here. A pagan festival was in progress, and when Julia refused to participate she was crucified; the gruesome legend relates that her breasts were then cut off and thrown onto a stone, from which sprang two springs, now enshrined in a chapel by the beach. To get there follow the sign on the right-hand side of the road before you enter the square, which points to the **La Fontaine de Ste-Julie**, down by the rocks.

You can **stay** in Nonza at *Auberge Patrizi* (☎95.37.82.16; ⑤; includes meal; closed mid-Oct to March), run from the big orange restaurant in the square. Made up of two village houses, the *Auberge* is an old-fashioned place where half-pension is obligatory, but the food is good and plentiful.

The Nebbio

Taking its name from the thick mists which sweep over the region, the **Nebbio** has for centuries been one of the most fertile parts of the island, producing honey, chestnuts and some of the island's finest wine. The Nebbio comprises the amphitheatre of rippled hills, vineyards and cultivated valleys that converge on **St-Florent**, a handful of kilometres due west of Bastia.

A bishopric until 1790, St-Florent is a chic coastal resort at the base of Cap Corse. It remains the Nebbio's chief town and best base, while villages such as **Olmeta-di-Tuda**, being close to Bastia, are lively and well-populated places. The wine produced around Patrimonio rivals that of Sartène. The two unmissable historic sites in this part of the island are the Pisan church of **Santa Maria Assunta**, just outside St-Florent, and the diminutive **San Michele de Murato**.

The only **public transport** serving Nebbio is the twice-daily bus that runs directly from Bastia to St-Florent.

St-Florent and around

Viewed from across the bay, **ST-FLORENT** (San Fiorenzu) appears as a bright line against the black tidal wave of the Tenda hills, the pale ancient houses seeming to rise straight out of the sea, overlooked by a huge circular **citadel**. It's a relaxing town, blessed with a decent beach and a good number of restaurants, but the key to its success is the **marina**, which has made St-Florent something of a low-key St-Tropez.

In Roman times, a town existed a kilometre east of the present village. Few traces remain of the settlement that grew up there, which in the fifteenth century was eclipsed by the port that developed around the new Genoese citadel. St-Florent prospered as one of Genoa's strongholds, and it was from here that Paoli set off for London in 1796, never to return.

Place des Portes, the centre of town life, has café tables facing the sea in the shade of plane trees, and in the evening fills with strollers and nonchalant boules players. In rue du Centre, which runs west off the square, parallel to the seafront and marina, you'll find some restaurants, a few shops and a couple of wine-tasting places – be sure to sample the sweet, maquis-scented muscat made around here. To reach the fifteenth-century circular **citadel** you climb to the end of rue du Centre and pass through the large wire gate. It's filled with pigeons, but does give a beautiful view of the hills of the Nebbio and the mountains of Cap Corse.

Just a kilometre to the east of the town off a small road running off place des Portes, on the original site of the Roman settlement of Nebbium, the **church of Santa Maria Assunta** – the so-called cathedral of the Nebbio – is a fine example of Pisan Romanesque architecture. Built of warm yellow limestone, the cathedral has a distinctly barn-like appearance – albeit a superlatively elegant one. Gracefully symmetrical blind arcades decorate the western facade, and at the entrance, twisting serpents and wild animals adorn the pilasters on each side of the door. The interior, too, appears deceptively simple. Carved shells, foliage and animals adorn the capitals of the pillars dividing the nave where, immediately to the right, you'll see a glass case containing the mummified figure of Saint Flor, a Roman soldier martyred in the third century.

Practicalities

Buses run from Bastia to St-Florent twice daily (except Sun), and arrive in the village car park. The journey takes one hour. For tourist information go to the **Centre Administratif** (Mon–Fri 9am–noon & 2–6pm; ☎95.37.06.04), which is on the Bastia road, next door to the *mairie*, about five minutes' walk from place des Portes.

St-Florent is a popular resort and **hotels** fill up quickly, especially at the height of summer when prior booking is essential. The elegant *Hôtel Europe* in place des Portes (☎95.37.00.33; ⑥) is the most attractive option. *Hôtel du Centre*, opposite the *Europe* (☎95.37.00.68; ③), has tiny rooms but an equally good view. All but the *Hôtel Europe* are closed during winter. A fair number of **campsites** are dotted about the coast, but are packed in August and closed out of season. *Camping U Pezzu*, rte de la Plage (☎95.37.01.65), is closest to town, 1km west on the small road which backs the beach. *Camping Kalliste*, 2km further on the same road (☎95.37.03.08), is clean and large, with its own beachside bar and restaurant.

St-Florent is renowned for its crayfish and red mullet, and a reasonably priced **restaurant** for excellent fish and Corsican specialities is *Le Cabistan* in the rue du Centre. More expensive is *La Marinuccia* at the far end of the same street, which serves the best fish in St-Florent and has a terrace jutting out into the sea. Otherwise *Pizzeria Citadel*, the fortress-shaped place just over the bridge south of the square, does very good pizzas and salads. The *Europe* is the most popular **café** in place des Portes. *Bar du Passage* opposite attracts a younger clientele, partly on account of its jukebox.

Patrimonio

As you leave St-Florent by the Bastia road, the first village you come to, after 6km, is **PATRIMONIO**, centre of the first Corsican wine region to gain *appellation controlée* status. Apart from the local muscat, which can be sampled in the village or at one of the *caves* along the route from St-Florent, Patrimonio's chief asset is the sixteenth-century **church of St-Martin**, occupying its own little hillock and visible for miles around. The colour of burnt sienna, it stands out vividly against the rich green vineyards. In a tiny garden close by stands a limestone statue-menhir known as U **Nativu**, a late megalithic piece dating from 800–900 BC. A carved T-shape on its front represents a breastbone, and two ears and a chin can also be made out.

Olmeta-di-Tuda to Murato

If you continue some 9km along the D82 from St-Florent, you come to the hamlet of **OLMETA-DI-TUDA**, which rises abruptly from the rocky slopes, with huge elm trees dominating the foreground and the distant peaks of Monte Astu creating a forbidding backdrop.

A further 3km along, the crossroads at the **Col de San Stefano** (349m) marks the entrance to the **Défilé de Lancone**, an exhilarating, precipitous descent that hits the main coast road 9km south of Bastia. Hewn out of the black rock, the Défilé is a road to be treated with respect – numerous little shrines along the way testify to the fatal smashes that have occurred here.

If you continue along the D5 instead of taking the Défilé, you'll soon pass the Pisan **church of San Michele de Murato**, which sits gracefully on a grassy ledge high above the hazy mountainous landscapes of the Nebbio. Built around 1280, this late Romanesque building is notable for its asymmetrical patterning of dark green serpentine and off-white marble. Outside, there's some sophisticated carving on the arches of the blind arcades and immediately beneath the roof, depicting gargoyles, wild beasts and human figures – look out for a relief on the north wall, showing an ashamed Eve reaching out to take the huge apple proffered by the serpent. Within the church you'll find less to catch the eye, though there's a faded fifteenth-century Annunciation frescoed on the arch of the apse. The church is always open to visitors.

The Balagne

Much of Corsica's northwest is taken up by the **Balagne**, a fertile region marked by a lush coastline and characterized by olive groves and a ribbon of ritzy private marinas and holiday villages, like **L'Île Rousse** and **Calvi**, which lie close to some remarkable beaches. The Balagne hinterland is a glorious landscape close to the borders of the *Parc Naturel Régional*, where the **Réserve Naturel de Scandola** gives the opportunity to witness wildlife and a geological freakshow close up.

L'Île Rousse

Developed by Pascal Paoli in the 1760s as a "gallows to hang Calvi", the port of **L'ÎLE ROUSSE** (Isula Rossa) simply doesn't convince as a Corsican town, its palm trees, smart shops, neat flower gardens and colossal pink seafront hotel creating an atmosphere that has more in common with the French Riviera. Pascal Paoli had great plans for his new town on the Haute-Balagne coast, which was laid out from scratch in 1758 as a port to export the olive oil produced in the Balagne region. A large part of the new port was built on a regular grid system, featuring lines of straight parallel streets quite at odds with the higgledy-piggledy nature of most Corsican villages and towns. Thanks to the busy trading of wine and oil, it soon began to prosper and, two and a half centuries later, still thrives as a successful port. These days, however, the main traffic consists of holidaymakers.

L'Île Rousse is easily accessible by **bus** from Bastia and Calvi, and the **train** stops here on the Calvi–Ponte-Leccia line.

Arrival and accommodation

The **train station** is on rte du Port, 500m south of where the ferries arrive. The Bastia–Calvi **bus** stops just south of place Paoli in the town's main thoroughfare, av Piccioni. The *SNCM* office is on av J-Calizi (☎95.60.09.56), and the **tourist office** on the south side of place Paoli (June–Sept daily 9am–noon & 2–7pm; ☎95.60.04.35).

Such a long season (May–Oct) means that L'Île Rousse fills up early in the year and it can be difficult to find a **hotel**, so be prepared to hunt around. Most places are modern buildings, more functional than personable.

HOTELS

L'Amiral, 5 bd de la Mer (☎95.60.28.05). Proximity to the beach is the main attraction of this hotel, although it has a bar terrace. Closed Nov–March. ③.

Napoléon Bonaparte, 3 pl Paoli (☎95.60.06.09). Garish converted palazzo which for years was the only luxury hotel on the island; it still has a certain old-fashioned appeal. Closed Nov–March. ②.

Santa Maria, in the port (☎95.60.13.49). Hardly an attractive locale, but this is one of the larger low-budget places. Rooms are adequate. ③.

Splendide, 4 rue Comte Valéry (☎95.60.00.24). Thirties-style building with a new swimming pool. Price includes breakfast. Twenty-percent reduction for stays of a week or more. ④.

The Town

All roads in L'Île Rousse lead to **place Paoli**, a shady square that's open to the sea and has as its focal point a fountain surmounted by a bust of "U Babbu di u Patria" (Grandfather of the Nation), one of many local tributes to Pascal Paoli. There's a Frenchified covered **market** at the entrance to the square, while on the west side rises the grim façade of the **church of the Immaculate Conception**, currently under large-scale restoration.

To reach the **Île de la Pietra**, the islet that gives the town its name, continue north, passing the station on your left. Once over the causeway connecting the islet to the mainland, you can walk through the crumbling mass of red granite as far as the lighthouse at the far end, from where the view of the town is spectacular, especially at sundown, when you get the full effect of the red glow of the rocks. Heading back along **A Marinella**, which follows the seafront behind the town beach, a ten-minute walk will bring you to the aquarium, the main sight in the town. The **Musée Océanographique** (April–Oct Mon–Fri 10.30am–1pm & 2–7pm; 35F), situated at the north end of the beach, publicizes itself as the "Grotte aux Requins", although the only members of the shark family on display are some timid dogfish. Nonetheless, the guided tour of tanks full of lobsters, conger eels, rays, octopuses and scores of other aquatic species is interesting, especially at feeding time, which can be a hair-raising experience.

Although L'Île Rousse has a decent beach, the most popular one hereabouts is **Plage de Rindara**, a fantastic duned strand with pale-green translucent water, 4km southwest of the town. Equally spectacular **Plage de Lozari**, a long semicircular sweep of white sand, lies 7km northeast of town. A decent road signposted "Lozari" leads down to the shore and a discreet holiday village, *De Lozari* (☎95.60.08.74), which offers upmarket accommodation and attracts big crowds in summer.

Eating and drinking

Tourism has taken its toll here, hence the abundance of mediocre **eating** places in the town. A few restaurants do stand out, however, some with classic gourmet menus and other Corsican places serving superb fresh seafood. The best cafés are found in place Paoli along the southern side.

Chez Paco, rue Paoli. Young inexpensive hang-out with tasty Spanish food and spicy fish dishes.

Le Grand Bleu, rue Napoléon. Brash decor but excellent and expensive food, mainly French fish dishes such as sea bass with fennel.

Le Grillon, av Paul Doumer. Popular and pricey French grill, whose *steak au Roquefort* is a dream.

L'Île d'Or, place Paoli. Bustling basic bistro, in a prime location for watching the *boules* players.

La Jonque, rue Paoli. Trendy, compact place serving Vietnamese food at reasonable prices.

A Merenda, rue Napoleon. One of the town's few Corsican places, with wholesome soups and stews, as well as fresh fish.

Calvi

Seen from the water, **CALVI** is a beautiful spectacle, with its three immense bastions topped by a crest of ochre buildings, sharply defined against a hazy backdrop of snow-capped mountains. Twenty kilometres west along the coast from L'Île Rousse, Calvi began as a fishing port on the site of the present-day *basse ville*, below the citadel, and remained just a cluster of houses and fishing shacks until the Pisans conquered the island in the tenth century. It wasn't until the arrival of the Genoese that the town became a stronghold when, in 1268, Giovaninello de Loreto, a Corsican nobleman, built a huge citadel on the windswept rock overlooking the port and named it Calvi. A fleet commanded by Nelson launched a brutal two-month attack on the town in the 1750s, and Nelson lost his eye; he left saying he hoped never to see the place again.

The French concentrated on developing Ajaccio and Bastia during the nineteenth century, and the town became primarily a military base, used as a point for smuggling arms to the mainland in World War II. A hang-out for European glitterati in the 1950s, Calvi now has the ambience of an old-fashioned English resort, the glamorous bars supplanted by souvenir shops and ice-cream stalls.

Arrival and accommodation

Ste-Catherine airport lies 6km south of Calvi (☎95.65.20.09); the only public transport into town is by taxi, which shouldn't cost more than 50F. The **train station** is on av de la République, close to the marina (☎95.65.00.61), where you'll find the **tourist office** on quai Landry (May–Oct Mon–Fri 9am–noon & 2–6pm, Sat 9am–noon; ☎95.65.16.67) – the staff will book rooms for a small fee. **Buses** from Bastia stop outside the station but those from Porto and Ajaccio use place Christophe-Colomb. You can find bus information at the *Agence de Beaux Voyages* on place de la Porteuse d'Eau (☎95.65.11.35). **Ferries** come in at the Port de Commerce at the centre of the *basse ville*, and the *SNCM* office is at quai Landry (☎95.65.01.38). You can rent **bikes** from *Location Ambrosini* on place Bel-Ombra, heading out of town towards Porto (☎95.65.02.13), and **cars** from *Aloha* (☎95.65.28.08), *Europcar* (☎95.65.10.19), or *Garage Luigi* (☎95.65.15.31), all at the airport.

Accommodation is easy to find in Calvi except during June's jazz festival. There are some excellent hotels, ranging from cheap *pensions* to more upmarket places. Those on a tight budget can choose between two youth hostels and several campsites within walking distance of the town.

HOTELS

Balanea, 6 rue Clemenceau (☎95.65.00.45). Grand place at the centre of the marina, with lavish rooms and excellent views of the citadel and sea. ④.

Belvedère, pl Christophe-Colomb (☎95.65.01.25). Large, simple rooms, in a good location in between the citadel and *basse ville*. ②.

Christophe Colomb, pl Christophe-Colomb (☎95.65.06.04). Spacious rooms with expansive views across the bay. Closed Nov–March. ④.

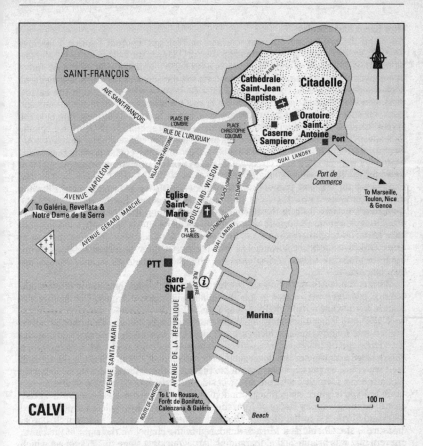

Grand Hotel, 3 bd Wilson (☎95.65.09.74). Old-fashioned luxury hotel in centre of town. Swish cocktail bar and restaurant. Closed mid-Oct to mid-March. ⑤.

Le Kalliste, 1 av du Commandant-Marche (☎95.65.09.81). Small dark rooms in the centre of town, but with its own restaurant. Closed Nov–March. ④.

YOUTH HOSTELS AND CAMPSITES

IYHF Corsotel youth hostel, 43 av de la République (☎95.65.33.72). Huge youth hostel in a prime position opposite the station and facing the sea. Very clean rooms for up to six people, some with balconies. Breakfast included. ①.

Relais International de la Jeunesse, 4km from the centre of town on the Route de Pietra-Maggiore (☎95.65.14.16). Follow the N197 for 2km, turn right at the sign for Pietra-Maggiore, and the hostel – two little houses with dormitories looking out over the gulf – is in the village another 2km further on. Breakfast included. ①.

Camping La Pinède, 1km east of Calvi between the beach and the N197 (☎95.65.17.00). Popular site in pine forest with bar and restaurant. April–Oct.

Camping-caravanning Bella Vista, 2km along the N197 from Calvi (☎95.65.11.76). A quiet and friendly site; to get to it, turn right at the sign to Pietra-Maggiore, and the campsite's another 1km along on the right-hand side. April–Oct.

The town and citadel

Social life in Calvi focuses on the restaurants and cafés of the **quai Landry**, a spacious seafront walkway linking the marina and the port. This is the best place to get the feel of the town, but as far as sights go, there's not a lot to the **basse ville**. At the far end of the quay, under the shadow of the citadel, stands the sturdy **Tour du Sel**, a medieval look-out post once used to store imported salt. If you strike up through the narrow passageways off quai Landry, you'll come to **rue Clemenceau**, where restaurants and souvenir shops are packed into every available space. In a small square giving onto the street stands the imposingly white **Ste-Marie-Majeure**, built in 1774, whose spindly bell tower rises elegantly above the cafés on the quay but whose interior contains nothing of interest. From the church's flank, a flight of steps connects with **boulevard Wilson**, a wide modern high street which rises to **place Christophe-Colomb**, point of entry for the **haute ville**, or citadel.

Beyond the ancient **gateway** to the citadel, with its inscription of the town's motto, you come immediately to the enormous **Caserne Sanpiero**, formerly the governor's palace. Built in the thirteenth century, when the great round tower was used as a dungeon, the **castle** was recently restored and is currently used for military purposes, and therefore closed to the public. The best way of seeing the rest of the citadel is to follow the ramparts, which connect three immense bastions. From each bastion the views across the sea, the Balagne and the Cinto Massif are magnificent.

Within the walls the houses are tightly packed along tortuous stairways and narrow passages that converge on the diminutive place d'Armes. Dominating the square is the **Cathédrale St-Jean-Baptiste**, set at the highest point of the promontory and sitting uncomfortably amid the ramshackle buildings. This chunky ochre edifice was founded in the thirteenth century, but was partly destroyed during the Turkish siege of 1553 and then suffered extensive damage twelve years later, when the powder magazine in the governors' palace exploded. It was rebuilt in the form of a Greek cross, as you see today. Inside, to the left of the entrance, are three elaborate alabaster fonts which date from 1568; beside the ostentatious marble altar stands a finely carved eighteenth-century wooden pulpit, and in the apse there's a seventeenth-century wooden statue of John the Baptist, framed by a solemn triptych dated 1498 and attributed to the obscure Genoese painter Barbagelata. The church's great treasure is the **Christ des Miracles**, housed in the chapel on the right of the choir; this crucifix was brandished at marauding Turks during a siege of 1553, an act which reputedly saved the day.

To the north of place d'Armes in rue de Fil stands the shell of the building that Calvi believes was **Christopher Columbus's birthplace**, as the plaque on the wall states, but the claim rides on pretty tenuous circumstantial evidence. The house itself was destroyed by Nelson's army during the siege of 1794, but as recompense a statue was erected on May 20, 1992, the 500th anniversary of his "discovery" of America; his alleged birthday, October 12, is now a public holiday in Calvi.

Calvi's outstanding **beach** sweeps right round the bay from the end of quai Landry, but most of the first kilometre or so is owned by bars which rent out sun loungers for a hefty price. To avoid these, follow the track behind the sand which will bring you to the start of a more secluded stretch. The sea might not be as sparklingly clear as at many other Corsican beaches, but it's warm, shallow and free of rocks.

Eating and drinking

Eating is a major pastime in Calvi, where you'll find a wide selection of restaurants and snack bars catering for all tastes. Fish restaurants predominate in the marina, where – at a price – you can eat excellent seafood fresh from the bay. It's cheaper to eat in the inland streets of *basse ville*, whose stairways and cramped forecourts hide a host of buzzing pizzerias and Corsican restaurants. **Cafés**, complete with raffia parasols, line the marina, becoming more expensive the nearer they are to the Tour du Sel.

CAFÉS AND BARS

Bar au Mal Assis, opposite the cathedral in the citadel. Café that's popular with locals.

Café des Marins, quai Landry. Looks like a huge boat inside, with portholes and a curvy bar. The best place for breakfast.

Café Rex, cnr bd Wilson/pl Christophe-Colombe. Full of singing locals and people waiting for the bus.

RESTAURANTS

U Casanu, 18 bd Wilson. Tasty and simple local dishes, inexpensive set menus and cosy little booths for the antisocial.

U Minellu, 3 bd Wilson. A friendly pizzeria with Corsican specialities at a moderate price.

Pizzeria La Galère, 6 rue des Anges. Unusual pasta dishes, such as tortelloni stuffed with aubergines and wild mushrooms. Trendy yet friendly.

Le San Carlu, pl St-Charles, off rue Clemenceau. Fine seafood, excellent paella, and menus at various reasonable prices. Nice garden terrace.

Le Santa-Maria, rue Clemenceau. Good-value four-course tourist menus. One of the few places you can eat *stifatu*, a local dish combining different meats rolled up.

Le Semiramis, av Paul-Doumer. Expensive, delicious fish dishes, couscous and desserts.

Chez Tao, rue St-Antoine, in the citadel. Expensive, legendary nightclub, now turned into a piano bar that serves excellent nouvelle cuisine and local fish dishes. Outstanding view of the bay.

Girolata and the Réserve Naturel de Scandola

Connected by a mere mule track to the rest of the island, and dwarfed by the plunging maquis-shrouded slopes, the tiny fishing haven of **GIROLATA**, 25km southwest of Calvi, has a dreamlike quality that's highlighted by the vivid red of the surrounding rocks. A short stretch of stony beach and a few houses are overlooked by a stately watchtower, built later in the seventeenth century in the form of a small castle by the Genoese and set high on the hills above the beach. There are no hotels, but *La Cabane du Berger* (☎95.20.16.98; ③), in the village above a good **restaurant**, is a reasonable **gîte d'étape**.

The **Réserve Naturel de Scandola** takes up the promontory west of Girolata, its name derived from the wooden tiles (*scandules*) that cover many of the island's mountain houses, but the area's rooflike rock formations are only part of its amazing geological repertoire. Its stacked slabs, towering pinnacles and gnarled claw-like outcrops were formed by volcanic eruptions 250 million years ago, and subsequent erosion has fashioned shadowy caves, grottoes and gashes in the rock. Scandola's colours are as remarkable as the shapes, the hues varying from the charcoal grey of granite to the incandescent rusty purple of porphyry.

The headland and its surrounding water were declared a nature reserve in 1975 and now support colonies of gulls and cormorants, dolphins, more than 450 types of seaweed and some remarkable fish such as the grouper, a species more commonly found in the caribbean. Scandola can be viewed only by **boat**, which means taking one of the daily excursions from Calvi and Porto. These leave from Calvi at 9am and Porto to 9.15am and 2.30pm (April–Oct), the first two stopping for two hours at Girolata (see p.935) and returning in the late afternoon. The later boat from Porto only stops for 45 minutes, but is a fascinating journey and well worth the 250F.

The GR20 runs close to the length of Corsica – 140km from Calenzana, 7km southeast of Calvi, to Conca near Porto-Vecchio in southern Corsica, through the *Parc Naturel Régional de la Corse* that takes up most of the island's hinterland. Despite the hardships of the trail, it's a very popular hike, with as many as a thousand walkers doing it at any one time – though many people cut the walk in half by starting at the Col de Vizzavona in the centre of the island, reached by the N193. It should only be attempted by those with sound experience of mountain-hiking, and it's essential to be prepared for sudden variations in climatic conditions. In some particularly hazardous parts of the route, the GR20 becomes more of a climb than a walk, with stanchions, cables and ladders driven into the rock as essential aids.

Practicable from mid-June until November, the GR20 is divided into fifteen stages of six to eight hours, each clearly marked by red and white paint flashes and starting and finishing at a mountain refuge. Booking isn't possible for these basic and often unstaffed huts, and meals are not available at them, so you need to stock up en route, either in the villages or at the main passes of Col de Vergio, Col de Vizzavona, Col de Bavella and Col de Verde, which have stores selling basic provisions – the first three also have restaurants.

Camping wild is forbidden in the *Parc Naturel*. An alternative to the refuges is to take farmhouse accommodation in **gîtes d'étapes** along the way, but you have to book these in advance. You can get current **details** from the main office of the *Parc Naturel Régional de la Corse* in rue Fiorella, Ajaccio (☎95.21.56.54), or enquire at the *mairie* in Calenzana, which has a subsidiary office (☎95.62.76.66).

Starting the round trip from Calvi, the first port of call is the **Baie d'Elbu**, where the rocks stand out red against a deep blue sea. Two kilometres south of here lies the **Punta Palazzu**, so called because of the soaring rocky towers that spring from the sea like a giant palace. Beyond here the boat weaves through the narrow straits by the Île **de Gargalo**, an islet created from volcanic lava where the most westerly point on Corsica is marked by a lighthouse.

Porto and around

The overwhelming proximity of the mountains, combined with the pervasive eucalyptus and spicy scent of the maquis, give **PORTO**, 30km south of Calvi, a uniquely intense, loaded atmosphere that makes it one of the most interesting places to stay on the west coast. Except for a watchtower built here by the Genoese in the second half of the sixteenth century, the site was only built upon with the onset of tourism since the 1950s; today the town is still so small that it can become claustrophobic in July and August and eerily deserted off-season.

The Town

Eucalyptus-bordered **route de la Marine** links the two parts of the resort. A strip of shops and hotels a kilometre from the sea makes up the actual village of Porto, but the main focus of activity is the small marina, located at the avenue's end. It's about a fifteen-minute walk from the marina up to the **Genoese Tower**, a square chimney-shaped structure that was cracked by an explosion in the seventeenth century, when the tower was used as an arsenal. An awe-inspiring view of the crashing sea and maquis-shrouded mountains makes it worth the short climb. The **beach** consists of a pebbly cove south beyond the shoulder of the massive rock supporting the tower. To reach it from the marina, follow the little road that skirts the rock, cross the wooden bridge which spans the River Porto on your left, then walk through the car park under the trees. Although it's rather exposed, and the sea very deep, the great crags overshadowing the shore give the place a vivid edge.

Practicalities

The **bus** from Calvi stops a little way north of the village, but leaves from the marina; Ajaccio is served by minibus, arriving in and leaving from the marina. There's also a **tourist office** in the village (June–Sept Mon–Fri 10am–noon & 2–6pm; ☎95.26.10.55). Information about and tickets for boat excusions to Scandola and the Calanche are available from *Boutique Anthony* in the marina (May–Oct Mon–Fri 9am–noon & 2–6pm). As for **hotels**, the most expensive places are found in the village, like the *Bella Vista*, three doors down from the bank (☎95.26.11.08; ②; mid-Oct to April), whose well-furnished rooms have balconies and an outstanding view of the mountains. *La Vaita*, next door to the supermarket (☎95.26.10.36; ③; closed Nov–March), is a long-established family-targeted place. The small and cosy *Le Golfe*, at the base of the rock in the marina (☎95.26.13.33; ③; closed Jan), has a small restaurant on the ground floor. The larger hotels cut their prices dramatically in September in order to entice the straggling tourists. The nearest **campsites** are just a bit farther inland from the village, with the *Camping les Oliviers* high on the slopes 1500m inland at the junction of the road to Ota (☎95.26.14.49), and *Camping Sole e Vista* close by (☎95.26.15.71).

Pizzerias and standard hotel-restaurants make up the bulk of **eating places** in Porto, with prices generally increasing the nearer you get to the tower. Try the moderately priced *Bar le Tour Genoise*, right opposite the tower, with snacks in the bar and a restaurant serving a lot of fresh fish and basic Corsican cuisine, or the expensive *Soleil Couchant*, at the foot of the tower, serving excellent pizzas. Just beyond the village at the junction of the Calvi and Evisa roads is *Le Moulin*, with delicious French food and some tasty regional dishes such as *sanglier en daube*, a rich wild boar stew.

The Calanche

The UNESCO-protected site of **the Calanche**, 5km southeast of Porto, takes its name from *calanca*, the Corsican word for creek or inlet, but the outstanding characteristics here are the vivid orange and pink rock masses and pinnacles which crumble into the dark blue sea. Liable to unusual patterns of erosion, these tormented rock formations and porphyry needles, some of which reach 300m above the sea, have long been associated with different animals and figures, of which the most famous is the *Tête de Chien* at the north end of the stretch of cliffs. Other figures and creatures conjured up include a Moor's head, a monocled bishop, a bear and a tortoise.

One way to see the fantastic cliffs of the Calanche is by boat from Porto; excursions leave daily in summer, cost 100F and last about an hour. Alternatively, you could drive along the corniche road which weaves through the granite archways on its way to Piana. Eight kilometres along the road from Porto, the *Roches Bleues*, once a restaurant but now abandoned, is a convenient landmark for walkers.

The Gorges de Spelunca

Spanning the two kilometres between the villages of Ota and Evisa, a few kilometres east of Porto, the **Gorges de Spelunca** are a formidable sight, with bare orange granite walls, a thousand metres deep in places, plunging into the foaming green torrent created by the confluence of the rivers Porto, Tavulella, Onca, Campi and Aitone. The sunlight, ricocheting across the rock walls, creates a sinister effect that's heightened by the dark jagged needles of the encircling peaks. The most dramatic part of the gorge can be seen from the road, which hugs the edge for much of its length.

EVISA's bright orange roofs emerge against a lush background of chestnut forests about 10km from Ota, on the eastern edge of the gorge, and the town makes the best base for hiking in the area. Situated 830m above sea level, the village caters well for hikers and makes a pleasant stop for a taste of mountain life.

The best place to **stay** is the cosy, rambling *Hôtel du Centre* (☎95.26.20.92; ③; closed Oct–June) opposite the statue in the centre of the village; the attached restaurant serves wholesome Corsican specialities. *Hôtel l'Aitone*, at the north exit to the village (☎95.26.20.04; ③; closed winter; closed mid-Nov to Dec), is a large country hotel with comfortable rooms, a swimming pool, and a reputation for gastronomic prowess. *Camping Paisolu d'Aitone* (☎95.26.20.39), 1km east of the village, is a smart all-year **campsite**.

An enjoyable short **walk** from Evisa runs down to the local chestnut wood beneath the village. About 250m west of the village a stone gateway leads into the wood, from where you soon emerge into a field of bracken. The view here embraces the Golfe de Porto, the Gorges de Spelunca and Ota. This is a good walk to do at sunset, when the colours can be amazingly vivid.

The five-kilometre walk from Evisa to Ota is basically easy-going, although from Ota you may well prefer to hitch back to Evisa rather than climb back up through the gorge. Follow the road west of the village as far as the cemetery, where a steep path marked "Ota–Evisa" descends into the gorge, through maquis interspersed with pines. Already you'll be able to see Ota, with the pink crags behind it. Continue through the mossy trees, past precipitous walls of bald grey rock, until you hit the river, and then follow it. About 45 minutes from Evisa, the Genoese Pont de Zaglia appears, a row of alders leaning across its cobbled walkway – a good place for a swim. Carry on for 2km and you will come out at the D124; past the two road bridges known as the Ponts d'Ota, carry on for 100m, then take the track on the left of the D124, following the orange paint marks. After 400m you'll rejoin the river, and another 800m will bring you to the Ponte Vecchio or Pont de Pianella, a perfectly restored Genoese bridge at the confluence of the Onca and the Porto, and another good bathing spot. Cross the bridge and turn left through the gate, carrying on along the river past two blades of rock, and climb up the hill into **OTA**.

Forêt d'Aitone

Thousands of soaring Laricio pines, some of them as much as 50m tall, make up the **Forêt d'Aitone**, just a few kilometres east of Evisa, the most beautiful forest in Corsica. It reaches 1391m at its highest point – the **Col de Salto** – and extends over ten square kilometres between Evisa and the **Col de Verghio**, the highest point in Corsica that's traversable by road. Well-worn tourist paths cross the forest at various points, but local wildlife still thrives here.

You can park 7km along the road from Evisa by the **Maison Forestière d'Aitone**, the forest headquarters and information centre (June–Sept 9am–noon & 2–6pm) and a starting-off point for walks in the area. One of the most popular short walks goes to the **Belvedère**, a great projecting rock 5km north of Evisa. To reach it, follow the signposted track leading into the forest, from beside a wide lay-by on the left-hand side of the road. The magnificent view across the valley takes in the rivers Aitone and Porto, rushing between high walls of copper-tinted rocks down to the Gorges de Spelunca. Another well-trekked route leads to the multiple **Cascades de la Valla Scarpa**, where the crystalline waters of the Aitone crash into a pool hollowed out by the falls. It's just fifteen minutes' walk from the *maison forestière*, signposted "*Piscines/les Cascades*", and it does become overcrowded in summer – though you don't have to walk much farther along the river to find more tranquil spots for a picnic and a swim.

If you want to reach the higher slopes, an hour's walk from the *maison forestière* will bring you to the **Col de Salto**, and a further three hours' heavy climbing along the same rocky track will bring you to **Col de Felce**, for a fantastic vista of the Golfe de Porto. For the more ambitious, the **Col de Cuccavera** – above the tree line at 1500m – can be attained by cutting north before the **Col de Felce**, striking right up the mountainside. Once you're this far up, you can make out hazy distant views of the Gorges d'Asco.

Just 4km beyond the *maison forestière*, the Col de Verghio (1477m) borders the remote district of the Niolo and marks the limit of the **Fôret de Valdo-Niello**. The *Castellacciu* **hotel** (☎95.26.20.09; ④; closed winter) doubles as a basic ski station, but these days there's rarely enough snow to keep it in use. The road is extremely rocky along the last stretch up to the building, where there's a **café** (May–Sept).

Cargèse

Sitting high above a deep blue bay on a cliff scattered with olive trees some 20km southwest of Porto, **CARGÈSE** (Carghjese) oozes a lazy charm that attracts hundreds of well-heeled summer residents to its pretty white houses and hotels.

Two churches stand on separate hummocks at the heart of the village; the **Catholic church** was built for the minority Corsican families in 1828 and is one of the latest examples of Baroque in Corsica, with a *trompe l'œil* ceiling that can't really compete with the view from the church's terrace. The **Greek Orthodox church** is the more interesting of the two, a large granite neo-Gothic edifice built in 1852 to replace a church that had become too small for the congregation. Inside, the outstanding feature is the iconostasis, a gift from a monastery in Rome, decorated with icons brought over from Greece with the original settlers in the late seventeenth century – the graceful Virgin and Child is thought to date from as far back as the twelfth century.

You can swim off the rocks beneath the hotel *Bel Mare* if you climb down the cliff through the gate just past the hotel. The nearest beach, **Plage de Pero**, is 2km north of Cargèse – walk up to the junction with the Piana road and take the left fork down to the sea. Overlooked by a Genoese tower, this white stretch of sand is the best beach in the area, and has a couple of bars. **Plage du Chiuni**, a further 2km along the same road, is much busier thanks to its windsurfing facilities and the presence of Club Med. A more secluded spot lies a kilometre south of the village at **Plage du Monachi**; this small, sandy cove is reached by climbing down the track at the side of the road past the little chapel on the cliff side.

There's a **tourist office** on rue Dr-Dragacci (Mon–Fri 9am–noon & 3–6pm), which can help find accommodation and sells tickets for summer boat trips to the Calanche (see p.937), costing about 150F. Buses for Ajaccio and Porto stop outside the post office, set back from the road in the main square, every day at 2pm.

All the best **hotels** are located within minutes of the centre, with the budget places at the top end of the village. *Hôtel de France* (☎95.26.41.07; ②), the large white building on the northern edge of the village, offers discounts in the autumn. Otherwise, there's *La Cyrnée* in the main square (☎95.26.40.03; ②; closed winter). If you'd rather be by the beach, try the *Thalassa* on Plage de Pero (☎95.26.40.08; ④; meal included; closed winter), an intimate little place with friendly owners. There's also a **campsite** on Plage de Pero.

There are a fair number of **restaurants** scattered about the village, as well as the standard pizzerias. *A Volta*, next to the Catholic church, offers an interesting menu, serving game and stuffed pasta on a spectacular terrace jutting out over the sea. The bizarre *Restaurant/Bar Le Select* in rue Dragacci is worth a visit for its fairy lights and accordion music; the food is mainly inexpensive French bistro food, plus pizzas. For a **drink**, go no further than the main square, where you can watch all the action from *Bar des Amis*, which has a pool table.

Ajaccio and around

Edward Lear claimed that on a wet day it would be hard to find so dull a place as **AJACCIO** (Aiacciu), a harsh judgement with an element of justice. The town has none of Bastia's sense of purpose and can seem to lack a definitive identity of its own, but it is a relaxed and good-looking place, with an exceptionally mild climate, a wealth of cafés, restaurants and shops, and a more welcoming attitude to tourists than you might find elsewhere in Corsica.

Although it's an attractive idea that Ajax once stopped here, the name of Ajaccio derives from the Roman *Adjaccium* ("place of rest"), a winter stop-off point for shepherds descending from the mountains to stock up on goods and sell their produce. This first settlement, to the north of the present town in the area called Castelvecchio, was destroyed by the Saracens in the tenth century, and modern Ajaccio grew up around the citadel that was founded in 1492. Napoléon gave Ajaccio international fame, but though the self-designated *Cité Impériale* is littered with statues and street names related to the Bonaparte family, you'll find the Napoleonic cult has a less dedicated following in his home town than you might imagine. The emperor is still considered by many Ajacciens as a self-serving Frenchman rather than as a Corsican, and his impact on the townscape of his birthplace wasn't enormous. Ajaccio remains memorable for the things that have long made it attractive – its battered old town, the pervasive scents of maquis and fresh coffee, and the encompassing view of its glorious bay.

And when you've had enough of city life, the nearby resort of **Porticcio** has a fine beach and a great nightlife; and there are more excellent beaches further south.

Arrival and accommodation

Ajaccio's **Campo dell'Oro airport** (☎95.21.07.07) is 6km south of town; three buses an hour provide a shuttle service into the centre, stopping on cours Napoléon, the main street. Other **buses** go to the *gare routière* next to the port de Commerce (☎95.21.06.30), a five-minute walk from the centre. **Ferries** also come in here, and the *SNCM* office is at quai Lherminier (☎95.29.66.88); the **gare SNCF** lies almost a kilometre east along bd Sampiero, a continuation of the port's quai l'Herminier. The **tourist office** is on the ground floor of the Hôtel de Ville (May–Oct Mon–Fri 9am–noon & 2–6pm, Sat 9am–noon; ☎95.21.40.87). You can rent **cars** from *Aloha* at the airport (☎95.20.52.00), *Avis*, 3 place de Gaulle (☎95.21.01.86), or *Hertz*, 8 cours Grandval (☎95.21.70.94), and **bikes** from *Leandri*, 4 rue Jean Pandolphi (☎95.76.01.49).

For **accommodation** you'll find a dearth of cheap hotels, but a fair amount of moderate to upmarket places.

Hotels

Bella Vista, 20 bd Lantivy (☎95.21.07.97). Large, imposing place offering views of the gulf. ③.

Colomba, 8 av de Paris (☎95.21.12.66). Cheapest place in Ajaccio but with only three rooms. Very central, opposite place de Gaulle. Third-floor reception. Closed winter. ②.

Fesch, 7 rue Cardinal Fesch (☎95.21.50.52). The most appealing hotel in Ajaccio, with sheepskin furnishings and medieval-style decor designed by Corsicada, a group of local artisans. Closed mid-Dec to mid-Jan. ④.

Du Golfe, 6 bd du Roi-Jerôme (☎95.21.47.64). Balconies overlooking the bay; televisions in every room; modern decor. Closed Feb. ⑥.

Kallysté, 51 cours Napoléon (☎95.51.34.45). Hotel with an international atmosphere. Rooms accommodate up to four; also rents studios with kitchenettes and TVs. Proprietor speaks English. ③.

Napoléon, 4 rue Lorenzo-Vero (☎95.21.30.01). Very plush hotel, 500m east of town centre. ⑥.

San Carlu, 8 bd Danielle-Casanova (☎95.21.13.84). Recently renovated hotel opposite the citadel, close to the beach, with its own parking facilities. Closed mid-Dec to mid-Jan. ④.

The Town

The core of the **old town** holds the most interest in Ajaccio: a cluster of ancient streets spreading north and south of **place Foch**, which opens out to the seafront by the port and the marina. Nearby **place de Gaulle** forms the town centre and is the source of the main thoroughfare, **cours Napoléon**, which extends parallel to the sea almost 2km to the northeast. West of place de Gaulle stretches the modern part of town fronted by the **beach**, overlooked at its northern end by the citadel.

Around place de Gaulle and the new town

Place de Gaulle – otherwise known as place du Diamant, after the Diamanti family who once owned much of the property in Ajaccio – is the most useful point of orientation, even if it's not much to look at, just a windy concrete platform surrounded by a shopping complex. The only noteworthy thing on the square is the huge bronze statue, a pompous lump commissioned by Napoléon III in 1865 showing Napoléon in Roman attire, surrounded by his four brothers on horseback.

A short way north of the square, **A Bandera** (Mon–Sat 10am–noon & 3–7pm; Oct–April Wed 2–6pm, Thurs & Fri 10am–noon & 2–6pm; 20F) is a small military museum with an unusually wide collection focusing on Bronze Age settlements, Moorish raids, the Wars of Independence and, finally, World War II and the Corsican resistance.

Devotees of Napoléon should take a stroll a kilometre up cours Grandval, the wide street rising west of place de Gaulle and ending in a square, the **Jardins du Casone**, where gaudily spectacular *son et lumière* shows take place in summer. An impressive **monument to Napoléon** dominates the square – a replica of the statue at Napoléon's burial place, Les Invalides in Paris, standing atop a huge pedestal inscribed with the names of his battles. Behind the monument lies a graffiti-bedaubed cave where Napoléon is supposed to have frolicked as a child.

Place Foch

Once the site of the town's medieval gate, **place Foch** lies at the heart of old Ajaccio. A delightfully shady square sloping down to the sea and lined with cafés and restaurants, it gets its local name – place des Palmiers – from the double row of huge palms bordering the central strip. Dominating the top end, a fountain of four marble lions provides a mount for the inevitable **statue of Napoléon**, this one by Ajaccien sculptor Maglioli. A humbler effigy occupies a niche high on the nearest wall – a figurine of Ajaccio's patron saint, **La Madonnuccia**, dating from 1656, a year in which Ajaccio's local council, fearful of infection from plague-struck Genoa, placed the town under the guardianship of the Madonna in a ceremony which took place on this spot.

At the northern end of place Foch is the **Hôtel de Ville** of 1826, with its prison-like wooden doors and barred windows. The first-floor **Salon Napoléonien** (Tues–Sat 10am–noon & 2–4pm; 5F) contains a replica of the ex-emperor's death mask in pride of place, along with a solemn array of Bonaparte family portraits and busts. A smaller medal room has a fragment from Napoléon's coffin and part of his dressing case, plus a model of the ship that brought him back from St-Helena, and a picture of the house where he died.

South of place Foch

An archway on the south side of place Foch, standing on the former dividing line between the poor district around the port and the bourgeoisie's territory, gives access to **rue Napoléon**, the main route through the latter quarter. Built on the promontory rising to the citadel, the secluded streets in this part of town – with their dusty buildings and busy workshops lit by flashes of sea or sky at the end of the alleys – retain more of a sense of the old Ajaccio than anywhere else.

Napoléon was born in the colossal **Maison Bonaparte** on place Letizia (Mon 2–6pm, Tues–Sat 9am–noon & 2–6pm, Sun 9am–noon; Oct–April Mon 2–6pm, Tues–Sat 10am–noon & 2–5pm, Sun 10am–noon; 20F), off the west side of rue Napoléon. The house passed to Napoléon's father in the 1760s and here he lived, with his wife and family, until his death. But in May 1793, the Bonapartes were driven from the house by Paoli's partisans, who stripped the place down to the floorboards. Requisitioned by the English in 1794, Maison Bonaparte became an arsenal and a lodging house for English officers until Napoléon's mother herself funded its

NAPOLÉON AND CORSICA

Napoléon Bonaparte was born in Ajaccio in 1769, a crucial year in the history of Corsica as the time the French took over the island from the Genoese. They made a thorough job of it, crushing Paoli's troops at Ponte Nuovo and driving the Corsican leader into exile (see p.957). Napoléon's father Carlo, a close associate of Paoli, fled the scene of the battle with his pregnant wife in order to escape the victorious French army. But Carlo's subsequent behaviour was quite different from that of his former leader – he came to terms with the French, becoming a representative of the newly styled Corsican nobility in the National Assembly, and using his contacts with the French governor to get a free education for his children.

At the age of nine, Napoléon was awarded a scholarship to the Brienne military academy, an institution specially founded to teach the sons of the French nobility the responsibilities of their status, and the young son of a Corsican Italian-speaking household used his time well, leaving Brienne to enter the exclusive École Militaire in Paris. At the age of sixteen he was commissioned into the artillery. When he was twenty the Revolution broke out in Paris and the scene was set for a remarkable career.

Always an ambitious opportunist, he obtained leave from his regiment, returned to Ajaccio, joined the local Jacobin club and – with his eye on a colonelship in the Corsican militia – promoted enthusiastically the interests of the Revolution. However, things did not quite work out as he had planned, for Pascal Paoli had also returned to Corsica.

Carlo Bonaparte had died some years before, and Napoléon was head of a family that had formerly given Paoli strong support. Having spent the last twenty years in London, Paoli was pro-English and had developed a profound distaste of revolutionary excesses. Napoléon's French allegiance and his Jacobin views antagonized the older man, and his military conduct didn't enhance his standing at all. Elected second-in-command of the volunteer militia, Napoléon was involved in an unsuccessful attempt to wrest control of the citadel from Royalist sympathizers. He thus took much of the blame when, in reprisal for the killing of one of the militiamen, several people were gunned down in Ajaccio, an incident which engendered eight days of civil war. In June 1793, Napoléon and his family were chased back to the mainland by the Paolists.

Napoléon promptly renounced any special allegiance he had ever felt for Corsica. He Gallicized the spelling of his name, preferring Napoléon to his baptismal Napoleone. And although he was later to speak with nostalgia about the scents of the Corsican countryside, he put the city of his birth fourth on the list of places he would like to be buried.

restoration. Owned by the state since 1923, the house now bears few traces of the Bonaparte family's existence.

One of the few original pieces of furniture left in the house is the wooden sedan chair in the hallway – Letizia was carried back from church on it when the prenatal Napoléon started giving her contractions. Upstairs, there's an endless display of portraits, miniatures, weapons, letters and documents. Amongst the highlights of the first room are a few maps of Corsica dating from the eighteenth century, some deadly "vendetta" daggers and two handsome pairs of pistols belonging to Napoléon's father. The next-door Alcove Room was, according to tradition, occupied by Napoléon in 1799 when he stayed here for the last time, while in the third room you can see the sofa upon which the future emperor first saw the light of day on August 15, 1769. Adjoining the heavily restored long gallery is a tiny room known as the Trapdoor Room, whence Letizia and her children made their getaway from the marauding Paolists.

Napoléon was baptized in 1771 in the **cathedral**, around the corner in rue Forcioli Conti. It was built in 1582 on a much smaller scale than intended due to lack of funds – an apology for its diminutive size is inscribed in a plaque inside, on the wall to the left as you enter. Inside, to the right of the door, stands the font where he was dipped at the age of 23 months; Napoléon's dying words are inscribed on a plaque adorning a pillar on the left; and his sister, Elisa Baciochi, donated the great marble altar in 1811. Before you go, take a look in the chapel to the left of the altar, which houses a gloomy Delacroix painting of the Virgin.

Musée Capitellu and the citadel

A left turn at the eastern end of rue Forcioli-Conti brings you onto bd Danielle-Casanova. Here, opposite the citadel, an elaborately carved capital marks the entrance to **Musée Capitellu** (May–Oct Mon–Wed 9am–noon & 2–6pm; 20F), a tiny museum mainly given over to offering a picture of domestic life in nineteenth-century Ajaccio. The house belonged to a wealthy Ajaccien family, the Baciochi, who were related to Napoléon through his sister's marriage. Amid the watercolour landscapes and marble busts, the glass display cases hold the most fascinating exhibits, including a rare edition of the first history of Corsica, written by Agostino Giustiniani, a bishop of the Nebbio who drowned in 1536, and the 1796 Code Corse, a list of laws set out by Louis XV for the newly occupied Corsica.

Opposite the museum, the restored **citadel**, a hexagonal fortress and tower stuck out on a wide promontory into the sea, is occupied by the military and usually closed to the public. Founded in the 1490s, the fort wasn't completed until the occupation of Ajaccio by Sampiero Corso and the powerful Marshall Thermes in 1553–58. The building overlooks the town beach, Plage St-François, a short curve of yellow sand which faces the expansive mountain-ringed bay. Several flights of steps lead down to the beach from boulevard Danielle Casanova.

North of place Foch

The dark narrow streets backing onto the port to the north of place Foch are Ajaccio's traditional trading ground, with the town's biggest market taking place every morning on bd du Roi-Jerôme. Behind here, the principal road leading north is rue Cardinal Fesch, a delightful meandering street lined with boutiques, cafés and restaurants. Halfway along the street, set back from the road behind iron gates, stands Ajaccio's best gallery, the **Musée Fesch** (Mon–Fri 9am–noon & 2–6pm, Sat 9am–noon; 25F). Cardinal Joseph Fesch was Napoléon's step-uncle and Bishop of Lyons, using his lucrative position to invest in large numbers of paintings, many of them looted by the French armies in Holland, Italy and Germany. His bequest to the town includes seventeenth-century French and Spanish masters, but it's the Italian paintings which are the chief attraction: Raphael, Titian, Bellini, Veronese and Botticelli all have a place here.

You'll need a separate ticket for the **Chapelle Impériale** (same hours; 10F), which stands across the courtyard from the museum. With its gloomy monochrome interior the chapel itself is unremarkable, and its interest lies in the crypt of various members of the Bonaparte family. It was the cardinal's dying wish that all the Bonaparte family be brought together under one roof, so the chapel was built in 1857 and the bodies subsequently ferried in.

Eating, drinking and nightlife

Restaurants in Ajaccio vary from basic bistros to trendy pizzerias and pricey fish restaurants, the majority of which are found in the old town. **Bars** and **cafés** jostle for pavement space along cours Napoléon, generally lined with young people checking out the promenaders, and on place de Gaulle, where old-fashioned cafés and *salons de thé* offer a more sedate scene. If you fancy a view of the bay, you can go to one of the flashy cocktail bars that line the seafront on bd Lantivy, but you'll pay more for the privilege.

What **nightlife** there is in Ajaccio consists chiefly of eating and drinking, although there are two cinemas and a few trashy discos to cater for the tourists and the more adventurous Ajacciens.

Bars and cafés

Le Canebière, 69 cours Napoléon. Smart, untouristy bar, at the quiet end of the street, away from shopping crowds.

A Cantina, 18 bd du Roi-Jerôme. Unpretentious place opposite the port, serving simple Corsican snacks such as *charcuterie* sandwiches and salads, as well as steaks and pasta.

Chjiami e Rispondi, 5 rue Dr-Versini. Candlelit nationalist bar; nightly cabaret and singing.

La Grisbi, top of rue Stephanopoli, off cours Napoléon. Small and intimate; a favourite with shopping Ajacciens.

Nord Sud, 12 pl de Gaulle. Elegant Art Nouveau *salon du thé*.

Bar Rade, 1 place Foch. Popular local café overlooking the boats.

Safari, 18 bd Lantivy. Enormous cocktail bar backing onto the beach; an evening hang-out.

Snack La Serre, 91 cours Napoléon. Popular place, serving good-value bistro dishes and snacks.

Restaurants

L'Amor Piattu, 8 pl de Gaulle. An expensive Corsican restaurant serving refined local dishes, such as an excellent fish soup. Closed Mon.

Le Boccaccio, 20 rue Roi-de-Rome. Good variety of Italian meat and pasta dishes.

Da Mamma, passage Guingette, off bd du Roi-Jerôme. Good Corsican food: roast wild boar, *canneloni al brocciu* and the like.

Chez Paolo, 8 rue Roi-de-Rome. The best pizzas in town at tables on the pavement.

Pizzeria Napoli, 3 rue Bonaparte. Tasty pizzas and regional specialities such as roast kid and Corsican lasagne. Lively place and open very late.

Le Point U, 30 rue Fesch. Reputedly Ajaccio's best restaurant. Serves renowned *aziminu* (fish soup) and gourmet French food. Closed Sun.

Chez Vlody, 6 rue Roi-de-Rome. Spicy Creole food and excellent salads, but pricey. Open late.

Discos and clubs

Casino, 5 bd Lantivy. Flashy and expensive Europop disco.

A Cassetta, 4 av Sebastiani. Nightclub with traditional Corsican singing as well as modern music.

Pennies, 13 rue Bonaparte. Popular nightclub hidden in the old town. Good music.

Around Ajaccio: Porticcio and beyond

The liveliest spot along the southern arm of the Golfe d'Ajaccio – known as La Rive Sud – is **PORTICCIO**, the largest and most established resort along this stretch, just a handful of kilometres southeast of Ajaccio. Once a hang-out for the rich and famous, the place has lost its elitist appeal and gets swamped by watersports enthusiasts and weekenders from Ajaccio when summer comes.

The village basically comprises a loop of modern hotels and shops dominated by a huge shopping complex – however, the **beach** is fabulous, a wide sandy stretch commanding a great view of the gulf. Come summer the place is overwhelmed by Ajacciens in a constant stream of cars, but on the other hand there's the compensation of the lively nightlife, as the cinemas and discos get cranked up for the holidaymakers.

A small **tourist office** (daily May–July 8.30am–noon & 3–6.30pm; Aug 8am–noon & 3–9pm; ☎95.25.01.01) in the shopping complex can be helpful for finding somewhere to stay. Much of the **accommodation** is aimed at monied types, but rooms are well priced at *Hôtel de Porticcio* (☎95.25.05.77; ③; closed Nov–April) at the cross-roads in the centre of the village. Otherwise, try *Isolella* (☎95.25.41.36; ①; Nov–March), 500m south of the village, a smaller place with balconied rooms. If you fancy splashing out, go to *Le Maquis* (☎95.25.05.55; ⑧), set in a secluded cove 2km south of Porticcio and done up like a Palladian villa. For **campers**, there's *Mare e Machja* (☎95.25.10.58), an open, pleasant site situated deep in the maquis up a track opposite the tourist office; the site has its own pool and pizzeria. *Camping Prunelli* (☎95.25.19.23) and *Camping Benista* (☎95.25.19.30) are other alternatives, both 1km north of the village, on opposite sides of the Ajaccio road. *Pizzeria l'Ostaria*, south of the centre on the main street, is the cheapest **eating** place around and boasts a terrace with a view. Another popular joint is the very Corsican *Crêperie Marie* on the road to Ajaccio, serving inexpensive and tasty crêpes.

South of Porticcio, the D55 narrows in its progress along the coast, a high bank of maquis screening expensive villas and private beaches from the passing cars. Some 5km along you'll come to **Plage d'Agosta**, a popular, wide, sandy beach sheltered in the south by the **Punta di Sette Nave**, a narrow, rocky headland crowned by the Tour de l'Isolella. A couple of **hotels** worth checking out are the *Agosta Plage* (☎95.25.40.26; ③; closed mid-Oct to March) overlooking the beach and *L'Isolella* (☎95.25.41.36; ④; closed Nov–March), which has a good restaurant.

By far the finest beach along this stretch and a less frenetic spot than Plage d'Agosta lies 2km to the south at **Plage de Ruppione**, a half-moon-shaped cove – perfect for sheltered swimming and snorkelling. **Campers** can stay here at the well-sited *Camping le Sud* (☎95.25.40.51), one of the less expensive campsites along this coast.

Sartène and around

A "town peopled by demons" is how German chronicler Gregorovius described **SARTÈNE** (Sarté) in the nineteenth century, and the town hasn't shaken off its hostile image, with a heavy presence of wealthy-looking Godfather types. On the other hand it's a smart, clean place, noticeably better groomed than many small Corsican towns, its principal income coming from Sartène wine – the best on the island. The town doesn't offer many diversions once you've explored the enclosed old town and prehistory museum, and the only time of year Sartène teems with tourists is at Easter for *U Catenacciu*, a Good Friday procession that packs the town with onlookers.

Close to Sartène are some of the island's best-known prehistoric sites, most notably **Filotsia**, dating back eight thousand years and largely swathed in mystery. The megaliths of **Cauria** and the **Alignement de Palaggiu** form Corsica's largest array of prehistoric standing stones.

The Town

Place Porta – its official name, place de la Libération, has never caught on – forms Sartène's nucleus. Once the arena for bloody quarrels, it's now a well-kept square opening onto a wide terrace that overlooks the rippling green valley of the Rizzanese. Flanking the south side of place Porta is the **church of Ste-Marie**, built in the 1760s but completely restored to a smooth granitic appearance. Inside the church, the only notable feature is the Baroque altar, a present from the town's Franciscan monastery, no longer in existence.

A flight of steps to the left of the **Hôtel de Ville**, formerly the governor's palace, leads to a ruined **lookout tower**, which is all that remains of the town's twelfth-century ramparts. This apart, the best of the old town is to be found behind the Hôtel de Ville in the **Santa Anna district**, a labyrinth of constricted passageways and ancient fortress-like houses that rarely give any signs of life. Featuring few windows and often linked to their neighbours by balconies, these houses are entered by first-floor doors which would have been approached by ladders – dilapidated staircases have replaced these necessary measures against unwelcome intruders. To the left of rue Frère-Bartoli are the strangest of all the vaulted passageways, where outcrops of rock block the paths between the ancient buildings. Just to the west of the Hôtel de Ville, signposted off the tiny place Maggiore, you'll find the **impasse Carababa**, a remarkable architectural puzzle of a passageway cut through the awkwardly stacked houses. A few steps away, at the western edge of the town, **place Angelo-Maria-Chiappe** offers a magnificent view of the Golfe du Valinco.

The town's main attraction is the **Musée de Préhistoire Corse**, set in a shady garden a short distance east of place Porta (Mon–Fri 9am–noon & 2–6pm; 25F). The museum is Corsica's centre for archeological research and packed with findings from digs throughout the island, such as neolithic and Torréen pottery fragments, bracelets from the Iron Age, and painted ceramics from the thirteenth to the sixteenth centuries.

Practicalities

If you're arriving in Sartène by **bus**, you'll be dropped at the top of rue Général-de-Gaulle. Just south of here, across place Porta, you'll find a tiny **tourist office** at 6 rue Borgo (summer only Mon–Fri 9am–noon & 2–6.30pm; ☎95.77.15.40).

The only **hotel** in Sartène itself *Les Roches* on rue Jean-Jaurès, a large family-run place on the west side of the old town (☎95.77.07.61; ③); it commands panoramic views of the Vallée du Rizzanese and has a restaurant that serves hearty Corsican food. At the delightful *Le Jardin des Orangers*, 1km west of town along the road to Propriano (☎95.77.02.72; ③; closed winter), you can rent studios and rooms. You could otherwise try the *Villa Piana*, 4km along the Bonifacio road (☎95.77.07.04; ③; closed Oct–March), an upmarket place overlooking the Golfe de Valinco – or simply stay in Propriano (see overleaf), which has a wider choice of accommodation. The nearest **campsite** lies 5km along the D69 to Castagna (☎95.77.11.58) – it offers a free bus service to and from Sartène.

As for **restaurants**, *U Catenacciu* on rue Capitaine-Benedetti, south of place Porta, serves pizzas and reasonably priced Corsican food in summer, while Sartène's young people hang out in *Pizza Porta* on cours Sœur-Amélie. *Crêperie Santa-Anna* in rue Frère-Bartoli serves up a good herby *crêpe du maquis*, and at 27 rue des Vôutes, the understated *Ghjuvan Micheli* has 65F menus. **Bars** cluster around place Porta, where *Au Bien Assis* has the best views across the valley, but the prices of its cocktails are extortionate.

The megalithic sites

Sparsely populated today, the rolling hills of the southwestern corner of Corsica arez rich in prehistoric sites. The megaliths of **Cauria**, standing in ghostly isolation 10km southwest from Sartène, comprise the Dolmen de Fontanaccia, the best-preserved dolmen on Corsica, and the nearby alignments of **Stantari** and **Renaggiu** have an impressive congregation of statue-menhirs.

More than 250 menhirs can be seen northwest of Cauria at **Palaggiu**, another rewardingly remote site. Equally wild is the coast hereabouts, with deep clefts and coves providing some excellent spots for diving and secluded swimming.

The only public transport in this region is the twice-daily Ajaccio–Bonifacio bus.

Cauria

To reach the **Cauria megalithic site**, you need to turn off the N196 about 2km outside Sartène, at the Col de l'Albitrina (291m), taking the D48 towards Tizzano. Four kilometres along this road a left turning brings you onto a winding road through vineyards, until eventually the **Dolmen de Fontanaccia** comes into view on the horizon, isolated in a clearing amidst a sea of maquis.

Known to the locals as the **Stazzona del Diavolu** (the Devil's Forge), a name that does justice to its enigmatic power, the Dolmen de Fontanaccia is in fact a burial chamber from around 2000 BC. This period was marked by a change in burial customs – whereas bodies had previously been buried in stone coffins in the ground, they were now placed above, in a mound of earth enclosed in a stone chamber. What you see today is the great stone table, comprising six huge granite blocks nearly two metres high, topped by a stone slab that has remained once the earth rotted away.

The twenty "standing men" of the **Alignement de Stantari**, 200m to the east of the dolmen, date from the same period. All are featureless except two which have roughly sculpted eyes and noses, with diagonal swords on their backs and sockets in their heads where horns would probably have been attached.

Across a couple of fields to the south is the **Alignement de Renaggiu**, a gathering of forty menhirs standing in rows amid a small shadowy copse, set against the enormous granite outcrop of Punta di Cauria. Some of the menhirs have fallen, but all face north to south, a fact that seems to rule out any connection with a sun-related cult.

Palaggiu

For the **Alignement de Palaggiu**, the largest concentration of menhirs in Corsica, you regain the D48 and continue south, keeping your eyes peeled for a clearing that emerges to the right of the roadside about 3km south of the junction for Cauria. Pass through the gate here (there are no signposts) and head in a straight line to get to the menhirs. The 258 menhirs, stretching in straight lines across the countryside like a battleground of soldiers, include three statue-menhirs with carved weapons and facial features – they are amidst the first line you come to. Dating from around 1800 BC, the statues give few clues as to their function, but it's a reasonable supposition that proximity to the sea was important – Grosjean's theory is that the statues were some sort of magical deterrent to invaders.

Propriano

Tucked into the narrowest part of the Golfe de Valinco, the small port of **PROPRIANO** (Prupria), 8km northwest of Sartène, has most of the area's hotels and campsites, and is handy for some good beaches as well as for the menhirs at Filitosa. Bracketed by the promontory of Scogliu Lungu, the fine natural harbour of Propriano's port was only developed at the beginning of this century and now handles ferries to the French mainland and Sardinia. For the nearest beach, head 1km north of town to the **Plage de Baracci**, a long sheltered stretch of sand which spans the narrowest part of the gulf. Just 3km further, the D157 branches off to the left and continues along the coast, which is built up with hotels and package-tour holiday blocks, until **Olmeto Plage**, 10km west, where an abundance of campsites are on offer (see opposite). You can only reach this last by car.

Practicalities

Ferries from France dock just five minutes' walk from where the **bus** stops at the top of rue du Général-de-Gaulle, the town's main street, and the *SNCM* office is on quai Commandant-Lherminier (☎95.76.04.36); the **tourist office** is at no. 17 (Mon–Fri 9am–noon & 2–6.30pm; Sat 9am–noon; ☎95.76.01.49).

For **accommodation** there's a reasonable choice of hotels in the centre of town, like the high-tech *Loft Hotel*, rue Jean Paul Pandolphi (☎95.76.17.48; ③; closed Feb), directly behind the port; the *Bellevue* on av Napoléon (☎95.76.01.86; ②) overlooks the marina and has the cheapest central rooms in town. If you have a car and the means, you could try the more alluring places along the coast, like the huge, modern complex of the *Abartello*, Olmeto Plage, 10km west of Propriano (☎95.74.04.73; ④; closed Nov–March), right on the beach and with chalets for rental. Propriano's **youth hostel** is 3km from Propriano on the road to Ajaccio (☎95.76.19.48; ①). **Campers** are well provided for in the area: for the best facilities try *Listinco*, 3km north along route de Baracci and with a swimming pool (☎95.76.19.17), or the cheaper *Corsica*, 4km towards Ajaccio, 1km beyond the hostel (☎95.76.00.57). At Olmeta Plage, the best site is *U libecciu* (☎95.74.01.28), the first place on the beach coming from Propriano, or you could try *Chez Antoine* (☎95.76.06.06) in Marinca d'Olmeto, north of the beach.

Cafés and **restaurants** are concentrated along the marina's av Napoléon, with *Resto Nicoli* just about the cheapest place to eat, with excellent omelettes. Also worth a look are *Le Cabanon* on rue des Pêcheurs, an excellent fish place at the south end of the marina towards the port and *L'Hippocampe* on rue Pandolphi behind the port, the best place for fresh fish at reasonable prices, with a quick turnover and a lively atmosphere.

Filitosa

Set deep in the countryside of the fertile Vallée du Taravo, the extraordinary **Station Préhistorique de Filitosa** (March–Oct daily 8am–7.30pm; 15F), 17km north of Propriano, is one of the most important prehistoric sites in the western Mediterranean, a wonderful array of statue-menhirs and prehistoric structures encapsulating some eight thousand years of history. There's no public transport to this site, but organized trips leave once a day from both Ajaccio (May–Sept; 100F for full day) and Propriano (June–Sept; 50F for half day). Vehicles can be left in the small car park in the hamlet of Filitosa, where you pay the entrance fee; from here it's a fifteen-minute walk to the site, which includes a café, a small museum and a workshop producing reproduction prehistoric ceramics.

The site was settled by neolithic farming people who lived here in rock shelters until the arrival of megalithic navigators from the East in about 3500 BC. These invaders were the creators of the menhirs, the earliest of which were possibly phallic symbols worshipped by an ancient fertility cult. When the Torréens conquered Filitosa around 1300 BC, they destroyed most of the menhirs, incorporating the broken stones into the area of dry-stone walling surrounding the site's two *torri* or towers, examples of which can be found all over the south of Corsica. The site remained undiscovered until a farmer stumbled across the ruins on his land in the late 1940s.

Filitosa V looms up on the right before you cross the stream. The largest statue-menhir on the island, it's an imposing sight, with clearly defined facial features and a sword and dagger outlined on the body. Beyond a sharp left turn lies the oppidum or central monument, its entrance marked by the eastern platform, thought to have been a lookout post. The cavelike structure sculpted out of the rock is the only evidence of neolithic occupation and is generally agreed to have been a burial mound. Straight ahead, the Torréen central monument comprises a scattered group of menhirs on a circular walled mound, surmounted by a dome and entered by a corridor of stone slabs and lintels. Nobody is sure of its exact function.

Nearby **Filitosa XIII** and **Filitosa IX**, implacable lumps of granite with long noses and round chins, are the most impressive menhirs on the site. Filitosa XIII is typical of the figures carved just before the Torréen invasion, with its vertical dagger carved in relief – **Filitosa VII** also has a clearly sculpted sword and shield. **Filitosa VI**, from the same period, is remarkable for its facial detail. On the eastern side of the central monument stand some vestigial Torréen houses, where fragments of ceramics dating from

5500 BC were discovered; they represent the most ancient finds on the site, and some of them are displayed in the museum.

The western monument, a two-roomed structure built underneath another walled mound, is thought to have been some form of Torréen religious building. Beyond here a meadow sweeps towards the River Barcajolo, on the other side of which five statue-menhirs are arranged in a wide semicircle beneath a thousand-year-old olive tree. A bank separates them from the quarry from which the megalithic sculptors hewed the stone for the menhirs – a granite block is marked ready for cutting.

In the **museum**, the major item is the formidable Scalsa Murta, a huge menhir dating from around 1400 BC and discovered at Olmeto. Like other statue-menhirs of this period, this one has two indents in the back of its head, which are thought to indicate that these figures would have been adorned with headdresses. Other notable exhibits are Filitosa XII, which has a hand and a foot carved into the stone, and Trappa II, a strikingly archaic face.

Bonifacio

BONIFACIO (Bonifaziu) enjoys a superbly isolated situation at Corsica's southern-most point, a narrow peninsula of dazzling white limestone creating a town site unlike any other on the island. Separated from the rest of the island by an expanse of maquis, Bonifacio has maintained a certain temperamental detachment from Corsica, and is distinctly more Italian than French in atmosphere. The old town, a maze of tortuous streets, retains Renaissance features found only here, and with Sardinia just a stone's throw away, much of the property in the area is owned by upper-echelon Italians. A haven for boats for centuries, the town's perfect natural harbour is nowadays a marina that attracts yachts from all around the Med, with a plethora of hotels and restaurants to cater for the thousands of summer visitors.

Such a place has its drawbacks: exorbitant prices, crowds in August, and a commercial cynicism that's atypical of Corsica. But Bonifacio is perhaps the island's best-looking maritime town, and you'll find it boasts a lively nightlife, culminating in the lively *Rencontres Méditérranéennes* music festival at the beginning of September.

Arrival and accommodation

Arriving by plane, you'll land at **Figari airport**, 17km north of Bonifacio (☎95.71.00.22). There's no bus service from here so you'll have to take a taxi into town – around 200F. If arriving by **bus** you will be dropped at the car park by the marina, close to most of the hotels. The **tourist office** is in rue des Deux Moulins (May–Oct Mon–Fri 9am–noon & 2–6pm, Sat 9am–noon; ☎95.73.11.88). You can rent a **car** from *Avis*, 20 quai Comparetti (☎95.73.01.28), *Hertz*, 3 quai du Commerce (☎95.73.02.47), or *Europcar*, by the Esso garage on the way into town coming from Sartène (☎95.73.10.99).

Finding a place to **stay** can be a chore, as Bonifacio's hotels are quickly booked up in the high season, so if you want to stay centrally make sure you ring in advance. You'll find the least expensive accommodation a little outside the marina on the road to Ajaccio, while campsites abound on the road to Porto-Vecchio.

Hotels

La Caravelle, 37 quai Comparetti (☎95.73.00.03). Stylish olde-worlde place with an excellent restaurant in a prime location. Closed mid-Oct to Easter. ⑤.

Hôtel des Étrangers, 4 av Sylvère Bohn (☎95.73.01.09). On the road to Ajaccio just past the port, this is the cheapest place in the south, gathering an interesting mix of travellers who compensate for the dull decor. Closed mid-Nov to March. ②.

Le Genovese, Quartier de la Citadelle (☎95.73.12.34). Deluxe hotel overlooking the port. Swimming pool and a fantastic view of the cliffs. ⑥.

Le Royal, 8 rue Fred Scamaroni (☎95.73.00.51). Above a modern bar in the *haute ville*. Bright, clean place with views of the citadel and the sea. ⑤.

Campsites

L'Araguina, av Sylvère Bohn, opposite the service station near *Hotel des Étrangers* (☎95.73.02.96). Closest place to town; gets overcrowded.

U Farniente, Pertamina, 3km along the road to Porto-Vecchio (☎95.73.05.47). Very flash, all mod cons – essential to book in summer.

Campo di Liccia, opposite *U Farniente* (☎95.73.03.09). Well shaded and large, so you're guaranteed a place.

U Pian del Fosse, rte de Santa Manza, 7km out of Bonifacio along the D58 (☎95.73.14.40). Very basic but cheaper than the rest.

The Town

Apart from the cafés, hotels and restaurants of quai Comparetti, the only attraction in the **basse ville** is the marina's **aquarium** (daily 10am–6pm; 15F), where blue lobsters are the star attractions. At the far end lies the port where ferries leave for Sardinia, and in between, a cluster of restaurants and shops lies at the foot of Montée Rastello, the steps up to the **haute ville**, where many of the houses are bordered by enormous battlements which, like the houses themselves, have been rebuilt many times – the most significant modifications were made by the French during their brief period of occupation following the 1554 siege, after they had reduced the town walls to rubble.

From the top of the Montée Rastello steps you can cross av Général-de-Gaulle to **Montée St-Roch**, which gives a stunning view of the white limestone cliffs and the huge lump of fallen rockface called the **Grain de Sable**. At the **Chapelle St-Roch**, built on the spot where the last plague victim died in 1528, more steps lead down to the tiny beach of **Sutta Rocca**, which is mainly frequented by divers.

At the top of the Montée St-Roch steps stands the drawbridge of the great **Porte des Gênes**, once the only entrance to the *haute ville*. Through the gate, in place d'Armes, you can see the **Bastion de l'Étendard** (daily 9am–noon, 2–6pm; 10F), sole remnant of the fortifications destroyed during the siege of 1554. A few paces further lies **rue des deux Empereurs**, where no. 22 features the flamboyant marble escutcheon of the Cattacciolo family, one of many such adornments on the houses of this quarter. Opposite stands the house in which Napoléon resided for eight months in 1793.

Cutting across to rue Palais du Garde brings you to the **church of Ste-Marie-Majeure**, originally Romanesque but restored in the eighteenth century, though the richly sculpted belfry dates from the fourteenth century. The façade is hidden by a loggia where the Genoese municipal officers used to dispense justice in the days of the republic. This church's treasure, a relic of the True Cross, was saved from a shipwreck in the Straits of Bonifacio; for centuries after, the citizens would take the relic to the edge of the cliff and pray for calm seas whenever storms raged. The relic is kept in the sacristy, along with an ivory cask containing relics of Saint Boniface, and you'll only be able to get a glimpse if you can find someone to open the room for you. The holy water stoup below it is a third-century sarcophagus, the sole Roman item in town.

Nearby **rue du Palais de Garde** is one of the handsomest streets in Bonifacio, with its closed arcades and double-arched windows separated by curiously stunted columns. The oldest houses along here did not originally have doors; the inhabitants used to climb up a ladder which they would pull up behind them to prevent a surprise attack, while the ground floor was used as a stable and grain store.

The **Jardin des Véstiges**, just a couple of minutes southeast of rue du Palais de Garde, is a good place to stop for a drink overlooking the white cliffs on both sides. South of here, rue Doria leads towards the Bosco (see below); at the end of this road a left down rue des Pachas will bring you to the **Torrione**, a 35-metre-high lookout post built in 1195 on the site of Count Bonifacio's castle. Descending the cliff from here, the **Escalier du Roi d'Aragon**'s 187 steps were said to have been built in one night by the Aragonese in an attempt to gain the town in 1420, but in fact they had already been in existence for some time and were used by the people to fetch water from a well.

The Bosco
To the west of the tower lies the **Bosco**, a quarter named after the wood that used to stand here in the tenth century. In those days a community of hermits dwelt here, but nowadays the limestone plateau is open and desolate. The only sign of life comes from the military training camp where young Corsicans sweat out their national service. The entrance to the Bosco is marked by the **church of St-Dominique**, a rare example of Corsican Gothic architecture – it was built in 1270, most probably by the Templars, and later handed over to the Dominicans.

Beyond the church, rue des Moulins leads on to the ruins of three **mills** dating from 1283, two of them decrepit, the third restored. Behind them stands a memorial to the 750 people who died when a troop ship named *Sémillante* ran aground here in 1855, on its way to the Crimea, one of the many disasters wreaked by the straits.

The tip of the plateau is occupied by the **Cimetière Marin**, its white crosses standing out sharply against the deep blue of the sea. Open until sundown, the cemetery is a fascinating place to explore, with its flamboyant mausoleums displaying a jumble of architectural ornamentations: stuccoed façades, Gothic arches, classical columns, even flashing lights. Next to the cemetery stands the **Couvent St-François**, allegedly founded after Saint Francis sought shelter in a nearby cave – the story goes that the convent was the town's apology to the holy man, over whom a local maid had nearly poured a bucket of slops. Immediately to the south, the **Esplanade St-François** commands breathtaking views across the bay to Sardinia.

Eating, drinking and nightlife

Eating possibilities in Bonifacio might seem unlimited, but it's best to avoid the chintzy restaurants in the marina, few of which merit their exorbitant prices – the places in the *haute ville* are less pretentious. The bars and cafés on quai Comparetti are the social focus for much of the day and in the evening.

Restaurants
Agora, 2 av de Carotola. Excellent pizzas, steaks and fish at reasonable prices; wonderful location overlooking the sea.

Le Guêpier, 7 rue Fred Scamaroni. Basic and inexpensive Corsican specialities.

Chez Jules La Stella d'Oro, 23 rue Doria, near Église St-Jean Baptiste. Very expensive but does delicious Corsican specialities, mainly fish.

La Main à la Pâtes, 1 pl Bonaparte. Expensive fresh pasta; view of cliffs and marina.

Royal, 1 av de Carotola. The best fish in town, but it's expensive.

Le Tiki, 3 rue de Palais du Garde. The cheapest place for snacks, salads and pasta. 55F menus.

Bars
L'Amphore, 16 quai Comparetti. Pool table and a youngish crowd.

Central, 4 rue Fred Scamaroni. Everyone comes here for a nightcap.

L'Émeraude, 5 quai Comparetti. Shady, relaxing bar close to the aquarium, with draught beer and ice creams.

Nearby beaches

The nearest accessible beach is the small and picturesque **Plage de la Catena**, a kilo-metre to the west – a track just before *Camping L'Araguina* (see p.951) leads down to it. For the best local beaches head northeast along the D58, where about 3km along there's a junction for a trio of beaches: the popular **Plage de Pianterella**, the dullest of the three; the adjacent **Plage de Sperone**, an excellent diving spot facing the islands of Cavallo and Lavezzi; and **Cala Lunga**, a lengthy stretch of sand, but not sparklingly clean. Further along the D58, a second right-hand turn leads to the hamlet of Gurgazu, on the southern edge of the Golfe de Santa Manza.

Stretching to the right is the **Plage de Santa Manza**, a narrow silver strip backed by a rough road. A better proposition is **Plage de Maora**, a wider beach with cleaner sand and a makeshift bar – reached by taking a left at the junction of the D60 and D58. The third beach of the gulf, **Plage de Balistra**, situated by a marshy lagoon, is less pleasant and not accessible from here; to get to it you need to follow the N198 north of Bonifacio for 12km, then take a right down a dirt track for 4km to the sea.

To reach the **Plage de la Rondinara**, an almost circular cove midway between Bonifacio and Porto-Vecchio, take the N198 north for about 10km, until a turning sign-posted "Camping Rondinara" appears suddenly to the right – the track to the sea is strewn with boulders, so you may prefer to walk the 3km. Sheltered by the Punta di Rondinara and backed by dunes, the small beach is a favourite with nudists.

Porto-Vecchio and around

Set on a hill above a deep and beautiful gulf, surrounded by gigantic outcrops of pink granite, **PORTO-VECCHIO** was rated by James Boswell as one of "the most distin-guished harbours in Europe". Now people flock to this town, 25km north of Bonifacio, for the fine outlying **beaches**: spectacular stretches of shoreline lie to the south of town, with Palombaggia the most popular and Golfe de Santa Giulia coming a close second, while to the north, the deep inlet of the Golfe de Porto-Vecchio boasts some luscious pine-backed strands.

The Town

Porto-Vecchio itself was founded in 1539 as a second Genoese stronghold on the east coast, Bastia being well established in the north. The location was perfect; close to the unexploited and fertile plain, the site benefited from secure high land and a sheltered gulf, although the mosquito population spread malaria and wiped out the first Ligurian settlers within months. Things began to take off mainly thanks to the cork industry, still thriving until this century. Today a third of Corsica's wine is exported from here, but most revenue comes from the rich tourists who descend on the town each year. Around the centre of town there's not much to see, apart from the well-preserved **fortress** and the small grid of **ancient streets** backing onto the main place de la République. East of the square you can't miss the **Porte Génoise**, which frames a delightful expanse of sea and through which you'll find the quickest route down to the modern marina, lined with cafés and hotels.

Practicalities

Buses from Bastia, Bonifacio and Ajaccio arrive at the marina. From here it's ten minutes' walk northeast to place de l'Hôtel de Ville, site of the efficient **tourist office** (May–Sept Mon–Sat 9am–1pm & 4–8pm; Sun 10am–noon & 5–7pm; ☎95.70.09.58), just west of place de la République. There is no public transport to any of the beaches.

Accommodation is easy to come by except in high summer. The cheapest place in town is the simple, family-run *Panorama*, 12 rue Jean Nicoli (☎95.70.07.96; ④), followed by the noisy, backpacker-friendly *Le Modern*, 10 cours Napoléon (☎95.70.06.36; ③; closed Oct–April). It's worth spending a bit extra for a place in the marina, like the pleasant *Goeland*, port de Plaisance (☎95.70.14.15; ⑤), or the *Roches Blanches*, port de Plaisance (☎95.70.06.96; ⑤; closed Nov–April), with rooms overlooking the sea. If you're **camping**, there's the well-equipped *Arutoli* on rte de l'Ospedale, 2km northwest of town along the D368 (☎95.70.12.73), with an enormous pool. *Les Amis de la Nature* is a basic site in a pine wood, 4km north of town (☎95.70.21.57).

For **eating**, try the moderately priced *Bistrot du Port*, a sailors' hang-out serving omelettes and steaks as well as good Corsican food, and expensive *La Marine*, with the best fish and seafood in town. Pizzerias and pasta places are found all over the centre, with *U Casteddu* just south of place de la République in rue Leandri, the locally popular and affordable *Les Milles Pâtes*, 4 rue Général-de-Gaulle, and *Le Tourisme* on place de la République, the cheapest place in town. *U Borgu*, rue Borgo, parallel to cours Napoléon in the old town, is cheap and cheerful, with a view over the hillside.

The route de Bavella

The D268 – the **route de Bavella** – is perhaps the most dramatic road in all Corsica, leading from unassuming **ZONZA**, 20km northwest of Porto-Vecchio and northeast towards the coast. It penetrates the **Forêt de Zonza**, a dense expanse of pine and chestnut trees as it rises steadily to the **Col de Bavella** (1218m). A towering statue of **Notre-Dame-des-Neiges** marks the pass itself, which has a bleak and blasted look, the flattened pines crouched from the wind, their jagged branches sharply black against the green-hued granite peaks. An amazing panorama of peaks and forests surrounds the col: to the northwest the serrated granite ridge of the **Cirque de Gio Agostino** is dwarfed by the pink pinnacles of the **Aiguilles de Bavella**; behind soars Monte Incudine; and the east is dominated by the ruddy shades of **Punta Tafonata** and the distant sea.

From this point it's a steep descent through what's left of the **Forêt de Bavella**, which still features some huge Laricio pines. The winding road offers numerous breathtaking glimpses of the Aiguilles de Bavella. About 10km from the Col de Bavella you'll come to the **Col de l'Arone** (608m), which offers stunning vistas of the mountains and the Forêt de Tova in the north.

If you want to **stay** locally, Zonza has a cluster of hotels, all with more than decent restaurants, such as *Le Tourisme*, set back on the west side of the Quenza road north of the village (☎95.78.67.72; ③; closed Nov–March), or *L'Aiglon* in the village centre (☎95.78.67.79; ③; closed Jan–April). The **Parc Naturel Régional office** is 500m north of the village (May–Sept daily 9am–noon & 3–5pm; ☎95.78.66.58).

Aléria

Built on the estuary at the mouth of the River Tavignano on the island's east coast, 40km southeast of Corte along the N200, **ALÉRIA** was first settled in 564 BC by a colony of Greek Phocaeans as a trading port for the copper and lead they mined from the land and the wheat, olives and grapes they farmed. After an interlude of Carthaginian rule, the Romans arrived in 259 BC, built a naval base and reestablished its importance in the Med. Aléria remained the east coast's principal town and port right up until the eighteenth century. Little is left of the historic town except Roman ruins and a thirteenth-century Genoese fortress, which stands high against a background of chequered fields and green vineyards. To the south, a strip of modern buildings straddling the main road makes up the modern town, but it's the village set on the hilltop just west of here which holds most interest.

The best plan is to begin with the **Musée Jerôme Carcopino** (Mon–Fri 9am–noon & 2–6pm; May–Sept 8am–noon & 2–7pm; 10F), housed in the Fort Matra and crammed with remarkable finds from the Roman site, including Hellenic and Punic coins, rings, belt links, elaborate oil lamps decorated with Christian symbols, an enormous Attic plate, and a second-century marble bust of Jupiter Ammon. Etruscan bronzes fill another room, with jewellery from the fourth to the second century BC.

It's a stone's throw from here to the **Roman site** (closes 30min before museum), where most of the excavation was done as recently as the 1950s, despite the fact that French novelist Prosper Merimée noticed signs of the Roman settlement during his survey of the island in 1830. Most of the site still lies beneath ground and is undergoing continuous excavation, but the *balneum* (bathhouse), the base of Augustus' triumphal arch, the foundations of the forum and traces of shops have already been unearthed.

First discovered was the arch, which formed the entrance to the governor's residence – the *praetorium* – on the western edge of the forum. In the adjacent *balneum*, a network of reservoirs and cisterns, the *caldarium* bears traces of the underground pipes that would have heated the room, and a patterned mosaic floor is visible inside the neighbouring chamber. To the north of the site lie the foundation walls of a large house, while at the eastern end of the forum the foundations of the temple can be seen, and at its northern edge, over a row of column stumps, are the foundations of the apse of an early Christian church.

Some traces of the **Greek settlement**, comprising the remains of an acropolis, have been discovered further to the east. It's believed that the main part of the town would have extended from the present site over to this acropolis and down to the Tavignano estuary. The port was located to the east of the main road, where the remnants of a second-century bathhouse have been found.

A saltwater lagoon, the **Étang de Diane** lies just north of the town and was formerly the town's port under the Romans. To get there you either take the narrow N200 at the Cateraggio crossroads, which will bring you to the beach and an oyster farm, or follow the main road north of Aléria for 4km until you reach a turning on the right, signposted *"Terra Vecchia"*. A narrow dirt track leads down to the banks of the lagoon, a glittering stretch of water with a lookout tower marking the northeastern edge. The best places to swim are from the sandy eastern banks, which also make a pleasant picnic spot.

Practicalities

If you decide to **stay**, there are a few hotels worth checking out: *Les Orangers* (☎95.57.00.31; ④) is the best place, situated 50m north of the Cateraggio crossroads in the centre of the modern part; *L'Atrachjata* (☎95.57.03.93; ③), a little further north, does good meals; *L'Empereur*, a big chalet-style building a little further up from *Les Orangers* (☎95.57.02.13; ②), is clean and comfortable. For budgeting travellers, *Le Petit Bosquet* (☎95.57.02.16; ②), 500m south of the Cateraggio crossroads, on the east side of the road, is a motel providing a decent bed.

Corte and central Corsica

Situated amidst mountains and gorges at the core of the island, **CORTE** (Corti), 40km east of Porto and 50km southwest of Bastia, has been the home of Corsican nationalism since the first National Constitution was drawn up here in 1731; it is also where Pascal Paoli, "U Babbu di u Patria" (father of the nation), formed the island's first democratic government later in the eighteenth century and set up the first

Corsican printing press and the Università di Corsica, the first university to be established on the island. For the outsider, Corte's charm is concentrated in the tranquil *ville haute*, where donkeys graze below the majestic citadel, amid deathly quiet cobbled streets.

Arrival and accommodation

Buses stop in the centre of town on cours Paoli (☎95.46.02.12), but the **gare SNCF** is at the foot of the hill near the university (☎95.46.00.97), from where it's a ten-minute uphill walk into town. If you're driving the best place to park is either at the top of av Jean-Nicoli, the road which leads into town from Ajaccio, or in place Paoli at the top of cours Paoli. Corte's **tourist office** (May–Oct daily 9am–noon & 2–6pm; ☎95.46.24.20) is inside the citadel in the *ville haute*. **Cars** can be rented from *Europcar*, 9 cours Paoli (☎95.46.02.79), or *Hertz*, c/o *Cyrnea Tourisme*, 9 av Xavier Luciani (☎95.46.24.62), and **bikes** from *Corte Location Service*, 4 cours Paoli (☎95.46.07.13).

Finding a place to **stay** shouldn't be too difficult, with some inexpensive places in the centre of town, rarely fully booked. You'll find the nearest campsites in the Vallée de la Restonica, about a kilometre out of town.

Hotels

Auberge de la Restonica, Vallée de la Restonica (☎95.46.20.13). Sumptuous comfort by the river, 1km southwest of town. It's best to book. ③.

Hôtel du Nord, 22 cours Paoli (☎95.46.00.68). Pleasant, clean place right in the centre. ③.

Hôtel de la Paix, 1 av Général-de-Gaulle (☎95.46. 06.72). Large, smart and central hotel set in an elegant part of town. Closed Nov–March. ④.

Porette, 6 av du 9-septembre (☎95.61.01.21). Close to the station and university; unprepossessing but open all year round. ②.

Hôtel de la Poste, 2 pl Padoue (☎95.46.01.37). Huge, shabby old place, but central and with lots of character. ②.

Campsites

L'Alivetu, faubourg St-Antoine (☎95.46.11.09). Well equipped but ugly, next to the university.

U Sognu, rte de la Restonica (☎95.46.09.07). Closest to the main town, at the foot of the valley. Has a view of the citadel and a recently opened restaurant.

U Tavignanu, chemin de Balini, Vallée du Tavignano (☎95.46.16.85). Basic camping in wild surroundings.

The Town

Corte is a very small town whose centre effectively consists of one street: **cours Paoli**, which runs from **place Paoli**, at the southern end, a tourist-friendly zone packed with cafés, restaurants and market stalls, to **place du Duc de Padoue**, an elegant square of nineteenth-century buildings. Its statue, a grim bronze lump by Bartholdi, designer of the Statue of Liberty, is of **Arrighi di Casanova**, a general whose service under Napoléon earned him the title of Duke of Padua; his ancestral home can be seen in place Poilu in the *ville haute*.

The old **ville haute** is next to the cours Paoli, reached by climbing one of the cobbled ramps on the west side of the cours or by taking the steep rue Scoliscia from place Paoli. **Place Gaffori**, the centre of the *ville haute*, is dominated by a statue of General Gian' Pietru Gaffori pointing vigorously towards the church in the midst of the square's restaurant tables. On the base of the statue a bas-relief depicts the siege of the Gaffori house by the Genoese, who attacked in 1750 when Gaffori was out of town and his wife Faustina was left holding the fort. Their house stands right behind, and you can clearly make out the bullet-marks made by the besiegers.

PASCAL PAOLI

Pascal Paoli was born in Morosaglia into a family of campaigners for Corsican independence. At the age of fourteen Pascal accompanied his father into exile in Naples, where the boy became a keen student of political enlightenment. At the time of Corsican leader Gaffori's assassination, Pascal was a 29-year-old sublieutenant in a Neapolitan regiment, but his brother Clemente was in the thick of the rebellion. Appointed one of four regents after Gaffori's death, Clemente invited his younger brother to take over the position of General of the Nation, a title he accepted in 1755 and was to hold for the next fourteen years.

Paoli's intention was to drive out the Genoese by force, but he wasn't an experienced soldier and was always short of the necessary supplies. He proved to be adept at the art of government, giving the island a democratic constitution which anticipated that of the United States of America, founding the university at Corte, building a navy strong enough to break the Genoese blockade, and establishing a mint, a printing press and an arms factory.

Then in 1768 the French moved in once more, this time intending to stay after having bought out the Genoese under the terms of the Treaty of Versailles. Determined to crush the rebels for good, the French overwhelmed the Corsican troops at Ponte Nuovo, whereupon Paoli went into exile in London.

In 1789, at the start of the French Revolution, the people of Corsica were declared to be subject to the same laws as the revolutionary state, and it was in this changed political climate that Paoli returned triumphantly to the island in the following year. Initially he sympathized with the new republicanism, but the Corsican Jacobites – the Bonaparte family amongst them – owed too much to France to have much sympathy with separatist politics. Disagreements came to a head with Paoli's arraignment in June 1793. His response was dramatic – setting up an independent government in Corte, he approached the British government for help. The British, driven out of Toulon by the French, were in search of a naval base in the area, and sent Sir Gilbert Elliot to evaluate the situation. English troops and naval forces quickly moved in and after some fighting – during which the future Admiral Nelson lost the sight in one eye – the French moved out. A new constitution was drawn up that gave Corsica an attachment to the English crown, but with a large degree of autonomy. It's questionable whether Paoli was ever entirely happy with the course of events, but he was in a difficult situation, as the guillotine was waiting for him if France ever regained control. There seems no doubt that he expected to be appointed viceroy of the island, and when Elliot was given the job things began to turn sour.

The parliament of 1795 elected Paoli as president, but Elliot objected; soon after, rioting was provoked by a rumour that Paoli's bust had been deliberately smashed at a ball given in the viceroy's honour. When the English began talking again to the republican French the game was over. In 1796 Paoli was persuaded to return to London, shortly before Elliot withdrew as Napoléon's army landed to secure the island for France.

Given a state pension, Paoli died in London in 1807 at the age of 82, a revered figure. He was initially buried in his place of exile – there's a bust of him in Westminster Abbey – but his body now lies in his birthplace.

Opposite the house is the **church of the Annunciation**, built in 1450 but restored in the seventeenth century. Inside, there's a delicately carved pulpit and a hideous wax statue of Saint Theophilus, patron of the town, on his death bed. The saint's birthplace – behind the church in place Théophile – is marked by the **Oratoire St-Théophile**, a large arcaded building which commands a magnificent view across the gorges of Tavignano and Restonica.

For the best view of the citadel, follow the signs uphill to the viewing platform, aptly named the **Belvédère**, which faces the medieval tower, suspended high above the town on its pinnacle of rock and dwarfed by the immense crags behind. The platform also gives a wonderful view of the converging rivers and encircling forest – a summer bar adds to the attraction. In **place du Poilu**, the forecourt to the citadel, stands the house of the di Casanova family, where Napoléon's father – a friend of the Casanovas – lived in 1768 when he was Pascal Paoli's secretary.

At the gates to the citadel stands the **Palais National**, a great, solid block of a mansion that's the sole example of Genoese civic architecture in Corte. Having served as the seat of Paoli's government for a while, it became the Università di Corsica in 1765. Run by Franciscan monks, it offered free education to all (Napoléon's father studied here), and the enlightened monks taught the contemporary social thought of philosophers such as Rousseau and Montesquieu as well as traditional subjects like theology, mathematics and law. The university closed in 1769 when the French took over the island after the Treaty of Versailles, not to be resurrected until 1981. Today several modern buildings have been added and it houses the *Institut Universitaire d'Études Corses*, dedicated to the study of Corsican history and culture.

Tickets for the **citadel** (April–Oct daily 9am–8pm; 10F) are sold at the tourist office. The only such fortress in the interior of the island, it served as a base for the Foreign Legion from 1962 until 1984, but now houses the **Fonds Régionale d'Arts Corses**, which holds exhibitions of contemporary Corsican artists.

The citadel is reached by a huge staircase of Restonica marble, which leads to the medieval tower known as the **Nid d'Aigle** (eagle's nest) at its highest point. The citadel, of which the tower is the only original part, was built by Vincentello d'Istria in 1420, and the barracks were added during the reign of Louis-Philippe. These were later converted into a prison, in use as recently as World War II, when the Italian occupiers incarcerated Corsican resistance fighters in tiny cells. Adjacent to the cells is a former **watchtower** which at the time of Paoli's government was inhabited by the hangman.

To complete a tour of the *ville haute*, take the steps to the left as you leave the citadel, crossing rue Colonel Feracci to arrive at the **Fontaine des Quatre Canons**, once the water supply for all the houses in the vicinity. From here you can either descend to the cours or carry on down rue Colonel Feracci for a look at the sixteenth-century **Chapelle Ste-Croix**, with a lavish Baroque interior and floor of Restonica marble.

Eating and drinking

Corte has a fair number of **restaurants** and more casual eating places, with the usual sprinkling of pizzerias and *crêperies*, nearly all of them on cours Paoli – place Gaffori is the only place in the *ville haute* with restaurants. The **bars** of cours Paoli are strictly for posing; place Paoli is more touristy but at least you can sit and drink in comfort.

Restaurants

Le Bips, 27 cours Paoli. The most popular restaurant in town. Excellent and inexpensive Corsican food, fresh fish, pasta and pizzas.

Le Gaffori, place Gaffori. The least expensive place in town, with 45F menus and loads of omelettes, salads and spaghetti. Local *charcuterie* especially good.

Le Passe Temps, 2 rampe Ste-Croix. Expensive *crêperie* in a restored vaulted building serving tasty variations on the normal fillings (like wild boar); also serves soups and fish.

Place a Piazetta, place Gaffori. Pleasant outdoor restaurant serving a mean lasagne with wild boar sauce and succulent trout. Closed winter.

Cafés and bars

Café de France, junction of cours Paoli and place Padoue. Pleasant café with a shady forecourt.

Le Pascal Paoli, place Paoli. Touristy place with inexpensive steaks and snacks.

Rex, cours Paoli. The best of the posy bars along this street.

Central Corsica

Central Corsica is a nonstop parade of stupendous scenery, and the best way to immerse yourself in it is to get onto the region's ever-expanding network of trails and forest roads. The ridge of granite mountains forming the spine of the island is closely followed by the epic GR20 (see p.936), a trail which can be picked up from various villages and is scattered with refuge huts, most of them offering no facilities except shelter. You don't have to be an athlete to enjoy the peaks of Monte Rotondo and Monte Incudine, however, and for the even less active there are plenty of roads penetrating deep into the forests of Vizzavona, la Restonica and Rospa Sorba, crossing lofty passes that provide exceptional views across the island.

The most popular attractions in the centre, though, are the magnificent gorges of la Restonica and Tavignano.

Gorges du Tavignano

A deep cleft of ruddy granite 5km to the west of Corte, the Gorges du Tavignano offers one of central Corsica's great walks, marked in yellow paint flashes alongside the broad cascading River Tavignano, and is only accessible on foot. You can pick up the trail from opposite the Chapelle Ste-Croix in Corte's *ville haute* and follow it as far as the Lac de Nino, 30km west of the town, where it joins the GR20. There's a refuge, *A Sega*, 15km along the route, but check at the Corte tourist office to make sure it's open.

The first part of the walk crosses a small chestnut wood before hugging the left bank of the Tavignano. Massive rocks, fringed by dense vegetation, border the river. Some 5km into the walk the gorge begins, the scenery becoming wilder the further you advance, with bare rock faces surging up on each side and boulders cluttering the path. Some 10km from Corte the gorge comes to an end – from here you either go on to Nino or take the branch up to the Col de l'Arinella (1592m), a further 7km to the northwest. Forming the watershed between the valleys of the Golo and the Tavignano, the col affords fantastic vistas of the Niolo.

Gorges de la Restonica and Monte Rotondo

The glacier-moulded rocks and deep pools of the Gorges de la Restonica make the D936 running southwest from Corte the busiest mountain road in Corsica – if you come in high summer, expect to see parked vehicles lining the road all the way up to the car park at the Bergeries de Grotelle, 15km from Corte. The gorges begin after 6km, just beyond where the route penetrates the Forêt de la Restonica, a glorious forest of chestnut, Laricio pine and the tough maritime pine endemic to Corte. Not surprisingly, it's a popular place to walk, picnic and bathe in the many pools fed by the cascading torrent of the River Restonica, easily reached by scrambling down the rocky banks.

The classic ascent of Monte Rotondo (2322m) begins at the Tragone bridge, opposite the *maison forestière* about 11km along the D623, and takes about five hours there and back. For a less strenuous expedition, continue along the road to the ramshackle huts of the Bergeries de Grotelle, one of which has been converted into a café, providing welcome refreshments before or after a trek. From here it's an hour's clearly marked hike to the Lac de Melo across a broad, sweeping, rocky slope. Enclosed by a moraine formed during the Ice Age, the lake is the lowest of the fifteen lakes of Monte Rotondo, and marks the point where the real mountains begin. It's a further thirty minutes to Lac de Capitello, which lies at a height of 1930m and is frozen over for eight months of the year; beyond here, the terrain is strictly for real climbers.

A relatively easy hike up Monte Rotondo begins 11km along the D623 from Corte, at the Pont de Tragone. Cross the bridge and take the first track to the left, following the wooden signs for the Bergeries de Timozzo refuge, which lies 1500m to the southwest. Beyond the Bergeries, continue to climb close to the Timozzo torrent, crossing over from one bank to another according to the difficulty of the terrain for about 200m, after which the rest of the walk is marked by cairns. Veering away from the torrent for a short distance, you soon rejoin it at a point where it forms a waterfall. Another 250m on and the black crest of rocks of the summit are visible. Roughly the same distance again brings you to the **Lac d'Oriente**, then another 1km leads to the foot of the great walls of rock which form the base of the mountain. Here a gully to your right helps you attain the small col which gives easy access to the top. You can take the route down by the **Pietra Piana refuge**, 2km south beyond the huge glacial **Lac de Lavu Bellebone**.

Venaco and Vivario

Immediately south of Corte you ascend into a landscape of lush chestnut forests that lasts as far as the **Col de Bellagranjo** (723m), before the road sweeps through **VENACO**, an elegant village of rusty buildings emerging from deep green verdure on the slopes of Monte Padro. You might want to halt here to admire the vistas – from the terrace of the Baroque church there's a spectacular view of the lower Vallée du Tavignano in the east.

About 5km from Venaco the road passes the **Pont de Vecchiu**, an arched stone bridge that flies over the River Vecchiu and under the iron bridge designed by Gustave Eiffel in 1888, putting the final touches to the Bastia–Ajaccio train line. The river's gorge is dominated by **VIVARIO**, a large innocuous village located at the junction of the routes to the **Forêt de Rospa Sorba** and the **Col de Verde**, and thus a good base for walkers, who stay here at the basic *Macchje Monte* (☎95.47.22.00; ③; closed Jan & Feb). Vivario's attraction lies in its forest setting, a savage environment that once supported its own wild man in the early nineteenth century. The only traversable spot across the **Gorge du Vecchiu**, a three-hour walk west of Vivario, is a three-metre jump still known as the **Saut du Sauvage**.

A shorter walk from Vivario takes you to the **Fort de Pasciolo**, an evocative ruin 1km south of the village beside the N193. Set in a wild site facing a great circle of peaks and overlooking the deep Gorge du Vecchiu, the fort was built around 1770 by the French, and was transformed into a prison to incarcerate the rebels of Fiumorbo.

Vezzani and around

East of Vivario, the D343 follows a tree-lined route around the side of Punta Muru mountain, soon passing through **MURACCIOLE**, where the view forms a pleasant prelude to the awe-inspiring panorama from the **Col de Morello** (824m), 2km north of the hamlet. From here, a rewarding half-hour walk goes to the Occhio-Vario, a rocky eminence providing an even more exceptional viewpoint – a narrow goat track leads north of the col to the point, which is marked by a white granite monument.

After the col, the road penetrates the **Forêt de Rospa-Sorba**, a glorious forest of Laricio pines and chestnut trees. Distant snowy peaks most of the year feature all along the meandering road, which swoops in a semicircle towards **VEZZANI**. Fantastically located under the high ridge of **Punta di a Ringhella**, this mountain village has a couple of hotels; *U Sambuccu* (☎95.44.03.38; ③) is the better and has a good restaurant.

Just 1km south of Vivario, the D69 cuts steeply east to the **Col de Sorba** (1311m), from where the panorama is stunning: in the foreground rise the needles of Kyrie Eleison, and to the south extend the forests of **Pietro Verde** and **Marmano**, with a towering backdrop formed by Monte d'Oro and Monte Renoso. Continuing south, the deteriorating and narrowing road descends through the forest to **GHISONI**, about 7km from the col. This large village, nestling in a vast hollow on a tributary of the River Fiumorbo, is dominated by **Monte Renoso**, and most people staying in the village's cheap and cheerful *Hôtel Kyrié* (☎95.57.60.33; ②) are here to climb the mountain.

Vizzavona and around

Monte d'Oro dominates the route south of Vivario to **VIZZAVONA**, about 10km away. Shielded by trees, the village is invisible from the main road, so keep your eyes peeled for a couple of tracks on the right, one of them signposted for the train station – the place where the legendary bandit Bellacoscia surrendered to the police at the age of 75 (see below). With its handful of *auberges* and restaurants, Vizzavona is an ideal place to spend a few days walking in the forest, although it gets crowded in summer.

If you want to **stay**, try the *Moderne* (☎95.47.21.12; ③) opposite the station, or the even less expensive *Beauséjour* (☎95.47.21.13; ②), a tiny place attached to the station, serving authentic Corsican cuisine. Even better is the *Monte d'Oro* (☎95.47.21.06; ④; closed Oct–April), a huge place in the hamlet of **LA FOCE**, deep in the forest 3km south along the main road, with a magnificent terrace looking out onto the mountain.

Forêt de Vizzavona

A glorious forest of beech and Laricio pine, the **Forêt de Vizzavona** is the most popular walking area in Corsica, thanks to the easy access by main road or train. A lot of people come here to tackle the ascent of 2389-metre-high **Monte d'Oro**, but there are many less demanding trails to follow, one of the most frequented of these being the walk to the **Cascade des Anglais**, connected to Vizzavona by a marked trail.

Less than a kilometre west of the hamlet of La Foce lies the highest pass on the Ajaccio–Bastia road, the **Col de Vizzavona** (1163m), usually jammed with picnickers. Fifteen minutes south of the col along the forest trail you come to a magnificent viewpoint over the forested peaks, with the ruins of the Genoese **Fort de Vizzavona** prominent on a rise in the valley below. You can reach the fort itself in just fifteen minutes along a wide path north of the picnic tables. A walk to **La Madonuccia** – a mound of scrambled rocks that's supposed to look like the Virgin – takes about thirty minutes from the col, following the trail signposted *"Bergeries des Pozzi"*, which branches off southeast. Another marked path from the col takes you to the **Fontaine de Vitulo**, the source of the Foce stream, which joins the River Gravona further down the mountain.

To get the best out of the forest, though, you should walk to **Col de Palmente** (1460m), a relatively strenuous four-hour there-and-back hike along the GR20 from the *maison forestière* just south of Vizzavona on the main road. The path winds through magnificent woodland before rising to the col, which affords fantastic views of Monte Renoso and the Forêt de Vizzavona.

Bocognano

From the Col de Vizzavona, the route winds southwards for 6km before reaching the appealing ochre cottages of **BOCOGNANO**. Set on a plateau amidst a chestnut forest, the village gives a perfect panorama of Monte d'Oro's pale grey domes, and is well placed for walks to the **Cascade du Voile de la Mariée**, where the River Gravona crashes from a height of 150m in a series of cascades. The best approach to the falls is a thirty-minute walk south from the main road 3km south of Bocognano.

Bocognano is indissolubly associated with Antoine and Jacques Bellacoscia, born here in 1817 and 1832. Antoine, the elder son, took to the maquis in 1848, having killed the mayor of the village after an argument over some land. With his brother he went on to commit several more murders in full view of the hapless gendarmes, yet remained at liberty thanks to the support of the local population. In 1871, Jacques and Antoine managed to gain a safe pass into Ajaccio to organize an expedition to fight for the French in the war with Prussia. They returned from the war with their reputations restored, and took up residence in the family home, from where they continued to flaunt the law. In 1888, the police finally succeeded in ousting them from their house, which was converted into a prison. Antoine eventually surrendered at Vizzavona station on June 25, 1892, whereupon he was acquitted and exiled to Marseille in true Corsican tradition. The fate of Jacques is unknown.

travel details

Trains

Ajaccio to: Bastia (4 daily; 4hr); Bocognano (4 daily; 45min); Calvi (2 daily; 3hr 30min); Corte (4 daily; 2hr); L'Île Rousse (2 daily; 3hr); Venaco (4 daily; 1hr 30min); Vizzavona (4 daily; 1hr).

Bastia to: Ajaccio (4 daily; 4hr); Bocognano (4 daily; 3hr); Calvi (2 daily; 3hr 30min); Corte (4 daily; 2hr); L'Île Rousse (2 daily; 3hr 15min); Venaco (4 daily; 2hr 15min); Vivario (4 daily; 3hr 15min); Vizzavona (4 daily; 3hr).

Calvi to: Ajaccio (2 daily; 4hr); Bastia (2 daily; 3hr 30min); Corte (2 daily; 2hr 30min); L'Île Rousse (2 daily; 30min).

Corte to: Ajaccio (4 daily; 2hr); Bastia (4 daily; 2hr); Bocognano (4 daily; 3hr 30min); Venaco (4 daily; 15min); Vivario (4 daily; 30min); Vizzavona (4 daily; 1hr).

L'Île Rousse to: Ajaccio (2 daily; 3hr 25min); Bastia (2 daily; 3hr); Corte (2 daily; 3hr).

Venaco to: Ajaccio (4 daily; 1hr 30min); Bastia (1hr 40min); Bocognano (4 daily; 40min); Corte (4 daily; 15min); Vivario (4 daily; 15min); Vizzavona (4 daily; 25min).

Vizzavona to: Ajaccio (4 daily; 1hr); Bastia (4 daily; 2hr 20min); Bocognano (4 daily; 10min); Corte (4 daily; 1hr 15min); Ponte Leccia (4 daily; 1hr 15min); Venaco (4 daily; 30min); Vivario (4 daily; 15min).

Buses

Ajaccio to: Bastia (2 daily; 3hr); Bonifacio (2 daily; 3hr); Corte (2 daily; 2hr); Evisa (3 daily; 1hr 30min); Porticcio (hourly; 20min); Porto (2 daily; 1hr 45min); Porto-Vecchio (2 daily; 3hr 30min); Propriano (2 daily; 2hr); Sagone (3 daily; 50 min); Sartène (2 daily; 2hr 20min); Vizzavona (2 daily; 1hr); Zonza (1 daily; 2hr).

Aléria to: Bastia (2 daily; 1hr 30min); Porto-Vecchio (2 daily; 1hr 30min).

Bastia to: Ajaccio (2 daily; 3hr); Calvi (1 daily; 3hr); Centuri (3 weekly in summer; 2hr); Corte (2 daily; 2hr); Erbalunga (6 daily; 20min); La Marana (2 daily; 30min); St-Florent (2 daily; 45min); Porto-Vecchio (2 daily; 3hr).

Bonifacio to: Ajaccio (2 daily; 3hr); Porto-Vecchio (2 daily; 30min); Propriano (2 daily; 1hr 15min); Sartène (2 daily; 1hr).

Calvi to: Bastia (1 daily; 3hr); Porto (1 daily; 2hr 30min); St-Florent (1 daily; 3hr).

Cargèse to: Ajaccio (2 daily; 1hr); Porto (2 daily; 30min).

Corte to: Ajaccio (2 daily; 2hr); Bastia (2 daily; 2hr).

Evisa to: Ajaccio (3 daily; 1hr 30min).

Porto to: Ajaccio (2 daily; 2hr); Calvi (1 daily; 2hr 30min); Cargèse (2 daily; 1hr).

Porto-Vecchio to: Ajaccio (2 daily; 3hr 20min); Bastia (2 daily; 2hr 30min); Bonifacio (4 daily; 30min); Propriano (2 daily; 1hr 30min); Sartène (2 daily; 1hr 20min).

Propriano to: Ajaccio (2 daily; 2hr); Bonifacio (2 daily; 1hr); Porto-Vecchio (2 daily; 1hr 30min); Sartène (2 daily; 20min).

Ferries – see pp.919–20

PART THREE

THE
CONTEXTS

HISTORICAL FRAMEWORK

EARLY CIVILIZATIONS

Traces of human existence are rare in France until about 50,000 BC. Thereafter, beginning with the "Mousterian civilization", they become ever more numerous, with an especially heavy concentration of sites in the Périgord region of the Dordogne. It was here, near the village of Les Eyzies, that remains were discovered of a late Stone Age people, subsequently dubbed "Cro-Magnon". Flourishing from around 25,000 BC, these cave-dwelling hunters seem to have developed quite a sophisticated culture, the evidence of which is preserved in the beautiful paintings and engravings on the walls of the region's caves.

By 10,000 BC human communities had spread out widely across the whole of France. The ice cap receded, the climate became warmer and wetter, and by about 7000 BC **farming and pastoral communities** had begun to develop. By 4500 BC, the first **dolmens** (megalithic stone tombs) showed up in Brittany; around 2000 BC copper made its appearance; and by 1800 BC the **Bronze Age** had arrived in the east and southeast of the country, and trade links had begun with Spain, central Europe and Wessex in Britain.

Significant population shifts occurred, too, around this time. Around 1200 BC the **Champs**

d'Urnes people, who buried their dead in sunken urns, began to make incursions from the east. By 900 BC, they had been joined by the **Halstatt people** who worked with iron and settled in Burgundy, Alsace and Franche-Comté near the principal ore **deposits**. At some point around 450 BC, the first Celts made an appearance in the region.

PRE-ROMAN GAUL

There were about 15 million people living in **Gaul**, as the Romans called what we know as France (and parts of Belgium), when Julius Cæsar arrived in 58 BC to complete the Roman conquest.

The southern part of this territory – more or less equivalent to modern **Provence** – had been a colony since 118 BC and exposed to the civilizing influences of Italy and Greece for much longer. **Greek colonists** had founded *Massalia* (Marseille) as far back as 600 BC. But even the inhabitants of the rest of the country, what the Romans called "long-haired Gaul", were far from shaggy barbarians. Though the economy was basically rural, the **Gauls** had established large **hilltop towns** by 100 BC, notably at Bibracte near Autun, where archeologists have identified separate merchants' quarters and so on.

The Gauls had also invented the barrel and soap and were skilful manufacturers. By 500 BC they were capable of making metal-wheeled carts, as was proved by the "chariot tombs" of **Vix**, where a young woman was found buried seated in a cart with its wheels pushed against the wall. She was wearing rich gold jewellery and lying next to Greek vases and Black Figure pottery, dating the burial at around 500 BC and revealing the extent of commercial relations. Interestingly, too, the Gauls' money was based on the gold *staters*, minted by Philip of Macedon.

ROMANIZATION

Gallic **tribal rivalries** made the Romans' job very much easier. And when at last they were able to unite under **Vercingétorix** in 52 BC, the occasion was their total and final defeat by **Julius Cæsar** at the battle of **Alésia**.

This event was one of the major turning points in the history of France. **Roman victory** fixed the frontier between Gaul and the

Germanic peoples at the Rhine. It saved Gaul from disintegrating because of internal dissension and made it a Latin province. During the five centuries of peace that followed, the Gauls farmed, manufactured and traded, became urbanized, embourgeoisied and educated – and learned Latin. Roman victory at Alésia laid the foundations of modern French culture and established them firmly enough to survive the centuries of chaos and destruction that followed the collapse of Roman power.

Augustus and **Claudius** were the emperors who set the process of **Romanization** going. *Lugdunum* (Lyon) was founded as the capital of Roman Gaul as early as 43 BC. Augustus founded numerous other cities – like Autun, Limoges and Bayeux – built roads, settled Roman colonists on the land and reorganized the entire administration. Gauls were incorporated into the Roman army and given citizenship; Claudius made it possible for them to hold high office and become members of the Roman Senate, blurring the distinction and resentment between colonizer and colonized. Vespasian secured the frontiers beyond the Rhine, thus ensuring a couple of hundred years of peace and economic expansion.

Serious **disruptions** of the Pax Romana only began in the third century AD. Oppressive aristocratic rule and an economic crisis turned the destitute peasantry into gangs of marauding brigands – precursors of the medieval *jacquerie*. But most devastating of all, there began a series of incursions across the Rhine frontier by various restless **Germanic tribes**, the Alemanni and Franks first, who pushed down as far as Spain, ravaging farmland and destroying towns.

In the fourth century the reforms of the emperor **Diocletian** secured some decades of respite from both internal and external pressures. Towns were rebuilt and fortified, an interesting development that foreshadowed feudalism and the independent power of the nobles since, due to the uncertainty of the times, big landed estates or *villae* tended to become more and more self-sufficient – economically, administratively and militarily.

By the fifth century, however, the Germanic invaders were back: **Alans**, **Vandals** and **Suevi**, with **Franks** and **Burgundians** in their wake. While the Roman administration assimilated them as far as possible, granting them land in return for military duties, they gradually achieved independence from the empire. Many Gauls, by now thoroughly Latinized, entered the service of the **Burgundian court of Lyon** or of the **Visigoth kings of Toulouse** as skilled administrators and advisors.

THE FRANKS AND CHARLEMAGNE

By 500 AD, the **Franks**, who gave their name to modern France, had become the dominant invading power. Their most celebrated king, **Clovis**, consolidated his hold on northern France and drove the Visigoths out of the southwest into Spain. In 507 he made the until-then insignificant little trading town of Paris his capital and became a Christian, which inevitably hastened the **Christianization** of Frankish society.

Under the succeeding **Merovingian** – as the dynasty was called – rulers, the kingdom began to disintegrate until in the eighth century the Pepin family, who were the Merovingians' chancellors, began to take effective control. In 732, one of their most dynamic scions, **Charles Martel**, reunited the kingdom and saved western Christendom from the northward expansion of Islam by defeating the Spanish Moors at the **battle of Poitiers**.

In 754 Charles' son, Pepin, had himself crowned king by the pope, thus inaugurating the **Carolingian dynasty** and establishing for the first time the principle of the divine right of kings. His son was **Charlemagne**, who extended Frankish control over the whole of what had been Roman Gaul, and far beyond. On Christmas Day in 800, he was crowned emperor of the **Holy Roman Empire**, though again, following his death, the kingdom fell apart in squabbles over who was to inherit various parts of his empire. At the Treaty of Verdun in 843, his grandsons agreed on a division of territory that corresponded roughly with the extent of contemporary France and Germany.

Charlemagne's administrative system had involved the royal appointment of counts and bishops to govern the various provinces of the empire. Under the destabilizing attacks of Normans/Norsemen/Vikings during the ninth century, Carolingian kings were obliged to delegate more power and autonomy to these **provincial governors**, whose lands, like **Aquitaine** and **Burgundy**, already had separate regional identities as a result of earlier invasions – the Visigoths in Aquitaine, the Burgundians in Burgundy, for example.

Gradually the power of these princes overshadowed that of the king, whose lands were confined to the Île-de-France. When the last Carolingian died in 987, it was only natural that they should elect one of their own number to take his place. This was Hugues Capet, founder of a dynasty that lasted until 1328.

THE RISE OF THE FRENCH KINGS

The years 1000 to 1500 saw the gradual extension and consolidation of the power of the **French kings**, accompanied by the growth of a centralized administrative system and bureaucracy. These objectives also determined their foreign policy, which was chiefly concerned with restricting papal interference in French affairs and checking the English kings' continuing involvement in French territory. While progress towards these goals was remarkably steady and single minded, there were setbacks, principally in the seesawing fortunes of the conflict with the English.

Surrounded by vassals much stronger than themselves, **Hugues Capet** and his successors remained weak throughout the eleventh century, though they made the most of their feudal rights. As dukes of the French, counts of Paris and anointed kings, they enjoyed a prestige their vassals dared not offend – not least because that would have set a precedent of disobedience for their own lesser vassals.

At the beginning of the twelfth century, having successfully tamed his own vassals in the Île-de-France, Louis VI had a stroke of luck. **Eleanor**, daughter of the powerful duke of Aquitaine, was left in his care on her father's death, so he promptly married her off to his son, the future Louis VII.

Unfortunately, the marriage ended in divorce and Eleanor immediately – in 1152 – remarried, to Henry of Normandy, shortly to become **Henry II** of England. Thus the **English** gained control of a huge chunk of French territory, stretching from the Channel to the Pyrenees. Though their fortunes fluctuated over the ensuing 300 years, the English rulers remained a perpetual thorn in the side of the French kings and a dangerous source of alliances for any rebellious French vassals.

Philippe Auguste (1180–1223) made considerable headway in undermining English rule by exploiting the bitter relations between Henry II and his three sons, one of whom was Richard the Lion Heart. But he fell out with Richard when they took part in the **Third Crusade** together. Luckily, Richard died before he was able to claw back Philippe's gains, and by the end of his reign Philippe had recovered all of Normandy and the English possessions north of the Loire.

For the first time, the royal lands were greater than those of any other French lord. The foundations of a systematic administration and civil service had been established in **Paris**, and Philippe had firmly and quietly marked his independence from the papacy by refusing to take any interest in the crusade against the heretic Cathars of Languedoc. When Languedoc and Poitou came under royal control in the reign of his son Louis VIII, France was by far the greatest power in western Europe.

THE HUNDRED YEARS' WAR

In 1328 the Capetian monarchy had its first succession crisis, which led directly to the ruinous **Hundred Years' War** with the English. Charles IV, last of the line, had only daughters as heirs, and when it was decided that France could not be ruled by a queen, the English king, **Edward III**, whose mother was Charles' sister, claimed the throne of France for himself.

The French chose **Philippe, Count of Valois**, instead, and Edward acquiesced for a time. But when Philippe began whittling away at his possessions in Aquitaine, Edward renewed his claim and embarked on war. Though, with its population of about twelve million, France was a far richer and more powerful country, its army was no match for the superior organization and tactics of the English. Edward won an outright victory at **Crécy** in 1346 and seized the port of Calais as a permanent bridgehead. Ten years later, his son, the Black Prince, actually took the French king, Jean le Bon, prisoner at the **Battle of Poitiers**.

Although by 1375 French military fortunes had improved to the point where the English had been forced back to Calais and the Gascon coast, the strains of war and administrative abuses, as well as the madness of Charles VI, caused other kinds of damage. In 1358 there were **insurrections** among the Picardy peasantry (the *Jacquerie*) and among the townspeople of Paris under the leadership of Étienne Marcel. Both were brutally repressed, as were subsequent risings in Paris in 1382 and 1412.

The consequences of the king's madness led to the formation of two rival factions, in the aftermath of the murder of his brother, the Duke of Orléans, by the Duke of Burgundy. The **Armagnacs** gathered round the young Orléans, and the other faction round the **Burgundys**. Both factions called in the English to help them, and in 1415 Henry V of England inflicted another crushing defeat on the French army at **Agincourt**. The Burgundians seized Paris, took the royal family prisoner and recognized Henry as heir to the French throne. When Charles VI died in 1422, Henry's brother, the Duke of Bedford, took over the government of France north of the Loire, while the young king Charles VII ineffectually governed the south from his refugee capital at Bourges.

At this point **Jeanne d'Arc** (Joan of Arc) arrived on the scene. In 1429 she raised the English siege of the crucial town of Orléans and had Charles crowned at Reims. Although Joan fell into the hands of the Burgundians, who sold her to the English, who tried and burnt her as a heretic, her dynamism and martyrdom raised French morale and tipped the scales against the English. Except for a toehold at Calais, they were finally driven from France altogether in 1453.

By the end of the century, **Dauphiné, Burgundy, Franche-Comté** and **Provence** were under royal control, and an effective standing army had been created. The taxation system had been overhauled, and France had emerged from the Middle Ages a rich, powerful state, firmly under the centralized authority of an absolute monarch.

THE WARS OF RELIGION

After half a century of self-confident but inconclusive pursuit of military *gloire* in Italy, brought to an end by the **Treaty of Cateau-Cambrésis** in 1559, France was plunged into another period of devastating internal conflict. The **Protestant** ideas of Luther and Calvin had gained widespread adherence among all classes of society, despite sporadic brutal attempts by François I and Henri II to stamp them out.

When **Catherine de Médicis**, acting as regent for Henri III, implemented a more tolerant policy, she provoked violent reaction from the ultra-Catholic faction led by the **Guise** family. Their massacre of a Protestant congregation coming out of church in March 1562 began a civil **war of religions** that, interspersed with ineffective truces and accords, lasted for the next thirty years.

Well organized and well led by the Prince de Condé and Admiral Coligny, the **Huguenots** – French Protestants – kept their end up very successfully, until Condé was killed at the battle of Jarnac in 1569. Three years later came one of the blackest events in the memory of French Protestants, even today: the **massacre of St Bartholomew's Day**. Coligny and three thousand Protestants who had gathered in Paris for the wedding of Marguerite, the king's sister, to the Protestant Henri of Navarre were slaughtered at the instigation of the Guises – a bloodbath was repeated across France, especially in the south and west where the Protestants were strongest.

In 1584 the king's son died, leaving his brother-in-law, **Henri of Navarre,** heir to the throne, to the fury of the Guises and their Catholic league, who seized Paris and drove out the king. In retaliation, Henri III murdered the Duc de Guise, and found himself forced into alliance with Henri of Navarre, whom the pope had excommunicated. In 1589 Henri III was himself assassinated, leaving Henri of Navarre to become Henri IV of France. It took another four years of fighting and the abjuration of his faith for the new king to be recognized. "Paris is worth a mass", he is reputed to have said.

Once on the throne Henri IV set about reconstructing and reconciling the nation. By the **Edict of Nantes** of 1598 the Huguenots were accorded freedom of conscience, freedom of worship in certain places, the right to attend the same schools and hold the same offices as Catholics, their own courts and the possession of a number of fortresses as a guarantee against renewed attack, the most important being La Rochelle and Montpellier.

KINGS, CARDINALS AND ABSOLUTE POWER

The main themes of the seventeenth century, when France was ruled by just two kings, **Louis XIII** (1610–43) and **Louis XIV** (1643–1715), were, on the domestic front, the strengthening of the centralized state embodied in the person of the king; and in external affairs, the securing of frontiers in the Pyrenees, on the Rhine and in the north, coupled with the attempt to prevent the unification of the territories of the Habsburg kings of Spain and Austria. Both kings had the good fortune to be served by capable, hard-working ministers dedicated to these objectives. Louis XIII had **Cardinal Richelieu** and Louis XIV had cardinals **Mazarin** and **Colbert**. Both reigns were disturbed in their early years by the inevitable aristocratic attempts at a *coup d'état*.

Having crushed revolts by Louis XIII's brother Gaston, Duke of Orléans, **Richelieu's** commitment to extending royal absolutism brought him into renewed conflict with the Protestants. Believing that their retention of separate fortresses within the kingdom was a threat to security, he attacked and took La Rochelle in 1627. Although he was unable to extirpate their religion altogether, Protestants were never again to present a military threat.

The other important facet of his domestic policy was the promotion of economic self-sufficiency – **mercantilism**. To this end, he encouraged the growth of the luxury craft industries, especially textiles, in which France was to excel right up to the Revolution. He built up the navy and granted privileges to companies involved in establishing **colonies** in North America, Africa and the West Indies.

In pursuing his foreign policy objectives, Richelieu adroitly kept France out of actual military involvement by paying substantial sums to the great Swedish king and general, Gustavus Adolphus, helping him to fund war against the Habsburgs in Germany. When in 1635, the French were finally obliged to commit their own troops, they made significant gains against the Spanish in the Netherlands, Alsace and Lorraine, and won Roussillon for France.

Richelieu died just a few months before Louis XIII in 1642. As Louis XIV was still an infant, his mother, Anne of Austria, acted as regent, served by Richelieu's protégé, **Cardinal Mazarin**, who was hated just as much as his predecessor by the traditional aristocracy and the *parlements*. These unelected bodies, which had the function of high courts and administrative councils, were protective of their privileges and angry that an upstart should receive such preferment. Spurred by these grievances, which were in any case exacerbated by the ruinous cost of the Spanish

wars, various groups in French society combined in a series of revolts, known as the **Frondes**.

The first Fronde, in 1648, was led by the *parlement* of Paris, which took up the cause of the hereditary provincial tax-collecting officials – a group that resented the supervisory role of the *intendants*, who had been appointed by the central royal bureaucracy to keep an eye on them. Paris rose in revolt but capitulated at the advance of royal troops. This was quickly followed by an aristocratic Fronde, supported by various peasant risings round the country. These revolts were suppressed easily enough. They were not really revolutionary movements but, rather, the attempts of various groups to preserve their privileges in the face of growing state power.

The economic pressures that contributed to their support were relieved when in 1659 Mazarin successfully brought the Spanish wars to an end with the **Treaty of the Pyrenees**, cemented by the marriage of Louis XIV and the daughter of Philip IV of Spain. On reaching the age of majority in 1661, **Louis XIV** declared that he was going to be his own man and do without a first minister. He proceeded to appoint a number of able ministers, with whose aid he embarked on a long struggle to modernize the administration.

The war ministers, Le Tellier and his son Louvois, provided Louis with a well-equipped and well-trained professional army that could muster some 400,000 men by 1670. But the principal reforms were carried out by **Colbert**, who set about streamlining the state's finances and tackling bureaucratic corruption. Although he was never able to overcome the opposition completely, he did manage to produce a surplus in state revenue. Attempting to compensate for deficiencies in the taxation system by stimulating trade, he set up a free-trade area in northern and central France, continued Richelieu's mercantilist economic policies, established the French East India Company, and built up the navy and merchant fleets with a view to challenging the world commercial supremacy of the Dutch.

These were all policies that the hard-working king was involved in and approved of. But in addition to his love of an extravagant court life at Versailles, which earned him the title of the **Sun King**, he had another obsession, ruinous to the state: the love of a prestigious military victory. There were sound political reasons for the **campaigns** he embarked on, but they did not help balance the budget.

Using his wife's Spanish connection, Louis demanded the cession of certain Spanish provinces in the Low Countries, and then embarked on a war against the Dutch in 1672. Forced to make peace at the **Treaty of Nijmegen** in 1678 by his arch-enemy, the Protestant William of Orange (later king of England), he nonetheless came out of the war with the annexation to French territory of **Franche-Comté**, plus a number of northern towns. In 1681 he simply grabbed Strasbourg, and got away with it.

In 1685, under the influence of his very Catholic mistress, Madame de Maintenon, the king removed all privileges from the **Huguenots** by revoking the Edict of Nantes. This incensed the Protestant powers, who combined under the auspices of the League of Augsburg. Another long and exhausting war followed, ending, most unfavourably to the French, in the **Peace of Rijswik** (1697).

No sooner was this concluded than Louis became embroiled in the question of who was to succeed the moribund Charles II of Spain. Both Louis and Leopold Habsburg, the Holy Roman Emperor, had married sisters of Charles. The prospect of Leopold acquiring the Spanish Habsburgs' possessions in addition to his own vast lands was not welcome to Louis or any other European power. When Charles died and it was discovered that he'd named Louis' grandson, Philippe, as his heir, there again was a shift in the balance of power that the English, Dutch and Austrians were not prepared to tolerate.

William of Orange, now king of England as well as ruler of the Dutch United Provinces, organized a Grand Alliance against Louis. The so-called **War of Spanish Succession** broke out and it went badly for the French, largely thanks to the brilliant generalship of the Duke of Marlborough. A severe winter in 1709 compounded the hardships with famine and bread riots at home, causing Louis to seek negotiations. The terms were too harsh for him and the war dragged on until 1713, leaving the country totally impoverished. The Sun King went out with scarcely a whimper.

LOUIS XV AND THE PARLEMENTS

While France remained in many ways a prosperous and powerful state, largely thanks to

colonial trade, the tensions between central government and traditional vested interests proved too great to be reconciled.

The *parlement* of Paris became more and more the focus of opposition to the royal will, bringing the country to a state of virtual ungovernability in the reign of **Louis XVI**. Meanwhile, the diversity of mutually irreconcilable interests sheltering behind that parliamentary umbrella came more and more to the fore, bringing the country to a climax of tension which would only be resolved in the turmoil of **Revolution**.

The next king, Louis XV, was two when his great-grandfather died. During the **Regency**, the traditional aristocracy and the *parlements*, who for different reasons hated Louis XIV's advisors, scrabbled – successfully – to recover a lot of their lost power and prestige. An experiment with government by aristocratic councils failed, and attempts to absorb the immense national debt by selling shares in an overseas trading company ended in a huge collapse. When the prudent and reasonable **Cardinal Fleury** came to prominence upon the regent's death in 1726, the nation's lot began to improve. The Atlantic seaboard towns grew rich on trade with the American and Caribbean colonies, though industrial production did not improve much and the disparity in wealth between the countryside and the growing towns continued to grow.

In the mid-century there followed more disastrous military ventures, including the **War of Austrian Succession** and the **Seven Years' War**, both of which were in effect contests with England for control of the colonial territories in America and India, contests that France lost. The need to finance the wars led to the introduction of a new tax, the Twentieth, which was to be levied on everyone. The *parlement*, which had successfully opposed earlier taxation and fought the crown over its religious policies, dug its heels in again. This led to renewed conflict over Louis' pro-Jesuit religious policy. The Paris *parlement* staged a strike, was exiled from Paris, then inevitably reinstated. Disputes about its role continued until the *parlement* of Paris was actually abolishèd in 1771, to the outrage of the privileged groups in society, which considered it the defender of their special interests.

The division between the *parlements* and the king and his ministers continued to sharpen during the reign of Louis XVI, which began in 1774. Attempts by the enlightened finance minister Turgot to cooperate with the *parlements* and introduce reforms to alleviate the tax burden on the poor produced only short-term results. The national debt trebled between 1774 and 1787. Ironically, the one radical attempt to introduce an effective and equitable tax system led directly to the Revolution. Calonne, finance minister in 1786, tried to get his proposed tax approved by an **Assembly of Notables**, a device that had not been employed for more than a hundred years. His purpose was to bypass the *parlement*, which could be relied on to oppose any radical proposal. The attempt backfired. He lost his position, and the *parlement* ended up demanding a meeting of the **Estates-General**, representing the nobles, the clergy and the bourgeoisie, as being the only body competent to discuss such matters. The town responded by exiling and then recalling the *parlement* of Paris several times. As law and order began to break down, it gave in and agreed to summon the Estates-General on May 17, 1789.

REVOLUTION

Against a background of deepening economic crisis and general misery, exacerbated by the catastrophic harvest of 1788, controversy focused on how the **Estates-General** should be constituted. Should they meet separately as on the last occasion — in 1614? This was the solution favoured by the *parlement* of Paris, a measure of its reactionary nature: separate meetings would make it easy for the privileged, namely the clergy and nobility, to outvote the Third Estate, the bourgeoisie. The king ruled that they should hold a joint meeting, with the Third Estate represented by as many deputies as the other two Estates combined, but no decisions were made about the order of voting.

On June 17, 1789, the **Third Estate** seized the initiative and declared itself the National Assembly. Some of the lower clergy and liberal nobility joined them. Louis XVI appeared to accept the situation, and on July 9 the Assembly declared itself the National Constituent Assembly. However, the king then tried to intimidate it by calling in troops, which unleashed the anger of the people of Paris, the *sans-culottes* (literally, "without trousers").

On July 14 the *sans-culottes* stormed the fortress of **the Bastille**, symbol of the oppressive nature of the *ancien régime*. Similar insurrections occurred throughout the country, accompanied by widespread peasant attacks on landowners' châteaux and the destruction of records of debt and other symbols of their oppression. On the night of August 4, the Assembly abolished the feudal rights and privileges of the nobility — a momentous shift of gear in the revolutionary process, although in reality it did little to alter the situation. Later that month they adopted the **Declaration of the Rights of Man**. In December church lands were nationalized, and the pope retaliated by declaring the Revolutionary principles impious.

Bourgeois elements in the Assembly tried to bring about a compromise with the nobility, with a view to establishing a constitutional monarchy, but these overtures were rebuffed. Emigré aristocrats were already working to bring about foreign invasion to overthrow the Revolution. In June 1791 the king was arrested trying to escape from Paris. The Assembly, following an initiative of the wealthier bourgeois **Girondin** faction, decided to go to war to protect the Revolution.

On August 10, 1792, the *sans-culottes* set up a **revolutionary Commune** in Paris and imprisoned the king. The Revolution was taking a radical turn. A new National Convention was elected and met on the day the ill-prepared Revolutionary armies finally halted the Prussian invasion at Valmy. A major rift swiftly developed between the **Girondins** and the **Jacobins** and *sans-culottes* over the abolition of the monarchy. The radicals carried the day. In January 1793, Louis XVI was executed. By June the Girondins had been ousted.

Counter-revolutionary forces were gathering in the provinces and abroad. A Committee of Public Safety was set up as chief organ of the government. Left-wing popular pressure brought laws on general conscription and price controls and a deliberate policy of de-Christianization. **Robespierre** was pressed onto the Committee as the best man to contain the pressure from the streets.

The Terror began. As well as ordering the death of the hated Marie-Antoinette, Robespierre felt strong enough to guillotine his opponents on both right and left. But the effect of so many rolling heads was to cool people's faith in the Revolution; by mid-1794, Robespierre himself was arrested and executed, and his fall marked the end of radicalism. More conservative forces gained control of the government, decontrolled the economy, repressed popular risings, limited the suffrage, and established a five-man executive Directory (1795).

THE RISE OF NAPOLÉON

In 1799, one **General Napoléon Bonaparte**, who had made a name for himself as commander of the Revolutionary armies in Italy and Egypt, returned to France and took power in a *coup d'état*. He was appointed First Consul, with power to choose officials and initiate legislation. He redesigned the tax system and created the Bank of France, replaced the power of local institutions by a corps of *préfets* answerable to himself, made judges into state functionaries – in short, laid the foundations of the modern French administrative system.

Though Napoléon upheld the fundamental reforms of the Revolution, the retrograde nature of his regime became more and more apparent with the proscription of the Jacobins, granting of amnesty to the emigrés and restoration of their unsold property, reintroduction of slavery in the colonies, recognition of the Church and so on. Although alarmingly revolutionary in the eyes of the rest of Europe, his Civil Code worked essentially to the advantage of the bourgeoisie. In 1804 he crowned himself **emperor** in the presence of the pope.

Decline, however, came only with military failure. After 1808, Spain – under the rule of Napoléon's brother – rose in revolt, aided by the British. This signalled a turning of the tide in the long series of dazzling military successes. The nation began to grow weary of the burden of unceasing war.

In 1812, Napoléon threw himself into the **Russian campaign**, hoping to complete his European conquests. He reached Moscow but the long retreat in terrible winter conditions annihilated his veteran *Grande Armée*. By 1814, he was forced to abdicate by a coalition of European powers, who installed Louis XVIII, brother of the decapitated Louis XVI, as monarch. In a last effort to recapture power, Napoléon escaped from exile in Elba and reorganized his armies, only to meet final defeat at **Waterloo** on June 18, 1815. Louis XVIII was restored to power.

THE RESTORATION AND 1830 REVOLUTION

The years following Napoléon's downfall were marked by a determined campaign, including the **White Terror**, on the part of those reactionary elements who wanted to wipe out all trace of the Revolution and restore the *ancien régime*. **Louis XVIII** resisted these moves and was able to appoint a moderate royalist minister, Decazes, under whose leadership the liberal faction that wished to preserve the Revolutionary reforms made steady gains. This process, however, was wrecked by the assassination of the Duc de Berry in an attempt to wipe out the Bourbon family. In response to reactionary outrage, the king dismissed Decazes. An attempted liberal insurrection was crushed and the four Sergeants of La Rochelle were shot by firing squad. Censorship became more rigid and education was once more subjected to the authority of the Church.

In 1824, Louis was succeeded by the thoroughly reactionary **Charles X**, who pushed through a law indemnifying emigré aristocrats for property lost during the Revolution. When the opposition won a majority in the elections of 1830, the king dissolved the Chamber and restricted the already narrow suffrage.

Barricades went up in the streets of Paris. Charles X abdicated and parliament was persuaded to accept **Louis-Philippe**, Duc d'Orléans, as king. On the face of it, divine right had been superseded by popular sovereignty as the basis of political legitimacy. The **1814 Charter**, which upheld Revolutionary and Napoleonic reforms, was retained, censorship abolished, the tricolour restored as the national flag, and suffrage widened.

However, the **Citizen King**, as he was called, had somewhat more absolutist notions about being a monarch. In the 1830s his regime survived repeated challenges from both attempted coups by reactionaries and some serious labour unrest in Lyon and Paris. The 1840s were calmer under the ministry of Guizot, the first Protestant to hold high office. It was at this time that **Algeria** was colonized.

Guizot, however, was not popular. He resisted attempts to extend the vote to enfranchise the middle ranks of the bourgeoisie. In 1846, economic crisis brought bankruptcies, unemployment and food shortages. Conditions were appalling for the growing urban working class, whose hopes of a more just future received a theoretical basis in the **socialist writings** and activities of Blanqui, Fourier, Louis Blanc and Proudhon, among others.

When the government banned an opposition "banquet", the only permissible form of political meeting, in February 1848, workers and students took to the streets. When the army fired on a demonstration and killed forty people, civil war appeared imminent. The Citizen King fled to England.

THE SECOND REPUBLIC

A provisional government was set up and a **republic** proclaimed. The government issued a right-to-work declaration and set up national workshops to relieve unemployment. The vote was extended to all adult males – an unprecedented move for its time.

All was not plain sailing, though. By the time elections were held in April, a new tax designed to ameliorate the financial crisis had antagonized the countryside. A massive conservative majority was re-elected, to the dismay of the radicals. Three days of bloody street fighting at the barricades followed, when General Cavaignac, who had distinguished himself in the suppression of Algerian resistance, turned the artillery on the workers. More than 1500 were killed and 12,000 arrested and exiled.

A reasonably democratic constitution was drawn up and elections called to choose a president. To everyone's surprise, Louis-Napoléon, nephew of the emperor, romped home. In spite of his liberal reputation, he restricted the vote again, censored the press and pandered to the Catholic Church. In 1852, following a coup and further street fighting, he had himself proclaimed Emperor Napoléon III.

NAPOLÉON III AND THE COMMUNE

Through the 1850s, **Napoléon III** ran an authoritarian regime whose most notable achievement was a rapid growth in industrial and economic power. Foreign trade trebled, the rail system grew enormously, and the first investment banks were established. In 1858, in the aftermath of an attempt on his life by an Italian patriot, the emperor suddenly embarked on a policy of **liberalization**, initially of the economy, which alienated much of the business class. Reforms included the right to form trade unions and to strike, an extension of public education, lifting of censorship, and the granting of ministerial "responsibility" under a government headed by the liberal opposition.

Disaster, however, was approaching on the diplomatic front. Involved in a conflict with Bismarck and the rising power of Germany, Napoléon III declared war. The French army was quickly defeated and the emperor himself taken prisoner in 1870. The result at home was a universal demand for the proclamation of a **third republic**. The German armistice agreement insisted on the election of a national assembly to negotiate a proper peace treaty. France lost Alsace and Lorraine and was obliged to pay hefty war reparations.

Outraged by the monarchist majority re-elected to the new Assembly and by the attempt of its chief minister, Thiers, to disarm the National Guard, the people of Paris created their own municipal government known as **the Commune** (see *Paris* chapter).

THE THIRD REPUBLIC

In 1889, the collapse of a company set up to build the Panama Canal involved several members of the government in a corruption scandal, which was one factor in the dramatic **Socialist gains** in the elections of 1893. More importantly, the urban working class was becoming more class-conscious under the influence of the ideas of Karl Marx. The strength of the movement, however, was undermined by divisions, the chief one being Jules Guesde's Marxian Party. Among the independent Socialists was **Jean Jaurès**, who joined with Guesde in 1905 to found the **Parti Socialiste**. The trade union movement, unified in 1895 as the **Confédération Générale du Travail** (CGT), remained aloof in its anarcho-syndicalist preference for direct action.

In 1894, **Captain Dreyfus**, a Jewish army officer, was convicted by court martial of spying for the Germans and shipped off to the penal colony of Devil's Island for life. It soon became clear that he had been framed – by the army itself, yet they refused to reconsider his case. The affair immediately became an issue between the Catholic right wing and the Republican left, with Jaurès, Émile Zola and Clemenceau coming out in favour of Dreyfus.

Charles Maurras, founder of the fascist *Action Française* – precursor of Europe's Blackshirts – took the part of the army.

Dreyfus was officially rehabilitated in 1904, his health ruined by penal servitude in the tropics. But in the wake of the affair the more radical element in the Republican movement had begun to dominate the administration, bringing the army under closer civilian control and dissolving most of the religious orders.

Although the country enjoyed a period of renewed prosperity in the years preceding World War I, there remained serious unresolved conflicts in the political fabric of French society. On the right was Maurras' lunatic fringe with its strong-arm *Camelots du Roi*, and on the left, the far bigger constituency of the working class – unrepresented in government. Although most workers now voted for it, the Socialist Party was not permitted to participate in bourgeois governments under the constitution of the Second International, to which it belonged. Several major strikes were brutally suppressed.

WORLD WAR I

With the outbreak of **World War I** in 1914, France found itself swiftly overrun by Germany and its allies, and defended by its old enemy, Britain. At home, the hitherto antimilitarist trade union and Socialist leaders (Jaurès was assassinated in 1914) rallied to the flag and to the forces.

The cost of the war was even greater for France than for the other participants because it was fought largely on French soil. Over a quarter of the eight million men called up were either killed or crippled; industrial production fell to 60 percent of the prewar level. This – along with memories of the Franco-Prussian war of 1870 – was the reason that the French were more aggressive than either the British or the Americans in seeking war reparations from the Germans.

In the **postwar struggle for recovery** the interests of the urban working class were again passed over, save for Clemenceau's eight-hour-day legislation in 1919. An attempted general strike in 1920 came to nothing, and the workers' strength was again undermined by the formation of new Catholic and Communist unions, and most of all by the irremediable split in the Socialist Party at the 1920 Congress of

Tours. The pro-Lenin majority formed the **French Communist Party**, while the minority faction, under the leadership of Léon Blum, retained the old SFIO title. The bitterness caused by this split has bedevilled the French left ever since. Both parties resolutely stayed away from government.

As the **Depression** deepened in the 1930s and Nazi power across the Rhine became more menacing, fascist thuggery and anti-parliamentary activity increased in France, culminating in a pitched battle outside the Chamber of Deputies in February 1934. The effect of this fascist activism was to unite the left, including the Communists led by the Stalinist Maurice Thorez, in the **Front Populaire**. When they won the 1936 elections with a handsome majority in the Chamber, there followed a wave of strikes and factory sit-ins – a spontaneous expression of working-class determination to get their just deserts after a century and a half of frustration.

Frightened by the apparently revolutionary situation, the major employers signed the **Matignon Agreement** with Blum, which provided for wage increases, nationalization of the armaments industry and partial nationalization of the Bank of France, a forty-hour week, paid annual leave, and collective bargaining on wages. These **reforms** were pushed through parliament, but when Blum tried to introduce exchange controls to check the flight of capital, the Senate threw the proposal out and he resigned. The left remained out of power, with the exception of coalition governments, until 1981. Most of the *Front Populaire's* reforms were promptly undone.

WORLD WAR II

The agonies of **World War II** were compounded for France by the additional traumas of **occupation, collaboration and Resistance** – in effect, a civil war.

After the 1940 defeat of the Anglo-French forces in France, **Maréchal Pétain**, a cautious and conservative veteran of World War I, emerged from retirement to sign an armistice with Hitler and head the collaborationist **Vichy government**, which ostensibly governed the southern part of the country, while the Germans occupied the strategic north and the Atlantic coast. Pétain's prime minister, Laval, believed it his duty to adapt France to the new authoritarian age heralded by the Nazi conquest of Europe.

There has been endless controversy over who collaborated, how much and how far it was necessary in order to save France from even worse sufferings. One thing at least is clear: Nazi occupation provided a good opportunity for the Maurras breed of out-and-out French fascist to go on the rampage, tracking down Communists, Jews, Resistance fighters, freemasons – indeed all those who, in their demonology, were considered "alien" bodies in French society.

While some Communists were involved in the **Resistance** right from the start, Hitler's attack on the Soviet Union in 1941 freed the remainder from ideological inhibitions and brought them into the movement on a large scale. Resistance numbers were further increased by young men taking to the hills to escape conscription as labour in Nazi industry. Général de Gaulle's radio appeal from London on June 18, 1940, rallied the French opposed to right-wing defeatism and resulted in the *Conseil National de la Résistance*, unifying the different Resistance groups in May 1943. The man to whom this task had been entrusted was Jean Moulin, shortly to be captured by the Gestapo and tortured to death by Klaus Barbie, who was convicted as recently as 1987 for his war crimes.

Although British and American governments found him irksome, **de Gaulle** was able to impose himself as the unchallenged spokesman of the Free French, leader of a government in exile, and to insist that the voice of France be heard as an equal in the Allied councils of war. Even the Communists accepted his leadership, though he was far from representing the kind of political interests with which they could sympathize.

Thanks, however, to his persistence, representatives of his provisional government moved into liberated areas of France behind the Allied advance after D-Day, thereby saving the country from what would certainly have been at least localized outbreaks of civil war. It was also thanks to his insistence that Free French units, notably General Leclerc's Second Armoured Division, were allowed to perform the psychologically vital role of being the first Allied troops to enter Paris, Strasbourg and other emotionally significant towns in France.

THE AFTERMATH OF WAR

France emerged from the war demoralized, bankrupt and bomb-wrecked. The only possible provisional government in the circumstances was de Gaulle's **Free French** and the *Conseil National de la Résistance*, which meant a coalition of left and right. As an opening move to deal with the shambles, coal mines, air transport and Renault cars were nationalized. But a new constitution was required and **elections**, in which French women voted for the first time, resulted in a large left majority in the new Constituent Assembly – which, however, soon fell to squabbling over the form of the new constitution. De Gaulle resigned in disgust. If he was hoping for a wave of popular sympathy, he didn't get it and retired to the country to sulk.

The constitution finally agreed on, with little enthusiasm in the country, was not much different from the discredited Third Republic. And the new **Fourth Republic** appropriately began its life with a series of short-lived coalitions. In the early days the foundations for welfare were laid, banks nationalized and trade union rights extended. With the exclusion of the Communists from the government in 1947, however, thanks to the Cold War and the carrot of American aid under the Marshall Plan, France found itself once more dominated by the right.

If the post-Liberation desire for political reform was quickly frustrated, the spirit that inspired it did bear fruit in other spheres. From being a rather backward and largely agricultural economy prewar, France in the 1950s achieved enormous industrial **modernization and expansion**, its growth rate even rivalling that of West Germany at times. In foreign policy France opted to remain in the US fold, but at the same time took the initiative in promoting closer **European integration**, first through the European Coal and Steel community and then, in 1957, through the creation of the European Economic Community (EC).

COLONIAL WARS

In its **colonial policy**, on the other hand, the Fourth Republic seemed firmly committed to nineteenth-century imperialism, despite the cosmetic reform of renaming the Empire the French Union.

On the surrender of Japan to the Allies in 1945, the north half of the French **Indochina** colony came under the control of Ho Chi Minh and his Communist organization Vietminh. Attempts to negotiate were bungled and there began an eight-year armed struggle which ended with French defeat at Dien Bien Phu and partition of the country at the Geneva Conference in 1954 – at which point the Americans took over in the south, with well-known consequences.

In that year, 1954, the government decided to create an **independent nuclear arsenal** and got embroiled in the horrendous **Algerian war of liberation**. If you want to take a charitable view, you can say that the situation was complicated from the French viewpoint by the legal fiction that Algeria was a *département*, an integral part of France, and by the fact that there were a million or so settlers or *pieds noirs* claiming to be French and there was oil in the south. But by 1958, half a million troops, most of them conscripts, had been committed to the war, with all the attendant horrors of torture, massacre of civilian populations and so forth.

When it began to seem in 1958 that the government would take a more liberal line towards Algeria, the hard-line rightists among the settlers and in the army staged a putsch and threatened to declare war on France. Général de Gaulle, waiting in the wings to resume his mission to save France, let it be known that in its hour of need and with certain conditions – ie stronger powers for the president – the country might call upon his help. Thus, on June 1, 1958, the National Assembly voted him full powers for six months and the Fourth Republic came to an end.

DE GAULLE'S PRESIDENCY

As prime minister, then president of the **Fifth Republic** – with powers as much strengthened as he had wished – **de Gaulle** wheeled and dealt with the *pieds noirs* and Algerian rebels, while the war continued. In 1961, a General Salan staged a military revolt and set up the OAS (secret army) organization to prevent a settlement. When his coup failed, his organization made several attempts on de Gaulle's life – thereby strengthening the feeling on the mainland that it was time to be done with Algeria.

This feeling was reinforced by an episode in the same year – covered up and censored until the 1990s – when between seventy and two hundred French Algerians were killed by the police in Paris. This "secret massacre" began with a peaceful demonstration in protest against police powers to impose a curfew on any place in France frequented by North Africans. The police it seems went mad – shooting at crowds, batoning protestors and then throwing their bodies into the Seine. For weeks corpses were recovered but the French media remained silent.

Eventually in 1962, a referendum gave an overwhelming yes to **Algerian independence**, and *pieds noirs* refugees flooded into France. Most of the rest of the French colonial empire had achieved independence by this time also, and the succeeding years were to see a resurgence of fascist and racist activity, both among the French "returnees" and the usual insular, anti-immigrant sectors.

De Gaulle's leadership was haughty and autocratic in style, more concerned with *gloire* and grandeur than the everyday problems of ordinary lives. His quirky strutting on the world stage greatly irritated France's partners. He blocked British entry to the EC, cultivated the friendship of the Germans, rebuked the US for its imperialist policies in Vietnam, withdrew from NATO, refused to sign a nuclear test ban treaty, and called for a "free Québec". If this projection of French influence pleased some, the very narrowly won presidential election of 1965 (in which Mitterrand was his opponent) showed that a good half of French voters would not be sorry to see the last of the general.

MAY 1968

Notwithstanding a certain domestic discontent, the sudden explosion of **May 1968** took everyone by surprise. Beginning with protests against the paternalistic nature of the education system by students at the University of Nanterre, the movement of revolt rapidly spread to the Sorbonne and out into factories and offices.

On the night of May 10, barricades went up in the streets of the Quartier Latin in Paris, and the CRS (riot police) responded by wading into everyone, including bystanders, and Red Cross volunteers with unbelievable ferocity. A **general strike** followed, and within a week more than a million people were out, with many factory occupations and professionals joining in with journalists striking for freedom of expression, doctors setting up new radically organized practices and so forth.

Autogestion – workers' participation – was the dominant slogan. More than specific demands for reform, there was a general feeling that all French institutions needed overhauling: they were too rigid, too hierarchical and too élitist.

De Gaulle seemed to lose his nerve and on May 27 he vanished from the scene. It turned out he had gone to assure himself of the support of the commander of the French army of the Rhine. On his return he appealed to the nation to elect him as the only effective barrier against left-wing dictatorship, and dissolved parliament. The frightened silent majority voted massively in his favour.

Although there were few short-term radical changes (except in education), the shockwaves of May 1968 continued to be felt over the next two decades. Women's liberation, ecology groups, a relaxing of the formality of French society, a lessening of authoritarianism – all these can be traced to the heady days of May.

AFTER DE GAULLE

Having petulantly staked his presidency on the outcome of yet another referendum (on a couple of constitutional amendments) and lost, de Gaulle once more took himself sulkily off to his country estate and retirement. He was succeeded as president by his business-orientated former prime minister, **Georges Pompidou**.

The new regime was devotedly capitalist, Pompidou hoping to eradicate the memory of 1968 in the creation of wealth, property and competition. His visions, however, had little time to reach reality. Having survived an election in 1972, Pompidou died, suddenly. His successor – and the 1974 presidential election winner by a narrow margin over the socialist François Mitterrand – was the former finance minister **Valéry Giscard d'Estaing**.

Having announced that his aim was to make France "an advanced liberal society", Giscard opened his term of office with some spectacular media coups, inviting Parisian trash collectors to breakfast and visiting prisons in Lyon. But aside from reducing the voting age to 18 and liberalizing divorce laws, the advanced liberal society did not make a lot of progress. In the wake of the 1974 oil crisis the government introduced economic austerity measures. Giscard fell out with his ambitious prime minister, **Jacques Chirac**, who set out to challenge the leadership with his own RPR Gaullist party. And in addition to his superior, monarchical style, Giscard further compromised his popularity by accepting diamonds from the (literally) child-eating emperor of the Central African Republic Bokassa, and by involvement in various other scandals.

The left seemed well placed to win the coming 1978 elections, when the fragile union between the Socialists and Communists cracked, the latter fearing their roles as the coalition's junior partners. The result was another right-wing victory, with Giscard able to form a new government, with the grudging support of the RPR. Law and order and immigrant controls were the dominant features of Giscard's second term.

THE POLITICAL PRESENT

1995 will be marked by the end of François Mitterrand's presidency. He has been the French head of state for fourteen years, presiding over two Socialist and two Gaullist governments. When he won the elections in 1981, he embodied all the hopes of a generation of socialists who had never seen their party in power. The last years of his presidency have seen him becoming ill and aged, with his reputation tarnished and his party's popularity reduced to the point where even its continued existence is in question.

The recession started to take hold during Mitterrand's presidency: official unemployment figures have passed three million, both the president and the Socialist Party have been touched by scandals and become deeply unpopular, while divisions in the Right have opened up. The French public seem to have lost faith in their rulers as a whole and lost interest in the old political debates. The Maastricht referendum in September 1992 cut across the Right–Left divide, following instead old and unchanged geographical and class divisions.

The European elections of 1994 saw huge numbers of votes going to mavericks opposing the established Left and Right parties: for example to the charismatic arch-spiv Bernard Tapie and the traditionalist, far-right Philippe de Villiers.

THE PARTIES IN POWER, 1981–95

The **Socialists** began their first five years in power under the prime ministership of **Pierre Mauroy**. In his cabinet were four Communist ministers: an alliance reflected in the government commitments to expanded state control of industry, high taxation for the rich, support for liberation struggles around the world, and a public spending programme to raise the living standards of the least well-off. By 1984, however, the government had done a complete volte-face with **Laurent Fabius** presiding over a cabinet of centrist to conser-

PARTIES AND POLITICIANS

ON THE LEFT

PS (Parti Socialist). The Socialist party of President **François Mitterrand**, divided into "Mitterrandists"; "Rocardians", who support **Michel Rocard** (prime minister 1988–91); "Jospians", followers of **Lionel Jospin**, who has served in every Socialist government; "Fabiusians" whose man is **Laurent Fabius** (prime minister 1984–86, and ousted by Rocard as party leader in 1993); and the left wingers who favour a new coalition with the Greens, the Communists and the *Mouvement des Radicaux de Gauche* (*MRG*). The one presidential candidate the party wanted was **Jacques Delors** (former president of the European Commission), but he declined, leaving the Socialists with no conceivable hope of holding onto the presidency. **Lionel Jospin** is a possible candidate for this miserable contest, as is **Jack Lang**, the former culture minister and a "champagne" socialist, who was thrown out of parliament for overspending in the 1993 elections. He is now an *MEP* (his campaign was backed by Moët et Chandon, Cartier and Yves St-Laurent). In 1994 the *PS* did well in local and by-elections, even winning a seat in Paris, though they fared very badly in the Europeans.

PCF (Parti Communist Français). **Robert Hue** has finally replaced the veteran Stalinist leader **Georges Marchais** as party leader. Hue has proposed a new broad coalition with progressive Greens, Socialists, community groups, churches etc, which forms a big break from the old line, but has probably come too late to get very far. The *PCF* remains influential with the country's trade unions and also in local government.

ON THE RIGHT

UDF (Union pour la Démocratie Française). Union of centre-right parties usually in alliance with *RPR* (see below), led by the aloof, aristo former president **Valéry Giscard d'Estaing**, who realizes he has no hope in the 1995 presidentials.

PR (Parti Républicain). Part of the *UDF* though many members want to form their own independent group. Key figure is **François Léotard**, culture minister under Chirac and defence minister

vative "socialist" ministers, clinging desperately to power.

The commitments had come to little. Attempts to bring private education under state control were defeated by mass protests in the streets; ministers were implicated in cover-ups and corruption; unemployment continued to rise. Any idea of peaceful and pro-ecological intent was dashed, as far as international opinion was concerned, by the French Secret Service's murder of a Greenpeace photographer on the *Rainbow Warrior* in New Zealand.

There were sporadic achievements – in labour laws and women's rights, notably – but no cohesive and consistent socialist line. The Socialists' 1986 election slogan was "Help – the Right is coming back", a bizarrely self-fulfilling tactic that they defended on the grounds of humour. For the unemployed and the low paid, for immigrants and their families, for women wanting the choice of whether to have children, for the young, the old and all those attached to certain civil liberties, the return of the Right was no laughing matter.

Throughout 1987 the chances of Mitterrand's winning the presidential election in 1988 seemed very slim. But **Chirac**'s economic policies of privatization and monetary control failed to deliver the goods. Millions of first-time investors in "popular capitalism" lost all their money on Black Monday. Terrorists planted bombs in Paris and took French hostages in Lebanon. Unemployment steadily rose and Chirac made the fatal mistake of flirting with the extreme right. Several leading politicians of the centre-right, among them Simone Weil, a concentration-camp survivor, denounced Chirac's concessions to Le Pen, and a new alignment of the centre started to emerge. **Mitterrand**, the grand old man of politics, with decades of experience, played off all the groupings of the Right in an all-but-flawless campaign, and won another mandate.

His party, however, did not fare so well in the parliamentary elections soon afterwards. The Socialists failed to achieve an absolute majority and Mitterrand's new prime minister, **Michel Rocard**, went for a centrist coalition, causing friction in the party grassroots for whom the Communists were still the natural partners. The *FN* lost all their seats, the consequence of an abandonment of

under Balladur, despite charges of corruption brought against him.

RPR **(Rassemblement pour la République)**. Gaullist, conservative party headed by **Jacques Chirac**, mayor of Paris, and prime minister 1986–88; standing against the odds-on favourite for the presidency is **Edouard Balladur**, prime minister since 1993 and an extremely popular leader. The other notable Gaullist is **Philippe de Villiers**, who ran against his party in the 1994 Euro elections with Jimmy Goldsmith and de Gaulle's grandson on an anti-European union ticket, and won 12 percent of the vote and is an independent candidate in the presidentials.

Charles Pasqua, home affairs minister under Chirac and Balladur, is another strong right-winger, and unlike the two prime ministers he has served, anti-Europe.

FN **(Front National)**. Extreme-right party led by arch-racist **Jean-Marie Le Pen** and his deputy **Bruno Méguet**. FN *députés* in the last parliament they sat in (1986–88, after which the voting system was changed to exclude them) included publishers of Hitler's speeches, Moonies and an octogenarian who as Paris councillor in 1943 voted full powers for Pétain's Vichy regime. The *FN* has 11 *MEPs* but its share of the vote dropped in 1994 local elections.

GREEN PARTIES

GE **(Génération Ecologie)**. One of the two green parties, led by **Brice Lalonde**, who served in the Socialist government of 1988–91 but switched allegiance in 1993 to the Gaullists and failed to win a local council seat in 1994. The party, like *Les Verts*, did very badly in the Euro elections, losing all its seats.

Les Verts. The other Greens, more "pure" than *GE*. All eight Green European seats were lost in 1994. Unofficial coalitions at the local level take place with left-wing socialists, anti-racists, reforming Communists etc. Many Greens now stand independently from *Les Verts* and *GE* (known together as *L'Ecologistes*).

proportional representation, but retained their popularity.

Rocard's ensuing **austerity measures** upset traditional Socialist supporters in the public-service sector, and nurses, civil servants, teachers and the like were quick to take industrial action. Additionally, though Chirac's programmes were halted, they were not reversed.

The 1980s ended with the most absurd blow-out of public funds ever – the **Bicentennial celebrations of the French Revolution**. They symbolized a culture industry spinning mindlessly around the vacuum at the centre of the French vision for the future. And they highlighted the contrast between the unemployed and homeless begging on the streets and the limitless cash available for prestige projects.

In 1991, Mitterrand sacked Michel Rocard and appointed **Edith Cresson** as prime minister. Initially the French were happy to have their first woman prime minister, who promised to wage economic war against the Germans and the Japanese. The Left, including the Communists, were pleased with Cresson's socialist credentials. But she soon began to turn a few heads with her comments about special charters for illegal immigrants; her dismissal of the stock exchange as a waste of time; her description of the Japanese as yellow ants and British males as homosexual; and by attacks on her own ministers. Cresson became the most unpopular prime minister in the history of the Fifth Republic. Cresson's worst move was to propose a tax on everyone's insurance contributions to pay for compensation to haemophiliacs infected with HIV. The knowing use of infected blood in transfusions in 1985 became one of the biggest scandals of the Socialist regime.

Pierre Bérégovoy succeeded Cresson in 1992. Universally known as *Béré*, and mocked for his bumbling persona, he survived strikes by farmers, dockers, car workers and nurses, the scandals touching the Socialists and the Maastricht referendum. But then a private loan was revealed from one Roger-Patrice Pelat, a friend of Mitterrand's accused of insider dealing. Mitterrand distanced himself from his prime minister, who then shot himself two months after losing the elections, leaving no note of explanation.

The new prime minister, **Edouard Balladur**, a fresh and fatherly face from the Right, started off with great popularity. A series of U-turns after demonstrations by *Air France* workers, teachers, farmers, fishermen and school pupils, and the state's rescue of the *Crédit Lyonnais* bank after spectacular losses, wiped away his successes over GATT and keeping the franc strong and inflation down. However, his standing has been restored, particularly following the rescue of hostages taken by Algerian fundamentalists, and because – unlike several members of his cabinet – his honesty has not been in question.

Balladur's home affairs minister, **Charles Pasqua** (who served in the same post under Chirac), is a right-winger with a strong anti-immigration and anti-immigrant line. In 1992, Pasqua joined forces with another senior Gaullist bully, Philippe Séguin, and the extreme *UDF* right-winger Philippe de Villiers, to oppose the Maastricht treaty. Opposition to the treaty also came from the *PCF*, the breakaway socialist Jean-Pierre Chèvenement and the Front National. Clearly, the long-established certainty of the absolute divide between Right and Left loyalties was no longer tenable. The actual voters divided along the lines of the poorer rural areas voting "No" and the rich urbanites voting "Yes". In Paris the "Yes" vote was overwhelming. Disillusionment with the established parties was confirmed in the 1994 Euro elections. The *RPR/UDF* lost votes to the anti-Europeans and for the *PS* it was a total disaster. Rocard had to resign as the party secretary – his attempts to "modernize" the party had failed.

Meanwhile Mitterrand totters on to the end of his presidential term (April 1995), looking less and less like the nation's favourite uncle. Two months after Bérégovoy's suicide, Réné Bousquet, a friend of Mitterrand's thought to have known shady secrets about the president, was murdered. The following year a secret service agent and close advisor and friend, Jacques Attali, had to resign from the European Bank for Reconstruction and Development for suspected filching of the bank's money. In January 1994, the Elysée Palace was caught phone-tapping a journalist from *Le Monde*.

On the twentieth anniversary of President Pompidou's death in April 1994, there was a wave of nostalgia for a time when "things were right and proper". A month later, a leading French businessman was arrested for corruption, and there have since been other corruption scandals touching business people and politicians. Cracks are opening up in the French establishment, the recession is biting and cynicism and nostalgia are the order of the day.

FOREIGN POLICY

Throughout the postwar years, France has maintained an independent and nationalist-orientated **foreign policy**, staying outside NATO and sustaining its own **nuclear arsenal**. For this, there has long been cross-party consensus, and indeed national pride.

The end of the Cold War does not seem to have changed matters. At the end of the 1980s Mitterrand said that France would finally sign the Nuclear Non-Proliferation Treaty, while giving the go-ahead for a new series of hydrogen warhead tests in the South Pacific. He has hosted international disarmament conferences in Paris while promising the French that their status as a nuclear power will not be threatened. Since 1992, the development of new ballistic missiles for the French nuclear submarine fleet has been underway. Increased defence spending of £70 billion was approved by both sides in parliament in 1994. Though Mitterrand has changed his mind on nuclear testing, Balladur is very much in favour.

In 1992 Mitterrand launched, with Chancellor Kohl, the "Eurocorps" of 40,000 troops based in Strasbourg. The two leaders claimed to be putting into practice the Maastricht accord on a joint European defence policy. Its relationship to NATO and the Western European Union is unclear and Britain's dismissive line is that the German half won't fight outside Europe and the French half won't fight inside.

In major conflicts France always tries to play a key role (and as one of the five permanent members of the UN Security Council, it gets a say). But high-profile diplomacy gives way to unprestigious military action, as in the Gulf War when the small French force was under American command. In the eyes of its allies, France puts its own trade interests before those of the West's and fails to share a proper concern with geopolitical issues. But Mitterrand's visit, under gunfire, to Sarajevo in July 1992 was universally applauded. The

French were also stronger on South African sanctions than the British government, and unlike the Americans, have admitted that their Indo-China war was a mistake. Mitterrand was the first Western head of state to visit Vietnam after the American's defeat, and has been instrumental in trying to find a solution in Cambodia. On the other hand, the French have been reluctant to commit troops for UN actions in former Yugoslavia. In 1994 a group of intellectuals ran a "Sarajevo" campaign to put Bosnia at the centre of the European debate; it included the philosophers Bernard-Henri Lévy and André Glucksmann, and it received considerable support. But the government's response after the elections, in a cynical move to deflect attention from domestic problems, was to suddenly decide to commit troops to Rwanda, whose previous murderous government they had supported and armed.

OVERSEAS TERRITORIES

Southeast Asia apart, the French have decolonized to a lesser extent than any other former powers. They maintain strong links with – and exercise much influence over – most of the former colonies in North and West Africa, as exemplified by their military forays into Chad and Zaire.

With France's remaining **overseas territories**, governments through the last two decades have said a resounding "no" to independence claims. When the Kanaks of **Nouvelle Calédonie** (New Caledonia, an island near New Zealand) rebelled against direct, unelected rule by Paris, Mitterrand responded with "autonomy" measures which kept defence, foreign affairs, law and order, control of the television, and education in the French governor's hands. Eventually, though, after a massacre by French settlers of indigenous tribe members in 1986, the situation proved too sensitive, and a referendum in 1988 committed France to granting independence in ten years' time.

Both the **New Zealand and Australian governments**, however, were warned to desist from their support for the island's independence – to stop meddling in French internal affairs as Paris sees it. Both countries have taken strong stands against the nuclear tests at **Mururoa** and felt the force of French economic muscle as a result. Meanwhile the subjugation of the Polynesian people to French interests, with slum dwellers surviving on subsistence while imported French goods decimate local economies, goes on and will no doubt continue, whether independence comes or not.

FRANCE AND EUROPE

As a founder member of the **European Union (EU)**, France sees itself very much at the centre – and very much in control – of developments. The French people were able to debate the **Maastricht treaty** at length, with almost non-stop discussion in the media in the weeks leading up to the referendum. Every voter received a copy of the treaty and the turn-out was very high at seventy percent. French national interests were the key motivating factor, with Mitterrand promising that a "Yes" vote would not affect French sovereignty in any way and the "No" campaigners claiming the contrary. Internal politics were also crucial – voting "yes" to support Mitterrand and the Socialists and vice versa, and "Yes" to oppose the *Front National* and the *RPR* extreme right-wingers. Perceived economic interests also played their part. What was missing in the debate was the actual concept of a unified Europe – the construction of a new European identity, the democracy of its governing structures, its relationship to eastern Europe and the Third World, its dominant ideology. For the French voter, the referendum was about France, not about Europe. The same was true of the 1994 European elections, when the turnout was much lower. De Villier's anti-Europe votes and Tapie's pro ones were again a reflection of the French political morass, not about a vision for Europe.

The city with the highest "Yes" vote for Maastricht was Strasbourg on the German border. The **French-German axis** has dominated the European Community with France well aware that its own political clout matched with German economic clout makes a powerful partnership. Maintaining the franc's position against the Deutschmark has been a major feature of French economic policy. Mitterrand has been keen for the French to forget the German occupation of France (he himself for a short time worked for the Vichy government before joining the Resistance), and on July 14, 1994, German troops joined the French army parade – at Mitterand's invitation. But a French psychosis still exists about World War II. Only very recently has Mitterrand stopped laying an official wreath on Pétain's grave, politicians are still questioned about their war activities, and war-crimes trials – like that of Paul Touvier, sentenced to life imprisonment – still continue to send tremors through the establishment. The main problem is that France and the French have never confessed to the extent of their collaboration and anti-semitism.

Unlike Chancellor Kohl, Mitterrand has been cautious about recognizing the newly emerging former **Soviet states**, and about the possible entry of east European countries to the EU. In this, he is responding to a deeply protectionist impulse in France. Meat imports from Poland, Hungary and Czechoslovakia were banned, after French farmers made their views clear with barricades of manure and burning tyres. New immigration laws turned many long-term residents from eastern Europe into illegal aliens. The close ties France once enjoyed with the countries of the old Soviet bloc have been severely strained. The power of French farmers has also forced France into highly unpopular positions with its trading partners over the last round of GATT talks.

The French stance over the GATT talks and the new strict laws governing the use of English reveal both the traditional Gaullist distrust of the Americans and French nationalism, along with a sense of insecurity, and a need for protective, inward-looking measures.

THE ECONOMY

The ambitious left-wing programme of the 1981–84 Socialist government was scuppered by the massive flight of capital, by bureaucracy, and by the opposition of half the country. When **Chirac** subsequently came to power, his **privatization programme** went much further than reversing the preceding Socialists' nationalizations – banks that de Gaulle took into the public sector after 1945 were sold off along with *Dassault*, the aircraft manufacturer, and *Elf-Aquitaine*, the biggest French oil company.

Workers attempting to protect their jobs found themselves being hauled before the law. The shock of Chirac's approach to the unions, which in France are mostly organized along political lines rather than by profession, galvanized the usually irreconcilably divided Communist *CGT*, Socialist *CFDT* and Catholic *FO* unions into finding common cause.

The return of the Socialists put further wholesale privatizations on hold – and brought an amnesty for trade unionists who had been prosecuted – but **Rocard** ruled out renationalization. Public spending was again increased, but not enough to compensate for all the jobs already lost. Rocard's centrist programme provoked a wave of strikes, but lay-offs continued in the mines, shipyards, transport industry and the denationalized industries.

For all this action, **unemployment** never became a key issue in the 1980s. When Chirac came to power in 1986 the official figures stood at 2.4 million. Under Balladur it has reached 3.3 million, 12.2 percent of the workforce. Adding young people palmed off with training schemes and older people forced into early retirement, the real figure is around 4.5 million. The school and university students' protest against reducing the national minimum wage for young people in 1994 brought the issue of unemployment to the top of the agenda.

No-one has any solutions, though Jacques Delors – to his credit – made unemployment a priority issue for the European Union. Public opinion in France has been supportive of the fishermen, farmers, *Air France* workers and students who have gone on strike, rioted or demonstrated. Large sums of money have been promised for better training schemes and retraining opportunities, but the costs of social security are taking their toll on the economy.

In industry, however, partial privatizations (a quarter of *Renault* has gone to *Volvo*; shares in *Total*, *Elf Aquitaine*, *Bull* and *Thompson* have been sold) and continuing state subsidies (much to the disgust of British EU commissioners) have allowed the big nationalized firms to weather the recession. Balladur's $13 billion privatization programme is keeping private business happy. The trade balance remains in surplus, the franc has not had to leave the ERM, and the public deficit is still much, much lower than in Britain.

Overall, France has fared well over the last decade, far better than Britain, thanks to keeping rampant monetarism at bay. **Inflation**, down to zero in 1990, has not passed four percent. Interest rates and the budget deficit have been kept low. The standard of living of those in full-time work is much higher than in Britain. French **hospitals** have been offering British NHS patients operations like hip replacements with less than a week's wait. The **education** budget has outstripped defence spending for the first time ever – after successful strikes by *lycée* students in 1990. And, unlike in Britain, no one has yet suggested taking water, energy, transport and communications out of state control. These are seen as legitimate national assets, whose subsidy is an assertion of French pride. The state and municipal building programme in Paris makes it look as if no-one has heard of the recession. But the people begging on the métro and living on the streets tell a different tale. The crunch is going to come and there will be many more confrontations between the state and the people.

NUCLEAR POWER AND THE GREEN PARTIES

Throughout the 1980s and early 1990s, the environmental movement in France grew from almost total nonexistence to having a minister in government and two green political parties that between them were able to take 15 percent of the vote. Brice Lalonde, founder of **Génération Écologie**, was appointed to Rocard's government as environmental minister in 1988, with his post upgraded to cabinet level in 1991. The other, more radical, green party, **Les Verts**, had eight MEPs. In 1993 the parties overcame their differences and agreed an electoral pact for the parliamentary elections, but Brice Lalonde's flirtation with the Gaullists caused a new rupture. Several green councillors now stand as independents and in the Euro elections all the seats were lost.

The two parties, and Brice Lalonde's period as minister, have however had a significant impact on green consciousness in France, and been effective in stopping major developments such as the damming of the Loire river and in introducing waste and pollution taxes.

But the bastion of **nuclear power** has yet to be breached. The PWR nuclear power station at Nogent-sur-Marne, on the doorstep of Paris, must be one of the closest nuclear reactors to a major population centre anywhere. The French nuclear industry is the world's second largest, and the biggest in proportion to its energy needs. It's a major exporter, and the question of its safety is hardly ever raised. In 1990, however, it was revealed that two nuclear waste dumps close to Paris, closed in the 1970s, were thirty times above the acceptable radioactivity levels. After initial denials, the Green parties' demands for an independent inquiry were met. In 1991 the *Assemblée Nationale* discussed legislation on high-level nuclear waste disposal. This was the first time any aspect of nuclear energy policy had ever been put before parliament. Plans for the new generation fast-breeder reactor, however – the *Super-Phénix* in central France – proceed apace, and that despite the 1993 accident at the Cadarache nuclear reactor in Provence.

THE IMMIGRATION ISSUE

From the mid-1950s to the mid-1970s a labour shortage in the French cities led to massive recruitment campaigns for workers in North Africa, Portugal, Spain, Italy and Greece. People were promised housing, free medical care, trips home and well-paid jobs. When they arrived in France, however, these **immigrants** found themselves paid half of what their French co-workers earned, accommodated in prison-style hostels, and sometimes poorer than they were at home. They had no vote, no automatic permit renewal, were subject to frequent racial abuse and assault and, until 1981, were forbidden to form their own associations.

The Socialist government lifted this ban, gave a ten-year automatic renewal for permits and even promised voting rights. Able to organize for the first time, immigrant workers staged protests at the racist basis of lay-offs in the major industries. The *Front National* responded with the age-old bogey of foreigners taking jobs from the French. The Gaullists joined in with the spectre of falling birth rates (a French obsession since 1945). Both benefited from these declarations in the 1986 elections.

Once in power, Chirac instituted a series of **anti-immigration laws** so extreme that they sparked unprecedented alliances. The Archbishop of Lyon and the head of the Muslim Institute in Paris together condemned their injustice. Human rights groups, churches and trade unions joined immigrants' groups in saying that France was on its way to becoming a police state. In 1992 the International Federation of Human Rights published a highly critical report on racism in the French police force in which they said that France "was not

the home of human rights". Natality measures and the position of women immigrants brought French feminists into the battle. **SOS Racisme** was born, an anti-racist organization appealing to young people, in particular to well-educated second- and third-generation immigrants, but it has failed to engage the most disenfranchised, the notorious *banlieue* (suburban) kids, who are seen by the middle classes as natural criminals.

On returning to power, the Socialists played electoral games with the immigration issue, reneged on the vote promise, and failed to tackle the social and economic deprivation of France's immigrant ghettoes. Polls showed over two-thirds of the adult French population to be in favour of deporting legal immigrants for any criminal offence, or for being unemployed for over a year. Le Pen's proposals that immigrants have second-class citizenship, segregated education and separate social security have received massive support.

This rampant racism struck such a chord that politicians of right and left jumped onto the bandwagon. Edith Cresson, while prime minister, said special planes should be chartered to deport illegal immigrants. Kofi Yamgname, the minister for integration and only black member of the Socialist cabinet, suggested that immigrants who maintained traditional habits should go home. On the right, Giscard has used the potent word "invasion" and said that citizenship should be based on blood ties, not on place of birth. Chirac talked of the "noise and smell" of immigrants, and a *UDF* senator compared the four million immigrants in France to the German occupation. All of which boosted the confidence of Jean-Marie Le Pen and of the current home affairs minister, Charles Pasqua, who has reintroduced random identity checks and clamped down on immigration.

The fate of immigrants and their French descendants has never been so precarious. Fury and frustration at discrimination, assault, abuse and economic deprivation has erupted into battles on the street. Several young blacks have died at the hands of the police, while the right-wing media have revelled in images of violent Arab youths. Confrontations in the poorest Paris suburbs have become commonplace, but mini-riots are far from being the sole outlet for the grievances of French blacks. Tent cities were erected by homeless Africans in the 13^e *arrondissement* and in Vincennes, bringing some public sympathy, but the current government has been very successful in distinguishing the "deserving" from the "undesirable undeserving". Organizations like *SOS Racisme* continue to campaign against discrimination in housing, jobs and the law, and when two Algerian boys were deported during the school pupil's actions in 1994, their release immediately became another popular demand.

NEW POLITICAL MOVEMENTS

With the Socialist Party firmly positioned towards the centre, and the Communist Party only beginning – rather late in the day – to open itself up to new debates, there has been a vacuum on the Left. Jean-Pierre Chevènement, a pacifist left-wing socialist who resigned as defence minister after the outbreak of the Gulf War, has left the *PS* to form his own grouping, the ***Mouvement des Citoyens***, which involves *Les Verts* and some reformers in the Communist

Party. But the most interesting potential new development was ***Le Mouvement***, a new political grouping initiated by Harlem Désir, the founder of *SOS Racisme*. It aimed to unite Arabs, Africans, Jews, Asians and West Indians in the demand for equal rights and allow joint membership with the Socialist, Green and Communist parties. Unfortunately it has failed to get beyond small local initiatives, and the issues of unemployment, poverty and resisting the neo-fascists have been appropriated by the charismatic and highly suspect Bernard Tapie, who has been declared bankrupt and cannot stand for office in France (though he remains an MEP) until 1999.

On the Right, well established alliances are under strain, mainly because of Europe. No party of the Left or Right has been immune from scandal – mostly of a financial nature. While it hasn't necessarily put the voters off particular individuals, there is a growing disillusionment and apathy and a sense that the choice now lies with a much more radical Left – or no Left at all – and a much more right-wing Right.

ART

From the **Middle Ages** to the twentieth century, France has held – with occasional gaps – a leading position in the history of European painting, with Paris, above all, attracting artists from the whole continent. The story of French painting is one of richness and complexity, partly due to this influx of foreign painters and partly due to the capital's stability as an artistic centre.

BEGINNINGS

In the late Middle Ages, the itinerant life of the nobles led them to prefer small and transportable works of art; splendidly **illuminated manuscripts** were much praised and the best painters, usually trained in Paris, continued to work on a small scale until the fifteenth century. In spite of the size of the illuminated image, painters made startling steps towards a realistic interpretation of the world, and in the exploration of new subject matters.

Many of these illuminators were also panel painters, foremost of whom was **Jean Fouquet** (c.1420–c.1481), born in Tours in the Loire valley and the central artistic personality of fifteenth-century France. Court painter to Charles VIII, Fouquet drew from both Flemish and Italian sources, utilizing the new fluid oil technique that had been perfected in Flanders, and concerning himself with the problem of representing space convincingly, much like his Italian contemporaries. Through this he moulded a

distinct personal style, combining richness of surface with broad, generalized forms and, in his feeling for volume and ordered geometric shapes, laying down principles that became intrinsic to French art for centuries to come, from Poussin to Seurat and Cézanne.

Two other fifteenth-century French artists deserve brief mention here, principally for the broad range of artistic expression they embody. **Emguerrand Quarton** (c.1410–c.1466) was the most famous Provençal painter of the time; his art, profoundly religious in subject as well as feeling, already shows the impact of the Mediterranean sun in the strong light that pervades his paintings. His *Pietà* in the Louvre is both stark and intensely poignant, while the *Coronation of the Virgin* that hangs at Villeneuve-lès-Avignon is a vast panoramic vision not only of heaven but also of a very real earth, in what ranks as one of the first city/landscapes in the history of French painting: Avignon itself is faithfully depicted and the Mont Ste-Victoire, later to be made famous by Cézanne, is recognizable in the distance.

The **Master of Moulins**, active in the 1480s and 1490s, was noticeably more northern in temperament, painting both religious altarpieces and portraits commissioned by members of the royal family or the fast-increasing bourgeoisie.

MANNERISM & ITALIAN INFLUENCE

At the end of the fifteenth and the beginning of the sixteenth centuries, the French invasion of Italy brought both artists and patrons into closer contact with the Italian Renaissance.

The most famous of the artists who were lured to France was **Leonardo da Vinci**, spending the last three years of his life (1516–19) at the court of François I. From the Loire valley, which until then had been his favourite residence, the French king moved nearer to Paris, where he had several palaces decorated. Italian artists were once again called upon and two of them, **Rosso** and **Primaticcio**, who arrived in France in 1530 and 1532, were to shape the artistic scene in France for the rest of the sixteenth century.

Both artists introduced to France the latest Italian style, **Mannerism**, a sometimes anarchic derivation of the High Renaissance of

Michelangelo and Raphael. Mannerism, with its emphasis on the fantastic, the luxurious and the large-scale decorative was eminently compatible with the taste of the court, and it was first put to the test in the revamping of the old Château de Fontainebleau.

There, a horde of French painters headed by the two Italians came to form what was subsequently called the **School of Fontainebleau**. Most French artists worked at Fontainebleau at some point in their career, or were influenced by its homogeneous style, but none stands out as a personality of any stature, and for the most part the painting of the time was dull and fanciful in the extreme.

Antoine Caron (c.1520–c.1600), who often worked for Catherine de Médicis, the widow of Henry II, contrived complicated allegorical paintings in which elongated figures are arranged within wide, theatre-like scenery packed with ancient monuments and Roman statues. Even the Wars of Religion, raging in the 1550s and 1560s, failed to rouse French artists' sense of drama, and representations of the many massacres then going on were detached and fussy in tone.

Portraiture tended to be more inventive. The portraits of **Jean Clouet** (c.1485–1541) and his son **François** (c.1510–72), both official painters to François I, combined sensitivity in the rendering of the sitter's features with a keen sense of abstract design in the arrangement of the figure, conveying with great clarity social status and giving clues to the sitter's profession. Though influenced by sixteenth-century Italian and Flemish portraits, their work remains nonetheless very French in its general sobriety.

THE SEVENTEENTH CENTURY

In the seventeenth century, Italy continued to be a source of inspiration for French artists, most of whom were drawn to Rome, at that time the most exciting artistic centre in Europe. There, two Italian artists especially dominated the scene in the first decade of the century: Michelangelo Merisi da Caravaggio and Annibale Carracci.

Caravaggio (d. 1610) often chose low-life subjects and treated them with remarkable realism, a realism that he extended to traditional religious subject matter and that he enhanced by using a strong, harsh lighting

technique. Although he had to flee Rome in great haste under sentence of murder in 1606, Caravaggio had already had a profound effect on the art of the age, both in terms of subjects and in his uncompromising use of realism.

Some French painters like **Moise Valentin** (c.1594–1632) worked in Rome and were directly influenced by Caravaggio; others, such as the great painter from Lorraine, **Georges de la Tour** (1593–1652), benefitted from his innovations at one remove, gaining inspiration from the Utrecht *Caravaggisti* who were active at the time in Holland. Starting with a descriptive realism in which naturalistic detail made for a varied painted surface, La Tour gradually simplified both forms and surfaces, producing deeply felt religious paintings in which figures appear to be carved out of the surrounding gloom by the magical light of a candle. Sadly, his output was very small – just some forty or so works in all.

Low-life subjects and attention to naturalistic detail were also important aspects of the work of the **Le Nain Brothers**, especially **Louis** (1593–1648), who depicted with great sympathy, but never with sentimentality, the condition of the peasantry. He chose moments of inactivity or repose within the lives of the peasants and his paintings achieve timelessness and monumentality by their very stillness.

The other Italian artist of influence, the Bolognese **Annibale Carracci** (d. 1609), impressed French painters not only with his skill as a decorator but, more tellingly, with his ordered, balanced landscapes, which were to prove of prime importance for the development of the classical landscape in general, and in particular for those painted by **Claude Lorrain** (1600–82).

Claude, who started work as a pastry cook, was born in Lorraine, near Nancy. He left France for Italy to practise his trade and worked in the household of a landscape painter in Rome, somehow persuading his master, who painted landscapes in the classical manner of Carracci, to let him abandon pastry for painting. Later he travelled to Naples, where the beauty of the harbour and bay made a lasting impression on him, the golden light of the southern port, and of Rome and its surrounding countryside, providing him with endless subjects of study which he drew, sketched and painted for the rest of his life. Claude's landscapes are airy compositions in which religious or mythological figures are lost within an idealized, Arcadian nature, bathed in a luminous, transparent light that, golden or silvery, lends a tranquil mood.

Landscapes, harsher and even more ordered, but also recalling the Arcadian mood of antiquity, were painted by the other French painter who elected to make Rome his home, **Nicolas Poussin** (1593–1665). Like Claude, Poussin selected his themes from the rich sources of Greek, Roman and Christian myths and stories, but unlike Claude, his figures are not subdued by nature but rather dominate it, in the tradition of the masters of the High Renaissance, such as Raphael and Titian, whom he greatly admired. During the working out of a painting Poussin would make small models, arrange them on an improvised stage and then sketch the puppet scene – which may explain why his figures often have a still, frozen quality. Poussin only briefly returned to Paris, called by the king, Louis XIII, to undertake some large decorative works quite unsuited to his style or character. Back in Rome he refined a style that became increasingly classical and severe.

Many other artists visited Italy but most returned to France, the luckiest to be employed at the court to boost the royal images of Louis XIII and XIV and the egos of their respective ministers, Richelieu and Colbert. **Simon Vouet** (1590–1649), **Charles Le Brun** (1619–90) and **Pierre Mignard** (1612–95) all performed that task with skill, often using ancient history and mythology to suggest flattering comparisons with the reigning monarch.

The official aspect of their works was parallelled by the creation of the new **Academy of Painting and Sculpture** in 1648, an institution that dominated the arts in France for the next few hundred years, if only by the way artists reacted against it. **Philippe de Champaigne** (1602–74), a painter of Flemish origin, alone stands out at the time as remotely different, removed from the intrigues and pleasures of the court and instead strongly influenced by the teaching and moral code of Jansenism, a purist and severe form of the Catholic faith. The apparent simplicity and starkness of his portraits hides an unusually perceptive understanding of his sitters' personalities. But it was the more courtly, fun-loving portraits and paintings by such artists as Mignard which were to influence most of the art of the following century.

THE EARLY EIGHTEENTH CENTURY

The semi-official art encouraged by the foundation of the Academy became more frivolous and lighthearted in the eighteenth century. The court at Versailles lost its attractions, and many patrons now were to be found among the hedonistic bourgeoisie and aristocracy living in Paris. History painting, as opposed to genre scenes or portraiture, retained its position of prestige, but at the same time the various categories began to merge and many artists tried their hands at landscape, genre, history, or decorative works, bringing aspects of one type into another. **Salons**, at which painters exhibited their works, were held with increasing frequency and bred a new phenomenon in the art world – the art critic. The philosopher **Diderot** was one of the first of these arbiters of taste, doers and undoers of reputations.

Possibly the most complex personality of the eighteenth century was **Jean-Antoine Watteau** (1684–1721). Primarily a superb draughtsman, Watteau's use of soft and yet rich, light colours showed how much he was struck by the great seventeenth-century Flemish painter Rubens. The open air scenes of flirtatious love painted by Rubens and by the eighteenth-century Venetian Giorgione provided Watteau with precedents for his own subtle depictions of dreamy couples (sometimes depictions of characters from the Italian Comedy) strolling in delicate, mythical landscapes. In some of these *Fêtes Galantes* and in pictures of solitary musicians or actors (*Gilles*), Watteau conveyed a mood of melancholy, loneliness and poignancy that was largely lacking in the works of his many imitators and followers (Nicolas Lancret, J. B. Pater).

The work of **François Boucher** (1703–70) was probably more representative of the eighteenth century: the pleasure-seeking court of Louis XV found the lightness of morals and colours in his paintings immensely congenial. Boucher's virtuosity is seen at its best in his paintings of women, always rosy, young and fantasy-erotic.

Jean-Honoré Fragonard (1732–1806) continued this exploration of licentious themes but with an exuberance, a richness of colour and a vitality (*The Swing*) that was a feast for the eyes and raised the subject to a glorification of love. Far more restrained were the paintings of **Jean-Baptiste-Siméon Chardin** (1699–1779), who specialized in homely genre scenes and still lifes, painted with a simplicity that belied a complex use of colours, shapes and space to promote a mood of stillness and tranquility. **Jean-Baptiste Greuze** (1725–1805) chose stories that anticipated reaction against the laxity of the times; the moral, at times sentimental, character of his paintings was all-pervasive, reinforced by a stage-like composition well suited to cautionary tales.

NEOCLASSICISM

This new seriousness became more severe with the rise of **Neoclassicism**, a movement for which purity and simplicity were essential components of the systematic depiction of edifying stories from the classical authors. Roman history and legends were the most popular subjects, and though **Jacques-Louis David** (1748–1825), a pupil of an earlier exponent of Neoclassicism, J. M. Vien, conformed to that to a certain extent, he was different in that he was also keenly sensitive to the changing mood and philosophies of his time and to the reaction against frivolity and self-indulgence. Many of his paintings are reflections of Republican ideals and of contemporary history, from the *Death of Marat* to events from the life of Napoléon who was his patron. For the emperor and his family, David painted some of his most successful portraits – *Madame Recamier* is not only an exquisite example of David's controlled use of shapes and space and his debt to antique Rome, but can also be seen as a paradigm of Neoclassicism.

Two painters, **Jean-Antoine Gros** (1771–1835) and **Baron Gérard** (1770–1837), followed David closely in style and in themes (portraits, Napoleonic history and legend) but often with a touch of softness and heroic poetry that pointed the way to Romanticism.

Jean-Auguste-Dominique Ingres (1780–1867) was a pupil of David; he also studied in Rome before coming back to Paris to develop the purity of line that was the essential and characteristic element of his art. His effective use of it to build up forms and bind compositions can be admired in conjunction with his recurrent theme of female nudes bathing, or in his magnificent and stately portraits that depict the nuances of social status.

ROMANTICISM

Completely opposed to the stress on drawing advocated by Ingres, two artists created, through their emphasis on colour, form and composition, pictures that look forward to the later part of the nineteenth century and the Impressionists. **Théodore Géricault** (1791–1824), whose short life was still dominated by the heroic vision of the Napoleonic era, explored dramatic themes of human suffering in such paintings as *The Raft of Medusa*, while his close contemporary, **Eugène Delacroix** (1798–1863), epitomized the **Romantic movement**, its search for emotions and its love of nature, power and change.

Delacroix was deeply aware of tradition, and his art was influenced, visually and conceptually, by the great masters of the Renaissance and the seventeenth and eighteenth centuries. In many ways he may be regarded as the last great religious and decorative French painter, but through his technical virtuosity, freedom of brushwork and richness of colours, he can also be seen as the essential forerunner of the Impressionists. For Delacroix there was no conflict between colour and design: David and Ingres saw these elements as separate aspects of creation, but Delacroix used colours as the basis and structure of his designs. His technical freedom was partly due to his admiration for two English painters, John Constable and his close friend, Richard Parkes Bonington, with whom he shared a studio for a few months. Bonington especially had a freshness of approach to colour and a free handling of paint, both of which had a strong impact on Delacroix. His numerous themes ranged from intimate female nudes, often with mysterious and erotic Middle Eastern overtones, to studies of animals and hunting scenes. Ancient and contemporary history supplied him with some of his most harrowing and dramatic paintings: *The Massacre at Chios* was based on an event that took place during the Greek War of Independence from the Turks, and *Liberty Guiding the People* was painted to commemorate the Revolution of 1830. Both paintings were his personal response to contemporary events and the human tragedies they entailed.

Other painters working in the Romantic tradition were still haunted by the Napoleonic legends, as well as by North Africa (Algeria) and the Middle East, which had become better known to artists and patrons alike during the Napoleonic wars. These were the subjects of paintings by **Horace Vernet** (1789–1863), **Jean-Louis-Ernest Meissonier** (1815–91) and **Théodore Chassériau** (1819–56).

Among their contemporaries was **Honoré Daumier** (1808–79): very much an isolated figure, influenced by the boldness of approach of caricaturists, he was content to depict everyday subjects such as a laundress or a third-class rail car – caustic commentaries on professions and politics that work as brilliant observations of the times.

THE NINETEENTH CENTURY

Some painters of the first part of the nineteenth century were fascinated by other themes. Nature, in its true state, unadorned by conventions, became a subject for study, and running parallel to this was the realization that painting could be the visual externalization of the artist's own emotions and feelings. These two aspects, which until this time had only been very tentatively touched upon, were now more fully explored and led directly to the innovations of the Impressionists and later painters.

Jean-Baptiste-Camille Corot (1796–1875) started to paint landscapes that were fresh, direct and influenced as much by the unpretentious and realistic country scenes of seventeenth-century Holland as by the balanced compositions of Claude. His loving and attentive studies of nature were much admired by later artists, including Monet.

At the same time a whole group of painters developed similar attitudes to landscape and nature. Helped greatly by the practical improvement of being able to buy oil paint in tubes rather than as unmixed pigments, they – known as the **Barbizon School** after the village on the outskirts of Paris round which they painted – soon discovered the joy and excitement of *plein-air* (open-air) painting.

Théodore Rousseau (1812–67) was their nominal leader, his paintings of forest undergrowth and forest clearings displaying an intimacy that came from the immediacy of the image. **Charles-François Daubigny** (1817–78), like Rousseau, often infused a sense of drama into his landscapes.

Jean-François Millet is perhaps the best-known associate of the Barbizon group, though he was more interested in the human figure than simple nature. Landscapes, however, were essential settings for his figures; indeed, his most famous pictures are those exploring the place of people in nature and their struggle to survive. *The Sower*, for instance, was a typical Millet theme, suggesting the heroic working life of the peasant. As is so often the case for painters touching on new themes or on ideas that are uncomfortable to the rich and powerful, Millet enjoyed little success during his lifetime, and his art was only widely recognized after his death.

The moralistic and romantic undertone in Millet's work was something that **Gustave Courbet** (1819–77) strove to avoid. Courbet was a socialist and his frank, outspoken attitude led to his being accused of taking part in the destruction of the column in place Vendôme in Paris after the outbreak of the Commune and, eventually, to his exile. After an initial resounding success in the Salon exhibition of 1849, he endured constant criticism from the academic world and patrons alike: scenes of ordinary life, such as the *Funeral at Orléans*, which he often chose to depict, were regarded as unsavoury and deliberately ugly.

But Courbet had a deep admiration for the old masters, especially for Rembrandt and the Spanish painters of the seventeenth and eighteenth centuries, and his link with tradition was probably one of the underlying themes of his large masterpiece, *The Studio*, which was emphatically rejected by the jury of the 1855 Exposition Universelle, and in which Courbet portrayed himself, surrounded by his model, his friends, colleagues and admirers, among them the poet Baudelaire. Courbet subsequently decided to hold a private exhibition of some forty of his works, writing at the same time a manifesto explaining his intentions of being true to his vision of the world and of creating "living art". Writing the word **Realism** in large letters on the door leading to the exhibition, he stated his intentions and gave a label to his art.

IMPRESSIONISM

Like Courbet, **Edouard Manet** (1832–83) was

strongly influenced by Spanish painters, whose works had become more easily accessible to artists when a large collection belonging to the Orléans family was confiscated by the state in 1848. Unlike Courbet, though, he never saw himself as a socialist or indeed as a rebel or avant-garde painter, yet his technique and interpretation of themes was quite new and shocked as many people as it inspired. Manet used bold contrasts of light and very dark colours, giving his paintings a forcefulness that critics often took for a lack of sophistication. And his detractors saw much to decry in his reworking of an old subject originally treated by the sixteenth-century Venetian painter, Giorgione, *Le Déjeuner sur l'herbe*. Manet's version was shocking because he placed naked and dressed figures together, and because the men were dressed in the costume of the day, implying a pleasure party too specifically contemporary to be "respectable".

Manet was not interested in painting moral lessons, however, and some of his most successful pictures are reflections of ordinary life in bars and public places, where respectability, as understood by the late-nineteenth-century bourgeoisie, was certainly lacking. To Manet, painting was to be enjoyed for its own sake and not as a tool for moral instruction – in itself an outlook on the role of art that was quite new, not to say revolutionary, and marked a definite break with the paintings of the past. With Manet the basis of our present expectations and understanding of modern art was set.

Although it is doubtful whether Manet either wanted or expected to assume the role of leader, **Claude Monet** (1840–1926) looked to the older artist as the painter in whose works the principles of **Impressionism** were first formulated. Born in Le Havre, Monet came in contact with **Eugène Boudin** (1824–98), whose colourful beach scenes anticipated the way the Impressionists approached colour. He then went to Paris to study under Charles Gleyre, a respected teacher in whose studio he met many of the people with whom he formulated his ideas. Monet soon discovered that, for him, light and the way in which it builds up forms and creates an infinity of colours was the element that governed all representations. Under the impact of Manet's bright hues and his unconventional attitude, "art for art's sake",

Monet soon began using pure colours side by side, blended together to create areas of brightness and shade.

In 1874, a group of some thirty artists exhibited together for the first time. Among them were some of the best-known names of this period of French art: Dégas, Monet, Renoir, Pissarro. One of Monet's paintings was entitled *Impression: Sun Rising*, a title that was singled out by the critics to ridicule the colourful, loose, and unacademic style of these young artists. Overnight they became, derisively, the "Impressionists".

Camille Pissarro (1830–1903) was slightly older than most of them and seems to have played the part of an encouraging father-figure, always keenly aware of any new development or new talent. Not a great innovator himself, Pissarro was a very gifted artist whose use of Impressionist technique was supplemented by a lyrical feeling for nature and its seasonal changes. But it was really with **Monet** that Impressionist theory ran its full course: he studied endlessly the impact of light on objects and the way in which it reveals colours. To understand this phenomenon better, Monet painted the same motif again and again under different conditions of light, at different times of the day, and in different seasons, producing whole series of paintings such as *Hay Stacks*, *Poplars* and, much later, his *Waterlilies*. In the late 1870s and the early 1880s many other artists helped formulate the new style, but few remained true to its principles for very long.

Auguste Renoir (1841–1919), who started life as a painter of porcelain, was swept away by Monet's ideas for a while, but soon felt the need to look again at the old masters and to emphasize the importance of drawing to the detriment of colour. Renoir regarded the representation of the female nude as the most taxing and rewarding subject that an artist could tackle. Like Boucher in the eighteenth century, Renoir's nudes are luscious, but they are rarely, if ever, erotic. They have a healthy, uncomplicated quality that was, in his later paintings, to become cloyingly, almost overpoweringly, sickly and sweet. Better were his portraits of women fully clothed, both for their obvious and innate sympathy and for their keen sense of design.

Edgar Degas (1834–1917) was yet another artist who, although he exhibited with the Impressionists, did not follow their precepts very closely. The son of a rich banker, he was trained in the tradition of Ingres: design and drawing were an integral part of his art, and whereas Monet was fascinated mainly by light, Degas wanted to express movement in all its forms. His pictures are vivid expressions of the body in action, usually straining under fairly exacting circumstances – dancers and circus *artistes* were among his favourite subjects, as well as more mundane depictions of laundresses and other working women.

Like so many artists of the day, Degas had his imagination fired by the discovery of **Japanese prints**, which could for the first time be seen in quantity. These provided him with new ideas of composition, not least in their asymmetry of design and the use of large areas of unbroken colour. **Photography**, too, had an impact, if only because it finally liberated artists from the task of producing accurate, exacting descriptions of the world.

Degas's extraordinary gift as a draughtsman was matched only by that of the Provençal aristocrat **Henri de Toulouse-Lautrec** (1864–1901). Toulouse-Lautrec, who had broken both his legs as a child, was unusually small, a physical deformity that made him particularly sensitive to free and vivacious movements. A great admirer of Degas, he chose similar themes: people in cafés and theatres, working women and variety dancers all figured large in his work. But unlike Degas, Toulouse-Lautrec looked at more than the body, and his work is scattered with social comment, sometimes sardonic and bitter. In his portrayal of Paris prostitutes, there is sympathy and kindness, and to study them better he lived in a brothel, revealing in his paintings the weariness and sometimes gentleness of these women.

POST-IMPRESSIONISM

Though a rather vague term, as it's difficult to date exactly when the backlash against Impressionism took place, **Post-Impressionism** represents in many ways a return to more formal concepts of painting – in composition, in attitudes to subject, and in drawing.

Paul Cézanne (1839–1906), for one, associated only very briefly with the Impressionists and spent most of his working life in relative isolation, obsessed with rendering, as objec-

tively as possible, the essence of form. He saw objects as basic shapes – cylinders, cones etc – and tried to give the painting a unity of texture that would force the spectator to view it not so much as representation of the world but rather as an entity in its own right, as an object as real and dense as the objects surrounding it. It was this striving for pictorial unity that led him to cover the entire surface of the picture with small, equal brushstrokes which made no distinction between the textures of a tree, a house, or the sky.

The detached, unemotional way in which Cézanne painted was not unlike that of the seventeenth-century artist, Poussin and he found a contemporary parallel in the work of **Georges Seurat**. Seurat (1859–91) was fascinated by current theories of light and colour, and he attempted to apply them in a systematic way, creating different shades and tones by placing tiny spots of pure colour side by side, which the eye could in turn fuse together to see the colours mixed out of their various components. This **pointillist** technique also had the effect of giving monumentality to everyday scenes of contemporary life.

While Cézanne, Seurat and, for that matter, the Impressionists, sought to represent the outside world objectively, several other artists – the **Symbolists** – were seeking a different kind of truth, through the subjective experience of fantasy and dreams. **Gustav Moreau** (1840–98) represented, in complex paintings, the intricate worlds of the romantic fairy tale, his visions expressed in a wealth of naturalistic details. The style of **Puvis de Chavannes** (1824–98) was more restrained and more obviously concerned with design and the decorative. And a third artist, **Odilon Redon** (1840–1916), produced some weird and visionary graphic work that especially intrigued Symbolist writers; his less frequent works in colour belong to the later part of his life.

The subjectivity of the Symbolists was of great importance to the art of **Paul Gauguin** (1843–1903). He started life as a stockbroker who collected Impressionist paintings, a Sunday artist who gave up his job in 1883 to dedicate himself to painting.

During his stay in Pont-Aven in Brittany, Gauguin worked with a number of artists who called themselves **the Nabis, Paul Serusier** and **Émile Bernard** among them; he began exploring ways of expressing concepts and emotions by means of large areas of colour and powerful forms, and developing a unique style that was heavily indebted to his knowledge of Japanese prints and of the tapestries and stained glass of medieval art. His search for the primitive expression of primitive emotions took him eventually to the South Sea islands and Tahiti, where he found some of his most inspiring subjects and painted some of his best-known canvases.

A similar derivation from Symbolist art and a wish to exteriorize emotions and ideas by means of strong colours, lines and shapes underlies the work of **Vincent Van Gogh** (1853–90), a Dutch painter who came to live in France. Like Gauguin, with whom he had an admiring but stormy friendship, Van Gogh started painting relatively late in life, lightening his palette in Paris under the influence of the Impressionists, and then heading south to Arles where, struck by the harshness of the Mediterranean light, he turned out such frantic expressionistic pieces as *The Reaper* and *Wheatfield with Crows*. In all his later pictures the paint is thickly laid on in increasingly abstract patterns that follow the shapes and tortuous paths of his deep inner melancholy.

Both Gauguin and Van Gogh saw objects and colours as means of representing ideas and subjective feelings. **Edouard Vuillard** (1868–1940) and **Pierre Bonnard** (1867–1947) combined this with Cézanne's insistence on unifying the surface and texture of the picture. The result was, in both cases, paintings of often intimate scenes in which figures and objects are blended together in a series of complicated patterns. In some of Vuillard's works, people dressed in checked material, for example, merge into the flowered wallpaper behind them, and in the paintings of Bonnard, the glowing design of the canvas itself is as important as what it's trying to represent.

THE TWENTIETH CENTURY

The twentieth century kicked off to a colourful start with the **Fauvist** exhibition of 1905, an appropriately anarchic beginning to a century which, in France above all, was to see radical changes in attitudes towards painting.

The painters who took part in the exhibition included, most influentially, **Henri Matisse** (1869–1954), **André Derain** (1880–1954), **Georges Rouault** (1871–1958) and **Albert Marquet** (1875–1947), and they were quickly nicknamed the Fauves (Wild Beasts) for their use of bright, wild colours that often bore no relation whatsoever to the reality of the object depicted. Skies were just as likely green as blue since, for the Fauves, colour was a way of composing, of structuring a picture, and not necessarily a reflection of real life.

Fauvism was just the beginning: the first decades of the twentieth century were times of intense excitement and artistic activity in Paris, and painters and sculptors from all over Europe flocked to the capital to take part in the liberation from conventional art that individuals and groups were gradually instigating.

Pablo Picasso (1881–1973) was one of the first, arriving here in 1900 from Spain and soon thereafter starting work on his first *Blue Period* paintings, which describe the sad and squalid life of intinerant actors in tones of blue. Later, while Matisse was experimenting with colours and their decorative potential, Picasso came under the sway of Cézanne and his organization of forms into geometrical shapes. He also learned from "primitive", and especially African, sculpture and out of these studies came a painting that heralded a definite new direction, not only for Picasso's own style but for the whole of modern art – *Les Demoiselles d'Avignon*. Executed in 1907, this painting combined Cézanne's analysis of forms with the visual impact of African masks.

It was from this semi-abstract picture that Picasso went on to develop the theory of **Cubism**, inspiring artists such as **Georges Braque** (1882–1963) and **Juan Gris** (1887–1927), another Spaniard, and formulating a whole new movement. The Cubists' aim was to depict objects not so much as they saw them but rather as they knew them to be: a bottle and a guitar were shown from the front, from the side, and from the back as if the eye could take in all at once every facet and plane of the object. Braque and Picasso first analysed forms into these facets (analytical Cubism), then gradually reduced them to series of colours and shapes (synthetic Cubism), among which a few recognizable symbols such as letters, fragments of newspaper and numbers appeared. The complexity of different planes overlapping one another made the deciphering of Cubist paintings sometimes difficult, and the very last phase of Cubism tended increasingly towards abstraction.

Spin-offs of Cubism were many: such movements as **Orphism**, headed by **Robert Delaunay** (1885–1941), who experimented not with objects but with the colours of the spectrum; and **Futurism**, which evolved first in Italy, then in Paris, and explored movement and the bright new technology of the industrial age. **Fernand Léger** (1881–1955), one of the main exponents of the so-called School of Paris, had also become acquainted with modern machinery during World War I, and he exploited his fascination with its smoothness and power to create geometric and monumental compositions of technical imagery that were indebted to both Cézanne and Cubism.

The war meanwhile had affected many artists: in Switzerland **Dada** was born out of the scorn artists felt for the petty bourgeois and nationalistic values that had led to the bloodshed, a nihilistic movement that sought to knock down all traditionally accepted ideas. It was best exemplified in the work of the Frenchman **Marcel Duchamp** (1887–1968), who selected ready-made, everyday objects and elevated them, without modification, to the rank of works of art by pulling them out of their ordinary context, or defaced such sacred cows as the Mona Lisa by decorating her with a moustache and an obscene caption.

Dada was also a literary movement, and through one of its main poets, André Breton, it led to the inception of **Surrealism**. It was the unconscious and its dark unchartered territories that interested the Surrealists: they derived much of their imagery from Freud and even experimented in words and images with free-association techniques.

Strangely enough, most of the "French" Surrealists were foreigners, primarily the German **Max Ernst** (1891–1976) and the Spaniards **Yves Tanguy** (1900–55) and **Salvador Dali** (1904–89). Mournful landscapes of weird, often terrifying images evoked the landscape of nightmares in often very precise details and with an anguish that went on to influence artists for years to come. Picasso, for instance, shocked by the massacre of the Spanish town of *Guernica* in 1936, drew greatly from Surrealism to produce the disquieting figures of his painting of the same name.

World War II put an end to the prominence of Paris as the artistic melting pot of Europe. Painters had rushed there at the beginning of the twentieth century and after World War I, contributing by their individuality, originality and different nationalities to the richness and constant renewal of artistic endeavour, but at the beginning of World War II they emigrated to the United States. And although many have since drifted back, artistic leadership has remained in New York. Still, desertion of Paris should not obscure the fact that over a span of some six centuries, French painters or painters trained in France produced some of the most significant monuments of European painting

Ann Rook

ARCHITECTURE

France's architectural legacy is rich and important, reflecting the power and personality of subsequent kings, the Church and the state, vying to outdo their peers with bold, lavish statements in brick and stone. Many architectural trends filtered into France from Italy – Romanesque, Renaissance and Baroque – but they have been refined and developed by the French. Rococo grew from Baroque, Neoclassicism came from the Renaissance, and Art Nouveau was a brilliant, confused jumble of Baroque features combined with the newly developed cast-iron industry. Architecture this century has produced two great names – Auguste Perret and Le Corbusier – but France's contemporary scene is still thriving, with a host of new developments throughout the country.

THE ROMANS

The south of France was colonized by the **Romans** by around 120 BC in order to expand their trading operations, and they set up substantial settlements at Marseille, Narbonne, Orange, Arles, Fréjus, Glanum near St-Rémy, and Nice, with a network of roads linking them.

The Romans were fine town planners, linking complexes of buildings with straight roads punctuated by decorative fountains, arches and colonnades. They built essentially in the Greek style, and their large, functional buildings were concerned more with strength and solidity than design. A number of substantial Roman building works survive: in **Nîmes** you can see the Maison Carrée, the best-preserved Roman temple still standing, and the Temple of Diana, one of just four vaulted Roman temples in Europe. Gateways remain at **Autun**, **Orange**, **Saintes** and **Reims**, and largely intact amphitheatres can be seen at **Nîmes** and **Arles**. The **Pont du Gard** aqueduct outside of Nîmes is still a magnificent and ageless monument of civil engineering, built to carry the town's fresh water over the gorge, and Orange has its massive theatre, with Europe's only intact Roman façade. There are excavated archeological sites at **Glanum** near St-Rémy, **Vaison-la-Romaine** and **Lyon**.

CAROLINGIAN AND ROMANESQUE

The Carolingian dynasty of Charlemagne attempted a revival of the symbols of civilized authority by recourse to Roman or "Romanesque" models. Of this era, practically nothing remains visible, though the motifs of arch and vault are carried on in their simplest forms; and the semicircular apse and the basilican plan of nave and aisles persists as the basis of the succeeding phases of Christian architecture. An interesting anomaly is the plan of the **church of St-Front** at Périgueux, a copy of St Mark's in Venice, brought by trading influence west along the Garonne in the early twelfth century.

Elsewhere development may be divided roughly north–south of the Loire. Southern **Romanesque** is naturally more Roman, with stone barrel vaults, aisleless naves and domes. **St-Trophime** at Arles (1150) has a porch directly derived from Roman models and, with the church at St-Gilles nearby, exhibits a delight in carved ornament peculiar to the south at this time. **Angoulême Cathedral** typifies the use of all these elements.

The south, too, was the readiest route for the introduction of new cultural developments, and it is here that the pointed arch and vault first appear – from Saracen sources – in churches such as **Notre-Dame** at Avignon, **Autun Cathedral**, and **Ste-Madeleine** at Vézelay (1089–1206), which contains the earliest pointed cross vault in France.

In the north of the country, the nave with aisles is more usual, together with the development of twin western towers to mask the end of the aisles. The **Abbaye-aux-Hommes** at Caen (1066–77) is typical. It contains the elements later developed as "Gothic", in piers, pillars, buttresses, arcades, ribbed vaults and spires. The best examples may be found in Normandy, and it is from here, with the introduction of the pointed arch from the south, that the Gothic style developed.

GOTHIC

The reasons behind the development of the **Gothic style** lie in the pursuit of sensations of the sublime; to achieve great height without apparent great weight would seem to imitate religious ambition. Its development in the north is partly due to the availability of good building stone and soft stone for carving, but perhaps more to the growth of royal aspiration and power based in the Île de France, which, allied with the papacy, stimulated the building of the great **cathedrals** of Paris, Bourges, Chartres, Laon, Le Mans, Reims and Amiens in the twelfth and thirteenth centuries.

The Gothic phase began with the building of the choir of the **abbey of St-Denis** near Paris in 1140, to run through to the end of the fifteenth century. Architecturally, it encompasses the development of wider, traceried windows of coloured glass, filling the wall spaces liberated by the refinement of vertical structure; the "rose" or wheel is an early and especially French feature in window tracery. The glass at Chartres shows better than anywhere the concerted architectural effect of these developments. Another distinctive element is the flying buttress outside the walls to resist the outward push of the vaulting.

In the south, as at Albi and Angers, the great churches are generally broader and simpler in plan and external appearance, with aisles often almost as high as the nave. Many secular buildings survive – some of the most notable the work of Viollet-le-Duc, the preeminent nineteenth-century restorer – and even whole towns, for example **Carcassonne** and **Aigues Mortes**; **Avignon** has the bridge and the papal palace.

Castles, of necessity, lent themselves less to the disappearing walls of the Gothic style. The **Château de Pierrefonds**, as restored by Viollet, may be taken as typical. The walls of many others disappeared by force, not whim,

as gunpowder made them obsolete and a more settled and subjugated order led to the development of château-palaces, such as **Châteaudun** (1441) and **Blois**. The **Château de Josselin** in Brittany is a marvellous example of the smaller fortresses that became common towards the end of the Gothic period. A series of colonial settlements, the *bastides*, or fortified towns, of the English occupation, remain in the Dordogne region and are a refreshing antidote to triumphal French bombast.

RENAISSANCE

Quite early in the sixteenth century the influence of the new style of the Italian Renaissance began to appear. Coupled with the persistence of Gothic traditions and the necessity of steep roofs and tall chimneys in a French climate, it appears immediately "Frenchified" rather than in its pure imported form. The châteaux of kings and courtiers round Paris and in the Loire Valley, such as **Blois, Chambord, Chenonceau and Fontainebleau**, exemplify this style, with their wholly un-Italian concentration of interest on the skyline and an elaboration of detail in the façades at the expense of the clear modelling of form. With the passing of time, however, the style became more purely classical.

The Louvre in Paris and the Château de Blois are notable examples of the developing **classicism**. The wing of the **Château de Blois** containing the famous staircase designed for François I in 1515 shows the beginning of an emphasis on horizontal lines and an overlay of Italian motifs on a basically Gothic form. The elevations, designed by **Mansart** in 1635, though distinctively French, are just as typically classical.

The **Louvre** even more embodies the whole history of the classical style in France, having been worked over by all the grand names of French architecture from Lescot in the early sixteenth century, via François Mansart and Claude Perrault in the seventeenth, to the later years of the nineteenth century. A recent turning point is the work of **I. M. Pei**, whose pyramid addition has proved a controversial departure from the Louvre's sober style.

It is unfortunate that the Renaissance style in France is chiefly seen in such structures as the Louvre and Versailles, which because of their scale can scarcely be experienced as buildings. That this is the case is largely due to the developing despotism and concentration of power under Louis XIII and XIV. But there was a lighter side to this. François Mansart, at **Blois** and **Maisons Lafitte** (1640), shows a certain suavity and elegance, which appears again in the eighteenth century in the town houses of the Rococo period, the generally reticent exteriors of which belie the vivacity and charm of the private life within.

On the other hand, **Claude Perrault** (1613–88), who designed the great colonnaded east front of the Louvre, gives an austere face to the official architecture of despotism, magnificent but far too imperial to be much enjoyed by common mortals. The high-pitched roofs, which had been almost universal until then, are replaced here by the classical balustrade and pediment, the style grand but cold and supremely secular. Art and architecture were at the time organized by boards and academies, and in the latter style and employment were strictly controlled by royal direction. Between 1643 and 1774 France was governed by two monarchs, who both ruled by the same maxim – absolute power. With such a limitation of ideas at the source of patronage, it is hardly surprising that there was a certain dullness to the era, at least in the acknowledged monuments of French architecture.

BAROQUE AND ROCOCO

In a similar way to the preceding century, the churches of the **seventeenth and eighteenth centuries** have a coldness quite different from the German and Flemish Baroque or the Italian. When the Renaissance style first appeared in the early sixteenth century, there was no great need for new church building, the country being so well endowed from the Gothic centuries. **St-Étienne-du-Mont** (1517–1620) and **St-Eustache** (1532–89), both in Paris, show how old forms persisted with only an overlay of the new style.

It is with the Jesuits in the seventeenth century that the Church embraced the new style to combat the forces of rational disbelief. In Paris the churches of the **Sorbonne** (1653) and **Val-de-Grâce** (1645) exemplify this, as do a good number of other grandiose churches in the **Baroque** style, through **Les Invalides** at the end of the seventeenth century to the **Panthéon** of the late eighteenth century. Here

is the Church triumphant rather than the state, but no more beguiling.

The architect of Les Invalides was **Jules Hardouin Mansart**, a product of the academy, who also greatly extended the palace of **Versailles** and so created the cinemascope view of France, with that seemingly endless horizon of royalty. As an antidote to this pomposity, the **Petit Trianon** at Versailles is as refreshing now as it was to Louis XV, who had it built in 1762 as a place of escape for his mistress. And even more so is this true of that other pearl formed of the grit of boredom in the enclosed world of Versailles – **La Petite Ferme,** where Marie-Antoinette played at being a milkmaid, which epitomizes the Arcadian and "picturesque" fantasy of the painters Boucher and Fragonard.

The lightness and charm that was undermining official grandeur with Arcadian fancies and Rococo decoration was, however, snuffed out by the Revolution. There is no real Revolutionary architecture, as the necessity of order and authority soon asserted itself and an autocracy every bit as absolute returned with Napoléon, drawing on the old grand manner but with a stronger trace of the stern old Roman. One architect, **Claude Ledoux**, was highly original and influential, both in England and Germany. And the visionary millennialist **Boullée** could also be said to be a child of revolutionary times, though it is likely that such men were inspired as much by the rediscovered plainness of the Greek Doric order as by radical politics.

In Paris it was not the democratic Doric but the imperial Corinthian order that re-emerged triumphant in the church of the **Madeleine** (1806) and, with the **Arc de Triomphe** like some colossal paperweight, reimposed the authority of academic architecture, in contrast to the fancy-dress architecture of contemporary Regency England.

THE NINETEENTH CENTURY

The restoration of legitimate monarchy after the **fall of Napoléon** stimulated a revival of interest in older Gothic and early Renaissance styles, which offered a symbol of dynastic reassurance not only to the state but also to the newly rich. So in the private and commercial architecture of the nineteenth century these earlier styles predominate – in mine-owners' villas and bankers' headquarters.

By the mid-nineteenth century, a neo-Baroque strain had established itself, a style exemplified by Charles Garnier's **Opéra** in Paris (1861–74), which, under the heading of Second Empire and with its associations of voluptuous good living, seductive painting and general "ooh-la-la", provides probably the most persistent image of France among the non-French – though you should avoid being blinded by Puritan distaste to the splendid spatial and decorative sensations that the style can arouse. Nineteenth-century French buildings are due for a reassessment and keener appreciation.

In addition to the correct, official classicism and the robust, exuberant and commercial Baroque, there is a third strand running through the nineteenth century that was ultimately more fruitful. The rational engineering approach, embodied in the official **School of Roads and Bridges** and invigorated by the teaching of Viollet-le-Duc, who reinterpreted Gothic style as pure structure, led to the development of new structural techniques out of which "modern" architectural style was born. Iron was the first significant new material, often used in imitation of Gothic forms and destined to be developed as an individual architectural style in America. In the **Eiffel Tower** (1889), France set up a potent symbol of things to come.

A more significantly French development was in the use of reinforced concrete towards the end of the century, most notably by **Auguste Perret**, whose 1903 apartment house at 25 rue Franklin, Paris 16^e, turns the concrete structure into a visible virtue and breaks with conventional façades. Changes in the patterns of work and travel were making the need for new urban planning very acute in such cities as Paris. Perret and other **modernists** were all for the high-rise buildings that were going to better the haphazard layouts in America by a rational integration to new street systems. Some of their designs for gigantic skyscraper avenues and suburban rings now look like totalitarian horror movie sets. But it was tradition, not charity, that blocked their projects at the time.

THE TWENTIETH CENTURY

The greatest proponent of the super New York scale, who also had genuine if mistaken concern for how people lived, was **Le Corbusier**, the most famous twentieth-century French archi-tect. His stature may now appear diminished by the ascendancy of a blander style in concrete boxing, as well as by the significant technical and social failures of his buildings and his total disregard for historic streets and monuments.

But while his manifesto, *"Vers une architecture moderne"*, sounds like a call to arms for a new and revolutionary movement, Le Corbusier would be perhaps more fairly assessed as the original, inimitable and highly individual artist he undoubtedly was. You should try to see some of his work – there's the **Cité Radieuse** in Marseille and plenty of examples in Paris – to make up your own mind about the man largely responsible for changing the face and form of buildings throughout the world.

One respect in which Paris at the turn of the century lagged behind London, Glasgow, Chicago and New York was in **underground transport**. First proposed in the 1870s, it took twenty years of furious debate before the Paris métro was finally realized in 1900. The design of the entrances was as controversial as every other aspect of the system, but the first commission went to **Hector Guimard**, renowned for his variations on the then current fashion in style. The whirling metal railings, Art Nouveau lettering and bizarre antennae-like orange lamps were his creation. Conservatives were less amused when it came to sites such as the Opéra: **Charles Garnier**, architect of that edifice, demanded classical marble and bronze porticoes for every station, and his line was followed, on a less grandiose scale, wherever the métro steps surfaced by a major monument. Thus Guimard was out of a job. Some of the early ones remain (**Place des Abbesses**, 18e, is one), as do some of the white-tiled interiors, replaced after World War II in central stations by bright paint with matching seats and display cases.

Art Nouveau designs also found their way on to buildings – the early department stores in Paris are the best example – but the new materials and simple geometry of the modern or International Style favoured the Art Deco look; again, you're most likely to come across them in the capital.

Skipping the miserable 1950s and 1960s buildings everywhere, France again becomes one of the most exciting patrons of international **contemporary architecture**. The **Centre Beaubourg**, by **Renzo Piano and Richard Rogers**, derided, adored and visited by millions, maximizes space by putting the service elements usually concealed in walls and floors on the outside. The visible ducts, cables and pipes are painted in accordance with the colour code of architectural plans. You might think the whole thing is a professional "in" joke, but Beaubourg is one of the great contemporary buildings in western Europe – for its originality, popularity and practicality.

In **housing**, new styles and forms are to be seen in city suburbs and vacation resorts, many of them disastrous and visually unappealing but interesting to look at when you don't have to live there. The latest state-funded projects confirm French seriousness about innovative design – in Paris, the Louvre pyramid, the **Porte de la Villette** complex and the new **National Library**; in Marseille, William Alsop's mammoth seat of regional government, and the postmodern **Futuroscope** cinema complex just outisde of Poitiers.

The country's ever-advancing transport network has provided sites for some of the most high-tech office building with state-of-the-art engineering in Europe, as at **Eurolille**, the complex around Lille's *TGV* station and in **Roissy**, around the Charles-de-Gaulle airport. The *TGV* **Satolas** station is another typical 1990s creation, both elegant and thrustingly optimistic.

But the French are also very good at preserving the past. Throughout the country you'll see far older period streets, medieval and Renaissance, that look as though they've never been touched. More often than not, the restoration has been carried out by the **Maisons de Compagnonage**, the old craft guilds which have maintained traditional building skills, handing them down as of old from master to apprentice (and never to women), in addition to taking on new industrial skills.

Above all, though, bear in mind the extent and variety of architecture in France and don't feel intimidated by the established sights. If the empty grandeur of the Loire châteaux is oppressive, there are numerous smaller country houses open to the public, and such municipal buildings as the **Hôtels de Ville** tend to offer some charm or amusement, even in the smallest towns.

It is also possible in France to experience whole towns as consistent places of architecture, not only Carcassonne and Aigues-Mortes, Dinan and Nancy, but villages off the main roads in which time seems to have stopped long ago. And, besides, from any hotel bedroom, you can simply delight in what Le Corbusier called "the magnificent play of forms seen in light", in the movement of morning sunlight over ordinary provincial tiles and chimneys.

Robin Salmon

BOOKS

Publishers are detailed below in the form of British publisher/American publisher, where both exist. Where books are published in one country only, UK or US follows the publisher's name.

Abbreviations: o/p (out of print); U.P. (University Press).

TRAVEL

James Boswell *An Account of Corsica, The Journal of a Tour to that Island and Memoirs of Pascal Paoli* (Williams & Norgate, UK, o/p). Typically robust and witty account of encounters with the Corsican people, including absorbing insights into the psychology of local hero Pascal Paoli. Excerpts published in *Journals of James Boswell* (Mandarin, UK).

Dorothy Carrington *Granite Island* (Penguin, UK/US). A fascinating and immensely comprehensive book, combining the writer's personal experiences with an evocative portrayal of historical figures and events. By far the best study of Corsica ever written in English.

Rodney Gallop *A Book of the Basques* (University of Nevada Press, UK/US, o/p). The classic study of Basque life before the twentieth century destroyed its particularity, by an English clergyman who learned Basque and adopted the country as his own.

Julian Green *Paris* (Marion Boyars, UK). A collection of very personal sketches and impressions of the city, by an American who has lived all his life in Paris, writes in French, and is considered one of the great French writers of the century. Bilingual text.

Richard Holmes *Fatal Avenue* (Pimlico, UK/US). The phrase is de Gaulle's. He used it to describe France's northeast frontier whose notorious topographical vulnerability has made it the natural route for invaders since time began. From the Channel to Alsace, Holmes relates the wars, the battles and the personalities to the ground and the places as they are today, from the Hundred Years' War to World War II. It is an exciting and informative read, the very best kind of guidebook.

Richard Holmes *Footsteps* (Penguin, UK/US). A marvellous mix of objective history and the personal and committed. Three-quarters of the book has to do with France. It includes an account of Holmes' own retracing, as a romantic eighteen-year-old in search of himself, of Robert Louis Stevenson's journey through the Cévennes; an account of his own excitement at the events of May 1968 in Paris, which leads him to investigate and reconstruct the experiences of the British in Paris during the 1789 Revolution, in particular of Mary Wollstonecraft; and finally, an investigation of the strange tormented life of the poet Gérard de Nerval.

Julian More *More about France: A Sentimental Journey* (Cape, UK). Entertaining tales of a lifetime's travel and sporadic residence, from the 1940s to the present, in Paris, Burgundy, Brittany, the Midi and Côte d'Azur.

Edwin Mullins *The Pilgrimage to Santiago* (Century/Taplinger, o/p). The main medieval pilgrim route to the shrine of Saint James (Santiago/Saint Jacques) began in Paris on rue St-Jacques. Mullins retraces the *Chemin* in this book, details the bizarre pilgrim industry that peaked in the twelfth to fifteenth centuries, and points you to the churches along the way. Fascinating stuff, treating architecture (rightfully) as social history.

Laurence Sterne *A Sentimental Journey Through France and Italy* (Oxford U.P., UK/US). By the author of *Tristram Shandy*, who, despite the title, never gets further than Versailles.

Robert Louis Stevenson *Travels with a Donkey* (Century/Biblio). Mile-by-mile account of Stevenson's twelve-day trek in the Haute Loire and Cévennes uplands with the donkey Modestine. Devotees of Stevenson's footpaths – and there are a surprising amount of both in France – might be interested in his first book, *Inland Voyage*, on the waterways of the north.

M. Uderzo and R. Goscinny *Asterix and the Goths* (Hodder/International Language Center). Take it as present-day French attitudes to their history, or as accurate portrayal of the Roman conquest – either way it's great reading.

Freda White *Three Rivers of France* (Faber, UK/US), *West of the Rhone* (o/p), *Ways of Aquitaine* (o/p). Freda White spent a great deal of time in France in the 1950s – before tourism came along to the backwater communities that were her interest. These are all evocative books, slipping in the history and culture painlessly, if not always too accurately.

HISTORY

THE MIDDLE AGES

Natalie Zemon Davis *The Return of Martin Guerre* (Harvard U.P., UK/US). A vivid account of peasant life in the sixteenth century and a perplexing and titillating hoax in the Pyrenean village of Artigat. Even better than the movie.

J.H. Huizinga *The Waning of the Middle Ages* (Penguin/Doubleday). Primarily a study of the culture of the Burgundian and French courts – but a masterpiece that goes far beyond this, building up meticulous detail to recreate the whole life and the mentality of the fourteenth and fifteenth centuries.

Emmanuel Le Roy Ladurie *Montaillou* (Penguin/Random House). Village gossip of who's sleeping with whom, tales of trips to Spain and details of work, all extracted by the Inquisition from Cathar peasants of the eastern Pyrenees in the fourteenth century, and stored away until the last decade in the Vatican archives. Though academic and heavy-going in places, most of this book reads like a novel.

Barbara Tuchman *A Distant Mirror* (Ballantine Books, UK/US, o/p). The history of the fourteenth century – plagues, wars, peasant uprisings and crusades – told through the life of a sympathetic French nobleman whose career takes him through England, Italy and Byzantium and finally ends in a Turkish prison.

REVOLUTIONS

Richard Cobb and Colin Jones (editors) *The French Revolution* (Simon & Schuster, UK/US). One of the best Bicentennial offerings with lots of pictures, texts of the time, and clear explanations by a host of historians.

Alfred Cobban *A History of Modern France* (3 vols: 1715–99, 1799–1871 and 1871–1962, Pelican, UK/US). Complete and very readable account of the main political, social and economic strands in French history from the death of Louis XIV to mid–de Gaulle.

Christopher Hibbert *The French Revolution* (Penguin/Morrow). Good, concise popular history of the period and events.

Alistair Horne *The Fall of Paris* (Penguin, UK/US). A very readable and humane account of the extraordinary period of the Prussian siege of Paris in 1870 and the ensuing struggles of the Commune.

Karl Marx *On the Paris Commune* (Lawrence and Wishart/Beekman Publications). Rousing prose from Karl, along with a history of the commune by Engels.

Peter McPhee *A Social History of France 1780–1880* (Routledge, UK/US). A scholarly work arguing that historians have underestimated the fundamental differences between how people lived and thought in 1880, compared with the time of the 1789 Revolution. He goes into such subjects as relations between men and women, education and reading material, the loss of diversity in rural France of languages and culture and changes in the physical environment.

Thomas Paine *The Rights of Man* (Penguin, UK/US). Written in 1791 in response to English conservatives' views on the situation in France, this reasoned and passionate tract expresses the ideas of both the American and French revolutions. It was immediately banned on publication, and its author charged with treason, but enough copies had crossed the Channel and been translated for Paine to be elected to the Convention by the people of Calais.

J.M. Thompson *The French Revolution* (Blackwell, UK/US). A detailed and passionate account, first published in 1943, but still the classic account in English.

Jean Tulard *Napoléon – The myth of the Saviour* (Methuen, UK). One of the classic French accounts of the rise and fall of the great man. It deals with the phenomenon rather than the details of character and personal life that appeal to so many biography readers.

NINETEENTH AND TWENTIETH CENTURIES

Marc Bloch *Strange Defeat* (Norton, US). Moving personal study of the reasons for France's defeat and subsequent caving-in to fascism. Found among the papers of this Sorbonne historian after his death at the hands of the Gestapo in 1942.

Dorothy Carrington *Napoleon and his Parents on the Threshold of History* (Viking/NAL-Dutton, o/p). Lucid study of Napoléon's early years in his native country.

Rupert Christiansen *Tales of the New Babylon, Paris 1869–1875* (Sinclair-Stevenson, UK). The compulsive and irresistible story of Paris in the last years of the Second Empire and the physical and social upheavals of the Prussian siege and the Commune. It is told both with a serious historical overview and through a mass of detail of the kind beloved of the tabloids: from gentlemen's problems in distinguishing between girls on the game and respectable women, to the sheer boredom of being besieged and the primitive form of microphotography used in the pigeon post.

Vincent Cronin *Napoleon* (Fontana, UK, o/p). Enthusiastic and accessible biography; you might still find copies of the recently deleted Penguin edition on the shelves.

H.R. Kedward *In Search of the Maquis: Rural Resistance in South France 1942–44* (Clarendon Press, UK/US). Slightly dry style, but full of fascinating detail about the brave and often mortal struggle of the countless ordinary people across France who fought to drive the Germans from their country.

François Maspero *Le Sourire du Chat* (translated as *Cat's Grin*, King Penguin, o/p). Semi-autobiographical novel of the young teenager Luc in Paris during the war with his adored elder brother in the Resistance, his parents taken to concentration camps as Paris is liberated, and everyone else busily collaborating. An intensely moving and revealing account of the war period.

David Thomson *Democracy in France since 1870* (Oxford U.P., o/p). An enquiry into why a country with such a strong socialist tradition should have had so many reactionary governments.

Barbara Tuchman *The Proud Tower* (Papermac/Bantam). Another work in her inimitable, readable style: this time a portrait of England, France, the US, Germany and Russia in the years 1890–1914. As far as France is concerned, there is a superb chapter on the extraordinary passions and enmities of the Dreyfus Affair which rocked French society between 1894 and 1899 and on the different currents in the rising socialist movement in the run-up to World War I, centring on the life of Jean Jaurès.

Paul Webster *Pétain's Crime: The full story of French collaboration in the Holocaust* (Macmillan, UK). The fascinating and alarming story of the Vichy regime's more than willing collaboration with the German authorities' campaign to implement the final solution in occupied France and the bravery of those, especially the Communist resistance, who attempted to prevent it. A mass of hitherto unpublished evidence.

Alexander Worth *France 1940–55* (Beacon Press, US). Extremely good and emotionally engaged portrayal of the most taboo period in French history – the Occupation, followed by the Cold War and colonial struggle years in which the same political tensions and heart-searchings were at play.

Theodore Zeldin *France 1845–1945: 5 vols* (Oxford U.P., UK/US). Five thematic volumes on all matters French. All good reads.

SOCIETY AND POLITICS

John Ardagh *France Today* (Penguin/Simon & Schuster). Comprehensive overview, covering food, film education and holidays as well as politics and economics – from a social democrat and journalistic position.

Roland Barthes *Mythologies* (Paladin/Hill & Wang). Brilliant analysis of how the ideas, prejudices and contradictions of French thought and behaviour manifest themselves – in food, wine, travel guides and other cultural offerings.

Simone de Beauvoir *The Second Sex* (Picador/Random House). One of the prime texts of western feminism, written in 1949, covering women's inferior status in history, literature, mythology, psychoanalysis, philosophy and everyday life. The style is dry and intellectual but the subject matter easily compensates.

Shari Benstock *Women of the Left Bank: Paris 1900–1940* (Virago, UK). Somewhat dry in an academic way, but full of information about the crucial female contribution to the expatriate literary scene in Paris and the founding of literary modernism.

Émilie Carles *Wild Herb Soup* (Gollancz/Norton). A moving and inspiring autobiography of a girl born and raised in the remote Alpine valley of the Névache near Briançon in the early years of the twentieth century. As well as giving an interesting account of peasant life, it records the development of social conscience and an extraordinary moral toughness as Émilie becomes aware of the brutality and harshness of peasant life, sees her brothers die in World War I, experiences Resistance in World War II, and finally finds herself, as an old lady, leading the campaign to stop the desecration of her beautiful natal valley by the construction of an autoroute.

Claire Duchen *Feminism in France: from May '68 to Mitterrand* (Routledge, UK/US). Charts the evolution of the women's movement through to its mid-80s crisis, clarifying the divergent political stances and feminist theory that informs the various groups, and placing them in the wider French political context.

Gisèle Halimi *Milk for the Orange Tree* (Quartet Books, UK). Born in Tunisia, daughter of an Orthodox Jewish family; ran away to Paris to become a lawyer; defender of women's rights, Algerian *FLN* fighters and all unpopular causes. A gutsy autobiographical story.

Patrick Marnham *Crime and the Académie Française* (Viking, UK). A very entertaining collection of essays and newspaper articles on some of the most bizarre, as well as mainstream, aspects of French life. Irreverent and sometimes very funny.

Paul Rambali *French Blues* (Heinemann/Trafalgar Square). Contemporary France – Minitel sex, structuralism, May '68, food, television and the rise of the Front National – experienced by a Londoner, already half-French, and gradually becoming a Parisian.

Gertrude Stein *The Autobiography of Alice B. Toklas* (Penguin, UK/US). The goings-on at Stein's famous salon in Paris. This most accessible of her works, written from the point of view of Stein's long-time companion, gives an amusing account of the Paris art and literary scene of the 1910s and 1920s.

Michel Tournier *The Golden Droplet* (Methuen Paperback, UK). A magical tale of a Saharan boy coming to Paris where strange adventures, against the backdrop of immigrant life in the slums, overtake him because he never drops his desert oasis view of the world.

Eugen Weber *My France* (Harvard U.P., US/UK). A collection of essays, fascinating and offbeat, about numerous aspects of French culture and politics. Some prior knowledge of mainstream French history is needed to make the most of them.

ART, ARCHITECTURE AND PHOTOGRAPHY

John Berger *Ways of Seeing* (BBC, UK). A book that can change how you look at paintings without making you feel ignorant or insensitive to the art.

Brassai *The Secret Paris of the Thirties* (Thames & Hudson, UK/US). Extraordinary photos of the capital's nightlife in the 1930s – brothels, music halls, street cleaners, transvestites and the underworld – each one a work of art and a familiar world to Brassai and his friend Henry Miller, who accompanied him on his night-time expeditions.

James Bromwich *The Roman Remains of Southern France* (Routledge, UK/US). The only comprehensive guide to the subject, detailed, well illustrated and approachable. In addition to accounts of the well-known sites, it will lead you off the map to all sorts of discoveries.

David J. Brown *Bridges* (Mitchell Beazley, UK). Not exclusively about France, but a very beautiful book about both the technical and aesthetic aspects of bridge building. Includes many French bridges from the Roman Pont-du-Gard to the Pont d'Avignon, Eiffel's constructions and the state-of-the-art Pont de Normandie across the Seine estuary.

Kenneth J. Comant *Carolingian and Romanesque Architecture, 800–1200* (Penguin, UK/US). Good European study with a focus on Cluny and the St-Jacques pilgrim route.

Norma Evenson *Paris: A Century of Change, 1878–1978* (Yale U.P., US). A large, illustrated volume that makes the development of urban planning and the fabric of Paris an enthralling subject – mainly because the author's ultimate concern is always with people, not panoramas.

Jacques-Henri Lartigue *Diary of a Century* (Penguin, UK/US). Book of pictures by a great

FRANCE IN LITERATURE

Listed below is a highly selective recommendation of works – mostly novels – that are rooted in the various French regions, and which would make good holiday reading.

For an overview of France-inspired authors – both French and foreign – **John Ardagh's** *Writers' France* (Hamish Hamilton, UK) is highly recommended: a knowing, beautifully illustrated guide.

PARIS AND AROUND

Charles Dickens *A Tale of Two Cities*
Gustave Flaubert *A Sentimental Education*
Victor Hugo *Les Misérables*
Henry Miller *Quiet Days in Clichy; Tropic of Cancer; Tropic of Capricorn*
Anais Nin *Journals 1917–1974*
George Orwell *Down and Out in Paris and London*
Georges Simenon Any *Maigret* thriller.
Emile Zola *Nana*

CALAIS TO CHAMPAGNE

Emile Zola *Germinal*

ALSACE, FRANCHE-COMTÉ AND JURA

John Berger *Pig Earth*
Colette *My Mother's House*
Stendhal *Scarlet and Black*

NORMANDY/BRITTANY

Honoré de Balzac *Les Chouans*
Colette *Ripening Seed*
Gustave Flaubert *Madame Bovary*
Pierre Loti *Pêcheur d'Islande*
Guy de Maupassant *Selected Short Stories*
Marcel Proust *Remembrance of Things Past*
Jean-Paul Sartre *La Nausée*

THE LOIRE

Alain Fournier *Le Grand Meaulnes*
Georges Sand *The Devil's Pool*
Rabelais *Gargantua and Pantagruel*
Zola *The Earth*

BURGUNDY

Gabriel Chevallier *Clochemerle*

ATLANTIC COAST

François Mauriac *Thérèse*

THE PYRENEES

Pierre Loti *Ramuntcho*

LANGUEDOC

Hannah Closs *High are the Mountains*

RHÔNE VALLEY AND PROVENCE

Alphonse Daudet *Letters from my Windmill; Tartarin de Tarascon* and *Tartarin of the Alps*
Lawrence Durrell *The Avignon Quintet*
Fréderic Mistral *Mireille*
Marcel Pagnol *Jean de Florette; Manon des Sources*
Emile Zola *Fortune of the Rougons*

CÔTE D'AZUR

Jean Anouilh *Point of Departure*
Colette *Collected Stories*
Alexandre Dumas *The Count of Monte Cristo*
F. Scott Fitzgerald *Tender is the Night*
Graham Greene *Loser Takes All*
Katherine Mansfield *Selected Short Stories*
Françoise Sagan *Bonjour Tristesse*

CORSICA

Gustave Flaubert *Memoires d'Un Fou*

photographer, from the day he was given a camera in 1901 through to the 1970s. It contains wonderful scenes of aristocratic leisure on Normandy and Côte d'Azur beaches and racetracks – plus his own diary commentary.

Edward Lucie-Smith *A Concise History of French Painting* (Thames & Hudson, UK/US). If you're after an art reference book, this will do as well as any . . . though there are of course hundreds of books on particular French art movements. Thames and Hudson also do useful introductions to Impressionism, Expressionism, Symbolism, etc.

William Mahder (editor), *Paris Arts: The '80s Renaissance* (Autrement, France). Illustrated, magazine-style survey of the French artistic scene now. The design and photos are reason enough in themselves to look it up. Fortunately, the French edition, *Paris Creation: Une Renaissance*, remains available; the English version now seems to be out of print.

Genevieve Moracchini-Mazel *Les Monuments Préchrétiens de la Corse* (o/p). An important work on Bronze Age Corsica, including an interpretation of the statue-menhirs of Filitosa.

J.P. Robert *Promenade dans le Paris Ancien* (Rotech, 2 vols). Two nostalgic collections of postcards and photographs of the 19th and 20th *arrondissements* of Paris, taken in the years around the turn of the century.

WALKING/HIKING

100 Walks in the French Alps (Hodder & Stoughton, UK). A very good guide to hiking in the Alps, detailing which walks are appropriate for different abilities.

Footpaths of Europe Series (16 titles; Robertson McCarta, UK). Route guides to most areas of France including Corsica, covering the system of GR footpaths, illustrated with 1:50,000 colour survey maps. These are English versions of the *Topoguides des Sentiers de Grande Randonnée* (CNSGR, Paris), which are widely available in France and themselves not hard to follow with a working knowledge of French.

Cicerone Walking Guides (Cicerone/Hunter). Neat, durable guides, with detailed route descriptions. Titles include *Tour of Mont Blanc; Chamonix-Mont Blanc; Tour of the Oisans (GR54); French Alps (GR5); The Way of Saint James (GR65); Tour of the Queyras; The Pyrenean Trail (GR10); Walks and Climbs in the Pyrenees.* All of these have information for hikers at all levels, though serious climbers should refer to the same publisher's *Rock Climbs in the Verdon* and *Rock Climbs in the Pyrenees.*

Haute-Savoie & Mont Blanc (Two Wheels, UK). The only English-language guide to mountain biking, detailing fifty off-road routes of varying difficulty in that region.

Robin G. Collomb *Corsica Mountains* (West Col, UK). Covers all the principal mountain peaks, with information on different approaches and ascents, backed up with diagrams.

Kev Reynolds *Walks and Climbs in the Pyrenees* (Cicerone Press, UK). The classic English guide for walking in the Pyrenees.

Georges Vernon *Haute Randonnée Pyrénées* (Club Alpin Français, Paris/Gastons-West Col). East-to-west description of the High Level route across the Pyrenees. Written in easy French, and published in English by Gastons-West Col.

OTHER SPECIALIST GUIDES

GAY

Gai Guide (Gai Pied, Paris). Listings (in French) of gay and lesbian clubs, saunas, restaurants, places to listen to music, and pick-up spots throughout the country. Not always up to date, but the best French gay guide on the market.

GREEN

Mary Davis *The Green Guide to France* (Green Print, UK). Definitely not the Michelin, this is a resource guide to French national parks and wildlife reserves, veggie restaurants, communes, communities and the like.

WORK

Mark Hempshell *Live and Work in France* (Vacation Work, UK). An invaluable guide for anyone considering residence or work in France; packed with ideas and advice on job hunting, bureaucracy, tax, health, etc.

Emplois d'Été en France (published in France; distributed in the UK by Vacation Work). Annual listings (in French) of thousands of summer jobs available in France.

Carol Pineau and Maureen Kelly *Working in France* (Frank Books, US). A practical guide, aimed at American readers, on how to get jobs in France, highlighting the cultural differences that affect job interviews and business practice generally.

FLOWERS

W. Lippert *Fleurs des Montagnes, Alpages et Forêts* (Miniguide Nathan Tout Terrain, Paris). Best palm-sized, colour guide if you want something to pack away with your gear in the mountains.

LANGUAGE

French can be a deceptively familiar language because of the number of words and structures it shares with English. Despite this, it's far from easy, though the bare essentials are not difficult to master and can make all the difference. Even just saying *"Bonjour Madame/Monsieur"* and then gesticulating will usually get you a smile and helpful service.

People working in tourist offices, hotels and so on, almost always speak English and tend to use it when you're struggling to speak French – be grateful, not insulted.

FRENCH PRONUNCIATION

One easy rule to remember is that **consonants** at the ends of words are usually silent. *Pas plus tard* (not later) is thus pronounced pa-plu-tarr. But when the following word begins with a vowel, you run the two together: *pas après* (not after) becomes pazapre.

Vowels are the hardest sounds to get right. Roughly:

a	as in h**a**t		*i*	as in mach**i**ne
e	as in g**e**t		*o*	as in h**o**t
é	between g**e**t and g**a**te		*o, au*	as in **o**ver
è	between g**e**t and g**u**t		*ou*	as in f**oo**d
eu	like the **u** in h**u**rt		*u*	as in a pursed-lip version of **u**se

More awkward are the **combinations** in/im, en/em, an/am, on/om, un/um at the ends of words, or followed by consonants other than n or m. Again, roughly:

in/im	like the **an** in **an**xious		*on/om*	like the **don** in **Don**caster said by
an/am, en/em	like the **don** in **Don**caster when			someone with a heavy cold
	said with a nasal accent		*un/um*	like the **u** in **u**nderstand

Consonants are much as in English, except that: ch is always sh, c is s, h is silent, th is the same as t, ll is like the y in yes, w is v, and r is growled (or rolled).

LEARNING MATERIALS

Rough Guide French Phrasebook (Rough Guides). Mini dictionary-style phrasebook with both English–French and French–English sections, along with cultural tips for tricky situations and a menu reader.

Mini French Dictionary (Harrap/Prentice Hall). French–English and English–French, plus a brief grammar and pronunciation guide.

Breakthrough French (Pan; book and two cassettes). Excellent teach-yourself course.

French and English Slang Dictionary (Harrap/Prentice Hall); ***Dictionary of Modern Colloquial French*** (Routledge). Both volumes are a bit large to carry, but they are the key to all you ever wanted to understand.

A Vous La France; Franc Extra; Franc-Parler (BBC Publications, UK; each has a book and two cassettes). BBC radio courses, running from beginners' to fairly advanced language.

A BRIEF GUIDE TO SPEAKING FRENCH

BASIC WORDS AND PHRASES

French nouns are divided into masculine and feminine. This causes difficulties with adjectives, whose endings have to change to suit the gender of the nouns they qualify. If you know some grammar, you will know what to do. If not, stick to the masculine form, which is the simplest – it's what we have done in this glossary.

today	*aujourd'hui*	that one	*celà*
yesterday	*hier*	open	*ouvert*
tomorrow	*demain*	closed	*fermé*
in the morning	*le matin*	big	*grand*
in the afternoon	*l'après-midi*	small	*petit*
in the evening	*le soir*	more	*plus*
now	*maintenant*	less	*moins*
later	*plus tard*	a little	*un peu*
at one o'clock	*à une heure*	a lot	*beaucoup*
at three o'clock	*à trois heures*	cheap	*bon marché*
at ten-thirty	*à dix heures et demie*	expensive	*cher*
at midday	*à midi*	good	*bon*
man	*un homme*	bad	*mauvais*
woman	*une femme*	hot	*chaud*
here	*ici*	cold	*froid*
there	*là*	with	*avec*
this one	*ceci*	without	*sans*

NUMBERS

1	*un*	11	*onze*	21	*vingt-et-un*	95	*quatre-vingt-quinze*
2	*deux*	12	*douze*	22	*vingt-deux*	100	*cent*
3	*trois*	13	*treize*	30	*trente*	101	*cent-et-un*
4	*quatre*	14	*quatorze*	40	*quarante*	200	*deux cents*
5	*cinq*	15	*quinze*	50	*cinquante*	300	*trois cents*
6	*six*	16	*seize*	60	*soixante*	500	*cinq cents*
7	*sept*	17	*dix-sept*	70	*soixante-dix*	1000	*mille*
8	*huit*	18	*dix-huit*	75	*soixante-quinze*	2000	*deux milles*
9	*neuf*	19	*dix-neuf*	80	*quatre-vingts*	5000	*cinq milles*
10	*dix*	20	*vingt*	90	*quatre-vingt-dix*	1,000,000	*un million*

DAYS AND DATES

January	*janvier*	November	*novembre*	August 1	*le premier août*
February	*février*	December	*décembre*	March 2	*le deux mars*
March	*mars*			July 14	*le quatorze juillet*
April	*avril*	Sunday	*dimanche*	November 23	*le vingt-trois*
May	*mai*	Monday	*lundi*		*novembre*
June	*juin*	Tuesday	*mardi*		
July	*juillet*	Wednesday	*mercredi*	1995	*dix-neuf-cent-*
August	*août*	Thursday	*jeudi*		*quatre-vingt-quinze*
September	*septembre*	Friday	*vendredi*	1996	*dix-neuf-cent-*
October	*octobre*	Saturday	*samedi*		*quatre-vingt-seize*

TALKING TO PEOPLE

When addressing people you should always use *Monsieur* for a man, *Madame* for a woman, *Mademoiselle* for a girl. Plain *bonjour* by itself is not enough. This isn't as formal as it seems, and it has its uses when you've forgotten someone's name or want to attract someone's attention.

Excuse me	*Pardon*	please	*s'il vous plaît*
Do you speak English?	*Vous parlez anglais?*	thank you	*merci*
		hello	*bonjour*
How do you say it in French?	*Comment ça se dit en Français?*	goodbye	*au revoir*
		good morning/ afternoon	*bonjour*
What's your name?	*Comment vous appelez-vous?*	good evening	*bonsoir*
My name is . . .	*Je m'appelle . . .*	good night	*bonne nuit*
I'm English/ Irish/Scottish Welsh/American/ Australian/ Canadian/ a New Zealander	*Je suis anglais[e]/ irlandais[e]/écossais[e]/ gallois[e]/américain[e]/ australien[ne]/ canadien[ne]/ néo-zélandais[e]*	How are you?	*Comment allez-vous? / Ça va?*
		Fine, thanks	*Très bien, merci*
		I don't know	*Je ne sais pas*
		Let's go	*Allons-y*
yes	*oui*	See you tomorrow	*A demain*
no	*non*	See you soon	*A bientôt*
I understand	*Je comprends*	Sorry	*Pardon, Madame/je m'excuse*
I don't understand	*Je ne comprends pas*		
Can you speak slower?	*S'il vous plaît, parlez moins vite*	Leave me alone (aggressive)	*Fichez-moi la paix!*
OK/agreed	*d'accord*	Please help me	*Aidez-moi, s'il vous plaît*

FINDING THE WAY

bus	*autobus, bus, car*	hitchhiking	*autostop*
bus station	*gare routière*	on foot	*à pied*
bus stop	*arrêt*	Where are you going?	*Vous allez où?*
car	*voiture*		
train/taxi/ferry	*train/taxi/ferry*	I'm going to . . .	*Je vais à . . .*
boat	*bâteau*	I want to get off at . . .	*Je voudrais descendre à . . .*
plane	*avion*		
train station	*gare (SNCF)*	the road to . . .	*la route pour . . .*
platform	*quai*	near	*près/pas loin*
What time does it leave?	*Il part à quelle heure?*	far	*loin*
		left	*à gauche*
What time does it arrive?	*Il arrive à quelle heure?*	right	*à droite*
		straight on	*tout droit*
a ticket to . . .	*un billet pour . . .*	on the other side of	*à l'autre côté de*
single ticket	*aller simple*	on the corner of	*à l'angle de*
return ticket	*aller retour*	next to	*à côté de*
validate your ticket	*compostez votre billet*	behind	*derrière*
		in front of	*devant*
valid for	*valable pour*	before	*avant*
ticket office	*vente de billets*	after	*après*
how many kilometres?	*combien de kilomètres?*	under	*sous*
		to cross	*traverser*
how many hours?	*combien d'heures?*	bridge	*pont*

QUESTIONS AND REQUESTS

The simplest way of asking a question is to start with *s'il vous plaît* (please), then name the thing you want in an interrogative tone of voice. For example:

| Where is there a bakery? | *S'il vous plaît, la boulangerie?* |
| Which way is it to the Eiffel Tower? | *S'il vous plaît, la route pour la tour Eiffel?* |

Similarly with requests:

| We'd like a room for two. | *S'il vous plaît, une chambre pour deux.* |
| Can I have a kilo of oranges? | *S'il vous plaît, un kilo d'oranges?* |

Question words

where?	*où?*	when?	*quand?*
how?	*comment?*	why?	*pourquoi?*
how many/	*combien?*	at what time?	*à quelle heure?*
how much?		what is/which is?	*quel est?*

ACCOMMODATION

a room for one/two people	*une chambre pour une/deux personnes*	do laundry	*faire la lessive*
a double bed	*un lit double*	sheets	*draps*
a room with a shower	*une chambre avec douche*	blankets	*couvertures*
a room with a bath	*une chambre avec salle de bain*	quiet	*calme*
		noisy	*bruyant*
For one/two/three nights	*Pour une/deux/trois nuits*	hot water	*eau chaude*
		cold water	*eau froide*
Can I see it?	*Je peux la voir?*	Is breakfast included?	*Est-ce que le petit déjeuner est compris?*
a room on the courtyard	*une chambre sur la cour*	I would like breakfast	*Je voudrais prendre le petit déjeuner*
a room over the street	*une chambre sur la rue*	I don't want breakfast	*Je ne veux pas de petit déjeuner*
first floor	*premier étage*	Can we camp here?	*On peut camper ici?*
second floor	*deuxième étage*	campsite	*un camping/terrain de camping*
with a view	*avec vue*	tent	*une tente*
key	*clef*	tent space	*un emplacement*
to iron	*repasser*	youth hostel	*auberge de jeunesse*

CARS

service station	*garage*	put air in the tyres	*gonfler les pneus*
service	*service*	battery	*batterie*
to park the car	*garer la voiture*	the battery is dead	*la batterie est morte*
car park	*un parking*	plugs	*bougies*
no parking	*défense de stationner/ stationnement interdit*	to break down	*tomber en panne*
		gas can	*bidon*
gas station	*poste d'essence*	insurance	*assurance*
fuel	*essence*	green card	*carte verte*
fill it up	*faire le plein*	traffic lights	*feux*
oil	*huile*	red light	*feu rouge*
air line	*ligne à air*	green light	*feu vert*

HEALTH MATTERS

doctor	*médecin*	stomachache	*mal à l'estomac*
I don't feel well	*Je ne me sens pas bien*	period	*règles*
medicines	*médicaments*	pain	*douleur*
prescription	*ordonnance*	it hurts	*ça fait mal*
I feel sick	*Je suis malade*	chemist	*pharmacie*
I have a headache	*J'ai mal à la tête*	hospital	*hôpital*

OTHER NEEDS

bakery	*boulangerie*	bank	*banque*
food shop	*alimentation*	money	*argent*
supermarket	*supermarché*	toilets	*toilettes*
to eat	*manger*	police	*police*
to drink	*boire*	telephone	*téléphone*
camping gas	*camping gaz*	cinema	*cinéma*
tobacconist	*tabac*	theatre	*théâtre*
stamps	*timbres*	to reserve/book	*réserver*

FRENCH AND ARCHITECTURAL TERMS: A GLOSSARY

These are either terms you'll come across in the guide, or come up against on signs, maps etc, while travelling round. For food items see *Basics*.

ABBAYE abbey

AMBULATORY passage round the outer edge of the choir of a church

APSE semicircular termination at the east end of a church

ARRONDISSEMENT district of a city

ASSEMBLÉE NATIONALE the French parliament

AUBERGE DE JEUNESSE (AJ) youth hostel

BAROQUE High Renaissance period of art and architecture, distinguished by extreme ornateness

BASTIDE medieval military settlement, constructed on a grid plan

BEAUX-ARTS fine arts museum (and school)

CAR coach, bus

CAROLINGIAN dynasty (and art, sculpture, etc) named after Charlemagne; mid-eighth to early tenth centuries

CFDT Socialist trade union

CGT Communist trade union

CHASSE GARDÉE hunting forbidden

CHÂTEAU mansion, country house, or castle

CHÂTEAU FORT castle

CHEMIN DE ST-JACQUES medieval pilgrim route to the shrine of St James at Santiago de Compostela in northwest Spain

CHEVET east end of a church

CIJ (*Centre d'Informations Jeunesse*) youth information centre

CLASSICAL architectural style incorporating Greek and Roman elements – pillars, domes, colonnades etc – at its height in France in the seventeenth century and revived, as **Neoclassical**, in the nineteenth century

CLERESTORY upper storey of a church, incorporating the windows

CONSIGNE left luggage

COUVENT convent, monastery

DÉGUSTATION tasting (wine or food)

DÉPARTEMENT county – more or less

DONJON castle keep

ÉGLISE church

ENTRÉE entrance

FERMETURE closing period

FLAMBOYANT florid form of Gothic (see below)

FN (Front National) fascist party led by Jean–Marie Le Pen

FO (Force Ouvrière) Catholic trade union

FOUILLES archaeological excavations

FRESQUE wall painting – durable through application to wet plaster

GALLO-ROMAIN period of Roman occupation of Gaul (first to fourth century AD)

GARE station; **ROUTIÈRE** – bus station; **SNCF** – train station

GAVE Pyrenean term for river

GÎTE D'ÉTAPE basic hostel accommodation primarily for walkers

HALLES covered market

HLM publicly subsidized housing

HÔTEL a hotel, but also an aristocratic townhouse or mansion

HÔTEL DE VILLE town hall

JOURS FÉRIÉS public holidays

MAIRIE town hall

MARCHÉ market

MEROVINGIAN dynasty (and art, etc), ruling France and parts of Germany from sixth to mid–eighth centuries

NARTHEX entrance hall of church

NAVE main body of a church

PCF Communist party of France

PIC peak

PLACE square

PORTE gateway

PRESQU'ÎLE peninsula

PS Socialist party

PTT post office

PUY peak or summit; a term particularly used in Massif Central and the southwest

QUARTIER district of a town

RELAIS ROUTIERS truckstop café-restaurants

RENAISSANCE art-architectural style developed in fifteenth-century Italy and imported to France in the sixteenth century by François I

RETABLE altarpiece

REZ DE CHAUSSÉE (RC) ground floor

RN (*Route Nationale*) main road

ROMANESQUE early medieval architecture distinguished by squat, rounded forms and naive sculpture, called Norman in Britain

RPR Gaullist party led by Jacques Chirac

SNCF (*Société Nationale des Chemins de Fer*) French railways

SORTIE exit

STUCCO plaster used to embellish ceilings, etc

SYNDICAT D'INITIATIVE Tourist information office; also known as *OT*, *OTSI* and *Maison du Tourisme*

TABAC bar or shop selling stamps, cigarettes, etc

TOUR tower

TRANSEPT transverse arms of a church

TYMPANUM sculpted panel above a church door

UDF centre-right party headed by Giscard d'Estaing

VAUBAN Seventeenth-century military architect – his fortresses still stand all over France

VOUSSOIR sculpted rings in arch over church door

ZONE BLEUE restricted parking zone

ZONE PIÉTONNE pedestrian precinct

MAP INDEX

direct orders from

Amsterdam	1-85828-086-9	£7.99	US$13.95	CAN$16.99
Andalucia	1-85828-094-X	8.99	14.95	18.99
Australia	1-85828-141-5	12.99	19.95	25.99
Bali	1-85828-134-2	8.99	14.95	19.99
Barcelona	1-85828-106-7	8.99	13.95	17.99
Berlin	1-85828-129-6	8.99	14.95	19.99
Brazil	1-85828-102-4	9.99	15.95	19.99
Britain	1-85828-208-X	12.99	19.95	25.99
Brittany & Normandy	1-85828-126-1	8.99	14.95	19.99
Bulgaria	1-85828-183-0	9.99	16.95	22.99
California	1-85828-181-4	10.99	16.95	22.99
Canada	1-85828-130-X	10.99	14.95	19.99
Corsica	1-85828-089-3	8.99	14.95	18.99
Costa Rica	1-85828-136-9	9.99	15.95	21.99
Crete	1-85828-132-6	8.99	14.95	18.99
Cyprus	1-85828-182-2	9.99	16.95	22.99
Czech & Slovak Republics	1-85828-121-0	9.99	16.95	22.99
Egypt	1-85828-075-3	10.99	17.95	21.99
Europe	1-85828-159-6	14.99	19.95	25.99
England	1-85828-160-1	10.99	17.95	23.99
First Time Europe	1-85828-210-1	7.99	9.95	12.99
Florida	1-85828-074-5	8.99	14.95	18.99
France	1-85828-124-5	10.99	16.95	21.99
Germany	1-85828-128-8	11.99	17.95	23.99
Goa	1-85828-156-3	8.99	14.95	19.99
Greece	1-85828-131-8	9.99	16.95	20.99
Greek Islands	1-85828-163-6	8.99	14.95	19.99
Guatemala	1-85828-045-1	9.99	14.95	19.99
Hawaii: Big Island	1-85828-158-X	8.99	12.95	16.99
Hawaii	1-85828-206-3	10.99	16.95	22.99
Holland, Belgium & Luxembourg	1-85828-087-7	9.99	15.95	20.99
Hong Kong	1-85828-066-4	8.99	13.95	17.99
Hungary	1-85828-123-7	8.99	14.95	19.99
India	1-85828-104-0	13.99	22.95	28.99
Ireland	1-85828-179-2	10.99	17.95	23.99
Italy	1-85828-167-9	12.99	19.95	25.99
Kenya	1-85828-043-5	9.99	15.95	20.99
London	1-85828-117-2	8.99	12.95	16.99
Mallorca & Menorca	1-85828-165-2	8.99	14.95	19.99
Malaysia, Singapore & Brunel	1-85828-103-2	9.99	16.95	20.99
Mexico	1-85828-044-3	10.99	16.95	22.99
Morocco	1-85828-040-0	9.99	16.95	21.99
Moscow	1-85828-118-0	8.99	14.95	19.99
Nepal	1-85828-190-3	10.99	17.95	23.99

In the UK, Rough Guides are available from all good bookstores, but can be obtained from Penguin by contacting: Penguin Direct, Penguin Books Ltd, Bath Road, Harmondsworth, West Drayton, Middlesex UB7 0DA; or telephone the credit line on 0181-899 4036 (9am–5pm) and ask for Penguin Direct. Visa, Access and Amex accepted. Delivery will normally be within 14 working days. Penguin Direct ordering facilities are only available in the UK and the USA. The availability and published prices quoted are correct at the time of going to press but are subject to alteration without prior notice.

around the world

New York	1-85828-171-7	9.99	15.95	21.99
Pacific Northwest	1-85828-092-3	9.99	14.95	19.99
Paris	1-85828-125-3	7.99	13.95	16.99
Poland	1-85828-168-7	10.99	17.95	23.99
Portugal	1-85828-180-6	9.99	16.95	22.99
Prague	1-85828-122-9	8.99	14.95	19.99
Provence	1-85828-127-X	9.99	16.95	22.99
Pyrenees	1-85828-093-1	8.99	15.95	19.99
Rhodes& the Dodecanese	1-85828-120-2	8.99	14.95	19.99
Romania	1-85828-097-4	9.99	15.95	21.99
San Francisco	1-85828-185-7	8.99	14.95	19.99
Scandinavia	1-85828-039-7	10.99	16.99	21.99
Scotland	1-85828-166-0	9.99	16.95	22.99
Sicily	1-85828-178-4	9.99	16.95	22.99
Singapore	1-85828-135-0	8.99	14.95	19.99
Spain	1-85828-081-8	9.99	16.95	20.99
St Petersburg	1-85828-133-4	8.99	14.95	19.99
Thailand	1-85828-140-7	10.99	17.95	24.99
Tunisia	1-85828-139-3	10.99	17.95	24.99
Turkey	1-85828-088-5	9.99	16.95	20.99
Tuscany & Umbria	1-85828-091-5	8.99	15.95	19.99
USA	1-85828-161-X	14.99	19.95	25.99
Venice	1-85828-170-9	8.99	14.95	19.99
Wales	1-85828-096-6	8.99	14.95	18.99
West Africa	1-85828-101-6	15.99	24.95	34.99
More Women Travel	1-85828-098-2	9.99	14.95	19.99
Zimbabwe & Botswana	1-85828-041-9	10.99	16.95	21.99
Phrasebooks				
Czech	1-85828-148-2	3.50	5.00	7.00
French	1-85828-144-X	3.50	5.00	7.00
German	1-85828-146-6	3.50	5.00	7.00
Greek	1-85828-145-8	3.50	5.00	7.00
Italian	1-85828-143-1	3.50	5.00	7.00
Mexican	1-85828-176-8	3.50	5.00	7.00
Portuguese	1-85828-175-X	3.50	5.00	7.00
Polish	1-85828-174-1	3.50	5.00	7.00
Spanish	1-85828-147-4	3.50	5.00	7.00
Thai	1-85828-177-6	3.50	5.00	7.00
Turkish	1-85828-173-3	3.50	5.00	7.00
Vietnamese	1-85828-172-5	3.50	5.00	7.00
Reference				
Classical Music	1-85828-113-X	12.99	19.95	25.99
Internet	1-85828-198-9	5.00	8.00	10.00
World Music	1-85828-017-6	16.99	22.95	29.99
Jazz	1-85828-137-7	16.99	24.95	34.99

Let's

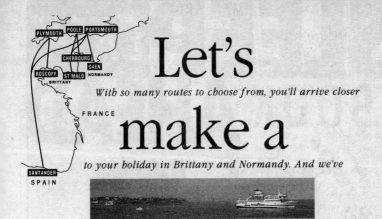

With so many routes to choose from, you'll arrive closer

make a

to your holiday in Brittany and Normandy. And we've

the fastest, shortest crossing to Spain, too. You'll discover luxurious

B≁line

cruise-ferries, convenient sailings, and you'll drive off in civilised

for the

ports, far nearer to where you'd like to be. So make a B-line for

best value

Brittany Ferries and you'll make a B-line for the perfect holiday.

routes.

For brochures **(01752) 269926**, *for bookings* **(01752) 221321** *or see your travel agent.*

Brittany Ferries
The Holiday Fleet

andy.

You are
A STUDENT

You travel
THE WORLD

You want
TO SAVE MONEY

Here's
how

The International
Student Identity Card

Available at Student Travel Offices Worldwide.

Entitles you to discounts and special services worldwide.